CAMBRIDGE
Learner's
Dictionary

CAMBRIDGE
UNIVERSITY PRESS

CAMBRIDGE UNIVERSITY PRESS
Cambridge, New York, Melbourne, Madrid, Cape Town, Singapore, São Paulo, Delhi

Cambridge University Press
The Edinburgh Building, Cambridge CB2 8RU, UK

http://www.cambridge.org
Information on this title: www.cambridge.org/9780521682022

First published 2001
Second edition 2004
Third edition 2007
3rd Printing 2008

Printed in Singapore by Green Giant Press

A catalogue record for this publication is available from the British Library

ISBN 978-0-521-681964 paperback
ISBN 978-0-521-682022 paperback + CD-ROM

Cambridge Learner's Dictionary

Managing Editor
Kate Woodford

Senior Commissioning Editor
Elizabeth Walter

Editorial Contributors
Melissa Good, Lucy Hollingworth, Kerry Maxwell,
Duncan O'Connor

Illustrations
David Shenton, Corinne Burrows, Ray Burrows
Eikon Illustrators Ltd

Previous edition:

Managing Editor
Elizabeth Walter

Lexicographers
Diane Cranz, Guy Jackson, Virginia Klein, Kerry Maxwell
Clea McEnery, Julie Moore, Martine Walsh, Sally Webber,
Kate Woodford

Editorial Contributors
Margit Aufterback, Jane Bottomley, Pat Bulhosen,
Rebecca Campbell, Carol Cassidy, Eric Fixmer, Lucy Hollingworth,
Tess Kaunhoven, Geraldine Mark, Mairi MacDonald,
Kate Mohideen, Diane Nicholls, Elizabeth Potter, Glennis Pye,
Mira Shapur, Penny Stock, Alison Tunley, Laura Wedgeworth,
Susannah Wintersgill

Cambridge Learner's Dictionary

Managing Editor
Kate Woodford

Senior Commissioning Editor
Elizabeth Walter

Editorial Contributors
Melissa Good, Lucy Hollingworth, Kerry Maxwell,
Duncan O'Connor

Illustrations
David Shenton, Corinne Burrows, Ray Burrows
Eikon Illustrators Ltd

Previous edition:

Managing Editor
Elizabeth Walter

Lexicographers
Diane Cranz, Guy Jackson, Virginia Klein, Kerry Maxwell,
Glennis McNew, Julie Moore, Martine Walsh, Sally Webber
Kate Woodford

Editorial Contributors
Maryn Aitchison, Jane Bottomley, Pat Bulhosen
Rebecca Campbell, Carol Cassidy, Eric Finch, Lucy Hollingworth,
Jess Kershaw, Geraldine Mark, Marti MacDonald,
Kate Mohideen, Diane Nicholls, Elizabeth Potter, Glennis Pye
Nina Prentice, Penny Stock, Alison Tunley, Laura Wedgeworth
Susannah Wintersgill.

Contents

Introduction

Welcome to the new, updated edition of the **Cambridge Learner's Dictionary** (3rd edition). You have in your hand the perfect dictionary for the intermediate and upper-intermediate learner of English, perfect for many reasons:

Clear word meanings (definitions)

You need to know what words mean. Our explanations of words are short, clear and accurate. Our definitions use only simple English that you will understand.

Help with grammar

You want to be able to speak and write English that is correct. Our grammar information is presented in a way that is clear and helpful and will show you how to avoid mistakes.

Natural-sounding examples

You want to know how to use words in a way that sounds natural. This dictionary contains over 27,000 examples. They show the context in which a word is most often said or written and the type of words that are often used with it.

Word partners (collocations)

Words that are often spoken or written together, for example, *a good buy* and *a big decision*, are called *word partners* or *collocations*. Knowing how to put the right words together is probably the most important skill for producing fluent, natural-sounding English. This dictionary has more information on word partners than any other dictionary at this level.

Keywords

You want to know which words are the most important to learn. The 2000 most important words in the English language are shown in blue with a key symbol **o-ᴹ** next to them.

New words

English is changing all the time. You can be confident that this dictionary is really up-to-date, with new words from many areas, such as technology, fashion and music.

Self-study

You want to be able to study English on your own. This dictionary has a centre section of 59 *Extra help pages* with lots of clear, useful information on important topics such as phrasal verbs and spelling. There are also 16 full-colour pages of pictures and photographs to help you increase your vocabulary.

Cambridge International Corpus and Cambridge Learner Corpus

All of the features described above were created using the *Cambridge International Corpus*, a collection of over *one billion* words of English. Only Cambridge dictionaries are produced using this amazing resource. The English in our corpus comes from many places, for example newspapers, best-selling novels, websites, magazines, TV programmes and recordings of people's everyday conversations. We store all this language in a huge database and use it to see how English is really used. The corpus gives us the evidence we need to be sure that what we say in the dictionary is accurate.

Another very valuable tool that we have is the *Cambridge Learner Corpus*, a large collection of exam scripts written by students taking Cambridge ESOL English exams around the world. This learner corpus shows which words cause problems for learners. By looking at it, we can see real problems that real learners have. That means we can add useful information – often in the form of *Common Learner Error Notes* to help you avoid them.

The *Cambridge Learner's Dictionary* is available with or without a CD-ROM. The CD-ROM contains everything that is in the dictionary plus some great extra features, such as spoken pronunciations in British and American accents, and the unique SMART thesaurus which gives synonym or topic lists for every single word in the dictionary and is a fantastic tool for building your vocabulary.

We know you will enjoy using the *Cambridge Learner's Dictionary*. Use it and see your English develop.

Visit the world's favourite learner dictionaries at:
http://dictionary.cambridge.org

How to use this dictionary

Finding a word

Each entry begins with the base form of the word.

language /ˈlæŋgwɪdʒ/ *noun* **1** COMMUNICATION [U] communication between people, usually using words *She has done research into how children acquire language.* **2** ENGLISH/SPANISH/ JAPANESE ETC [C] a type of communication used by the people of a particular country *How many languages do you speak?* **3** TYPE OF WORDS [U] words of a particular type, especially the words used by people in a particular job *legal language* ○ *the language of business* **4** COMPUTERS [C, U] a system of instructions that is used to write computer programs ➔See also: **body language, modern languages, second language, sign language.**

Words which are made of two separate words (compounds) are found in alphabetical order. The stress marks (',) show you which part of the word to say strongly.

language la‚boratory *UK* (*US* **'language ‚laboratory**) *noun* [C] a room in a college or school where you can use equipment to help you practise listening to and speaking a foreign language

When a word can be spelled another way, or when there is another word for it, this is shown.

dialogue (*also US* **dialog**) /ˈdaɪəlɒg/ *noun* [C, U] **1** the talking in a book, play, or film **2** a formal discussion between countries or groups of people

When two words have the same spelling but different parts of speech (e.g. a noun and a verb), they have separate entries.

interface¹ /ˈɪntəfeɪs/ *noun* [C] **1** a connection between two pieces of electronic equipment, or between a person and a computer *a simple user interface* **2** a situation, way, or place where two things can come together and have an effect on each other *the interface between technology and tradition*

interface² /ˈɪntəˌfeɪs/ *verb* [I, T] to communicate with people or electronic equipment, or to make people or electronic equipment communicate *We use email to interface with our customers.*

Some words which are formed from the main word are shown at the end of an entry. If a word is not formed with a regular pattern, or if its meaning is not easy to guess, it has its own explanation. See Word Beginnings and Endings on page 830.

fluent /'fluːənt/ *adjective* **1** able to use a language naturally without stopping or making mistakes *She is **fluent in** six languages.* **2** produced or done in a smooth, natural style *Hendrik speaks fluent English.* ● **fluency** /'fluːənsi/ *noun* [U] ● **fluently** *adverb*

Understanding an entry

Where a word has more than one meaning, the most frequent meaning is shown first.

Words which have several meanings have GUIDEWORDS to help you find the meaning you are looking for.

Example sentences, based on the *Cambridge International Corpus*, show how words are used in typical situations.

voice¹ /vɔɪs/ *noun* **1** SOUNDS [C] the sounds that you make when you speak or sing *I could hear voices in the next room.* ○ *Jessie has a beautiful singing voice.* ○ *Could you please **keep your voices down** (= speak more quietly)?* **2** **lose your voice** to become unable to speak, often because of an illness *She had a bad cold and was losing her voice.* **3** OPINION [C] someone's opinion about a particular subject *The programme gives people the opportunity to make their voices heard.* **4** PERSON [no plural] someone who expresses the opinions or wishes of a group of people *It's important that students have a voice on the committee.* ⊃See also: **the passive**.

Each word has a part of speech label (e.g. *noun, verb, adj*) For a list of the parts of speech, see inside the front cover.

Grammar labels tell you how a word is used. See grammar labels on page xiii.

say¹ /seɪ/ *verb* [T] **says**, *past* **said** **1** WORDS to speak words *"I'd like to go home," she said.* ○ *I couldn't hear what they were saying.* ○ *How do you say this word?* **2** TELL to tell someone about a fact, thought, or opinion [+ question word] *Did she say where she was going?* ○ [+ (that)] *The jury said that he was guilty.* **3** INFORMATION to give information in writing, numbers, or signs *My watch says one o'clock.* ○ *What do the papers say about the election?* **4** **say sth to yourself** to think something but not speak *"I hope she likes me," he said to himself.*

This symbol shows very frequent words which are important to learn.

Pronunciations use the International Phonetic Alphabet (IPA). There is a list of these symbols inside the back cover of the dictionary. The most difficult symbols are also explained at the bottom of each page.There is an explanation of the pronunciation system on page xvi.

Irregular inflections of words are clearly shown. There is a list of irregular verb inflections on page 827 and an explanation of regular inflections on page 825.

o→**speak** /spiːk/ *verb past tense* **spoke**, *past participle* **spoken** **1** [I] to say something using your voice *to speak loudly/quietly* ○ *There was complete silence - nobody spoke.* **2 speak to sb** *mainly UK* (*mainly US* **speak with sb**) to talk to someone *Could I speak to Mr Davis, please?* ○ *Have you spoken with your new neighbors yet?* **3 speak about/of sth** to talk about something *He refused to speak about the matter in public.* **4 speak English/French/German, etc** to be able to communicate in English/French/German, etc *Do you speak English?* **5** [I] to make a speech to a large group of people *She was invited to speak at a conference in Madrid.* **6 speak for/on behalf of sb** to express the feelings, opinions, etc of another person or of a group of people *I've been chosen to speak on behalf of the whole class.*

These labels show you when a word is used in British English or American English. See explanation of these labels on page xv.

These labels tell you how formal, informal, etc a word is. See explanation of all these labels on page xv.

o→**chat¹** /tʃæt/ *verb* [I] **chatting**, *past* **chatted** to talk with someone in a friendly and informal way *I wanted to **chat to** you **about** the party on Saturday.*
chat sb up *UK informal* to talk to someone in a way that shows them that you are sexually attracted to them

Learning more about a word

Cross references show you where you can find related information such as opposites, pictures, study pages, and idioms.

o→**ask** /ɑːsk/ *verb* **1** QUESTION [I, T] to say something to someone as a question which you want them to answer [+ **two objects**] *Can I **ask** you a few **questions**?* ○ *I **asked** him **about** his hobbies.* ○ [+ question word] *I asked why the plane was so late.* ○ *She asked whether I knew what Ian's plans were.* ○ *I asked him what time the party started.* ⊃See Common learner error at **question**. **2** WANT SOMETHING [I, T] to say something to someone because you want them to give you something *He's **asked for** a bike for his birthday.*

Words which are often used together (*collocations or word partners*) are shown in dark type in examples.

communicate /kə'mjuːnɪkeɪt/ *verb* [I, T] **1** to share information with others by speaking, writing, moving your body, or using other signals *We can now communicate instantly with people on the other side of the world.* **2** to talk about your thoughts and feelings, and help other people to understand them *He can't communicate with his parents.*

Some words are used as part of a phrase. This is shown clearly at the start of the definition.

Phrasal verbs come after the entry for the verb in alphabetical order

spell¹ /spel/ *verb past* **spelled** *also UK* **spelt** **1** [T] to write down or tell someone the letters which are used to make a word *How do you spell that?* ○ *Her name's spelt S-I-A-N.* **2** [I] If you can spell, you know how to write the words of a language correctly. *My grammar's all right, but I can't spell.* **3 spell disaster/trouble, etc** If something spells disaster, trouble, etc, you think it will cause something bad to happen in the future. *The new regulations could spell disaster for small businesses.*

spell sth out to explain something in a very clear way with details *They sent me a letter, spelling out the details of the agreement.*

Some words are used as part of an idiom. These are shown in dark type at the end of the entry.

message¹ /'mesɪdʒ/ *noun* [C] **1** a piece of written or spoken information which one person gives to another *Did you get my message?* ○ *I left her several messages, but she hasn't returned my call.* **2** the most important idea of a film, book, etc *The book conveys a complex message.* **3 get the message** *informal* to understand what someone wants you to do by their actions *Don't return any of his calls - he'll soon get the message and leave you alone.*

All our explanations use very simple words. Where we have had to use a more difficult word than usual, that word is explained in brackets.

express¹ /ɪk'spres/ *verb* [T] to show what you think or how you feel using words or actions *I'm simply expressing my opinion.* ○ [often reflexive] *You're not expressing yourself (= saying what you mean) very clearly.*

The information in the boxes

These word partner boxes give you information on words that are often spoken or written together, often called 'collocations' or 'word partners'. There are over 1000 of these boxes in this dictionary.

WORD PARTNERS FOR **text message**

get/send a text message • a text message **saying** sth • a text message **from/to** sb

These thesaurus boxes show you all the different words which have the same or a similar meaning. There are 80 of these boxes in this dictionary.

OTHER WAYS OF SAYING **talk**

The most common alternatives are **speak** and **say**: *Could you speak more quietly, please?* • *I couldn't hear what they were saying.*

The verb **chat** or the expression **have a chat** are often used if a person is talking with someone in a friendly, informal way: *We were just chatting about the party on Saturday.* • *Give me a call and we'll have a chat.*

If people talk for a long time about things that are not important, verbs such as **chatter**, **natter** (*UK, informal*), and the expression **have a natter** (*UK, informal*) are sometimes used: *She spent the morning chattering away to her friends.* • *We had a long natter over coffee.*

Common Learner Error notes based on the *Cambridge Learner Corpus* give extra information about words which often cause problems for learners.

COMMON LEARNER ERROR

mention

No preposition is normally needed after the verb **mention**.

He didn't mention the price.

He didn't mention about the price.

More information on using the dictionary

Grammar labels

When a word must *always* be used in a particular grammatical form, that form is shown at the beginning of the entry or the beginning of the meaning. Patterns which are common and typical, but are not *always* used, are given next to example sentences showing how they are used.

Nouns

C	countable noun	pencil, friend, house
U	uncountable noun, does not have a plural	water, advice, health
C, U	noun which can be countable or uncountable	ability, quantity, exercise ▶ *You should take some **exercise**.* ▶ *I do my **exercises** every morning.*
⊃	see also Extra help page **Countable and uncountable nouns**, on page Centre 20	
group	noun which refers to a group of people or things and can be used with either a singular or a plural verb	government, class, team ▶ *The French **team are** European champions.* ▶ *His **team is** top of the league.*
plural	plural noun, used with a plural verb	trousers, scissors, pliers
no plural	noun which can be used with a and an, but does not have a plural	rush, vicious circle, wait ▶ *Sorry, I'm in a **rush**.*
usually plural	noun usually used in the plural form	statistics, resources, regulations
usually singular	noun usually used in the singular form	mess, range, world

Verbs

I	intransitive verb, does not have an object	sleep, glance, fall ▶ *Anna's **sleeping**.*
T	transitive verb, must have an object	cure, hit, catch ▶ *Fiona **hit** her **sister**.*
I, T	verb that can be intransitive or transitive	sing, explain, drive ▶ *I always **sing** in the bath.* ▶ *He **sang** a love **song**.*
+ two objects	ditransitive verb, that has two objects	give, send, lend ▶ *She **gave** me the **keys**.*

| often passive | verb often used in the passive | allow
▶ *Smoking is not allowed in the restaurant.* |
| often reflexive | verb often used with a reflexive pronoun (myself, yourself, herself, etc) | defend
▶ *He can defend himself.* |

If a verb or a meaning of a verb is *always* **passive** (e.g. inundate, demote, affiliate) or *always* **reflexive** (e.g. brace, ingratiate, steel), the whole grammar pattern is shown at the beginning of the entry.

Some verb or meanings of verbs are **always followed by an adverb or preposition** (e.g. creep, flick, trickle). When this happens, common examples of adverbs and prepositions used are shown at the beginning of the entry or the meaning.

↻ see also Extra help page **Verb patterns**, on page Centre 27

Adjectives

always before noun	attributive adjective, always comes before the noun	major, basic, staunch ▶ *a staunch supporter*
never before noun	predicative adjective, used with verbs such as **be, seem, feel**	afraid, ready, done ▶ *She's afraid of water.*
always after noun	adjective always used directly after the noun	galore, proper, incarnate ▶ *the devil incarnate*

Other grammar patterns

The following patterns can refer to nouns, adjectives, and verbs:

+ that	the word is followed by a **that clause**, and the word **that** must be included	boast, assertion, evident ▶ *It was evident from her voice that she was upset.*
+ (that)	the word is followed by a **that clause** but the word **that** does not have to be used	hope, amazed, doubt ▶ *I hope that the bus won't be late.* *I hope the bus won't be late.*
+ doing sth	the word is followed by a verb in the –ing form	enjoy, busy, difficulty ▶ *I enjoy going to the beach.*
+ to do sth	the word is followed by a verb in the infinitive	confidence, careful, decide ▶ *I didn't have the confidence to speak up.*
+ for/of, etc + doing sth	the word is followed by a preposition (e.g. for/of) and then a verb in the –ing form	apologize, idea, guilty ▶ *She apologized for being late.*
+ question word	the word is followed by a question word (e.g. who, what, how)	ask, certain, clue ▶ *I'm not certain who to ask.*
used in questions and negatives	the word is used in questions and negative sentences	mind, much, yet ▶ *Do you mind if I come in?* *I haven't seen him yet.*

Usage labels

informal	used when you are speaking, or communicating with people you know but not normally in serious writing	brainy, freebie, goalie
formal	used in serious writing or for communicating with people about things like law or business	examination, moreover, purchase
very informal	used when you are talking to people you know well, and not usually in writing. Some of these words may offend people, and this is explained in the entry.	prat, barf, crap
spoken	a way of writing a word which is used in conversation	yeah, hey, eh
humorous	used in order to be funny or to make a joke	couch potato, snail mail
literary	used in books and poems, not in ordinary conversation	beloved, slumber, weep
old-fashioned	not used in modern English – you might find these words in books, used by older people, or used in order to be funny	gramophone, spectacles, farewell
trademark	the name of a product that is made by one company. Sometimes a trademark is used as a general word	Coke, Hoover, Sellotape

UK/US labels

The spelling used in definitions and examples in this dictionary is British English. However, American English is also explained clearly, and where there is a difference between British and American English, this is shown.

UK	only used in British English	pavement, petrol station
US	only used in American English	sidewalk, gas station
mainly UK	mainly used in British English, but sometimes in American English	lecturer, rubbish, nightdress
mainly US	mainly used in American English, but sometimes in British English	movie, apartment, semester
also UK	another word that can also be used in British English	truck (*also UK* lorry) ■ **truck** is used in Britain and US **lorry** is also used in Britain
also US	another word that can also be used in American English	railway (*also US* railroad) ■ **railway** is used in Britain and US **railroad** is also used in US

➲ see also Extra help page **UK and US English**, on page Centre 38

Pronunciation

All pronunciations use the International Phonetic Alphabet. There is a complete list of phonetic symbols inside the back cover.

Many phonetic symbols, e.g. /p/, /s/, /k/, sound exactly like the most common pronunciation of the letter they look like. Those that do not are explained at the bottom of every page of the dictionary.

Where more than one pronunciation is shown, the more common one is first, but both are often used.

British and American pronunciation

Most words are given only one pronunciation, which is acceptable in British and American English. There are some regular differences between British and American English which are not shown for every word.

The main ones are:

1 In American English, the **r** in words such as **hard** or **teacher** is pronounced, and in British English it is silent.

2 In American English, **t** and **tt** in words such as **later** and **butter**, are pronounced in a soft way, almost like a /d/ sound.

Where there is a big difference between British and American pronunciation, both forms are shown. The symbol ⑮ is shown before an American pronunciation, e.g. **schedule** /ˈʃedjuːl ⑮ ˈskedʒuːl/

Stress patterns

Stress patterns show you which parts of the word you should emphasize when you say them.

/ˈ/ shows the main emphasis on a word. For example, in the word **picture** /ˈpɪktʃəʳ/, you should emphasize the first part, and in the word **deny** /dɪˈnaɪ/ you should emphasize the second part.

/ˌ/ shows the second most important emphasis on the word. For example, in the word **submarine** /ˌsʌbməˈriːn/, the main emphasis is on the last part of the word, but you should also emphasize the first part of the word slightly.

Compound words (words made of two or more separate words) have their stress patterns shown on them. For example in the word **deˌsigner ˈbaby**, the main emphasis is on the first part of the second word, but you should also emphasize the first part of the first word slightly.

Strong forms and weak forms

Some common words (e.g. and, them, of) have strong forms and weak forms. The weak forms are more common.

For example, in the sentence '*I saw them leave.*', the weak form /ðəm/ would be used.

The strong form is used when you want to emphasize the word. For instance, in the sentence '*They said they saw me, but I didn't see them.*', the strong form /ðem/ would be used.

Regular inflections

All inflections (e.g. plurals, past tenses) that are not regular (= are not formed in the usual way) are shown at the entry for the word. The regular way of forming inflections is shown below.

Nouns

Most nouns form their plurals by adding –s
▶ *chair, chairs* ▶ *plate, plates*

Nouns which end in –s, –ss, –ch, –x, and –z, make their plurals by adding - es
▶ *mass, masses* ▶ *match, matches*

Nouns which end in a consonant (e.g. m, t, p) + –y, form their plurals by taking away the –y and adding –ies
▶ *baby, babies* ▶ *university, universities*

Adjectives

The comparative form of adjectives is used to show that someone or something has more of a particular quality than someone or something else. To make the regular comparative form, you either add –er to the end of the adjective, or use the word **more** before it.

The superlative form of adjectives is used to show that someone or something has more of a particular quality than anyone or anything else. To make the regular superlative form, you either add –est to the end of the adjective, or use the word **most** before it.

One-syllable adjectives usually form their comparative and superlative with –er and –est
▶ *small, smaller, smallest*

Two-syllable adjectives can all form their comparative and superlative with **more** and **most**.
▶ *complex, more complex, most complex*

Some two-syllable adjectives can use –er and –est too. The most common of these are:
■ adjectives ending in –y and –ow,
  ▶ *happy, noisy, shallow*
■ adjectives ending in –le,
  ▶ *able, noble, simple*
■ some other common two-syllable adjectives,
  ▶ *common, cruel, handsome, pleasant, polite, quiet, solid, wicked*

Three-syllable adjectives usually form their comparative and superlative with **more** and **most**
▶ *beautiful, more beautiful, most beautiful*

When you are using the –er, –est forms, if the adjective ends in –e, take away
the –e before adding the ending
▶ *pale, paler, palest*

If the adjective ends in –y, change this to –i before adding the ending
▶ *happy, happier, happiest*

Verbs

Regular verbs add the following endings:

for the **3rd person singular** add –s, or –es to verbs that end in –s, –ss, –ch, –x, and –z

for the **present participle** add –ing

for the **past tense** and the **past participle** add –ed
▶ *pack, packs, packing, packed*

For verbs ending in –e, take away the –e before adding the present participle, past tense, and past participle endings.
▶ *hate, hates, huting, hated*

For verbs ending in –y, for the third person singular take away the –y and add –ies, and for the past tense and past participle take away the –y and add –ied.
▶ *cry, cries, crying, cried*

New words

These three pages contain new words and phrases which have recently appeared in the English language or have recently become more popular. Many of these words and phrases will continue to be used in years to come while some may disappear from the language.

the arsenic hour *noun* [no plural] a busy time of day in a house with young children, especially the time after parents arrive home and before the evening meal *Here are some tips for preparing a meal during the arsenic hour.*

baby hunger *noun* [U] the strong wish to have a baby, especially among older women who have important jobs *Men's baby hunger is often not as great as women's.*

body lift *noun* [C] a medical operation that tightens loose skin on someone's body so that they look younger and more attractive *People sometimes have a body lift after they have lost a lot of weight.*

BOGOF *abbreviation for* buy one get one free: a supermarket offer in which you get two of something but only pay for one of them

caller-ID *noun* [U] a system that makes it possible for a telephone to show the telephone number of the person who is calling *Get caller-ID and then you don't have to answer the phone when he calls.*

Chelsea tractor *noun* [C] *humorous* a large four-wheel-drive (= a car with big wheels for driving on rough ground) which is only driven in a town *the Mums in their Chelsea tractors taking children to school*

chugger *noun* [C] someone who stands on the street on the street and asks people walking past to give money regularly to a charity

citizen journalist *noun* [C] someone who gives news stories to newspapers although it is not their job *Citizen journalists gave their accounts of the explosion.* • **citizen journalism** *noun* [U]

climate-friendly *adjective* Something that is climate-friendly does not cause any damage which will change the Earth's weather patterns. *climate-friendly technology* ○ *climate-friendly farming*

competitive compassion *noun* [U] when people give money to a charity (= an organization that helps people) because they want to seem kinder than other people *It was competitive compassion which led people to give so much money following the floods.*

cyberslacking *noun* [U] when people at work spend time sending emails to their friends and using the Internet for enjoyment instead of working *Cyberslacking is becoming a problem for many employers.* • **cyberslacker** *noun* [C]

data fast *noun* [C] a period of time when you do not use your computer, mobile phone, television, etc *If you want to feel less stressed, try a data fast.*

downtime *noun* [U] time when you relax and do not do very much. *We've had a busy weekend so I'm planning to have some downtime tomorrow.*

earworm *noun* [C] a song or part of a song that you hear again and again in your head *People who get the most earworms tend to listen to music frequently.*

e-dress *noun* [C] an email or website address *Please note the company's change of e-dress.*

ego surfing *noun* [U] searching on the Internet for your own name *Ego surfing is certainly easier if you have an unusual name.*

fat tax *noun* [C] a tax on food that is bad for your body and will make you fat *a fat tax on burgers and chips*

firefighting *noun* [U] when you spend all your time dealing with problems at work that need your immediate attention *I seem to be so busy firefighting that I never have time to do routine jobs.*

flexitarian *noun* [C] someone who does not eat meat or fish usually, but sometimes does *She*

| j yes | k cat | ŋ ring | ʃ she | θ thin | ð this | ʒ decision | dʒ jar | tʃ chip | æ cat | e bed | ə ago | ɪ sit | i cosy | ɒ hot | ʌ run | ʊ put |

eats chicken occasionally and describes herself as a flexitarian.

future-proof *verb* [T] to design software, a computer, etc so that it can still be used in the future, even when technology changes *Here are some tips for future-proofing your computer network.*

Googlewhacking *noun* [U] the activity of trying to find a set of words that will only produce one result when you use Google™ (= a computer program that finds information on the Internet) *Like a lot of bored office workers, I've done a bit of Googlewhacking in my time.*
• **Googlewhack** *noun* [C]

granny leave *noun* [U] a period of time when you do not go to work because you are looking after an old or ill parent *Small business owners are worried about the effect that granny leave will have on their businesses.*

greenwash *verb* [T] to make people believe that your company cares more about the environment than it really does *Many shoppers have been greenwashed by products claiming to be "natural" and "kind to the environment".*
• **greenwash** *noun* [C] *The government's latest initiative has been dismissed as a greenwash.*

grief tourist *noun* [C] someone who visits a place because something very bad has happened there *The site where the Twin Towers were in New York is a favourite destination for grief tourists.*

half birthday *noun* [C] the day that is exactly half a year from your birthday *If you need an excuse for a celebration, why not celebrate your half birthday?*

hand-me-up *noun* [C] something that you give to an older person because you no longer use it, or because you now have something better *My mobile phone is a hand-me-up from my son.*

ICE number *noun* [C] *abbreviation for* In Case of Emergency number: a telephone number that you store in your mobile phone under the name 'ICE' so that people know who to call if you are hurt in an accident *The emergency services are urging people to enter an ICE number on their mobile phones.*

infomania *noun* [U] when you cannot think clearly because you are spending too much time sending and reading emails and text messages *The study shows that there is a rise in infomania, with growing numbers of people obsessively checking their email.*

jobspill *noun* [U] when you spend time at home doing things that are part of your job *If your boss calls you at the weekend, that's jobspill.*

kidult *noun* [C] an adult who likes doing or buying things that are intended for children

latte factor *noun* [no plural] small amounts of money that you spend without thinking, which are a lot of money if you add them together *You could save $50 a week if you cut out the latte factor.*

metrosexual *noun* [C] a man who is sexually attracted to women but is also interested in fashion and the way he looks *The typical metrosexual is a young man, living in a city, with money to spend.* ⊃Compare **retrosexual**.

milk brain *noun* [U] the tired and confused feeling that many mothers of young babies have *Milk brain is a temporary effect brought on by lack of sleep.*

muffin top *noun* [C] fat on someone's stomach that you can see because it hangs over the top of their trousers *The appearance of muffin tops has increased with the fashion for low-cut trousers and short tops.*

phat *adjective* very good *informal The band had a really phat sound.*

podjacking *noun* [U] **1** when someone takes control of how a podcast (= a radio program stored in digital form) is sent to people so that people think it comes from him or her *There are steps you can take to avoid podjacking.* **2** the act of putting the cord from your MP3 player (= a piece of equipment that plays digital music) into someone else's MP3 player so that you can listen to or copy their music

regifting *noun* [U] when you give someone something which someone else gave to you as a present *Passing on gifts that we don't want or need, or regifting as it's now called, is becoming more acceptable.*

rendition *noun* [U] the practice of sending someone to another country to answer questions about a crime or to be put in prison *Since the terrorist attack of September 11, rendition has been carried out on a greater scale.*

rescue call *noun* [C] a call that you ask someone to make to your mobile phone at a particular time because you might need a reason to leave a place *Nancy was not sure that she would like her date so she arranged for a rescue call at 8pm.*

retrosexual *noun* [C] a man who is sexually attracted to women and is not interested in fashion or the way he looks *Retrosexuals would never use something like hair gel.* ⊃Compare **metrosexual**.

saviour sibling *UK* (*US* savior sibling) *noun* [C] a child who is born with particular genes which scientists have chosen so that he or she will be able to help treat an older brother or sister who has a disease *Baby James is a saviour sibling for his older brother John who has a life-threatening blood disorder.*

season creep *noun* [U] the fact that spring is coming earlier which may be caused by global warming (= the fact that the Earth is becoming warmer)

shouty *adjective* Someone who is shouty shouts a lot because they get angry very easily.

slow food *noun* [U] good food that is grown locally, cooked well, and eaten slowly so you can enjoy it *The slow food movement was created to combat fast food.*

splitter *noun* [C] someone who owns two homes, and spends some time in one home and some time in the other *Are you a splitter with a home in Britain and a home in Spain?*

springspotter *noun* [C] someone who looks for ideas, products, clothes, etc that are becoming fashionable, and tells people in business so they can develop new products *They have a team of springspotters who go round the neighbourhood and report back which trends and products are becoming popular.*

stealth tax *noun* [C] a new tax that is collected in a way that it is not very obvious, so people may not realise that they are paying it

Stepford *adjective* [always before noun] doing everything that someone tells you to, and not having any ideas of your own *a Stepford wife* ○ *Stepford employees*

stress puppy *noun* [C] someone who seems to enjoy stress (= worry caused by difficult situations), but complains about it often

supersize (*also* **supersized**) *adjective* describes something that is much bigger than normal *a supersize bacon cheeseburger*

Swiss army phone *noun* [C] a mobile phone that can do a lot of things such as play music, take photographs, etc

textual harassment *noun* [U] when someone sends rude or unpleasant text messages (= written messages sent from one mobile phone to another) to someone else *Textual harassment is becoming a popular way for school bullies to reach their victims day and night.*

TLA *noun* [C] *abbreviation for* three-letter abbreviation: a set of three letters that is a short form of a word or phrase *BBC and DVD are well-known TLAs.*

trouser *verb* [T] to get a large amount of money, especially money that should not be yours *She did all the work and yet her husband trousered the profits.*

ubersexual *noun* [C] a man who is sexually attracted to women, is kind, and wants to help other people *The ultimate ubersexual is confident and passionate about his beliefs.*

unibrow (*also* **monobrow**) *noun* [C] a line of hair that joins someone's eyebrows (= the lines of hair over the eyes) so that it looks as if they have one long eyebrow *If you have a unibrow should you pluck it, shave it, or leave it alone?*

universal release *noun* [C, U] when a new film becomes available in cinemas and on DVD on the same day *'Bubble' will be the movie industry's first universal release.* ○ *Universal release will increase audience and profits.*

Winterval *noun* [U] the time during the middle of winter when people celebrate Christmas and other festivals *The town renamed Christmas 'Winterval' in order to avoid offending non-Christians.*

zombie computer (*also* **zombie**) *noun* [C] a computer with a virus (= a program that is secretly put on a computer to cause damage) that makes it cause problems for other computers without the user knowing *50-80% of all email spam is sent by zombie computers.*

Aa

A, a /eɪ/ the first letter of the alphabet

o—**a** (*also* **an**) *strong form* /eɪ/ *weak form* /ə/ *determiner* **1** BEFORE NOUN used before a noun to refer to a single thing or person but not a particular thing or person or not one that you have referred to before *I need a new car.* ○ *I saw a woman speaking to him.* **2** ONE *one a hundred dollars* ○ *a dozen eggs* **3** EVERY/EACH every or each *A child needs love.* ○ *Take one tablet three times a (= each) day.* **4** TYPE used to say what type of thing or person something or someone is *It's a guinea-pig.* ○ *She's a doctor.* **5** AN ACTION used before some action nouns when referring to one example of the action *I'm just going to have a wash.* ○ *Take a look at this.* **6** TWO NOUNS used before the first of two nouns that are often used together *a cup and saucer* **7** AMOUNTS used before some phrases saying how much of something there is *a few days* ○ *a bit of sugar* **8** NAME used before a person's name when referring to someone you do not know *There's a Ms Leeming to see you.*

COMMON LEARNER ERROR

a or an?

Remember to use **an** in front of words which begin with a vowel sound. These are words which start with the letters a, e, i, o, u, or a sound like those letters.
a car, an orange, an hour

a- /eɪ/ *prefix* not, without *atypical* ○ *amoral*

aback /əˈbæk/ *adverb* **be taken aback** to be very surprised or shocked *I was rather taken aback by her honesty.*

abacus /ˈæbəkəs/ *noun* [C] a square object with small balls on wires, used for counting

WORD PARTNERS FOR *abandon*

be **forced to** abandon sth ● abandon an at-tempt/**effort/idea/plan/search**

abandon /əˈbændən/ *verb* [T] **1** to leave someone or something somewhere, sometimes not returning to get them *They were forced to abandon the car.* **2** to stop doing something before it is finished, or to stop following a plan, idea, etc *The match was abandoned because of rain.* ● **abandoned** *adjective* ● **abandonment** *noun* [U]

abate /əˈbeɪt/ *verb* [I] *formal* to become less strong *By the weekend, the storms had abated.*

abattoir /ˈæbətwɑːr/ *UK* (*UK/US* **slaughterhouse**) *noun* [C] a place where animals are killed for meat

abbey /ˈæbi/ *noun* [C] a group of buildings that is a home for monks or nuns (= religious men or women who live separately from other people)

abbreviate /əˈbriːvieɪt/ *verb* [T] to make a word or phrase shorter *The word 'street' is often abbreviated to 'St'.*

abbreviation /əˌbriːviˈeɪʃᵊn/ *noun* [C] a shorter form of a word or phrase, especially used in writing *A doctor is often called a 'GP', an abbreviation for 'general practitioner'.*

abdicate /ˈæbdɪkeɪt/ *verb* **1** [I] If a king or queen abdicates, they choose to stop being king or queen. **2 abdicate responsibility** *formal* to decide not to be responsible for something any more ● **abdication** /ˌæbdɪˈkeɪʃᵊn/ *noun* [C, U]

abdomen /ˈæbdəmən/ *noun* [C] *formal* the lower part of a person or animal's body, containing the stomach and other organs ● **abdominal** /æbˈdɒmɪnᵊl/ *adjective abdominal pains*

abduct /əbˈdʌkt/ *verb* [T] to take someone away illegally *He was abducted by a terrorist group.* ● **abduction** /əbˈdʌkʃᵊn/ *noun* [C, U]

aberration /ˌæbəˈreɪʃᵊn/ *noun* [C] *formal* a temporary change from what usually happens

abet /əˈbet/ *verb* **abetting**, *past* **abetted** ⊃See **aid**[2] and abet (sb).

abhor /əbˈhɔːr/ *verb* [T] **abhorring**, *past* **abhorred** *formal* to hate something or someone very much ● **abhorrence** /əbˈhɒrᵊns/ *noun* [U] *formal*

abhorrent /əbˈhɒrənt/ *adjective formal* morally very bad *an abhorrent crime*

abide /əˈbaɪd/ *verb* **can't abide sb/sth** to strongly dislike someone or something *I can't abide rudeness.*

abide by sth to obey a rule *Staff who refused to abide by the rules were fired.*

abiding /əˈbaɪdɪŋ/ *adjective* [always before noun] An abiding feeling or memory is one that you have for a long time. *My abiding memory is of him watering his plants in the garden.* ⊃See also: law-abiding.

WORD PARTNERS FOR *ability*

have/**lack/possess** ability ● **innate/remarkable/uncanny** ability

o—**ability** /əˈbɪləti/ *noun* [C, U] the physical or mental skill or qualities that you need to do something *athletic/academic ability* ○ [+ to do sth] *He had the ability to explain things clearly.* ○ *The report questions the technical ability of the staff.* ⊃Opposite **inability** ⊃Compare **disability**.

abject /ˈæbdʒekt/ *adjective* **1 abject misery/pov-erty/terror, etc** when someone is extremely un-happy, poor, afraid, etc **2** showing that you are very ashamed of what you have done *an abject apology*

ablaze /əˈbleɪz/ *adjective* [never before noun] burning strongly

o—**able** /ˈeɪbl/ *adjective* **1 be able to do sth** to have the ability to do something or the possibility of doing something *He'll be able to help you.* ⊃Opposite **be unable** to do sth. **2** clever or good at doing something *She's a very able student.* ● **ably** *adverb Robson, ably assisted by Ander-son, has completely rebuilt the team.*

able-bodied /ˌeɪblˈbɒdid/ *adjective* having all the physical abilities that most people have

abnormal /æbˈnɔːmᵊl/ *adjective* different from what is normal or usual, in a way which is strange or dangerous *abnormal behaviour/weather* ○ *They found abnormal levels of lead* in the water. ● abnormally *adverb* **abnormally high temperatures**

abnormality /ˌæbnɔːˈmælɪti/ *noun* [C, U] something abnormal, usually in the body *a genetic abnormality*

aboard /əˈbɔːd/ *adverb, preposition* on or onto a plane, ship, bus, or train *Welcome aboard flight BA109 to Paris.*

abode /əˈbəʊd/ *noun* [C] *formal* a home

abolish /əˈbɒlɪʃ/ *verb* [T] to officially end something, especially a law or system *National Service was abolished in Britain in 1962.* ● **abolition** /ˌæbəˈlɪʃ°n/ *noun* [U] *the abolition of slavery*

abominable /əˈbɒmɪnəbl/ *adjective* extremely bad *abominable behaviour* ● **abominably** *adverb*

Aboriginal /ˌæbəˈrɪdʒ°n°l/ *adjective* relating or belonging to the original race of people who lived in Australia ● **Aborigine** /ˌæbəˈrɪdʒ°ni/ *noun* [C] an Aboriginal person

abort /əˈbɔːt/ *verb* [T] **1** to stop a process before it has finished *The take-off was aborted due to bad weather.* **2** to end a pregnancy that is not wanted using a medical operation

abortion /əˈbɔːʃ°n/ *noun* [C, U] a medical operation to end a pregnancy when the baby is still too small to live *She had an abortion*

abortive /əˈbɔːtɪv/ *adjective* [always before noun] An abortive attempt or plan fails before it is complete.

abound /əˈbaʊnd/ *verb* [I] *formal* to exist in large numbers *Rumours abound about a possible change of leadership.*

o–about¹ /əˈbaʊt/ *preposition* **1** SUBJECT relating to a particular subject or person *a book about the Spanish Civil War* ○ *What was she talking about?* **2** DIRECTION *UK* (*US* around) to or in different parts of a place, often without purpose or order *We heard someone moving about outside.* **3** **what/how about ...? a** SUGGESTION used to make a suggestion *How about France for a holiday?* **b** OPINION used to ask for someone's opinion on a particular subject *What about Ann - is she nice?*

o–about² /əˈbaʊt/ *adverb* **1** APPROXIMATELY used before a number or amount to mean approximately *It happened about two months ago.* **2** DIRECTION *UK* (*US* around) to or in different parts of a place, often without purpose or order *She's always leaving her clothes lying about.* **3** NEAR *UK informal* (*US* around) If someone or something is about, they are near to the place where you are now. *Is Kate about?* **4 be about to do sth** to be going to do something very soon *I stopped her just as she was about to leave.*

o–above¹ /əˈbʌv/ *adverb, preposition* **1** HIGHER POSITION in or to a higher position than something else *There's a mirror above the washbasin.* ○ *I could hear music coming from the room above.* **2** MORE more than an amount or level *It says on the box it's for children aged three and above.* ○ *Rates of pay are above average.* **3** RANK in a more important or advanced position than someone else *Sally's a grade above me.* **4** TOO IMPORTANT too good or important for something *No one is above suspicion in this matter.* **5 above all** most importantly *Above*

uh, I'd like to thank everyone.

above² /əˈbʌv/ *adjective, adverb* higher on the same page *the above diagram* ○ *the address shown above*

a,bove 'board *adjective* [never before noun] honest and legal *We hired a lawyer to make sure the agreement was all above board.*

abrasive /əˈbreɪsɪv/ *adjective* **1** An abrasive substance is rough and can be used for rubbing surfaces, to make them clean or smooth. **2** speaking or behaving in a rude and unpleasant way *an abrasive manner*

abreast /əˈbrest/ *adverb* **1 keep (sb) abreast of sth** to make sure that you or someone else knows about the most recent changes in a subject or situation *I'll keep you abreast of any developments.* **2 two/three/four, etc abreast** If people who are moving are two/three, etc abreast, that number of people are next to each other, side by side. *They were cycling four abreast, completely blocking the road.*

abridged /əˈbrɪdʒd/ *adjective* An abridged book or other piece of writing has been made shorter. ⊃Opposite **unabridged**. ● **abridge** /əˈbrɪdʒ/ *verb* [T]

┌─────────────────────────────────────┐
│ ⊞ WORD PARTNERS FOR **abroad** │
└─────────────────────────────────────┘

go/live/travel/work abroad ● **a holiday/ trip** abroad

o–abroad /əˈbrɔːd/ *adverb* in or to a foreign country *He goes abroad a lot with his job.*

abrupt /əˈbrʌpt/ *adjective* **1** sudden and not expected *Our conversation came to an abrupt end.* **2** dealing with people in a quick way that is unfriendly or rude *She has a rather abrupt manner.* ● **abruptly** *adverb*

abscess /ˈæbses/ *noun* [C] a painful, swollen area on the body which contains a yellow liquid

abscond /əbˈskɒnd/ *verb* [I] *formal* to leave somewhere suddenly without permission because you want to escape, or because you have stolen something

┌─────────────────────────────────────┐
│ ⊞ WORD PARTNERS FOR **absence** │
└─────────────────────────────────────┘

a **lengthy/long/prolonged** absence ● an absence **from** sth ● **during/in** sb's absence

absence /ˈæbs°ns/ *noun* **1** [C, U] a time when you are not in a particular place *Lisa will be acting as manager in Phil's absence* (= while Phil is not here). ○ *A large number of absences from work are caused by back problems.* **2** [U] when something does not exist *In the absence of any proof, it is impossible to accuse her.*

absent /ˈæbs°nt/ *adjective* not in the place where you are expected to be, especially at school or work *He has been absent from school all week.*

absentee /ˌæbs°nˈtiː/ *noun* [C] someone who is not in a place where they should be ● **absenteeism** *noun* [U] when someone is often absent from work or school

absently /ˈæbs°ntli/ *adverb* without thinking about what you are doing *He stared absently at the television screen.*

| ɑː arm | ɜː her | iː see | ɔː saw | uː too | aɪ my | aʊ how | eə hair | eɪ day | əʊ no | ɪə near | ɔɪ boy | ʊə poor | aɪə fire | aʊə sour |

absent-minded /ˌæbsᵊnt'maɪndɪd/ adjective often forgetting things • **absent-mindedly** adverb • **absent-mindedness** noun [U]

absolute /'æbsəluːt/ adjective [always before noun] **1** complete absolute power/control ○ The party was an absolute disaster. **2** definite There was no **absolute proof** of fraud.

o⊶**absolutely** /ˌæbsə'luːtli/ adverb **1** completely The food was absolutely delicious. ○ There's absolutely nothing (= nothing at all) left for us to do here. **2** **Absolutely.** used to strongly agree with someone "Do you think it helped his career?" "Absolutely." **3** **Absolutely not.** used to strongly disagree with someone or to agree with something negative "Are you suggesting that we should just ignore the problem?" "No, absolutely not."

absolve /əb'zɒlv/ verb [T] formal to formally say that someone is not guilty of something, or to forgive someone

absorb /əb'zɔːb/ verb [T] **1** LIQUID If a substance absorbs a liquid, it takes it in through its surface and holds it. The fabric absorbs all the moisture, keeping your skin dry. **2** **be absorbed in sth** to give all your attention to something that you are doing Simon was so absorbed in his computer game, he didn't notice me come in. **3** REMEMBER to understand and remember facts that you read or hear It's hard to absorb so much information. **4** BECOME PART OF If something is absorbed into something else, it becomes part of it. The drug is quickly absorbed into the bloodstream.

absorbent /əb'zɔːbənt/ adjective An absorbent substance can take liquids in through its surface and hold them.

absorbing /əb'zɔːbɪŋ/ adjective very interesting an absorbing book/game

abstain /əb'steɪn/ verb [I] **1** formal to not do something that you enjoy because it is bad or unhealthy The doctor suggested that he abstain from alcohol. **2** to choose not to vote for or against something 63 members voted in favour, 39 opposed and 5 abstained. • **abstention** /əb'stenʃᵊn/ noun [C, U]

abstinence /'æbstɪnəns/ noun [U] formal when you do not do something that you enjoy because it is bad or unhealthy

abstract /'æbstrækt/ adjective **1** relating to ideas and not real things an abstract concept **2** Abstract art involves shapes and colours and not images of real things or people.

absurd /əb'zɜːd/ adjective very silly an absurd situation/suggestion • **absurdity** noun [C, U] • **absurdly** adverb

abundance /ə'bʌndəns/ noun [U, no plural] formal a lot of something an abundance of flowers ○ There was food in abundance (= a lot of food).

abundant /ə'bʌndənt/ adjective existing in large quantities an **abundant supply** of food • **abundantly** adverb

abuse[1] /ə'bjuːs/ noun **1** WRONG USE [C, U] when something is used for the wrong purpose in a way that is harmful or morally wrong drug/ alcohol abuse ○ abuse of public money **2** VIOLENCE [U] violent, cruel treatment of someone

child abuse ○ sexual abuse **3** LANGUAGE [U] rude and offensive words said to another person Rival fans shouted abuse at each other.

abuse[2] /ə'bjuːz/ verb [T] **1** VIOLENCE to treat someone cruelly and violently He was physically abused by his alcoholic father. **2** WRONG USE to use something for the wrong purpose in a way that is harmful or morally wrong to abuse alcohol **3** LANGUAGE to say rude and offensive words to someone The crowd started abusing him. • **abuser** noun [C]

abusive /ə'bjuːsɪv/ adjective saying rude and offensive words to someone an abusive phone call

abysmal /ə'bɪzmᵊl/ adjective very bad, especially of bad quality the team's abysmal performance last season • **abysmally** adverb

abyss /ə'bɪs/ noun [C] **1** a very bad situation which will not improve [usually singular] The country is sinking into an abyss of violence and bloodshed. **2** literary a very deep hole

academia /ˌækə'diːmiə/ noun [U] the people and organizations, especially universities, involved in studying

academic[1] /ˌækə'demɪk/ adjective **1** EDUCATION related to education, schools, universities, etc academic ability ○ It's the start of the academic year **2** SUBJECTS related to subjects which involve thinking and studying and not technical or practical skills academic subjects **3** CLEVER clever and good at studying **4** NOT REAL If what someone says is academic, it has no purpose because it relates to a situation that does not exist. The whole discussion is academic since management won't even listen to us. • **academically** adverb

academic[2] /ˌækə'demɪk/ noun [C] someone who teaches at a university or college, or is paid to study there

academy /ə'kædəmi/ noun [C] **1** a college which teaches people the skills needed for a particular job a military academy **2** an organization whose purpose is to encourage and develop an art, science, language, etc the Royal Academy of Music

accelerate /ək'seləreɪt/ verb **1** [I] to start to drive faster **2** [I, T] to start to happen more quickly, or to make something start to happen more quickly Inflation is likely to accelerate this year. • **acceleration** /ək,selə'reɪʃᵊn/ noun [U]

accelerator /ək'seləreɪtəʳ/ (also US **gas pedal**) noun [C] the part of a car which you push with your foot to make it go faster ⊃See colour picture Car on page Centre 7.

🧩 **WORD PARTNERS FOR accent**

have/speak with a [local/northern/strong, etc] accent • **lose** your accent • a **heavy/ strong/thick** accent

---

accent /'æksᵊnt/ noun [C] **1** PRONUNCIATION the way in which someone pronounces words, influenced by the country or area they come from, or their social class an American accent ○ a French accent **2** WRITTEN MARK a mark above a letter to show you how to pronounce it, for example (á) and (é) **3** WORD EMPHASIS the word or part of a word that you emphasize when you are speaking *In the word 'impossible' the **accent** is on the second syllable.* **4 the accent on sth** particular importance or attention that you give to something *a wonderful menu with the accent on fresh fish*

accentuate /ək'sentʃueɪt/ *verb* [T] to emphasize something so that people notice it *make-up to accentuate the eyes*

๐ᕀ**accept** /ək'sept/ *verb* **1** AGREE [I, T] to agree to take something that is offered to you *to accept an invitation/offer* ○ *He won't accept advice from anyone.* **2** ADMIT [T] to admit that something is true, often something unpleasant [+ (that)] *He refuses to accept that he's made a mistake.* **3** ALLOW TO JOIN [T] to allow someone to join an organization or become part of a group *She's been accepted by two universities.* **4 accept responsibility/blame** to admit that you caused something bad that happened *The company has now accepted responsibility for the accident.* **5** UNDERSTAND [T] to understand that you cannot change a very sad or unpleasant situation *The hardest part is accepting the fact that you'll never see that person again.*

COMMON LEARNER ERROR

accept or agree?

When you **accept** an invitation, job, or offer, you say yes to something which is offered. **Accept** is never followed by another verb.

They offered me the job and I've accepted it.

~~They offered me the job and I've accepted to take it.~~

When you **agree** to do something, you say that you will do something which someone asks you to do.

They offered me the job and I agreed to take it.

acceptable /ək'septəbl/ *adjective* **1** good enough *work of an acceptable standard* ○ *We still hope to find a solution which is acceptable to both sides.* **2** allowed or approved of *Smoking is less and less socially acceptable.* ⊃Opposite **unacceptable.** ● **acceptability** /ək,septə'bɪləti/ *noun* [U]

WORD PARTNERS FOR **acceptance**

sb/sth **gains/wins** acceptance ● **general/ growing / grudging / public** acceptance ● acceptance **of** sth

acceptance /ək'septəns/ *noun* [C, U] when you accept something *his **acceptance** of the award* ○ *There is a growing **public acceptance** of alternative medicine.*

accepted /ək'septɪd/ *adjective* agreed or approved by most people *an accepted spelling*

access¹ /'ækses/ *noun* [U] **1** when you have the right or opportunity to use or see something *I don't **have access** to that kind of information.* ○ *Do you have Internet access?* **2** the way in which you can enter a place or get to a place *The only access to the village is by boat.*

access² /'ækses/ *verb* [T] to find or see information, especially using a computer *You can access the files over the Internet.*

accessible /ək'sesəbl/ *adjective* **1** easy to find

or reach *Information such as this is freely **accessible** to the public.* ○ *The hotel is in a quiet but easily accessible part of the resort.* ⊃Opposite **inaccessible.** **2** easy to understand *They are attempting to make opera **accessible** to a wider audience.* ● **accessibility** /ək,sesə'bɪləti/ *noun* [U]

accessory /ək'ses³ri/ *noun* [C] **1** something extra which is not necessary but is attractive or useful [usually plural] *bathroom accessories* ○ *computer accessories* **2** *formal* someone who helps a criminal to commit a crime *an accessory to murder*

'access pro,vider *noun* [C] a company that makes you able to use the Internet, so that you can use email and see or show documents

WORD PARTNERS FOR **accident**

have/be involved in an accident ● an accident **happens/occurs** ● a **fatal/serious/ tragic** accident ● [killed, paralyzed, etc] **in** an accident ● a **car/traffic** accident

๐ᕀ**accident** /'æksɪd³nt/ *noun* [C] **1** something bad which happens that is not intended and which causes injury or damage *a car/traffic accident* ○ *She **had an accident** in the kitchen.* ○ *I didn't mean to spill his drink. It was an accident.* **2 by accident** without being intended *I deleted the wrong file by accident.*

accidental /,æksɪ'dent³l/ *adjective* not intended *accidental damage* ● **accidentally** *adverb She accidentally knocked over a glass of red wine.*

accident-prone /'æksɪd³nt,prəʊn/ *adjective* Someone who is accident-prone often has accidents.

acclaim /ə'kleɪm/ *noun* [U] praise from a lot of people *international/critical acclaim*

acclaimed /ə'kleɪmd/ *adjective* praised by a lot of people *the acclaimed singer and songwriter*

acclimatize (*also* UK **-ise**) /ə'klaɪmətaɪz/ *verb* [I, T] to start to feel happy with the weather, the way of life, etc in a new place, or to make someone do this ● **acclimatization** /ə,klaɪmətaɪ'zeɪʃ³n/ *noun* [U]

accolade /'ækəleɪd/ *noun* [C] *formal* a prize or praise given to someone because they are very good at something

accommodate /ə'kɒmədeɪt/ *verb* [T] **1** HAVE SPACE FOR to have enough space somewhere for a number of things or people *We need more roads to accommodate the increase in traffic.* **2** HELP to do what someone wants, often by providing them with something *He requires special equipment and, where possible, we've accommodated those needs.* **3** GIVE A HOME to provide someone with a place to live or stay *The athletes will be accommodated in a special Olympic village.*

accommodating /ə'kɒmədeɪtɪŋ/ *adjective* willing to change your plans in order to help people

accommodation /ə,kɒmə'deɪʃ³n/ *noun* [U] (*also* US **accommodations** [plural]) a place where you live or stay *rented accommodation* ○ *The price includes travel and accommodation.*

accompaniment /ə'kʌmp³nimənt/ *noun* **1** [C]

| ɑː **arm** | ɜː **her** | iː **see** | ɔː **saw** | uː **too** | aɪ **my** | aʊ **how** | eə **hair** | eɪ **day** | əʊ **no** | ɪə **near** | ɔɪ **boy** | ʊə **poor** | aɪə **fire** | aʊə **sour** |

formal something that is nice to eat or drink with a particular food or drink *salmon with an accompaniment of green salad* **2** [C, U] music that is played with the main instrument or with a singing voice *a song with piano accompaniment*

accompany /ə'kʌmpəni/ *verb* [T] **1** GO WITH *formal* to go somewhere with someone *We accompanied her back to her hotel.* **2** HAPPEN TOGETHER to happen or exist at the same time as something else *The teachers' book is accompanied by a video cassette.* **3** MUSIC to play a musical instrument with someone else who is playing or singing

accomplice /ə'kʌmplɪs/ *noun* [C] someone who helps a criminal to commit a crime

accomplish /ə'kʌmplɪʃ/ *verb* [T] to succeed in doing something good *I feel as if I've accomplished nothing all day.*

accomplished /ə'kʌmplɪʃt/ *adjective* having a lot of skill in art, music, writing, etc *an accomplished musician/painter*

accomplishment /ə'kʌmplɪʃmənt/ *noun* **1** [U] when you succeed in doing something good *Finishing the course gave me a great sense of accomplishment.* **2** [C] *formal* a skill in art, music, writing, etc

accord¹ /ə'kɔːd/ *noun* **1 of your own accord** If you do something of your own accord, you choose to do it and no one else forces you. *Luckily, she left of her own accord.* **2** [C] an official agreement, especially between countries *a peace/trade accord*

accord² /ə'kɔːd/ *verb* [T] *formal* to treat someone specially, usually by showing respect *the respect accorded to doctors*

accordance /ə'kɔːdəns/ *noun formal* **in accordance with sth** agreeing with a rule, law, or wish *Both companies have insisted that they were acting in accordance with the law.*

accordingly /ə'kɔːdɪŋli/ *adverb* in a way that is suitable *We'll wait until we hear the decision and act accordingly.*

o‑ **according to** /ə'kɔːdɪŋtuː/ *preposition* **1** as said by someone or shown by something *According to our records, she was absent last Friday.* **2** based on a particular system or plan *Children are allocated to schools according to the area in which they live.*

accordion /ə'kɔːdiən/ *noun* [C] a musical instrument with a folding centre part, and keyboards at both ends which you play by pushing the two ends together

accost /ə'kɒst/ *verb* [T] If someone you do not know accosts you, they move towards you and start talking to you in an unfriendly way.

WORD PARTNERS FOR *account*

1 give an account of sth • a brief/detailed/full account • an eye-witness/first-hand account • an account of sth

2 close/open an account • have an account with [name of bank] • a joint/personal/savings account • an account holder/number

---

account¹ /ə'kaʊnt/ *noun* [C] **1** REPORT a written

or spoken description of something that has happened *They gave conflicting accounts of the events.* ○ *The documents provide a detailed account of the town's early history.* **2** BANK (*also* **bank account**) an arrangement with a bank to keep your money there and to let you take it out when you need to *I paid the money into my account.* **3** SHOP an agreement with a shop or company that allows you to buy things and pay for them later **4 take sth into account; take account of sth** to consider something when judging a situation *You have to take into account the fact that he is less experienced when judging his performance.* **5 on account of sth** *formal* because of something *He doesn't drink alcohol on account of his health.* **6 by all accounts** as said by a lot of people *The party was, by all accounts, a great success.* **7 on my account** just for or because of me *Please don't change your plans on my account.* **8 on no account; not on any account** *UK* not for any reason or in any situation *On no account must these records be changed.* ⊃See also: checking account, current account, deposit account.

account² /ə'kaʊnt/ *verb*
account for sth **1** to be part of a total number of something *Oil accounts for 40% of Norway's exports.* **2** to be the reason for something, or to explain the reason for something *She was asked to account for the missing money.* ○ *He'd had an argument with Caroline this morning, which accounts for his bad mood.*

accountable /ə'kaʊntəbl/ *adjective* [never before noun] having to be responsible for what you do and able to explain your actions *Hospitals must be held accountable for their mistakes.* ○ *Politicians should be accountable to the public that elects them.* ⊃Opposite unaccountable. ● accountability /ə,kaʊntə'bɪləti/ *noun* [U]

accountancy /ə'kaʊntənsi/ *UK* (*US* **accounting**) *noun* [U] the job of being an accountant

accountant /ə'kaʊntənt/ *noun* [C] someone whose job is to keep or examine the financial records of a company or organization

accounts /ə'kaʊnts/ *noun* [plural] an official record of all the money a company or organization has received or paid

accreditation /ə,kredɪ'teɪʃ⁰n/ *noun* [U] official approval of an organization ● accredited /ə'kredɪtɪd/ *adjective* officially approved

accumulate /ə'kjuːmjəleɪt/ *verb* [I, T] to increase in amount over a period of time, or to make something increase over a period of time *The chemicals accumulate in your body.* ○ *to accumulate debts/wealth* ● accumulation /ə,kjuːmjə'leɪʃ⁰n/ *noun* [U]

accuracy /'ækjərəsi/ *noun* [U] how correct or exact something is *The new system should help to improve the accuracy of weather forecasts.*

accurate /'ækjərət/ *adjective* correct or exact *accurate information/measurements* ○ *She was able to give police a fairly accurate description of the man.* ○ *How accurate do you think these estimates are?* ⊃Opposite inaccurate. ● accurately *adverb*

A

WORD PARTNERS FOR ***accusation***

make an accusation • **deny/dismiss/face/reject** an accusation • a **false/wild** accusation • accusations **of** sth • an accusation **against** sb • an accusation **by/from** sb

accusation /ˌækjʊˈzeɪʃᵊn/ *noun* [C] when you say that someone has done something bad *He **made** a number of **accusations against** his former colleagues.*

o⊸**accuse** /əˈkjuːz/ *verb* [T] to say that someone has done something bad *He was falsely **accused of** murder.* ○ [+ of + doing sth] *She accused Andrew of lying to her.* • **accuser** *noun* [C]

the accused /əˈkjuːzd/ *noun formal* the person or people who are accused of a crime in a court of law

accusing /əˈkjuːzɪŋ/ *adjective* showing that you think someone is responsible for something bad *Why are you giving me that **accusing** look?* • **accusingly** *adverb She looked at me accusingly.*

accustom /əˈkʌstəm/ *verb*

accustom yourself to sth/doing sth to experience something often enough for it to seem normal to you

accustomed /əˈkʌstəmd/ *adjective* **accustomed to sth/doing sth** If you are accustomed to something, you have experienced it often enough for it to seem normal to you. *I've worked nights for years now so I've **grown accustomed to it**.*

ace[1] /eɪs/ *noun* [C] **1** a playing card with one symbol on it, that has the highest or lowest value in many games **2** when the first shot by a tennis player is too good for the other player to hit back

ace[2] /eɪs/ *adjective informal* very good

ache[1] /eɪk/ *noun* [C] a feeling of pain over an area of your body which continues for a long time *There's a **dull ache** in my right shoulder.* ➲See also: **stomach ache**.

ache[2] /eɪk/ *verb* [I] If a part of your body aches, it is painful. *My legs ache after all that exercise.*

o⊸**achieve** /əˈtʃiːv/ *verb* [T] to succeed in doing something good, usually by working hard *I've achieved my ambition* ○ *I've been working all day but I feel I've achieved nothing.* • **achievable** *adjective* possible to achieve ***achievable goals*** • **achiever** *noun* [C] *He's from a family of **high achievers*** (= very successful people).

WORD PARTNERS FOR ***achievement***

a **great/notable/outstanding/remarkable** achievement • sb's **crowning** achievement • **a sense of** achievement

achievement /əˈtʃiːvmənt/ *noun* **1** [C] something good that you achieve *This film is his **greatest achievement** to date.* **2** [U] when you succeed in doing something good, usually by working hard *You get such **a sense of achievement** when you finish the course.*

acid[1] /ˈæsɪd/ *noun* [C, U] one of several liquid substances which react with other substances, often burning or dissolving them *hydrochloric acid* • **acidity** /əˈsɪdəti/ *noun* [U]

acid[2] /ˈæsɪd/ *adjective* **1** (*also* **acidic** /əˈsɪdɪk/) containing acid, or having similar qualities to an acid *acid soil* ○ *an acid smell/taste* **2** **acid remark/comment, etc** an unkind remark that criticizes someone

ˌ**acid** ˈ**rain** *noun* [U] rain that contains chemicals from pollution and damages plants, etc

WORD PARTNERS FOR ***acknowledge***

be **generally/widely/universally** acknowledged • acknowledge sb/sth **as/to be** sth

acknowledge /əkˈnɒlɪdʒ/ *verb* [T] **1** ACCEPT to accept that something is true or exists **[+ (that)]** *He acknowledged that there was a problem.* **2** LETTER to tell someone, usually in a letter, that you have received something they sent you *Send a letter acknowledging receipt of his application.* **3** SAY HELLO to let someone know that you have seen them, usually by saying hello *She didn't even acknowledge my presence.*

acknowledgement (*also* **acknowledgment**) /əkˈnɒlɪdʒmənt/ *noun* **1** ACCEPT [C, U] when you accept that something is true or exists *There was no acknowledgement of the extent of the problem.* **2** LETTER [C] a letter telling you that someone has received something that you sent them **3** BOOK [C] something written at the front of a book by the author to thank people who have helped them [usually plural] *His name appears in the acknowledgements.*

acne /ˈækni/ *noun* [U] a skin problem that young people often have that causes spots on the face

acorn /ˈeɪkɔːn/ *noun* [C] an oval nut which grows on oak trees

acorn

acoustic /əˈkuːstɪk/ *adjective* **1** [always before noun] An acoustic musical instrument does not use electricity. *an **acoustic guitar*** **2** relating to sound and hearing

acoustics /əˈkuːstɪks/ *noun* [plural] the way in which the shape of a room affects the quality of sound *The acoustics of the hall were terrible.*

acquaintance /əˈkweɪntᵊns/ *noun* [C] someone who you know but do not know well *He's just a **business acquaintance**.*

acquainted /əˈkweɪntɪd/ *adjective* [never before noun] *formal* **1** If you are acquainted with someone, you have met them but do not know them well. *We're already acquainted - we met at Elaine's party.* **2** **be acquainted with sth** to know about something *I'm afraid I'm not yet acquainted with the system.*

acquiesce /ˌækwiˈes/ *verb* [I] *formal* to agree to something, often when you do not want to • **acquiescence** *noun* [U] *formal*

acquire /əˈkwaɪəʳ/ *verb* [T] **1** to get something *I managed to acquire a copy of the report.* **2** to learn something *to **acquire knowledge/skills***

acquisition /ˌækwɪˈzɪʃᵊn/ *noun* **1** [U] the process of learning or getting something *children's acquisition of language* **2** [C] something that you get, usually by buying it *And the hat - is that a **recent acquisition**?*

acquit /əˈkwɪt/ *verb* [T] **acquitting**, *past* **acquitted** If someone is acquitted of a crime, a court of law decides that they are not guilty. [often passive] Both men were **acquitted of murder.**

acquittal /əˈkwɪtəl/ noun [C, U] when a court of law decides that someone is not guilty of a crime

acre /ˈeɪkəʳ/ noun [C] a unit for measuring area, equal to 4047 square metres

acrid /ˈækrɪd/ adjective An acrid smell is unpleasant and causes a burning feeling in your throat.

acrimonious /ˌækrɪˈməʊniəs/ adjective involving a lot of anger, disagreement, and bad feelings **an acrimonious divorce** ● acrimony /ˈækrɪməni/ noun [U] angry, bad feelings between people

acrobat /ˈækrəbæt/ noun [C] someone who entertains people by performing difficult physical acts, such as walking on a wire high above the ground ● acrobatic /ˌækrəˈbætɪk/ adjective ● acrobatics /ˌækrəˈbætɪks/ noun [plural] the actions of an acrobat

acronym /ˈækrəʊnɪm/ noun [C] a word made from the first letters of other words AIDS is the acronym for 'acquired immune deficiency syndrome'.

o⤳**across** /əˈkrɒs/ adverb, preposition **1** SIDES from one side of something to the other I was walking across the road. ○ They've built a new bridge across the river. **2** OPPOSITE on the opposite side of There's a library just across the street. **3** MEASURE used after a measurement to show how wide something is The window measures two metres across.

acrylic /əˈkrɪlɪk/ adjective made of a material produced by a chemical process acrylic paint ○ an acrylic sweater

o⤳**act¹** /ækt/ verb **1** BEHAVE [I] to behave in a particular way to act responsibly ○ Jeff's been acting strangely recently. ○ Stop **acting like a child!** **2** DO SOMETHING [I] to do something, especially in order to solve a problem We have to act now to stop the spread of this disease. **3** PERFORM [I, T] to perform in a play or film He's acted in a number of successful Hollywood films.

act as sth **1** to do a particular job, especially one you do not normally do He was asked to act as an adviser on the project. **2** to have a particular effect Caffeine acts as a stimulant.

act sth out to perform the actions and words of a situation or story The children acted out a verse from their favourite poem.

act up If someone, especially a child, acts up, they behave badly.

WORD PARTNERS FOR **act**

an act of sth ● **commit** an act ● a **barbaric/cowardly** act ● a **criminal/terrorist** act

act² /ækt/ noun **1** DO [C] something that someone does **an act of terrorism/kindness** **2** LAW [C] a law made by a government an act of Congress/Parliament **3** THEATRE [C] one of the parts a play is divided into Her character doesn't appear until Act 2. **4** PERFORMERS [C] one or several performers who perform for a short while in a show a comedy **double act** **5** FALSE BEHAVIOUR [no plural] behaviour which hides your

real feelings or intentions Was she really upset or was that just an act? **6 in the act (of doing sth)** doing something wrong I caught him in the act of opening one of my letters. **7 get your act together** informal to organize your activities so that you can make progress **8 get in on the act** informal to become involved in something successful that someone else has started

acting¹ /ˈæktɪŋ/ adjective **acting chairman/director, etc** someone who does a job for a short time while the person who usually does it is not there

acting² /ˈæktɪŋ/ noun [U] the job of performing in plays and films He's trying to get into acting.

o⤳**action** /ˈækʃən/ noun **1** DO [C, U] something that you do She has to accept the consequences of her actions. ○ We must **take action** (= do something) before the problem gets worse. ○ So what do you think is the best **course of action** (= way of dealing with the situation)? ○ It was the first time I'd seen firemen **in action** (= doing a particular activity). **2** ACTIVITY [U] things which are happening, especially exciting or important things He likes films with a lot of action. ⊃Opposite **inaction**. **3 out of action** damaged or hurt and not able to operate or play sports They've got three players **out of action**. **4** legal action a legal process in a court They are planning to **take legal action against** the company. **5** FIGHTING [U] fighting in a war He was killed **in action** (= while fighting). **6** PROCESS [no plural] a movement or natural process The rocks are smoothed by the action of water. ⊃See also: **industrial action**, be all talk² (and no action).

action-packed /ˈækʃənˌpækt/ adjective An action-packed film or story has a lot of exciting events.

action 'replay UK (US **instant replay**) noun [C] when part of a film of a sporting event is shown again, often more slowly

activate /ˈæktɪveɪt/ verb [T] to make something start working The alarm can be activated by a laser beam.

o⤳**active** /ˈæktɪv/ adjective **1** INVOLVED very involved in an organization or planned activity He played an **active role** in the campaign. **2** BUSY doing a lot of things, or moving around a lot Even at the age of 80 she's still very active. **3** GRAMMAR An active verb or sentence is one in which the subject of the verb is the person or thing doing the action. For example 'Andy drove the car.' is an active sentence. ⊃Compare **passive**. **4** VOLCANO An active volcano could throw out rocks, fire, etc at any time.

actively /ˈæktɪvli/ adverb in a way that causes something to happen He **actively** encourages me to spend money.

activist /ˈæktɪvɪst/ noun [C] someone who tries to cause social or political change a **political activist** ● activism noun [U]

WORD PARTNERS FOR **activity**

do/perform an activity ● **frantic/strenuous** activity ● **outdoor/leisure** activity ● a **flurry of** activity

o⤳**activity** /ækˈtɪvəti/ noun **1** EVENT [C] something

which you do for enjoyment, especially an organized event *The centre offers a range of activities, such as cycling, swimming, and tennis.* **2** [WORK] [C, U] the work of a group or organization to achieve an aim *criminal/terrorist activities* **3** [MOVEMENT] [U] when a lot of things are happening or people are moving around *There was a sudden flurry of activity* (= short period of activity) *at the back of the hall.* ⊃Opposite **inactivity**.

o-**actor** /ˈæktəʳ/ *noun* [C] someone, especially a man, whose job is to perform in plays and films *What was the name of the actor who played the father?*

o-**actress** /ˈæktrəs/ *noun* [C] a woman whose job is to perform in plays and films

o-**actual** /ˈæktʃuəl/ *adjective* **1** real, not guessed or imagined *We were expecting about fifty people, though the actual number was a lot higher.* **2 in actual fact** *UK* really *It was due to start at ten, but in actual fact, it didn't begin until nearly eleven.*

COMMON LEARNER ERROR

actual or **current**?

Actual means 'real'. It does not mean 'happening now'.

His friends call him Jo-Jo, but his actual name is John.

Use **current** to talk about things which are happening or which exist now.

She started her current job two years ago.

o-**actually** /ˈæktʃuəli/ *adverb* **1** [TRUTH] used when you are saying what is the truth of a situation *He didn't actually say anything important.* ○ *I don't actually like seafood.* **2** [SURPRISE] used when you are saying something surprising *She sounds English but she's actually Spanish.* **3** [MISTAKE] *mainly UK* used when you are disagreeing with someone or saying no to a request *"You didn't tell me." "Actually, I did."* ○ *"Do you mind if I smoke?" "Actually, I'd rather you didn't."*

acumen /ˈækjəmən/ *noun* [U] the ability to make good judgments and decisions *business/political acumen*

acupuncture /ˈækjʊpʌŋktʃəʳ/ *noun* [U] a way of treating pain or illness by putting thin needles into different parts of the body

acute /əˈkjuːt/ *adjective* **1** [EXTREME] An acute problem or negative feeling is extreme. *There's an acute shortage of medical staff.* ○ *acute pain* ○ *acute anxiety* **2** [ANGLE] An acute angle is less than 90 degrees. **3** [QUICK TO NOTICE] quick to notice or understand things *an acute mind* ○ *Dogs rely on their acute sense of smell.*

acutely /əˈkjuːtli/ *adverb* very strongly *I was acutely aware of how Alex felt about the situation.*

AD /ˌeɪˈdiː/ *abbreviation for* Anno Domini: used to show that a particular year came after the birth of Christ *1066 AD*

ad /æd/ *noun* [C] an advertisement ⊃See also: **classified ad**.

adamant /ˈædəmənt/ *adjective* very sure of

what you think and not willing to change your opinion [+ (that)] *They are adamant that they have not broken any rules.* • **adamantly** *adverb*

Adam's apple /ˌædəmzˈæpl/ *noun* [C] the lump in a man's throat that you can see moving up and down when he speaks or swallows

adapt /əˈdæpt/ *verb* **1** [CHANGE BEHAVIOUR] [I] to change your behaviour so that it is suitable for a new situation *It takes time to adapt to a new working environment.* **2** [CHANGE SOMETHING] [T] to change something so that it is suitable for a different use or situation *Courses have to be adapted for different markets.* **3** [BOOK] [T] to change a book or play so that it can be made into a film or television programme *Both novels have been adapted for television.*

adaptable /əˈdæptəbl/ *adjective* able to change to suit different situations or uses • **adaptability** /əˌdæptəˈbɪləti/ *noun* [U]

adaptation /ˌædæpˈteɪʃⁿn/ *noun* **1** [C] a film, television programme, or play which has been made from a book **2** [C, U] the process or act of changing to suit a new situation *Evolution occurs as a result of adaptation to new environments.*

adapter (*also* **adaptor**) /əˈdæptəʳ/ *noun* [C] something that is used for connecting two or more pieces of electrical equipment to an electrical supply

o-**add** /æd/ *verb* **1** [PUT WITH] [T] to put something with something else *Add the eggs to the cream.* **2** [INCREASE] [I, T] to increase an amount or level *Then there's the service charge which adds another ten percent to the bill.* **3** [SAY MORE] [T] to say another thing [+ that] *She said she liked him but added that he was difficult to work with.* **4** [CALCULATE] [T] to put two or more numbers or amounts together to get a total ⊃See also: **add insult²** to injury.

add (sth) up to put numbers together in order to reach a total *When you add up everything we've spent, it's cost well over £200.*

not add up *informal* If something does not add up, you cannot believe it is true. *She gave me an explanation but somehow it doesn't add up.*

adder /ˈædəʳ/ *noun* [C] a small, poisonous snake

addict /ˈædɪkt/ *noun* [C] **1** someone who cannot stop taking a drug *a heroin/drug addict* **2** *informal* someone who likes something very much and does it or has it very often *a TV/computer game addict*

addicted /əˈdɪktɪd/ *adjective* **1** not able to stop taking a drug *He later became addicted to heroin.* **2** *informal* liking something very much and doing or having it too often *He's addicted to chocolate/football.*

WORD PARTNERS FOR addiction

fight/have/suffer from an addiction • **alcohol/drug/gambling** addiction • addiction **to sth**

addiction /əˈdɪkʃⁿn/ *noun* [C, U] when you cannot stop doing or taking something because you are addicted to it

addictive /əˈdɪktɪv/ *adjective* If something is

addictive, it makes you want more of it so that you become addicted. *Tobacco is highly addictive.*

addition /ə'dɪʃᵊn/ *noun* **1 in addition (to sth)** added to what already exists or happens, or more than you already do or have *In addition to teaching, she works as a nurse in the holidays.* **2** [U] the process of adding numbers or amounts together in order to get a total **3** [C] a new or extra thing which is added to something *Defender Matt Smith is the latest addition to the team.*

additional /ə'dɪʃᵊnᵊl/ *adjective* extra to what already exists *We plan to take on an additional ten employees over the next year.* ● **additionally** *adverb*

additive /'ædɪtɪv/ *noun* [C] a chemical which is added to food in order to make it taste or look better or to keep it fresh

add-on /'ædɒn/ *noun* [C] a piece of equipment that can be connected to a computer to give it an extra use

┌─────────────────────────────────────┐
│ ✂ **WORD PARTNERS FOR** *address*   │
│   │
│ **give** sb your address ● your **business/ home/work** address ● a **change of** address │
└─────────────────────────────────────┘

o╾**address¹** /ə'dres/ ⓤˢ /'ædres/ *noun* [C] **1** ⌈BUILDING DETAILS⌉ the details of where a building is, including the building number, road name, town, etc **2** ⌈ELECTRONIC⌉ a series of letters, signs, or numbers used to send email to someone or to reach a page of information on the Internet *an email/web address* **3** ⌈SPEECH⌉ a formal speech to a group of people ⇒See also: **forwarding address, public address system.**

address² /ə'dres/ *verb* [T] **1** ⌈BUILDING DETAILS⌉ to write a name or address on an envelope or parcel *A parcel arrived addressed to Emma.* **2** ⌈DEAL WITH⌉ to deal with a problem *We have to address the issue/problem before it gets worse.* **3** ⌈SPEAK⌉ *formal* to speak to someone, or to give a speech to an audience *Today she will be addressing a major conference in London.* **4 address sb as sth** *formal* to give someone a particular name or title when you speak or write to them *Do you think I should address him as 'Mr Benson' or 'Albert'?*

a'ddress ˌbook (*US* 'address ˌbook) *noun* [C] **1** a computer document that keeps a list of names and email addresses **2** a book in which you keep a list of names and addresses

adept /'ædept/ *adjective* good at doing something difficult *She's very adept at dealing with the media.*

adequate /'ædɪkwət/ *adjective* **1** enough *I didn't have adequate time to prepare.* **2** good enough, but not very good *The sound quality isn't exceptional but it's adequate for everyday use.* ⇒Opposite **inadequate.** ● **adequately** *adverb Make sure you are adequately equipped for the journey.*

adhere /əd'hɪəʳ/ *verb* [I] *formal* to stick to a surface

adhere to sth to obey a rule or principle *We always adhere strictly to the guidelines.*

adherence /əd'hɪərᵊns/ *noun* [U] *formal* when

someone obeys a set of rules or principles ● **adherent** *noun* [C] *formal* someone who obeys a particular set of rules, principles, etc

adhesive /əd'hiːsɪv/ *noun* [C] a substance used for sticking things together ● **adhesive** *adjective*

ad hoc /ˌæd'hɒk/ *adjective* not regular or planned, but happening only when necessary *We meet on an ad hoc basis.*

adjacent /ə'dʒeɪsᵊnt/ *adjective formal* If two things are adjacent, they are next to each other. *The fire started in an adjacent building.* ○ *They live in a house adjacent to the railway.*

o╾**adjective** /'ædʒɪktɪv/ *noun* [C] a word that describes a noun or pronoun. The words 'big', 'boring', 'purple', and 'obvious' are all adjectives. ● **adjectival** /ˌædʒɪk'taɪvᵊl/ *adjective* containing or used like an adjective *an adjectival phrase*

adjoining /ə'dʒɔɪnɪŋ/ *adjective* next to and joined to something *an adjoining room*

adjourn /ə'dʒɜːn/ *verb* [I, T] *formal* to stop a meeting, especially a legal process, for a period of time or until a later date *The judge adjourned the case until March 31.* ● **adjournment** *noun* [C]

adjudicate /ə'dʒuːdɪkeɪt/ *verb* [I, T] *formal* to make an official judgment or decision about a competition or disagreement *Occasionally, he has to adjudicate on a pensions matter.* ● **adjudication** /ə,dʒuːdɪ'keɪʃᵊn/ *noun* [U] ● **adjudicator** *noun* [C]

adjust /ə'dʒʌst/ *verb* **1** [T] to change something slightly so that it works better, fits better, or is more suitable *You can adjust the heat using this switch here.* ○ *The figures need to be adjusted for inflation.* **2** [I] to change the way you behave or think in order to suit a new situation *They found it hard adjusting to life in a new country.*

adjustable /ə'dʒʌstəbl/ *adjective* able to be changed slightly in order to suit different people or situations *an adjustable seat*

adjustment /ə'dʒʌstmənt/ *noun* [C, U] a slight change that you make to something so that it works better, fits better, or is more suitable *We've made a few adjustments to the schedule.*

ad lib /ˌæd'lɪb/ *verb* [I, T] to speak in public without having planned what to say *I had no script so I had to ad lib.*

admin /'ædmɪn/ *noun* [U] *UK short for* administration

administer /əd'mɪnɪstəʳ/ *verb* [T] **1** to organize or arrange something *The fund is administered by the Economic Development Agency.* **2** *formal* to give medicine or medical help to someone *to administer first aid*

administration /əd,mɪnɪ'streɪʃᵊn/ *noun* **1** [U] the work of organizing and arranging the operation of something, such as a company *The job involves a lot of administration.* **2** [C] *mainly US* the President and politicians who govern a country at a particular time, or a period of government *the Bush administration*

administrative /əd'mɪnɪstrətɪv/ *adjective* relating to the organization and management of

A

something *The work is largely administrative.*

administrator /əd'mɪnɪstreɪtəʳ/ *noun* [C] someone who helps to manage an organization

admirable /'ædməʳrəbl/ *adjective* If something is admirable, you respect or approve of it. *He has many admirable qualities.* • **admirably** *adverb*

admiral /'ædməʳrəl/ *noun* [C] an officer of very high rank in the navy

---
WORD PARTNERS FOR admiration

express/feel/have admiration • **enormous/ great / grudging / profound** admiration • admiration **for** sb
---

admiration /ˌædməˈreɪʃən/ *noun* [U] when you admire someone or something *My admiration for him grows daily.*

admire /əd'maɪəʳ/ *verb* [T] **1** to respect or approve of someone or something *You have to admire him for being so determined.* **2** to look at something or someone, thinking how attractive they are *We stood for a few minutes, admiring the view.* • **admirer** *noun* [C]

admissible /əd'mɪsəbl/ *adjective formal* allowed or acceptable, especially in a court of law *admissible evidence*

admission /əd'mɪʃən/ *noun* **1** MONEY [U] the money that you pay to enter a place *Art exhibition - admission free.* **2** TRUTH [C] when you agree that you did something bad, or that something bad is true *She is, by her own admission, lazy.* ○ *His departure was seen by many as an admission of guilt.* **3** PERMISSION [C, U] when someone is given permission to enter somewhere or to become a member of a club, university, etc *She's applied for admission to law school.*

OTHER WAYS OF SAYING **admit**

If a person admits that something bad is true, the verbs **accept** and **acknowledge** may be used: *I accept that things should have been done differently.* • *He refuses to acknowledge the problem.*

If a person admits that they have done something bad, the verb **confess** is often used: *Rawlinson finally confessed to the murder.*

The phrasal verbs **own up** and (*informal*) **fess up**, and the idiom **come clean** can also be used when a person admits that they have done something bad: *I decided to come clean about the broken vase.* • *Come on, own up - who's eaten the last sandwich?*

☛**admit** /əd'mɪt/ *verb* **admitting**, *past* **admitted 1** [I, T] to agree that you did something bad, or that something bad is true [+ doing sth] *Both men admitted taking illegal drugs.* ○ [+ to + doing sth] *She admitted to stealing the keys.* ○ *I was wrong - I admit it.* ○ [+ (that)] *He finally admitted that he couldn't cope.* **2** [T] to allow someone to enter somewhere, especially to take someone who is ill into hospital *UK to be admitted to hospital/ US to be admitted to the hospital* ○ *It says on the ticket 'admits 2'.*

admittance /əd'mɪtəns/ *noun* [U] permission to enter a place

admittedly /əd'mɪtɪdli/ *adverb* used when you are agreeing that something is true although you do not want to

admonish /əd'mɒnɪʃ/ *verb* [T] *formal* to gently tell someone that they have done something wrong

ado /ə'duː/ *noun* **without further/more ado** without waiting any more

adolescence /ˌædəl'esəns/ *noun* [U] the period of time in someone's life between being a child and an adult

adolescent /ˌædəl'esənt/ *noun* [C] a young person who is between being a child and an adult • **adolescent** *adjective*

adopt /ə'dɒpt/ *verb* **1** [I, T] to legally become the parents of someone else's child **2** [T] to accept or start using something new *We've adopted a new approach.* • **adopted** *adjective an adopted son* • **adoption** /ə'dɒpʃən/ *noun* [C, U]

adorable /ə'dɔːrəbl/ *adjective* very attractive, often because of being small *an adorable child*

adore /ə'dɔːʳ/ *verb* [T] **1** to love someone and have a very good opinion of them *Sarah adored her father.* **2** to like something very much *I adore travelling.* • **adoration** /ˌædə'reɪʃən/ *noun* [U]

adorn /ə'dɔːn/ *verb* [T] *formal* to decorate something *The room was adorned with flowers.* • **adornment** *noun* [C, U]

adrenalin (*also* **adrenaline**) /ə'dren³lɪn/ *noun* [U] a substance that your body produces when you are angry, excited, or frightened which makes your heart beat faster

adrift /ə'drɪft/ *adjective* **1** [never before noun] If a boat is adrift, it floats around in the water and is not tied to anything. **2** **come adrift** to become loose and not joined to anything

adulation /ˌædjʊ'leɪʃən/ *noun* [U] great praise and admiration for someone, often which they do not deserve

☛**adult¹** /'ædʌlt, ə'dʌlt/ *noun* [C] a person or animal that is not now a child

adult² /'ædʌlt, ə'dʌlt/ *adjective* **1** NOT A CHILD having finished growing *an adult male rat* **2** RELATING TO ADULTS [always before noun] for or relating to adults *adult education* ○ *adult life* **3** SEXUAL Adult books, films, etc show naked people or sexual acts and are not for children.

adultery /ə'dʌltəri/ *noun* [U] sex between a married person and someone who is not their husband or wife • **adulterous** *adjective*

adulthood /'ædʌlthʊd/ ⓤ /ə'dʌlthʊd/ *noun* [U] the part of your life when you are an adult

---
WORD PARTNERS FOR advance

medical/scientific/technological advances • a **major** advance • advances **in** sth
---

advance¹ /əd'vɑːns/ *noun* **1 in advance** before a particular time *You need to book your ticket at least 14 days in advance.* **2** PROGRESS [C, U] new discoveries and inventions *technological/ scientific advances* **3** MONEY [C] a payment given to someone before work has been completed, or before the usual time **4** FORWARD [C] a movement forward, especially by an army

advance² /əd'vɑːns/ *verb* **1** [I, T] to develop or

progress, or to make something develop or progress *He moved to New York with hopes of* ***advancing*** *his* ***career****.* **2** [I] to move forward to a new position, especially while fighting *Rebel soldiers* ***advanced on*** *the capital.*

advance[3] /əd'vɑːns/ *adjective* [always before noun] happening or ready before an event ***advance planning/warning*** ○ *an* ***advance booking***

advanced /əd'vɑːnst/ *adjective* **1** having developed or progressed to a late stage ***advanced technology*** ○ *The disease was at an* ***advanced stage.*** **2** at a higher, more difficult level *an advanced English course*

advancement /əd'vɑːnsmənt/ *noun* [C, U] progress ***career advancement*** ○ ***technological advancements***

advances /əd'vɑːnsɪz/ *noun* **sb's advances** things that someone says and does to try to start a sexual relationship with someone

WORD PARTNERS FOR ***advantage***

a **big/enormous/main/major** advantage • an **unfair** advantage • **take** advantage **of** sth • the advantage **of** sth

⊶**advantage** /əd'vɑːntɪdʒ/ *noun* [C, U] **1** something good about a situation that helps you *One of the* ***advantages of*** *living in town is having the shops so near.* **2** something that will help you to succeed *These new routes will give the airline a considerable* ***advantage over*** *its competitors.* ○ *If we could start early it would be* ***to our advantage*** (= help us to succeed). ➲Opposite **disadvantage**. **3 take advantage of sth** to use the good things in a situation *I thought I'd take advantage of the sports facilities while I'm here.* **4 take advantage of sb/sth** to treat someone badly in order to get what you want

advantageous /ˌædvən'teɪdʒəs/ *adjective* helping to make you more successful

advent /'ædvent/ *noun* **1 the advent of sth** the start or arrival of something new *the advent of the Internet* **2 Advent** the religious period before Christmas (= a Christian holiday) in the Christian year

WORD PARTNERS FOR ***adventure***

have an adventure • **be looking for** adventure • **a big/exciting** adventure • an adventure **holiday/playground**

⊶**adventure** /əd'ventʃəʳ/ *noun* [C, U] an exciting and sometimes dangerous experience *It's a film about the adventures of two friends travelling across Africa.* • **adventurer** *noun* [C]

adventurous /əd'ventʃᵊrəs/ *adjective* **1** willing to try new and often difficult things *I'm trying to be more adventurous with my cooking.* **2** exciting and often dangerous *He led an adventurous life.*

⊶**adverb** /'ædvɜːb/ *noun* [C] a word that describes or gives more information about a verb, adjective, phrase, or other adverb. In the sentences 'He ate quickly.' and 'It was extremely good.', 'quickly' and 'extremely' are both adverbs.

adversary /'ædvəsᵊri/ *noun* [C] *formal* someone who you are fighting or competing against

adverse /'ædvɜːs/ *adjective formal* **1 adverse conditions/effects/impact** things that cause problems or danger *adverse weather conditions* ○ *Pollution levels like these will certainly have an adverse effect on health.* **2 adverse comment/publicity/reaction, etc** something negative that is said or written about someone or something • **adversely** *adverb*

adversity /əd'vɜːsəti/ *noun* [C, U] *formal* an extremely difficult situation *She showed a great deal of courage* ***in adversity****.*

advert /'ædvɜːt/ *noun* [C] *UK* an advertisement

advertise /'ædvətaɪz/ *verb* **1** [I, T] to tell people about a product or service, for example in newspapers or on television, in order to persuade them to buy it *Companies are not allowed to advertise cigarettes on television any more.* **2** [I] to put information in a newspaper or on the Internet, asking for someone or something that you need *The university is* ***advertising for*** *administrative staff.* • **advertiser** *noun* [C] a company that advertises things

advertisement /əd'vɜːtɪsmənt/ [US] /ˌædvər'taɪzmənt/ *noun* [C] a picture, short film, song, etc which tries to persuade people to buy a product or service *a newspaper/television advertisement*

⊶**advertising** /'ædvətaɪzɪŋ/ *noun* [U] the business of trying to persuade people to buy products or services ***an advertising agency***

WORD PARTNERS FOR ***advice***

ask for/give/offer/provide/seek advice • **take** sb's advice • **bad/conflicting/expert/good** advice • advice **on/about** sth • **a piece of** advice

⊶**advice** /əd'vaɪs/ *noun* [U] suggestions about what you think someone should do or how they should do something *She* ***asked*** *me* ***for advice*** *about writing a book.* ○ *There's a booklet* ***giving advice on*** *how to set up your own club.* ○ *I* ***took*** *your* ***advice*** *and went home early.* ○ *Can I give you a* ***piece of advice****?*

COMMON LEARNER ERROR

advice

Remember that this word is not countable.

I need some advice.

~~*I need an advice.*~~

To make **advice** singular, say **a piece of advice**.

COMMON LEARNER ERROR

advice or advise?

Be careful not to confuse the noun **advice** with the verb **advise**.

I advise you to see a lawyer.

~~*I advice you to see a lawyer.*~~

advisable /əd'vaɪzəbl/ *adjective* [never before noun] If something is advisable, it will avoid problems if you do it. *It is advisable to book seats at least a week in advance.*

⊶**advise** /əd'vaɪz/ *verb* **1** [I, T] to make a suggestion about what you think someone should do or how they should do something [+ to do sth] *His doctor advised him to take time off work.* ○ *They* **advise** *the government* **on** *environmental matters.* ○ *The government is* **advising** **against** *travelling in the area.* ○ [+ that] *They're advising that children be kept out of the sun altogether.* **2** [T] *formal* to give someone official information about something *They were* **advised of** *their rights.*

adviser (*also* advisor) /əd'vaɪzə^r/ *noun* [C] someone whose job is to give advice about a subject *a financial adviser*

advisory¹ /əd'vaɪz^əri/ *adjective* **advisory committee/panel/board, etc** a group of people whose purpose is to give advice

advisory² /əd'vaɪz^əri/ *noun* [C] *US* an official announcement that contains advice, information, or a warning [usually plural] *weather/ travel advisories*

advocate¹ /'ædvəkeɪt/ *verb* [T] to express support for a particular idea or way of doing things *I certainly wouldn't advocate the use of violence.* ● **advocacy** /'ædvəkəsi/ *noun* [U] when someone advocates something

advocate² /'ædvəkət/ *noun* [C] **1** someone who supports a particular idea or way of doing things *He has always been* **an advocate of** *stricter gun controls.* **2** *UK* a lawyer who defends someone in court

A&E /ˌeɪənd'iː/ *UK* (*US* emergency room) *noun* [C, U] *abbreviation for* Accident and Emergency: the part of a hospital where people go when they are injured or ill and need treatment now

aerial¹ /'eəriəl/ *UK* (*US* antenna) *noun* [C] a piece of metal that is used for receiving television or radio signals ➪See colour picture **Car** on page Centre 7.

aerial² /'eəriəl/ *adjective* [always before noun] in or from the air, especially from an aircraft *an aerial photograph/view*

aerobic /eə'rəʊbɪk/ *adjective* Aerobic exercise is intended to make your heart stronger.

aerobics /eə'rəʊbɪks/ *noun* [U] physical exercises that you do to music, especially in a class *She goes to aerobics* (= to aerobics classes).

aerodynamic /ˌeərəʊdaɪ'næmɪk/ *adjective* having a shape that moves quickly through the air ● **aerodynamics** *noun* [U] the study of how objects move through the air

aeroplane *UK*, **airplane** *US*

aeroplane /'eərəpleɪn/ *UK* (*US* airplane) *noun* [C] a vehicle that flies and has an engine and wings

aerosol /'eərəsɒl/ *noun* [C] a metal container that forces a liquid out in small drops when you press a button

aerospace /'eərəʊspeɪs/ *noun* [U] the design and production of aircraft

aerosol

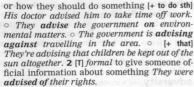

aesthetic (*also US* esthetic) /es'θetɪk/ *adjective* relating to beauty and the way something looks *the* **aesthetic appeal** *of cats* ● **aesthetically** *adverb*

aesthetics (*also US* esthetics) /es'θetɪks/ *noun* [U] the study of beauty, especially in art

AFAIK *internet abbreviation for* as far as I know: used when you believe that something is true, but you are not completely certain

afar /ə'fɑː^r/ *adverb literary* **from afar** from a long distance *He had admired her from afar.*

affable /'æfəbl/ *adjective* pleasant and friendly

affair /ə'feə^r/ *noun* **1** [C] a situation or set of related events, especially bad ones *The government's handling of the affair has been widely criticized.* **2** [C] a sexual relationship between two people when one or both of them is married to someone else *He's been* **having an affair** *with a woman at work.* **3 be sb's affair** If something is your affair, it is private and you do not want anyone else to be involved or know about it. ➪See also: love affair.

affairs /ə'feəz/ *noun* [plural] situations or subjects that involve you *He refused to discuss his financial affairs.* ➪See also: current affairs, state of affairs.

o▪**affect** /ə'fekt/ *verb* [T] **1** to influence someone or something, or cause them to change *It's a disease which affects many older people.* **2** to cause a strong emotion, especially sadness [often passive] *I was deeply affected by the film.* ➪See Common learner error at **effect**.

COMMON LEARNER ERROR

affect someone or something

Remember that you do not need a preposition after the verb **affect**.

The problem affects everyone.

~~The problem affects to everyone.~~

---

affectation /ˌæfek'teɪʃ^ən/ *noun* [C, U] a way of speaking or behaving that is not natural to someone

affected /ə'fektɪd/ *adjective* behaving or speaking in a way that is not natural or sincere

---

🧩 **WORD PARTNERS FOR** *affection*

show affection ● affection **for** sb ● a **display/show** of affection

---

affection /ə'fekʃ^ən/ *noun* [C, U] a feeling of liking or loving someone *Ann's* **affection for** *her grandfather was obvious.*

affectionate /ə'fekʃ^ənət/ *adjective* showing that you like or love someone *an affectionate*

A

little girl ○ *He's very affectionate.* ● **affectionately** *adverb*

affiliate /əˈfɪlieɪt/ *verb* be affiliated to/with sth to be officially connected to, or a member of, a larger organization *a college affiliated to the University of London* ● **affiliation** /əˌfɪliˈeɪʃən/ *noun* [C, U]

affinity /əˈfɪnəti/ *noun* 1 [no plural] a feeling that you like and understand someone or something *She seems to have a natural affinity for/with water.* 2 [C, U] a similarity *There are affinities between this poem and some of his earlier work.*

affirm /əˈfɜːm/ *verb* [T] *formal* to say that something is true *He gave a speech affirming the government's commitment to education.* ● **affirmation** /ˌæfəˈmeɪʃən/ *noun* [C, U]

affirmative /əˈfɜːmətɪv/ *adjective formal* In language, an affirmative word or phrase expresses the meaning 'yes'. *an affirmative answer*

affix /ˈæfɪks/ *noun* [C] a group of letters that you add to the beginning or the end of a word to make another word. In the word 'non-alcoholic', 'non-' is an affix. ⊃Compare **prefix**, **suffix**.

afflict /əˈflɪkt/ *verb* [T] *formal* If an illness or problem afflicts you, it makes you suffer. [often passive] *a country afflicted by civil war* ● **affliction** /əˈflɪkʃən/ *noun* [C, U] something that makes you suffer

affluent /ˈæfluənt/ *adjective* having a lot of money *affluent families/neighbourhoods* ● **affluence** /ˈæfluəns/ *noun* [U]

o⌐**afford** /əˈfɔːd/ *verb* [T] 1 **can afford** to have enough money to buy something or enough time to do something *I can't afford a new computer.* ○ [+ to do sth] *Can we afford to go away?* ○ *I'd love to come out but I can't afford the time.* 2 **can afford to do sth** If you can afford to do something, it is possible for you to do it without causing problems. *We can't afford to take that risk.*

COMMON LEARNER ERROR

afford to do something

When **afford** is followed by a verb, it is always in the to + infinitive form.

We can't afford to go on holiday this year.

~~We can't afford going on holiday this year.~~

affordable /əˈfɔːdəbl/ *adjective* cheap enough for most people *affordable housing/prices*

affront /əˈfrʌnt/ *noun* [C] something that is offensive or insulting to someone *He regarded the comments as an affront to his dignity.*

afield /əˈfiːld/ *adverb mainly UK* **far/further afield** away from the place where you are *We hired a car so we could travel further afield.*

afloat /əˈfləʊt/ *adjective* 1 floating on water 2 **stay afloat** to have enough money to continue a business *Many small business are struggling to stay afloat.*

afoot /əˈfʊt/ *adjective* [never before noun] being planned, or happening now *There are plans afoot to launch a new radio station.*

OTHER WAYS OF SAYING *afraid*

Other ways of saying 'afraid' are **frightened** and **scared**: *He's frightened that the other children will laugh at him.* ● *Gerry has always been scared of heights.*

If someone is extremely afraid, then you can use adjectives such as **petrified**, **terrified**, **panic-stricken** or the informal phrase **scared to death**: *I'm terrified of flying.* ● *She was panic-stricken when her little boy disappeared.* ● *He's scared to death of having the operation.*

If someone is afraid because they are worrying about something, then you can use adjectives such as **anxious**, **concerned**, **nervous**, or **worried**: *I'm worried that something will go wrong.* ● *All this waiting is making me feel anxious.*

If someone is afraid of something that might happen in the future, you can use the adjectives **apprehensive** or **uneasy**: *He's a bit apprehensive about living away from home.*

o⌐**afraid** /əˈfreɪd/ *adjective* [never before noun] 1 **I'm afraid** used to politely tell someone bad news or to politely disagree with someone *We haven't got any tickets left, I'm afraid.* ○ [+ (that)] *I'm afraid that I've broken your vase.* 2 frightened *She's afraid of water.* 3 worried that something bad might happen [+ (that)] *Many people are afraid that they might lose their jobs.* ○ [+ of + doing sth] *He was afraid of upsetting Clare.*

afresh /əˈfreʃ/ *adverb* If you do something afresh, you do it again in a different way. *Juan tore up the letter he was writing and started afresh.*

African /ˈæfrɪkən/ *adjective* relating or belonging to Africa *African art/music* ● **African** *noun* [C] someone from Africa

African-American /ˌæfrɪkənəˈmerɪkən/ (*also* **Afro-American** /ˌæfrəʊəˈmerɪkən/) *adjective* relating or belonging to American people whose families came from Africa in the past *the African-American community* ● **African-American** (*also* **Afro-American**) *noun* [C] *a 25-year-old African-American*

Afro-Caribbean /ˌæfrəʊkærɪˈbiːən/ *adjective UK* relating to people from the Caribbean whose families originally came from Africa *Afro-Caribbean art/music*

o⌐**after**[1] /ˈɑːftə/ *preposition* 1 [TIME/EVENT] when a time or event has happened *We went swimming after lunch.* ○ *Let's get the shopping. After that, we can have coffee.* 2 [LIST] following in order *H comes after G in the alphabet.* 3 [TIME] *US (UK/US* **past***)* used to say how many minutes past the hour it is *It's five after three.* 4 [BECAUSE OF] because of something that happened *I'll never trust her again after what she did to me.* 5 [DESPITE] despite *I can't believe he was so unpleasant after you gave him so much help.* 6 [FOLLOW] following someone or something *We ran after him, but he escaped.* 7 **after 5 minutes/2 weeks, etc** when five minutes, two weeks, etc have passed 8 **day after day/year**

| j yes | k cat | ŋ ring | ʃ she | θ thin | ð this | ʒ decision | dʒ jar | tʃ chip | æ cat | e bed | ə ago | ɪ sit | i cosy | ɒ hot | ʌ run | ʊ put |

after year, etc continuing for a long time, or happening many times *I'm bored with going to school day after day.* **9** NAMED FOR used when giving someone or something the same name as another person or thing *It was called the Biko building, after the famous South African.* **10 after all a** NOT EXPECTED used to say that something happened or was true although you did not expect it to happen or be true *Helen couldn't come to the party after all.* **b** EMPHASIZE TRUTH used to add information that shows that what you have just said is true *You can't expect to be perfect - after all, it was only your first lesson.* **11 be after sth** *informal* to be trying to get something *What type of job are you after?* **12 be after sb** *informal* to be looking for someone *The police are after him.*

○**after²** /ˈɑːftər/ *conjunction* at a later time than something else happens *We arrived after the game had started.* ○ *After further discussion, we decided to call the police.*

○**after³** /ˈɑːftər/ *adverb* later than someone or something else *He had the operation on Monday and I saw him the day after.*

▨▨▨ WORD PARTNERS FOR **aftermath**

in the aftermath of sth • the **immediate aftermath**

aftermath /ˈɑːftəmɑːθ/ *noun* [no plural] a situation that is the result of an accident, crime, or other violent event *There are calls for tighter airport security in the aftermath of last week's bombing.*

○**afternoon** /ˌɑːftəˈnuːn/ *noun* **1** [C, U] the time between the middle of the day, and the evening *I played tennis on Saturday afternoon.* ○ *The train arrives at 3 o'clock in the afternoon.* ○ *What are you doing this afternoon* (= today in the afternoon)? **2 (Good) afternoon.** used to say hello to someone in the afternoon

COMMON LEARNER ERROR

afternoon

If you talk about what happens in the afternoon, use the preposition **in**.

In the afternoon I phoned my girlfriend.

~~At the afternoon I phoned my girlfriend.~~

If you say a day of the week before 'afternoon', use the preposition **on**.

I'm going to the dentist on Tuesday afternoon.

aftershave /ˈɑːftəʃeɪv/ *noun* [C, U] a liquid with a pleasant smell that men put on their faces after shaving (= removing hair)

aftertaste /ˈɑːftəteɪst/ *noun* [C] the taste that a food or drink leaves in your mouth when you have swallowed it [usually singular] *a bitter/sweet aftertaste*

afterthought /ˈɑːftəθɔːt/ *noun* [C] something that you say or do later [usually singular] *She only asked me to the party as an afterthought.*

○**afterwards** /ˈɑːftəwədz/ (*also US* **afterward**) *adverb* at a later time, after something else has happened *I did my homework and went swimming afterwards.*

○**again** /əˈɡen/ *adverb* **1** once more *I'll ask her again.* ○ *I'll see you again next week.* **2** as before *Get some rest and you'll soon be well again.* **3 again and again** many times *He played the same song again and again.* **4 all over again** repeated from the beginning *We had to start all over again.* **5 then/there again** used when adding a fact to something you have just said *I failed my history test - but then again, I didn't do much studying for it.*

○**against** /əˈɡenst/ *preposition* **1** NOT AGREE disagreeing with a plan or activity *Andrew wants to change offices but I'm against it.* ○ *There were 70 votes for the new proposal and 30 against.* **2** COMPETE competing with or opposing someone or something *Liverpool is playing against AC Milan.* ○ *the fight against racism* **3** TOUCH touching something *Push the bed against the wall.* **4** PROTECT protecting you from something bad *Fresh fruit in the diet may protect against cancer.* **5** OPPOSITE DIRECTION in the opposite direction to the way something is moving *I was cycling against the wind.* **6 against the law/the rules** forbidden by a law or by rules *It's against the law to leave young children alone in the house.* **7 against sb's advice/wishes, etc** If you do something against someone's advice, wishes, etc, you do it although they have said you should not or must not. *He flew there against his doctor's advice.* **8 have sth against sb/sth** to have a reason not to like someone or something *I've got nothing against him personally, I just don't think he's the right man for the job.*

▨▨▨ WORD PARTNERS FOR **age**

reach the age **of** [18/60/75, etc] • **at/from** the age **of** [8/12/60, etc] • [8/25/70, etc] **years of** age • **at** sb's age • an age **limit**

○**age¹** /eɪdʒ/ *noun* **1** HOW OLD [C, U] the number of years that someone has lived, or that something has existed *The show appeals to people of all ages.* ○ *She left India at the age of 12.* ○ *Children under 10 years of age must be accompanied by an adult.* ⊃See Common learner error at **year**. **2** HISTORY [C] a period of history *the Ice Age* ○ *We're living in the age of electronic communication.* **3** OLD [U] when something is old *Some wines improve with age.* **4 under age** too young to do something legally ⊃See also: the **Middle Ages, old age.**

age² /eɪdʒ/ *verb* [I, T] *UK* **ageing**, *US* **aging**, *past* **aged** to become older or to make someone seem older *Dad has aged a lot recently.*

aged¹ /eɪdʒd/ *adjective* having a particular age *They have one daughter, aged three.* ⊃See also: **middle-aged.**

aged² /ˈeɪdʒɪd/ *adjective* old *an aged dog* ○ *improved health care for the aged*

'age ˌgroup *noun* [C] people of a particular age *job training for people in the 16-24 age group*

ageing¹ *UK* (*US* **aging**) /ˈeɪdʒɪŋ/ *adjective* becoming older *an ageing population*

ageing² *UK* (*US* **aging**) /ˈeɪdʒɪŋ/ *noun* [U] the process of becoming older *the ageing process*

'age ˌlimit *noun* [C] the age at which a person is allowed or not allowed to do something

| ɑː arm | ɜː her | iː see | ɔː saw | uː too | aɪ my | aʊ how | eə hair | eɪ day | əʊ no | ɪə near | ɔɪ boy | ʊə poor | aɪə fire | aʊə sour |

A

Eighteen is the legal age limit for buying alcohol.

agency /ˈeɪdʒᵊnsi/ *noun* [C] **1** a business that provides a service *an advertising agency* **2** an international organization or government department *an international development agency* ➲See also: **travel agency**.

WORD PARTNERS FOR ***agenda***

set (= decide) the agenda • be **off/on** the agenda • be **at the top of/high on** the agenda • the agenda **for** sth

agenda /əˈdʒendə/ *noun* [C] **1** a list of subjects that people will discuss at a meeting *There are several items **on the agenda**.* **2** important subjects that have to be dealt with *The issue of rail safety is back **on the political agenda**.*

agent /ˈeɪdʒᵊnt/ *noun* [C] **1** someone whose job is to deal with business for someone else *a literary agent* **2** (*also* **secret agent**) someone who tries to find out secret information, especially about another country ➲See also: **estate agent** *UK*, **real estate agent** *US*, **travel agent**.

ages /ˈeɪdʒɪz/ *noun* [plural] *informal* a very long time *I've been waiting here **for ages**.* ○ *It takes **ages** to cook.*

aggravate /ˈægrəveɪt/ *verb* [T] **1** to make a situation or condition worse *His comments only **aggravated the problem**.* **2** to annoy someone *She's starting to really aggravate me.* • **aggravating** *adjective* • **aggravation** /ˌægrəˈveɪʃᵊn/ *noun* [C, U]

aggregate /ˈægrɪgət/ *noun* [C, U] a total *(UK) Liverpool won 2-0 **on aggregate*** (= in total).

aggression /əˈgreʃᵊn/ *noun* [U] angry or violent behaviour towards someone *an act of aggression*

aggressive /əˈgresɪv/ *adjective* **1** behaving in an angry and violent way towards another person *aggressive behaviour* **2** using forceful methods and determined to succeed *an aggressive marketing campaign* • **aggressively** *adverb*

aggressor /əˈgresəʳ/ *noun* [C] someone who starts a fight or war with someone else

aggrieved /əˈgriːvd/ *adjective* upset or angry because someone has treated you unfairly

aghast /əˈgɑːst/ *adjective* [never before noun] very shocked *She looked at him aghast.*

agile /ˈædʒaɪl/ [US] /ˈædʒᵊl/ *adjective* **1** able to move your whole body easily and quickly **2** able to think quickly in an intelligent way *an agile mind* • **agility** /əˈdʒɪləti/ *noun* [U]

aging /ˈeɪdʒɪŋ/ *noun, adjective US spelling of* ageing

agitate /ˈædʒɪteɪt/ *verb* [I] to argue strongly about something in order to achieve social or political changes *They continued to **agitate for** changes to the legal system.* • **agitator** *noun* [C]

agitated /ˈædʒɪteɪtɪd/ *adjective* very anxious or upset *He seemed agitated, as if something was worrying him.* • **agitation** /ˌædʒɪˈteɪʃᵊn/ *noun* [U]

AGM /ˌeɪdʒiːˈem/ *UK* (*US* **annual meeting**) *noun* [C] *abbreviation for* Annual General Meeting: a meeting that happens once every year in which an organization discusses the past year's activities and chooses the people who will be in charge of the organization

agnostic /ægˈnɒstɪk/ *noun* [C] someone who believes that we cannot know if God exists or not • **agnostic** *adjective*

⊶**ago** /əˈgəʊ/ *adverb* **ten minutes/six years/a long time ago** used to refer to a time in the past *They moved to London ten years ago.*

agonize (*also UK* **-ise**) /ˈægənaɪz/ *verb* [I] to spend a lot of time worrying about a decision *Lee **agonized over** what to buy his girlfriend.*

agonizing (*also UK* **-ising**) /ˈægənaɪzɪŋ/ *adjective* causing you a lot of pain or worry *an agonizing choice*

agony /ˈægəni/ *noun* [C, U] extreme suffering, either physical or mental *She lay on the bed **in agony**.*

ˈagony ˌaunt *noun* [C] *UK* someone who gives advice on personal problems, in a newspaper or magazine

⊶**agree** /əˈgriː/ *verb* **agreeing**, *past* **agreed** **1** [SAME OPINION] [I, T] to have the same opinion as someone *I **agree with** you.* ○ *"She's definitely the right person for the job." "I agree."* ○ [+ (that)] *We all agreed that mistakes had been made.* ○ *We **agree about** most things.* **2** [SAY YES] [I] to say you will do something that someone asks you to do [+ to do sth] *She agreed to help him.* ➲See Common learner error at **accept** **3** [DECIDE] [I, T] to decide something with someone *We couldn't **agree on** what to buy.* ○ [+ to do sth] *They agreed to meet on Sunday.* ○ [+ (that)] *We agreed that they would deliver the sofa in the morning.* **4** [DESCRIPTION] [I] If two descriptions agree, they are the same. ➲Opposite **disagree**.

agree with sth to think that something is morally acceptable *I don't agree with hunting.*

agreeable /əˈgriːəbl/ *adjective formal* **1** pleasant or nice *an agreeable young man* ➲Opposite **disagreeable**. **2 be agreeable to sth** to be willing to do or accept something *If Harvey is agreeable to the proposal, we'll go ahead.* • **agreeably** *adverb*

WORD PARTNERS FOR ***agreement***

reach/sign an agreement • a **draft/written** agreement • an agreement **between** sb

⊶**agreement** /əˈgriːmənt/ *noun* **1** [C] a promise or decision made between two or more people *an international agreement* ○ *It was difficult to **reach an agreement**.* **2** [U] when people have the same opinion as each other *Not everyone was **in agreement**.* ➲Opposite **disagreement**.

agriculture /ˈægrɪkʌltʃəʳ/ *noun* [U] the work and methods of growing crops and looking after animals which are then used for food • **agricultural** /ˌægrɪˈkʌltʃᵊrᵊl/ *adjective*

agritourism /ˌægrɪˈtʊərɪzᵊm/ *noun* [U] the business of providing holidays for people on farms or in the countryside

aground /əˈgraʊnd/ *adverb* **run aground** If a ship runs aground, it cannot move because the water is not deep enough.

ah /ɑː/ *exclamation* **1** used to show sympathy or to show pleasure at seeing a baby or attractive animal *Ah, you poor thing!* ○ *Ah, look at that* *little kitten!* **2** used to show that you have just understood something *Ah, now I see what you're saying!*

aha /ə'hɑː/ *exclamation* used when you suddenly understand or find something *Aha! That's where I left my keys!*

ₒ▪**ahead** /ə'hed/ *adjective, adverb* **1** IN FRONT in front *The road ahead is very busy.* ○ *Rick walked ahead of us.* **2** FUTURE in the future *She has a difficult time ahead of her.* **3** MORE POINTS having more points than someone else in a competition *Barcelona was ahead after ten minutes.* **4** MORE PROGRESS making more progress than someone or something else *Sue is ahead of everyone else in French.* **5 go ahead** *informal* used to allow someone to do something *"Can I use your phone?" "Sure, go ahead."* **6 ahead of time/schedule** before the time that was planned *We finished the project ahead of schedule.* ⊃See also: be one **step**¹ ahead (of sb), be streets (**street**) ahead (of sb/sth), be ahead of your **time**¹.

-aholic /-ə'hɒlɪk/ *suffix* unable to stop doing or taking something *chocaholic* (= someone who cannot stop eating chocolate)

aid¹ /eɪd/ *noun* **1** [U] money, food, or equipment that is given to help a country or group of people *Emergency aid was sent to the flood victims.* ○ *aid workers* **2 in aid of sb/sth** *UK* in order to collect money for a group of people who need it *a concert in aid of famine relief* **3 with the aid of sth** using something to help you *She can walk with the aid of a stick.* **4 come/go to sb's aid** to go to someone and help them *Luckily a policeman came to my aid.* **5** [C] a piece of equipment that helps you to do something *teaching aids such as books and videos* ⊃See also: Band-Aid, first aid, visual aid.

aid² /eɪd/ *verb formal* **1** [T] to help someone **2 aid and abet (sb)** in law, to help someone do something that is illegal

aide /eɪd/ *noun* [C] someone whose job is to help someone important, especially in the government *a former aide to the President*

AIDS, Aids /eɪdz/ *noun* [U] *abbreviation for* acquired immune deficiency syndrome: a serious disease that destroys the body's ability to fight infection ⊃Compare HIV.

ailing /'eɪlɪŋ/ *adjective* weak or ill *an ailing company/economy*

ailment /'eɪlmənt/ *noun* [C] an illness *Treat minor ailments yourself.*

WORD PARTNERS FOR **aim**

achieve your aim ● sb's/sth's **main/ultimate** aim ● the aim **of** sth ● **with** the aim of doing sth

aim¹ /eɪm/ *noun* **1** [C] the purpose of doing something, and what you hope to achieve *The aim of the film was to make people laugh.* ○ [+ of + doing sth] *He went to Paris with the aim of improving his French.* **2 sb's aim** someone's ability to hit an object by throwing something or shooting at something **3 take aim** to point a weapon towards someone or something

aim² /eɪm/ *verb* **1 aim for/at sth; aim to do sth** to

intend to achieve something *I aim to arrive at three o'clock.* ○ *We're aiming for a 10% increase in sales.* **2 be aimed at sb** to be intended to influence or affect a particular person or group *advertising aimed at students* **3 be aimed at doing sth** to be intended to achieve a particular thing *a plan aimed at reducing traffic* **4** [I, T] to point a weapon towards someone or something *He aimed the gun at the lion.*

aimless /'eɪmləs/ *adjective* with no purpose ● **aimlessly** *adverb*

ain't /eɪnt/ *informal short for* am not, is not, are not, have not, or has not. This word is not considered correct by most people.

ₒ▪**air**¹ /eəʳ/ *noun* **1** GAS [U] the mixture of gases around the Earth which we breathe *air pollution* ○ *He went outside to get some fresh air* (= clean, cool air). **2 the air** the space above and around things *He fired his gun into the air.* **3** TRAVEL [U] travel in an aircraft *I like travelling by air.* ○ *air safety* **4** QUALITY [no plural] a particular appearance or quality *He has an air of authority.* **5 be on air** to be broadcasting on television or radio **6 clear the air** If an argument or discussion clears the air, people feel less angry or upset after it. **7 disappear/vanish into thin air** to suddenly disappear in a mysterious way **8 be up in the air** If something is up in the air, no decision has been made. *Our plans for the summer are still up in the air.* ⊃See also: a **breath** of fresh air, mid-air.

air² /eəʳ/ *verb* **1** BROADCAST [T] to broadcast something on radio or television **2 air your opinions/views, etc** to say what your opinions are *The meeting will give everyone a chance to air their views.* **3** ROOM [T] to make a room smell better by opening a door or window **4** CLOTHES [I, T] If clothes air, or if you air them, you hang them up with a lot of air all around them.

airbag /'eəbæg/ *noun* [C] a bag in the front of a car that protects people in an accident by filling with air *passenger/twin airbags*

airbase /'eəbeɪs/ *noun* [C] a military airport

airborne /'eəbɔːn/ *adjective* moving in, or carried by the air *airborne troops* ○ *an airborne virus*

'**air ˌcon** *noun* [U] *UK abbreviation for* air conditioning

'**air conˌditioner** *noun* [C] a machine that keeps the air cool in a building or a car

'**air conˌditioning** *noun* [U] a system that keeps the air cool in a building or car ● **air-conditioned** /'eəkən,dɪʃənd/ *adjective* having air conditioning *an air-conditioned office*

ₒ▪**aircraft** /'eəkrɑːft/ *noun* [C] *plural* aircraft a vehicle that can fly

'**aircraft ˌcarrier** *noun* [C] a ship on which aircraft can take off and land

airfare /'eəfeəʳ/ *noun* [C] the cost of a ticket to fly somewhere

airfield /'eəfiːld/ *noun* [C] a place where small or military aircraft can take off and land

'**air ˌforce** *noun* [C] the part of a country's military organization that uses aircraft to fight wars

'**air hoˌstess** *UK* (*UK/US* flight attendant) *noun*

[C] someone whose job is to serve passengers on an aircraft and to make sure that safety rules are obeyed

ˈairing ˌcupboard *noun* [C] *UK* a warm cupboard where you keep sheets, clean clothes, etc

airless /ˈeələs/ *adjective* An airless room does not have enough fresh air.

airlift /ˈeəlɪft/ *noun* [C] when people or things are moved by aircraft because it is too difficult or too slow to travel by road *an airlift of medical supplies* • **airlift** *verb* [T] [often passive] *Three small children were airlifted to safety.*

airline /ˈeəlaɪn/ *noun* [C] a company that provides regular flights to places

airliner /ˈeəlaɪnəʳ/ *noun* [C] a large plane for carrying people

airmail /ˈeəmeɪl/ *noun* [U] the sending of letters or parcels by plane *an airmail letter*

airman /ˈeəmən/ *noun* [C] *plural* **airmen** a man who flies an aircraft in a country's air force

airplane /ˈeəpleɪn/ *US* (*UK* **aeroplane**) *noun* [C] a vehicle that flies and has an engine and wings ➲See picture at **aeroplane**

⊶**airport** /ˈeəpɔːt/ *noun* [C] a place where planes take off and land, with buildings for passengers to wait in

ˈair ˌraid *noun* [C] an attack by military planes

airspace /ˈeəspeɪs/ *noun* [U] the sky above a country that belongs to that country

airstrike /ˈeəstraɪk/ *noun* [C] an attack by military planes

airtight /ˈeətaɪt/ *adjective* An airtight container does not allow air in or out.

ˌair traffic conˈtroller *noun* [C] the person in an airport who tells pilots when to take off and land their aircraft

airy /ˈeəri/ *adjective* An airy room or building is pleasant because it has a lot of space and air.

aisle

aisle /aɪl/ *noun* [C] a passage between the lines of seats or goods in a plane, church, supermarket, etc

ajar /əˈdʒɑːʳ/ *adjective* [never before noun] If a door is ajar, it is slightly open.

aka /ˌeɪkeɪˈeɪ/ *adverb abbreviation for* also known as: used when giving the name that a person is generally known by, after giving their real name *Peter Parker, aka Spiderman*

akin /əˈkɪn/ *adjective formal* **be akin to sth** to be similar to something

à la carte /ˌæləˈkɑːt/ *adjective, adverb* choosing food as separate items from a menu (= list of food), not as a meal with a fixed price

alacrity /əˈlækrəti/ *noun* [U] *formal* If you do something with alacrity, you do it in a very quick and willing way.

WORD PARTNERS FOR ***alarm***

an alarm **goes off/sounds** • **set off/trigger** an alarm • a **burglar/fire/smoke** alarm • a **car** alarm • an alarm **system**

alarm¹ /əˈlɑːm/ *noun* **1** [WARNING] [C] a loud noise that warns you of danger *a fire alarm* ○ *to set off an alarm* **2** [CLOCK] [C] (*also* **alarm clock**) a clock that makes a noise to wake you **3** [WORRY] [U] a sudden feeling of fear or worry that something bad might happen *There's no need for alarm - it is completely safe.* **4 raise the alarm** to warn someone of a dangerous situation *Her parents raised the alarm when she failed to return home.* ➲See also: **burglar alarm, false alarm.**

alarm² /əˈlɑːm/ *verb* [T] to make someone worried or frightened

aˈlarm ˌclock *noun* [C] a clock that makes a noise to wake you *I've set the alarm clock for six.*

alarm clock

alarmed /əˈlɑːmd/ *adjective* worried or frightened by something

alarming /əˈlɑːmɪŋ/ *adjective* making you feel worried or frightened *alarming news*

alas /əˈlæs/ *exclamation literary* used to show sadness

albeit /ɔːlˈbiːɪt/ *conjunction formal* although *He tried, albeit without success.*

albino /ælˈbiːnəʊ/ [US] /ælˈbaɪnəʊ/ *noun* [C] a person or animal with white skin, white hair or fur, and pink eyes

album /ˈælbəm/ *noun* [C] **1** several songs or pieces of music on a CD, a record, etc **2** a book in which you keep photographs, stamps, etc

alcohol /ˈælkəhɒl/ *noun* [U] **1** drinks such as wine and beer that can make you drunk **2** a liquid that has no colour and is in drinks that make you drunk

alcoholic¹ /ˌælkəˈhɒlɪk/ *noun* [C] someone who regularly drinks too much alcohol and cannot stop the habit

alcoholic² /ˌælkəˈhɒlɪk/ *adjective* **1** containing alcohol *alcoholic drinks* **2** [always before noun] regularly drinking too much alcohol and unable to stop the habit *She lived with her alcoholic father.*

alcoholism /ˈælkəhɒlɪzᵊm/ *noun* [U] the condition of being an alcoholic

alcove /ˈælkəʊv/ *noun* [C] a part of a wall in a room that is further back than the rest of the wall

ale /eɪl/ *noun* [C, U] a type of beer

alert¹ /əˈlɜːt/ *adjective* quick to notice and react to things around you *A young dog should be* *alert and playful.* ○ *Teachers need to be **alert to** sudden changes in students' behaviour.* • **alertness** *noun* [U]

alert² /ə'lɜːt/ *verb* [T] to warn someone of a possibly dangerous situation *Six hours later she still wasn't home so they alerted the police.*

alert³ /ə'lɜːt/ *noun* **1** [C] a warning about a possibly dangerous situation *a **bomb alert*** **2 be on full/red alert** to be expecting problems and ready to deal with them *Police in the region were on full alert against further attacks.*

'A ˌlevel *noun* [C] in England and Wales, an exam taken at the age of eighteen, or the qualification itself

algae /'ældʒiː/ *noun* [U, group] a plant with no stem or leaves that grows in or near water

algebra /'ældʒɪbrə/ *noun* [U] a type of mathematics in which numbers and amounts are shown by letters and symbols

alias¹ /'eɪliəs/ *noun* [C] a false name, especially one used by a criminal

alias² /'eɪliəs/ *preposition* used when giving the name that a person is generally known by, after giving their real name *Grace Kelly, alias Princess Grace of Monaco*

alibi /'ælɪbaɪ/ *noun* [C] proof that someone was not in the place where a crime happened and so cannot be guilty

alien¹ /'eɪliən/ *adjective* **1** strange and not familiar *The custom was totally **alien to** her.* **2** [always before noun] relating to creatures from another planet *an alien spacecraft*

alien² /'eɪliən/ *noun* [C] **1** a creature from another planet **2** *formal* someone who does not legally belong to the country where they live or work

alienate /'eɪliəneɪt/ *verb* [T] **1** to make someone stop supporting and liking you *The government's comments have alienated many teachers.* **2** to make someone feel that they are different and do not belong to a group *Disagreements can **alienate** teenagers **from** their families.* • **alienation** /ˌeɪliə'neɪʃᵊn/ *noun* [U]

alight¹ /ə'laɪt/ *adjective* [never before noun] *mainly UK* burning *Vandals **set** the car **alight** (= made it burn).*

alight² /ə'laɪt/ *verb* [I] *formal* to get out of a bus, train, etc *He alighted from the taxi.*

align /ə'laɪn/ *verb* **1** [T] to put things in an exact line or make them parallel **2 align yourself with sb; be aligned with sb** to support the opinions of a political group, country, etc *Many voters are not aligned with any party.* • **alignment** *noun* [C, U]

alike¹ /ə'laɪk/ *adjective* [never before noun] similar *The children look so alike.*

alike² /ə'laɪk/ *adverb* **1** in a similar way *We think alike.* **2** used to say that two people or groups are included *It is a disease which affects men and women alike.*

alimony /'ælɪməni/ *noun* [U] money that someone must pay regularly to their wife or husband after the marriage has ended

o⊸**alive** /ə'laɪv/ *adjective* [never before noun] **1** NOT DEAD living, not dead *Are your grandparents still alive?* **2** PLACE full of activity and excite-

ment *The bar was **alive with** the sound of laughter.* ○ *The city **comes alive** at night.* **3** CONTINUING continuing to exist *Local people are fighting to **keep** the language **alive**.* **4 be alive and kicking/well** to continue to be popular or successful *Despite rumours to the contrary, feminism is alive and kicking.*

o⊸**all¹** /ɔːl/ *pronoun, determiner* **1** EVERY ONE every person or thing in a group *We were all dancing.* ○ *I've watched all of the programmes in the series.* **2** WHOLE AMOUNT the whole amount of something *Who's eaten all the cake?* ○ *He spends all of his money on clothes.* **3** WHOLE TIME the whole of a period of time *all week/month/year* ○ *He's been studying all day.* **4** ONLY THING the only thing *All I remember is waking up in hospital.* **5 at all** in any way *He hasn't changed at all.* ○ *UK Can I help at all?* **6 in all** in total *There were twenty people at the meeting in all.*

COMMON LEARNER ERROR

all + period of time

You do not say 'the' when you use **all** + a period of time.
all day/morning/week/year/summer
~~all the day/morning/week/year/summer~~

o⊸**all²** /ɔːl/ *adverb* **1** completely or very *You're all wet!* ○ *I'm all excited now.* **2 all over a** in every place *Lee has travelled all over the world.* **b** finished *It was all over very quickly.* **3 2/5/8, etc all** used to say that two players or teams have the same number of points in a game *It was 3 all at half time.* **4 all along** from the beginning of a period of time *I said all along that it was a mistake.* **5 all but** almost *The film was all but over by the time we arrived.* **6 all the better/ easier/more exciting, etc** much better, easier, etc *The journey was all the more dangerous because of the bad weather.* **7 all in all** considering everything *All in all, I think she did well.*

Allah /'ælə/ *noun* the name of God for Muslims

allay /ə'leɪ/ *verb formal* **allay sb's concerns/fears/ suspicions, etc** to make someone feel less worried or frightened, etc *I tried to allay his fears about the interview.*

WORD PARTNERS FOR allegation

make/deny/face/investigate an allegation
• a **serious** allegation • an allegation **of** sth
• an allegation **against** sb

allegation /ˌælɪ'ɡeɪʃᵊn/ *noun* [C] when you say that someone has done something wrong or illegal, without proof that this is true *allegations of corruption* ○ [+ that] *He denied allegations that he had cheated.*

allege /ə'ledʒ/ *verb* [T] to say that someone has done something wrong or illegal, but not prove it [often passive] *The teacher is alleged to have hit a student.* ○ [+ (that)] *He alleges that Bates attacked him.*

alleged /ə'ledʒd/ *adjective* [always before noun] believed to be true, but not proved *an alleged attack* • **allegedly** /ə'ledʒɪdli/ *adverb He was arrested for allegedly stealing a car.*

allegiance /ə'liːdʒᵊns/ *noun* [U] loyalty and sup-

A

port *To become a citizen, you have to pledge/ swear allegiance to* (= say you will be loyal to) *the United States.*

allegory /'æligəri/ *noun* [C, U] a story, poem, or painting that has a hidden meaning, especially a moral one ● **allegorical** /,æli'gɒrikəl/ *adjective*

allergic /ə'lɜːdʒik/ *adjective* **1** [never before noun] having an allergy *I'm allergic to eggs.* **2** [always before noun] caused by an allergy *an allergic reaction*

allergy /'ælədʒi/ *noun* [C] a medical condition in which your body reacts badly to something that you eat, breathe, or touch *an allergy to dogs*

alleviate /ə'liːvieit/ *verb* [T] to make problems or suffering less extreme *She's been given some tablets to alleviate the pain.* ● **alleviation** /ə,liːvi'eiʃən/ *noun* [U]

alley /'æli/ (*also* alleyway /'æliwei/) *noun* [C] **1** a narrow road between buildings **2 be right up sb's alley** *US informal* (*UK* be right up sb's street) to be exactly the type of thing that someone knows about or likes to do

WORD PARTNERS FOR *alliance*

form an alliance ● an alliance **between** sb and sb ● an alliance **with** sb ● **in** alliance with sb

alliance /ə'laiəns/ *noun* [C] an agreement between countries or political parties to work together to achieve something *an alliance between France and Britain*

allied /'ælaid/ *adjective* **1** [always before noun] joined by a formal agreement *the allied powers* **2 be allied to/with sth** to be related to something *a group closely allied with the Green Party*

alligator /'æligeitə'/ *noun* [C] a big reptile with a long mouth and sharp teeth, that lives in lakes and rivers

alligator

all-night /'ɔːlnait/ *adjective* lasting all night *Tom was tired after his all-night party.*

allocate /'æləkeit/ *verb* [T] to give some time, money, space, etc to be used for a particular purpose *The government has promised to allocate extra money for health care.* ○ *More police time should be allocated to crime prevention.*

allocation /,æləkeiʃən/ *noun* **1** [C] an amount of money, time, space, etc that is allocated **2** [U] when money, time, space, etc is allocated *the allocation of money*

allot /ə'lɒt/ *verb* [T] allotting, *past* allotted to give someone a particular amount of something [often passive] *They were allotted seats on the front row.*

allotment /ə'lɒtmənt/ *noun* **1** [C] in Britain, a small area of land that people rent and grow vegetables and flowers on **2** [C, U] the process of sharing something, or the amount that you get *this year's allotment of funds*

all-out /'ɔːl,aut/ *adjective* [always before noun] complete and with as much effort as possible *an all-out battle/effort*

o⁻**allow** /ə'lau/ *verb* [T] **1** GIVE PERMISSION to give someone permission for something [often passive] *Smoking is not allowed in the restaurant.* ○ [+ to do sth] *You are not allowed to use calculators in the exam.* ○ [+ two objects] *Patients are not allowed visitors after nine o'clock.* **2** NOT PREVENT to not prevent something from happening [+ to do sth] *They have allowed the problem to get worse.* **3** MAKE POSSIBLE to make it possible for someone to do something [+ to do sth] *The extra money will allow me to upgrade my computer.* **4** TIME/MONEY to plan to use a particular amount of money, time, etc for something *You should allow three hours for the whole journey.*

COMMON LEARNER ERROR

allow or **let**?

Allow and let have similar meanings. Allow is used in more formal or official situations, especially when talking about rules and laws. Verb patterns - allow someone to do something / allow something to happen

The new legislation allows companies to charge for this service.

We can't allow this situation to continue.

Let is used in more informal and spoken situations. Verb patterns - let someone do something /let something happen.

Dad never lets anyone else drive his car.

She let her hair grow longer.

allow for sth to consider or include something when you are making plans *The journey should take two hours, allowing for delays.*

allowance /ə'lauəns/ *noun* [C] **1** money that you are given regularly, especially to pay for a particular thing *a clothing allowance* **2** an amount of something that you are allowed *The luggage allowance is 25 kilos.* **3 make allowances for sb/sth** to remember that someone has a disadvantage which is not their fault when you are judging their behaviour or work *They made allowances for the fact that he was ill.*

alloy /'æloi/ *noun* [C] a metal that is a mixture of two or more metals

o⁻**all 'right¹** (*also* alright) *adjective* [never before noun], *adverb* **1** GOOD good enough, although not very good *The hotel wasn't brilliant but it was all right.* ○ *It's a cheap wine but it tastes all right.* **2** SAFE safe or well *I'm all right thanks. How are you?* ○ *Did you get home all right last night?* **3 that's all right a** THANKS used as an answer when someone thanks you *"Thanks for cleaning the kitchen." "That's all right."* **b** SORRY something you say when someone says sorry to show that you are not angry *"I'm sorry - I forgot all about it." "That's all right."*

all 'right² (*also* **alright**) *exclamation* used to agree to a suggestion or request *"How about going out for dinner?" "All right."*

all-time /ˌɔːlˈtaɪm/ *adjective* [always before noun] If something is an all-time best/high/low, etc, it is the best/highest/lowest, etc it has ever been. *The president's popularity is at an all-time low.*

allude /əˈluːd/ *verb*
allude to sb/sth *formal* to refer to someone or something but not directly

allure /əˈljʊəʳ/ *noun* [U] an attractive or exciting quality *the allure of the city* ● **alluring** *adjective* attractive or exciting *an alluring image*

allusion /əˈluːʒᵊn/ *noun* [C, U] *formal* when you refer to someone or something but not directly *a play full of allusions to Shakespeare*

ally¹ /ˈælaɪ/ *noun* [C] **1** someone who supports you, especially when other people are against you **2** a country that has agreed to help another country, especially in a war

ally² /əˈlaɪ/ *verb*
ally yourself to/with sb to join someone and support them

almighty /ɔːlˈmaɪti/ *adjective* **1** [always before noun] very strong or forceful *All of a sudden I heard an almighty bang in the kitchen.* **2** having the power to do everything, like a god *Almighty God*

almond /ˈɑːmənd/ *noun* [C, U] a flat, oval nut, often used in cooking

⊶**almost** /ˈɔːlməʊst/ *adverb* **1** If something almost happens, it does not happen but it is very close to happening. *I almost missed the bus.* **2** **almost always/everyone/half, etc** not always/everyone/half, etc but very close to it *He's almost always late.*

⊶**alone** /əˈləʊn/ *adjective, adverb* **1** [never before noun] without other people *She lives alone.* **2** [always after noun] used to emphasize that only one person or thing is involved *Last year alone the company made a million dollars.* **3** **leave sb alone** to stop talking to someone or annoying them *Leave him alone, he's tired.* **4** **leave sth alone** to stop touching something *Leave your hair alone!* ⊃See also: **let** alone.

COMMON LEARNER ERROR

alone or **lonely**?

Alone means without other people. If you feel sad because you are alone, you are **lonely**.

Sometimes I like to be alone to think.

She has been very lonely since her husband died.

⊶**along¹** /əˈlɒŋ/ *preposition* **1** DIRECTION from one part of a road, river, etc to another *a romantic walk along the beach* **2** NEXT TO in a line next to something long *a row of new houses along the river* **3** PARTICULAR PLACE at a particular place on a road, river, etc *Somewhere along this road there's a garage.*

⊶**along²** /əˈlɒŋ/ *adverb* **1** forward *We were just walking along, chatting.* **2** **be/come along** to arrive somewhere *You wait ages for a bus and then three come along at once.* **3** **bring/take sb along** to take someone with you to a place *She*

asked if she could bring some friends along to the party. **4** **along with sb/sth** in addition to someone or something else *California along with Florida is probably the most popular American holiday destination.*

alongside /əˌlɒŋˈsaɪd/ *adverb, preposition* **1** next to someone or something *A car pulled up alongside ours.* **2** together with someone *She always enjoyed working alongside such famous actors.*

aloof /əˈluːf/ *adjective* **1** not friendly, especially because you think you are better than other people *He seems arrogant and aloof.* **2** not involved in something *He tried to remain aloof from family arguments.*

aloud /əˈlaʊd/ *adverb* in a way that other people can hear *to laugh aloud* ○ *The author read aloud from his new book.*

alphabet /ˈælfəbet/ *noun* [C] a set of letters used for writing a language *The English alphabet starts at A and ends at Z.*

alphabetical /ˌælfəˈbetɪkᵊl/ *adjective* arranged in the same order as the letters of the alphabet *Put the names in alphabetical order.* ● **alphabetically** *adverb*

alpine /ˈælpaɪn/ *adjective* [always before noun] existing in, or relating to high mountains *an alpine village*

⊶**already** /ɔːlˈredi/ *adverb* **1** before now, or before a particular time in the past *I've already told him.* ○ *By the time we arrived, he'd already left.* **2** used to say that something has happened earlier than you expected *I'm already full and I've only eaten one course.*

⊶**alright** /ɔːlˈraɪt/ *adjective, adverb, exclamation* another spelling of **all right**

⊶**also** /ˈɔːlsəʊ/ *adverb* in addition *She speaks French and also a little Spanish.* ○ *The book also has a chapter on grammar.*

altar /ˈɔːltəʳ/ *noun* [C] a table used for religious ceremonies, especially in a Christian church

alter /ˈɔːltəʳ/ *verb* [I, T] to change, or to make someone or something change *We've had to alter our plans.*

WORD PARTNERS FOR *alteration*

make alterations (to) sth ● a **major/minor/ slight** alteration ● an alteration **in/to** sth

alteration /ˌɔːltᵊrˈeɪʃᵊn/ *noun* [C, U] a change, or the process of changing something *We've made a few alterations to the kitchen.*

alternate¹ /ɔːlˈtɜːnət/ *adjective* **1** **alternate days/weeks/years, etc** one out of every two days, weeks, years, etc *I work alternate Saturdays.* **2** with first one thing, then another thing, and then the first thing again, etc *a dessert with alternate layers of chocolate and cream* **3** [always before noun] *US* An alternate plan, method, etc is one that you can use if you do not want to use another one. ● **alternately** *adverb*

alternate² /ˈɔːltəneɪt/ *verb* **1** [I] If two things alternate, one thing happens, then the other thing happens, then the first thing happens again, etc. *She alternates between cheerfulness and deep despair.* **2** **alternate sth with sth** to use or do one thing then another thing and then the first thing again, etc *They alternate classical pieces with more modern works.* • **alternating** *adjective alternating moods of anger and sadness*

alternative¹ /ɔːlˈtɜːnətɪv/ *noun* [C] one of two or more things that you can choose between *It's a low-fat **alternative to** butter.* ○ *After the public protests the government **had no alternative** but to change its policy.*

alternative² /ɔːlˈtɜːnətɪv/ *adjective* [always before noun] **1** (*also US* **alternate**) An alternative plan, method, etc is one that you can use if you do not want to use another one. *We can make **alternative arrangements** if necessary.* **2** different to what is usual or traditional ***alternative comedy*** ○ *an alternative lifestyle*

alternatively /ɔːlˈtɜːnətɪvli/ *adverb* used to give a second possibility *We could go there by train or, alternatively, I could drive us.*

alˌternative ˈmedicine *noun* [U] any way of trying to make an illness better that uses medicines or methods that are not normally used in Western medicine

⊶**although** /ɔːlˈðəʊ/ *conjunction* **1** despite the fact that *She walked home by herself, although she knew it was dangerous.* **2** but *He's coming to see us this evening, although I don't know exactly when.*

altitude /ˈæltɪtjuːd/ *noun* [C, U] the height of something above sea level *We were flying at an altitude of 8000 metres.*

alto /ˈæltəʊ/ *noun* [C] a woman or boy with a low singing voice

⊶**altogether** /ˌɔːltəˈɡeðəʳ/ *adverb* **1** [COMPLETELY] completely *The train slowed down and then stopped altogether.* ○ *I'm **not altogether** sure about the idea.* **2** [TOTAL] in total *There were twenty people there altogether.* **3** [GENERALLY] when you consider everything *Altogether, I'd say the party was a great success.*

aluminium /ˌæljəˈmɪniəm/ *UK* (*US* **aluminum** /əˈluːmɪnəm/) *noun* [U] a light, silver coloured metal used for making containers, cooking equipment, and aircraft parts *aluminium cans/foil*

OTHER WAYS OF SAYING *always*

If you are using **always** to mean 'again and again', then you could also use **constantly**, **continually**, **forever**, or the fixed expressions **time after time** or **all the time**: *He's **constantly/forever** losing his keys.* • *I'm fed up with you making excuses **all the time**.*

The word **invariably** is sometimes used as a more formal way of saying **always**, especially when talking about something bad which happens: *The train is **invariably** late.*

The fixed expression **without fail** can be used to show that someone always does something, even when it is difficult: *He visited her every Sunday **without fail**.*

⊶**always** /ˈɔːlweɪz/ *adverb* **1** [EVERY TIME] every time, or at all times *I always walk to work.* **2** [UNTIL NOW] at all times in the past *We've always lived here.* **3** [FOREVER] forever *I will always remember you.* **4** [MANY TIMES] again and again, usually in an annoying way [+ doing sth] *He's always losing his keys.* **5 can/could always do sth** used to suggest something *You can always stay with us if you miss your train.*

Alzheimer's (disease) /ˈæltshaɪməzdɪˌziːz/ *noun* [U] a brain disease mainly of old people which makes a person forget things and stops them from thinking clearly

⊶**a.m.** (*also* **am**) /ˌeɪˈem/ used to refer to a time between 12 o'clock in the night and 12 o'clock in the day *We're open from 9 a.m. to 5 p.m. daily.*

am *strong form* /æm/ *weak forms* /əm, m/ *present simple I of* be

amalgamate /əˈmælɡəmeɪt/ *verb* [I, T] If two or more organizations amalgamate, they join to become one, and if you amalgamate them, you make them do this. *a decision to **amalgamate with** another school* • **amalgamation** /əˌmælɡəˈmeɪʃᵊn/ *noun* [C, U]

amass /əˈmæs/ *verb* [T] *formal* to get a lot of money or information over a period of time *He **amassed a fortune** in the diamond trade.*

amateur¹ /ˈæmətəʳ/ *adjective* doing something as a hobby and not as your job *an amateur photographer*

amateur² /ˈæmətəʳ/ *noun* [C] **1** someone who does something as a hobby and not as their job **2** someone who is not good at what they do *I won't be giving them any more work - they're a bunch of amateurs.*

amateurish /ˈæmətᵊrɪʃ/ [US] /ˌæməˈtɜːrɪʃ/ *adjective* done without skill or attention

amaze /əˈmeɪz/ *verb* [T] to make someone very surprised *It amazes me how much energy that woman has*

amazed /əˈmeɪzd/ *adjective* extremely surprised *I was **amazed at** the price.* ○ [+ (that)] *I was amazed that Paul recognized me.*

amazement /əˈmeɪzmənt/ *noun* [U] extreme surprise *Jana looked at him **in amazement**.* ○ ***To his amazement** they offered him the job.*

amazing /əˈmeɪzɪŋ/ *adjective* very surprising [+ question word] *It's amazing how many people can't read.* • **amazingly** *adverb She looked amazingly well.*

ambassador /æmˈbæsədəʳ/ *noun* [C] the main official sent by the government of a country to represent it in another country *the French ambassador to Britain*

amber /ˈæmbəʳ/ *noun* [U] **1** a colour between yellow and orange **2** a hard, clear yellowish-brown substance, used for making jewellery • **amber** *adjective an amber traffic light*

ambience (*also* **ambiance**) /ˈæmbiəns/ *noun* [U, no plural] the qualities of a place and the way it makes you feel *Lighting adds a lot to the ambience of a room.*

ambiguity /ˌæmbɪˈɡjuːəti/ *noun* [C, U] when something has more than one possible meaning *Legal documents must be free of ambiguity.*

ambiguous /æmˈbɪɡjuəs/ *adjective* having more than one possible meaning *an ambiguous statement* • **ambiguously** *adverb*

A

WORD PARTNERS FOR *ambition*

have an ambition • **achieve/fulfil/realize** an ambition • a **burning/lifelong** ambition

⊶**ambition** /æm'bɪʃən/ *noun* **1** [C] something you want to achieve in your life *My ambition is to retire at forty.* **2** [U] a strong feeling that you want to be successful or powerful *My sister always had more ambition than me.*

ambitious /æm'bɪʃəs/ *adjective* **1** wanting to be successful or powerful *an ambitious young lawyer* **2** An ambitious plan will need a lot of work and will be difficult to achieve. *This is our most ambitious project so far.*

ambivalent /æm'bɪvələnt/ *adjective* having two different feelings about something *He was **ambivalent about** moving to London.* • **ambivalence** /æm'bɪvəlᵊns/ *noun* [U]

amble /'æmbl/ *verb* **amble along/around/through, etc** to walk somewhere in a slow and relaxed way *We ambled home across the fields.*

ambulance /'æmbjələns/ *noun* [C] a vehicle that takes people to hospital when they are ill or hurt *an ambulance driver*

ambush

ambush /'æmbʊʃ/ *verb* [T] to attack a person or vehicle after hiding somewhere and waiting for them to arrive [often passive] *The bus was ambushed by a gang of youths.* • **ambush** *noun* [C] *Two policemen were killed in a terrorist ambush.*

ameliorate /ə'mi:liᵊreɪt/ *verb* [T] *formal* to make a problem or bad situation better

amen /,ɑ:'men/ *exclamation* something that Christians say at the end of a prayer

amenable /ə'mi:nəbl/ *adjective* willing to do or accept something *She may be more **amenable to** the idea now.*

amend /ə'mend/ *verb* [T] to slightly change the words of a document [often passive] *The contract has now been amended.*

amendment /ə'mendmənt/ *noun* [C, U] a change in the words of a document, or the process of doing this *to **make an amendment to** the human rights law*

amends /ə'mendz/ *noun* **make amends** to do something nice for someone to show that you are sorry for something that you have done *I want to **make amends for** the worry I've caused you.*

amenity /ə'mi:nəti/ [US] /ə'menəti/ *noun* [C] a building, piece of equipment, or service that is provided for people's comfort or enjoyment [usually plural] *The campsite's amenities include a pool and three restaurants.*

American /ə'merɪkən/ *adjective* **1** relating to the United States of America *an American accent* **2 North/South American** relating to one or more of the countries of North/South America • **American** *noun* [C] someone who comes from the United States of America ➲See also: **Native American.**

A,merican 'football *UK* (*US* **football**) *noun* [U] a game for two teams of eleven players in which each team tries to kick, run with, or throw an oval ball across the opposing team's goal line ➲See colour picture **Sports 2** on page Centre 15.

A,merican 'Indian *adjective* relating or belonging to the original race of people who lived in North America • **American Indian** *noun* [C]

amiable /'eɪmiəbl/ *adjective* pleasant and friendly *an amiable young man* • **amiably** *adverb*

amicable /'æmɪkəbl/ *adjective formal* done in a friendly way, without arguments *an amicable agreement/divorce* • **amicably** *adverb*

amid /ə'mɪd/ (*also* **amidst** /ə'mɪdst/) *preposition formal* **1** while something else is happening *Security was increased **amid fears** of further terrorist attacks.* **2** among *a village set amid the hills*

amiss¹ /ə'mɪs/ *adjective* [never before noun] If something is amiss, there is something wrong. *I knew something was amiss when he didn't answer the door.*

amiss² /ə'mɪs/ *adverb* **1 would not go amiss** *UK* If something would not go amiss, it would be useful or nice in a particular situation. *A cup of coffee wouldn't go amiss.* **2 take it amiss** *UK* to feel upset by what someone says or does *I think she might take it amiss if I left early.*

ammonia /ə'məʊniə/ *noun* [U] a liquid or gas with a strong smell, used in substances for cleaning things

ammunition /,æmjə'nɪʃən/ *noun* [U] **1** a supply of bullets and bombs to be fired from guns **2** facts that you can use to criticize someone

amnesia /æm'ni:ʒə/ *noun* [U] a medical condition that makes you forget things

amnesty /'æmnəsti/ *noun* **1** [C, U] a time when a government allows political prisoners to go free **2** [C] a time when people can give weapons or drugs to the police, or admit that they have done something illegal, without being punished *to declare an amnesty*

⊶**among** /ə'mʌŋ/ (*also* **amongst** /ə'mʌŋst/) *preposition* **1** [IN THE MIDDLE] in the middle of something *He disappeared among the crowd.* **2** [IN A GROUP] in a particular group *The decision will not be popular among students.* ○ *I'm going to give you a minute to talk **amongst yourselves*** (= talk to each other). **3** [ONE OF A GROUP] to be one of a small group *He is among the top five tennis players in the country.* **4** [DIVIDE] to each one in a group *She divided the cake among the children.*

amoral /ˌeɪˈmɒrəl/ *adjective* not caring if what you are doing is morally wrong *an amoral person/act*

amorous /ˈæmərəs/ *adjective* full of love and sexual excitement *amorous adventures*

⊶**amount¹** /əˈmaʊnt/ *noun* **[C]** how much there is of something *The project will take a huge **amount of** time and money.*

COMMON LEARNER ERROR

amount of or **number of**?

Amount of is used with uncountable nouns.

I should reduce the amount of coffee I drink.

Did you use the right amount of flour?

Number of is used with countable nouns.

We don't know the number of people involved yet.

They received a large number of complaints.

amount² /əˈmaʊnt/ *verb*

amount to sth **1** to be the same as something, or to have the same effect as something *He gave what amounted to an apology on behalf of the company.* **2** to have a particular total *goods amounting to $800*

amp /æmp/ (*also* **ampere** /ˈæmpeər/) *noun* **[C]** a unit for measuring the strength of an electric current *a thirty-amp fuse*

ample /ˈæmpl/ *adjective* **1** enough, or more than enough *She's had **ample time** to get the work done.* **2** large *her ample bosom* • **amply** *adverb*

amplifier /ˈæmplɪfaɪər/ *noun* **[C]** a piece of electronic equipment that makes sounds louder

amplify /ˈæmplɪfaɪ/ *verb* **[T]** **1** to make a sound louder using electronic equipment **2** *formal* to make a feeling or opinion stronger or clearer • **amplification** /ˌæmplɪfɪˈkeɪʃən/ *noun* **[U]**

amputate /ˈæmpjəteɪt/ *verb* **[I, T]** to cut off someone's leg, arm, finger, etc in a medical operation *His leg was amputated at the knee.* • **amputation** /ˌæmpjəˈteɪʃən/ *noun* **[C, U]**

amuse /əˈmjuːz/ *verb* **[T]** **1** to make someone smile or laugh *I took him an article that I thought might amuse him.* **2** to keep someone interested and help them to have an enjoyable time **[often reflexive]** *I bought a magazine to amuse myself while I was on the train.*

amused /əˈmjuːzd/ *adjective* **1** showing that you think something is funny *an amused smile* ○ *She was very **amused by/at** your comments.* **2 keep sb amused** to keep someone interested and help them to have an enjoyable time *How do you keep an eight-year-old boy amused?*

amusement /əˈmjuːzmənt/ *noun* **1** **[U]** the feeling that you have when something makes you smile or laugh *I watched the performance **with** great **amusement**.* ○ ***To our amusement** the tent collapsed on top of them.* **2** **[C, U]** an enjoyable way of spending your time *I play the piano but just **for** my own **amusement**.*

aˈmusement ˌpark *noun* **[C]** a large park where you can ride on exciting machines

amusing /əˈmjuːzɪŋ/ *adjective* making you laugh or smile *an amusing letter*

⊶**an** *strong form* /æn/ *weak form* /ən/ *determiner* used instead of 'a' when the next word starts with a vowel sound *an apple* ○ *an hour* ➲See Common learner error at a.

anaemia *UK* (*US* **anemia**) /əˈniːmiə/ *noun* **[U]** a medical condition in which your blood does not contain enough red cells • **anaemic** *UK* (*US* **anemic**) /əˈniːmɪk/ *adjective*

anaesthetic *UK* (*US* **anesthetic**) /ˌænəsˈθetɪk/ *noun* **[C, U]** a drug that makes you unable to feel pain during an operation *The operation is done **under anaesthetic*** (= using anaesthetic). ➲See also: **general anaesthetic, local anaesthetic.**

anaesthetist *UK* (*US* **anesthetist**) /əˈniːsθətɪst/ [US] /əˈnesθətɪst/ *noun* **[C]** a doctor in a hospital who gives anaesthetics to people

anaesthetize *UK* (*US* **anesthetize**) /əˈniːsθətaɪz/ [US] /əˈnesθətaɪz/ *verb* **[T]** to give someone drugs that make them unable to feel pain

anagram /ˈænəɡræm/ *noun* **[C]** a word or phrase made by putting the letters of another word or phrase in a different order *'Team' is an anagram of 'meat'.*

anal /ˈeɪnəl/ *adjective* relating to the anus (= hole where solid waste comes out of the body)

analogous /əˈnæləɡəs/ *adjective formal* similar in some ways *It's often said that life is **analogous to** a journey.*

analogy /əˈnælədʒi/ *noun* **[C, U]** a comparison that shows how two things are similar *She **draws an analogy between** life's events and a game of chance.*

analyse *UK* (*US* **analyze**) /ˈænəlaɪz/ *verb* **[T]** to examine the details of something carefully, in order to understand or explain it *to analyse information* ○ *Blood samples were analysed in the laboratory.*

WORD PARTNERS FOR *analysis*

do an analysis • a **detailed** analysis • an analysis **of** sth • **send** sth **for** analysis

analysis /əˈnæləsɪs/ *noun* **[C, U]** *plural* **analyses** /əˈnæləsiːz/ the process of analysing something *a **detailed analysis*** ○ *A sample of soil was sent **for analysis**.*

analyst /ˈænəlɪst/ *noun* **[C]** someone whose job is to examine the details of a situation carefully, and give their opinion about it *a **financial/political analyst***

analytical /ˌænəlˈɪtɪkəl/ (*also* **analytic**) *adjective* examining the details of something carefully, in order to understand or explain it *analytical skills* ○ *an **analytical mind***

analyze /ˈænəlaɪz/ *verb* **[T]** *US spelling of* analyse

anarchist /ˈænəkɪst/ *noun* **[C]** someone who thinks that society should not be controlled by a government and laws

anarchy /ˈænəki/ *noun* **[U]** when there is no law or government, or when people ignore them • **anarchic** /ænˈɑːkɪk/ *adjective*

anatomy /əˈnætəmi/ *noun* **1** **[U]** the scientific study of the body and how its parts are arranged **2** **[C]** the body of a person or living thing **[usually singular]** *the female anatomy* • **anatomical** /ˌænəˈtɒmɪkəl/ *adjective*

ancestor /ˈænsestər/ *noun* **[C]** a relative who

lived a long time ago *My ancestors came from Ireland*. ● **ancestral** /æn'sestr°l/ *adjective*

ancestry /'ænsestri/ *noun* [C, U] your relatives who lived a long time ago, or the origin of your family *Americans of Japanese ancestry*

anchor¹ /'æŋkə'/
noun [C] **1** a heavy,
metal object that is
dropped into water
to stop a boat from
moving **2** *US* some-
one who reads the
news and announce-
ments on a tele-
vision or radio pro-
gramme

anchor

anchor² /'æŋkə'/ *verb*
1 BOAT [I, T] to stop a
boat from moving
by dropping a heavy
metal object into the
water **2** FASTEN [T] to make something or someone stay in one position by fastening them
firmly *We anchored ourselves to the rocks with
a rope*. **3** PROGRAMME [T] *US* to read the news or
announcements on television or radio as your
job

ancient /'eɪnʃ°nt/ *adjective* **1** [always before noun]
from a long time ago *ancient Greece/Rome* ○ *an
ancient building* **2** *humorous* very old *This
computer is ancient*.

COMMON LEARNER ERROR

ancient, former or old?

Ancient cannot be used to describe someone or something that existed in the recent past, but not now. Use
former instead.

He is a former pupil of mine.

~~He is an ancient pupil of mine.~~

Ancient means thousands or hundreds of years old. It
should not be used for people.

We need to provide care for old people.

~~We need to provide care for ancient people.~~

○**and** *strong form* /ænd/ *weak forms* /ənd, ən/ *conjunction* **1** JOIN used to join two words or two
parts of a sentence *tea and coffee* ○ *We were
tired and hungry*. **2** AFTER used to say that one
thing happens after another thing *I got dressed
and had my breakfast*. **3** SO *so The car
wouldn't start and I had to get a taxi*. **4** AFTER
VERB *mainly UK* used instead of 'to' after some
verbs, such as 'try' and 'go' *Try and eat something*. **5** NUMBERS used when saying or adding
numbers *It cost a hundred and twenty pounds*.
○ *UK Two and three equals five*. **6** EMPHASIZE
used between two words that are the same to
make their meaning stronger *The sound grew
louder and louder*.

anecdote /'ænɪkdəʊt/ *noun* [C] a short story
that you tell someone about something that
happened to you or someone else *a speech full
of anecdotes* ● **anecdotal** /ˌænɪk'dəʊt°l/ *adjective*
consisting of things that people have said, and
not facts *anecdotal evidence*

anemia /ə'ni:miə/ *noun* [U] *US spelling of*

anaemia (= a medical condition in which your
blood does not contain enough red cells)

anemic /ə'ni:mɪk/ *adjective US spelling of* anaemic (= having anemia)

anesthetic /ˌænəs'θetɪk/ *noun* [C, U] *US spelling
of* anaesthetic (= a drug that makes you unable
to feel pain during an operation)

anesthetist /ə'nesθətɪst/ *noun* [C] *US spelling of*
anaesthetist (= a doctor who gives anaesthetics to people)

anew /ə'nju:/ *adverb literary* If you do something anew, you do it again in a different way.
*Moving to another city gave me the chance to
start anew*.

angel /'eɪndʒ°l/ *noun* [C]
1 a spiritual creature
like a human with wings,
who some people believe
lives with God in heaven
2 a very good, kind
person *Be an angel and
get me a drink*. ● **angelic**
/æn'dʒelɪk/ *adjective* very
beautiful or good *an angelic child*

angel

WORD PARTNERS FOR *anger*

express/show anger ● **be trembling with**
anger ● anger **at/over** sth ● **in** anger ● **public**
anger ● **mounting/growing** anger

○**anger¹** /'æŋgə'/ *noun* [U] a strong feeling against
someone who has behaved badly, making you
want to shout at them or hurt them *public
anger at the terrorist killings* ○ *anger at/over
sth* ○ *He never once raised his voice in anger*.

anger² /'æŋgə'/ *verb* [T] to make someone angry
[often passive] *Students were angered by the college's decision*.

angle¹ /'æŋgl/ *noun*
[C] **1** SPACE a space
between two lines or
surfaces that meet
at one point, which
you measure in de-
grees *an angle of 90
degrees* **2** **at an angle**
not horizontal or
vertical, but sloping
*He wore his hat at
an angle*. **3** WAY OF
THINKING the way
you think about a
situation *Try look-
ing at the problem
from my angle*.
4 DIRECTION the dir-
ection from which you look at something *This
is the same building photographed from different angles*. ⊃See also: **right angle**.

angle

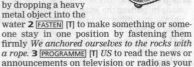

angle² /'æŋgl/ *verb* [T] to aim or turn something
in a direction that is not horizontal or vertical
She angled a shot into the corner of the court.
be angling for sth to try to get something
without asking for it in a direct way *Is he angling for an invitation?*

angler /'æŋglə'/ *noun* [C] someone who catches
fish as a hobby or sport

Anglican /ˈæŋglɪkən/ *adjective* belonging or relating to the Church of England (= the official church in England) ● **Anglican** *noun* [C]

angling /ˈæŋglɪŋ/ *noun* [U] the sport or hobby of catching fish

Anglo- /ˈæŋgləʊ-/ *prefix* of or connected with Britain or England *Anglo-Indian, Anglo-Saxon*

If someone is angry about something that has happened, you can say that they are **annoyed** or **irritated**: *He was a bit annoyed with her for being late.* ● *I was irritated that he didn't thank me.*

If someone is extremely angry, you can use adjectives such as **furious**, **irate**, or **livid**: *My boss was furious with me.* ● *Hundreds of irate passengers have complained to the airline about its poor service.*

If you are angry with a child, you might describe yourself as **cross**: *I'm cross with you for not telling me where you were going.*

The expression **up in arms** is sometimes used when people are angry about something they think is unfair: *Local people are up in arms over plans to close the local swimming pool.*

If someone suddenly becomes very angry, you can use the informal expressions **go crazy/mad**: *Dad went crazy/mad when he found out we'd broken the window.*

o─**angry** /ˈæŋgri/ *adjective* having a strong feeling against someone who has behaved badly, making you want to shout at them or hurt them *He's really angry at/with me for upsetting Sophie.* ○ *I don't understand what he's angry about.* ● **angrily** *adverb*

angst /æŋst/ *noun* [U] a strong feeling of worry and unhappiness *teenage angst*

anguish /ˈæŋgwɪʃ/ *noun* [U] extreme suffering, especially mental suffering *It's the anguish of knowing that I can do nothing to help.* ● **anguished** *adjective* [always before noun] *anguished parents*

angular /ˈæŋgjʊlə^r/ *adjective* An angular shape or object has a lot of straight lines and sharp points. *an angular face*

o─**animal¹** /ˈænɪm^əl/ *noun* [C] **1** [NOT A HUMAN] something that lives and moves but is not a person, bird, fish, or insect *a wild animal* ○ *She's a real animal lover.* **2** [NOT A PLANT] anything that lives and moves, including people, birds, etc *Are humans the only animals to use language?* **3** [CRUEL PERSON] *informal* a very cruel and violent person

animal² /ˈænɪm^əl/ *adjective* [always before noun] Animal qualities and feelings relate to your basic physical needs. *animal passion*

animate /ˈænɪmət/ *adjective formal* alive ⊃Opposite inanimate.

animated /ˈænɪmeɪtɪd/ *adjective* **1** showing a lot of interest and excitement *an animated conversation* **2** An animated film is one in which drawings and models seem to move.

animation /ˌænɪˈmeɪʃ^ən/ *noun* **1** [U] interest and excitement *She spoke with great animation.* **2** [C, U] an animated film, or the process of making animated films *a course in computer animation*

animosity /ˌænɪˈmɒsəti/ *noun* [C, U] when someone hates or feels angry towards someone else *There is no animosity between the two teams.*

ankle /ˈæŋkl/ *noun* [C] the part of your leg that is just above your foot ⊃See colour picture **The Body** on page Centre 13.

annex¹ /əˈneks/ *verb* [T] to start to rule or control an area or country next to your own ● **annexation** /ˌænekˈseɪʃ^ən/ *noun* [C, U]

annex² (*also UK* **annexe**) /ˈæneks/ *noun* [C] a building that is joined to a larger one

annihilate /əˈnaɪɪleɪt/ *verb* [T] **1** to destroy something completely *a city annihilated by an atomic bomb* **2** *informal* to defeat someone very easily ● **annihilation** /əˌnaɪɪˈleɪʃ^ən/ *noun* [U]

anniversary /ˌænɪˈvɜːs^əri/ *noun* [C] a date on which you remember or celebrate something that happened on that date one or more years ago *a wedding anniversary* ○ *the 40th anniversary of Kennedy's death* ⊃See also: silver wedding anniversary.

o─**announce** /əˈnaʊns/ *verb* [T] to tell people about something officially or with force or confidence *The company has announced plans to open six new stores.* ○ [+ (that)] *Halfway through dinner, he announced that he was going out.*

o─**announcement** /əˈnaʊnsmənt/ *noun* **1** [C] something that someone says officially, giving information about something *The Prime Minister made an unexpected announcement this morning.* **2** [no plural] when someone announces something

announcer /əˈnaʊnsə^r/ *noun* [C] someone who introduces programmes on the radio or television

annoy /əˈnɔɪ/ *verb* [T] to make someone slightly angry *He's always late and it's starting to annoy me.*

annoyance /əˈnɔɪəns/ *noun* [U] the feeling of being annoyed *He kept losing his keys, much to the annoyance of* (= which annoyed) *his wife.*

annoyed /ə'nɔɪd/ *adjective* slightly angry *I was a bit annoyed with/at Kathy for not coming.*

annoying /ə'nɔɪɪŋ/ *adjective* making you feel annoyed *an annoying habit/cough*

o⊷**annual**[1] /'ænjuəl/ *adjective* **1** happening or produced once a year *an annual meeting/report* **2** measured over a period of one year *annual rainfall* ● **annually** *adverb*

annual[2] /'ænjuəl/ *noun* [C] **1** a plant which grows, produces seed, and dies within one year **2** a book produced every year containing new information about the same subject

annulment /ə'nʌlmənt/ *noun* [C, U] *formal* when a court says officially that a marriage or agreement does not now exist and was never legal

anomaly /ə'nɒməli/ *noun* [C] *formal* something that is unusual or that does not seem right *There are some anomalies in the data.*

anonymity /,ænə'nɪməti/ *noun* [U] when someone's name is not given or known *She agreed to speak to a journalist but requested anonymity.*

anonymous /ə'nɒnɪməs/ *adjective* not giving a name *an anonymous phone call* ○ *The winner has asked to remain anonymous.* ● **anonymously** *adverb*

anorak /'æn³ræk/ *noun* [C] *UK* **1** a jacket with a hood (= part that covers your head) that protects you from rain and cold **2** *humorous* a boring person who is too interested in the details of a hobby and who is not good in social situations

anorexia /,æn³r'eksiə/ (*also* anorexia nervosa /æn³r,eksiən³:'vəʊsə/) *noun* [U] a mental illness in which someone refuses to eat and becomes very thin

anorexic /,æn³r'eksɪk/ *adjective* having the illness anorexia ● **anorexic** *noun* [C]

o⊷**another** /ə'nʌð³r/ *pronoun, determiner* **1** one more person or thing, or an additional amount *Would you like another piece of cake?* ○ *We can fit another person in my car.* **2** a different person or thing *I'm going to look for another job.* ○ *This one's slightly damaged - I'll get you another.*

COMMON LEARNER ERROR

another or **other**?

Another means 'one other' and is used with a singular noun. It is written as one word.
Would you like another cup of coffee?
~~Would you like other cup of coffee?~~

Other is used with a plural noun and means different things or people than the ones you are talking about.
She had other ambitions.
~~She had another ambitions.~~

o⊷**answer**[1] /'ɑːnsə³r/ *verb* **1** WORDS [I, T] to speak or write back to someone who has asked you a question or spoken to you *I asked when she was leaving but she didn't answer.* ○ *I must answer his letter.* **2** DOOR [I, T] to open the door when someone has knocked on it or rung a bell *I knocked several times but no one answered.* **3** TELEPHONE [I, T] to pick up the telephone receiver (= part that you hold to your ear) when it rings *Could someone answer the phone?* **4** TEST [T] to write or say something as a reply to a question in a test or competition

answer (sb) back If a child answers back, they reply rudely to an adult.

answer for sth 1 to be responsible for something, or punished for something *Do you think parents should have to answer for their children's behaviour?* **2** have a lot to answer for to be the main cause of something bad which has happened *"Why is violent crime on the increase?" " Well, I think television has a lot to answer for."*

WORD PARTNERS FOR answer

get/give/know/provide an answer ● a correct/simple/wrong answer ● the answer to sth

o⊷**answer**[2] /'ɑːnsə³r/ *noun* [C] **1** WORDS what you say or write back to someone who has asked you a question or spoken to you *I asked him if he was going but I didn't hear his answer.* ○ *Please give me your answer by next week.* **2** DOOR/TELEPHONE when someone answers the telephone or the door [usually singular] *I rang the bell but there was no answer.* **3** SOLUTION a way of solving a problem *It's a difficult situation and I don't know what the answer is.* **4** TEST the correct number or information given as a reply to a question in a test or competition *Did you get the answer to Question 6?*

answerphone /'ɑːnsə³fəʊn/ *UK* (*UK/US* answering machine) *noun* [C] a machine that records your message if you telephone someone and they do not answer *I left a message on her answerphone.*

ant /ænt/ *noun* [C] a small, black or red insect that lives in groups on the ground ⊃See picture at **insect**.

antagonism /æn'tæg³nɪz³m/ *noun* [U] feelings of strong disagreement or hate *There's a history of antagonism between the two teams.*

antagonistic /æn,tæg³n'ɪstɪk/ *adjective* strongly disagreeing with someone or something *He's antagonistic towards critics.*

antagonize (*also* UK -ise) /æn'tæg³naɪz/ *verb* [T] to make someone angry or unfriendly towards you *He's antagonized colleagues by making changes without discussing them.*

the Antarctic /æn'tɑːktɪk/ *noun* the very cold area around the South Pole ● **Antarctic** *adjective* [always before noun] *Antarctic wildlife*

antelope /'æntɪləʊp/ *noun* [C] an animal like a large deer with long horns

antenatal /,æntɪ'neɪt³l/ *UK* (*US* prenatal) *adjective* [always before noun] relating to pregnant women before their babies are born *an antenatal class*

antenna /æn'tenə/ *noun* [C] **1** *plural* antennae one of two long, thin parts on the head of an insect or sea creature, used for feeling things **2** *plural* antennae or antennas *US* (*UK* aerial) a piece of metal that is used for receiving television or radio signals ⊃See colour picture **Car** on page Centre 7.

anthem /'ænθəm/ *noun* [C] a song chosen by a country or organization to be sung on special occasions ⊃See also: **national anthem**.

anthology /æn'θɒlədʒi/ *noun* [C] a book which includes stories or poems written by different people *an anthology of Irish verse*

anthropology /ˌænθrə'pɒlədʒi/ *noun* [U] the scientific study of human development and society or different societies ● **anthropologist** /ˌænθrə'pɒlədʒɪst/ *noun* [C] ● **anthropological** /ˌænθrəpə'lɒdʒɪkəl/ *adjective*

anti- /ænti-/ *prefix* **1** opposed to or against *anti-terrorist laws, anti-American protesters* **2** opposite of or preventing *anti-clockwise movement, anti-lock brakes, anti-depressant drugs* ⊃Compare **pro-**.

antibiotic /ˌæntɪbaɪ'ɒtɪk/ *noun* [C] a medicine which cures infections by destroying harmful bacteria [usually plural] *He is on antibiotics for an ear infection.*

antibody /'æntɪˌbɒdi/ *noun* [C] a substance produced in your blood to fight disease

anticipate /æn'tɪsɪpeɪt/ *verb* [T] to expect something, or to prepare for something before it happens *to anticipate a problem* ○ [+ that] *We anticipate that prices will fall next year.*

anticipation /ænˌtɪsɪ'peɪʃən/ *noun* [U] **1** when you are waiting for something to happen, usually with excitement *The children were breathless with anticipation.* **2 in anticipation (of)** in preparation for something happening *She's even decorated the spare room in anticipation of your visit.*

anticlimax /ˌæntɪ'klaɪmæks/ *noun* [C, U] a disappointing experience, often one that you thought would be exciting before it happened or one that comes after a more exciting experience *After so much preparation, the party was a bit of an anticlimax.*

anti-clockwise /ˌæntɪ'klɒkwaɪz/ UK (US **counterclockwise**) *adjective, adverb* in the opposite direction to the way the hands (= that point to the numbers) of a clock move *Turn the knob anti-clockwise.* ⊃See picture at **clockwise**.

antics /'æntɪks/ *noun* [plural] unusual or bad behaviour that entertains or annoys people *He's well known for his antics on and off the tennis court.*

anti-depressant /ˌæntɪdɪ'presənt/ *noun* [C] a medicine for people who are depressed (= severely unhappy)

antidote /'æntɪdəʊt/ *noun* [C] **1 antidote to sth** an activity that stops something bad from harming you *Exercise is the best antidote to stress.* **2** a substance that stops another substance from damaging your body *a deadly poison with no antidote*

antipathy /æn'tɪpəθi/ *noun* [U] *formal* a strong feeling of dislike for someone *He is a private man with a deep antipathy to/towards the press.*

antiperspirant /ˌæntɪ'pɜːspərənt/ *noun* [C, U] a substance that prevents you from becoming wet under your arms when you are hot

antiquated /'æntɪkweɪtɪd/ *adjective* very old and not modern enough *an antiquated system*

antique /æn'tiːk/ *noun* [C] an object that is old, and often rare or beautiful *His home is full of valuable antiques.* ○ *an antique shop* ● **antique** *adjective antique furniture/china*

antiquity /æn'tɪkwəti/ *noun* **1** [U] *formal* the ancient past *the writers of antiquity* **2** [C] an ancient object [usually plural] *priceless Egyptian antiquities*

anti-Semitism /ˌæntɪ'semɪtɪzəm/ *noun* [U] when someone hates Jewish people, or treats them in a cruel or unfair way ● **anti-Semitic** /ˌæntɪsɪ'mɪtɪk/ *adjective*

antiseptic /ˌæntɪ'septɪk/ *noun* [C, U] a substance that you put on an injury to prevent infection ● **antiseptic** *adjective antiseptic cream*

anti-social /ˌæntɪ'səʊʃəl/ *adjective* **1** Anti-social behaviour harms or upsets the people around you. *Increasingly, smoking is regarded as an anti-social habit.* **2** An anti-social person does not like being with other people.

anti-spam /ˌæntɪ'spæm/ *adjective* [always before noun] used to stop people sending or receiving emails that are not wanted, especially advertisements *anti-spam legislation*

anti-terrorist /ˌæntɪ'terərɪst/ *adjective* intended to prevent or reduce terrorism (= the use of violence for political purposes) *anti-terrorist laws/legislation*

antithesis /æn'tɪθəsɪs/ *noun* [C] *plural* **antitheses** /æn'tɪθəsiːz/ *formal* the exact opposite [usually singular] *She is slim and shy - the antithesis of her sister.*

antler /'æntləʳ/ *noun* [C] a horn that looks like branches on the head of a male deer

anus /'eɪnəs/ *noun* [C] a hole where solid waste comes out of the body

---

WORD PARTNERS FOR anxiety

a cause/source of anxiety ● feelings/levels of anxiety ● anxiety about/over sth

---

anxiety /æŋ'zaɪəti/ *noun* [C, U] the feeling of being very worried *That explains his anxiety about her health.*

anxious /'æŋkʃəs/ *adjective* **1** worried and nervous *She's very anxious about her exams.* **2** wanting to do something or wanting something to happen [+ to do sth] *He's anxious to get home.* ○ [+ that] *I was anxious that no one else should know.* ● **anxiously** *adverb We waited anxiously by the phone.*

o--**any**[1] *strong form* /'eni/ *weak form* /əni/ *pronoun, determiner* **1** used in questions and negatives to mean 'some' *Is there any of that lemon cake left?* ○ *I haven't seen any of his films.* ○ *I asked Andrew for some change but he hasn't got any.* ⊃See Common learner error at **some**. **2** one of or each of a particular kind of person or thing when it is not important which *Any advice that you can give me would be greatly appreciated.* ○ *Any of those shirts would be fine.*

o--**any**[2] *strong form* /'eni/ *weak form* /əni/ *adverb* used in questions and negatives to emphasize a comparative adjective or adverb *Do you feel any better?* ○ *I can't walk any faster.* ○ *She couldn't wait any longer.*

A

o-**anybody** /'eni,bɒdi/ *pronoun* another word for anyone

anyhow /'enihaʊ/ (*also* anyway) *adverb* 1 MORE IMPORTANTLY used to give a more important reason for something that you are saying *I don't need a car and I can't afford one anyhow.* 2 DESPITE despite that *He hates carrots but he ate them anyhow.* 3 IN CONVERSATION used when you are returning to an earlier subject *Anyhow, as I said, I'll be away next week.* 4 CHANGING STATEMENT used when you want to slightly change something that you have just said *Boys aren't horrible - not all of them anyhow!*

,**any 'more** (*also* anymore) *adverb* If you do not do something or something does not happen any more, you have stopped doing it or it does not now happen. *This coat doesn't fit me any more, would you like to have it?*

o-**anyone** /'eniwʌn/ (*also* anybody) *pronoun* 1 used in questions and negatives to mean 'a person or people' *I didn't know anyone at the party.* ○ *Does anyone else* (= another person/other people) *want to come?* 2 any person or any people *Anyone can go - you don't have to be invited.*

anyplace /'enipleɪs/ *adverb* US anywhere

o-**anything** /'eniθɪŋ/ *pronoun* 1 used in questions and negatives to mean 'something' *I haven't got anything to wear.* ○ *Was there anything else* (= another thing) *you wanted to say?* 2 any object, event, or situation *We can do anything you like.* ○ *Tom will eat anything.* 3 **anything like** used in questions and negatives to mean 'at all similar to' *Does he look anything like his sister or brother?*

o-**anyway** /'eniweɪ/ (*also* anyhow) (*also* US anyways *spoken*) *adverb* 1 MORE IMPORTANTLY used to give a more important reason for something that you are saying *We can drive you to the station - we go that way anyway.* 2 DESPITE despite that *He hates carrots but he ate them anyway.* 3 IN CONVERSATION used when you are returning to an earlier subject *Anyway, as I said, I'll be away next week.* 4 CHANGING STATEMENT used when you want to slightly change something that you have just said *Boys aren't horrible - not all of them anyway!*

o-**anywhere** /'eniweəʳ/ (*also* US anyplace) *adverb* 1 in or to any place *Just sit anywhere.* ○ *I couldn't find a post office anywhere.* 2 used in questions and negatives to mean 'a place' *He doesn't have anywhere to stay.* ○ *Is there anywhere else you'd like to visit while you're here?* 3 **anywhere near sth** used in questions and negatives to mean 'close to being or doing something' *The house isn't anywhere near ready.* 4 **not get anywhere** *informal* to not make any progress *I tried discussing the problem with her but I didn't get anywhere.*

o-**apart** /ə'pɑːt/ *adverb* 1 SEPARATED separated by a space or period of time *Stand with your feet wide apart.* ○ *Our kids were born just eighteen months apart.* 2 INTO PIECES into separate, smaller pieces *My jacket is coming/falling apart.* 3 **apart from a** EXCEPT except for *Apart from Jodie, who hurt her leg, all the children*

were fine. **b** IN ADDITION in addition to *He works a ten-hour day and that's apart from the work he does at the weekend.*

apartheid /ə'pɑːtaɪt/ *noun* [U] in the past in South Africa, a political system in which white people had power over black people and made them live separately

o-**apartment** /ə'pɑːtmənt/ *noun* [C] *mainly US* a set of rooms for someone to live in on one level of a building or house

a'partment ,building *noun* [C] US a building which is divided into apartments

apathetic /,æpə'θetɪk/ *adjective* not interested in anything or willing to change things *Young people today are so apathetic about politics.*

apathy /'æpəθi/ *noun* [U] when someone is not interested in anything or willing to change things

ape /eɪp/ *noun* [C] a hairy animal like a monkey but with no tail and long arms

aperitif /ə,perə'tiːf/ *noun* [C] a small alcoholic drink before a meal

aperture /'æpətʃəʳ/ *noun* [C] a small hole, especially one that allows light into a camera

ape

apex /'eɪpeks/ *noun* [C] the highest part of a shape *the apex of a pyramid*

apiece /ə'piːs/ *adverb* each *Dolls from this period sell for £30 apiece.*

the apocalypse /ə'pɒkəlɪps/ *noun* in some religions, the final destruction of the world

apocalyptic /ə,pɒkə'lɪptɪk/ *adjective* showing or describing the destruction of the world *an apocalyptic vision of the future*

apologetic /ə,pɒlə'dʒetɪk/ *adjective* showing or saying that you are sorry about something *an apologetic smile* ○ *She was very apologetic about missing the meeting.*

apologize (*also* UK -ise) /ə'pɒlədʒaɪz/ *verb* [I] to tell someone that you are sorry about something you have done *The bank apologized for the error.* ○ *The pilot apologized to passengers for the delay.*

WORD PARTNERS FOR **apology**

demand/make/owe sb/**receive** an apology ● **accept** sb's apology ● **make no** apology **for** (doing) sth ● a **formal/full/public** apology ● an apology **for** sth ● an apology **to** sb

apology /ə'pɒlədʒi/ *noun* [C, U] something you say or write to say that you are sorry about something you have done *I have an apology to make to you - I opened your letter by mistake.* ○ *a letter of apology*

apostle /ə'pɒsl/ *noun* [C] one of the twelve men chosen by Jesus Christ to teach people about Christianity

apostrophe /ə'pɒstrəfi/ *noun* [C] 1 a mark (') used to show that letters or numbers are absent *I'm* (= I am) *hungry.* ○ *I graduated in '98* (= 1998). **2** a punctuation mark (') used before the letter 's' to show that something belongs to someone or something *I drove my brother's car.* ➲See Extra help page **Punctuation** on page Centre 33.

appal *UK* (*US* **appall**) /əˈpɔːl/ *verb* **[T]** **appalling,** *past* **appalled** to make someone extremely shocked or upset *The amount of violence on television appals me.* ○ *We were* ***appalled at/ by*** *her behaviour.* • **appalled** *adjective*

appalling /əˈpɔːlɪŋ/ *adjective* **1** shocking and very unpleasant *Many live in appalling conditions.* ○ *appalling injuries* **2** very bad *appalling behaviour/weather* • **appallingly** *adverb*

apparatus /ˌæpərˈeɪtəs/ [US] /ˌæpəˈrætəs/ *noun* **[C, U]** *plural* **apparatus** or **apparatuses** a set of equipment or tools used for a particular purpose *The diver wore breathing apparatus.*

apparel /əˈpærᵊl/ *noun* **[U]** *mainly US* clothes *children's/women's apparel*

apparent /əˈpærᵊnt/ *adjective* **1** obvious or easy to notice **[+ that]** *It soon became apparent that she had lost interest in the project.* ○ *Suddenly,* ***for no apparent reason*** (= without a reason) *he started screaming and shouting.* **2** **[always before noun]** seeming to exist or be true *I was a little surprised by her apparent lack of interest.*

🔑**apparently** /əˈpærəntli/ *adverb* **1** used to say that you have read or been told something although you are not certain it is true *Apparently it's going to rain today.* **2** used to say that something seems to be true, although it is not certain *There were two apparently unrelated deaths.*

apparition /ˌæpᵊrˈɪʃᵊn/ *noun* **[C]** *literary* a ghost

WORD PARTNERS FOR ***appeal***

issue/launch/make an appeal • **an appeal for sth**

appeal¹ /əˈpiːl/ *noun* **1** [REQUEST] **[C]** when a lot of people are asked to give money, information, or help *The appeal raised over £2 million for AIDS research.* **2** [QUALITY] **[U]** the quality in someone or something that makes them attractive or enjoyable *I've never understood the appeal of skiing.* **3** [LAW] **[C]** a request to a court of law to change a previous legal decision *He won his* ***appeal against*** *his five-year jail sentence.*

appeal² /əˈpiːl/ *verb* **[I]** **1** [REQUEST] to strongly request something, often publicly *The police have* ***appealed for*** *more information.* ○ *They* ***appealed to*** *the commission to keep the hospital open.* **2** [ATTRACT] to attract or interest someone *Cycling has never* ***appealed to*** *me.* **3** [FORMALLY ASK] to formally ask someone to change an official or legal decision *He is* ***appealing against*** *a ten year prison sentence.*

appealing /əˈpiːlɪŋ/ *adjective* attractive or interesting *The idea of living in Paris is very appealing.* • **appealingly** *adverb*

🔑**appear** /əˈpɪəʳ/ *verb* **[I]** **1** [SEEM] to seem to be a particular thing or have a particular quality *He appeared calm and relaxed.* ○ *She* ***appeared to be*** *crying.* ○ **[+ (that)]** ***It appears*** *that we were wrong about him.* **2** [BE SEEN] to start to be seen *He suddenly appeared in the doorway.* ○ *Then a bright light appeared in the sky.* ➲Opposite **disappear**. **3** [BECOME AVAILABLE] to start to exist or become available *Laptop computers first appeared in the 1990s.* ○ *The story appeared in all the major newspapers.* **4** **appear in/at/on, etc** to perform in a film, play, etc, or be seen in public *She appears briefly in the new Bond film.*

🔑**appearance** /əˈpɪərᵊns/ *noun* **1** [IN PUBLIC] **[C]** an occasion when someone appears in public *a television/* ***public appearance*** ○ *He* ***made*** *two* ***appearances*** *during his brief visit.* **2** [WAY YOU LOOK] **[no plural]** the way a person or thing looks *She's very concerned with her appearance.* **3** [ARRIVAL] **[no plural]** when you arrive somewhere or can be seen somewhere *Her appearance at the party was a surprise.* ➲Opposite **disappearance**. **4** [BECOMING AVAILABLE] **[no plural]** when something starts to exist or becomes available *The appearance of new products on the market has increased competition.*

appease /əˈpiːz/ *verb* **[T]** to avoid more arguments by doing what someone wants • **appeasement** *noun* **[U]**

appendicitis /əˌpendɪˈsaɪtɪs/ *noun* **[U]** an illness in which your appendix becomes larger than usual and painful

appendix /əˈpendɪks/ *noun* **[C]** **1** *plural* **appendixes** a small tube-shaped part inside the body below the stomach **2** *plural* **appendices** a separate part at the end of a book, article, etc which contains extra information

WORD PARTNERS FOR ***appetite***

give sb/**have** an appetite • **lose** your appetite • a **good/healthy/huge** appetite • **loss** of appetite

appetite /ˈæpɪtaɪt/ *noun* **[C, U]** **1** the feeling that makes you want to eat *All that walking has* ***given me an appetite.*** **2** **an appetite for sth** when you want something very much *his appetite for adventure* **3** **whet sb's appetite** to make someone want more of something

appetizer /ˈæpɪtaɪzəʳ/ *US* (*UK* **starter**) *noun* **[C]** something that you eat as the first part of a meal

appetizing (*also UK* **-ising**) /ˈæpɪtaɪzɪŋ/ *adjective* If food is appetizing, it looks or smells as if it will taste good.

applaud /əˈplɔːd/ *verb* **1** **[I, T]** to clap your hands to show that you have enjoyed a performance, talk, etc *The audience applauded loudly.* **2** **[T]** *formal* to approve of or admire something *Most people will surely applaud the decision.*

applause /əˈplɔːz/ *noun* **[U]** when people make a noise by clapping their hands to show they have enjoyed or approve of something

apple

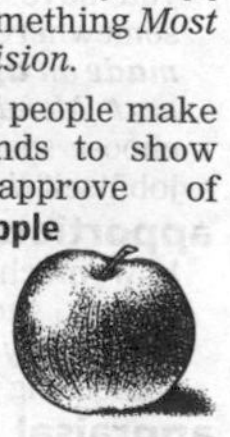

🔑**apple** /ˈæpl/ *noun* **[C]** a hard, round fruit with a green or red skin ➲See colour picture **Fruit and Vegetables** on page Centre 10 ➲See also: **Adam's apple**.

applet /'æplət/ *noun* [C] a small computer program that is automatically copied on to a computer when you look at a document that needs this program to make it work *You have to download an applet which records your payment details.*

appliance /ə'plaɪəns/ *noun* [C] a piece of electrical equipment with a particular purpose in the home *fridges, radios, and other **electrical appliances***

applicable /ə'plɪkəbl/ *adjective* affecting or relating to a person or situation *This law is only **applicable to** people living in Europe.*

applicant /'æplɪkənt/ *noun* [C] someone who asks for something officially, often by writing *There were over fifty **applicants for** the job.*

application /ˌæplɪ'keɪʃᵊn/ *noun* 1 [REQUEST] [C] an official request for something, usually in writing *an **application for** a bank loan* 2 [USE] [C, U] a way in which something can be used for a particular purpose *This technology has many practical applications.* 3 [COMPUTER PROGRAM] [C] a computer program designed for a particular purpose

appli'cation ,form *noun* [C] a form that you use to officially ask for something, for example a job

applied /ə'plaɪd/ *adjective* **applied mathematics/ science, etc** mathematics, science, or another subject which is studied for a practical use

apply /ə'plaɪ/ *verb* 1 [ASK] [I] to ask officially for something, often by writing *I've **applied for** a job.* ○ *He has **applied to** several companies.* 2 [AFFECT] [I] to affect or relate to a particular person or situation *This law only **applies to** married people.* 3 [USE] [T] to use something in a particular situation *The same method can be **applied to** other situations.* 4 [ON SURFACE] [T] to spread a substance on a surface *Apply the cream daily until the symptoms disappear.* 5 **apply yourself** to work hard *If he doesn't apply himself, he'll never pass his exams.*

appoint /ə'pɔɪnt/ *verb* [T] to officially choose someone for a job *He was **appointed as** company director last year.*

appointed /ə'pɔɪntɪd/ *adjective* **appointed date/time/place, etc** the date, time, place, etc that has been chosen for something to happen

> **WORD PARTNERS FOR *appointment***
>
> have/make an appointment • cancel/ keep/miss an appointment • an appointment with sb

o→**appointment** /ə'pɔɪntmənt/ *noun* 1 [C] a time you have arranged to meet someone or go somewhere *a doctor's/dental appointment* ○ *I made an **appointment** with my hairdresser for next Monday.* 2 [C, U] when you officially choose someone for an important job, or the job itself *the appointment of three new teachers*

apportion /ə'pɔːʃᵊn/ *verb* [T] *formal* 1 to choose how much of something a person or each person should have 2 **apportion blame/responsibility** to say who was responsible for something bad that happened

appraisal /ə'preɪzᵊl/ *noun* [C, U] when you examine someone or something and judge how good or successful they are *a critical appraisal*

appraise /ə'preɪz/ *verb* [T] to examine something and judge it *We need to stop and appraise the situation.*

appreciable /ə'priːʃəbl/ *adjective formal* large or important enough to be noticed *There's an **appreciable difference** in temperatures between the two regions.*

appreciate /ə'priːʃieɪt/ *verb* 1 [VALUE] [T] to understand how good something or someone is and be able to enjoy them *There's no point buying him expensive wines - he doesn't appreciate them.* 2 [GRATEFUL] [T] to feel grateful for something *I'd really appreciate your help.* 3 [UNDERSTAND] [T] to understand something about a situation, especially that it is complicated or difficult [+ (that)] *I appreciate that it is a difficult decision for you to make.* 4 [INCREASE] [I] *formal* to increase in value *Houses and antiques generally appreciate with time.*

appreciation /əˌpriːʃi'eɪʃᵊn/ *noun* [U] 1 [VALUE] when you understand how good something or someone is and are able to enjoy them *His appreciation of art increased as he grew older.* 2 [FEEL GRATEFUL] when you feel grateful for something *To show our appreciation, we've bought you a little gift.* 3 [UNDERSTANDING] when you understand something about a situation, especially that it is complicated or difficult *He has no appreciation of the size of the problem.* 4 [INCREASE] *formal* an increase in value

appreciative /ə'priːʃiətɪv/ *adjective* showing that you understand how good something is, or are grateful for something *an appreciative audience* • **appreciatively** *adverb*

apprehend /ˌæprɪ'hend/ *verb* [T] *formal* If the police apprehend someone, they catch them and take them away to ask them about a crime which they might have committed.

apprehension /ˌæprɪ'henʃᵊn/ *noun* [U] an anxious feeling about something that you are going to do *It's normal to feel a little apprehension before starting a new job.*

apprehensive /ˌæprɪ'hensɪv/ *adjective* feeling anxious about something that you are going to do *He's a bit **apprehensive about** living away from home.*

apprentice /ə'prentɪs/ *noun* [C] a person who is learning a job by working for someone who already has skills and experience

apprenticeship /ə'prentɪʃɪp/ *noun* [C, U] when someone learns the skills needed to do a job by working for someone who already has skills and experience

o→**approach¹** /ə'prəʊtʃ/ *noun* 1 [METHOD] [C] a way of doing something *Liam has a different **approach to** the problem.* ○ *We've decided to adopt/take a new approach.* 2 [ASKING] [C] when you speak or write to someone, often asking to buy something or offering them work 3 [COMING CLOSER] [U] when something or someone gets nearer, in distance or time *the approach of winter* 4 [PATH] [C] a path or route that leads to a place

o→**approach²** /ə'prəʊtʃ/ *verb* 1 [COME CLOSE] [I, T] to come close in distance or time *The train now* *approaching platform 2 is the 5.35 to London, Kings Cross.* ○ *Christmas is fast approaching.* **2** DEAL WITH [T] to deal with something *I'm not sure how to approach the problem.* **3** SPEAK TO SOMEONE [T] to speak or write to someone, often asking to buy something or offering them work *She's been approached by a modelling agency.*

COMMON LEARNER ERROR

approach

The verb **approach** is not normally followed by a preposition.

He approached the door.

~~He approached to the door.~~

---

approachable /əˈprəʊtʃəbl/ *adjective* friendly and easy to talk to

o—**appropriate**[1] /əˈprəʊpriət/ *adjective* suitable or right for a particular situation or person *Is this film appropriate for young children?* ⊃Opposite **inappropriate**. ● **appropriately** *adverb appropriately dressed*

appropriate[2] /əˈprəʊprieɪt/ *verb* [T] *formal* to take or steal something

---

WORD PARTNERS FOR **approval**

gain/get/receive/seek/win approval
● formal/full approval ● approval for sth

---

approval /əˈpruːvᵊl/ *noun* [U] **1** when you think that something or someone is good or right *I don't need his approval.* ⊃Opposite **disapproval**. **2** official permission *The project has now received approval from the government.*

o—**approve** /əˈpruːv/ *verb* **1** [T] to allow or officially agree to something *The council has approved plans for a new shopping centre.* **2** [I] to think that something is good or right *I don't approve of smoking.* ⊃Opposite **disapprove**.

approving /əˈpruːvɪŋ/ *adjective* showing that you think something is good or right *an approving smile* ⊃Opposite **disapproving**. ● **approvingly** *adverb*

approx *written abbreviation for* approximately

approximate[1] /əˈprɒksɪmət/ *adjective* not completely accurate but close *Do you have an approximate idea of when he's arriving?*

approximate[2] /əˈprɒksɪmeɪt/ (*also* approximate to) *verb* [T] *formal* to be almost the same as something ● **approximation** /əˌprɒksɪˈmeɪʃᵊn/ *noun* [C, U]

approximately /əˈprɒksɪmətli/ *adverb* close to a particular number or time although not exactly that number or time *The college has approximately 700 students.*

Apr *written abbreviation for* April

apricot /ˈeɪprɪkɒt/ *noun* [C] a small, soft, orange fruit

o—**April** /ˈeɪprᵊl/ (*written abbreviation* Apr) *noun* [C, U] the fourth month of the year

April 'Fool's Day *noun* 1 April, a day when people play tricks on people, then say 'April fool!'

apron /ˈeɪprən/ *noun* [C] a piece of clothing you wear when cooking to keep your clothes clean

apron

apt /æpt/ *adjective* **1** suitable for a particular situation *an apt description* **2 be apt to do sth** to often do something *He's apt to forget his keys.* ● **aptly** *adverb We stayed at the aptly named* (= suitably called) *Grand Hotel.*

WORD PARTNERS FOR **aptitude**

have/show an aptitude for (doing) sth ● a natural aptitude ● an aptitude test

---

aptitude /ˈæptɪtjuːd/ *noun* [C, U] a natural skill or an ability to do something well *He has an aptitude for learning languages.* ○ *an aptitude test*

aquarium /əˈkweəriəm/ *noun* [C] **1** a building where fish and other water animals are kept for people to visit **2** a glass container filled with water that fish are kept in

Aquarius /əˈkweəriəs/ *noun* [C, U] the sign of the zodiac which relates to the period of 21 January - 19 February, or a person born during this period ⊃See picture at **zodiac**.

aquatic /əˈkwætɪk/ *adjective* living or growing in water, or related to water *aquatic animals*

Arab /ˈærəb/ *adjective* relating or belonging to the people of the Middle East or North Africa whose families came from Arabia in the past *Arab countries* ● **Arab** *noun* [C] an Arab person

Arabic /ˈærəbɪk/ *noun* the language used by Arab peoples ● **Arabic** *adjective*

arable /ˈærəbl/ *adjective* suitable for or used for growing crops *arable land/farming*

arbiter /ˈɑːbɪtər/ *noun* [C] **1** someone who judges what is right or helps to solve an argument *Since you know more about the subject we thought we'd let you be the arbiter.* **2 arbiter of fashion/style/taste, etc** someone who decides what is beautiful or stylish

arbitrary /ˈɑːbɪtrᵊri/ *adjective* not based on a system or principles and often seeming unfair *an arbitrary decision* ○ *They are calling for an end to arbitrary arrests and torture.* ● **arbitrarily** /ˌɑːbɪˈtreᵊrᵊli/ *adverb*

arbitrate /ˈɑːbɪtreɪt/ *verb* [I, T] to officially help to solve an argument between two people or groups ● **arbitrator** *noun* [C]

arbitration /ˌɑːbɪˈtreɪʃᵊn/ *noun* [U] the process of solving an argument between people by helping them to agree to an acceptable solution *Most disputes of this sort tend to go to arbitration.*

arc /ɑːk/ *noun* [C] a curved line that looks like part of a circle

arcade /ɑːˈkeɪd/ *noun* [C] **1** a place where you can pay to play games on machines *an amusement arcade* **2** a passage, especially between shops, that is covered by a roof *a shopping arcade*

A

arch

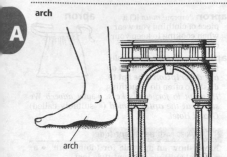

arch

arch¹ /ɑːtʃ/ *noun* [C] **1** a curved structure that usually supports something, for example a bridge or wall **2** the curved, middle part of your foot that does not touch the ground

arch² /ɑːtʃ/ *verb* [I, T] to be a curved shape or make something become a curved shape *The bridge arched over the river.*

archaeologist (*also US* **archeologist**) /ˌɑːkiˈɒlədʒɪst/ *noun* [C] someone who studies archaeology

archaeology (*also US* **archeology**) /ˌɑːkiˈɒlədʒi/ *noun* [U] the study of ancient cultures by looking for and examining their buildings, tools, and other objects ● **archaeological** (*also US* **archeological**) /ˌɑːkiəˈlɒdʒɪkəl/ *adjective*

archaic /ɑːˈkeɪɪk/ *adjective* very old and often not suitable for today *an archaic law*

archbishop /ˌɑːtʃˈbɪʃəp/ *noun* [C] a priest of the highest rank in some Christian churches, responsible for a very large area *Archbishop Desmond Tutu*

archeologist /ˌɑːkiˈɒlədʒɪst/ *noun* [C] *another US spelling of* archaeologist

archeology /ˌɑːkiˈɒlədʒi/ *noun* [U] *another US spelling of* archaeology

archery /ˈɑːtʃəri/ *noun* [U] a sport in which you shoot arrows *an archery competition*

architect /ˈɑːkɪtekt/ *noun* [C] someone who designs buildings

architecture /ˈɑːkɪtektʃəʳ/ *noun* [U] **1** the design and style of buildings *modern architecture* **2** the skill of designing buildings ● **architectural** /ˌɑːkɪˈtektʃərəl/ *adjective*

archive¹ /ˈɑːkaɪv/ *noun* [C] **1** a collection of historical documents that provides information about the past, or a place where they are kept *the national archives* **2** a place on a computer used to store information or documents that you do not need to use often

archive² /ˈɑːkaɪv/ *verb* [T] to store paper or electronic documents in an archive

the Arctic /ˈɑːktɪk/ *noun* the very cold area around the North Pole ● **Arctic** *adjective Arctic temperatures*

ardent /ˈɑːdᵊnt/ *adjective* [always before noun] enthusiastic or showing strong feelings *an ardent supporter of Arsenal* ● **ardently** *adverb*

arduous /ˈɑːdjuəs/ *adjective* needing a lot of effort to do *an arduous journey/task*

are *strong form* /ɑːʳ/ *weak form* /əʳ/ *present simple you/we/they of* be

○→**area** /ˈeəriə/ *noun* **1** REGION [C] a region of a country or city *an industrial area* ○ *a mountainous area* ○ *the London area* **2** PART [C] a part of a building or piece of land used for a particular purpose *a play/picnic area* **3** SUBJECT [C] a part of a subject or activity *Software is not really my area of expertise.* **4** SIZE [C, U] the size of a flat surface calculated by multiplying its width by its length ⊃See also: catchment area, no-go area.

ˈarea ˌcode *noun* [C] a set of numbers used at the beginning of all the telephone numbers in a particular area

arena /əˈriːnə/ *noun* [C] **1** a flat area with seats around where you can watch sports and other entertainments *an Olympic/sports arena* **2** in **the political/public, etc arena** involved in politics/the government, etc

○→**aren't** /ɑːnt/ **1** *short for* are not *We aren't going to the party.* **2** **aren't I?** *short for* am I not? *I am invited, aren't I?*

arguable /ˈɑːgjuəbl/ *adjective* **1 It is arguable that** it is possibly true that *It is arguable that the government has failed in this respect.* **2** If something is arguable, it is not certain if it is true. *It is arguable whether this method would even have succeeded.*

arguably /ˈɑːgjuəbli/ *adverb* possibly *He's arguably the greatest footballer in the world.*

○→**argue** /ˈɑːgjuː/ *verb* arguing, *past* argued **1** [I] to speak angrily to someone, telling them that you disagree with them *My parents are always arguing about money.* ○ *Kids, will you stop arguing with each other?* **2** [I, T] to give reasons to support or oppose an idea, action, etc [+ that] *He argued that cuts in military spending were necessary.* ○ *She argued for/against tax cuts.*

○→**argument** /ˈɑːgjəmənt/ *noun* [C] **1** an angry discussion with someone in which you both disagree *They had an argument about who should do the cleaning.* **2** a reason or reasons why you support or oppose an idea, action, etc *There are many arguments for/against nuclear energy.*

argumentative /ˌɑːgjəˈmentətɪv/ *adjective* often arguing or wanting to argue

aria /ˈɑːriə/ *noun* [C] a song that one person sings in an opera

arid /ˈærɪd/ *adjective* very dry and without enough rain for plants *an arid region/climate*

Aries /ˈeəriːz/ *noun* [C, U] the sign of the zodiac which relates to the period of 21 March - 20 April, or a person born during this period ⊃See picture at zodiac.

arise /əˈraɪz/ *verb* [I] *past tense* **arose**, *past participle* **arisen** 1 If a problem arises, it starts to happen. *The whole problem arose from a lack of communication.* 2 *literary* to get up, usually from a bed

aristocracy /ˌærɪˈstɒkrəsi/ *noun* [group] the highest social class, usually in countries which have or had a royal family

aristocrat /ˈærɪstəkræt/ *noun* [C] a member of the highest social class • **aristocratic** /ˌærɪstəˈkrætɪk/ *adjective an aristocratic family*

arithmetic /əˈrɪθmətɪk/ *noun* [U] when you calculate numbers, for example by multiplying or adding

o▪**arm¹** /ɑːm/ *noun* [C]
1 [BODY PART] the long part at each side of the human body, ending in a hand *He put his arms around her.* ○ *She was standing with her arms folded* (= with one arm crossed over the other). ➤See colour picture **The Body** on page Centre 13. **2 arm in arm** with your arm gently supporting or being supported by someone

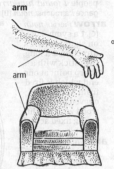
arm

arm

else's arm **3** [CLOTHES] the part of a piece of clothing that you put your arm in **4** [CHAIR] the part of a chair where your arm rests **5 twist sb's arm** *informal* to persuade someone to do something ➤See also: **arms**.

arm² /ɑːm/ *verb* [T] to give weapons to someone *The terrorists had **armed** themselves **with** automatic rifles.* ➤Opposite **disarm**.

armaments /ˈɑːməmənts/ *noun* [plural] military weapons and equipment *nuclear armaments*

armband /ˈɑːmbænd/ *noun* 1 [C] a strip of material worn around your upper arm *a black/reflective armband* **2 armbands** UK two plastic tubes that you fill with air and wear round the top of your arms when you are learning to swim

armchair /ˈɑːmˌtʃeəʳ/ *noun* [C] a comfortable chair with sides that support your arms ➤See colour picture **The Living Room** on page Centre 4.

armed /ɑːmd/ *adjective* 1 carrying or using weapons *armed guards/police* ○ *an armed robbery* (= robbery where guns are used) ➤Opposite **unarmed**. **2 armed with sth** carrying or knowing something that will be useful *I like to go to a meeting armed with the relevant facts.*

the ˌarmed ˈforces (*also the ˌarmed ˈservices*) *noun* [plural] a country's military forces, for example the army and the navy

armful /ˈɑːmfʊl/ *noun* [C] the amount that you can carry in your arms *an armful of books*

armistice /ˈɑːmɪstɪs/ *noun* [C] an agreement to stop fighting that is made between two countries *a two-week armistice*

armour UK (US **armor**) /ˈɑːməʳ/ *noun* [U] metal clothing which soldiers wore in the past to

protect them when fighting *a suit of armour*

armoured UK (US **armored**) /ˈɑːməd/ *adjective* covered with a protective layer of metal *an armoured vehicle*

armpit /ˈɑːmpɪt/ *noun* [C] the part of your body under your arm, where your arm meets your shoulder ➤See colour picture **The Body** on page Centre 13.

arms /ɑːmz/ *noun* [plural] **1** weapons *the sale of arms* **2 be up in arms** to be very upset and angry about something *Local residents are up in arms over plans to close the swimming pool.*

WORD PARTNERS FOR ***army***

join the army • be in the army

---

o▪**army** /ˈɑːmi/ *noun* [C] **1** a military force that fights wars on the ground *the British Army* **2** a group of people that is organized to do the same job *an army of cleaners/helpers*

aroma /əˈrəʊmə/ *noun* [C] a nice smell that usually comes from food or drink *the aroma of freshly baked bread* • **aromatic** /ˌærəʊˈmætɪk/ *adjective* having a nice smell *aromatic herbs* ○ *aromatic plants*

aromatherapy /əˌrəʊməˈθerəpi/ *noun* [U] a way of making a person who is ill better by rubbing pleasant-smelling oils into the skin or allowing them to smell the oils

arose /əˈrəʊz/ *past tense of* arise

o▪**around** /əˈraʊnd/ *adverb, preposition* **1** [IN A CIRCLE] (*also UK* round) on all sides of something *They sat around the table.* **2** [DIRECTION] (*also UK* round) to the opposite direction *He turned around and looked at her.* **3** [CIRCULAR MOVEMENT] (*also UK* round) in a circular movement *This lever turns the wheels around.* **4** [ALONG OUTSIDE] (*also UK* round) along the outside of something, not through it *You have to walk around the house to get to the garden.* **5** [TO A PLACE] (*also UK* round) to or in different parts of a place *I spent a year travelling around Australia.* **6** [SEVERAL PLACES] (*also UK* round) from one place or person to another *She passed a plate of biscuits around.* **7** [HERE] here, or near this place *Is Roger around?* **8** [EXISTING] present or available *Mobile phones have been around for years now.* **9** [APPROXIMATELY] used before a number or amount to mean 'approximately' *around four o'clock* ○ *around twenty thousand pounds* ➤See also: throw your **weight** around.

arousal /əˈraʊzᵊl/ *noun* [U] when someone is sexually excited

arouse /əˈraʊz/ *verb* [T] **1** to make someone have a particular feeling or reaction *It's a subject which has **aroused** a lot of **interest**.* **2** to make someone sexually excited

o▪**arrange** /əˈreɪndʒ/ *verb* [T] **1** to make the necessary plans and preparations for something to happen *to arrange a meeting* ○ *I'll **arrange for** a car to come and pick you up.* ○ [+ to do sth] *We've arranged to visit the house on Saturday afternoon.* **2** to put objects in a particular order or position *The books are arranged alphabetically by author.*

A

WORD PARTNERS FOR *arrangement*

have/make an arrangement • arrangements **for** sth • **alternative/necessary** arrangements

o➤**arrangement** /əˈreɪndʒmənt/ *noun* **1** [PLANS] [C] plans for how something will happen [usually plural] *We're meeting tomorrow to discuss* **arrangements for** *the competition.* ○ [+ to do sth] *I've* **made arrangements** *to go home this weekend.* **2** [AGREEMENT] [C, U] an agreement between two people or groups *We have an arrangement whereby we share the childcare.* ○ *Viewing is* **by prior arrangement. 3** [POSITION] [C] a group of objects in a particular order or position *a flower arrangement*

array /əˈreɪ/ *noun* [C] a large number of different things [usually singular] *There is* **a vast array of** *books on the subject.*

arrears /əˈrɪəz/ *noun* [plural] money that is owed and should have been paid before *mortgage/ rent arrears* ○ *He* **is** already **in arrears** with the rent.

o➤**arrest**[1] /əˈrest/ *verb* [T] If the police arrest someone, they take them away to ask them about a crime which they might have committed. *He was arrested for possession of illegal drugs.*

arrest

WORD PARTNERS FOR *arrest*

make an arrest • **resist** arrest • **be under** arrest • the arrest **of** sb • an arrest **for** [murder/drugs offences, etc]

arrest[2] /əˈrest/ *noun* [C, U] when the police take someone away to ask them about a crime which they might have committed *Police* **made** 20 **arrests** *at yesterday's demonstration.* ○ *He's* **under arrest** (= has been arrested). ⊃See also: house arrest.

o➤**arrival** /əˈraɪvəl/ *noun* **1** [ARRIVING] [U] when someone or something arrives somewhere *He first met Panos soon after his arrival in Greece.* ○ *There was a car waiting for him* **on arrival. 2** [BECOME AVAILABLE] [U] when something new is discovered or created or becomes available *The town grew rapidly with* **the arrival of** *the railway.* **3** [NEW PERSON/THING] [C] a new thing or person that has arrived *Two teachers were there to greet the* **new arrivals.**

o➤**arrive** /əˈraɪv/ *verb* [I] **1** to get to a place *When he first* **arrived in** *New York, he didn't speak a word of English.* ○ *We were the last to* **arrive at** *the station.* ○ *A letter* **arrived for** *you this morning.* **2** **arrive at an answer/decision/conclusion, etc** to find an answer to a problem or make a decision after a lot of discussion *We didn't* **arrive at** *any firm conclusions.* **3** to happen or start to exist *Summer had finally arrived.*

COMMON LEARNER ERROR

arrive somewhere

Be careful to choose the correct preposition after arrive.

You **arrive at** a place such as a building.
We arrived at the hotel just after 12 o'clock.

You **arrive in** a town, city or country.
They arrived in Tokyo on Wednesday.
When did David arrive in Australia?

You **arrive** home, here, or there. You do not use a preposition when **arrive** is used before these words.
We arrived home yesterday.
I had a lot of problems when I first arrived here.

arrogant /ˈærəgənt/ *adjective* believing that you are better or more important than other people *I found him arrogant and rude.* • **arrogance** /ˈærəgəns/ *noun* [U] • **arrogantly** *adverb*

arrow /ˈærəʊ/ *noun*
[C] **1** a symbol used on signs to show a direction **2** a long, thin stick with a sharp point at one end which is fired from a bow (= curved piece of wood with a tight string fixed at both ends)

arrow

arrow

arse /ɑːs/ *UK very informal* (*US* **ass**) *noun* [C] a person's bottom

arsenal /ˈɑːsənəl/ *noun* [C] a large collection of weapons

arsenic /ˈɑːsənɪk/ *noun* [U] a chemical element that is a very strong poison

arson /ˈɑːsən/ *noun* [U] the crime of intentionally burning something, such as a building • **arsonist** *noun* [C] someone who commits arson

o➤**art** /ɑːt/ *noun* **1** [U] the making or study of paintings, drawings, etc or the objects created *fine/ modern art* ○ *an* **art exhibition/gallery 2** [C, U] a skill in a particular activity *the* **art of** *conversation* ⊃See also: martial art, work of art.

artefact *UK* (*US* **artifact**) /ˈɑːtɪfækt/ *noun* [C] an object, especially something very old of historical interest *Indian artefacts*

artery /ˈɑːtəri/ *noun* [C] **1** one of the tubes in your body that carries blood from your heart **2** an important route for traffic

artful /ˈɑːtfəl/ *adjective* [always before noun] showing skill *an artful use of colour* • **artfully** *adverb*

arthritis /ɑːˈθraɪtɪs/ *noun* [U] an illness which causes the parts of the body where bones meet to become painful and often big • **arthritic** /ɑːˈθrɪtɪk/ *adjective an arthritic hip/knee*

artichoke /ˈɑːtɪtʃəʊk/ *noun* [C, U] a round, green vegetable with thick, pointed leaves covering the outside

article /ˈɑːtɪkl/ *noun* [C] **1** [WRITING] a piece of writing in a magazine, newspaper, etc **2** [OBJECT] an object, especially one of many *an* **article of clothing/furniture 3** [GRAMMAR] in grammar, used to mean the words 'the', 'a', or 'an' ⊃See also: definite article, indefinite article.

articulate[1] /ɑːˈtɪkjələt/ *adjective* able to express ideas and feelings clearly in words *She's an intelligent and highly articulate young woman.* ⇨Opposite **inarticulate**.

articulate² /ɑːˈtɪkjəleɪt/ *verb* **[T]** *formal* to express ideas or feelings in words *He articulates the views and concerns of the local community.* • **articulation** /ɑːˌtɪkjəˈleɪʃᵊn/ *noun* **[U]**

articulated /ɑːˈtɪkjəleɪtɪd/ *adjective* **[always before noun]** *mainly UK* An articulated vehicle is long and has two parts which are joined together to help it turn corners. *an **articulated** lorry*

artifact /ˈɑːtɪfækt/ *noun* **[C]** *US spelling of* artefact *Mayan artifacts*

artificial /ˌɑːtɪˈfɪʃᵊl/ *adjective* **1** not natural, but made by people *an artificial flower/lake* ○ *an artificial heart* **2** not sincere • **artificially** *adverb*

ˌartificial inˈtelligence *UK* (*US* **artiˌficial inˈtelligence**) *noun* **[U]** the study and development of computer systems which do jobs that previously needed human intelligence

artillery /ɑːˈtɪlᵊri/ *noun* **[U]** large guns, especially those fixed on wheels used by an army

artisan /ˌɑːtɪˈzæn/ [US] /ˈɑːrtəzᵊn/ *noun* **[C]** *old-fashioned* someone who does skilled work with their hands

🔑**artist** /ˈɑːtɪst/ *noun* **[C]** someone who creates art, especially paintings and drawings

artistic /ɑːˈtɪstɪk/ *adjective* **1** showing skill and imagination in creating things, especially in painting, drawing, etc *artistic talent* **2** **[always before noun]** relating to art *the artistic director of the theatre* • **artistically** *adverb*

artistry /ˈɑːtɪstri/ *noun* **[U]** great skill in creating or performing something, such as in writing, music, sport, etc

arts /ɑːts/ *noun* **1** **[plural]** (*also US* **liberal arts**) subjects of study which are not science, such as history, languages, etc *an arts subject/degree* **2** **the arts** activities such as painting, music, film, dance, and literature *public interest in the arts* ⇨See also: **the performing arts**.

artwork /ˈɑːtwɜːk/ *noun* **[U]** the pictures or patterns in a book, magazine, CD cover, etc

arty /ˈɑːti/ (*also US* **artsy** /ˈɑːtsi/) *adjective* knowing a lot about art, or wanting to appear as if you do

🔑**as** *strong form* /æz/ *weak form* /əz/ *preposition, conjunction* **1 as .... as** used to compare two things, people, amounts, etc *He's not as tall as his brother.* ○ *She earns three times as much as I do.* **2** [WHILE] used to describe two things happening at the same time or something happening at a particular time *He was shot in the back as he tried to escape.* ○ *I think your opinions change as you get older.* **3** [FOR THIS PURPOSE] used to describe the purpose, job, or appearance of something or someone *She **works as** a waitress.* ○ *It could be **used as** evidence against him.* **4** [LIKE] in the same way *This year, as in previous years, tickets sold very quickly.* **5** [IN THIS WAY] used to describe the way in which people see or think of something or someone *Most people think of nursing as a female occupation.* **6** [BECAUSE] because *You can go first as you're the oldest.* **7 as if/as though** used to describe how a situation seems to be *It looks as if it might rain.* **8 as for** used to talk about how another person or thing is affected by something *I was pleased. As for Emily, well, who cares what she thinks.* **9 as from/as of** *formal* starting from a particular time, date, etc *The new conditions are effective as of 15 May.* **10 as to** *formal* about *There's no decision as to when the work might start.*

asap /ˌeɪeseɪˈpiː/ *abbreviation for* as soon as possible

asbestos /æsˈbestɒs/ *noun* **[U]** a soft grey-white material which does not burn easily, once used in building

Asbo (*also* **ASBO**) /ˈæzbəʊ/ *UK abbreviation for* anti-social behaviour order: an official order that a person must stop doing something bad or not go somewhere or they might go to prison

ascend /əˈsend/ *verb* **[I, T]** *formal* to move up or to a higher position

ascendancy (*also* **ascendency**) /əˈsendənsi/ *noun* **[U]** *formal* a position of power, strength, or success ***in the ascendancy***

ascending /əˈsendɪŋ/ *adjective* **[always before noun]** starting with the lowest or smallest and becoming greater or higher *They announced the results **in ascending order**.*

ascent /əˈsent/ *noun* **1** [CLIMB] **[C]** when someone climbs or moves up *his first ascent of the mountain* **2** [BECOMING SUCCESSFUL] **[no plural]** when someone starts to become successful *The book describes his rapid ascent from truck driver to film star.* **3** [PATH UP] **[C]** a path or road which goes up a hill or mountain *a steep ascent*

ascertain /ˌæsəˈteɪn/ *verb* **[T]** *formal* to discover something **[+ question word]** *Police are still trying to ascertain whether last weekend's fire was started deliberately.*

ascribe /əˈskraɪb/ *verb*

ascribe sth to sth *formal* to say that something is caused by something else *She ascribes her success to hard work.*

ash /æʃ/ *noun* **1** **[U]** the soft, grey powder which remains when something has burnt *cigarette ash* **2** **[C]** a forest tree

🔑**ashamed** /əˈʃeɪmd/ *adjective* **1** feeling guilty or embarrassed about something you have done *You've got nothing to be **ashamed of**.* ○ **[+ to do sth]** *He was ashamed to admit his mistake.* **2 be ashamed of sb** to be angry and disappointed with a family member or friend because they have behaved badly *He was so rude to Phil - I was ashamed of him.*

ashes /ˈæʃɪz/ *noun* **sb's ashes** the powder that remains when a dead person's body has been burnt ***scatter her ashes***

ashore /əˈʃɔːʳ/ *adverb* onto land from the sea, a river, a lake, etc *We swam ashore.*

ashtray /ˈæʃˌtreɪ/ *noun* **[C]** a small, open container used to put cigarette ash and finished cigarettes in

Asian /ˈeɪʒᵊn/ *adjective* relating or belonging to Asia *Asian culture* • **Asian** *noun* **[C]** someone from Asia

aside¹ /əˈsaɪd/ *adverb* **1** in a direction to one side *I gave her a plate of food but she pushed it*

A

aside. **2** If you put or set something aside, you do not use it now, but keep it to use later. *We've put some money aside to pay for the children's education.* **3 aside from** except for *This document needs finishing but aside from that I think everything is done.*

aside² /ə'saɪd/ *noun* [C] something which you say quietly so that not everyone can hear it, often something funny *He said it as an aside and I don't think a lot of people heard it.* ○ *a comic aside*

o╾**ask** /ɑːsk/ *verb* **1** QUESTION [I, T] to say something to someone as a question which you want them to answer [+ two objects] *Can I ask you a few questions?* ○ *I asked him about his hobbies.* ○ [+ question word] *I asked why the plane was so late.* ○ *She asked whether I knew what Ian's plans were.* ○ *I asked him what time the party started.* ⊃See Common learner error at **question.** **2** WANT SOMETHING [I, T] to say something to someone because you want them to give you something *He's asked for a bike for his birthday.* **3** REQUEST [I, T] to say something to someone because you want them to do something [+ to do sth] *They've asked me to look after their dog while they're away.* ○ *She asked us to be quiet.* **4** INVITE [T] to invite someone to do something *She asked him out to lunch the next day.* **5** WANT PERMISSION [I, T] to say something to someone because you want to know if you can do something *Bruce asked if he could stay with us for a few days.* ○ [+ to do sth] *She asked to leave early.* **6** PRICE [T] to want a particular amount of money for something which you sell *How much are you asking for it?* ○ *They're asking a lot of money for that house.* **7 ask yourself sth** to think about something carefully *You've got to ask yourself whether it's what you really want.* **8 ask for it/trouble** *informal* to behave in a way that is likely to make something unpleasant happen to you or to cause you problems *His wife left him, but it seems to me he was asking for it.* ○ *Drinking and driving is asking for trouble.* **9 don't ask me** *informal* used to tell someone that you do not know the answer to a question and that you are surprised they have asked you. *Don't ask me why you left your last job!* **10 you may well ask** said to someone who has asked you a question that would be difficult or interesting to answer.

COMMON LEARNER ERROR

ask for

When you use **ask** with the meaning of saying you want someone to give you something, remember to use the preposition **for** before the thing that is wanted.

I'm writing to ask for information about your products.

I'm writing to ask information about your products.

askew /ə'skjuː/ *adjective* [never before noun] not straight *The picture was slightly askew.*

OTHER WAYS OF SAYING *asleep*

If someone starts to sleep, you can say that they **fall asleep**: *I fell asleep in front of the TV.*

If someone is completely asleep, you can say they are **fast asleep**: *You were fast asleep by the time I came to bed.*

The verbs **doze** and **snooze**, and the expression **have/take a nap** all mean 'to sleep, especially for a short time or during the day': *She's always dozing in front of the TV.* • *Granddad was snoozing in his chair.* • *Oliver is really tired so he's just taking a nap.*

The phrasal verbs **doze off** and (*informal*) **nod off** mean to start to sleep, especially during the day: *I must have nodded off after lunch.* • *She dozed off during the lecture.*

o╾**asleep** /ə'sliːp/ *adjective* **1 be asleep** to be sleeping *The children are asleep.* ○ *I was fast/ sound asleep* (= sleeping deeply). **2 fall asleep** to start sleeping *He fell asleep in front of the TV.*

asparagus /ə'spærəgəs/ *noun* [U] a vegetable consisting of a long, green stem with a pointed end

aspect /'æspekt/ *noun* [C] one part of a situation, problem, subject, etc *His illness affects almost every aspect of his life.*

asphalt /'æsfælt/ *noun* [U] a hard, black substance used to make roads and paths

asphyxiate /əs'fɪksieɪt/ *verb* **be asphyxiated** to die because you cannot breathe • **asphyxiation** /əs,fɪksi'eɪʃ°n/ *noun* [U]

WORD PARTNERS FOR *aspiration*

have aspirations to do sth/of doing sth • **high** aspirations • **dreams/hopes and** aspirations • aspirations **for** sth

aspiration /,æsp°r'eɪʃ°n/ *noun* [C, U] something you hope to achieve

aspire /ə'spaɪə'/ *verb* **aspire to sth; aspire to do sth** to hope to achieve something *He has never aspired to a position of power.*

aspirin /'æsp°rɪn/ *noun* [C, U] *plural* aspirin or aspirins a common drug used to reduce pain and fever

aspiring /ə'spaɪərɪŋ/ *adjective* **an aspiring actor/ politician/writer, etc** someone who is trying to become a successful actor/politician/writer, etc

ass /æs/ *noun* [C] **1** BOTTOM *US very informal* (*UK* arse) a person's bottom **2** PERSON *informal* a stupid person **3** ANIMAL *old-fashioned* a donkey (= animal like a small horse)

assailant /ə'seɪlənt/ *noun* [C] *formal* a person who attacks someone

assassin /ə'sæsɪn/ *noun* [C] a person who kills someone important or famous, often for money

assassinate /ə'sæsɪneɪt/ *verb* [T] to kill someone important or famous • **assassination** /ə,sæsɪ'neɪʃ°n/ *noun* [C, U]

assault /ə'sɔːlt/ *noun* [C, U] an attack *an assault on a police officer* ○ *sexual assault* • **assault** *verb* [T]

assemble /ə'sembl/ verb 1 [I, T] to join other people somewhere to make a group, or to bring people together into a group *They assembled in the meeting room after lunch.* 2 [T] to build something by joining parts together

assembly /ə'sembli/ noun 1 ⌐SCHOOL⌐ [C, U] *UK* a regular meeting of all the students and teachers at a school *morning assembly* 2 ⌐GROUP⌐ [C] a group of people, such as a government, who meet to make decisions, laws, etc *the national assembly* 3 ⌐BUILD⌐ [U] when you build something by joining parts together *The pack said 'assembly required'.*

assent /ə'sent/ noun [U] *formal* agreement or approval *Has she given her assent?* • assent verb [I] *formal* to agree to something

assert /ə'sɜːt/ verb 1 **assert yourself** to behave or speak in a strong, confident way *She has to learn to assert herself.* 2 **assert your authority/control/independence, etc** to do something to show other people that you have power 3 [T] *formal* to say that something is certainly true [+ that] *He asserts that she stole money from him while they were working together.*

assertion /ə'sɜːʃᵊn/ noun [C, U] *formal* when you say that something is certainly true [+ that] *I don't agree with his assertion that men are safer drivers than women.*

assertive /ə'sɜːtɪv/ adjective behaving or speaking in a strong, confident way *You need to be much more assertive.* • assertively adverb • assertiveness noun [U]

assess /ə'ses/ verb [T] to make a judgment about the quality, size, value, etc of something *The tests are designed to assess a child's reading skills.* • assessment noun [C, U]

asset /'æset/ noun [C] 1 a person, skill, or quality which is useful or helps you to succeed *He'll be a great asset to the team.* 2 something which a person or company owns which has a value [usually plural] *The company has $70 billion in assets.*

assiduous /ə'sɪdjuəs/ adjective *formal* showing a lot of effort and determination • assiduously adverb

assign /ə'saɪn/ verb [T] to give someone a particular job or responsibility [+ two objects] *UN troops were assigned the task of rebuilding the hospital.* ○ [often passive] *The case has been assigned to our most senior officer.*

assign sb to sth to give someone a particular job or place to work [often passive] *Which police officer has been assigned to this case?*

assignment /ə'saɪnmənt/ noun [C, U] a piece of work or job that you are given to do *a written assignment* ○ *He's on assignment in Brazil.*

assimilate /ə'sɪmɪleɪt/ verb *formal* 1 [T] to understand and remember new information 2 [I, T] to become part of a group, society, etc, or to make someone or something become part of a group, society, etc *The refugees have now assimilated into the local community.* • assimilation /ə,sɪmɪ'leɪʃᵊn/ noun [U]

assist /ə'sɪst/ verb [I, T] to help *The army arrived to assist in the search.* ○ *He's assisting the police with their investigation.*

assistance /ə'sɪstᵊns/ noun [U] *formal* help *financial/medical assistance* ○ *Can I be of any assistance?* (= Can I help you?) ○ *They have asked for financial assistance from the government.*

assistant /ə'sɪstᵊnt/ noun [C] 1 someone whose job is to help a person who has a more important job *an administrative assistant* ○ *assistant manager* 2 **a sales/shop assistant** *mainly UK* someone who helps customers in a shop *The sales assistant was very helpful.*

associate[1] /ə'səʊʃieɪt/ verb [T] to relate two things, people, etc in your mind *Most people associate this brand with good quality.*
associate with sb *formal* to spend time with someone
be associated with sth to be related to something or caused by something *There are many risks associated with smoking.*

associate[2] /ə'səʊʃiət/ noun [C] someone who you know because of work or business *She's a business associate of mine.*

associate[3] /ə'səʊʃiət/ adjective **associate director/editor/producer, etc** someone in a slightly less important position than the main person

association /ə,səʊʃi'eɪʃᵊn/ noun 1 [C] an organization of people with the same interests or with a particular purpose *the Football Association* 2 [C, U] a connection or relationship between two things or people 3 **in association with** working together with *The event was organized in association with the Sports Council.* ⊃See also: savings and loan association.

assorted /ə'sɔːtɪd/ adjective of different types *a box of assorted chocolates*

assortment /ə'sɔːtmənt/ noun [C] a group of different types of something *an assortment of vegetables*

assuage /ə'sweɪdʒ/ verb [T] *formal* to make unpleasant feelings less strong *The government tried to assuage the public's fears.* ○ *I'll take the kids out this afternoon and assuage my guilt for not having seen them all week.*

o-**assume** /ə'sjuːm/ verb [T] 1 to think that something is likely to be true, although you have no proof [+ (that)] *Everything was quiet when I got home so I assumed that you had gone out.* 2 **assume control/power/responsibility, etc** to take a position of control/power/responsibility, etc *He has assumed the role of spokesman for the group.* 3 **assume an air/expression, etc** *formal* to pretend to have a feeling that you do not have *He assumed an air of indifference though I knew how he really felt.* 4 **assume a false identity/name, etc** to pretend to be someone else *an assumed name*

⌐⌐⌐ **WORD PARTNERS FOR assumption**

make an assumption • be **based on** an assumption • a **basic/common/false/underlying** assumption • do sth **under the** assumption **that** • an assumption **about** sth

assumption /ə'sʌmpʃᵊn/ noun [C] 1 something that you think is true without having any proof *People tend to make assumptions about you when you have a disability.* ○ *These calculations are based on the assumption that prices will continue to rise.* **2 the assumption of power/responsibility, etc** when someone takes a position of power, responsibility, etc

assurance /əˈʃʊərᵊns/ *noun* **1** [C] a promise [+ that] *He gave us an assurance that it would not happen again.* **2** [U] confidence *He spoke with calm assurance.*

assure /əˈʃɔːʳ/ *verb* [T] **1** to tell someone that something is certainly true, especially so that they do not worry [+ (that)] *She assured them that she would be all right.* **2** to make something certain to happen *This loan should assure the company's future.*

assured /əˈʃʊəd/ *adjective* **1** showing skill and confidence *an assured performance* **2 be assured of sth** to be certain to get or achieve something in the future *They are now assured of a place in the final.* ⊃See also: self-assured.

asterisk /ˈæstᵊrɪsk/ *noun* [C] a written symbol in the shape of a star (*), often used to mark a particular word, phrase, etc

asthma /ˈæsmə/ *noun* [U] an illness which makes it difficult to breathe *She had an asthma attack.* ● **asthmatic** /æsˈmætɪk/ *adjective an asthmatic child*

astonish /əˈstɒnɪʃ/ *verb* [T] to make someone very surprised *Her quick recovery has astonished doctors.*

astonished /əˈstɒnɪʃt/ *adjective* very surprised *He was astonished at her behaviour.*

astonishing /əˈstɒnɪʃɪŋ/ *adjective* very surprising *It's astonishing that so many people believed his story.* ● **astonishingly** *adverb*

astonishment /əˈstɒnɪʃmənt/ *noun* [U] extreme surprise *The others stared at him in astonishment.* ○ *To my astonishment, he started laughing.*

astound /əˈstaʊnd/ *verb* [T] to make someone very surprised *The speed of her recovery has astounded doctors.*

astounded /əˈstaʊndɪd/ *adjective* very surprised *I'm astounded at/by these prices.*

astounding /əˈstaʊndɪŋ/ *adjective* very surprising *an astounding success* ● **astoundingly** *adverb*

astray /əˈstreɪ/ *adverb* **1 go astray** to get lost or go in the wrong direction *One of my bags went astray at the airport.* **2 lead sb astray** to encourage someone to do bad things that they should not do *He was led astray by his friends.*

astride /əˈstraɪd/ *adverb* If you sit or stand astride something, you have one foot on each side of it.

astro- /æstrəʊ-/ *prefix* relating to stars or outer space *astronomer* ○ *astrophysics*

astrology /əˈstrɒlədʒi/ *noun* [U] the study of the positions and movements of stars and planets to say how they might influence people's lives ● **astrologer** *noun* [C] someone who studies astrology ● **astrological** /ˌæstrəˈlɒdʒɪkəl/ *adjective*

astronaut /ˈæstrɔnɔːt/ *noun* [C] someone who travels into space

astronaut

astronomical /ˌæstrəˈnɒmɪkᵊl/ *adjective* **1** An astronomical amount is extremely large. *astronomical prices* **2** relating to astronomy ● **astronomically** *adverb*

astronomy /əˈstrɒnəmi/ *noun* [U] the scientific study of stars and planets ● **astronomer** *noun* [C] a scientist who studies astronomy

astute /əˈstjuːt/ *adjective* good at judging situations and making decisions which give you an advantage *an astute businesswoman* ○ *politically astute* ● **astutely** *adverb*

asylum /əˈsaɪləm/ *noun* **1** [U] when someone is allowed to stay somewhere because they are escaping danger in another country **2** [C] old-fashioned a hospital for people with a mental illness ⊃See also: political asylum.

aˈsylum ˌseeker *noun* [C] someone who leaves their country to escape from danger, and tries to get permission to live in another country

asymmetrical /ˌeɪsɪˈmetrɪkᵊl/ *adjective* not being exactly the same shape and size on both sides ● **asymmetry** /eɪˈsɪmɪtri/ *noun* [U]

o* **at** *strong form* /æt/ *weak form* /ət/ *preposition* **1** PLACE used to show the place or position of something or someone *We met at the station.* **2** TIME used to show the time something happens *The meeting starts at three.* **3** DIRECTION towards or in the direction of *She threw the ball at him.* **4** ABILITY used after an adjective to show a person's ability to do something *He's good at making friends.* **5** CAUSE used to show the cause of something, especially a feeling *We were surprised at the news.* **6** AMOUNT used to show the price, speed, level, etc of something *He denied driving at 120 miles per hour.* **7** ACTIVITY used to show a state or activity *a country at war* **8** INTERNET the @ symbol, used in email addresses to separate the name of a person, department, etc from the name of the organization or company

ate /eɪt, et/ *past tense of* eat

atheist /ˈeɪθiɪst/ *noun* [C] someone who believes that there is no god ● **atheism** *noun* [U]

athlete /ˈæθliːt/ *noun* [C] someone who is very good at a sport and who competes with others in organized events

athletic /æθˈletɪk/ *adjective* **1** strong, healthy, and good at sports **2** [always before noun] relating to athletes or to the sport of athletics

athletics /æθˈletɪks/ *UK* (*US* **track and field**) *noun* [U] the sports which include running, jumping, and throwing ⊃See colour picture **Sports 1** on page Centre 14.

-athon /-əθɒn/ *suffix* an event or activity that lasts a long time, usually to collect money for charity *a walkathon* (= a long walk)

atlas /ˈætləs/ *noun* [C] a book of maps *a road atlas* ○ *a world atlas*

ATM /ˌeɪtiːˈem/ *noun* [C] *mainly US abbreviation for* automated teller machine: a machine that you get money from using a plastic card

---

WORD PARTNERS FOR *atmosphere*

create an atmosphere • an atmosphere of [fear/trust, etc] • a **family/friendly/relaxed** atmosphere

---

atmosphere /ˈætməsfɪər/ *noun* **1** [no plural] the feeling which exists in a place or situation *a relaxed atmosphere* ○ *A lot of the kids are away from home for the first time so we create a nice, family atmosphere for them.* **2** the atmosphere the layer of gases around the Earth **3** [no plural] the air inside a room or other place *a smoky atmosphere*

atmospheric /ˌætməsˈferɪk/ *adjective* **1** [always before noun] relating to the air or to the atmosphere *atmospheric conditions/pressure* **2** creating a special feeling, such as mystery or romance *atmospheric music/lighting*

atom /ˈætəm/ *noun* [C] the smallest unit that an element can be divided into *A molecule of carbon dioxide (CO_2) has one carbon atom and two oxygen atioms.*

atomic /əˈtɒmɪk/ *adjective* **1** [always before noun] relating to atoms *an atomic particle* **2** using the energy created when an atom is divided *atomic power/weapons*

a,tomic 'bomb (*also* 'atom ,bomb) *noun* [C] a very powerful bomb which uses the energy created when an atom is divided

a,tomic 'energy *noun* [U] energy which is produced by dividing atoms

atop /əˈtɒp/ *preposition US* on the top of

atrium /ˈeɪtriəm/ *noun* [C] a large, central room with a glass roof in an office building, restaurant, etc

atrocious /əˈtrəʊʃəs/ *adjective* **1** extremely bad *atrocious weather* **2** violent and shocking *an atrocious crime*

atrocity /əˈtrɒsəti/ *noun* [C, U] when someone does something extremely violent and shocking *Soldiers have been committing atrocities against civilians.*

o—**attach** /əˈtætʃ/ *verb* [T] **1** to join or fix one thing to another *She attached a photograph to her letter.* **2 attach importance/value, etc to sb/sth** to think that someone or something has importance/value, etc *You attach too much importance to money.* **3** to include something as part of something else *There were too many conditions attached to the deal.* ⊃See also: no strings (**string**[1]) (attached).

attached /əˈtætʃt/ *adjective* **be attached to sb/sth** to like someone or something very much *I've become rather attached to my old car.*

attachment /əˈtætʃmənt/ *noun* **1** FEELING [C, U] a feeling of love or strong connection to someone or something *I wasn't aware of any romantic attachments.* **2** EMAIL [C] a computer file which is sent together with an email message *I wasn't able to open that attachment.* **3** EQUIPMENT [C] an extra part which can be added to a piece of equipment *There's a special attachment for cleaning in the corners.*

WORD PARTNERS FOR *attack*

1 launch/mount an attack • be **under** attack • a **bomb/terrorist** attack • an attack **on** sb/sth **2 launch/mount** an attack • be/come **under** attack • a **personal/scathing** attack • an attack **on** sb/sth

---

o—**attack**[1] /əˈtæk/ *noun* **1** VIOLENCE [C, U] a violent act intended to hurt or damage someone or something *a terrorist attack on the capital* **2** CRITICISM [C, U] when you say something to strongly criticize someone or something *a scathing attack on the president* **3** ILLNESS [C] a sudden, short illness *a nasty attack of flu* **4** SPORT [C, U] in games such as football, when the players in a team try to score points, goals, etc ⊃See also: counter-attack.

o—**attack**[2] /əˈtæk/ *verb* **1** VIOLENCE [I, T] to use violence to hurt or damage someone or something *He was attacked and seriously injured by a gang of youths.* **2** CRITICIZE [T] to strongly criticize someone or something *She attacked the government's new education policy.* **3** DISEASE [T] If a disease, chemical, etc attacks someone or something, it damages them. **4** SPORT [I, T] If players in a team attack, they move forward to try to score points, goals, etc.

attacker /əˈtækər/ *noun* [C] a person who uses violence to hurt someone *The police think she must have known her attacker.*

attain /əˈteɪn/ *verb* [T] to achieve something, especially after a lot of work *She's attained a high level of fitness.* • **attainable** *adjective* possible to achieve • **attainment** *noun* [C, U] when you achieve something

---

WORD PARTNERS FOR *attempt*

make an attempt • a **successful/unsuccessful** attempt • an attempt **at** sth/doing sth • an attempt **to** do sth • **in** an attempt to do sth

---

o—**attempt**[1] /əˈtempt/ *noun* [C] **1** when you try to do something *This is his second attempt at the exam.* ○ [+ to do sth] *They closed the road in an attempt to reduce traffic in the city.* **2 an attempt on sb's life** when someone tries to kill someone

o—**attempt**[2] /əˈtempt/ *verb* [T] to try to do something, especially something difficult [+ to do sth] *He attempted to escape through a window.*

attempted /əˈtemptɪd/ *adjective* **attempted murder/robbery, etc** when someone tries to commit a crime but does not succeed

---

OTHER WAYS OF SAYING *attend*

Instead of the verb 'attend', people usually say **come/go to**: *How many people came to the meeting?* • *He goes to church regularly.*

The verb **make** is sometimes used when someone is talking about whether or not they are able to attend an event: *I'm afraid I can't make the meeting this afternoon (= I will not be able to attend).*

The expression **make it** is also used, meaning 'to get to a place, even when there are problems': *The traffic was so bad we only just made it in time for the start of the film.*

---

attend /əˈtend/ *verb* [I, T] *formal* **1** to go to an event *to attend a concert/meeting* **2 attend a church/school, etc** to go regularly to a particular church/school, etc
attend to sb/sth *formal* to deal with something or help someone

attendance /əˈtendəns/ *noun* [C, U] **1** the number of people who go to an event, meeting, etc *falling attendance* **2** when you go somewhere such as a church, school, etc regularly *His attendance at school is very poor.* **3 in attendance** *formal* present at an event *They have doctors in attendance at every match.*

attendant /əˈtendənt/ *noun* [C] someone whose job is to help the public in a particular place *a parking attendant* ➔See also: **flight attendant.**

WORD PARTNERS FOR *attention*

pay attention (**to** sth/sb) • **give** sth attention • **have/hold/keep** sb's attention • **careful/full/special/undivided** attention

---

◦►**attention** /əˈtenʃ°n/ *noun* [U] **1** when you watch, listen to, or think about something carefully or with interest *Ladies and gentlemen, could I **have your attention**, please?* ○ *I was watching TV so you didn't have my full attention.* **2 pay attention (to sth)** to watch, listen to, or think about something carefully or with interest *You weren't paying attention to what I was saying.* **3 bring/draw (sb's) attention to sth/sb** to make someone notice something or someone *If I could just draw your attention to the second paragraph.* ○ *She's always trying to draw attention to herself.* **4 attract/get (sb's) attention** to make someone notice you *I waved at him to get his attention.* **5** treatment to deal with a problem *medical attention* ○ *This old engine needs a lot of attention.*

COMMON LEARNER ERROR

attention

Attention is usually followed by the preposition **to**.
You should pay attention to what she tells you.
We want to draw people's attention to the risks involved.

---

attentive /əˈtentɪv/ *adjective* listening or watching carefully and showing that you are interested *an attentive student* • **attentively** *adverb*

attest /əˈtest/ *verb* [I, T] *formal* to show or prove that something is true

attic /ˈætɪk/ *noun* [C] a room at the top of a house under the roof

attire /əˈtaɪəʳ/ *noun* [U] *old-fashioned* the clothes that you wear • **attired** *adjective* dressed in a particular way *suitably attired*

WORD PARTNERS FOR *attitude*

have/take a [positive/responsible, etc] attitude • a **casual/hostile/negative/positive** attitude • (sb's) attitude **to/towards** sth/sb

---

◦►**attitude** /ˈætɪtjuːd/ *noun* [C, U] how you think or feel about something and how this makes you behave *a **positive attitude*** ○ *He has a very*

*bad **attitude** to/towards work.*

attorney /əˈtɜːni/ *noun* [C] *US* a lawyer *a defense attorney* ➔See Common learner error at **lawyer** ➔See also: **district attorney.**

◦►**attract** /əˈtrækt/ *verb* [T] **1** to make people come to a place or do a particular thing by being interesting, enjoyable, etc *The castle attracts more than 300,000 visitors a year.* ○ *We need to attract more science graduates to teaching.* **2 attract attention/interest, etc** to cause people to pay attention/be interested, etc **3 be attracted to sb** to like someone, especially sexually, because of the way they look or behave *I was attracted to him straight away.* **4** If something attracts a substance or object, it causes it to move towards it. *Magnets attract metal.*

WORD PARTNERS FOR *attraction*

an **added/a big/**the **main/a major/**the **star** attraction • a **tourist** attraction • the attraction **of** sth • an attraction **for** sb

---

attraction /əˈtrækʃ°n/ *noun* **1** [C] something that makes people come to a place or want to do a particular thing *a tourist attraction* ○ *The opportunity to travel is one of the main attractions of this job.* **2** [U] when you like someone, especially sexually, because of the way they look or behave *physical attraction*

OTHER WAYS OF SAYING *attractive*

The adjectives **beautiful** and **lovely** are often used instead of 'attractive', and are used to describe both people and things: *His wife is very beautiful.* • *We drove through some really beautiful/lovely countryside.* • *You look lovely!*

If a person is attractive, we can say that they are **good-looking.** The adjective **handsome** is also sometimes used for men, and **pretty** for women: *He's certainly very good-looking.* • *Your daughter is very pretty.*

If someone is extremely attractive, you can say that they are **gorgeous** or **stunning**: *You look gorgeous in that dress!* • *Her daughter is absolutely stunning.*

If something is extremely attractive, you can say that it is **breathtaking, exquisite, stunning**, or **gorgeous**: *The views from the window were breathtaking.* • *These handmade decorations are exquisite.*

If a person or thing is attractive because of being small, you can say that they are **cute** or **sweet**: *He's got a really cute baby brother.* • *Look at that kitten - isn't she sweet?*

Adjectives such as **stylish** and **chic** can be used to describe something that has been made to look attractive and fashionable: *He took me to a very chic restaurant.* • *Their house is very stylish.*

◦►**attractive** /əˈtræktɪv/ *adjective* **1** beautiful or pleasant to look at *an attractive woman* ○ *I find him very attractive.* **2** interesting or useful *We want to make the club attractive to a wider range of people.* ➔Opposite **unattractive.**
• **attractively** *adverb* • **attractiveness** *noun* [U]

A

attributable /əˈtrɪbjətəbl/ *adjective* **attributable to sth** caused by something *A lot of crime is attributable to the use of drugs.*

attribute¹ /əˈtrɪbjuːt/ *verb*
attribute sth to sth to say that something is caused by something else *He attributes his success to hard work.*
attribute sth to sb to say that someone wrote, said, or made something *This drawing has been attributed to Picasso.*

attribute² /ˈætrɪbjuːt/ *noun* [C] a quality or characteristic that someone or something has *Her hair is her best attribute.*

attributive /əˈtrɪbjətɪv/ *adjective* An attributive adjective comes before the noun it describes. ⊃Compare predicative.

aubergine /ˈəʊbəʒiːn/ *UK* (*US* **eggplant**) *noun* [C, U] an oval, purple vegetable that is white inside ⊃See colour picture **Fruit and Vegetables** on page Centre 10.

auburn /ˈɔːbən/ *adjective* Auburn hair is red-brown.

auction /ˈɔːkʃən/ *noun* [C, U] a sale in which things are sold to the person who offers the most money • **auction** (*also* **auction off**) *verb* [T] to sell something at an auction

auctioneer /ˌɔːkʃənˈɪər/ *noun* [C] the person who is in charge of an auction

audacity /ɔːˈdæsəti/ *noun* [U] showing too much confidence in your behaviour in a way that other people find shocking or rude *And then he had the audacity to blame me for his mistake!* • **audacious** /ɔːˈdeɪʃəs/ *adjective*

audible /ˈɔːdəbl/ *adjective* If something is audible, you can hear it. *His voice was barely audible.* ⊃Opposite **inaudible**. • **audibly** *adverb*

⌗ **WORD PARTNERS FOR audience**

1 be **in** the audience • a **member of** the audience
2 reach an audience • sth's **target** audience • a **wide** audience

o⊷ **audience** /ˈɔːdiəns/ *noun* **1** [GROUP] [group] the people who sit and watch a performance at a theatre, cinema, etc *There were a lot of children in the audience.* **2** [TYPE] [group] the type of people who watch a particular TV show, read a particular book, etc *This magazine is aimed at a teenage audience.* **3** [MEETING] [C] *formal* a formal meeting with an important person *an audience with the Queen*

audio /ˈɔːdiəʊ/ *adjective* relating to the recording or playing of sound *audio equipment*

audio- /ɔːdiəʊ-/ *prefix* relating to hearing or sound *audiotape*

audit /ˈɔːdɪt/ *noun* [C] when an independent person examines all the financial records of a company to produce a report • **audit** *verb* [T] • **auditor** *noun* [C]

audition /ɔːˈdɪʃən/ *noun* [C] when someone does a short performance to try to get a job as an actor, singer, etc • **audition** *verb* [I]

auditorium /ˌɔːdɪˈtɔːriəm/ *noun* [C] the part of a theatre, hall, etc where people sit to watch a performance

Aug *written abbreviation for* August

augment /ɔːgˈment/ *verb* [T] *formal* to increase the size or value of something by adding something to it

o⊷ **August** /ˈɔːgəst/ (*written abbreviation* **Aug**) *noun* [C, U] the eighth month of the year

o⊷ **aunt** /ɑːnt/ (*also* **auntie, aunty** /ˈɑːnti/) *noun* [C] the sister of your mother or father, or the wife of your uncle ⊃See also: **agony aunt**.

au pair /ˌəʊˈpeər/ *noun* [C] a young person who goes to live with a family in another country and looks after their children, does work in their house, etc

aura /ˈɔːrə/ *noun* [C] a feeling which a person or place seems to have *an aura of mystery*

aural /ˈɔːrəl/ *adjective* relating to hearing

auspices /ˈɔːspɪsɪz/ *noun* **under the auspices of sb/sth** *formal* with the help or support of a person or organization *The conference was held under the auspices of the Red Cross.*

auspicious /ɔːˈspɪʃəs/ *adjective* If an event or time is auspicious, it makes you believe that something will be successful in the future. *an auspicious start*

austere /ɒsˈtɪər/ *adjective* **1** plain, simple, and without unnecessary decorations or luxuries *an austere room* **2** strict or severe *an austere woman* • **austerity** /ɒsˈterəti/ *noun* [U]

authentic /ɔːˈθentɪk/ *adjective* If something is authentic, it is real, true, or what people say it is. *authentic Italian food* • **authentically** *adverb* • **authenticity** /ˌɔːθenˈtɪsəti/ *noun* [U]

o⊷ **author** /ˈɔːθər/ *noun* [C] someone who writes a book, article, etc *a popular author of children's fiction*

authoritarian /ˌɔːθɒrɪˈteəriən/ *adjective* very strict and not allowing people freedom to do what they want *an authoritarian leader/regime*

authoritative /ɔːˈθɒrɪtətɪv/ *adjective* **1** An authoritative book, report, etc is respected and considered to be accurate. *an authoritative guide* **2** confident and seeming to be in control of a situation *an authoritative manner/voice*

o⊷ **authority** /ɔːˈθɒrəti/ *noun* **1** [POWER] [U] the official power to make decisions or to control other people *a position of authority* ○ [+ to do sth] *The investigators have the authority to examine all the company's records.* ○ *We need the support of someone in authority.* **2** [OFFICIAL GROUP] [C] an official group or government department with power to control particular public services *the local housing authority* **3** [QUALITY] [U] the quality of being confident and being able to control people *She has an air of authority.* **4** **an authority on sth** someone who has a lot of knowledge about a particular subject *She is an authority on seventeenth-century English literature.* ⊃See also: **local authority**.

authorize (*also UK* **-ise**) /ˈɔːθəraɪz/ *verb* [T] **1** to give official permission for something **2 be authorized to do sth** to be officially allowed to do something *Only managers are authorized to sign expense forms.* • **authorization** /ˌɔːθəraɪˈzeɪʃən/ *noun* [U]

autistic /ɔːˈtɪstɪk/ *adjective* Autistic children

have a mental illness which causes problems with communicating and forming relationships. *One child in 5000 is autistic.* ● **autism** /'ɔ:tɪzᵊm/ *noun* [U]

auto /'ɔ:təʊ/ *adjective US* relating to cars *the auto industry*

auto- /ɔ:təʊ-/ *prefix* **1** operating without being controlled by humans *autopilot* (= a comptuer that directs an aircraft) **2** self *an autobiography* (= a book that someone writes about their own life)

autobiography /ˌɔ:təʊbaɪˈɒɡrəfi/ *noun* [C] a book written by someone about their own life ● **autobiographical** /ˌɔ:təʊbaɪəʊˈɡræfɪkəl/ *adjective*

autograph /'ɔ:təɡrɑ:f/ *noun* [C] a famous person's name, written by that person ● **autograph** *verb* [T] *Her most treasured possession is an autographed photo of Elvis Presley.*

automate /'ɔ:təmeɪt/ *verb* [T] to control something using machines and not people ● **automated** *adjective a fully automated system* ● **automation** /ˌɔ:təˈmeɪʃᵊn/ *noun* [U]

automatic¹ /ˌɔ:təˈmætɪk/ *adjective* **1** MACHINE An automatic machine works by itself or with little human control. *automatic doors* **2** CERTAIN certain to happen as part of the normal process or system *You get an automatic promotion after two years.* **3** REACTION done as a natural reaction without thinking *My automatic response was to pull my hand away.* ● **automatically** *adverb*

automatic² /ˌɔ:təˈmætɪk/ *noun* [C] a car in which you do not have to change the gears (= parts that control how fast the wheels turn)

automobile /'ɔ:təməʊbi:l/ *noun* [C] *US* a car *the automobile industry*

automotive /ˌɔ:təˈməʊtɪv/ *adjective* [always before noun] relating to cars and car production *the automotive industry*

autonomous /ɔ:ˈtɒnəməs/ *adjective* independent and having the power to make your own decisions *an autonomous region/state*

autonomy /ɔ:ˈtɒnəmi/ *noun* [U] the right of a country or group of people to govern itself *Local councils need more autonomy.*

autopsy /'ɔ:tɒpsi/ *noun* [C] a medical examination of a dead body to discover the exact cause of death

○╼**autumn** /'ɔ:təm/ (*also US* **fall**) *noun* [C, U] the season of the year between summer and winter, when leaves fall from the trees *I'm starting a new job **in the autumn**.* ○ *autumn leaves* ● **autumnal** /ɔ:ˈtʌmnᵊl/ *adjective* typical of autumn

auxiliary /ɔ:ɡˈzɪliᵊri/ *adjective* providing extra help or support *an auxiliary nurse*

au‚xiliary 'verb *noun* [C] a verb which is used with another verb to form tenses, negatives, and questions. In English the auxiliary verbs are 'be', 'have', and 'do'.

avail /əˈveɪl/ *noun* **to no avail** without success, especially after a lot of effort *She sent more than 50 letters, but to no avail.*

be/become available ● **make** sth available ● **easily/freely/readily/widely** available ● **be available to** sb

○╼**available** /əˈveɪləbl/ *adjective* **1** If something is available, you can use it or get it. *This information is available free on the Internet.* ○ *The new drug is not yet **available to** the public.* **2** If someone is available, they are not busy and so are able to do something. *No one from the company was available to comment on the accident.* ⊃Opposite **unavailable**. ● **availability** /əˌveɪləˈbɪləti/ *noun* [U]

avalanche /'ævᵊlɑ:nʃ/ *noun* [C] **1** when a large amount of snow falls down the side of a mountain **2** **an avalanche of sth** a sudden, large amount of something, usually more than you can deal with *an avalanche of mail*

avalanche

avant-garde /ˌævɒŋˈɡɑ:d/ *adjective* If art, music, etc, is avant-garde, it is new and unusual in style.

avarice /'ævᵊrɪs/ *noun* [U] *formal* a strong feeling that you want a lot of money and possessions

Ave *written abbreviation for* avenue *132, Gainsborough Ave*

avenge /əˈvendʒ/ *verb* [T] *literary* to punish someone for doing something bad to you, your family, etc *He swore he would avenge his brother's death.*

avenue /'ævənju:/ *noun* [C] **1** (*written abbreviation* **Ave**) a wide road in a town or city, often with trees along it **2** a possible way of doing or achieving something *We have exhausted all other avenues of treatment.*

○╼**average¹** /'ævᵊrɪdʒ/ *adjective* **1** USUAL usual and like the most common type *an average person* ○ *an average day* **2** AMOUNT [always before noun] An average amount is calculated by adding some amounts together and then dividing by the number of amounts. *an average age/temperature* **3** NOT EXCELLENT not excellent, although not bad *The food was pretty average.*

○╼**average²** /'ævᵊrɪdʒ/ *noun* **1** [C] an amount calculated by adding some amounts together and then dividing by the number of amounts *They work an average of 30.5 hours per week.* **2** [C, U] the usual or typical amount *well above/below average* **3** **on average** usually, or based on an average *Female workers earn, on average, a third less than men.*

average³ /'ævᵊrɪdʒ/ *verb* [T] to reach a particular amount as an average *He averages about 20 points a game.*

averse /əˈvɜ:s/ *adjective* **1** **not be averse to sth** *UK humorous* to be happy or willing to do or have something *She's not averse to the occasional glass of champagne.* **2** **be averse to sth** *formal* to strongly dislike something

aversion /əˈvɜ:ʒᵊn/ *noun* **an aversion to** sth

when you strongly dislike something

avert /əˈvɜːt/ verb 1 **avert a crisis/disaster/war, etc** to prevent something bad from happening 2 **avert your eyes/face/gaze** to turn your head away so that you do not see something

avian flu /ˌeɪviənˈfluː/ noun [U] bird flu: an illness that kills birds and can sometimes pass from birds to people

aviary /ˈeɪviᵊri/ noun [C] a large cage for birds

aviation /ˌeɪviˈeɪʃᵊn/ noun [U] flying aircraft or producing aircraft *the aviation industry*

avid /ˈævɪd/ adjective very interested and enthusiastic *an avid reader* • **avidly** adverb

avocado /ˌævəˈkɑːdəʊ/ noun [C, U] a dark green, oval fruit which is pale green inside and is not sweet

ᴏ⃰**avoid** /əˈvɔɪd/ verb [T] 1 to stay away from a person, place, situation, etc *Try to avoid the city centre.* 2 to prevent something from happening *Book early to avoid disappointment.* 3 **avoid doing sth** to intentionally not do something *She managed to avoid answering my question.* • **avoidable** adjective possible to avoid ⊃Opposite **unavoidable.** • **avoidance** noun [U] when you avoid something

avoid doing something

When **avoid** is followed by a verb, the verb is always in the -ing form.

I avoided seeing him for several days.

~~I avoided to see him for several days.~~

await /əˈweɪt/ verb [T] formal 1 to wait for something *We are awaiting the results of the tests.* 2 If something awaits you, you will experience it in the future. *A surprise awaits her when she gets home.*

ᴏ⃰**awake¹** /əˈweɪk/ adjective 1 **be/lie/stay, etc awake** to not be sleeping *Is Tom awake yet?* ○ *The noise from the party kept me awake all night.* 2 **be wide awake** to be completely awake

awake² /əˈweɪk/ verb [I, T] past tense awoke past participle awoken literary to wake up, or make someone wake up

awaken /əˈweɪkᵊn/ verb 1 [T] formal to cause an emotion, feeling, etc *The song awakened painful memories.* 2 [I, T] literary to wake up, or make someone wake up

awakening /əˈweɪkᵊnɪŋ/ noun [no plural] 1 when you start to be aware of something or feel something 2 **a rude awakening** If you have a rude awakening, you have a shock when you discover the truth about a situation.

present/receive/win an award • an award **for** sth • an awards **ceremony** • an award **winner**

award¹ /əˈwɔːd/ noun [C] 1 a prize given to someone for something they have achieved *the award for best actress* ○ *to receive/win an award* 2 money given to someone because of a legal decision

award² /əˈwɔːd/ verb [T] to officially give some-

one something such as a prize or an amount of money [+ **two objects, often passive**] *He was awarded the Nobel Prize for Physics.*

ᴏ⃰**aware** /əˈweər/ adjective 1 **be aware of/that** to know about something *Are you aware of the risks involved?* ○ *She was **well** aware that he was married.* ⊃Opposite **unaware.** 2 interested in and knowing a lot about a particular subject *politically/socially aware*

create/increase/raise awareness • a **greater/growing/heightened/increased** awareness • **public** awareness • an awareness **about/of** sth • an awareness **among** [parents/students, etc]

awareness /əˈweənəs/ noun [U] when you know about something *Environmental awareness is increasing all the time.*

awash /əˈwɒʃ/ adjective **be awash with sth** UK (US **be awash in sth**) to have a lot of something, often too much *The sport is awash with money.*

ᴏ⃰**away¹** /əˈweɪ/ adverb 1 DIRECTION to or in a different place or situation *Go away and leave me alone.* ○ *We'd like to move **away from** the town centre.* 2 DISTANCE FROM at a particular distance from a place *The nearest town was ten miles away.* ○ *How far away is the station?* 3 NOT THERE not at the place where someone usually lives or works *Shirley's feeding the cat while we're away.* 4 SAFE PLACE into a usual or safe place *Can you put everything away when you've finished?* 5 **two weeks/five hours, etc away** at a particular time in the future *My exam's only a week away now.* 6 CONTINUOUS ACTION used after a verb to mean 'continuously' or repeatedly' *Chris was hammering away in the garden all day.* 7 GRADUALLY gradually disappearing until almost or completely gone *The snow has melted away.* 8 SPORT UK If a sports team is playing away, the game is at the place where the other team usually plays. ⊃See also: take your **breath** away, give the **game¹** away.

away² /əˈweɪ/ adjective [always before noun] UK in sports, an away game is played at the place where the other team usually plays.

awe /ɔː/ noun [U] 1 a feeling of great respect and sometimes fear *I was filled with awe at the sheer size of the building.* 2 **be in awe of sb** to feel great respect for someone *As children we were rather in awe of our grandfather.*

awe-inspiring /ˈɔːɪnspaɪərɪŋ/ adjective causing people to feel great respect or admiration

awesome /ˈɔːsəm/ adjective very great, large, or special and making you feel respect and sometimes fear *an awesome challenge/responsibility* ○ *The scenery was awesome.*

ᴏ⃰**awful** /ˈɔːfᵊl/ adjective 1 very bad, of low quality, or unpleasant *an awful place* ○ *The film was absolutely awful.* 2 **an awful lot (of sth)** informal a large amount *It cost an awful lot of money.*

awfully /ˈɔːfᵊli/ adverb very *awfully difficult/good*

awhile /əˈwaɪl/ adverb US for a short time *Let's wait awhile and see what happens.*

awkward /ˈɔːkwəd/ *adjective* **1** DIFFICULT difficult or causing problems *an awkward customer* ○ *an awkward question* **2** EMBARRASSING embarrassing and not relaxed *an awkward pause/silence* ○ *I'm in an awkward situation.* **3** NOT ATTRACTIVE moving in a way that is not attractive *His movements were slow and awkward.* ● **awkwardly** *adverb* *She fell awkwardly.* ● **awkwardness** *noun* [U]

awoke /əˈwəʊk/ *past tense of* awake

awoken /əˈwəʊkən/ *past participle of* awake

awry /əˈraɪ/ *adverb* **go awry** to not happen in the correct way *Suddenly everything started to go awry.*

axe¹ (*also US* **ax**) /æks/ *noun* [C] a tool consisting of a wooden handle with a sharp piece of metal at one end, used for cutting trees or wood

axe² (*also US* **ax**) /æks/ *verb* [T] to get rid of something or someone suddenly *The company has announced plans to axe 500 jobs.*

axes /ˈæksiːz/ *plural of* axis

axis /ˈæksɪs/ *noun* [C] *plural* **axes** /ˈæksiːz/ **1** an imaginary, central line around which an object turns **2** a line at the side or bottom of a graph (= picture showing measurements)

axle /ˈæksl/ *noun* [C] a long metal bar which connects two wheels on a vehicle

aye /aɪ/ *exclamation informal* yes, used especially in Scotland and the North of England

Bb

B, b /biː/ the second letter of the alphabet

BA /ˌbiːˈeɪ/ noun [C] abbreviation for Bachelor of Arts: a university or college qualification in an arts (= not science) subject which usually takes 3 or 4 years of study

baa /bɑː/ noun [C] the sound that a sheep makes

babble /ˈbæbl/ verb [I] to talk quickly in a way which is confused, silly, or has no meaning ● **babble** noun [U] the babble of voices

babe /beɪb/ noun [C] **1** very informal a young, attractive woman **2** literary a baby

WORD PARTNERS FOR baby

have/be expecting/give birth to a baby ● a baby is born ● a new/newborn baby

o―**baby** /ˈbeɪbi/ noun [C] **1** a very young child a baby girl/boy ○ baby clothes ○ Liz has had a baby. ○ Maria's expecting a baby (= she is pregnant). **2** a very young animal a baby bird

baby boom noun [C] a time when a lot of babies are born in a particular area the postwar baby boom

baby carriage noun [C] US a small vehicle with four wheels for carrying a baby

babyish /ˈbeɪbiɪʃ/ adjective Babyish behaviour is silly, like the behaviour of a young child.

babysit /ˈbeɪbisɪt/ verb [I, T] babysitting, past babysat to look after children while their parents are not at home ● **babysitter** noun [C] We'd like to come, but we can't get a babysitter. ● **babysitting** noun [U]

bachelor /ˈbætʃələr/ noun [C] **1** a man who is not married **2 Bachelor of Arts/Science/Education, etc** a university or college qualification which usually takes 3 or 4 years of study, or a person who has this qualification

o―**back¹** /bæk/ adverb **1** RETURNING where someone or something was before When do you go back to college? ○ I put it back in the cupboard. **2** BEHIND in a direction behind you Anna stepped back. ○ Flint leaned back in his chair. **3** REPLY as a reply or reaction to something UK to ring back/ US to call back ○ I signalled to her and she waved back. **4** STATE to the state something or someone was in before Hopefully things will get back to normal again now. ○ I'm sure we can put it back together again (= repair it). ○ Try to go back to sleep. **5** EARLIER at or to an earlier time We first met back in 1973. ○ Looking back, I think we did the right thing. **6** AWAY FROM in a direction away from something He pulled back the curtain. **7 back and forth** (also UK backwards and forwards) in one direction, then the opposite way, then in the original direction again many times He has to travel back and forth between London and Paris every week.

COMMON LEARNER ERROR

back to

Remember to use the preposition **to** when you are talking about returning to a place.

I haven't seen her since she went back to Korea.

~~I haven't seen her since she went back Korea.~~

o―**back²** /bæk/ noun [C] **1** NOT FRONT the part of something that is furthest from the front or in the opposite direction to the front He wrote his number down on the back of an envelope. ○ I always keep a blanket in the back of the car. **2** BODY the part of your body from your shoulders to your bottom back injuries/pain ○ He was lying on his back. ⊃See colour picture **The Body** on page Centre 13. **3** SEAT the part of a seat that you lean against when you are sitting the back of a chair **4 back to front** UK with the back part of something where the front should be You've got your trousers on back to front. **5 in back of** US behind They sat in back of us on the plane. **6 at/in the back of your mind** If you have a thought or idea at the back of your mind, you are always thinking about it. **7 behind sb's back** If you do something behind someone's back, you do it without them knowing, often in an unfair way. Have they been saying things about me behind my back? **8 be glad/happy, etc to see the back of sb/sth** UK to be pleased when someone leaves or something ends because you did not like them **9 be on sb's back** to remind someone again and again to do something, or to criticize someone in an annoying way **10 turn your back on sb/sth** to decide to stop having contact with someone or something, or to refuse to help someone She turned her back on Hollywood and went to live in Florida. ⊃See also: a pat² on the back, be (like) water¹ off a duck's back.

back³ /bæk/ verb **1** [T] to give support or help to a person, plan, or idea He backed Mr Clark in the recent election. **2** [T] to risk money by saying that you think a horse, team, etc will win a race, game, or competition in order to win more money if they do Many people are backing Holyfield to win the fight. **3 back (sth) away/into/out, etc** to move backwards or drive backwards She saw he had a gun and backed away.

back away to show that you do not support a plan or idea any more and do not want to be involved with it The government has backed away from plans to increase taxes.

back down to admit that you were wrong, or agree not to do something The council backed down over rent increases.

back off 1 to move away from someone, usually because you are afraid I saw the knife and backed off. **2** mainly US to stop supporting a plan The president has backed off from a threat to expel U.N. soldiers.

back out to decide not to do something you had planned or agreed to do Nigel backed out at the last minute, so we had a spare ticket.

back sb up 1 to support or help someone My family backed me up in my fight for compensation. **2** to say that someone is telling the

B

truth *Honestly, that's exactly what happened Claire'll back me up.*

back sth up 1 to prove that something is true [often passive] *His claims are backed up by recent research.* **2** to make an extra copy of computer information

back (sth) up to drive backwards

○**back⁴** /bæk/ *adjective* **1** [always before noun] at or near the back of something *back door/garden/page* ○ *I put it in the back pocket of my jeans.* **2 back road/street** a very small road or street that goes behind or between buildings ⊃See also: put sth on the back **burner.**

backache /'bækeɪk/ *noun* [C, U] a pain in your back *I suffer from backache.*

backbench /ˌbæk'bentʃ/ *adjective UK* **a backbench MP/politician, etc** a member of the government who does not have an important position ●**backbencher** *noun* [C] a backbench politician

the backbenches /ˌbæk'bentʃɪz/ *noun* [plural] *UK* the place where backbench politicians sit *He prefers to remain* **on the backbenches.**

backboard /'bækbɔːd/ *noun* [C] in basketball (= a sport), a board behind the metal ring that you have to throw the ball through to score ⊃See colour picture **Sports 2** on page Centre 15.

backbone /'bækbəʊn/ *noun* [C] **1** the main or strongest part of something *The car industry remains* **the backbone of** *the area's economy.* **2** the line of bones down the centre of your back

backdrop /'bækdrɒp/ *noun* [C] **1** the situation that an event happens in [usually singular] *The attack took place* **against a backdrop of** *rising tensions between the two communities.* **2** the painted cloth at the back of a stage in a theatre

backer /'bækəʳ/ *noun* [C] someone who supports a person or plan, especially by giving them money *financial backers*

backfire /ˌbæk'faɪəʳ/ *verb* [I] If something that you do backfires, it has the opposite result of what you wanted.

⟐ WORD PARTNERS FOR **background**

2 come from a [poor/different, etc] background ● sb's **family** background

background /'bækgraʊnd/ *noun* **1** SOUND [no plural] Sounds in the background are not the main sounds you can hear. *background music/noise* ○ *I could hear a baby crying in* **the background.** **2** PERSON [C] a person's education, family, and experience of life *She came* **from** *a middle-class background.* **3** PICTURE [C, U] the parts at the back of a picture, view, etc which are not the main things you look at *gold stars* **on** *a black background* **4** SITUATION [C] the situation that an event happens in, or things which have happened in the past which affect it [usually singular] *The talks are taking place* **against a background of** *economic uncertainty.* **5 in the background** If a person stays in the background, they try not to be noticed.

backhand /'bækhænd/ *noun* [C] when you hit a

ball with your arm across your body, in sports such as tennis

backing /'bækɪŋ/ *noun* [U] support, especially money, for a person or plan *financial backing* ○ *The proposal has the full backing of the government.*

backlash /'bæklæʃ/ *noun* [C] when people react against an idea which was previously popular [usually singular] a **backlash against** *the royal family*

backlog /'bæklɒg/ *noun* [C] work that should have been done earlier

backpack /'bækpæk/ **backpack**
noun [C] a bag that you carry on your back ⊃See picture at **luggage.** ● **backpacking** *noun* [U] *to go* **backpacking**
● **backpacker** *noun* [C]

backside /ˌbæk'saɪd/ ⑱ /'bæk,saɪd/ *noun* [C] *informal* the part of your body that you sit on

backslash /'bækslæʃ/ *noun* [C] the symbol '\', a symbol used in computer programs but rarely in Internet addresses ⊃Compare **forward slash.**

backstage /ˌbæk'steɪdʒ/ *adverb* in the area behind the stage in a theatre where performers get ready

backstroke /'bækstrəʊk/ *noun* [U] a style of swimming on your back

back-to-back /ˌbæktə'bæk/ *adjective, adverb* **1** If two people or things are back-to-back, their backs are touching or facing each other. *They stood back-to-back.* **2** If two things happen back-to-back, one happens after the other without a pause. *back-to-back interviews*

backtrack /'bæktræk/ *verb* [I] to say that you did not mean something you said earlier *The government has* **backtracked on** *its promises.*

backup /'bækʌp/ *noun* **1** [C, U] extra help, support, or equipment which is available if you need it *Medical staff are on call to* **provide** *backup in case of an emergency.* **2** [C] an extra copy of computer information *to* **make a** *backup*

backward /'bækwəd/ *adjective* **1** [always before noun] in the direction behind you a **backward** *glance* **2** less developed or slower to develop than normal *a backward country*

○**backwards** /'bækwədz/ (*also* **backward**) *adverb* **1** DIRECTION towards the direction behind you *She took a couple of steps backwards.* **2** EARLIER towards an earlier time or an earlier stage of development *Let's start with your most recent job and* **work backwards.** **3** OPPOSITE ORDER in the opposite order to what is usual *"Erehwon"* *is "nowhere" spelled backwards.* **4** WRONG WAY *(also UK* **back to front)** with the part that is usually at the front at the back *You've got your skirt on backwards.* **5 backwards and forwards** *UK (UK/US* **back and forth)** in one direction then the opposite way and back again many times *I have to drive backwards and forwards between here and Ipswich every day.* **6 bend**

over backwards to try extremely hard to help or to please someone [+ **to do sth**] *She bent over backwards to help him.*

backyard /ˌbækˈjɑːd/ noun [C] *US* the area behind a house

bacon /ˈbeɪkən/ noun [U] meat from a pig cut into long thin slices

bacteria /bækˈtɪəriə/ noun [plural] very small living things that sometimes cause disease ● **bacterial** adjective made from or caused by bacteria *bacterial infections*

ᴏ⊸**bad** /bæd/ adjective worse, worst 1 NOT PLEAS-ANT not pleasant *bad weather* ○ *My phone bill was even worse than I'd expected.* ○ *He's in a bad mood today.* 2 LOW QUAL-ITY of low quality *bad behaviour* ○ *The service was really bad.* ○ *He's always been bad at maths.* 3 SEVERE very serious or severe *a bad injury* ○ *the worst flooding for years* 4 NOT LUCKY not lucky, not convenient, or not happening how you would like *It was just bad luck that she heard us.* ○ *Is this a bad time to ask?* 5 **not bad** satisfactory *"There are about 10 people in a group." "Oh well, that's not bad."* ○ *That's not bad for such a small company.* 6 **be bad for sb/sth** to be harmful for someone or something *Looking at a computer screen for too long can be bad for your eyes.* 7 **feel bad about sth/doing sth** to feel guilty or sorry about something that has happened *I felt bad about letting her down.* 8 **too bad a** SYMPATHY mainly *US informal* used to say that you are sorry about a situation *"He didn't get the job." "Oh, that's too bad."* **b** CANNOT CHANGE informal used to say that nothing can be done to change a situation *I know you don't want to go but it's too bad, we have to.* 9 EVIL evil *She's a really bad person.* 10 NOT FRESH Bad food is not fresh and cannot be eaten. 11 PAINFUL [always before noun] If you have a bad arm, leg, heart, etc, there is something wrong with it and it is painful. ⊃See also: bad **blood**, be in sb's good/bad books (**book**¹).

baddie /ˈbædi/ noun [C] *mainly UK informal* a bad person in a film, book, etc

bade /bæd/ past tense of bid³

badge /bædʒ/ noun [C] 1 a piece of plastic, metal, etc which you wear on your clothes showing your name or the organization you work for 2 *UK* (*US* **button**) a piece of plastic, metal, etc with words or pictures on it that you wear on your clothes for decoration

badger /ˈbædʒəʳ/ noun [C] a wild animal with thick black and white fur that lives under the ground and comes out at night

ᴏ⊸**badly** /ˈbædli/ adverb worse, worst 1 very seriously *badly damaged/injured* 2 in a way that is of low quality or in an unpleasant way *to behave badly* ○ *They played badly in the first half.*

badminton /ˈbædmɪntən/ noun [U] a sport for two or four people in which you hit a shuttlecock (= a light object with feathers) over a net

bad-tempered /ˌbædˈtempəd/ adjective a bad-tempered person gets angry or annoyed easily *'Sam's been very bad-tempered recently, is something worrying him?'*

baffle /ˈbæfl/ verb [T] If something baffles you, you cannot understand it at all. [often passive] *The police were baffled by his disappearance.*

bags

handbag

rucksack *UK*,
backpack *US*

carrier bag *UK*,
grocery bag *US*

briefcase

ᴏ⊸**bag¹** /bæg/ noun [C] 1 CONTAINER a container made of paper, plastic, etc, used for carrying things *a paper/plastic bag* ○ *He packed his bags and left.* 2 FOR WOMAN (*also* **handbag**) *mainly UK* a bag with handles in which a woman carries her money, keys, etc 3 AMOUNT the amount a bag contains *It doesn't weigh more than a couple of bags of sugar.* 4 **bags of sth** *mainly UK informal* a large amount of something *There's bags of room.* 5 **bags** Bags under your eyes are areas of loose or dark skin. ⊃See also: carrier bag, let the **cat** out of the bag, shoulder bag, sleeping bag, tote bag

bag² /bæg/ verb [T] bagging, past bagged *informal* to get something, especially before other people have a chance to take it *Bag us some decent seats.*

bagel /ˈbeɪgᵊl/ noun [C] a type of bread made in the shape of a ring ⊃See picture at **bread.**

baggage /ˈbægɪdʒ/ noun [U] 1 all the cases and bags that you take with you when you travel *baggage reclaim* 2 feelings and experiences from the past that influence how you think and behave now *emotional baggage*

baggy /ˈbægi/ adjective Baggy clothes are big and loose.

bagpipes /ˈbægpaɪps/ noun [plural] a Scottish musical instrument that is played by blowing air into a bag and forcing it through pipes

baguette /bægˈet/ noun [C] a French-style loaf of bread that is long and thin and white *a ham and cheese baguette*

bail¹ /beɪl/ noun [U] when money is paid to a court so that someone can be released from prison until their trial *He was released on bail.* ○ *She was granted bail.*

bail² /beɪl/ verb **be bailed** If someone is bailed until a particular time, they can leave prison until then if they pay money to the court.

bail sb out 1 to help a person or organization by giving them money *Companies can't expect the government to keep bailing them out.* 2 to pay money to a court so that someone can be released from prison until their trial

bailiff /ˈbeɪlɪf/ noun [C] 1 *UK* someone whose job is to take away things people own when they owe money 2 *US* someone whose job is to guard prisoners in a court

bailout /ˈbeɪlaʊt/ *noun* [C] *mainly US* when a company is given money to solve its financial problems

bait¹ /beɪt/ *noun* [U, no plural] **1** food that is used to try to attract fish or animals so that you can catch them **2** something that you use to persuade someone to do something

bait² /beɪt/ *verb* [T] **1** to put food in or on something to try to catch fish or animals *a mouse trap baited with cheese* **2** to try to make someone angry by laughing at them or criticizing them

bake /beɪk/ *verb* [I, T] to cook something such as bread or a cake with dry heat in an oven *a baked apple* ➲See picture at **cook**.

ˌbaked ˈbeans *noun* [plural] beans cooked in a tomato (= soft, round, red fruit used like a vegetable) sauce and sold in tins (= metal containers) *baked beans on toast*

ˌbaked poˈtato *noun* [C] a potato baked and served with the skin (= outer layer) still on

baker /ˈbeɪkəʳ/ *noun* [C] someone who makes and sells bread, cakes, etc *Can you call at the baker's and get a loaf of bread?*

bakery /ˈbeɪkəri/ *noun* [C] a shop where you can buy bread, cakes, etc

baking /ˈbeɪkɪŋ/ *adjective informal* Baking weather is very hot.

WORD PARTNERS FOR ***balance***

1 keep/lose your balance • **knock/throw** sb **off** balance • sb's **sense of** balance
2 find/maintain/strike a balance • **redress** the balance • a **delicate** balance • a balance **between** sth and sth

balance¹ /ˈbæləns/ *noun* **1** [WEIGHT] [U] when the weight of someone or something is spread in such a way that they do not fall over *I lost my* ***balance*** *and fell off the bike.* ○ *The force of the explosion threw him* ***off balance*** (= it was difficult for him to stay standing). **2** [EQUAL] [U, no plural] when the correct amount of importance is given to each thing so that a situation is successful *We hope to* ***strike a balance between*** *police powers and the protection of citizens.* ➲Opposite **imbalance**. **3** [FAIR] [U] when you consider all the facts in a fair way *I felt his report lacked balance.* **4 on balance** used to give your opinion after you have considered all the facts about something *On balance, I'd prefer a woman dentist to a man.* **5** [MONEY] [C] the amount of money that you still have to pay, or that you have left to use [usually singular] *I always pay off the balance on my credit card each month.* **6 be/hang in the balance** If something hangs in the balance, nobody knows if it will continue to exist in the future or what will happen to it. *After a bad year, Judd's career hung in the balance.*

balance² /ˈbæləns/ *verb* **1** [I, T] to be in a position where you will not fall to either side, or to put something in this position *She was trying to balance a book on her head.* **2** [T] to give the correct amount of importance to each thing so that a situation is successful *I struggle to balance work and family commitments.* **3 balance the books/budget** to make sure that you do not spend more money than you get *If the business loses any more money, we won't be able to balance the books this year.*

balance sth against sth to compare the advantages and disadvantages of something *The ecological effects of the factory need to be balanced against the employment it provides.*

balanced /ˈbælənst/ *adjective* **1** considering all the facts in a fair way *a balanced discussion of his work* **2 a balanced diet/meal** a healthy mixture of different kinds of food *If you have a balanced diet, you are getting all the vitamins you need.* ➲See also: **well-balanced**.

ˌbalance of ˈpayments *noun* [no plural] *mainly UK* the difference between how much a country earns by selling things to other countries and how much it spends buying things from them

ˌbalance of ˈpower *noun* [no plural] the way in which power is divided between different people or groups *maintaining the balance of power in the European Union*

ˈbalance ˌsheet *noun* [C] a document that shows what a company has earned and what it has spent *We've had a good year's trading and are now looking at a very health balance sheet.*

balcony /ˈbælkəni/ *noun* [C] **1** a small area joined to the wall outside a room on a high level where you can stand or sit *We had drinks on the hotel balcony.* **2** the seats in an upper area of a theatre *Our seats are in row F of the balcony.*

bald

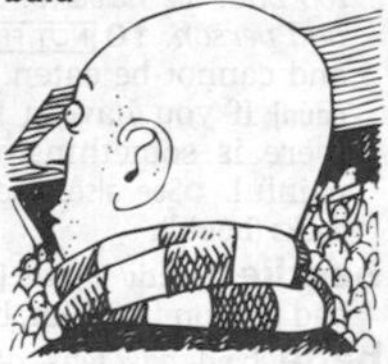

bald /bɔːld/ *adjective* **1** with little or no hair *John started to* ***go bald*** *at an early age.* ○ *I've got a* ***bald patch/spot***. **2** [always before noun] Bald facts or ways of saying things are very clear and are not intended to comfort you. *The bald truth is that we cannot afford to employ so many people.* •**baldness** *noun* [U]

balding /ˈbɔːldɪŋ/ *adjective* becoming bald *Eammon was plump and balding* (= becoming bald).

baldly /ˈbɔːldli/ *adverb* If you say something baldly, you say it in a very clear way which may upset the person you are speaking to. *"I don't love you any more," he said baldly.*

bale /beɪl/ *noun* [C] a large amount of something such as paper, cloth, or hay (= dried grass), that is tied together so that it can be stored or moved

baleful /ˈbeɪlfəl/ *adjective formal* evil or angry *a baleful look*

balk (*also UK* **baulk**) /bɔːlk/ [US] /bɔːk/ *verb* [I] to not want to do something that is unpleasant or difficult *Most people* ***balk at*** *paying these kind of prices for clothes.*

ball

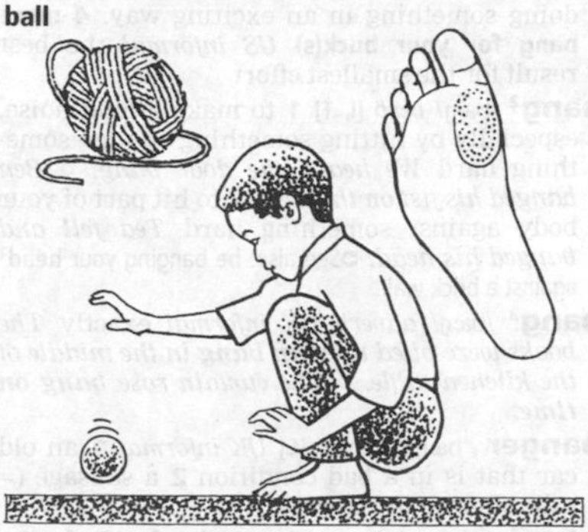

balloon

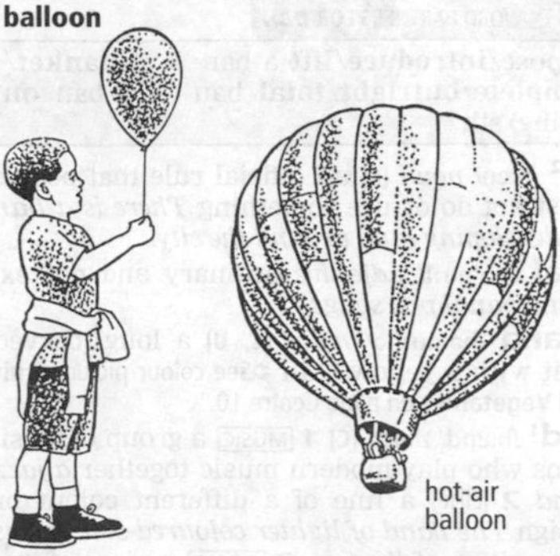

⊶ball /bɔːl/ *noun* [C] **1** a round object that you throw, kick, or hit in a game, or something with this shape *a tennis ball* ○ *a ball of string* ○ *The cat curled itself into a ball.* ○ *She* ***threw*** *a* ***ball*** *at me.* ○ *He* ***kicked*** *the* ***ball*** *hard into the net.* ○ *Just try to concentrate on* ***hitting*** *the* ***ball.*** **2** a large formal occasion where people dance*The colleges all hold summer balls.* ○ *a ball gown* **3 have a ball** *informal* to enjoy yourself very much *We had a ball in Miami.* **4 be on the ball** *informal* to be quick to understand and react to things *I didn't sleep well last night and I'm not really on the ball today.* **5 set/start the ball rolling** to begin an activity that involves a group of people *I've started the ball rolling by setting up a series of meetings.* ➲See also: **ball game, crystal ball.**

ballad /ˈbæləd/ *noun* [C] a song that tells a story, especially about love

ballerina /ˌbælᵊrˈiːnə/ *noun* [C] a female ballet dancer *She has devoted many years to her career as a ballerina.*

ballet /ˈbæleɪ/ [US] /bælˈeɪ/ *noun* **1** [DANCING] [U] a type of dancing that is done in a theatre and tells a story, usually with music *By the age of fifteen he had already performed in a professional ballet.* **2** [PERFORMANCE] [C] a particular story or performance of ballet dancing *Mary's favourite ballet was 'Giselle'.* **3** [DANCERS] [C] a group of ballet dancers who work together *the Royal Ballet*

ˈball ˌgame *noun* [C] **1** *US* a game of baseball (= where teams hit a ball and run round four fixed points), basketball (= where teams throw a ball through a high net), or American football *Hey, kids, let's go to a ball game tonight.* **2 a whole new ball game** *informal* (*also* **a different ball game**) a completely different situation from how things were before *We'd been climbing in Scotland, but the Himalayas were a whole new ball game.* ○ *I've worked in stressful environments before but this job is a different ball game.*

ballistic /bəˈlɪstɪk/ *adjective* **go ballistic** *informal* to suddenly become very angry *If your dad finds out you've been skipping school, he'll go ballistic.*

balloon¹ /bəˈluːn/ *noun* [C] a small coloured rubber bag that you fill with air to play with or to use as a decoration *Could you help me to* ***blow up*** *some* ***balloons?*** ○ *Millie's* ***balloon burst*** *and we had to buy her another.* ➲See also: **hot-air balloon.**

balloon² /bəˈluːn/ *verb* [I] to suddenly become much larger *I ballooned to 14 stone when I had my second baby.*

WORD PARTNERS FOR ***ballot***

hold a ballot • a ballot **on** sth • be **on** a ballot • *(UK)* ballot **papers** • a ballot **box**

ballot¹ /ˈbælət/ *noun* [C, U] a secret written vote *to* ***hold a ballot*** ○ *She was the only candidate* ***on the ballot*** (= available to vote for). ○ *UK* ***ballot papers*** ○ ***a ballot box*** (= box where votes are collected)

ballot² /ˈbælət/ *verb* [T] *mainly UK* to ask people to vote in a ballot so that you can find out their opinion about something *In July he will* ***ballot*** *his members* ***on*** *how they want to proceed.*

ballpark /ˈbɔːlpɑːk/ *noun* **1** [C] *US* a place where baseball (= game where teams hit a ball and run round four fixed points) is played and watched **2 ballpark estimate/figure** a number or amount that is not exact but should be near the correct number or amount *$3 million would be a ballpark figure for sales next year.*

ballpoint pen /ˌbɔːlpɔɪntˈpen/ *noun* [C] a pen with a very small ball in the end that rolls ink onto the paper

ballroom /ˈbɔːlruːm/ *noun* [C] a large room where dances are held

bamboo /bæmˈbuː/ *noun* [C, U] a tall plant with hard hollow stems, often used for making furniture

bamboo

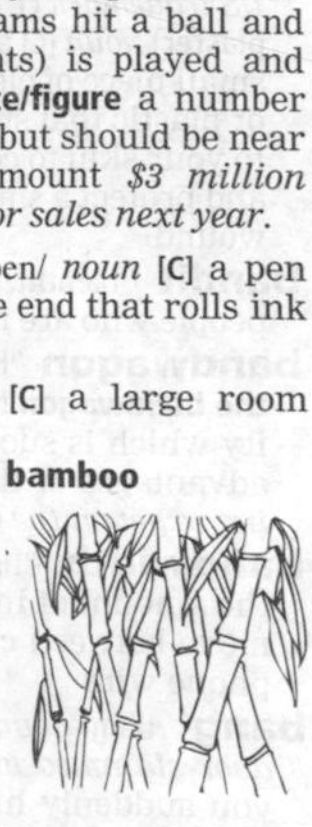

ban¹ /bæn/ *verb* [T] **banning** *past* **banned** to officially say that someone must not do something *A lot of people think boxing should be banned.* ○ **[+ from + doing sth]** *Ian's been banned from driving for 2 years.*

B

WORD PARTNERS FOR *ban*

impose/introduce/lift a ban • a blanket/complete/outright/total ban • a ban on (doing) sth

ban² /bæn/ *noun* [C] an official rule that people must not do or use something *There is a **ban** on developing land around the city.*

banal /bəˈnɑːl/ *adjective* ordinary and not exciting *banal pop songs*

oᴖ**banana** /bəˈnɑːnə/ *noun* [C, U] a long, curved fruit with a yellow skin ⊃See colour picture **Fruit and Vegetables** on page Centre 10.

oᴖ**band¹** /bænd/ *noun* [C] **1** [MUSIC] a group of musicians who play modern music together *a jazz band* **2** [LINE] a line of a different colour or design *The band of lighter coloured soil marks the position of the fort.* **3** [CIRCLE] a piece of material put around something *an **elastic band*** **4** [PEOPLE] a group of people who do something together *the Cathedral's band of regular worshippers* **5** [PART] *UK* one of the groups that something is divided into *the 20-25 age band* ⊃See also: **elastic band, rubber band.**

band² /bænd/ *verb*

band together to work with other people in order to achieve something *Companies banded together to keep prices high.* ⊃Opposite **disband.**

bandage¹ /ˈbændɪdʒ/ *noun* [C] a long piece of soft cloth that you tie around an injured part of the body

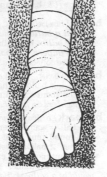
bandage

bandage² /ˈbændɪdʒ/ *verb* [T] to put a bandage around a wound or injury *I bandaged her wrist and took her to the doctor's.*

Band-Aid /ˈbændeɪd/ *US trademark* (*UK* **plaster**) *noun* [C] a small piece of cloth or plastic that sticks to your skin to cover and protect a small wound

bandit /ˈbændɪt/ *noun* [C] a thief who attacks people who are travelling in a wild place

bandwagon /ˈbændˌwægən/ *noun* **get/jump on the bandwagon** to become involved in an activity which is successful so that you can get the advantages of it yourself *Publishers are rushing to get on the CD-ROM bandwagon.*

bandwidth /ˈbændwɪtθ/ *noun* [usually singular] the amount of information per second that can move between computers connected by a telephone wire

bang¹ /bæŋ/ *noun* [C] **1** a sudden loud noise *The door slammed with a deafening bang.* **2** when you suddenly hit part of your body on something hard *a nasty bang on the head* **3 go out with a bang** *informal* If someone or something goes out with a bang, they stop existing or

doing something in an exciting way. **4 more bang for your buck(s)** *US informal* the best result for the smallest effort

bang² /bæŋ/ *verb* [I, T] **1** to make a loud noise, especially by hitting something against something hard *We heard the door bang.* ○ *Ben banged his fist on the desk.* **2** to hit part of your body against something hard *Ted fell and banged his head.* ⊃See also: be banging your **head¹** against a brick wall.

bang³ /bæŋ/ *adverb UK informal* exactly *The books were piled up **slap bang** in the middle of the kitchen table.* ○ *The curtain rose **bang on** time.*

banger /ˈbæŋəʳ/ *noun* [C] *UK informal* **1** an old car that is in a bad condition **2** a sausage (= tube of meat and spices)

bangle /ˈbæŋgl/ *noun* [C] a circle of stiff plastic, metal etc that people wear around the arm as jewellery

bangs /bæŋz/ *noun* [plural] *US* (*UK* **fringe** [C]) hair that is cut short and straight at the top of someone's face

banish /ˈbænɪʃ/ *verb* [T] **1** to send someone away from a place, often as a punishment [often passive] *He was **banished to** a remote Alaskan island.* **2** to make yourself stop thinking about something or feeling a particular way *Banish winter blues with a holiday in the sun!*

banister /ˈbænɪstəʳ/ *noun* [C] a long piece of wood that you can hold as you go up or down stairs

banjo /ˈbændʒəʊ/ *noun* [C] a musical instrument like a guitar with a round body

oᴖ**bank¹** /bæŋk/ *noun* [C] **1** [MONEY] an organization or place where you can borrow money, save money, etc *Most banks are reluctant to lend money to new businesses.* **2** [RIVER] the land along the side of a river *We found a shady spot on the river bank.* **3** [STORE] a place where a supply of something can be kept until it is needed *a blood bank* **4** [PILE] a large pile of snow, sand, or soil ⊃See also: **bottle bank, merchant bank, piggy bank.**

bank² /bæŋk/ *verb* **1** [I, T] to put or keep money in a bank *to bank a cheque* ○ *Who do you **bank with?*** ○ *I **bank at** the First National Bank.* **2** [I] When a plane banks, it flies with one wing higher than the other when turning.

bank on sb/sth to depend on someone doing something or something happening *Chrissie might arrive on time, but I wouldn't bank on it.*

bank aˌccount *noun* [C] an arrangement with a bank to keep your money there and take it out when you need to

banker /ˈbæŋkəʳ/ *noun* [C] someone who has an important job in a bank

ˌbank ˈholiday *noun* [C] *UK* an official holiday when all banks and most shops and offices are closed *Spring bank holiday*

banking /ˈbæŋkɪŋ/ *noun* [U] the business of operating a bank

banknote /ˈbæŋknəʊt/ *mainly UK* (*US* **bill**) *noun* [C] a piece of paper money

bankrupt¹ /ˈbæŋkrʌpt/ *adjective* unable to continue in business because you cannot pay your debts *He went bankrupt after only a year in business.* ○ *The recession has led to many small businesses going bankrupt.*

bankrupt² /'bæŋkrʌpt/ *verb* [T] to make someone bankrupt

bankruptcy /'bæŋkrəptsi/ *noun* [C, U] when a person or organization becomes bankrupt *Factories that continue to make losses could soon face bankruptcy.*

'bank ˌstatement *noun* [C] a piece of paper that shows how much money you have put into your bank account and how much you have taken out

banner /'bænər/ *noun* [C] a long piece of cloth, often stretched between poles, with words or a sign written on it

'banner ˌad *noun* [C] an advertisement that appears across the top of a page on the Internet

banquet /'bæŋkwɪt/ *noun* [C] a large formal dinner for a lot of people

banter /'bæntər/ *noun* [U] conversation which is funny and not serious

baptism /'bæptɪzᵊm/ *noun* [C, U] a Christian ceremony in which water is put on someone to show that they are a member of the Church

Baptist /'bæptɪst/ *adjective* belonging or relating to a Christian group which only believes in baptism for people who are old enough to understand what it means *the Baptist Church* • **Baptist** *noun* [C]

baptize (*also* UK **-ise**) /bæp'taɪz/ ⑩ /'bæptaɪz/ *verb* [T] to perform a baptism ceremony for someone

o▪bar¹ /bɑːr/ *noun* [C] **1** [DRINKING] a place where alcoholic drinks are sold and drunk, or the area behind the person serving the drinks *I met him in a bar in Soho.* **2** [BLOCK] a small block of something solid *a chocolate bar* ○ *gold bars* ⊃See colour picture **Pieces and Quantities** on page Centre 1. **3** [LONG PIECE] a long, thin piece of metal or wood *There were bars on the downstairs windows.* **4** [PREVENTING SUCCESS] UK something that prevents you doing something or having something *Lack of money should not be a bar to a good education.* **5** [MUSIC] one of the short, equal groups of notes that a piece of music is divided into *The band played the first few bars.* **6 the bar** lawyers (= people whose job is to know about the law and deal with legal situations) thought of as a group *Haughey was called to the bar* (= became a lawyer) *in 1949.* **7 behind bars** in prison

bar² /bɑːr/ *verb* [T] **barring**, *past* **barred 1** [PREVENT] to officially prevent someone doing something or going somewhere, or to prevent something happening [+ from + doing sth] *The court barred him from contacting his former wife.* **2** [KEEP OUT] to stop someone going into a place *A line of policemen barred the entrance to the camp.* **3** [CLOSE] to close and lock a door or gate

bar³ /bɑːr/ *preposition* **1** except *I've read all her books, bar one.* **2 bar none** used to emphasize that someone or something is the best *the best suspense writer going, bar none*

barbarian /bɑː'beəriən/ *noun* [C] someone who

behaves in a way which shows they are not well educated and do not care about the feelings of others

barbaric /bɑː'bærɪk/ *adjective* violent and cruel *a barbaric act of violence* • **barbarically** *adverb*

barbecue¹
/'bɑːbɪkjuː/ *noun* [C]
1 a party at which you cook food over a fire outdoors **2** a metal frame for cooking food over a fire outdoors

barbecue²
/'bɑːbɪkjuː/ *verb* [I, T] **barbecuing**, *past* **barbecued** to cook food on a barbecue *barbecued chicken wings*

barbed wire
/ˌbɑːbd'waɪər/ *noun* [U] strong wire with short, sharp points on it to keep people out of a place *a barbed wire fence*

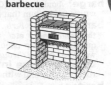
barbecue

barbed wire

barber /'bɑːbər/ *noun* [C] someone whose job is to cut men's hair *Dad goes to the barber's* (= the barber's shop) *once a month.*

'bar ˌcode *noun* [C] a row of black lines on something you buy, that a computer reads to find the price

bare¹ /beər/ *adjective* **1** [NO CLOTHES] not covered by clothes *a bare chest* ○ *She ran out into the road in her bare feet.* **2** [NOT COVERED] not covered by anything *bare floorboards* **3** [EMPTY] empty *a bare room* ○ *The cupboard was bare.* **4** [BASIC] including only the smallest amount that you need of something *The report just gave us the barest facts about the accident.* ○ *Tony's salary only covers the bare essentials for the family.* ⊃See also: with your bare hands (**hand¹**).

bare² /beər/ *verb* [T] to take away the thing that is covering something so that it can be seen *He bared his chest.* ○ *The dog bared its teeth.*

barefoot /beə'fʊt/ *adjective, adverb* not wearing any shoes or socks *They ran barefoot along the wet beach.*

barely /'beəli/ *adverb* only just *He was barely alive when they found him.*

barf /bɑːf/ *verb* [I] US *very informal* to vomit • **barf** *noun* [U]

⚐ WORD PARTNERS FOR *bargain*

get/pick up/snap up a bargain • a bargain **price** • bargain **hunting**

---

bargain¹ /'bɑːgɪn/ *noun* [C] **1** something that is sold for less than its usual price or its real value *At $8.95, it's a bargain.* **2** when you agree to something someone else wants so that they will agree to something you want *They were prepared to strike a bargain to avoid more fighting.* **3 into the bargain** mainly UK as well as everything else *Caffeine has no good effects on health and is mildly addictive into the bargain.*

bargain² /'bɑːgɪn/ *verb* [I] to try to make someone agree to something better for you *Do not hesitate to bargain over the price.*

bargain for/on sth to expect or be prepared for something *The stormy weather proved to be more than anybody bargained for.*

barge[1] /bɑːdʒ/ *noun* [C] a long, narrow boat with a flat bottom that is used to carry goods

barge[2] /bɑːdʒ/ *verb informal* **barge past/ through/ahead, etc** to walk somewhere quickly, pushing people or things out of the way *Fred barged through the crowd.*
barge in/barge into sth to walk into a room quickly and without being invited

baritone /'bærɪtəʊn/ *noun* [C] a man who sings in a voice that is quite low

bark[1] /bɑːk/ *noun* **1** [U] the hard substance that covers the surface of a tree **2** [C] the sound that a dog makes

bark[2] /bɑːk/ *verb* **1** [I] If a dog barks, it makes loud, short sounds. **2** [I, T] to say something loudly and quickly

barley /'bɑːli/ *noun* [U] a type of grain used for making food and alcoholic drinks

barmaid /'bɑːmeɪd/ *UK* (*US* **bartender**) *noun* [C] a woman who serves drinks in a bar

barman /'bɑːmən/ *UK* (*US* **bartender**) *noun* [C] *plural* **barmen** a man who serves drinks in a bar

bar mitzvah /,bɑː'mɪtsvə/ *noun* [usually singular] a religious ceremony for a Jewish boy when he reaches the age of 13

barmy /'bɑːmi/ *adjective UK informal* crazy or silly *What a barmy idea!*

barn /bɑːn/ *noun* [C] a large building on a farm where crops or animals can be kept

barometer /bə'rɒmɪtər/ *noun* [C] **1** a way of showing what people think or what the quality of something is *Car sales are viewed as a barometer of consumer confidence.* **2** a piece of equipment that shows when the weather will change

baron /'bærən/ *noun* [C] **1** a man of high social rank in the UK and other parts of Europe **2** a man who owns or controls a lot of a particular industry *a wealthy media baron*

baroness /'bærənes/ *noun* [C] a woman of the same rank as a baron or married to a baron, or a title given to a woman in the UK who has earned official respect *Baroness Thatcher*

baroque /bə'rɒk/ *adjective* relating to the style of art, building, and music that was popular in Europe in the 17th and early 18th century, and which had a lot of decoration

barracks /'bærəks/ *noun* [C] *plural* **barracks** a group of buildings where soldiers live

barrage /'bærɑːdʒ/ ⑥ /bə'rɑːdʒ/ *noun* **1** **a barrage of sth** a lot of questions, complaints, or criticisms *He faced a barrage of questions about his decision to leave the show.*
2 [C] a continuous attack with several big guns

barrel /'bærəl/ *noun* [C] **1** a large, round container for storing liquids such as oil or wine **2** the tube in a gun that the bullet shoots out of

barren /'bær³n/ *adjective* **1** Land that is barren does not produce crops. **2** *old-fashioned* A woman who is barren cannot have children.
● **barrenness** *noun* [U]

barricade[1] /,bærɪ'keɪd/ *noun* [C] something that is quickly put across a road or entrance to prevent people from going past *Police had erected a ten-foot barricade across the road.*

barricade[2] /,bærɪ'keɪd/ *verb* [T] to build a barricade somewhere [often reflexive] *They barricaded themselves in the building* (= built a barricade so that nobody could get to them).

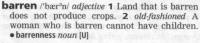

WORD PARTNERS FOR barrier

2 act as/be/create/serve as a barrier to sth ● break through/overcome/remove a barrier ● the biggest/the main/a major barrier ● [age/size, etc] is no barrier to sth ●

---

barrier /'bæriər/ *noun* [C] **1** a type of fence that prevents people from going into an area *Police erected barriers to hold back the crowd.* **2** something that prevents people from doing what they want to do *Shyness is a big barrier to making friends.* ⊃See also: **crash barrier**.

barring /'bɑːrɪŋ/ *preposition* if something does not happen *We should arrive at about five o'clock, barring accidents.*

barrister /'bærɪstər/ *noun* [C] in the UK, a lawyer (= someone whose job is to know about the law and deal with legal situations) who can work in the highest courts ⊃See Common learner error at **lawyer**.

barrow /'bærəʊ/ *UK* (*UK/US* **wheelbarrow**) a big, open container with a wheel at the front and handles that is used to move things, especially around in a garden

bartender /'bɑːˌtendər/ *US* (*UK* **barman/barmaid**) *noun* [C] someone who serves drinks in a bar

barter /'bɑːtər/ *verb* [I, T] to exchange goods or services for other goods or services, without using money

base[1] /beɪs/ *noun* [C] **1** [BOTTOM] the bottom part of something, or the part something rests on *I felt a sharp pain at the base of my thumb.* **2** [MAIN PART] the most important part of something, from which other things can develop *a solid economic base* **3** [PLACE] the main place where a person lives or works, or from where they do things *Keswick is an excellent base for exploring the Lake District.* **4** [ARMY] a place where people in the army or navy live and work *an American Air Force base* **5** [ORGANIZATION] the place where the main work of an organization is done *The company's European base is in Frankfurt.* **6** [SUBSTANCE] the main substance in a mixture *paints with an oil base* **7** [BASEBALL] one of the four places in baseball that a player must run to in order to win a point **8** **be off base** *US informal* to be wrong *In 1893, many of the forecasts about 1993 were way off base.* **9** **touch/cover all the bases** *mainly US* to deal with every part of a situation or activity

base[2] /beɪs/ *verb* **be based at/in, etc** If you are based at/in, etc a particular place, that is the main place where you live or work. *The company is based in Geneva.*

base sth on/upon sth If you base something on facts or ideas, you use those facts or ideas to develop it. *Her latest TV serial is based on a true story.*

o-**baseball** /ˈbeɪsbɔːl/ *noun* **1** [U] a game in which two teams try to win points by hitting a ball and running around four fixed points **2** [C] the ball used in this game ⊃See colour picture **Sports 2** on page Centre 15.

'**baseball ˌcap** *noun* [C] a type of hat with a long flat piece at the front to protect the eyes from the sun ⊃See colour picture **Clothes** on page Centre 9.

'**base ˌcamp** *noun* [C] the place from which people go to climb mountains

basement /ˈbeɪsmənt/ *noun* [C] a room or set of rooms that is below ground level in a building

bases /ˈbeɪsiːz/ *plural of* basis

bash¹ /bæʃ/ *verb* [T] *informal* **1** to hit someone or something hard *I bashed my arm on the car door as I got out.* **2 immigrant-bashing/lawyer-bashing/union-bashing, etc** when particular groups are criticized strongly and unfairly

bash² /bæʃ/ *noun* [C] *informal* **1** a party **2** a hard hit on something *a bash on the nose* **3 have a bash (at sth)** *UK informal* to try to do something *I've never been water-skiing but I'd love to have a bash at it.*

bashful /ˈbæʃfəl/ *adjective* shy and easily embarrassed • **bashfully** *adverb*

o-**basic** /ˈbeɪsɪk/ *adjective* **1** MAIN [always before noun] being the main or most important part of something *basic ideas/principles* **2** NECESSARY including or providing only the things that are most necessary *basic training/services/skills* **3** SIMPLE very simple, with nothing very special added *My software is pretty basic.*

o-**basically** /ˈbeɪsɪkᵊli/ *adverb* **1** in the most important ways *Frazier's films are basically documentaries.* ○ *The two PCs are basically the same.* **2** used to introduce a short explanation about something *Basically, what he's saying is that we need more time.*

the basics /ˈbeɪsɪks/ *noun* the most important facts, skills, or needs *the basics of computer technology*

basil /ˈbæzᵊl/ ⓤ /ˈbeɪzᵊl/ *noun* [U] a herb with a sweet smell

basin /ˈbeɪsᵊn/ *noun* [C] **1** BOWL *mainly UK* a bowl for liquids or food *a basin of water* **2** BATHROOM *UK* (*UK/US* **sink**) the bowl that is fixed to the wall in a bathroom, where you can wash your hands and face **3** LAND a low area of land from which water flows into a river

o-**basis** /ˈbeɪsɪs/ *noun* [C] *plural* **bases** /ˈbeɪsiːz/ **1 on a daily/monthly/regular, etc basis** how often something happens or is done *Meetings are held on a weekly basis.* **2 on a commercial/full-time/percentage, etc basis** the way something happens or is organized *Melissa's working on a part-time basis.* **3** the reason for something *Marks are awarded* **on the basis of** *progress and performance.* ○ *There is no legal basis for*

his claim. **4** a situation, fact, or idea from which something can develop *Dani's essay can serve as a basis for our discussion.*

bask /bɑːsk/ *verb* [I] to sit or lie in a place that is warm *Seals basked on the rocks.*

bask in sth to enjoy the way other people admire you *They basked in the glory victory had brought them.*

o-**basket** /ˈbɑːskɪt/ *noun* [C] **1** a container with a handle made of thin pieces of wood, wire, plastic, etc *a shopping basket* **2** when a player throws the ball through the net in basketball ⊃See also: wastepaper basket.

o-**basketball** /ˈbɑːskɪtbɔːl/ *noun* **1** [U] a game in which two teams try to win points by throwing a ball through a high net **2** [C] the large ball used in the game of basketball ⊃See colour picture **Sports 2** on page Centre 15.

bass /beɪs/ *noun* **1** VOICE [C] a man who sings with a very low voice **2** MUSIC [U] the lower half of the set of musical notes **3** INSTRUMENT [C, U] (*also* **double bass**) a large, wooden musical instrument with four strings that you play while standing up or sitting on a high chair **4** GUITAR [C, U] (*also* **ˌbass guiˈtar**) an electric guitar that makes a low sound

bassoon /bəˈsuːn/ *noun* [C] a long, wooden musical instrument that you blow through to make a low sound

bastard /ˈbɑːstəd/ *noun* [C] **1** an offensive word for a man you do not like **2** *old-fashioned* an offensive word for a child whose parents are not married

bastion /ˈbæstiən/ *noun* [C] a place, organization, etc where particular ideas or ways of doing things are protected *the last bastion of male chauvinism*

bat¹ /bæt/ *noun* [C] **1** a piece of wood used to hit the ball in some sports **2** a small animal like a mouse with wings that flies at night

bat² /bæt/ *verb* [I] batting, *past* batted to try to hit a ball with a bat *Rimmer batted well for Oxford.* ⊃See also: not bat an eyelid.

batch /bætʃ/ *noun* [C] a group of things or people that are dealt with at the same time or are similar in type *the university's first batch of students* ○ *Fry the aubergines in batches.*

bated /ˈbeɪtɪd/ *adjective* ⊃See with bated breath.

o-**bath**¹ /bɑːθ/ *noun* [C] **bath**

1 *UK* (*US* **bathtub**) the container that you sit or lie in to wash your body ⊃See colour picture **The Bathroom** on page Centre 3. **2** when you wash your body in a bath, or the water in the bath [usually singular] *I'll just have a quick bath.* ○ *UK She* **ran** *herself* **a bath** (= filled a bath with water).

bath² /bɑːθ/ *verb* [I, T] *UK* to wash yourself or someone else in a bath *Emma usually baths the kids about seven o'clock.*

bathe /beɪð/ *verb* **1** WASH YOURSELF [I, T] to wash

yourself or someone else in a bath *As a rule, I bathe every day.* **2** [PART OF BODY] [T] to wash part of someone's body, often because it is hurt *Bathe your eye with cool salty water.* **3** [SWIM] [I] *old-fashioned* to swim **4 be bathed in light** to look attractive in a beautiful light *The mountain was bathed in red-gold light from the setting sun.*

'**bathing ,suit** *noun* [C] a piece of clothing that you wear to swim in

bathrobe /'bɑːrəʊb/ *noun* [C] a soft coat that you wear before or after a bath

☞**bathroom** /'bɑːθruːm/ *noun* [C] **1** a room with a bath, sink (= bowl for washing), and often a toilet *an ensuite bathroom* (= a bathroom joined to a bedroom) ⊃See colour picture **The Bathroom** on page Centre 3. **2 go to the bathroom** *US* to use the toilet ⊃See Common learner error at **toilet**.

bathtub /'bɑːθtʌb/ *US* (*UK* **bath**) *noun* [C] the container that you sit or lie in to wash your body ⊃See colour picture **The Bathroom** on page Centre 3.

bat mitzvah /,bæt'mitsvə/ *noun* [usually singular] a religious ceremony for a Jewish girl when she reaches the age of 12 or 13

baton /'bætⁿn/ ⑩ /bə'tɑːn/ *noun* [C] **1** [STICK] a thin stick used to control the rhythm of a group of musicians **2** [POLICE] a thick stick that a police officer uses as a weapon **3** [RACE] a stick that a runner passes to the next person in a race

batsman /'bætsmən/ *noun* [C] *plural* **batsmen** *UK* the person who is trying to hit the ball in cricket *a former England batsman* ⊃See colour picture **Sports 2** on page Centre 15.

battalion /bə'tæliən/ *noun* [C] a large group of soldiers made from several smaller groups

batter¹ /'bætər/ *noun* **1** [U] a mixture of flour, milk, and often eggs used to make cakes and pancakes (= thin fried cakes), and to cover fish, etc before it is fried *Coat the fish pieces with beaten egg so that the batter sticks to them.* **2** [C] the person who is trying to hit the ball in baseball ⊃See colour picture **Sports 2** on page Centre 15.

batter² /'bætər/ *verb* [I, T] to hit someone or something repeatedly very hard *If you don't open up we'll batter the door down.* ○ *Waves battered against the rocks.*

battered /'bætəd/ *adjective* old and not in very good condition *a battered copy of her favourite novel*

battering /'bætərɪŋ/ *noun* [C] when someone or something is hit repeatedly, criticized strongly, or damaged badly [usually singular] *The prime minister has taken quite a battering this week.*

☞**battery** /'bætəri/ *noun* **1** [C] **battery** an object that provides electricity for things such as radios, toys, or cars *My car has got a flat battery* (= one that has no electricity left). **2** [U] *formal* the crime of hitting someone *assault and battery*

battle¹ /'bætl/ *noun* **1** [WAR] [C, U] a fight between two armies in a war *the Battle of Waterloo* ○ *Her grandfather was killed in battle* (= while fighting). **2** [POWER] [C] when two people or groups compete against each other or have an argument about something *a battle for control in the boardroom* ○ *The aid agency continues the battle against ignorance and superstition.* **3** [PROBLEMS/ILLNESS] [C] a fight against something that is hurting or destroying you *a long battle against cancer* **4 fight a losing battle** to try hard to do something when there is no chance that you will succeed *I try to control what my children watch on TV, but I think I'm fighting a losing battle.*

battle² /'bætl/ *verb* [I] to try very hard to do something that is difficult *Both teams are battling for a place in the Premier League.* ○ *Throughout the campaign Johnson was battling against severe health problems.*

baulk /bɔːk, bɔːlk/ *UK* (*UK/US* **balk**) *verb* [I] to not want to do something that is unpleasant or difficult *Most people would baulk at paying these kind of prices for clothes.*

bawl /bɔːl/ *verb* [I, T] *informal* to shout or cry loudly *The two girls were now bawling in unison.*

bay /beɪ/ *noun* **1** [C] an area of coast where the land curves in *a sandy bay* **2** [C] a part of a building or place that is used for a particular purpose *a parking bay* **3 keep/hold sth at bay** to prevent something unpleasant from coming near you or from happening *Gunmen kept police at bay for almost four hours.*

bayonet /'beɪənət/ *noun* [C] a knife that is fastened onto the end of a long gun

bazaar /bə'zɑːr/ *noun* [C] **1** a market in Eastern countries **2** a sale where goods are sold to raise money for a school, church, etc

B&B /,biːən'biː/ *noun* [C] *abbreviation for* bed and breakfast

BBC /,biːbiː'siː/ *noun abbreviation for* British Broadcasting Corporation: one of the main television and radio companies in the United Kingdom *a cookery programme on BBC2*

BC /biː'siː/ *abbreviation for* Before Christ: used to show that a particular year came before the birth of Christ *331 BC*

☞**be¹** *strong form* /biː/ *weak forms* /bi, bɪ/ *verb pres. participle* **being**, *past tense* **was**, *past participle* **been** **1** used to describe or give information about someone or something *I'm sixteen.* ○ *He's Andy.* ○ *Her mother is a teacher.* ○ *He's German.* ○ *They were very upset.* ○ *He was very ill last year.* ○ *I'm sorry I'm late.* ○ *They've been unlucky.* ○ *Be quiet!* **2 there is/there are/there was, etc** used to show that someone or something exists *There were about fifty people at the party.* ○ *Is there a bank near here?* **3** used to show the position of someone or something *It's been in the cupboard for months.* ○ *She's in the kitchen.* **4 it is/it was, etc** used to give a fact or your opinion about something *It's not surprising that she left him.* ○ *It's a good idea to keep a spare key somewhere safe.* ⊃See study page Be, do, go, have.

be² *strong form* /biː/ *weak forms* /bi, bɪ/ *auxiliary verb* **1** used with the present participle of other verbs to describe actions that are or were still continuing *Where are you going?* ○ *How long have you been sitting there?* ○ *He was standing by the window.* ○ *He's working at the moment.* **2** used with the present participle of other verbs, and sometimes after a modal verb, to describe actions that will happen in the future *I'm going to France next week.* ○ *I'll be coming back on Tuesday.* **3** used with the past participle of other verbs to form the passive *He was injured in a car crash.* ○ *The results will be announced next week.* **4** used in conditional sentences to say what might happen *If he were to offer me the job, I'd take it.* **5** used to say that someone must or should do something *You are not to see him again.* **6** *formal* used to show that something has been organized *They are to stay with us when they arrive.*

┌──────────────────────────────────┐
│ WORD PARTNERS FOR **beach** │
└──────────────────────────────────┘

on the beach ● a **sandy** beach ● a beach **house**

☞**beach** /biːtʃ/ *noun* [C] an area of sand or rocks next to the sea

beacon /ˈbiːkªn/ *noun* [C] a light on a hill or in a tower that warns people of something or is a signal or guide

bead /biːd/ *noun* [C] **1** a small, round ball of glass, plastic, or wood that is used for making jewellery *a necklace of coloured glass beads* **2** a small drop of liquid on a surface *beads of sweat*

beak /biːk/ *noun* [C] the hard part of a bird's mouth

beaker /ˈbiːkəʳ/ *noun* [C] *UK* a tall cup without a handle, usually made of plastic

beam¹ /biːm/ *noun* [C] **1** [LIGHT] a line of light shining from something *a laser beam* ⊃See picture at **light**. **2** [WOOD] a long, thick piece of wood, metal, or concrete that is used to support weight in a building or other structure **3** [SMILE] *UK* a big smile

beam² /biːm/ *verb* **1** [SMILE] [I] to smile very happily *The baby beamed at me.* **2** [SEND] [T] to send a television or radio signal **[often passive]** *The match was beamed live by satellite around the world.* **3** [SHINE] [I] If the sun or the moon beams, it shines brightly.

beamer /ˈbiːməʳ/ *noun* [C] a data projector: a machine that allows you to show words or images on a screen or wall

bean /biːn/ *noun* [C] **1** [SEED] a seed of some climbing plants, that is used as food *soya beans* **2** [VEGETABLE] a seed case of some climbing plants that is eaten as a vegetable *green beans* **3** [COFFEE/CHOCOLATE] a plant seed used to make coffee and chocolate *coffee beans* ⊃See also:

baked beans, runner bean.

bean curd /ˈbiːnkɜːd/ *noun* [U] tofu (= a soft, pale food made from the soya bean plant)

bear¹ /beəʳ/ *verb* [T] *past tense* **bore**, *past participle* **borne 1** [ACCEPT] to accept someone or something unpleasant *She couldn't bear the thought of him suffering.* ○ *I like her, but I can't bear her friends.* ○ **[+ to do sth]** *How can you bear to watch?* ○ *The pain was too much to bear.* **2 bear a resemblance/relation, etc to sb/sth** to be similar to someone or something *He bears a striking resemblance to his father.* **3** [CARRY] *formal* to carry something *He came in, bearing a tray of drinks.* **4** [WEIGHT] to support the weight of something *I don't think that chair will bear his weight.* **5 bear the responsibility/ cost, etc** to accept that you are responsible for something, you should pay for something, etc **6** [FEELING] to continue to have a bad feeling towards someone *They were rude to her in the past, but she's not the kind of woman who bears grudges* (= continues to be angry). **7** [HAVE CHILD] *formal* to give birth to a child *She has been told that she will never bear children.* **8** [NAME] to have or show a particular name, picture, or symbol *The shop bore his family name.* **9 bear left/right** to turn left or right *Bear right at the next set of traffic lights.* ⊃See also: bear fruit, grin and bear it.

bear sb/sth out to prove that someone is right or that something is true *The facts do not bear out his claims.*

bear with sb to be patient and wait while someone does something *If you'll bear with me a moment, I'll just find your details.*

bear² /beəʳ/ *noun* [C] a large, strong, wild animal with thick fur ⊃See also: polar bear, teddy bear.

bear

bearable /ˈbeərəbl/ *adjective* If an unpleasant situation is bearable, you can accept or deal with it. *Having her there made life at home more bearable for me.* ⊃Opposite **unbearable**.

beard /bɪəd/ *noun* [C] the hair that grows on a man's chin (= the bottom of his face) ● **bearded** *adjective* with a beard

bearer /ˈbeərəʳ/ *noun* [C] a person who brings or carries something *I am sorry to be the bearer of bad news.*

bearing /ˈbeərɪŋ/ *noun* **have a bearing on sth** to have an influence on something or a relationship to something *What you decide now could have a considerable bearing on your future.*

bearings /ˈbeərɪŋz/ *noun* **1 get/find your bearings a** to find out where you are *She looked at the sun to find her bearings.* **b** to become confident in a new situation *When you start a new job, it can take some time to get your bearings.* **2 lose your bearings** to become confused about where you are

beast /biːst/ *noun* [C] **1** *formal* an animal, especially a large or wild one *The room wasn't fit for man or beast.* **2** *old-fashioned* an annoying or cruel person *He was a beast to her during their marriage.*

beastly /ˈbiːstli/ *adjective old-fashioned* unkind or unpleasant

⊶**beat¹** /biːt/ *verb past tense* **beat**, *past participle* **beaten**, *also US* **beat 1** DEFEAT [T] to defeat someone in a competition *Our team beat Germany 3-1.* ➲See Common learner error at **win**. **2** HIT [I, T] to hit a person or animal hard many times *She beat the dog with a stick.* ○ *She was beaten to death.* **3** SOUND [I, T] to hit against something hard, making a continuous or regular sound *soldiers beating drums* ○ *We could hear the pigeons beating their wings.* ○ *Rain beat against the windows.* **4** GET RID OF [T] to get rid of something bad *measures to beat crime* ○ *I'm determined to beat this illness.* **5** HEART [I] When your heart beats, it makes regular movements and sounds. *By the time the doctor arrived, his heart had stopped beating.* **6** BE BETTER [T] to be better than something **[+ doing sth]** *Being at the youth club beats sitting at home.* **7 you can't beat sth** used to emphasize that something is best *You can't beat Pedro's for a great pizza.* **8 take a lot of/some, etc beating** to be so good or enjoyable that it is hard to find anything better *This ice cream takes some beating.* **9** FOOD [T] to mix food using hard, quick movements *Beat the egg whites until they are stiff.* **10 It beats me** *informal* something that you say when you do not understand a situation or someone's behaviour *It beats me why she goes out with him.* ➲See also: beat about the **bush**, beat/knock the (living) **daylights** out of sb, off the beaten **track¹**.

beat down If the sun beats down, it is very hot and bright.

beat sb down *UK* to persuade someone to charge you less for something

beat sb/sth off to manage to defeat someone who is attacking you

beat sb to sth to do something before someone else does it *I was going to ask her to the party, but you beat me to it.*

beat sb up to attack someone by hitting or kicking them many times *He beat up one of the other prisoners.*

beat² /biːt/ *noun* [C] **1** REGULAR SOUND a regular sound that is made by your heart or by something hitting a surface *a heart beat* ○ *the beat of a drum* **2** RHYTHM the main rhythm of a piece of music *loud music with a repetitive beat* **3** AREA the area of a town or city that a police officer walks around regularly *Having more police officers **on the beat*** (= walking around their beat) *should help to reduce crime.*

beating /ˈbiːtɪŋ/ *noun* **1** [C] when someone hits another person hard many times **2 take a beating** to be defeated, criticized, or damaged *Our team took a severe beating in the tournament.*

beautician /bjuːˈtɪʃən/ *noun* [C] someone whose job is to improve people's appearance by treatments to their hair, skin, etc

OTHER WAYS OF SAYING ***beautiful***

If a person (man or woman), is beautiful, we can say that they are **attractive** or **good-looking**. The adjective **handsome** is also sometimes used for men, and **pretty** for women: *Her husband is really **good-looking**.* ● *Your daughter is very **pretty**.*

If someone, especially a woman, is extremely beautiful, you can say that they are **gorgeous** or **stunning**: *You look **gorgeous** in that dress!* ● *I think she's **stunning**.*

The adjectives **breathtaking**, **lovely** and **gorgeous** are often used to describe scenery that is very beautiful. *The views from the window were **breathtaking**.* ● *We drove through some **gorgeous** countryside.*

The adjective **exquisite** is sometimes used to describe objects which are very beautiful and often delicate: *They do the most **exquisite** hand-made decorations.*

⊶**beautiful** /ˈbjuːtɪfəl/ *adjective* **1** very attractive *a beautiful woman* ○ *beautiful scenery* **2** very pleasant *beautiful music* ○ *It's a beautiful day* (= the sun is shining). ●**beautifully** *adverb a beautifully illustrated book*

WORD PARTNERS FOR ***beauty***

great/sheer/stunning beauty ● **natural** beauty ● beauty **products**

⊶**beauty** /ˈbjuːti/ *noun* **1** QUALITY [U] the quality of being beautiful *The whole area is famous for its **natural beauty**.* **2 the beauty of sth** the quality that makes something especially good or attractive *The beauty of the plan is that it won't cost anything.* **3 a beauty product/treatment** a product or treatment to make you more beautiful **4** EXCELLENT THING [C] *informal* something that is an excellent example of its type *That last goal was a beauty.* **5** WOMAN [C] *old-fashioned* a beautiful woman

ˈbeauty ˌsalon (*also US* **ˈbeauty ˌparlor**) *noun* [C] a place where you can have beauty treatments

ˈbeauty ˌspot *noun* [C] **1** *UK* a place in the countryside that is very beautiful **2** a small dark mark on someone's face

beaver /ˈbiːvər/ *noun* [C] an animal with brown fur, a long, flat tail, and sharp teeth, which builds dams (= walls made of pieces of wood) across rivers

became /bɪˈkeɪm/ *past tense of* become

⊶**because** /bɪˈkɒz, bɪˌkəz/ *conjunction* used to give a reason for something *I phoned because I needed to talk to you.*

⊶**because of** /bɪˈkɒzəv, bɪˌkəzəv/ *preposition* as a result of someone or something *We got into all this trouble because of you.*

beck /bek/ *noun* **be at sb's beck and call** to be always ready and willing to do what someone wants

beckon /ˈbekən/ *verb* **1** WAVE [I, T] to move your hand, head, etc to show someone that you would like them to come nearer *She **beckoned** to the waiter.* **2** BE LIKELY [I] to seem very likely to happen *A career as a lead guitarist* beckoned. **3** BE ATTRACTIVE [I] If a place beckons, it is very attractive to you, and you want to go there. *The bright lights of London beckoned.*

o-**become** /bɪˈkʌm/ *verb past tense* **became** *past participle* **become 1** **become available/rich/a writer, etc** to begin to be something *They became great friends.* ○ *She wants to become a teacher when she leaves school.* ○ *This style of skirt is becoming fashionable.* **2 what/whatever became of sb/sth** something you say when you want to know what has happened to someone *Whatever became of your friend Harry?*

WORD PARTNERS FOR *bed*

go to bed • be in /lie in/be tucked up in bed • get into/get out of bed • make the bed • be on the bed • share a bed • a double/single bed

---

o-**bed¹** /bed/ *noun* **1** FURNITURE [C, U] a piece of furniture that you sleep on *a single/double bed* ○ *What time did you go to bed last night?* ○ *She was lying in bed when I arrived.* ○ *He had only just got out of bed.* ○ *Have you made the bed* (= tidied the bed after you have slept in it)*?* **2** GROUND [C] a piece of ground that is used for growing plants, especially flowers *a flower bed* **3** BOTTOM [C] the ground at the bottom of the sea, a river, etc *the sea bed* ⊃See also: bunk beds.

ˌbed and ˈbreakfast (*also* B & B) *noun* [C] a small hotel or private house where you pay for a room to sleep in for the night and a meal in the morning

bedclothes /ˈbedkləʊðz/ *noun* [plural] the sheets and other pieces of cloth that cover you and keep you warm in bed

bedding /ˈbedɪŋ/ *noun* [U] **1** the sheets and other pieces of cloth that cover you and keep you warm in bed **2** material such as hay (= dried grass) that animals sleep on

bedraggled /bɪˈdrægld/ *adjective* untidy, and often wet and dirty

bedrock /ˈbedrɒk/ *noun* [U] *formal* a situation, idea, or principle that provides a strong base for something *Family life is **the bedrock** of a stable society.*

o-**bedroom** /ˈbedruːm/ *noun* [C] a room used for sleeping in

bedside /ˈbedsaɪd/ *noun* [no plural] **1** the area at the side of a bed *He was at her bedside in the hospital.* ○ *a bedside table/lamp* **2** **bedside manner** a doctor's ability to make the people they are treating feel comfortable *My surgeon has a wonderful bedside manner.*

bedsit /ˈbedsɪt/ *noun* [C] *UK* a rented room where you live, sleep, and cook your meals

bedspread /ˈbedspred/ *noun* [C] a cloth cover that is put over a bed

bedtime /ˈbedtaɪm/ *noun* [C, U] the time that you usually go to bed

bee /biː/ *noun* [C] a flying insect that has a yellow and black body and makes honey (= sweet, sticky food) *the queen bee*

beech /biːtʃ/ *noun* [C, U] a large tree with a smooth grey trunk (= main, vertical part) that produces small nuts

beef¹ /biːf/ *noun* [U] the meat of a cow *roast beef* ⊃See also: **ground beef**.

beef² /biːf/ *verb*
beef sth up to make something stronger or more important *The company wants to beef up its sales force by employing new graduates.*

beefburger /ˈbiːfˌbɜːgəʳ/ *UK* (*UK/US* **hamburger**) *noun* [C] very small pieces of meat that are pressed together into a round flat shape, cooked, and eaten between bread

beehive /ˈbiːhaɪv/ (*also* **hive**) *noun* [C] a special container where people keep bees

been /biːn, bɪn/ *verb* **have been to** to have gone to a place and come back *Have you ever been to Thailand?* ⊃Inflection of **be**.

beep /biːp/ *verb* **1** [I] If a machine beeps, it makes a short, high noise. **2** [I, T] If a car horn (= part you press to make a warning sound) beeps or if you beep it, it makes a loud noise. *Beep the horn to let me know that you're here.*
• **beep** *noun* [C]

beeper /ˈbiːpəʳ/ (*also UK* **bleeper**) *noun* [C] a small piece of electronic equipment that you carry which makes a short high sound when someone wants to talk to you

o-**beer** /bɪəʳ/ *noun* [C, U] an alcoholic drink made from grain, or a glass or container of this drink *a pint of beer*

beet /biːt/ *US* (*UK* **beetroot**) *noun* [C, U] a round, dark red vegetable, that is usually cooked and eaten cold

beetle /ˈbiːtl/ *noun* [C] an insect with a hard, usually black, shiny body

beetroot /ˈbiːtruːt/ *UK* (*US* **beet**) *noun* [C, U] a round, dark red vegetable, that is usually cooked and eaten cold

befall /bɪˈfɔːl/ *verb* [T] *past tense* **befell**, *past participle* **befallen** *formal* If something bad befalls you, it happens to you. *A dreadful misfortune has befallen the family.*

befit /bɪˈfɪt/ *verb* [T] **befitting**, *past* **befitted** *formal* to be suitable or right for someone or something *He was given a huge welcome, **as befits** such a hero.*

o-**before¹** /bɪˈfɔːʳ/ *preposition* **1** EARLIER earlier than something or someone *a week before Christmas* ○ *She arrived before me.* ○ [+ doing sth] *Think hard before accepting the offer.* **2** IN FRONT OF in a position in front of someone or something *I've never performed this before an audience.* ○ *He stood before her, shaking.* **3** PLACE at a place that you arrive at first when travelling towards another place *The hospital is just before the bridge.* **4** IN ORDER in front of someone or something in an order or a list *P comes before Q in the alphabet.* **5** IMPORTANCE treated as more important than someone or something *They always **put** the children's needs **before** their own.* **6** EXAMINATION being formally examined or considered by a group *He appeared before the court dressed in jeans.*

o-**before²** /bɪˈfɔːʳ/ *conjunction* **1** EARLIER earlier than the time when something happens *He was a teacher before he became famous.* ○ *Before I could warn him, he had fallen.* **2** TO AVOID STH in order to avoid something bad happening *Put that stick down before you hurt someone.* **3** UNTIL until *It took a few moments before I realized that he was lying.*

before³ /bɪˈfɔːʳ/ *adverb* at an earlier time, or on a previous occasion *I've never seen her before.* ○ *We had spoken on the phone a few days before.*

beforehand /bɪˈfɔːhænd/ *adverb* before a particular time or event *Did you know beforehand what they had planned to do?*

befriend /bɪˈfrend/ *verb* [T] *formal* to be friendly to someone, especially someone who needs support or help

beg /beg/ *verb* **begging**, *past* **begged 1** [I] to ask someone for food or money, because you do not have any *Young children were begging on the streets.* **2** [I, T] to make a very strong and urgent request *She begged him for help.* ○ [+ to do sth] *I begged her not to go.* ⊃See also: I beg your **pardon²**.

began /bɪˈgæn/ *past tense of* begin

beggar /ˈbegəʳ/ *noun* [C] a poor person who lives by asking other people for money and food

o⌐**begin** /bɪˈgɪn/ *verb* **beginning**, *past tense* **began**, *past participle* **begun 1** START TO DO [I, T] to start to do something [+ to do sth] *The children began to cry.* ○ [+ doing sth] *Have they begun building the wall yet?* ○ *She began her career as a journalist on a local newspaper.* **2** START TO HAPPEN [I] to start to happen *What time does the film begin?* **3 begin with sth** to have something at the start *Local phone numbers begin with 1223.* **4 to begin with a** AT THE START at the start of a situation *To begin with, the two girls got on well.* **b** GIVE REASON used to give the first important reason for something *To begin with, we can't leave the children alone.*

beginner /bɪˈgɪnəʳ/ *noun* [C] someone who is starting to do or learn something for the first time *I'm a complete beginner at yoga.*

o⌐**beginning** /bɪˈgɪnɪŋ/ *noun* [C] the first part of something or the start of something [usually singular] *We met at the beginning of 1998.* ○ *Things went well in the beginning.*

begrudge /bɪˈgrʌdʒ/ *verb* [T] **1** to feel upset because someone has something that you would like [+ two objects] *I don't begrudge him his success.* **2** to feel upset because you have to spend money on something or spend time doing something *They begrudge every penny that they have to spend on him.*

beguile /bɪˈgaɪl/ *verb* [T] *formal* to attract someone very much, sometimes in order to deceive them [often passive] *I can see how people are beguiled by his charm.* ○ *a beguiling smile*

begun /bɪˈgʌn/ *past participle of* begin

behalf /bɪˈhɑːf/ *noun* **on sb's behalf** If you do something on someone's behalf, you do it for them or instead of them. *We are campaigning on behalf of thousands of refugees.* ○ *Will you accept the prize on my behalf?*

o⌐**behave** /bɪˈheɪv/ *verb* [I] **1** to do or say things in a particular way *to behave badly/stupidly* ○ *They are behaving like children.* **2** (*also* **behave yourself**) to be polite and not make a

situation difficult *Try to behave.* ○ *The children can only come if they promise to behave themselves.* ⊃Opposite **misbehave**.

-behaved /bɪˈheɪvd/ *suffix* used after a word describing how someone behaves *a badly-behaved child* ⊃See also: **well-behaved**.

WORD PARTNERS FOR ***behaviour***

anti-social/bad/disruptive/good/normal behaviour

o⌐**behaviour** UK (US **behavior**) /bɪˈheɪvjəʳ/ *noun* [U] the way that you behave *good/bad behaviour* ○ *Did you notice anything odd about his behaviour?*

behavioural UK (US **behavioral**) /bɪˈheɪvjərəl/ *adjective* relating to behaviour *behavioural changes/problems*

behead /bɪˈhed/ *verb* [T] to cut someone's head off

beheld /bɪˈheld/ *past of* behold

o⌐**behind¹** /bɪˈhaɪnd/ *preposition* **1** BACK at or to the back of someone or something *Close the door behind you.* ○ *The pub is behind the train station.* **2** LESS SUCCESSFUL slower or less successful than someone or something *Our team is 3 points behind the winners.* ○ *The building work is already behind schedule* (= late). **3** CAUSING causing something, or responsible for something *What was the reason behind her decision to leave?* **4** SUPPORTING giving your help or support to someone *The group is 100 percent behind her.* **5** NOT AFFECTING If a bad experience or your own bad behaviour is behind you, it does not exist or affect your life now. *He's put his criminal past behind him.*

o⌐**behind²** /bɪˈhaɪnd/ *adverb* **1** BACK at or to the back of someone or something *Somebody grabbed me from behind.* **2** SLOWER slower or later than someone else, or than you should be *She's behind with the rent* (= is late to pay it). **3** PLACE in the place where someone or something was before *You go on ahead. I'll stay behind and tidy up.* ○ *When we got to the restaurant, I realized that I had left my purse behind.*

behind³ /bɪˈhaɪnd/ *noun* [C] *informal* the part of your body that you sit on

behold /bɪˈhəʊld/ *verb* [T] *past* beheld *literary* to see something

beige /beɪʒ/ *noun* [U] a pale brown colour ● **beige** *adjective* ⊃See colour picture **Colours** on page Centre 12.

being¹ /ˈbiːɪŋ/ *noun* **1** [C] a living person or imaginary creature *human beings* **2 come into being** to start to exist *The new law comes into being next month.* ⊃See also: **well-being**.

being² /ˈbiːɪŋ/ *present participle of* be

belated /bɪˈleɪtɪd/ *adjective* coming late, or later than expected *a belated attempt to win votes* ● **belatedly** *adverb* *Supermarkets have belatedly realized the purchasing power of mothers.*

belch¹ /beltʃ/ *verb* **1** [I] to make a sudden noise as air from your stomach comes out through your mouth **2** [T] (*also* **belch out**) to produce a lot of smoke, fire, gas, etc *tall chimneys belching smoke*

belch² /beltʃ/ noun [C] the noise you make when you belch *The baby let out a loud, satisfied belch.*

beleaguered /bɪˈliːɡəd/ adjective formal having a lot of problems *the beleaguered farming industry*

belfry /ˈbelfri/ noun [C] the tower of a church where the bells are hung

belie /bɪˈlaɪ/ verb [T] belying, past belied formal to give a wrong idea about something *His shy manner belied his very sharp mind.* ◦ *Her calm face belied the terror she was feeling.*

WORD PARTNERS FOR belief

a firm/mistaken/sincere/strong/widespread/widely-held belief • have/hold a belief • a belief in sth • in the belief that

---

o→**belief** /bɪˈliːf/ noun **1** [TRUE] [U, no plural] when you believe that something is true or real *It is a widely-held belief that smoking helps you lose weight.* ◦ *She married him in the belief that he would change.* ⊃Opposite **disbelief. 2** [IDEA] [C, U] an idea that you are certain is true *religious/political beliefs* **3** [EFFECTIVE] [U, no plural] the feeling that someone or something is effective or right *a belief in social justice* **4 beyond belief** too bad, good, difficult, etc to be real *The evil of this man is beyond belief.*

believable /bɪˈliːvəbl/ adjective If something is believable, you can believe that it could be true or real. *I didn't find any of the characters in the film believable* ⊃Opposite **unbelievable.**

o→**believe** /bɪˈliːv/ verb **1** [TRUE] [T] to think that something is true, or that what someone says is true [+ (that)] *They believe that their health has suffered because of the chemicals.* ◦ *Do you believe him?* ◦ *I can't believe that she wants to go out with me.* ⊃Opposite **disbelieve. 2** [THINK] [T] to think something, without being completely sure *'Is he coming out tonight?' 'I believe so.'* ◦ *The murderer is believed to be in his thirties.* **3** [RELIGION] [I] to have religious beliefs *She stopped believing after her son died.* **4 not believe your eyes/ears** to be very surprised when you see someone or something, or when you hear what someone says *I couldn't believe my ears when Dan said they were getting married.* **5 believe it or not** used to say that something is true although it seems surprising *He even remembered my birthday, believe it or not.*

believe in sth to be certain that something exists *I believe in life after death.*

believe in sth/doing sth to be confident that something is effective or right *He believes in saying what he thinks.*

believer /bɪˈliːvəʳ/ noun [C] **1** a person who has a religious belief **2 a firm/great/strong, etc believer in sth/doing sth** someone who has confidence in a particular idea or way of doing things *She's a firm believer in freedom of speech.*

belittle /bɪˈlɪtl/ verb [T] formal to say that someone or something is not very important or not very good *I certainly wouldn't want to belittle his achievements.*

bell

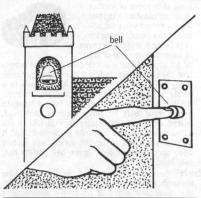

bell

o→**bell** /bel/ noun [C] **1** a hollow, metal object, shaped like a cup, that makes a ringing sound when you hit it *the sound of church bells ringing* **2** an electrical object that makes a ringing sound when you press a switch *Please ring the bell for attention* **3 give sb a bell** UK informal to telephone someone **4 ring a bell** If a word, especially a name, rings a bell, you think you have heard it before.

belligerent /bəˈlɪdʒ³rənt/ adjective wanting to fight or argue

bellow /ˈbeləʊ/ verb [I, T] to shout something in a loud voice • **bellow** noun [C]

belly /ˈbeli/ noun [C] informal your stomach (= organ where food is digested), or the front part of your body between your chest and your legs

'belly ˌbutton noun [C] informal the small, round, and usually hollow place on your stomach, where you were connected to your mother before birth

o→**belong** /bɪˈlɒŋ/ verb **1 belong in/on/there, etc** to be in the right place *That chair belongs in the dining room.* **2** [I] to feel happy and comfortable in a place or with a group of people *I never felt that I belonged there.*

o→**belong to sb** If something belongs to you, you own it. *This necklace belonged to my grandmother.*

belong to sth to be a member of a group or organization *We belong to the same youth club.*

belongings /bɪˈlɒŋɪŋz/ noun [plural] the things that you own *I took a few personal belongings with me.*

beloved /bɪˈlʌvɪd/ adjective literary very much loved *in memory of our beloved son*

o→**below** /bɪˈləʊ/ adverb, preposition **1** [POSITION] in a lower position than someone or something else *Send your answers to the address below* (= lower on the page or on a later page). **2** [LESS] less than an amount or level *The temperature there rarely drops below 22°C.* ◦ *His work is below average.* **3** [RANK] lower in rank *Monica is a grade below me.*

⊶**belt1** /belt/ *noun* [C] **1** [WAIST] a long, thin piece of leather, cloth, or plastic that you wear around your waist ➲See colour picture **Clothes** on page Centre 9. **2** [AREA] an area of a particular type of land, or an area where a particular group of people live *the* ***commuter belt*** ○ *a narrow belt of trees* **3** [MACHINE] part of a machine that moves in a circle to carry objects or to make a machine work *The car needs a new fan belt.* **4 have sth under your belt** to have already achieved, learnt, or done something important *At 18, she already has several victories under her belt.* **5 tighten your belt** to try to spend less money ➲See also: **conveyor belt, green belt, safety belt, seat belt.**

belt

belt2 /belt/ *verb informal* **1 belt along/down/through, etc** *UK* to move very fast *He came belting down the street.* **2** [T] to hit someone or something very hard

belt sth out to sing something very loudly

belt up *UK informal* used to tell someone to stop talking or making a noise

belying /bɪˈlaɪɪŋ/ *present participle of* belie

bemused /bɪˈmjuːzd/ *adjective* slightly confused *He seemed* ***bemused by*** *all the attention.*

bench /benʃ/ *noun* [C] **1** a long seat for two or more people, usually made of wood or metal *a park bench* **2 the bench a** in some sports, a place where players sit when they are not playing **b** a judge in court, or judges as a group *Please address your comments to the bench.*

benchmark /ˈbenʃmɑːk/ *noun* [C] a level of quality with which other things of the same type can be compared *Her performance set a new* ***benchmark for*** *ballet dancing.*

⊶**bend1** /bend/ *verb* [I, T] *past* **bent 1** to move your body or part of your body so that it is not straight *He was* ***bending over*** *to tie his shoelaces.* ○ *Bend your knees when lifting heavy objects.* **2** to become curved, or to make something become curved *The trees were bending in the wind.* ○ *The road bent sharply to the left.* ➲See also: bend over **backwards**, bend/stretch the rules (**rule1**).

WORD PARTNERS FOR ***bend***

a **sharp/tight** bend • a bend **in** sth

bend2 /bend/ *noun* [C] **1** a curved part of something *a* ***bend in*** *the road/river* **2 drive/send sb round the bend** *informal* to make someone very angry, especially by continuing to do something annoying ➲See also: **hairpin bend.**

beneath1 /bɪˈniːθ/ *adverb, preposition* **1** under something, or in a lower position than something *He hid the letter beneath a pile of papers.* ○ *She looked out of the window at the children playing beneath.* **2** If someone or something is beneath you, you think they are not good enough for you. *He thinks housework is beneath him.*

benefactor /ˈbenɪfæktəʳ/ *noun* [C] someone who gives money to help an organization or person

beneficial /ˌbenɪˈfɪʃəl/ *adjective* helpful or useful *Exercise is* ***beneficial to*** *almost everyone.*

beneficiary /ˌbenɪˈfɪʃəri/ *noun* [C] *formal* someone who receives money, help, etc from something or someone else *They were the* ***beneficiaries of*** *free education.*

WORD PARTNERS FOR ***benefit***

enjoy/have/offer/reap benefits • [the drawbacks/risks, etc] **outweigh** the benefits • **great/long-term/maximum/potential/tangible** benefit • **of** benefit **to** sb

benefit1 /ˈbenɪfɪt/ *noun* [C, U] **1** something that helps you or gives you an advantage *I've* ***had the benefit of*** *a happy childhood.* **2** money that the government gives to people who are ill, poor, not working, etc *unemployment benefit* **3 for sb's benefit** in order to help someone *We bought the piano for the children's benefit.* **4 give sb the benefit of the doubt** to choose to believe what someone tells you even though it may be wrong or a lie ➲See also: **child benefit, fringe benefit.**

benefit2 /ˈbenɪfɪt/ *verb* **benefiting**, *past* **benefited 1** [I] to be helped by something *The film* ***benefited from*** *the excellent acting by its stars.* **2** [T] to help someone *The charity supports activities that directly benefit children.*

benevolent /bɪˈnevələnt/ *adjective formal* kind, generous, and helpful • **benevolence** /bɪˈnevələns/ *noun* [U]

benign /bɪˈnaɪn/ *adjective* **1** not likely to kill you *a benign tumour* **2** kind, or not intending to harm anyone *a benign ruler*

bent1 /bent/ *adjective* **1** curved and not now straight or flat *The metal bars were bent and twisted.* **2 bent on sth/doing sth** determined to do something or get something *Both parties are bent on destroying each other's chances of winning.* **3** *UK informal* not honest *a bent policeman*

bent2 /bent/ *past of* bend

bequeath /bɪˈkwiːð/ *verb* [+ two objects] *formal* to formally arrange to give someone something after you die *He* ***bequeathed*** *his art collection* ***to*** *the city of Glasgow.*

bequest /bɪˈkwest/ *noun* [C] *formal* money or property that you have arranged for someone to get after you die

berate /bɪˈreɪt/ *verb* [T] *formal* to speak angrily to someone *She* ***berated*** *him* ***for*** *being late.*

bereaved /bɪˈriːvd/ *adjective* If you have been bereaved, someone you loved has died. *bereaved parents* ○ *The minister spoke quietly with* ***the bereaved.*** • **bereavement** *noun* [C, U] *formal*

bereft /bɪˈreft/ *adjective formal* **1 bereft of sth** completely without something *They were bereft of new ideas.* **2** [never before noun] alone and extremely sad *She was left bereft by his death.*

beret /ˈbereɪ/ [US] /bəˈreɪ/ *noun* [C] a round, flat hat made of soft material

berry /ˈberi/ *noun* [C] a small, round fruit on some plants and trees

berserk /bə'zɜːk/ adjective **go berserk** informal to become extremely angry or violent

berth /bɜːθ/ noun [C] **1** a bed on a boat or train **2** a place for a boat to stay in a port

beset /bɪ'set/ verb [T] formal If problems beset you, they cause you continuing difficulties. [often passive] The project has been **beset by problems** from the start.

beside /bɪ'saɪd/ preposition **1** next to someone or something, or very near them She knelt beside his bed. **2 be beside yourself (with sth)** to experience a powerful emotion He was beside himself with rage.

besides¹ /bɪ'saɪdz/ preposition in addition to something or someone Do you play any other sports besides football?

besides² /bɪ'saɪdz/ adverb **1** used to give another reason for something She won't mind if you're late - besides, it's not your fault. **2** in addition to Besides looking after the children, she also runs a successful business.

besiege /bɪ'siːdʒ/ verb **1 be besieged by/with sb** to have lots of people asking you questions or making demands The president was besieged by reporters. **2 be besieged by/with sth** to receive many demands or criticisms The radio station was besieged with calls from angry listeners. **3** [T] to surround a place with an army in order to attack it

o▪**best¹** /best/ adjective (superlative of good) better than any other She's one of our best students. ○ Give her my **best wishes**. ○ Susie's my **best friend** (= the friend I like more than any other). ○ What's the best way to get to Manchester from here? **⊃**See also: **second best**, the best/greatest **thing** since sliced bread.

o▪**best²** /best/ adverb (superlative of well) **1** most, or more than any other Which of the songs did you like best? **2** in the most suitable or satisfactory way I sleep best with the windows open.

best³ /best/ noun **1 the best** someone or something that is better than any other He's the best of the new players. **2 at best** used to show that the most positive way of considering something is still not good At best, only 50 per cent of babies born at 24 weeks will survive. **3 at his/ its, etc best** at the highest level of achievement or quality The article is an example of journalism at its best. **4 do/try your best** to make the greatest effort possible I did my best to persuade him. **5 bring out the best in sb** to cause someone's best qualities to show **6 make the best of sth** to try to be positive about a situation you do not like but cannot change Our hotel room is rather small, but we'll just have to make the best of it. **7 for the best** If something is for the best, it seems unpleasant now, but will improve a situation in the future. Divorce is always painful, but it really was for the best. **8 at the best of times** used to show that something is not good when it is the best it can be He's not exactly patient at the best of times. **9 have the best of both worlds** to have the advantages of two different situations Living in the country and working in the city you have the best of both worlds.

,best 'man noun [no plural] a man who stands next to the man who is getting married at the marriage ceremony and helps him

bestow /bɪ'stəʊ/ verb [T] formal to give someone an important present or a public reward for their achievements He won the Nobel Peace Prize, an honour also **bestowed on** two of his colleagues.

bestseller /,best'selər/ noun [C] a very popular book that many people have bought ●**best-selling** adjective [always before noun] best-selling authors

bet¹ /bet/ verb [I, T] betting, past bet **1** to risk money on the result of a game, competition, etc He lost all his money **betting** on horses. ○ [+ two objects + (that)] I bet him a dollar that I was right. **2 I bet** informal something that you say to show that you believe that something is true or will happen [+ (that)] I bet that he's forgotten my birthday again. **3 You bet!** mainly US informal used to say that you will do something with enthusiasm "Are you going to Pam's party?" "You bet!"

WORD PARTNERS FOR **bet**

have/place a bet **(on)** sth ● put a bet **on** sth
● lose/win a bet

bet² /bet/ noun [C] **1** when you risk money on the result of a game, competition, etc She won her **bet**. ○ He **put a bet on** Manchester United winning on Saturday. **2 a good bet** something that would be useful, clever, or enjoyable to do Putting your savings in a high-interest account would be a good bet. **3 your best bet** the best decision or choice Your best bet in terms of value would be the Regent Hotel. **4 hedge your bets** to avoid choosing one particular thing or action when it is not certain which is the right choice Journalists are hedging their bets on the likely outcome of the election. **5 a safe bet** something that you are certain will happen Wheeler is a safe bet for a place on the team.

betray /bɪ'treɪ/ verb [T] **1** PERSON to behave in a dishonest or cruel way to someone who trusts you When I heard what he had said about me, I felt betrayed. **2** SECRETS If you betray your country or an organization, you give secret information to its enemies or to other organizations. **3** EMOTION to show an emotion that you were trying to hide Her face was calm, but her hands betrayed her nervousness.

betrayal /bɪ'treɪəl/ noun [C, U] when you betray someone a betrayal of trust

o▪**better¹** /'betər/ adjective **1** (comparative of good) of a higher quality, more effective, or more enjoyable than something or someone else Jeff's been offered a better job in the States. ○ The sales figures were **better than** expected. ○ Her English has **got a lot better** (= improved) recently. **2** healthy, or less ill than before I feel much better. ○ I hope you **get better** soon. **3** the **bigger/brighter/hotter, etc the better** used to say that the bigger, brighter, hotter, etc something is, the more pleased you will be

o▪**better²** /'betər/ adverb **1** (comparative of well) to a greater degree, or in a more successful or effective way I'd like to get to know you better.

B

○ *Helen did much **better than** me in the exam.* **2 he/you, etc had better do sth** used in order to say what you think someone should do *You'd better hurry or you'll miss the train.* **3 know better** to have enough experience not to do something stupid or something that will not achieve anything *I thought she'd listen to me - I should have known better.*

better[3] /ˈbetəʳ/ *noun* **1 for the better** If a situation changes for the better, it improves. *Their relationship has changed for the better.* **2 get the better of sb** If a feeling gets the better of you, it becomes too strong to control. *Curiosity finally got the better of her and she opened the letter.*

better[4] /ˈbetəʳ/ *verb* **[T]** to do something better than it has been done before *He bettered his previous best time for a marathon.*

ˌbetter ˈoff *adjective* **[never before noun] 1** richer *We're a lot better off now that Jane's started work again.* **2** in a better situation *Simon's such an idiot - you'd be better off without him.* **3 you're better off doing sth** used to give advice *You're better off getting a taxi.*

⊶**between**[1] /bɪˈtwiːn/ *preposition* **1** [SPACE] in the space that separates two places, people, or things *The town lies halfway between Florence and Rome.* **2** [TIME] in the period of time that separates two events or times *The shop is closed for lunch between 12.30 and 1.30.* ○ *We'll be arriving sometine between 2.00 and 3.00.* **3** [INVOLVE] involving two or more groups of people *Tonight's game is between the New Orleans Saints and the Los Angeles Rams.* **4** [AMOUNT] used to show the largest and smallest amount or level of something *Between 50 and 100 people will lose their jobs.* **5** [CONNECT] connecting two or more places or things *There is a regular train service between Glasgow and Edinburgh.* **6** [SEPARATE] separating two or more things or people *the gap between rich and poor* ○ *What's the **difference between** these two cameras?* **7** [SHARE] shared by a particular number of people *We drank two bottles of wine between four of us.* **8** [AMOUNT] If something is between two amounts, it is larger than the first amount but smaller than the second. *The temperature will be between 20 and 25 degrees today.* **9** [CHOOSE] If you choose between two things, you choose one thing or the other. *If I had to choose between my career and my family it would be my family every time.*

between[2] /bɪˈtwiːn/ (*also* **in between**) *adverb* **1** in the space that separates two places, people, or things *The wood is in neat piles with newspaper placed between.* **2** in the period of time that separates two events or times *There's a train at 6.15 and one at 10.30 but nothing in between.*

beverage /ˈbevᵊrɪdʒ/ *noun* **[C]** *formal* a drink *hot and cold beverages*

beware /bɪˈweəʳ/ *verb* **[I]** used in order to warn someone to be careful ***Beware of** the dog.* ○ **[+ of + doing sth]** *You should beware of spending too long in the sun.*

bewildered /bɪˈwɪldəd/ *adjective* very confused and not sure what to do *She looked bewildered.*

• **bewilderment** *noun* **[U]** *He stared at me **in bewilderment**.*

bewildering /bɪˈwɪldᵊrɪŋ/ *adjective* making you feel confused *There was a bewildering range of subjects to choose from.*

bewitch /bɪˈwɪtʃ/ *verb* **[T]** If someone or something bewitches you, you find them extremely attractive and interesting. *a bewitching smile*

⊶**beyond**[1] /biˈɒnd/ *preposition* **1** [DISTANCE] on the other side of something *Our house is just beyond the bridge.* **2** [TIME] continuing after a particular time or date *A lot of people now live beyond the age of 80.* **3 beyond belief/repair/recognition, etc** impossible to believe/repair/recognize, etc *Steven had changed beyond all recognition.* **4** [NOT UNDERSTAND] *informal* If something is beyond you, you cannot understand it. *Computer studies is completely beyond me.* ○ *It's beyond me why anyone would want to buy that house.* **5** [EXCEPT] except for *She said very little beyond the occasional 'yes' and 'no'.* **6** [INVOLVING OTHERS] involving or affecting other things or people than the ones you have talked about *You should try to develop interests beyond the family.*

beyond[2] /biˈɒnd/ *adverb* **1** on the other side of something *From the top of the hill, we could see our house and the woods beyond.* **2** continuing after a particular time or date *The strike looks set to continue into March and beyond.*

bhangra /ˈbæŋgrə/ *noun* **[U]** a type of pop music based on traditional music from North India and Pakistan

bi- /baɪ-/ *prefix* two *bilingual* (= speaking two languages) ○ *bimonthly* (= happening twice in a month or once every two months)

biannual /baɪˈænjuəl/ *adjective* happening twice a year ➲Compare **biennial**.

bias /ˈbaɪəs/ *noun* **[C, U]** when you support or oppose someone or something in an unfair way because you are influenced by your personal opinions *a **bias towards/against** private education* ○ *The news channel has been accused of **bias in favour of** the government.*

biased /ˈbaɪəst/ *adjective* showing unfair support for or opposition to someone or something because of your personal opinions *to be **biased against/towards** younger workers*

bib /bɪb/ *noun* **[C]** a piece of cloth or plastic that is worn by young children when they are eating in order to stop their clothes getting dirty

bible /ˈbaɪbl/ *noun* **1 the Bible** the holy book of the Christian and Jewish religions **2 [C]** a copy of this book **3 [C]** a book or magazine that gives important information and advice about a particular subject *'Vogue' was regarded as the fashion student's bible.*

biblical /ˈbɪblɪkᵊl/ *adjective* relating to the Bible

bibliography /ˌbɪbliˈɒgrəfi/ *noun* **[C]** a list of books and articles on a particular subject

bicentenary /ˌbaɪsenˈtiːnᵊri/ [US] /baɪˈsentᵊneri/ *UK* (*US* **bicentennial** /ˌbaɪsenˈteniəl/) *noun* **[C]** the day or year that is 200 years after an important event *the bicentenary of Schubert's birth* ○ *bicentennial celebrations*

biceps /ˈbaɪseps/ *noun* [C] *plural* **biceps** the large muscle at the front of your upper arm

bicker /ˈbɪkəʳ/ *verb* [I] to argue about something that is not very important *They were bickering over which channel to watch.*

WORD PARTNERS FOR ***bicycle***

ride a bicycle • be **on** a bicycle • a bicycle **helmet**

⊶**bicycle** /ˈbaɪsɪkl/ *noun* [C] a vehicle with two wheels that you sit on and move by turning the two pedals (= parts you press with your feet) ➲See colour picture **Sports 2** on page Centre 15.

bicycle

WORD PARTNERS FOR ***bid***

launch/mount a bid • **in** a **(desperate)** bid to do sth • a bid **for** sth

bid¹ /bɪd/ *noun* [C] **1** [ATTEMPT] an attempt to achieve something *a successful **bid for** re-election* ○ [+ to do sth] *The council has banned cars from the city centre **in a bid** to reduce pollution.* **2** [BUY] an offer to pay a particular amount of money for something *I made a **bid** of $150 **for** the painting.* **3** [WORK] an offer to do work for someone for a particular amount of money *We put in a **bid for** the stadium contract.*

bid² /bɪd/ *verb* **bidding**, *past* **bid 1** [I, T] to offer to pay an amount of money for something *They **bid** $500 million **for** the company.* **2 bid for sth; bid to do sth** to try to do or obtain something *Five firms have bid for the contract.*

bid³ /bɪd/ *verb* **bidding**, *past tense* **bid** or **bade**, *past participle* **bid** or **bidden bid sb farewell/goodbye/good night, etc** *literary* to say goodbye, good night, etc *She bade her guests good night.*

bidder /ˈbɪdəʳ/ *noun* [C] someone who offers to pay a particular amount of money for something *The house will be sold to **the highest bidder*** (= the person who offers to pay the most).

bidding /ˈbɪdɪŋ/ *noun* [U] **1** when people offer to pay a particular amount of money for something **2 do sb's bidding** *literary* to do what someone tells you to do

bide /baɪd/ *verb* ➲See **bide your time¹**.

bidet /ˈbiːdeɪ/ [US] /bɪˈdeɪ/ *noun* [C] a small low bath that a person uses to wash their bottom and sex organs

biennial /baɪˈeniəl/ *adjective* happening every two years ➲Compare **biannual**.

⊶**big** /bɪg/ *adjective* **bigger** or **biggest 1** [SIZE] large in size or amount *I come from a big family.* ○ *We're looking for a bigger house.* **2** [IMPORTANT] important or serious *Tonight's big game is between Real Madrid and Manchester United.* ○ *Buying that car was a big mistake.* **3 your big brother/sister** *informal* your older brother/sister **4** [SUCCESSFUL] *informal* successful or popular *The programme's been **a big hit*** (= very popular) *with young children.* **5 make it big** *informal* to become very successful or famous

ˌ**big ˈbusiness** *noun* [U] **1** an activity that makes a lot of money *Football has become big business.* **2** large, powerful businesses

bigot /ˈbɪgət/ *noun* [C] a bigoted person

bigoted /ˈbɪgətɪd/ *adjective* A bigoted person has very strong, unfair opinions and refuses to consider different opinions. • **bigotry** /ˈbɪgətri/ *noun* [U] when someone is bigoted

big-ticket /ˈbɪgˌtɪkɪt/ *adjective* [always before noun] *US* Big-ticket items are expensive things to buy, such as cars or furniture.

ˌ**big ˈup** *verb* [T] *informal* to praise someone or something a lot, sometimes more than they deserve

⊶**bike** /baɪk/ *noun* [C] **1** *informal short for* bicycle **2** *informal short for* motorbike/motorcycle (= a vehicle with two wheels and an engine)

biker /ˈbaɪkəʳ/ *noun* [C] someone who rides a motorbike (= vehicle with two wheels and an engine)

bikini /bɪˈkiːni/ *noun* [C] a piece of clothing with two parts that women wear for swimming ➲See colour picture **Clothes** on page Centre 9.

bikini

bilateral /baɪˈlætᵊrᵊl/ *adjective* involving two groups or countries *bilateral talks/agreements/trade*

bile /baɪl/ *noun* [U] a bitter liquid made and stored in the body that helps to digest fat

bilingual /baɪˈlɪŋgwᵊl/ *adjective* using or able to speak two languages *a bilingual dictionary* ○ *She's bilingual.*

WORD PARTNERS FOR ***bill***

pay/settle a bill • a bill **comes to** [£100/$500, etc] • a bill **for** sth • an **electricity/gas/phone** bill

⊶**bill¹** /bɪl/ *noun* [C] **1** [PAYMENT] a piece of paper that tells you how much you must pay for something you have bought or for a service you have used *Have you **paid the** electricity **bill**?* **2** [LAW] a written plan for a law *Parliament will vote today on whether to pass the reform bill.* **3** [MONEY] *US* (*UK* **note**) a piece of paper money *a five dollar bill* **4** [ENTERTAINMENT] *UK* what is on at a cinema or theatre **5** [BEAK] a bird's beak

bill² /bɪl/ *verb* **1 be billed as sth** to be advertised with a particular description *The film was billed as a romantic comedy.* **2** [T] to give or send someone a bill asking for money that they owe for a product or service *He **billed** us for the materials.*

billboard /ˈbɪlbɔːd/ (*also UK* **hoarding**) *noun* [C] a large board used for advertising, especially by the side of a road

billfold /ˈbɪlfəʊld/ *US* (*UK/US* **wallet**) *noun* [C] a small, flat container for carrying paper money and credit cards (= plastic cards used for paying with)

billiards /ˈbɪliədz/ *noun* [U] a game in which two people try to hit coloured balls into holes around the edge of a table using long, thin sticks

billing /ˈbɪlɪŋ/ *noun* [U] **1** when people are sent letters to ask for payments **2 star/top billing** when a particular performer is shown as the most important person in a performance

billion /ˈbɪliən/ the number 1,000,000,000

billow /ˈbɪləʊ/ *verb* [I] to be moved and spread out by a current of air *Smoke billowed out of the building.*

bimbo /ˈbɪmbəʊ/ *noun* [C] *very informal* a young woman who is attractive but not intelligent

☞**bin** /bɪn/ *noun* [C] **1** *UK* (*US* **trash can**) a container that is used to put waste in *a rubbish/ wastepaper bin* ∘ *I threw it in the bin.* ➔See colour picture **The Office** on page Centre 5. **2** a container for storing things *a storage bin*

binary /ˈbaɪnᵊri/ *adjective* The binary system expresses numbers using only 1 and 0, and is especially used for computers.

bind¹ /baɪnd/ *verb* [T] *past* **bound 1** TIE to tie something together with string, rope, etc *His hands were bound behind his back.* **2** KEEP PROMISE to force someone to keep a promise *His contract binds him to working a six-day week.* **3** UNITE to unite people *Culture and language bind people together.* **4** BOOK to fasten together pages to make a book

bind² /baɪnd/ *noun* [no plural] *informal* **1** a difficult or unpleasant situation *a financial bind* **2** *UK* a job which uses a lot of your time *Cleaning the bathroom is a bind.*

binder /ˈbaɪndə/ *noun* [C] a strong cover for holding together pieces of paper

binding /ˈbaɪndɪŋ/ *adjective* A binding agreement, promise, etc cannot be broken or changed. *It's a legally binding contract.*

binge¹ /bɪndʒ/ *noun* [C] when you eat or drink too much or spend too much money in shops

binge² /bɪndʒ/ *verb* [I] **bingeing** or **binging** to eat too much food at one time *I've been bingeing on chocolate.*

'binge ˌdrinking *noun* [U] when someone drinks too much alcohol on one occasion ● **'binge ˌdrinker** *noun* [C]

bingo /ˈbɪŋgəʊ/ *noun* [U] a game in which people mark numbers on a card as they are called, and the person whose numbers are called first is the winner

binoculars /bɪˈnɒkjələz/ *noun* [plural] a piece of equipment for looking at things that are far away, made from two tubes with glass at the ends *a pair of binoculars*

binoculars

bio- /baɪəʊ-/ *prefix* relating to living things or human life *biodiversity* ∘ *bioethics*

biochemical /ˌbaɪəʊˈkemɪkᵊl/ *adjective* relating to the chemistry of living things

biochemistry /ˌbaɪəʊˈkemɪstri/ *noun* [U] the

study of the chemistry of living things such as plants, animals, or people ● **biochemist** *noun* [C] a scientist who studies biochemistry

biodegradable /ˌbaɪəʊdɪˈgreɪdəbl/ *adjective* Biodegradable substances decay naturally without damaging the environment.

biodiesel /ˈbaɪəʊˌdiːzl/ *noun* [U] fuel used in the engines of some vehicles that is made from vegetable oil or animal fat

bioethanol /ˌbaɪəʊˈeθənɒl/ *noun* [U] fuel used in the engines of some vehicles that is partly made from ethanol (= a chemical that comes from sugar)

biographer /baɪˈɒgrəfə/ *noun* [C] someone who writes the story of a particular person's life

biography /baɪˈɒgrəfi/ *noun* [C] the story of a person's life written by another person ● **biographical** /ˌbaɪəˈgræfɪkᵊl/ *adjective* about someone's life *biographical information*

biological /ˌbaɪəˈlɒdʒɪkᵊl/ *adjective* **1** relating to the study of living things such as plants and animals *biological sciences* **2** using living things or poisons made from living things *biological weapons* ● **biologically** *adverb*

biology /baɪˈɒlədʒi/ *noun* [U] the study of living things ● **biologist** *noun* [C] a scientist who studies biology

biopsy /ˈbaɪɒpsi/ *noun* [C] when a small number of cells are taken from a part of the body and examined to see if there is a disease

biotechnology /ˌbaɪəʊtekˈnɒlədʒi/ *noun* [U] the use of living cells and bacteria in chemical processes, especially in the food and medical industries

bioterrorism /ˌbaɪəʊˈterərɪzᵊm/ *noun* [U] when people use living things, such as bacteria, to hurt other people for political reasons ● **bioterrorist** *noun* [C]

bipartisan /baɪˈpɑːtɪzæn/ *adjective* involving two political parties *a bipartisan agreement*

birch /bɜːtʃ/ *noun* [C, U] a tree that has thin, smooth branches

☞**bird** /bɜːd/ *noun* [C] an animal that has wings and feathers and is usually able to fly

'bird ˌflu (*also* **avian flu**) *noun* [U] an illness that kills birds and can sometimes pass from birds to people

birdie /ˈbɜːdi/ *US* (*UK* **shuttlecock**) *noun* [C] a small object with feathers that is used like a ball in badminton (= a sport like tennis)

ˌbird of 'prey *noun* [C] *plural* **birds of prey** a large bird that kills smaller animals for food

bird-watching /ˈbɜːdˌwɒtʃɪŋ/ *noun* [U] the hobby of looking at birds

biro /ˈbaɪərəʊ/ *noun* [C, U] *UK trademark* a type of pen that has a very small metal ball at its end and a thin tube of ink inside

☞**birth** /bɜːθ/ *noun* **1 give birth** When a woman or an animal gives birth, she produces a baby from her body. *She gave birth to twins.* **2** [C, U] the time when a baby is born *a difficult birth* ∘ *Write your date of birth* (= the date when you were born) *here.* **3** [U] *literary* the beginning of something *the birth of modern science* **4 American/Italian, etc by birth** born in a particular place or having parents with a particular nationality

'birth cer,tificate noun [C] an official document that records when and where a person was born

'birth con,trol noun [U] methods of limiting the number of children you have

o**birthday** /'bɜːθdeɪ/ noun [C] the day on which someone was born, or the same date each year She is **celebrating** her seventieth **birthday**. ○ Happy Birthday! ○ a birthday cake/party

birthmark /'bɜːθmɑːk/ noun [C] a mark on someone's skin that has been there since they were born

birthplace /'bɜːθpleɪs/ noun [C] the place where someone was born

'birth ,rate noun [C] a measurement of the number of babies born in a particular period

o**biscuit** /'bɪskɪt/ noun [C] **1** UK (US cookie) a thin, flat cake that is dry and usually sweet ⊃See colour picture **Food** on page Centre 11. **2** US a small, soft, round bread

bisexual /baɪ'sekʃuəl/ adjective sexually attracted to both men and women

bishop /'bɪʃəp/ noun [C] a priest of high rank in some Christian churches the Bishop of Oxford

bison /'baɪsᵊn/ noun [C] plural bison a large, wild animal similar to a cow with long hair

bistro /'biːstrəʊ/ noun [C] an informal place to eat or drink, in a French style

o**bit¹** /bɪt/ noun [C] **1** SMALL AMOUNT a small amount or piece of something I wrote it down on a bit of paper. ○ There's a little bit more pasta left. ○ My favourite bit of the film is right at the end. ○ The books are falling to bits (= into separate parts). **2 a bit a** SLIGHTLY slightly It's a bit cold in here. ○ It was a bit too expensive. **b** SHORT TIME informal a short time I'll see you in a bit. ○ She lived in Italy for a bit. **3 a bit of a** change/fool/problem, etc a change, fool (= stupid person), problem, etc, but not an important or serious one I am a bit of a romantic. ○ It was a bit of a shock. **4 quite a bit** informal a lot He does quite a bit of travelling. ○ She is quite a bit older than him. **5 a bit much** informal more than is fair, or more than you can deal with It's a bit much to expect me to tidy up their mess. **6 bit by bit** gradually She saved up the money, bit by bit. **7 every bit as** used to emphasize that one thing is equally good, important, etc as something else The gardens are every bit as impressive as the castle itself. **8 bits and pieces** small things or jobs which are not connected or not very important We've packed most of it up now, there are just a few bits and pieces left. **9** COMPUTER a unit of information in a computer **10** HORSE a piece of metal which goes in the mouth of a horse to control it

bit² /bɪt/ past tense of bite

bitch¹ /bɪtʃ/ noun [C] **1** very informal an offen-

sive name for an unpleasant woman **2** a female dog

bitch² /bɪtʃ/ verb [I] very informal to talk in an unkind way about people She's always bitching about her boss.

bitchy /'bɪtʃi/ adjective If someone is bitchy, they are unkind about other people. a bitchy comment

o**bite¹** /baɪt/ verb past tense bit, past participle bitten **1** [I, T] to cut something using your teeth She bit into an apple. ○ He bites his fingernails. ○ He was bitten by a dog. **2** [I] to begin to have a bad effect Higher mortgage rates are beginning to bite. ⊃See also: bite the **bullet**, bite the **dust¹**. **3 come back to bite you** If a problem will come back to bite you, it will causes more trouble for you in the future if you do not solve it now.

bite² /baɪt/ noun **1** [C] a piece taken from food when you bite it She **took a bite** from her pizza. **2** [C] an injury caused when an animal or insect bites you mosquito bites **3 a bite** a small meal I just want to grab a bite to eat.

biting /'baɪtɪŋ/ adjective A biting wind or biting cold is extremely cold and hurts your skin.

bitten /'bɪtᵊn/ past participle of bite

bitter¹ /'bɪtəʳ/ adjective **1** ANGRY angry and upset because of something bad which has happened that you cannot forget I feel very bitter about my childhood. **2** HATE full of hate or anger a bitter argument/dispute **3** SOUR having a strong, sour, usually unpleasant taste **4** COLD extremely cold a bitter wind **5 to/until the bitter end** until something is completely finished, usually something unpleasant He was determined to stay right to the bitter end. **6** DISAPPOINTED making you feel very disappointed Losing the championship was a bitter disappointment. ● **bitterness** noun [U]

bitter² /'bɪtəʳ/ noun [U] UK a type of beer with a bitter taste

bitterly /'bɪtᵊli/ adverb **1** in a way which shows strong negative emotion such as anger or disappointment We were **bitterly disappointed** about the decision. **2** If it is bitterly cold, the weather is extremely and unpleasantly cold.

bizarre /bɪ'zɑːʳ/ adjective very strange and surprising bizarre behaviour ● **bizarrely** adverb

o**black¹** /blæk/ adjective **1** COLOUR being the colour of coal or of the sky on a very dark night a black jacket ⊃See colour picture **Colours** on page Centre 12. **2** PERSON Someone who is black has the dark skin typical of people from Africa. black athletes/Americans **3** OF BLACK PEOPLE relating to black people the black community **4** DRINK Black tea or coffee has no milk or cream added to it. **5** HUMOUR funny about unpleasant or frightening subjects black comedy **6** ANGRY angry He gave her a black look. **7** SITUATION If your situation or future is black, it is very bad. **8 black and blue** covered with bruises (= marks on your skin from being hit) **9 black and white** very clear or simple The issue of nuclear weapons is not black and white. ● **blackness** noun [U] ⊃See also: jet-black, pitch-black.

o**black²** /blæk/ noun **1** COLOUR [C, U] the colour of coal or of the sky on a very dark night She

B

always dresses in black (= in black clothes). ⊃See colour picture **Colours** on page Centre 12. **2** [PERSON] [C] a black person **3 in the black** If your bank account is in the black, it contains some money. **4 in black and white** a [PRINT] printed in a book, newspaper, or official document *Look at the contract - it's all there in black and white.* **b** [NO COLOUR] using or seeing no colours, but only black, white, and grey *I saw the original film in black and white.* ⊃See also: **jet-black**.

black³ /blæk/ *verb*
black out *informal* to suddenly become unconscious

blackberry /ˈblækbᵊri/ *noun* [C] a small, soft, dark purple fruit with seeds

Blackberry /ˈblækbᵊri/ *noun* [C] *trademark* a computer with no wires that fits in your hand and that you can use for documents, email and Internet access ● **Blackberry** *verb* [I] to use a Blackberry

blackbird /ˈblækbɜːd/ *noun* [C] a bird with black feathers and a yellow beak

blackboard /ˈblækbɔːd/ (*also US* **chalkboard**) *noun* [C] a large board with a dark surface that teachers write on with chalk (= soft, white rock) ⊃See colour picture **The Classroom** on page Centre 6.

ˌblack ˈbox *noun* [C] a small machine on an aircraft that people use to discover the reason for an aircraft accident

blackcurrant /ˌblækˈkʌrᵊnt/ *noun* [C] *UK* a very small, round, sour, dark purple fruit *blackcurrant juice/jelly*

blacken /ˈblækᵊn/ *verb* **1** [I, T] to become black or to make something become black *Storm clouds blackened the sky.* **2** [T] If you blacken someone's name, you say bad things about them.

ˌblack ˈeye *noun* [C] an eye that has a dark circle around it because it has been hit

ˌblack ˈhole *noun* [C] an area in outer space that sucks material and light into it from which it cannot escape

blacklist /ˈblæklɪst/ *verb* [T] to include someone on a list of people you think are bad or you will not deal with [often passive] *He was blacklisted by the banks and credit card companies.*

ˌblack ˈmagic *noun* [U] magic used for evil

blackmail /ˈblækmeɪl/ *noun* [U] when someone forces you to do something, or to pay them money, by saying they will tell another person something that you want to keep secret ● **blackmail** *verb* [T] [+ into + doing sth] *They used the photographs to blackmail her into spying for them.* ● **blackmailer** *noun* [C]

ˌblack ˈmarket *noun* [C] illegal trading of goods that are not allowed to be bought and sold or that there are not enough of for everyone who wants them *the black market in heroin*

blackout /ˈblækaʊt/ *noun* [C] **1** [UNCONSCIOUS] when someone suddenly becomes unconscious **2** [NO INFORMATION] when information is kept from people [usually singular] *a media/news blackout* **3** [NO ELECTRICITY] a failure in the

supply of electricity **4** [NO LIGHTS] a period during a war when no lights must show at night

blacksmith /ˈblæksmɪθ/ *noun* [C] someone whose job is to make things from metal, especially shoes for horses

bladder /ˈblædᵊr/ *noun* [C] the organ where waste liquid is stored before it leaves your body ⊃See also: **gall bladder**.

blade /bleɪd/ *noun* [C] **1** the flat, sharp, metal part of a knife, tool, or weapon **2** a long, narrow leaf of grass or a similar plant *a blade of grass* ⊃See also: **razor blade, shoulder blade**.

ₒ⁻**blame¹** /bleɪm/ *verb* [T] **1** to say or think that someone or something is responsible for something bad which has happened *Many people blame him for Tony's death.* ○ *Poor housing is to blame for many of their health problems.* ○ *They apologized for the delay and blamed it on technical problems.* **2 I don't blame him/them/you, etc** used to say that you understand and accept the reason for what someone is doing *"I think I'll go home early." "I don't blame you - you look really tired."*

> **WORD PARTNERS FOR blame**
>
> apportion blame ● get/shoulder/take the blame (for sth) ● lay/put the blame on sb/sth

blame² /bleɪm/ *noun* [U] when people say that someone or something is responsible for something bad *The manager should take the blame for the team's defeat.* ○ *They put the blame on faulty equipment.*

blameless /ˈbleɪmləs/ *adjective* not responsible for anything bad *They concluded that Lucy was entirely blameless.*

bland /blænd/ *adjective* **1** not interesting or exciting *bland statements* **2** If food is bland, it does not have much taste.

blank¹ /blæŋk/ *adjective* **1** with no writing, pictures, or sound *a blank page* ○ *a blank tape* ○ *The space for the date was left blank.* **2 go blank** If your mind goes blank, you suddenly cannot remember or think of something. **3** showing no feeling or understanding *a blank expression* ⊃See also: **point-blank**.

blank² /blæŋk/ *noun* **1** [C] an empty space on a piece of paper or form where information can be given *Just fill in the blanks.* **2 draw a blank** to be unable to get information, think of something, or achieve something *All their investigations have drawn a blank so far.*

ˌblank ˈcheque *UK* (*mainly US* ˌblank ˈcheck) *noun* [C] If you give someone a blank cheque, you allow them as much money as they want or need to do something.

blanket¹ /ˈblæŋkɪt/ *noun* [C] **1** a thick, warm cover that you sleep under **2** a thick layer of something *a blanket of cloud/snow*

blanket² /ˈblæŋkɪt/ *adjective* [always before noun] including or affecting everything *a blanket ban*

blanket³ /ˈblæŋkɪt/ *verb* [T] to completely cover something *The ground was blanketed with snow.*

blankly /ˈblæŋkli/ *adverb* without showing any

emotion or understanding *She just stared at me blankly.*

blare /bleə^r/ (*also* blare out) *verb* [I] to make a very loud noise *There was music blaring from his room.*

blasphemy /ˈblæsfəmi/ *noun* [U] something which you say or do that shows you do not respect God or a religion ● **blasphemous** /ˈblæsfəməs/ *adjective* expressing blasphemy

blast¹ /blɑːst/ *noun* 1 EXPLOSION [C] an explosion *a bomb blast* 2 AIR [C] a sudden strong movement of air *a blast of cold air/heat* 3 **full blast** If something is happening or working full blast, it is at its loudest, strongest, or fastest level. *The heating was on full blast.* 4 NOISE [C] a sudden loud noise *a blast on the trumpet* 5 ENJOYMENT [no plural] *US very informal* an exciting and enjoyable experience *Eric's party was a blast.*

blast² /blɑːst/ *verb* 1 NOISE [I, T] (*also* blast out) to make a very loud noise *rock music blasting from a stereo* 2 MOVE [I, T] to move through something or to hit something with force *Dixon blasted the ball past the goalkeeper.* 3 EXPLODE [I] to break through rock using explosives *They blasted a hole in the rock face.* 4 GUNS [T] to destroy a person or place with guns or bombs

blast off When a spacecraft blasts off, it leaves the ground to go into space.

blast³ /blɑːst/ *exclamation UK* used when you are annoyed at something *Blast! I forgot the keys.*

blast-off /ˈblɑːstɒf/ *noun* [U] when a spacecraft leaves the ground

WORD PARTNERS FOR *blatant*

a blatant **attempt** to do sth ● a blatant **disregard for** sth ● a blatant **lie**

blatant /ˈbleɪt³nt/ *adjective* very obvious, with no attempt to be honest or behave well *blatant lies/racism* ● **blatantly** *adverb*

blaze¹ /bleɪz/ *verb* [I] to burn or shine very brightly or strongly *The sun blazed down on the dry countryside.*

blaze² /bleɪz/ *noun* [C] 1 a large, strong fire *The blaze started in the hall.* 2 **a blaze of colour/lights etc** very bright colour, lights, etc *The tulips provided a blaze of colour outside her window.* 3 **a blaze of glory/publicity** a lot of public attention for a short time

blazer /ˈbleɪzə^r/ *noun* [C] a type of jacket, often worn as part of a school uniform

blazing /ˈbleɪzɪŋ/ *adjective* [always before noun] 1 very hot *a blazing log fire* 2 *UK* very angry *a blazing row*

bleach¹ /bliːtʃ/ *noun* [U] a strong chemical used for cleaning things or removing colour from things

bleach² /bliːtʃ/ *verb* [T] to remove the colour from something or make it lighter using chemicals *She's bleached her hair.*

bleak /bliːk/ *adjective* 1 If a situation is bleak, there is little or no hope for the future. *The future is looking bleak for small clubs struggling with debts.* 2 If a place is bleak, it is cold,

empty and not attractive. *a bleak landscape* ● **bleakness** *noun* [U]

bleary /ˈblɪəri/ *adjective* If you have bleary eyes, you cannot see clearly because you are tired or have just woken up.

bleat /bliːt/ *verb* [I] 1 to make the noise of a sheep or goat 2 to speak or complain in a weak and annoying way *She keeps bleating about her lack of money.* ● **bleat** *noun* [C]

bled /bled/ *past of* bleed

bleed /bliːd/ *verb* [I] *past* bled to have blood coming from a cut in your body ● **bleeding** *noun* [U] *Try to stop the bleeding.*

bleep /bliːp/ *noun* [C] a short, high electronic noise ● **bleep** *verb* [I]

bleeper /ˈbliːpə^r/ *UK* (*UK/US* beeper) *noun* [C] a small piece of electronic equipment which you carry that makes a sound when someone wants to speak to you

blemish /ˈblemɪʃ/ *noun* [C] a mark which spoils the appearance of someone or something

blend¹ /blend/ *verb* 1 [T] to mix two or more things together completely *Blend the ingredients into a smooth paste.* 2 [I, S] to combine two or more things *The team blends new, young players with more mature, experienced ones.*

blend in If something or someone blends in, they look or seem the same as the people or things around them and so are not easily noticed. *He blends in with the background.*

blend² /blend/ *noun* [C] a combination of two or more things *Their music is a blend of jazz and African rhythms.*

blender /ˈblendə^r/ *noun* [C] an electric machine for making soft foods into a smooth liquid ⊃See colour picture **The Kitchen** on page Centre 2.

bless /bles/ *verb* [T] 1 to ask God to help or protect someone or something, or to make it holy *The priest blessed their marriage.* 2 **be blessed with sth** to be lucky enough to have something good *He's blessed with a wonderful singing voice.* 3 **Bless you!** something you say when someone sneezes 4 **bless her/him/them, etc** *informal* used to show your affection for the person you are talking about *Peter, bless him, slept all the way through it.*

blessed /ˈblesɪd/ *adjective* [always before noun] 1 pleasant and wanted very much *The rain was a **blessed** relief.* 2 holy *the Blessed Virgin Mary*

blessing /ˈblesɪŋ/ *noun* 1 LUCK [C] something which is lucky or makes you happy *It is a blessing that no one was hurt.* 2 APPROVAL [U] approval that someone gives to a plan or action *Mr Newton has **given** his **blessing** for the plan.* 3 RELIGION [C, U] protection or help from God, or a prayer to ask for this 4 **a blessing in disguise** something that has a good effect, although at first it seemed that it would be bad 5 **a mixed blessing** something which has both good and bad effects

blew /bluː/ *past tense of* blow

blight /blaɪt/ *noun* [no plural] something which has a very bad effect on something, often for a long time *the blight of poverty/unemployment* ○ *He became **a blight** on their lives.* ● **blight**

verb [T] to cause damage to or have a bad effect on something *Injury has blighted his career.*

∘▪**blind¹** /blaɪnd/ *adjective* **1** not able to see *She went blind after an accident.* ○ *This project provides guide dogs for the blind.* **2 be blind to sth** to not notice something, or not want to notice something *Drivers who speed are often blind to the risks they cause.* **3 blind panic/rage/trust, etc** an extremely strong feeling that makes you do things without thinking **4 a blind corner/** UK a bend or corner on a road that is dangerous because you cannot see cars coming around it ● **blindness** *noun* [U] ⊃See also: **colour-blind**, turn a blind **eye¹** (to sth).

blind² /blaɪnd/ *verb* **1** [T] to make someone blind, either for always or for a short time [often passive] *I was blinded by the car head-lights.* **2 blind sb to sth** to make someone unable to understand the truth about someone or something *Love blinded her to all his faults.*

blind³ /blaɪnd/ *noun* [C] a cover that you pull down over a window ⊃See also: **venetian blind**.

‚**blind 'date** *noun* [C] a romantic meeting be-tween a man and a woman who have not met before

blindfold /'blaɪndfəʊld/ *noun* [C] a piece of cloth that you put over someone's eyes so they cannot see ● **blindfold** *verb* [T] to put a blindfold on someone

blinding /'blaɪndɪŋ/ *adjective* **1** A blinding light is extremely bright. **2** A blinding headache (= pain in the head) is extremely painful.

blindly /'blaɪndli/ *adverb* **1** not able to see or not noticing what is around you *Carly reached blindly for the light switch.* **2** not thinking about what you are doing *They just blindly fol-lowed orders.*

'**blind ‚spot** *noun* [C] **1** a difficulty in accepting or understanding a particular thing *She has a complete blind spot where relations with the press are concerned.* **2** the part of the road just behind you, that you cannot see when you are driving

blink /blɪŋk/ *verb* **1** [I, T] to open and close both of your eyes quickly **2** [I] If a light blinks, it goes on and off quickly. ● **blink** *noun* [C]

blinkered /'blɪŋkəd/ *adjective* not willing to consider new or different ideas *a blinkered attitude*

blip /blɪp/ *noun* [C] **1** a small, temporary, and usually negative change from what usually happens *The rise in unemployment may just be a blip.* **2** a small spot of light on an electronic screen, sometimes with a short, high sound

bliss /blɪs/ *noun* [U] complete happiness *My idea of bliss is lying on a sunny beach.* ● **blissful** *ad-jective* making you feel very happy *a blissful childhood* ● **blissfully** *adverb She seemed bliss-fully unaware of the chaos she had caused.*

blister¹ /'blɪstəʳ/ *noun* [C] a painful, raised area of skin with liquid inside, that you get if your skin has been rubbed or burned, or a similar area on a painted surface *My new sandals have given me blisters.*

blister² /'blɪstəʳ/ *verb* [I, T] to get or cause blisters

blistering /'blɪstəʳrɪŋ/ *adjective* **1** CRITICISM using

very strong criticism *a blistering attack* **2** HEAT extremely hot *blistering sunshine* **3** SPEED extremely fast *The economy has grown at a blistering pace.*

blithely /'blaɪðli/ *adverb* without thinking about what might happen *People were blithely ignoring warnings not to swim in the river.*

blitz¹ /blɪts/ *noun* [C] **1** a lot of activity to achieve something in a short time *We had a cleaning blitz before my parents came home.* **2 the Blitz** bomb attacks on British cities during the Second World War

blitz² /blɪts/ *verb* [T] **1** to defeat someone or something completely **2** to drop bombs on something

blizzard /'blɪzəd/ *noun* [C] a storm with strong winds and snow

bloated /'bləʊtɪd/ *adjective* **1** swollen because of air or liquid inside **2** feeling uncomfortable because you have eaten too much

blob /blɒb/ *noun* [C] a small amount of a thick liquid *a blob of cream/glue* ⊃See colour picture **Pieces and Quantities** on page Centre 1.

bloc /blɒk/ *noun* [C] a group of countries with similar political ideas, who work together *the communist bloc*

block

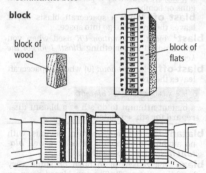

block of wood

block of flats

block¹ /blɒk/ *noun* [C] **1** PIECE a solid piece of something, usually in the shape of a square or rectangle *a block of ice/stone/wood* **2** DISTANCE US the distance along a street from where one road crosses it to the place where the next road crosses it *They only live two blocks away from the school.* **3** BUILDING a large building containing many apartments or offices UK *a block of flats* **4** GROUP OF BUILDINGS a square group of buildings or houses with roads on each side *Omar took the dog for a walk round the block.* **5** CANNOT THINK If you have a block about something, you cannot understand it or remember it. *I had a complete mental block about his name.* **6** STOP PROGRESS something that makes it difficult to move or make pro-gress **7** AMOUNT an amount or group of some-thing that is considered together *This block of seats is reserved.* ⊃See also: be a **chip¹** off the old block, **stumbling block**, **tower block**.

block² /blɒk/ *verb* [T] **1** CANNOT PASS (also **block up**) to prevent anyone or anything from pass-ing through a place *A fallen tree blocked the* road. ○ *The sink is blocked up.* ○ *a blocked drain* **2** STOP PROGRESS to stop something from happening or making progress *The council's blocked plans for a new supermarket.* **3** CANNOT SEE to be between someone and the thing they are looking at, so that they cannot see *A pillar was blocking my view.*

block sth off to close a road, path, or entrance so that people cannot use it *Police blocked off the road where the body was found.*

block sth out 1 to try to stop yourself thinking about something unpleasant *I've blocked out memories of the accident.* **2** to stop light or noise passing through something *Most sunscreens block out UVB radiation.*

blockade /blɒk'eɪd/ *noun* [C] when a government or soldiers stop goods or people from entering or leaving a place *The government imposed a blockade on oil trading.* ● **blockade** *verb* [T]

blockage /'blɒkɪdʒ/ *noun* [C] something that stops something else passing through *His death was caused by a blockage in his arteries.*

blockbuster /'blɒk,bʌstəʳ/ *noun* [C] *informal* a book, film, etc that is very popular and successful *a new blockbuster movie*

,**block 'capitals** *noun* [plural] letters in the form A, B, C, not a, b, c

blog /blɒg/ (*also* **weblog**) *noun* [C] a record of your thoughts that you put on the Internet for other people to read ● **blog** *verb* [I] ● **blogger** /'blɒgəʳ/ *noun* [C] a person who writes or reads a blog

bloke /bləʊk/ *noun* [C] *UK informal* a man *Jake's a nice bloke.*

blonde¹ (*also* **blond**) /blɒnd/ *adjective* **1** Blonde hair is pale yellow. **2** Someone who is blonde has pale yellow hair.

blonde² (*also* **blond**) /blɒnd/ *noun* [C] someone, especially a woman, who has pale yellow hair

---

WORD PARTNERS FOR ***blood***

donate/give blood (= allow blood to be taken from your body for someone else's body) ● a **drop/pool/trickle** of blood ● a blood **test**

---

o━**blood** /blʌd/ *noun* [U] **1** the red liquid that flows around your body *a blood test/sample* **2** the family or place that you come from *I've got some Spanish blood in me.* **3 be in your blood** If something is in your blood, you and other people in your family are interested in it or good at it. *Sailing is in my blood.* **4 bad blood** feelings of hate between people because of things that have happened in the past **5 in cold blood** in a cruel way, without showing any emotion *He shot three policemen in cold blood.* **6 new blood** new people in an organization who will provide new ideas and energy ⊃See also: your own flesh and blood.

bloodbath /'blʌdbɑːθ/ *noun* [no plural] an extremely violent event in which many people are killed

blood-curdling /'blʌd,kɜːdlɪŋ/ *adjective* extremely frightening *a blood-curdling scream*

'**blood ,donor** *noun* [C] someone who gives some of their blood for ill people who need it

'**blood ,group** *UK* (*UK/US* **blood type**) *noun* [C] one of the groups that human blood is divided into

bloodless /'blʌdləs/ *adjective* achieved without killing or violence *a bloodless coup*

'**blood ,pressure** *noun* [U] the force with which blood flows around your body *high/low blood pressure*

bloodshed /'blʌdʃed/ *noun* [U] when people are killed or injured in fighting *Peace talks have failed to end the bloodshed in the region.*

bloodshot /'blʌdʃɒt/ *adjective* Bloodshot eyes are red in the part that should be white.

'**blood ,sport** *noun* [C] a sport in which animals are killed

bloodstained /'blʌdsteɪnd/ *adjective* Something that is bloodstained has blood on it.

bloodstream /'blʌdstriːm/ *noun* [no plural] the flow of blood around your body

bloodthirsty /'blʌd,θɜːsti/ *adjective* enjoying using or watching violence

'**blood trans,fusion** *noun* [C] when blood is put into someone's body

'**blood ,type** (*also UK* **blood group**) *noun* [C] one of the groups that human blood is divided into

'**blood ,vessel** *noun* [C] one of the small tubes that blood flows through in your body

bloody¹ /'blʌdi/ *adjective* **1** covered in blood *bloody hands* **2** violent and involving a lot of blood and injuries *a bloody war*

bloody² /'blʌdi/ *adjective, adverb UK very informal* used to show anger or to emphasize what you are saying in a slightly rude way *I can't find my bloody keys.* ○ *We were bloody lucky to win.*

bloom¹ /bluːm/ *noun* **1** [C] a flower *beautiful, pink blooms* **2 in bloom** with flowers that are open *In June the roses are in bloom.*

bloom² /bluːm/ *verb* [I] **1** If a plant blooms, its flowers open. **2** to develop and become successful, happy, or healthy *Their romance bloomed while they were in Paris.*

blossom¹ /'blɒsəm/ *noun* [C, U] a small flower, or the small flowers on a tree or plant *cherry blossom*

blossom² /'blɒsəm/ *verb* [I] **1** If a tree blossoms, it produces flowers. **2** to develop and become successful or beautiful *She has blossomed into a world champion.*

blot¹ /blɒt/ *verb* [T] **blotting**, *past* **blotted** to dry wet marks using soft paper or a cloth

blot sth out 1 to stop yourself from thinking about something unpleasant *I've tried to blot out memories of my relationship with Dieter.* **2** If smoke or cloud blots out the sun, it prevents it from being seen.

blot² /blɒt/ *noun* **1** [C] a mark on something, made by ink or paint falling on it **2 a blot on sth** something that spoils something else *The financial scandal was a blot on his reputation.*

blotch /blɒtʃ/ *noun* [C] a mark on something, especially your skin ● **blotchy** (*also* **blotched**) *adjective* having blotches

'**blotting ,paper** *noun* [U] thick paper used for drying wet ink

---

| j yes | k cat | ŋ ring | ʃ she | θ thin | ð this | ʒ decision | dʒ jar | tʃ chip | æ cat | e bed | ə ago | ɪ sit | i cosy | ɒ hot | ʌ run | ʊ put |

blouse /blaʊz/ ⑩ /blaʊs/ *noun* [C] a piece of clothing like a shirt that women wear

o⁻**blow¹** /bləʊ/ *verb past tense* blew *past participle* blown **1** WIND [I] If the wind blows, it moves and makes currents of air. *A cool sea breeze was blowing.* **2** PERSON [I] to force air out through your mouth *She blew on her coffee before taking a sip.* **3** blow sth down/across/off, etc If the wind blows something somewhere, it makes it move in that direction. *The storm blew trees across the road.* **4** MOVE [I] to move in the wind *branches blowing in the breeze* **5** INSTRUMENT [I, T] to make a sound by forcing air out of your mouth and through an instrument *Ann blew a few notes on the trumpet.* **6** MAKE [T] to make shapes out of something by blowing it *to blow bubbles* **7** SPEND [T] *informal* to spend a lot of money quickly and without considering it seriously *Lou blew all her prize money on a diamond necklace.* **8** blow it/your chance(s) *informal* If you blow it or blow your chance, you lose an opportunity to do something by doing or saying the wrong thing. *Tom blew his chances of getting the job by arriving late for the interview.* **9** blow your nose to clear your nose by forcing air through it into a handkerchief (= piece of cloth or soft paper) **10** ELECTRICITY [I, T] If a piece of electrical equipment blows, it suddenly stops working because the electric current is too strong. ➔See also: blow your mind¹, blow/get sth out of proportion.

blow sb away *mainly US informal* to surprise or please someone very much *a movie that will blow you away*

blow (sth) out If a flame blows out, or if you blow it out, it stops burning because you or the wind have blown it.

blow over If a storm or an argument blows over, it ends.

blow (sb, sth) up to destroy something or kill someone with a bomb, or to be destroyed by a bomb *Terrorists blew up an office building in the city.*

blow sth up to fill something with air *blow up a balloon*

blow up 1 If a storm or an argument blows up, it starts suddenly. **2** *informal* to suddenly become very angry

blow² /bləʊ/ *noun* [C] **1** DISAPPOINTMENT a shock or disappointment *Losing his job was a terrible blow to him.* **2** HIT a hard hit with a hand or heavy object *He suffered serious blows to the head during the attack.* **3** INSTRUMENT when you blow something or blow into an instrument or other object *a blow on the whistle* **4** come to blows to fight or argue

blow-by-blow /ˌbləʊbaɪˈbləʊ/ *adjective* a blow-by-blow account/description a description of an event that gives all the details in the exact order that they happened

blow-dry /ˈbləʊdraɪ/ *verb* [T] to dry your hair in a particular style using a hairdryer (= electrical equipment for drying hair) ● blow-dry *noun* [no plural] *I had a cut and blow-dry.*

blown /bləʊn/ *past participle of* blow

blowout /ˈbləʊaʊt/ *noun* [C] **1** TYRE when a tyre suddenly explodes while a vehicle is still moving **2** MEAL/PARTY *informal* an expensive

meal or a big party **3** SPORT *US informal* when one team or player beats another easily in a sport

bludgeon /ˈblʌdʒ³n/ *verb* [T] to hit someone several times with a heavy object [often passive] *She was bludgeoned to death with a hammer.*

o⁻**blue¹** /bluː/ *adjective* **1** COLOUR being the same colour as the sky when there are no clouds *a dark blue jacket* ➔See colour picture **Colours** on page Centre 12. **2** SAD *informal* sad **3** SEX about sex *a blue joke/movie* ➔See also: black¹ and blue, once in a blue moon.

o⁻**blue²** /bluː/ *noun* **1** [C, U] the colour of the sky when there are no clouds ➔See colour picture **Colours** on page Centre 12. **2** out of the blue If something happens out of the blue, you did not expect it. *One day, completely out of the blue, I had a letter from her.*

bluebell /ˈbluːbel/ *noun* [C] a plant with small, blue flowers shaped like bells

blueberry /ˈbluːb³ri/ *noun* [C] a small, sweet, dark blue fruit that grows on bushes

blue-chip /ˌbluːˈtʃɪp/ *adjective* [always before noun] A blue-chip company or investment is considered certain to make a profit.

blue-collar /ˌbluːˈkɒlə³/ *adjective* [always before noun] A blue-collar worker does physical work, especially in a factory.

blueprint /ˈbluːprɪnt/ *noun* [C] a plan that shows how someone will design, build, or achieve something *a blueprint for political reform*

blues /bluːz/ *noun* [plural] **1** a type of slow, sad music that was developed by African-Americans *jazz and blues* **2** have/get the blues *informal* to feel or become sad

Bluetooth /ˈbluːtuːθ/ *noun* [U] *trademark* a technology that allows equipment such as computers and mobile phones to connect with no wires or cables *a Bluetooth headset*

bluff¹ /blʌf/ *verb* [I, T] to pretend you will do something or that you have knowledge, in order to force someone to do something *He won't really leave her - he's only bluffing.*

bluff² /blʌf/ *noun* **1** [C] an attempt to bluff **2** call sb's bluff to tell someone to do the thing they say they will do, because you do not think they will do it

blunder¹ /ˈblʌndə³/ *noun* [C] a serious and often stupid mistake *a series of financial blunders*

blunder² /ˈblʌndə³/ *verb* **1** [I] to make a serious mistake **2** blunder around/into, etc to move somewhere in a heavy way, as if you cannot see well *He blundered around, looking for the light switch.*

blunt¹ /blʌnt/ *adjective* **1** not sharp *a blunt knife* **2** saying exactly what you think without caring about people's feelings *a blunt letter* ● bluntness *noun* [U]

blunt² /blʌnt/ *verb* [T] **1** to make a feeling less strong *Mario's comments blunted everyone's enthusiasm.* **2** to make something less sharp

bluntly /ˈblʌntli/ *adverb* saying exactly what you think without caring about people's feelings

blur¹ /blɜː³/ *verb* [I, T] blurring, *past* blurred **1** to make the difference between two things less clear, or to make it difficult to see the exact truth about something *a book that blurs the distinction between reality and fiction* **2** to become difficult to see clearly, or to make something become difficult to see clearly *soft sunlight that blurred the edges of the mountains*

blur² /blɜːʳ/ *noun* [no plural] something that you cannot see or remember clearly *The accident happened so quickly that it's all a blur.*

blurb /blɜːb/ *noun* [C] a short description to advertise a product, especially a book

blurred /blɜːd/ *adjective* **1** (*also* blurry /ˈblɜːri/) not clear *a blurred photograph* ○ *blurred memories* **2** If your sight is blurred, you cannot see clearly. *blurred vision*

blurred

blurt /blɜːt/ (*also* blurt out) *verb* [T] to say something suddenly and without thinking, especially because you are excited or nervous *"Will you marry me?" he blurted.*

blush /blʌʃ/ *verb* [I] If you blush, your face becomes red, especially because you are embarrassed. *When he saw her, he **blushed with** shame.* ● blush *noun* [C]

blusher /ˈblʌʃəʳ/ *UK* (*US* blush) *noun* [U] red powder or cream that women put on their faces in order to make them more attractive ⊃See picture at **make up**.

bluster /ˈblʌstəʳ/ *verb* [I, T] to speak in a loud and angry way, often with little effect ● bluster *noun* [U]

blustery /ˈblʌstᵊri/ *adjective* very windy *a cold, blustery day*

boar /bɔːʳ/ *noun* [C] **1** a male pig **2** (*also* wild boar) a wild pig

board

board--

board¹ /bɔːd/ *noun* **1** [WOOD] [C] a long, thin, flat piece of wood *He nailed some boards across the broken window.* **2** [SURFACE] [C] a flat piece of wood, plastic, etc used for a particular purpose *an ironing board* ○ *a chopping board* **3** [IN-

[FORMATION] [C] a piece of wood, plastic, etc on a wall, where information can be put *Have you seen the poster on the board?* **4** [SCHOOL ROOM] [C] a surface on the wall of a school room that the teacher writes on *Copy down the sentences from the board.* **5** [GAMES] [C] a piece of wood, cardboard, etc for playing games on *a chess board* **6** [ORGANIZATION] [group] a group of people who officially control a company or organization, or a particular type of business activity *The board approved the sales plan.* ○ *the Gas/Tourist Board* **7 on board** on a boat, train, aircraft, etc **8** [MEALS] [U] meals that are provided when you stay in a hotel *bed and board* ○ *How much is a single room with **full board** (= all meals)?* **9 across the board** affecting everyone or every part of something *Jobs are likely to be lost across the board.* ⊃See also: bulletin board, diving board, drawing board, full board, half board, ironing board.

board² /bɔːd/ *verb* **1** [I, T] to get on a bus, boat, aircraft, etc *He boarded the train to London.* **2** [I] If an aircraft, train, etc is boarding, passengers are getting onto it. *The plane is now boarding at gate 26.*

board sth up to cover a door or window with wooden boards

boarder /ˈbɔːdəʳ/ *noun* [C] **1** [STUDENT] *UK* a student who lives at school **2** [PERSON] *US* (*UK* lodger) someone who pays for a place to sleep and meals in someone else's house **3** [SPORT] someone who goes snowboarding (= sport where you stand on a board to move over snow)

'board ,game *noun* [C] a game such as chess that is played on a board

'boarding ,house *noun* [C] a house where you pay for a room and meals

'boarding ,pass (*also* 'boarding ,card) *noun* [C] a piece of paper you must show to get on an aircraft

'boarding ,school *noun* [C] a school where students live and study

boardroom /ˈbɔːdruːm/ *noun* [C] a room where the people who control a company or organization have meetings

boast¹ /bəʊst/ *verb* **1** [I, T] to talk with too much pride about what you have done or what you own *I wish she would stop **boasting about** her exam results.* ○ *[+ that] Liam boasted that he owned two sports cars.* **2** [T] If a place boasts something good, it has it. *New York boasts some of the best museums in the world.*

boast² /bəʊst/ *noun* [C] something you are proud of and like to tell people about

boastful /ˈbəʊstfᵊl/ *adjective* talking with too much pride *boastful remarks*

o--**boat** /bəʊt/ *noun* **1** [C] a vehicle for travelling on water *a fishing boat* **2 be in the same boat** to be in the same unpleasant situation as other people *She complains that she doesn't have enough money, but we're all in the same boat.* **3 miss the boat** to be too late to get what you want *I'm afraid you've missed the boat. All the tickets have been sold.* **4 push the boat out** *UK* to spend a lot of money, especially when you are celebrating **5 rock the boat** to do or say something that changes a situation in a way that causes problems ⊃See also: **rowing boat**.

bob /bɒb/ *verb* [I] **bobbing**, *past* **bobbed** to move up and down quickly and gently *boats bobbing in the harbour*

bobby /'bɒbi/ *noun* [C] *UK informal old-fashioned* a police officer

'**bobby** ,**pin** *US* (*UK* **hairgrip**) *noun* [C] a small, thin piece of metal, used to fasten a woman's hair in position

bode /bəʊd/ *verb literary* **bode ill/well** to be a bad or good sign for the future *These religious differences do not bode well for their marriage.*

bodily[1] /'bɒdɪli/ *adjective* [always before noun] relating to a person's body *bodily strength*

bodily[2] /'bɒdɪli/ *adverb* If you move someone bodily, you lift or push them. *He carried her bodily out of the room.*

o⚊**body** /'bɒdi/ *noun* **1** [PERSON] [C] the whole physical structure of a person or animal *the human body* ⊃See colour picture **The Body** on page Centre 13. **2** [DEAD] [C] a dead person *Police found the body in a field.* **3** [NOT ARMS/LEGS] [C] the main part of a person or animal's body, not the head, arms, or legs *a dog with a thin body and short legs* **4** [GROUP] [group] an official group of people who work together *the sport's regulatory body* **5** [MAIN PART] [no plural] the main part of something *The body of the book is about his childhood.* **6** [AMOUNT] [no plural] a large amount of information *a body of research into AIDS* **7** [VEHICLE] [C] the main part of a vehicle *The body of the ship was not damaged.*

bodybuilding /'bɒdibɪldɪŋ/ *noun* [U] doing exercises with heavy weights to make your muscles big ● **bodybuilder** *noun* [C]

bodyguard /'bɒdigɑːd/ *noun* [C] someone whose job is to protect someone

'**body** ,**language** *noun* [U] the way you move your body, that shows people what you are feeling

bog[1] /bɒg/ *noun* [C, U] an area of soft, wet ground

bog[2] /bɒg/ *verb* **bogging**, *past* **bogged**
be bogged down to become so involved in something that you cannot do anything else *Try not to get too bogged down in details.*

boggle /'bɒgl/ *verb* **the mind boggles** *UK informal* (*US* **it boggles the mind** *informal*) something you say if something is difficult for you to accept, imagine, or understand *The mind boggles at the stupidity of some people.* ⊃See also: **mind-boggling**.

bogus /'bəʊgəs/ *adjective* pretending to be real *a bogus doctor* ○ *bogus documents* ○ *bogus claims*

bohemian /bəʊ'hiːmiən/ *adjective* typical of artists, musicians, etc, who live in a more informal way than most people

o⚊**boil**[1] /bɔɪl/ *verb* [I, T] [LIQUID] If a liquid boils, or if you boil it, it reaches the temperature where bubbles rise up in it and it produces steam. *boiling water* **2** [CONTAINER] If a container of liquid boils, or if you boil it, the liquid inside it reaches the temperature where bubbles rise up in it and it produces steam. *I've boiled the kettle.* **3** [COOK] to cook food in water that is boiling *Boil the pasta for 10 minutes.* ⊃See picture at **cook**.

boil down to sth If a situation or problem boils down to something, that is the main reason for it. *The problem boils down to one thing - lack of money.*

boil over **1** If a liquid that is being heated boils over, it flows over the side of the pan. **2** If a difficult situation or bad emotion boils over, it cannot be controlled any more and people start to argue or fight.

boil[2] /bɔɪl/ *noun* **1** **bring sth to the boil** to heat something until it starts to produce bubbles and steam *Bring the water to the boil, then add the rice.* **2** [C] a red swollen area on the skin that is infected

boiler /'bɔɪləʳ/ *noun* [C] a piece of equipment that provides hot water for a house

boiling /'bɔɪlɪŋ/ (*also* ,**boiling** '**hot**) *adjective informal* very hot *It's boiling in here!*

'**boiling** ,**point** *noun* [C] the temperature that a liquid boils at

boisterous /'bɔɪstᵊrəs/ *adjective* noisy and full of energy *a boisterous child* ● **boisterously** *adverb*

bold /bəʊld/ *adjective* **1** not frightened of taking risks *It was a bold decision to go and live abroad.* **2** strong in colour or shape *bold colours* ○ *a bold design* ● **boldly** *adverb* ● **boldness** *noun* [U]

bollard /'bɒlɑːd/ *noun* [C] *UK* a short thick post in a road, used to stop cars driving somewhere

bolster /'bəʊlstəʳ/ *verb* [T] to make something stronger by supporting or encouraging it *Strong sales are bolstering the economy.*

bolt[1] /bəʊlt/ *noun* [C] **1** a metal bar that you push across a door or window to lock it **2** a small piece of metal that is used with a nut (= metal piece with a hole in the middle) to fasten pieces of wood or metal together ⊃See picture at **tool** ⊃See also: the nuts (**nut**) and bolts.

bolt[2] /bəʊlt/ *verb* [T] **1** [FASTEN] to fasten two things together with a bolt *The seats in the cinema were bolted to the floor.* **2** [LOCK] to lock a door or window with a bolt **3** **bolt down/out/through, etc** to move suddenly and quickly *The cat bolted out of the door when it saw the dog.* **4** [EAT] (*also* **bolt down**) to eat something very quickly

,**bolt** '**upright** *adverb* sitting or standing with your back very straight

o⚊**bomb**[1] /bɒm/ *noun* [C] a weapon that explodes and causes damage *The bomb destroyed several office buildings in the city.* ⊃See also: **atomic bomb**.

bomb[2] /bɒm/ *verb* **1** [T] to attack a place using bombs *The factories were bombed during the war.* **2** **bomb along/down/through, etc** *UK informal* to move very quickly *A car came bomb-*

ing down the road.

bombard /bɒm'bɑːd/ *verb* [T] to continuously attack a place using guns and bombs • **bombardment** *noun* [C, U] *an **aerial bombardment***

bombard sb with sth to give someone too much information, ask them too many questions, etc

bomber /'bɒmər/ *noun* [C] **1** an aircraft that drops bombs **2** someone who puts a bomb somewhere

bombshell /'bɒmʃel/ *noun* [C] *informal* a piece of usually bad news that surprises you very much *He **dropped a bombshell** by announcing that he was quitting the sport.*

bona fide /ˌbəʊnə'faɪdi/ *adjective* real and honest *Make sure you are dealing with a bona fide company.*

bonanza /bə'nænzə/ *noun* [C] a situation in which many people are successful and get a lot of money *The rise in house prices meant that sellers enjoyed a bonanza.*

WORD PARTNERS FOR *bond*

create/forge/form/strengthen a bond • a close bond • a bond with sb/between sb and sb

---

bond¹ /bɒnd/ *noun* [C] **1** an interest, experience, or feeling that makes two things feel connected *A love of opera **created a bond between** them.* **2** an official document from a government or company to show that you have given them money that they will pay back with a certain amount of extra money

bond² /bɒnd/ *verb* **1** [I, T] If two things bond, they stick together, or if you bond them, you make them stick together. *This glue **bonds** wood and metal in seconds.* **2** [I] to develop a strong relationship with someone *Physical contact helps a mother **bond with** her baby.*

bondage /'bɒndɪdʒ/ *noun* [U] when someone is completely controlled by something or is a slave (= owned by the person they work for)

o⌐bone¹ /bəʊn/ *noun* **1** [C, U] one of the hard pieces that make the structure inside a person or animal *He broke a bone in his hand.* **2** a **bone of contention** something that people argue about **3** have a **bone to pick with sb** *informal* to want to talk to someone because you are annoyed about something they have done **4** make no bones about sth/doing sth to say what you think or feel, without being embarrassed *She made no bones about her reluctance to work with me.*

bone

bone² /bəʊn/ *verb* [T] to remove the bones from meat or fish

'bone ˌmarrow *noun* [U] the soft substance inside bones

bonfire /'bɒnfaɪər/ *noun* [C] a large fire outside, often used for burning waste

bonkers /'bɒŋkəz/ *adjective informal* crazy

bonnet /'bɒnɪt/ *noun* [C] **1** *UK* (*US* hood) the metal cover of a car's engine ⊃See colour picture **Car** on page Centre 7. **2** a hat that you tie under your face

bonus /'bəʊnəs/ *noun* [C] **1** an extra amount of money that you are given, especially because you have worked hard *All employees received a bonus of £500.* **2** another pleasant thing in addition to something you were expecting *The sunny weather was an **added bonus**.*

bony /'bəʊni/ *adjective* very thin, so that you can see or feel bones *bony elbows*

boo /buː/ *verb* [I, T] **booing**, *past* **booed** to shout the word "boo" to show that you do not like a speech, performance, etc • **boo** *noun* [C]

boob /buːb/ *noun* [C] *informal* **1** a woman's breast **2** a silly mistake

booby prize /'buːbiˌpraɪz/ *noun* [C] a prize that you get if you finish last in a competition

booby trap /'buːbiˌtræp/ *noun* [C] something dangerous, especially a bomb, that is hidden somewhere that looks safe • **booby-trap** *verb* [T] [often passive] *His car was booby-trapped.*

o⌐book¹ /bʊk/ *noun* **1** [C] a set of pages fastened together in a cover for people to read *a book about animals* **2** a book of stamps/tickets, etc a set of stamps, tickets, etc that are fastened together inside a cover **3** [C] a set of pages fastened together in a cover and used for writing on *an **address book*** **4** do sth by the book to do something exactly as the rules tell you **5** be in sb's good/bad books *UK informal* If you are in someone's good books, they are pleased with you, and if you are in their bad books, they are angry with you. ⊃See also: cookery book, take a leaf¹ out of sb's book, phone book, reference book.

o⌐book² /bʊk/ *verb* **1** ARRANGE [I, T] to arrange to use or do something at a particular time in the future *to book a ticket/hotel room* ○ *We've booked a trip to Spain for next month.* ○ *Sorry, the hotel is **fully booked** (= has no more rooms).* **2** CRIME [T] to officially accuse someone of a crime *Detectives **booked** him for resisting arrest.* **3** SPORT [T] *UK* If a sports official books you, they write an official record of something you have done wrong. *The referee **booked** two players **for** fighting during the game.*

book in/book into sth *UK* to say that you have arrived when you get to a hotel

book sb in/book sb into sth *mainly UK* to arrange for someone to stay at a hotel

bookcase /'bʊkkeɪs/ *noun* [C] a piece of furniture with shelves for putting books on ⊃See colour picture **The Living Room** on page Centre 4.

'book ˌclub *noun* [C] a group of people who meet regularly to talk about books they have read

bookie /'bʊki/ *noun* [C] *informal* someone whose job is to take and pay out money that people risk trying to guess the result of horse races, sports events, etc

---

| j yes | k cat | ŋ ring | ʃ she | θ thin | ð this | ʒ decision | dʒ jar | tʃ chip | æ cat | e bed | ə ago | ɪ sit | i cosy | ɒ hot | ʌ run | ʊ put |

accept/cancel/make/take a booking • an advance booking • a booking for sth • a booking fee/form

booking /'bʊkɪŋ/ noun [C, U] mainly UK an arrangement you make to have a hotel room, tickets, etc at a particular time in the future *advance booking*

bookkeeping /'bʊk,kiːpɪŋ/ noun [U] recording the money that an organization or business spends and receives • **bookkeeper** noun [C]

booklet /'bʊklət/ noun [C] a small, thin book that contains information *The tourist office has booklets about the area.*

bookmaker /'bʊk,meɪkəʳ/ noun [C] a bookie

bookmark¹ /'bʊkmɑːk/ noun [C] **1** something you put in a book so you can find the page you want **2** a record of an address on the Internet so that you can quickly find something again *Add this website to your bookmarks.*

bookmark² /'bʊkmɑːk/ verb [T] to make a record of the address of an Internet document in your computer so that you can find it again easily

books /bʊks/ noun [plural] the written financial records of a business or organization

bookseller /'bʊk,seləʳ/ noun [C] a person or company that sells books

bookshelf /'bʊkʃelf/ noun [C] plural **bookshelves** a shelf for holding books

bookshop /'bʊkʃɒp/ UK (US **bookstore** /'bʊkstɔːʳ/) noun [C] a shop that sells books

bookworm /'bʊkwɜːm/ noun [C] informal someone who enjoys reading very much

boom¹ /buːm/ noun [C] **1** a period when there is a big increase in sales or profits *an economic boom* ○ *The 1990's saw a boom in computer sales.* **2** a loud, deep sound ⊃See also: baby boom.

boom² /buːm/ verb [I] **1** If something is booming, it is increasing or becoming more successful or popular very quickly. *House prices are booming.* **2** to make a loud, deep sound, or to speak in a loud, deep voice

boomerang /'buːmˀræŋ/ noun [C] a curved piece of wood that comes back to you when you throw it

boon /buːn/ noun [C] something helpful that improves your life [usually singular] *Microwaves are a boon for busy people.*

give sb/sth a boost • receive a boost • a huge/major/massive/much-needed boost • a confidence/morale boost • a boost to sth • a boost for sb

boost¹ /buːst/ noun [C] something that makes you feel more confident and happy, or that helps something increase or improve *Increased tourism was a major boost to the local economy.*

boost² /buːst/ verb [T] to increase or improve something *Getting the job has boosted Elizabeth's confidence.*

booster /'buːstəʳ/ noun **1 a confidence/morale, etc booster** something that makes you feel happier or more confident **2** [C] an engine on a spacecraft that gives extra power for the first part of a flight

boot¹ /buːt/ noun [C] **1** a strong shoe that covers your foot and part of your leg *a pair of boots* ⊃See colour picture Clothes on pages Centre 8,9 . **2** UK (US **trunk**) a closed space at the back of a car for storing things in ⊃See colour picture Car on page Centre 7. **3 get/be given the boot** informal to be told that you must leave your job **4 too big for your boots** UK informal (US **too big for your britches** informal) behaving as if you are more important or more clever than you really are ⊃See also: car boot sale.

boot² /buːt/ verb [T] informal to kick someone or something
boot sb out informal to make someone leave a place or job

bootcut /'buːtkʌt/ adjective bootleg

booth /buːð/ noun [C] a small area that is separated from a larger public area, especially used for doing something privately *a telephone booth*

bootleg /'buːtleg/ (also **bootcut**) adjective bootleg trousers are wider at the bottom than at the knee • **bootlegs** noun [plural]

booty /'buːti/ noun [U] valuable things stolen by thieves or by an army in a war

booze¹ /buːz/ noun [U] informal alcoholic drinks

booze² /buːz/ verb [I] informal to drink alcohol

cross the border • across/on/over the border • the border between [France and Spain/Switzerland and Italy, etc] • [Germany's/Syria's, etc] border with [France/Lebanon, etc] • the [French/Mexican, etc] side of the border • border controls/guards

o⁻**border**¹ /'bɔːdəʳ/ noun [C] **1** the line that separates two countries or states *the border between France and Spain* ○ *We crossed the border from Canada into the US.* **2** a strip around the edge of something for decoration *white plates with a blue border*

border² /'bɔːdəʳ/ verb [T] **1** to form a line around the edge of something [often passive] *The fields are bordered by tall trees.* **2** to have a border with another country [often passive] *Spain is bordered by France and Portugal.*
border on sth to almost be a more extreme thing *Her anger bordered on aggression.*

borderline¹ /'bɔːdˀlaɪn/ adjective If something or someone is borderline, it is not clear if they are good enough or if they will succeed. *Borderline cases should take the exam again.*

borderline² /'bɔːdˀlaɪn/ noun [no plural] the point where one feeling, quality, level, etc ends and another one begins *My work was on the borderline between two grades.*

bore¹ /bɔːʳ/ verb **1** [T] to make someone feel bored *His war stories really bore me.* **2** [I, T] to make a hole in something hard with a tool

bore² /bɔːʳ/ noun **1** [C] someone who talks too

| ɑː arm | ɜː her | iː see | ɔː saw | uː too | aɪ my | aʊ how | eə hair | eɪ day | əʊ no | ɪə near | ɔɪ boy | ʊə poor | aɪə fire | aʊə sour |

much about things that are not interesting **2** [no plural] a situation or job that annoys you because it causes difficulties or is not interesting *It's a real bore not having a car.*

bore³ /bɔːʳ/ *past tense of* bear

o⌐**bored** /bɔːd/ *adjective* feeling tired and unhappy because something is not interesting or because you have nothing to do *I'm **bored with** doing homework.* ○ *We were **bored stiff** (= extremely bored) in her lessons.* ● **boredom** /ˈbɔːdəm/ *noun* [U] when you are bored *I nearly died of boredom.*

OTHER WAYS OF SAYING *boring*

We often use **bland** when describing food: *This sauce is really **bland**, it doesn't taste of anything.*

If a film, play, book, etc. or a person is boring, you can say that they are **dull**: *I find her writing a bit **dull**.*

Monotonous is often used about something that you listen to: *The teacher had a really **monotonous** voice and I almost fell asleep.*

When describing an activity, **tedious** is sometimes used: *You have to fill in various forms, which is a bit **tedious**.*

If speech or writing is boring because it is too long, we can describe it as **long-winded**: *He gave this really **long-winded** explanation about why he'd changed his mind.*

---

o⌐**boring** /ˈbɔːrɪŋ/ *adjective* not interesting or exciting *a boring job* ○ *The film was so boring, I fell asleep.*

COMMON LEARNER ERROR

bored or **boring**?

Bored is used to describe how someone feels about something.

He didn't enjoy the lesson because he was bored.

~~He didn't enjoy the lesson because he was boring.~~

If something or someone is **boring**, they make you feel bored.

The book was long and boring.

---

o⌐**born¹** /bɔːn/ *verb* **be born 1** When a person or animal is born, they come out of their mother's body and start to exist. *She was born in London in 1973.* ○ *an American-born writer* (= born in America) **2** If an idea is born, it starts to exist.

born² /bɔːn/ *adjective* **a born actor/leader/ teacher, etc** someone who has a natural ability to act, lead, teach, etc

born-again /ˌbɔːnəˈgen/ *adjective* **a born-again Christian** someone who has become a very enthusiastic member of the Christian religion

borne /bɔːn/ *past participle of* bear

borough /ˈbʌrə/ Ⓤ /ˈbɜːrəʊ/ *noun* [C] a town or part of a city

o⌐**borrow** /ˈbɒrəʊ/ *verb* **1** [USE] [T] to use something that belongs to someone else and give it back later *Can I borrow a pen please?* ○ *I borrowed*

*the book **from** my sister.* **2** [MONEY] [I, T] to take money from a bank or financial organization and pay it back over a period of time **3** [IDEA] [T] to take and use a word or idea *The English word 'rucksack' is **borrowed from** German.*

borrower /ˈbɒrəʊəʳ/ *noun* [C] someone who borrows money

bosom /ˈbʊzᵊm/ *noun* **1** [C] a woman's breasts **2** **a bosom buddy/pal, etc** a very good friend

o⌐**boss¹** /bɒs/ *noun* [C] someone who is responsible for employees and tells them what to do *I'll ask my boss if I can leave work early tomorrow.*

boss² /bɒs/ (*also* **boss about/around**) *verb* [T] to tell someone what they should do all the time *My older brother is always bossing me about.*

bossy /ˈbɒsi/ *adjective* always telling other people what to do ● **bossiness** *noun* [U]

botanist /ˈbɒtᵊnɪst/ *noun* [C] someone who studies plants

botany /ˈbɒtᵊni/ *noun* [U] the scientific study of plants ● **botanical** /bəˈtænɪkᵊl/ (*also* **botanic** /bəˈtænɪk/) *adjective* relating to botany

botch /bɒtʃ/ (*also* **botch up**) *verb* [T] to spoil something by doing it badly *a botched robbery*

o⌐**both** /bəʊθ/ *pronoun, determiner, quantifier* **1** used to talk about two people or things *The children both have red hair.* ○ **Both of my** *sisters are teachers.* ○ *Would you like cream, ice cream, or both?* **2** **both...and...** used to emphasize that you are talking about two people or things *Both Jack and his wife are keen chess players.* ⊃See also: have the **best³** of both worlds.

o⌐**bother¹** /ˈbɒðəʳ/ *verb* **1** [ANNOY] [T] to annoy someone by trying to get their attention when they do not want to see you or talk to you *Sorry to bother you, but could you spare any change?* **2** [WORRY] [T] to make someone feel worried or upset *Living on my own doesn't bother me at all.* **3** [DO] [I, T] to make the effort to do something [+ doing sth] *Don't bother making the bed - I'll do it later.* ○ [+ to do sth] *He didn't even bother to call.* **4** **can't be bothered** *informal* If you can't be bothered to do something, you are too lazy or tired to do it. [+ to do sth] *I can't be bothered to iron my clothes.* **5** **not bothered** *UK informal* If you are not bothered about something, it is not important to you and does not worry you. *"Do you want tea or coffee?" "Either, I'm not bothered."*

bother² /ˈbɒðəʳ/ *noun* [U] trouble or problems *"Are you sure you don't mind taking me?" "No, it's no bother, really!"*

bothered /ˈbɒðəd/ *adjective* [never before noun] If you are bothered about something, it is important to you and you are worried about it. *He's very **bothered about** what other people think.*

Botox /ˈbəʊtɒks/ *noun* [U] *trademark* Botulinum Toxin: a drug used in a person's face to make it look smooth and young ● **Botox** *verb* [T]

o⌐**bottle¹** /ˈbɒtl/ *noun* [C] a container for liquids, usually made of glass or plastic, with a narrow top *an empty bottle* ○ *a bottle of wine* ⊃See also: **hot-water bottle**.

bottle² /ˈbɒtl/ *verb* [T] to put liquid into a bottle [often passive] *This wine was bottled in France.*

○ *bottled beer/water*

bottle sth up to not allow yourself to show or talk about your feelings

bottle ‚bank *noun* [C] *UK* a large container outside, where you can put empty bottles so that the glass can be used again

bottleneck /'bɒtlnek/ *noun* [C] **1** something that causes a process to happen more slowly than it should **2** a narrow part of a road where traffic moves slowly

○**bottom¹** /'bɒtəm/ *noun* **1** LOWEST PART [C] the lowest part of something [usually singular] *Click on the icon at the bottom of the page.* **2** FLAT SURFACE [C] the flat surface on the lowest side of something [usually singular] *There was a price tag on the bottom of the box.* **3** LOWEST POSITION [no plural] the lowest position in a group, organization, etc *He got bad exam marks and is at the bottom of the class.* **4** SEA/RIVER ETC [no plural] the ground under a river, lake, or sea *Divers found the wreck on the bottom of the ocean.* **5** FURTHEST PART [no plural] the part of a road or area of land that is furthest from where you are *Go to the bottom of the road and turn left.* **6** PART OF THE BODY [C] the part of your body that you sit on **7 be at the bottom of sth** to be the cause of a problem or situation **8 get to the bottom of sth** to discover the truth about a situation ⊃See also: **rock bottom**, from **top¹** to bottom.

bottom² /'bɒtəm/ *adjective* [always before noun] in the lowest position *the bottom drawer*

bottomless /'bɒtəmləs/ *adjective* **a bottomless pit** a supply, especially of money, that has no limit

the ‚bottom 'line *noun* the most important fact in a situation *The bottom line is that if you don't work, you'll fail the test.*

bough /baʊ/ *noun* [C] *literary* a large branch on a tree

bought /bɔːt/ *past of* buy

boulder /'bəʊldəʳ/ *noun* [C] a very large rock

boulevard /'buːləvɑːd/ *noun* [C] a wide road in a city, usually with trees along it

bounce¹ /baʊns/ *verb* **1** BALL [I, T] to hit a surface and then move quickly away, or to make something do this *The ball bounced high into the air.* **2** JUMP [I] to jump up and down several times on a soft surface *The children loved bouncing on the bed.* **3 bounce along/around/into, etc** to move somewhere in a happy and energetic way *Sarah bounced into the room with a big smile on her face.* **4** NOT PAY [I, T] If a cheque (= piece of printed paper you write on to pay for things) bounces, or a bank bounces it, the bank will not pay it because there is not enough money in the account.

bounce back 1 to be successful or happy again after a failure, disappointment, etc *After a terrible start the team bounced back and won the game.* **2** If an email bounces back, it is returned to you because the address is not correct or there is a computer problem.

bounce² /baʊns/ *noun* [C, U] when something bounces, or the quality that makes something able to bounce

bouncer /'baʊnsəʳ/ *noun* [C] someone whose job is to stand at the door of a bar, party, etc and keep out people who are not wanted

bouncy /'baʊnsi/ *adjective* **1** happy and full of energy *She's very bouncy and confident.* **2** able to bounce *bouncy balls*

bound¹ /baʊnd/ *adjective* **1 bound to do sth** certain to do something, or certain to happen *You're bound to feel nervous before your driving test.* **2 bound up with sth** closely connected with something *A country's culture is bound up with its language and history.* **3** [never before noun] having a moral or legal duty to do something *The witness was bound by an oath to tell the truth.* **4** [never before noun] travelling towards a particular place *He was on a train bound for Berlin.*

bound² /baʊnd/ *verb* **bound across/down/into, etc** to move quickly with large steps or jumps *Guy bounded across the room to answer the phone.*

bound³ /baʊnd/ *noun* [C] a big jump ⊃See also: by/in leaps (**leap²**) and bounds.

bound⁴ /baʊnd/ *past of* bind

boundary /'baʊndᵊri/ *noun* [C] **1** a line that divides two areas or forms an edge around an area *The mountains mark the boundary between the two countries.* **2** a limit *Such violence is beyond the boundaries of civilized conduct.*

boundless /'baʊndləs/ *adjective* having no limit *He has boundless energy/enthusiasm.*

bounds /baʊndz/ *noun* **1** [plural] legal or social limits *They have overstepped the bounds of good taste.* **2 out of bounds** If a place is out of bounds, you are not allowed to go there. *The staff room is out of bounds to students.*

bounty /'baʊnti/ *noun* **1** [C, U] a large or generous amount of something **2** [C] an amount of money paid as a reward

bouquet /buˈkeɪ/ *noun* [C] flowers that are tied together in an attractive way

bourbon /'bɜːbən/ *noun* [C, U] a type of American whisky (= strong alcoholic drink)

bourgeois /'bɔːʒwɑː/ *adjective* typical of middle class people who are too interested in money and correct social behaviour *bourgeois values* ● **the bourgeoisie** /ˌbɔːʒwɑːˈziː/ *noun* [group] the middle class, that owns most of society's money

bout /baʊt/ *noun* [C] **1** a short period of activity or illness *a bout of depression* **2** a fight in boxing

boutique /buːˈtiːk/ *noun* [C] a small shop that sells fashionable clothes

bovine /'bəʊvaɪn/ *adjective* relating to cows

bow¹ /baʊ/ *verb* [I, T] to bend your head or body forward in order to show respect or to thank an audience *The actors all bowed after the performance.* ○ *We bowed our heads in prayer.*

bow out to leave a job or stop doing an activity, usually after a long time *He bowed out of politics at the age of 70.*

bow to sth/sb to do what someone else wants you to do *The government are refusing to bow to public pressure.*

bow² /baʊ/ *noun* [C] **1** when you bow *The actors came back on stage and took a bow.* **2** the front part of a ship

bow³ /bəʊ/ *noun* [C] **1** [KNOT] a knot with two curved parts and two loose ends, that is used to tie shoes or as decoration **2** [MUSIC] a long, thin piece of wood with hair stretched between the ends, used to play some musical instruments **3** [WEAPON] a piece of curved wood with string fixed to both ends, used for shooting arrows

bowel /baʊəl/ *noun* [C] the long tube that carries solid waste from your stomach out of your body [usually plural] *He's got trouble with his bowels.*

o→**bowl¹** /bəʊl/ *noun* [C] a round, deep dish used for holding soup and other food *a bowl of rice/ soup*

bowl² /bəʊl/ *verb* [I, T] **1** to roll a ball along a surface as part of a game **2** in cricket, to throw a ball to the person who has to hit it

bowler /'bəʊlə'/ *noun* [C] in cricket, the player who throws the ball so someone can hit it ⊃See colour picture **Sports 2** on page Centre 15.

bowler 'hat *UK* (*US* derby) *noun* [C] a round, hard, black hat worn by men, especially in the past

bowling /'bəʊlɪŋ/ *noun* [U] a game in which you roll a large ball along a wooden track in order to knock down bottle-shaped objects

bowls /bəʊlz/ *noun* [U] *UK* a game in which you roll large balls as close as possible to a smaller ball

bow 'tie *noun* [C] a piece of cloth around the neck in the shape of a bow that men sometimes wear, especially at formal events

o→**box¹** /bɒks/ *noun* **1** [CONTAINER] [C] a square or rectangular container *a cardboard box ○ a box of chocolates/matches* ⊃See picture at **container**. **2** [SQUARE SPACE] [C] a small square on a page that gives you information or where you write information *Tick the box if you would like more details.* **3** [SMALL PLACE] [C] a small area of a theatre, court, etc that is separate from where other people are sitting **4 the box** *informal* the television *What's on the box tonight?* ⊃See also: **phone box, post box, witness box.**

box² /bɒks/ *verb* **1** [I, T] to do the sport of boxing **2** [T] (*also* **box up**) to put something in a box *We boxed up the old books.*

box sb/sth in to move so close to someone or something that they cannot move [often passive] *When I returned I found that my car had been boxed in.*

boxer /'bɒksə'/ *noun* [C] someone who does the sport of boxing

boxers /'bɒksəz/ (*also* '**boxer ,shorts**) *noun* [plural] loose underwear worn by men ⊃See colour picture **Clothes** on page Centre 9.

boxing /'bɒksɪŋ/ *noun* [U] a sport in which two people hit each other while wearing big, leather gloves (= pieces of clothing for your hands) ⊃See colour picture **Sports 1** on page Centre 14.

boxing

'**Boxing ,Day** *noun* [C, U] 26 December, a public holiday in Britain and Canada

'**box ,office** *noun* [C] the place in a theatre, cinema, etc where you buy tickets

o→**boy¹** /bɔɪ/ *noun* **1** [C] a male child or young man *We've got three children - a boy and two girls.* **2 the boys** *informal* a group of male friends *Steve's gone out with the boys.*

boy² /bɔɪ/ (*also* **oh boy**) *exclamation* used when you are excited or pleased *Boy, that was good!*

'**boy ,band** *noun* [C] a pop music group made up of young men who sing and dance

boycott /'bɔɪkɒt/ *noun* [C] when someone refuses to buy, use, or do something because they do not approve of it *Environmental groups have called for a boycott of the company's products.* ● **boycott** *verb* [T] *Several countries boycotted the international peace talks.*

o→**boyfriend** /'bɔɪfrend/ *noun* [C] a man or boy who someone is having a romantic relationship with

boyhood /'bɔɪhʊd/ *noun* [U] the part of a male's life when they are a boy

boyish /'bɔɪɪʃ/ *adjective* like a boy *boyish charm*

,**Boy 'Scout** *UK* (*US* '**Boy ,Scout**) *noun* [C] a boy who belongs to an organization that teaches boys practical skills

bra /brɑː/ *noun* [C] a piece of woman's underwear that supports the breasts ⊃See colour picture **Clothes** on page Centre 9.

brace¹ /breɪs/ *verb* **brace yourself** to prepare for something difficult or unpleasant *I braced myself for bad news.*

brace² /breɪs/ *noun* [C] **1** something that supports or holds something in the correct position *He wore a neck brace for months after the accident.* **2** a wire object that some children wear to make their teeth straight

bracelet /'breɪslət/ *noun* [C] a piece of jewellery that you wear around your wrist ⊃See picture at **jewellery.**

braces /'breɪsɪz/ *UK* (*US* **suspenders**) *noun* [plural] two straps fixed to a pair of trousers that go over your shoulders and stop the trousers from falling down

bracing /breɪsɪŋ/ *adjective* Bracing weather or a bracing activity makes you feel cold but healthy and full of energy. *bracing sea air ○ a bracing walk*

bracket¹ /'brækɪt/ *noun* [C] **1** a group of people whose ages, taxes, etc are between two limits *Most heart attack victims are in the 45-65 age bracket.* **2** a piece of metal, wood, etc, that is fixed to a wall to support something, especially a shelf

bracket² /'brækɪt/ *verb* [T] **1** to put curved lines ( ) around words, phrases, numbers, etc to make them separate **2** to consider two or more people or things to be similar [often passive] *Canadian accents are often bracketed with American accents.*

brackets /'brækɪts/ (*also* **parentheses**) *noun* [plural] *UK* two curved lines ( ) used around extra information or information that should be considered as separate from the main part

brag /bræg/ *verb* [I] **bragging,** *past* **bragged** to talk with too much pride about what you have done or what you own *He's always **bragging** about how much money he earns.*

braid¹ /breɪd/ *noun* **1** [C] *US* (*UK* **plait**) a single piece of hair made by twisting three thinner pieces over and under each other **2** [U] a thin piece of cloth or twisted threads used for decorating clothes

braid² /breɪd/ *US* (*UK* **plait**) *verb* [T] to twist three pieces of hair over and under each other

braille /breɪl/ *noun* [U] a system of printing for blind people, using raised patterns that they read by touching

o▪**brain** /breɪn/ *noun* **1** [C] the organ inside your head that controls your thoughts, feelings, and movements *brain damage* **2** [C] *informal* an extremely intelligent person [usually plural] *This university attracts some of the **best brains** in the country.* **3 brains** intelligence *He has brains and good looks.* **4 have sth on the brain** *informal* to think or talk about something all the time *You've got football on the brain!* **5 the brains behind sth** *informal* the person who has planned and organized something successful *Anthony is the brains behind the project.*

brain

brainchild /'breɪntʃaɪld/ *noun* **the brainchild of sb** someone's new and clever idea or invention *The project is the brainchild of a well-known Japanese designer.*

brainstorm /'breɪnstɔːm/ *US* (*UK* **brainwave**) *noun* [C] a sudden, clever idea

brainstorming /'breɪnstɔːmɪŋ/ *noun* [U] when a group of people meet to develop new ideas *a **brainstorming** session*

brainwash /'breɪnwɒʃ/ *verb* [T] to make someone believe something by telling them that it is true many times [+ into + doing sth] *Advertising often brainwashes people into buying things they do not really need.* ● **brainwashing** *noun* [U]

brainwave /'breɪnweɪv/ *UK* (*US* **brainstorm**) *noun* [C] a sudden, clever idea

brainy /'breɪni/ *adjective informal* clever

WORD PARTNERS FOR **brake**

apply/hit/slam on the brakes ● the brakes **fail**

brake¹ /breɪk/ *noun* [C] **1** the part of a vehicle that makes it stop or go more slowly **2** something that stops or slows the progress of something *High inflation has **put the brakes on** economic growth.*

brake² /breɪk/ *verb* [I] to make a vehicle stop or move more slowly, using its brake

brake ,pedal *noun* [C] the part of a car which you push with your foot to make it go more slowly ⊃See colour picture **Car** on page Centre 7.

o▪**branch¹** /brɑːnʃ/ *noun* [C] **1** [TREE] one of the many parts of a tree that grows out from its trunk (= main, vertical part) ⊃See picture at **tree**.

2 [BUSINESS] one of several shops, offices, etc that are part of a company or organization *Lloyd's bank has branches all over the country.* **3** [SUBJECT] a part of a subject *Neurology is a branch of medicine.*

branch² /brɑːnʃ/ (*also* **branch off**) *verb* [I] If a road, path, etc branches, it separates into two or more roads, paths, etc.

branch out to start to do something different from what you usually do, especially in your job *After working in publishing, she branched out into journalism.*

brand¹ /brænd/ *noun* [C] **1** a product that is made by a particular company *Which brand of toothpaste do you use?* **2** a particular type of something *a team that plays a distinctive brand of football*

brand² /brænd/ *verb* [T] **1** to describe someone or something in a way that makes them seem bad *The media branded him a liar.* **2** to burn a mark on an animal to show who owns it

brandish /'brændɪʃ/ *verb* [T] to wave something in the air, especially a weapon *He came running into the room, brandishing a gun.*

'brand ,name *noun* [C] the special name that a company gives to a product

,brand 'new *adjective* completely new

brandy /'brændi/ *noun* [C, U] a strong alcoholic drink made from wine

brash /bræʃ/ *adjective* too confident *a brash young businessman*

brass /brɑːs/ *noun* [U] **1** a shiny yellow metal *a door with a brass handle* **2** the group of musical instruments made from brass *a brass band*

brat /bræt/ *noun* [C] a child who behaves badly *a spoilt brat*

bravado /brə'vɑːdəʊ/ *noun* [U] behaviour that is intended to make people admire you for your bravery and confidence

o▪**brave¹** /breɪv/ *adjective* showing no fear of dangerous or difficult situations *He died after a brave fight against cancer.* ● **bravely** *adverb*

brave² /breɪv/ *verb* [T] to deal with a dangerous or unpleasant situation in a brave way *Crowds braved the cold weather to watch the game.*

bravery /'breɪv°ri/ *noun* [U] when someone is brave

bravo /brɑː'vəʊ/ *exclamation* something you shout to show that you approve of something, for example a performance

brawl /brɔːl/ *noun* [C] a noisy fight, usually in public *a drunken brawl in a bar* ● **brawl** *verb* [I]

brazen /'breɪz°n/ *adjective* not feeling at all ashamed about your bad behaviour *a brazen cheat* ● **brazenly** *adverb*

BRB *internet abbreviation for* be right back: used when you stop taking part in a discussion on the Internet

WORD PARTNERS FOR **breach**

(a) breach **of sth** ● be **in** breach of sth ● a **flagrant** breach of sth

breach¹ /briːtʃ/ *noun* **1** [C, U] when someone breaks a rule, agreement, or law *a policy that* is **in breach of** international law o He was sued for **breach of** contract. **2** [C] formal a serious disagreement between two groups, countries, etc

breach² /briːtʃ/ verb [T] to break a rule, law, or agreement

bread

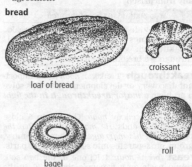

croissant

loaf of bread

bagel

roll

o--**bread** /bred/ noun [U] a basic food made by mixing and baking flour, water, and sometimes yeast (= substance that makes it rise) a **slice of bread** o a **loaf of** white **bread** ⊃See also: the best/greatest **thing** since sliced bread.

breadcrumbs /'bredkrʌmz/ noun [plural] very small pieces of dry bread, used in cooking

breadth /bretθ/ noun [U, no plural] **1** the distance from one side of something to the other side a swimming pool with a breadth of 10 metres and a length of 50 metres **2** sb's **breadth of experience/knowledge/interest**, etc the great number of different things that someone has done, knows, is interested in, etc ⊃See also: the **length** and breadth of sth.

breadwinner /'bred,wɪnəʳ/ noun [C] the person who earns the money in a family

break

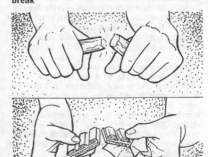

o--**break¹** /breɪk/ verb past tense **broke**, past participle **broken 1** [SEPARATE] [I, T] to separate into two or more pieces, or to make something separate into two or more pieces The vase fell on the floor and broke. o They had to break a window to get in. **2 break your arm/leg**, etc to damage a

bone in your arm/leg, etc Carolyn broke her leg in a skiing accident. **3** [NOT WORK] [I, T] If you break a machine, object, etc, or if it breaks, it stops working because it is damaged. Who broke the video? **4 break an agreement/promise/rule**, etc to not do what you should do according to an agreement/promise/rule, etc Police stopped him for breaking the speed limit. **5 break the law** to do something illegal **6 break the news to sb** to tell someone about something unpleasant that has happened **7 break the silence** to make a noise, speak, etc and end a period of silence The silence was broken by a sudden knock at the door. **8 break a habit/routine**, etc to stop doing something that you usually do **9 break a record** to do something faster, better, etc than anyone else He broke the world record for the 200m. **10** [REST] [I, T] to stop the activity you are doing to have a short rest Let's **break for** five minutes and have a drink. **11** [BECOME KNOWN] [I, T] If news or a story breaks, or if someone breaks it, it becomes known by the public for the first time. **12** [WEATHER] [I] UK If the weather breaks, it changes suddenly, and usually becomes worse. **13** [VOICE] [I] When a boy's voice breaks, it becomes deeper and sounds like a man's voice. **14** [WAVE] [I] When a wave breaks, it reaches its highest point as it moves towards the land, and then becomes flat and white. **15** [STORM] [I] If a storm breaks, it starts suddenly. **16 break even** to not make money but also not lose money **17 break free/loose** to suddenly escape or become separate from something **18 dawn/day breaks** When dawn (= early morning)/day breaks, the sky becomes lighter because the sun is rising. ⊃See also: break new **ground¹**, break sb's **heart**, break the **ice¹**, break the **mould¹**, break ranks (**rank¹**).

break away 1 to suddenly leave or escape from someone who is holding you **2** to stop being part of a group because you disagree with them Some members broke away to form a new political party.

break down 1 [MACHINE] If a machine or vehicle breaks down, it stops working. My car broke down on the way to work. **2** [COMMUNI-CATION] If a system, relationship, or discussion breaks down, it fails because there is a problem or disagreement. Their marriage broke down after only two years. **3** [CRY] to become very upset and start crying

break sth down to divide something into smaller, simpler parts

break in to get into a building or car using force, usually to steal something

break sth in to wear something new, usually shoes, for short periods of time to make them more comfortable

break into sth 1 to get into a building or car using force, usually to steal something **2** to suddenly start doing something The crowd broke into a cheer when he came on stage.

break (sth) off to separate a part from a larger piece, or to become separate from something He broke off a piece of chocolate.

break off to suddenly stop speaking or

B

doing something *She broke off in the middle of a sentence.*

break sth off to end a relationship *She broke off the engagement just two weeks before the wedding.*

break out 1 If a fire, war, disease, etc breaks out, it starts suddenly. *A fight broke out among the crowd.* **2** to escape from prison *to break out of jail* **3 break out in a rash/sweat, etc** to suddenly have spots or sweat (= salty liquid) appear on your skin

break through sth to force your way through something that is holding you back *Protesters broke through the barriers.*

break (sth) up to divide into many pieces, or to divide something into many pieces *The company has been broken up and sold.*

break up 1 If people break up, they stop having a relationship or stop working together. *He's just broken up with his girlfriend.* **2** UK When schools or colleges break up, the classes end and the holidays begin.

break² /breɪk/ *noun* [C] **1** STOP when you stop an activity for a short time, usually to rest or to eat *a coffee/tea break* ○ *Take a break and come back after lunch.* **2** HOLIDAY a holiday or period of time away from work, school, etc the *spring break* ○ *a weekend break to Paris* **3** OPPORTUNITY a lucky opportunity *His big break came when he was offered a part in a TV series.* **4** DAMAGE where something has separated in an accident *a break in the bone* **5 a break with sth** when you end a relationship, connection, or way of doing something *a break with tradition*

breakable /ˈbreɪkəbl/ *adjective* able to break easily *a breakable vase*

breakage /ˈbreɪkɪdʒ/ *noun* [C, U] when something has been broken *The delivery company must pay for any breakages.*

breakaway /ˈbreɪkəweɪ/ *adjective* **a breakaway group/republic/region, etc** a group/region, etc that has separated itself from a larger group or region because of a disagreement

breakdown /ˈbreɪkdaʊn/ *noun* [C] **1** ILLNESS (*also* **nervous breakdown**) a short period of mental illness when people are too ill to continue with their normal lives *to have a breakdown* **2** FAILURE when something such as communication or a relationship fails or ends *a breakdown in the peace talks* **3** EXPLANATION a short explanation of the details of something *I need a breakdown of the costs involved.* **4** NOT WORKING when a vehicle or machine stops working for a period of time

ꞏ**breakfast** /ˈbrekfəst/ *noun* [C] the food you eat in the morning after you wake up *She had breakfast in bed this morning.* ● **breakfast** *verb* [I] ⇨See also: **bed and breakfast, continental breakfast, English breakfast.**

break-in /ˈbreɪkɪn/ *noun* [C] when someone forces their way into a building or car, usually to steal something *There has been another break-in at the office.*

ꞏ**breaking point** *noun* [U] when a situation has become so bad that it cannot continue *Things had become so bad at work they'd*

almost **reached breaking point**.

breakneck /ˈbreɪknek/ *adjective* **breakneck speed/growth, etc** dangerously fast speed/growth, etc

breakout /ˈbreɪkaʊt/ *noun* [C] an escape, usually from prison

WORD PARTNERS FOR *breakthrough*

make/provide a breakthrough ● a breakthrough **comes** ● a **big/crucial/major/real** breakthrough ● a **medical/scientific** breakthrough ● a breakthrough **in** sth

breakthrough /ˈbreɪkθruː/ *noun* [C] an important discovery or development that helps solve a problem *a major breakthrough in the fight against cancer*

break-up /ˈbreɪkʌp/ *noun* [C] **1** when a close relationship ends *He moved away after the break-up of his marriage.* **2** when a country, group, etc separates into several smaller parts

breast /brest/ *noun* **1** [C] one of the two soft, round parts on a woman's chest **2** [C, U] the front part of a bird's body, or the meat from this area *chicken breast*

breast-feed /ˈbrestfiːd/ *verb* [I, T] *past* **breast-fed** If a woman breast-feeds, she gives a baby milk from her breast. ● **breast-feeding** *noun* [U]

breaststroke /ˈbreststrəʊk/ *noun* [U] a way of swimming in which you push your arms forward and then to the side, while you kick your legs backwards

breath /breθ/ *noun* **1** [U] the air that comes out of your lungs *His breath smells of garlic.* **2** [C] when air goes into or out of your lungs *She took a deep breath before she started.* **3 be out of breath** to be breathing quickly because you have been running, walking fast, etc **4 catch your breath; get your breath back** to rest for a short time until you can breathe regularly again **5 under your breath** If you say something under your breath, you say it very quietly so that other people cannot hear it. **6 hold your breath** to keep air in your lungs and not let it out *How long can you hold your breath under water?* **7 don't hold your breath** *humorous* something that you say in order to tell someone that an event is not likely to happen *He said he'd phone, but don't hold your breath.* **8 a breath of fresh air** someone or something that is new, different, and exciting **9 take your breath away** If something takes your breath away, you feel surprise and admiration because it is so beautiful or exciting. *The view from the window took my breath away.* **10 with bated breath** in an excited or anxious way *I waited with bated breath as the results were read out.*

COMMON LEARNER ERROR

breath or **breathe**?

Be careful not to confuse the noun **breath** with the verb **breathe**.

I was so excited, I could hardly breathe.

breathalyser /ˈbreθəlaɪzəʳ/ *noun* [C] UK a piece of equipment that tests your breath to measure how much alcohol you have had • **breath-alyse** *verb* [T] *UK* to measure the alcohol in someone's body using a breathalyser

o~**breathe** /briːð/ *verb* [I, T] to take air into and out of your lungs **breathe in/out** ○ **breathe deeply** ⊃See also: be breathing down sb's **neck**, not breathe a **word**[1].

breather /ˈbriːðər/ *noun* [C] *informal* a short rest *If you start to feel tired, take a breather.*

breathing /ˈbriːðɪŋ/ *noun* [U] when you take air into and out of your lungs *The doctor listened to my breathing.*

'**breathing ,space** *noun* [U] an opportunity to stop, relax, or think about things

breathless /ˈbreθləs/ *adjective* not able to breathe enough • **breathlessly** *adverb*

breathtaking /ˈbreθˌteɪkɪŋ/ *adjective* very beautiful or surprising **breathtaking views** • **breathtakingly** *adverb*

bred /bred/ *past of* breed

breed[1] /briːd/ *noun* [C] **1** a type of dog, sheep, pig, etc *a rare breed of cattle* **2** a type of person or thing *a new breed of bank*

breed[2] /briːd/ *verb past bred* /bred/ **1** [I] If animals breed, they produce young animals. **2** **breed chickens/horses/rabbits, etc** to keep animals in order to produce young animals **3** **breed contempt/ignorance, etc** to cause something to develop, especially something bad

breeder /ˈbriːdər/ *noun* [C] someone who keeps animals in order to produce young animals *a dog/horse breeder*

breeding /ˈbriːdɪŋ/ *noun* [U] **1** when animals produce young animals *the breeding season* **2** when someone keeps animals in order to produce young animals *horse breeding*

'**breeding ,ground** *noun* [C] **1** a place where something develops quickly, especially something bad *This estate is a breeding ground for crime.* **2** a place where animals breed

breeze[1] /briːz/ *noun* [C] a gentle wind *a cool breeze*

breeze[2] /briːz/ *verb informal* **breeze along/into/through, etc** to move somewhere quickly in a confident way and without worrying

breezy /ˈbriːzi/ *adjective* **1** with a slight wind *a cool, breezy day* **2** happy, confident, and enthusiastic *a cheerful, breezy style* • **breezily** *adverb*

brethren /ˈbreðrən/ *noun* [plural] members of an organized group, especially a religious group of men

brevity /ˈbrevəti/ *noun* [U] *formal* **1** when speech or writing is short and contains few words **2** when something lasts for a short time

brew[1] /bruː/ *verb* **1** [T] to make beer **2** [I, T] If you brew tea or coffee, you make it by adding hot water, and if it brews, it gradually develops flavour in hot water. **3 be brewing** If something bad is brewing, it is beginning to develop. *There is a row brewing over the plans.*

brew[2] /bruː/ *noun* [C] *informal* a drink made by brewing, such as beer or tea

brewer /ˈbruːər/ *noun* [C] a person or organization that makes beer

brewery /ˈbruːəri/ *noun* [C] a company that makes beer

WORD PARTNERS FOR **bribe**

accept/take a bribe • offer sb/pay a bribe • a **cash** bribe

bribe /braɪb/ *noun* [C] money or a present given to someone so that they will do something for you, usually something dishonest *The politician was accused of accepting bribes from businessmen.* • **bribe** *verb* [T] [+ to do sth] *He was bribed to give false evidence at the trial.*

bribery /ˈbraɪbəri/ *noun* [U] when someone is offered money or a present so that they will do something, usually something dishonest *bribery and corruption*

bric-a-brac /ˈbrɪkəˌbræk/ *noun* [U] a collection of small, decorative objects that have little value

brick /brɪk/ *noun* [C] a small, hard, rectangular block used for building walls, houses, etc *a brick wall* ⊃See also: be banging your **head**[1] against a brick wall.

brick

bricklayer /ˈbrɪkˌleɪər/ *noun* [C] someone whose job is to build houses, walls, etc with bricks

bridal /ˈbraɪdəl/ *adjective* [always before noun] relating to a woman who is getting married, or relating to a wedding *a bridal gown*

bride /braɪd/ *noun* [C] a woman who is getting married *the bride and groom*

bridegroom /ˈbraɪdgruːm/ (*also* groom) *noun* [C] a man who is getting married

bridesmaid /ˈbraɪdzmeɪd/ *noun* [C] a woman or girl who helps the bride on her wedding day

bridge

o~**bridge**[1] /brɪdʒ/ *noun* **1** STRUCTURE [C] a structure that is built over a river, road, etc so that people or vehicles can go across it *to go across/over a bridge* ○ *Brooklyn Bridge* **2** CONNECTION [C] something that connects two groups, organizations, etc and improves the relationship between them *After the war they tried to build bridges with neighbouring countries.* **3 the bridge of your nose** the hard part of your nose between your eyes **4 the bridge** the raised area of a ship where the controls are **5** GAME [U] a card game for four players **6 I'll/We'll cross that bridge when I/we come to it.**

| j yes | k cat | ŋ ring | ʃ she | θ thin | ð this | ʒ decision | dʒ jar | tʃ chip | æ cat | e bed | ə ago | ɪ sit | i cosy | ɒ hot | ʌ run | ʊ put |

something you say when you do not intend to worry about a possible problem now, but will deal with it if or when it happens

bridge² /brɪdʒ/ *verb* **bridge the gap/gulf, etc** to make the difference between two things smaller *This course is designed to **bridge the gap between** school and work.*

bridle /'braɪdl/ *noun* [C] a set of straps that you put on a horse's head to control it

brief¹ /briːf/ *adjective* **1** lasting only for a short time *a brief visit* **2** using only a few words *a brief description/statement* **3** **in brief** using only a few words *world news in brief* • **briefly** *adverb They discussed the matter briefly.*

brief² /briːf/ *verb* [T] to give someone instructions or information [**often passive**] *At the meeting reporters were **briefed on** the plans.*

brief³ /briːf/ *noun* [C] a set of instructions or information [**+ to do sth**] *My brief was to improve the image of the city.*

briefcase /'briːfkeɪs/ *noun* [C] a flat, rectangular case with a handle for carrying documents, books, etc ⊃See picture at **bag**.

briefing /'briːfɪŋ/ *noun* [C, U] a meeting when people are given instructions or information *a press briefing*

briefs /briːfs/ *noun* [**plural**] underwear that you wear on your bottom *a pair of briefs* ⊃See colour picture **clothes** on page Centre 9.

brigade /brɪ'geɪd/ *noun* [C] **1** a large group of soldiers **2** *UK humorous* a group of people with a particular characteristic or interest *the anti-smoking brigade* ⊃See also: **fire brigade**.

brigadier /ˌbrɪgə'dɪəʳ/ *noun* [C] a British army officer of high rank

⊶**bright** /braɪt/ *adjective* **1** [COLOUR] having a strong, light colour *bright yellow/blue* **2** [LIGHT] full of light or shining strongly *bright sunshine* **3** [INTELLIGENT] intelligent *He's a bright boy.* **4** [HAPPY] happy or full of hope *She's always so bright and cheerful.* • **brightly** *adverb* **brightly coloured** *flowers* • **brightness** *noun* [U]

brighten /'braɪtᵊn/ (*also* **brighten up**) *verb* [I, T] **1** to become lighter or more colourful, or to make something become lighter or more colourful *A picture or two would brighten up the room.* **2** to become happier, or to make someone become happier *She brightened up when she saw him.*

brilliant /'brɪliənt/ *adjective* **1** [GOOD] *UK* very good *We saw a brilliant film.* **2** [CLEVER] extremely clever *a brilliant scholar* **3** [LIGHT] full of light or colour *The sky was a brilliant blue.* • **brilliantly** *adverb* • **brilliance** /'brɪliəns/ *noun* [U]

brim¹ /brɪm/ *verb* **brimming**, *past* **brimmed** be **brimming with sth** to be full of something *Her eyes were brimming with tears.*

brim² /brɪm/ *noun* [C] **1** the flat part around the bottom of a hat **2** the top edge of a container *He **filled** my glass **to the brim**.*

brine /braɪn/ *noun* [U] salty water, often used for keeping food from decaying *olives in brine*

⊶**bring** /brɪŋ/ *verb* [T] *past* **brought 1** to take someone or something with you when you go somewhere *Did you bring an umbrella with you?* ○ [**+ two objects**] *He brought me some flowers.*

2 bring happiness/peace/shame, etc to cause happiness/peace/shame, etc *Money does not always bring happiness.* **3 can not bring yourself to do sth** to not be willing to do something because it is so unpleasant *He couldn't bring himself to talk to her.* ⊃See also: bring sb/sth to their knees (**knee**), bring sth to **light¹**.

bring or **take**?

Use **bring** to talk about moving something or someone towards the speaker or towards the place where you are now.

Did you bring any money?

I've brought you a present.

Use **take** to talk about moving something or someone away from the speaker or away from the place where you are now.

I can take you to the station.

Don't forget to take your umbrella.

bring sth about to make something happen *The Internet has **brought about** big changes in the way we work.*

bring sth back 1 to return from somewhere with something [**+ two objects**] *Can you bring me back some milk from the shop, please?* **2** to make someone think about something from the past *The photos brought back memories of our holiday.*

bring sb down to cause someone in a position of power to lose their job *This scandal could bring down the government.*

bring sth down to reduce the level of something *to bring down prices*

bring sth forward to change the date or time of an event so that it happens earlier than planned *I've brought forward the meeting to this week.*

bring sth in 1 to introduce something new, usually a product or a law *New safety regulations were brought in last year.* **2** to earn or make money *The film has brought in millions of dollars.*

bring sb in to ask someone to do a particular job *We need to bring in an expert to sort out this problem.*

bring sth off to succeed in doing something difficult *How did he manage to bring that off?*

bring sth on to make something happen, usually something bad [**often passive**] *Headaches are often brought on by stress.*

bring sth out 1 to produce something to sell to the public *They have just brought out a new, smaller phone.* **2** to make a particular quality or detail noticeable *Salt can help to bring out the flavour of food.*

bring sb together to cause people to be friendly with each other *The disaster brought the community closer together.*

bring sb up to look after a child and teach them until they are old enough to look after themselves *She was brought up by her grandparents.*

bring sth up 1 to start to talk about a particular subject *There are several points I'd* *like to bring up at tomorrow's meeting.* **2** *UK* to vomit something

brink /brɪŋk/ *noun* **be on the brink of sth** to be in a situation where something bad is going to happen very soon *The two countries are on the brink of war.*

brisk /brɪsk/ *adjective* quick and energetic *a* ***brisk walk*** • **briskly** *adverb*

bristle¹ /ˈbrɪsl/ *verb* [I] to show that you are annoyed about something *She* ***bristled at*** *the suggestion that it was her fault.*

bristle² /ˈbrɪsl/ *noun* [C, U] a short, stiff hair • **bristly** *adjective*

Brit /brɪt/ *noun* [C] *informal* someone who comes from Great Britain

British /ˈbrɪtɪʃ/ *adjective* relating to Great Britain or the United Kingdom

the British /ˈbrɪtɪʃ/ *noun* [plural] the people of Great Britain or the United Kingdom

Briton /ˈbrɪtᵊn/ *noun* [C] someone who comes from Great Britain

brittle /ˈbrɪtl/ *adjective* hard but able to be broken easily *brittle bones*

broach /brəʊtʃ/ *verb* **broach an idea/subject/topic, etc** to begin to talk about something, usually something difficult or embarrassing *I don't know how to broach the subject of money with him.*

broad /brɔːd/ *adjective* **1** wide ***broad shoulders*** ○ *a broad smile* **2 a broad range/variety, etc** a group that includes many different things or people *a broad range of subjects* **3 a broad outline/picture, etc** a general description, without detail *This is just a broad outline of the proposal.* **4** A broad accent (= way of speaking from a region) is very noticeable. *a broad Irish accent* **5 in broad daylight** during the day when it is light and people can see *He was attacked in broad daylight.*

broadband /ˈbrɔːdbænd/ *noun* [U] a system that allows large amounts of information to be sent very quickly between computers or other electronic equipment

broadcast¹ /ˈbrɔːdkɑːst/ *noun* [C] a television or radio programme *a news broadcast* • **broadcast** *adjective* [always before noun] relating to television or radio *broadcast news*

broadcast² /ˈbrɔːdkɑːst/ *verb* [I, T] *past* **broadcast**, *also US* **broadcasted** to send out a programme on television or radio [often passive] *The concert will be* ***broadcast live*** *next week.* • **broadcaster** *noun* [C] someone who speaks on radio or television as a job • **broadcasting** *noun* [U]

broaden /ˈbrɔːdᵊn/ *verb* [I, T] **1** to increase or make something increase and include more things or people *We need to broaden the range of services that we offer.* ○ *Travel* ***broadens your mind.*** **2** to become wider or make something become wider *Her smile broadened and she began to laugh.*

> WORD PARTNERS FOR ***broadly***
>
> broadly **in line with/similar** • broadly **welcome** sth

broadly /ˈbrɔːdli/ *adverb* in a general way and not including everything or everyone *The plans have been broadly accepted.*

broadsheet /ˈbrɔːdʃiːt/ *noun* [C] *UK* a large newspaper, usually considered to be more serious than smaller newspapers

broccoli /ˈbrɒkəli/ *noun* [U] a green vegetable with a thick stem

brochure /ˈbrəʊʃəʳ/ [US] /brəʊˈʃʊr/ *noun* [C] a thin book with pictures and information, usually advertising something *We looked at some* ***holiday brochures*** *last night.*

broil /brɔɪl/ *US* (*UK/US* **grill**) *verb* [T] to cook food using direct heat

broiler /ˈbrɔɪləʳ/ *US* (*UK/US* **grill**) *noun* [C] a piece of equipment used for cooking food under direct heat

broke¹ /brəʊk/ *adjective informal* **1 be broke** to not have any money **2 go broke** to lose all your money and have to end your business

broke² /brəʊk/ *past tense of* break

> OTHER WAYS OF SAYING ***broken***
>
> If a piece of equipment is broken (not working properly), you can use adjectives such as **dead**, **defunct**, or, informally, **bust** (*UK*): *You won't be able to watch the match, the telly's* ***bust***. • *The phone's* ***dead***, *there must be a problem with the line.*
>
> If a piece of equipment or machinery in a public place is broken, you can say that it is **out of order**: *The coffee machine was* ***out of order***.
>
> If a piece of equipment has broken, in informal situations you can use expressions like **have had it** and **give up the ghost**: *The kettle's* ***had it***, *you'll have to boil a pan of water.* • *I can't give you a lift - my car's* ***given up the ghost***.

⊶**broken¹** /ˈbrəʊkən/ *adjective* **1** damaged and separated into pieces *broken glass* ⊃Opposite **unbroken**. **2 a broken arm/leg, etc** an arm/leg, etc with a damaged bone **3** If a machine or piece of equipment is broken, it is not working. *The video's broken.* **4 a broken heart** when you are very sad because someone you love has ended a relationship with you **5 a broken home** a family in which the parents do not now live together **6 a broken promise** a promise that has not been kept **7 broken English/Spanish, etc** English/Spanish, etc that is spoken slowly and has a lot of mistakes in it

broken² /ˈbrəʊkən/ *past participle of* break

broken-down /ˌbrəʊkənˈdaʊn/ *adjective* not working or in bad condition *a broken-down vehicle*

broken-hearted /ˌbrəʊkənˈhɑːtɪd/ *adjective* very sad because someone you love has ended a relationship with you

broker¹ /ˈbrəʊkəʳ/ *noun* [C] **1** (*also* **stockbroker**) someone whose job is to buy and sell shares (= equal parts of a company's total value) **2 an insurance/mortgage, etc broker** someone who makes other people's financial arrangements for them

broker² /ˈbrəʊkəʳ/ *verb* [T] to arrange an agreement *The peace deal was brokered by the US.*

bronchitis /brɒŋˈkaɪtɪs/ *noun* [U] an illness in your lungs which makes you cough and have problems breathing

bronze¹ /brɒnz/ *noun* 1 [METAL] [U] a shiny orange-brown metal 2 [COLOUR] [U] an orange-brown colour 3 [PRIZE] [C] a bronze medal (= a small, round disc given to someone for finishing third in a competition) *He won a bronze in the 200m.*

bronze² /brɒnz/ *adjective* 1 made of bronze *a bronze statue* 2 being the colour of bronze

,**bronze 'medal** *noun* [C] a small, round disc given to someone for finishing third in a race or competition

brooch /brəʊtʃ/ *noun* [C] a piece of jewellery for women which is fastened onto clothes with a pin *a diamond brooch*

brood¹ /bruːd/ *noun* [C] a family of young birds or animals, all born at the same time

brood² /bruːd/ *verb* [I] to think for a long time about things that make you sad or angry *I wish he'd stop **brooding about** the past.*

brook /brʊk/ *noun* [C] a small stream

broom /bruːm/ *noun* [C] a brush with a long handle used for cleaning the floor ⊃See picture at **brush.**

broth /brɒθ/ *noun* [U] soup, usually made with meat *chicken broth*

brothel /ˈbrɒθəl/ *noun* [C] a building where prostitutes (= people who have sex for money) work

o-**brother** /ˈbrʌðər/ *noun* [C] 1 [RELATIVE] a boy or man who has the same parents as you *an older/younger brother* ○ *my big/little brother* 2 [MEMBER] a man who is a member of the same race, religious group, organization, etc 3 [RELIGION] (*also* Brother) a monk (= man who lives in a male religious group) *Brother Paul*

brotherhood /ˈbrʌðəhʊd/ *noun* 1 [C] a group of men who have the same purpose or religious beliefs 2 [U] friendship and loyalty, like the relationship between brothers

brother-in-law /ˈbrʌðərɪnlɔː/ *noun* [C] *plural* **brothers-in-law** the man married to your sister, or the brother of your husband or wife

brotherly /ˈbrʌðəli/ *adjective* [always before noun] relating to or typical of brothers *brotherly love*

brought /brɔːt/ *past of* bring

brow /braʊ/ *noun* [C] 1 the front part of your head between your eyes and your hair *He wiped the sweat from his brow.* 2 **brow of a hill/slope** *UK* the top part of a hill or slope

o-**brown** /braʊn/ *adjective* 1 being the same colour as chocolate or soil *a brown leather bag* ○ *dark brown hair/eyes* ⊃See colour picture Colours on page Centre 12. 2 having darker skin because you have been in the sun ●**brown** *noun* [C, U] the colour brown

brownfield /ˈbraʊnfiːld/ *adjective UK* describes land that was used for industry and where new buildings can be built *a brownfield site* ⊃Compare greenfield.

brownie /ˈbraʊni/ *noun* [C] a small, square cake made with chocolate and nuts

browse /braʊz/ *verb* 1 [INTERNET] [I, T] to look at information on the Internet *to browse the Internet/Web* 2 [READ] [I] to read a book, magazine, etc in a relaxed way and not in detail *She browsed through some travel brochures looking for ideas.* 3 [SHOP] [I] to walk around a shop and look at things without buying anything *I love browsing around bookshops.*

browser /ˈbraʊzər/ *noun* [C] 1 a computer program which allows you to look at pages on the Internet 2 someone who browses

bruise /bruːz/ *noun* [C] a dark area on your skin where you have been hurt *He suffered cuts and bruises after falling off his bike.* ●**bruise** *verb* [T] to cause someone or something to have a bruise [often passive] *He was badly bruised in the accident.* ●**bruising** *noun* [U]

brunette /bruːˈnet/ *noun* [C] a white woman with dark brown hair

brunt /brʌnt/ *noun* **bear/feel/take the brunt of sth** to experience the worst part of something *He took the brunt of the criticism.*

brushes

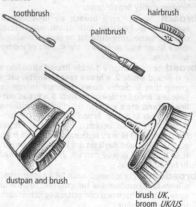

toothbrush

hairbrush

paintbrush

dustpan and brush

brush *UK*,
broom *UK/US*

brush¹ /brʌʃ/ *noun* 1 [C] an object made of short, thin pieces of plastic, wire, etc fixed to a handle and used to tidy hair, to clean, to paint, etc *a stiff wire brush* 2 [no plural] the action of using a brush *I need to **give** my hair a quick brush.* 3 **the brush of sth** when something touches you lightly *She felt the brush of his lips against her cheek.* 4 **a brush with sth** when you experience something, or almost experience something, especially something unpleasant *a brush with death*

brush² /brʌʃ/ *verb* [T] 1 to use a brush to clean or tidy something *to **brush** your hair/teeth* 2 **brush sth away/off, etc** to move something somewhere using a brush or your hand *He brushed the snow off his coat.* 3 **brush against/past sb/sth** to lightly touch someone or something as you move past *He brushed past me as he went up the stairs.*

brush sth aside/off to refuse to think about something seriously *He brushed aside her suggestion.*

brush up (on) sth to improve your skills

in something *I'm trying to brush up on my French before I go to Paris.*

brush-off /ˈbrʌʃɒf/ *noun informal* **give sb the brush-off** to be unfriendly to someone by not talking to them

brusque /bruːsk/ [US] /brʌsk/ *adjective* dealing with people in a quick way that is unfriendly or rude *a* ***brusque manner*** • **brusquely** *adverb*

brussel sprout /ˌbrʌsəlˈspraʊt/ [US] /ˈbrʌsəlˌspraʊt/ *noun* **[C]** a small, green vegetable which is round and made of leaves

brutal /ˈbruːtəl/ *adjective* very violent or cruel *a* ***brutal murder*** • **brutally** *adverb brutally murdered* ○ ***brutally honest*** • **brutality** /bruːˈtæləti/ *noun* **[C, U]**

brute¹ /bruːt/ *noun* **[C]** someone who behaves in a very violent and cruel way • **brutish** /ˈbruːtɪʃ/ *adjective* like a brute

brute² /bruːt/ *adjective* **brute force/strength** great force or strength

BSc /ˌbiːesˈsiː/ *UK* (*US* **BS** /biːˈes/) *noun* **[C]** *abbreviation for* Bachelor of Science: a university or college qualification in a science subject which usually takes 3 or 4 years of study *He has a BSc in computer science.*

BSE /ˌbiːesˈiː/ *noun* **[U]** *abbreviation for* bovine spongiform encephalopathy: a disease that kills cows by destroying their brains

BTW *Internet abbreviation for* by the way: used when you write some extra information that may or may not be related to what is being discussed

bubble¹ /ˈbʌbl/ *noun* **[C]** a ball of air or gas with liquid around it *an air bubble*

bubble² /ˈbʌbl/ *verb* **[I] 1** If a liquid bubbles, balls of air or gas rise to its surface. *The soup was bubbling on the stove.* **2 bubble (over) with confidence/enthusiasm, etc** to be full of a positive emotion or quality

ˈbubble ˌgum *noun* **[U]** a sweet that you chew and blow into a bubble

bubbly /ˈbʌbli/ *adjective* **1** happy and enthusiastic *a bubbly personality* **2** full of bubbles

buck¹ /bʌk/ *noun* **[C] 1** *US informal* a dollar (= US unit of money) *It cost me twenty bucks to get a new bike lock.* **2** a male rabbit or deer **3 pass the buck** to blame someone or to make them responsible for a problem that you should deal with yourself

buck² /bʌk/ *verb* **[I]** If a horse bucks, it kicks its back legs into the air.

bucket /ˈbʌkɪt/ *noun* **[C]** a round, open container with a handle used for carrying liquids *a bucket of water*

bucket

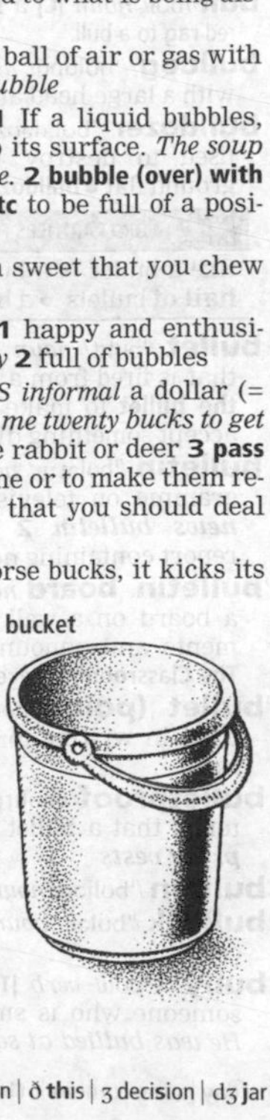

buckle¹ /ˈbʌkl/ *noun* **[C]** a metal object used to fasten the ends of a belt or strap *a silver buckle*

buckle² /ˈbʌkl/ *verb* **1** [FASTEN] **[I, T]** to fasten a belt or strap with a buckle **2** [BEND] **[I, T]** to bend, or to cause something to bend because of too much weight, heat, etc *His* ***legs buckled*** *as he reached the finishing line.* **3** [SUFFER] **[I]** to suffer and stop working effectively because of too many problems or too much work

buckle down to start working hard *I must* ***buckle down to*** *some work this afternoon.*

bud /bʌd/ *noun* **[C] 1** a part of a plant that develops into a leaf or a flower *In spring the trees are covered in buds.* **2 nip sth in the bud** to stop a small problem from getting worse by stopping it soon after it starts ➲See also: **taste buds**.

Buddha /ˈbʊdə/ [US] /ˈbuːdə/ *noun* the Indian holy man on whose life and teachings Buddhism is based

Buddhism /ˈbʊdɪzəm/ [US] /ˈbuːdɪzəm/ *noun* **[U]** a religion based on the teachings of Buddha

Buddhist /ˈbʊdɪst/ [US] /ˈbuːdɪst/ *noun* **[C]** someone who believes in Buddhism • **Buddhist** *adjective a Buddhist temple*

budding /ˈbʌdɪŋ/ *adjective* **[always before noun]** starting to develop well *a* ***budding romance***

buddy /ˈbʌdi/ *noun* **[C]** *informal* a friend *my best buddy*

budge /bʌdʒ/ *verb* **[I, T] 1** If something will not budge, or you cannot budge it, it will not move. *I've tried to open the window, but it won't budge.* **2** If someone will not budge, or you cannot budge them, they will not change their opinion.

budgerigar /ˈbʌdʒərɪɡɑːr/ *noun* **[C]** *UK* a budgie

WORD PARTNERS FOR *budget*

have a budget **of** [£30 000/$5000, etc] • be **on** a **tight** budget (= not have much money) • the budget **for** sth

🔑**budget¹** /ˈbʌdʒɪt/ *noun* **[C] 1** a plan that shows how much money you have and how you will spend it **2** the amount of money you have for something *an* ***annual budget*** *of £30 million* **3 the Budget** in the UK, when the government officially tells the public about its plans for taxes and spending • **budgetary** *adjective* **[always before noun]** relating to a budget

budget² /ˈbʌdʒɪt/ *verb* **[I, T]** to plan how much money you will spend on something *An extra £20 million has been* ***budgeted for*** *schools this year.*

budget³ /ˈbʌdʒɪt/ *adjective* **a budget hotel/price, etc** a very cheap hotel, price, etc

budgie /ˈbʌdʒi/ *noun* **[C]** *UK* a small, brightly coloured bird often kept as a pet

buff /bʌf/ *noun* **[C] a computer/film/wine, etc buff** someone who knows a lot about computers/films/wine, etc

buffalo /ˈbʌfələʊ/ *noun* **[C]** *plural* **buffaloes** or **buffalo** a large, wild animal, like a cow with horns *a herd of wild buffalo*

buffer /ˈbʌfər/ *noun* **[C]** something that helps protect someone or something from harm *I have some money saved to act as* ***a buffer against*** *unexpected bills.*

ˈbuffer ˌzone *noun* **[C]** an area created to separate two countries that are fighting

buffet¹ /ˈbʊfeɪ/ [US] /bəˈfeɪ/ *noun* **[C]** a meal in

which dishes of food are arranged on a table and you serve yourself *a cold buffet* ○ *a buffet lunch*

buffet[2] /'bʌfɪt/ *verb* [T] If something is buffeted by the weather, sea, etc, it is hit repeatedly and with force. [often passive] *The little boat was buffeted by the waves.*

'buffet ,car *noun* [C] *UK* the part of a train where you can buy something to eat or drink

buffoon /bə'fuːn/ *noun* [C] *old-fashioned* someone who does silly things

bug[1] /bʌg/ *noun* [C] **1** ILLNESS a bacteria or virus, or the illness that it causes *a flu/stomach bug* **2** COMPUTER a mistake in a computer program *This program is full of bugs.* **3** INSECT a small insect **4** EQUIPMENT a small, electronic piece of equipment used to secretly listen to people talking **5** **be bitten by the bug/get the bug** *informal* to develop a strong interest or enthusiasm for a particular activity *He's been bitten by the tennis bug.*

bug[2] /bʌg/ *verb* [T] bugging, *past* bugged **1** to hide a piece of equipment somewhere in order to secretly listen to people talking [often passive] *Their hotel room had been bugged.* **2** *informal* to annoy someone *He's been bugging me all morning.*

buggy /'bʌgi/ *noun* [C] **1** *UK* (*US* stroller) a chair on wheels which is used to move small children **2** a vehicle with two wheels that is pulled by a horse, especially in the past

bugle /'bjuːgl/ *noun* [C] a small, metal musical instrument that you play by blowing into it

o←**build**[1] /bɪld/ *verb past* built **1** [I, T] to make something by putting materials and parts together *build a house/wall* ○ *The bridge is built of steel and aluminium.* **2** [T] to create and develop something over a long time *They have built a solid friendship over the years.*

build sth into sth to make something a part of something else *There are video screens built into the back of the seats.*

build on sth to use a success or achievement as a base from which to achieve more success

build (sth) up to increase or develop, or to make something increase or develop *Traffic usually builds up in the late afternoon.*

build[2] /bɪld/ *noun* [C, U] the size and shape of a person's body *He's of medium build with short brown hair.*

builder /'bɪldəʳ/ *noun* [C] someone who makes or repairs buildings as a job

o←**building** /'bɪldɪŋ/ *noun* **1** [C] a structure with walls and a roof, such as a house, school, etc *an office building* **2** [U] the activity of putting together materials and parts to make structures *building materials* ⊃See also: apartment building.

'building so,ciety *UK* (*US* savings and loan association) *noun* [C] an organization similar to a bank which lends you money to buy a house

build-up /'bɪldʌp/ *noun* [U] **1** when something slowly increases [usually singular] *the build-up of traffic* **2** **the build-up to sth** *UK* the period of preparation before something happens *There*

was a lot of excitement in the build-up to the Olympics.

built /bɪlt/ *past of* build

built-in /,bɪlt'ɪn/ *adjective* [always before noun] included as part of the main structure of something *a computer with a built-in modem*

built-up /,bɪlt'ʌp/ *adjective* a built-up area has a lot of buildings

bulb /bʌlb/ *noun* [C] **1** (*also* light bulb) a glass object containing a wire which produces light from electricity *an electric light bulb* **2** a round root that some plants grow from *daffodil bulbs*

bulbous /'bʌlbəs/ *adjective* large and round in an unattractive way *a bulbous nose*

bulge[1] /bʌldʒ/ *verb* [I] to look larger and rounder or fuller than normal *Her bags were bulging with shopping.*

bulge[2] /bʌldʒ/ *noun* [C] a round, raised area on a surface

bulimia /bʊ'lɪmiə/ *noun* [U] a mental illness in which someone eats too much and then forces themselves to vomit ● **bulimic** *noun* [C], *adjective*

bulk /bʌlk/ *noun* **1** **in bulk** in large amounts *to buy in bulk* **2** **the bulk of sth** the largest part or most of something *He spends the bulk of his money on rent.* **3** [no plural] the large size of something or someone

bulky /'bʌlki/ *adjective* too big and taking up too much space

bull /bʊl/ *noun* [C] a male cow ⊃See also: be like a red rag to a bull.

bulldog /'bʊldɒg/ *noun* [C] a short, strong dog with a large head and neck

bulldozer /'bʊl,dəʊzəʳ/ *noun* [C] a heavy vehicle used to destroy buildings and make the ground flat ● **bulldoze** *verb* [T]

WORD PARTNERS FOR *bullet*

fire a bullet ● a bullet flies/lodges swh ● a hail of bullets ● a bullet hole/wound

bullet /'bʊlɪt/ *noun* **1** [C] a small, metal object that is fired from a gun *a bullet wound* **2** **bite the bullet** to make yourself do something or accept something difficult or unpleasant

bulletin /'bʊlətɪn/ *noun* [C] **1** a short news programme on television or radio *the evening news bulletin* **2** a regular newspaper or report containing news about an organization

'bulletin ,board *noun* [C] *US* (*UK* noticeboard) a board on a wall where you put advertisements and announcements ⊃See colour picture The Classroom on page Centre 6.

'bullet ,(point) *noun* [C] a small black circle used in writing to show separate items on a list

bulletproof /'bʊlɪtpruːf/ *adjective* made of material that a bullet cannot go through *bulletproof vests*

bullion /'bʊliən/ *noun* [U] blocks of gold or silver

bullock /'bʊlək/ *noun* [C] a young bull (= male cow)

bully[1] /'bʊli/ *verb* [T] to intentionally frighten someone who is smaller or weaker than you *He was bullied at school by some older boys.* ○

[+ into + doing sth] *She was bullied into leaving.*
• **bullying** *noun* [U] *Bullying is a problem in many schools.*

bully² /'buli/ *noun* [C] someone who intentionally frightens a person who is smaller or weaker than them

bum¹ /bʌm/ *noun* [C] **1** *UK informal* your bottom **2** *US informal* someone who has no home and no money

bum² /bʌm/ *verb* [T] **bumming**, *past* **bummed** *very informal* to ask someone for something, such as money or cigarettes, without intending to pay for them *Hey, could I bum a cigarette?*

bum around *informal* to spend time being lazy and doing very little

bum around sth *informal* to travel to different places and not do any work

bumbag /'bʌmbæg/ *UK (US* **fanny pack**) *noun* [C] a small bag fixed to a belt that you wear around your waist

bumblebee /'bʌmblbiː/ *noun* [C] a large, hairy bee (= flying insect)

bumbling /'bʌmblɪŋ/ *adjective* [always before noun] confused and showing no skill *a bumbling idiot*

bummer /'bʌmə'/ *noun* a **bummer** *informal* something unpleasant or annoying *That last exam was a real bummer.*

bump¹ /bʌmp/ *verb* **1** [T] to hurt part of your body by hitting it against something hard *I bumped my head on the door.* **2 bump into/ against sth** to hit your body, your car, etc against something by accident *He kept falling over and bumping into things.* **3 bump along/ over sth** to move in a vehicle over a surface that is not smooth *The bus bumped along the country road.*

bump into sb *informal* to meet someone you know when you have not planned to meet them *I bumped into an old school friend in town today.*

bump sb off *informal* to murder someone

bump² /bʌmp/ *noun* [C] **1** SURFACE a round, raised area on a surface *My bike hit a bump in the road.* **2** BODY a raised area on your body where it has been hurt by hitting something hard *a nasty bump on the head* **3** MOVEMENT when something hits something hard *I heard a bump upstairs.*

bumper¹ /'bʌmpə'/ *noun* [C] a bar fixed along the front or back of a vehicle to protect it in an accident *a front/rear bumper*

bumper² /'bʌmpə'/ *adjective* [always before noun] bigger or better than usual *a bumper year*

'**bumper** ,**sticker** *noun* [C] a sign that you stick on a car, often with a funny message on it

bumpy /'bʌmpi/ *adjective* **1** SURFACE A bumpy road or surface is not smooth but has raised areas on it. **2** JOURNEY A bumpy journey is uncomfortable because the vehicle moves around a lot. **3** SITUATION full of problems or sudden changes *We had a bumpy start.*

bun /bʌn/ *noun* [C] **1** CAKE *UK* a small, round cake *an iced bun* **2** BREAD a small, round piece of bread *a hamburger bun* **3** HAIR a hairstyle

in which the hair is arranged in a small, round shape on the back of the head

B

bunch¹ /bʌnʃ/ *noun* **1** [C] a number of things of the same type which are joined or held together *He handed me a bunch of flowers.* ↪See colour picture **Pieces and Quantities** on page Centre 1. **2** [C] *informal* a group of people [usually singular] *His friends are a nice bunch.* **3 a bunch of sth** *US informal* a large amount or number of something *There's a whole bunch of places I'd like to visit.*

bunch² /bʌnʃ/ *verb*

bunch (sb/sth) together/up to move close together so that you make a tight group, or to make someone or something do this [often passive] *We were all bunched up at the back of the room.*

bunch (sth) up If material bunches up, or if someone bunches it up, it moves into tight folds. [often passive] *My shirt's all bunched up at the back.*

bunches /'bʌnʃɪz/ *noun* [plural] *UK* a hairstyle in which the hair is tied together in two parts, one on each side of the head

bundle¹ /'bʌndl/ *noun* **1** [C] a number of things that are tied together *a bundle of letters/ clothes* **2 a bundle of energy/nerves** *informal* a very energetic or nervous person

bundle² /'bʌndl/ *verb* **1 bundle sb into/out of/ through sth** to push or carry someone somewhere quickly and roughly *He was bundled into the back of a car and driven away.* **2** to include an extra computer program or other product with something you sell

bundle sth up to tie a number of things together

bundle (sb) up to put warm clothes on yourself or someone else

bung /bʌŋ/ *verb* **bung sth in/on, etc** *UK informal* to put something somewhere in a quick, careless way *Shall I bung a chicken in the oven for dinner?*

bung sth up *UK informal* to cause something to be blocked so that it does not work in the way it should [often passive] *The toilet was bunged up with paper.*

bungalow /'bʌŋgələʊ/ *noun* [C] a house that has all its rooms on the ground floor

bungee jumping /'bʌndʒi,dʒʌmpɪŋ/ *(also* **bungy jumping**) *noun* [U] the sport of jumping from a very high place while tied to a long elastic rope, so that the rope pulls you back before you hit the ground

bungle /'bʌŋgl/ *verb* [T] to do something wrong in a very careless or stupid way *a bungled robbery* • **bungling** *noun* [U]

bunk /bʌŋk/ *noun* [C] a narrow bed in a ship, train, etc

'**bunk** ,**beds** *noun* [plural] two beds fixed together with one on top of the other

bunker /'bʌŋkə'/ *noun* [C] **1** an underground room where people go to be protected, especially from bombs **2** in golf, a hollow area filled with sand

bunny /ˈbʌni/ (also **'bunny ˌrabbit**) noun [C] a child's word for 'rabbit'

buoy[1] /bɔɪ/ noun [C] a floating object used in water to mark dangerous areas for boats

buoy[2] /bɔɪ/ verb **be buoyed (up) by sth** to feel happy or confident because of something *The team was buoyed up by their win last week.*

buoyant /ˈbɔɪənt/ adjective **1** [CONFIDENT] happy and confident *in a buoyant mood* **2** [BUSINESS] successful or making a profit *a buoyant economy* **3** [FLOATING] floating or able to float ● **buoyancy** /ˈbɔɪənsi/ noun [U]

WORD PARTNERS FOR burden

be/become a burden **on/to** sb ● carry the burden **of** sth ● ease/lighten/share the burden ● a **heavy** burden ● the burden of (doing) sth

---

burden /ˈbɜːdᵊn/ noun [C] something difficult or unpleasant that you have to deal with or worry about *the burden of responsibility* ○ *I'd hate to be a burden to you when I'm older.* ● **burden** verb [T] to give someone something difficult or unpleasant to deal with or worry about *Sorry to burden you with my problems.* ● **burdensome** adjective

bureau /ˈbjʊərəʊ/ noun [C] plural **bureaux** or US **bureaus** **1** [OFFICE] a department or office **2** [WRITING] UK a piece of furniture with drawers and a sloping top used for writing **3** [CLOTHES] US (UK **chest of drawers**) a piece of furniture with drawers for keeping clothes in

bureaucracy /bjʊəˈrɒkrəsi/ noun **1** [U] complicated rules and processes used by an organization, especially when they do not seem necessary *government bureaucracy* **2** [C, U] a government or organization in which there are a lot of officials in a lot of departments ● **bureaucrat** /ˈbjʊərəʊkræt/ noun [C] someone working in a bureaucracy ● **bureaucratic** /ˌbjʊərəʊˈkrætɪk/ adjective

burgeoning /ˈbɜːdʒᵊnɪŋ/ adjective growing very quickly *a burgeoning population*

burger /ˈbɜːgəʳ/ noun [C] a flat, round piece of food, usually made of meat, that is fried and served between pieces of bread *burger and fries* ○ *a veggie burger*

burglar /ˈbɜːgləʳ/ noun [C] someone who gets into buildings illegally and steals things

'burglar aˌlarm noun [C] something that makes a noise if someone tries to get into a building illegally

burglarize /ˈbɜːglᵊraɪz/ verb US burgle

burglary /ˈbɜːglᵊri/ noun [C, U] when someone gets into a building illegally and steals things

burgle /ˈbɜːgl/ UK (US **burglarize**) verb [T] to get into a building illegally and steal things [often passive] *They've been burgled twice recently.*

burial /ˈberiəl/ noun [C, U] when a dead body is put into the ground

burly /ˈbɜːli/ adjective A burly man is large and strong.

○~**burn**[1] /bɜːn/ verb past **burnt** or **burned 1** [DESTROY]

[I, T] to destroy something with fire, or to be destroyed by fire *I burnt all his letters.* ○ *The factory burned to the ground.* ○ *He dropped his cigarette and **burnt a hole in** his jacket.* **2** [FLAMES] [I] to produce flames *The fire's burning well.* **3** [COOK TOO LONG] [I, T] If you burn something that you are cooking, you cook it too much and if something you are cooking burns, it cooks too much. *Check the pizza - I think it's burning!* **4** **burn yourself/your fingers,** etc to be hurt by fire or heat *He burned his hand on the kettle.* **5** [ENERGY] [T] (also **burn up**) to use fuel to produce heat or energy *to burn calories/fuel* **6** [COPY] [T] to copy music, information or images onto a CD *He's burnt all his favourite records onto a CD.* **7** [SKIN] [I] to be very hot or sore *Her cheeks were burning.* **8 burn with anger/hatred,** etc to feel an emotion very strongly

burn (sth) down to destroy something, especially a building, by fire, or to be destroyed by fire *Their house burnt down while they were away on holiday.*

burn out If a fire burns out, it stops producing flames because nothing remains that can burn.

burn out phrasal verb to become ill or very tired from working too hard *If Olivia keeps working late every night, she will burn out.*

burn (sth) up to destroy something completely, or to be destroyed completely by fire or heat *The satellite will burn up when it enters the atmosphere.*

burn[2] /bɜːn/ noun [C] a place where fire or heat has damaged or hurt something *She has a nasty burn on her arm.*

burner /ˈbɜːnəʳ/ noun **1** [C] a piece of equipment used to burn or heat something **2 put sth on the back burner** to not deal with something now, but intend to deal with it at a later time

burning /ˈbɜːnɪŋ/ adjective **1** very hot *the burning heat of the midday sun* **2 burning ambition/desire,** etc a very strong need to do something **3 a burning issue/question** a subject or question that must be dealt with or answered quickly

burnout /ˈbɜːnaʊt/ noun [U] US extreme tiredness, usually caused by working too much

burnt[1] /bɜːnt/ adjective destroyed or made black by fire or heat *burnt toast*

burnt[2] /bɜːnt/ past of burn

burnt-out /ˌbɜːntˈaʊt/ (also **burned-out** /bɜːndˈaʊt/) adjective **1** A burnt-out car or building has been almost completely destroyed by fire. **2** informal tired and without enthusiasm because you have worked too hard *a burnt-out teacher*

burp /bɜːp/ verb [I] to let air from your stomach come out of your mouth in a noisy way ● **burp** noun [C]

burrow[1] /ˈbʌrəʊ/ verb [I] When an animal burrows, it digs a hole or passage in the ground to live in. *There are rabbits burrowing under the building.*

burrow[2] /ˈbʌrəʊ/ noun [C] a hole or passage in the ground dug by an animal to live in

burst[1] /bɜːst/ verb past burst **1** [I, T] If a container

---

bursts, or if you burst it, it breaks suddenly, so that what is inside it comes out. *A water **pipe** **burst** and flooded the cellar.* **2 burst in/out/ through, etc** to move somewhere suddenly and forcefully *Three masked men burst into the shop.* **3 burst into flames** to suddenly start burning **4 burst into laughter/tears, etc** to suddenly start laughing/crying, etc *She burst into tears and ran away.* **5 burst open** to open suddenly and with force **6 be bursting with confidence/joy, etc** to be full of an emotion or quality *She was bursting with pride.* **7 be bursting to do sth** *informal* to want to do something very much *I was bursting to tell him about the party.*

burst out 1 to suddenly say something loudly *'Don't go!' he burst out.* **2 burst out laughing/crying** to suddenly start laughing/ crying *I walked in and everyone burst out laughing.*

burst² /bɜːst/ *noun* **1 a burst of sth** a sudden large amount of noise, activity, etc *a burst of applause/laughter* **2** [C] when something breaks open and what is inside it comes out

bury /ˈberi/ *verb* [T] **1** to put a dead body into the ground [often passive] *He was buried next to his wife.* **2** to hide something in the ground or under something *buried treasure* ○ [often passive] *Two climbers were buried in the snow.* **3 bury your face/head in sth** to move your face/head somewhere where it is hidden *She buried her face in her hands.* **4 bury yourself in sth** to give all your attention to something *He buried himself in his work.* ⊃See also: bury the hatchet.

catch a bus • miss the bus • on a bus • by bus • a bus route

o→**bus** /bʌs/ *noun* [C] *plural* **buses** a large vehicle that carries passengers by road, usually along a fixed route *a school bus* ○ *I'll go home by bus.* • **bus** *verb* [T] *UK* **bussing**, *past* **bussed**, *US* **busing**, *past* **bused** to take a group of people somewhere in a bus ⊃See picture at **vehicle**.

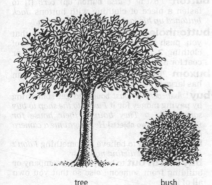

tree   bush

bush /bʊʃ/ *noun* **1** [C] a short, thick plant with a lot of branches *a rose bush* ○ *There was some-*

one hiding in the bushes. **2 the bush** wild parts of Australia or Africa where very few people live **3 beat about the bush** to avoid talking about something difficult or embarrassing

bushy /ˈbʊʃi/ *adjective* If hair or a plant is bushy, it has grown very thick. *bushy eyebrows*

busily /ˈbɪzɪli/ *adverb* in a busy, active way *He was busily writing notes.*

1 be in business • do business with sb • go into business • go out of business

o→**business** /ˈbɪznɪs/ *noun* **1** [TRADE] [U] the buying and selling of goods or services *The shop closed last year, but now they're back in business.* ○ *We do a lot of business with China.* ○ *His company has gone out of business* (= failed). **2** [ORGANIZATION] [C] an organization that sells goods or services *My uncle runs a small decorating business.* **3** [WORK] [U] work that you do to earn money *She's in Vienna on business* (= working). **4 a nasty/strange, etc business** an unpleasant/strange, etc situation **5 be sb's (own) business** to be something private that other people do not need to know **6 be none of sb's business** If something is none of someone's business, they do not need to know about it, although they want to, because it does not affect them. **7 mind your own business** used to tell someone in a rude way that you do not want them to ask about something private ⊃See also: big business, show business.

ˈbusiness ˌclass *noun* [U] a more expensive way of travelling by aircraft in which you sit in a separate part of the aircraft and are given better service • **business class** *adjective, adverb*

businesslike /ˈbɪznɪslaɪk/ *adjective* working in a serious and effective way *a businesslike manner*

businessman, businesswoman /ˈbɪznɪsmən, ˈbɪznɪsˌwʊmən/ *noun* [C] *plural* **businessmen** or **businesswomen** someone who works in business, usually in a high position in a company

busk /bʌsk/ *verb* [I] *UK* to perform music in a public place to get money from people walking past • **busker** *noun* [C]

ˈbus ˌstation (*also UK* coach station) *noun* [C] a building where a bus starts or ends its journey

ˈbus ˌstop *noun* [C] a place where buses stop to let passengers get on or off *I saw her waiting at the bus stop.* ⊃See Common learner error at **station**.

bust¹ /bʌst/ *verb* [T] *past* **bust**, *US* **busted** *informal* **1** to break or damage something *The cops had to bust the door down to get in.* **2** If the police bust someone, they catch them and accuse them of a crime. [often passive] *He was busted for selling drugs.*

bust² /bʌst/ *noun* [C] **1** a woman's breasts, or their size in relation to clothing *a 36-inch bust* **2** a model of someone's head and shoulders *a bronze bust of the Queen* **3 a drug bust** when the police catch people selling or using illegal drugs

bust³ /bʌst/ *adjective* **1 go bust** If a business

goes bust, it stops trading because it does not have enough money. *His company went bust, leaving huge debts.* **2** *UK informal* (*US* **busted** /'bʌstɪd/) broken *My phone's bust - can I use yours?*

bustle¹ /'bʌsl/ *verb* **1 bustle about/around/in, etc** to move around and do things in a quick, busy way *There were lots of shoppers bustling about.* **2 bustle with sth** to be full of people or activity *The town centre was bustling with people.*

bustle² /'bʌsl/ *noun* [U] people and activity *We left the bustle of the city behind us.*

bustling /'bʌslɪŋ/ *adjective* full of people and activity *a bustling city/street*

bust-up /'bʌstʌp/ *noun* [C] *UK informal* a serious disagreement *He left home after a big bust-up with his dad.*

●━**busy¹** /'bɪzi/ *adjective* **1** PERSON If you are busy, you are working hard, or giving your attention to a particular activity. *Mum was busy in the kitchen.* ○ [+ doing sth] *I was busy mowing the lawn.* ○ *I've got plenty of jobs to keep you busy.* ○ *He was too busy talking to notice us come in.* **2** PLACE A busy place is full of activity or people. *a busy restaurant/road* **3** TIME In a busy period you have a lot of things to do. *I've had a very busy week.* **4** TELEPHONE *US* (*UK* **engaged**) If a telephone line is busy, someone is using it.

busy² /'bɪzi/ *verb* **busy yourself** to spend time working or doing something *We busied ourselves in the kitchen preparing dinner.*

●━**but¹** *strong form* /bʌt/ *weak form* /bət/ *conjunction* **1** OPPOSITE INFORMATION used to introduce something new that you say, especially something which is different or the opposite from what you have just said *I'd drive you there, but I haven't got my car.* ○ *The tickets were expensive, but the kids really enjoyed it.* **2** EXPLAINING WHY used before you say why something did not happen or is not true *I was going to go to his party, but I was ill.* **3** SHOWING SURPRISE used to show that you are surprised about what someone has just said *'Tim is leaving.' 'But why?'* **4** CONNECTING PHRASES used to connect 'excuse me' or 'I'm sorry' with what you say next *Excuse me, but would you mind shutting the door?*

●━**but²** *strong form* /bʌt/ *weak form* /bət/ *preposition* except *Everyone but Andrew knows.* ○ *Can you buy me a sandwich? Anything but ham.* ○ *This is the last programme but one* (= the programme before the last).

but³ *strong form* /bʌt/ *weak form* /bət/ *adverb formal* only *We can but try.*

butcher¹ /'bʊtʃər/ *noun* [C] someone who prepares and sells meat

butcher² /'bʊtʃər/ *verb* [T] **1** to kill someone in a very violent way **2** to cut an animal into pieces of meat

butcher's /'bʊtʃəz/ *UK* (*US* 'butcher ,shop) *noun* [C] a shop that prepares and sells meat *I went to the butcher's to buy some sausages.*

butler /'bʌtlər/ *noun* [C] a man who opens the door, serves dinner, etc in a large house as a job

butt¹ /bʌt/ *noun* **1** BOTTOM [C] *US informal* your bottom *He just sits on his butt all day long.* **2** CIGARETTE [C] the end of a cigarette that is left after it is smoked *There were cigarette butts all over the floor.* **3** GUN [C] the end of the handle of a gun *the butt of a rifle* **4 a head butt** when you hit someone with the top, front part of your head **5 kick sb's butt** *US informal* to punish someone or defeat someone with a lot of force

butt² /bʌt/ *verb* [T] to hit something with the top, front part of your head *He butted me in the stomach.*

butt in to interrupt or join in a conversation or activity when the other people do not want you to *The interviewer kept butting in and wouldn't let me answer the question.*

●━**butter¹** /'bʌtər/ *noun* **1** [U] a soft, pale yellow food made from cream that you put on bread and use in cooking ➔See colour picture **Food** on page Centre 11. **2 butter wouldn't melt in sb's mouth** used to say that someone looks as if they would never do anything wrong ➔See also: **peanut butter**.

butter² /'bʌtər/ *verb* [T] to put a layer of butter on something *hot buttered toast*

butter sb up *informal* to be very nice to someone so that they will do what you want them to do

buttercup /'bʌtəkʌp/ *noun* [C] a small, bright yellow flower

butterfly /'bʌtəflaɪ/ *noun* **1** [C] an insect with large, patterned wings ➔See picture at **insect**. **2 have butterflies (in your stomach)** to feel very nervous about something that you are going to do

buttock /'bʌtək/ *noun* [C] one of the two sides of your bottom

button¹ /'bʌtən/ *noun* [C] **1** a small, round object that you push through a hole to fasten clothing *to do up/undo your buttons* **2** a switch that you press to control a piece of equipment *Press the play button to listen to your recording.* ➔See also: **belly button**.

button² /'bʌtən/ (*also* **button up**) *verb* [T] to fasten a piece of clothing with buttons *Jack buttoned up his jacket.* ➔Opposite **unbutton**.

buttonhole /'bʌtənhəʊl/ *noun* [C] **1** a hole that you push a button through on a piece of clothing **2** *UK* a flower worn on a jacket or coat for a special occasion

buxom /'bʌksəm/ *adjective* A buxom woman has large breasts.

●━**buy¹** /baɪ/ *verb* [T] *past* bought to get something by paying money for it *I went to the shop to buy some milk.* ○ *They bought their house for £14,000.* ○ [+ two objects] *He bought me a camera for my birthday.*

buy into sth to believe in something *I don't buy into all that dieting nonsense.*

buy sb/sth out to buy part of a company or building from someone else so that you own all of it

buy sth up to quickly buy a lot of something, often all that is available

buy² /baɪ/ *noun* **a good buy** when you buy something good for a cheap price *This coat was a really good buy.*

buyer /ˈbaɪəʳ/ *noun* [C] someone who buys something

buyout /ˈbaɪaʊt/ *noun* [C] when a group of people buy the company that they work for

buzz¹ /bʌz/ *noun* **1** [no plural] *informal* a feeling of excitement, energy, or pleasure *He gets a real buzz from going to the gym.* **2** [C] a continuous sound like a bee makes

buzz² /bʌz/ *verb* [I] **1** to make a continuous sound like a bee *I can hear something buzzing.* **2** to be full of activity or excitement *The crowd was buzzing with excitement.* **3 buzz about/ around, etc** to move around in a quick and busy way

buzzer /ˈbʌzəʳ/ *noun* [C] a piece of electronic equipment that makes a long sound as a signal *to press the buzzer*

buzzword /ˈbʌzwɜːd/ *noun* [C] a word or expression that has become fashionable, usually in a particular subject or group of people *a new political buzzword*

o•**by¹** *strong form* /baɪ/ *weak forms* /bɪ, bə/ *preposition* **1** DO used to show the person or thing that does something *She was examined by a doctor.* ○ *a painting by Van Gogh* **2** HOW through doing or using something *Can I pay by cheque?* ○ *We'll get there by car.* ○ [+ doing sth] *Open the file by clicking on the icon.* **3** HOLDING holding a particular part of someone or something *She grabbed me by the arm.* **4** NEAR near or next to something or someone *I'll meet you by the post office.* ○ *A small child stood by her side.* **5** NOT LATER not later than a particular time or date *Applications have to be in by the 31st.* **6** ACCORDING TO according to *By law you must be eighteen to purchase alcohol.* **7** PAST past *He sped by me on a motorcycle.* **8** AMOUNT used to show measurements or amounts *twelve by ten metres of floor space* ○ *Interest rates have been increased by 0.25%.* ○ *I'm paid by the hour.* **9 by accident/chance/**

mistake, etc as a result of an accident, chance, mistake, etc *I went to the wrong room by mistake.* **10 by day/night** during the day/night **11 day by day/little by little/one by one, etc** used in particular phrases to mean 'gradually' or 'in units of' *Day by day he grew stronger.*

o•**by²** /baɪ/ *adverb* past *A motorcycle sped by.*

o•**bye** /baɪ/ (*also* **bye-bye**) *exclamation* goodbye *Bye, see you tomorrow.*

by-election /ˈbaɪɪˌlekʃᵊn/ *noun* [C] an election in the UK to choose a new member of parliament for an area because the old one has left or died

bygone /ˈbaɪgɒn/ *adjective literary* **bygone age/ days/era, etc** a time in the past

bygones /ˈbaɪgɒnz/ *noun* **let bygones be bygones** something that you say to tell someone to forget about the unpleasant things in the past

bypass¹ /ˈbaɪpɑːs/ *noun* [C] **1** a road that goes around a town and not through it **2** a medical operation to make blood flow along a different route and avoid a damaged part of the heart *a coronary/heart bypass*

bypass² /ˈbaɪpɑːs/ *verb* [T] **1** to go around a place or thing and not through it *I was hoping to bypass the city centre.* **2** to avoid dealing with someone or something by dealing directly with someone or something else *They bypassed him and went straight to his manager.*

by-product /ˈbaɪˌprɒdʌkt/ *noun* [C] something that is produced when you are making or doing something else *Carbon monoxide is a by-product of burning.*

bystander /ˈbaɪˌstændəʳ/ *noun* [C] someone who is near the place where an event happens, but not directly involved in it *The gunman began firing at innocent bystanders.*

byte /baɪt/ *noun* [C] a unit for measuring the amount of information a computer can store, equal to 8 bits (= smallest unit of computer information)

Cc

C, c /siː/ the third letter of the alphabet

C *written abbreviation for* Celsius or centigrade: measurements of temperature *30°C*

c *written abbreviation for* circa (= used before a number or date which is not exact) *c. 1900*

cab /kæb/ *noun* **[C]** **1** *informal* a taxi *We **took a cab** to the theatre.* ○ *a cab driver* **2** the front part of a truck where the driver sits

cabaret /ˈkæbəreɪ/ *noun* **[C, U]** when someone entertains people with songs, jokes, etc in a bar or restaurant *He's appearing **in cabaret** at the Cafe Royal.*

cabbage /ˈkæbɪdʒ/ *noun* **[C, U]** a large, round vegetable that consists of a lot of thick leaves

cabbie /ˈkæbi/ *noun* **[C]** *informal* someone who drives a taxi

cabin /ˈkæbɪn/ *noun* **[C]** **1** [HOUSE] a small, simple house made of wood *a log cabin* **2** [SHIP] a small room to sleep in on a ship **3** [AIRCRAFT] the area where passengers sit on an aircraft

ˈcabin ˌcrew *noun* **[C]** the people on an aircraft who take care of the passengers as their job

cabinet /ˈkæbɪnət/ *noun* **1 the Cabinet** a group of people in a government who are chosen by and who advise the highest leader *a **Cabinet minister/member*** **2** **[C]** a cupboard with shelves or drawers to store or show things in *a **bathroom/medicine cabinet*** ➲See also: **filing cabinet.**

cable¹ /ˈkeɪbl/ *noun* **1** [WIRE] **[C, U]** a wire covered by plastic that carries electricity, telephone signals, etc *overhead **power cables*** **2** [ROPE] **[C, U]** thick wire twisted into a rope **3** [SYSTEM] **[U]** the system of sending television programmes or telephone signals along wires under the ground ***cable TV*** ○ *This channel is only available **on cable**.*

ˈcable ˌcar *noun* **[C]** a vehicle that hangs from thick cables and carries people up hills and mountains

ˌcable (TˈV) (*also* ˌ**cable ˈtelevision**) *noun* **[U]** a system of sending television pictures and sound along wires buried under the ground

cache /kæʃ/ *noun* **[C]** a secret supply of something *a **cache of weapons***

cachet /ˈkæʃeɪ/ [US] /kæʃˈeɪ/ *noun* **[U]** when something is admired or respected

cacophony /kəˈkɒfəni/ *noun* **[no plural]** a loud, unpleasant mixture of sounds

cactus /ˈkæktəs/ *noun* **[C]** *plural* **cacti** /ˈkæktaɪ/ or **cactuses** a plant with thick leaves for storing water and often sharp points that grows in deserts

cactus

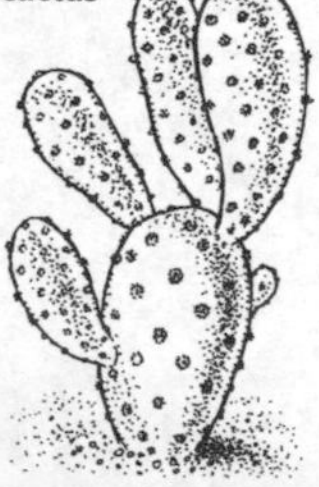

CAD /kæd/ *noun* **[U]** computer-aided design: the use of computers to design objects

caddie /ˈkædi/ *noun* **[C]** someone who carries the equipment for someone playing golf ➲See colour picture **Sports 2** on page Centre 15. • **caddie** *verb* **[I]** **caddying,** *past* **caddied** to be a caddie for someone

cadet /kəˈdet/ *noun* **[C]** a young person who is training to be in a military organization, the police, etc *an **army cadet***

caesarean (*also US* **cesarean**) /sɪˈzeəriən/ *noun* **[C]** an operation in which a baby is taken out of a woman through a cut in the front of her body

🔑**cafe** (*also* **café**) /ˈkæfeɪ/ [US] /kæˈfeɪ/ *noun* **[C]** a small restaurant where you can buy drinks and small meals

cafeteria /ˌkæfəˈtɪəriə/ *noun* **[C]** a restaurant where you collect and pay for your food and drink before you eat it *a school cafeteria*

caffeine /ˈkæfiːn/ *noun* **[U]** a chemical in coffee, tea, etc that makes you feel more awake

cage /keɪdʒ/ *noun* **[C]** a container made of wire or metal bars used for keeping birds or animals in *a **bird cage*** ➲See also: **rib cage.**

cage

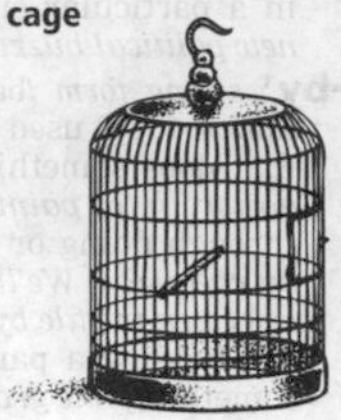

cagey /ˈkeɪdʒi/ *adjective* If someone is cagey, they are not very willing to give information, and you may think they are not honest. *He's very **cagey about** his past.*

cajole /kəˈdʒəʊl/ *verb* **[I, T]** to persuade someone to do something by being friendly or by promising them something **[+ into + doing sth]** *She cajoled me into helping with the dinner.*

🔑**cake** /keɪk/ *noun* **[C, U]** **1** a sweet food made from flour, butter, sugar, and eggs mixed together and baked *a chocolate/fruit cake* ○ *a **piece/slice of cake*** ○ *to bake/make a cake* ➲See colour picture **Food** on page Centre 11. **2 have your cake and eat it** to have or do two things that it is usually impossible to have or do at the same time ➲See also: the **icing** on the cake, be a **piece¹** of cake.

caked /keɪkt/ *adjective* **be caked in/with sth** to be covered with a thick, dry layer of something *His boots were caked in mud.*

calamity /kəˈlæməti/ *noun* **[C]** a sudden, bad event that causes a lot of damage or unhappiness *The next year brought with it a series of calamities.*

calcium /ˈkælsiəm/ *noun* **[U]** a chemical element in teeth, bones, and chalk (= a soft, white rock)

calculate /ˈkælkjəleɪt/ *verb* **1** **[T]** to discover an amount or number using mathematics *to calculate a cost/percentage* ○ *Have you calculated how much this is going to cost us?* **2 be calculated to do sth** to be intended to have a particular effect *His comments were calculated to embarrass the prime minister.*

calculated /ˈkælkjəleɪtɪd/ *adjective* based on careful thought or planning, not on emotion *a **calculated risk/decision***

calculating /'kælkjəleɪtɪŋ/ *adjective* Calculating people try to get what they want by thinking carefully and without emotion, and not caring about other people. *a cold, calculating criminal*

⟦WORD PARTNERS FOR **calculation**⟧

do/perform a calculation • a complex/precise/quick/rough calculation

calculation /ˌkælkjə'leɪʃ°n/ *noun* 1 [C, U] when you use mathematics to discover a number or amount *I did some quick calculations to see if I could afford to buy it.* 2 [U] when someone thinks very carefully about something without any emotion

calculator /'kælkjəleɪtə⟨r⟩/ *noun* [C] an electronic device that you use to do mathematical calculations *a pocket calculator*

calendar /'kæləndə⟨r⟩/ *noun* 1 [C] something that shows all the days, weeks, and months of the year 2 **the Christian/Jewish/Western, etc calendar** the system used to measure and arrange the days, weeks, months and special events of the year according to Christian/Jewish/Western, etc tradition 3 **the political/school/sporting, etc calendar** the events that are arranged during the year for a particular activity or organization

calf /kɑːf/ *noun* [C] *plural* **calves** /kɑːvz/ 1 a young cow 2 the back of your leg below your knee ⊃See colour picture **The Body** on page Centre 13.

calibre *UK* (*US* **caliber**) /'kælɪbə⟨r⟩/ *noun* [U] 1 the quality or level of ability of someone or something *The calibre of applicants was very high.* 2 the measurement across the inside of a gun, or across a bullet

CALL /kɔːl/ *abbreviation for* computer aided language learning: a way of learning languages using computers

⟦WORD PARTNERS FOR **call**⟧

make/get/take a call • give sb a call • a call from/to sb

o⧫**call²** /kɔːl/ *noun* [C] 1 ⟦TELEPHONE⟧ (*also* **phone call**) when you use the telephone *Give me a call at the weekend.* ○ *I got a call from Sue this morning.* 2 **a call for sth** a demand for something to happen *a call for action/peace* 3 ⟦VISIT⟧ a short visit *I thought I'd pay Gary a call.* 4 ⟦SHOUT⟧ when someone shouts something 5 ⟦BIRD⟧ a sound made by a bird or other animal 6 **sb's call** *informal* when someone can decide something *I don't mind what we do - it's your call.* 7 **call for sth** when people want or need a particular thing *There's not much call for interior designers round here.* 8 **be on call** to be ready to go to work if you are needed, as part of your job 9 **a close call** when something you do not want to happen nearly happens ⊃See also: be at sb's **beck and call**, **wake-up call**.

o⧫**call¹** /kɔːl/ *verb* 1 **be called sth** to have a particular name *a man called John* ○ *What's your dog called?* ○ *Their latest record is called "Ecstasy".* 2 ⟦GIVE NAME⟧ [+ two objects] to give someone or something a particular name *I want to call the baby Alex.* 3 ⟦DESCRIBE⟧ [+ two objects] to describe someone or something in a particular way *She called him a liar.* 4 ⟦ASK TO COME⟧ [T] to ask someone to come somewhere *She called me into her office.* 5 ⟦SHOUT⟧ [I, T] (*also* **call out**) to shout or say something in a loud voice *I thought I heard someone calling my name.* 6 ⟦TELEPHONE⟧ [I, T] to telephone someone *He called me every night while he was away.* ○ *Has anyone called the police?* ⊃See Common learner error at **phone**. 7 ⟦VISIT⟧ [I] (*also* **call by/in/round**) *UK* to visit someone for a short time *John called round earlier.* 8 **call an election/meeting, etc** to arrange for an election/meeting, etc to happen *The chairman has called an emergency meeting.* ⊃See also: call sb's **bluff²**, call it a **day**.

call back *UK* to go back to a place in order to see someone or collect something *I'll call back later to pick up the books.*

call (sb) back to telephone someone again, or to telephone someone who telephoned you earlier *I can't talk now - I'll call you back in ten minutes.*

call for sth 1 to demand that something happens *to call for a ban on guns* 2 to need or deserve a particular action or quality *You passed your test? This calls for a celebration!*

call for sb to go to a place in order to collect someone *I'll call for you at eight.*

call sth off 1 to decide that a planned event or activity will not happen because it is not possible, useful, or wanted now *The game has been called off because of the weather.* 2 to decide to stop an activity *Police have called off the search.*

call on sb to do sth to ask someone in a formal way to do something *He called on the rebels to stop fighting.*

call (sb) up *mainly US* to telephone someone *My dad called me up to tell me the good news.*

call sth up to find and show information on a computer screen *I'll just call up your account details.*

be called up to be ordered to join a military organization or asked to join an official team *He was called up soon after the war started.*

'call ˌcentre *noun* [C] *UK* a place where people use telephones to provide information to customers, or to sell goods or services

caller /'kɔːlə⟨r⟩/ *noun* [C] 1 someone who makes a telephone call *an anonymous caller* 2 *mainly UK* someone who visits for a short time

call-in /'kɔːlɪn/ *US* (*UK* **phone-in**) *noun* [C] a television or radio programme in which the public can ask questions or give opinions over the telephone

calling /'kɔːlɪŋ/ *noun* [C] a strong feeling that you should do a particular type of work *She found her true calling in teaching.*

callous /'kæləs/ *adjective* cruel and not caring about other people *a callous remark* • **callously** *adverb*

o⧫**calm¹** /kɑːm/ *adjective* 1 ⟦PERSON⟧ relaxed and not worried, frightened, or excited *a calm voice/manner* ○ *Try to stay calm - the doctor will be here soon.* 2 ⟦SEA⟧ If the sea is calm, it is still and has no large waves. 3 ⟦WEATHER⟧ If the weather

| j yes | k cat | ŋ ring | ʃ she | θ thin | ð this | ʒ decision | dʒ jar | tʃ chip | æ cat | e bed | ə ago | ɪ sit | i cosy | ɒ hot | ʌ run | ʊ put |

is calm, there are no storms or wind. ● **calm-ness** *noun* [U]

calm² /kɑːm/ *noun* [U] when people or conditions are calm

calm³ /kɑːm/ *verb* [T] to make someone stop feeling upset, angry, or excited *The police tried to calm the crowd.* ○ *a calming effect*

calm (sb) down to stop feeling upset, angry, or excited, or to make someone stop feeling this way *Calm down and tell me what's wrong.*

calmly /'kɑːmli/ *adverb* in a relaxed way *He spoke slowly and calmly.*

calorie /'kælᵊri/ *noun* [C] a unit for measuring the amount of energy food provides *I try to eat about 2000 calories a day.*

calves /kɑːvz/ *plural of* calf

camaraderie /ˌkæməˈrɑːdᵊri/ *noun* [U] special friendship felt by people who work together or experience something together

camcorder /'kæmˌkɔːdᵊ/ *noun* [C] a camera that you can hold in your hand and that takes moving pictures

came /keɪm/ *past tense of* come

camel /'kæmᵊl/ *noun* [C] a large animal that lives in the desert and has one or two humps (= raised parts on its back)

camel

cameo /'kæmiəʊ/ *noun* [C] when someone famous appears for a short time in a film or play *a cameo role*

o⁻**camera** /'kæmᵊrə/ *noun* [C] a piece of equipment used to take photographs or to make films *a digital camera* ○ *a television camera*

cameraman /'kæmᵊrəmæn/ *noun* [C] *plural* **cameramen** someone who operates a television camera or film camera as their job

camisole /'kæmɪsəʊl/ *noun* [C] a piece of women's underwear for the top half of the body, with thin straps that go over the shoulders *a lace camisole* ➔See colour picture **Clothes** at page Centre 9.

camouflage /'kæməflɑːʒ/ *noun* [U] when the colour or pattern on something is similar to the area around it making it difficult to see *a camouflage jacket* ● **camouflage** *verb* [T]

camp¹ /kæmp/ *noun* **1** [C] an area where people stay in tents for a short time, usually for a holiday **2 an army/prison/refugee, etc camp** an area containing temporary buildings or tents used for soldiers/prisoners/refugees (= people forced to leave their home), etc ➔See also: **base camp**, **concentration camp**.

camp² /kæmp/ (*also* **camp out**) *verb* [I] to stay in a tent or temporary shelter *We camped on the beach for two nights.*

campaign¹ /kæm'peɪn/ *noun* [C] **1** a series of organized activities or events intended to achieve a result *an advertising/election campaign* **2** a series of military attacks *a bombing campaign*

campaign² /kæm'peɪn/ *verb* [I] to organize a series of activities to try to achieve something *to campaign against/for something* ● **campaigner** *noun* [C] *an animal rights campaigner*

camper /'kæmpᵊ/ *noun* [C] **1** someone who stays in a tent on holiday **2** (*also* '**camper ,van**) a vehicle containing a bed, kitchen equipment, etc that you can live in

camping /'kæmpɪŋ/ *noun* [U] when you stay in a tent for a holiday *We're going camping in France this summer.* ○ *a camping trip*

camping or **campsite**?

Be careful not to use **camping**, the activity of staying in a tent, when you mean **campsite**, the area of ground where you do this.

campsite /'kæmpsaɪt/ (*also US* **campground** /'kæmpgraʊnd/) *noun* [C] an area where people can stay in tents for a holiday

campus /'kæmpəs/ *noun* [C, U] the land and buildings belonging to a college or university *I lived on campus in my first year.*

o⁻**can¹** *strong form* /kæn/ *weak forms* /kən, kn/ *modal verb past* **could 1** ⌈ABILITY⌉ to be able to do something *We can't pay the rent.* ○ *Can you drive?* **2** ⌈PERMISSION⌉ to be allowed to do something *You can't park here.* ○ *Can I go now?* **3** ⌈ASK⌉ used to ask someone to do or provide something *Can you tell her to meet me outside?* ○ *Can I have a drink of water?* **4** ⌈OFFER⌉ used to politely offer to do something *Can I carry those bags for you?* **5** ⌈POSSIBLE⌉ used to talk about what is possible *You can buy stamps from the shop on the corner.* ○ *Smoking can cause cancer.* **6** ⌈TYPICAL⌉ used to talk about how someone often behaves or what something is often like *She can be really rude at times.* **7** ⌈SURPRISE⌉ used to show surprise or lack of belief *You can't possibly be hungry already!* ○ *Can you believe it?* ➔See Extra help page **Modal verbs** on page Centre 22 .

can² /kæn/ *noun* [C] **1** a closed, metal container for food or liquids *a can of soup/beans* ○ *a can of paint* ➔See picture at **container**. **2 a can of worms** a situation which causes a lot of trouble for you when you start to deal with it ➔See also: **trash can**, **watering can**.

can³ /kæn/ *verb* [T] **canning** *past* **canned** to put food or drink into metal containers in a factory *canned tomatoes*

Canadian /kə'neɪdiən/ *adjective* relating to Canada ● **Canadian** *noun* [C] someone who comes from Canada

canal /kə'næl/ *noun* [C] an artificial river built for boats to travel along or to take water where it is needed

canary /kə'neᵊri/ *noun* [C] a small, yellow bird that sings

cancel /'kænsᵊl/ *verb* [T] *UK* **cancelling**, *past* **can-**

celled, US canceling, *past* canceled **1** to say that an organized event will not now happen [often passive] *The meeting has been cancelled.* **2** to stop an order for goods or services that you do not now want

cancel sth out If something cancels out another thing, it stops it from having any effect.

cancellation /ˌkænsəˈleɪʃᵊn/ *noun* [C, U] when someone decides that an event will not now happen or stops an order for something *a last-minute cancellation*

Cancer /ˈkænsəʳ/ *noun* [C, U] the sign of the zodiac which relates to the period of 22 June - 22 July, or a person born during this period ⊃See picture at **zodiac.**

cancer /ˈkænsəʳ/ *noun* [C, U] a serious disease that is caused when cells in the body grow in a way that is uncontrolled and not normal *breast/lung cancer* ○ *His wife died of cancer.* • **cancerous** *adjective a cancerous growth*

candid /ˈkændɪd/ *adjective* honest, especially about something that is unpleasant or embarrassing *She was very candid about her personal life in the interview.* • **candidly** *adverb*

candidacy /ˈkændɪdəsi/ *noun* [U] when someone is a candidate in an election

candidate /ˈkændɪdət/ *noun* [C] **1** one of the people taking part in an election or trying to get a job *a presidential candidate* **2** UK someone who is taking an exam

candle /ˈkændl/ *noun* [C] a stick of wax with string going through it that you burn to produce light ⊃See colour picture **The Living Room** on page Centre 4.

candle

candlelight /ˈkændllaɪt/ *noun* [U] light produced by a candle

candlestick /ˈkændlstɪk/ *noun* [C] an object that holds a candle

can-do /ˌkænˈduː/ *adjective informal* determined to deal with problems and achieve results *I really admire her can-do attitude.*

candour UK (US **candor**) /ˈkændəʳ/ *noun* [U] when you speak honestly, especially about something that is unpleasant or embarrassing

candy /ˈkændi/ *noun* [C, U] US a small piece of sweet food made from sugar, chocolate, etc *a box of candy* ○ *a candy bar*

cane¹ /keɪn/ *noun* **1** STEM [C, U] the long, hard, hollow stem of some plants, sometimes used to make furniture **2** WALK [C] a long stick used by people to help them walk **3** PUNISH [C] UK a long stick used in the past to hit children at school

cane² /keɪn/ *verb* [T] UK to hit someone, especially a school student, with a stick as a punishment

canine /ˈkeɪnaɪn/ *adjective* relating to dogs

canister /ˈkænɪstəʳ/ *noun* [C] a metal container for gases or dry things *a gas canister*

cannabis /ˈkænəbɪs/ *mainly UK* (*mainly US* **marijuana**) *noun* [U] a drug that some people smoke for pleasure and that is illegal in many countries *cannabis users*

canned /kænd/ (*also UK* **tinned**) *adjective* Canned food is sold in metal containers.

cannibal /ˈkænɪbᵊl/ *noun* [C] someone who eats human flesh • **cannibalism** *noun* [U]

cannon /ˈkænən/ *noun* [C] a very large gun, in the past one that was on wheels

ℴ**cannot** /ˈkænɒt/ *modal verb* the negative form of 'can' *I cannot predict what will happen.*

canny /ˈkæni/ *adjective* clever and able to think quickly, especially about money or business *a canny businessman*

canoe /kəˈnuː/ *noun* [C] a small, narrow boat with pointed ends that you move using a paddle (= stick with a wide, flat part) • **canoeing** *noun* [U] the activity of travelling in a canoe

canoe

canon /ˈkænən/ *noun* [C] a Christian priest who works in a cathedral (= large, important church) *the Canon of Westminster*

'can ˌopener (*also UK* **tin opener**) *noun* [C] a piece of kitchen equipment for opening metal food containers ⊃See colour picture **The Kitchen** on page Centre 2.

canopy /ˈkænəpi/ *noun* [C] a cover or type of roof for protection or decoration

can't /kɑːnt/ *modal verb* **1** *short for* cannot *I can't find my keys.* **2** used to suggest that someone should do something *Can't you ask Jonathan to help?*

canteen /kænˈtiːn/ *noun* [C] a restaurant in an office, factory, or school

canter /ˈkæntəʳ/ *verb* [I] When a horse canters, it runs quite fast. *Hattie cantered around the field.* • **canter** *noun* [no plural]

canvas /ˈkænvəs/ *noun* **1** [U] strong cloth used for making sails, tents, etc **2** [C] a piece of canvas used for a painting

canvass /ˈkænvəs/ *verb* **1** [I, T] to try to persuade people to vote for someone in an election *He's canvassing for the Labour party.* **2** [T] to ask people their opinion about something *The study canvassed the views of over 9000 people.*

canyon /ˈkænjən/ *noun* [C] a deep valley with very steep sides

cap¹ /kæp/ *noun* [C] **1** a hat with a flat, curved part at the front *a baseball cap* ⊃See colour picture **Clothes** on page Centre 9. **2** a small lid that covers the top or end of something ⊃See also: **skull cap.**

cap² /kæp/ *verb* [T] **capping**, *past* **capped 1** END to be the last and the best or worst event in a series of events *The party capped a wonderful week.* **2** LIMIT to put a limit on an amount of money that can be borrowed, charged, etc [often passive] *The interest rate has been capped at 5%.* **3** [COVER] to cover the top of something [often passive] *The mountains were capped with snow.*

capability /ˌkeɪpəˈbɪləti/ *noun* [C, U] the ability or power to do something [+ to do sth] *Both players have the capability to win this match.*

capable /ˈkeɪpəbl/ *adjective* **1** able to do things effectively and achieve results *She's a very capable young woman.* **2 capable of sth/doing sth** having the ability or qualities to be able to do something *She was capable of great cruelty.* ➲Opposite **incapable.**

capacity /kəˈpæsəti/ *noun* **1** [CONTAIN] [C, U] the largest amount or number that a container, building, etc can hold *The restaurant has **a capacity of** about 200.* ○ *The stadium was **filled to capacity*** (= completely full). **2** [PRODUCE] [U] the amount that a factory or machine can produce *The factory is operating **at full capacity*** (= producing as much as possible). **3** [ABILITY] [C] the ability to do, experience, or understand something *She has a great **capacity for** love.* **4** [JOB] [C] a position or job *He attended over 100 events last year **in his capacity as** mayor.*

cape /keɪp/ *noun* [C] **1** a loose coat without any sleeves that is fastened at the neck **2** a large area of land that goes out into the sea

caper /ˈkeɪpər/ *noun* [C] something that is done as a joke, or intended to entertain people *His new movie is a **comic caper**.*

capillary /kəˈpɪlᵊri/ [US] /ˈkæpəleri/ *noun* [C] a very thin tube that carries blood around the body

⊶**capital¹** /ˈkæpɪtᵊl/ *noun* **1** [CITY] [C] the most important city in a country or state, where the government is based *Paris is the capital of France.* **2** [MONEY] [U] an amount of money that you can use to start a business or to make more money **3** [LETTER] [C] (*also* ˌcapital ˈletter) a large letter of the alphabet used at the beginning of sentences and names ➲See Extra help page **Punctuation** on page Centre 33 ➲See also: **block capitals.**

capital² /ˈkæpɪtᵊl/ *adjective* **a capital crime/offence** a crime that can be punished by death

capitalism /ˈkæpɪtᵊlɪzᵊm/ *noun* [U] a political and economic system in which industry is owned privately for profit and not by the state

capitalist /ˈkæpɪtᵊlɪst/ *noun* [C] someone who supports capitalism • **capitalist** *adjective a capitalist society*

capitalize (*also UK* **-ise**) /ˈkæpɪtᵊlaɪz/ *verb* [T] to write something using capital letters, or starting with a capital letter

capitalize on sth to use a situation to achieve something good for yourself *He failed to capitalize on his earlier success.*

ˌ**capital ˈpunishment** *noun* [U] when someone is killed by the state for committing a serious crime

capitulate /kəˈpɪtjʊleɪt/ *verb* [I] to stop disagreeing or fighting with someone and agree to what they want • **capitulation** /kəˌpɪtjʊˈleɪʃᵊn/ *noun* [C, U]

cappuccino /ˌkæpʊˈtʃiːnəʊ/ *noun* [C, U] coffee made with milk that has been heated with steam to produce a lot of small bubbles

capricious /kəˈprɪʃəs/ *adjective* likely to suddenly change your ideas or behaviour

Capricorn /ˈkæprɪkɔːn/ *noun* [C, U] the sign of the zodiac which relates to the period of 23 December - 20 January, or a person born during this period ➲See picture at **zodiac.**

capsize /kæpˈsaɪz/ *verb* [I, T] If a boat capsizes, or if it is capsized, it turns over in the water. *A huge wave capsized the yacht.*

capsule /ˈkæpsjuːl/ *noun* [C] **1** a small container with medicine inside that you swallow **2** the part of a spacecraft that people live in

captain¹ /ˈkæptɪn/ *noun* [C] **1** [SHIP] the person in control of a ship or aircraft **2** [ARMY] an officer of middle rank in the army, navy, or air force **3** [SPORT] the leader of a team

captain² /ˈkæptɪn/ *verb* [T] to be the captain of a team, ship, or aircraft *He has captained the England cricket team three times.*

captaincy /ˈkæptɪnsi/ *noun* [U] when someone is the captain of a team

caption /ˈkæpʃᵊn/ *noun* [C] words written under a picture to explain it

captivate /ˈkæptɪveɪt/ *verb* [T] to interest or attract someone very much *She captivated film audiences with her beauty and charm.* • **captivating** *adjective a captivating performance*

captive¹ /ˈkæptɪv/ *adjective* **1** A captive person or animal is being kept somewhere and is not allowed to leave. **2 a captive audience/market** a group of people who have to watch something or have to buy something because they do not have a choice **3 hold/take sb captive** to keep someone as a prisoner, or make someone a prisoner *They were held captive for 32 days.*

captive² /ˈkæptɪv/ *noun* [C] someone who is kept as a prisoner

captivity /kæpˈtɪvəti/ *noun* [U] when a person or animal is kept somewhere and is not allowed to leave *lion cubs born **in captivity***

capture¹ /ˈkæptʃər/ *verb* [T] **1** [PRISONER] to catch someone and make them your prisoner *Two soldiers were captured by the enemy.* **2** [CONTROL] to get control of a place with force *Rebel troops have captured the city.* **3** [GET] to succeed in getting something when you are competing against other people *The Green Party has captured 12% of the vote.* **4** [DESCRIBE] to show or describe something successfully using words or pictures *His book really captures the spirit of the place.* **5 capture sb/sth on camera/film, etc** to record someone or something on camera/film, etc **6 capture sb's attention/imagination** to make someone very interested or excited *The campaign has really captured the public's imagination.* **7 capture sb's heart** to make someone love you *She captured the hearts of the nation.*

capture² /ˈkæptʃər/ *noun* [U] **1** when someone is caught and made a prisoner *He shot himself to avoid capture.* **2** when someone gets control of a place with force *the capture of the city by foreign troops*

WORD PARTNERS FOR *car*

drive/park/start a car • a car **breaks down** • **by** car • a car **accident/crash** • a car **driver**

⊶**car** /kɑːʳ/ *noun* [C] **1** a vehicle with an engine, four wheels, and seats for a small number of passengers *She goes to work* ***by car****.* ○ *Where did you* ***park your car****?* ➲See colour picture **Car** on page Centre 7. **2** *US* a part of a train in which passengers sit, eat, sleep, etc *the dining car* ➲See also: **buffet car, cable car, estate car, sports car.**

caramel /ˈkærəmᵊl/ *noun* [C, U] sugar that has been heated until it turns brown and that is used to add colour and flavour to food, or a sweet made from sugar, milk, and butter

carat (*also US* **karat**) /ˈkærət/ *noun* [C] a unit for measuring how pure gold is, or how much jewels (= valuable stones) weigh *22 carat gold*

caravan /ˈkærəvæn/ *noun* [C] **1** *UK* a vehicle which people can live in on holiday and which is pulled by a car *a* ***caravan site*** **2** a group of people with animals or vehicles who travel together across a desert

carbohydrate /ˌkɑːbəʊˈhaɪdreɪt/ *noun* [C, U] a substance in food such as sugar, potatoes, etc that gives your body energy

carbon /ˈkɑːbᵊn/ *noun* [U] a chemical element present in all animals and plants and in coal and oil

carbonated /ˈkɑːbəneɪtɪd/ *adjective* Carbonated drinks contain a lot of small bubbles.

ˌcarbon ˈcopy *noun* [C] **1** a copy of a written document that is made using carbon paper (= thin paper covered in carbon) **2** an exact copy of something *He's a* ***carbon copy of*** *his father.*

carbon dioxide /ˌkɑːbᵊndaɪˈɒksaɪd/ *noun* [U] a gas that is produced when people and animals breathe out, or when carbon is burned

ˈcarbon ˌemissions *noun* [plural] carbon dioxide and carbon monoxide made by things such as factories or cars that burn carbon and cause pollution

carbon monoxide /ˌkɑːbᵊnməˈnɒksaɪd/ *noun* [U] a poisonous gas that is produced by burning some types of fuel, especially petrol (= fuel for cars)

ˌcarbon ˈneutral *adjective* not producing carbon emissions *a carbon netral fuel/home/lifestyle*

ˈcarbon ˌpaper *noun* [U] thin paper that is covered on one side with carbon (= a black substance) and is used for making copies of written documents

ˌcar ˈboot sale *noun* [C] *UK* an event where people sell things they no longer want from the backs of their cars

carburettor *UK* (*US* **carburetor**) /ˌkɑːbəˈretəʳ/ [US] /ˈkɑːbəreɪtər/ *noun* [C] the part of an engine that mixes fuel and air which are then burned to provide power

carcass /ˈkɑːkəs/ *noun* [C] the body of a dead animal

carcinogen /kɑːˈsɪnədʒᵊn/ *noun* [C] a substance that can cause cancer (= a disease when cells in your body grow in an uncontrolled way) • **carcinogenic** /ˌkɑːsɪnəʊˈdʒenɪk/ *adjective carcinogenic chemicals*

⊶**card** /kɑːd/ *noun* **1** [MESSAGE] [C] a folded piece of stiff paper with a picture on the front and a message inside that you send to someone on a special occasion *a* ***birthday card*** **2** [INFORMATION] [C] a piece of stiff paper or plastic that has information printed on it *a library card* **3** [GAME] [C] (*also* **playing card**) one of a set of 52 pieces of stiff paper with numbers and pictures used for playing games *UK a pack of cards/ US a deck of cards* ○ *We spent the evening* ***playing cards*** (= playing games using cards). **4** [PAPER] [U] *UK* thick, stiff paper **5** [WITHOUT ENVELOPE] [C] a postcard (= card with a picture on one side that you send without an envelope) **6** [COMPUTER] a part inside a computer which controls how the computer operates *a graphics/sound card* **7 be on the cards** *UK* (*US* **be in the cards**) to be likely to happen *Do you think marriage is on the cards?* **8 put/lay your cards on the table** to tell someone honestly what you think or plan to do ➲See also: **cash card, charge card, Christmas card, credit card, debit card, phone card, smart card, swipe card, trump card, wild card.**

cardboard /ˈkɑːdbɔːd/ *noun* [U] thick, stiff paper that is used for making boxes

cardiac /ˈkɑːdiæk/ *adjective* [always before noun] relating to the heart *cardiac surgery* ○ ***cardiac arrest*** (= when the heart stops beating)

cardigan /ˈkɑːdɪgən/ *noun* [C] a piece of clothing, often made of wool, that covers the top part of your body and fastens at the front ➲See colour picture **Clothes** on page Centre 8.

cardinal¹ /ˈkɑːdɪnᵊl/ *noun* [C] a priest with a high rank in the Catholic Church *Cardinal Basil Hume*

cardinal² /ˈkɑːdɪnᵊl/ *adjective* [always before noun] *formal* extremely important or serious *One of the* ***cardinal rules*** *of business is know what your customer wants.*

ˌcardinal ˈnumber (*also* **cardinal**) *noun* [C] a number such as 1, 2, 3, etc that shows the quantity of something

⊶**care¹** /keəʳ/ *verb* **1** [I, T] to think that something is important and to feel interested in it or worried about it *He* ***cares*** *deeply* ***about*** *the environment.* ○ [+ question word] *I don't care how long it takes - just get the job done.* **2** [I] to love someone *Your parents are only doing this because they* ***care about*** *you.* ○ *I knew that Amy still* ***cared for*** *me.* **3 I/he, etc couldn't care less** *informal* used to emphasize that someone is not interested in or worried about something or someone [+ question word] *I couldn't care less what people think.* **4 Who cares?** *informal* used to emphasize that you do not think something is important *"Manchester United will be in the final if they win this match." "Who cares?"* **5 Would you care for sth/to do sth?** *formal* used to ask someone if they want something or want to do something *Would you care for a drink?* ○ *Would you care to join us for dinner?*

care for sb/sth to look after someone or something, especially someone who is young, old, or ill *The children are being cared for by a relative.*

not care for sth/sb *formal* to not like something or someone *I don't care for modern music.*

WORD PARTNERS FOR care

take care of sb • need/provide/receive care • constant/long-term care • in/under sb's care

---

care² /keə^r/ *noun* 1 [PROTECTION] [U] the process of looking after something or someone, especially someone who is young, old, or ill *skin/hair care* ○ *A small baby requires constant care.* 2 [ATTENTION] [U] If you do something with care, you give a lot of attention to it so that you do not make a mistake or damage anything. *She planned the trip with great care.* ○ *Fragile - please handle with care.* 3 **take care** to give a lot of attention to what you are doing so that you do not have an accident or make a mistake *The roads are very icy so take care when you drive home.* 4 **Take care!** *informal* used when saying goodbye to someone *See you soon, Bob - take care!* 5 [WORRY] [C] a feeling of worry *He was sixteen years old and didn't have a care in the world* (= had no worries). 6 **in care** *UK* Children who are in care are looked after by government organizations because their parents cannot look after them. *She was put/taken into care at the age of twelve.* 7 **take care of sb/sth** to look after someone or something *My parents are going to take care of the house while we're away.* 8 **take care of sth/doing sth** to be responsible for dealing with something *I did the cooking while Guy took care of the washing up.* ⊃See also: intensive care.

WORD PARTNERS FOR career

begin/embark on/launch a career • follow/pursue a career • a career in sth • a career change • career opportunities/prospects

---

career¹ /kə'rɪə^r/ *noun* [C] 1 a job that you do for a long period of your life and that gives you the chance to move to a higher position and earn more money *a successful career in marketing* 2 the time that you spend doing a particular job *She began her acting career in TV commercials.* ⊃See Common learner error at **work.**

career² /kə'rɪə^r/ *verb* **career down/into/off, etc** *UK* to move quickly and in an uncontrolled way *The train careered off a bridge and plunged into the river.*

carefree /'keəfriː/ *adjective* without any worries or problems *a carefree childhood*

careful /'keəf^əl/ *adjective* giving a lot of attention to what you are doing so that you do not have an accident, make a mistake, or damage something *careful planning/consideration* ○ **Be careful**, *Michael - that knife's very sharp.* ○ [+ to do sth] *We were careful to avoid the midday sun.* • **carefully** *adverb a carefully prepared speech*

OTHER WAYS OF SAYING careful

If someone is careful to avoid risks or danger, you can describe them as **cautious**: *She's a very cautious driver.*

The expression **play (it) safe** also means 'to be careful to avoid risks': *I think I'll play it safe and get the earlier train.*

If someone does something in a very careful way, paying great attention to detail, you can use adjectives such as **meticulous**, **methodical**, and **painstaking**: *This book is the result of years of meticulous/painstaking research.*

---

caregiver /'keə,gɪvə^r/ *US* (*UK* carer) *noun* [C] someone who looks after a person who is young, old, or ill

careless /'keələs/ *adjective* not giving enough attention to what you are doing *It was very careless of you to forget your passport.* ○ *He was fined £250 for careless driving.* • **carelessly** *adverb* • **carelessness** *noun* [U]

carer /'keərə^r/ *UK* (*US* caregiver) *noun* [C] someone who looks after a person who is young, old, or ill

caress /kə'res/ *verb* [T] to touch someone in a gentle way that shows that you love them • **caress** *noun* [C]

caretaker /'keə,teɪkə^r/ *noun* [C] 1 someone whose job is to look after a large building, such as a school 2 *US* someone who looks after a person who is young, old, or ill

cargo /'kɑːgəʊ/ *noun* [C, U] *plural* **cargoes** goods that are carried in a vehicle *a cargo of oil* ○ *a cargo ship/plane*

caricature /'kærɪkətʃʊə^r/ *noun* [C] a funny drawing or description of someone, especially someone famous, which makes part of their appearance or character more noticeable than it really is • **caricature** *verb* [T]

caring /'keərɪŋ/ *adjective* kind and supporting other people *She's a very caring person.*

carjacking /'kɑː,dʒækɪŋ/ *noun* [C, U] the crime of attacking someone who is driving and stealing their car • **carjacker** *noun* [C] someone who commits the crime of carjacking

carnage /'kɑːnɪdʒ/ *noun* [U] *formal* when a lot of people are violently killed or injured

carnation /kɑː'neɪʃ^ən/ *noun* [C] a small flower with a sweet smell that is usually white, pink, or red

carnival /'kɑːnɪv^əl/ *noun* [C] 1 a public celebration where people wear special clothes and dance and play music in the roads 2 *US* a place of outside entertainment where there are machines you can ride on and games that can be played for prizes

carnivore /'kɑːnɪvɔː^r/ *noun* [C] an animal that eats meat • **carnivorous** /kɑː'nɪv^ərəs/ *adjective* eating meat

carol /'kær^əl/ (*also* Christmas carol) *noun* [C] a song that people sing at Christmas

carousel /,kærə'sel/ *noun* [C] 1 a moving strip where passengers collect their bags at an airport 2 *mainly US* a machine that goes round

---

and round and has toy animals or cars for children to ride on

carp[1] /kɑːp/ *noun* [C, U] *plural* carp a large fish that lives in lakes and rivers, or the meat of this fish

carp[2] /kɑːp/ *verb* [I] to complain continually about things that are not important *He's always carping about how badly organized the office is.*

'car ,park UK (US parking lot) *noun* [C] a place where vehicles can be parked

carpenter /'kɑːpəntər/ *noun* [C] a person whose job is making and repairing wooden objects

carpentry /'kɑːpəntri/ *noun* [U] making and repairing wooden objects

carpet /'kɑːpɪt/ *noun* **1** [C, U] thick material for covering floors, often made of wool *a new living room carpet* ○ *UK fitted carpets* (= carpets that cover floors from wall to wall) **2 a carpet of sth** a thick layer of something that covers the ground *a carpet of snow* ● **carpet** *verb* [T] to put carpet on the floor of a room *The stairs were carpeted.* ⊃See also: **the red carpet.**

carriage /'kærɪdʒ/ *noun* **1** [TRAIN] [C] UK one of the separate parts of a train where the passengers sit *The front carriage of the train is for first-class passengers only.* **2** [WITH HORSE] [C] a vehicle with wheels that is pulled by a horse **3** [GOODS] [U] UK the cost of transporting goods ⊃See also: **baby carriage.**

carriageway /'kærɪdʒweɪ/ *noun* [C] UK one of the two sides of a motorway or main road *an accident on the southbound carriageway* ⊃See also: **dual carriageway.**

carrier /'kæriər/ *noun* [C] **1** [TRANSPORT] a person, vehicle, or machine that transports things from one place to another **2** [DISEASE] a person who has a disease that they can give to other people without suffering from it themselves **3** [COMPANY] a company that operates aircraft ⊃See also: **aircraft carrier, letter carrier.**

'carrier ,bag *noun* [C] UK a large paper or plastic bag with handles that you are given in a shop to carry the things that you have bought ⊃See picture at **bag.**

carrot /'kærət/ *noun* **1** [C, U] an orange-coloured vegetable that is long and thin and grows in the ground ⊃See colour picture **Fruit and Vegetables** on page Centre 10. **2** [C] *informal* something that is offered to someone in order to encourage them to do something **3 carrot and stick** If you use a carrot-and-stick method, you offer someone rewards if they do something and say you will punish them if they do not.

o─**carry** /'kæri/ *verb* **1** [HOLD] [T] to hold something or someone with your hands, arms, or on your back and take them from one place to another *He was carrying my bags.* **2** [TRANSPORT] [T] to move someone or something from one place to another *The plane was carrying 30 passengers.* ○ *Strong currents carried them out to sea.* **3** [HAVE WITH YOU] [T] to have something with you in a pocket, bag, etc *She still carries his photo in her purse.* **4** [DISEASE] [T] to have a disease that you might give to someone else *Mosquitoes carry malaria and other infectious diseases.*

5 [PART] [T] to have something as a part or a result *of something All cigarette advertising must carry a government health warning.* ○ *Murder still carries the death penalty there.* **6** [SOUND] [I] If a sound or someone's voice carries, it can be heard a long way away. *The sound of the explosion carried for miles.* **7** [SUPPORT] [T] to support the weight of something *Is the ice thick enough to carry my weight?* ○ *The weight of the cathedral roof is carried by two rows of pillars.* **8** [DEVELOP] [T] to develop something in a particular way *She carried her diet to extremes.* **9 be carried** to be formally accepted by people voting at a meeting *The motion was carried by 210 votes to 160.* ⊃See also: carry **weight.**

be carried away to be so excited about something that you do not control what you say or do *There's far too much food - I'm afraid I got a bit carried away.*

carry sth off to succeed in doing or achieving something difficult *It's not an easy part to act but he carried it off brilliantly.*

carry on to continue doing something [+ doing sth] *The doctors have warned him but he just carries on drinking.* ○ *Carry on with your work while I'm gone.* ○ *Daphne is carrying on the family tradition by becoming a lawyer.*

carry out sth to do or complete something, especially something that you have said you would do or that you have been told to do *I was only carrying out orders.* ○ *Nigel is carrying out research on early Islamic art.*

carryall /'kæriɔːl/ US (UK holdall) *noun* [C] a large bag for carrying clothes ⊃See picture at luggage.

cart[1] /kɑːt/ *noun* [C] **1** a vehicle with two or four wheels that is pulled by an animal and used for carrying goods **2** US (UK trolley) a metal structure on wheels that is used for carrying things ⊃See picture at trolley ⊃See also: go-cart.

cart[2] /kɑːt/ *verb informal* **cart sb/sth around/ away/off, etc** to take someone or something somewhere *I've had to cart the kids around with me all day* ○ *I've been carting these letters around with me all week, and I still haven't posted them.*

carte blanche /,kɑːt'blɑːnʃ/ *noun* [U] complete freedom to do what you want [+ to do sth] *She was given carte blanche to make whatever changes she wanted.*

cartel /kɑː'tel/ *noun* [C] a group of companies who join together to control prices and limit competition

cartilage /'kɑːtɪlɪdʒ/ *noun* [C, U] a strong elastic substance found where two bones connect in the human body *Owen has a torn cartilage in his right knee.*

carton /'kɑːtən/ *noun* [C] a container for food and drink that is made from strong, stiff paper or plastic *a carton of milk/fruit juice* ⊃See picture at **container.**

cartoon

cartoon /kɑːˈtuːn/ *noun* [C] **1** a film made using characters that are drawn and not real *Mickey Mouse and other famous* **cartoon characters** **2** a funny drawing, especially in a newspaper or magazine ● **cartoonist** *noun* [C] someone whose job is to draw cartoons

cartridge /ˈkɑːtrɪdʒ/ *noun* [C] **1** a small container that is used in a larger piece of equipment and can be easily replaced *an ink cartridge* **2** a tube containing an explosive substance and a bullet for use in a gun

carve /kɑːv/ *verb* [I, T] **1** to make an object, a shape, or a pattern by cutting wood, stone, etc *The statue was carved out of stone.* ○ *They had carved their initials into the tree.* **2** to cut a large piece of cooked meat into smaller pieces **3 carve (out) a niche/career/role, etc for yourself** to be successful in a particular job or activity
carve sth up to divide something into smaller parts, in a way that people do not approve of *The countryside has been carved up and sold to property developers.*

carving /ˈkɑːvɪŋ/ *noun* **1** [C] an object or a pattern that has been carved **2** [U] the activity of carving an object or pattern *wood carving*

cascade /kæsˈkeɪd/ *verb* [I] to fall quickly and in large amounts *Water cascaded from the rocks above.* ● **cascade** *noun* [C] *literary* a large amount of something, especially something falling or hanging *a cascade of golden hair*

○ⁿ**case** /keɪs/ *noun* **1** [SITUATION] [C] a particular situation or example of something *People were imprisoned, and, in some cases, killed for their beliefs.* ○ *We usually ask for references, but in your case it will not be necessary.* ○ *The whole film is based on a case of mistaken identity.* **2** [COURT OF LAW] [C] something that is decided in a court of law *a libel/criminal/divorce case* ○ *He lost his case.* **3** [CRIME] [C] a crime that police are trying to solve *a murder case* ○ *Police in the town have investigated 50 cases of burglary in the past month.* **4** [ILLNESS] [C] an illness, or somebody with an illness *4,000 new cases of the disease are diagnosed every year.* **5 be the case** to be true *Bad diet can cause tiredness, but I don't think that's the case here.* **6** [REASONS] [C] facts or reasons that prove a particular opinion [usually singular] *There is a*

strong **case for/against** bringing in the new legislation. ○ *mainly UK He* **put the case for** *more funding very convincingly.* **7** [CONTAINER] [C] a container for storing or protecting something *a pencil case* ○ *a cigarette case* **8** [BAG] [C] *UK another word for* suitcase (= a rectangular bag or container with a handle which you use for carrying clothes in when you are travelling) **9 (just) in case** because something might happen, or might have happened *I don't think that it's going to rain, but I'll bring a raincoat just in case.* **10 in any case** used to give another reason for something that you are saying, or that you have done *I don't want to go skiing and, in any case, I can't afford it.* **11 in that case/in which case** because that is the situation/if that is the situation *"Peter's coming tonight." "Oh, in that case, I'll stay in."* **12 be a case of doing sth** to be necessary to do something *We know that we're right. It's just a case of proving it.* **13 in case of sth** *formal* when something happens, or in preparation for when something happens *We keep a bucket of water backstage, in case of fire.* **14 a case in point** a good example of something *Supermarkets often charge too much for goods. Bananas are a case in point.* **15 be/get on sb's case** *informal* to criticize someone in an annoying way because of something that they have done *She's always on my case about something.* **16 be on the case** *UK informal* to be doing what needs to be done ⊃See also: lower case, upper case.

case ˈhistory *noun* [C] a record of what happens to a particular person *The study used case histories from 500 teenage boys.*

ˈcase ˌstudy *noun* [C] a report about a particular person or thing, to show an example of a general principle

WORD PARTNERS FOR *cash*

pay (in) cash ● [£50/$100, etc] in cash ● a cash **machine** ● cash **payments**

○ⁿ**cash¹** /kæʃ/ *noun* [U] **1** money in the form of coins or notes (= paper money) *I'm taking £50 in cash.* ○ *Are you paying by cheque or in cash?* **2** *informal* money in any form *She's a bit short of cash at the moment.* ○ *a cash prize* ⊃See also: e-cash, hard cash.

cash² /kæʃ/ *verb* **cash a cheque** to exchange a cheque (= piece of paper printed by a bank and used to pay for things) for coins or paper money
cash in on sth to get money or another advantage from an event or a situation, often in an unfair way *Her family have been accused of cashing in on her death.*

cashback /ˈkæʃbæk/ *noun* [U] *UK* money that you can take from your bank account when you pay in a shop with a bank card *£50 cashback*

ˈcash ˌcard *noun* [C] *UK* a plastic card that you use to get money from a machine

ˈcash ˌcrop *noun* [C] a crop that is grown to be sold

ˈcash ˌdesk *noun* [C] *UK* the place in a shop where you pay for the things you buy

| ɑː arm | ɜː her | iː see | ɔː saw | uː too | aɪ my | aʊ how | eə hair | eɪ day | əʊ no | ɪə near | ɔɪ boy | ʊə poor | aɪə fire | aʊə sour |

cashew /ˈkæʃuː, kəˈʃuː/ (*also* ˈ**cashew ˌnut**) *noun* [C] a curved nut that you can eat

cashflow /ˈkæʃfləʊ/ *noun* [U] the movement of money in and out of a business or bank account *strong cashflow*

cashier /kæʃˈɪəʳ/ *noun* [C] someone whose job is to receive and pay out money in a shop, bank, restaurant, etc

ˈ**cash maˌchine** (*also UK* **cashpoint**) *noun* [C] a machine, usually in a wall outside a bank, that you can get money from using a plastic card

cashmere /ˈkæʃmɪəʳ/ [US] /ˈkæʒmɪr/ *noun* [U] a type of very soft, expensive wool

cashpoint /ˈkæʃpɔɪnt/ *UK* (*UK/US* **cash machine**) *noun* [C] a machine, usually in a wall outside a bank, that you can get money from using a plastic card

ˈ**cash ˌregister** *noun* [C] a machine that is used in shops for keeping money in, and for recording everything that is sold

casino /kəˈsiːnəʊ/ *noun* [C] a place where card games and other games of risk are played for money

cask /kɑːsk/ *noun* [C] a strong, round, wooden container that is used for storing alcoholic drinks

casket /ˈkɑːskɪt/ *noun* [C] **1** *UK* a small, decorated box that is used for keeping valuable objects **2** *US* (*UK/US* **coffin**) a box in which a dead body is buried

casserole /ˈkæsᵊrəʊl/ *noun* **1** [C, U] a mixture of meat or beans with liquid and vegetables cooked for a long time in the oven **2** [C] (*also* ˈ**casserole ˌdish**) a large, heavy container with a lid, that is used for cooking casseroles

cassette /kəˈset/ *noun* [C] a flat, plastic case containing a long piece of magnetic material that is used to record and play sound or pictures *a video cassette*

caˈssette ˌplayer *noun* [C] a machine that plays cassettes of music or sound

caˈssette reˌcorder *noun* [C] a machine that is used for playing cassettes of music or sound and for recording music or sound onto cassettes

cast¹ /kɑːst/ *verb* [T] *past* **cast** **1** [ACTOR] to choose an actor for a particular part in a film or play [often passive] *Why am I always* ***cast as*** *the villain?* **2** [THROW] *literary* to throw something **3** [LIGHT] *literary* to send light or shadow (= dark shapes) in a particular direction *The moon cast a white light into the room.* **4 cast doubt/suspicion on sb/sth** to make people feel less sure about or have less trust in someone or something *A leading scientist has cast doubts on government claims that the drug is safe.* **5 cast a/your vote** to vote **6 cast a spell on sb a** [ATTRACT] to seem to use magic to attract someone *The city had cast a spell on me and I never wanted to leave.* **b** [MAGIC] to use magic to make something happen to someone **7** [METAL] to make an object by pouring hot metal into a container of a particular shape ➲See also: cast/run your/an **eye¹** over sth, cast/shed **light¹** on sth, cast a **pall²** over sth, cast a **shadow¹** over sth.

cast off If a boat casts off, it leaves.

WORD PARTNERS FOR ***cast***

[a play/film, etc] **features** a cast • the cast **includes** sb • the cast **of** sth • **a member of** the cast

cast² /kɑːst/ *noun* **1** [group] all the actors in a film or play *The cast are in rehearsal at the moment.* **2** [C] a hard cover used to keep a broken bone in the correct position until it gets better

castaway /ˈkɑːstəweɪ/ *noun* [C] someone who is left on an island, or in a place where there are few or no other people, after their ship has sunk

caste /kɑːst/ *noun* [C, U] a system of dividing Hindu society into social groups, or one of these groups *the caste system*

castigate /ˈkæstɪgeɪt/ *verb* [T] *formal* to criticize someone severely

cast-iron /ˈkɑːstˌaɪən/ *adjective* **1** [always before noun] able to be trusted completely, or impossible to doubt *I need a cast-iron guarantee that the work will be finished on time.* **2** made of cast iron

ˌ**cast ˈiron** *noun* [U] a type of very hard iron

⊶**castle** /ˈkɑːsl/ *noun* [C] a large, strong building with towers and high walls, that was built in the past to protect the people inside from being attacked

castle

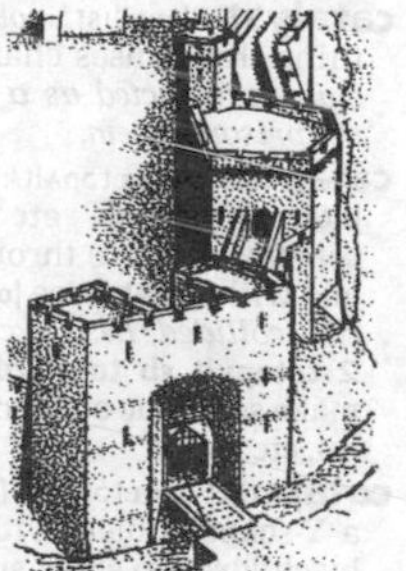

cast-off /ˈkɑːstɒf/ *noun* [C] a piece of clothing or other item that you give to someone because you do not want it any more [usually plural] *This dress is another of my sister's cast-offs.*

castrate /kæsˈtreɪt/ [US] /ˈkæstreɪt/ *verb* [T] to remove the testicles (= organs that produce sperm) of a man or male animal •**castration** /kæsˈtreɪʃᵊn/ *noun* [U]

casual /ˈkæʒjuəl/ *adjective* **1** [NOT PLANNED] [always before noun] not planned, or without particular meaning or importance *a casual remark/acquaintance/meeting* **2** [RELAXED] relaxed and not seeming very interested in someone or something *a casual manner/approach* ○ *She's much too casual about her work.* **3** [CLOTHING] Casual clothing is comfortable and not suitable for formal occasions. **4** [WORK] [always before noun] *mainly UK* Casual work is not regular or fixed. ***casual labour/workers***

casually /ˈkæʒjuəli/ *adverb* **1** in a relaxed way, or not seeming to be interested in someone or something *I asked as casually as I could if she was going to be at the party.* **2** If you dress casually, you do not dress in a formal way.

casualty /ˈkæʒjuəlti/ *noun* **1** [INJURED] [C] someone who is injured or killed in an accident or war *Both sides in the conflict have promised to try to avoid civilian casualties.*

2 BADLY AFFECTED [C] someone or something that is badly affected by something that happens *The health service has been the biggest casu-alty of government cuts.* **3** HOSPITAL [U] *UK* (*US* **emergency room**) the part of a hospital where people go when they have been injured or have urgent illnesses so that they can be treated immediately

╼**cat** /kæt/ *noun* [C] **1** a small animal with fur, four legs and a tail that is kept as a pet **2** a large, wild animal that is related to the cat, such as the lion **3** **let the cat out of the bag** to tell people secret information, often without intending to

cataclysmic /ˌkætəˈklɪzmɪk/ *adjective* sudden, shocking, and violent *cataclysmic changes/events*

catalogue¹ (*also US* catalog) /ˈkætəlɒg/ *noun* [C] **1** a book with a list of all the goods that you can buy from a shop, or of all the books, paintings, etc that you can find in a place *a clothing catalogue* **2** a catalogue of disasters/errors/fail-ures, etc a series of bad events

catalogue² (*also US* catalog) /ˈkætəlɒg/ *verb* [T] cataloguing, *past* catalogued to make a list of things, especially in order to put it in a cata-logue

catalyst /ˈkætəlɪst/ *noun* [C] someone or some-thing that causes change *Recent riots and sui-cides have acted as a catalyst for change in the prison system.*

catapult¹ /ˈkætəpʌlt/ *verb* **1** **catapult sb/sth into/out/through, etc** to make someone or something move through the air very quickly and with great force [often passive] *When the two cars collided, he was catapulted out of his seat.* **2** **catapult sb to stardom/into the lead, etc** to make someone suddenly very famous, success-ful, etc

catapult² /ˈkætəpʌlt/ *UK* (*US* **slingshot**) *noun* [C] a Y-shaped object with a piece of elastic used by children to shoot small stones

cataract /ˈkætərækt/ *noun* [C] an area of someone's eye with a disease that gradually prevents them from seeing correctly

catarrh /kəˈtɑːʳ/ *noun* [U] *UK* the thick sub-stance that is produced in your nose and throat when you have a cold

catastrophe /kəˈtæstrəfi/ *noun* [C, U] an ex-tremely bad event that causes a lot of suffering or destruction *After the drought, the country is facing environmental catastrophe.*

catastrophic /ˌkætəˈstrɒfɪk/ *adjective* causing a lot of suffering or destruction

o╼**catch¹** /kætʃ/ *verb past* caught **1** GET HOLD [T] to stop someone or something that is moving through the air by getting hold of it *Try to catch the ball.* ○ *She fell backwards but he caught her in his arms.* **2** STOP ESCAPING [T] to find and stop a person or animal who is trying to escape *He ran after his attacker but couldn't catch him.* ○ *Did you catch many fish today?* **3** CRIMINAL [T] If the police catch a criminal, they find them and take them away. *These terrorists must be caught.* **4** ILLNESS [T] to get an illness or disease *I think I've caught a cold.* **5** TRANSPORT [T] to get on a bus, train, etc in

order to travel somewhere *You can catch the bus from the top of the hill.* **6** DISCOVER [T] to dis-cover someone who is doing something wrong or something secret [+ doing sth] *I caught her listening outside the door.* ○ *informal You won't catch me wearing* (= I never wear) *a tie.* **7** STICK [I, T] to stick somewhere, or to make something stick somewhere *My dress caught on the door handle as I was leaving.* **8** COLLECT [T] to collect something that is falling *I used a bucket to catch the drips.* **9** BE IN TIME [T] to manage to be in time to see or do something *I only caught the end of the programme.* **10** HEAR [T] to hear or understand something correctly *I'm sorry. I didn't catch your name.* **11** **catch fire** to start burning **12** **be/get caught** to be unable to avoid something unpleasant *I got caught in the rain.* **13** **catch the sun** *UK* to burn your skin in the sun *You've caught the sun on your shoulders.* **14** **catch sight of sth** to see something suddenly, often only for a short time *He caught sight of himself in the mirror.* **15** HIT [T] *UK* to hit something or someone *The ball flew across the garden, and caught me on the chin.* ⊃See also: catch sb's eye¹, catch sb off guard¹.

catch on 1 to become popular *I wonder if the game will catch on with young people?* **2** *in-formal* to understand something, especially after a long time *It took him a while to catch on to what we meant.*

catch sb out *UK* to trick someone so that they make a mistake

catch (sb/sth) up 1 to reach someone or something that is in front of you, by going faster than them *We soon caught up with the car in front.* **2** to reach the same level or qual-ity as someone or something else *She's doing extra work to catch up with the rest of the class.*

catch up to learn or discuss the most recent news *Let's meet for a chat - I need to catch up on all the gossip.*

catch up on/with sth to do something that you did not have time to do earlier *After the exams, I need to catch up on some sleep.*

catch up with sb If something bad that you have done or that has been happening to you catches up with you, it begins to cause problems for you. *I can feel the stress of the last few weeks beginning to catch up with me.*

be/get caught up in sth to become in-volved in a situation, often without wanting to *How did the paper get caught up in a legal dis-pute?*

catch² /kætʃ/ *noun* [C] **1** WITH HANDS when some-one catches something that is moving through the air *a brilliant catch* **2** FISH the amount of fish that someone has caught **3** PROBLEM a hidden problem or difficulty with something *He's offering us a free flight? There must be a catch.* **4** LOCK a part on something that fastens it and keeps it closed *a safety catch*

Catch-22 /ˌkætʃtwentiˈtuː/ *noun* [C] an im-possible situation: you cannot do one thing until you have done another thing, but you cannot do the other thing until you have done the first thing *a Catch-22 situation*

catching /'kætʃɪŋ/ *adjective* [never before noun] If an illness or a mood is catching, other people can get it from you.

catchment area /'kætʃmənt,eəriə/ *noun* [C] *UK* the area around a school or a hospital, where most of the students or patients come from

catchphrase /'kætʃfreɪz/ *noun* [C] a phrase which is often repeated by a particular organization or person, and becomes connected with them

catchy /'kætʃi/ *adjective* A catchy song, tune, or phrase is easy to remember.

categorical /ˌkætə'gɒrɪkᵊl/ *adjective* If someone is categorical about what they say, they say it with force and are completely certain about it. *a categorical assurance/denial* • **categorically** *adverb* *They have denied categorically that they were involved in the conspiracy.*

categorize (*also UK* -ise) /'kætəgᵊraɪz/ *verb* [T] to divide people or things into groups of similar types *The books are categorized according to subject.*

category /'kætəgᵊri/ *noun* [C] a group of people or things of a similar type *Our customers fall into two main categories: retired people and housewives.*

cater /'keɪtᵊr/ *verb* [I, T] to provide and often serve food and drinks for a particular event *How many are we catering for at the wedding reception?*

cater for sb/sth *mainly UK* to provide what is wanted or needed by a particular group of people *The club caters for children between the ages of 4 and 12.*

cater to sb/sth to give people exactly what they want, usually something that people think is wrong *This legislation simply caters to unacceptable racist opinions.*

caterer /'keɪtᵊrᵊr/ *noun* [C] a person or company that provides food and drinks for particular events, or for an organization

catering /'keɪtᵊrɪŋ/ *noun* [U] providing food and drinks for people *Who did the catering for the party?*

caterpillar
/'kætəpɪlᵊr/ *noun* [C] a small, long animal with many legs that eats leaves

caterpillar

cathartic /kə'θɑːtɪk/ *adjective* A cathartic experience or event helps you to express and get rid of strong emotions.

cathedral /kə'θiːdrᵊl/ *noun* [C] the largest and most important church in a particular area

Catholic /'kæθᵊlɪk/ (*also* Roman Catholic) *adjective* belonging or relating to the part of the Christian religion that has the Pope (= a very important priest) as its leader *a Catholic priest/school* • **Catholic** *noun* [C] *I think he's a Catholic.*

the ˌCatholic 'Church *noun* the Catholic religion and all the people who believe in it

Catholicism /kə'θɒlɪsɪzᵊm/ (*also* ˌRoman Ca'tholicism) *noun* [U] the beliefs of the Catholic religion

catsup /'kætsəp/ *noun* [U] *another US spelling of* ketchup (= a thick, red sauce that is eaten cold with food)

cattle /'kætl/ *noun* [plural] male and female cows, kept on a farm for their milk and meat

catty /'kæti/ *adjective informal* intending to hurt someone by saying unkind things *I don't like her catty remarks.*

catwalk /'kætwɔːk/ *noun* [C] the narrow, raised path that people walk along in a fashion show

Caucasian /kɔː'keɪʒən/ *adjective* belonging to a race of people with white or pale skin • **Caucasian** *noun* [C] a Caucasian person

caught /kɔːt/ *past of* catch

cauldron /'kɔːldrᵊn/ *noun* [C] *literary* a large, round metal pot that is used for cooking over a fire

cauliflower /'kɒlɪ,flaʊᵊr/ *noun* [C, U] a large, round, white vegetable with thick, green leaves around the outside ⊃See colour picture **Fruit and Vegetables** on page Centre 10.

WORD PARTNERS FOR *cause*

a **common/leading/probable/root** cause • **discover/establish/identify** the cause of sth • the **main** cause

---

∘→**cause¹** /kɔːz/ *noun* 1 [MAKES HAPPEN] [C] someone or something that makes something happen *The police are still trying to establish the cause of the fire.* ○ *She died of natural causes.* 2 [REASON] [U] a reason to feel something or to behave in a particular way *He's never given me any cause for concern.* 3 [PRINCIPLE] [C] a principle or aim that a group of people support or fight for *The money will all go to a good cause.*

∘→**cause²** /kɔːz/ *verb* [T] to make something happen *The hurricane caused widespread damage.* ○ *Most heart attacks are caused by blood clots.* ○ [+ two objects] *I hope the children haven't caused you too much trouble.* ○ [+ to do sth] *What caused the washing machine to blow up?*

causeway /'kɔːzweɪ/ *noun* [C] a raised path or road over a wet area

caustic /'kɔːstɪk/ *adjective* 1 A caustic remark is extremely unkind and intended to upset or criticize someone. 2 Caustic chemicals can burn things.

WORD PARTNERS FOR *caution*

advise/exercise/urge caution • **extreme/great** caution • do sth **with** caution • caution **in** doing sth

---

caution¹ /'kɔːʃᵊn/ *noun* 1 [U] great care and attention not to take risks or get into danger *Travellers have been advised to exercise caution when passing through the region.* ○ *I would treat anything he says with extreme caution* (= not be too quick to believe it). 2 [C] *UK* when a police officer or other person in authority warns you that you will be punished if you do something bad again **3 throw caution to the wind** to take a risk ➲See also: err on the side[1] of caution.

caution² /ˈkɔːʃᵊn/ *verb* **1** [I, T] *formal* to warn someone of something [often passive] *They were* ***cautioned against*** *buying shares in the company.* **2** [T] *UK* If police caution people, they are given a spoken warning that they will be punished next time.

cautionary /ˈkɔːʃᵊnᵊri/ *adjective* intended to warn or advise someone *a* ***cautionary tale***

cautious /ˈkɔːʃəs/ *adjective* taking care to avoid risks or danger *She is cautious about lending money to anyone.* • **cautiously** *adverb*

cavalier /ˌkævᵊlˈɪəʳ/ *adjective formal* without caring about other people or about a dangerous or serious situation *a* ***cavalier attitude***

the cavalry /ˈkævᵊlri/ *noun* [U, group] soldiers who fight on horses

cave¹ /keɪv/ *noun* [C] a large hole in the side of a cliff (= straight, high rock next to the sea), mountain, or under the ground

cave² /keɪv/ *verb*

cave in 1 If a ceiling, roof, or other structure caves in, it breaks and falls into the space below. **2** to agree to something that you were against before, after someone has persuaded you or made you afraid *The company has finally* ***caved in to*** *the demands of the unions.*

caveat /ˈkæviæt/ *noun* [C] *formal* something you say which warns that there is a limit on a general announcement made earlier

cavern /ˈkævᵊn/ *noun* [C] a large cave

caviar (*also* **caviare**) /ˈkæviɑːʳ/ *noun* [U] the eggs of a large fish, eaten as a food and usually very expensive

cavity /ˈkævəti/ *noun* [C] **1** a hole or a space inside something solid or between two surfaces **2** a hole in a tooth

cavort /kəˈvɔːt/ *verb* [I] to jump, dance, or move about in an excited way

cc /ˌsiːˈsiː/ **1** *abbreviation for* carbon copy: used on a letter or email to show that you are sending a copy to other people **2** *abbreviation for* cubic centimetre: a unit for measuring the volume of something *a 750cc motorcycle*

CCTV /ˌsiːsiːtiːˈviː/ *noun* [U] *abbreviation for* closed circuit television: a system of television cameras filming in shops and public places so that people can watch and protect those places *CCTV cameras*

⊶**CD** /ˌsiːˈdiː/ *noun* [C] *abbreviation for* compact disc: a small disc on which music or information is recorded ➲See colour picture **The Office** on page Centre 5.

ˌC'D ˌburner *noun* [C] a machine that can record information onto a CD

ˌC'D ˌplayer *noun* [C] a machine that is used for playing music CDs

CD-R /ˌsiːdiːˈɑːʳ/ *noun* [C] *abbreviation for* compact disc recordable: an empty compact disc for recording information only once using special comptuer equipment

⊶**CD-ROM** /ˌsiːdiːˈrɒm/ *noun* [C] *abbreviation for* compact disc read-only memory: a CD that holds large amounts of information that can be read by a computer

CD-RW /ˌsiːdiːɑːˈdʌbljuː/ *noun* [C] *abbreviation for* compact disc rewritable: an empty compact disc for recording and changing information using special computer equipment

ˌC'D ˌwriter *noun* [C] a CD burner

cease /siːs/ *verb* [I, T] *formal* to stop [+ doing sth] *He ordered his men to cease firing.* ○ [+ to do sth] *Her behaviour never ceases to amaze me.*

ceasefire /ˈsiːsfaɪəʳ/ *noun* [C] an agreement between two armies or groups to stop fighting

ceaseless /ˈsiːsləs/ *adjective formal* continuous *the ceaseless movement of the sea* • **ceaselessly** *adverb*

cedar /ˈsiːdəʳ/ *noun* [C, U] a tall, evergreen (= with leaves that do not fall off in winter) tree, or the red wood of this tree

cede /siːd/ *verb* [T] *formal* to give something such as land or power to another country or person, especially because you are forced to

ceiling /ˈsiːlɪŋ/ *noun* [C] **1** the surface of a room which you can see when you look above you **2** a limit on the amount that can be paid for something *They have set a* ***ceiling on*** *pay rises.*

celeb /sɪˈleb/ *noun* [C] *informal* a celebrity (= famous person)

⊶**celebrate** /ˈseləbreɪt/ *verb* [I, T] to do something enjoyable because it is a special day, or because something good has happened *Do you celebrate Christmas in your country?*

celebrated /ˈseləbreɪtɪd/ *adjective* famous for a special ability or quality *She is* ***celebrated for*** *her wit.*

WORD PARTNERS FOR ***celebration***

anniversary / birthday / New Year celebrations • be a **cause for** celebration • sth **calls for** a celebration • a celebration **to mark/of** sth • **in** celebration **of** sth

celebration /ˌseləˈbreɪʃᵊn/ *noun* [C, U] when you celebrate a special day or event *Let's buy some champagne* ***in celebration of*** *her safe arrival.* ○ *You've passed? This* ***calls for a celebration****.*

celebratory /ˌseləˈbreɪtᵊri/ [US] /ˈseləbrətɔːri/ *adjective* done to celebrate something or wanting to celebrate something *a celebratory dinner* ○ *in a celebratory mood*

celebrity /səˈlebrəti/ *noun* [C] a famous person

celery /ˈselᵊri/ *noun* [U] a vegetable with long, pale green stems, often eaten in salads ➲See colour picture **Fruit and Vegetables** on page Centre 10.

celestial /səˈlestiəl/ *adjective literary* relating to heaven or the sky

celibate /ˈseləbət/ *adjective* Someone who is celibate does not have sex. • **celibacy** /ˈseləbəsi/ *noun* [U] when you do not have sex

cell /sel/ *noun* [C] **1** the smallest living part of an animal or a plant *brain/cancer cells* **2** a small room in a prison or police station where a prisoner is kept

cellar /ˈseləʳ/ *noun* [C] a room under the floor of a building ➲See also: **salt cellar**.

cellist /ˈtʃelɪst/ *noun* [C] someone who plays the cello

cello /ˈtʃeləʊ/ *noun* [C] a large, wooden musical instrument with four strings that you hold between your knees to play

Cellophane /ˈseləfeɪn/ *noun* [U] *trademark* thin, transparent material that is used for wrapping goods, especially flowers and food

cell phone /ˈselfəʊn/ (*also* **cellular phone**) *noun* [C] *US* a mobile phone

cellular /ˈseljələʳ/ *adjective* **1** relating to animal or plant cells *cellular damage* **2** [always before noun] relating to cellular phones *cellular companies/communications*

ˌcellular ˌphone (*also* **cell phone** /ˈselfəʊn/) *noun* [C] a mobile phone ➲See picture at **telephone**. *cellular phone accessories*

cellulite /ˈseljəlaɪt/ *noun* [U] fat that looks like small lumps below the skin, especially on the upper legs *I can't seem to get rid of my cellulite.*

cellulose /ˈseljələʊs/ *noun* [U] a substance in plants that is used to make some paper and plastics

Celsius /ˈselsiəs/ (*written abbreviation* **C**) *noun* [U] a measurement of temperature in which water freezes at 0° and boils at 100°

Celtic /ˈkeltɪk/ *adjective* relating to the people of Ireland, Scotland, and Wales *Celtic art/music*

cement¹ /sɪˈment/ *noun* [U] a grey powder used in building which is mixed with water and sand or stones to make a hard substance

cement² /sɪˈment/ *verb* [T] **1** to make something such as a relationship, a belief, or a position stronger *It was the holiday that really cemented our friendship.* **2** (*also* **cement over**) to cover something with cement

cemetery /ˈsemətri/ *noun* [C] a place where dead people are buried

censor /ˈsensəʳ/ *verb* [T] to examine books, documents, or films and remove parts of them that are offensive or not allowed by rules [often passive] *The book was heavily censored before publication.* • **censor** *noun* [C]

censorship /ˈsensəʃɪp/ *noun* [U] when a book, film, newspaper, or other information is censored *political/state censorship*

censure /ˈsensjəʳ/ *verb* [T] *formal* to criticize someone formally for something that they have done • **censure** *noun* [U] *formal*

census /ˈsensəs/ *noun* [C] when people in a country are officially counted and information is taken about them

⊶**cent** /sent/ *noun* [C] a coin or unit of money with a value of 1⁄100 of a dollar (= US unit of money); ¢ *The newspaper costs sixty-five cents.*

centenary /senˈtiːnᵊri/ [US] /ˈsentᵊneri/ (*also US* **centennial** /senˈteniəl/) *noun* [C] the day or year that is 100 years after an important event *This year, there will be many concerts to mark the centenary of the composer's death.*

⊶**center** /ˈsentəʳ/ *noun, verb US spelling of* centre

centerpiece /ˈsentəpiːs/ *noun* [C] *US spelling of* centrepiece

centi-, cent- /senti-, sent-/ *prefix* hundred *a centimetre* ○ *a century*

centigrade /ˈsentɪgreɪd/ (*written abbreviation* **C**) *noun* [U] a measurement of temperature in which water freezes at 0° and boils at 100°

centilitre /ˈsentɪˌliːtəʳ/ *UK* (*US* **centiliter**) (*written abbreviation* **cl**) *noun* [C] a unit for measuring liquid, equal to 0.01 litres

⊶**centimetre** *UK* (*US* **centimeter**) (*written abbreviation* **cm**) /ˈsentɪˌmiːtəʳ/ *noun* [C] a unit for measuring length, equal to 0.01 metres

⊶**central** /ˈsentrᵊl/ *adjective* [POSITION] in or near the centre of a place or object *central Africa/America* ○ *The roof is supported by a central column.* **2** [ORGANIZATION] [always before noun] controlled or organized in one main place *central authorities/government* ○ *the US central bank* **3** [IMPORTANT] main or most important *a central character/figure* ○ *Her role is* **central to** *the film.* **4** [CITY] in the main part of a town or city • **centrally** *adverb*

ˌcentral ˈheating *noun* [U] a system of heating a building by warming air or water in one place and carrying it to different rooms in pipes

centralize (*also UK* **-ise**) /ˈsentrᵊlaɪz/ *verb* [T] If a country or organization is centralized, it is controlled from one place. [often passive] *centralized control/government* • **centralization** /ˌsentrᵊlaɪˈzeɪʃᵊn/ *noun* [U]

⊶**centre¹** *UK* (*US* **center**) /ˈsentəʳ/ *noun* **1** [MIDDLE] [C] the middle point or part of something *She stood in the centre of the room.* ○ *Cars are not allowed in the town centre.* **2** [PLACE] [C] a place or a building used for a particular activity *a health/advice centre* ○ *a centre for the homeless* **3** [BUSINESS] [C] a place where a lot of a particular activity or business takes place *an industrial centre* **4** [POLITICAL] [no plural] (*also* **the centre**) a political position with opinions that are not extreme *His political views are left of centre.* **5 be the centre of attention** to receive more attention than anyone or anything else ➲See also: **community centre, garden centre, shopping centre.**

centre² *UK* (*US* **center**) /ˈsentəʳ/ *verb* [T] to put something in the middle of an area

centre around/on sb/sth to have someone or something as the main part of a discussion or activity *The dispute centres on racial issues.*

ˌcentre of ˈgravity *noun* [C] *plural* **centres of gravity** the point in an object where its weight is balanced

centrepiece *UK* (*US* **centerpiece**) /ˈsentəpiːs/ *noun* [C] **1** the most important or attractive part of something *The employment programme is the centrepiece of the government's economic strategy.* **2** a decoration that is put in the middle of a dinner table

WORD PARTNERS FOR *century*

in the [17th/21st, etc] century • **the early/mid/late** [15th/19th, etc] century • **the turn of the** century (= the time around the end of one century and the beginning of the next)

⊶**century** /ˈsenʃᵊri/ *noun* [C] a period of 100 years, especially used in giving dates *the twentieth century*

CEO /ˌsiːiːˈəʊ/ *noun* [C] *abbreviation for* chief

executive officer: the person with the most important job in a company

ceramics /sə'ræmɪks/ *noun* **[plural]** objects that are made by shaping and heating clay • **ceramic** *adjective* made by shaping and heating clay *a ceramic pot*

cereal /'sɪəriəl/ *noun* **[C, U]** **1** a plant that is grown to produce grain for food *cereal crops* **2** a food that is made from grain and eaten with milk, especially in the morning ***breakfast cereals*** ➲See colour picture **Food** on page Centre 11.

cerebral /'serəbrᵊl/ *adjective formal* **1** Cerebral films, books, etc need a lot of thought to understand them, and cerebral people think a lot. **2** **[always before noun]** relating to the brain *cerebral arteries*

ceremonial /ˌserɪ'məʊniəl/ *adjective* relating to a ceremony • **ceremonially** *adverb*

WORD PARTNERS FOR ***ceremony***

attend/hold a ceremony • **at** a ceremony • an **award/marriage/wedding** ceremony

ceremony /'serɪməni/ *noun* **1** **[C]** a formal event that is performed on important social or religious occasions *a **marriage/wedding ceremony*** ○ *an **award ceremony*** **2** **[U]** formal behaviour, words, and actions that are part of a ceremony

🔑**certain** /'sɜːtᵊn/ *adjective* **1** [NO DOUBT] **[never before noun]** completely sure of something, or knowing without doubt that something is true **[+ (that)]** *I feel absolutely certain that you're doing the right thing.* ○ **[+ question word]** *Nobody was certain how the accident had happened.* ○ *He was quite **certain about/of** the thief's identity.* ➲Opposite **uncertain**. **2** **know/say for certain** to know something without doubt *We don't know for certain whether she's coming.* **3** [SURE TO HAPPEN] sure to happen, to do something, or to be true **[+ (that)]** *It now looks certain that she will resign.* ○ **[+ to do sth]** *She is certain to do well in the exams.* ○ *How can we **make certain that*** (= do something to be sure that) *she sees the note?* **4** [PARTICULAR] **[always before noun]** used to refer to a particular person or thing without naming or describing them exactly *The museum is only open at certain times of the day.* **5** **a certain** used before a noun to mean existing, but difficult to describe the exact quality or amount *He's got a certain charm.* **6** **certain of** *formal* used to refer to some of a group of people or things *Certain of you already know the news.*

🔑**certainly** /'sɜːtᵊnli/ *adverb* **1** used to emphasize something and show that there is no doubt about it *Their team certainly deserved to win.* ○ *"Are your parents paying for dinner?" "I certainly hope so."* ○ *"Do you regret what you said?" "**Certainly not!**"* **2** used to agree to a request *"Could you pass the salt, please?" "Certainly."*

certainty /'sɜːtᵊnti/ *noun* **1** **[U]** when you are completely sure about something *I can't say **with any certainty** what time she left.* **2** **[C]** something that is very likely to happen or cannot be doubted *There are no absolute certainties in life.*

certificate /sə'tɪfɪkət/ *noun* **[C]** an official document that gives details to show that something is true *a **death/marriage certificate*** ○ *an **exam certificate*** ➲See also: **birth certificate**.

certify /'sɜːtɪfaɪ/ *verb* **[T]** **1** [TRUTH] *formal* to say in a formal or official way that something is true or correct **[+ (that)]** *I certify that the information I have given is true.* ○ *She was **certified dead** on arrival at the hospital.* **2** [CERTIFICATE] to give someone a certificate to say that they have completed a course of study *a certified accountant* **3** [HEALTH] to say officially that someone has a mental illness

certitude /'sɜːtɪtjuːd/ *noun* **[U]** *formal* when you feel certain about something

cervix /'sɜːvɪks/ *noun* **[C]** the narrow entrance to a woman's womb • **cervical** /sə'vaɪkᵊl, 'sɜːvɪkᵊl/ *adjective cervical cancer*

cesarean /sɪ'zeəriən/ *noun* **[C]** *US spelling of* caesarean

cessation /ses'eɪʃᵊn/ *noun* **[C, U]** *formal* when something, especially violence, stops *the cessation of hostilities*

cf used in writing when you want the reader to make a comparison between the subject being discussed and something else

CFC /ˌsiːef'siː/ *noun* **[C]** *abbreviation for* chlorofluorocarbon: a type of gas used in fridges (= containers for keeping food cold) and aerosols (= containers for making liquids come out in small drops), which damages the layer of gases around the Earth

chafe /tʃeɪf/ *verb* **1** **[I]** to feel angry because of rules and limits *He **chafed against/at** the narrow academic approach of his school.* **2** **[I, T]** to make part of the body painful by rubbing, or to become painful because of being rubbed

chagrin /'ʃægrɪn/ [US] /ʃə'grɪn/ *noun* **[U]** anger or disappointment caused by something that does not happen the way you wanted it ***To** his parents' **chagrin**, he had no intention of becoming a lawyer.*

chain

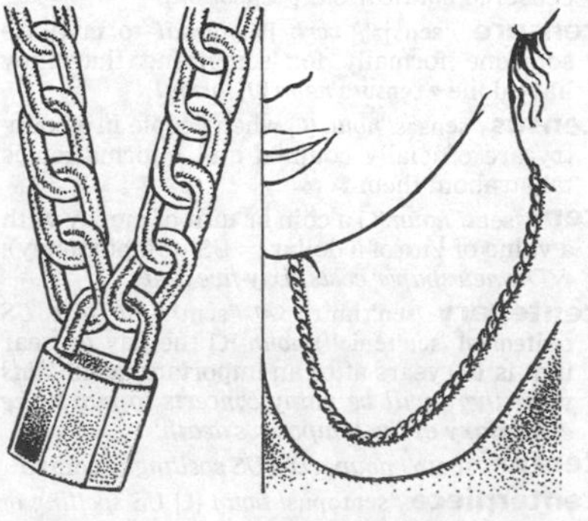

chain¹ /tʃeɪn/ *noun* **1** [METAL RINGS] **[C, U]** a line of metal rings connected together *a bicycle chain* ○ *She wore a gold chain around her neck.* ○ *The hostages were kept **in chains**.* **2** [BUSINESS] **[C]** a number of similar shops, restaurants, etc owned by the same company *a chain of hotels/ supermarkets* **3** [EVENTS] [C] a series of things that happen one after the other *His arrival set off a surprising chain of events.*

chain² /tʃeɪn/ (*also* chain up) *verb* [T] to fasten someone or something to someone or something else using a chain *I chained my bike to a lamppost.* ○ *You shouldn't keep a dog chained up like that.*

chain re'action *noun* [C] a series of events where each one causes the next one to happen

chain-smoke /'tʃeɪnsməʊk/ *verb* [I, T] to smoke cigarettes one after another ● **chain smoker** *noun* [C]

'chain ,store *noun* [C] one of a group of similar shops owned by the same company

o→**chair¹** /tʃeəʳ/ *noun* [C] **1** [FURNITURE] a seat for one person, with a back, usually four legs, and sometimes two arms ⊃See also colour picture **The Office** on page Centre 5. **2** [MEETING] someone who controls a meeting or organization [usually singular] *All questions should be addressed to the chair.* **3** [UNIVERSITY] a very important position in a university department, or the person who has this position ⊃See also: **the electric chair.**

chair² /tʃeəʳ/ *verb* [T] to control a meeting or organization *I've been asked to chair the finance committee.*

chairman, chairwoman /'tʃeəmən, 'tʃeə,wʊmən/ *noun* [C] *plural* **chairmen** *or* **chairwomen** a man/woman who controls a meeting, company, or other organization

chairperson /'tʃeə,pɜːsᵊn/ *noun* [C] someone who controls a meeting, company, or other organization

chalet /'ʃæleɪ/ ⓤ /ʃæl'eɪ/ *noun* [C] a small wooden house, often in a mountain area, or for people who are on holiday

chalk¹ /tʃɔːk/ *noun* **1** [U] a type of soft, white rock **2** [C, U] a small stick of chalk that is used for writing and drawing *a piece of chalk* ⊃See colour picture **The Classroom** on page Centre 6. **3 be like chalk and cheese** *UK* If two people are like chalk and cheese, they are completely different from each other.

chalk² /tʃɔːk/ *verb* [T] *UK* to write something with a piece of chalk
chalk sth up to achieve something *Thierry Henry's chalked up thirty-five goals for Arsenal this season.*

chalkboard /'tʃɔːkbɔːd/ *US (UK/US* blackboard*)* *noun* [C] a large board with a dark surface that teachers write on with chalk

chalky /'tʃɔːki/ *adjective* made of chalk, or similar to chalk

WORD PARTNERS FOR *challenge*
face/pose/present/relish a challenge ● a big/formidable/serious/tough challenge

o→**challenge¹** /'tʃælɪndʒ/ *noun* **1** [DIFFICULT] [C, U] something that is difficult and that tests someone's ability or determination *Finding a decision that pleases everyone is the challenge which now faces the committee.* **2** [INVITATION] [C] an invitation to compete in a game or a fight *I'm sure Paul will race you. He never refuses a*

challenge. **3** [DISAGREEMENT] [C] an expression of disagreement with ideas, rules, or someone's authority *a challenge to the authority of the President*

challenge² /'tʃælɪndʒ/ *verb* [T] **1** to express disagreement with ideas, rules, or someone's authority *The election results are being challenged.* **2** to invite someone to compete in a game or fight *He challenged Smith to a fight.*

challenger /'tʃælɪndʒəʳ/ *noun* [C] someone who competes in a game, competition, or election, often to win a position that someone else has *There are five challengers for the title.*

challenging /'tʃælɪndʒɪŋ/ *adjective* difficult to do in a way that tests your ability or determination *This has been a challenging three years for us all.*

chamber /'tʃeɪmbəʳ/ *noun* [C] **1** [ROOM] a room used for an official or special purpose *a debating chamber* ○ *a burial chamber* **2** [PARLIAMENT] one of the groups that a parliament is divided into *the upper/lower chamber* **3** [MACHINE/BODY] a closed space in a machine or in your body *the left chamber of the heart* ⊃See also: **gas chamber.**

chambermaid /'tʃeɪmbəmeɪd/ *noun* [C] a woman whose job is to clean and tidy hotel bedrooms

'chamber ,music *noun* [U] music that is written for a small group of musicians

,chamber of 'commerce *noun* [C] *plural* **chambers of commerce** an organization of business people who work together to improve business in their local area

champ /tʃæmp/ *noun* [C] *informal short for* champion

champagne /ʃæm'peɪn/ *noun* [U] French white wine with lots of bubbles in it which people often drink to celebrate something

champagne

o→**champion¹** /'tʃæmpiən/ *noun* [C] **1** a person, animal, or team that wins a competition *a boxing champion* ○ *the world champions* **2** someone who supports, defends, or fights for a person, belief, or principle *a champion of human rights* ⊃See also: **reigning champion.**

champion² /'tʃæmpiən/ *verb* [T] to support, defend, or fight for a person, belief, or principle *She championed the cause of free speech.*

championship /'tʃæmpiənʃɪp/ *noun* [C] **1** a competition to find the best team or player in a particular game or sport *The world championship will be held in this country next year.* **2** the position of being a champion *She is current holder of our tennis championship.*

WORD PARTNERS FOR *chance*
a chance of sth ● a fifty-fifty chance ● a fair/good/slim chance

o→**chance¹** /tʃɑːns/ *noun* **1** [POSSIBILITY] [C, U] the possibility that something will happen [+ (that)] *There's a chance that she'll still be there.* ○ *She has little chance of passing the exam.* ○ *Is there* *any chance of a drink?* **2** OPPORTUNITY [C] the opportunity to do something [+ to do sth] *I didn't get a chance to speak to you at the party.* ○ *I hope you've had the chance to look around the exhibition.* ○ *Give me a chance to prove that I can do the work.* ○ *Going on a world cruise is the chance of a lifetime* (= an opportunity which only comes once in your life). **3** LUCK [U] when something happens because of luck, or without being planned *I saw her by chance in the shop.* **4** RISK [C] a risk *I'm delivering my work by hand. I'm not taking any chances.* **5 by any chance** used to ask in a polite way whether something is possible or true *You're not Spanish by any chance, are you?* **6 stand a chance** to have a chance of success or of achieving something *He stands a good chance of winning the election.* **7 chances are** it is likely [+ (that)] *Chances are that he'll refuse.* **8 No chance!/ Not a chance!** used to emphasize that there is no possibility of something happening *"Do you think she'd go out with me?" "No chance!"* **9 fat chance** *informal* used to say that you do not think that something is likely to happen *"Do you think we'll win?" "Fat chance."* ⊃See also: off-chance, outside chance.

chance² /tʃɑːns/ *verb* [T] *informal* to take a risk by doing something

chance³ /tʃɑːns/ *adjective* [always before noun] A chance event is not planned or expected. *a chance meeting*

chancellor /'tʃɑːnsələʳ/ *noun* [C] **1** GOVERNMENT the leader of the government in some countries *the German chancellor* **2** UNIVERSITY the person with the highest position in some universities **3** MONEY (*also* ˌChancellor of the Ex'chequer) *UK* the person in the British government who makes decisions about taxes and government spending

chandelier /ˌʃændə'lɪəʳ/ *noun* [C] a large light that hangs from the ceiling that is made of many small lights or candles and small pieces of glass

○━**change¹** /tʃeɪndʒ/ *verb* **1** DIFFERENT [I, T] to become different, or to make someone or something become different *I hadn't seen her for twenty years, but she hadn't changed a bit.*

○ *The course changed my life.* ○ *She's **changed from** being a happy, healthy child to being ill all the time.* **2** FROM ONE THING TO ANOTHER [I, T] to stop having or using one thing, and start having or using another *The doctor has recommended changing my diet.* ○ *I'll have to ask them if they can change the time of my interview.* **3** CLOTHES [I, T] to take off your clothes and put on different ones *He **changed out of** his school uniform **into** jeans and a T-shirt.* ○ *Is there somewhere I can **get changed**?* **4** JOURNEY [I, T] to get off a bus, plane, etc and catch another, in order to continue a journey *I have to change trains at Bristol.* **5** IN SHOP [T] *UK* to take something you have bought back to a shop and exchange it for something else *If the dress doesn't fit, can I **change** it **for** a smaller one?* **6** MONEY [T] to get or give someone money in exchange for money of a different type *Where can I change my dollars?* ○ *Can you change a £20 note for two tens?* **7** BED [T] to take dirty sheets off a bed and put on clean ones *to change the bed/sheets* **8** BABY [T] to put a clean nappy (= thick cloth worn on a baby's bottom) on a baby ⊃See also: chop¹ and change, change hands (hand¹), change your tune¹.

change sth around/round to move objects such as furniture into different positions

change over *UK* to stop using or having one thing and start using or having something else *We've just **changed over from** gas central heating to electric.*

○━**change²** /tʃeɪndʒ/ *noun* **1** DIFFERENCE [C, U] when something becomes different, or the result of something becoming different *We need to make a few changes to the design.* ○ *There is no change in the patient's condition* (= the illness has not got better or worse). ○ *How can we bring about social change?* **2** FROM ONE THING TO ANOTHER [C, U] when you stop having or using one thing and start having or using another *This country needs a change of government.* ○ *I've notified the school of our change of address.* **3** NEW EXPERIENCE [C] something that you enjoy because it is a new experience [usually singular] *Going abroad for our anniversary would make a lovely change.* ○ *It's nice to eat together as a family for a change.* **4** MONEY [U] the money that you get back when you pay more for something than it costs *There's your receipt and £3 change.* **5** COINS [U] coins, not paper money *Have you got any change for the parking meter?* ○ *Have you got change for £5* (= can you give me £5 in coins in return for paper money)? **6 a change of clothes** a set of clean clothes that you can put on if you need to take off the ones you are wearing **7 a change of heart** If you have a change of heart, you change your opinion or feelings about something. ⊃See also: small change.

changeable /'tʃeɪndʒəbl/ *adjective* often changing, or likely to change

changeover /'tʃeɪndʒ,əʊvəʳ/ noun [C] a change from one system or situation to another [usually singular] *the changeover from the old computer system to the new one*

'changing ,room noun [C] UK a room in a shop where you can try clothes, or a room where you change into clothes to do sport

o-w**channel¹** /'tʃænᵊl/ noun [C] 1 TELEVISION a television or radio station (= broadcasting company) 2 PASSAGE a long, narrow passage for water or other liquids to flow along *an irrigation channel* 3 COMMUNICATION a way of communicating with people or getting something done *a channel of communication* 4 the Channel (*also* the ,English 'Channel) the narrow area of water between England and France 5 RIVER a part of a river or sea that is deep and wide enough for ships to travel along *a navigable channel*

channel² /'tʃænᵊl/ verb [T] UK channelling, past channelled, US channeling, past channeled 1 to direct water along a particular route *The waste water is channelled through this pipe.* 2 to use money or energy for a particular purpose *We've channelled all our resources into this project.*

the ,Channel 'Tunnel noun the three long passages under the English Channel between England and France

chant¹ /tʃɑːnt/ verb [I, T] 1 to repeat or sing a word or phrase many times, often shouting *The demonstrators chanted anti-racist slogans.* 2 to sing a religious song or prayer using a very simple tune

chant² /tʃɑːnt/ noun [C] 1 a word or phrase that is repeated many times 2 a religious song or prayer that is sung using a very simple tune

Chanukah /'hɑːnəkə/ noun [C, U] Hanukkah

cause chaos • descend into/be thrown into chaos • be in chaos • total/utter chaos

chaos /'keɪɒs/ noun [U] a situation where there is no order at all and everyone is confused *The country's at war and everything is in chaos.*

chaotic /keɪ'ɒtɪk/ adjective in a state of chaos *a chaotic situation*

chap /tʃæp/ noun [C] UK informal a man

chapel /'tʃæpᵊl/ noun [C] a small church, or a room used as a church in a building

chaperone¹ (*also* chaperon) /'ʃæpᵊrəʊn/ noun [C] an older person who goes somewhere with a younger person in order to make sure they behave well, especially a woman in the past who went with a younger woman who was not married

chaperone² (*also* chaperon) /'ʃæpᵊrəʊn/ verb [T] to go somewhere with someone as their chaperone *to chaperone the school disco*

chaplain /'tʃæplɪn/ noun [C] a priest in the army, a school, a hospital, or a prison

chapter /'tʃæptəʳ/ noun [C] 1 one of the parts that a book is divided into 2 a period of time when something happens in history or in someone's life *an interesting chapter in Spanish history*

5 a colourful / lovable / shady / strong / unsavoury character • a real character

o-w**character** /'kærəktəʳ/ noun 1 QUALITIES [C, U] the combination of qualities and personality that makes one person or thing different from others *It's not in her character to be jealous* (= she would not usually be jealous). ○ *It would be very out of character* (= not typical) *of her to lie.* ○ *The character of the village has changed since the road was built.* 2 STORY [C] a person in a book, film, etc *a cartoon character* 3 GOOD QUALITIES [U] qualities that are interesting or unusual *a hotel of character* 4 PERSON [C] *informal* a particular kind of person *an unpleasant character* 5 INTERESTING PERSON [C] an interesting or funny person whose behaviour is different from most people's *Your granny's a real character.* 6 WRITING [C] a letter, sign, or number that you use when you are writing or printing *Chinese characters*

characteristic¹ /,kærəktə'rɪstɪk/ noun [C] a typical or obvious quality that makes one person or thing different from others *a national characteristic* ○ *Does he have any distinguishing physical characteristics?*

characteristic² /,kærəktə'rɪstɪk/ adjective typical of someone or something *Grey stone is characteristic of buildings in that area.* ⊃Opposite uncharacteristic. • characteristically adverb

characterization (*also* UK -isation) /,kærəktᵊraɪ'zeɪʃᵊn/ noun [U] the way that people are described in a play, book, etc

characterize (*also* UK -ise) /'kærəktᵊraɪz/ verb [T] 1 to be typical of someone or something [often passive] *Her behaviour in class has been characterized by rudeness and laziness.* 2 to describe or show someone or something in a particular way *Historians have characterized the age as a period of great change.*

charade /ʃə'rɑːd/ ⑳ /ʃə'reɪd/ noun [C] a situation which is clearly false, but where people behave as if it is true or serious *The interview was just a charade.*

charcoal /'tʃɑːkəʊl/ noun [U] a hard, black substance that is produced by burning wood without much air, and that is used as fuel or for drawing

make a charge • at no extra/free of/without charge • a charge for sth • a charge of [£10/$12, etc] • a small charge

o-w**charge¹** /tʃɑːdʒ/ noun 1 MONEY [C, U] the amount of money that you have to pay for something, especially for an activity or a service *bank charges* ○ *There's no charge for children under 14.* ○ *He repaired the computer free of charge* (= it did not cost anything). 2 be in charge to be the person who has control of or is responsible for someone or something *She's in charge of a team of 20 people.* ○ *Who's in charge of organizing the music for the party?* 3 take charge to take control of or make yourself responsible for something *I was happy to*

let her take charge of paying all the bills.
4 CRIME [C] a formal police statement saying that someone is accused of a crime *to bring/press charges* ○ *She was arrested on charges of theft and forgery.* **5** ACCUSE [C] when you accuse someone of something *This is a serious charge to make against your colleagues.* **6** ATTACK [C] an attack in which people or animals run forward suddenly **7 reverse the charges** *UK* (*US* **call collect**) to make a telephone call that is paid for by the person who receives it ⊃See also: **service charge.**

o━**charge**² /tʃɑːdʒ/ *verb* **1** ASK TO PAY [I, T] to ask someone to pay an amount of money for something, especially for an activity or a service **[+ two objects]** *They are going to charge motorists a tax to drive into the city centre.* ○ *How much do you charge for delivery?* **2** ACCUSE [T] If the police charge someone, they accuse them officially of a crime. **[often passive]** *He was charged with assault.* **3** ATTACK [I, T] to attack someone or something by moving forward quickly *The bull looked as if it was about to charge.* **4 charge around/into/through, etc** to run from one place to another *The children charged around the house.* **5** ELECTRICITY [I, T] to put electricity into something

'**charge ‚card** *noun* [C] a small plastic card that allows you to buy something and pay for it at a particular date in the future

charged /tʃɑːdʒd/ *adjective* A situation or a subject that is charged causes strong feelings or arguments. *a highly charged debate*

chariot /'tʃæriət/ *noun* [C] a vehicle with two wheels that was used in races and fights in ancient times and was pulled by a horse

charisma /kə'rɪzmə/ *noun* [U] a natural power which some people have to influence or attract people ● **charismatic** /ˌkærɪz'mætɪk/ *adjective*

charitable /'tʃærɪtəbl/ *adjective* **1** [always before noun] A charitable event, activity, or organization gives money, food, or help to people who need it. **2** kind, and not judging other people in a severe way ● **charitably** *adverb*

> ┌──────────────────────────────────────┐
> │ ⬚⬚⬚ **WORD PARTNERS FOR *charity*** │
> └──────────────────────────────────────┘
> **donate/give** sth **to** charity ● [money, etc] **goes to** charity ● do sth **for** charity ● a charity **for** [homeless people/sick children, etc] ● a charity **event** (= an event to raise money for a charity)

charity /'tʃærɪti/ *noun* **1** ORGANIZATION [C, U] an official organization that gives money, food, or help to people who need it *The raffle will raise money for charity.* ○ *A percentage of the company's profits go to charity.* **2** MONEY/HELP [U] money, food, or other help that is given to people *I won't accept charity from anybody.* **3** KINDNESS [U] kindness towards other people *an act of charity*

'**charity ‚shop** *UK* (*US* **thrift shop**) *noun* [C] a shop which sells goods given by the public, especially clothes, to make money for a particular charity

charlatan /'ʃɑːlətⁿn/ *noun* [C] someone who pretends to have skills or knowledge that they do not have

charm¹ /tʃɑːm/ *noun* **1** [C, U] a quality that makes you like someone or something *The building had a certain charm.* **2** [C] an object that you keep or wear because you believe that it is lucky *a lucky charm*

charm² /tʃɑːm/ *verb* [T] to attract someone or persuade someone to do something because of your charm **[often passive]** *We were charmed by his boyish manner.*

charmed /tʃɑːmd/ *adjective* very lucky, or managing to avoid danger *The young boy had led a charmed life.*

charmer /'tʃɑːmə'/ *noun* [C] *informal* someone who knows how to be charming in order to attract people or persuade them to do things

charming /'tʃɑːmɪŋ/ *adjective* pleasant or attractive *a charming smile/place* ● **charmingly** *adverb*

charred /tʃɑːd/ *adjective* black from having been burned *charred wreckage*

chart¹ /tʃɑːt/ *noun* **1** [C] a drawing which shows information in a simple way, often using lines and curves to show amounts *a sales chart* **2 the charts** an official list of the most popular songs each week **3** [C] a map of the sea or the sky

chart² /tʃɑːt/ *verb* [T] **1** to watch and record information about something over a period of time *The documentary charted the progress of the war.* **2** to make a map of an area of land, sea, or sky

charter¹ /'tʃɑːtə'/ *noun* [C] a formal, written description of the principles, activities, and purpose of an organization

charter² /'tʃɑːtə'/ *verb* [T] to rent a vehicle, especially an aircraft *The holiday company chartered a plane to fly us all home.*

charter³ /'tʃɑːtə'/ *adjective* **a charter flight/company/plane, etc** using aircraft paid for by travel companies for their customers

chartered /'tʃɑːtəd/ *adjective* [always before noun] *UK* having the necessary qualifications to work in a particular profession *a chartered accountant/surveyor*

chase

chase¹ /tʃeɪs/ *verb* **1** [I, T] to run after someone or something in order to catch them *The dog was chasing a rabbit.* **2 chase sb/sth away/off/out, etc** to run after a person or animal to make them leave a place *I chased the cat away.*

3 [T] *UK* to try very hard to get something *There are hundreds of graduates* ***chasing*** *very few* ***jobs****.*

chase² /tʃeɪs/ *noun* **1** [C] when you go after someone or something quickly in order to catch them *a high speed* ***car chase*** **2 give chase** to go after someone or something quickly in order to catch them

chasm /ˈkæzᵊm/ *noun* [C] **1** a long, deep, narrow hole in rock or ice **2** a very large difference between two opinions or two groups of people

chassis /ˈʃæsi/ *noun* [C] *plural* **chassis** /ˈʃæsiz/ the structure of a vehicle that the outer metal is fixed onto

chaste /tʃeɪst/ *adjective* not having had sex, or without sexual thoughts or intentions *a chaste relationship*

chasten /ˈtʃeɪsᵊn/ *verb* [T] *formal* to make someone feel ashamed by making them understand that they have failed or done something wrong **[often passive]** *The team were chastened by their defeat.* • **chastening** *adjective*

chastise /tʃæsˈtaɪz/ *verb* [T] *formal* to criticize or punish someone

chastity /ˈtʃæstəti/ *noun* [U] when someone does not have sex

o¬**chat¹** /tʃæt/ *verb* [I] **chatting**, *past* **chatted** to talk with someone in a friendly and informal way *I wanted to* ***chat to*** *you* ***about*** *the party on Saturday.*

chat sb up *UK informal* to talk to someone in a way that shows them that you are sexually attracted to them

WORD PARTNERS FOR *chat*

have a chat • a chat **about** sth • a **good/little/long/quick** chat • a chat **with** sb

o¬**chat²** /tʃæt/ *noun* [C, U] a friendly, informal conversation

chateau /ˈʃætəʊ/ [US] /ʃæˈtəʊ/ *noun* [C] *plural* **chateaux** a large house or castle in France

ˈchat ˌroom *noun* [C] a place on the Internet where you can use email for discussions with other people

ˈchat ˌshow *UK* (*US* **talk show**) *noun* [C] a television or radio programme where people are asked questions about themselves

chatter /ˈtʃætəʳ/ *verb* [I] **1** to talk for a long time about things that are not important **2** If your teeth chatter, they knock together because you are cold or frightened. • **chatter** *noun* [U]

chatty /ˈtʃæti/ *adjective* **1** liking to talk **2** A piece of writing that is chatty has a friendly and informal style. *a chatty letter/style*

chauffeur /ˈʃəʊfəʳ/ [US] /ʃəʊˈfɜːr/ *noun* [C] someone whose job is to drive a car for someone else • **chauffeur** *verb* [T]

chauvinist /ˈʃəʊvənɪst/ *noun* [C] **1** (*also* **male chauvinist**) a man who believes that men are better or more important than women **2** someone who believes that their country or race is better or more important than other countries or races • **chauvinism** *noun* [U] the beliefs and behaviour of chauvinists

chav /tʃæv/ *noun* [C] *UK informal* a young person who dresses in cheap clothes and jewellery that are intended to look expensive, and who does not look clever *He was dressed in the chav's uniform of baseball cap, gold chains and very bright white trainers.*

OTHER WAYS OF SAYING *cheap*

If something is cheap enough for most people to be able to buy, you can say that it is **affordable**, **inexpensive**, or **reasonable**: *There's very little* ***affordable*** *housing around here.* • *They sell* ***inexpensive*** *children's clothes.* • *I thought the food in the canteen was very* ***reasonable****.*

The adjective **cut-price** is sometimes used to describe something that is cheaper than usual: *We managed to get* ***cut-price*** *tickets the day before the show.*

A piece of equipment that is cheap to use is often described as **economical**: *I need a car that's reliable and* ***economical****.*

o¬**cheap¹** /tʃiːp/ *adjective* **1** [NOT EXPENSIVE] not expensive, or costing less than usual *I got a cheap flight to Spain at the last minute.* ○ *It will be a lot cheaper to go by bus.* ○ *During times of high unemployment, there is a pool of cheap labour for employers to draw from.* **2** [PAY LESS] where you have to pay less than usual or less than you expect *Are there any cheap restaurants around here?* ○ *I go to the cheapest hairdresser's in town.* **3** [LOW QUALITY] low in price and quality *I bought some cheap wine for cooking with.* ○ *He bought some cheap shoes that fell apart after a couple of months.* **4** [PERSON] *US* not willing to spend money *He's so cheap he didn't even buy me a card for my birthday.*

cheap² /tʃiːp/ *adverb informal* **1** for a low price *You'll* ***get*** *the table* ***cheap*** *if you buy the chairs too.* **2 be going cheap** *UK* to be offered for sale for less money than is usual **3 not come cheap** to be expensive *Good carpets don't come cheap.* ○ *If you want a qualified accountant, their services don't come cheap.*

cheaply /ˈtʃiːpli/ *adverb* for a low price *You can buy some goods more cheaply in America.* ○ *The shop round the corner does repairs very cheaply.*

cheat¹ /tʃiːt/ *verb* [I, T] to behave in a way that is not honest or fair in order to win something or to get something *She was caught (UK)* ***cheating in*** *her French exam/ (US)* ***cheating on*** *her French exam.* ○ *He* ***cheats at*** *cards.*

cheat on sb to have a secret sexual relationship with someone who is not your usual sexual partner *She found out that he'd been cheating on her.*

cheat sb out of sth to get something that belongs to someone else by deceiving them *He claimed that his brother had cheated him out of his inheritance.*

cheat² /tʃiːt/ *noun* [C] **1** someone who cheats **2** special instructions or information which someone can use to help them play a computer game more effectively

check in

○⌐**check¹** /tʃek/ *verb* **1** EXAMINE [I, T] to examine something in order to make sure that it is correct or the way it should be [+ (that)] *I went to check that I'd locked the door.* ○ *Have you checked your facts?* ○ *I knelt down beside the body and checked for a pulse.* **2** FIND OUT [I, T] to find out about something [+ question word] *I'll check whether Peter knows about the party.* **3** ASK [I] to ask someone for permission to do something *I'd like to stay overnight, but I need to check with my parents.* **4** STOP [T] to stop something bad from increasing or continuing *The government needs to find a way to check rising inflation.* **5** MARK [T] *US* (*UK* tick) to put a mark on an answer to show that it is correct, or by an item on a list to show that you have dealt with it **6** LEAVE [T] *US* to leave your coat, bags, or other possessions temporarily in someone's care ⊃See also: double-check.

check in 1 to go to the desk at an airport in order to say that you have arrived and to get the number of your seat *We have to check in three hours before the flight leaves.* **2** to go to the desk at a hotel in order to say that you have arrived, and to get the key to your room

check sth off *US* (*UK* tick sth off) to put a mark next to a name or an item on a list to show that it is correct, or that it has been dealt with

check (up) on sb/sth to try to discover how something is progressing or whether someone is doing what they should be doing *My boss is always checking up on me.*

check out to leave a hotel after paying your bill

check sth out 1 INFORMATION *informal* to examine something or get more information about it in order to be certain that it is true, safe, or suitable *We'll need to check out his story.* **2** GO TO SEE *informal* to go to a place in order to see what it is like *Let's check out that new dance club.* **3** BOOKS *mainly US* to borrow books from a library

WORD PARTNERS FOR check

do/make a check • a rigorous check • a final/last-minute/random/routine check • safety/security checks • a check of/on sth

check² /tʃek/ *noun* **1** EXAMINATION [C] an examination of something in order to make sure that it is correct or the way it should be *We do safety checks on all our equipment.* **2** BANK [C] *US spelling of* cheque (= a piece of paper printed by a bank that you use to pay for things) **3** RESTAURANT [C] *US* (*UK* bill) a list that you are given in a restaurant showing how much your meal costs **4** MARK [C] *US* (*UK* tick) a mark (check) that shows that an answer is correct, or that you have dealt with something on a list **5** PATTERN [C, U] a pattern of squares of different colours **6** hold/keep sth in check to control something that could increase too quickly or become too large or powerful *We need to keep our spending in check.* ⊃See also: rain check.

checkbook /'tʃekbʊk/ *noun* [C] *US spelling of* chequebook (= a book of papers printed by a bank that you use to pay for things)

checked /tʃekt/ *adjective* with a pattern of squares of different colours *a checked shirt/tablecloth*

checkers /'tʃekəz/ *US* (*UK* draughts) *noun* [U] a game that two people play by moving flat, round objects around on a board of black and white squares

check-in /'tʃekɪn/ *noun* [C] the place at an airport where you go to say that you have arrived for your flight, or the act of going to the check-in to say that you have arrived for your flight *a check-in counter/desk*

'**checking ac,count** *US* (*UK* current account) *noun* [C] a bank account which you can take money out of at any time

checklist /'tʃeklɪst/ *noun* [C] a list of things that you should think about, or that you must do

checkmate /'tʃekmeɪt/ *noun* [U] the final position in the game of chess when your king cannot escape and you have lost the game

checkout /'tʃekaʊt/ *noun* [C] **1** (*also US* 'check-out ,counter) the place in a large shop, especially a food shop, where you pay for your goods *a supermarket checkout* **2** the place on an Internet website where you order and pay for things *After you've chosen what you want, click here to go to checkout.*

checkpoint /'tʃekpɔɪnt/ *noun* [C] a place where people and vehicles are stopped and examined *a military/police checkpoint*

check-up /'tʃekʌp/ *noun* [C] a general medical examination to see if you are healthy *I'm going to the doctor for a check-up.*

cheddar /'tʃedər/ *noun* [U] a type of hard, yellow cheese

cheek /tʃiːk/ *noun* **1** [C] the soft part of your face below your eye *Tears ran down his cheeks.* ⊃See colour picture The Body on page Centre 13. **2** [U, no plural] *mainly UK* rude behaviour that shows that you do not respect someone [+ to do sth] *She had the cheek to ask me to pay for her!*

cheekbone /'tʃiːkbəʊn/ *noun* [C] one of the two bones below your eyes

cheeky /'tʃiːki/ *adjective UK* slightly rude or behaving without respect, but often in a funny

way *He's got such a **cheeky** grin.* ● **cheekily**
adverb

cheer¹ /tʃɪəʳ/ *verb* **1** [I, T] to shout loudly in
order to show your approval or to encourage
someone *The crowd stood up and cheered at the
end of the concert.* **2 be cheered by sth** to feel
happier or encouraged because of something

cheer sb on to shout loudly in order to encourage someone in a competition

cheer (sb) up to stop feeling sad, or to
make someone feel happier *Cheer up. It's not
the end of the world.*

cheer sth up to make a place look brighter
or more attractive

cheer² /tʃɪəʳ/ *noun* [C] a shout of approval or encouragement

cheerful /'tʃɪəfʲl/ *adjective* **1** happy *I'm not feeling very cheerful today.* **2** bright and pleasant
to look at *a bright and cheerful room* ● **cheer-
fully** *adverb* ● **cheerfulness** *noun* [U]

cheering¹ /'tʃɪərɪŋ/ *noun* [U] shouts of encouragement and approval

cheering² /'tʃɪərɪŋ/ *adjective* Something cheering encourages you and makes you feel happier. *We received some cheering news.*

cheerleader /'tʃɪə,liːdəʳ/ *noun* [C] a girl, especially in the United States, who leads the
crowd in shouting encouragement to a team
who are playing a sport

cheers /tʃɪəz/ *exclamation* **1** something friendly
that you say before you start to drink alcohol
with someone **2** *UK informal* thank you

cheery /'tʃɪəri/ *adjective* bright and happy *a
cheery wave/smile* ● **cheerily** *adverb*

o─**cheese** /tʃiːz/ *noun* **1** [C, U] a food that is made
from milk, is usually white or yellow, and can
be either hard or soft *a cheese sandwich* ⊃See
colour picture **Food** on page Centre 11. **2 Say cheese!**
something that you say to make someone
smile when you are taking their photograph
⊃See also: be like **chalk¹** and cheese, **cottage cheese,
cream cheese.**

cheesecake /'tʃiːzkeɪk/ *noun* [C, U] a sweet cake
made with soft, white cheese on a biscuit base

cheesy /'tʃiːzi/ *adjective informal* **1** not fashionable and of low quality *cheesy music* **2 a cheesy
grin** a wide smile that is not always sincere

cheetah /'tʃiːtə/ *noun* [C] a large, wild cat that
has black spots and can run very fast

chef /ʃef/ *noun* [C] someone who is the main
cook (= person who cooks) in a hotel or a
restaurant

chemical¹ /'kemɪkʲl/ *adjective* relating to chemistry or chemicals *a chemical reaction* ○ *chemical weapons* ● **chemically** *adverb*

o─**chemical²** /'kemɪkʲl/ *noun* [C] a basic substance
that is used in chemistry or produced by
chemistry

chemist /'kemɪst/ *noun* [C] **1** *UK* (*US* **pharmacist**)
someone whose job is to prepare and sell
drugs in a shop **2** a scientist who does work
involving chemistry

chemistry /'kemɪstri/ *noun* [U] the scientific
study of substances and how they change
when they combine

chemist's /'kemɪsts/ *UK* (*US* **drugstore**) *noun* [C]

a shop where you can buy drugs, soap, beauty
products, etc

chemotherapy /,kiːməʊ'θerəpi/ (*also* **chemo**)
noun [U] the treatment of a disease using chemicals *Chemotherapy is used to treat many types
of cancer.*

WORD PARTNERS FOR ***cheque***

pay by cheque ● a cheque **bounces** ● **write** a
cheque ● a cheque **for** [£50/£200, etc]

o─**cheque** *UK* (*US* **check**) /tʃek/ *noun* [C] a piece of
paper printed by a bank that you use to pay
for things *a **cheque** for £1500* ○ *Are you **paying
by cheque**?* ⊃See also: blank cheque, traveller's
cheque.

chequebook *UK* (*US* **checkbook**) /'tʃekbʊk/
noun [C] a book of cheques

'cheque ,card *noun* [C] a small plastic card
from your bank which you show when you
write a cheque

cherish /'tʃerɪʃ/ *verb* [T] **1** to love someone or
something very much and take care of them
2 If you cherish an idea, hope, memory, etc, it
is very important to you.

cherry /'tʃeri/ *noun* [C] a small, round red or
black fruit with a large seed inside

cherub /'tʃerəb/ *noun* [C] a small child with a
beautiful, round face and wings who appears
in religious paintings

chess /tʃes/ *noun* [U] a game that two people
play by moving differently shaped pieces
around a board of black and white squares *a
chess set*

chest /tʃest/ *noun* [C] **1** the front of your body
between your neck and your waist *a hairy
chest* ○ *chest pains* ⊃See colour picture **The Body** on
page Centre 13. **2** a strong, usually wooden, container with a lid, used for keeping things in *a
treasure chest* **3 get sth off your chest** *informal*
to tell someone about something that you have
been worried or angry about for a long time

chestnut /'tʃesnʌt/ *noun* **1** [C] a nut that has a
shiny, red-brown surface and is white inside,
or the tree that produces these nuts *roasted
chestnuts* **2** [C, U] a dark red-brown colour ⊃See
also: horse chestnut.

,chest of 'drawers *UK* (*US* **bureau**) *noun* [C] a
piece of furniture with drawers for keeping
clothes in

chew /tʃuː/ *verb* [I, T] **1** to crush food between
your teeth before you swallow it **2** to repeatedly bite something without swallowing it *to
chew gum*

chew sth over to think carefully about
something, or to discuss it

'chewing ,gum *noun* [U] a sweet substance
that you chew but do not swallow

chewy /'tʃuːi/ *adjective* Chewy food needs to be
chewed a lot before you can swallow it.

chic /ʃiːk/ *adjective* fashionable and attractive *a
chic restaurant*

chick /tʃɪk/ *noun* [C] a baby bird, especially a
baby chicken

o─**chicken¹** /'tʃɪkɪn/ *noun* **1** [C] a bird kept on a
farm for its meat and eggs **2** [U] the meat of a

C

chicken *a chicken sandwich*

chicken^{2} /ˈtʃɪkɪn/ *verb*

chicken out *informal* to decide not to do something because you are too nervous

ˈchicken ˌpox *noun* [U] a children's disease that causes a fever and red spots on the skin

ˈchick ˌflick *noun* [C] *humorous* a film about romantic relationships or other subjects that interest women

ˈchick ˌlit *noun* [C] *humorous* a book about romantic relationships or other subjects that interest women

chief^{1} /tʃiːf/ *adjective* [always before noun] **1** most important *The wonderful weather was our* ***chief reason*** *for coming here.* **2** highest in rank *chief economic adviser to the government*

chief^{2} /tʃiːf/ *noun* [C] **1** the leader of a group of people *tribal chiefs* **2** a person who controls other people in an organization *police chiefs*

ˌchief exˈecutive (*also* **chief executive officer**) *noun* [C] the person with the most important job in a company

chiefly /ˈtʃiːfli/ *adverb* mainly *magazines intended chiefly for teenagers*

chieftain /ˈtʃiːftᵊn/ *noun* [C] the leader of a tribe (= group of people with the same language and customs)

chiffon /ˈʃɪfɒn/ [US] /ʃɪˈfɑːn/ *noun* [U] a soft, thin cloth used for making women's clothes

⊶**child** /tʃaɪld/ *noun* [C] *plural* **children** **1** a young person who is not yet an adult *an eight-year-old child ○ How many children are there in your class?* **2** someone's son or daughter, also when they are adults *Both our children have grown up and moved away.* ➲See also: **only child**.

ˈchild aˌbuse *noun* [U] when adults treat children in a cruel or violent way

ˌchild ˈbenefit *noun* [U] money that the British government pays every week to families with children

childbirth /ˈtʃaɪldbɜːθ/ *noun* [U] the process during which a baby is born *His mother died* ***in childbirth***.

childcare /ˈtʃaɪldkeəʳ/ *noun* [U] when someone looks after children while their parents are working

WORD PARTNERS FOR ***childhood***

spend your childhood swh/doing sth • **early** childhood • **in** (sb's) childhood • a **happy/lonely/unhappy** childhood • a childhood **friend**/sb's childhood **sweetheart** • childhood **memories**

childhood /ˈtʃaɪldhʊd/ *noun* [C, U] the part of your life when you are a child

childish /ˈtʃaɪldɪʃ/ *adjective* **1** Childish behaviour is silly, like that of a small child. *Don't be so childish!* **2** typical of a child *childish handwriting* • **childishly** *adverb* • **childishness** *noun* [U]

childless /ˈtʃaɪldləs/ *adjective* A childless person has no children.

childlike /ˈtʃaɪldlaɪk/ *adjective* Childlike people are like children in some ways, such as trusting people or behaving in a natural way.

childminder /ˈtʃaɪldˌmaɪndəʳ/ *noun* [C] *UK* someone whose job is to look after children while their parents are working

⊶**children** /ˈtʃɪldrən/ *plural of* child

ˈchild ˌsupport *noun* [U] money that someone gives the mother or father of their children when they do not live with them

chili /ˈtʃɪli/ *noun US spelling of* chilli

chill^{1} /tʃɪl/ *verb* [I, T] to become cold, or to make someone or something become cold *Chill the wine before serving.*

chill out *informal* to relax completely, or not allow things to upset you *Chill out, Dad - if we miss this train there's always another one.*

chill^{2} /tʃɪl/ *noun* **1** [COLD] [no plural] a cold feeling *There is a definite chill in the air.* **2** [FEAR] [C] a sudden frightened feeling *The scream* ***sent a chill down my spine.*** **3** [ILLNESS] [C] *UK* a cold (= common illness that makes you sneeze) that is not very bad

chilli *UK* (*US* **chili**) /ˈtʃɪli/ *noun plural* **chillies** **1** [C, U] a small, thin, red or green vegetable that tastes very hot *chilli powder* **2** [U] a spicy dish of beans, meat, and chillies

chilling /ˈtʃɪlɪŋ/ *adjective* very frightening *a chilling tale*

chilly /ˈtʃɪli/ *adjective* **1** unpleasantly cold *a chilly evening* **2** unfriendly *He gave me a chilly look.*

chime /tʃaɪm/ *verb* [I, T] If a bell or clock chimes, it rings. • **chime** *noun* [C]

chime in to suddenly say something in order to add your opinion to a conversation *"Quite right too!" Tony chimed in.*

chimney /ˈtʃɪmni/ *noun* [C] a wide pipe that allows smoke from a fire to go out through the roof

chimney

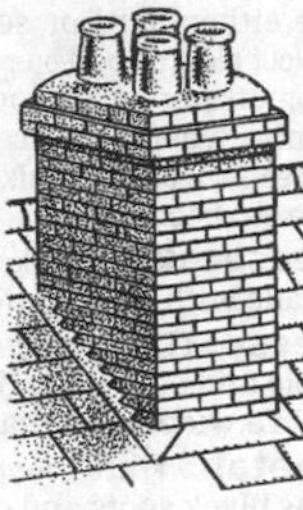

ˈchimney ˌsweep *noun* [C] someone whose job is to clean inside a chimney, using long brushes

chimpanzee /ˌtʃɪmpᵊnˈziː/ (*also* **chimp** /tʃɪmp/ *informal*) *noun* [C] an African animal like a large monkey

chin /tʃɪn/ *noun* [C] the bottom part of your face, below your mouth ➲See colour picture **The Body** on page Centre 13.

china /ˈtʃaɪnə/ *noun* [U] **1** the hard substance that plates, cups, bowls, etc are made from *a china teapot* **2** cups, plates, bowls, etc that are made from china

chink /tʃɪŋk/ *noun* [C] **1** a small, narrow opening in something **2** a short ringing sound that is made when glass or metal objects touch each other

chip^{1} /tʃɪp/ *noun* [C] **1** [POTATO] *UK* (*US* **french fry**) a long, thin piece of potato that is cooked in oil [usually plural] *fish and chips* ➲See colour picture **Food** on page Centre 11. **2** [IN BAG] *US* (*UK* **crisp**) a very thin, dry, fried slice of potato [usually plural] *barbecue flavoured potato chips* ⇒See colour picture **Food** on page Centre 11. **3** [COMPUTER] a microchip (= very small part of a computer that stores information) **4** [SMALL PIECE] a small piece that has broken off something *wood chips* **5** [HOLE] a place where a small piece has broken off something *This cup has a chip in it.* **6 be a chip off the old block** *informal* to be very similar to your mother or father **7 have a chip on your shoulder** *informal* to blame other people for something bad that has happened to you and continue to feel angry about it *She's always had a real chip on her shoulder because she didn't go to university.*

chip² /tʃɪp/ *verb* [T] **chipping,** *past* **chipped** to break a small piece off something *Henman may have chipped a bone in his wrist.* ○ *a chipped plate*

chip in *informal* to interrupt a conversation in order to say something *I'll start and you can all chip in with your comments.*

chip in (sth) If several people chip in, they each give money to buy something together. *We all chipped in to buy our teacher a present.*

chip and 'PIN *noun* [U] a way to pay for goods and services using a credit card (= a small plastic card that allows you to buy things) and a secret number

chiropodist /kɪˈrɒpədɪst/ UK (US **podiatrist**) *noun* [C] someone whose job is to treat problems with people's feet

chirp /tʃɜːp/ *verb* [I] If birds or insects chirp, they make short, high sounds. ● **chirp** *noun* [C]

chirpy /ˈtʃɜːpi/ *adjective* UK *informal* happy and active *Why's Ben so chirpy this morning?*

chisel /ˈtʃɪzᵊl/ *noun* [C] a tool with a sharp end that you use for cutting and shaping wood or stone ⇒See picture at **tool.**

chivalrous /ˈʃɪvᵊlrəs/ *adjective* A chivalrous man behaves very politely towards women. ● **chivalry** *noun* [U] polite behaviour towards women

chives /tʃaɪvz/ *noun* [plural] a plant with long, thin leaves used in cooking to give a flavour similar to onions

chlorine /ˈklɔːriːn/ *noun* [U] a gas with a strong smell, used to make water safe to drink and swim in

o--**chocolate** /ˈtʃɒkᵊlət/ *noun* **1** [SUBSTANCE] [U] a sweet, brown food that is usually sold in a block *a bar of chocolate* ○ *milk chocolate* ○ *a chocolate cake* **2** [SWEET] [C] a small piece of sweet food covered in chocolate *a box of chocolates* **3** [DRINK] [C, U] a sweet drink made with chocolate and hot milk

WORD PARTNERS FOR choice

have/make a choice ● give/offer sb a choice ● a good / informed / obvious / popular/ stark/wide/wrong choice ● a choice be-tween sth ● by choice ● have (no) choice

o--**choice¹** /tʃɔɪs/ *noun* **1** [RIGHT] [U, no plural] when you can choose between two or more things *If I had a choice, I'd give up work.* ○ *He had no choice but to accept their offer.* ○ *I'm single by choice* (= because I want to be). **2** [DECISION] [C] the decision to choose one thing or person and

---

not someone or something else *In the past women had to **make a choice between** a career or marriage.* **3** [THINGS TO CHOOSE FROM] [U, no plural] the things or people you can choose from *The dress is available in a **choice of** colours.* ○ *The evening menu offers **a wide choice** of dishes.* **4** [CHOSEN ONE] [C] the person or thing that someone has chosen [usually singular] *Harvard was not his **first** choice.* ○ *The winner got £1000 to give to the charity **of her** choice.* ⇒See also: **multiple choice.**

choice² /tʃɔɪs/ *adjective* [always before noun] of very good quality *the choicest cuts of meat*

choir /kwaɪᵊr/ *noun* [group] a group of people who sing together *a school/church choir*

choke¹ /tʃəʊk/ *verb* **1** [I, T] If you choke, or if something chokes you, you stop breathing because something is blocking your throat. *Children can **choke on** peanuts.* **2** [T] (*also* **choke up**) to fill something such as a road or pipe so that nothing can pass through [often passive] *The roads were choked with traffic.*

choke sth back to try not to show how angry or upset you are *She ran to the door, choking back the tears.*

choke (sb) up to become unable to speak because you are starting to cry *I can't watch that movie without choking up.*

choke² /tʃəʊk/ *noun* [C] a piece of equipment that controls the amount of air going into a car engine

cholera /ˈkɒlᵊrə/ *noun* [U] a serious disease that affects the stomach and bowels, usually caused by dirty water or food

cholesterol /kəˈlestᵊrɒl/ *noun* [U] a type of fat in your body that can cause heart disease if you have too much

OTHER WAYS OF SAYING **choose**

The verbs **pick** and **select** are often used when someone chooses someone or some-thing after thinking carefully: *He's been picked for the school football team.* ● *We've selected three candidates.*

In more informal situations, the phrasal verbs **go for, opt for,** or **decide on** are sometimes used: *I've decided on blue walls for the bathroom.* ● *I think I'll go for the chocolate cake.* ● *Mike's opted for early retirement.*

The verbs **opt** and **decide** can also be used when someone chooses to do something: *Most people opt to have the operation.* ● *I've decided to take the job.*

o--**choose** /tʃuːz/ *verb past tense* **chose,** *past parti-ciple* **chosen 1** [I, T] to decide which thing you want *I helped my sister choose a name for her baby.* ○ *They have to **choose between** earning a living or getting an education.* ○ *There were lots of books to **choose from.*** ○ [+ question word] *How did you choose which school to go to?* ○ *Adam was **chosen as** team captain.* **2 choose to do sth** to decide to do something *Manuela chose to take a job in Paris.*

choosy /ˈtʃuːzi/ *adjective* difficult to please be-cause of being very exact about what you like *a choosy customer*

chop

chop¹ /tʃɒp/ *verb* **chopping**, *past* **chopped** **1** [T] (*also* **chop up**) to cut something into small pieces *Chop an onion finely.* **2 chop and change** *UK informal* to keep changing your opinions, activities, or job
chop sth down to cut through something to make it fall down
chop sth off to cut off part of something with a sharp tool

chop² /tʃɒp/ *noun* [C] **1** a flat piece of meat with a bone in it *a lamb chop* **2** a quick, hard hit with a sharp tool or with the side of your hand

chopper /'tʃɒpəʳ/ *noun* [C] **1** *informal* a helicopter (= aircraft with turning parts on top) **2** a heavy tool with a sharp edge for cutting wood, meat, etc

choppy /'tʃɒpi/ *adjective* Choppy water has a lot of small waves.

chopsticks /'tʃɒpstɪks/ *noun* **[plural]** thin sticks used for eating food in East Asia

choral /'kɔːrəl/ *adjective* Choral music is written for a choir (= group of people who sing).

chord /kɔːd/ *noun* **1** [C] two or more musical notes that are played at the same time **2 strike a chord (with sb)** If something strikes a chord with you, you like it or are interested in it because it is connected with your own life or opinions. ⊃See also: vocal cords.

chore /tʃɔːʳ/ *noun* [C] a boring job that you must do *I find cooking a real chore.*

choreograph /'kɒriəɡrɑːf/ *verb* [T] **1** to arrange an event or series of events carefully *a carefully choreographed publicity stunt* **2** to design the dances for a performance ● **choreographer** /ˌkɒri'ɒɡrəfəʳ/ *noun* [C]

choreography /ˌkɒri'ɒɡrəfi/ *noun* [U] the process of designing dances for a performance

chorus¹ /'kɔːrəs/ *noun* **1** SONG [C] the part of a song that is repeated several times **2** SINGING GROUP **[group]** a large group of people who sing together **3** IN A SHOW **[group]** a group of dancers and singers in a show who do not have the main parts **4 a chorus of approval/demands/protest, etc** something that a lot of people say at the same time

chorus² /'kɔːrəs/ *verb* [T] *UK* If two or more

people chorus something, they say it at the same time.

chose /tʃəʊz/ *past tense of* choose

chosen /'tʃəʊzən/ *past participle of* choose

Christ /kraɪst/ (*also* **Jesus Christ**) *noun* the Jewish holy man believed by Christians to be the Son of God, and on whose life and teachings Christianity is based

christen /'krɪsən/ *verb* [T] to give a baby a name at a Christian ceremony and make them a member of the Christian Church **[often passive]** *She's being christened in June.* ○ *She was christened Maria.*

christening /'krɪsənɪŋ/ *noun* [C] a ceremony where someone is christened

Christian /'krɪstʃən/ *noun* [C] someone who believes in Christianity *a Christian charity organization* ● **Christian** *adjective*

Christianity /ˌkrɪsti'ænəti/ *noun* [U] a religion based on belief in God and the life and teachings of Jesus Christ, and on the Bible

'Christian ˌname *noun* [C] your first name, not your family name

⊶**Christmas** /'krɪsməs/ *noun* [C, U] the Christian period of celebration around 25 December, when Christians celebrate the birth of Jesus Christ and people give each other presents, or the day itself *We're going to my mother's for Christmas.* ○ **Merry Christmas!** ○ *the Christmas holidays* ○ *Christmas dinner* ⊃See also: Father Christmas.

'Christmas ˌcard *noun* [C] a decorated card that you send to someone at Christmas

ˌChristmas 'carol *UK* (*US* **'Christmas ˌcarol**) *noun* [C] a song that people sing at Christmas

ˌChristmas 'cracker *noun* [C] a coloured paper tube with a small toy inside, that people in the UK pull open at Christmas

ˌChristmas 'Day *noun* [C, U] 25 December, the day on which Christians celebrate the birth of Jesus Christ

ˌChristmas 'Eve *noun* [C, U] the day before Christmas Day

'Christmas ˌtree *noun* [C] a real or artificial tree that people decorate inside their home for Christmas

chrome /krəʊm/ *noun* [U] a hard, shiny metal that is used to cover objects *chrome bath taps*

chromosome /'krəʊməsəʊm/ *noun* [C] the part of a cell that controls what an animal or plant is like

chronic /'krɒnɪk/ *adjective* A chronic illness or problem continues for a long time. *a chronic shortage of nurses* ○ *chronic back pain* ● **chronically** *adverb*

chronicle¹ /'krɒnɪkl/ *noun* [C] a written record of things that happened in the past

chronicle² /'krɒnɪkl/ *verb* [T] to make a record of something, or give details of something *The book chronicles his life as an actor.*

chronological /ˌkrɒnə'lɒdʒɪkəl/ *adjective* arranged in the order in which events happened ● **chronologically** *adverb*

chubby /'tʃʌbi/ *adjective* pleasantly fat *the*

baby's chubby legs

chuck /tʃʌk/ *verb* [T] *informal* to throw something *Don't just chuck your coat on the floor!*

chuck sth away/out *informal* to throw something away *I chucked out all my old clothes.*

chuck sth in *UK informal* to stop doing something because it is boring

chuck sb out *informal* to force someone to leave a place *Pierre was chucked out of school for starting a fight.*

chuckle /'tʃʌkl/ *verb* [I] to laugh quietly • **chuckle** *noun* [C]

chug /tʃʌg/ *verb* **chugging**, *past* **chugged** **chug across/along/up, etc** If a vehicle chugs somewhere, it moves slowly, making a low, regular noise with its engine. *a boat chugging across the lake*

chum /tʃʌm/ *noun* [C] *informal* a friend • **chummy** *adjective* friendly

chunk /tʃʌŋk/ *noun* [C] **1** a large piece of something *a chunk of cheese* ⊃See colour picture **Pieces and Quantities** on page Centre 1. **2** a large part of something *I spend a big chunk of my money on clothes.*

chunky /'tʃʌŋki/ *adjective* **1** A chunky person is short and heavy. **2** big, thick, and heavy *chunky shoes*

🧩 WORD PARTNERS FOR **church**

go to church • in church • a church **service**

o⚬**church** /tʃɜːtʃ/ *noun* **1** [C, U] a building where Christians go to worship God *We used to go to church every Sunday morning.* **2** [C] (*also* **Church**) one of the different groups that make up the Christian religion *the Anglican Church* ⊃See also: **the Catholic Church**.

churchgoer /'tʃɜːtʃˌgəʊər/ *noun* [C] someone who goes to church regularly

churchyard /'tʃɜːtʃjɑːd/ *noun* [C] the land around a church, often where people are buried

churn¹ /tʃɜːn/ *verb* **1** SURFACE [T] (*also* **churn up**) to mix something, especially liquids, with great force *The sea was churned up by heavy winds.* **2** STOMACH [I] If your stomach is churning, you feel sick, usually because you are nervous. **3** BUTTER [T] to mix milk until it becomes butter

churn sth out *informal* to produce large quantities of something very quickly

churn² /tʃɜːn/ *noun* [C] **1** a container that you fill with milk and mix to make butter **2** *UK* a tall metal container for storing and transporting milk

chute /ʃuːt/ *noun* [C] **1** a long thin structure that people or things can slide down *a water chute* **2** *informal short for* parachute

chutney /'tʃʌtni/ *noun* [U] a mixture of fruit, vegetables, sugar, and vinegar that you eat with meat or cheese

the CIA /ˌsiːaɪ'eɪ/ *noun abbreviation for* Central Intelligence Agency: the department of the US government that collects secret information about people and organizations

the CID /ˌsiːaɪ'diː/ *noun abbreviation for* Criminal Investigation Department: the part of the British police force that deals with serious crimes

cider /'saɪdər/ *noun* [C, U] **1** *UK* a drink made from apples that contains alcohol **2** *US* a drink made from apples that contains no alcohol

cigar /sɪ'gɑːr/ *noun* [C] a thick tube made from rolled tobacco leaves, that people smoke

o⚬**cigarette** /ˌsɪgə'ret/ *noun* [C] a thin tube of paper filled with tobacco, that people smoke

cilantro /sɪ'læntrəʊ/ *US* (*UK/US* **coriander**) *noun* [U] a herb that is used in cooking

cinder /'sɪndər/ *noun* [C] a small piece of coal, wood, etc that has been burned

o⚬**cinema** /'sɪnəmə/ *noun* **1** [C] *UK* (*US* **movie theater**) a building where you go to watch films **2** [U] the art or business of making films *an article about French cinema*

cinnamon /'sɪnəmən/ *noun* [U] a brown spice that is used in cooking

circa /'sɜːkə/ *formal* (*written abbreviation* **c**) *preposition* used before a date to show that something happened at about that time *Gainsborough's painting 'The Cottage Door' (circa 1780)*

o⚬**circle¹** /'sɜːkl/ *noun* **1** [C] a round, flat shape like the letter O, or a group of people or things arranged in this shape *We all sat on the floor in a circle.* ⊃See picture at **shape**. **2** [C] a group of people with family, work, or social connections *a close circle of friends* ○ *a technical term used in medical circles.* **3** **the circle** *UK* the seats in the upper area of a theatre ⊃See also: **inner circle**, **traffic circle**, **vicious circle**.

circle² /'sɜːkl/ *verb* **1** [I, T] to move in a circle, often around something *Birds circled above the trees.* **2** [T] to draw a circle around something *Circle the answer you think is correct.*

circuit /'sɜːkɪt/ *noun* [C] **1** TRACK a path, route, or sports track that is shaped like a circle **2** ELECTRIC a complete circle that an electric current travels around **3** EVENTS a regular series of places or events that people involved in a particular activity go to [usually singular] *the tennis circuit* ⊃See also: **short-circuit**.

circular¹ /'sɜːkjələr/ *adjective* **1** shaped like a circle *a circular rug* **2** A circular journey takes you around in a circle, back to the place where you started. *a circular walk*

circular² /'sɜːkjələr/ *noun* [C] a letter or advertisement that is sent to a lot of people at the same time

circulate /'sɜːkjəleɪt/ *verb* **1** INFORMATION [I] If information circulates, a lot of people hear about it. *Rumours are circulating that the mayor is going to resign.* **2** SEND INFORMATION [T] to give or send information to a group of people *A copy of the report was circulated to each director.* **3** MOVE [I, T] to move around or through something, or to make something move around or through something *Hot water circulates through the pipes.*

circulation /ˌsɜːkjə'leɪʃən/ *noun* **1** BLOOD [U] the movement of blood around your body *Exercise improves your circulation.* **2** INFORMATION [U] when something such as information, money, or goods pass from one person to another *Police have warned there are a lot of fake £50 notes in circulation.* **3** [NEWSPAPERS] [no plural] the number of copies of a newspaper or magazine that are sold each day, week, etc

circumcize (*also UK* -ise) /'sɜ:kəmsaɪz/ *verb* [T] to cut off the skin at the end of a boy's or man's penis, or cut off part of a girl's sex organs ● **circumcision** /,sɜ:kəm'sɪʒᵊn/ *noun* [C, U] when someone is circumcised

circumference /sə'kʌmfᵊrᵊns/ *noun* [C, U] the distance around the edge of a circle or round object *The lake is 250km in circumference.*

circumspect /'sɜ:kəmspekt/ *adjective formal* careful about things you do or say

---
WORD PARTNERS FOR *circumstances*

in/under [any/certain/difficult/normal, etc] circumstances ● **in / under** the circumstances ● the circumstances **of/surrounding** sth ● **exceptional/normal/unforeseen** circumstances

---

circumstances /'sɜ:kəmstænsɪz/ *noun* [plural] **1** facts or events that make a situation the way it is *I think they coped very well under the circumstances.* ○ *We oppose capital punishment in/under any circumstances.* **2 under no circumstances** used to say that something must never happen *Under no circumstances should you approach the man.*

circumstantial /,sɜ:kəm'stænʃᵊl/ *adjective* **circumstantial evidence** information about a crime that makes you believe that something is true, but does not prove it

circumvent /,sɜ:kəm'vent/ *verb* [T] *formal* to find a way of avoiding something, especially a law or rule

circus /'sɜ:kəs/ *noun* [C] a show in which a group of people and animals perform in a large tent

cistern /'sɪstən/ *noun* [C] a large container to store water, especially one that supplies water to a toilet ⊃See colour picture **The Bathroom** on page Centre 3.

citadel /'sɪtədᵊl/ *noun* [C] a strong castle that was used in the past to protect people when their city was attacked

cite /saɪt/ *verb* [T] *formal* **1** to mention something as an example or proof of something else *The doctor cited the case of a woman who had died after taking the drug.* **2** *US* to order someone to go to court because they have done something wrong [often passive] *A local farmer was cited for breaking environmental standards.*

WORD PARTNERS FOR *citizen*

a citizen **of** [Paris/Tokyo, etc] ● your **fellow** citizens ● **decent/law-abiding** citizens

---

citizen /'sɪtɪzᵊn/ *noun* [C] **1** someone who lives in a particular town or city *the citizens of Berlin* **2** someone who has a legal right to live in a particular country *My husband became a British citizen in 1984.* ⊃See also: **senior citizen.**

citizenship /'sɪtɪzᵊnʃɪp/ *noun* [U] the legal right to be a citizen of a particular country *British/French citizenship*

citrus fruit /'sɪtrəs,fru:t/ *noun* [C, U] an orange, lemon, or similar fruit

◦**city** /'sɪti/ *noun* **1** [C] a large town *the city of Boston* ○ *the city centre* **2 the City** *UK* the part of London where the large financial organizations have their offices ⊃See also: **inner city.**

civic /'sɪvɪk/ *adjective* [always before noun] relating to a city or town and the people who live there *civic leaders* ○ *The opera house was a source of great civic pride* (= people in the city were proud of it).

civil /'sɪvᵊl/ *adjective* **1** [PEOPLE] [always before noun] relating to the ordinary people or things in a country and not to military or religious organizations *They married in a civil ceremony.* **2** [LAW] [always before noun] relating to private arguments between people and not criminal cases *a civil court* **3** [POLITE] polite in a formal way *He and his ex-wife can't even have a civil conversation.*

,**civil engi'neering** *noun* [U] the planning and building of roads, bridges, and public buildings

civilian /sɪ'vɪliən/ *noun* [C] someone who is not a member of a military organization or the police

civility /sɪ'vɪləti/ *noun* [U] polite behaviour

civilization (*also UK* -isation) /,sɪvᵊlaɪ'zeɪʃᵊn/ *noun* **1** [C, U] human society with its developed social organizations, or the culture and way of life of a society at a particular period of time *ancient civilizations* ○ *Nuclear war could mean the end of civilization.* **2** [U] when people have an advanced and comfortable way of life *modern civilization*

civilize (*also UK* -ise) /'sɪvᵊlaɪz/ *verb* [T] to educate a society so that it becomes more advanced and organized

civilized (*also UK* -ised) /'sɪvᵊlaɪzd/ *adjective* **1** A civilized society is advanced and has well-developed laws and customs. *A fair justice system is an important part of civilized society.* **2** polite and calm *Let's discuss this in a civilized manner.*

,**civil 'liberties** *noun* [plural] the freedom people have to do, think, and say what they want

,**civil 'rights** *noun* [plural] the rights that everyone in a country has

,**civil 'servant** *noun* [C] someone who works in the Civil Service

the ,Civil 'Service *noun* the government departments and the people who work in them

,**civil 'war** *noun* [C, U] a war between groups of people who live in the same country

cl *written abbreviation for* centilitre (= a unit for measuring liquid) *a 75 cl bottle of wine*

clad /klæd/ *adjective literary* covered or dressed in something *He came to the door clad only in a towel.*

◦**claim¹** /kleɪm/ *verb* **1** [SAY] [T] to say that something is true, although you have not proved it [+ (that)] *She claimed that the dog attacked her.* ○ [+ to do sth] *He claims to have seen a ghost.* **2 claim credit/responsibility/success, etc** to say that you have done or achieved something *No* one has claimed responsibility for yesterday's bomb attack. ⊃Opposite **disclaim**. **3** DEMAND [I, T] to ask for something because it belongs to you or you have the right to have it *She claimed $2,500 in travel expenses.* ○ *If no one claims the watch, then you can keep it.* **4** KILL [T] If an accident, war, etc claims lives, people are killed because of it. *The floods claimed over 200 lives.*

WORD PARTNERS FOR **claim**

make a claim • **deny / dismiss / reject** a claim • a **false** claim • a claim **by** sb

o—**claim²** /kleɪm/ *noun* [C] **1** ANNOUNCEMENT when someone says that something is true, although it has not been proved [+ (that)] *She rejected claims that she had lied.* **2** DEMAND an official demand for something you think you have a right to *a claim for compensation* **3** RIGHT a right to have something *You don't have any claim to the land.* **4** lay claim to sth *formal* to say that something is yours or that you have done something **5** sb's/sth's claim to fame a reason why someone or something is known *My main claim to fame is meeting the President.*

clam¹ /klæm/ *noun* [C] a small sea creature with a shell in two parts, that you can eat

clam² /klæm/ *verb* clamming, *past* clammed

clam up *informal* to suddenly stop talking, usually because you are embarrassed or nervous *He was afraid he would clam up in front of the TV camera.*

clamber /ˈklæmbə'/ *verb* **clamber into/over/up, etc** to climb somewhere with difficulty, especially using your hands and feet *The children clambered into the boat.*

clammy /ˈklæmi/ *adjective* unpleasantly wet and sticky *clammy hands*

clamour¹ UK (US **clamor**) /ˈklæmə'/ *verb* **clamour for sth; clamour to do sth** to ask for something continuously in a loud or angry way *Fans were clamouring for their autographs.*

clamour² UK (US **clamor**) /ˈklæmə'/ *noun* [no plural] **1** a demand for something, or a complaint about something that is made by a lot of people *the public's clamour for organic food* **2** a loud, continuous noise made by people talking or shouting *We heard the clamour of voices in the street outside.*

clamp¹ /klæmp/ *noun* [C] **1** a piece of equipment that is used for holding things together tightly **2** UK a metal cover that is put on the wheel of a car so you cannot move it if you have parked in an illegal place

clamp² /klæmp/ *verb* **1** **clamp sth around/over/ to, etc** to put something in a particular position and hold it there tightly *He clamped his hand over her mouth.* **2** **clamp sth onto/to/together, etc** to fasten two things together using a clamp **3** [T] UK to fasten a metal cover on the wheel of a car to stop it moving because it has been parked in an illegal place

clamp down to do something strict to try to stop or limit an activity *Local police have clamped down on teenage drinking.*

clampdown /ˈklæmpdaʊn/ *noun* [C] a strict attempt to stop or limit an activity [usually singular] *a clampdown on inner city pollution*

clan /klæn/ *noun* [C] a large group of families who are all related to each other, especially in Scotland

clandestine /klænˈdestɪn/ *adjective formal* secret and often illegal *a clandestine meeting*

clang /klæŋ/ *verb* [I, T] If something metal clangs, it makes a loud ringing sound, or if you clang it, you make it do this. *The gate clanged shut behind me.* • **clang** *noun* [C]

clank /klæŋk/ *verb* [I] If metal objects clank, they make a low noise when they hit each other. *The bracelets on her arm clanked as she moved.* • **clank** *noun* [C]

clap

clap¹ /klæp/ *verb* clapping, *past* clapped **1** [I, T] to hit your hands together, often repeatedly, especially in order to show that you enjoyed a performance *The crowd clapped and cheered for more.* **2** **clap sb on the back/shoulder** to hit someone on the back or shoulder in a friendly way **3** [T] to put something somewhere suddenly *She clapped her hands over her ears and refused to listen.*

clap² /klæp/ *noun* **1** [no plural] when you hit your hands together, often repeatedly *Let's give our winning contestant a big clap.* **2** a clap of thunder a sudden, loud sound that is made by thunder

claret /ˈklærət/ *noun* [U] UK red wine from the area of France around Bordeaux

clarify /ˈklærɪfaɪ/ *verb* [T] to make something easier to understand by explaining it *The law aims to clarify building regulations.* • clarification /ˌklærɪfɪˈkeɪʃ³n/ *noun* [C, U]

clarinet /ˌklærɪˈnet/ *noun* [C] a musical instrument like a long, black tube, that you play by blowing into it and pressing metal keys

clarity /ˈklærəti/ *noun* [U] the quality of being clear and easy to understand

clash¹ /klæʃ/ *verb* **1** FIGHT [I] to fight or argue *Government troops clashed with rebel soldiers.* ○ *Many young people clash with their parents over what time they must be home at night.* **2** COLOUR [I] If colours or styles clash, they do not look good together. *You can't wear pink lipstick - it clashes with your dress.* **3** EVENT [I] UK If two events clash, they happen at the same time so that you cannot go to them both. *Emma's party **clashes with** my brother's wedding.* **4** NOISE **[I, T]** to make a loud noise by hitting metal objects together

clash² /klæʃ/ *noun* **[C] 1** FIGHT a fight or argument *There were violent **clashes between** the police and demonstrators.* **2** DIFFERENCE when ideas or qualities are very different, and this causes problems *a **clash of personalities*** **3** SOUND a loud sound that is made when metal objects hit each other *the **clash of pans** in the sink*

clasp¹ /klɑːsp/ *verb* **[T]** to hold something or someone tightly *He clasped his daughter in his arms.*

clasp² /klɑːsp/ *noun* **1 [C]** a small metal object that is used to fasten a bag, belt, or piece of jewellery **2** [no plural] a tight hold

☞**class¹** /klɑːs/ *noun* **1** STUDENTS **[C]** a group of students who have lessons together *Katie and Sarah are in the same class at school.* **2** LESSON **[C, U]** a period of time in which students are taught something *My first class starts at 8.30.* ○ *He was told off for talking in class* (= during the lesson). **3** SOCIAL GROUP **[C, U]** one of the groups in a society with the same social and economic position, or the system of dividing people into these groups *Class is still very much a feature of English society.* **4** QUALITY **[C]** a group into which people or things are put according to their quality *When it comes to mathematics, he's in a different class to his peers.* ○ *second-class mail* **5** SIMILARITY **[C]** a group of similar or related things, especially plants and animals **6** STYLE **[U]** *informal* the quality of being stylish or fashionable *a player with real class* ➔See also: **middle class, upper class, working class.**

class² /klɑːs/ *verb* **class sb/sth as sth** to put someone or something in a particular group according to their qualities *The tower is classed as a historic monument.*

classic¹ /ˈklæsɪk/ *adjective* **1** POPULAR A classic book, film, etc is one that has been popular for a long time and is considered to be of a high quality. *the classic film 'Gone with the Wind'* **2** TRADITIONAL having a traditional style that is always fashionable *a classic black jacket* **3** TYPICAL typical

classic² /ˈklæsɪk/ *noun* **[C]** a classic book, film, etc

classical /ˈklæsɪkᵊl/ *adjective* **1 classical music** serious music by people like Mozart and Stravinsky *Do you prefer classical music or pop music?* **2** traditional in style *classical and*

modern dance **3** relating to ancient Greece and Rome *classical literature*

classically /ˈklæsɪkᵊli/ *adverb* **1** in a traditional style *a **classically trained** actor* **2** in a typical style *a classically English tea room*

classics /ˈklæsɪks/ *noun* **[U]** the study of ancient Greece and Rome, especially the language, literature, and history

classification /ˌklæsɪfɪˈkeɪʃᵊn/ *noun* **[C, U]** the process of putting people or things into groups by their type, size, etc, or one of these groups *the classification of plants*

classified /ˈklæsɪfaɪd/ *adjective* Classified information is officially kept secret by a government. *classified documents/information*

classified 'ad *noun* **[C]** a small advertisement that you put in a newspaper if you want to buy or sell something

classify /ˈklæsɪfaɪ/ *verb* **[T]** to put people or things into groups by their type, size, etc [often passive] *A third of the population has been **classified as** poor.* ○ *The books are **classified** by subject.*

classmate /ˈklɑːsmeɪt/ *noun* **[C]** someone who is in your class at school or college

☞**classroom** /ˈklɑːsruːm/ *noun* **[C]** a room in a school where students have lessons ➔See colour picture **The Classroom** on page Centre 6.

classy /ˈklɑːsi/ *adjective informal* stylish and fashionable

clatter /ˈklætəʳ/ *verb* **1 [I]** If something clatters, it makes a lot of noise when it hits something hard. **2 clatter about/around/down, etc** to move somewhere in a very noisy way *I could hear Sue clattering about upstairs.* • **clatter** *noun* [no plural] *He dropped his spoon **with a clatter**.*

clause /klɔːz/ *noun* **[C] 1** a part of a legal document *a clause in a contract* **2** a group of words containing a subject and a verb, that is usually only part of a sentence ➔See also: **relative clause, subordinate clause.**

claustrophobia /ˌklɒstrəˈfəʊbiə/ *noun* **[U]** fear of being in a small or crowded place

claustrophobic /ˌklɒstrəˈfəʊbɪk/ *adjective* **1** feeling very anxious when you are in a small or crowded place **2** A claustrophobic place makes you feel anxious because it is very small or crowded. *a claustrophobic room*

claw

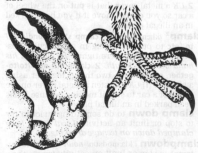

claw¹ /klɔː/ *noun* **[C]** one of the sharp, curved

nails on the feet of some animals and birds

claw² /klɔː/ *verb* [I, T] If a person or animal claws something, they try to get hold of it or damage it with their nails or claws. *He clawed at the rope, trying to free himself.*

claw sth back *mainly UK* to try to get back something that you had before *The party is desperately trying to claw back support.*

clay /kleɪ/ *noun* [U] a type of heavy soil that becomes hard when dry, used for making things such as bricks and containers *a clay pot*

o⌐**clean¹** /kliːn/ *adjective* 1 [NOT DIRTY] not dirty *clean hands* ○ *clean clothes* 2 [NO SEX] not about sex *a clean joke* 3 [NO CRIME] showing that you have not done anything illegal *a clean driving licence* 4 [FAIR] fair and honest *a clean election/fight* 5 **come clean** *informal* to tell the truth about something that you have been keeping secret

o⌐**clean²** /kliːn/ *verb* [I, T] to remove the dirt from something *I spent the morning cleaning the house.* ⊃See also: **dry clean**, **spring clean**.

clean sth out 1 to take everything out of a room, car, container, etc and clean the inside of it 2 *informal* to steal everything from a place

clean (sb/sth) up to make a person or place clean and tidy *We have to clean up before we leave.*

clean³ /kliːn/ *adverb informal* used to emphasize that something is done completely *The bullet went clean through his helmet.*

clean-cut /ˌkliːn'kʌt/ *adjective* Someone who is clean-cut has a tidy appearance.

cleaner /'kliːnəʳ/ *noun* 1 [C] someone whose job is to clean houses, offices, public places, etc 2 [C, U] a substance used for cleaning things *carpet/oven cleaner* 3 **the cleaner's** a shop where clothes are cleaned with chemicals ⊃See also: **vacuum cleaner**.

cleanliness /'klenlɪnəs/ *noun* [U] the state of being clean, or the practice of keeping things clean

cleanly /'kliːnli/ *adverb* in a quick and tidy way *The branch broke cleanly away from the tree.*

cleanse /klenz/ *verb* [T] to clean your face or an injured part of your body

cleanser /'klenzəʳ/ *noun* [C, U] a substance for cleaning, especially your face

o⌐**clear¹** /klɪəʳ/ *adjective* 1 [UNDERSTAND] easy to understand *clear instructions* 2 [HEAR/SEE] easy to hear, read, or see *These photos are very clear.* ○ *Can we make the sound any clearer?* 3 [NO DOUBT] not possible to doubt *The evidence against him was clear.* ○ [+ (that)] *It was clear that Leif was angry.* ○ *Ella made it clear that she didn't like James.* 4 [CERTAIN] [never before noun] certain about something *Are you clear about how to get there?* ○ [+ question word] *I'm not very clear why she phoned.* 5 [NOT BLOCKED] not covered or blocked by anything *a clear road* ○ *a clear desk* 6 [WITHOUT CLOUDS] A clear sky does not have any clouds. 7 [TRANSPARENT] easy to see through *clear water* ○ *clear glass* ⊃See also: the **coast¹** is clear, **crystal clear**.

clear² /klɪəʳ/ *verb* 1 [EMPTY] [T] to remove all the objects or people from a place *clear a room/*

shelf ○ *Police cleared the building because of a bomb threat.* 2 [WEATHER] [I] If the sky or weather clears, the clouds and rain disappear. 3 [NOT GUILTY] [T] to prove that someone is not guilty of something that they were accused of *The jury cleared him of murder.* 4 [MONEY] [I] If a cheque (= printed paper used to pay for things) clears, the money goes from one person's bank account to another person's bank account. 5 [GO OVER] [T] to jump over something without touching it *The horse easily cleared the fence.* 6 [GIVE PERMISSION] [T] to give or get permission to do something *You have to clear it with the headteacher if you want a day off school.* ⊃See also: clear the **air¹**.

clear sth away to make a place tidy by removing things from it, or putting them where they should be *The children are not very good at clearing away their toys.*

clear off *UK informal* used to tell someone to go away immediately

clear sth out to tidy a place by getting rid of things that you do not want

clear (sth) up 1 *mainly UK* to make a place tidy by removing things from it or putting them where they should be *Dad was clearing up in the kitchen.* 2 to make an illness better *Antibiotics will clear up the infection.*

clear sth up to give an explanation for something, or to deal with a problem or argument *Before we sign the contract, there are a few points we should clear up.*

clear up *informal* If the weather clears up, the cloud and rain disappears.

clear³ /klɪəʳ/ *adverb* 1 away from something so that you are not touching it *Stand clear of the doors, please.* 2 **steer clear of sb/sth** to avoid someone or something because they are unpleasant or dangerous

clear⁴ /klɪəʳ/ *noun* 1 **in the clear a** not responsible for a mistake or crime **b** *UK* not in a difficult situation or having problems any more

clearance /'klɪərəns/ *noun* [C, U] 1 [PERMISSION] permission from someone in authority *The company needs to get government clearance for the deal.* 2 [DISTANCE] the distance that is needed for one thing to avoid touching another thing 3 [REMOVING THINGS] when waste or things you do not want are removed from a place

clear-cut /ˌklɪə'kʌt/ *adjective* very certain or obvious *The issue is not very clear-cut.*

clearing /'klɪərɪŋ/ *noun* [C] a small area in the middle of a forest, where there are no trees

o⌐**clearly** /'klɪəli/ *adverb* 1 [EASY] in a way that is easy to see, hear, read, or understand *He spoke very clearly.* 2 [CERTAIN] used to show that you think something is obvious or certain *Clearly he's very talented.* 3 [NOT CONFUSED] If you think clearly, you are not confused.

cleavage /'kliːvɪdʒ/ *noun* [C, U] the area between a woman's breasts

cleaver /'kliːvəʳ/ *noun* [C] a heavy knife with a large, square blade *a meat cleaver*

clef /klef/ *noun* [C] a sign written at the beginning of a line of music, that shows how high or low the notes are

clemency /'klemənsi/ *noun* [U] *formal* when a

judge, king, etc decides not to punish someone severely although they have committed a crime

clench /klenʃ/ *verb* [T] to close your hands or teeth very tightly, or to hold something tightly *Dan **clenched his fists**.*

clergy /'klɜːdʒi/ *noun* [plural] priests or religious leaders *a member of the clergy*

clergyman /'klɜːdʒɪmən/ *noun* [C] *plural* **clergymen** a man who is a member of the clergy

cleric /'klerɪk/ *noun* [C] a member of the clergy

clerical /'klerɪkəl/ *adjective* **1** relating to work done in an office *a clerical assistant* **2** relating to priests or religious leaders

clerk /klɑːk/ [US] /klɜːrk/ *noun* [C] **1** someone who works in an office or bank, keeping records and doing general office work *a bank clerk* **2** *US* someone who sells things in a shop *a store/sales clerk*

OTHER WAYS OF SAYING *clever*

The adjectives **intelligent** and **smart** are common alternatives to 'clever': *She's a highly **intelligent** woman.* • *He's one of the **smartest** kids in the class.*

Young people who are clever are sometimes described as **bright**: *Jacob was a very **bright** boy.*

The adjective **brainy** is used in informal contexts, especially by young people when describing other young people: *Ask Louisa to help you - she's really **brainy**.*

Someone who is extremely clever is sometimes described as **brilliant** or **gifted**: *William was a **brilliant/gifted** scholar.*

⊶**clever** /'klevər/ *adjective* **1** able to learn and understand things quickly and easily *a clever student* **2** designed in an effective and intelligent way *a clever idea* ○ *a clever tool* • **cleverly** *adverb a cleverly designed toy* • **cleverness** *noun* [U]

cliché /'kliːʃeɪ/ [US] /kliː'ʃeɪ/ *noun* [C] something that people have said or done so much that it has become boring or has no real meaning

⊶**click**[1] /klɪk/ *verb* **1** [SOUND] [I, T] to make a short, sharp sound, or to use something to make this sound *The door clicked shut behind him.* **2** [COMPUTER] [I, T] to press on part of a computer mouse (= small computer control) to make the computer do something *To start the program, **click on** its icon.* **3** [PEOPLE] [I] *informal* If two people click, they like each other immediately. **4** [IDEA] [I] *informal* to suddenly understand something *Suddenly everything clicked and I realized where I'd met him.* ➲See also: **double-click**, snap your fingers (**finger**[1]).

click[2] /klɪk/ *noun* [C] a short, sharp sound *the click of a switch*

client /klaɪənt/ *noun* [C] someone who pays someone else for services or advice

clientele /ˌkliːɒn'tel/ *noun* [group, no plural] the regular customers of a business *The new bar aims to attract a younger clientele.*

cliff /klɪf/ *noun* [C] an area of high, steep rocks beside the sea

cliff

climactic /klaɪ'mæktɪk/ *adjective* [always before noun] *literary* A climactic event or time is one in which important or exciting things happen.

WORD PARTNERS FOR *climate*

2 create a climate **of** [fear/trust, etc] • **in a** climate • **in the current/in the present** climate • the **political/social** climate

climate /'klaɪmət/ *noun* **1** [C, U] the weather conditions that an area usually has *a hot, dry climate* **2** [C] the situation, feelings, and opinions that exist at a particular time [usually singular] *the **political/social climate*** ○ *Terrorism **creates a climate of** fear.*

'climate ˌchange *noun* [C, U] the way the Earth's weather is changing

climatic /klaɪ'mætɪk/ *adjective formal* relating to the weather conditions that an area usually has *climatic change*

WORD PARTNERS FOR *climax*

build up to/come to/reach a climax • **a dramatic/exciting/fitting/thrilling** climax • the climax **of** sth

climax[1] /'klaɪmæks/ *noun* [C] the most exciting or important part of something [usually singular] *The **climax of** her career was winning a gold medal.* ➲Opposite **anticlimax**.

climax[2] /'klaɪmæks/ *verb* [I, T] to reach the most important or exciting part *The festival **climaxed with/in** a huge fireworks display.*

climb

He climbed a tree. They went climbing.

⊶**climb** /klaɪm/ *verb* **1** [PERSON] [I, T] (*also* **climb up**) to go up something, or onto the top of something ***climb a ladder/tree/mountain*** ○ *He climbed up on a chair to change the light bulb.* **2 climb into/out of/through, etc** to move somewhere using your hands and legs *The child climbed into the back of the car.* **3** [NUMBER] [I] If a price, number, or amount climbs, it increases. *Profits climbed 11% last quarter.* **4** [MOVE HIGHER] [I] to move to a higher position *The road climbs quite steeply.* ● **climb** *noun* [C] *a long/steep/uphill climb*

climb down *UK informal* to change your opinion or admit that you are wrong *The government has been forced to climb down over the issue of increased taxes.*

climbdown /'klaɪmdaʊn/ *noun* [C] *UK* when someone admits that they were wrong about something or have changed their opinion *an embarrassing climbdown by the government*

climber /'klaɪmə'/ *noun* [C] someone who climbs mountains, hills, or rocks as a sport

climbing /'klaɪmɪŋ/ *noun* [U] the sport of climbing mountains, hills, or rocks *rock/mountain climbing* ○ *climbing boots*

clinch /klɪnʃ/ *verb* [T] *informal* **1** to finally get or win something *clinch a deal* **2 clinch it** *informal* to make someone finally decide what to do *When he said the job was in Paris, that clinched it for me.*

cling /klɪŋ/ *verb* [I] *past* **clung 1** to hold someone or something tightly, especially because you are frightened *She was found clinging to the ledge.* ○ *I clung on to his hand in the dark.* **2** to stick to something *His damp hair clung to his forehead.*

cling (on) to sth to try very hard to keep something *He clung on to power for ten more years.*

cling to sth to refuse to stop believing or hoping for something *He clung to the belief that his family were alive.*

clingfilm /'klɪŋfɪlm/ *UK trademark* (*US* **plastic wrap**) *noun* [U] thin, transparent plastic used for wrapping or covering food

clingy /'klɪŋi/ *adjective mainly UK* always wanting to be with someone and not wanting to do things alone *a clingy child*

clinic /'klɪnɪk/ *noun* [C] a place where people go for medical treatment or advice *an eye/skin clinic*

clinical /'klɪnɪk³l/ *adjective* **1** [always before noun] relating to medical treatment and tests *clinical trials/research* **2** only considering facts and not influenced by feelings or emotions *a clinical approach/attitude* ● **clinically** *adverb*

clinician /klɪ'nɪʃ³n/ *noun* [C] a doctor who treats ill people and does not just study diseases

clink /klɪŋk/ *verb* [I, T] If pieces of glass or metal clink, they make a short ringing sound when they touch, and if you clink them, you make them do this. ● **clink** *noun* [C]

clip¹ /klɪp/ *noun* [C] **1** a small metal or plastic object used for holding things together **2** a short part of a film or television programme that is shown at a different time *They showed clips from Spielberg's new movie.* **3 a clip round the ear/earhole** *UK informal* a quick hit on the side of someone's head ⊃See also: **paper clip**.

clip² /klɪp/ *verb* **clipping**, *past* **clipped 1** [FASTEN] [I, T] to fasten things together with a clip, or to be fastened in this way *Clip the microphone to*

the collar of your jacket. **2** [CUT] [T] to cut small pieces from something *Jamie was outside clipping the hedge.* ○ *I'm always clipping recipes out of magazines.* **3** [HIT] [T] to hit something quickly and lightly *The plane clipped a telephone line and crashed.* ○ *He clipped the edge of the kerb with his front tyre.*

clipart /'klɪpɑːt/ *noun* [U] small pictures which are stored on a computer and can be easily added to a document *The site links to about 24 other sites offering clipart* ○ *a clipart collection/library*

clipboard /'klɪpbɔːd/ *noun* [C] **1** a board with a clip at the top that holds paper in position for writing on *A woman with a clipboard stopped us in the street to ask us some questions.* **2** an area for storing information in a computer when you are moving it from one document to another *You draw the shape somewhere on your worksheet, click on it and copy it to the clipboard.*

clipped /klɪpt/ *adjective* If someone speaks in a clipped voice, their words sound quick, short, and not friendly.

clippers /'klɪpəz/ *noun* [plural] a tool used to cut small pieces off something *hedge clippers*

clipping /'klɪpɪŋ/ *noun* [C] **1** (*also UK* **cutting**) an article or picture that has been cut out of a newspaper or magazine *a collection of newspaper clippings about the princess* **2** a small piece that has been cut off something [usually plural] *grass clippings*

clique /kliːk/ *noun* [C] a small group of people who spend a lot of time together and are unfriendly to people who are not in the group

cloak /kləʊk/ *noun* **1** [C] a loose coat without sleeves that hangs down from your shoulders **2 a cloak of sth** *literary* something that is intended to cover or hide the truth of something else *a cloak of secrecy/mystery*

cloakroom /'kləʊkruːm/ *noun* [C] **1** a room where you leave your coat at a theatre, school, etc **2** *UK old-fashioned* a toilet in a public building

clobber /'klɒbə'/ *verb* [T] *informal* **1** to hit someone **2** to affect someone very badly *a policy that has clobbered people on low incomes*

o⁻**clock¹** /klɒk/ *noun* [C] **1** a piece of equipment that shows you what time it is, usually in a house or on a building *She could hear the hall clock ticking.* ⊃See colour picture **The Living Room** on page Centre 4. **2** *UK* a piece of equipment in a vehicle for measuring how far it has travelled *a car with 63,000 kilometres on the clock* **3 around/round the clock** all day and all night *Rescue teams are working round the clock to search for survivors of the earthquake.* **4 race/work against the clock** to do something as fast as you can in order to finish before a particular time **5 turn/put the clock back** *UK* to make a situation the same as it was at an earlier time ⊃See also: **alarm clock, grandfather clock**.

clock² /klɒk/ *verb*

clock sth up to achieve a particular number or amount of something *Yuri has clocked up 5,500 flying hours.*

clockwise

clockwise   anti-clockwise *UK*,
                   counterclockwise *US*

clockwise /'klɒkwaɪz/ *adjective, adverb* in the
same direction as the hands (= parts that point
to the numbers) on a clock move ⊃Opposite
anti-clockwise *UK*, **counterclockwise** *US*.

clockwork /'klɒkwɜːk/ *noun* **1** [U] a system of
machinery that starts when you turn a handle
or key *a clockwork toy* **2 (as) regular as clockwork** extremely regularly *The bell rang at 8
a.m., regular as clockwork.* **3 run/go like clockwork** to happen exactly as planned, with no
problems

clog /klɒg/ (*also* **clog up**) *verb* [I, T] clogging, *past*
clogged to fill something so that nothing can
pass through it, or to be filled in this way [often
passive] *The plughole was clogged with hair.*

clogs /klɒgz/ *noun* [plural] shoes made from wood,
or shoes with a wooden sole (= bottom part)

cloister /'klɔɪstər/ *noun* [C] a covered stone passage around the edges of a garden in a church
or religious building

clone¹ /kləʊn/ *noun* [C] **1** an exact copy of a
plant or animal that scientists make by removing one of its cells **2** *informal* someone or
something that is very similar to someone or
something else

clone² /kləʊn/ *verb* [T] to create a clone of a plant
or animal *Scientists have already cloned a
sheep.* • **cloning** *noun* [U] *animal/human cloning*

o━**close¹** /kləʊz/ *verb* [I, T] **1** DOOR/WINDOW ETC If
something closes, it moves so that it is not
open, and if you close something, you make it
move so that it is not open. *Jane closed the
window.* ○ *Lie down and close your eyes.* ○ *Suddenly the door closed.* **2** PUBLIC PLACE If a shop,
restaurant, public place, etc closes, people
cannot go in it. *The supermarket closes at 8
p.m.* **3** ORGANIZATION (*also* **close down**) If a business or organization closes, or if someone or
something closes it, it stops operating. *Many
factories have closed in the last ten years.* **4** END
to end, or to end something *She closed the meeting with a short speech.* ⊃See Common learner error
at **open**.

close (sth) down If a business or organization closes down, or if someone or something closes it down, it stops operating.

close in If people close in, they gradually get
nearer to someone, usually in order to attack
them or stop them escaping. *Police closed in
on the demonstrators.*

close sth off to put something across the
entrance to a place in order to stop people
entering it *Police quickly closed off the area.*

o━**close²** /kləʊs/ *adjective* **1** DISTANCE near in distance *His house is close to the sea.* **2** TIME near
in time *It was close to lunchtime when we arrived.* **3** FRIENDLY If people are close, they know
each other very well and like each other a lot.
close friends ○ *I'm very close to my brother.*
4 RELATIVE [always before noun] A close relative is
someone who is directly related to you, for
example your mother, father, or brother.
5 RELATIONSHIP seeing or talking with someone
a lot *Our school has close links with a school
in China.* ○ *I'm still in close contact with my
school friends.* **6 be/come close to doing sth** to
almost achieve or do something *We are close to
reaching an agreement.* **7 be close to sth** If
someone or something is close to a particular
state, they are almost in that state. *She was
close to tears.* **8** COMPETITION A close game,
competition, etc is one in which people's
scores are nearly the same. **9** CAREFUL [always
before noun] looking at or listening to someone
or something very carefully *On close inspection, you could see that the painting was a
fake.* ○ *Keep a close watch on the children* (=
watch them carefully). **10** WEATHER Close
weather is too warm and there is not enough
fresh air. • **closeness** *noun* [U] ⊃See also: a close
call², a close **shave²**.

o━**close³** /kləʊs/ *adverb* **1** near in distance *He
stayed close to his mother.* ○ *Come a bit closer.*
○ *We walked close behind them.* ○ *There's a
great beach close by* (= near). **2** near in time
The time for change is coming closer.

close⁴ /kləʊz/ *noun* **1** [no plural] the end of something *They finally reached an agreement at the
close of a week of negotiations.* ○ *The year was
drawing to a close.*

close⁵ /kləʊs/ *noun* [C] (*also* **Close**) used in the
name of a road that cars can only enter from
one end *They live at 7 Kingswear Close.*

o━**closed** /kləʊzd/ *adjective* **1** BUSINESS/SHOP not
open for business *We went to the library but it
was closed.* **2** NOT OPEN not open *The door was
closed.* ○ *Her eyes were closed.* **3** NOT ACCEPTING
IDEAS not wanting to accept new ideas, people,
customs, etc *a closed mind* ⊃See Common learner
error at **open**.

,**closed-circuit 'television** *noun* [C, U] a
system of hidden cameras that take pictures of
people in public places, used to help prevent
crime

close-knit /,kləʊs'nɪt/ *adjective* A close-knit
group of people is one in which everyone helps
and supports each other. *a close-knit family/
community*

closely /'kləʊsli/ *adverb* **1** CAREFULLY If you look
at or listen to something closely, you look at it
or listen to it very carefully. **2** CONNECTED If
two things are closely connected, related, etc,
they are very similar to each other or there is
a relationship between them. *The two languages are closely related.* ○ *I saw a cat that
closely resembles ours.* **3** VERY NEAR in a way
that is very near in distance or time *Elke came
into the room, closely followed by her children.*
4 WORK If you work closely with someone, you
work together a lot. *Nurses work closely with*

other medical staff.

closet¹ /'klɒzɪt/ US (UK **wardrobe**) *noun* [C] a large cupboard for keeping clothes in ⊃See also: have a **skeleton** in the cupboard/closet.

closet² /'klɒzɪt/ *adjective* a **closet intellectual/liberal/socialist, etc** someone who hides their true opinions or way of life

close-up /'kləʊsʌp/ *noun* [C] a photograph of someone or something that is taken by standing very close to them

closing /'kləʊzɪŋ/ *adjective* [always before noun] The closing part of an event or period of time is the final part of it. *Owen scored a goal in the closing minutes of the game.*

WORD PARTNERS FOR **closure**

face/be threatened with closure • **save** sth **from** closure • the closure **of** sth

closure /'kləʊʒəʳ/ *noun* 1 [C, U] when a business, organization, etc stops operating *factory closures* ○ *The company announced the closure of its Paris office.* 2 [U] the feeling that a sad or unpleasant experience has now finished so that you can think about and do other things

clot¹ /klɒt/ *noun* [C] 1 a lump that forms when a liquid, especially blood, becomes almost solid 2 *UK informal* a stupid person

clot² /klɒt/ *verb* [I, T] clotting, *past* clotted to form clots, or to make clots form

cloth /klɒθ/ *noun* 1 [U] material made from cotton, wool, etc, and used, for example, to make clothes or curtains *a piece of cloth* 2 [C] a piece of cloth used for cleaning or drying things

COMMON LEARNER ERROR

cloth, clothes or clothing?

The most usual word for the things you wear is **clothes**. **Clothing** is slightly more formal, and often used for particular types of clothes. **Cloth** is the material that clothes are made from. Do not try to make a plural 'cloths' - it is an uncountable noun.

I put my clothes on.

~~I put my cloth on.~~

They gave us money for food and clothing.

~~They gave us money for food and cloths.~~

clothe /kləʊð/ *verb* [T] to supply clothes for someone

clothed /kləʊðd/ *adjective* wearing clothes *fully clothed*

WORD PARTNERS FOR **clothes**

put on/take off/wear clothes • **change** your clothes

o--**clothes** /kləʊðz/ *noun* [plural] items such as shirts and trousers that you wear on your body *She was wearing her sister's clothes.* ○ *to put on/take off your clothes* ⊃See colour picture **Clothes** on pages Centre 8, 9.

COMMON LEARNER ERROR

clothes

Remember that **clothes** is plural. If you want to talk about one particular thing that you wear, use the expression **piece/item of clothing**.

I need some new clothes.

He bought two or three pieces of clothing.

clothesline /'kləʊðzlaɪn/ *noun* [C] a rope for hanging wet clothes on until they dry

'clothes ˌpeg UK (US **clothespin** /'kləʊðzpɪn/) *noun* [C] a short piece of wood or plastic that is used to hold clothes on a rope while they dry

clothing /'kləʊðɪŋ/ *noun* [U] clothes, especially of a particular type *outdoor/protective clothing*

cloud¹ /klaʊd/ *noun* **cloud**
1 [C, U] a white or grey mass that floats in the sky, made of small water drops *rain/storm clouds* 2 [C] a mass of gas or very small pieces of something floating in the air *a cloud of dust/smoke* 3 **be under a cloud** If someone is under a cloud, they are not trusted or not popular because people think they have done something bad. • **cloudless** *adjective* without clouds

cloud² /klaʊd/ *verb* 1 [T] to make someone confused, or make something harder to understand *to cloud someone's judgment/vision* 2 [I, T] If something transparent clouds, it becomes hard to see through, and if something clouds it, it makes it hard to see through.

cloud over to become covered with clouds

cloudy /'klaʊdi/ *adjective* 1 When it is cloudy, there are clouds in the sky. 2 A cloudy liquid is not transparent. *cloudy water*

clout /klaʊt/ *noun* 1 [U] power and influence over other people *As mayor, he has political clout.* 2 [C] *UK informal* a heavy blow made with the hand

clove /kləʊv/ *noun* [C] 1 a small, dark-brown, dried flower that is used as a spice 2 one separate part in a root of garlic (= plant with a strong taste used in cooking)

clover /'kləʊvəʳ/ *noun* [U] a small plant that has three round leaves and round flowers

clown¹ /klaʊn/ *noun* **clown**
[C] 1 a performer who has special clothes and a painted face and makes people laugh 2 a silly person

clown² /klaʊn/ (*also* **clown around**) *verb* [I] to behave in a silly way in order to make people laugh

WORD PARTNERS FOR **club**

belong to/join a club • a **member of** a club

o--**club¹** /klʌb/ *noun* [C] 1 ORGANIZATION an organization for people who want to take part in a sport or social activity together, or the build-

ing they use for this *a fitness/football club*
2 GOLF (*also* **golf club**) a long, thin stick used to hit the ball in golf ⊃See colour picture **Sports 2** on page Centre 15. **3** WEAPON a heavy stick used as a weapon **4** DANCE a place open late at night where people can dance **5 clubs** playing cards with black shapes like three leaves on them *the ten of clubs* ⊃See also: **fan club**.

club² /klʌb/ *verb* **clubbing**, *past* **clubbed 1** [T] to hit a person or animal with a heavy stick **2 go clubbing** *mainly UK* to go to clubs where there is music and dancing

club together *UK* If a group of people club together to buy something, they share the cost of it.

clubhouse /'klʌbhaʊs/ *noun* [C] a building that the members of a club use for social activities or for changing their clothes

cluck /klʌk/ *verb* [I] to make the sound that a chicken makes ● **cluck** *noun* [C]

clue /kluː/ *noun* [C] **1** a sign or a piece of information that helps you to solve a problem or answer a question *Police are searching the area for clues to the murder.* ○ *I can't remember who wrote it. Give me a clue.* **2 not have a clue** *informal* to be completely unable to guess, understand, or deal with something [+ question word] *I haven't a clue what you're talking about.*

clued 'up *adjective UK* knowing all the most important information about something *He's very clued up on the law.*

clueless /'kluːləs/ *adjective informal* A clueless person does not know anything about a particular subject.

clump /klʌmp/ *noun* [C] a group of plants growing closely together *a clump of grass*

clumsy /'klʌmzi/ *adjective* **1** PERSON Clumsy people move in a way that is not controlled or careful enough, and often knock or damage things. **2** BEHAVIOUR If you behave in a clumsy way, you upset people because you are not careful about their feelings. *a clumsy attempt to be friendly* **3** OBJECT Clumsy objects are large, not attractive, and often difficult to use. ● **clumsily** *adverb* ● **clumsiness** *noun* [U]

clung /klʌŋ/ *past of* cling

cluster¹ /'klʌstəʳ/ *noun* a group of similar things that are close together *a cluster of galaxies*

cluster² /'klʌstəʳ/ *verb* **cluster around/round/together, etc** to form a close group *Photographers clustered round the film star.*

clutch¹ /klʌtʃ/ *verb* [T] to hold something tightly *She clutched a coin.*

clutch at sth to try very hard to hold something *She clutched wildly at the branch.*

clutch² /klʌtʃ/ *noun* **1** [C] the part of a car or truck that you press with your foot when you change gear (= part that controls how fast the wheels turn) ⊃See colour picture **Car** on page Centre 7. **2** [C, U] when someone holds or tries to hold something tightly **3 sb's clutches** If you are in someone's clutches, they control you, often in an evil way.

clutter¹ /'klʌtəʳ/ (*also* **clutter up**) *verb* [T] to

cover a surface, or to fill a place with things that are not tidy or well organized [often passive] *Every shelf is cluttered with ornaments.*

clutter² /'klʌtəʳ/ *noun* [U] a lot of objects that are not tidy or well organized *I've got too much clutter on my desk.*

cm *written abbreviation for* centimetre (= a unit for measuring length)

Co 1 *written abbreviation for* Company (= name of business) *Williams & Co* **2** *written abbreviation for* County (= area with own local government) *Co. Wexford*

co- /kəʊ-/ *prefix* with or together *a co-author* ○ *to coexist*

c/o *written abbreviation for* care of: used when you send a letter to someone who will give it to the person you are writing to

coach¹ /kəʊtʃ/ *noun* [C] **1** BUS *UK* a comfortable bus used to take groups of people on long journeys *a coach trip* **2** PERSON someone whose job is to teach people to improve at a sport, skill, or school subject *a football/tennis coach* **3** OLD VEHICLE a vehicle with wheels that is pulled by horses

coach² /kəʊtʃ/ *verb* [T] to teach someone so they improve at a sport, skill, or in a school subject ● **coaching** *noun* [U]

coach ,station *UK* (*UK/US* **bus station**) *noun* [C] a building where a bus starts or ends its journey

coal /kəʊl/ *noun* **1** [U] a hard, black substance that is dug from under the ground and burnt as fuel *a lump of coal* **2 coals** pieces of coal, usually burning

coalition /ˌkəʊə'lɪʃən/ *noun* [C] two or more political parties that have joined together, usually to govern a country *to form a coalition* ○ *a coalition government*

coal ,mine *noun* [C] (*also UK* **colliery**) a place where people work digging coal from under the ground

coarse /kɔːs/ *adjective* **1** rough and thick, or not in very small pieces *coarse cloth* ○ *coarse breadcrumbs* **2** not polite *coarse language* ● **coarsely** *adverb*

⚬ **coast¹** /kəʊst/ *noun* [C, U] **1** the land beside the sea *The island lies off the North African coast* (= in the sea near North Africa). ○ *They live on the east coast of Scotland.* **2 coast to coast** from one side of a country to the other **3 the coast is clear** If the coast is clear, you can do something or go somewhere because there is nobody who might see you.

coast² /kəʊst/ *verb* [I] **1** to progress or succeed without any effort or difficulty *Pakistan coasted to a four-wicket victory over Australia.* **2** to move forward in a vehicle without using the engine, usually down a hill

coastal /'kəʊstəl/ *adjective* situated on or relating to the coast *a coastal town/resort*

coastguard /'kəʊstɡɑːd/ *noun* [C] a person or the organization responsible for preventing accidents and illegal activities in the sea near a coast

coastline /'kəʊstlaɪn/ *noun* [C, U] the part of the land along the edge of the sea *a rocky coastline*

⊶**coat**[1] /kəʊt/ *noun* [C] **1** [CLOTHES] a piece of clothing with sleeves that you wear over your other clothes, especially when you go outside *a fur/winter coat* **2** [FUR] the fur that covers an animal's body **3** [LAYER] a layer of a substance such as paint *a coat of paint/varnish*

coat[2] /kəʊt/ *verb* [T] to cover something with a thin layer of something *Stir the rice until it is **coated with** butter.*

ˈ**coat ˌhanger** *noun* [C] a wire, wooden, or plastic object for hanging clothes on

coating /ˈkəʊtɪŋ/ *noun* [C] a thin layer that covers the surface of something *a protective/non-stick coating*

coax /kəʊks/ *verb* [T] to persuade someone in a gentle way [+ into + doing sth] *She coaxed me into joining the group.*

cobble[1] /ˈkɒbl/ *verb*
cobble sth together to make something quickly and not very carefully

cobble[2] /ˈkɒbl/ *noun* [C] a rounded stone used on the surface of an old-fashioned road • **cobbled** *adjective* made with cobbles ***cobbled streets***

cobbler /ˈkɒbləʳ/ *noun* [C] *mainly UK old-fashioned* someone whose job is to make or repair shoes

cobblestone /ˈkɒblstəʊn/ *noun* [C] a rounded stone that is used on the surface of an old-fashioned road

cobra /ˈkəʊbrə/ *noun* [C] a poisonous snake that makes the skin of its neck wide and flat when it is going to attack

cobweb /ˈkɒbweb/ *noun* [C] a structure of fine threads made by a spider (= insect with eight legs) to catch insects

cobweb

Coca Cola /ˌkəʊkəˈkəʊlə/ *noun* [U] *trademark* a sweet, dark-brown drink with lots of bubbles

cocaine /kəʊˈkeɪn/ *noun* [U] an illegal drug, often used in the form of white powder

cock[1] /kɒk/ *noun* [C] an adult male chicken

cock[2] /kɒk/ *verb* [T] to move part of the body up or to the side *to cock an ear/eyebrow*
cock sth up *UK informal* to do something wrong or badly *I really cocked up my exams.*

cockerel /ˈkɒkᵊrᵊl/ *noun* [C] *UK* a young male chicken

cockney /ˈkɒkni/ *noun* **1** [U] a type of English spoken in East London **2** [C] someone who speaks Cockney

cockpit /ˈkɒkpɪt/ *noun* [C] the part of an aircraft or racing car that contains the controls

cockroach /ˈkɒkrəʊtʃ/ *noun* [C] a large, brown or black insect that can live in houses and places where food is prepared

cocktail /ˈkɒkteɪl/ *noun* **1** [MIXTURE] [C] a mixture of powerful substances *a cocktail of drugs/chemicals* **2** [DRINK] [C] an alcoholic drink made from two or more kinds of drink mixed together *a cocktail bar/party* **3** [DISH] [C, U] a cold dish containing small pieces of food mixed together *a prawn cocktail ○ fruit cocktail*

cock-up /ˈkɒkʌp/ *noun* [C] *UK informal* a stupid mistake or failure

cocky /ˈkɒki/ *adjective* confident in an annoying way

cocoa /ˈkəʊkəʊ/ *noun* [U] **1** a dark-brown powder produced from a type of bean, used to make chocolate **2** a drink made by mixing cocoa powder with hot milk

coconut /ˈkəʊkənʌt/ *noun* [C] a very large nut with a hard, hairy shell, a white part that you eat, and liquid in the centre

cocoon /kəˈkuːn/ *noun* [C] a cover that protects some insects as they develop into adults

cod /kɒd/ *noun* [C, U] *plural* **cod** a large sea fish which can be eaten as food

code /kəʊd/ *noun* **1** [SECRET MESSAGE] [C, U] a set of letters, numbers, or signs that are used instead of ordinary words to keep a message secret *It was written **in code**. ○ They were trying to **break*** (= understand) *the enemy's code.* **2** [TELEPHONE] [C] *UK* (*UK/US* **area code**) a set of numbers used at the beginning of all the telephone numbers in a particular area **3** [RULES] [C] a set of rules on how to behave or how to do things *a code of conduct/practice ○ The club has a strict **dress code*** (= rules about what you wear). ➲See also: **bar code, zip code.**

coded /ˈkəʊdɪd/ *adjective* written or sent in code ***a coded message/warning***

codeine /ˈkəʊdiːn/ *noun* [U] a medicine used to reduce pain

co-ed /ˌkəʊˈed/ [US] /ˈkəʊˌed/ *adjective* with both male and female students

coerce /kəʊˈɜːs/ *verb* [T] *formal* to make someone do something that they do not want to do [+ into + doing sth] *Employees said they were coerced into signing the agreement.* • **coercion** /kəʊˈɜːʃᵊn/ *noun* [U]

coexist /ˌkəʊɪgˈzɪst/ *verb* [I] If two things or groups coexist, they exist at the same time or together, although they may be very different. *Can science and religion coexist?* • **coexistence** *noun* [U]

⊶**coffee** /ˈkɒfi/ *noun* **1** [C, U] a hot drink made from dark beans which are made into a powder, or a cup of this drink **2** [U] the beans from which coffee is made, or the powder made from these beans *instant coffee*

ˈ**coffee ˌtable** *noun* [C] a low table in a room where people sit ➲See colour picture **The Living Room** on page Centre 4.

coffers /ˈkɒfəz/ *noun* [plural] a supply of money that a group or organization has and can spend *government/party coffers*

coffin /ˈkɒfɪn/ (*also US* **casket**) *noun* [C] a box in which a dead body is buried ➲See also: the final **nail**[1] in the coffin.

cog /kɒg/ *noun* [C] a part shaped like a tooth on the edge of a wheel in a machine, that makes another wheel turn

cogent /ˈkəʊdʒᵊnt/ *adjective* A cogent argument, reason, or explanation is one which people will believe because it is clear and careful.

cognac /ˈkɒnjæk/ *noun* [U] good quality French brandy (= strong alcoholic drink)

cognitive /'kɒgnətɪv/ *adjective* [always before noun] *formal* relating to how people think, understand, and learn

cohabit /kəʊ'hæbɪt/ *verb* [I] *formal* If two people cohabit, they live together and are sexual partners but are not married. • **cohabitation** /kəʊ,hæbɪ'teɪʃᵊn/ *noun* [U]

coherent /kəʊ'hɪərᵊnt/ *adjective* **1** A coherent argument, plan, etc is clear, and each part of it has been carefully considered. **2** If someone is coherent, you can understand what they say. ⊃Opposite **incoherent**. • **coherence** /kəʊ'hɪərᵊns/ *noun* [U] • **coherently** *adverb*

cohesion /kəʊ'hiːʒᵊn/ *noun* [U] when the members of a group or society are united *The country needs greater social cohesion.* • **cohesive** /kəʊ'hiːsɪv/ *adjective* united and working together effectively *a cohesive unit/group*

cohort /'kəʊhɔːt/ *noun* [C] someone who supports someone else, especially a political leader *the prime minister's cohorts*

coil¹ /kɔɪl/ *noun* [C] a long piece of wire, rope, etc curled into several circles *a coil of rope*

coil² /kɔɪl/ (*also* **coil up**) *verb* [I, T] to twist something into circles, or to become twisted into circles *Her hair was coiled in a bun on top of her head.*

coin¹ /kɔɪn/ *noun* **1** [C] a flat, usually round, piece of metal used as money *a pound coin* **2 toss a coin** to throw a coin into the air so that it turns over several times, and see which side it lands on, often in order to make a decision

coin² /kɔɪn/ *verb* [T] **1** to be the first person who uses a new word or phrase **2 to coin a phrase** something you say before using a common expression *Still, to coin a phrase, there is light at the end of the tunnel.*

coincide /,kəʊɪn'saɪd/ *verb* [I] **1** to happen at the same time as something else *The band's American tour coincided with the release of their second album.* **2** When people's opinions or ideas coincide, they are the same.

WORD PARTNERS FOR **coincidence**

by coincidence • an **amazing / happy / remarkable/strange/unfortunate** coincidence • **mere/pure** coincidence • **it's no** coincidence **that**

coincidence /kəʊ'ɪnsɪdᵊns/ *noun* [C, U] when two very similar things happen at the same time but there is no reason for it *an amazing/strange coincidence* ○ *It was pure coincidence that we both married dentists.* • **coincidental** /kəʊ,ɪnsɪ'dentᵊl/ *adjective* happening by coincidence *The similarities are coincidental.* • **coincidentally** /kəʊ,ɪnsɪ'dentᵊli/ *adverb*

Coke /kəʊk/ *noun* [C, U] *trademark short for* Coca Cola (= a sweet, dark-brown drink with lots of bubbles)

Col *written abbreviation for* Colonel (= an officer of high rank in the army or air force)

cola /'kəʊlə/ *noun* [U] a sweet, dark-brown drink with lots of bubbles ⊃See also: Coca Cola.

colander /'kɒləndəʳ/ *noun* [C] a bowl with small holes in it used for washing food or separating water from food after cooking ⊃See colour picture

The Kitchen on page Centre 2.

OTHER WAYS OF SAYING **cold**

If the weather outside or the temperature inside is very cold, you can use the adjectives **bitter** or **freezing**: *Wrap up warmly - it's bitter outside!* • *It's absolutely freezing in here!*

If the weather, especially the wind, is so cold that it is unpleasant to be in, the adjectives **biting** and **icy** are sometimes used: *A biting/icy wind blew in her face as she opened the door.*

The adjective **chilly** is often used to describe weather or temperatures that feel slightly cold and unpleasant: *It's a bit chilly in here - can you turn the heater on?*

If the temperature feels cold but pleasant, you can say that it is **cool**: *That's a nice cool breeze.*

Cold weather in autumn or winter that is dry and pleasant is sometimes described as **crisp**: *We walked through the forest on a crisp autumn day.*

⟶**cold¹** /kəʊld/ *adjective* **1** [TEMPERATURE] having a low temperature *cold water/weather* ○ *This soup has gone cold.* ○ *My hands are getting cold.* **2** [UNFRIENDLY] unfriendly or showing no emotion *a cold stare/voice* ○ *She became quite cold and distant with me.* **3** [FOOD] served cold *cold roast beef* • **coldness** *noun* [U] ⊃See also: in cold **blood**, get cold feet (**foot¹**).

WORD PARTNERS FOR **cold**

catch/have a cold • a **bad/heavy/stinking** (= very bad) cold

cold² /kəʊld/ *noun* **1** [C] a common illness which makes you sneeze and makes your nose produce liquid *I've got a cold.* ○ *He caught a bad cold at school.* **2 the cold** cold weather or temperatures **3 leave sb out in the cold** to not allow someone to be part of a group or activity

cold³ /kəʊld/ *adverb* **1 be out cold** *informal* to be unconscious *I hit my head and was out cold for two minutes.* **2** completely and immediately *I offered him £10 but he turned me down cold.*

cold-blooded /,kəʊld'blʌdɪd/ *adjective* showing no emotion or sympathy *a cold-blooded killer*

cold-hearted /,kəʊld'hɑːtɪd/ *adjective* feeling no kindness or sympathy towards other people

coldly /'kəʊldli/ *adverb* in a way that is not friendly or emotional *He looked at me coldly.*

colic /'kɒlɪk/ *noun* [U] When a baby has colic, it has a bad pain in the stomach.

collaborate /kə'læbᵊreɪt/ *verb* [I] **1** When two or more people collaborate, they work together to create or achieve the same thing. *Didn't you collaborate with him on one of your books?* **2** to help people who are an enemy of your country or government *He was accused of collaborating with the enemy.* • **collaborator** *noun* [C]

collaboration /kə,læbə'reɪʃ³n/ *noun* **1** [C, U] when two or more people work together to create or achieve the same thing, or a product of this *The show was a result of **collaboration between** several museums.* **2** [U] when someone helps an enemy country or government

collage /kɒl'ɑːʒ/ *noun* [C, U] a picture made by sticking small pieces of paper or other materials onto a surface, or the process of making pictures like this

collapse¹ /kə'læps/ *verb* **1** FALL [I] When someone collapses, they fall down, usually because they are ill or weak. **2** OBJECT [I, T] to fall down or towards the inside, or to make a structure or object fall down or towards its inside *The roof collapsed under the weight of snow.* **3** FAIL [I] to fail to work or succeed *The peace talks have collapsed.*

collapse² /kə'læps/ *noun* [C, U] **1** the sudden failure of a system, organization, business, etc **2** when a person or structure becomes too weak to stand and suddenly falls

collapsible /kə'læpsɪbl/ *adjective* able to be folded or made flat in order to be stored or carried *a collapsible table/boat*

collar¹ /'kɒlə³/ *noun* [C] **1** the part of a shirt, coat, etc that is usually folded over and goes round your neck *a shirt collar* ⊃See picture at **jacket**. **2** a narrow piece of leather or plastic that you fasten round the neck of an animal

collar² /'kɒlə³/ *verb* [T] *informal* to find someone and stop them going somewhere, often so that you can talk to them about something

collarbone /'kɒləbəʊn/ *noun* [C] a bone between the base of your neck and your shoulder

collateral /kə'læt³r³l/ *noun* [U] things that you agree to give someone if you are not able pay back money you have borrowed from them *I used my car **as collateral** for a loan.*

o--**colleague** /'kɒliːg/ *noun* [C] someone that you work with

o--**collect¹** /kə'lekt/ *verb* **1** BRING TOGETHER [T] to get things from different places and bring them together *Police collected a good deal of information during the investigation.* ∘ *Would you **collect up** the books please, Joanne?* **2** KEEP [T] to get and keep things of one type such as stamps or coins as a hobby *She collects dolls.* **3** GO TO GET [T] *UK* to go to a place and bring someone or something away from it *She collects Anna **from** school at three o'clock.* **4** MONEY [I, T] to ask people to give you money for something, for example a charity (= organization that helps people) *I'm collecting on behalf of Oxfam.* **5** RECEIVE [T] to receive money that you are owed *You can begin to collect a pension at age 62.* **6** COME TOGETHER [I] to come together in a single place *Journalists collected outside the palace.* **7 collect yourself/your thoughts** to get control over your feelings and thoughts

collect² /kə'lekt/ *adjective, adverb US* When you telephone collect or make a collect telephone call, the person you telephone pays for the call.

collected /kə'lektɪd/ *adjective* **1** [always before noun] brought together in one book or series of books *His collected poems were published in 1928.* **2** showing control over your feelings *Jane was very **calm and collected**.*

🧩 WORD PARTNERS FOR **collection**

amass/display/have a collection • an exten-sive/large/priceless/private collection

o--**collection** /kə'lekʃ³n/ *noun* **1** OBJECTS [C] a group of objects of the same type that have been collected by one person or in one place *a private art collection* **2** TAKING AWAY [U] when something is taken away from a place *rubbish collection* **3** MONEY [C] an amount of money collected from several people *We **had a collection for** Emily's gift.* **4** GROUP [C] a group of things or people *There's quite a **collection of** toothbrushes in the bathroom.*

collective¹ /kə'lektɪv/ *adjective* involving, felt by, or owned by everyone in a group *collective responsibility*

collective² /kə'lektɪv/ *noun* [C] a business that is owned and controlled by the people who work in it

collectively /kə'lektɪvli/ *adverb* as a group *She has a staff of four who collectively earn almost $200,000.*

collector /kə'lektə³/ *noun* [C] **1** someone whose job is to collect tickets or money from people *a tax collector* **2** someone who collects objects because they are interesting or beautiful *a collector of modern art*

🧩 WORD PARTNERS FOR **college**

go to college • be at college • a college **course/ lecturer/student**

o--**college** /'kɒlɪdʒ/ *noun* **1** EDUCATION [C, U] *UK* a place where students are educated when they are between 16 and 18 years old, or after they have finished school *a sixth-form college* ∘ *a teacher-training college* **2** UNIVERSITY [C, U] *US* a university **3** PART OF UNIVERSITY [C] a part of a university that has its own teachers and students *Cambridge/Oxford colleges* ⊃See also: **community college**, **junior college**.

collegiate /kə'liːdʒiət/ *adjective* relating to or belonging to a college or its students *collegiate sports*

collide /kə'laɪd/ *verb* [I] When two objects collide, they hit each other with force, usually while moving. *The car **collided with** a van.*

colliery /'kɒljəri/ *UK* (*UK/US* **coal mine**) *noun* [C] a place where people work digging coal from under the ground

🧩 WORD PARTNERS FOR **collision**

avoid/be involved in a collision • [a car/ train, etc] is in a collision **with** sth • a head-on collision • a collision **between** sth and sth

collision /kə'lɪʒ³n/ *noun* **1** [C] an accident that happens when two vehicles hit each other with force **2 be on a collision course** If two people or groups are on a collision course, they are doing or saying things that are certain to cause a serious disagreement or fight between them.

collocation /ˌkɒləˈkeɪʃən/ *noun* [C] **1** a word or phrase that sounds natural and correct when it is used with another word or phrase *In the phrase 'a hard frost', 'hard' is a collocation of 'frost', and 'strong' would not sound natural.* **2** the combination of words formed when two or more words are frequently used together in a way that sounds natural *The phrase 'a hard frost' is a collocation.*

colloquial /kəˈləʊkwiəl/ *adjective* Colloquial words or expressions are informal. *colloquial speech* ● **colloquially** *adverb*

collude /kəˈluːd/ *verb* [I] *formal* to do something secretly with another person or group, in order to deceive or cheat others *The company colluded with competitors to fix prices.* ● **collusion** /kəˈluːʒən/ *noun* [U] *He was accused of being in collusion with the terrorists.*

colon /ˈkəʊlɒn/ *noun* [C] **1** a mark (:) used before a list, an example, an explanation, etc ⊃See Extra help page **Punctuation** on page Centre 33. **2** the lower part of a person's bowels

colonel /ˈkɜːnəl/ *noun* [C] an officer of high rank in the army or air force

colonial /kəˈləʊniəl/ *adjective* [always before noun] relating to colonialism or a colony (= country controlled by another country) *colonial rule/ government*

colonialism /kəˈləʊniəlɪzəm/ *noun* [U] the system in which powerful countries control other countries

colonize (*also UK* -ise) /ˈkɒlənaɪz/ *verb* [T] **1** to send people to live in and govern another country [often passive] *Burundi was first colonized by the Germans.* **2** to start growing or living in large numbers in a place *Weeds quickly colonize areas of cleared ground.* ● **colonist** /ˈkɒlənɪst/ *noun* [C] someone who goes to colonize a country ● **colonization** /ˌkɒlənaɪˈzeɪʃən/ *noun* [U]

colony /ˈkɒləni/ *noun* [C] **1** COUNTRY a country or area controlled in an official, political way by a more powerful country *a French/British colony* **2** GROUP a group of animals, insects, or plants living together in a particular place *a colony of ants* **3** PEOPLE a group of people with the same interests or job who live together *an artists' colony*

○▪**color** /ˈkʌlər/ *noun, verb US spelling of* colour

colored /ˈkʌləd/ *adjective US spelling of* coloured

colorful /ˈkʌləfəl/ *adjective US spelling of* colourful

coloring /ˈkʌlərɪŋ/ *noun* [U] *US spelling of* colouring

colorless /ˈkʌlələs/ *adjective US spelling of* colourless

colossal /kəˈlɒsəl/ *adjective* extremely large *colossal amounts of money*

○▪**colour¹** *UK* (*US* color) /ˈkʌlər/ *noun* **1** RED/BLUE ETC [C, U] red, blue, green, yellow, etc *Green is my favourite colour.* ○ *What colour shall I paint the kitchen?* ⊃See colour picture **Colours** on page Centre 12. **2** FILM/TV ETC [U] using or showing all the colours, not only black and white *Why didn't he shoot the film in colour?* **3** SKIN [U] the colour of a person's skin, which shows

their race **4** FACE [U] healthy pink skin on someone's face *The colour drained from her cheeks.* **5** INTEREST [U] interesting or exciting qualities or parts *We added your story for a bit of local colour.* **6** **with flying colours** with a very high score or with great success *He passed the entrance exam with flying colours.* ⊃See also: primary colour.

colour² *UK* (*US* color) /ˈkʌlər/ *verb* **1** [I, T] to become a particular colour, or to make something a particular colour *He drew a heart and coloured it red.* ○ *Fry the onions until they start to colour.* **2** [T] to affect what someone does, says, or feels [often passive] *Her views are coloured by her own bad experiences.*

colour sth in to fill an area with colour using paint, pens, etc

colour-blind *UK* (*US* color-blind) /ˈkʌləblaɪnd/ *adjective* unable to see the difference between particular colours

coloured *UK* (*US* colored) /ˈkʌləd/ *adjective* **1** having or producing a colour or colours *coloured lights/cloth* **2** an old-fashioned way of describing someone from a race with dark skin that is now considered offensive

colourful *UK* (*US* colorful) /ˈkʌləfəl/ *adjective* **1** having bright colours *a colourful painting* **2** interesting and unusual *a colourful character*

colouring *UK* (*US* coloring) /ˈkʌlərɪŋ/ *noun* [U] **1** the colour of something, especially an animal or person's skin, hair, and eyes *The boys have their father's colouring.* **2** a substance that is used to colour something *food/ artificial colouring*

colourless (*US* colorless) /ˈkʌlələs/ *adjective* **1** without any colour *a colourless liquid* **2** without the qualities that make someone or something interesting and unusual

colt /kəʊlt/ *noun* [C] a young male horse

column

column /ˈkɒləm/ *noun* [C] **1** TALL POST a tall, solid, usually stone post which is used to support a roof or as decoration in a building *a stone/marble column* **2** NEWSPAPER a regular article in a newspaper or magazine on a particular subject or by the same writer **3** PRINT one of the blocks of print into which a page of a newspaper, magazine, or dictionary is divided **4** NUMBERS ETC any block of numbers or words written one under the other **5** a

column of sth something with a tall, narrow shape *A column of smoke rose from the chimney.* **6** PEOPLE MOVING a long line of moving people or vehicles *a column of refugees* ⇒See also: **gossip column**.

columnist /'kɒləmnɪst/ *noun* [C] someone who writes a regular article for a newspaper or magazine *a sports/gossip columnist*

.com /dɒt'kɒm/ *internet abbreviation for* company: used in some Internet addresses which belong to companies or businesses *www.google.com*

coma /'kəʊmə/ *noun* [C] when someone is not conscious for a long time [usually singular] *She has been in a coma for over a week.*

comb[1] /kəʊm/ *noun* [C] a flat piece of metal or plastic with a row of long, narrow parts along one side, that you use to tidy your hair

comb [image]

comb[2] /kəʊm/ *verb* [T] **1** to tidy your hair using a comb **2** to search a place very carefully *Investigators combed through the wreckage.*

combat[1] /'kɒmbæt/ *noun* [C, U] a fight, especially during a war *The aircraft was shot down in combat.*

🔧 WORD PARTNERS FOR **combat**

combat **crime/global warming/racism/ terrorism** • combat **the effects** of sth • combat **a problem** • combat **the threat of** sth • combat **the rise in** [crime, etc.]

combat[2] /'kɒmbæt/ *verb* [T] **combatting**, *past* **combatted**, **combating**, *past* **combated** to try to stop something unpleasant or harmful from happening or increasing *new measures to combat the rise in crime*

combatant /'kɒmbət°nt/ *noun* [C] *formal* someone who fights in a war

combative /'kɒmbətɪv/ *adjective formal* eager to fight or argue

o→**combination** /ˌkɒmbɪ'neɪʃ°n/ *noun* **1** [C, U] a mixture of different people or things *Strawberries and cream - a perfect combination!* ○ *We won through a combination of luck and skill.* ○ *This drug can be safely used in combination with other medicines.* **2** [C] a set of numbers or letters in a particular order which is needed to open some types of locks *a combination lock*

o→**combine** /kəm'baɪn/ *verb* **1** [I, T] to become mixed or joined, or to mix or join things together *My wages combined with your savings should just pay for it.* ○ *The band combines jazz rhythms and romantic lyrics.* **2** [T] to do two or more activities at the same time *I don't know how she combines working with studying.*

combined /kəm'baɪnd/ *adjective* [always before noun] joined together *the combined effects of poverty and disease*

combine harvester /ˌkɒmbaɪn'hɑːvɪstə'/ (*also* **combine**) *noun* [C] a large farm machine which cuts a crop and separates the grain from the stem

combustion /kəm'bʌstʃ°n/ *noun* [U] the process of burning

o→**come** /kʌm/ *verb past tense* **came**, *past participle* **come 1** MOVE TOWARDS [I] to move or travel towards a person who is speaking or towards the place that they are speaking about *Come and see what I've done.* ○ *Can you come to my party?* ○ *The rain came down heavily.* ○ *Here comes Adam* (= Adam is coming). **2** ARRIVE [I] to arrive somewhere or go to a place *I'll come and see you later.* ○ [+ to do sth] *I've come to see Mr Curtis.* ○ *Dad will come for you at six.* ○ *We came to a crossroads.* **3** GO WITH SOMEONE [I] to go somewhere with the person who is speaking *Come for a walk with us.* ○ *We're going to the cinema. Do you want to come?* **4 come after/first/last, etc** to have or achieve a particular position in a race, competition, list, etc *Our team came third.* ○ *Sunday comes after Saturday.* **5 come past/to/up to, etc** to reach a particular length, height, or depth *The water came up to my waist.* **6 come apart/off, etc** to become separated or removed from something *The book came apart in my hands.* ○ *The handle came off.* ○ *My shoelaces have come undone.* ○ *The door came open.* **7 come easily/easily/naturally** to be very easy for someone *Singing came naturally to Louise.* **8** HAPPEN [I] to happen *Spring has come early.* ○ *The worst problems are still to come.* **9 how come** *Informal* used to ask why or how something has happened *How come you didn't go to the party?* **10 come and go** to exist or happen somewhere for a short time and then go away *The feeling of nausea comes and goes.* **11** BE AVAILABLE [I] to be available in a particular size, colour, etc *The table comes in three different sizes.* ○ *Furniture like this doesn't come cheap.* **12 come to do sth** to start to do something *I have come to rely on acupuncture.* ○ *This place has come to be known as 'Pheasant Corner'.* **13 when it comes to sth/doing sth** used to introduce a new idea that you want to say something about *When it comes to baking cakes, she's an expert.* **14 come to think of it** used to say that you have just thought of something *Come to think of it, I've got two batteries that you can have upstairs.* ⇒See also: **come to blows** (**blow**[2]), I'll/We'll cross that **bridge**[1] when I/we come to it., come **clean**[1], if/when it comes to the **crunch**[1], come (back) down to **earth**[1], come under **fire**[1], deliver/come up with the **goods**, come to **grief**, come/get to grips (**grip**[1]) with sth, come to **light**[1], come into your/its **own**[1], not be/come up to **scratch**[2], come to your senses (**sense**[1]), come/turn up trumps (**trump**).

come about to happen, or start to happen *How did the idea for an arts festival come about?*

come across sb/sth to meet someone or discover something by chance *I came across a lovely little restaurant in the village.*

come across 1 to seem to be a particular type of person *He came across as shy.* **2** If an idea or emotion comes across, it is expressed clearly and people understand it. *His bitterness comes across in his poetry.*

come along 1 ARRIVE to arrive or appear at a place *A taxi never comes along when you need* one. **2** GO WITH SOMEONE to go somewhere with someone *We're going to the cinema. Do you want to come along?* **3** EXIST to start to exist *I gave up climbing when my first child came along.* **4 be coming along** to be developing or making progress

come around 1 VISIT to visit someone at their house **2** AGREE to change your opinion about something, or agree to an idea or a plan that you were against *I'm sure she'll come around to our view eventually.* **3** EVENT If an event that happens regularly comes around, it happens, or is going to happen soon. *Thanksgiving has come around again.* **4** BECOME CONSCIOUS to become conscious again after an accident or medical operation

come back 1 to return to a place *I've just come back from the dentist's.* **2** If a style or a fashion comes back, it becomes popular again. *Miniskirts are coming back into fashion.*

come back to sb If something comes back to you, you remember it. *Suddenly, the horror of the accident came back to me.*

come between sb to harm the relationship between two or more people *I won't let anything come between me and my children.*

come by sth to get something, especially something that is unusual or difficult to find *Cheap organic food is still difficult to come by.*

come down 1 to break and fall to the ground *A lot of trees came down in the storm.* **2** If a price or a level comes down, it becomes lower. *Prices always come down after Christmas.* **3** to decide that you support a particular person or side in an argument, etc *The government has come down on the side of military action.*

come down on sb to punish or criticize someone *The police are coming down hard on people for not paying parking fines.*

come down to sth/doing sth If a situation, problem, decision, etc comes down to something, then that is the thing that will influence it most.

come down with sth *informal* to get an illness *I came down with the flu at Christmas.*

come forward to offer to help someone or to give information *We need witnesses to come forward with information about the attack.*

○▪**come from sth** to be born, obtained from, or made somewhere *She comes from Poland.* ○ *Milk comes from cows.*

come from sth/doing sth to be caused by something *"I feel awful." "That comes from eating too many sweets."*

come in 1 ENTER to enter a room or building *Do you want to come in for a cup of tea?* **2** FASHION If a fashion or a product comes in, it becomes available or becomes popular. *Flared trousers came in during the seventies.* **3** BE RECEIVED If news, information, a report, etc comes in, it is received. *News is just coming in about the explosion.* **4 come in first/second, etc** to finish a race or a competition in first/second, etc position **5** SEA If the tide (= regular change in the level of the sea) comes in, the sea moves towards the beach or coast. **6** BE INVOLVED *informal* used to describe how someone is involved in a situation, story, or plan *We need people to help clean up, and that's where you come in.*

come in for sth If someone comes in for criticism, praise, etc, they are criticized, praised, etc.

come into sth 1 to get money from someone who has died *Just after I left university, I came into a bit of money.* **2 come into it** *UK informal* to influence a situation *Money doesn't come into it.*

come of sth/doing sth to happen as a result of something *Did anything come of all those job applications?*

come off 1 to happen successfully *His attempt to impress us all didn't quite come off.* **2 come off badly/best/well, etc** to be in a bad or good position at the end of a fight, argument, etc *She usually comes off best in an argument.* **3 Come off it!** *informal* used to tell someone that you do not agree with them or do not believe them *Oh, come off it! I saw you take it!*

come on 1 START to start to happen or work *The heating comes on at six in the morning.* ○ *I've got a cold coming on.* **2** MAKE PROGRESS to make progress *How's your new novel coming on?* **3 Come on!** *informal* **4** ENCOURAGEMENT used to encourage someone to do something, to hurry, to try harder, etc *Come on! We're going to be late.* **5** DISAGREEMENT used to tell someone that you do not agree with them, do not believe them, etc *Come on Bob! You made the same excuse last week.*

come out 1 BECOME AVAILABLE If a book, record, film, etc comes out, it becomes available for people to buy or see. *When does their new album come out?* **2** SUN When the sun, the moon, or a star comes out, it appears in the sky. **3** BECOME KNOWN to become known *The truth about him will come out in the end.* **4** SOCIAL EVENT *UK* to go somewhere with someone for a social event *Would you like to come out for a drink?* **5** RESULT If you describe how something comes out at the end of a process or activity, you say what it is like. *How did your chocolate cake come out?* **6** INFORMATION If results or information come out, they are given to people. *The exam results come out in August.* **7** BE REMOVED If dirt or a mark comes out of something, it disappears when you clean it. *Will this red wine stain come out?* **8** PHOTOGRAPH If a photograph comes out, the picture can be seen clearly. *The photos didn't come out very well.* **9** BE SAID If something that you say comes out in a particular way, you say it in that way. *I wanted to tell her that I loved her, but it came out all wrong.* **10** TELL to tell people that you are homosexual (= sexually attracted to people of the same sex) **11 come out against/in favour of sth** to say publicly that you oppose or support something

come out in sth If you come out in a skin disease, it appears on your skin.

come out of sth If something comes out of a process or event, it is one of the results. *I hope something good can come out of this mess.*

come out with sth to say something suddenly that is not expected

come over 1 to come to a place, move from one place to another, or move towards someone *Are your family **coming over from** Greece for the wedding?* **2** to seem to be a particular type of person *Henry **came over as** a real enthusiast.*

come over sb If a feeling comes over you, you suddenly experience it. *I don't usually get so angry. I don't know what came over me.*

come round UK **1** VISIT to visit someone at their house *You must come round to the flat for dinner some time.* **2** AGREE to change your opinion about something, or agree to an idea or a plan that you were against **3** EVENT If an event that happens regularly comes round, it happens, or is going to happen soon. *I can't believe that winter has come round already.* **4** BECOME CONSCIOUS to become conscious again after an accident or medical operation

come through 1 If information or a result comes through, you receive it. *Have the results of the tests come through yet?* **2** If an emotion comes through, other people can notice it. *His nervousness came through when he spoke.*

come through (sth) to manage to get to the end of a difficult or dangerous situation *We've had some hard times, but we've come through them.*

come to to become conscious again after an accident or medical operation

come to sb If a thought or idea comes to you, you suddenly remember it or start to think about it.

come to sth 1 to be a particular total when numbers or amounts are added together *That comes to £50, please.* **2 come to a decision/conclusion/arrangement, etc** to make a decision or decide what to think about something **3** to reach a particular state or situation, especially a bad one *You won't **come to** any harm.*

come under sth 1 come under attack/criticism/scrutiny, etc to be attacked, criticized, examined, etc **2** to be controlled or dealt with by a particular authority *Water rates come under local government control.* **3** to be in a particular part of a book, list, etc *Hairdressers come under 'beauty salons' in the Yellow Pages.*

come up 1 MOVE TOWARDS to move towards someone *After the concert, he came up to me to ask for my autograph.* **2** BE DISCUSSED to be discussed or suggested *The issue of security came up at the meeting yesterday.* **3** OPPORTUNITY If a job or opportunity comes up, it becomes available. **4** PROBLEM If a problem or difficult situation comes up, it happens. **5 be coming up** to be happening soon *My exams are coming up next month.* **6** SUN OR MOON When the sun or the moon comes up, it rises. **7** COMPUTER If information comes up on a computer screen, it appears there.

come up against sb/sth to have to deal with a problem or difficulty *She came up against a lot of sexism in her first engineering job.*

come up to sth to reach the usual or necessary standard *This essay doesn't **come up** to your usual **standards**.*

come up with sth to think of a plan, an idea, or a solution to a problem *We need to come up with a good scheme to make money.*

comeback /'kʌmbæk/ noun [C] a successful attempt to become powerful, important, or famous again *She's **made a comeback** with her first new album for twenty years.*

comedian /kə'miːdiən/ noun [C] someone who entertains people by telling jokes

comedown /'kʌmdaʊn/ noun [C] informal a situation that is not as good as one you were in before [usually singular] *Cleaning windows is a bit of a comedown after his last job.*

comedy /'kɒmədi/ noun [C, U] entertainment such as a film, play, etc which is funny *The film is a romantic comedy.*

comet /'kɒmɪt/ noun [C] an object in space that leaves a bright line behind it in the sky

comfort¹ /'kʌmfət/ noun **1** NO PAIN [U] a pleasant feeling of being relaxed and free from pain *Now you can watch the latest films **in the comfort of** your sitting room.* **2** FOR SADNESS [U] when you feel better after being worried or sad *What she said brought me great comfort.* **3** ENOUGH MONEY [U] when you have a pleasant life with enough money for everything that you need *He can afford to retire and live in comfort for the rest of his life.* **4 a comfort to sb** someone or something that helps you when you are anxious or sad *The children have been a great comfort to me since his death.* **5** PLEASANT THING [C] something that makes your life easy and pleasant [usually plural] *Good dark chocolate is one of life's little comforts.* ⊃Opposite **discomfort.**

comfort² /'kʌmfət/ verb [T] to make someone feel better when they are anxious or sad •**comforting** adjective *He said a few comforting words.*

o—**comfortable** /'kʌmftəbl/ adjective **1** NOT CAUSING PAIN Comfortable furniture, clothes, rooms, etc make you feel relaxed and do not cause any pain. *comfortable shoes ○ We had a comfortable journey.* **2** PERSON If you are comfortable, you are relaxed and have no pain. ***Make yourself comfortable** while I fetch you a drink.* ⊃Opposite **uncomfortable. 3** WITHOUT WORRIES If you are comfortable in a situation, you do not have any worries about it. *I don't feel comfortable about leaving the children here alone.* **4** MONEY having enough money for everything that you need *a comfortable retirement* **5** WIN If you win a game or competition by a comfortable amount, you win easily. *a comfortable lead/victory* •**comfortably** adverb

comforter /'kʌmfətə/ US (UK **duvet**) noun [C] a cover filled with feathers or warm material, that you sleep under

'comfort ˌzone noun [C] a situation that you know well and in which you are relaxed and confident *Owen thought about deep-sea diving but decided it was outside his comfort zone.*

comfy /'kʌmfi/ adjective informal comfortable

comic¹ /'kɒmɪk/ adjective funny *a comic actor*

comic² /'kɒmɪk/ noun [C] **1** (also **'comic ˌbook**) a magazine with stories told in pictures **2** someone who entertains people by telling jokes

comical /'kɒmɪkəl/ *adjective* funny in a strange or silly way *He looked so comical in that hat.* ● **comically** *adverb*

comic strip *noun* [C] a set of pictures telling a story, usually in a newspaper

coming¹ /'kʌmɪŋ/ *noun* **1 the coming of sth** the arrival of something *the coming of spring* **2 comings and goings** people's movements to and from a particular place over a period of time

coming² /'kʌmɪŋ/ *adjective* [always before noun] a coming time or event will come or happen soon *the coming elections* ⊃See also: **up-and-coming.**

comma /'kɒmə/ *noun* [C] a mark (,) used to separate parts of a sentence, or to separate the items in a list ⊃See Extra help page **Punctuation** on page Centre 33. ⊃See also: **inverted commas.**

command¹ /kə'mɑːnd/ *noun* **1** CONTROL [U] control over someone or something and responsibility for them *The soldiers were **under the command of** a tough sergeant-major.* ○ *Jones was **in command** (= the leader).* **2** ORDER [C] an order to do something **3** KNOWLEDGE [no plural] knowledge of a subject, especially a language *She **had a good command** of French and Italian.* **4 be at sb's command** to be ready to obey someone's orders **5** COMPUTER [C] an instruction to a computer

command² /kə'mɑːnd/ *verb formal* **1** [T] to control someone or something and tell them what to do *He commanded the armed forces.* **2** [I, T] to order someone to do something [+ to do sth] *The officer commanded his men to shoot.* **3 command attention/loyalty/respect, etc** to deserve and get attention, loyalty, respect, etc from other people

commandeer /ˌkɒmən'dɪər/ *verb* [T] *formal* to take something, especially for military use *The ships were commandeered as naval vessels.*

commander /kə'mɑːndər/ *noun* [C] an officer who is in charge of a military operation, or an officer of middle rank in the navy

commanding /kə'mɑːndɪŋ/ *adjective* [always before noun] in a very successful position and likely to win or succeed *He has a **commanding lead** in the championships.*

commandment /kə'mɑːndmənt/ *noun* [C] one of the ten important rules of behaviour given by God in the Bible

commando /kə'mɑːndəʊ/ *noun* [C] a soldier who is part of a small group who make surprise attacks

commemorate /kə'meməreɪt/ *verb* [T] to do something to show you remember an important person or event in the past with respect *a ceremony to commemorate the battle* ● **commemoration** /kəˌmemə'reɪʃən/ *noun* [U] *a march **in commemoration of** the war of independence*

commemorative /kə'memərətɪv/ *adjective* intended to commemorate a person or event *a commemorative coin*

commence /kə'mens/ *verb* [I, T] *formal* to begin something ● **commencement** *noun* [C, U] *formal* the beginning of something

commend /kə'mend/ *verb* [T] *formal* to praise someone or something [often passive] *His courage was commended by the report.* ● **commendation** /ˌkɒmen'deɪʃən/ *noun* [C, U]

commendable /kə'mendəbl/ *adjective* deserving praise *Anne Marie showed commendable modesty.*

WORD PARTNERS FOR **comment**

make a comment ● **make no** comment ● **do** sth **without** comment ● a comment **about/ on** sth

⊶**comment¹** /'kɒment/ *noun* [C, U] **1** something that you say or write that shows what you think about something *He **made** negative **comments** to the press.* **2 No comment.** used to say that you do not want to answer someone's question

⊶**comment²** /'kɒment/ *verb* [I, T] to make a comment *My mum always **comments on** what I'm wearing.* ○ [+ that] *He commented that the two essays were very similar.*

commentary /'kɒməntəri/ *noun* **1** [C, U] a spoken description of an event on the radio or television while the event is happening *the football commentary* **2** [U, no plural] a discussion or explanation of something *a **commentary on** American culture*

commentator /'kɒmənteɪtər/ *noun* [C] someone who describes an event on the radio or television while it is happening *a **sports commentator***

commerce /'kɒmɜːs/ *noun* [U] the activities involved in buying and selling things ⊃See also: **chamber of commerce, e-commerce.**

commercial¹ /kə'mɜːʃəl/ *adjective* **1** relating to buying and selling things **2** intended to make a profit *commercial television* ● **commercially** *adverb*

commercial² /kə'mɜːʃəl/ *noun* [C] an advertisement on the radio or television

commercialism /kə'mɜːʃəlɪzəm/ *noun* [U] when making money is the most important aim of an activity

commercialized (*also* UK **-ised**) /kə'mɜːʃəlaɪzd/ *adjective* organized to make profits *Christmas has become so commercialized.* ● **commercialization** /kəˌmɜːʃəlaɪ'zeɪʃən/ *noun* [U]

commiserate /kə'mɪzəreɪt/ *verb* [I] to express sympathy to someone who is sad or has had bad luck

commission¹ /kə'mɪʃən/ *noun* **1** GROUP OF PEOPLE [group] an official group of people who have been chosen to find out about something and say what they think should be done about it **2** PIECE OF WORK [C, U] when you arrange for someone to do a piece of work for you such as painting, writing, or making something **3** MONEY [C, U] money given to someone when they sell something *The staff receive 5% **commission on** everything that they sell.* ○ *Many estate agents work **on commission**.*

commission² /kə'mɪʃən/ *verb* [T] to arrange for someone to do a piece of work [+ to do sth] *I've been commissioned to write a song for their wedding.*

commissioner /kə'mɪʃənəʳ/ *noun* [C] a member of a commission or someone with an important government job in a particular area

⊶**commit** /kə'mɪt/ *verb* [T] **committing**, *past* **committed 1** [CRIME] to do something that is considered wrong, or that is illegal *He was sent to prison for a **crime** that he didn't **commit**. ○ to **commit suicide/adultery*** **2** [DECISION] to make a firm decision that you will do something *He **committed himself to** helping others.* **3 not commit yourself** to refuse to express an opinion about a particular subject **4** [MONEY/TIME] If you commit money, time, energy, etc to something, you use it to try to achieve something. *The government has **committed** thousands of pounds **to** the research.*

WORD PARTNERS FOR ***commitment***

make a commitment • **fulfil/honour/meet** a commitment • a commitment **to** sth

⊶**commitment** /kə'mɪtmənt/ *noun* **1** [PROMISE] [C] a promise or firm decision to do something *Players must **make a commitment to** daily training.* **2** [LOYALTY] [U] when you are willing to give your time and energy to something that you believe in *We are looking for someone with talent, enthusiasm, and commitment.* **3** [ACTIVITY] [C] something that you must do that takes your time *I've got too many **commitments** at the moment.*

committed /kə'mɪtɪd/ *adjective* loyal and willing to give your time and energy to something that you believe in *a committed Christian ○ She's **committed to** the job.*

committee /kə'mɪti/ *noun* [group] a group of people who have been chosen to represent a larger organization and make decisions for it

commodity /kə'mɒdəti/ *noun* [C] a product that you can buy or sell

⊶**common**[1] /'kɒmən/ *adjective* **1** [USUAL] happening often or existing in large numbers *Injuries are common in sports such as hockey.* ⊃Opposite **uncommon**. **2** [SHARED] belonging to or shared by two or more people or things *a common goal/interest ○ English has some features **common to** many languages.* **3 common knowledge** something that a lot of people know [+ that] *It's common knowledge that he spent time in jail.* **4** [ORDINARY] [always before noun] not special in any way *The herbs all have **common names** and Latin names.* **5** [LOW CLASS] *UK* typical of a low social class *My mum thinks dyed blonde hair is really common.*

common[2] /'kɒmən/ *noun* **1 have sth in common** to share interests, experiences, or other characteristics with someone or something *Sue and I don't have much in common.* **2 in common with sb/sth** in the same way as someone or something *In common with many working mothers, she feels guilty towards her children.* **3** [C] a large area of grass in a town or village which everyone is allowed to use

ˌcommon 'ground *noun* [U] shared interests, beliefs, or ideas *It's difficult for me to **find** any **common ground** with my dad.*

common-law /ˌkɒmən'lɔː/ *adjective* [always before noun] A common-law wife or husband is someone who is not married, but has lived with their partner for a long time as if they were married.

commonly /'kɒmənli/ *adverb* often or usually *These caterpillars are **commonly found** on nettles.*

commonplace /'kɒmənpleɪs/ *adjective* [never before noun] happening often or existing in large numbers, and so not considered special or unusual

the Commons /'kɒmənz/ (*also* **the House of Commons**) *noun* one of the two parts of the British parliament, with elected members who make laws

ˌcommon 'sense *noun* [U] the natural ability to be practical and to make good decisions *The children shouldn't be in any danger as long as they use their common sense.*

the Commonwealth /'kɒmənwelθ/ *noun* Britain and the group of countries that used to be in the British Empire (= ruled by Britain)

commotion /kə'məʊʃən/ *noun* [U, no plural] a sudden period of noise and confused or excited movement *He looked up to see what all the commotion was about.*

communal /'kɒmjʊnəl/ [US] /kə'mjuːnəl/ *adjective* belonging to or used by a group of people *a communal changing room*

commune /'kɒmjuːn/ *noun* [C] a group of people who live together, sharing the work and the things they own

communicate /kə'mjuːnɪkeɪt/ *verb* [I, T] **1** to share information with others by speaking, writing, moving your body, or using other signals *We can now **communicate** instantly **with** people on the other side of the world.* **2** to talk about your thoughts and feelings, and help other people to understand them *He can't **communicate with** his parents.*

WORD PARTNERS FOR ***communication***

communication **between** sb and sb • **in** communication **with** sb • a **means of** communication • a **breakdown in** communication • communication **skills**

⊶**communication** /kəˌmjuːnɪ'keɪʃən/ *noun* **1** [U] the act of communicating with other people *The school is improving **communication between** teachers and parents. ○ We are **in** direct **communication with** Moscow.* **2** [C] *formal* a message sent to someone by letter, email, telephone, etc

communications /kəˌmjuːnɪ'keɪʃənz/ *noun* [plural] the different ways of sending information between people and places, such as post, telephones, computers, and radio *the communications industry*

communicative /kə'mjuːnɪkətɪv/ *adjective* willing to talk to people and give them information

communion /kə'mjuːniən/ *noun* [U] (*also* **Communion**) the Christian ceremony in which people eat bread and drink wine, as symbols of Christ's body and blood

communiqué /kə'mjuːnɪkeɪ/ [US] /kəˌmjuːnɪ'keɪ/ *noun* [C] an official announcement

communism, Communism /'kɒmjənɪzᵊm/
noun [U] a political system in which the
government controls the production of all
goods, and where everyone is treated equally

communist, Communist /'kɒmjənɪst/ *noun*
[C] someone who supports communism ● **communist** *adjective a communist country/leader*

community /kə'mju:nəti/ *noun* 1 [C] the people
living in a particular area *a rural/small community* 2 [group] a group of people with the
same interests, nationality, job, etc *the business/Chinese community*

com'munity ,centre UK (US **community
center**) *noun* [C] a place where people who live
in an area can meet together to play sport, go
to classes, etc

com,munity 'college *noun* [C, U] US a two-year college where students can learn a skill
or prepare to enter a university

com,munity 'service *noun* [U] work that
someone who has committed a crime does to
help other people instead of going to prison

commute /kə'mju:t/ *verb* [I] to regularly travel
between work and home ● **commuter** *noun* [C]

compact[1] /kəm'pækt/ *adjective* small and including many things in a small space

compact[2] /kəm'pækt/ *verb* [T] to press something together so that it becomes tight or solid

,compact 'disc *noun* [C] a CD (= a disc for recorded music or information)

companion /kəm'pænjən/ *noun* [C] someone
who you spend a lot of time with or go somewhere with *a travelling companion*

companionship /kəm'pænjənʃɪp/ *noun* [U] the
feeling of having friends around you

establish/found/set up/start up a company

☞**company** /'kʌmpəni/ *noun* 1 [BUSINESS] [C] an
organization which sells goods or services *a
software/telephone company* 2 [PEOPLE] [U] when
you have a person or people with you *I enjoy
his company.* ○ *I didn't realize that you had
company.* 3 **keep sb company** to stay with
someone so that they are not alone 4 **be good
company** to be a pleasant or interesting person
to spend time with 5 [PERFORMERS] [C] a group of
performers such as actors or dancers *the
Royal Shakespeare Company* ⊃See also: **limited
company**.

comparable /'kɒmpᵊrəbl/ *adjective* similar in
size, amount, or quality to something else *Our
prices are comparable to those in other shops.*

comparative[1] /kəm'pærətɪv/ *adjective* 1 **comparative comfort/freedom/silence, etc** a situation which is comfortable/free/silent, etc
when compared to another situation or to
what is usual *I enjoyed the comparative calm of
his flat after the busy office.* 2 comparing similar things *a comparative study of two poems*

comparative[2] /kəm'pærətɪv/ *noun* [C] the form
of an adjective or adverb that is used to show
that someone or something has more of a
particular quality than someone or something
else. For example 'better' is the comparative of

'good' and 'smaller' is the comparative of
'small'. ⊃Compare **superlative**.

comparatively /kəm'pærətɪvli/ *adverb* **comparatively cheap/easy/little, etc** cheap/easy/
little, etc when compared to something else or
to what is usual

☞**compare** /kəm'peəʳ/ *verb* 1 [T] to examine the
ways in which two people or things are different or similar *The teachers are always comparing me with/to my sister.* 2 [I] to be as
good as something else *This product compares
well with more expensive brands.* 3 **compared
to/with sb/sth** used when saying how one
person or thing is different from another *This
room is very tidy compared to mine.* ⊃See also:
compare notes (**note**[1]).

compare sb/sth to sb/sth to say that
someone or something is similar to someone
or something else

draw/make a comparison ● a comparison
between sth and sth ● a comparison of sth
(with) sth ● by/in comparison (with) sth

☞**comparison** /kəm'pærɪsᵊn/ *noun* [C, U] 1 when
you compare two or more people or things
*They published a comparison of schools in the
area.* ○ *She's so tall that he looks tiny by/in
comparison.* 2 **There's no comparison.** used to
say that someone or something is much better
than someone or something else

compartment /kəm'pɑ:tmənt/ *noun* [C] 1 one
of the separate areas inside a vehicle, especially a train *The first class compartment is at
the front of the train.* 2 a separate part of a container, bag, etc *a fridge with a small freezer
compartment*

compass /'kʌmpəs/
noun [C] a piece of
equipment which
shows you which direction you are going in

compasses
/'kʌmpəsɪz/ *noun* [plural]
UK (US **compass** [C]) a
piece of equipment
which is used for
drawing circles

compass

compassion
/kəm'pæʃᵊn/ *noun* [U] a
feeling of sympathy
for people who are
suffering

compassionate /kəm'pæʃᵊnət/ *adjective* showing compassion

compatible /kəm'pætɪbl/ *adjective* 1 [EQUIPMENT]
compatible equipment can be used together
*This keyboard is compatible with all of our
computers.* 2 [PEOPLE] If people are compatible,
they like each other and are happy to spend
time together. 3 [IDEAS] *formal* compatible ideas
or situations can exist together *Such policies
are not compatible with democratic government.* ● **compatibility** /kəm,pætə'bɪləti/ *noun* [U]

compatriot /kəm'pætriət/ *noun* [C] *formal*
someone who comes from the same country

compel /kəm'pel/ *verb* compelling, *past* compelled *formal* **compel sb to do sth** to force someone to do something [often passive] *He felt compelled to resign from his job.*

compelling /kəm'pelɪŋ/ *adjective* **1** very exciting or interesting and making you want to watch, listen, etc *a compelling story* **2** If a reason, argument, etc is compelling, it makes you believe it or accept it because it is so strong. *compelling evidence*

compensate /'kɒmpənseɪt/ *verb* **1** [T] to pay someone money because you are responsible for injuring them or damaging something *Victims of the crash will be compensated for their injuries.* **2** [I, T] to reduce the bad effect of something, or make something bad become something good *Nothing will ever compensate for his lost childhood.*

compensation /ˌkɒmpən'seɪʃᵊn/ *noun* **1** [U] money that you pay to someone because you are responsible for injuring them or damaging something *Most of the workers have won compensation for losing their jobs.* **2** [C, U] something you get to make you feel better when you have suffered something bad *Free food was no compensation for a very boring evening.*

compete /kəm'piːt/ *verb* [I] **1** to take part in a race or competition *She's competing for a place in next year's Olympics.* **2** to try to be more successful than someone or something else *It's difficult for small shops to compete with/against the big supermarkets.*

competent /'kɒmpɪtᵊnt/ *adjective* able to do something well *a competent swimmer/teacher* ● **competence** /'kɒmpɪtᵊns/ *noun* [U] the ability to do something well ● **competently** *adverb*

WORD PARTNERS FOR **competition**

1 enter/go in for/take part in a competition ● hold a competition ● win a competition
2 fierce/intense/stiff competition ● competition between sb and sb ● competition for sth

o~**competition** /ˌkɒmpə'tɪʃᵊn/ *noun* **1** [C] an organized event in which people try to win a prize by being the best, fastest, etc *to enter a competition* **2** [U] when someone is trying to win something or be more successful than someone else *There's a lot of competition between computer companies.* ○ *Applicants face stiff competition for university places this year.* **3** the competition people who you are competing against, especially in business

competitive /kəm'petɪtɪv/ *adjective* **1** [SITUATION] involving competition *competitive sports* ○ *a highly competitive industry* **2** [PERSON] wanting to win or to be more successful than other people *She's very competitive.* **3** [PRICES/SERVICES] Competitive prices, services, etc are as good as or better than other prices, services, etc. ● **competitively** *adverb* ● **competitiveness** *noun* [U]

competitor /kəm'petɪtəʳ/ *noun* [C] a person, team, or company that is competing with others

compilation /ˌkɒmpɪ'leɪʃᵊn/ *noun* [C] a recording, book, or film containing a collection of things from many different recordings, books, or films *I've got a CD compilation of her best singles.*

compile /kəm'paɪl/ *verb* [T] to collect information and arrange it in a book, report, or list *He's currently compiling a dictionary of musical terms.*

complacent /kəm'pleɪsᵊnt/ *adjective* feeling so satisfied with your own abilities or situation that you do not feel that you need to try any harder *We can't afford to become too complacent about our work.* ● **complacency** *noun* [U] when someone is complacent *There's really no room for complacency.* ● **complacently** *adverb*

OTHER WAYS OF SAYING **complain**

The verbs **grumble**, **moan** and (*UK, informal*) **whinge** are sometimes used when someone is complaining about things which are not important: *She's always grumbling about something.* ● *He's forever moaning about his work.* ● *I hope you don't think I'm just whingeing.*

If someone, especially a child, complains in an annoying way, the verb **whine** is often used: *Stop whining, Tom - it's not that bad!*

The expression **kick up a fuss** is sometimes used in informal contexts, especially when someone is complaining that something has not happened in the way they wanted: *If the food doesn't come soon, I'm going to kick up a fuss.*

o~**complain** /kəm'pleɪn/ *verb* [I] to say that something is wrong or that you are annoyed about something *Lots of people have complained about the noise.* ○ [+ that] *He's always complaining that nobody listens to him.* ○ *I complained to the manager about the state of the toilets.* ○ *He treats her so badly and yet she never complains.*

COMMON LEARNER ERROR

complain about something

Be careful to choose the correct preposition after **complain**.

I am writing to complain about the trip.

~~I am writing to complain for the trip.~~

~~I am writing to complain on the trip.~~

complain of sth to tell other people that something is making you feel ill *She's been complaining of a headache all day.*

WORD PARTNERS FOR **complaint**

make/investigate/receive a complaint ● a complaint about sb/sth ● a complaint against sb ● a formal/official/written complaint ● a letter of complaint ● have cause for/grounds for complaint

o~**complaint** /kəm'pleɪnt/ *noun* **1** [NOT SATISFACTORY] [C, U] when someone says that something is wrong or not satisfactory *a letter of complaint* ○ *I wish to* **make a complaint**. **2** ANNOYING THING [C] something that makes you complain *My only complaint was the lack of refreshments*. **3** ILLNESS [C] an illness *a stomach complaint*

complement¹ /'kɒmplɪmənt/ *noun* [C] **1** MAKE GOOD something that makes something else seem good, attractive, or complete *This wine is the perfect* **complement** *to the meal*. **2** TOTAL NUMBER the total amount or number of something that is needed to complete a group *Do we have* **a full complement** *of players for Saturday's match?* **3** GRAMMAR a word or phrase which comes after the verb and gives more information about the subject of the verb

complement² /'kɒmplɪment/ *verb* [T] to make something else seem good or attractive *The music complements her voice perfectly.*

complementary /ˌkɒmplɪ'mentˀri/ *adjective* **1** Things which are complementary are good or attractive together. *complementary colours/flavours* **2** **complementary medicine/treatment, etc** ways of treating medical problems which people use instead of or in addition to ordinary medicine *The clinic offers complementary therapies such as homeopathy.*

complete¹ /kəm'pliːt/ *adjective* **1** WHOLE with all parts the **complete works** *of Oscar Wilde* ○ *The report comes* **complete with** (= including) *diagrams and colour photographs.* **2** TOTAL [always before noun] used to emphasize what you are saying *a complete waste of time* **3** FINISHED finished *Our final report is almost complete.*

o-**complete²** /kəm'pliːt/ *verb* [T] **1** FINISH to finish doing or making something *The palace took 15 years to complete.* **2** MAKE STH WHOLE to provide the last part needed to make something whole *Complete the sentence with one of the adjectives provided.* **3** WRITE to write all the details asked for on a form or other document

o-**completely** /kəm'pliːtli/ *adverb* in every way or as much as possible *I completely forgot that you were coming.*

completion /kəm'pliːʃˀn/ *noun* [U] when something that you are doing or making is finished *The stadium is due for completion in 2008.* ○ *They will be paid* **on completion of** *the job.*

o-**complex¹** /'kɒmpleks, kəm'pleks/ *adjective* involving a lot of different but connected parts in a way that is difficult to understand *complex details/issues* ○ *The situation is very complex.* ● **complexity** /kəm'pleksəti/ *noun* [C, U] when something is complex *the complexities of life*

complex² /'kɒmpleks/ *noun* [C] **1** a group of buildings or rooms that are used for a particular purpose *a sports/housing complex* **2** a mental problem which makes someone anxious or frightened about something *an inferiority complex*

complexion /kəm'plekʃˀn/ *noun* [C] **1** the colour and appearance of the skin on someone's face *a clear complexion* **2** the way something seems to be *This new information*

puts a *completely different* **complexion** *on the situation.*

compliance /kəm'plaɪəns/ *noun* [U] *formal* when people obey an order, rule, or request *The work was done* **in compliance with** *planning regulations.*

compliant /kəm'plaɪənt/ *adjective* Compliant people are willing to do what other people want them to. *I haven't asked her yet but I'm hoping she will be compliant.*

complicate /'kɒmplɪkeɪt/ *verb* [T] to make something more difficult to deal with or understand *These new regulations just complicate matters further.*

o-**complicated** /'kɒmplɪkeɪtɪd/ *adjective* involving a lot of different parts, in a way that is difficult to understand *a complicated problem/process* ○ *The instructions were too complicated for me.*

complication /ˌkɒmplɪ'keɪʃˀn/ *noun* [C] **1** something which makes a situation more difficult *There were a few complications that we had to deal with.* **2** a new medical problem that develops when you are already ill *Eye problems can be a complication of diabetes.*

complicity /kəm'plɪsəti/ *noun* [U] *formal* when someone is involved in doing something wrong

compliment¹ /'kɒmplɪmənt/ *noun* **1** [C] something that you say or do to show praise or admiration for someone *She was always paying him compliments.* ○ *He told me I had a firm manner and I took it* **as a compliment**. **2** **with the compliments of sb** *formal* used by someone to express good wishes when they give you something free, for example in a restaurant *Please accept this champagne with the compliments of the manager.*

compliment² /'kɒmplɪment/ *verb* [T] to praise or express admiration for someone *He complimented me on my writing.*

complimentary /ˌkɒmplɪ'mentˀri/ *adjective* **1** praising or expressing admiration for someone *a complimentary report* ○ *She was very complimentary about your handling of the situation.* **2** given free, especially by a business *a complimentary glass of wine*

comply /kəm'plaɪ/ *verb* [I] to obey an order, rule, or request *The pilot* **complied with** *instructions to descend.*

component /kəm'pəʊnənt/ *noun* [C] one of the parts of something, especially a machine *The factory supplies electrical components for cars.*

compose /kəm'pəʊz/ *verb* **1** PARTS [T] to be the parts that something consists of [often passive] *The committee* **was composed of** *elected leaders and citizens.* **2** MUSIC [I, T] to write a piece of music **3** **compose yourself** to make yourself calm again after being angry or upset **4** WRITING [T] to write a speech, letter, etc, thinking carefully about the words to use *Laura was composing a letter of sympathy.*

composed /kəm'pəʊzd/ *adjective* calm and in control of your emotions

composer /kəm'pəʊzəʳ/ noun [C] someone who writes music

composite /'kɒmpəzɪt/ adjective consisting of several different parts *a composite image of the killer*

composition /ˌkɒmpə'zɪʃᵊn/ noun 1 PARTS [U] the parts, substances, etc that something consists of *the composition of the atmosphere* 2 MUSIC [C] a piece of music that someone has written 3 WRITING MUSIC [U] the process or skill of writing music *He taught composition at Columbia University.* 4 WRITING [C, U] a short piece of writing about a particular subject, done by a student 5 ARRANGEMENT [U] the way that people or things are arranged in a painting or photograph

compost /'kɒmpɒst/ noun [U] a mixture of decayed leaves and plants that is added to the soil to improve its quality *a compost heap*

composure /kəm'pəʊʒəʳ/ noun [U] when you feel or look calm and confident *to keep/lose your composure*

compound¹ /'kɒmpaʊnd/ noun [C] 1 MIXTURE a substance that is a combination of two or more elements *Water is a compound of hydrogen and oxygen.* 2 AREA an area of land with a group of buildings surrounded by a fence or wall *a prison compound* 3 GRAMMAR (also **compound noun/verb/adjective**) a noun, verb, or adjective that is made by two or more words used together. For example, 'golf club' is a compound.

compound² /kəm'paʊnd/ verb [T] to make a problem or difficult situation worse *Severe drought has compounded food shortages in the region.*

compère /'kɒmpeəʳ/ noun [C] *UK* someone whose job is to introduce performers on television, radio, or in a theatre

comprehend /ˌkɒmprɪ'hend/ verb [I, T] *formal* to understand *I was too young to comprehend what was happening.*

comprehensible /ˌkɒmprɪ'hensəbl/ adjective easy to understand *Computer manuals should be easily comprehensible.*

comprehension /ˌkɒmprɪ'henʃᵊn/ noun 1 [U] the ability to understand something *It's beyond my comprehension* (= I can't understand) *how anyone could be so cruel.* 2 [C, U] *UK* a test to see how well students understand written or spoken language *a reading comprehension*

comprehensive¹ /ˌkɒmprɪ'hensɪv/ adjective including everything *a comprehensive study of the subject* • **comprehensively** adverb completely *We were comprehensively beaten in the finals.*

comprehensive² /ˌkɒmprɪ'hensɪv/ (also **compre'hensive ˌschool**) noun [C] a school in Britain for students aged 11 to 18 of all levels of ability

compress /kəm'pres/ verb [T] 1 to make something smaller, especially by pressing it, so that it uses less space or time *compressed air* ○ *The course compresses two years' training into six months.* 2 to use a special program to make information on a computer use less space • **compression** /kəm'preʃᵊn/ noun [U]

comprise /kəm'praɪz/ verb [T] *formal* 1 to consist of particular parts or members *The orchestra was comprised of amateur and professional musicians.* 2 to form part of something, especially a larger group *Women comprise 15% of the police force.*

╔═══ WORD PARTNERS FOR **compromise** ═══

accept/come to/find/reach a compromise • a compromise **between** sth and sth • a compromise **on** sth • a compromise **agreement/deal/solution**

compromise¹ /'kɒmprəmaɪz/ noun [C, U] when you agree to something which is not exactly what you want *We need to reach a compromise over this issue.* ○ *Decorating is usually a compromise between taste and cost.*

compromise² /'kɒmprəmaɪz/ verb 1 AGREE [I] to agree to something that is not exactly what you want *The president may be willing to compromise in order to pass the bill.* ○ *I never compromise on fresh ingredients.* 2 **compromise yourself** to do something dishonest or embarrassing that makes people stop admiring you 3 BELIEFS [T] to do something that does not agree with what you believe in *I refuse to compromise my principles.* 4 HARM [T] *formal* to have a harmful effect on something *The trial has been seriously compromised by sensational media coverage.*

compromising /'kɒmprəmaɪzɪŋ/ adjective A compromising situation, photograph, etc makes people think you have done something wrong. *The press printed compromising photographs of the princess and her bodyguard.*

compulsion /kəm'pʌlʃᵊn/ noun 1 [C] a strong wish to do something, often something that you should not do 2 [U] when you are forced to do something *We were under no compulsion to attend.*

compulsive /kəm'pʌlsɪv/ adjective 1 A compulsive habit is something that you do a lot because you want to so much that you cannot control yourself. *a compulsive eating disorder* 2 a **compulsive eater/gambler/liar, etc** someone who is unable to stop eating, lying, etc, despite knowing that they should stop 3 so interesting or exciting that you cannot stop reading, playing, or watching it *This documentary about life in prison makes compulsive viewing.* • **compulsively** adverb

compulsory /kəm'pʌlsᵊri/ adjective If something is compulsory, you must do it because of a rule or law.

o-**computer** /kəm'pjuːtəʳ/ noun [C] an electronic machine that can store and arrange large amounts of information *We've put all our records on computer.* ○ *computer software* ⇒See colour picture **The Office** on page Centre 5.

com,puter aided de'sign ⇒See CAD.

computerize (also UK -ise) /kəm'pjuːtᵊraɪz/ verb [T] to use a computer to do something that was done by people or other machines before *a computerized accounts system* • **computerization** /kəmˌpjuːtᵊraɪ'zeɪʃᵊn/ noun [U]

com,puter 'literate adjective able to understand and use computer systems

computing /kəm'pjuːtɪŋ/ *noun* [U] the study or use of computers *a degree in computing*

comrade /'kɒmreɪd/ ⑳ /'kɑːmræd/ *noun* [C] **1** *literary* a friend, especially someone who fights with you in a war **2** a word used by some members of trade unions (= organizations which represent people who do a particular job) or other Socialist organizations to talk to or about each other

comradeship /'kɒmreɪdʃɪp/ *noun* [U] the feeling of friendship between people who live or work together, especially in a difficult situation

con¹ /kɒn/ *verb* [T] **conning**, *past* **conned** *informal* to trick someone, especially in order to take money from them *Thieves conned him out of his life savings.* ○ *She felt she had been conned into buying the car.*

con² /kɒn/ *noun* [C] *informal* a trick to get someone's money, or make them do what they want

'con ,artist *noun* [C] someone who tricks people into giving them money or valuable things

concave /'kɒnkeɪv/ *adjective* A concave surface curves inwards. *a concave lens*

conceal /kən'siːl/ *verb* [T] to hide something *The listening device was concealed in a pen.* ○ *She could barely conceal her irritation.* ● **concealment** *noun* [U] when something is hidden

concede /kən'siːd/ *verb* **1** [T] to admit that something is true, even though you do not want to [+ (that)] *Even the company chairman concedes that the results are disappointing.* **2** [I, T] to allow someone to have something, even though you do not want to *The government will not concede to rebel demands.* **3** **concede defeat** to admit that you have lost a fight, argument, game, etc

conceit /kən'siːt/ *noun* [U] when you are too proud of yourself and your actions

conceited /kən'siːtɪd/ *adjective* too proud of yourself and your actions ● **conceitedly** *adverb*

conceivable /kən'siːvəbl/ *adjective* possible to imagine or to believe *every conceivable kind of fruit* ○ [+ (that)] *It is just conceivable that the hospital made a mistake.* ● **conceivably** *adverb*

conceive /kən'siːv/ *verb* **1** BABY [I, T] to become pregnant **2** IMAGINE [I, T] to be able to imagine something *I cannot conceive of anything more horrible.* **3** IDEA [T] to think of an idea or plan *The original idea for the novel was conceived in Rome.*

o⁻**concentrate** /'kɒns³ntreɪt/ *verb* **1** [I] to think very carefully about something you are doing and nothing else *Be quiet - I'm trying to concentrate.* ○ *I can't concentrate on my work. It's too noisy here.* **2** **be concentrated around/in/on, etc** to be present in large numbers or amounts in a particular area *Most of the fighting was concentrated in the mountains.*

concentrate on sth to use most of your time and effort to do something *She gave up her job to concentrate on writing a novel.*

concentrated /'kɒnsəntreɪtɪd/ *adjective* **1** [always before noun] using a lot of effort to succeed at one particular thing *a concentrated*

effort to finish the work **2** A concentrated liquid has had most of the water removed. *concentrated tomato puree*

concentration /,kɒns³n'treɪʃ³n/ *noun* **1** [U] the ability to think carefully about something you are doing and nothing else **2** [C, U] a large number or amount of something in the same place *high concentrations of minerals*

concen'tration ,camp *noun* [C] a prison where large numbers of people are kept in very bad conditions, especially for political reasons

concentric /kən'sentrɪk/ *adjective* Concentric circles have the same centre but are different sizes.

concept /'kɒnsept/ *noun* [C] an idea or principle *the concept of free speech*

conception /kən'sepʃ³n/ *noun* **1** [C, U] an idea about what something is like or a way of understanding something **2** [U] when a woman or animal becomes pregnant

conceptual /kən'septʃuəl/ *adjective formal* based on ideas *a conceptual model*

concern¹ /kən'sɜːn/ *verb* [T] **1** INVOLVE to involve someone or be important to them *Environmental issues concern us all.* **2** WORRY to worry or upset someone *What really concerns me is her lack of experience.* **3** BE ABOUT If a story, film, etc concerns a particular subject, it is about that subject. **4** **concern yourself** to become involved with doing something *You needn't concern yourself with the travel arrangements.*

concern² /kən'sɜːn/ *noun* **1** WORRY [C, U] a feeling of worry about something, or the thing that is worrying you *I have concerns about his health.* **2** IMPORTANT THING [C, U] something that involves or affects you or is important to you *Our primary concern is safety.* **3** BUSINESS [C] a company or business *The perfume factory was a family concern.*

o⁻**concerned** /kən'sɜːnd/ *adjective* **1** worried [+ that] *I am very concerned that class sizes seem to be growing.* ○ *People are becoming more concerned about what they eat.* ⭲Opposite **unconcerned. 2** [never before noun] involved in something or affected by it *A letter will be sent out to everyone concerned.* **3** **as far as sb is concerned** used to show what someone thinks about something *As far as our customers are concerned, price is the main consideration.* **4** **as far as sth is concerned** used to tell someone what you are talking about *As far as college is concerned, everything is fine.*

concerning /kən'sɜːnɪŋ/ *preposition* about

something *I've had a letter concerning my tax payments.*

o̶**concert** /ˈkɒnsət/ *noun* [C] a performance of music and singing *a pop concert*

concerted /kənˈsɜːtɪd/ *adjective* [always before noun] done with a lot of effort, often by a group of people working together *Iceland has made a concerted effort to boost tourism.*

concerto /kənˈtʃeətəʊ/ *noun* [C] a piece of music for one main instrument and an orchestra (= large group of musicians) *a piano concerto*

concession /kənˈseʃᵊn/ *noun* 1 AGREEMENT [C, U] something that you agree to do or give to someone in order to end an argument *Both sides will have to make concessions.* 2 BUSINESS [C] a special right to use buildings or land or to sell a product in a particular area *a concession to develop oil fields in the north* 3 LOW PRICE [C] *UK* a reduction in the price of a ticket for a particular group of people such as students, people without a job, or old people

conciliation /kənˌsɪliˈeɪʃᵊn/ *noun* [U] *formal* the process of trying to end an argument

conciliatory /kənˈsɪliətᵊri/ *adjective formal* If people behave in a conciliatory manner, they try to make people stop being angry with them. *a conciliatory approach*

concise /kənˈsaɪs/ *adjective* 1 giving a lot of information clearly in a few words 2 A concise book is small. *a concise history of France* ● **concisely** *adverb* ● **conciseness** *noun* [U]

conclude /kənˈkluːd/ *verb* 1 END [I, T] *formal* to end something such as a meeting, speech, or piece of writing by doing or saying one last thing *The concert concluded with a firework display.* ○ *I would like to conclude by thanking you all for attending.* 2 DECIDE [T] to decide something after studying all the information about it very carefully [+ that] *The report concluded that the drug was safe.* 3 COMPLETE [T] to complete something, especially an agreement or a business arrangement *talks aimed at concluding the peace treaty*

concluding /kənˈkluːdɪŋ/ *adjective* [always before noun] last in a series of things *Don't miss tonight's concluding episode.*

WORD PARTNERS FOR **conclusion**

draw/reach a conclusion ● come to the conclusion that ● sth leads (you) to the conclusion that

o̶**conclusion** /kənˈkluːʒᵊn/ *noun* 1 OPINION [C] the opinion you have after considering all the information about something *I've come to the conclusion that we'll have to sell the car.* 2 END [C] the final part of something *the dramatic conclusion of the film* ○ *The case should finally be brought to a conclusion* (= end) *this week.* 3 in conclusion used to introduce the last part of a speech or piece of writing *In conclusion, I would like to thank our guest speaker.* 4 ARRANGEMENT [U] when something is arranged or agreed formally *the conclusion of peace talks* 5 jump to conclusions to guess the facts about a situation without having enough information ⊃See also: foregone conclusion.

conclusive /kənˈkluːsɪv/ *adjective* proving that something is true *conclusive evidence/proof* ● **conclusively** *adverb* *Tests have proved conclusively that the drugs are effective.*

concoct /kənˈkɒkt/ *verb* [T] 1 to invent a story or explanation in order to deceive someone *He had concocted a web of lies.* 2 to make something unusual, especially food, by mixing things together ● **concoction** /kənˈkɒkʃᵊn/ *noun* [C] *a concoction of meringue, ice cream, and fresh strawberries*

concourse /ˈkɒŋkɔːs/ *noun* [C] a large room or open area inside a building such as an airport or station

concrete¹ /ˈkɒŋkriːt/ *noun* [U] a hard substance that is used in building and is made by mixing sand, water, small stones, and cement (= grey powder that is mixed with water and becomes hard when it dries) *concrete blocks*

concrete² /ˈkɒŋkriːt/ *adjective* 1 certain or based on facts *concrete evidence/proof* 2 existing in a real form that can be seen or felt *concrete achievements/actions* ○ *concrete objects*

concrete³ /ˈkɒŋkriːt/ *verb* [T] *UK* to cover something with concrete

concur /kənˈkɜːʳ/ *verb* [I] concurring, *past* concurred *formal* to agree *The new report concurs with previous findings.*

concurrent /kənˈkʌrᵊnt/ *adjective* happening or existing at the same time *three concurrent prison sentences* ● **concurrently** *adverb* ↖

concussed /kənˈkʌst/ *adjective* [never before noun] If someone is concussed, they are suffering from concussion.

concussion /kənˈkʌʃᵊn/ *noun* [C, U] a slight injury to the brain that is caused by being hit on the head and makes you feel tired or sick

condemn /kənˈdem/ *verb* [T] 1 to say very strongly that you think something is wrong or very bad *The Prime Minister was quick to condemn the terrorists.* 2 to say that a building must be destroyed because it is not safe enough for people to use

condemn sb to sth 1 to say what the punishment of someone who is guilty of a serious crime will be *He was condemned to death.* 2 to make someone suffer in a particular way *Poor education condemns many young people to low-paid jobs.*

condemnation /ˌkɒndemˈneɪʃᵊn/ *noun* [C, U] when you say very strongly that you think something is wrong or very bad *widespread condemnation of the war*

condensation /ˌkɒndenˈseɪʃᵊn/ *noun* [U] small drops of water that form when warm air touches a cold surface

condense /kənˈdens/ *verb* 1 AIR [I, T] If hot air or a gas condenses, it changes into a liquid as it becomes colder. 2 WORDS [T] to make something such as a speech or piece of writing shorter *You need to condense your conclusion into a single paragraph.* 3 LIQUID [T] to make a liquid thicker by taking some of the water out of it *condensed milk*

condescend /ˌkɒndɪˈsend/ *verb* **condescend to**

do sth *humorous* to agree to do something even though you think you are too important to do it **condescend to sb** to treat someone as though you are better or more important than them

condescending /ˌkɒndɪˈsendɪŋ/ *adjective* showing that you think that you are better or more important than someone else *a condescending smile* • **condescendingly** *adverb*

condescension /ˌkɒndɪˈsenʃᵊn/ *noun* [U] when you behave as though you are better or more important than someone else

⊶**condition¹** /kənˈdɪʃᵊn/ *noun* **1** STATE [U, no plural] the state that something or someone is in *My bike's a few years old but it's **in really good condition**.* ○ *He's **in no condition*** (= not well enough) *to travel.* **2** AGREEMENT [C] something that must happen or be agreed before something else can happen *One of the conditions of the contract is that we can't keep pets.* **3 on condition that** only if *Visitors are allowed in the gardens on condition that they don't touch the plants.* **4** ILLNESS [C] an illness *a serious heart condition* **5 conditions** the physical situation that people are in ***working/living conditions*** ○ *severe **weather conditions***

condition² /kənˈdɪʃᵊn/ *verb* [T] **1** to make a person or animal behave in a particular way by influencing the way they think [often passive, + to do sth] *The boys were conditioned to be aggressive.* **2** to put a special liquid on your hair to make it soft and healthy

conditional /kənˈdɪʃᵊnᵊl/ *adjective* **1** If an offer or agreement is conditional, it will only happen if something else is done first. *Their fee is **conditional on** the work being completed by January.* ➲Opposite **unconditional**. **2** A conditional sentence usually begins with 'if' and says that something must be true or happen before something else can be true or happen.

conditioner /kənˈdɪʃᵊnəʳ/ *noun* [C, U] a liquid that you use when you wash your hair to make it soft

conditioning /kənˈdɪʃᵊnɪŋ/ *noun* [U] when a person or animal is made to behave in a particular way *social/physical conditioning* ➲See also: **air conditioning**.

condo /ˈkɒndəʊ/ *noun* [C] *US informal short for* condominium

condolence /kənˈdəʊləns/ *noun* [C, U] *formal* sympathy for the family or friends of a person who has recently died *Please **offer my condolences** to your father.*

condom /ˈkɒndɒm/ (US) /ˈkɑːndəm/ *noun* [C] a thin rubber covering that a man wears on his penis during sex to stop a woman becoming pregnant, or to protect against diseases

condominium /ˌkɒndəˈmɪniəm/ *noun* [C] *US* a building containing apartments which are owned by the people living in them, or one of these apartments

condone /kənˈdəʊn/ *verb* [T] to accept or allow behaviour that is wrong *His comments appeared to condone drug abuse.*

conducive /kənˈdjuːsɪv/ *adjective* making something possible or likely to happen *Such a noisy environment was not **conducive to** a good night's sleep.*

conduct¹ /ˈkɒndʌkt/ *noun* **1** [U] the way someone behaves *a code of conduct* (= rules about how to behave) **2 conduct of sth** the way someone organizes or does something *He was criticized for his conduct of the inquiry.*

WORD PARTNERS FOR ***conduct***

conduct an **experiment** / an **interview** / an **inquiry** / an **investigation** / **research** / a **survey**

conduct² /kənˈdʌkt/ *verb* **1** DO [T] to organize or do something *They're **conducting a survey**.* **2** MUSIC [I, T] to stand in front of a group of musicians and control their performance **3** HEAT [T] If a substance conducts electricity or heat, it allows electricity or heat to go through it. **4 conduct yourself** to behave in a particular way *She conducted herself with great dignity.* **5** LEAD [T] *formal* to lead someone to a place *I was conducted to a side room.*

conductor /kənˈdʌktəʳ/ *noun* [C] **1** MUSIC someone who stands in front of a group of musicians or singers and controls their performance **2** BUS *UK* someone whose job is to sell or check tickets on a bus, train, etc **3** TRAIN *US* (*UK* **guard**) someone whose job is to be responsible for a train and the people who work on it **4** HEAT a substance that allows electricity or heat to go through it

cone /kəʊn/ *noun* [C] **1** a solid shape with a round or oval base which narrows to a point, or an object which has this shape *a row of **traffic cones*** **2** a container for ice cream (= sweet, frozen food) that you can eat

confectionery /kənˈfekʃᵊnᵊri/ *noun* [U] *mainly UK* sweet food like sweets and chocolate

confederacy /kənˈfedᵊrəsi/ (*also* **confederation** /kənˌfedəˈreɪʃən/) *noun* [C] an organization of smaller groups who have joined together for business or political purposes

confer /kənˈfɜːʳ/ *verb* **conferring**, *past* **conferred** **1** [I] to discuss something with other people before making a decision *I'll need to **confer with** my lawyers.* **2** [T] *formal* to give someone something, especially an official title, an honour, or an advantage

WORD PARTNERS FOR ***conference***

attend/hold a conference • a conference **on** sth • **at** a conference • a conference **centre** • **a sales** conference

conference /ˈkɒnfᵊrᵊns/ *noun* [C] **1** a large, formal meeting, often lasting a few days, where people discuss their work, politics, subjects they are studying, etc *the annual **sales conference*** **2** a small, private meeting for discussion of a particular subject ➲See also: **press conference**.

ˈconference ˌcall *noun* [C] a telephone call among three or more people in different places

confess /kənˈfes/ *verb* [I, T] **1** to admit that you have done something wrong or something that you feel guilty about [+ to + doing sth] *The man has confessed to stealing the painting.* ○ *Rawlinson finally **confessed to** the murder.*

2 to tell a priest or God about all the wrong things that you have done

confession /kənˈfeʃən/ noun [C, U] **1** when you admit that you have done something wrong or illegal *Following his arrest, Sutcliffe has made a full confession to the police.* **2** when someone tells a priest all the wrong things they have done *to go to confession*

confetti /kənˈfeti/ noun [U] small pieces of coloured paper that you throw when celebrating something such as a marriage

confidant, confidante /ˈkɒnfɪdænt/ noun [C] a person you can talk to about your feelings and secrets

confide /kənˈfaɪd/ verb [I, T] to tell a secret to someone who you trust not to tell anyone else [+ that] *Holly confided to me that she was ill.*
confide in sb to tell someone who you trust about things that are secret or personal

┌─────────────────────────────────────┐
│ 🧩 WORD PARTNERS FOR **confidence** │
└─────────────────────────────────────┘

1 grow in/lack/lose confidence • sth gives you confidence • do sth with confidence • a lack of confidence
2 express/lose/restore confidence (in sth) • have [complete/every/little/no] confidence in sb/sth • consumer/public confidence • confidence in sth

⚬**confidence** /ˈkɒnfɪdəns/ noun **1** [ABILITY] [U] when you are certain of your ability to do things well *He's a good student, but he lacks confidence.* ○ [+ to do sth] *His training has given him the confidence to deal with any problem that arises.* **2** [TRUST] [U] trusting someone's ability or believing that something will produce good results *Kate's new to the job, but I've got every confidence in her.* **3** [SECRET] [C] something secret that you tell someone *to exchange confidences* **4 in confidence** If you tell something to someone in confidence, you do not want them to tell anyone else.

⚬**confident** /ˈkɒnfɪdənt/ adjective **1** certain about your ability to do things well *a confident grin* ○ *He feels confident of winning.* **2** being certain that something will happen [+ (that)] *Doctors are confident that she'll recover.* ● confidently adverb ⇒See also: self-confident.

confidential /ˌkɒnfɪˈdenʃəl/ adjective secret, especially in an official situation *Of course, these documents are strictly confidential.* ● confidentially adverb ● confidentiality /ˌkɒnfɪdenʃiˈæləti/ noun [U]

confine /kənˈfaɪn/ verb [T] to prevent someone from leaving a place or to prevent something from spreading [often passive] *He was confined to a prison cell for several days.*
be confined to sth/sb to only exist in a particular area or group of people *The flooding was confined to the basement.*
confine sb/sth to sth to limit an activity *Please confine your discussion to the topic.*

confined /kənˈfaɪnd/ adjective [always before noun] A confined space is very small.

confinement /kənˈfaɪnmənt/ noun [U] when someone is kept in a room or area, usually by force ⇒See also: solitary confinement.

confines /ˈkɒnfaɪnz/ noun [plural] the outer limits of edges of something

confirm /kənˈfɜːm/ verb [T] **1** to say or show that something is true [+ (that)] *His wife confirmed that he'd left the house at 9 to make an arrangement certain Flights should be confirmed 48 hours before departure.* **3 be confirmed** to become a member of the Christian Church at a special ceremony

confirmation /ˌkɒnfəˈmeɪʃən/ noun [C, U] **1** an announcement or proof that something is true or certain *You'll receive written confirmation of your reservation within five days.* **2** a special ceremony in which someone becomes a full member of the Christian Church

confirmed /kənˈfɜːmd/ adjective a confirmed atheist/bachelor/pessimist, etc someone who has behaved in a particular way for a long time and is not likely to change

confiscate /ˈkɒnfɪskeɪt/ verb [T] to take something away from someone, especially as a punishment ● confiscation /ˌkɒnfɪˈskeɪʃən/ noun [C, U]

┌─────────────────────────────────────┐
│ 🧩 WORD PARTNERS FOR **conflict** │
└─────────────────────────────────────┘

resolve a conflict • be in/come into conflict with sb • a conflict between sb and sb • a conflict over sth • an area of/source of conflict

conflict¹ /ˈkɒnflɪkt/ noun [C, U] **1** [DISAGREEMENT] serious disagreement *The Government was in conflict with the unions over pay.* ○ *The peasants often came into conflict with the landowners.* **2** [FIGHTING] fighting between groups or countries *armed conflict* **3** [DIFFERENCE] when two or more different things cannot easily exist together *the conflict between science and religion* **4 a conflict of interest** a situation where someone cannot make fair decisions because they are influenced by something

conflict² /kənˈflɪkt/ verb [I] If things such as beliefs, needs, or facts conflict, they are very different and cannot easily exist together or both be true. *Her views on raising children conflict with mine.* ○ *There were conflicting accounts of how the fight started.*

conflicted /kənˈflɪktɪd/ adjective [never before noun] confused because you have two feelings or opinions about something that are opposite

conform /kənˈfɔːm/ verb [I] to behave in the way that most other people behave
conform to/with sth to obey a rule or to do things in a traditional way *All our toys conform with safety standards.*

conformity /kənˈfɔːməti/ noun [U] **1** behaving in the way that most other people behave **2 conformity to/with sth** formal following rules or traditional ways of doing things

confound /kənˈfaʊnd/ verb [T] If something confounds someone, it makes them surprised and confused, because they cannot explain it. *The growth in the economy continues to confound the experts.*

confront /kənˈfrʌnt/ verb [T] **1** [ACCUSE] to tell someone something, or show them something to try to make them admit they have done something wrong *Confronted with the evidence, she broke down and confessed.* **2 be confronted by/with sth** to be in a difficult situation, or to be shown something which may cause difficulties *We are confronted by the possibility of war.* **3** FRIGHTEN to stand in front of someone in a frightening way *He was confronted by two masked men.* **4** DEAL WITH to see that a problem exists and try to deal with it *First, they must confront their addiction.*

confrontation /ˌkɒnfrʌnˈteɪʃ⁰n/ *noun* [C, U] a fight or argument

confrontational /ˌkɒnfrʌnˈteɪʃ⁰n⁰l/ *adjective* intentionally causing fighting or an argument *a confrontational style of management*

◦ᴀ**confuse** /kənˈfjuːz/ *verb* [T] **1** to make someone unable to think clearly or understand something *These advertisements simply confused the public.* **2** to think that one person or thing is another person or thing *I don't see how anyone could confuse me with my mother!*

◦ᴀ**confused** /kənˈfjuːzd/ *adjective* **1** unable to think clearly or to understand something *Sorry, I'm completely confused.* ○ *The politicians themselves are confused about what to do.* **2** not clear *The witnesses gave confused accounts of what happened.*

confusing /kənˈfjuːzɪŋ/ *adjective* difficult to understand *I found the instructions very confusing.*

WORD PARTNERS FOR **confusion**

sth **causes/creates/leads to** confusion • confusion **surrounds** sth • do sth **in** confusion • **widespread** confusion • confusion **about/over** sth

◦ᴀ**confusion** /kənˈfjuːʒ⁰n/ *noun* **1** NOT UNDERSTAND [C, U] when people do not understand what is happening or what they should do *There was a lot of confusion about what was actually going on.* **2** THOUGHT [U] a feeling of not being able to think clearly *He could see the confusion on Marion's face.* **3** BETWEEN SIMILAR THINGS [U] when you think that one person or thing is another **4** SITUATION [U] a situation which is confusing because there is a lot of noise and activity *In the confusion, several prisoners tried to escape.*

congeal /kənˈdʒiːl/ *verb* [I] If a liquid congeals, it becomes thick and almost solid. *congealed fat*

congenial /kənˈdʒiːniəl/ *adjective formal* pleasant and friendly *congenial company*

congenital /kənˈdʒenɪt⁰l/ *adjective* Congenital diseases or problems are ones that people have from when they are born. *a congenital heart defect*

congested /kənˈdʒestɪd/ *adjective* full or blocked, especially with traffic *The roads are very congested.*

congestion /kənˈdʒestʃ⁰n/ *noun* [U] when something is full or blocked, especially with traffic *traffic congestion*

conglomerate /kənˈɡlɒm⁰rət/ *noun* [C] a large company that is made up of several smaller companies

congratulate /kənˈɡrætʃʊleɪt/ *verb* [T] to tell someone that you are happy because they have done something good or something good has happened to them *Did you congratulate Cathy on her engagement?*

congratulations /kənˌɡrætʃʊˈleɪʃ⁰nz/ *exclamation* something that you say when you want to congratulate someone *Congratulations on doing an outstanding job.* ○ *I hear you're getting married. Congratulations!*

congregate /ˈkɒŋɡrɪɡeɪt/ *verb* [I] to come together in a group *Young people congregated on street corners.*

congregation /ˌkɒŋɡrɪˈɡeɪʃ⁰n/ *noun* [group] a group of people meeting to worship in church

congress /ˈkɒŋɡres/ *noun* **1** [C] a large meeting of the members of one or more organizations *an international congress on art history* **2 Congress** the group of people who make laws in the United States. Congress consists of the Senate and the House of Representatives.

congressional /kənˈɡreʃ⁰n⁰l/ *adjective* [always before noun] relating to the United States Congress *a congressional committee*

congressman, congresswoman /ˈkɒŋɡresmən, ˈkɒŋɡreswʊmən/ *noun* [C] *plural* **congressmen** or **congresswomen** a man or woman who is a member of the United States Congress *a congressman from Ohio*

conical /ˈkɒnɪk⁰l/ *adjective* Conical objects have a wide, round base, sloping sides and a pointed top.

conifer /ˈkɒnɪfəʳ/ *noun* [C] a tree with cones (= hard, brown, oval objects) and thin green leaves that stay green all winter

conjecture /kənˈdʒektʃəʳ/ *noun* [C, U] *formal* guessing about something without real evidence *Exactly what happened that night is still a matter for conjecture.* • **conjecture** *verb* [I, T] *formal* [+ (that)] *Some people conjectured that it was an attempt to save money.*

conjugal /ˈkɒndʒʊɡ⁰l/ *adjective formal* relating to marriage

conjugate /ˈkɒndʒʊɡeɪt/ *verb* [T] to add different endings to a verb in order to produce all its different forms • **conjugation** /ˌkɒndʒʊˈɡeɪʃ⁰n/ *noun* [C, U]

conjunction /kənˈdʒʌŋkʃ⁰n/ *noun* **1** [C] A word that is used to connect phrases or parts of a sentence. For example the words 'and', 'because', and 'although' are conjunctions. **2 in conjunction with sth/sb** working, used, or happening with something or someone else

conjure /ˈkʌndʒəʳ/ *verb*

conjure sth up 1 to make a picture or idea appear in someone's mind *Familiar tunes can help us conjure up memories of the past.* **2** to make something in a quick and clever way, especially food

conjurer /ˈkʌndʒərəʳ/ *noun* [C] another spelling of conjuror

conjuring /ˈkʌndʒərɪŋ/ *noun* [U] performing magic to entertain people *a conjuring trick*

conjuror /ˈkʌndʒərəʳ/ *noun* [C] a person who performs magic to entertain people

conman /ˈkɒnmæn/ *noun* [C] a man who tricks

people into giving him money or valuable things

o▪**connect** /kəˈnekt/ *verb* **1** JOIN [I, T] to join two things or places together *Ferries connect the mainland with the islands.* ○ *Connect up the printer to your computer.* **2** INVOLVE [T] to see or show that two or more people or things are involved with each other *There is no evidence to connect him with the crime.* **3** TRAVEL [I] If buses, trains, aircraft, etc connect, they arrive at a particular time so that passengers can get off one and onto another. *Can you get me a connecting flight?* **4** TELEPHONE [T] to make it possible for two people to talk to each other on the telephone ⊃Opposite **disconnect**.

connected /kəˈnektɪd/ *adjective* **1** If people or things are connected, there is a relationship between them. *The hospital is connected to the University of Rochester.* ○ *He remained closely connected with the Metropolitan Museum until his death.* ⊃Opposite **unconnected**. **2** If two things are connected, they are joined together. *The Red Sea is connected to the Mediterranean by the Suez Canal.* ⊃Opposite **disconnected** ⊃See also: **well-connected**.

┌─────────────────────────────┐
│ ▪▪▪ WORD PARTNERS FOR *connection* │
│   │
│ have a/no connection with sb/sth • a │
│ close/direct connection • a connection be- │
│ tween sth and sth • a connection with sth │
└─────────────────────────────┘

o▪**connection** /kəˈnekʃ⁰n/ *noun* **1** RELATIONSHIP [C, U] a relationship between people or things *The connection between smoking and heart disease is well known.* ○ *He denied having any connection with the terrorists.* **2** JOINING THINGS [C, U] something that joins things together *Many companies now offer free connection to the Internet.* **3** TRAVEL [C] a train, bus, or aircraft that leaves a short time after another arrives, so that people can continue their journey *The train was half an hour late and I missed my connection.* **4** in connection with used to say what something is about *A man has been arrested in connection with last month's murder.*

connections /kəˈnekʃ⁰nz/ *noun* [plural] important or powerful people who you know and who will help you *He has a lot of connections in Washington.*

connive /kəˈnaɪv/ *verb* [I] to work secretly to do something wrong or illegal, or to allow something wrong or illegal to happen *Journalists accused the government of conniving in drug smuggling.*

connoisseur /ˌkɒnəˈsɜːʳ/ *noun* [C] someone who knows a lot about and enjoys good food, wine, art, etc

connotation /ˌkɒnəˈteɪʃ⁰n/ *noun* [C, U] the feelings or ideas that words give in addition to their meanings *The word 'second-hand' has connotations of poor quality.*

conquer /ˈkɒŋkəʳ/ *verb* **1** [I, T] to take control of a country or to defeat people by war *Peru was conquered by the Spanish in 1532.* **2** [T] to succeed in stopping or dealing with a bad feeling or a difficult problem *He has finally conquered his fear of spiders.*

conqueror /ˈkɒŋk⁰rəʳ/ *noun* [C] someone who has conquered a country or its people

conquest /ˈkɒŋkwest/ *noun* [C, U] when someone takes control of a country, area, or situation *the Roman conquest of Britain*

conscience /ˈkɒnʃ⁰ns/ *noun* **1** [C, U] the part of you that makes you feel guilty when you have behaved badly *a guilty conscience* ○ *My conscience is clear* (= I do not feel guilty) *because I've done nothing wrong.* **2** be on your conscience If something is on your conscience, it is making you feel guilty.

conscientious /ˌkɒnʃiˈenʃəs/ *adjective* always doing your work with a lot of care *a conscientious student* • **conscientiously** *adverb*

conscientious objector /ˌkɒnʃi‚enʃəsəbˈsʒektəʳ/ *noun* [C] someone who refuses to work in the armed forces because they think war is wrong

conscious /ˈkɒnʃəs/ *adjective* **1** be conscious of/that to know that something is present or that something is happening *I'm very conscious that a lot of people disagree with me.* **2** a conscious decision/choice/effort, etc a decision, choice, effort, etc that you make intentionally *Did you make a conscious decision to lose weight?* ⊃Opposite **subconscious**. **3** awake and able to think and notice things *He's still conscious but he's very badly injured.* ⊃Opposite **unconscious**. • **consciously** *adverb* ⊃See also: **self-conscious**.

-conscious /ˈkɒnʃəs/ *suffix* used at the end of words to mean 'thinking that something is important' *a safety-conscious mother* ○ *fashion-conscious teenagers*

consciousness /ˈkɒnʃəsnəs/ *noun* **1** [U] when someone is awake and can think and notice things *He lost consciousness* (= stopped being conscious) *for several minutes.* ○ *I want to be here when she regains consciousness* (= becomes conscious again). **2** [no plural] when someone knows about something *There's a growing consciousness about environmental issues among young people.*

conscript¹ /ˈkɒnskrɪpt/ *noun* [C] someone who has been made to join the army

conscript² /kənˈskrɪpt/ *verb* [T] to make someone join the army [often passive] *During World War I, he was conscripted into the Russian army.*

conscription /kənˈskrɪpʃ⁰n/ *noun* [U] a system in which people are made to join the army

consecrate /ˈkɒnsɪkreɪt/ *verb* [T] to make a place or object holy in a religious ceremony • **consecration** /ˌkɒnsɪˈkreɪʃ⁰n/ *noun* [U] *a consecration ceremony*

consecutive /kənˈsekjʊtɪv/ *adjective* Consecutive events, numbers, or periods of time come one after the other. *the third consecutive day of rain* • **consecutively** *adverb*

consensus /kənˈsensəs/ *noun* [U, no plural] when all the people in a group agree about something *to reach a consensus* ○ *The general consensus is that we should wait and see what happens.*

consent¹ /kənˈsent/ *noun* [U] **1** permission for

someone to do something *You can't come without your parents' consent.* **2 by common consent** *UK* used to say that everyone agrees about something *He is, by common consent, the most talented actor in Hollywood.*

consent² /kən'sent/ *verb* [I] to agree to do something, or to allow someone to do something [+ to do sth] *They eventually consented to let us enter.*

WORD PARTNERS FOR *consequence*

face/live with/suffer the consequences • **as a consequence (of** sth) • a **direct** consequence • **devastating/dire/disastrous/ serious** consequences • the consequences **of** sth

---

◦▪**consequence** /'kɒnsɪkwəns/ *noun* **1** [C] the result of an action or situation, especially a bad result *The ship capsized, with disastrous consequences.* ○ *If you make him angry, you'll have to suffer the consequences.* **2 of little/no consequence** *formal* not important *The money was of little consequence to Tony.*

consequent /'kɒnsɪkwənt/ *adjective* [always before noun] *formal* happening as a result of something *the closure of the factory and the consequent loss of 400 jobs*

consequently /'kɒnsɪkwəntli/ *adverb* as a result *She was the child of two models and, consequently, she was very tall.*

conservation /ˌkɒnsə'veɪʃən/ *noun* [U] **1** the protection of nature *wildlife conservation* ○ *conservation groups* **2** when you are careful not to waste energy, water, etc

conservationist /ˌkɒnsə'veɪʃənɪst/ *noun* [C] someone who believes that people should protect nature

conservatism /kən'sɜːvətɪzəm/ *noun* [U] conservative actions and beliefs

conservative /kən'sɜːvətɪv/ *adjective* **1** not trusting sudden changes or new ideas *Older people tend to be very conservative.* **2 a conservative estimate/guess** a guess about a number or amount that is probably lower than the true number or amount

Conservative /kən'sɜːvətɪv/ *noun* [C] someone who supports the Conservative Party in the UK *the Conservative candidate/MP*

the Con'servative ˌParty *noun* [group] one of the three main political parties in the UK

conservatory /kən'sɜːvətri/ *noun* [C] a room attached to a house that has windows all around it and a glass roof

conserve /kən'sɜːv/ *verb* [T] **1** to use something in a way that does not waste it *Insulating the walls will help to conserve heat.* **2** to prevent harm or damage to animals or places

◦▪**consider** /kən'sɪdər/ *verb* **1** [T] to think carefully about a decision or something you might do *Have you considered surgery?* ○ [+ doing sth] *We're considering buying a new car.* **2** [T] to think about particular facts when you are making a decision about something *If you buy an old house, you have to consider the cost of repairs.* **3 consider sb/sth (to be) sth; consider that** to have a particular opinion about someone or

something [often reflexive] *I don't consider myself to be a great athlete.*

considerable /kən'sɪdərəbl/ *adjective* large or important enough to have an effect *a considerable amount of money* ○ *The damage has been considerable.* • **considerably** *adverb Rates of pay vary considerably.*

considerate /kən'sɪdərət/ *adjective* kind and helpful *a polite and considerate child* ⊃Opposite **inconsiderate.**

WORD PARTNERS FOR *consideration*

1 an **important/the main/a major** consideration • **environmental / financial / political** considerations
2 careful/serious consideration • be **under** consideration • be **worthy of** consideration

---

consideration /kənˌsɪdər'eɪʃən/ *noun* **1** [IMPORTANT FACT] [C] something that you have to think about when you make decisions or plans *Safety is our main consideration.* **2** [CAREFUL THOUGHT] [U] when you think about something very carefully *After careful consideration, we have decided to offer you the job.* ○ *Several options are under consideration* (= being considered). **3** [KINDNESS] [U] when you are kind to people or think about their feelings *They always treated me with consideration.* **4 take sth into consideration** to think about something when you make a decision or plan

considered /kən'sɪdəd/ *adjective* **1** [always before noun] A considered opinion or decision is based on careful thought. *It is our considered opinion that he should resign.* **2 all things considered** used when you are giving your opinion about something after thinking carefully about all the facts *All things considered, I think we made the right choice.*

considering /kən'sɪdərɪŋ/ *preposition, conjunction* used for saying that you have a particular opinion about something, because of a particular fact about it *She's fairly fit considering her age.* ○ *Considering she'd only been there once before, she did well to find the way.*

consign /kən'saɪn/ *verb*
consign sb/sth to sth *formal* to get rid of someone or something or to put them in an unpleasant place or situation *They were consigned to a life of poverty.*

consignment /kən'saɪnmənt/ *noun* [C] an amount of goods that is being sent somewhere *a ship carrying a small consignment of rice*

consist /kən'sɪst/ *verb*
consist of sth to be formed or made from two or more things *a dessert consisting of fruit and cream*

consistency /kən'sɪstənsi/ *noun* **1** [U] when someone always behaves or performs in a similar way or when something always happens in a similar way *The team has won a few matches but lacks consistency.* **2** [C, U] how thick or smooth a liquid is *Beat the mixture to a smooth consistency.*

consistent /kən'sɪstənt/ *adjective* **1** always behaving or happening in a similar, usually positive, way *consistent effort/improvement* **2 consistent with sth** *formal* having the same principles as something else, or agreeing with other facts *His account of events is entirely consistent with the video evidence.* • **consistently** *adverb The President has consistently denied the rumours.*

consolation /ˌkɒnsə'leɪʃᵊn/ *noun* [C, U] something that makes you feel better about a bad situation *If it's any consolation, I failed my driving test too.*

console¹ /kən'səʊl/ *verb* [T] to make someone who is sad feel better *I tried to console her but she just kept crying.*

console² /'kɒnsəʊl/ *noun* [C] an object that contains the controls for a piece of equipment *a video game console*

consolidate /kən'sɒlɪdeɪt/ *verb* 1 [I, T] to make sure that you become more powerful, or that success and achievements continue strongly *It will take him some time to consolidate his position in the banking world.* 2 [T] to combine several things, especially businesses, so that they become more effective, or to be combined in this way *He consolidated his businesses into one large company.* • **consolidation** /kənˌsɒlɪ'deɪʃᵊn/ *noun* [U]

consonant /'kɒnsᵊnənt/ *noun* [C] a letter of the alphabet that is not a vowel

consort /kən'sɔːt/ *verb*
consort with sb to spend time with a bad person *They claimed he had been consorting with drug dealers.*

consortium /kən'sɔːtiəm/ *noun* [C] *plural* **consortiums** or **consortia** an organization consisting of several businesses or banks *an international consortium of airlines*

conspicuous /kən'spɪkjuəs/ *adjective* very easy to notice *His army uniform made him very conspicuous.* • **conspicuously** *adverb His wife was conspicuously absent.*

conspiracy /kən'spɪrəsi/ *noun* [C, U] when a group of people secretly plan to do something bad or illegal [+ to do sth] *a conspiracy to overthrow the government*

conspirator /kən'spɪrətəʳ/ *noun* [C] someone who secretly plans with other people to do something bad or illegal

conspire /kən'spaɪəʳ/ *verb* 1 [I] to join with other people to secretly plan to do something bad or illegal [+ to do sth] *He was convicted of conspiring to blow up the World Trade Center.* ○ *The king accused his advisers of conspiring against him.* 2 **conspire against sb; conspire to do sth** If events or a situation conspire against you, they cause problems for you. *Circumstances had conspired to ruin her plans.*

constable /'kʌnstəbl/ *noun* [C] a British police officer of the lowest rank

constant /'kɒnstənt/ *adjective* 1 happening a lot or all the time *machines that are in constant use* 2 staying at the same level *The temperature remained constant.* • **constantly** *adverb He's constantly changing his mind.*

constellation /ˌkɒnstə'leɪʃᵊn/ *noun* [C] a group of stars

consternation /ˌkɒnstə'neɪʃᵊn/ *noun* [U] a feeling of shock or worry

constipated /'kɒnstɪpeɪtɪd/ *adjective* unable to empty your bowels as often as you should

constipation /ˌkɒnstɪ'peɪʃᵊn/ *noun* [U] when you are constipated

constituency /kən'stɪtjuənsi/ *noun* [C] an area of a country which elects someone to represent it in the government, or the people who live there

constituent /kən'stɪtjuənt/ *noun* [C] 1 one of the parts or substances that something is made of *Methane is the main constituent of natural gas.* 2 someone who lives in a particular constituency

constitute /'kɒnstɪtjuːt/ *verb* [T] to be or form something *This defeat constitutes a real setback for their championship hopes.*

constitution /ˌkɒnstɪ'tjuːʃᵊn/ *noun* [C] 1 the set of laws and principles that a country's government must obey *the US Constitution* ○ *Britain has no written constitution.* 2 the state of someone's health *a strong/weak constitution*

constitutional /ˌkɒnstɪ'tjuːʃᵊnᵊl/ *adjective* relating to the constitution of a country *a constitutional crisis*

constrain /kən'streɪn/ *verb* [T] to control something by limiting it *regulations that constrain industry* ○ [often passive] *I'm constrained by decisions made in the past.*

constraint /kən'streɪnt/ *noun* [C] something that limits what you can do *budget constraints* ○ *There are constraints on the medicines doctors can prescribe.*

constrict /kən'strɪkt/ *verb* 1 [T] to limit someone's freedom to do what they want to or be the way they want to *His creativity was constricted by the political regime he lived under.* 2 [I, T] to become narrower or tighter, or to make something narrower or tighter *The blood vessels constricted.* • **constriction** /kən'strɪkʃᵊn/ *noun* [U]

construct /kən'strʌkt/ *verb* [T] to build something from several parts *The building was constructed in 1930.*

construction /kən'strʌkʃᵊn/ *noun* 1 [BUILDING WORK] [U] the work of building houses, offices, bridges, etc *railway construction* ○ *construction work* 2 [LARGE BUILDING] [C] something large that is built *a large steel construction* 3 [WORDS] [C] The construction of a sentence or phrase is the way the words are arranged.

constructive /kən'strʌktɪv/ *adjective* helpful or useful *constructive advice/criticism* • **constructively** *adverb*

construe /kən'struː/ *verb* [T] construing, *past* construed to understand something in a particular way *Her comments could be construed as patronizing.*

consul /'kɒnsᵊl/ *noun* [C] someone whose job is to work in a foreign country taking care of the people from their own country who go or live there

consular /'kɒnsjʊləʳ/ *adjective* [always before noun] relating to a consul or a consulate *consular officials*

consulate /'kɒnsjʊlət/ *noun* [C] the offices

where a consul works *the Cuban consulate in Mexico City*

consult /kən'sʌlt/ *verb* [T] **1** to go to a particular person or book to get information or advice *For more information, consult your travel agent.* **2** to discuss something with someone before you make a decision *Why didn't you consult me about this?*

consultancy /kən'sʌltᵊnsi/ *noun* **1** [C] a company that gives advice on subjects it knows a lot about *a management/recruitment consultancy* **2** [U] the activity of giving advice on a particular subject

consultant /kən'sʌltᵊnt/ *noun* [C] **1** someone who advises people about a particular subject *a tax consultant* **2** UK a hospital doctor who is an expert in a particular area of medicine

consultation /ˌkɒnsᵊl'teɪʃᵊn/ *noun* **1** [C] a meeting to discuss something or to get advice *a medical consultation* **2** [U] when you discuss something with someone in order to get their advice or opinion about it *After consultation with his lawyers, he decided to abandon the case.*

consultative /kən'sʌltətɪv/ *adjective* A consultative group or document gives advice about something.

consume /kən'sjuːm/ *verb* [T] **1** USE to use something such as a product, energy, or fuel *These lights don't consume much electricity.* **2** EAT OR DRINK *formal* to eat or drink something **3** be consumed with/by sth to have so much of a feeling that it affects everything you do *a dancer consumed by ambition* **4** FIRE If fire consumes something, it completely destroys it.

WORD PARTNERS FOR **consumer**

consumer **choice/confidence/demand/protection/spending**

consumer /kən'sjuːməʳ/ *noun* [C] someone who buys or uses goods or services *These price cuts are good news for consumers.*

consumerism /kən'sjuːmərɪzᵊm/ *noun* [U] buying and selling things, especially when this is an important part of a society's activities

consummate¹ /'kɒnsəmeɪt/ *verb* [T] to make a marriage or relationship complete by having sex ● consummation /ˌkɒnsə'meɪʃᵊn/ *noun* [U]

consummate² /kən'sʌmət, 'kɒnsəmət/ *adjective* [always before noun] *formal* having great skill *a consummate professional* ○ *consummate ease/skill*

consumption /kən'sʌmʃᵊn/ *noun* [U] **1** the amount of something that someone uses, eats, or drinks *China's total energy consumption* **2** when someone uses, eats, or drinks something *products sold for personal consumption*

WORD PARTNERS FOR **contact**

be in/get in/keep in/stay in contact (with sb) ● lose/make contact (with sb) ● have no contact with sb ● close/regular contact

contact¹ /'kɒntækt/ *noun* **1** COMMUNICATION [U] when you communicate with someone, especially by speaking to them *We keep in close contact with our grandparents.* ○ *Jo and I are determined not to lose contact.* ○ *"Have you been in contact with Andrew recently?" "Only by telephone."* ○ *I'm still in contact with her - we write a couple of times a year.* **2** TOUCH [U] when two people or things are touching each other *She dislikes any kind of physical contact.* ○ *Wash your hands if they come into contact with chemicals.* ○ *Have you been in contact with (= touched or been very near) anyone with the disease?* **3** PERSON [C] someone you know who may be able to help you because of their job or position *business contacts* ○ *If you need more stationery, I've got a good contact in a local printing firm.* **4** EYE [C] (*also* contact lens) a small piece of plastic that you put on your eye to make you see more clearly ⊃See also: **eye contact**.

contact² /'kɒntækt/ *verb* [T] to telephone, email or write to someone *I've been trying to contact you for days.*

'contact ˌlens UK (US ˌcontact 'lens) *noun* [C] a small piece of plastic that you put on your eye to make you see more clearly *I usually wear contact lenses, but I sometimes wear glasses when my eyes are tired.*

contagious /kən'teɪdʒəs/ *adjective* **1** A contagious disease is one that you can get if you touch someone who has it. *The infection is highly contagious, so don't let anyone else use your towel.* **2** A contagious feeling spreads quickly amongst people. *Her excitement was contagious.*

○┅**contain** /kən'teɪn/ *verb* [T] **1** INSIDE If one thing contains another, it has it inside it. *a box containing a diamond ring* **2** PART to have something as a part *Does this drink contain alcohol?* **3** CONTROL to control something by stopping it from spreading *The police were unable to contain the fighting.* **4** EMOTION to control your emotions *He could barely contain his anger.* ○ [often reflexive] *I could not contain myself any longer.* ○ *She could no longer contain her anger and shouted at him uncontrollably.*

COMMON LEARNER ERROR

contain or **include**?

Use **contain** to talk about objects which have something else inside them.

This folder contains important letters.

This soup contains garlic and onions.

Use **include** to say that something or someone is a part of something else.

The team includes two new players.

The price of the ticket includes insurance and tax.

container

a box of cereal

a bag of crisps

a carton of milk

a tube of toothpaste

a bag of peanuts

a can of drink

a tin of sardines *UK*, a can of sardines *US*

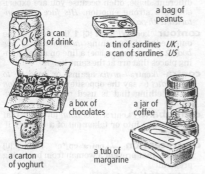

a box of chocolates

a jar of coffee

a carton of yoghurt

a tub of margarine

container /kənˈteɪnəʳ/ *noun* [C] an object such as a box or a bottle that is used for holding something

contaminate /kənˈtæmɪneɪt/ *verb* [T] to make something dirty or poisonous *contaminated drinking water* • **contamination** /kənˌtæmɪˈneɪʃən/ *noun* [U]

contemplate /ˈkɒntəmpleɪt/ *verb* [T] to think about something for a long time or in a serious way [+ **doing sth**] *I'm contemplating changing my name.* ○ *He even contemplated suicide.* • **contemplation** /ˌkɒntəmˈpleɪʃən/ *noun* [U]

contemporary¹ /kənˈtempᵊrᵊri, kənˈtempəri/ *adjective* **1** of the present time *contemporary music* **2** [always before noun] existing or happening at the same time as something *Most contemporary accounts of the event have been destroyed.*

contemporary² /kənˈtempᵊrᵊri, kənˈtempəri/ *noun* [C] Someone's contemporaries are the people who live at the same time as them. *Shakespeare and his contemporaries*

WORD PARTNERS FOR **contempt**

treat sb/sth **with** contempt • **deep/open/ utter** contempt • **have nothing but** contempt **for** sb/sth • sb's contempt **for** sb/sth

contempt /kənˈtempt/ *noun* **1** [U] a strong feeling that you do not respect someone or something *He has utter contempt for anyone with power.* **2 contempt of court** behaviour that is illegal because it does not obey the rules of a law court

contemptible /kənˈtemptəbl/ *adjective* ex-

tremely bad, because of being dishonest or cruel

contemptuous /kənˈtemptʃuəs/ *adjective* showing contempt • **contemptuously** *adverb*

contend /kənˈtend/ *verb* **1** [T] *formal* to say that something is true [+ **(that)**] *His lawyers contend that he is telling the truth.* **2** [I] to compete with someone to try to win something *one of the groups contending for power*
contend with sth to have to deal with a difficult or unpleasant situation *I have enough problems of my own to contend with.*

contender /kənˈtendəʳ/ *noun* [C] someone who competes with other people to try to win something *a leading contender for an Oscar*

content¹ /ˈkɒntent/ *noun* [no plural] **1** the information or ideas that are talked about in a book, speech, film, etc *The content of the article was controversial.* **2** the amount of a particular substance that something contains *Most soft drinks have a high sugar content.*

content² /kənˈtent/ *adjective* happy or satisfied *Not content with second place, Jeff played only to win.* ○ [+ **to do sth**] *I was content to stay home and read.*

content³ /kənˈtent/ *verb*
content yourself with sth to do something or have something although it is not exactly what you want *Since it rained we had to content ourselves with playing cards.*

contented /kənˈtentɪd/ *adjective* satisfied, or making you feel satisfied ⊃Opposite **discontented**. • **contentedly** *adverb*

contention /kənˈtenʃən/ *noun* **1** OPINION [C] *formal* a belief or opinion *There's a general contention that too much violence is shown on TV.* **2** COMPETITION [U] when people or groups compete for something *Johnson is back in contention for the championships.* **3** DISAGREEMENT [U] arguments and disagreements ⊃See also: a **bone¹** of contention.

contentious /kənˈtenʃəs/ *adjective* likely to make people argue *a contentious issue*

contentment /kənˈtentmənt/ *noun* [U] the feeling of being happy or satisfied

contents /ˈkɒntents/ *noun* [plural] **1** THINGS INSIDE all of the things that are contained inside something *Please empty out the contents of your pockets.* **2** INFORMATION the information or ideas that are written in a book, letter, document, etc *the contents of his will* **3** BOOK a list in a book that tells you what different parts the book contains *a table of contents*

WORD PARTNERS FOR **contest**

be in/enter a contest • **win** a contest • a **close** contest • a contest **between** sb and sb • a contest **for** sth

contest¹ /ˈkɒntest/ *noun* [C] a competition or election

contest² /kənˈtest/ *verb* [T] **1** to say formally that something is wrong or unfair and try to have it changed *Mr Hughes went back to court to contest the verdict.* **2** to compete for something *a keenly contested match*

contestant /kənˈtestᵊnt/ *noun* [C] someone who

competes in a contest

context /'kɒntekst/ *noun* [C, U] **1** all the facts, opinions, situations, etc relating to a particular thing or event *This small battle is important in the context of Scottish history.* **2** other words that were said or written at the same time as the word or words you are talking about *Taken out of context, her remark sounded like an insult.*

o⊸**continent** /'kɒntɪnənt/ *noun* [C] one of the seven main areas of land on the Earth, such as Asia, Africa, or Europe

continental /ˌkɒntɪ'nentəl/ *adjective* relating to a continent *the continental US*

Continental /ˌkɒntɪ'nentəl/ *adjective mainly UK* relating to Europe, but not Britain

,continental 'breakfast *noun* [C] a breakfast (= morning meal) consisting of fruit juice, coffee, and bread

the Continent /'kɒntɪnənt/ *noun UK* the main part of land in Europe, not including Britain

contingency /kən'tɪndʒənsi/ *noun* [C] **1** an event or situation that might happen in the future, especially one which could cause problems *a contingency fund/plan* (= money or a plan that can be used if there are problems) **2** a contingency fee money that lawyers (= people who advise people about the law and deal with legal situations) charge, which is a share of what the person they represent has won

contingent¹ /kən'tɪndʒ³nt/ *noun* [group] **1** a group of people from the same country, organization, etc who are part of a much larger group **2** a group of soldiers who are part of a larger military group

contingent² /kən'tɪndʒ³nt/ *adjective* **contingent on sth** depending on something else in order to happen *Buying the new house was contingent on selling the old one.*

continual /kən'tɪnjuəl/ *adjective* happening again and again over a long period of time *I can't work with these continual interruptions.* • **continually** *adverb* Dad *continually complains about money.*

continuation /kənˌtɪnju'eɪʃ³n/ *noun* **1** [C] something that comes after an event, situation, or thing to make it continue or go further *Today's meeting will be a continuation of yesterday's talks.* **2** [U, no plural] when something continues to exist, happen, or be used *the continuation of their partnership*

o⊸**continue** /kən'tɪnjuː/ *verb* continuing, *past* continued **1** [I, T] to keep happening, existing, or doing something [+ to do sth] *It continued to snow heavily for three days.* ○ *Ann continued working part-time until June.* **2** [T] to start doing or saying something again, after stopping for a short period *We'll have to continue this discussion tomorrow.* **3** continue along/down/up, etc to go further in a particular direction

continued /kən'tɪnjuːd/ *adjective* [always before noun] still happening, existing, or done *his continued success*

continuity /ˌkɒntɪ'njuːəti/ *noun* [U] the state of

continuing for a long period of time without being changed or stopped

continuous¹ /kən'tɪnjuəs/ *adjective* **1** happening or existing without stopping *continuous pain* ○ *ten years of continuous service in the army* **2** The continuous form of a verb is used to show that an action is continuing to happen. The sentence 'He was eating lunch.' is in the continuous form. • **continuously** *adverb* Their *baby cried continuously all afternoon.*

the continuous /kən'tɪnjuəs/ *noun* the continuous form of the verb

contort /kən'tɔːt/ *verb* [I, T] If your face or body contorts, or you contort it, you twist it into a different shape, often because you are experiencing a strong emotion. *His face was contorted with pain.*

contour /'kɒntʊəʳ/ *noun* [C] **1** the shape of the outer edge of something *the contours of her body* **2** (*also* 'contour ,line) a line on a map joining places that are at the same height

contra- /kɒntrə-/ *prefix* against or opposite *to contradict* (= say the opposite) ○ *contraception* (= something that is used to prevent pregnancy)

contraband /'kɒntrəbænd/ *noun* [U] goods that are brought into or taken out of a country illegally

contraception /ˌkɒntrə'sepʃ³n/ *noun* [U] methods that prevent a woman from becoming pregnant

contraceptive /ˌkɒntrə'septɪv/ *noun* [C] a drug or object that prevents a woman from becoming pregnant

WORD PARTNERS FOR **contract**
enter into/negotiate/sign a contract • breach/break/end/terminate a contract • in a contract • the terms of a contract • a contract between sb and sb /with sb

o⊸**contract¹** /'kɒntrækt/ *noun* [C] a legal agreement between two people or organizations, especially one that involves doing work for a particular amount of money

contract² /kən'trækt/ *verb* **1** REDUCE [I, T] to become smaller or shorter, or to make something do this *The wood contracts in dry weather.* **2** DISEASE [T] *formal* to get a serious disease *She contracted malaria while living abroad.* **3** AGREEMENT [I, T] to make a legal agreement with someone to do work or to have work done for you [+ to do sth] *He's been contracted to perform in five shows.*

contract out sth to make a formal arrangement for other people to do work that you are responsible for *They've contracted out the cleaning to a private firm.*

contraction /kən'trækʃ³n/ *noun* **1** MUSCLE [C] a strong, painful movement of the muscles that a woman has when she is having a baby *She was having contractions every ten minutes.* **2** WORD [C] a short form of a word or group of words 'Won't' is a contraction of 'will not'. **3** REDUCTION [U] when something becomes smaller or shorter

contractor /kən'træktəʳ/ *noun* [C] a person or

company that supplies goods or does work for other people

contractual /kən'træktʃuəl/ *adjective* relating to or stated in a contract (= legal agreement) *a contractual dispute*

contradict /ˌkɒntrə'dɪkt/ *verb* 1 [T] If two things that are said or written about something contradict each other, they are so different that they cannot both be true. *His account of the accident contradicts the official government report.* 2 [I, T] to say that what someone else has just said is wrong

contradiction /ˌkɒntrə'dɪkʃⁿn/ *noun* 1 [C] a big difference between two things that are said or written about the same subject, or between what someone says and what they do *There is a clear contradiction between what she says and what she does.* 2 [U] when you say that what someone has just said is wrong 3 **a contradiction in terms** a phrase that is confusing because it contains words that seem to have opposite meanings *An honest politician - isn't that a contradiction in terms?*

contradictory /ˌkɒntrə'dɪktⁿri/ *adjective* If two statements about the same subject or two actions by the same person are contradictory, they are very different.

contraption /kən'træpʃⁿn/ *noun* [C] a machine or object that looks strange or complicated

contrary¹ /'kɒntrⁿri/ *noun* 1 **to the contrary** saying or showing the opposite *She claimed she hadn't been involved, despite evidence to the contrary.* 2 **on the contrary** used to show that the opposite of what has just been said is true *"You're a vegetarian, aren't you?" "On the contrary, I love meat."*

contrary² /'kɒntrⁿri/ *adjective* 1 opposite or very different *a contrary opinion/view* 2 **contrary to sth** opposite to what someone said or thought *Contrary to popular belief, bottled water is not always better than tap water.* **b** If something is contrary to a rule, it does not obey that rule.

🧩 **WORD PARTNERS FOR *contrast***

a **complete/sharp/striking** contrast ● the contrast **between** sth and sth ● in **direct/marked/sharp/stark** contrast (**to** sth)

---

o⃝**contrast¹** /'kɒntrɑːst/ *noun* [C, U] 1 an obvious difference between two people or things *The contrast between their lifestyles couldn't be greater.* ○ *The busy north coast of the island is in sharp contrast to the peaceful south.* 2 **by/in contrast** used to show that someone or something is completely different from someone or something else *She's quite petite, in contrast with her tall sister.*

contrast² /kən'trɑːst/ *verb* 1 [T] to compare two people or things in order to show the differences between them *If you contrast his early novels with his later work, you can see how his writing has developed.* 2 [I] If one thing contrasts with another, it is very different from it. *The sharpness of the lemons contrasts with the sweetness of the honey.*

contrasting /kən'trɑːstɪŋ/ *adjective* very different *contrasting colours/styles*

contravene /ˌkɒntrə'viːn/ *verb* [T] *formal* to do something that is forbidden by a law or rule ● **contravention** /ˌkɒntrə'venʃⁿn/ *noun* [C, U] *By accepting the money, she was in contravention of company rules.*

o⃝**contribute** /kən'trɪbjuːt, 'kɒntrɪbjuːt/ *verb* [I, T] 1 to give something, especially money, in order to provide or achieve something together with other people *I contributed $20 towards Andrea's present.* 2 to write articles for a newspaper, magazine, or book *She contributes to several magazines.*

contribute to sth to be one of the causes of an event or a situation *Smoking contributed to his early death.*

o⃝**contribution** /ˌkɒntrɪ'bjuːʃⁿn/ *noun* [C] 1 something that you do to help produce or develop something, or to help make something successful *She has made a major contribution to our work.* 2 an amount of money that is given to help pay for something *a generous contribution to charity*

contributor /kən'trɪbjutⁿr/ *noun* [C] 1 ARTICLE someone who writes articles for a newspaper, magazine, or book 2 MONEY someone who gives something, especially money, together with other people 3 CAUSE one of the causes of something *Speeding is a major contributor to road accidents.*

contributory /kən'trɪbjutⁿri/ *adjective* helping to cause something

contrive /kən'traɪv/ *verb* [T] *formal* to manage to do something difficult, or to make something happen, by using your intelligence or by tricking people [+ to do sth] *They contrived to meet in secret.*

contrived /kən'traɪvd/ *adjective* Something that is contrived seems false and not natural.

o⃝**control¹** /kən'trəʊl/ *noun* 1 POWER [U] the power to make a person, organization, or object do what you want *The new teacher has no control over the class.* ○ *The police are in control of the situation.* ○ *He lost control of the vehicle.* 2 RULE [U] the power to rule or govern an area *Soldiers took control of the airport.* 3 **under control** being dealt with successfully *Don't worry - everything's under control.* ○ *I couldn't keep my drinking under control.* 4 **out of control** If something or someone is out of control, you cannot influence, limit, or direct them. 5 RULE [C, U] a rule or law that limits something *The government has introduced tighter immigration controls.* 6 CALM [U] the ability to be calm *It took a lot of control to stop myself hitting him.* 7 EQUIPMENT [C] a switch or piece of equipment that you use to operate a machine or vehicle *Where's the volume control on your stereo?* 8 OFFICIAL PLACE [C, U] a place where something official, usually a document, is checked *passport/immigration control* ⊃See also: **birth control, remote control, self-control**.

o⃝**control²** /kən'trəʊl/ *verb* [T] controlling, *past* controlled 1 MAKE SB DO STH to make a person, organization, or object do what you want *This switch controls the temperature.* ○ *Can't you control your dogs?* 2 LIMIT to limit the number, amount, or increase of something *Fire crews* *struggled to control the blaze.* **3** RULE to rule or govern an area *The whole area is controlled by rebel forces.* **4** EMOTION to stop yourself expressing strong emotions or behaving in a silly way *He can't control his temper.*

con'trol ,freak *noun* [C] *informal* someone who wants to control everything about a situation and does not want other people to be involved

controller /kən'trəʊlə^r/ *noun* [C] someone who directs the work of other people *a marketing controller*

controversial /ˌkɒntrə'vɜːʃ^əl/ *adjective* causing a lot of disagreement or argument *a controversial decision/issue*

┌─────────────────────────────────────┐
│ 🧩 WORD PARTNERS FOR **controversy** │

sth **attracts** / **causes** / **provokes** / **sparks** controversy • the controversy **surrounding** sth • **bitter** / **continuing** / **furious** controversy • controversy **about/over** sth • be **at the centre of** a controversy
└─────────────────────────────────────┘

controversy /'kɒntrəvɜːsi/ *noun* [C, U] a lot of disagreement and argument about something *There is a lot of controversy over mobile phone towers.*

conundrum /kə'nʌndrəm/ *noun* [C] a problem or question that is difficult to solve

convalescence /ˌkɒnvə'les^əns/ *noun* [U] the period of time when you rest and get better after a serious illness • **convalesce** *verb* [I]

convene /kən'viːn/ *verb* [I, T] *formal* to arrange a meeting, or to meet for a meeting *The committee convenes three times a year.*

convenience /kən'viːniəns/ *noun* **1** [U] when something is easy to use and suitable for what you want to do *the convenience of credit cards* **2** [C] something that makes life easier *Fortunately for Adam, his new house has every modern convenience.*

con'venience ,food *noun* [C] food that can be prepared quickly and easily

con'venience ,store *noun* [C] *mainly US* a shop that sells food, drinks, etc, and is usually open late

convenient /kən'viːniənt/ *adjective* **1** easy to use or suiting your plans well *When would be a convenient time to meet?* **2** near or easy to get to *The new supermarket is very convenient for me.* • **conveniently** *adverb*

convent /'kɒnvənt/ *noun* [C] a building where nuns (= religious women) live and pray together *enter a convent*

convention /kən'venʃ^ən/ *noun* **1** MEETING [C] a large formal meeting of people with the same interest or work *the Democratic Party convention* **2** CUSTOM [C, U] a usual and accepted way of behaving or doing something *In many countries it is the convention to wear black at funerals.* **3** AGREEMENT [C] a formal agreement between countries *an international convention on human rights*

conventional /kən'venʃ^ən^əl/ *adjective* **1** Conventional people are traditional and not willing to try new ideas. **2** Conventional objects or ways of doing things are the usual ones which have been used for a long time. *conventional*

farming/medicine **3** conventional **arms/forces/ warfare**, etc not involving the use of nuclear weapons **4** conventional **wisdom** what most people believe ⊃Opposite **unconventional**

conventionally /kən'venʃ^ən^əli/ *adverb* in a traditional way *He dressed conventionally in a suit and tie.*

converge /kən'vɜːdʒ/ *verb* [I] **1** COME TOGETHER If lines, roads, or rivers converge, they meet at a particular point. **2** FORM GROUP to move towards a particular point and form a group there *The protesters converged on the town square.* **3** BECOME SIMILAR If ideas, interests, or systems converge, they become more similar to one another. • **convergence** *noun* [U]

┌─────────────────────────────────────┐
│ 🧩 WORD PARTNERS FOR **conversation** │

engage in/have/join in/strike up a conversation • **make** conversation • a **brief** / **casual** / **long** / **polite** / **private** conversation • a conversation **about** sth • a conversation **between** sb
└─────────────────────────────────────┘

⚬**conversation** /ˌkɒnvə'seɪʃ^ən/ *noun* [C, U] a talk between two or more people, usually an informal one *a telephone conversation* ◦ *We had a conversation about football.* • **conversational** *adjective* relating to or like a conversation *a conversational style*

converse /kən'vɜːs/ *verb* [I] *formal* to talk with someone

conversely /'kɒnvɜːsli/ *adverb* used to introduce something that is different to something you have just said *Dark lipsticks make your mouth look smaller. Conversely, light shades make it larger.*

conversion /kən'vɜːʒ^ən/ *noun* [C, U] **1** when the appearance, form, or purpose of something is changed *the country's conversion to democracy* **2** when someone changes to a new religion or belief *her conversion to Christianity*

convert¹ /kən'vɜːt/ *verb* **1** [I, T] to change the appearance, form, or purpose of something *The old warehouse was converted into offices.* ◦ *How do you convert miles into kilometres?* **2** [I, T] to change to a new religion, belief, etc, or to make someone do this *When did he convert to Islam?*

convert² /'kɒnvɜːt/ *noun* [C] someone who has been persuaded to change to a different religion or belief *a Catholic convert*

convertible¹ /kən'vɜːtəbl/ *adjective* able to be converted

convertible² /kən'vɜːtəbl/ *noun* [C] a car with a folding roof

convex /kɒn'veks/ *adjective* A convex surface curves out. *a convex mirror/lens*

convey /kən'veɪ/ *verb* [T] **1** to communicate information, feelings, or images to someone *She always conveys a sense of enthusiasm for her work.* **2** to transport something or someone to a particular place

conveyor belt /kən'veɪə,belt/ *noun* [C] a continuous moving piece of rubber or metal used to transport objects from one place to another

convict¹ /kən'vɪkt/ *verb* [T] to decide officially in a court of law that someone is guilty of a

| ɑː arm | ɜː her | iː see | ɔː saw | uː too | aɪ my | aʊ how | eə hair | eɪ day | əʊ no | ɪə near | ɔɪ boy | ʊə poor | aɪə fire | aʊə sour |

particular crime [often passive] *He was con-victed of murder.* ○ *a convicted criminal*

convict² /'kɒnvɪkt/ *noun* [C] someone who is in prison because they are guilty of a particular crime

conviction /kən'vɪkʃ°n/ *noun* **1** [C] when someone is officially found to be guilty of a particular crime *He already had two convictions for burglary.* **2** [C, U] a strong opinion or belief *religious/moral convictions*

convince /kən'vɪns/ *verb* [T] **1** to make someone believe that something is true [+ that] *He tried to convince me that I needed a new car.* ○ *She convinced the jury of her innocence.* **2** to persuade someone to do something [+ to do sth] *I convinced her to go to the doctor's.*

convinced /kən'vɪnst/ *adjective* completely certain about something [+ (that)] *I'm convinced that he's made a mistake.*

convincing /kən'vɪnsɪŋ/ *adjective* **1** able to make you believe that something is true or right *a convincing argument* **2** a **convincing win/victory** a win or victory where the person or team that wins is much better than the people they are competing against ● **convincingly** *adverb*

convoluted /'kɒnvəluːtɪd/ *adjective formal* extremely complicated and difficult to understand *a convoluted argument/story*

convoy /'kɒnvɔɪ/ *noun* [C] a group of vehicles or ships that travel together

convulsion /kən'vʌlʃ°n/ *noun* [C] a sudden uncontrollable movement of muscles in your body, caused by illness or drugs

coo /kuː/ *verb* [I] *cooing, past* cooed **1** to make a soft, low sound, like a pigeon (= large, grey bird) **2** to speak in a soft, low voice

cook

bake

fry

boil

grill   roast

o- **cook¹** /kʊk/ *verb* **1** [I, T] to prepare food and usually heat it *Who's cooking this evening?* ○ *She cooked the meat in oil and spices.* **2** [I] If food cooks, it is heated until it is ready to eat. *The rice is cooking.* ● **cooked** *adjective* not raw

  cook sth up *informal* to invent a story, plan, etc, usually dishonestly

cook² /kʊk/ *noun* [C] someone who prepares and cooks food

cookbook /'kʊkbʊk/ (*also UK* **cookery book**) *noun* [C] a book containing instructions for preparing food

cooker /'kʊkəʳ/ *UK* (*UK/US* **stove**) *noun* [C] a piece of equipment used to cook food *an electric cooker* ᴐSee also: **pressure cooker.**

cookery /'kʊk°ri/ *noun* [U] *UK* preparing or cooking food

'**cookery ˌbook** *UK* (*UK/US* **cookbook**) *noun* [C] a book containing instructions for preparing food

o-**cookie** /'kʊki/ *noun* [C] **1** *US* (*also UK* **biscuit**) a thin, flat cake that is dry and usually sweet ᴐSee colour picture **Food** on page Centre 11. **2** a piece of information stored on your computer which contains information about all the Internet documents you have looked at

o-**cooking** /'kʊkɪŋ/ *noun* [U] **1** preparing or cooking food *I do most of the cooking.* **2** a style of preparing food *vegetarian/French cooking* ● **cooking** *adjective* [always before noun] suitable to cook with *cooking oil/apples*

o-**cool¹** /kuːl/ *adjective* **1** COLD slightly cold, but not too cold *a cool breeze/day* ○ *cool water* **2** GOOD *informal* good, stylish, or fashionable *He looks really cool in those sunglasses.* **3** CALM calm and not emotional *She seemed cool and confident* **4** UNFRIENDLY unfriendly **5** be cool with sth *informal* to be happy to accept a situation or suggestion *She seemed cool and confident* **4** UNFRIENDLY unfriendly **5** be cool with sth *informal* to be happy to accept a situation or suggestion *I'm cool with that.* ● **coolness** *noun* [U]

cool² /kuːl/ *verb* [I, T] **1** to become less hot, or make something become less hot *Allow the bread to cool before slicing it.* **2** If emotions or relationships cool, or if something cools them, they become less strong.

  cool (sb/sth) down/off 1 to become less hot, or to make someone or something become less hot *We went for a swim to cool off.* **2** to become calmer, or to make someone become calmer

cool³ /kuːl/ *noun* **1 the cool** a cool temperature *the cool of the early morning* **2 keep your cool** to remain calm **3 lose your cool** to suddenly become very angry

cool⁴ /kuːl/ *exclamation informal* used when you like something or agree to something

coolly /'kuːlli/ *adverb* without showing emotion or interest *Her colleagues reacted coolly to the idea.*

coop¹ /kuːp/ *noun* [C] a cage for birds such as chickens

coop² /kuːp/ *verb*

  coop sb up to keep a person or animal in a small area [often passive] *We've been cooped up in a plane all day.*

co-op /'kəʊɒp/ *noun* [C] *informal short for* co-operative²

cooperate (*also UK* **co-operate**) /kəʊ'ɒp°reɪt/ *verb* [I] **1** to work together with someone in order to achieve the same aim *Witnesses are cooperating with detectives.* ○ *Several countries are cooperating in the relief effort.* **2** to help someone or do what they ask *We can get there early as long as the children will cooperate.*

cooperation (*also* UK **co-operation**) /kəʊˌɒpəˈreɪʃ³n/ *noun* [U] when you work together with someone or do what they ask you *international cooperation* ○ *The clubs work in close cooperation with the Football Association.*

cooperative¹ (*also* UK **co-operative**) /kəʊˈɒp³rətɪv/ *adjective* **1** willing to help or do what people ask *a cooperative and polite employee* **2** involving people working together to achieve the same aim *a cooperative relationship* ● **cooperatively** *adverb*

cooperative² (*also* UK **co-operative**) /kəʊˈɒp³rətɪv/ *noun* [C] a business or organization owned and managed by the people who work in it

coordinate (*also* UK **co-ordinate**) /kəʊˈɔːdɪneɪt/ *verb* [T] to make different people or things work together effectively, or to organize all the different parts of an activity *My manager is coordinating the new project.*

coordination (*also* UK **co-ordination**) /kəʊˌɔːdɪˈneɪʃ³n/ *noun* [U] **1** when you organize the different parts of an activity or make people or things work together effectively *The President called for closer coordination between business and government.* **2** the ability to make different parts of your body move together in a controlled way *Dancing helps develop balance and coordination.*

coordinator (*also* UK **co-ordinator**) /kəʊˈɔːdɪneɪtəʳ/ *noun* [C] someone who organizes the different parts of an activity or makes people or things work together effectively

cop /kɒp/ *noun* [C] *mainly US informal* a police officer *a traffic cop*

cope /kəʊp/ *verb* [I] to deal quite successfully with a difficult situation *How do you cope with stress?*

copier /ˈkɒpiəʳ/ *mainly US* (*UK/US* **photocopier**) *noun* [C] a machine which produces copies of documents by photographing them

copious /ˈkəʊpiəs/ *adjective* [always before noun] in large amounts *They drank copious amounts of wine.* ● **copiously** *adverb*

copper /ˈkɒpəʳ/ *noun* **1** [METAL] [U] a soft, red-brown metal, used in electrical equipment and to make coins, etc *copper wire* **2** [MONEY] [C] UK a brown coin with a low value **3** [POLICE] [C] UK *informal* a police officer

ꙮ**copy¹** /ˈkɒpi/ *noun* [C] **1** something that is made to look exactly like something else *Always make copies of important documents.* **2** a single book, newspaper, etc of which many have been produced *Four million copies of the book were sold in the first year.* ⊃See also: **carbon copy**.

ꙮ**copy²** /ˈkɒpi/ *verb* **1** [PRODUCE] [T] to produce something that is similar or exactly the same as something else *Copy the file onto disk.* ○ *The design was copied from the American model.* **2** [BEHAVE] [T] to behave like someone else *He likes to copy his older brother.* **3** [CHEAT] [I, T] to cheat by looking at and using someone else's work *She copied his answers.*

copy sth out UK If you copy out a piece of writing, you write it out again on a piece of paper.

copy sb in on sth *phrasal verb* If you copy somebody in on something, you give them a copy of something, usually an email, that you have written for somebody else. *Please copy me in on your email to Dr White.*

copyright /ˈkɒpiraɪt/ *noun* [C, U] the legal right to control the use of an original piece of work such as a book, play, or song *The book is protected by copyright.*

coral /ˈkɒrəl/ *noun* [U] a hard, usually pink or white substance produced by a type of very small sea animal *a coral reef*

cord /kɔːd/ *noun* **1** [C, U] **1** thick string, or a piece of this **2** (*also UK* **flex**) a piece of wire covered in plastic, used to connect electrical equipment to a power supply *an electrical cord* ○ *a telephone cord* ⊃See also: **umbilical cord**.

cordial /ˈkɔːdiəl/ *adjective* polite and friendly *a cordial invitation* ● **cordially** *adverb*

cordless /ˈkɔːdləs/ *adjective* able to operate without an electrical cord *a cordless phone*

cordon¹ /ˈkɔːd³n/ *noun* [C] a line of police, soldiers, vehicles, etc around an area, protecting it or keeping people out

cordon² /ˈkɔːd³n/ *verb*
cordon sth off If the police, army, etc cordon off an area, they stop people from entering it.

cords /kɔːdz/ *noun* [plural] *informal* trousers made from corduroy

corduroy /ˈkɔːdərɔɪ/ *noun* [U] thick, cotton cloth with raised parallel lines on the outside *a corduroy jacket*

core /kɔːʳ/ *noun* **1** [IMPORTANT PART] [no plural] the most important part of a system or principle *core values* ○ *Better health care was at the core of the senator's campaign.* **2** [FRUIT] [C] the hard, central part of certain fruits, such as apples, which contains the seeds **3** [PLANET] [no plural] the centre of a planet *the Earth's core* ⊃See also: **hard core**.

coriander /ˌkɒriˈændəʳ/ (*also US* **cilantro**) *noun* [U] a herb that is used in cooking

cork /kɔːk/ *noun* **1** [U] a light material obtained from the bark (= outer layer) of a particular type of tree **2** [C] a small cylindrical piece of this material put in the top of a bottle, especially a wine bottle, to close it

corkscrew /ˈkɔːkskruː/ *noun* [C] a piece of equipment used for pulling corks out of wine bottles

corn /kɔːn/ *noun* [U] **1** *mainly UK* a crop of grain, or the seed from this crop used to make flour or feed animals *fields of corn* **2** US (*UK* **sweetcorn**) a tall plant with yellow seeds that are cooked and eaten as a vegetable ⊃See colour picture **Fruit and Vegetables** on page Centre 10.

ꙮ**corner¹** /ˈkɔːnəʳ/ *noun* [C] **1** [POINT] the point or area where two lines, walls, or roads meet *There was a television in the corner of the room.* ○ *The pub is on/at the corner of Ross Street and Mill Road.* **2** [PLACE] a part of a larger area, often somewhere quiet or far away *He lives in a beautiful corner of northern Cali-*

fornia. **3** FOOTBALL a kick or hit taken from the corner of the field in some games, especially football **4 from/out of the corner of your eye** If you see something out of the corner of your eye, you just see it, but do not look at it directly. **5 around/round the corner** going to happen soon **6 cut corners** to do something in the quickest or cheapest way, often harming the quality of your work

corner² /'kɔːnəʳ/ *verb* **1** [T] to force a person or animal into a situation or place from which it is hard to escape *His attackers cornered him in a dark alley.* **2 corner the market** to become so successful at selling or making a particular product that almost no one else sells or makes it

cornerstone /'kɔːnəstəʊn/ *noun* [C] something very important that something else depends on *Freedom of speech is* **the cornerstone of** *democracy.*

cornflakes /'kɔːnfleɪks/ *noun* [plural] a food made from corn (= grain) and eaten with milk for breakfast (= morning meal)

corny /'kɔːni/ *adjective informal* repeated too often to be interesting or funny *a corny joke*

coronary¹ /'kɒrənʳri/ *adjective* relating to the heart *coronary heart disease*

coronary² /'kɒrənʳri/ *noun* [C] a heart attack (= when the heart stops working normally)

coronation /,kɒrə'neɪʃʳn/ *noun* [C] a ceremony at which someone is officially made king or queen

coroner /'kɒrənəʳ/ *noun* [C] an official who examines the causes of someone's death, usually if it was violent or sudden

Corp *noun* [C] *written abbreviation for* corporation (=used after the name of a large company in the United States)

corporal /'kɔːpʳrʳl/ *noun* [C] a soldier of low rank in the army or air force

corporal 'punishment *noun* [U] physical punishment, especially of children, usually by hitting with the hand or a stick

corporate /'kɔːpʳrət/ *adjective* [always before noun] relating to a large company or group *corporate finance*

corporation /,kɔːpʳr'eɪʃʳn/ *noun* [C] a large company or group of companies

corps /kɔːʳ/ *noun* [C] *plural* **corps 1** a group of people involved in the same job *the press/ diplomatic corps* **2** a special part of a military force *the Air Corps*

corpse /kɔːps/ *noun* [C] a dead person's body

o‑**correct¹** /kə'rekt/ *adjective* **1** accurate, or having no mistakes *Check that you have the correct information.* ○ *Was that the correct answer?* **2** suitable for a particular situation *correct behaviour* ○ *Have you got the correct number of players for the match?* ● **correctly** *adverb* ● **correctness** *noun* [U] ↪See also: **politically correct**.

COMMON LEARNER ERROR

correct or **right**?

Correct means 'accurate' or 'without mistakes'.
All the details were correct.

Right is another word for 'correct'. It also means 'suitable' or 'morally acceptable'.
Be careful to choose the right word.

I don't think it's right for parents to hit their children.

Remember that **correct** does not mean 'good'.
The hotel was cheap but good.
~~The hotel was cheap but correct.~~

correct² /kə'rekt/ *verb* [T] **1** MAKE RIGHT to make a mistake or problem right or better *The new software finds and corrects any errors on the hard disk.* **2** IMPROVE to improve the quality of something *These contact lenses will help to correct your vision.* **3** SHOW MISTAKE to show someone the mistakes in something they have said or written *Our teacher normally corrects our pronunciation.*

WORD PARTNERS FOR **correction**

make a correction ● a **minor / small** correction ● a correction **to** sth

o‑**correction** /kə'rekʃʳn/ *noun* [C, U] a change to make something right or better, or when you make such a change *She made some corrections before handing in the essay.*

corrective /kə'rektɪv/ *adjective formal* intended to improve or correct something *corrective surgery/lenses*

correlate /'kɒrəleɪt/ *verb* [I, T] If facts or pieces of information correlate, they are connected to each other and influence each other, and if you correlate them, you show their connections.

WORD PARTNERS FOR **correlation**

a **clear/close/direct/high/strong** correlation ● a correlation **between** sth and sth

correlation /,kɒrə'leɪʃʳn/ *noun* [C] a connection between two or more things, usually where one causes or influences the other *The research showed a* **close correlation between** *smoking and lung cancer.*

correspond /,kɒrɪ'spɒnd/ *verb* [I] **1** to be the same or very similar *The newspaper story does not* **correspond with/to** *what really happened.* **2** to communicate with someone by writing letters

correspondence /,kɒrɪ'spɒndəns/ *noun* **1** [U] letters or emails from one person to another, or the activity of writing and receiving letters or emails *business correspondence* **2** [C, U] when there is a connection or similarity between two or more things

correspondent /,kɒrɪ'spɒndʳnt/ *noun* [C] **1** someone who reports news for newspapers, television, or radio, usually from another country **2** someone who writes letters regularly

corresponding /,kɒrɪ'spɒndɪŋ/ *adjective* [always before noun] similar or related *Draw a line between the words with corresponding meanings.*

corridor /'kɒrɪdɔːʳ/ *noun* [C] a passage in a

building or train with rooms on one or both sides

corroborate /kəˈrɒbᵊreɪt/ *verb* [T] *formal* to say something or provide information that supports what someone says *A witness corroborated his account of the accident.* • **corroboration** /kəˌrɒbəˈreɪʃᵊn/ *noun* [U]

corrode /kəˈrəʊd/ *verb* **1** [I, T] If metal corrodes, or rain or chemicals corrode it, it is slowly damaged by them. *Rain corroded the metal pipes.* **2** [T] to slowly damage someone or something *He was corroded by guilt.* • **corrosion** /kəˈrəʊʒᵊn/ *noun* [U] • **corrosive** /kəˈrəʊsɪv/ *adjective Acid rain is **highly corrosive**.*

corrugated /ˈkɒrəgeɪtɪd/ *adjective* [always before noun] Corrugated metal or cardboard has parallel rows of folds that look like waves. *a corrugated iron roof*

corrupt[1] /kəˈrʌpt/ *adjective* **1** dishonest or illegal *a corrupt government* **2** If information on a computer is corrupt, it has been damaged or spoiled. *corrupt files*

corrupt[2] /kəˈrʌpt/ *verb* [T] **1** to make someone or something become dishonest or immoral [often passive] *He was corrupted by power and money.* **2** to damage information on a computer

corruption /kəˈrʌpʃᵊn/ *noun* [U] **1** dishonest or immoral behaviour, usually by people in positions of power *He was arrested for corruption and bribery.* **2** when you cause someone or something to become dishonest or immoral *the corruption of innocent young children*

corset /ˈkɔːsət/ *noun* [C] a tight piece of underwear worn by women to make themselves look thinner, especially in the past

cosmetic /kɒzˈmetɪk/ *adjective* **1** intended to improve your appearance **2** involving only small changes or improvements that will not solve a problem *Critics claimed that the changes were only cosmetic.*

cosmetics /kɒzˈmetɪks/ *noun* [plural] substances that you put on your face or body to improve your appearance

cosˌmetic ˈsurgery *noun* [U] a medical operation to make someone more attractive

cosmic /ˈkɒzmɪk/ *adjective* relating to the whole universe *cosmic rays*

cosmopolitan /ˌkɒzməˈpɒlɪtᵊn/ *adjective* **1** consisting of people and things from many different countries *London is a very **cosmopolitan city**.* **2** having experience of many different countries or cultures *a dynamic, cosmopolitan businesswoman*

the cosmos /ˈkɒzmɒs/ *noun* the whole universe

> WORD PARTNERS FOR ***cost***
>
> the cost **of** sth • **at a cost of** [£500/$1000, etc] • the **high/low** cost of sth • **cover the cost of** (doing) sth • **cut/reduce** costs • **at no extra** cost • the cost **of living**

🔑**cost[1]** /kɒst/ *noun* **1** [C, U] the amount of money that you need to buy or do something *The cruise ship was built **at a cost of** $400 million.* ○ *Software is included **at no extra cost**.* ○ *The **cost of living** (= the cost of food, clothes, etc) has increased.* **2** [no plural] something that you give or lose, in order to get or achieve something else *He rescued four people **at the cost of** his own life.* **3** **at all costs** If something must be done at all costs, it is very important that it is done. *We have to succeed at all costs.* **4** **to your cost** *UK* because of a bad experience you have had *An ankle injury can last a long time, as I know to my cost.*

🔑**cost[2]** /kɒst/ *verb past* **cost** **1** [T] If something costs a particular amount of money, you have to pay that in order to buy or do it. *How much do these shoes cost?* ○ [+ to do sth] ***It costs** $5 to send the package by airmail.* ○ [+ two objects] *It's going to cost me a lot of money to buy a new car.* **2** [+ two objects] to make someone lose something *His lazy attitude cost him his job.*

cost[3] /kɒst/ *verb* [T] to calculate the amount of money needed to do or make something *The building work has been costed at $30,000.*

co-star[1] /ˈkəʊstɑːʳ/ *noun* [C] one of two famous actors who both have important parts in a particular film

co-star[2] /kəʊˈstɑːʳ/ [US] /ˈkəʊstɑːr/ *verb* **co-starring**, *past* **co-starred** **1** [T] If a film, play, etc co-stars two or more famous actors, they are in it. **2** [I] to be in a film, play, etc with another famous actor *Hugh Grant **co-stars with** Julia Roberts in 'Notting Hill'.*

cost-cutting /ˈkɒstˌkʌtɪŋ/ *noun* [U] actions that reduce the amount of money spent on something ***cost-cutting measures/strategies***

cost-effective /ˌkɒstɪˈfektɪv/ *adjective* If something is cost-effective, it achieves good results for little money.

costly /ˈkɒstli/ *adjective* **1** expensive [+ to do sth] *It would be too costly to build a swimming pool.* **2** causing a lot of problems, or causing you to lose something important *a costly mistake*

costume /ˈkɒstjuːm/ *noun* **1** [C, U] a set of clothes that someone wears to make them look like someone or something else, for example in a play *actors in costume* ○ *He arrived at the party dressed in a gorilla costume.* **2** [U] a set of clothes that are typical of a particular country or time in history *Japanese national costume* ➲See also: **swimming costume**.

cosy *UK* (*US* **cozy**) /ˈkəʊzi/ *adjective* comfortable and warm

cot /kɒt/ *UK* (*US* **crib**) *noun* [C] a bed with high sides for a baby

ˈcot ˌdeath *UK* (*US* **SIDS**) *noun* [C, U] the sudden death of a sleeping baby for no obvious reason

cottage /ˈkɒtɪdʒ/ *noun* [C] a small house, usually in the countryside

ˌcottage ˈcheese *noun* [U] a soft, white cheese with small lumps in it

cotton[1] /ˈkɒtᵊn/ *noun* [U] **1** [CLOTH] cloth or thread that is produced from the cotton plant *a cotton shirt/dress* **2** [PLANT] a plant that produces a soft, white substance used for making thread and cloth **3** [FOR CLEANING] *US* (*UK* **cotton wool**) a soft mass of cotton, usually used for cleaning your skin ➲See colour picture **The Bathroom** at page Centre 3.

,cotton 'wool *UK* (*US* **cotton**) *noun* [U] a soft mass of cotton, usually used for cleaning your skin ⊃See colour picture **The Bathroom** on page Centre 3.

couch¹ /kautʃ/ *noun* [C] a long, comfortable piece of furniture that two or more people can sit on

couch² /kautʃ/ *verb* **be couched in/as sth** to be expressed in a particular way *His explanation was couched in technical language.*

'couch po,tato *noun* [C] *UK humorous* a person who is not active and spends a lot of time watching television

o↝**cough¹** /kɒf/ *verb* [I] to make air come out of your throat with a short sound

cough sth up to make something come out of your lungs or throat by coughing *Doctors were worried when she started coughing up blood.*

cough (sth) up *informal* to give money to someone although you do not want to

cough² /kɒf/ *noun* [C] **1** when you cough, or the sound this makes **2** an illness that makes you cough a lot *Uwe has a nasty cough.* ⊃See also: **whooping cough.**

o↝**could** *strong form* /kud/ *weak form* /kəd/ *modal verb* **1** [CAN] used as the past form of 'can' to talk about what someone or something was able to do *I couldn't see what he was doing.* ○ *You said we could watch television when we'd finished our homework.* **2** [POSSIBLE] used to talk about what is possible or might happen *The baby could arrive any day now.* ○ *This kind of crime could easily be prevented.* ○ *She could have* (= might have) *been seriously injured.* **3** [ASK] used to ask someone politely to do or provide something *Could you lend me £5?* **4** [ASK PERMISSION] used to ask politely for permission to do something *Could I speak to Mr Davis, please?* **5** [SUGGEST] used to make a suggestion *You could try painting it a different colour.* **6 I could (have)** used when you feel so happy, sad, angry, etc that you would like to do something *I was so grateful I could have kissed her!* ⊃See Extra help page **Modal verbs** on page Centre 22.

o↝**couldn't** /'kudªnt/ *short for* could not *I couldn't understand what he was saying.*

o↝**could've** /'kudəv/ *short for* could have *It could've been much worse.*

council, Council /'kaunsªl/ *noun* [C] **1** a group of people who are elected to control a town, city, or area *Edinburgh City Council* ○ *a council meeting* **2** a group of people who are elected or chosen to give advice or make decisions *the Medical Research Council* **3 a council house/flat** in the UK a house or flat that is owned by a city or town council and rented to people

'council e,state *UK* (*US* **housing project**) *noun* [C] a part of a city with council houses and flats (= homes owned by a council and rented to people) *a Birmingham council estate*

councillor *UK* (*US* **councilor**) /'kaunsªlər/ *noun* [C] a member of a town, city, or area council

counsel¹ /'kaunsªl/ *noun* **1** [C] a lawyer (= someone who advises people about the law and deals with legal situations) who speaks for someone in court **2** [U] *literary* advice

counsel² /'kaunsªl/ *verb* [T] *UK* **counselling**, *past* **counselled**, *US* **counseling**, *past* **counseled 1** *formal* to advise someone to do something [+ **to do sth**] *Lawyers had counselled him not to say anything.* **2** to give advice to someone who has problems

counselling *UK* (*US* **counseling**) /'kaunsªlɪŋ/ *noun* [U] the job or process of listening to someone and giving them advice about their problems *a counselling service*

counsellor *UK* (*US* **counselor**) /'kaunsªlər/ *noun* [C] someone whose job is to listen to people and give them advice about their problems

o↝**count¹** /kaunt/ *verb* **1** [CALCULATE] [T] to see how many people or things there are *I counted the money on the table.* **2** [SAY NUMBERS] [I] to say numbers in their correct order *Can you count to twenty in French?* **3** [CONSIDER] [T] to think of someone or something in a particular way *She counted Tim as her closest friend.* ○ *You should count yourself lucky you weren't hurt.* **4** [IMPORTANT] [I] to be important *I believe that health and happiness count more than money.* ○ *Doesn't my opinion count for anything?* **5** [INCLUDE] [T] to include something or someone in a calculation *There are 1500 people at my school, counting teachers.* **6** [RF ACCEPTED] [I] to be accepted or allowed as part of something *I've been to sixteen different countries, but I only spent half an hour in Luxembourg, so that doesn't really count.*

count against sb/sth to make someone or something more likely to fail *She's got the qualifications for the job, but her lack of experience will count against her.*

count sb in to include someone in an activity *If you're going for a pizza, you can count me in.*

count on sb to be confident that you can depend on someone *I can always count on my parents to help me.*

count on sth to expect something to happen and make plans based on it *I didn't count on so many people coming to the party.*

count sth out to count coins or pieces of paper money one by one as you put them down *She counted out five crisp $20 bills.*

count sb out to not include someone in an activity

count towards sth to be part of what is needed to complete something or achieve something *This essay counts towards my exam result.*

count up sb/sth to add together all the people or things in a group

count² /kaunt/ *noun* **1** [NUMBER] [C] when you count something, or the total number you get after counting [usually singular] *At the last count there were 410 club members.* **2 lose count** to forget how many of something there is *I've lost count of the number of times she's arrived late.* **3 on all/both/several, etc counts** in all, both, several, etc parts of a situation, argument, etc *I had been wrong on both counts.* **4** [RANK] [C] (*also* **Count**) a man of high social rank in some European countries **5** [CRIME] [C] one of the times that someone has been accused of a particular crime *He was charged* *with two counts of assault.* ⊃See also: **pollen count.**

countable noun /ˌkaʊntəbˀlˈnaʊn/ (*also* **'count ˌnoun**) *noun* [C] a noun that has both plural and singular forms ⊃See Extra help page **Countable and uncountable nouns** on page Centre 20.

countdown /ˈkaʊntdaʊn/ *noun* [C] the time just before an important event when people are counting the time until it happens [usually singular] *The countdown to the Olympics has begun.*

countenance¹ /ˈkaʊntᵊnəns/ *noun* [C] *literary* the appearance or expression of someone's face

countenance² /ˈkaʊntᵊnəns/ *verb* [T] *formal* to accept that something should happen *They will not countenance building a new apartment.*

counter¹ /ˈkaʊntəʳ/ *noun* [C] **1** [IN A SHOP] the place in a shop, bank, etc, where people are served *The woman **behind the counter** took his money.* **2** [SURFACE] *US* a flat surface in a kitchen on which food can be prepared **3** [DISC] a small disc used in some games that are played on a board

counter² /ˈkaʊntəʳ/ *verb* [T] **1** to prevent something or reduce the bad effect that it has *This skin cream claims to counter the effects of sun damage.* **2** to say something to show that what someone has just said is not true *"Of course I love him," Clare countered.*

counter³ /ˈkaʊntəʳ/ *adverb* **be/run counter to sth** to have the opposite effect to something else *The new road plans run counter to the government's aim of reducing pollution.*

counter- /ˈkaʊntəʳ-/ *prefix* opposing or as a reaction to *a counter-attack* (= an attack on someone who has attacked you)

counteract /ˌkaʊntᵊrˈækt/ *verb* [T] to reduce the bad effect that something else has *drugs that counteract the side effects of sea sickness*

counter-attack /ˈkaʊntərəˌtæk/ *noun* [C] an attack that you make against someone who has attacked you in a sport, war, or argument ● **counter-attack** *verb* [I, T]

counterclockwise /ˌkaʊntəˈklɒkwaɪz/ *US* (*UK* **anti-clockwise**) *adjective, adverb* in the opposite direction to the way the hands (= parts that point to the numbers) of a clock move ⊃See picture at **clockwise.**

counterfeit /ˈkaʊntəfɪt/ *adjective* made to look like the real thing, in order to trick people *counterfeit money/jewellery*

counterpart /ˈkaʊntəpɑːt/ *noun* [C] someone or something that has the same job or position as someone or something in a different place or organization

counterproductive /ˌkaʊntəprəˈdʌktɪv/ *adjective* having the opposite effect from the one you want

countess /ˈkaʊntɪs/ *noun* [C] a woman who has a high social rank in some European countries, especially the wife of an earl or count (= man of high social rank) *the Countess of Abingdon*

countless /ˈkaʊntləs/ *adjective* [always before noun] very many *The song has been played countless times on the radio.*

ᵒ᪻**country¹** /ˈkʌntri/ *noun* **1** [C] an area of land that has its own government, army, etc *European countries* **2 the country a** the areas that are away from towns and cities **b** the people who live in a country *The country was shocked by the President's decision.*

COMMON LEARNER ERROR

country, land, nation, or **state?**

Country is the most general word which means 'an area of land'. It usually means an area of land with its own government and people.

China, Japan, and other countries in Asia

Nation is used to talk about a country, especially when you mean the people or the culture of that country.

The nation celebrated the 100th anniversary of independence.

State is used to talk about a country as a political or official area. Some countries are divided into political units that are also called **states.**

Belgium became an independent state in 1830.

America is divided into 50 states.

the State of Florida

Land means an area of ground, not an area with its own government.

We bought some land to build a house on.

country² /ˈkʌntri/ *adjective* [always before noun] in or relating to the areas that are away from towns and cities *country roads/hotels*

countryman /ˈkʌntrɪmən/ *noun* [C] *plural* **countrymen** someone from the same country as you

ˌcountry 'music (*also* ˌcountry and 'western) *noun* [U] a style of popular music from the southern and western US

countryside /ˈkʌntrɪsaɪd/ *noun* [U] land that is not in towns or cities and has farms, fields, forests, etc ⊃See Common learner error at **nature.**

county /ˈkaʊnti/ *noun* [C] an area of Britain, Ireland, or the US that has its own local government

coup /kuː/ *noun* [C] **1** (*also* **coup d'état** /ˌkuːdeɪˈtɑː/) when a group of people suddenly takes control of a country using force *a military coup* **2** an important achievement, often one that was not expected *The award is a major coup for the university.*

ᵒ᪻**couple¹** /ˈkʌpl/ *noun* **1** [no plural] two or a few *I went to New York with **a couple of** friends.* ○ *The weather has improved over the last couple of weeks.* **2** [C] two people who are married or having a romantic relationship *a married couple*

couple² /ˈkʌpl/ *verb* **coupled with sth** combined with something else *Concern about farming methods, coupled with health awareness, have led to a fall in meat consumption.*

coupon /ˈkuːpɒn/ *noun* [C] **1** a piece of printed paper that you can use to buy something at a cheaper price or to get something free *Collect 10 coupons to get a free meal.* **2** a printed form in a magazine or newspaper, that you use to send for information, enter a competition, etc

WORD PARTNERS FOR *courage*

have the courage to do sth • **show** courage • sth **takes** courage • **great/immense/personal** courage

courage /'kʌrɪdʒ/ *noun* [U] **1** the ability to deal with dangerous or difficult situations without being frightened [+ to do sth] *She didn't have the courage to tell him the truth.* **2 pluck up the courage (to do sth)** to decide to do something that you were too frightened to do before

courageous /kə'reɪdʒəs/ *adjective* brave • **courageously** *adverb*

courgette /kɔː'ʒet/ *UK* (*US* zucchini) *noun* [C, U] a long, green vegetable which is white inside

courier /'kʊriəʳ/ *noun* [C] **1** someone whose job is to take and deliver documents and parcels **2** *UK* someone whose job is to look after people who are on holiday

o▪**course** /kɔːs/ *noun* **1 of course a** [YES] used to say 'yes' and emphasize your answer *"Can you help me?" "Of course!"* **b** [OBVIOUS] used to show that what you are saying is obvious or already known *Of course, the Olympics are not just about money.* **2 of course not** used to say 'no' and emphasize your answer *"Do you mind if I borrow your pen?" "Of course not."* **3** [LESSONS] [C] a series of lessons about a particular subject *She did a ten-week course in computing.* **4** [PART OF MEAL] [C] a part of a meal *a three-course dinner* **5** [SPORT] [C] an area used for horse races or playing golf *a golf course* **6** [MEDICINE] [C] *mainly UK* a fixed number of regular medical treatments *a course of antibiotics* **7** [ROUTE] [C, U] the direction in which a ship, aircraft, etc is moving *During the storm, the boat was blown off course* (= in the wrong direction). **8** [ACTION] [C] (*also* **course of 'action**) something that you can do in a particular situation *I think the best course of action would be to write to him.* **9 during/in/over the course of sth** during a particular time or activity *In the course of the interview she mentioned her previous experience.* **10 in due course** at a suitable time in the future *The results will be sent to you in due course.* **11** [DEVELOPMENT] [no plural] the way something develops, usually over a long time *Nuclear weapons have changed the course of modern history.* **12 in the course of time** *UK* gradually, or over a period of time **13 be on course for sth/to do sth** *UK* to be very likely to succeed at something **14 run its course** If something runs its course, it continues naturally until it has finished. ⊃See also: be on a **collision** course, **crash course**, be **par** for the course.

coursebook /'kɔːsbʊk/ *noun* [C] *UK* a book used by students when they do a particular course of study

coursework /'kɔːswɜːk/ *noun* [U] *UK* work done by students as part of their course of study

o▪**court¹** /kɔːt/ *noun* [C, U] **1** [LAW] the place where a judge decides whether someone is guilty of a crime *The suspect appeared in court charged with robbery.* ○ *You can take them to court* (= make them be judged in court) *if they don't pay.* **2 the court** the judge and group of people at a trial who decide whether someone is guilty of a crime **3** [SPORT] an area for playing particular sports *a tennis/basketball court* **4** [ROYAL HOUSE] the official home of a king or queen and the people who live with them ⊃See also: **High Court**, the **supreme court**.

court² /kɔːt/ *verb* **1** [PLEASE] [T] to try to please someone because you want them to support you or join you *Adams is being courted by several football clubs.* **2** [TRY TO GET] [T] to try to get or achieve something *to court investment/publicity* **3** [RELATIONSHIP] [I, T] *old-fashioned* to have a romantic relationship with someone you hope to marry **4 court controversy/danger/disaster, etc** to behave in a way that risks bad results

courteous /'kɜːtiəs/ *adjective* polite and showing respect • **courteously** *adverb*

courtesy /'kɜːtəsi/ *noun* **1** [U] behaviour that is polite and shows respect, or a polite action or remark *The hotel treats all guests with courtesy.* ○ [+ to do sth] *He didn't even have the courtesy to thank me.* **2 (by) courtesy of sb/sth** If you have something courtesy of someone, they have allowed you to have it. *The photograph is courtesy of the Natural History Museum.*

courthouse /'kɔːthaʊs/ *noun* [C] *plural* courthouses /'kɔːthaʊzɪz/ *mainly US* a building with law courts inside it

courtier /'kɔːtiəʳ/ *noun* [C] someone who spent a lot of time in the home of a king or queen in the past

court-martial¹ /ˌkɔːt'mɑːʃ°l/ *noun* [C] a military court, or a trial in a military court

court-martial² /ˌkɔːt'mɑːʃ°l/ *verb* [T] to judge someone in a military court

'court ˌorder *noun* [C] an instruction from a law court that someone must do or not do something

courtroom /'kɔːtrʊm/ *noun* [C] the room where a judge and other people decide whether someone is guilty of a crime

courtship /'kɔːtʃɪp/ *noun* [C, U] *formal* the time when people have a romantic relationship with the intention of getting married

courtyard /'kɔːtjɑːd/ *noun* [C] an open area by a building with walls or buildings around it

o▪**cousin** /'kʌz°n/ *noun* [C] the child of your aunt or uncle

couture /kuː'tjʊəʳ/ *noun* [U] the design, making, and selling of expensive and fashionable clothes

cove /kəʊv/ *noun* [C] a place on the coast where the land curves in

covenant /'kʌv°nənt/ *noun* [C] a formal written agreement

o▪**cover¹** /'kʌvəʳ/ *verb* [T] **1** [PUT] to put something over something else, in order to protect or hide it *They covered him with a blanket.* ○ *He covered his face with his hands.* ⊃Opposite un-cover. **2** [LAYER] to form a layer on the surface of something *Snow covered the trees.* ○ *My legs were covered in/with mud.* **3** [DISTANCE] to travel a particular distance *We covered 700 kilometres in four days.* **4** [AREA] to be a particular size or area *The town covers an area of 10* square miles. **5** INCLUDE to include or deal with a subject or piece of information *The book covers European history from 1789-1914.* **6** REPORT to report on an event for a newspaper, television programme, etc *Dave was asked to cover the Olympics.* **7** MONEY to be enough money to pay for something *£100 should cover the cost of the repairs.* **8** FINANCIAL PROTECTION to provide financial protection if something bad happens *travel insurance that covers accident and injury* ⊃See also: touch/cover all the bases (**base**[1]).

cover sth up to put something over something else, in order to protect or hide it

cover (sth) up to stop people from discovering the truth about something bad *She tried to cover up her mistakes.*

☞**cover²** /'kʌvəʳ/ *noun* **1** BOOK [C] the outer part of a book, magazine, etc, that protects the pages *Her picture was on the cover of 'Vogue' magazine.* **2** PROTECTION [C] something you put over something else, usually to protect it *an ironing board cover* ○ *a lens cover* **3** FINANCIAL [U] financial protection so that you get money if something bad happens *The policy provides £50,000 accidental damage cover.* **4** FROM WEATHER/ATTACK [U] protection from bad weather or an attack *They took cover under some trees until the rain stopped.* **5** FOR ILLEGAL ACTIVITY [C] something used to hide a secret or illegal activity *The club is used as a cover for a gang of car thieves.*

coverage /'kʌvrɪdʒ/ *noun* [U] **1** the way a newspaper, television programme, etc reports an event or subject *There is live coverage of the game on cable TV.* **2** *mainly US* financial protection so that you get money if something bad happens

coveralls /'kʌvərɔːlz/ *US* (*UK* **overalls**) *noun* [plural] a piece of clothing that you wear over your clothes to keep them clean while you are working

covering /'kʌvərɪŋ/ *noun* [C] a layer that covers something *a thick covering of snow*

covering 'letter *UK* (*US* 'cover ,letter) *noun* [C] a letter that you send with something to explain what it is or to give more information about it

covers /'kʌvəz/ *noun* [plural] the sheets and other layers of cloth on your bed that keep you warm

covert /'kəʊvɜːt/ *adjective* done in a secret way *covert police operations* ● **covertly** *adverb*

cover-up /'kʌvərʌp/ *noun* [C] an attempt to prevent people finding out the truth about a crime or a mistake *Police denied accusations of a cover-up.*

'cover ,version *noun* [C] a recording of a song already recorded by someone else *a cover version of 'Let It Be'*

covet /'kʌvɪt/ *verb* [T] *formal* to want something very much, especially something that someone else has

☞**cow** /kaʊ/ *noun* [C] **1** a large farm animal kept for milk or meat **2** *UK informal* an offensive word for a woman

coward /kaʊəd/ *noun* [C] someone who is not

brave and tries to avoid dangerous or difficult situations

cowardice /'kaʊədɪs/ *noun* [U] behaviour that shows that someone is not brave

cowardly /'kaʊədli/ *adjective* behaving in a way that shows you are not brave

cowboy /'kaʊbɔɪ/ *noun* [C] **1** a man whose job is to look after cattle (= animals such as cows) in the US, and who usually rides a horse **2** *UK informal* someone who does their job badly or who is dishonest in business *cowboy builders*

'cowboy ,boots *noun* [C] a type of boots with pointed toes, first worn by cowboys ⊃See colour picture **Clothes** on page Centre 9.

'cowboy ,hat *noun* [C] a type of hat with a hight top and a wide lower edge, first worn by cowboys

cower /kaʊəʳ/ *verb* [I] to bend down or move back because you are frightened

co-worker /,kəʊ'wɜːkəʳ/ *noun* [C] *mainly US* someone that you work with

coy /kɔɪ/ *adjective* **1** not wanting to give people information about something *Nigel's very coy about how much he earns.* **2** pretending to be shy *a coy look* ● **coyly** *adverb*

coyote /kaɪ'əʊti/ *noun* [C] a wild animal similar to a dog, that lives in North America

cozy /'kəʊzi/ *adjective US* spelling of cosy

crab /kræb/ *noun* [C, U] a sea creature with ten legs and a round, flat body covered by a shell, or the meat from this animal

crack¹ /kræk/ *verb* **1** BREAK [I, T] to break something so that it does not separate, but very thin lines appear on its surface, or to become broken in this way *The concrete had started to crack.* ○ *cracked dishes* **2** EGG/NUT [T] to open an egg or nut by breaking its shell **3** HIT [T] to hit a part of your body against something hard, by accident *He cracked his head on the cupboard door.* **4** SOLVE [T] *informal* to solve a difficult problem *It took three months to crack the enemy's code.* **5** **get cracking** *informal* to start doing something quickly **6** LOSE CONTROL [I] to lose control of your emotions and be unable to deal with a situation *He finally cracked after years of stress.* **7** NOISE [I, T] to make a sudden, short noise, or to cause something to make this noise **8** **crack a joke** to tell a joke **9** **not all it's cracked up to be** *informal* (*also* **not as good as it's cracked up to be** *informal*) not as good as people think or say *Being an actor isn't all it's cracked up to be.*

crack down to start dealing with bad or illegal behaviour in a more severe way *Police are cracking down on crime in the area.*

crack up *informal* to become mentally ill

crack (sb) up *informal* to suddenly laugh a lot, or to make someone suddenly laugh a lot

crack² /kræk/ *noun* **1** LINE [C] a line on the surface of something that is damaged *Several cups had cracks in them.* **2** NARROW SPACE [C] a narrow space between two parts of something or between two things *I could see sunlight through a crack in the curtains.* **3** DRUG [U] an illegal drug that is very harmful **4** NOISE [C] a sudden, short noise *a crack of thunder* **5** JOKE [C] an unkind joke or remark *He was*

always **making cracks about** my weight.
6 have/take a crack at sth informal to try to do something I've never put up shelves before, but I'll have a crack at it. **7 the crack of dawn** very early in the morning He gets up at the crack of dawn.

crack³ /kræk/ adjective [always before noun] of the highest quality a crack regiment

crackdown /'krækdaʊn/ noun [C] when bad or illegal behaviour is dealt with in a very severe way, in order to stop it happening The police are having **a crackdown** on speeding.

cracker /'krækə^r/ noun **1** FOOD [C] a dry biscuit that you eat with cheese **2** CHRISTMAS [C] (also **Christmas cracker**) a coloured paper tube with a small toy inside, that people pull open at Christmas (= a Christian holiday) in the UK **3** GOOD [no plural] UK informal someone or something that is very good

crackle /'krækl/ verb [I] to make a lot of short, dry noises A fire crackled in the hearth.
● **crackle** noun [no plural]

cradle¹ /'kreɪdl/ noun **1** BED [C] a baby's bed, especially one that swings from side to side **2** TELEPHONE the part of a telephone that holds the receiver (= the part of a telephone that you hold in your hand and use to listen and speak) **3** MOBILE PHONE a small stand that holds a mobile phone **4 the cradle of sth** the place where something started Massachusetts, the cradle of the American Revolution

cradle² /'kreɪdl/ verb [T] to hold someone or something in a careful, gentle way He **cradled** her **in** his arms.

craft¹ /krɑːft/ noun **1** [C, U] an activity in which you make something using a lot of skill, especially with your hands traditional crafts such as weaving **2** [C] plural craft a boat

craft² /krɑːft/ verb [T] to make something using a lot of skill [often passive] a bowl that was beautifully crafted from wood

craftsman /'krɑːftsmən/ noun [C] plural crafts-men someone who uses special skill to make things, especially with their hands ● **craftsman-ship** noun [U] skill at making things

crafty /'krɑːfti/ adjective clever at getting what you want, especially by deceiving people ● **craftily** adverb

crag /kræg/ noun [C] a high, rough mass of rock that sticks up from the land around it

cram /kræm/ verb cramming, past crammed **1 cram sth between/in/into, etc** to force things into a small space The refugees were crammed into the truck. **2** [I] to study a lot before an exam

crammed /kræmd/ adjective completely full of people or things crammed commuter trains ○ The room was **crammed with** boxes.

cramp¹ /kræmp/ noun [C, U] a sudden, strong pain in a muscle that makes it difficult to move I've got cramp in my legs.

cramp² /kræmp/ verb ➪See cramp sb's style¹.

cramped /kræmpt/ adjective A cramped room, building, etc is unpleasant because it is not big enough.

cranberry /'krænb^əri/ noun [C] a small, red berry (= soft fruit) with a sour taste

crane¹ /kreɪn/ noun [C] **1** a large machine used for lifting and moving heavy things **2** a bird with long legs and a long neck

crane² /kreɪn/ verb [I, T] to stretch your neck, in order to see or hear something

crank /kræŋk/ noun [C] **1** informal someone with strange ideas or behaviour **2** a handle that you turn to make a machine work

cranny /'kræni/ noun ➪See every nook and cranny.

crap¹ /kræp/ noun [U] very informal a very impolite word for something that you think is wrong or bad He was talking a lot of crap!

crap² /kræp/ UK (UK/US crappy /'kræpi/) adjective crapper, crappest very informal a very impolite word for describing things that are very bad in quality a crap car/job

crash¹ /kræʃ/ noun [C] **1** VEHICLE an accident in which a vehicle hits something a car/plane crash **2** NOISE a sudden, loud noise made when something falls or breaks I heard a crash and hurried into the kitchen. **3** COMPUTER when a computer or computer system sud-denly stops working **4** BUSINESS when the value of a country's businesses suddenly falls by a large amount He lost a lot of money in the stock market crash of 1929.

crash² /kræʃ/ verb **1** VEHICLE [I, T] If a vehicle crashes, it hits something by accident, and if you crash a vehicle, you make it hit something by accident. The van skidded and **crashed into** a tree. ○ Rick crashed his dad's car. **2** COM-PUTER [I] If a computer or computer system crashes, it suddenly stops working. **3 crash against/on/through, etc** to hit something and make a loud noise The waves crashed against the rocks. **4** LOUD NOISE [I] to make a sudden, loud noise Thunder crashed overhead. **5** MONEY [I] If a financial market crashes, prices suddenly fall by a large amount.

'crash ,barrier noun [C] UK a fence along the middle or edge of a road for preventing acci-dents

'crash ,course UK (US ,crash 'course) noun [C] a course that teaches you a lot of basic facts in a very short time

'crash ,helmet noun [C] a hard hat that pro-tects your head when you ride a motorcycle

crass /kræs/ adjective showing that you do not understand or care about other people's feel-ings a crass remark

crate /kreɪt/ noun [C] a large box used for carry-ing or storing things

crater /'kreɪtə^r/ noun [C] **1** the round, open part at the top of a volcano **2** a big hole in the ground The explosion left a crater in the road.

crave /kreɪv/ verb [T] to want something very

much *a child who craves affection* ● **craving** *noun* [C] a strong feeling that you want or need a particular thing *She had a craving for chocolate.*

crawl¹ /krɔːl/ *verb*

crawl

1 PERSON [I] to move on your hands and knees *I crawled under the desk to plug the lamp in.*
2 ANIMAL [I] If an insect crawls, it uses its legs to move. *There's an ant crawling up your leg.* **3** TRAFFIC [I] If traffic crawls, it moves extremely slowly. *We were crawling along at 10 miles per hour.* **4** TRY TO PLEASE [I] *UK informal* to try to please someone because you want them to like you or help you *My brother is always crawling to Mum.* **5 be crawling with sb/sth** to be full of insects or people in a way that is unpleasant *The kitchen's crawling with ants.*

crawl² /krɔːl/ *noun* **1** [no plural] a very slow speed *Traffic slowed to a crawl.* **2** [U] a style of swimming in which you move your arms over your head and kick with straight legs

crayon /'kreɪɒn/ *noun* [C] a stick of coloured wax used for drawing

craze /kreɪz/ *noun* [C] something that is very popular for a short time

crazed /kreɪzd/ *adjective* behaving in a dangerous and uncontrolled way *a crazed gunman*

⟐**crazy** /'kreɪzi/ *adjective* **1** stupid or strange *a crazy idea* ○ *I was crazy not to take that job.* **2** annoyed or angry *The children are driving me crazy* (= making me annoyed). ○ *Dad went crazy when I told him what had happened.* **3 be crazy about sb/sth** to love someone very much, or to be very interested in something *Mia's crazy about baseball.* **4 go crazy** to become very excited about something *When he came on stage the audience went crazy.* **5 like crazy** *informal* If you do something like crazy, you do a lot of it, or do it very quickly. *We worked like crazy to get everything finished.*
● **crazily** *adverb* ● **craziness** *noun* [U]

creak /kriːk/ *verb* [I] If something such as a door or a piece of wood creaks, it makes a long noise when it moves. *creaking floorboards*
● **creak** *noun* [C] ● **creaky** *adjective* A creaky door, stair, etc creaks.

⟐**cream¹** /kriːm/ *noun* **1** FOOD [U] a thick, yellowish-white liquid that is taken from milk *raspberries and cream* **2** FOR SKIN [C, U] a soft substance that you rub into your skin to make it softer or less painful *face/hand cream* **3** COLOUR [U] a yellowish-white colour **4 the cream of sth** the best people or things in a particular group *the cream of Milan's designers* ⊃See also: **ice cream.**

cream² /kriːm/ *adjective* being a yellowish-white colour

cream³ /kriːm/ *verb*
cream sth/sb off *UK* to take away the best part of something, or the best people in a group, and use them for your own advantage

‚cream ¹cheese *noun* [U] smooth, soft, white cheese

creamy /'kriːmi/ *adjective* like cream or containing cream *creamy sauce/soup*

crease¹ /kriːs/ *noun* [C] a line on cloth or paper where it has been folded or crushed

crease² /kriːs/ *verb* [I, T] If cloth, paper, etc creases, or if you crease it, it gets a line in it where it has been folded or crushed. *Cotton creases very easily.*

⟐**create** /kri'eɪt/ *verb* [T] to make something happen or exist *The project will create more than 500 jobs.* ○ *The heavy snow created further problems.*

creation /kri'eɪʃᵊn/ *noun* **1** PROCESS [U] when someone makes something happen or exist *the creation of a new political party* **2** PRODUCT [C] something that someone has made *The museum contains some of his best creations.* **3** UNIVERSE [U] (*also* **Creation**) in many religions, when God made the universe and everything in it

creative /kri'eɪtɪv/ *adjective* good at thinking of new ideas or using imagination to create new and unusual things *Her book is full of creative ways to decorate your home.* ● **creatively** *adverb* ● **creativity** /ˌkriːeɪ'tɪvəti/ *noun* [U] the ability to produce new ideas or things using skill and imagination

creator /kri'eɪtəʳ/ *noun* **1** [C] someone who invents or makes something **2 the Creator** God

creature /'kriːtʃəʳ/ *noun* [C] anything that lives but is not a plant *Dolphins are very intelligent creatures.*

creche /kreʃ/ *noun* [C] *UK* a place where babies and young children are looked after while their parents do something else

credence /'kriːdᵊns/ *noun* **add/give/lend credence to sth** to make a story, theory, etc seem more likely to be true *The letters lend credence to the idea that he had an unhappy life.*

credentials /krɪ'denʃᵊlz/ *noun* [plural] **1** skills and experience that show you are suitable for a particular job or activity *academic credentials* **2** documents that prove who you are

---

WORD PARTNERS FOR *credibility*

gain/lose credibility ● sth **damages/destroys/restores/undermines** sb's credibility ● sb **lacks** credibility

---

credibility /ˌkredə'bɪləti/ *noun* [U] when someone can be believed and trusted *This decision has damaged the President's credibility.*

credible /'kredəbl/ *adjective* able to be trusted or believed *credible evidence*

credit¹ /'kredɪt/ *noun* **1** PAYMENT [U] a way of buying something in which you arrange to pay for it at a later time *We offer interest-free credit on all new cars.* ○ *He bought most of the furniture on credit.* **2** PRAISE [U] praise that is given to someone for something they have done *I did most of the work but Dan got all the credit!* ○ *We should give her credit for her honesty.* ○ *I can't take full credit for this meal - Sam helped.* **3 be a credit to sb/sth** to do something that makes a person or organization

proud of you *Giorgio is a credit to his family.*
4 to sb's credit If something is to someone's
credit, they deserve praise for it. *To his credit,
Bill never blamed her for the incident.* **5 have
sth to your credit** to have achieved something
*By the age of 25, she had five novels to her
credit.* **6 in credit** having money in your bank
account **7** MONEY [C] an amount of money that
you put into your bank account ⊃Opposite **debit.**
8 COURSE [C] a unit that shows you have completed part of a college course

credit² /'kredɪt/ *verb* [T] **1** to add money to
someone's bank account **2** to believe that
something is true *Dean's getting married! Who
would have credited it?*
    credit sth to sb to say that someone is re-
sponsible for something good *an idea credited
to Isaac Newton*
    credit sb with sth to believe that someone
has a particular quality *Credit me with some
intelligence!*
    credit sb with sth/doing sth to say that
someone is responsible for something good
*She is credited with making the business a suc-
cess.*

creditable /'kredɪtəbl/ *adjective* Something
that is creditable deserves praise. *a creditable
performance*

'credit ,card *noun* [C] a small plastic card that
allows you to buy something and pay for it
later *He paid by credit card.*

'credit ,limit *noun* [C] the largest amount of
money that a person can borrow with a credit
card (= a small plastic card that allows you to
buy something and pay for it later) *a £500
credit limit*

creditor /'kredɪtəʳ/ *noun* [C] a person or organization that someone owes money to

the credits /'kredɪts/ *noun* [plural] a list of
people who made a film or television programme

creed /kriːd/ *noun* [C] a set of beliefs, especially
religious beliefs that influence your life

creek /kriːk/ *noun* [C] **1** *UK* a narrow area of
water that flows into the land from a sea or
river **2** *mainly US* a stream or narrow river

creep¹ /kriːp/ *verb past* crept **1 creep along/in/
out, etc** to move very quietly and carefully *I
crept out of the room.* **2 creep across/in/into, etc**
to gradually start to exist or appear *Problems
were beginning to creep into their relationship.*
3 creep along/down/through, etc to move somewhere very slowly *The convoy crept along in
the darkness.*
    creep up on sb 1 to surprise someone by
moving closer to them from behind *Don't creep
up on me like that!* **2** If a feeling or state creeps
up on you, it happens gradually so that you do
not notice it. *Old age just creeps up on you.*

creep² /kriːp/ *noun* [C] **1** *UK* someone who you
do not like because they are nice to people in a
way that is not sincere **2** someone who you
think is unpleasant

creeps /kriːps/ *noun* **give sb the creeps** *informal*
to make someone feel frightened or nervous
These old buildings give me the creeps.

creepy /'kriːpi/ *adjective informal* strange and

frightening *a creepy story/person*

cremate /krɪ'meɪt/ *verb* [T] to burn a dead body
● **cremation** /krɪ'meɪʃᵊn/ *noun* [C, U] the ceremony
where someone is cremated

crematorium /,kremə'tɔːriəm/ (*also US* crema-
tory /'kriːmətɔːri/) *noun* [C] a place where people
are cremated

crept /krept/ *past of* creep

crescendo /krɪ'ʃendəʊ/ *noun* [C] when a noise
or piece of music gradually gets louder

crescent /'kresᵊnt/ *noun* **1** [C] a curved shape
that is narrow at each end and wider in the
middle *the pale crescent of the moon* **2 Crescent**
used in the names of streets that have a
curved shape *57 Park Crescent*

crest /krest/ *noun* [C] **1** TOP the highest part of a
hill or wave **2** FEATHERS the feathers that point
upwards on a bird's head **3** DESIGN a design
used as the symbol of a school, important
family, etc

crestfallen /'krest,fɔːlᵊn/ *adjective* disappointed or sad

crevasse /krɪ'væs/ *noun* [C] a deep, wide crack,
especially in ice

crevice /'krevɪs/ *noun* [C] a small, narrow crack,
especially in a rock

crew /kruː/ *noun* [group] **1** the people who work
together on a ship, aircraft, or train *a crew
member* **2** a team of people with special skills
who work together *Fire and ambulance crews
were at the scene.*

crewman /'kruːmæn/ *noun* [C] *plural* crewmen a
member of the crew of a ship or aircraft

crib /krɪb/ *US* (*UK* cot) *noun* [C] a bed with high
sides for a baby

cricket /'krɪkɪt/ *noun* **1** [U] a game in which two
teams of eleven people try to score points by
hitting a ball and running between two
wickets (= sets of three wooden sticks) *a
cricket ball/bat* ⊃See colour picture **Sports 2** on
page Centre 15. **2** [C] an insect that jumps and
makes a noise by rubbing its wings together

cricketer /'krɪkɪtəʳ/ *noun* [C] someone who
plays cricket, especially as their job

WORD PARTNERS FOR ***crime***

commit a crime ● **combat/reduce/fight**
crime ● a **minor** / **petty** / **terrible** / **violent**
crime

o-**crime** /kraɪm/ *noun* **1** [U] illegal activities *violent crime* ○ *tough new measures to fight
crime* **2** [C] something someone does that is illegal *He committed a serious crime.* ⊃See also:
war crime.

criminal¹ /'krɪmɪnᵊl/ *adjective* **1** [always before
noun] relating to crime *criminal activity* ○ *He
has a criminal record* (= the police have an
official record of his crimes). **2** *informal* very
bad or morally wrong *It's criminal that people
are having to wait so long for hospital treatment.* ● **criminally** *adverb*

criminal² /'krɪmɪnᵊl/ *noun* [C] someone who has
committed a crime *a dangerous/violent
criminal*

criminologist /,krɪmɪ'nɒlədʒɪst/ *noun* [C] someone who studies crime and criminals

crimson /ˈkrɪmzᵊn/ *noun* [U] a dark red colour • **crimson** *adjective*

cringe /krɪndʒ/ *verb* [I] **1** to feel very embarrassed about something *Jan* ***cringed at*** *the sight of her father dancing.* **2** to move away from something because you are frightened

crinkle /ˈkrɪŋkl/ *verb* [I, T] to become covered in small lines or folds, or to make something become covered in small lines or folds • **crinkly** *adjective* Something that is crinkly has crinkles in it.

cripple¹ /ˈkrɪpl/ *verb* [T] **1** to injure someone so that they cannot use their arms or legs **[often passive]** *His son was crippled by a riding accident.* **2** to damage something very badly and make it weak or not effective **[often passive]** *a country crippled by war*

cripple² /ˈkrɪpl/ *noun* [C] *old-fashioned* an offensive word for someone who cannot use their legs or arms in a normal way

crippling /ˈkrɪplɪŋ/ *adjective* **1** **[always before noun]** A crippling illness makes someone unable to use their arms or legs in a normal way. **2** causing great damage *a crippling storm*

🔑**crisis** /ˈkraɪsɪs/ *noun* [C, U] *plural* **crises** /ˈkraɪsiːz/ a situation or time that is extremely dangerous or difficult *an economic/financial crisis* ○ *The country's leadership is* ***in crisis.*** ➲See also: **mid-life crisis.**

crisp¹ /krɪsp/ *adjective* **1** [FOOD] Crisp food is pleasantly hard. *a crisp apple* ○ *crisp pastry* **2** [MATERIAL] Crisp cloth or paper money is clean and looks new, with no folds. *a crisp linen shirt* **3** [WEATHER] Crisp weather is pleasantly cold and dry. *a crisp autumn day* **4** [QUICK] A crisp way of talking or behaving is quick and confident. **5** [IMAGE] A crisp image is very clear.

crisp² /krɪsp/ *UK* (*US* **chip**) *noun* [C] a very thin slice of potato that has been cooked in oil and is eaten cold **[usually plural]** *a packet of crisps* ➲See colour picture **Food** on page Centre 11.

crispy /ˈkrɪspi/ *adjective* Crispy food is pleasantly hard and easy to bite through. *crispy bacon*

criss-cross /ˈkrɪskrɒs/ *verb* [I, T] If something criss-crosses an area, it crosses it several times in different directions. **[often passive]** *The forest is criss-crossed with paths and tracks.*

criterion /kraɪˈtɪəriən/ *noun* [C] *plural* **criteria** a fact or level of quality that you use when making a choice or decision **[+ for + doing sth]** *We have strict criteria for deciding which students will receive a grant.*

critic /ˈkrɪtɪk/ *noun* [C] **1** someone who says that they do not approve of someone or something *an* ***outspoken critic*** *of the government* **2** someone whose job is to give their opinion of a book, play, film, etc *a theatre/film critic*

critical /ˈkrɪtɪkᵊl/ *adjective* **1** [NOT PLEASED] saying that someone or something is bad or wrong *a critical report* ○ *He is very* ***critical of*** *the way I work.* **2** [IMPORTANT] very important for the way things will happen in the future *a critical decision* **3** [SERIOUS] extremely serious or dangerous *The doctors said her condition was critical and she might not survive.* **4** [OPINIONS] giving judgments and opinions on books, plays, films, etc *a critical study of Tennyson's work* • **critically** *adverb*

WORD PARTNERS FOR *criticism*

sb/sth **attracts/draws/faces/sparks** criticism • **deflect/dismiss** criticism • **fierce/stinging/strong** criticism • criticism **of** sb/sth • criticism **from** sb

🔑**criticism** /ˈkrɪtɪsɪzᵊm/ *noun* **1** [C, U] when you say that something or someone is bad *Plans to close the hospital* ***attracted*** *strong public* ***criticism.*** **2** [U] when someone gives their judgments and opinions on books, plays, films, etc *literary criticism*

criticize (*also UK* **-ise**) /ˈkrɪtɪsaɪz/ *verb* [I, T] to say that something or someone is bad **[often passive, + for + doing sth]** *The film was criticized for being too violent.*

critique /krɪˈtiːk/ *noun* [C] a report that says what is good and bad about something

croak /krəʊk/ *verb* **1** [I, T] to talk or say something in a low, rough voice [I] *"I don't feel well," he croaked.* **2** [I] If a bird or frog (= green jumping animal) croaks, it makes a deep, low sound.

crochet /ˈkrəʊʃeɪ/ [US] /krəʊˈʃeɪ/ *verb* [I, T] to make clothes and other items using wool and a special needle with a hook at one end

crockery /ˈkrɒkᵊri/ *noun* [U] plates, cups, and other dishes, especially those made from clay

crocodile /ˈkrɒkədaɪl/ *noun* [C] a big reptile with a long mouth and sharp teeth, that lives in lakes and rivers

crocus /ˈkrəʊkəs/ *noun* [C] a small yellow, purple, or white spring flower

croissant /ˈkwæsɒŋ/ [US] /kwɑːˈsɒŋ/ *noun* [C] a soft, curved piece of bread, eaten for breakfast ➲See picture at **bread.**

crony /ˈkrəʊni/ *noun* [C] *informal* one of a group of friends who help each other, especially in a way that is not fair **[usually plural]** *He gave his cronies all the best jobs.*

crook /krʊk/ *noun* **1** [C] *informal* a criminal or someone who cheats people **2 the crook of your arm** the inside part of your arm where it bends

crooked /ˈkrʊkɪd/ *adjective* **1** not straight *crooked teeth* **2** *informal* not honest *a crooked politician*

croon /kruːn/ *verb* [I, T] to sing in a soft, low, romantic voice

crop¹ /krɒp/ *noun* **1** [C] a plant such as a grain, fruit, or vegetable that is grown in large amounts by farmers **2** [C] the amount of plants of a particular type that are produced at one time *We had a record crop of grapes this year.* **3 a crop of sth** a group of the same type of things or people that exist at the same time *He's one of the current crop of young Italian artists.* ➲See also: **cash crop.**

crop² /krɒp/ *verb* **cropping,** *past* **cropped** **1** [T] to cut something so that it is short **2** [I] *UK* If a plant crops, it produces fruit, flowers, etc.

crop up to happen or appear suddenly *The*

*same old problems **kept cropping up**.*

cropper /ˈkrɒpəʳ/ *noun* **1 come a cropper a** to fall over *The horse came a cropper at the first fence.* **b** to fail in an embarrassing way, or to make an embarrassing mistake

croquet /ˈkrəʊkeɪ/ [US] /krəʊˈkeɪ/ *noun* [U] a game played on grass, in which you hit a ball with a wooden hammer through curved wires pushed into the ground

⊶ **cross¹** /krɒs/ *verb* **1** [FROM ONE SIDE TO ANOTHER] [I, T] to go from one side of something to the other side *It's not a good place to **cross** the road.* **2** [LINE/BORDER] [I, T] to travel over a border or line into a different area, country, etc *They **crossed** from Albania **into** Greece.* **3** [MEET AND GO ACROSS] [I, T] If two lines, roads, etc cross, they go over or across each other. **4 cross your arms/fingers/legs** to put one of your arms, fingers, or legs over the top of the other **5 cross yourself** to touch your head, chest, and both shoulders as a sign to God **6** [ANIMAL/PLANT] [T] to mix two breeds of animal or plant to produce a new breed **7** [MAKE SOMEONE ANGRY] [T] to make someone angry by refusing to do what they want you to do ➲See also: I'll/We'll cross that **bridge¹** when I/we come to it., **criss-cross**, **double-cross**, keep your fingers (**finger¹**) crossed, cross your **mind¹**.

cross sth off (sth) to remove a word from a list by drawing a line through it *Did you cross her name off the guest list?*

cross sth out to draw a line through something that you have written, usually because it is wrong *Cross out that last sentence.*

⊶ **cross²** /krɒs/ *noun* **1** [WOOD] [C] two pieces of wood that cross each other, on which people were left to die as a punishment in the past **2** [SYMBOL] [C] an object in the shape of a cross, used as a symbol of the Christian religion **3** [MARK] [C] a written mark (x), used for showing where something is, or that something that has been written is wrong **4 a cross between sth and sth** a mixture of two different things or people *The dog is a cross between a terrier and a rottweiler.* **5** [SPORT] [C] when someone kicks or hits the ball across the field in sport, especially football

cross³ /krɒs/ *adjective* annoyed or angry *Don't be cross with me!*

cross- /krɒs-/ *prefix* **1** across *cross-border* **2** including different groups or subjects *a cross-party committee* (= one formed from many political parties) ○ *cross-cultural*

crossbar /ˈkrɒsbɑːʳ/ *noun* [C] **1** the post at the top of a goal in games such as football *Owen hit the crossbar.* **2** the metal tube that joins the front and back of a bicycle

cross-border /ˈkrɒsˌbɔːdəʳ/ *adjective* [always before noun] between different countries, or involving people from different countries *cross-border trade*

cross-Channel /ˌkrɒsˈtʃænəl/ *adjective* [always before noun] connecting or happening between England and France *a **cross-Channel** ferry/route*

cross-country /ˌkrɒsˈkʌntri/ *adjective* [always before noun], *adverb* **1** across fields and countryside *cross-country running/skiing* **2** from one side of a country to the other side

cross-examine /ˌkrɒsɪgˈzæmɪn/ *verb* [T] to ask someone a lot of questions about something they have said, in order to discover if it is true, especially in a court of law • **cross-examination** /ˌkrɒsɪgˌzæmɪˈneɪʃən/ *noun* [U]

cross-eyed /krɒsˈaɪd/ *adjective* A cross-eyed person has both eyes looking in towards their nose.

crossfire /ˈkrɒsfaɪəʳ/ *noun* **1** [U] bullets fired towards you from different directions *Civilians died when a bus was **caught in crossfire** between government and rebel troops.* **2 be caught in the crossfire** to be involved in a situation where people around you are arguing

crossing /ˈkrɒsɪŋ/ *noun* [C] **1** [WHERE PEOPLE CROSS] a place where people can go across a road, river, etc **2** [SEA JOURNEY] a journey across water **3** [WHERE LINES CROSS] a place where roads, railways, etc cross each other ➲See also: **grade crossing, level crossing, zebra crossing.**

cross-legged /ˌkrɒsˈlegɪd/ *adverb* **sit cross-legged** to sit on the floor with your knees wide apart and one foot over the other foot

ˌcross ˈpurposes *noun* **at cross purposes** If two people are at cross purposes, they do not understand each other because they are talking about different things but do not know this.

ˌcross ˈreference *noun* [C] a note in a book that tells you to look somewhere else in the book for more information about something

crossroads /ˈkrɒsrəʊdz/ *noun* [C] *plural* **crossroads** **1** a place where two roads cross each other **2** a time when you have to make an important decision that will affect your future life *I felt I was **at a crossroads** in my life.*

cross-section /ˈkrɒssekʃən/ *noun* [C] **1** a small group of people or things that represents all the different types in a larger group *a **cross-section** of society* **2** something that has been cut in half so that you can see the inside, or a picture of this *a cross-section of a human heart*

crosswalk /ˈkrɒswɔːk/ *US* (*UK* **pedestrian crossing**) *noun* [C] a special place on a road where traffic must stop if people want to cross

crossword /ˈkrɒswɜːd/ (*also* **ˈcrossword ˌpuzzle**) *noun* [C] a game in which you write words which are the answers to questions in a pattern of black and white squares

crotch /krɒtʃ/ (*also UK* **crutch**) *noun* [C] the part of your body between the tops of your legs, or the part of a piece of clothing that covers this area

crouch /kraʊtʃ/ (*also* **crouch down**) *verb* [I] to move your body close to the ground by bending your knees *I crouched behind the chair to avoid being seen.*

crow¹ /krəʊ/ *noun* **1** [C] a large black bird that makes a loud noise **2 as the crow flies** when measured in a straight line *It's about 50 miles from London to Cambridge as the crow flies.*

crow² /krəʊ/ *verb* [I] **1** to talk in a proud and annoying way about something you have done *Donald wouldn't stop **crowing about** his exam results.* **2** If a cock (= male chicken) crows, it makes a loud noise, usually in the early morning.

WORD PARTNERS FOR **crowd**

a crowd **gathers** • a crowd **of** [people/tourists, etc] • **in** a crowd

---

crowd[1] /kraʊd/ noun **1** [C] a large group of people who are together in one place *A large crowd had gathered to wait for the princess.* ○ *Shop early and avoid the crowds.* **2** [no plural] *informal* a group of friends or people with similar interests *the art/theatre crowd*

crowd[2] /kraʊd/ verb [T] **1** to stand together in large numbers *Protesters crowded the streets.* **2** to stand too close to someone *Don't crowd me!*

crowd around/round (sb/sth) If a group of people crowd around or crowd around someone or something, they stand very close all around them. *Everyone crowded around my desk.*

crowd in/crowd (sb) into sth If a large group of people crowd into somewhere, they all go there and fill the place.

crowd sb out to prevent someone or something from succeeding or existing to by being much more successful than them or by being present in much larger numbers *Large national companies often crowd out smaller local businesses.*

crowded /kraʊdɪd/ adjective very full of people *a crowded room/train*

crown[1] /kraʊn/ noun **1** KING/ QUEEN [C] a round object made of gold and jewels (= valuable stones) that a king or queen wears on their head **2** TOP [C] the top of a hat, head, or hill **3** the **Crown** used to refer to the power or government of a king or queen *All this land belongs to the Crown.* **4** TOOTH [C] an artificial top that is put on a damaged tooth

crown[2] /kraʊn/ verb [T] **1** MAKE KING/QUEEN to put a crown on someone's head in an official ceremony that makes them a king or queen [often passive] *Queen Elizabeth II of England was crowned in 1952.* **2** ON TOP *literary* to be on top of something else *A large domed ceiling crowns the main hall.* **3** BEST PART to be the best or most successful part of something *a book that crowned his successful writing career*

crowning /kraʊnɪŋ/ adjective [always before noun] more important, beautiful, etc than anything else *It was the **crowning achievement** of his political career.*

crucial /kruːʃəl/ adjective extremely important or necessary *a crucial decision/question* ○ *Her work has been **crucial to** the project's success.* ● **crucially** adverb

crucifix /kruːsɪfɪks/ noun [C] a model of a cross with Jesus Christ on it

crucifixion /ˌkruːsəˈfɪkʃən/ noun [C, U] in the past, when someone was fastened to a cross and left to die *the crucifixion of Christ*

crucify /ˈkruːsɪfaɪ/ verb [T] **1** in the past, to fasten someone to a cross and leave them to

die **2** *informal* to criticize someone or something in a cruel and damaging way [often passive] *The film has been crucified by the media.*

crude /kruːd/ adjective **1** made or done in a simple way and without much skill *a crude device/weapon* **2** rude and offensive *a crude comment/remark* ● **crudely** adverb

crude 'oil (*also* crude) *noun* [U] oil in its natural state before it has been treated

○ᴡ**cruel** /ˈkruːəl/ adjective **crueller, cruellest** or **crueler, cruelest** extremely unkind, or causing people or animals to suffer *a cruel joke* ○ *Many people think hunting is **cruel to** animals.* ● **cruelly** adverb

cruelty /ˈkruːəlti/ noun [C, U] cruel behaviour or a cruel action *laws against **cruelty to** animals*

cruise[1] /kruːz/ noun [C] a holiday on a ship, sailing from place to place

cruise[2] /kruːz/ verb **1** [I] to move in a vehicle at a speed that does not change *The plane is cruising at 500 miles per hour.* **2** [I] to go on a cruise **3 cruise to success/victory, etc** *informal* to win a competition easily

cruise 'missile *UK* (*US* 'cruise ˌmissile) *noun* [C] a weapon that flies through the air, and which often carries nuclear weapons

cruiser /ˈkruːzəʳ/ noun [C] **1** a large military ship used in wars **2** (*also* 'cabin ˌcruiser) a motor boat with a room for people to sleep in

'cruise ˌship (*also* 'cruise ˌliner) *noun* [C] a large ship like a hotel, which people travel on for pleasure

crumb /krʌm/ noun **1** [C] a very small piece of bread, cake, etc **2 a crumb of sth** a very small amount of something

crumble /ˈkrʌmbl/ verb **1** [I, T] to break into small pieces, or to make something break into small pieces *Buildings crumbled as the earthquake struck.* **2** [I] If a relationship, system, or feeling crumbles, it fails or ends. *His first marriage crumbled after only a year.*

crummy /ˈkrʌmi/ adjective *informal* unpleasant, or of bad quality *a crummy job* ○ *a crummy hotel*

crumple /ˈkrʌmpl/ verb **1** [I, T] If something such as paper or cloth crumples, it becomes crushed, and if you crumple it, you crush it until it is full of folds. *a crumpled shirt* **2** [I] If someone's face crumples, they suddenly look very sad or disappointed.

crumple sth up to crush a piece of paper until it is full of folds

crunch[1] /krʌnʃ/ noun **1** [C] the sound of something being crushed [usually singular] *the crunch of dried leaves under our feet* **2 if/when it comes to the crunch** if/when a situation becomes serious or you have to make an important decision

crunch[2] /krʌnʃ/ verb **1** [I, T] to make a noise by chewing hard food *She was **crunching on** an apple.* **2** [I] to make a sound as if something is being crushed *The gravel crunched under our feet.*

crunchy /ˈkrʌntʃi/ adjective Crunchy food is hard and makes a noise when you eat it.

🧩 **WORD PARTNERS FOR *crusade***

launch/mount a crusade • be **on** a crusade • a **moral/personal** crusade • a crusade **against/for** sth

crusade /kru:'seɪd/ *noun* [C] a determined attempt to change or achieve something that you believe in strongly • **crusader** *noun* [C] someone who is involved in a crusade

crush¹ /krʌʃ/ *verb* [T] **1** to press something so hard that it is made flat or broken into pieces *Her car was crushed by a falling tree.* **2** to defeat someone or something completely *government attempts to crush protests* ○ *a crushing defeat*

crush² /krʌʃ/ *noun* **1** [no plural] a crowd of people forced to stand close together because there is not enough room *Many people fell over in the crush.* **2** [C] *informal* a strong temporary feeling of love for someone *Tim **has a crush on** Jennifer.*

crust /krʌst/ *noun* [C, U] **1** the hard outer surface of bread or other baked foods **2** a hard, dry layer on the surface of something

crusty /'krʌsti/ *adjective* **1** unfriendly and becoming annoyed very easily **2** Something that is crusty has a hard outer layer. *crusty bread*

crutch /krʌtʃ/ *noun* [C] **1** a stick that you put under your arm to help you walk if you have injured your leg or foot [usually plural] *Charles was **on crutches** (= walking with crutches) for six weeks.* **2** *UK (UK/US* **crotch***)* the part of your body between the tops of your legs, or the part of a piece of clothing that covers this area

crux /krʌks/ *noun* **the crux (of sth)** the main or most important part of a problem, argument, etc

cry

o⭐**cry**¹ /kraɪ/ *verb* **1** [I] to produce tears from your eyes, usually because you are sad, angry, or hurt *My baby brother cries all the time.* **2** [I, T] to speak or say something loudly *"Look at this!" cried Raj.* ⊃See also: cry your eyes (**eye**¹) out, a **shoulder**¹ to cry on.

be crying out for sth *informal* to need something very much *a school that's crying out for more money*

cry out (sth) to shout or make a loud noise because you are frightened, hurt, etc *She cried out in terror.*

cry² /kraɪ/ *noun* **1** [C] a shout, especially one that shows that someone is frightened, hurt, etc *a cry of horror/joy/pain* **2** [C] a sound that a particular animal or bird makes *an eagle's cry* **3 have a cry** to produce tears from your eyes, usually because you are sad, angry, or hurt **4 be a far cry from sth** to be very different from something *Her luxury mansion is a far cry from the house she grew up in.*

crying /'kraɪɪŋ/ *adjective* **1 a crying need for sth** *mainly UK* a need that is very urgent *There's a crying need for more nurses.* **2 it's a crying**

shame used to say that you think a situation is very wrong

crypt /krɪpt/ *noun* [C] a room under a church, especially one where people are buried

cryptic /'krɪptɪk/ *adjective* mysterious and difficult to understand *a cryptic comment/message* • **cryptically** *adverb*

crystal /'krɪst³l/ *noun* **1** ROCK [C, U] a type of transparent rock **2** GLASS [U] a type of high quality glass *a crystal vase* **3** SHAPE [C] a piece of a substance that has become solid, with a regular shape *ice crystals*

crystal 'ball *noun* [C] a large, glass ball that some people believe you can look into to see what will happen in the future

crystal 'clear *adjective* very obvious and easy to understand *She made her feelings crystal clear to me.*

CU *internet abbreviation for* see you: used when saying goodbye at the end of an email or text message

cub /kʌb/ *noun* [C] a young bear, fox, lion, etc

cube¹ /kju:b/ *noun* **1** [C] a solid object with six square sides of the same size *Cut the cheese into small cubes.* ⊃See picture at **shape**. **2 the cube of sth** the number you get when you multiply a particular number by itself twice *The cube of 3 is 27.* ⊃See also: **ice cube**.

cube² /kju:b/ *verb* [T] **1** to multiply a particular number by itself twice *5 cubed is 125.* **2** to cut something into cubes

cubic /'kju:bɪk/ *adjective* **cubic centimetre/inch/metre, etc** a unit of measurement that shows the volume (= length multiplied by width multiplied by height) of something *a reservoir that holds 22 million cubic metres of water*

cubicle /'kju:bɪkl/ *noun* [C] a small space with walls around it, that is separate from the rest of a room *a shower cubicle*

cuckoo /'kʊku:/ *noun* [C] a small bird that makes a sound like its name and puts its eggs into other birds' nests

cucumber /'kju:kʌmbə/ *noun* [C, U] a long, green vegetable that you eat raw in salads ⊃See colour picture **Fruit and Vegetables** on page Centre 10.

cuddle /'kʌdl/ *verb* [I, T] to put your arms around someone to show them that you love them *Her mother cuddled her until she stopped crying.* • **cuddle** *noun* [C]

cuddle up to sit or lie very close to someone *The children **cuddled up to** me to keep warm.*

cuddly /'kʌdli/ *adjective* soft and pleasant to hold close to you

cue /kju:/ *noun* **1** ACTION/EVENT [C] an action or event that is a sign that something should happen *The final goal was the cue for celebration.* **2** SIGNAL [C] a signal that tells someone to start speaking or doing something when acting in a play, film, etc **3 on cue** If something happens on cue, it happens at exactly the right time. *Then, **right on cue**, Andrew appeared at the door.* **4 take your cue from sb/sth** to copy what someone else does *I took my cue from the others and left.* **5** STICK [C] a long, straight stick used to hit the balls in games like snooker (= a

---

| j yes | k cat | ŋ ring | ʃ she | θ thin | ð this | ʒ decision | dʒ jar | tʃ chip | æ cat | e bed | ə ago | ɪ sit | i cosy | ɒ hot | ʌ run | ʊ put |

game played with small coloured balls on a table)

cuff /kʌf/ *noun* [C] **1** the bottom part of a sleeve that goes around your wrist ⊃See picture at **jacket**. **2 off the cuff** If you speak off the cuff, you do it without having planned what you will say.

cuisine /kwɪz'iːn/ *noun* [U] a style of cooking *French/international cuisine*

cul-de-sac /'kʌldəsæk/ *noun* [C] a short road with houses which is blocked at one end

culinary /'kʌlɪnᵊri/ *adjective* [always before noun] *formal* related to food and cooking *culinary equipment*

cull /kʌl/ *verb* [T] to kill some of the animals in a group, especially the weakest ones, to limit their numbers ● **cull** *noun* [C]

cull sth from sth to collect ideas or information from several different places [often passive] *The book is culled from over 800 pages of his diaries.*

culminate /'kʌlmɪneɪt/ *verb formal* **1 culminate in/with sth** to finish with a particular event, or reach a final result after gradual development and often a lot of effort *His career culminated with the post of ambassador to NATO.* **2** [T] *US* to be the final thing in a series of events *The discovery of a body culminated two days of desperate searching.* ● **culmination** /ˌkʌlmɪ'neɪʃᵊn/ *noun* [no plural] *This discovery is the culmination of years of research.*

culpable /'kʌlpəbl/ *adjective formal* deserving to be blamed for something bad ● **culpability** /ˌkʌlpə'bɪləti/ *noun* [U]

culprit /'kʌlprɪt/ *noun* [C] **1** someone who has done something wrong **2** something that is responsible for a bad situation *In many of these illnesses, stress is the main culprit.*

cult /kʌlt/ *noun* [C] **1** someone or something which has become very popular with a particular group of people *a cult figure/movie* **2** a religious group whose ideas are considered strange by many people

cultivate /'kʌltɪveɪt/ *verb* [T] **1** to prepare land and grow crops on it *This shrub is cultivated in Europe as a culinary herb.* **2** to try to develop or improve something *She has cultivated an image as a tough negotiator.* ● **cultivation** /ˌkʌltɪ'veɪʃᵊn/ *noun* [U]

cultivated /'kʌltɪveɪtɪd/ *adjective* A cultivated person has had a good education and knows a lot about art, books, music, etc.

cultural /'kʌltʃᵊrᵊl/ *adjective* **1** relating to the habits, traditions and beliefs of a society *cultural diversity/identity* **2** relating to music, art, theatre, literature, etc *cultural events* ● **culturally** *adverb*

o▬**culture** /'kʌltʃəʳ/ *noun* **1** SOCIETY [C, U] the habits, traditions, and beliefs of a country, society, or group of people *American/Japanese culture* ○ *It's a good opportunity for children to learn about other cultures.* **2** ARTS [U] music, art, theatre, literature, etc *popular culture* **3** BIOLOGY [C, U] the process of growing living things, especially bacteria (= very small living things that can cause disease), for scientific purposes, or the bacteria produced by this process

cultured /'kʌltʃəd/ *adjective* A cultured person knows a lot about music, art, theatre, etc.

'**culture ˌshock** *noun* [U] the feeling of confusion someone has when they go to a new and very different place

-cum- /kʌm/ used between two nouns to describe something which combines the two things *a kitchen-cum-dining room* (= room which is used as a kitchen and a dining room)

cumbersome /'kʌmbəsəm/ *adjective* **1** large and difficult to move or use *cumbersome safety equipment* **2** slow and not effective *cumbersome bureaucracy*

cumulative /'kjuːmjələtɪv/ *adjective* reached by gradually adding one thing after another *a cumulative score*

cunning /'kʌnɪŋ/ *adjective* clever at getting what you want, especially by tricking people *a cunning plan/ploy* ● **cunning** *noun* [U] ● **cunningly** *adverb*

cup

o▬**cup** /kʌp/ *noun* [C] **1** CONTAINER a small, round container with a handle on the side, used to drink from *a cup of tea/coffee* **2** SPORT a prize given to the winner of a competition, or the name of the competition *the World Cup* **3** COOKING *mainly US* a measurement of amounts of food used in cooking ⊃See also: **egg cup**.

cup² /kʌp/ *verb* [T] **cupping**, *past* **cupped** to make your hands into the shape of a cup, or to hold something with your hands in this shape

o▬**cupboard** /'kʌbəd/ *noun* [C] a piece of furniture with a door on the front and shelves inside, used for storing things ⊃See colour picture **The Kitchen** on page Centre 2 ⊃See also: have a **skeleton** in the cupboard.

curate /'kjʊərət/ *noun* [C] a person who works for the Church of England and whose job is to help the vicar (= priest in a particular area)

curator /kjʊə'reɪtəʳ/ *noun* [C] a person who is in charge of a museum (= a building where you can look at objects, such as art or old things)

curb¹ /kɜːb/ *verb* [T] to limit or control something *to curb crime/inflation*

curb² /kɜːb/ *noun* [C] **1** something which limits or controls something *They are proposing a curb on tobacco advertising.* **2** *US* spelling of **kerb** (= the line of stones at the edge of a path next to the road)

curdle /'kɜːdl/ *verb* [I, T] If a liquid curdles, or if you curdle it, it gets thicker and develops lumps. *Heat the sauce slowly or it will curdle.*

WORD PARTNERS FOR *cure*

find/look for a cure • a cure for sth • the
search for a cure

cure[1] /kjʊəʳ/ *noun* [C] **1** something that makes
someone with an illness healthy again *They
are trying to find a cure for cancer.* **2** a solution to a problem

cure[2] /kjʊəʳ/ *verb* [T] **1** to make someone with an
illness healthy again *Getting a better chair
completely cured my back problems.* **2** to solve
a problem *the fight to cure social inequality*

curfew /'kɜːfjuː/ *noun* [C] a time, especially at
night, when people are not allowed to leave
their homes

WORD PARTNERS FOR *curiosity*

arouse/satisfy sb's curiosity • (do sth) out
of curiosity • mild/natural curiosity • curiosity about sth

curiosity /ˌkjʊəriˈɒsəti/ *noun* **1** [U] the feeling of
wanting to know or learn about something *My
curiosity got the better of me and I opened the
envelope.* ○ *Just out of curiosity, how did you
get my address?* **2** [C] something strange or unusual

curious /'kjʊəriəs/ *adjective* **1** wanting to know
or learn about something *I was curious about
his life in India.* ○ *I was curious to know what
would happen next.* **2** strange or unusual *The
house was decorated in a curious style.* • **curiously** *adverb She looked at him curiously.*

curl[1] /kɜːl/ *noun* [C] something with a small,
curved shape, especially a piece of hair *a child
with blonde curls*

curl[2] /kɜːl/ *verb* [I, T] to make something into the
shape of a curl, or to be this shape *The cat
curled its tail around its body.*

curl up 1 to sit or lie in a position with your
arms and legs close to your body *She curled up
and went to sleep.* **2** If something flat, such as a
piece of paper, curls up, the edges start to
curve up.

curly /'kɜːli/ *adjective* shaped like a curl, or with
many curls *curly hair*

currant /'kʌrənt/ *noun* [C] a small, black dried
fruit used in cooking, especially in cakes

currency /'kʌrənsi/ *noun* **1** [C, U] the units of
money used in a particular country *foreign
currency* **2** [U] when an idea is believed or accepted by many people *This view is gaining
currency within the government.* ⊃See also: **hard
currency**.

o-- **current**[1] /'kʌrənt/ *adjective* happening or exist-
ing now *What is your current address?* ⊃See
Common learner error at **actual**. • **currently** *adverb
The factory currently employs 750 people.*

current[2] /'kʌrənt/ *noun* **1** [C] the natural flow of
air or water in one direction *a current of air
○ dangerous/strong currents* **2** [C, U] the flow of
electricity through a wire *an electrical current*

,**current ac'count** UK (US **checking account**)
noun [C] a bank account which you can take
money out of at any time

,**current af'fairs** UK (US ,**current e'vents**) *noun*
[plural] important political or social events

which are happening in the world at the present time

curriculum /kəˈrɪkjələm/ *noun* [C] *plural* **curric-
ula** or **curriculums** all the subjects taught in a
school, college, etc or on an educational course
the school curriculum

curry /'kʌri/ *noun* [C, U] a type of food from India,
made of vegetables or meat cooked with hot
spices

curse[1] /kɜːs/ *noun* [C] **1** MAGIC magic words
which are intended to bring bad luck to someone *to put a curse on someone* **2** RUDE WORDS a
rude or offensive word or phrase **3** PROBLEM
something that causes harm or unhappiness,
often over a long period of time *Traffic is one
of the curses of modern living.*

curse[2] /kɜːs/ *verb* **1** [I] to use rude or offensive
words *He cursed angrily under his breath.* **2** [T]
to express anger towards someone or something *He cursed himself for not telling David
about it earlier.* **3 be cursed by/with sth** to have
something which causes problems over a long
period of time

cursor /'kɜːsəʳ/ *noun* [C] a symbol on a computer
screen which shows the place where you are
working

cursory /'kɜːsəri/ *adjective* [always before noun]
formal done quickly and without much care *a
cursory glance*

curt /kɜːt/ *adjective* If something you say or
write is curt, it is short and not very polite.
• **curtly** *adverb*

curtail /kɜːˈteɪl/ *verb* [T] *formal* to reduce, limit,
or stop something *to curtail spending* • **curtail-
ment** *noun* [U]

curtain /'kɜːtən/ *noun* [C] a piece of material
which hangs down to cover a window, stage,
etc *to draw the curtains* (= open or close
them) ○ *The curtain goes up* (= the performance starts) *at 8 o'clock .* ⊃See colour picture **The
Living Room** on page Centre 4.

curtsey (*also* **curtsy**) /'kɜːtsi/ *noun* [C] a movement where a girl or woman puts one foot
behind the other and bends her knees, especially to show respect to a king or queen • **curtsey** *verb* [I]

curve[1] /kɜːv/ *noun* [C] a line which bends round
like part of a circle *a road with gentle curves*

curve[2] /kɜːv/ *verb* [I, T] to move in a curve, form
a curve, or make something into the shape of a
curve *The road curves to the left.* ○ *a chair with
a curved back* ⊃See picture at **flat**.

cushion[1] /'kʊʃən/ *noun* [C] **1** a cloth bag filled
with something soft which you sit on or lean
against to make you comfortable ⊃See colour picture **The Living Room** on page Centre 4. **2** something which protects you from possible problems *Overseas savings provide a cushion
against tax rises at home.*

cushion[2] /'kʊʃən/ *verb* [T] **1** to reduce the bad
effects of something *attempts to cushion the
impact of unemployment* **2** to protect something, especially part of the body, with something soft *Soft grass cushioned his fall.*

cushy /'kʊʃi/ *adjective informal* very easy *a
cushy job*

custard /'kʌstəd/ *noun* **1** [U] a sweet, yellow sauce made from milk and eggs, usually eaten hot with sweet food *apple pie and custard* **2** [C, U] a soft baked mixture made from milk, eggs, and sugar *a custard pie/tart*

custodial /kʌs'təudiəl/ *adjective* If someone is given a custodial sentence (= punishment), they are sent to prison.

custodian /kʌs'təudiən/ *noun* [C] **1** *formal* a person who takes care of something valuable or important *He's the grandson of Oscar Wilde and custodian of his private papers.* **2** *US* someone whose job is to look after a building, especially a school *the custodian of a museum/castle*

> **WORD PARTNERS FOR custody**
>
> be **awarded/given** custody (of sb) • **have/win** custody (of sb)

custody /'kʌstədi/ *noun* [U] **1** the legal right to look after a child, especially when parents separate *When they divorced, it was Nicola who won custody of their two children.* **2** when someone is kept in prison, usually while they are waiting for a trial in court *He is being held in custody in Los Angeles charged with assault.* ○ *He was taken into custody by Mexican authorities.*

> **WORD PARTNERS FOR custom**
>
> an **ancient/local/traditional** custom • the custom **of** doing sth

custom /'kʌstəm/ *noun* **1** [C, U] a habit or tradition *I wasn't familiar with the local customs.* ○ *Many of the ancient customs are still observed today.* **2** [U] when people buy things from shops or businesses *Free gifts are a good way of attracting custom.* ○ *Most of our custom comes from tourists nowadays.* ○ *If we don't give good service, people will take their custom elsewhere.*

custom- /'kʌstəm/ *prefix* used before another word to mean 'specially designed for a particular person or purpose' *custom-built* ○ *custom-designed*

customary /'kʌstəm³ri/ *adjective* normal or expected for a particular person, situation, or society [+ to do sth] *It is customary for the chairman to make the opening speech.* ○ *She's not her customary (= usual) cheerful self today.* • **customarily** /ˌkʌstə'mer³li/ *adverb*

o→**customer** /'kʌstəmər/ *noun* [C] a person or organization that buys goods or services from a shop or business *a satisfied customer* ○ *Mrs Wilson is one of our regular customers.*

customise *UK* (*US* **customize**) /'kʌstəmaɪz/ *verb* [T] to change something to make it suitable for a particular person or purpose *Our language courses are customised to each student.*

customs /'kʌstəmz/ *noun* [U] the place where your bags are examined when you are going into a country, to make sure you are not carrying anything illegal *customs officials* ○ *to go through customs*

cut

o→**cut¹** /kʌt/ *verb* cutting, *past* cut **1** ⟦KNIFE⟧ [I, T] to use a knife or other sharp tool to divide something, remove part of something, or make a hole in something *Cut the meat into small pieces.* ○ *He cut the piece of wood in half.* ○ *I had my hair cut last week.* ○ *She cut off all the diseased buds.* **2** ⟦REDUCE⟧ [T] to reduce the size or amount of something *Prices have been cut by 25%.* ○ *The company is cutting 50 jobs.* **3** ⟦INJURE⟧ [T] to injure yourself on a sharp object which makes you bleed *She cut her finger on a broken glass.* **4** ⟦REMOVE⟧ [T] to remove part of a film or piece of writing *The film was too long so they cut some scenes.* ⊃See also: cut corners (**corner¹**), cut it/things **fine²**, have your **work²** cut out.

cut across sth 1 to go from one side of an area to the other instead of going round it *If we cut across this field, it will save time.* **2** If a problem or subject cuts across different groups of people, all of those groups are affected by it or interested in it.

cut back (sth) to reduce the amount of money being spent on something *We have had to cut back on training this year.*

cut sth down to make a tree or other plant fall to the ground by cutting it near the bottom

cut down (sth) to eat or drink less of something, or to reduce the amount or number of something *My doctor says I should cut down on cigarettes.*

cut sb off to stop someone speaking by interrupting them or putting the telephone down *She cut me off in the middle of our conversation.*

cut sb/sth off 1 to prevent people from reaching or leaving a place, or to separate them from other people [often passive] *The whole village was cut off by flooding.* ○ *She lives abroad and feels very cut off from her family.* **2** to stop providing something such as electricity or food supplies [often passive] *If we*

| ɑː arm | ɜː her | iː see | ɔː saw | uː too | aɪ my | aʊ how | eə hair | eɪ day | əʊ no | ɪə near | ɔɪ boy | ʊə poor | aɪə fire | aʊə sour |

don't pay the gas bill, we'll be cut off.
cut sth out 1 to remove something or form a shape by cutting, usually something made of paper or cloth *She cut out his picture from the magazine.* **2** to stop eating or drinking something, usually to improve your health *I've cut out red meat from my diet.* **3 Cut it out!** *informal* something you say to tell someone to stop doing something annoying **4 not be cut out to be sth/not be cut out for sth** to not have the right qualities for something *I'm not really cut out to be a nurse.*
cut out If an engine, machine, or piece of equipment cuts out, it suddenly stops working.
cut sth/sb out to not let someone share something or be included in something
cut sth up 1 to cut something into pieces **2 be cut up** *UK informal* to be very upset about something *He was very cut up when his brother died.*
cut² /kʌt/ *noun* [C] **1** [INJURY] an injury made when the skin is cut with something sharp *He suffered cuts and bruises in the accident.* **2** [OPENING] an opening made with a sharp tool *She **made a cut** in the material.* **3** [REDUCTION] a reduction in the number or amount of something *tax/job cuts* ○ *The workers were angry about the cut in pay.* **4** [MEAT] a piece of meat from a particular part of an animal *an expensive cut of beef* **5** [SHARE] a share of something, usually money *My family owns the company, so we get a cut of the profits.* **6 an electricity/power, etc cut** when the supply of something is stopped **7** [HAIR] (*also* **haircut**) the style in which your hair has been cut ⊃See also: **shortcut**.
,**cut and 'paste** *verb* [I, T] cutting and pasting *past* **cut** and **pasted** to move words or pictures from one place to another in a computer document

⟐⟐ WORD PARTNERS FOR ***cutback***

make cutbacks • **drastic/severe/sharp** cutbacks • cutbacks **in** sth

cutback /'kʌtbæk/ *noun* [C] a reduction of something, usually to save money *The company has **made cutbacks** and closed one of its factories.*
cute /kjuːt/ *adjective* **1** attractive *a cute baby* **2** *US informal* clever in a way that is annoying or rude *He thinks it's cute to tell dirty jokes.*
cutlery /'kʌtl°ri/ *UK* (*US* **silverware**) *noun* [U] knives, forks, and spoons
cutlet /'kʌtlət/ *noun* [C] a small piece of meat still joined to the bone *a lamb cutlet*
cut-price /'kʌt,praɪs/ *mainly UK* (*US* **cut-rate**) *adjective* [always before noun] cheaper than usual *cut-price tickets*
cutters /'kʌtəz/ *noun* [plural] a tool for cutting something *wire cutters*
cut-throat *mainly UK* (*also US* **cutthroat**) /'kʌtθrəʊt/ *adjective* a cut-throat business or other situation is where people will do anything to succeed and do not care if they hurt others *the cut-throat world of journalism*
cutting¹ /'kʌtɪŋ/ *noun* [C] **1** a piece cut from a plant and used to grow a new plant **2** *UK* (*UK/US* **clipping**) an article or picture that has been

cut out of a newspaper or magazine
cutting² /'kʌtɪŋ/ *adjective* If something you say or write is cutting, it is unkind. *a cutting remark*
cutting-edge /,kʌtɪŋ'edʒ/ *adjective* very modern and with all the newest developments *cutting-edge design/technology*
CV /,siː'viː/ *UK* (*US* **résumé**) *noun* [C] a document which describes your qualifications and the jobs you have done, which you send to an employer that you want to work for
cwt *written abbreviation for* hundredweight (= a unit for measuring weight, equal to 50.8 kilograms in the UK and 45.36 kilograms in the US)
cyanide /'saɪənaɪd/ *noun* [U] a very strong poison
cyber- /saɪbəʳ/ *prefix* relating to electronic communications, especially the Internet *cyberspace*
cybercafe /'saɪbə,kæfeɪ/ *noun* [C] a place where customers can buy food and drink and use computers to search for information on the Internet
cyberspace /'saɪbə,speɪs/ *noun* [U] the Internet, considered as an imaginary area where you can communicate with people and find information
cycle¹ /'saɪkl/ *noun* [C] **1** a series of events which happen in a particular order and are often repeated *the **life cycle** of a moth* **2** a bicycle ⊃See also: life cycle.
cycle² /'saɪkl/ *verb* [I] to ride a bicycle ● **cycling** *noun* [U] ⊃See colour picture **Sports 2** on page Centre 15. ● **cyclist** *noun* [C] someone who rides a bicycle
'**cycle ,helmet** *noun* [C] a hard hat that protects your head when you ride a bicycle ⊃See colour picture **Clothes** on page Centre 9.
cyclical /'sɪklɪk°l/ *adjective* happening in a regular and repeated pattern *the cyclical nature of the country's history*
cyclone /'saɪkləʊn/ *noun* [C] a violent storm with very strong winds which move in a circle
cylinder /'sɪlɪndəʳ/ *noun* [C] **1** a shape with circular ends and long, straight sides, or a container or object shaped like this *an oxygen cylinder* ⊃See picture at **shape**. **2** a part in a car or machine's engine which is shaped like a tube, and where another part moves up and down
cylindrical /sə'lɪndrɪk°l/ *adjective* having the shape of a cylinder
cymbal /'sɪmb°l/ *noun* [C] a musical instrument like a metal plate which is played by being hit with a stick or another cymbal
cynic /'sɪnɪk/ *noun* [C] a cynical person
cynical /'sɪnɪk°l/ *adjective* believing that people are only interested in themselves and are not sincere *Many people have become cynical about politicians.* ● **cynically** *adverb* ● **cynicism** /'sɪnɪsɪz°m/ *noun* [U] cynical beliefs
cyst /sɪst/ *noun* [C] a small lump containing liquid that can grow under your skin
cystic fibrosis /,sɪstɪkfaɪ'brəʊsɪs/ *noun* [U] a

serious disease which causes the lungs and other organs to become blocked

czar (*also UK* **tsar**) /zɑːʳ/ *noun* [C] **1** a male Russian ruler before 1917 **2** *informal* a powerful official who makes important decisions for the government about a particular activity *a drugs czar*

Dd

D, d /diː/ the fourth letter of the alphabet

dab /dæb/ verb [I, T] dabbing past dabbed to touch something with quick, light touches, or to put a substance on something with quick, light touches *She **dabbed** at her eyes with a tissue.* ● dab noun [C] a small amount of something *a **dab** of lipstick*

DAB /ˌdiːeɪˈbiː/ noun [U] abbreviation for digital audio broadcasting: an electronic system for sending radio or television information using signals in the form of numbers

dabble /ˈdæbl/ verb [I] to try something or take part in an activity in a way that is not serious *I only **dabble** in politics.* ○ *He **dabbled** with drugs at university.*

o--**dad** /dæd/ noun [C] informal father *Can I go to the park, Dad?*

daddy /ˈdædi/ noun [C] a word for 'father', used especially by children

daffodil /ˈdæfədɪl/ noun [C] a yellow flower that usually grows in spring

daffodil

daft /dɑːft/ adjective UK informal silly *That's a **daft** idea.*

dagger /ˈdægəʳ/ noun [C] a short knife, used as a weapon

o--**daily¹** /ˈdeɪli/ adjective [always before noun], adverb **1** happening or produced every day or once a day *a **daily** newspaper* ○ *The shop is open **daily** from 8 a.m. to 6 p.m.* **2** relating to one single day *They are paid on a **daily** basis.* **3** daily life the usual things that happen to you every day *Shootings are **part of daily life** in the region.*

daily² /ˈdeɪli/ noun [C] a newspaper that is published every day except Sunday

dainty /ˈdeɪnti/ adjective small, attractive, and delicate *dainty feet* ● daintily adverb

dairy¹ /ˈdeəri/ noun [C] **1** a place where milk is stored and cream and cheese are made **2** a company which sells milk and products made of milk

dairy² /ˈdeəri/ adjective [always before noun] relating to milk or products made using milk *dairy products* ○ *dairy cattle*

daisy /ˈdeɪzi/ noun [C] a small flower with white petals and a yellow centre that often grows in grass

dam /dæm/ noun [C] a strong wall built across a river to stop the water and make a lake ● dam verb [T] damming, past dammed to build a dam across a river

o--**damage¹** /ˈdæmɪdʒ/ noun [U] harm or injury *He suffered brain **damage** in the car crash.* ○ *The strong wind caused serious **damage to** the roof.*

o--**damage²** /ˈdæmɪdʒ/ verb [T] to harm or break something *Many buildings were **damaged** in the storm.* ○ *Smoking can seriously **damage** your health.* ● damaging adjective harmful *the **damaging** effects of pollution*

damages /ˈdæmɪdʒɪz/ noun [plural] money that a person or organization pays to someone because they have harmed them or something that belongs to them *She was **awarded** £400 **in** damages.*

dame /deɪm/ noun [C] **1** a title used in the UK before the name of a woman who has been officially respected *Dame Agatha Christie* **2** US informal old-fashioned a woman

damn¹ /dæm/ (also damned /dæmd/) adjective [always before noun] informal used to express anger *He didn't listen to a **damn** thing I said.*

damn² /dæm/ (also damn it) exclamation used to express anger or disappointment *Damn! I've forgotten the tickets.*

damn³ /dæm/ (also damned /dæmd/) adverb informal *He worked damn hard to win.*

damn⁴ /dæm/ noun not give a damn informal to not be interested in or worried about someone or something *I don't give a damn what people think.*

damn⁵ /dæm/ verb **1** damn him/it/you, etc used to express anger about someone or something *Stop complaining, damn you!* **2** [T] to strongly criticize someone or something *He was damned by the media.*

damning /ˈdæmɪŋ/ adjective criticizing someone or something very strongly, or showing clearly that someone is guilty *damning evidence* ○ *a **damning** report on education standards*

damp /dæmp/ adjective slightly wet, usually in an unpleasant way *damp clothes/grass* ○ *It was cold and damp outside.* ● damp (also dampness) noun [U] when something is slightly wet

dampen /ˈdæmpən/ (also damp) verb [T] **1** to make something less strong *Nothing you can say will **dampen** her enthusiasm.* **2** to make something slightly wet

damper /ˈdæmpəʳ/ noun put a damper on sth to stop an occasion from being enjoyable *The accident put a damper on their holiday.*

o--**dance¹** /dɑːns/ verb [I, T] to move your feet and body to the rhythm of music *She's dancing with Steven.* ○ *Can you dance the tango?* ● dancer noun [C] ● dancing noun [U]

o--**dance²** /dɑːns/ noun **1** MOVING [C] when you move your feet and body to music *I had a*

D

dance with my dad. **2** STEPS [C] a particular set of steps or movements to music *My favourite dance is the tango.* **3** EVENT [C] a social event where people dance to music **4** ACTIVITY [U] the activity or skill of dancing *a dance school*

dandelion /'dændɪlaɪən/ *noun* [C] a yellow wild flower

dandruff /'dændrʌf/ *noun* [U] small pieces of dead skin in someone's hair or on their clothes

---

WORD PARTNERS FOR **danger**

face danger • pose a danger • great/serious danger • be in danger • be in danger of sth

---

◦**danger** /'deɪndʒər/ *noun* **1** [C, U] the possibility that someone or something will be harmed or killed, or that something bad will happen *the dangers of rock climbing* ○ *The soldiers were in serious danger.* ○ *We were in danger of missing our flight.* **2** [C] something or someone that may harm you *Icy roads are a danger to drivers.*

OTHER WAYS OF SAYING **dangerous**

If something is extremely dangerous, you can use the adjectives **hazardous**, **perilous** or **treacherous**: *Ice had made the roads treacherous.* • *Heavy rain is causing hazardous driving conditions.* • *A perilous journey through the mountains was their only escape route.*

Substances which are dangerous are often described as **harmful** or **hazardous**: *Please be aware that these chemicals are harmful/hazardous to human health.*

If something is dangerous because something bad might happen, you can say that it is **risky**: *Surgery at his age would be too risky.*

◦**dangerous** /'deɪndʒərəs/ *adjective* If someone or something is dangerous, they could harm you. *a dangerous chemical* • **dangerously** *adverb dangerously close to the edge*

dangle /'dæŋgl/ *verb* **1** [I, T] to hang loosely, or to hold something so that it hangs loosely *Electrical wires were dangling from the ceiling.* **2** [T] to offer someone something they want in order to persuade them to do something *They dangled the possibility of a job in Paris in front of him.*

dank /dæŋk/ *adjective* wet, cold, and unpleasant *a dark, dank basement*

dapper /'dæpər/ *adjective* A dapper man looks stylish and tidy.

dare¹ /deər/ *verb* **1** **dare (to) do sth** to be brave enough to do something *I didn't dare tell Dad that I'd scratched his car.* **2** **dare sb to do sth** to try to make someone do something dangerous *She dared her friend to climb onto the roof.* **3** **Don't you dare** *informal* used to tell someone angrily not to do something *Don't you dare hit your sister!* **4** **How dare she/you, etc** used to express anger about something someone has done *How dare you talk to me like that!* **5** **I dare say** (*also* **I daresay**) used when you think that

something is probably true or will probably happen *I dare say she'll change her mind.*

dare² /deər/ *noun* [C] something that you do to prove that you are not afraid [usually singular] *She climbed down the cliff for a dare.*

daredevil /'deə,devəl/ *noun* [C] someone who enjoys doing dangerous things *We watched racing-car drivers doing daredevil stunts.*

daren't /deənt/ UK short for dare not *I daren't tell my wife how much it cost.*

daring /'deərɪŋ/ *adjective* brave and taking risks *a daring escape* ○ *She was wearing a rather daring* (= sexually exciting) *skirt that only just covered her bottom.* • **daring** *noun* [U]

◦**dark¹** /dɑːk/ *adjective* **1** NO LIGHT with no light or not much light *It's a bit dark in here.* ○ *It doesn't get dark until 9 o'clock in the evening.* **2** NOT PALE nearer to black than white in colour *dark blue/green* ○ *dark clouds* ○ *He's got dark hair and blue eyes.* **3** PERSON having black or brown hair or brown skin *A short, dark woman with glasses.* **4** BAD frightening or unpleasant *a dark period in human history*

◦**dark²** /dɑːk/ *noun* **1** **the dark** when there is no light somewhere *I don't like going out alone in the dark.* ○ *He's scared of the dark.* **2** **before/after dark** before/after it becomes night *She doesn't let her children out after dark.* **3** **be in the dark** to not know about something that other people know about *I'm completely in the dark about all this.* ⊃See also: a **shot¹** in the dark.

darken /'dɑːkən/ *verb* [I, T] **1** to become dark or make something dark *a darkened room* ○ *The sky darkened as thick smoke billowed from the blazing oil well.* **2** If someone's mood darkens, or if something darkens it, they suddenly feel less happy.

darkly /'dɑːkli/ *adverb* in a frightening or mysterious way *"He might not be what he seems," she said darkly.*

darkness /'dɑːknəs/ *noun* [U] when there is little or no light *He stumbled around in the darkness looking for the light switch.* ○ *There was a power cut and the house was in darkness.*

darling¹ /'dɑːlɪŋ/ *noun* [C] used when you speak to someone you love *Would you like a drink, darling?*

darling² /'dɑːlɪŋ/ *adjective* [always before noun] loved very much *my darling daughter*

darn¹ /dɑːn/ US informal (*also* **darned** /dɑːnd/) *adjective* [always before noun], *adverb* used to emphasize what you are saying, or to show that you are annoyed *I'm too darn tired to care.*

darn² /dɑːn/ *verb* [I, T] to repair a piece of clothing by sewing across a hole with thread *to darn socks*

dart¹ /dɑːt/ *noun* [C] a small arrow used in the game of darts or as a weapon *a tranquilizer dart*

dart² /dɑːt/ *verb* **dart between/in/out, etc** to run or move somewhere quickly and suddenly *A cat darted across the street.*

darts

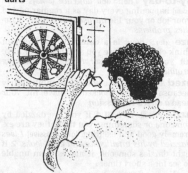

darts /dɑːts/ *noun* [U] a game played by throwing small arrows at a round board

dash¹ /dæʃ/ *verb* **1** [I] to go somewhere quickly *She dashed downstairs when she heard the phone.* ○ *I must dash. I've got to be home by 7 p.m.* **2 dash sb's hopes** to destroy someone's hopes *Saturday's 2-0 defeat dashed their hopes of reaching the final.* **3 dash (sth) against/on, etc** *literary* to hit or throw something with great force, usually causing damage *Waves dashed against the cliffs.*

dash sth off *UK* to write something very quickly *She dashed off a letter to her solicitor.*

dash² /dæʃ/ *noun* **1** [RUN] [no plural] when you run somewhere very quickly *As the rain started, we made a dash for shelter.* **2** [AMOUNT] [C] a small amount of something, often food *Add a dash of milk to the sauce.* **3** [MARK] [C] a mark (–) used to separate parts of sentences ⊃See Extra help page **Punctuation** on page Centre 33.

dashboard /'dæʃbɔːd/ *noun* [C] the part facing the driver at the front of a car with controls and equipment to show things such as speed and temperature ⊃See colour picture **Car** on page Centre 7.

dashing /'dæʃɪŋ/ *adjective* A dashing man is attractive in a confident and exciting way.

analyse/collect data • data on sth

o⊸**data** /'deɪtə/ *noun* [U] **1** information or facts about something *financial data* **2** information in the form of text, numbers, or symbols that can be used by or stored in a computer

database /'deɪtəbeɪs/ *noun* [C] information stored in a computer in an organized structure so that it can be searched in different ways *a national database of missing people*

'**data pro,jector** (beamer) *noun* [C] a machine that allows you to show words or images on a screen or wall

make/fix/set a date • at a future/at a later date • the date of sth • sb's date of birth

o⊸**date¹** /deɪt/ *noun* [C] **1** [PARTICULAR DAY] a particular day of the month or year *"What's the date today?" "It's the fifth."* ○ *Please give your name, address and date of birth.* **2** [ARRANGED TIME] a time when something has been arranged to happen *Let's make a date to have lunch.* ○ *We agreed to finish the report at a later date.* **3 to date** *formal* up to the present time *This novel is his best work to date.* **4** [GOING OUT] a romantic meeting when two people go out somewhere, such as to a restaurant or to see a film *He's asked her out on a date.* **5** [PERSON] someone who you are having a romantic meeting with *Who's your date for the prom?* **6** [FRUIT] a sticky brown fruit with a long seed inside ⊃See also: **blind date, sell-by date.**

date² /deɪt/ *verb* **1** [MEET] [I, T] to regularly spend time with someone you have a romantic relationship with *We've been dating for six months.* **2** [WRITE] [T] to write the day's date on something *a letter dated March 13th* **3** [TIME] [T] to say how long something has existed or when it was made *Scientists have dated the bones to 10,000 BC.* **4** [NOT MODERN] [I, T] to stop seeming modern, or to make something not seem modern *Clothes like these date really quickly.*

date back to have existed a particular length of time or since a particular time *This house dates back to 1650.*

date from sth to have existed since a particular time *The castle dates from the 11th century.*

dated /'deɪtɪd/ *adjective* not modern *This film seems a bit dated today.*

'**date ,rape** *noun* [C] when someone is raped (= forced to have sex when they do not want to) by someone they know, or someone they have arranged to meet

daub /dɔːb/ *verb* [T] to put a lot of a substance like paint on a surface in a careless way, often to write words or draw pictures *The walls have been daubed with graffiti.*

o⊸**daughter** /'dɔːtəʳ/ *noun* [C] your female child

daughter-in-law /'dɔːtərɪnlɔː/ *noun* [C] *plural* **daughters-in-law** your son's wife

daunt /dɔːnt/ *verb* [T] If someone is daunted by something, they are worried because it is difficult or frightening. **[often passive]** *I was a bit daunted by the idea of cooking for so many people.*

daunting /'dɔːntɪŋ/ *adjective* If something is daunting, it makes you worried because it is difficult or frightening. *a daunting challenge/task*

dawdle /'dɔːdl/ *verb* [I] to walk very slowly, or do something very slowly in a way that wastes time *Stop dawdling! You'll be late for school!*

dawn¹ /dɔːn/ *noun* [U] **1** the early morning when light first appears in the sky *We woke at dawn.* **2 the dawn of sth** *literary* the time when something began *the dawn of civilization* ⊃See also: the **crack²** of dawn.

dawn² /dɔːn/ *verb* [I] If a day or a period of time dawns, it begins. *The day of her party dawned at last.*

dawn on sb If a fact dawns on you, you become aware of it after a period of not being aware of it. [+ that] *It suddenly dawned on them that Mary had been lying.*

◦⊶**day** /deɪ/ *noun* **1** [24 HOURS] [C] a period of 24 hours *the days of the week* ○ *January has 31 days.* ○ *I saw her the day before yesterday.* **2** [LIGHT HOURS] [C, U] the period during the day when there is light from the sun *a bright, sunny day* ○ *We've been travelling all day.* **3** [WORK HOURS] [C] the time that you usually spend at work or school *She's had a very busy day at the office.* **4 the other day** a few days ago *I saw Terry the other day.* **5 day after day** every day for a long period of time *Day after day they marched through the mountains.* **6 one day** used to talk about something that happened in the past *One day, I came home to find my windows smashed.* **7 one day/some day/one of these days** used to talk about something you think will happen in the future *One of these days I'll tell her what really happened.* **8 days a** [PERIOD] used to talk about a particular period of time when something happened or existed *in my younger days* **b** [LONG TIME] a long time *I haven't seen Jack for days.* **9 these days** used to talk about the present time *I don't go out much these days.* **10 in those days** used to talk about a period in the past *In those days, boys used to wear short trousers.* **11 the old days** a period in the past **12 call it a day** *informal* to stop doing something, especially working *It's almost midnight - let's call it a day.* **13 it's early days** UK something that you say when it is too early to know what will happen *Both teams are at the bottom of the league, but it's early days yet.* **14 make sb's day** to make someone very happy *Go on, ask him to dance - it'll make his day!* **15 save the day** to do something that solves a serious problem ⊃See also: **April Fool's Day, Boxing Day, Christmas Day,** at the **end¹** of the day, **field day, Independence Day, Mother's Day, New Year's Day, open day, polling day, Valentine's Day.**

daybreak /'deɪbreɪk/ *noun* [U] the time in the morning when light first appears in the sky

daycare /'deɪkeəʳ/ *noun* [U] care provided during the day for people who cannot look after themselves, especially young children or old people *a daycare centre*

daydream /'deɪdriːm/ *verb* [I] to have pleasant thoughts about something you would like to happen ● **daydream** *noun* [C]

daylight /'deɪlaɪt/ *noun* **1** [U] the natural light from the sun **2 in broad daylight** used to emphasize that something happens when it is light and people can see *He was attacked in broad daylight.*

daylights /'deɪlaɪts/ *noun* **1 beat/knock the (living) daylights out of sb** *informal* to hit someone very hard many times **2 scare/frighten the (living) daylights out of sb** *informal* to frighten someone very much

,**day re'turn** *noun* [C] UK a ticket for a bus or train when you go somewhere and come back on the same day *a day return to Norwich*

daytime /'deɪtaɪm/ *noun* [U] the period of the day when there is light from the sun, or the period when most people are at work *daytime television* ○ *a daytime telephone number*

day-to-day /ˌdeɪtə'deɪ/ *adjective* [always before noun] happening every day as a regular part of your job or your life *the usual day-to-day activities/problems*

daze /deɪz/ *noun* **in a daze** when you cannot think clearly because you are shocked or have hit your head *The survivors were walking around in a daze.*

dazed /deɪzd/ *adjective* not able to think clearly because you are shocked or have hit your head *a dazed expression*

dazzle /'dæzl/ *verb* [T] **1** If you are dazzled by someone or something, you think they are extremely good and exciting. [often passive] *I was dazzled by his intelligence and good looks.* **2** If light dazzles someone, it makes them unable to see for a short time.

dazzling /'dæzlɪŋ/ *adjective* **1** extremely good and exciting *a dazzling display/performance* **2** A dazzling light is so bright that you cannot see for a short time after looking at it. *a dazzling white light*

de- /di-/ *prefix* to take something away *deforestation* (= when the trees in an area are cut down) ○ *deseed*

deacon /'diːkən/ *noun* [C] an official in some Christian churches

◦⊶**dead¹** /ded/ *adjective* **1** [NOT ALIVE] not now alive *She's been dead for 20 years now.* ○ *He was shot dead by a masked intruder.* ○ *There were three children among the dead.* ⊃See Common learner error at **die. 2** [EQUIPMENT] If a piece of equipment is dead, it is not working. *a dead battery* ○ *The phone suddenly went dead.* **3** [QUIET] *informal* If a place is dead, it is too quiet and nothing interesting is happening there. **4** [COMPLETE] [always before noun] complete *We waited in dead silence as the votes were counted.* **5** [BODY] mainly UK If part of your body is dead, you cannot feel it. *My arm's gone dead.* **6 wouldn't be caught/seen dead** *informal* If someone wouldn't be caught dead in a place or doing something, they would never go there or do it, usually because it would be too embarrassing. [+ doing sth] *I wouldn't be caught dead wearing a bikini.* **7 drop dead** *informal* to die very suddenly

dead² /ded/ *adverb* **1** *informal* extremely or completely UK *The exam was dead easy.* ○ US *His advice was dead wrong.* **2 be dead set against sth/doing sth** to oppose something strongly *My parents were dead set against us getting married.* **3 stop dead** to suddenly stop moving or doing something

dead³ /ded/ *noun* **the dead of night/winter** the middle of the night/winter

deadbeat /'dedbiːt/ *noun* [C] US *informal* someone who does not pay their debts *a deadbeat dad*

deaden /'dedⁿn/ *verb* [T] to make something less painful or less strong *She gave me an injection to deaden the pain.*

,**dead 'end** *noun* [C] **1** a road which is closed at one end **2** a situation in which it is impossible to make progress *The peace talks have reached a dead end.* ● **dead-end** /ˌded'end/

adjective a **dead-end job/relationship** ○ a **dead-end street**

,**dead 'heat** *noun* [C] when two people finish a race at exactly the same time

WORD PARTNERS FOR **deadline**

set a deadline • **meet/miss** a deadline • a **tight** deadline • the deadline **for** (doing) sth

deadline /'dedlaɪn/ *noun* [C] a time by which something must be done ○ *meet/miss a dead-line* ○ *The deadline for entering the competition is tomorrow.*

deadlock /'dedlɒk/ *noun* [U] a situation in which it is impossible to make progress or to reach a decision *The talks have reached dead-lock.* ○ *There have been several attempts to break the deadlock.* • **deadlocked** *adjective*

deadly¹ /'dedli/ *adjective* likely to cause death *a deadly virus* ○ *a deadly weapon*

deadly² /'dedli/ *adverb* **deadly dull/serious, etc** extremely dull/serious, etc

deadpan /'dedpæn/ *adjective* looking or sounding serious when you are telling a joke *a dead-pan expression*

deaf /def/ *adjective* **1** unable to hear *Many deaf people learn to lip read.* ○ *He goes to a school for the deaf.* **2 be deaf to sth** to refuse to listen to something • **deafness** *noun* [U] ⊃See also: fall on deaf ears (ear), **tone-deaf.**

deafening /'def°nɪŋ/ *adjective* extremely loud *a deafening noise*

WORD PARTNERS FOR **deal**

agree/do/make/strike a deal • **negotiate/sign** a deal • a deal **between** [two people/companies, etc] • a deal **with** sb

deal¹ /diːl/ *noun* **1** [C] an arrangement or an agreement, especially in business *The police refused to do/make/strike a deal with the terrorists.* **2** [C] the price you pay for something, and what you get for your money *I got a really good deal on my new car.* **3 a good/great deal** a lot *A great deal of time and effort went into arranging this party.*

deal² /diːl/ *verb* [I, T] *past* dealt to give cards to players in a game *Whose turn is it to deal?*

deal in sth to buy and sell particular goods as a business *a shop dealing in rare books*

o~**deal with sth 1** to take action in order to achieve something or to solve a problem *Can you deal with this gentleman's complaint?* **2** to be about a particular subject *The programme dealt with teenage pregnancy.*

deal with sb/sth to do business with a person or organization *I usually deal with the accounts department.*

deal with sb to meet or talk to someone, especially as part of your job *She's used to dealing with foreign customers.*

dealer /'diːlə⁰/ *noun* [C] **1** a person or company that buys and sells things for profit *a car dealer* ○ *a drug dealer* **2** a person who gives out cards to players in a game

dealership /'diːləʃɪp/ *noun* [C] a business that sells cars, usually cars made by a particular company *a Ford/Toyota dealership*

dealings /'diːlɪŋz/ *noun* [plural] activities involving other people, especially in business *Have you had any dealings with their London office?*

dealt /delt/ *past of* deal

dean /diːn/ *noun* [C] **1** an official in a college or university **2** an official in charge of a large church or group of churches

o~**dear¹** /dɪə⁰/ *adjective* **1** [IN LETTERS] used at the beginning of a letter, before the name of the person you are writing to *Dear Amy* ○ *Dear Mrs Simpson* ○ *Dear Sir/Madam* **2** [LIKED] [always before noun] A dear person is someone who you know and like very much. *my dear Peter* ○ *He's one of my dearest friends.* **3** [EXPENSIVE] *UK* expensive **4 dear to sb/sb's heart** If something is dear to someone or dear to their heart, it is very important to them. *The charity was very dear to his heart.*

dear² /dɪə⁰/ *exclamation* **oh dear** used to express surprise and disappointment *Oh dear! I forgot my keys!*

dear³ /dɪə⁰/ *noun* [C] used to address someone in a friendly way, especially a child or someone you love *Don't cry, my dear.* ○ *Yes, dear?*

dearly /'dɪəli/ *adverb* very much *I would dearly love to visit Rome again.*

dearth /dɜːθ/ *noun formal* **a dearth of sth** when there are not many or not enough of something available *a dearth of new homes*

WORD PARTNERS FOR **death**

bleed/choke/freeze/starve to death • be **beaten / crushed / stabbed / trampled** to death • sb's **premature/sudden/tragic/untimely** death • death **from** sth

o~**death** /deθ/ *noun* **1** [C, U] the end of life *Do you believe in life after death?* ○ *We need to reduce the number of deaths from heart attacks.* ○ *a death threat* **2 to death** until you die *He was beaten to death by a gang of youths.* **3 put sb to death** to kill someone as a punishment [often passive] *She was put to death for her beliefs.* **4 frightened/bored, etc to death** *informal* extremely frightened/bored, etc *She's scared to death of dogs.*

deathbed /'deθbed/ *noun* **on your deathbed** very ill and going to die soon

deathly /'deθli/ *adjective, adverb* extreme in a way which is unpleasant *a deathly silence* ○ *Her face turned deathly pale.*

'**death ,penalty** *noun* [C] the legal punishment of death for a crime

,**death 'row** *noun* **on death row** in prison and waiting to be killed as a punishment for a crime

'**death ,sentence** *noun* [C] a legal punishment of death for a crime

'**death ,toll** *noun* [C] the number of people who die because of an event such as a war or an accident *The death toll from the earthquake has risen to 1500.*

'**death ,trap** *noun* [C] something that is very dangerous and could cause death *That old factory across the road is a real death trap.*

debase /dɪ'beɪs/ *verb* [T] *formal* to reduce the

value or quality of something *They argue that money has debased football.*

debatable /dɪˈbeɪtəbl/ *adjective* If something is debatable, it is not certain if it is true or not. *It's **debatable whether** a university degree will help you in this job.*

debate¹ /dɪˈbeɪt/ *noun* [C, U] discussion or argument about a subject *a political debate* ○ *There has been a lot of public **debate on** the safety of food.*

D

debate² /dɪˈbeɪt/ *verb* **1** [I, T] to discuss a subject in a formal way *These issues need to be debated openly.* **2** [T] to try to make a decision about something [+ question word] *I'm still debating whether to go out tonight or not.*

debilitating /dɪˈbɪlɪteɪtɪŋ/ *adjective formal* A debilitating illness or problem makes you weak and unable to do what you want to do. *the debilitating effects of flu*

debit¹ /ˈdebɪt/ *noun* [C] money taken out of a bank account, or a record of this ⇨Opposite **credit** ⇨See also: **direct debit**.

debit² /ˈdebɪt/ *verb* [T] to take money out of a bank account as a payment for something *Twenty pounds has been debited from my account.*

ˈdebit ˌcard *noun* [C] a plastic card used to pay for things directly from your bank account

debris /ˈdebriː/ [US] /dəˈbriː/ *noun* [U] broken pieces of something *Debris from the aircraft was scattered over a wide area.*

WORD PARTNERS FOR ***debt***

be in/fall into/get into/run into debt • **get out of** debt • **clear/pay off/repay/settle** a debt

⊶**debt** /det/ *noun* **1** [C] an amount of money that you owe someone *She's working in a bar to try to **pay off** her **debts**.* **2** [U] when you owe money to someone *We don't want to **get into debt**.* ○ *He's heavily **in debt**.* **3 be in sb's debt** to feel grateful to someone who has helped you or given you something

debtor /ˈdetəʳ/ *noun* [C] someone who owes money

ˈdebt reˌlief *noun* [U] when a bank tells a person, a company or a government that they do not have to pay back the money they owe the bank

debut /ˈdeɪbjuː/ [US] /deɪˈbjuː/ *noun* [C] when someone performs or presents something to the public for the first time *She **made her debut** as a pianist in 1975.* ○ *This is the band's **debut album**.*

Dec *written abbreviation for* December

⊶**decade** /ˈdekeɪd/ *noun* [C] a period of ten years

decadence /ˈdekədᵊns/ *noun* [U] when you do or have things only for your own pleasure or behave in an immoral way • **decadent** *adjective a decadent lifestyle*

decaf /ˈdiːkæf/ *noun* [C, U] *informal short for* decaffeinated coffee

decaffeinated /dɪˈkæfɪneɪtɪd/ *adjective* Decaffeinated tea or coffee is made by removing the caffeine (= chemical which makes you feel more awake).

decay /dɪˈkeɪ/ *verb* [I] to gradually become bad or weak or be destroyed, often because of natural causes like bacteria or age *decaying leaves* ○ *Sugar makes your teeth decay.* • **decay** *noun* [U] when something decays ***tooth decay*** ○ *Many of the buildings had **fallen into decay**.*

deceased /dɪˈsiːst/ *adjective formal* **1** dead *the deceased man's belongings* **2 the deceased** someone who has died *The police have not yet informed the family of the deceased.*

deceit /dɪˈsiːt/ *noun* [U] when someone tries to make someone believe something that is not true • **deceitful** *adjective deceitful behaviour*

deceive /dɪˈsiːv/ *verb* [T] to make someone believe something that is not true *The company deceived customers by selling old computers as new ones.*

⊶**December** /dɪˈsembəʳ/ (*written abbreviation* **Dec**) *noun* [C, U] the twelfth month of the year

decency /ˈdiːsᵊnsi/ *noun* [U] behaviour that is good, moral, and acceptable in society *a sense of decency* ○ *She didn't even **have the decency to** tell me she wasn't coming.*

decent /ˈdiːsᵊnt/ *adjective* **1** [SATISFACTORY] of a satisfactory quality or level *He earns a decent salary.* ○ *I haven't had a decent cup of coffee since I've been here.* **2** [HONEST] honest and morally good *Decent people have had their lives ruined by his behaviour.* ○ *She should **do the decent thing** and apologize.* **3** [CLOTHES] [never before noun] wearing clothes *Can I come in? Are you decent?* • **decently** *adverb*

decentralize (*also UK* **-ise**) /diːˈsentrəlaɪz/ *verb* [T] to move the control of an organization or a government from a single place to several smaller places • **decentralization** /diːˌsentrᵊlaɪˈzeɪʃᵊn/ *noun* [U]

deception /dɪˈsepʃᵊn/ *noun* [C, U] when someone makes someone believe something that is not true *He was found guilty of obtaining money by deception.*

deceptive /dɪˈseptɪv/ *adjective* If something is deceptive, it makes you believe something that is not true. *Appearances can be deceptive.* • **deceptively** *adverb*

decibel /ˈdesɪbel/ *noun* [C] a unit for measuring how loud a sound is

OTHER WAYS OF SAYING ***decide***

If someone is deciding a time or an amount, especially an exact date or price, the verbs **fix** and **set** are often used: *The price has been **set/fixed** at $10.* • *Have you **set/fixed** a date for the wedding?*

If someone makes a final and certain decision about a plan, date, etc., the verb **finalize** is sometimes used: *We've chosen a venue, but we haven't **finalized** the details yet.*

The verb **settle** and the phrasal verb **settle on/upon** are also often used when someone is making a final decision: *Have you **settled on** a place to live yet?* • *Right then, we're going to Spain. That's **settled**.*

The fixed expression **make up your mind** is often used to mean 'to decide': *I like them both - I just can't **make up my mind** which one to pick.* • *Have you **made up your mind*** *whether you're going?*

If someone is unable to decide between two choices, in informal situations you can use the expression **be torn between** something **and** something else: *I'm **torn between** the fish pie **and** the beef.*

⊶**decide** /dɪˈsaɪd/ *verb* **1** [I, T] to choose something after thinking about several possibilities [+ question word] *I haven't decided whether or not to tell him.* ○ [+ to do sth] *She's decided to take the job.* ○ [+ (that)] *The teachers decided that the school would take part in the competition.* **2** [T] to be the reason or situation that makes a particular result happen *This match will decide the tournament.* **3 deciding factor** the thing that helps to make the final decision

decide on sth/sb to choose something or someone after thinking carefully *I've decided on blue walls for the bathroom.*

decided /dɪˈsaɪdɪd/ *adjective* [always before noun] certain, obvious, or easy to notice *She had a decided advantage over her opponent.* • **decidedly** *adverb That exam was decidedly more difficult than the last one.*

deciduous /dɪˈsɪdjuəs/ *adjective* A deciduous tree has leaves that drop off every autumn.

decimal¹ /ˈdesɪməl/ *adjective* involving counting in units of 10 *a decimal system*

decimal² /ˈdesɪməl/ *noun* [C] a number less than one that is written as one or more numbers after a point *The decimal 0.5 is the same as the fraction* (= 1/2). ➲See Extra help page **Numbers** on page Centre 30.

ˌdecimal ˈplace *UK* (*US* ˈ**decimal** ˌ**place**) *noun* [C] the position of a number after a decimal point *The number is accurate to three decimal places.*

ˌdecimal ˈpoint *UK* (*US* ˈ**decimal** ˌ**point**) *noun* [C] the point (.) that is used to separate a whole number and a decimal

decimate /ˈdesɪmeɪt/ *verb* [T] *formal* to destroy large numbers of people or things *Populations of endangered animals have been decimated.*

decipher /dɪˈsaɪfəʳ/ *verb* [T] to discover what something says or means *It's sometimes difficult to **decipher** his **handwriting**.*

WORD PARTNERS FOR ***decision***

come to/make/reach a decision • a **big/difficult/final/important/unanimous/wise** decision • a decision **about/on** sth

⊶**decision** /dɪˈsɪʒən/ *noun* [C] a choice that you make about something after thinking about several possibilities *She has had to **make** some very difficult **decisions**.* ○ [+ to do sth] *It was his decision to leave.* ○ *The committee should **come to/reach a** final **decision** by next week.*

decisive /dɪˈsaɪsɪv/ *adjective* **1** strongly affecting how a situation will progress or end *a **decisive goal/victory*** **2** making decisions quickly and easily *You need to be more decisive.* ➲Opposite **indecisive**. • **decisively** *adverb* • **decisiveness** *noun* [U]

deck¹ /dek/ *noun* [C] **1** [SHIP/BUS/PLANE] one of the floors of a ship, bus, or aircraft *The children like to sit on the top deck of the bus.* **2 on deck** on the top floor of a ship that is not covered **3** [CARDS] *US* (*UK* **pack**) a collection of cards that you use to play a game **4** [MACHINE] a machine that you use to play records or tapes (= plastic cases containing magnetic material used to record sounds) *a tape deck*

deck² /dek/ *verb*

be decked out to be decorated with something, or dressed in something special *The bar was decked out with red and yellow flags.*

deckchair /ˈdektʃeəʳ/ *noun* [C] a folding chair that you use outside

declaration /ˌdekləˈreɪʃən/ *noun* [C] an announcement, often one that is written and official *a declaration of independence*

declare /dɪˈkleəʳ/ *verb* [T] **1** to announce something publicly or officially *to declare war* ○ [+ that] *Scientists have declared that this meat is safe to eat.* **2** to officially tell someone the value of goods you have bought, or the amount of money you have earned because you might have to pay tax *Have you got anything to declare?*

WORD PARTNERS FOR ***decline***

be **in** decline • a **sharp/steady/steep** decline • a decline **in** sth

decline¹ /dɪˈklaɪn/ *noun* [C, U] when something becomes less in amount, importance, quality, or strength *a steady **decline in** sales/standards*

decline² /dɪˈklaɪn/ *verb* **1** [I, T] *formal* If you decline something, you refuse it politely. *She **declined** his **offer** of a lift.* ○ [+ to do sth] *He **declined to comment**.* **2** [I] to become less in amount, importance, quality, or strength *Sales of records have declined steadily.*

decode /ˌdiːˈkəʊd/ *verb* [T] to discover the meaning of a message that is in code (= secret system of communication)

decoder /diːˈkəʊdəʳ/ *noun* [C] a piece of equipment that allows you to receive particular television signals

decompose /ˌdiːkəmˈpəʊz/ *verb* [I] If a dead person, animal, or plant decomposes, it decays and is gradually destroyed. *a decomposing body*

decor /ˈdeɪkɔːʳ/ [US] /deɪˈkɔːr/ *noun* [U, no plural] the style of decoration and furniture in a room or building

OTHER WAYS OF SAYING ***decorate***

The verbs **refurbish**, **renovate** and **revamp** are common alternatives to 'decorate' when you are talking about improving the appearance of a room or building: *The University library is currently being **refurbished**.* • *They were in the process of **renovating** an old barn.* • *The restaurant has recently been **revamped**.*

Another alternative used in more informal situations is the phrasal verb **do up**: *He's bought an old cottage and is gradually **doing** it **up**.*

decorate

ꙮ**decorate** /'dek³reɪt/ *verb* **1** [T] to make something look more attractive by putting things on it or around it *They decorated the room with balloons for her party.* **2** [I, T] to put paint or paper on the walls or other surfaces of a room or building *The whole house needs decorating.* **3 be decorated** to be given a medal (= small, metal disc) as official respect for military action *He was decorated for bravery.*

decoration /ˌdek³'reɪʃ³n/ *noun* **1** ATTRACTIVE THING [C, U] when you make something look more attractive by putting things on it or around it, or something that you use to do this *Christmas decorations* ○ *She hung some pictures around the room for decoration.* **2** PAINT [U] when the walls or other surfaces of rooms or buildings are covered with paint or paper *This place is badly in need of decoration.* **3** OFFICIAL RESPECT [C] an official sign of respect such as a medal (= small, metal disc)

decorative /'dek³rətɪv/ *adjective* making something or someone look more attractive *decorative objects*

decorator /'dek³reɪtə³/ *noun* [C] **1** *UK* someone whose job is to put paint or paper on the walls and other surfaces of rooms or buildings **2** *US* someone whose job is to design the appearance of rooms in houses and buildings

decorum /dɪ'kɔːrəm/ *noun* [U] *formal* behaviour which is considered to be polite and correct

decoy /'diːkɔɪ/ *noun* [C] someone or something used to lead a person or animal to a place so that they can be caught

⬚ WORD PARTNERS FOR **decrease**

a **marked/significant/slight** decrease ● a decrease **in** sth ● a decrease **of** [5%/1000, etc]

decrease /dɪ'kriːs/ *verb* [I, T] to become less, or to make something become less *During the summer months, rainfall decreases.* ●**decrease** /'diːkriːs/ *noun* [C, U] *There has been a **decrease in** the number of violent crimes.* ⊃Opposite increase.

The verbs **lessen**, **lower**, and **reduce**, and the phrasal verb **bring down** are often used when someone decreases an amount or level: *They've just lowered the age at which you can join.* ● *Exercise reduces the chance of heart disease.* ● *They are bringing down their prices.*

The verbs **drop** and **fall**, and the phrasal verbs **go down** and **come down** are often used when a level or amount decreases: *Unemployment has dropped/fallen from 8% to 6% in the last year.* ● *Prices always come/go down after Christmas.*

If a level or amount decreases very quickly, the verbs **plummet** and **plunge** are sometimes used: *Temperatures last night plummeted/plunged below zero.*

If the size of something decreases, the verb **shrink** is sometimes used. The verb **contract** is used in technical contexts: *Forests have shrunk to almost half the size they were 20 years ago.* ● *As the metal cools, it contracts.*

decree /dɪ'kriː/ *noun* [C] an official order or decision from a government or leader *a presidential/royal decree* ●**decree** *verb* [T] decreeing, *past* decreed

decrepit /dɪ'krepɪt/ *adjective* old and in very bad condition *a decrepit building*

decrypt /dɪ'krɪpt/ *verb* [T] to change electronic information from a secret system of letters, numbers, or symbols back into a form that people can understand

dedicate /'dedɪkeɪt/ *verb* **1 dedicate your life/ yourself to sth** to give most of your energy and time to something *She has dedicated her life to helping others.* **2 dedicate sth to sb** to say that something you have made or done is to show your love or respect for someone [often passive] *This book is dedicated to my daughter.*

dedicated /'dedɪkeɪtɪd/ *adjective* **1** believing that something is very important and giving a lot of time and energy to it *a dedicated teacher* **2** designed to be used for a particular purpose *a dedicated word processor*

dedication /ˌdedɪ'keɪʃ³n/ *noun* **1** [U] when you are willing to give a lot of time and energy to something because you believe it is very important *She thanked the staff for their dedication and enthusiasm.* **2** [C] when someone says that something has been made or done to show love and respect for someone else *a dedication to the poet's mother*

deduce /dɪ'djuːs/ *verb* [T] to decide that something is true using the available information [+ (that)] *From the contents of his shopping basket, I deduced that he was single.*

deduct /dɪ'dʌkt/ *verb* [T] to take an amount or a part of something away from a total *The company will deduct tax from your earnings.* ○ *Marks are deducted for spelling mistakes.*

deduction /dɪ'dʌkʃ³n/ *noun* [C, U] **1** an amount or a part of something is taken away from a total, or the amount that is taken *tax deductions* **2** when you decide that something

is true using the available information

deed /diːd/ noun [C] **1** formal something that you do good deeds ○ I judge a person by their deeds, not their words. **2** a legal document recording an agreement, especially saying who owns something [usually plural] Where do you keep the deeds to the house?

deem /diːm/ verb [T] formal to judge or consider something in a particular way The book was deemed to be unsuitable for children.

deep

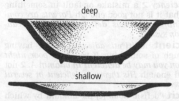

deep

shallow

o--**deep**¹ /diːp/ adjective **1** TOP TO BOTTOM having a long distance from the top to the bottom The water is a lot deeper than it seems. **2** FRONT TO BACK having a long distance from the front to the back How deep are the shelves? **3 one metre/6ft, etc deep** one metre/6 ft, etc from the top to the bottom, or from the front to the back This end of the pool is two metres deep. **4** FEELING A deep feeling is very strong. deep affection/regret **5** SOUND A deep sound is low. a deep voice **6** SERIOUS serious and difficult for most people to understand a deep and meaningful conversation **7 a deep sleep** when someone is sleeping in a way that makes it difficult to wake them up **8** COLOUR A deep colour is strong and dark. deep brown eyes **9 take a deep breath** to fill your lungs with air Take a deep breath and relax. **10 deep in thought/conversation** giving all of your attention to what you are thinking or talking about, and not noticing anything else ⊃See also: throw sb in at the deep end¹, be in deep water¹.

o--**deep**² /diːp/ adverb **1** a long way into something from the top or outside They travelled deep into the forest. **2 deep down** If you know or feel something deep down, you are certain that it is true, or you feel it strongly although you do not admit it or show it. Deep down, I knew that I was right. **3 go/run deep** If a feeling or a problem goes deep, it is very strong or serious and has existed for a long time.

deepen /ˈdiːpᵊn/ verb [I, T] **1** to become deeper, or to make something become deeper The sky deepened to a rich, dark blue. **2** to become worse, or to make something become worse a deepening crisis

,**deep 'freeze** UK (US 'deep ˌfreeze) noun [C] another word for freezer (= a large container in which food can be frozen and stored)

deep-fried /ˌdiːpˈfraɪd/ adjective fried in a lot of oil

deeply /ˈdiːpli/ adverb **1** very much I have fallen deeply in love with her. **2 breathe deeply** to fill your lungs with air

deep-seated /ˌdiːpˈsiːtɪd/ (also deep-rooted)

adjective strongly felt or believed and difficult to change deep-seated fears/problems

deer

deer /dɪər/ noun [C] plural deer a large, wild animal that is sometimes hunted for food and which has antlers (= long horns) if it is male

deface /dɪˈfeɪs/ verb [T] to spoil the appearance of something, especially by writing or painting on it Several posters have been defaced with political slogans.

default¹ /dɪˈfɔːlt/ noun **1** [no plural] what exists or happens usually if no changes are made **2 by default** If something happens by default, it happens only because something else does not happen. No one else stood in the election, so he won by default. ● default adjective [always before noun] The default font size is 10.

default² /dɪˈfɔːlt/ verb [I] to not do what you have made an agreement to do, especially paying back money you have borrowed They have defaulted on their debt repayments.

o--**defeat**¹ /dɪˈfiːt/ verb [T] **1** to win against someone in a fight or competition She was defeated by an Australian player in the first round of the tournament. **2** to make someone or something fail The crime bill was narrowly defeated in parliament.

o--**defeat**² /dɪˈfiːt/ noun **1** [C, U] when someone loses against someone else in a fight or competition The Chicago Cubs have suffered their worst defeat of the season. **2** [no plural] when someone or something is made to fail the defeat of apartheid

defeatism /dɪˈfiːtɪzᵊm/ noun [U] behaviour or thoughts that show that you do not expect to be successful

defeatist /dɪˈfiːtɪst/ adjective behaving in a way that shows that you do not expect to be successful a defeatist attitude ● defeatist noun [C]

defect¹ /ˈdiːfekt/ noun [C] a fault or problem with someone or something a birth defect ○ A mechanical defect caused the plane to crash. ● defective /dɪˈfektɪv/ adjective having a fault or problem defective goods

defect² /dɪˈfekt/ verb [I] to leave your country or organization and go to join an enemy country or competing organization *He **defected to** the West.* • **defection** /dɪˈfekʃᵊn/ *noun* [C, U] when someone defects • **defector** *noun* [C]

WORD PARTNERS FOR **defence**

2 mount/put up a defence • an effective/spirited/strong/vigorous defence • defence against sth • [argue, etc.] in defence of sth

defence UK (US **defense**) /dɪˈfens/ *noun* 1 MILITARY [U] the weapons and military forces that a country uses to protect itself against attack *Government spending on defence is increasing.* ○ *the defence minister/industry* 2 PROTECTION [C, U] protection, or something that provides protection against attack or criticism *the body's defences against infection* ○ *She argued strongly **in defence of** her actions.* 3 **come to sb's defence** to support someone when they are being criticized 4 **the defence** [group] the lawyers in a court who work in support of the person who is accused of a crime *He was cross-examined by the defence.* ○ *a **defence lawyer*** 5 SPORT [C, U] the part of a sports team which tries to prevent the other team from scoring points ⇒See also: **self-defence**.

defenceless UK (US **defenseless**) /dɪˈfensləs/ *adjective* weak and unable to protect yourself from attack *a small, defenceless child*

✧**defend** /dɪˈfend/ *verb* 1 PROTECT [T] to protect someone or something from being attacked, especially by fighting *The army was sent in to **defend** the country **against** enemy attack.* ○ [often reflexive] *She tried to defend herself with a knife.* 2 SUPPORT [T] to support someone or something that is being criticized *The newspaper's editor **defended** his **decision** to publish the photos.* 3 LAW [T] to try to show in a court that someone is not guilty of a crime *He has hired two lawyers to defend him in court.* 4 SPORT [I, T] to try to stop the other sports team from scoring points 5 **defend a championship/title, etc** to try to win a match or competition that you have won before • **defender** *noun* [C]

defendant /dɪˈfendənt/ *noun* [C] the person in a court who is accused of a crime

✧**defense** /dɪˈfens/ *noun US spelling of* defence

defenseless /dɪˈfensləs/ *adjective US spelling of* defenceless

defensive¹ /dɪˈfensɪv/ *adjective* 1 CRITICISM quick to protect yourself from being criticized *He's very **defensive about** his weight.* 2 SPORT mainly US A defensive player in a sports team tries to stop the other team scoring points. 3 ATTACK done or used to protect someone or something from attack • **defensively** *adverb*

defensive² /dɪˈfensɪv/ *noun* **on the defensive** ready to protect yourself because you are expecting to be criticized or attacked

defer /dɪˈfɜː/ *verb* [T] **deferring**, *past* **deferred** to arrange for something to happen at a later time *The payments can be deferred for three months.*

deference /ˈdefᵊrᵊns/ *noun* [U] polite behaviour that shows that you respect someone or something • **deferential** /ˌdefᵊˈrenʃᵊl/ *adjective*

defiance /dɪˈfaɪəns/ *noun* [U] when you refuse

to obey someone or something *an **act of defiance***

defiant /dɪˈfaɪənt/ *adjective* refusing to obey someone or something *a defiant child* • **defiantly** *adverb*

WORD PARTNERS FOR **deficiency**

2 a glaring / major / serious / severe deficiency • a deficiency in sth

deficiency /dɪˈfɪʃᵊnsi/ *noun* [C, U] 1 when you do not have enough of something *a vitamin deficiency* 2 a mistake or fault in something so that it is not good enough *Parents are complaining of serious **deficiencies in** the education system.*

deficient /dɪˈfɪʃᵊnt/ *adjective* 1 not having enough of something *If you have poor night vision you may be **deficient in** vitamin A.* 2 not good enough *His theory is deficient in several respects.*

deficit /ˈdefɪsɪt/ *noun* [C] the amount by which the money that you spend is more than the money that you receive *a **budget deficit***

defile /dɪˈfaɪl/ *verb* [T] *formal* to spoil someone or something that is pure, holy, or beautiful

define /dɪˈfaɪn/ *verb* [T] 1 to say exactly what something means, or what someone or something is like *Your duties are clearly defined in the contract.* 2 to show the outer edges or shape of something *It has sharply defined edges.*

✧**definite** /ˈdefɪnət/ *adjective* 1 certain, fixed, and not likely to change *We need a definite answer by tomorrow.* 2 clear and obvious *There has been a definite improvement in her behaviour.*

definite ˈarticle *noun* [C] in grammar, used to mean the word 'the' ⇒Compare **indefinite article**.

✧**definitely** /ˈdefɪnətli/ *adverb* without any doubt *This book is definitely worth reading.* ○ *"Do you want to come?" "Yes, definitely."*

definition /ˌdefɪˈnɪʃᵊn/ *noun* 1 [C] an explanation of the meaning of a word or phrase *a dictionary definition* 2 [U] how clear an image of something is in a photograph or on a screen *high definition TV*

definitive /dɪˈfɪnətɪv/ *adjective* 1 certain, clear, and not likely to change *a **definitive answer*** 2 A definitive book or piece of work is the best of its type. *the definitive guide to London* • **definitively** *adverb*

deflate /dɪˈfleɪt/ *verb* 1 [I, T] to let all the air or gas out of something, or to become emptied of air or gas *to deflate a balloon/tyre* 2 [T] to make someone lose confidence or feel less important [often passive] *They were totally deflated by losing the match.*

deflect /dɪˈflekt/ *verb* 1 [I, T] to make something change direction by hitting or touching it, or to change direction after hitting something *The ball was deflected into the corner of the net.* 2 **deflect attention/blame/criticism, etc** to cause attention/blame/criticism, etc to be directed away from you • **deflection** /dɪˈflekʃᵊn/ *noun* [C, U]

deforestation /diːˌfɒrɪˈsteɪʃᵊn/ *noun* [U] when

all the trees in a large area are cut down

deformed /dɪˈfɔːmd/ *adjective* with a shape that has not developed normally *deformed hands* • **deform** /dɪˈfɔːm/ *verb* [T]

deformity /dɪˈfɔːməti/ *noun* [C, U] when a part of the body has not developed in the normal way, or with the normal shape

defraud /dɪˈfrɔːd/ *verb* [T] to obtain money from someone illegally by being dishonest

defrost /ˌdiːˈfrɒst/ *verb* [I, T] **1** If food defrosts, it becomes warmer after being frozen, and if you defrost it, you make it become warmer after being frozen. *You need to defrost the fish before you can cook it.* **2** If you defrost a fridge or freezer (= machines that keep food cold), you make them warmer and remove the ice, and if they defrost, they become warmer and the ice melts.

deft /deft/ *adjective* quick and showing great skill *a **deft movement/touch*** • **deftly** *adverb formal*

defunct /dɪˈfʌŋkt/ *adjective* not working or existing now

defuse /ˌdiːˈfjuːz/ *verb* [T] **1** to make a difficult or dangerous situation calmer *He made a joke to **defuse** the **tension**.* **2** to prevent a bomb from exploding by removing the fuse (= part that starts the explosion)

defy /dɪˈfaɪ/ *verb* **1** [T] to refuse to obey someone or something *Some of these children openly defy their teachers.* **2 defy belief/description/explanation, etc** to be impossible to believe, describe, explain, etc *His attitude defies belief.* **3 defy sb to do sth** to tell someone to do something that you think will be impossible *I defy you to prove that I'm wrong.*

degenerate¹ /dɪˈdʒenəreɪt/ *verb* [I] to become worse *The protest soon **degenerated into** violence.* • **degeneration** /dɪˌdʒenəˈreɪʃən/ *noun* [U]

degenerate² /dɪˈdʒenərət/ *adjective* having low moral principles

degrade /dɪˈgreɪd/ *verb* [T] **1** to treat someone without respect and as if they have no value *They think the advert degrades women.* **2** to damage the quality or condition of something • **degradation** /ˌdegrəˈdeɪʃən/ *noun* [U]

degrading /dɪˈgreɪdɪŋ/ *adjective* treating people without respect and as if they have no value *degrading work*

o→**degree** /dɪˈgriː/ *noun* **1** [TEMPERATURE] [C] a unit for measuring temperature, shown by the symbol ° written after a number **2** [ANGLE] [C] a unit for measuring angles, shown by the symbol ° written after a number **3** [QUALIFICATION] [C] a qualification given for completing a university course *She has a **degree in** physics.* **4** [AMOUNT] [C, U] an amount or level of something *I agree with you **to a degree*** (= in some ways but not completely). ➲See also: **master¹**'s (degree).

dehydrated /ˌdiːhaɪˈdreɪtɪd/ *adjective* not having enough water in your body

dehydration /ˌdiːhaɪˈdreɪʃən/ *noun* [U] when you do not have enough water in your body

deign /deɪn/ *verb* **deign to do sth** to do something that you think you are too important to do

deity /ˈdeɪɪti/ Ⓤⓢ /ˈdiːəti/ *noun* [C] *formal* a god or goddess (= female god)

deja vu /ˌdeɪʒɑːˈvuː/ *noun* [U] a feeling that you have already experienced exactly what is happening now *She suddenly had a strong **sense of deja vu**.*

dejected /dɪˈdʒektɪd/ *adjective* unhappy and disappointed *He looked tired and dejected.* • **dejection** /dɪˈdʒekʃən/ *noun* [U]

o→**delay¹** /dɪˈleɪ/ *verb* **1** [I, T] to make something happen at a later time than originally planned or expected *Can you delay your departure until next week?* **2** [T] to cause someone or something to be slow or late [often passive] *I was delayed by traffic.*

WORD PARTNERS FOR ***delay***

a brief / short / slight delay • **a considerable / lengthy / long** delay • **cause** delays • **experience/face/suffer** delays

o→**delay²** /dɪˈleɪ/ *noun* [C, U] when you have to wait longer than expected for something to happen, or the time that you have to wait *An accident caused long **delays** on the motorway.*

delectable /dɪˈlektəbl/ *adjective formal* extremely nice, especially to eat

delegate¹ /ˈdelɪgət/ *noun* [C] someone who is sent somewhere to represent a group of people, especially at a meeting

delegate² /ˈdelɪgeɪt/ *verb* [I, T] to give someone else part of your work or some of your responsibilities

delegation /ˌdelɪˈgeɪʃən/ *noun* **1** [C] a group of people who have been chosen to represent a much larger group of people *a delegation of Chinese officials* **2** [U] when you give someone else part of your work or some of your responsibilities

delete /dɪˈliːt/ *verb* [T] to remove something, especially from a computer's memory *All names have been deleted from the report.* • **deletion** /dɪˈliːʃən/ *noun* [C, U]

deli /ˈdeli/ *noun* [C] *short for* delicatessen

deliberate¹ /dɪˈlɪbərət/ *adjective* **1** done intentionally, or planned *This was a **deliberate attempt** by them to deceive us.* **2** careful and without hurry *Her movements were calm and deliberate.*

deliberate² /dɪˈlɪbəreɪt/ *verb* [I, T] to consider something carefully before making a decision *They deliberated for ten hours before reaching a decision.*

o→**deliberately** /dɪˈlɪbərətli/ *adverb* intentionally, having planned to do something *He deliberately lied to the police.*

deliberation /dɪˌlɪbəˈreɪʃən/ *noun* [C, U] careful thought or talk about a subject before a decision is made *The jury began deliberations on Thursday.*

delicacy /ˈdelɪkəsi/ *noun* **1** [FOOD] [C] a special food, usually something rare or expensive **2** [GENTLE QUALITY] [U] the quality of being soft, light, or gentle **3** [EASY TO DAMAGE] [U] when something is easy to damage or break

4 NEEDING CARE [U] when something needs to be treated very carefully *You need to be very tactful because of the delicacy of the situation.* **5** ATTRACTIVE [U] when something has a thin, attractive shape

delicate /ˈdelɪkət/ *adjective* **1** GENTLE soft, light, or gentle *a delicate flavour* ○ *a delicate shade of pink* **2** EASY TO DAMAGE easy to damage or break *a delicate china cup* **3** NEEDING CARE needing to be dealt with very carefully *I need to discuss a very delicate matter with you.* **4** ATTRACTIVE having a thin, attractive shape *delicate hands* • **delicately** *adverb*

delicatessen /ˌdelɪkəˈtesⁿn/ *noun* [C] a shop, or a part of a shop which sells cheeses, cooked meats, salads, etc

delicious /dɪˈlɪʃəs/ *adjective* If food or drink is delicious, it smells or tastes extremely good. *This soup is absolutely delicious.* • **deliciously** *adverb*

delight¹ /dɪˈlaɪt/ *noun* **1** [U] happiness and excited pleasure *The children screamed with delight.* **2** [C] someone or something that gives you pleasure *She is a delight to have around.*

delight² /dɪˈlaɪt/ *verb* [T] to make someone feel very pleased and happy *The new discovery has delighted scientists everywhere.*

delight in sth/doing sth to get a lot of pleasure from something, especially something unpleasant *She seems to delight in making him look stupid.*

delighted /dɪˈlaɪtɪd/ *adjective* very pleased [+ to do sth] *I'd be delighted to accept your invitation.* ○ *They are delighted with their new car.*

delightful /dɪˈlaɪtfⁿl/ *adjective* very pleasant, attractive, or enjoyable *We had a delightful evening.* • **delightfully** *adverb*

delinquency /dɪˈlɪŋkwənsi/ *noun* [U] criminal or bad behaviour, especially by young people

delinquent /dɪˈlɪŋkwənt/ *noun* [C] a young person who behaves badly, usually by committing crimes • **delinquent** *adjective delinquent behaviour*

delirious /dɪˈlɪriəs/ *adjective* **1** speaking or thinking in a confused way, often because of a fever or drugs **2** extremely happy *delirious fans* • **deliriously** *adverb*

deliver /dɪˈlɪvəʳ/ *verb* **1** [I, T] to take things such as letters, parcels, or goods to a person or place *They can deliver the sofa on Wednesday.* **2** [I, T] to achieve or do something that you have promised to do, or that people expect you to do *The company failed to deliver the high quality service that we expect.* **3** **deliver a speech/talk, etc** to speak formally to a group of people *She delivered the speech on national TV.* **4** **deliver a baby** to help take a baby out of its mother when it is being born ⊃See also: deliver/come up with the **goods**.

delivery /dɪˈlɪvəri/ *noun* [C, U] **1** when someone takes things such as letters, parcels, or goods to a person or place *Is there a charge for delivery?* **2** when a baby is born and comes out of its mother *Susannah's husband was present at the delivery.*

delta /ˈdeltə/ *noun* [C] a low, flat area of land where a river divides into smaller rivers and goes into the sea *the Nile delta*

delude /dɪˈluːd/ *verb* [T] to make someone believe something that is not real or true [often reflexive, + into + doing sth] *She deluded herself into thinking she could win.* • **deluded** *adjective* believing things that are not real or true

deluge¹ /ˈdeljuːdʒ/ *noun* [C] **1** a very large amount of something that suddenly arrives *They have received a deluge of complaints.* **2** a sudden, large amount of rain, or a flood

deluge² /ˈdeljuːdʒ/ *verb* **be deluged with/by sth** to receive very large amounts of something suddenly *Our switchboard was deluged with calls last night.*

delusion /dɪˈluːʒⁿn/ *noun* [C, U] when someone believes something that is not true [+ (that)] *She is **under the delusion** that her debts will just go away.*

deluxe /dəˈlʌks/ *adjective* luxurious and of very high quality *a deluxe hotel*

delve /delv/ *verb* **delve in/into/inside, etc** to search in a container to try to find something *He delved in his pocket and pulled out a pen.*

delve into sth to examine something carefully in order to discover more information about someone or something *I don't like to delve too deeply into his past.*

o⌐**demand¹** /dɪˈmɑːnd/ *noun* **1** [U, no plural] a need for something to be sold or supplied *There's an increasing **demand for** cheap housing.* **2** [C] a strong request *They received a final **demand** for payment.* **3** **in demand** wanted or needed in large numbers *Good teachers are always in demand.*

o⌐**demand²** /dɪˈmɑːnd/ *verb* [T] **1** to ask for something in a way that shows that you do not expect to be refused *I demanded an explanation.* ○ [+ that] *The survivors are demanding that the airline pays them compensation.* ⊃See Common learner error at **ask**. **2** to need something such as time or effort *This job demands a high level of concentration.*

demanding /dɪˈmɑːndɪŋ/ *adjective* needing a lot of your time, attention, or effort *a very demanding job*

demands /dɪˈmɑːndz/ *noun* [plural] the difficult things that you have to do *the demands of modern life* ○ *His new job **makes** a lot of **demands on** him* (= he has to work very hard).

demeaning /dɪˈmiːnɪŋ/ *adjective* If something is demeaning, it makes you feel that you are not respected. *Some people consider beauty competitions demeaning to women.*

demeanour UK (US **demeanor**) /dɪˈmiːnəʳ/ *noun* [C] the way that someone looks, seems, and behaves *a quiet, serious demeanour*

demented /dɪˈmentɪd/ *adjective* mentally ill, or behaving in a very strange way without any control

dementia /dɪˈmenʃə/ *noun* [U] a mental illness suffered especially by old people

demi- /demi-/ *prefix* half, partly *demitasse* (= a small coffee cup) o *demigod* (= a creature that is part god and part human)

demise /dɪˈmaɪz/ *noun* **1** [no plural] when something ends, usually because it has stopped being popular or successful *the demise of apartheid* **2 sb's demise** someone's death

demo¹ /ˈdeməʊ/ *noun* [C] **1** an example of a product, given or shown to someone to try to make them buy it *a software demo* **2** *UK short for* demonstration (= political march) *a student demo*

demo² /ˈdeməʊ/ *verb* [T] to show something and explain how it works *We need someone to demo a new piece of software.*

an **emerging/new** democracy • **in** a democracy

o-**democracy** /dɪˈmɒkrəsi/ *noun* [C, U] a system of government in which people elect their leaders, or a country with this system

democrat /ˈdeməkræt/ *noun* [C] **1** someone who supports democracy **2 Democrat** someone who supports the Democratic Party in the US *the Democrat candidate* ➔See also: Liberal Democrat.

democratic /ˌdeməˈkrætɪk/ *adjective* **1** following or supporting the political system of democracy *a democratic society/government* **2** where everyone has equal rights and can help to make decisions *a democratic discussion/debate* • **democratically** *adverb a democratically elected government*

the Demo'cratic ,Party *noun* [group] one of the two main political parties in the US

demolish /dɪˈmɒlɪʃ/ *verb* [T] **1** to destroy something such as a building *The factory is dangerous, and will have to be demolished.* **2** to show that an idea or argument is wrong *He completely demolished my argument.*

demolition /ˌdeməˈlɪʃən/ *noun* [C, U] when something such as a building is destroyed *the demolition of dangerous buildings*

demon /ˈdiːmən/ *noun* [C] an evil spirit

demonic /dɪˈmɒnɪk/ *adjective* evil

demonstrable /dɪˈmɒnstrəbl/ *adjective* Something that is demonstrable can be shown to exist or be true. *a demonstrable fact* • **demonstrably** *adverb*

o-**demonstrate** /ˈdemənstreɪt/ *verb* **1** [PROVE] [T] to show or prove that something exists or is true [+ that] *The survey clearly demonstrates that tourism can have positive benefits.* **2** [SHOW HOW] [T] to show someone how to do something, or how something works *She demonstrated how to use the new software.* **3** [EXPRESS] [T] to express or show that you have a feeling, quality, or ability *He has demonstrated a genuine interest in the project.* **4** [MARCH] [I] to march or stand with a group of people to show that you disagree with or support someone or something *Thousands of people gathered to demonstrate against the new proposals.*

hold/organize/stage a demonstration • **go on/take part in** a demonstration • a **mass** demonstration • a demonstration **against** sth

demonstration /ˌdemənˈstreɪʃən/ *noun* **1** [MARCH] [C] when a group of people march or stand together to show that they disagree with or support someone or something *They're taking part in a **demonstration against** the causes of climate change.* **2** [SHOWING HOW] [C, U] showing how to do something, or how something works *We asked the sales assistant to give us a **demonstration**.* **3** [PROOF] [C, U] proof that something exists or is true *This disaster is a clear demonstration of the need for tighter controls.*

demonstrative /dɪˈmɒnstrətɪv/ *adjective* willing to show your feelings, especially your affection

demonstrator /ˈdemənstreɪtər/ *noun* [C] a person who marches or stands with a group of people to show that they disagree with or support someone or something

demoralized (*also UK* -ised) /dɪˈmɒrəlaɪzd/ *adjective* having lost your confidence, enthusiasm, and hope *After the match, the players were tired and demoralized.* • **demoralizing** *adjective* making you lose your confidence, enthusiasm, and hope *a demoralizing defeat* • **demoralize** /dɪˈmɒrəlaɪz/ *verb* [T]

demote /dɪˈməʊt/ *verb* **be demoted** to be moved to a less important job or position, especially as a punishment • **demotion** /dɪˈməʊʃən/ *noun* [C, U]

demotivated /ˌdiːˈməʊtɪveɪtɪd/ *adjective* not having any enthusiasm for your work

demure /dɪˈmjʊər/ *adjective* If a young woman is demure, she is quiet and shy. • **demurely** *adverb*

den /den/ *noun* [C] **1** [ANIMAL'S HOME] the home of some wild animals *a lions' den* **2** [ILLEGAL ACTIVITY] a place where secret and illegal activity happens *a gambling den* **3** [ROOM] *mainly US* a room in your home where you relax, read, watch television, etc

issue a denial • a **categorical/emphatic/strenuous/vehement** denial • denial **of** sth

denial /dɪˈnaɪəl/ *noun* **1** [C, U] when you say that something is not true *a denial of his guilt* **2** [U] not allowing someone to have or do something *the denial of medical treatment*

denigrate /ˈdenɪgreɪt/ *verb* [T] to criticize and not show much respect for someone or something

denim /ˈdenɪm/ *noun* [U] thick, strong, cotton cloth, usually blue, which is used to make clothes *a denim jacket*

denomination /dɪˌnɒmɪˈneɪʃən/ *noun* [C] **1** a religious group which has slightly different beliefs from other groups which share the same religion **2** the value of a particular coin, piece of paper money, or stamp

denote /dɪˈnəʊt/ *verb* [T] to be a sign of some-

D

thing *The colour red is used to denote passion or danger.*

denounce /dɪˈnaʊns/ *verb* [T] to publicly criticize someone or something, or to publicly accuse someone of something *They've been denounced as terrorists.*

dense /dens/ *adjective* **1** with a lot of people or things close together *dense forest* **2** If cloud, smoke, etc is dense, it is thick and difficult to see through. *dense fog* ● **densely** *adverb a densely populated area*

density /ˈdensɪti/ *noun* [C, U] **1** the number of people or things in a place when compared with the size of the place *The area has a high population density.* **2** the relationship between the weight of a substance and its size *bone density*

dent¹ /dent/ *noun* [C] **1** a hollow area in a hard surface where it has been hit *The car door had a dent in it.* **2** a reduction in something *The cost of repairs made a serious dent in my savings.*

dent² /dent/ *verb* [T] **1** to create a hollow area in the hard surface of something by hitting it *The side of the car was dented in the accident.* **2** to reduce someone's confidence or positive feelings about something *The defeat did little to dent her enthusiasm.*

dental /ˈdentˀl/ *adjective* relating to teeth *dental treatment*

dental floss /ˈdentˀl.flɒs/ *noun* [U] a thin thread which is used for cleaning between the teeth

dentist /ˈdentɪst/ *noun* [C] someone who examines and repairs teeth *I've got an appointment at the dentist's (= where the dentist works) tomorrow.* ● **dentistry** *noun* [U] the subject or job of examining and repairing teeth

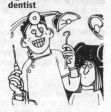
dentist

dentures /ˈdentʃəz/ *noun* [plural] false teeth

denunciation /dɪˌnʌnsiˈeɪʃˀn/ *noun* [C, U] when you publicly criticize someone or something, or publicly accuse someone of something

◦•**deny** /dɪˈnaɪ/ *verb* [T] **1** to say that something is not true, especially something that you are accused of [+ (that)] *He never denied that he said those things.* ○ [+ doing sth] *He denies murdering his father.* **2** to not allow someone to have or do something [often passive] *These children are being denied access to education.*

deodorant /diˈəʊdˀrˀnt/ *noun* [C, U] a substance that you put on your body to prevent or hide unpleasant smells

depart /dɪˈpɑːt/ *verb* [I] *formal* to leave a place, especially to start a journey to another place *The train to Lincoln will depart from platform 9.* ○ *He departed for Paris on Tuesday.*

◦•**department** /dɪˈpɑːtmənt/ *noun* [C] a part of an organization such as a school, business, or government which deals with a particular area of work *the sales department* ○ *head of the*

English department ⟩See also: **police department.**

departmental /ˌdiːpɑːtˈmentˀl/ *adjective* relating to a department *the departmental budget*

de'partment ˌstore *noun* [C] a large shop divided into several different parts which sell different types of things

◦•**departure** /dɪˈpɑːtʃər/ *noun* [C, U] **1** when someone or something leaves a place, especially to start a journey to another place *the departure of flight BA117* ○ *This fare is valid for weekday departures from Manchester.* **2** a change from what is expected, or from what has happened before *This film is a major departure from his previous work.*

◦•**depend** /dɪˈpend/ *verb* **it/that depends** used to say that you are not certain about something because other things affect your answer [+ question word] *"Are you coming out tonight?" "It depends where you're going."*

depend on something

Be careful to choose the correct preposition after **depend**.

I might go on Friday, it depends on the weather.

~~I might go on Friday, it depends of the weather.~~

~~I might go on Friday, it depends from the weather.~~

depend on/upon sb/sth 1 NEED to need the help of someone or something in order to exist or continue as before *She depends on her son for everything.* ○ *The city's economy depends largely on the car industry.* **2** BE INFLUENCED BY If something depends on someone or something, it is influenced by them, or changes because of them. [+ question word] *The choice depends on what you're willing to spend.* **3** TRUST to be able to trust someone or something to help, or to do what you expect [+ to do sth] *You can always depend on Andy to keep his promises.*

dependable /dɪˈpendəbl/ *adjective* able to be trusted and very likely to do what you expect *the team's most dependable player*

dependant *UK* (*US* **dependent**) /dɪˈpendənt/ *noun* [C] someone, usually a child, who depends on you for financial support

dependence /dɪˈpendəns/ (*also* **dependency** /dɪˈpendəntsi/) *noun* [U] when you need someone or something all the time in order to exist or continue as before *Our society needs to reduce its dependence on the car.*

dependent¹ /dɪˈpendənt/ *adjective* **1** needing the help of someone or something in order to exist or continue as before *She's completely dependent on her parents for money.* **2 dependent on/upon sth** influenced by or decided by something *The amount of tax you pay is dependent on how much you earn.*

dependent² /dɪˈpendənt/ *noun* [C] *US* spelling of dependant

depict /dɪˈpɪkt/ *verb* [T] to represent someone or something in a picture or story *The cartoon depicts the president as a vampire.* ● **depiction** /dɪˈpɪkʃˀn/ *noun* [C, U]

deplete /dɪˈpliːt/ *verb* [T] to reduce the amount of something, especially a natural supply *Alcohol depletes the body of B vitamins.* • **depletion** /dɪˈpliːʃᵊn/ *noun* [U]

deplorable /dɪˈplɔːrəbl/ *adjective* very bad or morally wrong

deplore /dɪˈplɔːʳ/ *verb* [T] *formal* to feel or express strong disapproval of something *We deeply deplore the loss of life.*

deploy /dɪˈplɔɪ/ *verb* [T] to move soldiers or equipment to a place where they can be used when they are needed • **deployment** *noun* [U] *the deployment of nuclear weapons*

deport /dɪˈpɔːt/ *verb* [T] to force a foreign person to leave a country *Thousands of illegal immigrants are **deported from** the US every year.* • **deportation** /ˌdiːpɔːˈteɪʃᵊn/ *noun* [C, U] *He now faces deportation back to his native country.*

depose /dɪˈpəʊz/ *verb* [T] to remove a ruler or leader from their position of power • **deposed** *adjective the deposed president*

WORD PARTNERS FOR ***deposit***

pay/put down a deposit • a deposit **of** [£500/$300, etc] • a deposit **on** sth

deposit[1] /dɪˈpɒzɪt/ *noun* [C] **1** [BUYING] a payment that you make immediately when you decide to buy something, as proof that you will really buy it *They've **put down a deposit on** a house.* **2** [BANK] an amount of money that you pay into a bank *to **make a deposit*** **3** [SUBSTANCE] a layer of a substance that has developed from a natural or chemical process *deposits of iron ore* **4** [RENT] an amount of money that you pay when you rent something, and that is given back to you when you return it without any damage

deposit[2] /dɪˈpɒzɪt/ *verb* [T] **1** [PUT DOWN] to put something down somewhere *He deposited his books on the table.* **2** [MONEY] to put money into a bank or valuable things into a safe place *She deposited $150,000 in a Swiss bank account.* **3** [SUBSTANCE] to leave something lying on a surface, as a result of a natural or chemical process

deˈposit acˌcount *noun* [C] *UK* a bank account that pays interest on the money you put into it and that you use for saving

depot /ˈdepəʊ/ *noun* [C] **1** [VEHICLES] a place where trains, trucks, or buses are kept **2** [GOODS] a building where supplies of goods are stored **3** [STATION] *US* a small bus or train station

depraved /dɪˈpreɪvd/ *adjective* morally bad • **depravity** /dɪˈprævəti/ *noun* [U]

depreciate /dɪˈpriːʃieɪt/ *verb* [I] to lose value over a period of time *New computers depreciate in value very quickly.* • **depreciation** /dɪˌpriːʃiˈeɪʃᵊn/ *noun* [U]

depress /dɪˈpres/ *verb* [T] **1** to make someone feel very unhappy, especially about the future *This place really depresses me.* **2** to reduce the value or level of something, especially in business *Competition between stores has depressed prices.*

depressed /dɪˈprest/ *adjective* **1** very unhappy, often for a long time *She has been feeling very depressed since her marriage broke up.* **2** A depressed country, area, or economy does not have enough jobs or business activity. *an economically depressed area*

depressing /dɪˈpresɪŋ/ *adjective* making you feel unhappy and without any hope for the future *The news is very depressing.*

depression /dɪˈpreʃᵊn/ *noun* [C, U] **1** when you feel very unhappy, or a mental illness that makes you feel very unhappy *Nearly three million people **suffer from depression** every year.* **2** a time when there is not much business activity *The stock market crash marked the start of a severe depression.*

deprive /dɪˈpraɪv/ *verb*

deprive sb/sth of sth to take something important or necessary away from someone or something *They were deprived of food for long periods.* • **deprivation** /ˌdeprɪˈveɪʃᵊn/ *noun* [C, U] ***sleep deprivation***

deprived /dɪˈpraɪvd/ *adjective* not having enough food, money, and the things that you need to have a normal life *children from **deprived backgrounds***

dept *written abbreviation for* department (= a part of an organization or government)

WORD PARTNERS FOR ***depth***

a depth **of** [6 metres/8 inches, etc] • [5cm/7 inches, etc] **in** depth • **at/to** a depth of [5 metres/6 inches, etc]

depth /depθ/ *noun* **1** [TOP TO BOTTOM] [C, U] the distance from the top of something to the bottom *The lake reaches a maximum **depth of** 292 metres.* ○ *Dig a hole 10 cm **in depth**.* ➲See picture at **length**. **2** [FRONT TO BACK] [C, U] the distance from the front to the back of something **3** [AMOUNT] [U] how much someone knows or feels about something *She was amazed at the depth of his knowledge.* **4 in depth** giving all the details *With access to the Internet, students can do their homework in greater depth.* **5 be out of your depth** to not have the knowledge, experience or skills to deal with a particular subject or situation

depths /depθs/ *noun* [plural] **1** a position far below the surface or far into something ***the depths of** the forest* **2** the worst period of something *the **depths of despair***

deputy /ˈdepjəti/ *noun* [C] someone who has the second most important job in an organization *the deputy Prime Minister*

derail /dɪˈreɪl/ *verb* **1** [I, T] If a train derails, or is derailed, it comes off the railway tracks. **2** [T] If you derail plans, you prevent them from happening. • **derailment** *noun* [C, U]

deranged /dɪˈreɪndʒd/ *adjective* behaving in a way that is not normal, especially when suffering from a mental illness

derby /ˈdɑːbi/ [US] /ˈdɜːrbi/ *noun* [C] **1** *mainly UK* a type of sports competition *a fishing/motorcycle derby* **2 Derby** a type of horse race **3** *US* (*UK* **bowler hat**) a round, hard, black hat worn by men, especially in the past

deregulate /ˌdiːˈregjəleɪt/ *verb* [T] to remove

national or local government controls from a business *The government plans to deregulate the banking industry.* ● **deregulation** /ˌdiːregjəˈleɪʃ³n/ *noun* [U]

derelict /ˈderəlɪkt/ *adjective* A derelict building or piece of land is not used any more and is in a bad condition. *a derelict house*

deride /dɪˈraɪd/ *verb* [T] *formal* to talk about someone or something as if they are ridiculous and do not deserve any respect *Her novel, once derided by critics, is now a classic.*

derision /dɪˈrɪʒ³n/ *noun* [U] when you talk about someone or something as if they are ridiculous and do not deserve respect *The novel was greeted with derision.*

derisive /dɪˈraɪsɪv/ *adjective* showing derision towards someone or something

derisory /dɪˈraɪs³ri/ *adjective* 1 so small that it seems ridiculous *a derisory sum of money* 2 cruel and making someone feel stupid *derisory remarks*

derivation /ˌderɪˈveɪʃ³n/ *noun* [C, U] the origin of something, such as a word, from which another form has developed, or the new form itself

derivative /dɪˈrɪvətɪv/ *noun* [C] a form of something, such as a word, that has developed from another form

derive /dɪˈraɪv/ *verb*
derive (sth) from sth 1 to come from or be developed from something *The name derives from Latin.* 2 **derive comfort/pleasure, etc from sth** to get a positive feeling or advantage from someone or something *I derive great pleasure from gardening.*

dermatitis /ˌdɜːməˈtaɪtɪs/ *noun* [U] a condition which makes your skin red and painful

derogatory /dɪˈrɒgət³ri/ *adjective* showing strong disapproval and not showing any respect for someone *He was derogatory comments/remarks about her appearance.*

descend /dɪˈsend/ *verb* [I, T] *formal* to move or go down *We descended four flights of stairs.*
be descended from sb/sth to be related to a person or creature that lived a long time ago

descendant /dɪˈsendənt/ *noun* [C] someone who is related to someone who lived a long time ago *She is a direct descendant of Queen Victoria.*

descent /dɪˈsent/ *noun* [C, U] 1 a movement down *The plane began its descent into Heathrow.* 2 **of Irish/French, etc descent** being related to people who lived in the past in Ireland/France, etc

o⇤**describe** /dɪˈskraɪb/ *verb* [T] to say what someone or something is like *Neighbours described her as a shy, quiet girl.* ○ [+ question word] *I tried to describe what I had seen.*

o⇤**description** /dɪˈskrɪpʃ³n/ *noun* 1 [C, U] something that tells you what someone or something is like *I gave the police a description of*

the stolen jewellery. 2 **of any/every/some description** of any/every/some type *They sell plants of every description.*

descriptive /dɪˈskrɪptɪv/ *adjective* describing something, especially in a detailed, interesting way

desert¹ /ˈdezət/ *noun* [C, U] a large, hot, dry area of land with very few plants *the Sahara Desert*

desert² /dɪˈzɜːt/ *verb* 1 PERSON [T] to leave someone and never come back *He deserted his family.* 2 PLACE [T] to leave a place, so that it is empty *People are deserting the countryside to work in towns.* 3 ARMY [I, T] to leave the army without permission ● **desertion** /dɪˈzɜːʃ³n/ *noun* [U]

deserted /dɪˈzɜːtɪd/ *adjective* If a place is deserted, it has no people in it. *a deserted street*

deserter /dɪˈzɜːtə³/ *noun* [C] someone who leaves the army without permission

desert ˈisland *noun* [C] a tropical island where no one lives, far from any other places

o⇤**deserve** /dɪˈzɜːv/ *verb* [T] If you deserve something good or bad, it should happen to you because of the way you have behaved. *The school deserves praise for the way it has raised standards.* ○ [+ to do sth] *He deserves to be locked up for life.* ● **deservedly** *adverb*

deserving /dɪˈzɜːvɪŋ/ *adjective* If something or someone is deserving, people should help or support them. *The children's charity is a deserving cause.*

o⇤**design**¹ /dɪˈzaɪn/ *noun* 1 PLANNING [U] the way in which something is planned and made *There was a fault in the design of the aircraft.* 2 DRAWING [C] a drawing which shows how an object, machine, or building will be made *Engineers are working on the new designs.* 3 DECORATION [C] a pattern or decoration 4 PROCESS [U] the process of making drawings to show how something will be made *a course in art and design* ⊃See also: interior design.

o⇤**design**² /dɪˈzaɪn/ *verb* [T] 1 to draw or plan something before making it *She designs furniture.* 2 **be designed to do sth** to have been planned or done for a particular purpose *The new law is designed to protect children.*

designate /ˈdezɪgneɪt/ *verb* [T] *formal* to choose someone or something for a particular purpose or duty *The area has been designated as a nature reserve.* ● **designation** /ˌdezɪgˈneɪʃ³n/ *noun* [C, U]

designer¹ /dɪˈzaɪnə³/ *noun* [C] someone who draws and plans how something will be made *a fashion designer*

designer² /dɪˈzaɪnə³/ *adjective* **designer jeans/sunglasses, etc** clothes or objects made by a fashionable designer

deˌsigner ˈbaby *noun* [C] a baby with some characteristics chosen by its parents and doctors using gene therapy (= the science of changing genes in order to stop or prevent a disease)

desirable /dɪˈzaɪərəbl/ *adjective* If something is desirable, it is very good or attractive and most people would want it. *A good education is highly desirable.* ⊃Opposite undesirable.

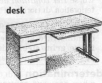

WORD PARTNERS FOR desire

express/have a desire to do sth • a burning/strong desire • a desire for sth

---

desire¹ /dɪˈzaɪəʳ/ noun **1** [C, U] a strong feeling that you want something [+ to do sth] *I have no desire to have children.* ○ *There is a strong desire for peace among the people.* **2** [U] when you are sexually attracted to someone

desire² /dɪˈzaɪəʳ/ verb [T] *formal* to want something *You can have whatever you desire.*

desired /dɪˈzaɪəd/ adjective **the desired effect/result/shape, etc** the effect/result/shape, etc that is wanted *Her medicine seems to have had the desired effect.*

o⌐**desk** /desk/ noun [C] a table that you sit at to write or work, often with drawers ⊃See also: **cash desk** ⊃See colour picture **The Office** on page Centre 5.

desk

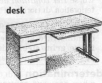

desktop /ˈdesktɒp/ noun [C] **1** COMPUTER SCREEN a computer screen that contains icons (= symbols that represent programs, information or equipment) and which is usually used as a place to start and finish computer work **2** COMPUTER (*also* **desktop computer**) a computer that is small enough to fit on a desk **3** SURFACE the top of a desk

desktop 'publishing noun [U] producing finished designs for pages of books or documents using a small computer and printer (= machine for printing)

desolate /ˈdesəlʌt/ adjective **1** A desolate place is empty and makes you feel sad. *a desolate landscape* **2** lonely and unhappy *She felt desolate when he left.* • **desolation** /ˌdesəˈleɪʃən/ noun [U]

WORD PARTNERS FOR despair

abject/complete/utter despair • in despair

---

despair¹ /dɪˈspeəʳ/ noun [U] a feeling of having no hope *She shook her head in despair.*

despair² /dɪˈspeəʳ/ verb [I] to feel that you have no hope *Don't despair - things will improve.* ○ [+ of + doing sth] *He had begun to despair of ever finding a job.* • **despairing** adjective

despatch¹ UK (UK/US **dispatch**) /dɪˈspætʃ/ verb [T] *formal* to send someone or something somewhere *They despatched a police car to arrest him.*

despatch² UK (UK/US **dispatch**) /dɪˈspætʃ/ noun **1** [U] when someone or something is sent somewhere *the despatch of troops* **2** [C] an official report that someone in a foreign country sends to their organization

desperate /ˈdespᵊrət/ adjective **1** WITHOUT HOPE feeling that you have no hope and are ready to do anything to change the situation you are in *He was absolutely desperate and would have tried anything to get her back.* **2** NEEDING SOMETHING needing or wanting something very much *By two o'clock I was desperate for some-*

thing to eat. **3** BAD A desperate situation is very bad or serious. *The economy is in a really desperate situation.* • **desperately** adverb • **desperation** /ˌdespᵊˈreɪʃən/ noun [U]

despicable /dɪˈspɪkəbl/ adjective very unpleasant or cruel *a despicable act/crime*

despise /dɪˈspaɪz/ verb [T] to hate someone or something and have no respect for them *The two groups despise each other.*

o⌐**despite** /dɪˈspaɪt/ preposition **1** used to say that something happened or is true, although something else makes this seem not probable *I'm still pleased with the house despite all the problems we've had.* ○ [+ doing sth] *He managed to eat lunch despite having had an enormous breakfast.* **2 despite yourself** If you do something despite yourself, you do it although you did not intend to.

despondent /dɪˈspɒndənt/ adjective unhappy and having no enthusiasm • **despondency** noun [U]

despot /ˈdespɒt/ noun [C] a very powerful person, especially someone who treats people cruelly

dessert

dessert /dɪˈzɜːt/ noun [C, U] sweet food that is eaten after the main part of a meal *We had ice cream for dessert.*

dessertspoon /dɪˈzɜːtspuːn/ noun [C] UK a medium-sized spoon used for eating or measuring food, or the amount this spoon can hold

destabilize (*also* UK **-ise**) /ˌdiːˈsteɪbᵊlaɪz/ verb [T] to cause change in a country or government so that it loses its power or control *a plot to destabilize the government*

destination /ˌdestɪˈneɪʃən/ noun [C] the place where someone or something is going *Spain is a very popular holiday destination.*

destined /ˈdestɪnd/ adjective **be destined for sth; be destined to do sth** to be certain to be something or do something in the future *She was destined for a brilliant future.*

destiny /ˈdestɪni/ noun **1** [C] the things that will happen to someone in the future *At last she feels in control of her own destiny.* **2** [U] a power that some people believe controls what will happen in the future *Nick said it was destiny that we met.*

destitute /ˈdestɪtjuːt/ adjective so poor that you

do not have the basic things you need to live, such as food, clothes, or money ● **destitution** /ˌdestɪ'tjuːʃᵊn/ *noun* [U]

o▪**destroy** /dɪ'strɔɪ/ *verb* [T] to damage something so badly that it does not exist or cannot be used *Many works of art were destroyed in the fire.*

destroyer /dɪ'strɔɪəʳ/ *noun* [C] a small, fast ship that is used in a war

destruction /dɪ'strʌkʃᵊn/ *noun* [U] when something is destroyed *We are all responsible for the destruction of the forest.* ● **destructive** /dɪ'strʌktɪv/ *adjective* causing a lot of damage *the destructive power of nuclear weapons* ⊃See also: **self-destructive**.

detach /dɪ'tætʃ/ *verb* [T] to take a part of something off so that it is separate *Please complete and detach the form below and return it to the school.* ● **detachable** *adjective*

detached /dɪ'tætʃt/ *adjective* **1** *UK* A detached building is not joined to another building. **2** If someone is detached, they do not feel involved with someone or emotional about something. ⊃See also: **semi-detached**.

detachment /dɪ'tætʃmənt/ *noun* **1** [U] when someone does not feel involved in a situation *He spoke with cool detachment.* **2** [C] a small group of soldiers with a particular job to do

o▪**detail¹** /'diːteɪl/ ⑩ /dɪ'teɪl/ *noun* [C, U] **1** a fact or piece of information about something *Please send me details of your training courses.* ○ *She didn't include very much detail in her report.* **2 in detail** including every part of something *He explained it all in great detail.* **3 go into detail** to include all the facts about something

detail² /'diːteɪl/ ⑩ /dɪ'teɪl/ *verb* [T] to describe something completely, giving all the facts

detailed /'diːteɪld/ *adjective* giving a lot of information *a detailed account/description*

detain /dɪ'teɪn/ *verb* [T] to keep someone somewhere and not allow them to leave, especially in order to ask them about a crime *Three men were detained by police for questioning.*

detect /dɪ'tekt/ *verb* [T] to discover or notice something, especially something that is difficult to see, hear, smell, etc *This special camera can detect bodies by their heat.*

detection /dɪ'tekʃᵊn/ *noun* [U] **1** when someone notices or discovers something *the early detection of cancer* **2** when the police discover information about a crime

detective /dɪ'tektɪv/ *noun* [C] someone, especially a police officer, whose job is to discover information about a crime

detector /dɪ'tektəʳ/ *noun* [C] a piece of equipment used to discover something, especially something that is difficult to see, hear, smell, etc *a smoke detector*

detente /ˌdeɪ'tɒnt/ *noun* [U] *formal* when countries become friendly with each other after a period of not being friendly

detention /dɪ'tenʃᵊn/ *noun* **1** [U] when someone is officially kept somewhere and not allowed to leave **2** [C, U] when a student is kept in school after the other students leave, as a punishment

deter /dɪ'tɜːʳ/ *verb* [T] **deterring**, *past* **deterred** to make someone less likely to do something, or to make something less likely to happen *We have introduced new security measures to deter shoplifters.* ○ [+ from + doing sth] *Higher fuel costs could deter people from driving their cars.*

detergent /dɪ'tɜːdʒᵊnt/ *noun* [C, U] a liquid or powder that is used to clean things

deteriorate /dɪ'tɪəriᵊreɪt/ *verb* [I] to become worse *Her condition deteriorated rapidly.* ● **deterioration** /dɪˌtɪəriᵊ'reɪʃᵊn/ *noun* [U]

determination /dɪˌtɜːmɪ'neɪʃᵊn/ *noun* [U] when someone continues trying to do something, although it is very difficult *Andy Murray will need great determination and skill to win this match.*

determine /dɪ'tɜːmɪn/ *verb* [T] **1** to discover the facts or truth about something [+ question word] *The doctors are still unable to determine what is wrong.* **2** to decide what will happen [+ question word] *Her exam results will determine which university she goes to.*

o▪**determined** /dɪ'tɜːmɪnd/ *adjective* wanting to do something very much, and not letting anyone stop you [+ to do sth] *He's determined to win this match.*

determiner /dɪ'tɜːmɪnəʳ/ *noun* [C] a word that is used before a noun or adjective to show which person or thing you are referring to. For example 'my' in 'my old car' and 'that' in 'that man' are determiners.

deterrent /dɪ'terᵊnt/ *noun* [C] something that stops people doing something because they are afraid of what will happen if they do *They've installed a security camera as a deterrent to thieves.* ● **deterrent** *adjective* *a deterrent effect*

detest /dɪ'test/ *verb* [T] to hate someone or something very much

detonate /'detᵊneɪt/ *verb* [I, T] to explode or make something explode *The bomb was detonated safely by army officers and no one was hurt.* ● **detonation** /ˌdetᵊ'neɪʃᵊn/ *noun* [C, U]

detonator /'detᵊneɪtəʳ/ *noun* [C] a piece of equipment that makes a bomb explode

detour /'diːtʊəʳ/ *noun* [C] a different, longer route to a place that is used to avoid something or to visit something *Several roads were closed, so we had to take a detour.*

detox /'diːtɒks/ *noun* [U] *informal* treatment to clean out your blood, stomach, etc and get rid of bad substances such as drugs

detract /dɪ'trækt/ *verb*

detract from sth to make something seem less good than it really is, or than it was thought to be

detriment /'detrɪmənt/ *noun* **to the detriment**

of sth causing damage to something *He was working very long hours, to the detriment of his health.* • **detrimental** /ˌdetrɪˈmentəl/ *adjective a detrimental effect*

devaluation /ˌdiːvæljuˈeɪʃən/ *noun* [C, U] when the value of something is reduced *the devaluation of the dollar*

devalue /ˌdiːˈvæljuː/ *verb* [T] **devaluing**, *past* **devalued 1** to make something less valuable, especially a country's money *to devalue the pound* **2** to make someone or something seem less important than they really are

devastate /ˈdevəsteɪt/ *verb* [T] to destroy or damage something very badly *A recent hurricane devastated the city.* • **devastation** /ˌdevəˈsteɪʃən/ *noun* [U]

devastated /ˈdevəsteɪtɪd/ *adjective* **1** very shocked and upset *She was devastated when her husband died.* **2** completely destroyed

devastating /ˈdevəsteɪtɪŋ/ *adjective* **1** making someone very shocked and upset *Despite the devastating news, no one is giving up hope.* **2** causing a lot of damage or destruction *The fire has had a devastating effect on the local wildlife.*

devastatingly /ˈdevəsteɪtɪŋli/ *adverb* extremely *devastatingly funny/handsome*

o‑**develop** /dɪˈveləp/ *verb* **1** CHANGE [I, T] to grow or change and become more advanced, or to make someone or something do this *The baby develops inside the mother for nine months.* ○ *He's developing into a very good tennis player.* **2** MAKE [T] to make something new such as a product *Scientists are developing new drugs all the time.* **3** ILLNESS [T] to start to have something, such as an illness, problem, or feeling *Shortly after take-off the plane developed engine trouble.* **4** HAPPEN [I] to start to happen or exist *Further problems may develop if you do not deal with this now.* **5** FILM [T] to use special chemicals on a piece of film to make photographs appear *I need to get my holiday photos developed.* **6** BUILD [T] to build houses, factories, shops, etc on a piece of land

developed /dɪˈveləpt/ *adjective* a **developed country/nation, etc** a country with an advanced level of technology, industry, etc ⊃Opposite un-developed.

developer /dɪˈveləpər/ *noun* [C] a person or company that buys land and builds houses, factories, shops, etc

WORD PARTNERS FOR **development**

encourage/monitor/restrict development • dramatic/major/rapid development • in/under development

o‑**development** /dɪˈveləpmənt/ *noun* **1** CHANGE [C, U] when someone or something grows or changes and becomes more advanced *The nurse will do some tests to check on your child's development.* ○ *There have been some major developments in technology recently.* **2** MAKE [C, U] when something new is made *the development of new drugs* **3** START [U] when something starts to happen or exist *Smoking encourages the development of cancer.* **4** BUILD [U] when new houses, factories, shops, etc, are built on

an area of land *land suitable for development* **5** BUILDINGS [C] an area of land with new houses, factories, shops, etc on it *a new housing development* **6** EVENT [C] something new that happens and changes a situation *Have there been any more developments since I left?* **7** PHOTOGRAPH [U] when someone makes photographs from a film

deviant /ˈdiːviənt/ *adjective* different to what most people think is normal or acceptable, usually relating to sexual behaviour • **deviant** *noun* [C]

deviate /ˈdiːvieɪt/ *verb* [I] to do something in a different way from what is usual or expected *The aircraft **deviated from** its original flight plan.*

deviation /ˌdiːviˈeɪʃən/ *noun* [C, U] when something is different to what is usual, expected, or accepted by most people *sexual deviation*

device /dɪˈvaɪs/ *noun* **1** [C] a piece of equipment that is used for a particular purpose *A pager is a small, electronic device for sending messages.* **2** leave someone to their own devices to leave someone to do what they want to do *With both parents out at work, the kids were often left to their own devices.*

devil /ˈdevəl/ *noun* **1 the Devil** the most powerful evil spirit, according to the Christian and Jewish religions **2** [C] an evil spirit **3** [C] *informal* someone who behaves badly **4 lucky/poor, etc devil** *informal* used to describe a person **5 speak/talk of the devil** *informal* something that you say when someone you have been talking about suddenly appears

devilish /ˈdevəlɪʃ/ *adjective* evil or bad *a devilish smile* • **devilishly** *adverb* very *a devilishly difficult puzzle*

devious /ˈdiːviəs/ *adjective* clever in a way that is bad and not honest *a devious mind*

devise /dɪˈvaɪz/ *verb* [T] to design or invent something such as a system, plan, or piece of equipment

devoid /dɪˈvɔɪd/ *adjective* **devoid of sth** *formal* completely without a quality *His voice was devoid of emotion.*

devolution /ˌdiːvəˈluːʃən/ *noun* [U] when power moves from a central government to local governments

devolve /dɪˈvɒlv/ *verb* **devolve sth to sb/sth** *formal* to give power or responsibility to a person or organization at a lower or more local level

devote /dɪˈvəʊt/ *verb* **devote sth to sb/sth 1** to use time, energy, etc for a particular purpose *She devotes most of her free time to charity work.* **2** to use a space or area for a particular purpose [often passive] *Most of the magazine was devoted to coverage of the soap star's wedding.*

devoted /dɪˈvəʊtɪd/ *adjective* loving or caring very much about someone or something *She's absolutely **devoted to** her grandchildren.* • **devotedly** *adverb*

devotee /ˌdevəʊˈtiː/ *noun* [C] someone who likes something or someone very much *a **devotee** of classical music*

devotion /dɪ'vəʊʃ°n/ *noun* [U] **1** great love or loyalty for someone or something *She will always be remembered for her devotion to her family.* **2** strong religious belief or behaviour

devour /dɪ'vaʊəʳ/ *verb* [T] **1** to eat something quickly because you are very hungry **2** to read something quickly and enthusiastically

devout /dɪ'vaʊt/ *adjective* extremely religious *a devout Catholic/Muslim* ● **devoutly** *adverb*

dew /djuː/ *noun* [U] drops of water that form on surfaces outside during the night

dexterity /dek'sterəti/ *noun* [U] skill at doing something, especially using your hands *manual dexterity*

diabetes /ˌdaɪə'biːtiːz/ *noun* [U] a serious medical condition in which your body cannot control the level of sugar in your blood ● **diabetic** /ˌdaɪə'betɪk/ *adjective* ● **diabetic** /ˌdaɪə'betɪk/ *noun* [C] someone who has diabetes

diabolical /ˌdaɪə'bɒlɪk°l/ *adjective* extremely bad

diagnose /'daɪəgnəʊz/ *verb* [T] to say what is wrong with someone who is ill [often passive] *She was diagnosed with/as having cancer last year.*

diagnosis /ˌdaɪəg'nəʊsɪs/ *noun* [C, U] *plural* **diagnoses** when a doctor says what is wrong with someone who is ill

diagnostic /ˌdaɪəg'nɒstɪk/ *adjective* **diagnostic methods/tests, etc** methods/tests, etc that help you discover what is wrong with someone or something

diagonal /daɪ'æg°n°l/ *adjective* **1** A diagonal line is straight and sloping and not horizontal or vertical. *a tie with diagonal stripes* **2** going from the top corner of a square to the bottom corner on the other side ● **diagonally** *adverb*

diagram /'daɪəgræm/ *noun* [C] a simple picture showing what something looks like or explaining how something works

dial¹ /daɪəl/ *noun* [C] **1** TIME/MEASUREMENT the round part of a clock, watch, or machine that shows you the time or other measurement **2** BUTTON a round part on a piece of equipment such as a television or radio that you turn to operate it, make it louder, etc **3** TELEPHONE the ring of holes with numbers that you turn on the front of an old telephone

dial² /daɪəl/ *verb* [I, T] *UK* **dialling**, *past* **dialled**, *US* **dialing**, *past* **dialed** to make a telephone call to a particular number *Dial 0 for the operator.*

dialect /'daɪəlekt/ *noun* [C, U] a form of a language that people speak in a particular part of a country

'dialog ,box *noun* [C] a window (= a separate area on a computer screen) that appears and gives the person using the computer infor-

mation about what they are doing

dialogue (*also US* **dialog**) /'daɪəlɒg/ *noun* [C, U] **1** the talking in a book, play, or film **2** a formal discussion between countries or groups of people

dial-up /'daɪəlʌp/ *adjective* [always before noun] Dial-up computer systems and equipment and Internet services use a telephone connection to reach them. ⊃Compare **broadband**.

diameter /daɪ'æmɪtəʳ/ *noun* [C, U] a straight line that goes from one side of a circle to the other side and through the centre, or the length of this line *The cake was about 30 centimetres in diameter.*

diamond /'daɪəmənd/ *noun*
1 STONE [C, U] a very hard, transparent stone that is extremely valuable and is often used in jewellery *a diamond ring* **2** SHAPE [C] a shape with four straight sides of equal length that join to form two large angles and two small angles **3** BASEBALL [C] the field where baseball is played **4** **diamonds** playing cards with red, diamond shapes on them *the queen of diamonds*

diamond

diaper /'daɪəpəʳ/ *US* (*UK* **nappy**) *noun* [C] a thick piece of paper or cloth worn by a baby on its bottom

diaphragm /'daɪəfræm/ *noun* [C] the large muscle between your lungs and your stomach

diarrhoea *UK* (*US* **diarrhea**) /ˌdaɪə'rɪə/ *noun* [U] an illness in which your solid waste is more liquid than usual, and comes out of your body more often

◦▪ **diary** /'daɪəri/ *noun* [C] **1** a book containing spaces for all the days and months of the year, in which you write meetings and other things that you must remember **2** a book in which you write each day about your personal thoughts and experiences *She kept a diary of her trip to Egypt.*

dice¹ /daɪs/ *noun* [C] *plural* **dice** a small object with six equal square sides, each with between one and six spots on it, used in games *Roll the dice to see who starts the game.*

dice² /daɪs/ *verb* [T] to cut food into small, square pieces *diced onions*

dicey /'daɪsi/ *adjective informal* possibly dangerous or involving a risk

dichotomy /daɪ'kɒtəmi/ *noun* [C] *formal* the difference between two completely opposite ideas or things *the dichotomy between good and evil*

dictate /dɪk'teɪt/ *verb* **1** [I, T] to say or read

something for someone to write down *Tony was busy **dictating** letters to his secretary.* **2** [T] to decide or control what happens [+ question word] *The weather will dictate where we hold the party.*

dictate to sb to tell someone what to do, often in a way that annoys them *I'm 15 years old - you can't dictate to me any more.*

dictation /dɪk'teɪʃ³n/ *noun* **1** [U] when someone speaks or reads something for someone else to write down **2** [C, U] when a teacher says or reads something for students to write down as a test

dictator /dɪk'teɪtə³/ *noun* [C] a leader who has complete power in a country and has not been elected by the people *For many years they were under a **dictator**.* ● **dictatorial** /ˌdɪktə'tɔːriəl/ *adjective*

dictatorship /dɪk'teɪtəʃɪp/ *noun* [C, U] a country or system of government with a dictator as leader

o﹣**dictionary** /'dɪkʃ³n³ri/ *noun* [C] a book that contains a list of words in alphabetical order with their meanings explained or written in another language

o﹣**did** /dɪd/ *past tense of* do

o﹣**didn't** /'dɪd³nt/ *short for* did not

o﹣**die** /daɪ/ *verb* dying, *past* died **1** [I] to stop living *Many of the refugees **died** of hunger.* ○ *She **died from** brain injuries after a road accident.* **2 be dying for sth; be dying to do sth** *informal* to very much want to have, eat, drink, or do something *I'm **dying** for a drink.* **3 to die for** *informal* If something is to die for, it is extremely good. *Their chocolate cake is to die for.* ➎See also: die **hard²**.

died or **dead**?

Be careful not to confuse the verb and adjective forms of these words. **Died** is the past of the verb 'to die', which means 'to stop living'.

*My cat **died** last week.*

Dead is an adjective and is used to talk about people or things which are not alive.

*My cat is **dead**.*

die away If something, especially a sound, dies away, it gradually becomes less strong and then stops. *The sound of his footsteps gradually died away.*

die down If something, especially noise or excitement, dies down, it gradually becomes less loud or strong until it stops. *It was several minutes before the applause died down.*

die off If a group of plants, animals, or people dies off, all of that group dies over a period of time.

die out to become more and more rare and then disappear completely *Dinosaurs **died out** about 65 million years ago.* ○ *The custom has long since died out.*

diehard /'daɪhɑːd/ *adjective* [always before noun] supporting something in a very determined way and refusing to change *a **diehard** fan*

diesel /'diːz³l/ *noun* **1** [U] fuel used in the engines of some vehicles, especially buses and trucks **2** [C] a vehicle that uses diesel in its engine

WORD PARTNERS FOR **diet**

be on/go on a diet ● **follow/stick to** a diet ● **a special /strict** diet

diet¹ /daɪət/ *noun* **1** [C, U] the type of food that someone usually eats **2** [C] when someone eats less food, or only particular types of food, because they want to become thinner, or because they are ill *No cake for me, thanks - I'm **on a diet**.*

diet² /daɪət/ *verb* [I] to eat less food so that you become thinner

differ /'dɪfə³/ *verb* [I] **1** to be different *How does the book **differ from** the film?* ○ *These computers **differ** quite a lot **in** price.* **2** to have a different opinion *Economists **differ on** the cause of inflation.*

WORD PARTNERS FOR **difference**

know/tell the difference ● a **big/fundamental/important/obvious** difference ● a difference **between** [sth **and** sth]

o﹣**difference** /'dɪf³r³ns/ *noun* **1** WAY [C, U] the way in which two people or things are not the same *What's the **difference between** an ape and a monkey?* **2** QUALITY [U] when two people or things are not the same **3** AMOUNT [C, U] the amount by which one thing or person is different from another *There's a big **difference** in age between them.* **4** DISAGREEMENT [C] a disagreement or different opinion *They must try to resolve their **differences** peacefully.* **5 make a/any difference** to have an effect on a situation *Painting the walls white has made a big difference to this room.*

difference

When you want to talk about how something or someone has changed, use the preposition **in**.

*The graph shows the difference **in** sales this year.*

~~*The graph shows the difference of sales this year.*~~

OTHER WAYS OF SAYING **different**

If something is different from what people normally expect, you can say that it is **unusual**: *Carina - that's quite an **unusual** name.*

The adjective **alternative** is often used to describe something which is different to something else but can be used instead of it: *The hotel's being renovated, so we're looking for an **alternative** venue.*

If something is very different and separate from other things, you can describe it as **distinct** or **distinctive**: *She's got really distinctive handwriting.* ● *The word has* *three **distinct** meanings.*

The preposition **unlike** is often used to compare people or things that are very different from each other: *Dan's actually quite nice, **unlike** his father.* ● *The furniture was **unlike** anything she had ever seen.*

○→**different** /ˈdɪf³r³nt/ *adjective* **1** not the same as someone or something else *Jo's very **different** from her sister, isn't she?* ○ *UK The house is **different to** how I expected it to be.* **2** [always before noun] used to talk about separate things or people of the same type *I had to go to three different shops to find the book she wanted.* ● **differently** *adverb* ⊃See also: a whole new **ball game.**

<hr>

COMMON LEARNER ERROR

different

Different is usually followed by the preposition **from**. In British English people also use **to**.

Anne is very different to her younger sister.

In American English people also use **than**, but teachers prefer students to use **from**.

<hr>

differential /ˌdɪf³ˈrenʃ³l/ *noun* [C] a difference between amounts of things *differentials in pay/wealth*

differentiate /ˌdɪf³ˈrenʃieɪt/ *verb* **1** [I, T] to understand or notice how two things or people are different from each other *He can't **differentiate between** blue and green.* **2** [T] to make someone or something different *We need to **differentiate** ourselves **from** the competition.* ● **differentiation** /ˌdɪf³renʃiˈeɪʃ³n/ *noun* [U]

and determination: *This has been a **challenging** time for us all.* ● *I found the course very **challenging**.*

You say **easier said than done** about something that is impossible or very difficult to do: *I suppose I should stop smoking but it's **easier said than done**.*

○→**difficult** /ˈdɪfɪk³lt/ *adjective* **1** not easy and needing skill or effort to do or understand *Japanese is a difficult language for Europeans to learn.* ○ *This game is too **difficult for me**.* [+ to do sth] *It's difficult to think with all that noise.* **2** not friendly or easy to deal with *a difficult teenager*

<hr>

WORD PARTNERS FOR **difficulty**

create/experience/have difficulty ● **great/ serious** difficulty ● **with/without** difficulty

<hr>

○→**difficulty** /ˈdɪfɪk³lti/ *noun* **1** [U] when something is not easy to do or understand [+ in + doing sth] *He was **having difficulty** in breathing because of the smoke.* ○ [+ doing sth] *I **had difficulty** finding somewhere to park.* ○ *She had twisted her ankle and was walking **with difficulty**.* **2** [C] something that is not easy to deal with *The company is having some **financial difficulties** at the moment.*

<hr>

COMMON LEARNER ERROR

have difficulty doing something

You can say you **have difficulty doing** something or **have difficulty in doing** something.

She has difficulty walking.

She has difficulty in walking.

~~I have difficulty to walk.~~

<hr>

diffident /ˈdɪfɪd³nt/ *adjective* shy and without any confidence *a diffident young man* ● **diffidence** /ˈdɪfɪd³ns/ *noun* [U]

diffuse /dɪˈfjuːz/ *verb*   **dig** [I, T] to spread, or to make something spread over a large area, or to a large number of people

○→**dig¹** /dɪg/ *verb* **digging** *past* **dug** **1** [I, T] to break or move the ground with a tool, machine, etc *Digging the garden is good exercise.* **2 dig a hole/ tunnel, etc** to make a hole in the ground by moving some of the ground or soil away *They've dug a huge hole in the road.* ⊃See also: dig the/up **dirt¹** on sb.

dig in/dig into sth *informal* to start eating food *Dig in, there's plenty for everyone.*

dig (sth) into sb/sth to press or push hard into someone or something, or to press something hard into someone or something *A stone was digging into my heel.*

dig sb/sth out to get someone or something out of somewhere by digging

dig sth out to find something that you have not seen or used for a long time *Mum dug out some old family photographs to show me.*

dig sth up 1 TAKE OUT to take something out of the ground by digging *Could you dig up a few potatoes for dinner?* **2** BREAK GROUND to break the ground or make a hole in the ground with a tool, machine, etc *They're digging up the road outside my house.* **3** INFORMATION to discover information that is secret or forgotten by searching very carefully *See if you can dig up anything interesting about his past.*

dig² /dɪɡ/ noun **1** REMARK [C] something that you say to annoy or criticize someone *He was having a dig at me.* **2** PLACE [C] a place where people are digging in the ground looking for ancient things to study *an archaeological dig* **3** PUSH [no plural] *informal* a quick, hard push *a dig in the ribs*

digest /daɪˈdʒest/ verb [T] **1** to change food in your stomach into substances that your body can use **2** to read and understand new information *You need to give me time to digest this report.* ● **digestible** adjective easy to digest

digestion /daɪˈdʒestʃən/ noun [U] when your body changes food in your stomach into substances that it can use

digestive /daɪˈdʒestɪv/ adjective [always before noun] relating to digestion *the digestive system*

digger /ˈdɪɡəʳ/ noun [C] a large machine that is used to lift and move soil, or a person who digs

Digibox /ˈdɪdʒɪbɒks/ noun [C] *trademark* a piece of electronic equipment that allows you to watch digital broadcasts (= television sounds and pictures sent as signals in the form of numbers) on an ordinary television

digit /ˈdɪdʒɪt/ noun [C] any of the numbers from 0 to 9, especially when they form part of a longer number *a seven digit telephone number*

digital /ˈdɪdʒɪtəl/ adjective **1** using an electronic system that changes sounds or images into signals in the form of numbers before it stores them or sends them *digital television* **2** A digital clock or watch shows the time in the form of numbers.

digital 'camera noun [C] a type of camera that records images that you can use and store on a computer

dignified /ˈdɪɡnɪfaɪd/ adjective calm, serious and behaving in a way that makes people respect you *a quiet, dignified woman*

dignitary /ˈdɪɡnɪtəri/ noun [C] someone with an important, official position *a group of visiting dignitaries*

dignity /ˈdɪɡnəti/ noun [U] calm and serious behaviour that makes people respect you *He behaved with great dignity and courage.*

digress /daɪˈɡres/ verb [I] to start talking about something that is not related to what you were talking about before ● **digression** /daɪˈɡreʃən/ noun [C, U]

digs /dɪɡz/ noun [plural] *UK informal* a room in someone's house that you pay rent to live in

dike (also **dyke**) /daɪk/ noun **1** a wall built to stop

water from a sea or river going onto the land **2** *UK* a passage that has been dug to take water away from fields

dilapidated /dɪˈlæpɪdeɪtɪd/ adjective A dilapidated building or vehicle is old and in bad condition. ● **dilapidation** /dɪˌlæpɪˈdeɪʃən/ noun [U]

dilate /daɪˈleɪt/ verb [I, T] If a part of your body dilates, or if you dilate it, it becomes wider or more open. *The drug causes your pupils to dilate.* ● **dilation** /daɪˈleɪʃən/ noun [U]

🧩 WORD PARTNERS FOR **dilemma**

face/have/be in a dilemma ● sth poses/presents a dilemma ● a moral dilemma ● a dilemma for sb ● a dilemma about/over sth

dilemma /dɪˈlemə/ noun [C] when you have to make a difficult choice between two things you could do *She's still in a dilemma about whether she should go or not.*

diligence /ˈdɪlɪdʒəns/ noun [U] when you work hard with care and effort

diligent /ˈdɪlɪdʒənt/ adjective working hard with care and effort *a diligent student* ● **diligently** adverb

dilute /daɪˈluːt/ verb [T] to make a liquid thinner or weaker by adding water or another liquid to it ● **dilute** adjective

dim¹ /dɪm/ adjective dimmer, dimmest **1** not bright or clear *He could hardly see her in the dim light.* **2** a dim memory/recollection, etc when you can remember something slightly, but not very well **3** *UK informal* stupid *He's nice, but a bit dim.* ● **dimly** adverb *a dimly lit room*

dim² /dɪm/ verb [I, T] dimming, past dimmed to become less bright, or to make something become less bright *He dimmed the lights and turned up the music.*

dime /daɪm/ noun [C] **1** a US or Canadian coin with a value of 10 cents **2** a dime a dozen *mainly US informal* easy to find and very ordinary *Millionaires are now a dime a dozen.*

🧩 WORD PARTNERS FOR **dimension**

add/give a [new/extra, etc] dimension (to sth) ● an added/extra/new dimension

dimension /ˌdaɪˈmenʃən/ noun [C] **1** a particular part of a situation, especially something that affects how you think or feel *Music has added a new dimension to my life.* **2** a measurement of the length, width, or height of something

diminish /dɪˈmɪnɪʃ/ verb [I, T] to become less, or to make something become less *Your pain should diminish gradually after taking these tablets.*

diminutive /dɪˈmɪnjʊtɪv/ adjective formal extremely small *a diminutive figure*

dimple /ˈdɪmpl/ noun [C] a small hollow place on your skin, often one that appears on your face when you smile ● **dimpled** adjective

din /dɪn/ noun [no plural] a lot of loud, unpleasant noise

dine /daɪn/ verb [I] formal to eat dinner *On Saturday we dined with friends.*

dine out *formal* to eat your evening meal in a restaurant

diner /'daɪnəʳ/ *noun* [C] **1** someone who is eating in a restaurant **2** *mainly US* a small, informal restaurant

dinghy /'dɪŋi/ *noun* [C] a small boat *an inflatable dinghy*

dingy /'dɪndʒi/ *adjective* dirty and not bright *a dingy basement*

'dining ,room *noun* [C] a room where you eat your meals in a house or hotel

◦⃔**dinner** /'dɪnəʳ/ *noun* [C, U] the main meal of the day that people usually eat in the evening

'dinner ,jacket *UK* (*US* **tuxedo**) *noun* [C] a black or white jacket that a man wears on a very formal occasion

dinner jacket *UK*, tuxedo *US*

dinosaur /'daɪnəsɔːʳ/ *noun* [C] a very large animal that used to live millions of years ago

dinosaur

diocese /'daɪəsɪs/ *noun* [C] the area controlled by a bishop (= an important Christian official)

dip¹ /dɪp/ *noun* **1** FOOD [C, U] a thick sauce that you can put pieces of food into before you eat them *a blue cheese dip* **2** SURFACE [C] a lower area on a surface *a sudden dip in the road* **3** AMOUNT [C] a sudden fall in the level or amount of something *a dip in profits* **4** SWIM [C] *informal* a short swim

dip² /dɪp/ *verb* **dipping**, *past* **dipped** **1** [T] to put something into a liquid for a short time *She dipped the brush into the paint.* **2** [I] to become lower in level or amount *The number of students taking sciences has dipped sharply.*

dip into sth 1 *UK* to read small parts of a book or magazine *It's the sort of book you can dip into now and then.* **2** to spend part of a supply of money that you have been keeping *I had to dip into my savings to pay for the repairs.*

diphtheria /dɪp'θɪəriə/ *noun* [U] a very serious disease of the throat

diphthong /'dɪfθɒŋ/ *noun* [C] a sound made by two vowels which are said together

diploma /dɪ'pləʊmə/ *noun* [C] a qualification from a school, college, or university, or an official document showing that someone has completed a course of study *a diploma in art and design*

diplomacy /dɪ'pləʊməsi/ *noun* [U] **1** dealing with the relationships between governments *international diplomacy* **2** skill in dealing with people well and not upsetting them *She showed great tact and diplomacy in the meeting.*

diplomat /'dɪpləmæt/ *noun* [C] someone whose job is to live in another country and to keep a good relationship between their government and that country's government

diplomatic /ˌdɪplə'mætɪk/ *adjective* **1** [always before noun] relating to diplomacy or diplomats *diplomatic relations* **2** good at dealing with people without upsetting them *That's a very diplomatic answer.* • **diplomatically** *adverb*

dire /daɪəʳ/ *adjective* very serious or bad *He's in dire need of help.*

◦⃔**direct¹** /dɪ'rekt/, /daɪ'rekt/ *adjective* **1** STRAIGHT going straight from one place to another without turning or stopping *We went by the most direct route.* **2** NOTHING BETWEEN with no other person or thing involved or between *There is a direct link between smoking and cancer.* **3** CLEAR saying clearly and honestly what you think *a direct answer* ↪Opposite **indirect**.

direct² /dɪ'rekt/, /daɪ'rekt/ *adverb* going straight from one place to another without turning or stopping *Several airlines now fly direct from Heathrow to Vancouver.*

direct³ /dɪ'rekt/, /daɪ'rekt/ *verb* **1** FILM/PLAY [T] to tell the actors in a film or play what to do *a film directed by Alfred Hitchcock* **2** **direct sth against/at/towards, etc sb/sth** to aim something at someone or something *The demonstrators' anger was directed at the police.* **3** ROUTE [T] to show or tell someone how to get to a place *Can you direct me to the manager's office please?* **4** ORGANIZE [T] to organize and control the way something is done *He directed the building of the new art gallery.* **5** **direct sb to do sth** *formal* to officially order someone to do something *They directed us not to discuss the matter.*

,direct 'debit *noun* [C, U] an arrangement that allows an organization to take money from your bank account at regular times to pay for goods or services *I pay my bills by direct debit.*

◦⃔**direction** /dɪ'rekʃən/ *noun* **1** WAY [C] the way that someone or something is going or facing *The car sped away in the direction of the airport.* ○ *I think we're going in the wrong direction.* **2** **in sb's direction** towards someone *She keeps looking in my direction.* **3** DEVELOPMENT [C] the way that someone or something changes or develops *Our careers have gone in very different directions.* **4** CONTROL [U] control or instructions *Under his direction the com-*

pany has doubled its profits. **5** PURPOSE **[U]** knowing what you want to do *According to his teachers, he **lacks direction**.*

directions /dɪˈrekʃⁿnz/ *noun* **[plural]** instructions that tell you how to get to a place, or how to do something *We stopped to **ask for directions**.* ○ *Just **follow** the **directions** on the label.*

directive /dɪˈrektɪv/ *noun* **[C]** *formal* an official instruction *The government has **issued** new directives on food hygiene.*

directly /dɪˈrektli/ *adverb* **1** with no other person or thing involved or between *Why don't you **speak to** him **directly**?* **2 directly after/ behind/opposite, etc** exactly or immediately after/behind/opposite, etc *She was sitting directly opposite me.* **3** clearly and honestly

directness /dɪˈrektnəs/ *noun* **[U]** when someone is clear and honest in their speech or behaviour *He liked her directness and simplicity.*

ˌdirect ˈobject *noun* **[C]** the direct object of a transitive verb is the person or thing that is affected by the action of the verb. In the sentence 'I bought a new car yesterday.', 'a new car' is the direct object. ⊃Compare **indirect object**.

director /dɪˈrektər/ *noun* **[C]** **1** an important manager in an organization or company *Meet the new **sales director**.* **2** someone who tells the actors in a film or play what to do ⊃See also: **funeral director, managing director.**

directorate /dɪˈrektⁿrət/ *noun* **[C]** a part of a government or other organization with responsibility for a particular activity

directory /dɪˈrektⁿri/ *noun* **[C]** a book or list of names, numbers, or other facts ⊃See also: **telephone directory.**

dirt¹ /dɜːt/ *noun* **[U]** **1** an unpleasant substance that makes something not clean *You've got some **dirt** on your trousers.* **2** soil or rough ground *a **dirt road/track*** **3 dig the/up dirt on sb** *informal* to try to discover bad things about someone to stop other people admiring them

dirt² /dɜːt/ *adverb* **dirt cheap/poor** extremely cheap/poor

> OTHER WAYS OF SAYING *dirty*
>
> If something is extremely dirty, you can say it is **filthy**: *Wash your hands before supper - they're **filthy**!*
>
> If someone or something looks dirty and untidy, you can say that they are **scruffy** or **messy**: *He's the typical **scruffy** student.* ● *Ben's bedroom is always really **messy**.*
>
> If something is covered in dirt and needs washing, the adjectives **grimy** and **grubby** are often used: *Don't' wipe your **grimy** hands on that clean towel!* ● *He was wearing an old pair of jeans and a **grubby** T-shirt.*
>
> The adjective **soiled** is sometimes used to describe material that is dirty: ***Soiled** tablecloths should be soaked in detergent.*
>
> If a place is extremely dirty and unpleasant, the adjective **squalid** is sometimes used: *The prisoners lived in **squalid** conditions.*

o⚬**dirty¹** /ˈdɜːti/ *adjective* **1** NOT CLEAN not clean

dirty clothes ○ *dirty dishes* **2** OFFENSIVE talking about sex in a way that some people find offensive *dirty books/jokes* **3** DISHONEST dishonest or unfair *a **dirty business*** ⊃See also: do sb's dirty **work².**

dirty² /ˈdɜːti/ *verb* **[T]** to make something dirty

dis- /dɪs-/ *prefix* not or the opposite of *dishonest* ○ *disbelief* ○ *to disagree*

disability /ˌdɪsəˈbɪləti/ *noun* **[C, U]** an illness, injury, or condition that makes it difficult for someone to do the things that other people do

disable /dɪˈseɪbl/ *verb* **[T]** **1** If someone is disabled by an illness or injury, it makes it difficult for them to live in the way that most other people do. **[often passive]** *Some children were permanently **disabled** by the bomb.* **2** to stop a piece of equipment from working *The thieves must have **disabled** the alarm system.*

disabled /dɪˈseɪbld/ *adjective* having an illness, injury, or condition that makes it difficult to do the things that other people do *They are demanding equal rights for **the disabled**.*

> WORD PARTNERS FOR *disadvantage*
>
> **have/face** a disadvantage ● a **big**/the **main**/ a **major**/a **serious** disadvantage ● a disadvantage **of/to** (doing) sth ● a disadvantage **for** sb ● the **advantages** and disadvantages **(of** sth)

disadvantage /ˌdɪsədˈvɑːntɪdʒ/ *noun* **1** **[C]** something which makes a situation more difficult, or makes you less likely to succeed *One **disadvantage** of living in the country is the lack of public transport.* **2 at a disadvantage** having problems that other people do not have *Being shy puts him **at a disadvantage**.*

disadvantaged /ˌdɪsədˈvɑːntɪdʒd/ *adjective* Disadvantaged people are poor and do not have many opportunities. *economically disadvantaged children*

disaffected /ˌdɪsəˈfektɪd/ *adjective* disappointed with someone or something and not supporting them as you did before *disaffected voters* ● **disaffection** /ˌdɪsəˈfekʃⁿn/ *noun* **[U]**

o⚬**disagree** /ˌdɪsəˈɡriː/ *verb* **[I]** disagreeing, *past* disagreed to have a different opinion from someone else about something *I **disagree with** most of what he said.* ○ *Experts **disagree about/on** the causes of the disease.*

disagreeable /ˌdɪsəˈɡriːəbl/ *adjective* *formal* unpleasant *a **disagreeable** old man*

disagreement /ˌdɪsəˈɡriːmⁿnt/ *noun* **[C, U]** when people have a different opinion about something or have an argument *They **had** a **disagreement about/over** money.* ○ *There is a lot of **disagreement among** doctors on this matter.*

disallow /ˌdɪsəˈlaʊ/ *verb* **[T]** to officially refuse to accept something because the rules have been broken *The goal was **disallowed** by the referee.*

o⚬**disappear** /ˌdɪsəˈpɪər/ *verb* **[I]** **1** NOT SEE to become impossible to see *She watched him **dis-***

appear into the crowd. **2** [GO] to suddenly go somewhere else and become impossible to find *Her husband disappeared in 1991.* **3** [STOP EXISTING] to stop existing *These flowers are disappearing from our countryside.* • **disappearance** /ˌdɪsəˈpɪərᵊns/ *noun* [C, U] *Police are investigating the girl's disappearance.* ⊃See also: disappear/vanish into thin **air**[1].

disappoint /ˌdɪsəˈpɔɪnt/ *verb* [T] to make someone feel unhappy because someone or something was not as good as they had expected *We don't want to disappoint the fans.*

OTHER WAYS OF SAYING ***disappointed***

If someone feels very disappointed about something that has happened, you can use the adjectives **disheartened** or, in informal situations, (*UK*) **gutted**: *He was very **disheartened** by the results of the test.* • *Nick's absolutely **gutted** that he's been dropped from the team.*

If a person disappoints someone by not doing what they agreed to do, then the phrasal verb **let down** is sometimes used: *John had promised to go but he **let** me **down** at the last minute.*

A situation which makes someone feel disappointed is often described as a **letdown**: *After all that planning the party was a bit of a **letdown**.*

An **anti-climax** is a disappointing experience, often one that you thought would be exciting before it happened or one that comes after a more exciting experience: *After so much preparation, the party itself was a bit of an **anticlimax**.*

disappointed /ˌdɪsəˈpɔɪntɪd/ *adjective* unhappy because someone or something was not as good as you hoped or expected, or because something did not happen [+ (that)] *I was very disappointed that he didn't come.* ○ *I'm really **disappointed in** you.*

disappointing /ˌdɪsəˈpɔɪntɪŋ/ *adjective* making you feel disappointed *a disappointing performance/result* • **disappointingly** *adverb a disappointingly small audience*

disappointment /ˌdɪsəˈpɔɪntmənt/ *noun* **1** [U] the feeling of being disappointed *She couldn't hide her disappointment when she lost.* **2** [C] someone or something that disappoints you *I'm sorry I'm such **a disappointment to** you.*

disapproval /ˌdɪsəˈpruːvᵊl/ *noun* [U] when you think that someone or something is bad or wrong

disapprove /ˌdɪsəˈpruːv/ *verb* [I] to think that someone or something is bad or wrong *Her family **disapproved of** the marriage.* • **disapproving** *adjective* showing that you think someone or something is bad or wrong *a disapproving look*

disarm /dɪˈsɑːm/ *verb* **1** [I, T] to give up your weapons, or to take away someone else's weapons *Both sides have agreed to disarm.* **2** [T] to make someone feel less angry *His smile disarmed her.*

disarmament /dɪˈsɑːməmənt/ *noun* [U] when a country or group gets rid of some or all of its weapons ***nuclear disarmament***

disarming /dɪˈsɑːmɪŋ/ *adjective* behaving in a way that stops people feeling angry with you or criticizing you *a **disarming smile***

disarray /ˌdɪsᵊrˈeɪ/ *noun* [U] when something is untidy and not organized *The house was **in** complete **disarray**.*

WORD PARTNERS FOR ***disaster***

bring/cause/prevent disaster • disaster **happens/strikes** • a **complete/major/terrible/unmitigated** disaster • a **natural** disaster

disaster /dɪˈzɑːstəʳ/ *noun* **1** [DAMAGE] [C] something that causes a lot of harm or damage *floods and other **natural disasters*** **2** [FAILURE] [C] a failure or something that has a very bad result *His idea was a total disaster.* **3** [BAD SITUATION] [U] an extremely bad situation *The holiday ended in disaster.*

disastrous /dɪˈzɑːstrəs/ *adjective* extremely bad ***disastrous consequences*** ○ *a disastrous week*

disband /dɪsˈbænd/ *verb* [I, T] *formal* to stop working together as a group, or to stop a group from working together

disbelief /ˌdɪsbɪˈliːf/ *noun* [U] when you do not believe that something is true or real *She shook her head **in disbelief**.*

disbelieve /ˌdɪsbɪˈliːv/ *verb* [T] to not believe someone or something

disc (*also US* **disk**) /dɪsk/ *noun* [C] **1** [SHAPE] a flat, round shape or object **2** [RECORDING] a record or CD **3** [BACK] a piece of cartilage (= strong material in the body) between the bones in your back ⊃See also: **compact disc**.

discard /dɪˈskɑːd/ *verb* [T] to throw something away *discarded food wrappers*

discern /dɪˈsɜːn/ *verb* [T] *formal* to see or recognize something • **discernible** *adjective There was **no discernible difference** between them.*

discerning /dɪˈsɜːnɪŋ/ *adjective* having or showing good judgment, especially about style and quality *a discerning customer/reader*

discharge[1] /dɪsˈtʃɑːdʒ/ *verb* [T] **1** to allow someone to leave a hospital or prison, or to order or allow someone to leave an organization such as the army [often passive] *She was **discharged from** the army yesterday.* **2** If a liquid or gas is discharged from something, it comes out of it.

discharge[2] /ˈdɪstʃɑːdʒ/ *noun* [C, U] **1** [LEAVE] when someone is officially allowed or ordered to leave somewhere such as a prison, hospital, or the army **2** [COME OUT] when a liquid or gas comes out of something *the discharge of carbon dioxide* **3** [SUBSTANCE] a liquid or gas that comes out of something

disciple /dɪˈsaɪpl/ *noun* [C] someone who follows the ideas and teaching of someone, especially of a religious leader

disciplinarian /ˌdɪsəplɪˈneəriən/ *noun* [C] someone who is very strict and gives punishments when people break rules

disciplinary /ˌdɪsəˈplɪnᵊri/ [US] /ˈdɪsəplɪneri/ *adjective* [always before noun] relating to punishment for someone who has broken rules *disciplinary action*

enforce / establish / restore discipline • firm/harsh/rigorous discipline • lax/ poor discipline

discipline[1] /'dɪsəplɪn/ *noun* 1 CONTROL [U] when people's behaviour is controlled using rules and punishments *There should be better discipline in schools.* 2 SELF CONTROL [U] when you can control your own behaviour carefully *I don't have enough discipline to save money.* 3 KNOWLEDGE [C] *formal* a particular subject of study *the scientific disciplines* ⊃See also: self-discipline.

discipline[2] /'dɪsəplɪn/ *verb* [T] 1 to punish someone [often passive] *He was disciplined for missing a training session.* 2 to teach someone to behave in a controlled way [often reflexive] *You have to learn to discipline yourself.*

disciplined /'dɪsəplɪnd/ *adjective* behaving in a very controlled way *the most disciplined army in the world*

disc jockey (*also* DJ) *noun* [C] someone who plays music on the radio or at discos

disclaim /dɪs'kleɪm/ *verb* [T] *formal* to say that you know nothing about something, or are not responsible for something *The terrorists disclaimed responsibility for the bomb.*

disclaimer /dɪs'kleɪmə[r]/ *noun* [C] when someone officially says that they are not responsible for something

disclose /dɪs'kləʊz/ *verb* [T] *formal* to give new or secret information to someone *He refused to disclose details of the report.*

disclosure /dɪs'kləʊʒə[r]/ *noun* [C, U] when someone gives people new or secret information

disco /'dɪskəʊ/ *noun* [C] a place or event where people dance to pop music

discoloured UK (*US* discolored) /dɪs'kʌləd/ *adjective* If something is discoloured, it has become a less attractive colour than it was originally. *discoloured teeth*

discomfort /dɪs'kʌmfət/ *noun* 1 PAIN [U] slight pain *You may feel some discomfort for a few days.* 2 MENTAL FEELING [U] when you feel slightly embarrassed or anxious 3 SITUATION [C, U] a physically uncomfortable situation

disconcert /ˌdɪskən'sɜːt/ *verb* [T] to make someone feel confused or anxious [often passive] *She was disconcerted by his questions.*

disconcerting /ˌdɪskən'sɜːtɪŋ/ *adjective* making you feel confused or anxious *a disconcerting silence* • disconcertingly *adverb*

disconnect /ˌdɪskə'nekt/ *verb* [T] to separate two things that are joined or connected, especially a piece of equipment and a power supply *Switch off the machine before disconnecting it from the power supply.*

disconnected /ˌdɪskə'nektɪd/ *adjective* not joined in any way *disconnected thoughts*

discontent /ˌdɪskən'tent/ *noun* [U] unhappiness about a situation *There is growing discontent with this government.* • discontented *adjective*

discontinue /ˌdɪskən'tɪnjuː/ *verb* [T] discontinuing, *past* discontinued to stop producing or providing something such as a product or service [often passive] *I'm afraid this model has been discontinued.*

discord /'dɪskɔːd/ *noun* [U] disagreement between people

discount[1] /'dɪskaʊnt/ *noun* [C, U] a reduction in price *They offer a 10 percent discount on rail travel for students.*

discount[2] /dɪ'skaʊnt/ *verb* [T] 1 to ignore something because you do not believe that it is true or that it will happen *You shouldn't discount the possibility of him coming back.* 2 to reduce the price of something *discounted goods/rates*

discourage /dɪ'skʌrɪdʒ/ *verb* 1 discourage sb from doing sth to try to persuade someone not to do something *a campaign to discourage people from smoking* 2 [T] to try to prevent something from happening *a campaign to discourage smoking* 3 [T] to make someone less confident or enthusiastic about something *I didn't mean to discourage her.* • discouragement *noun* [U] ⊃Opposite encourage.

discouraged /dɪ'skʌrɪdʒd/ *adjective* having lost your confidence or enthusiasm for something *to feel discouraged*

discouraging /dɪ'skʌrɪdʒɪŋ/ *adjective* making you feel less enthusiastic or confident about something *discouraging results*

o- **discover** /dɪ'skʌvə[r]/ *verb* [T] 1 FIND to find something *The body was discovered in a ditch.* 2 FIRST to be the first person to find something important *Who discovered America?* 3 GET INFORMATION to get information about something for the first time [+ (that)] *She discovered that he had been married three times before.* ○ [+ question word] *Have they discovered what was causing your headaches?*

discoverer /dɪ'skʌvərə[r]/ *noun* [C] someone who is the first person to find something important

make a discovery • a chance/new discovery • the discovery of sth

discovery /dɪ'skʌvə[r]i/ *noun* 1 [C, U] when someone discovers something *the discovery of bones in the garden* ○ *Scientists have made some important discoveries about genetics recently.* 2 [C] something or someone that is discovered

discredit /dɪ'skredɪt/ *verb* [T] to make someone or something appear bad and lose the respect of other people *They're always looking for ways to discredit her.*

discreet /dɪ'skriːt/ *adjective* careful not to cause embarrassment or attract too much attention, especially by keeping something secret *Can I trust you to be discreet?* ⊃Opposite indiscreet. • discreetly *adverb*

discrepancy /dɪ'skrepə[n]si/ *noun* [C, U] when two things that should be the same are different *There is a slight discrepancy between the two statements.*

discrete /dɪ'skriːt/ *adjective* separate and different *a word that has two discrete meanings*

discretion /dɪ'skreʃ[ə]n/ *noun* [U] 1 when someone is careful not to cause embarrassment or attract too much attention, especially by keeping something secret *You can rely on my discretion.* ⊃Opposite **indiscretion.** **2** the right to decide something *Students can be expelled at the discretion of the head teacher* (= if the head teacher decides it).

discretionary /dɪˈskreʃ°n°ri/ *adjective* decided by officials and not fixed by rules *Judges have great discretionary powers.*

discriminate /dɪˈskrɪmɪneɪt/ *verb* [I] **1** to treat someone unfairly because of their sex, race, religion, etc *The company was accused of discriminating against people on the basis of age.* **2** to notice a difference between two things *Police dogs are very good at discriminating between different smells.*

discriminating /dɪˈskrɪmɪneɪtɪŋ/ *adjective* good at judging what is good quality *a discriminating shopper*

WORD PARTNERS FOR *discrimination*

face/suffer discrimination • **age/racial/ sex** discrimination • discrimination **against** sb

discrimination /dɪˌskrɪmɪˈneɪʃ°n/ *noun* [U] when someone is treated unfairly because of their sex, race, religion, etc *racial/sex discrimination* ○ *discrimination against older workers*

discus /ˈdɪskəs/ *noun* [C] a round, flat, heavy object that people throw as a sport

o-=**discuss** /dɪˈskʌs/ *verb* [T] to talk about something with someone and tell each other your ideas or opinions *Have you discussed this matter with anyone else?*

discuss

Discuss is not followed by a preposition.
We discussed the plans for the wedding.
~~We discussed about the plans for the wedding.~~
You can discuss something with someone.
Can I discuss this report with you?

WORD PARTNERS FOR *discussion*

have/hold a discussion • a **heated/lengthy** discussion • a discussion **about** sth • be **under** discussion

o-=**discussion** /dɪˈskʌʃ°n/ *noun* [C, U] when people talk about something and tell each other their ideas or opinions *They were having a discussion about football.* ○ *Several ideas are still under discussion* (= being discussed).

disdain /dɪsˈdeɪn/ *noun* [U] when you dislike someone or something and think that they do not deserve any respect *His disdain for politicians is obvious.* • **disdainful** *adjective disdainful remarks* • **disdainfully** *adverb*

WORD PARTNERS FOR *disease*

be affected by/have/suffer from a disease • contract/develop a disease • cure/ detect/diagnose/treat a disease • a chronic/deadly/hereditary/infectious disease

o-=**disease** /dɪˈziːz/ *noun* [C, U] an illness caused by an infection or by a failure of health and not by an accident *heart disease* ○ *an infectious disease* • **diseased** *adjective* affected by a disease *a diseased lung*

disembark /ˌdɪsɪmˈbɑːk/ *verb* [I] *formal* to leave a ship, boat, or aircraft *All passengers must disembark in Vancouver.* • **disembarkation** /ˌdɪsɪmbɑːˈkeɪʃ°n/ *noun* [U]

disembodied /ˌdɪsɪmˈbɒdid/ *adjective* seeming not to have a body or not to be connected to a body *a disembodied voice*

disenchanted /ˌdɪsɪnˈtʃɑːntɪd/ *adjective* disappointed with something that you thought was good in the past *He became disenchanted with politics.* • **disenchantment** *noun* [U]

disengage /ˌdɪsɪnˈgeɪdʒ/ *verb* [I, T] to become separated from something, or to make two things become separate from each other *He gently disengaged his hand from hers.*

disentangle /ˌdɪsɪnˈtæŋgl/ *verb* [T] **1** to separate someone or something that is connected to something else in a complicated way *He disentangled himself from her arms.* **2** to separate things such as pieces of string, hair, or wire that have become twisted together

disfigure /dɪsˈfɪgəʳ/ *verb* [T] to spoil someone's or something's appearance [often passive] *Her face was disfigured by a huge scar.*

disgrace¹ /dɪsˈgreɪs/ *verb* [T] to make people stop respecting you or your family, team, etc by doing something very bad

disgrace² /dɪsˈgreɪs/ *noun* [U] **1** when someone does something very bad that makes people stop respecting them or their family, team, etc *They were sent home in disgrace.* **2 be a disgrace** to be very bad [+ that] *It's a disgrace that money is being wasted like this.* **3 be a disgrace to sb/sth** to be so bad or unacceptable that you make people stop respecting a particular group, activity, etc *You are a disgrace to your profession.*

disgraced /dɪsˈgreɪst/ *adjective* A disgraced person has lost other people's respect because they have done something very bad. *a disgraced politician*

disgraceful /dɪsˈgreɪsf°l/ *adjective* very bad *disgraceful behaviour* • **disgracefully** *adverb*

disgruntled /dɪsˈgrʌntld/ *adjective* angry and upset *Disgruntled workers have decided to go on strike.*

disguise¹ /dɪsˈgaɪz/ *noun* [C, U] clothes and other things that you wear to change the way you look so that people cannot recognize you *She usually goes out in disguise to avoid being bothered by the public.* ⊃See also: a **blessing** in disguise.

disguise² /dɪsˈgaɪz/ *verb* **1 disguise yourself/ your voice, etc** to change your appearance/ voice, etc so that people cannot recognize you *He managed to escape by disguising himself as a woman.* **2 be disguised as sb/sth** to be wearing clothes and other things that make you look like someone or something else **3** [T] to hide something such as a feeling or opinion *She couldn't disguise her disappointment.*

disgust¹ /dɪs'gʌst/ *noun* [U] a very strong feeling of dislike or disapproval *She walked out in disgust.*

disgust² /dɪs'gʌst/ *verb* [T] If something disgusts you, it makes you feel extreme dislike or disapproval. *These pictures disgust me.*

disgusted /dɪs'gʌstɪd/ *adjective* feeling extreme dislike or disapproval of something *I'm totally disgusted with your behaviour.*

disgusting /dɪs'gʌstɪŋ/ *adjective* extremely unpleasant *What's that disgusting smell?*

o→**dish**¹ /dɪʃ/ *noun* [C] **1** a curved container for eating or serving food from *a baking/serving dish* **2** food that is prepared in a particular way as part of a meal *a chicken/vegetarian dish* **3** the dishes dirty plates, bowls, and other objects for cooking or eating food *Who's going to wash the dishes?*

dish² /dɪʃ/ *verb*
dish sth out *informal* to give or say things to people without thinking about them carefully

dishcloth /'dɪʃklɒθ/ *noun* [C] a cloth used for washing dirty dishes

disheartened /dɪs'hɑːtᵊnd/ *adjective* disappointed or without hope *She was very disheartened by the results of the test.*

disheartening /dɪs'hɑːtᵊnɪŋ/ *adjective* making you feel disappointed or without hope *a disheartening experience*

dishevelled UK (US **disheveled**) /dɪ'ʃevᵊld/ *adjective* very untidy *dishevelled hair*

dishonest /dɪ'sɒnɪst/ *adjective* not honest and likely to lie or do something illegal ●**dishonestly** *adverb* ●**dishonesty** *noun* [U] when someone is not honest

dishonour¹ UK (US **dishonor**) /dɪ'sɒnᵊʳ/ *noun* [U] when people stop respecting you because you have done something bad ●**dishonourable** *adjective* bad or not deserving respect *dishonourable conduct*

dishonour² UK (US **dishonor**) /dɪ'sɒnᵊʳ/ *verb* [T] to show no respect for someone or something by behaving badly *He felt that he had dishonoured his country.*

dish ˌsoap US (UK **washing-up liquid**) *noun* [U] a thick liquid soap used to wash pans, plates, knives and forks etc.

dishtowel /'dɪʃtaʊəl/ US (UK **tea towel**) *noun* [C] a cloth that is used for drying plates, dishes, etc *Pass me a dishtowel and I'll dry the dishes.*

dishwasher /'dɪʃˌwɒʃᵊʳ/ *noun* [C] a machine that washes plates, glasses and other kitchen equipment *I'll load the dishwasher.* ➸See colour picture **The Kitchen** on page Centre 2.

disillusion /ˌdɪsɪ'luːʒᵊn/ *verb* [T] to cause someone to discover that something they believed is not true

disillusioned /ˌdɪsɪ'luːʒᵊnd/ *adjective* feeling disappointed because something is not as good as you thought it was *She says she's disillusioned with the music business.*

disillusionment /ˌdɪsɪ'luːʒᵊnmənt/ (*also* **disillusion**) *noun* [U] the disappointment someone feels when they discover something is not as good as they thought it was *There's growing disillusionment with the government.*

disinfect /ˌdɪsɪn'fekt/ *verb* [T] to clean something with a chemical that destroys bacteria

disinfectant /ˌdɪsɪn'fektənt/ *noun* [C, U] a chemical substance that destroys bacteria

disintegrate /dɪ'sɪntɪgreɪt/ *verb* [I] **1** to break into a lot of small pieces **2** to become much worse *The situation is disintegrating into total chaos.* ●**disintegration** /dɪˌsɪntɪ'greɪʃᵊn/ *noun* [U]

disinterested /dɪ'sɪntrəstɪd/ *adjective* not involved in a situation and so able to judge it without supporting a particular side *a disinterested observer*

disjointed /dɪs'dʒɔɪntɪd/ *adjective* having words or ideas that are not in a clear order *a disjointed conversation*

WORD PARTNERS FOR **disk**

save/write sth **to** disk ● **on** a disk ● disk space

o→**disk** /dɪsk/ *noun* [C] **1** another US spelling of **disc** **2** a piece of computer equipment that records and stores information electronically *How much disk space is there?* ➸See colour picture **The Office** on page Centre 5 ➸See also: **floppy disk, hard disk.**

'disk ˌdrive *noun* [C] the part of a computer that allows the person using the computer to store and read information from a disk

diskette /dɪ'sket/ *noun* [C] a small, flat, plastic object that you put in your computer to record and store information electronically

dislike¹ /dɪ'slaɪk/ *verb* [T] to not like someone or something *Why do you dislike her so much?* ○ [+ doing sth] *I dislike ironing intensely.*

dislike² /dɪ'slaɪk/ *noun* [C, U] when you do not like someone or something *a dislike of cold weather* ○ *I took an instant dislike to her* (= disliked her immediately).

dislocate /'dɪsləʊkeɪt/ *verb* [T] If you dislocate a part of your body, the bones move away from their correct position. *I think you've dislocated your shoulder.* ○ *a dislocated hip* ●**dislocation** /ˌdɪsləʊ'keɪʃᵊn/ *noun* [U]

dislodge /dɪ'slɒdʒ/ *verb* [T] to move something away from a fixed position

disloyal /dɪ'slɔɪəl/ *adjective* not loyal or not supporting someone who you should support *I don't want to be disloyal to my friend.* ●**disloyalty** *noun* [U] *They accused her of disloyalty.*

dismal /'dɪzməl/ *adjective* very bad or unpleasant and making you feel unhappy *What dismal weather.* ○ *That was a dismal performance.* ●**dismally** *adverb* *I tried to cheer her up, but failed dismally* (= completely failed).

dismantle /dɪ'smæntl/ *verb* [T] **1** to take something apart so that it is in several pieces *He's specially trained to dismantle bombs.* **2** to get rid of a system or organization

dismay /dɪ'smeɪ/ *noun* [U] a feeling of unhappiness and disappointment *To our dismay, it started raining.*

dismayed /dɪ'smeɪd/ *adjective* unhappy and disappointed [+ to do sth] *I was dismayed to discover that he'd lied to me.*

D

dismember /dɪˈsmembəʳ/ *verb* [T] to cut the arms and legs off the body of a person or animal *a dismembered body*

dismiss /dɪˈsmɪs/ *verb* [T] **1** NOT CONSIDER to refuse to consider an idea or opinion *The committee dismissed the idea as rubbish.* **2** MAKE LEAVE to officially make someone leave their job [often passive] *Anyone who breaks company rules will be dismissed.* **3** ALLOW TO LEAVE to give someone official permission to leave *The bell rang and the teacher dismissed the class.*

dismissal /dɪˈsmɪsᵊl/ *noun* **1** [U] when someone refuses to consider an idea or opinion **2** [C, U] when an employer officially makes someone leave their job

dismissive /dɪˈsmɪsɪv/ *adjective* treating something as if it is not important *Alexander's so dismissive of all my suggestions.* • **dismissively** *adverb*

dismount /dɪˈsmaʊnt/ *verb* [I] *formal* to get off a horse or bicycle

disobedience /ˌdɪsəʊˈbiːdiəns/ *noun* [U] when someone refuses to do what someone in authority tells them to do

disobedient /ˌdɪsəʊˈbiːdiənt/ *adjective* refusing to do what someone in authority tells you to do *a disobedient child*

disobey /ˌdɪsəʊˈbeɪ/ *verb* [T] to not do what you are told to do by someone in authority *How dare you disobey me!*

disorder /dɪˈsɔːdəʳ/ *noun* **1** ILLNESS [C] a disease or mental problem *a blood disorder* **2** BAD BEHAVIOUR [U] uncontrolled, bad behaviour, especially by large groups of people *crime and disorder* **3** NOT ORGANIZED [U] when things are untidy or confused and not organized *His financial affairs are in complete disorder.* ⊃See also: **eating disorder**.

disordered /dɪˈsɔːdəd/ *adjective* confused and not organized *a disordered mind*

disorderly /dɪˈsɔːdᵊli/ *adjective* **1** behaving badly by being noisy or violent *He was charged with being drunk and disorderly.* **2** untidy

disorganized (*also UK* -ised) /dɪˈsɔːɡənaɪzd/ *adjective* **1** not planned or organized well *The competition was completely disorganized.* **2** not good at planning or organizing things

disorient /dɪˈsɔːriənt/ (*also UK* **disorientate** /dɪˈsɔːriənteɪt/) *verb* [T] to make someone not know where to go or what to do

disoriented /dɪˈsɔːriəntɪd/ (*also UK* **disorientated** /dɪˈsɔːriənteɪtɪd/) *adjective* confused and not knowing where to go or what to do *Whales become disoriented in shallow water.*

disown /dɪˈsəʊn/ *verb* [T] to say that you do not want to have any involvement or connection with someone *Even his parents have disowned him.*

disparage /dɪˈspærɪdʒ/ *verb* [T] to say that you think someone or something is not very good [often passive] *He is often disparaged by the critics.*

disparaging /dɪˈspærɪdʒɪŋ/ *adjective* criticizing someone or something *She's always making disparaging remarks.*

disparate /ˈdɪspᵊrət/ *adjective* *formal* completely different *people from disparate cultures*

disparity /dɪˈspærəti/ *noun* [C, U] *formal* difference, usually relating to the money people earn or their position

dispatch¹ (*also UK* **despatch**) /dɪˈspætʃ/ *verb* [T] *formal* to send someone or something somewhere *They dispatched a police car to arrest him.*

dispatch² (*also UK* **despatch**) /dɪˈspætʃ/ *noun* **1** [U] when someone or something is sent somewhere *the dispatch of troops* **2** [C] an official report that someone in a foreign country sends to their organization

dispel /dɪˈspel/ *verb* [T] **dispelling**, *past* **dispelled** to get rid of a feeling, thought, or belief *The president appeared on TV to dispel rumours that he was dying.*

dispensary /dɪˈspensᵊri/ *noun* [C] a place where medicines are given out

dispensation /ˌdɪspenˈseɪʃᵊn/ *noun* [C, U] special permission to do something [+ to do sth] *The court would not grant him a dispensation to visit his children.*

dispense /dɪˈspens/ *verb* [T] to give something out *a machine that dispenses drinks and snacks* **dispense with sth/sb** to stop using something or someone, or to get rid of something or someone, usually because you do not need them

dispenser /dɪˈspensəʳ/ *noun* [C] a machine that you can get something from *a cash/drink/soap dispenser*

disperse /dɪˈspɜːs/ *verb* [I, T] to separate and go in different directions, or to make something do this *We waited until the crowds had dispersed.* • **dispersal** *noun* [U]

dispirited /dɪˈspɪrɪtɪd/ *adjective* unhappy and without hope

displace /dɪˈspleɪs/ *verb* [T] **1** to take the place of someone or something *Many of these workers will be displaced by modern technology.* **2** to make someone or something leave their usual place or position *The earthquake displaced thousands of people.* • **displacement** *noun* [U]

display¹ /dɪˈspleɪ/ *noun* **1** ARRANGEMENT [C] a collection of objects or pictures arranged for people to look at *a display of children's paintings* **2** **on display** If something is on display, it is there for people to look at. *Many old aircraft are on display at the museum.* **3** SHOW a performance or show for people to watch *a firework display* **4** ON SCREEN [C, U] when something is shown electronically such as on a computer screen *The display problems might be due to a shortage of disk space.* **5** **a display of affection/anger, etc** when someone behaves in a way that shows they have a particular feeling *There's never much display of affection between them.*

display² /dɪˈspleɪ/ *verb* **1** ARRANGE [T] to arrange something somewhere so that people can see it *There were some family photographs displayed on his desk.* **2** ON SCREEN [I, T] to show something electronically such as on a computer screen *The text can be **displayed** and edited on screen.* **3** FEELING [T] to show how you feel by your expression or behaviour *He never **displayed** any interest in girls.*

displease /dɪ'spliːz/ *verb* [T] *formal* to make someone annoyed or unhappy • **displeased** *adjective*

displeasure /dɪ'spleʒə^r/ *noun* [U] *formal* when someone is annoyed or unhappy about something *She expressed great **displeasure** at his behaviour.*

disposable /dɪ'spəʊzəbl/ *adjective* intended to be used only once and then thrown away *a disposable camera/razor*

disposable 'income UK (US **dis,posable 'income**) *noun* [C, U] the amount of money that you have available to spend after tax, rent and other basic things that you must pay for

disposal /dɪ'spəʊz^əl/ *noun* [U] **1** when you get rid of something, especially by throwing it away *waste **disposal*** ∘ *the disposal of hazardous substances* **2 at sb's disposal** available for someone to use *We will have a car at our disposal for the whole trip.*

dispose /dɪ'spəʊz/ *verb*
  dispose of sth to get rid of something, especially by throwing it away

disposed /dɪ'spəʊzd/ *adjective formal* **1 be disposed to do sth** to be willing or likely to do something *I tried to tell her but she didn't seem disposed to listen.* **2 be favourably/well, etc disposed towards sth** to like or approve of something *She seems well disposed towards the idea.*

disposition /ˌdɪspə'zɪʃ^ən/ *noun* [C] the type of character someone has *a cheerful/nervous disposition*

disproportionate /ˌdɪsprə'pɔːʃ^ənət/ *adjective* too large or small in comparison to something else *There are a **disproportionate** number of girls in the class.* • **disproportionately** *adverb*

disprove /dɪ'spruːv/ *verb* [T] to prove that something is not true

have/be involved in a dispute • resolve/settle a dispute • a bitter/long-running dispute • a dispute about/over sth

dispute¹ /'dɪspjuːt/ *noun* [C, U] a disagreement, especially one that lasts a long time *A man stabbed his neighbour in a **dispute** over noise.*

dispute² /dɪ'spjuːt/ *verb* [T] to disagree with something someone says [+ (that)] *I'm not disputing that the drug has benefits.*

disqualify /dɪ'skwɒlɪfaɪ/ *verb* [T] to stop someone from being in a competition or doing some other activity because they have done something wrong [often passive] *She was **disqualified** from the race after a drugs test.* • **disqualification** /dɪˌskwɒlɪfɪ'keɪʃ^ən/ *noun* [U]

disquiet /dɪ'skwaɪət/ *noun* [U] *formal* when people are anxious or worried about something *His health has been causing disquiet.*

blatant/callous/flagrant/total disregard • disregard for/of sb/sth

disregard¹ /ˌdɪsrɪ'gɑːd/ *noun* [U, no plural] when someone does not care about or show any interest in someone or something *His behaviour shows a total **disregard** for other people.*

disregard² /ˌdɪsrɪ'gɑːd/ *verb* [T] to ignore something *She chose to disregard my advice.*

disrepair /ˌdɪsrɪ'peə^r/ *noun* [U] when a building is in a bad condition because someone has not taken care of it *The Fitzwilliams' house has fallen into disrepair.*

disreputable /dɪs'repjətəbl/ *adjective* not respected or trusted by people *a disreputable company*

disrepute /ˌdɪsrɪ'pjuːt/ *noun* **bring sb/sth into disrepute** *formal* to cause people not to respect or trust someone or something *Corrupt policemen are bringing the law into disrepute.*

disrespect /ˌdɪsrɪ'spekt/ *noun* [U] when someone does not show any respect or behave politely towards someone or something *a disrespect for authority*

disrespectful /ˌdɪsrɪ'spektf^əl/ *adjective* being rude and not showing any respect *Don't be **disrespectful** to your mother.* • **disrespectfully** *adverb*

disrupt /dɪs'rʌpt/ *verb* [T] to interrupt something and stop it continuing as it should *He disturbs other children and disrupts the class.* • **disruption** /dɪs'rʌpʃ^ən/ *noun* [C, U] *the disruption of services* • **disruptive** *adjective disruptive behaviour*

dissatisfaction /dɪsˌsætɪs'fækʃ^ən/ *noun* [U] when you are not pleased or happy with something *He expressed his **dissatisfaction** with the legal system.*

dissatisfied /dɪs'sætɪsfaɪd/ *adjective* not pleased or happy with something *a dissatisfied customer* ∘ *Please let us know if you are **dissatisfied** with our service.*

dissect /daɪ'sekt/ *verb* [T] to cut something into pieces for scientific study *We had to dissect a rat in biology.* • **dissection** /daɪ'sekʃ^ən/ *noun* [U]

disseminate /dɪ'semɪneɪt/ *verb* [T] to spread information or ideas *They are using their website to disseminate political propaganda.* • **dissemination** /dɪˌsemɪ'neɪʃ^ən/ *noun* [U]

dissent /dɪ'sent/ *noun* [U] when someone does not agree with something *There is a lot of dissent within the Church about women priests.* • **dissent** *verb* [I] to not agree with other people about something • **dissenter** *noun* [C]

dissertation /ˌdɪsə'teɪʃ^ən/ *noun* [C] a very long piece of writing done as part of a course of study *She's writing a **dissertation** on American poetry.*

disservice /ˌdɪs'sɜːvɪs/ *noun* [no plural] when something causes harm to someone or something *Bad teaching **does a great disservice** to children.*

dissident /'dɪsɪd^ənt/ *noun* [C] someone who criticizes their government in a public way

D

political dissidents

dissimilar /ˌdɪsˈsɪmɪləʳ/ *adjective* different *Her hair is not dissimilar to yours* (= is similar to yours).

dissipate /ˈdɪsɪpeɪt/ *verb* [I, T] to disappear, or to make something disappear *The heat gradually dissipates into the atmosphere.*

dissociate /dɪˈsəʊʃieɪt/ *verb* **dissociate yourself from sb/sth** to say that you do not have any connection or involvement with someone or something *He's trying to dissociate himself from his former friends.*

dissolution /ˌdɪsəˈluːʃⁿn/ *noun* [U] when an organization or an official arrangement ends

dissolve /dɪˈzɒlv/ *verb* **1** [I, T] If a solid dissolves, it becomes part of a liquid, and if you dissolve it, you make it become part of a liquid. *These tablets dissolve in water.* **2** [T] to end an organization or official arrangement [often passive] *Their marriage was dissolved in 1996.* **3 dissolve into laughter/tears, etc** to suddenly start to laugh/cry, etc

dissuade /dɪˈsweɪd/ *verb* [T] to persuade someone not to do something [+ from + doing sth] *We tried to dissuade him from leaving.*

WORD PARTNERS FOR **distance**

a **large/long/short/small/vast** distance • a [short/long, etc] distance **from** [a place] • the distance **between** sth and sth

o⊷**distance¹** /ˈdɪstⁿns/ *noun* **1** [C, U] the length of the space between two places or things *We're only a short distance from my house.* ○ *He calculated the distance between the Earth and the Sun.* ○ *Are the shops within walking distance?* **2** [no plural] somewhere that is far away, but close enough for you to see or hear the things that are there *I could see Mary in the distance.* ○ *From a distance, it sounded like a bell ringing.*

distance² /ˈdɪstⁿns/ *verb* **distance yourself from sb/sth** to say or show that you are not connected or involved with someone or something *She has tried to distance herself from the book.*

distant /ˈdɪstⁿnt/ *adjective* **1** [FAR AWAY] far away in space or time *distant galaxies* ○ *the distant sound of traffic* ○ *We hope to see you in the not too distant future.* **2** [RELATIVE] A distant relative is not very closely related to you. *a distant cousin* **3** [NOT FRIENDLY] [never before noun] not friendly *She seemed cold and distant.* • **distantly** *adverb* **distantly related**

distaste /dɪˈsteɪst/ *noun* [U] when you dislike something and think it is unpleasant *I have developed a distaste for meat.*

distasteful /dɪˈsteɪstfⁿl/ *adjective* unpleasant or offensive *I find this advertisement extremely distasteful.* • **distastefully** *adverb*

distil UK (US distill) /dɪˈstɪl/ *verb* [T] distilling, *past* distilled to make a liquid stronger or more pure by heating it until it changes into a gas and then changing it into a liquid again *distilled water* • **distillation** /ˌdɪstɪˈleɪʃⁿn/ *noun* [U] • **distillery** /dɪˈstɪlⁿri/ *noun* [C] a place where strong alcoholic drinks are produced

distinct /dɪˈstɪŋkt/ *adjective* **1** [DIFFERENT] different and separate *This word has three distinct meanings.* **2** [HEAR/SEE] easy to hear, see, or smell *The voices gradually became louder and more distinct.* ⊃Opposite **indistinct**. **3** [CLEAR] [always before noun] clear and certain *There's been a distinct improvement in your work.* • **distinctly** *adverb*

WORD PARTNERS FOR **distinction**

draw/make a distinction • a **clear** distinction • a distinction **between** sth and sth

distinction /dɪˈstɪŋkʃⁿn/ *noun* [C, U] **1** a difference between two similar things *the distinction between spoken and written language* **2** a quality or fact that makes someone or something special or different *wines of distinction* ○ *He has the distinction of being the youngest player in the World Cup finals.*

distinctive /dɪˈstɪŋktɪv/ *adjective* Something that is distinctive is easy to recognize because it is different from other things. *a distinctive style of writing* • **distinctively** *adverb*

distinguish /dɪˈstɪŋgwɪʃ/ *verb* **1** [RECOGNIZE DIFFERENCES] [I, T] to recognize the differences between two people, ideas, or things *Children must learn to distinguish between right and wrong.* ○ *People have difficulty distinguishing Tracy from her twin sister Mary.* **2** [SHOW DIFFERENCES] [T] to make one person or thing seem different from another *His great skill distinguishes him from the rest of the team.* **3** [SEE/HEAR] [T] to be able to see, hear, or understand something **4 distinguish yourself** to do something so well that people notice and admire you • **distinguishable** *adjective*

distinguished /dɪˈstɪŋgwɪʃt/ *adjective* famous, praised, or admired *a distinguished writer*

distort /dɪˈstɔːt/ *verb* [T] **1** to change the shape, sound, or appearance of something so that it seems strange *It's a bad recording - the microphone distorted our voices.* **2** to change information so that it is not true or realistic *Newspapers distorted the truth about their marriage.* • **distorted** *adjective* • **distortion** /dɪˈstɔːʃⁿn/ *noun* [C, U] *a gross distortion of the facts*

distract /dɪˈstrækt/ *verb* [T] to make someone stop giving their attention to something *Stop distracting me - I'm trying to finish my essay.*

distracted /dɪˈstræktɪd/ *adjective* anxious and unable to think carefully

distraction /dɪˈstrækʃⁿn/ *noun* **1** [C, U] something that makes you stop giving your attention to something else *The phone calls were a constant distraction.* **2 drive sb to distraction** UK to make someone very annoyed

distraught /dɪˈstrɔːt/ *adjective* extremely upset and unhappy

WORD PARTNERS FOR **distress**

deep/great distress • to sb's distress • be **in** distress

distress¹ /dɪˈstres/ *noun* [U] **1** the feeling of being extremely upset or worried *The newspaper reports caused her a great deal of distress.* **2** when someone or something is in danger and needs help *an aircraft **in distress***

distress² /dɪˈstres/ *verb* [T] to make someone feel very upset or worried ● **distressing** *adjective a distressing experience*

distribute /dɪˈstrɪbjuːt/ *verb* [T] **1** to give something out to people or places *The books will be distributed free to local schools.* **2** to supply goods to shops and companies *The company manufactures and distributes computer equipment worldwide.*

distribution /ˌdɪstrɪˈbjuːʃᵊn/ *noun* **1** [U] when something is supplied or given out to people or places *the sale and distribution of videos* **2** [U, no plural] the way something is divided and shared in a group or area *the distribution of wealth*

distributor /dɪˈstrɪbjətəʳ/ *noun* [C] a person or organization that supplies goods to shops and companies

district /ˈdɪstrɪkt/ *noun* [C] a part of a city or country, either an official area or one that is known for having a particular characteristic or business *the fashion district of New York*

district atˈtorney *(abbreviation DA) noun* [C] *US* a lawyer who works for the government of a particular district

distrust /dɪˈstrʌst/ *noun* [U] when you do not trust someone or something ● **distrust** *verb* [T]

disturb /dɪˈstɜːb/ *verb* [T] **1** [INTERRUPT] to interrupt what someone is doing by making noise or annoying them *Don't disturb him, he needs to sleep.* **2** [UPSET] to make someone feel anxious or upset *Some scenes are violent and may disturb younger viewers.* **3** [CHANGE] to change something by touching it or moving it from its original position

disturbance /dɪˈstɜːbᵊns/ *noun* **1** [C, U] something that interrupts what you are doing, especially something loud or annoying **2** [C] when people fight or shout

disturbed /dɪˈstɜːbd/ *adjective* not thinking or behaving normally because of mental or emotional problems

disturbing /dɪˈstɜːbɪŋ/ *adjective* unpleasant in a way that makes people feel anxious or upset *disturbing images* ● **disturbingly** *adverb*

disused /dɪsˈjuːzd/ *adjective* not used now *a disused warehouse* ● **disuse** /dɪsˈjuːs/ *noun* [U] when something is not used *to fall into disuse*

ditch¹ /dɪtʃ/ *noun* [C] a long, narrow hole in the ground next to a road or field, which water can flow through

ditch² /dɪtʃ/ *verb* [T] *informal* to get rid of someone or something that you do not need or want now *He ditched his girlfriend when she got pregnant.*

dither /ˈdɪðəʳ/ *verb* [I] to spend too much time trying to make a decision *Stop dithering and tell me which one you want!*

ditto¹ /ˈdɪtəʊ/ *adverb* used to agree with something that has been said, or to avoid repeating something that has been said

ditto² /ˈdɪtəʊ/ *noun* [C] a mark (") used instead of words to show that you are repeating what is written above it

ditty /ˈdɪti/ *noun* [C] a short, simple song

diva /ˈdiːvə/ *noun* [C] a successful and famous female singer

Divali /dɪˈvɑːli/ *noun* [U] Diwali (= a Hindu festival)

dive

dive¹ /daɪv/ *verb* [I] *past tense* **dived**, *also US* **dove** *past participle* **dived** **1** [JUMP IN] to jump into water with your head and arms going in first *He dived off the side of the boat into the sea.* **2** [SWIM] to swim under water, usually with breathing equipment **3** **dive into/over/under, etc** to move somewhere quickly *He heard footsteps and dived under the table.* **4** [FLY] to fly down through the air very quickly *Suddenly the plane dived to the ground.* **5** [VALUE] If a value or price dives, it suddenly becomes less.

dive² /daɪv/ *noun* [C] **1** [JUMP] a jump into water with your arms and head going in first **2** [MOVEMENT] a quick movement somewhere **3** [VALUE] when the value or price of something suddenly becomes less *Share prices **took a dive** today.* **4** [PLACE] *informal* a place such as a bar which is considered to be dirty or of low quality

diver /ˈdaɪvəʳ/ *noun* [C] someone who swims under water, usually with breathing equipment *a deep sea diver*

diverge /daɪˈvɜːdʒ/ *verb* [I] to be different, or to go or develop in a different direction *Over the years our interests have diverged.* ● **divergence** *noun* [C, U]

diverse /daɪˈvɜːs/ *adjective* including many different types *a diverse collection of music*

diversify /daɪˈvɜːsɪfaɪ/ *verb* [I, T] If a business diversifies, it starts making new products or offering new services. *Many designers are diversifying into casual wear.* ● **diversification** /daɪˌvɜːsɪfɪˈkeɪʃᵊn/ *noun* [U]

diversion /daɪˈvɜːʃᵊn/ *noun* **1** [CHANGE] [C, U] when something is sent somewhere different from where it was originally intended to go *the diversion of money to other projects* **2** [ROUTE] [C] *UK* (*US* **detour**) a different route that is used because a road is closed **3** [ATTENTION] [C] something that takes your attention away from

D

something else *John **created a diversion** while the rest of us escaped.* **4** ENTERTAINMENT [C] an activity you do for entertainment or pleasure *Reading is a pleasant diversion.*

diversity /daɪˈvɜːsəti/ *noun* [U] when many different types of things or people are included in something *ethnic diversity*

divert /daɪˈvɜːt/ *verb* **1** [T] to send someone or something somewhere different from where they were expecting to go *The plane was **diverted to** Stansted because of engine trouble.* **2 divert sb's attention/thoughts, etc** to take someone's attention away from something

⚬**divide** /dɪˈvaɪd/ *verb* **1** SEPARATE [I, T] to separate into parts or groups, or to make something separate into parts or groups *We **divided up into** teams of six.* ○ *Each school year is divided into two semesters.* **2 divide sth (up) among/between sb** to separate something into parts and give a part to each person in a group *The prize money will be divided equally among the winners.* **3** PLACE [T] to separate a place into two areas *An ancient wall divides the city.* **4** NUMBERS [I, T] to calculate how many times a number can go into another number *12 **divided by** 6 equals 2.* **5** DISAGREE [T] to cause people to disagree about something [often passive] *Council members were **divided over** plans to build a new stadium.*

dividend /ˈdɪvɪdend/ *noun* [C] an amount of money paid regularly to someone who owns shares in a company from the company's profits

divine /dɪˈvaɪn/ *adjective* relating to or coming from God or a god

diving /ˈdaɪvɪŋ/ *noun* [U] **1** the activity or sport of swimming under water, usually using special breathing equipment **2** the activity or sport of jumping into water with your arms and head going in first ⊅See also: scuba diving.

ˈ**diving ˌboard** *noun* [C] a raised board next to a swimming pool that you jump from into the water

divisible /dɪˈvɪzəbl/ *adjective* **divisible by 2/7/50, etc** able to be divided by 2/7/50, etc

division /dɪˈvɪʒᵊn/ *noun* **1** SEPARATED [U] when something is separated into parts or groups, or the way that it is separated *the equal division of labour among workers* **2** ORGANIZATION [C] one of the groups in a business or organization *the sales division* **3** DISAGREEMENT [C, U] when people disagree about something *a division over the issue of free medical care* **4** CALCULATION [U] when you calculate how many times one number goes into another number

divisive /dɪˈvaɪsɪv/ *adjective* causing disagreements between people *a divisive issue*

🧩 WORD PARTNERS FOR ***divorce***

get a divorce • a divorce **from** sb • divorce **proceedings/rate/settlement**

divorce /dɪˈvɔːs/ *noun* [C, U] when two people officially stop being married *My parents are **getting a divorce.*** • divorce *verb* [I, T] *She's divorcing her husband.*

divorcée /dɪˌvɔːˈsiː/ ⓤ /-ˈseɪ/ *noun* [C] a person,

usually a woman, who is divorced

divorced /dɪˈvɔːst/ *adjective* **1** married before but not married now **2 get divorced** to officially stop being married *My parents got divorced when I was seven.* ⊅See Common learner error at **married.**

divulge /daɪˈvʌldʒ/ *verb* [T] to give secret or private information to someone

Diwali /dɪˈwɑːli/ (*also* Divali) *noun* [C, U] a Hindu holiday in October/November that celebrates light and the new year

DIY /ˌdiːaɪˈwaɪ/ *noun* [U] *UK abbreviation for* do it yourself: when you do building, decorating, or repairs in your own home

dizzy /ˈdɪzi/ *adjective* feeling like everything is turning round, so that you feel ill or as if you might fall

DJ /ˈdiːˌdʒeɪ/ (*also* disc jockey) *noun* [C] someone who plays music on the radio or at discos

DNA /ˌdiːenˈeɪ/ *noun* [U] a chemical in the cells of living things which contains genetic information

⚬**do¹** *strong form* /duː/ *weak form* /də/ *auxiliary verb* **1** QUESTIONS/NEGATIVES used with another verb to form questions and negative phrases *Do you need any help?* ○ *When does the next bus leave?* ○ *I don't know.* **2** MAKE QUESTION used in a phrase at the end of a sentence to make it into a question *Sarah lives near here, doesn't she?* **3** AVOID REPEATING used to avoid repeating a verb that has just been used *"I hate that song." "So do I."* ○ *My sister reads a lot more than I do.* **4** EMPHASIZE used to emphasize the main verb *He does like you, he's just shy.* ○ *Do come and visit us soon.*

⚬**do²** /duː/ *verb past tense* did, *past participle* done **1** ACTION/JOB [T] to perform an action or job *Go upstairs and do your homework.* ○ *What are you doing this weekend?* ○ *What does she do?* (= What is her job?) **2** MAKE [T] to make or prepare something *Our printer does copies black and white copies.* **3 do badly/well, etc** to be unsuccessful/successful, etc *Sam did very well in her exams.* **4 do biology/French/history, etc** *UK* to study biology/French/history, etc **5 do your hair/make-up, etc** to make your hair/make-up, etc look nice **6 do sb good** to have a good effect on someone *A holiday would do you good.* **7 do damage/harm, etc** to cause damage/harm, etc *Luckily the fire didn't do much damage.* **8 will do** will be satisfactory *You don't have to pay now, next week will do.* **9** SPEED [T] to travel at a particular speed *For most of the journey we were doing 70 miles an hour.*

COMMON LEARNER ERROR

do or make?

Do usually means to perform an activity or job.
I should do more exercise.
~~I should make more exercise.~~

Make usually means to create or produce something.
Did you make the dress yourself?
~~Did you do the dress yourself?~~

do away with sth to get rid of something, or to stop using something *We may do away with the school uniform soon.*

do away with sb *informal* to kill someone

do sb in *informal* **1** to make someone extremely tired *All that exercise has done me in.* **2** to attack or kill someone

do sth over *US* to do something again because you did not do it well the first time

do sth up **1** *mainly UK* to fasten something *Do your coat up. It's cold outside.* **2** to repair or decorate a building so that it looks attractive

do with sth used to ask where someone put something *What did you do with my keys?*

do with sb/sth **1 could do with sb/sth** to need or want someone or something *I could do with a few days off work.* **2 be/have to do with sb/sth** to be about or connected with someone or something *My question has to do with yesterday's homework.*

do without (sb/sth) to manage without having someone or something *Jack's the kind of player we can't do without.*

do[3] /duː/ *noun* [C] *UK informal* a party *Are you going to the Christmas do?*

docile /ˈdəʊsaɪl/ [US] /ˈdɑːsəl/ *adjective* A docile person or animal is quiet and easily controlled.

dock[1] /dɒk/ *noun* **1** [C] the place where ships stop and goods are taken off or put on **2 the dock** *UK* (*US* **the stand**) the place in a law court where the person who is accused of a crime sits

dock[2] /dɒk/ *verb* **1** [I, T] If a ship docks, it arrives at a dock. **2 dock sb's pay/wages** to take away part of the money you pay someone, usually as a punishment

WORD PARTNERS FOR ***doctor***

consult/see a doctor • **go to the doctor's** • a doctor's **appointment**

⊶**doctor[1]** /ˈdɒktəʳ/ *noun* **1** [C] a person whose job is to treat people who have an illness or injury *I have to **go to the doctor's** for a check-up.* ○ *He went back to see Doctor Jones when the pain got worse.* ○ *Is it serious, Doctor?* **2 Doctor of Philosophy/Divinity, etc** someone who has the most advanced type of qualification from a university ➲See also: **spin doctor**.

doctor[2] /ˈdɒktəʳ/ *verb* [T] to change something, usually in a dishonest way *The photo in his passport had been doctored.*

doctorate /ˈdɒktərət/ *noun* [C] the most advanced type of qualification from a university *Jennifer has a **doctorate in** physics from Cambridge.*

doctrine /ˈdɒktrɪn/ *noun* [C, U] a belief or set of beliefs taught by a religious or political group *Christian doctrine*

WORD PARTNERS FOR ***document***

draw up/produce a document • **in** a document • a document **about/concerning/on** sth

⊶**document** /ˈdɒkjəmənt/ *noun* [C] **1** a piece of paper with official information on it *Please sign and return the insurance documents enclosed.* **2** a piece of text produced electronically on a computer *How do I create a new document?*

documentary /ˌdɒkjəˈmentəri/ *noun* [C] a film or television programme that gives facts about a real situation or real people *a TV documentary about the Russian Revolution*

documentation /ˌdɒkjəmenˈteɪʃən/ *noun* [U] **1** pieces of paper containing official information **2** the instructions written for a piece of computer software or equipment

docusoap /ˈdɒkjuːsəʊp/ *noun* [C] *UK* an entertaining television programme about the lives of real people who live in the same place or who do the same thing

doddle /ˈdɒdl/ *noun UK* **be a doddle** *informal* to be very easy *This computer's a doddle to use.*

dodge[1] /dɒdʒ/ *verb* **1** [I, T] to move quickly to avoid someone or something *He managed to **dodge past** the security guard.* **2** [T] to avoid talking about something or doing something you should do *The minister dodged questions about his relationship with the actress.*

dodge[2] /dɒdʒ/ *noun* [C] when you avoid something, usually in a dishonest way *a tax dodge*

dodgy /ˈdɒdʒi/ *adjective UK informal* bad, or not able to be trusted *His friend's a bit dodgy.*

doe /dəʊ/ *noun* [C] a female deer

⊶**does** *strong form* /dʌz/ *weak form* /dəz/ *present simple he/she/it of* do

⊶**doesn't** /ˈdʌzənt/ *short for* does not *Keith doesn't like mushrooms or garlic.*

⊶**dog[1]** /dɒg/ *noun* [C] an animal with fur, four legs and a tail that is kept as a pet, or trained to guard buildings and guide blind people *Let's take the dog for a walk.* ➲See also: **guide dog, hot dog**.

dog[2] /dɒg/ *verb* [T] **dogging**, *past* **dogged** to cause someone or something trouble for a long time **[often passive]** *His football career has been dogged by injury.*

dog-eared /ˈdɒgɪəd/ *adjective* If a piece of paper or a book is dog-eared, its corners are folded and torn from being touched a lot.

dogged /ˈdɒgɪd/ *adjective* **[always before noun]** continuing to do or believe in something, although it is difficult ***dogged determination*** • **doggedly** *adverb*

doghouse /ˈdɒghaʊs/ *noun* **1** [C] *US* (*UK* **kennel**) a small building for a dog to sleep in **2 be in the doghouse** If you are in the doghouse, you have done something to make people angry or annoyed with you.

dogma /ˈdɒgmə/ *noun* [C, U] a belief or set of beliefs that people are expected to accept as the truth, without ever doubting them ***political dogma***

dogmatic /dɒgˈmætɪk/ *adjective* not willing to accept other ideas or opinions because you think yours are right

dogsbody /ˈdɒgzbɒdi/ *noun* [C] *UK* someone who has to do boring jobs for someone else

doing /ˈduːɪŋ/ *noun* **1 be sb's doing** to have been done or caused by someone *The problem is not all his doing.* **2 take some/a lot of doing** *in-*

D

formal to be difficult to do *It took some doing to convince him to come.*

doldrums /ˈdɒldrəmz/ *noun* **in the doldrums 1** If a business or job is in the doldrums, it is not very successful and nothing new is happening in it. *a career in the doldrums* **2** *UK* sad and with no energy or enthusiasm

dole /dəʊl/ *verb*
dole sth out to give something, especially money, to several people or in large amounts

the dole /dəʊl/ *noun* *UK* money that the government gives someone when they are unemployed *He's been on the dole for years.*

doleful /ˈdəʊlfəl/ *adjective* very sad *doleful eyes*

doll /dɒl/ *noun* [C] a child's toy that looks like a small person

⚬**dollar** /ˈdɒlər/ *noun* [C] the unit of money used in the US, Canada, and some other countries; $ *a hundred dollars/$100* ○ *a dollar bill*

dollop /ˈdɒləp/ *noun* [C] a lump or mass of a soft substance, usually food *a dollop of cream*

dolphin /ˈdɒlfɪn/ *noun* [C] an intelligent animal that lives in the sea, breathes air, and looks like a large, smooth, grey fish

domain /dəʊˈmeɪn/ *noun* [C] **1** a particular area, activity, or subject that someone controls or deals with *The garden is his domain.* ○ *This information should be in the public domain* (= known by the public). **2** an address on the Internet where email can be sent or documents shown

do'main ,name *noun* [C] the part of an email or website address that shows the name of the organization that the address belongs to

dome /dəʊm/ *noun* [C] a curved, round roof of a building • **domed** *adjective a domed roof*

domestic /dəˈmestɪk/ *adjective* **1** HOME relating to the home and family relationships *domestic violence* ○ *What are his domestic arrangements?* **2** COUNTRY inside one country and not international *a domestic flight* **3** ANIMAL A domestic animal is kept as a pet.

domesticated /dəˈmestɪkeɪtɪd/ *adjective* **1** A domesticated animal is kept as a pet or lives on a farm. **2** A domesticated person is able or willing to do cleaning, cooking, and other jobs in the home.

domesticity /ˌdɒmesˈtɪsəti/ *noun* [U] life at home looking after a house and family

dominance /ˈdɒmɪnəns/ *noun* [U] power, influence, and control *the company's dominance in the software industry*

dominant /ˈdɒmɪnənt/ *adjective* **1** main or most important *Her mother was the dominant influence in her life.* **2** strongest and wanting to take control *a dominant older brother*

dominate /ˈdɒmɪneɪt/ *verb* [I, T] **1** to control or have power over someone or something *The US continues to dominate the world politically.* **2** to be the largest, most important, or most noticeable part of something *The cathedral dominates the skyline.*

🧩 WORD PARTNERS FOR **domination**

global/world domination • domination **of** sth • domination **over** sb/sth

domination /ˌdɒmɪˈneɪʃən/ *noun* [U] great power and control over someone or something else *world domination*

domineering /ˌdɒmɪˈnɪərɪŋ/ *adjective* trying to control people too much *a domineering mother*

dominion /dəˈmɪnjən/ *noun* [U] *formal* the power and right to control someone or something *God has dominion over all his creatures.*

domino /ˈdɒmɪnəʊ/ *noun* [C] *plural* **dominoes** a small, rectangular object that has spots on it, used in a game • **dominoes** *noun* [U] a game played using dominoes

don /dɒn/ *verb* [T] **donning**, *past* **donned** *formal* to put on a piece of clothing such as a coat or hat

donate /dəʊˈneɪt/ *verb* [T] **1** to give money or goods to a person or organization that needs help *Four hundred new computers were donated to the college.* **2** to allow some of your blood or part of your body to be used for medical purposes

🧩 WORD PARTNERS FOR **donation**

make a donation • a donation **of** [$50/food/clothing, etc] • a donation **to** sb/sth

donation /dəʊˈneɪʃən/ *noun* [C, U] when money or goods are given to help a person or organization *Would you like to make a donation?*

⚬**done**[1] /dʌn/ *adjective* **1** finished or completed *Did you get your essay done in time?* **2** cooked enough *The potatoes aren't quite done yet.* ⟴See also: easier (**easy**[2]) said than done, **well-done**.

done[2] /dʌn/ *exclamation* something that you say to show that you accept someone's offer *"I'll give you 50 pounds for the whole lot." "Done!"*

done[3] /dʌn/ *past participle of* do

donkey /ˈdɒŋki/ *noun* [C] **1** an animal that looks like a small horse with long ears **2 for donkey's years** *UK informal* for a long time

donkey

'donkey ,work *noun* [U] *UK informal* the most boring or difficult parts of a job

donor /ˈdəʊnər/ *noun* [C] **1** someone who gives some of their blood or part of their body to be used for medical purposes **2** someone who gives money or goods to a person or organization that needs help *Ten thousand dollars was given by an anonymous donor.* ⟴See also: blood donor.

⚬**don't** /dəʊnt/ *short for* do not *Please don't talk during the exam.*

donut /ˈdəʊnʌt/ *noun* [C] *another US spelling of* doughnut (= a small, round, fried cake)

doodle /ˈduːdl/ *verb* [I, T] to draw little pictures or patterns on something without thinking about it • **doodle** *noun* [C]

doodle

doom /duːm/ *noun* [U] **1** death, destruction, and other unpleasant events that cannot be avoided *a horrible sense of doom* **2 doom and gloom** unhappiness and feeling no hope for the future *Life's not all doom and gloom, you know.*

| ɑː arm | ɜː her | iː see | ɔː saw | uː too | aɪ my | aʊ how | eə hair | eɪ day | əʊ no | ɪə near | ɔɪ boy | ʊə poor | aɪə fire | aʊə sour |

doomed /duːmd/ *adjective* certain to fail, die, or have problems *Their marriage was doomed from the start.*

WORD PARTNERS FOR *door*

close/open/shut/slam a door • knock on a door • be at the door

---

o⌐**door** /dɔːʳ/ *noun* [C] **1** the part of a building, room, vehicle, or piece of furniture that you open or close to get inside it or out of it *the front door* ○ *the back door* ○ *a sliding door* ○ *the car door* ○ *Please **shut the door** behind you.* ○ *I can't **open the door**.* ○ *There's someone **at the door**.* **2** the space in a wall where you enter a building or room *He led us through the door to the rear of the building.* **3 behind closed doors** privately and not in public *Most of the deals were done behind closed doors.* **4 two/three, etc doors away** in a place that is two/three, etc houses away *We live just a few doors away from the Smiths.* ⊃See also: **trap door**.

doorbell /ˈdɔːbel/ *noun* [C] a button that you press next to a door that makes a noise to let someone know that you are there

doorknob /ˈdɔːnɒb/ *noun* [C] a round object on a door that you hold and turn to open or close it

doorman /ˈdɔːmən/ *noun* [C] *plural* **doormen** a man who stands near the doors of a large building such as a hotel to watch and help the visitors

doormat /ˈdɔːmæt/ *noun* [C] **1** a piece of thick material on the floor by a door used to clean your shoes before entering a building **2** *informal* someone who allows other people to treat them very badly *He may be selfish and insensitive, but she is a bit of a doormat.*

doorstep /ˈdɔːstep/ *noun* [C] **1** a step in front of the door of a building **2 on your doorstep** very near to where you live *They have the Rocky Mountains on their doorstep.*

door-to-door /ˌdɔːtəˈdɔːʳ/ *adjective* [always before noun], *adverb* **1** going from one house or building to another *The hotel offers a **door-to-door service** to the airport.* **2** going to every house in an area *a **door-to-door salesman***

doorway /ˈdɔːweɪ/ *noun* [C] an entrance to a building or room through a door *She waited **in the doorway** while I ran back inside.*

dope¹ /dəʊp/ *noun informal* **1** [U] an illegal drug taken for pleasure, especially cannabis (= drug that you smoke) **2** [C] *US informal* a stupid or silly person

dope² /dəʊp/ *verb* **1** [T] to give a drug to a person or animal, usually so that they become sleepy **2 be doped up** to have a lot of a drug in your body affecting your behaviour

dork /dɔːk/ *noun* [C] *mainly US informal* a stupid or silly person

dormant /ˈdɔːmənt/ *adjective* not active or developing now, but possibly active in the future *a dormant volcano*

dormitory /ˈdɔːmɪtᵊri/ (*also* **dorm** *informal*) *noun* [C] **1** a large bedroom with a lot of beds, especially in a school **2** *US* (*UK* **hall of residence**) a large building at a college or university where students live

dosage /ˈdəʊsɪdʒ/ *noun* [C] how much medicine you should take and how often you should take it *the recommended daily dosage*

WORD PARTNERS FOR *dose*

a **high/low** dose • a **fatal/lethal** dose • a dose **of** sth

---

dose /dəʊs/ *noun* [C] **1** a measured amount of medicine that is taken at one time or during a period of time *What is the recommended dose?* ○ *a **lethal dose*** **2 a dose of sth** an amount of something, often something unpleasant *a dose of bad news* ● **dose** *verb* [T] to give someone a drug or medicine

dosh /dɒʃ/ *noun* [U] *UK informal* money

doss /dɒs/ (*also* **doss down**) *verb* [I] *UK informal* to sleep somewhere temporarily, such as on the floor *Can I doss at your house tonight?*

doss about/around *UK informal* to spend your time doing very little

dossier /ˈdɒsɪeɪ/ *noun* [C] a set of documents that contain information about a particular person or subject *The officers **compiled a dossier** on the case.*

dot¹ /dɒt/ *noun* **1** [C] a small, round mark or spot *a pattern of blue and green dots* **2** [U] *spoken* the spoken form of '.' in an internet address *dot co dot uk* (= .co.uk) **3 on the dot** at that exact time *We have to leave at 7.30 on the dot.*

dot² /dɒt/ *verb* [T] **dotting**, *past* **dotted 1** to put a dot or dots on something **2** (*also* **dot around**) to be spread across an area *The company has 43 hotels dotted around the UK.*

dot.com /ˌdɒtˈkɒm/ (*also* **dotcom**) *noun* [C] a company that does most of its business on the Internet *a dot.com company/millionaire*

dote /dəʊt/ *verb*

dote on sb to love someone completely and believe that they are perfect *She absolutely dotes on that little boy.*

doting /ˈdəʊtɪŋ/ *adjective* [always before noun] extremely loving and caring *doting parents*

dotted 'line *noun* **1** [C] a line of printed dots on a piece of paper **2 sign on the dotted line** to make an agreement official by writing your name on it

dotty /ˈdɒti/ *adjective UK* slightly crazy *a dotty old woman*

o⌐**double¹** /ˈdʌbl/ *adjective* **1** ⟨TWO PARTS⟩ having two parts of the same type or size *double doors* ○ *My number is four, two, six, double two, five* (= 426225). **2** ⟨TWICE THE SIZE⟩ twice the amount, number, or size of something *a double vodka* ○ *a double hamburger* **3** ⟨FOR TWO⟩ made to be used by two people *a double bed/room*

double² /ˈdʌbl/ *verb* [I, T] to increase and become twice the original size or amount, or to make something do this *Our house has almost doubled in value.*

double (up) as sth If something doubles

up as something else, it also has the purpose of that thing. *The school's gymnasium doubles up as a dining room.*

double back to turn and go back in the direction that you have come from

double (sb) over/up to suddenly bend your body forward, usually because of pain or laughter, or to make someone do this

double³ /'dʌbl/ *noun* **1** [C, U] something that is twice the usual amount, number, or size **2 sb's double** someone who looks exactly the same as someone else

double⁴ /'dʌbl/ *determiner* twice as much or as many *Our new house is double the size of our old one.*

double-barrelled UK (US **double-barreled**) /ˌdʌbl'bærəld/ *adjective* **1** A double-barrelled gun has two of the cylindrical parts that bullets come out of. **2** UK A double-barrelled name is two names joined together.

,**double 'bass** *noun* [C] a wooden musical instrument with four strings, like a very large violin (= instrument you hold against your neck), that you play while standing up or sitting on a high chair

,**double 'bed** *noun* [C] a bed big enough for two people to sleep in

double-breasted /ˌdʌbl'brestɪd/ *adjective* A double-breasted jacket or coat has two sets of buttons to fasten at the front.

double-check /ˌdʌbl'tʃek/ *verb* [I, T] to examine something again so that you are certain it is safe or correct

double-click /ˌdʌbl'klɪk/ *verb* [I, T] to quickly press a button twice on a mouse (= small computer control) to make something happen on a computer screen *Double-click on the icon to start the program.*

double-cross /ˌdʌbl'krɒs/ *verb* [T] to deceive someone who you should be helping

double-decker /ˌdʌbl'dekəʳ/ *noun* [C] UK a tall bus with two levels *a double-decker bus*

double-glazing /ˌdʌbl'gleɪzɪŋ/ *noun* [U] UK windows that have two layers of glass to keep a building warm or quiet

doubles /'dʌblz/ *noun* [U] a game, especially tennis, in which two people play together against two other people

,**double 'standard** *noun* [C] when people are given different treatment in an unfair way [usually plural] *Critics accused the government of double standards in its policies.*

,**double 'take** *noun* [C] when you quickly look at someone or something a second time because you cannot believe you have seen something or heard something [usually singular] *He did a double take when he saw her.*

doubly /'dʌbli/ *adverb* twice as much, or very much more *It is doubly important to drink plenty of water when it's hot.*

◦⌐**doubt¹** /daʊt/ *noun* **1** [C, U] when you are not certain about something, or do not trust some-

one or something *I have some **doubts about** his ability to do the job.* **2 have no doubt** to be certain [+ (that)] *I have no doubt that I made the right decision.* **3 there's no doubt** it is certain [+ (that)] *There is no doubt that he's a good player.* **4 be in doubt** to not be certain *The future of the project is in doubt.* **5 cast doubt on sth** to make something seem uncertain *Witnesses have cast doubt on the suspect's innocence.* **6 without (a) doubt** certainly *She is without doubt a great musician.* **7 no doubt** used to say that something is very likely *No doubt she'll spend the money on new clothes.* ⊃See also: give sb the **benefit¹** of the doubt, beyond/without a **shadow¹** of a doubt.

◦⌐**doubt²** /daʊt/ *verb* [T] **1** to feel uncertain about something or think that something is not probable [+ (that)] *I doubt that I'll get the job.* ○ *I doubt if/whether he'll win.* **2** to not believe someone or something *Do you have any reason to doubt her?*

doubtful /'daʊtfᵊl/ *adjective* **1** not probable *It's doubtful if/whether he'll be able to come.* ○ [+ (that)] *It's doubtful that anyone survived the fire.* **2** not feeling certain about something ● **doubtfully** *adverb*

doubtless /'daʊtləs/ *adverb* probably *He will doubtless be criticized by journalists.*

dough /dəʊ/ *noun* [U] a thick mixture of flour and liquid used to make foods such as bread or pastry

doughnut (*also US*   **doughnut**
donut) /'dəʊnʌt/ *noun*
[C] a small, round,
fried cake, some-
times with a hole in
the middle

dour /dʊəʳ/, /daʊəʳ/ *adjective* unfriendly and serious *a dour expression*

douse /daʊs/ *verb* [T] **1** to pour a lot of liquid over someone or something *The dessert was doused with brandy and set alight.* **2** to stop a fire burning by putting a lot of water on it *to douse the flames/fire*

dove¹ /dʌv/ *noun* [C] a white bird, sometimes used as a symbol of peace

dove² /dəʊv/ *US past tense of* dive

dowdy /'daʊdi/ *adjective* plain and not fashionable *a dowdy skirt*

◦⌐**down¹** /daʊn/ *adverb, preposition* **1** LOWER PLACE towards or in a lower place *The kids ran down the hill to the gate.* ○ *I bent down to have a look.* **2** LEVEL/AMOUNT towards or at a lower level or amount *Can you turn the music down?* ○ *Slow down so they can see us.* **3** SURFACE moving from above and onto a surface *I sat down and turned on the TV.* ○ *Put that box down on the floor.* **4** DIRECTION in or towards a particular direction, usually south *Pete's moved down to London.* **5 down the road/river, etc** along or further along the road/river, etc *There's another pub further down the street.* **6 note/write, etc sth down** to write something on a piece of paper *Can I just take down your phone number?* **7** STOMACH inside your stomach *He's had food poisoning and can't keep anything* *down.* **8 be down to sb** *UK* to be someone's responsibility or decision *I've done all I can now, the rest is down to you.* **9 come/go down with sth** to become ill *The whole family came down with food poisoning.* **10 down under** *informal* Australia, or in Australia

down² /daʊn/ *adjective* [never before noun] **1** sad *What's the matter? You look a bit down today.* **2** If a computer or machine is down, it is temporarily not working. *The network was down all morning.*

down³ /daʊn/ *noun* [U] soft feathers, often used as a warm filling for bed covers ➲See also: **ups and downs.**

down⁴ /daʊn/ *verb* [T] *informal* to drink something quickly

down-and-out /ˌdaʊnən'aʊt/ *adjective* If someone is down-and-out, they have no money, possessions, or opportunities. • **down-and-out** *noun* [C]

downcast /'daʊnkɑːst/ *adjective* **1** sad or disappointed **2** If someone's eyes are downcast, they are looking down.

downgrade /ˌdaʊn'greɪd/ *verb* [T] to move someone or something to a less important position *My job's been downgraded.*

downhearted /ˌdaʊn'hɑːtɪd/ *adjective* sad or disappointed

downhill¹ /ˌdaʊn'hɪl/ *adverb* **1** towards the bottom of a hill or slope *It's so much easier cycling downhill.* **2 go downhill** to gradually become worse *After his wife died, his health started to go downhill.*

downhill² /ˌdaʊn'hɪl/ *adjective* **1** leading down towards the bottom of a hill or slope *downhill skiing* **2 be all downhill; be downhill all the way** to be much easier *From now on it will be all downhill.*

download¹ /ˌdaʊn'ləʊd/ [US] /'daʊnˌloʊd/ *verb* [T] to copy computer programs, music or other information electronically, usually from a large computer to a small one *You can **download** this software free **from** their website.* • **downloadable** *adjective* able to be downloaded ***downloadable files/images***

download² /'daʊnləʊd/ *noun* [C] a computer program, music or other information that has been or can be downloaded

downmarket /ˌdaʊn'mɑːkɪt/ *adjective UK* cheap and low quality

ˌ**down 'payment** *noun* [C] the first amount of money that you pay when you buy something expensive and pay over a period of time ***a down payment on** a house*

downplay /ˌdaʊn'pleɪ/ *verb* [T] to make something seem less important or bad than it really is *The report downplays the risks of nuclear power.*

downpour /'daʊnpɔːʳ/ *noun* [C] when it suddenly rains a lot

downright /'daʊnraɪt/ *adverb* **downright dangerous/rude/ugly, etc** extremely dangerous/rude/ugly, etc

downside /'daʊnsaɪd/ *noun* [no plural] the disadvantage of a situation *The **downside of** living in a city is all the pollution.*

downsize /'daʊnˌsaɪz/ *verb* [I, T] to make a company or organization smaller by reducing the number of people who work there • **downsizing** *noun* [U]

Down's syndrome /'daʊnzˌsɪndrəʊm/ *noun* [U] a medical condition in which a person is born with low mental ability, a flat face, and sloping eyes

downstairs /ˌdaʊn'steəz/ *adverb* on or to a lower level of a building *She **went downstairs** to see who was at the door.* • **downstairs** *adjective a downstairs bathroom*

downstream /ˌdaʊn'striːm/ *adverb* in the direction that the water in a river is moving in

down-to-earth /ˌdaʊntu'ɜːθ/ *adjective* practical and realistic

downtown /ˌdaʊn'taʊn/ *adjective* [always before noun], *adverb US* in or to the central part or main business area of a city *downtown Chicago*

downtrodden /'daʊnˌtrɒdᵊn/ *adjective* treated badly and without respect from other people *downtrodden workers*

downturn /'daʊntɜːn/ *noun* [C] when a business or economy becomes less successful *There has been a sharp **downturn in** sales.*

downwards (*also US* **downward**) /'daʊnwədz/ *adverb* towards a lower place or level *The road slopes downwards to the river.* • **downward** *adjective* ➲See also: **a downward spiral.**

downwind /ˌdaʊn'wɪnd/ *adjective, adverb* in the direction that the wind is blowing

dowry /'daʊri/ *noun* [C] money that a woman's family gives to the man she is marrying in some cultures

doze /dəʊz/ *verb* [I] to sleep lightly *Grandma was dozing in front of the TV.*

doze off to gradually start sleeping, usually during the day *He dozed off during the film.*

dozen /'dʌzᵊn/ *noun, determiner* **1** twelve, or a group of twelve *There were about a dozen people at the party.* **2 dozens** *informal* a lot *She's got **dozens of** friends.* ➲See also: **a dime a dozen.**

⊶**Dr** *written abbreviation for* doctor *an appointment with Dr Paul Thomas*

drab /dræb/ *adjective* without colour and boring to look at *drab, grey buildings*

draconian /drə'kəʊniən/ *adjective* very severe *draconian laws*

draft¹ /drɑːft/ *noun* **1** [C] a piece of writing or a plan that is not yet in its finished form *He made several changes to the **first draft**.* **2 the draft** *US* when people are told that they must join the armed forces **3** [C] *US spelling of* draught (= a current of cold air in a room)

WORD PARTNERS FOR ***draft***

draft **a constitution/legislation/a letter/a proposal**

draft² /drɑːft/ *verb* [T] **1** to produce a piece of writing or a plan that you intend to change later *to **draft a letter*** **2** to order someone to join the armed forces

draft sb in/draft sb into sth *UK* to

bring someone somewhere to do a particular job *Extra police were drafted in to stop the demonstration.*

draftsman *US* (*UK* draughtsman) /'drɑːftsmən/ *noun* [C] *plural* draftsmen someone who draws detailed drawings as plans for something

drafty /'drɑːfti/ *adjective US spelling of* draughty

drag[1] /dræg/ *verb* dragging, *past* dragged **1 drag sth/sb across/along/over, etc** to pull something or someone along the ground somewhere, usually with difficulty *The table was too heavy to lift, so we had to drag it across the room.* **2 drag sb along/out/to, etc** to make someone go somewhere they do not want to go *I have to drag myself out of bed every morning.* **3** [T] to move something somewhere on a computer screen using a mouse (= small computer control) **4** [I] (*also* drag on) to continue for too much time in a boring way ⊃See also: drag your feet (**foot**[1]).

drag sb down *UK* If an unpleasant situation drags someone down, it makes them feel unhappy or ill.

drag sb into sth to force someone to become involved in an unpleasant or difficult situation *I don't want to be dragged into this argument.*

drag sth out to make something continue for more time than is necessary

drag[2] /dræg/ *noun* **1 in drag** *informal* If a man is in drag, he is wearing women's clothes. **2 be a drag** *informal* to be boring and unpleasant *Cleaning the house is such a drag.* **3** [C] when you breathe in smoke from a cigarette *He took a drag on his cigarette.*

dragon /'drægən/ *noun* [C] a big, imaginary creature which breathes out fire

dragonfly /'drægənflaɪ/ *noun* [C] an insect with long wings and a thin, colourful body, often seen flying near water ⊃See picture at **insect**.

dragon

drain[1] /dreɪn/ *verb* **1** [REMOVE LIQUID] [T] to remove the liquid from something, usually by pouring it away *Drain the pasta and add the tomatoes.* **2** [FLOW AWAY] [I] If something drains, liquid flows away or out of it. **3** [MAKE TIRED] [T] to make someone very tired *The long journey drained him.* **4** [DRINK] [T] If you drain a glass or cup, you drink all the liquid in it.

drain[2] /dreɪn/ *noun* **1** [C] a pipe or hole that takes away waste liquids or water *She poured the dirty water down the drain.* **2 a drain on sth** something that uses or wastes a lot of money or energy **3 down the drain** *informal* If money or work goes down the drain, it is wasted.

drainage /'dreɪnɪdʒ/ *noun* [U] the system of water or waste liquids flowing away from somewhere into the ground or down pipes

drained /dreɪnd/ *adjective* If someone is drained, they are extremely tired.

drainpipe /'dreɪnpaɪp/ *noun* [C] a pipe that carries waste water away from a building

■ WORD PARTNERS FOR *drama*

3 a drama unfolds • high drama • human drama

drama /'drɑːmə/ *noun* **1** [PLAY] [C] a play in a theatre or on television or radio *a historical drama* **2** [PLAYS/ACTING] [U] plays and acting generally *modern drama* **3** [EXCITEMENT] [C, U] when something exciting happens *There was a lot of drama in the courtroom.*

'drama ˌqueen *noun* [C] *informal* someone who gets far too upset or angry over small problems

dramatic /drə'mætɪk/ *adjective* **1** [SUDDEN] very sudden or noticeable *a dramatic change/improvement* **2** [EXCITING] full of action and excitement *a dramatic rescue* **3** [THEATRE] [always before noun] relating to plays and acting **4** [BEHAVIOUR] showing your emotions in a very obvious way because you want other people to notice you *Stop being so dramatic!* • **dramatically** *adverb*

dramatist /'dræmətɪst/ *noun* [C] someone who writes plays

dramatize (*also UK* -ise) /'dræmətaɪz/ *verb* [T] **1** to make an event or situation seem more exciting than it really is *The media tends to dramatize things.* **2** to change a story so that it can be performed as a play • **dramatization** /ˌdræmətaɪ'zeɪʃən/ *noun* [C, U]

drank /dræŋk/ *past tense of* drink

drape /dreɪp/ *verb* **1 drape sth across/on/over, etc** to put something such as cloth or a piece of clothing loosely over something *He draped his jacket over the chair and sat down to eat.* **2 be draped in/with sth** to be loosely covered with a cloth *The coffin was draped in a flag.*

drapes /dreɪps/ *noun* [plural] *mainly US* long, heavy curtains

drastic /'dræstɪk/ *adjective* Drastic action or change is sudden and extreme. *drastic reductions in price* • **drastically** *adverb*

draught[1] *UK* (*US* draft) /drɑːft/ *noun* [C] a current of cold air in a room

draught[2] *UK* (*US* draft) /drɑːft/ *adjective* **draught beer/lager, etc** a drink that comes from a large container and not from a can or bottle

draughts /drɑːfts/ *UK* (*US* checkers) *noun* [U] a game that two people play by moving flat, round objects around on a board of black and white squares

draughtsman *UK* (*US* draftsman) /'drɑːftsmən/ *noun* [C] *plural* draughtsmen someone who draws detailed drawings as plans for something

draughty *UK* (*US* drafty) /'drɑːfti/ *adjective* having currents of cold air blowing through *a draughty old building*

o--**draw**[1] /drɔː/ *verb past tense* drew, *past participle* drawn **1** [PICTURE] [I, T] to produce a picture by making lines or marks, usually with a pen or pencil *She drew a picture of a tree.* **2 draw sth/sb across/back/over, etc** to pull something or someone gently in a particular direction *He* took her hand and drew her towards him. **3 draw into/out/away, etc** to move somewhere, usually in a vehicle *The train drew into the station.* **4 draw the curtains** to pull curtains open or closed **5 draw (sb's) attention to sth/sb** to make someone notice someone or something *I don't want to draw too much attention to myself.* **6** ATTRACT [T] to attract someone to a place or person *Thousands of tourists are drawn to the city every year.* **7** SPORT [I, T] *UK* to finish a game or competition with each team or player having the same score *England drew 2-2 against Italy.* **8** TAKE OUT [T] to take something out of a container or your pocket, especially a weapon *He drew a knife and started threatening me.* **9 draw near/close** to become nearer in space or time *Her birthday's drawing nearer every day.* **10 draw (a) breath** to breathe in air *She drew a deep breath and started her speech.* **11** MONEY [T] (*also* **draw out**) to take money from your bank account **12 draw to a close/end** to be almost finished **13 draw conclusions** to make judgments after considering an subject or situation **14 draw a comparison/distinction** to say that there is a similarity or difference between two things ⇒See also. draw a **blank²**, draw the **line¹** at sth, draw a **veil** over sth.

draw back to move away from someone or something, usually because you are surprised or frightened

draw sb/sth into sth to make someone or something become involved in a difficult or unpleasant situation *I'm not going to be drawn into this argument.*

draw on sth to use information or your knowledge or experience of something to help you do something *His novels draw heavily on his childhood.*

draw sth up to prepare something, usually a plan, list, or an official agreement, by writing it

draw² /drɔː/ *noun* [C] **1** *mainly UK* when a game or competition finishes with each player or team having the same score *The match ended in a draw.* **2** (*also US* **drawing**) a competition that is decided by choosing a particular ticket or number *the National Lottery draw* ⇒See also: the **luck** of the draw.

drawback /'drɔːbæk/ *noun* [C] a problem or disadvantage *The only* **drawback with** *this camera is the price.*

drawer /drɔː/ *noun* [C] a container like a box without a lid that is part of a piece of furniture and that slides in and out *She* **opened** *the drawer and took out a knife.* ⇒See also: **chest** of drawers.

drawing /'drɔːɪŋ/ *noun* **1** PICTURE [C] a picture made with a pencil or pen *There were some children's drawings pinned up on the wall.* **2** ACTIVITY [U] the skill or activity of making pictures using a pencil or pen *Do you want to*

do some drawing? **3** NUMBER/TICKET [C] *US* (*UK/ US* **draw**) a competition that is decided by choosing a particular ticket or number

'drawing ,board *noun* **back to the drawing board** If you go back to the drawing board, you have to start planning a piece of work again because the first plan failed.

'drawing ,pin *UK* (*US* **thumbtack**) *noun* [C] a pin with a wide, flat top, used for fastening pieces of paper to a wall

'drawing ,room *noun* [C] *old-fashioned* a room in a large house used for sitting in and talking with guests

drawl /drɔːl/ *noun* [no plural] a lazy way of speaking that uses long vowel sounds • **drawl** *verb* [I]

drawn¹ /drɔːn/ *adjective* looking very tired or ill *She looked pale and drawn after the operation.* ⇒See also: horse-drawn.

drawn² /drɔːn/ *past participle of* draw

drawn-out /,drɔːn'aʊt/ *adjective* continuing for longer than you think is necessary *long, drawn-out negotiations*

dread¹ /dred/ *verb* **1** [T] to feel worried or frightened about something that has not happened yet *I'm dreading the first day at my new school.* ○ [+ doing sth] *I dread seeing him again.* **2 I dread to think** *UK* used to say that you do not want to think about something because it is too worrying *I dread to think what could have happened if we hadn't been wearing seat belts.*

dread² /dred/ *noun* [U, no plural] a strong feeling of fear or worry [+ of + doing sth] *a dread of being lonely*

dreadful /'dredfₑl/ *adjective* extremely bad or unpleasant *a dreadful mistake* ○ *a dreadful man*

dreadfully /'dredfₑli/ *adverb* **1** *mainly UK formal* very *I'm dreadfully sorry.* **2** very badly *The children behaved dreadfully.*

dreadlocks /'dredlɒks/ *noun* [plural] a hairstyle in which the hair is twisted together in lengths and is never brushed

o→**dream¹** /driːm/ *noun* **1** [C] a series of events and images that happen in your mind while you are sleeping *a bad dream* ○ *I had a very strange dream last night.* **2** [C] something that you want to happen although it is not very likely *It was his dream to become an actor.* **3 be in a dream** *UK* to not notice things that are around you because you are thinking about something else **4 beyond your wildest dreams** bigger or better than anything you could imagine or hope for **5 like a dream** If something or someone does something like a dream, they do it very well.

o→**dream²** /driːm/ *verb past* **dreamed** or **dreamt** **1** [I, T] to experience events and images in your mind while you are sleeping [+ (that)] *Last night I dreamed that I was flying.* **2** [I, T] to imagine something that you would like to happen [+ of + doing sth] *I dream of living on a desert island.* ○ [+ (that)] *He never dreamed that one day he* *would become President.* **3 wouldn't dream of doing sth** used to say that you would not do something because you think it is wrong or silly

dream sth up to think of an idea or plan, usually using a lot of imagination *Who dreams up these new designs?*

dream³ /driːm/ *adjective* **dream house/job/car, etc** the perfect house/job/car, etc

dreamer /ˈdriːməʳ/ *noun* [C] someone who is not practical and thinks about things that are not likely to happen

dreamy /ˈdriːmi/ *adjective* **1** seeming to be in a dream and thinking about pleasant things instead of what is happening around you *She had a dreamy look in her eyes.* **2** very pleasant *a dreamy dessert* ● **dreamily** *adverb*

dreary /ˈdrɪəri/ *adjective* boring and making you feel unhappy *a rainy, dreary day* ○ *a dreary job*

dredge /dredʒ/ *verb* [T] to clean the bottom of a lake or river by removing dirt, plants, or rubbish

dredge sth up to talk about something bad or unpleasant that happened in the past

dregs /dregz/ *noun* **1** [plural] the part of a drink at the bottom of a glass or other container that usually contains small solid bits **2 the dregs of society/humanity** people who you think are extremely bad or unimportant

drench /drenʃ/ *verb* [T] to make something or someone completely wet [often passive] *He was completely drenched by the time he got home.*

☞**dress¹** /dres/ *verb* **1** [I, T] to put clothes on yourself or someone else *I usually get dressed before having breakfast.* ⊃Opposite **undress**. **2** [I] to wear a particular type, style, or colour of clothes *Ali always dresses smartly for work.* ○ [often passive] *She was dressed in black.* **3 dress a burn/cut/wound, etc** to clean an injury and put a covering over it to protect it

---

COMMON LEARNER ERROR

be/get dressed

Be careful to use the correct preposition. You do not always need one.

I got dressed and went to school.

Are you dressed yet?

He was dressed in a black suit.

~~He was dressed with a black suit.~~

---

dress up 1 to put on formal clothes for a special occasion **2** to wear special clothes in order to change your appearance, usually for a game or party *He dressed up as Superman for the party.*

☞**dress²** /dres/ *noun* **1** [C] a piece of clothing for women or girls which covers the top of the body and hangs down over the legs *She was wearing a short, black dress.* ⊃See colour picture **Clothes** on page Centre 8. **2** [U] a particular style of clothes *casual/formal dress* ⊃See also: **fancy dress**.

dresser /ˈdresəʳ/ *noun* [C] **1** mainly US a piece of bedroom furniture with a mirror and drawers for keeping clothes in **2** UK a piece of furni-

ture consisting of a cupboard with shelves above for keeping plates, cups, and other kitchen equipment

dressing /ˈdresɪŋ/ *noun* **1** [C, U] a sauce, especially a mixture of oil and vinegar for salad **2** [C] a covering that protects an injury

'dressing ,gown UK (US **robe**) *noun* [C] a piece of clothing, like a long coat, that you wear at home when you are not dressed

'dressing ,room *noun* [C] a room where actors or sports teams get dressed before a performance or game

'dressing ,table *noun* [C] mainly UK a piece of bedroom furniture like a table with a mirror and drawers

dressy /ˈdresi/ *adjective* Dressy clothes are suitable for a formal occasion.

drew /druː/ *past tense of* draw

dribble /ˈdrɪbl/ *verb* **1** [MOUTH] [I] If someone dribbles, a small amount of liquid comes out of their mouth and goes down their face. *Babies dribble a lot.* **2** [LIQUID] [I, T] If a liquid dribbles, it falls slowly in small amounts, and if you dribble a liquid, you pour it so it falls slowly in small amounts. *Dribble some oil over the vegetables.* **3** [SPORT] [I, T] to move a ball along by using your hand to hit it against the ground or kicking it several times ● **dribble** *noun* [C, U]

dried /draɪd/ *past of* dry

drier /ˈdraɪəʳ/ *noun* [C] *another spelling of* dryer (= a machine for drying wet things)

drift¹ /drɪft/ *verb* **1 drift across/down/towards, etc** to be moved slowly somewhere by currents of wind or water *Smoke drifted across the rooftops.* **2 drift in/out/into, etc** to move somewhere slowly *Guests were drifting out onto the terrace.* **3** [I] to get into a situation or job without having any particular plan *He drifted into acting after university.* **4** [I] If snow or leaves drift, they are blown into piles by the wind.

drift apart If two people drift apart, they gradually become less friendly and the relationship ends.

drift off to gradually start to sleep *I drifted off during the lecture.*

drift² /drɪft/ *noun* **1** [C] slow, gradual movement from one place to another *the drift of people into Western Europe* **2 catch/get sb's drift** to understand the general meaning of what someone is saying **3** [C] a pile of snow or leaves that has been blown somewhere

drill¹ /drɪl/ *noun* **1** [TOOL] [C] a tool or machine for making holes in a hard substance *an electric drill* ⊃See picture at **tool**. **2** [FOR LEARNING] [C, U] a teaching method in which students repeat something several times to help them learn it *We do lots of drills to practise pronunciation.* **3 an emergency/fire, etc drill** when you practise what to do in an emergency/fire, etc **4** [SOLDIERS] [C, U] when soldiers do training for marching

drill² /drɪl/ *verb* **1** [I, T] to make a hole in a hard substance using a special tool *Billy drilled a hole in the wall.* ○ *The engineers were drilling for oil.* **2** [T] to make someone repeat something several times so that they learn it

drily /'draɪli/ *adverb another spelling of* dryly (= in a serious voice but trying to be funny)

o▪**drink**[1] /drɪŋk/ *verb past tense* drank, *past participle* drunk **1** [I, T] to put liquid into your mouth and swallow it *Would you like something to drink?* ○ *He was drinking a glass of milk.* **2** [I] to drink alcohol, usually regularly *She doesn't smoke or drink.*
drink to sb/sth to hold your glass up before drinking from it, in order to wish someone or something good luck or success
drink (sth) up to finish your drink completely *Drink up! We've got to leave soon.*

WORD PARTNERS FOR **drink**

have a drink ● a drink of [water/milk, etc]
● a **hot/cold** drink

o▪**drink**[2] /drɪŋk/ *noun* **1** [C] a liquid or an amount of liquid that you drink *a hot/cold drink* ○ *Can I have a drink of water please?* **2** [C, U] alcohol, or an alcoholic drink *Do you fancy a drink tonight to celebrate?* ⊃See also: **soft drink.**

drink-driving /ˌdrɪŋk'draɪvɪŋ/ *UK* (*US* **drunk driving**) *noun* [U] driving a vehicle after drinking too much alcohol *He was convicted of drink-driving.*

drinker /'drɪŋkəʳ/ *noun* **1** [C] someone who regularly drinks alcohol *He's a **heavy drinker** (= he drinks a lot of alcohol).* **2 a coffee/tea/wine, etc drinker** someone who regularly drinks a particular drink

drinking /'drɪŋkɪŋ/ *noun* [U] when someone drinks alcohol

'**drinking ˌwater** *noun* [U] water that is safe for people to drink

drip[1] /drɪp/ *verb* dripping, *past* dripped **1** [I, T] If a liquid drips, it falls in drops or you make it fall in drops. *There was water dripping from the ceiling.* **2** [I] to produce drops of liquid *The candle's dripping.*

drip[2] /drɪp/ *noun* **1** DROP [C] a drop of liquid that falls from something **2** SOUND [no plural] the sound or action of a liquid falling in drops **3** MEDICAL [C] *UK* (*US* **IV**) a piece of medical equipment used for putting liquids into your body *The doctor's put him **on a drip.***

o▪**drive**[1] /draɪv/ *verb past tense* drove, *past participle* driven **1** CONTROL VEHICLE [I, T] to make a car, bus, or train move, and control what it does *She's learning to drive.* ○ *He drives a red sports car.* **2** TRAVEL [I, T] to travel somewhere in a car, or to take someone somewhere in a car *My friend drove me home last night.* **3 drive sb out/away/ from, etc** to force someone to leave a place *The supermarket has driven many small shops out of the area.* **4 drive sb crazy/mad/wild, etc** to make someone feel crazy, annoyed, or excited *That noise is driving me mad.* **5 drive sb to sth; drive sb to do sth** to make someone have a bad feeling or do something bad *The arguments and violence drove her to leave home.* **6 drive sth into/through/towards, etc** to push something somewhere by hitting it hard *He drove the nail into the wall with a hammer.* **7** MAKE WORK [T] to provide the power or energy that makes someone or something work [often passive] *She was driven by greed and ambition.*

⊃See also: drive/send sb round the **bend**[2], drive sb up the **wall.**

COMMON LEARNER ERROR

drive or **ride?**

You **drive** a car, truck, or bus.
She drives an expensive sports car.
You **ride** a bicycle, motorcycle, or horse.
My brother is learning to ride a bicycle.
~~My brother is learning to drive a bicycle.~~

be driving at sth used to ask what someone really means *Just what are you driving at?*
drive off to leave in a car

WORD PARTNERS FOR **drive**

go for a drive

drive[2] /draɪv/ *noun* **1** JOURNEY [C] a journey in a car *The drive from Boston to New York took 4 hours.* **2** GROUND [C] the area of ground that you drive on to get from your house to the road *You can park on the drive.* **3** COMPUTER [C] a part of a computer that can read or store information *a DVD drive* ○ *Save your work **on the C: drive.*** **4** EFFORT [C] when someone makes a great effort to achieve something [+ to do sth] *The government started a drive to improve standards in schools.* **5** ENERGY [U] energy and determination to achieve things *She has drive and ambition.*

drive-by /'draɪvbaɪ/ *adjective* describes something that someone does when they are inside a vehicle that is moving *a drive-by shooting*

drive-in /'draɪvɪn/ *noun* [C] *mainly US* a cinema or restaurant that you can visit without getting out of your car

drivel /'drɪvəl/ *noun* [U] nonsense *He was talking complete drivel.*

driven /'drɪvən/ *past participle of* drive

WORD PARTNERS FOR **driver**

a **bus/taxi/train/truck** driver ● the driver of sth

o▪**driver** /'draɪvəʳ/ *noun* [C] someone who drives a vehicle *a bus/train driver* ⊃See also: **engine driver.**

'**driver's ˌlicense** *US* (*UK* **driving licence**) *noun* [C] an official document that allows you to drive a car

drive-through /'draɪvθruː/ *noun* [C] a place where you can get some type of service by driving through, without needing to get out of your car *a drive-through restaurant*

driveway /'draɪvweɪ/ *noun* [C] the area of ground that you drive on to get from your house to the road

driving[1] /'draɪvɪŋ/ *noun* [U] when you drive a car, or the way someone drives

driving[2] /'draɪvɪŋ/ *adjective* **1 driving rain/snow** rain or snow that is falling very fast and being blown by the wind **2 the driving force** a person or thing that has a very strong effect and makes something happen *She was the **driving force behind** the project.*

'driving ,licence *UK* (*US* **driver's license**) *noun* [C] an official document that allows you to drive a car

drizzle /'drɪzl/ *noun* [U] light rain • **drizzle** *verb* [I]

drone¹ /drəʊn/ *verb* [I] to make a continuous, low sound, like an engine *I could hear traffic droning in the distance.*
drone on to talk for a long time in a very boring way *I wish he'd stop droning on about school.*

drool /druːl/ *verb* [I] If a person or animal drools, liquid comes out of the side of their mouth.
drool over sb/sth to look at someone or something in a way that shows you think they are very attractive

droop /druːp/ *verb* [I] to hang down, often because of being weak, tired, or unhappy *He was tired and his eyelids were starting to droop.*

⊶**drop¹** /drɒp/ *verb* drop-ping, *past* dropped
1 LET FALL [T] to let something you are carrying fall to the ground *She tripped and dropped the vase.* **2** FALL [I] to fall *The ball dropped to the ground.* **3** BECOME LESS [I] If a level or amount drops, it becomes less. *Unemployment has dropped from 8% to 6% in the last year.* **4** TAKE [T] (*also* **drop off**) to take someone or something to a place, usually by car as you travel somewhere else *I can drop you at the station on my way to work.* **5** STOP ACTIVITY [T] If you drop a plan, activity, or idea, you stop doing or planning it. *Plans for a new supermarket have been dropped.* ◦ *When we heard the news, we **dropped everything** (= stopped what we were doing) and rushed to the hospital.* **6** STOP INCLUDING [T] to decide to stop including someone in a group or team *The coach dropped me from the team.* **7** **drop it/the subject** to stop talking about something, especially because it is annoying or upsetting someone **8** VOICE [I, T] If your voice drops, or if you drop your voice, you talk more quietly. ⊃See also: be dropping like flies (**fly²**).

drop by/in to visit someone for a short time, usually without arranging it before *I dropped in on George on my way home from school.*
drop sb/sth off to take someone or something to a place, usually as you travel somewhere else
drop off 1 *informal* to start to sleep *She dropped off in front of the TV.* **2** If the amount, number, or quality of something drops off, it becomes less. *The demand for mobile phones shows no signs of dropping off.*
drop out to stop doing something before you have completely finished *He **dropped out** of school at 14.*

⊶**drop²** /drɒp/ *noun* **1** LIQUID [C] a small, round shaped amount of liquid *I felt a few drops of rain.* ⊃See colour picture **Pieces and Quantities** on page Centre 1. **2** REDUCTION [no plural] when the level or amount of something becomes less *There has been a **drop in** crime recently.* **3** SMALL AMOUNT [no plural] a small amount of a liquid you can drink *Would you like a drop more milk?* **4** DISTANCE [no plural] a vertical distance down from somewhere to the ground *It's a drop of about 50 metres from the top of the cliff.*

'drop-down ,menu *noun* [C] a pop-up menu: a list of choices on a computer screen which is hidden until you choose to look at it

dropout /'drɒpaʊt/ *noun* [C] **1** a student who leaves school or university before they have completely finished *a high-school dropout* **2** someone who does not want to have a job, possessions, etc because they do not want to be like everyone else

droppings /'drɒpɪŋz/ *noun* [plural] solid waste from birds and some small animals *rabbit droppings*

drought /draʊt/ *noun* [C, U] a long period when there is no rain and people do not have enough water *A severe drought ruined the crops.*

drove /drəʊv/ *past tense of* drive

droves /drəʊvz/ *noun* **in droves** If people do something in droves, they do it in large numbers.

drown /draʊn/ *verb* **1** [I, T] to die because you are under water and cannot breathe, or to kill someone in this way *Two people drowned in a boating accident yesterday.* **2** [T] (*also* **drown out**) If a loud noise drowns the sound of something else, it prevents that sound from being heard. *His voice was drowned out by the traffic.*

drowning /'draʊnɪŋ/ *noun* [C, U] when someone dies because they are under water and cannot breathe

drowsy /'draʊzi/ *adjective* feeling tired and wanting to sleep *The sun was making me drowsy.* • **drowsily** *adverb* • **drowsiness** *noun* [U]

drudgery /'drʌdʒ³ri/ *noun* [U] work that is very boring

⊶**drug¹** /drʌg/ *noun* [C] **1** an illegal substance that people take to make them feel happy [usually plural] *He started **taking/using drugs** such as heroin and cocaine.* ◦ *Greg is **on drugs** (= he uses drugs regularly).* ◦ *a drug dealer* **2** a chemical substance used as a medicine *Scientists are developing a new drug to treat cancer.* ⊃See also: hard drugs.

drug² /drʌg/ *verb* [T] drugging, *past* drugged to give someone a chemical substance that makes them sleep or stop feeling pain *He drugged his victims before robbing them.*

'drug ,addict *noun* [C] someone who cannot stop taking drugs

drugstore /'drʌgstɔːʳ/ *US* (*UK* **chemist's**) *noun* [C] a shop that sells medicines and also things such as soap and beauty products

drum¹ /drʌm/ *noun* [C] **1** a round, hollow, musical instrument that you hit with your hands or with sticks *Anna **plays the drums***. **2** a large, round container for holding substances such as oil or chemicals

drum

drum² /drʌm/ *verb* [I, T] **drumming**, *past* **drummed** to hit something several times and make a sound like a drum, or to make something do this *the sound of rain drumming on the roof* ○ *She drummed her fingers nervously on the desk.*

drum sth into sb to make someone remember or believe an idea or fact by repeating it to them many times [often passive] *The importance of good manners was drummed into me by my father.*

drum up sth to increase interest in something or support for something *He was trying to **drum up** some **enthusiasm** for his idea.*

drummer /'drʌməʳ/ *noun* [C] someone who plays a drum

drunk¹ /drʌŋk/ *adjective* unable to behave or speak normally because you have drunk too much alcohol *Isabella usually **gets drunk** at parties.*

drunk² /drʌŋk/ *past participle of* drink

drunken /'drʌŋkən/ *adjective* [always before noun] drunk, or involving people who are drunk *a drunken man* ○ *drunken behaviour* ● **drunkenly** *adverb* ● **drunkenness** *noun* [U]

o⌐**dry¹** /draɪ/ *adjective* **drier, driest** or **dryer, dryest 1** NOT WET Something that is dry does not have water or liquid in it or on its surface. *dry paint* ○ *Is your hair dry yet?* **2** NO RAIN with no or not much rain *a dry summer* **3** HAIR/SKIN Dry skin or hair does not feel soft or smooth. *My lips feel really dry.* **4** WINE Dry wine is not sweet. **5** BORING If a book, talk, or subject is dry, it is not interesting. **6** FUNNY saying something in a serious way but trying to be funny *a dry sense of humour* ● **dryness** /'draɪnəs/ *noun* [U]

dry² /draɪ/ *verb* [I, T] to become dry, or to make something become dry *He dried his hands on a towel.* ⊃See also: blow-dry.

dry (sb/sth) off to make someone or something dry, or to become dry, especially on the surface [often reflexive] *I dried myself off with a towel and got dressed.*

dry (sth) out to become dry, or to make something become dry

dry (sth) up *mainly UK* to make plates, cups, etc dry with a cloth after they have been washed

dry up 1 If a supply of something dries up, it ends. *The work dried up and he went out of business.* **2** If a river or lake dries up, the water in it disappears.

,dry 'clean *verb* [T] to clean clothes using a special chemical and not with water ● **dry**

cleaner's *noun* [C] a shop where you can have your clothes cleaned this way ● **dry cleaning** *noun* [U]

dryer (*also* **drier**) /'draɪəʳ/ *noun* [C] a machine for drying wet things, usually clothes or hair ⊃See also: **tumble dryer**.

dryly (*also* **drily**) /'draɪli/ *adverb* If you say something dryly, you say it in a serious way but you are trying to be funny.

dual /'djuːəl/ *adjective* [always before noun] having two parts, or having two of something *dual nationality*

,dual 'carriageway *noun* [C] *UK* a road that consists of two parallel roads, so that traffic travelling in opposite directions is separated by a central strip of land

dub /dʌb/ *verb* [T] **dubbing**, *past* **dubbed 1** to give someone or something an unofficial or funny name [often passive] *He was dubbed 'Big Ears' by the media.* **2** to change the language in a film or television programme into a different language [often passive] *The film was **dubbed** into English.*

dubious /'djuːbiəs/ *adjective* **1** thought not to be completely true, honest, or legal *dubious evidence* ○ *a man with a dubious reputation* **2** not certain that something is good or true *He's **dubious about** the benefits of acupuncture.* ● **dubiously** *adverb*

duchess /'dʌtʃɪs/ *noun* [C] a woman of very high social rank in some European countries *the Duchess of Windsor*

duck

duck¹ /dʌk/ *noun* [C, U] a bird with short legs that lives in or near water, or the meat from this bird ⊃See also: be (like) **water¹** off a duck's back.

duck² /dʌk/ *verb* **1** [I, T] to move your head or body down quickly to avoid being hit or seen *Billy ducked behind a car when he saw his teacher.* **2** [T] *informal* to avoid something that is difficult or unpleasant *He managed to **duck** the issue.*

duck out of sth to avoid doing something that other people are expecting you to do [+ doing sth] *She was trying to **duck out of** doing her homework.*

duct /dʌkt/ *noun* [C] **1** a tube in the body that a liquid substance can flow through *a tear duct* **2** a tube or passage for air or wires that is part of the structure of a building *a heating duct*

D

dud /dʌd/ *noun* [C] something that does not work correctly ● **dud** *adjective*

dude /duːd/ *noun* [C] *mainly US very informal* a man *a cool dude*

☞**due¹** /djuː/ *adjective* **1** ⌈EVENT⌉ [never before noun] expected or planned [+ to do sth] *He was due to fly back this morning.* ○ *Her book is due out* (= expected to be published) *next week.* ○ *When is the baby due* (= expected to be born)? **2 due to sth** because of something *The train was late due to snow.* **3** ⌈MONEY⌉ [never before noun] Money that is due is owed to someone and must be paid. *The rent is due today.* **4** ⌈DESERVE⌉ Something that is due to you is something that is owed to you or something you deserve. *He didn't get the praise and recognition that was due to him.* **5** ⌈BEHAVIOUR⌉ [always before noun] *formal* correct and suitable *He was fined for driving without due care and attention.* ➲Opposite **undue**. **6 be due for sth** If you are due for something, it should happen very soon. *I'm due for a check-up at the dentist's.*

due² /djuː/ *noun* **give sb their due** something that you say when you want to describe someone's good qualities after they have done something wrong or after you have criticized them *Joe's a bit slow but, to give him his due, he does work hard.*

due³ /djuː/ *adverb* **due east/north/south/west, etc** directly east/north/south/west, etc *sail/fly due south*

duel /ˈdjuːəl/ *noun* [C] **1** a type of fight in the past between two people with weapons, used as a way of deciding an argument *He challenged him to a duel.* **2** an argument or competition between two people or groups

dues /djuːz/ *noun* [plural] money that you must pay to be a member of an organization *annual dues*

duet /djuˈet/ *noun* [C] a piece of music for two people to perform together

dug /dʌɡ/ *past of* dig

duke /djuːk/ *noun* [C] a man of very high social rank in some parts of Europe *the Duke of Beaufort*

dull¹ /dʌl/ *adjective* **1** ⌈BORING⌉ not interesting *a dull place* ○ *a dull person* **2** ⌈NOT BRIGHT⌉ not bright *dull colours* ○ *dull weather* **3** ⌈SOUND⌉ A dull sound is not loud or clear. *a dull thud* **4** ⌈PAIN⌉ [always before noun] A dull pain is not strong. *a dull ache* ● **dullness** *noun* [U] ● **dully** *adverb*

dull² /dʌl/ *verb* [T] to make a feeling or quality become less strong *He's on morphine to dull the pain.*

duly /ˈdjuːli/ *adverb formal* at the correct time, in the correct way, or as you would expect *I ordered it over the Internet and within a few days, it duly arrived.* ○ *I was duly impressed.*

dumb /dʌm/ *adjective* **1** *mainly US informal* stupid *a dumb idea/question* ○ *He's too dumb to understand.* **2** physically unable to talk **3 be struck dumb** to be unable to speak because you are so shocked or angry ● **dumbly** *adverb*

dumbfounded /ˌdʌmˈfaʊndɪd/ *adjective* extremely surprised

dummy¹ /ˈdʌmi/ *noun* [C] **1** ⌈BABY EQUIPMENT⌉ *UK* (*US* **pacifier**) a small, rubber object that a baby sucks to stop it crying **2** ⌈STUPID PERSON⌉ *mainly US informal* a stupid person *She's no dummy.* **3** ⌈MODEL⌉ a model of a person

dummy² /ˈdʌmi/ *adjective* [always before noun] not real but made to look real *dummy weapons*

dump¹ /dʌmp/ *verb* **1** [T] to put something somewhere to get rid of it, especially in a place where you should not put it *The company was fined for illegally dumping toxic chemicals.* **2 dump sth on/in/down, etc** to put something somewhere quickly and carelessly *Henri dumped his bag on the table and went upstairs.*

dump² /dʌmp/ (*also UK* **tip**) *noun* [C] **1** a place where people take things that they do not want *We took our old mattress to the dump.* **2** *informal* a place that is dirty and untidy *His room is a dump.*

dumpling /ˈdʌmplɪŋ/ *noun* [C] a round mixture of fat and flour that has been cooked in boiling liquid *stew and dumplings*

dumps /dʌmps/ *noun* **be down in the dumps** *informal* to be unhappy *He looks a bit down in the dumps.*

Dumpster /ˈdʌmpstər/ *US trademark* (*UK* **skip**) *noun* [C] a very large, metal container for big pieces of rubbish

dumpy /ˈdʌmpi/ *adjective informal* short and fat

dune /djuːn/ (*also* **sand dune**) *noun* [C] a hill of sand in the desert or on the coast

dung /dʌŋ/ *noun* [U] solid waste from a large animal

dungarees /ˌdʌŋɡəˈriːz/ *UK* (*US* **overalls**) *noun* [plural] trousers with a part that covers your chest and straps that go over your shoulders

dungeon /ˈdʌndʒən/ *noun* [C] a dark, underground prison, used in the past

dunk /dʌŋk/ *verb* [T] to quickly put something into liquid and take it out again *He dunked the roll in his soup.*

dunno /dəˈnəʊ/ *informal* **I dunno** I do not know.

duo /ˈdjuːəʊ/ *noun* [C] two people who perform together *a comedy/pop duo*

dupe /djuːp/ *verb* [T] to trick someone [often passive, + into + doing sth] *He was duped into paying $4000 for a fake painting.*

duplicate¹ /ˈdjuːplɪkeɪt/ *verb* [T] **1** to make an exact copy of something *The document has been duplicated.* **2** to do something that has already been done, in exactly the same way *Ajax hope to duplicate last year's success.* ● **duplication** /ˌdjuːplɪˈkeɪʃən/ *noun* [U]

duplicate² /ˈdjuːplɪkət/ *noun* **1** [C] something that is an exact copy of something else *I lost my passport and had to get a duplicate.* **2 in duplicate** If a document is in duplicate, there are two copies of it. ● **duplicate** *adjective a duplicate key*

duplicity /djuˈplɪsəti/ *noun* [U] when you dishonestly tell different people different things

durable /ˈdjʊərəbl/ *adjective* remaining in good condition for a long time *durable goods* ○ *a fabric that is comfortable and durable* ● **durability** /ˌdjʊərəˈbɪləti/ *noun* [U]

duration /djʊə'reɪʃ°n/ *noun* [U] *formal* the amount of time that something lasts *The singer remained in the hotel **for the duration** of his stay in the UK.*

duress /dju'res/ *noun formal* **under duress** If you do something under duress, you do it because someone is forcing you to. *a confession made under duress*

o-=**during** /'djʊərɪŋ/ *preposition* **1** for the whole of a period of time *Emma's usually at home during the day.* **2** at a particular moment in a period of time *We'll arrange a meeting some time during the week.*

during or **for**?

Use **during** to talk about a period of time when something happens.

I'm at work during the day, so it's better to phone in the evening.

Please don't take photos during the performance.

Use **for** to say how long something happens or continues, for example 'for two hours', 'for three days'.

I've been in Cambridge for six months now.

We waited for an hour and then left.

~~We waited during an hour and then left.~~

dusk /dʌsk/ *noun* [U] the time in the evening when it starts to become dark *As dusk fell, we headed back to the hotel.*

dust¹ /dʌst/ *noun* [U] **1** a powder of dirt or soil that you see on a surface or in the air *He drove off in a cloud of dust.* **2 bite the dust** *informal* to die, fail, or stop existing **3 the dust settles** If the dust settles after an argument or big change, the situation becomes calmer. *Let the dust settle a bit before you make any decisions about the future.*

dust² /dʌst/ *verb* [I, T] to remove dust from something *I tidied and dusted the shelves.*

dustbin /'dʌstbɪn/ UK (US **garbage can**) *noun* [C] a large container for rubbish kept outside your house

duster /'dʌstər/ *noun* [C] UK a cloth used for removing dust (= powder of dirt) from furniture and other objects

dustman /'dʌstmən/ UK (US **garbage man**) *noun* [C] *plural* UK **dustmen** someone whose job is to remove rubbish from containers outside people's houses

dustpan /'dʌstpæn/ *noun* [C] a flat container with a handle, used with a brush for removing dirt from a floor *Get the **dustpan and brush** and I'll sweep this up.* ⊃See picture at **brush**.

dusty /'dʌsti/ *adjective* covered with dust (= powder of dirt) *a dusty old chair* ○ *dusty streets*

dutiful /'dju:tɪf°l/ *adjective* doing everything that you should do in your position or job *a dutiful son* • **dutifully** *adverb*

o-=**duty** /'dju:ti/ *noun* [C, U] **1** RIGHT THING TO DO something that you must do because it is morally or legally right *a **moral duty*** ○ [+ to do sth] *Rail companies **have a duty** to provide safe transport.* **2** JOB something you do as part of your job or because of your position *professional/official duties* **3 on/off duty** If a doctor, police officer, etc is on duty, they are working, and if they are off duty, they are not working. **4** TAX tax that you pay on something you buy

duty-free /,dju:ti'fri:/ *adjective* Duty-free goods are things that you can buy and bring into a country without paying tax.

duvet /'dju:veɪ/ ⑬ /du:'veɪ/ UK (US **comforter**) *noun* [C] a cover filled with feathers or warm material that you sleep under

DVD /,di:vi:'di:/ *noun* [C] *abbreviation for* digital versatile disc: a small disc for storing music, films and information *a **DVD player/drive*** ○ *Is this film available **on DVD**?*

dwarf¹ /dwɔ:f/ *noun* [C] **1** an imaginary creature like a little man, in children's stories *Snow White and the Seven Dwarves* **2** an offensive word for someone who is very short • **dwarf** *adjective* A dwarf animal or plant is much smaller than the normal size.

dwarf² /dwɔ:f/ *verb* [T] If something dwarfs other things, it is very big and makes them seem small. [often passive] *The hotel is dwarfed by skyscrapers.*

dwell /dwel/ *verb past* **dwelt** or **dwelled** **dwell in/among/with, etc** *literary* to live somewhere **dwell on/upon sth** to keep thinking or talking about something, especially something bad or unpleasant *I don't want to dwell on the past.*

dweller /'dwelər/ *noun* **an apartment/city/country, etc dweller** someone who lives in an apartment/city/the country, etc

dwelling /'dwelɪŋ/ *noun* [C] *formal* a house or place to live in

dwindle /'dwɪndl/ *verb* [I] to become smaller or less *The number of students in the school has dwindled to 200.* ○ *Our savings slowly dwindled away.* ○ *dwindling supplies of oil*

dye¹ /daɪ/ *noun* [C, U] a substance that is used to change the colour of something

dye² /daɪ/ *verb* [T] **dyeing**, *past* **dyed** to change the colour of something by using a dye *He dyed his hair pink last week.*

dying /'daɪɪŋ/ *present participle of* die

dyke (*also* **dike**) /daɪk/ *noun* [C] **1** a wall built to stop water from a sea or river going onto the land **2** UK a passage that has been dug to take water away from fields

dynamic /daɪ'næmɪk/ *adjective* **1** ACTIVE full of ideas, energy, and enthusiasm *a dynamic, young teacher* ○ *dynamic leadership* **2** CHANGING continuously changing or moving *a dynamic economy* **3** PRODUCING MOVEMENT A dynamic force makes something move. • **dynamically** *adverb*

dynamics /daɪ'næmɪks/ *noun* **1** [plural] the way that parts of a situation, group, or system affect each other *political dynamics* ○ *The dy-*

namics of family life have changed greatly.
2 [U] the scientific study of the movement of objects

dynamism /'daɪnəmɪzᵊm/ *noun* [U] the quality of being dynamic

dynamite /'daɪnəmaɪt/ *noun* [U] **1** a type of explosive *a stick of dynamite* **2** *informal* someone or something that is very exciting, powerful, or dangerous *an issue that is political dynamite*

dynasty /'dɪnəsti/ ⑩ /'daɪnəsti/ *noun* [C] a series of rulers who are all from the same family *the Ming dynasty*

dysentery /'dɪsᵊntᵊri/ *noun* [U] an infectious disease which causes severe problems with the bowels, making solid waste become liquid

dysfunctional /dɪs'fʌŋkʃᵊnᵊl/ *adjective formal* not behaving, working, or happening in the way that most people think is normal *a dysfunctional family/childhood*

dyslexia /dɪ'sleksiə/ *noun* [U] a condition affecting the brain that makes it difficult for someone to read and write ● **dyslexic** /dɪ'sleksɪk/ *adjective* having dyslexia

Ee

E, e /iː/ the fifth letter of the alphabet

e- /iː-/ *prefix* electronic, usually relating to the Internet *an e-ticket* o *e-commerce*

o--**each** /iːtʃ/ *pronoun, determiner* every one in a group of two or more things or people when they are considered separately *A player from each of the teams volunteered to be captain.* o *The bill is £36 between the four of us, that's £9 each.*

,each 'other *pronoun* used to show that each person in a group of two or more people does something to the others *The kids are always arguing with each other.*

eager /ˈiːgəʳ/ *adjective* wanting to do or have something very much *Sam was eager to go home and play on his computer.* • **eagerly** *adverb an eagerly awaited announcement* • **eagerness** *noun* [U]

eagle

eagle /ˈiːgl/ *noun* [C] a large, wild bird with a big, curved beak, that hunts smaller animals

o--**ear** /ɪəʳ/ *noun* **1** [C] one of the two organs on your head that you hear with *The child whispered something in her mother's ear.* ⊃See colour picture **The Body** on page Centre 13. **2** [C] the top part of some crop plants, which produces grain *an ear of wheat/corn* **3 have an ear for sth** to be good at hearing, repeating, or understanding a particular type of sound *He has no ear for music.* **4 fall on deaf ears** If advice or a request falls on deaf ears, people ignore it. **5 play it by ear** to decide how to deal with a situation as it develops **6 play sth by ear** to play a piece of music by remembering the notes

earache /ˈɪəreɪk/ *noun* [C, U] pain in your ear *I've got (UK) earache/(US) an earache.*

eardrum /ˈɪədrʌm/ *noun* [C] a part inside your ear made of thin, tight skin that allows you to hear sounds

earl /ɜːl/ *noun* [C] a man of high social rank in the UK *the Earl of Northumberland*

earlobe /ˈɪələʊb/ *noun* [C] the soft part at the bottom of your ear

o--**early** /ˈɜːli/ *adjective, adverb* earlier, earliest **1** *near*

the beginning of a period of time, process, etc *the early 1980s* o *It is too early to say whether he will recover completely.* **2** before the usual time or the time that was arranged *early retirement* o *The plane arrived ten minutes early.* **3 at the earliest** used after a time or date to show that something will not happen before then *Building will not begin until July at the earliest.* **4 early on** in the first stage or part of something *I lost interest quite early on in the book.* ⊃See also: it's early days (**day**).

earmark /ˈɪəmɑːk/ *verb* [T] to decide that something, especially money, will be used for a particular purpose [often passive] *More than $7 million has been earmarked for schools in the area.* o *The land is earmarked for development.*

o--**earn** /ɜːn/ *verb* **1** GET MONEY [I, T] to get money for doing work *She earns more than £40,000 a year.* **2 earn a/your living** to work to get money for the things you need **3** DESERVE [T] to get something that you deserve because of your work, qualities, etc *As a teacher you have to earn the respect of your students.* **4** PROFIT [T] to make a profit *an account that earns a high rate of interest*

WORD PARTNERS FOR **earner**

high/low/top earners • **wage** earners

earner /ˈɜːnəʳ/ *noun* [C] **1** someone who earns money *a high earner* **2** *UK informal* a product or service that earns you money *She has a nice little earner making curtains.*

earnest /ˈɜːnɪst/ *adjective* **1** very serious and sincere *an earnest young man* o *an earnest effort* **2 in earnest** If something begins to happen in earnest, it really starts to happen in a serious way. *The research will begin in earnest early next year.* **3 be in earnest** to be very serious about something and mean what you are saying • **earnestly** *adverb* • **earnestness** *noun* [U]

earnings /ˈɜːnɪŋz/ *noun* [plural] money that you get from working

earphones /ˈɪəfəʊnz/ *noun* [plural] a piece of electronic equipment that you put on your ears so that you can listen privately to radio, recorded music, etc

earring /ˈɪərɪŋ/ *noun* [C] a piece of jewellery that you wear on or through your ear [usually plural] *diamond earrings*

earring

earshot /ˈɪəʃɒt/ *noun* **be out of/within earshot** If you are out of earshot, you are too far away to hear something, and if you are within earshot, you are close enough to hear something.

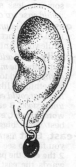

o--**earth** /ɜːθ/ *noun* **1** PLANET [no plural] (*also* the Earth) the planet that we live on **2** SUBSTANCE [U] soil or ground *a mound of earth* **3** ELECTRICAL WIRE [C] *UK* (*US* ground) a

---

| j yes | k cat | ŋ ring | ʃ she | θ thin | ð this | ʒ decision | dʒ jar | tʃ chip | æ cat | e bed | ə ago | ɪ sit | i cosy | ɒ hot | ʌ run | ʊ put |

wire that makes electrical equipment safer
4 cost/charge, etc the earth *UK informal* to
cost/charge, etc an extremely large amount of
money **5 come (back) down to earth** to start
dealing with life and problems again after you
have had a very exciting time *Have you come
back down to earth since the wedding?* **6 how/
what/why, etc on earth** *informal* used when you
are extremely surprised, confused, or angry
about something *Why on earth didn't you tell
me before?*

earthly /'ɜːθli/ *adjective* **1 no earthly doubt/
reason/use, etc** used to emphasize that there is
not any doubt/reason/use, etc *There's no
earthly reason why you should feel guilty.* **2**
literary relating to this world and not any
spiritual life *earthly powers*

WORD PARTNERS FOR earthquake

an earthquake **hits/strikes** [a place] • a
devastating/major/massive/powerful
earthquake

earthquake /'ɜːθkweɪk/ *noun* [C] a sudden
movement of the Earth's surface, often causing severe damage *A powerful earthquake
struck eastern Turkey last night.*

earthy /'ɜːθi/ *adjective* **1** referring to sex and
the human body in a direct way *earthy jokes*
2 similar to soil in colour, smell, or taste

earwig /'ɪəwɪg/ *noun* [C] a small dark-brown
insect with two curved parts on its tail

ease¹ /iːz/ *noun* **1** [U] If you do something with
ease, it is very easy for you to do it. *Gary
passed his exams **with ease**.* ○ *I'm amazed at
the ease with which he learnt the language.*
2 at ease feeling relaxed and comfortable *I felt
completely at ease with him.* **3 ill at ease** feeling
anxious

ease² /iːz/ *verb* **1** [I, T] to become less severe, or
to make something become less severe *The
new road should ease traffic problems in the village.* **2 ease sb/sth back/out/up, etc** to move
someone or something gradually and gently to
another position [often reflexive] *Tom eased himself back in his chair.*
ease off/up **1** STOP to gradually stop or
become less *The storm is easing off.* **2** WORK
LESS to start to work less or do things with less
energy *As he got older, he started to ease up a
little.* **3** TREAT LESS SEVERELY to start to treat
someone less severely *I wish his supervisor
would ease up on him a bit.*

easel /'iːzªl/ *noun* [C] something
used to support a painting
while you paint it

☞**easily** /'iːzɪli/ *adverb* **1** with no
difficulty *She makes friends
easily.* **2** used to emphasize that
something is likely *A comment
like that could easily be misunderstood.* **3 easily the best/
worst/biggest, etc** certainly the
best/worst/biggest, etc

☞**east, East** /iːst/ *noun* **1** [U] the direction that
you face to see the sun rise *Which way's east?*
2 the east the part of an area that is further towards the east than the rest **3 the East** the

countries of Asia, especially Japan and China
● **east** *adjective New York is **east of** Chicago.*
● **east** *adverb* towards the east *They sailed east.*
⊃See also: **the Middle East.**

Easter /'iːstər/ *noun* [C, U] the Christian period of
celebration around Easter Sunday (= the special Sunday in March or April on which Christians celebrate Jesus Christ's return to life)

'**Easter ,egg** *noun* [C] a chocolate egg that
people give and receive at Easter

easterly /'iːstªli/ *adjective* **1** towards or in the
east *The river flows in an easterly direction.*
2 An easterly wind comes from the east. *a
strong, easterly breeze*

☞**eastern, Eastern** /'iːstªn/ *adjective* [always
before noun] **1** in or from the east part of an
area *eastern Europe* **2** in or from the countries
of Asia *Eastern philosophy* ○ *an Eastern religion*

easterner, Easterner /'iːstªnər/ *noun* [C]
mainly US someone from the east part of a
country or area

,**Easter 'Sunday** (*also* ,Easter 'Day) *noun* [C, U]
the special Sunday in March or April on
which Christians celebrate Jesus Christ's
return to life

eastward, eastwards /'iːstwəd, 'iːstwədz/
adverb towards the east ● **eastward** *adjective an
eastward direction*

OTHER WAYS OF SAYING easy

If something is easy to do or understand, we
often use the adjectives **simple** or **straightforward**: *The recipe is so **simple**, you just
mix all the ingredients together.* ● *It seems
like a fairly **straightforward** task.*

If a machine or system is easy to use, we
often describe it as **user-friendly**: *This
latest version of the software is much more
user-friendly.*

In informal situations there are also some
fixed expressions you can use to say that
something is very easy to do, for example:
*(UK) This machine's **a doddle** to use.* ● *My
last exam was **a piece of cake**.* ● *Once we
reached the main road the journey was **plain
sailing**.*

☞**easy¹** /'iːzi/ *adjective* **1** not difficult *an easy
choice* ○ *He thought the exam was very easy.* ○
[+ to do sth] *It's easy to see why he's so popular.*
2 relaxed and comfortable *She has a very easy
manner.* **3 I'm easy** *informal* used to say that
you do not mind which choice is made

COMMON LEARNER ERROR

easy or **easily**?

Remember, **easy** is an adjective and usually describes a
noun.

an easy question

The exam was easy.

Easily is an adverb and usually describes a verb.

You should pass the exam easily.

~~You should pass the exam easy.~~

easy² /'i:zi/ *adverb* **1 take it/things easy** to relax and not use too much energy *After his heart attack, he had to take things easy for a while.* **2 go easy on sb** *informal* to treat someone in a gentle way and not be so strict *Go easy on the boy - he's only young.* **3 go easy on sth** *informal* to not eat or use too much of something *Go easy on the chips, there aren't many left.* **4 easier said than done** used to say that something seems like a good idea but it would be difficult to do *I do want to ask her out, but it's easier said than done.*

easy-going /ˌi:zi'gəʊɪŋ/ *adjective* relaxed and not easily upset or worried

---

OTHER WAYS OF SAYING *eat*

A more formal alternative is the verb **consume**: *He consumes vast quantities of bread with every meal.*

If someone eats something quickly because they are very hungry, the verb **devour** is sometimes used: *The children devoured a whole packet of biscuits.*

The phrasal verbs **bolt down**, **gobble up**, and **wolf down** are also used to describe the action of eating something very quickly: *He gobbled up his food before anyone else had started.* • *I gave her a plate of pasta and she wolfed it down.*

The verb **scoff** (**scarf** *US*) can be used in informal situations when someone eats a lot of something very quickly: *Who scoffed/scarfed all the cake?*

The verb **snack** means 'to eat a little food between main meals': *I've been snacking on biscuits and chocolate all afternoon.*

To **eat out** is to eat in a restaurant. *I thought we could eat out tonight.*

The phrasal verb **pick at** is sometimes used when someone eats only a little of something: *He didn't feel hungry, and sat at the table picking at his food.*

The phrasal verb **tuck into** means 'to start to eat something with enthusiasm': *I was just about to tuck into a huge bowl of ice cream.*

⌐**eat** /i:t/ *verb past tense* **ate**, *past participle* **eaten** **1** [I, T] to put food into your mouth and then swallow it *Who ate all the cake?* ○ *I haven't eaten since breakfast.* ○ *Let's have something to eat* (= some food). **2** [I] to eat a meal *We usually eat in the kitchen.* ⊃See also: have your **cake** and eat it.

eat away at sb If a memory or bad feeling eats away at someone, it makes them feel more and more unhappy.

eat away at sth to gradually damage or destroy something

eat into sth to use or take away a large part of something valuable, such as money or time *The high cost of living in London is eating into my savings.*

eat out to eat at a restaurant ⊃See colour picture **Phrasal Verbs** on page Centre 16.

eat (sth) up to eat all the food you have

been given *Be a good boy and eat up your spinach.*

eat up sth to use or take away a large part of something valuable, such as money or time *Cities are eating up more and more farmland.*

eater /'i:tər/ *noun* **a big/fussy/meat, etc eater** someone who eats in a particular way or eats a particular food

eatery /'i:tªri/ *noun* [C] *informal* a restaurant

'eating di,sorder *noun* [C] a mental illness in which someone cannot eat normal amounts of food

eaves /i:vz/ *noun* [plural] the edges of a roof where it is wider than the walls

eavesdrop /'i:vzdrɒp/ *verb* [I] **eavesdropping**, *past* **eavesdropped** to secretly listen to a conversation *He stood outside the door eavesdropping on their conversation.* • **eavesdropper** *noun* [C]

eBay /'i:beɪ/ *noun* [U] *trademark* a website that allows users to buy and sell things online

ebb¹ /eb/ *noun* **1 the ebb (tide)** when the sea flows away from the land **2 be at a low ebb** If someone's enthusiasm, confidence, etc is at a low ebb, it is much less than before. *Staff morale is at a low ebb.* **3 ebb and flow** the way in which the level of something regularly becomes higher or lower in a situation *the ebb and flow of the economy*

ebb² /eb/ *verb* [I] **1** (*also* ebb away) to gradually disappear *She watched her father's life slowly ebbing away.* **2** When the tide ebbs, the sea flows away from the land.

ebony /'ebªni/ *noun* [U] hard black wood

ebullient /ɪ'bʊliənt/ *adjective* energetic, enthusiastic, and excited *an ebullient personality*

e-business /'i:ˌbɪznɪs/ *noun* [C, U] the business of buying and selling goods and services on the Internet, or a company which does this

e-cash /'i:kæʃ/ *noun* [U] money in an electronic form, used for buying goods and services on the Internet

eccentric¹ /ɪk'sentrɪk/ *adjective* behaving in a strange and unusual way *an eccentric professor* ○ *eccentric behaviour* • **eccentrically** *adverb* • **eccentricity** /ˌeksen'trɪsəti/ *noun* [U] when someone is eccentric

eccentric² /ɪk'sentrɪk/ *noun* [C] someone who is eccentric *a harmless eccentric*

ecclesiastical /ɪˌkli:zi'æstɪkªl/ *adjective* relating to the Christian Church *ecclesiastical law/history*

echelon /'eʃəlɒn/ *noun formal* **the lower/upper echelons** the people at the lower/upper level of a large organization or society *the upper echelons of government/management*

echinacea /ˌekɪ'neɪʃə/ *noun* [U] a plant that is used as a medicine, especially to help your body fight illness

echo¹ /'ekəʊ/ *verb* **echoing**, *past* **echoed 1** [I] If a sound echoes, or a place echoes with a sound, you hear the sound again because you are in a large, empty space. *Their voices echoed around the room.* **2** [T] to repeat something that someone else has said because you agree with it *This report echoes some of the earlier research I've read.*

E

echo² /ˈekəʊ/ noun [C] plural **echoes** **1** a sound that you hear more than once because you are in a big, empty space **2** something that is very much like something else and makes you think of it [usually plural] *There are echoes of Shakespeare's work in the play.*

eclectic /ekˈlektɪk/ adjective including many different styles and types *an eclectic mix*

eclipse¹ /ɪˈklɪps/ noun [C] when the sun is covered by the moon, or the moon is covered by the Earth's shadow (= dark area) *a solar/lunar eclipse*

eclipse² /ɪˈklɪps/ verb [T] **1** to make another person or thing seem much less important, good, or famous [often passive] *Braque was somewhat eclipsed by Picasso.* **2** to make an eclipse of the moon or sun

eco- /iːkəʊ-/ prefix relating to the environment *eco-friendly cleaning products*

eco-friendly /ˌiːkəʊˈfrendli/ adjective describes a product that is designed so that it does not damage the environment *eco-friendly washing powder*

ecological /ˌiːkəˈlɒdʒɪkᵃl/ adjective relating to ecology or to the environment *an ecological disaster* ● **ecologically** adverb

eco,logical ˈfootprint noun [C] the amount of the earth's energy that someone or something uses *You can reduce your ecological footprint by cycling more and driving less.*

ecology /iˈkɒlədʒi/ noun [U, no plural] the relationship between living things and the environment, or the scientific study of this ● **ecologist** noun [C] someone who studies ecology

e-commerce /ˈiːˌkɒmɜːs/ noun [U] the buying and selling of goods and services on the Internet *E-commerce is becoming an important part of the economy.*

➤ **economic** /ˌiːkəˈnɒmɪk/, /ˌekəˈnɒmɪk/ adjective **1** [always before noun] relating to trade, industry, and money *economic growth* ○ *economic policies* **2** making a profit, or likely to make a profit *It's not economic to produce goods in small quantities.* ⊃Opposite **uneconomic.** ● **economically** adverb *The country would benefit economically from reform.*

economical /ˌiːkəˈnɒmɪkᵃl/, /ˌekəˈnɒmɪkᵃl/ adjective not using a lot of money, fuel, etc *I need a car that's economical and reliable.* ● **economically** adverb

,**economic ˈmigrant** noun [C] a person who leaves their home country to live in another country with better work or living conditions

economics /ˌiːkəˈnɒmɪks/ noun [U] the study of the way in which trade, industry, and money are organized ● **economist** /ɪˈkɒnəmɪst/ noun [C] someone who studies economics ⊃See also: home economics.

economize (also UK **-ise**) /ɪˈkɒnəmaɪz/ verb [I] to use less of something because you want to save money

➤ **economy** /ɪˈkɒnəmi/ noun **1** [C] the system by which a country produces and uses goods and money *the German/US economy* ○ *a global economy* **2** [C, U] when someone or something does not use much money, fuel, etc *The car's design combines comfort with economy.* ○ UK *We'll need to **make** some **economies** when I stop work.*

e'**conomy ,class** noun [U] the cheapest and least comfortable seats on an aircraft ● e'conomy ,class adjective, adverb

ecosystem /ˈiːkəʊˌsɪstəm/ noun [C] all the living things in an area and the way they affect each other and the environment *Tourism is damaging the fragile ecosystem of the Great Barrier Reef.*

ecotourism /ˈiːkəʊtʊərɪzᵃm/ noun [U] the business of providing holidays for people so that they can help local people and not damage the environment

eco-warrior /ˈiːkəʊˌwɒriəʳ/ noun [C] someone who tries to stop activities which damage the environment

ecstasy /ˈekstəsi/ noun **1** [U] a feeling of extreme happiness *She danced about in ecstasy.* **2 Ecstasy** an illegal drug that makes you feel happier and more active

ecstatic /ɪkˈstætɪk/ adjective extremely happy ● **ecstatically** adverb

ecumenical /ˌekjuˈmenɪkᵃl/ adjective encouraging different types of Christian churches to unite *an ecumenical service*

eczema /ˈeksɪmə/ noun [U] a medical condition which makes areas of skin become red and dry

➤ **edge¹** /edʒ/ noun **1** [C] the part around something that is furthest from the centre *Rick was sitting on the edge of the bed.* ○ *She ran down to the water's edge.* **2** [C] the part of a blade of a knife or tool that cuts *a sharp/cutting edge* **3** **have the edge on/over sb/sth** to be slightly better than someone or something else **4 be on edge** to be nervous or worried *Sorry for shouting - I'm a bit on edge today.* **5 take the edge off sth** to make something unpleasant have less of an effect on someone *Have an apple. It'll take the edge off your hunger.*

edge² /edʒ/ verb **1** edge (sth) up/down/past, etc to move somewhere gradually, or to make something move somewhere gradually *She edged her way through the crowd of reporters.* **2** [T] to put something around the edge of something else as a decoration *The cloth was edged with gold.*

edgeways /ˈedʒweɪz/ UK (US **edgewise** /ˈedʒwaɪz/) adverb with the narrowest part going first *We should be able to get the sofa through edgeways.* ⊃See also: not get a **word¹** in edgeways.

edgy /ˈedʒi/ adjective nervous *David was starting to feel a bit edgy.*

edible /ˈedɪbl/ adjective safe to eat and not harmful *edible berries* ⊃Compare **inedible.**

edict /ˈiːdɪkt/ noun [C] formal an official order from someone in authority

edifice /ˈedɪfɪs/ noun [C] formal a very large building

edit /ˈedɪt/ verb [T] to prepare text, film, etc by

deciding what to include and making mistakes correct

edition /ɪ'dɪʃ³n/ *noun* [C] **1** a book, newspaper, etc that is one of several that are the same and were produced at the same time *a new edition* ○ *The paperback edition costs £7.95.* **2** a radio or television programme that is one of a series

editor /'edɪtə'/ *noun* [C] **1** someone whose job is to prepare text, film, etc by deciding what to include and making mistakes correct **2** someone who is in charge of a newspaper or magazine

editorial¹ /,edɪ'tɔːriəl/ *adjective* [always before noun] **1** relating to editors or editing *editorial skills* **2** written by or expressing the opinions of a newspaper editor *editorial pages*

editorial² /,edɪ'tɔːriəl/ (*US* **op-ed**) *noun* [C] an article in a newspaper expressing the editor's opinion

educate /'edʒʊkeɪt/ *verb* [T] **1** to teach someone at a school or college [often passive] *She was educated at the Perse School.* **2** to give people information about something so that they understand it better *This is part of a campaign to educate people about the dangers of smoking.*

educated /'edʒʊkeɪtɪd/ *adjective* **1** Someone who is educated has learned a lot at school or university and has a good level of knowledge. **2 an educated guess** a guess that is probably correct because you have enough knowledge about something ⊃See also: **well-educated**.

┌─────────────────────────────────────┐
│ WORD PARTNERS FOR *education* │
└─────────────────────────────────────┘

continue/have/provide/receive education
● **compulsory/good** education

o→**education** /,edʒʊ'keɪʃ³n/ *noun* [U, no plural] the process of teaching and learning in a school or college, or the knowledge that you get from this *We expect a good standard of education for our children.* ● **educational** *adjective* providing education, or relating to education *the educational system* ● **educationally** *adverb* ⊃See also: **further education, higher education**.

┌─────────────────────────────────────┐
│ COMMON LEARNER ERROR │
└─────────────────────────────────────┘

education or **upbringing?**

If you want to talk about the way your parents treated you when you were growing up, you should use **upbringing**, not 'education'.
My parents were old-fashioned, and my upbringing was rather strict.

eel /iːl/ *noun* [C] a long fish that looks like a snake

eerie /'ɪəri/ *adjective* unusual and slightly frightening *an eerie silence* ● **eerily** *adverb* ● **eeriness** *noun* [U]

┌─────────────────────────────────────┐
│ WORD PARTNERS FOR *effect* │
└─────────────────────────────────────┘

have/produce an effect ● an **adverse/ beneficial/devastating/harmful/profound** effect ● an effect **on** sb/sth ● the effects **of** sth

o→**effect¹** /ɪ'fekt/ *noun* **1** [C, U] a change, reaction, or result that is caused by something *The accident had a huge effect on her life.* ○ *We don't know the long-term effects of this drug.* **2 in**

effect used to say what the real situation is *This means, in effect, that the plan has been scrapped.* **3 come/go into effect** to start being used *New food safety rules come into effect on Monday.* **4 take effect** to start to produce results or changes *The anaesthetic takes effect in about ten minutes.* **5 to that effect** used to say that you are giving the general meaning of something but not the exact words *He said he was bored with school or something to that effect.* **6 a sound/special/visual, etc effect** a sound, image, etc that is created artificially ⊃See also: **side effect**.

┌─────────────────────────────────────┐
│ COMMON LEARNER ERROR │
└─────────────────────────────────────┘

affect or **effect?**

Be careful not to confuse these two words.
Affect is a verb which means to cause a change.
Pollution seriously affects the environment.

Use the noun **effect** to talk about the change, reaction, or result caused by something.
Global warming is one of the effects of pollution.

effect² /ɪ'fekt/ *verb* [T] *formal* to make something happen *The civil rights movement effected a huge change in America.*

o→**effective** /ɪ'fektɪv/ *adjective* **1** successful or achieving the result that you want *effective management* ○ *What is the most effective way of teaching grammar?* **2 become/be effective** If changes, laws, etc become effective, they officially start. **3** [always before noun] used to say what the real situation is although officially it is different *Bernardo has effective control of the company.* ⊃Opposite **ineffective**. ● **effectiveness** *noun* [U]

effectively /ɪ'fektɪvli/ *adverb* **1** in a way that is successful and achieves what you want *Teachers need to be able to communicate ideas effectively.* **2** used when you describe what the real result of a situation is *His illness effectively ended his career.*

effects /ɪ'fekts/ *noun* [plural] *formal* possessions *my personal effects*

effeminate /ɪ'femɪnət/ *adjective* An effeminate man behaves or looks like a woman.

efficiency /ɪ'fɪʃ³nsi/ *noun* [U] when someone or something uses time and energy well, without wasting any *fuel efficiency*

efficient /ɪ'fɪʃ³nt/ *adjective* working well and not wasting time or energy *an efficient person/organization* ○ *Email is a quick and efficient way of contacting people.* ⊃Opposite **inefficient**. ● **efficiently** *adverb*

effigy /'efɪdʒi/ *noun* [C] a model of a person *Protesters burned effigies of the president.*

┌─────────────────────────────────────┐
│ WORD PARTNERS FOR *effort* │
└─────────────────────────────────────┘

make an effort ● **require/take** effort ● a **big/brave / concerted / frantic / valiant** effort ● **in** an effort to do sth

o→**effort** /'efət/ *noun* **1** [C, U] an attempt to do something [+ to do sth] *We huddled together in an effort to keep warm.* **2** [U] the energy that you need to do something *I put a lot of effort into* *organizing the party.* ○ [+ **to do sth**] *It would take too much effort to tidy my bedroom.* **3 be an effort** to be difficult or painful *After his accident, walking was an effort.*

effortless /'efətləs/ *adjective* achieved without any special or obvious effort *effortless grace/style* ● **effortlessly** *adverb*

effusive /ɪ'fjuːsɪv/ *adjective* showing a lot of enthusiasm or approval for someone or something, often too much

EFL /ˌiːef'el/ *noun* [U] *abbreviation for* English as a Foreign Language: the teaching of English to students whose first language is not English

o⁺**e.g.** (*also* eg) /ˌiː'dʒiː/ used to give an example of what you mean *crime writers, e.g. Agatha Christie and Ruth Rendell*

egalitarian /ɪˌɡælɪ'teəriən/ *adjective formal* believing that everyone should have the same freedom and opportunities

o⁺**egg¹** /eɡ/ *noun* **1** FOOD [C, U] an oval object produced by a female chicken, that you eat as food *a boiled/fried egg* ⊃See colour picture **Food** on page Centre 11. **2** BABY [C] an oval object with a hard shell that contains a baby bird, insect, or other creature *The bird lays* (= produces) *its eggs in a nest.* **3** FEMALE CELL [C] a cell inside a female person or animal that can develop into a baby **4 have egg on your face** to seem stupid because of something you have done ⊃See also: **Easter egg, scrambled eggs.**

egg² /eɡ/ *verb*
egg sb on to encourage someone to do something, usually something that is wrong, stupid, or dangerous *Two girls were fighting outside the club, egged on by a group of friends.*

'egg ,cup *noun* [C] a small container for holding a boiled egg while you eat it

eggplant /'eɡplɑːnt/ *US* (*UK* aubergine) *noun* [C, U] an oval, purple vegetable that is white inside ⊃See colour picture **Fruit and Vegetables** on page Centre 10.

ego /'iːɡəʊ, 'eɡəʊ/ *noun* [C] your opinion of yourself *He has a huge ego.*

egocentric /ˌiːɡəʊ'sentrɪk/ *adjective* interested only in yourself

egotism /'iːɡəʊtɪzᵊm/ (*also* egoism /'iːɡəʊɪzᵊm/) *noun* [U] when someone thinks that they are very important and is not interested in other people ● **egotist** *noun* [C] ● **egotistic** /ˌiːɡəʊ'tɪstɪk/ (*also* egotistical /ˌiːɡəʊ'tɪstɪkəl/) *adjective*

egregious /ɪ'ɡriːdʒəs/ *adjective formal* extremely bad or shocking in an obvious way *an egregious example of racism*

eh? /eɪ/ *exclamation UK informal spoken* **1** used to ask someone to repeat something because you did not hear or understand it *"You're looking tired." "Eh?" "I said, you're looking tired."* **2** used to show interest or surprise at something *Sue's had a baby girl, eh?*

Eid /iːd/ *noun* the name of two Muslim festivals. The more important one celebrates the end of Ramadan.

o⁺**eight** /eɪt/ the number 8

o⁺**eighteen** /ˌeɪ'tiːn/ the number 18 ● **eighteenth** 18th written as a word

o⁺**eighth¹** /eɪtθ/ 8th written as a word

eighth² /eɪtθ/ *noun* [C] one of eight equal parts of something; ⅛

o⁺**eighty** /'eɪti/ **1** the number 80 **2 the eighties** the years from 1980-1989 **3 be in your eighties** to be aged between 80 and 89 ● **eightieth** 80th written as a word

either¹ /'aɪðəʳ, 'iːðəʳ/ *conjunction* **either... or** used when you are giving a choice of two or more things *Either call me tonight or I'll speak to you tomorrow.*

o⁺**either²** /'aɪðəʳ, 'iːðəʳ/ *pronoun, determiner* **1** one of two people or things when it is not important which *"Would you like red or white wine?" - "Oh, either."* ○ *Ask Dom or Andrew, either of them will help you.* **2** both *People were smoking on either side* (= at both sides) *of me.* ○ *You can use the train or the bus, either way it'll take an hour.*

o⁺**either³** /'aɪðəʳ, 'iːðəʳ/ *adverb* used in negative sentences to mean that something else is also true *The menu is boring and it's not cheap either.* ⊃See Common learner error at **not.**

eject /ɪ'dʒekt/ *verb* **1** LEAVE PLACE [T] *formal* to make someone leave a place, usually using force [often passive] *He was ejected from the courtroom for shouting.* **2** LEAVE MACHINE [I, T] to come out of a machine when a button is pressed, or to make something do this *How do you eject the tape?* **3** LEAVE AIRCRAFT [I] to leave an aircraft in an emergency by being pushed out while still in your seat

eke /iːk/ *verb*
eke sth out 1 to use something slowly or carefully because you only have a small amount of it **2 eke out a living/existence** to earn only just enough money to pay for things you need *He ekes out a living by cleaning windows.*

elaborate¹ /ɪ'læbᵊrət/ *adjective* complicated, detailed, or made carefully from many parts *an elaborate system/scheme* ○ *an elaborate design* ● **elaborately** *adverb*

elaborate² /ɪ'læbᵊreɪt/ *verb* [I, T] to explain something and give more details *He wouldn't elaborate on the details.* ● **elaboration** /ɪˌlæbə'reɪʃᵊn/ *noun* [U]

elapse /ɪ'læps/ *verb* [I] *formal* If time elapses, it passes. *Two years have elapsed since the attack.*

elastic¹ /ɪ'læstɪk/ *adjective* Something that is elastic can stretch and return to its original size. *Your skin is more elastic when you are young.* ● **elasticity** /ˌiːlæs'tɪsəti/ *noun* [U] the quality of being elastic

elastic² /ɪ'læstɪk/ *noun* [U] a type of rubber that returns to its original size and shape after you stretch it

e,lastic 'band *UK* (*UK/US* rubber band) *noun* [C] a thin circle of rubber used to hold things together

elated /ɪ'leɪtɪd/ *adjective* extremely happy and excited *We were elated by/at the news.* ● **elation** /ɪ'leɪʃᵊn/ *noun* [U]

elbow¹ /'elbəʊ/ *noun* [C] the part in the middle of your arm where it bends ⊃See colour picture **The Body** on page Centre 13.

elbow² /'elbəʊ/ *verb* [T] to push someone with

your elbow, especially so you can move past them *He **elbowed his way through** the crowds of shoppers.*

'elbow ,room *noun* [U] space to move easily

elder[1] /'eldə^r/ *adjective* **elder brother/daughter/ sister, etc** the older of two brothers/daughters/sisters, etc ⊃See Common learner error at **old**.

elder[2] /'eldə^r/ *noun* **1 the elder** the oldest of two people *He's the elder of two sons.* **2 your elders** people older than you *I was taught to respect my elders.* **3** [C] an important, respected, older member of a group

elderly /'eldə^oli/ *adjective* a more polite word for 'old', used to describe people *an elderly man* ○ *Children should show respect for the elderly.*

eldest /'eldɪst/ *adjective* **eldest child/daughter/ brother, etc** the oldest child/daughter/brother, etc *My eldest brother is a doctor.* ○ *Susan is the eldest of three sisters.*

e-learning /'iːˌlɜːnɪŋ/ *noun* [U] electronic learning: the business of providing courses online for students so that they can study and learn from home

elect /ɪ'lekt/ *verb* **1** [T] to choose someone for a particular job or position by voting [often passive] *She was **elected to** the US Senate in 2004.* ○ *He was elected president in 1997.* **2 elect to do sth** *formal* to choose to do something *The children elected to stay with their mother.* ⊃See also: re-elect.

◦᱃**election** /ɪ'lekʃ^on/ *noun* [C, U] a time when people vote in order to choose someone for a political or official job *a presidential election* ○ *Who do you think will **win the election**?* ○ *Will you **stand/run for election** again this year?* ⊃See also: by-election, general election, re-election.

e'lection ,day *US* (*UK* polling day) *noun* [C] the day when people vote in an election

electoral /ɪ'lekt^or^ol/ *adjective* [always before noun] relating to elections *the **electoral system*** ○ *electoral reform*

electorate /ɪ'lekt^orət/ *noun* [group] the people who are allowed to vote in an election *the British electorate*

◦᱃**electric** /ɪ'lektrɪk/ *adjective* **1** EQUIPMENT Electric lights, tools, etc work using electricity. *an electric light/heater* **2** SUPPLY supplying electricity *an electric socket* ○ *electric current* **3** EXCITING full of excitement and emotion *The atmosphere backstage was electric.*

electrical /ɪ'lektrɪk^ol/ *adjective* **1** Electrical goods or equipment work using electricity. *electrical appliances/goods* **2** relating to the production and supply of electricity *Fernando is studying to be an electrical engineer.*

the e,lectric 'chair *noun* a chair used in parts of the US to kill a criminal using electricity

electrician /ɪˌlek'trɪʃ^on/ *noun* [C] someone whose job is to put in, check, or repair electrical wires and equipment

◦᱃**electricity** /ɪˌlek'trɪsəti/ *noun* [U] a type of energy that can produce light and heat, or make machines work *The electricity has been turned off.* ○ *an electricity bill*

e,lectric 'shock *noun* [C] a sudden, painful feeling that you get when electricity flows through your body

electrify /ɪ'lektrɪfaɪ/ *verb* [T] **1** to make people who are watching something feel very excited *She electrified the crowd with her fantastic performance.* **2** to supply something with electricity *an electrified railway*

electrocute /ɪ'lektrəkjuːt/ *verb* [T] to kill someone by causing electricity to flow through their body [often passive] *He was electrocuted while playing on a railway line.* • **electrocution** /ɪˌlektrə'kjuːʃ^on/ *noun* [U]

electrode /ɪ'lektrəʊd/ *noun* [C] the point where an electric current enters or leaves something such as a battery (= object which provides electricity)

electron /ɪ'lektrɒn/ *noun* [C] an extremely small piece of an atom with a negative electrical charge

◦᱃**electronic** /ɪˌlek'trɒnɪk/ *adjective* **1** Electronic equipment consists of things such as computers, televisions, and radios. **2** Electronic music, games, etc use electronic equipment. • **electronically** *adverb*

electronics /ɪˌlek'trɒnɪks/ *noun* [U] the science of making electronic equipment *the electronics industry*

elegance /'elɪgəns/ *noun* [U] when someone or something is stylish or attractive in their appearance or behaviour

elegant /'elɪgənt/ *adjective* stylish or attractive in appearance or behaviour *an elegant dining room* ○ *She's a very elegant woman.* • **elegantly** *adverb*

element /'elɪmənt/ *noun* **1** PART [C] a part of something *This book has all the elements of a good detective story.* **2 an element of sth** a small amount of an emotion or quality *There's an element of truth in what she says.* **3** PEOPLE [C] a group of people of a particular type *The disruptive element on the committee voted against the proposal.* **4** SIMPLE SUBSTANCE [C] a simple substance which cannot be reduced to smaller chemical parts *Iron is one of the elements of the Earth's crust.* **5** HEAT [C] the part of a piece of electrical equipment which produces heat **6 be in your element** to be happy because you are doing what you like doing and what you are good at *I'm in my element at a children's party.*

elementary /ˌelɪ'ment^ori/ *adjective* **1** basic *I only have an elementary knowledge of physics.* ○ *an elementary mistake* **2** relating to the early stages of studying a subject *students at elementary level*

ele'mentary ,school *US* (*UK* primary school)

noun [C] a school for children from the ages of five to eleven

elements /ˈelɪmənts/ *noun* **the elements** the weather, especially bad weather *Shall we* ***brave the elements*** *and go out for a walk?*

elephant

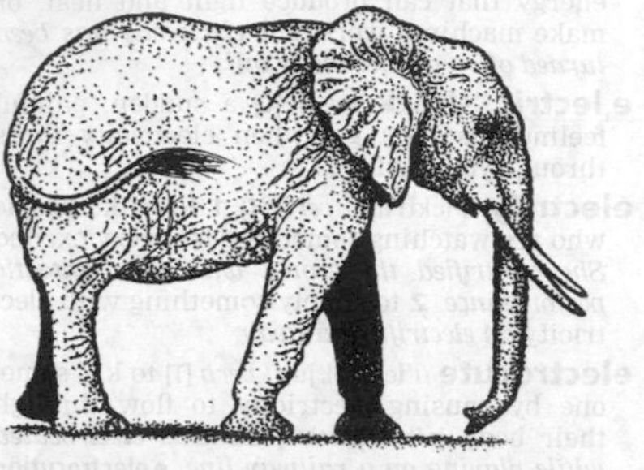

elephant /ˈelɪfənt/ *noun* [C] a very large, grey animal with big ears and a very long nose

elevate /ˈelɪveɪt/ *verb formal* **1 be elevated to sth** to be given a more important position *She has been elevated to deputy manager.* ○ *an elevated position* **2** [T] to move something to a higher level or height *High stress levels elevate blood pressure.* ○ *Try to keep your leg elevated.*

elevation /ˌelɪˈveɪʃən/ *noun* **1** [C] the height of a place above the level of the sea *The hotel is situated at an elevation of 1000m.* **2** [U] *formal* when someone or something is given a more important position *his sudden* ***elevation to*** *stardom*

elevator /ˈelɪveɪtər/ *US* (*UK* **lift**) *noun* [C] a machine that carries people up and down in tall buildings

o→**eleven** /ɪˈlevən/ the number 11 • **eleventh** 11th written as a word

elf /elf/ *noun* [C] *plural* **elves** a small person with pointed ears who has magic powers in children's stories

elicit /ɪˈlɪsɪt/ *verb* [T] *formal* to get information or a reaction from someone *You have to ask the right questions to* ***elicit*** *the* ***information*** *you want.*

eligible /ˈelɪdʒəbl/ *adjective* **1** If you are eligible to do something, you can do it because you are in the right situation. [+ to do sth] *Only people over 18 are eligible to vote.* ○ *You might be* ***eligible for*** *a grant for your studies.* ⊃Opposite **ineligible. 2** If someone who is not married is eligible, they would be a good husband or wife because they are rich, attractive, etc. *an eligible young bachelor* • **eligibility** /ˌelɪdʒəˈbɪləti/ *noun* [U]

eliminate /ɪˈlɪmɪneɪt/ *verb* [T] **1** to remove something from something, or get rid of something *The doctor advised me to* ***eliminate*** *salt* ***from*** *my diet.* **2** to defeat someone so that they cannot go any further in a competition [often passive] *She was eliminated after the first round of the tournament.*

elimination /ɪˌlɪmɪˈneɪʃən/ *noun* **1** [U] when you eliminate someone or something **2 a process of elimination** when you remove all possible answers to something until only one remains

elite /ɪˈliːt/ *noun* [group] the richest, most powerful, or best educated group in a society *a member of the elite* ○ *an elite group*

elitism /ɪˈliːtɪzəm/ *noun* [U] when a small group of rich, powerful, or educated people are given an advantage in a situation • **elitist** *adjective elitist attitudes*

elm /elm/ *noun* [C, U] a large tree which loses its leaves in winter

elocution /ˌeləˈkjuːʃən/ *noun* [U] the skill of speaking in a careful, clear way

elongated /ˈiːlɒŋgeɪtɪd/ [US] /iːˈlɒŋgeɪtɪd/ *adjective* longer and thinner than usual

elope /ɪˈləʊp/ *verb* [I] to leave home secretly with someone in order to get married

eloquent /ˈeləkwənt/ *adjective* expressing ideas clearly and in a way that influences people *the most eloquent speaker at the conference* • **eloquence** /ˈeləkwəns/ *noun* [U] when someone or something is eloquent • **eloquently** *adverb*

o→**else** /els/ *adverb* **1** [IN ADDITION] in addition to someone or something *Would you like* ***anything else*** *to eat?* ○ ***What else*** *did he say?* **2** [DIFFERENT] different from someone or something *I don't like it here. Let's go* ***somewhere else.*** ○ *I didn't say that. It must have been* ***someone else.*** **3** [OTHER] other things or people *I forgot my toothbrush, but I remembered* ***everything else.*** **4 or else a** [COMPARE] used to compare two different things or situations *He talks to her all the time, or else he completely ignores her.* **b** [IF NOT] used to say what will happen if another thing does not happen *We must be there by six, or else we'll miss the beginning.* **5 if all else fails** if no other plan is successful *If all else fails, you're welcome to stay at our house overnight.*

elsewhere /ˌelsˈweər/ *adverb* in or to another place *The report studies economic growth in Europe and elsewhere.* ○ *If we can't find it here, we'll have to* ***go elsewhere.***

ELT /ˌiːelˈtiː/ *noun* [U] *abbreviation for* English Language Teaching: the teaching of English to students whose first language is not English

elucidate /ɪˈluːsɪdeɪt/ *verb* [T] *formal* to explain something, or make it clear

elude /ɪˈluːd/ *verb* [T] *formal* **1** [NOT ACHIEVE] If something that you want eludes you, you do not succeed in achieving it. *The gold medal continues to elude her.* **2** [NOT BE CAUGHT] to not be caught by someone *He eluded the police for years before he was arrested.* **3** [NOT REMEMBER] If a piece of information eludes you, you cannot remember it.

elusive /ɪˈluːsɪv/ *adjective* difficult to describe, find, achieve, or remember *The answers to these questions remain as elusive as ever.*

elves /elvz/ *plural of* elf

'em /əm/ *informal spoken short for* them

emaciated /ɪˈmeɪsieɪtɪd/ *adjective* very thin and weak because of being ill or not eating enough food

get/send an email ● by email ● in an email
● an email address/attachment

o╍**email** (*also* e-mail) /'i:meɪl/ *noun* 1 [U] a system
for sending messages electronically, especially
from one computer to another using the Internet *You can contact me by email.* ○ *What's
your email address?* 2 [C, U] a message sent
electronically *I got an email from Danielle
yesterday.* ● email *verb* [T] to send a message
using email ⊃See Extra help page **Emailing and
texting on page Centre 37**.

emanate /'emənert/ *verb formal*
emanate from sth to come from something *Strange noises emanated from the room
next door.*

emancipate /ɪ'mænsɪpeɪt/ *verb* [T] *formal* to
give people more freedom or rights by removing social, legal, or political controls that
limit them *emancipated women* ● **emancipation**
/ɪ,mænsɪ'peɪʃᵊn/ *noun* [U]

embalm /ɪm'bɑːm/ *verb* [T] to use oils and chemicals to prevent a dead body from decaying

embankment /ɪm'bæŋkmənt/ *noun* [C] an artificial slope built from soil or stones to stop
floods, or to support a road or railway *a railway embankment*

embargo /ɪm'bɑːgəʊ/ *noun* [C] *plural* embargoes
an order by a government to stop trade with
another country *an arms/oil embargo* ○ *We
will not lift* (= stop) *the trade embargo until
they end this war.*

embark /ɪm'bɑːk/ *verb* [I] to get on a ship, boat,
or aircraft to begin a journey ⊃Opposite disembark.
embark on/upon sth to start something
new or important *You're never too old to
embark on a new career.*

embarrass /ɪm'bærəs/ *verb* [T] to make someone feel ashamed or shy *My dad's always embarrassing me in front of my friends.*

embarrassed /ɪm'bærəst/ *adjective* feeling
ashamed or shy *She felt embarrassed about
undressing in front of the doctor.* ○ [+ to do sth] *I
was too embarrassed to admit that I was scared.*

embarrassing /ɪm'bærəsɪŋ/ *adjective* making
you feel embarrassed *an embarrassing defeat*
○ *What has been your most embarrassing
moment?* ● **embarrassingly** *adverb The play was
embarrassingly bad.*

acute/great/huge embarrassment ● a **source
of** embarrassment ● the embarrassment **of**
doing sth

embarrassment /ɪm'bærəsmənt/ *noun* 1 [U]
when you feel embarrassed *He blushed with
embarrassment.* ○ *Her behaviour has caused
great embarrassment to her family.* 2 [C] something or someone that makes you feel embarrassed *He is becoming an embarrassment to
the government.*

embassy /'embəsi/ *noun* [C] the official group of
people who live in a foreign country and
represent their government there, or the

building where they work

embedded /ɪm'bedɪd/ *adjective* 1 fixed into the
surface of something *A small piece of glass was
embedded in his finger.* 2 If an emotion, attitude, etc is embedded in someone or something, it is a very strong and important part of
them. *A sense of guilt was deeply embedded in
my conscience.*

embellish /ɪm'belɪʃ/ *verb* [T] to make something more beautiful or interesting by adding
something to it *Sebastian embellished the story
with lots of dramatic detail.* ● **embellishment**
noun [C, U]

embers /'embəz/ *noun* [plural] pieces of wood or
coal that continue to burn after a fire has no
more flames

embezzle /ɪm'bezl/ *verb* [T] to steal money that
belongs to the company or organization that
you work for ● **embezzlement** *noun* [U]

embittered /ɪm'bɪtəd/ *adjective* very angry
about unfair things that have happened to
you

emblazoned /ɪm'bleɪz²nd/ *adjective* decorated
in a very obvious way with something such as
a name or a design *Her T-shirt was emblazoned with the company logo.*

emblem /'embləm/ *noun* [C] a picture, object, or
symbol that is used to represent a person,
group, or idea *The rose is the national emblem
of England.*

embodiment /ɪm'bɒdɪmənt/ *noun* the **embodiment of sth** If someone or something is the embodiment of a particular idea or quality, they
express or represent it exactly. *The mother in
the story is the embodiment of evil.*

embody /ɪm'bɒdi/ *verb* [T] to represent an idea
or quality exactly *He embodies the values of
hard work and fair play.*

embrace[1] /ɪm'breɪs/ *verb* 1 HOLD [I, T] If you
embrace someone, you put your arms around
them, and if two people embrace, they put
their arms around each other. 2 ACCEPT [T] to
accept new ideas, beliefs, methods, etc in an
enthusiastic way *We are always eager to embrace the latest technology.* 3 INCLUDE [T] *formal*
to include a number of things *The report em
braces a wide range of opinions.*

embrace[2] /ɪm'breɪs/ *noun* [C] when you put
your arms around someone *He held her in a
passionate embrace.*

embroider /ɪm'brɔɪdəʳ/ *verb* 1 [I, T] to decorate
cloth by sewing small patterns or pictures
onto it 2 [T] to add imaginary details to a story
to make it more interesting *They accused him
of embroidering the facts.*

embroidery /ɪm'brɔɪd²ri/ *noun* [U] 1 the activity of sewing small patterns or pictures onto
things 2 decoration on cloth made by sewing
small patterns or pictures onto it

embroil /ɪm'brɔɪl/ *verb formal* be embroiled in
sth to be involved in an argument or difficult
situation *We don't want to become embroiled in
a dispute over ownership.*

embryo /'embriəʊ/ *noun* [C] a human or an
animal that is starting to develop in its
mother's uterus

| j yes | k cat | ŋ ring | ʃ she | θ thin | ð this | ʒ decision | dʒ jar | tʃ chip | æ cat | e bed | ə ago | ɪ sit | i cosy | ɒ hot | ʌ run | ʊ put |

embryonic

embryonic /ˌembriˈɒnɪk/ *adjective* starting to develop *The project is still at an embryonic stage.*

emerald /ˈemərₐld/ *noun* **1** [C] a bright green stone used in jewellery **2** [U] (*also* ˌemerald ˈgreen) a bright green colour ● **emerald** *adjective*

emerge /ɪˈmɜːdʒ/ *verb* [I] **1** [COME OUT] to appear from somewhere or come out of somewhere *A figure emerged from the shadows.* **2** [BECOME KNOWN] to become known *It emerged that she had lied to her employers.* **3** [DIFFICULT SITUATION] to reach the end of a difficult situation *They emerged victorious from the fight.* ● **emergence** *noun* [U]

> ### WORD PARTNERS FOR *emergency*
> **cope with/respond to** an emergency ● a **major/real** emergency ● **in** an emergency

emergency /ɪˈmɜːdʒ³nsi/ *noun* [C] a serious or dangerous situation that needs immediate action *You should only ring this number in an emergency.* ○ *an emergency exit*

eˈmergency ˌbrake *US* (*UK* handbrake) *noun* [C] a stick inside a car that you can pull up to stop the car from moving ➪See colour picture **Car** on page Centre 7.

eˈmergency ˌroom *US* (*UK* casualty) *noun* [C] the part of a hospital where people go when they have been injured or have urgent illnesses so that they can be treated immediately

eˌmergency ˈservices *noun* [plural] the organizations who deal with accidents and urgent problems such as fire, illness, or crime

emerging /ɪˈmɜːdʒɪŋ/ *adjective* [always before noun] starting to exist or develop *emerging economies/markets*

emigrant /ˈemɪgrənt/ *noun* [C] someone who leaves their own country to go and live in another one

emigrate /ˈemɪgreɪt/ *verb* [I] to leave your own country to go and live in another one *We're thinking of emigrating to New Zealand.* ● **emigration** /ˌemɪˈgreɪʃ³n/ *noun* [U]

eminent /ˈemɪnənt/ *adjective* famous, respected, or important *an eminent historian* ● **eminence** /ˈemɪnəns/ *noun* [U] ➪See also: **preeminent.**

eminently /ˈemɪnəntli/ *adverb formal* very *He is eminently qualified for the job.*

emission /ɪˈmɪʃ³n/ *noun* [C, U] when gas, heat, light, etc is sent out into the air, or an amount of gas, heat, light, etc that is sent out *Carbon dioxide emissions will be reduced by 20%.*

emit /ɪˈmɪt/ *verb* [T] emitting, *past* emitted to send out gas, heat, light, etc into the air *The machine emits a high-pitched sound when you press the button.*

emoticon /ɪˈməʊtɪkɒn/ *noun* [C] an image such as :-) which looks like a face when you look at it from the side, made using keyboard symbols and used in emails to express emotions ➪See Extra help page **Emailing and texting** on page Centre 37.

> ### WORD PARTNERS FOR *emotion*
> **display / experience / feel / show** emotion ● **deep/powerful/strong** emotion

emotion /ɪˈməʊʃ³n/ *noun* [C, U] a strong feeling such as love or anger, or strong feelings in general *He finds it hard to express his emotions.* ○ *She was overcome with emotion and burst into tears.*

emotional /ɪˈməʊʃ³n³l/ *adjective* **1** [EMOTIONS] relating to emotions *a child's emotional development* **2** [STRONG FEELINGS] showing strong feelings, or making people have strong feelings *an emotional speech* ○ *After the argument, I was feeling confused and emotional.* **3** [PERSON] An emotional person shows their emotions very easily or very often. ● **emotionally** *adverb*

emotive /ɪˈməʊtɪv/ *adjective* making people feel strong emotions *Animal experimentation is a very emotive issue.*

empathy /ˈempəθi/ *noun* [U] the ability to imagine what it must be like to be in someone's situation ● **empathize** (*also UK* -ise) /ˈempəθaɪz/ *verb* [I] to feel empathy with someone *I think people find it easy to empathize with the main character.*

emperor /ˈempərəʳ/ *noun* [C] the male ruler of an empire (= group of countries ruled by one person or government) *Emperor Charlemagne*

emphasis /ˈemfəsɪs/ *noun* [C, U] *plural* emphases /ˈemfəsiːz/ **1** particular importance or attention that you give to something *Schools are starting to place/put greater emphasis on passing exams.* **2** the extra force that you give to a word or part of a word when you are saying it *The emphasis is on the final syllable.*

emphasize (*also UK* -ise) /ˈemfəsaɪz/ *verb* [T] to show that something is especially important or needs special attention *The government is emphasizing the importance of voting in the election.* ○ [+ that] *He emphasized that the driver was not to blame for the accident.*

emphatic /ɪmˈfætɪk/ *adjective* done or said in a strong way and without any doubt *an emphatic victory* ● **emphatically** *adverb*

empire /ˈempaɪəʳ/ *noun* [C] **1** a group of countries that is ruled by one person or government **2** a large group of businesses that is controlled by one person or company *a publishing empire*

empirical /ɪmˈpɪrɪk³l/ *adjective formal* based on experience or scientific experiments and not only on ideas *empirical evidence* ● **empirically** *adverb*

employ /ɪmˈplɔɪ/ *verb* [T] **1** If a person or company employs someone, they pay that person to work for them. *The company employs 2500 staff.* ○ [+ to do sth] *They employ her to look after their children.* **2** *formal* to use something *Companies employ clever tactics to persuade us to buy their products.*

employee /ɪmˈplɔɪiː/ *noun* [C] someone who is paid to work for a person or company

employer /ɪmˈplɔɪəʳ/ *noun* [C] a person or company that pays people to work for them

> ### WORD PARTNERS FOR *employment*
> **find/offer/provide/seek** employment ● **gainful/paid/temporary** employment ● **be in** employment ● **full-time/part-time** employment

o⌐**employment** /ɪm'plɔɪmənt/ noun [U] **1** when someone is paid to work for a person or company *full-time/part-time employment* ○ *It is not easy to find employment in the country-side.* ○ *employment opportunities/rights* ⊃Compare unemployment. **2** formal the use of something *the employment of capital punishment*

empower /ɪm'paʊəʳ/ verb **1** [T] to give someone the confidence, skills, freedom, etc to do something [+ to do sth] *Education empowers people to take control of their lives.* **2** be empowered to do sth to have the legal or official right to do something

empress /'emprəs/ noun [C] the female ruler, or the wife of a male ruler, of an empire (= group of countries ruled by one person or government) *Empress Josephine*

o⌐**empty**[1] /'empti/ adjective **1** If something is empty, it does not contain any things or people. *an empty house/street* ○ *empty bottles/ glasses* ○ *The train was completely empty when it reached London.* ⊃See picture at full. **2** having no meaning or value *an empty promise/ threat* ● emptiness noun [U]

empty[2] /'empti/ verb **1** [T] (*also* empty out) If you empty a container, or if you empty the things inside it, you remove everything from it. *He emptied the dirty water into the sink.* **2** [I] to become empty *The room emptied rapidly when the fire started.*

empty-handed /ˌempti'hændɪd/ adjective without bringing or taking anything *We can't go to the party empty-handed.*

emulate /'emjəleɪt/ verb [T] formal to try to be like someone or something that you admire or that is successful *They hope to emulate the success of other software companies.*

emulsion /ɪ'mʌlʃən/ noun [U] paint used to cover walls, ceilings, etc

enable /ɪ'neɪbl/ verb [T] to make someone able to do something, or to make something possible [+ to do sth] *This money has enabled me to buy a new computer.*

-enabled /ɪ'neɪbᵊld/ suffix **1** having the necessary equipment or system to use something *Bluetooth-enabled mobile phones* **2** used or made possible by using a particular thing *voice-enabled software*

enact /ɪ'nækt/ verb [T] **1** to make something into a law [often passive] *When was this legislation enacted?* **2** formal to perform a story or play ● enactment noun [U]

enamel /ɪ'næmᵊl/ noun [U] **1** a hard, shiny substance that is used to decorate or protect metal or clay **2** the hard, white substance that covers your teeth

enamoured UK formal (US enamored) /ɪ'næməd/ adjective be enamoured of/with sb/sth to like someone or something very much

enc (*also* encl) written abbreviation for enclosed: used at the end of a business letter to show that there is something else in the envelope

encapsulate /ɪn'kæpsjəleɪt/ verb [T] to express or show the most important facts about something *The film encapsulates the essence of that period.*

encase /ɪn'keɪs/ verb formal be encased in sth to be completely covered in something *The outside walls are encased in concrete.*

enchanted /ɪn'tʃɑːntɪd/ adjective **1** If you are enchanted by something, you like it very much. *She was enchanted by the Scottish landscape.* **2** affected by magic *an enchanted forest*

enchanting /ɪn'tʃɑːntɪŋ/ adjective very nice *What an enchanting child!*

encircle /ɪn'sɜːkl/ verb [T] formal to form a circle around something [often passive] *The house is encircled by a high fence.*

enclave /'enkleɪv/ noun [C] a place which is different from the area that is around it because its people have a different language or culture *an Italian enclave in Switzerland*

enclose /ɪn'kləʊz/ verb [T] **1** to send something in the same envelope or parcel as something else *I enclose a map of the area.* **2** to be all around something and separate it from other things or places ● enclosed adjective *He doesn't like enclosed spaces.*

enclosure /ɪn'kləʊʒəʳ/ noun [C] a small area of land that has a wall or fence around it

encompass /ɪn'kʌmpəs/ verb [T] to include a lot of things, ideas, places, etc *Their albums encompass a wide range of music.*

encore /'ɒŋkɔːʳ/ noun [C] an extra song or piece of music that is performed at the end of a show because the audience shout for it

encounter[1] /ɪn'kaʊntəʳ/ verb [T] **1** to experience something unpleasant *We encountered quite a few problems at the beginning.* **2** literary to meet someone, especially when you do not expect it

▨▨▨ WORD PARTNERS FOR **encounter**

have an encounter   ● a **chance** encounter ● an encounter **with** sb

encounter[2] /ɪn'kaʊntəʳ/ noun [C] a meeting, especially one that happens by chance

o⌐**encourage** /ɪn'kʌrɪdʒ/ verb [T] **1** to make someone more likely to do something, or make something more likely to happen [+ to do sth] *My parents encouraged me to try new things.* ○ *Cutting back plants will encourage growth.* **2** to give someone confidence or hope *My parents encouraged me when things weren't going well at school.* ⊃Opposite discourage. ● encouragement noun [C, U] *Children need lots of encouragement from their parents.*

encouraged /ɪn'kʌrɪdʒd/ adjective having more confidence or hope about something *We were very encouraged by his exam results.*

encouraging /ɪn'kʌrɪdʒɪŋ/ adjective making you feel more hope and confidence *The team's performance was very encouraging.* ⊃Opposite discouraging. ● encouragingly adverb

encroach /ɪn'krəʊtʃ/ verb

encroach on/upon sth to gradually take away someone's rights, power, etc, or get control of something, often without being noticed *My job is starting to encroach on my family life.*

encrusted /ɪn'krʌstɪd/ adjective covered with something hard, for example dirt or stones *My trousers were encrusted with mud.*

E

encrypt /ɪnˈkrɪpt/ *verb* [T] to change electronic information into a secret system of letters, numbers, or symbols • **encryption** *noun* [U]

encyclopedia (*also* *UK* **encyclopaedia**) /ɪnˌsaɪkləˈpiːdiə/ *noun* [C] a book or a set of books containing facts about a lot of subjects

end¹ /end/ *noun* **1** [FINAL PART] [no plural] the final part of something such as a period of time, activity, or story *I'll pay you at the end of next month.* ○ *I didn't meet him until the end of the course.* ○ *a film with a twist at the end* **2** [FURTHEST PART] [C] the furthest part or final part of a place or thing *They live at the other end of the street.* ○ *They were standing at opposite ends of the room.* **3** [STOP] [C] when something stops happening [usually singular] *They are calling for an end to the violence.* **4 in the end** finally, after something has been thought about or discussed a lot **5 come to an end** to finish **6 put an end to sth** to make something stop happening or existing *He's determined to put an end to these rumours.* **7 bring sth to an end** to make something finish *The stories in the newspaper brought her career to a sudden end.* **8 no end** *informal* a lot *I've had no end of trouble finding a hotel room.* **9 for hours/days, etc on end** for days, hours, etc without stopping *He waited by the telephone for hours on end.* **10** [INTENTION] [C] an intention or purpose *She only has one end in mind.* **11 be at a loose end** to have nothing to do *Come and visit us if you're at a loose end over the weekend.* **12 at the end of the day** *UK* something that you say before you give the most important fact of a situation *At the end of the day, what matters is that you're safe.* **13 at the end of your tether** (*also US* **at the end of your rope**) so tired, annoyed, or worried by something that you do not feel that you can deal with it **14 get (hold of) the wrong end of the stick** to not understand a situation correctly *My mum got the wrong end of the stick and thought that Jim was my boyfriend.* **15 make ends meet** to have just enough money to pay for the things that you need *I've taken a second job in the evenings just to make ends meet.* **16 not be the end of the world** If something is not the end of the world, it will not cause very serious problems. *It won't be the end of the world if I don't get the job.* **17 be on/at the receiving end of sth** If you are on the receiving end of something, you suffer something unpleasant when you have done nothing to deserve it. *They are often on the receiving end of verbal abuse from angry customers.* **18 throw sb in at the deep end** to make someone start a new and difficult job or activity without helping them or preparing them for it ➔See also: **dead end**, **light¹** at the end of the tunnel, **odds** and ends, the **tail¹** end of sth, the **West End**, be at your **wits'** end.

◦▪**end²** /end/ *verb* [I, T] to finish or stop, or to make something finish or stop *What time does the concert end?* ○ *These talks do not look likely to end the war.*

end in/with sth to finish in a particular way *The evening ended in a big argument.*

end up to finally be in a particular place or situation *I never thought he'd end up in prison.* ○ [+ doing sth] *He always ends up doing what Alan wants to do.* ○ *She'll end up pregnant.*

endanger /ɪnˈdeɪndʒəʳ/ *verb* [T] to put someone or something in a situation where they might be harmed or seriously damaged *He would never do anything to endanger the children's lives.*

endangered /ɪnˈdeɪndʒəd/ *adjective* **endangered birds/plants/species, etc** animals or plants which may soon not exist because there are very few now alive

endear /ɪnˈdɪəʳ/ *verb*

endear sb to sb If a quality in someone's character, or their behaviour endears them to you, it makes you like them.

endearing /ɪnˈdɪərɪŋ/ *adjective* An endearing quality is one that makes people like you.

endeavour *UK formal* (*US* **endeavor**) /ɪnˈdevəʳ/ *verb* **endeavour to do sth** to try very hard to do something *I endeavoured to help her, but she wouldn't let me.* • **endeavour** *noun* [C, U] *human/artistic endeavour*

endemic /enˈdemɪk/ *adjective formal* If something unpleasant is endemic in a place or among a group of people, there is a lot of it there. *Corruption is endemic in some parts of the police force.*

ending /ˈendɪŋ/ *noun* [C] **1** the last part of a story *I hope this film has a happy ending.* **2** a part added to the end of a word *To make the plural of 'dog', you add the plural ending '-s'.*

endive /ˈendaɪv/ *noun* [C, U] a plant with bitter green leaves that are eaten in salads

endless /ˈendləs/ *adjective* continuing for a long time and never finishing, or never seeming to finish *He seems to think that I have an endless supply of money.* • **endlessly** *adverb*

endorse /ɪnˈdɔːs/ *verb* [T] *formal* to say publicly that you support a person or action [often passive] *The idea was endorsed by a majority of members.* • **endorsement** *noun* [C, U]

endow /ɪnˈdaʊ/ *verb formal* **1 be endowed with sth** to have a particular quality or characteristic *The country is richly endowed with natural resources.* **2** [T] to give a large amount of money to a college, hospital, etc

end-product /ˈendˌprɒdʌkt/ *noun* [C] the thing that you get at the end of a process or activity

endurance /ɪnˈdjʊərəns/ *noun* [U] the ability to keep doing something difficult, unpleasant, or painful for a long time *a race to test athletes' endurance*

endure /ɪnˈdjʊəʳ/ *verb* [T] *formal* to suffer something difficult, unpleasant, or painful *She's already had to endure three painful operations on her leg.*

enduring /ɪnˈdjʊərɪŋ/ *adjective* existing for a long time *the enduring popularity of cartoons*

◦▪**enemy** /ˈenəmi/ *noun* **1** [C] a person who you

dislike or oppose *I try not to **make any en-emies**.* **2** [group] a country or army that your country or army is fighting against in a war *enemy forces/territory*

energetic /ˌenə'dʒetɪk/ *adjective* having or involving a lot of energy *an energetic young woman* ○ *Aerobics is too energetic for me.* ● **energetically** *adverb*

WORD PARTNERS FOR **energy**

expend/have/save/waste energy ● boundless/high/restless/surplus energy

ₒ⸝**energy** /'enədʒi/ *noun* [C, U] **1** the power and ability to be very active without becoming tired *Looking after children takes up a lot of time and energy.* ○ [+ to do sth] *I didn't even have the energy to get out of bed.* **2** the power that comes from electricity, gas, etc *nuclear energy* ○ *energy conservation* ⇒See also: **atomic energy**.

enforce /ɪn'fɔːs/ *verb* [T] **1** to make people obey a rule or law *It is the duty of the police to enforce the law.* **2** to make a particular situation happen, or to make people accept it *The new teacher failed to enforce discipline.* ● **enforcement** *noun* [U] *law enforcement*

engage /ɪn'geɪdʒ/ *verb* [T] *formal* **1** to interest someone in something and keep them thinking about it *The debate about food safety has engaged the whole nation.* **2** to employ someone [+ to do sth] *I have engaged a secretary to deal with all my paperwork.*
  engage in sth to take part in something
  engage sb in sth If you engage someone in conversation, you start a conversation with them.

engaged /ɪn'geɪdʒd/ *adjective* **1** If two people are engaged, they have formally agreed to marry each other. *When did they **get engaged?*** **2** *UK* If a telephone line or a toilet is engaged, it is already being used.

WORD PARTNERS FOR **engagement**

announce/break off your engagement ● your engagement to sb ● an engagement party/ring

engagement /ɪn'geɪdʒmənt/ *noun* [C] **1** an agreement to get married to someone *an engagement ring* **2** an arrangement to meet someone or do something at a particular time

engaging /ɪn'geɪdʒɪŋ/ *adjective* pleasant, interesting, or attractive *She has a very engaging personality.*

engender /ɪn'dʒendər/ *verb* [T] *formal* to make people have a particular feeling or make a situation exist to exist *We want to engender loyalty to our products.*

WORD PARTNERS FOR **engine**

start/switch on/switch off/turn off the engine

ₒ⸝**engine** /'endʒɪn/ *noun* [C] **1** the part of a vehicle that uses energy from oil, electricity, or steam to make it move *a diesel/petrol engine* **2** the part of a train that pulls it along ⇒See also: **fire engine**, **search engine**.

'**engine ˌdriver** *UK* (*US* **engineer**) *noun* [C] someone whose job is to drive a train

engineer[1] /ˌendʒɪ'nɪər/ *noun* [C] **1** someone whose job is to design, build, or repair machines, engines, roads, bridges, etc *a mechanical/structural engineer* ○ *a software engineer* **2** *US* someone whose job is to drive a train

engineer[2] /ˌendʒɪ'nɪər/ *verb* [T] to arrange for something to happen, especially in a clever and secret way [often passive] *Giancarlo was convinced that the accident had been engineered by his enemies.*

engineering /ˌendʒɪ'nɪərɪŋ/ *noun* [U] the work of an engineer, or the study of this work *mechanical engineering* ⇒See also: **civil engineering**, **genetic engineering**.

English[1] /'ɪŋglɪʃ/ *noun* **1** [U] the language that is spoken in the UK, the US, and in many other countries *American/British English* ○ *Do you speak English?* **2** **the English** [plural] the people of England

English[2] /'ɪŋglɪʃ/ *adjective* **1** relating to the English language *an English teacher* **2** relating to England *English law*

ˌ**English 'breakfast** *noun* [C] *UK* a dish including cooked meat and eggs, eaten as the first meal of the day

ˌ**English 'muffin** *US* (*UK* **muffin**) *noun* [C] a small, round, flat bread that is often eaten hot with butter ⇒See picture at **muffin**.

engrave /ɪn'greɪv/ *verb* [T] to cut words or pictures into the surface of metal, stone, etc *He gave her a silver pen engraved with her name.* ● **engraver** *noun* [C]

engraving /ɪn'greɪvɪŋ/ *noun* [C] a picture printed from an engraved piece of metal or wood

engrossed /ɪn'grəʊst/ *adjective* giving all your attention to something *He was so engrossed in what he was doing that he didn't hear the bell.*

engrossing /ɪn'grəʊsɪŋ/ *adjective* very interesting, and needing all your attention *an engrossing book*

engulf /ɪn'gʌlf/ *verb* [T] **1** to surround or cover someone or something completely [often passive] *The house was quickly engulfed in flames.* **2** to affect a place or a group of people quickly and strongly *Panic is threatening to engulf the country.*

enhance /ɪn'hɑːns/ *verb* [T] *formal* to improve something *Winning that award greatly enhanced her reputation.* ● **enhancement** *noun* [C, U] when something is improved

enigma /ɪ'nɪgmə/ *noun* [C] someone or something that is mysterious and difficult to understand *She is a complete enigma to me.*

enigmatic /ˌenɪg'mætɪk/ *adjective* mysterious and impossible to understand completely

ₒ⸝**enjoy** /ɪn'dʒɔɪ/ *verb* [T] **1** If you enjoy something, it gives you pleasure. *I hope you enjoy your meal.* ○ [+ doing sth] *I really enjoyed being with him.* **2** **enjoy yourself** to get pleasure from something that you are doing *Everyone eventually relaxed and began to enjoy themselves.* **3** *formal* to have or experience something good

E

such as success *His play enjoyed great success on Broadway.*

A more formal way of saying 'enjoy' is **relish**: *Jonathan always relishes a challenge.*

When someone enjoys a situation or activity very much, you can use the phrasal verbs **lap up** or **revel in**: *He lapped up all the attention they gave him.* • *She revelled in her role as team manager.*

If someone enjoys doing something that other people think is unpleasant, the phrasal verb **delight in** is sometimes used: *She seems to delight in making other people look stupid.*

The verb **savour** (*UK*) (**savor** *US*) is sometimes used when someone enjoys something slowly so that they can appreciate it as much as possible: *It was the first chocolate he'd had for over a year, so he savoured every mouthful.*

When someone enjoys themselves very much, in informal situations you can use the expression **have a ball**: *We had a ball in Miami.*

enjoy doing something

When **enjoy** is followed by a verb, the verb must be in the -*ing* form.
My parents enjoy walking in the mountains.
~~My parents enjoy to walk in the mountains.~~

enjoyable /ɪn'dʒɔɪəbl/ *adjective* An enjoyable event or experience gives you pleasure. *We had a very enjoyable evening.*

enjoyment /ɪn'dʒɔɪmənt/ *noun* [U] when you enjoy something *She gets a lot of enjoyment from music.*

enlarge /ɪn'lɑːdʒ/ *verb* [I, T] to become bigger or to make something become bigger [often passive] *I want to get this photo enlarged.* ○ *an enlarged liver*
  enlarge on/upon sth *formal* to give more details about something that you have said or written

enlargement /ɪn'lɑːdʒmənt/ *noun* [C, U] when something is enlarged, or something that has been enlarged *I'm going to get an enlargement of this wedding photo.*

enlighten /ɪn'laɪt³n/ *verb* [T] *formal* to give someone information about something, so that they understand a situation *He believes he has a duty to enlighten the public on these matters.*

enlightened /ɪn'laɪt³nd/ *adjective* having practical, modern ideas and ways of dealing with things *an enlightened attitude*

enlightening /ɪn'laɪt³nɪŋ/ *adjective* giving you more information and understanding about something *an enlightening book*

enlist /ɪn'lɪst/ *verb* **1 enlist the help/support of sb** to ask for and get help or support from

someone *They are hoping to enlist the support of local politicians.* **2** [I] to join the army, navy, etc

enliven /ɪn'laɪv³n/ *verb* [T] to make something more interesting *The children's arrival enlivened a boring evening.*

en masse /ɒn'mæs/ *adverb* If a group of people do something en masse, they do it together as a group. *They surrendered en masse.*

enmity /'enməti/ *noun* [U] *formal* a strong feeling of hate

enormity /ɪ'nɔːməti/ *noun* **the enormity of sth** how big or important something is *He hadn't realized the enormity of the problem.*

◦•**enormous** /ɪ'nɔːməs/ *adjective* extremely large *This living room is enormous.*

enormously /ɪ'nɔːməsli/ *adverb* extremely *an enormously popular show*

◦•**enough¹** /ɪ'nʌf/ *pronoun, quantifier* **1** as much as is necessary *They had enough fuel for one week.* ○ [+ to do sth] *Have you had enough to eat?* **2** as much as or more than you want *I've got enough work at the moment, without being given any more.* **3 have had enough** to want something to stop because it is annoying you *I've had enough of your excuses.* **4 that's enough** used to tell someone to stop behaving badly

◦•**enough²** /ɪ'nʌf/ *adverb* **1** as much as is necessary [+ to do sth] *Are you old enough to vote?* ○ *You're not going fast enough.* **2** slightly, but not very *He's nice enough, but I don't really want to go out with him.* **3 funnily/oddly/strangely enough** although it may seem strange *I was dreading the party, but I really enjoyed it, funnily enough.*

enquire *UK* (*UK/US* inquire) /ɪn'kwaɪə^r/ *verb* [I, T] to ask someone for information about something *"Are you staying long?" she enquired.* ○ *I'm enquiring about dentists in the area.* • enquirer *UK* (*UK/US* inquirer) *noun* [C]
  enquire after sb *UK formal* to ask someone for information about someone else's health and what they are doing, in order to be polite
  enquire into sth *formal* to try to discover the facts about something

enquiring *UK* (*UK/US* inquiring) /ɪn'kwaɪərɪŋ/ *adjective* [always before noun] **1** always wanting to learn new things *an enquiring mind* **2** An enquiring expression on your face shows that you want to know something.

make/receive an enquiry • an enquiry **about** sth

enquiry *UK* (*UK/US* inquiry) /ɪn'kwaɪəri/ *noun* **1** QUESTION [C] *formal* a question that you ask when you want more information *We receive a lot of enquiries about tax issues.* **2** OFFICIAL PROCESS [C] an official process to discover the facts about something bad that has happened *The hospital is holding an enquiry into the accident.* **3** ASKING QUESTIONS [U] *formal* the process of asking questions in order to get information

enrage /ɪn'reɪdʒ/ *verb* [T] to make someone very angry [often passive] *Farmers are enraged by the* *government's refusal to help.*

enrich /ɪn'rɪtʃ/ *verb* [T] to improve the quality of something by adding something to it [often passive] *Our culture has been enriched by the many immigrants who live here.* • **enrichment** *noun* [U]

enrol *UK* (*US* enroll) /ɪn'rəʊl/ *verb* [I, T] **enrolling**, *past* **enrolled** to become or make someone become an official member of a course, college, or group *I've (UK)* **enrolled on**/*(US)* **enrolled in** *a creative writing course.* • **enrolment** *UK* (*US* **enrollment**) *noun* [C, U]

en route /ˌɒn'ruːt/ *adverb* on the way to or from somewhere *We stopped in Monaco en route to Switzerland.*

ensemble /ɒn'sɒmbəl/ *noun* [C] a small group of musicians or actors who regularly play or perform together

enshrined /ɪn'ʃraɪnd/ *verb formal* **be enshrined in sth** If a political or social right is enshrined in something, it is protected by being included in it. *These fundamental human rights are enshrined in the constitution.*

enslave /ɪn'sleɪv/ *verb* [T] *formal* to control someone and keep them in a bad situation [often passive] *These workers are enslaved by poverty.*

ensue /ɪn'sjuː/ *verb* [I] **ensuing**, *past* **ensued** *formal* to happen after something, often as a result of it • **ensuing** *adjective* [always before noun] *the ensuing hours/months*

en suite /ˌɒn'swiːt/ *adjective UK* An en suite bathroom is directly connected to a bedroom.

ensure /ɪn'ʃɔːʳ/ *verb* [T] *formal* to make certain that something is done or happens [+ (that)] *Please ensure that all examination papers have your name at the top.*

entail /ɪn'teɪl/ *verb* [T] to involve something *What exactly does the job entail?*

entangled /ɪn'tæŋgld/ *adjective* **1** involved with someone or something so that it is difficult to escape *I don't know how I ever got entangled in this relationship.* **2** caught in something such as a net or ropes *The dolphin had become entangled in the fishing net.*

o--**enter** /'entəʳ/ *verb* **1** [PLACE] [I, T] to come or go into a place *The police entered by the back door.* ○ *She is accused of entering the country illegally.* **2** [INFORMATION] [T] to put information into a computer, book, or document *You have to enter a password to access this information.* **3** [COMPETITION] [I, T] to take part in a competition, race, or exam, or to arrange for someone else to do this *Are you going to enter the photography competition?* **4** [ORGANIZATION] [T] to become a member of a particular organization, or start working in a particular type of job *She didn't enter the legal profession until she was 40.* **5** [PERIOD OF TIME] [T] to begin a period of time *The violence is now entering its third week.*

COMMON LEARNER ERROR

enter a place

You do not need to use a preposition after **enter**.
I entered the classroom.
~~I entered in the classroom.~~

Be careful not to use **enter** with vehicles.
The children got on the bus.
~~The children entered the bus.~~

enter into sth to start to become involved in something, especially a discussion or agreement *He refused to enter into any discussion.*

enterprise /'entəpraɪz/ *noun* **1** [BUSINESS] [C] a business or organization *a state-owned enterprise* **2** [PLAN] [C] a difficult and important plan *Putting on the concert will be a joint enterprise between the two schools.* **3** [QUALITY] [U] when someone is enthusiastic and willing to do something new and clever, although there are risks involved *The scheme shows imagination and enterprise.* ⊃See also: **free enterprise**.

enterprising /'entəpraɪzɪŋ/ *adjective* enthusiastic and willing to do something new, clever, and difficult *The film was made by an enterprising group of students.*

entertain /ˌentə'teɪn/ *verb* **1** [INTEREST] [T] to keep someone interested and help them to have an enjoyable time *We hired a clown to entertain the children.* **2** [GUEST] [I, T] to invite someone to be your guest and give them food, drink, etc *We don't entertain as much as we used to.* **3** [THINK ABOUT] *formal* to consider or be willing to accept an idea or suggestion *He had never even* **entertained the idea** *of her returning.*

entertainer /ˌentə'teɪnəʳ/ *noun* [C] someone whose job is to entertain people by singing, telling jokes, etc

entertaining /ˌentə'teɪnɪŋ/ *adjective* interesting and helping someone to have an enjoyable time *an entertaining and informative book*

o--**entertainment** /ˌentə'teɪnmənt/ *noun* [C, U] shows, films, television, or other performances or activities that entertain people *popular entertainment* ○ *There is* **live entertainment** *in the bar every night.*

enthral *UK* (*US* enthrall) /ɪn'θrɔːl/ *verb* [T] **enthralling**, *past* **enthralled** to keep someone's interest and attention completely [often passive] *The children were enthralled by the circus.* • **enthralling** *adjective* keeping someone's interest and attention completely

enthuse /ɪn'θjuːz/ *verb* [I] to express excitement about something or great interest in it *She couldn't stop enthusing about the film.*

enthusiasm /ɪn'θjuːziæzᵊm/ *noun* [U] when you feel very interested in something and would very much like to be involved in it *She has always had a lot of* **enthusiasm for** *her work.*

enthusiast /ɪn'θjuːziæst/ *noun* [C] someone who is very interested in and involved with a particular activity or subject *Akbar is such a sports enthusiast.*

enthusiastic /ɪnˌθjuːzi'æstɪk/ *adjective* showing enthusiasm *The teacher was very* **enthusiastic about** *my project.* • **enthusiastically** *adverb*

entice /ɪn'taɪs/ *verb* [T] to persuade someone to do something by offering them something pleasant [+ to do sth] *Supermarkets use all sorts of tricks to entice you to buy things.* • **enticing** *adjective* Something which is enticing attracts you by offering you something pleasant.

entire /ɪn'taɪəʳ/ *adjective* **[always before noun]** whole or complete *She spent her entire life caring for other people.*

entirely /ɪn'taɪəli/ *adverb* completely *I'm not entirely convinced that it will work.*

entirety /ɪn'taɪərəti/ *noun* **in its entirety** with all parts included *This is the first time that the book has been published in its entirety.*

entitle /ɪn'taɪtl/ *verb* **1 entitle sb to (do) sth** to give someone the right to do or have something **[often passive]** *I'm entitled to apply for citizenship.* **2 [T]** to give something a particular title *a lecture entitled "Language, Learning and Literacy"*

entitlement /ɪn'taɪtlmənt/ *noun* **[C, U]** when you have the right to do or have something

entity /'entɪti/ *noun* **[C]** something which exists apart from other things *They want the area recognized as a **separate political entity**.*

entourage /'ɒntʊrɑːʒ/ [US] /ɒntʊ'rɑːʒ/ *noun* **[group]** the group of people who travel with an important or famous person *She arrived with her usual entourage of dancers and musicians.*

WORD PARTNERS FOR ***entrance***

the **back/front/main** entrance • **at** the entrance • the entrance **to** sth

⊶**entrance** /'entrəns/ *noun* **1** [DOOR] **[C]** a door or other opening which you use to enter a building or place *They must have used the **back entrance to** the building.* ○ *I'll meet you **at the main entrance**.* **2** [COMING IN] **[C]** when someone comes into or goes into a place, especially in a way that makes people notice them *The whole room went quiet when he **made his entrance**.* **3** [RIGHT] **[U]** the right to enter a place or to join an organization, college, etc *Entrance is free, but you have to pay for your drinks.*

entranced /ɪn'trɑːnst/ *adjective* If you are entranced by someone or something, you cannot stop watching them because they are very interesting or very beautiful. *The children were entranced by the puppet show.*

entrant /'entrənt/ *noun* **[C]** someone who enters a competition, organization, or examination

entreat /ɪn'triːt/ *verb* **[T]** *formal* to try very hard to persuade someone to do something

entrenched /ɪn'trenʃt/ *adjective* Entrenched ideas are so fixed or have existed for so long that they cannot be changed. *These **attitudes** are firmly **entrenched** in our culture.*

entrepreneur /ˌɒntrəprə'nɜːʳ/ *noun* **[C]** someone who starts their own business, especially when this involves risks • **entrepreneurial** *adjective an entrepreneurial spirit*

entrust /ɪn'trʌst/ *verb* **[T]** to make someone responsible for doing something or looking after something **[often passive]** *I **was entrusted with** the task of organizing the party.*

WORD PARTNERS FOR ***entry***

allow/gain/refuse entry • entry **into/to** [a place]

⊶**entry** /'entri/ *noun* **1** [COMING IN] **[U]** when you come into or go into a place *She was **refused entry** to the US.* ○ *Police **gained entry** by breaking a window.* **2** [JOINING/TAKING PART] **[U]** when you join an organization or take part in a competition *Are there lots of exams for **entry into** the legal profession?* ○ *an entry form* **3** [COMPETITION WORK] **[C]** a piece of work that you do to try to win a competition *The first ten correct entries will receive a prize.* **4** [PIECE OF INFORMATION] **[C]** one of the pieces of information or writing that is recorded in a book such as a dictionary, or in a computer system *a diary entry* **5** [ADDING INFORMATION] **[U]** when someone puts information into something such as a computer system ***data entry***

entwined /ɪn'twaɪnd/ *adjective* **1** twisted together or twisted around something *Their arms were entwined.* **2** unable to be separated *My fate is entwined with his.*

enumerate /ɪ'njuːməreɪt/ *verb* **[T]** *formal* to name each thing on a list

envelop /ɪn'veləp/ *verb* **[T]** to completely cover something **[often passive]** *The farm was enveloped in fog.*

envelope /'envələʊp/ *noun* **[C]** a flat paper container for a letter ➲See colour picture **The Office** on page Centre 5.

enviable /'enviəbl/ *adjective* If someone is in an enviable situation, you wish that you were also in that situation. *She's in the **enviable position** of being able to choose who she works for.*

envious /'enviəs/ *adjective* wishing that you had what someone else has *She was **envious of** his successful career.* • **enviously** *adverb*

WORD PARTNERS FOR ***environment***

damage/harm/pollute/protect the environment

⊶**environment** /ɪn'vaɪərᵊnmənt/ *noun* **1 the environment** the air, land, and water where people, animals, and plants live *The new road may cause damage to the environment.* ➲See Common learner error at **nature**. **2 [C]** the situation that you live or work in, and how it influences how you feel *We are working in a very competitive environment.*

environmental /ɪnˌvaɪərᵊn'mentᵊl/ *adjective* relating to the environment *environmental damage* ○ *an environmental disaster* • **environmentally** *adverb environmentally damaging chemicals*

environmentalist /ɪnˌvaɪərᵊn'mentᵊlɪst/ *noun* **[C]** someone who tries to protect the natural environment from being damaged

enˌvironmentally 'friendly *adjective* not damaging the environment *environmentally-friendly washing powder*

envisage /ɪn'vɪzɪdʒ/ *mainly UK* (*mainly US* **envision** /ɪn'vɪʒən/) *verb* **[T]** to imagine something happening, or think that something is likely to happen *The police don't envisage any trouble at the festival.*

envoy /'envɔɪ/ *noun* **[C]** someone who is sent to represent their government in another country

envy[1] /ˈenvi/ *noun* **1** [U] the feeling that you wish you had something that someone else has *I watched with envy as he climbed into his brand new sports car.* **2 be the envy of sb** to be liked and wanted by someone *Her new office was the envy of the whole company.*

envy[2] /ˈenvi/ *verb* [T] to wish that you had something that someone else has *I envy her good looks.* ○ [+ two objects] *I don't envy him that job.*

enzyme /ˈenzaɪm/ *noun* [C] a chemical substance produced by living cells which makes particular chemical reactions happen in animals and plants

ephemeral /ɪˈfemᵊrᵊl/ *adjective* lasting for only a short time

epic /ˈepɪk/ *noun* [C] a story or film which is very long and contains a lot of action • **epic** *adjective an epic journey*

epidemic /ˌepɪˈdemɪk/ *noun* [C] when a large number of people get the same disease over the same period of time *the AIDS epidemic*

epilepsy /ˈepɪlepsi/ *noun* [U] a brain disease which can make someone become unconscious and have fits (= when you shake in an uncontrolled way)

epileptic /ˌepɪˈleptɪk/ *noun* [C] someone who suffers from epilepsy • **epileptic** *adjective*

epilogue /ˈepɪlɒg/ *noun* [C] a speech or piece of writing that is added to the end of a play or book

epiphany /ɪˈpɪfᵊni/ *noun* [U] *literary* a moment when you suddenly understand or become aware of something

episode /ˈepɪsəʊd/ *noun* [C] **1** one programme of a series shown on television *Did you see last week's episode of Lost?* **2** a single event or period of time *an important* ***episode in British history***

epitaph /ˈepɪtɑːf/ *noun* [C] words that are written to remember a dead person, usually on the stone where they are buried

epitome /ɪˈpɪtəmi/ *noun* **be the epitome of sth** to be a perfect example of a quality or type of thing *The hotel was the epitome of luxury.*

epitomize (*also UK* **-ise**) /ɪˈpɪtəmaɪz/ *verb* [T] to be a perfect example of a quality or type of thing *She epitomizes elegance and good taste.*

epoch /ˈiːpɒk/ [US] /ˈepək/ *noun* [C] *plural* **epochs** a long period of time in history

eponymous /ɪˈpɒnɪməs/ *adjective* [always before noun] *literary* An eponymous character in a play, book, etc, has the same name as the title.

⊶**equal**[1] /ˈiːkwəl/ *adjective* **1** the same in amount, number, or size *The sides are of equal length.* ○ *One metre is* ***equal to*** *39.37 inches.* **2 equal opportunities/rights, etc** opportunities/rights, etc that are the same for everyone without anyone having an unfair advantage ➲Opposite **unequal**.

equal[2] /ˈiːkwəl/ *verb* [T] *UK* **equalling**, *past* **equalled**, *US* **equaling**, *past* **equaled 1** to have the same value, size, etc as something else, often shown using a symbol (=) *Two plus two equals four.* **2** to be as good as someone or something else *She equalled her own world record in the race.*

equal[3] /ˈiːkwəl/ *noun* [C] someone who has the same ability, opportunities, or rights as someone else *The teacher treats us all as equals.*

WORD PARTNERS FOR ***equality***

racial/sexual/social equality • equality **between sb and sb**

equality /ɪˈkwɒləti/ *noun* [U] when everyone is equal and has the same opportunities, rights, etc ***racial/sexual equality*** ○ ***equality between men and women*** ➲Opposite **inequality**.

equalize (*also UK* **-ise**) /ˈiːkwᵊlaɪz/ *verb* **1** [I] *UK* to get the point in a game or competition that makes your score the same as the other team or player **2** [T] to make things or people equal

⊶**equally** /ˈiːkwəli/ *adverb* **1** [SAME DEGREE] to the same degree or level *an equally important question* ○ *She did* ***equally well in the competition*** *last year.* **2** [SAME AMOUNTS] into amounts or parts that are the same size *She shared the money equally between the four children.* **3** [SAME WAY] If you treat people equally, you treat everyone in the same way so that no one has an unfair advantage.

ˈequal ˌsign (*also* **ˈequals ˌsign**) *noun* [C] the symbol =, used to show that two things are the same in value, size, meaning, etc

equanimity /ˌekwəˈnɪməti/ *noun* [U] *formal* the ability to react calmly, especially in difficult situations

equate /ɪˈkweɪt/ *verb* [T] to consider one thing to be the same as or equal to another thing *Many people* ***equate*** *wealth* ***with*** *happiness.*

equation /ɪˈkweɪʒᵊn/ *noun* [C] when you show that two amounts are equal using mathematical symbols

equator /ɪˈkweɪtəʳ/ *noun* [U] the imaginary line around the Earth that divides it into equal north and south parts • **equatorial** /ˌekwəˈtɔːriəl/ *adjective* relating to the equator

equestrian /ɪˈkwestriən/ *adjective* relating to riding horses *She has a new job at an equestrian centre.*

equi- /ekwɪ-/ *prefix* equal, equally *equidistant* (= the same distance from two or more places)

equip /ɪˈkwɪp/ *verb* **equipping**, *past* **equipped 1 be equipped with sth** to include the things that are needed for a particular purpose *The new trains are equipped with all the latest technology.* **2** [T] to give someone the skills they need to do a particular thing [+ **to do sth**] *The course didn't really equip me to be a journalist.*

WORD PARTNERS FOR ***equipment***

install/operate/use equipment • **modern/necessary/specialist** equipment • equipment for sth

⊶**equipment** /ɪˈkwɪpmənt/ *noun* **1** [U] the things that are used for a particular activity or purpose *kitchen/office equipment* ○ *electrical equipment* (= equipment that uses electricity) **2 a piece of equipment** a tool or object used for a particular activity or purpose

COMMON LEARNER ERROR

equipment

Remember you cannot make **equipment** plural. Do not say 'equipments'.

The computer room has all the equipment you need.

equitable /ˈekwɪtəbl/ *adjective formal* treating everyone in an equal way *a fair and equitable voting system* • **equitably** *adverb*

equity /ˈekwɪti/ *noun* [U] *formal* when everyone is treated fairly and equally *pay equity* ➲Compare **inequity**.

equivalent[1] /ɪˈkwɪvələnt/ *adjective* equal in amount, value, importance, or meaning *The UK's Brit Awards are roughly* ***equivalent to*** *the Oscars.*

equivalent[2] /ɪˈkwɪvələnt/ *noun* [C] something that has the same value, importance, size, or meaning as something else *She won the* ***equivalent of*** *$5 million.*

er /ɜːr/ *exclamation UK spoken* (*US* **uh**) something that you say while you are thinking what to say next *Well, er, I'm not too sure about that.*

ER /ˌiːˈɑːr/ *noun* [C] *US abbreviation for* emergency room: the part of a hospital where people go when they have been injured or have urgent illnesses so that they can be treated immediately

era /ˈɪərə/ *noun* [C] a period of time in history that is special for a particular reason *the Victorian era* ○ *a new era of peace*

eradicate /ɪˈrædɪkeɪt/ *verb* [T] *formal* to destroy or completely get rid of something such as a social problem or a disease • **eradication** /ɪˌrædɪˈkeɪʃən/ *noun* [U]

erase /ɪˈreɪz/ [US] /ɪˈreɪs/ *verb* [T] to completely remove words, music, pictures, etc that are written or stored on a computer or other piece of equipment *I accidentally erased the tape she lent me.*

eraser /ɪˈreɪzər/ [US] /ɪˈreɪsər/ *US* (*UK* **rubber**) *noun* [C] **1** a small object which is used to remove pencil marks from paper **2** an object which is used to remove marks from a blackboard (= a large dark board that teachers write on) ➲See colour picture **The Classroom** on page Centre 6.

erect[1] /ɪˈrekt/ *adjective* straight and standing up *She stood very erect, with her hands behind her back.*

erect[2] /ɪˈrekt/ *verb* [T] *formal* to build or put up a structure *When was this building erected?*

erection /ɪˈrekʃən/ *noun* **1** [C] when a penis becomes harder and bigger than usual **2** [C, U] *formal* when a structure is built or put up, or the building itself

erode /ɪˈrəʊd/ *verb* **1** [I, T] If soil, stone, etc erodes or is eroded, it is gradually damaged and removed by the sea, rain, or wind. **[often passive]** *The coastline is slowly being eroded by the sea.* **2** [T] *formal* to gradually destroy a good quality or situation *Reports of corruption have eroded people's confidence in the police.* • **erosion** /ɪˈrəʊʒən/ *noun* [U] *soil erosion*

erotic /ɪˈrɒtɪk/ *adjective* making you feel strong sexual feelings, or involving sexual love *an erotic film* • **erotically** *adverb*

err /ɜːr/ *verb* [I] *formal* to make a mistake or do something that is wrong ➲See also: err on the side[1] of caution.

errand /ˈerənd/ *noun* [C] a short journey in order to buy or do something for someone *I've got to* ***run*** *a few* ***errands*** *this morning before we go.*

errant /ˈerənt/ *adjective* **[always before noun]** An errant person has behaved badly. *an errant husband*

erratic /ɪˈrætɪk/ *adjective* often changing suddenly and not regular *His behaviour is becoming more and more erratic.* • **erratically** *adverb*

erroneous /ɪˈrəʊniəs/ *adjective formal* not correct *an erroneous answer*

WORD PARTNERS FOR *error*

make/correct an error • a **fundamental/glaring** error • **do** sth **in** error • **human** error

⊶**error** /ˈerər/ *noun* [C, U] a mistake, especially one that can cause problems *a computer error/* ***human error*** ○ *to* ***make an error*** ○ *The documents were destroyed* ***in error*** (= by mistake) *by the police.*

erupt /ɪˈrʌpt/ *verb* [I] **1** [VOLCANO] If a volcano erupts, it suddenly throws out smoke, fire, and melted rocks. **2** [HAPPEN] to happen suddenly or violently ***Violence erupted*** *in the city on Friday night.* **3** [PERSON] to suddenly become very excited or angry, or start to shout *The whole stadium erupted when he scored the second goal.* • **eruption** /ɪˈrʌpʃən/ *noun* [C, U] *a* ***volcanic eruption***

escalate /ˈeskəleɪt/ *verb* **1** [I, T] If a violent or bad situation escalates or is escalated, it quickly becomes worse or more serious. *The fight quickly* ***escalated into*** *a riot.* **2** [I] to rise or increase quickly *Airline* ***prices escalate*** *during the holiday season.* • **escalation** /ˌeskəˈleɪʃən/ *noun* [C, U] *an* ***escalation in*** *violence*

escalator /ˈeskəleɪtər/ *noun* [C] moving stairs that take people from one level of a building to another *We* ***took*** *the* ***escalator*** *down to the basement.*

escapade /ˌeskəˈpeɪd/ *noun* [C] an exciting and sometimes dangerous experience

⊶**escape**[1] /ɪˈskeɪp/ *verb* **1** [GET AWAY] [I] to succeed in getting away from a place where you do not want to be *The two killers* ***escaped from*** *prison last night.* **2** [AVOID] [I, T] to avoid a dangerous or unpleasant situation *to* ***escape capture/injury*** **3** [FORGET] [T] If something such as a name escapes you, you cannot remember it. *The* ***name*** *of her book* ***escapes*** *me at the moment.* **4** [NOT NOTICE] [T] If something escapes your notice or attention, you do not notice or see it. *Nothing that goes on in this office* ***escapes*** *her* ***attention.*** **5** [GAS/LIQUID] [I] If a gas or liquid escapes from a pipe or container, it comes out, especially when it should not. • **escaped** *adjective an escaped prisoner*

attempt/make/plan an escape • a **lucky/ remarkable** escape • an escape **from** sth/sb

o-**escape²** /ɪˈskeɪp/ *noun* **1** [C, U] when someone succeeds in getting out of a place or a dangerous or bad situation **2 a narrow escape** when someone almost dies or almost has a very bad experience **3** [U, no plural] something that helps you to forget about your usual life or problems *I love old movies, they're such an escape from the real world.* ⊃See also: **fire escape**.

es'cape ˌ(key) (*written abbreviation* Esc) *noun* [C] the key on a computer keyboard which allows you to leave a particular screen or program *If you press the escape key, you will return to the main menu.*

escapism /ɪˈskeɪpɪzᵊm/ *noun* [U] entertainment or imagination that helps you to forget about your work and your problems • **escapist** *adjective escapist literature*

escort¹ /ˈeskɔːt/ *noun* **1** [C, U] a person or vehicle that goes somewhere with someone to protect or guard them *She was driven to court under police escort.* **2** [C] a person who goes with someone else to a social event, sometimes for payment

escort² /ɪˈskɔːt/ *verb* [T] to go somewhere with someone, often to protect or guard them *He offered to escort me home.*

Eskimo /ˈeskɪməʊ/ *noun* [C, U] *plural* Eskimos or Eskimo old fashioned another word for* Inuit (= a group of people who live in the cold, northern areas of North America, Russia, and Greenland, or a member of this group) *an Eskimo village*

ESL /ˌiːesˈel/ *noun* [U] *abbreviation for* English as a Second Language: the teaching of English to students whose first language is not English, but who live in a country where it is the main language

o-**especially** /ɪˈspeʃᵊli/ *adverb* **1** more than other things or people, or much more than usual *He's always making comments about her appearance, especially her weight.* ○ *She's especially interested in American poetry.* **2** for one particular person, purpose, or reason *I cooked this meal especially for you.* ⊃See Common learner error at **specially**.

espionage /ˈespiənɑːʒ/ *noun* [U] the activity of discovering secret information about a country or company that is fighting or competing against your *industrial espionage*

espouse /ɪˈspaʊz/ *verb* [T] *formal* to support a belief or way of life

espresso /esˈpresəʊ/ *noun* [C, U] strong, black coffee

do/write an essay • **in** an essay • an essay **on** sth

o-**essay** /ˈeseɪ/ *noun* [C] a short piece of writing about a particular subject, especially one written by a student *He wrote an essay on modern Japanese literature.*

essence /ˈesᵊns/ *noun* **1** [U, no plural] the basic or most important idea or quality of something *The essence of his argument is that we should not eat meat.* **2** [C, U] a strong liquid, usually made from a plant or flower, that is used to add a flavour or smell to something *vanilla essence*

o-**essential** /ɪˈsenʃᵊl/ *adjective* **1** very important and necessary *Computers are an essential part of our lives.* ○ *Fibre is essential for a healthy digestive system.* ○ [+ to do sth] *It is essential to arrive early for the show.* ○ [+ (that)] *It is absolutely essential that she gets this message.* **2** the most basic and important *There's one essential point I think you've forgotten.*

essentially /ɪˈsenʃᵊli/ *adverb* used when you are emphasizing the basic facts about something *What he is saying is essentially true.*

esˌsential 'oil *noun* [C, U] a strong oil made from a plant which contains its smell or other special qualities

essentials /ɪˈsenʃᵊlz/ *noun* [plural] the most important or necessary things

establish /ɪˈstæblɪʃ/ *verb* **1** START [T] to start a company or organization that will continue for a long time [often passive] *The brewery was established in 1822.* **2 establish sb/sth as sth** to put someone or something into a successful and lasting position [often reflexive] *He quickly established himself as a talented actor.* **3 establish communication/relations, etc** to start having a relationship or communicating with another company, country, or organization *The two countries have only recently established diplomatic relations.* **4** DECIDE [T] to decide something *Our first step must be to establish priorities for the weeks ahead.* **5** DISCOVER [T] to find out information or prove something [+ question word] *The police are trying to establish how she died.* • **established** *adjective*

establishment /ɪˈstæblɪʃmənt/ *noun* **1** [C] an organization or business **2** [U] when an organization, school, business, etc is started *the establishment of a new national bank* **3 the Establishment** the people and organizations that have most power and influence in a country **4 the legal/medical, etc establishment** the group of people with most influence in a particular area of work or activity

estate /ɪˈsteɪt/ *noun* [C] **1** LAND a large area of land in the countryside that is owned by one person or organization *a country estate* **2** BUILDINGS *UK* an area with a lot of buildings of the same type *an industrial estate* **3** POSSESSIONS the possessions and money that someone owns when they die ⊃See also: **housing estate, real estate**.

es'tate ˌagent *UK* (*US* real estate agent) *noun* [C] someone who sells buildings and land as their job

es'tate ˌcar *UK* (*US* station wagon) *noun* [C] a big car with a large space for bags behind the back seat

esteem /ɪˈstiːm/ *noun* [U] *formal* respect and admiration for someone *My father was held in high esteem by everyone who knew him.* ⊃See also: **self-esteem**.

esteemed /ɪˈstiːmd/ *adjective formal* respected

and admired *a **highly esteemed** professor*

esthetic /es'θetɪk/ *adjective another US spelling of* aesthetic (= relating to beauty and the way something looks) • **esthetically** *adverb*

esthetics /es'θetɪks/ *noun* [U] *another US spelling of* aesthetics (= the study of beauty)

WORD PARTNERS FOR ***estimate***

an **accurate/rough** estimate • an estimate of sth • **give** sb an estimate

estimate¹ /'estɪmət/ *noun* [C] **1** a guess of what a size, value, amount, etc might be *a **rough estimate*** **2** a written document saying how much it will probably cost to do a job *Can you **give** me an **estimate** for the work?*

⊶**estimate²** /'estɪmeɪt/ *verb* [T] to guess the cost, size, value, etc of something [+ **that**] *They estimate that a hundred people were killed in the accident.* ○ *The number of dead **is estimated at** a hundred.* • **estimated** *adjective an estimated cost*

estimation /ˌestɪ'meɪʃ°n/ *noun* [U] your opinion of someone or something *He is a total genius, **in my estimation**.*

estranged /ɪ'streɪndʒd/ *adjective formal* **1** not now communicating with a friend or a member of your family, because you have argued **2** not now living with your husband or wife *a dispute with his estranged wife* • **estrangement** *noun* [C, U]

estrogen /'iːstrədʒ°n/ [US] /'estrədʒ°n/ *noun* [U] *US spelling of* oestrogen (= a chemical substance in a woman's body)

estuary /'estjʊəri/ *noun* [C] the wide part of a river where it goes into the sea

⊶**etc** /et'set°rə/ *abbreviation for* et cetera: used at the end of a list to show that other things or people could also be added to it

etch /etʃ/ *verb* [I, T] to cut lines on a hard surface to make a picture or words

eternal /ɪ'tɜːn°l/ *adjective* continuing forever, or seeming to continue forever ***eternal youth*** • **eternally** *adverb I will be **eternally grateful** to you.*

eternity /ɪ'tɜːnəti/ *noun* **1** [U] time that continues forever, especially after death **2 an eternity** *informal* a very long time *It **seemed like an eternity** until she came back.*

ethereal /ɪ'θɪəriəl/ *adjective* very delicate and light and almost seeming not to be from this world • **ethereally** *adverb*

ethic /'eθɪk/ *noun* [no plural] a belief or idea that influences the way you think or behave

ethical /'eθɪk°l/ *adjective* **1** relating to what is right or wrong *The book raises some serious ethical questions.* **2** morally correct and good *He dealt with this case in a completely professional and ethical manner.* ⊃Opposite **unethical**. • **ethically** *adverb*

ethics /'eθɪks/ *noun* [plural] ideas and beliefs about what type of behaviour is morally right and wrong *a **code of ethics*** ○ *the ethics of genetic engineering*

ethnic /'eθnɪk/ *adjective* relating to a particular race of people ***ethnic minorities***

ethnic cleansing /ˌeθnɪk'klenzɪŋ/ *noun* [U] the use of violence to remove everyone of a particular race or religion from a country

ethos /'iːθɒs/ *noun* [no plural] the ideas and beliefs of a particular person or group

e-ticket /'iːˌtɪkɪt/ *noun* [C] a ticket, usually for someone to travel on an aircraft, that is held on a computer and is not printed on paper

etiquette /'etɪket/ *noun* [U] rules about what is polite and correct behaviour

etymology /ˌetɪ'mɒlədʒi/ *noun* [U] the study of the history and origin of words and their meanings • **etymological** /ˌetɪmə'lɒdʒɪk°l/ *adjective* • **etymologically** *adverb*

the EU /ˌiː'juː/ *noun abbreviation for* the European Union: a European political and economic organization that encourages business and good relationships between the countries that are members

euphemism /'juːfəmɪz°m/ *noun* [C, U] a polite word or phrase that is used to avoid saying something embarrassing or offensive *'Passed away' is a **euphemism for** 'died'.* • **euphemistic** /ˌjuːfə'mɪstɪk/ *adjective* • **euphemistically** *adverb*

euphoria /juː'fɔːriə/ *noun* [U] a feeling of extreme happiness and excitement • **euphoric** /juː'fɒrɪk/ *adjective*

euro /'jʊərəʊ/ *noun* [C] a unit of money used in European countries that belong to the European Union (= a European political and economic organization); €

Euro- /jʊərəʊ-/ *prefix* relating to Europe *Europop* (= pop music from Europe)

European /ˌjʊərə'piːən/ *adjective* relating or belonging to Europe *European countries/languages* ○ *the European Parliament* • **European** *noun* [C] *Many Europeans speak English.*

the ˌEuropean 'Union (*also* **the EU**) *noun* a European political and economic organization that encourages business and good relationships between the countries that are members

euthanasia /ˌjuːθə'neɪziə/ *noun* [U] when someone who is very old or very ill is killed so that they do not suffer any more ***voluntary euthanasia***

evacuate /ɪ'vækjueɪt/ *verb* [T] to move people from a dangerous place to somewhere safer *The police quickly evacuated the area after the bomb threat.* • **evacuation** /ɪˌvækju'eɪʃ°n/ *noun* [C, U] *the evacuation of civilians from the war zone*

evacuee /ɪˌvækju'iː/ *noun* [C] someone who is evacuated from a place to somewhere safer

evade /ɪ'veɪd/ *verb* **1** [T] to avoid something or someone, especially in a dishonest way *to **evade capture*** ○ *to evade paying tax* **2 evade the issue/question, etc** to intentionally not talk about something or not answer something

evaluate /ɪ'væljueɪt/ *verb* [T] *formal* to consider or study something carefully and decide how good or bad it is • **evaluation** /ɪˌvælju'eɪʃ°n/ *noun* [C, U]

evangelical /ˌiːvæn'dʒelɪk°l/ *adjective* Evangelical Christians believe that faith in Jesus Christ and studying the Bible are more important than religious ceremonies.

evaporate /ɪ'væp°reɪt/ *verb* **1** [I, T] If a liquid

evaporates or is evaporated, it changes into steam. **2** [I] If feelings evaporate, they disappear. ● **evaporation** /ɪˌvæpəˈreɪʒ³n/ *noun* [U]

evasion /ɪˈveɪʒ³n/ *noun* [C, U] when you avoid something, especially in a dishonest way *tax evasion*

evasive /ɪˈveɪsɪv/ *adjective* **1** trying to avoid talking about something *He was very evasive about his past.* ○ *an evasive answer* **2** take **evasive action** to do something to avoid an accident or bad situation ● **evasively** *adverb* ● **evasiveness** *noun* [U]

eve /iːv/ *noun* **1 Christmas Eve/New Year's Eve** the day or night before Christmas Day/New Year's Day **2 the eve of sth** the time just before something important happens *They were married in Washington on the eve of the Second World War.*

even¹ /ˈiːv³n/ *adjective* **1** FLAT flat, level, or smooth *Find an even surface to work on.* ⊃Opposite **uneven**. **2** NOT CHANGING An even temperature or rate is regular and does not change very much. **3** NUMBER An even number is a number which can be exactly divided by two, for example four, six, or eight. ⊃Opposite **odd**. **4** MONEY *informal* not now owing someone money *If you pay for my cinema ticket, we'll be even.* **5** COMPETITION An even race or competition is one that both players, teams, or people involved have an equal chance of winning. **6 get even (with sb)** *informal* If you get even with someone who has done something bad to you, you do something bad to them.

even² /ˈiːv³n/ *adverb* **1** used to emphasize something that is surprising *Everyone danced, even Mick.* **2 even better/faster/smaller, etc** used when comparing things, to emphasize the difference *I think Alex is going to be even taller than his father.* **3 even if** used to emphasize that a particular situation would not change what you have just said *I would never eat meat, even if I was really hungry.* **4 even though** although *He still smokes, even though he's got asthma.* **5 even so** used to emphasize that something surprising is true despite what you have just said *Car prices have gone down a lot, but even so, we couldn't afford to buy one.*

even³ /ˈiːv³n/ *verb*
even (sth) out to become equal, or to make something equal *Sometimes I pay and sometimes Tom does - it usually evens out in the end.*

WORD PARTNERS FOR **evening**

this/tomorrow/yesterday evening ● in the evening

o-**evening** /ˈiːvnɪŋ/ *noun* **1** [C, U] the part of the day between the afternoon and the night *Are you doing anything this evening?* ○ *I go to band practice on Monday evenings.* ○ *We usually eat our main meal in the evening.* **2 (Good) evening.** something that you say when you meet someone in the evening

evenly /ˈiːv³nli/ *adverb* **1** into equal amounts, or in a regular way *They decided to divide the prize money evenly between them.* **2 evenly matched** Two people or teams who are evenly matched are equally good, or have an equal

chance of winning.

WORD PARTNERS FOR **event**

an event **happens/occurs/takes place** ● **witness** an event ● a **dramatic/major/rare/tragic** event ● **recent** events

o-**event** /ɪˈvent/ *noun* [C] **1** something that happens, especially something important or unusual *Local people have been shocked by recent events in the town.* **2** a race, party, competition, etc that has been organized for a particular time *a social/sporting event* **3 in the event** *UK* used to emphasize what did happen when it was not what you had expected *In the event, we didn't need the extra money.* **4 in the event of sth** *formal* if something happens *An airbag could save your life in the event of an accident.* **5 in any event** whatever happens *I'm not sure if I'm coming on Friday, but in any event, I'll see you next week.* ⊃See also: **non-event**.

eventful /ɪˈventf³l/ *adjective* full of interesting or important events *a very eventful day/journey* ○ *the most eventful time of her life*

eventual /ɪˈventʃuəl/ *adjective* [always before noun] happening or existing at the end of a process or period of time *the eventual winner of the competition*

o-**eventually** /ɪˈventʃuəli/ *adverb* in the end, especially after a long time *We all hope that an agreement can be reached eventually.*

o-**ever** /ˈevə³/ *adverb* **1** at any time *Have you ever been skiing?* ○ *No one ever calls me any more.* **2 better/faster/happier, etc than ever** better/faster/happier, etc than at any time before **3 hardly ever** almost never *We hardly ever go out these days.* **4 ever since** always since that time *We met at school and have been friends ever since.* **5 ever so/ever such a** *UK* very/a very *She's ever so pretty.* **6 for ever** *UK/US* forever) always in the future *I'm not going to live here for ever.* **7 ever-changing/growing/increasing, etc** always changing/growing/increasing, etc

evergreen /ˈevəɡriːn/ *adjective* An evergreen plant has green leaves that do not fall off in winter. ● **evergreen** *noun* [C] a plant with leaves that do not fall off in winter

everlasting /ˌevəˈlɑːstɪŋ/ *adjective* continuing for a long time or always *everlasting love*

evermore /ˌevəˈmɔː³/ *adverb* *literary* always in the future

o-**every** /ˈevri/ *determiner* **1** EACH each one of a group of people or things *He knows the name of every child in the school.* ○ *Every one of the paintings was a fake.* **2** HOW OFTEN used to show that something is repeated regularly *He goes to Spain every summer.* **3** POSSIBLE as much as is possible *I'd like to wish you every success in your new job.* ○ *Every effort is being made to rectify the problem.* **4 every now and then/every so often** sometimes, but not often *We still meet up every now and then.* **5 one in every five/ten, etc** used to show how many people or things in a group are affected by or involved in something *One in three marriages now ends in divorce.*

⊶**everybody** /'evri,bɒdi/ *pronoun* another word for everyone *Everybody was asking after you.* ○ *Everybody I know seems to like his music.*

everyday /'evrideɪ/ *adjective* [always before noun] normal, usual, or happening every day *Computers are now part of everyday life.*

⊶**everyone** /'evriwʌn/ (*also* **everybody**) *pronoun* **1** every person *Everyone agreed with the decision.* ○ *Everyone gets fed up with their job from time to time.* **2 everyone else** every other person *Everyone else was wearing jeans.*

everyplace /'evripleɪs/ *adverb* US another word for everywhere *Everyplace I looked I saw people I knew.*

⊶**everything** /'evriθɪŋ/ *pronoun* **1** all things or each thing *They lost everything in the fire.* ○ *What's the matter Nick, is everything all right?* **2 everything else** all the other things *The meat tasted strange, but everything else was okay.* **3 be/mean everything** to be the most important part of someone's life *His children mean everything to him.* ○ *Of course, money isn't everything.*

⊶**everywhere** /'evriweəʳ/ *adverb* in or to every place *I've looked everywhere, but I still can't find that letter.* ○ *Everywhere I look I see things that remind me of Brendan.*

evict /ɪ'vɪkt/ *verb* [T] to legally force someone to leave the house they are living in *They were evicted after complaints from their neighbours.* ● **eviction** /ɪ'vɪkʃən/ *noun* [C, U]

WORD PARTNERS FOR **evidence**

compelling / conclusive / hard / strong / scientific evidence ● evidence of sth

⊶**evidence** /'evidəns/ *noun* [U] **1** something that makes you believe that something is true or exists *evidence of global warming* ○ [+ that] *There is no scientific evidence that the drug is addictive.* **2** information that is given or objects that are shown in a court of law to help to prove if someone has committed a crime *He was arrested despite the lack of evidence against him.* ○ *Fresh evidence suggests that he was wrongly accused of the crime.* **3 give evidence** UK to give information and answer questions in a court of law *She was called to give evidence at his trial.* **4 be in evidence** *formal* to be noticeable

evident /'evidənt/ *adjective formal* obvious to everyone and easy to see or understand [+ that] *It was evident from his voice that he was upset.* ⊃See also: self-evident.

evidently /'evidəntli/ *adverb* **1** used to say that something can easily be noticed *Evidently he didn't want the job or he would have made a little effort to keep it.* ○ *He evidently likes her.* **2** used to say that something seems probable from the information you have *The intruder evidently got in through an open window.*

evil¹ /'iːvəl/ *adjective* very cruel, bad, or harmful *an evil monster*

evil² /'iːvəl/ *noun* [C, U] something that is very bad and harmful *The theme of the play is the*

battle between **good and evil.** ⊃See also: the lesser of two evils.

evocative /ɪ'vɒkətɪv/ *adjective* making you remember or imagine something that is pleasant *evocative music* ○ **evocative of** the sea

evoke /ɪ'vəʊk/ *verb* [T] to make someone remember something or feel an emotion *The story evoked memories of my childhood.*

evolution /ˌiːvə'luːʃən/ *noun* [U] **1** the way in which living things gradually change and develop over millions of years *Darwin's theory of evolution* **2** a gradual process of change and development *the evolution of language* ● **evolutionary** *adjective*

evolve /ɪ'vɒlv/ *verb* **1** [I] to develop from other forms of life over millions of years **2** [I, T] to develop or make something develop, usually gradually *rapidly evolving technology*

ewe /juː/ *noun* [C] a female sheep

ex /eks/ *noun* [C] *informal* someone who used to be your husband, wife, or partner *My ex and his new wife live abroad.*

ex- /eks-/ *prefix* from before *an ex-boyfriend* ○ *an ex-boss*

exacerbate /ɪg'zæsəbeɪt/ *verb* [T] to make something worse *Sunny weather exacerbates the effects of pollution.*

⊶**exact¹** /ɪg'zækt/ *adjective* completely correct in every detail *I'm afraid I can't give you the exact details of the show yet.* ○ *They've lived here a long time - 25 years* **to be exact.** ● **exactness** *noun* [U]

exact² /ɪg'zækt/ *verb* [T] *formal* to demand and get something from someone

exacting /ɪg'zæktɪŋ/ *adjective* needing a lot of effort and attention *an exacting training schedule*

⊶**exactly** /ɪg'zæktli/ *adverb* **1** COMPLETELY CORRECT used when you are giving or asking for information that is completely correct *What exactly seems to be the problem?* ○ *The train got in at exactly ten o'clock.* **2** EMPHASIS used to emphasize what you are saying *I found a dress that's exactly the same colour as my shoes.* **3** AGREEMENT something you say when you agree completely with someone *"Surely they should have told us about this problem sooner?" "Exactly."* **4 not exactly** used to say that something is not completely true *"Do you live here?" "Not exactly, I'm staying with friends."* **5 not exactly easy/new/clear, etc** *informal* used to say that a description is completely untrue *Let's face it, we're not exactly rich, are we?*

exaggerate /ɪg'zædʒəreɪt/ *verb* [I, T] to make something seem larger, better, worse, etc than it really is *Don't exaggerate - it didn't cost that much!*

WORD PARTNERS FOR **exaggeration**

a **gross/slight** exaggeration • an exaggeration **of** sth

exaggeration /ɪgˌzædʒ³r'eɪʃ³n/ noun [C, U] when you describe something as larger, better, worse, etc than it really is *a gross exaggeration of the facts*

exalted /ɪg'zɔːltɪd/ adjective formal very highly respected, or with a very high position

WORD PARTNERS FOR **exam**

do/*(UK)* sit/take an exam • fail/pass an exam • exam results

o▪**exam** /ɪg'zæm/ noun [C] **1** an official test of how much you know about something, or how well you can do something *a maths exam ○ to fail/pass an exam ○ (UK) to sit/(UK/US) to take (= do) an exam* **2** US a series of medical tests *an eye exam*

COMMON LEARNER ERROR

take/sit an exam

To **take an exam** means to do an official test. 'Sit' is slightly more formal than 'take' in this phrase and is only used in the UK.
We have to take an exam at the end of the course.
~~We have to write an exam at the end of the course.~~
If you **pass an exam**, you are successful because you get a good mark. If you **fail an exam**, you are not successful because you get a bad mark.

examination /ɪgˌzæmɪ'neɪʃ³n/ noun **1** [C, U] when someone looks at something very carefully *a medical examination ○ a close examination of the facts* **2** [C] formal an exam *a written examination*

examine /ɪg'zæmɪn/ verb [T] **1** LOOK AT to look at someone or something very carefully, especially to try to discover something *She picked up the knife and examined it closely. ○ He was examined by a doctor as soon as he arrived.* **2** TEST formal to test someone to see how much they know or how well they can do something *You'll be examined in three main areas: speaking, listening, and reading comprehension.* **3** CONSIDER to consider a plan or an idea carefully *They have called a special meeting to examine the proposal.* ⊃See also: cross-examine.

examiner /ɪg'zæmɪnəʳ/ noun [C] someone who tests how much you know about something, or how well you can do something

WORD PARTNERS FOR **example**

a **classic/good/prime** example • an example **of** sth

o▪**example** /ɪg'zɑːmpl/ noun **1** [C] something that is typical of the group of things that you are talking about *This is a good example of medieval Chinese architecture.* **2 for example** used to give an example of what you are talking about *Some people, students for example, can get cheaper tickets.* **3** [C] someone or something

that is very good and should be copied *He is a very good example to the rest of the class.* **4 set an example** to behave in a way that other people should copy

exasperate /ɪg'zæsp³reɪt/ verb [T] to annoy someone a lot

exasperated /ɪg'zæsp³reɪtɪd/ adjective extremely annoyed *He's become increasingly exasperated with the situation.*

exasperating /ɪg'zæsp³reɪtɪŋ/ adjective extremely annoying

exasperation /ɪgˌzæspə'reɪʃ³n/ noun [U] when you feel extremely annoyed with someone or something

excavate /'ekskəveɪt/ verb [I, T] to dig in the ground, especially with a machine, or to look for objects from the past *These Roman coins were excavated from a site in Cambridge.* • excavation /ˌekskə'veɪʃ³n/ noun [C, U]

exceed /ɪk'siːd/ verb **1** [T] to be more than a particular number or amount *Sales have exceeded $1 million so far this year.* **2 exceed the speed limit** to drive faster than you are allowed to according to the law

exceedingly /ɪk'siːdɪŋli/ adverb formal very *He was clever, attractive, and exceedingly rich.*

excel /ɪk'sel/ verb excelling, past excelled formal **1** [I] to be very good at something *Paula always excelled in languages at school.* **2 excel yourself** to do something better than you usually do

o▪**excellent** /'eks³l³nt/ adjective very good, or of a very high quality *Thank you, that was an excellent meal.* • excellently adverb • excellence /'eks³l³ns/ noun [U]

o▪**except** /ɪk'sept/ preposition, conjunction not including a particular fact, thing, or person *The boat sails from Oban every day except Sunday. ○ Everyone passed the exam except for Rory. ○ [+ (that)] So nothing changed, except that Anna saw her son less and less.*

excepted /ɪk'septɪd/ adjective [always after noun] formal not included *Everybody who was asked, myself excepted, said no.*

excepting /ɪk'septɪŋ/ preposition not including

exception /ɪk'sepʃ³n/ noun **1** [C, U] someone or something that is not included in a rule, group, or list *There are exceptions to every rule. ○ I like all kinds of movies, with the exception of horror films. ○ All our pupils, without exception, have access to the Internet. ○ Her films are always popular and this one is no exception.* **2 make an exception** to not treat someone or something according to the usual rules *They don't usually take cheques, but they said they'd make an exception in my case.* **3 take exception to sth** formal to be annoyed or insulted by something

exceptional /ɪk'sepʃ³n³l/ adjective **1** extremely good *an exceptional student* **2** very unusual and not likely to happen very often *Visitors are only allowed in exceptional circumstances.* • exceptionally adverb *an exceptionally gifted pianist*

excerpt /'eksɜːpt/ noun [C] a short piece from a book, film, piece of music, etc

| j yes | k cat | ŋ ring | ʃ she | θ thin | ð this | ʒ decision | dʒ jar | tʃ chip | æ cat | e bed | ə ago | ɪ sit | i cosy | ɒ hot | ʌ run | ʊ put |

excess¹ /ɪkˈses/ *noun* **1** [U, no plural] more of something than is usual or needed *An excess of oil on the markets has caused prices to fall sharply.* **2 in excess of sth** more than a particular amount or level *He earns in excess of £60,000 a year.* **3 do sth to excess** to do something too much *He occasionally has a beer, but he never drinks to excess.*

excess² /ɪkˈses/ *adjective* [always before noun] more than is usual or allowed *We had to pay £100 for excess baggage.*

excesses /ɪkˈsesɪz/ *noun* [plural] extreme, harmful, or immoral actions or behaviour

excessive /ɪkˈsesɪv/ *adjective* more than is necessary or wanted *They accused the police of using excessive force.* ● **excessively** *adverb*

exchange¹ /ɪksˈtʃeɪndʒ/ *noun* **1** GIVING [C, U] when you give something to someone and they give you something else *an exchange of ideas/information* ○ *They were given food and shelter in exchange for work.* **2** STUDENTS [C] an arrangement by which students and teachers from one country go to stay with students and teachers in another **3** CONVERSATION [C] a short conversation or argument *There were angry exchanges between the police and demonstrators.* ⊃See also: **the stock exchange**.

exchange² /ɪksˈtʃeɪndʒ/ *verb* **1** [T] to give something to someone and receive something similar from them *It's traditional for the two teams to exchange shirts after the game.* **2** [T] to take something back to the shop where you bought it and change it for something else *Could I exchange this shirt for a larger size, please?* **3 exchange looks/smiles/words, etc** If two people exchange looks, smiles, words, etc, they look at each other, smile at each other, talk to each other, etc.

exˈchange ˌrate *noun* [C] the amount of another country's money that you can buy with a particular amount of your own country's money

excise /ˈeksaɪz/ *noun* [U] government taxes that must be paid on some things that are made or sold in a particular country

excitable /ɪkˈsaɪtəbl/ *adjective* easily becoming excited *a very excitable child/puppy*

excite /ɪkˈsaɪt/ *verb* [T] **1** to make someone feel very happy and enthusiastic *Try not to excite the children too much.* **2** *formal* to cause a particular reaction in someone *This product has excited a great deal of interest.*

o⁻**excited** /ɪkˈsaɪtɪd/ *adjective* feeling very happy and enthusiastic *happy, excited faces* ○ *The children are getting really excited about the party.* ● **excitedly** *adverb*

COMMON LEARNER ERROR

excited or **exciting**

Excited is used to describe how someone feels.
She was very excited about the visit.
~~She was very exciting about the visit.~~

Exciting is used to describe the thing that makes you excited.
I've had some exciting news!

WORD PARTNERS FOR excitement

cause/feel excitement ● excitement **mounts** ● **great/wild** excitement ● excitement **about/at/over** sth

o⁻**excitement** /ɪkˈsaɪtmənt/ *noun* [U] when people feel very happy and enthusiastic *The competition is causing a lot of excitement.*

OTHER WAYS OF SAYING exciting

If something is so exciting that it holds your attention completely, you can say that it is **gripping** or **riveting**: *The book was gripping - I couldn't put it down.* ● *I found the film absolutely riveting.*

Sports and outdoor activities which are exciting are often described as **exhilarating**: *I find skiing absolutely exhilarating.*

The adjective **action-packed** is often used to describe a story or period of time which is full of exciting events: *We had an action-packed weekend in Berlin.* ● *The film is described as 'an action-packed thriller'.*

An exciting atmosphere is sometimes described as **electric**: *The atmosphere backstage was electric.*

Vibrant is often used to describe places which are exciting: *This is one of Europe's most vibrant cities.*

o⁻**exciting** /ɪkˈsaɪtɪŋ/ *adjective* making you feel very happy and enthusiastic *an exciting football match* ○ *You're going to Africa on safari? How exciting!*

exclaim /ɪksˈkleɪm/ *verb* [I, T] to say something suddenly and loudly because you are surprised, annoyed, excited, etc *"How terrible!" she exclaimed.*

exclamation /ˌekskləˈmeɪʃ^ən/ *noun* [C] something that you say loudly and suddenly because you are surprised, angry, excited, etc *an exclamation of delight*

exclaˈmation ˌmark (*also US* exclaˈmation ˌpoint) *noun* [C] a mark (!) used at the end of a sentence that expresses surprise, excitement, or shock, or that is a greeting or an order ⊃See Extra help page **Punctuation** on page Centre 33 .

exclude /ɪksˈkluːd/ *verb* [T] **1** KEEP OUT to not allow someone or something to take part in an activity or enter a place [often passive] *Women are still excluded from the club.* **2** NOT INCLUDE to intentionally not include something *The insurance cover excludes particular medical conditions.* **3** POSSIBILITY to decide that something is certainly not true or possible *We can't exclude the possibility that he is dead.*

excluding /ɪksˈkluːdɪŋ/ *preposition* not including *That's $600 per person for seven days, excluding travel costs.*

exclusion /ɪksˈkluːʒ^ən/ *noun* **1** [C, U] when someone or something is not allowed to take part in an activity or to enter a place *the exclusion of disruptive pupils* ⊃Opposite **inclusion**. **2 to the exclusion of sth** If you do something to the exclusion of something else, you do it so much that you have no time to do anything else.

exclusive¹ /ɪksˈkluːsɪv/ *adjective* **1** expensive and only for people who are rich or of a high social class *an exclusive private club* **2 exclusive of sth** not including something *The price of the meal is exclusive of drinks.* ⊃Opposite **inclusive. 3** not shared with another person, organization, newspaper, etc *an exclusive interview*

exclusive² /ɪksˈkluːsɪv/ *noun* [C] a news story that appears in only one newspaper or on one television programme

exclusively /ɪksˈkluːsɪvli/ *adverb* only *an exclusively female audience*

excrement /ˈekskrəmənt/ *noun* [U] *formal* solid waste that comes out of the bottom of a person or animal

excrete /ɪkˈskriːt/ *verb* [I, T] to get rid of waste substances from the body • **excretion** /ɪkˈskriːʃən/ *noun* [C, U]

excruciating /ɪkˈskruːʃieɪtɪŋ/ *adjective* very bad or painful *Her illness causes her excruciating pain.* • **excruciatingly** *adverb an excruciatingly embarrassing situation*

excursion /ɪkˈskɜːʒən/ *noun* [C] a short journey made by a group of people for pleasure *We've booked to go on an excursion to Pompeii.*

excusable /ɪkˈskjuːzəbl/ *adjective* easy to forgive ⊃Opposite **inexcusable.**

excuse¹ /ɪkˈskjuːz/ *verb* [T] **1** FORGIVE to forgive someone for something that is not very serious *Please excuse my appearance, I've been painting.* ○ [+ for + doing sth] *She asked him to excuse her for being so rude.* **2** NOT DO to say that someone does not have to do something that they usually have to do *Could I be excused from football training today?* **3** EXPLAIN to be given as a reason for someone's bad behaviour, so that it does not seem so bad *Nothing can excuse what he did.* **4 excuse me a** ATTRACTING ATTENTION used to politely get someone's attention *Excuse me, does this bus go to Oxford Street?* **b** SAYING SORRY used to say sorry for something that you do without intending to *Oh, excuse me, did I take your seat?* • **excusable** *adjective*

WORD PARTNERS FOR **excuse**

have/make/offer/think up an excuse • a feeble/good excuse

o-**excuse²** /ɪkˈskjuːs/ *noun* [C] **1** a reason that you give to explain why you did something wrong [+ for + doing sth] *I hope he's got a good excuse for being so late.* **2** a false reason that you give to explain why you do something *Nick was just looking for an excuse to call her.*

execute /ˈeksɪkjuːt/ *verb* [T] **1** to kill someone as a legal punishment *He was executed for murder.* **2** *formal* to do something, such as follow a plan or order *to execute a deal/plan*

execution /ˌeksɪˈkjuːʃən/ *noun* **1** [C, U] when someone is killed as a legal punishment **2** [U] when you do something, such as follow a plan or order *He was killed in the execution of his duties as a soldier.*

executioner /ˌeksɪˈkjuːʃənər/ *noun* [C] someone whose job is to execute criminals

executive¹ /ɪɡˈzekjətɪv/ *adjective* [always before noun] **1** relating to making decisions and managing businesses *an executive director* **2** suitable for people who have important jobs in business *Peter always stays in the executive suite.*

executive² /ɪɡˈzekjətɪv/ *noun* **1** [C] someone who has an important job in a business *a company executive* **2 the executive** *mainly UK* the people who have the power to make decisions in an organization

exemplary /ɪɡˈzempləri/ *adjective formal* very good and suitable to be copied by people *Sarah's behaviour is always exemplary.*

exemplify /ɪɡˈzemplɪfaɪ/ *verb* [T] *formal* to be or give a typical example of something

exempt¹ /ɪɡˈzempt/ *adjective* [never before noun] with special permission not to have to do something or pay something *The first £4,000 that you earn is exempt from tax.*

exempt² /ɪɡˈzempt/ *verb* [T] *formal* to officially say that someone does not have to do something or pay for something [often passive] *Students are exempted from payment.* • **exemption** /ɪɡˈzempʃən/ *noun* [C, U]

exercise

WORD PARTNERS FOR **exercise**

do/get/take exercise • daily/gentle/regular/strenuous exercise • a form of exercise

o-**exercise¹** /ˈeksəsaɪz/ *noun* **1** PHYSICAL ACTIVITY [C, U] physical activity that you do to make your body strong and healthy *Swimming is my favourite form of exercise.* ○ *Let's do some stretching exercises to start with.* **2** TEST [C] a piece of written work that helps you learn something *For your homework, please do exercise 3 on page 24.* **3** ACTIVITY WITH PURPOSE [C] an activity which is intended to achieve a particular thing *The whole point of the exercise was to get people to share their ideas.* ○ *a team-building exercise.* **4** MILITARY [C] a set of actions that a group of soldiers do to practise their skills *The cadets are out on military exer-*

cises. **5** [USE] [U] *formal* the use of something such as a power or right

exercise[2] /'eksəsaɪz/ *verb* **1** [I, T] to do physical activities to make your body strong and healthy *I try to exercise every day.* **2** [T] *formal* to use a power, right, or ability *You should always exercise your right to vote.*

exert /ɪg'zɜːt/ *verb* **1** [T] to use something such as authority, power, influence, etc in order to make something happen *My parents exerted a lot of pressure on me to do well at school.* **2 exert yourself** to use a lot of physical or mental energy to do something *She was too ill to exert herself much.*

exertion /ɪg'zɜːʃᵊn/ *noun* [C, U] when you use a lot of physical or mental energy to do something *I get out of breath with any kind of physical exertion.*

exhale /eks'heɪl/ *verb* [I, T] *formal* to send air out of your lungs ⊃Opposite **inhale.**

exhaust[1] /ɪg'zɔːst/ *verb* [T] **1** [SUPPLY] to finish all of the supply of something *How long will it be before the world's fuel supplies are exhausted?* **2** [TIRED] to make someone very tired **3** [SUBJECT] to say everything possible about a subject *We seem to have exhausted that topic of conversation.*

exhaust[2] /ɪg'zɔːst/ *noun* **1** [U] the waste gas from a vehicle's engine **exhaust fumes 2** [C] (*also* **exhaust pipe**) *mainly UK* the pipe that waste gas from a vehicle's engine flows through ⊃See colour picture **Car** on page Centre 7.

exhausted /ɪg'zɔːstɪd/ *adjective* very tired

exhausting /ɪg'zɔːstɪŋ/ *adjective* making you feel very tired *What an exhausting day!*

exhaustion /ɪg'zɔːstʃᵊn/ *noun* [U] when you are extremely tired *The tennis star was suffering from exhaustion.*

exhaustive /ɪg'zɔːstɪv/ *adjective* complete and including everything *an exhaustive account of the incident*

ex'haust ˌpipe *mainly UK* (*also US* **tailpipe**) *noun* [C] the pipe that waste gas from a vehicle's engine flows through

exhibit[1] /ɪg'zɪbɪt/ *verb* **1** [I, T] to show objects such as paintings to the public *She's exhibiting her roses at the local flower show.* **2** [T] *formal* to show a feeling, quality, or ability *The crew exhibited great courage when the plane crashed.*

exhibit[2] /ɪg'zɪbɪt/ *noun* [C] an object such as a painting that is shown to the public *a museum exhibit* ● **exhibitor** *noun* [C] someone who shows something that they own or have made to the public

exhibition /ˌeksɪ'bɪʃᵊn/ *noun* **1** [C, U] when objects such as paintings are shown to the public *There's a new exhibition of sculpture on at the city gallery.* ○ *an exhibition centre* **2** [C] when someone shows a particular skill or quality that they have to the public

exhibitionist /ˌeksɪ'bɪʃᵊnɪst/ *noun* [C] someone who tries to attract attention to themselves with their behaviour ● **exhibitionism** /ˌeksɪ'bɪʃᵊnɪzᵊm/ *noun* [U] behaviour which tries to attract attention

exhilarated /ɪg'zɪlᵊreɪtɪd/ *adjective* very excited and happy

exhilarating /ɪg'zɪlᵊreɪtɪŋ/ *adjective* making you feel very excited and happy *There's nothing more exhilarating than water-skiing.*

exhilaration /ɪgˌzɪlᵊr'eɪʃᵊn/ *noun* [U] when you feel very excited and happy

exhort /ɪg'zɔːt/ *verb* [T] *formal* to strongly encourage someone to do something ● **exhortation** /ˌegzɔː'teɪʃᵊn/ *noun* [C, U]

exile /'eksaɪl/, /'egzaɪl/ *noun* **1** [U] when someone has to leave their home and live in another country, often for political reasons *He spent the war years in exile in New York.* ○ *The King was forced into exile.* **2** [C] someone who is forced to live in another country *She lived the rest of her life as an exile in the UK.* ● **exile** *verb* [T] to force someone to leave their home and live in another country, often for political reasons ● **exiled** *adjective*

⚬ **exist** /ɪg'zɪst/ *verb* [I] **1** to be real or present *Poverty still exists in this country.* **2** to live in difficult conditions *You can't exist without water for more than a week.*

> **WORD PARTNERS FOR existence**
>
> **come into/go out of** existence ● be **in** existence ● **the** existence **of** sth

existence /ɪg'zɪstᵊns/ *noun* **1** [U] when something or someone exists *She never doubted the existence of God.* ○ *The theatre company that we started is still in existence today.* ○ *When did the Football League come into existence (=* begin to exist)*?* **2** [C] a particular way of life *We could have a much more peaceful existence in the countryside.*

existing /ɪg'zɪstɪŋ/ *adjective* [always before noun] which exist or are used at the present time *Existing schools will have to be expanded to accommodate the extra students.* ⊃See also: **pre-existing.**

⚬ **exit**[1] /'eksɪt/ *noun* [C] **1** [DOOR] the door or gate which you use to leave a public building or place *a fire exit* ○ *an emergency exit* **2** [LEAVING] when someone leaves a place *Sue made a quick exit when she saw Mick come in.* **3** [ROAD] a road which you use to leave a motorway (= wide, fast road) or roundabout (= place where three or more main roads meet) *Take the third exit at the next roundabout.*

exit[2] /'eksɪt/ *verb* [I, T] **1** to stop using a program on a computer *Press escape to exit the game.* **2** *formal* to leave a place or a competition

'exit ˌstrategy *noun* [C] a plan that you use to get out of a difficult situation *A good politician will plan his exit strategy before announcing his retirement from office.*

exodus /'eksədəs/ *noun* [no plural] when a large number of people all leave a place together *There has been a mass exodus of workers from the villages to the towns.*

exonerate /ɪg'zɒnᵊreɪt/ *verb* [T] *formal* to say that someone is not guilty of doing something that they have been blamed for [often passive] *He was exonerated of all blame by the investigation.* ● **exoneration** /ɪgˌzɒnᵊ'reɪʃᵊn/ *noun* [U]

exorbitant /ɪgˈzɔːbɪtᵊnt/ *adjective* Exorbitant prices or costs are much too high.

exorcism /ˈeksɔːsɪzᵊm/ *noun* [C, U] when an evil spirit is exorcized

exorcize (*also UK* -ise) /ˈeksɔːsaɪz/ *verb* [T] **1** to make evil spirits leave a person or place by saying special prayers and having a special ceremony **2** to get rid of something such as a bad memory *She moved to Paris to try to exorcize the past.*

exotic /ɪgˈzɒtɪk/ *adjective* unusual, interesting, and often foreign *exotic fruits*

expand /ɪkˈspænd/ *verb* [I, T] to increase in size or amount, or to make something increase *We are hoping to expand our range of products.*

expand on sth to give more details about something that you have said or written *She mentioned a few ideas, but she didn't expand on them.*

expanse /ɪkˈspæns/ *noun* [C] a large, open area of land, sea, or sky *a vast expanse of water*

expansion /ɪkˈspænʃᵊn/ *noun* [U] when something increases in size or amount *the rapid expansion of the software industry*

expansive /ɪkˈspænsɪv/ *adjective formal* very happy to talk to people in a friendly way *He was in an expansive mood on the night of the party.*

expatriate /ɪkˈspætriət/ (*also UK* **expat** /ˌekˈspæt/ *informal*) *noun* [C] someone who does not live in their own country ● **expatriate** *adjective*

o⌐**expect** /ɪkˈspekt/ *verb* **1** [T] to think that something will happen [+ to do sth] *He didn't expect to see me.* ○ [+ (that)] *I expect that she'll be very angry about this.* **2** be expecting sb/sth to be waiting for someone or something to arrive *I'm expecting a letter from my sister.* **3** [T] to think that someone should behave in a particular way or do a particular thing [+ to do sth] *You will be expected to work some weekends.* **4 I expect** *mainly UK informal* used to show that you think that something is likely to be true *I expect Isabel's told you about me?* ○ *"Will you be coming to the party?" " I expect so."* **5 be expecting** to be going to have a baby *I'm expecting my first baby in May.* ⊃See Common learner error at **wait**.

expectancy /ɪkˈspektᵊnsi/ *noun* [U] when you think that something pleasant or exciting is going to happen *An air of expectancy filled the room.* ⊃See also: **life expectancy**.

expectant /ɪkˈspektᵊnt/ *adjective* **1** thinking that something pleasant or exciting is going to happen *the children's expectant faces* **2 an expectant mother/father, etc** someone who is going to have a baby soon ● **expectantly** *adverb*

WORD PARTNERS FOR **expectation**

have high/have low expectations ● live up to/meet (sb's) expectations ● expectations of sth

expectation /ˌekspekˈteɪʃᵊn/ *noun* **1** [C] when you expect good things to happen in the future [usually plural] *The holiday lived up to all our expectations* (= was as good as we expected).

○ *My parents had high expectations for me* (= expected me to be successful). **2** [C, U] when you expect something to happen *He had gone away and there was no expectation of his return.*

expedient¹ /ɪkˈspiːdiənt/ *adjective formal* An expedient action achieves a useful purpose, although it may not be moral. *It might be expedient not to pay him until the work is finished.* ● **expediency** /ɪkˈspiːdiənsi/ *noun* [U] when something is expedient *an issue of political expediency*

expedient² /ɪkˈspiːdiənt/ *noun* [C] *formal* a useful or clever action

expedite /ˈekspɪdaɪt/ *verb* [T] *formal* to make an action or process happen more quickly

expedition /ˌekspɪˈdɪʃᵊn/ *noun* [C] an organized journey, especially a long one for a particular purpose *Peary led the first expedition to the North Pole.* ○ *a shopping expedition*

expel /ɪkˈspel/ *verb* [T] **expelling**, *past* **expelled 1** to make someone leave a school, organization, or country because of their behaviour [often passive] *He was expelled from school for hitting another student.* **2** *formal* to force air, gas, or liquid out of something

expend /ɪkˈspend/ *verb* [T] *formal* to use effort, time, or money to do something [+ doing sth] *You expend far too much energy doing things for other people.* ○ *Governments expend a lot of resources on war.*

expendable /ɪkˈspendəbl/ *adjective* If someone or something is expendable, people can do something or deal with a situation without them. *He considers his staff as temporary and expendable.*

expenditure /ɪkˈspendɪtʃəʳ/ *noun* [U] *formal* **1** the total amount of money that a government or person spends *The government's annual expenditure on arms has been reduced.* **2** when you use energy, time, or money

o⌐**expense** /ɪkˈspens/ *noun* **1** [C, U] the money that you spend on something *You have to pay your own medical expenses.* ○ *He eventually found her the car she wanted, at great expense* (= cost him a lot of money). **2 at the expense of sth** If you do one thing at the expense of another, doing the first thing harms the second thing. *He spent a lot of time at work, at the expense of his marriage.* **3 at sb's expense a** If you do something at someone's expense, they pay for it. *We went on holiday at my father's expense.* **b** in order to make someone look stupid *Stop making jokes at my expense.*

expenses /ɪkˈspensɪz/ *noun* [plural] money that you spend when you are doing your job, that your employer will pay back to you *travel expenses* ○ *They pay us two hundred pounds a week, plus expenses.*

o⌐**expensive** /ɪkˈspensɪv/ *adjective* costing a lot of money *expensive jewellery* ○ [+ to do sth] *It's too expensive to go out every night.* ⊃Opposite **inexpensive**. ● **expensively** *adverb* *expensively dressed*

WORD PARTNERS FOR ***experience***

gain/have/lack experience • **good/previous/useful/wide** experience • experience **in/of** sth • **from** experience • **in my** experience

⊶**experience**[1] /ɪk'spɪəriəns/ *noun* **1** [U] knowledge that you get from doing a job, or from doing, seeing, or feeling something *Do you have any **experience of** working with children?* ○ *He knows **from experience** not to play with fire.* ○ ***In my experience**, people smile back if you smile at them.* **2** [C] something that happens to you that affects how you feel *My trip to Australia was an experience I'll never forget.*

experience[2] /ɪk'spɪəriəns/ *verb* [T] If you experience something, it happens to you, or you feel it. *It was the worst pain I had ever experienced.*

experienced /ɪk'spɪəriənst/ *adjective* having skill and knowledge because you have done something many times *Karsten's a very experienced ski instructor.* ⊃Opposite **inexperienced**.

WORD PARTNERS FOR ***experiment***

conduct/do/perform an experiment • an experiment **on** sth

⊶**experiment**[1] /ɪk'sperɪmənt/ *noun* [C] a test, especially a scientific one, that you do in order to learn something or discover if something is true *to **conduct/do/perform** an **experiment*** ○ *They're conducting **experiments on** hamster cells to test the effects of the drug.*

experiment[2] /ɪk'sperɪment/ *verb* [I] **1** to try something in order to discover what it is like *Did he ever **experiment with** drugs?* **2** to do an experiment ***Experimenting on** mice can give us an idea of the effect of the disease in humans.* • **experimentation** /ɪkˌsperɪmen'teɪʃ^{ə}n/ *noun* [U]

experimental /ɪkˌsperɪ'ment^{ə}l/ *adjective* relating to tests, especially scientific ones • **experimentally** *adverb*

⊶**expert**[1] /'ekspɜːt/ *noun* [C] someone who has a lot of skill in something or a lot of knowledge about something *He's **an expert on** Japanese literature.*

expert[2] /'ekspɜːt/ *adjective* [**always before noun**] having a lot of skill in something or knowing a lot about something *I need some **expert advice** on investments.* ○ *What's your **expert opinion**?* • **expertly** *adverb He carved the roast expertly.*

expertise /ˌekspɜː'tiːz/ *noun* [U] skill *the technical expertise of the engineers*

expire /ɪk'spaɪə^{r}/ *verb* [I] If a legal document or agreement expires, you can no longer use it. *Your contract expired six months ago.*

expiry /ɪk'spaɪəri/ *noun* [U] *UK* the end of a period when something can be used *What's **the expiry date** on your passport?*

⊶**explain** /ɪk'spleɪn/ *verb* [I, T] to make something clear or easy to understand by giving reasons for it or details about it [+ **question word**] *Can you explain why you did this?* ○ *Can you ex**plain to** me how this mobile phone works?* ○ [+ **(that)**] *He explained that he was going to stay with his sister.* • **explaining** *noun* [U] when you have to explain or give a good reason for your actions *You'll **have a lot of explaining to do** when dad finds out what happened.*

COMMON LEARNER ERROR

explain something

Explain is followed by the thing you are explaining.

I'll explain the situation.

Remember to use the preposition **to** before a person.

I'll explain the situation to my parents.

~~*I'll explain the situation my parents.*~~

OTHER WAYS OF SAYING ***explain***

If someone is explaining something in order to make it easier for someone else to understand, you can use the verb **clarify**: *Let me just **clarify** what I mean here.*

The verb **define** is sometimes used when explaining exactly what something means: *Your responsibilities are clearly **defined** in the contract.*

If something is being explained clearly in writing, the phrasal verb **set out** is sometimes used: *Your contract will **set out** the terms of your employment.*

If something is being explained in great detail, the phrasal verb **spell out** is often used: *They sent me a letter, **spelling out** the details of the agreement.*

WORD PARTNERS FOR ***explanation***

demand/give/have/offer an explanation • **a clear/possible/satisfactory/simple** explanation • an explanation **for** sth

⊶**explanation** /ˌeksplə'neɪʃ^{ə}n/ *noun* [C, U] the details or reasons that someone gives to make something clear or easy to understand *What's your **explanation for** the team's poor performance?* ○ *Could you give me a quick **explanation** of how it works?*

explanatory /ɪk'splænət^{ə}ri/ *adjective* giving an explanation about something *There are **explanatory notes** with the diagram.* ⊃See also: **self-explanatory**.

expletive /ɪk'spliːtɪv/ [US] /'eksplətɪv/ *noun* [C] *formal* a swear word (= word which people think is rude or offensive)

explicable /ɪk'splɪkəbl/ *adjective formal* Something that is explicable can be explained. ⊃Opposite **inexplicable**.

explicit /ɪk'splɪsɪt/ *adjective* **1** clear and exact *She was very **explicit about** her plans.* ○ *He made no **explicit references** to Tess.* **2** showing or talking about sex or violence in a very detailed way *a **sexually explicit** film* • **explicitly** *adverb She **explicitly stated** that she did not want her name to be revealed.*

⊶**explode** /ɪk'spləʊd/ *verb* **1** [I, T] If something such as a bomb explodes, it bursts (= breaks suddenly from inside) with noise and force, and if you explode it, you make it burst with noise and force. *One of the bombs did not explode.* **2** [I] to suddenly start shouting because you are very angry

exploit[1] /ɪkˈsplɔɪt/ *verb* [T] **1** to not pay or reward someone enough for something [**often passive**] *I felt as though I was being exploited.* **2** to use or develop something for your advantage *We are not fully exploiting all the resources that we have.* • **exploitation** /ˌeksplɔɪˈteɪʃᵊn/ *noun* [U] *the exploitation of child workers*

exploit[2] /ˈeksplɔɪt/ *noun* [C] something unusual, brave, or interesting that someone has done [**usually plural**] *Have you heard about her amazing exploits travelling in Africa?*

exploratory /ɪkˈsplɒrətᵊri/ *adjective* done in order to discover or learn about something *an exploratory expedition to Antarctica* ○ *an exploratory operation*

explore /ɪkˈsplɔːʳ/ *verb* **1** [I, T] to go around a place where you have never been in order to find out what is there *The children love exploring.* ○ *The best way to explore the countryside is on foot.* **2** [T] to think about something very carefully before you make a decision about it *We're exploring the possibility of buying a holiday home.* • **exploration** /ˌekspləˈreɪʃᵊn/ *noun* [C, U] *She's always loved travel and exploration.*

explorer /ɪkˈsplɔːrəʳ/ *noun* [C] someone who travels to places where no one has ever been in order to find out what is there

o⌐**explosion** /ɪkˈspləʊʒᵊn/ *noun* [C] **1** when something such as a bomb explodes *Forty people were killed in the explosion.* **2** when something increases suddenly by a large amount *the recent population explosion*

explosive[1] /ɪkˈspləʊsɪv/ *adjective* **1** An explosive substance or piece of equipment can cause explosions. *The explosive device was hidden in a suitcase.* **2** An explosive situation or subject causes strong feelings, and may make people angry or violent. *a highly explosive political issue*

explosive[2] /ɪkˈspləʊsɪv/ *noun* [C] a substance or piece of equipment that can cause explosions

exponent /ɪkˈspəʊnənt/ *noun* [C] someone who supports a particular idea or belief, or performs a particular activity *The early exponents of votes for women suffered greatly.*

export[1] /ˈekspɔːt/ *noun* **1** [C] a product that you sell in another country *Scottish beef exports to Japan* **2** [U] the business of sending goods to another country in order to sell them there *the export of industrial goods* ⊃Opposite **import**.

export[2] /ɪkˈspɔːt/ *verb* [I, T] **1** to send goods to another country in order to sell them there *Singapore exports large quantities of rubber.* ⊃Opposite **import**. **2** If you export information from a computer, you copy it to another place. • **exporter** *noun* [C] *Brazil is the world's largest exporter of coffee.*

expose /ɪkˈspəʊz/ *verb* [T] **1** HIDDEN THING to remove what is covering something so that it can be seen *Our bodies need to be exposed to sunlight in order to make vitamin D.* **2** BAD THING to make public something bad or something that is not honest *The review exposed widespread corruption in the police force.* **3** be

exposed to sth to experience something or be affected by something because you are in a particular situation or place *It was the first time I'd been exposed to violence.* **4** PHOTOGRAPHY to allow light to reach a piece of camera film in order to produce a photograph

exposed /ɪkˈspəʊzd/ *adjective* having no protection from bad weather *an exposed cliff*

exposure /ɪkˈspəʊʒəʳ/ *noun* **1** EXPERIENCING [U] when someone experiences something or is affected by it because they are in a particular situation or place *There is a risk of exposure to radiation.* ○ *Many young children now have exposure to computers in the home.* **2** MAKING PUBLIC [C, U] when something bad that you have done is made public *She was threatened with exposure by a journalist.* **3** MEDICAL [U] a serious medical condition that is caused by being outside in very cold weather **4** PHOTOGRAPH [C] a single photograph on a piece of film *This film has 24 exposures.*

expound /ɪkˈspaʊnd/ *verb* [I, T] *formal* to give a detailed explanation of something *He's always expounding on what's wrong with the world.* ○ *She uses her newspaper column to expound her views on environmental issues.*

o⌐**express**[1] /ɪkˈspres/ *verb* [T] to show what you think or how you feel using words or actions *I'm simply expressing my opinion.* ○ [**often reflexive**] *You're not expressing yourself* (= saying what you mean) *very clearly.*

express[2] /ɪkˈspres/ *adjective* **1** **an express service/train, etc** a service, train, etc that is much faster than usual **2** **an express aim/intention/purpose, etc** a clear and certain aim, intention, purpose, etc *You came here with the express purpose of causing trouble.*

express[3] /ɪkˈspres/ (*also* ex'press ˌtrain) *noun* [C] a fast train *I took the express to London.*

o⌐**expression** /ɪkˈspreʃᵊn/ *noun* **1** LOOK [C] the look on someone's face showing what they feel or think *your facial expression* ○ *He had a sad expression on his face.* **2** PHRASE [C] a phrase that has a special meaning *'A can of worms' is an expression meaning a difficult situation.* **3** SHOWING THOUGHTS [C, U] when you say what you think or show how you feel using words or actions *As an expression of our disapproval, we will no longer use his shop.*

expressive /ɪkˈspresɪv/ *adjective* showing your feelings *a very expressive face*

expressly /ɪkˈspresli/ *adverb formal* **1** If you say something expressly, you say it in a clear way, so that your meaning cannot be doubted. *I expressly stated that I did not want any visitors.* **2** If something is expressly for a particular reason or person, it is for that reason or person only. *The picture was painted expressly for me.*

expressway /ɪkˈspreswei/ *US* (*UK* **motorway**) *noun* [C] a long, wide road, usually used by traffic travelling fast over long distances

expulsion /ɪkˈspʌlʃᵊn/ *noun* [C, U] when someone is made to leave their school, organization, or country because of their behaviour *They threatened him with expulsion from school.*

exquisite /ɪkˈskwɪzɪt/ *adjective* very beautiful or perfect *a garden of exquisite flowers* ● **exquisitely** *adverb* *an exquisitely dressed woman*

extend /ɪkˈstend/ *verb* 1 MAKE BIGGER [T] to make something bigger or longer *We're going to extend our kitchen.* 2 MAKE LAST [T] to make an activity, agreement, etc last for a longer time *They have extended the deadline by one week.* 3 **extend from/into/over, etc** to continue or stretch over a particular area of land or period of time *Will the building work extend into next week?* 4 STRETCH OUT [T] to stretch out a part of your body *She smiled and extended her hand.* 5 **extend an invitation/thanks, etc to sb** *formal* to give someone an invitation, thanks, etc *I'd like to extend a warm welcome to our guests.*

extension /ɪkˈstenʃᵊn/ *noun* [C] 1 PART OF A BUILDING a new room or rooms that are added to a building *You could build an extension onto the back of the house.* 2 EXTRA TIME extra time that you are given to do or use something *You might be able to get an extension on your visa.* 3 TELEPHONE a telephone that is connected to the main telephone in an office or other large building *Call me on extension 213.*

extensive /ɪkˈstensɪv/ *adjective* large in amount or size *an extensive art collection* ○ *The hurricane caused extensive damage.* ● **extensively** *adverb* *I have travelled extensively in Europe.*

WORD PARTNERS FOR **extent**

the **full/true** extent of sth ● **to such** an extent ● the extent **of** sth

extent /ɪkˈstent/ *noun* 1 [no plural] the size or importance of something *They are just beginning to realize the **full extent** of the damage.* ○ *Her face was injured **to such an extent** (= so much) that he didn't recognize her.* 2 **to some extent/to a certain extent** in some ways *I was, to some extent, responsible for the accident.*

exterior /ɪkˈstɪəriᵊr/ *noun* [C] the outside part of something or someone [usually singular] *The exterior of the house was painted white.* ● **exterior** *adjective* [always before noun] *an exterior wall* ⊃Opposite **interior**.

exterminate /ɪkˈstɜːmɪneɪt/ *verb* [T] to kill a large group of people or animals ● **extermination** /ɪkˌstɜːmɪˈneɪʃᵊn/ *noun* [C, U]

external /ɪkˈstɜːnᵊl/ *adjective* 1 relating to the outside part of something *the **external walls** of the house* ○ *The ointment is **for external use only** (= it must not be put inside the body).* 2 coming from or relating to another country, group, or organization *All exams are marked by an **external examiner**.* ⊃Opposite **internal**. ● **externally** *adverb*

extinct /ɪkˈstɪŋkt/ *adjective* If a type of animal is extinct, it does not now exist.

extinction /ɪkˈstɪŋkʃᵊn/ *noun* [U] when a type of animal no longer exists *Many species of animal are threatened with extinction.*

extinguish /ɪkˈstɪŋgwɪʃ/ *verb* [T] *formal* to stop something burning or giving out light *The fire took two hours to extinguish.*

extinguisher /ɪkˈstɪŋgwɪʃᵊr/ (*also* **fire extinguisher**) *noun* [C] a piece of equipment shaped like a tube, which is used to spread a substance onto a fire to stop it burning

extol /ɪkˈstəʊl/ *verb* [T] **extolling**, *past* **extolled** to say that you think that something is very good *He always **extols the virtues of** (= praises) French cooking.*

extort /ɪkˈstɔːt/ *verb* [T] to get money from someone by saying that you will harm them ● **extortion** /ɪkˈstɔːʃᵊn/ *noun* [U]

extortionate /ɪkˈstɔːʃᵊnət/ *adjective* Extortionate prices or costs are very high.

o▪**extra¹** /ˈekstrə/ *adjective* more, or more than usual *Can I invite a few extra people?* ○ *She's been babysitting to earn some extra cash.*

WORD PARTNERS FOR **extra**

an **added/hidden/optional** extra

extra² /ˈekstrə/ *noun* [C] 1 something that costs more when you buy goods or pay for a service *The hi-fi comes with **optional extras** such as headphones and remote control.* 2 an actor in a film who does not have a main part and usually plays someone in a crowd

extra³ /ˈekstrə/ *adverb* more than usual *Do you get paid extra for working late?*

extra- /ekstrə-/ *prefix* outside of or in addition to *extracurricular activities* (= activities that are in addition to the usual school work)

extract¹ /ɪkˈstrækt/ *verb* [T] *formal* 1 to take something out, especially using force *He's going to the dentist's to have a tooth extracted.* 2 to get the money, information, etc that you want from someone who does not want to give it to you *They were not able to extract a confession from her.*

extract² /ˈekstrækt/ *noun* [C] 1 a particular part of a book, poem, etc that is chosen so that it can be used in a discussion, article, etc *The teacher read out **an extract from** 'Brave New World'.* 2 a substance taken from a plant, flower, etc and used especially in food or medicine *pure vanilla extract*

extraction /ɪkˈstrækʃᵊn/ *noun* 1 [C, U] when something is taken out, especially using force 2 **of Chinese/Italian, etc extraction** having a family whose origin is Chinese, Italian, etc

extradite /ˈekstrədaɪt/ *verb* [T] to send someone back to the country where they are accused of a crime, so that a court there can decide if they are guilty [often passive] *The suspects were **extradited to the UK.*** ● **extradition** /ˌekstrəˈdɪʃᵊn/ *noun* [C, U]

extraneous /ɪkˈstreɪniəs/ *adjective* not directly connected to something *extraneous information/noise*

extraordinary /ɪkˈstrɔːdᵊnᵊri/ *adjective* very special, unusual, or strange *an extraordinary tale of courage* ○ *She was an extraordinary* *young woman.* • **extraordinarily** *adverb Their last album was extraordinarily successful.*

extravagant /ɪkˈstrævəgənt/ *adjective* **1** costing too much or spending a lot more money than you need to *the* ***extravagant lifestyle*** *of a movie star* **2** too unusual and extreme to be believed or controlled *the* ***extravagant claims*** *made by cosmetics companies* • **extravagance** /ɪkˈstrævəgəns/ *noun* **[C, U]** when someone or something is extravagant • **extravagantly** *adverb*

extravaganza /ɪkˌstrævəˈgænzə/ *noun* **[C]** a large, exciting, and expensive event or entertainment *a three-hour extravaganza of country music*

extreme¹ /ɪkˈstriːm/ *adjective* **1** SERIOUS the most unusual or most serious possible *extreme weather conditions* ○ ***In extreme cases****, the disease can lead to blindness.* **2** VERY LARGE very large in amount or degree *extreme pain* ○ *extreme wealth* **3** OPINIONS having such strong opinions or beliefs that most people cannot agree with you *extreme views* ○ *the extreme right* **4** FURTHEST **[always before noun]** at the furthest point of something *in the extreme south of the island*

extreme² /ɪkˈstriːm/ *noun* **[C]** the largest possible amount or degree of something *Anna's moods went* ***from one extreme to another*** (= first she was very happy, then she was very unhappy). ○ *Coach Wilson* ***took*** *our training* ***to extremes*** (= made us train extremely hard).

⊶**extremely** /ɪkˈstriːmli/ *adverb* very, or much more than usual *extremely beautiful*

exˌtreme ˈsports *noun* **[C, U]** a game or activity which people do that is dangerous *extreme sports such as bungee jumping and snowboarding*

extremist /ɪkˈstriːmɪst/ *noun* **[C]** someone who has such strong opinions or beliefs that most people cannot agree with them • **extremism** /ɪkˈstriːmɪzᵊm/ *noun* **[U]** • **extremist** *adjective*

extremities /ɪkˈstremətiz/ *noun* **[plural]** the end parts of your body such as your hands and feet

extremity /ɪkˈstreməti/ *noun formal* **1 [C]** the part of something that is furthest from the centre *at the north-west extremity of Europe* **2 [U]** when a feeling is very strong or a bad situation very serious

extricate /ˈekstrɪkeɪt/ *verb* **extricate yourself from sth** to get yourself out of a difficult situation or unpleasant place *I didn't know how to extricate myself from such an embarrassing situation.*

extrovert /ˈekstrəvɜːt/ *noun* **[C]** someone who is very confident and likes being with other people ➲Opposite **introvert.** • **extrovert** *adjective an extrovert personality* ➲Opposite **introverted.**

exuberant /ɪgˈzjuːbᵊrᵊnt/ *adjective* full of happiness, excitement, and energy *a warm and exuberant personality* • **exuberance** /ɪgˈzjuːbᵊrᵊns/ *noun* **[U]**

exude /ɪgˈzjuːd/ *verb* **[T]** If you exude love, confidence, pain, etc, you show that you have a lot of that feeling.

exult /ɪgˈzʌlt/ *verb* **[I]** to show great pleasure, especially at someone else's defeat or failure *She seems to* ***exult in*** *her power.* • **exultation** /ˌegzʌlˈteɪʃᵊn/ *noun* **[U]**

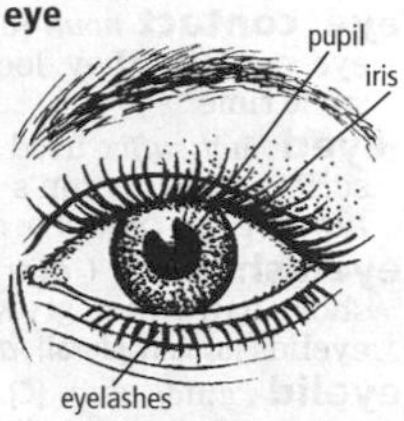

⊶**eye¹** /aɪ/ *noun* **1** SEEING **[C]** one of the two organs in your face, which you use to see with *Sara has black hair and brown eyes.* ○ *She* ***closed*** *her* ***eyes*** *and fell off to sleep.* **2** NEEDLE **[C]** the small hole at the end of a needle, that you put the thread through **3 have an eye for sth** to be good at noticing a particular type of thing *Your son has a very good eye for detail.* **4 keep your/an eye on sb/sth** to watch or look after someone or something *Could you keep an eye on this pan of soup for a moment?* **5 have your eye on sth** *informal* to want something and intend to get it *Jane's got her eye on that new advertising job.* **6 can't keep/take your eyes off sb/sth** to be unable to stop looking at someone or something because they are so attractive or interesting *He couldn't take his eyes off her all night.* **7 lay/set eyes on sb/sth** to see someone or something for the first time *They fell in love the moment they laid eyes on each other.* **8 look sb in the eye/eyes** to look at someone in a direct way, without showing fear or shame *Look me in the eye and say that you didn't steal it.* **9 in sb's eyes** in someone's opinion *In my parents' eyes, I'll always be a child.* **10 cast/run your/an eye over sth** *UK* to look at something quickly, often in order to give your opinion about it *Would you cast an eye over our work so far?* **11 catch sb's eye a** GET SOMEONE'S ATTENTION to get someone's attention by looking at them *I tried to catch her eye, but she had already turned away.* **b** BE NOTICED to be attractive or different enough to be noticed by people *It was the colour of his jacket that caught my eye.* **12 cry your eyes out** If someone cries their eyes out, they cry a lot about a problem or situation. **13 keep your eyes open/peeled (for sb/sth)** to watch carefully for someone or something *Keep your eyes peeled, he should be here any minute.* **14 keep an eye out for sb/sth** to watch carefully for someone or something to appear *Keep an eye out for the delivery van.* **15 see eye to eye (with sb)** If two people see eye to eye, they agree with each other. **16 turn a blind eye (to sth)** to choose to ignore something that you know is wrong or illegal **17 with your eyes open** knowing about all of the problems that could happen if you do something *I went into this marriage with my eyes open.* ➲See also: **black eye.**

eye² /aɪ/ *verb* **[T] eyeing,** *also US* **eying,** *past* **eyed** to look at someone or something with interest *The two women eyed each other suspiciously.*

eyeball /ˈaɪbɔːl/ *noun* **[C]** the whole of the eye, that has the shape of a small ball

eyebrow /ˈaɪbraʊ/ *noun* **[C]** the thin line of hair that is above each eye ➲See colour picture **The Body** on page Centre 13.

eye-catching /ˈaɪˌkætʃɪŋ/ *adjective* attractive, interesting, or different enough to be noticed *an eye-catching poster*

ˈeye ˌcontact *noun* [U] *UK* If two people make eye contact, they look at each other at the same time.

-eyed /aɪd/ *suffix* used at the end of a word describing a person's eyes *Both sisters are brown-eyed.* ⊃See also: cross-eyed, wide-eyed.

eyelash /ˈaɪlæʃ/ (*also* lash) *noun* [C] one of the short hairs that grow from the edge of your eyelids [usually plural] *false eyelashes*

eyelid /ˈaɪlɪd/ *noun* [C] **1** the piece of skin that covers your eyes when you close them **2 not bat an eyelid** to not react to something unusual

eyeliner /ˈaɪˌlaɪnəʳ/ *noun* [C, U] a coloured substance, usually contained in a pencil, which you put in a line above or below your eyes in order to make them more attractive ⊃See

picture at **make up.**

eye-opener /ˈaɪˌəʊpᵊnəʳ/ *noun* [C] something that surprises you and teaches you new facts about life, people, etc *Living in another country can be a real eye-opener.*

eyeshadow /ˈaɪʃædˌəʊ/ *noun* [C, U] a coloured cream or powder which you put above or around your eyes in order to make them more attractive

eyesight /ˈaɪsaɪt/ *noun* [U] the ability to see *My eyesight is getting worse.*

eyesore /ˈaɪsɔːʳ/ *noun* [C] a building, area, etc that looks ugly compared to the things that are around it

eyewitness /ˌaɪˈwɪtnɪs/ (*also* witness) *noun* [C] someone who saw something such as a crime or an accident happen *Eyewitnesses saw two men running away from the bank.*

Ff

F, f /ef/ the sixth letter of the alphabet

F *written abbreviation for* Fahrenheit (= a measurement of temperature) *a body temperature of 98.6°F*

FA /ˌefˈeɪ/ *noun abbreviation for* Football Association: the national organization for football in England *the FA Cup*

fable /ˈfeɪbl/ *noun* [C] a short, traditional story, usually involving animals, which is intended to show people how to behave *Aesop's fables*

fabric /ˈfæbrɪk/ *noun* **1** [C, U] cloth *a light/woollen fabric* **2 the fabric of sth a** the basic way in which a society or other social group is organized *The family is part of* ***the fabric of society***. **b** *UK* the walls, floor, and roof of a building

fabricate /ˈfæbrɪkeɪt/ *verb* [T] to invent facts, a story, etc in order to deceive someone *He claims that the police* ***fabricated evidence*** *against him.* • **fabrication** /ˌfæbrɪˈkeɪʃ^ən/ *noun* [C, U]

fabulous /ˈfæbjələs/ *adjective* extremely good *They've got a fabulous house.* ○ *We had an absolutely fabulous holiday.* • **fabulously** *adverb* extremely *Her family is* ***fabulously wealthy***.

facade (*also* **façade**) /fəˈsɑːd/ *noun* [C] **1** a false appearance ***Behind*** *that amiable* ***facade****, he's a deeply unpleasant man.* **2** the front of a large building *the gallery's elegant 18th century facade*

🔑**face**[1] /feɪs/ *noun* **1** [C] the front part of the head where the eyes, nose, and mouth are, or the expression on this part *She's got a long, thin face.* ○ *I can't wait to see her face when she opens the present.* **2 make a face** (*also UK* **pull a face**) to show with your face that you do not like someone or something *The baby made a face every time I offered her some food.* **3 make faces** to make silly expressions with your face in order to try and make people laugh **4 sb's face falls/lights up** someone starts to look disappointed/happy *His face fell when I said that she wasn't coming.* **5 to sb's face** If you say something unpleasant to someone's face, you say it to them directly, when you are with them. *If you've got something to say, say it to my face.* **6** the front or surface of something *the north face of the cliff* ○ *a clock face* **7 in the face of sth** while having to deal with a difficult situation or problem *She refused to leave him, in the face of increasing pressure from friends and family.* **8 on the face of it** used when you are describing how a situation seems on the surface *On the face of it, it seems like a bargain, but I bet there are hidden costs.* **9 keep a straight face** to manage to stop yourself from smiling or laughing *I can never play jokes on people because I can't keep a straight face.* **10 lose/save face** to do something so that people stop respecting you/still respect you *He seemed more interested in saving face than telling the truth.* ➲See also: have **egg**[1] on your face, a **slap**[2] in the face.

🔑**face**[2] /feɪs/ *verb* [T] **1** [DIRECTION] to be or turn in a particular direction *The room faces south.* ○ *She turned to face him.* **2** [PROBLEM] If you face a problem, or a problem faces you, you have to deal with it. **[often passive]** *This is one of the many problems faced by working mothers.* **3 can't face sth/doing sth** to not want to do something or deal with something because it is so unpleasant *I had intended to go for a run, but now I just can't face it.* **4** [ACCEPT] to accept that something unpleasant is true and start to deal with the situation *She's going to have to* ***face the fact that*** *he's not coming back to her.* **5 let's face it** something that you say before you say something that is unpleasant but true *Let's face it, none of us are getting any younger.* **6** [PUNISHMENT] If you face something unpleasant, especially a punishment, then it might happen to you. *If found guilty, the pair face fines of up to $40,000.* **7** [DEAL WITH] to deal with someone when the situation between you is difficult *How can I face him now that he knows what I've done?* **8** [COMPETITION] to play against another player or team in a competition, sport, etc *We face Spain in the semifinal.* ➲See also: face the **music**.

face up to sth to accept that a difficult situation exists

facelift /ˈfeɪslɪft/ *noun* [C] **1** medical treatment which makes the skin of your face tighter so that you look younger *She looks like she's* ***had a facelift***. **2** when you improve a place and make it look more attractive *The council is planning a £6 million facelift for the old harbour area.*

facet /ˈfæsɪt/ *noun* [C] one part of a subject, situation, etc that has many parts *She has many* ***facets to*** *her personality.*

facetious /fəˈsiːʃəs/ *adjective* trying to make a joke or a clever remark in a way that annoys people

face-to-face /ˌfeɪstəˈfeɪs/ *adjective, adverb* directly, meeting someone in the same place *We need to talk face-to-face.* ○ *She* ***came face-to-face with*** *the gunman as he strode into the playground.*

ˌface ˈvalue *noun* **take sth at face value** to accept the way that something first appears without thinking about what it really means *You can't just take everything you read in the papers at face value.*

facial /ˈfeɪʃ^əl/ *adjective* of or on the face ***facial expressions/hair***

facile /ˈfæsaɪl/ [US] /ˈfæsəl/ *adjective formal* A facile remark is too simple and has not been thought about enough.

facilitate /fəˈsɪlɪteɪt/ *verb* [T] *formal* to make something possible or easier *I will do everything in my power to facilitate the process.*

> WORD PARTNERS FOR ***facilities***
>
> **offer/provide** facilities • facilities **for** sb/(doing) sth • **sports** facilities

facilities /fəˈsɪlətiz/ *noun* **[plural]** buildings, equipment, or services that are provided for a particular purpose ***sports/washing facilities*** ○ *childcare facilities*

facility /fə'sɪləti/ *noun* [C] **1** a part of a system or machine which makes it possible to do something *This phone has a memory facility.* **2** a place where a particular activity happens *a new medical facility*

☞ WORD PARTNERS FOR **fact**

accept / face up to / establish / explain / ignore a fact • the fact remains • an important / interesting / simple / undeniable fact • the facts about sth • know for a fact

---

☞**fact** /fækt/ *noun* **1** TRUE THING [C] something that you know is true, exists, or has happened *I'm not angry that you drove my car, it's just the fact that you didn't ask me first.* ○ *No decision will be made until we know all the facts.* ○ *He knew for a fact* (= was certain) *that Natalie was lying.* **2** REAL THINGS [U] real events and experiences, not things that are imagined *It's hard to separate fact from fiction in what she says.* **3 in fact/in actual fact/as a matter of fact a** EMPHASIZING TRUTH used to emphasize what is really true *I was told there were some tickets left, but in actual fact they were sold out.* **b** MORE INFORMATION used when giving more information about something *"Is Isabel coming?" "Yes. As a matter of fact, she should be here soon."* **4 the fact (of the matter) is** used to tell someone that something is the truth *I wouldn't usually ask for your help, but the fact is I'm desperate.* **5 the facts of life** details about sexual activity and the way that babies are born *Does he know the facts of life?*

faction /'fækʃⁿn/ *noun* [C] a small group of people who are part of a larger group, and oppose the ideas of everyone else

☞**factor** /'fæktəʳ/ *noun* [C] **1** one of the things that has an effect on a particular situation, decision, event, etc *Money was an important factor in their decision to move.* **2** a number that another larger number can be divided by exactly *5 is a factor of 10.*

☞**factory** /'fæktⁿri/ *noun* [C] a building or group of buildings where large amounts of products are made or put together *a textile factory*

factual /'fæktʃuəl/ *adjective* using or consisting of facts • **factually** *adverb factually correct/incorrect*

faculty /'fækⁿlti/ *noun* **1** [C] a natural ability to hear, see, think, move, etc **2 the English/law/ science, etc faculty** a particular department at a college or university, or the teachers in that department **3 the faculty** *US* all of the teachers at a school or college

fad /fæd/ *noun* [C] something that is fashionable to do, wear, say, etc for a short period of time *the latest health fad*

fade /feɪd/ *verb* **1** [I, T] If a colour or a sound fades, or if something fades it, it become less bright or strong. *The music began to fade.* ○ *The walls had been faded by the sun.* **2** [I] (*also* **fade away**) to slowly disappear, lose importance, or become weaker *With time, memories of that painful summer would fade away.*

faeces *UK* (*US* **feces**) /'fiːsiːz/ *noun* [plural] *formal* solid waste that comes out of the bottom of a person or animal

fag /fæg/ *noun* [C] *UK informal* a cigarette

Fahrenheit /'færⁿnhaɪt/ (*written abbreviation* F) *noun* [U] a measurement of temperature in which water freezes at 32° and boils at 212°

☞**fail¹** /feɪl/ *verb* **1** NOT SUCCEED [I] to not be successful *Dad's business failed after just three years.* ○ *She keeps failing in her attempt to lose weight.* **2 fail to do sth** to not do what is necessary or expected *John failed to turn up for football practice yesterday.* **3** EXAM [I, T] to not pass a test or an exam, or to decide that someone has not passed *I'm worried about failing my driving test.* **4** STOP WORKING [I] to stop working normally, or to become weaker *Two of the plane's engines had failed.* **5** NOT HELPING [T] to stop being helpful or useful to someone when they need you *The government is failing the poor and unemployed.* **6 I fail to see/understand** used to show that you do not accept something [+ question word] *I fail to see why you cannot work on a Sunday.*

fail² /feɪl/ *noun* **without fail** If you do something without fail, you always do it, also when it is difficult. *I go to the gym every Monday and Thursday without fail.*

failing¹ /'feɪlɪŋ/ *noun* [C] a bad quality or fault that someone or something has *Despite one or two failings, he's basically a nice guy.*

failing² /'feɪlɪŋ/ *preposition* **failing that** if something is not possible or does not happen *Our goal is to move out by January, or failing that, by March.*

☞ WORD PARTNERS FOR **failure**

admit/end in failure • be doomed to failure • an abject / complete / humiliating / total failure

---

☞**failure** /'feɪljəʳ/ *noun* **1** NO SUCCESS [U] when someone or something does not succeed *Their attempt to climb Everest ended in failure.* **2** PERSON/ACTION [C] someone or something that does not succeed *All my life I've felt like a failure.* **3 failure to do sth** when you do not do something that you must do or are expected to do *Failure to pay within 14 days will result in prosecution.* **4** NOT WORKING [C, U] when something does not work, or stops working as well as it should **heart failure** ○ *All trains were delayed due to a power failure.*

faint¹ /feɪnt/ *adjective* **1** slight and not easy to notice, smell, hear, etc *a faint smell of smoke* ○ *faint laughter coming from next door* **2 feel faint** to feel very weak and as if you might fall down *Seeing all the blood made me feel faint.* **3 faint hope/praise/chance, etc** very little hope, praise, chance, etc *a faint hope of winning the gold medal* **4 not have the faintest idea** used to emphasize that you do not know something [+ question word] *I haven't the faintest idea what you're talking about.*

faint² /feɪnt/ *verb* [I] to suddenly become unconscious for a short time, usually falling down onto the floor *After the long journey, she fainted with exhaustion.*

faintly /'feɪntli/ *adverb* slightly *faintly embarrassed*

| ɑː arm | ɜː her | iː see | ɔː saw | uː too | aɪ my | aʊ how | eə hair | eɪ day | əʊ no | ɪə near | ɔɪ boy | ʊə poor | aɪə fire | aʊə sour |

o━**fair¹** /feəʳ/ adjective **1** EQUAL treating everyone in the same way, so that no one has an advantage *a fair trial ○ That's not fair. You always go first!* **2** RIGHT acceptable or right *a fair deal ○ We'd like to move abroad, but it's just not fair on the children.* ⊃Opposite **unfair. 3** HAIR/SKIN having pale skin or a light colour of hair *a boy with fair hair and blue eyes* ⊃Opposite **dark. 4 a fair amount/distance/size, etc** quite a large amount, distance, size, etc *There's still a fair bit of work to be done on the house.* **5** WEATHER sunny and not raining *Tomorrow will be fair, with some early morning frost.* **6** AVERAGE not very good but not very bad *He has a **fair chance** of winning.* **7 fair enough** UK informal used to say that you agree, or think that something is acceptable *"He'll only work on Sunday if he gets paid extra." "Fair enough."* ⊃See also: fair play², have your (fair) share² of sth.

fair² /feəʳ/ noun fair [C] **1** an event outside where you can ride large machines for pleasure and play games to win prizes **2** an event where people show and sell goods or services relating to a particular business or hobby *a **trade fair***

fair³ /feəʳ/ adverb **1 play fair** to do something in a fair and honest way *All I ask is that they play fair.* **2 fair and square** in an honest way and without any doubt *We won the match fair and square.*

fairground /'feəgraʊnd/ noun [C] an outside area that is used for fairs

fair-haired /,feə'heəd/ adjective having a light colour of hair *a fair-haired child*

o━**fairly** /'feəli/ adverb **1** more than average, but less than very *a fairly big family ○ fairly quickly* **2** done in a fair way *treating people fairly*

fairness /'feənəs/ noun [U] when you treat everyone in the same way, so that no one has an advantage

fair 'trade noun [U] a way of buying and selling products that makes certain that the original producer receives a fair price *fair trade coffee/chocolate* ⊃Compare **free trade.** ● **fairly traded** adverb

fairy /'feəri/ noun [C] a small, imaginary creature that looks like a person with wings, and has magic powers *All the little girls were dressed up as fairies.*

fairy

fairytale /'feəriteɪl/ adjective [always before noun] happy and beautiful, like something in a fairy tale *But this was no fairytale romance. ○ They had what can only be de-*

scribed as *a fairytale wedding.*

'**fairy ,tale** noun [C] a story told to children which involves magic, imaginary creatures, and a happy ending

faith /feɪθ/ noun **1** TRUST [U] the belief that someone or something is good, right, and able to be trusted *Have **faith in** me. I won't let you down.* **2** STRONG BELIEF [U] strong belief in a god or gods *Throughout her illness, she never lost her **faith** in God.* **3** RELIGION [C] a religion *the Jewish and Christian faiths* **4 in good faith** If you act in good faith, you believe that what you are doing is good, honest, or legal.

faithful /'feɪθfᵊl/ adjective **1** RELATIONSHIP If your husband, wife, or partner is faithful, they do not have a sexual relationship with anyone else. *a faithful husband ○ They remained **faithful to** each other throughout their long marriage.* **2** LOYAL always loyal *his trusted and faithful servant* **3** NOT CHANGED not changing any of the original details, facts, style, etc *Does the film adaptation stay **faithful** to the novel?* ⊃Opposite **unfaithful.** ● **faithfulness** noun [U]

faithfully /'feɪθfᵊli/ adverb **1** in a faithful way **2 Yours faithfully** used to end a formal letter to someone whose name you do not know

fake¹ /feɪk/ adjective not real, but made to look or seem real *fake fur ○ a fake passport*

fake² /feɪk/ noun [C] **1** a copy of something that is intended to look real or valuable and deceive people *Experts say that the painting is a fake.* **2** someone who pretends to have particular skills or qualities so that they can deceive people or get their admiration

fake³ /feɪk/ verb [T] **1** to copy something in order to deceive people *faked documents* **2** to pretend that you have a particular feeling or emotion *He said he was feeling sick, but he was just **faking** it.*

falcon /'fɔːlkᵊn/ noun [C] a large bird that eats small animals and is often taught to hunt by people

o━**fall¹** /fɔːl/ verb [I] past tense **fell** past participle **fallen 1** MOVE DOWN to move down towards the ground *Huge drops of rain were **falling from** the sky. ○ By winter, all the leaves had **fallen off** the trees.* **2** STOP STANDING to suddenly go down and hit the ground without intending to *She **fell off** her bike and broke her arm.* **3** BECOME LESS to become less in number or amount *Housing prices have **fallen by** 15% since last year. ○ Temperatures are expected to **fall from** 15°C to 9°C.* **4** BECOME WORSE to become worse, or start to be in a bad situation or condition *Education standards are continuing to fall. ○ Empty for 30 years, the building had **fallen into ruin** (= become very damaged).* **5** BECOME ... asleep/ill/still, etc *I fell asleep on the*

sofa watching TV. **6 darkness/night falls** *literary* used to say that it is becoming dark **7** LOSE POWER to lose power and start to be controlled by a different leader *In 1453 the city fell to the Turks.* **8** HANG DOWN to hang down *Her long blonde hair fell softly over her shoulders.* ⊃See also: fall on deaf ears (**ear**), fall **flat³**, fall **foul¹** of sb/sth, go/fall to pieces (**piece¹**), fall into **place¹**, fall **prey¹** to sth, fall by the **wayside**.

COMMON LEARNER ERROR

fall and **feel**

Be careful not to confuse the past forms of the verbs **fall** and **feel**.

The past tense of **fall** is **fell**.

Chris fell off the ladder and broke his arm.

The past tense of **feel** is **felt**.

I felt really happy and relaxed.

fall apart 1 to break into pieces *My poor old boots are falling apart.* **2** to start having problems that you cannot deal with *Their relationship fell apart after they moved to Detroit.*

fall back on sb/sth to use someone or something when other things have failed, or when there are no other choices *We've been saving up the past few years, to have something to fall back on.*

fall behind to not do something fast enough, or not do something by a particular time *Lucy's been falling behind in her homework again.*

fall for sb to suddenly have strong, romantic feelings about someone

fall for sth to be tricked into believing something that is not true *He told me he owned a mansion in Spain and I fell for it.*

fall in If a roof or ceiling falls in, it drops to the ground because it is damaged.

fall off If the amount, rate, or quality of something falls off, it becomes smaller or lower. *Demand for new cars is falling off.*

fall on sth to happen on a particular day or date *New Year's Day falls on a Tuesday this year.*

fall out *UK* to argue with someone and stop being friendly with them *Have you and Sam fallen out with each other again?*

o⁻**fall over** If someone or something falls over, they fall to the ground or onto their side. *The fence fell over in the wind.* ⊃See colour picture **Phrasal Verbs** on page Centre 16.

fall through If a plan or agreement falls through, it fails to happen.

WORD PARTNERS FOR fall

a **dramatic / sharp / steep** fall • a fall **in** sth

o⁻**fall²** /fɔːl/ *noun* **1** AMOUNT [C] when the number or amount of something becomes smaller *There's been a sharp fall in prices.* **2** MOVEMENT [C] when someone or something moves down to the ground *a heavy fall of snow* **3** SEASON [C, U] *US* (*UK/US* autumn) the season of the year between summer and winter, when leaves fall from the trees *He started a new job in the fall.* **4** DEFEAT [no plural] when a city,

government, leader, etc loses power or control *the fall of communism*

fallacy /ˈfæləsi/ *noun* [C, U] a belief that is not true or correct *It's a fallacy that problems will disappear if you ignore them.*

fallen /ˈfɔːlən/ *past participle of* fall

fallible /ˈfæləbl/ *adjective* able to make mistakes *We place our trust in doctors, but even they are fallible.* ⊃Opposite **infallible**. • **fallibility** /ˌfæləˈbɪləti/ *noun* [U]

fallout /ˈfɔːlaʊt/ *noun* [U] the radiation (= powerful and dangerous energy) from a nuclear explosion

fallow /ˈfæləʊ/ *adjective* If land is left fallow, it is not planted with crops, in order to improve the quality of the soil.

o⁻**false** /fɔːls/ *adjective* **1** NOT TRUE not true or correct *a false name* ○ *Many rumours about her life were later proved to be false.* **2** NOT REAL not real, but made to look or seem real *false teeth* ○ *false documents* **3** NOT SINCERE not sincere or expressing real emotions *false promises* • **falsely** *adverb*

ˌfalse aˈlarm *noun* [C] an occasion when people believe that something dangerous is happening, but it is not *Fire engines rushed to the scene, but it was a false alarm.*

falsehood /ˈfɔːlshʊd/ *noun* [C] *formal* a lie

ˌfalse ˈstart *noun* [C] an occasion when you try to start an activity, event, or process, but fail and have to stop *The after-school club finally opened this term, after several false starts.*

falsify /ˈfɔːlsɪfaɪ/ *verb* [T] to change important information, especially in documents, in order to deceive people

falter /ˈfɔːltəʳ/ *verb* [I] **1** to stop being confident, powerful, or successful *In the late 1980s his career began to falter.* **2** to pause, make mistakes, or seem weak when you are talking or moving *Her voice didn't falter once during the ceremony.* ○ *a few faltering steps*

fame /feɪm/ *noun* [U] when you are known by many people because of your achievements, skills, etc *fame and fortune* ○ *She first rose to fame as a pop star at the age of 16.* ⊃See also: sb's/sth's **claim²** to fame.

famed /feɪmd/ *adjective* famous, especially for having particular qualities *It is a city famed for its ski slopes and casinos.*

o⁻**familiar** /fəˈmɪliəʳ/ *adjective* **1** easy to recognize because of being seen, met, heard, etc before *It's nice to see a few familiar faces* (= people that I recognize) *around here.* ○ *This street doesn't look familiar to me.* **2 be familiar with sth** to know about something or have experienced it many times before *Anyone who's familiar with his poetry will find the course easy.* ⊃Opposite **unfamiliar**. **3** friendly and very informal *He doesn't like to be too familiar with his staff.*

familiarity /fəˌmɪliˈærəti/ *noun* [U] **1** a good knowledge of something, or experience of doing or using it *Her familiarity with computers is very impressive.* **2** friendly and informal behaviour

familiarize (*also UK* -ise) /fəˈmɪliəraɪz/ *verb*

familiarize sb/yourself with sth to teach someone more about something new, or try to understand more about it yourself *We spent a few minutes familiarizing ourselves with the day's schedule.*

have/raise/start/support a family • a big/close/happy family • your close/extended/immediate family

o►**family** /'fæmᵊli/ *noun* 1 RELATED PEOPLE [group] a group of people who are related to each other, such as a mother, a father, and their children *Her (UK) family are/(US) family is originally from Ireland.* ○ *a family business* 2 CHILDREN [C] the children in a family [usually singular] *Single parents have to raise a family on their own.* ○ *Paul and Alison are hoping to start a family soon.* 3 PLANTS/ANIMALS [C] a group of similar types of plants or animals that are related to each other

'**family ,name** *noun* [C] the name that is used by all the members of a family

,**family 'planning** *noun* [U] controlling how many children you have by using contraceptives (= pills or objects that prevent a woman from becoming pregnant)

,**family 'tree** *noun* [C] a drawing that shows the relationships between the different members of a family, especially over a long period of time

famine /'fæmɪn/ *noun* [C, U] when people living in a particular area do not have enough food for a long time causing suffering and death

o►**famous** /'feɪməs/ *adjective* known or recognized by many people *a famous actress* ○ *New York is a city famous for its shopping and nightlife.* ⊃See also: world-famous.

famously /'feɪməsli/ *adverb* 1 **get on famously (with sb)** to have a very friendly relationship with someone 2 in a way that is famous

fan

a big/huge fan • a fan of sb/sth • football/soccer fans

o►**fan¹** /fæn/ *noun* [C] 1 someone who admires and supports a famous person, sport, type of music, etc *More than 15,000 Liverpool fans* attended Saturday's game. ○ *He's a big fan of country music.* 2 something that is used to move the air around so that it feels cooler, such as a machine or an object that you wave with your hand *an electric fan* ○ *There was no air conditioning, just a ceiling fan turning slowly.*

fan² /fæn/ *verb* [T] **fanning** *past* **fanned** to move the air around with a fan or something used like a fan, to make it feel cooler [often reflexive] *The spectators sat in the bright sun, fanning themselves with newspapers.*

fan out If a group of people fan out, they move out in different directions from a single point.

fanatic /fə'nætɪk/ *noun* [C] someone whose interest in something or enthusiasm for something is extreme • **fanatical** *adjective* extremely enthusiastic about something *She's fanatical about football.* ○ *Nathaniel's enthusiasm for aerobics was almost fanatical.* • **fanaticism** /fə'nætɪsɪzᵊm/ *noun* [U]

fanciable /'fænsiəbl/ *adjective* UK informal sexually attractive *This Solomon bloke, is he fanciable?*

fanciful /'fænsɪfᵊl/ *adjective* Something that is fanciful comes from someone's imagination and so is probably not true or real. *a fanciful story*

'**fan ,club** *noun* [C] an organization for the people who support and admire a particular singer, actor, sports team, etc *a member of the official Elvis Presley fan club*

fancy¹ /'fænsi/ *verb* [T] 1 WANT UK to want to have or do something *Do you fancy a drink?* ○ [+ doing sth] *We fancy going to the Caribbean for our holiday.* 2 PERSON UK informal to feel sexually attracted to someone *I fancied him the first time I saw him.* 3 **fancy (that)!** UK informal used to show that you are surprised or shocked by something [+ doing sth] *Fancy seeing you here!* ○ *He's going out with Marie? Well fancy that!* 4 THINK formal to think that something is true [+ (that)] *I fancy that he was smiling, but I can't be sure.*

fancy² /'fænsi/ *adjective* 1 Fancy things and places are expensive and fashionable. *a fancy restaurant* 2 with lots of decoration, or very complicated *fancy cakes*

fancy³ /'fænsi/ *noun* 1 **take a fancy to sb/sth** to start to like someone or something a lot *Marina had taken a fancy to her.* 2 **take sb's fancy** If something or someone takes your fancy, you find them interesting or attractive. *We can go anywhere that takes your fancy.*

,**fancy 'dress** *noun* [U] UK special clothes that people wear for a party, which make them look like a different person *a fancy dress party* ○ *When I saw Simon looking like that, I thought he was in fancy dress.*

fanfare /'fænfeəʳ/ *noun* [C] a short, loud tune played on a trumpet (= metal musical instrument) to announce an important person or event

fang

fang

fang /fæŋ/ *noun* [C] a long, sharp tooth of an animal such as a dog or a snake

'fanny ,pack *US* (*UK* bumbag) *noun* [C] a small bag fixed to a belt that you wear around your waist

fantasize (*also UK* -ise) /'fæntəsaɪz/ *verb* [I, T] to imagine something that you would like to happen, but is not likely to happen *We used to fantasize about becoming famous actresses.*

fantastic /fæn'tæstɪk/ *adjective* **1** GOOD *informal* very good *I've had a fantastic time.* **2** LARGE *informal* A fantastic amount or number of something is very large. *They're making fantastic amounts of money.* **3** STRANGE very strange and probably not true *fantastic stories about monsters and witches*

fantastically /fæn'tæstɪkᵊli/ *adverb* extremely *fantastically rich*

WORD PARTNERS FOR **fantasy**

have fantasies **about** /**of** (doing) sth • **sexual** fantasies • a fantasy **world**
---

fantasy /'fæntəsi/ *noun* [C, U] a situation or event that you imagine, which is not real or true

FAQ /,efeɪ'kjuː/ *noun* [C] *abbreviation for* frequently asked question: something that many people ask when they use the Internet or a computer program, or a file (= collection) of these questions with their answers

o=**far¹** /fɑːʳ/ *adverb* farther, farthest *or* further, furthest **1** used to talk about how distant something is *It's the first time I've been so far away from home.* ○ *How far is it to the supermarket?* ○ *Bournemouth is not far from Poole.* ○ *In the summer the herds move farther north.* **2** a long time *How far back can you remember?* ○ *We need to plan further ahead.* **3 far better/cheaper/more, etc** much better, cheaper, more, etc *Young people are far more independent these days.* **4 far too difficult/expensive/late, etc** much too difficult, expensive, late, etc *His trousers were far too tight.* **5 as far as I know** *informal* used to say what you think is true, although you do not know all the facts *As far as I know, they haven't reached a decision yet.* **6 as**

far as sb is concerned used to say what someone's opinion is *It's all over as far as I'm concerned.* **7 as far as sth is concerned** used to say what you are talking about *As far as sport's concerned, I like tennis and football.* **8 by far** used to emphasize that something is the biggest, the best, etc *This is his best film by far.* **9 far from sth** certainly not something *The situation is far from clear.* **10 far from doing sth** certainly not doing something *Far from being pleased, he was embarrassed by the praise.* **11 far from it** *informal* used to tell someone that something is certainly not true *He's not handsome - far from it.* **12 as far as possible** as much as is possible *We try to buy organic food as far as possible.* **13 go so far as to do sth** to take the extreme action of doing something *He even went so far as to stop her using the telephone.* **14 go too far** to behave in a way that upsets or annoys other people **15 how far** used to talk about how true something is *How far do politicians represent the views of ordinary people?* **16 so far** until now *So far, we haven't made much progress.* **17 so far so good** *informal* used to say that something has gone well until now **18 not go (very) far** If something such as money does not go far, you cannot do very much with it. *£1 doesn't go very far these days.*

o=**far²** /fɑːʳ/ *adjective* farther, farthest *or* further, furthest **1** [always before noun] describes the part of something that is most distant from you or from the centre *His office is at the far end of the corridor.* ○ *They live in the far south of the country.* **2 the far left/right** used to describe political groups whose opinions are very extreme ⊃See also: be a far **cry²** from sth.

faraway /,fɑːrə'weɪ/ *adjective* **1** [always before noun] *literary* a long distance away *faraway places* **2 a faraway look/expression** an expression on someone's face that shows that they are not thinking about what is happening around them *He had a faraway look in his eyes.*

farce /fɑːs/ *noun* **1** [no plural] a serious event or situation that becomes ridiculous because it is so badly organized *The meeting was a complete farce.* **2** [C] a funny play in which a lot of silly things happen • **farcical** /'fɑːsɪkᵊl/ *adjective* like a farce

---
WORD PARTNERS FOR **fare**

a **return**/**single** fare • the fare **to** [Seattle/Moscow, etc]
---

fare¹ /feəʳ/ *noun* [C] the price that you pay to travel on an aircraft, train, bus, etc *air/train fares*

fare² /feəʳ/ *verb formal* **fare well/badly/better, etc** used to say how well or badly someone or something does in a particular situation *All the children fared well in the exams.*

farewell /,feə'wel/ *exclamation* old-fashioned goodbye • **farewell** *noun* [C] when someone says goodbye *a sad farewell* ○ *a farewell party*

far-fetched /,fɑː'fetʃt/ *adjective* difficult to believe and not likely to be true *The idea is not as far-fetched as it might sound.*

farm

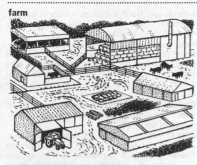

o⁻**farm¹** /fɑːm/ noun [C] an area of land with fields and buildings that is used for growing crops and keeping animals as a business *a dairy farm ○ farm animals/buildings*

farm² /fɑːm/ verb [I, T] to grow crops or keep animals as a business *Only 2% of the country's farmland is farmed organically.*

o⁻**farmer** /ˈfɑːməʳ/ noun [C] someone who owns or looks after a farm

farmhouse /ˈfɑːmhaʊs/ noun [C] plural **farmhouses** /ˈfɑːmhaʊzɪz/ the house on a farm where the farmer lives

farming /ˈfɑːmɪŋ/ noun [U] working on a farm or organizing the work there

farmland /ˈfɑːmlænd/ noun [U] land which is used for or suitable for farming

farmyard /ˈfɑːmjɑːd/ noun [C] an area of ground with farm buildings around it

far-off /ˌfɑːʳˈɒf/ adjective *literary* a long distance away or a long time in the past or future *far-off lands*

far-reaching /ˌfɑːʳˈriːtʃɪŋ/ adjective Far-reaching acts, events, or ideas have very big effects. *far-reaching changes in the education system*

farsighted /ˈfɑːˌsaɪtɪd/ US (UK **long-sighted**) adjective able to see objects which are far away, but not things which are near to you

fart /fɑːt/ verb [I] *very informal* to release gas from the bowels through the bottom • **fart** noun [C]

farther /ˈfɑːðəʳ/ adjective, adverb (comparative of far) more distant *I couldn't walk any farther.*

farthest /ˈfɑːðɪst/ adjective, adverb (superlative of far) most distant *They walked to the farthest edge of the garden.*

fascinate /ˈfæsɪneɪt/ verb [T] to interest someone a lot *Science has always fascinated me.*

fascinated /ˈfæsɪneɪtɪd/ adjective extremely interested *They were absolutely fascinated by the game.*

fascinating /ˈfæsɪneɪtɪŋ/ adjective extremely interesting *I found the movie fascinating.*

fascination /ˌfæsɪˈneɪʃᵊn/ noun [U, no plural] when you find someone or something fascinating *Her fascination with fashion started at an early age.*

fascism, Fascism /ˈfæʃɪzᵊm/ noun [U] a political system in which the government is extremely powerful and controls people's lives

fascist /ˈfæʃɪst/ noun [C] **1** (*also* **Fascist**) someone who supports fascism **2** someone who you do not like because they try to control other people's behaviour • **fascist** adjective *a fascist dictator/regime*

o⁻**fashion¹** /ˈfæʃᵊn/ noun **1** STYLE [C, U] the most popular style of clothes, appearance, or behaviour at a particular time *Long hair is back in fashion for men. ○ Fur coats have gone out of fashion.* **2** BUSINESS [U] making and selling clothes *the fashion industry* **3** WAY [no plural] *formal* the way in which someone does something *Verity told the story in a very amusing fashion.*

fashion² /ˈfæʃᵊn/ verb [T] *formal* to make something *jewellery fashioned from recycled metal*

fashionable /ˈfæʃᵊnəbl/ adjective popular at a particular time *fashionable clothes* ○ *[+ to do sth] It's no longer fashionable to smoke.* ⊃Opposite **unfashionable.** • **fashionably** adverb *fashionably dressed*

OTHER WAYS OF SAYING **fast**

If you want to use fast as an adjective, a very common alternative is **quick**: *I tried to catch him, but he was too **quick** for me.*

If something is done fast, without waiting, you can use the adjectives **prompt** or **speedy**: *A **prompt** reply would be very much appreciated.* • *He made a **speedy** recovery.*

If something is done too fast, without thinking carefully, the adjectives **hasty** and **hurried** are often used: *I don't want to make a **hasty** decision.* • *We left early after a **hurried** breakfast.*

A fast walk is often described as **brisk**: *We took a **brisk** walk through the park.*

The adjective **rapid** is often used to describe fast growth or change: *The 1990's were a period of **rapid** change/growth.*

If you want to use fast as an adverb, a very common alternative is **quickly**: *The problem needs to be sorted out as **quickly** as possible.*

If someone does something very fast, in informal situations you can use the expressions **in a flash** and **like a shot**: *I'll be back **in a flash.*** • *There was an almighty crash and he got up **like a shot.***

o⁻**fast¹** /fɑːst/ adjective **1** moving, happening, or doing something quickly *fast cars* ○ *a fast swimmer* ○ *Computers are getting faster all the time.* **2** [never before noun] If a clock or watch is fast, it shows a time that is later than the correct time. ⊃See also: a fast **track¹** (to sth).

o⁻**fast²** /fɑːst/ adverb **1** moving or happening

quickly *We ran as fast as we could.* ○ *You'll have to act fast.* **2 fast asleep** completely asleep (= sleeping) **3** in a firm or tight way *He tried to get away, but she held him fast.* ⊃See also: **thick¹** and fast.

fast³ /fɑːst/ *verb* [I] to eat nothing, or much less than you usually eat for a period of time ● **fast** *noun* [C]

⊶**fasten** /ˈfɑːsᵊn/ *verb* **1** [I, T] to close or fix something together, or to become closed or fixed together *Fasten your seat belts.* ○ *This dress fastens at the side.* **2 fasten sth on/to/together, etc** to fix one thing to another *He fastened the rope to a tree.* ⊃Opposite **unfasten.**

fastener /ˈfɑːsᵊnəʳ/ *noun* [C] something that is used to close or fix things together

,**fast 'food** *noun* [U] hot food that can be served very quickly in a restaurant because it is already prepared *fast food restaurants*

fast-forward /ˌfɑːstˈfɔːwəd/ *verb* [I, T] If you fast-forward a recording, or if it fast-forwards, you make it play at very high speed so that you get to the end more quickly. ● **fast-forward** *noun* [U]

fastidious /fæsˈtɪdiəs/ *adjective* Someone who is fastidious wants every detail of something to be correct and perfect.

⊶**fat¹** /fæt/ *adjective* **fatter, fattest 1** Someone who is fat weighs too much. *She eats all the time but never gets fat.* **2** thick or large *a fat book* ⊃See also: fat **chance¹.**

fat² /fæt/ *noun* **1** [U] the substance under the skin of people and animals that keeps them warm *body fat* **2** [C, U] a solid or liquid substance like oil that is taken from plants or animals and used in cooking *animal/vegetable fat* ⊃See also: **saturated fat.**

fatal /ˈfeɪtᵊl/ *adjective* **1** A fatal accident or illness causes death. *a fatal car crash* **2** Fatal actions have very bad effects. *a fatal error* ● **fatally** *adverb fatally injured*

fatalism /ˈfeɪtᵊlɪzᵊm/ *noun* [U] the belief that people cannot change events, and that bad events cannot be avoided ● **fatalistic** /ˌfeɪtᵊlˈɪstɪk/ *adjective*

fatality /fəˈtæləti/ *noun* [C] *formal* the death of a person caused by violence or an accident

,**fat 'cat** *noun* [C] someone who has a lot of money, especially someone in charge of a company *fat cat bosses/directors*

fate /feɪt/ *noun* **1** [C] what happens to someone, especially something bad *His fate is now in the hands of the jury.* **2** [U] a power that

some people believe decides what will happen *I believe it was fate that caused us to meet again.* ⊃See also: **quirk** of fate.

fated /ˈfeɪtɪd/ *adjective* [never before noun] If something that happens or someone's actions are fated, they are decided by a power that controls events, and cannot be avoided. [+ to do sth] *I seem fated to meet him wherever I go.* ⊃See also: **ill-fated.**

fateful /ˈfeɪtfᵊl/ *adjective* A fateful event has an important and usually bad effect on the future. *a fateful decision*

⊶**father¹** /ˈfɑːðəʳ/ *noun* **1** [C] your male parent **2 Father** the title of some Christian priests *Father O'Brian* **3 the father of sth** the man who invented or started something *Descartes is known as the father of modern philosophy.*

father² /ˈfɑːðəʳ/ *verb* [T] *formal* to become a male parent *He fathered three children.*

,**Father 'Christmas** *noun* [no plural] *UK* a kind, fat, old man in red clothes who people say brings presents to children at Christmas

'**father ,figure** *noun* [C] an older man who gives you advice and support like a father

fatherhood /ˈfɑːðəhʊd/ *noun* [U] being a father

father-in-law /ˈfɑːðərɪnlɔː/ *noun* [C] *plural* **fathers-in-law** the father of your husband or wife

fathom¹ /ˈfæðəm/ (*also UK* **fathom out**) *verb* [T] to be able to understand something after thinking about it a lot [+ question word] *No one could fathom why she had left so early.*

fathom² /ˈfæðəm/ *noun* [C] a unit for measuring the depth of water, equal to 1.8 metres

fatigue /fəˈtiːg/ *noun* [U] when you feel very tired ● **fatigued** *adjective*

fatigues /fəˈtiːgz/ *noun* [plural] special clothes that soldiers wear when they are fighting or working

fatten /ˈfætᵊn/ *verb* [T] to make animals fatter so that they can be eaten

fatten sb/sth up to give a thin person or animal lots of food so that they become fatter

fattening /ˈfætᵊnɪŋ/ *adjective* Fattening food can make you fat. *I don't eat chips, they're too fattening.*

fatty /ˈfæti/ *adjective* Fatty foods contain a lot of fat.

fatuous /ˈfætjuəs/ *adjective* very stupid and not deserving your attention or respect *a fatuous comment/remark*

faucet /ˈfɔːsɪt/ *US* (*UK/US* **tap**) *noun* [C] an object at the end of a pipe which you turn to control the flow of water ⊃See picture at **tap** ⊃See colour picture **The Kitchen** on page Centre 2.

⊶**fault¹** /fɔːlt/ *noun* **1 sb's fault** If something bad that has happened is someone's fault, they are responsible for it. *She believes it was the doctor's fault that Peter died.* **2 at fault** responsible for something bad that has happened *I was at fault and I would like to apologize.* **3** [C] something that is wrong with something or with someone's character *The car has a serious design fault.* **4 find fault with sb/sth** to criticize someone or something, especially without good reasons

fault or mistake?

Use **fault** for explaining who is responsible when something bad happens.

It's my fault that the car was stolen. I left the window open.

~~It's my mistake the car was stolen. I left the window open.~~

Use **mistake** for talking about something that you did or thought which was wrong.

I still make lots of mistakes in my essays.

~~I still make lots of faults in my essays.~~

fault² /fɔːlt/ *verb* [T] to find a reason to criticize someone or something *I can't fault the way that they dealt with the complaint.*

faultless /'fɔːltləs/ *adjective* perfect, or without any mistakes *a faultless performance*

faulty /'fɔːlti/ *adjective* not working correctly *faulty brakes/wiring*

fauna /'fɔːnə/ *noun* [group] all the animals that live in a particular area *the flora and fauna of the area*

favour¹ UK (US favor) /'feɪvəʳ/ *noun* **1** HELP [C] something that you do to help someone *Could you do me a favour please?* ○ *I wanted to ask you a favour.* **2 be in favour of sth** to agree with or approve of a plan or idea *Most people are in favour of reducing traffic in cities.* **3 in favour of sb/sth** If you refuse or get rid of someone or something in favour of someone or something else, you choose them instead. *They dropped him from the team in favour of a much younger player.* **4 in sb's favour a** ADVANTAGE If something is in your favour, it helps you to win or succeed. *Both sides have strong arguments in their favour.* **b** WINNING If a game, vote, or judgement is in someone's favour, they win. *The final score ‚ was 16-10 in England's favour.* **5** LIKE [U] *formal* when people like something or someone *Her work never found favour among the critics.* **6 be in favour/out of favour** to be popular/unpopular *He has fallen out of favour recently.*

favour² UK (US favor) /'feɪvəʳ/ *verb* [T] **1** to choose or prefer one possibility [often passive] *These are the running shoes favoured by marathon runners.* **2** to act unfairly by treating one person better than another *She always felt that her parents favoured her brother.*

favourable UK (US favorable) /'feɪvʳrəbl/ *adjective* **1** showing that you like or approve of someone or something, or making you like or approve of them *She made a very favourable impression on us.* **2** making something more likely to be successful *favourable weather conditions* ⊃Opposite **unfavourable**. • **favourably** UK (US favorably) *adverb*

o⁻**favourite¹** UK (US favorite) /'feɪvʳrət/ *adjective* [always before noun] Your favourite person or

thing is the one that you like best. *What's your favourite band?*

favourite² UK (US favorite) /'feɪvʳrət/ *noun* [C] **1** a person or thing that you like more than all others *These chocolates are my favourites.* **2** the person or animal that is most likely to win a competition *The Dallas Cowboys are now favourites to win.*

favouritism UK (US favoritism) /'feɪvʳrətɪzᵊm/ *noun* [U] unfairly treating one person or group better than another

fawn¹ /fɔːn/ *noun* **1** [C] a young deer **2** [U] a light brown colour

fawn² /fɔːn/ *verb*
fawn on/over sb to praise someone or be nice to someone in a way that is false in order to get something or to make them like you

fax¹ /fæks/ *noun* **1** DOCUMENT [C] a document that is sent or received using a special machine and a telephone line *I got a fax from them this morning.* **2** SYSTEM [U] the system of sending or receiving documents using a special machine and a telephone line *Some products can be ordered by fax.* **3** MACHINE [C] (*also* **'fax ‚machine**) a machine that is used to send and receive faxes ⊃See colour picture **The Office** on page Centre 5.

fax² /fæks/ *verb* [T] to send documents using a fax machine [+ two objects] *Can you fax me a price list?*

the FBI /ˌefbiːˈaɪ/ *noun abbreviation for* the Federal Bureau of Investigation: one of the national police forces in the US that is controlled by the central government *He is wanted by the FBI for fraud.*

allay/calm/cause/heighten fear • hold no
fear for sb • great/morbid/widespread fear
• fear of sth

o⁻**fear¹** /fɪəʳ/ *noun* **1** [C, U] a strong, unpleasant feeling that you get when you think that something bad, dangerous, or frightening might happen *She was trembling with fear.* ○ *Unlike the rest of us, Dave had no fear of snakes.* ○ [+ (that)] *There are fears that the disease will spread to other countries.* **2 for fear of sth/doing sth** because you are worried about something/doing something *I didn't want to move for fear of waking her up.*

fear² /fɪəʳ/ *verb* [T] **1** to be worried or frightened that something bad might happen or might have happened [+ (that)] *Police fear that the couple may have drowned.* **2** to be frightened of something or someone unpleasant *Most older employees fear unemployment.* **3 fear the worst** If you fear the worst, you are frightened that an unpleasant situation will become much worse. *When there was no sign of the children, rescuers feared the worst.*

fear for sth/sb to be worried about something, or to be worried that someone is in danger *Her parents fear for her safety* (= worry that she may not be safe).

fearful /'fɪəfᵊl/ *adjective formal* **1** frightened or worried [+ of + doing sth] *Many women are fearful of travelling alone.* **2** [always before noun] UK very bad *Nigel has a fearful temper.* ● **fearfully** *adverb*

fearless /ˈfɪələs/ *adjective* not frightened of anything *a fearless fighter* ● **fearlessly** *adverb*

fearsome /ˈfɪəsəm/ *adjective* very frightening *a fearsome opponent*

feasible /ˈfiːzəbl/ *adjective* possible to do *a feasible plan* ○ [+ to do sth] *It may be feasible to clone human beings, but is it ethical?* ● **feasibility** /ˌfiːzəˈbɪləti/ *noun* [U]

feast¹ /fiːst/ *noun* [C] a large meal, especially to celebrate something special *a wedding feast*

feast² /fiːst/ *verb*
feast on sth to eat a lot of food and enjoy it very much

feat /fiːt/ *noun* **1** [C] an act or achievement that shows great skill or strength *The Eiffel Tower is a remarkable feat of engineering.* **2 be no mean feat** used when you want to emphasize that an act or achievement is very difficult *Learning to ski at 60 is no mean feat!*

feather /ˈfeðəʳ/ *noun* [C] one of the soft, light things that grow from and cover a bird's skin ● **feathery** *adjective* like feathers *feathery leaves*

╔═══════════════════════════════════╗
WORD PARTNERS FOR feature

a **distinguishing/important/notable** feature ● a **redeeming** feature ● a feature **of** sth ● a **new** feature
╚═══════════════════════════════════╝

◦ᴀ**feature¹** /ˈfiːtʃəʳ/ *noun* [C] **1** PART a typical quality, or important part of something *This phone has several new features.* **2** FACE Someone's features are the parts of their face that you notice when you look at them. *His eyes are his best feature.* **3** NEWSPAPER a special article in a newspaper or magazine, or a special television programme *a double-page feature on global warming*

feature² /ˈfiːtʃəʳ/ *verb* [T] to include someone or something as an important part *a new movie featuring Bruce Willis*
feature in sth to be an important part of something

feature film *noun* [C] a film that is usually 90 or more minutes long

◦ᴀ**February** /ˈfebruʳri/ (*written abbreviation* **Feb**) *noun* [C, U] the second month of the year

feces /ˈfiːsiːz/ *noun* [plural] *US spelling of* faeces

feckless /ˈfekləs/ *adjective* A feckless person is not willing to work or take responsibility for their actions.

fed /fed/ *past of* feed

federal /ˈfedʳrʳl/ *adjective* [always before noun] **1** relating to the central government, and not to the government of a region, of some countries such as the United States *the federal government* ○ *a federal agency/employee* **2** A federal system of government consists of a group of regions that is controlled by a central government.

federal holiday *US* (*UK/US* national holiday) *noun* [C] a day when most people in a country do not have to work

federalism /ˈfedʳrʳlɪzʳm/ *noun* [U] a political system in which separate states are organized

under a central government ● **federalist** *noun* [C] someone who supports federalism

federation /ˌfedʳrˈeɪʃʳn/ *noun* [C] a group of organizations, countries, regions, etc that have joined together to form a larger organization or government *the International Tennis Federation*

fed 'up *adjective informal* [never before noun] annoyed or bored by something that you have experienced for too long *I'm fed up with my job.*

fee /fiː/ *noun* [C] an amount of money that you pay to do something, to use something, or to get a service *an entrance fee* ○ *university fees*

feeble /ˈfiːbl/ *adjective* **1** extremely weak *She became too feeble to get out of bed.* **2** not very good or effective *a feeble argument/excuse* ● **feebly** *adverb*

◦ᴀ**feed¹** /fiːd/ *verb past* **fed 1** GIVE FOOD [T] to give food to a person, group, or animal *I fed Simone's cat while she was away.* **2** EAT FOOD [I] If an animal or a baby feeds, it eats. *The caterpillars feed on cabbage leaves.* **3** SUPPLY [T] to supply something such as information to a person or a machine, especially in a regular or continuous way *We fed them false information about our plans.* ⊃See also: breast-feed.

feed² /fiːd/ *noun* **1** [U] food for animals that are not kept as pets *cattle/chicken feed* **2** [C] *UK* (*US* **feeding**) a meal for a baby or an animal *He has three feeds during the night.*

╔═══════════════════════════════════╗
WORD PARTNERS FOR feedback

get/give/provide feedback ● **negative/positive** feedback ● feedback **on** sth ● feedback **from** sb
╚═══════════════════════════════════╝

feedback /ˈfiːdbæk/ *noun* [U] an opinion from someone about something that you have done or made *negative/positive feedback* ○ *We've had lots of feedback on these new products from our customers.*

◦ᴀ**feel¹** /fiːl/ *verb past* **felt 1** EXPERIENCE [I, T] to experience an emotion or a physical feeling *You shouldn't feel embarrassed about making a mistake.* ○ *I felt a sharp pain in my side when I stood up.* ○ *"Are you feeling better?" "Yes, thanks, I feel fine now."* **2 feel better/different/strange, etc; feel like/as if** If you describe the way a place, situation, or object feels, you say how it seems to you, or what your experience of it is like. *It felt strange to see him again after so long.* ○ *The house feels empty without the children.* ○ *This shirt feels tight under my arms.* ○ *I feel as if I've known you for ages.* **3 feel like sb/sth** to seem to be similar to a type of person, thing, or situation *My feet feel like blocks of ice.* ○ *I felt like a fool when I saw what everyone else was wearing.* **4** OPINION [I, T] to think something or have an opinion [+ (that)] *I feel that he's the best person for the job.* ○ *Do you feel strongly* (= have strong opinions) *about it?* **5** TOUCH [I, T] to touch something, especially with your hands, in order to examine it *He felt her ankle to see if it was broken.* **6 feel like sth/doing sth** to want something, or want to do something *I feel like some chocolate.* ○ *Jane felt like crying.* **7** BE AWARE [T] to be aware of something *You could feel the tension*

in the room. ○ *I could feel them watching me.*
⊃See Common learner error at **fall** ⊃See also: feel
free¹, feel the **pinch**², be/feel under the **weather**¹.
feel for sb to feel sorry for someone because they are very unhappy, or in a difficult
situation

feel² /fiːl/ *noun* **1** [no plural] the way that something seems, or feels when you touch it *I love
the feel of silk against my skin.* ○ *His art has a
very modern feel to it.* **2 a feel for sth** *informal*
the ability to do something or use something
well *Once you get a feel for it, using the mouse
is easy.* ○ *Claire has a feel for this kind of work.*

feel-good /'fiːlgʊd/ *adjective* causing happy
feelings about life *a feel-good story*

OTHER WAYS OF SAYING *feeling*

A very common alternative to the noun 'feeling' is **emotion**: *He finds it hard to express
his emotions.*

The nouns **pang** or **stab** are sometimes used
to describe a sudden, strong, bad feeling:
*Amelia felt a sharp pang of jealousy when
she saw her.* ● *He felt a stab of regret as he
looked at his son.*

A small amount of a sad feeling is often described as a **tinge**: *It was with a tinge of sadness that she finally said goodbye.*

---

o⁻**feeling** /'fiːlɪŋ/ *noun* **1** [EMOTION] [C, U] emotion
guilty feelings ○ *a feeling of joy/sadness* ○ *Her
performance was completely lacking in feeling.*
2 [PHYSICAL] [C, U] when you feel something physical *I had a tingling feeling in my fingers.*
○ *Pablo lost all feeling* (= could not feel anything) *in his feet.* **3** [OPINION] [C] an opinion or
belief *My feeling is that we should wait until
they come back.* **4 have/get a feeling (that)...** to
think that something is likely *I had a feeling
he'd be there.* ○ *I get the feeling that he doesn't
like me.* **5 bad/ill feeling** when people are upset
or angry with each other

🧩 **WORD PARTNERS FOR *feelings***

express/hide/show your feelings ● **hurt**
sb's feelings ● **mixed/strong** feelings

---

feelings /'fiːlɪŋz/ *noun* **1** [plural] Your feelings
are your beliefs and emotions. *You can't hide
your feelings from me.* **2 hurt sb's feelings** to
make someone feel unhappy

feet /fiːt/ *plural of* foot

feign /feɪn/ *verb* [T] *formal* If you feign an emotion, illness, etc, you pretend to have it. *He
feigned illness to avoid having to work.*

feisty /'faɪsti/ *adjective* active, confident and
determined *a feisty young woman*

feline /'fiːlaɪn/ *adjective* relating to cats, or like
a cat

fell¹ /fel/ *verb* [T] **1** to cut down a tree **2** to knock
someone down *He was felled with a single
punch.*

fell² /fel/ *past tense of* fall

fella (*also* feller) /'felə/ *noun* [C] *informal* a man

fellow¹ /'feləʊ/ *noun* [C] **1** [MAN] *old-fashioned* a
man *a big fellow with broad shoulders* **2** [COL-](continued)

[LEGE] someone whose job is to teach or study a
particular subject at some colleges or universities *She's a research fellow at St Peter's
college.* **3** [MEMBER] a member of an official
organization for a particular subject or job

fellow² /'feləʊ/ *adjective* **fellow countrymen/students, etc** used to describe people who share
your interests or situation *She's earned enormous respect from her fellow artists.*

fellowship /'feləʊʃɪp/ *noun* **1** [JOB] [C] a job
teaching or studying a particular subject at
some colleges or universities *a research fellowship at Harvard* **2** [FEELING] [U] a friendly feeling
among people **3** [GROUP] [C] a group of people
who share the same interests or beliefs

felon /'felən/ *noun* [C] someone who is guilty of
a serious crime in the US *a convicted felon*

felony /'feləni/ *noun* [C, U] a serious crime in the
US *to commit a felony*

felt¹ /felt/ *noun* [U] a soft, thick cloth that is
made from wool, hair, or fur that has been
pressed together

felt² /felt/ *past of* feel

felt-tip 'pen *noun* [C] a pen with a point made
of soft material, usually with brightly coloured ink for colouring pictures

o⁻**female¹** /'fiːmeɪl/ *adjective* belonging to or relating to women, or to the sex that can produce eggs or have babies *a female athlete/employee* ○ *a female butterfly/elephant* ○ *Is it male
or female?*

female² /'fiːmeɪl/ *noun* [C] a person or animal
that belongs to the sex that can produce eggs
or have babies *Our dog's just had puppies -
three males and two females.*

feminine /'femɪnɪn/ *adjective* **1** showing qualities that people generally think are typical of
women *a feminine voice* ○ *feminine beauty* **2** in
some languages, belonging to a group of nouns
or adjectives that have the same grammatical
behaviour. The other groups are 'masculine'
and 'neuter'.

femininity /,femɪ'nɪnəti/ *noun* [U] when someone shows qualities that people generally
think are typical of women

feminism /'femɪnɪzᵊm/ *noun* [U] the belief that
women should have the same economic,
social, and political rights as men ● **feminist**
noun [C] someone who supports feminism *a
radical feminist* ● **feminist** *adjective* feminist
literature

fence¹ /fens/ *noun* [C]
1 a wood, wire, or
metal structure that
divides or goes around
an area *a garden/electric fence* **2 sit on the
fence** to wait before
you choose between
two possibilities ⊃See
also: **picket fence**.

fence

fence² /fens/ *verb* [I] to
take part in the sport
of fencing

fence sth in to build a fence around an area
fence sth off to separate one area from an-

other by building a fence

fencing /ˈfensɪŋ/ *noun* [U] **1** the sport of fighting with thin swords (= weapons like long knives) **2** fences, or the material that is used to make them

fend /fend/ *verb*
fend for yourself to take care of yourself without help
fend sb/sth off to defend yourself against someone or something that is attacking you or annoying you *They managed to fend off their attackers with rocks and sticks.*

fender /ˈfendəʳ/ *noun* [C] **1** [CAR] *US* (*UK* **wing**) one of the parts at each corner of a car above the wheels **2** [BICYCLE] *US* (*UK* **mudguard**) a curved piece of metal or plastic fixed above a wheel of a bicycle or motorcycle to prevent water or dirt from hitting the legs of the person who is riding it **3** [FIREPLACE] *UK* a low, metal structure around an open fireplace which stops the coal or wood from falling out

feng shui /ˌfʌŋˈʃweɪ/ *noun* [U] an ancient Chinese belief that the way your house is built and the way that you arrange objects affects your success, health, and happiness

fennel /ˈfenəl/ *noun* [U] a plant whose base can be eaten, and whose leaves and seeds are used as a spice in cooking

ferment¹ /fəˈment/ *verb* [I, T] If food or drink ferments, or if you ferment it, the sugar in it changes into alcohol because of a chemical process. *wine fermenting in barrels* • **fermentation** /ˌfɜːmenˈteɪʃən/ *noun* [U]

ferment² /ˈfɜːment/ *noun* [U] *formal* excitement or disagreement caused by change or a difficult situation

fern /fɜːn/ *noun* [C] a green plant with long stems, narrow leaves like feathers, and no flowers

fern

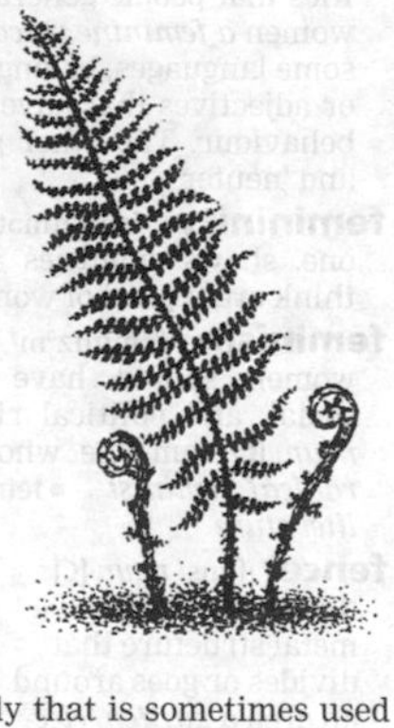

ferocious /fəˈrəʊʃəs/ *adjective* extremely angry, violent, or forceful *a ferocious dog* ○ *a ferocious attack* • **ferociously** *adverb*

ferocity /fəˈrɒsəti/ *noun* [U] extreme violence or force *a storm of incredible ferocity*

ferret¹ /ˈferɪt/ *noun* [C] a small animal with a long, thin body that is sometimes used to hunt rabbits

ferret² /ˈferɪt/ *verb*
ferret sth out to find something after searching carefully for it

Ferris wheel /ˈferɪsˌwiːl/ *noun* [C] an entertainment consisting of a large wheel that turns slowly with seats for people to sit in

ferry¹ /ˈferi/ *noun* [C] a boat that regularly carries passengers and vehicles across an area of water ***a car/passenger ferry***

ferry² /ˈferi/ *verb* [T] to regularly carry passengers or goods from one place to another in a vehicle

fertile /ˈfɜːtaɪl/ [US] /ˈfɜːrtəl/ *adjective* **1** Fertile land or soil produces a lot of healthy plants. **2** If people or animals are fertile, they are able to have babies. **3 fertile ground (for sth)** a situation or place where an idea, activity, etc is likely to succeed **4 a fertile imagination** If someone has a fertile imagination, they have lots of interesting and unusual ideas. • **fertility** /fəˈtɪləti/ *noun* [U]

fertilize (*also UK* **-ise**) /ˈfɜːtɪlaɪz/ *verb* [T] **1** to cause an egg to start to develop into a young animal or baby by combining it with a male cell *Once an egg is fertilized it becomes an embryo.* **2** to put a natural or chemical substance on land in order to make plants grow well • **fertilization** /ˌfɜːtɪlaɪˈzeɪʃən/ *noun* [U]

fertilizer (*also UK* **-iser**) /ˈfɜːtɪlaɪzəʳ/ *noun* [C, U] a natural or chemical substance that you put on land in order to make plants grow well

fervent /ˈfɜːvənt/ *adjective* showing sincere and enthusiastic beliefs or feelings ***a fervent supporter of animal rights*** • **fervently** *adverb*

fervour *UK* (*US* **fervor**) /ˈfɜːrvəʳ/ *noun* [U] extremely strong beliefs or feelings ***religious/patriotic fervour***

fess /fes/ *verb*
fess up *informal* to admit that you have done something bad *He eventually **fessed up to** having spilt coffee on it.*

fest /fest/ *noun mainly US* **a beer/film/jazz, etc fest** a special event where people can enjoy a particular activity or thing

fester /ˈfestəʳ/ *verb* [I] **1** If a bad feeling or situation festers, it becomes worse over a period of time. *Hatred between the two groups has festered for years.* **2** If an injury festers, it becomes infected. *a festering wound*

festival /ˈfestɪvəl/ *noun* [C] **1** a series of special events, performances, etc that often takes place over several days ***a dance/music festival*** ○ *the Berlin Film Festival* **2** a special day or period when people celebrate something, especially a religious event *the Jewish festival of Hanukkah*

festive /ˈfestɪv/ *adjective* happy and enjoyable because people are celebrating ***a festive mood/occasion*** ○ *What are you doing for the festive season* (= Christmas)*?* • **festivity** /fesˈtɪvəti/ *noun* [U] when people are happy and celebrating

festivities /fesˈtɪvətiz/ *noun* [plural] events that people organize in order to celebrate something *holiday festivities*

festoon /fesˈtuːn/ *verb* [T] to cover something with objects, especially decorations [often passive] *The balcony was **festooned with** flags and ribbons.*

fetch /fetʃ/ *verb* [T] **1** to go to another place to get something or someone and bring them back *Can you fetch my glasses from the bedroom?* **2** If something fetches a particular amount of money, it is sold for that amount. *The painting is expected to fetch $50,000 in the auction.*

fetching /ˈfetʃɪŋ/ *adjective* attractive *That scarf looks rather fetching on you.*

fête /feɪt/ *noun* [C] **1** *UK* an event that is held outside and includes competitions, games, and things for sale *a village fête* **2** *US* a special event to celebrate someone or something ● **fête** *verb* [T] to publicly celebrate someone, often by having a special party [often passive] *She was fêted by audiences all over the world.*

fetish /ˈfetɪʃ/ *noun* [C] **1** a strong sexual interest in something unusual *a rubber fetish* **2** something that someone spends too much time thinking about or doing *a fetish for cleanliness*

fetus /ˈfiːtəs/ *noun* [C] *US spelling of* foetus (= a young human or animal that is still developing inside its mother) ● **fetal** /ˈfiːtᵊl/ *adjective US spelling of* foetal

feud /fjuːd/ *noun* [C] a serious and sometimes violent argument between two people or groups that continues for a long period ● **feud** *verb* [I] *The families have been feuding for years.*

feudal /ˈfjuːdᵊl/ *adjective* relating to a social system in the past in which people worked and fought for a lord (= a man of high rank) in exchange for land and protection ● **feudalism** *noun* [U]

fever /ˈfiːvəʳ/ *noun* **1** [C, U] when someone's body temperature rises because they are ill *a high/ slight fever* **2** [U] when people are very excited about something *Election fever has gripped the nation.* ⊃See also: glandular fever, hay fever.

feverish /ˈfiːvᵊrɪʃ/ *adjective* **1** having a fever *I feel a bit feverish.* **2** Feverish activity is done quickly, often because of excitement or fear. *The rescuers worked at a feverish pace.* ● **feverishly** *adverb* *They worked feverishly to put out the fire.*

'fever ˌpitch *noun* **reach fever pitch** If emotions reach fever pitch, they become so strong that they are difficult to control.

o⚬**few** /fjuː/ *quantifier* **1** a few some, or a small number of *It'll be here in a few minutes.* ○ *I met a few of the other employees at my interview.* **2** quite a few/a good few quite a large number of *Quite a few people have had the same problem.* **3** not many, or only a small number of *We get few complaints.* ○ *Few of the children can read or write yet.* ○ *Very few people can afford to pay those prices.* ⊃See Common learner error at less. **4** few and far between not happening or existing very often *Opportunities like this are few and far between.*

fiancé /fiˈɒnseɪ/ *noun* [C] A woman's fiancé is the man that she has promised to marry.

fiancée /fiˈɒnseɪ/ *noun* [C] A man's fiancée is the woman that he has promised to marry.

fiasco /fiˈæskəʊ/ *noun* [C] a complete failure, especially one that embarrasses people *My last dinner party was a complete fiasco.*

fib /fɪb/ *noun* [C] *informal* a small lie that is not very important *Don't tell fibs.* ● **fib** *verb* [I] fibbing *past* fibbed to say something that is not true

fibre *UK* (*US* fiber) /ˈfaɪbəʳ/ *noun* **1** CLOTH [C, U] cloth made from thin threads twisted together *Man-made fibres like nylon are easy to wash.* **2** THIN THREAD [C] one of the thin threads that forms a substance such as cloth *The fibres are woven into fabric.* **3** FOOD [U] the substance in plants which cannot be digested and helps food pass through your body *Broccoli is a good source of fibre.* **4** BODY [C] a structure like a thread in your body *muscle/nerve fibres*

fibreglass *UK* (*US* fiberglass) /ˈfaɪbəglɑːs/ *noun* [U] a light material made by twisting together glass or plastic threads

fickle /ˈfɪkl/ *adjective* Someone who is fickle often changes their opinion about things.

fiction /ˈfɪkʃᵊn/ *noun* **1** [U] literature and stories about imaginary people or events *What's the best-selling children's fiction title?* ⊃Opposite nonfiction. **2** [U, no plural] something that is not true or real ⊃See also: science fiction.

fictional /ˈfɪkʃᵊnᵊl/ *adjective* existing only in fiction *a fictional character*

fictitious /fɪkˈtɪʃəs/ *adjective* invented and not real or true *a fictitious name*

fiddle¹ /ˈfɪdl/ *verb* [T] *UK informal* to change something dishonestly in order to get money *She was fined for fiddling her travel expenses.*
fiddle (about/around) with sth 1 to touch or move things with your fingers because you are nervous or bored *Stop fiddling with your hair!* **2** to make small changes to something to try to make it work *He fiddled with the wires to get the radio working again.*

fiddle² /ˈfɪdl/ *noun* [C] **1** *informal* a violin (= a wooden musical instrument with strings) **2** *UK* a dishonest way to get money *a tax fiddle*

fiddler /ˈfɪdləʳ/ *noun* [C] someone who plays the violin (= a wooden musical instrument with strings)

fiddly /ˈfɪdli/ *adjective UK* difficult to do because the parts involved are small *Repairing a watch is very fiddly.*

fidelity /fɪˈdeləti/ *noun* [U] loyalty, especially to a sexual partner ⊃Opposite infidelity.

fidget /ˈfɪdʒɪt/ *verb* [I] to keep making small movements with your hands or feet because you are nervous or bored *Cecilia fidgeted all the way through the job interview.* ● **fidgety** *adjective*

o⚬**field**¹ /fiːld/ *noun* **1** LAND [C] an area of land used for growing crops or keeping animals *a wheat field* ○ *a field of cows* **2** SPORT [C] an area of grass where you can play a sport *a football field* **3** AREA OF STUDY [C] an area of study or activity *He's an expert in the field of biochemistry.* **4** IN RACE/BUSINESS [no plural] the people who are competing in a race, activity, or business *We lead the field in genetic research.* **5** a gas/oil field an area of land containing gas or oil **6 a gravitational/magnetic field** an area affected by a particular physical force ⊃See also: paddy field, playing field.

field² /fiːld/ *verb* **1** [I, T] to try to catch or stop a ball after it has been hit in a game such as cricket or baseball *Are we fielding or batting?* **2** [T] to send out a team or player to play in a game *Brazil fielded a strong team in the World Cup.* **3 field questions/telephone calls** to answer or deal with questions/telephone calls

'**field ,day** *noun* **have a field day** to have the opportunity to do a lot of something you want to do, especially to criticize someone *The press had a field day when they found out about the scandal.*

fielder /ˈfiːldəʳ/ *noun* [C] a player who tries to catch or stop the ball in games such as cricket or baseball

'**field ,hockey** *US* (*UK* hockey) *noun* [U] a team game played on grass where you hit a small ball with a long, curved stick

,**field 'marshal** *UK* (*US* '**field ,marshal**) *noun* [C] an officer of the highest rank in the British army

fiend /fiːnd/ *noun* [C] **1** an evil or cruel person **2** someone who is very interested in a particular thing

fiendish /ˈfiːndɪʃ/ *adjective* **1** evil or cruel *a fiendish attack* **2** very difficult or complicated *a fiendish crossword* • **fiendishly** *adverb mainly UK* extremely *fiendishly clever/difficult*

fierce /fɪəs/ *adjective* **1** violent or angry *a fierce attack* ○ *a fierce dog* **2** very strong or powerful *fierce winds/storms* ○ *There is fierce competition between car manufacturers.* • **fiercely** *adverb*

fiery /ˈfaɪəri/ *adjective* **1** showing strong emotion, especially anger *a fiery temper* **2** bright or burning like a fire *a fiery sunset*

ℴ⁻**fifteen** /ˌfɪfˈtiːn/ *the number 15* • **fifteenth** 15th written as a word

fifth¹ /fɪfθ/ 5th written as a word

fifth² /fɪfθ/ *noun* [C] one of five equal parts of something; ⅕

ℴ⁻**fifty** /ˈfɪfti/ **1** the number 50 **2 the fifties** the years from 1950 to 1959 **3 be in your fifties** to be aged between 50 and 59 • **fiftieth** 50th written as a word

fifty-fifty /ˌfɪftiˈfɪfti/ *adjective, adverb informal* **1** shared equally between two people *Let's divide the bill fifty-fifty.* **2 a fifty-fifty chance** If something has a fifty-fifty chance, it is equally likely to happen or not to happen. *We have a fifty-fifty chance of winning the match.*

fig /fɪɡ/ *noun* [C] a dark, sweet fruit with lots of seeds, that is often eaten dried

fig. *written abbreviation for* figure (= a picture or drawing in a book or document, usually with a number) *See fig. 1.*

ℴ⁻**fight¹** /faɪt/ *verb past* **fought 1** USE FORCE [I, T] When people fight, they use physical force to try to defeat each other. *Two men were arrested for fighting outside a bar.* ○ *Sam's always fighting with his little brother.* **2** JOIN WAR [I, T] to take part in a war *Millions of young men fought in World War I.* **3** ARGUE [I]

to argue *We've got to stop fighting in front of the children.* **4** TRY TO STOP [I, T] to try hard to stop something bad happening *He fought against racism.* ○ *New measures have been introduced to fight crime.* **5** TRY TO ACHIEVE [I] to try hard to achieve something you want or think is right *They are fighting for their freedom.* ○ [+ to do sth] *He had to fight very hard to keep his job.* **6 be fighting for your life** to be trying very hard to stay alive when you are very ill or badly injured ⊃See also: fight a losing battle¹.

fight back to defend yourself when someone or something attacks you or causes problems for you

---

WORD PARTNERS FOR *fight*

a fight **with** sb • **get into/have/pick/start** a fight • **lose/win** a fight

---

ℴ⁻**fight²** /faɪt/ *noun* [C] **1** PHYSICAL FORCE when people use physical force to hurt or attack others *He's always getting into fights.* **2** EFFORT a determined effort to achieve or stop something *She was very active in the fight against drugs.* ○ *Join us in our fight for freedom!* ○ [+ to do sth] *This year has brought some good news in the fight to save the whales.* **3** ARGUMENT an argument *I don't want to have a fight over this.* **4** SPORT a boxing competition

fighter /ˈfaɪtəʳ/ *noun* [C] **1** (*also* '**fighter ,plane**) a fast military aircraft that can attack other aircraft *a fighter pilot* **2** someone who fights in a war or as a sport

fighting /ˈfaɪtɪŋ/ *noun* [U] when people fight, usually in a war *Thousands of civilians were killed in the fighting.*

figment /ˈfɪgmənt/ *noun* **a figment of sb's imagination** something that someone believes is real but that only exists in their imagination

figurative /ˈfɪgʲərətɪv/ *adjective* **1** A figurative meaning of a word or phrase is a more imaginative meaning developed from the usual meaning. **2** Figurative art shows people, places, or things in a similar way to how they look in real life. • **figuratively** *adverb*

WORD PARTNERS FOR *figure*

4 a **key/leading/major/prominent** figure • a **public** figure

---

ℴ⁻**figure¹** /ˈfɪgəʳ/ *noun* [C] **1** SYMBOL a symbol for a number *Write down the amount in words and figures.* ○ *He's now being paid a six-figure salary.* **2 single/double, etc figures** numbers from 0 to 9/numbers from 10 to 99, etc **3** AMOUNT a number that expresses an amount, especially in official documents *Government figures show a rise in unemployment.* **4** TYPE OF PERSON a particular type of person, often someone important or famous *a mysterious figure* ○ *Lincoln was a major figure in American politics.* **5** PERSON a person that you cannot see clearly *I could see two figures in the distance.* **6** BODY SHAPE the shape of someone's body, usually an attractive shape *She's got a good figure for her age.* **7** PICTURE (*written abbreviation* fig.) a picture or drawing in a book or document, usually with a number *Look at the graph shown in Figure 2.* ➲See also: **father figure**.

figure² /ˈfɪgəʳ/ *verb* **1** [I] to be a part of something, or to appear in something *Love **figures in** most pop songs.* **2** [T] to decide something after thinking about it [+ (that)] *I figured that it was time to tell her the truth.* **3 that/it figures** *informal* something you say when you expected something to happen *"I've run out of money, mum." "That figures."*

figure sth/sb out to finally understand something or someone after a lot of thought [+ question word] *I never could figure out what she saw in him.*

figurehead /ˈfɪgəhed/ *noun* [C] a leader who has no real power

ˌ**figure of ˈspeech** *noun* [C] *plural* **figures of speech** words that are used together in an imaginative way to mean something different from their usual meaning

WORD PARTNERS FOR ***file***

1 hold/keep a file **on** sb/sth
2 close/create/download/open/save a file

⊶**file¹** /faɪl/ *noun* **1** [INFORMATION] [C] a collection of information and documents about someone or something *The school **keeps files on** all its pupils.* **2** [COMPUTER] [C] a collection of information such as text, pictures, or computer programs stored together electronically with a single name *Do you want to **download** all these **files**?* **3** [CONTAINER] [C] a box or folded piece of thick paper used to put documents in *He keeps all his bank statements in a file.* ➲See colour picture **The Office** on page Centre 5, **The Classroom** on page Centre 6. **4 on file** If information is on file, it is recorded and stored somewhere. **5** [TOOL] [C] a small tool with a rough edge that is used to make a surface smooth *a **nail file*** **6 in single file** in a line with one person following the other ➲See also: the **rank¹** and file.

file² /faɪl/ *verb* **1** [PAPER] [T] (*also* **file away**) to put documents into an ordered system of boxes or files where you can easily find them again *She filed all her tax returns under T.* **2** [LAW] [T] (*also* **file for**) to officially state that you are going to take someone to court *His wife's **filing for divorce**.* **3** [RUB] [T] to rub something with a rough tool in order to make it smooth **4 file along/into/through, etc** to walk somewhere in a line, one behind the other *The audience slowly filed back to their seats.*

ˈ**file ˌsharing** *noun* [U] the activity of putting a file onto a special place on your computer so that many other people can copy it, look at it, or use it by using the Internet

filet /fɪˈleɪ/ *noun* [C] *another US spelling of* **fillet** (= a piece of meat or fish with the bones taken out)

ˈ**filing ˌcabinet** (*also US* ˈ**file ˌcabinet**) *noun* [C] a piece of office furniture with deep drawers for storing documents ➲See colour picture **The Office** on page Centre 5.

⊶**fill¹** /fɪl/ *verb* **1** [MAKE FULL] [I, T] (*also* **fill up**) to make a container or space full, or to become full *He filled the bucket with water.* ○ *I made a drink while the bath was filling.* **2** [TAKE SPACE] [T] If people or things fill a place, there are a lot of them in it. *The streets were **filled with** tourists.* ○ *Dark clouds filled the sky.* **3** [BE NOTICEABLE] [T] If light, sound, or a smell fills a place, you can easily notice it. *The smell of smoke filled the room.* **4 fill sb with anger/joy/pride, etc** to make someone feel very angry/happy/proud, etc *The thought of losing him filled her with fear.* **5 fill a post/position/vacancy** to take a new a job *They still haven't found anyone to fill the vacancy.* **6 fill a need/gap/demand** to provide something that people need or want

fill sth in/out to write the necessary information on an official document *to **fill in** a **form/questionnaire***

fill (sth) up to become full, or to make something become full *The restaurant soon filled up with people.*

fill² /fɪl/ *noun* **your fill** as much of something as you want or need *I've **had my fill of** living in the city.*

fillet (*also US* **filet**) /ˈfɪlɪt/ [US] /fɪˈleɪ/ *noun* [C] a piece of meat or fish with the bones taken out

filling

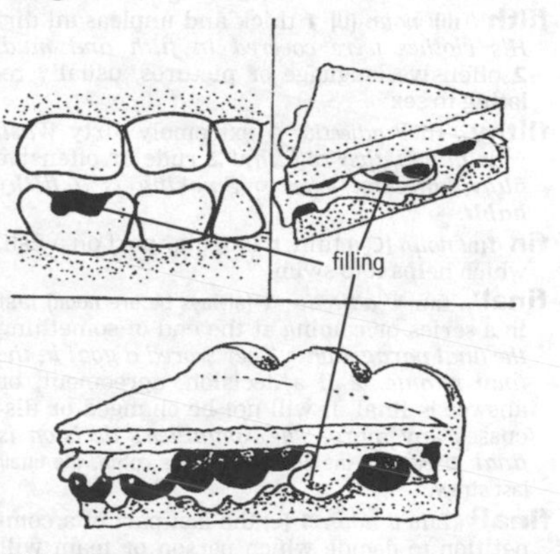

filling¹ /ˈfɪlɪŋ/ *noun* **1** [C, U] food that is put inside things such as cakes, pastry, pieces of bread, etc *What sort of filling do you want in your sandwich?* **2** [C] a hard substance that fills a hole in a tooth

filling² /ˈfɪlɪŋ/ *adjective* Food that is filling makes your stomach feel full. *This soup is very filling.*

ˈ**filling ˌstation** *noun* [C] a petrol station (= place where you can buy fuel for your car)

WORD PARTNERS FOR ***film***

make a film • a film **about** sb/sth • **in** a film • a **horror** film • a **classic** film • the film **industry**

⊶**film¹** /fɪlm/ *noun* **1** [PICTURES] [C] (*also US* **movie**) a story shown in moving pictures, shown at the cinema or on television *'Titanic' was one of the most popular Hollywood **films** ever **made**.* **2** [MATERIAL] [C, U] special thin plastic used for making photographs or moving pictures, or a length of this *I need to buy another* **roll of film**. **3** ⌐LAYER⌐ [no plural] a thin layer of something on a surface *A thick film of grey dust covered the furniture.*

film² /fɪlm/ *verb* [I, T] to record moving pictures with a camera, usually to make a film for the cinema or television *Most of the scenes were filmed in a studio.* ● **filming** *noun* [U]

film-maker *UK* (*US* **filmmaker**) /'fɪlmmeɪkəʳ/ *noun* [C] someone who makes films for the cinema or television

'film ,star *noun* [C] a famous cinema actor or actress

filter¹ /'fɪltəʳ/ *verb* **1** [T] to pass a liquid or gas through a piece of equipment in order to remove solid pieces or other substances *The water was filtered to remove any impurities.* **2 filter down/in/through, etc** to gradually appear or become known *News is filtering in of an earthquake in Mexico.*
filter sth out to remove a particular substance from a liquid or gas

filter² /'fɪltəʳ/ *noun* [C] a piece of equipment that you pass a liquid or gas through in order to remove particular substances *a coffee filter*

filth /fɪlθ/ *noun* [U] **1** thick and unpleasant dirt *His clothes were covered in filth and mud.* **2** offensive language or pictures, usually relating to sex

filthy /'fɪlθi/ *adjective* **1** extremely dirty *Wash your hands, they're filthy!* **2** rude or offensive *filthy language/jokes* ○ *Smoking is a filthy habit.*

fin /fɪn/ *noun* [C] a thin, triangular part on a fish, which helps it to swim

○⌐**final¹** /'faɪnəl/ *adjective* **1** [always before noun] last in a series or coming at the end of something *the final paragraph* ○ *They scored a goal in the final minute.* **2** If a decision, agreement, or answer is final, it will not be changed or discussed any more. *The committee's decision is final.* ○See also: the final **nail¹** in the coffin, the final/ last straw.

final² /'faɪnəl/ *noun* **1** [C] the last part of a competition to decide which person or team will be the winner *the European Cup Final* ○ *The finals will be shown on TV.* **2 finals** exams taken at the end of a university course

finale /fɪ'nɑːli/ *noun* [C] the last part of a show, event, or piece of music

finalist /'faɪnəlɪst/ *noun* [C] a person or team in the last part of a competition

finalize (*also UK* **-ise**) /'faɪnəlaɪz/ *verb* [T] to make a final and certain decision about a plan, date, etc *to finalize arrangements/details*

○⌐**finally** /'faɪnəli/ *adverb* **1** ⌐AFTER A LONG TIME⌐ after a long time or some difficulty *After months of looking, he finally found a job.* **2** ⌐LAST POINT⌐ used to introduce the last point or idea *Finally, I'd like to thank everyone for coming this evening.* **3** ⌐CERTAINLY⌐ in a way that will not be changed *The date of the wedding hasn't been finally decided yet.*

finance¹ /'faɪnæns/ *noun* **1** [U] the control of how large amounts of money should be spent **2** [U] the money that is needed to support a business *Who put up the finance for the project?* **3 sb's finances** the money which a person, company, or country has *You must learn how to manage your own finances.*

finance² /'faɪnæns/ *verb* [T] to provide the money needed to do something *Who's financing the project?*

○⌐**financial** /faɪ'nænʃəl/ *adjective* relating to money or how money is managed *a financial adviser* ○ *She's having some financial difficulties at the moment.* ● **financially** *adverb Many students are still financially dependent on their parents.*

finch /fɪnʃ/ *noun* [C] a small singing bird with a short beak

---

OTHER WAYS OF SAYING **find**

A common alternative to 'find' is the verb **discover**: *The victim's wallet was discovered in a ditch.* ● *I finally discovered the letters in a drawer.*

If someone finds the exact position of someone or something, in formal situations the verb **locate** is sometimes used: *Police are still trying to locate the suspect.*

If someone finds something that has been secret or hidden, then the verbs **uncover** or **unearth** are sometimes used: *Reporters uncovered/unearthed evidence of corruption.*

The phrasal verbs **come across** and **stumble across/on** are used when someone finds something by chance: *I stumbled on these photographs when I was cleaning out my desk.* ● *We came across a lovely little restaurant in the village.*

If someone finds something or someone after looking carefully in different places, you can use the verb **trace** or the phrasal verb **track down**: *Police have so far failed to trace/ track down the missing woman.*

○⌐**find¹** /faɪnd/ *verb* [T] *past* **found 1** ⌐DISCOVER WHEN SEARCHING⌐ to discover something or someone that you have been searching for *I can't find my glasses and I've looked everywhere.* ○ *Police found the missing girl at a London railway station.* ○ [+ two objects] *Has he found himself a place to live yet?* **2** ⌐DISCOVER BY CHANCE⌐ to discover something or someone by chance *The body was found by a man walking his dog.* **3** ⌐BECOME AWARE⌐ to become aware that something exists, or has happened *I came home to find that my cat had had kittens.* **4 find the energy/money/time, etc** to have or get enough energy/money/time, etc to do something *Where do you find the energy to do all these things?* **5 find sb/sth easy/boring/funny, etc** to think or feel a particular way about someone or something *I still find exams very stressful.* **6 find yourself somewhere/doing sth** to become aware that you have gone somewhere or done something without intending to *I suddenly found myself making everyone's lunch.* **7 be found** to exist or be present somewhere *Vitamin C is found in oranges and other citrus fruit.* **8 find sb guilty/not guilty** to judge that someone is guilty or not guilty in a law court [often passive] *She was found guilty of murder.*

o┅**find (sth) out** to get information about something, or to learn a fact for the first time *I must find out the train times.* ○ [+ question word] *Peter was shocked when he found out what we had done.* ⇒See Common learner error at **know.**

find² /faɪnd/ *noun* [C] something or someone valuable, interesting, or useful that you discover [usually singular] *This hotel was a real find.*

finding /ˈfaɪndɪŋ/ *noun* [C] a piece of information that has been discovered as a result of an official study [usually plural] *The findings of this research will be published next year.*

o┅**fine¹** /faɪn/ *adjective* 1 WELL well, healthy, or happy *"How are you?" "I'm fine thanks. And you?"* ○ *I had a cold last week, but I'm fine now.* 2 GOOD good or good enough *"Is the soup hot enough?" "Yes, it's fine."* 3 EXCELLENT excellent, or of very good quality *fine wines* ○ *He's a fine musician.* 4 **(that's) fine** used to agree with a suggestion, idea, decision, etc *"Shall we meet at 8 o'clock?" "Yes, that's fine by me."* 5 THIN thin or made of very small pieces *fine, brown hair* ○ *fine sand* 6 SUNNY sunny and not raining *If it's fine, we could have a picnic.* 7 **the finer details/points, etc of sth** the more detailed or more difficult parts of an argument, idea, etc

fine² /faɪn/ *adverb informal* 1 very well or without any problems *"How did your exam go?" "It went fine thanks."* 2 **cut it/things fine** to leave yourself only just enough time to do something *Twenty minutes to get to the station? That's cutting it a bit fine!*

fine³ /faɪn/ *verb* [T] to make someone pay an amount of money as a punishment for breaking a law or rule [often passive] *He was fined £500 for dangerous driving.*

⟦ WORD PARTNERS FOR **fine** ⟧

face/get/receive a fine ● **pay** a fine ● a **heavy/hefty/stiff** fine ● a **parking** fine

fine⁴ /faɪn/ *noun* [C] an amount of money that you must pay for breaking a law or rule *a parking fine* ○ *The court gave her two weeks to pay the fine.*

finely /ˈfaɪnli/ *adverb* 1 into small pieces *Finely chop the garlic.* 2 very exactly *a finely tuned machine*

o┅**finger¹** /ˈfɪŋɡəʳ/ *noun* 1 [C] one of the five, long, separate parts at the end of your hand, including your thumb ⇒See colour picture **The Body** on page Centre 13. 2 **have green fingers** UK (US **have a green thumb**) to be good at gardening and making plants grow well 3 **keep your fingers crossed** *informal* to hope that things will happen in the way that you want them to *Let's keep our fingers crossed that it doesn't rain.* 4 **not lift a finger** *informal* to not help someone do something, usually because you are too lazy *He never lifts a finger to help with the housework.* 5 **put your finger on sth** to understand exactly why a situation is the way it is *Something was wrong, but I couldn't put my finger on it.* 6 **snap your fingers** (*also UK* **click your fingers**) to press your thumb and middle finger to-

gether until the finger hits your hand and makes a short sound ⇒See also: **index finger.**

finger² /ˈfɪŋɡəʳ/ *verb* [T] to touch or feel something with your fingers

fingernail /ˈfɪŋɡəneɪl/ *noun* [C] the hard, thin part on the top of the end of your finger

fingerprint /ˈfɪŋɡəprɪnt/ *noun* [C] the mark made on something by the pattern of curved lines on the end of someone's finger *The police found fingerprints all over the murder weapon.*

fingertip /ˈfɪŋɡətɪp/ *noun* 1 [C] the end of your finger 2 **at your fingertips** if you have something at your fingertips, you can get it and use it very easily. *He had all the information he needed at his fingertips.*

⟦ OTHER WAYS OF SAYING **finish** ⟧

The verb **end** is a common alternative to 'finish' when it means 'stop': *What time does the concert end?*

When someone finishes doing or making something, the verb **complete** is sometimes used: *Have you completed all the questions?* ● *The project took 5 years to complete.*

If someone finishes something quickly and easily, especially food or a piece of work, in informal situations you can use the phrasal verb **polish off**: *He's just polished off two huge bowls of pasta.*

The phrasal verb **wind up** is sometimes used when an activity is gradually finishing: *It's time to wind up the game now.*

o┅**finish¹** /ˈfɪnɪʃ/ *verb* 1 COMPLETE [I, T] to complete something, or come to the end of an activity *When I finish my homework, can I watch TV?* ○ [+ doing sth] *Have you finished reading that book yet?* 2 END [I] to end *The meeting should finish at five o'clock.* 3 USE COMPLETELY [T] (*also* **finish off**) to eat, drink, or use something completely *They finished their drinks and left the bar.* 4 **finish first/second, etc** to be in the first/ second, etc winning position at the end of a race or competition

finish sth off 1 to complete the last part of something that you are doing *I have to finish off this report by Friday.* 2 to eat, drink, or use the last part of something *Would you like to finish off the pizza?*

finish up *mainly UK* to finally be in a particular place, state, or situation, usually without having planned it *I only went for two days, but finished up staying for a week.*

finish with sth to stop using or needing something *Have you finished with the newspaper?*

finish with sb *UK* to stop having a romantic relationship with someone

finish² /ˈfɪnɪʃ/ *noun* [C] 1 the end of a race, or the last part of something *a close/exciting finish* ○ *I enjoyed the film from start to finish.* 2 the way the surface of something feels or looks *The table has a smooth, shiny finish.*

finished /ˈfɪnɪʃt/ *adjective* 1 completed *How much does the finished product cost?* ⇒Opposite **unfinished.** 2 **be finished** If you are finished, you have completed something. *I hope I'll be fin-*

ished before 5 p.m.

fir /fɜːʳ/ (*also* **'fir ,tree**) *noun* [C] a tree with thin, straight leaves shaped like needles that do not fall in winter

fire

o-**fire¹** /faɪəʳ/ *noun* **1** FLAME [U] heat, light, and flames that are produced when something burns **2 catch fire** to start burning *The car crashed and caught fire.* **3 on fire** burning *That house is on fire.* **4 set fire to sth; set sth on fire** to make something start burning, usually to cause damage *Enemy troops set fire to the village.* **5** EVENT [C] when something burns in a way that causes damage and cannot be controlled *Three people were killed in the fire.* ○ *It took the firefighters two hours to put the fire out* (= stop it burning). **6** NATURAL HEAT [C] a pile of wood, coal, etc that is burning to produce heat *We sat by the fire.* ○ *They put up the tents and lit a fire.* **7 an electric/gas fire** UK a piece of equipment that uses electricity/gas to heat a room **8** SHOOTING [U] the shooting of guns and other weapons *The soldiers opened fire* (= started shooting). **9 come under fire** to be criticized *The government has come under fire for closing the hospital.*

fire² /faɪəʳ/ *verb* **1** [I, T] to shoot a bullet from a gun *She fired three shots at him.* **2** [T] *informal* to tell someone they must leave their job [often passive] *I was fired for being late.* **3 fire sb's imagination** to make someone very excited or interested in something **4 fire questions at sb** to ask someone questions quickly one after the other

fire sb up to make someone excited or angry *We got all fired up for the match.*

'fire a,larm *noun* [C] a device such as a bell that warns the people in a building that the building is on fire *If you hear the fire alarm, you must leave the building immediately.*

firearm /faɪrɑːm/ *noun* [C] a gun that you can carry easily

'fire bri,gade UK (US **'fire de,partment**) *noun* [C] an organization of people whose job is to stop fires burning

'fire ,engine *noun* [C] a vehicle for carrying firefighters and equipment for stopping large fires

'fire es,cape *noun* [C] a set of metal stairs on the outside of a building which allows people to leave if there is an emergency

'fire ex,tinguisher *noun* [C] a piece of equip-

ment kept inside buildings which is used to stop small fires

firefighter /ˈfaɪəfaɪtəʳ/ *noun* [C] someone whose job is to stop fires burning

fireman /ˈfaɪəmən/ *noun* [C] *plural* **firemen** a man whose job is to stop fires burning

fireplace /ˈfaɪəpleɪs/ *noun* [C] a space in the wall of a room where you can have a fire, or the structure around this space ⊃See colour picture **The Living Room** on page Centre 4.

fireside /ˈfaɪəsaɪd/ *noun* [U] the area next to a fireplace

'fire ,station *noun* [C] the building where fire engines are kept, and firefighters wait for emergencies

firewall /ˈfaɪəwɔːl/ *noun* [C] a system that stops other people looking at information on your computer while it is connected to the Internet

firewood /ˈfaɪəwʊd/ *noun* [U] wood that is used for burning on a fire

fireworks

firework /ˈfaɪəwɜːk/ *noun* [C] a small object that explodes to produce a loud noise and bright colours and is often used to celebrate special events *a firework display*

'firing ,squad *noun* [C] a group of soldiers who are ordered to shoot and kill a prisoner

firm¹ /fɜːm/ *adjective* **1** NOT SOFT not soft, but not completely hard *A firm bed is better for your back.* **2** FIXED [always before noun] certain or fixed and not likely to change *We don't have any firm plans for the weekend yet.* ○ *I'm a firm believer in equal rights.* **3** STRONG strong and tight *a firm handshake/grip* **4** STRICT strict and making certain that people do what you want *You've got to be firm with children.* ● **firmly** *adverb* ● **firmness** *noun* [U]

firm² /fɜːm/ *noun* [C] a company that sells goods or services *a law firm*

o-**first¹** /fɜːst/ *adjective* **1** BEFORE coming before all others *Who was the first person to arrive at* *the party?* ○ *He was nervous on his first day at school.* ○ *They went abroad last year for the first time since having children.* **2** NUMBER 1st written as a word **3** IMPORTANT most important *Sheila won first prize in the photo competition.* ⊃See also: in the first **place**¹.

o-**first²** /fɜːst/ *adverb* **1** BEFORE before everything or everyone else *I can go to the cinema, but I've got to do my homework first.* ○ *Jason came first in the 400 metres* (= he won). **2** FIRST TIME for the first time *I first heard the song on the radio.* ○ *He first started playing the piano at school.* **3 at first** at the beginning of a situation or period of time *At first I thought she was unfriendly, but actually she is just shy.* **4 first; first of all a** BEGINNING SENTENCE used to introduce the first idea, reason, etc in a series *First, I think we have to change our marketing strategy.* **b** BEFORE EVERYTHING before doing anything else *First of all check you have all the correct ingredients.* **5 come first** to be the most important person or thing *Her career always comes first.* **6 put sb/sth first** to consider someone or something to be the most important thing *Most couples put their children first when sorting out their problems.* **7 First come, first served.** something you say when there is not enough of something for everyone and only the first people who ask for it will get it

o-**first³** /fɜːst/ *noun, pronoun* **1 the first** the first person, people, thing, or things *Hillary and Norgay were the first to climb Everest.* **2 be a first** to be something that has never happened before *Man walking on the moon was a first in space history.* **3** [C] the highest exam result that you can achieve at the end of a university course in the UK

,**first 'aid** *noun* [U] basic medical treatment that you give someone who is ill or injured in an emergency *The policeman gave him first aid before the ambulance arrived.*

first-class /ˌfɜːstˈklɑːs/ *adjective* **1** relating to the best and most expensive available service, especially when travelling or sending something somewhere *a first-class ticket* ○ *a first-class stamp* **2** of very good quality *It was a first-class restaurant.* ● **first class** *adverb* *How much is it to send this letter first class?*

,**first 'floor** *noun* [no plural] **1** *UK* the level of a building directly above the ground level **2** *US* (*UK* **ground floor**) the level of a building on the same level as the ground

firsthand /ˌfɜːstˈhænd/ *adjective, adverb* experienced, seen, or learnt directly *Police heard firsthand accounts of the accident from witnesses.* ○ *firsthand experience*

'**first ,language** *noun* [C] the language that someone learns to speak first *Madeleine's first language is French, but she also knows English and German.*

firstly /ˈfɜːstli/ *adverb* used to introduce the first idea, reason, etc in a series *The aim of this activity is firstly to have fun, and secondly to keep fit.*

'**first ,name** *noun* [C] the name that people who know you call you and that comes before your family name

the ,first 'person *noun* the form of a verb or pronoun that is used when people are speaking or writing about themselves. For example, 'I' and 'we' are first person pronouns.

first-rate /ˌfɜːstˈreɪt/ *adjective* extremely good *a first-rate team/writer*

fiscal /ˈfɪskəl/ *adjective* relating to government money, especially taxes

o-**fish¹** /fɪʃ/ *noun plural* **fish** or **fishes 1** [C] an animal that lives only in water and swims using its tail and fins (= thin, triangular parts) *Are there any fish in the pond?* **2** [U] fish eaten as food *fish and chips* ⊃See colour picture **Food** on page Centre 11.

> ### COMMON LEARNER ERROR
>
> fish or fishes?
>
> Fish is the usual plural of fish.
>
> *I caught six fish in the river.*
>
> ~~I caught six fishes in the river.~~
>
> Fishes is sometimes used to talk about different types of fish.

fish² /fɪʃ/ *verb* [I] to try to catch fish *They're fishing for tuna.*

fish sth out *informal* to pull or take something out of a bag or pocket, especially after searching

fisherman /ˈfɪʃəmən/ *noun* [C] *plural* **fishermen** someone who catches fish as a job or as a hobby

fishing /ˈfɪʃɪŋ/ *noun* [U] the sport or job of catching fish *Dad loves to go fishing.*

'**fish ,slice** *noun* [C] *UK* a kitchen tool with a wide, flat end used for lifting and serving food ⊃See colour picture **The Kitchen** on page Centre 2.

fishy /ˈfɪʃi/ *adjective* **1** smelling or tasting like fish **2** making you feel that someone is lying or something dishonest is happening *His story sounds a bit fishy to me.*

fist /fɪst/ *noun* [C] a hand closed into a ball with the fingers and thumb curled tightly together *He banged his fist down angrily on the table.*

fist

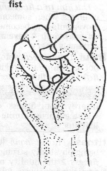

o-**fit¹** /fɪt/ *verb* **fitting** *past* **fitted 1** RIGHT SHAPE [I, T] to be the right shape or size for someone or something *These trousers don't fit any more.* ○ *I can't find a lid to fit this jar.* **2 fit (sth) in/ through/under, etc** If people or things fit somewhere, or if you can fit them somewhere, that place is big enough for them. *How many people can you fit in your car?* ○ *This radio is small enough to fit into my pocket.* **3** PUT [T] *mainly UK* to put or fix something somewhere *You ought to fit a smoke alarm in the kitchen.* **4** SAME [I, T] to be the same as or like something *She seems to fit the* *police description.* **5** [SUITABLE] [T] to be suitable for something *The punishment should fit the crime.*

COMMON LEARNER ERROR

fit or suit?

Remember that the verb **fit** means to be the right shape or size.

This jacket doesn't fit me. It's too tight.

Use the verb **suit** when you want to say that something is right for someone or makes them look more attractive.

That dress looks lovely. Red really suits you.

Life in the big city didn't suit him.

~~Life in the big city didn't fit him.~~

---

fit in to feel that you belong to a particular group and are accepted by them *He doesn't fit in with the other pupils in his class.*

fit sb/sth in to find the time to see someone or do something *The dentist can fit you in on Tuesday morning.*

fit in with sth If one activity or event fits in with another, they exist or happen together in a way that is convenient. *The party is in June. Does that fit in with your holiday plans?*

fit² /fɪt/ *adjective* **fitter, fittest 1** of a good enough quality or suitable type for a particular purpose [+ to do sth] *Is this water fit to drink?* ○ *She's not in a fit state to drive.* **2** healthy, especially because you exercise regularly *He's very fit for his age.* ⊃Opposite **unfit. 3 do sth as you see/think fit** to do something that you feel is the right thing to do, although other people might disapprove *You must spend the money as you see fit.*

fit³ /fɪt/ *noun* **1 a good/loose/tight, etc fit** when something fits someone or somewhere well, loosely, tightly, etc *These shoes are a perfect fit.* **2** [C] a sudden, uncontrolled period of doing something or feeling something *a coughing fit* ○ *I hit him in a fit of anger.* **3** [C] a short period of illness when someone cannot control their movements and becomes unconscious *to have an epileptic fit* **4 have a fit** *informal* to become extremely angry

fitful /'fɪtf°l/ *adjective* stopping and starting and not happening in a regular or continuous way *fitful sleep* ● **fitfully** *adverb*

WORD PARTNERS FOR **fitness**

improve your fitness ● sb's fitness **level(s)** ● a fitness **programme/regime/test** ● **physical** fitness

fitness /'fɪtnəs/ *noun* [U] **1** the condition of being physically strong and healthy *physical fitness* **2** the quality of being suitable for a particular purpose, job, course of study, etc *The purpose of the exercise is to judge a soldier's fitness for combat.*

fitted /'fɪtɪd/ *adjective* **1** *UK* made or cut to fill a particular space exactly *fitted carpets/kitchens* **2** Fitted clothes fit tightly to your body. *a fitted jacket*

fitting /'fɪtɪŋ/ *adjective* suitable or right for a particular situation *The promotion was a fit-*

ting reward for all his hard work.

fittings /'fɪtɪŋz/ *noun* [plural] *mainly UK* **1** parts that are fixed to a piece of furniture or equipment *a circular bath with gold fittings* **2** things that are fixed to the walls, floors, and ceilings inside a house but that can be moved

๐ᵐ**five** /faɪv/ the number 5

fiver /'faɪvəʳ/ *noun* [C] *UK informal* a piece of paper money worth £5 *You owe me a fiver.*

five-star /faɪv'stɑːʳ/ *adjective* describes a hotel of very high quality

๐ᵐ**fix¹** /fɪks/ *verb* [T] **1** [REPAIR] to repair something *My watch is broken - can you fix it?* **2** [DECIDE] to decide a certain and exact date, price, plan, etc *Let's fix a day to have lunch together.* ○ *The price has been fixed at $10.* **3 fix sth onto/to/under, etc** to fasten something in a particular place *They fixed the bookcase to the wall.* **4** [PREPARE] to prepare a drink or meal [+ two objects] *I'll fix you a sandwich.* **5** [CHEAT] to do something dishonest to make certain that a competition, race, or election is won by a particular person [often passive] *People are saying that the elections were fixed.*

fix sth up 1 *UK* to arrange a meeting, date, event, etc *Can we fix up a date for the next meeting?* **2** to repair or change something in order to improve it *He fixes up old cars.*

fix sb up to provide someone with something that they need *My uncle has fixed me up with a summer job.*

fix² /fɪks/ *noun* **1 a quick fix** a way of solving a problem easily *There is no quick fix for unemployment.* **2 be in a fix** to be in a difficult situation **3** [C] *informal* an amount of an illegal drug or something that you want very much *Cath needs her fix of chocolate every day.*

fixation /fɪk'seɪʃ°n/ *noun* [C] a very strong interest in a particular person or thing *She's got an unhealthy fixation with her weight.*

fixed /fɪkst/ *adjective* **1** decided already and not able to be changed *a fixed price* ○ *Is the date of the wedding fixed yet?* **2** fastened somewhere and not able to be moved

fixture /'fɪkstʃəʳ/ *noun* [C] **1** a piece of furniture or equipment that is fixed inside a house or building and is usually sold with it [usually plural] *It comes with the usual fixtures and fittings.* **2** *UK* a sports event that is arranged for a particular day

fizz /fɪz/ *noun* [U] bubbles of gas in a liquid or the sound that they make ● **fizz** *verb* [I]

fizzle /'fɪzl/ *verb*

fizzle out to gradually end in a disappointing way *Their relationship soon fizzled out when they got back from holiday.*

fizzy /'fɪzi/ *adjective* A fizzy drink has lots of bubbles of gas in it.

flabbergasted /'flæbəgɑːstɪd/ *adjective informal* extremely surprised

flabby /'flæbi/ *adjective* having too much loose fat on your body *flabby arms/thighs*

flag¹ /flæg/ *noun* [C] a piece of

fizzy

cloth with a special design and colours, that is fixed to a pole as the symbol of a country or group *the French flag* ○ *There was a flag flying above the castle.* ○ *The guard waved his flag and the train pulled away from the station.*

flag² /flæg/ *verb* [I] **flagging** *past* **flagged** to become tired or less interested in something *The players started to flag towards the end of the game.*

flag sth down to make a vehicle stop by waving at the driver *I managed to flag down a passing police car.*

flagrant /'fleɪɡrənt/ *adjective* shocking because of being so obviously wrong or bad *a flagrant disregard for the law* ● **flagrantly** *adverb*

flagship /'flæɡʃɪp/ *noun* [C] a product or service that is the best and most admired that a company has

flail /fleɪl/ (*also* **flail about/around**) *verb* [I, T] to wave or move your arms and legs about energetically and in an uncontrolled way *The wasp came towards us and Howard started flailing his arms around.*

flair /fleəʳ/ *noun* **1** [no plural] a natural ability to do something well *She has a flair for languages.* **2** [U] when you do something in an exciting and interesting way *He played with great imagination and flair.*

flak /flæk/ *noun* [U] *informal* criticism *The government took a lot of flak for breaking its election promises.*

flake¹ /fleɪk/ *noun* [C] a small, flat, thin piece of something *flakes of paint/snow*

flake² /fleɪk/ *verb* [I] to come off in small, flat, thin pieces *The paint was flaking off the walls.* ● **flaky** *adjective* coming off easily in small, flat, thin pieces *dry, flaky skin*

flake off

flamboyant
/flæm'bɔɪənt/ *adjective*
1 A flamboyant person is loud, stylish, and confident. *a flamboyant pop star* **2** Flamboyant clothes or colours are very bright and noticeable. ● **flamboyance** /flæm'bɔɪəns/ *noun* [U]

WORD PARTNERS FOR *flame*

be in flames ● **burst into/go up in** flames ● flames **spread**

flame¹ /fleɪm/ *noun* [C, U] **1** hot, bright, burning gas produced by something on fire *Smoke and flames were pouring out of the burning factory.* ○ *The whole building was soon in flames* (= burning). ○ *The car crashed and burst into flames* (= suddenly started burning). **2** an angry email

flame² /fleɪm/ *verb* [I, T] to send an angry email to someone

flaming /'fleɪmɪŋ/ *adjective* [always before noun] **1** BURNING burning with a bright light *a flaming building* **2** BRIGHT very bright in colour or light *flaming red hair* **3** ANNOYED *UK informal* used to emphasize something when you are annoyed *What a flaming idiot!*

flamingo /flə'mɪŋɡəʊ/ *noun* [C] a large bird with long, thin legs and pink feathers that lives near water in some hot countries

flammable /'flæməbl/ (*also* **inflammable**) *adjective* Flammable liquids, gases, or materials burn very easily.

flan /flæn/ *noun* [C, U] a round, open pastry base filled with something such as fruit, or cheese and vegetables *cheese and onion flan*

flank¹ /flæŋk/ *verb* **be flanked by sb/sth** to have someone or something at the side or at each side *The President was flanked by police officers.*

flank² /flæŋk/ *noun* [C] **1** the side of the body of an animal or person from the chest to the hips **2** the side of an army when it is ready to fight

flannel /'flænᵊl/ *noun* **1** [U] soft, warm cloth for making clothes *flannel pyjamas* **2** [C] *UK* (*US* **washcloth**) a small cloth that you use to wash your face and body ⊃See colour picture **The Bathroom** on page Centre 3.

flap¹ /flæp/ *noun* **1** [C] a piece of cloth or material fixed along one edge to cover or close an opening **2** [C, U] *US* when someone is worried or excited, or a situation that causes them to feel this way *The President's remarks caused a huge flap.* **3** **be/get in a flap** *mainly UK informal* to be or become worried or excited

flap² /flæp/ *verb* **flapping** *past* **flapped 1** WINGS [T] If a bird flaps its wings, it moves them up and down. **2** MOVE [I] If something such as cloth or paper flaps, the side that is not fixed to something moves around, especially in the wind. *The curtains were flapping around in the breeze.* **3** WORRY [I] *UK informal* to become worried or excited about something *Don't flap! We've got plenty of time to get to the airport.*

flare¹ /fleəʳ/ (*also* **flare up**) *verb* [I] **1** If something bad such as anger or pain flares or flares up, it suddenly starts or gets worse. *Violence flared up between football fans yesterday.* **2** to suddenly burn brightly, usually for a short time *The rocket flared in the sky and disappeared into space.*

flare² /fleəʳ/ *noun* [C] **1** a piece of safety equipment that produces a bright signal when you are lost or injured **2** a sudden, bright light

flared /fleəd/ *adjective* wide at the bottom *flared trousers*

flash¹ /flæʃ/ *verb* **1** [I, T] to shine brightly and suddenly, or to make something shine in this way *The doctor flashed a light into my eye.* ○ *Lightning flashed across the sky.* **2** [I, T] (*also* **flash up**) to appear for a short time, or to make something appear for a short time *An icon flashed up on the screen.* **3** **flash by/past/through**, etc to move somewhere fast *The motorcycle flashed past us and around the corner.* **4** **flash (sb) a look/smile, etc** to look, smile, etc at someone quickly *She flashed him a smile as he came in.*

flash back If your mind or thoughts flash back to something that happened in the past, you suddenly remember it. *Her mind flashed back to the day of their divorce.*

flash² /flæʃ/ *noun* 1 [BRIGHT LIGHT] [C] a sudden bright light *The bomb exploded in a flash of yellow light.* 2 [CAMERA] [C, U] a piece of camera equipment that produces a bright light when you take a photograph in a dark place 3 [SUDDEN EXPERIENCE] [C] a sudden experience of something such as a feeling or idea *a flash of anger* ○ *I had a flash of inspiration.* **4 in a flash** immediately, or very quickly *I'll be back in a flash.* **5 a flash in the pan** a sudden success that does not continue

flashback /'flæʃbæk/ *noun* [C] 1 when you suddenly remember something that happened in the past, usually something bad 2 part of a film or book that goes back in time to something that happened before the main story began *The novel began with a flashback to the hero's experience in the war.*

flashlight /'flæʃlaɪt/ *US* (*UK* **torch**) *noun* [C] an electric light that you can hold in your hand

flashy /'flæʃi/ *adjective* looking too bright, big, and expensive, in a way that is intended to get attention *flashy gold jewellery*

flask

flask *UK*, Thermos *US*

flask

flask /flɑːsk/ *noun* [C] 1 [HOT DRINKS] *UK* (*UK/US* **Thermos**) a special container that keeps drinks hot or cold *a flask of coffee* 2 [ALCOHOL] a flat bottle that is used to carry alcohol in your pocket *Tobias uses his grandfather's silver hip flask.* 3 [SCIENCE] a glass container with a wide base and a narrow opening used in science

WORD PARTNERS FOR flat

in a flat ● a **block of** flats ● a **one-bedroom/two-bedroom** flat ● a **basement** flat

◦▪**flat¹** /flæt/ *mainly UK* (*mainly US* **apartment**) *noun* [C] a set of rooms to live in, with all the

rooms on one level of a building *a large block of flats*

flat

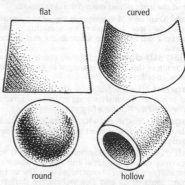

flat

curved

round

hollow

◦▪**flat²** /flæt/ *adjective* **flatter, flattest** 1 [SMOOTH] smooth and level, with no curved, high, or hollow parts *a flat surface* ○ *The countryside around here is very flat.* 2 [WITHOUT EMOTION] without any energy, interest, or emotion *Her voice sounded very flat.* 3 [WITHOUT AIR] If a tyre is flat, it does not contain enough air. 4 [WITHOUT GAS] If a drink is flat, it does not contain enough bubbles of gas. 5 [WITHOUT POWER] *UK* If a battery (= object which provides electricity) is flat, it does not contain any more electrical power. **6 a flat price/rate, etc** a price/rate, etc which is the same for everyone and does not change *He charges a flat rate of £15 an hour.* **7 B flat/E flat, etc** the musical note that is between the note B/E, etc and the note below it 8 [TOO LOW] A flat musical note sounds unpleasant because it is slightly lower than it should be. 9 [LOW] Flat shoes do not raise your feet far from the ground.

flat³ /flæt/ *adverb* or **flatter** or **flattest** 1 in a horizontal or level position on a surface *She spread the cloth flat across the kitchen table.* **2 flat out** using all your energy or effort *We've all been working flat out to finish the project on time.* **3 in 5 minutes/30 seconds, etc flat** in exactly and only 5 minutes, 30 seconds, etc *He showered and got dressed in 10 minutes flat.* **4 fall flat** If an event or joke falls flat, it fails to have the effect that you wanted, such as making people laugh.

flatly /'flætli/ *adverb* 1 **flatly deny/refuse, etc** to say something in a direct and certain way *He flatly refused to answer our questions.* 2 without showing any emotion or interest *"He's gone," she said flatly.*

flatmate /'flætmeɪt/ *mainly UK* (*US* **roommate**) *noun* [C] someone who you share a flat with

flatpack /'flætpæk/ *adjective* used to describe furniture that is sold in pieces inside a flat box, ready to be put together *a flatpack table*

flat-screen T'V *noun* [C] a type of television with a screen that is very thin and shows a very clear picture

flatten /'flæt°n/ verb [I, T] to become flat or to make something become flat *Roll out the dough into balls and flatten them slightly.*

flatter /'flætə'/ verb **1** [T] to say nice things to someone in order to make them feel attractive or important, sometimes in a way that is not sincere *The interviewer flattered him about his recent work.* **2 be flattered** to feel very pleased and proud *She was flattered by his attention.* **3** [T] to make someone look more attractive than usual *That new hairstyle really flatters you.* **4 flatter yourself** to believe something good about yourself, although it might not be true *He flatters himself that he's a good driver.*

flattering /'flætərɪŋ/ adjective making you look more attractive than usual *a flattering picture*

flattery /'flæt°ri/ noun [U] when you say nice things to someone, often because you want something from that person

flaunt /flɔ:nt/ verb [T] to make your success, money, beauty, etc very obvious so that people notice it and admire you *Although he's a millionaire, he doesn't flaunt his wealth.*

> **WORD PARTNERS FOR flavour**
>
> have a [mild/spicy/strong, etc] flavour • a delicate/delicious flavour

flavour¹ UK (US **flavor**) /'fleɪvə'/ noun **1** [C, U] the taste of a particular type of food or drink *We sell 50 different flavours of ice cream.* ○ *Add some salt to give the soup more flavour.* **2** [no plural] a particular quality or style that something has *New York City has a very international flavour.*

flavour² UK (US **flavor**) /'fleɪvə'/ verb **1** [T] to give a particular taste to food or drink [often passive] *This sauce is flavoured with garlic and herbs.* **2 cheese/chocolate, etc -flavoured** tasting of cheese/chocolate, etc *lemon-flavoured sweets*

flavouring UK (US **flavoring**) /'fleɪvərɪŋ/ noun [C, U] something that is added to food or drink to give it a particular taste

flaw /flɔ:/ noun [C] a mistake or bad characteristic that stops someone or something from being perfect *There's a flaw in your reasoning.* • **flawed** adjective *a flawed argument*

flawless /'flɔ:ləs/ adjective with no mistakes or bad characteristics *a flawless complexion* • **flawlessly** adverb

flea /fli:/ noun [C] a small, jumping insect that lives on animals or people and drinks their blood

'flea ,market noun [C] a market where you can buy old or used things cheaply

fleck /flek/ noun [C] a mark, or a very small piece of something *His shirt was covered in flecks of paint.*

fledgling /'fledʒlɪŋ/ adjective [always before noun] A fledgling company, country, or organization is new and not yet developed. *a fledgling business/democracy*

flee /fli:/ verb [I, T] fleeing past fled to leave a place quickly because you are in danger or are

afraid *Police think the suspect has now fled the country.*

fleece /fli:s/ noun [C, U] **1** a warm, soft, light jacket, or the material used to make it *My jacket is lined with fleece.* **2** the thick covering of wool on a sheep

fleet /fli:t/ noun [C] **1** a group of ships, or all of the ships in a country's navy **2** a group of vehicles that are owned and controlled by one person or organization *a fleet of aircraft/cars*

flesh /fleʃ/ noun [U] **1** the soft part of a person's or animal's body between the skin and bones **2 in the flesh** in real life and not on television or in a film *She looks much taller in the flesh.* **3** the soft part of a fruit or vegetable which you can eat **4 your own flesh and blood** a member of your family • **fleshy** adjective fat or thick, or with a lot of flesh

flew /flu:/ past tense of fly

flex¹ /fleks/ verb [T] to bend a part of your body so that the muscle becomes tight

flex² /fleks/ UK (UK/US **cord**) noun [C, U] a piece of wire covered in plastic, that is used to connect electrical equipment to a power supply

flexible /'fleksɪbl/ adjective **1** able to change or be changed easily according to the situation *I'd like a job with more flexible working hours.* ○ *I'm fairly flexible – I can go anytime to suit you.* **2** A flexible substance can bend easily without breaking. • **flexibility** /ˌfleksɪ'bɪləti/ noun [U]

flick¹ /flɪk/ verb **1 flick sth into/off/over, etc** to move something somewhere suddenly and quickly through the air, usually with your fingers *He quickly flicked the crumbs off the table.* **2 flick down/out/towards, etc** to make a sudden, quick movement somewhere *His eyes flicked between her and the door.* **3 flick a switch** to move a switch in order to make electrical equipment start or stop working

flick sth on/off to move a switch in order to make electrical equipment start/stop working

flick through sth to look quickly at the pages of a magazine, book, etc *As I was flicking through the magazine an article caught my eye.*

flick² /flɪk/ noun [C] a sudden, quick movement *With a flick of her wrist, she threw the pebble into the water.*

flicker¹ /'flɪkə'/ verb [I] **1** to shine with a light that is sometimes bright and sometimes weak *a candle flickering in the window* **2** to appear for a short time or make a sudden movement somewhere *A smile flickered across her face.*

flicker² /'flɪkə'/ noun [no plural] **1** when a light is sometimes bright and sometimes weak *the soft flicker of candlelight* **2** a slight, brief feeling or expression of an emotion *a flicker of hope*

flier (also **flyer**) /'flaɪə'/ noun [C] **1** a small piece of paper advertising a business, show, event, etc **2** someone who flies, especially a passenger on an aircraft

flies /flaɪz/ UK (UK/US **fly**) noun [plural] the part where trousers open and close at the front

✺**flight** /flaɪt/ noun 1 JOURNEY [C] a journey in an
aircraft *The flight to Chicago took 4 hours.*
2 AIRCRAFT [C] an aircraft that carries passengers from one place to another *Flight 102 is
ready for boarding at Gate 3.* 3 MOVEMENT [U]
when something flies or moves through the
air *an eagle in flight* 4 **a flight of stairs/steps** a
set of stairs

'**flight at,tendant** noun [C] someone whose
job is to look after passengers on an aircraft

flimsy /ˈflɪmzi/ adjective 1 thin and not solid or
strong *a flimsy cardboard box* 2 A flimsy argument, excuse, etc is weak and difficult to believe. *I'm sick of his flimsy excuses for being
late.*

flinch /flɪnʃ/ verb [I] 1 to make a sudden movement backwards because you are afraid or in
pain *She didn't flinch when the nurse cleaned
the wound.* 2 to avoid doing something that is
unpleasant *Nick never flinches from difficult
decisions.*

fling¹ /flɪŋ/ verb past flung **fling sth around/
across/down, etc** to throw or move something
suddenly and with a lot of force *She flung her
arms around his neck.*

fling² /flɪŋ/ noun [C] 1 a sexual relationship that
is short and not serious *She had a fling with
someone last summer.* 2 a short period of time
when you have a lot of enjoyment or pleasure
This is my last fling before the exams.

flint /flɪnt/ noun [C, U] a very hard, grey stone
that can be used to produce a flame

flip /flɪp/ verb flipping past flipped 1 [I, T] to turn or
make something turn onto a different side, or
so that it is the wrong way up *to flip a coin/
pancake* ○ *The boat flipped right over.* 2 [I] informal to become uncontrollably angry, crazy,
or excited *Dad completely flipped when he saw
the car.*

flip through sth to look quickly at the
pages of a magazine, book, etc

'**flip ,chart** noun [C] large pieces of paper
attached to a board on legs, which you write
or draw on when you are talking to a group of
people

,**flip-'flop** /ˈflɪpˌflɒp/ (*US also* thong) noun [usually
plural] a type of shoe, often made of rubber,
with a V-shaped strap in between the big toe
and the toe next to it ⊃See colour picture **Clothes**
on page Centre 9.

flippant /ˈflɪpᵊnt/ adjective without respect or
not serious *a flippant remark* • flippantly
adverb • flippancy /ˈflɪpᵊnsi/ noun [U]

flipper /ˈflɪpəʳ/ noun [C] 1 a part like a wide, flat
arm without fingers that some sea animals use
for swimming 2 a long, flat, rubber shoe that
you use when swimming under water

flipping /ˈflɪpɪŋ/ adjective [always before noun] UK
informal used to emphasize something ,or to
show slight anger *Where are my flipping keys?*

the '**flip ,side** noun the opposite, less good, or
less popular side of something

flirt¹ /flɜːt/ verb [I] to behave as if you are sexually attracted to someone, usually not in a
very serious way *She was flirting with a guy
at the bar.*

flirt with sth 1 to be interested in an idea,
activity, etc but not seriously, or for only a
short time *He flirted with the idea of becoming a priest.* 2 **flirt with danger/disaster, etc**
to risk experiencing something bad • flirtation
/flɜːˈteɪʃᵊn/ noun [C, U] *It was a harmless flirtation and nothing more.*

flirt² /flɜːt/ noun [C] someone who often flirts
with people

flirtatious /flɜːˈteɪʃəs/ adjective behaving as if
you are sexually attracted to someone, usually
not in a very serious way

flit /flɪt/ verb flitting past flitted **flit about/around/
in and out, etc** to fly or move quickly from one
place to another *Birds were flitting from tree to
tree.*

float

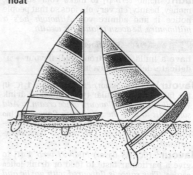

float   sink

float¹ /fləʊt/ verb 1 LIQUID [I, T] to stay on the
surface of a liquid instead of sinking, or to
make something do this *I like floating on my
back in the pool.* 2 AIR [I] to stay in the air, or
move gently through the air *A balloon floated
across the sky.* 3 BUSINESS [I, T] to start selling a
company's shares to the public 4 **float sb's
boat** informal to interest someone *Georgia
likes William, but he just doesn't float my boat.*

float² /fləʊt/ noun [C] 1 VEHICLE a large, decorated vehicle that is used in public celebrations
2 WATER an object that floats on water, used in
fishing or when learning to swim 3 BUSINESS
when you float a business

flock¹ /flɒk/ noun [group] 1 a group of birds or
sheep *a flock of geese* 2 a group of people led by
one person *a flock of children/visitors*

flock² /flɒk/ verb [I] to move or come together in
large numbers *Tourists are flocking to the
beaches.* ○ [+ to do sth] *People flocked to hear
him speak.*

flog /flɒg/ verb [T] flogging past flogged 1 to hit
someone repeatedly as a punishment with
something such as a stick 2 UK informal to sell
something quickly or cheaply *I had to flog the
car to pay my bills.* • flogging noun [C, U]

| ɑː arm | ɜː her | iː see | ɔː saw | uː too | aɪ my | aʊ how | eə hair | eɪ day | əʊ no | ɪə near | ɔɪ boy | ʊə poor | aɪə fire | aʊə sour |

flood

flood¹ /flʌd/ *verb* [I, T] **1** If a place floods or is flooded, it becomes covered in water. [**often passive**] *The town was flooded when the river burst its banks.* ○ *I left the taps running and flooded the bathroom.* **2** to fill or enter a place in large numbers or amounts *Light flooded the room.* ○ *Shoppers flooded into the store.* ● **flooding** *noun* [U] *There is widespread flooding in the South.*

be flooded with sth to receive so many letters, telephone calls, etc that you cannot deal with them

WORD PARTNERS FOR flood

catastrophic / devastating floods ● flood damage/victims/warnings

o-**flood²** /flʌd/ *noun* **1** [C] when a lot of water covers an area that is usually dry, especially when a river becomes too full **2** [C] a large number or amount of things or people that arrive at the same time *a flood of letters/calls* **3** in floods of tears *UK* crying a lot

floodgates /ˈflʌdɡeɪts/ *noun* **open the floodgates** to make it possible for a lot of people to do something

floodlights /ˈflʌdlaɪts/ *noun* [**plural**] powerful lights used to light up sports fields or the outside of buildings at night ● **floodlit** /ˈflʌdlɪt/ *adjective* lit up by floodlights

o-**floor** /flɔːʳ/ *noun* **1** SURFACE [C] a surface that you walk on inside a building *a wooden/tiled floor* ○ *I must sweep the kitchen floor.* **2** BUILDING [C] a particular level of a building *the second/third floor* **3** BOTTOM [no plural] the ground or surface at the bottom of something *the forest/sea floor* **4** AREA [C] an area where a particular activity happens *a dance floor* ⊃See also: **first floor, ground floor, shop floor.**

floorboard /ˈflɔːbɔːd/ *noun* [C] a long, narrow, flat board that forms part of a wooden floor in a building

flooring /ˈflɔːrɪŋ/ *noun* [U] the material used to make or cover a floor *vinyl flooring*

flop¹ /flɒp/ *verb* [I] flopping *past* flopped **1 flop down/into/onto, etc** to fall or sit somewhere suddenly in a heavy or relaxed way *He flopped down on the sofa.* **2** to hang loosely *Her hair kept flopping in her eyes.* **3** *informal* If a film, product, plan, etc flops, it is not successful.

flop² /flɒp/ *noun* [C] *informal* **1** something that is not a success *The party was a bit of a flop.* **2** a movement towards the ground, or the noise someone or something makes as they fall down *She fell onto the bed with a flop.*

floppy /ˈflɒpi/ *adjective* soft and loose or hanging down loosely *floppy hair* ○ *a floppy hat*

,**floppy 'disk** (*also* **floppy**) *noun* [C] a small disk inside a flat, square piece of plastic used for storing information electronically from a computer

flora /ˈflɔːrə/ *noun* [U, group] the plants that grow naturally in a particular area *Scotland's flora and fauna*

floral /ˈflɔːrºl/ *adjective* [**always before noun**] made from flowers or relating to flowers *a floral arrangement/pattern*

florist /ˈflɒrɪst/ *noun* [C] **1** someone who sells and arranges flowers in a shop **2** (*also* **florist's**) a shop that sells flowers

flotation /fləʊˈteɪʃªn/ *noun* **1** [C, U] when a company's shares are sold to the public for the first time **2** [U] when something or someone floats on or in liquid

flounder /ˈflaʊndəʳ/ *verb* [I] **1** MOVEMENT to make wild movements with your arms or body, especially because you are trying not to sink **2** NOT KNOW to not know what to do or say *When he resigned, the team was left floundering.* **3** FAIL If a relationship, organization, or plan flounders, it fails or begins to experience problems. *By 1993 Fletcher's marriage was floundering.*

flour /flaʊəʳ/ *noun* [U] a powder made from grain that is used to make bread, cakes, and other food

flourish¹ /ˈflʌrɪʃ/ *verb* **1** [I] to grow or develop well *a flourishing tourist industry* **2** [T] to wave something around in the air

flourish² /ˈflʌrɪʃ/ *noun* [no plural] when someone does something in a special and noticeable way *The waiter handed me the menu with a flourish.*

flout /flaʊt/ *verb* [T] to intentionally not obey or accept something *to flout the law/rules*

flow¹ /fləʊ/ *verb* [I] **1** If something such as a liquid flows, it moves somewhere in a smooth, continuous way. *The river flows from the Andes to the ocean.* **2** If words, ideas, or conversations flow, they continue in an easy and relaxed way without stopping. *At dinner, the conversation flowed freely.*

flow² /fləʊ/ *noun* **1** [no plural] when something such as a liquid moves somewhere in a smooth, continuous way *the flow of blood* ○ *the flow of information* **2 go with the flow** *informal* to do or accept what other people are doing because it is the easiest thing to do *Just relax and go with the flow!* ⊃See also: **ebb¹** and **flow.**

WORD PARTNERS FOR flower

a bouquet/bunch of flowers ● wild flowers ● cut/fresh flowers ● dried flowers

o-**flower¹** /flaʊəʳ/ *noun* **1** [C] the attractive, coloured part of a plant where the seeds grow *a bunch of flowers* **2** [C] a type of plant that produces flowers *spring/wild flowers* **3 be in flower** When plants are in flower, they have flowers on them. **4 the flower of sth** *literary* the best part of something *the flower of our nation's youth*

flower² /ˈflaʊəʳ/ *verb* [I] to produce flowers *These pansies flower all summer.*

'flower ˌbed *noun* [C] an area of soil in a garden that you grow flowers in

flowery /ˈflaʊəri/ *adjective* **1** (*also* **flowered** /ˈflaʊəd/) decorated with a pattern of flowers *a flowery dress* **2** Flowery language contains unnecessarily complicated and unusual words.

flowing /ˈfləʊɪŋ/ *adjective* **1** hanging down in a long, loose way *flowing robes/hair* **2** produced in a smooth, continuous, or relaxed style *flowing lines*

flown /fləʊn/ *past participle of* fly

fl oz *written abbreviation for* fluid ounce (= a unit for measuring liquid)

flu /fluː/ *noun* [U] an illness like a very bad cold, that makes you feel hot and weak *I had the flu last week.*

fluctuate /ˈflʌktʃueɪt/ *verb* [I] to keep changing, especially in level or amount *Oil prices have fluctuated wildly in recent weeks.* • **fluctuation** /ˌflʌktʃuˈeɪʃᵊn/ *noun* [C, U] *fluctuations in house prices*

fluent /ˈfluːənt/ *adjective* **1** able to use a language naturally without stopping or making mistakes *She is fluent in six languages.* **2** produced or done in a smooth, natural style *Hendrik speaks fluent English.* • **fluency** /ˈfluːənsi/ *noun* [U] • **fluently** *adverb*

fluff¹ /flʌf/ *noun* [U] small, loose bits of wool or other soft material *There's a piece of fluff on your jacket.*

fluff² /flʌf/ *verb* [T] *informal* to fail to do something successfully *I had a great chance to score but I fluffed it.*

fluff sth out/up to make something appear bigger or fuller by hitting or shaking it so that it contains more air *I'll fluff up your pillows for you.*

fluffy /ˈflʌfi/ *adjective* made or covered with soft fur or cloth *a fluffy toy*

fluid¹ /ˈfluːɪd/ *noun* [C, U] a liquid *cleaning fluid* ○ *Drink plenty of fluids.*

fluid² /ˈfluːɪd/ *adjective* **1** LIQUID able to flow easily like liquid **2** CHANGING likely or able to change *a fluid situation* **3** SMOOTH smooth and continuous *fluid movements*

ˌfluid 'ounce (*written abbreviation* **fl oz**) *noun* [C] a unit for measuring liquid, equal to 0.0284 litres in the UK and 0.0296 litres in the US

fluke /fluːk/ *noun* [C, U] something good that happens only because of luck or chance *That first goal was just a fluke.*

flume /fluːm/ *noun* [C] a large tube for people to slide down at a swimming pool

flung /flʌŋ/ *past of* fling

fluorescent /flɔːˈresᵊnt/ *adjective* **1** Fluorescent lights are very bright, tube-shaped, electric lights, often used in offices. **2** Fluorescent colours, clothes, etc are very bright and can be seen in the dark. *fluorescent pink* ○ *a*

fluorescent jacket

fluoride /ˈflɔːraɪd/ *noun* [U] a chemical that helps to prevent tooth decay *Dentists recommend fluoride toothpaste.*

flurry /ˈflʌri/ *noun* [C] **1** a sudden, short period of activity, interest, or excitement *a flurry of phone calls* **2** a sudden, short period of snow and wind

flush¹ /flʌʃ/ *verb* **1** [I, T] If you flush a toilet, or if it flushes, its contents empty and it fills with water again. **2 flush sth away/down/out, etc** to get rid of something by pushing it somewhere with lots of water, such as down a toilet **3** [I] If you flush, your face becomes red and hot, usually because you are embarrassed or angry.

flush sb/sth out to force a person or animal to come out from where they are hiding

flush² /flʌʃ/ *noun* [C] **1** when your face becomes hot and red *a hot flush* **2 a flush of excitement/pleasure, etc** a sudden feeling of excitement/pleasure, etc

flush³ /flʌʃ/ *adjective* [never before noun] **1** at the same level as another surface *I want the door flush with the wall.* **2** *informal* rich *flush with cash*

flustered /ˈflʌstəd/ *adjective* upset and confused *She arrived very late, looking flustered.*

flute /fluːt/ *noun* [C] a musical instrument in the shape of a tube that is held out to the side and played by blowing across a hole near one end

flutter¹ /ˈflʌtəʳ/ *verb* **1** [I, T] to move quickly and gently up and down or from side to side in the air, or to make something move in this way *The flag was fluttering in the breeze.* **2 flutter about/around/down, etc** to move somewhere quickly and gently, usually without any particular purpose *There were several moths fluttering around the light.*

flutter² /ˈflʌtəʳ/ *noun* [C] **1** MOVEMENT a quick, gentle movement *the flutter of wings* **2** EMOTION a state of excitement or worry *a flutter of excitement* **3** RISK MONEY *UK informal* when you risk money on the result of a game, competition, etc

flux /flʌks/ *noun* [U] continuous change *The housing market is still in a state of flux.*

◦➤**fly¹** /flaɪ/ *verb past tense* **flew** *past participle* **flown** **1** MOVE THROUGH AIR [I] When a bird, insect, aircraft, etc flies, it moves through the air. *The robin flew up into a tree.* ○ *The plane was flying at 5000 feet.* **2** TRAVEL [I] to travel through the air in an aircraft *I'm flying to Delhi tomorrow.* **3** CONTROL AIRCRAFT [I, T] to control an aircraft *She learned to fly at the age of 18.* **4** TAKE/SEND [T] to take or send people or goods somewhere by aircraft [often passive] *She was flown to hospital by helicopter.* **5 fly along/down/past, etc** to move somewhere very quickly *He grabbed some clothes and flew down the stairs.* **6 send sb/sth flying** to cause someone or something to move through the air suddenly, usually in an accident **7** LEAVE [I] *UK* to leave suddenly *I must fly - I'm late for work.* **8 let fly (at sb/sth)** *mainly UK informal* to start shouting angrily or attacking someone **9** TIME [I] If time flies, it passes very quickly. **10** FLAG [I, T] If you fly a flag, or a flag is flying, it is fixed to a rope or pole and raised in the air. • **flying** *noun* [U] *Ben's afraid of flying.* ⊃See also: as the **crow**[1] flies, fly off the **handle**[2].

fly about/around If ideas or remarks are flying about, they are being passed quickly from one person to another and causing excitement. *All kinds of rumours are flying around about the school closing.*

fly into a rage/temper to suddenly become very angry *He flies into a rage over the smallest thing.*

fly[2] /flaɪ/ *noun* 1 [C] A small insect with two wings *There was a fly buzzing around in the kitchen.* ⊃See picture at **insect**. 2 [C] (*also UK* **flies** [plural]) the part where trousers open and close at the front *a button/zip fly* 3 **fly on the wall** If you say that you would like to be a fly on the wall in a certain situation, you mean that you would like to be there secretly to see and hear what happens. 4 **a fly-on-the-wall documentary/film** a television programme or film in which people do not act but are recorded in real situations, sometimes without knowing 5 **be dropping like flies** to be dying or becoming ill in large numbers *Half the office seems to have got this flu bug they're dropping like flies.* 6 **wouldn't hurt a fly** If you say that someone wouldn't hurt a fly, you mean that they are very gentle and would never do anything to injure or upset anyone.

flyer (*also* **flier**) /ˈflaɪər/ *noun* [C] 1 a small piece of paper advertising a business, show, event, etc *She's handing out flyers in the shopping centre.* 2 someone who flies, especially a passenger on an aircraft *a frequent flyer* ⊃See also: **high-flyer**.

flying /ˈflaɪɪŋ/ *adjective* [always before noun] 1 A flying creature or object moves or is able to move through the air. *flying ants* 2 **a flying visit** *UK* a very brief visit ⊃See also: with flying colours (**colour**[1]).

flyover /ˈflaɪˌəʊvər/ *UK* (*US* **overpass**) *noun* [C] a bridge that carries a road over another road

FM /ˌef'em/ *noun* [U] a system of radio signals used for broadcasting programmes

foal /fəʊl/ *noun* [C] a young horse

foam /fəʊm/ *noun* [U] 1 [BUBBLES] a mass of small, white bubbles on the surface of a liquid 2 [PRODUCT] a thick substance of small, white bubbles used as a cleaning or beauty product *shaving foam* 3 [FILLING] a soft substance used to fill furniture and other things

focal point /ˈfəʊkəlˌpɔɪnt/ *noun* [no plural] the thing that attracts most of your attention or interest in a place, picture, etc *The fireplace is the focal point of the room.*

focus[1] /ˈfəʊkəs/ *verb* focusing *past* focused 1 [T] If you focus a camera or something else that you look through, you make small changes to it until you can see something clearly. 2 [I, T] If you focus your eyes, or your eyes focus, they change so that you can see clearly. *Give your eyes time to focus in the darkness.*

focus (sth) on sth to give a lot of attention to one particular subject or thing *The research focused on men under thirty.*

focus[2] /ˈfəʊkəs/ *noun* 1 **the focus of sth** the person or thing that is getting most attention in a situation or activity *the focus of our attention* ○ *He is the focus of a police investigation.* 2 [U] when you give special attention to something *Their main focus must be on reducing crime.* 3 **in focus** If an image is in focus, you are able to see it clearly. 4 **out of focus** If an image is out of focus, you are not able to see it clearly.

focus group *noun* [group] a group of people who are brought together to discuss what they think about something such as a new product

fodder /ˈfɒdər/ *noun* [U] food such as dried grass for animals that are kept on farms *cattle/sheep fodder*

foe /fəʊ/ *noun* [C] *literary* an enemy

foetus *UK* (*US* **fetus**) /ˈfiːtəs/ *noun* [C] a young human or animal that is still developing inside its mother • **foetal** *UK* (*US* **fetal**) /ˈfiːtəl/ *adjective* *foetal development*

fog /fɒg/ *noun* [U] thick cloud just above the ground or sea that makes it difficult to see

foggy /ˈfɒgi/ *adjective* 1 with fog *a foggy day* 2 **not have the foggiest (idea)** *informal* to not know anything about something [+ question word] *I haven't the foggiest idea what you're talking about.*

foible /ˈfɔɪbl/ *noun* [C] a slightly unusual or annoying habit [usually plural] *Married couples must learn to accept each other's little foibles.*

foil[1] /fɔɪl/ *noun* 1 [U] metal made into very thin sheets like paper and used mainly for covering food *(UK) aluminium foil/(US) aluminum foil* 2 **a foil for sb/sth** a person or thing that shows or emphasizes how different someone or something else is

foil[2] /fɔɪl/ *verb* [T] to stop a crime, plan, etc from succeeding, or to stop someone doing what they want to do [often passive] *The plot was foiled by undercover police officers.*

fold[1] /fəʊld/ *verb* 1 [MATERIAL] [T] If you fold paper, cloth, etc, you bend it so that one part of it lies flat on top of another part. *He folded the letter in half.* 2 [FURNITURE] [I, T] (*also* **fold up**) to make something such as a chair or table smaller or flatter by closing it or bending it together *a folding chair* ⊃Opposite **unfold**. 3 [BUSINESS] [I] *informal* If a business folds, it fails and is unable to continue. *The restaurant folded last year.* 4 **fold your arms** to bend your arms across your chest, with one crossing over the other *He sat with his arms folded.*

fold[2] /fəʊld/ *noun* [C] 1 a line or mark where paper, cloth, etc was or is folded *Make a fold across the centre of the card.* 2 a thick part where something folds or hangs over itself [usually plural] *folds of skin/fabric*

folder /'fəuldə'/ noun [C] **1** a piece of plastic or thick paper folded down the middle and used to store loose papers ⇒See colour picture **The Office** on page Centre 5. **2** a place on a computer where particular files (= documents, pictures, etc) are kept

foliage /'fəuliɪdʒ/ noun [U] the leaves on a plant

folk¹ /fəuk/ noun **1** [plural] UK informal (US **folks**) people *country folk* ○ *old folk* **2** sb's **folks** informal someone's parents *We always spend Christmas with my folks.* **3** [U] folk music

folk² /fəuk/ adjective **folk art/dancing, etc** the traditional style of art, dancing, etc among a particular group of people

F 'folk ,music noun [U] music written and played in a traditional style

○ᴀ**follow** /'fɒləu/ verb **1** GO [I, T] to move behind someone or something and go where they go, sometimes secretly *She followed me into the kitchen.* **2** HAPPEN [I, T] to happen or come after something *There was a bang, followed by a cloud of smoke.* **3 follow a path/road, etc** to travel along a path, road, etc *Follow the main road down to the traffic lights.* **4 follow instructions/orders/rules, etc** to do what the instructions, orders, rules, etc say you should do *I followed your advice and stayed at home.* **5 follow sb's example/lead** to copy someone's behaviour or ideas **6** UNDERSTAND [I, T] to understand something *Could you say that again? I didn't quite follow.* **7** BE INTERESTED [T] to be interested in an event or activity *I followed the trial closely.* **8 as follows** used to introduce a list or description **9 it follows that** used to say that if one thing is true, another thing will also be true *He's big, but it doesn't follow that he's strong.* ⇒See also: follow in sb's footsteps (**footstep**), follow **suit¹**.

follow on *mainly UK* to happen or exist as the next part of something *This report follows on from my earlier study.*

follow sth through to do something as the next part of an activity or period of development, usually to make certain that it is completed or successful

follow sth up to discover more about a situation or take further action in connection with it

follower /'fɒləuə'/ noun [C] someone who believes in a particular person or set of ideas *a follower of Jesus*

following¹ /'fɒləuɪŋ/ adjective **1 the following day/morning, etc** the next day, morning, etc **2 the following** what comes next, often used to introduce a list, report, etc *The following is an extract from her diary: Today I stayed in bed all day.*

following² /'fɒləuɪŋ/ noun [no plural] a group of people who follow a leader, sport, etc, or admire a particular performer *He has a large and loyal following.*

following³ /'fɒləuɪŋ/ preposition after or as a result of *He died on October 23rd, following several years of illness.*

follow-up /'fɒləuʌp/ noun [C] something that is done to continue or complete something that was done before *a follow-up meeting*

fond /fɒnd/ adjective **1 be fond of sb/sth** to like someone or something *to be fond of animals/ music* ○ [+ doing sth] *He's not very fond of dancing.* **2** [always before noun] expressing or causing happy feelings *fond memories* **3 a fond hope/belief, etc** something that you wish were true, but probably is not ● **fondly** adverb ● **fondness** noun [C, U] *We both have a fondness for cricket.*

fondle /'fɒndl/ verb [T] to touch and rub part of someone's body, in a loving or sexual way

font /fɒnt/ noun [C] **1** a set of letters and symbols that are printed in a particular design and size *What size font are you using?* **2** a container in a church which holds the water for a baptism (= Christian ceremony)

WORD PARTNERS FOR **food**

cold/hot/savoury/sweet food ● baby/cat/ dog food ● canned / frozen / organic / processed food

○ᴀ**food** /fuːd/ noun [C, U] something that people and animals eat, or plants absorb, to keep them alive *baby/dog food* ○ *His favourite food is pizza.* ⇒See colour picture **Food** on page Centre 11 ⇒See also: fast food, junk food.

foodie /'fuːdi/ noun [C] informal someone who loves food and knows a lot about it

'food ,mile noun [C] a unit for measuring how far food travels from where it is made or grown to where it is eaten *People are becoming more concerned about how many food miles their produce has travelled.*

'food ,poisoning noun [U] an illness caused by eating food containing harmful bacteria

'food ,processor noun [C] a piece of electrical equipment with a sharp blade, for cutting and mixing food ⇒See colour picture **The Kitchen** on page Centre 2.

foodstuff /'fuːdstʌf/ noun [C] formal a substance used as food or to make food [usually plural] *They need basic foodstuffs like rice and corn.*

fool¹ /fuːl/ noun **1** [C] a stupid person *I was a fool to trust him.* **2 make a fool (out) of sb** to try to make someone look stupid intentionally *She was always trying to make a fool out of me in front of my friends.* **3 make a fool of yourself** to behave in a silly or embarrassing way *I got drunk and started singing and making a fool of myself.* **4 act/play the fool** UK to behave in a silly way, usually in order to make people laugh *Joe is always playing the fool in class.*

fool² /fuːl/ verb **1** [T] to trick someone *Don't be fooled by his appearance.* ○ [+ into + doing sth] *He fooled the old man into giving him the money.* **2 you could have fooled me** informal something that you say when you do not believe what someone says about something that you saw or experienced yourself *"I wasn't cross." "Really? You could have fooled me."*

fool around/about to behave in a silly way or have a good time *Stop fooling around - this is serious!*

fool with sb/sth mainly US to deal with someone or something that could be dangerous in a stupid or careless way

foolhardy /ˈfuːlˌhɑːdi/ *adjective* taking or involving silly and unnecessary risks *a foolhardy decision*

foolish /ˈfuːlɪʃ/ *adjective* silly and not wise [+ to do sth] *It would be foolish to ignore his advice.* • **foolishly** *adverb* • **foolishness** *noun* [U]

foolproof /ˈfuːlpruːf/ *adjective* A foolproof method, plan, or system is certain to succeed and not fail.

o⌐**foot**[1] /fʊt/ *noun* **1** [C] *plural* **feet** one of the two flat parts on the ends of your legs that you stand on *bare feet* ○ *He stepped on my foot.* ⊃See colour picture **The Body** on page Centre 13. **2** [C] *plural* **foot** or **feet** (*written abbreviation* ft) a unit for measuring length, equal to 0.3048 metres or 12 inches *Alex is about 6 feet tall.* ⊃See Extra help page **Measurements** on page Centre 31. **3 the foot of sth** the bottom of something such as stairs, a hill, a bed, or a page *Put the notes at the foot of the page.* **4 on foot** If you go somewhere on foot, you walk there. ⊃See Common learner error at **walk**. **5 be on your feet** to be standing and not sitting *I'm exhausted, I've been on my feet all day.* **6 put your feet up** to relax, especially by sitting with your feet supported above the ground **7 set foot in/on sth** to go into a place or onto a piece of land *He told me never to set foot in his house again.* **8 get/rise to your feet** to stand up after you have been sitting *The audience rose to their feet.* **9 drag your feet** to deal with something slowly because you do not really want to do it **10 get cold feet** to suddenly become too frightened to do what you had planned to do, especially something important **11 get/start off on the wrong foot** to start a relationship or activity badly *He got off on the wrong foot with my parents by arriving late.* **12 not put a foot wrong** UK to not make any mistakes **13 put your foot down** to tell someone in a strong way that they must do something or must stop doing something **14 put your foot in it** UK (US **put your foot in your mouth**) to say something silly or embarrassing, without intending to **15 stand on your own two feet** to do things for yourself without wanting or needing anyone else to help you

foot[2] /fʊt/ *verb* **foot the bill** to pay for something *Why should taxpayers have to foot the bill?*

footage /ˈfʊtɪdʒ/ *noun* [U] film of an event *news/TV footage*

▓▓▓ WORD PARTNERS FOR **football**

play football • a football **club** / **match** / **player/team** • a **game** of football

o⌐**football** /ˈfʊtbɔːl/ *noun* **1** ⎡UK GAME⎤ [U] UK (UK/US **soccer**) a game in which two teams of players kick a round ball and try to score goals *a game of football* ○ *a football match/team* ⊃See colour picture **Sports 2** on page Centre 15. **2** ⎡US GAME⎤ [U] US (UK **American football**) a game in which two teams of players try to kick, run with, or throw an oval ball across each other's goal line ⊃See colour picture **Sports 2** on page Centre 15. **3** ⎡BALL⎤ [C] a large ball for kicking, especially in football • **footballer** *noun* [C] UK someone who plays football, especially as their job

• **footballing** *adjective* [always before noun] relating to or playing football *his footballing career*

foothills /ˈfʊthɪlz/ *noun* [plural] the lower hills next to a mountain or line of mountains

foothold /ˈfʊthəʊld/ *noun* [C] **1** a place where it is safe to put your foot when you are climbing **2** a safe position from which you can make more progress, for example in business *We are still trying to gain a foothold in the Japanese market.*

footing /ˈfʊtɪŋ/ *noun* **1** [no plural] when you are standing on a surface firmly *I lost my footing and fell.* **2 be on an equal/firm, etc footing** to be in an equal/safe, etc position or situation

footnote /ˈfʊtnəʊt/ *noun* [C] extra information that is printed at the bottom of a page

footpath /ˈfʊtpɑːθ/ *noun* [C] *mainly UK* a path or track for people to walk along, especially in the countryside *a public footpath*

footprint /ˈfʊtprɪnt/ *noun* [C] **1** a mark made by a foot or shoe [usually plural] *The police found some footprints in the mud.* **2** the amount of space on a surface that something needs, especially a computer ⊃Compare **ecological footprint**.

footstep /ˈfʊtstep/ *noun* **1** [C] the sound of a foot hitting the ground when someone walks [usually plural] *I heard footsteps behind me and quickly turned round.* **2 follow in sb's footsteps** to do the same job or the same things in your life as someone else, especially a member of your family *He followed in his father's footsteps and became an actor.*

footwear /ˈfʊtweəʳ/ *noun* [U] shoes, boots, and other things that you wear on your feet

o⌐**for**[1] *strong form* /fɔːʳ/ *weak form* /fəʳ/ *preposition* **1** ⎡GIVEN/USED⎤ intended to be given to or used by someone or something *I've bought a few clothes for the new baby.* ○ *parking for residents only* **2** ⎡PURPOSE⎤ having a particular purpose *a cream for dry skin* ○ *What are those large scissors for?* **3** ⎡BECAUSE OF⎤ because of or as a result of something [+ doing sth] *I got fined for travelling without a ticket.* ○ *Scotland is famous for its spectacular countryside.* **4** ⎡TIME/DISTANCE⎤ used to show an amount of time or distance *We drove for miles before we found a phone box.* ○ *I've been living with my parents for a few months.* ⊃See Common learner error at **during**. **5** ⎡GET⎤ in order to get or achieve something *I've sent off for an application form.* ○ *We had to wait for a taxi.* **6** ⎡HELP⎤ in order to help someone *I'll carry those bags for you.* **7** ⎡OCCASION⎤ on the occasion of *We're having a party for Jim's 60th birthday.* **8** ⎡AT A TIME⎤ at a particular time *I've booked a table for 9 o'clock.* **9** ⎡IN EXCHANGE⎤ in exchange for something, especially an amount of money *How much did you pay for your computer?* ○ *I'd like to change it for a smaller one.* **10** ⎡SUPPORT⎤ supporting or agreeing with someone or something *Who did you vote for?* ○ *There were 16 people for the motion and 14 against.* **11** ⎡REPRESENT⎤ representing or working with a country, organization, etc *He plays football for Cambridge United.* ○ *She works for a charity.* **12** ⎡TOWARDS⎤ towards or in the direction of *Just follow the signs for the airport.* **13** ⎡COMPARE⎤ when compared to a

particular fact *She's quite tall for her age.*
14 MEANING meaning or representing something *What's the German word for 'cucumber'?*
15 RESPONSIBILITY used to say whose responsibility something is *I can't tell you whether you should go or not - that's for you to decide.* **16 for all** despite *For all her qualifications, she's useless at the job.* **17 for all I care/know** used to say that a fact is not important to you *He could be married by now, for all I care.* **18 for now** used to say that something should happen or be done now but can be changed later *Just put everything on the table for now.* **19 be for it** *UK informal (UK/US be in for it)* to be in trouble *If Hilary finds out I'll be for it!*

forage /'fɒrɪdʒ/ *verb* [I] to move about searching for things you need, especially food *Chimpanzees spend most of the day foraging for fruit, leaves, and insects.*

foray /'fɒreɪ/ *noun* [C] when you try to do something that is not familiar to you, or go somewhere different, for a short time *In 2004, she made her first foray into politics.*

forbid /fə'bɪd/ *verb* [T] forbidding *past tense* **forbade** *past participle* **forbidden** **1** to order someone not to do something, or to say that something must not happen [+ to do sth] *I forbid you to see that boy again.* ○ [often passive, + from + doing sth] *He is forbidden from leaving the country.* **2 God/Heaven forbid!** something you say when you hope that something will not happen [+ (that)] *God forbid that he should die during the operation.* ● **forbidden** *adjective* not allowed by an official rule *Smoking is strictly forbidden in this area.*

forbidding /fə'bɪdɪŋ/ *adjective* looking unpleasant, unfriendly, or frightening *a cold and forbidding landscape*

WORD PARTNERS FOR **force**

exert/use force • **brute/sheer** force • **do** sth **by** force • **the** force **of** sth

⚬**force¹** /fɔːs/ *noun* **1** POWER [U] physical power or strength *The force of the explosion shattered every window in the street.* ○ *The army has seized power by force.* **2** ORGANIZED GROUP [C] a group of people organized to work together for a particular purpose, for example in military service *the Royal Air Force* ○ *a skilled work force* **3** INFLUENCE [C, U] power and influence, or a person or thing that has it *the forces of good/evil* **4 in/into force** If a law, rule, etc is in force, it is being used, and if it comes into force, it starts to be used. *The new law came into force in April.* **5 be out in force** to be somewhere in large numbers *Photographers were out in force at the palace today.* **6 a force to be reckoned with** a very powerful person or organization **7 join forces** When two people or groups join forces, they act or work together. [+ to do sth] *She joined forces with her sister-in-law to set up a restaurant.* ⊃See also: **air force, the armed forces, market forces, police force, task force**.

⚬**force²** /fɔːs/ *verb* [T] **1** to make someone do something that they do not want to do [+ to do sth] *The hijacker forced the pilot to fly to New York.* ○ [often passive] *She was forced out of the*

race by a knee injury. **2** to make an object move or open by physical strength or action *They had to force the lock.* ○ *She forced the window open.*

forceful /'fɔːsfᵊl/ *adjective* expressing opinions strongly and demanding attention or action *a forceful manner/personality* ● **forcefully** *adverb* to argue forcefully

forcible /'fɔːsəbl/ *adjective* A forcible action is done using force. *forcible entry/arrest* ● **forcibly** *adverb* *Thousands of people were forcibly removed from their homes.*

fore /fɔːʳ/ *noun* **to the fore** in or to an important or popular position *The band first came to the fore in the late 1990s.*

forearm /'fɔːrɑːm/ *noun* [C] the lower part of your arm between your hand and your elbow (= the place where it bends)

foreboding /fɔː'bəʊdɪŋ/ *noun* [U, no plural] a feeling that something very bad is going to happen *a sense of foreboding*

WORD PARTNERS FOR **forecast**

a forecast of sth • an **economic** forecast • a **gloomy** forecast

forecast¹ /'fɔːkɑːst/ *noun* [C] a report saying what is likely to happen in the future *economic forecasts* ⊃See also: **weather forecast**.

forecast² /'fɔːkɑːst/ *verb* [T] *past* **forecast** or **forecasted** to say what you expect to happen in the future *In 2001 a serious earthquake was forecast for the area.* ● **forecaster** *noun* [C] *a weather forecaster*

forecourt /'fɔːkɔːt/ *noun* [C] *UK* a large area with a hard surface at the front of a building *a garage forecourt*

forefather /'fɔːˌfɑːðəʳ/ *noun formal* sb's **forefathers** someone's relatives who lived a long time ago

forefinger /'fɔːˌfɪŋgəʳ/ *noun* [C] the finger next to your thumb

forefront /'fɔːfrʌnt/ *noun* **be at/in the forefront of sth** to have an important position or job in an area of activity *The company is at the forefront of developing new technology.*

forego /fɔː'gəʊ/ *verb* [T] **foregoing** *past tense* **forewent** *past participle* **foregone** another spelling of **forgo** (= to decide not to have or do something you want)

foregone con'clusion *noun* [no plural] a result that is obvious before it happens [+ (that)] *It was a foregone conclusion that he'd go into politics.*

the foreground /ðəˈfɔːgraʊnd/ *noun* **1** the area of a view or picture which seems closest to you *There's a seated figure in the foreground of the painting.* **2** the subject or person that people give most attention to *Environmental issues have recently moved to the foreground.*

forehand /'fɔːhænd/ *noun* [C] when you hit the ball in sports such as tennis with your arm held out on the side that you hold the racket (= object to hit balls with) *a forehand volley*

forehead /'fɔːhed/ *noun* [C] the part of your face between your eyes and your hair ⊃See colour picture **The Body** on page Centre 13.

o⊷**foreign** /'fɒrɪn/ *adjective* **1** belonging to or coming from another country, not your own *a foreign language/student* ○ *foreign cars/films* **2** [always before noun] relating to or dealing with countries that are not your own *foreign policy* ○ *the Foreign Minister* **3 be foreign to sb** to be something you know nothing about or do not understand *The concept of loyalty is completely foreign to him.*

foreigner /'fɒrɪnəʳ/ *noun* [C] someone from another country

foreman /'fɔːmən/ *noun* [C] *plural* **foremen** someone who leads a group of workers *a factory foreman*

foremost /'fɔːməʊst/ *adjective, adverb formal* most important *He's one of the country's foremost experts on military law.*

forename /'fɔːneɪm/ *noun* [C] *UK formal* your first name, which comes before your family name

forensic /fə'rensɪk/ *adjective* [always before noun] relating to scientific methods of solving crimes *forensic evidence/medicine* ○ *a forensic scientist*

forerunner /'fɔː,rʌnəʳ/ *noun* [C] an earlier, less developed example *the forerunner of the modern car*

foresee /fɔː'siː/ *verb* [T] **foreseeing** *past tense* **foresaw** *past participle* **foreseen** to expect a future situation or event *I don't foresee any problems in the future.*

foreseeable /fɔː'siːəbl/ *adjective* **for/in the foreseeable future** as far in the future as you can imagine *Prices will remain high for the foreseeable future.*

foreshadow /fɔː'ʃædəʊ/ *verb* [T] *formal* to show or warn that something bigger, worse, or more important is coming

foresight /'fɔːsaɪt/ *noun* [U] when you know or can judge what will happen or what you will need in the future *She had the foresight to book her flight early.*

foreskin /'fɔːskɪn/ *noun* [C, U] the loose skin that covers the end of a penis

o⊷**forest** /'fɒrɪst/ *noun* [C, U] a large area of trees growing closely together *pine forest* ● **forested** *adjective* covered by forest *heavily forested areas*

forest

forestall /fɔː'stɔːl/ *verb* [T] to prevent something from happening by taking action before it does *to forestall an attack/crisis*

forestry /'fɒrɪstri/ *noun* [U] the work of looking after or making forests

foretell /fɔː'tel/ *verb* [T] *past* **foretold** *formal* to say what is going to happen in the future

forever /fə'revəʳ/ *adverb* **1** [IN FUTURE] for all time in the future *I'll love you forever.* **2** [A LONG TIME]

informal used to emphasize that something takes a long time *The journey home took forever.* **3** [OFTEN] used to emphasize that something happens often *She is forever helping people.*

foreword /'fɔːwɜːd/ *noun* [C] a short piece of writing at the front of a book that introduces the book or its writer

forfeit /'fɔːfɪt/ *verb* [T] to lose the right to do something or have something because you have done something wrong *They have forfeited the right to live in society.*

forgave /fə'geɪv/ *past tense of* forgive

forge[1] /fɔːdʒ/ *verb* [T] **1** to make an illegal copy of something in order to deceive people *a forged passport* **2** to develop a good relationship with someone or something *The group forged friendships that have lasted more than twenty years.*

forge ahead to suddenly make a lot of progress with something *The organizers are forging ahead with a programme of public events.*

forge[2] /fɔːdʒ/ *noun* [C] a place where metal objects are made by heating and shaping metal

forgery /'fɔːdʒəri/ *noun* **1** [C] an illegal copy of a document, painting, etc **2** [U] the crime of making an illegal copy of something

The expression **slip someone's mind** is often used informally when someone forgets to do something: *I meant to tell you that he'd phoned, but it completely slipped my mind.*

If a word is **on the tip of your tongue**, you have forgotten it but think that you will very soon remember it: *Oh, what was that film called? - it's on the tip of my tongue.*

If something such as a name **escapes** you, you cannot remember it: *The name of her book escapes me at the moment.*

o⊷**forget** /fə'get/ *verb* **forgetting** *past tense* **forgot** *past participle* **forgotten 1** [NOT REMEMBER] [I, T] to be unable to remember a fact, something that happened, or how to do something *I've forgotten his name.* ○ [+ (that)] *Don't forget that Lucy and John are coming this weekend.* ○ *He'd completely forgotten about their quarrel.* ○ [+ question word] *You never forget how to ride a bike.* **2** [NOT DO] [I, T] to not remember to do something [+ to do sth] *Dad's always forgetting to take his pills.* **3** [NOT BRING] [T] to not bring something with you because you did not remember it *Oh no, I've forgotten my passport.* **4** [STOP THINKING] [T] (*also* **forget about**) to stop thinking about someone or something *I'll never forget him for as long as I live.* **5 forget it** used to tell someone not to worry about something as it is not important **6 I forget** used instead of 'I have forgotten' *I forget when we last saw him.* **7 forget yourself** to do or say something that is not acceptable in a particular situation *She completely forgot herself and started screaming at him.*

forgetful /fə'getfʰl/ *adjective* often forgetting things *She's 84 now and getting a bit forgetful.*

• **forgetfulness** *noun* [U]

ᴏ⸰**forgive** /fəˈgɪv/ *verb past tense* **forgave** *past participle* **forgiven** 1 [I, T] to decide not to be angry with someone or not to punish them for something they have done *I've apologized, but I don't think she'll ever forgive me.* ○ [often reflexive] *Mike would never forgive himself if anything happened to the children.* ○ [+ for + doing sth] *Jane never forgave her mother for lying to her.* 2 **forgive me** used before you ask or say something that might seem rude *Forgive me for asking, but how much did you pay for your bag?* 3 **sb could be forgiven for doing sth** used to say that you can understand if someone might think, believe, or do something

WORD PARTNERS FOR **forgiveness**

ask (for)/beg (for) forgiveness • forgiveness for sth

forgiveness /fəˈgɪvnəs/ *noun* [U] when you forgive someone for something they have done

forgiving /fəˈgɪvɪŋ/ *adjective* ready to forgive someone for something they have done

forgo /fɔːˈgəʊ/ *verb* [T] **forgoing** *past tense* **forwent** *past participle* **forgone** *formal* to decide not to have or do something, although you want to have it or do it *She had to forgo her early ambition to be a writer.*

forgot /fəˈgɒt/ *past tense of* forget

forgotten /fəˈgɒtən/ *past participle of* forget

ᴏ⸰**fork**¹ /fɔːk/ *noun* [C] 1 [FOOD] a small object with three or four points and a handle, that you use to pick up food and eat with *a knife and fork* 2 [DIGGING] a tool with a long handle and three or four points, used for digging and breaking soil into pieces *a garden fork* 3 [ROAD] a place where a road or river divides into two parts *Turn right when you reach a fork in the road.*

fork² /fɔːk/ *verb* [I] If a road or river forks, it divides into two parts.

fork sth out UK (US **fork sth over**) *informal* to pay or give money for something, especially when you do not want to

forlorn /fəˈlɔːn/ *adjective* lonely and unhappy *The captured soldiers looked forlorn and helpless.* • **forlornly** *adverb*

ᴏ⸰**form**¹ /fɔːm/ *noun* 1 [TYPE] [C] a type of something or way of doing something *Swimming is the best form of exercise.* 2 [PAPER] [C] a printed document with spaces for you to write information *Please fill in/out the form using black ink.* 3 **the form of sth** the particular way in which something exists *The novel is written in the form of a series of letters.* 4 [SPORT] [U] In sport, someone's form is how well or badly they are performing. *The team seems to have lost its form lately.* 5 **be in/on/off form** UK If someone is in form or on form, they are feeling or performing well, and if they are off form they are not feeling or performing well. *Harry was on good form last night.* 6 [SCHOOL GROUP] [C] UK (US **grade**) a school class or group of classes for students of the same age or ability *He's in the third form.* 7 [SHAPE] [C] the body or shape of someone or something 8 [GRAMMAR] [C] a way of writing or saying a word that shows if it is singular or plural, past or present, etc

The plural form of 'sheep' is 'sheep'. ᴐSee also: application form, sixth form.

ᴏ⸰**form²** /fɔːm/ *verb* 1 [BEGIN] [I, T] to begin to exist, or to make something begin to exist [often passive] *We are learning more about how stars are formed.* ○ *A crowd formed in the street.* 2 [SHAPE] [I, T] to take or to make something take a particular shape *Form the dough into little balls.* ○ *The children formed into lines.* 3 [COMBINE] [T] to make something by combining different parts *In English you form the present participle by adding -ing to the verb.* 4 [START] [T] to start an organization or business *Brown formed her own company eleven years ago.* 5 [BE] [T] to be the thing talked about or be part of it *The Alps form a natural barrier between Italy and Switzerland.* 6 **form an opinion/impression, etc** to begin to have a particular opinion or idea about something because of the information you have *I formed the impression that she wasn't really interested.*

ᴏ⸰**formal** /ˈfɔːməl/ *adjective* 1 [SERIOUS] used about clothes, language, and behaviour that are serious and not friendly or relaxed *a formal dinner party* ○ *I felt I needed to look more formal for the interview.* 2 [OFFICIAL] [always before noun] public or official *a formal announcement/apology* 3 [IN SCHOOL] [always before noun] Formal education, training, etc happens in a school or college. *Tom had little formal schooling.*

formality /fɔːˈmæləti/ *noun* 1 [C] something that the law or an official process says must be done *There are certain legal formalities to be completed.* 2 [U] formal and polite behaviour *the formality of a royal funeral*

formally /ˈfɔːməli/ *adverb* 1 officially *The deal will be formally announced on Tuesday.* ○ *Nothing has been formally agreed yet.* 2 in a polite way *They shook hands formally.*

format¹ /ˈfɔːmæt/ *noun* [C] the way something is designed, arranged, or produced *This year's event will have a new format.*

format² /ˈfɔːmæt/ *verb* [T] **formatting** *past* **formatted** 1 to prepare a computer disk so that information can be stored on it 2 to organize and design the words on a page or document

formation /fɔːˈmeɪʃən/ *noun* 1 [U] the development of something into a particular thing or shape *the formation of a crystal* 2 [C, U] when something has a particular shape or things are arranged in a particular way *rock/cloud formations* ○ *The planes flew overhead in formation* (= in a pattern).

formative /ˈfɔːmətɪv/ *adjective* relating to the time when your character and opinions are developing *She spent her formative years in New York.*

former /ˈfɔːmər/ *adjective* [always before noun] happening, existing, or true in the past but not now *the former Soviet Union* ○ *former President Bill Clinton*

the former /ˈfɔːmər/ *noun* the first of two people or things that have just been talked about

formerly /ˈfɔːməli/ *adverb* in the past *The European Union was formerly called the Euro-*

pean Community.

formidable /'fɔːmɪdəbl/ *adjective* **1** Someone who is formidable is strong and a bit frightening. *a formidable woman* **2** difficult and needing a lot of effort or thought *a formidable task*

formula /'fɔːmjələ/ *noun* [C] *plural* formulas or formulae **1** [METHOD] a plan or method that is used to achieve something *There's no magic formula for success.* **2** [RULE] a set of letters, numbers, or symbols that are used to express a mathematical or scientific rule **3** [LIST] a list of the substances that something is made of

formulate /'fɔːmjəleɪt/ *verb* [T] **1** to develop all the details of a plan for doing something *They formulated a plan to save the company.* **2** to say what you think or feel after thinking carefully *to formulate an answer/reply* ● formulation /,fɔːmjə'leɪʃ°n/ *noun* [C, U]

forsake /fə'seɪk/ *verb* [T] *past tense* forsook *past participle* forsaken *formal* **1** to leave someone, especially when they need you *He felt he couldn't forsake her when she was so ill.* **2** to stop doing or having something *He decided to forsake politics for journalism.*

fort /fɔːt/ *noun* [C] a strong building that soldiers use to defend a place

forth /fɔːθ/ *adverb literary* out of a place or away from it *The knights rode forth into battle.*

forthcoming /,fɔːθ'kʌmɪŋ/ *adjective* **1** [SOON] [always before noun] *formal* going to happen soon *the forthcoming election/visit* **2** [OFFERED] [never before noun] If money or help is forthcoming, it is offered or given. *He insisted that no more money would be forthcoming.* **3** [WILLING] [never before noun] willing to give information *Elaine wasn't very forthcoming about her love life.*

forthright /'fɔːθraɪt/ *adjective* saying what you think honestly and clearly *They dealt with all our questions in a very forthright manner.*

forthwith /,fɔːθ'wɪθ/ *adverb formal* immediately *to cease forthwith*

fortifications /,fɔːtɪfɪ'keɪʃ°nz/ *noun* [plural] strong walls, towers, etc that are built to protect a place

fortify /'fɔːtɪfaɪ/ *verb* [T] **1** to build strong walls, towers, etc around a place to protect it *a fortified city/town* **2** to make someone feel stronger physically or mentally *She had a sandwich to fortify herself before going on.*

fortitude /'fɔːtɪtjuːd/ *noun* [U] *formal* when you are brave and do not complain about pain or problems

fortnight /'fɔːtnaɪt/ *noun* [C] *UK* two weeks [usually singular] *a fortnight's holiday* ○ *We usually get together about once a fortnight.* ● **fortnightly** *adverb UK* happening every two weeks *a fortnightly meeting*

fortress /'fɔːtrəs/ *noun* [C] a castle or other strong building built to defend a place

fortunate /'fɔːtʃ°nət/ *adjective* lucky [+ to do sth] *I'm very fortunate to be alive.* ○ [+ (that)] *It was fortunate that someone was available to take over.* ⊃Opposite **unfortunate**.

o-**fortunately** /'fɔːtʃ°nətli/ *adverb* happening because of good luck *Fortunately, no one was*

hurt in the accident. ⊃Opposite **unfortunately**.

fortune /'fɔːtʃuːn/ *noun* **1** [C] a lot of money *She made a fortune selling her story to the newspapers.* **2** [C, U] the good or bad things that happen to you [usually plural] *The family's fortunes changed almost overnight.* **3** tell sb's fortune to say what is going to happen to someone in the future

fortune-teller /'fɔːtʃuːn,telə'/ *noun* [C] someone who tells you what will happen to you in the future

o-**forty** /'fɔːti/ *the number* 40 ● fortieth 40th written as a word

forum /'fɔːrəm/ *noun* [C] a situation or meeting in which people can exchange ideas and discuss things *We are establishing a forum for debate/discussion.*

o-**forward¹** /'fɔːwəd/ (*also* forwards) *adverb* **1** [DIRECTION] towards the direction that is in front of you *She leaned forward to make sure I could hear her.* **2** [FUTURE] towards the future *I always look forward, not back.* **3** [PROGRESS] used to say that something is making good progress *This is a big step forward for democracy.*

forward² /'fɔːwəd/ *adjective* **1** forward motion/movement, etc movement towards the direction that is in front of you **2** forward planning/thinking, etc when you plan or think about something for the future **3** Someone who is forward is too confident or too friendly with people they do not know.

forward³ /'fɔːwəd/ *verb* [T] to send a letter, email, etc that you have received to someone else *Could you forward my mail to me while I'm away?* ⊃See also: fast-forward.

forward⁴ /'fɔːwəd/ *noun* [C] a player in a sport such as football who plays near the front and tries to score goals

forwarding a'ddress *noun* [C] a new address that letters and parcels should be sent to

forward-looking /'fɔːwədlʊkɪŋ/ *adjective* planning for the future and using new ideas or technology *a forward-looking plan/policy*

forwards /'fɔːwədz/ *adverb* another word for forward

'forward ,slash (*also* slash) *noun* [C] the symbol '/', a symbol used in Internet addresses and used to show where on a computer files are kept ⊃Compare backslash.

forwent /fɔː'went/ *past simple of* forgo

fossil /'fɒs°l/ *noun* [C] part of an animal or plant from thousands of years ago, preserved in rock

'fossil ,fuel *noun* [C, U] a fuel such as coal or oil that is obtained from under the ground

foster¹ /'fɒstə'/ *verb* [T] **1** to encourage a particular feeling, situation, or idea to develop *The growth of the Internet could foster economic development worldwide.* **2** to look after a child as part of your family for a time, without becoming their legal parent

foster² /ˈfɒstəʳ/ *adjective* **1 foster home/mother/parent, etc** the home where a child who is fostered lives, or the person or people who foster a child **2 foster child/daughter/son, etc** a child who is fostered

fought /fɔːt/ *past of* fight

foul¹ /faʊl/ *adjective* **1** very dirty, or with an unpleasant smell *the foul smell of rotting fish* **2** very bad or unpleasant *foul weather* ○ *She's in a foul mood.* **3 foul language/words** very rude and offensive words **4 fall foul of sb/sth** *UK* to do something which causes you to be in trouble

foul² /faʊl/ *verb* **1** [T] to make something very dirty *The beaches had been fouled by dogs.* **2** [I, T] to do something that is against the rules in a sport *He was fouled as he was about to shoot at goal.*

foul sth up *informal* to spoil something completely *The travel company completely fouled up our holiday.*

WORD PARTNERS FOR ***foul***

commit a foul • a foul **against/on** sb

foul³ /faʊl/ *noun* [C] something that someone does in a sport that is not allowed by the rules

ˌfoul ˈplay *noun* [U] when someone's death is caused by a violent crime *Police do not suspect foul play at present.*

found¹ /faʊnd/ *verb* [T] **1** to start an organization, especially by providing money *The company was founded in 1861.* **2** to base something on a set of ideas or beliefs [often passive] *a society **founded on** principles of equality*

found² /faʊnd/ *past of* find

foundation /faʊnˈdeɪʃᵊn/ *noun* **1** [IDEA] [C] the idea or principle that something is based on *Jefferson's document **formed the foundation** of a new nation.* **2** [STARTING] [U] when an organization, state, or country is established *the foundation of a new state* **3** [ORGANIZATION] [C] an organization that gives money for a particular purpose *the Mental Health Foundation* **4 foundations** [plural] *UK* (*US* **foundation** [C]) the part of a building, road, bridge, etc that is under the ground and supports it *concrete foundations* **5** [MAKE-UP] [U] make-up that is worn all over the face to give it a smooth appearance **6 be without foundation; have no foundation** If something is without foundation, there is no proof that it is true. *The allegations are completely without foundation.* **7 lay the foundation(s) for/of sth** to provide the conditions that make it possible for something to happen *His reforms laid the foundation of future greatness.*

founˈdation ˌcourse *UK* (*US* **introductory course**) *noun* [C] a college or university course on a subject that students take to prepare them for a more advanced course on that subject *a foundation course in physics*

founder /ˈfaʊndəʳ/ *noun* [C] someone who establishes an organization

foundry /ˈfaʊndri/ *noun* [C] a place where metal or glass is melted and made into objects

fountain /ˈfaʊntɪn/ *noun* [C] a structure that forces water up into the air as a decoration

fountain

ˈfountain ˌpen *noun* [C] a pen that you fill with ink

⊶**four** /fɔːʳ/ the number 4

four-by-four /ˌfɔːbaɪˈfɔːʳ/ a four-wheel drive

fours /fɔːz/ **on all fours** with your hands and knees on the ground

foursome /ˈfɔːsəm/ *noun* [C] a group of four people *We could go out as a foursome.*

⊶**fourteen** /ˌfɔːˈtiːn/ the number 14 • **fourteenth** 14th written as a word

fourth¹ /fɔːθ/ 4th written as a word

fourth² /fɔːθ/ *US* (*UK/US* **quarter**) *noun* [C] one of four equal parts of something; ¼

ˌFourth of Juˈly (*also* **Independence Day**) *noun* [U] 4 July, a national holiday in the US to celebrate the country's freedom from Great Britain in 1776

ˌfour-wheel ˈdrive (*written abbreviation* **4WD**) *noun* [C] a vehicle with an engine that supplies power to all four wheels so that it can drive easily over rough ground • **ˌfour-wheel ˈdrive** *adjective a four-wheel drive car*

fowl /faʊl/ *noun* [C] *plural* **fowl** or **fowls** a bird that is kept for its eggs and meat, especially a chicken

fox /fɒks/ *noun* [C] a wild animal like a dog with red-brown fur, a pointed nose, and a long thick tail

foyer /ˈfɔɪeɪ/ [US] /ˈfɔɪər/ *noun* [C] a room at the entrance of a hotel, theatre, cinema, etc

fracas /ˈfrækɑː/ [US] /ˈfreɪkəs/ *noun* [no plural] a noisy fight or argument

WORD PARTNERS FOR ***fraction***

2 a **minute/small/tiny** fraction of sth • a fraction of sth

fraction /ˈfrækʃᵊn/ *noun* [C] **1** a number less than 1, such as ½ or ¾ ➲See Extra help page **Numbers** on page Centre 30. **2** a very small number or amount *a fraction of a second* • **fractionally** *adverb* by a very small amount *Harry is fractionally taller than Ben.*

fracture /ˈfræktʃəʳ/ *verb* [T] to break something hard such as a bone, or a piece of rock *She's fractured her ankle.* • **fracture** *noun* [C]

fragile /ˈfrædʒaɪl/ [US] /ˈfrædʒᵊl/ *adjective* **1** easily broken, damaged, or destroyed *a fragile china cup* ○ *a fragile economy* **2** physically or emotionally weak *a fragile little girl* • **fragility** /frəˈdʒɪləti/ *noun* [U]

fragment¹ /ˈfrægmənt/ *noun* [C] a small piece of something *fragments of pottery*

fragment² /frægˈment/ *verb* [I, T] to break something into small parts, or to be broken in this way *The opposition has fragmented into a number of small groups.* • **fragmented** *adjective a fragmented society*

fragrance /ˈfreɪgrəns/ *noun* [C, U] **1** a pleasant smell *the delicate fragrance of roses* **2** a substance which people put on their bodies to make themselves smell nice *a new fragrance for men*

fragrant /ˈfreɪɡrənt/ *adjective* with a pleasant smell *fragrant flowers*

frail /freɪl/ *adjective* not strong or healthy *a frail old lady*

frailty /ˈfreɪlti/ *noun* [C, U] when someone is physically or morally weak

frame

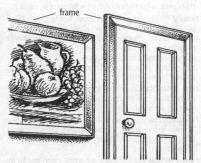
frame

frame¹ /freɪm/ *noun* [C] **1** PICTURE a structure that goes around the edge of something such as a door, picture, window, or mirror *a picture frame* ◦ *a window frame* **2** STRUCTURE the basic structure of a building, vehicle, or piece of furniture that other parts are added onto *a bicycle frame* **3** BODY the shape of someone's body *his large/small frame* **4 frame of mind** the way someone feels at a particular time *She was in a much more positive frame of mind today.*

frame² /freɪm/ *verb* [T] **1** PICTURE to put something such as a picture into a frame *I'm going to frame this and put it on the wall.* **2** EDGE to form an edge to something in an attractive way *Dark hair framed her face.* **3** CRIME to intentionally make it seem as if someone is guilty of a crime [often passive] *He claimed he had been framed by the police.* **4** EXPRESS *formal* to express something choosing your words carefully *I tried to frame a suitable reply.*

frames /freɪmz/ *noun* [plural] the plastic or metal structure that holds together a pair of glasses

create/develop/establish/provide a framework • a framework for (doing) sth

framework /ˈfreɪmwɜːk/ *noun* [C] **1** a system of rules, ideas, or beliefs that is used to plan or decide something *a legal framework for resolving disputes* **2** the basic structure that supports something such as a vehicle or building and gives it its shape

franchise /ˈfrænʃaɪz/ *noun* **1** [C] the right to sell a company's products or services in a particular area using the company's name *a fast food franchise* ◦ *a franchise holder* **2** [U] the legal right to vote in elections

frank /fræŋk/ *adjective* speaking honestly and saying what you really think *a full and frank discussion* ◦ *To be frank, I don't really want to see him.* • **frankness** *noun* [U]

frankfurter /ˈfræŋkfɜːtəʳ/ *noun* [C] a long, thin sausage (= tube of meat and spices), often eaten with bread

frankly /ˈfræŋkli/ *adverb* in an honest and direct way *Quite frankly, I think you're making a big mistake.*

frantic /ˈfræntɪk/ *adjective* **1** done in a fast and excited way and not calm or organized *a frantic search* **2** very worried or frightened *frantic calls for help* ◦ *I got home to find Joe frantic with worry.* • **frantically** *adverb Laura was searching frantically for her keys.*

fraternal /frəˈtɜːn²l/ *adjective* like or relating to a brother

fraternity /frəˈtɜːnəti/ *noun* **1** [U] a feeling of friendship between people **2** [C] in the US, a social organization of male college students

commit fraud • a fraud case / charge / investigation

fraud /frɔːd/ *noun* **1** [U] when someone does something illegal in order to get money *credit card fraud* **2** [C] someone who deceives people by pretending to be someone or something that they are not

fraudulent /ˈfrɔːdjələnt/ *adjective formal* dishonest and illegal *fraudulent insurance claims* • **fraudulently** *adverb*

fraught /frɔːt/ *adjective* **1 fraught with danger/ difficulties, etc** full of danger/difficulties, etc *The present situation is fraught with danger.* **2** *mainly UK* causing worry, or feeling worried *a fraught silence*

fray¹ /freɪ/ *verb* **1** [I, T] If material or clothing frays, or if it is frayed, the threads at the edge break and become loose. **2** [I] If your temper (= mood) frays or your nerves fray, you gradually become annoyed or upset. *After hours of waiting, tempers were beginning to fray.*

fray

fray

fray² /freɪ/ *noun* **enter/ join, etc the fray** to start taking part in an argument or fight *The time had come for the US to enter the fray.*

freak¹ /friːk/ *noun* [C] **1** *informal* someone who is very interested in a particular subject or activity *My brother's a bit of a computer freak.* **2** someone who looks strange or behaves in a strange way *They made me feel like a freak.*

freak² /friːk/ *adjective* **a freak accident/storm, etc** A freak event is one that is very unusual.

freak³ /friːk/ (*also* **freak out**) *verb* [I, T] *informal* to suddenly become very angry, frightened, or surprised, or to make someone do this *I hated* *that film, it totally freaked me out.*

freckle /'frekl/ *noun* [C] a very small, brown spot on your skin from the sun • **freckled** *adjective*

o‑**free¹** /friː/ *adjective* **1** [NOT CONTROLLED] able to live, happen, or exist without being controlled by anyone or anything *free trade* ○ *a free society* ○ [+ to do sth] *People should be free to say what they think.* **2** [NO COST] not costing any money *a free sample of perfume* ○ *Entry is free for children under 12.* ○ *The unemployed get their prescriptions free of charge.* **3** [NOT A PRISONER] not in prison or in a cage *He opened the cage and set the birds free.* **4** [NOT BUSY] not busy doing anything *Are you free this evening?* ○ *I don't have much free time.* **5** [NOT USED] not being used by anyone *Is this seat free?* **6 free from/of sth** not containing or having anything harmful or unpleasant *a life free from pain* **7 feel free** something that you say in order to tell someone that they are allowed to do something [+ to do sth] *Please feel free to ask questions.* ⊅See also: duty-free, a free **hand¹**, free rein, tax-free, toll-free.

free² /friː/ *adverb* **1** without cost or payment *Children under five travel free.* ○ *He offered to do it for free.* **2** in a way that is not tied, limited, or controlled *She broke free from his grasp and ran away.*

o‑**free³** /friː/ *verb* [T] freeing *past* freed **1** [ALLOW TO LEAVE] to allow someone to leave a prison or place where they have been kept *The last hostages were finally freed yesterday.* **2** [GET OUT] to get someone out of a situation or place that they cannot escape from *Firefighters worked for two hours to free the driver from the wreckage.* **3** [TAKE AWAY] to help someone by taking something unpleasant away from them *The book's success freed her from her financial worries.* **4** [MAKE AVAILABLE] (*also* **free up**) to make something available for someone to use *I need to free up some space for these files.*

-free /friː/ *suffix* used at the end of words to mean 'without' or 'not containing' *sugarfree gum* ○ *an interest-free loan*

freebie /'friːbi/ *noun* [C] *informal* something that you are given, usually by a company, and do not have to pay for

Freecycle /'friːsaɪkl/ *verb* [T, I] *trademark* to use a local Freecycle email group to give away things that you do not want now • **freecycler** *noun* [C]

o‑**freedom** /'friːdəm/ *noun* **1** [C, U] the right to live in the way you want, say what you think, and make your own decisions without being controlled by anyone else *religious freedom* ○ *freedom of choice/speech* ○ [+ to do sth] *You have the freedom to do what you want to do.* **2 freedom from sth** a situation in which you are not suffering because of something unpleasant or harmful *freedom from fear/poverty* **3** [U] when someone is no longer a prisoner

free 'enterprise *noun* [U] when trade and business is allowed to operate without much control from the government

free 'kick *noun* [C] a kick that a player in a football match is allowed to take after a player from the other team has broken the rules

freelance /'friːlɑːns/ *adjective, adverb* working for several different organizations, and paid according to the hours you work *a freelance photographer* ○ *Most of our producers work freelance.* • **freelance** *verb* [I] • **freelancer** *noun* [C]

freely /'friːli/ *adverb* **1** without being controlled or limited *For the first time in months she could move freely.* ○ *Exotic foods are freely available in supermarkets.* **2** If you freely admit something, you are very willing to agree that it is true. *I freely admit that I was wrong about him.*

free 'market *noun* [no plural] when the government does not control prices and trade *a free-market economy*

freephone /'friːfəʊn/ *UK* (*US* **toll-free**) *adjective* [always before noun] A freephone number is a telephone number that you can connect to without paying.

free-range /ˌfriːˈreɪndʒ/ *adjective* relating to or produced by farm animals that are allowed to move around outside and are not kept in cages *free-range eggs*

freesheet /'friːʃiːt/ *noun* [C] a free newspaper

free 'speech *noun* [U] the right to express your opinions in public

free 'trade *noun* [C] a way to buy and sell products between countries, without limits on the amount of goods that can be bought and sold, and without special taxes on the goods ⊅Compare **fair trade**.

freeware /'friːweə'/ *noun* [U] computer software that you do not have to pay for, for example from the Internet

freeway /'friːweɪ/ *US* (*UK* **motorway**) *noun* [C] a long, wide road, usually used by traffic travelling fast over long distances

free 'will *noun* **1** [U] when people choose and decide what they want to do in their own lives **2 do sth of your own free will** to do something because you want to, not because someone forces you to *She had gone there of her own free will.*

o‑**freeze¹** /friːz/ *verb* past tense **froze** past participle **frozen 1** [ICE] [I, T] If something freezes or is frozen, it becomes hard and solid because it is very cold. *The river had frozen overnight.* ○ *Water freezes at 0° Celsius.* **2** [FOOD] [I, T] to make food last a long time by making it very cold and hard *You can freeze any cakes that you have left over.* **3** [PERSON] [I] to feel very cold *One of the climbers froze to death on the mountain.* **4** [NOT MOVE] [I] to suddenly stop moving, especially because you are frightened *She saw someone outside the window and froze.* **5** [LEVEL] [T] to fix the level of something such as a price or rate so that it does not increase

freeze² /friːz/ *noun* **1** [LEVEL] [C] when the level of something such as a price or rate is fixed so that it does not increase *a pay freeze* **2** [PROCESS]

[C] when a process is stopped for a period of time *an immediate freeze on all new building in the city* **3** COLD [no plural] *informal* a period of extremely cold weather

freezer /'fri:zər/ *noun* [C] a large container operated by electricity in which food can be frozen and stored ⊃See colour picture **The Kitchen** on page Centre 2.

freezing¹ /'fri:zɪŋ/ *adjective informal* very cold *It's absolutely freezing in here.*

freezing² /'fri:zɪŋ/ *noun* [U] the temperature at which water freezes *It was five degrees **below/above** freezing.*

'freezing ˌpoint *noun* [C, U] the temperature at which a liquid freezes

freight /freɪt/ *noun* [U] goods that are carried by trains, trucks, ships, or aircraft

freighter /'freɪtər/ *noun* [C] a large ship or aircraft that carries goods

'french ˌfries *US* (*UK* chips) *noun* [plural] long, thin pieces of potato that have been cooked in hot oil ⊃See colour picture **Food** on page Centre 11.

ˌFrench 'knickers *noun* [plural] women's loose underwear that covers all the bottom ⊃See colour picture **Clothes** on page Centre 9.

ˌFrench 'windows (*also* ˌFrench 'doors) *noun* [plural] a pair of glass doors that usually open into a garden

frenetic /frə'netɪk/ *adjective* fast and exciting in an uncontrolled way *a frenetic pace* ○ *frenetic activity*

frenzied /'frenzɪd/ *adjective* wild and uncontrolled *a frenzied dance*

frenzy /'frenzi/ *noun* [U, no plural] when you are so excited, nervous, or anxious that you cannot control what you are doing *She hit him in a frenzy of rage.*

frequency /'fri:kwənsi/ *noun* [C, U] **1** the number of times something happens in a particular period, or the fact that something happens often or a large number of times *The frequency of attacks seems to have increased recently.* **2** the rate at which a sound wave or radio wave is repeated *the very high frequencies of a television signal*

o--**frequent¹** /'fri:kwənt/ *adjective* happening often *He is a frequent visitor to the US.*

frequent² /frɪ'kwent/ ⊛ /'fri:kwent/ *verb* [T] to go to a place often *a bar frequented by criminals*

o--**frequently** /'fri:kwəntli/ *adverb formal* often *a frequently asked question*

o--**fresh** /freʃ/ *adjective* **1** DIFFERENT new or different from what was there before *We're looking for fresh ideas.* ○ *They decided to move abroad and make a fresh start.* **2** NOT OLD Fresh food has been produced or collected recently and has not been frozen, dried, etc. *fresh fruit/vegetables* ○ *fresh bread* **3** CLEAN/COOL smelling clean or feeling pleasantly cool *a fresh breeze* ○ *a fresh smell* **4 fresh air** air outside buildings that is clean and cool *Let's go outside and get some fresh air.* **5 fresh water** water from lakes, rivers, etc that has no salt in it **6** NOT TIRED having a lot of energy and not feeling tired *We got up the next day feeling fresh and relaxed.* **7** SKIN Fresh skin looks healthy. *a fresh com-*

plexion **8** RECENT recently made or done and not yet changed by time *The memory of the accident is still very fresh in my mind.* **9 fresh from/out of sth** having just left a place *The new French teacher's fresh out of college.* ● **freshness** *noun* [U] ⊃See also: a **breath** of fresh air.

freshen /'freʃən/ *verb*
freshen up to quickly wash yourself so that you feel clean *Would you like to freshen up before dinner?*
freshen sth up to make something look cleaner and more attractive *A coat of paint would help to freshen this place up.*

fresher /'freʃər/ *noun* [C] *UK informal* a student in the first year of university

freshly /'freʃli/ *adverb* recently *freshly baked bread*

freshman /'freʃmən/ *noun* [C] *plural* **freshmen** *US* a student in the first year of a course at a US college, university, or high school (= school for students aged 15 to 18)

freshwater /'freʃˌwɔːtər/ *adjective* relating to water that is not salty *freshwater fish*

fret /fret/ *verb* [I] **fretting**, *past* **fretted** to be anxious or worried *There's no point in **fretting about** what you cannot change.* ● **fretful** *adjective* anxious and unhappy

Fri *written abbreviation for* Friday

friar /'fraɪər/ *noun* [C] a member of a religious group of men

friction /'frɪkʃən/ *noun* [U] **1** when a surface rubs against something, often making movement more difficult **2** when people argue or disagree, often over a long period of time *There's a lot of **friction between** my wife and my mother.*

o--**Friday** /'fraɪdeɪ/ (*written abbreviation* Fri) *noun* [C, U] the day of the week after Thursday and before Saturday ⊃See also: **Good Friday.**

fridge /frɪdʒ/ *noun* [C] a large container that uses electricity to keep food cold ⊃See colour picture **The Kitchen** on page Centre 2.

fridge-freezer /ˌfrɪdʒ'fri:zər/ *noun* [C] a piece of equipment for storing food that has two parts: a *fridge* (= a part that keeps food cold) and a *freezer* (= a part that keeps food frozen)

fried /fraɪd/ *adjective* cooked in hot oil or fat *a fried egg* ⊃See also: **deep-fried.**

⊞ WORD PARTNERS FOR *friend*

sb's **best** friend ● a **close/good** friend ● a **family** friend ● an **old** friend ● a friend **of mine**

OTHER WAYS OF SAYING ***friend***

The words **chum**, **mate** (*UK*), and **pal** are all informal words for 'friend': *Pete was there with a couple of his **mates**.*

An **old friend** is someone you have known and liked for many years: *Rachel is one of my **oldest friends**.*

An **acquaintance** is someone you know, but do not know well: *He had a few business **acquaintances**.*

A **confidant** is a friend whom you can talk to about your feelings and secrets: *Sarah* *was my **confidant** throughout this period and I told her everything.*

A group of friends with similar interests are sometimes described informally as a **crowd**: *"Who was there?" "Oh, you know, Dave, Fiona and all that **crowd**."*

The informal word **crony** is sometimes used disapprovingly to describe one of a group of friends who help each other in an unfair way: *He always gives his **cronies** all the best jobs.*

⌐**friend** /frend/ *noun* [C] **1** someone who you know well and like *Sarah's my **best friend** (= the friend I like most).* ○ *Gordon is a **friend of** mine.* **2 an old friend** someone who you have known and liked for a long time **3 be friends (with sb)** to know and like someone *I have been friends with Jo for years.* **4 make friends (with sb)** to begin to know and like someone *He's shy and finds it difficult to make friends.*

⌐**friendly¹** /'frendli/ *adjective* **1** behaving in a pleasant, kind way towards someone *a friendly face/smile* ○ *The other students have been very **friendly** to us.* ↻Opposite **unfriendly**. **2 be friendly with sb** to know and like someone *She's **friendly** with a lot of the people on her course.* ● **friendliness** *noun* [U]

friendly² /'frendli/ *noun* [C] *UK* a sports match that is not part of an official competition

-friendly /'frendli/ *suffix* **1** used at the end of words to mean 'not harmful' *environmentally-friendly detergent* **2** used at the end of words to mean 'suitable for particular people to use' *a family-friendly restaurant* ↻See also: **user-friendly**.

┌─────────────────────────────┐
│ WORD PARTNERS FOR **friendship** │
└─────────────────────────────┘

strike up a friendship ● a **close** friendship ● sb's friendship **with** sb ● a friendship **between** sb and sb

friendship /'frendʃɪp/ *noun* [C, U] when two people are friends *a **close friendship***

fries /fraɪz/ *mainly US* (*also UK* **chips**) *noun* [plural] long, thin pieces of potato that have been cooked in hot oil

frieze /friːz/ *noun* [C] an area of decoration along a wall

frigate /'frɪɡət/ *noun* [C] a small, fast military ship

fright /fraɪt/ *noun* [U, no plural] a sudden feeling of shock and fear *That dog **gave me a** terrible **fright**.* ○ *She screamed **in fright** when she saw him.*

⌐**frighten** /'fraɪtᵊn/ *verb* [T] to make someone afraid or nervous *It frightens me when he drives so fast.* ↻See also: scare/frighten the (living) **daylights** out of sb, scare/frighten sb out of their **wits**.
frighten sb away/off to make a person or animal afraid or nervous so that they go away or they do not go somewhere

⌐**frightened** /'fraɪtᵊnd/ *adjective* afraid or nervous *I've always been **frightened of** going to the dentist.* ○ [+ (that)] *Gerry was frightened that people would laugh at him.*

The adjectives **afraid** and **scared** are common alternatives to 'frightened': *She's very **afraid** of dogs.* ● *Gerry has always been **scared** of heights.*

If someone is extremely frightened, then you can use adjectives like **petrified**, **terrified**, **panic-stricken**, or the informal phrase **scared to death**: *I'm **terrified** of flying.* ● *She was **panic-stricken** when her little boy disappeared.* ● *He's **scared to death** of having the operation.*

If someone is frightened because they are worrying about something, then you can use the adjectives **afraid** and **worried**: *I'm **afraid/worried** that something will go wrong.*

If someone is frightened about something that might happen in the future, you can use the adjectives **apprehensive** or **uneasy**: *He's a bit **apprehensive** about living away from home.*

⌐**frightening** /'fraɪtᵊnɪŋ/ *adjective* making you feel afraid or nervous *a very frightening film* ● **frighteningly** *adverb*

frightful /'fraɪtᵊl/ *adjective* *UK old-fashioned* very bad *The house was in a frightful mess.*

frightfully /'fraɪtᵊli/ *adverb* *UK old-fashioned* very *They're frightfully rich, you know.*

frigid /'frɪdʒɪd/ *adjective* **1** not enjoying sexual activity, usually said about a woman **2** *literary* not friendly or emotional

frill /frɪl/ *noun* **1** [C] a strip of material with a lot of folds which is used to decorate the edge of cloth **2 frills** extra things that are added to something to make it nicer or more attractive, but that are not really necessary *a cheap, no frills airline service*

frilly /'frɪli/ *adjective* with a lot of frills *a frilly dress*

fringe¹ /frɪndʒ/ *noun* [C] **1** [HAIR] *UK* (*US* **bangs** [plural]) hair that is cut short and straight at the top of someone's face **2** [DECORATION] loose threads that hang along the edge of cloth as a decoration **3** [EDGE] the outside edge of an area, group, or subject and not the main part

fringe² /frɪndʒ/ *verb* **be fringed with sth** If a place or object is fringed with something, that thing forms a border along the edge. *The river is fringed with wild flowers.*

fringe³ /frɪndʒ/ *adjective* [always before noun] not belonging to the main part of a group, activity, or subject *fringe politics/theatre*

fringe 'benefit *noun* [C] something extra that you get from your employer in addition to money [usually plural] *fringe benefits such as private health care*

frisk /frɪsk/ *verb* **1** [T] to move your hands over someone's body to discover if they have a weapon, drugs, etc. **2** [I] to run and jump happily like a young animal

frisky /'frɪski/ *adjective* energetic and wanting

to be active or play *a frisky puppy*

fritter /ˈfrɪtəʳ/ *verb*
fritter sth away to waste money or time on something that is not important

frivolity /frɪˈvɒləti/ *noun* [C, U] when people are being silly and not being serious

frivolous /ˈfrɪvələs/ *adjective* silly and not serious • **frivolously** *adverb*

frizzy /ˈfrɪzi/ *adjective* Frizzy hair has a lot of very small, tight curls.

fro /frəʊ/ *adverb* ⊃See to³ and fro.

frog /frɒg/ *noun* [C] a small, green animal with long back legs for jumping that lives in or near water

frogman /ˈfrɒgmən/ *noun* [C] *plural* **frogmen** someone whose job is to swim under water wearing a rubber suit and using special breathing equipment *Police frogmen are searching the lake.*

o⇥**from** *strong form* /frɒm/ *weak form* /frəm/ *preposition* **1** STARTING PLACE used to show the place, time, or level that someone or something started at *Did you walk all the way from Bond Street?* ○ *The museum is open from 9.30 to 6.00, Tuesday to Sunday.* ○ *Prices start from £5,595.* **2** HOME used to say where someone was born, or where someone lives or works *His mother's originally from Poland.* ○ *Our speaker tonight is from the BBC.* **3** DISTANCE used to say how far away something is *Their holiday cottage is about 15 kilometres from the coast.* **4** GIVING used to say who gave or sent something to someone *Have you had a Christmas card from Faye yet?* **5** REMOVING If you take something from a person, place, or amount, you take it away. *Two from ten leaves eight.* ○ *We had to borrow some money from my father to pay the bill.* **6** PRODUCED used to say where something was produced or grown *These vegetables are fresh from the garden.* **7** MATERIAL used to say what something is made of *juice made from oranges* **8** AVOID used to show something that you want to avoid or prevent *There's a bar across the front to prevent you from falling out.* **9** POSITION used to show where you are when you look at something or how you see something *The view from the top was absolutely breathtaking.* **10** REASON used to say why you think or believe something *I guessed from her accent that she must be French.* ○ *From what I've heard, the new exam is going to be a lot more difficult.* **11** CAUSE used to say what causes something *Deaths from heart disease continue to rise every year.* ○ *He was rushed to hospital suffering from severe burns.* **12** COMPARE used when you are saying how similar or different two things, people, or places are *University is very different from school.* **13** **a week/six months/ten years, etc from now** a week/six months/ten years, etc after the time when you are speaking *Who knows what we'll all be doing five years from now?* **14** **from now/then, etc on** starting now/then, etc and continuing into the future *They were good friends from that day on.*

o⇥**front¹** /frʌnt/ *noun* **1 the front a** MOST IMPORTANT SIDE the side of something that is most import-

ant or most often seen because it faces forward *You need to write the address clearly on the front of the envelope.* ○ *There was blood on the front of his shirt.* **b** FORWARD PART the part of something that is furthest forward *We asked to sit in the front of the plane.* ○ *He was standing right at the front.* **2** **in front a** FURTHER FORWARD further forward than someone or something else *She started a conversation with the man sitting in front of her.* **b** WINNING winning in a game or competition *By half time the Italians were well in front.* **3** **in front of a** NEAR close to the front part of something *He parked the car in front of the house.* **b** SEEING/HEARING where someone can see or hear you *Please don't swear in front of the children.* **4** BEHAVIOUR [C] when someone behaves in a way that hides how they really feel [usually singular] *Many parents decide to stay together, putting up a front for the children's sake.* **5** ILLEGAL ACTIVITY [C] an organization or activity that is used to hide a different, illegal activity [usually singular] *Police discovered the restaurant was just a front for a drugs operation.* **6** **the front** an area of land where soldiers fight during a war *Thousands of young men were sent to the front to fight.* **7** **on the business/jobs/politics, etc front** in a particular area of activity *How are things on the work front at the moment?* **8** WEATHER [C] a line where warm air meets cold air affecting the weather *A cold front is moving across the Atlantic.*

o⇥**front²** /frʌnt/ *adjective* [always before noun] in or at the front of something *the front door/garden* ○ *the front page of the newspaper*

frontal /ˈfrʌntºl/ *adjective* **1** relating to the front of something **2** **a frontal attack/assault** when you criticize or attack someone or something in a very strong and direct way

frontier /frʌnˈtɪəʳ/ *noun* **1** [C] a line or border between two countries **2** **the frontiers of sth** the limits of what is known or what has been done before in an area of knowledge or activity *the frontiers of science and technology*

front 'line *noun* **1** **the front line a** the place where soldiers fight in a war **b** a position of direct and important influence *doctors working in the front line of medicine* • **front-line** /ˈfrʌntlaɪn/ *adjective* [always before noun] *front-line troops*

front-page /ˈfrʌntˌpeɪdʒ/ *adjective* **front-page news/story, etc** news that is very important and suitable for the front page of a newspaper

front-runner /ˌfrʌntˈrʌnəʳ/ ⓤ /ˈfrʌntˌrʌnəʳ/ *noun* [C] the person or organization that will most probably win something

frost¹ /frɒst/ *noun* **1** [U] a thin, white layer of ice that forms on surfaces, especially at night, when it is very cold **2** [C] when the temperature is cold and water freezes *We're expecting a hard frost tonight.*

frost² /frɒst/ *US* (*UK/US* **ice**) *verb* [T] to cover a cake with frosting (= sweet mixture used to cover cakes)

frostbite /ˈfrɒstbaɪt/ *noun* [U] when extreme cold injures your fingers and toes

frosted /ˈfrɒstɪd/ *adjective* Frosted glass has a

special surface so that you cannot see through it.

frosting /ˈfrɒstɪŋ/ US (UK/US **icing**) *noun* [U] a sweet mixture used to cover or fill cakes, made from sugar and water or sugar and butter

frosty /ˈfrɒsti/ *adjective* **1** very cold, with a thin layer of white ice covering everything *a frosty morning* **2** not friendly *She gave me a very frosty look.*

froth /frɒθ/ *noun* [U] small, white bubbles such as on the surface of a liquid • **froth** *verb* [I] • **frothy** *adjective* ***frothy coffee***

frown¹ /fraʊn/ *verb* [I] to make your face show that you are annoyed or worried by moving your eyebrows (= lines of hair above your eyes) *She frowned when I mentioned his name.*

frown on/upon sth to think that something is wrong and that you should not do it [often passive] *Smoking is frowned upon in many public places.*

frown² /fraʊn/ *noun* [C] the expression on your face when you frown *He looked at me with a puzzled frown.*

froze /frəʊz/ *past tense of* freeze

frozen¹ /ˈfrəʊzᵊn/ *adjective* **1** [FOOD] Frozen food has been made so that it will last a long time by freezing. *frozen peas* **2** [WATER] turned into ice *The pond was frozen and people were skating on it.* **3** [PERSON] *informal* extremely cold *Is there any heating in here? I'm frozen!*

frozen² /ˈfrəʊzᵊn/ *past participle of* freeze

frugal /ˈfruːgᵊl/ *adjective* careful not to spend very much money

WORD PARTNERS FOR ***fruit***

dried/fresh fruit • **a piece of** fruit • fruit **juice** • **citrus/tropical** fruit

⊶**fruit** /fruːt/ *noun* **1** [C, U] something such as an apple or orange that grows on a tree or a bush, contains seeds, and can be eaten as food ***dried/fresh fruit*** ○ *fruit juice* ➲See colour picture **Fruit and Vegetables** on page Centre 10. **2 the fruit(s) of sth** the good result of someone's work or actions *This book is the fruit of 15 years' research.* **3 bear fruit** If something that someone does bears fruit, it produces successful results. *Our decision is just beginning to bear fruit.* ➲See also: **citrus fruit**.

fruitful /ˈfruːtfᵊl/ *adjective* producing good or useful results *Sophie and Jacintha had a very fruitful discussion.*

fruition /fruˈɪʃᵊn/ *noun* [U] *formal* when a plan or an idea really begins to happen, exist, or be successful *The plan never really **came to fruition**.*

fruitless /ˈfruːtləs/ *adjective* not successful or achieving good results *a long and **fruitless** search*

fruity /ˈfruːti/ *adjective* smelling or tasting of fruit *a fruity wine/taste*

frustrate /frʌsˈtreɪt/ [US] /ˈfrʌstreɪt/ *verb* [T] **1** to make someone feel annoyed because things are not happening in the way that they want, or in the way that they should *It really frustrates me when she arrives late for meetings.* **2** to prevent someone from achieving something, or to prevent something from happening *They have frustrated all our attempts to find a solution to this problem.*

frustrated /frʌsˈtreɪtɪd/ [US] /ˈfrʌstreɪtɪd/ *adjective* annoyed because things are not happening in the way that you want, or in the way that they should *I'm very **frustrated at/with** my lack of progress.*

frustrating /frʌsˈtreɪtɪŋ/ [US] /ˈfrʌstreɪtɪŋ/ *adjective* making you feel frustrated *a frustrating situation*

WORD PARTNERS FOR ***frustration***

sheer frustration • **in** frustration • frustration **at (doing) sth**

frustration /frʌsˈtreɪʃᵊn/ *noun* [C, U] the feeling of being annoyed because things are not happening in the way that you want, or in the way that they should *I could sense his **frustration at** not being able to help.*

fry /fraɪ/ *verb* [I, T] to cook something in hot oil or fat or to be cooked in hot oil or fat *Fry the onions in a little butter.* ➲See picture at **cook**.

ˈ**frying ˌpan** *noun* [C] a flat, metal pan with a long handle that is used for frying food ➲See colour picture **The Kitchen** on page Centre 2.

ft *written abbreviation for* foot (= a unit for measuring length)

fudge¹ /fʌdʒ/ *noun* [U] a soft sweet food made from butter, sugar, and milk

fudge² /fʌdʒ/ *verb informal* **1** [T] *UK* to avoid making a decision or giving a clear answer about something *The government continues to **fudge the issue**.* **2** [I, T] *US* to slightly cheat, often by not telling the exact truth *He **fudged** on his income tax return.*

WORD PARTNERS FOR ***fuel***

fuel **bills / consumption / prices / supplies** • fuel **efficiency**

⊶**fuel¹** /ˈfjuːəl/ *noun* [C, U] a substance that is burned to provide heat or power *The plane ran out of fuel and had to land at sea.*

fuel² /ˈfjuːəl/ *verb* [T] *UK* **fuelling** *past* **fuelled** *US* **fueling** *past* **fueled** to make people's ideas or feelings stronger, or to make a situation worse *Newspaper reports are **fuelling fears** about GM foods.*

fugitive /ˈfjuːdʒətɪv/ *noun* [C] someone who is escaping or hiding from the police or from a dangerous situation

fulfil *UK* (*US* **fulfill**) /fʊlˈfɪl/ *verb* **fulfilling** *past* **fulfilled** **1 fulfil a duty/promise/responsibility, etc** to do something that you have promised to do or that you are expected to do *He has failed to fulfil his duties as a father.* **2 fulfil an ambition/dream/goal, etc** to do something that you really wanted to do **3 fulfil a function/need/role, etc** to do something that is necessary or useful *You seem to fulfil a very useful role in the organization.* **4 fulfil criteria/requirements/qualifications, etc** to have all the qualities that are wanted or needed for something *You have to fulfil certain requirements to qualify for the competition.*

fulfilled /fʊlˈfɪld/ *adjective* feeling happy that you are receiving everything that you want from your life ⊃Opposite **unfulfilled**.

fulfilling /fʊlˈfɪlɪŋ/ *adjective* If something is fulfilling, it satisfies you and makes you happy. *a fulfilling job*

fulfilment UK (US **fulfillment**) /fʊlˈfɪlmənt/ *noun* [U] **1** a feeling of pleasure because you are receiving or achieving what you want *I hope that you'll find happiness and fulfilment in your life together.* **2** when someone does something necessary or something that they have wanted or promised to do *Being here is the fulfilment of a lifelong ambition.*

o⌐**full**[1] /fʊl/ *adjective* **1** NO MORE POSSIBLE If a container or a space is full, it contains as many things or people as possible or as much of something as possible. *We couldn't get in, the cinema was full.* ○ *The shelves were full of books.* **2** A LOT containing a lot of things or people or a lot of something *The room was full of people.* ○ *His face was full of anger.* **3** COMPLETE [always before noun] complete and including every part *Please give your full name and address.* **4** full **speed/strength/volume, etc** the greatest speed, strength, volume, etc possible *We were driving at full speed.* ○ *She got full marks in the test.* **5** **be full of yourself** to think that you are very important **6** **be full of sth** to be talking or thinking a lot about a particular thing *He's full of stories about his holiday.* **7** FOOD *informal (also UK* **full up**) having eaten enough food *No more for me, thanks, I'm full.* **8** **a full face/figure** a face or body shape that is large and round ⊃See also: have your hands (**hand**[1]) full, be in full **swing**[2].

full   empty

full[2] /fʊl/ *noun* **1** **in full** completely and with nothing missing *The speech will be published in full in tomorrow's newspaper.* **2** **to the full** *mainly UK* as much or as well as possible *She certainly lived life to the full.*

full-blown /ˈfʊlˌbləʊn/ *adjective* completely developed *a full-blown crisis* ○ *a full-blown disease*

full 'board *noun* [U] UK when all your meals are provided in a hotel

full-fledged /ˌfʊlˈfledʒd/ US (UK **fully-fledged**) *adjective* [always before noun] having finished developing, studying, or establishing yourself

full-grown /ˌfʊlˈgrəʊn/ *adjective* A full-grown person, animal, or plant has developed completely, and is not expected to grow more. *a full-grown man*

full 'house *noun* [C] when all the seats in a place such as a theatre or cinema are full

full-length /ˌfʊlˈleŋθ/ *adjective* **1** **a full-length book/film, etc** a book or film that is the usual

length and not shorter *a full-length feature film* **2** **a full-length mirror/photograph, etc** a mirror or image that shows a person's whole body from the head to the feet **3** **a full-length coat/dress/skirt, etc** a long piece of clothing that reaches to your feet

full 'moon *noun* [no plural] the moon when it appears as a complete circle

full-on /fʊlˈɒn/ *adjective* **1** very great or to the greatest degree *full-on luxury* **2** very serious and enthusiastic, often in a way which annoys other people

full-page /ˌfʊlˈpeɪdʒ/ *adjective* [always before noun] filling a complete page in a newspaper or magazine *a full-page ad*

full-scale /ˌfʊlˈskeɪl/ *adjective* [always before noun] **1** very large or serious and involving everything that is possible or expected *The violence has developed into a full-scale war.* **2** A full-scale model is the same size as the original thing that it is representing.

full 'stop UK (US **period**) *noun* [C] a mark (.) used at the end of a sentence, or to show that the letters before it are an abbreviation ⊃See Extra help page **Punctuation** on page Centre 33.

full-time /ˌfʊlˈtaɪm/ *adjective* happening or working for the whole of the working week and not only part of it *a full-time job/course* • full-time *adverb* *She works full-time for the council.*

o⌐**fully** /ˈfʊli/ *adverb* completely *The restaurant was fully booked.* ○ *He is fully aware of the dangers involved.*

fully-fledged /ˌfʊliˈfledʒd/ UK (US **full-fledged**) *adjective* [always before noun] having finished developing, studying, or establishing yourself *I won't be a fully-fledged doctor until after the exams.*

fumble /ˈfʌmbl/ *verb* [I] to use your hands with difficulty to try to get hold of something or find something *She fumbled in her bag for her glasses.*

fume /fjuːm/ *verb* [I] to be extremely angry, especially in a quiet way *A week later, she was still fuming about his behaviour.*

fumes /fjuːmz/ *noun* [plural] strong, unpleasant, and often dangerous gas or smoke *car exhaust fumes*

WORD PARTNERS FOR **fun**

have fun • good/great fun • be no fun • for fun

o⌐**fun**[1] /fʌn/ *noun* [U] **1** enjoyment or pleasure, or something that gives you enjoyment or pleasure *She's great fun to be with.* ○ *Have fun!* (= enjoy yourself) ○ *It's no fun having to work late every night.* **2** **for fun/for the fun of it** for pleasure and not for any other reason **3** **make fun of sb/sth** to make a joke about someone or something in an unkind way *The other children at school used to make fun of his hair.*

fun[2] /fʌn/ *adjective* enjoyable or entertaining *There are lots of fun things to do here.*

F

○ᵘ**function¹** /'fʌŋkʃən/ *noun* [C] **1** the purpose of something or someone *Each button has a different function.* **2** a large, formal party or ceremony *a charity function*

function² /'fʌŋkʃən/ *verb* [I] to work or operate *The operation should help his lungs to function properly again.*

function as sth to have a particular purpose *The spare bedroom also functions as a study.*

functional /'fʌŋkʃənəl/ *adjective* **1** designed to be practical or useful and not only attractive *functional clothing* **2** operating or working correctly *The system is not yet fully functional.*

'**function ,key** (*written abbreviation* F) *noun* [C] one of the keys on a computer keyboard which has the letter F and a number on it and that makes the computer do particular jobs *Press F4 to print.*

○ᵘ**fund** /fʌnd/ *noun* **1** [C] an amount of money collected, saved, or provided for a purpose *a pension fund* **2** **funds** [plural] money needed or available to spend on something *The charity closed down due to **lack of funds**.* ● **fund** *verb* [T] to provide money for an event, activity, or organization *Who is the project funded by?*

fundamental /ˌfʌndə'mentəl/ *adjective* relating to the most important or main part of something *a fundamental change/difference* ○ *Training is **fundamental** to success.* ● **fundamentally** *adverb The world has changed fundamentally over the last century.*

fundamentalism /ˌfʌndə'mentəlɪzəm/ *noun* [U] the belief that the traditions and rules of a religion should be followed exactly

fundamentalist /ˌfʌndə'mentəlɪst/ *noun* [C] someone who believes that the rules of their religion should be followed exactly ● **fundamentalist** *adjective*

fundamentals /ˌfʌndə'mentəlz/ *noun* [plural] the main principles, or most important parts of something

funding /'fʌndɪŋ/ *noun* [U] money given by a government or organization for an event or activity *The company received state funding for the project.*

fundraiser /'fʌndˌreɪzər/ *noun* [C] a person or an event that collects money for a particular purpose

fundraising /'fʌndˌreɪzɪŋ/ *noun* [U] when you collect money for a particular purpose *a fundraising event*

○ᵘ**funeral** /'fjuːnərəl/ *noun* [C] a ceremony for burying or burning the body of a dead person

'**funeral ,director** *UK* (*US* '**funeral di,rector**) *noun* [C] someone whose job is to organize funerals and prepare dead bodies to be buried or burned

fungus /'fʌŋgəs/ *noun* [C, U] *plural* **fungi** or **funguses** a type of plant without leaves and without green colouring which gets its food from other living or decaying things

funk /fʌŋk/ *noun* [U] a style of popular music with a strong rhythm that is influenced by African and jazz music

funky /'fʌŋki/ *adjective informal* **1** fashionable in an unusual and noticeable way *She's got some very funky clothes.* **2** Funky music has a strong rhythm, and is good to dance to.

funnel /'fʌnəl/ *noun*
[C] **1** a tube with a wide part at the top that you use to pour liquid or powder into something that has a small opening **2** a metal pipe on the top of a ship or train which smoke comes out of

funnel

funnily /'fʌnɪli/ *adverb UK* **funnily enough** although it seems strange and surprising *Funnily enough, I was just thinking about you when you called.*

○ᵘ**funny** /'fʌni/ *adjective* **1** making you smile or laugh *a funny story* ○ *It's not funny. Don't laugh!* **2** strange or unusual and not what you expect *This chicken tastes a bit funny.*

○ᵘ**fur** /fɜːr/ *noun* **1** [U] the thick hair that covers the bodies of some animals like cats and rabbits **2** [C, U] the skin of an animal covered in thick hair and used for making clothes, or a piece of clothing made from this

furious /'fjʊəriəs/ *adjective* **1** extremely angry

*He's **furious at** the way he's been treated.* ○ *My boss was **furious with** me.* **2** very energetic or fast *a furious attack* • **furiously** *adverb*

furlong /ˈfɜːlɒŋ/ *noun* **[C]** a unit of length used in horse races equal to 201 metres

furnace /ˈfɜːnɪs/ *noun* **[C]** a container which is heated to a very high temperature and used to heat buildings, melt metal, or burn things

furnish /ˈfɜːnɪʃ/ *verb* **[T]** to put furniture into a room or building *They have furnished the room very simply.*

furnish sb with sth *formal* to provide someone with something *Can you furnish me with any further information?*

furnished /ˈfɜːnɪʃt/ *adjective* If a room or building is furnished, there is furniture in it.

furnishings /ˈfɜːnɪʃɪŋz/ *noun* **[plural]** the furniture, curtains and other decorations in a room or building

WORD PARTNERS FOR ***furniture***

a **piece of** furniture • **garden/office** furniture • **antique** furniture

⊶**furniture** /ˈfɜːnɪtʃəʳ/ *noun* **[U]** objects such as chairs, tables, and beds that you put into a room or building *antique furniture*

COMMON LEARNER ERROR

furniture

Remember you cannot make **furniture** plural. Do not say 'furnitures'.

I want to buy some new furniture for my bedroom.

furore /fjʊəˈrɔːri/ *UK* (*US* **furor** /ˈfjʊrɔːr/) *noun* **[no plural]** a sudden, excited, or angry reaction to something by a lot of people *The book **caused a furore** when it was published.*

furrow¹ /ˈfʌrəʊ/ *noun* **[C]** **1** a deep line cut into a field that seeds are planted in **2** a deep line on someone's face, especially above their eyes

furrow² /ˈfʌrəʊ/ *verb* **furrow your brow** to make deep lines appear on your face above your eyes *He furrowed his brow as he struggled to think of a solution.*

furry /ˈfɜːri/ *adjective* covered with fur or with something that feels like fur

further¹ /ˈfɜːðəʳ/ *adverb* **1** more *He refused to discuss the matter further.* ○ *Have you **got any further*** (= achieved any more) *with your research?* **2** (*comparative of* far) at or to a place or time that is a longer distance away *Let's walk a bit further down the road.*

further² /ˈfɜːðəʳ/ *adjective* **[always before noun]** more or extra *For further details about the offer, call this number.* ○ *We will let you know if there are any further developments.*

COMMON LEARNER ERROR

further or **farther**?

Further means the same as **farther** when you are talking about distance.

We walked further down the street.

We walked farther down the street.

In all other situations you should use **further**.

Petrol prices have increased further.

For further information contact our office.

further³ /ˈfɜːðəʳ/ *verb* **[T]** to make something develop or become more successful *He'll do anything to **further** his **career**.*

ˌ**further eduˈcation** *noun* **[U]** *UK* education at a college for people who have left school but are not at a university

furthermore /ˌfɜːðəˈmɔːʳ/ [US] /ˈfɜːrðərmɔːr/ *adverb* in addition to what has just been said

furthest /ˈfɜːðɪst/ *adjective, adverb* (*superlative of* far) most distant

furtive /ˈfɜːtɪv/ *adjective* doing something secretly, or done secretly, so that people do not notice *He gave her a **furtive glance** as soon as his wife left the room.* • **furtively** *adverb*

fury /ˈfjʊəri/ *noun* **[U, no plural]** extreme anger *He could hardly control his fury.*

fuse¹ /fjuːz/ *noun* **[C]** **1** a small object that stops electrical equipment working if there is too much electricity going through it *The **fuse has blown**. You'll have to change it.* ○ *a **fuse box*** **2** the part of a bomb or other explosive object that starts the explosion ***Light the fuse**, and then stand back.*

fuse² /fjuːz/ *verb* **[I, T]** **1** *UK* If a piece of electrical equipment fuses, or if you fuse it, it stops working because there is too much electricity going through it. *You've **fused** the **lights**.* **2** to join or become combined *The bones of a baby's skull are not properly fused at birth.*

fuselage /ˈfjuːzəlɑːʒ/ *noun* **[C]** the main body of an aircraft

fusion /ˈfjuːʒən/ *noun* **[C, U]** when two or more things join or become combined *nuclear fusion* ○ *She describes her music as a fusion of folk and rock.*

fuss¹ /fʌs/ *noun* **1** **[U, no plural]** when people become excited, annoyed, or anxious about something, especially about something unimportant *What's all the fuss about?* ○ *They were **making** a big **fuss** over nothing.* **2** **kick up/make a fuss** to complain about something *If they don't bring our food soon, I'll have to kick up a fuss.* **3** **make a fuss of/over sb** to give someone a lot of attention and treat them well *My uncle Bradley always makes a big fuss of the children.*

fuss² /fʌs/ *verb* **[I]** to worry too much or get too excited, especially about unimportant things *Please don't fuss, Mum. Everything's under control.*

fuss over sb/sth to give someone or something too much attention because you want to show that you like them

fussy /ˈfʌsi/ *adjective* **1** [NOT LIKING] only liking particular things and very difficult to please *She's a very **fussy eater**.* **2** [CAREFUL] too careful about unimportant details **3** [TOO COMPLICATED] If something is fussy, it is too complicated in design and has too many details.

futile /ˈfjuːtaɪl/ [US] /ˈfjuːtəl/ *adjective* certain not to have a successful effect or result *a futile attempt to escape* • **futility** /fjuːˈtɪləti/ *noun* **[U]**

when something is futile

futon /ˈfuːtɒn/ *noun* [C] a flat bed filled with soft material that can be used on the floor or on a wooden base, or folded into a seat

---

WORD PARTNERS FOR *future*

the **distant/foreseeable/near** future • **plan for/predict** the future • **in the** future

---

o–**future**[1] /ˈfjuːtʃəʳ/ *noun* **1 the future a** [TIME TO COME] the time which is to come *He likes to plan for the future.* ○ *They hope to get married in the near future* (= soon). **b** [GRAMMAR] In grammar, the future is the form of the verb used to talk about something that will happen. **2 in future** UK (*mainly US* **in the future**) beginning from now *In future, I'll be more careful about who I lend my bike to.* **3** [WHAT WILL HAPPEN] [C] what will happen to someone or something in the time which is to come *We need to discuss the future of the company.* **4** [SUCCESS] [U, no plural] the chance of continuing to exist or succeed *She's got a very promising future ahead of her.*

o–**future**[2] /ˈfjuːtʃəʳ/ *adjective* [always before noun] **1** happening or existing in the time which is to come *future plans* ○ *in future years* ○ *What will we leave for future generations?* **2 future tense** the form of the verb which is used to talk about something that will happen

the ˌfuture ˈperfect *noun* the form of the verb which is used to show that an action will have been completed before a particular time in the future. The sentence 'I'll probably have left by then.' is in the future perfect.

futuristic /ˌfjuːtʃəˈrɪstɪk/ *adjective* very modern and strange and seeming to come from some imagined time in the future *a futuristic steel building*

fuzzy /ˈfʌzi/ *adjective* **1** confused and not clear *We could only get a fuzzy picture on the television.* **2** covered in soft, short hairs, or material like this *a fuzzy kitten* ○ *fuzzy slippers*

FYI *internet abbreviation for* for your information: used when you send someone a document or tell them something you think they should know about

---

Gg

G, g /dʒiː/ the seventh letter of the alphabet

g *written abbreviation for* gram (= a unit for measuring weight)

gabble /ˈgæbl/ *verb* [I, T] *UK informal* to talk quickly or in a way that people cannot understand *He gabbled something in Italian.*

gable /ˈgeɪbl/ *noun* [C] the top end of a wall of a building where two sloping parts of a roof meet at a point

gadget /ˈgædʒɪt/ *noun* [C] a small piece of equipment that does a particular job, especially a new type *a **kitchen gadget***

Gaelic /ˈgeɪlɪk, ˈgælɪk/ *noun* [U] a language spoken in parts of Scotland and Ireland • **Gaelic** *adjective* relating to Gaelic or to the Gaelic culture of Scotland and Ireland

gaffe /gæf/ *noun* [C] when someone says or does something embarrassing without intending to *The minister has **made** a series of embarrassing **gaffes**.*

gag¹ /gæg/ *verb* **gagging** *past* **gagged 1** [COVER MOUTH] [T] to fasten something over someone's mouth so that they cannot speak *The owners of the house were found **bound and gagged** in the cellar.* **2** [STOP INFORMATION] [T] to prevent someone from giving their opinion or giving information about something *The government is trying to gag the press over the issue.* **3** [ALMOST VOMIT] [I] to feel that you are going to vomit *The sight of the body made him gag.* **4 be gagging for sth** *UK informal* to want something or want to do something very much *I'm gagging for a coffee.*

gag² /gæg/ *noun* [C] **1** *informal* a joke or funny story **2** something that is fastened over someone's mouth to stop them speaking

gaggle /ˈgægl/ *noun* [C] a group of people, especially when they are noisy *a gaggle of newspaper reporters*

gaiety /ˈgeɪəti/ *noun* [U] *old-fashioned* happiness or excitement

gaily /ˈgeɪli/ *adverb old-fashioned* in a happy way

⊶**gain¹** /geɪn/ *verb* **1** [GET] [T] to get something useful or positive *The country gained independence in 1948.* ○ *You'll gain a lot of experience working there.* **2 gain by/from sth** to get an advantage or something valuable from something *Who stands to gain from the will?* **3** [INCREASE] [T] to increase in something such as size, weight, or amount *He's gained a lot of weight in the last few months.* **4** [CLOCK] [I, T] If a clock or a watch gains, it works too quickly and shows a time that is later than the real time. ➲See also: gain/lose **ground¹**, get/gain the upper **hand¹**.

gain on sb/sth to get nearer to someone or something that you are chasing *Quick! They're gaining on us.*

gain² /geɪn/ *noun* [C, U] **1** when you get something useful or positive ***financial gain*** **2** an increase in something such as size, weight, or amount

gait /geɪt/ *noun* [C] someone's particular way of walking *I recognized his gait from a distance.*

gala /ˈgɑːlə/ [US] /ˈgeɪlə/ *noun* [C] a special social event, performance, or sports competition *a gala concert*

galaxy /ˈgæləksi/ *noun* [C] a very large group of stars held together in the universe

gale /geɪl/ *noun* [C] a very strong wind

gall¹ /gɔːl/ *noun* **have the gall to do sth** to be rude enough to do something that is not considered acceptable *I can't believe he had the gall to complain.*

gall² /gɔːl/ *verb* [T] to annoy someone *What galls me is that he escaped without punishment.* • **galling** *adjective* annoying *It's particularly galling for me that she gets paid more than I do.*

gallant /ˈgælənt/ *adjective literary* **1** brave *a gallant attempt to rescue a drowning man* **2** polite and kind, especially to women • **gallantly** *adverb* • **gallantry** *noun* [U] when someone is gallant

ˈgall ˌbladder *noun* [C] an organ in the body that contains a substance that helps you to digest food

gallery /ˈgælᵊri/ *noun* [C] **1** a room or building that is used for showing paintings and other art to the public *a museum and **art gallery*** **2** a floor at a higher level that looks over a lower floor inside a large room or building *The courtroom has a **public gallery**.*

galley /ˈgæli/ *noun* [C] a kitchen in a ship or aircraft

gallon /ˈgælən/ *noun* [C] a unit for measuring liquid, equal to 4.546 litres in the UK and 3.785 litres in the US ➲See Extra help page **Measurements** on page Centre 31

gallop /ˈgæləp/ *verb* [I] If a horse gallops, it runs very fast. • **gallop** *noun* [no plural]

gallows /ˈgæləʊz/ *noun* [C] *plural* **gallows** a wooden structure used in the past to hang criminals from to kill them

galore /gəˈlɔːʳ/ *adjective* [always after noun] in large amounts or numbers *There are bargains galore at the new supermarket.*

galvanize (*also UK* **-ise**) /ˈgælvənaɪz/ *verb* [T] to make someone suddenly decide to do something *His words **galvanized** the team **into** action.*

gamble¹ /ˈgæmbl/ *verb* [I, T] to risk money on the result of a game, race, or competition *He gambled away all of our savings.* • **gambler** *noun* [C] • **gambling** *noun* [U]

gamble on sth to take a risk that something will happen

WORD PARTNERS FOR ***gamble***

take a gamble • a gamble **backfires/pays off** • a gamble **on** sth

gamble² /ˈgæmbl/ *noun* [C] a risk that you take that something will succeed *Buying this place was a big **gamble**, but it seems to have **paid off**.*

G

╔╗ WORD PARTNERS FOR **game**

play a game • lose/win a game • a game of [chess/football, etc] • a **computer** game

℗**game¹** /geɪm/ *noun* **1** [ACTIVITY] [C] an entertaining activity or sport that people play, usually needing some skill and played according to rules *a computer game* ○ *Do you want to play a different game?* **2** [OCCASION] [C] a particular competition, match, or occasion when people play a game *Would you like a game of chess?* ○ *Who won yesterday's game?* **3 games** *UK* organized sports that children do at school *I always hated games at school.* ○ *a games teacher* **4 the European/Commonwealth, etc Games** a special event where there are lots of competitions for different sports **5** [SECRET PLAN] [C] *UK informal* a secret plan *What's your game?* **6** [ANIMALS] [U] wild animals and birds that are hunted for food or sport **7 give the game away** *UK* to spoil a surprise or joke by letting someone know something that should have been kept secret **8 play games** to not deal with a situation seriously or honestly *Someone's life is in danger here - we're not playing games.* ⊃See also: **ball game, board game, the Olympic Games, video game.**

game² /geɪm/ *adjective* to be willing to do new things, or things that involve a risk *She's game for anything.*

Gameboy /'geɪmbɔɪ/ *noun* [C] *trademark* a small machine that you play computer games on and that you can carry with you

gamekeeper /'geɪmˌkiːpər/ *noun* [C] someone whose job is to look after wild animals and birds that are going to be hunted

gamepad /'geɪmpæd/ *noun* [C] a device that you hold in your hands and use to control a computer game or video game (= a game in which you make pictures move on a screen)

gamer /'geɪmər/ *noun* [C] someone who plays games, especially computer games

'**game ˌshow** *noun* [C] a programme on television in which people play games to try to win prizes

gammon /'gæmən/ *noun* [U] *UK* a type of meat from a pig, usually cut in thick slices

gamut /'gæmət/ *noun* [no plural] the whole group of things that can be included in something *The film explores the whole gamut of emotions from despair to joy.*

╔╗ WORD PARTNERS FOR **gang**

in a gang • a gang of sth • a gang leader/member

gang¹ /gæŋ/ *noun* [C] **1** [YOUNG PEOPLE] a group of young people who spend time together, usually fighting with other groups and behaving badly *a member of a gang* ○ *gang violence* **2** [CRIMINALS] a group of criminals who work together *a gang of armed robbers* **3** [FRIENDS] *informal* a group of young friends

gang² /gæŋ/ *verb*

gang up against/on sb to form a group to attack or criticize someone, usually un-

fairly *Some older girls have been ganging up on her at school.*

gangly /'gæŋgli/ (*also* **gangling**) *adjective* tall and thin *a gangly youth*

gangrene /'gæŋgriːn/ *noun* [U] the death and decay of a part of the body because blood is not flowing through it

gangster /'gæŋstər/ *noun* [C] a member of a group of violent criminals

gangway /'gæŋweɪ/ *noun* [C] **1** *UK* a space that people can walk down between two rows of seats in a vehicle or public place **2** a board or stairs for people to get on and off a ship

gaol /dʒeɪl/ *noun* [C, U] *another UK spelling of* jail (= a place where criminals are kept as a punishment)

gap

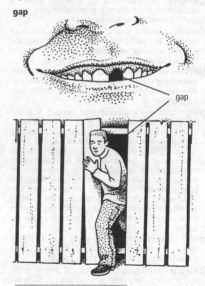

gap

╔╗ WORD PARTNERS FOR **gap**

2 bridge/close/narrow the gap • the gap **between** sth and sth

℗**gap** /gæp/ *noun* [C] **1** [SPACE] an empty space or hole in the middle of something, or between two things *There's quite a big gap between the door and the floor.* ○ *The sun was shining through a gap in the curtains.* **2** [DIFFERENCE] a difference between two groups of people, two situations, etc *an age gap* ○ *This course bridges the gap between school and university.* **3** [ABSENT THING] something that is absent and stops something from being complete *There are huge gaps in my memory.* **4 a gap in the market** an opportunity for a product or service that does not already exist **5** [TIME] a period of time when nothing happens, or when you are doing something different from usual *I decided to go back to teaching after a gap of 10 years.* ⊃See also: **the generation gap.**

gape /geɪp/ *verb* [I] **1** to look at someone or

something with your mouth open because you are so surprised *We stood there **gaping** in wonder **at** the beautiful landscape.* **2** to be wide open

gaping /ˈɡeɪpɪŋ/ *adjective* **a gaping hole/wound, etc** a hole/wound, etc that is open very wide

ˈgap ˌyear *noun* **[C]** *UK* a year between leaving school and starting university which you usually spend travelling or working

⊶**garage** /ˈɡærɑːʒ/ [US] /ɡəˈrɑːʒ/ *noun* **[C] 1** a small building, often built next to a house, that you can put a car in **2** a business that repairs or sells cars, and sometimes also sells fuel

garbage /ˈɡɑːbɪdʒ/ *US* (*UK* **rubbish**) *noun* **[U] 1** things that you throw away because you do not want them **2** something that you think is nonsense, wrong, or very bad quality *How can you listen to that garbage on the radio!*

ˈgarbage ˌcan *US* (*UK* **dustbin**) *noun* **[C]** a large container for waste kept outside your house

ˈgarbage colˌlector *US* (*UK* **dustman**) *noun* **[C]** someone whose job is to remove the waste from containers left outside houses

ˈgarbage ˌman *noun* **[C]** *US another word for* garbage collector

garbled /ˈɡɑːbəld/ *adjective* Garbled words or messages are not clear and are very difficult to understand.

⊶**garden** /ˈɡɑːdᵊn/ *noun* **1 [C]** *UK* (*US* **yard**) an area of ground belonging to a house, often containing grass, flowers, or trees *the **front/back garden*** ○ *Dad's outside **in the garden**.* **2 gardens [plural]** a park or large public area where plants and flowers are grown • **garden** *verb* **[I]** to work in a garden, growing plants and making it look attractive *gardening gloves/tools*

ˈgarden ˌcentre *noun* **[C]** *UK* a place that sells things for gardens such as plants and tools

gardener /ˈɡɑːdᵊnəʳ/ *noun* **[C]** someone who works in a garden, growing plants and making it look attractive

gardening /ˈɡɑːdᵊnɪŋ/ *noun* **[U]** the job or activity of growing a garden and keeping it attractive *gardening gloves/tools*

gargle /ˈɡɑːɡl/ *verb* **[I]** to move liquid or medicine around in your throat without swallowing, especially to clean it or stop it feeling painful

garish /ˈɡeərɪʃ/ *adjective* unpleasantly bright in colour, or decorated too much *a garish red jacket*

garlic /ˈɡɑːlɪk/ *noun* **[U]** a vegetable like a small onion with a very strong taste and smell *a **clove of garlic*** ⮊See colour picture **Fruit and Vegetables** on page Centre 10.

garment /ˈɡɑːmənt/ *noun* **[C]** *formal* a piece of clothing

garnish /ˈɡɑːnɪʃ/ *verb* **[T]** to decorate food with something such as herbs or pieces of fruit *salmon **garnished with** herbs and lemon* • **garnish** *noun* **[C]**

garrison /ˈɡærɪsᵊn/ *noun* **[C]** a group of soldiers living in a particular area or building to defend it

garter /ˈɡɑːtəʳ/ *noun* **[C]** a piece of elastic that holds up a woman's stockings (= very thin pieces of clothing that cover a woman's foot and leg)

⊶**gas¹** /ɡæs/ *noun* **1** [SUBSTANCE] **[C, U]** a substance in a form like air and not solid or liquid *poisonous gases* **2** [FUEL] **[U]** a substance in a form like air used as a fuel for heating and cooking *(UK) a gas cooker/(US) a gas stove* **3** [CAR FUEL] **[U]** *US* (*UK* **petrol**) a liquid fuel used in cars *half a tank of gas* **4** [STOMACH] **[U]** *US* (*UK* **wind**) gas or air in your stomach that makes you feel uncomfortable and sometimes makes noises **5 the gas** *US informal* the part of a car which you push with your foot to make it go faster *We'd better **step on the gas*** (= drive faster). ⮊See also: **natural gas, tear gas.**

gas² /ɡæs/ *verb* **[T] gassing** *past* **gassed** to poison or kill someone with gas

ˈgas ˌchamber *noun* **[C]** a room that is filled with poisonous gas to kill people

gash /ɡæʃ/ *noun* **[C]** a long, deep wound or cut • **gash** *verb* **[T]**

ˈgas ˌmask *noun* **[C]** a cover you wear over your face to protect you from breathing poisonous gas

gasoline /ˈɡæsᵊliːn/ *US* (*UK* **petrol**) *noun* **[U]** *another word for* gas (= a liquid fuel used in cars)

gasp /ɡɑːsp/ *verb* **[I] 1** to make a noise by suddenly breathing in because you are shocked or surprised *She gasped in horror as the car spun out of control.* **2** to breathe loudly and with difficulty trying to get more air *He clutched his heart, **gasping for breath**.* • **gasp** *noun* **[C]** *a gasp of surprise*

ˈgas ˌpedal *US* (*UK/US* **accelerator**) *noun* **[C]** the part of a car which you push with your foot to make it go faster

ˈgas ˌstation *US* (*UK* **petrol station**) *noun* **[C]** a place where you can buy petrol (= fuel for cars)

gastric /ˈɡæstrɪk/ *adjective* relating to the stomach *gastric ulcers*

gastronomic /ˌɡæstrəˈnɒmɪk/ *adjective* relating to good food and cooking

⊶**gate** /ɡeɪt/ *noun* **[C] 1** the part of a fence or outside wall that opens and closes like a door *Please **shut the gate**.* **2** the part of an airport where passengers get on or off an aircraft *The flight to Dublin is now boarding at gate 8.*

gateau /ˈɡætəʊ/ [US] /ɡæˈtəʊ/ *noun* **[C, U]** *plural* **gateaux** *UK* a large cake, usually filled and decorated with cream

gatecrash /ˈɡeɪtkræʃ/ *verb* **[I, T]** to go to a party or private event without an invitation • **gatecrasher** *noun* **[C]** someone who gatecrashes

gateway /ˈɡeɪtweɪ/ *noun* **1 [C]** an opening in a fence or outside wall that is closed with a gate **2 the gateway to sth** the way to get into something or somewhere *the gateway to the North*

⊶**gather** /ˈɡæðəʳ/ *verb* **1** [MAKE A GROUP] **[I, T]** to join other people somewhere to make a group, or to bring people together into a group *Crowds of fans gathered at the stadium for the big match.* **2** [COLLECT] **[T]** to collect several things together, often from different places or people *They interviewed 1000 people to gather data on TV viewing habits.* ○ *She **gathered** her things to-*

gether and left. **3** [THINK] [T] to think something is true because you have heard or seen information about it *From what I can gather, they haven't sold their house yet.* **4 gather speed/ strength/support, etc** to increase in speed/ strength/support, etc

gathering /ˈɡæðərɪŋ/ *noun* [C] a party or a meeting when many people get together as a group *a family gathering*

gaudy /ˈɡɔːdi/ *adjective* unpleasantly bright in colour or decoration *a gaudy pink sweatshirt with gold embroidery*

gauge¹ /ɡeɪdʒ/ *verb* [T] **1** to make a judgment about a situation or about what someone thinks or feels [+ question word] *It's impossible to gauge what her reaction will be.* **2** to measure a distance, size, or amount

gauge² /ɡeɪdʒ/ *noun* [C] **1** a way of judging something such as a situation or what someone thinks or feels *Street interviews aren't an accurate gauge of public opinion.* **2** a method or piece of equipment that you use to measure something *a fuel gauge*

gaunt /ɡɔːnt/ *adjective* very thin, especially because of being ill or old *a pale, gaunt face*

gauntlet /ˈɡɔːntlət/ *noun* **1** [C] a long, thick glove (= piece of clothing for your hand) **2 run the gauntlet** to have to deal with a lot of people who are criticizing or attacking you **3 throw down the gauntlet** to invite someone to argue, fight, or compete with you

gauze /ɡɔːz/ *noun* [U] thin, transparent cloth, especially used to cover injuries

gave /ɡeɪv/ *past tense of* give

gawp /ɡɔːp/ *UK* (*US* **gawk** /ɡɔːk/) *verb* [I] to look at someone or something with your mouth open because you are shocked or surprised *He just stood there gawping at me.*

o━**gay**¹ /ɡeɪ/ *adjective* **1** homosexual *Have you told your parents you're gay yet?* ○ *a gay bar/club* **2** *old-fashioned* very happy and enjoying yourself

gay² /ɡeɪ/ *noun* [C] someone who is homosexual, especially a man *equal rights for gays and lesbians*

gaze /ɡeɪz/ *verb* **gaze at/into, etc** to look for a long time at someone or something or in a particular direction *They gazed into each other's eyes.* • **gaze** *noun* [no plural]

GB *written abbreviation for* gigabyte (= a unit for measuring the amount of information a computer can store) *a 4 GB hard drive*

GCSE /ˌdʒiːsiːesˈiː/ *noun* [C] *abbreviation for* General Certificate of Secondary Education: in the UK, an exam taken by students at the age of sixteen, or the qualification itself *Mary's got nine GCSEs.*

GDP /ˌdʒiːdiːˈpiː/ *noun* [U] *abbreviation for* Gross Domestic Product: the total value of goods and services that a country produces in a year ⊃Compare GNP.

gear¹ /ɡɪəʳ/ *noun* **1** [C] a set of parts in a motor vehicle or bicycle that control how fast the

wheels turn [usually plural] *a mountain bike with 21 gears* ○ *to change gear* **2 first/second/third, etc gear** a particular position of the gears in a motor vehicle or bicycle that controls how fast the wheels turn *The lights turned green, but I couldn't get into first gear.* **3** [U] the clothes and equipment used for a particular purpose *sports/swimming gear*

gear² /ɡɪəʳ/ *verb*

gear sth to/towards sb/sth to design or organize something so that it is suitable for a particular purpose, situation, or group of people [often passive] *These advertisements are geared towards a younger audience.*

gear (sb/sth) up to prepare for something that you have to do, or to prepare someone else for something [often reflexive] *I'm trying to gear myself up for the exams.*

gearbox /ˈɡɪəbɒks/ *noun* [C] the set of gears in a motor vehicle and the metal box that contains them

ˈgear ˌlever *UK* (*US* **gearshift** /ˈɡɪəʃɪft/) *noun* [C] a stick with a handle that you move to change gear in a vehicle ⊃See colour picture **Car** on page Centre 7.

gearstick /ˈɡɪəstɪk/ *noun* [C] *UK another word for* gear lever

GED /ˌdʒiːiːˈdiː/ *noun* [C] *abbreviation for* General Equivalency Diploma: an official document in the US that is given to someone who did not complete high school (= school for students aged 15 to 18) but who has passed a government exam instead

geek /ɡiːk/ *noun* [C] *informal* a man who is boring and not fashionable • **geeky** *adjective informal a geeky guy with a beard and glasses*

geese /ɡiːs/ *plural of* goose

geezer /ˈɡiːzəʳ/ *noun* [C] *UK very informal* a man *an old geezer*

gel /dʒel/ *noun* [C, U] a thick, clear, liquid substance, especially a product used to style hair *hair gel* ○ *shower gel*

gelatine *UK* /ˈdʒelətiːn/ (*US* **gelatin** /ˈdʒelətɪn/) *noun* [U] a clear substance made from animal bones, often used to make food thicker

gem /dʒem/ *noun* [C] **1** a valuable stone, especially one that has been cut to be used in jewellery **2** *informal* someone or something that you like very much and think is very special

Gemini /ˈdʒemɪnaɪ/ *noun* [C, U] the sign of the zodiac which relates to the period of 23 May - 21 June, or a person born during this period ⊃See picture at **zodiac**.

gender /ˈdʒendəʳ/ *noun* [C, U] **1** the state of being male or female **2** the division of nouns, pronouns and adjectives into masculine, feminine and neuter types

gene /dʒiːn/ *noun* [C] a part of a cell that is passed on from a parent to a child and that controls particular characteristics

o━**general**¹ /ˈdʒenərəl/ *adjective* **1** [NOT DETAILED] not detailed, but including the most basic or necessary information *These leaflets contain some general information about the school.* ○ *I've got a general idea of how it works.* **2** MOST PEOPLE [always before noun] relating to or involving all or most people, things, or places *There seems to be general agreement on this matter.* **3** NOT LIMITED [always before noun] including a lot of things or subjects and not limited to only one or a few *general knowledge* **4 in general a** CONSIDERING EVERYTHING considering the whole of someone or something, and not just a particular part of them *I still have a sore throat, but I feel much better in general.* **b** USUALLY usually, or in most situations *In general, the weather here stays sunny.*

general² /'dʒenᵊrᵊl/ *noun* [C] an officer of very high rank in the army or air force

general anaes'thetic *UK* (*US* **general anesthetic**) *noun* [C, U] a substance that is used to stop someone being conscious when they have an operation so that they do not feel any pain

general e'lection *noun* [C] a big election in which the people living in a country vote to decide who will represent them in the government

---

WORD PARTNERS FOR *generalization*

make a generalization ● a **broad/gross/ sweeping** generalization

---

generalization (*also UK* **-isation**) /,dʒenᵊrᵊlaɪ-'zeɪʃᵊn/ *noun* [C, U] when someone says something very basic that is often true but not always true

generalize (*also UK* **-ise**) /'dʒenᵊrᵊlaɪz/ *verb* [I] to say something very basic that is often true but not always true

o--**generally** /'dʒenᵊrᵊli/ *adverb* **1** USUALLY usually, or in most situations *I generally wake up early.* **2** AS A WHOLE considering the whole of someone or something, and not just a particular part of them *The police said that the crowd was generally well-behaved.* **3** BY MOST PEOPLE by most people, or to most people *He is generally believed to be their best player.*

general prac'titioner (*also* **GP**) *noun* [C] a doctor who sees people in the local area and treats illnesses that do not need a hospital visit

generate /'dʒenᵊreɪt/ *verb* [T] **1** to cause something to exist *to generate income/profit* ○ *This film has generated a lot of interest.* **2** to produce energy *Many countries use nuclear fuels to generate electricity.*

generation /,dʒenᵊ'reɪʃᵊn/ *noun* **1** PEOPLE [C] all the people in a society or family who are approximately the same age *the older/ younger generation* ○ *This is the story of three generations of women.* **2** TIME [C] a period of about 25 to 30 years, the time it takes for a child to become an adult and take the place of their parents in society *Our family has lived in this village for generations.* **3** PRODUCT [C] a product when it is at a particular stage of development *a new generation of computers* **4** ENERGY [U] the production of energy *the generation of electricity*

the gener'ation ,gap *noun* when young people and old people do not understand each other because of their age difference

generator /'dʒenᵊreɪtᵊr/ *noun* [C] a machine that produces electricity

generic /dʒə'nerɪk/ *adjective* **1** relating to a whole group of things or type of thing **2** A generic product such as a drug is not sold with the name of the company that produced it.

generosity /,dʒenᵊ'rɒsəti/ *noun* [U] the quality of being generous

o--**generous** /'dʒenᵊrəs/ *adjective* **1** giving other people a lot of money, presents, or time in a kind way *a very generous man* **2** larger than usual or than expected *a generous portion* ● **generously** *adverb*

'gene ,therapy *noun* [C] the science of changing genes (= parts of cells which control particular characteristics) in order to stop or prevent a disease

genetic /dʒə'netɪk/ *adjective* relating to genes (= parts of cells which control particular characteristics) *a rare genetic disorder* ○ *genetic research* ● **genetically** *adverb*

ge,netically 'modified *adjective* Genetically modified plants or animals have had some of their genes (= parts of cells which control particular characteristics) changed.

ge,netic engi'neering *noun* [U] when scientists change the genes (= parts of cells which control particular characteristics) in the cells of plants or animals

genetics /dʒə'netɪks/ *noun* [U] the scientific study of genes (= parts of cells which control particular characteristics)

genial /'dʒiːniəl/ *adjective* kind and friendly

genitals /'dʒenɪtᵊlz/ *noun* [plural] the sexual organs

genius /'dʒiːniəs/ *noun* **1** [C] someone who is extremely intelligent or extremely good at doing something *Einstein was a genius.* **2** [U] the quality of being extremely intelligent or extremely good at doing something *Einstein's genius*

genocide /'dʒenəsaɪd/ *noun* [U] the intentional killing of a large group of people who belong to a particular race or country

genre /'ʒɒnrə/ *noun* [C] a type of art or writing with a particular style *a literary/musical genre*

gent /dʒent/ *noun* [C] *informal short for* gentleman

genteel /dʒen'tiːl/ *adjective* very polite, especially in an artificial way ● **gentility** /,dʒen'tɪləti/ *noun* [U]

o--**gentle** /'dʒentl/ *adjective* **1** KIND kind and careful not to hurt or upset anyone or anything *My mother was such a gentle, loving person.* **2** NOT STRONG not strong or severe *a mild soap that is gentle on your skin* ○ *a gentle breeze* **3** SLOPE A gentle slope or climb is not steep. ● **gently** *adverb* ● **gentleness** *noun* [U]

gentleman /'dʒentlmən/ *noun* [C] *plural* **gentlemen 1** a man who behaves politely and treats people with respect *He was a perfect gentleman.* **2** a polite word for 'man', used especially when talking to or about a man you do not know *There's a gentleman here to see you.*

the gents /ðə dʒents/ *noun* [group] *UK informal* a toilet in a public place for men ⊃See Common learner error at **toilet.**

oᵈ**genuine** /'dʒenjuɪn/ *adjective* **1** If a person or their feelings are genuine, they are sincere and honest. *He shows a genuine concern for the welfare of his students.* **2** If something is genuine, it is really what it seems to be. *a genuine gold necklace* • **genuinely** *adverb*

genus /'dʒiːnəs/, /'dʒenəs/ *noun* [C] *plural* **genera** a group of animals or plants that have the same characteristics

geo- /dʒiːəu-/ *prefix* relating to the earth *geothermal* (= of or connected with the heat inside the Earth)

geography /dʒi'ɒɡrəfi/ *noun* [U] the study of all the countries of the world, and of the surface of the Earth such as the mountains and seas • **geographer** *noun* [C] someone who studies geography • **geographical** /ˌdʒiːəu'ɡræfɪkəl/ (*also* **geographic** /ˌdʒiːəu'ɡræfɪk/) *adjective* • **geographically** *adverb*

geology /dʒi'ɒlədʒi/ *noun* [U] the study of rocks and soil and the physical structure of the Earth • **geological** /ˌdʒiːəu'lɒdʒɪkəl/ *adjective geological formations* • **geologist** *noun* [C] someone who studies geology

geometric /ˌdʒiːəu'metrɪk/ (*also* **geometrical**) *adjective* **1** having a regular shape such as a circle or triangle, or having a pattern made of regular shapes **2** relating to geometry

geometry /dʒi'ɒmɪtri/ *noun* [U] a type of mathematics that deals with points, lines, angles and shapes

geriatric /ˌdʒeri'ætrɪk/ *adjective* relating to very old people *geriatric patients* ∘ *a geriatric hospital* • **geriatrics** *noun* [U] care and medical treatment for very old people

germ /dʒɜːm/ *noun* **1** [C] a very small living thing that causes disease *Wash your hands before cooking so that you don't spread germs.* **2** the germ of sth the beginning of something *the germ of a brilliant idea*

,**German 'measles** (*also* **rubella**) *noun* [U] a disease which causes red spots on your skin

germinate /'dʒɜːmɪneɪt/ *verb* [I, T] If a seed germinates or is germinated, it begins to grow. • **germination** /ˌdʒɜːmɪ'neɪʃᵊn/ *noun* [U]

gerund /'dʒerᵊnd/ *noun* [C] a noun made from the form of a verb that ends with -ing, for example 'fishing' in 'John loves fishing.'

gesticulate /dʒes'tɪkjəleɪt/ *verb* [I] to move your hands and arms around to emphasize what you are saying or to express something

WORD PARTNERS FOR *gesture*

2 a **grand/token** gesture • a gesture **of** [friendship/goodwill, etc] • a **nice** gesture

gesture¹ /'dʒestʃəʳ/ *noun* [C] **1** a movement you make with your hand, arm, or head to express what you are thinking or feeling *He made a rude gesture at the crowd.* **2** something you do to show people how you feel about a person or situation *It would be a nice gesture to invite her to dinner.*

gesture² /'dʒestʃəʳ/ *verb* [I] to point at something or express something using your hand, arm, or head *He gestured towards the window.*

oᵈ**get**¹ /get/ *verb* getting, *past tense* **got**, *past participle* **got** *or US* **gotten 1** OBTAIN [T] to obtain or buy something *I need to get some bread on the way home.* ∘ [+ two objects] *I'll try to get you a ticket.* **2** BRING [T] to go somewhere and bring back someone or something *Wait here while I get the car.* **3** RECEIVE [T] to receive something or be given something *Did you get anything nice for your birthday?* ∘ *Guy still hasn't got my email yet.* **4** UNDERSTAND [T] to understand something *He never gets any of my jokes.* **5** get into/off/through, etc to move somewhere *Get over here right now!* **6** get sth into/down/out, etc to move something somewhere *Could you get that bowl down from the shelf for me?* **7** get here/there/to the bank, etc to arrive somewhere *What time do you normally get home from work?* **8** get sb/sth to do sth to make someone or something do something *Sorry, I couldn't get the window to shut properly.* **9** get to do sth to have an opportunity to do something *I never get to sit in the front seat.* **10** get ill/rich/wet, etc to become ill/rich/wet, etc *We should go. It's getting late.* **11** get caught/killed/married, etc to have something done to you **12** get sth painted/repaired, etc to arrange for someone to do something for you, usually for money *I need to get my hair cut.* **13** get cancer/flu/malaria, etc to become ill or develop an illness *I feel like I'm getting a cold.* **14** get a bus/train, etc to travel somewhere on a bus/train, etc *Maybe we should get a taxi home.* **15** get the phone/door *informal* to answer someone calling on the telephone or waiting at the door *Can you get the phone?*

COMMON LEARNER ERROR

got or **gotten**?

The past participle of the verb 'get' is **got** in British English and **gotten** in American English.

Have you got my email yet? (UK)

Have you gotten my email yet? (US)

get about *UK* (*US* **get around**) **1** TRAVEL to travel to a lot of places **2** MOVE to be able to go to different places without difficulty, especially if you are old or ill **3** INFORMATION If news or information gets about, a lot of people hear about it.

get sth across to successfully communicate information to other people *This is the message that we want to get across to the public.*

get ahead to be successful in the work that you do *It's tough for any woman who wants to get ahead in politics.*

get along *mainly US* (*mainly UK* **get on**) **1** If two or more people get along, they like each other and are friendly to each other. *I don't really get along with my sister's husband.* **2** to deal with a situation, especially successfully *I wonder how Michael's getting along in his new job?*

get around sth (*also UK* **get round sth**) to find a way of dealing with or avoiding a problem *Our lawyer found a way of getting around the adoption laws.*

get around to sth (*also UK* **get round to**

sth) to do something that you have intended to do for a long time *I finally got around to calling her yesterday.*

get at sb *UK informal* to criticize someone in an unkind way

be getting at sth *informal* If you ask someone what they are getting at, you are asking them what they really mean.

get at sth to be able to reach or get something *He can't get at it up there.*

get away 1 to leave or escape from a place or person, often when it is difficult to do this *We walked to the next beach to get away from the crowds.* **2** to go somewhere to have a holiday, especially because you need to rest *We decided to go up to Scotland to get away from it all* (= have a relaxing holiday).

get away with sth to succeed in doing something bad or wrong without being punished or criticized *He shouldn't treat you like that. Don't let him get away with it.*

get back to return to a place after you have been somewhere else *By the time we got back to the hotel, Lydia had already left.*

get sth back If you get something back, something that you had before is given to you again. *I wouldn't lend him anything, you'll never get it back.*

get sb back *informal* to do something unpleasant to someone because they have done something unpleasant to you

get back to sb to talk to someone, usually on the telephone, to give them some information they have asked for or because you were not able to speak to them before

get back to sth to start doing or talking about something again *Anyway, I'd better get back to work.*

get behind If you get behind with work or payments, you have not done as much work or paid as much money as you should by a particular time.

get by to be able to live or deal with a situation with difficulty, usually by having just enough of something you need, such as money *I don't know how he gets by on so little money.*

get sb down to make someone feel unhappy *All this uncertainty is really getting me down.*

get sth down to write something, especially something that someone has said

get down to sth to start doing something seriously and with a lot of attention and effort *Before we get down to business, I'd like to thank you all for coming today.*

get in 1 ENTER to succeed in entering a place, especially a building *They must have got in through the bathroom window.* **2** PERSON ARRIVING to arrive at your home or the place where you work *What time did you get in last night?* **3** VEHICLE ARRIVING If a train or other vehicle gets in at a particular time, that is when it arrives. *Our flight's getting in later than expected.* **4** BE CHOSEN to succeed in being chosen or elected for a position in a school or other organization *He wanted to go to Oxford but he didn't get in.*

get into sth 1 to succeed in being chosen

or elected for a position in a school or other organization **2** to become interested in an activity or subject, or start being involved in an activity *How did you get into journalism?*

get into sb If you do not know what has got into someone, you do not understand why they are behaving strangely.

o⌐**get off (sth) 1** to leave a bus, train, aircraft, or boat *We should get off at the next stop.* ⊃See colour picture **Phrasal Verbs** on page Centre 16. **2** to leave the place where you work, usually at the end of the day *What time do you get off work?*

Get off! *UK informal* something that you say in order to tell someone to stop touching someone or something

get (sb) off (sth) to avoid being punished for something you have done wrong, or to help someone avoid getting punished for something they have done wrong *He got off with a £20 fine.*

get off on sth *informal* If you get off on something, it makes you feel very excited, especially in a sexual way.

get off with sb *UK informal* to begin a sexual relationship with someone

o⌐**get on (sth)** to go onto a bus, train, aircraft, or boat *I think we got on the wrong bus.* ⊃See colour picture **Phrasal Verbs** on page Centre 16.

be getting on *informal* **1** to be old **2** *mainly UK* If time is getting on, it is becoming late.

get on *mainly UK* (*mainly US* **get along**) **1** If two or more people get on, they like each other and are friendly to each other. *I never knew that Karen didn't get on with Sue.* **2** to deal with a situation, especially successfully *How's Frank getting on in his new job?*

get on with sth to continue doing something, especially work *Get on with your homework now, Linda.*

get onto sth to start talking about a subject after discussing something else *How did we get onto this subject?*

get out 1 MOVE OUT to move out of something, especially a vehicle *I'll get out when you stop at the traffic lights.* **2** DIFFERENT PLACES to go out to different places and meet people in order to enjoy yourself *She doesn't get out so much now that she's got the baby.* **3** NEWS If news or information gets out, people hear about it although someone is trying to keep it secret.

get (sb) out to escape from or leave a place, or to help someone do this *I left the door open and the cat got out.*

get out of sth to avoid doing something that you should do, often by giving an excuse *You're just trying to get out of doing the housework!*

get sth out of sb to persuade or force someone to tell or give you something *He was determined to get the truth out of her.*

get sth out of sth to enjoy something or think that something is useful *It was an interesting course but I'm not sure I got much out of it.*

get over sth 1 to begin to feel better after being unhappy or ill *It took her months to get*

G

over the shock of Richard leaving. **2 can't/
couldn't get over sth** *informal* to be very
shocked or surprised about something *I can't
get over how different you look with short hair.*

get sth over with to do and complete
something difficult or unpleasant that must be
done *I'll be glad to get these exams over with.*

get round *UK* (*US* **get around**) If news or information gets round, a lot of people hear
about it.

get round sth *UK* (*US* **get around sth**) to find
a way of dealing with or avoiding a problem

get round sb *UK* to persuade someone to
do what you want by being kind to them

get through to manage to talk to someone
on the telephone *I tried to ring earlier, but I
couldn't get through.*

get through to sb to succeed in making
someone understand or believe something *I
just don't seem to be able to get through to him
these days.*

get through sth 1 to deal with a difficult
or unpleasant experience successfully, or to
help someone do this *If I can just get through
my exams I'll be so happy.* **2** *mainly UK* to
finish doing or using something *We got
through a whole jar of coffee last week.*

get to sb *informal* to make someone feel
upset or angry *I know he's annoying, but you
shouldn't let him get to you.*

get together 1 to meet in order to do
something or spend time together *Jan and I
are getting together next week for lunch.* **2** to
begin a romantic relationship *She got together
with Phil two years ago.*

o⊷**get (sb) up** to wake up and get out of bed, or
to make someone do this *I had to get up at five
o'clock this morning.* ⊃See colour picture **Phrasal
Verbs** on page Centre 16.

get up to stand up *The whole audience got up
and started clapping.*

get up to sth *UK* to do something, especially something that other people think is
wrong *She's been getting up to all sorts of mischief lately.*

getaway /'getəweɪ/ *noun* [C] when someone
leaves a place quickly, especially after
committing a crime *They had a car waiting
outside so they could* **make** *a quick getaway.*

get-together /'gettəgeðə/ *noun* [C] an informal meeting or party *We have a big family
get-together every year.*

ghastly /'gɑːstli/ *adjective* very bad or unpleasant *a ghastly mistake* ○ *a ghastly man*

ghetto /'getəʊ/ *noun* [C] *plural* **ghettos** or **ghettoes**
an area of a city where people of a particular
race or religion live, especially a poor area

ghost /gəʊst/ *noun*
1 [C] the spirit of a
dead person which
appears to people
who are alive *Do
you believe in
ghosts?* ○ *a ghost
story* **2** **give up the
ghost** *UK humorous*
If a machine gives
up the ghost, it stops

ghost

working completely. ● **ghostly** *adverb a ghostly
figure*

'**ghost ,town** *noun* [C] a town where few or no
people now live

ghoul /guːl/ *noun* [C] an evil spirit

GI /,dʒiː'aɪ/ *noun* [C] a soldier in the US army

giant¹ /'dʒaɪənt/ *adjective* [always before noun] extremely big, or much bigger than other simi-
lar things *a giant spider*

giant² /'dʒaɪənt/ *noun* [C] **1** an imaginary man
who is much bigger and stronger than ordinary men **2** a very large and important company or organization *a media/software giant*

gibberish /'dʒɪbᵊrɪʃ/ *noun* [U] something that
someone says that has no meaning or that
cannot be understood

gibe /dʒaɪb/ *noun* [C] *another spelling of* jibe (= an
insulting remark)

giddy /'gɪdi/ *adjective* feeling as if you cannot
balance and are going to fall

o⊷**gift** /gɪft/ *noun* [C] **1** something that you give to
someone, usually for a particular occasion *a
birthday/wedding gift* **2** a natural ability or
skill *She has a gift for design.*

gifted /'gɪftɪd/ *adjective* A gifted person has a
natural ability or is extremely intelligent. *a
gifted athlete* ○ *a school for gifted children*

'**gift ,token/,voucher** *UK* (*US* **gift certificate**)
noun [C] a card with an amount of money
printed on it which you exchange in a shop for
goods that cost that amount of money *a £20 gift
voucher*

gig /gɪg/ *noun* [C] *informal* a performance of pop
or rock music

gigabyte /'gɪgəbaɪt/ (*written abbreviation* **GB**)
noun [C] a unit for measuring the amount of information a computer can store, equal to
1,000,000,000 bytes

gigantic /dʒaɪ'gæntɪk/ *adjective* extremely big *a
gigantic teddy bear*

giggle /'gɪgl/ *verb* [I] to laugh in a nervous or
silly way *She started giggling and couldn't
stop.* ● **giggle** *noun* [C]

gilded /'gɪldɪd/ *adjective* covered with a thin
layer of gold or gold paint *a gilded frame/
mirror/table*

gill /gɪl/ *noun* [C] an organ on each side of a fish
or other water creature which it uses to
breathe

gilt /gɪlt/ *noun* [U] a thin covering of gold or gold
paint ● **gilt** *adjective*

gimmick /'gɪmɪk/ *noun* [C] something that is
used only to get people's attention, especially
to make them buy something *a* **marketing/
publicity gimmick** ● **gimmicky** *adjective*

gin /dʒɪn/ *noun* [C, U] a strong alcoholic drink
which has no colour

ginger¹ /'dʒɪndʒər/ *noun* [U] a pale brown root
with a strong taste used as a spice in cooking
ginger cake

ginger² /'dʒɪndʒər/ *adjective* *UK* Ginger hair is
an orange-brown colour. *She's got ginger hair
and freckles.*

ginger³ /'dʒɪŋgər/ *noun* [C] *UK informal* an offensive word for a person with red hair

gingerly /'dʒɪndʒ°li/ *adverb* slowly and carefully *He lowered himself gingerly into the freezing water.*

gipsy /'dʒɪpsi/ *noun* [C] *another UK spelling of* gypsy (= a member of a race of people who travel from place to place, especially in Europe)

giraffe /dʒɪ'rɑːf/ *noun* [C] a large African animal with a very long neck and long, thin legs

giraffe

girder /'gɜːdəʳ/ *noun* [C] a long, thick piece of metal that is used to support bridges or large buildings

o━**girl** /gɜːl/ *noun* **1** [C] a female child or young woman *We have three children - a boy and two girls.* **2** **the girls** a group of female friends *I'm going out with the girls tonight.*

o━**girlfriend** /'gɜːlfrend/ *noun* [C] **1** a woman or girl who someone is having a romantic relationship with *Have you met Steve's new girlfriend?* **2** a female friend, especially of a woman

girth /gɜːθ/ *noun* [C, U] the measurement around something round, such as someone's waist

gist /dʒɪst/ *noun* **the gist of sth** the main point or meaning of something without the details

Very common alternatives to 'give' are verbs such as **offer**, **provide**, and **supply**: *This booklet **provides** useful information about local services.* • *Your doctor should be able to **offer** advice.* • *The lake **supplies** the whole town **with** water.*

The verb **donate** is often used when someone gives money or goods to an organisation that needs help: *Four hundred pounds has been **donated** to the school book fund.*

If one of many people gives something, especially money, in order to provide something, the verb **contribute** is used: *I **contributed** twenty dollars towards Jamie's present.*

If you put something from your hand into someone else's hand, you can use verbs such as **pass** and **hand**: *Could you **hand** me that book, please?* • *He **passed** a note to her during the meeting.*

The phrasal verb **pass on** is often used when you ask someone to give something to someone else: *Could you **pass** this **on** to Laura when you've finished reading it?*

If something like a prize or an amount of money is given in an official way, you can use verbs like **award** or **present**: *She was **presented** with a bouquet of flowers and a cheque for £500.* • *He was **awarded** the Nobel Prize for Physics.*

o━**give**[1] /gɪv/ *verb past tense* **gave**, *past participle* **given** **1** [PROVIDE] [+ two objects] to provide someone with something *Her parents gave her a car for her birthday.* ○ *Do you **give** money to charity?* ○ *Could you give me a lift to the station, please?* **2** [PUT NEAR] [+ two objects] to put something near someone or in their hand so that they can use it or look at it *Can you give me that pen?* ○ *He poured a cup of coffee and gave it to Isabel.* **3** [ALLOW] [+ two objects] to allow someone to have a right or an opportunity *We didn't really give him a chance to explain.* **4** [TELL] [T] to tell someone something *The woman refused to give her name.* ○ [+ two objects] *Can you give Jo a message?* **5** [CAUSE] [+ two objects] to cause someone to have or feel something *I hope he hasn't given you any trouble.* ○ *This news will **give** hope to thousands of sufferers.* **6** [ALLOW TIME] [+ two objects] to allow someone or something a particular amount of time *I'm nearly ready - just give me a few minutes.* **7** [PAY MONEY] [+ two objects] to pay someone a particular amount of money for something *I gave him £20 for his old camera.* **8** [DO] [T] to perform an action *to give a cry/shout* ○ [+ two objects] *He gave her a kiss on the cheek.* **9** **give sb a call/ring** to telephone someone *Why don't you just give him a call?* **10** **give a performance/speech, etc** to perform or speak in public *Tony gave a great speech.* **11** **give a party** to have a party *Claire's giving a birthday party for Eric.* **12** [MOVE] [I] to bend, stretch, or break because of too much weight **13** **give way** *UK* (*US* **yield**) to stop in order to allow other vehicles to go past before you drive onto a bigger road

give sth away 1 to give something to someone without asking for any money *They're giving away a CD with this magazine.* **2** to let someone know a secret, often without intending to *The party was meant to be a surprise, but Caroline gave it away.*

give sth back to return something to the person who gave it to you *Has she given you those books back yet?*

give in 1 to finally agree to what someone wants after a period when you refuse to agree *We will never **give in to** terrorists' demands.* **2** to accept that you have been beaten and agree to stop competing or fighting *Don't worry – I'm not going to give in.*

give sth in *UK* to give a piece of written work or a document to someone for them to read, judge, or deal with *I have to give my essay in on Monday.*

give off sth to produce heat, light, a smell, or a gas *The fire was giving off a lot of smoke.*

give sth out to give something to a large number of people *He gave out copies of the report at the end of the meeting.*

give out If a machine or part of your body gives out, it stops working correctly. *She read until her eyes gave out.*

give up (sth) 1 If you give up a habit such as smoking, or give up something unhealthy such as alcohol, you stop doing it or having it. *I gave up smoking two years ago.* **2** to stop doing something before you have completed it,

G

usually because it is too difficult [+ **doing sth**] *I've given up trying to help her.*

give up sth to stop doing a regular activity or job *Are you going to give up work when you have your baby?*

give up to stop trying to think of the answer to a joke or question *Do you give up?*

give it up for sb *phrasal verb* used to ask people to clap their hands to show that they like a performance *Ladies and gentlemen, give it up for the star of our show, Amy Jones!*

give yourself up to allow the police or an enemy to catch you

give up on sb to stop hoping that someone will do what you want them to do *The doctors have given up on him.*

give up on sth to stop hoping that something will achieve what you want it to achieve

⚬**give²** /gɪv/ *noun* **1** [U] when something can bend or move from its normal shape to take extra weight or size **2 give and take** when people reach agreement by letting each person have part of what they want

giveaway /ˈgɪvəweɪ/ *noun* **1** [C] something that is given to people free **2** [no plural] something that makes it easy for people to guess something

given¹ /ˈgɪvⁿn/ *adjective* **1** [always before noun] already arranged or agreed *They can only stay for a given amount of time.* **2 any given day/ time/week, etc** any day/time/week, etc *About 4 million women are pregnant in the US at any given time.*

given² /ˈgɪvⁿn/ *preposition* when you consider *Given the force of the explosion, it's a miracle they survived.*

given³ /ˈgɪvⁿn/ *past participle of* give

glacial /ˈgleɪsiəl/ ⓤⓢ /ˈgleɪʃⁿl/ *adjective* [always before noun] relating to glaciers or ice *glacial lakes*

glacier /ˈglæsiəʳ/ ⓤⓢ /ˈgleɪʃər/ *noun* [C] a large mass of ice that moves very slowly, usually down a slope or valley

⚬**glad** /glæd/ *adjective* [never before noun] **1** happy about something [+ (that)] *She's very glad that she left.* ○ [+ to do sth] *I'm so glad to see you.* **2** very willing to do something [+ to do sth] *She's always glad to help.* **3 be glad of sth** *formal* to be grateful for something *I was glad of a few days off before going back to work.*

gladly /ˈglædli/ *adverb* willingly or happily *I would gladly pay extra for better service.*

glamorize (*also* UK **-ise**) /ˈglæmⁿraɪz/ *verb* [T] to make something seem glamorous

glamorous /ˈglæmⁿrəs/ *adjective* attractive in an exciting and special way *a glamorous woman* ○ *a glamorous lifestyle*

glamour (*also* US **glamor**) /ˈglæməʳ/ *noun* [U] the quality of being attractive, exciting and special *the glamour of Hollywood*

glance¹ /glɑːns/ *verb* **1 glance at/around/towards, etc** to look somewhere for a short time *He glanced at his watch.* **2 glance at/over/ through, etc** to read something quickly *She glanced through the newspaper.*

glance² /glɑːns/ *noun* **1** [C] a quick look *She had a quick glance around the restaurant.* **2 at a glance** If you see something at a glance, you see it very quickly or immediately.

gland /glænd/ *noun* [C] an organ in the body that produces a particular chemical substance or liquid

glandular fever /ˌglændjʊləˈfiːvəʳ/ UK (US **mononucleosis**) *noun* [U] an infectious disease that makes your glands swell and makes you feel tired

glare¹ /gleəʳ/ *noun* **1** [U] strong, bright light that hurts your eyes *I get a lot of glare from my computer screen.* **2** [C] a long, angry look **3 the glare of publicity/the media, etc** when someone gets too much attention from newspapers and television

glare² /gleəʳ/ *verb* [I] to look at someone in an angry way

glaring /ˈgleərɪŋ/ *adjective* **1 a glaring error/mistake/omission, etc** a very noticeable mistake or problem **2 glaring light/sun, etc** light which is too strong and bright

glass

glass

The window is made of glass.

glasses

⚬**glass** /glɑːs/ *noun* **1** [U] a hard, transparent substance that objects such as windows and bottles are made of ***broken glass*** ○ *glass jars* **2** [C] a container made of glass that is used for drinking *Would you like **a glass of** water?* ⊃See also: **magnifying glass, stained glass**.

glasses /ˈglɑːsɪz/ *noun* [plural] a piece of equipment with two transparent parts that you wear in front of your eyes to help you see better *a **pair of glasses*** ○ *She was wearing glasses.*

glassy /ˈglɑːsi/ *adjective* **1** A glassy surface is smooth and shiny like glass. **2** Glassy eyes show no expression and seem not to see anything.

glaze¹ /gleɪz/ *verb* 1 [EYES] [I] (*also* glaze over) If someone's eyes glaze or glaze over, they stop showing any interest or expression because they are bored or tired. 2 [CLAY] [T] to cover the surface of objects made of clay with a liquid that makes them hard and shiny when they are baked 3 [FOOD] [T] to put a liquid on food to make it shiny and more attractive 4 [GLASS] [T] to put glass in a window or door

glaze² /gleɪz/ *noun* [C, U] 1 a liquid that is put on objects made of clay to make them hard and shiny when they are baked 2 a liquid that is put on food to make it shiny and attractive

gleam¹ /gliːm/ *verb* [I] to shine in a pleasant, soft way *a gleaming new car*

gleam² /gliːm/ *noun* [no plural] 1 when something shines in a pleasant, soft way *the gleam of sunlight on the frozen lake* 2 an expression in someone's eyes *She had a strange gleam in her eye.*

glean /gliːn/ *verb* [T] to discover information slowly or with difficulty [often passive] *Some useful information can be gleaned from this study.*

glee /gliː/ *noun* [U] a feeling of great happiness, usually because of your good luck or someone else's bad luck *Rosa began laughing with glee.* • **gleeful** *adjective* • **gleefully** *adverb*

glib /glɪb/ *adjective* using words in a way that is clever and confident, but not sincere

glide /glaɪd/ *verb* **glide along/into/over, etc** to move somewhere smoothly and quietly *The train slowly glided out of the station.*

glider /ˈglaɪdər/ *noun* [C] an aircraft that has no engine and flies on air currents • **gliding** *noun* [U] the activity of flying in a glider ⊃See also: hang glider, hang gliding.

glimmer¹ /ˈglɪmər/ *noun* 1 **a glimmer of happiness/hope, etc** a small sign of something good 2 [C] when a light shines in a weak way

glimmer² /ˈglɪmər/ *verb* [I] to shine in a weak way

WORD PARTNERS FOR **glimpse**

catch/get a glimpse • a **brief/fleeting** glimpse • a glimpse **of** sb/sth

glimpse /glɪmps/ *noun* [C] when you see something or someone for a very short time *He caught/got a glimpse of her as she got into the car.* • **glimpse** *verb* [T] to see something or someone for a very short time *She glimpsed him out of the corner of her eye.*

glint /glɪnt/ *noun* [no plural] 1 when your eyes shine with excitement or because you are going to do something bad *She had a wicked glint in her eye.* 2 when something shines or reflects light for a short time • **glint** *verb* [I]

glisten /ˈglɪsən/ *verb* [I] If something glistens, it shines, often because it is wet. *Their faces were glistening with sweat.*

glitch /glɪtʃ/ *noun* [C] *informal* a mistake or problem that stops something from working correctly *technical glitches*

glitter¹ /ˈglɪtər/ *verb* [I] to shine with small flashes of light *Snow glittered on the mountains.* ○ *Her necklace glittered in the firelight.*

glitter² /ˈglɪtər/ *noun* [U] 1 very small, shiny pieces of metal used for decoration 2 when something seems exciting and attractive

glittering /ˈglɪtərɪŋ/ *adjective* 1 shining with small flashes of light *glittering jewels* 2 successful and exciting *a glittering party/career*

glitz /glɪts/ *noun* [U] when something is attractive, exciting and shows money in an obvious way • **glitzy** *adjective a glitzy nightclub*

gloat /gləʊt/ *verb* [I] to show pleasure at your success or at someone else's failure *His enemies were gloating over his defeat.*

global /ˈgləʊbəl/ *adjective* relating to the whole world *the global problem of nuclear waste* • **globally** *adverb*

globalization /ˌgləʊbəlaɪˈzeɪʃən/ *noun* [U] 1 the increase of business around the world, especially by big companies operating in many countries 2 when things all over the world become more similar *the globalization of fashion/youth culture*

global 'warming *noun* [U] when the air around the world becomes warmer because of pollution

globe /gləʊb/ *noun*
1 **the globe** the world *This event is being watched by 200 million people around the globe.* 2 [C] a model of the world shaped like a ball with a map of all the countries on it

globe

globule /ˈglɒbjuːl/ *noun* [C] a small, round mass or lump of a liquid substance *a globule of oil*

gloom /gluːm/ *noun* [U] 1 a feeling of unhappiness and of not having any hope *an atmosphere of gloom* 2 when it is dark, but not completely dark

gloomy /ˈgluːmi/ *adjective* 1 [NEGATIVE] very negative about a situation *a gloomy report* ○ *The outlook is fairly gloomy.* 2 [DARK] dark in an unpleasant way *a small, gloomy room* 3 [UNHAPPY] unhappy and without hope *a gloomy face* • **gloomily** *adverb*

glorify /ˈglɔːrɪfaɪ/ *verb* [T] 1 to describe or represent something in a way that makes it seem better or more important than it really is *films that glorify violence* 2 to praise someone, especially God

glorious /ˈglɔːriəs/ *adjective* 1 beautiful or wonderful *We had four days of glorious sunshine.* ○ *glorious colours* 2 deserving praise and respect *a glorious career* • **gloriously** *adverb*

glory¹ /ˈglɔːri/ *noun* [U] 1 when people praise and respect you for achieving something important 2 great beauty *The castle has been restored to its former glory.*

glory² /ˈɡlɔːri/ *verb*
glory in sth to enjoy something and be very proud of it

gloss¹ /ɡlɒs/ *noun* 1 [PAINT] [U] paint that creates a shiny surface 2 [SHINE] [U] shine on a surface 3 [EXPLANATION] [C] a short explanation of a word or phrase in a text

gloss² /ɡlɒs/ *verb* [T] to give a short explanation of a word or phrase
gloss over sth to avoid discussing something, or to discuss something without any details in order to make it seem unimportant

glossary /ˈɡlɒsºri/ *noun* [C] a list of difficult words with their meanings like a small dictionary, especially at the end of a book

glossy /ˈɡlɒsi/ *adjective* 1 smooth and shiny *glossy hair* 2 Glossy magazines and pictures are printed on shiny paper. *a glossy brochure*

glove /ɡlʌv/ *noun* [C] a piece of clothing which covers your fingers and hand *a pair of gloves* ⊃See colour picture **Clothes** on page Centre 9.

'glove com,partment (*also* **glove box**) *noun* [C] a small cupboard in the front of a car, used to hold small things

glow¹ /ɡləʊ/ *noun* [no plural] 1 a soft, warm light *the warm glow of the moon* 2 when your face feels or appears warm and healthy *Sam's face had lost its rosy glow.* 3 **a glow of happiness/pride, etc** a strong feeling of being happy/proud, etc

glow² /ɡləʊ/ *verb* [I] 1 to produce a soft, warm light *toys which glow in the dark* 2 to have a warm and healthy appearance *Her eyes were bright and her cheeks were glowing.* 3 **glow with happiness/pride, etc** to feel very happy, proud, etc *Glowing with pride, she showed me her painting.*

glower /ˈɡlaʊəʳ/ *verb* [I] to look at someone in a very angry way *The woman glowered at her husband.*

WORD PARTNERS FOR **glowing**

a glowing **reference/report/tribute** • in glowing **terms**

glowing /ˈɡləʊɪŋ/ *adjective* praising someone a lot *She got a glowing report from her teacher.*

glucose /ˈɡluːkəʊs/ *noun* [U] a type of sugar

glue¹ /ɡluː/ *noun* [U] a substance used to stick things together *Put a bit of glue on both edges and hold them together.* ⊃See colour picture **The Classroom** on page Centre 6.

glue² /ɡluː/ *verb* [T] **glueing gluing** *past* **glued** to stick something to something else with glue *Do you think you can glue this vase back together?*
be glued to sth to be watching something, especially television *The kids were glued to the TV all morning.*

glum /ɡlʌm/ *adjective* unhappy *Why are you looking so glum today?* • **glumly** *adverb*

glut /ɡlʌt/ *noun* [C] more of something than is needed [usually singular] *There is a glut of houses for sale in this area.*

glutton /ˈɡlʌtºn/ *noun* 1 [C] someone who eats too much 2 **be a glutton for punishment** to enjoy doing things that are unpleasant or

difficult *You've said you'll look after Isobel's children too? You're a glutton for punishment!*

gluttony /ˈɡlʌtºni/ *noun* [U] when someone eats too much

gm *written abbreviation for* gram (= a unit for measuring weight)

GM /ˌdʒiːˈem/ *adjective abbreviation for* genetically modified: genetically modified plants or animals have had some of their genes (= parts of cells which control particular characteristics) changed. *GM foods*

GMO /ˌdʒiːemˈəʊ/ *noun* [U] *abbreviation for* genetically modified organism: a plant or animal in which scientists have changed the genes (= a part of a cell that controls particular characteristics)

GMT /ˌdʒiːemˈtiː/ *noun* [U] *abbreviation for* Greenwich Mean Time: the time at Greenwich in London, which is used as an international measurement for time

gnarled /nɑːld/ *adjective* rough and twisted, usually because of being old *a gnarled tree trunk*

gnat /næt/ *noun* [C] a small flying insect that can bite you

gnaw /nɔː/ *verb* [I, T] to bite something with a lot of small bites *He was gnawing on a bone.*
gnaw at sb to make someone feel more and more anxious or annoyed *Doubt kept gnawing at him.*

gnome /nəʊm/ *noun* [C] an imaginary little man with a pointed hat *a garden gnome*

GNP /ˌdʒiːenˈpiː/ *noun* [U] *abbreviation for* gross national product: the total value of goods and services produced in a country in a year, including the profits made in foreign countries ⊃Compare GDP.

⚬ **go¹** /ɡəʊ/ *verb* [I] going, *past tense* went, *past participle* gone 1 [MOVE] to move or travel somewhere *I'd love to go to America.* ○ *We went into the house.* ○ *Are you going by train?* 2 [DO SOMETHING] to move or travel somewhere in order to do something *Let's go for a walk.* ○ [+ doing sth] *We're going camping tomorrow.* 3 [DISAPPEAR] to disappear or no longer exist *When I turned round the man had gone.* 4 **go badly/well, etc** to develop in a particular way *My exams went really badly.* 5 [CONTINUE] to continue to be in a particular state *We won't let anyone go hungry.* 6 [WORKING] to work correctly *Did you manage to get the car going?* 7 [STOP WORKING] to stop working correctly *Her hearing is going, so speak loudly.* 8 [MATCH] If two things go, they match each other. *That jumper doesn't go with those trousers.* 9 [TIME] If time goes, it passes. *The day went very quickly.* 10 [SONG] to have a particular tune or words *I can't remember how it goes.* 11 [SOUND/MOVEMENT] to make a particular sound or movement *My dog goes like this when he wants some food.* 12 **not go there** to not think or talk about a subject that makes you feel bad *"Then there's the guilt I feel about leaving my child with another woman." "Don't even go there!"*

go, gone, and been

Gone is the usual part participle of the verb **go**. Sometimes you use the past participle **been** when you want to say that you have gone somewhere and come back, or to say that you have visited somewhere.

Paul has gone to the hospital this morning (= he is still there).

Paul has been to the hospital this morning (= he went and has come back).

He has gone to New York (= he is still there).

Have you ever been to New York? (= Have you ever visited New York?)

---

go about sth to start to do something or deal with something *What's the best way to go about this?*

go after sb to chase or follow someone in order to catch them *He ran away, but the police went after him.*

go against sth If something goes against a rule or something you believe in, it does not obey it or agree with it. *It goes against my principles to lie.*

go against sb If a decision or vote goes against someone, they do not get the result that they needed. *The judge's decision went against us.*

go ahead 1 to start to do something *We have permission to go ahead with the project.* **2** something that you say to someone to give them permission to do something *"Can I borrow your book?" "Yes, go ahead."* ● **go-ahead** *noun* **get/give the go-ahead**

go along 1 *UK* to go to a place or event, usually without much planning *I might go along to the party after work.* **2** to continue doing something *I'll tell you the rules as we go along.*

go along with sth/sb to support an idea, or to agree with someone's opinion *She'll never go along with this idea.*

go around (*also UK* **go round**) **1** to be enough for everyone in a group *There aren't enough chairs to go around.* **2 go around doing sth** to spend your time behaving badly or doing something that is unpleasant for other people *She's been going around telling people I'm stupid.*

go at sth *UK informal* to start doing something with a lot of energy and enthusiasm *There were a lot of dishes to wash so we went at it straight away.*

o▴**go away 1** [LEAVE] to leave a place *Go away - I'm busy.* **2** [HOLIDAY] to leave your home in order to spend time in a different place, usually for a holiday *They're going away for a few weeks in the summer.* **3** [DISAPPEAR] to disappear *That smell seems to have gone away.*

go back to return to a place where you were or where you have been before *When are you going back to London?*

go back on sth to not do something that you promised you would do *I never go back on my word* (= not do what I said I would do).

go back to sb to start a relationship again with a person who you had a romantic relationship with in the past *Jim's gone back to his ex-wife.*

go back to sth to start doing something again that you were doing before *It's time to go back to work now.*

go by 1 If time goes by, it passes. *The days went by really slowly.* **2** to move past *A green sports car went by.*

go by sth to use information about something to help you make a decision about the best thing to do *You can't go by anything she says.*

go down 1 [BECOME LESS] to become lower in level *Interest rates are going down at the moment.* **2** [SUN] When the sun goes down, it moves down in the sky until it cannot be seen any more. **3** [COMPUTER] If a computer goes down, it stops working. **4** [REMEMBER] to be considered or remembered in a particular way *This will go down as one of the most exciting soccer matches ever played.* ○ *(UK) I don't think my plan will go down well at all.*

go down with sth *UK informal* to become ill, usually with an illness that is not very serious *Our whole class went down with the flu.*

go for sth 1 [CHOOSE] to choose something *What sort of printer are you going to go for?* **2** [HAVE] *informal* to try to have or achieve something *He'll be going for his third straight Olympic gold medal in the 200-meter dash.* ○ *If you want it, go for it* (= do what you need to do in order to have or achieve it). **3** [GET] to try to get something *He tripped as he was going for the ball.* **4** [MONEY] If something goes for a particular amount of money, it is sold for that amount.

go for sb to attack someone *He suddenly went for me with a knife.*

go in to enter a place *I looked through the window, but I didn't actually go in.*

go in for sth to like a particular activity *I don't really go in for sports.*

go into sth 1 [START] to start to do a particular type of work *What made you decide to go into politics?* **2** [DESCRIBE] to describe, discuss, or examine something in a detailed way *She didn't go into any detail about the job.* **3** [BE USED] If an amount of time, money, or effort goes into a product or activity, it is used or spent creating that product or doing that activity. *A lot of effort has gone into producing this play.*

go off 1 [LEAVE] to leave a place and go somewhere else *She's gone off to the pub with Tony.* **2** [FOOD] *UK informal* If food goes off, it is not good to eat any more because it is too old. **3** [STOP] If a light or machine goes off, it stops working. *The heating goes off at 10 o'clock.* **4** [EXPLODE] If a bomb or gun goes off, it explodes or fires. **5** [MAKE NOISE] If something that makes a noise goes off, it suddenly starts making a noise. *His car alarm goes off every time it rains.*

go off sb/sth *UK* to stop liking someone or something *I've gone off fish recently.*

go on 1 [LAST] to last for a particular period of time *The film seemed to go on forever.* **2** [CONTINUE] to continue doing something [+ doing sth] *We can't go on living like this.* **3 go on to do sth**

to do something else in the future *He went on to win the final.* **4** [HAPPEN] to happen *What's going on?* **5** [TALK] *UK* to talk in an annoying way about something for a long time *I wish she'd stop **going on about** her boyfriend.* **6** [TALK AGAIN] to start talking again after stopping for a short time *He paused and then went on with his story.* **7 Go on** *informal* something that you say to encourage someone to do something *Go on, what happened next?*

go on sth to use a piece of information to help you discover or understand something *Her first name was all we had to go on.*

⚬▪**go out 1** [LEAVE] to leave a place in order to go somewhere else *Are you going out tonight?* **2** [LIGHT/FIRE] If a light or something that is burning goes out, it stops producing light or heat. *It took ages for the fire to go out.* **3** [RELATIONSHIP] If two people go out together, they have a romantic relationship with each other. *I've been going out with him for a year.*

go over *US* to be thought of in a particular way *I wonder how my speech will go over this afternoon.*

go over sth to talk or think about something in order to explain it or make certain that it is correct *Let's go over the plan one more time.*

go round *UK* (*UK/US* **go around**) **1** to be enough for everyone in a group *There aren't enough chairs to go round.* **2 go round doing sth** to spend your time behaving badly or doing something that is unpleasant for other people *She's been going round telling people I'm stupid.*

go through sth 1 [EXPERIENCE] to experience a difficult or unpleasant situation *She's going through a difficult time with her job.* **2** [EXAMINE] to carefully examine the contents of something or a collection of things in order to find something *A customs officer went through my suitcase.* **3** [USE] to use a lot of something *I've gone through two boxes of tissues this week.*

go through If a law, plan, or deal goes through, it is officially accepted or approved.

go through with sth to do something unpleasant or difficult that you have planned or promised to do *He was too scared to go through with the operation.*

go under If a company or business goes under, it fails financially.

go up 1 [INCREASE] to become higher in level *House prices keep going up.* **2** [BE FIXED] If a building or sign goes up, it is fixed into position. **3** [EXPLODE] to suddenly explode *There was a loud bang, and then the building went up in flames.*

go without (sth) to not have something that you usually have *They went without food for four days.*

go² /gəʊ/ *noun* [C] *plural* **goes 1** *UK* when someone tries to do something *I had a go at catching a fish.* ○ *If you think you might like skiing, why don't you give it a go* (= try to do it)? **2** *mainly UK* someone's turn to do something *Throw the dice Jane, it's your go.* **3 have a go at sb** *UK* to criticize someone angrily *My mother's always having a go at me about my hair.*

4 make a go of sth to try to make something succeed, usually by working hard

goad /gəʊd/ *verb* [T] to make someone angry or annoyed so that they react in the way that you want [+ into + doing sth] *They tried to goad us into attacking the police.*

> **WORD PARTNERS FOR goal**
>
> **1 score** a goal • the **winning** goal
> **3 set** yourself a goal • **achieve** a goal

⚬▪**goal** /gəʊl/ *noun* [C] **1** [POINT] a point scored in sports such as football when a player sends a ball or other object into a particular area, such as between two posts *He scored two goals in the second half.* **2** [AREA] in some sports, the area between two posts where players try to send the ball ⊃See colour picture **Sports 2** on page Centre 15. **3** [AIM] something you want to do successfully in the future *Andy's goal is to run in the New York Marathon.*

goalie /ˈgəʊli/ *noun* [C] *informal short for* goalkeeper

goalkeeper
/ˈgəʊlˌkiːpər/ (*also US*
goaltender
/ˈgəʊlˌtendər/) *noun*
[C] the player in a
sport such as football who tries to
stop the ball going
into the goal ⊃See
colour picture **Sports 2**
on page Centre 15.

goalkeeper

goalpost
/ˈgəʊlpəʊst/ *noun* [C] either of the two posts that are each side of the area where goals are scored in sports such as football ⊃See colour picture **Sports 2** on page Centre 15.

goat /gəʊt/ *noun* [C] an animal with horns which is kept for the milk it produces

gobble /ˈgɒbl/ (*also* **gobble up/down**) *verb* [T] *informal* to eat food very quickly

gobbledygook (*also* **gobbledegook**)
/ˈgɒbldiˌguːk/ *noun* [U] *informal* nonsense or very complicated language that you cannot understand

go-between /ˈgəʊbɪˌtwiːn/ *noun* [C] someone who talks and gives messages to people who will not or cannot talk to each other

goblin /ˈgɒblɪn/ *noun* [C] a short, ugly, imaginary creature who behaves badly

go-cart (*also UK* **go-kart**) /ˈgəʊkɑːt/ *noun* [C] a small, low racing car with no roof or windows

⚬▪**god** /gɒd/ *noun* **1 God** in Jewish, Christian, or Muslim belief, the spirit who created the universe and everything in it, and who rules over it **2** [C] a spirit, especially a male one, that people pray to and who has control over parts of the world or nature *the ancient Greek gods and goddesses* **3 (Oh) (my) God!** *informal* used to emphasize how surprised, angry, shocked, etc you are *Oh my God! The car has been stolen.* **4 thank God** *informal* something you say when you are happy because something bad did not happen *Thank God nobody was hurt in the accident.*

godchild /'gɒdtʃaɪld/ noun [C] plural **godchildren** a child who has godparents (= people who take responsibility for the child's moral and religious development)

goddess /'gɒdes/ noun [C] a female spirit that people pray to and who has control over parts of the world or nature

godfather /'gɒdfɑːðəʳ/ noun [C] a man who is responsible for the moral and religious development of another person's child

godforsaken /'gɒdfəˌseɪkⁿn/ adjective [always before noun] informal A godforsaken place is very unpleasant and usually far from other places.

godlike /'gɒdlaɪk/ adjective having qualities that make someone admired and respected as if they were a god or God

godmother /'gɒdˌmʌðəʳ/ noun [C] a woman who is responsible for the moral and religious development of another person's child

godparent /'gɒdˌpeəʳⁿnt/ noun [C] a person who is responsible for the moral and religious development of another person's child

godsend /'gɒdsend/ noun [no plural] something good which happens unexpectedly, usually when you really need it *The lottery win was a godsend for her.*

goes /gəʊz/ present simple he/she/it of go

goggles /'gɒglz/ noun [plural] special glasses which fit close to your face to protect your eyes *a pair of goggles* ⊃See colour picture **Sports** 1 on page Centre 14.

🧩 WORD PARTNERS FOR **going**

hard/heavy/slow/tough going

---

going¹ /'gəʊɪŋ/ noun 1 DIFFICULTY [U] how easy or difficult something is *I found the exam quite hard going.* 2 GROUND [U] the condition of the ground for walking, riding, etc 3 LEAVING [no plural] when someone leaves somewhere *His going came as a big surprise.*

going² /'gəʊɪŋ/ adjective **the going price/rate, etc** the usual amount of money you would expect to pay for something *What's the going rate for babysitting these days?* ⊃See also: **easy-going.**

going³ /'gəʊɪŋ/ present participle of go

goings-on /ˌgəʊɪŋz'ɒn/ noun [plural] informal unusual events or activities *There are some strange goings-on in that house.*

go-kart /'gəʊkɑːt/ noun [C] another UK spelling of go-cart (= a small, low racing car with no roof or windows)

o⌐**gold¹** /gəʊld/ noun 1 [U] a valuable, shiny, yellow metal used to make coins and jewellery 2 [C, U] a gold medal (= a small, round disc given to someone for winning a race or competition)

o⌐**gold²** /gəʊld/ adjective 1 made of gold *gold coins* 2 being the colour of gold *gold paint*

golden /'gəʊldⁿn/ adjective 1 being a bright yellow colour *bright golden hair* 2 literary made of gold or like gold *a golden ring* 3 a **golden opportunity** a very exciting and valuable opportunity

---

golden 'wedding noun [C] the day when two people have been married for 50 years

goldfish /'gəʊldfɪʃ/ noun [C] plural **goldfish** or **goldfishes** a small, orange fish that is often kept as a pet

gold 'medal noun [C] a small, round disc given to someone for winning a race or competition *to win an Olympic gold medal*

'gold ˌmine noun [C] 1 a place where gold is taken from the ground 2 something that provides you with a lot of money

o⌐**golf** /gɒlf/ noun [U] a game on grass where players try to hit a small ball into a series of holes using a long, thin stick ● **golfer** noun [C] ⊃See colour picture **Sports** 2 on page Centre 15.

golf

'golf ˌball noun [C] a small hard white ball used for playing golf

'golf ˌclub noun [C] 1 a place where people can play golf 2 a long, thin stick used to play golf ⊃See colour picture **Sports** 2 on page Centre 15.

'golf ˌcourse noun [C] an area of land used for playing golf

gone /gɒn/ past participle of go

gong /gɒŋ/ noun [C] a metal disc which makes a loud sound when you hit it with a stick

gonna /'gɒnə/ informal short for going to

goo /guː/ noun [U] a thick, sticky substance

o⌐**good¹** /gʊd/ adjective better, best 1 PLEASANT enjoyable, pleasant, or interesting *a good book* ○ *Did you have a good time at the party?* 2 HIGH QUALITY of a high quality or level *She speaks good French.* ○ *The food at this restaurant is very good.* 3 SUCCESSFUL successful, or able to do something well *Anne's a good cook.* ○ *She's very good at geography.* 4 KIND kind or helpful *a good friend* ○ *My granddaughter is very good to me.* 5 HEALTHY something that you say when a person asks how you are *"Hi, how are you?" "I'm good, thanks."* 6 POSITIVE having a positive or useful effect *Exercise is good for you.* 7 SUITABLE suitable or satisfactory *When would be a good time to phone?* 8 BEHAVIOUR A good child or animal behaves well. 9 MORALLY RIGHT morally right *a good person* ○ *He sets a good example to the rest of the class.* 10 COMPLETE complete and detailed *She got a good look at the robbers.* 11 LARGE used to emphasize the number, amount, quality, etc of something *There's a good chance he'll pass the exam.* 12 SATISFACTION something you say when you are satisfied or pleased about something or when you agree with something *Oh good, he's arrived at last.* 13 **Good God/grief/heavens!, etc** used to express surprise or shock *Good heavens! It's already 11 p.m.* 14 **a good 20 minutes/30 miles, etc** not less than 20 minutes/30 miles, etc and probably a bit more ⊃See also: be in sb's good/bad books (**book¹**), it's a good **job**, for good **measure¹**, stand sb in good **stead**. 15 **good to go** informal be ready to go *I'll get my coat and then I'm good to go.*

good or **well**?

Good is an adjective and is used to describe nouns.
She's a good cook.
Her children had a good education.

Well is an adverb and is used to describe verbs.
She cooks well.
Her children were well educated.

good² /gʊd/ *noun* **1** [U] something that is an advantage or help to a person or situation *It's hard work, but it's for your own good.* **2 be no good/not any good** to not be useful, helpful, or valuable **3 do sb good** to be useful or helpful to someone *A holiday will do you good.* **4** [U] what people think is morally right *Children don't always understand the difference between **good** and **bad**.* **5 for good** forever *When he was 20, he left home for good.* ⊃See also: do sb a/the **world**¹ of good.

good after'noon *exclamation* something you say to greet someone when you meet them in the afternoon

goodbye /gʊd'baɪ/ *exclamation* something you say when you leave someone or when they leave you *Goodbye Vicki! See you next week.*

good 'evening *exclamation* something you say to greet someone in the evening

Good 'Friday *noun* [C, U] the Friday before Easter (= a Christian holiday), a day when Christians remember the death of Jesus Christ

good-humoured *UK* (*US* **good-humored**) /ˌgʊd'hjuːməd/ *adjective* pleasant and friendly

goodies /'gʊdiz/ *noun* [plural] *informal* special or nice things that you will enjoy *She gave the children some sweets and other goodies.*

good-looking /ˌgʊd'lʊkɪŋ/ *adjective* If someone is good-looking, they have an attractive face. *a good-looking woman*

good 'looks *noun* [plural] an attractive face

good 'morning *exclamation* something you say to greet someone when you meet them in the morning

good-natured /ˌgʊd'neɪtʃəd/ *adjective* pleasant and friendly *a good-natured smile/crowd*

goodness /'gʊdnəs/ *noun* **1** [U] the quality of being good *She believes in the goodness of human nature.* **2 my goodness** *informal* something you say when you are surprised *My goodness, he's a big baby, isn't he?* **3 thank goodness** *informal* something you say when you are happy because something bad did not happen *Thank goodness that dog didn't bite you.* **4 for goodness sake** used when you are annoyed or when you want something to happen quickly *For goodness sake, come in out of the rain.*

good 'night *exclamation* something you say

when you leave someone or when they leave you in the evening or when someone is going to bed

goods /gʊdz/ *noun* **1** [plural] items which are made to be sold *radios, stereos and other electrical goods* **2 deliver/come up with the goods** If you deliver the goods, you do what people hope you will do.

goodwill /gʊd'wɪl/ *noun* [U] kind, friendly, or helpful feelings towards other people *He gave them a thousand pounds as a **gesture of good-will**.*

goody-goody /'gʊdi,gʊdi/ *noun* [C] *informal* someone who tries too hard to be good, usually to parents or teachers

gooey /'guːi/ *adjective* soft and sticky *a sweet, gooey sauce*

goof /guːf/ (*also* **goof up**) *verb* [I] *US informal* to make a silly mistake

goof around *US* to spend your time doing silly or unimportant things

goof off *US* to avoid doing any work

goofy /'guːfi/ *adjective mainly US* silly *a goofy sense of humour*

Google¹ /'guːgl/ *noun trademark* a popular Internet search engine (= a computer program which finds things on the Internet by looking for words which you have typed in)

Google² /'guːgl/ *verb* [T] to use the Google search engine

goose /guːs/ *noun* [C, U] *plural* **geese** a large water bird similar to a duck, or the meat from this bird

gooseberry /'gʊzbªri/ ⑲ /'guːsberi/ *noun* [C] a small, sour, green fruit with a hairy skin

goose ,pimples (*also* **'goose ,bumps**) *noun* [plural] small, raised lumps that appear on your skin when you are cold or frightened

gore¹ /gɔːʳ/ *noun* [U] blood, usually from a violent injury

gore² /gɔːʳ/ *verb* [T] If an animal gores someone, it injures them with its horn.

gorge¹ /gɔːdʒ/ *noun* [C] a narrow and usually steep valley

gorge² /gɔːdʒ/ *verb* **gorge (yourself) on sth** to eat food until you cannot eat any more *She gorged herself on chocolate biscuits.*

gorgeous /'gɔːdʒəs/ *adjective* very beautiful or pleasant *You look gorgeous in that dress.*

gorilla /gə'rɪlə/ *noun* [C] a big, black, hairy animal, like a large monkey

gorse /gɔːs/ *noun* [U] a bush with yellow flowers and sharp, pointed leaves

gory /'gɔːri/ *adjective* involving violence and blood *a gory murder*

gosh /gɒʃ/ *exclamation* used to express surprise or shock *Gosh! I didn't realize it was that late.*

gosling /'gɒzlɪŋ/ *noun* [C] a young goose (= large water bird)

gospel /'gɒspªl/ *noun* **1** TEACHING [no plural] the teachings of Jesus Christ *to **preach the gospel*** **2** BOOK [C] one of the four books in the Bible that tells the life of Jesus Christ **3 the gospel truth** something that is completely true **4** [MUSIC] [U] a style of Christian music, originally sung by black Americans

---

WORD PARTNERS FOR *gossip*

a **bit of/piece of** gossip • **juicy** (= interesting) gossip

---

gossip[1] /ˈgɒsɪp/ *noun* **1** [U] conversation or reports about other people's private lives that might or might not be true *an interesting piece of gossip* **2** [C] someone who likes to talk about other people's private lives

gossip[2] /ˈgɒsɪp/ *verb* [I] to talk about other people's private lives *They were **gossiping about** her boss.*

'gossip ,column *noun* [C] an article appearing regularly in a newspaper giving information about famous people's private lives

got /gɒt/ *past of* get

gotta /ˈgɒtə/ *informal short for* got to

gotten /ˈgɒtᵊn/ *US past participle of* get

gouge /gaʊdʒ/ *verb* [T] to make a hole or long cut in something *He accidentally gouged a hole in the wall*
gouge sth out to remove something by digging or cutting it out of a surface, often violently

gourmet[1] /ˈgʊəmeɪ/ *noun* [C] someone who enjoys good food and drink and knows a lot about it

gourmet[2] /ˈgʊəmeɪ/ *adjective* [always before noun] relating to good food and drink *a gourmet meal*

govern /ˈgʌvᵊn/ *verb* **1** [I, T] to officially control a country *The country is now governed by the Labour Party.* ○ *a **governing body*** **2** [T] to influence or control the way something happens or is done *There are rules that govern how teachers treat children.*

governess /ˈgʌvᵊnəs/ *noun* [C] a woman employed to teach the children in a family at home

---

WORD PARTNERS FOR *government*

bring **down** / **elect** / **form** / **overthrow** a government • a **democratic/elected** government • be **in** government

---

o~**government** /ˈgʌvᵊnmənt/ *noun* **1** [group] the group of people who officially control a country *The Government has cut taxes.* **2** [U] the method or process of governing a country *a new style of government* • **governmental** /ˌgʌvᵊnˈmentᵊl/ *adjective* relating to government

governor /ˈgʌvᵊnə/ *noun* [C] someone who is officially responsible for controlling a region, city, or organization *a prison/school governor* ○ *the Governor of Texas*

gown /gaʊn/ *noun* [C] **1** a woman's dress, usually worn on formal occasions *a silk gown* **2** a loose piece of clothing like a coat worn for a particular purpose *a hospital gown* ⊃See also: **dressing gown.**

GP /ˌdʒiːˈpiː/ *noun* [C] *abbreviation for* general practitioner: a doctor who sees people in the local area and treats illnesses that do not need a hospital visit

GPS /ˌdʒiːpiːˈes/ *noun* [U] *abbreviation for* Global Positioning System: a system of computers and satellites (= equipment that is sent into space around the Earth to receive and send signals) that work together to tell a user where they are

o~**grab**[1] /græb/ *verb* [T] grabbing, *past* grabbed **1** [TAKE SUDDENLY] to take hold of something or someone suddenly *He grabbed my arm and pulled me away.* **2** [DO QUICKLY] *informal* to eat, do, or get something quickly because you do not have much time *I grabbed a sandwich on the way to the station.* **3 grab sb's attention** *informal* to attract someone's attention **4** [TAKE OPPORTUNITY] If someone grabs a chance or opportunity, they take it quickly and with enthusiasm.
grab at sb/sth to try to get hold of someone or something quickly, with your hand

grab[2] /græb/ *noun* **1 make a grab for sth/sb** to try to take hold of something or someone suddenly *He made a grab for the gun.* **2 up for grabs** *informal* If something is up for grabs, it is available to anyone who wants to try to get it. *Ten free concert tickets are up for grabs.*

grace[1] /greɪs/ *noun* [U] **1** [MOVEMENT] the quality of moving in a smooth, relaxed, and attractive way *She moved with grace and elegance.* **2** [POLITENESS] the quality of being pleasantly polite *He **had the grace to** apologize for his mistake the next day.* **3 with good grace** in a willing and happy way *He accepted the failure with good grace.* **4 a month's/week's, etc grace** an extra month/week, etc you are given before something must be paid or done **5** [PRAYER] a prayer of thanks said before or after a meal *to say grace*

grace[2] /greɪs/ *verb* [T] When a person or object graces a place or thing, they make it more attractive. *Her face has graced the covers of magazines across the world.*

graceful /ˈgreɪsfᵊl/ *adjective* **1** moving in a smooth, relaxed, and attractive way, or having a smooth, attractive shape *graceful movements* ○ *a graceful neck* **2** behaving in a polite and pleasant way • **gracefully** *adverb*

gracious /ˈgreɪʃəs/ *adjective* **1** behaving in a pleasant, polite, calm way *He was gracious enough to thank me.* **2** comfortable and with a good appearance and quality *gracious homes/ living* **3 Good/Goodness gracious!** used to express polite surprise • **graciously** *adverb*

grade[1] /greɪd/ *noun* [C] **1** [SCORE] a number or letter that shows how good someone's work or performance is *Steve never studies, but he always gets good grades.* ○ *(UK) Carla got a grade A in German.* **2** [LEVEL] a level of quality, size, importance, etc *I applied for a position a grade higher than my current job.* **3** [SCHOOL GROUP] *US* a school class or group of classes for students of the same age or ability *My son is in fifth grade.* **4 make the grade** to perform well enough to succeed *He wanted to get into the team but he didn't make the grade.*

grade[2] /greɪd/ *verb* [T] **1** to separate people or things into different levels of quality, size, importance, etc *The fruit is washed and then graded by size.* **2** *US* (*UK* mark) to give a score to a student's piece of work *to grade work/ papers/exams*

'grade ,crossing *US (UK* **level crossing)** *noun* [C] a place where a railway crosses a road

'grade ,school *noun* [C, U] *US* a school for the first six to eight years of a child's education

gradient /'greɪdiənt/ *noun* [C] how steep a slope is *a steep/gentle gradient*

o⁻**gradual** /'grædʒuəl/ *adjective* happening slowly over a period of time *a gradual change/ improvement*

o⁻**gradually** /'grædʒuəli/ *adverb* slowly over a period of time *Gradually he began to get better.*

graduate¹ /'grædʒuət/ *noun* [C] **1** *UK* someone who has studied for and received a degree (= qualification) from a university *a science graduate* **2** *US* someone who has studied for and received a degree (= qualification) from a school, college, or university *a high-school graduate*

graduate² /'grædʒueɪt/ *verb* **1** [I] to complete your education successfully at a university, college, or, in the US, at school *He graduated from Cambridge University in 2005.* **2 graduate to sth** to move up to something more advanced or important

graduated /'grædʒueɪtɪd/ *adjective* divided into levels or stages *a graduated scale*

graduation /ˌgrædʒu'eɪʃᵊn/ *noun* [C, U] when you receive your degree (= qualification) for completing your education or a course of study *a graduation ceremony*

graffiti

graffiti /grə'fiːti/ *noun* [U] writing or pictures painted on walls and public places, usually illegally

graft¹ /grɑːft/ *noun* **1** SKIN/BONE [C] a piece of skin or bone taken from one part of a body and joined to another part *a skin/bone graft* **2** PLANT [C] a piece cut from one plant and joined onto another plant **3** WORK [U] *UK informal* work *hard graft*

graft² /grɑːft/ *verb* **1** SKIN/BONE [T] to join a piece of skin or bone from one part of the body to another part **2** PLANT [T] to join a piece cut from one plant onto another plant **3** WORK [I] *UK informal* to work hard

grain /greɪn/ *noun* **1** SEED [C, U] a seed or seeds from types of grass which are eaten as food

grains of wheat/rice **2** PIECE [C] a very small piece of something *a grain of sand/sugar* **3** QUALITY [no plural] a very small amount of a quality *There isn't **a grain of truth** in her story.* **4 the grain** the natural direction and pattern of lines which you can see in wood or material *to cut something along/against the grain* **5 go against the grain** If something goes against the grain, you would not normally do it because it would be unusual or morally wrong. ➭See also: take sth with a pinch of **salt¹**.

gram *(also UK* **gramme)** *(written abbreviation* **g, gm)** /græm/ *noun* [C] a unit for measuring weight, equal to 0.001 kilograms

o⁻**grammar** /'græmᵊʳ/ *noun* **1** [U] the way you combine words and change their form and position in a sentence, or the rules or study of this **2** [C] *mainly UK* a book of grammar rules

'grammar ,school *noun* [C, U] **1** in the UK, a school which clever children over 11 years old can go to if they pass a special exam *Manchester Grammar School* **2** *US* another way of *saying* elementary school (= a school for children from the ages of five to eleven)

grammatical /grə'mætɪkᵊl/ *adjective* relating to grammar, or obeying the rules of grammar *grammatical rules* ○ *a grammatical sentence* ● **grammatically** *adverb*

gramme /græm/ *noun* [C] another UK spelling of gram

gramophone /'græməfəʊn/ *noun* [C] *old-fashioned* a machine for playing music

gran /græn/ *noun* [C] *UK informal short for* grandmother

grand¹ /grænd/ *adjective* **1** LARGE very large and special *a grand hotel* ○ *the Grand Canal* **2** IMPORTANT rich and important, or behaving as if you are *a grand old lady* **3** GOOD *informal* very good or enjoyable

grand² /grænd/ *noun* [C] *plural* **grand** *informal* one thousand dollars or pounds *The holiday cost me two grand.*

grandad /'grændæd/ *noun* [C] *another UK spelling of* granddad

grandchild /'græntʃaɪld/ *noun* [C] *plural* **grandchildren** the child of your son or daughter

granddad /'grændæd/ *noun* [C] *mainly UK informal* grandfather

granddaughter /'grænd,dɔːtəʳ/ *noun* [C] the daughter of your son or daughter

grandeur /'grændjəʳ/ *noun* [U] the quality of being very large and special or beautiful *the grandeur of the hills*

o⁻**grandfather** /'grænd,fɑːðəʳ/ *noun* [C] the father of your mother or father

,grandfather 'clock *noun* [C] a clock in a very tall, wooden case

grandiose /'grændiəʊs/ *adjective* large or detailed and made to appear important, often in an unnecessary and annoying way *grandiose plans*

grandly /'grændli/ *adverb* in a very important way, or as if you are very important

grandma /'grænmɑː/ *noun* [C] *informal another word for* grandmother

grandmother /'grænd,mʌðər/ noun [C] the mother of your mother or father

grandpa /'grændpɑː/ noun [C] informal another word for grandfather

grandparent /'grænd,peərᵊnt/ noun [C] the parent of your mother or father

grand pi'ano noun [C] a very large piano, usually used in public performances

grand prix /,grɒn'priː/ noun [C] (plural **grands prix**) one of a series of important international races for very fast cars the Italian Grand Prix

grand 'slam noun [C] when you win all the important competitions that are held in one year for a particular sport

grandson /'grændsʌn/ noun [C] the son of your son or daughter

grandstand /'grændstænd/ noun [C] a large, open structure containing rows of seats, used for watching sporting events

granite /'grænɪt/ noun [U] a type of very hard, grey rock

granny /'græni/ noun [C] informal another word for grandmother

grant¹ /grɑːnt/ verb **1** [T] formal to give or allow someone something, usually in an official way [+ two objects] to grant someone a licence/visa **2** [T] formal to admit or agree that something is true She's a good-looking woman, I grant you. **3** take sb/sth for granted to not show that you are grateful for someone or something, and forget that you are lucky to have them Most of us take our freedom for granted. **4** take it for granted to believe that something is true without checking or thinking about it [+ (that)] I took it for granted that we'd be invited.

grant² /grɑːnt/ noun [C] an amount of money provided by a government or organization for a special purpose They received a **research grant** for the project.

granule /'grænjuːl/ noun [C] a small, hard piece of a substance coffee granules • **granulated** /'grænjəleɪtɪd/ adjective **granulated sugar**

grape /greɪp/ noun [C] a small, round, green, purple or red fruit that grows in large, close groups and is often used to make wine a **bunch of grapes** ⊃See colour picture Fruit and Vegetables on page Centre 10.

grapefruit /'greɪpfruːt/ noun [C, U] plural grapefruit or grapefruits a large, round, yellow fruit with a sour taste

grapevine /'greɪpvaɪn/ noun **hear sth on/ through the grapevine** to hear news from someone who heard the news from someone else

graph /grɑːf/ noun [C] a picture with measurements marked on it as lines or curves, used to compare different things or show the development of something

graph

graphic /'græfɪk/ adjective A graphic description or image is extremely clear and detailed. The film contains **graphic violence**. • **graphically** adverb

graphical user 'interface noun [C] a way of arranging information on a computer screen that is easy to understand because it uses pictures and symbols as well as words

graphic de'sign noun [U] the art of designing pictures and text for books, magazines, advertisements, etc

graphics /'græfɪks/ noun [plural] images shown on a computer screen

graphite /'græfaɪt/ noun [U] a soft, grey-black form of carbon used in pencils

grapple /'græpl/ verb

grapple with sth to try to deal with or understand something difficult

grapple with sb to hold onto someone and fight with them

grasp¹ /grɑːsp/ verb [T] **1** to take hold of something or someone firmly He grasped my hand enthusiastically. **2** to understand something I find these mathematical problems difficult to grasp.

grasp at sth to quickly try to get hold of something

grasp² /grɑːsp/ noun [no plural] **1** [UNDERSTAND] when you understand something He **has an excellent grasp** of English. **2** [HOLD] when you hold onto someone or something I tried to pull him out but he slipped from my grasp. **3** [ABILITY] the ability to obtain or achieve something Victory is **within** our grasp.

grasping /'grɑːspɪŋ/ adjective wanting much more of something than you need, especially money a grasping, greedy man

grass /grɑːs/ noun **1** [U] a common plant with narrow green leaves that grows close to the ground in gardens and fields to **mow/cut the grass** ○ We lay on the grass in the sunshine. **2** [C] a particular type of grass ornamental grasses

grasshopper /'grɑːs,hɒpər/ noun [C] a green insect which jumps about using its long back legs
grasshopper

grass 'roots noun [plural] ordinary people in a society or political organization and not the leaders

grassy /'grɑːsi/ adjective covered with grass a grassy slope/meadow

grate¹ /greɪt/ verb **1** [T] to break food such as cheese into small, thin pieces by rubbing it against a grater (= kitchen tool with holes) grated cheese/carrot **2** [I] to make an unpleasant noise when rubbing against something *The chair grated against the floor*.

grate on sb/sth If someone's voice or behaviour grates on you, it annoys you.

grate² /greɪt/ *noun* [C] a metal structure for holding the wood or coal in a fireplace

The adjective **appreciative** is sometimes used to show that someone is grateful, or you can use the verb **appreciate** to express the same idea: *I'm really appreciative of all the help you've given me.* • *I really appreciate all the help you've given me.*

The expression **be glad of** is another alternative: *We were very glad of some extra help.*

The expression **be indebted to** is a more formal way of saying that someone is very grateful for something: *I'm indebted to my parents for all their love and support.*

The adjectives **thankful** or **relieved** are often used when a person is grateful that something bad did not happen: *I'm just thankful/relieved that she's safe and well.*

If a person is grateful that someone has done something kind, the adjective **touched** is sometimes used: *She was really touched that he remembered her birthday.*

✒**grateful** /ˈgreɪtfºl/ *adjective* feeling or showing thanks *I'm really grateful to you for all your help*. ⭢Opposite **ungrateful**. • **gratefully** *adverb All donations gratefully received*.

grater /ˈgreɪtəʳ/ *noun* [C] a kitchen tool with a surface full of holes with sharp edges, used to grate (= break into small pieces) foods such as cheese ⭢See colour picture **The Kitchen** on page Centre 2.

gratify /ˈgrætɪfaɪ/ *verb* [T] *formal* to please someone or satisfy their wishes or needs *I was gratified by their decision.* ○ *a gratifying result* • **gratification** /ˌgrætɪfɪˈkeɪʃºn/ *noun* [U]

grating /ˈgreɪtɪŋ/ *noun* [C] a flat structure made of long, thin pieces of metal crossing each other over a hole in the ground or a window

gratitude /ˈgrætɪtjuːd/ *noun* [U] the feeling or quality of being grateful *I would like to express my deep gratitude to all the hospital staff*.

gratuitous /grəˈtjuːɪtəs/ *adjective* unnecessary and done without a good reason *gratuitous violence*

gratuity /grəˈtjuːəti/ *noun* [C] *formal* an extra amount of money given to someone to thank them for providing a service

✒**grave¹** /greɪv/ *noun* [C] a place in the ground where a dead body is buried

grave² /greɪv/ *adjective* very serious *grave doubts* ○ *a grave mistake* • **gravely** *adverb*

gravel /ˈgrævºl/ *noun* [U] small pieces of stone used to make paths and road surfaces

gravestone /ˈgreɪvstəʊn/ *noun* [C] a stone that shows the name of a dead person who is buried under it

graveyard /ˈgreɪvjɑːd/ *noun* [C] an area of land

where dead bodies are buried, usually next to a church

gravitate /ˈgrævɪteɪt/ *verb*

gravitate to/towards sth/sb to be attracted to something or someone, or to move in the direction of something or someone

gravitational /ˌgrævɪˈteɪʃºnºl/ *adjective* relating to gravity *gravitational force*

gravity /ˈgrævəti/ *noun* [U] **1** the force that makes objects fall to the ground or that pulls objects towards a planet or other body *the laws of gravity* **2** *formal* when something is very serious *You don't seem to realize the gravity of the situation*. ⭢See also: **centre of gravity**.

gravy /ˈgreɪvi/ *noun* [U] a warm, brown sauce made from the fat and liquid that comes from meat when it is being cooked

✒**gray** /greɪ/ *noun, adjective* [C, U] US spelling of grey

graying /ˈgreɪɪŋ/ *adjective* US spelling of greying (= having hair that is becoming grey or white)

graze¹ /greɪz/ *verb* **1** EAT [I] When cows or other animals graze, they eat grass. *Cattle grazed in the meadow.* **2** INJURE [T] (*UK/US* **skin**) to injure your skin by rubbing it against something rough *I fell and grazed my knee.* **3** TOUCH [T] to touch or move lightly along the surface or edge of something *A bullet grazed his cheek*.

graze² /greɪz/ *noun* [C] *mainly UK* an injury on the surface of your skin caused by rubbing against something *She has a nasty graze on her elbow.*

grease¹ /griːs/ *noun* [U] **1** a substance such as oil or fat **2** a substance like thick oil that is put on parts in an engine or machine to make them move more smoothly

grease² /griːs/ *verb* [T] to put fat or oil on or in something

greasy /ˈgriːsi/ *adjective* containing or covered with fat or oil *greasy food/fingers*

✒**great** /greɪt/ *adjective* **1** EXCELLENT very good *We had a great time.* ○ *I've had a great idea!* **2** IMPORTANT important or famous *a great statesman/novelist* **3** LARGE large in amount, size, or degree *a great crowd of people* **4** EXTREME extreme *great success/difficulty* **5** great big/long, etc very big/long, etc *I gave her a great big hug.* **6** a great many a large number • **greatness** *noun* [U] ⭢See also: go to great lengths (**length**) to do sth, set great **store¹** by sth, the best/greatest **thing** since sliced bread.

great- /greɪt/ *prefix* **1** great-grandfather/-grandmother the father/mother of your grandfather or grandmother **2** great-aunt/-uncle the aunt/uncle of your mother or father **3** great-grandchild/-granddaughter, etc the child/daughter, etc of your grandson or granddaughter **4** great-niece/-nephew the daughter/son of your niece or nephew

greatly /ˈgreɪtli/ *adverb* very much *I greatly admire your paintings.* ○ *All of us will miss her greatly.*

greed /griːd/ *noun* [U] when you want a lot more food, money, etc, than you need

greedy /ˈgriːdi/ *adjective* wanting a lot more food, money, etc, than you need *greedy, selfish* people ○ *They were* **greedy** *for money.* ● **greedily** *adverb* ● **greediness** *noun* [U]

Greek /griːk/ *adjective* relating to the culture, language, or people of Greece or ancient Greece

o⁻**green¹** /griːn/ *adjective* **1** COLOUR being the same colour as grass *The traffic lights turned green.* ⊃See colour picture **Colours** on page Centre 12. **2** ENVIRONMENT [always before noun] relating to nature and protecting the environment *a green activist/campaigner* **3** GRASS covered with grass or other plants *green spaces* **4** NOT EXPERIENCED *informal* having little experience or understanding *I was very green when I joined the company.* **5 be green with envy** to wish very much that you had something that another person has ⊃See also: **have green fingers** (**finger¹**), **green light**.

o⁻**green²** /griːn/ *noun* **1** COLOUR [C, U] the colour of grass ⊃See colour picture **Colours** on page Centre 12. **2** GOLF [C] a special area of very short, smooth grass on a golf course *the 18th green* **3** VILLAGE [C] an area of grass in the middle of a village

'**green ,belt** *noun* [C] an area of land around a city or town where no new building is allowed

,**green 'card** *noun* [C] an official document allowing a foreigner to live and work in the US permanently

greenery /'griːn³ri/ *noun* [U] green leaves, plants, or branches

greenfield /'griːnfiːld/ *adjective UK* describes land where there were no buildings before, or buildings on land that have never had buildings *a greenfield site* ⊃Compare **brownfield**.

greengrocer /'griːnˌɡrəʊsə'/ *noun* [C] *UK* **1 greengrocer's** a shop where you buy fruit and vegetables **2** someone who sells fruit and vegetables

greenhouse /'griːnhaʊs/ *noun* [C] *plural* **greenhouses** /'griːnhaʊzɪz/ a building made of glass for growing plants in

the 'greenhouse ef,fect *noun* the gradual warming of the Earth's surface caused by an increase in pollution and gases in the air

'**greenhouse ,gas** *noun* [C] a gas which causes the greenhouse effect, especially carbon dioxide (= a gas produced when carbon is burned)

,**green 'light** *noun* [no plural] permission to do something [+ to do sth] *They've been given the green light to build two new supermarkets.*

the 'Green ,Party *noun* [group] a political party whose main aim is to protect the environment *Green party policies*

greens /griːnz/ *noun* [plural] green leaves that are cooked and eaten as a vegetable

greet /griːt/ *verb* [T] **1** to welcome someone *He greeted me at the door.* **2** to react to something in a particular way [often passive] *His story was greeted with shrieks of laughter.*

greeting /'griːtɪŋ/ *noun* [C] *formal* something friendly or polite that you say or do when you meet or welcome someone

gregarious /grɪ'ɡeəriəs/ *adjective* If you are gregarious, you enjoy being with other people.

grenade /grə'neɪd/ *noun* [C] a small bomb that

is thrown or fired from a weapon

grew /gruː/ *past tense of* grow

o⁻**grey¹** *UK* (*US* **gray**) /greɪ/ *adjective* **1** COLOUR being a colour that is a mixture of black and white *grey clouds* ⊃See colour picture **Colours** on page Centre 12. **2** HAIR having hair that has become grey or white *She went grey in her thirties.* **3** WEATHER cloudy and not bright *a cold, grey morning* **4** BORING not interesting or attractive *Life was grey and tedious.* **5 grey area** something which people are not certain about, usually because there are no clear rules for it

o⁻**grey²** *UK* (*US* **gray**) /greɪ/ *noun* [C, U] a colour that is a mixture of black and white ⊃See colour picture **Colours** on page Centre 12.

greyhound /'greɪhaʊnd/ *noun* [C] a thin dog with short hair that runs very fast, sometimes in races

greying *UK* (*US* **graying**) /'greɪɪŋ/ *adjective* having hair that is becoming grey or white

grid /grɪd/ *noun* **1** PATTERN [C] a pattern or structure made from horizontal and vertical lines crossing each other to form squares *a grid system of roads* **2** POWER [no plural] a system of connected wires used to supply electrical power to a large area *the National Grid* **3** MAP [C] a pattern of squares with numbers or letters used to find places on a map

gridlock /'grɪdlɒk/ *noun* [U] when the traffic cannot move in any direction because all of the roads are blocked with cars

grief /griːf/ *noun* **1** [U] great sadness, especially caused by someone's death **2 Good grief!** *informal* something that you say when you are surprised or annoyed **3 come to grief** *informal* to suddenly fail or have an accident **4 cause/ give sb grief** *informal* to annoy someone or cause trouble or problems for them

grievance /'griːv³ns/ *noun* [C] *formal* a complaint, especially about unfair behaviour

grieve /griːv/ *verb* **1** [I] to feel or express great sadness, especially when someone dies *He is still grieving for his wife.* **2** [T] *formal* to make someone feel very sad

grievous /'griːvəs/ *adjective formal* very serious *grievous injuries* ● **grievously** *adverb*

grill¹ /grɪl/ *noun* [C] **1** (*also US* **broiler**) a piece of equipment which cooks food using direct heat from above ⊃See colour picture **The Kitchen** on page Centre 2. **2** a flat, metal structure used to cook food over a fire

grill² /grɪl/ *verb* [T] **1** (*also US* **broil**) to cook food using direct heat *Grill the fish for 2 to 3 minutes on each side.* ⊃See picture at **cook. 2** to ask someone questions continuously and for a long time *After my arrest, I was grilled by the police for two days.*

grille /grɪl/ *noun* [C] a metal structure of bars built across something to protect it

grim /grɪm/ *adjective*, **grimmer**, **grimmest 1** BAD worrying and bad *grim news* ○ *The future looks grim.* **2** SERIOUS sad and serious *a grim expression* **3** UNPLEASANT A grim place is ugly and unpleasant. ● **grimly** *adverb*

grimace /'grɪməs/ *verb* [I] to make your face

show an expression of pain or unhappiness *He grimaced at the bitter taste.* ● **grimace** *noun* [C]

grime /graɪm/ *noun* [U] dirt that covers a surface *The walls were covered in grime.* ● **grimy** *adjective* covered in dirt *grimy hands*

grin /grɪn/ *verb* grinning *past* grinned **1** [I] to smile a big smile *He grinned at me from the doorway.* **2 grin and bear it** to accept an unpleasant or difficult situation because there is nothing you can do to improve it ● **grin** *noun* [C] *She had a big grin on her face.*

grind[1] /graɪnd/ *verb* [T] *past* ground **1** to keep rubbing something between two rough, hard surfaces until it becomes a powder *to grind coffee* **2** to rub a blade against a hard surface to make it sharp **3 grind your teeth** to rub your teeth together, making an unpleasant sound **grind sb down** to gradually make someone lose hope, energy, or confidence

grind[2] /graɪnd/ *noun* [no plural] *informal* work or effort that is boring and unpleasant and makes you tired because it does not change *the daily grind*

grinder /ˈgraɪndəʳ/ *noun* [C] a machine used to rub or press something until it becomes a powder *a coffee grinder*

▨▨▨ WORD PARTNERS FOR *grip*

loosen/release/tighten your grip ● sb's grip **on** sth

grip[1] /grɪp/ *noun* [no plural] **1** when you hold something tightly *She tightened her grip on my arm.* **2** control over something or someone *He has a firm grip on the economy.* **3 come/get to grips with sth** to understand and deal with a problem or situation *It's a difficult subject to get to grips with.* **4 get a grip (on yourself)** to make an effort to control your emotions and behave more calmly

grip[2] /grɪp/ *verb* [T] gripping *past* gripped **1** HOLD to hold something tightly *She gripped his arm.* **2** INTEREST to keep someone's attention completely *This trial has gripped the whole nation.* **3** EMOTION When an emotion grips you, you feel it very strongly. [often passive] *He was gripped by fear.*

gripe /graɪp/ *verb* [I] *informal* to complain, often in an annoying way ● **gripe** *noun* [C]

gripping /ˈgrɪpɪŋ/ *adjective* If something is gripping, it is so interesting that it holds your attention completely. *a gripping story*

grisly /ˈgrɪzli/ *adjective* very unpleasant, especially because death or blood is involved *a grisly murder*

grit[1] /grɪt/ *noun* [U] **1** very small pieces of stone or sand *I've got a bit of grit in my eye.* **2** the quality of being brave and determined

grit[2] /grɪt/ *verb* [T] gritting *past* gritted to put grit onto a road surface when the road has ice on it ⊃See also: grit your teeth (**teeth**).

gritty /ˈgrɪti/ *adjective* **1** showing unpleasant details about a situation in a way that seems very real *a gritty drama* ○ *gritty realism* **2** brave and determined *gritty determination*

groan /grəʊn/ *verb* [I] to make a long, low sound such as when expressing pain, unhappiness,

etc *He collapsed, groaning with pain.* ● **groan** *noun* [C]

grocer /ˈgrəʊsəʳ/ *noun* **1 grocer's** *UK* a shop that sells food and other products used in the home **2** [C] someone who owns or works in a grocer's

groceries /ˈgrəʊsəriz/ *noun* [plural] goods bought to be used in the home such as food and cleaning products

grocery /ˈgrəʊsəri/ (*also US* '**grocery ˌstore**) *noun* [C] a shop that sells food and products used in the home

groggy /ˈgrɒgi/ *adjective informal* unable to think or act quickly because you have just woken up, been ill, etc *I felt a bit groggy after the operation.*

groin /grɔɪn/ *noun* [C] the area where the legs join the rest of the body near the sexual organs *He pulled a muscle in his groin.*

groom[1] /gruːm/ *verb* [T] **1** to prepare someone carefully for a special position or job *He's being groomed for stardom.* **2** to clean and brush an animal's fur

groom[2] /gruːm/ *noun* [C] **1** (*also* **bridegroom**) a man who is getting married **2** someone who cleans and looks after horses

groove /gruːv/ *noun* [C] a long, narrow line that has been cut into a surface

grope /grəʊp/ *verb* [I, T] to try to get hold of something with your hand, usually when you cannot see it *I groped in my bag for my keys.* **2 grope your way along/through, etc** to move somewhere with difficulty, feeling with your hands because you cannot see clearly *We groped our way through the smoke to the exit.* **grope for sth** to try to think of the right words or the right way to express something *He groped for the words to tell her.*

gross[1] /grəʊs/ *adjective* **1** TOTAL A gross amount of money has not had taxes or other costs taken from it. *gross earnings/profit* **2** SERIOUS [always before noun] *formal* very serious or unacceptable *gross misconduct* **3** UNPLEASANT *informal* very unpleasant *Oh, yuck. That's really gross.*

gross[2] /grəʊs/ *verb* [T] to earn a particular amount of money as a total before tax or other costs are taken from it *The film grossed $250 million.*

grossly /ˈgrəʊsli/ *adverb* extremely *grossly unfair/exaggerated*

grotesque /grəʊˈtesk/ *adjective* strange and unpleasant, especially in a ridiculous or slightly frightening way *a grotesque image* ● **grotesquely** *adverb*

grotto /ˈgrɒtəʊ/ *noun* [C] a small cave

○-**ground**[1] /graʊnd/ *noun* **1 the ground** the surface of the Earth *I sat down on the ground.* **2** SOIL [U] the soil in an area *soft/stony ground* **3** AREA [C] an area of land used for a particular purpose or activity *a football ground* **4** KNOWLEDGE [U] an area of knowledge, information, interest, or experience *He had to go over the same ground several times before I understood it.* **5 break new ground** to do something that is different to anything that has been done before **6 gain/lose ground** to become more/less popular and accepted *The idea is gradually gaining ground.* **7 get (sth) off the ground** If a plan or activity gets off the ground, or if you get it off the ground, it starts or succeeds. *He worked hard at getting the project off the ground.* **8 stand your ground** to refuse to change your opinion or move your position despite attempts to make you **9 suit sb down to the ground** *UK* to be exactly right or suitable for someone *That job would suit you down to the ground.* **10 be thin on the ground** *UK* to exist only in small numbers or amounts ⊃See also: breeding ground, common ground.

ground² /graʊnd/ *verb* **1 be grounded** If a vehicle that travels on water or in the air is grounded, it cannot or may not leave the ground. *The aircraft was grounded by fog.* **2 be grounded in sth** *formal* to be based firmly on something *Fiction should be grounded in reality.*

ground³ /graʊnd/ *past of* grind

ground 'beef *US* (*UK* mince) *noun* [U] beef (= meat from a cow) that has been cut into very small pieces by a machine

groundbreaking /'graʊnd,breɪkɪŋ/ *adjective* based on or containing completely new ideas *groundbreaking research*

ground 'floor *UK* (*US* first floor) *noun* [C] the level of a building which is on the ground

grounding /'graʊndɪŋ/ *noun* [no plural] knowledge of the basic facts and principles of a subject *The course gave me a good grounding in bookkeeping.*

groundless /'graʊndləs/ *adjective* Groundless fears, worries, etc have no reason or facts to support them.

ground ,rules *noun* [plural] the basic rules or principles for doing something

grounds /graʊndz/ *noun* [plural] **1** the reason for doing or believing something *He resigned on medical grounds.* ○ *I refused on the grounds that* (= because) *it was too risky.* **2** the land around and belonging to a particular building or organization *We strolled around the hospital grounds.*

groundwork /'graʊndwɜːk/ *noun* [U] work or events that prepare for something that will be done or produced in the future *The project is laying the groundwork for a new approach to research.*

ground 'zero *noun* [U] **1** the exact place where a nuclear bomb explodes **2** the place in New York City where the World Trade Center stood before it was destroyed in an attack on September 11, 2001

o─**group¹** /gruːp/ *noun* [C] **1** a number of people or things that are together in one place or are connected *She went camping with a small group of friends.* **2** a few musicians or singers who perform together, usually playing popular music *a pop group* ⊃See also: age group,

blood group, focus group, peer group, pressure group.

group² /gruːp/ *verb* [I, T] to form a group or put people or things into a group or groups *The children are grouped according to their ability.*

grouping /'gruːpɪŋ/ *noun* [C] a group of people or things that have the same aims or qualities *regional groupings*

grouse¹ /graʊs/ *noun* [C] **1** *plural* grouse a small, fat, brown bird that some people hunt for food **2** a small complaint about something

grouse² /graʊs/ *verb* [I] to complain about something

grove /ɡrəʊv/ *noun* [C] a small group of trees *an olive grove*

grovel /'ɡrɒvəl/ *verb* [I] *UK* grovelling *past* grovelled *US* groveling *past* groveled **1** to try very hard to be nice to someone important so that they will be nice to you or forgive you *She grovelled to the producer to get that part.* **2** to move around on your hands and knees *He was grovelling around on the floor.*

o─**grow** /ɡrəʊ/ *verb past tense* grew, *past participle* grown **1** DEVELOP [I] to develop and become bigger or taller as time passes *Children grow very quickly.* **2** PLANT [I, T] If a plant grows, or you grow it, it develops from a seed to a full plant. *These shrubs grow well in sandy soil.* **3** INCREASE [I] to increase *The number of people living alone grows each year.* **4** grow tired/old/calm, etc to gradually become tired/old/calm, etc *The music grew louder and louder.* **5** HAIR [I, T] If your hair or nails grow, or if you grow them, they get longer.

grow into sb/sth to develop into a particular type of person or thing

grow into sth If a child grows into clothes, they gradually become big enough to wear them.

grow on sb If someone or something grows on you, you start to like them. *I didn't like her at first but she's grown on me over the years.*

grow out of sth 1 If children grow out of clothes, they gradually become too big to wear them. *Adam's grown out of his shoes.* **2** to stop doing something as you get older *He still bites his nails, but hopefully he'll grow out of it.*

o─**grow up 1** to become older or an adult *She grew up in New York.* **2** to develop or become bigger or stronger *A close friendship had grown up between them.*

grower /'ɡrəʊəʳ/ *noun* [C] someone who grows fruit or vegetables to sell to people

growing /'ɡrəʊɪŋ/ *adjective* increasing *A growing number of people are choosing to live alone.*

growl /ɡraʊl/ *verb* [I] If a dog or similar animal growls, it makes a deep, angry noise in its throat. • growl *noun* [C]

grown¹ /ɡrəʊn/ *adjective* a grown man/woman an adult, used especially when they are not behaving like an adult

grown² /ɡrəʊn/ *past participle of* grow

grown-up¹ /'ɡrəʊnʌp/ *noun* [C] an adult, used especially when talking to children *Ask a grown-up to cut the shape out for you.*

grown-up² /,ɡrəʊn'ʌp/ *adjective* with the physical and mental development of an adult *Jenny has a grown-up son of 24.*

WORD PARTNERS FOR *growth*

encourage/slow/stimulate/stunt growth
● healthy/long-term/low/rapid/slow/
steady growth ● a growth in sth

☞**growth** /grəʊθ/ *noun* **1** [U, no plural] when something grows, increases, or develops *population growth* ○ *A balanced diet is essential for healthy growth.* **2** [C] something that grows on your skin or inside your body, that should not be there

grub /grʌb/ *noun* **1** [U] *informal* food **2** [C] a young, developing insect which has a fat, white tube shape

grubby /'grʌbi/ *adjective* quite dirty *a grubby little boy*

grudge[1] /grʌdʒ/ *noun* [C] a feeling of dislike or anger towards someone because of something they have done in the past *He is not the type of person to bear a grudge against anyone.*

grudge[2] /grʌdʒ/ *verb* [T] to not want to spend time or money or to give something to someone *He grudged the time he spent in meetings.*

grudging /'grʌdʒɪŋ/ *adjective* done against your will, in a way that shows you do not want to do it *He treated her with grudging respect.* ● **grudgingly** *adverb*

gruelling *UK* (*US* **grueling**) /'gruːəlɪŋ/ *adjective* Gruelling activities are very difficult and make you very tired. *a gruelling bicycle race*

gruesome /'gruːsəm/ *adjective* very unpleasant or violent, usually involving injury or death *a gruesome murder*

gruff /grʌf/ *adjective* sounding unfriendly *a gruff voice* ● **gruffly** *adverb*

grumble /'grʌmbl/ *verb* [I] to complain about something in a quiet but angry way *She's always grumbling about something.* ● **grumble** *noun* [C]

grumpy /'grʌmpi/ *adjective* easily annoyed and often complaining *a grumpy old man* ● **grumpily** *adverb* ● **grumpiness** *noun* [U]

grunt /grʌnt/ *verb* **1** [I, T] to make a short, low sound instead of speaking, usually when you are angry or in pain **2** [I] If a pig grunts, it makes short, low sounds. ● **grunt** *noun* [C]

guarantee[1] /,gærən'tiː/ *verb* [T] **guaranteeing** *past* **guaranteed 1** to promise that something is true or will happen *Every child is guaranteed a place at a local school.* ○ [+ (that)] *We can't guarantee that it will arrive in time.* **2** If a company guarantees its products, it makes a written promise to repair them or give you a new one if they have a fault.

guarantee[2] /,gærən'tiː/ *noun* [C, U] **1** a written promise made by a company to repair one of its products or give you a new one if it has a fault *a three-year guarantee* ○ *I'm afraid this camera is no longer under guarantee.* **2** a promise that something will be done or will happen [+ (that)] *There's no guarantee that it actually works.*

guard[1] /gɑːd/ *noun* **1** PROTECT [C] someone whose job is to make certain someone does not

escape or to protect a place or another person *a security guard* ○ *prison guards* **2** SOLDIERS [no plural] a group of soldiers or police officers who are protecting a person or place **3** TRAIN [C] (*also* **conductor**) someone who is in charge of a train **4** THING [C] something that covers or protects someone or something *a fire guard* **5** **be on guard; stand guard** to be responsible for protecting a place or a person *Armed police stood guard outside the house.* **6** **be under guard** to be kept in a place by a group of people who have weapons *The suspect is now under guard in the local hospital.* **7** **catch sb off guard** to surprise someone by doing something when they are not ready to deal with it **8** **be on (your) guard** to be ready to deal with something difficult that might happen *Companies were warned to be on their guard for suspicious packages.*

guard[2] /gɑːd/ *verb* [T] **1** to protect someone or something from being attacked or stolen *Soldiers guarded the main doors of the embassy.* **2** to watch someone and make certain that they do not escape from a place *Five prison officers guarded the prisoners.*

guard against sth to try to make certain that something does not happen by being very careful *Regular exercise helps guard against heart disease.*

guarded /'gɑːdɪd/ *adjective* careful not to give too much information or show how you really feel *a guarded response* ● **guardedly** *adverb*

guardian /'gɑːdiən/ *noun* [C] **1** someone who is legally responsible for someone else's child *The consent form must be signed by the child's parent or guardian.* **2** a person or organization that protects laws, principles, etc ● **guardianship** *noun* [U]

guerrilla /gə'rɪlə/ *noun* [C] a member of an unofficial group of soldiers fighting to achieve their political beliefs *guerrilla warfare*

☞**guess**[1] /ges/ *verb* **1** [I, T] to give an answer or opinion about something without having all the facts *Can you guess how old he is?* **2** [I, T] to give a correct answer without having all the facts *"You've got a promotion!" "Yes, how did you guess?"* ○ [+ (that)] *I'd never have guessed that you two were related.* **3** **I guess** used when you think that something is probably true or likely *I've known her for about 12 years, I guess.* **4** **I guess so/not** used when you agree/disagree but are not completely certain about something **5** **Guess what?** something you say when you have some surprising news for someone *Guess what? I'm pregnant.*

WORD PARTNERS FOR *guess*

have/hazard/make/take a guess ● a rough
guess ● at a guess ● a guess as to/at sth

☞**guess**[2] /ges/ *noun* [C] **1** an attempt to give the right answer when you are not certain what it is *How old do you think John is? Go on,* (*UK*) *have a guess/*(*US*) *take a guess.* ○ *At a guess, I'd say there were about 70 people there.* **2** an opinion that you have formed by guessing *My guess is they'll announce their engagement soon.* **3** **be anybody's guess** *informal* to be something that no one can be certain about *What happens after the election is anybody's guess.*

guesswork /'gesw3:k/ *noun* [U] when you try to find an answer by guessing

∘⸚**guest** /gest/ *noun* [C] **1** VISITOR someone who comes to visit you in your home, at a party, etc *We've got some guests coming this weekend.* **2** HOTEL someone who is staying in a hotel *The hotel has accommodation for 200 guests.* **3** TV a famous person who takes part in a television programme or other entertainment *Our special guest tonight is George Michael.* **4 Be my guest.** something you say when you give someone permission to use something or do something

guesthouse /'gesthaus/ *noun* [C] a small cheap hotel

GUI /'gu:i/ *noun* [C] graphical user interface: a way of arranging information on a computer screen that is easy to understand because it uses pictures and symbols as well as words

guidance /'gaɪdᵊns/ *noun* [U] help or advice *Students make choices about their future, with the guidance of their teachers.*

guide¹ /gaɪd/ *noun* [C] **1** PERSON someone whose job is to show interesting places to visitors, or to help people get somewhere *a tour guide* **2** BOOK a book that gives information about something or tells you how to do something *a hotel/restaurant guide* ○ *a user's guide* **3** PLAN something that helps you plan or decide what to do [usually singular] *Parents use this report as a guide when choosing schools for their children.* **4 Guide** (*also* ˌGirl 'Guide) a girl who belongs to an organization in the UK that teaches practical things like living outside, and how to work as part of a team **5 the Guides** an organization in the UK that teaches girls practical skills and how to work as part of a team

guide² /gaɪd/ *verb* [T] **1** to help someone or something go somewhere *He gently guided her back to her seat.* **2** to tell someone what they should do *Rosemary had no one to guide her as a teenager.*

guidebook /'gaɪdbʊk/ *noun* [C] a book that gives visitors information about a particular place

'**guide ˌdog** (*also* US **seeing eye dog**) *noun* [C] a dog that is trained to help blind people

guidelines /'gaɪdlaɪnz/ *noun* [plural] advice about how to do something *government guidelines on tobacco advertising*

guild /gɪld/ *noun* [C] an organization of people who have the same job or interests *the Designers' Guild*

guile /gaɪl/ *noun* [U] *formal* clever but sometimes dishonest behaviour that you use to deceive someone

guillotine /'gɪlətiːn/ *noun* [C] a piece of equipment used to cut off criminals' heads in the past ● **guillotine** *verb* [T]

guilt /gɪlt/ *noun* [U] **1** FEELING the strong feeling of shame that you feel when you have done something wrong *He was overcome with guilt over what he had done.* **2** ILLEGAL the fact that someone has done something illegal *The prosecution must convince the jury of his guilt.* **3** WRONG the responsibility for doing something bad

guilt-ridden /'gɪltrɪdᵊn/ *adjective* feeling very guilty

∘⸚**guilty** /'gɪlti/ *adjective* **1** ashamed because you have done something wrong [+ about + doing sth] *I feel so guilty about not going to see them.* **2** having broken a law *They found her guilty* (= decided that she was guilty of a crime). ○ *They found him guilty of rape.* ● **guiltily** *adverb* ● **guiltiness** *noun* [U]

guinea pig /'gɪni,pɪg/ *noun* [C] **1** a small animal with fur and no tail that people sometimes keep as a pet **2** *informal* someone who is used in a test for something such as a new medicine or product

guise /gaɪz/ *noun* [C] *formal* what something seems to be, although it is not *Banks are facing new competition in the guise of supermarkets.*

guitar /gɪ'tɑːʳ/ *noun* [C]   **guitar** a musical instrument with strings that you play by pulling the strings with your fingers or a piece of plastic *an electric guitar*

guitarist /gɪ'tɑːrɪst/ *noun* [C] someone who plays the guitar, especially as their job

gulf /gʌlf/ *noun* [C] **1** a large area of sea that has land almost all the way around it *the Arabian Gulf* **2** an important difference between the opinions or situations of two groups of people *There is a growing gulf between the rich and the poor.*

gull /gʌl/ (*also* **seagull**) *noun* [C] a white or grey bird that lives near the sea and has a loud cry

gullible /'gʌlɪbl/ *adjective* Someone who is gullible is easily tricked because they trust people too much. *How could you be so gullible?*

gully /'gʌli/ *noun* [C] a narrow valley which is usually dry except after a lot of rain

gulp /gʌlp/ *verb* **1** DRINK/EAT [T] (*also* **gulp down**) to drink or eat something quickly *I just had time to gulp down a cup of coffee before I left.* **2** BREATHE [I, T] to breathe in large amounts of air **3** SWALLOW [I] to swallow suddenly, sometimes making a noise, because you are nervous or surprised ● **gulp** *noun* [C] *He took a large gulp of tea.*

gum¹ /gʌm/ *noun* **1** MOUTH [C] the hard, pink part inside your mouth that your teeth grow out of [usually plural] *Protect your teeth and gums by visiting your dentist regularly.* ○ *gum dis-*

ease **2** [SWEET] [U] (*also* **chewing gum**) a sweet substance that you chew (= bite repeatedly) but do not swallow *a stick of gum* **3** [STICKY] [U] a sticky substance like glue, used for sticking papers together ⊃See also: **bubble gum**.

gum² /gʌm/ *verb* [T] **gumming** *past* **gummed** *UK* to stick things together using glue

ᴑ**gun¹** /gʌn/ *noun* **1** [C] a weapon that you fire bullets out of **2 jump the gun** to do something too soon, before you have thought about it carefully **3 stick to your guns** *informal* to refuse to change your ideas although other people try to make you ⊃See also: **machine gun**.

gun² /gʌn/ *verb* **gunning**, *past* **gunned**
   gun sb down to shoot someone and kill them or injure them badly

gunboat /'gʌnbəʊt/ *noun* [C] a small ship used during a war

gunfire /'gʌnfaɪəʳ/ *noun* [U] when guns are fired, or the noise that this makes

gunman /'gʌnmən/ *noun* [C] *plural* **gunmen** a criminal with a gun

gunner /'gʌnəʳ/ *noun* [C] a soldier or sailor whose job is to fire a large gun

gunpoint /'gʌnpɔɪnt/ *noun* **at gunpoint** with someone aiming a gun towards you *The hostages are being **held at gunpoint**.*

gunpowder /'gʌn,paʊdəʳ/ *noun* [U] an explosive powder

gunshot /'gʌnʃɒt/ *noun* [C] when a gun is fired *I heard a gunshot and rushed into the street.* ○ *gunshot wounds to the chest*

gurgle /'gɜːgl/ *verb* [I] to make a sound like bubbling liquid *The baby was gurgling happily.* • **gurgle** *noun* [C]

guru /'guːruː/ *noun* [C] **1** someone whose opinion you respect because they know a lot about a particular thing **2** a teacher or leader in the Hindu religion

gush¹ /gʌʃ/ *verb* [I, T] **1** If liquid gushes from an opening, it comes out quickly and in large amounts. *He ran down the street, blood gushing from a wound in his neck.* **2** to praise someone so much that they do not believe you are sincere *"Darling! I'm so excited!" she gushed.*

gush² /gʌʃ/ *noun* [C] **1** a large amount of liquid or gas that flows quickly **2** a sudden feeling of a particular emotion

gust /gʌst/ *verb* [I] If winds gust, they blow strongly. *Winds gusting to 50 mph brought down power cables.* • **gust** *noun* [C] *a gust of air* • **gusty** *adjective*

gusto /'gʌstəʊ/ *noun* **with gusto** with a lot of energy and enthusiasm *Everyone joined in the singing with great gusto.*

gut¹ /gʌt/ *noun* [C] the tube in your body that takes food from your stomach to be passed out as waste

gut² /gʌt/ *adjective* **gut reaction/feeling/instinct** a reaction, feeling, etc that you feel certain is right, although you have no reason to think so *I had a gut feeling that Travis was going to come back.*

gut³ /gʌt/ *verb* [T] **gutting** *past* **gutted 1** to remove the organs from inside a fish or other animal **2** to completely destroy or remove the inside of a building *A fire gutted the local bookshop last week.*

guts /gʌts/ *noun* [plural] *informal* **1** the bravery and determination that is needed to do something difficult or unpleasant *It **took guts** to stand up and tell her boss how she felt.* **2** the organs inside a person or animal's body **3 hate sb's guts** *informal* to dislike someone very much

gutsy /'gʌtsi/ *adjective* brave and determined *a gutsy performance*

gutted /'gʌtɪd/ *adjective* *UK informal* very disappointed and upset [+ (that)] *Neil's absolutely gutted that he's been dropped from the team.*

gutter /'gʌtəʳ/ *noun* [C] **1** a long, open pipe that is fixed to the edge of a roof to carry water away **2** the edge of a road where water flows away

ᴑ**guy** /gaɪ/ *noun informal* **1** [C] a man *What a nice guy!* **2 guys** used when you are talking to or about two or more people *Come on, you guys, let's go home.*

guzzle /'gʌzl/ *verb* [I, T] *informal* to eat or drink a lot of something quickly *Who's guzzled all the beer?*

gym /dʒɪm/ *noun* **1** [C] a building with equipment for doing exercises *Nick goes to the gym three times a week.* **2** [U] exercises done inside, especially as a school subject

gymnasium /dʒɪm'neɪziəm/ *noun* [C] a gym

gymnast /'dʒɪmnæst/ *noun* [C] someone who does gymnastics *an Olympic gymnast*

gymnastics /dʒɪm'næstɪks/ *noun* [U] a sport in which you do physical exercises on the floor and on different pieces of equipment, often in competitions

gymnastics

gynaecologist *UK* (*US* **gynecologist**) /,gaɪnə'kɒlədʒɪst/ *noun* [C] a doctor who treats medical conditions that only affect women

gynaecology *UK* (*US* **gynecology**) /,gaɪnə'kɒlədʒi/ *noun* [U] the study and treatment of diseases and medical conditions that only affect women • **gynaecological** /,gaɪnəkə'lɒdʒɪkəl/ *adjective*

gypsy (*also UK* **gipsy**) /'dʒɪpsi/ *noun* [C] a member of a race of people who travel from place to place, especially in Europe *a gypsy caravan*

Hh

H, h /eɪtʃ/ the eighth letter of the alphabet

ha /hɑː/ *exclamation* something you say when you are surprised or pleased

WORD PARTNERS FOR *habit*

get **into**/get **out of** the habit of doing sth • **have/kick** a habit • an **annoying/bad/good** habit • do sth **from/out of/through** habit

o▬**habit** /ˈhæbɪt/ *noun* **1** [REGULAR ACTIVITY] [C, U] something that you do regularly, almost without thinking about it *He's just eating out of habit - he's not really hungry.* **2 be in/get into the habit of doing sth** to be used/get used to doing something regularly *We don't want the children to get into the habit of watching a lot of TV.* **3** [BAD ACTIVITY] [C, U] something that you often do that is bad for your health or is annoying *He has some really nasty habits.* ○ *We offer help to alcoholics who want to kick the habit.* **4** [CLOTHING] [C] a long, loose piece of clothing worn by some religious groups *a monk's habit*

habitable /ˈhæbɪtəbl/ *adjective* A habitable building is in good enough condition to live in.

habitat /ˈhæbɪtæt/ *noun* [C] the natural environment of an animal or plant

habitation /ˌhæbɪˈteɪʃən/ *noun* [U] when people live in a place *This place is not fit for **human habitation**.*

habitual /həˈbɪtʃuəl/ *adjective* **1** usual or typical *an habitual expression/gesture* **2** doing something often because it is a habit *a habitual drug user* • **habitually** *adverb*

hack¹ /hæk/ *verb* [I, T] **1** to cut something roughly into pieces *The victim had been hacked to death.* **2** to use a computer to illegally get into someone else's computer system and read the information that is kept there *Two British youths were caught **hacking** into government computers.*

hack² /hæk/ *noun* [C] *informal* someone who produces low quality writing for books, newspapers, etc

hacker /ˈhækər/ *noun* [C] someone who illegally gets into someone else's computer system

o▬**had** *strong form* /hæd/ *weak forms* /həd, əd, d/ *verb* **1** *past of* have **2 be had** *informal* to be tricked or made to look silly *I think I've been had - this camera doesn't work.*

haddock /ˈhædək/ *noun* [C, U] *plural* haddock a fish that lives in northern seas and is eaten as food

o▬**hadn't** /ˈhædənt/ *short for* had not *I hadn't seen Megan since college.*

haemophilia UK (US hemophilia) /ˌhiːməˈfɪliə/ *noun* [U] a serious disease in which the flow of blood from someone's body cannot be stopped when they are hurt • **haemophiliac** UK (US

hemophiliac) *noun* [C] someone who has haemophilia

haemorrhage UK (US hemorrhage) /ˈhemərɪdʒ/ *noun* [C, U] when someone suddenly loses a lot of blood *a brain haemorrhage*

haemorrhoids UK (US hemorrhoids) /ˈhemərɔɪdz/ *noun* [plural] painful swollen tissue around the opening of a person's bottom

haggard /ˈhægəd/ *adjective* Someone who is haggard has a thin face with dark marks around their eyes because they are ill or tired.

haggle /ˈhægl/ *verb* [I] to argue, especially about the price of something *I spent 20 minutes haggling over the price of a leather bag.*

ha 'ha *exclamation* used in writing to represent the sound someone makes when they laugh

hail¹ /heɪl/ *noun* **1** [U] small, hard pieces of frozen rain that fall from the sky **2 a hail of bullets/stones/bottles, etc** a lot of bullets/stones/bottles, etc that are fired or thrown at the same time

hail² /heɪl/ *verb* **1** [T] to call or wave to someone to get their attention *She stepped into the road and hailed a taxi.* **2 it hails** If it hails, small, hard pieces of frozen rain fall from the sky.
hail sb/sth as sth to say publicly and enthusiastically that someone or something is something very good
hail from to come from a particular place

o▬**hair** /heər/ *noun* **1** [U] the thin, thread-like parts that grow on your head *a girl with long, fair hair* **2** [C] one of the thin thread-like parts that grow on a person's or animal's skin *My black skirt was covered in cat hairs.* **3 let your hair down** *informal* to relax and enjoy yourself **4 pull/tear your hair out** to be very anxious about something *When they still weren't home by midnight, I was pulling my hair out.* **5 split hairs** to argue about small details that are not important ⊃See also: pubic hair.

hairbrush /ˈheəbrʌʃ/ *noun* [C] a brush that you use to make your hair look tidy ⊃See picture at brush.

haircut /ˈheəkʌt/ *noun* [C] **1** when someone cuts your hair *I really need a haircut.* **2** the style in which your hair has been cut

hairdo /ˈheəduː/ *noun* [C] *informal* the style in which someone arranges their hair

hairdresser /ˈheəˌdresər/ *noun* **1** [C] someone whose job is to wash, cut, colour, etc people's hair **2 hairdresser's** the place where you go to have your hair washed, cut, coloured, etc

hairdryer /ˈheəˌdraɪər/ *noun* [C] a piece of electrical equipment for drying your hair with hot air

-haired /-ˈheəd/ *suffix* used after a word describing someone's hair *a red-haired woman* ○ *a short-haired cat* ⊃See also: fair-haired.

hairgrip /ˈheəgrɪp/ UK (US bobby pin) *noun* [C] a small, thin piece of metal, used to fasten a woman's hair in position

hairline /ˈheəlaɪn/ *noun* **1** [C] the place at the top of your face where your hair starts growing **2 a hairline crack/fracture** a very thin line where something hard such as a bone or cup is broken

hairpin /ˈheəpɪn/ *noun* [C] a piece of metal shaped like a U, used to fasten a woman's hair in position

,**hairpin 'bend** *UK* (*US* ,**hairpin 'turn**) *noun* [C] a bend shaped like a U on a steep road

hair-raising /ˈheəˌreɪzɪŋ/ *adjective* frightening but in an enjoyable way *It was a rather hair-raising journey down the mountain road.*

hairstyle /ˈheəstaɪl/ *noun* [C] the style in which someone arranges their hair *Do you like my new hairstyle?*

hairy /ˈheəri/ *adjective* **1** covered in hair *a hairy chest* ○ *hairy legs* **2** *informal* frightening or dangerous *There were some rather hairy moments during the race.* ● **hairiness** *noun* [U]

hajj (*plural* hajjes), *also* haj (*plural* hajes) /hædʒ/ *noun* [C] the religious journey to Mecca which all Muslims try to make at least once in their life

halal /hælˈæl/ *adjective* Halal meat is prepared according to Islamic law.

hale /heɪl/ *adjective* **hale and hearty** healthy and full of life

◦**half**[1] /hɑːf/ *noun, determiner plural* **halves** **1** [C, U] one of two equal parts of something; ½ *Rice is eaten by half of the world's population.* ○ *Divide the lemons into halves.* ○ *It'll take half an hour to get there.* ○ *Jenny lived in Beijing for a year and a half.* **2 break/cut/split sth in half** to divide something into two equal parts *Divide the dough in half and roll it out into two circles.* **3 decrease/increase, etc sth by half** to make something smaller/larger, etc by half its size *The drug reduces the risk of stroke by half.* **4 half past one/two/three, etc** *mainly UK* 30 minutes past one o'clock/two o'clock/three o'clock, etc *We got back to our hotel at half past seven.* **5 half one/two/three, etc** *UK informal* 30 minutes past one o'clock/two o'clock/three o'clock, etc *"What time does it start?" "About half six."* **6 go halves with sb** *informal* to divide the cost of something with someone *Shall we go halves on a present for Laura?* **7 half the fun/time/pleasure, etc** *informal* a large part of the enjoyment/time, etc *Kids today - parents don't know where they are half the time.* **8 not half as good/bad/exciting, etc** *informal* to be much less good/bad/exciting, etc than something else *Her new book's not half as good as the last one.*

half[2] /hɑːf/ *adverb* partly, but not completely *half empty/full* ○ *Sophia is half Greek and half Spanish* (= she has one Greek parent and one Spanish parent). ○ *She was only half aware of what was happening.*

,**half 'board** *noun* [U] *mainly UK* the price for a room in a hotel, which includes breakfast and dinner

half-brother /ˈhɑːfˌbrʌðər/ *noun* [C] a brother who is the son of only one of your parents

half-hearted /ˌhɑːfˈhɑːtɪd/ *adjective* without much effort or interest *a half-hearted attempt* ● **half-heartedly** *adverb*

half-sister /ˈhɑːfˌsɪstər/ *noun* [C] a sister who is

the daughter of only one of your parents

half-term /ˌhɑːfˈtɜːm/ *noun* [C, U] *UK* a short holiday in the middle of a school term (= one of the periods the school year is divided into)

half-time /ˌhɑːfˈtaɪm/ *noun* [U] a short period of rest between the two halves of a game

halfway /ˌhɑːfˈweɪ/ *adjective, adverb* at an equal distance between two places, or in the middle of a period of time *the halfway point* ○ *He was released halfway through his prison sentence.*

◦**hall** /hɔːl/ *noun* [C] **1** (*also* hallway /ˈhɔːlweɪ/) a room or passage in a building, which leads to other rooms **2** a large room or building where meetings, concerts, etc are held *The Albert Hall* ○ *The disco will be held in the school hall.* ⊃See also: **town hall**.

hallmark /ˈhɔːlmɑːk/ *noun* [C] **1** an official mark that is put on something made of silver or gold to prove that it is real **2** a quality or method that is typical of a particular type of person or thing *Simplicity is a hallmark of his design.*

hallo *UK* (*UK/US* hello) /həˈləʊ/ *exclamation* **1** used to greet someone *Hallo, Chris, how are things?* **2** used to start a conversation on the telephone *Hallo, this is Alex.*

,**hall of 'residence** *UK* (*US* dormitory) *noun* [C] *plural* **halls of residence** a building where university or college students live

hallowed /ˈhæləʊd/ *adjective* **1** respected and considered important *a hallowed tradition* **2** made holy by a priest *the hallowed ground of the churchyard*

Halloween /ˌhæləʊˈiːn/ *noun* [U] the night of 31 October when children dress in special clothes and people try to frighten each other

hallucinate /həˈluːsɪneɪt/ *verb* [I] to see things that are not really there, because you are ill or have taken an illegal drug

hallucination /həˌluːsɪˈneɪʃən/ *noun* [C, U] when you see things that are not really there because you are ill or have taken an illegal drug

halo /ˈheɪləʊ/ *noun* [C] a gold circle of light that is shown around the head of a holy person in a painting

WORD PARTNERS FOR *halt*

bring sth to/come to a halt ● an abrupt/grinding/sudden halt

halt[1] /hɒlt/ *noun* **1** [no plural] when something stops moving or happening *The car came to a halt just inches from the edge of the cliff.* ○ *News of the accident brought the party to a halt.* **2 call a halt to sth** to officially order something to stop *The government has called a halt to all new building in the area.*

halt[2] /hɒlt/ *verb* [I, T] *formal* to stop or make something stop *The council ordered that work on the project should be halted immediately.*

halting /ˈhɒltɪŋ/ *adjective* stopping often while you are saying or doing something, especially because you are nervous *He spoke quietly, in halting English.*

halve /hɑːv/ *verb* **1** [T] to divide something into two equal parts *Peel and halve the potatoes.* **2** [I, T] If you halve something, or if it halves, it

| ɑː arm | ɜː her | iː see | ɔː saw | uː too | aɪ my | aʊ how | eə hair | eɪ day | əʊ no | ɪə near | ɔɪ boy | ʊə poor | aɪə fire | aʊə sour |

is reduced to half the size it was before. *They have almost halved the price of flights to New York.*

ham /hæm/ *noun* [C, U] meat from a pig's back or upper leg *a ham sandwich*

hamburger /'hæm,bɜːɡəʳ/ *noun* **1** [C] a round, flat shape of meat which is cooked in hot oil and eaten between round pieces of bread *a hamburger and fries* **2** [U] *US* (*UK* mince) beef (= meat from a cow) that is cut into very small pieces

hamlet /'hæmlət/ *noun* [C] a very small village

hammer¹ /'hæməʳ/ *noun* [C] a **hammer** tool with a heavy, metal part at the top that you use to hit nails into something ⊃See picture at **tool**.

hammer² /'hæməʳ/ *verb* [I, T] to hit something with a hammer

hammer sth into sb to repeat something to someone a lot of times until they remember it

hammer on sth to hit something many times, making a lot of noise *They were woken up by someone hammering on the door.*

hammer sth out to finally agree on a plan, business agreement, etc after arguing about the details for a long time

hammering /'hæmᵊrɪŋ/ *noun* **1** [U] the noise made by hitting something with a hammer or hitting something hard with your hands **2** [no plural] *UK informal* a very bad defeat

hammock /'hæmək/ *noun* [C] a large piece of cloth or strong net that you hang between two trees or poles to sleep on

hamper¹ /'hæmpəʳ/ *verb* [T] to make it difficult for someone to do something *The police investigation was hampered by a lack of help from the community.*

hamper² /'hæmpəʳ/ *noun* [C] a large basket (= container made of thin pieces of wood) with a lid *a picnic hamper*

hamster /'hæmstəʳ/ *noun* [C] a small animal with soft fur and no tail that is often kept as a pet

hamstring¹ /'hæmstrɪŋ/ *noun* [C] a tendon (= part that connects a muscle to a bone) at the back of the upper part of your leg *a hamstring injury*

hamstring² /'hæmstrɪŋ/ *verb* [T] *past* **hamstrung** to make it difficult for a person, team, or organization to do something

o-ᴧ**hand**¹ /hænd/ *noun* **1** [ARM] [C] the part of your body on the end of your arm that has fingers and a thumb *Take your hands out of your pockets.* ⊃See colour picture **The Body** on page Centre 13. **2 take sb by the hand** to get hold of someone's hand *Bill took her by the hand and led her into the garden.* **3 hand in hand** holding each other's hand *The young couple walked hand in hand by the lake.* **4 hold hands** to hold each other's hand **5 at hand** near in time or space *Teachers are always close at hand to give help to any child who needs it.* **6 by hand** done or made by a person instead of a machine *This sweater has to be washed by hand.* **7 in hand**

being worked on or dealt with now *Despite the pressures we are determined to get on with the job in hand.* **8 be in sb's hands** to be in someone's control or care *The matter is now in the hands of my solicitor.* **9 on hand** (*also UK* **to hand**) near to someone or something, and ready to help or be used when necessary *Extra supplies will be on hand, should they be needed.* **10 at the hands of sb** If you suffer at the hands of someone, they hurt you or treat you badly. **11** [CLOCK] [C] one of the long, thin pieces that point to the numbers on a clock or watch **12** [CARDS] [C] the set of playing cards that one player has been given in a game **13 a hand** some help, especially to do something practical *Could you give me a hand with these suitcases?* ○ *I think Matthew might need a hand with his homework.* **14 on the one hand ... on the other hand** used when you are comparing two different ideas or opinions *On the one hand, computer games develop many skills, but on the other, they mean kids don't get enough exercise.* **15 hands off** *informal* used to tell someone not to touch something *Hands off - that's mine!* **16 change hands** to be sold by someone and bought by someone else *The hotel has changed hands twice since 1982.* **17 a free hand** permission to make your own decisions about how you want to do something **18 get out of hand** to become difficult to control *It was the end of term and the children were getting a little out of hand.* **19 go hand in hand** If two things go hand in hand, they exist together and are connected with each other. **20 have your hands full** to be very busy *Shelley has her hands full with three kids under 5.* **21 get/lay your hands on sth** to find something *I wanted to give you that report but I haven't managed to lay my hands on it yet.* **22 get/gain the upper hand** to get into a stronger position than someone else so that you are controlling a situation *Government troops are gradually gaining the upper hand over the rebels.* **23 with your bare hands** without using a weapon or tool **24 wring your hands** to press your hands together because you are upset or worried about something

hand² /hænd/ *verb* **1** [+ two objects] to give something to someone *Could you hand me that book, please?* **2 you have to hand it to sb** *informal* used when you want to show that you admire someone *You have to hand it to Mick, he's done a good job on that kitchen.*

hand sth back to return something to the person who gave it to you

hand sth down **1** to give toys, clothes, books, etc to children who are younger than you in your family **2** to pass traditions from older people to younger ones *a custom handed down through the generations*

hand sth in to give something to someone in a position of authority *Have you handed your history essay in yet?*

hand sth out to give something to all the people in a group *A girl was handing out leaflets at the station.*

hand sb/sth over to give someone or something to someone else *The hijacker was* *handed over to the French police.*

-hand /hænd/ ⊃See **left-hand, right-hand, second-hand**.

handbag /'hændbæg/ *mainly UK* (*mainly US* **purse**) *noun* [C] a bag carried by a woman with her money, keys, etc inside ⊃See picture at **bag**.

handbook /'hændbʊk/ *noun* [C] a book that contains information and advice about a particular subject *a teacher's handbook*

handbrake /'hændbreɪk/ *UK* (*US* **emergency brake**) *noun* [C] a stick inside a car that you can pull up to stop the car from moving ⊃See colour picture **Car** on page Centre 7.

handcuffs
/'hændkʌfs/ *noun*
[plural] two metal
rings that are joined
by a chain and are
put on a prisoner's
wrists (= lower arm)

handcuffs

-handed /'hændɪd/
suffix ⊃See **empty-handed, heavy-handed, left-handed, red-handed, right-handed, single-handed.**

handful /'hændfʊl/ *noun* **1** [C] the amount of something that you can hold in one hand **2 a handful of sth** a small number of people or things *Only a handful of people came to the meeting.* **3 a handful** *informal* someone who is difficult to control, especially a child

handgun /'hændɡʌn/ *noun* [C] a small gun that you can hold in one hand

hand-held /'hændheld/ *adjective* describes something that is designed to be held and used easily with one or two hands *a hand-held computer/device*

handicap /'hændɪkæp/ *noun* [C] *old-fashioned* **1** something that is wrong with your mind or body permanently *a mental/physical handicap* **2** something that makes it more difficult for you to do something *I found not having a car quite a handicap in the countryside.*

handicapped /'hændɪkæpt/ *adjective old-fashioned* not able to use part of your body or your mind because it has been damaged in some way *mentally/physically handicapped*

handicraft /'hændɪkrɑːft/ *noun* **1** [C] an activity that involves making things with your hands and that needs skill and artistic ability **2 handicrafts** things that people make with their hands *a sale of handicrafts*

handiwork /'hændɪwɜːk/ *noun* [U] something that someone makes or does *Georgina put down the brush and stood back to* **admire** *her* **handiwork**.

handkerchief /'hæŋkətʃiːf/ *noun* [C] a small piece of cloth or soft paper that you use to dry your eyes or nose

⦿ **handle**[1] /'hændl/ *verb* [T] DEAL WITH **1** to deal with something *He handled the situation very well.* ○ *This office handles thousands of enquiries every day.* **2** TOUCH to touch, hold, or pick up something *You must wash your hands before handling food.* **3** BUY to buy and sell goods *He's been charged with* **handling stolen goods**.

handle

handles

handle[2] /'hændl/ *noun* **1** [C] the part of something that you use to hold it or open it *a door handle* ○ *the handle on a suitcase* **2 fly off the handle** *informal* to suddenly become very angry

handlebars /'hændlbɑːz/ *noun* [plural] the metal bars at the front of a bicycle or motorcycle that you hold onto to control direction

handler /'hændlə[r]/ *noun* [C] someone whose job is to deal with or control a particular type of thing *a police dog handler*

'hand ,luggage *noun* [U] small bags that you can carry onto an aircraft with you when you travel

handmade /,hænd'meɪd/ *adjective* made by hand instead of by machine

handout /'hændaʊt/ *noun* [C] **1** money or food that is given to people who are poor *Increasing numbers of people are dependent on government handouts.* **2** a copy of a document that is given to all the people in a class or meeting

handpicked /,hænd'pɪkt/ *adjective* carefully chosen for a particular purpose or job *a handpicked audience*

handset /'hændset/ *noun* [C] **1** the outer part of a mobile phone **2** the part of a telephone that you hold in front of your mouth and against your ear

,hands 'free *adjective* describes a piece of equipment, especially a telephone, that you can use without needing to hold it in your hand

handshake /'hændʃeɪk/ *noun* [C] the action of taking someone's right hand and shaking it when you meet or leave each other

handsome /'hændsəm/ *adjective* **1** A handsome man is attractive. *tall, dark and handsome* **2 a handsome profit/sum, etc** a large amount of money

hands-on /,hændz'ɒn/ *adjective* physically doing something and not only studying it or watching someone else do it *hands-on experience*

handwriting /'hænd,raɪtɪŋ/ *noun* [U] the way that someone forms the letters when they write with a pen or pencil

handwritten /,hænd'rɪtᵊn/ *adjective* written with a pen or pencil *a handwritten letter*

handy /'hændi/ *adjective* **1** useful or easy to use *a handy container/tool* **2 come in handy** *informal* to be useful at some time in the future *Don't throw those jars away - they might come in handy.* **3** *UK informal* near to a place *It's a nice house and it's **handy** for the station.* **4 be handy with sth** to be good at using something, usually a tool *Alessandro's very handy with a paintbrush.*

handyman /'hændimæn/ *noun* [C] *plural* **handymen** someone who is good at making things or repairing them

o→**hang**[1] /hæŋ/ *verb past* **hung 1** FASTEN [I, T] to fasten something so that the top part is fixed but the lower part is free to move, or to be fastened in this way *He **hung** his coat **on** the hook behind the door.* **2** *past also* **hanged** KILL [I, T] to kill someone by putting a rope around their neck and making them drop, or to die in this way **3** IN AIR [I] to stay in the air for a long time *Thick fog hung over the town.* ⊃See also: be/hang in the **balance**[1], hang your **head**[1] (in shame).

hang around *informal* (*also UK* **hang about**) **1** to spend time somewhere, usually without doing very much *There's nowhere for teenagers to go, so they just **hang around on street corners**.* **2 hang around with sb** to spend time with someone

hang on 1 *informal* to wait for a short time *Hang on - I'm almost finished.* **2** to hold something tightly *Hang on, we're going over a big bump here.*

hang onto sth *informal* to keep something *You should hang onto that - it might be worth something.*

hang out *informal* to spend a lot of time in a particular place or with a particular group of people

hang up to finish a conversation on the telephone by putting the phone down

hang sth up to put something such as a coat somewhere where it can hang *You can hang up your jacket over there.*

hang[2] /hæŋ/ *noun* **get the hang of sth** *informal* to gradually learn how to do or use something

hangar /'hæŋgə'/ *noun* [C] a large building where aircraft are kept

hanger /'hæŋə'/ (*also* **coat hanger**) *noun* [C] a wire, wooden, or plastic object for hanging clothes on

'**hang ˌglider** *noun* [C] a structure covered in cloth that you hold onto and float through the air

'**hang ˌgliding** *noun* [U] the sport of flying using a structure covered in cloth that you hang from

hangover /'hæŋəʊvə'/ *noun* [C] If you have a hangover, you feel ill because you drank too much alcohol the evening before.

hanker /'hæŋkə'/ *verb*

hanker after/for sth to want something very much, especially over a long period of time

hankie (*also* **hanky**) /'hæŋki/ *noun* [C] *informal short for* handkerchief

Hanukkah (also **Chanukah**) /'hɑːnəkə/ *noun* [C, U] a Jewish religious holiday lasting for eight

days in December

haphazard /ˌhæp'hæzəd/ *adjective* not planned, organized, controlled, or done regularly *The whole examination process seemed completely haphazard.* ● **haphazardly** *adverb*

hapless /'hæpləs/ *adjective literary* having bad luck

o→**happen** /'hæp²n/ *verb* [I] **1** If an event or situation happens, it exists or starts to be done, usually by chance. *Were you anywhere nearby when the accident happened?* ○ *We can't let a mistake like this happen again.* **2** to be the result of an action, situation, or event that someone or something experiences *Did you hear what **happened to** Jamie last night?* ○ *What happens if we can't get enough tickets?* **3 happen to do sth** to do something by chance *If you **happen to** see Peter, say "hi" for me.* ○ *You don't **happen to** know her phone number, do you?* **4 as it happens; it so happens** something that you say in order to introduce a surprising fact *As it happens, her birthday is the day after mine.*

happen on/upon sth/sb to find something or meet someone without planning to

happening /'hæp²nɪŋ/ *noun* [C] something that happens, often a strange event that is difficult to explain

happily /'hæpɪli/ *adverb* **1** HAPPY in a happy way *happily married* **2** WILLING in a way that is very willing *I'd happily drive you to the airport.* **3** LUCKY having a good or lucky result *Happily, the operation was a complete success.*

WORD PARTNERS FOR *happiness*

find happiness

happiness /'hæpɪnəs/ *noun* [U] the feeling of being happy

OTHER WAYS OF SAYING *happy*

A person who seems happy may be described as **cheerful**: *She's always very cheerful.*

If someone is happy because of something, they may be described as **pleased** or **glad**, and if they are extremely happy because of something, they may be described as **delighted**: *He was **pleased** that she had come back.* ● *I was so **glad** to see her.* ● *They are **delighted** with their new car.*

If someone is extremely happy and excited, they may be described as **ecstatic** or **elated**: *The new president was greeted by an **ecstatic** crowd.* ● *We were **elated** at the news.*

o→**happy** /'hæpi/ *adjective* **1** PLEASED pleased and in a good mood, especially because something good has happened *I'm glad you've finally found someone who **makes** you **happy**.* ○ *Jean seems much happier now that she's moved out.* **2 happy to do sth** to be willing to do something *I'd be very happy to help, if you need a hand.* **3** SHOWING HAPPINESS making you feel happy, or expressing happiness *Did the book have a **happy ending**?* **4** SATISFIED satisfied and not worried *Are you **happy with** your exam re-sults?* ○ *I'm not very **happy about** you travel-ling alone at night.* **5 Happy Birthday/New Year, etc** something friendly that you say to some-one on a special day or holiday *Happy Christ-mas!* ⊃Opposite **unhappy**.

happy-go-lucky /ˌhæpigəʊˈlʌki/ *adjective* not worried and not having any responsibilities

'happy ˌhour *noun* [usually singular] a period of time, usually in the early evening, when a bar (= a place where alcoholic drinks are sold and drunk) sells drinks more cheaply than usual

ˌhappy 'slapping *noun* [U] when a group of young people attack someone and photograph their attack with mobile phones

harass /ˈhærəs, həˈræs/ *verb* [T] to continue to annoy or upset someone over a period of time

harassed /ˈhærəst/ *adjective* tired and feeling anxious *harassed passengers*

WORD PARTNERS FOR *harassment*

be subjected to / suffer harassment
• racial/sexual harassment • harassment
of sb

---

harassment /ˈhærəsmənt/ *noun* [U] behaviour that annoys or upsets someone *sexual harassment*

harbour

harbour¹ *UK* (*US* **harbor**) /ˈhɑːbəʳ/ *noun* [C] an area of water near the coast where ships are kept and are safe from the sea

harbour² *UK* (*US* **harbor**) /ˈhɑːbəʳ/ *verb* [T] **1** If you harbour doubts, hopes, thoughts, etc, you feel or think about them for a long time. *He harboured dreams of one day becoming a pro-fessional footballer.* **2** to hide someone or something bad *to **harbour** a criminal*

○ᴗhard¹ /hɑːd/ *adjective* **1** FIRM firm and stiff, and not easy to press or bend *a hard surface* ○ *The seats in the waiting room were hard and un-comfortable.* **2** DIFFICULT difficult to do or understand [+ to do sth] *It must be hard to study with all this noise.* ○ *Quitting my job was the hardest decision I ever had to make.* **3** WITH EFFORT using or done with a lot of effort *the long, **hard struggle*** ○ *With a bit of **hard work** and determination we might still finish on time.* **4** UNPLEASANT full of problems and difficult to deal with *My grandparents had a very **hard** life.* **5** NOT KIND not gentle or kind *She had a cold, hard look in her eyes.* **6 be hard on sb a**

CRITICIZE to criticize someone too much or treat them unfairly *You shouldn't be so hard on yourself.* **b** MAKE UNHAPPY to make someone un-happy by causing them problems *Our divorce has been particularly hard on the children.* **7 be hard on sth** to damage something or make it have problems *Stress can be hard on any relationship.* **8 do/learn sth the hard way** to do or learn something by experiencing a lot of problems or difficulty ⊃See also: give sb a hard time¹.

○ᴗhard² /hɑːd/ *adverb* **1** with a lot of effort *She tried very **hard** but she wasn't quite fast enough.* ○ *You'll have to **work harder,** if you want to pass this exam.* **2** with a lot of force *It's been raining hard all day.* ○ *She kicked the ball as hard as she could.* **3 die hard** If a belief, custom, or habit dies hard, it is very difficult to change. *I'm afraid that **old habits die hard.*** **4 hit sb hard** *UK* If a situation or experi-ence hits you hard, it makes you so upset that you have difficulty dealing with it.

hardback /ˈhɑːdbæk/ *noun* [C] a book that has a thick, stiff cover

hard-boiled /ˌhɑːdˈbɔɪld/ *adjective* A hard-boiled egg has been boiled with its shell on, until the inside is solid.

ˌhard 'cash *noun* [U] coins and paper money

ˌhard 'copy *UK* (*US* **'hard ˌcopy**) *noun* [C, U] in-formation from a computer that has been printed on paper

hardcore (*also* **hard-core**) /ˈhɑːdˌkɔː/ *adjective* **1** extremely loyal to someone or something, and not willing to change *a **hard-core** follow-ing* **2** Hardcore magazines, films, etc show very active or offensive sexual acts. *hardcore pornography*

ˌhard 'core *noun* [no plural] a small group of people in society or an organization who are very active and determined not to change *a hard core of activists*

ˌhard 'currency *noun* [U] money that is valu-able and can be exchanged easily because it comes from a powerful country

ˌhard 'disk *noun* [C] a hard drive

'hard ˌdrive (*also* **hard disk**) *noun* [C] the part inside a computer that is not removed and stores very large amounts of information

ˌhard 'drugs *noun* [plural] very strong, illegal drugs

harden /ˈhɑːdᵊn/ *verb* [I, T] **1** to become hard and stiff, or to make something become hard and stiff *This island is formed from volcanic lava that has hardened into rock.* **2** to stop feeling emotions about someone or something, so that you seem less kind, gentle, or weak *hardened criminals*

hard-headed /ˌhɑːdˈhedɪd/ *adjective* very determined, and not willing to be influenced by your emotions *a hard-headed manager*

hard-hearted /ˌhɑːdˈhɑːtɪd/ *adjective* not caring how other people feel

hard-hitting /ˌhɑːdˈhɪtɪŋ/ *adjective* A hard-hit-ting speech, report, article, etc is very severe or criticizes someone or something a lot.

| ɑː arm | ɜː her | iː see | ɔː saw | uː too | aɪ my | aʊ how | eə hair | eɪ day | əʊ no | ɪə near | ɔɪ boy | ʊə poor | aɪə fire | aʊə sour |

,**hard 'line** *noun* [no plural] when someone is very strict and severe *Judge Tucker has a reputation for taking a hard line on criminals.* ● **hardline** /ˌhɑːdˈlaɪn/ *adjective* a **hardline policy** on illegal immigrants ○ a hardline stance on drug abuse

o⌐**hardly** /ˈhɑːdli/ *adverb* **1** almost not, or only a very small amount *I was so tired that I could hardly walk.* ○ *We've hardly ever spoken to each other.* ○ *There's hardly any food left in the fridge.* **2** used to emphasize that you think something is not likely, true, possible, etc *I hardly think she'll want to talk to me now that I have a new girlfriend.* ○ *You can hardly expect a pay-rise when you've only been working for a company for a month.*

COMMON LEARNER ERROR

hardly or **hard**

When you mean 'with a lot of effort or force', you should use the adverb **hard**, not 'hardly'.
We worked very hard.
~~We worked very hardly.~~

---

hard-nosed /ˌhɑːdˈnəʊzd/ *adjective* very determined, and not willing to be influenced by your emotions *a hard-nosed lawyer*

hard-pressed /ˌhɑːdˈprest/ *adjective* **1** be **hard-pressed to do sth** to not be able to do something, or have difficulty doing something *You'd be hard-pressed to find a better worker than Jeff.* ○ *Most people would be hard-pressed to name more than five or so members of the government.* **2** having problems because you are poor *hard-pressed farmers*

WORD PARTNERS FOR *hardship*

suffer hardship ● **economic/financial/ physical** hardship

hardship /ˈhɑːdʃɪp/ *noun* [C, U] a problem or situation that makes you suffer a lot, especially because you are very poor *They have suffered years of financial hardship.*

,**hard 'shoulder** UK (US **shoulder**) *noun* [C] the area on the edge of a main road where a car can stop in an emergency

,**hard 'up** *adjective informal* not having enough money

hardware /ˈhɑːdweəʳ/ *noun* [U] **1** the machines or equipment that your computer system is made from, not the programs ⊃Compare **software 2** tools and strong equipment, such as those used in the home or garden *a large hardware store*

hard-working /ˌhɑːdˈwɜːkɪŋ/ *adjective* doing a job seriously and with a lot of effort *She's a very hard-working student.*

hardy /ˈhɑːdi/ *adjective* strong enough to deal with bad conditions or difficult situations *Goats are very hardy animals.* ○ *A few hardy souls continue to swim in the sea in the middle of winter.*

hare /heəʳ/ *noun* [C] an animal like a large rabbit that can run very fast and has long ears

harem /ˈhɑːriːm/ ⑱ /ˈherəm/ *noun* [C] a group of women who live with or are married to one

man in some Muslim societies, or the place where these women live

WORD PARTNERS FOR *harm*

cause/do (sb/sth) harm ● **not come to** any harm ● **great/serious/untold** harm ● **harm to** sb

o⌐**harm**¹ /hɑːm/ *noun* **1** [U] hurt or damage *Smoking can cause serious harm to the lungs.* ○ *Alan would never do anyone any harm.* **2 not come to any harm** to not be hurt or damaged **3 not do any harm** to not be a bad thing to do and possibly be a good thing [+ to do sth] *It wouldn't do any harm to have another look.* **4 there's no harm in doing sth** used to say that something is not a bad thing to do and could possibly have a good effect *I suppose there's no harm in trying.* **5 not mean any harm** to not intend to hurt someone or damage something *I never meant him any harm, I just wanted him to leave me alone.* **6 out of harm's way** safe from a dangerous place or situation

o⌐**harm**² /hɑːm/ *verb* [T] to hurt someone or damage something *Thankfully no one was harmed in the accident.*

harmful /ˈhɑːmfʳl/ *adjective* causing or likely to cause harm *Doctors believe that smoking is harmful to your health.*

harmless /ˈhɑːmləs/ *adjective* **1** not able or not likely to cause any hurt or damage *Taken in small doses, this drug is completely harmless.* **2** not likely to shock or upset people *Their jokes seemed harmless enough.* ● **harmlessly** *adverb*

harmonica /hɑːˈmɒnɪkə/ *noun* [C] a small musical instrument that you blow into as you move it across your mouth

harmonious /hɑːˈməʊniəs/ *adjective* **1** friendly and peaceful *a harmonious business relationship* **2** having or making a pleasant sound

harmonize (*also UK* -**ise**) /ˈhɑːmənaɪz/ *verb* [I, T] **1** to be suitable together, or to make different people, plans, situations, etc suitable for each other *The gardens had been designed to harmonize with the natural landscape.* **2** to sing or play music in harmony

harmony /ˈhɑːməni/ *noun* **1** [U] when people are peaceful and agree with each other, or when different things seem right or suitable together *living together in peace and harmony* **2** [C, U] a pleasant sound in music, made by playing or singing a group of different notes together

harness¹ /ˈhɑːnɪs/ *noun* [C] **1** a set of straps fastened around a horse's body and connecting it to a vehicle that it will pull **2** a set of strong, flat ropes that fasten equipment to your body or fasten you to a vehicle to prevent you from moving too much *All climbers must wear safety harnesses and helmets.*

harness² /ˈhɑːnɪs/ *verb* [T] **1** to put a harness on a horse, or to connect a horse to a vehicle using a harness **2** to control something so that you can use its power or qualities for a particular purpose

harp¹ /hɑːp/ *noun* [C] a large wooden musical

H

instrument with many strings that you play with your fingers

harp² /hɑːp/ *verb*
harp on (about sb/sth) to talk about someone or something too much

harpoon /ˌhɑːˈpuːn/ *noun* [C] a weapon with a sharp point, used especially for hunting whales (= large sea animals)

harrowing /ˈhærəʊɪŋ/ *adjective* making you feel extremely frightened or upset *a harrowing experience*

harsh /hɑːʃ/ *adjective* **1** CRUEL cruel, unkind, or unpleasant in a way that seems unfair *harsh criticism/punishment* ○ *Taking him out of the game was bit harsh.* **2** DIFFICULT very cold, dangerous, or unpleasant and difficult to live in *harsh conditions* **3** STRONG too strong, bright, loud, etc *harsh chemicals* ○ *harsh lighting* ● **harshly** *adverb* ● **harshness** *noun* [U]

harvest¹ /ˈhɑːvɪst/ *noun* **1** [C, U] when crops are cut and collected from fields **2** [C] the quality or amount of crops that are collected

harvest² /ˈhɑːvɪst/ *verb* [I, T] to cut and collect crops when they are ready

☞**has** *strong form* /hæz/ *weak forms* /həz, əz, z/ *present simple he/she/it of* have

has-been /ˈhæzbiːn/ *noun* [C] *informal* someone who was famous or important in the past but is now ignored

hash /hæʃ/ *noun* **make a hash of sth** *UK informal* to do something very badly

hashish /ˈhæʃiːʃ/ (*also* hash) *noun* [U] an illegal drug that is usually smoked for pleasure

☞**hasn't** /ˈhæz²nt/ *short for* has not *It hasn't rained for three weeks.*

hassle¹ /ˈhæsl/ *noun* [C, U] **1** something that is annoying because it is difficult or unpleasant to do *I don't want to drive - it's such a hassle finding a place to park.* **2** an argument or fight *They aren't giving you any hassle, are they?*

hassle² /ˈhæsl/ *verb* [T] to annoy someone, especially by asking them something again and again *Isabella's always hassling me about money.*

⬛ WORD PARTNERS FOR **haste**

indecent/undue haste ● **in** sb's haste ● **do** sth **in** haste

haste /heɪst/ *noun* [U] when you are in a hurry and do something more quickly than you should *In their haste to escape, they left behind all their belongings.*

hasten /ˈheɪs²n/ *verb* **1** [T] to make something happen faster than usual **2 hasten to do sth** to hurry to do or say something *I was not, I hasten to add, the only male there.*

hasty /ˈheɪsti/ *adjective* done very quickly, usually too quickly and without thinking enough *a hasty decision/remark* ● **hastily** *adverb*

☞**hat** /hæt/ *noun* [C] something you wear to cover your head, for fashion or protection *a cowboy hat* ⊃See also: **bowler hat, top hat.**

hatch¹ /hætʃ/ *verb* **1** [I, T] If an egg hatches or is hatched, it is broken open by a baby creature such as a bird, fish, or snake being born.

2 hatch a plan/plot, etc to plan something secretly, especially something bad *He hatched a plot to kill his wife.*

hatch² /hætʃ/ *noun* [C] a small door or opening, especially in a ship, aircraft, or spacecraft *an escape hatch*

hatchback /ˈhætʃbæk/ *noun* [C] a car that has a large door at the back, which you lift up to open

hatchet /ˈhætʃɪt/ *noun* **1** [C] a small axe (= tool for cutting wood) **2 bury the hatchet** to forget about your arguments and become friends with someone again

☞**hate¹** /heɪt/ *verb* [T] **1** to dislike someone or something very much *They've hated each other since they were kids.* ○ [+ doing sth] *He hates going to the dentist's.* ○ [+ to do sth] *I hate to see you look so upset.* **2** used to emphasize that you are sorry you have to do something *I hate to interrupt, John, but we need to leave.* ⊃See also: hate sb's **guts.**

hate² /heɪt/ *noun* [U] when you dislike someone or something very much ⊃See also: **pet hate.**

hateful /ˈheɪtf²l/ *adjective* extremely unpleasant or unkind *She called me the most hateful names.*

⬛ WORD PARTNERS FOR **hatred**

deep/intense hatred ● **racial** hatred ● **hatred of** sb/sth

hatred /ˈheɪtrɪd/ *noun* [U] when you dislike someone or something very much *He developed an intense hatred of all women.*

'hat ˌtrick *noun* [C] when a player or team has three successes, one after the other, especially three goals in a game

haughty /ˈhɔːti/ *adjective* showing that you think you are much better or more important than other people *a haughty young actress* ● **haughtily** *adverb*

haul¹ /hɔːl/ *verb* [T] to pull something somewhere slowly and with difficulty *They hauled the piano into the living room.*

haul² /hɔːl/ *noun* **1** [C] an amount of something that has been stolen or that is owned illegally *a haul of arms/drugs* **2 be a long haul** to be difficult and take a long time

haulage /ˈhɔːlɪdʒ/ *noun* [U] *UK* the business of moving things by road or railway *a road haulage firm*

haunt¹ /hɔːnt/ *verb* [T] **1** If a ghost haunts a place, it appears there often. *a haunted house* **2** If an unpleasant memory or feeling haunts you, you think about or feel it often. [often passive] *He was haunted by memories of the war.*

haunt² /hɔːnt/ *noun* [C] a place that someone visits often *Regents Park is one of my favourite haunts in London.*

haunting /ˈhɔːntɪŋ/ *adjective* beautiful, but in a sad way *the haunting beauty of Africa*

☞**have¹** *strong form* /hæv/ *weak forms* /həv, əv, v/ *auxiliary verb* used with the past participle of another verb to form the present and past perfect tenses *Have you seen Roz?* ○ *I've passed my test.* ○ *He hasn't visited London before.* ○ *It would have been better to tell the truth.* ○ *He's* *been working in France for two years now.* ○ *I had met his wife before.*

o▪**have²** /hæv/ *modal verb* **have to do sth; have got to do sth 1** to need to do something or be forced to do something *I have to go to Manchester tomorrow.* ○ *Do we have to finish this today?* ○ *They've had to change their plans.* **2** used when you are telling someone how to do something *You've got to type in your name, then your password.* **3** used to say that you feel certain that something is true or will happen *Interest rates have to come down at some point.* ○ *There's* (= there has) *got to be a better way of doing this.* ⊃See Extra help page **Modal verbs** on page Centre 22 .

o▪**have³** *strong form* /hæv/ *weak forms* /həv/, /əv/, v/ *verb past* had **1** OWN [T] (*also* have got) to own something *I have two horses.* ○ *Laura has got beautiful blue eyes.* **2** HOLD [T] used to say that someone is holding something, or that someone or something is with them *He had a pen in his hand.* ○ *She had a baby with her.* **3** BE ILL [T] (*also* have got) If you have a particular illness, you are suffering from it. *Have you ever had the measles?* **4** EAT/DRINK [T] to eat or drink something *We are having dinner at 7 o'clock.* ○ *Can I have a drink of water?* **5 have a bath/ sleep/walk, etc** used with nouns to say that someone does something *Can I have a quick shower?* ○ *Let Mark have a try.* **6 have difficulty/fun/problems, etc** used with nouns to say that someone experiences something *We had a great time in Barcelona.* **7 have a baby** to give birth to a baby **8 have sth done** If you have something done, someone does it for you. *I'm having my hair cut tomorrow.* ○ *We had the carpets cleaned.* **9 have had it** to be broken or not working well *I think the car engine's had it.* **10 have it in for sb** to dislike someone and want to cause problems for them *She really has it in for me - I don't know what I've done to offend her.* **11 have it out (with sb)** to talk to someone about something they have done which makes you angry, in order to try to solve the problem

have (got) sth on to be wearing something *She only had a bikini on.*

have sb on *UK* to make someone think that something is true, as a joke *He's not really angry - he's just having you on.*

have sth out to have something removed from your body *I'm having two teeth out next week.*

haven /ˈheɪvᵊn/ *noun* [C] a safe place *a haven for wildlife*

o▪**haven't** /ˈhævᵊnt/ *short for* have not *I haven't finished eating.*

WORD PARTNERS FOR *havoc*

cause/create/wreak havoc ● play havoc with sth

havoc /ˈhævək/ *noun* [U] a very confused and possibly dangerous situation *The snow has caused havoc on Scotland's roads today.*

hawk /hɔːk/ *noun* [C] a large hunting bird

hay /heɪ/ *noun* [U] dried grass for animals to eat

hay ˌfever *noun* [U] an illness caused by a bad reaction to plants that some people get in the summer, especially affecting the nose and eyes

haystack /ˈheɪstæk/ *noun* [C] a large pile of hay

hazard¹ /ˈhæzəd/ *noun* **1** [C] something that is dangerous *a fire hazard* ○ *a health hazard* **2 an occupational hazard** something unpleasant that sometimes happens to people who do a particular job

hazard² /ˈhæzəd/ *verb* **hazard a guess** to risk guessing something *I don't know where he is, but I'd be willing to hazard a guess.*

hazardous /ˈhæzədəs/ *adjective* dangerous *hazardous chemicals*

haze /heɪz/ *noun* [U] when the air is not very clear because of something such as heat or smoke, making it difficult to see well

hazel /ˈheɪzᵊl/ *adjective* green-brown in colour *hazel eyes*

hazy /ˈheɪzi/ *adjective* **1** If the air is hazy, it is not very clear because of something such as heat or smoke, making it difficult to see well. *a hazy day* **2** not remembering things clearly *He has only a hazy recollection of what happened.*

o▪**he** *strong form* /hiː/ *weak form* /hi/ *pronoun* used as the subject of the verb when referring to someone male who has already been talked about *"When is Paul coming?" "He'll be here in a minute."*

o▪**head¹** /hed/ *noun* [C] **1** BODY the part of your body above your neck which contains your brain, eyes, ears, mouth, nose, etc and on which your hair grows *He fell and hit his head on the table.* ⊃See colour picture **The Body** on page Centre 13. **2** MIND your mind *All these thoughts were going round in my head.* **3** ORGANIZATION the person who is in charge of an organization *Her father is the head of an oil company* **4** SCHOOL (*also* ˌhead ˈteacher) *UK* the person in charge of a school *You'll have to ask the head if you can have a day off school.* **5** FRONT/TOP the front or top part of something *Who is that at the head of the table?* **6 £10/$6, etc a head** costing £10/$6, etc for each person *The meal costs £20 a head.* **7 heads** the side of a coin that has a picture of someone's head on it *Heads or tails?* **8 be banging your head against a brick wall** to try, say, or ask for something repeatedly but to be unable to change a situation **9 come to a head** If a problem or disagreement comes to a head, it becomes so bad that you have to start dealing with it. **10 go over sb's head** to be too difficult for someone to understand *All this talk about philosophy went right over my head.* **11 go to your head** If something that you have achieved goes to your head, it makes you too proud. *Fame and fortune had gone to his head.* **12 hang your head (in shame)** to look ashamed or embarrassed **13 keep your head** to stay calm in a difficult situation **14 lose your head** to stop being calm in a difficult situation **15 raise/rear its ugly head** If a problem or something unpleasant raises its ugly head, it becomes a problem that people have to deal with. **16 laugh/shout/scream, etc your head off** to laugh/shout/scream, etc very much and very loudly ⊃See also: hit the **nail¹** on the head, a **roof**

head, off the **top**[1] of your head.

/hed/ *verb* **1 head back/down/towards, etc** ...ove in a particular direction *They headed* ...k to the shore. **2** LEAD [T] to lead an organ- ...zation or group [often passive] *The company is headed by a young entrepreneur.* **3** FRONT/TOP [T] to be at the front or top of something *Jo headed a very short list of candidates.* **4** HIT [T] to hit a ball with your head *Owen headed the ball straight into the back of the net.*

be heading for sth to be likely to get or experience something soon *Those children are heading for trouble.*

head off to start a journey or leave a place

headache /'hedeɪk/ *noun* [C] pain inside your head *I've got a bad headache.* ⊃See also: **splitting headache.**

headhunt /'hedhʌnt/ *verb* [T] to persuade some- one to leave their job for a job with a different company *She was headhunted by a rival firm.* • **headhunter** *noun* [C]

heading /'hedɪŋ/ *noun* [C] words at the top of a piece of writing that tell you what it is about

headlight /'hedlaɪt/ *noun* [C] one of the two large lights on the front of a car ⊃See picture at **light.**

headline /'hedlaɪn/ *noun* **1** [C] the title of a newspaper story that is printed in large letters above it *a front-page headline* **2 the headlines** the main stories in newspapers, on television, etc *That story was in the headlines all over the world.*

headlong /'hedlɒŋ/ *adverb* quickly and dir- ectly *The plane plunged headlong into the sea.*

headmaster /ˌhed'mɑːstəʳ/ UK (US **principal**) *noun* [C] a man who is in charge of a school

headmistress /ˌhed'mɪstrəs/ UK (US **principal**) *noun* [C] a woman who is in charge of a school

head 'office *noun* [usually singular] the most important office of a company, or the people who work there *Head office handles all com- plaints made against the company.*

head 'on *adverb* **1** If two vehicles hit each other head on, the front parts hit each other as they are moving forward. **2** If you deal with something head on, you deal with it directly, although it is difficult. • **head-on** /ˌhed'ɒn/ *ad- jective a head-on collision*

headphones
/'hedfəʊnz/ *noun* [plural] a piece of equipment that you wear over your ears so that you can listen to music without anyone else hearing it *a pair of head- phones*

headphones

headquarters
/'hedˌkwɔːtəz/ *noun* [group] *plural* head- quarters the place from where an organ- ization is controlled *police headquarters*

headset /'hedset/ *noun* [C] a piece of equipment

that you wear over your ears so that you can hear things, especially one with a microphone (= a piece of equipment that you speak into) attached to it *a mobile phone headset*

head 'start *noun* [C] an advantage that some- one has over other people *Caroline's language skills should give her a head start over/on other people applying for the job.*

headstone /'hedstəʊn/ *noun* [C] a stone that shows the name of a dead person who is buried under it

headstrong /'hedstrɒŋ/ *adjective* extremely determined *a headstrong young girl*

headteacher /ˌhed'tiːtʃəʳ/ UK (US **principal**) *noun* [C] the person in charge of a school

headway /'hedweɪ/ *noun* **make headway** to make progress in what you are doing *The builders aren't making much headway with our new house.*

heady /'hedi/ *adjective* having a powerful effect on the way you feel, for example by making you feel excited *a heady experience*

heal /hiːl/ (*also* **heal up**) *verb* [I, T] If a wound or broken bone heals, it becomes healthy again, and if something heals it, it makes it healthy again. *The wound on his head had begun to heal.* • **healer** *noun* [C] someone who makes ill people well again using something such as prayer or magic

WORD PARTNERS FOR **health**

> **damage/improve** sb's health • **excellent/ good/ill/poor** health • **be in** [good/bad, etc] health

health /helθ/ *noun* [U] **1** the condition of your body *to be in good/poor health* ○ *Regular exer- cise is good for your health.* **2** how successful and strong something is *the financial health of the business* ⊃See also: **the National Health Service.**

health-care /'helθˌkeəʳ/ *noun* [U] the set of ser- vices provided by a country or an organiza- tion for treating people who are ill

health 'service *noun* [C] UK the National Health Service: the system providing a free medical service in the UK

healthy /'helθi/ *adjective* **1** PHYSICALLY STRONG physically strong and well *Sue is a normal healthy child.* **2** GOOD good for your health *a healthy diet* **3** SUCCESSFUL successful and strong *a healthy economy* ⊃Opposite **unhealthy.**

COMMON LEARNER ERROR

healthy or **health**?

Remember not to use 'healthy' as a noun. If you need a noun, use **health**.

She has some health problems.

~~She has some healthy problems.~~

WORD PARTNERS FOR **heap**

> a heap **of** sth • **in** a heap

heap[1] /hiːp/ *noun* **1** [C] an untidy pile of things *a heap of rubbish* **2 heaps of sth** *informal* a lot of something *He's got heaps of money.*

heap² /hiːp/ *verb informal* **1** [T] to put things into an untidy pile *He heaped more food onto his plate.* **2 heap criticism/insults/praise, etc on sb** to criticize/insult/praise, etc someone a lot

oa**hear** /hɪəʳ/ *verb past heard* **1** [SOUND] [I, T] to be aware of a sound through your ears *I could hear his voice in the distance.* ○ *I can't hear - can you turn the sound up?* **2** [INFORMATION] [I, T] to be told some information *When did you first hear about this?* ○ *Have you heard the news? Jane's back.* ○ [+ (that)] *I hear that you're leaving.* **3** [LAW] [T] If a judge hears a case, they listen to it in a law court, to decide if someone is guilty or not. **4 will not hear of sth** If someone will not hear of something, they will not allow it. *I wanted to pay for her meal but she wouldn't hear of it.*

hear from sb to receive a letter, telephone call, or other message from someone *Have you heard from Sue recently?*

have heard of sb/sth to know that someone or something exists *I've never heard of her.*

hearing /'hɪərɪŋ/ *noun* **1** [U] the ability to hear sounds *He lost his hearing when he was a child.* **2** [C] a meeting in a law court when a judge hears the facts of a case *The preliminary hearing will take place next week.* **3 a fair hearing** If you get a fair hearing, someone listens to your opinion.

hearing-impaired /'hɪərɪŋɪmˌpeəd/ *adjective* A person who is hearing-impaired cannot hear or cannot hear well. ⊃Compare **deaf**.

hearsay /'hɪəseɪ/ *noun* [U] things that people have told you and that may or may not be true *Everything we heard was based on hearsay and rumour.*

hearse /hɜːs/ *noun* [C] a large car that is used to take a dead body to a funeral

⬚ WORD PARTNERS FOR *heart*

your heart **beats** • heart **disease/failure** • a heart **condition/problem**

heart

oa**heart** /hɑːt/ *noun* **1** [ORGAN] [C] the organ inside your chest that sends blood around your body *Isabel's heart was beating fast.* ○ *heart disease/failure* **2** [CENTRE] [no plural] the centre of something *Her office is in the heart of Tokyo.* **3 the heart of sth** the most important part of something *We need to get to the heart of the matter.* **4** [FEELINGS] [C, U] someone's deepest feel-

ings and true character *She has a kind heart.* **5** [SHAPE] [C] a shape that is used to mean love **6 hearts** playing cards with red, heart shapes on them **7 at heart** used to say what someone is really like *I'm just a kid at heart.* **8 in your heart** used to say what you really think *In his heart he felt they were wrong.* **9 with all your heart** used to say that you feel something very strongly *I thank you with all my heart.* **10 not have the heart to do sth** to decide not to do something that would make someone unhappy **11 learn/know, etc sth by heart** to be able to remember all of something **12 break sb's heart** to make someone very unhappy **13 heart and soul** used to say that you give all your attention and enthusiasm to something *She threw herself into teaching heart and soul.* ⊃See also: a **change²** of heart.

heartache /'hɑːteɪk/ *noun* [C, U] extreme sadness *joys and heartaches*

'heart at,tack *noun* [C] when someone's heart suddenly stops working correctly, sometimes causing death *I think he's had a heart attack.*

heartbeat /'hɑːtbiːt/ *noun* [C, U] the regular movement of the heart as it moves blood around the body

heartbreaking /'hɑːtˌbreɪkɪŋ/ *adjective* causing extreme sadness *heartbreaking news*

heartbroken /'hɑːtˌbrəʊkⁿn/ *adjective* If you are heartbroken, you feel extremely sad about something that has happened.

-hearted /-'hɑːtɪd/ ⊃See **broken-hearted, cold-hearted, half-hearted, hard-hearted, light-hearted.**

heartened /'hɑːtⁿnd/ *adjective* feeling happier because of something *We all felt heartened by the news.* ⊃Opposite **disheartened.**

heartening /'hɑːtⁿnɪŋ/ *adjective* making you feel happier *heartening news* ⊃Opposite **disheartening.**

'heart ,failure *noun* [U] when someone's heart stops working, often causing death

heartfelt /'hɑːtfelt/ *adjective* Heartfelt feelings and words are strong and sincere. *heartfelt thanks/gratitude*

hearth /hɑːθ/ *noun* [C] the floor around a fireplace *hearth and home*

heartily /'hɑːtɪli/ *adverb* **1** with a lot of enthusiasm *We all laughed heartily at the joke.* **2** completely or very much *I am heartily sick of the situation.*

heartland /'hɑːtlænd/ *noun* [C] the place where an activity or belief is strongest *the traditional heartland of the motor industry*

heartless /'hɑːtləs/ *adjective* cruel and not caring about other people

heart-to-heart /,hɑːttə'hɑːt/ *noun* [C] a serious conversation between two people in which they talk honestly about their feelings

hearty /'hɑːti/ *adjective* **1** friendly and full of energy *a hearty laugh/welcome* **2** Hearty meals are large and satisfy you.

⬚ WORD PARTNERS FOR *heat*

generate/give out heat • **intense/searing** heat

d noun **1** HOT [U] the quality of being warm *the heat of summer* **2 the heat** it is very hot *I don't really like the heat.* TEMPERATURE [U, no plural] the temperature of _ething Cook on a low heat._ **4 the heat** US (UK **the heating**) the system that keeps a building warm *Could you turn the heat up a little.* **5** RACE [C] a competition, especially a race, which decides who will be in the final event **6 in the heat of the moment** If you do or say something in the heat of the moment, you do or say it without thinking because you are angry or excited. ⊃See also: **dead heat.**

heat² /hi:t/ (*also* **heat up**) *verb* [I, T] to make something become hot or warm, or to become hot or warm *I'll just heat up some soup.*

heated /'hi:tɪd/ *adjective* **1** made warm or hot **2 a heated argument/debate, etc** an angry or excited argument

heater /'hi:tər/ *noun* [C] a machine that heats air or water

heath /hi:θ/ *noun* [C] an open area of land covered with wild plants and rough grass

heather /'heðər/ *noun* [C, U] a small plant with purple or white flowers that grows on hills

heating /'hi:tɪŋ/ *UK* (*US* **heat**) *noun* [U] the system that keeps a building warm ⊃See also: **central heating.**

heatwave /'hi:tweɪv/ *noun* [C] a period of time, usually a few days or weeks, when the weather is much hotter than usual

heave /hi:v/ *verb* **1** [I, T] to move something heavy using a lot of effort *He heaved the bag on to his shoulder.* **2** [I] to move up and down *Her chest heaved as she started to cry.* **3 heave a sigh of relief** to breathe out loudly because you are pleased that something bad has not happened ● **heave** *noun* [C]

heaven /'hevən/ *noun* [U] **1** according to some religions, the place where good people go when they die **2** *informal* something very nice that gives you great pleasure *This cake is absolute heaven.*

heavenly /'hevənli/ *adjective* **1** [always before noun] relating to heaven *the heavenly kingdom* **2** *informal* very nice *a heavenly day*

heavens /'hevənz/ *noun* **1 the heavens** *literary* the sky **2 (Good) Heavens!** used when you are surprised or annoyed *Heavens, what's the matter?*

heavily /'hevɪli/ *adverb* **1** a lot or to a great degree *She's heavily involved in politics.* **2 drink/smoke heavily** to drink/smoke a lot **3 rain/snow heavily** to rain/snow a lot **4** using a lot of force *to breathe heavily*

o~**heavy** /'hevi/ *adjective* **1** WEIGHING A LOT Heavy objects weigh a lot. *heavy bags* ○ *heavy machinery/equipment* **2** HOW MUCH used to say how much someone or something weighs *How heavy are you?* ○ *Oxygen is sixteen times heavier than hydrogen.* **3** A LOT large in amount or degree *heavy traffic* ○ *heavy costs* **4 a heavy drinker/smoker** someone who drinks/smokes a lot **5 heavy snow/rain** when a lot of snow/rain falls **6** FORCE using a lot of force *a heavy blow* ○ *heavy breathing* **7** SERIOUS *informal* serious *The discussion got a bit too heavy.* **8 heavy**

going *mainly UK* too serious or difficult *I found the book very heavy going.*

heavy-handed /ˌhevi'hændɪd/ *adjective* using too much force in dealing with people

heavy 'metal *noun* [U] a type of very loud, modern music

heavyweight /'heviweɪt/ *noun* [C] **1** a fighter such as a boxer who is in the heaviest weight group *the heavyweight champion of the world* **2** someone who is powerful and important *a political heavyweight*

Hebrew /'hi:bru:/ *noun* [U] the language used in the Jewish religion and in Israel ● **Hebrew** *adjective*

hectare /'hekteər/ *noun* [C] a unit for measuring area, equal to 10,000 square metres

hectic /'hektɪk/ *adjective* extremely busy and full of activity *a hectic day/week*

o~**he'd** /hi:d/ **1** *short for* he had *We knew he'd taken the money.* **2** *short for* he would *No one thought he'd get the job.*

hedge¹ /hedʒ/ *noun* [C] a row of bushes growing close together, often used to divide land into separate areas

hedge

hedge² /hedʒ/ *verb* [I, T] to avoid giving a direct answer ⊃See also: hedge your bets (bet²).

hedgehog /'hedʒhɒg/ *noun* [C] a small animal whose body is covered with sharp spines

hedgerow /'hedʒrəʊ/ *noun* [C] *UK* a row of bushes and small trees along the edge of a field or road

heed¹ /hi:d/ *verb* [T] *formal* to pay attention to some advice or a warning *Officials failed to heed his warning.*

heed² /hi:d/ *noun formal* **take heed of sth** to pay attention to something, especially some advice or a warning

heel /hi:l/ *noun* [C] **1** the back part of your foot ⊃See colour picture **The Body** on page Centre 13. **2** the part of a shoe that is under your heel *high heels*

hefty /'hefti/ *adjective informal* very large *a hefty bill/fine* ○ *a hefty woman with dyed hair*

WORD PARTNERS FOR **height**

grow to/reach a height of sth ● be [3 metres, etc] **in** height

o~**height** /haɪt/ *noun* **1** HOW TALL [C, U] how tall or high something or someone is *a man of average height* ○ *The tower measures 27.28 metres in height.* **2** HOW FAR UP [C, U] how far above the ground something is *The aircraft was flying at a height of about 6000 metres.* **3** TALL [U] being tall *People always make comments about his height.* **4 the height of sth** the strongest or most important part of something *I met him when he was at the height of his fame.*

heighten /'haɪtən/ *verb* [I, T] to increase or make something increase *heightened aware-*

ness ○ [often passive] *The book's success was heightened by the scandal.*

heights /haɪts/ *noun* **1** [plural] high places *I've always been afraid of heights.* **2 new heights** when something is better or more successful than ever before *Our athletes have reached new heights of sporting glory.*

heinous /'heɪnəs/ *adjective formal* very bad and shocking *heinous crimes*

heir /eəʳ/ *noun* [C] a person who will have the legal right to someone's money and possessions when they die *He is the **heir to** a huge fortune.*

heiress /'eəres/ *noun* [C] a woman who will have the legal right to someone's money and possessions when they die

held /held/ *past of* hold

helicopter

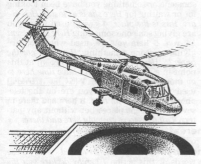

helicopter /'helɪkɒptəʳ/ *noun* [C] an aircraft which flies using long, thin parts on top of it that turn round and round very fast

helium /'hiːliəm/ *noun* [U] a gas that is lighter than air and that will not burn *a helium balloon*

o-**he'll** /hiːl/ *short for* he will *He'll be home soon.*

o-**hell** /hel/ *noun* **1** [U] according to some religions, the place where bad people go when they die **2** [U] *informal* an experience that is very unpleasant *It's been hell working with him.* **3 the hell** *informal* used to emphasize something in a rude or angry way *What the hell are you doing here?* **4 a/one hell of a** *informal* used to say that someone or something is very good, big, etc *a hell of a noise* ○ *He's one hell of a tennis player.* **5 from hell** *informal* used to say that someone or something is extremely bad *We had the holiday from hell.* **6 like hell** *informal* very much *It's raining like hell out there.*

hellish /'helɪʃ/ *adjective informal* extremely bad or unpleasant *a hellish place/journey*

o-**hello** (*also UK* hallo) /hel'əʊ/ *exclamation* **1** used to greet someone *Hello, Chris, how are things?* **2** used to start a conversation on the telephone *Hello, this is Alex.*

helm /helm/ *noun* **1** [C] the part that you use to direct a boat or ship **2 at the helm** controlling a group or organization *With Lewis at the helm we are certain of success.*

helmet /'helmət/ *noun* [C] a hard hat that protects your head *a cycling helmet* ➔See also: **crash helmet** ➔See colour picture **Sports 2** on page Centre 15.

helmet

OTHER WAYS OF SAYING *help*

The verbs **aid** and **assist** are more formal alternatives to 'help': *The army arrived to **assist** in the search.* ● *The project is designed to **aid** poorer countries.*

If two or more people help each other in order to achieve the same thing, verbs such as **collaborate** or **cooperate** are sometimes used: *Several countries are **collaborating/cooperating** in the relief effort.*

The verb **benefit** is sometimes used when someone is helped by something: *We have **benefited** greatly from the new facilities.*

If someone is asking for help, in informal situations the expression **give** someone **a hand** is sometimes used: *Do you think you could **give** me **a hand** with these heavy boxes?*

o-**help¹** /help/ *verb* **1** [I, T] to make it easier for someone to do something [+ (to) do sth] *Shall I help you to set the table?* ○ *Dad always **helps** me **with** my homework.* **2** [I, T] to make something easier or better [+ to do sth] *When you're nervous or frightened, it helps to breathe slowly and deeply.* **3 can't/couldn't help sth** to be unable to stop yourself doing something or to stop something happening [+ doing sth] *I couldn't help thinking about what had happened.* ○ *He couldn't help it, he slipped.* **4 help yourself (to sth)** to take something, especially food or drink, without asking *Please help yourself to some coffee.*

help (sb) out to help someone, especially by giving them money or working for them *Carol's been helping out in the shop this week.*

WORD PARTNERS FOR *help*

ask for/need/offer/provide/refuse help ● a **big/great** help ● **extra/professional** help

o-**help²** /help/ *noun* **1** [U] when someone helps another person *I was too embarrassed to **ask for** help.* ○ *Do you want any help?* **2** [no plural] something or someone that helps *Dave has been a great help to me.* **3 with the help of sth** using something *We assembled the computer with the help of the manual.*

help³ /help/ *exclamation* something that you shout when you are in danger

'**help ˌdesk** *noun* [C] a service which provides help to the people who use a computer network (= a group of computers that share information and programs)

helper /'helpəʳ/ *noun* [C] someone who helps another person to do something

helpful /'helpfəl/ *adjective* **1** useful *helpful advice/comments* **2** willing to help *The staff here are very helpful.* ➔Opposite **unhelpful.** ● **helpfully** *adverb* ● **helpfulness** *noun* [U]

helping /ˈhelpɪŋ/ *noun* [C] an amount of food given to one person at one time *She gave me a very large helping of pasta.*

helpless /ˈhelpləs/ *adjective* not able to defend yourself or do things without help *a helpless animal/child* • **helplessly** *adverb*

helpline /ˈhelplaɪn/ *noun* [C] *UK* a telephone number that you can ring for help or information *If you have any questions about any of our products, just call our helpline.*

hem /hem/ *noun* [C] the edge of a piece of clothing or cloth that has been folded under and sewn • **hem** *verb* [T] hemming *past* hemmed to sew a hem on a piece of clothing or cloth

hem sb in to prevent someone from moving, or from doing what they want to do

hemisphere /ˈhemɪsfɪəʳ/ *noun* [C] one half of the Earth *birds of the northern hemisphere*

hemophilia /ˌhiːməˈfɪliə/ *noun* [U] *US spelling of* haemophilia (= a serious disease in which the flow of blood from someone's body cannot be stopped when they are hurt)

hemophiliac /ˌhiːməˈfɪliæk/ *noun* [C] *US spelling of* haemophiliac (= someone who has haemophilia)

hemorrhage /ˈhemərɪdʒ/ *noun* [C, U] *US spelling of* haemorrhage (= when someone suddenly loses a lot of blood)

hemorrhoids /ˈhemərɔɪdz/ *noun* [plural] *US spelling of* haemorrhoids (= painful swollen tissue around the opening of a person's bottom)

hemp /hemp/ *noun* [U] a plant that is used for making rope, cloth, and the drug cannabis

hen /hen/ *noun* [C] a female bird, especially a chicken

hence /hens/ *adverb* **1** for this reason *He's got an interview today, hence the suit.* **2** **three weeks/two months, etc hence** *formal* three weeks/two months, etc from this time

henceforth /ˌhensˈfɔːθ/ *adverb formal* from this time *Henceforth only English may be spoken in this classroom.*

henchman /ˈhenʃmən/ *noun* [C] *plural* henchmen someone who does unpleasant jobs for a powerful person

'hen ˌnight (*also* 'hen ˌparty) *noun* [C] a party for women only, usually one held for a woman before she gets married ⊃Compare **stag night**.

hepatitis /ˌhepəˈtaɪtɪs/ *noun* [U] a serious disease that affects your liver (= the organ that cleans your blood)

○━**her¹** *strong form* /hɜːʳ/ *weak forms* /həʳ, əʳ/ *pronoun* **1** used after a verb or preposition to refer to someone female who has already been talked about *Where's Kath - have you seen her?* **2** used to refer to a country or ship *God bless HMS Victoria and all who sail in her.*

○━**her²** *strong form* /hɜːʳ/ *weak form* /həʳ/ *determiner* belonging to or relating to someone female who has already been talked about *That's her house on the corner.* ○ *It's not her fault.*

herald¹ /ˈherəld/ *verb* [T] to be a sign that a particular event will happen soon *Thick black clouds heralded rain.*

herald² /ˈherəld/ *noun* [C] a sign that a particu-

lar event will happen soon *A fall in unemployment was the herald of economic recovery.*

herb /hɜːb/ ⑩ /ɜːrb/ *noun* [C] a plant that is used in cooking to add flavour to food or used in medicines • **herbal** /ˈhɜːbºl/ *adjective* herbal medicine

herd¹ /hɜːd/ *noun* [C] a large group of animals such as cows that live and eat together *a herd of cattle/deer*

herd² /hɜːd/ *verb* [T] If people or animals are herded somewhere, they are moved there in a group. [often passive] *The passengers were quickly herded onto a bus.*

○━**here** /hɪəʳ/ *adverb* **1** IN THIS PLACE in the place where you are *Does Jane live near here?* ○ *Come here!* **2** GETTING ATTENTION used to bring someone's attention to someone or something *Look, here's our bus.* ○ *Here, put this on.* **3** **here you are/ here he is, etc** used when you see someone or something you have been looking for or waiting for *Here she is at last.* ○ *Here we are, this is the place.* **4** GIVING used when you are giving someone something *Here's a present for you.* **5** **Here you are.** used when you are giving someone something *"Have you got the paper?" "Here you are."* **6** AT THIS POINT at this point in a discussion *I don't have time here to go into all the arguments.* **7** ON THE TELEPHONE used when saying who you are on the telephone *Hello, it's Tim here.* **8** **here and there** in several different places but without any pattern *Tall trees were growing here and there.*

hereafter /ˌhɪərˈɑːftəʳ/ *adverb formal* from now or after this time

hereby /ˌhɪəˈbaɪ/ *adverb formal* with these words or this action *I hereby declare you the winner.*

hereditary /hɪˈredɪtºri/ *adjective* **1** passed to a child from its parents before birth *Depression is often hereditary.* **2** passed from parent to child as a right *a hereditary title*

heredity /hɪˈredəti/ *noun* [U] the way in which mental or physical qualities pass from parent to child

heresy /ˈherəsi/ *noun* [C, U] a belief which is against what a group or society generally believe to be right or good

heretic /ˈherətɪk/ *noun* [C] someone with a belief which is against what a group or society generally believe to be right or good • **heretical** /həˈretɪkºl/ *adjective*

heritage /ˈherɪtɪdʒ/ *noun* [U] the buildings, paintings, customs, etc which are important in a culture or society because they have existed for a long time *our architectural/cultural heritage*

hermit /ˈhɜːmɪt/ *noun* [C] someone who chooses to live alone and away from other people

hernia /ˈhɜːniə/ *noun* [C] a medical condition in which an organ pushes through the muscle which is around it

WORD PARTNERS FOR **hero**

a **local/national** hero • an **unsung** hero

○━**hero** /ˈhɪərəʊ/ *noun* [C] *plural* heroes **1** someone who does something brave or good which people respect or admire them for *He became a national hero for his part in the revolution.* **2** the main male character in a book or film who is usually good *the hero of her new novel*

heroic /hɪˈrəʊɪk/ *adjective* **1** very brave *a heroic figure* ○ *a heroic act/deed* **2** If someone makes a heroic effort to do something, they work very hard to try to do it. *In spite of England's heroic efforts, they lost the match.* ● **heroically** *adverb*

heroics /hɪˈrəʊɪks/ *noun* [plural] actions which seem brave but are stupid because they are dangerous

heroin /ˈherəʊɪn/ *noun* [U] a very strong drug which some people use illegally for pleasure *a heroin addict*

heroine /ˈherəʊɪn/ *noun* [C] **1** the main female character in a book or film, who is usually good *the heroine of the film 'Alien'* **2** a woman who does something brave or good which people respect or admire her for

heroism /ˈherəʊɪzᵊm/ *noun* [U] very brave behaviour *an act of heroism*

herring /ˈherɪŋ/ *noun* [C, U] a small, silver-coloured fish which lives in the sea and is eaten as food ⊃See also: red herring.

o=**hers** /hɜːz/ *pronoun* the things that belong or relate to someone female who has already been talked about *That's Ann's coat over there - at least I think it's hers.* ○ *I borrowed it from a friend of hers.*

o=**herself** /həˈself/ *pronoun* **1** the reflexive form of the pronoun 'she' *She kept telling herself that nothing was wrong.* **2** used to emphasize the pronoun 'she' or the particular female person you are referring to *She decorated the cake herself.* **3 (all) by herself** alone or without anyone else's help *She managed to put her shoes on all by herself.* **4 (all) to herself** for her use only *Mum's got the house to herself this weekend.*

hertz /hɜːts/ (*written abbreviation* Hz) *noun* [C] *plural* hertz a unit for measuring the number of cycles (= events which are repeated) that happen every second, used especially in electronics

o=**he's** /hiːz/ **1** *short for* he is *He's my best friend.* **2** *short for* he has *Sam must be tired - he's been dancing all night!*

hesitant /ˈhezɪtᵊnt/ *adjective* If you are hesitant, you do not do something immediately or quickly because you are nervous or not certain. *Patricia was hesitant about returning to her home town.* ● **hesitantly** *adverb* ● **hesitancy** *noun* [U]

hesitate /ˈhezɪteɪt/ *verb* **1** [I] to pause before doing something, especially because you are nervous or not certain *Richard hesitated before answering.* **2 not hesitate to do sth** to be very willing to do something because you are certain it is right *They would not hesitate to call the police at the first sign of trouble.*

▦▦ WORD PARTNERS FOR *hesitation*

without hesitation ● a **brief/momentary/moment's/slight** hesitation

hesitation /ˌhezɪˈteɪʃᵊn/ *noun* **1** [C, U] when you pause before doing something, especially because you are nervous or not certain *After a moment's hesitation, he unlocked the door.* ○ *Any hesitation on the part of the government will be seen as weakness.* **2 have no hesitation in doing sth** when you are very willing to do something because you know it is the right thing to do *He had no hesitation in signing for the team.* ○ *I have no hesitation in recommending Ms Shapur for the job.*

heterogeneous /ˌhetᵊrəʊˈdʒiːniəs/ *adjective formal* consisting of parts or things of different types *a heterogeneous sample of people* ○ *Switzerland is a heterogeneous confederation of 26 self-governing cantons.*

heterosexual /ˌhetᵊrəʊˈsekʃuᵊl/ *adjective* sexually attracted to people of the opposite sex *heterosexual sex/relationships* ● **heterosexual** *noun* [C]

H

het up /hetˈʌp/ *adjective* [never before noun] *UK informal* worried and upset *Why are you getting so het up about this?* ○ *There's no need to get so het up about a few dirty dishes in the sink!*

hexagon /ˈheksəgən/ *noun* [C] a flat shape with six sides of the same length ● **hexagonal** /hekˈsægᵊnᵊl/ *adjective* shaped like a hexagon *a hexagonal building/object*

hey /heɪ/ *exclamation spoken* used to get someone's attention or to show that you are interested, excited, angry, etc *Hey, Helen, look at this!* ○ *Hey, wait a minute!* ○ *Hey! what are you doing with my car!* ○ *Hey, come on! It's not that bad.*

heyday /ˈheɪdeɪ/ *noun* [no plural] the time when something or someone was most successful or popular *In its heyday, the company employed over a thousand workers.* ○ *In their heyday, they sold as many records as all the other groups in the country put together.*

o=**hi** /haɪ/ *exclamation* hello *Hi! How's it going?* ○ *Hi there!* ○ *Hi, how're you doing?* ○ *Hi, Gemma! Didn't think I'd see you here.*

hiatus /haɪˈeɪtəs/ *noun* [no plural] *formal* a short pause in which nothing happens or is said *The company expects to resume production of the vehicle again after a two-month hiatus.* ○ *He has been writing now for 30 years, except for a brief hiatus in the early 1990s.*

hibernate /ˈhaɪbəneɪt/ *verb* [I] If an animal hibernates, it goes to sleep for the winter. *The turtle hibernates in a shallow burrow for six months of the year.* ● **hibernation** /ˌhaɪbəˈneɪʃᵊn/ *noun* [U] *Bears go into hibernation in the autumn.*

hiccup (*also* hiccough) /ˈhɪkʌp/ *noun* [C] **1** a quick noise you make in your throat when a muscle in your chest moves suddenly [usually plural] *I got hiccups from drinking too quickly.* **2** a small, temporary problem *I'm afraid there's been a slight hiccup.*

hide

H

ᵒ⁻**hide¹** /haɪd/ *verb past tense* hid, *past participle* hidden **1** THING [T] to put something in a place where it cannot be seen or found *I hid the money in a vase.* ○ [often passive] *She kept the diary hidden in a drawer.* **2** PERSON [I] (*also* hide yourself) to go to a place where you cannot be seen or found *She ran off and hid behind a tree.* **3** FEELING/INFORMATION [T] to keep a feeling or information secret *He couldn't hide his embarrassment.* ○ *I feel sure that there's something about her past that she's trying to hide from me.*

hide² /haɪd/ *noun* [C, U] the skin of an animal which is used for making leather

hide-and-seek /,haɪdən'siːk/ *noun* [U] a children's game in which one child hides and the others try to find them

hideaway /'haɪdəweɪ/ *noun* [C] a place where you go to hide or to be alone

hideous /'hɪdiəs/ *adjective* very ugly *a hideous monster* • **hideously** *adverb The accident left him hideously scarred.*

hideout /'haɪdaʊt/ *noun* [C] a place where you go to hide, especially from the police or if you are in danger

hiding /'haɪdɪŋ/ *noun* be in hiding; go into hiding to hide in a place, especially from the police or if you are in danger

hierarchy /'haɪərɑːki/ *noun* [C] a system or organization in which people or things are arranged according to their importance • **hierarchical** /,haɪə'rɑːkɪkəl/ *adjective a hierarchical structure*

hieroglyphics /,haɪərəʊ'glɪfɪks/ *noun* [plural] a system of writing which uses pictures instead of words, especially used in ancient Egypt

hi-fi /'haɪfaɪ/ *noun* [C] a set of electronic equipment for playing music, consisting of a CD player, radio, etc

ᵒ⁻**high¹** /haɪ/ *adjective* **1** TALL having a large distance from the bottom to the top *a high building/mountain* **2** ABOVE GROUND a large distance above the ground or the level of the sea *a high shelf/window* ○ *The village was high up in the mountains.* **3** MEASUREMENT used to say how big the distance is from the top of something to the bottom, or how far above the ground something is *How high is it?* ○ *It's ten metres high.* **4** AMOUNT great in amount, size, or level *a high temperature* ○ *high prices/costs* ○ *The car sped away at high speed.* **5** VERY GOOD very good *high standards/quality* **6** IMPORTANT important, powerful, or at the top level of something *a high rank* ○ *Safety is our highest priority.* **7** DRUGS If someone is high, they are behaving in an unusual way because they have taken an illegal drug. **8** SOUND A high sound or note is near the top of the set of sounds that people can hear. **9** high in sth If a food is high in something, it contains a lot of it. *Avoid foods that are high in salt.*

ᵒ⁻**high²** /haɪ/ *adverb* **1** at or to a large distance above the ground *We flew high above the city.* ○ *He threw the ball high into the air.* **2** at or to a large amount or level *Temperatures rose as high as 40 degrees.*

high³ /haɪ/ *noun* [C] **1** the top amount or level which something reaches *Computer ownership has reached an all-time high* (= more people own computers than ever before). **2** a feeling of excitement or happiness [usually singular] *The players are still on a high from their last match.*

highbrow /'haɪbraʊ/ *adjective* A highbrow book, film, etc is serious and intended for very intelligent or well-educated people.

high-class /,haɪ'klɑːs/ *adjective* of very good quality *a high-class hotel*

,**High 'Court** *noun* [C] the most important law court in some countries *a High Court judge*

,**higher edu'cation** *noun* [U] education at a college or university

high-flyer (*also* high-flier) /,haɪ'flaɪə'/ *noun* [C] someone who is very successful or who is likely to be very successful, especially in business • **high-flying** *adjective*

,**high 'heels** (*also* **heels**) *noun* [plural] women's shoes with heels raised high off the ground ● **high-heeled** *adjective*

the 'high ,jump *noun* a sports event in which people try to jump over a bar which gets higher and higher during the competition つSee colour picture **Sports 1** on page Centre 14.

highlands /ˈhaɪləndz/ *noun* [plural] an area with a lot of mountains *the Scottish highlands* ● **highland** /ˈhaɪlənd/ *adjective* in or relating to the highlands *a highland village*

high-level /ˌhaɪˈlevᵊl/ *adjective* involving important or powerful people *high-level meetings/talks*

░░░ WORD PARTNERS FOR *highlight*

highlight a **danger/need/issue/problem** ● highlight **the need for** sth

---

highlight¹ /ˈhaɪlaɪt/ *verb* [T] **1** to emphasize something or make people notice something *to highlight a problem/danger* ○ *The report highlights the need for stricter regulations.* **2** to make something a different colour so that it is more easily noticed, especially written words

highlight² /ˈhaɪlaɪt/ *noun* [C] the best or most important part of something *The boat trip was one of the highlights of the holiday.*

highlighter /ˈhaɪˌlaɪtəʳ/ *noun* [C] a pen with bright, transparent ink which is used to emphasize words in a book, article, etc つSee colour picture **The Office** on page Centre 5.

o-ᴡ**highly** /ˈhaɪli/ *adverb* **1** very or to a large degree *a highly effective treatment* ○ *It is highly unlikely that they will succeed.* **2** at a high level *a highly paid worker* **3** **to speak/think highly of sb/sth** to have or express a very good opinion of someone or something

Highness /ˈhaɪnəs/ *noun* **Her/His/Your Highness** used when you are speaking to or about a royal person *Thank you, Your Highness.*

high-pitched /haɪˈpɪtʃt/ *adjective* **1** A voice that is high-pitched is higher than usual. **2** describes a noise that is high and sometimes also loud or unpleasant *a high-pitched whine*

high-powered /ˌhaɪˈpaʊəd/ *adjective* very important or responsible *a high-powered executive/job*

high-profile /ˌhaɪˈprəʊfaɪl/ *adjective* A high-profile person or event is known about by a lot of people and receives a lot of attention from television, newspapers, etc. *a high-profile campaign/case*

high-rise /ˈhaɪˌraɪz/ *adjective* A high-rise building is very tall and has a lot of floors.

'**high ,school** *noun* [C, U] a school in the US which children go to between the ages of 14 and 18 *I played violin when I was in high school.* ○ *a high-school student/teacher*

'**high ,street** *noun* [C] UK the main road in the centre of a town where there are a lot of shops

high-tech (*also* UK **hi-tech**) /ˌhaɪˈtek/ *adjective* using or involved with the most recent and advanced electronic machines, computers, etc *high-tech companies/industry* つCompare **low-tech.**

highway /ˈhaɪweɪ/ *noun* [C] mainly US a main road, especially between two towns or cities

hijack /ˈhaɪdʒæk/ *verb* [T] to take control of an aircraft during a journey, especially using violence [often passive] *The jumbo jet was hijacked by terrorists.* ● **hijacker** *noun* [C] ● **hijacking** *noun* [C, U]

hike¹ /haɪk/ *noun* [C] a long walk, usually in the countryside

hike² /haɪk/ *verb* [I] to go for a long walk in the countryside ● **hiker** *noun* [C] ● **hiking** *noun* [U] *to go hiking in the mountains*

hilarious /hɪˈleəriəs/ *adjective* extremely funny *They all thought the film was hilarious.* ● **hilariously** *adverb* **hilariously funny**

hilarity /hɪˈlærəti/ *noun* [U] when people laugh very loudly and think something is very funny

o-ᴡ**hill** /hɪl/ *noun* [C] a raised area of land, smaller than a mountain *They climbed up the hill to get a better view.*

hillside /ˈhɪlsaɪd/ *noun* [C] the sloping side of a hill

hilly /ˈhɪli/ *adjective* having a lot of hills *hilly countryside*

hilt /hɪlt/ *noun* **to the hilt** very much or as much as is possible *Mark borrowed to the hilt to pay for his new car.*

ᴜ-ᴡ**him** *strong form* /hɪm/ *weak form* /ɪm/ *pronoun* used after a verb or preposition to refer to someone male who has already been talked about *Where's Serge - have you seen him?*

o-ᴡ**himself** /hɪmˈself/ *pronoun* **1** the reflexive form of the pronoun 'he' *John always cuts himself when he's shaving.* **2** used to emphasize the pronoun 'he' or the particular male person you are referring to *Do you want to speak to Dr Randall himself or his secretary?* ○ *He made the bookcase himself.* **3** **(all) by himself** alone or without anyone else's help *Joe made that snowman all by himself.* **4** **(all) to himself** for his use only *Tim wants a desk all to himself.*

hind /haɪnd/ *adjective* **a hind foot/leg** a foot/leg at the back of an animal

hinder /ˈhɪndəʳ/ *verb* [T] to make it difficult to do something or for something to develop [often passive] *His performance at the Olympics was hindered by a knee injury.*

hindrance /ˈhɪndrəns/ *noun* [C] something or someone that makes it difficult for you to do something *Large class sizes are a hindrance to teachers.*

hindsight /ˈhaɪndsaɪt/ *noun* [U] the ability to understand an event or situation only after it has happened *With hindsight, I should have taken the job.*

Hindu /ˈhɪnduː/ *noun* [C] someone who believes in Hinduism ● **Hindu** *adjective a Hindu temple*

Hinduism /ˈhɪnduːɪzᵊm/ *noun* [U] the main religion of India, based on belief in many gods and the belief that when someone dies their spirit returns to life in another body

hinge¹ /ˈhɪndʒ/ *noun* [C] a metal fastening that joins the edge of a door, window, or lid to something else and allows you to open or close it

hinge² /ˈhɪndʒ/ *verb*
hinge on sth to depend completely on

---

something *Her career hinges on the success of this project.*

hint¹ /hɪnt/ *noun* **1** [C] when you say something that suggests what you think or want, but not in a direct way *He **dropped** (= made) several hints that he wanted a CD player for his birthday.* **2** [C] a small piece of advice *The magazine gives lots of **useful hints** on how to save money.* **3 a hint of sth** a small amount of something *There was a hint of anger in her voice.*

hint² /hɪnt/ *verb* [I, T] to suggest something, but not in a direct way [+ (that)] *He hinted that he wants to retire next year.* ○ *She **hinted at** the possibility of moving to America.*

hip¹ /hɪp/ *noun* [C] one of the two parts of your body above your leg and below your waist ⊃See colour picture **The Body** on page Centre 13.

hip² /hɪp/ *adjective informal* fashionable

hip-hop /ˈhɪphɒp/ *noun* [U] a type of pop music with songs about problems in society and words that are spoken and not sung

hippie /ˈhɪpi/ (*also UK* **hippy**) *noun* [C] someone who believes in peace and love and has long hair, especially someone who was young in the 1960s

hippo /ˈhɪpəʊ/ *noun* [C] *short for* hippopotamus

hippopotamus /ˌhɪpəˈpɒtəməs/ *noun* [C] *plural* **hippopotamuses** or **hippopotami** a very large animal with a thick skin that lives near water in parts of Africa

o⊶**hire¹** /haɪəʳ/ *verb* [T] **1** *UK* (*US* **rent**) to pay money in order to use something for a short time *They hired a car for a few weeks.* ⊃See Common learner error at **rent**. **2** to begin to employ someone *We hired a new secretary last week.*

hire sth out *UK* to allow someone to borrow something from you in exchange for money *The shop hires out electrical equipment.*

hire² /haɪəʳ/ *noun* [U] *UK* when you arrange to use something by paying for it *The price includes flights and **car hire**.* ○ *Do you have bikes **for hire**?*

o⊶**his¹** *strong form* /hɪz/ *weak form* /ɪz/ *determiner* belonging to or relating to someone male who has already been talked about *Alex is sitting over there with his daughter.* ○ *It's not his fault.*

o⊶**his²** /hɪz/ *pronoun* the things that belong or relate to someone male who has already been talked about *That's Frank's coat over there - at least I think it's his.* ○ *I borrowed them from a friend of his.*

Hispanic /hɪˈspænɪk/ *adjective* relating or belonging to people whose families came from Spain or Latin America in the past • **Hispanic** *noun* [C] a Hispanic person

hiss /hɪs/ *verb* **1** [I] to make a long noise like the letter 's' *The gas hissed through the pipes.* **2** [T] to speak in an angry or urgent way *"Will you be quiet," she hissed.* • **hiss** *noun* [C] a sound like the letter 's'

hissy (fit) /ˈhɪsi,fɪt/ *noun* [C] *informal* a sudden strong feeling of anger that someone cannot

control *David, of course, **threw a hissy fit** when he found out.*

historian /hɪˈstɔːriən/ *noun* [C] someone who studies or writes about history

historic /hɪˈstɒrɪk/ *adjective* important in history or likely to be important in history *historic buildings* ○ *a historic day/moment*

historical /hɪˈstɒrɪkᵊl/ *adjective* relating to events or people in the past, or the study of history *a historical novel* ○ *historical documents* • **historically** *adverb*

o⊶**history** /ˈhɪstᵊri/ *noun* **1** PAST [U] the whole series of events in the past which relate to the development of a country, subject, or person *The Civil War was a terrible time in American history.* **2** SUBJECT [U] the study of events in the past *He's very interested in modern European history.* ○ *a history book* **3 a history of sth** If you have a history of a particular problem or illness, you have already suffered from it. *a man with a history of drug addiction* **4** DESCRIPTION [C] a description or record of events in the past relating to someone or something *The doctor read through his **medical history**.* ⊃See also: **case history**, **natural history**.

COMMON LEARNER ERROR

history or story?

History is events that happened in the past.
He's studying history at university.

A **story** is a description of real or imaginary events, often told to entertain people.
The story is about two friends travelling across India.

hit

o⊶**hit¹** /hɪt/ *verb* **hitting**, *past tense* **hit** HAND [T] to touch something quickly and with force using your hand or an object in your hand *She hit him on* *the head with her tennis racket.* **2** TOUCH [T] to touch someone or something quickly and with force, usually causing injury or damage *The car skidded and hit a wall.* ○ *As she fell, she hit her head on the pavement.* **3** AFFECT [I, T] to affect something badly [often passive] *The economy has been hit by high unemployment.* **4** REACH [T] to reach a place, position, or state *Our profits have already hit $1 million.* **5** THINK [T] *informal* If an idea or thought hits you, you suddenly think of it. *The idea for the book hit me in the middle of the night.* **6 hit it off** *informal* If people hit it off, they like each other and become friendly immediately. ⊃See also: hit sb **hard²**, hit the **jackpot**, hit the **nail¹** on the head, hit the **roof**.

hit back to criticize or attack someone who has criticized or attacked you *The President hit back at journalists who said he was a liar.*

hit on/upon sth to have a good idea, especially one which solves a problem *We hit upon the idea of writing to the mayor to ask for his help.*

> WORD PARTNERS FOR *hit*
>
> a **big/massive/smash** hit • a hit **CD/single**

hit² /hɪt/ *noun* [C] **1** SONG/FILM a very successful song, film, book, etc *The film 'Titanic' was a big hit.* **2** PERSON/THING a popular person or thing *The chocolate cake was a big hit with the children.* **3** TOUCH when you touch something or when something touches you quickly and with force **4** INTERNET a request to see a document on the Internet that is then counted to calculate the number of people looking at the page

hit-and-miss /ˌhɪtˀnˈmɪs/ *UK* (*US* hit or miss) *adjective* not planned, but happening by chance

hit-and-run /ˌhɪtˀnˈrʌn/ *adjective* A hit-and-run accident is when the driver of a vehicle hits and injures someone, but then drives away without helping.

hitch¹ /hɪtʃ/ *noun* [C] a small problem *The ceremony went without a hitch.*

hitch² /hɪtʃ/ *verb* **1 hitch a lift/ride** to get a free ride in someone's vehicle, by standing next to the road and waiting for someone to pick you up **2** [T] (*also US* hitch up) to fasten something to an object or vehicle *They hitched the caravan to the car.*

hitch sth up to pull up a piece of clothing

hitchhike /ˈhɪtʃhaɪk/ *verb* [I] to get free rides in people's vehicles by standing next to the road and waiting for someone to pick you up • hitchhiker *noun* [C]

hi-tech *UK* (*UK/US* high-tech) /ˌhaɪˈtek/ *adjective* using or involved with the most recent and advanced electronic machines, computers, etc

hitherto /ˌhɪðəˈtuː/ *adverb formal* until now, or until a particular point in time

HIV /ˌeɪtʃaɪˈviː/ *noun* [U] *abbreviation for* human immunodeficiency virus: a virus which causes AIDS (= a serious disease that destroys the body's ability to fight infection)

hive /haɪv/ *noun* **1** [C] (*also* beehive) a special container where people keep bees **2 a hive of activity** a place where people are busy and working hard

HIV-positive /ˌeɪtʃaɪviːˈpɒzətɪv/ *adjective* If a person is HIV-positive, they are infected with HIV although they might not have AIDS.

hiya /ˈhaɪjə/ *exclamation informal* a way to say hello to someone you know well *Hiya, Mike, how are you doing?*

hm (*also* hmm) /həm/ *spoken* something you say when you pause while talking or when you are uncertain *"Which one do you like best?" "Hmm. I'm not sure."*

hoard /hɔːd/ *verb* [T] to collect and store a large supply of something, often secretly *He hoarded antique books in the attic.* ○ *During the war, people hoarded food and supplies.* • hoard *noun* [C] a large, secret supply or collection of something *Police found a hoard of stolen jewellery in the car.*

hoarding /ˈhɔːdɪŋ/ *UK* (*UK/US* billboard) *noun* [C] a large board used for advertising, especially by the side of a road

hoarse /hɔːs/ *adjective* If you are hoarse, your voice sounds rough when you speak, often because you are ill. *The teacher was hoarse from shouting.* • hoarsely *adverb*

hoax /həʊks/ *noun* [C] when someone tries to make people believe something which is not true *The police said the bomb threat was a hoax.*

hob /hɒb/ *noun* [C] *UK* the flat part on top of an oven where you heat food in pans ⊃See colour picture **The Kitchen** on page Centre 2.

hobble /ˈhɒbl/ *verb* [I] to walk with small, uncomfortable steps, especially because your feet hurt

hobby /ˈhɒbi/ *noun* [C] an activity that you enjoy and do regularly when you are not working *Do you have any hobbies?*

hockey /ˈhɒki/ *noun* [U] **1** *UK* (*US* field hockey) a team game played on grass where you hit a small ball with a long, curved stick **2** *US* (*UK/US* ice hockey) a team game played on ice where you hit a small, hard object with a long, curved stick ⊃See colour picture **Sports 1** on page Centre 14.

hoe /həʊ/ *noun* [C] a garden tool with a long handle used for removing weeds (= plants you do not want)

hog¹ /hɒg/ *noun* [C] *mainly US* a large pig

hog² /hɒg/ *verb* [T] hogging *past* hogged *informal* to use or keep all of something for yourself *Stop hogging the newspaper! I want to read it too.*

hoist /hɔɪst/ *verb* [T] to raise something, sometimes using a rope or machine *They slowly hoisted the flag.*

∘⋆**hold¹** /həʊld/ *verb past* held **1** IN HAND [T] to have something in your hand or arms *He was holding a glass of wine.* ○ *They were holding hands and kissing.* **2** KEEP IN POSITION [T] to keep something in a particular position *Can you hold the door open please?* ○ *Hold your hand up if you know the answer.* ○ *The frame was held* *together with screws.* **3** ORGANIZE [T] to organize an event *to hold talks/an election* **4** CONTAIN [T] to contain something or to be able to contain a particular amount of something *The bucket holds about 10 litres.* **5** JOB OR QUALIFICATION [T] to have a particular job, position, or qualification *She held the post of treasurer.* **6** COMPETITION [T] to have a particular position in a competition *to hold the world record* ○ *to hold the lead* **7** STORE [T] to store documents, information, etc in a particular place *The documents are held in the local library.* **8** PRISONER [T] to keep someone as a prisoner *Police held the suspect overnight.* ○ *The hijackers are holding them hostage/prisoner.* **9** ARMY [T] If soldiers hold a place, they control it. *Rebel troops held the village.* **10 hold an opinion/belief/view** to believe something *They held the view that corporal punishment was good for children.* **11 hold a conversation** to have a conversation **12 hold sb's attention/interest** to keep someone interested in something *The film held my attention from beginning to end.* **13** TELEPHONE [I, T] to wait on the telephone until someone can speak to you *Her line's busy. Would you like to hold?* ○ *Hold the line, please.* **14** NOT BREAK [I] to not break *The rope held.* **15 Hold it!** *informal* used to tell someone to wait or stop doing something *Hold it! I've forgotten my coat.* **16 hold shares** to own shares (= small, equal parts of the value of a company) **17 hold your breath a** STOP BREATHING to intentionally stop breathing for a time **b** WAIT to wait for something to happen, often feeling anxious **18 hold your nose** to close your nose with your fingers to avoid smelling something unpleasant ➋See also: hold your own[1].

hold sth against sb to like someone less because they have done something wrong or behaved badly *It was his mistake, but I won't hold it against him.*

hold sb/sth back 1 to prevent someone or something from moving forward *The police held back the protesters.* **2** to prevent someone or something from making progress *She felt that having children would hold her back.*

hold sth back 1 to stop yourself showing an emotion *She couldn't hold back the tears.* **2** to not give information to someone

hold sth/sb down 1 to stop someone moving or escaping *It took three officers to hold down the suspect.* **2** to keep the cost of something at a low level *to hold down prices/wages* **3 hold down a job** to keep a job *It's difficult for mothers to hold down a full-time job.*

hold off (sth/doing sth) to wait before doing something *They are holding off making a decision until next week.*

hold on *informal* **1** to wait *Hold on! I'll just check my diary.* **2** to hold something or someone firmly with your hands or arms *Hold on tight!*

hold onto sth/sb to hold something or someone firmly with your hands or arms *Hold onto the rope and don't let go.*

hold onto/on to sth to keep something you have *It was a tough election, but they held onto their majority.*

hold sth out to move your hand or an object in your hand towards someone *She held out her glass for some more wine.*

hold out 1 If a supply of food or money holds out, you have enough for a particular period of time. **2** to continue to defend yourself against an attack *The city is still holding out against rebel troops.*

hold out for sth to wait until you get what you want *I decided to hold out for a better offer.*

hold sth up to prevent something from falling down *The tent was held up by ropes.*

hold sth/sb up to make something or someone slow or late *Sorry I'm late. I got held up in traffic.*

hold up sth to try to steal money from a bank, shop, or vehicle using force

hold² /həʊld/ *noun* **1** WITH HANDS [C] when you hold something or someone, or the way you do this *Keep a tight hold on your tickets.* **2 catch/grab/take, etc hold of sth/sb** to start holding something or someone *He tried to escape, but I grabbed hold of his jacket.* **3 get hold of sth/sb** to obtain something, or to manage to speak to someone *I got hold of a copy at the local library.* ○ *I rang three times, but couldn't get hold of her.* **4 on hold a** DO IN FUTURE If a plan or activity is on hold, it will not be done until a later time. *The project is on hold until we get more money.* **b** TELEPHONE waiting to speak to someone on the telephone *His secretary put me on hold.* **5 keep hold of sth** to keep something *Keep hold of this. You might need it later.* **6 hold on/over sth/sb** power or control over something or someone *Their company has a strong hold on the computer market.* **7** SPACE [C] an area on a ship or aircraft for storing things *a cargo hold* ➋See also: get (hold of) the wrong end[1] of the stick.

holdall /ˈhəʊldɔːl/ *UK* (*US* **carryall**) *noun* [C] a large bag for carrying clothes ➋See picture at luggage.

holder /ˈhəʊldəʳ/ *noun* [C] someone who officially owns something *the world record holder* ○ *passport holders* ➋See also: title-holder.

holding /ˈhəʊldɪŋ/ *noun* [C] part of a company which someone owns

hold-up *UK* (*US* **holdup**) /ˈhəʊldʌp/ *noun* [C] **1** something that slows you down or makes you late *There were several hold-ups on the motorway.* **2** when someone steals money from a bank, shop, or vehicle using force

⊶**hole¹** /həʊl/ *noun* **1** [C] a hollow space in something, or an opening in a surface *a bullet hole* ○ *There's a hole in the roof.* ○ *We dug a hole to plant the tree.* **2 a rabbit/mouse, etc hole** a hollow space where a rabbit/mouse, etc lives **3** a small, hollow space in the ground that you try to hit a ball into in a game of golf

hole² /həʊl/ *verb*

hole up *informal* (*also* **be holed up**) to stay or hide somewhere

WORD PARTNERS FOR *holiday*

book/go on/have a holiday • a **summer** holiday • be **on** holiday

o-¤**holiday**[1] /'hɒlədeɪ/ *noun* 1 NO WORK [C, U] *UK* (*US* **vacation**) a time when you do not have to go to work or school *My aunt looks after us during the school holidays.* 2 VISIT [C, U] *UK* (*US* **vacation**) a long visit to a place away from where you live, for pleasure *a skiing/walking holiday* ○ *Are you going on holiday this year?* 3 DAY [C] an official day when you do not have to go to school or work *a public holiday* ⊃See also: bank holiday, federal holiday, national holiday, package holiday, summer holiday.

holiday[2] /'hɒlədeɪ/ *UK* (*US* **vacation**) *verb* [I] to have your holiday somewhere *We usually holiday in Spain.*

holidaymaker /'hɒlədeɪˌmeɪkər/ *noun* [C] *UK* someone who is away from home on holiday

holiness /'həʊlɪnəs/ *noun* [U] the quality of being holy

holistic /həʊ'lɪstɪk/ *adjective* dealing with or treating the whole of something or someone and not just some parts

holler /'hɒlər/ *verb* [I] *US informal* to shout or call loudly • **holler** *noun* [C]

hollow[1] /'hɒləʊ/ *adjective* **1** having a hole or empty space inside *a hollow shell/tube* ⊃See picture at flat. **2** without meaning or real feeling *a hollow victory* ○ *a hollow laugh* **3 hollow cheeks/eyes** If someone has hollow cheeks/eyes, their face seems to curve in around these areas.

hollow[2] /'hɒləʊ/ *noun* [C] a hole or empty space in something, or a low area in a surface

hollow

hollow[3] /'hɒləʊ/ *verb* **hollow sth out** to make an empty space inside something

holly /'hɒli/ *noun* [U] a green bush with sharp, pointed leaves and small, red fruit

Hollywood /'hɒliwʊd/ *noun* the centre of the US film industry

holocaust /'hɒləkɔːst/ *noun* [C] when a very large number of people are killed and things destroyed, such as in a war or fire *a nuclear holocaust*

hologram /'hɒləgræm/ *noun* [C] a photograph or image which appears to be solid and have depth when light shines on it in a particular way

holster /'həʊlstər/ *noun* [C] a leather container for carrying a gun on your body

holy /'həʊli/ *adjective* **1** relating to a religion or a god *the holy city of Jerusalem* **2** very religious or pure *a holy man*

homage /'hɒmɪdʒ/ *noun* **pay homage to sb** to show your respect for someone, especially by praising them in public *Fans paid homage to the actress who died yesterday.*

WORD PARTNERS FOR *home*

go home • be **at** home

o-¤**home**[1] /həʊm/ *noun* **1** [C, U] the place where you live or feel you belong *I tried to ring him, but he wasn't at home.* ○ *He left home* (= stopped living with his family) *when he was eighteen.* **2** [C] a place where people who need special care live *a children's home* ○ *My grandmother lives in a home now.* **3 feel at home** to feel happy and confident in a place or situation *After a month she felt at home in her new job.* **4 make yourself at home** to behave in a relaxed way in a place, as if it was your own home *Take off your coat and make yourself at home.* **5 the home of sth/sb** the place where you usually find something or someone, or where they come from *France, the home of good food* ⊃See also: nursing home, stately home.

COMMON LEARNER ERROR

home

When you use verbs of movement with **home**, for example 'go' or 'come', you do not need to use a preposition.

What time did you go home?

I'll call you as soon as I get home.

When you use the verbs **be** or **stay** with **home**, you can use the preposition **at**.

I was at home all afternoon.

I'll stay at home to look after the children.

Let's stay home and watch a movie. (mainly US)

o-¤**home**[2] /həʊm/ *adverb* **1** to the place where you live *He didn't come home until midnight.* ○ *I went home to visit my parents.* **2** at or in the place someone lives *Will you be home tomorrow evening?*

home[3] /həʊm/ *adjective* **1 sb's home address/ phone number, etc** an address/telephone number, etc for the place where someone lives **2** FOR/FROM HOME made or used in the place where someone lives *home cooking* ○ *a home computer* **3** SPORT relating to a sporting event happens *The home team won 2-0.* **4** COUNTRY relating to things in your own country *home affairs*

home[4] /həʊm/ *verb* **home in on sth/sb** to give a lot of attention to something or someone *The report only homes in on the negative points.*

homeboy /'həʊmbɔɪ/ (*also* **homey**) *noun* [C] *mainly US informal* a boy or man who is a close friend or who is from your own town

homecoming /'həʊmˌkʌmɪŋ/ *noun* [C, U] when someone returns home, usually after being away for a long time

home eco'nomics *noun* [U] a school subject in which you learn how to cook and sew

home-grown /ˌhəʊm'grəʊn/ *adjective* **1** from your own garden *home-grown vegetables* **2** If someone or something is home-grown, they belong to or were developed in your own country. *Our football team has many home-grown players.*

homeland /ˈhəʊmlænd/ *noun* [C] the country where you were born

homeless /ˈhəʊmləs/ *adjective* without a place to live *10,000 people were made homeless by the floods.* ○ *They're opening a new shelter for* **the homeless.** ● **homelessness** *noun* [U] *Homelessness has become a real problem in the capital.*

homely /ˈhəʊmli/ *adjective* **1** *UK* A homely place is simple, but comfortable and pleasant. *It's a small restaurant with a homely atmosphere.* **2** *(US)* Someone who is homely is not very attractive.

homemade (*also UK* **home-made**) /ˌhəʊmˈmeɪd/ *adjective* made at home and not bought from a shop *homemade bread/cookies*

homeopathy /ˌhəʊmiˈɒpəθi/ *noun* [U] a way of treating illnesses using very small amounts of natural substances ● **homeopathic** /ˌhəʊmiəʊˈpæθɪk/ *adjective a* **homeopathic remedy**

homeowner /ˈhəʊmˌəʊnəʳ/ *noun* [C] someone who owns the house that they live in

'home ˌpage *noun* [C] the first page that you see when you look at a website on the Internet

ˌhome 'shopping *noun* [U] when someone buys goods from a magazine, a television programme or a website

homesick /ˈhəʊmsɪk/ *adjective* feeling sad because you are away from your home *She went to France to be an au pair but had to come home because she was so homesick.* ● **homesickness** *noun* [U]

homestead /ˈhəʊmsted/ *noun* [C] *mainly US* a house and area of land usually used as a farm

hometown *US* (*UK/US* ˌhome 'town) /ˌhəʊmˈtaʊn/ *noun* [C] the town or city that you come from

homeward /ˈhəʊmwəd/ *adjective, adverb* towards home *the homeward journey* ○ *The next day we were* **homeward bound**, *hoping to return one day.*

◦⤚**homework** /ˈhəʊmwɜːk/ *noun* [U] **1** work which teachers give students to do at home *Have you done your homework yet?* **2 do your homework** to prepare carefully for a situation *It was clear that she had done her homework before the meeting.*

homey¹ /ˈhəʊmi/ *US* (*UK* **homely**) *adjective* A homey place is simple, but comfortable and pleasant.

homey² /ˈhəʊmi/ (*also* **homeboy**) *noun* [C] *mainly US informal* a boy or man who is a close friend or who is from your own town

homicide /ˈhɒmɪsaɪd/ *noun* [C, U] *US* the crime of killing someone *There were over 400 homicides in Chicago last year.* ● **homicidal** /ˌhɒmɪˈsaɪd³l/ *adjective* likely to murder someone *a homicidal maniac*

homogeneous /ˌhɒməˈdʒiːniəs, ˌhəʊm*ə*ˈdʒiː-niəs/ *adjective formal* consisting of parts or members that are all the same *The village was*

a fairly homogeneous community.

homophobia /ˌhəʊməˈfəʊbiə/ *noun* [U] hate of homosexual people ● **homophobic** *adjective* hating homosexual people

homosexual /ˌhəʊmə*ʊ*ˈsekʃu³l/ *adjective* sexually attracted to people of the same sex ● **homosexual** *noun* [C] someone who is homosexual ● **homosexuality** /ˌhəʊmə*ʊ*ˌsekʃu³ˈæləti/ *noun* [U] the quality of being homosexual

hone /həʊn/ *verb* [T] to improve something and make it perfect *an opportunity for you to* **hone** *your skills*

◦⤚**honest** /ˈɒnɪst/ *adjective* **1** sincere and telling the truth *If you want my* **honest opinion**, *I think your hair looks awful.* **2** not likely to lie, cheat, or steal *an honest man* ⊃Opposite **dishonest.** **3 to be honest** *informal* used to express your real opinion *To be honest, I didn't really enjoy the party.*

honestly /ˈɒnɪstli/ *adverb* **1** EMPHASIZE used to emphasize that you are telling the truth *Thanks, but I honestly couldn't eat another piece of cake.* **2** HONEST in an honest way **3** ANNOYED used to show that you are annoyed or do not approve of something *Honestly! He should have been here hours ago.*

honesty /ˈɒnɪsti/ *noun* **1** [U] the quality of being honest **2 in all honesty** used when you are saying what you really think or feel about something *In all honesty, I'd rather not go.* ⊃Opposite **dishonesty.**

honey /ˈhʌni/ *noun* **1** [U] a sweet, sticky food that is made by bees ⊃See colour picture **Food** on page Centre 11. **2** [C] *mainly US* a name that you call someone you love or like very much

WORD PARTNERS FOR *honeymoon*

be **on** (your) honeymoon ● a honeymoon **couple**

honeymoon /ˈhʌnimuːn/ *noun* [C] a holiday taken by two people who have just got married *We went to Paris on our* **honeymoon.** ● **honeymooner** *noun* [C]

honk /hɒŋk/ *verb* [I, T] to make a short sound with your car's horn (= part you press to make a warning noise) *The lorry driver* **honked** *his* **horn** *at me.*

honor /ˈɒnəʳ/ *noun, verb US spelling of* honour

honorable /ˈɒn³rəbl/ *adjective US spelling of* honourable

honorary /ˈɒn³rəri/ *adjective* **1** given as a reward to show respect *He was given an* **honorary degree** *from Cambridge University.* **2** If you have an honorary job, you are not paid for it. *the honorary chairman*

honour¹ *UK* (*US* **honor**) /ˈɒnəʳ/ *noun* **1** RESPECT [U] when people respect you because you have done what you believe is honest and right, or the quality of doing this *a man of honour* ○ *The soldiers fought for the honour of their country.* ⊃Opposite **dishonour.** **2 in honour of sb/ sth** in order to celebrate or show great respect for someone or something *a banquet in honour of the President* **3** PRIDE [no plural] something which makes you feel proud and pleased [+ to do sth] *It's an honour to be team captain.* ○ [+ of + doing sth] *I had the great honour of meeting the King.* **4** REWARD [C] something that you give to someone in public to show respect for them and their achievements *She was granted the Order of Merit - one of the nation's highest honours.* **5 Her/His/Your Honour** used when you are speaking to or about a judge **6 honours** A qualification or university course with honours is of a very high level. *an honours degree*

honour² *UK* (*US* honor) /'ɒnə'/ *verb* **1** [T] to show great respect for someone or something, usually in public [often passive] *He was honoured for his bravery.* ○ *She was honoured with an Oscar.* **2 honour an agreement/contract/promise, etc** to do what you agreed or promised to do ⊃Opposite **dishonour**.

honourable /'ɒnərəbl/ *adjective UK* **1** (*US* honorable) honest and fair, or deserving praise and respect *a decent, honourable man* ⊃Opposite **dishonourable**. **2 the Honourable a** a title used before the name of some important government officials **b** a title used in the UK before the name of certain people of high social rank • **honourably** *adverb*

hood /hʊd/ *noun* [C] **1** a part of a coat or jacket that covers your head and neck *a waterproof jacket with a hood* ⊃See colour picture **Clothes** on page Centre 8. **2** *US* (*UK* **bonnet**) the metal part that covers a car engine ⊃See colour picture **Car** on page Centre 7.

hooded /'hʊdɪd/ *adjective* having or wearing a hood *a hooded sweatshirt* ○ *hooded figures*

hoodie /'hʊdi/ (*also* hoody) *noun* [C] a sweatshirt (= a piece of clothing made of soft cotton which covers the top of your body) with a hood (= part which covers your head) ⊃See colour picture **Clothes** on page Centre 8.

hoof /huːf/ *noun* [C] *plural* hooves *or* hoofs the hard part on the foot of a horse and some other large animals

hook¹ /hʊk/ *noun* [C] **1** a curved piece of metal or plastic used for hanging something on, or a similar object used for catching fish *His coat was hanging from a hook on the door.* **2 off the hook** If a telephone is off the hook, the part you speak into is not in its correct position, so the telephone will not ring. **3 a left/right hook** when you hit someone hard with your left/right hand **4 get/let sb off the hook** *informal* to allow someone to escape from a difficult situation or to avoid doing something that they do not want to do

hook² /hʊk/ *verb* **1** [T] to fasten something with a hook, hang something on a hook, or catch something with a hook **2 be/get hooked on sth a** to like or start to like doing something very much and want to do it all the time *He's completely hooked on computer games.* **b** If you are hooked on a drug, you cannot stop taking it. • **hooked** *adjective* shaped like a hook *a hooked nose*

hook sth/sb up to connect a machine to a power supply or to another machine, or to connect someone to a piece of medical equipment

hooligan /'huːlɪgən/ *noun* [C] someone who behaves badly or violently and causes damage in a public place • **hooliganism** *noun* [U]

hoop /huːp/ *noun* [C] a ring made of metal, plastic, or wood

hooray (*also* hurrah) /hʊ'reɪ/ *exclamation* something that you shout when you are happy, excited, etc or when you approve of someone or something *Hip, hip, hooray!*

hoot¹ /huːt/ *noun* **1** [C] a short sound made by an owl (= bird) or by a car horn (= warning equipment) **2 a hoot of laughter** when someone laughs loudly **3** [no plural] *informal* something or someone that is very funny *The film was an absolute hoot.*

hoot² /huːt/ *verb* **1** [I, T] *mainly UK* to make a short sound with your car's horn (= part you press to make a warning noise) *The van driver hooted his horn impatiently.* **2** [I] If an owl (= bird) hoots, it makes a low 'oo' sound. **3 hoot with laughter** to laugh a lot very loudly

Hoover /'huːvə'/ *mainly UK trademark* (*UK/US* vacuum cleaner) *noun* [C] an electric machine which cleans floors by sucking up dirt • **hoover** *verb* [I, T]

hooves /huːvz/ *plural of* hoof

hop¹ /hɒp/ *verb* [I] hopping, *past* hopped **1** ONE FOOT to jump on one foot or to move about in this way **2** ANIMAL If a small animal, bird, or insect hops, it moves by jumping on all of its feet at the same time. *Rabbits were hopping across the field.* **3** MOVE QUICKLY *informal* to go somewhere quickly or get into or out of a vehicle quickly *to hop on a plane/train*

hop² /hɒp/ *noun* **1** [C] a short jump, especially on one leg **2 a short hop** *informal* a short journey or distance *London to Paris is only a short hop by plane.*

o-**hope¹** /həʊp/ *verb* **1** [I, T] to want something to happen or be true [+ (that)] *I hope that the bus won't be late.* ○ *We had hoped for better weather than this.* ○ *"Do you think it's going to rain?" "I hope not!"* ○ *"Is he coming?" "I hope so."* **2 hope to do sth** to intend to do something *Dad hopes to retire next year.*

> **WORD PARTNERS FOR** *hope*
>
> bring / give / give up / hold out / lose / offer hope • fresh/great/renewed/vain hope • hope of sth/doing sth

o-**hope²** /həʊp/ *noun* **1** [C, U] a positive feeling about the future, or something that you want to happen *a message full of hope* ○ *What are your hopes and dreams for the future?* ○ [+ of + doing sth] *Young people are growing up in our cities without any hope of getting a job.* **2 sb's best/last/only hope** the best/last/only person or thing that can help you and make you succeed *Doctors say his only hope is a transplant.* **3 in the hope of/that** because you want something good to happen [+ doing sth] *She went to Paris in the hope of improving her French.* **4 pin your hopes on sb/sth** to hope that someone or something will help you achieve what you want

hopeful /'həʊpfʰl/ *adjective* **1** feeling positive

about a future event or situation *Many teenagers do not feel **hopeful about** the future.* ○ [+ (that)] *Police are still **hopeful that** they will find the missing family.* **2** If something is hopeful, it makes you feel that what you want to happen will happen. *There are **hopeful signs** that she will make a full recovery.* ● **hopefulness** *noun* [U] ● **hopeful** *noun* [C] someone who hopes to succeed, especially in the entertainment business *a **young hopeful***

o⁻**hopefully** /ˈhəʊpfəli/ *adverb* **1** used, often at the start of a sentence, to express what you would like to happen *Hopefully it won't rain.* **2** in a hopeful way *"Are there any tickets left?"* she asked *hopefully.*

hopeless /ˈhəʊpləs/ *adjective* **1** VERY BAD very bad and not likely to succeed or improve *a hopeless situation* ○ *They searched for survivors, but it was **hopeless**.* **2** NOT ABLE very bad at a particular activity *Dad's a hopeless cook.* ○ *I'm **hopeless at** sports.* **3** NOT POSITIVE feeling no hope *She was depressed and felt totally **hopeless about** the future.* ● **hopelessness** *noun* [U] *the hopelessness of the situation*

hopelessly /ˈhəʊpləsli/ *adverb* extremely, or in a way that makes you lose hope *hopelessly lost* ○ *They met at university and fell **hopelessly in** love.*

hops /hɒps/ *noun* [plural] the flowers of a plant that are used to make beer

horde /hɔːd/ *noun* [C] a large group of people *There was a **horde of** tourists outside Buckingham Palace.*

horizon /həˈraɪzᵊn/ *noun* **1** [C] the line in the distance where the sky seems to touch the land or sea **2 broaden/expand/widen your horizons** to increase the number of things that you know about, have experienced, or can do *Travelling certainly broadens your horizons.* **3 on the horizon** likely to happen soon *Economic recovery is on the horizon.*

horizontal/vertical

horizontal stripes

vertical stripes

horizontal /ˌhɒrɪˈzɒntᵊl/ *adjective* level and flat, or parallel to the ground or to the bottom of a page *a horizontal line/stripe* ● **horizontally** *adverb*

hormone /ˈhɔːməʊn/ *noun* [C] one of several chemicals produced in your body that influence its growth and development ● **hormonal** /hɔːˈməʊnᵊl/ *adjective a **hormonal imbalance***

horn /hɔːn/ *noun* [C] **1** ANIMAL one of the two hard, pointed growths on the heads of cows, goats, and some other animals **2** EQUIPMENT a piece of equipment used to make a loud sound as a warning or signal *a car horn* ○ *The taxi driver **hooted** his **horn**.* **3** MUSIC a curved musical instrument that you blow into to make a sound *the French horn*

horoscope /ˈhɒrəskəʊp/ *noun* [C] a description of what someone is like and what might happen to them in the future, based on the position of the stars and planets when they were born

horrendous /həˈrendəs/ *adjective* extremely unpleasant or bad *She suffered horrendous injuries in the accident.* ● **horrendously** *adverb* extremely or extremely badly *horrendously expensive*

horrible /ˈhɒrəbl/ *adjective* very unpleasant or bad *What's that horrible smell?* ○ *That was a horrible thing to say to your sister.* ● **horribly** *adverb* extremely, or in a very bad or unpleasant way *His plan went horribly wrong.*

horrid /ˈhɒrɪd/ *adjective* very unpleasant or unkind

horrific /hɒrˈɪfɪk/ *adjective* very bad and shocking *a horrific accident/crime* ○ *horrific injuries* ● **horrifically** *adverb*

horrify /ˈhɒrɪfaɪ/ *verb* [T] to make someone feel very shocked [often passive] *I was horrified to hear about your accident.* ● **horrifying** *adjective*

horror /ˈhɒrəʳ/ *noun* **1** [C, U] a strong feeling of shock or fear, or something that makes you feel shocked or afraid *She watched **in horror** as the car skidded across the road.* **2 a horror film/movie/story** a film or story that entertains people by shocking or frightening them

o⁻**horse** /hɔːs/ *noun* [C] a large animal with four legs, which people ride or use to pull heavy things

horseback /ˈhɔːsbæk/ *noun* **1 on horseback** riding a horse *police on horseback* **2 horseback riding** US (UK **horse riding**) the sport or activity of riding a horse ⊃See colour picture **Sports 1** on page Centre 14.

horse ˈchestnut *noun* [C] a tree that produces shiny, brown nuts in thick green shells with sharp points, or one of these nuts

horse-drawn /ˈhɔːsdrɔːn/ *adjective* [always before noun] A horse-drawn vehicle is pulled by a horse.

horseman, horsewoman /ˈhɔːsmən, ˈhɔːsˌwʊmən/ *noun* [C] *plural* **horsemen** or **horsewomen** a man/woman who rides horses well

horsepower /ˈhɔːsˌpaʊəʳ/ (*written abbreviation* **hp**) *noun* [U] a unit for measuring the power of an engine

horse ˈracing *noun* [U] the sport where people race on horses, usually to win money

horse ˈriding UK (US **ˈhorseback ˌriding**) *noun* [U] the sport or activity of riding a horse ⊃See colour picture **Sports 1** on page Centre 14.

horseshoe /ˈhɔːsʃuː/ *noun* [C] a U-shaped piece of metal that is nailed to a horse's foot

horticulture /ˈhɔːtɪkʌltʃəʳ/ *noun* [U] the study or activity of growing plants ● **horticultural**

/ˌhɔːtɪˈkʌltʃ°rºl/ *adjective* relating to gardening

hose /həʊz/ *noun* **1** [C] (*also UK* **hosepipe** /ˈhəʊzpaɪp/) a long pipe made of rubber or plastic and used for directing water somewhere, usually onto a garden or fire **2** [plural] (*also* **pantyhose**) *US* a piece of women's clothing made of very thin material that covers the legs and bottom

hospice /ˈhɒspɪs/ *noun* [C] a place where people who are dying live and are cared for

hospitable /hɒsˈpɪtəbl/ *adjective* A hospitable person or place is friendly, pleasant, and welcomes visitors.

WORD PARTNERS FOR *hospital*

be **admitted to/discharged from** hospital • be (UK) **in**/(US) **in the** hospital

---

o₋**hospital** /ˈhɒspɪt°l/ *noun* [C, U] a place where ill or injured people go to be treated by doctors and nurses *He was (UK)* **in hospital**/(US) **in the hospital** *for two weeks.*

hospitalize (*also UK* -ise) /ˈhɒspɪt°laɪz/ *verb* [T] to take someone to hospital and keep them there for treatment [often passive] *My wife was often hospitalized for depression.*

host¹ /həʊst/ *noun* **1** PARTY [C] someone who organizes a party and invites the guests **2** TELEVISION [C] someone who introduces the guests on a radio or television programme *a talk show host* **3** PLACE [C] a country or city that provides the place and equipment for an organized event *Australia played host to the Olympics in 2000.* **4** COMPUTERS a company that hosts websites on the Internet **5 a host of sth** a large number of people or things *I've got a whole host of questions to ask you.*

host² /həʊst/ *verb* [I] **1** to be the host of an event *to host a party/dinner* **2** to provide the computer equipment and programs that allow a website to operate on the Internet

hostage /ˈhɒstɪdʒ/ *noun* **1** [C] someone who is kept as a prisoner and may be hurt or killed in order to force other people to do something **2 take/hold sb hostage** to catch or keep someone as a prisoner *Two tourists were held hostage by terrorists.*

hostel /ˈhɒst°l/ *noun* [C] a place like a cheap hotel, where you can live when you are away from home or have no home *a hostel for the homeless* ○ *a student hostel* ➔See also: **youth hostel**.

hostess /ˈhəʊstɪs/ *noun* [C] **1** a woman who organizes a party and invites the guests **2** a woman who introduces the guests on a television programme ➔See also: **air hostess**.

hostile /ˈhɒstaɪl/ *adjective* **1** unfriendly and not liking or agreeing with something *Some politicians were very hostile to the idea.* **2** unpleasant or not suitable for living or growing *a hostile climate*

WORD PARTNERS FOR *hostility*

arouse/provoke hostility • **open** hostility • hostility **to/towards** sb

---

hostility /hɒsˈtɪləti/ *noun* **1** [U] unfriendly, angry behaviour that shows that you dislike someone *hostility towards outsiders* **2** [U] when you strongly disagree with something or someone *There is still open hostility to the idea.* **3 hostilities** [plural] *formal* fighting in a war

o₋**hot¹** /hɒt/ *adjective* **hotter, hottest 1** VERY WARM having a high temperature *a hot summer's day* ○ *a hot drink/meal* ○ *I'm too hot in this jacket.* **2** SPICY Hot food contains strong spices which cause a burning feeling in your mouth. *Be careful. The chilli sauce is very hot.* **3** EXCITING *informal* exciting or interesting *Hollywood's hottest new actress* **4 a hot issue/topic** a subject which people discuss and have strong feelings about *The legalization of drugs is a hot topic.* ➔See also: **piping hot, red-hot**.

hot² /hɒt/ *verb* **hotting** *past* **hotted**
hot up *UK informal* If a situation or event hots up, it becomes more exciting and more things start to happen.

hot-'air bal,loon *noun* [C] a very large balloon filled with hot air, that has a container below it where people can travel ➔See picture at **balloon**.

hotbed /ˈhɒtbed/ *noun* [C] a place where there is a lot of a particular activity, usually something bad *The government was a hotbed of corruption.*

,**hot 'chocolate** *noun* [C, U] a hot, sweet drink with a chocolate flavour

'**hot ,dog** *noun* [C] a cooked sausage (= tube of meat and spices) that you usually eat inside bread

---

WORD PARTNERS FOR *hotel*

at/in a hotel • a hotel **guest/room** • a **luxury** hotel

---

o₋**hotel** /həʊˈtel/ *noun* [C] a place where you pay to stay when you are away from home *We spent our honeymoon in a luxury hotel.* ○ *a hotel room*

hotelier /həʊˈteliəʳ/ ⓤ/həʊˈtəljər/ *noun* [C] someone who owns or is in charge of a hotel

hotline /ˈhɒtlaɪn/ *noun* [C] a telephone number that you can ring for help or information *Ring our 24-hour hotline for advice.*

hotly /ˈhɒtli/ *adverb* **1** in an angry or excited way *He hotly denied the rumours.* **2 hotly contested** If a race, election or other competition is hotly contested, everyone is trying very hard to win it.

,**hot-'water bottle** *noun* [C] a flat, rubber container that you fill with hot water to keep you warm

hound¹ /haʊnd/ *noun* [C] a dog that is used when people hunt animals

hound² /haʊnd/ *verb* [T] to follow someone and annoy them by asking questions or taking photographs [often passive] *She is always being hounded by photographers.*

o₋**hour** /aʊəʳ/ *noun* **1** [C] a period of time equal to 60 minutes *half an hour* ○ *It's a six-hour flight.* ○ *The job pays $5 an hour.* **2** [C] the period of time when a particular activity happens or when a shop or public building is open [usually plural] *working hours* ○ *Our opening hours*

---

are from 8 to 6. ○ *I've got to go to the bank (UK) in my* **lunch hour***/ (US) on my lunch hour.* **3 hours** *informal* a long time *I* **spent hours** *doing my homework.* **4 the hour** the point when a new hour begins *The train leaves at two minutes past the hour.* ○ *My watch beeps* **on the hour.** **5 all hours** very late at night, until early morning, or almost all the time *Our neighbours are up till all hours every night, playing loud music.* **6 the early/small hours** the hours between midnight and the time that the sun rises ⊃See also: **rush hour.**

COMMON LEARNER ERROR

hour or **time**?

An **hour** is a period of 60 minutes.
The journey takes about three hours.
We went for a 2-hour walk.

Time is measured in hours and minutes. We use **time** to refer to a particular point during the day or night, or to say when something happens.
What time do you get up in the morning?
There's only one bus at that time of night.
Remember to use **time** not 'hour' when you are talking about what time it is.
"What time is it?" "2 o'clock".
~~*"What hour is it?" "2 o'clock".*~~

---

hourly /ˈaʊəli/ *adjective, adverb* **1** happening every hour *There is an hourly bus service.* **2** for each hour *an hourly rate/wage*

WORD PARTNERS FOR *house*

build/buy/rent/sell a house • a **detached/semi-detached/terraced** house

---

⚬**house**¹ /haʊs/ *noun plural* **houses** /ˈhaʊzɪz/ **1** [BUILDING] [C] a building where people live, usually one family or group *a three-bedroomed house* ○ *We went to my aunt's house for dinner.* **2** [PEOPLE] [no plural] the people who live in a house *The baby's screaming woke the* **whole house** *up.* **3** [PLACE FOR ACTIVITY] [C] the place where a particular business or activity happens *an opera house* ○ *a publishing house* **4 the House** a group of people which makes a country's laws, or the place where they meet *the House of Commons/Representatives* ○ *The House voted on the proposals.* **5** [THEATRE] [C] the people watching a performance or the area where they sit [usually singular] *The actors played to a* **full house***.* **6 on the house** If food or drink is on the house in a bar or restaurant, it is free. ⊃See also: **boarding house, full house, row house, terraced house, the White House.**

house² /haʊz/ *verb* [T] **1** to give a person or animal a place to live *This development will house over 100 families.* **2** to provide space for something *The museum houses a huge collection of paintings.*

house ar'rest *noun* **under house arrest** when you are kept as a prisoner in your own home

houseboat /ˈhaʊsbəʊt/ *noun* [C] a boat that people can live on

housebound /ˈhaʊsbaʊnd/ *adjective* unable to leave your home because you are too ill or old

household¹ /ˈhaʊshəʊld/ *noun* [C] a family or group of people who live together in a house *Many households own more than one television.*

household² /ˈhaʊshəʊld/ *adjective* **1** [always before noun] connected with or belonging to a home *household bills/expenses* ○ *household products/goods* **2 a household name** someone or something that everyone knows *Her TV roles made her a household name in the UK.*

householder /ˈhaʊshəʊldəʳ/ *noun* [C] *UK* someone who owns or rents a house

'house ˌhusband *noun* [C] a man who takes care of the house and children while his wife or partner earns money for the family

housekeeper /ˈhaʊsˌkiːpəʳ/ *noun* [C] someone who is paid to clean and cook in someone else's house

housekeeping /ˈhaʊsˌkiːpɪŋ/ *noun* [U] the cleaning and cooking that you do in your home

'house ˌ(music) *noun* [U] a type of electronic pop music with a strong beat for dancing

ˌHouse of 'Commons *noun* [no plural] one of the two parts of the British parliament, with elected members who make laws

ˌHouse of 'Lords *noun* [no plural] one of the two parts of the British parliament, with members who are chosen by the government

ˌHouse of Repre'sentatives *noun* [no plural] a group of politicians elected by people in the US to make laws

ˌHouses of 'Parliament *noun* [plural] the House of Commons and the House of Lords, or the building in London where they meet

'house ˌwarming *noun* [C] a party to celebrate moving into a new house

housewife /ˈhaʊswaɪf/ *noun* [C] *plural* **housewives** /ˈhaʊswaɪvz/ a woman who stays at home to cook, clean, and take care of her family

housework /ˈhaʊswɜːk/ *noun* [U] the work that you do to keep your house clean *I can't stand doing housework.*

housing /ˈhaʊzɪŋ/ *noun* [U] buildings for people to live in *a shortage of local housing*

'housing eˌstate *UK* (*US* **'housing deˌvelopment**) *noun* [C] an area with a large number of houses that were built at the same time

hover /ˈhɒvəʳ/ *verb* [I] **1** to stay up in the air but without moving anywhere *A helicopter hovered overhead.* **2** If you hover, you stand and wait near someone or something. *A waiter hovered at the table ready to take our order.*

hovercraft /ˈhɒvəkrɑːft/ *noun* [C] a boat that moves across the surface of land or water supported by a large cushion (= soft container) of air

⚬**how**¹ /haʊ/ *adverb* **1** [WAY] used to ask about the way something happens or is done *How did he die?* ○ *How does she manage to keep the house so tidy?* **2** [QUANTITY] used to ask about quantity, size, or age *How big is the house?* ○ *How old are they?* ○ *How much* (= what price) *was that dress?* **3** [EMPHASIZE] used before an adjective or adverb to emphasize it *I was amazed at how quickly she finished.* **4** [HEALTH] used to ask

---

| ɑː arm | ɜː her | iː see | ɔː saw | uː too | aɪ my | aʊ how | eə hair | eɪ day | əʊ no | ɪə near | ɔɪ boy | ʊə poor | aɪə fire | aʊə sour |

about someone's health *How are you feeling today?* **5** SITUATION used to ask about the success or progress of a situation *How's everything going?* ○ *How was the exam?* **6 How are you?** used to ask someone if they are well and happy *"How are you Jane?" - "Oh, not so bad thanks."* **7 How about..?** used to make a suggestion *How about a drink?* ○ [+ doing sth] *How about going to the cinema?* **8 How come?** *informal* used to ask about the reason for something, especially when you feel surprised about it *"Kate's gone to the party on her own." "How come?"* **9 How strange/stupid/weird, etc. is that?** said to mean that something is strange/ stupid, etc. ⊃See also: know-how.

how or what?

In these expressions we use **what**. Be careful not to use 'how'.

what something is called

I don't know what it's called in English.

~~I don't know how it's called in English.~~

what something/someone looks like

I'd like to see what it looks like before I buy it.

What does your brother look like?

how² /haʊ/ *conjunction* used to talk about the way that something happens or is done [+ to do sth] *I don't know how to turn the video on.*

o→**however¹** /haʊ'evəʳ/ *adverb* **1 however cold/difficult/slowly, etc** used to say that it does not make any difference how cold/difficult/ slowly, etc *We're not going to get there in time, however fast we drive.* **2** used when you are about to say something which is surprising compared with what you have just said *He had always been a successful businessman. Recently, however, things have not been going well for him.* **3** *UK* used to ask about how something happened when the person asking feels surprised *However did you manage to persuade her?*

however² /haʊ'evəʳ/ *conjunction* in any way *However you look at it, it's still a mess.* ○ *You can do it however you like.*

howl /haʊl/ *verb* [I] **1** ANIMAL If a dog or wolf (= wild animal like a dog) howls, it makes a long, sad sound. **2** MAKE SOUND to make a loud sound, usually to express pain, sadness, or another strong emotion *He howled in pain.* ○ *The audience was howling with laughter.* **3** WIND If the wind howls, it blows hard and makes a lot of noise. ● **howl** *noun* [C]

hp *written abbreviation for* horsepower (= a unit for measuring the power of an engine)

HQ /ˌeɪtʃ'kjuː/ *noun* [C, U] *abbreviation for* headquarters (= the place from where an organization is controlled)

hr *written abbreviation for* hour

HRH /ˌeɪtʃɑːr'eɪtʃ/ *abbreviation for* His/Her Royal Highness: used when speaking to or about a royal person

HTH *internet abbreviation for* hope this helps: used when you send someone information you

think is useful, especially when you answer a question

HTML /ˌeɪtʃtiːem'el/ *abbreviation for* hypertext markup language: a way of marking text so that it can be seen on the Internet

http /ˌeɪtʃtiːtiː'piː/ *abbreviation for* hypertext transfer protocol: a set of instructions made by a computer program that allows your computer to connect to an Internet document

hub /hʌb/ *noun* [C] **1** a place that is the centre of a particular activity [usually singular] *Silicon Valley has become the **hub** of the electronics industry.* **2** the round part in the centre of a wheel

huddle¹ /'hʌdl/ (*also* huddle together/up) *verb* [I] to move closer to other people, or to hold your arms and legs close to your body, usually because you are cold or frightened *They huddled around the fire to keep warm.*

huddle² /'hʌdl/ *noun* [C] a group of people or things that are standing close together

hue /hjuː/ *noun* [C] *literary* a colour

huff¹ /hʌf/ *verb* **huff and puff** *informal* to breathe loudly, especially because you have been exercising

huff² /hʌf/ *noun* **in a huff** *informal* angry with someone *Mum's in a huff because I didn't call yesterday.*

hug¹ /hʌg/ *verb* hugging, *past* hugged **1** [I, T] to put your arms around someone and hold them tightly, usually because you love them *They hugged and kissed each other.* **2** [T] to stay very

hug

close to the edge of something *The road hugs the coast for several miles.*

hug² /hʌg/ *noun* [C] when you put your arms around someone and hold them tightly *She gave me a big hug before she left.*

o→**huge** /hjuːdʒ/ *adjective* extremely large *a huge house*

hugely /'hjuːdʒli/ *adverb* extremely *hugely popular/successful*

huh /hʌ/ *exclamation informal* used to ask a question, or to express surprise, anger, etc *So, you're leaving, huh?*

hull /hʌl/ *noun* [C] the main part of a ship that is mostly under water

hullo *UK* (*UK/US* hello) /hə'ləʊ/ *exclamation* **1** used to greet someone *Hullo, Chris, how are things?* **2** used to start a conversation on the telephone *Hullo, this is Alex.*

hum /hʌm/ *verb* humming, *past* hummed **1** [I, T] to sing without opening your mouth *She hummed to herself as she walked to school.* **2** [I] to make a continuous, low sound *The computers were humming in the background.* **3 be humming** If a place is humming, it is busy and full of activity. ● **hum** *noun* [C] a low, continuous sound *the hum of traffic*

o→**human¹** /'hjuːmən/ *adjective* **1** relating to people or their characteristics *the human body*

○ *human behaviour* ○ *The accident was caused by* **human error** (= a person's mistake). **2 be only human** to not be perfect *Of course Tom makes mistakes - he's only human.*

human² /'hjuːmən/ (*also* ˌhuman 'being) *noun* [C] a man, woman, or child *The disease affects both humans and animals.*

humane /hjuːˈmeɪn/ *adjective* kind, especially towards people or animals that are suffering *They fought for more humane treatment of prisoners of war.* ⊃Opposite **inhumane**. ● **humanely** *adverb*

humanism /'hjuːmənɪzᵊm/ *noun* [U] a belief system based on human needs and values and not on a god or religion ● **humanist** *noun* [C] ● **humanistic** /ˌhjuːməˈnɪstɪk/ *adjective*

humanitarian /hjuːˌmænɪˈteəriən/ *adjective* connected with improving people's lives and reducing suffering *The UN is sending* **humanitarian aid** *to the refugees.*

humanities /hjuːˈmænɪtiz/ *noun* [plural] subjects that you study which are not connected with science, such as literature and history

humanity /hjuːˈmænɪti/ *noun* [U] **1** ALL PEOPLE all people *The massacre was a* **crime against humanity**. **2** KINDNESS kindness and sympathy towards others ⊃Opposite **inhumanity**. **3** BEING HUMAN the condition of being human

humankind /ˌhjuːmənˈkaɪnd/ *noun* [U] all the people in the world

humanly /'hjuːmənli/ *adverb* **humanly possible** able to be done by people *Doctors did everything humanly possible to save her life.*

ˌhuman 'nature *noun* [U] feelings, qualities, and behaviour that are typical of most people *It's human nature to want to be loved.*

the ˌhuman 'race *noun* all the people in the world

ˌhuman re'sources *UK* (*US* ˌhuman 'resources) *noun* [U] the department of an organization that deals with finding new people to work there, keeping records about all the organization's employees, and helping them with any problems

ˌhuman 'rights *noun* [plural] the basic rights that every person should have, such as justice and the freedom to say what you think *international laws protecting human rights* ○ *the human rights group Amnesty International*

humble¹ /'hʌmbl/ *adjective* **1** not proud or not believing that you are important *He's very humble about his success.* **2** poor or of a low social rank *She rose from* **humble beginnings** *to become Prime Minister.* ● **humbly** *adverb*

humble² /'hʌmbl/ *verb* [T] to make someone understand that they are not as important or special as they think they are *She was humbled by the unexpected defeat.* ● **humbling** *adjective* a **humbling experience**

humdrum /'hʌmdrʌm/ *adjective* boring and ordinary *a humdrum existence*

humid /'hjuːmɪd/ *adjective* Humid air or weather is hot and slightly wet. *a hot and humid climate*

humidity /hjuːˈmɪdəti/ *noun* [U] a measurement of how much water there is in the air

humiliate /hjuːˈmɪlieɪt/ *verb* [T] to make someone feel stupid or ashamed *How could you humiliate me in front of all my friends!* ● **humiliated** *adjective* *Sue felt completely humiliated.* ● **humiliation** /hjuːˌmɪliˈeɪʃᵊn/ *noun* [C, U]

humiliating /hjuːˈmɪlieɪtɪŋ/ *adjective* making you feel stupid or ashamed *a humiliating defeat*

humility /hjuːˈmɪləti/ *noun* [U] the quality of not being proud or not thinking that you are better than other people

humor /'hjuːmər/ *noun, verb* US spelling of humour

humorless /'hjuːmələs/ *adjective* US spelling of humourless

humorous /'hjuːmᵊrəs/ *adjective* funny, or making you laugh *a humorous book* ● **humorously** *adverb*

WORD PARTNERS FOR *humour*
a **sense** of humour ● a **dry/wry** humour

---

humour¹ *UK* (*US* humor) /'hjuːmər/ *noun* [U] **1** ABILITY the ability to laugh and recognize that something is funny *He's got a great* **sense of humour**. **2** FUNNY QUALITY the quality of being funny, or things that are funny *His speech was full of humour.* **3** MOOD *formal* the way you are feeling, or your mood **good humour**

humour² *UK* (*US* humor) /'hjuːmər/ *verb* [T] to do what someone wants so that they do not become annoyed or upset *Carol applied for the job just to humour me.*

humourless *UK* (*US* humorless) /'hjuːmələs/ *adjective* unable to laugh and recognize when something is funny, or being without funny qualities

hump /hʌmp/ *noun* [C] **1** a round, raised area on a road or other surface **2** a round, hard part on an animal's or person's back *a camel's hump*

hunch¹ /hʌnʃ/ *noun* [C] a feeling or guess that something might be true, when there is no proof *I* **had a hunch** *that he would get the job.*

hunch² /hʌnʃ/ *verb* [I] to stand or sit with your shoulders and back curved forward *Sitting* **hunched over** *a computer all day can cause back problems.*

hunchback /'hʌnʃbæk/ *noun* [C] someone with a large lump on their back, which makes them lean forward

⊶**hundred** /'hʌndrəd/ **1** the number 100 **2** **hundreds** *informal* a lot *Hundreds of people wrote in to complain.*

hundredth¹ /'hʌndrədθ/ 100th written as a word

hundredth² /'hʌndrədθ/ *noun* [C] one of a hundred equal parts of something; 1/100, .01 *a hundredth of a second*

hundredweight /'hʌndrədweɪt/ (*written abbreviation* cwt) *noun* [C] *plural* hundredweight a unit for measuring weight, equal to 50.8 kilograms in the UK and 45.36 kilograms in the US

hung /hʌŋ/ *past of* hang

hunger /'hʌŋgər/ *noun* **1** FEELING [U] the feeling

you have when you need to eat *The children were almost crying with hunger by the time we got home.* **2** NOT ENOUGH FOOD [U] when you do not have enough food *Many of the refugees died of hunger.* **3** WISH [no plural] a strong wish for something *a hunger for success/knowledge*

'**hunger ˌstrike** *noun* [C, U] when someone refuses to eat in order to show that they strongly disagree with something *The prisoners went on hunger strike.*

hungover /ˌhʌnˈəʊvəʳ/ *adjective* feeling ill after drinking too much alcohol the day before *He was hungover and in a bad mood.*

o━**hungry** /ˈhʌŋgri/ *adjective* **1** wanting or needing food *I'm hungry. What's for supper?* ○ *Are you hungry?* ○ *I hope you're hungry – there's loads of food.* **2 go hungry** to not have enough food to eat *In an ideal world, nobody should go hungry.* **3 be hungry for sth** to have a strong wish for something *The journalists were hungry for more details of the accident.* • **hungrily** *adverb*

hunk /hʌŋk/ *noun* [C] **1** *informal* an attractive man who is often young and has a strong body **2** a piece of something, usually large and not flat or smooth *a hunk of bread* ○ *a great hunk of cheese* ➋See colour picture **Pieces and Quantities** on page Centre 1.

hunt¹ /hʌnt/ *verb* [I, T] **1** to chase and kill wild animals *to hunt deer/rabbits* **2** to search for something *The children hunted for sea shells on the beach.* ○ *I spent the morning hunting for Heather's photos.* • **hunter** *noun* [C] a person who hunts wild animals

hunt sb/sth down to search everywhere for someone or something until you find them *He was eventually hunted down and brought to justice.*

hunt² /hʌnt/ *noun* [C] **1** a search for something or someone *a job hunt* ○ *The detective leading the hunt for the killer spoke at the news conference.* **2** when people chase and kill wild animals *a fox/deer hunt* ➋See also: **witch-hunt**.

hunting /ˈhʌntɪŋ/ *noun* [U] the sport of chasing and killing animals *fox-hunting* ○ *She's very much against hunting of any sort.*

hurdle¹ /ˈhɜːdl/ *noun* [C] **1** a bar or fence that people or horses jump over in a race *He cleared the first four hurdles but fell at the fifth.* **2** a problem or difficulty that you have to deal with in order to be able to make progress *Getting a work permit was the first hurdle to overcome.*

hurdle² /ˈhɜːdl/ *verb* [I, T] to jump over something, such as a bar or a fence, when you are running • **hurdler** *noun* [C]

hurl /hɜːl/ *verb* **1** [T] to throw something with a lot of force, usually in an angry or violent way *The demonstrators hurled stones at police.* **2 hurl abuse/insults, etc at sb** to shout something at someone in a rude or angry way

hurrah (*also* **hooray**) /həˈrɑː/ *exclamation* something that you shout when you are happy, excited, etc, or when you approve of someone or something *Hurrah! Ian's won!*

hurricane /ˈhʌrɪkən/ *noun* [C] a violent storm with very strong winds

hurried /ˈhʌrid/ *adjective* done more quickly than normal *a hurried explanation/meeting* • **hurriedly** *adverb*

o━**hurry¹** /ˈhʌri/ *verb* [I, T] to move or do things more quickly than normal or to make someone do this *to hurry away/home* ○ *Please hurry, the train is about to leave.* ○ [+ to do sth] *We had to hurry to get there on time.*

hurry up to start moving or doing something more quickly *Hurry up! We're going to be late.*

hurry² /ˈhʌri/ *noun* **1 be in a hurry** If you are in a hurry, you want or need to do something quickly. *If you're in a hurry, it's better to take a taxi.* **2 be in no hurry; not be in any hurry** If you are in no hurry to do something, either you do not need to do it soon or you do not really want to do it . [+ to do sth] *They are in no hurry to sign a contract.*

o━**hurt¹** /hɜːt/ *verb past* **hurt 1** CAUSE PAIN [T] to cause someone pain or to injure them *Simon hurt his knee playing football.* ○ [often reflexive] *She hurt herself when she slipped on an icy step.* **2** BE PAINFUL [I] If a part of your body hurts, it is painful. *My eyes really hurt.* ○ [+ to do sth] *It hurts to walk on it.* **3** UPSET [I, T] to cause emotional pain to someone *Her comments about my work really hurt.* **4** AFFECT [T] to have a harmful effect on something *His chances of re-election were hurt by allegations of corruption.* **5 it won't/wouldn't hurt (sb) to do sth** *informal* used to say that someone should do something *It wouldn't hurt to get there a bit earlier than usual.* ➋See also: wouldn't hurt a **fly²**.

hurt² /hɜːt/ *adjective* [never before noun] **1** injured or in pain *Several people were seriously hurt in the accident.* ○ *Put that knife away before someone gets hurt.* **2** upset or unhappy *She was deeply hurt by what he said.*

hurt³ /hɜːt/ *noun* [U] emotional pain *She has caused a lot of hurt.*

hurtful /ˈhɜːtfəl/ *adjective* Hurtful behaviour or remarks make someone feel upset. *hurtful comments/remarks*

hurtle /ˈhɜːtl/ *verb* [I] to move very quickly in a way which is not controlled and may be dangerous *The explosion sent pieces of glass and metal hurtling through the air.*

o━**husband** /ˈhʌzbənd/ *noun* [C] the man you are married to *Janet's husband is in the Navy.*

hush¹ /hʌʃ/ *exclamation* used to tell someone to be quiet, especially if they are crying *It's okay. Hush now and wipe your eyes.*

hush² /hʌʃ/ *noun* [no plural] a period of silence *A hush fell over the room.* ●**hushed** *adjective a hushed atmosphere/crowd*

hush³ /hʌʃ/ *verb* [T] to make someone be quiet
hush sth up to keep something secret, especially from the public, because it could cause embarrassment or trouble *The whole affair was hushed up by the management.*

hush-hush /ˌhʌʃˈhʌʃ/ *adjective informal* If something is hush-hush, it is kept secret. *The project's all very hush-hush.*

husky¹ /ˈhʌski/ *adjective* **1** A husky voice is low and rough but usually sounds attractive. **2** *US* A husky man or boy is big and strong.

husky² /ˈhʌski/ *noun* [C] a large, strong dog that is used to pull heavy things across snow

hustle¹ /ˈhʌsl/ *verb* **1** [T] to make someone move somewhere, especially by pushing them quickly *The security men hustled him out of the back door.* **2** [I, T] *informal* to try to persuade someone, especially to buy something, often illegally *to hustle for business/customers*

hustle² /ˈhʌsl/ *noun* **hustle and bustle** busy movement and noise, especially where there are a lot of people *He wanted to escape the hustle and bustle of city life.*

hustler /ˈhʌslər/ *noun* [C] someone who tries to persuade people to give them what they want, especially in order to make money illegally

hut /hʌt/ *noun* [C] a small, simple building, often made of wood *a mountain hut*

hybrid /ˈhaɪbrɪd/ *noun* [C] **1** a plant or animal that is produced from two different types of plant or animal **2** something, for example a machine, which is made using ideas or parts from two different things **3** (*also* hybrid car) a vehicle with an engine that uses both petrol (= a liquid fuel made from oil) and another type of energy, usually electricity or batteries ●**hybrid** *adjective*

hydrant /ˈhaɪdrənt/ *noun* [C] a pipe, especially at the side of the road, which is connected to the water system and is used to get water to stop fires *a fire hydrant*

hydraulic /haɪˈdrɔːlɪk/ *adjective* operated using the force of water or another liquid

hydro- /haɪdrəʊ-/ *prefix* relating to water *hydroponic* (= a method of growing plants in water)

hydroelectric /ˌhaɪdrəʊɪˈlektrɪk/ *adjective* using the force of water to create electricity *hydroelectric power*

hydrogen /ˈhaɪdrədʒən/ *noun* [U] a gas that combines with oxygen to form water

WORD PARTNERS FOR *hygiene*

standards of hygiene   ●   **dental/personal** hygiene

hygiene /ˈhaɪdʒiːn/ *noun* [U] the process of keeping things clean, especially to prevent disease *health and hygiene regulations* ○ **dental/personal hygiene** ●**hygienic** /haɪˈdʒiːnɪk/ *adjective* very clean, so that bacteria cannot spread

hymn /hɪm/ *noun* [C] a song sung by Christians in church to praise God

hype¹ /haɪp/ *noun* [U] when people talk a lot

about something, especially in newspapers, on television, etc, and make it seem more important or exciting than it really is *media hype* ○ *There's been a lot of* **hype about/surrounding** *his latest film.*

hype² /haɪp/ (*also* hype up) *verb* [T] to make something seem more important or exciting than it really is by talking about it a lot, especially in newspapers, on television, etc *It's being* **hyped as** *the musical event of the year.* ●**hyped** *adjective*

hyper /ˈhaɪpər/ *adjective informal* Someone who is hyper has more energy than is normal and is very excited.

hyper- /haɪpər/ *prefix* having a lot of or too much of a quality *hyperactive* ○ *hypersensitive* (= more than normally sensitive)

hyperactive /ˌhaɪpərˈæktɪv/ *adjective* Someone who is hyperactive has more energy than is normal, gets excited easily, and cannot stay still or think about their work. *hyperactive children* ● **hyperactivity** /ˌhaɪpərækˈtɪvəti/ *noun* [U]

hyperbole /haɪˈpɜːbəli/ *noun* [U] *formal* when you describe something as much better, more important, etc than it really is

hyperlink /ˈhaɪpəlɪŋk/ *noun* [C] a connection that lets you move easily between two computer documents or two pages on the Internet

hypermarket /ˈhaɪpəˌmɑːkɪt/ *noun* [C] a very large shop, usually outside the centre of town

hypertext /ˈhaɪpətekst/ *noun* [U] a way of joining a word or image to another page, document, etc on the Internet or in another computer program so that you can move from one to the other easily

hyphen /ˈhaɪfən/ *noun* [C] a mark (-) used to join two words together, or to show that a word has been divided and continues on the next line ⊃See Extra help page **Punctuation** on page Centre 33. ● **hyphenated** *adjective* written with a hyphen

hypnosis /hɪpˈnəʊsɪs/ *noun* [U] a mental state like sleep, in which a person's thoughts can be easily influenced by someone else *Police placed witnesses* **under hypnosis** *in an effort to gain additional information.* ● **hypnotic** /hɪpˈnɒtɪk/ *adjective*

hypnotize (*also* UK **-ise**) /ˈhɪpnətaɪz/ *verb* [T] to place someone in a mental state like sleep, in which their thoughts can be easily influenced ● **hypnotist** *noun* [C] someone who hypnotizes people ● **hypnotism** /ˈhɪpnətɪzᵊm/ *noun* [U] when someone is hypnotized

hypochondriac /ˌhaɪpəˈkɒndriæk/ *noun* [C] someone who worries about their health more than is normal, although they are not really ill ● **hypochondria** /ˌhaɪpəʊˈkɒndriə/ *noun* [U]

hypocrisy /hɪˈpɒkrəsi/ *noun* [C, U] when someone pretends to believe something that they do not really believe or that is the opposite of what they do or say at another time

hypocrite /ˈhɪpəkrɪt/ *noun* [C] someone who pretends to believe something that they do not really believe or that is the opposite of what they do or say at another time ● **hypocritical** /ˌhɪpəʊˈkrɪtɪkᵊl/ *adjective* ● **hypocritically** *adverb*

hypothermia /ˌhaɪpəʊˈθɜːmiə/ *noun* [U] a serious illness caused by someone's body becoming too cold

hypothesis /haɪˈpɒθəsɪs/ *noun* [C] *plural* **hypotheses** /haɪˈpɒθəsiːz/ a suggested explanation for something which has not yet been proved to be true

hypothetical /ˌhaɪpəˈθetɪkəl/ *adjective* A hypothetical situation or idea has been suggested but does not yet really exist or has not been proved to be true.

hysteria /hɪˈstɪəriə/ *noun* [U] extreme fear, excitement, anger, etc which cannot be controlled *mass hysteria*

hysterical /hɪˈsterɪkəl/ *adjective* **1** If someone is hysterical, they cannot control their feelings or behaviour because they are extremely frightened, angry, excited, etc. *hysterical laughter* ○ *As soon as Wendy saw the blood, she became hysterical.* **2** *informal* extremely funny ●**hysterically** *adverb* *They all thought it was hysterically funny.*

hysterics /hɪˈsterɪks/ *noun* **1** [plural] uncontrolled behaviour **2** in hysterics *informal* laughing so much that you cannot stop

Hz *written abbreviation for* hertz (= a unit of measurement used in electronics)

Ii

I, i /aɪ/ the ninth letter of the alphabet

◦⁓**I** /aɪ/ *pronoun* used when the person speaking or writing is the subject of the verb *I had lunch with Glen yesterday.* ○ *Did I tell you I saw Annie yesterday?* ○ *Chris and I have been married for twelve years.* ⊃See Common learner error at **me**.

◦⁓**ice¹** /aɪs/ *noun* [U] **1** water that has frozen and become solid *Gerry slipped on the ice and broke his arm.* ○ *I've put a couple of bottles of champagne on ice* (= in a bucket of ice to get cold). **2 break the ice** to make people who have not met before feel relaxed with each other, often by starting a conversation *I made what I hoped was an amusing remark to break the ice.*

ice² /aɪs/ (*also US* **frost**) *verb* [T] to cover a cake with icing (= sweet mixture used to cover cakes) *an iced bun*

iceberg /'aɪsbɜːɡ/ *noun* [C] a very large piece of ice that floats in the sea ⊃See also: be the **tip¹** of the iceberg.

ice 'cream UK (US **'ice ˌcream**) *noun* [C, U] a sweet food made from frozen milk or cream and sugar *chocolate/vanilla ice cream*

'ice ˌcube *noun* [C] a small block of ice that you put into drinks to make them cold

'ice ˌhockey (*also US* **hockey**) *noun* [U] a game played on ice in which two teams try to hit a small hard object into a goal using long curved sticks ⊃See colour picture **Sports 1** on page Centre 14.

ˌice 'lolly /aɪs'loli/ UK (US **Popsicle** *trademark*) *noun* [C] a sweet, fruit-flavoured piece of ice on a small stick

'ice ˌrink *noun* [C] an area of ice, usually inside a building, which is prepared for people to ice skate on

'ice ˌskate *noun* [C] a boot with a metal part on the bottom, used for moving across ice ● **ice skate** *verb* [I] to move across ice using ice skates ● **ice skating** *noun* [U] the activity or sport of moving across ice using ice skates ⊃See colour picture **Sports 1** on page Centre 14.

icicle /'aɪsɪkl/ *noun* [C] a long, thin piece of ice that hangs down from something

icicles

icing /'aɪsɪŋ/ *noun* [U] **1** (*also US* **frosting**) a sweet mixture used to cover or fill cakes, made from sugar and water or sugar and butter *chocolate butter icing* **2 the icing on the cake** something that makes a good situation better *He was delighted to get the article published and the £100 payment was the icing on the cake.*

icon

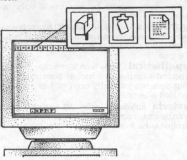

icon /'aɪkɒn/ *noun* [C] **1** a small picture on a computer screen that you choose in order to make the computer do something *Click on the print icon.* **2** a person or thing that is famous because it represents a particular idea or way of life *a cultural/fashion/national icon*

ICT /ˌaɪsiː'tiː/ *noun* [U] *abbreviation for* information and communication technology: the use of computers and other electronic equipment to store and send information

icy /'aɪsi/ *adjective* **1** [WITH ICE] covered in ice *icy roads* **2** [COLD] extremely cold *an icy wind* ○ *icy water* **3** [WITHOUT EMOTION] without showing any emotion *an icy look/stare* ● **icily** *adverb*

◦⁓**I'd** /aɪd/ **1** *short for* I had *Everyone thought I'd gone.* **2** *short for* I would *I'd like to buy some stamps, please.*

ID /ˌaɪ'diː/ *noun* [C, U] *abbreviation for* identification: an official document that shows or proves who you are *When you apply, you'll need to show some form of ID, such as a passport or driving licence.*

I.'D. ˌcard *noun* [C] an identity card

WORD PARTNERS FOR *idea*

come up with/have an idea ● a **bad/ bright/brilliant/good/stupid** idea

---

OTHER WAYS OF SAYING ***idea***

An idea about how to do something is often described as a **plan**, **thought** or **suggestion**: *The **plan** is to hire a car when we get there.* ● *Have you got any **suggestions** for improvements?* ● *Have you had any **thoughts** on presents for your mother?*

A sudden, clever idea is sometimes described as a **brainwave** in the UK and **brainstorm** in the US: *I wasn't sure what to do and then I had a **brainwave** - I could ask Anna for help.*

The noun **theory** is sometimes used to describe a set of ideas intended to explain something: *He was giving a lecture on Darwin's **theory** of evolution.*

◦⁓**idea** /aɪ'dɪə/ *noun* **1** [SUGGESTION] [C] a suggestion or plan *"Why don't we ask George?" "That's a good idea."* ○ [+ for + doing sth] *Stevens ex-*

plained his ideas for improving production. ○ [+ to do sth] *It was Kate's idea to hire a car.* **2** [THOUGHT] [U, no plural] an understanding, thought, or picture in your mind [+ of + doing sth] *Clive soon got used to the idea of having children around the house again.* ○ [+ (that)] *I don't want them to get the idea that we're not interested.* **3 have no idea** to not know *Beth had no idea where he'd gone.* **4** [OPINION] [C] an opinion or belief *My husband and I have very different ideas about school discipline.* **5** [AIM] [no plural] the aim or purpose of something *The idea is to give local people a chance to voice their opinions.* ⊃See also: not have the foggiest (foggy) (idea).

ideal¹ /aɪˈdɪəl/ *adjective* perfect, or the best possible *an ideal candidate/solution* ○ *The book is ideal for children aged 4 to 6.* ○ *In an ideal world, you wouldn't need to use a keyboard at all.*

ideal² /aɪˈdɪəl/ *noun* **1** [C] a belief about the way you think something should be *democratic ideals* ○ *They are committed to the ideal of equality.* **2** [no plural] a perfect thing or situation *The ideal would be to have a house in the country and a flat in the city too.*

idealism /aɪˈdɪəlɪzᵊm/ *noun* [U] the belief that your ideals can be achieved, often when this does not seem likely to others ● **idealist** *noun* [C] a person who believes that it is possible to achieve your ideals ● **idealistic** /aɪˌdɪəˈlɪstɪk/ *adjective*

ideally /aɪˈdɪəli/ *adverb* **1** used to describe how something would be in a perfect situation *Ideally, I'd like to work at home.* **2** in a perfect way *She seemed ideally suited for the job.*

identical /aɪˈdentɪkᵊl/ *adjective* exactly the same *The two rooms were almost/virtually identical.* ○ *She found a dress identical to the one in the picture.* ● **identically** *adverb*

i,dentical 'twin *noun* [C] one of two babies who are born at the same time from the same egg, and look exactly the same

identifiable /aɪˌdentɪˈfaɪəbl/ *adjective* If someone or something is identifiable, you can recognize them and say or prove who or what they are. *clearly/readily identifiable*

a form/a means/proof of identification

identification /aɪˌdentɪfɪˈkeɪʃᵊn/ *noun* [U] **1** when you recognize and can name someone or something *Most of the bodies were badly burned, making identification almost impossible.* **2** an official document that shows or proves who you are *an identification card/number*

o-. **identify** /aɪˈdentɪfaɪ/ *verb* [T] **1** [RECOGNIZE] to recognize someone or something and say or prove who or what they are *The gunman in Wednesday's attack has been identified as Lee Giggs, an unemployed truck driver.* **2** [NAME] to tell people who someone is *My informant asked not to be identified.* **3** [DISCOVER] to find a particular thing or all the things of a particular group *You need to identify your priorities.*

identify sb/sth with sb/sth to connect one person or thing with another *As a politician he was identified with liberal causes.*

identify with sb/sth to feel that you are similar to someone, and can understand them or their situation because of this

2 cultural/national/personal identity ● a sense of identity

identity /aɪˈdentəti/ *noun* [C, U] **1** who someone is *Police are trying to establish the identity of a woman seen walking away from the accident.* **2** the things that make one person or group of people different from others *cultural/national identity*

i'dentity ,card *noun* [C] a piece of paper or a card that shows your name, photograph and information to prove who you are

ideological /ˌaɪdɪəˈlɒdʒɪkᵊl/ *adjective* based on or relating to a particular set of ideas or beliefs *ideological conflicts/disagreements* ● **ideologically** *adverb*

ideology /ˌaɪdɪˈɒlədʒi/ *noun* [C, U] a set of ideas or beliefs, especially about politics *socialist ideology*

idiom /ˈɪdiəm/ *noun* [C] a group of words used together with a meaning that you cannot guess from the meanings of the separate words ⊃See Extra help page **Idioms** on page Centre 26. ● **idiomatic** /ˌɪdiəˈmætɪk/ *adjective idiomatic language*

idiosyncratic /ˌɪdiəsɪŋˈkrætɪk/ *adjective* An idiosyncratic quality or way of behaving is typical of only one person and is often strange or unusual. ● **idiosyncrasy** /ˌɪdiəˈsɪŋkrəsi/ *noun* [C] an idiosyncratic habit or way of behaving

idiot /ˈɪdiət/ *noun* [C] a stupid person or someone who is behaving in a stupid way *Like an idiot, I believed him.* ● **idiocy** /ˈɪdiəsi/ *noun* [C, U] stupid behaviour ● **idiotic** /ˌɪdiˈɒtɪk/ *adjective* stupid *an idiotic grin/idea* ● **idiotically** *adverb*

idle¹ /ˈaɪdl/ *adjective* **1** [NOT WORKING] not working or being used *The factory has stood idle for over a year.* **2** [NOT SERIOUS] [always before noun] not serious or having no real purpose *idle gossip* ○ *This is no idle threat.* **3** [LAZY] lazy and not willing to work *He knows what has to be done, he's just bone idle* (= extremely lazy). ● **idleness** *noun* [U] ● **idly** *adverb* *We cannot stand idly by* (= not do anything) *and let this plan go ahead.*

idle² /ˈaɪdl/ *verb* **1** [ENGINE] [I] If an engine or machine idles, it runs slowly but does not move or do any work. **2** [STOP WORKING] [T] *US* to stop someone or something working or being used, often because there is not enough work to do *The closure of the plant idled about 300 workers.* **3** [TIME] [I] to spend time doing nothing *We saw her idling in the school grounds.*

idle sth away to waste time doing nothing *I idled away a few hours watching TV.*

idol /ˈaɪdᵊl/ *noun* [C] **1** someone that you admire and respect very much *a pop/sporting idol* **2** a picture or object that people pray to as part of their religion ● **idolize** (*also UK* -ise) *verb* [T] to admire and respect someone very much

idyllic /ɪˈdɪlɪk/ *adjective* An idyllic place or experience is extremely pleasant, beautiful, or peaceful. *an **idyllic** childhood* ○ *an **idyllic** existence*

i.e. (*also* ie) /ˌaɪˈiː/ used to explain exactly what you are referring to or what you mean *The price must be more realistic, i.e. lower.*

⌐**if¹** /ɪf/ *conjunction* **1** DEPEND used to say that something will happen only after something else happens or is true *We'll have the party in the garden if the weather's good.* ○ *If you eat up all your dinner you can have some chocolate.* **2** MIGHT used to talk about something that might happen or be true *What will we do if this doesn't work?* **3** WHETHER whether *I wonder if he'll get the job.* **4** ALWAYS used to mean always or every time *If you mention his mother, he always cries.*

if² /ɪf/ *noun* [C] *informal* something which is not certain or not yet decided *There are still a lot of ifs.* ○ *There are **no ifs and buts** (= no doubts or excuses) about it - we'll have to start again.*

iffy /ˈɪfi/ *adjective informal* **1** not completely good, honest, or suitable *The milk smells a bit iffy.* **2** not certain or decided *Simon's still kind of iffy about going to Colombia.*

igloo /ˈɪɡluː/ *noun* [C]   igloo
a house made of
blocks of hard snow

ignite /ɪɡˈnaɪt/ *verb*
formal **1** [I, T] to start
to burn or make
something start to
burn *A spark ignited
the fumes.* **2** [T] to
start an argument
or fight

ignition /ɪɡˈnɪʃ³n/
noun **1** [no plural] the
part of a car that
starts the engine *He
turned the key in the
ignition.* ➔See colour
picture **Car** on page Centre 7. **2** [U] *formal* when something makes something start to burn

ignominious /ˌɪɡnəˈmɪniəs/ *adjective formal* making you feel embarrassed or ashamed *an ignominious defeat* ● **ignominiously** *adverb*

ignorance /ˈɪɡn³r³ns/ *noun* [U] when someone does not have enough knowledge, understanding, or information about something *There is still widespread **ignorance about** the disease.* ○ *I was shocked by her total **ignorance of** world history.*

ignorant /ˈɪɡn³r³nt/ *adjective* **1** not having enough knowledge, understanding, or information about something *He was a newcomer to Formula One and **ignorant of** many of the circuits.* **2** *UK* not polite or showing respect *an ignorant lout*

⌐**ignore** /ɪɡˈnɔːʳ/ *verb* [T] to pay no attention to something or someone *They just ignored him and carried on with the game.* ○ *We cannot afford to ignore the fact that the world's population is increasing rapidly.*

IIRC *internet abbreviation for* if I remember correctly

il- /ɪl-/ *prefix* not *illegal* ○ *illegible*

A common alternative is the adjective **sick**: *He was off work **sick** last week.*

In informal situations in the UK, you can also use the adjectives **poorly** and **rough**: *What's the matter, Sophie - are you feeling **poorly**?* ● *I felt really **rough** after eating that curry.*

A more formal adjective meaning 'ill' is **unwell**: *I've felt a little **unwell** all week.*

If you want to say that someone feels slightly ill, in informal situations you can also use the expressions **be/feel under the weather** and **be/feel below par**: *I don't think I'll be coming to the party- I'm a bit **under the weather**.*

⌐**ill¹** /ɪl/ *adjective* **1** not feeling well, or suffering from a disease *critically/seriously ill* ○ *Mark had been **feeling ill** for a couple of days.* ➔See Common learner error at **sick**. **2** [always before noun] *formal* bad *ill health* ○ *He suffered no **ill effects** from his fall.* ➔See also: ill at **ease**¹.

ill² /ɪl/ *noun* [C] *formal* a problem [usually plural] *social and economic ills*

ill³ /ɪl/ *adverb formal* **1** badly *Many of the nurses were **ill prepared** to deal with such badly burned patients.* **2 can ill afford (to do) sth** If you can ill afford to do something, it is likely to make things difficult for you if you do it. *This is a match United can ill afford to lose.* **3 speak ill of sb** *formal* to say bad things about someone

I'll /aɪl/ *short for* I shall/I will *I'll be there at 6:00.*

ill- /ɪl-/ *prefix* in a way which is bad or not suitable *ill-prepared* ○ *an ill-judged remark*

ill-advised /ˌɪlədˈvaɪzd/ *adjective* not wise, and likely to cause problems in the future

ill-conceived /ˌɪlkənˈsiːvd/ *adjective* badly planned or not wise

⌐**illegal** /ɪˈliːɡ³l/ *adjective* not allowed by law *illegal drugs/weapons* ○ [+ to do sth] *It is illegal to sell cigarettes to anyone under 16.* ● **illegally** *adverb an illegally parked car*

il‚legal ˈimmigrant (*also US* il‚legal ˈalien) *noun* [C] someone who goes to live or work in another country when they do not have the legal right to

illegible /ɪˈledʒəbl/ *adjective* Illegible writing is difficult or impossible to read.

illegitimate /ˌɪlɪˈdʒɪtəmət/ *adjective* **1** An illegitimate child is born to parents who are not married to each other. **2** not legal, honest, or fair *an illegitimate use of council funds* ● **illegitimacy** /ˌɪlɪˈdʒɪtəməsi/ *noun* [U]

ill-equipped /ˌɪlɪˈkwɪpt/ *adjective* **1** not having the necessary equipment **2** not having the necessary ability or qualities to do something [+ to do sth] *These teachers were ill-equipped to deal with rowdy students.*

ill-fated /ˌɪlˈfeɪtɪd/ *adjective* unlucky and often unsuccessful *an ill-fated expedition to the South Pole*

ill-fitting /ˌɪlˈfɪtɪŋ/ *adjective* Ill-fitting clothes do not fit well.

ill-gotten /ˌɪl'gɒtᵊn/ *adjective literary* obtained in a dishonest or illegal way *He deposited his **ill-gotten gains** in foreign bank accounts.*

illicit /ɪ'lɪsɪt/ *adjective* not legal or not approved of by society *an illicit love affair*

ill-informed /ˌɪlɪn'fɔːmd/ *adjective* without enough knowledge or information *an ill-informed decision*

illiterate /ɪ'lɪtᵊrət/ *adjective* not able to read or write

> ☆ **WORD PARTNERS FOR *illness***
>
> **cause / develop / have / recover from / treat** an illness • a **critical/minor/rare/serious/terminal** illness

o▪**illness** /'ɪlnəs/ *noun* **1** [C] a disease of the body or mind *a **serious/terminal illness*** ○ *He died at the age of 83 after a long illness.* **2** [U] when you are ill

illogical /ɪ'lɒdʒɪkᵊl/ *adjective* not based on careful thought *It would be illogical for them to stop at this stage.*

illuminate /ɪ'luːmɪneɪt/ *verb* [T] **1** to shine lights on something *The paintings and sculptures are illuminated by spotlights.* **2** to explain something clearly or make it easier to understand • **illumination** /ɪˌluːmɪ'neɪʃᵊn/ *noun* [C, U] *formal*

illuminating /ɪ'luːmɪneɪtɪŋ/ *adjective* giving you new information about something or making it easier to understand *a most illuminating discussion*

illusion /ɪ'luːʒᵊn/ *noun* **1** [C, U] an idea or belief that is not true *He **had no illusions about** his talents as a singer.* ○ *We are not **under any illusion** - we know the work is dangerous.* **2** [C] something that is not really what it seems to be *There is a large mirror at one end to **create the illusion** of more space.* ⊃See also: **optical illusion**.

illustrate /'ɪləstreɪt/ *verb* [T] **1** to give more information or examples to explain or prove something *to illustrate a point/problem* ○ [+ question word] *This new discovery illustrates how little we know about early human history.* **2** to draw pictures for a book, magazine, etc *an illustrated children's book*

illustration /ˌɪlə'streɪʃᵊn/ *noun* **1** [C] a picture in a book, magazine, etc *a full-page colour illustration* **2** [C, U] an example that explains or proves something *This is another **illustration** of the power of the media.*

illustrator /'ɪləstreɪtə/ *noun* [C] a person whose job is to draw or paint pictures for books

illustrious /ɪ'lʌstriəs/ *adjective formal* famous and well respected *an illustrious career*

ill 'will *noun* [U] bad feelings between people because of things that happened in the past

o▪**I'm** /aɪm/ *short for* I am

im- /ɪm-/ *prefix* not *impossible* ○ *immortal*

> ☆ **WORD PARTNERS FOR *image***
>
> **create/project** an image • sb's/sth's **public** image • an **image of** sth

o▪**image** /'ɪmɪdʒ/ *noun* **1** PUBLIC [C, U] the way that other people think someone or something is *The aim is to improve the **public image** of the police.* **2** PICTURE [C] a picture, especially on film or television or in a mirror *television images of starving children* **3** IDEA [C] a picture in your mind or an idea of how someone or something is *I have an image in my mind of the way I want the garden to look.*

imagery /'ɪmɪdʒᵊri/ *noun* [U] the use of words or pictures in books, films, paintings, etc to describe ideas or situations

imaginable /ɪ'mædʒɪnəbl/ *adjective* possible to think of *ice cream of every imaginable flavour* ⊃Opposite **unimaginable**.

imaginary /ɪ'mædʒɪnᵊri/ *adjective* not real but imagined in your mind *The story takes place in an imaginary world.*

> ☆ **WORD PARTNERS FOR *imagination***
>
> **have/lack/show** imagination • **use** your imagination • **capture** sb's imagination • a **fertile/vivid** imagination

o▪**imagination** /ɪˌmædʒɪ'neɪʃᵊn/ *noun* **1** [C] the part of your mind that creates ideas or pictures of things that are not real or that you have not seen [usually singular] *There's nothing out here - it's just your imagination.* **2** [U] the ability to create ideas or pictures in your mind *The job needs someone with creativity and imagination.* ⊃See also: not by any **stretch²** of the imagination.

imaginative /ɪ'mædʒɪnətɪv/ *adjective* **1** Something which is imaginative is new or clever and often unusual. *an imaginative use of colour* **2** Someone who is imaginative is able to create new and interesting ideas or things. *a highly imaginative poet* • **imaginatively** *adverb*

o▪**imagine** /ɪ'mædʒɪn/ *verb* [T] **1** CREATE to create an idea or picture of something in your mind [+ doing sth] *Imagine being able to do all your shopping from your armchair.* ○ [+ question word] *You can imagine how pleased I was when the letter arrived.* **2** BELIEVE to believe that something is probably true *I imagine he must be under a lot of pressure at the moment.* **3** NOT REAL to think that you hear or see something which does not really exist *I can't hear anything - you must be imagining it.*

imaging /'ɪmɪdʒɪŋ/ *noun* [U] the process of producing an exact picture of something, especially on a computer screen *computer/digital imaging*

imbalance /ˌɪm'bæləns/ *noun* [C] when two things which should be equal or are normally equal are not *There is a huge economic **imbalance between** the two countries.*

imbue /ɪm'bjuː/ *verb imbuing past imbued*
imbue sb/sth with sth *formal* to fill someone or something with a particular feeling, quality, or idea *His poetry is imbued with deep religious feeling.*

IMHO *internet abbreviation for* in my humble opinion: used when you tell someone your opinion

o▪**imitate** /'ɪmɪteɪt/ *verb* [T] to copy the way someone or something looks, sounds, or behaves

She tried to imitate the way the models walked. • **imitator** *noun* [C]

WORD PARTNERS FOR ***imitation***

a **cheap/convincing/good/pale** imitation • an imitation **of** sb/sth

imitation /ˌɪmɪˈteɪʃᵊn/ *noun* **1** [C] a copy of something that is made to look like the real thing *It wasn't a genuine Gucci handbag, just **a cheap imitation**.* ○ ***imitation leather*** **2** [C, U] when someone copies the way another person speaks or behaves *He does a very good **imitation of** the Prime Minister.*

immaculate /ɪˈmækjələt/ *adjective* **1** perfectly clean and tidy or in perfect condition *an immaculate garden/room* **2** perfect and without any mistakes *an **immaculate performance*** • **immaculately** *adverb*

immaterial /ˌɪməˈtɪəriəl/ *adjective* If something is immaterial, it is not important because it does not affect a situation.

immature /ˌɪməˈtjʊəʳ/ *adjective* **1** not behaving in a way which is as wise and calm as people expect from someone your age *Some of the boys are quite immature for their age.* **2** not completely developed *immature cells* • **immaturity** *noun* [U]

immeasurable /ɪˈmeʒᵊrəbl/ *adjective* very large or extreme and so impossible to measure *the immeasurable pain of losing a child* • **immeasurably** *adverb His confidence has grown immeasurably since he got the job.*

⊶**immediate** /ɪˈmiːdiət/ *adjective* **1** [WITHOUT WAITING] happening or done without waiting or very soon after something else *The government has promised to take **immediate action**.* ○ *The drugs will have an **immediate effect**.* **2** [IMPORTANT NOW] important now and needing attention *Our **immediate concern** is getting food and water to the refugees.* **3** [CLOSEST] [always before noun] closest to something or someone *Police cleared people from the **immediate area** following the bomb warning.* **4 the immediate future** the period of time that is coming next **5 sb's immediate family** someone's closest relatives, such as their parents, children, husband, or wife

⊶**immediately¹** /ɪˈmiːdiətli/ *adverb* **1** now or without waiting or thinking about something *The cause of the problem wasn't **immediately obvious**.* **2** next to something, or close to something in time *There are fields immediately behind the house.* ○ *Cole scored again **immediately after** half-time.*

immediately² /ɪˈmiːdiətli/ *conjunction UK* as soon as *Immediately I saw her I knew something terrible had happened.*

immense /ɪˈmens/ *adjective* extremely big *immense pressure/value* ○ *Health care costs the country **an immense amount of** money.*

immensely /ɪˈmensli/ *adverb* extremely *immensely powerful/popular*

immerse /ɪˈmɜːs/ *verb* **1 be immersed in sth; immerse yourself in sth** to be or become completely involved in something, so that you do not notice anything else **2** [T] to put something in a liquid so that it is completely covered • **immersion** /ɪˈmɜːʃᵊn/ *noun* [U]

immigrant /ˈɪmɪgrənt/ *noun* [C] someone who comes to live in a different country ➲See also: **illegal immigrant**.

immigration /ˌɪmɪˈgreɪʃᵊn/ *noun* [U] **1** when someone comes to live in a different country ***immigration policy*** **2** the place where people's official documents are checked when they enter a country at an airport, port, border, etc ***immigration control*** • **immigrate** /ˈɪmɪgreɪt/ *verb* [I] to come to live in a different country

imminent /ˈɪmɪnənt/ *adjective* coming or happening very soon ***imminent danger***

immobile /ɪˈməʊbaɪl/ [US] /ɪˈməʊbᵊl/ *adjective* not moving or not able to move • **immobility** /ˌɪməʊˈbɪləti/ *noun* [U]

immoral /ɪˈmɒrᵊl/ *adjective* morally wrong *immoral behaviour* • **immorality** /ˌɪməˈræləti/ *noun* [U]

immortal /ɪˈmɔːtᵊl/ *adjective* **1** living or lasting forever *an immortal soul/God* **2** famous or remembered for a very long time *Then he uttered the **immortal line** - "My name is Bond".* • **immortality** /ˌɪmɔːˈtæləti/ *noun* [U]

immortalize (*also UK* **-ise**) /ɪˈmɔːtᵊlaɪz/ *verb* [T] to make someone or something famous for a long time

immune /ɪˈmjuːn/ *adjective* **1** [PROTECTED] [never before noun] If you are immune to a disease, you will not get it. *Once you've had the virus, you are **immune to** it.* **2** [BODY SYSTEM] [always before noun] relating to the way your body fights disease *an **immune deficiency/response*** **3** [NOT AFFECTED] [never before noun] not affected by a particular type of behaviour or emotion *He is **immune to** flattery.* **4** [NOT PUNISHED] [never before noun] not able to be punished or damaged by something *His diplomatic passport makes him **immune from** prosecution.*

imˈmune ˌsystem *noun* [C] the cells and tissues in your body that fight against infection [usually singular] *Vitamins help **boost*** (= make stronger) ***your immune system***.

immunity /ɪˈmjuːnəti/ *noun* [U] when you are immune, especially to disease or from legal action ***diplomatic immunity*** ○ *The vaccine gives you lifelong **immunity to** the virus.*

immunize (*also UK* **-ise**) /ˈɪmjənaɪz/ *verb* [T] to make a person or animal immune by giving them special medicine *He was **immunized against** measles as a child.* • **immunization** /ˌɪmjənaɪˈzeɪʃᵊn/ *noun* [C, U] *a programme of mass immunization*

IMO *Internet abbreviation for* in my opinion: used when you want to give an opinion

WORD PARTNERS FOR ***impact***

have/make an impact • a **major/negative/significant** impact • an impact **on** sth

impact¹ /ˈɪmpækt/ *noun* **1** [no plural] the effect that a person, event, or situation has on someone or something *Latino singers **have had a major impact on** pop music this year.* **2** [U] the force or action of one object hitting another

The missile explodes ***on impact*** (= when it hits another object).

impact² /ɪm'pækt/ (*also* **impact on/upon)** *verb* **[T]** *mainly US* to affect something or someone *Rising interest rates are sure to* ***impact on*** *the housing market.*

impair /ɪm'peəʳ/ *verb* **[T]** *formal* to harm something and make it less good **[often passive]** *When you're tired your* ***judgment*** *is* ***impaired.*** • **impairment** *noun* **[C, U]** when something is impaired ***mental/physical impairment***

impaired /ɪm'peəd/ *adjective* **visually/hearing impaired** unable to see or hear as well as most people

impale /ɪm'peɪl/ *verb* **[T]** to push a sharp object through something or someone

impart /ɪm'pɑːt/ *verb* **[T]** *formal* **1** to communicate information or knowledge to someone *I have disappointing* ***news to impart.*** **2** to give something a particular feeling, quality, or taste *Preservatives can impart colour and flavour to a product.*

impartial /ɪm'pɑːʃᵊl/ *adjective* not supporting or preferring any person, group, plan, etc more than others ***impartial advice*** ○ *A trial must be fair and impartial.* • **impartiality** /ɪm,pɑːʃi'æləti/ *noun* **[U]** when someone or something is impartial

impassable /ɪm'pɑːsəbl/ *adjective* If roads or paths are impassable, vehicles cannot move along them.

WORD PARTNERS FOR ***impasse***

break/reach an impasse • an impasse **in** sth

impasse /'æmpæs/ [US] /'ɪmpæs/ *noun* **[U]** a situation in which it is impossible to make any progress *He is determined to* ***break*** (= end) ***the impasse*** *in the peace process.*

impassioned /ɪm'pæʃᵊnd/ *adjective* showing and expressing strong emotion ***an impassioned plea/speech***

impassive /ɪm'pæsɪv/ *adjective* An impassive person or face shows no emotion. • **impassively** *adverb*

impatience /ɪm'peɪʃᵊns/ *noun* **[U]** when someone is impatient

impatient /ɪm'peɪʃᵊnt/ *adjective* **1** easily annoyed by someone's mistakes or because you have to wait *I do get* ***impatient with*** *the children when they won't do their homework.* **2** **[never before noun]** wanting something to happen as soon as possible *People are increasingly* ***impatient for*** *change in this country.* • **impatiently** *adverb We waited impatiently for the show to begin.*

impeccable /ɪm'pekəbl/ *adjective* perfect and with no mistakes *She speaks impeccable English.* • **impeccably** *adverb* ***impeccably dressed***

impede /ɪm'piːd/ *verb* **[T]** *formal* to make it difficult or impossible for someone or something to move or make progress *A broken-down car is impeding the flow of traffic.*

impediment /ɪm'pedɪmənt/ *noun* **[C]** **1** *formal* something that makes it difficult or impossible for someone or something to move or make progress *Cramped classrooms are an* ***impediment to*** *learning.* **2** a problem that makes speaking, hearing, or moving difficult ***a speech impediment***

impel /ɪm'pel/ *verb* **[T]** **impelling** *past* **impelled** *formal* to make you feel that you must do something **[+ to do sth]** *Harry felt impelled to tell the truth.*

impending /ɪm'pendɪŋ/ *adjective* **[always before noun]** An impending event will happen soon and is usually bad or unpleasant. ***impending disaster/doom*** ○ *I've just heard about the* ***impending departure*** *of our chairman.*

impenetrable /ɪm'penɪtrəbl/ *adjective* **1** impossible to understand *impenetrable jargon* **2** impossible to see through or go through *impenetrable fog*

imperative¹ /ɪm'perətɪv/ *adjective* **1** *formal* When an action or process is imperative, it is extremely important that it happens or is done. **[+ (that)]** *It is imperative that I speak with him at once.* **2** An imperative form of a verb is used to express an order. In the sentence 'Stop the machine!', the verb 'stop' is an imperative verb.

imperative² /ɪm'perətɪv/ *noun* **[C]** **1** something that must happen, exist, or be done *a moral/political imperative* **2** the imperative form of a verb

imperceptible /,ɪmpə'septəbl/ *adjective* not able to be noticed or felt *She heard a faint, almost imperceptible cry.* • **imperceptibly** *adverb*

imperfect /ɪm'pɜːfɪkt/ *adjective* not perfect and with some mistakes *an imperfect solution* • **imperfectly** *adverb*

the imperfect /ɪm'pɜːfɪkt/ (*also* **the im,perfect 'tense)** *noun* The form of the verb that is used to show an action in the past which has not been completed. In the sentence 'We were crossing the road', 'were crossing' is in the imperfect.

imperfection /,ɪmpə'fekʃᵊn/ *noun* **[C, U]** when something or someone is not perfect *Make-up can hide small skin imperfections.*

imperial /ɪm'pɪəriəl/ *adjective* **1** **[always before noun]** relating or belonging to an empire (= group of countries ruled by one person or government) or the person who rules it *imperial rule* ○ *the imperial family* **2** The imperial system of measurement uses units based on measurements such as inches, pints, and ounces.

imperialism /ɪm'pɪəriəlɪzᵊm/ *noun* **[U]** **1** when one government or person rules a group of other countries *the age of imperialism* **2** when one country has a lot of power or influence over others ***cultural/economic imperialism*** • **imperialist** *adjective* relating to imperialism

imperil /ɪm'perᵊl/ *verb* **[T]** *UK* **imperilling** *past* **imperilled**, *US* **imperiling** *past* **imperiled** *formal* to put someone or something in a dangerous situation

imperious /ɪm'pɪəriəs/ *adjective formal* showing that you think that you are important and expect others to obey you ***an imperious manner***

impersonal /ɪmˈpɜːsᵊnᵊl/ *adjective* not being friendly towards people or showing any interest in them *a cold and impersonal letter*

impersonate /ɪmˈpɜːsᵊneɪt/ *verb* [T] to copy the way someone looks and behaves in order to pretend to be them or to make people laugh *Impersonating a police officer is a serious offence.* ● **impersonation** /ɪmˌpɜːsᵊnˈeɪʃᵊn/ *noun* [C, U] *He did an impersonation of Bill Clinton.* ● **impersonator** *noun* [C] *an Elvis impersonator*

impertinent /ɪmˈpɜːtɪnənt/ *adjective formal* rude or not showing respect *an impertinent remark*

impervious /ɪmˈpɜːviəs/ *adjective* **1** not affected by something *She was impervious to the pain.* **2** *formal* Impervious material does not let liquid into or through it. *impervious rock*

impetuous /ɪmˈpetʃuəs/ *adjective* done or acting quickly and without thinking carefully *an impetuous outburst*

WORD PARTNERS FOR *impetus*

give/provide [new, fresh, added, etc] impetus **to** sth ● the impetus **behind/for** sth

---

impetus /ˈɪmpɪtəs/ *noun* [U] **1** something that makes an activity or process happen or continue with more speed and energy *His visit gave new impetus to the peace process.* **2** a physical force that makes an object start or continue to move

impinge /ɪmˈpɪndʒ/ *verb formal*
  impinge on/upon sb/sth to affect or limit someone or something *How does your religious commitment impinge upon your professional life?*

implacable /ɪmˈplækəbl/ *adjective formal* determined not to change the strong feelings you have against someone or something *implacable opposition/hostility*

implant¹ /ˈɪmplɑːnt/ *noun* [C] an object placed inside part of your body in an operation, to improve your appearance or treat a medical condition *breast implants*

implant² /ɪmˈplɑːnt/ *verb* [T] to place something into someone's body in a medical operation *Two embryos were implanted in her womb.*

implausible /ɪmˈplɔːzəbl/ *adjective* difficult to believe or imagine *an implausible explanation*

implement¹ /ˈɪmplɪment/ *verb* [T] *formal* to make a law, system, plan, etc start to happen or operate *Our new computerized system will soon be fully implemented.* ● **implementation** /ˌɪmplɪmenˈteɪʃᵊn/ *noun* [U]

implement² /ˈɪmplɪmənt/ *noun* [C] a tool *a garden/farm implement*

implicate /ˈɪmplɪkeɪt/ *verb* [T] to show that someone or something is involved in something bad, especially a crime [often passive] *Two senior officers are implicated in the latest drugs scandal.*

WORD PARTNERS FOR *implication*

have implications **for** sth ● **far-reaching/profound/serious** implications ● the implications **of** sth

---

implication /ˌɪmplɪˈkeɪʃᵊn/ *noun* **1** [EFFECT] [C] a result or effect that seems likely in the future [usually plural] *financial/health implications* ○ *This scheme has serious implications for the local economy.* **2** [SUGGESTION] [C, U] when you seem to suggest something without saying it directly *The implication was that the school had to do much better or it would be closed.* **3** [INVOLVEMENT] [U] when something or someone is implicated in something bad

implicit /ɪmˈplɪsɪt/ *adjective* **1** suggested but not stated directly *an implicit threat* ○ *We interpreted his silence as implicit agreement.* **2** complete *implicit faith/trust* ● **implicitly** *adverb I trust him implicitly.*

implore /ɪmˈplɔː/ *verb* [T] *literary* to ask for something in a serious and emotional way [+ to do sth] *I implored him to let the child go.*

imply /ɪmˈplaɪ/ *verb* [T] to suggest or show something, without saying it directly [+ (that)] *Hang on, are you implying that I'm fat?* ○ *an implied criticism*

impolite /ˌɪmpᵊlˈaɪt/ *adjective formal* not polite

import¹ /ɪmˈpɔːt/ *verb* [T] **1** to bring something into your country from another country for people to buy *We import about 20 percent of our food.* **2** to copy information from one computer or computer program to another *to import data* ○ *imported files* ⊃Opposite **export**. ● **importation** /ˌɪmpɔːˈteɪʃᵊn/ *noun* [U] ● **importer** *noun* [C]

import² /ˈɪmpɔːt/ *noun* **1** [C] a product which is imported from another country [usually plural] *Japanese/American imports* **2** [U] when you import goods *a ban on the import of beef* ⊃Opposite **export**.

WORD PARTNERS FOR *importance*

central/great/major/paramount/the utmost/vital importance ● **emphasize/stress** the importance of sth ● **attach** (great) importance **to** sth ● the importance **of** sth

---

☞**importance** /ɪmˈpɔːtᵊns/ *noun* [U] how important someone or something is *He emphasized the importance of following safety procedures.* ○ *She attaches a lot of importance to personal possessions* (= she thinks they are important).

OTHER WAYS OF SAYING *important*

Adjectives such as **big**, **major** and **significant** are often used to mean 'important' in this sense: *This is a big game tonight – if Manchester lose, they're out of the championship.* ● *This is a major decision so we'd better get it right.* ● *Did he make any significant changes to my suggestions?*

Someone or something **of note** is important or famous: *Did she say anything of note at the meeting?*

A person who is important and famous is sometimes described as **eminent**, **prominent**, or **great**: *Her father was an eminent historian.*

☞**important** /ɪmˈpɔːtᵊnt/ *adjective* **1** valuable, useful, or necessary *My family is very import-*

ant to me. ○ [+ to do sth] *Listen, Donna has something important to say.* **2** having a lot of power, influence, or effect *an important person/decision* ➜Opposite **unimportant**. ● **importantly** *adverb They provided hot showers and, more importantly, clean clothes.*

impose /ɪmˈpəʊz/ *verb* [T] **1** to officially order that a rule, tax, punishment, etc will happen *to impose a ban/tax* ○ *The judge imposed the death penalty on both men.* **2** to force someone to accept a belief or way of living *I don't want them to impose their religious beliefs on my children.*

impose on sb to ask or expect someone to do something that may give them extra work or trouble *I hate to impose on you, but could I stay the night?*

imposing /ɪmˈpəʊzɪŋ/ *adjective* looking big and important in a way that people admire *He was an imposing figure - tall and broad-chested.*

imposition /ˌɪmpəˈzɪʃən/ *noun* **1** [U] when you impose something *the imposition of a fine* **2** [C] the cause of extra work or trouble for someone else *It's a bit of an imposition, but could you take me to the airport?*

o⌐**impossible** /ɪmˈpɒsəbl/ *adjective* **1** If an action or event is impossible, it cannot happen or be done. *an impossible task* ○ *He finds walking almost impossible.* ○ [+ to do sth] *It was impossible to sleep because of the noise.* **2** very difficult to deal with *You're putting me in an impossible position.* ● **impossibility** /ɪmˌpɒsəˈbɪləti/ *noun* [C, U] when something is impossible [usually singular] *I can't do it - it's a physical impossibility.*

the impossible /ɪmˈpɒsəbl/ *noun* something that it is not possible to have or achieve

impossibly /ɪmˈpɒsəbli/ *adverb* extremely, in a way that is very difficult to achieve or deal with *a picture of an impossibly pretty woman*

impostor (*also* **imposter**) /ɪmˈpɒstəʳ/ *noun* [C] someone who pretends to be someone else in order to deceive people

impotent /ˈɪmpətənt/ *adjective* **1** An impotent man is unable to have sex because his penis does not become or stay hard. **2** not having the power or strength to do anything to change a situation *When your child is ill, you feel so impotent.* ● **impotence** /ˈɪmpətəns/ *noun* [U]

impound /ɪmˈpaʊnd/ *verb* [T] If the police or someone in authority impounds something that belongs to you, for example your car, they take it away because you have broken the law.

impoverished /ɪmˈpɒvərɪʃt/ *adjective formal* **1** poor or made poor *an impoverished country/family* **2** made worse or weaker *culturally/emotionally impoverished*

impractical /ɪmˈpræktɪkəl/ *adjective* **1** METHOD/IDEA Impractical ideas, methods, etc cannot be used or done easily. **2** PERSON Impractical people are not good at making, repairing, or planning things. **3** MATERIAL/CLOTHING not suitable for using in normal situations *I love high heels but they're rather impractical.*

imprecise /ˌɪmprɪˈsaɪs/ *adjective* not accurate or exact *an imprecise description*

impress /ɪmˈpres/ *verb* [T] to make someone

admire or respect you *I was impressed by her professionalism.* ○ *Sarah was hoping to impress him with her cooking.*

impress sth on sb to make someone understand the importance of something *He tried to impress the importance of hygiene on them.*

▨▨▨ WORD PARTNERS FOR ***impression***

convey/**create**/**give**/**make** an impression ● **get** an impression ● be **under** an impression ● a **distinct**/**false**/**favourable**/**indelible**/**lasting**/**misleading** impression

o⌐**impression** /ɪmˈpreʃən/ *noun* **1** OPINION [no plural] an idea, feeling, or opinion about something or someone [+ (that)] *I got/had the impression that he was bored.* ○ *Monica gives the impression of being shy.* ○ *Remember that it makes a bad impression if you're late.* ○ *I think Mick was under the impression that* (= thought that) *we were married.* **2** COPY [C, U] when you copy the way a particular person or animal speaks or behaves, often to make people laugh *He does a brilliant impression of the president.* **3** MARK [C] a mark left when an object is pressed into something soft

impressionable /ɪmˈpreʃənəbl/ *adjective* easy to influence *impressionable young people*

impressive /ɪmˈpresɪv/ *adjective* Someone or something that is impressive makes you admire and respect them. *an impressive performance/view* ● **impressively** *adverb*

imprint /ˈɪmprɪnt/ *noun* **1** [C] a mark left when an object is pressed into something soft *The steps showed the imprint of his boots in the snow.* **2** [no plural] the effect that something leaves behind *Much of the house still bears the imprint of her personality.*

imprison /ɪmˈprɪzən/ *verb* [T] to put someone in prison or keep them as a prisoner [often passive] *Taylor was imprisoned in 1969 for burglary.* ● **imprisonment** *noun* [U]

improbable /ɪmˈprɒbəbl/ *adjective* **1** not likely to be true or to happen **2** surprising *Shirley seemed an improbable choice for a supermodel.* ● **improbably** *adverb*

impromptu /ɪmˈprɒmptjuː/ *adjective, adverb* not planned or prepared *an impromptu performance/party*

improper /ɪmˈprɒpəʳ/ *adjective formal* not correct, suitable, honest, or acceptable *improper conduct* ● **improperly** *adverb The court ruled that he had acted improperly.*

impropriety /ˌɪmprəˈpraɪəti/ *noun* [U] *formal* behaviour that is not correct, suitable, or honest *The enquiry found no evidence of financial impropriety.*

o⌐**improve** /ɪmˈpruːv/ *verb* [I, T] to get better or to make something better *Scott's behaviour has improved a lot lately.* ○ *Every year thousands of students come to London to improve their English.* ○ *improved earnings/productivity*

improve on sth to do something in a better way or with better results than before *I hope our team can improve on last Saturday's performance.*

If something improves after a period of doing badly, you can use the verbs **rally** and **recover**: *The team played badly in the first half but rallied in the second.* ● *We are still waiting for the economy to recover.*

The phrasal verbs **look up** and **pick up** can be used informally to say that a situation is improving: *Our financial situation is looking up.* ● *Business is really beginning to pick up.*

The phrasal verb **work on** means 'to try to improve something': *You need to work on your technique.*

The verb **refine** can be used when someone improves something by making small changes: *A team of experts spent several months refining the software.*

WORD PARTNERS FOR **improvement**

a **continuous/dramatic/gradual/significant/slight** improvement ● **bring about/ notice/produce/show** an improvement ● an improvement **in/to** sth

○ **improvement** /ɪm'pruːvmənt/ *noun* [C, U] when something gets better or when you make it better *There's been a noticeable improvement in her work this term.* ○ *He's a definite improvement on her last boyfriend.* ○ *Sadly, Olivia's health has shown no improvement.*

improvise /'ɪmprəvaɪz/ *verb* [I, T] **1** to make or do something without any preparation, using only the things that are available *For a football, we improvised with some rolled-up socks.* **2** to play music or say words that you are inventing, not reading or remembering ● **improvisation** /ˌɪmprəvaɪ'zeɪʃ°n/ *noun* [C, U]

WORD PARTNERS FOR **impulse**

resist an impulse ● sb's **first** impulse

impulse /'ɪmpʌls/ *noun* **1** [C] a sudden feeling that you must do something, without thinking about the results [usually singular] *Her first impulse was to run away.* **2 on impulse** suddenly and without thinking first *I tend to act on impulse.* **3** [C] a short signal that carries information through a system, for example an electrical system or the nerves in your body

impulsive /ɪm'pʌlsɪv/ *adjective* Impulsive people do things suddenly, without planning or thinking carefully, but because they want to. ● **impulsively** *adverb*

impunity /ɪm'pjuːnəti/ *noun formal* **with impunity** without being punished *Criminal gangs are terrorizing the city with apparent impunity.*

impure /ɪm'pjʊəʳ/ *adjective* not pure, but mixed with other substances ● **impurity** *noun* [C, U] when something is impure or a substance that is impure

○ **in¹** /ɪn/ *preposition* **1** POSITION inside or towards the inside of a container, place, or area *There's milk in the fridge.* ○ *a shop in South London* ○ *He put his hand in his pocket.* **2** DURING during part or all of a period of time *We're going to Italy in April.* ○ *I started working here in 1993.* **3** USING TIME needing or using no more than a particular amount of time *I'll be ready in a few minutes.* **4** PART OF part of something *Who's the woman in the painting?* ○ *There's a few spelling mistakes in your essay.* **5** JOB involved in a particular kind of job *a career in publishing/politics* **6** SUBJECT connected with a particular subject *a degree in philosophy* ○ *advances in medical science* **7** WEARING wearing *Do you know that man in the grey suit?* **8** EXPRESSED expressed or written in a particular way *Complete the form in black ink.* ○ *She spoke to him in Russian.* **9** ARRANGED arranged in a particular way *We sat down in a circle.* ○ *Is this list in alphabetical order?* **10** EXPERIENCE experiencing an emotion or condition *She's in a bad mood this morning.* ○ *The kitchen's in a terrible state.* **11 in all** used to show the total amount of something *Some of the children came, so there were 15 of us in all.*

○ **in²** /ɪn/ *adverb* **1** INTO A SPACE into an area or space from the outside of it *He rushed in halfway through the meeting.* ○ *Annie opened the car door and threw her luggage in.* **2** AT A PLACE at the place where a person usually lives or works *I phoned, but she wasn't in.* ○ *Could you ask him to ring me when he gets in?* **3** TRAIN/ PLANE If a train, plane, etc is in, it has arrived at the place it was going to. *My train gets in at 17.54.* **4** SENT given or sent to someone official in order to be read *Applications must be in by 28th February.* **5** TOWARDS LAND If the sea or a ship moves close to land *Let's go - the tide is coming in.* **6 be in for sth** *informal* If someone is in for a surprise, treat, shock, etc, it will happen to them soon. *If he thinks looking after a baby is easy, he's in for a shock.* **7 be in on sth** *informal* If you are in on something, you know about it or are involved in it. *Were you in on the surprise?* ○ *Please let me in on (= tell me) the secret.* **8** SPORT UK In cricket and similar sports, if a person or team is in, they are taking a turn to play. **9 be in for it** *informal (also UK be for it)* to be in trouble

in³ /ɪn/ *adjective informal* fashionable or popular *Pink is in this season.*

in⁴ /ɪn/ *noun* **the ins and outs of sth** the details of a particular subject *the ins and outs of the legal system*

in⁵ *(also* **in.***) written abbreviation for* inch (= a unit for measuring length)

in- /ɪn-/ *prefix* not *inaccurate* ○ *insensitive*

inability /ˌɪnə'bɪləti/ *noun* [no plural] when you are unable to do something

inaccessible /ˌɪnək'sesəbl/ *adjective* impossible or extremely difficult to get to *The plane crashed in a mountain area that was totally inaccessible to vehicles.*

inaccurate /ɪn'ækjərət/ *adjective* not correct or exact *inaccurate information/figures* ● **inaccuracy** /ɪn'ækjərəsi/ *noun* [C, U] when something is not correct or exact *His book contains historical inaccuracies.*

inaction /ɪn'ækʃ°n/ *noun* [U] when people do not take any action, especially about a problem

This announcement follows months of inaction and delay.

inactive /ɪnˈæktɪv/ *adjective* not active or working *Beetle grubs stay inactive underground until spring.* • **inactivity** /ˌɪnækˈtɪvəti/ *noun* [U] when something or someone is not active or working *a period of inactivity*

inadequacy /ɪˈnædɪkwəsi/ *noun* 1 [C, U] when something or someone is not good enough or not of a high enough quality *feelings of inadequacy* ○ *He pointed out several inadequacies in the present system.* 2 [U] when there is not enough of something *The basic problem is the inadequacy of our school budget.*

inadequate /ɪˈnædɪkwət/ *adjective* 1 not good enough or too low in quality *inadequate facilities/training* ○ *Our equipment is totally inadequate for a job like this.* 2 not enough *inadequate funds* • **inadequately** *adverb*

inadvertent /ˌɪnədˈvɜːtənt/ *adjective* not done intentionally *an inadvertent error* • **inadvertently** *adverb I had inadvertently picked up the wrong keys.*

inadvisable /ˌɪnədˈvaɪzəbl/ *adjective* likely to cause problems *It is inadvisable for women to travel alone in this region.*

inane /ɪˈneɪn/ *adjective* very silly and annoying *an inane question*

inanimate /ɪˈnænɪmət/ *adjective* not alive *an inanimate object*

inappropriate /ˌɪnəˈprəʊpriət/ *adjective* not suitable *inappropriate behaviour* ○ *It would be inappropriate for me to comment, without knowing the facts.* • **inappropriately** *adverb*

inarticulate /ˌɪnɑːˈtɪkjələt/ *adjective* unable to express clearly what you feel or mean in words

inasmuch as /ɪnəzˈmʌtʃˌəz/ *conjunction formal* used to introduce a phrase which explains the degree to which something you have just said is true *They were strict about our appearance inasmuch as we weren't allowed to wear jewellery or make-up.*

inaudible /ɪˈnɔːdəbl/ *adjective* impossible to hear *His voice was almost inaudible.*

inaugural /ɪˈnɔːgjərəl/ *adjective* [always before noun] An inaugural speech, meeting, etc is the first one of a new organization or leader. *the President's inaugural address*

inaugurate /ɪˈnɔːgjəreɪt/ *verb* [T] 1 to have a ceremony to celebrate an important person starting a new job, a new building opening, etc *Ronald Reagan was inaugurated in 1981.* 2 *formal* to start a new system or organization *He inaugurated a programme to fight tuberculosis.* • **inauguration** /ɪˌnɔːgjəˈreɪʃən/ *noun* [C, U] *the inauguration of the Lord Mayor*

in-box (*also* **inbox**) /ˈɪnbɒks/ *noun* [C] 1 the place on a computer where email messages are sent 2 *US* (*UK* **in-tray**) a container where you keep letters and documents that need to be dealt with

Inc. *written abbreviation for* incorporated (= used after the name of some companies) *Macmillan Inc.*

incalculable /ɪnˈkælkjələbl/ *adjective* too big to

measure *The hurricane's cost in human terms is incalculable.*

incapable /ɪnˈkeɪpəbl/ *adjective* **incapable of sth/doing sth** not able to do something or to feel a particular emotion *He's incapable of controlling his temper.*

incapacitate /ˌɪnkəˈpæsɪteɪt/ *verb* [T] *formal* to make someone too ill or weak to work or do things normally [often passive] *He was incapacitated by illness.* • **incapacity** /ˌɪnkəˈpæsəti/ *noun* [U] when you cannot do something because you do not have the ability or you are too weak

incarcerate /ɪnˈkɑːsəreɪt/ *verb* [T] *formal* to put and keep someone in prison [often passive] *Marks was incarcerated for robbery.* • **incarceration** /ɪnˌkɑːsərˈeɪʃən/ *noun* [U]

incarnate /ɪnˈkɑːnət/ *adjective* [always after noun] in human form *He was acting like the devil incarnate.*

incarnation /ˌɪnkɑːˈneɪʃən/ *noun* 1 [C] a particular form of something or someone that is changing or developing *In their new incarnation, the band have acquired a female singer.* 2 **the incarnation of sth** the physical form of a god or quality *the incarnation of evil/freedom* 3 [C] a particular life, in religions which believe we have many lives

incendiary /ɪnˈsendiəri/ *adjective* [always before noun] designed to cause a fire *an incendiary bomb/device*

incense /ˈɪnsens/ *noun* [U] a substance which burns with a strong, sweet smell, often used in religious ceremonies

incensed /ɪnˈsenst/ *adjective* extremely angry

have/provide an incentive • an **added/ powerful/strong** incentive • an incentive **for** sb

incentive /ɪnˈsentɪv/ *noun* [C, U] something that encourages you to act in a particular way [+ to do sth] *People had little incentive to save.* ○ *The government should provide incentives for young people to stay in school.*

inception /ɪnˈsepʃən/ *noun* [no plural] *formal* the time when an organization or official activity began *Ivana has directed the project since its inception.*

incessant /ɪnˈsesənt/ *adjective* continuous, especially in a way that is annoying or unpleasant *incessant rain/noise* • **incessantly** *adverb The phone rang incessantly.*

incest /ˈɪnsest/ *noun* [U] sex that is illegal because it is between closely related people, for example a father and daughter

incestuous /ɪnˈsestjuəs/ *adjective* 1 involving sex between people who are closely related 2 involving a group of people who are not interested in people or things outside the group *Universities can be very incestuous places.*

o⌐**inch¹** /ɪntʃ/ *noun* [C] 1 (*written abbreviation* **in.**) a unit for measuring length, equal to 2.54 centimetres ⮡See Extra help page **Measurements** on page Centre 31. 2 **not budge/give an inch** *in-*

formal to refuse to change your opinions **3 to be every inch sth** to be a particular kind of person in every way *He is every inch a gentleman.*

inch² /ɪnʃ/ *verb* **inch closer/forward/up, etc** to move somewhere slowly or by very small amounts

incidence /ˈɪnsɪd³ns/ *noun* [C] how often something happens, especially something bad [usually singular] *There's a high **incidence** of crime in the area.*

incident /ˈɪnsɪd³nt/ *noun* [C] *formal* an event, especially one that is bad or unusual *Police are investigating the incident.*

incidental /ˌɪnsɪˈdent³l/ *adjective* less important than the thing something is connected with or part of *The lyrics here are **incidental** to the music.*

incidentally /ˌɪnsɪˈdent³li/ *adverb* used when you say something that is not as important as the main subject of conversation but is connected to it *Incidentally, talking of Stephen, have you met his girlfriend?*

incinerator /ɪnˈsɪn³reɪtə³/ *noun* [C] a machine that is used to burn waste, especially harmful materials

incipient /ɪnˈsɪpiənt/ *adjective* [always before noun] *formal* just beginning *incipient wrinkles*

incision /ɪnˈsɪʒ³n/ *noun* [C] *formal* an opening that is made in something with a sharp tool, especially in someone's body during an operation

incisive /ɪnˈsaɪsɪv/ *adjective* showing an ability to think quickly and clearly and deal with situations effectively *incisive questions*

incite /ɪnˈsaɪt/ *verb* [T] to do or say something that encourages people to behave violently or illegally *They denied inciting the crowd to violence.* • **incitement** *noun* [C, U] when someone does or says something that incites people

incl *written abbreviation for* including or inclusive

inclination /ˌɪnklɪˈneɪʃ³n/ *noun* [C, U] a feeling that you want to do something [+ to do sth] *She showed little **inclination** to leave.*

incline¹ /ɪnˈklaɪn/ *verb* [T] *formal* If you incline your head, you bend your neck so that your face bends down.
incline to/towards sth *formal* to think that a belief or opinion is probably correct *I incline to the view that peace can be achieved.*

incline² /ˈɪnklaɪn/ *noun* [C] *formal* a slope *a steep/gentle incline*

inclined /ɪnˈklaɪnd/ *adjective* [never before noun] **1 be inclined to think/believe/agree, etc** to have an opinion, but not a strong opinion *I'm inclined to agree with you.* **2 inclined to do sth** a

often behaving in a particular way *Tom is inclined to be forgetful.* **b** wanting to do something *No one seemed inclined to help.* **3 artistically/technically, etc inclined** having natural artistic/technical, etc ability *She's very bright, but not academically inclined.*

ℴ⁻**include** /ɪnˈkluːd/ *verb* [T] **1** to have something or someone as part of something larger or more general, such as a group, price, or process *His books include the best-selling novel 'The Foundling'.* ○ *The price includes flights and three nights' accommodation.* ⊃See Common learner error at **contain**. **2** to allow someone to take part in an activity [often passive] *Local residents were **included in** the initial planning discussions.* ⊃Opposite **exclude**.

ℴ⁻**including** /ɪnˈkluːdɪŋ/ *preposition* used to show that someone or something is part of a larger group, amount, or process *Fourteen people, including a prison warden, were killed.* ○ *It's £24.99, including postage and packing.*

inclusion /ɪnˈkluːʒ³n/ *noun* [C, U] when you include someone or something, especially in a group, amount, or event *Her self-portrait was chosen for inclusion in the exhibition.* ⊃Opposite **exclusion**.

inclusive /ɪnˈkluːsɪv/ *adjective* **1** [COST] An inclusive price or amount includes everything. *Prices are **inclusive** of flights and accommodation.* **2** [NUMBERS] [always after noun] including the first and last date or number stated *The course will run from October 19 to November 13, inclusive.* **3** [PEOPLE] Inclusive groups try to include many different types of people. *Our aim is to create a fairer, more inclusive society.* ⊃Opposite **exclusive**.

incoherent /ˌɪnkəʊˈhɪər³nt/ *adjective* not using clear words or ideas, and difficult to understand *His statement to the police was rambling and incoherent.* • **incoherence** /ˌɪnkəʊˈhɪər³ns/ *noun* [U]

ℴ⁻**income** /ˈɪŋkʌm/ *noun* [C, U] money that you earn by working, investing, or producing goods *families on **low incomes*** ○ *Tourism accounts for 25% of the country's national income.* ⊃See Common learner error at **pay**.

income sup,port *noun* [U] in the UK, money that is paid by the government to people who have very little or no income

income ,tax *noun* [C, U] tax that you have to pay on your income

incoming /ˈɪnˌkʌmɪŋ/ *adjective* [always before noun] coming into a place or starting a job *incoming phone calls/mail* ○ *the incoming government*

incomparable /ɪnˈkɒmp³rəbl/ *adjective* too good to be compared with anything or anyone else *incomparable beauty*

incompatible /ˌɪnkəmˈpætəbl/ *adjective* **1** too different to exist or live together *He regarded being a soldier as **incompatible with** his*

Christian faith. **2** If equipment or software is incompatible with other equipment or software, it will not work with it. ● **incompatibility** /ˌɪnkəmˌpætəˈbɪləti/ *noun* [U] when two people or things are incompatible

incompetent /ɪnˈkɒmpɪtᵊnt/ *adjective* not able to do your job, or things that you are expected to do, successfully *incompetent managers* ● **incompetence** /ɪnˈkɒmpɪtᵊns/ *noun* [U]

incomplete /ˌɪnkəmˈpliːt/ *adjective* not finished, or having one or more parts missing *Decisions were made on the basis of incomplete information.* ● **incompleteness** *noun* [U]

incomprehensible /ɪnˌkɒmprɪˈhensəbl/ *adjective* impossible to understand *The instructions are almost incomprehensible.* ○ *His behaviour is quite incomprehensible to me.*

incomprehension /ɪnˌkɒmprɪˈhenʃᵊn/ *noun* [U] *formal* when you do not understand something *She looked at Ludovic in total incomprehension.*

inconceivable /ˌɪnkənˈsiːvəbl/ *adjective* impossible to imagine [+ that] *I find it inconceivable that she could be a killer.*

inconclusive /ˌɪnkənˈkluːsɪv/ *adjective* not leading to a definite decision or result *inconclusive evidence/results* ○ *The battle was inconclusive.*

incongruous /ɪnˈkɒŋɡruəs/ *adjective formal* strange or not suitable for a particular situation *Bill was an incongruous sight, standing on the beach in his suit.*

inconsequential /ɪnˌkɒnsɪˈkwenʃᵊl/ *adjective formal* not important *inconsequential remarks*

inconsiderate /ˌɪnkənˈsɪdᵊrət/ *adjective* not caring about other people's situations or the way they feel *It was very inconsiderate of you to keep us all waiting.*

WORD PARTNERS FOR *inconsistency*

(an) **apparent/glaring** inconsistency ● (an) inconsistency **in** sth

inconsistency /ˌɪnkənˈsɪstᵊnsi/ *noun* [C, U] when something is inconsistent *The report was full of errors and inconsistencies.*

inconsistent /ˌɪnkənˈsɪstənt/ *adjective* **1** not staying the same in quality or behaviour *His homework is very inconsistent.* **2** not having the same principles as something else, or not agreeing with other facts *The story Robert told his mother is totally inconsistent with what he told me.*

inconspicuous /ˌɪnkənˈspɪkjuəs/ *adjective* not noticeable or attracting attention *Emma tried to make herself as inconspicuous as possible.*

incontinent /ɪnˈkɒntɪnənt/ *adjective* not able to control when urine or faeces come out of your body

incontrovertible /ˌɪnˌkɒntrəˈvɜːtəbl/ *adjective formal* certainly true *incontrovertible evidence/proof*

inconvenience /ˌɪnkənˈviːniəns/ *noun* [C, U] when something is inconvenient, or something that is inconvenient *The Director apologized for any inconvenience caused.* ○ [usually singular] *Having to wait for ten minutes was a* *minor inconvenience.* ● **inconvenience** *verb* [T] *There were complaints from travellers inconvenienced by delays and cancellations.*

inconvenient /ˌɪnkənˈviːniənt/ *adjective* involving or causing difficulty, such as unexpected changes or effort *I'm sorry, I seem to have called at an inconvenient time.*

incorporate /ɪnˈkɔːpᵊreɪt/ *verb* [T] to include something as part of another thing *He began to incorporate dance and mime into his plays.* ● **incorporation** /ɪnˌkɔːpᵊrˈeɪʃᵊn/ *noun* [U]

Incorporated /ɪnˈkɔːpᵊreɪtɪd/ (*written abbreviation* Inc.) *adjective* used after the name of companies which have been organized in a particular legal way *They formed their own company, Broadcast Music Incorporated.*

incorrect /ˌɪnkᵊrˈekt/ *adjective* not correct *His answers were incorrect.* ● **incorrectly** *adverb My name is spelled incorrectly on your list.*

incorrigible /ɪnˈkɒrɪdʒəbl/ *adjective* having particular faults and impossible to change

OTHER WAYS OF SAYING *increase*

The verbs **grow** and **rise** are common alternatives to 'increase': *The number of people living alone grows each year.* ● *Prices rose by ten percent.*

The phrasal verb **go up** is often used when prices increase: *House prices keep going up.* ● *The price of fuel has gone up by 5p a litre.*

If something suddenly increases by a large amount, you can use verbs such as **escalate**, **rocket**, or **soar**: *Crime in the city has escalated in recent weeks.* ● *Building costs have rocketed by seventy percent.* ● *House prices have soared this year.*

If someone makes something increase in size or amount, you can use verbs like **expand** or **extend**: *We're hoping to expand/extend our range of products.*

The verb **maximize** is sometimes used when someone tries to increase something as much as possible: *We need to maximize profits.*

o⌐**increase**[1] /ɪnˈkriːs/ *verb* [I, T] to get bigger or to make something bigger in size or amount *Eating fatty food increases the risk of heart disease.* ○ *Exports of computers have increased by 15% since January.* ○ *increased demand/competition* ⊃Opposite **decrease**.

WORD PARTNERS FOR *increase*

a **dramatic/sharp/significant/slight/substantial** increase ● an increase **in** sth

o⌐**increase**[2] /ˈɪnkriːs/ *noun* **1** [C, U] when the number, size, or amount of something gets bigger *a price/tax increase* ○ *We are seeing an increase in standards of living.* **2 on the increase** If something is on the increase, it is happening more often. *Violent crime is on the increase.* ⊃Opposite **decrease**.

COMMON LEARNER ERROR

increase in or increase of?

Use **increase in** before the thing which is increasing.

an increase in profits/sales

an increase in the number of AIDS cases

Use **increase** of before the size of the increase.

an increase of 30%

---

increasingly /ɪnˈkriːsɪŋli/ adverb more and more *increasingly important* ○ *Increasingly, education is seen as a right, not a privilege.*

⊶**incredible** /ɪnˈkredɪbl/ adjective **1** informal very good, exciting, or large *We had an incredible time that summer.* ○ *an incredible noise* **2** too strange to be believed *an incredible story*

incredibly /ɪnˈkredɪbli/ adverb **1** informal extremely *The team played incredibly well.* **2** in a way that is difficult to believe *Incredibly, no one was hurt.*

incredulous /ɪnˈkredjələs/ adjective not able to believe something *He looked incredulous when I told him the results.* ● **incredulity** /ˌɪnkrəˈdjuːləti/ noun [U] ● **incredulously** adverb

increment /ˈɪnkrəmənt/ noun [C] formal one of a series of increases *pay increments*

incremental /ˌɪnkrəˈmentᵊl/ adjective formal increasing by small amounts *incremental changes*

incriminate /ɪnˈkrɪmɪneɪt/ verb [T] to make someone seem guilty of a crime or to show that they are guilty [often reflexive] *He refused to answer questions on the grounds that he might incriminate himself.*

incriminating /ɪnˈkrɪmɪneɪtɪŋ/ adjective Something that is incriminating makes someone seem guilty of a crime. *incriminating evidence/remarks*

incubator /ˈɪŋkjubeɪtᵊr/ noun [C] a heated container that provides the right conditions for a baby born too early, or for very young birds, animals, or eggs

incumbent¹ /ɪnˈkʌmbənt/ noun [C] formal someone who has an official job, especially a political one *the previous incumbent*

incumbent² /ɪnˈkʌmbənt/ adjective **1 be incumbent on/upon sb to do sth** formal to be someone's duty or responsibility to do something **2** [always before noun] holding an official job, especially a political one *the incumbent president*

incur /ɪnˈkɜːr/ verb [T] incurring past incurred formal to experience something unpleasant as a result of something you have done *to incur debts* ○ *I am sorry to have incurred his anger.*

incurable /ɪnˈkjʊərəbl/ adjective impossible to cure *an incurable disease*

incursion /ɪnˈkɜːʃᵊn/ noun [C] formal a sudden attack or entry into an area that belongs to other people *incursions into enemy territory*

indebted /ɪnˈdetɪd/ adjective **1 be indebted to sb** to be very grateful to someone *I'm indebted to my parents for all their support.* **2** having a debt to pay *indebted countries* ● **indebtedness** noun [U]

indecent /ɪnˈdiːsᵊnt/ adjective showing or consisting of sexual behaviour, language, etc which is unacceptable to most people *indecent photographs* ● **indecency** /ɪnˈdiːsᵊnsi/ noun [U] in-

decent behaviour, or when something is indecent ● **indecently** adverb

indecision /ˌɪndɪˈsɪʒᵊn/ noun [U] when you cannot make a decision *a moment of indecision*

indecisive /ˌɪndɪˈsaɪsɪv/ adjective not good at making decisions, or not producing a decision *She was weak and indecisive.*

indeed /ɪnˈdiːd/ adverb **1** EMPHASIS used to add emphasis after 'very' followed by an adjective or adverb *For a four-year-old, her vocabulary is very good indeed.* ○ *Thank you very much indeed.* **2** REACTION used when someone has said something that surprises, interests, or annoys you *"She asked if you were married." "Did she, indeed?"* **3** TRUE used to emphasize that something is true or that you agree with it *"He sounds a very interesting man." "He is indeed."* **4** MORE formal used when you say more to support or develop what has already been said *For such creatures speed is not important, indeed it is counterproductive.*

indefatigable /ˌɪndɪˈfætɪɡəbl/ adjective formal never becoming tired *She was indefatigable in promoting her cause.*

indefensible /ˌɪndɪˈfensəbl/ adjective completely wrong, and so impossible to defend or support *Racism is morally indefensible.*

indefinable /ˌɪndɪˈfaɪnəbl/ adjective difficult to describe or explain *an indefinable atmosphere of tension*

indefinite /ɪnˈdefɪnət/ adjective with no fixed time, size, end, or limit *an indefinite period*

in,definite 'article noun [C] in grammar, a phrase used to mean the words 'a' or 'an' ⊃Compare **definite article.**

indefinitely /ɪnˈdefɪnətli/ adverb for a period of time for which no end has been fixed *His visit has been postponed indefinitely.*

indelible /ɪnˈdeləbl/ adjective **1** impossible to forget *an indelible impression/image* **2** impossible to wash away or remove *indelible ink*

indemnity /ɪnˈdemnəti/ noun formal **1** [U] protection against possible damage or punishment **2** [C, U] money paid or promised to you if something valuable to you is lost or damaged *indemnity insurance*

indentation /ˌɪndenˈteɪʃᵊn/ noun [C] a mark, cut, or hole in the surface of something

WORD PARTNERS FOR *independence*
2 achieve/gain independence ● independence **from** sth

⊶**independence** /ˌɪndɪˈpendəns/ noun [U] **1** when someone looks after themselves and does not need money, help, or permission from other people *My parents gave me a lot of independence.* ○ *Many old people are afraid of losing their independence.* **2** when a country has its own government and is not ruled by another country *Mexico gained its independence from Spain in 1821.*

Inde'pendence ,Day (also Fourth of July) noun 4 July, a national holiday in the US to celebrate the country's freedom from Great Britain in 1776

o→**independent**[1] /ˌɪndɪˈpendənt/ *adjective* **1** RULE not controlled or ruled by anyone else *an independent state/company* ○ *The group is **independent of** any political party.* **2** NEED not wanting or needing anyone else to help you or do things for you *She's a proud, independent woman.* **3** INFLUENCE not influenced by anyone or anything else *an independent expert/study* ● **independently** *adverb to operate independently*

independent[2] /ˌɪndɪˈpendənt/ *noun* [C] a politician who does not belong to a political party

in-depth /ˈɪnˌdepθ/ *adjective* [always before noun] involving or considering all the details of something *in-depth knowledge*

indescribable /ˌɪndɪˈskraɪbəbl/ *adjective* so good, bad, large, etc that it is impossible to describe *an indescribable feeling* ○ *indescribable agony*

indestructible /ˌɪndɪˈstrʌktəbl/ *adjective* impossible to destroy or break

indeterminate /ˌɪndɪˈtɜːmɪnət/ *adjective* impossible to know *a large woman of indeterminate age*

index[1] /ˈɪndeks/ *noun* [C] **1** LIST *plural* **indexes** an alphabetical list of subjects or names at the end of a book, which show what page they are found in the text *Look up 'heart disease' in the index.* **2** INFORMATION *plural* **indexes** a collection of information stored on a computer or on cards in alphabetical order **3** SYSTEM *plural* **indices** or **indexes** a system for comparing different values and recording changes, especially in financial markets *the retail price index*

index[2] /ˈɪndeks/ *verb* [T] to make an index for text or information, or arrange it in an index

'index ˌfinger *noun* [C] the finger next to your thumb

Indian /ˈɪndiən/ *noun* [C] **1** someone from India **2** an American Indian (= one of the original race of people who lived in North America) ○See also: **West Indian**.

indicate /ˈɪndɪkeɪt/ *verb* **1** SHOW [T] to show that something exists or is likely to be true [+ (that)] *Recent evidence indicates that the skeleton is about 3 million years old.* **2** SAY [T] to say something or give a signal to show what you mean or what you intend to do *He has indicated his intention to resign.* **3** POINT [T] to point to someone or something *He indicated a man in a dark coat.* **4** SIGNAL [I, T] *UK* to show that you intend to turn left or right when you are driving *The driver turned right without indicating.*

WORD PARTNERS FOR *indication*

a **clear/good/strong** indication ● an indication **of** sth

indication /ˌɪndɪˈkeɪʃən/ *noun* [C, U] **1** a sign showing that something exists or is likely to be true [+ (that)] *There are **strong indications** that the case will be referred to the Court of Appeal.* **2** a sign showing what someone means or what they intend to do *Helen's face gave no **indication** of what she was thinking.*

indicative[1] /ɪnˈdɪkətɪv/ *adjective formal* **1 be indicative of sth** to be a sign that something exists, is true, or is likely to happen *These statistics are indicative of a widespread problem.* **2** An indicative form of a verb is used to express a fact or action.

indicative[2] /ɪnˈdɪkətɪv/ *noun* [no plural] the indicative form of a verb

WORD PARTNERS FOR *indicator*

a **good/reliable/useful** indicator ● an indicator **of** sth

indicator /ˈɪndɪkeɪtər/ *noun* [C] **1** a fact, measurement, or condition that shows what something is like or how it is changing *With some goods, cost is the most reliable **indicator of** quality.* **2** *UK* (*US* **turn signal**) a light that flashes on a vehicle to show that the driver intends to turn right or left ○See colour picture **Car** on page Centre 7.

indict /ɪnˈdaɪt/ *verb* [T] *formal* to accuse someone officially of a crime [often passive] *Pound was indicted for treason.*

indictment /ɪnˈdaɪtmənt/ *noun* **1** [C] something which shows the bad things which a person or system is responsible for *The novel is a scathing **indictment of** the slave trade.* **2** [C, U] when someone is legally indicted, or the official document or process for doing this

indie /ˈɪndi/ *noun* [C, U] *informal* a small independent music company or film producer *indie music/bands*

WORD PARTNERS FOR *indifference*

callous/casual/cold indifference ● indifference **to/towards** sth

indifference /ɪnˈdɪfərəns/ *noun* [U] when you do not care about something or have any particular opinions about it *He had an air of indifference about him.*

indifferent /ɪnˈdɪfərənt/ *adjective* **1** not caring about or interested in someone or something *They are **indifferent to** the plight of the unemployed.* **2** neither good nor bad *an indifferent performance*

indigenous /ɪnˈdɪdʒɪnəs/ *adjective* having always lived or existed in a place *indigenous peoples* ○ *The kangaroo is **indigenous to** Australia.*

indigestion /ˌɪndɪˈdʒestʃən/ *noun* [U] pain which you feel when your stomach is unable to digest food correctly

indignant /ɪnˈdɪgnənt/ *adjective* angry because you have been treated badly or unfairly *Consumers are **indignant at/about** the high prices charged by car dealers.* ● **indignantly** *adverb*

indignation /ˌɪndɪgˈneɪʃən/ *noun* [U] when someone is indignant *His voice was trembling with indignation.*

indignity /ɪnˈdɪgnəti/ *noun* [C, U] a situation which makes you lose respect or look silly, or the feeling of shame and embarrassment it gives you [+ doing sth] *Hugo and Bob suffered the **indignity** of being searched like common criminals.*

indigo /ˈɪndɪgəʊ/ *noun* [U] a blue-purple colour ● **indigo** *adjective*

indirect /ˌɪndɪˈrekt/ *adjective* **1** NOT CONNECTED not directly caused by or connected with something *Indirect effects of the fighting include disease and food shortages.* **2** NOT OBVIOUS hidden, or not taken or given in a way that is obvious *indirect taxes/costs* ○ *an indirect criticism* **3** NOT STRAIGHT not going straight from one place or person to another *an indirect route* ● **indirectly** *adverb*

indirect 'object *noun* [C] The indirect object of a verb with two objects is the person or thing that is affected by the result of the action of the verb. In the sentence 'Give Val some cake.', 'Val' is the indirect object. ⊃Compare direct object.

indiscreet /ˌɪndɪˈskriːt/ *adjective* saying or doing things which let people know things that should be secret *indiscreet remarks* ● **indiscretion** /ˌɪndɪˈskreʃᵊn/ *noun* [C, U]

indiscriminate /ˌɪndɪˈskrɪmɪnət/ *adjective* not planned or controlled in a responsible or careful way *the indiscriminate use of pesticides* ● **indiscriminately** *adverb* *The gunman fired indiscriminately into the crowd.*

indispensable /ˌɪndɪˈspensəbl/ *adjective* completely necessary *an indispensable tool/ guide* ○ *She quickly became indispensable to him.*

indisputable /ˌɪndɪˈspjuːtəbl/ *adjective* obviously and certainly true *an indisputable fact*

indistinct /ˌɪndɪˈstɪŋkt/ *adjective* not clear *His words became indistinct.*

indistinguishable /ˌɪndɪˈstɪŋgwɪʃəbl/ *adjective* impossible to see or hear as different or separate *Many toy pistols are indistinguishable from real guns.*

individual¹ /ˌɪndɪˈvɪdʒuəl/ *adjective* **1** [always before noun] considered separately from other things in a group *Read out the individual letters of each word.* **2** given to or relating to one particular person or thing *We deal with each case on an individual basis.*

individual² /ˌɪndɪˈvɪdʒuəl/ *noun* [C] **1** a person, especially when considered separately and not as part of a group *We try to treat our students as individuals.* **2** *informal* a person with a special characteristic, usually one you dislike *a ruthless individual*

individualism /ˌɪndɪˈvɪdʒuəlɪzᵊm/ *noun* [U] the quality of being different from other people

individualist /ˌɪndɪˈvɪdʒuəlɪst/ *noun* [C] someone who likes to behave or do things differently from other people ● **individualistic** /ˌɪndɪˌvɪdʒuəˈlɪstɪk/ *adjective* behaving or doing things differently from other people

individuality /ˌɪndɪˌvɪdʒuˈæləti/ *noun* [U] the quality of being different from others *The houses had no character and no individuality.*

individually /ˌɪndɪˈvɪdʒuəli/ *adverb* separately and not as a group *He apologized to each person individually.*

indoctrinate /ɪnˈdɒktrɪneɪt/ *verb* [T] to make someone accept your ideas and beliefs by repeating them so often that they do not consider any others *They try to indoctrinate young people with their religious beliefs.* ● **indoctrin-**

ation /ɪnˌdɒktrɪˈneɪʃᵊn/ *noun* [U] *political indoctrination*

indoor /ˌɪnˈdɔːʳ/ *adjective* [always before noun] happening, used, or existing in a building *an indoor swimming pool*

indoors /ˌɪnˈdɔːz/ *adverb* into or inside a building *If you're feeling cold, we can go indoors.*

induce /ɪnˈdjuːs/ *verb* [T] **1** PERSUADE *formal* to persuade someone do something [+ to do sth] *Nothing would induce me to marry that man!* **2** CAUSE *formal* to cause a particular condition *High doses of the drug may induce depression.* **3** BABY to give a woman a drug to make her have a baby earlier than she would naturally

inducement /ɪnˈdjuːsmənt/ *noun* [C, U] *formal* something that someone offers you to try to persuade you to do something *They offered me more money as an inducement to stay.*

induct /ɪnˈdʌkt/ *verb* [T] *formal* to accept someone officially as a member of an organization *He was inducted into the army in 1943.*

induction /ɪnˈdʌkʃᵊn/ *noun* [C, U] when someone is officially accepted into a new job or an organization *a two-week induction course*

indulge /ɪnˈdʌldʒ/ *verb* **1** [I, T] to let yourself do or have something that you enjoy but which may be bad for you *They indulged in a bit of gossip.* ○ [often reflexive] *Go on, indulge yourself! Have another chocolate.* **2** [T] to let someone do or have anything they want *Their children are dreadfully indulged.*

indulgence /ɪnˈdʌldʒᵊns/ *noun* **1** [U] when you eat or drink too much or do anything you want **2** [C] something that you do or have because you want to, not because you need it *Silk sheets are one of my indulgences.*

indulgent /ɪnˈdʌldʒᵊnt/ *adjective* If you are indulgent to someone, you give them anything they want and do not mind if they behave badly. *an indulgent father* ● **indulgently** *adverb* *She smiled indulgently at her son.* ⊃See also: self-indulgent.

∘⁻**industrial** /ɪnˈdʌstriəl/ *adjective* **1** connected with industry *the industrial revolution* **2** with a lot of factories *an industrial city such as Sheffield*

in,dustrial 'action *noun* [U] *UK* when workers stop working or do less work because they want better pay or conditions

in,dustrial es'tate *UK* (*US* **industrial park**) *noun* [C] an area where there are a lot of factories and businesses

industrialist /ɪnˈdʌstriəlɪst/ *noun* [C] someone who owns or has an important position in a large industrial company

industrialization /ɪnˌdʌstriəlaɪˈzeɪʃᵊn/ *noun* [U] the process of developing industries in a country *Japan's rapid industrialization*

industrialized (*also UK* -**ised**) /ɪnˈdʌstriəlaɪzd/ *adjective* Industrialized countries have a lot of industry. *the industrialized nations*

in'dustrial ,park *US* (*UK* **industrial estate**) *noun* [C] an area where there are a lot of factories and businesses

in,dustrial tri'bunal *noun* [C] in the UK, a type of law court that decides on disagreements between companies and their workers

industrious /ɪnˈdʌstriəs/ *adjective formal* Industrious people work hard. • **industriously** *adverb*

o-**industry** /ˈɪndəstri/ *noun* **1** [U] the production of goods in factories *heavy industry* **2** [C] all the companies involved in a particular type of business *the entertainment industry*

inedible /ɪˈnedɪbl/ *adjective* not suitable for eating *The meat was inedible.*

ineffective /ˌɪnɪˈfektɪv/ *adjective* If something is ineffective, it does not work well. • **ineffectively** *adverb* • **ineffectiveness** *noun* [U]

ineffectual /ˌɪnɪˈfektʃuᵊl/ *adjective* Ineffectual people or actions do not achieve much. *a weak and ineffectual president* • **ineffectually** *adverb*

inefficient /ˌɪnɪˈfɪʃᵊnt/ *adjective* Inefficient people or things waste time, money, or effort, and do not achieve as much as they should. *an inefficient heating system* • **inefficiently** *adverb* • **inefficiency** /ˌɪnɪˈfɪʃᵊnsi/ *noun* [C, U]

ineligible /ɪˈnelɪdʒəbl/ *adjective* not allowed to do something or have something [+ to do sth] *Foreign residents are ineligible to vote.* ○ *Non-graduates are ineligible for this position.* • **ineligibility** /ɪˌnelɪdʒəˈbɪləti/ *noun* [U]

inept /ɪˈnept/ *adjective* unable to do something well *socially inept* ○ *She was totally inept at telling jokes.* • **ineptly** *adverb* • **ineptitude** /ɪˈneptɪtjuːd/ *noun* [U]

inequality /ˌɪnɪˈkwɒləti/ *noun* [C, U] when some groups in a society have more advantages than others *inequality between the sexes*

inequity /ɪˈnekwəti/ *noun* [C, U] when something is unfair, or something that is unfair *inequities in the health care system*

inert /ɪˈnɜːt/ *adjective formal* **1** Inert substances do not produce a chemical reaction when another substance is added. *inert gases* **2** not moving *Vanessa lay inert on the sofa.* • **inertly** *adverb*

inertia /ɪˈnɜːʃə/ *noun* [U] **1** NO CHANGE when a situation remains the same or changes very slowly *the inertia of larger organizations* **2** LAZY when you are too lazy to do anything *International inertia could lead to a major disaster in the war zone.* **3** FORCE the physical force that keeps something in the same position or moving in the same direction

inescapable /ˌɪnɪˈskeɪpəbl/ *adjective* An inescapable fact cannot be ignored. *Racial discrimination is an inescapable fact of life for some people.* • **inescapably** *adverb*

inevitable /ɪˈnevɪtəbl/ *adjective* **1** If something is inevitable, you cannot avoid or prevent it. [+ (that)] *It was inevitable that his crime would be discovered.* **2 the inevitable** something that

cannot be prevented *Eventually the inevitable happened and he had a heart attack.* • **inevitably** *adverb Inevitably, there was a certain amount of fighting between the groups.* • **inevitability** /ɪˌnevɪtəˈbɪləti/ *noun* [U]

inexcusable /ˌɪnɪkˈskjuːzəbl/ *adjective* Inexcusable behaviour is too bad to be forgiven. *His rudeness was inexcusable.* • **inexcusably** *adverb*

inexhaustible /ˌɪnɪgˈzɔːstəbl/ *adjective* existing in very large amounts that will never be finished *The Internet is an inexhaustible source of information.*

inexorable /ɪˈneksᵊrəbl/ *adjective formal* continuing without any possibility of being stopped *the inexorable progress of civilization* • **inexorably** *adverb These events led inexorably to war.*

inexpensive /ˌɪnɪkˈspensɪv/ *adjective* cheap but of good quality *inexpensive children's clothes*

inexperience /ˌɪnɪkˈspɪəriəns/ *noun* [U] when you do not know how to do something because you have not done it or experienced it much before *The accident was probably caused by the driver's inexperience.*

inexperienced /ˌɪnɪkˈspɪəriənst/ *adjective* without much experience or knowledge of something *Abigail Kennedy was young and inexperienced.*

inexplicable /ˌɪnɪkˈsplɪkəbl/ *adjective* so strange or unusual that you cannot understand or explain it *To me his behaviour was quite inexplicable.* • **inexplicably** *adverb*

inextricably /ˌɪnɪkˈstrɪkəbli/ *adverb* If things are inextricably connected, they are so closely connected that you cannot separate them. *His story is inextricably linked with that of his brother.*

infallible /ɪnˈfæləbl/ *adjective* always right, true, or correct *infallible evidence of guilt* ○ *They're experts, but they're not infallible.* • **infallibility** /ɪnˌfæləˈbɪləti/ *noun* [U]

infamous /ˈɪnfəməs/ *adjective* famous for being bad *The area became infamous for its slums.*

infancy /ˈɪnfənsi/ *noun* **1** [U] when you are a baby or a very young child *Their fourth child died in infancy.* **2 in its infancy** Something that is in its infancy has only just begun to develop. *In the 1950s, space travel was in its infancy.*

infant /ˈɪnfənt/ *noun* [C] *formal* a baby or very young child

infantile /ˈɪnfəntaɪl/ *adjective* behaving like a young child in a way that seems silly *Don't be so infantile.*

infantry /ˈɪnfəntri/ *noun* [U, group] soldiers who fight on foot

infatuated /ɪnˈfætjueɪtɪd/ *adjective* If you are infatuated with someone, you feel extremely strongly attracted to them. *As the weeks passed he became totally infatuated with her.* • **infatuation** /ɪnˌfætjuˈeɪʃᵊn/ *noun* [C, U]

infect /ɪnˈfekt/ *verb* [T] **1** DISEASE to give someone a disease [often passive] *Thousands of people were infected with the virus.* **2** PLACE/SUBSTANCE If a place, wound, or substance is infected, it contains bacteria or other things that can cause disease. [often passive] *The wound became infected.* ○ *infected water/meat* ⊃Compare **disinfect**. **3** FEELING to make other people feel the same way as you do [often passive] *They became infected by the general excitement.*

◦⁻**infection** /ɪnˈfekʃᵊn/ *noun* [C, U] a disease in a part of your body that is caused by bacteria or a virus *an ear/throat infection*

infectious /ɪnˈfekʃəs/ *adjective* **1** An infectious disease can be passed from one person to another. **2** Infectious laughter or feelings quickly spread from one person to another. *infectious enthusiasm*

infer /ɪnˈfɜːʳ/ *verb* [T] inferring *past* inferred *formal* to guess that something is true because of the information that you have [+ (that)] *I inferred from the number of cups that he was expecting visitors.*

inference /ˈɪnfᵊrᵊns/ *noun* [C] *formal* a fact that you decide is true because of the information that you have *What inferences can we draw from this?*

inferior¹ /ɪnˈfɪəriəʳ/ *adjective* not good, or not so good as someone or something else *I've never felt inferior to anyone.* ○ *They're selling inferior products at inflated prices.* ● **inferiority** /ɪnˌfɪəriˈɒrəti/ *noun* [U] when something is not as good as another thing, or when someone feels they are not as good as other people

inferior² /ɪnˈfɪəriəʳ/ *noun* [C] someone who is considered to be less important than other people

inferno /ɪnˈfɜːnəʊ/ *noun* [C] *literary* a very large hot fire

infertile /ɪnˈfɜːtaɪl/ @ /ɪnˈfɜːrtᵊl/ *adjective* **1** An infertile person or animal cannot have babies. **2** Infertile land is not good enough for plants to grow well there. ● **infertility** /ˌɪnfəˈtɪləti/ *noun* [U] when a person or piece of land is infertile

infest /ɪnˈfest/ *verb* [T] If insects, animals, weeds (= plants you do not want), etc infest a place, they cause problems by being there in large numbers. [often passive] *The hotel was infested with cockroaches.*

infidelity /ˌɪnfɪˈdeləti/ *noun* [C, U] when someone who is married or in a relationship has sex with someone who is not their wife, husband, or regular partner

infighting /ˈɪnˌfaɪtɪŋ/ *noun* [U] arguments between the members of a group *political infighting between the parties*

infiltrate /ˈɪnfɪltreɪt/ *verb* [T] to secretly join a group or organization so that you can learn more about them *A journalist managed to infiltrate the gang of drug dealers.* ● **infiltration** /ˌɪnfɪlˈtreɪʃᵊn/ *noun* [C, U] ● **infiltrator** *noun* [C]

infinite /ˈɪnfɪnət/ *adjective* **1** extremely large or great *She took infinite care with the painting.* **2** without limits or without an end *God's power is infinite.*

infinitely /ˈɪnfɪnətli/ *adverb* very or very much *Travel is infinitely more comfortable now than it used to be.*

infinitive /ɪnˈfɪnətɪv/ *noun* [C] the basic form of a verb that usually follows 'to'. In the sentence 'Harriet decided to leave.', 'to leave' is an infinitive.

infinity /ɪnˈfɪnəti/ *noun* [U] **1** time or space that has no end **2** a number that is larger than all other numbers

infirm /ɪnˈfɜːm/ *adjective formal* weak or ill, especially because of being old *They are building houses for the elderly and infirm.*

infirmary /ɪnˈfɜːmᵊri/ *noun* [C] **1** *UK formal* used in the name of some hospitals *Leicester Royal Infirmary* **2** *mainly US* a room in a school, prison, etc where people go when they are ill

infirmity /ɪnˈfɜːməti/ *noun* [C, U] *formal* when someone is weak and unhealthy, or the illness they have

inflame /ɪnˈfleɪm/ *verb* [T] to cause or increase strong emotions *These brutal attacks have inflamed passions in a peaceful country.*

inflamed /ɪnˈfleɪmd/ *adjective* If part of your body is inflamed, it is red and often painful and swollen. *The drug is used to treat inflamed joints.*

inflammable /ɪnˈflæməbl/ *adjective* Inflammable liquids, gases, or materials burn very easily.

inflammation /ˌɪnfləˈmeɪʃᵊn/ *noun* [C, U] a red, painful, and often swollen area in or on a part of your body

inflammatory /ɪnˈflæmətᵊri/ *adjective* intended or likely to cause anger or hate *inflammatory statements/speeches*

inflatable /ɪnˈfleɪtəbl/ *adjective* An inflatable object has to be filled with air before you can use it. *an inflatable boat*

inflate /ɪnˈfleɪt/ *verb* **1** [I, T] to fill something with air or gas, or to become filled with air or gas **2** [T] to make something such as a number, price, etc larger

inflated /ɪnˈfleɪtɪd/ *adjective* Inflated prices, costs, numbers, etc are higher than they should be. *Prices in the tourist shops are somewhat inflated.*

◦⁻**inflation** /ɪnˈfleɪʃᵊn/ *noun* [U] the rate at which prices increase, or a continuing increase in prices *low/rising inflation*

inflationary /ɪnˈfleɪʃᵊnᵊri/ *adjective* likely to make prices rise

inflection /ɪnˈflekʃᵊn/ *noun* [C, U] **1** the way the end of a word changes to show tense, plural forms, etc **2** the way that your voice goes up and down when you speak, for example to show that you are asking a question

inflexible /ɪnˈfleksəbl/ *adjective* **1** Inflexible rules, opinions, beliefs, etc do not change easily. *a cold and inflexible man* **2** Inflexible materials do not bend easily. ● **inflexibility** /ɪnˌfleksəˈbɪləti/ *noun* [U]

inflict /ɪnˈflɪkt/ *verb* [T] to make someone suffer by doing something unpleasant to them *I would never have inflicted such suffering on you.*

in-flight /ˈɪnˌflaɪt/ *adjective* [always before noun] happening or available during a flight *in-flight entertainment*

WORD PARTNERS FOR *influence*

exert/have/wield influence • bad/considerable/disruptive/good/powerful influence • influence **on/over** sb/sth • be **under** the influence **of** sb/sth

•►**influence**[1] /'ɪnfluəns/ *noun* **1** [C, U] the power to affect how someone thinks or behaves, or how something develops *The drug companies have a lot of influence on doctors.* **2** [C] someone or something that has an effect on another person or thing *His grandfather was a strong influence on him.*

•►**influence**[2] /'ɪnfluəns/ *verb* [T] to affect or change how someone or something develops, behaves, or thinks *Many factors influence a film's success.* ○ [often passive] *Were you influenced by anybody when you were starting your career?*

influential /,ɪnflu'enʃ°l/ *adjective* having a lot of influence *an influential figure in modern jazz*

influenza /,ɪnflu'enzə/ *noun* [U] *formal* flu (= an illness like a very bad cold, that makes you feel hot and weak)

influx /'ɪnflʌks/ *noun* [C] the arrival of a lot of people or things at the same time [usually singular] *The 1990s saw an influx of foreign players into British football.*

info /'ɪnfəʊ/ *noun* [U] *informal short for* information

inform /ɪn'fɔːm/ *verb* [T] **1** to tell someone about something *If he calls me again, I shall inform the police.* ○ [+ (that)] *He informed us that we would have to leave.* **2** to give someone information about something [often passive] *Patients should be informed about the risks.* ○ *He keeps his parents informed of his whereabouts.*

inform against/on sb to tell the police about something illegal that someone has done *The terrorists said that anyone caught informing on them would be killed.*

informal /ɪn'fɔːm°l/ *adjective* **1** relaxed and friendly *an informal discussion/meeting* **2** suitable for normal situations *informal clothes* ○ *informal language* • **informality** /,ɪnfɔː'mæləti/ *noun* [U] • **informally** *adverb*

informant /ɪn'fɔːmənt/ *noun* [C] someone who gives information to another person *Our survey is based on over 200 informants.*

•►**information** /,ɪnfə'meɪʃ°n/ *noun* [U] facts about a situation, person, event, etc *a vital piece of information* ○ *Police are urging anyone with information about the crime to contact them.*

COMMON LEARNER ERROR

information

Remember you cannot make **information** plural. Do not say 'informations'.

Could you send me some information about your courses?

For more information contact our office.

That's the only piece of information we've been able to find out.

WORD PARTNERS FOR *information*

accurate/confidential/detailed/further/useful information • access/exchange/gather/give/need/provide information • information **about/on** sth

OTHER WAYS OF SAYING *information*

The plural noun **details** is often used to describe facts or pieces of information grouped together: *Please send me details of your training courses.*

The plural nouns **directions** and **instructions** are often used to talk about information which describes how to do something: *Just follow the directions/instructions on the label.*

The plural noun **directions** is also used to mean 'information about how to get to a place': *We had to stop and ask for directions.*

The noun **data** is sometimes used to describe information in the form of facts and numbers: *Our consultants have been collecting financial data.*

Written information about a subject is sometimes described as **literature**: *Some literature on our current policy is enclosed.*

infor,mation tech'nology *noun* [U] (*abbreviation* IT) the use of computers and other electronic equipment to store and send information

informative /ɪn'fɔːmətɪv/ *adjective* containing a lot of useful facts *a very informative lecture*

informed /ɪn'fɔːmd/ *adjective* having a lot of information or knowledge about something *informed choice/decision* ⊃ See also: well-informed.

informer /ɪn'fɔːməʳ/ *noun* [C] someone who secretly gives information to the police about a crime

infraction /ɪn'frækʃ°n/ *noun* [C, U] *formal* when someone breaks a rule or the law

infrared /,ɪnfrə'red/ *adjective* Infrared light feels warm but cannot be seen.

infrastructure /'ɪnfrə,strʌktʃəʳ/ *noun* [C] the basic systems, such as transport and communication, that a country or organization uses in order to work effectively [usually singular] *The country's infrastructure is in ruins.*

infrequent /ɪn'friːkwənt/ *adjective* not happening very often • **infrequently** *adverb*

infringe /ɪn'frɪndʒ/ *verb* [T] **1** *formal* to break a law or rule *They infringed building regulations.* **2** (*also* infringe on) to limit someone's rights or freedom *This law infringes on a citizen's right to bear arms.* • **infringement** *noun* [C, U] *an infringement of copyright*

infuriate /ɪn'fjʊərieɪt/ *verb* [T] to make someone very angry *What really infuriated me was the fact that he'd lied.* • **infuriating** *adjective* extremely annoying

infuse /ɪn'fjuːz/ *verb* **1** [T] *formal* to fill someone or something with a lot of a particular emotion or quality [often passive] *His work is infused with a love for tradition.* **2** [I, T] to put something into a liquid so that its taste goes into the liquid

infusion /ɪnˈfjuːʒ°n/ *noun* [C, U] *formal* when one thing is added to another thing to make it stronger or better *an infusion of cash*

ingenious /ɪnˈdʒiːniəs/ *adjective* very clever and involving new ideas, equipment, or methods *an ingenious idea/scheme/solution* ● **ingeniously** *adverb*

ingenuity /ˌɪndʒɪˈnjuːəti/ *noun* [U] skill at inventing things or finding new ways to solve problems

ingest /ɪnˈdʒest/ *verb* [T] *formal* to eat or drink something ● **ingestion** *noun* [U]

ingrained /ɪnˈɡreɪnd/ *adjective* **1** Ingrained beliefs, behaviour, problems, etc have existed for a long time and are difficult to change. *For most of us, watching television is a deeply ingrained habit.* **2** Ingrained dirt has got under the surface of something and is difficult to remove.

ingratiate /ɪnˈɡreɪʃieɪt/ *verb* **ingratiate yourself (with sb)** to try to make people like you by doing things to please them ● **ingratiating** *adjective* Ingratiating behaviour is done to try to make people like you. *an ingratiating smile/manner*

ingratitude /ɪnˈɡrætɪtjuːd/ *noun* [U] when someone is not grateful for something

ingredient /ɪnˈɡriːdiənt/ *noun* [C] **1** one of the different foods that a particular type of food is made from **2** one of the parts of something successful *Trust is an essential ingredient in a successful marriage.*

inhabit /ɪnˈhæbɪt/ *verb* [T] *formal* to live in a place [often passive] *an area inhabited by artists and writers*

inhabitant /ɪnˈhæbɪt°nt/ *noun* [C] someone who lives in a particular place *a city with 10 million inhabitants*

inhabited /ɪnˈhæbɪtɪd/ *adjective* An inhabited place or building has people living in it. *Is the island inhabited?*

inhale /ɪnˈheɪl/ *verb* [I, T] *formal* **1** to breathe air, smoke, or gas into your lungs **2** *US informal* to eat something very quickly *Slow down, you're inhaling that pizza!*

inherent /ɪnˈher°nt/ *adjective* existing as a natural and basic part of something *The desire for freedom is inherent in all people.* ● **inherently** *adverb* There's nothing inherently wrong with his ideas.

inherit /ɪnˈherɪt/ *verb* [T] **1** FROM DEAD PERSON to receive possessions or money from someone who has died *In 1842 he inherited a small estate near Liverpool.* **2** QUALITY to have the same physical or mental characteristics as one of your parents or grandparents *Miranda has inherited her father's red hair.* **3** PROBLEM If you inherit a problem, situation, or belief, it is passed on to you by someone who had it before. *The mayor will inherit a city hopelessly in debt.*

inheritance /ɪnˈherɪt°ns/ *noun* [C, U] money or

possessions that someone gives you when they die *Nick has sold off much of his inheritance.*

inhibit /ɪnˈhɪbɪt/ *verb* [T] **1** to make the progress or growth of something slower *a product which inhibits the growth of harmful bacteria* **2** to make it more difficult for someone to do something *Their threats inhibited witnesses from giving evidence.*

inhibited /ɪnˈhɪbɪtɪd/ *adjective* not confident enough to say or do what you want

inhibition /ˌɪnhɪˈbɪʃ°n/ *noun* [C, U] a feeling of embarrassment or worry that prevents you from saying or doing what you want *The whole point about dancing is to lose all your inhibitions.*

inhospitable /ˌɪnhɒsˈpɪtəbl/ *adjective* **1** An inhospitable place is not pleasant or easy to live in because it is too hot, cold, etc. *the world's most inhospitable deserts* **2** not friendly towards people who are visiting you

in-house /ˌɪnˈhaʊs/ *adjective, adverb* done in the offices of a company or organization by employees of that company *in-house training of staff*

inhuman /ɪnˈhjuːmən/ *adjective* extremely cruel *the inhuman treatment of prisoners*

inhumane /ˌɪnhjuːˈmeɪn/ *adjective* treating people or animals in a cruel way *inhumane experiments on monkeys* ● **inhumanely** *adverb*

inhumanity /ˌɪnhjuːˈmænəti/ *noun* [U] extremely cruel behaviour *the inhumanity of war*

initial[1] /ɪˈnɪʃ°l/ *adjective* [always before noun] first, or happening at the beginning *My initial reaction was one of anger.*

initial[2] /ɪˈnɪʃ°l/ *noun* [C] the first letter of a name [usually plural] *His initials are S.G.M.*

initial[3] /ɪˈnɪʃ°l/ *verb* [T] UK **initialling** *past* **initialled** US **initialing** *past* **initialed** to write your initials on something

initialize /ɪˈnɪʃ°laɪz/ *verb* [T] to make a computer program ready to use

initially /ɪˈnɪʃ°li/ *adverb* at the beginning *The situation was worse than they initially thought.*

initiate /ɪˈnɪʃieɪt/ *verb* [T] **1** to make something begin [often passive] *The reforms were initiated by Gorbachev.* **2** to make someone a member of a group or organization in a special ceremony, or to show someone how to do an activity *At the age of 50, he was initiated into the priesthood.* ● **initiation** /ɪˌnɪʃiˈeɪʃ°n/ *noun* [C, U]

initiative /ɪˈnɪʃətɪv/ *noun* **1** [C] a plan or activity that is done to solve a problem or improve a situation *a new government initiative to reduce crime* **2** [U] the ability to make decisions and do things without needing to be told what to do *We need someone who can work on their own initiative* (= without anyone telling them what to do). **3 take the initiative** to be the first person to do something that solves a problem or improves a situation *Jackson had taken the initiative and prepared a report.*

inject /ɪnˈdʒekt/ *verb* [T] 1 DRUG to put a drug into someone's body using a needle *Phil's diabetic and has to inject himself with insulin every day.* 2 IMPROVE to add a good quality to something *The new teacher has injected a bit of enthusiasm into the school.* 3 MONEY to provide a large amount of money for a plan, service, organization, etc *The government plans to inject £100 million into schools.*

injection

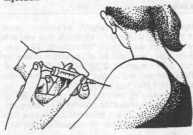

injection /ɪnˈdʒekʃən/ *noun* 1 [C, U] when someone puts a drug into your body using a needle *an injection of insulin* 2 [C] when a large amount of money is provided for a plan, service, organization, etc *The university has welcomed the $5 million cash injection.*

injunction /ɪnˈdʒʌŋkʃən/ *noun* [C] an official order from a court that prevents someone from doing something *The courts have issued an injunction to prevent the book from being published.*

o-n**injure** /ˈɪndʒər/ *verb* [T] to hurt a person, animal, or part of your body *She injured her ankle when she fell.*

injured /ˈɪndʒəd/ *adjective* hurt *Fortunately, no one was seriously injured in the accident.*

WORD PARTNERS FOR *injury*

a fatal / major / minor / serious injury • cause / prevent / receive / recover from/suffer an injury • an injury to sth

o-n**injury** /ˈɪndʒəri/ *noun* [C, U] damage to someone's body in an accident or attack *head injuries* ○ *The passenger in the car escaped with minor injuries.* ⊃See also: add insult[2] to injury.

injustice /ɪnˈdʒʌstɪs/ *noun* [C, U] a situation or action in which people are treated unfairly *the fight against racial injustice*

ink /ɪŋk/ *noun* [C, U] a coloured liquid that you use for writing, printing, or drawing

inkling /ˈɪŋklɪŋ/ *noun* have an inkling to think that something might be true or might happen *She had absolutely no inkling that we were planning the party.*

inland[1] /ˈɪnlənd/ *adjective* [always before noun] Inland areas, lakes, towns, etc are a long way from the coast.

inland[2] /ɪnˈlænd/ *adverb* towards the middle of a country and away from the coast

in-laws /ˈɪnlɔːz/ *noun* [plural] *informal* the parents of your husband or wife, or other people in their family

inlet /ˈɪnlet/ *noun* [C] a narrow part of a sea, river, or lake where it flows into a curve in the land

in-line 'skate *noun* [C] (*also* **rollerblades** [plural]) a boot with a single line of wheels on the bottom, used for moving across the ground ⊃See colour picture **Sports** 1 on page Centre 14.

inmate /ˈɪnmeɪt/ *noun* [C] someone who lives in a prison or in a hospital for people with mental illnesses

inn /ɪn/ *noun* [C] a small hotel in the countryside

innate /ɪˈneɪt/ *adjective* An innate quality or ability is one that you were born with, not one you have learned. *He has an innate desire to win.* • **innately** *adverb*

inner /ˈɪnər/ *adjective* [always before noun] 1 on the inside, or near the middle of something *The monastery is built around an inner courtyard.* ⊃Opposite **outer**. 2 Inner feelings, thoughts, etc are ones that you do not show or tell other people. *a profound sense of inner peace*

inner 'circle *noun* [C] the small group of people who control an organization, political party, etc *The statement was made by a member of the President's inner circle.*

inner 'city *noun* [C] the part of a city that is closest to the centre, often where buildings are in a bad condition and there are social problems *a plan to tackle rising crime in inner cities* • **inner-city** /ˈɪnəˌsɪti/ *adjective* [always before noun] *inner city schools*

innermost /ˈɪnəməʊst/ *adjective* [always before noun] 1 Your innermost feelings, thoughts, etc are the most private ones that you do not want other people to know about. 2 *formal* closest to the middle of something

inning /ˈɪnɪŋ/ *noun* [C] one of the nine playing periods in a baseball game

innings /ˈɪnɪŋz/ *noun* [C] *plural* **innings** the period of time in a game of cricket when one player or one team hits the ball

innit /ˈɪnɪt/ *exclamation* UK *very informal* used to change a statement into a question *It's wrong, innit.*

WORD PARTNERS FOR *innocence*

proclaim/protest/prove sb's innocence

innocence /ˈɪnəsəns/ *noun* [U] 1 when someone is not guilty of a crime *She fought to prove her son's innocence.* 2 when someone does not have much experience of life and does not know about the bad things that happen *the innocence of childhood*

o-n**innocent** /ˈɪnəsənt/ *adjective* 1 NOT GUILTY not guilty of committing a crime *He claims to be innocent of the crime.* 2 NO EXPERIENCE not having much experience of life and not knowing about the bad things that happen *an innocent young woman* 3 NOT DESERVED used to emphasize that someone who was hurt had done nothing wrong *Several innocent civilians were killed in the bombing.* 4 NOT INTENDED TO HARM not intended to harm or upset anyone *It was an innocent mistake.* • **innocently** *adverb*

innocuous /ɪˈnɒkjuəs/ *adjective* not likely to

upset or harm anyone *The parcel looked innocuous enough.* • **innocuously** *adverb*

innovation /ˌɪnəʊˈveɪʃᵊn/ *noun* [C, U] a new idea or method that is being tried for the first time, or the use of such ideas or methods *the latest innovations in education*

innovative /ˈɪnəvətɪv/ [US] /ˈɪnəveɪtɪv/ *adjective* using new methods or ideas *an **innovative approach** to programme making*

innovator /ˈɪnəveɪtəʳ/ *noun* [C] someone who uses or designs new methods or products

innuendo /ˌɪnjuˈendəʊ/ *noun* [C, U] *plural* **innuendoes** or **innuendos** a remark that intentionally suggests something about sex, or something unpleasant about someone, without saying it directly *The advertisement was criticized for its **sexual innuendo**.*

innumerable /ɪˈnjuːmᵊrəbl/ *adjective* very many, or too many to count *She has innumerable problems.*

inoffensive /ˌɪnəˈfensɪv/ *adjective* not likely to upset anyone or make them angry *an inoffensive colour*

inordinate /ɪˈnɔːdɪnət/ *adjective formal* much more than is usual or suitable *James seems to spend an **inordinate amount** of time on his computer.* • **inordinately** *adverb*

inorganic /ˌɪnɔːˈgænɪk/ *adjective* not being or consisting of living things *inorganic waste*

in-patient /ˈɪnˌpeɪʃᵊnt/ *noun* [C] someone who stays in hospital for one or more nights while they are receiving treatment

input¹ /ˈɪnpʊt/ *noun* **1** [IDEAS] [C, U] ideas, money, effort, etc that you put into an activity or process in order to help it succeed *Input from students is used to develop new and exciting courses.* **2** [ELECTRICAL] [C, U] electrical energy that is put into a machine to make it work **3** [COMPUTER] [U] information that is put into a computer

input² /ˈɪnpʊt/ *verb* [T] **inputting** *past* **inputted** or **input** to put information into a computer

WORD PARTNERS FOR ***inquest***

hold an inquest • an inquest **into** sth

inquest /ˈɪŋkwest/ *noun* [C] a legal process to discover the cause of an unexpected death *There will be an **inquest into** the deaths of the three men.*

inquire *formal* (*also UK* **enquire**) /ɪnˈkwaɪəʳ/ *verb* [I, T] to ask someone for information about something *If you like languages, why don't you **inquire about** French classes in your area?* ○ [+ question word] *Vronsky inquired whether the picture was for sale.* • **inquirer** (*also UK* **enquirer**) *noun* [C]

inquire after sb *UK formal* to ask someone for information about someone else's health and what they are doing, in order to be polite *Jane inquired after your mother.*

inquire into sth *formal* to try to discover the facts about something *a report inquiring into the causes of the region's housing problem*

inquiring (*also UK* **enquiring**) /ɪnˈkwaɪərɪŋ/ *adjective* [always before noun] **1** always wanting to learn new things *an **inquiring mind*** **2** An inquiring expression on your face shows that you want to know something. *He gave her **an inquiring look**.* • **inquiringly** *adverb She looked at her mother inquiringly.*

WORD PARTNERS FOR ***inquiry***

make/receive an inquiry • an inquiry **about** sth

inquiry (*also UK* **enquiry**) /ɪnˈkwaɪəri/ *noun* **1** [QUESTION] [C] *formal* a question that you ask when you want more information *The company has received a lot of **inquiries about** its new Internet service.* **2** [OFFICIAL PROCESS] [C] an official process to discover the facts about something bad that has happened *There will be an official **inquiry into** the train crash.* **3** [ASKING QUESTIONS] [U] *formal* the process of asking questions in order to get information *Inquiry into the matter is pointless - no one will tell you anything.*

inquisitive /ɪnˈkwɪzətɪv/ *adjective* wanting to discover as much as you can about things *an inquisitive child* ○ *She could see inquisitive faces looking out the windows.* • **inquisitively** *adverb* • **inquisitiveness** *noun* [U]

inroads /ˈɪnrəʊdz/ *noun* **make inroads (into/on sth)** to start to become successful by getting sales, power, votes, etc that someone else had before *Women have made great inroads into the male-dominated legal profession.* ○ *The government is making inroads into the unemployment problem.*

the ˌins and ˈouts *noun* all the details and facts about something *Tolya is someone who knows **the ins and outs of** the music industry.* ○ *I can use a computer, but I don't understand the ins and outs of how they work.*

insane /ɪnˈseɪn/ *adjective* **1** seriously mentally ill *a hospital for the **criminally insane*** **2** very silly or stupid *an insane decision* • **insanely** *adverb Her husband was **insanely jealous** and hated her seeing other men.*

insanity /ɪnˈsænəti/ *noun* [U] **1** when someone is seriously mentally ill *He was found not guilty by reason of insanity.* **2** when something is extremely stupid *It would be insanity to expand the business at the moment.*

insatiable /ɪnˈseɪʃəbl/ *adjective* always wanting more of something *an **insatiable appetite/desire/hunger** for power* ○ *There was an **insatiable demand** for pictures of Princess Diana.* • **insatiably** *adverb*

inscribe /ɪnˈskraɪb/ *verb* [T] *formal* to write words in a book or cut them on an object [often passive] *The child's bracelet was inscribed with the name 'Amy'.* ○ *The wall of the church was inscribed with the names of the dead from the Great War.*

inscription /ɪnˈskrɪpʃᵊn/ *noun* [C, U] words that are written or cut in something *The inscription on the gravestone was almost illegible.*

insects

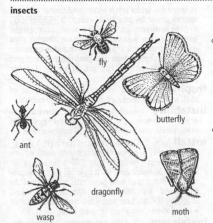

fly

butterfly

ant

dragonfly

wasp

moth

o→**insect** /'ɪnsekt/ noun [C] a small creature with six legs, for example a bee or a fly

insecticide /ɪn'sektɪsaɪd/ noun [C, U] a chemical that is used for killing insects

insecure /ˌɪnsɪ'kjʊər/ adjective **1** having no confidence in yourself and what you can do *a shy, insecure teenager* **2** not safe or protected *Many of our staff are worried because their jobs are insecure.* ● **insecurely** adverb ● **insecurity** /ˌɪnsɪ'kjʊərəti/ noun [U]

insensitive /ɪn'sensətɪv/ adjective **1** not noticing or not caring about other people's feelings *an insensitive remark* ○ *He was completely insensitive to Maria's feelings.* **2** not able to feel something, or not affected by it *She was insensitive to the pain.* ● **insensitively** adverb ● **insensitivity** /ɪn,sensə'tɪvəti/ noun [U]

inseparable /ɪn'sepʳrəbl/ adjective **1** formal Two things that are inseparable are so closely connected that you cannot consider them separately. *Rossetti's work was inseparable from his life.* **2** People who are inseparable are always together because they are such good friends. ● **inseparably** adverb

insert¹ /ɪn'sɜːt/ verb [T] formal **1** to put something into something else *Insert the coin in the slot.* **2** to add something to the middle of a document or piece of writing *He inserted a new paragraph.* ● **insertion** /ɪn'sɜːʃʳn/ noun [C, U]

insert² /'ɪnsɜːt/ noun [C] something that is made to go inside or into something else *The leaflet is designed as an insert for a magazine.*

inshore /ˌɪn'ʃɔːr/ adjective, adverb near or towards the coast *inshore waters*

o→**inside¹** /ˌɪn'saɪd/ noun **1 the inside** the part of something that is under its surface *I cleaned the inside of the oven.* **2 inside out** If a piece of clothing is inside out, the part that is usually outside is on the inside. *Harry, you've got your sweater on inside out again.* **3 know sth inside out** to know everything about something

inside² /ˌɪn'saɪd/ adjective **1** [always before noun] in or on the part of something under its surface *Put your wallet in the inside pocket of your jacket.* **2 inside information/knowledge**, etc information that is only known by people who are part of an organization, group, etc

o→**inside³** /ˌɪn'saɪd/ preposition **1** CONTAINER in or into a room, building, container, etc *There were some keys inside the box.* ○ *Luckily, no one was inside the house when the fire started.* **2** TIME in less than a particular length of time *The doctor's promised to be here inside an hour.* **3** ORGANIZATION in an organization, group, etc and not known or happening outside it *rumours of disputes inside the company*

o→**inside⁴** /ˌɪn'saɪd/ adverb **1** CONTAINER in or into a room, building, container, etc *I'm freezing, let's go back inside.* **2** FEELING If you have a feeling inside, people do not know about it if you do not tell them. *She looked calm but was feeling nervous inside.* **3** PRISON informal in prison

insider /ɪn'saɪdər/ noun [C] someone who knows about a business or organization because they are part of it *Industry insiders say they are surprised by the company's success.* ⊃Compare outsider.

insides /ˌɪn'saɪdz/ noun [plural] informal your stomach

insidious /ɪn'sɪdiəs/ adjective having harmful effects that happen gradually so you do not notice them for a long time *the insidious effects of pollution* ● **insidiously** adverb ● **insidiousness** noun [U]

WORD PARTNERS FOR **insight**

gain/give/provide an insight **into** sth ● a **fascinating/rare/unique/valuable** insight

insight /'ɪnsaɪt/ noun [C, U] the ability to understand what something is really like, or an example of this *The book **provides** a fascinating **insight into** the world of art.*

insignia /ɪn'sɪgniə/ noun [C] plural insignia a piece of cloth or a symbol that shows someone's military rank or official position

insignificant /ˌɪnsɪg'nɪfɪkᵊnt/ adjective not important or large enough to consider or worry about *insignificant differences* ● **insignificance** /ˌɪnsɪg'nɪfɪkᵊns/ noun [U] ● **insignificantly** adverb

insincere /ˌɪnsɪn'sɪər/ adjective pretending to feel something that you do not really feel, or not meaning what you say *an insincere apology* ● **insincerely** adverb ● **insincerity** /ˌɪnsɪn'serəti/ noun [U]

insinuate /ɪn'sɪnjueɪt/ verb [T] to suggest that something bad is true without saying it directly [+ that] *She insinuated that Perez had lied.* ● **insinuation** /ɪn,sɪnju'eɪʃᵊn/ noun [C, U]

insipid /ɪn'sɪpɪd/ adjective not interesting, exciting, or colourful *a dull, insipid man* ○ *The soup was rather insipid.* ● **insipidly** adverb

o→**insist** /ɪn'sɪst/ verb [I, T] **1** to say firmly that something is true, especially when other people do not believe you [+ (that)] *Mia insisted that she and Carlo were just friends.* **2** to demand that something must be done or that you must have a particular thing *The school **insists on** good behaviour from its students.* ○ [+ on + doing sth] *Frank insisted on doing all the* work himself. ○ [+ (that)] *Gerlinde insisted that I stay for dinner.*

insistence /ɪnˈsɪstᵊns/ *noun* [U] **1** when you demand that something must be done or that you must have a particular thing [+ that] *his insistence that his children should have a good education* ○ *Clare's* **insistence on** *a vegetarian diet caused arguments with her mother.* **2** when you say firmly that something is true, especially when other people do not believe you [+ that] *Jane was in trouble despite her insistence that she had done nothing wrong.*

insistent /ɪnˈsɪstᵊnt/ *adjective* firmly saying that something is true or must be done [+ that] *Pedro is absolutely insistent that Sinda should be invited too.* ● **insistently** *adverb*

insofar as /ɪnsəʊˈfɑːr‚əz/ *conjunction formal* to the degree that *The story is based insofar as possible on notes made by Scott himself.*

insolent /ˈɪnsᵊlənt/ *adjective formal* rude and not showing respect *an insolent reply* ● **insolence** /ˈɪnsᵊləns/ *noun* [U] ● **insolently** *adverb*

insoluble /ɪnˈsɒljəbl/ *adjective* **1** An insoluble problem, mystery, etc is impossible to solve. **2** An insoluble substance does not dissolve when you put it in liquid.

insomnia /ɪnˈsɒmniə/ *noun* [U] when you find it difficult to sleep ● **insomniac** /ɪnˈsɒmniæk/ *noun* [C] someone who often finds it difficult to sleep

inspect /ɪnˈspekt/ *verb* [T] **1** to officially visit a building or organization, in order to check that everything is correct and legal *Schools will be inspected regularly to maintain standards.* **2** to look at something very carefully *Clara inspected her make-up in the mirror.*

WORD PARTNERS FOR ***inspection***

carry out an inspection ● an inspection **of** sth

inspection /ɪnˈspekʃᵊn/ *noun* [C, U] **1** an official visit to a building or organization to check that everything is correct and legal *Fire officers* **carried out an inspection** *of the building.* **2** when you look at something carefully *On closer* **inspection** (= when looked at more carefully)*, the painting was discovered to be a fake.*

inspector /ɪnˈspektər/ *noun* [C] **1** someone whose job is to check that things are being done correctly *a factory inspector* **2** a police officer of middle rank

inspiration /ˌɪnspᵊrˈeɪʃᵊn/ *noun* **1** [C, U] someone or something that gives you ideas for doing something *Africa has long been a source of* **inspiration for** *his painting.* **2** [C] a sudden good idea about what you should do **3 be an inspiration to sb** to be so good that someone else admires you and is encouraged by your behaviour *The way she has dealt with her illness is an inspiration to us all.*

inspire /ɪnˈspaɪər/ *verb* [T] **1** [ENCOURAGE] to make someone feel that they want to do something and can do it [+ to do sth] *A drama teacher at school had inspired Sam to become an actor.* **2** [FEELING] to make someone have a particular feeling or reaction *Robson's first task will be to*

inspire *his team* **with** *some confidence.* ○ *He* **inspires** *great loyalty in his staff.* **3** [PROVIDE IDEA] to give someone an idea for a book, play, painting, etc [often passive] *a television drama that was inspired by a true story* ● **inspiring** *adjective* giving you new ideas and making you feel you want to do something *an inspiring teacher* ○ *an inspiring book*

inspired /ɪnˈspaɪəd/ *adjective* showing a lot of skill and good ideas *an inspired performance*

instability /ˌɪnstəˈbɪləti/ *noun* [U] when a situation or someone's behaviour changes a lot and you do not know what will happen next

install (*also UK* instal) /ɪnˈstɔːl/ *verb* [T] **1** [EQUIPMENT] to put a piece of equipment somewhere and make it ready to use *The school has installed a burglar alarm.* **2** [PERSON] to give someone an important and powerful job *She will be* **installed as** *Managing Director in May.* **3** [COMPUTER] to put software onto a computer ● **installation** /ˌɪnstəˈleɪʃᵊn/ *noun* [C, U]

instalment *UK* (*US* installment) /ɪnˈstɔːlmənt/ *noun* [C] **1** a regular payment that you make, for example each month, in order to pay for something *You can pay for your computer in six monthly instalments.* **2** one of the parts of a story that you can see every day or week in a magazine or on television *Don't miss next week's exciting instalment.*

instance /ˈɪnstəns/ *noun* **1 for instance** for example *Many teenagers earn money, for instance by babysitting or cleaning cars.* **2** [C] an example of a particular type of event, situation, or behaviour *There have been several* **instances of** *violence in the school.*

o→**instant¹** /ˈɪnstənt/ *adjective* **1** happening immediately *The book was an instant success in the US.* **2** Instant food or drink is dried, usually in the form of a powder, and can be made quickly by adding hot water. *instant coffee* ⊃See also: instant replay.

instant² /ˈɪnstənt/ *noun* [C] a moment *Take a seat, I'll be with you in an instant.*

instantaneous /ˌɪnstənˈteɪniəs/ *adjective* happening immediately *The Internet offers almost instantaneous access to vast amounts of information.* ● **instantaneously** *adverb*

instantly /ˈɪnstəntli/ *adverb* immediately *A car hit them, killing them both instantly.*

instant messaging /ˌɪnstənt ˈmesɪdʒɪŋ/ *noun* [U] a system on the Internet which makes it possible to send messages quickly between two people using the system

‚**instant 'replay** *US* (*UK* action replay) *noun* [C] when part of a film of a sporting event is shown again, often more slowly

o→**instead** /ɪnˈsted/ *adverb* in the place of someone or something else *If you don't want pizza, we can have pasta instead.* ○ *I'm going swimming on Monday* **instead of** *Friday now.* ○ [+ of + doing sth] *Why don't you help instead of just complaining?*

instigate /ˈɪnstɪɡeɪt/ *verb* [T] *formal* to make something start to happen *Carolyn had instigated divorce proceedings.* ● **instigation** /ˌɪnstɪˈɡeɪʃᵊn/ *noun* [U] ● **instigator** *noun* [C]

instil UK (US **instill**) /ɪnˈstɪl/ verb [T] **instilling** past **instilled** to make someone have a particular feeling or idea *He's a manager with great skill at instilling confidence in/into his players.*

WORD PARTNERS FOR ***instinct***

follow/trust your instincts • instinct **tells** sb sth • sb's **first/gut** instinct

instinct /ˈɪnstɪŋkt/ noun [C, U] the way someone naturally reacts or behaves, without having to think or learn about it [+ to do sth] *a mother's instinct to protect her children*

instinctive /ɪnˈstɪŋktɪv/ adjective behaving or reacting naturally and without thinking *Her instinctive response was to fight back.* • **instinctively** adverb

institute[1] /ˈɪnstɪtjuːt/ noun [C] an organization where people do a particular kind of scientific, educational, or social work *the Massachusetts Institute of Technology*

institute[2] /ˈɪnstɪtjuːt/ verb [T] formal to start a plan, law, system, etc *Major reforms were instituted in the company's finance department.*

institution /ˌɪnstɪˈtjuːʃᵊn/ noun [C] **1** ORGANIZATION a large and important organization, such as a university or bank *one of the country's top medical institutions* **2** PLACE a building where people are sent so they can be looked after, for example a prison or hospital **3** TRADITION a custom that has existed for a long time *the institution of marriage* • **institutional** adjective relating to an institution

instruct /ɪnˈstrʌkt/ verb [T] **1** to officially tell someone to do something [+ to do sth] *Staff are instructed not to use the telephones for personal calls.* **2** formal to teach someone about something *She is there to instruct people in the safe use of the gym equipment.*

o--**instruction** /ɪnˈstrʌkʃᵊn/ noun **1** [C] something that you have been told to do [+ to do sth] *I had strict instructions to call them as soon as I arrived home.* **2** [U] formal the activity of teaching or training someone, or the information you are being taught *religious instruction*

WORD PARTNERS FOR ***instructions***

follow the instructions • **give** instructions • **detailed/full** instructions • instructions **on** sth

instructions /ɪnˈstrʌkʃᵊnz/ noun [plural] information that explains how to do or use something *Are there any instructions on how to load the software? ○ I just followed the instructions that you gave me.*

instructive /ɪnˈstrʌktɪv/ adjective providing useful information *an instructive discussion* • **instructively** adverb

instructor /ɪnˈstrʌktər/ noun [C] someone who teaches a particular sport or activity *a driving instructor*

o--**instrument** /ˈɪnstrəmənt/ noun [C] **1** TOOL a tool that is used for doing something *scientific instruments* **2** MUSIC an object that is used for playing music, for example a piano or drum **3** EQUIPMENT a piece of equipment that is used for measuring speed, light, fuel level, etc **4** FOR

ACHIEVING SOMETHING someone or something that is used for achieving something *The Internet is a very powerful instrument of communication.* ⊃See also: **wind instrument**.

instrumental /ˌɪnstrəˈmentᵊl/ adjective **1** be **instrumental in sth/doing sth** to be one of the main people or things that make something happen *Mikan was instrumental in establishing professional basketball in the US.* **2** involving only musical instruments, and no singing

insubordinate /ˌɪnsəˈbɔːdᵊnət/ adjective not willing to obey rules or people in authority • **insubordination** /ˌɪnsəˌbɔːdɪˈneɪʃᵊn/ noun [U]

insubstantial /ˌɪnsəbˈstænʃᵊl/ adjective not very large, strong, or good *The meal was rather insubstantial.*

insufferable /ɪnˈsʌfᵊrəbl/ adjective extremely annoying or unpleasant *insufferable arrogance* • **insufferably** adverb

insufficient /ˌɪnsəˈfɪʃᵊnt/ adjective not enough *insufficient information ○* [+ to do sth] *Her income is insufficient to support a family.* • **insufficiently** adverb

insular /ˈɪnsjələr/ adjective only interested in your own country, life, etc and not willing to accept new ideas or people • **insularity** /ˌɪnsjəˈlærəti/ noun [U]

insulate /ˈɪnsjəleɪt/ verb [T] **1** to cover something with a special material so that heat, electricity, or sound cannot escape through it **2** to protect someone from unpleasant experiences or bad influences *parents who want to insulate their children from real life*

insulation /ˌɪnsjəˈleɪʃᵊn/ noun [U] **1** a special material used for insulating something such as a wall, roof, or building **2** when you insulate something, or when something is insulated

insulin /ˈɪnsjəlɪn/ noun [U] a substance produced by the body that controls the amount of sugar in your blood

insult[1] /ɪnˈsʌlt/ verb [T] to say or do something to someone that is rude and offensive *How dare you insult me in front of my friends!* • **insulting** adjective rude and offensive *an insulting remark*

insult[2] /ˈɪnsʌlt/ noun [C] **1** a rude and offensive remark or action *They were shouting insults at each other. ○ His comments are an insult to the victims of the war.* **2 add insult to injury** to make someone's bad situation worse by doing something else to upset them

WORD PARTNERS FOR ***insurance***

take out insurance • insurance **against** [sickness / fire, etc] • an insurance **company/ policy/premium** • **car/travel** insurance

insurance /ɪnˈʃʊərᵊns/ noun [U] an agreement in which you pay a company money and they pay your costs if you have an accident, injury, etc *car/travel insurance ○ an insurance policy*

insure /ɪnˈʃʊər/ verb [T] to buy insurance from a company, or to provide insurance for someone *I need to get my car insured. ○ The policy in-*

sures you against damage and theft.

insurmountable /ˌɪnsəˈmaʊntəbl/ *adjective* impossible to deal with *an insurmountable problem/task*

insurrection /ˌɪnsəˈrekʃ°n/ *noun* [C, U] when a group of people use force to try to get control of a government

intact /ɪnˈtækt/ *adjective* not damaged or destroyed *Many of the old buildings are still intact.*

intake /ˈɪnteɪk/ *noun* [C] **1** the amount of food or drink that you take into your body [usually singular] *Reducing your salt intake can help to lower blood pressure.* **2** *UK* the group of people who start working or studying somewhere at the same time *a new intake of students*

intangible /ɪnˈtændʒəbl/ *adjective* An intangible feeling or quality exists but you cannot describe or prove it.

integral /ˈɪntɪgrəl/ *adjective* necessary and important as part of something *The Internet has become an integral part of modern life.*

integrate /ˈɪntɪgreɪt/ *verb* **1** [I, T] to become part of a group or society, or to help someone do this *After a few weeks of training he was fully integrated into the team.* **2** [T] to combine two or more things to make something more effective *plans to integrate the two schools* • **integration** /ˌɪntɪˈgreɪʃ°n/ *noun* [U]

integrity /ɪnˈtegrəti/ *noun* [U] honesty and the ability to do or know what is morally right *a woman of great integrity*

intellect /ˈɪnt°lekt/ *noun* [C, U] the ability to learn and understand something, and to form ideas, judgments, and opinions about what you have learned *His energy and intellect are respected by many people.*

intellectual¹ /ˌɪnt°lˈektjuəl/ *adjective* **1** using or relating to your ability to think and understand things *intellectual work* ○ *intellectual and physical development* **2** interested in learning and in thinking about complicated ideas *She's very intellectual.* • **intellectually** *adverb*

intellectual² /ˌɪnt°lˈektjuəl/ *noun* [C] someone who enjoys studying and thinking about complicated ideas

◦=**intelligence** /ɪnˈtelɪdʒ°ns/ *noun* [U] **1** the ability to learn, understand, and think about things *a child of low intelligence* **2** secret information about the governments of other countries, or the group of people who get this information *military intelligence* ⊃See also: artificial intelligence.

◦=**intelligent** /ɪnˈtelɪdʒ°nt/ *adjective* able to learn and understand things easily *a highly intelligent young woman* • **intelligently** *adverb*

intelligible /ɪnˈtelɪdʒəbl/ *adjective* able to be understood ⊃Opposite unintelligible.

◦=**intend** /ɪnˈtend/ *verb* **1** [T] to want and plan to do something [+ to do sth] *How long are you intending to stay in Paris?* ○ [+ doing sth] *I don't*

intend seeing him again. **2** be intended for sb; be intended as sth to be made, designed, or provided for a particular person or purpose *The book is intended for anyone who wants to learn more about the Internet.*

intense /ɪnˈtens/ *adjective* **1** extreme or very strong *intense heat/pain* **2** Intense people are very serious, and usually have strong emotions or opinions. • **intensely** *adverb* *Clare disliked him intensely.* • **intensity** *noun* [U]

intensify /ɪnˈtensɪfaɪ/ *verb* [I, T] to become greater, more serious, or more extreme, or to make something do this *The fighting has intensified in the past week.*

intensive /ɪnˈtensɪv/ *adjective* involving a lot of work in a short period of time *ten weeks of intensive training* • **intensively** *adverb*

in,tensive 'care *noun* [U] the part of a hospital used for treating people who are seriously ill or very badly injured

intent¹ /ɪnˈtent/ *noun* [U, no plural] *formal* **1** when you want and plan to do something [+ to do sth] *It had not been his intent to hurt anyone.* **2** to/ for all intents (and purposes) in all the most important ways *To all intents and purposes, the project was a disaster.*

intent² /ɪnˈtent/ *adjective* **1** be intent on sth/ doing sth to be determined to do or achieve something *She seems intent on winning this year's tennis tournament.* **2** giving a lot of attention to something *She had an intent look on her face.* • **intently** *adverb*

◦=**intention** /ɪnˈtenʃ°n/ *noun* [C, U] something that you want and plan to do [+ to do sth] *She announced her intention to resign.* ○ [+ of + doing sth] *I have no intention of seeing him again.*

intentional /ɪnˈtenʃ°n°l/ *adjective* planned or intended *I'm sorry if I said something that offended you. It really wasn't intentional.* • **intentionally** *adverb*

inter- /ɪntə°-/ *prefix* between or among *international* ○ *an interdepartmental meeting*

interact /ˌɪntərˈækt/ *verb* [I] **1** to talk and do things with other people *At school, teachers say he interacted well with other students.* **2** If two things interact, they have an effect on each other. *We are looking at how these chemicals interact.*

interaction /ˌɪntərˈækʃ°n/ *noun* [C, U] **1** the activity of talking and doing things with other people, or the way you do this *Our work involves a lot of interaction with the customers.* **2** when two or more things combine and have an effect on each other

interactive /ˌɪntərˈæktɪv/ *adjective* **1** Interactive computer programs, games, etc involve the person using them by reacting to the way they use them. **2** involving communication between people

intercept /ˌɪntəˈsept/ *verb* [T] to stop someone or something before they are able to reach a particular place *Johnson intercepted the pass* *and went on to score the third goal.* ● **interception** /ˌɪntəˈsepʃ³n/ *noun* [C, U]

interchangeable /ˌɪntəˈtʃeɪndʒəbl/ *adjective* If things are interchangeable, you can exchange them because they can be used in the same way. *interchangeable words* ● **interchangeably** *adverb*

intercom /ˈɪntəkɒm/ *noun* [C] an electronic system used for communicating with people in different parts of a building, aircraft, ship, etc *A stewardess asked over the intercom if there was a doctor on board.*

intercontinental /ˌɪntəˌkɒntɪˈnent³l/ *adjective* in or between two continents *an intercontinental flight*

intercourse /ˈɪntəkɔːs/ (*also* **sexual intercourse**) *noun* [U] *formal* when a man puts his penis into a woman's vagina

WORD PARTNERS FOR *interest*

develop/generate/have/show/take an interest ● a **genuine/keen/passionate/strong** interest ● an interest **in** sth ● be of interest

o→**interest¹** /ˈɪntrəst/ *noun* **1** [FEELING] [U, no plural] the feeling of wanting to give attention to something or discover more about it *Mark had an interest in the media and wanted to become a journalist.* ○ *After a while he simply lost interest in* (= stopped being interested) *his studies.* ○ *Bindi felt that her father didn't take much of an interest in her* (= he was not very interested). **2** [ACTIVITY/SUBJECT] [C] something you enjoy doing, studying, or experiencing *We share a lot of the same interests, particularly music and football.* **3** [MONEY YOU PAY] [U] the extra money that you must pay to a bank, company, etc which has lent you money *low interest rates* **4** [MONEY YOU EARN] [U] the money you earn from keeping your money in a bank account **5** [QUALITY] [U] a quality that makes you think something is interesting *Would this book be of any interest to you?* **6** [ADVANTAGE] [C, U] something that gives someone or something an advantage *A union looks after the interests of its members.* **7 be in sb's interest(s)** to help someone and give them an advantage *It may not be in your interests to change jobs so soon.* **8 in the interest(s) of sth** in order to achieve a particular situation or quality *In the interest of safety, passengers are advised to wear their seat belts at all times.* **9** [LEGAL RIGHT] [C] *formal* the legal right to own or receive part of a building, company, profits, etc ⊃See also: **self-interest, vested interest.**

interest² /ˈɪntrəst/ *verb* [T] If someone or something interests you, you want to give them your attention and discover more about them. *History doesn't really interest me.*

o→**interested** /ˈɪntrəstɪd/ *adjective* **1** [never before noun] wanting to give your attention to something and discover more about it *Sarah's only interested in boys, CDs, and clothes.* ○ [+ to do sth] *I'd be interested to find out more about the course.* ⊃Opposite **uninterested. 2** [never before noun] wanting to do, get, or achieve something [+ in + doing sth] *Mark said he's interested in*

buying your bike. **3 interested parties/groups** people who will be affected by a situation ⊃Opposite **disinterested.**

OTHER WAYS OF SAYING *interesting*

You can use **absorbing** or **gripping** to describe a game, book, film, etc. which is so interesting that it keeps your attention completely: *I found the book absolutely gripping - I couldn't put it down.* ● *It was a very absorbing film.*

A game, book, TV programme, etc. which is so interesting that you cannot stop playing, reading, or watching it, may be described as **compulsive**: *I found the whole series compulsive viewing.*

Fascinating is often used to describe someone or something you have seen or heard that you have found extremely interesting: *The history of the place was absolutely fascinating.* ● *He's fascinating on the subject.*

If something or someone is interesting because they seem mysterious and make you want to know more about them, you can say that they are **intriguing**: *It's a very intriguing situation.*

o→**interesting** /ˈɪntrəstɪŋ/ *adjective* Someone or something that is interesting keeps your attention because they are unusual, exciting, or have lots of ideas. *an interesting person* ○ *The museum was really interesting.* ○ [+ to do sth] *It'll be interesting to see what Mum thinks of John's new girlfriend.*

COMMON LEARNER ERROR

interesting or **interested**?

Interested is used to describe how someone feels about a person or thing.

I'm interested in theatre.

~~I'm interesting in theatre.~~

If a person or thing is **interesting**, they make you feel interested.

It was an interesting film.

COMMON LEARNER ERROR

interesting

Interesting does not mean 'useful'. Use a word like **useful, beneficial** or **valuable** instead.

This course could be very useful for my colleagues.

~~This course could be very interesting for my colleagues.~~

'**interest ˌrate** *noun* [C] the per cent of an amount of money which is charged by a bank or other financial company

interface¹ /ˈɪntəfeɪs/ *noun* [C] **1** a connection between two pieces of electronic equipment, or between a person and a computer *a simple user interface* **2** a situation, way, or place where two things can come together and have an effect on each other *the interface between technology and tradition*

interface² /'ɪntəˌfeɪs/ *verb* [I, T] to communicate with people or electronic equipment, or to make people or electronic equipment communicate *We use email to **interface with** our customers.*

☞**interfere** /ˌɪntə'fɪəʳ/ *verb* [I] to try to control or become involved in a situation, in a way that is annoying *I know he's worried about us, but I wish he wouldn't interfere.* ○ *You shouldn't **interfere in** other people's business.*

interfere with sth 1 to prevent something from working effectively or from developing successfully *I try not to let my dancing classes interfere with my schoolwork.* 2 If something interferes with radio or television signals, it stops you from getting good pictures or sound.

interference /ˌɪntə'fɪərᵊns/ *noun* [U] 1 when someone tries to interfere in a situation *There have been claims of too much political **interference in** education.* 2 noise or other electronic signals that stop you from getting good pictures or sound on a television or radio

interim¹ /'ɪntᵊrɪm/ *adjective* [always before noun] temporary and intended to be used or accepted until something permanent exists *an interim solution* ○ *an **interim government***

interim² /'ɪntᵊrɪm/ *noun* **in the interim** in the time between two particular periods or events

interior /ɪn'tɪəriəʳ/ *noun* [C] the inside part of something *the grand interior of the hotel* ⊃Opposite **exterior**.

in,terior de'sign *noun* [U] the job of choosing colours, designs, etc for the inside of a house or room ● **interior designer** *noun* [C] someone whose job is to do interior design

interjection /ˌɪntə'dʒekʃᵊn/ *noun* [C] an exclamation or sudden expression of your feelings. For example 'Hey' in 'Hey you!' is an interjection.

interlude /'ɪntəluːd/ *noun* [C] a period of time between two events, activities, etc *a brief interlude of peace*

intermediary /ˌɪntə'miːdiəri/ *noun* [C] someone who works with two people or groups to help them agree on something important

intermediate /ˌɪntə'miːdiət/ *adjective* 1 between the highest and lowest levels of knowledge or skill *intermediate students* 2 between two different stages in a process *intermediate steps towards achieving our goal*

interminable /ɪn'tɜːmɪnəbl/ *adjective* lasting a very long time, in a way that is boring *an interminable train journey* ● **interminably** *adverb*

intermission /ˌɪntə'mɪʃᵊn/ *noun* [C] a short period between the parts of a play, performance, etc

intermittent /ˌɪntə'mɪtᵊnt/ *adjective* stopping and starting again for short periods of time *intermittent rain* ● **intermittently** *adverb*

intern¹ /'ɪntɜːn/ *noun* [C] US 1 a young doctor who works in a hospital to finish their medical education 2 a student who learns about a particular job by doing it for a short period of time ● **internship** *noun* [C] the time when someone is an intern

intern² /ɪn'tɜːn/ *verb* [T] to put someone in prison for political reasons, especially during a war ● **internment** *noun* [U] when someone is interned

internal /ɪn'tɜːnᵊl/ *adjective* 1 INSIDE A PLACE happening or coming from inside a particular country, group, or organization *an internal report* ○ *internal disputes* 2 BODY inside your body *internal injuries* 3 PLACE inside a country, building, area, etc *an internal flight* ○ *internal walls* ⊃Opposite **external**. ● **internally** *adverb*

☞**international¹** /ˌɪntə'næʃᵊnᵊl/ *adjective* relating to or involving two or more countries *international politics* ○ *an international team of scientists* ● **internationally** *adverb*

international² /ˌɪntə'næʃᵊnᵊl/ *noun* [C] UK a game of sport involving two or more countries, or a player in one of these games *a one-day international in South Africa*

the inter,national com'munity *noun* countries of the world considered or acting together as a group *The international community expressed shock at the terrorist attacks.*

☞**the Internet** /'ɪntənet/ *noun* (*also* **the Net**) the system that connects computers all over the world and allows people who use computers to look at websites (= electronic documents) *She found a lot of information **on the Internet**.* ○ *a company that provides cheap **Internet access*** ⊃See Extra help page **The Web and the Internet** on page Centre 36.

'internet ,cafe *noun* [C] a place where customers can buy food and drink and use computers to search for information on the Internet

'Internet ,dating *noun* [U] a way to meet people for possible romantic relationships, in which you look at descriptions of people on a website and arrange to meet them if you like them

interplay /'ɪntəpleɪ/ *noun* [U] the effect that two or more things have on each other *I'm interested in the **interplay between** Latin and English.*

interpret /ɪn'tɜːprɪt/ *verb* 1 [T] to explain or decide what you think a particular phrase, performance, action, etc means *His comments were **interpreted as** an attack on the government.* 2 [I, T] to change what someone has said into another language *We had to ask the guide to interpret for us.*

interpretation /ɪnˌtɜːprɪ'teɪʃᵊn/ *noun* 1 [C, U] an explanation or opinion of what something means *traditional interpretations of the Bible* 2 [C] the way someone performs a particular play, piece of music, etc *a beautiful interpretation of Swan Lake*

interpreter /ɪnˈtɜːprɪtəʳ/ *noun* [C] someone whose job is to change what someone else is saying into another language

interrogate /ɪnˈterəgeɪt/ *verb* [T] to ask someone a lot of questions, often with great force *Police have arrested and interrogated the two suspects.* • **interrogation** /ɪnˌterəˈgeɪʃ³n/ *noun* [C, U] *twelve hours of brutal interrogation* • **interrogator** *noun* [C]

interrogative /ˌɪntəˈrɒgətɪv/ *noun* [C] a word or sentence used when asking a question. For example 'Who' and 'Why' are interrogatives. • **interrogative** *adjective*

o⌐**interrupt** /ˌɪntəˈrʌpt/ *verb* **1** [I, T] to stop someone while they are talking or doing something, by saying or doing something yourself *I was trying to work but the children were interrupting me.* **2** [T] to stop an action or activity, usually for a short period of time *In 1998, a leg injury interrupted his sporting career.*

WORD PARTNERS FOR *interruption*

a **brief/short** interruption • **without** interruption • an interruption **in/of** sth

interruption /ˌɪntəˈrʌpʃ³n/ *noun* [C, U] when an action or activity is interrupted, or something that interrupts someone or something

intersect /ˌɪntəˈsekt/ *verb* [I, T] If two things such as lines or roads intersect, they go across each other at a particular point.

intersection /ˌɪntəˈsekʃ³n/ *noun* [C] *US* (*UK* junction) the place where two roads meet or cross each other

interspersed /ˌɪntəˈspɜːst/ *adjective* **interspersed with sth** having something in several places among something else *farmland interspersed with forests and lakes*

interstate /ˈɪntəˌsteɪt/ *adjective* [always before noun] relating to, or involving two or more US states *interstate commerce/travel* ○ *an interstate highway*

interval /ˈɪntəv³l/ *noun* **1** [C] a period of time between two actions, activities, or events *After an interval of three days the peace talks resumed.* **2 at intervals** repeated after a particular period of time or particular distance *Patients were injected with the drug at four-hour intervals* (= every four hours). **3** [C] *UK* (*UK/US* intermission) a short period of time between the parts of a play, performance, etc

intervene /ˌɪntəˈviːn/ *verb* [I] **1** BECOME INVOLVED to become involved in a situation in order to try to stop a fight, argument, problem, etc *Government officials refused to intervene in the recent disputes.* ○ [+ to do sth] *Harris intervened to stop the attack.* **2** INTERRUPT to interrupt someone who is talking *"Mr Lawrence," the judge intervened, "please be silent."* **3** PREVENT If something intervenes, it stops something or prevents it from happening. *She was going to marry Barratt but tragedy intervened.*

intervening /ˌɪntəˈviːnɪŋ/ *adjective* **the intervening months/period/years, etc** the time between two events *In the intervening years, his*

illness had become a lot worse.

intervention /ˌɪntəˈvenʃ³n/ *noun* [C, U] when someone intervenes, especially to prevent something from happening *Without medical intervention, the child would have died.*

WORD PARTNERS FOR *interview*

2 an **exclusive/frank/in-depth** interview • **conduct/do/give/have** an interview • an interview **with** sb

o⌐**interview¹** /ˈɪntəvjuː/ *noun* [C] **1** JOB/COURSE a meeting in which someone asks you questions to see if you are suitable for a job or course *I had an interview last week for a job in London.* **2** NEWS a meeting in which someone is asked questions for a newspaper article, television show, etc *an exclusive interview with Madonna* **3** POLICE a meeting in which the police ask someone questions to see if they have committed a crime

interview² /ˈɪntəvjuː/ *verb* [T] to ask someone questions in an interview *Police are interviewing a 43-year-old man in connection with the murder.* ○ *So far we've interviewed five applicants for the Managing Director's job.* • **interviewer** *noun* [C]

interviewee /ˌɪntəvjuˈiː/ *noun* [C] someone who is being interviewed

intestine /ɪnˈtestɪn/ *noun* [C] a long tube that carries food from your stomach • **intestinal** /ˌɪntesˈtaɪnəl/ /ɪnˈtestɪnəl/ *adjective* relating to your intestine

intimacy /ˈɪntɪməsi/ *noun* [U] when you have a very special friendship or sexual relationship with someone

intimate¹ /ˈɪntɪmət/ *adjective* **1** PRIVATE private and personal *intimate details of her family life* ○ *intimate conversations* **2** RELATIONSHIP having a special relationship with someone who you like or love very much *an intimate friend* **3** SMALL If a place or event is intimate, it is small in a way that feels comfortable or private. *an intimate hotel* **4 an intimate knowledge/understanding of sth** when you know all of the facts about something or about how it works • **intimately** *adverb*

intimate² /ˈɪntɪmeɪt/ *verb* [T] *formal* to suggest that something is true without saying it directly *She has intimated that she might resign.*

intimidate /ɪnˈtɪmɪdeɪt/ *verb* [T] to intentionally frighten someone, especially so that they will do what you want • **intimidation** /ɪnˌtɪmɪˈdeɪʃ³n/ *noun* [U]

intimidated /ɪnˈtɪmɪdeɪtɪd/ *adjective* frightened or nervous because you are not confident in a situation *Older people can feel very intimidated by computers.* • **intimidating** *adjective* making you feel intimidated *I find speaking in front of a crowd very intimidating.*

o⌐**into** /ˈɪntə, ˈɪntuː/ *preposition* **1** IN towards the inside or middle of something *Stop running around and get into bed!* ○ *He's gone into a shop across the road.* **2** CHANGE used to show when a person or thing changes from one form or condition to another *We're planning to turn the smallest bedroom into an office.* ○ *Her last*

novel was translated into nineteen languages.
3 ABOUT involving or about something *an investigation into the cause of the fire* **4** TOWARDS in the direction of something or someone *She was looking straight into his eyes.* **5** HIT moving towards something or someone and hitting them *I backed the car into the garden wall.* **6 be into sth** *informal* to be very interested in something *Kate's really into classical music.* **7** DIVIDE used when dividing one number by another *What's 5 into 125?*

intolerable /ɪnˈtɒlˀrəbl/ *adjective* too bad or unpleasant to deal with or accept *an intolerable situation* ● **intolerably** *adverb*

intolerance /ɪnˈtɒlˀr²ns/ *noun* [U] when someone is intolerant *religious intolerance*

intolerant /ɪnˈtɒlˀr²nt/ *adjective* refusing to accept any opinions, beliefs, customs, etc that are different from your own

intonation /ˌɪntəˈneɪʃˀn/ *noun* [C, U] the way your voice goes up and down when you speak

intoxicated /ɪnˈtɒksɪkeɪtɪd/ *adjective* **1** *formal* drunk **2** *literary* very excited or enthusiastic about someone or something ● **intoxicating** *adjective* making you intoxicated ● **intoxication** /ɪnˌtɒksɪˈkeɪʃˀn/ *noun* [U]

intra- /ɪntrə-/ *prefix* within *an intranet*

intranet /ˈɪntrənet/ *noun* [C] a system that connects the computers in a company or organization so that people can share information and send messages

intransitive /ɪnˈtrænsətɪv/ *adjective* An intransitive verb does not have an object. In the sentence 'John arrived first.', 'arrived' is an intransitive verb. ➞See Extra help page **Verb patterns** on page Centre 27. ➞Compare **transitive**.

intravenous /ˌɪntrəˈviːnəs/ *adjective* Intravenous medicines or drugs are put directly into your veins (= tubes that carry your blood). ● **intravenously** *adverb*

in-tray /ˈɪntreɪ/ *UK* (*US* **in-box**) *noun* [C] a container where you keep letters and documents that need to be dealt with ➞See colour picture **The Office** on page Centre 5.

intrepid /ɪnˈtrepɪd/ *adjective* brave and willing to do dangerous things *intrepid travellers*

intricacy /ˈɪntrɪkəsi/ *noun* **1 the intricacies of sth** the complicated details of something *a booklet explaining the intricacies of the game's rules* **2** [U] the quality of being intricate *the intricacy of the stone carvings*

intricate /ˈɪntrɪkət/ *adjective* having many small or complicated parts and details *an intricate pattern* ● **intricately** *adverb*

intrigue¹ /ɪnˈtriːɡ/ *verb* [T] intriguing *past* intrigued If someone or something intrigues you, they interest you very much. *Ancient Egyptian art has always intrigued me.*

intrigue² /ˈɪntriːɡ/ *noun* [C, U] a secret, clever plan to deceive someone or do something bad *a tale of romance, intrigue, and betrayal*

intriguing /ɪnˈtriːɡɪŋ/ *adjective* very interesting *an intriguing story*

intrinsic /ɪnˈtrɪnsɪk/ *adjective* [always before noun] An intrinsic quality or thing forms part of the basic character of something or someone.

*Drama is an **intrinsic part** of the school's curriculum.* ● **intrinsically** *adverb*

⚬ **introduce** /ˌɪntrəˈdjuːs/ *verb* [T] **1** SOMETHING NEW to make something exist, happen, or be used for the first time *CD players were first introduced in 1983.* ○ *We have introduced a new training schedule for employees.* **2** MEETING PEOPLE to tell someone another person's name the first time that they meet *He took me round the room and **introduced** me **to** everyone.* ○ [often reflexive] *Emma introduced herself and they shook hands.* **3** TO AN AUDIENCE to tell an audience who is going to speak to them or perform for them *I'd like to introduce Rachel Elliott who is our speaker this evening.*

introduce sb to sth to help someone experience something for the first time *His father introduced him to the pleasures of good food.*

⚬ **introduction** /ˌɪntrəˈdʌkʃˀn/ *noun* **1** SOMETHING NEW [U] when you make something exist, happen, or be used for the first time *the introduction of a minimum wage* **2** BOOK [C] the first part of a book or speech **3** BASIC KNOWLEDGE [C] a book or course which provides basic knowledge about a subject *an introduction to psychology* **4** FIRST EXPERIENCE [no plural] the first time someone experiences something *It was our first **introduction to** great poetry.* **5** FIRST MEETING [C] when you tell someone another person's name the first time that they meet [usually plural] *Can you do the introductions?* **6** TO AN AUDIENCE [C, U] when you tell an audience who is going to speak to them or perform for them *My next guest needs no introduction.*

introductory /ˌɪntrəˈdʌktˀri/ *adjective* **1 an introductory chapter/essay/message, etc** a part that comes at the beginning of a piece of writing or a speech and explains what will come later **2 an introductory book/course/lesson, etc** something that provides basic information about a subject *an introductory course in economics* **3 an introductory discount/fare/offer, etc** something that you get when you start buying something or using a service

introspective /ˌɪntrəʊˈspektɪv/ *adjective* thinking a lot about your own thoughts and feelings, in a way that is not always good for you ● **introspection** /ˌɪntrəʊˈspekʃˀn/ *noun* [U]

introvert /ˈɪntrəʊvɜːt/ *noun* [C] someone who is quiet and shy and prefers to be alone ● **introverted** *adjective* *an introverted child* ➞Opposite **extrovert**.

intrude /ɪnˈtruːd/ *verb* [I] to become involved in a situation which people want to be private *They should not have **intruded on** the family's grief.*

intruder /ɪnˈtruːdəʳ/ *noun* [C] someone who enters a place where they are not allowed to be, often to commit a crime

WORD PARTNERS FOR *intrusion*

an **unwarranted/unwelcome** intrusion
● an intrusion **into/on** sth

intrusion /ɪnˈtruːʒˀn/ *noun* [C, U] when someone becomes involved in a situation which people want to be private *She could not bear the* *intrusion into her private life.*

intrusive /ɪnˈtruːsɪv/ *adjective* If something or someone is intrusive, they become involved in things which should be private. *The magazine published intrusive pictures of the princess's family.*

intuition /ˌɪntjuˈɪʃᵊn/ *noun* [C, U] the feeling that you know something without being able to explain why *Her approach to childcare is based on intuition.*

intuitive /ɪnˈtjuːɪtɪv/ *adjective* using intuition *He has an intuitive understanding of animals.* • **intuitively** *adverb*

Inuit /ˈɪnuɪt/ *noun* [C, U] *plural* **Inuit** or **Inuits** a group of people who live in the cold, northern areas of North America, Russia, and Greenland, or a member of this group

inundate /ˈɪnʌndeɪt/ *verb* **be inundated with/by sth** to receive so much of something that you cannot deal with it *Laura was inundated with flowers, cards, and other gifts.*

invade /ɪnˈveɪd/ *verb* **1** [I, T] to enter a country by force in order to take control of it *Portugal was invaded by the French in 1807.* **2** [T] to enter a place in large numbers *Every summer the town is invaded by tourists.* **3 invade sb's privacy** to become involved in someone's private life when they do not want you to

invader /ɪnˈveɪdəʳ/ *noun* [C] someone who enters a country by force in order to take control of it

invalid¹ /ˈɪnvəlɪd/ *noun* [C] someone who is so ill that they have to be looked after by other people

invalid² /ɪnˈvælɪd/ *adjective* **1** An invalid document, ticket, law, etc is not legally or officially acceptable. **2** An invalid argument is not correct.

invaluable /ɪnˈvæljuəbl/ *adjective* extremely useful *Her contacts in government **proved invaluable** to the company.*

invariably /ɪnˈveəriəbli/ *adverb* always *The train is invariably packed.*

invasion /ɪnˈveɪʒᵊn/ *noun* **1** [C, U] when an army enters a country by force in order to take control of it **2 an invasion of privacy** becoming involved in someone's private life when they do not want you to

⊶**invent** /ɪnˈvent/ *verb* [T] **1** to design or create something that has never existed before *We've invented a new game.* **2** to think of a story or explanation in order to deceive someone *She invented an excuse to leave.*

⊶**invention** /ɪnˈvenʃᵊn/ *noun* **1** [C] something that has been designed or created for the first time **2** [U] when someone designs or creates something new *the invention of printing*

inventive /ɪnˈventɪv/ *adjective* full of clever and interesting ideas *inventive designs* • **inventively** *adverb* • **inventiveness** *noun* [U]

inventor /ɪnˈventəʳ/ *noun* [C] someone who designs and makes new things

inventory /ˈɪnvᵊntri/, /ɪnˈventᵊri/ *noun* [C] a list of all the things that are in a place

invert /ɪnˈvɜːt/ *verb* [T] *formal* to turn something upside-down, or put something in the opposite order from how it usually is

inverted commas /ɪnˌvɜːtɪdˈkɒməz/ *noun* [plural] *UK* a pair of marks (" ") or (' ') used before and after a group of words to show that they are spoken or that someone else originally wrote them ➲See Extra help page **Punctuation** on page Centre 33.

invest /ɪnˈvest/ *verb* **1** [I, T] to give money to a bank, business, etc, or buy something, because you hope to get a profit *He's **invested** over a million pounds **in** the city's waterfront restoration project.* **2** [T] to use a lot of time, effort, or emotions because you want to succeed *I think she **invests** too much time and energy **in** her career.*

invest in sth to buy something because you think it will be useful *Dad's decided to invest in a computer.*

investigate /ɪnˈvestɪgeɪt/ *verb* [I, T] to try to discover all the facts about something, especially a crime or accident *He has been questioned by detectives investigating Jenkins' murder.*

WORD PARTNERS FOR ***investigation***

carry out/conduct/launch an investigation • a **detailed/full/thorough** investigation • an investigation **into** sth • be **under** investigation

investigation /ɪnˌvestɪˈgeɪʃᵊn/ *noun* [C, U] when officials try to discover all the facts about something, especially a crime or an accident *Police have begun an **investigation into** his death.* ○ *The cause of the fire is still **under investigation*** (= being investigated).

investigative /ɪnˈvestɪgətɪv/ [US] /ɪnˈvestɪgeɪtɪv/ *adjective* trying to discover all the facts about something ***investigative journalists***

investigator /ɪnˈvestɪgeɪtəʳ/ *noun* [C] someone who tries to discover all the facts about something, especially as their job

investment /ɪnˈvestmənt/ *noun* **1** [C, U] the money that you put in a bank, business, etc in order to make a profit, or the act of doing this *Businesses need to increase their **investment in** new technology.* **2** [C] something that you do or have, in order to have more in the future *Going to college is an **investment in** the future.*

investor /ɪnˈvestəʳ/ *noun* [C] someone who puts money in a bank, business, etc in order to make a profit

inveterate /ɪnˈvetᵊrət/ *adjective* **an inveterate liar/gambler/reader, etc** someone who does something very often

invigorating /ɪnˈvɪgəreɪtɪŋ/ *adjective* making you feel very healthy and energetic *a long, invigorating walk* • **invigorate** *verb* [T] to make you feel very healthy and energetic

invincible /ɪnˈvɪnsəbl/ *adjective* If someone or something is invincible, it is impossible to defeat or destroy them. *The French army seemed invincible.*

invisible /ɪnˈvɪzəbl/ *adjective* Someone or something that is invisible cannot be seen. *invisible particles called electrons* ○ *The house was invisible from the road.* • **invisibility** /ɪnˌvɪzəˈbɪləti/ *noun* [U]

WORD PARTNERS FOR **invitation**

accept/decline/turn down an invitation
• an invitation to sth

o⌐**invitation** /ˌɪnvɪˈteɪʃ°n/ noun 1 INVITING SOMEONE [C, U] when someone invites you to do something or go somewhere *an invitation to dinner* ○ [+ to do sth] *He has accepted their invitation to visit China.* 2 PIECE OF PAPER [C] a piece of paper or card that invites someone to an event 3 CAUSE RESULT [no plural] something that is likely to cause a particular result, especially a bad one *It is an invitation to violence.*

o⌐**invite¹** /ɪnˈvaɪt/ verb [T] 1 SOCIAL EVENT to ask someone to come to a social event *They've invited us to the wedding.* 2 ASK OFFICIALLY to officially ask someone to do something [+ to do sth] *I was invited to appear on television.* 3 REACTION to do something that is likely to cause a particular reaction or result, especially a bad one *Unconventional ideas often invite attack.*

COMMON LEARNER ERROR

invite someone to something

If you are talking about a social event, use the preposition **to**.

She invited me to the party.

~~She invited me for the party.~~

~~She invited me at the party.~~

If you are talking about a meal, you can use **to** or **for**.

He invited me for dinner/to dinner.

If you are talking about a particular type of food, or inviting someone for a particular activity, use **for**.

I was invited for an interview.

They invited her for a pizza.

invite sb in to ask someone to come into your house *The neighbours invited us in for coffee.*

invite sb over (*also UK* invite sb round) to invite someone to come to your house

invite² /ˈɪnvaɪt/ noun [C] informal an invitation

inviting /ɪnˈvaɪtɪŋ/ adjective pleasant and attractive *an inviting smile* ○ *The room looked cosy and inviting.* • **invitingly** adverb

invoice¹ /ˈɪnvɔɪs/ noun [C] a list that shows you how much you owe someone for work they have done or for goods they have supplied

invoice² /ˈɪnvɔɪs/ verb [T] to send someone an invoice

invoke /ɪnˈvəʊk/ verb [T] formal to use a law, rule, etc to support what you are saying or doing *The President may invoke federal law to stop the strike.*

involuntary /ɪnˈvɒlənt°ri/ adjective An involuntary movement or action is something you do but cannot control. *an involuntary shudder* • **involuntarily** adverb

o⌐**involve** /ɪnˈvɒlv/ verb [T] 1 NECESSARY PART If a situation or activity involves something, that thing is a necessary part of it. *The trips often involve a lot of walking.* ○ *There are a lot of risks involved.* 2 AFFECT/INCLUDE to affect or include someone or something in an activity *an*

event *involving hundreds of people* 3 TAKE PART to make someone be part of an activity or process *I prefer teaching methods that actively involve students in learning.*

o⌐**involved** /ɪnˈvɒlvd/ adjective 1 be/get involved (in/with sth) to do things and be part of an activity or event *How did you get involved in acting?* 2 be/get involved with sb to have a sexual or romantic relationship with someone *She got involved with a boy from college.* 3 complicated *a long and involved story*

WORD PARTNERS FOR **involvement**

close/direct/personal involvement • involvement in sth

o⌐**involvement** /ɪnˈvɒlvmənt/ noun [U] when someone or something is involved in an activity or event *He denies any involvement in the attack.*

inward¹ /ˈɪnwəd/ adjective 1 [always before noun] towards the centre or the inside of something 2 **inward investment** UK money from foreign companies that is put into businesses in your own country 3 [always before noun] inside your mind and not shown to other people *inward feelings.* ⊃Opposite **outward**.

inward² /ˈɪnwəd/ (*also UK* inwards) adverb towards the inside or the centre *The door slowly opened inward.*

inwardly /ˈɪnwədli/ adverb in your mind without anyone else seeing or knowing *She smiled inwardly.* ⊃Opposite **outwardly**.

in-your-face /ˌɪnjeˈfeɪs/ (*also* in-yer-face) adjective informal describes something that is done in a forceful way that intends to shock people *in-your-face television advertising*

iodine /ˈaɪədiːn/ noun [U] a chemical element found in sea water, and used in some medicines

IOU /ˌaɪəʊˈjuː/ noun [C] abbreviation for I owe you: a piece of paper saying that you will pay back money you owe

IOW Internet abbreviation for in other words: used when you want to express something in a different way in order to explain it clearly

IPA /ˌaɪpiːˈeɪ/ noun [U] abbreviation for International Phonetic Alphabet: a system of symbols for showing how words are spoken

iPod /ˈaɪpɒd/ noun [C] trademark one of a group of small electronic devices for storing and playing music

IQ /ˌaɪˈkjuː/ noun [C, U] abbreviation for intelligence quotient: a person's intelligence when measured by a special test *a high/low IQ*

ir- /ɪr-/ prefix not irregular ○ irresponsible

irate /aɪˈreɪt/ adjective extremely angry *Hundreds of irate passengers have complained to the airline.*

iris /ˈaɪərɪs/ noun [C] 1 a tall plant with purple, yellow, or white flowers 2 the coloured part of your eye

Irish¹ /ˈaɪərɪʃ/ adjective relating to Ireland *Irish music/culture* ○ *Irish whisky*

Irish² /ˈaɪərɪʃ/ noun 1 [U] the language that is spoken in some parts of Ireland 2 **the Irish**

[plural] the people of Ireland

o-**iron**[1] /aɪən/ *noun* **1** [U] a dark grey metal used to make steel (= very strong metal) and found in small amounts in blood and food *an iron bar/ gate* **2** [C] a piece of electrical equipment that you use for making clothes flat and smooth ⊃See also: cast iron, wrought iron.

iron[2] /aɪən/ *verb* [I, T] to make clothes flat and smooth using an iron *I need to iron a shirt to wear tomorrow.*

iron sth out to solve a problem or difficulty *We're still trying to iron out a few problems with the computer system.*

iron[3] /aɪən/ *adjective* [always before noun] extremely strong and determined *a man of iron will* ⊃See also: cast-iron.

ironic /aɪəˈrɒnɪk/ *adjective* **1** saying something that you do not mean, as a joke *ironic comments* **2** An ironic situation is strange because it is the opposite of what you expected. [+ that] *It's ironic that she was hurt by the very person she's trying to help.* ● **ironically** *adverb*

ironing /ˈaɪənɪŋ/ *noun* [U] **1** the activity of making clothes flat and smooth using an iron (= a piece of electrical equipment) *John was doing the ironing.* **2** the clothes that are waiting to be ironed, or those that have just been ironed *a basket full of ironing*

ironing board *noun* [C] a narrow table that you use for ironing

irony /ˈaɪərəni/ *noun* **1** [C, U] a situation that is strange because it is the opposite of what you expected *The irony is that now he's retired, he's busier than ever.* **2** [U] a type of humour in which people say something they do not mean

irrational /ɪˈræʃ°n°l/ *adjective* Irrational feelings and actions are based on your emotions and not on good reasons. *irrational behaviour* ○ *an irrational fear of flying* ● **irrationality** /ɪˌræʃ°nˈæləti/ *noun* [U] ● **irrationally** *adverb*

irreconcilable /ɪˌrek°nˈsaɪləbl/ *adjective formal* Irreconcilable beliefs, opinions, etc are so different that no agreement is possible. *Irreconcilable differences led to their divorce.*

irregular /ɪˈregjələ°/ *adjective* **1** [TIME] Irregular actions or events happen with a different amount of time between each one. *an irregular heartbeat* ○ *They met at irregular intervals.* **2** [SHAPE] not smooth or straight, or having parts that are different sizes *an irregular coastline* **3** [GRAMMAR] not following the general rules in grammar *irregular verbs/plurals* **4** [BEHAVIOUR] *UK formal* slightly illegal, or not done in the usual and acceptable way *He led a very irregular life.* ● **irregularity** /ɪˌregjəˈlærəti/ *noun* [C, U] ● **irregularly** *adverb*

irrelevant /ɪˈreləv°nt/ *adjective* not important in a particular situation *The car had faults but these were irrelevant to the crash.* ● **irrelevance** /ɪˈreləv°ns/ *noun* [C, U] something that is irrelevant, or the quality of being irrelevant ● **irrelevantly** *adverb*

irreparable /ɪˈrep°rəbl/ *adjective* Irreparable damage, harm, injury, etc is so bad that it can never be repaired. ● **irreparably** *adverb*

irreplaceable /ˌɪrɪˈpleɪsəbl/ *adjective* Someone

or something that is irreplaceable is so valuable or special that you could not get another one like them.

irrepressible /ˌɪrɪˈpresəbl/ *adjective* **1** always happy and energetic **2** An irrepressible feeling is impossible to control. *an irrepressible urge to travel* ● **irrepressibly** *adverb*

irresistible /ˌɪrɪˈzɪstəbl/ *adjective* **1** extremely attractive and impossible not to like or want *an irresistible smile* **2** too powerful to control or ignore *irresistible pressure* ○ *an irresistible desire to run away* ● **irresistibly** *adverb*

irrespective /ˌɪrɪˈspektɪv/ *adverb* **irrespective of sth** used to say that something does not affect a situation *Everyone should be treated equally, irrespective of skin colour.*

irresponsible /ˌɪrɪˈspɒnsəbl/ *adjective* not thinking about the possible bad results of what you are doing *an irresponsible attitude* ● **irresponsibility** /ˌɪrɪˌspɒnsəˈbɪləti/ *noun* [U] ● **irresponsibly** *adverb*

irreverent /ɪˈrev°r°nt/ *adjective* not showing any respect for people or traditions that are usually respected *irreverent humour* ● **irreverence** /ɪˈrev°r°ns/ *noun* [U] when someone or something is irreverent ● **irreverently** *adverb*

irreversible /ˌɪrɪˈvɜːsəbl/ *adjective* Something that is irreversible cannot be changed back to how it was before. *Smoking has caused irreversible damage to his lungs.* ● **irreversibly** *adverb*

irrevocable /ɪˈrevəkəbl/ *adjective formal* impossible to change or stop *irrevocable decisions* ● **irrevocably** *adverb*

irrigate /ˈɪrɪɡeɪt/ *verb* [T] to provide water for an area of land so that crops can be grown ● **irrigation** /ˌɪrɪˈɡeɪʃ°n/ *noun* [U]

irritable /ˈɪrɪtəbl/ *adjective* becoming annoyed very easily *Jack's been irritable all day.* ● **irritability** /ˌɪrɪtəˈbɪləti/ *noun* [U] ● **irritably** *adverb*

irritant /ˈɪrɪt°nt/ *noun* [C] **1** someone or something that makes you feel annoyed **2** a substance that makes part of your body hurt

irritate /ˈɪrɪteɪt/ *verb* [T] **1** to annoy someone *His comments really irritated me.* **2** to make a part of your body hurt *The smoke irritated her eyes.* ● **irritation** /ˌɪrɪˈteɪʃ°n/ *noun* [C, U]

irritated /ˈɪrɪteɪtɪd/ *adjective* annoyed *Ben began to get increasingly irritated by/at her questions.* ○ [+ that] *I was irritated that he didn't thank me.*

irritating /ˈɪrɪteɪtɪŋ/ *adjective* making you feel annoyed *an irritating habit* ● **irritatingly** *adverb*

o-**is** *strong form* /ɪz/ *weak form* /z/ *present simple he/ she/it of* be

Islam /ˈɪzlɑːm/ *noun* [U] a religion based on belief in Allah, on the Koran, and on the teachings of Mohammed *The followers of Islam are called Muslims.*

Islamic /ɪzˈlæmɪk/ *adjective* related to Islam *Islamic art* ○ *an Islamic country*

o-**island** /ˈaɪlənd/ *noun* [C] an area of land that has water around it *the Caribbean island of Grenada* ○ *the Hawaiian Islands* ● **islander** *noun* [C] someone who lives on an island ⊃See also: desert island.

isle /aɪl/ *noun* [C] an island, often used in the name of a particular island *the British Isles*

⚬**isn't** /ˈɪzᵊnt/ *short for* is not *Mike isn't coming with us.*

isolate /ˈaɪsᵊleɪt/ *verb* [T] to separate someone or something from other people or things *Scientists have been able to isolate the gene responsible for causing the illness.* ○ *He had been isolated from other prisoners.*

isolated /ˈaɪsᵊleɪtɪd/ *adjective* **1** a long way from other places *an isolated village in the mountains* **2** alone and not having help or support from other people *Kazuo felt very isolated at his new school.* **3 an isolated case/example/incident, etc** an event, action, etc that happens only once

isolation /ˌaɪsᵊlˈeɪʃᵊn/ *noun* **1** [U] the state of being separate from other people, places, or things *the country's economic isolation from the rest of the world* **2 in isolation** alone, or separately from other people, places, or things *These poems cannot be considered in isolation.* **3** [U] a feeling of being lonely *I had this awful sense of isolation.*

ISP /ˌaɪesˈpiː/ *noun* [C] *abbreviation for* Internet service provider: a company that connects your computer to the Internet, and lets you use email and other services

⊞ WORD PARTNERS FOR *issue (noun)*

a **contentious** / **important** / **key** / **major** / **thorny** issue • **address** / **discuss** / **raise** / **resolve** an issue • the issue **of** sth

⚬**issue¹** /ˈɪʃuː/ *noun* **1** [C] an important subject or problem that people are discussing *the issues of race and social class* ○ *political issues* ○ *Chris has raised a very important issue.* **2** [C] the newspaper, magazine, etc that is produced on a particular day *Have you seen the latest issue of Computer World?* **3 at issue** most important in what is being discussed *The point at issue is what is best for the child.* **4 take issue (with sb/sth)** to disagree with what someone says or writes *I would take issue with you on that.* **5 have issues with sth** to often be sad, anxious or angry because of something *A very high proportion of women diet frequently and have issues with their bodies.*

⊞ WORD PARTNERS FOR *issue (verb)*

issue an **order/statement/warning** • issue **guidelines/instructions**

issue² /ˈɪʃuː/ *verb* [T] *issuing past* issued **1** to say something officially *The Prime Minister will issue a statement tomorrow.* ○ *Police issued a warning about the dangers of playing near water.* **2** to officially give something to someone *to issue a passport/ticket/invitation* ○ *All members will be issued with a membership card.*

IT /ˌaɪˈtiː/ *noun* [U] *abbreviation for* information technology: the use of computers and other electronic equipment to store and send information

⚬**it** /ɪt/ *pronoun* **1** THING used to refer to the thing, situation, or idea that has already been talked about *"Have you seen my bag?" "It's in the hall."* **2** DESCRIPTION used before certain adjectives, nouns, or verbs to introduce an opinion or description of a situation *It's unlikely that she'll arrive on time.* **3** SUBJECT/OBJECT used with certain verbs that need a subject or object but do not refer to a particular noun *It costs less if you travel at the weekend.* ○ *I liked it in Scotland.* **4** TIME/WEATHER used with the verb 'be' in sentences giving the time, date, weather or distances *It rained all day.* ○ *What time is it?* **5** SEEM used as the subject of verbs such as 'seem', 'appear' and 'look' *It seemed unfair to leave her at home.* **6** EMPHASIZE used to emphasize one part of a sentence *It's the children I'm concerned about, not me.* **7 it's sb/sth** used to say the name of a person or thing when the person you are speaking to does not know *It's your Dad on the phone.*

italics /ɪˈtælɪks/ *noun* [plural] a style of writing or printing in which the letters slope to the right • *italic adjective* written in italics

itch¹ /ɪtʃ/ *verb* **1** [I] If a part of your body itches, it feels uncomfortable and you want to rub it with your nails. *Woollen sweaters make my arms itch.* **2 be itching to do sth** *informal* to want to do something very much *You could tell that they were itching to leave.*

itch² /ɪtʃ/ *noun* [C] an uncomfortable feeling on your skin that makes you want to rub it with your nails *I've got an itch in the middle of my back.*

itching /ˈɪtʃɪŋ/ *noun* [U] when a part of your body itches *a lotion to stop itching*

itchy /ˈɪtʃi/ *adjective* If a part of your body is itchy, it feels uncomfortable and you want to rub it with your nails. *an itchy nose* • *itchiness noun* [U]

⚬**it'd** /ˈɪtəd/ **1** *short for* it would *It'd be great if we could meet next week.* **2** *short for* it had *It'd taken us an hour to find Bruce's house.*

⚬**item** /ˈaɪtəm/ *noun* [C] **1** a single thing in a set or on a list *the last item on the list* ○ *Various stolen items were found.* **2** a piece of news on television or radio, or in a newspaper *a small item on the back page of the local newspaper*

itemize (*also UK* **-ise**) /ˈaɪtəmaɪz/ *verb* [T] to list things separately, often including details about each thing *an itemized phone bill*

itinerant /aɪˈtɪnᵊrᵊnt/ *adjective* [always before noun] *formal* travelling from one place to another *an itinerant preacher*

itinerary /aɪˈtɪnᵊrᵊri/ *noun* [C] a list of places that you plan to visit on a journey *The President's itinerary includes visits to Boston and New York.*

⚬**it'll** /ˈɪtᵊl/ *short for* it will *It'll take about twenty minutes to get there.*

⚬**it's** /ɪts/ **1** *short for* it is *"What time is it?" "It's one o'clock."* **2** *short for* it has *It's been a long day and I'm tired.*

⚬**its** /ɪts/ *determiner* belonging to or relating to the thing that has already been talked about *The house has its own swimming pool.*

⚬**itself** /ɪtˈself/ *pronoun* **1** REFLEXIVE the reflexive form of the pronoun 'it' *The cat licked itself* *clean.* **2** EMPHASIS used to emphasize the particular thing you are referring to *The garden is enormous but the house itself is very small.* **3 (all) by itself a** ALONE alone *The dog was in the house by itself for several days.* **b** AUTOMATIC automatically *The heating comes on by itself.* **4 in itself** as the only thing being talked about and nothing else *You've managed to complete the course - that in itself is an achievement.*

ITV /ˌaɪtiːˈviː/ *noun abbreviation for* Independent Television: one of the main television companies in the United Kingdom *There's a good film on ITV tonight.*

IV /ˌaɪˈviː/ *US* (*UK* **drip**) *noun* [C] a piece of medical equipment used for putting liquids into your body

o→ **I've** /aɪv/ *short for* I have *I've decided not to go.*

IVF /ˌaɪviːˈef/ *noun* [U] *abbreviation for* in vitro fertilization: a treatment to make a woman pregnant in which an embryo (= a human that is starting to develop into a baby) is put into her womb (= the organ inside a woman's body where a baby grows)

ivory /ˈaɪvᵊri/ *noun* [U] a hard, white substance from the tusks (= long teeth) of some animals, such as elephants (= large, grey animals)

ivy /ˈaɪvi/ *noun* [U] a dark green plant that often grows up walls

ivy

J, j /dʒeɪ/ the tenth letter of the alphabet

jab¹ /dʒæb/ *verb* [I, T] **jabbing** *past* **jabbed** to push something quickly and hard into or towards another thing *He jabbed a finger into her back.*

jab² /dʒæb/ *noun* [C] **1** a quick, hard push into or towards something **2** *UK informal* an injection (= when a drug is put in your body with a needle) *a flu jab*

jack¹ /dʒæk/ *noun* [C] **1** a piece of equipment for lifting a heavy object such as a car **2** a playing card that comes between a ten and a queen *the jack of diamonds*

jack² /dʒæk/ *verb*

jack sth in *UK informal* to stop doing something, especially a job *She's jacked in her job.*

jack sth up *informal* to increase a price or rate suddenly and by a large amount

jackal /ˈdʒækəl/ *noun* [C] a wild dog that hunts in groups

jacket

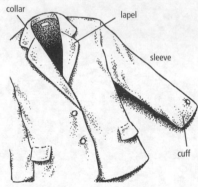
collar
lapel
sleeve
cuff

o--**jacket** /ˈdʒækɪt/ *noun* [C] a short coat *a leather jacket* ⊃See colour picture **Clothes** on page Centre 8 ⊃See also: **dinner jacket, life jacket, strait-jacket.**

ˌjacket poˈtato *noun* [C] *plural* **jacket potatoes** *UK* a potato that has been baked in the oven with its skin on

jack-knife¹ /ˈdʒæknaɪf/ *noun* [C] *plural* **jack-knives** a knife with a blade that can be folded away into the handle

jack-knife² /ˈdʒæk,naɪf/ *verb* [I] If a large truck jack-knifes, the front part turns round to face the back in a way that is not controlled.

jackpot /ˈdʒækpɒt/ *noun* **1** [C] an amount of money that is the largest prize anyone can win in a competition **2 hit the jackpot** to be very successful, especially by winning or earning a lot of money

Jacuzzi /dʒəˈkuːzi/ *noun* [C] *trademark* a bath or pool that produces bubbles in the water

jade /dʒeɪd/ *noun* [U] a green stone used in making jewellery

jaded /ˈdʒeɪdɪd/ *adjective* tired or bored with something, especially because you have done it too much *a jaded traveller*

jagged /ˈdʒægɪd/ *adjective* very rough and sharp *jagged rocks*

jaguar /ˈdʒægjuə²/ *noun* [C] a large, wild cat that lives in Central and South America

WORD PARTNERS FOR jail

be released from/be sent to jail • in jail • a jail sentence

jail¹ (*also UK* gaol) /dʒeɪl/ *noun* [C, U] a place where criminals are kept as a punishment *He ended up in jail.*

jail² /dʒeɪl/ *verb* [T] to put someone in a jail [often passive] *He was jailed for two years.*

jailer /ˈdʒeɪlə²/ *noun* [C] someone who guards prisoners in a jail

jam¹ /dʒæm/ *noun* **1** [C, U] (*also US* jelly) a sweet food made from fruit that you spread on bread *a jar of strawberry jam* ⊃See colour picture **Food** on page Centre 11. **2** [C] (*also* traffic jam) a line of cars, trucks, etc that are moving slowly or not moving *We were stuck in a jam for hours.*

jam² /dʒæm/ *verb* **jamming** *past* **jammed 1 jam sth in/into/on, etc** to push something somewhere firmly and tightly *She jammed her hands into her pockets.* **2** [STUCK] [I, T] to get stuck or make something get stuck *The machine keeps jamming.* **3** [FILL] [T] to fill a place completely [often passive] *The streets were jammed with cars.* **4** [STOP RADIO] [T] to send a signal that stops a radio being able to broadcast

jamboree /ˌdʒæmbəˈriː/ *noun* [C] a big celebration or party

Jan *written abbreviation for* January

jangle /ˈdʒæŋgl/ *verb* [I, T] If small metal objects jangle, they hit together making a ringing noise, and if you jangle them, you make them make this noise. *He was jangling his keys.* • **jangle** *noun* [C]

janitor /ˈdʒænɪtə²/ *noun* [C] *US* someone whose job is to look after a building *the school janitor*

o--**January** /ˈdʒænju²ri/ (*written abbreviation* **Jan**) *noun* [C, U] the first month of the year

jar¹ /dʒɑː²/ *noun* [C] a glass container used for storing food *a jar of coffee/jam* ⊃See picture at **container.**

jar² /dʒɑː²/ *verb* **jarring** *past* **jarred** [I, T] to move suddenly, hitting something and causing pain or damage *The movement jarred his injured leg.*

jar on sb *UK* to annoy someone *Her voice jars on me.*

jargon /ˈdʒɑːgən/ *noun* [U] words and phrases used by particular groups of people that are difficult for other people to understand *legal jargon*

jaundice /ˈdʒɔːndɪs/ *noun* [U] a disease that makes your eyes and skin yellow

jaundiced /ˈdʒɔːndɪst/ *adjective* having a negative opinion of something because of bad things that have happened to you *a jaundiced* *view of marriage*

jaunt /dʒɔːnt/ *noun* [C] a short, enjoyable journey *a pleasant jaunt*

jaunty /'dʒɔːnti/ *adjective* happy and confident *a jaunty walk*

javelin /'dʒævəlɪn/ *noun* **1** [C] a long, pointed stick that you throw as a sport **2 the javelin** a sport in which you throw a javelin as far as you can ⊃See colour picture **Sports 1** on page Centre 14.

jaw /dʒɔː/ *noun* [C] **1** either of the two bones in your mouth that contain your teeth ⊃See colour picture **The Body** on page Centre 13. **2 sb's jaw drops** If someone's jaw drops, their mouth opens because they are very surprised.

jazz /dʒæz/ *noun* [U] music with a strong beat that is often played without written music *a jazz band*

┌─────────────────────────────────────┐
│ WORD PARTNERS FOR *jealous*   │
└─────────────────────────────────────┘
make sb jealous • **insanely/madly** jealous • jealous **of** sb/sth

jealous /'dʒeləs/ *adjective* **1** unhappy and angry because you want something that someone else has *His new bike was **making** his friends **jealous**.* ○ *Steve has always been **jealous of** his brother's good looks.* **2** upset and angry because someone you love seems too interested in another person *a jealous husband* • **jealously** *adverb*

jealousy /'dʒeləsi/ *noun* [U] jealous feelings

∘⟹**jeans** /dʒiːnz/ *noun* [plural] trousers made from denim (= a strong, usually blue, material) *a pair of jeans* ⊃See colour picture **Clothes** on page Centre 8.

Jeep /dʒiːp/ *noun* [C] *trademark* a strongly built vehicle with big wheels that is used for driving over rough ground

jeer /dʒɪəʳ/ *verb* [I, T] to laugh and shout insults at someone *The crowd outside his house jeered as he left.* • **jeer** *noun* [C]

Jell-O /'dʒeləʊ/ *noun* [U] *US trademark* jelly

jelly /'dʒeli/ *noun* [C, U] **1** *UK* (*US* **Jell-O**) a soft but solid sweet food that shakes when you move it *jelly and ice cream* **2** *US* (*UK/US* **jam**) a sweet food made from fruit that you spread on bread

jellyfish /'dʒelifɪʃ/ *noun* [C] *plural* jellyfish a sea creature with a clear body that may sting you (= put poison into your skin)

jeopardize (*also* *UK* **-ise**) /'dʒepədaɪz/ *verb* [I] to put something in a situation where there is a risk of failing or being harmed *Bad weather could jeopardize all our plans.*

jeopardy /'dʒepədi/ *noun* **in jeopardy** in danger of failing or being harmed *If the factory closes, local jobs will be in jeopardy.*

jerk¹ /dʒɜːk/ *verb* [I, T] to move very quickly and suddenly, or to make something move like this *The truck jerked forward.*

jerk² /dʒɜːk/ *noun* [C] **1** a quick, sudden movement *a sudden jerk of the head* **2** *mainly US informal* a stupid or annoying person

jerky /'dʒɜːki/ *adjective* Jerky movements are quick and sudden. • **jerkily** *adverb*

jersey /'dʒɜːzi/ *noun* **1** [C] a piece of clothing which covers the top of your body and is pulled on over your head **2** [U] soft wool or cotton cloth used for making clothes

jest /dʒest/ *noun* **in jest** said as a joke

Jesus Christ /,dʒiːzəs'kraɪst/ *noun* the Jewish holy man believed by Christians to be the Son of God, and on whose life and teachings Christianity is based

jet¹ /dʒet/ *noun* [C] **1** an aircraft that flies very fast ⊃See also: **jumbo jet**. **2** water or gas that is forced out of something in a thin, strong line

jet² /dʒet/ *verb* [I] *jetting past* jetted **jet in/off, etc** to fly somewhere in an aircraft *She jetted off to Athens for a week.*

jet-black /,dʒet'blæk/ *noun* [U] a very dark black colour • **jet-black** *adjective* *jet-black hair*

'**jet ,engine** *noun* [C] an engine that makes an aircraft fly very fast

'**jet ,lag** *noun* [U] when you feel tired because you have just travelled a long distance on an aircraft

jettison /'dʒetɪsən/ *verb* [T] **1** to get rid of something you do not want or need *The station has jettisoned educational broadcasts.* **2** If an aircraft or a ship jettisons something, it throws it off to make itself lighter.

jetty /'dʒeti/ *noun* [C] a wooden structure at the edge of the sea or a lake where people can get on and off boats

Jew /dʒuː/ *noun* [C] someone whose religion is Judaism, or who is related to the ancient people of Israel

jewel /'dʒuːəl/ *noun* [C] a valuable stone that is used to make jewellery

jeweller *UK* (*US* **jeweler**) /'dʒuːələ/ *noun* [C] someone whose job is to sell or make jewellery

jewellery *UK*, **jewelry** *US*

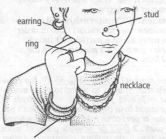

earring • stud

ring

necklace

bracelet

jewellery *UK* (*US* **jewelry**) /'dʒuːəlri/ *noun* [U] objects made from gold, silver, and valuable stones that you wear for decoration

Jewish /'dʒuːɪʃ/ *adjective* relating or belonging to the Jews *Jewish history/law*

jibe (*also* **gibe**) /dʒaɪb/ *noun* [C] an insulting

remark *He kept making **jibes** at me about my weight.*

jig /dʒɪg/ *noun* [C] a traditional, quick dance, or the music it is danced to

jiggle /'dʒɪgl/ *verb* [I, T] to make quick, short movements from side to side or to make something else move like this

jigsaw /'dʒɪgsɔː/ (*also* 'jigsaw ,puzzle) *noun* [C] a picture in many small pieces that you put together as a game

jingle¹ /'dʒɪŋgl/ *noun* [C] **1** a short song that is used to advertise a product on the radio or television **2** a sound made when small metal objects hit against each other

jingle² /'dʒɪŋgl/ *verb* [I, T] to make the sound of small metal objects hitting against each other *a pocket full of jingling coins*

jinx /dʒɪŋks/ *noun* [C] someone or something that brings bad luck *There seems to be **a jinx on** this school.* ● **jinx** *verb* [T]

jitters /'dʒɪtəz/ *noun* [plural] a nervous feeling *Hospitals give me **the jitters**.*

jittery /'dʒɪtᵊri/ *adjective* nervous *She gets quite **jittery about** exams.*

Jnr *UK* (*UK/US* **Jr**) *written abbreviation for* junior (= the younger of two men in a family with the same name)

WORD PARTNERS FOR job

a **dead-end/full-time/good/part-time/temporary** job ● **apply for/create/do/find/get/lose** a job ● a job **as** sth

OTHER WAYS OF SAYING job

A more formal alternative is the noun **occupation**: *Please fill in your name, age and **occupation**.*

The nouns **post** and **position** are often used to talk about a particular job within an organisation: *She's applied for a part-time teaching **post/position**.*

The noun **career** is sometimes used to describe a job that a person does for a long period in their life: *She's had a very successful **career** in marketing.*

A **placement** (*UK*) (**internship** *US*) is a job that someone does for a short time in order to learn more about a particular kind of work: *He's got a year's **placement** in the medical labs.*

◦▪**job** /dʒɒb/ *noun* [C] **1** PAID EMPLOYMENT the regular work that you do in order to earn money *She got a **job** in publishing.* ○ *Hundreds of workers could **lose** their **jobs**.* ○ *Why don't you **apply for** a part-time job?* ➔See Common learner error at **work. 2** PIECE OF WORK a piece of work that you have to do *cooking, cleaning and other household jobs* **3** RESPONSIBILITY something that is your responsibility *It's my job to water the plants.* **4 make a bad/good, etc job of sth** *UK* to do sth badly/well, etc **5 do a good/excellent, etc job** to do something well/very well, etc *She did a great job of organizing the event.* **6 out of a job** without a job *How long have you been out of a job?* **7 do the job** If something does the job,

it is suitable for a particular purpose. *Here, this knife should do the job.* **8 it's a good job** *UK informal* If it is a good job that something happened, it is lucky that it happened. [+ (that)] *It's a good job that Jo was there to help you.* **9 just the job** *UK* If something is just the job, it is exactly what you want or need.

'**job de,scription** *noun* [C] a list of the things you must do in your work

jobless /'dʒɒbləs/ *adjective* without a job *young jobless people*

jobshare /'dʒɒbʃeᵊr/ *verb* [I] *UK* If two people jobshare, they do one job between them, working at different times. ● **jobshare** *noun* *UK*

jockey /'dʒɒki/ *noun* [C] someone who rides horses in races ➔See also: **disc jockey**.

jog /dʒɒg/ *verb* jogging, *past* jogged **1** [I] to run slowly for exercise *I jog through the park every morning.* **2** [T] to hit something gently by mistake *He jogged her arm.* **3 jog sb's memory** to cause someone to remember something *They hoped the photographs would jog his memory.* ● **jog** *noun* [no plural] *Let's go for a jog.* ● **jogging** *noun* [U]

jogger /dʒɒgᵊr/ *noun* [C] someone who runs for exercise

◦▪**join**¹ /dʒɔɪn/ *verb* **1** BECOME MEMBER [T] to become a member of a group or organization *He joined the army when he was eighteen.* **2** DO WITH OTHERS [T] to do something or go somewhere with someone *Would you like to join us for dinner?* **3** FASTEN [T] to fasten or connect things together *Join the ends together with strong glue.* **4** MEET [I, T] to meet at a particular point *The Mississippi River and the Missouri join near St Louis.* **5 join a line** (*also UK* join a queue) to go and stand at the end of a row of people waiting for something ➔See also: **join forces** (**force**¹).

COMMON LEARNER ERROR

join

Join is not followed by a preposition when it is used in expressions such as 'join a company'.

He joined the team in 1998.

~~He joined to the team in 1998.~~

join in (sth) to become involved in an activity with other people *We're playing cards. Would you like to join in?*

join up to become a member of the army or other military group

join² /dʒɔɪn/ *noun* [C] *UK* the place where two or more things are fastened together

joined-up /ˌdʒɔɪn'dʌp/ *adjective UK* **1 joined-up writing** a style of writing where each letter in a word is connected to the next one **2 joined-up thinking** thinking about a complicated problem in an intelligent and original way, and considering everything that is connected with it

joint¹ /dʒɔɪnt/ *adjective* [always before noun] belonging to or done by two or more people *a joint statement* ○ *The project was a joint effort by all the children in the class.* ● **jointly** *adverb*

joint² /dʒɔɪnt/ *noun* [C]
1 BODY PART a place in your body where two bones meet *the knee joint* **2** MEAT *UK* a large piece of meat, usually cooked in the oven *a joint of beef* **3** CONNECTION a place where parts of a structure or machine are connected

joint

4 PLACE *informal* a place where something is sold, especially a restaurant or bar *a pizza joint*

joint ˈventure *noun* [C] a business activity that involves two or more companies working together

 WORD PARTNERS FOR *joke*

crack/make/tell a joke • a dirty/sick joke • a joke **about** sth

o↤**joke¹** /dʒəʊk/ *noun* **1** [C] something which someone says to make people laugh, usually a short story with a funny ending *to **tell/make** a joke* **2** be a joke *informal* to not be serious or not deserve respect *The investigation was a joke.* **3** be no joke to be serious or difficult *It's no joke driving on icy roads.* **4** take a joke to understand and accept a trick without becoming angry or upset ⊃See also: practical joke.

joke² /dʒəʊk/ *verb* **1** [I] to say funny things, or not be serious *She always **jokes about** her husband's cooking.* **2** You must be joking!/You're joking! *informal* something you say to show that you are surprised by what someone has said, or do not believe it is true • jokingly *adverb*

joker /ˈdʒəʊkəʳ/ *noun* [C] **1** someone who likes saying or doing funny things **2** one of a set of playing cards which can be used instead of another card in some games

jolly¹ /ˈdʒɒli/ *adjective* happy or enjoyable *We had a jolly evening.*

jolly² /ˈdʒɒli/ *adverb old-fashioned* very *a jolly good idea*

jolt¹ /dʒəʊlt/ *noun* [C] **1** a sudden, violent movement *With a **sudden jolt** the train started moving again.* **2** an unpleasant shock or surprise *The reminder that he was dead **gave** her **a jolt**.*

jolt² /dʒəʊlt/ *verb* [I, T] to move suddenly and forcefully, or to make someone or something do this *The bus stopped suddenly and the passengers were jolted forward.*

jostle /ˈdʒɒsl/ *verb* [I, T] to push other people in order to get somewhere in a crowd
jostle for sth to try hard to get something *Thousands of companies are jostling for business on the Internet.*

jot /dʒɒt/ *verb* [T] jotting *past* jotted to write something quickly *She **jotted** a **note** to Sue.*
jot sth down to write something quickly on a piece of paper so that you remember it *I **jotted down** some **notes** during his speech.*

journal /ˈdʒɜːnºl/ *noun* [C] **1** a magazine containing articles about a particular subject

a medical journal **2** a book in which you regularly write about what has happened to you

journalism /ˈdʒɜːnºlɪzºm/ *noun* [U] the work of writing articles for newspapers, magazines, television, or radio

o↤**journalist** /ˈdʒɜːnºlɪst/ *noun* [C] someone whose job is journalism

journalistic /ˌdʒɜːnºlˈɪstɪk/ *adjective* relating to journalism or typical of journalism

 WORD PARTNERS FOR *journey*

an **arduous/long/perilous/short** journey • **begin/complete/embark on/go on/make** a journey

o↤**journey** /ˈdʒɜːni/ *noun* [C] when you travel from one place to another *a car/train journey* ○ *We take games for the children when we **go on** long **journeys**.* ⊃See Common learner error at **travel**.

jovial /ˈdʒəʊviəl/ *adjective* happy and friendly *a jovial man*

joy /dʒɔɪ/ *noun* **1** HAPPINESS [U] a feeling of great happiness *the joy of winning* **2** PLEASURE [C] something or someone that makes you feel very happy *She's a joy to work with.* **3** SUCCESS [U] *UK informal* success *I tried ringing for a plumber, but had **no joy**.*

joyful /ˈdʒɔɪfºl/ *adjective* very happy, or making people feel very happy *joyful news* • joyfully *adverb*

joyous /ˈdʒɔɪəs/ *adjective literary* extremely happy, or making people extremely happy • joyously *adverb*

joypad /ˈdʒɔɪpæd/ *noun* [C] a gamepad

joyriding /ˈdʒɔɪˌraɪdɪŋ/ *noun* [U] stealing cars and driving them fast and dangerously • joyride /ˈdʒɔɪraɪd/ *noun* [C] *They took the car for a joyride.* • joyrider *noun* [C]

joystick /ˈdʒɔɪstɪk/ *noun* [C] a vertical handle you move to control a computer game, machine, or aircraft

JP /ˌdʒeɪˈpiː/ *noun* [C] *abbreviation for* Justice of the Peace: a judge in a small or local court of law

JPEG /ˈdʒeɪpeg/ *noun* **1** [U] *abbreviation for* joint photographics experts group: a system for making electronic pictures use less space **2** [C] a type of computer file (= collection of information) that contains pictures or photographs

Jr (*also UK* **Jnr**) *written abbreviation for* junior (= the younger of two men in a family with the same name) *John F. Kennedy, Jr.*

jubilant /ˈdʒuːbɪlənt/ *adjective* feeling or showing great happiness, usually because of a success *jubilant United supporters* • jubilation /ˌdʒuːbɪˈleɪʃºn/ *noun* [U] a feeling of great happiness and success

jubilee /ˈdʒuːbɪliː/ *noun* [C] a celebration of an important event in the past, usually one which happened 25 or 50 years ago *a **golden jubilee*** (= 50 years) ○ *a **silver jubilee*** (= 25 years)

Judaism /ˈdʒuːdeɪɪzºm/ *noun* [U] the religion of the Jewish people, based on belief in one God and on the laws contained in the Torah

judge¹ /dʒʌdʒ/ *noun* [C] **1** someone who controls a trial in court, decides how criminals should be punished, and makes decisions about legal things *Judge Moylan* ○ *The judge ruled that they had acted correctly.* **2** someone who decides which person or thing wins a competition *the Olympic judges* **3 a bad/good, etc judge of sth** someone who is usually wrong, usually right, etc when they judge something *a good judge of character*

◦**judge²** /dʒʌdʒ/ *verb* **1** DEVELOP OPINION [I, T] to have or develop an opinion about something or someone, usually after thinking carefully [+ question word] *I can't judge whether he's telling the truth or not.* ○ *You shouldn't judge people on their appearances.* ○ *He was judged guilty/ insane.* **2 judging by/from** used to express the reasons why you have a particular opinion *She must be popular judging by the number of letters that she receives.* **3** COMPETITION [I, T] to decide the winner or results of a competition *I've been asked to judge the art contest.* **4** BAD OPINION [I, T] to have a bad opinion of someone's behaviour, often because you think you are better than them *What gives you the right to judge people?* **5** GUESS [T] to try to guess something, especially a measurement *I find it difficult to judge distances.*

◦**judgment** (*also* judgement) /dʒʌdʒmənt/ *noun* **1** OPINION [C, U] an opinion about someone or something that you decide on after thinking carefully *The inspector needs to make a judgment about how the school is performing.* **2** ABILITY [U] the ability to make good decisions or to be right in your opinions *to have good/ bad judgment* **3** LEGAL DECISION [C, U] an official legal decision, usually made by a judge

judgmental (*also* UK judgemental) /dʒʌdʒ'mentəl/ *adjective* quick to criticize people

judicial /dʒuː'dɪʃəl/ *adjective* relating to a court of law or the legal system *a judicial inquiry*

the judiciary /dʒuː'dɪʃəri/ *noun* all the judges in a country

judicious /dʒuː'dɪʃəs/ *adjective* done or decided carefully and with good judgment

judo /dʒuːdəʊ/ *noun* [U] a sport from Japan in which two people try to throw each other to the ground

jug /dʒʌg/ *noun* [C] a container with a handle used for pouring out liquids *a jug of water*

juggle /dʒʌgl/ *verb*
1 [T] to try to do several things at once, when it is difficult to have enough time *Many women have to juggle work and family.* **2** [I, T] to keep two or more objects such as balls in the air by throw-

jug

ing them repeatedly, usually in order to entertain people

juggler /dʒʌglər/ *noun* [C] someone who juggles objects to entertain people

◦**juice** /dʒuːs/ *noun* [C, U] the liquid that comes from fruit or vegetables ⊃See also: orange juice.

juices /dʒuːsɪz/ *noun* [plural] the liquid that comes from cooked meat

juicy /dʒuːsi/ *adjective* **1** full of juice *juicy apples* **2** interesting because of shocking or personal information *juicy gossip*

jukebox /dʒuːkbɒks/ *noun* [C] a machine, usually in a bar, which plays a song when you put money into it

◦**July** /dʒʊ'laɪ/ *noun* [C, U] the seventh month of the year ⊃See also: Fourth of July.

jumble¹ /dʒʌmbl/ *noun* [no plural] a confused mixture or group of things *Her handbag is a jumble of pens, make-up, and keys.*

jumble² /dʒʌmbl/ (*also* jumble up) *verb* [T] to mix things together in an untidy way [often passive] *Elizabeth's clothes were all jumbled up in the suitcase.*

'jumble ,sale UK (US rummage sale) *noun* [C] a sale of old items, especially clothes, usually to make money for an organization

jumbo /dʒʌmbəʊ/ *adjective* [always before noun] extra large *a jumbo bag of sweets*

,jumbo 'jet *noun* [C] a very large aircraft for carrying passengers

◦**jump¹** /dʒʌmp/ *verb* **1** INTO AIR [I] to push your body up and away from the ground using your feet and legs *The children were jumping up and down with excitement.* ○ *I jumped over the log.* ○ *They jumped into the water.* **2 jump into/ up, etc** to move somewhere suddenly and quickly *She jumped into a taxi and rushed to the station.* **3** GO OVER [T] to move over something by moving up into the air *The horse jumped the last fence.* **4** INCREASE [I, T] to suddenly increase by a large amount *House prices have jumped by 20%.* **5** FEAR [I] to make a sudden movement because you are frightened or surprised *Her scream made me jump.* ⊃See also: get/jump on the bandwagon, jump to conclusions (conclusion), jump the gun¹, jump the queue.

jump at sth to take an opportunity to have or do something in a very willing and excited way *He jumped at the chance to join the band.*

jump² /dʒʌmp/ *noun* [C] **1** when you push your body up into the air using your feet and legs *He won with a jump of 8.5 metres.* **2** a sudden increase in the amount of something *a jump in profits* ⊃See also: the high jump, the long jump.

jumper /dʒʌmpər/ *noun* [C] **1** UK (US/UK sweater) a warm piece of clothing which covers the top of your body and is pulled on over your head **2** US (UK pinafore) a loose dress with no sleeves that is worn over other clothes such as a shirt

'jump ,rope US (UK skipping rope) *noun* [C] a rope that you move over your head and then jump over as you move it under your feet

jumpy /dʒʌmpi/ *adjective* nervous or anxious

the junction **of** sth and sth ● a **railway/road** junction ● a **busy** junction

junction /'dʒʌŋkʃ°n/ noun [C] UK the place where two roads or railway lines meet or cross each other *The accident happened at a busy road junction.* ⊃See also: **T-junction.**

juncture /'dʒʌŋktʃər/ noun [C] formal a particular point in an event or period of time

o--**June** /dʒuːn/ noun [C, U] the sixth month of the year

jungle /'dʒʌŋgl/ noun [C, U] an area of land, usually in tropical countries, where trees and plants grow close together

junior¹ /'dʒuːniər/ adjective 1 [LOW RANK] low or lower in rank *a junior minister/senator* 2 [YOUNG PEOPLE] for or relating to young people *a junior tennis tournament* 3 [NAME] mainly US (written abbreviation **Jr**) used at the end of a man's name to show that he is the younger of two men in the same family who have the same name *Hello, I'd like to speak to Mr Anderson Junior, please.*

junior² /'dʒuːniər/ noun 1 **be 10/20, etc years sb's junior** to be 10, 20, etc years younger than someone *My wife is 8 years my junior.* 2 [C] a student in their third year of study at an American college or high school (= school for 15-18 year olds) 3 [C] UK a child who goes to a junior school

,**junior ,college** noun [C, U] a two-year college in the US where students can learn a skill or prepare to enter a university

,**junior 'high school** (also ,junior 'high) noun [C, U] a school in the US or Canada for children who are 12 to 15 years old

,**junior ,school** noun [C, U] a school in the UK for children who are 7 to 11 years old

junk /dʒʌŋk/ noun [U] informal old things which have little value

,**junk ,food** noun [U] food which is unhealthy but is quick and easy to eat

junkie /'dʒʌŋki/ noun [C] informal 1 someone who cannot stop taking illegal drugs 2 someone who wants something or wants to do something very much *a publicity junkie*

,**junk ,mail** noun [U] letters sent by companies to advertise their goods and services

junta /'dʒʌntə/ noun [C] a military government that has taken power in a country by force

Jupiter /'dʒuːpɪtər/ noun [no plural] the planet that is fifth from the Sun, after Mars and before Saturn

jurisdiction /,dʒʊərɪs'dɪkʃ°n/ noun [U] the legal power to make decisions and judgments *The school is **under the jurisdiction** of the local council.*

juror /'dʒʊərər/ noun [C] a member of a jury

be **on** a jury

o--**jury** /'dʒʊəri/ noun [group] 1 a group of people in a court of law who decide if someone is guilty or not 2 a group of people who decide the winner of a competition

o--**just¹** strong form /dʒʌst/ weak form /dʒəst/ adverb 1 [ONLY] only *I'll just have a small piece.* ○ *He just wants to win.* ○ *The film is not just about love.* 2 [RECENTLY] a very short time ago *I've just been on a trip to France.* ○ *We've only just begun.* 3 [EMPHASIS] used to emphasize something you say *I just can't bear it!* 4 [ALMOST NOT] UK almost not *This dress **only just** fits.* 5 [EXACTLY] exactly *Tim looks just like his father.* ○ *This carpet would be **just right** for my bedroom.* 6 [ALMOST NOW] now or very soon *I'm just coming!* 7 **just before/over/under, etc** a little before/over/under, etc something else *It costs just over $10.* ○ *She left just before Michael.* 8 **just about** almost *I think I've remembered just about everything.* 9 **be just about to do sth** to be going to do something very soon *I was just about to phone you.* 10 **just as bad/good/tall, etc (as sb/sth)** equally bad/good/tall, etc *He's just as talented as his brother.* 11 **I/you/we, etc will just have to do sth** used to say that there is nothing else someone can do *You'll just have to wait.* 12 **just as** at the same time as *She woke up just as we got there.* 13 **it's just as well** used to say that it is lucky that something happened *It's just as well we brought an umbrella.* ⊃See also: just the **job.**

just² /dʒʌst/ adjective fair or morally right *a just society* ⊃Opposite **unjust.** ● **justly** adverb

fight **for/seek** justice ● justice **for** sb

justice /'dʒʌstɪs/ noun 1 [FAIR BEHAVIOUR] [U] behaviour or treatment that is fair and morally correct *She tried to bring about fairness and justice for all.* ⊃Opposite **injustice.** 2 [LAW] [U] the system of laws which judges or punishes people *the **criminal justice system*** 3 [JUDGE] [C] US someone who judges in a court of law 4 **bring sb to justice** to catch a criminal and decide if they are guilty or not 5 **do sb/sth justice; do justice to sb/sth** to show the best or real qualities of something or someone *This postcard doesn't do justice to the wonderful scenery.*

,**Justice of the 'Peace** noun [C] someone who acts as a judge in a small or local court of law

justifiable /'dʒʌstɪfaɪəbl/ adjective having a good reason *justifiable anger* ● **justifiably** adverb

justification /,dʒʌstɪfɪ'keɪʃ°n/ noun [C, U] a reason for something *There's no **justification** for treating her so badly.*

justified /'dʒʌstɪfaɪd/ adjective fair or having a good reason *justified criticism* ○ *He's perfectly **justified in** asking for a larger salary.* ⊃Opposite **unjustified.**

justify /'dʒʌstɪfaɪ/ verb [T] to give a good enough reason to make something seem acceptable *I don't know how they can justify those ticket prices.*

jut /dʒʌt/ verb jutting past jutted **jut into/out, etc** If something juts out, it comes out further than the edge or surface around it. *The rocks jutted out into the sea.*

juvenile¹ /ˈdʒuːvᵊnaɪl/ *adjective* **1** [always before noun] by, for, or relating to young people *juvenile crime* **2** behaving in a silly way as if you were a young child

juvenile² /ˈdʒuːvᵊnaɪl/ *noun* [C] especially in law, a young person

juvenile de'linquent *noun* [C] a young criminal

juxtapose /ˌdʒʌkstəˈpəʊz/ *verb* [T] *formal* to place very different things or people close to each other *The exhibition juxtaposes paintings with black and white photographs.* ● **juxtaposition** /ˌdʒʌkstəpəˈzɪʃᵊn/ *noun* [C, U]

Kk

K, k /keɪ/ the eleventh letter of the alphabet

K /keɪ/ *abbreviation for* kilobyte: a unit for measuring the amount of information a computer can store

kaleidoscope /kəˈlaɪdəskəʊp/ *noun* **1** [C] a tube-shaped toy you look through which contains mirrors and pieces of coloured glass that make patterns **2** [no plural] a mixture of different things *The fashion show was a kaleidoscope of colours.*

kangaroo /ˌkæŋɡəˈruː/ *noun* [C] a large Australian animal that moves by jumping on its back legs

karat /ˈkærət/ *noun* [C] *another US spelling of* carat (= a unit for measuring how pure gold is, or how much valuable stones weigh)

karate /kəˈrɑːti/ *noun* [U] a sport from Japan in which people fight using fast, hard hits with the hands or feet

karma /ˈkɑːmə/ *noun* [U] in some religions, the actions of a person in this life or earlier lives, which influence their future

kayak /ˈkaɪæk/ *noun* [C] a light, narrow boat, usually for one person, which you move using a paddle (= stick with a wide, flat part) • **kayaking** *noun* [U] the activity of travelling in a kayak

kebab /kɪˈbæb/ (*also* **shish kebab**) *noun* [C] small pieces of meat or vegetables cooked on a long, thin stick

keel¹ /kiːl/ *noun* [C] a long piece of wood or metal at the bottom of a boat that helps it to balance

keel² /kiːl/ *verb*
keel over to fall over suddenly

o→**keen** /kiːn/ *adjective* **1** [INTERESTED] very interested or enthusiastic *a keen golfer/photographer* ○ *He's very keen on travelling.* **2** [WANTING TO DO] wanting to do something very much [+ to do sth] *The shop is keen to attract new customers.* **3** [VERY GOOD] very good or well developed *a keen sense of smell* • **keenness** *noun* [U] • **keenly** *adverb*

OTHER WAYS OF SAYING *keep*

If someone keeps something somewhere until they need it, the verb **store** is sometimes used: *I've **stored** all Helen's books in the attic.*

The verb **stash** (*informal*) and the phrasal verb **stash away** (*informal*) are sometimes used if someone keeps a lot of something in a secret place: *His money was **stashed** (away) in a cupboard.*

The verb **save** is often used when someone keeps something to use in the future: *I have* some really good chocolates that I've been **saving** for a special occasion.

The phrasal verbs **hang onto** and **hold onto** are also often used when someone keeps something that they might need in the future: *You should **hang/hold onto** that picture - it might be worth something.*

o→**keep¹** /kiːp/ *verb past* **kept 1** [HAVE] [T] to have something permanently or for the whole of a period of time *You can keep that dress if you like it.* ○ *He borrowed my bike and kept it all week.* **2 keep sth in/on, etc** to regularly store something in a particular place *I think he keeps his keys in the desk drawer.* ○ *We'll keep your application on file.* **3 keep doing sth** to continue to do something, or to do something repeatedly *I keep telling her not to leave her clothes on the floor.* ○ *He keeps hitting me.* **4 keep (sb/sth) awake/clean/safe, etc** to remain in a particular state or make someone or something remain in a particular state *He goes jogging twice a week to keep fit.* ○ *He keeps his car spotlessly clean.* **5 keep sb/sth in/inside, etc** to make someone or something stay in the same place *They will keep her at home for a few more days.* **6** [MAKE DO STH] [T] to make someone do something that stops them doing something else [+ doing sth] *She kept me talking for ages.* ○ *Sorry to keep you waiting.* ○ *Don't let me keep you from your work.* **7 keep a secret** to not tell anyone a secret **8 keep a promise/your word, etc** to do what you have promised to do **9 keep an appointment** to meet someone when you have arranged to meet them **10** [MAKE LATE] [T] to make someone arrive later than they planned *I was expecting you at six - what kept you?* **11** [WRITE] [T] to write down something in order to remember it *to keep records/notes* **12** [FOOD] [I] If food or drink keeps, it remains fresh. **13** [PROVIDE MONEY] [T] to provide enough money for someone to live *I can't keep a family on that salary.* **14** [ANIMALS] [T] to have and look after animals *Our neighbours keep pigs.* **15 keep sb going** to provide what someone needs for a short period of time *Dinner is at eight, but I had an apple to keep me going.* ⊃See also: keep your **cool³**, keep a straight **face¹**, keep your fingers (**finger¹**) crossed, put/keep sb in the **picture¹**, keep a low **profile¹**, keep a tight **rein** on sb/sth, keep tabs (**tab**) on sb/sth, keep sb on their toes (**toe¹**).

keep at sth to continue working hard at something difficult *Learning a language is hard but you've just got to keep at it.*

keep (sb/sth) away to not go somewhere or near something, or to prevent someone from going somewhere or near something *I told them to keep away from the edge of the cliff.*

keep (sb/sth) back to not go near something, or to prevent someone or something from going past a particular place *Barriers were built to keep back the flood water.*

keep sth back to not tell someone everything you know about a situation or an event *I was sure she was keeping something back.*

keep sth down 1 to stop the number, level, or size of something from increasing *I have to exercise to keep my weight down.* **2** to be able to eat or drink without vomiting

keep sb/sth from doing sth to prevent someone or something from doing something

keep sth from sb to not tell someone about something *Is there something you're keeping from me?*

keep sb in to make a child stay inside as a punishment, or to make someone stay in hospital

keep (sb/sth) off sth to not go onto an area, or to stop someone or something going onto an area *Keep off the grass.*

keep sth off (sb/sth) to stop something touching or harming someone or something *He put a cloth over the salad to keep the flies off.*

keep on doing sth to continue to do something, or to do something again and again *She kept on asking me questions the whole time.*

keep on UK to continue to talk in an annoying way about something *I wish he wouldn't keep on about how much he earns.*

keep (sb/sth) out to not go into a place, or to stop someone or something from going into a place *He locked the room and put up a sign asking people to keep out.*

keep to sth 1 to stay in one particular area *We kept to main roads all the way.* **2** to do what you have promised or planned to do *I think we should keep to our original plan.*

keep sth to sth If you keep something to a particular number or amount, you make sure it does not become larger than that. *I'm trying to keep costs to a minimum.*

keep sth to yourself to keep something secret and not tell anyone else about it

keep up 1 [SAME SPEED] to move at the same speed as someone or something that is moving forward so that you stay level with them *She was walking so fast I couldn't keep up with her.* **2** [MAKE PROGRESS] to increase or make progress at the same speed as something or someone else so that you stay at the same level as them *Prices have been rising very fast and wages haven't kept up.* **3** [UNDERSTAND] to be able to understand or deal with something that is happening or changing very fast *I feel it's important to keep up with current events.*

keep sth up to not allow something that is at a high level to fall to a lower level *Make sure you eat properly - you've got to keep your strength up.*

keep (sth) up to continue without stopping or changing, or to continue something without allowing it to stop or change *People are having difficulties keeping up the repayments on their loans.*

keep² /kiːp/ *noun* [no plural] the money needed to pay for someone to eat and live in a place *He earns his keep working in a garage.*

keeper /ˈkiːpəʳ/ *noun* [C] **1** someone who looks after a place and the things, people, or animals there *a park keeper* **2** *informal* short for goal-keeper (= the player in a sport such as football who tries to stop the ball going into the goal)

keeping /ˈkiːpɪŋ/ *noun* **1 for safe keeping** in order to keep something safe *She put the money into a bank for safe keeping.* **2 in keep-**

ing with sth suitable or right for a situation, style, or tradition *The antique desk was in keeping with the rest of the furniture in the room.*

keg /keg/ *noun* [C] a large, round container used for storing beer

kennel /ˈkenᵊl/ *noun* [C] **1** a small building for a dog to sleep in **2** US (UK **kennels**) a place where dogs are cared for while their owners are away

kennel

kept /kept/ *past of* keep

kerb UK (US **curb**) /kɜːb/ *noun* [C] the line of stones at the edge of a pavement (= raised path that people walk on) next to the road

kernel /ˈkɜːnᵊl/ *noun* [C] the part of a nut or seed inside the hard shell which you can usually eat

kerosene /ˈkerəsiːn/ US (UK **paraffin**) *noun* [U] oil used for heating and in lamps (= equipment that produces light)

ketchup /ˈketʃʌp/ *noun* [U] a thick sauce made from tomatoes (= round, red fruit) that is eaten cold with food

kettle /ˈketl/ *noun* [C] a metal or plastic container with a lid, used for boiling water *Charlotte put the kettle on to make some tea.* ➲See colour picture **The Kitchen** on page Centre 2.

🧩 **WORD PARTNERS FOR key**

a **bunch of/set of** keys • the key **for/to** sth • a **car** key

---

key¹ /kiː/ *noun* [C]

1 [FOR LOCKS] a piece of metal cut into a particular shape and used for locking things such as doors, or for starting an engine *I've lost my car keys.* **2** [METHOD] a way of explaining or achieving something *Hard work is the key to success.* **3** [KEYBOARD] one of the parts you press with your fingers on a keyboard or musical instrument to produce letters, numbers, or to make a sound **4** [MUSIC] a set of musical notes based on one particular note *the key of D major* **5** [SYMBOLS] a list which explains the symbols on a map or picture **6** [ANSWERS] a list of answers to an exercise or game ➲See also: under **lock²** and **key**.

keys

key

key² /kiː/ *adjective* very important in influencing or achieving something *a key factor*

key³ /kiː/ *verb*

key sth in to put information into a computer or machine using a keyboard

keyboard /ˈkiːbɔːd/ *noun* [C] **1** a set of buttons on a computer, which you press to make it work, or the rows of keys on a piano ➲See colour picture **The Office** on page Centre 5. **2** an electrical

---

musical instrument similar to a piano

keyhole /ˈkiːhəʊl/ *noun* [C] a hole in a lock where you put a key

keynote /ˈkiːnəʊt/ *noun* [C] the most important part of an event, idea, or speech, or something that is emphasized strongly *the keynote speech/speaker*

keypad /ˈkiːpæd/ *noun* [C] a set of buttons with numbers on them used to operate a television, telephone, etc

'key ˌring *noun* [C] a metal ring used for keeping keys together

kg *written abbreviation for* kilogram (= a unit for measuring weight)

khaki /ˈkɑːki/ *noun* [U] a pale green-brown colour, often worn by soldiers ● **khaki** *adjective* ⇒See colour picture Colours on page Centre 12.

kibbutz /kɪˈbʊts/ *noun* [C] *plural* kibbutzim a place in Israel where people live and work together, often a farm or a factory

o⊷**kick¹** /kɪk/ *verb* **1** [I, T] to hit or move something or someone with your foot *The boys were kicking a ball back and forth.* ○ *They tried to kick the door down.* **2** [I] to move your feet and legs forwards or backwards quickly and with force *I kicked at them and screamed for help.* **3 kick yourself** *informal* to be very annoyed with yourself for doing something stupid or wrong *I could have kicked myself for saying that.* ⇒See also: be alive and kicking/well.

be kicking about/around *informal* If something is kicking about, it is in a particular place, but nobody is using it or paying attention to it. *We've probably got a copy of the document kicking around the office.*

kick in *informal* to start to be effective or to happen *The new tax rate kicks in next month.*

kick off When a football match or other event kicks off, it starts. **2** to start to get angry or complain

kick (sth) off *informal* When you kick off a discussion or activity, you start it.

kick sb out *informal* to force someone to leave a place or organization *His wife kicked him out.*

kick² /kɪk/ *noun* **1** [C] when you kick something with your foot *He gave her a kick in the ribs.* **2** [C] *informal* a special feeling of excitement and energy *She gets a kick out of performing live.* **3 a kick in the teeth** used when someone treats you badly or unfairly, especially when you need or expect support *This latest pay award amounts to a kick in the teeth.* ⇒See also: free kick.

kickback /ˈkɪkbæk/ *noun* [C] *US* money given to someone, especially illegally, for providing help, a job, or a piece of business

kickboxing /ˈkɪkˌbɒksɪŋ/ *noun* [U] a sport in which two people fight by hitting each other with their hands and kicking each other with their feet

kick-off /ˈkɪkɒf/ *noun* [C, U] the time when a football match begins

o⊷**kid¹** /kɪd/ *noun* [C] **1** *informal* a child or young person *school kids* **2** a young goat

kid² /kɪd/ *verb* [I, T] kidding *past* kidded **1** to make a

joke, or to trick someone with a joke **2** to deceive or trick someone into believing something [often reflexive] *You've got to stop kidding yourself. She's not coming back.*

kiddie /ˈkɪdi/ *noun* [C] *informal* a child

kidnap /ˈkɪdnæp/ *verb* [T] kidnapping *past* kidnapped to take someone away using force, usually to obtain money in exchange for releasing them ● **kidnap** *noun* [C] *a kidnap victim/attempt* ● **kidnapper** *noun* [C]

kidnapping /ˈkɪdnæpɪŋ/ *noun* [C, U] when someone is kidnapped

kidney /ˈkɪdni/ *noun* [C] one of the two organs in your body which remove waste from the blood and produce urine

o⊷**kill¹** /kɪl/ *verb* **1** DEATH [I, T] to cause someone or something to die *Sunday's bomb killed 19 people.* ○ *Their son was killed in a road accident.* **2 sb will kill sb** *informal* used to say that someone will be very angry with someone else *Dad will kill me for being late.* **3** END [T] to stop an activity or experience completely *His remark killed the conversation.* **4** CAUSE PAIN [T] *informal* to cause you a lot of pain or effort *My feet are killing me.* ○ *It wouldn't kill you to tidy up occasionally.* ⇒See also: kill time¹.

kill sth/sb off to stop something or someone from existing any more *Lack of funding is killing off local theatres.*

kill² /kɪl/ *noun* **1** [no plural] when an animal is killed **2 go/move in for the kill** to prepare to defeat someone completely or to kill them

killer /ˈkɪləʳ/ *noun* [C] someone who kills, or a disease, substance, or animal that kills *Cancer and heart disease are the UK's biggest killers.* ⇒See also: serial killer.

killing /ˈkɪlɪŋ/ *noun* **1** [C] a murder, or when someone or something is killed *the killing of civilians* **2 make a killing** *informal* to make a lot of money very quickly

kiln /kɪln/ *noun* [C] a large oven for baking bricks and other clay objects until they are hard

kilo /ˈkiːləʊ/ *noun* [C] *short for* kilogram

kilo- /ˈkɪlə-/ *prefix* a thousand *a kilometre* ○ *a kilogram*

kilobyte /ˈkɪləbaɪt/ (*written abbreviation* K) *noun* [C] a unit for measuring the amount of information a computer can store, equal to 1024 bytes

kilogram (*also* *UK* **kilogramme**) (*written abbreviation* kg) /ˈkɪləgræm/ *noun* [C] a unit for measuring weight, equal to 1000 grams

o⊷**kilometre** *UK* (*US* **kilometer**) (*written abbreviation* km) /kɪˈlɒmɪtəʳ, ˈkɪləˌmiːtəʳ/ *noun* [C] a unit for measuring distance, equal to 1000 metres

kilowatt /ˈkɪləwɒt/ (*written abbreviation* kW) *noun* [C] a unit for measuring electrical power, equal to 1000 watts

kilt /kɪlt/ *noun* [C] a traditional Scottish skirt for men, made of heavy material with close vertical folds at the back

kin /kɪn/ *noun* [plural] *formal* the members of your family ⇒See also: next of kin.

o⊷**kind¹** /kaɪnd/ *noun* **1** [C] a type of thing or person *What kind of music do you like?* ○ *All* *kinds of people come to our church.* ○ *Older kids like board games and that kind of thing.* ○ *Her travel company was the first of its kind* (= the first one like it). **2 some kind of** used to talk about something when you are not sure of its exact type *She has some kind of disability.* **3 kind of** *informal* used when you are trying to explain or describe something, but you cannot be exact *It's kind of unusual.* **4 of a kind** used to describe something that exists but is not very good *The school had a swimming pool of a kind, but it was too small for most classes to use.*

kind² /kaɪnd/ *adjective* Kind people do things to help others and show that they care about them. *Your mother was very kind to us.* ○ *It was very kind of you to come and see me.* ⊃Opposite **unkind.**

kinda /'kaɪndə/ *mainly US informal short for* kind of *I'm kinda busy right now.*

kindergarten /'kɪndə,gɑːtən/ *noun* [C, U] **1** in the UK, a school for children under five **2** in the US, a class in school for children aged five

kind-hearted /,kaɪnd'hɑːtɪd/ *adjective* having a kind character *a kind-hearted family man*

kindly¹ /'kaɪndli/ *adverb* **1** in a kind or generous way *She kindly offered to cook me lunch.* **2** *formal* used in instructions to mean 'please', usually when you are annoyed *Would you kindly get out of my car?* **3 not take kindly to sth** to not like something that someone says or does *He doesn't take kindly to criticism.*

kindly² /'kaɪndli/ *adjective* old-fashioned kind *a kindly old gentleman*

kindness /'kaɪndnəs/ *noun* [C, U] when someone is kind *Thanks for all your kindness this morning.*

king /kɪŋ/ *noun* [C] **1** RULER a male ruler in some countries *King Richard II* ○ *the kings and queens of England* **2** BEST PERSON the best or most important person in a particular activity *He's the new king of pop music.* **3** PLAYING CARD a playing card with a picture of a king on it *the king of spades*

kingdom /'kɪŋdəm/ *noun* **1** [C] a country with a king or queen *the Kingdom of Belgium* **2 the animal/plant kingdom** all animals or plants considered together

kingfisher /'kɪŋ,fɪʃəʳ/ *noun* [C] a small, brightly coloured bird which catches fish from rivers and lakes

king-size (*also* **king-sized**) /'kɪŋsaɪz/ *adjective* very big *a king-size bed* ○ *a king-size duvet* ○ *king-size cigarettes*

kink /kɪŋk/ *noun* [C] a bend in something long and thin *There was a kink in the cassette tape.*

kinky /'kɪŋki/ *adjective informal* involving strange or unusual sexual behaviour *kinky underwear*

kiosk /'kiːɒsk/ *noun* [C] a small building with a window where things like tickets or newspapers are sold *There's a kiosk on the street corner where they sell train tickets.*

kip /kɪp/ *noun* [C, U] *UK informal* a short period of sleep *I might have a kip this afternoon* ○ *Why don't you go home and try to get some kip?* ● **kip** *verb* [I] **kipping** *past* **kipped**

kipper /'kɪpəʳ/ *noun* [C] *UK* a type of fish that has been cut open and dried over smoke

kiss¹ /kɪs/ *verb* [I, T] **kiss** to press your lips against another person's lips or skin to show love or affection *He kissed her cheek.* ○ *Len kissed Samantha goodbye at the front gate.*

kiss² /kɪs/ *noun* [C] **1** an act of kissing someone *She ran up and gave me a big kiss.* ○ *Do you remember your first kiss?* **2 give sb the kiss of life** *UK* to help to keep someone who has stopped breathing alive by blowing into their mouth

kit /kɪt/ *noun* **1** COLLECTION [C] a collection of things kept in a container ready for a particular use *a first-aid/tool kit* **2** CLOTHES [C, U] *UK* a set of clothes worn for sport or military service *Don't forget your football kit.* **3** PARTS [C] a set of parts which you put together to make something *He's making a model car from a kit.*

kitchen /'kɪtʃɪn/ *noun* [C] a room used to prepare and cook food in *I was in the kitchen, making dinner, at the time.* ⊃See colour picture **The Kitchen** on page Centre 2.

kite /kaɪt/ *noun* [C] a toy made of paper or cloth which flies in the air on the end of a long string *We spent the morning flying a kite in the local park.*

kitsch /kɪtʃ/ *noun* [U] decorative objects or

pieces of art that are ugly, silly, or have little value

kitten /ˈkɪtᵊn/ *noun* [C] a young cat

kitty /ˈkɪti/ *noun* [C] an amount of money consisting of a share from everyone in a group, used for a special purpose [usually singular] *We all put money into a kitty to pay for drinks.*

kiwi /ˈkiːwiː/ (*also* ˈkiwi ˌfruit) *noun* [C] a small, green fruit with black seeds and brown, hairy skin

km *written abbreviation for* kilometre (= a unit for measuring distance)

---

knack /næk/ *noun* [no plural] a special skill, or the ability to use or do something easily *a knack for remembering faces* ○ *She has the knack of making people feel comfortable.*

knackered /ˈnækəd/ *adjective UK informal* extremely tired

knead /niːd/ *verb* [T] to press and shape the mixture for making bread firmly and repeatedly with your hands

o⇥**knee** /niː/ *noun* [C] **1** the middle part of your leg where it bends *a knee injury* ⇨See colour picture **The Body** on page Centre 13. **2** the part of a pair of trousers that covers the knee **3 bring sb/sth to their knees** to destroy or defeat someone or something *The war brought the country to its knees.*

kneecap /ˈniːkæp/ *noun* [C] the round bone at the front of your knee

knee-deep /ˌniːˈdiːp/ *adjective* **1** reaching as high as someone's knees *knee-deep in cold water* **2 be knee-deep in sth** to have a lot of something to deal with *I'm knee-deep in paperwork.*

knee-jerk /ˈniːdʒɜːk/ *adjective* **a knee-jerk reaction/response, etc** an immediate reaction that does not allow you time to consider something carefully

kneel

kneel /niːl/ *verb* [I] *past* knelt *or* kneeled to go down into or stay in a position where one or both of your knees are on the ground *She knelt down beside the child.*

knew /njuː/ *past tense of* know

knickers /ˈnɪkəz/ *UK* (*US* panties) *noun* [plural] women's underwear that covers the bottom ⇨See Common learner error at **underwear.**⇨See colour picture **Clothes** on page Centre 9.

---

o⇥**knife¹** /naɪf/ *noun* [C] *plural* knives a sharp tool or weapon for cutting, usually with a metal blade and a handle *a knife and fork*

knife² /naɪf/ *verb* [T] to attack someone using a knife ⇨See also: jack-knife.

knight¹ /naɪt/ *noun* [C] **1** a man of high social rank who fought as a soldier on a horse in the past **2** a man who has been given the title 'Sir' by the King or Queen in the UK

knight² /naɪt/ *verb* **be knighted** to be given a knighthood

knighthood /ˈnaɪthʊd/ *noun* [C] the title of 'Sir' given to someone by the King or Queen in the UK

knit /nɪt/ *verb* [I, T] knitting, *past tense* knitted, *past participle* knitted (*UK*) knit (*US*) to make clothes using wool and two long needles to join the wool into rows *She was knitting him a jumper.*

knit

knitting /ˈnɪtɪŋ/ *noun* [U] when something is being knitted or the thing that is being knitted *She put down her knitting.*

knitwear /ˈnɪtweəʳ/ *noun* [U] knitted clothes

knob /nɒb/ *noun* **1** [C] a round handle, or a round button on a machine *a door knob* ○ *Turn the black knob to switch on the radio.* **2 a knob of butter** *UK* a small lump of butter

o⇥**knock¹** /nɒk/ *verb* **1** [MAKE NOISE] [I] to make a noise by hitting something, especially a door, with your closed hand in order to attract someone's attention *There's someone knocking at/on the door.* ○ *Please knock before entering.* **2** [HIT] [T] to hit something or someone and make them move or fall down *He accidentally knocked the vase off the table.* ○ *I knocked over the mug.* **3** [CRITICIZE] [T] *informal* to criticize someone or something, often unfairly *She knocks every suggestion I make.* **4 Knock it off!** *informal* something you say when you want someone to stop doing something that is annoying you ⇨See also: beat/knock the (living) daylights out of sb.

COMMON LEARNER ERROR

knock

Be careful to use the correct prepositions. You do not always need one.
The policeman knocked on/knocked at the door.
~~Listen! There is someone knocking to the door.~~
Knock before you come in.

---

knock sth back *UK informal* to drink alcohol very quickly

knock sb down *UK* to hit someone with a vehicle and injure or kill them [often passive] *She was knocked down by a bus.*

knock sb/sth down *US* to cause someone or something to fall to the ground by hitting them

K

knock sth down to destroy a building or part of a building

knock off *informal* to stop working, usually at the end of a day *I don't knock off until six.*

knock sth off (sth) to take a particular amount away from something, usually a price *The manager knocked $5 off because it was damaged.*

knock sb out 1 to make someone become unconscious, usually by hitting them on the head *He was knocked out halfway through the fight.* **2** to defeat a person or team in a competition so they cannot take part any more [often passive] *The French team were knocked out in the semifinal.*

knock² /nɒk/ *noun* [C] **1** a sudden short noise made when something or someone hits a surface *a knock at/on the door* **2** when someone or something is hit, sometimes causing damage or injury *a knock on the head*

knocker /ˈnɒkəʳ/ *noun* [C] a metal object fixed to the outside of a door which visitors use to knock

knock-on /ˌnɒkˈɒn/ *adjective* UK **a knock-on effect** When an event or situation has a knock-on effect, it causes another event or situation. *Cutting schools' budgets will have a knock-on effect on teachers' jobs.*

knockout /ˈnɒkaʊt/ *noun* [C] in boxing, when one person hits the other hard and they become unconscious

knot¹ /nɒt/ *noun* **1** [C] a place where pieces of string, rope, etc have been tied together **2** [C] a unit for measuring the speed of the wind, ships, or aircraft **3 tie the knot** *informal* to get married

knot² /nɒt/ *verb* [T] **knotting** *past* **knotted** to tie knots in pieces of string, rope, etc

oʻ**know¹** /nəʊ/ *verb past tense* **knew,** *past participle* **known 1** [HAVE INFORMATION] [I, T] to have knowledge or information about something in your mind *"How old is she?" "I don't know."* ○ *Andrew knows a lot about computers.* ○ [+ question word] *Do you know where the station is?* ○ [+ (that)] *He knew that she was lying.* **2** [BE FAMILIAR WITH] [T] to be familiar with a person, place, or thing because you have met them, been there, used it, etc before *I've known Tim since primary school.* ○ *I grew up in Brussels so I know it well.* ○ *Since moving to London, I've got to know* (= become familiar with) *some nice people.* **3** [BE ABLE] [T] to be able to do something [+ question word] *Do you know how to ski?* ○ *I only know* (= understand and speak) *a little Spanish.* **4 let sb know** to tell someone something *Let me know if you're going to the party.* **5** [GUESS CORRECTLY] [T] to guess something correctly *I knew she'd arrive late.* ○ *I should have known he wouldn't come.* **6** [UNDERSTAND] [I, T] to

understand and agree with someone *I know what you mean about Pete - I wouldn't trust him at all.* **7 be known as sth** to be called *California is also known as the Sunshine State.* **8 have known sth** to have had experience of something *I've never known the weather be so hot.* **9 know better (than to do sth)** to have the intelligence or judgment not to do something *She should have known better than to eat so much. No wonder she feels sick now.* **10 I know a** [AGREEING] used when you agree with something someone has just said *"It's a lovely day, isn't it?" "I know - let's hope it lasts."* **b** [NEW IDEA] used when you have an idea *I know - let's go to Helen's house.* **11 you know a** used to emphasize that someone does know what you are referring to *You know, he's the one with curly hair.* **b** something that you say while you are thinking what to say next *It's, you know, supposed to be a surprise.* **c** used to emphasize what you are saying *I'm not an idiot, you know.* **12 as far as I know** used to say that you think something is true, but cannot be sure *As far as I know, he's never been in prison.* **13 you never know** used to say that something could be possible although it does not seem likely *You never know - you might win the lottery.* **14 before you know it** very soon *We'll be there before you know it.* ⊃See also: know sth **inside¹** out, learn/know the ropes (**rope¹**), know your **stuff¹**.

meet, get to know and know

When you **meet someone**, you see or speak to them for the first time. When you **get to know someone**, you learn more about them and after this you can say that you **know** them.

I met Nick on holiday.

~~I know Nick on holiday.~~

We got to know each other and became good friends.

~~We knew each other and became friends.~~

How long have you known Nick?

~~How long have you got to know Nick?~~

know or find out?

To **know** something means to already have information about something.

Kelly knows what time the train leaves.

His parents already know about the problem.

To **find out** something means to learn new information for the first time.

Can you find out what time the train leaves?

His parents were angry when they found out about the problem.

know of sth/sb to have heard of something or someone and have a little information about them *I know of a good restaurant near the station.*

know² /nəʊ/ *noun* **be in the know** to have knowledge about something which not everyone knows *People in the know were sure the film* *would win an Oscar.*

know-how /ˈnəʊhaʊ/ *noun* [U] practical skill and knowledge *technical know-how*

knowing /ˈnəʊɪŋ/ *adjective* A knowing smile, look, etc shows that you know what another person is really thinking. *He gave me a knowing wink.*

knowingly /ˈnəʊɪŋli/ *adverb* **1** If you knowingly do something, you mean to do it although it is wrong. **2** showing that you know what another person is really thinking *He smiled knowingly.*

> **WORD PARTNERS FOR *knowledge***
>
> common / detailed / firsthand / poor / thorough knowledge • knowledge about/of sth • have/gain/impart knowledge

o-**knowledge** /ˈnɒlɪdʒ/ *noun* **1** [U, no plural] information and understanding that you have in your mind *He has a detailed knowledge of naval history.* ○ *He took the car without my knowledge* (= I did not know). **2 to (the best of) sb's knowledge** used to say that someone thinks that something is true, but cannot be sure *To the best of my knowledge, she's never worked abroad.*

COMMON LEARNER ERROR

knowledge

Remember you cannot make **knowledge** plural. Do not say 'knowledges'.

I have some knowledge of French and German.

knowledgeable /ˈnɒlɪdʒəbl/ *adjective* knowing a lot *He's very knowledgeable about art.*

known¹ /nəʊn/ *adjective* recognized or known about by most people *He's a member of a known terrorist organization.* ⊃Opposite un-

known ⊃See also: well-known.

known² /nəʊn/ *past participle of* know

knuckle¹ /ˈnʌkl/ *noun* [C] one of the parts of your finger where it bends ⊃See also: a **rap**¹ on/ across/over the knuckles.

knuckle² /ˈnʌkl/ *verb*

knuckle down to start to work or study hard

koala /kəʊˈɑːlə/ (*also* koˈala ˌbear) *noun* [C] an Australian animal like a small bear with grey fur which lives in trees and eats leaves

koala

the Koran /kɒrˈɑːn/ ⓤ /kəˈræn/ *noun* the holy book of Islam

kosher /ˈkəʊʃəʳ/ *adjective* Kosher food is prepared according to Jewish law.

kph *written abbreviation for* kilometres per hour: a unit for measuring speed *a car travelling at 100 kph*

kudos /ˈkjuːdɒs/ *noun* [U] praise and respect for what you have done

kung fu /kʌŋˈfuː/ *noun* [U] a sport from China in which people fight using their hands and feet

Kurdish /ˈkɜːdɪʃ/ *adjective* belonging or relating to a Muslim people living in parts of Turkey, Iran, Iraq, etc • **Kurd** /kɜːd/ *noun* [C] a Kurdish person

kW (*also* **kw**) *written abbreviation for* kilowatt (= a unit for measuring electrical power)

K

Ll

L, l /el/ the twelfth letter of the alphabet

l *written abbreviation for* litre (= a unit for measuring liquid)

lab /læb/ *noun* [C] *short for* laboratory (= a room used for scientific work)

label[1] /ˈleɪbᵊl/ *noun* [C] **1** [INFORMATION] a small piece of paper or other material which gives information about the thing it is fixed to *There should be washing instructions on the label.* **2** [WORD] a word or phrase that is used to describe the qualities of someone or something, usually in a way that is not fair *He seems to be stuck with the label of 'troublemaker'.* **3** [MUSIC] (*also* **record label**) a company that records and sells music *They've just signed a deal with a major record label.*

label[2] /ˈleɪbᵊl/ *verb* [T] *UK* **labelling**, *past* **labelled**, *US* **labeling**, *past* **labeled** **1** to fix a small piece of paper or other material to something which gives information about it *All food has to be labelled with 'best before' or 'use by' dates.* **2** to describe the qualities of someone or something using a word or phrase, usually in a way that is not fair [often passive] *They've been unfairly* ***labelled as*** *criminals.*

labor /ˈleɪbəʳ/ *noun, verb US spelling of* labour

laboratory /ləˈbɒrətᵊri/ [US] /ˈlæbrətɔːri/ *noun* [C] a room used for scientific work *research laboratories* ○ *a computer laboratory* ➲See also: **language laboratory**.

laborer /ˈleɪbᵊrəʳ/ *noun* [C] *US spelling of* labourer *a day laborer*

laborious /ləˈbɔːriəs/ *adjective* Laborious work is very difficult and needs a lot of effort. *a* ***laborious task***

labors /ˈleɪbəz/ *noun* [plural] *US spelling of* labours *You want to earn something for your labors.*

ˈlabor ˌunion *US* (*UK/US* **trade union**) *noun* [C] an organization that represents people who do a particular job

labour[1] *UK* (*US* **labor**) /ˈleɪbəʳ/ *noun* **1** [WORK] [U] work, especially the type of work that needs a lot of physical effort ***manual labour*** **2** [WORKERS] [U] people who work ***cheap/skilled labour*** **3** [BIRTH] [C, U] the stage of pregnancy when a woman has pain in her stomach because the baby is coming out *to be* ***in labour***/ ***go into labour*** ○ ***labour pains*** **4** **Labour** [group] *short for* the Labour Party *I voted Labour* (= for the Labour party) *at the last election.* ○ *a Labour MP* **5** **a labour of love** work that you do because you like it, not because you are paid for it

labour[2] *UK formal* (*US* **labor**) /ˈleɪbəʳ/ *verb* [I] to work hard *He laboured night and day to get the house finished on time.*

labourer *UK* (*US* **laborer**) /ˈleɪbᵊrəʳ/ *noun* [C] a worker who uses a lot of physical effort in their job *a farm labourer*

the ˈLabour ˌParty *noun* [group] one of the three main political parties in the UK

labours (*US* **labors**) /ˈleɪbəz/ *noun* [plural] **sb's labours** work done with a lot of effort *He earned a mere $15 for his labours.*

lace[1] /leɪs/ *noun* **1** [U] a delicate cloth with patterns of holes *a lace curtain* **2** [C] a string used to tie shoes *to tie/untie your laces*

lace[2] /leɪs/ *verb*

lace sth up to fasten something with laces *He laced up his boots.*

be laced with sth If food or drink is laced with alcohol or a drug, a small amount has been added to it. *coffee laced with brandy*

lacerate /ˈlæsᵊreɪt/ *verb* [T] *formal* to make deep cuts in someone's skin *a lacerated arm* ○ *The man's face was severely lacerated in the accident.* • **laceration** /ˌlæsᵊrˈeɪʃᵊn/ *noun* [C] *formal* a cut

WORD PARTNERS FOR ***lack***

a complete/distinct/marked/total lack of sth • **an apparent** lack of sth

🔑**lack**[1] /læk/ *noun* **lack of sth** not having something, or not having enough of something *a lack of food/money*

🔑**lack**[2] /læk/ *verb* **1** [T] to not have something, or not have enough of something *She really lacks confidence.* ○ *What we lack in this house is space to store things.* **2** **be lacking** If something that you need is lacking, you do not have enough of it. *Enthusiasm has been sadly lacking these past few months at work.* **3** **be lacking in sth** to not have a quality *He's totally lacking in charm of any sort.*

lacklustre *UK* (*US* **lackluster**) /ˈlækˌlʌstəʳ/ *adjective* without energy or excitement *a* ***lacklustre performance***

laconic /ləˈkɒnɪk/ *adjective formal* using very few words to express yourself *laconic humour/wit*

lacquer /ˈlækəʳ/ *noun* [U] a clear, hard substance which is painted on wood or metal to protect it

lad /læd/ *noun* [C] *UK* a boy or young man *a nice young lad* ○ *(informal) He's having a night out with* ***the lads*** (= his male friends).

ladder /ˈlædəʳ/ *noun* [C] a piece of equipment which is used to reach high places, consisting of short steps fixed between two long sides ➲See also: the first/highest/next, etc **rung**[1] of the ladder.

ladder

laddish /ˈlædɪʃ/ *adjective UK* rude, noisy and typical of the way that young men behave in groups

laden /ˈleɪdᵊn/ *adjective* **be laden with sth** to be holding a

L

lot of something *She staggered home, laden with shopping.*

the ladies /'leɪdiz/ *noun* [group] *UK* a toilet in a public place for women *Where's the ladies?* ⊃See Common learner error at **toilet.**

'ladies' ,room *noun* [C] *US* a room in a public place where there are women's toilets ⊃See Common learner error at **toilet.**

ladle /'leɪdl/ *noun* [C] a large, deep spoon, used to serve soup ⊃See colour picture **The Kitchen** on page Centre 2.

o-**lady** /'leɪdi/ *noun* **1** [C] a polite way of saying 'woman' *There's a young lady here to see you.* ○ *Ladies and gentlemen, can I have your attention please?* **2 Lady** a title used before the name of some women of high social rank in the UK *Lady Alison Weir*

ladybird /'leɪdibɜːd/ *UK* (*US* **ladybug** /'leɪdibʌg/) *noun* [C] a small flying insect which is usually red with black spots

lag¹ /læg/ (*also* **time lag**) *noun* [C] a period of time between two things happening *You have to allow for a time lag between order and delivery.* ⊃See also: **jet lag.**

lag² /læg/ *verb* lagging, *past* lagged
lag behind (sb/sth) 1 to move more slowly than someone or something else so that you are behind them **2** to achieve less than someone or something else *Britain is lagging far behind the rest of Europe on this issue.*

lager /'lɑːgəʳ/ *noun* [C, U] a pale yellow beer *A pint of lager, please.*

lagoon /lə'guːn/ *noun* [C] a lake that contains sea water

laid /leɪd/ *past of* lay

laid-back /,leɪd'bæk/ *adjective informal* very relaxed and not seeming worried about anything *a laid-back style of teaching* ○ *He's very laid-back.*

lain /leɪn/ *past participle of* lie¹

laissez-faire /,leɪseɪ'feəʳ/ *adjective* allowing things to happen and not trying to control them *a laissez-faire attitude*

o-**lake** /leɪk/ *noun* [C] a large area of water which has land all around it *Lake Windermere*

lamb /læm/ *noun* **1** [C] a young sheep *a newborn lamb* ○ *a lamb's-wool sweater* **2** [U] meat from a young sheep *grilled lamb chops* ○ *roast leg of lamb* ⊃See also: **mutton** dressed as lamb.

lame /leɪm/ *adjective* **1** A lame excuse or explanation is one that you cannot believe. *He said he didn't go because it was raining, which is a pretty lame excuse if you ask me.* **2** A lame animal or person cannot walk because they have an injured foot or leg. *a lame horse*

lament /lə'ment/ *verb* [I, T] *formal* to say that you are disappointed about a situation *He was lamenting the fact that so few people read fiction nowadays.*

lamentable /'læməntəbl/ *adjective formal* extremely bad *a lamentable performance*

lamp /læmp/ *noun* [C] a piece of equipment that produces light *a table lamp* ○ *an oil lamp* ⊃See colour picture **The Living Room** on page Centre 4.

lamppost /'læmppəʊst/ *noun* [C] a tall post with a light at the top, which you see on roads where there are houses

lampshade /'læmpʃeɪd/ *noun* [C] a decorative cover for an electric light ⊃See colour picture **The Living Room** on page Centre 4.

LAN /læn/ *noun* [C] *abbreviation for* local area network: a system that connects the computers of people who work in the same building

o-**land¹** /lænd/ *noun* **1** [AREA] [U] an area of ground *agricultural land* ○ *undeveloped land* ⊃See Common learner error at **country. 2** [NOT SEA] [U] the surface of the Earth that is not sea *to travel over land and sea* **3** [COUNTRY] [C] *literary* a country *a land of ice and snow* ⊃See also: **no-man's land.**

COMMON LEARNER ERROR

land or **country**?

Land is only used to mean 'country' in literary writing or poems. In ordinary speech or writing, it is better to use country.

I enjoyed visiting their country.

~~I enjoyed visiting their land.~~

o-**land²** /lænd/ *verb* **1** [I, T] If an aircraft lands, it arrives on the ground after a journey, and if you land it, you make it arrive on the ground. *We should land in Madrid at 7 a.m.* ○ *He managed to land the helicopter on the cliff.* **2 land in/on, etc** If an object or person lands somewhere, they fall to the ground there. *She landed flat on her back.* **3** [T] to get something, usually something good *He's just landed a new job at an agency in London.*

land sb in sth to cause someone to be in a difficult situation *His remarks have landed him in a lot of trouble with the association.*

land sb with sth If something lands you with problems, it causes problems for you. *The project's failure has landed him with debts of over £50,000.*

landfill /'lændfɪl/ *noun* [C] a place where waste is buried in the ground *a landfill site*

landing /'lændɪŋ/ *noun* [C] **1** an arrival on the ground, usually of an aircraft or boat *They had to make an emergency landing in Chicago.* **2** the area of floor at the top of a set of stairs

landlady /'lænd,leɪdi/ *noun* [C] a woman who you rent a room or house from

landline /'lændlaɪn/ *noun* [C] a telepone that is not a mobile phone

landlord /'lændlɔːd/ *noun* [C] a man who rent a room or house from

landmark /'lændmɑːk/ *noun* [C] **1** a building that you can easily recognize, especially one that helps you to know where you are *a historic landmark* **2** an event which is famous or important in the history of something *His speech was a landmark in the history of civil rights.*

landmine /'lændmaɪn/ *noun* [C] a bomb which is hidden in the ground

landowner /'lændəʊnəʳ/ *noun* [C] someone who owns a lot of land *a wealthy landowner*

L

landscape /ˈlændskeɪp/ *noun* [C] the appearance of an area of land, especially in the countryside *The cathedral dominates the landscape for miles around.*

landslide /ˈlændslaɪd/ *noun* [C] **1** when rocks and soil slide down a mountain or hill **2** an easy victory in an election *a **landslide defeat/victory***

> WORD PARTNERS FOR ***lane***
>
> **in** the [inside/fast, etc] lane • the **fast/slow** lane

lane /leɪn/ *noun* [C] **1** [PART] part of a road or track that is separated from the other parts, usually by a painted line *the inside/middle/outside lane ○ the **fast/slow lane*** **2** [ROAD] a narrow road, usually in the countryside *We drove down a winding country lane.* **3** [BOATS/AIRCRAFT] a route that is regularly used by boats or aircraft *It's one of the world's busiest shipping lanes.*

> WORD PARTNERS FOR ***language***
>
> **learn/speak** a language • **foreign** languages • **foul/native/official/strong** language

⊶**language** /ˈlæŋɡwɪdʒ/ *noun* **1** [COMMUNICATION] [U] communication between people, usually using words *She has done research into how children acquire language.* **2** [ENGLISH/SPANISH/JAPANESE ETC] [C] a type of communication used by the people of a particular country *How many **languages** do you **speak**?* **3** [TYPE OF WORDS] [U] words of a particular type, especially the words used by people in a particular job *legal language ○ the language of business* **4** [COMPUTERS] [C, U] a system of instructions that is used to write computer programs ➲See also: **body language, modern languages, second language, sign language.**

ˈ**language laˌboratory** *UK* (*US* ˈ**language ˌlaboratory**) *noun* [C] a room in a college or school where you can use equipment to help you practise listening to and speaking a foreign language

languid /ˈlæŋɡwɪd/ *adjective literary* moving or speaking slowly and with little energy, often in an attractive way *a languid manner/voice*

languish /ˈlæŋɡwɪʃ/ *verb* [I] *formal* **languish at/in, etc sth** to stay in an unpleasant or difficult situation for a long time *to languish in jail*

lanky /ˈlæŋki/ *adjective informal* A lanky person is very tall and thin.

lantern /ˈlæntən/ *noun* [C] a light that can be carried, usually with a candle inside it *a paper lantern*

lap¹ /læp/ *noun* [C] **1** Your lap is the top part of your legs when you are sitting down. *Sit on my lap and I'll read you a story.* **2** one journey around a circular race track *He's two laps behind the leaders.*

lap² /læp/ *verb* **lapping**, *past* **lapped lap against/on, etc sth** If water laps against something, it touches it gently in waves.

lap sth up *informal* to enjoy something very much *He loved all the attention - he was lapping it up!*

lapel /ləˈpel/ *noun* [C] the part of a collar that is folded against the front of a shirt or jacket *wide lapels* ➲See picture at **jacket**.

> WORD PARTNERS FOR ***lapse***
>
> a **momentary** lapse • a lapse **in/of** sth

lapse¹ /læps/ *noun* [C] **1** a period of time when something fails to happen as it should *a memory lapse ○ It is thought that the accident was caused by a **lapse of** concentration.* **2** a period of time passing between two things happening *a **time lapse**/a **lapse of time** ○ He turned up again after a lapse of two years.*

lapse² /læps/ *verb* [I] If an arrangement lapses, it stops existing because of the amount of time that has passed. *I've allowed my membership to lapse.*

lapse into sth If you lapse into something, you change to a different, and usually bad, condition. *to lapse into silence*

laptop /ˈlæptɒp/ *noun* [C] a computer that is small enough to be carried around and used where you are sitting

laptop

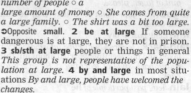

⊶**large** /lɑːdʒ/ *adjective* **1** big in size or amount *a large number of people ○ a large amount of money ○ She comes from quite a large family. ○ The shirt was a bit too large.* ➲Opposite **small**. **2 be at large** If someone dangerous is at large, they are not in prison. **3 sb/sth at large** people or things in general *This group is not representative of the population at large.* **4 by and large** in most situations *By and large, people have welcomed the changes.*

largely /ˈlɑːdʒli/ *adverb* mainly *Their complaints have been largely ignored.*

large-scale /ˌlɑːdʒˈskeɪl/ *adjective* involving a lot of people or happening in big numbers *a large-scale development ○ large-scale redundancies*

lark /lɑːk/ *noun* [C] a small brown bird that is known for its beautiful singing

larva /ˈlɑːvə/ *noun* [C] *plural* **larvae** /ˈlɑːviː/ the form of some creatures, for example insects, before they develop into a different form *insect larvae*

lasagne *UK* (*US* **lasagna**) /ləˈzænjə/ [US] /ləˈzɑːnjə/ *noun* [U] a type of Italian food consisting of flat pieces of pasta with layers of meat and sauce in between

laser /ˈleɪzəʳ/ *noun* [C] a strong beam of light that has medical and technical uses *a **laser beam** ○ **laser surgery***

ˈ**laser ˌprinter** *noun* [C] a printer (= a machine which is connected to a computer and which produces writing or pictures) which uses a laser (= a strong beam of light) to produce very clear writing or pictures

lash¹ /læʃ/ *verb* **1** [I, T] If wind or rain lashes against something, the wind or rain is very strong and hits or blows hard against it. *Rain lashed against the window.* **2 lash sth down/together, etc** to tie something firmly to something else

lash out 1 to suddenly hit someone *He lashed out and caught her on the side of the face.* **2** to criticize someone angrily *The protestor lashed out at the government for refusing to take action.*

lash² /læʃ/ *noun* [C] a hit with a whip (= long, thin piece of leather) *He was given forty lashes.*

lashes /ˈlæʃɪz/ *noun* [plural] the small hairs on the edges of your eye

lass /læs/ *noun* [C] *UK informal* a girl or a young woman *a young lass*

○ʷ**last¹** /lɑːst/ *adjective, determiner* **1** MOST RECENT [always before noun] the most recent *What was the last film you saw?* ○ *It's rained for the last three days.* **2** ONE BEFORE PRESENT [always before noun] The last book, house, job, etc is the one before the present one. *I liked his last book but I'm not so keen on this latest one.* **3** FINAL happening or coming at the end *It's the last room on the left.* ○ *That's the last programme of the series.* ○ *I was the last one to arrive.* ○ *"How did she get on in her race?" "She was last."* **4** REMAINING [always before noun] only remaining *Who wants the last piece of cake?* **5 the last person/thing, etc** the least expected or wanted person or thing *Three extra people to feed - that's the last thing I need!* ○ *He's the last person you'd expect to see at an aerobics class.* ⊃Opposite **first** ⊃See also: be on its last legs (**leg**), the final/last straw, have the last **word¹**.

○ʷ**last²** /lɑːst/ *adverb* **1** after everything or everyone else *I wasn't expecting to win the race but I didn't think I'd come last!* ○ *We've still got to check the figures but we'll do that last.* **2** used to talk about the most recent time you did something *When did you last see her?* **3 last but not least** something that you say to introduce the last person or thing on a list *This is Jeremy, this is Cath and, last but not least, this is Eva.* ⊃Opposite **first**.

○ʷ**last³** /lɑːst/ *noun, pronoun* **1 the last** a person or thing that comes after all the others [+ to do sth] *We were the last to get there.* **2 the last of sth** the only part of something that remains *We've just finished the last of the wine.* **3 the day/week/year before last** the day, week, or year before the one that has just finished **4 at (long) last** finally *At last, I've found a pair of jeans that actually fit.* **5 the last I heard** used before saying a piece of information about someone that you previously heard *The last I heard, they were selling their house.*

○ʷ**last⁴** /lɑːst/ *verb* [I, T] **1** to continue to happen, exist, or be useful *How long will the meeting last?* ○ *We don't get much sun - enjoy it while it lasts!* ○ *The batteries only last about five hours.* **2** to be enough for a period of time *I've only got £30 to last me till the end of the month.* ○ *We've got enough food to last another week.*

last-ditch /ˌlɑːstˈdɪtʃ/ *adjective* **a last-ditch attempt/effort** a final attempt to solve a problem

that you have failed to solve several times before *a last-ditch effort to prevent war*

lasting /ˈlɑːstɪŋ/ *adjective* continuing to exist for a long time *lasting damage* ○ *a lasting friendship*

lastly /ˈlɑːstli/ *adverb* finally *And lastly, I'd like to thank everyone who took part in the event.*

last-minute /ˌlɑːstˈmɪnɪt/ *adjective* done at the last possible time *I was just doing some last-minute preparations.*

ˌ**last 'name** *noun* [C] the name that you and other members of your family all have

latch¹ /lætʃ/ *noun* [C] **1** a small piece of metal on a door that you move down so that the door will stay closed **2** a type of lock for a door that you need a key to open from the outside

latch² /lætʃ/ *verb*

latch on *informal* to begin to understand something *It took me ages to latch on to what she was saying.*

○ʷ**late** /leɪt/ *adjective, adverb* **1** AFTER THE USUAL TIME after the usual time or the time that was arranged *I was late for work this morning.* ○ *We got there too late and all the tickets had been sold.* ○ *We had a late lunch.* **2** NEAR END OF PERIOD near the end of a period of time *It was built in the late nineteenth century.* ○ *It was late at night.* ○ *Marsha is in her late twenties.* **3 it's late** something that you say when it is near the end of a day *It's late - I really should be going.* ○ *It's getting late and I'm a bit tired.* **4** DEAD [always before noun] not now alive *the late Mrs Walker* **5 of late** *formal* recently *We've scarcely seen him of late.*

lately /ˈleɪtli/ *adverb* recently *I haven't been feeling so well lately.* ○ *Lately, I've been walking to work.*

latent /ˈleɪtᵊnt/ *adjective* A feeling or quality that is latent exists now but is hidden or not yet developed. *latent hostility/racism*

later /ˈleɪtəʳ/ *adjective* **1** after some time *I might arrange it for a later date.* **2** more recent *I'm not so familiar with his later work.*

later (on) *adverb* after some time *I'm off now - see you later.* ○ *If you're busy now we could do it later on.*

latest¹ /ˈleɪtɪst/ *adjective* [always before noun] most recent *the latest fashions/news/technology*

latest² /ˈleɪtɪst/ *noun* **1 the latest in sth** the most recent of its type *This is the latest in a series of terrorist attacks in the region.* **2 at the latest** If you tell someone to do something by a particular time at the latest, you mean they must do it before that time. *She said to be there by 8 o'clock at the latest.*

lather /ˈlɑːðəʳ/ *noun* **1** [U] small white bubbles that are produced when soap is used with water **2 get into a lather** *informal* to become anxious or upset about something

Latin /ˈlætɪn/ *noun* [U] the language used by ancient Romans ● **Latin** *adjective*

ˌ**Latin A'merican** *adjective* relating or belonging to the countries of South and Central America, and Mexico ● **Latin American** *noun* [C] a Latin American person

Latino /ləˈtiːnəʊ/ *noun* [C] *US* someone who lives

in the US whose family came from Latin America

latitude /ˈlætɪtjuːd/ *noun* **1** [C, U] the distance of a place north or south of the Equator (= imaginary line around the Earth's middle), measured in degrees *The latitude of Helsinki is approximately 60 degrees north.* **2** [U] *formal* freedom to do what you want *She should be allowed the latitude to choose the people she wants.*

latte /ˈlæteɪ/ [US] /ˈlɑːteɪ/ *noun* [C, U] a drink of coffee made from espresso (= strong coffee) and milk

latter /ˈlætəʳ/ *adjective* [always before noun] *formal* near the end of a period *the* ***latter half*** *of the twentieth century* ○ *She had moved to California in the* ***latter part*** *of the year.* ○ *She is now in the* ***latter stages*** *of the disease.*

the latter /ˈlætəʳ/ *noun* the second of two people or things that have just been talked about *She offered me more money or a car, and I chose the latter.*

latterly /ˈlætəli/ *adverb UK formal* recently *She started her career in radio, but latterly she has been working in television.*

laudable /ˈlɔːdəbl/ *adjective formal* A laudable idea or action deserves admiration, even if it is not successful. *a* ***laudable aim/ambition/goal*** ○ *a* ***laudable attempt/effort***

L

⊶**laugh¹** /lɑːf/ *verb* [I] to smile while making sounds with your voice that show you are happy or think something is funny *I laughed til I had tears in my eyes.* ○ *I could hear you laughing all the way down the corridor.* ○ *You never* ***laugh at*** *my jokes.* ○ *She really* ***makes*** *me* ***laugh***. ○ *It's very rare that a book is so good you* ***laugh out loud***. ○ *It was so funny, we* ***burst out laughing*** (= laughed suddenly and loudly). ⇨See also: be no laughing **matter¹**.

laugh at sb/sth to show that you think someone or something is stupid *I can't go into work looking like this - everyone will laugh at me.* ○ *He seemed offended – I think he thought we were laughing at him.*

laugh sth off to laugh about something unpleasant so that it seems less important *He was upset by the criticism though he tried to laugh it off at the time.* ○ *I can usually laugh off his comments.*

laugh² /lɑːf/ *noun* [C] **1** the act or sound of laughing *a loud/nervous laugh* ○ *She has a very distinctive laugh.* ○ *At the time, I was embarrassed, but I* ***had a good laugh*** (= laughed a lot) *about it later.* **2 be a (good) laugh** *UK informal* to be funny *You'd like David - he's a good laugh.* **3 for a laugh** *informal* If you do something for a laugh, you do it because you think it will be funny. *Just for a laugh, I pretended that I'd forgotten it was his birthday.*

laughable /ˈlɑːfəbl/ *adjective* If something is laughable, it is stupid and you cannot believe it or respect it. *Most people thought his suggestions were laughable.*

ˈlaughing ˌstock *noun* [no plural] someone who does something very stupid which makes other people laugh at them *If I wear this hat, I'll be the laughing stock of the party!*

WORD PARTNERS FOR *laughter*

burst into laughter • **roar** with laughter • be **in fits of** laughter

⊶**laughter** /ˈlɑːftəʳ/ *noun* [U] the sound or act of laughing *I heard the sound of laughter in the room next door.* ○ *The crowd* ***roared with laughter*** (= laughed very loudly).

launch¹ /lɔːnʃ/ *verb* [T] **1** [SEND] to send a spacecraft or bomb into the sky, or a ship into the water *to* ***launch a rocket/satellite*** ○ *to* ***launch a boat/fleet*** **2** [BEGIN] to begin an important activity *to* ***launch an attack/inquiry/investigation*** **3** [NEW PRODUCT] If a company launches a product or service, it makes it available for the first time. *The book was launched last February.* ○ *The airline will launch its new transatlantic service next month.*

launch into sth to start saying or criticizing something with a lot of anger or energy *Then he launched into a verbal attack on her management of the situation.*

launch² /lɔːnʃ/ *noun* [C] **1** [SENDING] the launching of a spacecraft, ship, or weapon *Poor weather delayed the space shuttle's launch.* **2** [BEGINNING] the beginning of an activity *The campaign's launch was a well-publicized event.* **3** [NEW PRODUCT] the time when a new product or service becomes available *The film's launch attracted a lot of Hollywood stars.* **4** [BOAT] a large boat with a motor *a police launch*

launder /ˈlɔːndəʳ/ *verb* [T] to hide the fact that an amount of money has been made illegally by putting the money into legal bank accounts or businesses *to* ***launder*** *drug* ***money*** • **laundering** *noun* [U] ***money laundering***

launderette /ˌlɔːndəʳret/ *UK* (*US* **laundromat** /ˈlɔːndrəmæt/ *trademark*) *noun* [C] a place where you pay to use machines that wash and dry your clothes

laundry /ˈlɔːndri/ *noun* [U] clothes, sheets, etc that need to be washed *to* ***do the laundry*** ○ *a* ***laundry basket***

ˈlaundry deˌtergent *noun* [C, U] *US* washing powder

laurels /ˈlɒrəlz/ *noun* [plural] **rest on your laurels** to be so satisfied with what you have achieved that you make no effort to improve *Just because you've passed your exams, that's no reason to rest on your laurels.*

lava /ˈlɑːvə/ *noun* [U] hot melted rock that comes out of a volcano

lavatory /ˈlævətəri/ [US] *noun* [C] *formal mainly UK* a toilet *to go to the lavatory* ○ *public lavatories* ⇨See Common learner error at toilet.

lavender /ˈlævəndəʳ/ *noun* [U] a plant with purple flowers and a strong, pleasant smell *lavender oil*

lavish¹ /ˈlævɪʃ/ *adjective* showing that a lot of money has been spent *a lavish meal/party*

• **lavishly** *adverb a lavishly illustrated book*
lavish² /ˈlævɪʃ/ *verb*
lavish sth on sb/sth to give a large amount of money, presents, attention, etc to someone or something *They have lavished more than £6 million on the new stadium.*

WORD PARTNERS FOR **law**

break/enforce/obey/pass a law • the law **forbids/prohibits/requires** sth • a law **against** sth • be **against** the law

o-**law** /lɔː/ *noun* **1 the law** the system of official rules in a country *You're breaking the law.* ○ *It's against the law* (= illegal) *not to wear seat belts.* ○ *It's their job to enforce the law.* **2 by law** If you have to do something by law, it is illegal not to do it. *They have to provide a contract by law.* **3** RULE [C] an official rule in a country *There are laws against drinking in the street.* ○ *They led the fight to impose laws on smoking.* **4 law and order** the obeying of laws in society *a breakdown in law and order* **5** SUBJECT [U] the subject or job of understanding and dealing with the official laws of a country *to study/practise law* ○ *a law school/firm* ○ *a specialist in civil/criminal law* **6** ALWAYS TRUE [C] something that is always true in science, mathematics, etc. *the laws of nature/physics* ○ *the law of averages/gravity* **7 lay down the law** to repeatedly tell people what they should do, without caring about how they feel *People are fed up with him laying down the law the whole time.* ○See also: brother-in-law, common-law, daughter-in-law, father-in-law, in-laws, martial law, mother-in-law, sister-in-law, son-in-law.
law-abiding /ˈlɔːəˌbaɪdɪŋ/ *adjective* A law-abiding person always obeys the law. *a law-abiding citizen*
lawful /ˈlɔːfəl/ *adjective* allowed by the law *He was going about his lawful business as a press photographer.*
lawmaker /ˈlɔːˌmeɪkəʳ/ *noun* [C] *US* someone who makes laws *state lawmakers*
lawn /lɔːn/ *noun* [C] an area of grass that is cut *to mow the lawn*
ˈ**lawn ˌmower** *noun* [C] a machine that you use to cut grass
lawsuit /ˈlɔːsuːt/ *noun* [C] a legal complaint against someone that does not usually involve the police *The tenants have filed a lawsuit against their landlord.*
o-**lawyer** /ˈlɔɪəʳ/ *noun* [C] someone whose job is to understand the law and deal with legal situations *I want to see my lawyer before I say anything else.*

COMMON LEARNER ERROR

lawyer, solicitor, barrister, attorney

In Britain, **lawyers** are divided into two types, **solicitors** and **barristers**. **Solicitors** give advice on legal subjects and work in the lower courts of law. **Barristers** can represent people in the higher courts of law. In America, there is only one type of lawyer, who is sometimes called an **attorney**.

lax /læks/ *adjective* not careful enough or not well controlled *They seem to have a very lax attitude towards security.*
o-**lay¹** /leɪ/ *verb past* laid **1 lay sth down/in/on, etc** to put something down somewhere carefully *She laid the baby on the bed.* ○ *He laid the tray down on the table.* **2** [T] to put something into its correct position *to lay a carpet* ○ *to lay bricks* **3 lay eggs** If an animal lays eggs, it produces them out of its body. **4 lay the blame on sb** to blame someone, usually when this is not fair *You always lay the blame on me!* **5 lay the table** *UK* to put plates, knives, forks, etc on the table to prepare for a meal ○See also: put/lay your cards (**card**) on the table, lay the **foundation**(s) for/of sth, get/lay your hands (**hand¹**) on sth, lay down the law.

COMMON LEARNER ERROR

lay and lie

Be careful not to confuse these verbs.
Lay means 'put down carefully' or 'put down flat'. This verb is always followed by an object. **Laying** is the present participle. **Laid** is the past simple and the past participle.
She laid the papers on the desk.
Lie means 'be in a horizontal position' or 'be in a particular place'. This verb is irregular and is never followed by an object. **Lying** is the present participle. **Lay** is the past simple and **lain** is the past participle.
The papers were lying on the desk.
~~The papers were laying on the desk.~~
I lay down and went to sleep.
~~I laid down and went to sleep.~~
The regular verb **lie** means 'not say the truth'.
He lied to me about his age.

lay sth down 1 to officially make new rules, or to officially say how something must be done *The committee has laid down guidelines for future cases.* **2** If someone lays down their weapons, they stop fighting. *It is hoped the two sides will lay down their arms and return to peace.*
lay into sb *informal* to attack or criticize someone *They started laying into me for no reason.*
lay sb off to stop employing someone, usually because there is no more work for them [often passive] *Thirty more people were laid off last week.*
lay sth on to provide something for a group of people *They're laying on free buses to and from the concert.*
lay sth out 1 to arrange something on a surface *He'd laid his tools out all over the kitchen floor.* **2** to explain something clearly, usually in writing *I've just laid out some proposals.*
lay² /leɪ/ *adjective* [always before noun] **1** involved in religious activities, but not trained as a priest *a lay preacher* **2** not having special or detailed knowledge of a subject *a lay person/audience*
lay³ /leɪ/ *past tense of* lie¹

lay-by /'leɪbaɪ/ *noun* [C] *UK* a small area where cars can stop at the side of a road

○━**layer** /leɪəʳ/ *noun* [C] an amount of a substance covering a surface, or one of several amounts of substance, each on top of the other *the outer/top layer* ○ *Place alternate layers of pasta and meat sauce in a shallow dish.* ○ *The shelf was covered in a thick layer of dust.* • layer *verb* [T] [often passive] *The potatoes are layered with onion.* ➔See also: the ozone layer.

layer

layers

layman /'leɪmən/ (*also* **layperson**) *noun* [C] *plural* **laymen** someone who does not have special knowledge of a subject *Could you please explain that in layman's terms* (= in a simple way)?

layoff /'leɪɒf/ *noun* [C] the ending of someone's job by an employer, usually because there is no more work [usually plural] *Several hundred more layoffs are planned next month.*

layout /'leɪaʊt/ *noun* [C] the way that something is arranged *Do you like the new layout of the kitchen?*

○━**lazy** /'leɪzi/ *adjective* **1** Someone who is lazy does not like working or using any effort. *You lazy thing!* ○ *He's too lazy to make his bed in the morning.* **2** slow and relaxed *a lazy morning/weekend* • **lazily** *adverb* • **laziness** *noun* [U]

lb *written abbreviation for* pound (= a unit for measuring weight)

LCD /ˌelsiː'diː/ *noun* [C] *abbreviation for* liquid crystal display: a screen for showing words or pictures which uses a liquid and an electric current *LCD TV*

○━**lead¹** /liːd/ *verb past* **led** /led/ **1** TAKE SOMEONE [I, T] to show someone where to go, usually by taking them to a place or by going in front of them *She led them down the hall.* ○ *We followed a path that led us up the mountain.* ○ *You lead and we'll follow.* ○ *I'll lead the way* (= go first to show the route). **2** lead into/to/towards etc If a path or road leads somewhere, it goes there. *That path leads to the beach.* **3** BE WINNING [I, T] to be winning a game *They were leading by 11 points at half-time.* ○ *The Lions lead the Hawks 28-9.* **4** BE THE BEST [T] to be better than anyone else *I still believe that we lead the world in acting talent.* **5** CONTROL [T] to be in control of a group, country, or situation *to lead a discussion* ○ *Is this man really capable of leading the country?* ○ *Shearer led his team to victory.* **6** lead sb to do sth to cause someone to do or think something *What led you to think*

that? ○ *I was led to believe that breakfast was included.* **7** lead a busy/normal/quiet, etc life to live in a particular way *He was able to lead a normal life despite his illness.* **8** lead sb to a conclusion to cause you to think that something is probably true *So you thought I was leaving, did you? What led you to that conclusion?*

lead to sth to cause something to happen or exist *A poor diet can lead to health problems in later life.*

lead up to sth to happen before an event *The shops are always busy in the weeks leading up to Christmas.*

○━**lead²** /liːd/ *noun* **1** WINNING [no plural] a winning position during a race or other situation where people are competing *She's in the lead* (= winning). ○ *France has just taken the lead* (= started to win). ○ *a three-goal lead* **2** FILM/PLAY [C] the main person in a film or play *She plays the lead in both films.* **3** DOG [C] *UK* (*US* leash) a chain or piece of leather fixed to a dog's collar so that it can be controlled *Dogs must be kept on a lead at all times.* **4** ELECTRICITY [C] *UK* (*US* cord) the wire that connects a piece of electrical equipment to the electricity supply **5** INFORMATION [C] information about a crime that police are trying to solve *Police are chasing up a new lead.*

lead³ /liːd/ *adjective* [always before noun] The lead performer or lead part in a performance is the main performer or part. *the lead singer* ○ *Who played the lead role?*

lead⁴ /led/ *noun* **1** [U] a soft, heavy, grey, poisonous metal used for roofs, pipes, etc *a lead pipe* ○ *lead-free petrol/gasoline* **2** [C, U] the black part inside a pencil

○━**leader** /'liːdəʳ/ *noun* [C] **1** a person in control of a group, country, or situation *a religious leader* ○ *Who's the leader of the Democratic Party in the Senate?* **2** someone or something that is winning during a race or other situation where people are competing *He's fallen two laps behind the leaders.* ○ *Microsoft is a world leader in software design.*

leadership /'liːdəʃɪp/ *noun* **1** [U] the job of being in control of a group, country, or situation *the leadership of the Conservative party* ○ *leadership skills/qualities* ○ *a leadership contest* **2** [group] the people in control of a group, country, or situation *There is growing discontent with the leadership.*

leading /'liːdɪŋ/ *adjective* [always before noun] very important or most important *He's a leading Hollywood producer.*

leaf

○━**leaf¹** /liːf/ *noun* [C] *plural* **leaves** /liːvz/ **1** a flat, green part of a

L

plant that grows from a stem or branch *an oak leaf* ○ *a lettuce leaf* ○ *the falling leaves* **2 take a leaf out of sb's book** *mainly UK* to copy something good that someone else does **3 turn over a new leaf** to start to behave in a better way *I've tried to turn over a new leaf since starting this job.*

leaf² /liːf/ *verb*
leaf through sth to turn the pages of a book or magazine and look at them quickly *She lay on the sofa, leafing through glossy magazines.*

leaflet /ˈliːflət/ *noun* [C] a piece of folded paper or a small book which contains information *I picked up a useful leaflet on how to fill in tax forms.*

leafy /ˈliːfi/ *adjective* [always before noun] A leafy place is pleasant and quiet with a lot of trees. *a leafy lane/suburb*

league /liːg/ *noun* **1** [C] a group of teams which compete against each other in a sport *top/ bottom of the league* ○ *major/minor league baseball* ○ *Who won the league championship this year?* **2 be in league with sb** to be secretly working or planning something with someone, usually to do something bad **3 not be in the same league as sb/sth** *informal* to not be as good as someone or something *It's a nice enough restaurant but it's not in the same league as Rossi's.*

leak¹ /liːk/ *verb* **1** [I, T] If a liquid or gas leaks, it comes out of a hole by accident, and if a container leaks, it allows liquid or gas to come out when it should not. *Water had leaked all over the floor.* ○ *The bottle must have leaked because the bag's all wet.* **2** [T] If someone leaks secret information, they intentionally tell people about it. *Details of the report had been leaked to the press.*
leak out If secret information leaks out, people find out about it.

leak² /liːk/ *noun* [C] **1** a hole in something that a liquid or gas comes out of, or the liquid or gas that comes out *I think we may have a leak in the roof.* ○ *a gas leak* **2** the act of intentionally telling people a secret

leakage /ˈliːkɪdʒ/ *noun* [U] the problem of a liquid or gas coming out of something when it should not

leaky /ˈliːki/ *adjective informal* Something that is leaky has a hole in it and liquid or gas can get through. *a leaky boat/roof*

o— **lean¹** /liːn/ *verb past* leaned (*also UK*) leant /lent/
lean (sth) back/forward/out, etc to move the top part of your body in a particular direction *She leaned forward and whispered in my ear.* ○ *Lean your head back a bit.*
lean (sth) against/on sth to sit or stand with part of your body touching something as a support *He leaned against the wall.* ○ *She leaned her head on his shoulder.*
lean sth against/on sth to put something against a wall or other surface so that it is supported *Lean the ladder against the wall.*
lean on sb/sth to use someone or something to help you, especially in a difficult situation *Her mother had always leaned on her for support.*

lean² /liːn/ *adjective* **1** thin and healthy *lean and fit* **2** Lean meat has very little fat on it.

leaning /ˈliːnɪŋ/ *noun* [C] a belief or idea [usually plural] *I don't know what his political leanings are.*

leap¹ /liːp/ *verb past* leapt /lept/ or leaped **1 leap into/out of/up, etc** to suddenly move somewhere *He leapt out of his car and ran towards the house.* ○ *I leapt up to answer the phone.* **2 leap off/over/into, etc** to jump somewhere *She leapt over the wall and disappeared down the alley.*
leap at sth to accept the chance to have or do something with enthusiasm *I'd leap at the opportunity to work in Japan.*

WORD PARTNERS FOR **leap** (noun)

a leap **in** sth ● a leap **of** [75%/5 million, etc] ● a leap **forward**

leap² /liːp/ *noun* [C] **1** a sudden improvement or increase *There was a big leap in profits last year.* ○ *This represents a great leap forward in technology.* **2** a big jump *He finished third in the long jump with a leap of 26 feet.* **3 by/in leaps and bounds** If progress or growth happens in leaps and bounds, it happens very quickly. ⮑See also: **quantum leap**.

leap ˌyear *noun* [C] a year that happens every four years, in which February has 29 days instead of 28

o— **learn** /lɜːn/ *verb past* learned (*also UK*) learnt /lɜːnt/ **1** GET SKILL [I, T] to get knowledge or skill in a new subject or activity *I learned Russian at school.* ○ *"Can you drive?" "I'm learning."* ○ *She's learned a lot about computers in the last three months.* ○ [+ to do sth] *I'm learning to play the piano.* **2** REMEMBER [T] to make yourself remember a piece of writing by reading or repeating it many times *I don't know how actors learn all those lines.* **3** UNDERSTAND [I, T] to start to understand that you must change the way you behave [+ (that)] *She'll have to learn that she can't have everything she wants.* ○ *The good thing is, he's not afraid to learn from his mistakes.* ⮑See also: learn your lesson, learn/know the ropes (**rope¹**).

COMMON LEARNER ERROR

learn, teach, or study?

To **learn** is to get new knowledge or skills.
I want to learn how to drive.

When you **teach** someone, you give them new knowledge or skills.
My dad taught me how to drive.
~~My dad learnt me how to drive.~~

When you **study**, you go to classes, read books, etc to try to understand new ideas and facts.
He is studying biology at university.

learn about/of sth to hear facts or information that you did not know *We only learned about the accident later.*

learned /ˈlɜːnɪd/ *adjective formal* Someone who is learned has a lot of knowledge from reading and studying. *He was a very learned man.*

learner /'lɜːnəʳ/ *noun* [C] someone who is getting knowledge or a new skill *learners of English*

learning /'lɜːnɪŋ/ *noun* [U] the process of getting knowledge or a new skill *language learning*

'learning ,curve *noun* [C] how quickly or slowly someone learns a new skill *I've been on a steep learning curve since I started my new job.*

WORD PARTNERS FOR *lease*

renew/sign/take a lease • a lease of/on sth

---

lease¹ /liːs/ *noun* [C] **1** a legal agreement in which you pay money in order to use a building or a piece of land for a period of time *We signed a three-year lease when we moved into the house.* **2** give sb/sth a new lease of life *UK* (*also US* give sb/sth a new lease on life) **a** to make someone feel happy or healthy after a period of illness or sadness *The operation has given her a new lease of life.* **b** to improve something that was old so that it works much better

lease² /liːs/ *verb* [T] to use a building or piece of land, or to allow someone to use a building or piece of land, in exchange for money *We want to lease some office space in the centre of town.* ○ *The council eventually leased the land to a local company.*

leash /liːʃ/ (*also UK* lead) *noun* [C] a chain or piece of leather fixed to a dog's collar so that it can be controlled

☞**least¹** /liːst/ *adverb* **1** less than anyone or anything else *Which car costs least?* ○ *I chose the least expensive dish on the menu.* ○ *No one, least of all* (= especially not) *James, is going to be angry with you.* **2** at least **a** as much as, or more than, a number or amount *You'll have to wait at least an hour.* **b** something that you say when you are telling someone about an advantage in a bad situation *It's a small house but at least there's a garden.* **c** used to say that someone should give a small amount of help although they do not intend to give a lot *Even if you didn't want to send a present, you could at least have sent a card.* **d** something that you say in order to correct something you said that was wrong *I've seen that film. At least, I saw the beginning then I fell asleep.* **3** not least *formal* especially *The whole trip was fascinating, not least because of the people I met.* **4** not in the least not at all *I don't mind staying at home, not in the least.* ➔See also: last² but not least.

least² /liːst/ *quantifier* **1** the smallest amount *She earns the least money of all of us.* ○ *Jake had more experience than anyone else and I probably had the least.* **2** to say the least used to emphasize that you could have said something in a much stronger way *We were surprised, to say the least.*

leather /'leðəʳ/ *noun* [U] the skin of animals that is used to make things such as shoes and bags *a leather jacket*

☞**leave¹** /liːv/ *verb past* left /left/ **1** GO AWAY [I, T] to go away from a place or a situation, either permanently or for a temporary period *I'm* leaving work early this afternoon. ○ *What time does the bus leave?* ○ *They left for Paris last night.* ○ *"Does Trevor still work there?" "No, he left."* (= he does not work there now). ○ *She left school at 16.* **2** END RELATIONSHIP [I, T] to end a relationship with a husband, wife, or partner and stop living with them *I'll never leave you.* ○ *She left him for a younger man.* **3** NOT TAKE [T] to not take something with you when you go away from a place, either intentionally or by accident *Why don't you leave your jacket in the car?* ○ *She'd left a note for him in the kitchen.* ○ *That's the second umbrella I've left on the train!* **4** NOT USE ALL [T] to not use all of something *They'd drunk all the wine but they'd left some food.* ○ *Are there any biscuits left?* **5** REMAIN [T] to make a permanent mark *The operation may leave a scar.* **6** leave sth open/on/off, etc to cause something to stay in a particular condition *Who left the window open?* **7** DO LATER [T] to do something later that you could do immediately *Don't leave your packing till the night before you go.* **8** GIVE [T] to arrange for someone to receive something after you die *His aunt left him a lot of money.* ○ *He left the house to Julia.* **9** leave sb alone to stop speaking to or annoying someone *Leave me alone! I'm trying to work.* **10** leave sth alone to stop touching something *Leave your hair alone!* ➔See also: leave someone to their own devices (device), leave/make your mark¹.

leave sb/sth behind to leave a place without taking something or someone with you *We were in a hurry and I think I must have left my keys behind.*

leave behind sth; leave sth behind (sb) to cause a situation to exist after you have left a place *The army left a trail of destruction behind them.*

leave sth for/to sb to give someone the responsibility for dealing with something *I've left the paperwork for you.*

leave sb/sth out to not include someone or something *I've made a list of names - I hope I haven't left anyone out.*

be left out If someone feels left out, they are unhappy because they have not been included in an activity. *The older children had gone upstairs to play and she felt left out.*

be left over If an amount of money or food is left over, it remains when the rest has been used or eaten. *There was a lot of food left over from the party.*

WORD PARTNERS FOR *leave*

annual / maternity / paternity / sick leave
• on leave • leave from [work/your job, etc]

---

leave² /liːv/ *noun* [U] a period of time when you do not go to work *She's on maternity/sick leave.*

leaves /liːvz/ *plural of* leaf

lecherous /'letʃ°rəs/ *adjective* A lecherous man shows too much interest in sex, in a way that is unpleasant.

lecture¹ /'lektʃəʳ/ *noun* [C] **1** a formal talk given to a group of people in order to teach them about a subject *We went to a lecture on Italian*

---

art. ○ *Do you know who's* **giving the lecture** *this afternoon?* **2** an angry or serious talk given to someone in order to criticize their behaviour *My dad* **gave** *me* **a lecture on** *smoking last night.*

lecture² /'lektʃə^r/ *verb* **1** [I] to give a formal talk to a group of people, often at a university *She travelled widely throughout North America* **lecturing on** *women's rights.* ○ *For ten years she* **lectured in** *law.* **2** [T] to talk angrily to someone in order to criticize their behaviour *Stop lecturing me!* ○ *His parents used to* **lecture** *him* **on** *his table manners.*

lecturer /'lektʃə^rə^r/ *noun* [C] *mainly UK* someone who teaches at a university or college *a* **lecturer in** *psychology* ○ *a senior lecturer*

COMMON LEARNER ERROR

lecturer or **teacher**?

In American English, **lecturer** is formal, and **teacher** or **professor** is usually used instead.

---

led /led/ *past of* lead

ledge /ledʒ/ *noun* [C] a long, flat surface that comes out under a window or from the side of a mountain *The birds landed on a ledge about halfway up the cliff.*

leek /liːk/ *noun* [C, U] a long white and green vegetable that smells and tastes similar to an onion

leer /lɪə^r/ *verb* [I] to look at someone in an unpleasant and sexually interested way *He was always* **leering at** *female members of staff.* ● **leer** *noun* [C]

leery /'lɪəri/ *adjective US* worried and not able to trust someone *I've gotten more* **leery of** *the media.*

leeway /'liːweɪ/ *noun* [U] freedom to do what you want *My current boss* **gives** *me much more* **leeway**.

left¹ /left/ *adjective, adverb* on or towards the side of your body that is to the west when you are facing north [always before noun] *Step forward on your left leg.* ○ *She had a diamond earring in her left ear.* ○ *Turn left at the end of the corridor.* ⊃Opposite **right**.

WORD PARTNERS FOR left *(noun)*

on the left ● be **to** sb's left ● the left **of** sth

---

left² /left/ *noun* **1** [no plural] the left side *Ned's the man sitting* **on** *my* **left** *in that photo.* ○ *Jean's house is last* **on** *the* **left. 2 the Left/left** political groups which believe that power and money should be shared more equally among people *The proposals were sharply criticized by the Left.* ⊃Opposite **right**.

left³ /left/ *past of* leave

left 'click *verb* [I] to press the button on the left of a computer mouse (= a small piece of equipment that you move with your hand to control what the computer does)

left 'field *noun US informal* **in/from/out of left field** strange and not expected *His question*

came out of left field, and I didn't know what to say.

left-hand /ˌleft'hænd/ *adjective* [always **before noun**] on the left *a* **left-hand** *drive car* (= car which you drive sitting on the left-hand side) ○ *The swimming pool is on* **the left-hand side** *of the road.*

left-handed /ˌleft'hændɪd/ *adjective* Someone who is left-handed uses their left hand to do most things. *Are you left-handed?*

leftist /'leftɪst/ *adjective* supporting the ideas of parties on the political left *leftist politics/ideas*

leftover /'left,əʊvə^r/ *adjective* [always **before noun**] Leftover food remains after a meal. *If there's any leftover food we can take it home with us.* ● **leftovers** *noun* [plural] food which remains after a meal *We've been eating up the leftovers from the party all week.*

left-wing /ˌleft'wɪŋ/ *adjective* supporting the ideas of parties on the political left *a left-wing newspaper* ● **left-winger** *noun* [C]

leg

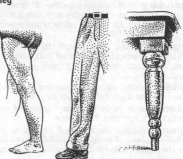

o= **leg** /leg/ *noun* [C] **1** PART OF BODY one of the parts of the body of a human or animal that is used for standing and walking *He broke his leg in the accident.* ○ *There were cuts on her arms and legs.* ○ *She had bare legs and wore only a light summer dress.* ⊃See colour picture **The Body** on page Centre 13. **2** FOOD the meat of an animal's leg eaten as food *a chicken leg* **3** FURNITURE one of the vertical parts of a chair, table, etc that is on the floor *a chair/table leg* **4** CLOTHES the part of a pair of trousers that covers one of your legs *He rolled up his* **trouser legs** *and waded into the water.* **5** PART OF JOURNEY one part of a journey or competition *the first/second/third leg of the journey* **6 not have a leg to stand on** to have no chance of proving that something is true *If you don't have a witness, you don't have a leg to stand on.* **7 be on its last legs** *informal* If a machine is on its last legs, it will stop working soon because it is so old. *We've had the same oven for twenty years now and it really is on its last legs.* **8 stretch your legs** *informal* to go for a walk

legacy /'legəsi/ *noun* [C] **1** a situation that was caused by something from an earlier time *The war has left a* **legacy of** *hatred.* **2** money or buildings, etc that you receive after someone dies

---

o-**legal** /ˈliːɡəl/ *adjective* **1** relating to the law *legal action/advice* ○ *the legal profession/system* **2** allowed by law *Is it legal to carry a handgun?* ➲Opposite **illegal**. ● **legally** *adverb Children under sixteen are not legally allowed to buy cigarettes.*

ˌlegal ˈaid *noun* [U] a system that provides free advice about the law to people who are too poor to pay for it

legality /liːˈɡæləti/ *noun* [U] the legal quality of a situation or action *Some board members have questioned the legality of the proposal.*

legalize /ˈliːɡəlaɪz/ *verb* [T] to make something legal *How many Americans want to legalize drugs?* ● **legalization** /ˌliːɡəlaɪˈzeɪʃən/ *noun* [U] *the legalization of abortion*

legend /ˈledʒənd/ *noun* **1** [C, U] an old story or set of stories from ancient times *the legends of King Arthur* ○ *She's writing a book on Greek legend.* **2** [C] a famous person *a living legend* ○ *Jazz legend, Ella Fitzgerald, once sang in this bar.*

legendary /ˈledʒəndəri/ *adjective* **1** from a legend (= old story) *a legendary Greek hero* **2** very famous *He became editor of the legendary Irish journal, 'The Bell'.*

leggings /ˈleɡɪŋz/ *noun* [plural] tight trousers which are made of soft material that stretches and are worn mainly by women *a pair of leggings*

legible /ˈledʒəbl/ *adjective* If writing is legible, you can read it easily. ➲Opposite **illegible**.

legion /ˈliːdʒən/ *noun* [C] a large group of soldiers that forms part of an army

legions /ˈliːdʒənz/ *noun* [plural] **legions of sb** large numbers of people *He failed to turn up for the concert, disappointing the legions of fans waiting outside.*

legislate /ˈledʒɪsleɪt/ *verb* [I] If a government legislates, it makes a new law. *We believe it is possible to **legislate against** racism.* ○ *It's hard to **legislate for*** (= make a law that will protect) *the ownership of an idea.*

WORD PARTNERS FOR *legislation*

introduce/pass legislation ● a **piece of** legislation ● legislation **on** sth

legislation /ˌledʒɪˈsleɪʃən/ *noun* [U] a law or a set of laws *Most people want tougher environmental legislation but large corporations continue to oppose it.*

legit /ləˈdʒɪt/ *adjective informal short for* legitimate *This had better be legit.*

legitimate /lɪˈdʒɪtəmət/ *adjective* **1** allowed by law *Sales of illegal CDs now exceed those of legitimate recordings.* ➲Opposite **illegitimate**. **2** A legitimate complaint or fear can be understood or believed. *People have expressed **legitimate fears** about the spread of the disease.* ● **legitimately** *adverb*

leisure /ˈleʒər/ [US] /ˈliːʒər/ *noun* [U] **1** the time when you are not working ***leisure activities*** ○ *Try to spend your **leisure time** doing activities you really enjoy.* **2 at your leisure** If you do something at your leisure, you do it when you have the time. *Take it home and read it at your leisure.*

ˈleisure ˌcentre *UK* a building with a swimming pool and places where you can play sports

leisurely /ˈleʒəli/ [US] /ˈliːʒərli/ *adjective* in a relaxed way without hurrying ***a leisurely stroll***

lemon /ˈlemən/ *noun* [C, U] an oval, yellow fruit that has sour juice ***a slice of lemon*** ○ ***lemon juice*** ➲See colour picture **Fruit and Vegetables** on page Centre 10.

lemon

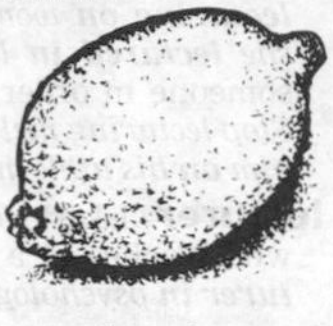

lemonade /ˌleməˈneɪd/ *noun* [C, U] **1** *UK* a cold drink with a lemon flavour that is sweet and has bubbles **2** *mainly US* a cold drink that is made from lemon juice, water, and sugar

o-**lend** /lend/ *verb past* **lent** /lent/ **1** [+ two objects] to give something to someone for a period of time, expecting that they will then give it back to you *She lent me her car for the weekend.* ○ *I do have a bike but I've **lent it to** Sara.* **2** [I, T] If a bank lends money, it gives money to someone who then pays the money back in small amounts over a period. *The bank refused to lend us money for another mortgage.*

COMMON LEARNER ERROR

lend and **borrow**

Be careful not to confuse these two verbs. **Lend** means to give something to someone for a period of time.

It was raining so she lent me her umbrella.

Borrow means to use something which belongs to someone else and give it back later.

Can I borrow your umbrella? It's raining.

~~*Can I lend your umbrella? It's raining.*~~

lend itself to sth *formal* to be suitable for a particular purpose *The old system doesn't lend itself to mass production.*

lend sth to sb/sth *formal* to add a quality to something or someone *We will continue to lend support to our allies.*

lender /ˈlendər/ *noun* [C] a person or organization that lends money to people *mortgage lenders*

WORD PARTNERS FOR *length*

the length **of** sth ● [20m/3cm, etc] **in** length

o-**length** /leŋθ/ *noun* **1** [DISTANCE] [C, U] the measurement or distance of something from one end to the other *The carpet is over three metres **in length**.* ○ *The length of the bay is roughly 200 miles.* ➲See Extra help page **Measure-**

length

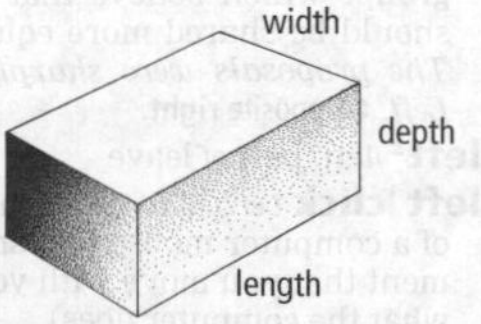

ments on page Centre 31 . **2** TIME [C, U] the amount of time something takes *the length of a film/play/speech* ○ *Sitting still for any length of time is quite hard for most children.* **3** WRITING [C, U] the amount of writing in a book or document *He's written books of various lengths on the subject.* **4 at length** If you talk about something at length, you talk for a long time. *We discussed both topics at length.* **5** PIECE [C] a long piece of something *a length of cloth/cord/rope* **6 go to great lengths to do sth** to try very hard to achieve something *He'll go to great lengths to get what he wants.* **7 the length and breadth of sth** in every part of a place *They travelled the length and breadth of Scotland together.*

lengthen /'leŋθən/ *verb* [I, T] to become longer or to make something longer *lengthening waiting lists*

lengthy /'leŋθi/ *adjective* continuing for a long time *a lengthy discussion/process*

lenient /'liːniənt/ *adjective* A lenient punishment is not severe. *He asked the judge to pass a lenient sentence.*

lens /lenz/ *noun* [C] a curved piece of glass in cameras, glasses, and scientific equipment used for looking at things ⊃See also: **contact lens**, **zoom lens**.

lent /lent/ *past of* lend

Lent /lent/ *noun* [U] the religious period before Easter (= a Christian holiday), in which some Christians do not allow themselves something that they usually enjoy *She's given up chocolate for Lent.*

lentil /'lentⁿl/ *noun* [C] a very small dried bean which is cooked and eaten *lentil soup*

Leo /'liːəʊ/ *noun* [C, U] the sign of the zodiac which relates to the period of 23 July - 22 August, or a person born during this period ⊃See picture at **zodiac.**

leopard

leopard /'lepəd/ *noun* [C] a large, wild animal of the cat family, with yellow fur and dark spots

leper /'lepəʳ/ *noun* [C] a person who has leprosy

leprosy /'leprəsi/ *noun* [U] a serious skin disease which can destroy parts of the body

lesbian /'lezbiən/ *noun* [C] a woman who is sexually attracted to other women *a lesbian affair*

o-ω**less¹** /les/ *adverb* **1** not as much *I'm trying to exercise more and eat less.* ○ *Plastic bottles are*

less expensive to produce. **2 less and less** If something happens less and less, it gradually becomes smaller in amount or not so frequent. *I find I'm eating less and less red meat.*

o-ω**less²** /les/ *quantifier* a smaller amount *She gets about £50 a week or less.* ○ *I was driving at less than 20 miles per hour.* ○ *Tuberculosis is less of a threat these days.* ○ *I prefer my coffee with a little less sugar.*

COMMON LEARNER ERROR

less or fewer?

Less is used before uncountable nouns.
I should eat less fat.

Fewer is used before countable nouns.
I should smoke fewer cigarettes.

-less /-ləs/ *suffix* changes a noun into an adjective meaning 'without' *homeless people* ○ *a meaningless statement* ○ *a hopeless situation*

lessen /'lesⁿn/ *verb* [I, T] to become less or to make something less *Exercise and a healthy diet lessen the chance of heart disease.*

lesser /'lesəʳ/ *adjective* **1** not as large, important, or of such good quality *The price increase was due to labour shortages and,* **to a lesser extent**, *the recent earthquake.* ○ *He faces the lesser charge of assault.* **2 the lesser of two evils** the less bad of two bad things *I suppose I regard the Democratic candidate as the lesser of two evils.*

lesser-known /ˌlesə'nəʊn/ *adjective* not as popular or famous as something else *We stayed on one of the lesser-known Greek islands.*

WORD PARTNERS FOR lesson

have/take lessons • **give** sb a lesson

o-ω**lesson** /'lesⁿn/ *noun* [C] **1** a period of time when a teacher teaches people *The best way to improve your game is to take lessons.* ○ *She gives French lessons.* ○ *Lessons start at 9 a.m.* **2** an experience which teaches you how to behave better in a similar situation in the future *My parents made me pay back all the money, and it was a lesson I never forgot.* **3 learn your lesson** to decide not to do something again because it has caused you problems in the past *I'm not going out without my umbrella again - I've learnt my lesson!* **4 teach sb a lesson** to punish someone so that they will not behave badly again *The next time she's late, go without her. That should teach her a lesson.*

o-ω**let** /let/ *verb* [T] letting, *past* let **1** ALLOW to allow someone to do something, or to allow something to happen *Let them play outside.* ○ *Don't let the camera get wet.* ○ *We had a whole year go by before we tried again.* ⊃See Common learner error at **allow.** **2 let sb/sth in/past/through, etc** to allow someone or something to move to a particular place *They won't let us past the gate.* ○ *I won't let him near my children.* ○ *The roof lets in a lot of rain.* **3 let's** something that you say when you are making a suggestion *Let's eat out tonight.* **4 let me/us** something that you say when you are offering to help someone *Let* *me carry your cases.* **5** [BUILDING] If you let a building or part of a building, you allow someone to live there and they give you money. *I let the top floor of my house to a student.* **6 Let's see/Let me see** something that you say when you are trying to remember something or calculate something *Let's see - there are five people and only three beds.* ○ *It must have been - let me see - three years ago.* **7 Let's say** something that you say when you are suggesting a possible situation or action *Let's say we'll meet back here in an hour.* **8 let sb know (sth)** to tell someone something **[+ question word]** *I'll let you know when we've fixed a date for the meeting.* **9 let (sth) go** to stop holding something *I let go of the rope.* **10 let yourself go a** [LESS ATTRACTIVE] to allow yourself to become less attractive or healthy **b** [RELAX] to relax completely and enjoy yourself *It's a party - let yourself go!* **11 let's face it** something that you say when the truth is unpleasant but must be accepted *Let's face it, we're not getting any younger.* **12 let alone** used to emphasize that something is more impossible than another thing *You couldn't trust her to look after your dog, let alone your child.* ➲See also: let the **cat** out of the bag, let your **hair** down, get/let sb off the **hook**[1], let off **steam**[1].

let sb down to disappoint someone by failing to do what you agreed to do *I promised to go to the party with Jane and I can't let her down.*

let sb in to allow someone to enter a room or building, often by opening the door *Could you go down and let Darren in?*

let yourself in for sth to become involved in an unpleasant situation without intending to *Do you realize how much work you're letting yourself in for?*

let sb off to not punish someone who has done something wrong, or to not punish them severely *I'll let you off this time, but don't ever lie to me again.* ○ *The judge* ***let*** *her* ***off with*** (= only punished her with) *a fine.*

let on to tell someone about something secret *She* ***let on to*** *a friend that she'd lied in court.*

let sb/sth out to allow a person or animal to leave somewhere, especially by opening a locked or closed door

let up If bad weather or an unpleasant situation lets up, it stops or improves. *I hope the rain lets up for the weekend.*

letdown /ˈletdaʊn/ *noun* **[no plural]** *informal* a disappointment *After all I'd heard about the film it was a bit of a letdown when I finally saw it.*

lethal /ˈliːθəl/ *adjective* able to cause death

lethargic /ləˈθɑːdʒɪk/ *adjective* When you feel lethargic, you have no energy and you do not want to do anything. • **lethargy** /ˈleθədʒi/ *noun* **[U]** the feeling of being tired and having no energy

WORD PARTNERS FOR ***letter***

get/receive/send/write a letter • **in** a letter • a letter **from/to** sb

o- **letter** /ˈletər/ *noun* **[C]** **1** a written message that you send to someone, usually by post *I got a letter from Paul this morning.* **2** a symbol that is used in written language and that represents a sound in that language *the letter K* ➲See also: **covering letter.**

letterbox /ˈletəbɒks/ *noun* **[C]** *UK* **1** a small hole in a door that letters are put through **2** (*US* **mailbox**) a large, metal container in a public place where you can post letters

ˈletter ˌcarrier *US* (*UK* **postman**) *noun* **[C]** someone who takes and brings letters and parcels as a job

lettuce /ˈletɪs/ *noun* **[C]** a plant with green leaves, which is eaten in salads ➲See colour picture **Fruit and Vegetables** on page Centre 10.

leukaemia *UK* (*US* **leukemia**) /luːˈkiːmiə/ *noun* **[U]** a serious disease in which a person's body produces too many white blood cells

levee /ˈlevi/ *noun* **[C]** a wall made of land or other materials that is built next to a river to stop the river from flooding (= covering everywhere in water)

WORD PARTNERS FOR ***level***

the level **of** sth • **at** a [high/low, etc] level

o- **level**[1] /ˈlevəl/ *noun* **[C]** **1** [HEIGHT] the height of something *the water level* **2** [AMOUNT] the amount or number of something *Chess requires a high level of concentration.* **3** [ABILITY] someone's ability compared to other people *Students at this level need a lot of help.* **4** [FLOOR] a floor in a building *The store had three levels.* ➲See also: **A level,** a level **playing field, sea level.**

level[2] /ˈlevəl/ *adjective* **1** **[never before noun]** at the same height *I got down till my face was* ***level with*** *his.* **2** flat or horizontal *Make sure the camera is level before you take the picture.*

level[3] /ˈlevəl/ *verb* **[T]** *UK* **levelling,** *past* **levelled,** *US* **leveling,** *past* **leveled** **1** to make something flat *He levelled the wet cement before it set.* **2** to completely destroy a building *Artillery fire levelled the town.*

level sth against/at sb to say that someone has done something wrong **[often passive]** *Charges of corruption have been levelled against him.*

level sth at sb to aim a gun at someone or something *He levelled the gun at my head.*

level off/out to stop rising or falling and stay at the same level *Road deaths have levelled off since the speed limit was lowered.*

ˌlevel ˈcrossing *UK* (*US* **grade crossing**) *noun* **[C]** a place where a railway crosses a road

lever /ˈliːvər/ [US] /ˈlevər/ *noun* **[C]** **1** a handle that you push or pull to make a machine work **2** a long bar that you use to lift or move something by pressing one end

leverage /ˈliːvərɪdʒ/ [US] /ˈlevərɪdʒ/ *noun* **[U]** the power to influence people in order to get what you want

levy /ˈlevi/ *verb* **levy a charge/fine/tax, etc** to officially demand money **[often passive]** *A new tax was* ***levied on*** *consumers of luxury goods.*

lewd /luːd/ *adjective* sexual in a way that is unpleasant *lewd comments/gestures*

liability /ˌlaɪə'bɪləti/ *noun* **1** [U] when you are legally responsible for something *They have admitted liability for the damage caused.* **2** [no plural] someone or something that is likely to cause you a lot of trouble *Wherever we go she upsets someone - she's a real liability.*

liable /'laɪəbl/ *adjective* **1 be liable to do sth** to be likely to do something *He's liable to make a fuss if you wake him.* **2** legally responsible *Corporate officials are liable for the safety of their employees.*

liaise /li'eɪz/ *verb* [I] to speak to other people at work in order to exchange information with them *Our head office will liaise with the suppliers to ensure delivery.*

liaison /li'eɪzⁿn/ *noun* **1** COMMUNICATION [U] communication between people or groups that work with each other **2** PERSON [C] *US* someone who helps groups to communicate effectively with each other *She served as an informal liaison between employees and management.* **3** RELATIONSHIP [C] a short sexual relationship between people who are not married

liar /'laɪə/ *noun* [C] someone who tells lies

Lib Dem /lɪb'dem/ *noun* [C] *short for* Liberal Democrat

libel /'laɪbl/ *noun* [U] writing which contains bad information about someone which is not true *Tabloid magazines are often sued for libel.*

liberal /'lɪbⁿrⁿl/ *adjective* **1** accepting beliefs and behaviour that are new or different from your own *a liberal attitude* **2** Liberal political ideas emphasize the need to make new laws as society changes and the need for government to provide social services. ● **liberal** *noun* [C] someone who is liberal

liberal 'arts *US* (*UK/US* arts) *noun* [plural] subjects of study which are not science, such as history, languages, etc

Liberal 'Democrat *noun* [C] **1 the Liberal Democrats** one of the three main political parties in the UK *He's the leader of the Liberal Democrats.* **2** someone who supports the Liberal Democrats

liberally /'lɪbⁿrⁿli/ *adverb* in large amounts *fruit liberally sprinkled with sugar*

liberate /'lɪbⁿreɪt/ *verb* [T] to help someone or something to be free *Troops liberated the city.* ● **liberation** /ˌlɪbⁿr'eɪʃⁿn/ *noun* [U] *the invasion and liberation of France*

liberated /'lɪbⁿreɪtɪd/ *adjective* not following traditional ways of behaving or old ideas *a liberated woman*

liberating /'lɪbⁿreɪtɪŋ/ *adjective* making you feel that you can behave in exactly the way that you want to *Taking all your clothes off can be a very liberating experience.*

liberty /'lɪbⁿti/ *noun* [C, U] **1** the freedom to live, work, and travel as you want to *Many would willingly fight to preserve their liberty.* **2 be at liberty to do sth** *formal* to be allowed to do something *I'm not at liberty to discuss the matter at present.* **3 take the liberty of doing sth** *formal* to do something that will have an effect on someone else, without asking their permission *I took the liberty of booking theatre seats*

for us. ⊃See also: **civil liberties.**

Libra /'liːbrə/ *noun* [C, U] the sign of the zodiac which relates to the period of 23 September - 22 October, or a person born during this period ⊃See picture at **zodiac.**

librarian /laɪ'breəriən/ *noun* [C] someone who works in a library

o— **library** /'laɪbrⁿri/ *noun* [C] a room or building that contains a collection of books and other written material that you can read or borrow

lice /laɪs/ *plural of* **louse**

┌─────────────────────────────────┐
│ 🧩 **WORD PARTNERS FOR *licence*** │
└─────────────────────────────────┘

apply for/hold/issue a licence ● a licence for sth

licence *UK* (*US* **license**) /'laɪsⁿns/ *noun* [C] an official document that allows you to do or have something *a hunting licence* ○ *a marriage licence* ⊃See also: **driving licence, off-licence.**

license /'laɪsⁿns/ *verb* [T] to give someone official permission to do or have something [often passive, + to do sth] *Undercover agents are licensed to carry guns.*

licensed /'laɪsⁿnst/ *adjective* **1** *mainly US* officially approved *a licensed physician* **2** A licensed bar or restaurant is officially allowed to serve alcoholic drinks.

'license ,plate *US* (*UK* **number plate**) *noun* [C] an official metal sign with numbers and letters on the front and back of a car ⊃See colour picture **Car** on page Centre 7.

lick¹ /lɪk/ *verb* [T] to move your tongue across the surface of something *to lick your lips* ○ *We licked the chocolate off our fingers.*

lick

lick² /lɪk/ *noun* **1** [C] when you lick something [usually singular] *Here, have a lick of my ice cream.* **2 a lick of paint** *UK informal* If you give a wall or other surface a lick of paint, you paint it.

lid /lɪd/ *noun* [C] the top part of a container that can be removed in order to put something in or take something out

o— **lie¹** /laɪ/ *verb* [I] lying, *past tense* lay, *past participle* lain **1 lie in/on, etc** to be in a horizontal or flat position on a surface *to lie in bed* ○ *to lie on a beach* ○ *to lie on your side* ○ *The pen lay on the desk.* ○ *She had lain where she fell until morning.* **2 lie below/in/on/to, etc** to be in a particular place *The river lies 30 km to the south of the city.* ⊃See Common learner error at **lay.**

lie around 1 *informal* to spend time lying down and doing very little *We spent a week by the sea, lying around on the beach.* **2** If things are lying around, they are left in an untidy way in places where they should not be. *He's always leaving money lying around.*

lie back to lower the top half of your body from a sitting position to a lying position *Lie back and relax.*

lie down to move into a position in which

your body is flat, usually in order to sleep or rest *I'm not feeling well - I'm going to lie down.* ➲See colour picture **Phrasal Verbs** on page Centre 16.

lie in *UK* to stay in bed in the morning later than usual *Ottolie lay in till eleven o'clock this morning.*

lie in sth to exist or be found in something *Her strength lies in her faith.*

lie with sb If the responsibility or blame for something lies with someone, it is their responsibility. *The final decision lies with me.*

⊶**lie²** /laɪ/ *verb* **[I] lying,** *past* **lied** to say or write something that is not true in order to deceive someone *Are you **lying to** me?* ○ *He **lied about** his qualifications for the job.*

⊶**lie³** /laɪ/ *noun* **[C]** something that you say or write which you know is not true *I **told a lie** when I said I liked her haircut.* ➲See also: **white lie.**

lie-in /ˈlaɪˌɪn/ *noun* **[no plural]** *UK* when you stay in bed in the morning longer than usual *I **had** a long **lie-in** this morning.*

lieu /luː/ *noun* **in lieu of sth** *formal* instead of something *She took the money in lieu of the prize.*

lieutenant /lefˈtenənt/ [US] /luːˈtenənt/ *noun* **[C]** an officer of middle rank in the army, navy, or air force *first/second lieutenant*

WORD PARTNERS FOR ***life***

have/lead/live a [charmed/normal, etc] life • **spend** your life (doing sth) • **a part** of sb's life

⊶**life** /laɪf/ *noun plural* **lives** /laɪvz/ **1** [ANIMALS/PLANTS] **[U]** living things and their activities *human/marine life* ○ *Is there life in outer space?* **2** [PERSON'S EXISTENCE] **[C]** the existence of a person *How many lives will be lost to AIDS?* **3** [TIME] **[C, U]** the time between a person's birth and their death *I'm not sure I want to **spend** the rest of my **life** with him.* ○ ***Life's too short** to worry about stuff like that.* ○ *Unfortunately, accidents are **part of life**.* ○ *He **had** a happy **life**.* **4** [WAY OF LIVING] **[C, U]** a way of living *You **lead** an exciting **life**.* **5 family/private/sex, etc life** one part of someone's existence *My private life is nobody's business but mine.* **6** [ACTIVITY] **[U]** energy and activity *She was always bubbly and **full of life**.* ○ *I looked through the window but couldn't see any **signs of life*** (= people moving). **7** [ACTIVE PERIOD] **[no plural]** the amount of time that a machine, system, etc exists or can be used *Careful use will prolong the life of your machine.* **8 bring sth to life/come to life** to make something more real or exciting, or to become more real or exciting **9 That's life.** something you say which means bad things happen and you cannot prevent them *You don't get everything you want but that's life, isn't it?* **10 Get a life!** *informal* something you say to a boring person when you want them to do more exciting things *Surely you're not cleaning the house on Saturday night? Get a life!* ➲See Common learner error at **live** ➲See also: the facts (**fact**) of life, give sb the **kiss²** of life, give sb/sth a new **lease¹** of life, **shelf life, walk²** of life.

lifeboat /ˈlaɪfbəʊt/ *noun* **[C]** a small boat that is used to help people who are in danger at sea

ˈlife ˌcoach *noun* **[C]** someone whose job is to teach people how to solve problems and make decisions in their daily life

ˈlife ˌcycle *noun* **[C]** the changes that happen in the life of an animal or plant

ˈlife exˌpectancy *noun* **[C, U]** the number of years that someone is likely to live

lifeguard /ˈlaɪfgɑːd/ *noun* **[C]** someone at a swimming pool or beach whose job is to help people who are in danger in the water

ˈlife inˌsurance (*UK* **ˈlife aˌssurance**) *noun* **[U]** a system of payments to an insurance company (= a company that will pay money) that will pay money to your family when you die

ˈlife ˌjacket *noun* **[C]** a piece of equipment that you wear on the upper part of your body to help you float if you fall into water

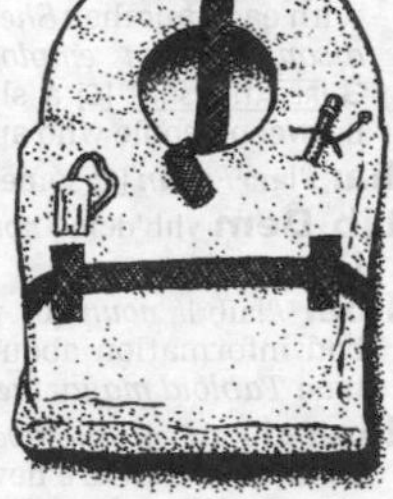

life jacket

lifeless /ˈlaɪfləs/ *adjective* **1** without life *his lifeless body* **2** without energy or feeling *a lifeless performance*

lifelike /ˈlaɪflaɪk/ *adjective* If something is lifelike, it looks real. *a lifelike portrait/sculpture*

lifeline /ˈlaɪflaɪn/ *noun* **[C]** something that helps you when you are in a difficult or dangerous situation *For a lot of old people who live on their own, the telephone is a lifeline.*

lifelong /ˌlaɪfˈlɒŋ/ *adjective* **[always before noun]** for all of your life *a **lifelong friend/interest***

ˌlife ˈpeer *noun* **[C]** someone who has been officially respected in the UK by being given an important title, for example 'Lord', 'Lady' or 'Baroness'

ˈlife ˌsentence (*informal* **life [U]**) *noun* **[C]** the punishment of spending a very long time, or the rest of your life, in prison

lifespan /ˈlaɪfspæn/ *noun* **[C]** the amount of time that a person lives or a thing exists

lifestyle /ˈlaɪfstaɪl/ *noun* **[C]** the way that you live *a **healthy lifestyle***

life-threatening /ˈlaɪfθretᵊnɪŋ/ *adjective* likely to cause death ***life-threatening conditions/diseases***

lifetime /ˈlaɪftaɪm/ *noun* **[C]** the period of time that someone is alive **[usually singular]** *We'll see such huge changes **in our lifetime**.*

⊶**lift¹** /lɪft/ *verb* **1** [UP] **[T]** to put something or someone in a higher position *Could you help me lift this table, please?* ○ *She **lifted** the baby **up** and put him in his chair.* **2** [WEATHER] **[I]** If fog lifts, it disappears. *By noon the fog had lifted and the day turned hot.* **3** [RULES] **[T]** to stop a rule *The government had already **lifted** the **ban** on beef imports.* **4** [STEAL] **[T]** *informal* to steal or copy something *Entire paragraphs of his thesis were* *lifted from other sources.* ⊃See also: not lift a finger[1].

o-π**lift²** /lɪft/ *noun* [C] **1** MACHINE *UK* (*US* **elevator**) a machine that carries people up and down in tall buildings *Shall we use the stairs or take the lift?* **2** RIDE a free ride somewhere, usually in a car [usually singular] *Can you give me a lift to the airport?* **3** MOVE when you move someone or something up to a higher position

lift-off /'lɪftɒf/ *noun* [C] the moment when a spacecraft leaves the ground

ligament /'lɪgəmənt/ *noun* [C] a piece of strong tissue in the body that holds bones together *ankle/knee ligaments* ○ *torn ligaments*

WORD PARTNERS FOR **light**

light **shines** • a **beam/ray/shaft** of light • a **bright** light

---

light

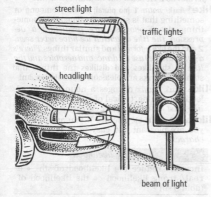

street light

traffic lights

headlight

beam of light

---

o-π**light¹** /laɪt/ *noun* **1** [U] the brightness that shines from the sun, from fire, or from electrical equipment, allowing you to see things *bright/dim light* ○ *fluorescent/ultraviolet light* ○ *a beam/ray of light* ○ *Light was streaming in through the open door.* **2** [C] a device which produces light *car lights* ○ *to switch/turn the light on* ○ *They must be in bed - I can't see any lights on anywhere.* **3** a light a flame from a match, etc used to make a cigarette start burning *Have you got a light, please?* **4 set light to sth** *UK* to make something start burning **5 in the light of sth** (*also US* **in light of sth**) If something is done or happens in the light of facts, it is done or happens because of those facts. *The drug has been withdrawn in the light of new research.* **6 bring sth to light** If information about something bad is brought to light, it is discovered. *The trial brought to light numerous contradictions in his story.* **7 cast/shed light on sth** to help people understand a situation *We were hoping you might be able to shed some light on the matter.* **8 come to light** If information about something bad comes to light, it is discovered. **9 light at the end of the tunnel** something which makes you believe that an unpleasant situation will soon

end ⊃See also: **green light**, **street light**, **tail light**, **traffic light**.

o-π**light²** /laɪt/ *adjective* **1** NOT HEAVY not heavy *light clothing/machinery* ○ *I can carry both bags - they're quite light.* **2** NOT MUCH small in amount *light rain/snow* ○ *I only had a light lunch.* **3** NOT STRONG not strong or not forceful *a light breeze* ○ *a light embrace* **4** PALE Light colours are pale. *light brown/green* ○ *a light blue cardigan* **5** NOT SERIOUS easy to understand and not serious *light entertainment* ○ *I'm taking some light reading on holiday.* **6 make light of sth** to talk or behave as if you do not think a problem is serious **7 it is light** bright from the sun *Let's go now while it's still light.* • **lightness** *noun* [U]

light³ /laɪt/ *verb past* **lit** or **lighted 1** [I, T] to start to burn, or to make something start to burn *to light a candle/cigarette/fire* ○ *The wood was damp and wouldn't light.* **2** [T] to produce light somewhere so that you can see things [often passive] *The room was lit by a single light bulb.* ○ *Burning buildings lit up the sky.*

light up If your face or your eyes light up, you suddenly look happy or excited. *His eyes lit up when you mentioned her name.*

light (sth) up to make a cigarette, etc start burning *He made himself a coffee and lit up a cigarette.*

'light ,bulb *noun* [C] a glass object containing a wire which produces light from electricity

light bulb

lighten /'laɪtᵊn/ *verb* **1** [I, T] If a serious situation lightens, it becomes less serious, and if something or someone lightens it, they make it less serious. *Her mood lightened a bit when I asked about her holiday.* ○ *He tried to lighten the atmosphere by telling a joke.* **2 lighten the burden/load** to reduce the amount of work or trouble someone has to deal with **3** [I, T] to become less dark, or to make something less dark *The sun had lightened her hair.*

lighten up *informal* to become more relaxed and less serious *I wish she'd lighten up a bit.*

lighter /'laɪtə/ *noun* [C] a small object that produces a flame and is used to make cigarettes start burning

light-hearted /,laɪt'hɑːtɪd/ *adjective* not serious *a light-hearted remark*

lighthouse /'laɪthaus/ *noun* [C] *plural* **lighthouses** /'laɪthauzɪz/ a tall building on the coast containing a large light which warns ships that there are rocks

lighthouse

lighting /'laɪtɪŋ/ *noun* [U] the light created by electrical equipment, candles, etc *soft lighting*

lightly /'laɪtli/ *adverb* **1** gently *He kissed her lightly on the cheek.* **2** not much *lightly* *cooked vegetables* **3 not do sth lightly** to think carefully about something before you do it, knowing that it is serious *It's not a decision that I take lightly.* **4 get off lightly** (*also UK* **escape lightly**) to have less trouble or punishment than you expected

be **struck by** lightning • a **bolt/flash** of lightning • **thunder and** lightning

lightning /ˈlaɪtnɪŋ/ *noun* [U] a sudden flash of light in the sky during a storm *thunder and lightning* ○ *He was struck by lightning and killed.*

lights /laɪts/ (*also* ˈtraffic ˌlights) *noun* [plural] a set of red, green, and yellow lights that is used to stop and start traffic

lightweight /ˈlaɪtweɪt/ *adjective* not weighing much *a lightweight jacket for the summer* • **lightweight** *noun* [C] a sportsman such as a boxer who is not in the heaviest weight group

o→**like**[1] /laɪk/ *preposition* **1** [SIMILAR] similar to or in the same way as someone or something *They were acting like children.* ○ *He looks like his father.* ○ *It sounded like Harry.* **2 What is sb/sth like?** something you say when you want someone to describe someone or something *I haven't met him - what's he like?* ○ *So what's your new dress like?* **3 What are you like?** *UK* used when someone has said or done something silly *You've bought another jacket? What are you like?* **4** [TYPICAL] If behaviour is like someone, it is typical of the way that they behave. *It's just like Anita to miss her train.* ○ *It's not like Tim to be late.* **5** [FOR EXAMPLE] for example *She looks best in bright colours, like red and pink.*

If a person likes someone or something very much, you can use the verbs **love** and **adore**: *I adore/love seafood.* • *Oliver loves animals.* • *Kate adored her grandfather.*

The expressions **think the world of** someone and **have a soft spot for** someone can also be used when a person likes someone very much: *I've always had a soft spot for Rebecca ever since she was tiny.* • *Annabel's like a daughter to him, he thinks the world of her.*

The expression **be fond of** is sometimes used to talk about someone or something that someone likes: *She's very fond of Chinese food.* • *I think she's very fond of you.*

The phrasal verbs **grow on** and **take to/ warm to** can be used when someone starts to like someone or something: *I wasn't sure about the colour at first, but it's growing on me.* • *For some reason, I just didn't take/ warm to him.*

The expressions **take a shine to** or **take a liking to** are sometimes used when someone immediately likes a person: *I think he's taken a bit of a shine to you.*

o→**like**[2] /laɪk/ *verb* [T] **1** to enjoy something or feel

that someone or something is pleasant [+ doing sth] *I just like playing with my computer.* ○ [+ to do sth] *I like to paint in my spare time.* ○ *He really likes her.* ○ *What do you like about him?* ⊃Opposite **dislike**. **2 not like to do sth/not like doing sth** to not usually do something because you think it is wrong *I don't like to criticize her too much.* **3 would like sth** to want something [+ to do sth] *I'd like to think about it.* ○ *I'd like some chips with that, please.* **4 Would you like...?** used to offer someone something *Would you like a drink?* ○ [+ to do sth] *Would you like to eat now?* **5 if you like a** used to say 'yes' when someone suggests a plan *"Shall I come?" "If you like."* **b** used when you offer someone something *If you like I could drive you there.* **6 How do you like sb/sth?** used to ask someone for their opinion *How do you like my new shoes?*

o→**like**[3] /laɪk/ *conjunction* **1** *informal* in the same way as *Do it exactly like I told you to.* **2** *US informal* as if *He acted like he didn't hear me.*

like[4] /laɪk/ *noun* **1** [no plural] *formal* someone or something that is similar to someone or something else *Economists are predicting a depression, the like of which we have never seen.* **2 and the like** *informal* and similar things *There's a gym that they use for dance and aerobics and the like.* **3 sb's likes and dislikes** the things that someone thinks are pleasant and not pleasant

-like /-laɪk/ *suffix* changes a noun into an adjective meaning 'typical of or similar to' *childlike trust* ○ *a cabbage-like vegetable*

likeable /ˈlaɪkəbl/ *adjective* If you are likeable, you are pleasant and easy to like. *a likeable character*

increase/reduce the likelihood **of** sth • a **real/strong** likelihood • the likelihood **of** (doing) sth

likelihood /ˈlaɪklihʊd/ *noun* [U] the chance that something will happen *There's not much likelihood of that happening.*

o→**likely**[1] /ˈlaɪkli/ *adjective* **1** expected [+ to do sth] *Do remind me because I'm likely to forget.* ○ [+ (that)] *It's likely that he'll say no.* **2** probably true *the most likely explanation* ⊃Opposite **unlikely**.

likely[2] /ˈlaɪkli/ *adverb* **1** probably *She'll most likely come without him.* **2 Not likely!** *UK informal* used to say that you will certainly not do something *"So are you coming running with me?" "Not likely!"*

liken /ˈlaɪk[ə]n/ *verb*
liken sth/sb to sth/sb *formal* to say that two people are similar or two things are similar *She's been likened to a young Elizabeth Taylor.*

likeness /ˈlaɪknəs/ *noun* [C, U] being similar in appearance *There's a definite family likeness around the eyes.*

likewise /ˈlaɪkwaɪz/ *adverb* *formal* in the same way *Water these plants twice a week and likewise the ones in the bedroom.* ○ *Watch what she does and then do likewise.*

liking /ˈlaɪkɪŋ/ *noun* **1** [no plural] a feeling that you like someone or something *He has a **liking** for young women.* **2 take a liking to sb** to like someone immediately *He obviously took a liking to her.* **3 be too bright/sweet, etc for your liking** to be brighter/sweeter, etc than you like **4 be to sb's liking** *formal* to be the way that someone prefers something *Is the wine to your liking, sir?*

lilac /ˈlaɪlək/ *noun* [C, U] a small tree that has sweet-smelling purple, pink, or white flowers

lily /ˈlɪli/ *noun* [C] a plant with large, bell-shaped flowers that are often white

limb /lɪm/ *noun* [C] **1** a leg or an arm of a person **2** a large branch of a tree

lime /laɪm/ *noun* **1** [FRUIT] [C, U] a small, green fruit that is sour like a lemon **2** [TREE] [C] (*also* 'lime ,tree) a large tree that has pale green leaves and yellow flowers **3** [SUBSTANCE] [U] a white substance that is found in water and soil and is used to improve the quality of soil **4** [COLOUR] [U] (*also* ,lime 'green) a bright colour that is a mixture of yellow and green ⊃See colour picture **Colours** on page Centre 12. ● **lime** (*also* lime-green) *adjective*

the limelight /ˈlaɪmlaɪt/ *noun* attention from the public *She's been **in the limelight** for most of her career.*

⟦⟧ WORD PARTNERS FOR **limit**

an **age/height/speed/time** limit ● a **legal/ maximum/strict/upper** limit ● **exceed/ impose** a limit ● a limit **on/to** sth

o⌐**limit¹** /ˈlɪmɪt/ *noun* [C] **1** the largest amount of something that is possible or allowed *a time limit* ○ *Is there a **limit on** the amount of money you can claim?* ○ *There's a **limit to** how much time we can spend on this.* **2 be over the limit** *UK* to have more alcohol in your blood than is legally allowed while driving **3 within limits** avoiding behaviour that is extreme or silly *You can wear what you want, within limits.* **4 off limits** If an area is off limits, you are not allowed to enter it. ⊃See also: **speed limit**.

o⌐**limit²** /ˈlɪmɪt/ *verb* [T] to control something so that it is less than a particular amount or number *We'll have to **limit** the number of guests.*

be limited to sth to only exist in a particular area *Racial problems are certainly not limited to the south.*

limit sb to sth to only allow someone a particular amount or number of something [often passive] *We're limited to two pieces of luggage each.* ○ [often reflexive] *I try to limit myself to two glasses of wine a day.*

limitation /ˌlɪmɪˈteɪʃⁿn/ *noun* [C, U] when something is controlled so that it is less than a particular amount or number *the limitation of free speech* ○ *You can't write everything you want to because of space limitations.*

limitations /ˌlɪmɪˈteɪʃⁿnz/ *noun* [plural] things that someone is not good at doing *Both films show her limitations as an actress.*

limited /ˈlɪmɪtɪd/ *adjective* small in amount or number *a **limited** choice* ○ *limited resources* ⊃Opposite **unlimited**.

,limited 'company *noun* [C] a company, especially one in the UK, whose owners only have to pay part of the money they owe if the company fails financially

limousine /ˌlɪməˈziːn/ (*also* limo /ˈlɪməʊ/) *noun* [C] a large, expensive car, usually for rich or important people *a chauffeur-driven limousine*

limp¹ /lɪmp/ *adjective* soft and weak *a **limp** handshake* ○ *a limp lettuce*

limp² /lɪmp/ *verb* [I] to walk with difficulty because one of your legs or feet is hurt ● **limp** *noun* [no plural] *She walks with a limp.*

⟦⟧ WORD PARTNERS FOR **line**

draw a line ● a **diagonal/horizontal/ straight/vertical** line

o⌐**line¹** /laɪn/ *noun* **1** [MARK] [C] a long, thin mark *a horizontal/straight/vertical line* ○ *Sign your name on the dotted line.* ○ ***Draw a line** around your hand.* **2** [ROW] [C] a row of people or things *a line of trees* ○ *We formed two lines, men on one side and women on the other.* **3** [ROPE ETC] [C] a piece of rope or wire with a particular purpose *a clothes/fishing line* **4** [TELEPHONE] [C] the connection between two telephones *I've got Neil **on the line** for you* (= waiting to speak to you) ○ *I'll be with you in a moment - could you **hold the line*** (= wait), *please?* **5** [WAITING] [C, U] *US* (*UK* queue) a row of people waiting for something, one behind the other *We were **standing in line** for hours to get tickets.* **6** [SONG/POEM] [C] a row of words on a page, for example in a song or poem *The same line is repeated throughout the poem.* **7 lines** the words spoken by an actor in a performance *I don't know how actors remember all their lines.* **8** [OPINION] [C] the official opinion of an organization [usually singular] *the government's **line on** immigration* **9 along the lines of sth** based on and similar to something *He gave a talk along the lines of the one he gave in Oxford.* **10 sb's line of reasoning/thinking, etc** your reasons for believing that something is true or right **11** [PRODUCT] [C] a type of product that a company sells *They're advertising a new **line in** garden furniture.* **12** [DIRECTION] [C] the direction that something moves in *He can't kick the ball in a straight line.* **13 lines** the marks that older people have on their faces, when the skin is loose **14** [BORDER] [C] *US* a border between two areas *the New York state line* **15 be on the line** If someone's job is on the line, they may lose it. **16 be in line for sth** to be likely to get something good, especially a job **17 be in line with sth** to be similar to and suitable for something *a pay increase in line with inflation* **18 draw the line at sth** to never do something because you think it is wrong *I swear a lot but even I draw the line at certain words.* **19 toe the (party) line** to do what someone in authority tells you to do although you may not agree with it ⊃See also: **the bottom line, dotted line, front line, hard line**.

line² /laɪn/ *verb* [T] **1** to form a row along the side of something *Trees and cafes lined the street.* **2 be lined with sth** If a piece of clothing is lined with a material, its inside is covered

with it. *a jacket lined with fur*

line (sb/sth) up to stand in a row, or to arrange people or things in a row *Books were neatly lined up on the shelves.*

line sb/sth up to plan for something to happen *What future projects have you lined up?*

ˈline ˌmanager *noun* [C] *mainly UK* the person who manages another person in a company or business

linen /ˈlɪnɪn/ *noun* [U] **1** an expensive cloth that is like rough cotton *a linen jacket* **2** pieces of cloth that you use to cover tables and beds *bed linen*

liner /ˈlaɪnəʳ/ *noun* [C] a large ship like a hotel, which people travel on for pleasure *a cruise/ocean liner*

linesman /ˈlaɪnzmən/ *noun* [C] *plural* **linesmen** in a sport, someone who watches to see if a ball goes into areas where it is not allowed *The linesman pointed to the corner flag.*

linger /ˈlɪŋgəʳ/ *verb* [I] to stay somewhere for a long time *The smell from the fire still lingered hours later.* ○ *After the play had finished, we lingered for a while in the bar hoping to catch sight of the actors.*

lingerie /ˈlɒnʒəri/ [US] /ˌlɑːnʒəˈreɪ/ *noun* [U] women's underwear

lingering /ˈlɪŋgərɪŋ/ *adjective* [always before noun] lasting a long time ***lingering doubts*** ○ *The defeat ends any lingering hopes she might have had of winning the championship.*

linguist /ˈlɪŋgwɪst/ *noun* [C] someone who is good at learning foreign languages, or someone who studies or teaches linguistics

linguistic /lɪŋˈgwɪstɪk/ *adjective* [always before noun] relating to language or linguistics *She's studying the linguistic development of young children.*

linguistics /lɪŋˈgwɪstɪks/ *noun* [U] the scientific study of languages

lining /ˈlaɪnɪŋ/ *noun* [C, U] a material or substance that covers the inside of something *a coat/jacket lining* ○ *the lining of the stomach*

WORD PARTNERS FOR ***link***

discover/establish/find a link • a **close/direct/strong** link • a link **between** sth and sth • a link **with** sth

⊶**link¹** /lɪŋk/ *noun* [C] **1** [CONNECTION] a connection between two people, things, or ideas *There's a* ***direct link between*** *diet and heart disease.* ○ *Their* ***links with*** *Britain are still strong.* **2** [CHAIN] one ring of a chain **3** [INTERNET] (*also* **hyperlink**) a connection between documents or areas on the Internet *Click on this link to visit our online bookstore.*

link² /lɪŋk/ *verb* [T] to make a connection between two or more people, things, or ideas [often passive] *Both men have been* ***linked with*** *the robberies.* ○ *The drug has been* ***linked to*** *the deaths of several athletes.*

link (sb/sth) up If two or more things or people link up, or if you link them up, they form a connection so that they can operate or work together. *Each house will be linked up with the new communications network.*

lion

lion /laɪən/ *noun* [C] a large, wild animal of the cat family, with light brown fur ➲See also: **sea lion.**

⊶**lip** /lɪp/ *noun* [C] **1** one of the two soft, red edges of the mouth *He licked his lips.* ➲See colour picture **The Body** on page Centre 13. **2** the edge of a container that liquid is poured from

lip-read /ˈlɪpriːd/ *verb* [I, T] *past* **lip-read** to understand what someone is saying by looking at the way their mouth moves • **lip-reading** *noun* [U]

lip-service /ˈlɪpsɜːvɪs/ *noun* [no plural] **give/pay lip-service to sth** *informal* to say that you support an idea or plan, but not do anything to help it succeed

lipstick /ˈlɪpstɪk/ *noun* [C, U] a coloured substance that women put on their lips ➲See picture at **make up.**

lipstick

liqueur /lɪˈkjʊəʳ/ *noun* [C] a strong, sweet alcoholic drink which people usually drink a little of at the end of a meal

⊶**liquid** /ˈlɪkwɪd/ *noun* [C, U] a substance, for example water, that is not solid and that can be poured easily • **liquid** *adjective* *liquid fuel/nitrogen*

liquidate /ˈlɪkwɪdeɪt/ *verb* [T] to close a business because it has no money left • **liquidation** /ˌlɪkwɪˈdeɪʃən/ *noun* [C, U] *The store* ***went into liquidation.***

liquid-crystal display /ˌlɪkwɪdˌkrɪstəldɪˈspleɪ/ *noun* [C] LCD

liquor /ˈlɪkəʳ/ *noun* [U] *US* a strong alcoholic drink

ˈliquor ˌstore *US* (*UK* **off-licence**) *noun* [C] a shop that sells alcoholic drink

lisp /lɪsp/ *noun* [C] a way of speaking where 's' and 'z' sound like 'th' • **lisp** *verb* [I]

WORD PARTNERS FOR ***list***

compile/draw up/make/write a list • a list **of** sth • **on** a list • a **shopping** list

⊶**list¹** /lɪst/ *noun* [C] a series of names, numbers, or items that are written one below the other *a* ***shopping list*** ○ *Is your name* ***on the list?*** ○ ***Make a list*** *of everything you need.* ➲See also: **mailing list, waiting list.**

list² /lɪst/ *verb* [T] to make a list, or to include something in a list *All participants' names are listed alphabetically.*

⊶**listen** /ˈlɪsən/ *verb* [I] **1** to give attention to someone or something in order to hear them *What* *kind of music do you* **listen to***?* ○ *She does all the talking - I just sit and listen.* ○ *You haven't listened to a word I've said.* ○ *Listen, if you need money, I'm happy to lend you some.* **2** to accept someone's advice *I told you she wouldn't like it but you wouldn't listen to me!*

COMMON LEARNER ERROR

listen, listen to, or hear?

Use **hear** when you want to say that sounds, music, etc come to your ears. You can **hear** something without wanting to.

I could hear his music through the wall.

Use **listen** to say that you pay attention to sounds or try to hear something.

The audience listened carefully.

Ssh! I'm listening!

Use **listen to** when you want to say what it is that you are trying to hear.

The audience listened to the speaker.

Ssh! I'm listening to the radio!

listen (out) for sth to try to hear something *Could you listen out for the phone while I'm upstairs?*
listen in to secretly listen to a conversation, especially a telephone conversation
Listen up! *mainly US* something you say to tell people to listen to you *Okay, everyone, listen up! I have an announcement to make.*
listener /ˈlɪsᵊnəʳ/ *noun* [C] someone who listens *The new radio station already has twelve million listeners.* ○ *She's a* **good listener** (= she gives you all her attention when you speak).
lit /lɪt/ *past of* light
liter /ˈliːtəʳ/ *noun* [C] *US spelling of* litre
literacy /ˈlɪtᵊrəsi/ *noun* [U] the ability to read and write
literal /ˈlɪtᵊrᵊl/ *adjective* The literal meaning of a word or phrase is its real or original meaning. *the* **literal meaning***/sense*
literally /ˈlɪtᵊrᵊli/ *adverb* **1** having the real or original meaning of a word or phrase *They were responsible for literally millions of deaths.* **2** *informal* used to emphasize what you are saying *He missed that kick literally by miles!*
literary /ˈlɪtᵊrᵊri/ *adjective* relating to literature, or typical of the type of language that is used in literature **literary criticism**
literate /ˈlɪtᵊrət/ *adjective* able to read and write ⊃Opposite **illiterate.**
o⋅**literature** /ˈlɪtrətʃəʳ/ *noun* [U] **1** books, poems, etc that are considered to be art *classical/modern literature* **2** written information about a subject *There is very little literature on the disease.*
o⋅**litre** UK (*US* liter) (*written abbreviation* I) /ˈliːtəʳ/ *noun* [C] a unit for measuring liquid

WORD PARTNERS FOR *litter*

drop litter ● a piece of litter ● a litter bin

litter¹ /ˈlɪtəʳ/ *noun* **1** [U] pieces of paper and other waste that are left in public places **2** [C] a group of baby animals that are from the same mother and born at the same time *a litter of kittens/puppies*
litter² /ˈlɪtəʳ/ *verb* [T] If things litter an area, they cover parts of it in an untidy way. *Clothes littered the floor.*
be littered with sth to contain a lot of something *The whole book is littered with errors.*
o⋅**little¹** /ˈlɪtl/ *adjective* **1** [SMALL] small in size or amount *a little bag/box/town* ○ *She's so little.* ○ *It costs* **as little as** *one dollar.* ○ *I might have* **a little bit of** *cake.* **2** [SHORT] [always before noun] short in time or distance *Sit down for a little while.* ○ *Let's have a little break.* **3** [NOT IMPORTANT] [always before noun] not important *It's only a little problem.* ○ *I'm having a little trouble with my back.* **4** [YOUNG] [always before noun] young and small *She was my little sister and I looked after her.* ⊃See Common learner error at **small.**
o⋅**little²** /ˈlɪtl/ *quantifier* **1** not much or not enough *He has little chance of winning.* ○ *There's so little choice.* **2 a little sth** a small amount of something *It just needs a little effort.*

COMMON LEARNER ERROR

little

When **little** is used as a quantifier, it can only be used with uncountable nouns.

o⋅**little³** /ˈlɪtl/ *pronoun* **1** not much, or not enough *We did very little on Sunday.* **2 a little** a small amount *I only know a little about my grandparents.* ○ *"More dessert?" "Just a little, please."*
o⋅**little⁴** /ˈlɪtl/ *adverb* not much or not enough *She ate very little at dinner.* ○ *a little-known fact*
o⋅**live¹** /lɪv/ *verb* **1** [I] to be alive *She only lived a few days after the accident.* ○ *I hope I live to see my grandchildren.* **2 live at/in/near, etc** to have your home somewhere *They live in New York.* ○ *We live near each other.* ○ *Where do you live?* **3** [I, T] to spend your life in a particular way *Many people are living in poverty.* **4 I'll never live it down!** *humorous* something you say about an embarrassing experience that other people will not forget
live for sth/sb to have something or someone as the most important thing in your life *I love dancing - I just live for it.*
live on to continue to live *She lived on well into her nineties.*
live on sth 1 Money that you live on is the money you use to buy the things that you need. *We lived on very little when we were students.* **2** to only eat a particular type of food *All summer we live on hamburgers and hot dogs.*
live together If two people live together, they live in the same home and have a sexual relationship, but are not married.
live up to sth to be as good as someone hopes *Did your trip to China live up to your expectations?*
live with sb to live in the same home as someone and have a sexual relationship with them although you are not married
live with sth to accept a difficult or un-

pleasant situation *It's a problem she's going to have to live with.*

⚬**live²** /laɪv/ *adjective* **1** [LIFE] having life *Millions of live animals are shipped around the world each year.* **2** [ELECTRICITY] A live wire has electricity in it. **3** [BROADCAST] A live radio or television programme is seen or heard as it happens. *live coverage* ○ *a live broadcast* **4** [AUDIENCE] A live performance or recording of a performance is done with an audience. *a live concert* **5** [BOMB] A live bomb has not yet exploded.

live³ /laɪv/ *adverb* broadcast at the same time that something happens *We'll be bringing the match to you live on Wednesday.*

COMMON LEARNER ERROR

live or life

Live cannot be used as a noun. The correct noun to use is life.

It was the best day of my life.

livelihood /ˈlaɪvlihʊd/ *noun* [C, U] the way that you earn the money you need for living *The farm is his livelihood.*

lively /ˈlaɪvli/ *adjective* full of energy and interest *a lively conversation/debate* ○ *a lively child* ● **liveliness** *noun* [U]

liver /ˈlɪvəʳ/ *noun* **1** [C] a large organ in your body that cleans your blood **2** [U] the liver of an animal that is eaten by people

lives /laɪvz/ *plural of* life

livestock /ˈlaɪvstɒk/ *noun* [U] animals that are kept on a farm

livid /ˈlɪvɪd/ *adjective* very angry

living¹ /ˈlɪvɪŋ/ *noun* **1** [C] the money that you earn from your job [usually singular] *to earn/ make a living* ○ *What does he do for a living* (= how does he earn money)? **2** **country/ healthy, etc living** the way in which you live your life ⊃See also: **standard of living**.

living² /ˈlɪvɪŋ/ *adjective* [always before noun] **1** alive now *He's probably the best known living photographer.* **2** alive *living organisms* ○ *living things* ⊃See also: beat/knock the (living) **daylights** out of sb, scare/frighten the (living) **daylights** out of sb.

'living ˌroom (*also UK* **sitting room**) *noun* [C] the room in a house where people sit to relax and, for example, watch television ⊃See colour picture **The Living Room** on page Centre 4.

lizard /ˈlɪzəd/ *noun* [C] a small animal with thick skin, a long tail, and four short legs

load¹ /ləʊd/ *noun* **1** [C] something that is carried, often by a vehicle *We were behind a truck carrying a load of coal.* **2** **a load/loads** *informal* a lot of something *There were loads of people there.* ○ *Have some more food - there's loads.* **3** **a load of rubbish/nonsense, etc** *UK informal* nonsense

load² /ləʊd/ *verb* **1** [I, T] (*also* **load up**) to put a lot of things into a vehicle or machine *Bring the car up to the door and I'll start loading up.* ○ *to load the dishwasher/washing machine* ⊃Opposite **unload**. **2** [T] to put film in a camera or bullets in a gun

be loaded down with sth to have too

much to carry, or too much work to do *I was loaded down with shopping.*

be loaded with sth to contain a lot of something *Most fast foods are loaded with fat.*

-load /ləʊd/ *suffix* used at the end of a word to describe an amount of something that is being carried *a truckload of soldiers*

loaded /ˈləʊdɪd/ *adjective* **1** A loaded gun, or similar weapon, has a bullet in it. **2** [never before noun] *informal* very rich

ˌloaded 'question *noun* [C] a question which makes you answer in a particular way

loaf /ləʊf/ *noun* [C] *plural* **loaves** /ləʊvz/ bread that has been baked in one large piece so that it can be cut into smaller pieces *a loaf of bread* ⊃See picture at **bread**.

WORD PARTNERS FOR **loan**

apply for/repay/take out a loan ● a bank load

⚬**loan¹** /ləʊn/ *noun* **1** [C] money that someone has borrowed *a bank loan* ○ *He repaid the loan within two years.* **2** **be on loan** If something is on loan, someone is borrowing it. *Both paintings are on loan from the city museum.*

loan² /ləʊn/ *verb* [+ two objects] to lend something to someone *I was glad to loan my old books to her.* ○ *My dad loaned me the money.*

loath /ləʊθ/ *adjective* **be loath to do sth** *formal* to not want to do something because it will cause problems *I'm loath to spend it all.*

loathe /ləʊð/ *verb* [T] to hate someone or something ● **loathing** *noun* [U] a feeling of hating someone or something

loaves /ləʊvz/ *plural of* loaf

lobby¹ /ˈlɒbi/ *noun* [C] **1** a room at the main entrance of a building, often with doors and stairs that lead to other parts of the building *a hotel lobby* **2** a group of people who try to persuade the government to do something *the anti-smoking lobby*

lobby² /ˈlɒbi/ *verb* [I, T] to try to persuade the government to do something *They're lobbying for changes to the law.*

lobster /ˈlɒbstəʳ/ *noun* [C, U] a sea creature that has two claws (= sharp, curved parts) and eight legs, or the meat of this animal

⚬**local¹** /ˈləʊkəl/ *adjective* relating to an area near you *the local school/newspaper/radio station* ● **locally** *adverb* *locally grown vegetables*

local² /ˈləʊkəl/ *noun* [C] **1** someone who lives in the area you are talking about **2** **sb's local** *UK informal* a bar that is near someone's home

ˌlocal anaes'thetic *UK* (*US* **local anesthetic**) *noun* [C, U] a substance that is put into a part of your body so that you do not feel pain there *The procedure is carried out under local anaesthetic.*

ˌlocal au'thority *noun* [group] the group of people who govern a small area of a country *Local authorities are looking for new ways to promote investment.*

ˌlocal 'time *noun* [U] the official time in an area or country *We will shortly be landing in London, where the local time is 3.15.*

locate /ləʊˈkeɪt/ *verb* [T] *formal* **1** to find the exact position of someone or something *Police are still trying to locate the suspect.* **2 be located in/near/on, etc** to be in a particular place *Both schools are located in the town.*

WORD PARTNERS FOR *location*

at/in a [remote/secret, etc] location • the location **of** sth

---

location /ləʊˈkeɪʃᵊn/ *noun* **1** [C] a place or position *They haven't yet decided on **the location** of the new store.* **2 on location** If a film or television programme is made on location, it is made at a place suitable to the story.

loch /lɒk, lɒx/ *noun* [C] a lake in Scotland *Loch Lomond*

o━**lock¹** /lɒk/ *verb* **1** [I, T] to fasten something with a key, or to be fastened with a key *Did you lock the door? ○ If you shut the door it will lock automatically.* ⊃Opposite **unlock.** **2 lock sth/sb away/in, etc** to put something or someone in a place or container that is fastened with a key *She locked herself in her bedroom. ○ Most of my jewellery is locked away in a safe.* **3** [I] to become fixed in one position *I tried to move forward but the wheels had locked.*

lock sb in/out to prevent someone from entering/leaving a room or building by locking the door

lock (sth) up to lock all the doors and windows of a building when you leave it

lock sb up to put someone in prison or a hospital for people who are mentally ill

---

WORD PARTNERS FOR *lock (noun)*

fit a lock • a lock **on** sth • a **safety** lock

---

o━**lock²** /lɒk/ *noun* [C] **1** the thing that is used to close a door, window, etc, and that needs a key to open it *I heard someone turn a key in the lock. ○ safety locks* **2** a place on a river with gates to allow boats to move to a different water level **3 under lock and key** kept safely in a room or container that is locked *I tend to keep medicines under lock and key because of the kids.*

locker /ˈlɒkəʳ/ *noun* [C] a small cupboard in a public place where your personal possessions can be kept *a gym/luggage/school locker*

ˈlocker ˌroom *noun* [C] a room where you change your clothes and leave those and other personal possessions in a locker

locomotive /ˌləʊkəˈməʊtɪv/ *noun* [C] the part of a train that makes it move *a steam locomotive*

lodge¹ /lɒdʒ/ *noun* [C] a small house in the country that is used especially by people on holiday *a hunting/mountain/ski lodge*

lodge² /lɒdʒ/ *verb* **1 lodge in/on, etc** to become stuck somewhere *The bullet had lodged near his heart.* ⊃Compare **dislodge. 2 lodge at/with, etc** to live in someone's home and give them money for it **3 lodge a claim/complaint/protest, etc** to officially complain about something *He lodged an official complaint against the officers responsible.*

lodger /ˈlɒdʒəʳ/ *UK* (*US* **boarder**) *noun* [C] someone who pays for a place to sleep and meals in someone else's house

lodgings /ˈlɒdʒɪŋz/ *noun* [plural] *mainly UK* a room in someone's home that you pay money to live in *temporary lodgings*

loft /lɒft/ *noun* [C] **1** the space under the roof of a house or other building **2** *US* space where someone lives or works in a building that used to be a factory

log¹ /lɒg/ *noun* [C] **1** a thick piece of wood that has been cut from a tree **2** a written record of events, often on a ship or aircraft

log² /lɒg/ *verb* [T] *logging past* logged to make a written record of events, often on a ship or aircraft *to log an accident*

log in/on to connect a computer to a system of computers by typing your name, usually so that you can start working

log off/out to stop a computer being connected to a computer system, usually when you want to stop working

loggerheads /ˈlɒgəhedz/ *noun* **be at loggerheads (with sb)** If two people or groups are at loggerheads, they disagree strongly about something. *He is at loggerheads with the Prime Minister over public spending.*

WORD PARTNERS FOR *logic*

the logic **behind/in/of** sth

---

logic /ˈlɒdʒɪk/ *noun* [U] the use of reason, or the science of using reason *It was difficult to understand the **logic behind** his argument.*

logical /ˈlɒdʒɪkᵊl/ *adjective* using reason *a logical choice/conclusion* ⊃Opposite **illogical.** • **logically** *adverb*

login /ˈlɒgɪn/ *noun* [C, U] a box that appears on your computer screen when you start to use a computer which is connected to a computer system

logistics /ləˈdʒɪstɪks/ *noun* **the logistics of sth/doing sth** the practical arrangements for something *We could all use the one car but I'm not sure about the logistics of it.*

logo /ˈləʊgəʊ/ *noun* [C] a design or symbol used by a company to advertise its products *a corporate logo*

loiter /ˈlɔɪtəʳ/ *verb* [I] to stand in a place or walk slowly around without any purpose *A gang of youths were loitering outside the cinema.*

LOL *internet abbreviation for* laughing out loud: used when you think something is very funny

lollipop /ˈlɒlipɒp/ (*also UK* **lolly** /ˈlɒli/) *noun* [C] a large, hard sweet on a stick

lollipop

lone /ləʊn/ *adjective* [always before noun] alone *lone parents ○ the lone survivor*

o━**lonely** /ˈləʊnli/ *adjective* **1** unhappy because you are not with other people *She gets lonely now that the kids have all left home.* ⊃See Common learner error at **alone. 2** A lonely place is a long way from where people live. • **loneliness** *noun* [U]

loner /ˈləʊnəʳ/ *noun* [C] someone who likes to be

alone *He was always a bit of a loner at school.*

lonesome /ˈləʊnsəm/ *adjective US* lonely

o=**long¹** /lɒŋ/ *adjective* **1** [DISTANCE] having a large distance from one end to the other *long, brown hair* ○ *a long dress* ○ *It's a long way to travel to work.* **2** [TIME] continuing for a large amount of time *a long film/meeting* ○ *Have you been waiting a long time?* **3** [HOW LONG] used when asking for or giving information about the distance or time of something *It's about three metres long.* ○ *Most of the concerts are over three hours long.* ○ *Do you know how long the film is?* **4** [BOOK] A long book or other piece of writing has a lot of pages or words. *a long article/letter* ⊃See also: in the long/short **run²**.

o=**long²** /lɒŋ/ *adverb* **1** for a long time *We didn't have to wait long for the train.* ○ *The band played long into the night.* **2 as long as** used when you are talking about something that must happen before something else can happen *You can play football as long as you do your homework first.* **3 before long** soon *He'll be home before long.* **4 long ago** If something happened long ago, it happened a great amount of time ago. **5 no longer/not any longer** not now *He no longer works here.*

long³ /lɒŋ/ *noun* [U] a large amount of time *She won't be away for long.*

long⁴ /lɒŋ/ *verb formal* **long for sth; long to do sth** to want something very much *She longed to see him again.*

long-distance /ˌlɒŋˈdɪstəns/ *adjective* travelling or communicating between two places that are a long way apart *a long-distance race* ○ *a long-distance phone call*

long-haul /ˈlɒŋˌhɔːl/ *adjective* [always before noun] travelling a long distance *a long-haul flight*

longing /ˈlɒŋɪŋ/ *noun* [U, no plural] a feeling of wanting something or someone very much *He gazed at her, his eyes full of longing.* ○ *a longing for his homeland* ● **longingly** *adverb She looked longingly at the silk dresses.*

longitude /ˈlɒndʒɪtjuːd/ *noun* [U] the distance of a place east or west of an imaginary line from the top to the bottom of the Earth, measured in degrees

the ˈlong ˌjump *noun* a sports event where people try to jump as far as possible

long-life /ˌlɒŋˈlaɪf/ *adjective UK* Long-life drink or food has been treated so that it will last a long time. *long-life milk*

long-lost /ˈlɒŋˌlɒst/ *adjective* **long-lost friend/cousin, etc** a friend or relative that you have not seen for a long time

long-range /ˌlɒŋˈreɪndʒ/ *adjective* [always before noun] **1** relating to a time in the future *a long-range weather forecast* **2** able to be sent long distances *a long-range bomber/missile*

ˈlong ˌshot *noun* [C] *informal* something that is not likely to succeed *It's a long shot, but you could try phoning him at home.*

long-sighted /ˌlɒŋˈsaɪtɪd/ *UK* (*US* **farsighted**) *adjective* able to see objects which are far away but not things which are near to you

long-standing /ˌlɒŋˈstændɪŋ/ *adjective* having

existed for a long time *a long-standing relationship*

long-suffering /ˌlɒŋˈsʌfᵊrɪŋ/ *adjective* A long-suffering person has been very patient for a long time about all the trouble that someone has caused them. *Bill and his long-suffering wife*

long-term /ˌlɒŋˈtɜːm/ *adjective* continuing a long time into the future *the problem of long-term unemployment*

long-winded /ˌlɒŋˈwɪndɪd/ *adjective* If what someone says or writes is long-winded, it is boring because it is too long. *a long-winded explanation*

loo /luː/ *noun* [C] *UK informal* toilet *I'll just go to the loo.* ⊃See Common learner error at **toilet**.

o=**look¹** /lʊk/ *verb* **1** [I] to turn your eyes in the direction of something or someone so that you can see them *Look at the picture on page two.* ○ *He was looking out of the window.* ○ *I looked around and there she was.* **2** [I] to try to find someone or something *I'm looking for my keys.* ○ *I've looked everywhere but I can't find my bag.* **3 look nice/strange, etc; look like/as if** used to describe the appearance of a person or thing *That food looks nice.* ○ *You look tired, my love.* ○ *Do I look silly in this hat?* ○ *He looked like a drug addict.* **4 it looks like; it looks as if** used to say that something is likely to happen *It looks like there'll be three of us.* ○ *It looks as if he isn't coming.* **5 be looking to do sth** to plan to do something *I'm looking to start my own business.* **6 Look!** something you say when you are annoyed and you want people to know that what you are saying is important *Look, I've had enough of your complaints.* ⊃See also: look the **part¹**.

COMMON LEARNER ERROR

look, see, or watch?

See means to notice people and things with your eyes.

She saw a big spider and screamed.

Did you see anyone you knew at the party?

Look (at) is used when you are trying to see something or someone. Look cannot be followed by an object.

I've looked everywhere, but can't find my keys.

He looked at the map to find the road.

~~He looked the photographs.~~

Watch means to look at something for a period of time, usually something which moves or changes.

He watched television all evening.

I watched them playing football.

o=**look after sb/sth** to take care of someone or something by keeping them healthy or in a good condition *Could you look after the children while I'm out?*

look ahead to think about something that will happen in the future and plan for it

look at sth 1 [THINK] to think about a subject carefully so that you can make a decision about it *Management is looking at ways of cutting costs.* **2** [READ] to read something *Can you look at my essay sometime?* **3** [EXPERT] If an expert looks at something, they examine it.

Did you get the doctor to look at your knee?
4 OPINION to consider something in a particular way *If I'd been a mother I might have looked at things differently.*
look back to remember something in the past *He **looked back** on his childhood with affection.*
look down on sb to think that someone is less important than you
o▸**look forward to sth/doing sth** to feel happy and excited about something that is going to happen *I'm really looking forward to seeing him.*

look forward to

Remember always to use the preposition **to** when you use this verb.
We are looking forward to your visit.
~~We are looking forward your visit.~~

look into sth to examine the facts about a situation *They are looking into the causes of the accident.*
look on to watch something happen but not become involved in it
look on sb/sth to think about someone or something in a particular way *We look on him almost as our own son.*
Look out! something you say when someone is in danger *Look out - there's a car coming!*
look out for sb/sth to try to notice someone or something *Look out for Anna while you're there.*
look over sth to examine something quickly *I'm just looking over what you've written so far.*
look through sth to read something quickly *I've looked through a few catalogues.*
look up to become better *Our financial situation is looking up.*
look sth up to look at a book or computer in order to find information *I looked it up in the dictionary.*
look up to sb to respect and admire someone *Georgia looks up to Lidia.*

WORD PARTNERS FOR **look** (noun)

have/take a look • a **close/good** look • a look **at** sb/sth

o▸**look²** /lʊk/ *noun* **1** SEE [C] when you look at someone or something [usually singular] *Take a look at these pictures.* ○ *You've got your photos back - can I **have a look**?* **2** **have/take a look** when you try to find something *I've had a look in the drawer but I can't find my passport.* **3** FACE [C] an expression on someone's face *She had a worried look on her face.* ○ *She gave me a questioning look.* **4** FASHION [no plural] a style or fashion *the new look for the summer* **5** **the look of sb/sth** the appearance of someone or something *I like the look of that new music programme they're advertising.* **6** **sb's looks** a person's appearance, especially how attractive they are ⊃See also: **good looks.**

lookalike /'lʊkəlaɪk/ *noun* [C] *informal* someone who looks very similar to a famous person *an Elvis lookalike*
look-in /'lʊkɪn/ *noun* UK *informal* **not get a look-in** to get no chance to achieve what you want or to succeed in something *He played so well, nobody else got a look-in.*
lookout /'lʊkaʊt/ *noun* **1** [C] a person who watches for danger and warns other people **2** **be on the lookout** to be continuing to search for something or someone *I'm always on the lookout for interesting new recipes.*
loom¹ /luːm/ *verb* [I] **1** to appear as a large, sometimes frightening shape *Dark storm clouds loomed on the horizon.* **2** If an unpleasant event looms, it is likely to happen soon. *The threat of closure looms over the workforce.*
loom² /luːm/ *noun* [C] a machine for making cloth by weaving together (= crossing over) threads
loony /'luːni/ *noun* [C] *informal* someone who behaves in a crazy way *The man's a complete loony.* ●**loony** *adjective informal* crazy *loony ideas*
loop¹ /luːp/ *noun* [C] a circle of something long and thin, such as a piece of string or wire
loop² /luːp/ *verb* **loop sth around/over, etc sth** to make something into the shape of a loop *Loop the rope around your waist.*

WORD PARTNERS FOR **loophole**

a loophole **in** sth • a **legal** loophole

loophole /'luːphəʊl/ *noun* [C] a mistake in an agreement or law which gives someone the chance to avoid having to do something
o▸**loose** /luːs/ *adjective* **1** NOT FIXED not firmly fixed *There were some loose wires hanging out of the wall.* ○ *One of my buttons is loose.* **2** CLOTHES large and not fitting tightly *a loose dress/ sweater* **3** FREE An animal that is loose is free to move around. *Two lions escaped and are still loose.* **4** NOT EXACT not exact *It's only a loose translation of the poem.* ●**loosely** *adverb The film is **based** very loosely (= not exactly) on the novel.* ⊃See also: be at a loose **end¹.**

loose or lose?

Be careful, these two words look and sound similar but have completely different meanings.
Loose is an adjective, meaning not fixed or not tight.
These trousers are a bit loose.
Be careful not to use **loose** when you really mean the verb **lose**.
I hope he doesn't lose his job.
~~I hope he doesn't loose his job.~~

loosen /'luːsᵊn/ *verb* [I, T] to become loose or make something loose *He loosened his tie.*
loosen up to become more relaxed with other people *After a while he loosened up.*
loot¹ /luːt/ *verb* [I, T] to steal from shops and houses during a war or period of fighting

Rioters looted the capital.

loot² /luːt/ *noun* [U] goods which have been stolen

lop /lɒp/ *verb* **lopping** *past* **lopped**

lop sth off to cut off something in one quick movement *I lopped off the biggest branches.*

lopsided /ˌlɒpˈsaɪdɪd/ [US] /ˈlɒpsaɪdɪd/ *adjective* with one side lower than the other *a lopsided grin*

loquacious /ləʊˈkweɪʃəs/ *adjective formal* talking a lot

lord /lɔːd/ *noun* **1** [C, U] (*also* **Lord**) a man of high social rank, or a title given to a man who has earned official respect, in the UK *Lord Lichfield* **2 the Lord** God or Christ **3 Good Lord!** *informal* something you say when you are surprised or angry *Good Lord! Is that the time?* ➲See also: **House of Lords**.

the Lords /lɔːdz/ (*also* **House of Lords**) *noun* [group] one of the two parts of the British parliament, with members who are chosen by the government

lorry /ˈlɒri/ *UK* (*UK/US* **truck**) *noun* [C] a large road vehicle for carrying goods from place to place ➲See picture at **vehicle**.

⊶**lose** /luːz/ *verb past* **lost** **1** [NOT FIND] [T] to not be able to find someone or something *I've lost my passport.* ○ *She's always losing her car keys.* **2** [NOT HAVE] [T] to stop having someone or something that you had before *She lost a leg in a car accident.* ○ *I hope he doesn't lose his job.* ○ *He lost his mother* (= his mother died) *last year.* **3** [HAVE LESS] [T] to have less of something than you had before *She's lost a lot of weight.* ○ *He's losing his hair.* ○ *She lost a lot of blood in the accident.* ○ *to lose your memory* **4** [NOT WIN] [I, T] If you lose a game, the team or person that you are playing against wins. *Chelsea lost by a goal.* ○ *They're losing 3-1.* ○ *They hadn't lost an election in 15 years.* **5 lose faith/interest/patience, etc** to stop feeling something good *I'm rapidly losing interest in the whole subject.* ○ *He kept on crying and I lost my patience.* **6** [TIME] [T] If you lose a number of hours or days, you cannot work during this time. *Four million hours were lost last year through stress-related illnesses.* **7** [CLOCK] [T] If a clock loses time, it goes slower than it should. **8** [CONFUSE] [T] *informal* to confuse someone so that they do not understand something *No, you've lost me there - can you explain that again?* ○ *He lost me five minutes into the lecture.* **9** [GET RID OF] *informal* to take something away, usually because it looks bad. *Lose the belt, Andrea, it looks ridiculous with that dress.* **10 lose your balance** to fall because you are leaning too much to one side *I was cycling and I took a corner too sharply and lost my balance.* **11 lose count of sth** to forget the exact number *I've lost count of how many times I've called her.* **12 lose your life** to die *Millions of young men lost their lives in the war.* **13 be losing it** *informal* to start to become crazy *I can't even remember my own telephone number - I think I must be losing it.* **14 lose it** *informal* to stop being able to control your emotions and suddenly start to laugh, shout or cry *I was trying so hard to stay calm but in the end I just lost it.* ➲See Common learner error at **loose** ➲See also: fight a losing **battle¹**, lose your **cool³**, lose/save **face¹**, gain/lose **ground¹**, lose **sight¹** of sth, lose **sleep²** over sth.

COMMON LEARNER ERROR

lose or miss?

Usually you **miss** something which happens, such as an event, a train leaving, or an opportunity.

I do not want to miss my class.

~~*I do not want to lose my class.*~~

Usually you **lose** a thing.

I've lost my umbrella.

lose out to not have an advantage that someone else has

loser /ˈluːzəʳ/ *noun* [C] **1** someone who does not win a game or competition *The losers of both games will play each other for third place.* **2** *informal* someone who is not successful in anything they do *I'd been made redundant, my wife was divorcing me and I felt like such a loser.*

WORD PARTNERS FOR ***loss***

2 make/suffer a loss • a loss **of** [$50,000/£3 million, etc]

⊶**loss** /lɒs/ *noun* **1** [NOT HAVING] [C, U] when you do not have someone or something that you had before, or when you have less of something than before *loss of income/memory* ○ *blood/hair/weight loss* ○ *job losses* **2** [MONEY] [C, U] when a company spends more money than it earns *Both companies* ***suffered losses*** *this year.* **3** [DISADVANTAGE] [no plural] a disadvantage caused by someone leaving an organization *It would be a great* ***loss to*** *the department if you left.* **4 be at a loss** to not know what to do or say [+ to do sth] *I'm at a loss to explain his disappearance.* **5 a sense of loss** sadness because someone has died or left **6** [DEATH] [C, U] the death of a person *They never got over the loss of their son.*

⊶**lost¹** /lɒst/ *adjective* **1** [PERSON] not knowing where you are or where you should go *I* ***got lost*** *on the way.* **2** [OBJECT] If something is lost, no one knows where it is. *Things tend to* ***get lost*** *when you move house.* ○ *Lost: black cat with white paws.* **3** [NEW SITUATION] not knowing what to do in a new situation *It was his first day in the office and he seemed a bit lost.* **4 be lost without sb/sth** *informal* to be unable to live or work without someone or something *She's lost without her computer.* **5 be lost on sb** If a joke or remark is lost on someone, they do not understand it. **6 Get lost!** *informal* an impolite way of telling someone to go away ➲See also: **long-lost**.

lost² /lɒst/ *past of* lose

ˌlost ˈproperty *noun* [U] *UK* things that people have left in public places which are kept somewhere until the owners can collect them

o-**lot** /lɒt/ *noun* **1 a lot; lots** a large number or amount of people or things *There were **a lot of** people outside the building.* ○ *He earns **lots of** money.* ○ *I've got a lot to do this morning.* ⊃See Common learner error at **many**. **2 a lot better/older/ quicker, etc** much better/older/quicker, etc *It's a lot better than the old system.* ○ *It's a lot quicker by train.* **3 the lot** *UK informal* all of an amount or number *I made enough curry for three people and he ate the lot.* **4** GROUP [C] *UK* a group of people or things that you deal with together *I've already done one lot of washing.* **5** AREA [C] *US* an area of land *a parking lot* ○ *an empty lot* **6** SALE [C] something being sold at an auction (= sale where things are sold to the people who pay the most) *Lot 3: a Victorian chest.* **7 sb's lot** the quality of someone's life and the type of experiences they have *They've done much to improve the lot of working people.*

COMMON LEARNER ERROR

a lot of sth

Remember to use the preposition **of** before the thing that there is a large number of.

A lot of people enjoy travelling to other countries.

~~A lot people enjoy travelling to other countries.~~

lotion /'ləʊʃ⁰n/ *noun* [C, U] a liquid that you put on your skin to make it soft or healthy *suntan lotion* ○ *body lotion*

lottery /'lɒt⁰ri/ *noun* [C] a way of making money by selling numbered tickets to people who then have a chance of winning a prize if their number is chosen *the national lottery*

o-**loud¹** /laʊd/ *adjective* **1** making a lot of noise *a loud noise* ○ *a **loud voice*** ○ *a loud explosion* **2** Loud clothes are too bright or have too many colours. ● **loudly** *adverb She was speaking very loudly.*

loud² /laʊd/ *adverb* **1** loudly *Can you speak a bit louder?* **2 out loud** If you say or read something out loud, you say or read it so that other people can hear you.

loudspeaker /ˌlaʊd'spiːkə⁰/ ⓤⓢ /'laʊd,spiːkə⁰/ *noun* [C] a piece of equipment used for making voices or sounds louder

lounge¹ /laʊndʒ/ *noun* [C] **1** *UK* the room in a home where you sit and relax **2** *US* a room in a hotel, theatre, airport, etc where people can relax or wait

lounge² /laʊndʒ/ *verb*
lounge about/around (sth) to spend your time in a relaxed way, doing very little *Most days were spent lounging around the pool.*

louse /laʊs/ *noun* [C] *plural* **lice** /laɪs/ a very small insect that lives on the bodies or in the hair of people or animals

lousy /'laʊzi/ *adjective informal* very bad *lousy food/service* ○ *I **felt lousy** when I woke up this morning.*

lout /laʊt/ *noun* [C] a man who behaves in a rude or violent way

lovable (*also* **loveable**) /'lʌvəbl/ *adjective* A

person or animal that is lovable has qualities which make them easy to love.

o-**love¹** /lʌv/ *verb* [T] **1** ROMANCE/SEX to like someone very much and have romantic or sexual feelings for them *Last night he told me he loved me.* ○ *I've only ever loved one woman.* **2** FRIENDS/ FAMILY to like a friend or a person in your family very much *I'm sure he loves his kids.* **3** ENJOY to enjoy something very much or have a strong interest in something *He loves his music.* ○ *She loves animals.* ○ **[+ doing sth]** *I love eating out.* **4 I'd love to** used to say that you would very much like to do something that someone is offering *"I wondered if you'd like to meet up sometime?" "I'd love to."*

WORD PARTNERS FOR **love** (noun)

in love **with** sb ● **fall** in love ● **madly** in love ● **brotherly/unconditional** love

o-**love²** /lʌv/ *noun* **1** ROMANCE/SEX [U] when you like someone very much and have romantic or sexual feelings for them *He's **madly in love with** (= he loves) her.* ○ *I was 20 when I first **fell in love** (= started to love someone).* ○ *a love song/story* **2 make love** to have sex **3** PERSON [C] someone who you like very much and have a romantic or sexual relationship with *He was my first love.* **4** FRIENDS/FAMILY [U] when you like a friend or person in your family very much *Nothing is as strong as the love you have for your kids.* **5** INTEREST [C, U] something that interests you a lot *his love of books* **6 Love from; All my love** something you write at the end of a letter to a friend or someone in your family *Love from Mum.* ○ *All my love, Louise.* **7** SPEAKING TO SOMEONE *mainly UK* You call someone 'love' to show affection or to be friendly. *"Margot?" "Yes, love."* ○ *Two portions of chips please, love.* **8** SPORTS [U] in games such as tennis, a score of zero *She's leading by two sets to love.* ⊃See also: a **labour¹** of love.

'**love af,fair** *noun* [C] a romantic or sexual relationship

loveless /'lʌvləs/ *adjective* without love *She was trapped in a **loveless marrage**.*

'**love ,life** *noun* the romantic relationships in a person's life *How's your love life these days?*

o-**lovely** /'lʌvli/ *adjective* **1** pleasant or enjoyable *We had a **lovely** day together.* ○ *What lovely weather.* **2** very attractive *a lovely dress/ house/village* ○ *You look lovely!*

lover /'lʌvə⁰/ *noun* **1** [C] If two people are lovers, they have a sexual relationship but they are not married. *She had a string of lovers before her marriage finally broke up.* **2 a book/cat/ dog, etc lover** someone who is very interested in books/cats/dogs, etc *She's a real cat lover.*

loving /'lʌvɪŋ/ *adjective* showing a lot of affection and kindness towards someone *a loving relationship* ○ *a loving father* ● **lovingly** *adverb*

o-**low¹** /ləʊ/ *adjective* **1** NOT HIGH near the ground, not high *low aircraft* ○ *a low fence* **2** LEVEL below the usual level *a low income* ○ *low temperatures/prices* ○ *a low number* ○ *Fish is very **low in** (= has little) fat.* **3** SOUND deep or quiet *a low voice* ○ *a low note* **4** LIGHTS If lights are low, they are not bright. *We have very low lighting in the main room.* **5** UNHAPPY unhappy and without energy *Illness of any sort can leave you feeling low.* ⊃See also: be at a low ebb¹, keep a low **profile**¹.

low² /ləʊ/ *adverb* **1** in or to a low position or level *low-paid workers* ○ *Turn the oven on low.* **2** with deep notes *You can sing lower than me.*

low³ /ləʊ/ *noun* a new/record/all-time, etc low the lowest level *Temperatures in the region hit a record low yesterday.*

low-alcohol /ˌləʊˈælkəhɒl/ *adjective* A low-alcohol drink has less alcohol in it than the normal type. *low-alcohol beer*

low-calorie /ˌləʊˈkælˀri/ (*abbreviation* **low-cal, lo-cal**) *adjective* A low-calorie food or drink will not make you fat because it has fewer calories (= units for measuring the amount of energy a food provides) than normal food or drink.

low-cut /ˌləʊˈkʌt/ *adjective* describes a piece of clothing that does not cover the top part of a woman's chest *a low-cut dress*

the lowdown /ˈləʊdaʊn/ *noun informal* the most important information about something *Jenny will give you the lowdown on what happened at yesterday's meeting.*

lower¹ /ˈləʊəʳ/ *adjective* being the bottom part of something *I've got a pain in my lower back.* ○ *She bit her lower lip.*

lower² /ˈləʊəʳ/ *verb* [T] **1** to move something to a low position *They lowered the coffin into the grave.* **2** to reduce the amount of something *I'll join if they lower the entrance fee.*

lower 'case *noun* [U] letters of the alphabet which are not written as capital letters, for example a, b, c

low-fat /ˌləʊˈfæt/ *adjective* Low-fat foods do not contain much fat. *low-fat cheese* ○ *a low-fat diet*

low-key /ˌləʊˈkiː/ *adjective* not attracting attention *The wedding reception itself was surprisingly low-key.*

lowly /ˈləʊli/ *adjective* not important or respected *He took a lowly job in an insurance firm.*

low-rise /ˈləʊˌraɪz/ *adjective* describes trousers in which the top part of the trousers ends below the person's waist

low-tech /ˌləʊˈtek/ *adjective* Something that is low-tech does not use the most recent technology. ⊃Compare high-tech.

loyal /lɔɪəl/ *adjective* always liking and supporting someone or something, sometimes when other people do not *a loyal supporter* ○ *She's very loyal to her friends.* ⊃Opposite disloyal. ● **loyally** *adverb*

loyalties /ˈlɔɪəltiz/ *noun* [plural] a feeling of support for someone *My loyalties to my family come before work.*

loyalty /ˈlɔɪəlti/ *noun* [U] the quality of being loyal *Your loyalty to the company is impressive.* ⊃Opposite disloyalty.

lozenge /ˈlɒzɪndʒ/ *noun* [C] a sweet which you suck to make your throat feel better

LP /ˌelˈpiː/ *noun* [C] a record that has about 25 minutes of music on each side

LPG /ˌelpiːˈdʒiː/ *noun* [U] *abbreviation for* liquid petroleum gas: a type of fuel used for heating, cooking and in some vehicles *Ben converted his car to run on LPG.*

L-plate /ˈelpleɪt/ *noun* [C] *UK* a red and white 'L' symbol on the car of someone learning to drive

Ltd *written abbreviation for* limited company (= used after the name of some companies) *Pinewood Supplies Ltd*

lubricant /ˈluːbrɪkənt/ *noun* [C, U] a liquid, such as oil, which is used to make the parts of an engine move smoothly together

lubricate /ˈluːbrɪkeɪt/ *verb* [T] to put a lubricant on something ● **lubrication** /ˌluːbrɪˈkeɪʃˀn/ *noun* [U]

lucid /ˈluːsɪd/ *adjective* **1** clear and easy to understand *a lucid account* **2** able to think and speak clearly *In a lucid moment, she spoke about her son.* ● **lucidly** *adverb*

┌─────────────────────────────┐
│ WORD PARTNERS FOR **luck**
│ bad/beginner's/good/rotten luck ● bring/
│ wish sb luck ● curse your luck ● a stroke of
│ luck
└─────────────────────────────┘

◦→ **luck** /lʌk/ *noun* [U] **1** good and bad things caused by chance and not by your own actions *It was just luck that I asked for a job at the right time.* ○ *Then I met this gorgeous woman and I couldn't believe my luck.* ○ *He seems to have had a lot of bad luck in his life.* **2** success *Have you had any luck* (= succeeded in) *finding your bag?* ○ *He's been trying to find work but with no luck so far.* **3** be in luck *informal* to be able to have or do what you want *"Do you have any tuna sandwiches?" "You're in luck - there's one left."* **4** Good luck! something you say to someone when you hope that they will be successful *Good luck with your exam!* **5** Bad/Hard luck! used to show sympathy when someone is unsuccessful or unlucky *"They've run out of tickets for the Arctic Monkeys concert." "Oh, bad luck!"* **6** the luck of the draw If something is the luck of the draw, it is the result of chance and you have no control over it. ⊃See also: a stroke¹ of luck.

◦→ **lucky** /ˈlʌki/ *adjective* **1** having good things happen to you *"I'm going on holiday." "Lucky you!"* ○ *The lucky winner will be able to choose from three different holidays.* ○ [+ to do sth] *You're lucky to have such a nice office to work in.* **2** If an object is lucky, some people believe that it gives you luck. *I chose six - it's my lucky number.* ⊃Opposite unlucky. ● **luckily** *adverb* *Luckily I had some money with me.* ⊃See also: happy-go-lucky.

lucrative /ˈluːkrətɪv/ *adjective* If something is lucrative, it makes a lot of money. *a lucrative contract/job/offer*

ludicrous /ˈluːdɪkrəs/ *adjective* stupid *a ludicrous idea/suggestion* ● **ludicrously** *adverb*

lug /lʌg/ *verb* [T] **lugging**, *past* **lugged** *informal* to carry or pull a heavy object *You don't want to lug your suitcase across London.*

luggage

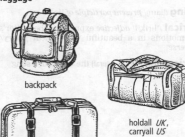

backpack

holdall *UK*,
carryall *US*

suitcase

luggage /ˈlʌɡɪdʒ/ *noun* [U] bags and cases that you carry with you when you are travelling ⊃See also: **hand luggage**.

lukewarm /ˌluːkˈwɔːm/ *adjective* **1** A liquid which is lukewarm is only slightly warm. *Dissolve yeast and one tablespoon of sugar in lukewarm water.* **2** showing little interest or enthusiasm *She seemed rather lukewarm about the idea.*

lull¹ /lʌl/ *verb* [T] to make someone feel calm and make them want to sleep *Soft music lulled him to sleep.*

lull sb into sth/doing sth to make someone feel safe so that you can then trick them

lull² /lʌl/ *noun* [C] a short period of calm in which little happens *a lull in the conversation/traffic*

lullaby /ˈlʌləbaɪ/ *noun* [C] a song which you sing to children to make them sleep

lumber¹ /ˈlʌmbər/ *verb* **lumber along/around/off, etc** to move slowly with heavy steps *The bear lumbered off into the forest.*

be lumbered with sth/sb *mainly UK* to have to deal with something or someone that you do not want to *I've been lumbered with my neighbours' cat while they're away.*

lumber² /ˈlʌmbər/ *US* (*UK* timber) *noun* [U] wood that is used for building

lumberjack /ˈlʌmbədʒæk/ *noun* [C] a person whose job is to cut down trees in a forest

luminary /ˈluːmɪnəri/ *noun* [C] *formal* a famous person who is respected for their skills or knowledge

luminous /ˈluːmɪnəs/ *adjective* Something that is luminous shines in the dark.

lump¹ /lʌmp/ *noun* [C] **1** a piece of a solid substance with no particular shape *a lump of coal* ○ *You don't want lumps in the sauce.* ⊃See colour picture **Pieces and Quantities** on page Centre 1. **2** a hard piece of tissue under the skin caused by injury or illness *She found a lump in her breast.*

lump² /lʌmp/ *verb*
lump sth/sb together to put different groups together and think about them or deal

with them in the same way *American and Canadian authors tend to be lumped together.*

lump ˈsum *noun* [C] a large amount of money given as a single payment *She received a tax-free lump sum on leaving the company.*

lumpy /ˈlʌmpi/ *adjective* covered with or containing lumps (= bits of solid substance) *a lumpy sauce*

lunacy /ˈluːnəsi/ *noun* [U] stupid behaviour that will have bad results *It was lunacy spending all that money.*

lunar /ˈluːnər/ *adjective* [always before noun] relating to the moon

lunatic /ˈluːnətɪk/ *noun* [C] someone who behaves in a crazy way *He drives like a lunatic.*

WORD PARTNERS FOR *lunch*

eat/have lunch • have sth for lunch • a light lunch

ᴏ⁻**lunch¹** /lʌnʃ/ *noun* [C, U] a meal that you eat in the middle of the day ⊃See also: **packed lunch**.

lunch² /lʌnʃ/ *verb* [I] to eat lunch

luncheon /ˈlʌnʃən/ *noun* [C] *formal* lunch

lunchtime /ˈlʌnʃtaɪm/ *noun* [C, U] the time when lunch is eaten

lung /lʌŋ/ *noun* [C] one of the two organs inside your chest that are used for breathing *lung cancer*

lurch /lɜːtʃ/ *verb* **lurch forward/towards, etc** to suddenly move in a way that is not controlled *The car lurched forward before hitting the tree.*

lure¹ /lʊər/ *verb* [T] to persuade someone to go somewhere or do something by offering them something exciting *It seems that he was lured into a trap.* ○ *They had been lured to the big city by the promise of high wages.*

lure² /lʊər/ *noun* [U] the power to attract people *the lure of fame/power/money*

lurid /ˈlʊərɪd/ *adjective* **1** shocking in a way that involves sex or violence *lurid details/stories* **2** too brightly coloured *a lurid green miniskirt*

lurk /lɜːk/ *verb* [I] **1** to wait somewhere secretly, especially before doing something bad *Someone was lurking in the shadows.* **2** to enter a chat room (= place on the Internet for email discussions) and read what other people have written without them knowing you are there ● **lurker** *noun* [C]

lush /lʌʃ/ *adjective* A lush area has a lot of healthy grass, plants, or trees.

lust¹ /lʌst/ *noun* [U] **1** a strong feeling of sexual attraction to someone **2** when you want something very much *a lust for power*

lust² /lʌst/ *verb*
lust after sb to feel strong sexual attraction for someone
lust after sth to want something very much *to lust after fame/power*

Lutheran /ˈluːθərən/ *adjective* belonging or relating to a Christian group based on the teachings of Martin Luther ● **Lutheran** *noun* [C]

luxurious /lʌɡˈʒʊəriəs/ *adjective* very comfortable and expensive *a luxurious hotel* ○ *luxurious fabrics*

luxury /ˈlʌkʃəri/ *noun* **1** COMFORT/PLEASURE [U]

great comfort or pleasure from expensive or beautiful things *to live in luxury* ⚬ *a luxury apartment/car* **2** NOT NECESSARY [C] something expensive that you enjoy but do not need *It's nice to buy people the little luxuries that they wouldn't buy themselves.* **3** RARE PLEASURE [U, no plural] something which gives you a lot of pleasure but which you cannot often do *A day off*

work is such a luxury.

lying /ˈlaɪɪŋ/ *present participle of* lie[1,2]

lyrical /ˈlɪrɪkᵊl/ *adjective* expressing the writer's emotions in a beautiful way *lyrical poetry/ verse*

lyrics /ˈlɪrɪks/ *noun* [plural] the words of a song

Mm

M, m /em/ the thirteenth letter of the alphabet

m *written abbreviation for* metre (= a unit of length)

MA /ˌemˈeɪ/ *noun* [C] *abbreviation for* Master of Arts: a higher university qualification in an arts (= not science) subject

ma'am /mæm, mɑːm/ *US short for* madam *Can I help you, Ma'am?*

mac /mæk/ *noun* [C] *UK* a coat that you wear in the rain ➲See colour picture **Clothes** on page Centre 8.

macabre /məˈkɑːbrə/ *adjective* strange and frightening, and often connected with death *a macabre story*

macaroni /ˌmækᵊrˈəʊni/ *noun* [U] pasta that is shaped like small tubes

machete /məˈʃeti/ *noun* [C] a large knife with a wide blade

machinations /ˌmæʃɪˈneɪʃᵊnz/ *noun* [plural] complicated and secret plans and activities *political machinations*

> WORD PARTNERS FOR ***machine***
>
> **operate/use** a machine • **turn off/turn on** a machine • do sth **by** machine • a machine **for** doing sth

⊶**machine** /məˈʃiːn/ *noun* [C] **1** [EQUIPMENT] a piece of equipment with moving parts that uses power to do a particular job *a fax machine* ○ *a coffee machine* ○ *Clothes are generally sewn **by machine** these days.* **2** [GROUP] a group of people all working together to achieve the same result *a political/war machine* **3** [COMPUTER] a computer ➲See also: **answerphone, cash machine, sewing machine, slot machine, vending machine, washing machine.**

maˈchine ˌgun *noun* [C] a gun that fires a lot of bullets very quickly

machine-readable /məˌʃiːnˈriːdəbl/ *adjective* able to be understood by a computer *a machine-readable dictionary*

machinery /məˈʃiːnᵊri/ *noun* [U] **1** machines, often large machines *industrial/farm machinery* **2** the system that a group of people uses to achieve something *the machinery of government*

macho /ˈmætʃəʊ/ Ⓤⓢ /ˈmɑːtʃəʊ/ *adjective informal* Men who are macho emphasize their traditional male qualities, such as physical strength, and do not show emotion.

mackerel /ˈmækrᵊl/ *noun* [C, U] *plural* **mackerel** or **mackerels** a type of sea fish, or the meat from this fish

mackintosh /ˈmækɪntɒʃ/ *noun* [C] *old-fashioned* a mac

macro- /mækrəʊ-/ *prefix* large or on a large scale *macroeconomics* (= the study of financial systems at a national level)

⊶**mad** /mæd/ *adjective* **1** [CRAZY] *informal* stupid or crazy [+ to do sth] *You're mad to walk home alone at night.* **2** [ANGRY] *mainly US* angry *Were your parents **mad at** you when you came home late?* **3 go mad a** [ANGRY] to become very angry *Dad'll go mad when he finds out you took the car.* **b** [EXCITED] to suddenly become very excited *When the band arrived on stage, the crowd went mad.* **4** [ILL] mentally ill **5** [NOT CONTROLLED] not controlled *We made a **mad dash** for the exit.* **6 be mad about sb/sth** *informal* to love something or someone *Jo's mad about skiing.* **7 like mad a** [QUICKLY] If you run, work, etc like mad, you do it very quickly and with a lot of energy. **b** [PAIN] If something hurts like mad, it hurts a lot.

> **COMMON LEARNER ERROR**
>
> **mad** or **mentally ill**?
>
> If someone has mental health problems, it is not polite to say that they are **mad**, use **mentally ill** instead.

madam /ˈmædəm/ *noun formal* **1** (*also* **Madam**) You call a woman 'madam' when you are speaking to her politely. *This way, madam.* **2 Madam** You write 'Madam' at the beginning of a formal letter to a woman when you do not know her name. *Dear Madam, I am writing to...*

made /meɪd/ *past of* make

-made /meɪd/ *suffix* ➲See **man-made, ready-made, self-made, tailor-made.**

madhouse /ˈmædhaʊs/ *noun* [C] *informal* a place where there is a lot of uncontrolled noise and activity

madly /mædli/ *adverb* **1** with a lot of energy and enthusiasm *We cheered madly as the team came out onto the field.* **2 be madly in love** to love someone very much

madman, madwoman /ˈmædmən, ˈmædˌwʊmən/ *noun* [C] *plural* **madmen** or **madwomen** a crazy person *He was running around **like a madman**.*

madness /ˈmædnəs/ *noun* [U] **1** stupid or dangerous behaviour *It would be madness to give up your job when you've just bought a house.* **2** mental illness

maestro /ˈmaɪstrəʊ/ *noun* [C] someone who is very good at something, especially playing music

the mafia /ˈmæfiə/ Ⓤⓢ /ˈmɑːfiə/ *noun* a large group of organized criminals *Drug-smuggling activities have been linked to the Mafia.*

⊶**magazine** /ˌmægəˈziːn/ *noun* [C] a thin book published every week or month, that has shiny, colourful pages with articles and pictures *a fashion/news magazine*

magazine

maggot /ˈmægət/ *noun* [C] a small insect with a soft body and no legs that often lives in decaying food

⊶**magic¹** /ˈmædʒɪk/ *noun* [U] **1** [SPECIAL POWERS]

| j **yes** | k **cat** | ŋ **ring** | ʃ **she** | θ **thin** | ð **this** | ʒ **decision** | dʒ **jar** | tʃ **chip** | æ **cat** | e **bed** | ə **ago** | ɪ **sit** | i **cosy** | ɒ **hot** | ʌ **run** | ʊ **put** |

special powers that can make things happen that seem impossible *Do you believe in magic?* **2** ENTERTAINMENT clever actions intended to entertain people, often making objects appear and disappear **3** SPECIAL QUALITY a quality that makes something or someone seem special or exciting *No one could fail to be charmed by the magic of this beautiful city.* **4 as if by magic** in a way that is surprising and impossible to explain *Food would appear on the table every day, as if by magic.* ➜See also: **black magic**.

magic² /'mædʒɪk/ *adjective* **1** with special powers *a magic spell/wand* **2** relating to magic *a magic trick* **3 magic moments** special and exciting experiences

magical /'mædʒɪkᵊl/ *adjective* **1** with special powers *Diamonds were once thought to have magical powers.* **2** special or exciting *It was a magical night.* ● **magically** *adverb I knew my problems would not just magically disappear.*

magician /mə'dʒɪʃᵊn/ *noun* [C] **1** someone who entertains people by performing magic tricks **2** a character in old stories who has magic powers

magistrate /'mædʒɪstreɪt/ *noun* [C] a type of judge (= person who decides what punishments should be given) who deals with less serious crimes

magnate /'mægneɪt/ *noun* [C] someone who is rich and successful in business *a business/media magnate*

magnesium /mæg'niːziəm/ *noun* [U] a metallic element that burns very brightly, used to make fireworks (= explosives used to entertain people)

magnet /'mægnət/ **magnet** *noun* **1** [C] an iron object that makes pieces of iron or steel (= metal made with iron) move towards it **2 be a magnet for sb** If a place or event is a magnet for people, a lot of people go there. *Airports are a magnet for thieves.*

magnetic /mæg'netɪk/ *adjective* **1** with the power of a magnet *a magnetic field* **2 magnetic tape/disk/storage, etc** equipment for storing information from a computer **3** having a character that attracts people to you

magnificent /mæg'nɪfɪsᵊnt/ *adjective* very good or very beautiful *a magnificent view* ● **magnificently** *adverb*

magnify /'mægnɪfaɪ/ *verb* [T] **1** to make an object look larger than it is by looking through special equipment *The cells are first magnified under a microscope.* **2** to make a bad situation worse *All your problems are magnified when you're ill.*

magnifying glass *noun* [C] a piece of curved

glass which makes objects look larger than they are

magnitude /'mægnɪtjuːd/ *noun* [U] *formal* the large size or importance of something *People were still unaware of the magnitude of the problem.*

mahogany /mə'hɒgᵊni/ *noun* [U] a dark, redbrown wood used to make furniture

maid /meɪd/ *noun* [C] a woman who works as a servant in a hotel or in someone's home

maiden¹ /'meɪdᵊn/ *noun* [C] *literary old-fashioned* a young woman who is not married

maiden² /'meɪdᵊn/ *adjective* **a maiden flight/voyage** the first journey of a new aircraft or ship

maiden name *noun* [C] the family name that a woman has before she gets married

mail¹ /meɪl/ *noun* [U] **1** letters and parcels that are brought by post **2** *mainly US* the system by which letters and parcels are taken and brought *Send it by mail.* ○ *The letter is in the mail.* ➜See also: **email, junk mail, snail mail, surface mail, voice mail**.

mail² /meɪl/ *verb* [T] *mainly US* to send a letter or parcel or email something *Could you mail it to me?*

mailbox /'meɪlbɒks/ *noun* [C] *US* **1** a small box outside your home where letters are delivered **2** (*UK* **letterbox, post box**) a large, metal container in a public place where you can post letters

mailing list *noun* [C] a list of names and addresses that an organization uses in order to send information to people

mailman /'meɪlmæn/ *US* (*UK* **postman**) *noun* [C] *plural* **mailmen** a man who takes and brings letters and parcels as a job

mail order *noun* [U] a way of buying goods by ordering them from a catalogue (= book) and receiving them by post

maim /meɪm/ *verb* [T] to injure someone permanently *Thousands of innocent people have been killed or maimed by landmines.*

main¹ /meɪn/ *adjective* [always before noun] **1** most important or largest *the main problem/reason* ○ *The main airport is 15 miles from the capital.* **2 the main thing** the most important fact in a situation *You're happy and that's the main thing.*

main² /meɪn/ *noun* **1** [C] **gas/water main** a pipe that carries gas or water to a building **2 in the main** generally or mostly *Her friends are teachers in the main.*

main course *noun* [C] the largest or most important part of a meal

mainframe /'meɪnfreɪm/ *noun* [C] a large, powerful computer which many people can use at the same time

mainland /'meɪnlənd/ *noun* **the mainland** the main part of a country, not including the islands around it *A daily ferry links the islands to the mainland.* ● **mainland** *adjective* [always before noun] *mainland Britain*

mainly /'meɪnli/ *adverb* mostly or to a large degree *The waitresses are mainly French.*

main 'road *noun* [C] a large road which leads from one town to another *Stay on the main road for about three miles and you'll be there.*

mainstay /ˈmeɪnsteɪ/ *noun* **a/the mainstay of sth** the most important thing or activity *Cattle farming is still the mainstay of the country's economy.*

the mains /meɪnz/ *noun* [group] *UK* **1** the system of pipes or wires that carries gas, water, or electricity to a building *The house isn't connected to the mains yet.* **2** the place inside a building where you can connect a machine to a supply of electricity *Is the cooker turned off at the mains?*

mainstream /ˈmeɪnstriːm/ *noun* **the mainstream** the beliefs or way of living accepted by most people *The party is now in the mainstream of politics.* • **mainstream** *adjective* [always before noun] *mainstream culture/politics*

maintain /meɪnˈteɪn/ *verb* [T] **1** NOT CHANGE to make a situation or activity continue in the same way *The army has been brought in to maintain order in the region.* **2** CONDITION to keep a building or area in good condition *A large house is very expensive to maintain.* **3** SPEAK TRUTH *formal* to say that you are certain something is true [+ (that)] *He has always maintained that he is innocent.*

maintenance /ˈmeɪntᵊnəns/ *noun* [U] **1** the work that is done to keep something in good condition *car maintenance* ○ *I want a garden that's very low maintenance* (= easy to look after). **2** *UK* regular amounts of money that someone must pay after they have left their family so that the family still has money to live *child maintenance*

maize /meɪz/ *UK* (*US* **corn**) *noun* [U] a tall plant with yellow seeds that are eaten as food

majestic /məˈdʒestɪk/ *adjective* very beautiful or powerful in a way that people admire *majestic scenery*

majesty /ˈmædʒəsti/ *noun* **1** [U] the quality of being majestic *the majesty of the pyramids* **2** **His/Her/Your Majesty** used when you are speaking to or about a king or queen *His Majesty King Edward VII*

o-**major¹** /ˈmeɪdʒər/ *adjective* **1** [always before noun] more important or more serious than other things or people of a similar type *a major problem/issue* ○ *a major city* ○ *America has played a major role in the peace process.* **2** in music, belonging to a key (= set of musical notes) which often produces a happy sound ⊃Opposite **minor**.

major² /ˈmeɪdʒər/ *noun* [C] **1** *US* the most important subject that a college or university student studies, or the student who is studying *What's your major?* ○ *Diane's an English major.* **2** an officer of middle rank in the army or air force

major³ /ˈmeɪdʒər/ *verb*
major in sth If you major in a subject, it is

the most important part of your course at a college or university.

o-**majority** /məˈdʒɒrəti/ *noun* **1** [no plural] more than half of a group of people or things *The majority of people in this country own their houses.* ○ *The vast majority of smokers claim they would like to give up.* **2** **be in a/the majority** to be larger than other similar groups *Women are in the majority in the publishing world.* **3** [C] in an election, the difference between the number of votes for the winner, and the votes for the party that came second *Labour has a strong majority.* ⊃Opposite **minority**.

o-**make¹** /meɪk/ *verb* [T] *past* **made 1** CREATE to produce or create something *Shall I make some coffee?* ○ *They've made a film about her life.* ⊃See Common learner error at **do**. **2 make a promise/remark/mistake, etc** to promise something, to say something, to do something wrong, etc *We have to make a decision today.* ○ *You're making a big mistake.* ○ *She made some useful suggestions.* **3 make sb do sth** to force someone to do something *You can't make me go.* **4 make sb/sth happy/sad/difficult, etc** to cause someone or something to become happy, sad, difficult, etc *You've made me very happy.* ○ *This is the song that made her a star.* **5** GO TO to be able to go to an event *I'm afraid I can't make the meeting this afternoon.* **6** EARN MONEY If you make an amount of money, you earn it. *He makes £20,000 a year.* **7** NUMBERS If two or more numbers make a particular amount, that is the amount when they are added together. *That makes $40 altogether.* **8** PERSONAL QUALITIES [T] to have the right qualities to become a father or mother or to do a particular job *Andy would make a good teacher.* **9** GIVE A JOB [+ two objects] to give someone a particular job *They made her a director of the company.* **10 make an appointment** to arrange to do something at a particular time *I've made an appointment with the doctor.* **11 make the bed** to make the sheets and covers on a bed tidy **12 make time** to leave enough time to do something although you are busy [+ to do sth] *You must make time to do your homework.* **13 make do (with)** to accept that something is less good than you would like *If we can't get a bigger room we'll have to make do with this.* **14 make it a** ARRIVE to manage to arrive at a place *Will we make it in time for the film?* **b** SUCCEED to be successful *Very few actors actually make it.*

make for sth to move towards a place *He got up and made for the exit.*

make sth into sth to change something into something else *We're going to make the spare room into an office.*

make of sb/sth If you ask someone what they make of someone or something, you want to know their opinion about that person or thing. *What do you make of this letter?*

make off with sth *informal* to steal something

make sth/sb out to be able to see, hear, or understand something or someone *We could just make out a building through the trees.*

make out sth to say something that is not true [+ (that)] *He made out that he'd been living in Boston all year.*

make out *US informal* **1** to deal with a situation, usually in a successful way *How is Jake making out in his new school?* **2** to kiss and touch someone in a sexual way

make it up to sb to do something good for someone because you have done something bad to them in the past *I'm sorry I missed your birthday. I'll make it up to you, I promise.*

make sth up to say or write something that is not true *I made up some story about having to go and see my sick mother.*

make up sth to form the whole of an amount *Women make up nearly 50% of medical school entrants.*

make up to become friendly with someone again after you have argued with them *Have you made up with Daryl yet?*

make up for sth to reduce the bad effect of something, or make something bad become something good *I hope this money will make up for the inconvenience.*

make² /meɪk/ *noun* [C] the name of a company that makes a particular product *I like your stereo. What make is it?*

make-believe /'meɪkbɪ,liːv/ *noun* [U] when you pretend that something is real *Disneyland creates a world of make-believe.*

makeover /'meɪk,əʊvəʳ/ *noun* [C] when you suddenly improve your appearance by wearing better clothes, cutting your hair, etc *to have a makeover*

maker /'meɪkəʳ/ *noun* [C] the person or company that makes a product *makers of top quality electrical products*

makeshift /'meɪkʃɪft/ *adjective* [always before noun] temporary and low quality *makeshift shelters*

make-up

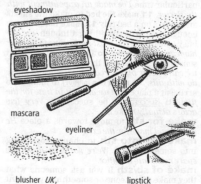

eyeshadow
mascara
eyeliner
blusher *UK*, blush *US*
lipstick

make-up, makeup /'meɪkʌp/ *noun* [U] coloured substances that a woman puts on her face in order to make herself more attractive *to put on/take off make-up* ○ *She doesn't wear much make-up.*

making /'meɪkɪŋ/ *noun* [U] **1** the process of making or producing something *There's an article on the making of a television series.* ○ *the art of film making* **2** be a sth/sb in the making to be likely to develop into a particular thing or type of person *What we're seeing is a disaster in the making.* **3** have the makings of sth to seem likely to develop into something *She has the makings of a great violinist.*

malaria /mə'leəriə/ *noun* [U] a serious disease that you can get in hot countries if a mosquito (= small insect) bites you

ᵒᵃ**male¹** /meɪl/ *adjective* belonging to or relating to the sex that cannot have babies *a male colleague* ⊃Opposite **female**.

male² /meɪl/ *noun* [C] a male person or animal *In 1987, 27 percent of adult males smoked.*

male 'chauvinist *noun* [C] a man who believes that men are better or more important than women

malice /'mælɪs/ *noun* [U] when you want to harm or upset someone *There was no malice in her comments.*

malicious /mə'lɪʃəs/ *adjective* intended to harm or upset someone *malicious gossip*

malignant /mə'lɪgnənt/ *adjective* A malignant tumour (= group of diseased cells) is one that could cause death.

mall /mɔːl/ (*also* **shopping mall**) *noun* [C] a large, covered shopping area

malleable /'mæliəbl/ *adjective* **1** easy to bend or make into a different shape **2** *formal* easily influenced and controlled

mallet /'mælɪt/ *noun* [C] a tool like a hammer with a large, flat end made of wood or rubber ⊃See picture at **tool**.

malnutrition /,mælnju:'trɪʃᵊn/ *noun* [U] a serious illness caused by too little food

malpractice /,mæl'præktɪs/ *noun* [U] when a doctor, lawyer, etc does not do one of their duties or makes a mistake at work *medical malpractice*

malt /mɔːlt/ *noun* [U] a substance made from grain that is used to make drinks, for example beer and whisky (= strong alcoholic drink)

mama /mə'mɑː/ *noun* [C] *mainly US* a child's word for 'mother'

mammal /'mæmᵊl/ *noun* [C] an animal that feeds its babies on milk from its body

mammoth /'mæməθ/ *adjective* very large *a mammoth task/project*

ᵒᵃ**man¹** /mæn/ *noun plural* **men** **1** [C] an adult male human *a young/tall man* ○ *men and women* **2** [U] used to refer to both men and women *Man is still more intelligent than the cleverest robot.* ⊃See also: **best man**, **garbage man**, **no-man's land**, **the man/person, etc in the street**.

man² /mæn/ *verb* [T] **manning**, *past* **manned** to be present somewhere, especially in order to operate a machine *The emergency room is manned 24 hours a day.*

ᵒᵃ**manage** /'mænɪdʒ/ *verb* **1** DO SUCCESSFULLY [I, T]

to do something or deal with something successfully *Will you be able to manage on your own?* ○ **[+ to do sth]** *Anyway, we managed to get there on time.* **2** CONTROL **[T]** to be in control of an office, shop, team, etc *He used to manage the bookshop on King Street.* **3** USE TIME/MONEY **[T]** to use or organize your time or money *He's no good at managing his money.* **4** HAVE ENOUGH MONEY **[I]** to have enough money to live *How can anyone manage on such a low income?*

manageable /ˈmænɪdʒəbl/ *adjective* easy to control *Are they going to reduce classes to a more manageable size?*

management **of** sth • management **skills** • **middle/senior** management

o•**management** /ˈmænɪdʒmənt/ *noun* **1** **[U]** being in control of an office, shop, team, etc *management skills/training* **2** **[group]** the people who are in control of an office, shop, team, etc *middle/senior* management

o•**manager** /ˈmænɪdʒəʳ/ *noun* **[C]** someone in control of an office, shop, team, etc *a sales manager* ○ *She's the manager of the local sports club.*

managerial /ˌmænəˈdʒɪəriəl/ *adjective* relating to a manager or management *managerial skills*

managing di'rector *noun* **[C]** *mainly UK* the main person in control of a company

mandate /ˈmændeɪt/ *noun* **[C]** *formal* support for action given to someone by the people voting for them *The electorate have given them a clear mandate for social reform.*

mandatory /ˈmændətᵊri/ *adjective formal* If something is mandatory, it must be done.

mane /meɪn/ *noun* **[C]** the long, thick hair that grows on the necks of animals such as horses or lions

maneuver[1] *US* (*UK* **manoeuvre**) /məˈnuːvəʳ/ *noun* **[C] 1** a movement that needs care or skill **2** a clever action, usually done to trick someone *a political/tactical maneuver*

maneuver[2] *US* (*UK* **manoeuvre**) /məˈnuːvəʳ/ *verb* **[I, T]** to move with care or skill *I find big cars difficult to maneuver.*

mangled /ˈmæŋɡld/ *adjective* badly crushed and damaged *a mangled body*

mango /ˈmæŋɡəʊ/ *noun* **[C]** *plural* **mangoes** or **mangos** a tropical fruit that has a green skin and is orange inside

manhood /ˈmænhʊd/ *noun* **[U]** the qualities related to being a man and not a boy

mania /ˈmeɪniə/ *noun* **[U]** extreme enthusiasm or interest *football mania*

maniac /ˈmeɪniæk/ *noun* **[C]** *informal* someone who behaves in an extreme or uncontrolled way *a sex maniac* ○ *He drives like a maniac.*

manic /ˈmænɪk/ *adjective* behaving in an excited and uncontrolled way

manicure /ˈmænɪkjʊəʳ/ *noun* **[C, U]** when someone makes your hands look attractive by cleaning and cutting your nails, etc

manifest[1] /ˈmænɪfest/ *verb* **[T]** *formal* to show a quality or condition **[often reflexive]** *Grief manifests itself in a number of different ways.*

manifest[2] /ˈmænɪfest/ *adjective* **[always before noun]** *formal* obvious *Sarah's manifest lack of interest*

manifestation /ˌmænɪfesˈteɪʃᵊn/ *noun* **[C, U]** *formal* something which shows that a quality or condition exists *one of the manifestations of the disease*

manifesto /ˌmænɪˈfestəʊ/ *noun* **[C]** when a political group says publicly what it intends to do

manipulate /məˈnɪpjəleɪt/ *verb* **[T]** to control someone or something in a clever way so that they do what you want them to do *She knows how to manipulate the press.* • **manipulation** /məˌnɪpjəˈleɪʃᵊn/ *noun* **[U]**

manipulative /məˈnɪpjələtɪv/ *adjective* A manipulative person controls people in a clever and unpleasant way. *a devious, manipulative little boy*

mankind /mænˈkaɪnd/ *noun* **[U]** all people, considered as a group *the history of mankind*

manly /ˈmænli/ *adjective* having the qualities and appearance that people think a man should have *a deep, manly voice*

man-made /ˌmænˈmeɪd/ *adjective* not natural, but made by people *man-made fibres* ○ *a man-made lake*

manned /mænd/ *adjective* A place or vehicle that is manned has people working in it. *a manned space flight*

2 in a [similar/traditional/professional, etc] manner • the manner **of** sth

o•**manner** /ˈmænəʳ/ *noun* **[no plural] 1** the way in which a person talks and behaves with other people *an aggressive/friendly manner* **2** the way something happens or something is done *They dealt with the problem in a very efficient manner.*

mannerism /ˈmænᵊrɪzᵊm/ *noun* **[C]** something strange that someone often does with their face, hands, or voice, and that is part of their personality

manners /ˈmænəz/ *noun* **[plural]** polite ways of behaving with other people *bad/good manners* ○ *table manners*

1 carry out/perform a manoeuvre

manoeuvre[1] *UK* (*US* **maneuver**) /məˈnuːvəʳ/ *noun* **[C] 1** a movement that needs care or skill **2** a clever action, usually done to trick someone *a political/tactical manoeuvre*

manoeuvre[2] *UK* (*US* **maneuver**) /məˈnuːvəʳ/ *verb* **[I, T]** to move with care or skill *I find big cars difficult to manoeuvre.*

manpower /ˈmæn,paʊəʳ/ *noun* **[U]** the people needed or available to do a job *a manpower shortage*

mansion /ˈmænʃᵊn/ *noun* **[C]** a very large house

manslaughter /ˈmænˌslɔːtəʳ/ *noun* [U] the crime of killing someone without intending to kill them

mantelpiece /ˈmæntəlpiːs/ (*also US* **mantel**) *noun* [C] the shelf above a fireplace (= place in a room where wood, etc is burned) *There was an old family photo **on the mantelpiece**.* ➲See colour picture **The Living Room** on page Centre 4.

mantra /ˈmæntrə/ *noun* [C] an idea or belief that people often say but do not think about *the mantra of 'democratic reform'*

manual¹ /ˈmænjuəl/ *adjective* using your hands *manual labour/work* ○ *a manual control/gearbox* ● **manually** *adverb*

manual² /ˈmænjuəl/ *noun* [C] a book that tells you how to use something or do something

manufacture /ˌmænjəˈfæktʃəʳ/ *verb* [T] to produce something, usually in large numbers in a factory *Local industries manufacture plastic products, boats, and clothing.* ● **manufacture** *noun* [U] *the manufacture of computers/margarine/plastic*

manufacturer /ˌmænjəˈfæktʃərəʳ/ *noun* [C] a company that manufactures something *a shoe manufacturer*

manufacturing /ˌmænjəˈfæktʃərɪŋ/ *noun* [U] the production of something, usually in large numbers in a factory *car/food manufacturing*

manure /məˈnjʊəʳ/ *noun* [U] solid waste from animals that is used to make plants grow well *cow/horse manure*

manuscript /ˈmænjəskrɪpt/ *noun* [C] a piece of writing or music that has been written, but not published

🔑**many** /ˈmeni/ *pronoun, quantifier* **1** used mainly in negative sentences and questions to mean 'a large number of' *I don't have many clothes.* ○ *Were there many cars on the road?* ○ *I've got **so many** things to do this morning.* ○ *You've given me **too many** potatoes* (= more than I want). ○ *There aren't **as many** people here **as** last year.* **2 how many** used in questions to ask about the number of something *How many hours a week do you work?* ○ *How many do you want?* **3 as many as** used before a number or amount to show that the number or amount is large *As many as 6000 people may have been infected with the disease.*

COMMON LEARNER ERROR

many, much, or a lot of?

Many is used with countable nouns in negative sentences and questions. **Much** is used with uncountable nouns in negative sentences and questions.

Do you have many friends?

I don't earn much money.

A lot of can be used to mean **much** or **many**. In positive sentences it sounds formal to use **much** or **many**. You can use **a lot of** instead.

There was much enthusiasm for the project.

There was a lot of enthusiasm for the project.

Maori /ˈmaʊəri/ *adjective* relating or belonging to the original group of people who lived in New Zealand *Maori culture* ● **Maori** *noun* [C] a Maori person

WORD PARTNERS FOR *map*

read a map ● a **detailed** map ● a map **of** sth ● be **(marked) on** a map ● a **road** map

map /mæp/ *noun* [C] a picture that shows where countries, towns, roads, rivers, etc are *a **road map*** ○ *a large-scale **map** of Europe*

map

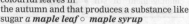

maple /ˈmeɪpl/ *noun* [C, U] a tree that has colourful leaves in the autumn and that produces a substance like sugar *a **maple leaf*** ○ ***maple syrup***

Mar *written abbreviation for* March

mar /mɑːʳ/ *verb* [T] **marring** *past* **marred** *formal* to spoil something **[often passive]** *The evening was marred by Meg's appalling behaviour.*

marathon /ˈmærəθən/ *noun* [C] **1** a race in which people run for about 26 miles/42 km *the London marathon* ○ *a marathon runner* **2** a very long event *a dance marathon*

marble /ˈmɑːbl/ *noun* [U] hard, smooth stone which is often used for decoration *green/pink marble* ○ *a marble statue*

march¹ /mɑːtʃ/ *noun* [C] **1** an organized walk by a group to show that they disagree with something *to **go on a march*** **2** the special type of walking that soldiers do

march² /mɑːtʃ/ *verb* [I] **1** to walk somewhere as a group to show that you disagree with something *They marched to London to protest against health cuts.* **2** When soldiers march, they walk together with regular steps. **3 march off/up/down, etc** to walk somewhere fast, often because you are angry

🔑**March** /mɑːtʃ/ (*written abbreviation* **Mar**) *noun* [C, U] the third month of the year

mare /meəʳ/ *noun* [C] a female horse

margarine /ˌmɑːdʒəˈriːn/ [US] /ˈmɑːrdʒərɪn/ *noun* [U] a yellow substance made from vegetable oil which you put on bread and use in cooking

margin /ˈmɑːdʒɪn/ *noun* [C] **1** the difference between two amounts of time, money, etc, usually between people in a competition *to win by a narrow/wide margin* ○ *He took third place **by a margin of** seven minutes.* **2** an empty space down the side of a page of writing *You can make notes **in the margin**.* **3 a margin of error** the amount by which a calculation can be wrong but still produce a good result *a margin of error of 5 percent*

marginal /ˈmɑːdʒɪnəl/ *adjective* small and not important *a marginal effect/improvement*

marginalize (*also UK* -ise) /ˈmɑːdʒɪnəlaɪz/ *verb* [T] to treat someone or something as if they are not important **[often passive]** *The poorest countries are increasingly marginalized from the world economy.*

marginally /ˈmɑːdʒɪnəli/ *adverb* by a small amount *marginally more expensive*

a piece of . . .

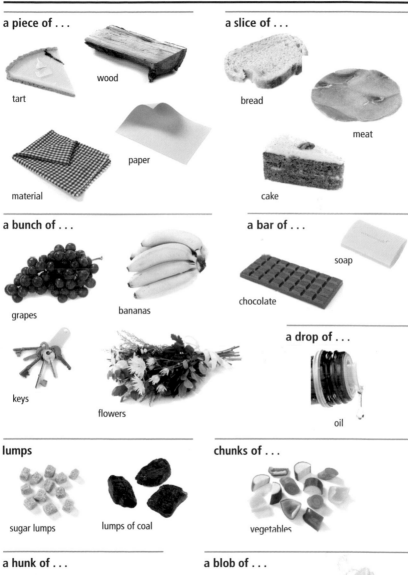

tart

wood

paper

material

a slice of . . .

bread

meat

cake

a bunch of . . .

grapes

bananas

keys

flowers

a bar of . . .

soap

chocolate

a drop of . . .

oil

lumps

sugar lumps

lumps of coal

chunks of . . .

vegetables

a hunk of . . .

bread

cheese

a blob of . . .

cream

THE KITCHEN

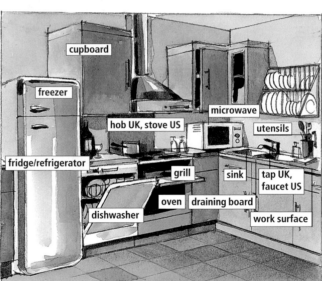

chopping board

toaster

bread bin UK, bread box US

tin opener UK, can opener US

food processor

grater

oven glove

kettle

blender

cupboard

freezer

microwave

hob UK, stove US

utensils

fridge/refrigerator

grill

sink

tap UK, faucet US

oven

draining board

dishwasher

work surface

coffee maker

teapot

sieve

colander

cake tin UK, cake pan US

rolling pin

baking tray UK, baking pan US

saucepan

ladle

scales UK, scale

frying pan

flan dish

whisk

fish slice UK, spatula US

measuring spo

THE BATHROOM

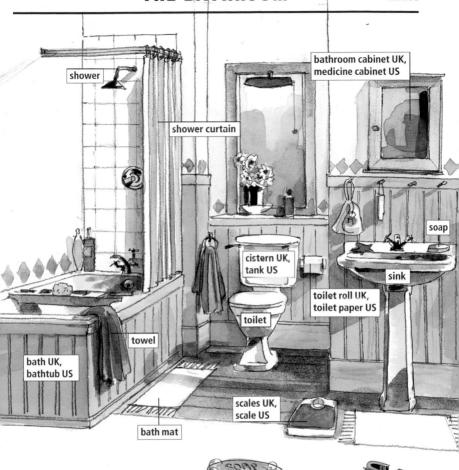

shower

shower curtain

bathroom cabinet UK, medicine cabinet US

soap

cistern UK, tank US

sink

toilet roll UK, toilet paper US

toilet

towel

bath UK, bathtub US

scales UK, scale US

bath mat

toothbrush

soap

nail brush

toothpaste

cotton wool UK, cotton US

flannel UK, washcloth US

razor

electric razor

THE LIVING ROOM

picture

window

mirror

ornaments

curtain

windowsil

mantelpiece

radiator

bookcase

TV

cushion

sofa

fireplace

vase

coffee table

rug

armchair

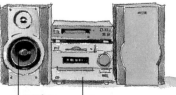

remote control

video UK, VCR US

candles

lampshad

speaker   stereo

clock

lamp

timetable UK, schedule US

board rubber UK, eraser US

blackboard

chalk

whiteboard

whiteboard mar

noticeboard UK, bulletin board US

teacher

pupil

pen

ruler

exercise book

textbook

file

chair

glue

Sellotape UK, Scotch tape US

rubber UK, eraser US

satchel

pencil

scissors

pencil sharpener

desk

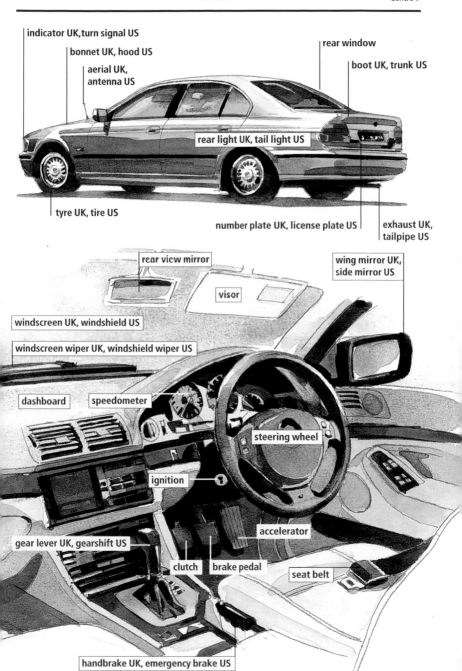

indicator UK, turn signal US

bonnet UK, hood US

aerial UK, antenna US

rear window

boot UK, trunk US

rear light UK, tail light US

tyre UK, tire US

number plate UK, license plate US

exhaust UK, tailpipe US

rear view mirror

wing mirror UK, side mirror US

visor

windscreen UK, windshield US

windscreen wiper UK, windshield wiper US

dashboard

speedometer

steering wheel

ignition

accelerator

gear lever UK, gearshift US

clutch

brake pedal

seat belt

handbrake UK, emergency brake US

CLOTHES

jacket

cardigan

sweater

halter top

trousers UK
pants US

jeans

skirt

miniskirt

suit

salwar kameez

t-shirt

dress

shorts

pyjamas

slippers

sweatshirt

fur collar

coat

hood

mac UK
raincoat US

boots

jacket

hoodie

tie

waistcoat UK
vest US

shirt

sweatshirt

gloves

scarves
(one scarf)

trousers UK
pants US

shoes

bra

tracksuit UK
sweats US

boxers

briefs

bikini

swimming
trunks UK
swimsuit US

trunks

French knickers

pants UK panties US

underpants

swimming
costume UK
swimsuit US

briefs

cycle helmet

camisole

socks

sunglasses

sun visor

tights UK

belt

flip-flops

mules

baseball cap

trainers UK sneakers US

ankle
boots

sun hat

cowboy boots

sandals

boots

FRUITS AND VEGETABLES

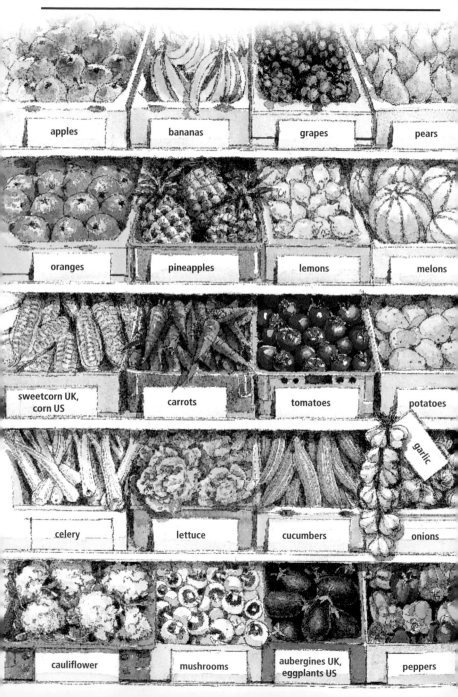

apples

bananas

grapes

pears

oranges

pineapples

lemons

melons

sweetcorn UK, corn US

carrots

tomatoes

potatoes

celery

lettuce

cucumbers

onions

garlic

cauliflower

mushrooms

aubergines UK, eggplants US

peppers

roll UK,
sandwich US

sandwich UK & US

soup

biscuits UK,
cookies US

cake

salad

vegetables

pizza

rice

chips UK,
french fries US

cereal

pasta

honey

jam

crisps UK,
chips US

peanuts

egg

butter

fish

yoghurt

cheese

meat

COLOURS

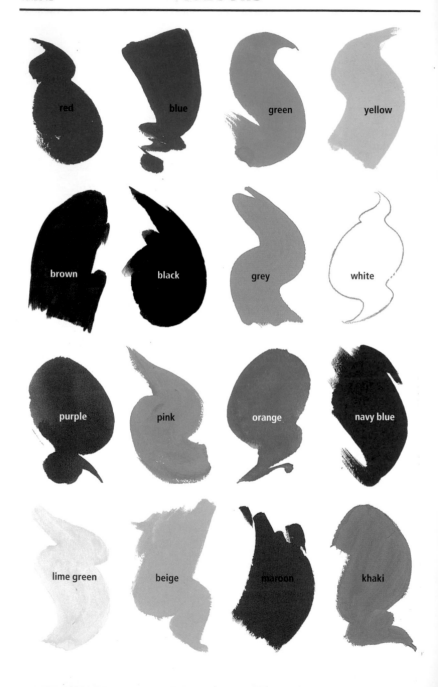

red

blue

green

yellow

brown

black

grey

white

purple

pink

orange

navy blue

lime green

beige

maroon

khaki

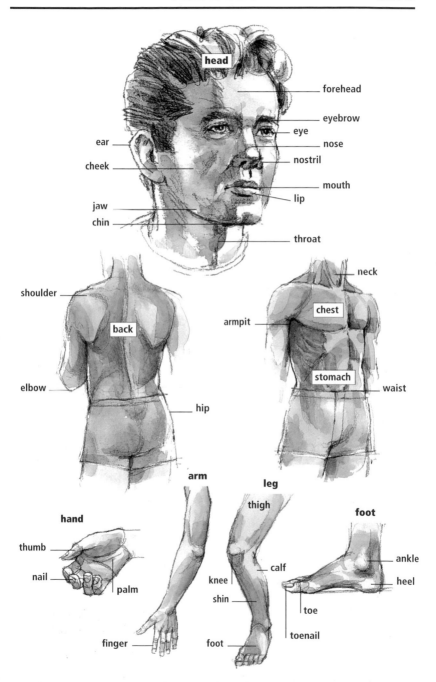

head

forehead

eyebrow

eye

nose

ear

nostril

cheek

mouth

jaw

lip

chin

throat

neck

shoulder

chest

back

armpit

stomach

elbow

waist

hip

arm

leg

thigh

hand

foot

thumb

ankle

calf

nail

heel

knee

palm

shin

toe

finger

foot

toenail

SPORTS

skiing

goggles

pole

skis

athletics UK, track and field US

javelin

running

high jump

boxing

boxing gloves

ring

snowboarding

snowboard

ice hockey

puck

elbow pads

rollerblading

rollerblades/in-line skates

ice skating

skateboarding

skate

knee pads

skateboard

swimming

cap

lane

goggles

horse riding UK, horseback riding US

reins

rider

saddle

football UK, soccer US
referee / goal / goalkeeper

American football UK, football US
goal post / helmet

rugby

golf
cup / club / caddie

basketball
backboard / basket

cricket
batsman / bowler / stumps

baseball
cap / pitcher / glove/mitt / batter

tennis
racket / net

cycling
helmet / bicycle

volleyball
net

PHRASAL VERBS

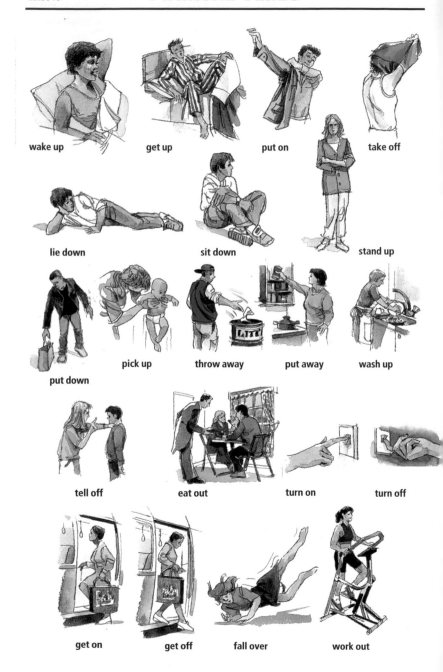

wake up

get up

put on

take off

lie down

sit down

stand up

pick up

throw away

put away

wash up

put down

tell off

eat out

turn on

turn off

get on

get off

fall over

work out

Extra help pages

Checking your work

There are many ways that this dictionary can help you avoid common mistakes.

Common Learner Error notes

Words which often cause difficulty for learners of English have special common learner error notes explaining how to use them correctly. These are all based on the *Cambridge Learner Corpus*.

1 Correct the following sentences by looking at the *Common Learner Error* notes for the underlined word:

1 The new rule <u>affects</u> to everyone.
2 What <u>hour</u> is it?
3 It's <u>quiet</u> hot in here.
4 He did an interesting <u>speech</u>.

Grammar

Always check the grammar of the words you want to use. There is an explanation of all the grammar labels on page xiii, and the Extra help pages on **Countable and uncountable nouns** and **Verb patterns** will help you too.

Using the right words

Look carefully at the example sentences, which will show you typical ways of using words. When a word is used with another word extremely often we call it a *collocation* or *word partners*. These collocations or word partners are shown in dark type.

2 Fill in the gaps in these sentences by looking at examples at the entry for the underlined word:

1 You must ___ your <u>homework</u> before you go out.
2 Shall we ___ a <u>taxi</u> to the station?
3 He has no <u>chance</u> ___ getting there on time.
4 I'm ___ rather <u>ill</u> this morning.

➲ See also Extra help pages
Punctuation on page Centre 33, **Spelling** on page Centre 34,
What is a collocation/word partner? on page Centre 41

3 Below is a piece of writing by a candidate taking PET (the Preliminary English Test). It was taken from the *Cambridge Learner Corpus*. There are ten mistakes in it. Can you find them and correct them?

The name of this place is Milan, and it is one of the most important Italian cities. You will find Milan in the north of Italy and you can get there by car, train, or plane, but about me travelling by car is the best solution.
I suggest you to visit Milan not only because it's full of people but also for its historical buildings.
I decided to go in Milan because I desired seeing the Duomo, and the Castello Sforsesco, and I must say you that they are incredibles. I hope that you decide to go to Milan the next summer.
I look forward to see you very soon, with love, Luca
PS Besides in Milan there are a lots of pubs and discos where I know many interesting persons

Classroom language

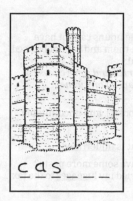

Asking about words

What does 'fierce' mean?

How do you say ___ in English?

How do you spell 'castle'?

How do you pronounce this word?

What's the past tense/past participle of 'lie'?

Can you give me an example?

Could you say that again, please?

Asking about activities

I'm sorry, I don't understand what we have to do.

Can you repeat the instructions please?

Could you repeat that, please?

Could you speak more slowly, please?

Could I borrow a pen/pencil, etc, please?

Can you lend me a pen/pencil, please?

How long do we have to do this?

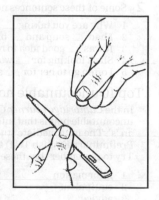

Classroom instructions

Open your books at page 40.

Turn to page 6.

Close your books.

Work in pairs/groups of three, four etc.

Listen to the tape, then try to answer the questions.

Write the answers on a piece of paper.

Work with your partner.

Look up these words in your dictionary.

No talking, please.

Hand in your homework as you leave.

Countable and uncountable nouns

Nouns can be countable or uncountable.

Countable nouns can have *a/an* or *the* before them and can be used both in the singular and the plural:
▶ *There's a plate, three spoons and a cup on the table.*

Uncountable nouns cannot have *a/an* before them and cannot be used in the plural:
▶ *We have rice and some cheese but we haven't any wine.*

In this dictionary, countable nouns have the symbol [C], and uncountable nouns have the symbol [U].

1 Are these sentences correct? Look up the noun that is <u>underlined</u>.

1 We get a lot of English <u>homeworks</u>.
2 I've got some <u>sands</u> in my shoe.
3 They bought some new <u>equipment</u>.
4 Can I have some more <u>pasta</u>?
5 She carried my <u>luggages</u> to the taxi.

2 Some of these sentences need 'a' or 'an' in the gaps. Put them in if necessary.

1 Why are you taking ___ umbrella? It's not raining.
2 I had ___ soup and ___ bread roll for lunch.
3 It was ___ good idea to have a party.
4 She's looking for ___ work in Madrid.
5 I often go to her for ___ advice.

Top 10 uncountable noun errors

In the *Cambridge Learner Corpus* these are the ten most common uncountable nouns that intermediate students try to pluralize by adding an 's'. The intermediate students were taking exams such as PET (the Preliminary English Test) and FCE (the First Certificate in English). Try to remember that these nouns cannot be used in the plural.

1 information	5 transport	8 knowledge
2 equipment	6 homework	9 countryside
3 advice	7 paper (= material	10 stuff
4 furniture	used for writing on)	

Some and *any*

You can use **some** and **any** with plural countable nouns:
▶ *There are some cakes left. Are there any biscuits?*

You can use **some** and **any** with uncountable nouns:
▶ *I'd like some sugar in my coffee. Is there any water in the jug?*

3 Fill in the gaps with a noun from the box:

chair	suitcase	fly	rice	furniture
day	weather	accidents	luggage	

1 There's a ___ in my soup.
2 I have to buy some ___ for my new house.
3 I haven't got much ___ with me. Just this bag.
4 It's a sunny ___ today.
5 There weren't any ___ on the roads yesterday.

Much, many, a lot of, a few

> You can use **many** and **a few** with plural countable nouns:
> ▶ Did you take **many photographs?**
> ▶ I've got **a few friends** who live in London.

> You can use **much** with uncountable nouns:
> ▶ I haven't got **much news** to tell you.

> You can use **a lot of** with both plural countable nouns and with uncountable nouns:
> ▶ Did you take **a lot of photographs?**
> ▶ I haven't got **a lot of news** to tell you.

4 Which of the underlined words in parts of these sentences is right? Put a circle around the correct part.

1 Hurry up! We haven't got <u>many</u>/<u>a lot of</u> time.
2 I don't eat <u>much</u>/<u>many</u> chocolate.
3 I didn't take <u>much</u>/<u>many</u> photographs.
4 I don't listen to <u>much</u>/<u>many</u> classical music.

Nouns which can be both countable and uncountable

> Some nouns can be used both countably and uncountably:
> ▶ a fish/fish, a glass/glass, a hair/hair, a chocolate/chocolate

> When we use these nouns countably we refer to particular things:
> ▶ There are **some glasses** on the table.
> ▶ I caught **a fish** at the lake.

> When we use these nouns uncountably we refer to the thing in general:
> ▶ Careful. There's broken **glass** on the floor.
> ▶ I'd like **fish** and chips for dinner.

5 Look at the items below. How many of them can be used both countably and uncountably?

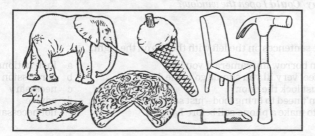

Modal verbs

A modal verb is a verb, for example 'can', 'might', or 'must' that is used before
another verb to show that something is possible, necessary, etc.
Here are some of the uses and meanings of modal verbs.
For a more detailed description, use a good grammar book.

> Here are the main modal verbs of English:
>
> **can   could   may   might   must   ought   shall   will   would**
>
> We also use *need* and *have to* as modal verbs.

Same word, different use

Each modal verb has more than one use. For example, look at these two
sentences with **can**. The use is explained in brackets.
▶ *I **can** swim.* (ability)
▶ ***Can** you carry this bag for me?* (request)

1 The dictionary helps you decide which meaning of the verb is used.
     Look at the modal verb 'can'. How many meanings can you find?

Expressing instructions, advice, permission, and necessity

> to give instructions or to say that something is necessary
> ▶ *You **must** wear a helmet when riding a bike.*
> ▶ *You **mustn't** smoke in here.*
> ▶ *I **have to** be at the dentist at 3 o'clock.*
> ▶ *You **needn't** shut the door.*
>
> ....
> to give advice or to express a strong opinion
> ▶ *You **should/ought to** go to bed if you're tired.*
> ▶ *She **shouldn't** worry about me.*
>
> ....
> to give and ask for permission
> ▶ *She **can** borrow my dress.*
> ▶ ***Can/May/Could** I open the window?*

2 Match the sentences on the left with the use on the right:

1	You can borrow my camera if you like.	a	instructions
2	If you feel very ill you should go to the doctor.	b	permission
3	You must lock the door.	c	necessary
4	You don't need to bring food – just something to drink.	d	advice
5	I need to make a phone call before I go out.	e	not necessary

Expressing degrees of certainty

> In the speaker's opinion, John has the car:
> ► *The car's not here – John **must** have taken it.*

> The speaker thinks this is Clare's sister but is not sure:
> ► *She **might/could** be Clare's sister. She looks very like her.*

> The speaker thinks this is not possible:
> ► *She **can't** be his mother – she's younger than me.*

> The speaker is sure she will do it:
> ► *If she's promised to do it she**'ll** do it.*

> The speaker is not sure if it will rain:
> ► *It **might/could** rain. It's getting cloudy.*

3 Fill in the gaps in these sentences with a word from the list on the right:

1 He ___ be a hairdresser. His hair's a mess.   a may
2 'Do you think Joanna will call?'   b won't
  'Who knows? She ___ do.'   c must
3 She ___ ever come back – I know she won't.   d can't
4 Her hair's all wet – it ___ be raining.   e might
5 'It's 1–1 and there are five minutes to play.
  We ___ still win.'

Forming modal verbs

Modal verbs are very different from other verbs of English:

The forms of the verbs do not change, for example there is no -s in the third person of the present tense.
► *I **can** speak Spanish and she **can** speak Portuguese.*

They are always followed by a main verb and cannot be used as a main verb by themselves.
► *I **must make** a phone call. / We **won't wait** for you.*

They do not use *do* and *did* to form questions, negatives, and short answers.
► *'He **wouldn't** steal anything, would he?' 'Oh yes he **would**.'*

MODAL VERB	SHORT FORM	NEGATIVE	SHORT FORM
can		cannot	can't
could		could not	couldn't
may		may not	
might		might not	mightn't
must		must not	mustn't
ought to		ought not to	oughtn't to
shall		shall not	shan't
will	'll	will not	won't
would	'd	would not	wouldn't

Phrasal verbs

What are phrasal verbs?

A phrasal verb is a verb followed by one or two adverbs or prepositions.
Here are some examples:

get up   break down   look after   run out   look forward to

It is usually impossible to guess the meaning of phrasal verbs just
from knowing the meaning of the verb and the adverb or preposition.
For example, 'give up something' means to stop doing or using something.
It has nothing to do with giving things.

Finding phrasal verbs

In this dictionary, phrasal verbs follow the entry for the main verb, and are in
alphabetical order. For instance, the phrasal verb 'lose out' comes after all the
meanings of the verb 'lose'.

1 How many phrasal verbs can you find in the dictionary formed with the
following verbs?

1 drag   2 hand   3 pack   4 make

2 Use the dictionary to help you fill in the gaps in the sentences below to make
phrasal verbs.

1 If you carry ____ spending like that you'll have no money left.
2 I nodded ____ after lunch.
3 The brakes suddenly seized ____.
4 It took him a long time to get ____ her death.

> Of course, verbs are often used with their normal meanings with adverbs and
> prepositions too, e.g.:
> ▶ *I went into the room.*
> ▶ *He put the book on the shelf.*
>
> These are not phrasal verbs. They are just the normal meanings explained at
> the entries for the verbs, adverbs, and prepositions.

Phrasal verbs with more than one meaning

One phrasal verb can have more than one meaning.
Often, the meanings are not related:
▶ *Just **pick up** the phone and ring her!* (*pick-up*=lift)
▶ *She **picks up** languages really easily.* (*pick-up*=learn)

3 Write two sentences for each of these phrasal verbs, using different
meanings for each sentence:

turn out   catch on   come under sth   fall apart

The grammar of phrasal verbs

Some phrasal verbs have objects, some do not, and some sometimes have objects and sometimes do not. This is shown in the way the phrasal verb is written in the dictionary. The way the phrasal verb is written also shows you whether the object is a person, a thing, or an action.

Phrasal verbs that do not need an object are shown like this:

check in	▶ *You need to **check in** three hours before the flight.*
drift off	▶ *The room was so hot I could feel myself beginning to **drift off**.*

Phrasal verbs that need an object are shown like this:

pack sth in	▶ *I **packed in** my job to go travelling.*
pack sb off	▶ *They **packed him off** to school in Paris.*

Note that **sth** means 'something', and **sb** means 'someone'.

Phrasal verbs where an object is sometimes used and sometimes not used are shown like this:

pack (sth) up	▶ *I **packed up** all my **belongings** and left the house.*
	▶ *Could you help me **pack up**?*

Prepositions following phrasal verbs

Many phrasal verbs are often followed by particular prepositions.
These are shown in bold letters in the dictionary.
▶ *He **dressed up as** a ghost.*

4   Fill in the gaps in these sentences with the correct prepositions.

1   She stood in ____ her boss while he was sick.
2   Just carry on ____ your work.
3   She looked back ____ her days as a student with nostalgia.
4   He's always going on ____ his car.
5   We will have to cut back ____ our spending.

Idioms

Idioms are groups of words that have a meaning which is different from
the usual meanings of the words in them. It is often impossible to guess what
they mean. They are used in all types of language, but especially in informal
situations. Idioms often have a stronger meaning than ordinary words.
For example, 'be at loggerheads with someone' has more emphasis than
'be arguing with someone', but they mean the same thing.

Finding idioms in this dictionary

Most idioms are found at the entry for the first noun in the idiom.
(A noun is a word that is the name of a thing, person, or place.)

1 Underline the first noun in each idiom on the left.
    Then match each idiom with its meaning on the right.

    1 be up to your neck in sth   a try to do something you cannot achieve
    2 the final nail in the coffin   b be very busy
    3 fight a losing battle   c have nothing to do
    4 be at a loose end   d not laugh
    5 keep a straight face   e something that causes failure

If the idiom does not contain a
noun, try the first verb (word for
doing things) or adjective (word
for describing things). But don't
worry if you do not know where to
look for an idiom. If you look in
the wrong place, you will find an
arrow telling you where to go.

> **breathe** /briːð/ *verb* [I, T] to take air
> into and out of your lungs *breathe
> in/out* • *breathe deeply* ⊃ *See also:*
> be breathing down sb's **neck**, not
> breathe a **word**¹.

2 The following sentences all use idioms that contain a part of the body. Choose
    a body part from the box below to complete each sentence.

    | head   face   arm   leg   ear |

    1 The accident was clearly his fault – he doesn't have a __ to stand on.
    2 Most of her lecture went over my __.
    3 Dad might lend you his camera if you twist his __.
    4 I've never taught this class before, so I'll have to play it by __.
    5 When I saw his hat, I could hardly keep a straight __.

Verb patterns

Some verbs must have something (an object) after them: ▶ *She put **the cup** on the table.* ▶ *Did you **bring** any **money**?* These verbs are 'transitive' verbs. They are marked in the dictionary with a [T].	Other verbs don't need anything after them: ▶ *He **fell**.* ▶ *They don't want to **stay**.* These verbs are 'intransitive' verbs. They are marked in the dictionary with an [I].

Some verbs can be both transitive and intransitive:
▶ *Did you **see the moon** last night?* [T]　　▶ *Can you move, please?*
　　　　　　　　　　　　　　　　　　　　　　　*I can't **see**.* [I]
▶ *Did you **pay the bill**?* [T]　　　　　　　　▶ *Have you **paid**?* [I]

1 Look up these verbs in the dictionary to find out if they are transitive or intransitive or both.

1 like	3 drive	5 tell	7 hate	9 fall
2 hear	4 smoke	6 explain	8 play	10 hit

Sometimes a verb has to be followed by other grammar words or grammar patterns, for example a preposition, an infinitive verb, or a verb ending -ing:

　　　　　　　　*I **apologized** to her.*
[+ to do sth]　　*I **promise** to help you.*
[+ doing sth]　　*Have you **finished reading** the newspaper?*
[+ (that)]　　　*He **told** me (that) it was safe.*

If you are not sure what type of grammar to use after a verb, look up the word in the dictionary. There is a full explanation of all the grammar codes on page xiii.

2 Can you describe what follows these verbs? Match the underlined parts on the left with a description from the list on the right.

1 He's always **complaining** <u>that</u> nobody listens to him.	a　+ to do sth
2 Did she **say** <u>where</u> she was going?	b　+ two objects
3 He doesn't **like** <u>watching</u> TV.	c　+ that
4 They **want** <u>to go</u> shopping.	d　+ doing sth
5 He **brought** <u>me some flowers</u>.	e　+ question word

3 Write a sentence using each of these verbs and the patterns that are shown in the following grammar codes.

1 forget	+ [that]	4 start	+ to do sth
2 tell	+ question word	5 sell	+ two objects
3 like	+ doing sth		

Word formation

Here are some ways of building words in English.

Prefixes

Prefixes are added to the beginning of words to change their meaning.
There is a list of common prefixes in the appendices at the end of this book.

Here are some common prefixes that are used before adjectives to give
opposite and often negative meanings:

dis-	dissimilar	When you learn a new adjective try to find out
il-	illegal	if its opposite is formed with a prefix and write
im-	impossible	down the two words together, for example:
in-	inexpensive	**happy unhappy**
ir-	irregular	
un-	unhappy	

The prefixes **un-** and **dis-** combine with verbs to form the opposite of
the action of the verb.

▶ *She appeared from behind a door.*

▶ *I covered the food with a cloth.*

▶ *He **disappeared** through the window.*

▶ *They brushed away the dirt to **uncover** a box.*

1 Match the prefixes on the left to the adjectives and verbs on the right to make new words.

1	un-	4	im-	lock	legal
2	dis-	5	ir-	responsible	agree
3	il-			possible	

2 Now use the words you have made to fill in the gaps in the sentences below.

1 Which key do I need to ___ this door?
2 The tide is so strong it's ___ to swim against it.
3 It is ___ to drive without a licence.
4 I ___ with her views on immigration.
5 Leaving the children alone was a very ___ thing to do.

3 There are many other prefixes used in English. Match the prefix on the left with the meaning on the right. Then form new words by choosing a suitable word from the box to combine with each prefix.

1	multi-	a	half
2	semi-	b	in favour of
3	anti-	c	former (not now)
4	pro-	d	not enough
5	ex-	e	many
6	post-	f	against
7	over-	g	after
8	under-	h	too much

president	war
cooked	racial
graduate	worked
circle	democracy

Suffixes

Suffixes are used at the ends of words. There is a list of suffixes in the appendices at the end of this book. Here are some common ones:

-er **-or**	■ for people who do activities and for things that have a particular function	worker, swimmer, golfer, driver, actor, sailor, conductor; tin opener, screwdriver, hanger, projector
-ist	■ for people with certain beliefs ■ who play musical instruments ■ for some professions	Buddhist, socialist violinist, pianist, guitarist journalist, pharmacist, artist
-ness	to make nouns from adjectives	happiness, sadness, rudeness
-(t)ion	to make nouns from verbs	education, television, pollution
-ment	to make nouns from verbs	improvement, government
Note: Adding a suffix to a word sometimes changes its pronunciation. Look at how the stress changes in these words: **pho**tograph → pho**to**grapher **edu**cate → edu**ca**tion		

Noun, verb, adjective?

Most suffixes can tell you whether a word is a noun, verb or adjective.
This table shows some common ones:

adjectives	-able, -al, -ful, -ible, -ive, -less, -ous, -y	washable, natural, beautiful, flexible, active, helpless, adventurous, happy
nouns	-al -ance, -(t)ion, -ence, -hood, -ity, -ment, -ness, -ship	performance, reduction, independence, parenthood, similarity, enjoyment, politeness, friendship, arrival
verb	-en, -ify, -ize	harden, solidify, modernize
Note: -al can be used to make nouns, e.g. arrival, and adjectives, e.g. comical		

4 Use suffixes to change the following adjectives and verbs into nouns.

1 rude	4 ignorant
2 create	5 hilarious
3 prefer	6 develop

Numbers

Saying numbers

Don't forget to say 'and' after hundreds:
▶ *569*   *five hundred and sixty nine*
▶ *7,892*   *seven thousand, eight hundred and ninety two*
▶ *4,680,022 four million, six hundred and eighty thousand and twenty two*

Parts of numbers: decimals and fractions

For decimals we say each number separately after the point (.):
▶ *2.5*   *two point five*   ▶ *3.65*   *three point six five*
▶ *22.33 twenty two point three three*

For fractions we say:
▶ *2¼*   *two and a quarter*   ▶ *⅕*   *one fifth*
▶ *5¾*   *five and three quarters*

Remember we use ordinal numbers for most fractions but not for ½, ¼, ¾:
▶   *⅜*   *three eighths*   ▶   *⅓*   *a third or one third*

▶ *1/12*   *a twelfth or one twelfth*

Percentages and other symbols

Here are some other symbols used with numbers:

%	percent	45%	*forty five percent*
°	degree	22°C	*twenty two degrees Celsius*
		70°F	*seventy degrees Fahrenheit*
+	addition	6 + 2 = 8	*six plus two is/equals eight*
−	subtraction	6 − 2 = 4	*six minus two is/equals four*
×	multiplication	6 × 3 = 18	*six times three/six multiplied by three is/equals eighteen*
÷	division	24 ÷ 4 = 6	*twenty four divided by four is/equals six*

Saying 0

'0' can be said in different ways. It is usually said as 'oh' or 'zero' ('zero' is especially used in American English). Here are some ways of saying '0':

MATHS: 0.65 (UK): *nought point six five*, (US): *zero point six five*
FOOTBALL: 6–0 (UK): *six nil*, (US): *six to zero*
TENNIS: 15–0 *fifteen love*
TELEPHONE NUMBER: 965703 *nine six five seven oh three*
(also US English *seven zero three*)

Measurements

Metric and imperial measurements

The international system of metric units of measurement is not used in the US.
It is used in Britain, but many people still use the older system of imperial
units such as pounds, feet, and gallons.

Some units have the same name but mean different amounts in Britain
and the US.

IMPERIAL	METRIC	IMPERIAL	METRIC
1 inch (in)	2.5 centimetres (cm)	1 ounce (oz)	28 gram (g)
1 foot (ft)	30 centimetres	1 pound (lb)	450 gram
	(100 cm = 1 metre (m))		
1 yard (yd)	90 centimetres	1 pint	(UK) 0.6 litres (US) 0.5 litres
1 mile (m)	2.2 kilometres (km)	1 gallon	(UK) 4.5 litres (US) 3.8 litres

Saying how tall you are

Most people in Britain and the US say their height in imperial units.
▶ *I'm **six feet** tall.*   ▶ *I'm **five foot seven**.* (often written 5' 7")

Saying how much you weigh

In Britain, people usually say their weight in stones and pounds.
There are fourteen pounds in a stone.
▶ *I weigh **nine stone three**.* (Note that you do not have to say 'pounds'.)
▶ *I weigh **seven and a half stone**.*

In the US, people usually say their weight in pounds.
▶ *I weigh **160 pounds**.*

Talking about measurements

We normally use adjectives to talk or ask about measurements:
▶ *The box is 30cm **long**.*   ▶ *How **tall** is David?*

We can also use nouns, but they are more formal:
▶ *The **length** of the box is 30cm.*   ▶ *What is David's **height**?*

height	deep	length	width	depth	high	long	wide

1 Look at the words in the box. Decide which are adjectives and
which are nouns. Use them to complete the table below.

	QUESTION	ANSWER	FORMAL
1	How wide is it?	It's 5m ___ .	The ___ of the x is 5m.
2	How ___ is it?	It's 50m long.	The length of the x is 50m.
3	How deep is it?	It's 10m deep.	The ___ of the x is 10m.
4	How ___ is it?	It's 70m ___ .	The height of the x is 70m.

Pronunciation

Pronouncing words in English can be very difficult. Often, words are not written the way they are pronounced. The phonetic symbols after each word in the dictionary show you how to say each word. There is an explanation of all these symbols inside the back cover, and more information about the pronunciation system on page xvi.

Some of the symbols are pronounced in the same way as the letter they look like, e.g. /b/ sounds like 'b' in 'bad'. All the others are explained at the bottom of every page in the dictionary.

1 Look at these words and match them with their pronunciations.

1	cough	a	/'sɪnəmə/
2	throw	b	/θruː/
3	through	c	/sɪŋ/
4	cup	d	/kɒf/
5	cinema	e	/θrəʊ/
6	sing	f	/kʌp/

2 All these words are names of animals. Write the name of the animal next to the phonetic symbols.

1	/məʊl/	3	/hɔːs/	5	/laɪən/
2	/dʒɪˈrɑːf/	4	/ʃiːp/	6	/tʃɪmp/

Silent letters

Many words in English contain letters that are not pronounced, for example the 't' in 'listen' /lɪsn/.

3 Which is the silent letter in each of these words?

1	know	3	island	5	two
2	honest	4	wrong	6	talk

Word stress

In English, it is very important to put the stress on the right part of the word. The symbol / ' / shows you where to put the main stress. (Some words have another, less important stress too.)

purple /'pɜːpl/	**important** /ɪmˈpɔːtənt/	**difficult** /'dɪfɪkəlt/

4 Put a circle around the part of each word that has the main stress.

1	brother	3	photographer	5	computer
2	education	4	below	6	necessary

Punctuation

	Uses	Examples
capital letter	■ the first letter of a sentence	*Football is very popular in Britain.*
	■ for countries, nationalities, languages, religions, names of people, places, events, organizations, trademarks, days, months, titles	Portugal, Africa, Russian, Islam, Joanne, John, Dubai, Geneva, the World Trade Fair, Jaguar, the Internet, Sunday, February, Mr / Mrs / Ms / Dr / Professor
	■ for titles of books, films, etc.	*Matrix Reloaded*
	■ for abbreviations	OPEC, AIDS, WWF
full stop UK/ period US	■ the end of a sentence	*I'm going for a walk.*
	■ sometimes after an abbreviation	Marton Rd./Mrs. White/Dr. Evans
question mark	■ after a direct question	*What's your name?*
exclamation mark	■ at the end of a sentence to express surprise, shock, etc.	*I can't believe it!*
	■ to indicate a loud sound	Ouch! Yes!
comma	■ between items in a list	*I need some peas, butter, sugar and eggs.*
	■ to show a pause in a long sentence	*They didn't want to eat before I'd arrived, but I was an hour late.*
	■ when you want to add extra information	*The woman, who I'd met last week, waved as she went past.*
apostrophe	■ for missing letters	don't, I'll, it's (it is)
	■ for possessives	Paul's bike
	Note: words ending in 's' don't need another 's' added	James' house
colon	■ to introduce a list or a quotation in a sentence	*You need the following: paint, brushes, water, cloths.*
semi-colon	■ to separate two parts of a sentence	*I spoke to Linda on Monday; she can't come to the meeting tomorrow.*
hyphen	■ to join two words together	blue-black
	■ to show that a word has been divided and continues on the next line	*Everyone in the room was horri-fied by the news.*
dash	■ to separate parts of sentences	*The car – the one with the broken window – was parked outside our house.*
quotation marks/UK also inverted commas	■ to show that words are spoken	'I'm tired,' she said. 'Let's go,' he suggested.
	■ to show that someone else originally wrote the words	*She had described the school as 'not attracting the best pupils'.*

Spelling

Because of its history, the English language does not have simple spelling rules.
Often words are not written exactly as they sound, so it is important to check the
spelling of any new word and to copy it down correctly.

Top 10 learner spelling errors

In the *Cambridge Learner Corpus* these are the ten most common spelling errors
made by intermediate students taking exams such as PET (the Preliminary
English Test) and FCE (the First Certificate in English).

1	**accommodation**	double **c** and double **m**
2	**restaurant**	remember the two vowels (**au**) after the **t**
3	**advertisement**	don't forget the **e** in the middle (-**is**ement)
4	**because**	remember **au** after the **c**
5	**which**	remember the **h** after the **w**
6	**beautiful**	remember the three vowels (**eau**) after the **b**
7	**different**	double **f** and remember the **e** after the second **f**
8	**environment**	remember the **n** before -**ment**
9	**especially**	this word starts with **esp**
10	**opportunity**	double **p** and remember the **r** before the first **t**

Regular inflections

There are many rules you can learn which will help a lot with your spelling.
Look at page xvii, which explains the rules for regular inflections (e.g. plurals,
past tenses).

1 Write the plural of these nouns.

   1 house   2 watch   3 brick   4 minute   5 fax   6 loss

Word beginnings

Even the first letter of a word can sometimes be difficult to guess.

c Some words beginning with **c** sound as though they begin with **s**.
  ▶ *cell, centre, circle*

ps Words beginning with **ps** sound as though they start with **s**.
  ▶ *pseudonym, psychiatrist*

ph Words beginning with **ph** sound as though they start with **f**.
  ▶ *philosophy, phone, physical*

Same or similar sound, different spelling

Some words in English have the same or very similar sounds, but are spelled differently.

2 Choose the correct word from the pair on the right to fill in the gaps.

1 I don't know ___ he will come. weather/whether
2 It's ___ a long way to my brother's house. quite/quiet
3 ___ of these pictures do you like best? Which/Witch
4 They didn't have ___ coats with them. their/there
5 We stayed in a cottage by the ___. see/sea

Doubling consonants

Some adjectives have a double consonant at the end when they make the comparative form with **-er** and the superlative form with **-est**. When this happens, it is clearly shown in the entry for those adjectives.

> o•**big** /bɪg/ *adjective* **bigger, biggest 1** SIZE
> large in size or amount *I come from a big family.* • *We're looking for a bigger house.*

Some verbs have a double consonant when they make the present participle or the past tense and past participle. This is also shown clearly in the entry for those verbs.

> **acquit** /əˈkwɪt/ *verb* [T] **acquitting** *past* **acquitted** If someone is acquitted of a crime, a court of law decides that they are not guilty. **[often passive]** *Both men were* **acquitted of** *murder.*

A lot of verbs ending in **l** (e.g. travel, level) have a double consonant in UK English, and a single consonant in US English. This is also shown in the entry for those verbs.

3 Fill in the gaps in the sentences below with the correct inflection of the word on the right. Be careful not to double the consonant where it is not correct to do so.

1 It's usually ___ than this in the summer. (hot)
2 The use of mobile phones is ___ on aircraft. (ban)
3 The concert was the ___ I've ever been to. (loud)
4 I'm ___ to find my way around the city. (begin)
5 I'm tired of ___ ten hours a day. (work)

British and American children learn this rhyme to help them with their spelling:

'**I** before **E**, except after **C**.'

▶ *friend, receive*

The Web and the Internet

The Web or the World Wide Web (www) refers to all the websites (= electronic documents) that you can look at using the Internet. The Internet or the Net is the system that connects computers all over the world and allows computer users to look at websites. The Internet has become a part of many people's lives and has generated many new words. Here are a few important ones:

Online
To be online is to be connected to the Internet or to be available on the Internet. To go online is to start to connect your computer to the Internet.

Modems
A modem is a piece of equipment that allows you to send information from a computer through a cable or a telephone line.

Moving around on the www
You can use your mouse to click on links (= connections between the documents or areas on the Internet), to go to a different website, or to move from one part of a website to another.

Websites
Websites usually consist of a series of web pages. The main page on a website is called the homepage. If you know the web address or URL of a website you can type it in at the top of the screen. Otherwise you can use a search engine. A search engine is the software which allows you to search for information on the Internet by typing in one or two words. To surf or to surf the Web is to look at many different websites, often without knowing where you are going next or what you are looking for.

Blogs
A blog is part of a website where someone describes what they do every day or what they think about different subjects. A blogger is someone who writes a blog.

Podcasts
A podcast is a recording from the Internet that you can listen to on your computer or MP3 player. You can also sign up to (= say that you want to receive) a podcast which is then updated (= new information is added to it) through the Internet when you plug your MP3 player into your computer.

Downloading and uploading
If you download an image, video, music, etc., you copy it onto your computer using the Internet. To upload something is to copy something from your computer onto a website or other place where, through the Internet, many people can use it.

Filesharing
Filesharing is the activity of putting a file from your computer onto a special place on your computer so that other people can, through the Internet, copy it, look at it, or use it.

Emailing and texting

Emails are usually shorter and more informal than letters and people sometimes use abbreviations and 'smileys' in them. **Smileys** (also called '**emoticons**') are images which look like faces when you see them from the side. They are made using keyboard symbols and are used to express emotions. Text messages are even shorter and more informal and usually use abbreviations. Here are some frequently used smileys and abbreviations:

Smileys

:-)	I'm happy or smiling
:-(	I'm unhappy or angry
:-D	I'm laughing
>:-(	I'm very angry
:-|	I'm bored
:-o	I'm surprised or shouting
:-@	I'm screaming
:-*	I'm sending you a kiss
;-)	I'm only joking
:-p	I'm smirking (= smiling in an unpleasant or unkind way)
:-b	I'm sticking my tongue out at you

Abbreviations

AFAIK	as far as I know	IMHO	in my humble opinion
AFK	away from keyboard	IOU	I owe you
ASAP	as soon as possible	JIT	just in time
BAK	back at keyboard	LOL	lots of love
BCNU	be seeing you	L8R	later
BF	boyfriend	MSG	message
B4	before	OIC	oh, I see
B4N	bye for now	OTOH	on the other hand
BRB	be right back	PDQ	pretty damn quick
BTW	by the way	PLS	please
C	see	R	are
CU	See you!	SPK	speak
CUL8R	See you later!	TAFN	that's all for now
FWIW	for what it's worth	THX	thanks
FYA	for your amusement	TIA	thanks in advance
FYI	for your information	2DAY	today
GF	girlfriend	2MORO	tomorrow
GR8	great	2NITE	tonight
GSOH	good sense of humour	TTFN	ta-ta for now (= goodbye)
GTG	got to go	U	you
ILU	I love you	WAN2	want to
IMO	in my opinion	WKND	weekend
		X	kiss

UK and US English

Although English in the UK and the US is very similar, there are a lot of differences in vocabulary, spelling, grammar, and pronunciation.

This dictionary shows you when there are differences.
For a full explanation of the UK and US labels, see page xv.

Vocabulary

Many common words for items we see or use every day are different in UK and US English.

1 The words on the left are UK English. Match each one with a US word from the list on the right.

1 aubergine	4 windscreen	a elevator	d eggplant
2 wardrobe	5 queue	b truck	e closet
3 lift	6 lorry	c windshield	f line

In informal language there are lots of differences between UK and US English.

2 The <u>underlined</u> word in each sentence is used in UK English only.
Replace it with a word from the list on the right which would be understood in both UK and US English.

1 I got it from a <u>bloke</u> at work.	a complaining
2 I'm feeling rather <u>poorly</u> today.	b man
3 I wish he'd stop <u>whingeing</u> and do some work.	c weak
4 I was <u>gutted</u> when I heard I hadn't got the job.	d disappointed
5 My brother's too <u>weedy</u> to climb that tree.	e ill

Spelling

3 Look at these pairs of words. Which is the UK spelling and which is the US spelling?

1 labour/labor	3 offence/offense	5 metre/meter
2 center/centre	4 color/colour	6 traveller/traveler

Pronunciation

In this dictionary, words which are pronounced very differently in UK and US English have both pronunciations shown at the word. The US pronunciation follows the symbol ⓤⓢ.

4 Which of these words have different pronunciations in UK and US English?

1 peach	4 ballet
2 schedule	5 zebra
3 colour	6 bicycle

> **albino** /æl'biːnəʊ/ ⓤⓢ /æl'baɪnəʊ/ *noun* [C] a person or animal with white skin, white hair or fur, and pink eyes

Writing letters

Formal letters

> 47 Abrahams Rd
> Cambridge
> CB4 3AL
>
> 20 January 2006
>
> Ms R Perry
> Evening News
> 107 Wolfs Way
> Newtown
> NT7 0PE
>
> Dear Ms Perry ❶
>
> I am ❸ writing to enquire about ❷ the possibility of holiday work with your company this summer. I am very interested in gaining some experience working for a newspaper.
>
> For the last two years I have been editor of the student magazine at my school. Next year I am planning to do a one-year course in newspaper journalism.
>
> I have good computer skills and accurate written English.
>
> I very much hope you have a vacancy for me. I enclose a copy of my CV and look forward to hearing from you soon. ❹
>
> Yours sincerely, ❶
>
> Anna Thompson

❶ If you know the name of the person you are writing to, but the letter is formal, end the letter: *Yours sincerely.*

If you do not know the name of the person you are writing to, begin the letter: *Dear Sir/Madam* and end it: *Yours faithfully.*

❷ Other ways of beginning a formal letter:
- ▶ *I am writing to inform you of/that ...*
- ▶ *I am writing to complain about ...*
- ▶ *I am writing regarding your advertisement ...*
- ▶ *Please send me ...*
- ▶ *Further to my letter of June 1st ...*

❸ You should not use contractions (e.g. I'm, I'd) in a formal letter.

❹ Other ways of ending a formal letter:
- ▶ *Thank you in advance for your help.*
- ▶ *Wishing you all the best for the future.*

continued on next page

Informal letters

47 Abrahams Rd
Cambridge
CB4 3AL

20 January 2006

Dear Julia,

It was lovely to chat to you the other day. ❶ It seems ages since we last met. We're so excited that you're finally coming over to see us. In fact, John's going to take those two weeks off work so he can spend more time with us.

By the way, could you bring some photos of your family? I'd love to see them.

We're both really looking forward to seeing you. ❷

Love, ❸
Anna

❶ Other ways of starting an informal letter:
  ▶ *Thanks for your letter.*
  ▶ *How are you?*
  ▶ *I hope you're well.*
  ▶ *Sorry it's been so long since I last wrote.*
  ▶ *It was lovely to hear from you.*

❷ Other ways of ending an informal letter:
  ▶ *Drop me a line soon.*
  ▶ *Write soon.*
  ▶ *Take care.*
  ▶ *Do keep in touch.*
  ▶ *Give my love to Paul.*
  ▶ *Hope to hear from you soon.*

❸ Before your name, you write:

  to close friends:
  ▶ *love from*
  ▶ *all my love*
  ▶ *lots of love*

  to less close friends:
  ▶ *best wishes*
  ▶ *all the best*
  ▶ *yours*
  ▶ *kind regards*

What is a collocation/word partner?

A **collocation** is two or more words which native speakers of a language often say or write together. In the boxes in the a-z part of this dictionary we call them **'word partners'**. They are important for natural sounding English. For example, a native speaker of English would say:
*He **made** a **mistake**.*

But would **not** say:
*He **did** a **mistake**.*

This is because **mistake** collocates with **make** but it does not collocate with **do**.

If you want to speak natural-sounding English, you need to remember important collocations so that you can put the right words together in your speaking and writing. This will make your English easier to understand.

What types of collocation are there?

Verbs and nouns
There are verb + noun collocations. For example:
take a photo   **have** fun   **make** a decision

Or noun + verb collocations. For example:
an accident **happens**   disaster **strikes**   a problem **arises**

Adjectives and nouns
There are adjective + noun collocations. For example:
heavy traffic   a **written** agreement   a **useful** skill

Nouns and prepositions
There are noun + preposition collocations. For example:
an answer **to** sth   an argument **with** sb   a choice **between** sth and sth

Or preposition + noun collocations. For example:
by mistake   **in** pain   be **of** interest

Collocations are sometimes used with a lot of words in the same topic. For example, in the topic 'clothes' the collocation 'wear' is used with words such as 'jeans', 'skirt', 'shirt', etc.

Here are twelve topics in which the same collocations are used with many different words. On the pages that follow, you will find the most important collocations for these topics. These are very useful collocations to learn.

1	Age	7	Meals
2	Clothes	8	Months
3	Crimes	9	Musical instruments
4	Days of the week	10	Seasons
5	Illnesses	11	Software
6	Languages	12	Subjects for study

1 Age

• be [15/30/50, etc.] **years old**
She's only four years old.

• be **in your** [30s/40s/50s, etc.]
Many women now have children in their thirties.

• *formal* [32/57/70, etc.] **years of age**
The prices apply to children between 2 and 15 years of age.

• [a man/woman/daughter, etc] **of** [20/30/65, etc.]
She has a son of 10 and a daughter of 8.

• **about** [17/40/65, etc.]
Their son must be about 25 now.

• **approaching/nearly** [50/60/70, etc.]
I would think he's approaching 70. • *She's nearly twenty and still lives with her parents.*

• **over**/**under** [18/35/80, etc.]
You have to be over 21 to get in the club. • *People under 18 are not allowed to drive.*

• **over the age of/under the age of**
You must be over the age of 16 to buy cigarettes. • *We don't sell alcohol to anyone under the age of 18.*

• *humorous* **be the wrong side of** [40/50/60, etc.] = be older than 40, 50, 60, etc.
She's the wrong side of 50 but she's still attractive.

2 Clothes

• **wear** [jeans/a skirt/a shirt, etc.]
I wear a uniform for work.

• **in** sth/be **dressed in** sth/**wearing** sth
He was dressed in a grey suit. • *She was wearing a green dress.* • *a woman in a red coat*

• **have** [a dress/skirt/T-shirt, etc.] **on**
I only had a thin shirt on.

• **put on/take off** [your dress/jeans/coat, etc.]
Put your hat on – it's cold. • *She took off her coat.*

• **do up/fasten/undo/unfasten** [your skirt/belt/coat, etc.]
Fasten your coat. • *She undid her jacket and took it off.*

• **loose/tight** [jeans/T-shirt, etc.]
He was wearing a pair of tight black jeans. • *Wear loose clothes in hot weather.*

3 Crimes

• be **accused of/charged with** (doing) sth
He appeared in court, accused of stabbing a man. • *He has been charged with the murder of a 10-year-old girl.*

• **face charges of** [murder/burglary, etc.]
He arrived in the country to face charges of theft and kidnapping.

• **confess to/admit** (doing) sth
She confessed to the murder. • *He admitted driving while drunk.*

• **deny** (doing) sth
*He has **denied** murdering his girlfriend.*

• be **convicted of/found guilty of** (doing) sth
*Jenkins was **convicted of** murdering his mother in 1998.* • *Bates was **found guilty of** assault.*

• be **arrested for/jailed for** (doing) sth
*She was **arrested for** shoplifting.* • *He was **jailed for** stealing cars.*

• **investigate** [a murder, assault, etc.]
*Police are **investigating** the murder of a young mother.*

• the [murder/rape, etc.] **of** sb
*The murder **of** the 85-year-old woman has shocked everyone.*

• a [crime/murder/rape, etc.] **victim**
*The organization offers help to rape **victims**.*

• a [murder/rape, etc.] **inquiry/investigation**
*Police have a launched a murder **inquiry** after a woman's body was found.*

• a [murder/rape, etc.] **case**
*The police still have 110 unsolved rape **cases**.*

• a **brutal** [murder/attack/rape, etc.]
*He was jailed for the **brutal** rape of a teenage girl.*

4 Days of the week

• **on** [Monday/Tuesday, etc.]
*I'm going to London **on** Friday.*

• **on** [Mondays/Tuesdays, etc.] (= every Monday/Tuesday, etc.)
*She works **on** Wednesdays and Fridays.*

• **every** [Saturday/Tuesday, etc.]
*I have a piano lesson **every** Saturday.*

• **last/next** [Wednesday/Thursday, etc.]
*The meeting was **last** Monday.* • *It's my birthday **next** Tuesday.*

• **the following** [Tuesday/Friday, etc.]
*She went into hospital on Friday for an operation **on the following** Monday.*

• [Monday/Friday, etc.] **afternoon/evening/morning/night**
*I have to work on Monday **morning**.* • *I'm going to a party on Friday **night**.*

5 Illnesses

• **have (got)/suffer from** [a cold/cancer, etc.]
I've got a really bad cold. • *He was **suffering from** flu.*

• be **diagnosed with** [AIDS/a brain tumour/cancer, etc.]
*In 2001, she **was diagnosed with** breast cancer.*

• **catch** [a cold/chickenpox/measles, etc.]
*I **caught** chickenpox from one of the children.*

• **develop** [cancer/an infection/asthma, etc.]
*People who smoke are more likely to **develop** cancer.*

• **go down with** [flu/a stomach upset, etc.]
He went down with flu two days before we were due to leave.

• **shake off** [a cold, flu, etc.]
I've had a cold for two weeks now and I can't shake it off.

• **Cure/treat** [a cold/infection/cancer, etc.]
Scientists are searching for a drug to cure colds. • *Antibiotics can be used to treat some throat infections.*

• [AIDS/asthma/cancer, etc.] **sufferers**
The drug offers new hope to cancer sufferers.

6 Languages

• **speak** [French/Italian/Arabic, etc.]
She speaks very good Russian.

• **learn/study** [Cantonese/Urdu/Spanish, etc.]
I'm learning German at school. • *She wants to study Icelandic at university.*

• **in** [Danish/Mandarin/Portuguese, etc.]
All the signs were in French.

• **fluent/be fluent in** [German/Japanese/Russian, etc.]
He speaks fluent Italian. • *Anna is fluent in Japanese.*

• **broken** (= not good and full of mistakes) [French/Italian/Spanish, etc.]
I tried to make myself understood in broken French.

• a [French/Latin/Russian, etc.] **teacher**
She's a Spanish teacher at the local school.

7 Meals

• **eat/have** [breakfast/lunch, etc.]
More workers are eating lunch at their desks. • *He was sitting in a café having lunch.*

• **make/prepare** [breakfast/lunch, etc.]
He was in the kitchen making lunch. • *She'd prepared a lovely meal for us.*

• **have** sth **for** [lunch/dinner, etc.]
I had toast for breakfast. • *What did you have for dinner?*

• **serve** [breakfast/lunch, etc.]
Breakfast is served in the hotel restaurant between 7 and 9.30am.

• **skip** [breakfast/lunch, etc.] (= not eat breakfast, lunch, etc.)
I was late for school so I had to skip breakfast.

• a **big/light** [breakfast/lunch, etc.]
He always eats a big breakfast. • *I usually have a light lunch.*

• an **early/late** [breakfast/lunch, etc.]
We had an early lunch and then set off. • *I got up at 11am and had a late breakfast.*

• a **leisurely/quick** [breakfast/lunch, etc.]
They enjoyed a leisurely lunch on the hotel terrace. • *We set off early after a quick breakfast.*

• **at/over** [lunch/dinner, etc.]
*He didn't say a word **at** breakfast.* • *We discussed it **over** dinner.*

8 Months

• **in** [December/March, etc.]
*My birthday's **in** July.*

• **on** [August 24th/May 12th, etc.]
*Her birthday's **on** August 24th.*

• **early/mid/late** [January/June, etc.]
*The weather is usually very nice in **early** July.* • *By **late** May, the situation had improved.*

• **the beginning of/the end of** [May/October, etc.]
*The work should be finished by **the beginning of** April.* • *He's coming at **the end of** November.*

• **last/next** [May/June, etc.]
*They got married **last** December.* • *The elections will be held **next** June.*

9 Musical instruments

• **play the/play** [guitar/piano, etc.]
*He **plays** saxophone in a band.* • *She was **playing the** violin.*

• **learn (to play) the** [flute/violin, etc.]
*John's **learning** the clarinet.*

• **on the/on** [drums/violin, etc.]
*Sam was **on the** trumpet and Jim was **on the** saxophone.*

• **a** [piano/guitar, etc.] **lesson/player/teacher**
*I'm having piano **lessons**.* • *He's a great guitar **player**.*

10 Seasons

• **during the/in the/in** [spring/summer, etc.]
*We're very busy **during the** summer.* • *The park is open for longer **in** summer.* • *It often snows **in the** winter.*

• **through the/throughout the** [summer/winter, etc.]
*The plant produces flowers **throughout the** summer.*

• **early/late** [autumn/spring, etc.]
*Sow the seeds in **early** spring.* • *It was a cold night in **late** autumn.*

• **last/next** [winter/summer, etc.]
*The book was published **last** autumn.* • *They're getting married **next** summer.*

• **the depths of winter/the height of spring/summer**
*He never wears a coat, even in **the depths of winter**.* • *It was **the height of summer** and very hot.*

• **the** [spring/summer, etc.] **of** [1995/2004, etc.]
*He had a heart attack in **the** summer **of** 2002.*

• **the** [summer/winter, etc.] **months**
*In the **winter** months, people visit the area to ski.*

11 Software

• **download** [files/music/software, etc.]
*You can just **download** the software from the Internet.*

• **install/uninstall** [a program/software, etc.]
*Follow the on-screen instructions to **install** the program. • **Uninstall** the software if you want to free up more disk space.*

• **run** [a program, etc.]
*Click on the icon to **run** the program.*

• **copy/paste** [a file, etc.]
***Copy** the file onto the C-drive.*

• **develop** [software/a program, etc.]
*The software was **developed** in the US.*

12 Subjects for study

• **do/study** [physics/German, etc.]
*I'm **doing** French and German this year. • Amy's **studying** law at Cambridge University.*

• **have a degree in** [French/history/law, etc.]
*She **has a degree in** chemistry.*

• a [geography/history/maths, etc.] **class/course/lesson**
*He fell asleep in the geography **class**. • The college offers language and computer **courses**. • She's having French **lessons**.*

• a [history/maths, etc.] **lecturer/student/teacher**
*Our English **teacher** is called Mrs Jackson. • She's a maths **lecturer** at the university.*

Speaking naturally
1: language for different situations

These pages will help you to speak naturally, like people who have spoken English since they were children. They give you the phrases (= groups of words that are often used together) that you need in lots of different situations. Try to learn theses phrases.

1 Saying hello	5 Asking if you can have something	8 Inviting someone
2 Saying goodbye	6 Offering something	9 What to say when someone thanks you
3 When someone says sorry	7 Offering to help someone	
4 Asking if you can do something		

1 Saying hello

There are other ways to say hello to someone as well as the usual 'Hello' or, 'Hello, how are you?' Here are a few:

Hello/Hi, **how are you doing?**

Hello/Hi, **how's it going?**

Hello/Hi, **how are things?**

Answering

If you are well or happy

Fine, thanks. How are you?

Good, thanks. And you?

Not so bad, thanks. How are you doing?

If you are not well or happy

Not too good today.

Not brilliant, actually.

So-so.

2 Saying goodbye

Other ways to say 'goodbye' informally to friends and family:

Bye. **Catch you later!**

Bye. **See you later!**

See you!

3 When someone says sorry

If someone says they are sorry about something they have done, you can say one of these:

It doesn't matter.

That's all right!

Don't worry about it!

4 Asking if you can do something

Is it all right if I open a window?

Do you mind if I smoke?

May I sit here?

Saying 'yes'

Please do!

Be my guest!

Sure. Go ahead!

Saying 'no'

Actually I'd rather you didn't.

I'd rather you didn't, if you don't mind.

I'd rather you didn't – I'm sorry.

5 Asking if you can have something

May I take this chair?

Could I have a hand-out, please?

Saying 'yes'

Yes, of course!

Please do!

Be my guest!

Help yourself!

Feel free!

Saying 'no'

I'm sorry – that's the only one I've got.

I'm afraid I need it myself.

6 Offering something

Can I get you something to drink?

Would you like something to drink?

Saying 'yes'

Saying 'no'

Yes, please. A coffee *would be great.*

No, thanks. *I'm fine.*

I'd love a coffee, thanks.

No, *I'm all right,* thanks.

7 Offering to help someone

Can I help you with your bags?

Would you like some help with your bags?

Let me help you with your bags.

Saying 'yes'

Saying 'no'

Thanks, **that would be great.**

It's all right, thanks. I can manage.

Thanks, **that's a great help.**

I'm fine, thanks.

Yes, thanks, **if you don't mind.**

8 Inviting someone

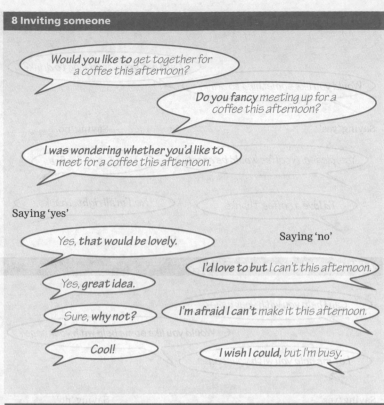

Would you like to get together for a coffee this afternoon?

Do you fancy meeting up for a coffee this afternoon?

I was wondering whether you'd like to meet for a coffee this afternoon.

Saying 'yes'

Yes, **that would be lovely.**

Yes, **great idea.**

Sure, why not?

Cool!

Saying 'no'

I'd love to but I can't this afternoon.

I'm afraid I can't make it this afternoon.

I wish I could, but I'm busy.

9 What to say when someone thanks you …

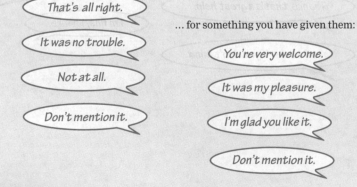

… for something you have done:

That's all right.

It was no trouble.

Not at all.

Don't mention it.

… for something you have given them:

You're very welcome.

It was my pleasure.

I'm glad you like it.

Don't mention it.

Speaking naturally
2: conversation exercises

These pages contain twelve longer conversations that take place in different situations. There are gaps in the conversations. Under each conversation you will find some phrases (= groups of words which are often used together). Try to find the right phrases to fill the gaps. Then try to learn these phrases. Again, they will help your English to sound natural, like the English that native speakers of English use.

1 Making an appointment	7 Asking someone how their family are
2 Making phone calls	8 Talking about where you come from
3 Invitations	9 Talking about your plans (for the weekend and for your holiday)
4 Apologizing (saying you are sorry)	10 Talking about the past weekend
5 At the restaurant	11 Cancelling an arrangement
6 Visiting someone's house	12 When someone tells you news (good and bad)

1 Making an appointment

Complete the dialogue with the phrases below:

Making an appointment with a doctor
Mark: I'd like to (1) _____ Dr Parker, please.
Receptionist: Right, let me see. The first appointment available is 3.30, Wednesday.
Mark: I'm afraid Wednesday is no good. (2) _____ on Friday?
Receptionist: 4.20 on Friday?
Mark: Yes, that's fine - (3) _____
Receptionist: What's the name, please?
Mark: Mark Klein, (4) _____ K-L-E-I-N.
Receptionist: So, that's 4.20 on Friday with Dr Parker.

a. I'll take that
b. make an appointment to see
c. Do you have anything
d. that's spelt

2 Making phone calls

Complete the dialogues with the phrases below:

An informal call
Su: Hello.
Anna: Hello, can I speak to Jane, please?
Su: I'm afraid she's not here at the moment. (1) _____
Anna: Yes, please. It's Anna Morris calling. Could you ask her to call me when she gets back?
Su: Sure. (2) _____
Anna: I think so but I'll give it to you anyway. It's 0209 435876.
Su: Ok, (3) _____
Anna: Thanks very much.
Su: Bye.

Anna: Goodbye.

A business call
Receptionist: Good morning. Smith and Dawson. (4)_____
John: Hello. Could I speak to Sylvie Roberts, please?
Receptionist: Certainly. (5)_____
John: It's John Wilson.
Receptionist: OK. (6)_____

a. I'll just put you through.
b. Does she have your number?
c. I'll ask her to call you when she gets in.
d. How can I help you?
e. Could I ask who's calling, please?
f. Can I take a message?

3 Invitations

Complete the dialogues with the phrases below:

Saying 'yes' to an invitation
Sasha: I was wondering whether you'd like to come over for dinner one
    evening.
Nihal: Yes, thank you (1) _____
Sasha: Are you free on Thursday evening?
Nihal: Yes. (2) _____
Sasha: About 7 o'clock?
Nihal: Yes, thanks, that would be great. (3) _____
Sasha: OK, see you on Thursday, then.
Nihal: (4) _____

a. I'll put it in my diary.
b. What sort of time?
c. I'd love to.
d. I'll look forward to it.

Saying 'no' politely to an invitation
Tomas: Suki, would you like to join us for dinner this evening?
Suki: I'd love to but (1)_____ - I'm meeting a friend.
Tomas: That's a shame.
Suki: Yes, (2) _____
Tomas: Maybe another time, then?
Suki: (3)_____

a. I'd love to have come otherwise.
b. Definitely.
c. I'm afraid I can't

4 Apologizing (saying you are sorry)

Complete the dialogues with the phrases below:

Vikram: Maria, (1)_____ I said I'd call you last night, and I completely forgot.
Maria: Oh, (2) _____ It doesn't matter. I know you're really busy.
Vikram: (3)_____ - it just completely slipped my mind.
Maria: Really, Vikram, it doesn't matter. (4)_____

a. Don't give it another thought.
b. Don't worry about it.
c. I owe you an apology.
d. I feel really bad about it

5 At the restaurant

Complete the dialogues with the phrases below:

Before the meal
Waiter: Good evening.
Alexandra: Good evening. (1)_____
Waiter: (2) _____
Alexandra: Non-smoking, please.
Waiter: Take a seat near the window.
Alexandra: Thanks. (3) _____ and wine list, please?

a. Smoking or non-smoking?
b. Could we see the menu
c. A table for two, please?

Ordering the meal
Waiter: Are you (1)_____
Alexandra: Yes, I think so. (2) _____salmon, please.
Waiter: And for you, madam?
Danielle: Do you have (3)_____
Waiter: Yes, we have several dishes without meat, at the bottom of the menu.
Danielle: Ah yes, I'll have the mushroom tart, please.
Waiter: Okay. (4) _____
Danielle: Yes, one mixed salad, please.
Waiter: (5)_____
Danielle: A bottle of house red and some mineral water, please.
Waiter: (6)_____
Danielle: Sparkling, please.
Waiter: (7)_____
Danielle: Yes, thank you.

a. a vegetarian option?
b. I'll have the
c. Any side dishes with that?
d. And to drink?
e. ready to order?
f. Is that everything?
g. Sparkling or still?

During the meal
Waiter: (1)_____
Alexandra: Yes, thanks. (2)_____bread, please?
Waiter: Certainly. And (3)_____wine?
Alexandra: No thanks, but could we have another bottle of sparkling mineral water?

a. Could we have some more
b. Is everything all right for you?
c. can I get you any more

After the meal
Waiter: (1)_____
Danielle: Yes, thanks. It was lovely.
Waiter: Good. (2)_____More coffee?
Danielle: No thanks. (3)_____
Waiter: Of course.

a. Would you like anything else?
b. Could we have the (*UK*) bill/(*US*) check, please?
c. Did you enjoy your meal?

6 Visiting someone's house

Complete the dialogues with the phrases below:
Ethan arrives at Lidia's house to have dinner.

Welcoming someone
Lidia: Hello. (1)_____
Ethan: Hello. (2)_____
Lidia: Not at all. Perfect timing. (3)_____
Ethan: Thank you.
Lidia: (4)_____
Ethan: No, not at all. We've brought you these flowers.
Lidia: Oh, (5)_____ They're beautiful - thank you!

a. I'm sorry we're late.
b. Did you have any problems finding us?
c. Lovely to see you.
d. you shouldn't have!
e. Let me take your coats.

Saying goodbye
Ethan: It's been a lovely evening. (1)_____
Lidia: Not at all. (2)_____ Thank you for coming.
Ethan: We'll see you soon. (3)_____
Lidia: That would be great. See you soon. (4)_____
Ethan: Thanks. Bye!
Lidia: Bye!

a. You must come over to us next time.
b. Thank you very much for having us.
c. It's been a pleasure.
d. Drive carefully

7 Asking someone how their family are

Complete the dialogue with the phrases below:

Luis: Juan, hello!
Juan: Hello Luis, how are you?
Luis: (1)_____, thanks, and you?
Juan: Fine. How's the family?
Luis: (2)_____, thanks. Julia has just been promoted at work.
Juan: (3)_____
Luis: Yes, she's very pleased.
Juan: Do (4)_____
Luis: Yes, I will. By the way, (5)_____, how is your father these days?
Juan: He's much better, thank you.
Luis: That's good. (6)_____ , won't you?
Juan: Yes, I will. Thanks. (7)_____
Luis: Nice to see you too.

a. They're doing well
b. tell her I was asking after her.
c. Not too bad
d. Good for her!
e. Give him my regards when you see him
f. I was meaning to ask you
g. Nice to see you.

8 Talking about where you come from

Complete the dialogue with the phrases below:

Jude: So (1)_____, Thomas?
Thomas: I'm from Germany.
Jude: (2)_____ in Germany?
Thomas: From the north – Osnabrück. Do you know it?
Jude: No, I've been to Karlsruhe but I don't know the north of Germany at all.
Thomas: (3)_____ Where are you from?
Jude: (4)_____ Edinburgh but I live in London now.
Thomas: (5)_____ London?
Jude: North London – a place called Hampstead . (6)_____
Thomas: Yes, I know the name but I've never been there.

a. Have you heard of it?
b. What about you?
c. Where are you from
d. I'm originally from
e. Whereabouts
f. Which part of

9 Talking about your plans...

Complete the dialogues with the phrases below:

...for the weekend

Akbar: (1)_____ this weekend?
Carolina: (2) _____ Just having (3)_____ at home. How about you?
Akbar: We're going to visit my brother in Paris.
Carolina: Paris? That'll be nice. (4)_____
Akbar: Yes, it should be good.

a. a quiet weekend
b. What are you doing
c. Are you looking forward to it?
d. Nothing special.

...for your (*UK*) holiday (*US*) vacation

Georgia: (1)_____ this summer?
Leo: Yes, we're going camping in France. How about you?
Georgia: (2)_____ yet but (3)_____ Switzerland for a couple of weeks.
Leo: Switzerland. We went there last year and really enjoyed it. (4)_____

a. I think you'll like it.
b. we're thinking of going to
c. Are you going away
d. We haven't booked anything

10 Talking about the past weekend

Complete the dialogue with the phrases below:

Ava: (1)_____
Owen: Yes, thanks - very good. Did you?
Ava: Yes, it was nice.
Owen: Did you (2)_____
Ava: No not really – we just (3)_____ How about you?
Owen: We went to the coast on Saturday.
Ava: (4)_____
Owen: It was really nice. The weather was perfect.
Ava: (5)_____

a. Sounds great!
b. Did you have a good weekend?
c. do anything special?
d. had a quiet one.
e. How was that?

TALK! Talk! TALK! TALK! TALK! Talk! TALK! TALK! TALK! Talk! TALK! Talk!

11 Cancelling an arrangement

Complete the dialogue with the phrases below:

Marta: I'm really sorry , Michel, but (1)_____ dinner tonight. (2) _____
Michel: Oh what a shame. (3) _____
Marta: Can we arrange it for another time?
Michel: Yes, (4) _____
Marta: Next week sometime would be great. (5) _____
Michel: Don't worry about it – it's not a problem.

a. Something's come up.
b. I'm going to have to cancel
c. I'm free most evenings next week.
d. Never mind.
e. I'm really sorry about tonight.

12 When someone tells you news

Complete the dialogues with the phrases below:

Good news
James: I've just heard that I've got the job.
Erin: (1) _____
James: Thank you!
Erin: Well done! (2) _____
James: Yes, I am. It's really good news.
Erin: I'm so pleased for you, James – you deserve it.
James: Thank you – (3) _____

Bad news
Conor: I'm afraid I won't be able to make it to the party tonight.
I've got to work.
Patrice: Oh no, (4) _____ You were really looking forward to it.
Conor: Yes, I'm really disappointed.
Patrice: (5) _____ Is there no way round it?

a. You must be really pleased.
b. what a shame!
c. that's very kind.
d. Congratulations!
e. I bet you are.

Answer key

Checking your work

1 **1** The new rule affects everyone.
   2 What time is it?
   3 It's quite hot in here.
   4 He made/gave an interesting speech.
2 **1** do **2** take **3** of **4** feeling
3 The name of this place is Milan, and it is one of
   the most important Italian cities. You will find
   Milan in the north of Italy and you can get there
   by car, train, or plane, but **I think/in my
   opinion**, travelling by car is the best solution. I
   suggest **visiting/you visit** Milan, not only
   because it's full of people but also for its
   historical buildings.
   I decided **to** go to Milan because **I wanted to**
   see the Duomo and the Castello Sforsesco, and
   I must **tell you** that they are **incredible**. I
   hope that you decide to go to Milan **next
   summer**.
   I look forward to **seeing** you very soon, with
   love, Luca
   PS Besides, in Milan there are **a lot of** pubs
   and discos where I know many interesting
   people.

Countable and uncountable nouns

1 **1** homework **2** sand **3** ✓
   4 ✓ **5** luggage
2 **1** an **2** —, a **3** a **4** — **5** —
3 **1** fly **2** furniture **3** luggage **4** day
   5 accidents
4 **1** a lot of **2** much **3** many **4** much
5 duck, ice cream, lipstick, pizza

Modal verbs

1 7
2 **1** b **2** d **3** a **4** e **5** c
3 **1** d **2** e **3** b **4** c **5** a

Phrasal verbs

1 **1** drag: 3 **2** hand: 5 **3** pack: 3
   4 make: 12
2 **1** on **2** off **3** up **4** over
3 your own answers
4 **1** for **2** with **3** on **4** about **5** on

Idioms

1 **1** neck: b **2** nail: e **3** battle: a **4** end: c
   5 face: d
2 **1** leg **2** head **3** arm **4** ear **5** face

Verb patterns

1 **1** T **2** I,T **3** I,T **4** I,T **5** T
   6 I,T **7** T **8** I,T **9** I **10** T
2 **1** c **2** e **3** d **4** a **5** b
3 your own answers

Word formation

1 **1** unlock **2** disagree **3** illegal
   4 impossible **5** irresponsible
2 **1** unlock **2** impossible **3** illegal
   4 disagree **5** irresponsible
3 **1** e, multiracial **2** a, semicircle
   3 f, anti-war **4** b, pro-democracy
   5 c, ex-president **6** g, postgraduate
   7 h, overworked **8** d, under-cooked
4 **1** rudeness **2** creation **3** preference
   4 ignorance **5** hilarity **6** development

Measurements

1 wide, width **2** long **3** depth
4 high, high

Pronunciation

1 **1** d **2** e **3** b **4** f **5** a **6** c
2 **1** mole **2** giraffe **3** horse **4** sheep
5 lion **6** chimp
3 **1** k **2** h **3** s **4** w **5** w **6** l
4 **1** **bro**ther **2** edu**ca**tion **3** pho**tog**rapher
4 be**low** **5** com**pu**ter **6** **ne**cessary

Spelling

1 **1** houses **2** watches **3** bricks
4 minutes **5** faxes **6** losses
2 **1** whether **2** quite **3** which **4** their
5 sea
3 **1** hotter **2** banned **3** loudest
4 beginning **5** working

UK and US English

1 **1** d **2** e **3** a **4** c **5** f **6** b
2 **1** b **2** e **3** a **4** d **5** c
3 in each case, UK comes first
1 labour/labor
2 centre/center **3** offence/offense
4 colour/color **5** metre/meter
6 traveller/traveler
4 schedule, ballet, zebra

Speaking naturally
2: conversation exercises

1 **1** b **2** c **3** a **4** d
2 An informal call
1 f **2** b **3** c
A business call
4 d **5** e **6** a
3 Saying 'yes' to an invitation
1 c **2** b **3** a **4** d
Saying 'no' politely to an invitation
1 c **2** a **3** b
4 **1** c **2** b **3** d **4** a
5 Before the meal
1 c **2** a **3** b
Ordering the meal
1 e **2** b **3** a **4** c **5** d **6** g **7** f
During the meal
1 h **2** a **3** c
After the meal
1 c **2** a **3** b
6 Welcoming someone
1 c **2** a **3** e **4** b **5** d
Saying goodbye
1 b **2** c **3** a **4** d
7 **1** c **2** a **3** d **4** b **5** f **6** e **7** g
8 **1** c **2** e **3** b **4** d **5** f **6** a
9 For this weekend
1 b **2** d **3** a **4** c
For a (*UK*) holiday/(*US*) vacation
1 c **2** d **3** b **4** a
10 **1** b **2** c **3** d **4** e **5** a
11 **1** b **2** a **3** d **4** c **5** e
12 Good news
1 d **2** a **3** c
Bad news
4 b **5** e

marijuana /ˌmærɪ'wɑːnə/ *mainly US* (*mainly UK* **cannabis**) *noun* [U] a drug that some people smoke for pleasure and that is illegal in many countries

marina /mə'riːnə/ *noun* [C] an area of water where people keep their boats

marinate /'mærɪneɪt/ (*also* **marinade** /ˌmærɪ'neɪd/) *verb* [T] to add a mixture of oil, wine, herbs, etc to food before cooking it ● **marinade** /ˌmærɪ'neɪd/ *noun* [C, U]

marine¹ /mə'riːn/ *adjective* [always before noun] found in the sea, or relating to the sea *marine creatures/life* ○ *marine biology*

marine² /mə'riːn/ *noun* [C] a soldier who has been trained to fight at sea and on land *the Marine Corps*

marital /'mærɪtəl/ *adjective* [always before noun] relating to marriage *marital problems*

marital ˌstatus *noun* [U] whether or not someone is married *The form asks for personal information such as name, date of birth and marital status.*

maritime /'mærɪtaɪm/ *adjective* [always before noun] relating to ships and sea travel *a maritime museum*

🧩 WORD PARTNERS FOR *mark*

leave/make a mark ● a mark **on** sth ● **dirty marks**

o▪**mark¹** /mɑːk/ *noun* 1 [AREA] [C] an area of dirt, damage, etc that is left on something *You've got a black mark on your nose.* ○ *He's left dirty marks all over the carpet.* 2 [SCORE] [C] a number or letter that is written on a piece of work, saying how good the work is *She always gets good marks in English.* 3 [LEVEL] [no plural] a particular level, degree, distance, etc *They've just passed the 5000m mark.* ○ *Interest rates are somewhere around the seven percent mark.* 4 **a mark of sth** a sign or proof that something exists *a mark of genius* ○ *There was a minute's silence everywhere as a mark of respect.* 5 **leave/make your mark** to do something that makes you successful or makes people notice you 6 **On your marks. Get set. Go!** something that you say to start a running race 7 **be wide of the mark** to not be correct or accurate ➌See also: **punctuation mark, quotation marks.**

o▪**mark²** /mɑːk/ *verb* 1 [HAPPEN] [T] If an event marks the beginning, end, etc of something, it causes it, or happens at the same time as it. *His death marks the end of an era in television.* 2 [CELEBRATE] [T] If you mark an occasion, you do something to celebrate it. *They've declared Tuesday a national holiday to mark the 10th anniversary of Independence.* 3 [SHOW A PLACE] [T] to show where something is by drawing or putting something somewhere *I've marked my street on the map for you.* 4 [GIVE RESULTS] [I, T] to check a piece of work or an exam, showing mistakes and giving a letter or number to say how good it is *to mark essays* 5 [DIRTY] [T] to leave an area of dirt on something

mark sth out to show the shape or position of something by drawing a line around it

marked /mɑːkt/ *adjective* very noticeable *There has been a marked improvement since last year.* ● **markedly** *adverb*

marker /'mɑːkər/ *noun* [C] 1 (*also* 'marker ˌpen) a thick pen used especially for writing on boards *a black felt marker* ➌See colour picture **The Classroom** on page Centre 6. 2 a sign that shows where something is

market

🧩 WORD PARTNERS FOR *market*

3 the market **is booming/is growing** ● a market **collapses** ● the market **in** sth

o▪**market¹** /'mɑːkɪt/ *noun* [C] 1 [SELLING PLACE] a place where people go to buy or sell things, often outside *a cattle/fish/flower market* ○ *a market stall* 2 [SHOP] *US* a supermarket (= large shop that sells food) 3 [BUSINESS] the buying and selling of something *the insurance/personal computer market* 4 [BUYING GROUP] all the people who want to buy a particular product, or the area where they live *South America is our largest market.* ○ *Is there a market for (= will people buy) second-hand jewellery?* 5 **on the market** available to buy *His house has been on the market for over a year.* ➌See also: **black market, flea market, free market, niche market, the stock exchange.**

market² /'mɑːkɪt/ *verb* [T] to try to sell products using advertising or other ways of making people want to buy them *Their products are very cleverly marketed.*

marketable /'mɑːkɪtəbl/ *adjective* Marketable products or skills are easy to sell because people want them.

ˌmarket 'forces *noun* [plural] the way that prices and wages are influenced by how many people want to buy a particular product and how much is available

marketing /'mɑːkɪtɪŋ/ *noun* [U] the work of encouraging people to buy a product or service *a career in marketing/sales and marketing*

marketplace /'mɑːkɪtpleɪs/ *noun* 1 **the marketplace** in business, the buying and selling of products *We have to learn to compete in the international marketplace.* 2 [C] an area in a town where there is a market

ˌmarket re'search *noun* [U] the activity of finding out what people like about products and what new things they want to buy *a market research company*

ˈmarket ˌshare *noun* [C] the number of things that a company sells compared with the number of things of the same type that other companies sell

markings /ˈmɑːkɪŋz/ *noun* [plural] the shapes and colours on an animal or bird *The spider is easily distinguished by the orange and black markings on its back.* ○ *distinctive markings*

mark-up /ˈmɑːkʌp/ *noun* [C] the amount by which the price of something is increased before it is sold again *The usual mark-up on clothes is around 20%.*

marmalade /ˈmɑːməleɪd/ *noun* [U] a sweet, soft food made with oranges or lemons and often eaten on toast (= cooked bread)

maroon¹ /məˈruːn/ *noun* [U] a dark red-purple colour ● **maroon** *adjective* ➲See colour picture **Colours** on page Centre 12.

maroon² /məˈruːn/ *verb* **be marooned** to be left somewhere where you cannot get away *The army was called in on Wednesday to help rescue millions of people marooned by the floods.*

marquee /mɑːˈkiː/ *noun* [C] *UK* **1** a large tent used for parties, shows, etc *We had our wedding in a marquee.* **2** *US* a large sign over a cinema or theatre that says what films or shows are playing

WORD PARTNERS FOR *marriage*

sb's marriage **breaks up/fails** ● sb's marriage **to** sb ● a **happy** marriage

⊶**marriage** /ˈmærɪdʒ/ *noun* **1** [C, U] the legal relationship of a man and a woman being a husband and a wife ***a happy marriage*** **2** [C] the ceremony where people become a husband and a wife ***a marriage ceremony/certificate***

⊶**married** /ˈmærid/ *adjective* **1** A married man or woman has a wife or husband. ***a married couple*** ○ *She's been* ***married to*** *David for nearly ten years.* ○ *As far as I know they're very* ***happily married****.* ➲Opposite **unmarried**. **2 get married** to begin a legal relationship with someone as their husband or wife *We got married last year.*

marrow /ˈmærəʊ/ *noun UK* **1** [C, U] a large vegetable which has dark green skin and is white on the inside **2** [U] (*also* **bone marrow**) the soft substance inside bones

⊶**marry** /ˈmæri/ *verb* **1** [I, T] to begin a legal relationship with someone as their husband or wife ***Will you marry me?*** ○ *He never married.* **2** [T] to officially make people become a husband and a wife in a ceremony *We were married by our local vicar.*

Mars /mɑːz/ *noun* [no plural] the planet that is fourth from the Sun, after the Earth and before Jupiter

marsh /mɑːʃ/ *noun* [C, U] an area of soft, wet land

marshal /ˈmɑːʃəl/ *noun* [C] **1** someone who helps to organize or control a large public event *race marshals* **2** an important officer in police or fire departments in the US ➲See also: **field marshal**.

marshmallow /ˌmɑːʃˈmæləʊ/ [US] /ˈmɑːrʃˌmæləʊ/ *noun* [C, U] a soft, white food made from sugar

martial art /ˌmɑːʃəlˈɑːt/ *noun* [C] traditional Japanese or Chinese skills of fighting, done as sports in western countries

martial law /ˌmɑːʃəlˈlɔː/ *noun* [U] the control of a country by its army instead of by its usual leaders *to declare martial law*

Martian /ˈmɑːʃən/ *noun* [C] in stories, someone from the planet Mars

martyr /ˈmɑːtər/ *noun* [C] someone who dies for their beliefs *a Catholic martyr* ● **martyrdom** *noun* [U]

marvel¹ /ˈmɑːvəl/ *noun* [C] something really surprising, exciting, or good *a marvel of modern technology*

marvel² /ˈmɑːvəl/ *verb* [I] *UK* **marvelling** *past* **marvelled** *US* **marveling** *past* **marveled** to admire something very much *I'm just* ***marvelling at*** *your skills.*

marvellous *UK* (*US* **marvelous**) /ˈmɑːvələs/ *adjective* extremely good *What a marvellous idea!* ● **marvellously** *UK* (*US* **marvelously**) *adverb*

Marxism /ˈmɑːksɪzəm/ *noun* [U] the political and economic ideas of Karl Marx

Marxist /ˈmɑːksɪst/ *adjective* relating to Marxism *Marxist ideology* ● **Marxist** *noun* [C] someone who supports Marxism

mascara /mæsˈkɑːrə/ *noun* [U] a dark substance that you put on your eyelashes (= hairs that grow above and below your eyes) to make them look longer and thicker ➲See picture at **make up**.

mascot /ˈmæskɒt/ *noun* [C] a toy or a child that a person or a team takes with them to bring them luck *He's our* ***lucky mascot****.*

masculine /ˈmæskjəlɪn/ *adjective* **1** having qualities that are typical of men *a masculine appearance/voice* **2** in some languages, belonging to a group of nouns or adjectives that have the same grammatical behaviour. The other groups are 'feminine' and 'neuter'.

masculinity /ˌmæskjəˈlɪnəti/ *noun* [U] the qualities that are typical of men

mash /mæʃ/ *verb* [T] to crush food until it is soft *(UK) mashed potato/ (US) mashed potatoes*

mask

mask¹ /mɑːsk/ *noun* [C] a covering for the face that protects, hides, or decorates the person wearing it ➲See also: **gas mask**.

mask² /mɑːsk/ *verb* [T] to prevent something

from being noticed *I've had to put some flowers in there to* **mask** *the smell.*

masked /mɑːskt/ *adjective* wearing a mask *a masked gunman*

masochism /'mæsəkɪzᵊm/ *noun* [U] when people get pleasure from being hurt • **masochist** *noun* [C] someone who gets pleasure from being hurt

masochistic /ˌmæsəˈkɪstɪk/ *adjective* getting pleasure from being hurt *masochistic behaviour*

masonry /'meɪsᵊnri/ *noun* [U] the parts of a building that are made of bricks or stone

masquerade /ˌmæskᵊrˈeɪd/ *verb*
masquerade as sb/sth to pretend to be someone or something *She's just a teacher masquerading as an academic.*

mass¹ /mæs/ *noun* **1** [C] a solid lump with no clear shape *The sauce was now a sticky mass in the bottom of the pan.* **2 a mass of sth** a large amount or number of something *She had a mass of blond curls.* **3** [U] in physics, the amount of substance that something contains *One litre of water has a mass of one kilogram.* **4 masses** *informal* a large amount or number of something *I've got masses of work to do.* **5 the masses** the ordinary people who form the largest part of society *He failed to win the support of the masses.*

mass² /mæs/ *adjective* [always before noun] involving a lot of people *mass destruction/unemployment* ○ *a mass murderer*

mass³ /mæs/ *verb* [I, T] *formal* to come together somewhere in large numbers, or make people or things do this *Over 20,000 demonstrators massed in the town's main square.*

Mass, mass /mæs/ *noun* [C, U] a religious ceremony in some Christian churches in which people eat bread and drink wine *to go to Mass*

massacre /'mæsəkəʳ/ *noun* [C] the killing of a lot of people *He ordered the massacre of over 2,000 women and children.* • **massacre** *verb* [T] *Hundreds of civilians were massacred in the raid.*

massage /'mæsɑːdʒ/ ⑱ /məˈsɑːdʒ/ *noun* [C, U] the activity of rubbing or pressing parts of someone's body in order to make them relax or to stop their muscles hurting *to have a massage* ○ *She gave me a foot massage.* • **massage** *verb* [T] *Would you massage my shoulders?*

massive /'mæsɪv/ *adjective* very big *a massive building* ○ *massive debts*

mass-market /ˌmæsˈmɑːkɪt/ *adjective* describes something that is made to be sold to as many people as possible • **'mass ˌmarket** *noun* [C]

the ˌmass 'media *noun* [group] newspapers, television, and radio

mass-produced *adjective* describes something that is made cheaply in very large numbers, using factory machines • **mass-produce** *verb* [T]

mast /mɑːst/ *noun* [C] **1** a tall pole on a boat that supports its sails **2** a tall metal pole that sends out television, radio or mobile phone signals

master¹ /'mɑːstəʳ/ *noun* [C] **1** IN CHARGE In the past, a servant's master was the man that they worked for. **2** TEACHER *old-fashioned* a male teacher *the Latin master* **3** SKILL someone who does something very well *He was a master of disguise.* **4** FOR COPYING a document or recording from which copies can be made **5 Master of Arts/Science, etc** a higher university qualification which usually takes 1 or 2 more years of study after your first qualification, or a person who has this qualification **6 Master's (degree)** a higher university qualification *to study for a Master's degree* **7 Master** *formal* a title for a boy, used before his family name or full name *Master Thomas Mills*

master² /'mɑːstəʳ/ *verb* [T] to learn how to do something well *to master a technique* ○ *He lived for several years in Italy but never quite mastered the language.*

master³ /'mɑːstəʳ/ *adjective* [always before noun] having the skills for a particular job *a master chef/craftsman*

masterful /'mɑːstəfᵊl/ *adjective* done with great skill *a masterful display of golf*

mastermind /'mɑːstəmaɪnd/ *verb* [T] to plan every detail of a complicated event or activity and make sure that it happens *He allegedly masterminded both bomb attacks in the region.* • **mastermind** *noun* [C] *It is thought he was the* **mastermind behind** (= the person who planned) *last year's bombing campaign.*

masterpiece /'mɑːstəpiːs/ *noun* [C] a painting, book, or film that is generally considered to be of excellent quality *'Mona Lisa' is widely regarded as Leonardo da Vinci's masterpiece.*

mastery /'mɑːstᵊri/ *noun* **1 mastery of sth** great skill or understanding of something *his mastery of the Japanese language* **2 mastery of/over sth** control over something *The two countries battled for mastery over the region.*

masturbate /'mæstəbeɪt/ *verb* [I] to make yourself feel sexually excited by touching your sexual organs • **masturbation** /ˌmæstəˈbeɪʃᵊn/ *noun* [U]

mat /mæt/ *noun* [C] **1** a piece of thick material that you put on the floor, often in order to protect it *There's a mat by the door for you to wipe your feet on.* **2** a small piece of plastic or other material that you put on a table so that hot plates and liquid will not damage it

WORD PARTNERS FOR **match**

play/lose/win a match • a match against sb
• in a match

o⟶**match¹** /mætʃ/ *noun* **1** GAME [C] a sports competition in which two people or teams compete against each other *a football/tennis match* **2** FIRE [C] a thin, wooden stick which produces a flame when you rub one end of it against a rough surface *a box of matches* **3** ATTRACTIVE [no plural] If something is a good match for something else, it looks attractive next to it, usually because it is the right colour. *The curtains look nice - they're a perfect match for the sofa.* **4** RELATIONSHIP [no plural] If two people who are having a relationship are a good match, they are very suitable for each other. **5 be no match for sb/sth** to not be as good as someone or something else *Gibson ran well but was no match for the young Italian.*

match² /mætʃ/ *verb* **1** [BE THE SAME] **[I, T]** If two things match, they are the same colour or type. *That jacket matches your skirt perfectly.* ○ *I can't find anything to match my green shirt.* ○ *Your socks don't match.* ○ *Traces of blood found on Walker's clothing matched the victim's blood type.* **2** [CHOOSE] **[T]** to choose someone or something that is suitable for a particular person, activity, or purpose *In the first exercise, you have to* ***match*** *the famous person* ***to*** *their country of origin.* **3** [BE AS GOOD AS] **[T]** to be as good as someone or something else *It would be difficult to match the service this airline gives to its customers.* ○ *She'd given such a brilliant talk – it will be difficult to match it.*

match up If two pieces of information match up, they are the same. *Their accounts of what happened that evening didn't match up.*

match sb/sth up to choose someone or something that is suitable for a particular person, activity, or purpose *They look at your interests and try to* ***match you up with*** *someone suitable.*

match up to sth to be as good as something else *Nothing that he wrote after this point ever matched up to his early work.* ○ *It was the perfect holiday and nothing since has matched up to it.*

M

matchbox /ˈmætʃbɒks/ *noun* **[C]** a small box containing matches

matching /ˈmætʃɪŋ/ *adjective* **[always before noun]** having the same colour or pattern as something else *She wore purple shorts and a matching T-shirt.*

mate¹ /meɪt/ *noun* **[C]** **1** [FRIEND] *UK informal* a friend *She's my* ***best mate****.* ○ *Pete was there with a couple of mates.* ○ *I'll ask one of my mates if they can help out.* **2** [TALKING TO A MAN] *UK informal* You call a man 'mate' when you are speaking to him informally. *Thanks, mate.* **3** [ANIMAL] an animal's sexual partner

mate² /meɪt/ *verb* **[I]** When animals mate, they have sex in order to produce babies. *They mate in the spring.*

material¹ /məˈtɪəriəl/ *noun* **1** [SUBSTANCE] **[C, U]** a solid substance from which things can be made *building materials* ○ *Crude oil is used as the* ***raw material*** *for making plastics.* **2** [CLOTH] **[C, U]** cloth for making clothes, curtains, etc *Her dress was made of a soft, silky material.* **3** [INFORMATION] **[U]** the facts or ideas in a piece of writing *I'm collecting material for an article that I'm writing.* ○ *Please state clearly on your entry if you do not wish to receive promotional material from other companies.*

material² /məˈtɪəriəl/ *adjective* relating to money and possessions and not emotions or thoughts *the* ***material world*** ○ ***Material wealth*** *has never interested him.*

materialism /məˈtɪəriəlɪzᵊm/ *noun* **[U]** the belief that having money and possessions is the most important thing in life • **materialistic** /məˌtɪəriəˈlɪstɪk/ *adjective* believing in materialism *a materialistic society*

materialize (*also UK* **-ise**) /məˈtɪəriəlaɪz/ *verb* **[I]** If something does not materialize, it does not happen. *She was promised a promotion but it never materialized.*

materials /məˈtɪəriəlz/ *noun* **[plural]** the equipment that you need for a particular activity *teaching/writing materials*

maternal /məˈtɜːnᵊl/ *adjective* **1** like a mother *I've never had much of a* ***maternal instinct*** (= wish to have children). **2** **[always before noun]** A maternal relation is part of your mother's family. *He's my maternal grandfather.*

maternity /məˈtɜːnəti/ *adjective* **[always before noun]** related to pregnancy and birth *maternity clothes*

maternity leave /məˈtɜːnəti,liːv/ *noun* **[U]** a period of weeks or months that a mother spends away from her usual job so that she can look after a new baby

math /mæθ/ *noun* **[U]** *US short for* mathematics

mathematical /ˌmæθᵊmˈætɪkᵊl/ *adjective* relating to mathematics *a mathematical formula/equation* • **mathematically** *adverb*

mathematician /ˌmæθᵊməˈtɪʃᵊn/ *noun* **[C]** someone who studies mathematics

mathematics /mæθᵊmˈætɪks/ *noun* **[U]** *formal* the study or science of numbers and shapes

maths /mæθs/ *noun* **[U]** *UK short for* mathematics

matinée /ˈmætɪneɪ/ [US] /mætəˈneɪ/ *noun* **[C]** an afternoon performance of a play or film

matrimony /ˈmætrɪməni/ *noun* **[U]** *formal* the state of being married

matron /ˈmeɪtrᵊn/ *noun* **[C]** **1** [NURSE] *UK old-fashioned* a female nurse in a school, or a female nurse who is in charge of other nurses in a hospital **2** [WOMAN] *US* a married woman, especially one who is old or a widow (= woman whose husband has died) **3** [PRISON/SCHOOL] *US* a woman who is a manager at some hospitals, schools, prisons, etc

matt *UK* (*US* **matte**) /mæt/ *adjective* not shiny *a matt photograph* ○ *matt paint*

WORD PARTNERS FOR ***matter***

consider/discuss/pursue/raise/resolve a matter • **on** the matter (of sth)

matter¹ /ˈmætəʳ/ *noun* **1** [SUBJECT] **[C]** a subject or situation that you need to think about, discuss, or deal with *I've been thinking about this matter for a long time.* ○ *He denied any knowledge of the matter.* ○ ***To make matters worse,*** *our car broke down!* **2** [SUBSTANCE] **[U]** In science, matter is the physical substances that exist in the universe. **3** [TYPE OF THING] **[U]** a particular type of substance or thing *vegetable matter* ○ *printed matter* **4** **what's the matter** used to ask or talk about the reason for a problem *What's the matter with your leg?* **5** **there's something/nothing the matter** used to say that there is/is not a problem ***There's something the matter with*** *the washing machine.* **6** **a matter of days/weeks/feet, etc** used in expressions describing how small an amount or period of time is *The aircraft missed each other by a matter of feet*. **7 a matter of confidence/ luck/waiting, etc** If something is a matter of confidence/luck/waiting, etc, that is what you need for it to happen. *Learning languages is just a matter of hard work*. **8 no matter how/ what/when, etc** used to emphasize that something cannot be changed *I never manage to lose any weight, no matter how hard I try*. **9 as a matter of fact** used to emphasize that something is true, especially when it is surprising *As a matter of fact, I used to live next door to him*. **10 a matter of course** If something happens as a matter of course, it always happens as part of the normal process or system. *Babies were tested for the disease as a matter of course*. **11 a matter of life and/or death** a serious situation where people could die *Getting water to these people is a matter of life and death*. **12 it's only a matter of time** If you say that it is only a matter of time before something happens, you are sure it will happen but you do not know when. **13 be no laughing matter** If a subject is no laughing matter, it is serious and not something that people should joke about. ⊃See also: **subject matter**.

o-**matter²** /'mætə°/ *verb* [I] to be important, or to affect what happens *It doesn't matter to me whether he comes or not*. ○ *"I've forgotten to bring your book back." "It doesn't matter – there's no hurry."*

matter-of-fact /ˌmætərəv'fækt/ *adjective* not showing emotion when you talk about something *a matter-of-fact tone/manner* ● **matter-of-factly** *adverb*

matting /'mætɪŋ/ *noun* [U] strong, rough material for covering floors

mattress /'mætrəs/ *noun* [C] the soft, comfortable part of a bed that you lie on

mature¹ /mə'tjʊə°/ *adjective* **1** completely grown or developed *sexually mature* ○ *mature trees* **2** Mature people behave like adults in a way which shows they are well developed emotionally. *She seems very mature for thirteen*. ⊃Opposite **immature**.

mature² /mə'tjʊə°/ *verb* [I] **1** [AGE] to become completely grown or developed **2** [BEHAVIOUR] to start to behave in a more mature way *Girls mature sooner than boys*. **3** [MONEY] If an investment (= money you have given to a bank or a company in order to make a profit) matures, you receive the money you have made from it.

ma,ture 'student *noun* [C] a college or university student who is older than the usual age

maturity /mə'tjʊərəti/ *noun* [U] **1** the quality of behaving like an adult, in a way which shows that you are well developed emotionally *She shows remarkable maturity for a child of 13*. **2** when someone or something is completely grown or developed *Penguins reach maturity in late summer*.

maul /mɔːl/ *verb* [T] **1** If you are mauled by an animal, you are injured by its teeth or claws (= the sharp parts of its feet). [often passive] *He was mauled by a lion*. **2** to criticize someone or something very badly [often passive] *His film*

was mauled by critics.

mausoleum /ˌmɔːsə'liːəm/ *noun* [C] a building where dead people are buried

mauve /məʊv/ *noun* [U] a pale purple colour ● **mauve** *adjective*

maverick /'mævʳɪk/ *noun* [C] someone who thinks and behaves in an unusual way *a maverick cop/politician*

max¹ /mæks/ *adjective* **1** *informal for* maximum (= the largest amount allowed or possible), often used after numbers *The trip should take 30 minutes max*. **2 to the max** *informal* as much as possible *He lived life to the max*.

max² *verb*

max out *informal* to use all that is available of something, especially money *We maxed out our credit cards when we bought all that new furniture*.

maxim /'mæksɪm/ *noun* [C] a phrase which gives advice *Our company works on the maxim that small is beautiful*.

maximize (*also UK* -**ise**) /'mæksɪmaɪz/ *verb* [T] to increase something as much as you can *to maximize profits*

o-**maximum¹** /'mæksɪməm/ *adjective* [always before noun] The maximum amount of something is the largest amount that is allowed or possible. *the maximum temperature/speed* ⊃Opposite **minimum**.

> 🧩 WORD PARTNERS FOR **maximum**
>
> **reach** a maximum ● a maximum **of** [10/50%, etc] ● **up to** a maximum [**of** 10/50%, etc]

maximum² /'mæksɪməm/ *noun* [no plural] the largest amount that is allowed or possible *The school has a maximum of 30 students per class*.

o-**may** /meɪ/ *modal verb* **1** used to talk about what is possibly true or will possibly happen *There may be other problems that we don't know about*. ○ *I think I may have a cold*. **2** *formal* used to ask or give permission *May I be excused, please?* ○ *You may begin*. **3 may (well) ... but** used to show that the first thing you say is not important when compared to another fact *It may be cheap but it's not very good*. ⊃See Extra help page **Modal verbs** on page Centre 22.

> **COMMON LEARNER ERROR**
>
> may be or maybe?
>
> May be is written as two separate words when be is used as a verb. Here may is being used as a modal verb.
> *I may be late this evening*.
> ~~I maybe late this evening.~~
> Maybe is an adverb, and is written as one word.
> *Maybe we should do it tomorrow*.
> ~~May be we should do it tomorrow.~~

o-**May** /meɪ/ *noun* [C, U] the fifth month of the year

o-**maybe** /'meɪbi/ *adverb* **1** possibly *Maybe we're too early*. ○ *It could take a month, or maybe more, to complete*. **2** used to suggest something *Maybe Ted would like to go*.

mayhem /'meɪhem/ *noun* [U] a situation in which there is no order or control *With five kids running around, it was complete mayhem.*

mayonnaise /ˌmeɪə'neɪz/ *noun* [U] a thick, cold, white sauce that is made from eggs and oil

mayor /meəʳ/ *noun* [C] the person who is elected to be the leader of the group that governs a town or city

maze /meɪz/ *noun* [C] a complicated system of paths where you can easily become lost

MB *written abbreviation for* megabyte (= a unit for measuring the amount of information a computer can store) *This program needs 8 MB of hard-disk space.*

MBA /ˌembiː'eɪ/ *noun* [C] *abbreviation for* Master of Business Administration: an advanced degree in business, or a person who has this degree *a Harvard MBA*

McCoy /mə'kɔɪ/ *noun* **the real McCoy** *informal* the real thing, and not a copy or something similar *Cheap sparkling wines cannot be labelled 'champagne' - it has to be the real McCoy.*

MD /ˌem'diː/ *abbreviation for* Doctor of Medicine

☛**me** /miː/ *pronoun* used after a verb or preposition to refer to the person who is speaking or writing *She gave me some money.* ○ *She never gave it to me.* ○ *Lydia is three years younger than me.* ○ *It wasn't me!*

me or I?

Me is used after 'than', 'as', or 'be'. It would sound very formal if you used **I**.

She's taller than me.

David is not as tall as me.

"Who's there?" "It's me."

~~*"Who's there?" "It's I."*~~

Sometimes **me** is used with another noun as the subject of a sentence, especially in informal English.

Jane and me went to the cinema yesterday. (informal)

Jane and I went to the cinema yesterday.

meadow /'medəʊ/ *noun* [C] a field of grass, often with flowers

meagre *UK* (*US* **meager**) /'miːgəʳ/ *adjective* not enough in amount *a meagre ration/salary*

☛**meal** /miːl/ *noun* [C] **1** when you eat, or the food that you eat at that time *a three-course meal* **2** **make a meal of sth** *UK* to spend more time and energy doing something than is necessary *A simple apology will do. There's no need to make a meal of it!* ⊃See also: a **square²** meal.

mealtime /'miːltaɪm/ *noun* [C] when you eat *These days I only see him at mealtimes.*

☛**mean¹** /miːn/ *verb* [T] *past* **meant** /ment/ **1** MEANING to have a particular meaning *What does 'perpendicular' mean?* ○ *The red light means*

stop. **2** EXPRESS to intend to express a fact or opinion *I didn't mean that as a criticism.* ○ *What exactly do you mean by 'old-fashioned'?* **3** **mean to do sth** to intend to do something *I didn't mean to hurt her.* **4** RESULT to have a particular result *These changes will mean better health care for everyone.* ○ [+ (that)] *It doesn't mean that you can stop working.* **5** SERIOUS to be serious about something that you have said *I'll take that sandwich away if you don't eat it properly - I mean it!* **6** IMPORTANT to have an important emotional effect on someone *You don't know what it means to me to get this letter.* ○ *Their support has meant a lot to us.* **7** **have been meaning to do sth** to have been wanting and planning to do something *I've been meaning to call you for weeks.* **8** **be meant to do sth** If you are meant to do something, that is what you should do in order to behave correctly. *You're meant to shake the bottle first.* **9** **mean well** to intend to behave in a kind way *I know my parents mean well, but I wish they wouldn't interfere.* **10** **I mean a** CONTINUING SENTENCE something that people often say before they continue their sentence *I mean, I don't dislike her.* **b** CORRECTING YOURSELF something that you say in order to correct yourself *We went there in May - I mean June.*

mean² /miːn/ *adjective* **1** UNKIND unkind and unpleasant *I thought my sister was being mean to me.* **2** NOT GENEROUS *mainly UK* A mean person does not like spending money, especially on other people. *He's too mean to buy her a ring.* **3** VIOLENT *mainly US* A mean person or animal is strong and violent, and makes people frightened. *He's a big, mean guy.* **4** GOOD [always before noun] *informal* very good *I make a mean spaghetti.* **5** AVERAGE [always before noun] In mathematics, a mean number is an average number. *Their mean age at death was 84.6.* **6** **no mean** used to describe something very difficult *Setting up a business in two days was no mean feat* (= was a difficult thing to do).

mean³ /miːn/ *noun* [no plural] *formal* the average

meander /mi'ændəʳ/ *verb* **1** **meander along/around/through, etc** If a river, a road, or a line of something meanders, it has many curves. *The coast road meanders along the beach for miles.* **2** **meander around/from/off, etc** to move around with no clear purpose *We meandered around town for a couple of hours.*

☛**meaning** /'miːnɪŋ/ *noun* **1** [C, U] The meaning of words, signs, or actions is what they express or represent. *The word 'squash' has several meanings.* ○ *The meaning of her gesture was clear.* **2** [U, no plural] purpose or emotional importance *Philippa felt that her life had no meaning.*

meaningful /'miːnɪŋfəl/ *adjective* **1** USEFUL useful, serious, or important *a meaningful discussion* **2** WITH MEANING having a clear meaning which people can understand *a meaning-*

ful comparison/conclusion **3** [LOOK] intended to show a meaning, often secretly *a meaningful look* • **meaningfully** *adverb*

meaningless /'mi:nɪŋləs/ *adjective* without any meaning or purpose *He produced yet another set of meaningless statistics.*

┌─────────────────────────────────┐
│ 🔲 **WORD PARTNERS FOR means**   │
│   │
│ **(as) a means of (doing) sth** • **the means by** │
│ **which** sth happens/sb does sth │
└─────────────────────────────────┘

o-ᴀ**means** /mi:nz/ *noun* **1** [C] *plural* means a way of doing something *We had no means of communication.* ○ *It was a means of making money.* **2** [plural] money *We don't have the means to buy the house.* **3 by no means; not by any means** not at all *I'm not an expert by any means.* **4 by all means** something that you say when you are agreeing to let someone do something *I have a copy of the report on my desk. By all means have a look at it.*

means-tested /'mi:nztestɪd/ *adjective mainly UK* If an amount of money or an activity such as education is means-tested, it is only given to people who are poor enough. *means-tested benefits*

meant /ment/ *past of* mean

meantime /'mi:n,taɪm/ *noun* **in the meantime** in the time between two things happening, or while something else is happening *Your computer won't be arriving till Friday. In the meantime, you can use Julie's.*

o-ᴀ**meanwhile** /'mi:n,waɪl/ *adverb* in the time between two things happening, or while something else is happening *The mother is ill. The child, meanwhile, is living with foster parents.*

measles /'mi:zlz/ *noun* [U] an infectious disease which covers your skin in small, red spots ⊃See also: German measles.

measurable /'meʒ°rəbl/ *adjective* If something is measurable, it is big enough to be measured. *Extra training has led to measurable improvements in performance.* ⊃Opposite **immeasurable**.

o-ᴀ**measure**[1] /'meʒəʳ/ *verb* **1** [JUDGE] [T] to judge the quality, effect, importance, or value of something *We will soon be able to measure the results of these policy changes.* ○ *They measured the performance of three different engines.* **2** [FIND SIZE] [T] to find the size, weight, amount, or speed of something *I've measured all the windows.* ○ *The distances were measured in kilometres.* **3** [BE SIZE] [I] to be a certain size *a whale measuring around 60 feet in length*

measure sth out to weigh or measure a small amount of something and remove it from a larger amount *Use a hot spoon to measure out honey into a bowl.*

measure up to be good enough, or as good as something or someone else *He did not measure up to the requirements of the job.*

o-ᴀ**measure**[2] /'meʒəʳ/ *noun* **1** [C] a way of achieving something or dealing with a situation *This arrangement is only a temporary measure.* ○ *We must take preventative measures to stop the spread of the disease.* ○ *security measures* **2 a measure of sth** a good way of judging something *Ticket sales are not necessarily a measure*

of the show's popularity. **3 a/some measure of sth** *formal* an amount of something *Bulletproof vests give some measure of protection.* **4** [U] a way of measuring something *The basic units of measure we use are distance, time, and mass.* **5 for good measure** as well as something you have already done or given to someone *They stole his passport and wallet, and for good measure beat him unconscious.* ⊃See also: **tape measure**.

o-ᴀ**measurement** /'meʒəmənt/ *noun* **1** [PROCESS] [U] the process of measuring something **2** [SIZE] [C] the size and shape of something *I've taken measurements of all the rooms.* **3** [WAY OF MEASURING] [U] a way of measuring something *SI units are the standard units of measurement used all over the world.*

o-ᴀ**meat** /mi:t/ *noun* [U] muscles and other soft parts of animals, used as food *I don't eat meat.* ○ *red/white meat* ⊃See colour picture **Food** on page Centre 11.

mecca /'mekə/ *noun* [no plural] a place where particular groups of people like to go because they feel happy there *His Indiana bookstore became a mecca for writers and artists.*

mechanic /mɪ'kænɪk/ *noun* [C] someone whose job is to repair machines *a car mechanic*

mechanical /mɪ'kænɪk°l/ *adjective* **1** relating to or operated by machines *a mechanical engineer* ○ *a mechanical device* **2** If you do something in a mechanical way, you do it without emotion or without thinking about it. *a mechanical performance* • **mechanically** *adverb*

mechanics /mɪ'kænɪks/ *noun* [U] the study of physical forces on objects and their movement

mechanism /'mekənɪz°m/ *noun* [C] **1** a part of a piece of equipment that does a particular job *The clock's winding mechanism had broken.* **2** a system for achieving something, or the way that a system works *We need a mechanism for resolving this sort of dispute.*

mechanized (*also UK* -ised) /'mekənaɪzd/ *adjective* A mechanized organization or activity uses machines. *mechanized farming/production*

medal /'med°l/ *noun* [C] a metal disc given as a prize in a competition or given to someone who has been very brave *a bronze medal* ○ *an Olympic medal* ⊃See also: **gold medal, silver medal**.

medallist *UK* (*US* **medalist**) /'med°lɪst/ *noun* [C] someone who has received a medal in a sports event *an Olympic medallist*

meddle /'medl/ *verb* [I] to try to influence people or change things that are not your responsibility *He's always meddling in other people's business.*

the media /'mi:diə/ *noun* [group] television, newspapers, magazines, and radio considered as a group *media coverage/attention* ○ *The issue has been much discussed in the media.* ⊃See also: the **mass media**.

mediaeval /medi'i:v°l/ *adjective another spelling of* medieval (= relating to the period in Europe between about AD 500 and AD 1500)

median /'mi:diən/ *adjective* [always before noun] in

M

mathematics, relating to the middle number or amount in a series *the median age/income*

mediate /'mi:dieɪt/ *verb* [I, T] to try to find a solution between two or more people who disagree about something *Negotiators were called in to* **mediate between** *the two sides.* ● mediation /,mi:di'eɪʃ³n/ *noun* [U]

mediator /'mi:dieɪtə³r/ *noun* [C] someone who mediates between people who disagree about something

medic /'medɪk/ *noun* [C] *informal* 1 a medical student or doctor 2 *US* someone who does medical work in a military organization

o→**medical¹** /'medɪk³l/ *adjective* relating to medicine and different ways of curing illness *medical treatment* ○ *a medical student* ○ *She has a medical condition that makes it hard for her to work.* ● medically *adverb*

medical² /'medɪk³l/ *UK* (*US* physical) *noun* [C] an examination of your body by a doctor to find out if you are healthy

medicated /'medɪkeɪtɪd/ *adjective* A medicated substance contains medicine. *medicated soap*

medication /,medɪ'keɪʃ³n/ *noun* [C, U] medicine that is used to treat an illness *He's on medication to control his depression.*

medicinal /mə'dɪsɪn³l/ *adjective* Medicinal substances are used to cure illnesses. *I keep some brandy for medicinal purposes.*

> ⚒ WORD PARTNERS FOR **medicine**
>
> take medicine ● a medicine for sth

medicine

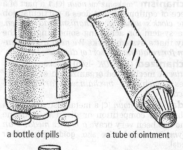

a bottle of pills   a tube of ointment

a bottle of medicine   a box of tablets

o→**medicine** /'medɪs³n/ *noun* 1 [C, U] a substance used to cure an illness or injury *cough medicine* ○ *Have you* **taken** *your* **medicine** *today?* 2 [U] the science of curing and preventing illness and injury *to study medicine* ○ *western/ Chinese medicine*

medieval (*also* mediaeval) /,medi'i:v³l/ *adjective* relating to the period in Europe between about AD 500 and AD 1500 *medieval literature/art*

mediocre /,mi:di'əʊkə³r/ *adjective* not good in quality *The acting was mediocre.* ● mediocrity /,mi:di'ɒkrəti/ *noun* [U]

meditate /'medɪteɪt/ *verb* [I] 1 to think calm thoughts for a long period in order to relax or as a religious activity *I meditate twice a day.* 2 *formal* to think seriously about something *He* **meditated on** *the consequences of his decision.* ● meditation /,medɪ'teɪʃ³n/ *noun* [U] *Let's spend a few moments in quiet meditation.*

the Mediterranean /,medɪt³r'eɪniən/ *noun* the sea that has southern Europe, northern Africa, and the Middle East around it, or the countries around this sea ● Mediterranean *adjective a Mediterranean climate/island*

o→**medium¹** /'mi:diəm/ *adjective* in the middle of a group of different amounts or sizes *people of medium weight* ○ *She bought a medium-sized car.* ○ *The shirt comes in small, medium, and large.*

medium² /'mi:diəm/ *noun* [C] *plural* media or mediums a way of communicating or expressing something *the medium of television/radio* ○ *The Internet has become yet another medium for marketing.*

medium-term /'mi:diəm,tɜ:m/ *adjective* continuing into the future for a time that is neither short nor long *The medium-term outlook remains favourable.*

medley /'medli/ *noun* [C] a mixture of different items, especially songs *She sang a medley of show tunes.*

meek /mi:k/ *adjective* Someone who is meek is quiet and does not argue with others. ● meekly *adverb*

o→**meet¹** /mi:t/ *verb past* met /met/ 1 [COME TOGETHER] [I, T] to come to the same place as someone else by arrangement or by chance *We met for coffee last Sunday.* ○ *I met my old English teacher while trekking in the Alps.* ○ *Each student meets with an adviser at the start of the school year.* 2 [INTRODUCE] [I, T] to see and speak to someone for the first time *I've always wanted to meet a movie star.* ○ *"This is Helen." "Pleased to meet you."* ➾See Common learner error at know. 3 [GROUP] [I] If a group of people meet, they come to a place in order to do something. *The shareholders meet once a year to discuss profits.* 4 [PLACE] [T] to wait at a place for someone or something to arrive *They met me at the airport.* 5 [ENOUGH] [T] to be a big enough amount or of a good enough quality for something *This old building will never meet the new fire regulations.* ○ *Can your product meet the needs of a wide range of consumers?* 6 [ACHIEVE] [T] to be able to achieve something *He met every goal he set for himself.* ○ *to meet a deadline* 7 [JOIN] [I, T] to join something *There's a large crack* *where the ceiling meets the wall.* ➲See also: make ends (**end¹**) meet.

meet or **visit**?

You **meet** a person, but not a place or thing.

I met John's parents for the first time last week.

You **visit** a person, place, or thing.

I visited my aunt today.

We visited Paris and the Eiffel Tower.

meet up 1 to meet another person in order to do something together *I met up with a few friends yesterday.* **2** If roads or paths meet up, they join at a particular place. *This path meets up with the main road.*
meet with sth to cause a particular reaction or result *Both proposals have met with fierce opposition.* ○ *(formal) I trust the arrangements meet with your approval* (= I hope that you like them).
meet² /miːt/ *noun* [C] US a sports competition *a swim/track meet* ○ *His final jump set a new meet record.*

WORD PARTNERS FOR *meeting*

arrange/attend/chair/convene/have/ hold a meeting • an emergency/private/ recent/urgent meeting • a meeting between sb • be in a meeting

o→**meeting** /ˈmiːtɪŋ/ *noun* [C] **1** an event where people come together for a reason, usually to discuss something *We're having a meeting on Monday to discuss the problem.* ○ *He's in a meeting - I'll ask him to call you back later.* **2** UK a sporting competition *an international meeting*
mega- /meɡə-/ *prefix* **1** *informal* extremely *megarich* (= extremely rich) **2** one million *40 megabytes*
megabyte /ˈmeɡəbaɪt/ (*written abbreviation* MB) *noun* [C] a unit for measuring the amount of information a computer can store, equal to 1,000,000 bytes
megaphone /ˈmeɡəfəʊn/ *noun* [C] a thing that you hold in your hand and speak into to make your voice louder
megapixel /ˈmeɡəˌpɪksəl/ *noun* [C] one million pixels (= small points that form part of the image on a comptuer screen), used to describe the amount of detail in images made by a digital camera, computer screen, etc
megawatt /ˈmeɡəwɒt/ *noun* [C] a unit for measuring electrical power, equal to 1,000,000 watts
melancholy /ˈmelənkɒli/ *adjective formal* sad *a melancholy expression* •**melancholy** *noun* [U] *formal* a feeling of sadness
melanoma /ˌmeləˈnəʊmə/ *noun* [C] a type of skin cancer (= a serious disease) that appears as a coloured mark on the skin
melee /ˈmeleɪ/ *noun* [C] a situation where many people are behaving in a noisy, confused, and sometimes violent way *In the melee his jaw was broken.*
mellow¹ /ˈmeləʊ/ *adjective* **1** pleasant and soft *a*

mellow voice ○ *a mellow flavour/wine* **2** calm and relaxed *After a few drinks, he became very mellow.*
mellow² /ˈmeləʊ/ *verb* [I, T] to become more relaxed and gentle, or to make someone become more relaxed and gentle *Age has mellowed him.*
melodic /məˈlɒdɪk/ *adjective* Melodic music has a pleasant tune, and melodic sounds are pleasant and like music.
melodrama /ˈmeləʊˌdrɑːmə/ *noun* [C, U] a story in which the characters show much stronger emotions than in real life
melodramatic /ˌmeləʊdrəˈmætɪk/ *adjective* showing much stronger emotions than are necessary for a situation *Don't be so melodramatic! It's only a scratch.*
melody /ˈmelədi/ *noun* [C] a song or tune
melon /ˈmelən/ *noun* [C, U] a large, round, sweet fruit with a thick, green or yellow skin and a lot of seeds ➲See colour picture **Fruit and Vegetables** on page Centre 10.
o→**melt** /melt/ *verb* **1** [I, T] If something melts, it changes from a solid into a liquid because of heat and if you melt something, you heat it until it becomes liquid. *The sun soon melted the ice on the pond.* ○ *The chocolate had melted in my pocket.* ○ *melted cheese* **2** [I] to start to feel love or sympathy, especially after feeling angry *When he smiles at me, I just melt.* ➲See also: **butter¹** wouldn't melt in sb's mouth.
melt away to disappear *Then I saw her and all my fears just melted away.*
melt sth down If you melt something down, especially a metal object, you heat it until it changes to liquid.
meltdown /ˈmeltdaʊn/ *noun* [C, U] **1** *informal* a situation of complete failure and no control *economic meltdown* **2** a serious accident in which nuclear fuel melts through its container and escapes into the environment
'melting ˌpot *noun* [C] a place where people of many different races and from different countries live together
o→**member** /ˈmembər/ *noun* [C] a person who belongs to a group or an organization *family/ staff members* ○ *He was a member of the university rowing club.*
ˌMember of ˈParliament *noun* [C] *plural* Members of Parliament a person who has been elected to represent people in their country's parliament

WORD PARTNERS FOR *membership*

apply for membership • membership (UK) of/(US) in sth • a membership card/fee

membership /ˈmembəʃɪp/ *noun* **1** [C, U] the state of belonging to a group or an organization *I've applied for membership of the union.* ○ *a membership card/fee* **2** [group] the people who belong to a group or an organization *Union membership is now over three million and rising.*
membrane /ˈmembreɪn/ *noun* [C] a thin sheet of tissue that covers some parts inside the body

M

memento /mɪˈmentəʊ/ *noun* [C] *plural* **mementos** or **mementoes** an object that you keep to remember a person, place, or event

memo /ˈmeməʊ/ *noun* [C] a written message sent from one member of an organization to another

memoirs /ˈmemwɑːz/ *noun* [plural] a written story of a person's own life and experiences

memorabilia /ˌmemᵊrəˈbɪliə/ *noun* [plural] objects relating to famous people or events that people collect *an auction of pop memorabilia*

memorable /ˈmemᵊrəbl/ *adjective* If an occasion is memorable, you will remember it for a long time because it is so good. *a memorable performance* ● **memorably** *adverb*

memorandum /ˌmemᵊrˈændəm/ *noun plural* **memoranda** *formal* a memo

memorial /məˈmɔːriəl/ *noun* [C] an object, often made of stone, that is built to help people remember an important person or event *a war memorial* ○ *a memorial service*

memorize (*also UK* **-ise**) /ˈmemᵊraɪz/ *verb* [T] to learn something so that you remember it exactly *I've memorized all my friends' birthdays.*

---

have a **bad/good** memory ● have a [good, amazing, etc] memory **for** sth ● a **photographic** memory

---

⟶**memory** /ˈmemᵊri/ *noun* **1** [ABILITY] [C, U] your ability to remember *John has an amazing memory for historical facts.* ○ *She had a photographic memory* (= was able to remember every detail). **2** [THOUGHT] [C] something that you remember [usually plural] *I have fond memories of my childhood.* **3** [MIND] [C, U] the part of your mind that stores what you remember *He recited the poem from memory.* **4 in memory of sb** If you do something in memory of a dead person, you do it to show your respect or love for them. *They built a statue in memory of those who died in the fire.* **5** [COMPUTING] [C, U] the part of a computer where information and instructions are stored, or the amount of information that can be stored there *You need 32 megabytes of memory to run this software.*

'**Memory ,Stick** *noun* [C] *trademark* a small electronic device designed to store information that can be put into a computer, mobile phone, etc

men /men/ *plural of* man

menace¹ /ˈmenɪs/ *noun* **1** [C] something that is likely to cause harm [usually singular] *Drunk drivers are a menace to everyone.* **2** [U] a dangerous quality that makes you think someone is going to do something bad *His eyes were cold and filled with menace.*

menace² /ˈmenɪs/ *verb* [T] *formal* to cause harm to someone or something, or be likely to cause harm *Hurricane Bonnie continues to menace the east coast.*

menacing /ˈmenɪsɪŋ/ *adjective* making you think that someone is going to do something bad *a menacing gesture/voice*

mend¹ /mend/ *verb* [T] to repair something that is broken, torn, or not working correctly *I've*

---

mended that hole in your skirt for you.

mend² /mend/ *noun* **be on the mend** *informal* If you are on the mend, your health is improving after an illness.

mendacious /menˈdeɪʃəs/ *adjective formal* not telling the truth

menial /ˈmiːniəl/ *adjective* Menial work is boring, and not well paid or respected. *a menial job/task*

meningitis /ˌmenɪnˈdʒaɪtɪs/ *noun* [U] a serious infectious disease that affects a person's brain and spinal cord (= the nerves in your back)

menopause /ˈmenəʊpɔːz/ *noun* [U] the time, usually between the ages of 45 and 55, when a woman gradually stops having periods (= monthly blood from the uterus)

'**men's ,room** *noun* [C] *US* a room in a public place where there are men's toilets ⊃See Common learner error at **toilet**.

menstrual /ˈmenstruəl/ *adjective* [always before noun] *formal* relating to menstruating *a menstrual cycle*

menstruate /ˈmenstrueɪt/ *verb* [I] *formal* to have a monthly flow of blood from the uterus ● **menstruation** /ˌmenstruˈeɪʃᵊn/ *noun* [U]

⟶**mental** /ˈmentᵊl/ *adjective* [always before noun] relating to the mind, or involving the process of thinking *mental health/illness* ●**mentally** *adverb a mentally ill person*

mentality /menˈtæləti/ *noun* [C] a person's opinions or way of thinking *I can't understand the mentality of people who hunt animals for fun.*

⟶**mention¹** /ˈmenʃᵊn/ *verb* [T] **1** to briefly speak or write about something or someone *I'll mention your ideas to Caroline.* ○ *She didn't mention her daughter.* ○ [+ (that)] *He mentioned that he liked skydiving.* **2 not to mention** used to emphasize the importance of something that you are adding to a list *The resort has great hotels and restaurants, not to mention some of the best skiing in the region.*

---

mention

No preposition is normally needed after the verb **mention**.

He didn't mention the price.

~~He didn't mention about the price.~~

---

deserve/get/be worth a mention ● **make no** mention **of** sth ● a **brief/passing/special** mention ● mention **of** sth

---

mention² /ˈmenʃᵊn/ *noun* [C] a brief remark *The report made no mention of the problem.*

mentor /ˈmentɔːʳ/ *noun* [C] *formal* an experienced person who gives help and advice to someone with less experience

⟶**menu** /ˈmenjuː/ *noun* [C] **1** a list of food and drinks that you can order in a restaurant *a lunch/dinner menu* ○ *I ordered the most expensive thing on the menu* (= available in the restaurant). **2** a list that appears on a com-

---

puter screen of the choices available in a computer program *a pop-up menu*

'menu ,bar *noun* [C] a long, narrow area, usually at the top of a computer screen, that contains computer menus

'menu ,option *noun* [C] one of the choices on a computer menu

meow /miː'aʊ/ *noun* [C] *US spelling of* miaow (= the sound that a cat makes)

MEP /ˌemiː'piː/ *noun* [C] *abbreviation for* Member of European Parliament: a person who represents an area of a European country in the European Parliament *the MEP for Glasgow*

mercenary[1] /'mɜːsᵊnᵊri/ *noun* [C] a soldier who fights for any country or organization who pays them

mercenary[2] /'mɜːsᵊnᵊri/ *adjective* interested only in getting money or an advantage from a situation

merchandise /'mɜːtʃᵊndaɪz/ *noun* [U] *formal* goods that are traded, or sold in shops *We stock a broad range of merchandise.*

merchandising /'mɜːtʃᵊndaɪzɪŋ/ *noun* [U] the selling of products relating to films, television programmes, and famous people

merchant[1] /'mɜːtʃᵊnt/ *noun* [C] *formal* someone whose job is buying and selling goods, usually in large amounts *a wine/grain merchant*

merchant[2] /'mɜːtʃᵊnt/ *adjective* [always before noun] relating to trading of large amounts of goods *a merchant ship/seaman*

,merchant 'bank *noun* [C] a bank that organizes investments in companies or lends money to them ● **merchant banker** *noun* [C]

mercifully /'mɜːsɪfᵊli/ *adverb informal* used to show that you are pleased that something unpleasant has been avoided *Her illness was mercifully short.*

merciless /'mɜːsɪləs/ *adjective* cruel, or showing no kindness *a merciless attack* ○ *She was merciless in her criticism of his work.* ● **mercilessly** *adverb*

Mercury /'mɜːkjᵊri/ *noun* [no plural] the planet that is closest to the Sun, before Venus

mercury /'mɜːkjᵊri/ *noun* [U] a heavy, silver-coloured metal that is liquid at ordinary temperatures

WORD PARTNERS FOR ***mercy***

ask for/beg for/plead for mercy   ● **show (no)** mercy

mercy /'mɜːsi/ *noun* [U] **1** kindness that makes you forgive someone, usually someone that you have authority over *The judge showed no mercy.* **2 be at the mercy of sth/sb** to not be able to protect yourself from something or someone that you cannot control *Farmers are often at the mercy of the weather.*

mere /mɪᵊ/ *adjective* [always before noun] **1** used to emphasize that something is not large or important *It costs a mere twenty dollars.* ○ *The mere thought of* (= Just thinking about) *eating octopus makes me feel sick.* **2 the merest** used to emphasize that something is small, often when it has an important effect *She's*

upset by *the merest hint of criticism.*

merely /'mɪᵊli/ *adverb* **1** used to emphasize that you mean exactly what you are saying and nothing more *I'm not arguing with you - I'm merely explaining the problem.* **2** used to emphasize that something is not large, important, or effective when compared to something else *The medicine doesn't make you better, it merely stops the pain.*

merge /mɜːdʒ/ *verb* [I, T] If two or more things merge, they combine or join, and if you merge two or more things, you combine or join them. *The two companies merged, forming the largest brewery in Canada.* ○ *The city's smaller libraries will be merged into a large, central one.*

merger /'mɜːdʒᵊr/ *noun* [C, U] when two or more companies or organizations join together

meringue /mᵊ'ræŋ/ *noun* [C, U] a light, sweet food that is made by baking the white part of an egg mixed with sugar

merit[1] /'merɪt/ *noun* [C, U] *formal* good qualities which deserve praise *His ideas have merit.* ○ *We debated the merits of using television in the classroom.* ○ *Every application has to be judged on its own merits* (= judged by considering the qualities of each).

merit[2] /'merɪt/ *verb* [T] *formal* to be important enough to receive attention or punishment *Her crimes were serious enough to merit a prison sentence.*

mermaid /'mɜːmeɪd/ *noun* [C] an imaginary creature that lives in the sea and has the upper body of a woman and the tail of a fish

merry /'meri/ *adjective* showing enjoyment and happiness *a merry laugh* ○ **Merry Christmas!** ● **merrily** *adverb*

mesh[1] /meʃ/ *noun* [C, U] material that is like a net and is made of wire, plastic, or thread *a wire mesh fence*

mesh[2] /meʃ/ *verb* [I] If two or more things mesh, they are suitable for each other. *Her ideas mesh well with our plans for the future.*

WORD PARTNERS FOR ***mess***

make a mess   ● **clean up/clear up** a mess   ● **be in** a mess

o▪**mess**[1] /mes/ *noun* [C] **1** UNTIDY Someone or something that is a mess, or is in a mess, is dirty or untidy. [usually singular] *My hair's such a mess!* ○ *The house is in a mess.* ○ *Don't make a mess in the kitchen!* **2** DIFFICULT a confused or difficult situation [usually singular] *She told me that her life was a mess.* ○ *If he hadn't lied, he wouldn't be in this mess now.* **3 make a mess of** sth to damage or spoil something *He made a mess of his first marriage.* **4** MILITARY a place where members of the armed forces eat [usually singular] *the officers' mess*

mess[2] /mes/ *verb*

mess about/around *informal* **1** to waste time, often by doing things that are not important *Stop messing around and do your homework!* **2** to spend time playing and doing things with no particular purpose *I can spend hours messing around with my computer.*

mess sb about/around *UK informal* to

treat someone badly, often by not doing something that you have promised

mess about/around with sth *informal* to use or treat something in a careless or harmful way *Who's been messing around with my computer?*

mess sth up **1** to make something untidy or dirty *I hate wearing hats - they always mess up my hair.* **2** to spoil something, or to do something badly *Don't try to cook lunch by yourself - you'll only mess it up.*

mess with sb/sth *informal* to become involved with someone or something dangerous *If you mess with drugs, you're asking for trouble.*

WORD PARTNERS FOR ***message***

get/leave/send/take a message • a message for/from sb

⊶**message¹** /ˈmesɪdʒ/ *noun* [C] **1** a piece of written or spoken information which one person gives to another *Did you* ***get my message?*** ○ *I* ***left*** *her several* ***messages****, but she hasn't returned my call.* **2** the most important idea of a film, book, etc *The book conveys a complex message.* **3 get the message** *informal* to understand what someone wants you to do by their actions *Don't return any of his calls - he'll soon get the message and leave you alone.*

message² /ˈmesɪdʒ/ *verb* [T] to send someone an email or text message (= a written message sent from one mobile phone to another)

M

ˈmessage ˌboard *noun* [C] a place on a website where you can leave messages for other people to read

messenger /ˈmesɪndʒəʳ/ *noun* [C] someone who takes a message between two people

the Messiah /məˈsaɪə/ *noun* **1** Jesus Christ **2** the leader that Jews believe God will send them

Messrs /ˈmesəz/ *noun formal* a title used before the names of two or more men *Messrs Davis and Dixon led the discussion on tax reform.*

messy /ˈmesi/ *adjective* **1** untidy or dirty *messy hair* ○ *a messy house/car* ○ *My son's bedroom is always messy.* **2** unpleasant and complicated *Ian's just gone through a* ***messy divorce****.*

met /met/ *past of* meet

metabolism /məˈtæbəlɪzəm/ *noun* [C] all the chemical processes in your body, especially the ones that use food

⊶**metal** /ˈmetəl/ *noun* [C, U] a usually hard, shiny material such as iron, gold, or silver which heat and electricity can travel through *scrap metal* ○ *Metals are used for making machinery and tools.* ○ *a metal sheet/bar* • **metallic** /məˈtælɪk/ *adjective* having a quality that is similar to metal *a metallic paint/taste* ➲See also: **heavy metal**.

metamorphosis /ˌmetəˈmɔːfəsɪs/ *noun plural* **metamorphoses** /metəˈmɔːfəsiːz/ **1** [C] a gradual change into something very different *The past year has seen a complete metamorphosis of the country's economy.* **2** [U] in biology, the process by which the young forms of some animals, such as insects, develop into very different adult forms *Caterpillars changing into butterflies is an example of metamorphosis.*

metaphor /ˈmetəfəʳ/ *noun* [C, U] a way of describing something by comparing it with something else which has some of the same qualities *She used a computer metaphor to explain how the human brain works.* • **metaphorical** /ˌmetəˈfɒrɪkəl/ *adjective* using a metaphor

mete /miːt/ *verb* **meting** *past* **meted**

mete sth out *formal* to punish someone [often passive] *Long jail sentences are* ***meted out*** *to drug smugglers.*

meteor /ˈmiːtiəʳ/ *noun* [C] a rock from outer space which becomes very hot and burns brightly in the sky at night as it enters Earth's atmosphere (= air surrounding Earth)

meteoric /ˌmiːtiˈɒrɪk/ *adjective* If the development of something is meteoric, it happens very quickly or causes great success. *a meteoric career* ○ *The band's rise to fame was meteoric.*

meteorite /ˈmiːtiəraɪt/ *noun* [C] a piece of rock from outer space which has fallen on Earth's surface

meteorological /ˌmiːtiərəˈlɒdʒɪkəl/ *adjective* [always before noun] relating to the scientific study of weather

meteorologist /ˌmiːtiərˈɒlədʒɪst/ *noun* [C] someone who studies weather, especially to say how it will be in the near future • **meteorology** *noun* [U] the scientific study of weather

⊶**meter** /ˈmiːtəʳ/ *noun* [C] **1** a piece of equipment for measuring the amount of something such as electricity, time, or light *a gas/water meter* ○ *a parking/taxi meter* **2** *US spelling of* metre

methadone /ˈmeθədəʊn/ *noun* [U] a drug for treating people who want to stop using heroin (= an illegal drug)

methane /ˈmiːθeɪn/ [US] /ˈmeθeɪn/ *noun* [U] a gas that has no colour or smell, used for cooking and heating

WORD PARTNERS FOR ***method***

an **alternative/new/reliable/simple/traditional** method • **develop/devise/use** a method

⊶**method** /ˈmeθəd/ *noun* [C] a way of doing something, often one that involves a system or plan *What's the best* ***method of/for*** *solving this problem?* ○ *traditional teaching methods*

methodical /məˈθɒdɪkəl/ *adjective* careful and well organized, using a plan or system *a methodical researcher* • **methodically** *adverb*

Methodist /ˈmeθədɪst/ *adjective* belonging or relating to a Christian group that was started by John Wesley • **Methodist** *noun* [C]

methodological /ˌmeθədəlˈɒdʒɪkəl/ *adjective* relating to a methodology *methodological problems*

methodology /ˌmeθəˈdɒlədʒi/ *noun* [C, U] the system of methods used for doing, teaching, or studying something

meticulous /məˈtɪkjələs/ *adjective* very careful, and giving great attention to detail *This book is the result of meticulous research.*

• **meticulously** *adverb*

me time /ˈmiːtaɪm/ *noun* [U] *informal* time when you can do exactly what you want

o-**metre** *UK* (*US* **meter**) /ˈmiːtəʳ/ *noun* **1** [C] (*written abbreviation* **m**) a unit for measuring length, equal to 100 centimetres *Our bedroom is five metres wide.* ○ *She finished third in the women's 400 metres* (= running race). **2** [C, U] a pattern of rhythm in poetry

metric /ˈmetrɪk/ *adjective* The metric system of measurement uses units based on the gram, metre, and litre.

ˌmetric ˈton *noun* [C] a unit for measuring weight, equal to 1000 kilograms

metro¹ /ˈmetrəʊ/ *noun* [C] an underground railway system in a large city *the Paris metro*

COMMON LEARNER ERROR

metro, subway, or **underground?**

All these words mean an underground railway system in a large city. **Metro** is the most general word. The usual word in British English is **underground.** In American English it is **subway.**

the Paris metro

the London underground

the New York subway

metro² /ˈmetrəʊ/ *adjective* [always before noun] *US informal* relating to a large city and the towns around it *the New York metro area*

metropolis /məˈtrɒpəlɪs/ *noun* [C] a very large city, often the capital of a country or region

metropolitan /ˌmetrəˈpɒlɪtᵊn/ *adjective* [always before noun] relating to a large city *a metropolitan area/council*

mg *written abbreviation for* milligram (= a unit for measuring weight)

miaow *UK* (*US* **meow**) /ˌmiːˈaʊ/ *noun* [C] the sound that a cat makes

mice /maɪs/ *plural of* mouse

mickey /ˈmɪki/ **take the mickey (out of sb)** *UK informal* to laugh at someone and make them seem silly

micro- /maɪkrəʊ-/ *prefix* very small *a microchip* ○ *microscopic* (= very small)

microbe /ˈmaɪkrəʊb/ *noun* [C] a very small organism, often a bacterium that causes disease

microchip /ˈmaɪkrəʊtʃɪp/ *noun* [C] a very small part of a computer or machine which does calculations or stores information

microcosm /ˈmaɪkrəʊˌkɒzᵊm/ *noun* [C] *formal* a place, group of people, or situation that has the same characteristics as a larger one *The town is a microcosm of French culture.*

microphone /ˈmaɪkrəfəʊn/ *noun* [C] a piece of electrical equipment for recording or broadcasting sounds, or for making sounds louder

microprocessor /ˌmaɪkrəʊˈprəʊsesəʳ/ [US] /ˈmaɪkrəʊˌprɑːsesər/ *noun* [C] the part of a computer that controls all the other parts

WORD PARTNERS FOR ***microscope***

under a microscope • through a microscope

microscope /ˈmaɪkrəskəʊp/ *noun* [C] a piece of scientific equipment which uses lenses (= pieces of curved glass) to make very small objects look bigger

microscope

microscopic /ˌmaɪkrəˈskɒpɪk/ *adjective* extremely small and needing a microscope to be seen, or using a microscope to see something *microscopic organisms/particles*

microwave¹ /ˈmaɪkrəʊweɪv/ *noun* [C] **1** (*also* **microˌwave ˈoven**) an electric oven that uses waves of energy to cook or heat food ⊃See colour picture **The Kitchen** on page Centre 2. **2** a very short wave similar to a radio wave that is used for sending information and cooking

microwave² /ˈmaɪkrəʊweɪv/ *verb* [T] to cook or heat food using a microwave oven

mid- /mɪd-/ *prefix* the middle of *mid-March* ○ *mid-afternoon*

mid-air /ˌmɪdˈeəʳ/ *noun* **in mid-air** in the air or sky *She jumped up and caught the ball in mid-air.* • **mid-air** *adjective* [always before noun] *a mid-air collision*

midday /ˌmɪdˈdeɪ/ *noun* [U] 12 o'clock in the middle of the day, or the period around this time *the heat of the midday sun*

o-**middle¹** /ˈmɪdl/ *noun* **1 the middle** the central part, position, or point in time *We used to live just outside Boston but now we live right* (= exactly) ***in the middle.*** ○ *The letter should arrive by the middle of next week.* **2 be in the middle of doing sth** to be busy *I can't talk now - I'm in the middle of cooking a meal.* **3 your middle** *informal* your waist, or your waist and stomach *He wrapped the towel round his middle.* **4 in the middle of nowhere** a long way from places where people live *His car broke down in the middle of nowhere.*

o-**middle²** /ˈmɪdl/ *adjective* [always before noun] **1** in a central position *The middle layer is made of plastic.* ○ *Our company rents the middle warehouse.* **2** neither high nor low in importance or amount *middle managers*

middle-aged /ˌmɪdlˈeɪdʒd/ *adjective* in the middle of your life before you are old *a middle-aged couple/man/woman*

the ˌMiddle ˈAges *noun* the period in European history between the end of the Roman Empire and the start of the Renaissance

ˌmiddle ˈclass *noun* [group] a social group that consists of well-educated people, such as doctors, lawyers, and teachers, who have good jobs and are neither very rich nor very poor • **middle-class** /ˌmɪdlˈklɑːs/ *adjective* belonging or

M

relating to the middle class *a middle-class suburb*

the ˌMiddle ˈEast *noun* a group of countries in the area where Africa, Asia, and Europe meet • **Middle Eastern** *adjective* relating to the Middle East *Middle Eastern cuisine*

middleman /ˈmɪdlmæn/ *noun* [C] *plural* **middlemen** someone who buys goods from one person and sells them to someone else for a higher price *Selling direct from the factory* ***cuts out the middleman.***

ˌmiddle ˈname *noun* [C] an extra name between someone's first and family names *Do you have a middle name?*

ˈmiddle ˌschool *noun* [C] a school in the US for children usually between the ages of 11 and 14

midget /ˈmɪdʒɪt/ *noun* [C] someone who is very small

the Midlands /ˈmɪdləndz/ *noun* the central area of England which includes several large industrial cities

ˌmid-life ˈcrisis *noun* [C] *plural* **mid-life crises** a period in the middle of your life when you lose confidence in your abilities and worry about the future

midnight /ˈmɪdnaɪt/ *noun* [U] 12 o'clock at night *He died shortly after midnight.* ○ *They both left the party* ***at midnight***

midriff /ˈmɪdrɪf/ *noun* [C] the front of your body between your chest and waist *She was wearing a short top which revealed a bare midriff.*

midst /mɪdst/ *noun* **1 in the midst of sth** in the middle of something, usually an event or activity **[+ of + doing sth]** *Can I phone you back? I'm in the midst of cooking dinner.* **2 in your midst** among the group of people that you belong to *Residents are protesting about a convicted murderer living in their midst.*

midsummer /ˌmɪdˈsʌməʳ/ *noun* [U] the longest day of the year, or the period around this

midway /ˌmɪdˈweɪ/ *adverb* **1 midway between sth and sth** at the middle point between two places or things *Leeds is midway between London and Edinburgh.* **2 midway through sth** at the middle point of an activity or a period of time *He scored the third goal midway through the second half.*

midweek /ˌmɪdˈwiːk/ *noun* [U] the middle of the week, usually from Tuesday to Thursday • **midweek** *adjective, adverb* **[always before noun]** in the middle of the week *a midweek game/match* ○ *Flights are cheaper if you travel midweek.*

the Midwest /ˌmɪdˈwest/ *noun* the northern central area of the United States • **Midwestern** *adjective* **[always before noun]** relating to the Midwest *Midwestern values*

midwife /ˈmɪdwaɪf/ *noun* [C] *plural* **midwives** /ˈmɪdwaɪvz/ a nurse who has had special training to help women give birth

midwifery /mɪdˈwɪfəri/ *noun* [U] the work of a midwife

midwinter /ˌmɪdˈwɪntəʳ/ *noun* [U] the shortest day of the year, or the period around this

⊶**might¹** /maɪt/ *modal verb* **1** used to talk about what will possibly happen *It might be finished by Thursday.* ○ *She might not come.* **2** used to talk about what is possibly true *I think Isabel might be pregnant.* ○ *The rain might have stopped by now.* **3 you might like/want to** *UK formal* used to politely suggest something *You might want to try a different approach next time.* ➲See Extra help page **Modal verbs** on page Centre 22.

might² /maɪt/ *noun* [U] *formal* great strength or power ***economic/military might*** ○ *She pushed the door* ***with all her might*** (= with as much force as possible).

mightn't /ˈmaɪtᵊnt/ *mainly UK formal short for* might not *It mightn't be true.*

might've /ˈmaɪtəv/ *short for* might have *The children might've seen her in the park.*

mighty¹ /ˈmaɪti/ *adjective* very powerful or successful *In their next game they're playing the mighty Redskins.*

mighty² /ˈmaɪti/ *adverb mainly US informal* very *It's mighty tempting to stay in bed on a rainy morning.*

migraine /ˈmaɪgreɪn/ *noun* [C, U] a very bad pain in the head, often one that makes you vomit

migrant /ˈmaɪgrᵊnt/ *noun* [C] someone who goes to live in a different place in order to find work *migrant labour/workers*

migrate /maɪˈgreɪt/ [US] /ˈmaɪgreɪt/ *verb* [I] **1** When birds, fish, or animals migrate, they travel from one place to another at the same time each year. *Many birds migrate from Europe to African forests for the winter.* **2** When people migrate, they move to another place, often a different country, in order to find work and a better life. *Between 1900 and 1914, 3.1 million people* ***migrated to*** *the US from central Europe.* • **migration** /maɪˈgreɪʃᵊn/ *noun* [C, U]

migratory /ˈmaɪgreɪtᵊri/ [US] /ˈmaɪgrətɔːri/ *adjective* **[always before noun]** relating to birds, fish, or animals that migrate

mike /maɪk/ *noun* [C] *informal short for* microphone

mild /maɪld/ *adjective* **1** [WEATHER] When weather is mild, it is less cold than you would expect. *a* ***mild winter*** **2** [ILLNESS] When an illness is mild, it is not as serious as it could be. *My doctor said I had a mild form of pneumonia.* **3** [WEAK] not having a strong effect *a mild taste* ○ *a mild detergent* **4** [KIND] calm and gentle *He has a very mild manner.*

mildly /ˈmaɪldli/ *adverb* **1** slightly *I find his films mildly amusing.* **2 to put it mildly** something you say when an opinion is not expressed as strongly as it should be *The building is unsafe, to put it mildly.*

⊶**mile** /maɪl/ *noun* [C] **1** a unit for measuring distance, equal to 1609 metres or 1760 yards *The nearest station is two miles from here.* ○ *It's a five-mile walk to the next village.* ○ *The latest high-speed trains can travel at 140* ***miles per hour.*** ➲See Extra help page **Measurements** on page Centre 31. **2 miles** a very long distance *We drove for miles along dusty roads.* ○ *Her cottage is* ***miles from*** *the nearest village.*

mileage /'maɪlɪdʒ/ noun 1 DISTANCE [C, U] the number of miles that a vehicle has travelled since it was new *low mileage* 2 FUEL [C, U] the number of miles a vehicle can travel using a particular amount of fuel 3 ADVANTAGE [U] *informal* an advantage got from something *There's no mileage in taking your employer to court.*

milestone /'maɪlstəʊn/ noun [C] an important event in the history or development of something or someone *Passing my driving test was an important milestone for me.*

militant¹ /'mɪlɪtənt/ adjective expressing strong support for a political or social idea, and willing to use extreme or violent methods to achieve it *a militant group/organization* • **militancy** /'mɪlɪtənsi/ noun [U] when someone is militant

militant² /'mɪlɪtənt/ noun [C] a militant person

o⟶**military**¹ /'mɪlɪtri/ adjective relating to the army, navy, or air force *military action/ service*

the military² /'mɪlɪtri/ noun a country's army, navy, and air force

militia /mɪ'lɪʃə/ noun [C] a group of people who have been trained as soldiers but are not part of a country's official army • **militiaman** noun [C] *plural* **militiamen** a member of a militia

o⟶**milk**¹ /mɪlk/ noun [U] a white liquid produced by women and other female animals, such as cows, for feeding their babies *a carton of milk* ○ *breast milk* ⊃See also: **skimmed milk**.

milk² /mɪlk/ verb [T] 1 to get as much money or as many advantages as possible from a person or situation *She milked her grandfather for all his savings.* 2 to take milk from a cow using your hands or a machine

milkman /'mɪlkmən/ noun [C] *plural* **milkmen** a man whose job is bringing milk to people's homes early in the morning

milkshake /'mɪlkʃeɪk/ noun [C, U] a sweet drink made of milk and chocolate or fruit *a banana milkshake*

milky /'mɪlki/ adjective 1 containing milk, often a lot of it *milky coffee/tea* 2 similar to milk *a milky liquid*

the Milky Way /ðə,mɪlki'weɪ/ noun the group of very many stars which includes the sun

mill¹ /mɪl/ noun [C] 1 FLOUR a machine for crushing grain into flour, or a building with this machine *a flour mill* 2 POWDER a small machine used in the kitchen for crushing things such as coffee beans into a powder *a coffee/ pepper mill* 3 MATERIAL a factory where one material or substance is made *a cotton/wool-len mill* ○ *a paper/steel mill*

mill² /mɪl/ verb [T] to use a machine to crush something into a powder *freshly milled black pepper*

mill about/around (sth) When people mill around, they come together in a place, usually to wait for someone or something.

millennium /mɪ'leniəm/ noun [C] *plural* **millennia** 1 a period of 1000 years, often calculated from the date when Christ is thought to have been born 2 **the Millennium** the change

from the year 1999 to 2000 in the Western calendar *Where did you celebrate the Millennium?*

milli- /mɪli-/ prefix a thousandth *a millisecond*

milligram /'mɪlɪgræm/ (*written abbreviation* mg) noun [C] a unit for measuring weight, equal to 0.001 grams

millilitre *UK* (*US* **milliliter**) (*written abbreviation* ml) /'mɪlɪ,liːtəʳ/ noun [C] a unit for measuring liquid, equal to 0.001 litres

millimetre *UK* (*US* **millimeter**) (*written abbreviation* mm) /'mɪlɪ,miːtəʳ/ noun [C] a unit for measuring length, equal to 0.001 metres

o⟶**million** /'mɪljən/ 1 the number 1,000,000 2 **millions** *informal* a lot *I've seen that film millions of times.*

millionaire /,mɪljə'neəʳ/ noun [C] a very rich person who has money and possessions to the value of at least one million pounds or dollars *His father is a millionaire with homes in New York and Paris.*

millionth¹ /'mɪljənθ/ 1,000,000th written as a word

millionth² /'mɪljənθ/ noun [C] one of a million equal parts of something; ¹/₁,₀₀₀,₀₀₀; .000001

mime /maɪm/ verb [I, T] to act or tell a story without speaking, using movements of your hands and body, and expressions on your face *Pop stars often mime* (= pretend to sing while their song is played) *on TV.* • **mime** noun [C, U] *a mime artist*

mimic¹ /'mɪmɪk/ verb [T] mimicking *past* mimicked 1 to copy the way someone talks and behaves, usually to make people laugh *He's always getting into trouble for mimicking his teachers.* 2 to have the same behaviour or qualities as something else *The drug mimics the effects of a natural hormone.*

mimic² /'mɪmɪk/ noun [C] someone who is good at mimicking other people *He's a really good mimic.*

mince¹ /mɪns/ *UK* (*US* **ground beef**) noun [U] meat, usually from a cow, which has been cut into very small pieces by a machine

mince² /mɪns/ verb [T] to cut food into small pieces in a machine *minced beef/onions*

mincemeat /'mɪnsmiːt/ noun [U] 1 a spicy, sweet mixture of apples, dried fruit, and nuts, which have been cut into small pieces 2 **make mincemeat of sb** *informal* to defeat someone very easily

mince 'pie noun [C] *UK* a small pastry filled with mincemeat that is eaten mainly at Christmas

o⟶**mind**¹ /maɪnd/ noun [C] 1 someone's memory or their ability to think, feel emotions, and be aware of things *For some reason her words stuck in my mind.* ○ *She has a very logical mind.* 2 **have sth on your mind** to think or worry about something *Jim has a lot on his mind at the moment.* 3 **bear/keep sb/sth in mind** to remember someone or something that may be useful in the future *I'll keep you in mind if another job comes up.* ○ [+ (that)] *Bear in mind that there's a bank holiday next week.* 4 **make your mind up** to make a decision [+ question

M

word] *I haven't made up my mind whether to go yet.* **5 change your mind** to change a decision or opinion *We've changed our minds about selling the house.* **6 come/spring to mind** If an idea comes to mind, it is the first thing you think of. *I was thinking about who might be suitable for this job, and your name came to mind.* **7 put your mind to sth** to give your full attention to something *You could win if you put your mind to it.* **8 be out of your mind** *informal* to be crazy or very stupid **9 be out of your mind with worry/grief, etc** to be very worried or upset **10 blow your mind** *informal* If something blows your mind, you are very excited or surprised by it. *There was one scene in the film that really blew my mind.* **11 cross your mind** If an idea crosses your mind, you think about it for a short time. [+ (that)] *It never crossed my mind* (= I never thought) *that she might be married.* **12 be in two minds** *UK* (*US* **be of two minds**) to have difficulty making a decision *I'm in two minds about accepting his offer.* **13 put/set sb's mind at rest** to say something to someone to stop them worrying *I was really worried about the tests, but talking to the doctor put my mind at rest.* **14 slip your mind** If something slips your mind, you forget it. **15 speak your mind** to say exactly what you think without worrying if it will upset anyone *She has very strong opinions and she's not afraid to speak her mind.* ⊃See also: at/in the **back**² of your mind, **frame**¹ of mind, give sb a **piece**¹ of your mind, a **weight** off your mind.

mind² /maɪnd/ *verb* **1** |BE ANNOYED| [I, T] to be annoyed or worried by something *Do you think he'd mind if I borrowed his book?* ○ [+ doing sth] *Tim won't mind lending you his car.* ○ *I don't seem to mind doing all the driving.* ○ *I don't mind taking her* (= I am willing to take her) *if you're too busy.* **2** |LOOK AFTER| [T] to look after someone or something *Who's minding the baby?* **3 do you mind/would you mind** something you say when politely asking someone to do something *Do you mind not smoking in here, please?* ○ *Would you mind if I borrowed your phone?* **4** |BE CAREFUL| [T] something you say when telling someone to be careful with something dangerous *Mind the iron - it's still very hot!* **5 never mind a** |DO NOT WORRY| something that you say to tell someone that something is not important *"I forgot to bring any money." "Never mind, you can pay me next week."* **b** |IMPOSSIBLE| something you say to emphasize that something is impossible *I can't afford to buy a bike, never mind a car!* **6 mind you** something you say before saying the opposite of what you have just said *We had a lovely holiday in France. Mind you, the weather was appalling.*

Mind out! *UK* something you say to warn someone about a danger or to tell them to move *Mind out - this plate's very hot!*

mind-boggling /'maɪnd,bɒglɪŋ/ *adjective informal* difficult to accept, imagine, or understand *The amount of information available on the Internet is mind-boggling.*

-minded /'maɪndɪd/ ⊃See absent-minded, narrow-minded, open-minded, single-minded.

minder /'maɪndəʳ/ *noun* [C] *UK* someone who physically protects a famous, important, or very rich person

mindless /'maɪndləs/ *adjective* stupid and done without a good reason *mindless violence*

ᵒ⁻**mine¹** /maɪn/ *pronoun* the things that belong or relate to the person who is speaking or writing *I borrowed them from a friend of mine.* ○ *"Whose book is this?" "It's mine."* ○ *Can I use your pen? Mine's not working.*

ᵒ⁻**mine²** /maɪn/ *noun* [C] **1** an underground system of holes and passages where people dig out coal or other minerals **2** a bomb hidden in the ground or water which explodes when it is touched ⊃See also: **gold mine**.

mine³ /maɪn/ *verb* **1** [I, T] to dig out of the ground minerals such as coal, metals, and valuable stones *Tin was mined in this area for hundreds of years.* ○ *He made his fortune **mining for** gold and diamonds.* **2** [T] to put mines (= bombs) in the ground or water *The southern coast was heavily mined during the war.*

minefield /'maɪnfiːld/ *noun* [C] **1** a situation with many complicated problems *a **legal minefield*** **2** an area of land or sea where bombs have been hidden

miner /'maɪnəʳ/ *noun* [C] someone who works in a mine *a coal miner*

mineral /'mɪn³r³l/ *noun* [C] **1** a valuable or useful substance that is dug out of the ground *The region's rich mineral deposits include oil, gold, and aluminium.* **2** a chemical that your body needs to stay healthy

'mineral ,water *noun* [C, U] water which is taken from the ground and contains chemicals that are good for your health

mingle /'mɪŋgl/ *verb* **1** [I, T] to mix, or be mixed *The smell of fresh coffee **mingled with** cigarette smoke.* **2** [I] to meet and talk to a lot of people at a party or similar event *The party will be a good opportunity for you to **mingle with** the other students.*

mini- /mɪni-/ *prefix* small *a miniskirt* (= very short skirt) ○ *a minibus*

miniature¹ /'mɪnətʃəʳ/ *adjective* [always before noun] extremely small *a miniature camera*

miniature² /'mɪnətʃəʳ/ *noun* **1** [C] a very small copy of an object *You can buy miniatures of the statue in the museum shop.* **2 in miniature** If something is in miniature, it is a very small copy of something else.

minibus /'mɪnɪbʌs/ *noun* [C] a small bus with seats for about ten people

minimal /'mɪnɪm³l/ *adjective* very small in amount *Damage to the building was minimal.* ● minimally *adverb*

minimize (*also UK* **-ise**) /'mɪnɪmaɪz/ *verb* [T] to make the amount of something that is unpleasant or not wanted as small as possible *Airport staff are trying to minimize the inconvenience caused to passengers.*

ᵒ⁻**minimum¹** /'mɪnɪməm/ *adjective* [always before noun] The minimum amount of something is the smallest amount that is allowed, needed, or possible. *How much is the **minimum wage**?* ○ *There is a **minimum charge** of $5 for postage.* ⊃Opposite **maximum**.

WORD PARTNERS FOR *minimum*

a minimum **of** [5/2%, etc] • **keep** sth **to** a minimum • an **absolute/bare** minimum • **with the** minimum of sth

⊶**minimum²** /ˈmɪnɪməm/ *noun* **[no plural]** the smallest amount that is allowed, needed, or possible *The judge sentenced him to **a minimum of** five years in prison.* ○ *Please **keep** noise **to** an absolute **minimum**.*

mining /ˈmaɪnɪŋ/ *noun* **[U]** the industrial process of digging coal or other minerals out of the ground

miniscule /ˈmɪnɪskjuːl/ *adjective* a common spelling of 'minuscule' that is not correct

miniskirt /ˈmɪniˌskɜːt/ *noun* **[C]** a very short skirt ➲See colour picture **Clothes** on page Centre 8.

minister /ˈmɪnɪstəʳ/ *noun* **[C] 1** a politician who is responsible for a government department or has an important position in it *a finance/health minister* **2** a priest in some Christian churches *a Baptist/Methodist minister* ➲See also: **prime minister**.

ministerial /ˌmɪnɪˈstɪəriəl/ *adjective* relating to a government minister *a **ministerial job/post***

ministry /ˈmɪnɪstri/ *noun* **1 [C]** a government department which is responsible for a particular subject *the Ministry of Defence* ○ *a Foreign Ministry spokesman* **2 the ministry** the job of being a priest

minivan /ˈmɪnivæn/ *noun* **[C]** *US* a people carrier (= large, high car for many people)

mink /mɪŋk/ *noun* **[C, U]** a small animal with valuable fur which is used to make expensive coats, or the fur from this animal *a mink coat*

minor¹ /ˈmaɪnəʳ/ *adjective* **1** not important or serious *a minor offence* ○ *Most of the passengers suffered only minor injuries.* **2 [always before noun]** in music, belonging to a key (= set of musical notes) that often produces a sad sound ➲Opposite **major**.

minor² /ˈmaɪnəʳ/ *noun* **[C]** *formal* someone who is too young to have the legal responsibilities of an adult

WORD PARTNERS FOR *minority*

be **in** a minority • a **sizeable/small/substantial/tiny** minority • a minority **of** sth

⊶**minority** /maɪˈnɒrəti/ *noun* **1 [no plural]** a part of a group which is less than half of the whole group, often much less *The violence was caused by a **small minority** of football supporters.* ○ *I voted to accept the proposal, but I was **in the minority**.* ➲Opposite **majority**. **2 [C]** a group of people whose race is different from the race of most of the people where they live **[usually plural]** *ethnic minorities*

mint¹ /mɪnt/ *noun* **1** [SWEET] **[C]** a sweet with a fresh, strong taste **2** [HERB] **[U]** a plant whose leaves are used to add flavour to food and drinks **3** [FACTORY] **[C]** a factory which produces coins for the government

mint² /mɪnt/ *verb* **[T]** to produce a coin for the government

minus¹ /ˈmaɪnəs/ *preposition* **1** used when the second of two numbers should be taken away from the first *Five minus three is two.* **2** *informal* without something that should be there *She arrived at the meeting minus her briefcase.*

minus² /ˈmaɪnəs/ *adjective* **1 [always before noun]** A minus number is less than zero. *The temperature last night was minus ten.* **2 A minus/B minus, etc** used with scores given to written work meaning 'slightly lower than' *I got an A minus for my last essay.*

minus³ /ˈmaɪnəs/ *noun* **[C] 1** (*also* **ˈminus ˌsign**) the sign which shows that the second of two numbers should be taken away from the first, or that a number is less than zero, shown by the symbol '–' **2** a problem or difficulty *It isn't easy having a child but the pluses outweigh the minuses.*

minuscule /ˈmɪnəskjuːl/ *adjective* extremely small *The cost of vaccination is minuscule compared to the cost of treating the disease.*

⊶**minute¹** /ˈmɪnɪt/ *noun* **[C] 1** [60 SECONDS] a period of time equal to 60 seconds *She was ten minutes late for her interview.* ○ *"Did you have a good holiday?" "Yes, thanks. I enjoyed every minute of it."* ○ *a thirty-minute journey* **2** [SHORT TIME] a very short period of time *It'll only take **a minute** to call him.* ○ *I'll be with you **in a minute**.* ○ *She died **within minutes of*** (= very soon after) *the attack.* **3 (at) any minute** very soon *Her train should be arriving any minute.* **4 the last minute** the latest time possible *The concert was cancelled at the last minute.* **5 the minute (that)** as soon as *I'll tell you the minute we hear any news.* **6 Wait/Just a minute; Hold on a minute. a** [WAIT] used when asking someone to wait for a short time *Just a minute - I've left my coat in the restaurant.* **b** [DISAGREEING] used when you disagree with something that someone has said or done *Hold on a minute, Pete! I never said you could borrow my car.*

minute² /maɪˈnjuːt/ *adjective* **1** extremely small *a minute amount/quantity* **2 [always before noun]** done in great detail *He explained everything **in minute detail**.*

the minutes /ˈmɪnɪts/ *noun* **[plural]** an official record of what is said and decided during a meeting *Michael has kindly agreed to **take the minutes*** (= write them down).

miracle /ˈmɪrəkl/ *noun* **[C] 1** something that is very surprising or difficult to believe *an economic miracle* ○ **[+ (that)]** *It's a miracle that he's still alive.* ○ *a **miracle cure*** **2** an event which should be impossible and cannot be explained by science

miraculous /mɪˈrækjələs/ *adjective* very surprising or difficult to believe *John's made a **miraculous recovery** from his illness.* • **miraculously** *adverb*

mirage /ˈmɪrɑːʒ/ [US] /mɪˈrɑːʒ/ *noun* **[C]** when hot air produces an image of water in a desert or on a road

⊶**mirror¹** /ˈmɪrəʳ/ *noun* **[C]** a piece of glass with a shiny metallic material on one side which produces an image of anything that is in front of it *a bathroom mirror* ○ *He looked at his reflection **in the mirror**.* ➲See colour picture **The**

M

Living Room on page Centre 4 ⊃See also: rear-view mirror, wing mirror.

mirror[2] /ˈmɪrəʳ/ *verb* [T] to be similar to or represent something *Our newspaper mirrors the opinions of ordinary people.*

mirth /mɜːθ/ *noun* [U] *formal* laughter or happiness *a source of mirth*

mis- /mɪs-/ *prefix* not or badly *mistrust* ○ *to misbehave*

misadventure /ˌmɪsədˈventʃəʳ/ *noun* **1** [U] *UK formal* when someone is killed by accident and no one is legally responsible for the death *The coroner recorded a verdict of death by misadventure.* **2** [C] an unlucky event

misanthrope /ˈmɪsᵊnθrəʊp/ *noun* [C] *formal* someone who hates people in general and avoids being with them

misapprehension /ˌmɪsæprɪˈhenʃᵊn/ *noun* [C] *formal* a idea or opinion about someone or something that is wrong [+ that] *He was labouring under the misapprehension* (= wrongly believed) *that she loved him.*

misbehave /ˌmɪsbɪˈheɪv/ *verb* [I] to behave badly ● **misbehaviour** *UK* (*US* **misbehavior**) *noun* [U] bad behaviour

misc *written abbreviation for* miscellaneous

miscalculate /mɪsˈkælkjəleɪt/ *verb* [I, T] **1** to make a mistake when calculating something *I think I've miscalculated how much wine we'll need for the party.* **2** to make a bad decision because you do not completely understand a situation *If she thinks Mike will support her plan, then she's seriously miscalculated.* ● **miscalculation** /ˌmɪskælkjəˈleɪʃᵊn/ *noun* [C, U]

miscarriage /ˈmɪsˌkærɪdʒ/ *noun* [C, U] **1** when a baby is born too early and dies because it has not developed enough *She had a miscarriage after her car accident.* **2 miscarriage of justice** when a court makes a wrong or unfair decision *His conviction was a miscarriage of justice.*

miscarry /mɪˈskæri/ *verb* [I, T] to give birth to a baby too early so that it dies

miscellaneous /ˌmɪsᵊlˈeɪniəs/ *adjective* [always before noun] consisting of a mixture of several different things *The plumber tried to charge me fifty pounds for miscellaneous items.*

mischief /ˈmɪstʃɪf/ *noun* [U] behaviour, usually of a child, which is slightly bad but not serious

mischievous /ˈmɪstʃɪvəs/ *adjective* behaving in a way that is slightly bad but not serious *a mischievous grin* ○ *a mischievous five-year-old* ● **mischievously** *adverb*

misconceived /ˌmɪskənˈsiːvd/ *adjective* If a plan is misconceived, it is not suitable or has not been thought about carefully.

⬚ WORD PARTNERS FOR *misconception*

be **based on** a misconception ● a **common/popular** misconception ● a misconception **about** sth

misconception /ˌmɪskənˈsepʃᵊn/ *noun* [C] when your understanding of something is wrong [+ that] *It's a common misconception that older workers cannot learn to use new technology.*

misconduct /mɪsˈkɒndʌkt/ *noun* [U] *formal* when someone in a position of responsibility behaves in a way that is morally wrong or breaks rules while doing their job *professional misconduct*

misdemeanour *UK* (*US* **misdemeanor**) /ˌmɪsdɪˈmiːnəʳ/ *noun* [C] **1** behaviour that is bad or not moral *political/sexual misdemeanours* **2** *US* a crime which is not serious

misdirect /ˌmɪsdɪˈrekt/ *verb* [T] to use money or people's skills in a way that is not suitable [often passive] *Large quantities of money and expertise have been misdirected.*

miserable /ˈmɪzᵊrəbl/ *adjective* **1** [SAD] unhappy *I just woke up feeling miserable.* **2** [NOT PLEASANT] very unpleasant or bad, and causing someone to feel unhappy *Some families are living in miserable conditions.* **3** [NOT ENOUGH] *informal* A miserable amount is too small to be acceptable. *She offered me a miserable £50 for my old computer.*

miserably /ˈmɪzᵊrəbli/ *adverb* **1** in a way that causes disappointment or suffering *miserably low wages* ○ *Every job application that I've made has failed miserably* (= has been extremely unsuccessful). **2** in a very unhappy way *"I feel so ill," said Rachel miserably.*

misery /ˈmɪzᵊri/ *noun* [C, U] **1** great suffering or unhappiness *The war brought misery to millions of people.* ○ *Her husband's drinking is making her life a misery.* **2 put sb out of their misery** to stop someone worrying by telling them what they want to know

misfire /mɪsˈfaɪəʳ/ *verb* [I] When something that you do misfires, it does not have the result that you intended. *His joke misfired badly, and he was forced to make a public apology.*

misfit /ˈmɪsfɪt/ *noun* [C] someone with strange or unusual behaviour who is not accepted by other people *a social misfit*

misfortune /mɪsˈfɔːtʃuːn/ *noun* [C, U] bad luck, or an unlucky event [+ to do sth] *He had the misfortune to fall in love with a married woman.*

⬚ WORD PARTNERS FOR *misgiving*

express/have misgivings ● **grave/serious/strong** misgivings ● misgivings **about** sth

misgiving /mɪsˈgɪvɪŋ/ *noun* [C] a feeling of doubt or worry about a future event [usually plural] *She has serious misgivings about giving birth at home.*

misguided /mɪsˈgaɪdɪd/ *adjective* not likely to succeed because of a bad judgment or understanding of a situation *The government's policy seems to me completely misguided.*

mishandle /mɪsˈhændl/ *verb* [T] to deal with a problem or situation badly *The murder investigation was mishandled from the beginning.*

mishap /ˈmɪshæp/ *noun* [C, U] an accident or unlucky event which usually is not serious *They suffered a series of mishaps during the trip.*

misinform /ˌmɪsɪnˈfɔːm/ *verb* [T] to give someone false information [often passive] *I'm afraid you've been misinformed about your exam results.*

misinterpret /ˌmɪsɪnˈtɜːprɪt/ *verb* [T] to understand something in the wrong way [often passive] *He claims his speech was deliberately misinterpreted by journalists.*

misjudge /mɪsˈdʒʌdʒ/ *verb* [T] **1** to form a wrong opinion about a person or situation *We believe that the government has seriously misjudged the public mood.* **2** to guess an amount or distance wrongly

misjudgment (*also UK* **misjudgement**) /mɪsˈdʒʌdʒmənt/ *noun* [C, U] when you form a wrong opinion or make a wrong guess *Her outspoken criticism of her boss was a serious misjudgment.*

mislay /mɪˈsleɪ/ *verb* [T] *past* **mislaid** /mɪˈsleɪd/ *formal* to lose something for a short time by forgetting where you put it *I seem to have mislaid my car keys.*

mislead /mɪˈsliːd/ *verb* [T] *past* **misled** /mɪˈsled/ to make someone believe something that is untrue by giving them information that is wrong or not complete [often passive] *She claims the public was misled by the government.*

misleading /mɪˈsliːdɪŋ/ *adjective* making someone believe something that is untrue *misleading information/statements*

mismanage /ˌmɪsˈmænɪdʒ/ *verb* [T] to control or organize something badly *He accused the government of mismanaging the crisis.* • **mismanagement** *noun* [U] when something is badly organized or controlled

misnomer /mɪˈsnəʊməʳ/ *noun* [C] a name which is not suitable for the person or thing that it refers to [usually singular] *It's a misnomer to call young car thieves 'joyriders'.*

misogynist /mɪˈsɒdʒənɪst/ *noun* [C] a man who dislikes women very much • **misogynistic** /mɪˌsɒdʒənˈɪstɪk/ (*also* **misogynist**) *adjective* expressing a great dislike of women *a misogynistic attitude/writer*

misogyny /mɪˈsɒdʒɪni/ *noun* [U] a great dislike of women

misplaced /mɪˈspleɪst/ *adjective* If you have a misplaced feeling or belief, it is wrong because you have not understood the situation correctly. ***misplaced loyalty/trust***

misprint /ˈmɪsprɪnt/ *noun* [C] a mistake made in the printing of a newspaper or book *The article is full of misprints.*

misread /mɪsˈriːd/ *verb* [T] *past* **misread** /mɪsˈred/ **1** to make a mistake when you are reading something *He misread the cooking instructions on the packet.* **2** to not understand something correctly *Philippa completely **misread** the **situation**.*

misrepresent /ˌmɪsreprɪˈzent/ *verb* [T] to say things that are not true about someone or something *He claims that the article misrepresented his views.* • **misrepresentation** /ˌmɪsreprɪzenˈteɪʃən/ *noun* [C, U]

⊶**miss¹** /mɪs/ *verb* **1** [FEEL SAD] [T] to feel sad about someone that you do not see now or something that you do not have or do now *I'll miss you when you go.* ○ [+ doing sth] *He misses having a room of his own.* **2** [NOT GO TO] [T] to not go to something *I missed my class this morning.* **3** [NOT SEE/HEAR] [T] to not see or hear something or someone *Sorry, I missed that, could you repeat it please?* ○ *We missed the first five minutes of the film.* **4** [NOT HIT] [I, T] to not hit or catch something as you intended *It should have been such an easy goal and he missed.* **5** [TOO LATE] [T] to arrive too late to get on a bus, train, or aircraft *If I don't leave now, I'll miss my train.* ➲See Common learner error at **lose**. **6** [NOT NOTICE] [T] to not notice someone or something *It's the big house on the corner - you can't miss it.* **7 miss a chance/opportunity** to not use an opportunity to do something *You can't afford to miss a chance like this.* **8 miss the point** to not understand something correctly ➲See also: miss the **boat**.

COMMON LEARNER ERROR

miss or lack?

Be careful not to confuse the verb **lack** with **miss**. **Lack** means to not have something, or to not have enough of something.

Our town lacks a cinema.

~~*Our town misses a cinema.*~~

miss sb/sth out *UK* to not include someone or something

miss out to not do or have something that you would enjoy or something that other people do or have *I got there late and **missed out on** all the fun.*

miss² /mɪs/ *noun* **1** [C] when you do not hit or catch something as you intended **2 give sth a miss** *UK informal* to not do an activity *I think I'll give aerobics a miss this evening.* **3 a near miss** something bad which does not happen but almost happens

⊶**Miss** /mɪs/ *noun* a title for a girl or woman who is not married, used before her family name or full name *Miss Olivia Allenby* ○ *Tell Miss Russell I'm here.* ➲See Common learner error at **Mr**.

misshapen /mɪsˈʃeɪpən/ *adjective* not the correct or normal shape

missile /ˈmɪsaɪl/ [US] /ˈmɪsəl/ *noun* [C] **1** an explosive weapon which can travel long distances through the air *nuclear missiles* ○ *a missile attack* **2** an object which is thrown through the air to hit someone or something

WORD PARTNERS FOR *missing*

go missing • **report** sb missing • missing from sth

⊶**missing** /ˈmɪsɪŋ/ *adjective* **1** If someone or something is missing, you cannot find them because they are not in their usual place. *Have you found those missing documents?* ○ *Her daughter **went missing** a week ago.* **2** not included in something *There are a couple of things **missing from** the list.*

mission /ˈmɪʃən/ *noun* [C] **1** [JOB] an important job, usually travelling somewhere *I'll be going on a fact-finding **mission** to Paris next week.* **2** [GROUP] an official group of people who are sent somewhere, usually to discover information about something *a trade mission* **3** [JOURNEY] an important journey which a spacecraft or military aircraft goes on **4** PUR-POSE someone's duty or purpose in life *Her mission in life was to help the poor.*

missionary /'mɪʃᵊnᵊri/ *noun* [C] someone who travels to another country to teach people about the Christian religion

missive /'mɪsɪv/ *noun* [C] *literary* a letter or message

misspell /mɪs'spel/ *verb* [T] *past* **misspelled** or *UK* **misspelt** to spell something wrongly

mist¹ /mɪst/ *noun* [C, U] small drops of water in the air which makes it difficult to see objects which are not near *Gradually the mist cleared and the sun began to shine.*

mist² /mɪst/ *verb*

mist over/up If a glass surface mists over, it becomes covered with very small drops of water so that you cannot see through it easily.

WORD PARTNERS FOR *mistake*

correct/make/repeat a mistake • a **big/ costly/fatal/serious/terrible** mistake • **by** mistake

◦▪**mistake¹** /mɪ'steɪk/ *noun* [C] **1** something that you do or think which is wrong *a spelling mistake* ○ *He made a lot of mistakes in his written test.* ○ [+ to do sth] *It would be a big mistake to leave school.* ○ [+ of + doing sth] *She made the mistake of giving him her phone number.* **2 by mistake** If you do something by mistake, you do it without intending to. *I picked up someone else's book by mistake.*

COMMON LEARNER ERROR

mistake

Remember to use the correct verb with this word.

*I always **make** mistakes in my essays.*

~~I always do mistakes in my essays.~~

OTHER WAYS OF SAYING *mistake*

A common alternative is the noun **error**: *He admitted that he'd made an **error**.* • *The letter contained a number of typing **errors**.*

A stupid mistake is sometimes described as a **blunder**: *The company was struggling after a series of financial **blunders**.*

A mistake which causes confusion is often described as a **mix-up**: *There was a **mix-up** with the bags at the airport.*

An embarrassing mistake that someone makes when they are talking is sometimes described as a **gaffe**: *I made a real **gaffe** by calling her 'Emma' which is the name of his previous girlfriend.*

The noun **oversight** is sometimes used to describe a mistake which someone makes by forgetting to do something: *The payment was delayed because of an **oversight** in the accounts department.*

mistake² /mɪ'steɪk/ *verb* [T] *past tense* **mistook**, *past participle* **mistaken** to not understand something correctly *Sorry, I think you mistook my meaning.*

mistake sb/sth for sb/sth to confuse someone or something with someone or something else *People sometimes mistake him for a girl.*

mistaken /mɪ'steɪkᵊn/ *adjective* If you are mistaken, or you have a mistaken belief, you are wrong about something. *If you think you can behave like that, you are mistaken.* • **mistakenly** *adverb I **mistakenly** (= wrongly) **thought** he had left.*

Mister /'mɪstər/ *noun* [U] *US informal* used when calling or talking to a man that you do not know *Hey Mister, you forgot your suitcase!*

mistletoe /'mɪsltəʊ/ *noun* [U] a plant with white berries (= small, round fruit) which is often used as a decoration at Christmas

mistook /mɪ'stʊk/ *past tense of* mistake

mistreat /mɪs'triːt/ *verb* [T] to treat a person or animal in a bad or cruel way *A local farmer has been accused of mistreating horses.* • **mistreatment** *noun* [U] when people or animals are badly or cruelly treated

mistress /'mɪstrəs/ *noun* [C] a woman who has a sexual relationship with a man who is married to someone else

mistrust /mɪ'strʌst/ *noun* [U] when you do not believe or have confidence in someone or something *They have a deep mistrust of strangers.* • **mistrust** *verb* [T]

misty /'mɪsti/ *adjective* If the weather is misty, there is a cloud of small drops of water in the air, which makes it difficult to see objects which are not near. *a cold and misty morning*

misunderstand /ˌmɪsʌndə'stænd/ *verb* [T] *past* **misunderstood** **1** to not understand someone or something correctly *He misunderstood the question completely.* **2 be misunderstood** If someone is misunderstood, other people do not understand that they have good qualities.

misunderstanding /ˌmɪsʌndə'stændɪŋ/ *noun* **1** [C, U] when someone does not understand something correctly *There must have been a misunderstanding.* **2** [C] a slight disagreement

misuse /ˌmɪs'juːz/ *verb* [T] to use something in the wrong way or for the wrong purpose *He misused his position to obtain money dishonestly.* • **misuse** /ˌmɪs'juːs/ *noun* [C, U] *the misuse of drugs/power*

mite /maɪt/ *noun* [C] **1** an extremely small insect with eight legs *dust mites* **2** *informal* a small child *You're so cold, you poor little mite!* **3 a mite** *mainly UK informal* slightly *He seemed a mite embarrassed.*

mitigate /'mɪtɪgeɪt/ *verb* [T] to reduce the harmful effects of something • **mitigation** /ˌmɪtɪ'geɪʃᵊn/ *noun* [U]

mitigating /'mɪtɪgeɪtɪŋ/ *adjective* **mitigating circumstances/factors** facts that make something bad that someone has done seem less bad or less serious

mitt /mɪt/ *noun* [C] a thick leather glove (= cover for the hand) used for catching a baseball ⊃See colour picture **Sports 2** on page Centre 15.

◦▪**mix¹** /mɪks/ *verb* **1** COMBINE SUBSTANCES [I, T] If two or more substances mix, they combine to make one substance, and if you mix two or more substances, you combine them to make one substance. ***Mix** the powder **with** water to form a paste.* ○ *Put the chocolate, butter, and egg in a bowl and **mix** them all **together**.* ○ *Oil and water don't mix.* **2** [COMBINE QUALITIES ETC] **[I, T]** to have or do two or more qualities, styles, activities, etc at the same time *a feeling of anger mixed with sadness* **3** [MEET] **[I]** to meet and talk to people *She enjoys going to parties and **mixing with** people.*

mix sth/sb up to confuse two people or things by thinking that one person or thing is the other person or thing *People often mix them up because they look so similar.*

mix sth up to cause a group of things to be untidy or badly organized *The books were all mixed up in a box.*

WORD PARTNERS FOR ***mix***

a mix **of** sth • an **ethnic/racial/social** mix

mix² /mɪks/ *noun* **1** **[C]** a combination of things or people, often in a group **[usually singular]** *There's a good **mix of** nationalities in the class.* **2** **[C, U]** a powder to which you add liquid in order to make something *cake mix*

mixed /mɪkst/ *adjective* **1** made of a combination of different people or things *a racially mixed area* ○ *a mixed salad* **2 mixed feelings** If you have mixed feelings about something, you are pleased and not pleased at the same time. ➲See also: a mixed **blessing**.

mixed-race /mɪkstˈreɪs/ *adjective* describes a person whose parents are of different races (= the groups that people are divided into according to their physical characteristics)

ˌmixed ˈup *adjective informal* **1** confused *I got a bit mixed up and thought we were supposed to be there at eight.* **2 be mixed up in sth** to be involved in an activity that is bad or illegal **3 be mixed up with sb** to be involved with someone who has a bad influence on you *Her son got mixed up with the wrong people.*

mixer /ˈmɪksəʳ/ *noun* **[C]** a machine that mixes things *an electric mixer*

🔑**mixture** /ˈmɪkstʃəʳ/ *noun* **1** **[C, U]** a substance made of other substances that have been combined *Add milk to the mixture and stir until smooth.* **2** **[no plural]** when there is a combination of two or more ideas, qualities, styles, etc *Their house is decorated in a mixture of styles.*

mix-up /ˈmɪksʌp/ *noun* **[C]** *informal* when there is a mistake because things are confused **[usually singular]** *There was a mix-up with the bags at the airport.*

ml *written abbreviation for* millilitre (= a unit for measuring liquid)

mm *written abbreviation for* millimetre (= a unit for measuring length)

moan /məʊn/ *verb* **[I]** **1** to complain or speak in a way that shows you are unhappy *She's always **moaning about** something.* **2** to make a low sound, especially because you are in pain *He lay on the floor moaning.* • **moan** *noun* **[C]**

mob¹ /mɒb/ *noun* **[C]** a large group of people that is often violent or not organized *an angry mob*

mob² /mɒb/ *verb* **[T]** **mobbing** *past* **mobbed** If a group of people mob someone, they get close to them, often to get their photograph or signature. **[often passive]** *She was mobbed by photographers as she left the hotel.*

mobile¹ /ˈməʊbaɪl/ [US] /ˈməʊbəl/ *adjective* able to move or be moved easily *a mobile home* ➲Opposite **immobile**.

🔑**mobile²** /ˈməʊbaɪl/ [US] /ˈməʊbiːl/ *noun* **[C]** **1** a mobile phone **2** a decoration made of objects on threads that hang down and move in the air

🔑**ˌmobile ˈphone** *noun* **[C]** a telephone that you can carry everywhere with you

mobile phone

mobilize (*also UK* -ise) /ˈməʊbɪlaɪz/ *verb* **1** **[T]** to organize a group of people so that they support or oppose something or someone *He's trying to **mobilize support** for the strike.* **2** **[I, T]** *formal* to prepare for a war *The forces were fully mobilized for action.* • **mobilization** /ˌməʊbɪlaɪˈzeɪʃᵊn/ *noun* **[U]**

mock¹ /mɒk/ *verb* **[I, T]** to laugh at someone or something in an unkind way *The older kids mocked him whenever he made a mistake.*

mock² /mɒk/ *adjective* **[always before noun]** not real but appearing or pretending to be exactly like something *a **mock exam*** ○ ***mock surprise*** ○ *mock leather*

mockery /ˈmɒkᵊri/ *noun* **[U]** **1** when someone laughs at someone or something in an unkind way **2 make a mockery of sth** to make something seem stupid *The latest outbreak of fighting makes a mockery of the peace process.*

modal verb /ˈməʊdəlˌvɜːb/ (*also* **modal**) *noun* **[C]** a verb, for example 'can', 'might', or 'must', that is used before another verb to show that something is possible, necessary, etc ➲See Extra help page **Modal verbs** on page Centre 22.

mode /məʊd/ *noun* **[C]** *formal* a way of doing something *a mode of transport*

🔑**model¹** /ˈmɒdᵊl/ *noun* **[C]** **1** [PERSON] someone whose job is to wear fashionable clothes, be in photographs, etc in order to advertise things *a fashion model* **2** [COPY] a smaller copy of a real object, often used to show how something works or what it looks like **3** [EXAMPLE] someone or something that is an example for others to copy *a model of good behaviour* **4** [DESIGN] a design of machine or car that is made by a particular company *I think her car is a slightly older model.* ➲See also: **role model**.

model² /ˈmɒdᵊl/ *verb* **[I, T]** *UK* **modelling**, *past* **modelled**, *US* **modeling**, *past* **modeled** to wear clothes in fashion shows, magazines, etc as a model

be modelled on sth to be based on the design of something else *The house is modelled on a 16th century castle.*

model yourself on sb to try to make yourself very similar to someone else *He models himself on Mohammed Ali.*

M

modem /'məʊdem/ *noun* [C] a piece of equipment that is used to send information from a computer through a telephone line, cable or other link ➔See Extra help page **The Web and the Internet** on page Centre 36..

moderate¹ /'mɒdᵊrət/ *adjective* **1** average in size or amount and not too much *Eating a moderate amount of fat is healthy.* **2** not extreme, especially relating to political opinions *a moderate political group* • **moderately** *adverb*

moderate² /'mɒdᵊrət/ *noun* [C] someone who does not have extreme political opinions

moderate³ /'mɒdᵊreɪt/ *verb* [T] to make something less extreme *He's trying to moderate his drinking.*

moderation /,mɒdᵊr'eɪʃᵊn/ *noun* **1 in moderation** If you do something in moderation, you do not do it too much. *I only drink alcohol in moderation now.* **2** [U] when you control your feelings or actions and stop them from becoming extreme

◦⁻**modern** /'mɒdᵊn/ *adjective* **1** relating to the present time and not to the past *modern society* ○ *the stresses of modern life* **2** using the newest ideas, design, technology, etc and not traditional *modern art/architecture* ○ *modern medicine* • **modernity** /mɒd'ɜ:nəti/ *noun* [U] *formal* when something is modern

modern-day /'mɒdᵊndeɪ/ *adjective* [always before noun] relating to the present time and not to the past *a modern-day version of Shakespeare*

modernize (*also UK* -**ise**) /'mɒdᵊnaɪz/ *verb* [I, T] to make something more modern or to become more modern *We really need to modernize our image.* • **modernization** /,mɒdᵊnaɪ'zeɪʃᵊn/ *noun* [U]

,**modern 'languages** *noun* [plural] languages that are spoken now such as Spanish or German

modest /'mɒdɪst/ *adjective* **1** not large in size or amount, or not expensive *a modest amount of money* ○ *Their house is quite modest in size.* **2** If you are modest, you do not talk in a proud way about your skills or successes. *He's very modest about his achievements.* • **modestly** *adverb*

modesty /'mɒdɪsti/ *noun* [U] when you do not talk in a proud way about your skills or successes

modicum /'mɒdɪkəm/ *noun formal* **a modicum of sth** a small amount of something *a modicum of success*

modification /,mɒdɪfɪ'keɪʃᵊn/ *noun* [C, U] a small change to something *We've made a few modifications to the system.*

modifier /'mɒdɪfaɪᵊr/ *noun* [C] in grammar, a word that describes or limits the meaning of another word

modify /'mɒdɪfaɪ/ *verb* [T] **1** to change something in order to improve it [often passive] *The plans will have to be modified to reduce costs.* ○ *genetically modified food* **2** In grammar, a word that modifies another word describes or limits the meaning of that word. *Adjectives modify nouns.*

module /'mɒdju:l/ *noun* [C] **1** *UK* a part of a university or college course **2** a part of an object

that can operate alone, especially a part of a spacecraft

mogul /'məʊɡᵊl/ *noun* [C] an important, powerful person *media/movie moguls*

Mohammed /mə'hæmɪd/ *noun* the Arab holy man on whose life and teachings Islam is based

moist /mɔɪst/ *adjective* slightly wet *Keep the soil moist but not wet.* ○ *It was a lovely, moist cake.* • **moisten** /'mɔɪsᵊn/ *verb* [I, T] to make something slightly wet, or to become slightly wet

moisture /'mɔɪstʃᵊr/ *noun* [U] very small drops of water in the air or on a surface

moisturizer (*also UK* -**iser**) /'mɔɪstʃᵊraɪzᵊr/ *noun* [C, U] a substance which you put on your skin to make it less dry • **moisturize** (*also UK* -**ise**) /'mɔɪstʃᵊraɪz/ *verb* [T] to put moisturizer on your skin

molasses /məʊ'læsɪz/ (*also UK* **treacle**) *noun* [U] a sweet, thick, dark liquid used in sweet dishes

mold /məʊld/ *noun, verb US spelling of* mould

moldy /'məʊldi/ *adjective US spelling of* mouldy

mole /məʊl/ *noun* [C] **1** ⎡SKIN⎤ a small, dark mark on the skin **2** ⎡ANIMAL⎤ a small animal with black fur that digs holes in the soil and lives under the ground **3** ⎡PERSON⎤ *informal* someone who gives other organizations or governments secret information about the organization where they work

molecule /'mɒlɪkju:l/ *noun* [C] the smallest unit of a substance, consisting of one or more atoms

molehill /'məʊlhɪl/ *noun* [C] ➔See make a **mountain** out of a molehill.

molest /məʊ'lest/ *verb* [T] to hurt or attack someone in a sexual way *He was accused of molesting children.* • **molestation** /,məʊles'teɪʃᵊn/ *noun* [U]

mom /mɒm/ *US* (*UK* **mum**) *noun* [C] *informal* mother *My mom phoned last night.* ○ *Can we go now, Mom?*

◦⁻**moment** /'məʊmənt/ *noun* **1** [C] a very short period of time *I'll be back in a moment.* **2 For a moment** I thought it was Anna. ○ *Could you wait a moment?* **2** [C] a point in time *Just at that moment, the phone rang.* **3 at the moment** now *I'm afraid she's not here at the moment.* **4 for the moment** If you do something for the moment, you are doing it now but might do something different in the future. **5 the moment (that)** as soon as *I'll call you the moment I hear anything.* **6 have a senior/blond, etc moment** *informal* to behave, for a short time, in a way which shows you are old, silly, etc *I've just had a senior moment – I couldn't remember why I'd gone into the kitchen.* ➔See also: on the **spur²** of the moment.

momentarily /'məʊməntᵊrᵊli/ *adverb* for a very short time *I momentarily forgot his name.*

momentary /'məʊməntᵊri/ *adjective* lasting for a very short time *a momentary lapse of memory*

momentous /məʊ'mentəs/ *adjective* A momentous decision, event, etc is very important because it has a big effect on the future.

gain/gather/lose momentum • **keep up/ maintain** the momentum • the momentum **for/of** sth

momentum /məʊˈmentəm/ *noun* [U] **1** when something continues to move, increase, or develop *to* ***gain/gather*** *momentum* ○ *The players seemed to* ***lose*** *momentum halfway through the game.* **2** in science, the force that makes something continue to move

momma /ˈmɒmə/ *noun* [C] *US another word for* mommy

mommy /ˈmɒmi/ *US* (*UK* **mummy**) *noun* [C] *informal* a word for 'mother', used especially by children *I want my mommy!* ○ *Can I have some candy, Mommy?*

Mon *written abbreviation for* Monday

monarch /ˈmɒnək/ *noun* [C] a king or queen

monarchy /ˈmɒnəki/ *noun* **1** [U, no plural] when a country is ruled by a king or queen **2** [C] a country that is ruled by a king or queen

monastery /ˈmɒnəstˑri/ *noun* [C] a building where men live as a religious group

monastic /məˈnæstɪk/ *adjective* relating to a monk (= religious man) or a monastery

o→**Monday** /ˈmʌndeɪ/ (*written abbreviation* Mon) *noun* [C, U] the day of the week after Sunday and before Tuesday

monetary /ˈmʌnɪtˑri/ *adjective* relating to money

borrow / earn / lend / make / pay / raise / save /spend money

o→**money** /ˈmʌni/ *noun* [U] the coins or banknotes (= pieces of paper with values) that are used to buy things *How much money have you got?* ○ *He* ***spends*** *all his* ***money*** *on clothes and CDs.* ○ *The company's not* ***making*** (= earning) *any money at the moment.* ⊃See also: pocket money.

¹**money ˌorder** *US* (*UK* **postal order**) *noun* [C] an official piece of paper bought at a post office that you can send instead of money

mongrel /ˈmʌŋgrˑl/ *noun* [C] a dog that is a mix of different breeds

monies /ˈmʌniz/ *noun* [plural] *formal* amounts of money

monitor¹ /ˈmɒnɪtˑr/ *noun* [C] **1** [SCREEN] a screen that shows information or pictures, usually connected to a computer *a colour monitor* ⊃See colour picture **The Office** on page Centre 5. **2** [MA-CHINE] a machine, often in a hospital, that measures something such as the rate that your heart beats *a* ***heart monitor*** **3** [PERSON] someone who watches something to make certain that it is done correctly or fairly *a human rights monitor*

monitor² /ˈmɒnɪtˑr/ *verb* [T] to watch something carefully and record your results *to monitor progress*

monk /mʌŋk/ *noun* [C] a member of a group of religious men living apart from other people

monkey /ˈmʌŋki/ *noun* [C] a hairy animal with a long tail that lives in hot countries and climbs trees

mono- /mɒnəʊ-/ *prefix* one or single *monolingual* ○ *a monologue*

monochrome /ˈmɒnəkrəʊm/ *adjective* A monochrome image is only in black, white, and grey and not in colour.

monogamy /məˈnɒgəmi/ *noun* [U] when someone has a sexual relationship with only one person • **monogamous** *adjective* relating to monogamy *a* ***monogamous relationship***

monolingual /ˌmɒnəʊˈlɪŋgwˑl/ *adjective* using only one language *monolingual dictionaries*

monolithic /ˌmɒnəʊˈlɪθɪk/ *adjective* large and powerful

monologue (*also US* **monolog**) /ˈmɒnˑlɒg/ *noun* [C] a long speech by one person, often in a performance

mononucleosis /ˌmɒnəʊˌnjuːkliˈəʊsɪs/ *US* (*UK* **glandular fever**) *noun* [U] an infectious disease that makes your glands (= small organs in your body) swell and makes you feel tired

monopolize (*also UK* **-ise**) /məˈnɒpˑlaɪz/ *verb* [T] to control a situation by being the only person or organization involved in it

monopoly /məˈnɒpˑli/ *noun* [C] **1** when a company or organization is the only one in an area of business or activity and has complete control of it *They* ***have a monopoly on*** *the postal service.* **2** a company or other organization that has a monopoly in a particular industry

monosyllabic /ˌmɒnəʊsɪˈlæbɪk/ *adjective* using only short words such as 'yes' or 'no', usually because you do not want to talk

monotonous /məˈnɒtˑnəs/ *adjective* If something is monotonous, it is boring because it stays the same. *a* ***monotonous voice*** ○ *monotonous work* • **monotonously** *adverb*

monsoon /mɒnˈsuːn/ *noun* [C] the season when there is heavy rain in Southern Asia

monster /ˈmɒnstˑr/ *noun* [C] an imaginary creature that is large, ugly, and frightening

monstrous /ˈmɒnstrəs/ *adjective* **1** very bad or cruel *a* ***monstrous crime*** **2** like a monster

o→**month** /mʌnθ/ *noun* [C] **1** one of the twelve periods of time that a year is divided into *last/next month* ○ *Your birthday's this month, isn't it?* **2** a period of approximately four weeks *I saw him about three months ago.*

monthly /ˈmʌnθli/ *adjective, adverb* happening or produced once a month *a monthly meeting* ○ *a monthly magazine*

monument /ˈmɒnjəmənt/ *noun* [C] **1** a building or other structure that is built to make people remember an event in history or a famous person *a national monument* ○ *They built the statue as* ***a monument to*** *all the soldiers who died.* **2** an old building or place that is important in history *an ancient monument*

monumental /ˌmɒnjəˈmentˑl/ *adjective* very large *a* ***monumental task***

moo /muː/ *noun* [C] the sound that a cow makes • **moo** *verb* [I] **mooing** *past* **mooed**

M

| j yes | k cat | ŋ ring | ʃ she | θ thin | ð this | ʒ decision | dʒ jar | tʃ chip | æ cat | e bed | ə ago | ɪ sit | i cosy | ɒ hot | ʌ run | ʊ put |

o─**mood** /muːd/ *noun* **1** [C, U] the way someone
feels at a particular time *to be **in** a good/bad
mood* ○ *The **public mood** changed dramatically after the bombing.* **2 be in a mood** to not be
friendly to other people because you are feeling angry **3 be in the mood for sth/to do sth** to
want to do or have something *I'm not really in
the mood for shopping at the moment.* **4 be in
no mood for sth/to do sth** to not want to do
something with someone else, often because
you are angry with them **5** [C] in grammar,
one of the different ways a sentence is being
used, for example to give an order, express a
fact, etc *the indicative/imperative mood*

moody /ˈmuːdi/ *adjective* If someone is moody,
they are often unfriendly because they feel
angry or unhappy. ● **moodily** *adverb* ● **moodi-
ness** *noun* [U]

o─**moon** /muːn/ *noun* **1 the moon** the round object
that shines in the sky at night and moves
around the Earth **2 crescent/full/new moon** the
shape made by the amount of the moon that
you can see at a particular time **3** [C] a round
object like the moon that moves around another planet **4 once in a blue moon** rarely *We
only go out once in a blue moon.* **5 be over the
moon** *UK* to be very pleased about something
*"I bet she was pleased with her results." "She
was over the moon."*

moonlight /ˈmuːnlaɪt/ *noun* [U] light that
comes from the moon *In the moonlight she
looked even more beautiful.* ● **moonlit** *adjective*
[always before noun] with light from the moon

moor /mɔːr/ *noun* [C] an open area in the
countryside that is covered with rough grass
and bushes [usually plural] *the Yorkshire Moors*

moose /muːs/ *noun* [C] *plural* **moose** a large deer
that comes from North America

moot point /ˌmuːtˈpɔɪnt/ *noun* [C] a subject
that people cannot agree about

mop[1] /mɒp/ *noun* [C] a piece of equipment used
for cleaning floors that has a long handle and
thick strings at one end

mop[2] /mɒp/ *verb* [T] **mopping** *past* **mopped** to use a
mop *to **mop** the floor*

mop sth up to use a cloth or mop to remove
liquid from a surface

o─**moral**[1] /ˈmɒrəl/ *adjective* **1** [always before noun] relating to beliefs about what is right or wrong
moral standards/values ○ *a moral issue*
2 behaving in a way that most people think is
correct and honest *He's a very moral person.*
⊃Opposite **immoral** ⊃Compare **amoral**. ● **morally**
adverb **morally wrong**

moral[2] /ˈmɒrəl/ *noun* [C] something you learn
from a story or event about how to behave *The
moral of the story is never to lie.*

morale /məˈrɑːl/ *noun* [U] the amount of confidence or hope for the future that people feel
*The pay increase should help to **improve** staff
morale.*

morality /məˈræləti/ *noun* [U] ideas and beliefs
about what is right or wrong

morals /ˈmɒrəlz/ *noun* [plural] principles of good
behaviour *He doesn't care what he does, he has
no morals at all.*

moral su'pport *noun* [U] help and encouragement *Roz has said she'll come with me for
moral support.*

morbid /ˈmɔːbɪd/ *adjective* showing too much
interest in unpleasant things such as death *a
morbid fascination with death*

o─**more**[1] /mɔːr/ *quantifier* **1** something in addition
to what you already have *Would anyone like
some more food?* ○ *I need a bit more money.* **2** a
greater number or amount of people or things
*There are a lot more people here today than
yesterday.* ○ *He knows more about computers
than I do.* **3 more and more** an increasing
number *More and more people are choosing not
to get married.* ⊃See also: **any more**.

more

The opposite of **more** is **fewer** for countable nouns and
less for uncountable nouns.

He takes more exercise now.

He takes less exercise now.

He smokes fewer cigarettes.

o─**more**[2] /mɔːr/ *adverb* **1 more beautiful/difficult/
interesting, etc** used to show that someone or
something has a greater amount of a quality
than someone or something else *It's **more**
expensive **than** the others.* ○ *She's far more intelligent than her sister.* **2** used to show that
something happens a greater number of times
than before *We eat out a lot **more than** we used
to.* **3 more or less** almost *We've more or less finished work on the house.* **4 more and more**
as time passes *It's becoming more and more difficult to pass the exam.* ⊃See also: **any more**.

more

More is used to form the comparative of many adjectives
and adverbs that have two or more syllables.

a more expensive hotel

Could you drive more slowly please?

~~an expensiver hotel~~

The opposite of the adverb **more** is **less**.

a less expensive hotel

moreover /mɔːrˈəʊvər/ *adverb formal* also *It is
a cheap and, moreover, effective way of dealing
with the problem.*

morgue /mɔːg/ *noun* [C] a building or room
where dead bodies are prepared and kept
before a funeral

Mormon /ˈmɔːmən/ *adjective* belonging or relating to a Christian group that was started in

the US by Joseph Smith ● **Mormon** *noun* [C]

o-**morning** /'mɔːnɪŋ/ *noun* [C, U] **1** the first half of the day, from the time when the sun rises or you wake up until the middle of the day *a beautiful/sunny/wet morning* ○ *Friday morning* ○ *tomorrow morning* ○ *I got up late this morning.* **2 in the morning a** during the early part of the day *I listen to the radio in the morning.* **b** tomorrow morning *I'll pack my bags in the morning.* **3 3,4, etc o'clock in the morning** 3,4, etc o'clock in the night *My car alarm went off at 3 o'clock in the morning.* ○ *The murder took place at four o'clock in the morning.* **4 (Good) morning.** used to say hello to someone in the morning *Good morning, Elizabeth. How are you today?*

moron /'mɔːrɒn/ *noun* [C] *informal* a very stupid person *Some moron smashed into my car yesterday.* ● **moronic** /mɔːˈrɒnɪk/ *adjective informal* stupid

morose /məˈrəʊs/ *adjective* If someone is morose, they are not friendly or happy and they talk very little. *Why are you so morose these days?*

morphine /'mɔːfiːn/ *noun* [U] a powerful drug that is used to reduce pain

morsel /'mɔːsəl/ *noun* [C] a small piece of something *a morsel of food* ○ *The prisoners ate every last morsel.*

mortal¹ /'mɔːtəl/ *adjective* **1** not living forever *All men are mortal.* ⊃Opposite **immortal.** **2 mortal danger/fear/terror, etc** extreme danger/fear/terror, etc, because you could die *We live in mortal dread of further attacks.* ● **mortally** *adverb* **mortally wounded**

mortal² /'mɔːtəl/ *noun* [C] *literary* a human being

mortality /mɔːˈtæləti/ *noun* [U] **1** the number of deaths at a particular time or in a particular place *Infant mortality is much higher in the poorest areas of the city.* ○ *the mortality rate* **2** the way that people do not live forever *Her death made him more aware of his own mortality.*

mortar /'mɔːtəʳ/ *noun* **1** [C] a heavy gun that fires explosives high into the air *a mortar attack/bomb* **2** [U] a mixture of substances, for example sand and water, that is used between bricks or stones to keep them together

mortgage /'mɔːgɪdʒ/ *noun* [C] money that you borrow to buy a home *a monthly mortgage payment* ○ *They took out a £40,000 mortgage (= they borrowed £40,000) to buy the house.*

mortified /'mɔːtɪfaɪd/ *adjective* very embarrassed

mortify /'mɔːtɪfaɪ/ *verb* **be mortified** to feel very embarrassed or upset about something *I told her she'd upset John and she was mortified.*

mortuary /'mɔːtʃu³ri/ *noun* [C] a building or room where dead bodies are prepared and kept before a funeral

mosaic

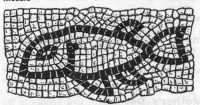

mosaic /məʊˈzeɪɪk/ *noun* [C, U] a picture or pattern that is made with small pieces of coloured stone, glass, etc

Moslem /'mɒzləm/ *noun* [C] another spelling of Muslim (= someone who believes in Islam) ● **Moslem** *adjective*

mosque /mɒsk/ *noun* [C] a building where Muslims say their prayers

mosquito /məˈskiːtəʊ/ *noun* [C] *plural* **mosquitoes** a small flying insect that sucks your blood, sometimes causing malaria (= a serious disease) *mosquito bites*

moss /mɒs/ *noun* [C, U] a very small, green plant that grows on the surface of rocks, trees, etc

o-**most**¹ /məʊst/ *adverb* **1 the most attractive/ important/popular, etc** used to show that someone or something has the greatest amount of a quality *She's the most beautiful girl I've ever seen.* ○ *There are various reasons but this is the most important.* **2** more than anyone or anything else *Which subject do you like most?* ○ *Sam enjoyed the swings most of all.*

o-**most**² /məʊst/ *quantifier* **1** almost all of a group of people or things *Most people think he's guilty.* ○ *Most of our students walk to school.* **2** a larger amount than anyone or anything else *This one costs the most.* ○ *Which of you earns most?* **3 the most** the largest number or amount possible *That's the most I can pay you.* **4 make the most of sth** to take full advantage of something because it may not last long *We should make the most of this good weather.* **5 at (the) most** not more than a particular amount or number *The journey will take an hour at the most.*

o-**mostly** /'məʊstli/ *adverb* mainly or most of the time *She reads mostly romantic novels.*

motel /məʊˈtel/ *noun* [C] a hotel for people who are travelling by car

moth /mɒθ/ *noun* [C] an insect with large wings that often flies at night and is attracted to light ⊃See picture at **insect.**

o-**mother** /'mʌðəʳ/ *noun* [C] **1** your female parent *a single mother* ○ *My mother and father are divorced.* **2 Mother** the title of an important nun (= woman who lives in a female religious group) *Mother Teresa* ⊃See also: **surrogate mother.**

motherhood /'mʌðəhʊd/ *noun* [U] when someone is a mother

mother-in-law /'mʌðərɪn,lɔː/ *noun* [C] *plural* **mothers-in-law** the mother of your husband or wife

motherly /'mʌðəli/ *adjective* A **motherly** woman is like a mother, usually because she is kind and looks after people.

'Mother's ,Day *noun* [C, U] a Sunday in the spring when people give their mothers presents to show their love

,mother 'tongue *noun* [C] the first language that you learn when you are a child

motif /məʊ'tiːf/ *noun* [C] a small design used as a decoration on something *a floral motif*

motion¹ /'məʊʃ³n/ *noun* **1** [MOVEMENT] [U] when or how something moves *The motion of the boat made him feel sick.* **2** [ACTION] [C] a single action or movement *She made a motion with her hand.* **3** [SUGGESTION] [C] a suggestion that you make in a formal meeting or court of law *to propose/oppose a motion* **4 set sth in motion** to make something start to happen **5 go through the motions** to do something that you have to do without enthusiasm ⊃See also: **slow motion.**

motion² /'məʊʃ³n/ *verb* **motion (for/to) sb to do sth** to make a movement as a sign for someone to do something *She motioned him to sit down.*

motionless /'məʊʃ³nləs/ *adjective* not moving *He stood motionless in the middle of the road.*

motivate /'məʊtɪveɪt/ *verb* [T] **1** to make someone enthusiastic about doing something [+ to do sth] *Teaching is all about motivating people to learn.* **2** to cause someone to behave in a particular way [often passive] *Some people are motivated by greed.* ● **motivated** *adjective a racially motivated crime* ○ *a very motivated student* (= one who works hard and wants to succeed)

motivation /,məʊtɪ'veɪʃ³n/ *noun* **1** [U] enthusiasm for doing something *There is a lack of motivation among the staff.* **2** [C] the need or reason for doing something *What was the motivation for the attack?*

motivational /,məʊtɪ'veɪʃ³n³l/ *adjective* [always before noun] giving you encouragement to do something *a motivational speaker*

motive /'məʊtɪv/ *noun* [C] a reason for doing something *The police don't yet know the motive for the killing.*

motor¹ /'məʊtə*/ *noun* [C] the part of a machine or vehicle that changes electricity or fuel into movement and makes it work *an electric motor*

motor² /'məʊtə*/ *adjective* [always before noun] re-

lating to cars *motor racing*

motorbike /'məʊtəbaɪk/ *noun* [C] a vehicle with two wheels and an engine

motorcycle /'məʊtə,saɪkl/ *noun* [C] a motorbike

motoring /'məʊtərɪŋ/ *adjective* [always before noun] *UK* relating to driving *a motoring offence*

motorist /'məʊtərɪst/ *noun* [C] someone who drives a car

'motor ,racing *noun* [U] the sport of driving extremely fast and powerful cars around a track

motorway /'məʊtəweɪ/ *UK* (*US* **freeway, expressway, interstate**) *noun* [C] a long, wide road, usually used by traffic travelling fast over long distances

mottled /'mɒtld/ *adjective* A **mottled** pattern has a mixture of dark and light areas. *mottled skin*

motto /'mɒtəʊ/ *noun* [C] a short phrase that expresses someone's purpose or beliefs *Her motto is, "Work hard, play hard".*

mould¹ *UK* (*US* **mold**) /məʊld/ *noun* **1** [U] a green or black substance that grows in wet places or on old food **2** [C] a container that is used to make something in a particular shape *a chocolate mould* **3 break the mould** to do something differently after it has been done in the same way for a long time

mould² *UK* (*US* **mold**) /məʊld/ *verb* [T] to make a soft substance a particular shape *moulded plastic*

mouldy *UK* (*US* **moldy**) /'məʊldi/ *adjective* covered with mould *mouldy cheese*

mound /maʊnd/ *noun* [C] **1** a large pile of something *a mound of clothes waiting to be ironed* **2** a higher area of soil, like a small hill *an ancient burial mound*

Mount /maʊnt/ *noun* [C] used in the names of mountains *Mount Everest*

mount /maʊnt/ *verb* **1 mount a campaign/challenge/protest, etc** to arrange a series of organized activities that will achieve a particular result **2** [INCREASE] [I] to increase in amount or level *Tension in the room was mounting.* **3 mount sth on/to, etc** to fix an object onto something *They've mounted a camera on the wall by the door.* **4** [GO UP] [T] to go up something *to mount the stairs* **5** [RIDE] [T] to get on a horse or bicycle ⊃Opposite **dismount.**

mount up to gradually become a large amount *My homework is really mounting up this week.*

◦⁻**mountain**
/'maʊntɪn/ *noun* [C]
1 a very high hill *to climb a mountain* ○ *a mountain range* **2** *informal* a large pile of something *There's a mountain of papers on my desk.* **3 make**

mountain

a mountain out of a molehill to deal with a small problem as if it were a big problem

'mountain ,bike *noun* [C] a bicycle with

thick tyres, originally made for people to ride on hills and rough ground

mountainous /'mauntɪnəs/ *adjective* A mountainous area has a lot of mountains.

mourn /mɔːn/ *verb* [I, T] to feel very sad because someone has died *He **mourned for** his dead son every day.*

mourner /'mɔːnər/ *noun* [C] someone at a funeral *chief mourners*

mournful /'mɔːnfəl/ *adjective* very sad *a mournful voice* • **mournfully** *adverb*

mourning /'mɔːnɪŋ/ *noun* [U] when someone mourns the death of someone else *a **period of** mourning* ○ *Barbara's **in mourning** for her husband.*

mouse

mouse /maus/ *noun* [C] *plural* **mice** **1** a small piece of equipment connected to a computer that you move with your hand to control what the computer does **2** a small animal with fur and a long, thin tail

'mouse ,mat *noun* [C] a flat piece of material on which you move the mouse of your computer

mousse /muːs/ *noun* [C, U] **1** a soft, cold food that is often sweet and usually has eggs or cream in it *chocolate mousse* **2** a substance that you put in your hair so that it stays in a particular shape

moustache (*also* US **mustache**) /məˈstɑːʃ/ Ⓤ /ˈmʌstæʃ/ *noun* [C] a line of hair that some men grow above their mouths

moustache

mousy (*also* **mousey**) /ˈmausi/ *adjective* **1** Mousy hair is light brown. **2** A mousy person is shy and not very interesting.

◻◻◻ WORD PARTNERS FOR **mouth**

close/open your mouth • **in** your mouth

o-**mouth** /mauθ/ *noun* [C] **1** the part of the face that is used for eating and speaking ○See colour picture **The Body** on page Centre 13. **2 mouth of a cave/tunnel, etc** the opening or entrance of a cave/tunnel, etc **3 mouth of a river** where a river goes into the sea ○See also: **butter¹** wouldn't melt in sb's mouth.

mouthful /'mauθful/ *noun* [C] the amount of food or drink that you can put into your mouth at one time

mouthpiece /'mauθpiːs/ *noun* [C] a person, newspaper, etc that expresses the opinions of the government or a political group

mouthwash /'mauθwɒʃ/ *noun* [U] a liquid used to make your mouth clean and fresh

movable /'muːvəbl/ *adjective* able to be moved

o-**move¹** /muːv/ *verb* **1** CHANGE PLACE [I] If a person or an organization moves, they go to a different place to live or work. *Eventually, he **moved** to Germany.* ○ *She's **moving into** a new apartment.* ○ *Our children have all **moved away**.* **2** POSITION [I, T] to change place or position, or to make something change place or position *We **moved** the chairs **to** another room.* ○ *Someone was **moving around** upstairs.* **3 move ahead/along/forward, etc** to make progress with something that you have planned to do *The department is **moving ahead** with changes to its teaching programme.* **4** ACTION [I] to take action [+ **to do sth**] *The company **moved** swiftly to find new products.* **5** TIME [T] to change the time or order of something *We need to **move** the meeting back a few days.* **6** FEELING [T] to make someone have strong feelings of sadness or sympathy [**often passive**] *I was deeply **moved** by his speech.* ○ *Many people were **moved to tears** (= were so sad they cried).* ○Compare **unmoved**. **7 move house** *UK* to leave your home in order to live in a new one **8 get moving** *informal* to hurry

COMMON LEARNER ERROR

move or **travel**?

Move means to change position or put something in a different position.

*Could you **move** back a bit, please?*

*Why don't you **move** the table over there?*

Travel means to go from one place to another, usually in a vehicle.

*Most people **travel** to work by car.*

move in to begin living in a new home *She's just **moved in with** her boyfriend.* ○ *They want to **move in together** before they get married.*
move on 1 NEW PLACE to leave the place where you are staying and go somewhere else *After three days in Madrid we thought we'd **move on**.* **2** NEW ACTIVITY to start doing a new activity *I'd done the same job for ten years and felt it was time to **move on**.* **3** NEW SUBJECT to change from one subject to another when you are talking or writing *Let's **move on to** the next topic.*
move out to stop living in a particular home
move over to change the place where you are sitting or standing so that there is space for someone else to sit or stand

move² /muːv/ *noun* [C] **1** ACTION something that you do in order to achieve something or to make progress in a situation *"I've told her*

M

she's got to find somewhere else to live." " Good move!" ○ *The latest policies are clearly a move towards democracy.* ○ *a good career move* **2** NEW HOME/OFFICE when you go to live or work in a different place *The move will cost us a lot of money.* **3 make a move** MOVE to change from one place or position to another *He made a move as if to leave.* **b** LEAVE *UK informal* to leave somewhere *I'd better make a move or I'll be late.* **4 get a move on** *informal* to hurry *Come on, get a move on!*

○ⁿ**movement** /'muːvmənt/ *noun* **1** GROUP [C] a group of people with the same beliefs who work together to achieve something *the women's movement* ○ *the labour movement* **2** CHANGE [C] a change or development in the way people think or behave *a movement towards democracy* **3** POSITION [C, U] a change of position or place *His movements were rather clumsy.* **4** MUSIC [C] a part of a piece of music *The symphony opens with a slow movement.* **5 sb's movements** what someone is doing during a particular period of time *I don't know his movements this week.*

WORD PARTNERS FOR **movie**

make/see/watch a movie ● **in** a movie

○ⁿ**movie** /'muːvi/ *noun* [C] *US* **1** a film **2 the movies** *US* (*UK* **the cinema**) a cinema, or group of cinemas *What's playing at the movies?* ○ *Why don't we go to the movies tonight?*

'movie ,star *noun* [C] a famous movie actor or actress

'movie ,theater *US* (*UK* **cinema**) *noun* [C] a building where you go to watch films

moving /'muːvɪŋ/ *adjective* **1** causing strong feelings of sadness or sympathy *a moving tribute* **2** [always before noun] A moving object is one that moves. *a moving target*

mow /məʊ/ *verb* [T] *past tense* **mowed** *past participle* **mown** or **mowed** to cut grass using a machine *to mow the lawn*

mower /'məʊəʳ/ (*also* **lawn mower**) *noun* [C] a machine that you use to cut grass

MP /ˌemˈpiː/ *noun* [C] *abbreviation for* Member of Parliament: someone who has been elected to the government of the United Kingdom

MP3 /ˌempiːˈθriː/ *noun* [C, U] a computer file (= collection of information) which stores good-quality sound in a small amount of space, or the technology that makes this possible

MP'3 ,player *noun* [C] a piece of electronic equipment or a computer program for playing music that has been stored as MP3 files (= collections of information)

mph *written abbreviation for* miles per hour: a unit for measuring speed *a 30 mph speed limit*

MPV /ˌempiːˈviː/ *UK* (*US* **minivan**) *noun* [C] *abbreviation for* multi-purpose vehicle: a large, high car which can carry more people than a normal car

○ⁿ**Mr** /'mɪstəʳ/ *noun* a title for a man, used before his family name or full name *Good morning, Mr Smith.* ○ *This package is addressed to Mr Gordon Harper.*

COMMON LEARNER ERROR

Mr, Mrs, Ms, Miss

All these titles are used before someone's name.

Mr is used for men. **Mrs** is used for women who are married. **Miss** is used for girls or for women who are not married. **Ms** is used for women and does not show if a woman is married. Many prefer to use this title to **Miss** or **Mrs**.

We do not use these titles on their own as a way of speaking to someone. Usually, we use no name.

Can I help you?

Can I help you, Mrs?

MRI /ˌemɑːrˈaɪ/ *noun* [C] *abbreviation for* magnetic resonance imaging: a system that produces electronic pictures of the organs inside a person's body

○ⁿ**Mrs** /'mɪsɪz/ *noun* a title for a married woman, used before her family name or full name *Hello, Mrs. Jones.* ○ *Please send your application to the finance director, Mrs Laura Fox.*

MRSA /ˌemɑːresˈeɪ/ *noun abbreviation for* Methicillin Resistant Staphylococcus Aureus: a type of bacteria (= very small living things that cause disease) that is often found in hospitals and can make people very ill

○ⁿ**Ms** /mɪz/ *noun* a title for a woman, used before her family name or full name *Ms Holly Fox*

MS /ˌemˈes/ *noun* [U] *abbreviation for* multiple sclerosis (= a serious disease that gradually makes it difficult for a person to see, speak, or move)

MSc /ˌemesˈsiː/ *noun* [C] *abbreviation for* Master of Science: a higher university qualification in a science subject

MTV /ˌemtiːˈviː/ *noun* [U] *trademark abbreviation for* Music Television: an organization that broadcasts pop music around the world

○ⁿ**much¹** /mʌtʃ/ *quantifier* **1** QUESTION In questions, 'much' is used to ask about the amount of something. *Was there much food there?* ○ *How much money will I need for the taxi?* **2** NEGATIVE In negative sentences, 'much' is used to say that there is not a large amount of something. *She doesn't earn much money.* ○ *Pete didn't say much at dinner.* ○ *"Is there any coffee left?" "Not much."* **3 too much/so much** a large amount of something, often more than you want *I'd love to come, but I've got too much work.* ○ *We were having so much fun, I didn't want to go home.* **4** A LOT OF *formal* a lot of *Much work remains to be done.* ○ *Much of his evidence was unreliable.* **5 not much of a sth** used when you want to say that a person or thing is a bad example of something *I'm not much of a cook.* **6 not be up to much** *UK informal* to be of bad quality *Her latest novel isn't up to much.* ⊃See Common learner error at **many**.

○ⁿ**much²** /mʌtʃ/ *adverb* more, most **1** often or a lot *Do you go to London much?* ○ *I don't like curry very much.* **2** used before comparative adjectives (= adjectives like 'better' and 'smaller', that are used to compare things) to mean 'a lot' *Their old house was much bigger.* ○ *That's a much more sensible idea.* ○ *"Is her*

---

new car faster than her old one?" "Oh yes, much." ○ You look so much slimmer – have you lost weight?

muck¹ /mʌk/ noun [U] informal dirt You've got muck on your shoes.

muck² /mʌk/ verb
muck about/around mainly UK informal to behave stupidly and waste time Stop mucking around, will you! ○ Don't muck around with those knives, Josh.
muck sth up informal to do something badly, or to spoil something I mucked up the interview.

mucus /ˈmjuːkəs/ noun [U] a thick liquid produced inside the nose and other parts of the body Dairy products such as milk are said to increase mucus production.

o⊶mud /mʌd/ noun [U] a thick liquid mixture of soil and water, or this mixture after it has dried He'd been playing football and was covered in mud. ○ You've got mud all over your boots.

muddle¹ /ˈmʌdl/ noun [C, U] a situation of confusion or bad organization There was a big muddle over who was buying the tickets. ○ I'm in such a muddle with these bills. ○ We got ourselves in a terrible muddle with the paperwork.

muddle² /ˈmʌdl/ verb **get sb/sth muddled up** to think that a person or thing is someone or something else I often get Jonathan and his brother muddled up. ○ She gets a lot of words muddled up.
muddle through (sth) to manage to do something although you do not know how to do it well None of us has any formal training but somehow we muddle through.
muddle sth up to arrange things in the wrong order Please don't muddle up those books - I've just sorted them out.

muddled /ˈmʌdld/ adjective **1** A person who is muddled is confused. He became increasingly muddled as he grew older. ○ muddled thinking **2** Things that are muddled are badly organized. He left his clothes in a muddled pile in the corner.

muddy /ˈmʌdi/ adjective covered by or containing mud (= mixture of soil and water) a muddy stream ○ muddy boots ○ You've made the kitchen floor all muddy.

mudguard /ˈmʌdgɑːd/ UK (US fender) noun [C] a curved piece of metal or plastic fixed above a wheel of a bicycle or motorcycle to prevent water or dirt from hitting the person's legs a **front/rear mudguard**

muesli /ˈmjuːzli/ noun [U] a mixture of grains, dried fruit and nuts that people eat with milk in the morning I had my usual bowl of muesli for breakfast.

muffin

muffin UK,
English muffin US

muffin

muffin /ˈmʌfɪn/ noun [C] **1** a small, sweet cake a blueberry muffin **2** UK (US **English muffin**) a small, round, flat bread that is often eaten hot with butter toasted muffins

muffle /ˈmʌfl/ verb [T] to make a noise quieter and less clear The pillow muffled her screams. ● **muffled** adjective Muffled sounds cannot be heard clearly. a **muffled sound/voice** ○ a muffled scream/cry

muffler /ˈmʌflər/ US (UK **silencer**) noun [C] a part of a vehicle that reduces noise

mug¹ /mʌg/ noun [C] **1** a large cup with straight sides usually used for hot drinks a coffee mug ○ a steaming mug of tea **2** informal someone who is stupid and easily deceived I was such a mug to think he'd pay me back.

mug² /mʌg/ verb [T] mugging, past mugged to attack and rob someone in a public place [often passive] He was mugged as he walked across the park. ● **mugger** noun [C] someone who mugs people

mugging /ˈmʌgɪŋ/ noun [C, U] when someone is attacked in a public place and money, etc stolen from them

muggy /ˈmʌgi/ adjective When the weather is muggy, it is unpleasantly warm and the air contains a lot of water. a muggy afternoon

Muhammad /məˈhæməd/ noun another spelling of Mohammed (= the Arab holy man on whose life and teachings Islam is based)

mule /mjuːl/ noun [C] an animal whose mother is a horse and whose father is a donkey (= animal like a small horse)

mules /mjuːlz/ noun [plural] women's shoes that have no back ⊃See colour picture **Clothes** on page Centre 9.

mull /mʌl/ verb
mull sth over to think carefully about something for a long time, often before you make a decision

mullah /ˈmʌlə/ noun [C] a Muslim religious teacher or leader

multi- /mʌlti-/ prefix many a multi-millionaire ○ a multi-storey car park

multicultural /ˌmʌltiˈkʌltʃərəl/ adjective including people of different races and religions a **multicultural society**

multilingual /ˌmʌltiˈlɪŋgwəl/ adjective using or speaking more than two languages

M

multimedia /ˌmʌltiˈmiːdiə/ *adjective* [always before noun] Multimedia computers and programs use sound, pictures, film, and text. *multimedia software/technology*

multinational¹ /ˌmʌltiˈnæʃᵊnᵊl/ *adjective* active in several countries, or involving people from several countries *a multinational company/corporation*

multinational² /ˌmʌltiˈnæʃᵊnᵊl/ *noun* [C] a large company that produces goods or services in several countries

multiple¹ /ˈmʌltɪpl/ *adjective* with several parts *multiple injuries*

multiple² /ˈmʌltɪpl/ *noun* [C] a number that can be divided by another number an exact number of times *Nine is a multiple of three.*

,multiple 'choice *adjective* A multiple choice exam or question gives you different answers and you choose the correct one.

multiple sclerosis /ˌmʌltɪplskləˈrəʊsɪs/ *noun* [U] a serious disease that gradually makes it difficult for a person to see, speak, or move

multiplex /ˈmʌltipleks/ *noun* [C] a cinema which has separate screens and shows different films at the same time

multiplication /ˌmʌltɪplɪˈkeɪʃᵊn/ *noun* [U] the process of multiplying a number with other numbers

multiply /ˈmʌltɪplaɪ/ *verb* **1** [I, T] to increase by a large number, or to cause something to increase by a large number *In warm weather, germs multiply rapidly.* **2** [T] to add one number to itself a particular number of times *Three multiplied by six equals eighteen.*

multi-purpose /ˌmʌltiˈpɜːpəs/ *adjective* describes something that can be used in many different ways *a multi-purpose cleaning fluid*

multiracial /ˌmʌltiˈreɪʃᵊl/ *adjective* involving people from different races *a multiracial society*

multi-storey /ˌmʌltiˈstɔːri/ *UK* (*US* multistory) *adjective* describes a building with many floors *(UK) a multi-storey car park/(US) a multistory office building*

multitasking /ˌmʌltiˈtɑːskɪŋ/ *noun* [U] the ability of a person to do more than one thing at a time *It's often said that women are very good at multitasking.*

multitude /ˈmʌltɪtjuːd/ *noun* [C] *formal* a large number of people or things *a multitude of problems/questions*

◦⊶**mum** /mʌm/ *UK* (*US* mom) *noun* [C] *informal* mother *I asked my mum but she said no.* ○ *Can we go now, Mum?*

mumble /ˈmʌmbl/ *verb* [I, T] to speak too quietly and not clearly enough for someone to understand you *He mumbled something about it being a waste of time.*

mummy /ˈmʌmi/ *noun* [C] **1** *UK informal* (*US* mommy) a word for 'mother', used especially by children *Come here, Mummy!* ○ *My mummy and daddy came too.* **2** a dead body covered in cloth, especially from ancient Egypt

mumps /mʌmps/ *noun* [U] an illness that children get which makes the throat and neck swell *to have mumps*

munch /mʌnʃ/ *verb* [I, T] to eat something in a noisy way *She was sitting on the lawn munching an apple.*

mundane /mʌnˈdeɪn/ *adjective* ordinary, or not interesting *a mundane task/life*

municipal /mjuːˈnɪsɪpᵊl/ *adjective* [always before noun] relating to the government of a town or city *a municipal council/election*

munitions /mjuːˈnɪʃᵊnz/ *noun* [plural] bombs, guns, and other military equipment *a munitions factory*

mural /ˈmjʊərᵊl/ *noun* [C] a picture that is painted on a wall

> ▨▨ WORD PARTNERS FOR **murder**
>
> **commit** (a) murder ● the murder **of** sb ● a murder **charge / investigation / victim / weapon**

◦⊶**murder¹** /ˈmɜːdəʳ/ *noun* [C, U] **1** the crime of intentionally killing someone *to commit murder* ○ *She was charged with attempted murder.* ○ *a murder charge/trial* **2 be murder** *informal* to be unpleasant or cause difficulty *Driving in Chicago at rush hour is murder.*

◦⊶**murder²** /ˈmɜːdəʳ/ *verb* [T] to kill someone intentionally and illegally [often passive] *He was murdered by a former employee.*

murderer /ˈmɜːdᵊrəʳ/ *noun* [C] someone who has committed murder *a convicted murderer*

murderous /ˈmɜːdᵊrəs/ *adjective* [always before noun] likely to kill someone, or wanting to kill them *a murderous dictator/regime*

murky /ˈmɜːki/ *adjective* **1** secret, and involving dishonest or illegal activities *He has a murky past as an arms dealer.* ○ *the murky world of drug dealing* **2** dirty and dark *murky water*

murmur¹ /ˈmɜːməʳ/ *verb* [I, T] to speak quietly so that you can only be heard by someone near you *"Go to sleep now," she murmured.* ○ *He murmured a few words of sympathy.*

murmur² /ˈmɜːməʳ/ *noun* [C] the sound of something being said quietly *I could hear the low murmur of voices from behind the door.*

◦⊶**muscle¹** /ˈmʌsl/ *noun* **1** [C, U] one of many pieces of tissue in the body that are connected to bones and which produce movement by becoming longer or shorter *aching joints and muscles* ○ *stomach/thigh muscles* ○ *I think I may have pulled* (= injured) *a muscle.* **2** [U] the ability to control or influence people *political/military muscle*

muscle² /ˈmʌsl/ *verb*

muscle in to force yourself into an activity in which other people do not want you to be involved *How can we stop him muscling in on this project?*

muscular /ˈmʌskjələʳ/ *adjective* **1** having firm, strong muscles *muscular legs/arms* **2** relating to muscles *muscular aches/pains*

muse /mjuːz/ *verb* [I] *formal* to think carefully about something for a long time *I was just musing about relationships.*

◦⊶**museum** /mjuːˈziːəm/ *noun* [C] a building where you can look at important objects connected with art, history, or science *a museum of modern art*

mush /mʌʃ/ *noun* [U] *informal* food that is unpleasantly soft and wet, usually because it has been cooked for too long

mushroom[1] /ˈmʌʃruːm/ *noun* [C] a type of fungus (= organism like a plant) with a short stem and a round top, some types of which can be eaten *pasta with wild mushrooms*

mushroom

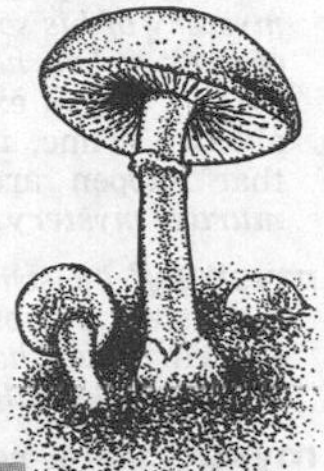

mushroom[2] /ˈmʌʃruːm/ *verb* [I] to increase or develop very quickly *mushrooming costs*

WORD PARTNERS FOR ***music***

compose/listen to/play music • **a piece of** music • **dance/pop/classical** music • **put on** some music

⊶**music** /ˈmjuːzɪk/ *noun* [U] **1** a pattern of sounds that is made by playing instruments or singing, or a recording of this ***pop/dance music*** ○ ***classical music*** ○ *He likes* ***listening to music****.* ○ *Could you* ***put on*** *some* ***music****?* ○ *a music festival* ○ *a music lesson/teacher* **2** written signs which represent sounds that can be sung or played with instruments *I never learnt to* ***read music*** (= understand written music). **3 face the music** to accept punishment or criticism for something bad that you have done ➲See also: **chamber music, country music, folk music.**

musical[1] /ˈmjuːzɪkəl/ *adjective* **1** [always before noun] relating to music *a* ***musical instrument*** **2** good at playing music *She comes from a very musical family.* • **musically** *adverb*

musical[2] /ˈmjuːzɪkəl/ *noun* [C] a play or film in which singing and dancing tell part of the story *a Broadway/Hollywood musical*

musician /mjuːˈzɪʃən/ *noun* [C] someone who plays a musical instrument, often as a job *a talented jazz/classical musician*

Muslim (*also* **Moslem**) /ˈmʊzlɪm/ [US] /ˈmʌzləm/ *noun* [C] someone who believes in Islam • **Muslim** *adjective a Muslim family*

muslin /ˈmʌzlɪn/ *noun* [U] a very thin cotton cloth

mussel /ˈmʌsəl/ *noun* [C] a small sea creature that has a black shell in two parts and that can be eaten

⊶**must**[1] *strong form* /mʌst/ *weak forms* /məst, məs/ *modal verb* **1** [NECESSARY] used to say that it is necessary that something happens or is done *The meat must be cooked thoroughly.* ○ *You mustn't show this letter to anyone else.* ○ *I must get some sleep.* **2** [LIKELY] used to show that you think something is very likely or certain to be true *You must be exhausted.* ○ *She must be very wealthy.* **3** [SUGGEST] used to show that you think it is a good idea for someone to do something *You must come and stay with us some time.* ➲See Extra help page **Modal verbs** on page Centre 22.

must[2] /mʌst/ *noun* **be a must** *informal* If something is a must, it is very important to have or do it. *The restaurant has become so popular that reservations are a must.*

mustache /məˈstɑːʃ/ [US] /ˈmʌstæʃ/ *noun* [C] *another US spelling of* moustache (= a line of hair above the mouth)

mustard /ˈmʌstəd/ *noun* [U] a thick, spicy, yellow or brown sauce often eaten in small amounts with meat *a teaspoon of mustard*

muster /ˈmʌstər/ (*also* **muster up**) *verb* [T] to get enough support, bravery, or energy to do something difficult *I hope she* ***musters*** *the* ***courage*** *to invite him for dinner.*

⊶**mustn't** /ˈmʌsənt/ *short for* must not *You mustn't let her know I'm coming.*

musty /ˈmʌsti/ *adjective* smelling old and slightly wet in an unpleasant way *a musty room* ○ *the* ***musty smell*** *of old books*

mutant /ˈmjuːtənt/ *noun* [C] an organism or cell that is different from others of the same type because of a change in its genes *a mutant virus*

mutation /mjuːˈteɪʃən/ *noun* [C, U] a permanent change in the genes of an organism, or an organism with such a change *The disease is caused by a mutation in a single gene.*

mute /mjuːt/ *adjective* **1** expressed in thoughts but not in speech or writing *The president has* ***remained mute*** *about whether he will resign.* ○ *I gazed at her in* ***mute admiration****.* **2** unable to speak for physical or mental reasons *a school for deaf and mute children*

muted /ˈmjuːtɪd/ *adjective* **1** [FEELING] not strongly expressed *a* ***muted response/reaction*** ○ ***muted criticism*** **2** [SOUND] A muted sound is quieter than usual. ***muted voices*** **3** [COLOUR] [always before noun] A muted colour is not bright or easily noticed.

mutilate /ˈmjuːtɪleɪt/ *verb* [T] to damage someone's body violently and severely, often by cutting off a part of it *a* ***mutilated body/corpse*** • **mutilation** /ˌmjuːtɪˈleɪʃən/ *noun* [C, U]

mutiny /ˈmjuːtɪni/ *noun* [C, U] when a group of people, usually soldiers or sailors, refuse to obey orders, often because they want to be in control themselves • **mutiny** *verb* [I] to take part in a mutiny

mutt /mʌt/ *noun* [C] *informal* a dog that is a mixture of different breeds (= types)

mutter /ˈmʌtər/ *verb* [I, T] to speak quietly so that your voice is difficult to hear, often when complaining about something *She walked past me,* ***muttering to herself****.* ○ *He muttered* ***something about*** *the restaurant being too expensive.* • **mutter** *noun* [C]

mutton /ˈmʌtən/ *noun* [U] **1** meat from an adult sheep *a leg/shoulder of mutton* **2 mutton dressed as lamb** *UK informal* an older woman who wears clothes that would be more suitable for a young woman

mutual /ˈmjuːtʃuəl/ *adjective* **1** When two or more people have a mutual feeling, they have the same opinion about each other. ***mutual admiration/respect*** ○ *He doesn't like her, and I suspect* ***the feeling's mutual****.* **2** When two or more people have a mutual friend or interest, they have the same one. *Andrew and Jean*

M

*were introduced to each other by a **mutual friend**.*

mutually /ˈmjuːtʃuəli/ *adverb* You use mutually before an adjective when the adjective describes all sides of a situation. *a **mutually dependent** relationship ○ Being attractive and intelligent are not **mutually exclusive** (= someone can be attractive and intelligent).*

muzzle[1] /ˈmʌzl/ *noun* [C] **1** the mouth and nose of a dog, or a covering put over these to prevent the dog biting **2** the open end of the long cylindrical part of a gun

muzzle[2] /ˈmʌzl/ *verb* [T] **1** to put a muzzle on a dog **2** to prevent someone expressing their own opinions

⚬**my** /maɪ/ *determiner* belonging to or relating to the person who is speaking or writing *Tom's my older son. ○ It's not my fault. ○ My house is near the station.*

MYOB *Internet abbreviation for* mind your own business: used in emails and text messages to say rudely that you do not want to talk about something

myriad /ˈmɪriəd/ *adjective literary* very many *myriad problems* ● myriad *noun* [C] *literary Digital technology resulted in **a myriad of** (= many) new TV channels.*

⚬**myself** /maɪˈself/ *pronoun* **1** the reflexive form of the pronouns 'me' or 'I' *I've bought myself a new coat. ○ I looked at myself in the mirror.* **2** used to emphasize the pronoun 'I', especially when the speaker wants to talk about their actions and not someone else's *I'll tell her myself. ○ Jack always drinks red wine but I prefer white myself.* **3** (all) by myself alone or without anyone else's help *I live by myself in a small flat. ○ Mummy, I got dressed all by myself.* **4** (all) to myself for my use only *I'll have the flat all to myself this weekend.*

mysterious /mɪˈstɪəriəs/ *adjective* **1** strange or unknown, and not explained or understood *a mysterious stranger ○ the mysterious death of her son* **2** refusing to talk about something and behaving in a secretive way *Nick is being very mysterious about where he's going on holiday.* ● mysteriously *adverb to disappear/vanish mysteriously*

WORD PARTNERS FOR ***mystery***

explain/solve/unravel a mystery ● the mystery surrounding sth ● an unexplained/unsolved mystery ● the mystery of sth ● be a mystery to sb

mystery[1] /ˈmɪstᵊri/ *noun* **1** [C, U] something strange or unknown that cannot be explained or understood *an **unsolved mystery** ○ He never gave up hope that he would **solve the mystery** of his son's disappearance. ○ He's out of work, so how he pays his rent is **a mystery to me** (= I cannot explain it).* **2** [C] a story, often about a crime, in which the strange events that happen are explained at the end *a murder mystery*

mystery[2] /ˈmɪstᵊri/ *adjective* [always before noun] A mystery person or thing is one who is unknown. *I saw her with a mystery man in a restaurant last night.*

mystic /ˈmɪstɪk/ *noun* [C] someone who attempts to be united with God through prayer

mystical /ˈmɪstɪkᵊl/ (*also* mystic) *adjective* **1** relating to the religious beliefs and activities of mystics **2** involving magical or spiritual powers that are not understood

mysticism /ˈmɪstɪsɪzᵊm/ *noun* [U] the religious beliefs and activities of mystics

mystify /ˈmɪstɪfaɪ/ *verb* [T] If something mystifies someone, they cannot understand or explain it because it is confusing or complicated. [often passive] *I was mystified by the decision.*

mystique /mɪˈstiːk/ *noun* [U] a mysterious quality that makes a person or thing seem interesting or special *the mystique of the princess*

WORD PARTNERS FOR ***myth***

2 debunk/dispel/explode a myth (= show that an idea is not true) ● a common/popular myth ● the myth of sth

myth /mɪθ/ *noun* [C] **1** an ancient story about gods and brave people, often one that explains an event in history or the natural world *a Greek myth* **2** an idea that is not true but is believed by many people *It's a myth that men are better drivers than women.*

mythical /ˈmɪθɪkᵊl/ (*also* mythic) *adjective* **1** existing in a myth *a mythical character* **2** imaginary or not true

mythology /mɪˈθɒlədʒi/ *noun* [U] myths, often those relating to a single religion or culture *classical mythology ○ the mythology of the ancient Greeks* ● mythological /ˌmɪθᵊlˈɒdʒɪkᵊl/ *adjective*

Nn

N, n /en/ the fourteenth letter of the alphabet

N/A (*also US* NA) *written abbreviation for* not applicable: used on official forms to show that you do not need to answer a question

naff /næf/ *adjective UK informal* silly and not fashionable *naff lyrics*

nag /næg/ *verb* [I, T] **nagging** *past* **nagged** to keep criticizing or giving advice to someone in an annoying way *They keep nagging me about going to university.*
nag (away) at sb If doubts or worries nag at you, you think about them all the time. *The same thought has been nagging away at me since last week.*

nagging /ˈnægɪŋ/ *adjective* [always before noun] Nagging doubts or worries make you worried and you cannot forget them. *a nagging doubt*

◌**nail¹** /neɪl/ *noun* [C] **1** a thin piece of metal with a sharp end, used to join pieces of wood together *a hammer and nails* **2** the hard surface at the end of your fingers and toes *fingernails/toenails* ○ *to cut your nails* ○ *nail clippers/scissors* ○ *Stop biting your nails.* **3** hit the nail on the head to describe exactly what is causing a situation or problem **4** the final nail in the coffin an event which causes the failure of something that had already started to fail *This latest evidence could be the final nail in the coffin for Jackson's case.*

nail

nail² /neɪl/ *verb* **1** nail sth down/on/to, etc to fasten something with nails *There was a 'private property' sign nailed to the tree.* **2** [T] *mainly US informal* to catch someone who has committed a crime *They eventually **nailed** him for handling stolen goods.*
nail sb down to make someone give you exact details or a decision about something
nail sth down *US* to understand something completely, or to describe something correctly *We haven't been able to nail down the cause of the fire yet.*

ˈnail ˌbrush *noun* [C] a small brush, used for cleaning your nails ⊃See colour picture **The Bathroom** on page Centre 3.

ˈnail ˌpolish (*also UK* **ˈnail ˌvarnish**) *noun* [U] paint that you put on your nails

naive /naɪˈiːv/ *adjective* If someone is naive, they believe things too easily and do not have enough experience of the world. *I was much younger then, and very naive.* • **naively** *adverb I naively believed that we would be treated as equals.* • **naivety** /naɪˈiːvəti/ *noun* [U] the quality of being naive

◌**naked** /ˈneɪkɪd/ *adjective* **1** not wearing clothes or not covered by anything *a naked thigh/shoulder* ○ *He was **stark naked** (= completely naked).* **2** [always before noun] A naked feeling or quality is not hidden, although it is bad. *naked aggression* **3** the naked eye If something can be seen by the naked eye, it is big enough to be seen without special equipment.

◌**name¹** /neɪm/ *noun* **1** [C] the word or group of words that is used to refer to a person, thing, or place *What's your name?* ○ *My name's Alexis.* ○ *I can't remember the name of the street he lives on.* ○ *He didn't mention her **by name** (= he did not say her name).* **2** in the name of sth If bad things are done in the name of something, they are done in order to help that thing succeed. *So much blood has been spilt in the name of religion.* **3** a bad/good name If things or people have a bad/good name, people have a bad/good opinion of them. *Their behaviour gives us all a bad name.* **4** call sb names to use impolite or unpleasant words to describe someone **5** make a name for yourself to become famous or respected by a lot of people **6** the name of the game the main purpose or most important part of an activity *Popularity is the name of the game in television.* ⊃See also: **brand name, Christian name, family name, first name, last name, maiden name, middle name.**

◌**name²** /neɪm/ *verb* [T] **1** ⌜GIVE A NAME⌝ to give someone or something a name [+ two objects] *We named our first son Mike.* ○ *A young boy named Peter answered the phone.* **2** ⌜SAY NAME⌝ to say what the name of someone or something is [often passive] *The dead man has been **named as** John Kramer.* ○ *She cannot be named for legal reasons.* **3** ⌜ANNOUNCE⌝ to announce who has got a new job or won a prize [+ two objects] *She has been named manager of the new Edinburgh branch.* **4** you name it something that you say which means anything you say or choose *I've never seen such a wide selection. You name it, they've got it.* **5** name and shame *UK* to publicly say that a person or business has done something wrong
name sb after sb to give someone the same name as someone else *We named him after my wife's brother.*

nameless /ˈneɪmləs/ *adjective* If someone or something is nameless, they have no name or their name is not known. *a nameless soldier* ⊃Compare **unnamed.**

namely /ˈneɪmli/ *adverb* a word used when you are going to give more detail about something you have just said *She learned an important lesson from failing that exam, namely that nothing is ever certain.*

namesake /ˈneɪmseɪk/ *noun* [C] **your namesake** someone who has the same name as you

nan /næːn/ *noun* [C] *UK informal* grandmother

nanny /ˈnæni/ *noun* [C] someone whose job is to look after a family's children

nano- /ˈnænəʊ-/ *prefix* **1** extremely small *nano-*

N

technology **2** one billionth (= a thousand millionth) *a nanosecond*

nap /næp/ *noun* [C] a short sleep *He likes to have/ take a nap after lunch.* • **nap** *verb* [I] napping, *past* napped

nape /neɪp/ *noun* [C] the back of your neck

napkin /'næpkɪn/ (*also UK* **serviette**) *noun* [C] a piece of cloth or paper used when you eat to keep your clothes clean and to clean your mouth and hands *a paper napkin*

nappy /'næpi/ *UK* (*US* **diaper**) *noun* [C] a thick piece of paper or cloth worn by a baby on its bottom ***disposable nappies*** ○ *to* **change a nappy**

narcissism /'nɑːsɪsɪzᵊm/ *noun* [U] *formal* great interest in and pleasure at your own appearance and qualities • **narcissistic** /,nɑːsɪ'sɪstɪk/ *adjective* If people or their actions are narcissistic, they show narcissism.

narcotic /nɑː'kɒtɪk/ *noun* [C] a drug that stops you feeling pain or makes you sleep, and that is addictive (= difficult to stop using)

narrate /nə'reɪt/ *verb* [T] *formal* to tell the story in a book, film, play, etc *'Peter and the Wolf,' narrated by actress Glenn Close* • **narration** /nə'reɪʃᵊn/ *noun* [U] *formal*

narrative /'nærətɪv/ *noun* [C] *formal* a story or description of a series of events

narrator /nə'reɪtᵊr/ *noun* [C] the person who tells the story in a book, film, play, etc

narrow

wide

o⌐**narrow¹** /'nærəʊ/ *adjective* **1** Narrow things measure a small distance from one side to the other. *a narrow lane/street* ○ *a narrow tie* **2** including only a small number *He has* **very narrow interests.** **3** **a narrow defeat/victory** If you have a narrow defeat/victory, you only just lose/win. **4** **a narrow escape** If you have a narrow escape, you only just avoid danger.

narrow² /'nærəʊ/ *verb* [I, T] **1** to become less wide or to make something less wide *The road has been narrowed to one lane.* **2** to become less or to make something become less *to narrow the gap between rich and poor*

narrow sth down to make something, for example a list or a choice, smaller and clearer by removing the things that are less important

We've managed to narrow the list down to four.

narrowly /'nærəʊli/ *adverb* only by a small amount *A tile fell off the roof,* **narrowly missing** *my head.*

narrow-minded /,nærəʊ'maɪndɪd/ *adjective* not willing to accept new ideas or opinions different from your own

nasal /'neɪzᵊl/ *adjective* relating to the nose *the* **nasal passages**

nascent /'næsᵊnt/, /'neɪsᵊnt/ *adjective formal* starting to develop *a nascent democracy*

nasty /'nɑːsti/ *adjective* **1** [BAD] very bad *a nasty shock/surprise* ○ *a nasty smell/taste* ○ *a nasty cut/burn* **2** [UNKIND] unkind *She's always being* **nasty to** *her little brother.* **3** [ANGRY] very angry or violent *When I asked for the money, he turned really nasty.* • **nastiness** *noun* [U]

⁙⁙⁙ WORD PARTNERS FOR *nation*

a   **civilized/industrialized/poor/powerful** nation • **govern/lead** a nation • **across** the nation • a nation **of** sth

---

o⌐**nation** /'neɪʃᵊn/ *noun* [C] a country or the people living in a country *Asian nations* ○ *industrial nations* ○ *The entire nation mourned her death.* ○ *a nation of dog lovers.* ⊅See Common learner error at **country** ⊅See also: **the United Nations**.

o⌐**national¹** /'næʃᵊnᵊl/ *adjective* **1** relating to the whole of a country *to threaten* **national security** ○ *a sense of national identity* ○ *a national newspaper* ○ **national elections** ○ *His income is way above the national average.* ○ *Gambling is a national pastime* (= many people do it) *here.* **2** [always before noun] connected with the traditions of a particular nation *national dress/customs* • **nationally** *adverb*

national² /'næʃᵊnᵊl/ *noun* [C] someone who officially belongs to a particular country *a British/ Chinese national*

national 'anthem *noun* [C] the official song of a country, played at public events

the ,National 'Health Service *noun* the system providing free medical services in the UK

,national 'holiday (*also US* **federal holiday**) *noun* [C] a day when most people in a country do not have to work

,National In'surance *noun* [U] the system in the UK in which people regularly pay money to the government in order to help people who are ill or have no work

nationalism /'næʃᵊnᵊlɪzᵊm/ *noun* [U] **1** a feeling of pride in your own country **2** the belief that a particular area should have its own government *Welsh nationalism*

nationalist /'næʃᵊnᵊlɪst/ *noun* [C] someone who wants a particular area to have its own government

nationalistic /,næʃᵊnᵊl'ɪstɪk/ *adjective* having a lot of pride, often too much pride, in your own country *nationalistic fervour*

nationality /,næʃᵊn'æləti/ *noun* [C, U] If you have American/British/Swiss, etc nationality, you are legally a member of that country. *What nationality is she?* ○ *She has* **dual nationality** (= nationality of two countries).

| ɑː arm | ɜː her | iː see | ɔː saw | uː too | aɪ my | aʊ how | eə hair | eɪ day | əʊ no | ɪə near | ɔɪ boy | ʊə poor | aɪə fire | aʊə sour |

nationalize /'næʃᵊnᵊlaɪz/ *verb* [T] If private companies are nationalized, the government takes control of them. ● **nationalization** /,næʃᵊnᵊlaɪ'zeɪʃᵊn/ *noun* [U]

,**national 'park** *noun* [C] a large area of park for use by the public, usually an area of special beauty

,**national 'service** *noun* [U] the period of time young people in some countries have to spend in the army

nationwide /,neɪʃᵊn'waɪd/ *adjective, adverb* including all parts of a country *a nationwide campaign* ○ *Surveys have been carried out nationwide.*

native¹ /'neɪtɪv/ *adjective* **1** [BORN IN] [always before noun] Your native town or country is the place where you were born. *It was a custom in his native Algeria.* ○ *She is a native-born Texan.* **2** [LANGUAGE] [always before noun] Your native language is the first language you learn. **3** [PEOPLE] [always before noun] relating to the people who lived in a country first, before other people took control of it *the native inhabitants/population* **4** [ANIMALS AND PLANTS] Native animals or plants live or grow naturally in a place, and have not been brought from somewhere else. *a large bird native to Europe*

native² /'neɪtɪv/ *noun* [C] **1** someone who was born in a particular place *He's a native of Texas.* **2** an old-fashioned and often offensive word for a person who lived in a country, for example an African country, before Europeans went there

,**Native A'merican** *adjective* relating or belonging to the original group of people who lived in North America ● **Native American** *noun* [C]

,**native 'speaker** *noun* [C] someone who speaks a language as their first language

NATO (*also UK* Nato) /'neɪtəʊ/ *noun abbreviation for* North Atlantic Treaty Organization: an international military organization formed in 1949 to improve the defence of Western Europe

natter /'nætər/ *verb* [I] *mainly UK informal* to talk about things that are not important ● **natter** *noun* [no plural] *UK* to **have a natter**

o⌐**natural** /'nætʃᵊrᵊl/ *adjective* **1** [NATURE] Something that is natural exists or happens because of nature, not because it was made or done by people. *natural gas/resources* ○ *natural beauty* ○ *to die of natural causes* (= because you are ill or old) ○ *This product contains only natural ingredients.* **2** [NORMAL] normal or expected *a natural impulse/instinct* ○ *It's perfectly natural to feel nervous.* ⊃Opposite **unnatural. 3** [FROM BIRTH] If you have a natural characteristic, it is something you have been born with. *a natural talent* ○ *She's a natural athlete/blonde.* ● **naturalness** *noun* [U]

,**natural 'gas** *noun* [U] a gas that is found under the ground and is used for cooking and heating

,**natural 'history** *noun* [U] the study of animals and plants

naturalist /'nætʃᵊrᵊlɪst/ *noun* [C] someone who studies animals and plants

naturalistic /,nætʃᵊrᵊl'ɪstɪk/ *adjective* Naturalistic art, writing, or acting tries to show things as they really are.

naturalize /'nætʃᵊrᵊlaɪz/ *verb* **be naturalized** to officially become a member of another country *a naturalized US citizen* ● **naturalization** /,nætʃᵊrᵊlaɪ'zeɪʃᵊn/ *noun* [U]

naturally /'nætʃᵊrᵊli/ *adverb* **1** [AS EXPECTED] as you would expect *Naturally, he was very disappointed.* **2** [NORMALLY] in a normal way *Relax and try to behave naturally.* **3** [FROM BIRTH] having been born with a characteristic *naturally aggressive/funny/slim* **4** [NATURE] Something that exists or happens naturally is part of nature and not made or done by people. *Organic tomatoes are grown naturally without chemical fertilizers.*

,**natural 'sciences** *noun* [plural] sciences that relate to the physical world such as biology, chemistry, and physics

,**natural se'lection** *noun* [U] the way that plants and animals die when they are weak or not suitable for the place where they live, while stronger ones continue to exist

---

WORD PARTNERS FOR *nature*

? in sb's nature ● [happy/optimistic, etc.] by nature

---

o⌐**nature** /'neɪtʃər/ *noun* **1** [PLANTS AND ANIMALS] [U] all the plants, creatures, substances, and forces that exist in the universe, which are not made by people *the laws of nature* ○ *I like to get out and enjoy nature.* ○ *a nature trail* **2** [CHARACTER] [no plural] someone's character *I didn't think it was in his nature to behave like that.* **3** [TYPE] [no plural] *formal* type *What exactly is the nature of your business?* ○ *I don't like hunting and things of that nature.* ⊃See also: **human nature, second nature.**

COMMON LEARNER ERROR

nature, the environment and countryside

Nature means all the things in the world which exist naturally and were not created by people.

He's interested in wildlife and anything to do with nature.

The environment means the land, water, and air that animals and plants live in. It is usually used when talking about the way people use or damage the natural world.

The government has introduced new policies to protect the environment.

Countryside means land where there are no towns or cities.

I love walking in the countryside.

'**nature re,serve** *noun* [C] a place where animals and plants live and are protected

naught *old-fashioned* (*also UK* nought) /nɔːt/ *noun* [U] nothing

naughty /'nɔːti/ *adjective* **1** If a child is naughty, they behave badly. *a naughty little boy/girl* **2** a word used humorously to describe things that are sexual *naughty films/magazines*

nausea /'nɔːziə/ *noun* [U] the unpleasant feeling

of wanting to vomit *She was hit by a sudden wave of nausea.*

nauseating /ˈnɔːsieɪtɪŋ/ *adjective* If something is nauseating, it makes you want to vomit. *a nauseating smell*

nauseous /ˈnɔːsiəs/ *adjective* If you feel nauseous, you feel like you might vomit, and if something is nauseous, it makes you want to vomit.

nautical /ˈnɔːtɪkᵊl/ *adjective* relating to boats or sailing *a nautical mile*

naval /ˈneɪvᵊl/ *adjective* [always before noun] relating to the navy *a naval base/officer*

navel /ˈneɪvᵊl/ *noun* [C] the small, round, and usually hollow place on your stomach, where you were connected to your mother before birth

navigable /ˈnævɪgəbl/ *adjective* If an area of water is navigable, it is wide, deep, and safe enough to sail a boat on.

navigate /ˈnævɪgeɪt/ *verb* 1 [WITH MAP] [I, T] to find the right direction to travel by using maps or other equipment *He navigated the ship back to Plymouth.* ○ *We navigated using a map and compass.* ○ *I drive and he navigates.* 2 [BOAT] [T] to successfully sail along an area of water 3 [DIFFICULT JOURNEY] [T] to find your way through a difficult place *We had to navigate several flights of stairs.* 4 [SYSTEM] [T] to successfully use a complicated system *to navigate a website* ● **navigation** /ˌnævɪˈgeɪʃᵊn/ *noun* [U] ● **navigator** *noun* [C] a person who navigates

navy /ˈneɪvi/ *noun* 1 **the Navy** ships and soldiers used for fighting wars at sea *to be in the navy* 2 [U] (*also* ˌnavy 'blue) a very dark blue colour ⊃See colour picture **Colours** on page Centre 12.

Nazi /ˈnɑːtsi/ *noun* [C] someone who supported the ideas of Hitler in Germany in the 1930s and 1940s *Nazi propaganda*

nb, NB /ˌenˈbiː/ used to tell the reader that a particular piece of information is very important

o➤**near¹** /nɪəʳ/ *adverb, preposition* 1 [DISTANCE] not far away in distance *Could you come a bit nearer, please?* ○ *I stood near the window.* ○ *Are you going anywhere near the post office?* 2 be/come near to doing sth to almost achieve or do something *This is the nearest I've ever got to winning anything.* ○ *He came near to punching him.* 3 [STATE] If something or someone is near a particular state, they are almost in that state. *She looked near exhaustion.* ○ *She was near to tears* (= almost crying) *when I told her.* 4 [TIME] not far away in time *She shouldn't be partying so near her exams.* ○ *We can decide nearer the time.* 5 [SIMILAR] similar *The feelings I had were near hysteria.* ○ *He is Russia's nearest thing to a rock legend.* 6 nowhere near not close in distance, amount, time, or quality *It wasn't me - I was nowhere near him.* ○ *That's nowhere near enough for six people.* ○ *It was nowhere near as difficult as I thought it would be.* 7 near enough almost *The books were ordered near enough alphabetically.*

o➤**near²** /nɪəʳ/ *adjective* 1 not far away in distance or time *The school's very near.* ○ *The nearest garage is 10 miles away.* ○ *The baby's due date*

was getting nearer. 2 **in the near future** at a time that is not far away *Space travel may become very common in the near future.* ⊃See also: a near **miss²**.

near³ /nɪəʳ/ *verb* [T] to get close to something in distance or time *The building work is nearing completion at last.*

nearby /nɪəˈbaɪ/ *adjective, adverb* not far away *a nearby town/village*

o➤**nearly** /ˈnɪəli/ *adverb* 1 almost *It's nearly three weeks since I last saw her.* ○ *Nearly all the food had gone when I arrived.* ○ *She nearly drowned when she was eight.* ○ *I'll be with you in a minute - I've nearly finished.* 2 not nearly (as/so) a lot less *It's not nearly as expensive as I thought.*

nearsighted /ˌnɪəˈsaɪtɪd/ *US* (*UK* short-sighted) *adjective* If you are nearsighted, you cannot see things very well if they are too far away.

neat /niːt/ *adjective* 1 [TIDY] tidy and clean *He always looks very neat and tidy.* 2 [GOOD] *US informal* good *That's really neat.* ○ *What a neat idea.* 3 [ALCOHOL] A neat alcoholic drink is drunk on its own, and not mixed with any other liquid.

neatly /ˈniːtli/ *adverb* in a tidy way *neatly dressed* ○ *a neatly folded pile of clothes*

necessarily /ˌnesəˈserᵊli/ *adverb* not necessarily not for certain *That's not necessarily true.* ○ *I know she doesn't say much, but it doesn't necessarily mean she's not interested.*

The verbs **need** and **require** and the modal verb **must** are very commonly used to show that something is necessary: *The meat must be cooked thoroughly.* ● *Does she have the skills needed/required for work of that sort?*

If something is very important and necessary, you can use adjectives such as **essential**, **fundamental**, and **indispensable**: *Some understanding of grammar is essential/fundamental to learning a language.* ● *This book is an indispensable resource for teachers.*

The expression **be a must** is sometimes used in informal situations to describe things that are very necessary to have or do: *If you live in the country a car is a must.*

o➤**necessary** /ˈnesəsᵊri/ *adjective* needed in order to achieve something [+ to do sth] *Is it really necessary to give so much detail?* ○ *Does he have the necessary skills and experience?* ○ *The police are prepared to use force, if necessary.* ⊃Opposite **unnecessary**.

necessitate /nəˈsesɪteɪt/ *verb* [T] *formal* to make something necessary

out of necessity ● the necessity for/of sth ● financial necessity

necessity /nəˈsesəti/ *noun* 1 [U] the need for something *There's no financial necessity for her to work.* ○ *Sewing is something I do out of necessity, not for pleasure.* 2 [C] something you need *Most people seem to consider a car a necessity, not a luxury.*

○—**neck** /nek/ *noun* [C] **1** the part of the body between your head and your shoulders *He was wearing a gold chain around his neck.* ➔See colour picture **The Body** on page Centre 13. **2** the part of a piece of clothing that goes around your neck *a polo-neck/V-neck jumper* **3** **be breathing down sb's neck** to watch what someone does all the time in a way that annoys them *The last thing I want is a boss breathing down my neck.* **4** **neck and neck** If two people who are competing are neck and neck, they are very close and either of them could win. **5** **be up to your neck (in sth)** to be very busy ➔See also: **polo neck**, by the **scruff** of the/your neck.

necklace /'nekləs/ *noun* [C] a piece of jewellery that you wear around your neck *a pearl necklace* ➔See picture at **jewellery**.

neckline /'neklaɪn/ *noun* [C] the shape made by the edge of a dress or shirt at the front of the neck *a low neckline*

nectar /'nektə^r/ *noun* [U] a sweet liquid produced by plants and collected by bees

nectarine /'nektə^rri:n/ *noun* [C] a soft, round fruit which is sweet and juicy and has a smooth red and yellow skin

née /neɪ/ *adjective* [always before noun] a word used to introduce the family name that a woman had before she got married *Margaret Hughes, née Johnson*

○—**need**[1] /ni:d/ *verb* [T] **1** If you need something, you must have it, and if you need to do something, you must do it. *I need some new shoes.* ○ *The country still desperately needs help.* ○ [+ to do sth] *If there's anything else you need to know, just give me a call.* ○ *We need you to look after the children for us.* **2** **don't need to do sth/ needn't do sth** used in order to say that someone does not have to do something or should not do something *You didn't need to come all this way.* ○ *You don't need to be frightened.* ○ *She needn't have taken him to the hospital.* **3** If something needs something to be done to it, that thing should be done in order to improve it. *Do the clothes on this chair need washing?* ○ *The car needs to be serviced.* **4** **There needs to be sth** used to say that something is necessary *There needs to be more funding for education in this country.*

COMMON LEARNER ERROR

needed or **necessary**?

It is not usual to use 'needed' as an adjective. We usually say **necessary** instead.

He gave us the necessary information.

~~He gave us the needed information.~~

📖 WORD PARTNERS FOR *need* (noun)

identify a need • **meet** a need (= provide what is needed) • **a need for** sth

○—**need**[2] /ni:d/ *noun* **1** [no plural] something that is necessary to have or do *There's an urgent need for more medical supplies.* ○ [+ to do sth] *Is there any need to change the current system?*

○ *There's really no need for that sort of behaviour.* **2** **be in need of sth** to need something *My car's in desperate need of repair.*

needle /'ni:dl/ *noun*

[C] **1** MEDICAL the thin, sharp, metal part of a piece of medical equipment used to take blood out of the body, or to put medicine or drugs in **2** SEWING a thin, pointed metal object with a small hole at one end for thread, used for sewing *a needle and thread* **3** MEASURING a thin, pointed piece of metal or plastic that moves to point to numbers on equipment used for measuring things ➔See also: **pins and needles**

needle

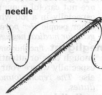

needless /'ni:dləs/ *adjective* not necessary *a needless expense* ○ **Needless to say** (= as you would expect), *it rained the whole time we were there.* • **needlessly** *adverb*

○—**needn't** /'ni:d^ənt/ *short for* need not *You needn't have come.*

needs /ni:dz/ *noun* [plural] the things you need in order to have a good life *her emotional needs* ○ *The city is struggling to meet the needs of its homeless people.*

needy /'ni:di/ *adjective* Needy people do not have enough money. *The mayor wants to establish permanent housing for the needy.*

negate /nɪ'geɪt/ *verb* [T] *formal* to make something lose its effect or value • **negation** /nɪ'geɪʃ^ən/ *noun* [U] *formal*

○—**negative**[1] /'negətɪv/ *adjective* **1** NO ENTHUSIASM not having enthusiasm or positive opinions about something *negative feelings* ○ *Many people have a negative attitude towards ageing.* **2** BAD A negative effect is bad and causes damage to something. *Terrorist threats have had a very negative impact on tourism.* **3** MEDICINE If the result of a test to prove if someone is pregnant or ill is negative, that person is not pregnant or ill. **4** NUMBERS A negative number is less than zero. **5** GRAMMAR In language, a negative word or phrase expresses the meaning 'no' or 'not'.

negative[2] /'negətɪv/ *noun* [C] **1** a piece of film from which a photograph can be produced, where dark areas look light and light areas look dark **2** a word or phrase which expresses the meaning 'no' or 'not'

negatively /'negətɪvli/ *adverb* **1** without enthusiasm or positive opinions to **react/respond negatively** **2** with a bad effect *negatively affected*

negativity /ˌnegə'tɪvəti/ *noun* [U] when you do not feel enthusiastic or positive about things

neglect[1] /nɪ'glekt/ *verb* [T] **1** to not give enough care or attention to something or someone *to neglect your appearance/the garden* ○ [often passive] *Some of these kids have been badly neglected in the past.* ○ *neglected children* **2** **neglect to do sth** to not do something, often intentionally *He neglected to mention the fact that we could lose money on the deal.*

neglect[2] /nɪ'glekt/ *noun* [U] when you do not

N

give enough care or attention to something or someone *to suffer years of neglect*

negligence /'neglɪdʒəns/ *noun* [U] when you are not careful enough in something you do, especially in a job where your actions affect other people *Her parents plan to sue the surgeon for medical negligence.*

negligent /'neglɪdʒənt/ *adjective* not giving enough care or attention to a job or activity, especially where your actions affect someone else *The report found him negligent in his duties.*

negligible /'neglɪdʒəbl/ *adjective* small and not important *a negligible effect/result*

negotiable /nɪ'gəʊʃiəbl/ *adjective* If something is negotiable, it is not completely fixed, and can be changed after discussion. *The January deadline is not negotiable.*

negotiate /nɪ'gəʊʃieɪt/ *verb* 1 [I, T] to try to make or change an agreement by discussion *to negotiate with employers about working conditions* 2 [T] to successfully move around, through, or past something *to negotiate your way around/through a city* • **negotiator** *noun* [C] *a peace negotiator*

🧩 WORD PARTNERS FOR *negotiation*

enter into/be in negotiations • negotiations **break down/fail** • negotiations **about/on/over** sth • negotiations **with** sb • negotiations **between** sb and sb

negotiation /nɪ,gəʊʃi'eɪʃən/ *noun* [C, U] when people try to make or change an agreement by discussion *Peace negotiations are due to start.*

Negro /'niːgrəʊ/ *noun* [C] *plural* **Negroes** *old-fashioned* a word that means a black person, which some people think is offensive

⚬ᴬ **neighbour** UK (US **neighbor**) /'neɪbəʳ/ *noun* [C] 1 someone who lives very near you, especially in the next house *Our **next-door neighbours** are always arguing.* 2 someone or something that is near or next to someone or something else *The French make more films than their European neighbours.*

neighbourhood UK (US **neighborhood**) /'neɪbəhʊd/ *noun* [C] an area of a town or city that people live in *I grew up in a very poor neighbourhood.* ○ *Are there any good restaurants **in the neighbourhood** (= in this area)?*

neighbouring UK (US **neighboring**) /'neɪbʳrɪŋ/ *adjective* [always before noun] near or next to somewhere *neighbouring countries/villages*

⚬ᴬ **neither¹** /'naɪðəʳ, 'niːðəʳ/ *adverb* used to say that a negative fact is also true of someone or something else *Jerry doesn't like it, and neither do I.* ○ *She's not very tall and neither is her husband.*

⚬ᴬ **neither²** /'naɪðəʳ, 'niːðəʳ/ *pronoun, determiner* not either of two people or things *Luckily, neither child was hurt in the accident.* ○ **Neither of** us had ever been to London before. ○ *They gave us two keys, but neither worked.*

⚬ᴬ **neither³** /'naɪðəʳ, 'niːðəʳ/ *conjunction* **neither ... nor** used when a negative fact is true of two people or things or when someone or something does not have either of two qualities *Neither he nor his mother would talk to the police.*

○ *Their performance was neither entertaining nor educational.*

COMMON LEARNER ERROR

Neither...nor

This expression can be used with a singular or plural verb.

Neither Jack nor Philip likes/like football.

neo- /'niːəʊ-/ *prefix* new *neo-facists*

neon /'niːɒn/ *noun* [U] a gas that produces bright, colourful light when electricity passes through it, often used in signs *neon lights/signs*

nephew /'nefjuː/ *noun* [C] the son of your brother or sister, or the son of your husband's or wife's brother or sister

Neptune /'neptjuːn/ *noun* [no plural] the planet that is eighth from the Sun, after Uranus and before Pluto

nerd /nɜːd/ *noun* [C] *informal* someone, especially a man, who is not fashionable and who is interested in boring things • **nerdy** *adjective informal* boring and not fashionable

nerve /nɜːv/ *noun* 1 PART OF THE BODY [C] one of the threads in your body which carry messages between your brain and other parts of the body *the optic nerve* ○ *nerve cells/endings* 2 BEING BRAVE [no plural] the quality of being brave [+ to do sth] *I haven't got the nerve to tell him I'm leaving.* ○ *He lost his nerve and couldn't go through with it.* 3 RUDENESS [no plural] the rudeness necessary to do something you know will upset someone *You've **got a nerve**, coming here!* ○ [+ to do sth] *I can't believe she **had the nerve** to talk to me after what happened.* 4 **hit/touch a (raw) nerve** to upset someone by talking about a particular subject

nerve-racking /'nɜːv,rækɪŋ/ *adjective* If an experience is nerve-racking, it makes you very nervous. *a nerve-racking experience*

🧩 WORD PARTNERS FOR *nerves*

suffer from nerves • **calm/settle/steady** your nerves

nerves /nɜːvz/ *noun* [plural] 1 the state of being nervous *I need something to **calm my nerves**.* ○ *I always **suffer from nerves** before a match.* 2 **steady/strong nerves** the ability to be calm in difficult situations *You need a cool head and steady nerves for this job.* 3 **get on sb's nerves** to annoy someone, especially by doing something again and again *If we spend too much time together we end up getting on each other's nerves.*

⚬ᴬ **nervous** /'nɜːvəs/ *adjective* 1 worried and anxious *a **nervous cough/laugh*** ○ *She's very **nervous about** her driving test.* 2 [always before noun] relating to the nerves in the body *a nervous disorder*

COMMON LEARNER ERROR

nervous, agitated or **irritable?**

Nervous means 'worried or frightened'. It does not mean 'angry' or 'upset'.

I get very nervous if I have to speak in public.

If you want to describe someone who cannot control their voice and movements because they are anxious and upset, use **agitated**.

He was very agitated and aggressive.

If you want to describe someone who becomes annoyed easily, use **irritable** or **bad-tempered**.

She was tired and irritable.

ˌnervous 'breakdown *noun* [C] a short period of mental illness when people are too ill to continue with their normal lives

nervously /ˈnɜːvəsli/ *adverb* in a worried and anxious way *to giggle/laugh nervously* • **nervousness** *noun* [U]

ˈnervous ˌsystem *noun* [C] your brain and all the nerves in your body which control your feelings and actions *a disease of the central nervous system*

nest¹ /nest/ *noun* [C] a home built by birds for their eggs and by some other creatures to live in *a birds'/wasps' nest*

nest² /nest/ *verb* [I] to live in a nest or build a nest

nestle /ˈnesl/ *verb* **1 nestle (sth) against/in/on, etc** to rest yourself or part of your body in a comfortable, protected position *The cat was nestling in her lap.* **2 nestle beneath/between/ in, etc** If a building, town, or object nestles somewhere, it is in a protected position, with bigger things around it. *a village nestled in the Carpathian mountains*

net

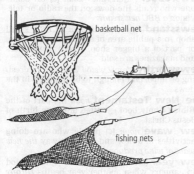

basketball net

fishing nets

net¹ /net/ *noun* **1** [U] material made of crossed threads with holes in them **2** [C] something made with a piece of net, for example for catching fish or insects, or for sports *a fishing net* ○ *a tennis/basketball net* **3 the Net** short for the Internet ⊃See also: **safety net**.

net² (*also UK* **nett**) /net/ *adjective* A net amount of money has had costs such as tax taken away from it. *a net income/profit of £10,000*

net³ /net/ *verb* [T] netting, *past* netted **1** to get an amount of money as profit *One trader netted a bonus of £1 million.* **2** to hit, throw, or kick a ball into a net *He netted a great penalty.*

netball /ˈnetbɔːl/ *noun* [U] a game usually played by teams of women, where a ball is thrown from player to player and goals are scored by throwing the ball through a high net

netting /ˈnetɪŋ/ *noun* [U] material made of crossed threads or wires with holes between them *wire netting*

nettle /ˈnetl/ *noun* [C] a wild plant whose leaves hurt you if you touch them

📇 WORD PARTNERS FOR **network**

build/create/establish/form a network • a network **of** sth • a **rail/road** network

network¹ /ˈnetwɜːk/ *noun* [C] **1** SYSTEM a system or group of connected parts *a rail/ road network* ○ *a network of cables/tunnels* **2** PEOPLE a group of people who know each other or who work together *a large network of friends* **3** COMPANY a large television or radio company that broadcasts programmes in many areas

network² /ˈnetwɜːk/ *verb* **1** [I] to use social events to meet people who might be useful for your business **2** [T] to connect computers together so that they can share information and programs

networking /ˈnetwɜːkɪŋ/ *noun* [U] **1** when you use social events to meet people who might be useful for your business **2** when you connect computers together so that they can share programs and information

neural /ˈnjʊərəl/ *adjective* [always before noun] relating to the nerves in your body *neural activity*

neurology /njʊəˈrɒlədʒi/ *noun* [U] the study of the system of nerves in people's bodies • **neurological** /ˌnjʊərəˈlɒdʒɪkᵊl/ *adjective* Neurological illnesses affect the nerves in people's bodies. • **neurologist** /njʊəˈrɒlədʒɪst/ *noun* [C] a doctor who deals with neurological illnesses

neuron /ˈnjʊərɒn/ *noun* [C] a nerve cell which carries messages between your brain and other parts of your body

neurosis /njʊəˈrəʊsɪs/ *noun* [C] *plural* neuroses /njʊəˈrəʊsiːz/ a mental illness, often causing you to worry too much about something

neurotic /njʊəˈrɒtɪk/ *adjective* If you are neurotic, you worry about things too much.

neuter /ˈnjuːtəʳ/ *adjective* in some languages, belonging to a group of nouns or adjectives that have the same grammatical behaviour. The other groups are 'masculine' and 'feminine'.

neutral¹ /ˈnjuːtrᵊl/ *adjective* **1** independent and not supporting any side in an argument, fight, or competition *neutral ground/territory* ○ *He decided to remain neutral on the issue.* **2** Neutral colours are not strong or bright.

neutral² /ˈnjuːtrᵊl/ *noun* [U] In driving, neutral is the position of the gears (= parts of a vehicle that control how fast the wheels turn) when they are not connected. *to be in neutral*

neutrality /njuːˈtræləti/ *noun* [U] the state of being independent and not supporting any side in an argument, war, etc *The Queen is famous for her neutrality.* ○ *political neutrality*

neutron /ˈnjuːtrɒn/ *noun* [C] a part of an atom which has no electrical charge (= the electricity something stores or carries)

N

never /ˈnevəʳ/ *adverb* **1** not ever, not one time *"Have you ever been to Australia?" "No, never."* ○ *I've never even thought about that before.* ○ *She'll never be able to have children.* ○ *He just walked out of the door one day and never came back.* ○ *He never worked again after the accident.* **2** used to emphasize something negative *I never knew you lived around here.* ○ *I never realized how hard she worked.*

never-ending /ˌnevəˈrˈendɪŋ/ *adjective* If something is never-ending, it continues for ever. *The housework in this place is just never-ending.*

nevertheless /ˌnevəðəˈles/ *adverb* despite that *I knew a lot about the subject already, but her talk was interesting nevertheless.*

new /njuː/ *adjective* **1** [DIFFERENT] different from before *I need some new shoes.* ○ *Have you met Fiona's new boyfriend?* ○ *He's starting his new job on Monday.* ○ *We're always looking for new ways to improve our services.* ○ *I've decided to take a new approach to the problem.* **2** [RECENTLY MADE] recently made *Their house is quite new - it's about five years old.* ○ *The factory will provide hundreds of new jobs for the area.* **3** [NOT KNOWN BEFORE] not known before *to discover a new gene/star* **4 be new to sb** If a situation or activity is new to you, you have not had experience of it before. *You'll have to be patient as this is all new to me.* **5 be new to sth** If you are new to a situation or activity, you have only recently started experiencing it. *I'm new to the job.* ➲See also: a whole new **ball game**, new **blood**, **brand new**, break new **ground**[1], new **heights**, turn over a new **leaf**[1], give sb/sth a new **lease**[1] of life.

newborn /ˌnjuːˈbɔːn/ *adjective* [always before noun] A newborn baby has just been born. • **newborn** *noun* [C] a newborn baby

newcomer /ˈnjuːˌkʌməʳ/ *noun* [C] someone who has only recently arrived or started doing something *Elizabeth's a relative **newcomer to** the area.*

new-found /ˈnjuːˌfaʊnd/ *adjective* [always before noun] A new-found quality or ability has started recently. *This success is a reflection of their new-found confidence.*

newly /ˈnjuːli/ *adverb* recently *a **newly married** couple* ○ *newly-built houses*

WORD PARTNERS FOR ***news***

the latest news • **hear/listen to/see/watch** the news • **in/on** the news

news /njuːz/ *noun* [U] **1 the news** the announcement of important events on television, radio, and in newspapers *the **local/national news*** ○ *to **watch** the 6 o'clock **news*** ○ *Did you see that report about child labour **on the news** last night?* ○ *a **news bulletin/report*** ○ *There's been a lot in the news about the issue recently.* **2** new information *Have you **had** any **news** about your job yet?* ○ *I've got some **good news** for you.* ○ *Any news from John?* **3 be news to sb** *informal* to be a surprise to someone *He's leaving? Well that's certainly news to me.* **4 be bad/good news for sb** to affect someone badly/well *This weather is bad news for farmers.*

newsagent /ˈnjuːzˌeɪdʒənt/ *noun* [C] *UK* **1 newsagent's** a shop that sells newspapers, magazines, and things like sweets and cigarettes **2** someone who owns or works in a newsagent's

newscast /ˈnjuːzkɑːst/ *noun* [C] *US* a television or radio broadcast of the news *the evening newscast*

newscaster /ˈnjuːzkɑːstəʳ/ *noun* [C] someone who reads the news on the radio or television

newsgroup /ˈnjuːzgruːp/ *noun* [group] a collection of messages on the Internet that people write about a particular subject *a political newsgroup*

newsletter /ˈnjuːzˌletəʳ/ *noun* [C] a regular report with information for people who belong to an organization or who are interested in a particular subject *a monthly newsletter about business and the environment*

newspaper /ˈnjuːsˌpeɪpəʳ/ [US] /ˈnuːzˌpeɪpəʳ/ *noun* **1** [C] large, folded sheets of paper which are printed with the news and sold every day or every week *a **local/national newspaper*** ○ *I read about his death **in the newspaper**.* ○ *a **newspaper article/headline*** **2** [U] paper from newspapers *The cups were wrapped in newspaper.*

newsprint /ˈnjuːzprɪnt/ *noun* [U] cheap, low quality paper used to print newspapers

newsreader /ˈnjuːzˌriːdəʳ/ *noun* [C] *UK* someone who reads the news on the radio or television *a BBC newsreader*

newsstand /ˈnjuːzstænd/ *noun* [C] *US* a small shop in a public area of a building or station, or part of a bigger shop, where newspapers and magazines are sold

newsworthy /ˈnjuːzˌwɜːði/ *adjective* interesting or important enough to be included in the news

the ˌNew ˈTestament *noun* the part of the Bible (= holy book) written after the birth of Jesus Christ

ˌnew ˈwave *noun* [C] people who are doing activities in a new and different way *the new wave of wine producers*

ˌnew ˈyear (*also* New Year) *noun* [C] the period in January when another year begins ***Happy New Year!*** ○ *We're going away **in the new year**.*

ˌNew ˌYear's ˈDay *noun* [C, U] 1 January, the first day of the year and a public holiday in many countries

ˌNew ˌYear's ˈEve *noun* [C, U] 31 December, the last day of the year

next[1] /nekst/ *adjective* **1 next week/year/Monday, etc** the week/year/Monday, etc that follows the present one *I'm planning to visit California next year.* ○ *Are you doing anything next Wednesday?* ○ *Next time, ask my permission before you borrow the car.* **2** The next time, event, person, or thing is the one nearest to now or the one that follows the present one. *What time's the next train to London?* ○ *We're* *going to be very busy for the next few months.* **3** The next place is the one nearest to the present one. *She only lives in the next village.* ○ *Turn left at the next roundabout.* **4 the next best thing** the thing that is best, if you cannot have or do the thing you really want *Coaching football is the next best thing to playing.* **5 the next thing I knew** used to talk about part of a story that happens in a sudden and surprising way *A car came speeding round the corner, and the next thing I knew I was lying on the ground.*

⊶**next²** /nekst/ *adverb* **1** immediately after *You'll never guess what happened next.* ○ *Where shall we go next?* **2** The time when you next do something is the first time you do it again. *Could you get some coffee when you next go to the supermarket?*

⊶**next³** /nekst/ *preposition* **next to sth/sb** very close to something or someone, with nothing in between *Come and sit next to me.* ○ *The factory is right next to a residential area.*

⊶**next⁴** /nekst/ *pronoun* **1** the person or thing that follows the present person or thing *Who's next to see the nurse?* ○ *Blue roses?* ***Whatever next?*** (= What other strange things might happen?) **2 the weekend/week/Thursday, etc after next** the weekend/week/Thursday, etc that follows the next one

ˌnext ˈdoor *adjective, adverb* in the next room, house, or building *What are your* ***next-door neighbours*** *like?* ○ *That's the old man who lives* ***next door*** *to Paul.*

ˌnext of ˈkin *noun* [C] *plural* **next of kin** *formal* the person you are most closely related to *The names of the dead cannot be released until their next of kin have been notified.*

the NHS /ˌeneɪtʃˈes/ *noun abbreviation for* the National Health Service: the system providing free medical services in the UK *Did she get it done privately or* ***on the NHS?***

nib /nɪb/ *noun* [C] the pointed end of a pen, where the ink comes out

nibble /ˈnɪbl/ *verb* [I, T] to eat something by taking very small bites or to bite something gently *He was nibbling a biscuit.*

> **OTHER WAYS OF SAYING *nice***
>
> If a person is nice because they are kind to other people, you can say that they are **kind** or **sweet**: *She's a very* ***kind*** *person.* • *Thank you so much for the card - it was very* ***sweet*** *of you!*
>
> If something that you do is nice, you can describe it as **fun**, **enjoyable**, or **lovely**: *We had a really* ***lovely*** *day at the beach.* • *You'd have liked the party - it was* ***fun****.*
>
> If something is nice to look at, then adjectives such as **attractive**, **beautiful**, **pleasant**, **lovely**, and **pretty** are often used: *There's some* ***beautiful*** *countryside in Yorkshire.* • *That's a* ***pretty*** *dress you're wearing.*
>
> If food tastes nice, then we can say that it is **delicious** or **tasty**: *This chicken soup is absolutely* ***delicious****.*

⊶**nice** /naɪs/ *adjective* **1** pleasant *They live in a nice old house on Market Street.* ○ *We could go to the coast tomorrow, if the weather's nice.* ○ **[+ to do sth]** *It was very nice to meet you.* ○ **[+ doing sth]** *Nice talking to you.* **2** kind and friendly *He seems like a really nice guy.* ○ *She's always been very* ***nice to*** *me.* **3 nice and sth** *informal* used to emphasize a positive quality *nice and clean* ○ *This chair's nice and comfy.* ○ *It's nice and warm in here!*

nicely /ˈnaɪsli/ *adverb* **1** well *That table would fit nicely in the bedroom.* ○ *His business is* ***doing very nicely.*** **2** in a pleasant way *nicely dressed*

niche /niːʃ/ [US] /nɪtʃ/ *noun* [C] **1** a job or activity that is very suitable for someone *After years of job dissatisfaction, he's at last* ***found his niche*** *in financial services.* **2** a hollow space cut into a wall

ˌniche ˈmarket *noun* [C] when a product or service is only sold to a small number of people

nick¹ /nɪk/ *verb* [T] **1** [STEAL] *UK informal* to steal something *She got caught nicking CDs from Woolworth's.* **2** [CATCH] *UK informal* If the police nick someone, they catch that person because they have committed a crime. **[often passive]** *He got nicked for handling stolen goods.* **3** [CUT] to make a small cut in something without intending to *He nicked himself shaving.*

nick² /nɪk/ *noun* **1** [C] *mainly UK informal* a prison or police station *They spent the night* ***in the nick.*** **2** [C] a small cut *He has a little nick on his cheek.* **3 in bad/good nick** *UK informal* in bad/good condition *It's not a new car but it's in pretty good nick.* **4 in the nick of time** just before it was too late *The ambulance arrived in the nick of time.*

nickel /ˈnɪkl/ *noun* **1** [C] a US or Canadian coin with a value of 5 cents **2** [U] a silver-white metal that is often mixed with other metals

nickname /ˈnɪkneɪm/ *noun* [C] a name used informally instead of your real name *His behaviour has earned him the nickname 'Mad Dog'.* •**nickname** *verb* **[+ two objects]** *They nicknamed her 'The Iron Lady'.*

nicotine /ˈnɪkətiːn/ *noun* [U] a poisonous chemical substance in tobacco

niece /niːs/ *noun* [C] the daughter of your brother or sister, or the daughter of your husband's or wife's brother or sister

nifty /ˈnɪfti/ *adjective informal* well-designed and effective *a nifty piece of software* ○ ***a nifty little*** *device*

nigger /ˈnɪgəʳ/ *noun* [C] a very offensive word for a black person

niggle /ˈnɪgl/ *verb* **1** [I, T] to worry or annoy someone slightly for a long time *a* ***niggling injury*** **2 niggle about/over, etc** *UK* to complain about things which are not very important *She kept niggling about the extra work.* •**niggle** *noun* [C]

nigh /naɪ/ *adverb* **1** *literary* near *The end of the world is nigh.* **2 well nigh/nigh on** *old-fashioned* almost *Our family has lived here well nigh two hundred years.*

spend the night • **at** night • **in** the night • **the middle of** the night • **last** night

o-=**night** /naɪt/ *noun* [C, U] **1** DARK the time in every 24 hours when it is dark and people usually sleep *I didn't get any sleep **last night**.* ○ *It's warm during the day, but it can get quite cold **at night**.* ○ *The phone rang in the **middle of the night**.* ○ *We stayed up almost all night talking.* ○ *Tim's working nights this week.* **2** EVENING the period from the evening to the time when you go to sleep *Did you have a good time **last night**?* ○ *Are you doing anything **on Friday night**?* **3** SAYING THE TIME used to describe the hours from the evening until just after 12 midnight *They're open from 7 in the morning until 10 o'clock at night.* **4 have an early/a late night** to go to bed early/late **5 a night out** an evening spent away from home doing something enjoyable *a night out at the theatre* **6 Good night.** You say 'Good night' to someone who is going to bed. *Good night, sleep well.* ⊃See also: the **dead³** of night/winter.

nightclub /ˈnaɪtklʌb/ *noun* [C] a place where you can dance and drink at night

nightdress /ˈnaɪtdres/ *noun* [C] *mainly UK* a loose dress that women wear in bed

nightfall /ˈnaɪtfɔːl/ *noun* [U] the time in the evening when it gets dark

nightgown /ˈnaɪtgaʊn/ *noun* [C] a loose dress that women wear in bed

nightie /ˈnaɪti/ *noun* [C] a loose dress that women wear in bed

nightingale /ˈnaɪtɪŋgeɪl/ *noun* [C] a small brown bird which sings very well

nightlife /ˈnaɪtlaɪf/ *noun* [U] entertainment for the night such as bars, restaurants, and theatres *What's the nightlife like around here?*

nightly /ˈnaɪtli/ *adjective* [always before noun], *adverb* happening every night *the nightly news* ○ *The show, lasting ninety minutes, will be broadcast nightly from Monday to Friday.*

an **absolute/complete/living/total** nightmare • be sb's **worst** nightmare • the nightmare **of** (doing) sth • a nightmare **for** sb

nightmare /ˈnaɪtmeəʳ/ *noun* [C] **1** a very unpleasant experience *The traffic can be a real nightmare after 4.30.* **2** a frightening dream

ˈnight ˌschool *noun* [U] classes for adults that are taught in the evening

nightstick /ˈnaɪtstɪk/ *US* (*UK* truncheon) *noun* [C] a short stick that police officers carry to use as a weapon

night-time /ˈnaɪttaɪm/ *noun* [U] the period of time when it is dark at night

nil /nɪl/ *noun* [U] **1** *UK* In sports results, nil means 'zero'. *Germany beat England three nil* (= 3-0). **2** not existing *The chances of that happening are virtually nil.*

nimble /ˈnɪmbl/ *adjective* able to move quickly and easily *nimble fingers*

o-=**nine** /naɪn/ the number 9

o-=**nineteen** /ˌnaɪnˈtiːn/ the number 19 • **nineteenth** 19th written as a word

nine-to-five /ˌnaɪntəˈfaɪv/ *adj, adv* describes work that begins at nine o'clock in the morning and ends at five o'clock, which are the hours that people work in many offices from Monday to Friday *She's tired of **working nine-to-five**.* ○ *a nine-to-five job*

o-=**ninety** /ˈnaɪnti/ **1** the number 90 **2 the nineties** the years from 1990 to 1999 **3 be in your nineties** to be aged between 90 and 99 • **ninetieth** 90th written as a word

ninth¹ /naɪnθ/ 9th written as a word

ninth² /naɪnθ/ *noun* [C] one of nine equal parts of something; ⅑

nip /nɪp/ *verb* nipping, *past* nipped **1 nip down/out/up, etc** *UK informal* to go somewhere quickly and for a short time *I'm just nipping down the road to get a paper.* **2** [T] If something nips you, it gives you a small, sharp bite. *His parrot nipped him on the nose.* ⊃See also: nip sth in the bud.

nipple /ˈnɪpl/ *noun* [C] the small, circular area of slightly darker, harder skin in the centre of each breast in women, or on each side of the chest in men

nirvana /nɪəˈvɑːnə/ *noun* [U] a state of perfection

nitrate /ˈnaɪtreɪt/ *noun* [C, U] a chemical that is used on crops to make them grow better

nitrogen /ˈnaɪtrədʒən/ *noun* [U] a gas that has no colour or smell and is the main part of air

the nitty-gritty /ˌnɪtiˈgrɪti/ *noun* the important details of a subject or activity *English teachers should concentrate on **the nitty-gritty** of teaching grammar.*

o-=**no¹** /nəʊ/ *exclamation* **1** something that you say in order to disagree, give a negative answer, or say that something is not true *"Have you seen Louise?" "No, I haven't."* ○ *"Have you ever been to Ireland?" "No."* ○ *"Can I have some more cake?" "No, you'll be sick."* ○ *"He's really ugly." "No he isn't!"* **2** something that you say to agree with something that is negative *"He's not very bright, is he?" "No, I'm afraid not."* **3 Oh no!** something that you say when you are shocked and upset *Oh no! It's gone all over the carpet!*

o-=**no²** /nəʊ/ *determiner* **1** not any *There were no signposts anywhere.* ○ *I had no difficulty getting work.* ○ *There was no mention of money.* **2** a word used to say that something is forbidden *No smoking.* ○ *There was no talking in her classes.* **3 There's no doing sth** something that you say when an action is impossible *There's no pleasing some people* (= nothing that you do will make them happy).

no³ /nəʊ/ *adverb* **no ... than** not any *The work should be done no later than Friday.* ○ *There were no more than ten people there.*

no. *written abbreviation for* number

nobility /nəʊˈbɪləti/ *noun* **1 the nobility** [group] the people from the highest social group in a society **2** [U] the quality of being noble

noble¹ /ˈnəʊbl/ *adjective* **1** honest, brave, and kind *a noble gesture* **2** belonging to the highest social group of a society

noble² /'nəʊbl/ *noun* [C] a person of the highest social group in some countries

nobleman, noblewoman /'nəʊblmən, 'nəʊbl,wʊmən/ *noun* [C] *plural* **noblemen** or **noblewomen** someone belonging to the highest social group in some countries

nobly /'nəʊbli/ *adverb* in a brave or generous way *She nobly offered to sell her jewellery.*

o- **nobody** /'nəʊbədi/ *pronoun* no person *There was nobody I could talk to.* ○ *Nobody's listening.* ○ *Sally helped me, but* ***nobody else*** *bothered.*

nocturnal /nɒk'tɜːnəl/ *adjective* **1** Nocturnal animals and birds are active at night. **2** happening at night *nocturnal activities/habits*

nod /nɒd/ *verb* [I, T] **nodding** *past* **nodded** to move your head up and down as a way of agreeing, to give someone a sign, or to point to something *They nodded enthusiastically at the proposal.* ○ *Barbara nodded in approval.* • **nod** *noun* [C] *He* ***gave a nod*** *of approval.*

nod off *informal* to start sleeping

nodule /'nɒdjuːl/ *noun* [C] a small lump, especially on a plant or someone's body

no-fault /'nəʊfɔːlt/ *adjective* [always before noun] *US* No-fault laws or systems are ones where it is not important who is responsible for what has happened. *no-fault insurance*

,no-go 'area *noun* [C] *mainly UK* an area, usually in a city, where it is too dangerous to go because there is a lot of violent crime there

WORD PARTNERS FOR ***noise***

background noise • a **deafening/faint/loud/strange** noise • **hear/make** a noise

o- **noise** /nɔɪz/ *noun* [C, U] a sound, often a loud, unpleasant sound *a deafening/loud noise* ○ *Stop* ***making so much noise!*** ○ *The engine's making funny noises.* ○ *There is some* ***background noise*** *on the recording.* ○ *I had to shout above the noise of the party.*

'noise poll,ution *noun* [U] noise, often from traffic, which upsets people where they live or work

o- **noisy** /'nɔɪzi/ *adjective* Noisy people or things make a lot of noise. *A crowd of noisy protesters gathered in the square.* ○ *We've had problems with noisy neighbours.* • **noisily** *adverb*

nomad /'nəʊmæd/ *noun* [C] a member of a group of people who move from one place to another instead of living in the same place all the time • **nomadic** /nəʊ'mædɪk/ *adjective* Nomadic people move from place to place.

'no-man's ,land *noun* [U, no plural] an area of land which no one owns or controls, especially in a war

nominal /'nɒmɪnəl/ *adjective* **1** existing officially, but not in reality *a nominal leader* **2** A nominal sum of money is a small amount of money. *a* ***nominal charge/fee***

nominally /'nɒmɪnəli/ *adverb* officially but not in reality *nominally Catholic areas*

nominate /'nɒmɪneɪt/ *verb* [T] **1** to officially suggest a person for a job or a position in an organization, or to suggest a person or their work for a prize [often passive] *Judges are nominated by the governor.* ○ *The film was* ***nominated for*** *an Academy Award.* ○ *He was* ***nominated as*** *best actor.* **2** to choose someone for a job or to do something *He has* ***nominated*** *his brother* ***as*** *his heir.* ○ [+ to do sth] *Two colleagues were nominated to attend the conference.*

WORD PARTNERS FOR ***nomination***

make/receive/seek/win a nomination • a nomination **as/for** sth

nomination /,nɒmɪ'neɪʃən/ *noun* [C, U] **1** the act of officially suggesting a person for a job or their work for a prize *to* ***seek/win*** *a* ***nomination*** ○ *He won the Democratic* ***nomination for*** *mayor of Chicago.* ○ *She has just* ***received*** *her fourth Oscar* ***nomination.*** **2** the choice of someone for a job or to do something *They did everything they could to defeat his nomination to be surgeon general.*

nominee /,nɒmɪ'niː/ *noun* [C] a person or a piece of work which has been nominated

non- /nɒn-/ *prefix* not or the opposite of *non-alcoholic drinks* ○ *non-smokers*

non-alcoholic /,nɒnælkə'hɒlɪk/ *adjective* describes a drink that does not contain alcohol

nonchalant /'nɒnʃələnt/ [US] /,nɑːnʃə'lɑːnt/ *adjective* calm and not worried *a nonchalant shrug* • **nonchalantly** *adverb*

noncommittal /,nɒnkə'mɪtəl/ *adjective* not showing your opinion about something *a noncommittal expression/response*

nondescript /'nɒndɪskrɪpt/ *adjective* not interesting *a nondescript building/man*

o- **none** /nʌn/ *quantifier* **1** not any ***None of*** *them smoke.* ○ *In 1992, the company had 2,700 part-time workers. Today it has none.* ○ *There were only three births here in March and* ***none at all*** *in April.* ○ *He asked if there was any hope. I told him frankly that there was none.* **2 none too clean/clever/pleased, etc** not at all clean/clever/pleased, etc *His handkerchief was none too clean.* **3 none the happier/poorer/wiser, etc** not any happier/poorer/wiser, etc than before *She must have explained the theory three times, but I'm still none the wiser.*

nonetheless /,nʌnðə'les/ *adverb* despite what has just been said *He was extremely rude in meetings. Nonetheless, his arguments found some support.*

non-event /,nɒnɪ'vent/ *noun* [no plural] *informal* an event that was not as exciting or interesting as you expected it to be *Her party was a bit of a non-event.*

non-existent /,nɒnɪg'zɪstənt/ *adjective* not existing *We knew our chances of success were non-existent.*

nonfiction /,nɒn'fɪkʃən/ *noun* [U] writing about things which are true *nonfiction books/titles*

no-no /'nəʊnəʊ/ *noun* [C] *informal* something that is forbidden or not socially acceptable *Cardigans are a fashion no-no this season.*

no-nonsense /,nəʊ'nɒnsəns/ *adjective* [always

before noun] not having or allowing others to have any silly ideas or behaviour *a no-non-sense approach to child rearing*

nonplussed /ˌnɒn'plʌst/ *adjective* extremely surprised

non-profit-making /ˌnɒn'prɒfɪtˌmeɪkɪŋ/ *UK* (*US* **nonprofit**) *adjective* A non-profit-making organization does not make money from its activities.

nonsense /'nɒns²ns/ *noun* [U] **1** If something someone has said or written is nonsense, it is silly and not true. *She talks such nonsense sometimes.* ○ *That's a load of nonsense.* ○ *It's nonsense to suggest they could have cheated.* **2** silly behaviour *Will you stop this childish nonsense!* **3 make a nonsense of sth** *UK* to spoil something or make it seem stupid *Cuts to the text made a nonsense of the play.*

non-smoker /ˌnɒn'sməʊkəʳ/ *noun* [C] a person who does not smoke

non-smoking /ˌnɒn'sməʊkɪŋ/ *adjective* A non-smoking area is one where people are not allowed to smoke.

non-starter /ˌnɒn'stɑːtəʳ/ *noun* [C] *informal* something that will not be successful *The amount of money needed makes his project a non-starter.*

non-stop /ˌnɒn'stɒp/ *adjective, adverb* without stopping or resting *non-stop flights from Britain to the West Indies* ○ *We've been talking non-stop the whole way.*

non-violent /ˌnɒn'vaɪələnt/ *adjective* not using violent methods *non-violent action/protests* ○ *non-violent crimes/offenders*

noodles /'nuːdlz/ *noun* [plural] thin pieces of pasta (= food made from flour, eggs, and water)

nook /nʊk/ *noun* **every nook and cranny** every part of a place *I know every nook and cranny of this place.*

noon /nuːn/ *noun* [U] 12 o'clock in the middle of the day *He has until noon to act.* ○ *The service will be held at 12 noon.*

⊶**no one** *pronoun* no person *No one bothered to read the report.* ○ *No one knows where he is now.* ○ *There was no one there.* ○ *No one else makes puddings like my Mum.*

noose /nuːs/ *noun* [C] a piece of rope tied in a circle, used to catch animals or to hang (= kill) people

⊶**nor** /nɔːʳ/ *adverb, conjunction* **1 neither...nor...** used after 'neither' to introduce the second thing in a negative sentence *Strangely, neither James nor Emma saw what happened.* ○ *He neither spoke nor moved.* **2 nor can I/nor do you, etc** *mainly UK* used after something negative to say that the same thing is true for someone or something else *"I don't like cats." "Nor do I."* ○ *"I won't get to see him tomorrow." "Nor will Tom."* ○ *She couldn't speak a word of Italian and nor could I.*

Nordic /'nɔːdɪk/ *adjective* from or relating to the North European countries of Sweden, Denmark, Norway, Finland, and Iceland

norm /nɔːm/ *noun* **1 the norm** the usual way that something happens *Short-term job contracts are the norm nowadays.* **2** [C] an accepted way of behaving in a particular society [usually plural] *cultural/social norms*

⊶**normal** /'nɔːm²l/ *adjective* usual, ordinary, and expected *to lead a normal life* ○ *It's perfectly normal to feel some degree of stress at work.* ○ *It's normal for couples to argue now and then.* ○ *Now that trains are running again things are back to normal.*

normality /nɔː'mæləti/ (*also US* **normalcy** /'nɔːməlsi/) *noun* [U] a situation in which everything is happening normally *a return to normality*

⊶**normally** /'nɔːməli/ *adverb* **1** usually *Normally, I start work around nine o'clock.* **2** in the ordinary way that you would expect *Both lungs are now functioning normally.*

north

⊶**north, North** /nɔːθ/ *noun* [U] **1** the direction that is on your left when you face towards the rising sun *The stadium is to the north of the city.* **2 the north** the part of an area that is further towards the north than the rest *She's from the north of England.* ●**north** *adjective a north wind* ●**north** *adverb* towards the north *I live north of the river.* ○ *We're going to visit Paul's family up north.*

northbound /'nɔːθbaʊnd/ *adjective* going or leading towards the north

northeast, Northeast /ˌnɔːθ'iːst/ *noun* [U] **1** the direction between north and east **2 the northeast** the northeast part of a country ●**northeast, Northeast** *adjective, adverb*

northeastern, Northeastern /ˌnɔːθ'iːstən/ *adjective* in or from the northeast

northerly /'nɔːð²li/ *adjective* **1** towards or in the north *Canada's most northerly point* **2** A northerly wind comes from the north.

⊶**northern, Northern** /'nɔːð²n/ *adjective* in or from the north part of an area *Northern Eng-*

land ∘ _a northern accent_

northerner, Northerner /'nɔːðnə/ _noun_ [C] someone from the north part of a country

northernmost /'nɔːðənməʊst/ _adjective_ The northernmost part of an area is the part furthest to the north.

north-facing /'nɔːθ,feɪsɪŋ/ _adjective_ [always before noun] positioned towards the north _a north-facing slope_

the ˌNorth ˈPole _noun_ the point on the Earth's surface which is furthest north

northward, northwards /'nɔːθwəd/, /'nɔːθwədz/ _adverb_ towards the north ●**northward** _adjective a northward direction_

northwest, Northwest /ˌnɔːθ'west/ _noun_ [U] **1** the direction between north and west **2 the northwest** the northwest part of a country ●**northwest, Northwest** _adjective, adverb_

northwestern, Northwestern /ˌnɔːθ-ˈwestən/ _adjective_ in or from the northwest

o⇥**nose¹** /nəʊz/ _noun_ [C] **1** the part of your face through which you breathe and smell _a big/broken nose_ ∘ _She paused to **blow her nose** (=_ breathe out hard to empty it into a piece of cloth). ⊅See colour picture **The Body** on page Centre 13. **2 get up sb's nose** _UK informal_ to annoy someone _That man really gets up my nose_ **3 poke/stick your nose into sth** _informal_ to show too much interest in a situation that does not involve you _You shouldn't go sticking your nose into other people's business!_ **4 thumb your nose at sth/sb** to show that you do not respect rules, laws, or powerful people **5 turn your nose up at sth** to not accept something because you do not think it is good enough for you _He turned his nose up at my offer of soup, saying he wanted a proper meal._ **6 under your nose** If something bad happens under your nose, it happens close to you but you do not notice it.

nose² /nəʊz/ _verb_
  nose about/around (sth) _informal_ to look around a place, often in order to find something _I caught him nosing around in my office._

nosebleed /'nəʊzbliːd/ _noun_ [C] **have a nosebleed** to have blood coming from your nose

nosedive /'nəʊzdaɪv/ _verb_ [I] to fall very quickly in value _The economy nosedived after the war._ ●**nosedive** _noun_ [C]

nosey /'nəʊzi/ _another spelling of_ nosy

nostalgia /nɒs'tældʒə/ _noun_ [U] a feeling of happiness mixed with sadness when you think about things that happened in the past _his nostalgia for his college days_

nostalgic /nɒs'tældʒɪk/ _adjective_ feeling both happy and sad when you think about things that happened in the past _Talking about those holidays has made me feel quite nostalgic._

nostril /'nɒstrəl/ _noun_ [C] one of the two holes at the end of your nose ⊅See colour picture **The Body** on page Centre 13.

nosy /'nəʊzi/ _adjective_ always trying to find out private things about other people _nosy neighbours_ ∘ _Don't be so nosy!_

o⇥**not** /nɒt/ _adverb_ **1** used to form a negative phrase after verbs like 'be', 'can', 'have', 'will', 'must', etc, usually used in the short form 'n't' in speech _I won't tell her._ ∘ _I can't go._ ∘ _He hasn't eaten yet._ ∘ _Don't you like her?_ ∘ _It isn't difficult (= It is easy)._ ∘ _The service isn't very good (= it is bad)._ ∘ _You're coming, aren't you?_ ∘ _I will not tolerate laziness._ **2** used to give the next word or group of words a negative meaning _I told you not to do that._ ∘ _I like most vegetables but not cabbage._ ∘ _"Come and play football, Dad." "Not now, Jamie."_ ∘ _"Whose are these?" "Not mine."_ **3** used after verbs like 'be afraid', 'hope', 'suspect', etc in short, negative replies _"Do you think it's going to rain?" "I hope not."_ ∘ _"Have you finished?" "I'm afraid not."_ **4 certainly/hopefully not** used after an adverb in short, negative replies _"She's not exactly poor, is she?" "Certainly not."_ ∘ _"We won't need much money, will we?" "Hopefully not."_ **5 not at all** used instead of 'no' or 'not' to emphasize what you are saying _"I hope this won't cause you any trouble." "No, not at all."_ ∘ _I'm not at all happy about it._ **6 Not at all.** used as a polite reply after someone has thanked you _"Thanks for all your help." "Not at all."_ **7 if not** used to say what the situation will be if something does not happen _I hope to see you there but, if not, I'll call you._ **8 or not** used to express the possibility that something might not happen _Are you coming or not?_ **9 not a/one** used to emphasize that there is nothing of what you are talking about _Not one person came to hear him talk._ ∘ _"You haven't heard from Nick, have you?" "Not a word."_

COMMON LEARNER ERROR

not ... either

The words **not ... either** are used to add another piece of negative information.

I'd forgotten my credit card and I didn't have any cash either.

~~_I'd forgotten my credit card and I didn't have any cash neither._~~

Helen didn't enjoy it either.

~~_Helen didn't enjoy it too._~~

---

notable /'nəʊtəbl/ _adjective_ If someone or something is notable, they are important or interesting. _a notable achievement_

notably /'nəʊtəbli/ _adverb_ used to emphasize an important example of something _Florida is well known for many of its fruits, notably oranges and grapefruits._

notation /nəʊ'teɪʃən/ _noun_ [U] a system of written symbols used especially in mathematics or to represent musical notes

notch¹ /nɒtʃ/ _noun_ [C] **1** a level of quality or amount _Interest rates have moved up another notch._ **2** a cut in the shape of the letter V on the edge or surface of something

notch² /nɒtʃ/ _verb_
  notch up sth to achieve something _He has notched up a total of 34 goals this season._

N

⚬**note¹** /nəʊt/ *noun* **1** LETTER [C] a short letter *He
left a note on her desk.* ○ *Did you get my note?*
2 INFORMATION [C] words that you write down
to help you remember something *She studied
her notes before the exam.* ○ *Let me make a
note of* (= write) *your phone number.* ○ *The
doctor took notes* (= wrote information) *while
I described my symptoms.* **3** EXPLANATION [C] a
short explanation or an extra piece of information that is given at the bottom of a page or
at the back of a book *See note 3, page 37.* **4** FEEL-
ING [no plural] a particular feeling or mood *a
sad/serious/positive note* ○ *His speech had
just the right note of sympathy.* **5** MUSIC [C] a
single musical sound or the symbol that represents it **6** MONEY [C] *UK* (*US* bill) a piece of
paper money *a ten-pound note* **7** take note (of
sth) to pay careful attention to something
Make sure you take note of what she says. **8** sb/
sth of note *formal* someone or something
famous or important *A medieval church is the
only monument of note in the town.* **9** compare
notes If two people compare notes, they tell
each other what they think about something
that they have both done. *We compared notes
about our experiences in China.*

note² /nəʊt/ *verb* [T] **1** to notice something *She
noted a distinct chill in the air.* ○ [+ (that)] *We
noted that their idea had never been tried.* **2** to
say or write something *In the article, she notes
several cases of medical incompetence.*
note down sth to write something so that
you do not forget it *I noted down the telephone
number for the police.*

notebook /'nəʊtbʊk/ *noun* [C] **1** a book with
empty pages that you can write in **2** a small
computer that can be carried around and used
anywhere

noted /'nəʊtɪd/ *adjective* important or famous *a
noted artist* ○ *He was noted for his modern approach to architecture.*

'notepad (com,puter) *noun* [C] a very small
computer that you can carry easily

notepaper /'nəʊt,peɪpəʳ/ *noun* [U] paper that
you write letters on

noteworthy /'nəʊt,wɜːði/ *adjective* If someone
or something is noteworthy, they are important or interesting. *a noteworthy example*

⚬**nothing** /'nʌθɪŋ/ *pronoun* **1** not anything *I've
had nothing to eat since breakfast.* ○ *He
claimed that he did nothing wrong.* ○ *He had
nothing in his pockets.* ○ *There was nothing
else* (= no other thing) *I could do to help.* ○ *She
did nothing but criticize* (= criticized a lot).
2 not something important or of value *He's a
dangerous person - human life means nothing
to him.* ○ *A thousand pounds is nothing to a
woman of her wealth.* **3** for nothing without a
successful result *I've come all this way for
nothing.* **4** be nothing to do with sb If something is or has nothing to do with you, you
have no good reason to know about it or be involved with it. *I wish he wouldn't offer advice
on my marriage - it's nothing to do with him.*
5 have nothing to do with sb/sth to have no
connection or influence with someone or
something *He made his own decision - I had
nothing to do with it.* **6** to say nothing of sth
used to emphasize other problems you have
not talked about *Most wild otters have disappeared from populated areas, to say nothing
of wilderness areas.* **7** nothing of the sort used
to emphasize that something is not true *He
said that he was a legitimate businessman - in
fact, he was nothing of the sort.* **8** It was nothing. a polite reply to someone who has thanked
you for doing something "Thank you so much
for helping out." "Oh, it was nothing." **9** be
nothing if not sth used to emphasize a quality
The senator was nothing if not honest (= he was
very honest). **10** stop at nothing to be willing
to do anything in order to achieve something
*He will stop at nothing to get what he
wants.*

nothingness /'nʌθɪŋnəs/ *noun* [U] a state
where nothing exists

⚬**notice¹** /'nəʊtɪs/ *verb* [I, T] to see something and
be aware of it *If the sign's too small, no one will
notice it.* ○ [+ (that)] *I noticed that he walked
with a limp.* ○ *I noticed him because he was behaving strangely.* ○ *Did you notice anything
odd about her?*

notice² /'nəʊtɪs/ *noun* **1** SIGN [C] a sign giving
information about something *The notice said
that the pool was closed for repairs.* ○ *Have you
seen any notices about the new sports club?*
2 WARNING [U] a warning that something will
happen *I had to give my landlord a month's
notice before moving.* ○ *How much notice do you
have to give your employer before you leave?*
3 at short notice *UK* (*US* on short notice) only a
short time before something happens **4** ATTEN-
TION [U] attention *I didn't take any notice of* (=
give attention to) *his advice.* ○ *It has come to
our notice* (= we became aware) *that you are
being overcharged for your insurance.* **5** hand/
give in your notice to tell your employer that
you are going to stop working for them *I
handed in my notice yesterday.* ○ *If my job
doesn't improve I'm going to give in my
notice.*

noticeable /'nəʊtɪsəbl/ *adjective* easy to see or
be aware of *There was a noticeable difference
in his behaviour after the injury.* ●**noticeably**
*adverb She was quite noticeably thinner after
the illness.*

noticeboard /'nəʊtɪsbɔːd/ *UK* (*US* bulletin
board) *noun* [C] a board on a wall where you put
advertisements and announcements *I saw the
ad on the noticeboard.* ○ *They've just put up a
sign on the noticeboard.* ⊃See colour picture The
Classroom on page Centre 6.

notify /'nəʊtɪfaɪ/ *verb* [T] *formal* to officially tell
someone about something *You should notify
the police if you are involved in a road accident.*
○ [+ (that)] *The court notified her that her trial*

date had been postponed. ● **notification** /ˌnəʊtɪfɪˈkeɪʃⁿn/ *noun* [C, U]

notion /ˈnəʊʃⁿn/ *noun* [C] an idea or belief *The notion of sharing is unknown to most two-year-olds.*

notoriety /ˌnəʊtⁿrˈaɪəti/ *noun* [U] when someone is famous for something bad *He **gained** notoriety for his racist speeches.*

notorious /nəʊˈtɔːriəs/ *adjective* famous for something bad *a notorious criminal* ○ *She was notorious for her bad temper.* ● **notoriously** *adverb* *Mount Everest is a notoriously difficult mountain to climb.*

notwithstanding /ˌnɒtwɪθˈstændɪŋ/ *adverb, preposition formal* despite *Injuries notwithstanding, he won the semi-final match.*

nought /nɔːt/ *noun* [C, U] **1** *UK* the number 0 **2** *old-fashioned* (*mainly US* **naught**) nothing

o⌐**noun** /naʊn/ *noun* [C] a word that refers to a person, place, object, event, substance, idea, feeling, or quality. For example the words 'teacher', 'book', 'development', and 'beauty' are nouns. ⊃See also: **countable noun, proper noun, uncountable noun.**

nourish /ˈnʌrɪʃ/ *verb* [T] *formal* to provide living things with food in order to make them grow or stay healthy *Mammals provide milk to nourish their young.*

nourishing /ˈnʌrɪʃɪŋ/ *adjective* Nourishing food makes you healthy.

nourishment /ˈnʌrɪʃmənt/ *noun* [U] *formal* the food that you need to stay alive and healthy

Nov *written abbreviation for* November

WORD PARTNERS FOR *novel*

read/write a novel ● a novel by sb ● a novel about sth ● in a novel

novel¹ /ˈnɒvⁿl/ *noun* [C] a book that tells a story about imaginary people and events *Have you read any good novels lately?* ● **novelist** *noun* [C] someone who writes novels

novel² /ˈnɒvⁿl/ *adjective* new or different from anything else

novelty /ˈnɒvⁿlti/ *noun* **1** QUALITY [U] the quality of being new or unusual *The fashion industry relies on novelty, and photographers are always looking for new faces.* **2** NEW THING [C] an object, event, or experience that is new or unusual *Tourists are still a novelty on this remote island.* **3** CHEAP TOY [C] a cheap toy or unusual object, often given as a present

o⌐**November** /nəʊˈvembə⁻/ (*written abbreviation* **Nov**) *noun* [C, U] the eleventh month of the year

novice /ˈnɒvɪs/ *noun* [C] someone who is beginning to learn how to do something *I've never used a computer before - I'm a complete novice.*

o⌐**now¹** /naʊ/ *adverb* **1** AT PRESENT at the present time *She's finished her degree and now she teaches English.* ○ *Do you know where Eva is **right now** (= at this moment)?* **2** IMMEDIATELY immediately *Come on, Andreas, we're going home now.* ○ *I don't want to wait - I want it now!* **3** LENGTH OF TIME used to show the length of time that something has been happening, from the time it began until the present *I've lived in Cambridge for two years now.* **4** IN

SPEECH used when you start to tell someone something *Now, I have been to Glasgow many times before.* ○ ***Now then,** would anyone else like to ask a question?* **5 just now** a very short time ago *When I came in just now, everyone was laughing.* ○ *Who was that woman who was speaking just now?* **6 (every) now and then/again** If something happens now and then, it happens sometimes but not very often. *I love chocolate, but I only eat it now and then.* **7 any day/minute/time, etc** used to say that something will happen very soon *We're expecting our second child any day now.*

o⌐**now²** /naʊ/ (*also* **now that**) *conjunction* as a result of a new situation *Now that I've got a car I can visit her more often.* ○ *You should help in the house more, now you're older.*

o⌐**now³** /naʊ/ *pronoun* the present time or moment *Now isn't a good time to speak to him.* ○ *She'd kept calm until now.* ○ *I'll be more careful **from now on** (= from this moment and always in the future).*

nowadays /ˈnaʊədeɪz/ *adverb* at the present time, especially when compared to the past *Everything seems more expensive nowadays.*

o⌐**nowhere** /ˈnəʊweə⁻/ *adverb* **1** not anywhere *The room was very crowded - there was nowhere to sit.* ○ *We had **nowhere else** to go.* **2 out of nowhere** If someone or something appears out of nowhere, it appears suddenly or unexpectedly. *The car came out of nowhere and we had to swerve to miss it.* **3 get/go nowhere** *informal* to fail to make any progress or achieve anything *They're getting nowhere on this project.* **4 get you nowhere** If something gets you nowhere, it does not help you to succeed. *Bad manners will get you nowhere.*

noxious /ˈnɒkʃəs/ *adjective* [always before noun] *formal* poisonous or harmful *noxious fumes/gases*

nozzle /ˈnɒzl/ *noun* [C] a narrow, hollow object which is fixed to a tube and which helps you to control the liquid or air that comes out

o⌐**n't** /ənt/ *short for* not *She isn't* (= is not) *going.* ○ *I can't* (= cannot) *hear you.* ○ *They didn't* (= did not) *believe me.*

nuance /ˈnjuːɑːns/ *noun* [C] a very slight difference in meaning, appearance, sound, etc *a subtle nuance* ○ *Linguists explore the nuances of language.*

o⌐**nuclear** /ˈnjuːkliə⁻/ *adjective* [always before noun] **1** relating to the energy that is released when the nucleus (= central part) of an atom is divided *nuclear weapons/waste* ○ *a **nuclear power plant* ***2** relating to the nucleus (= central part) of an atom *nuclear physics*

nuclear re'actor *noun* [C] a large machine which uses nuclear fuel to produce power

nucleus /ˈnjuːkliəs/ *noun* [C] *plural* **nuclei** /ˈnjuːkliaɪ/ **1** the central part of an atom or cell **2** the central or most important part of a group or idea *Senior coaches handpicked the nucleus of the team.*

nude¹ /njuːd/ *adjective* not wearing any clothes *Our children were running around the garden **in the nude** (= not wearing any clothes).*

N

nude² /njuːd/ *noun* [C] a painting or other piece of art that shows a nude person

nudge /nʌdʒ/ *verb* [T] to gently push someone or something *She nudged me towards the door.* • **nudge** *noun* [C] *I gave him a nudge.*

nudism /ˈnjuːdɪzᵊm/ *noun* [U] when someone wears no clothes when they are outside with other people, etc • **nudist** *noun* [C] someone who practices nudism

nudity /ˈnjuːdəti/ *noun* [U] when you are wearing no clothes *Some people are offended by* ⊶ *nudity.*

nugget /ˈnʌgɪt/ *noun* [C] **1** a small amount of something good *nuggets of wisdom* **2** a small, round piece of a solid substance *gold nuggets*

nuisance /ˈnjuːsᵊns/ *noun* [C] **1** a person, thing, or situation that annoys you or causes problems for you *Not being able to use my computer is a real nuisance.* **2 make a nuisance of yourself** to annoy someone or cause problems for them

nullify /ˈnʌlɪfaɪ/ *verb* [T] *formal* **1** to make something lose its effect *Advances in medicine have nullified the disease's effect.* **2** to say officially that something has no legal power *The judge could nullify the entire trial.*

numb /nʌm/ *adjective* **1** If a part of your body is numb, you cannot feel it. *My fingers and toes were numb with cold.* **2** If you are numb with a bad emotion, you are so shocked that you are not able to think clearly. *I was numb with grief after his death.*

⊶**number¹** /ˈnʌmbəʳ/ *noun* **1** [SYMBOL] [C] a symbol or word used in a counting system or used to show the position or order of something *Think of a number smaller than 100.* ○ *The Prime Minister lives at number 10, Downing Street.* ○ *Look at item number three on your agenda.* **2** [GROUP OF NUMBERS] [C] a group of numbers that represents something *What's your phone number?* ○ *Each person receives a membership number when they join.* **3** [AMOUNT] [C] an amount *a small number of* (= a few) ○ *a large number of* (= many) ○ *There were a number of* (= several) *soldiers present at the rally.* ○ *Scientists have noticed a drop in the number of song birds in Britain.* ⊃See Common learner error at **amount** ⊃See also: **cardinal number, ordinal number, phone number, telephone number.**

COMMON LEARNER ERROR

number

We use the adjectives **large** and **small** with the word **number**, not 'big' and 'little'.

A large number of people attended the concert.

~~A big number of people attended the concert.~~

number² /ˈnʌmbəʳ/ *verb* [T] **1** to give something a number [often passive] *Each volume was numbered and indexed.* **2** If people or things number a particular amount, there are that many of them. *Our company's sales force numbered over 5,000.*

ˈnumber ˌplate UK (US **license plate**) *noun* [C] an official metal sign with numbers and letters on the front and back of a car ⊃See colour picture

Car on page Centre 7.

numeral /ˈnjuːmᵊrᵊl/ *noun* [C] a symbol used to represent a number ⊃See also: **Roman numeral.**

numerical /njuːˈmerɪkl/ *adjective* [always before noun] relating to or expressed by numbers *The exams were filed in numerical order.*

numerous /ˈnjuːmᵊrəs/ *adjective formal* many *He is the author of numerous articles.*

nun /nʌn/ *noun* [C] a member of a group of religious women living apart from other people

⊶**nurse¹** /nɜːs/ *noun* [C] someone whose job is to care for ill and injured people

nurse² /nɜːs/ *verb* [T] **1** [CARE FOR] to care for a person or animal that is ill *We nursed the injured sparrow back to health.* **2** [FEED] US to feed a baby milk from its mother's breast *She nursed her son until he was a year old.* **3** [INJURY] to try to cure an illness or injury by resting *He was nursing a broken nose.* **4** [EMOTION] to think about an idea or an emotion for a long time *She nursed a great hatred towards her older sister.*

nursery /ˈnɜːsᵊri/ *noun* [C] **1** a place where babies and young children are looked after without their parents **2** a place where plants are grown and sold

ˈnursery ˌrhyme *noun* [C] a short poem or song for young children

ˈnursery ˌschool *noun* [C] a school for very young children

nursing /ˈnɜːsɪŋ/ *noun* [U] the job of being a nurse

ˈnursing ˌhome *noun* [C] a place where old people live to receive medical care

nurture /ˈnɜːtʃəʳ/ *verb* [T] *formal* **1** to encourage or support the development of someone or something *He was an inspiring leader who nurtured the talents of his colleagues.* **2** to look after, feed, and protect young children, animals, or plants *The rains nurtured the newly planted crops.*

⊶**nut** /nʌt/ *noun* [C] **1** [FOOD] the dry fruit of some trees which grows in a hard shell, and can often be eaten *a brazil/cashew nut* **2** [METAL] a piece of metal with a hole in it through which you put a bolt (= metal pin) to hold pieces of wood or metal together ⊃See picture at **tool.** **3** [KEEN] *informal* a person who is keen on a particular subject or hobby *She's a real sports nut.* **4 the nuts and bolts** the basic parts of a job or an activity *Law school can teach you theory, but it can't teach you the nuts and bolts of the profession.*

nutrient /ˈnjuːtriənt/ *noun* [C] *formal* any substance that animals need to eat and plants need from the soil in order to live and grow *A healthy diet should provide all your essential nutrients.*

nutrition /njuːˈtrɪʃᵊn/ *noun* [U] the food that you eat and the way that it affects your health *Good nutrition is essential for growing children.* • **nutritional** *adjective* relating to nutrition *Some snacks have little nutritional value.*

nutritionist /njuːˈtrɪʃᵊnɪst/ *noun* [C] someone who gives advice on the subject of nutrition

nutritious /njuːˈtrɪʃəs/ *adjective* Nutritious

| ɑː arm | ɜː her | iː see | ɔː saw | uː too | aɪ my | aʊ how | eə hair | eɪ day | əʊ no | ɪə near | ɔɪ boy | ʊə poor | aɪə fire | aʊə sour |

food contains substances that your body needs to stay healthy. *a nutritious meal*

nuts /nʌts/ *adjective informal* **1** crazy *They thought I was nuts to go parachuting.* **2 go nuts** to become very excited, angry, or upset *If I don't have a holiday soon, I'll go nuts.*

nutshell /'nʌtʃel/ *noun* **in a nutshell** something that you say when you are describing something using as few words as possible *The answer, in a nutshell, is yes.*

nutty /'nʌti/ *adjective* **1** *informal* crazy *nutty ideas* **2** Something nutty tastes of nuts.

nylon /'naɪlɒn/ *noun* [U] a strong, artificial material used to make clothes, ropes, etc *nylon stockings* ○ *a nylon shirt/bag*

nymph /nɪmf/ *noun* [C] in Greek and Roman stories, a spirit in the form of a young girl who lives in trees, rivers, mountains, etc

Oo

O, o /əʊ/ the fifteenth letter of the alphabet

oak /əʊk/ noun [C, U] a large tree found in northern countries, or the wood of this tree

OAP /ˌəʊeɪˈpiː/ noun [C] *UK abbreviation for* old-age pensioner: a person who regularly receives money from the state because they are too old to work

oar /ɔːʳ/ noun [C] **1** a long pole with a wide, flat end that you use to move a boat through water **2 stick/put your oar in** *UK informal* to involve yourself in a discussion or situation when other people do not want you to

oasis /əʊˈeɪsɪs/ noun [C] *plural* oases /əʊˈeɪsiːz/ **1** a place in the desert where there is water and where plants grow **2** a place that is much calmer and more pleasant than what is around it *The cafe was an oasis in the busy, noisy city.*

oath /əʊθ/ noun **1** [C] a formal promise *an oath of allegiance* ○ *They refused to take an oath of* (= to promise) *loyalty to the king.* **2 under oath** If someone is under oath, they have promised to tell the truth in a law court. *He denied under oath that he was involved in the crime.*

oats /əʊts/ noun [plural] grain which people eat or feed to animals

obedience /əʊˈbiːdɪəns/ noun [U] when someone is willing to do what they are told to do *He demanded complete obedience from his soldiers.* ➔Opposite **disobedience**. ● **obedient** /əʊˈbiːdɪənt/ *adjective* willing to do what you are told to do *an obedient child/dog* ➔Opposite **disobedient**.

obese /əʊˈbiːs/ *adjective* extremely fat ● **obesity** noun [U] when someone is obese

o▬**obey** /əʊˈbeɪ/ verb [I, T] to do what you are told to do by a person, rule, or instruction *He gave the command, and we obeyed.* ➔Opposite **disobey**.

obfuscate /ˈɒbfʌskeɪt/ verb [T] *formal* to make something harder to understand or less clear

obituary /əʊˈbɪtʃʊəri/ noun [C] a report in a newspaper that gives details about a person who has recently died

o▬**object¹** /ˈɒbdʒɪkt/ noun **1** [C] a thing that you can see or touch but that is usually not alive *a bright, shiny object* **2 the object of sth** the purpose of something *The object of the game is to score more points than the opposing team.* **3 the object of sb's affection/desire, etc** the cause of someone's feelings *He's the object of my affection.* **4** in grammar, the person or thing that is affected by the action of the verb ➔See also: **direct object, indirect object**.

object² /əbˈdʒekt/ verb [I] to feel or say that you do not like or do not approve of something or someone *We objected to his unreasonable demands.* ○ *Would anyone object if I were to leave early?* ➔See also: **conscientious objector**.

🧩 WORD PARTNERS FOR *objection*

lodge/make/raise/voice an objection
● have no objections ● a serious/strong objection ● an objection to sth

objection /əbˈdʒekʃən/ noun [C, U] when someone says that they do not like or approve of something or someone *Our main objection to the new factory is that it's noisy.* ○ *I have no objections, if you want to stay an extra day.*

objectionable /əbˈdʒekʃənəbl/ *adjective formal* very unpleasant

objective¹ /əbˈdʒektɪv/ noun [C] something that you are trying to achieve *His main objective was to increase profits.*

objective² /əbˈdʒektɪv/ *adjective* only influenced by facts and not by feelings *I try to be objective when I criticize someone's work.*

🧩 WORD PARTNERS FOR *obligation*

feel/have an obligation to do sth ● carry out/fulfil/meet an obligation ● be under an obligation

obligation /ˌɒblɪˈgeɪʃən/ noun [C, U] something that you do because it is your duty or because you feel you have to *a moral/legal obligation* ○ *to fulfil an obligation* ○ *He was under no obligation to answer any questions.* ○ [+ to do sth] *Parents have an obligation to make sure that their children receive a proper education.*

obligatory /əˈblɪgətʳri/ *adjective* If something is obligatory, you must do it because of a rule, or because everyone else does it. *obligatory military service*

oblige /əˈblaɪdʒ/ verb **1 be obliged to do sth** to be forced to do something *Sellers are not legally obliged to accept the highest offer.* **2** [I, T] *formal* to be helpful *The manager was only too happy to oblige.*

obliged /əˈblaɪdʒd/ *adjective* **1 feel obliged to do sth** to think that you must do something *They helped us when we moved so I feel obliged to do the same.* **2** *formal old-fashioned* grateful or pleased *Thank you, I'm much obliged to you.*

oblique /əʊˈbliːk/ *adjective formal* not expressed in a direct way *an oblique comment* ● **obliquely** *adverb formal*

obliterate /əˈblɪtʳreɪt/ verb [T] to destroy something completely [often passive] *The town was obliterated by bombs.*

oblivion /əˈblɪvɪən/ noun [U] **1** when something is not remembered *to disappear into oblivion* **2** when you are not aware of what is happening around you *He drank himself into oblivion.*

oblivious /əˈblɪvɪəs/ *adjective* not aware of something *She seemed completely oblivious to what was happening around her.*

obnoxious /əbˈnɒkʃəs/ *adjective* very unpleasant or rude *He was loud and obnoxious.*

obscene /əbˈsiːn/ *adjective* **1** relating to sex in a way that is unpleasant or shocking *an obscene gesture* ○ *obscene language* **2** An obscene amount of something is morally wrong because it is too large. *obscene profits*

obscenity /əb'senəti/ *noun* **1** [U] when something is sexually shocking *obscenity laws/ trials* **2** [C] a sexually shocking word or expression [usually plural] *He was shouting obscenities at people walking by.*

obscure¹ /əb'skjʊəʳ/ *adjective* **1** not known by many people *an obscure figure/writer* **2** difficult to understand *His answers were obscure and confusing.*

obscure² /əb'skjʊəʳ/ *verb* [T] **1** to prevent something from being seen or heard [often passive] *The moon was partially obscured by clouds.* **2** to make something difficult to understand *He deliberately obscured details of his career in the army.*

obscurity /əb'skjʊərəti/ *noun* [U] when something or someone is not known by many people *to fade into obscurity* ○ *He rose from relative obscurity to worldwide recognition.*

obsequious /əb'si:kwiəs/ *adjective formal* too willing to praise or obey someone

observance /əb'zɜ:vᵊns/ *noun* [C, U] *formal* when someone obeys a law or follows a religious custom *strict observance of the law* ○ *religious observances*

observant /əb'zɜ:vᵊnt/ *adjective* good or quick at noticing things *He's very observant.*

observation /ˌɒbzə'veɪʃᵊn/ *noun* **1** [U] when someone watches someone or something carefully *The doctor wants to keep him under observation for a week.* ○ *to have good powers of observation* (= to be good at noticing things) **2** [C] a remark about something that you have noticed *He made an interesting observation.*

observatory /əb'zɜ:vətri/ *noun* [C] a building that is used by scientists to look at stars and planets

observe /əb'zɜ:v/ *verb* [T] **1** [WATCH] to watch someone or something carefully *Children learn by observing adults.* **2** [NOTICE] *formal* to notice something **3** [SAY] *formal* to make a remark about something you have noticed *"It's still raining," he observed.* **4** [OBEY] to obey a law, rule, or religious custom *to observe the law*

observer /əb'zɜ:vəʳ/ *noun* [C] **1** someone who watches people and events as a job *a UN observer* ○ *a political observer* **2** someone who sees something *a casual observer*

obsess /əb'ses/ *verb* [I, T] If something or someone obsesses you, or if you obsess about something or someone, you think about them all the time. *She used to obsess about her weight.*

obsessed /əb'sest/ *adjective* **be obsessed by/ with sb/sth** to think about someone or something all the time *to be obsessed with money/ sex*

obsession /əb'seʃᵊn/ *noun* [C, U] someone or something that you think about all the time *an unhealthy obsession with death* ○ *a lifelong/ national obsession*

obsessive /əb'sesɪv/ *adjective* thinking too much about something, or doing something too much *obsessive behaviour* ○ *He's obsessive about his health.* • **obsessively** *adverb*

obsolete /'ɒbsᵊli:t/ *adjective* not used now *obsolete equipment* ○ *Will books become obsolete because of computers?*

obstacle /'ɒbstəkl/ *noun* [C] something that makes it difficult for you to go somewhere or to succeed at something *to overcome an obstacle* ○ *His refusal to talk is the main obstacle to peace.*

obstetrician /ˌɒbstə'trɪʃᵊn/ *noun* [C] a doctor who looks after pregnant women and helps in the birth of children

obstinate /'ɒbstɪnət/ *adjective* not willing to change your ideas or behaviour although you are wrong *He's a very rude and obstinate man.*

obstruct /əb'strʌkt/ *verb* [T] **1** to be in a place that stops someone or something from moving or stops someone from seeing something *to obstruct the traffic* ○ *There was a pillar obstructing our view.* **2** to try to stop something from happening or developing *to obstruct a police investigation* • **obstruction** /əb'strʌkʃᵊn/ *noun* [C, U] *Your car's causing an obstruction.* ○ *the obstruction of justice*

obtain /əb'teɪn/ *verb* [T] *formal* to get something *to obtain permission* ○ *He obtained a law degree from the University of California.* • **obtainable** *adjective* If something is obtainable, you can get it. *This information is easily obtainable on the Internet.*

⚬ᴑ**obvious** /'ɒbviəs/ *adjective* easy to understand or see *an obvious choice/answer* ○ [+ (that)] *It's obvious that he doesn't really care about her.*

⚬ᴑ**obviously** /'ɒbviəsli/ *adverb* in a way that is easy to understand or see *They're obviously in love.* ○ *Obviously we want to start as soon as possible.*

⚬ᴑ**occasion** /ə'keɪʒᵊn/ *noun* **1** [C] a time when something happens *a previous/separate occasion* ○ *We met on several occasions to discuss the issue.* ⊃See Common learner error at **possibility**. **2** [C] an important event or ceremony *a special occasion* ○ *She bought a new dress for the occasion.* **3** **on occasion(s)** sometimes, but not often *I only drink alcohol on occasion.*

occasional /ə'keɪʒᵊnᵊl/ *adjective* not happening often *He still plays the occasional game of football.* • **occasionally** *adverb They only meet occasionally.*

the occult /'ɒkʌlt/ *noun* the study of magic or mysterious powers

occupant /'ɒkjəpənt/ *noun* [C] *formal* someone who lives or works in a room or building *the occupant of No. 46*

occupation /ˌɒkjə'peɪʃᵊn/ *noun* **1** [JOB] [C] *formal* your job *You have to give your name, age, and occupation on the application form.* ⊃See Common learner error at **work**. **2** [CONTROL] [U] when an army moves into a place and takes control of it *a military occupation* **3** [HOBBY] [C] *formal* something that you do in your free time

occupational /ˌɒkjəˈpeɪʃᵊnᵊl/ *adjective* relating to your job *an occupational hazard*

occupied /ˈɒkjəpaɪd/ *adjective* **1** being used by someone *All of these seats are occupied.* ⊃Opposite **unoccupied. 2** busy doing something or thinking about something *There was enough to keep us occupied.*

occupier /ˈɒkjəpaɪəʳ/ *noun* [C] *UK* someone who lives or works in a room or building

occupy /ˈɒkjəpaɪ/ *verb* [T] **1** [FILL] to fill a place or period of time *His book collection occupies most of the room.* ○ *The baby seems to occupy all our time.* **2** [LIVE] to live or work in a room or building *They occupy the second floor of the building.* **3** [CONTROL] to move into a place and take control of it *The troops eventually occupied most of the island.*

◦•**occur** /əˈkɜːʳ/ *verb* [I] occurring *past* occurred **1** *formal* to happen, often without being planned *According to the police, the shooting occurred at about 12.30 a.m.* **2** occur in/among, etc sth/sb to exist or be present in a particular place or group of people *Minerals occur naturally in the Earth's crust.* ○ *The disease mainly occurs in women over 40.*

occur to sb to suddenly think of something [+ (that)] *It had never occurred to me that he might be lying.*

WORD PARTNERS FOR *occurrence*

a **common/everyday/rare/regular** occurrence

occurrence /əˈkʌrᵊns/ *noun* [C] something that happens *a common/everyday occurrence*

ocean /ˈəʊʃᵊn/ *noun* **1** [no plural] the sea *to swim in the ocean* **2** [C] one of the five main areas that the sea is divided into *the Pacific Ocean*

◦•**o'clock** /əˈklɒk/ *adverb* **one/two/three, etc o'clock** used after the numbers one to twelve to mean exactly that hour when you tell the time *It was ten o'clock when we got home.*

Oct *written abbreviation for* October

octagon /ˈɒktəgən/ *noun* [C] a flat shape with eight equal sides

octave /ˈɒktɪv/ *noun* [C] the space between two musical notes that are eight notes apart

◦•**October** /ɒkˈtəʊbəʳ/ (*written abbreviation* Oct) *noun* [C, U] the tenth month of the year

octopus /ˈɒktəpəs/ *noun* [C] a sea creature with eight long arms

octopus

odd /ɒd/ *adjective* **1** [STRANGE] strange or unusual *I always thought there was something odd about her.* ○ *It's a bit odd that he didn't come.* **2** [NOT OFTEN] [always before noun] not happening often *He does odd jobs here*

and there. **3** [SEPARATED] [always before noun] being one of a pair when the other item is missing *an odd sock* **4** [APPROXIMATELY] used after a number to mean approximately *There are thirty odd kids in the class.* **5** [NUMBER] An odd number does not produce a whole number when it is divided by two.

oddity /ˈɒdɪti/ *noun* [C] someone or something that is strange or unusual *He's always been a bit of an oddity.*

oddly /ˈɒdli/ *adverb* in a strange way *He's been behaving very oddly lately.* ○ *Oddly enough, business was good during the bad weather months.*

WORD PARTNERS FOR *odds*

the odds **of/on** sth happening • the odds are **(stacked) against** sb

odds /ɒdz/ *noun* [plural] **1** the probability that something will happen *What are the odds of winning the top prizes?* ○ *I'm afraid the odds are against us.* **2** against all (the) odds If you do or achieve something against all the odds, you succeed although you were not likely to. *We won the game against all odds.* **3** be at odds with sb/sth to not agree with someone or something *His remark was at odds with our report.* **4** odds and ends *informal* a group of small objects of different types which are not valuable or important

odious /ˈəʊdiəs/ *adjective formal* very unpleasant *an odious little man*

odour *UK* (*US* odor) /ˈəʊdəʳ/ *noun* [C] a smell, often one that is unpleasant *body odour*

odyssey /ˈɒdɪsi/ *noun* [C] *literary* a long, exciting journey

oestrogen *UK* (*US* estrogen) /ˈiːstrəʊdʒᵊn/ ⑫ /ˈestrədʒən/ *noun* [U] a chemical substance in a woman's body

◦•**of** *strong form* /ɒv/ *weak form* /əv/ *preposition* **1** [BELONG] belonging or relating to someone or something *a friend of mine* ○ *the colour of her hair* ○ *part of the problem* **2** [AMOUNT] used after words which show an amount *a kilo of apples* ○ *both of us* ○ *a handful of raisins* **3** [NUMBER] used with numbers, ages and dates *a boy of six* ○ *a decrease of 10%* ○ *the 14th of February 2005* **4** [CONTAIN] containing *a glass of milk* ○ *sacks of rubbish* **5** [MADE] made or consisting of *dresses of lace and silk* **6** [ADJECTIVE/VERB] used to connect particular adjectives and verbs with nouns *frightened of spiders* ○ *smelling of garlic* **7** [SHOW] showing someone or something *a map of the city centre* **8** [CAUSE] showing a reason or cause *He died of a heart attack.* **9** [POSITION] showing position or direction *the front of the queue* ○ *a small town north of Edinburgh* **10** [ACTION/FEELING] used after nouns describing actions or feelings to mean 'done to' or 'experienced by' *the destruction of the rain forest* ○ *the suffering of millions* **11** [WRITTEN] written or made by *the collected works of William Shakespeare*

◦•**of course** /əvˈkɔːs/ *adverb* **1** used to say 'yes' and emphasize your answer *'Can you help me?'* *'Of course!'* **2** used to show that what you are saying is obvious or already known *The rain* meant, of course, that the match was cancelled. ○ *Of course, the Olympics are not just about money.* **3 of course not** used to say 'no' and emphasize your answer *'Do you mind if I borrow your pen?' 'Of course not.'*

o▪**off¹** /ɒf/ *adverb, preposition* **1** NOT TOUCHING not touching or connected to something or not on a surface *Keep off the grass! ○ A button came off my coat.* **2** AWAY away from a place or position *He ran off to find his friend. ○ I'll be off (= will go) soon.* **3** NOT OPERATING not operating or being used *Make sure you switch your computer off.* **4** NEAR near to a building or place *an island off the coast of Spain* **5** PRICE If a price has a certain amount of money off, it costs that much less than the usual price. *These jeans were $10 off.* **6** DISTANCE/TIME far in distance or time *My holidays seem a long way off.* **7 go off sth/sb** *UK* to stop liking something or someone *I've gone off meat.* **8** NOT AT WORK not at work *I had 6 months off when my son was born.* ⊃See also: the **cuff**, **on²** and **off**.

off² /ɒf/ *adjective* [never before noun] **1** NOT CORRECT not correct *Our sales figures were off by ten percent.* **2** FOOD If food or drink is off, it is not now fresh and good to eat or drink. *This milk smells off.* **3** NOT AT WORK not at work *He's off today - I think he's ill.* ⊃See also: **off-chance**.

offal /ˈɒfl/ *noun* [U] organs from the inside of animals that are killed for food

,**off 'balance** *adjective, adverb* If someone or something is off balance, they are in a position where they are likely to fall or be knocked down. *to knock/throw someone off balance*

off-chance /ˈɒftʃɑːns/ *noun* *UK informal* **on the off-chance** hoping that something may be possible, although it is not likely *I went to the station on the off-chance that she'd be there.*

,**off 'duty** *adjective* When an official such as a police officer is off duty, they are not working.

⌐⌐┐ WORD PARTNERS FOR **offence**

cause/give/take offence • **grave** offence

o▪**offence** *UK* (*US* **offense**) /əˈfens/ *noun* **1** [U] when something rude makes someone upset or angry *to cause/give offence ○ Many people take offence at swearing.* **2** [C] a crime *a criminal offence ○ He committed several serious offences.*

o▪**offend** /əˈfend/ *verb* **1** [T] to make someone upset or angry [often passive] *I was deeply offended by her comments.* **2** [I] *formal* to commit a crime *If she offends again, she'll go to prison.*

offender /əˈfendər/ *noun* [C] someone who has committed a crime *a sex offender ○ a young offender*

o▪**offense** /əˈfens/ *noun* *US spelling of* offence

o▪**offensive¹** /əˈfensɪv/ *adjective* **1** likely to make people angry or upset *an offensive remark* ⊃Opposite **inoffensive**. **2** used for attacking *an offensive weapon* • **offensively** *adverb*

offensive² /əˈfensɪv/ *noun* [C] an attack *It's time to launch a major offensive against terrorism.*

o▪**offer¹** /ˈɒfər/ *verb* **1** ASK [+ two objects] to ask someone if they would like something *They offered me a job. ○ Someone should offer that old lady a seat.* **2** SAY YOU WILL DO [I, T] to say that you are willing to do something [+ to do sth] *He offered to get me a cab. ○ Polly has offered to help out with the preparations.* **3** AGREE TO PAY [T] to say that you will pay a particular amount of money [+ two objects] *I offered him £500 for the car. ○ Police have offered a $1,000 reward for information.* **4** PROVIDE [T] to give or provide something *to offer advice ○ The hotel offers a wide range of facilities. ○ What sort of services do you offer?*

⌐⌐┐ WORD PARTNERS FOR **offer**

accept/make/receive/turn down an offer • a **generous/tempting** offer • an offer **of** sth

o▪**offer²** /ˈɒfər/ *noun* [C] **1** ASK when you ask someone if they would like something *an offer of help ○ a job offer ○ to accept/refuse an offer* **2** PAYMENT an amount of money that you say you will pay for something *The highest offer anyone has made so far is £150.* **3** CHEAP a cheap price or special arrangement for something you are buying *This special offer ends on Friday.* **4 on offer a** CHEAP at a cheaper price than usual *Are these jeans still on offer?* **b** AVAILABLE available to do or have *We were amazed at the range of products on offer. ○ You should find out about the services on offer.*

offering /ˈɒfərɪŋ/ *noun* [C] something that you give to someone *a peace offering*

offhand¹ /ˌɒfˈhænd/ *adjective* not friendly or polite *He was a bit offhand with me.*

offhand² /ˌɒfˈhænd/ *adverb* immediately, without thinking about something *I don't know offhand how much it will cost. ○ I couldn't say offhand how long the process will take.*

o▪**office** /ˈɒfɪs/ *noun* **1** PLACE [C] a room or building where people work *an office worker ○ I never get to the office before nine.* ⊃See colour picture **The Office** on page Centre 5. **2** INFORMATION [C] a room or building where you can get information, tickets, or a particular service *a ticket office ○ the tourist office* **3** JOB [U] an important job in an organization *Some people think he has been in office for too long. ○ She held the office of mayor for eight years.* ⊃See also: **box office**, the **Oval Office**, **post office**, **register office**, **registry office**.

'**office ,building** (*also UK* **office block**) *noun* [C] a large building which contains offices *The town centre is full of office buildings.*

'**office ,hours** *noun* [plural] the hours during the day when people who work in offices are usually at work *I'm available during normal office hours.*

officer /ˈɒfɪsər/ *noun* [C] **1** MILITARY someone with an important job in a military organization *an army/naval officer* **2** GOVERNMENT someone who works for a government department *a customs officer ○ a prison officer*

O

3 [POLICE] a police officer *a uniformed officer* ⊃See also: **probation officer.**

o➤**official¹** /əˈfɪʃᵊl/ *adjective* **1** [APPROVED] approved by the government or someone in authority *the official language of Singapore* ○ *an official document* **2** [JOB] [always before noun] relating to the duties of someone in a position of authority *the official residence of the ambassador* ○ *an official visit* **3** [KNOWN] known to the public *It's official - they're getting married!* **4** [NOT TRUE] [always before noun] An official explanation or statement is one that is given, but which may not be true. *The official reason for the delay is bad weather.* ⊃Opposite **unofficial.**
● **officially** *adverb The new hospital was officially opened yesterday.*

official² /əˈfɪʃᵊl/ *noun* [C] someone who has an important position in an organization such as the government *a senior official* ○ *a UN official*

offing /ˈɒfɪŋ/ *noun* **be in the offing** If something is in the offing, it will happen or be offered soon. *He thinks there might be a promotion in the offing.*

off-licence /ˈɒflaɪsᵊns/ *UK* (*US* **liquor store**) *noun* [C] a shop that sells alcoholic drink

offline /ɒfˈlaɪn/ (*also* **off-line**) *adjective, adverb* A computer is offline when it is not connected to a central system, or not connected to the Internet.

off-peak /ˌɒfˈpiːk/ *adjective* not at the most popular and expensive time *an off-peak phone call*

offset /ˌɒfˈset/ *verb* [T] **offsetting** *past* **offset** If one thing offsets another thing, it has the opposite effect and so creates a more balanced situation. [often passive] *The costs have been offset by savings in other areas.*

offshore /ˌɒfˈʃɔːʳ/ *adjective* [always before noun] **1** in the sea and away from the coast *an offshore island* **2** An offshore bank or bank account is based in another country and so less tax has to be paid. *an offshore account/trust*

offside /ˌɒfˈsaɪd/ (*also US* **offsides**) *adjective* [always before noun] In sports such as football, a player who is offside is in a position that is not allowed.

offspring /ˈɒfsprɪŋ/ *noun* [C] *plural* **offspring** *formal* the child of a person or animal *to produce offspring*

off-the-cuff /ˌɒfðəˈkʌf/ *adjective* An off-the-cuff remark is one that is not planned.

o➤**often** /ˈɒfᵊn, ˈɒftᵊn/ *adverb* **1** many times or regularly *I often see her there.* ○ *He said I could visit as often as I liked.* ○ *How often* (= How many times) *do you go to the gym?* ○ *I don't see her very often.* **2** If something often happens or is often true, it is normal for it to happen or it is usually true. *Headaches are often caused by stress.* ○ *Brothers and sisters often argue.*

ogre /ˈəʊɡəʳ/ *noun* [C] an unpleasant, frightening person

o➤**oh** /əʊ/ *exclamation* **1** used before you say something, often before replying to what someone has said *"Ian's going." "Oh, I didn't realize."* ○ *"I'm so sorry." "Oh, don't worry."* **2** used to show an emotion or to emphasize your opinion about something *Oh, no! I don't believe it!* ○ *"I don't think I can come." "Oh, that's a shame."* ○ *Oh, how sweet of you!*

o➤**oil** /ɔɪl/ *noun* [U] **1** a thick liquid that comes from under the Earth's surface that is used as a fuel and for making parts of machines move smoothly *an oil company* ○ *an oil well* **2** a thick liquid produced from plants or animals that is used in cooking *vegetable oil* ⊃See also: **crude oil, olive oil.**

oilfield /ˈɔɪlfiːld/ *noun* [C] an area under the ground where oil is found *an offshore oilfield*

oil ˌpainting *noun* [C] a picture made using paint which contains oil

oil ˌspill *noun* [C] when oil has come out of a ship and caused pollution

oily /ˈɔɪli/ *adjective* containing a lot of oil or covered with oil *oily fish* ○ *oily hands*

oink /ɔɪnk/ *noun* [C] the sound that a pig makes

ointment /ˈɔɪntmənt/ *noun* [C, U] a smooth, thick substance that is used on painful or damaged skin

okay¹ (*also* **OK**) /əʊˈkeɪ/ *exclamation* **1** used when agreeing to do something or when allowing someone to do something *"Let's meet this afternoon." "Okay."* ○ *"Can I use the car?" "Okay."* **2** used before you start speaking, especially to a group of people *Okay, I'm going to start by showing you a few figures.*

o➤**okay²** *informal* (*also* **OK**) /əʊˈkeɪ/ *adjective, adverb* **1** [GOOD] good or good enough *Is your food okay?* ○ *It was okay, but it wasn't as good as his last film.* **2** [SAFE] safe or healthy *Is your grandmother okay now?* **3** [ALLOWED] allowed or acceptable *Is it okay if I leave early today?* ○ [+ to do sth] *Is it okay to smoke in here?*

o➤**old** /əʊld/ *adjective* **1** [LIVED LONG] having lived or existed for a long time *an old man/woman* ○ *an old house* ○ *We're all getting older.* ○ *Children should show some respect for the old.* **2** [USED A LOT] having been used or owned for a long time *You might get dirty so wear some old clothes.* **3** [AGE] used to describe or ask about someone's age *How old are you?* ○ *She'll be 3 years old this month.* ⊃See Common learner error at **year.** **4 an old friend/enemy, etc** someone who has been your friend/enemy, etc for a long time *I met an old friend who I was at college with.* **5** [BEFORE] [always before noun] used before or in the past *I think the old system was better in many ways.*

COMMON LEARNER ERROR

older, oldest, elder, eldest

Older and **oldest** are the comparative and superlative forms of the adjective 'old'.

I'm four years older than my sister.

Pedro is the oldest student in the class.

The adjectives **elder** and **eldest** are only used before nouns. They are usually used when you are comparing members of a family.

My elder brother is a doctor.

Mary has three sons. Her eldest boy is called Mark.

,old 'age *noun* [U] the period of time when you are old

,old-age 'pension *noun* [U] *UK* money that people receive regularly from the government when they are old and have stopped working

,old-age 'pensioner *noun* [C] *UK* someone who gets an old-age pension

olden /'əʊldən/ *adjective* **in the olden days/in olden times** a long time ago

o--**old-fashioned** /ˌəʊld'fæʃənd/ *adjective* not modern *old-fashioned clothes/furniture*

oldie /'əʊldi/ *noun* [C] *informal* an old song or film, or an old person *a golden oldie*

old-style /'əʊldstaɪl/ *adjective* [always before noun] used or done in the past *old-style politics*

the ,Old 'Testament *noun* the part of the Bible (= holy book) written before the birth of Jesus Christ

the 'Old ,World *noun* Asia, Africa, and Europe

olive /'ɒlɪv/ *noun* 1 [C] a small green or black fruit with a bitter taste that is eaten or used to produce oil 2 [U] (*also* ,olive 'green) a colour that is a mixture of green and yellow ● **olive** (*also* **olive-green**) *adjective*

'olive ,oil *noun* [U] oil produced from olives, used for cooking or on salads

-**ology** /-ɒlədʒi/ *suffix* makes a noun meaning 'the study of something' *psychology* (= the study of the mind) ○ *sociology* (= the study of society)

the Olympic Games /ðiːə'lɪmpɪkˌɡeɪmz/ (*also* the Olympics) *noun* [plural] an international sports competition that happens every four years ● **Olympic** *adjective* [always before noun] relating to the Olympic Games *She broke the Olympic record.*

ombudsman /'ɒmbʊdzmən/ *noun* [C] *plural* ombudsmen someone who deals with complaints that people make against the government or public organizations

omelette /'ɒmlət/ (*also US* omelet) *noun* [C] a food made with eggs that have been mixed and fried, often with other foods added *a mushroom and cheese omelette*

a **bad/good/lucky** omen ● an omen **of** [death/disaster/good fortune,etc] ● an omen **for** sb/sth

omen /'əʊmən/ *noun* [C] a sign of what will happen in the future *a good/bad omen*

ominous /'ɒmɪnəs/ *adjective* making you think that something bad is going to happen *an ominous sign* ○ *ominous clouds*

a **glaring/serious/surprising** omission ● sb/sth's omission **from** sth ● the omission **of** sb/sth

omission /əʊ'mɪʃən/ *noun* [C, U] when something has not been included but should have been *There are some serious omissions in the book.*

omit /əʊ'mɪt/ *verb* omitting *past* omitted 1 [T] to not include something [often passive] *He was omitted from the team because of his behaviour.* 2 **omit to do sth** *mainly UK formal* to not do something *She omitted to mention where she was going.*

o--**on**¹ /ɒn/ *preposition* 1 SURFACE on a surface of something *We put all of our medicine on a high shelf.* 2 PLACE in a particular place *the diagram on page 2* ○ *I met her on a ship.* 3 RECORDING/PERFORMANCE used to show the way in which something is recorded or performed *What's on television tonight?* 4 TOUCHING used to show what happens as a result of touching something *I cut myself on a knife.* 5 SUBJECT about *a book on pregnancy* 6 MONEY/TIME used to show what money or time is used for *I've wasted too much time on this already.* ○ *She refuses to spend more than £20 on a pair of shoes.* 7 NEXT TO next to or along the side of *The post office is on Bateman Street.* 8 DATE/DAY used to show the date or day when something happens *He's due to arrive on 14 February.* ○ *I'm working on my birthday.* 9 USING using something *I spoke to Mum on the phone.* 10 AFTER happening after something and often because of it *The Prince was informed on his return to the UK.* 11 TRANSPORT used to show some methods of travelling *Did you go over on the ferry?* ○ *Sam loves travelling on buses.* 12 FOOD/FUEL/DRUGS used to show something that is used as food, fuel, or a drug *This radio runs on batteries.* ○ *I can't drink wine because I'm on antibiotics.* 13 **be on a committee/panel,** etc to be a member of a group or organization *She's on the playgroup committee.* 14 **have/carry sth on you** to have something with you *Do you have your driving licence on you?* 15 **be on me/him,** etc *informal* used to show who is paying for something *This meal is on me.*

o--**on**² /ɒn/ *adverb* 1 CONTINUE used to show that an action or event continues *The old tradition lives on.* ○ *It was a complicated situation that dragged on for weeks.* 2 WEAR If you have something on, you are wearing it. *She's got a black coat on.* ○ *Why don't you put your new dress on?* 3 WORKING working or being used *The heating has been on all day.* 4 TRAVEL into a bus, train, plane, etc *Amy got on in Stamford.* 5 HAPPENING happening or planned *I've got a lot on at the moment.* ○ *Have you checked what's on at the cinema?* 6 **on and off** (*also* off and on) If something happens on and off during a period of time, it happens sometimes. *They've been seeing each other on and off since Christmas.*

o--**once**¹ /wʌns/ *adverb* 1 ONE TIME one time *It's only snowed once or twice this year.* ○ *I go swimming once a week* (= one time every week). 2 NOT NOW in the past, but not now *This house once belonged to my grandfather.* 3 **once again** again *Once again I'm left with all the washing up.* 4 **all at once** suddenly *All at once he stood up and walked out of the room.* 5 **at once a** IMMEDIATELY immediately *I knew at once that I would like it here.* **b** AT SAME TIME at the same time *They all started talking at once.* 6 **once in a while** sometimes but not often *He plays tennis once in a while.* 7 **once and for all**

O

| j yes | k cat | ŋ ring | ʃ she | θ thin | ð this | ʒ decision | dʒ jar | tʃ chip | æ cat | e bed | ə ago | ɪ sit | i cosy | ɒ hot | ʌ run | ʊ put |

If you do something **once and for all**, you do it now so that it does not have to be dealt with again. *Let's get to the bottom of this matter once and for all!* **8 once more** one more time *If you say that once more, I'm going to leave.* **9 for once** used to mean that something is happening that does not usually happen *For once, I think I have good news for him.* **10 once upon a time** used at the beginning of a children's story to mean that something happened a long time ago ⊃See also: once in a blue **moon**.

∘ᴿ**once²** /wʌns/ *conjunction* as soon as *Once I've found somewhere to live, I'll send you my new address.* ∘ *We'll send your tickets once we've received your cheque.*

oncoming /'ɒn,kʌmɪŋ/ *adjective* [always before noun] Oncoming vehicles are coming towards you.

∘ᴿ**one¹** /wʌn/ the number 1 ⊃See also: back to **square¹** one.

∘ᴿ**one²** /wʌn/ *pronoun* **1** used to refer to a particular person or thing in a group that has already been talked about *I've just made some scones, do you want one?* ∘ *Throw those gloves away and get some new ones.* ∘ *Chris is* **the one** *with glasses.* **2** *formal* any person in general *One ought to respect one's parents.* **3 one at a time** separately *Eat them one at a time.* **4 one by one** separately, with one thing happening after another *One by one the old buildings have been demolished.* **5 one another** each other *How can they reach an agreement if they won't talk to one another?* **6 (all) in one** combined into a single thing *It's a CD player and cassette deck all in one.*

∘ᴿ**one³** /wʌn/ *determiner* **1** PARTICULAR PERSON/THING used to refer to a particular person or thing in a group *One drawback is the cost of housing in the area.* ∘ **One** *of our daughters has just got married.* **2** FUTURE TIME used to refer to a time in the future which is not yet decided *We must have a drink together one evening.* **3** TIME IN PAST at a particular time in the past *I first met him one day in the park.* **4** ONLY only *He's the one person you can rely on in this place.* **5** WITH ADJECTIVE mainly US used to emphasize an adjective *That's one big ice cream you've got there!* **6 one or two** a few *I'd like to make one or two suggestions.* ⊃See also: put sth to one **side¹**, be one **step¹** ahead (of sb).

one-man /,wʌn'mæn/ *adjective* [always before noun] with only one person doing something *a one-man show*

,**one-night 'stand** *noun* [C] when two people have sex just after they meet but do not then have a relationship

one-off /,wʌn'ɒf/ *adjective* [always before noun] *UK* only happening once *a* **one-off payment** ● **one-off** *noun* [C] *UK* something that only happens once *His Olympic victory was not just a one-off.*

one-on-one /,wʌnɒn'wʌn/ *adjective, adverb* mainly *US* only including two people

onerous /'əʊnᵊrəs/ *adjective formal* difficult and needing a lot of effort *an onerous task*

oneself /wʌn'self/ *pronoun formal* the reflexive form of the pronoun 'one' when it refers to the

person speaking or people in general *How else should one protect oneself and one's family?*

one-sided /,wʌn'saɪdɪd/ *adjective* **1** If a competition is one-sided, one team or player is much better than the other. *a one-sided contest/game* **2** only considering one opinion in an argument in a way that is unfair *a one-sided view*

one-time /'wʌntaɪm/ *adjective* [always before noun] A one-time position or job is one that you had or did in the past, but not now. *a one-time friend/minister*

one-to-one /,wʌntə'wʌn/ *adjective, adverb* mainly *UK* only including two people *She's having private lessons on a one-to-one basis.*

one-way /,wʌn'weɪ/ *adjective* If a road is one-way, you can only drive on it in one direction. *a one-way street*

,**one-way 'ticket** *US* (*UK* **single**) *noun* [C] A one-way ticket for a journey can only be used to travel in one direction and not for returning. *a one-way ticket to Memphis*

ongoing /'ɒn,gəʊɪŋ/ *adjective* [always before noun] still happening *an ongoing process/investigation*

onion /'ʌnjən/ *noun* [C, U] a round vegetable with layers that has a strong taste and smell ⊃See colour picture **Fruit and Vegetables** on page Centre 10 ⊃See also: spring **onion**.

∘ᴿ**online** /,ɒn'laɪn/ *adjective, adverb* connected to a system of computers, especially the Internet *online services* ∘ *to* **go online** (= start using the Internet) ∘ *Most newspapers are now available online.* ⊃See Extra help page **The Web and the Internet** on page Centre 36.

onlooker /'ɒn,lʊkəʳ/ *noun* [C] someone who watches something happening without becoming involved in it *a crowd of onlookers*

∘ᴿ**only¹** /'əʊnli/ *adverb* **1** NOT MORE not more than a particular size or amount *It'll only take a few minutes.* ∘ *She's only fifteen.* **2** NO ONE/NOTHING ELSE not anyone or anything else *The offer is available to UK residents only.* **3** RECENTLY used to mean that something happened very recently *She's* **only just** *finished writing it.* **4 not only ... (but) also** used to say that one thing is true and another thing is true too, especially a surprising thing *Not only did he turn up late, he also forgot his books.*

∘ᴿ**only²** /'əʊnli/ *adjective* [always before noun] used to mean that there are not any others *This could be our only chance.* ∘ *You're the only person here I know.*

only³ /'əʊnli/ *conjunction* used to introduce a statement which explains why something you have just said cannot happen or is not completely true *I'd phone him myself only I know he's not there at the moment.*

'**only ,child** *noun* [C] *plural* **only children** someone who has no brothers or sisters

on-screen /'ɒnskriːn/ *adjective, adverb* appearing on a computer or television screen

onset /'ɒnset/ *noun* **the onset of sth** the beginning of something, usually something unpleasant *the onset of cancer*

| ɑː arm | ɜː her | iː see | ɔː saw | uː too | aɪ my | aʊ how | eə hair | eɪ day | əʊ no | ɪə near | ɔɪ boy | ʊə poor | aɪə fire | aʊə sour |

open

The window is open.

WORD PARTNERS FOR *onslaught*

launch/mount an onslaught • an onslaught **against/on** sb

onslaught /ˈɒnslɔːt/ *noun* [C] when someone attacks or criticizes someone or something *It is unlikely that his forces could withstand an allied onslaught for very long.* ○ *Scotland's onslaught on Wales in the second half earned them a 4-1 victory.*

o⟶**onto** (*also* **on to**) /ˈɒntuː/ *preposition* **1** used to show movement into or on a particular place *The sheep were loaded onto trucks.* ○ *Can you get back onto the path?* ○ *I slipped as I stepped onto the platform* ○ *I've been having problems loading this software onto my computer.* **2 hold/grip, etc onto sth** to hold something *Hold onto my hand before we cross the road.* ○ *Grip onto the hand-rail as you climb the stairs.* **3** used to show that you are starting to talk about a different subject *Can we move onto the next item on the agenda?* **4 be onto sb** to know that someone has done something wrong or illegal *She knows we're onto her and she's trying to get away.* ○ *Who **put** the police **onto** (= told the police about) her?* **5 be onto sth** to know or discover something useful or important *Researchers think they may be onto something big.* ○ *You're onto a good thing with this buy-one-get-one-free offer at the shop.* ○ *Can you **put** me **onto** (= tell me about) a good dentist?*

the onus /ˈəʊnəs/ *noun formal* the responsibility for doing something *The onus is on parents to make sure their children attend school.* ○ *The onus is on the landlord to ensure that the property is habitable.*

onward /ˈɒnwəd/ (*also* **onwards**) *adverb* **1 from the 1870s/March/6.30 pm, etc onwards** beginning at a time and continuing after it *I'm usually at home from 5 o'clock onward.* **2** If you move onwards, you continue to go forwards. *We sailed onwards in a north-westerly direction.*

oops /uːps/ *exclamation* something you say when you make a mistake or have a slight accident *Oops! I've spilled my coffee.* ○ *Oops! I've typed two L's by mistake.*

ooze /uːz/ *verb* **1** [I, T] If a liquid oozes from something or if something oozes a liquid, the liquid comes out slowly. *Blood was oozing out of the wound.* ○ *The waiter brought her a massive pizza oozing (with) cheese.* **2** [T] *informal* to show a lot of a quality *to **ooze charm***

opaque /əʊˈpeɪk/ *adjective* **1** If an object or substance is opaque, you cannot see through it. *We need opaque glass for the bathroom window.* **2** *formal* difficult to understand *I find her poetry rather opaque.*

op-ed /ɒpˈed/ *US* (*UK* **editorial**) *adjective* [always before noun] describes a piece of writing in a newspaper in which a writer gives an opinion about a subject *an **op-ed article/page***

The book is open.

o⟶**open¹** /ˈəʊpən/ *adjective* **1** [NOT CLOSED] not closed or fastened *an **open** door/window* ○ *Someone had left the gate wide open.* ○ *Is there a bottle of wine already open?* ○ *A magazine was lying open on her lap.* **2** [DOING BUSINESS] A shop or business is open during the time it is available for business or serving customers. *Most shops are open on Sundays now.* **3** [COMPUTERS] If a computer document or program is open, it is ready to be read or used. **4** [WITHOUT BUILDINGS] [always before noun] An open area of land has no buildings on it or near it. *large **open** spaces* **5** [NOT COVERED] [always before noun] without a roof or cover *an **open** courtyard* **6** [FOR EVERYONE] If a place or event is open, everyone can go to it or become involved in it. *an **open** debate* ○ *Are the gardens **open** to the public?* **7** [HONEST] An open person is honest and does not hide their feelings. **8** [NOT HIDDEN] [always before noun] Open feelings, usually negative ones, are not hidden. *open hostility/rivalry* **9** [NOT DECIDED] If a decision or question is open, it has not yet been decided. *We don't have to make a firm arrangement now. Let's **leave it open**.* **10 have/keep an open mind** to wait until you know all the facts before you form an opinion about something or judge someone *The cause of the fire is still unclear and we are keeping an **open mind**.* **11 open to discussion/suggestions, etc** willing to consider a discussion/suggestions, etc *This is only a proposal. I'm open to suggestions.* **12 open to abuse/criticism, etc** likely to be abused/criticized, etc *The system is wide open to abuse.* ⊃See also: with your eyes (**eye¹**) open.

COMMON LEARNER ERROR

open and close

Be careful not to confuse the adjective and verb forms of these words.

The adjectives are **open** and **closed**.

Is the supermarket open on Sunday?

The museum is closed today.

The verbs are **open** and **close**.
The supermarket opens at 8 a.m.
The museum closes at 5 p.m. today.

◦▪**open²** /ˈəʊpᵊn/ *verb* **1** NOT CLOSED [I, T] If something opens, it changes to a position that is not closed, and if you open it, you make it change to a position that is not closed. *to open a door/window* ○ *The gate won't open.* ○ *Don't open your eyes yet.* **2** REMOVE COVER [T] to remove part of a container or parcel so that you can see or use what it contains *Karen opened the box and looked inside.* ○ *Why don't you open the envelope?* ○ *I can't open this bottle.* **3** PREPARE FOR USE [I, T] If an object opens, the parts that are folded together move apart, and if you open it, you make the parts that are folded together move apart. *Shall I open the umbrella?* ○ *Open your books at page 22.* **4** START WORK [I] If a shop or office opens at a particular time of day, it starts to do business at that time. *What time does the bank open?* **5** COMPUTERS [T] to make a computer document or program ready to be read or used **6** START OFFICIALLY [I, T] If a business or activity opens, it starts officially for the first time, and if you open it, you make it start officially for the first time. *That restaurant's new - it only opened last month.* ○ *Several shops have opened up in the last year.* **7** MAKE AVAILABLE [T] to allow people to use a road or area *They opened up the roads again the day after the flooding.* **8 open an account** to make an arrangement to keep your money with a bank *Have you opened a bank account yet?* ⊃See also: open the floodgates.

open (sth) up 1 to create a new opportunity or possibility *A teaching qualification can open up many more career opportunities.* **2** to open the lock on the door of a building *The caretaker opens up the school every morning at seven.*

open up to start to talk more about yourself and your feelings *I've tried to get him to open up to me, but with no success.*

the open /ˈəʊpᵊn/ *noun* **1 in the open** outside *We spent the night in the open.* **2 bring sth out into the open** to tell people information that was secret [often passive] *It's time this issue was brought out into the open.*

open-air /ˌəʊpənˈeəʳ/ *adjective* [always before noun] An open-air place does not have a roof. *an open-air swimming pool*

'**open ,day** *noun* [C] *UK* a day when people can visit a school or organization to see what happens there

open-ended /ˌəʊpənˈendɪd/ *adjective* An open-ended activity or situation does not have a planned ending. *We are not willing to enter into open-ended discussions.*

opener /ˈəʊpənəʳ/ *noun* [C] **1 bottle/can/tin, etc opener** a piece of kitchen equipment used to open bottles/cans, etc **2** someone or something that begins a series of events, usually in sports ⊃See also: eye-opener.

opening¹ /ˈəʊpənɪŋ/ *noun* [C] **1** HOLE a hole or space that something or someone can pass through *We found an opening in the fence and*

climbed through. **2** START the beginning of something *The opening of the opera is quite dramatic.* **3** CEREMONY a ceremony at the beginning of an event or activity *I've been invited to the opening of the new exhibition on Tuesday.* **4** OPPORTUNITY a job or an opportunity to do something *There's an opening for an editorial assistant in our department.*

opening² /ˈəʊpənɪŋ/ *adjective* [always before noun] happening at the beginning of an event or activity *the opening night* ○ *her opening remarks*

openly /ˈəʊpᵊnli/ *adverb* without hiding any of your thoughts or feelings *He talks quite openly about his feelings.*

open-minded /ˌəʊpᵊnˈmaɪndɪd/ *adjective* willing to consider ideas and opinions that are new or different to your own

openness /ˈəʊpᵊnnəs/ *noun* [U] when someone is honest about their thoughts and feelings *I appreciated his openness.*

open-plan /ˌəʊpᵊnˈplæn/ *adjective* describes a room or a building without many walls *an open-plan office*

opera /ˈɒpᵊrə/ *noun* [C, U] a musical play in which most of the words are sung *to go to the opera* ○ *opera singers* ○ *an opera house* (= building for opera) ●**operatic** /ˌɒpᵊrˈætɪk/ *adjective* relating to opera *an operatic society*

◦▪**operate** /ˈɒpᵊreɪt/ *verb* **1** ORGANIZATION [I, T] If an organization or business operates, it is working, and if you operate it, you manage it and make it work. *Our company is operating under very difficult conditions at present.* **2** MACHINE [I, T] If a machine operates, it does what it is designed to do, and if you operate it, you make it do what it is designed to do. *You have to be trained to operate the machinery.* **3** TREATMENT [I] to treat an illness or injury by cutting someone's body and removing or repairing part of it *Did they have to operate on him?*

'**operating ,room** *US* (*UK* operating theatre) *noun* [C] a room in a hospital where doctors do operations

'**operating ,system** *noun* [C] computer software that controls how different parts of a computer work together

'**operating ,theatre** *UK* (*US* operating room) *noun* [C] a room in a hospital where doctors do operations

WORD PARTNERS FOR **operation**

have/undergo an operation ● **do/perform** an operation ● an operation **on** sb/sb's [hand/knee, etc] ● a **major/minor** operation

◦▪**operation** /ˌɒpᵊrˈeɪʃᵊn/ *noun* [C] **1** MEDICAL TREATMENT when a doctor cuts someone's body to remove or repair part of it *a heart/lung operation* ○ *a major/minor operation* ○ *My son's got to have an operation.* **2** ORGANIZATION an organization or business *a large commercial operation* **3** ACTIVITY an activity that is intended to achieve a particular purpose *a military/peacekeeping operation* ○ *a joint operation by French and Spanish police* **4 in operation** If a machine or system is in operation, it is working or being used. *The new rail link is now in operation.* ◦ *Most of the machines are now back in operation.*

operational /ˌɒpᵊr'eɪʃᵊnᵊl/ *adjective* **1** If a system is operational, it is working. *The service becomes fully operational next June.* **2** [always before noun] relating to a particular activity *operational control/responsibility*

operative¹ /'ɒpᵊrᵊtɪv/ *adjective formal* working or being used *The agreement will not become operative until all members have signed.*

operative² /'ɒpᵊrᵊtɪv/ *noun* [C] *mainly US* someone who does secret work for a government or other organization *a former CIA operative*

operator /'ɒpᵊreɪtᵊr/ *noun* [C] **1** ⃞TELEPHONE⃞ someone who helps to connect people on a telephone system *Why don't you call the operator?* **2** ⃞MACHINE⃞ someone whose job is to use and control a machine or vehicle *a computer operator* **3** ⃞BUSINESS⃞ a company that does a particular type of business *a tour operator*

🧩 WORD PARTNERS FOR *opinion*

express/hold/voice an opinion • a **favourable/low/personal/poor/strong** opinion • sb's opinion **about/on** sth • **in** sb's opinion

◦━**opinion** /ə'pɪnjən/ *noun* **1** [C] a thought or belief about something or someone *What's your opinion about/on the matter?* ◦ *He has fairly strong opinions on most subjects.* ◦ *In my opinion* (= I think) *he's the best football player we have in this country.* ◦ *I asked Christopher his opinion on the subject.* ◦ *Caroline, I'd like your opinion on a matter.* **2** public opinion the thoughts and beliefs that most people have about a subject *Eventually, the government will have to take notice of public opinion.* **3** have a high/low opinion of sb/sth to think that someone or something is good/bad *He has a low opinion of doctors.*

opinionated /ə'pɪnjəneɪtɪd/ *adjective* being too certain that your strong opinions are correct *I found him arrogant and opinionated.*

o'pinion ˌpoll *noun* [C] when people are asked questions to discover what they think about a subject *The latest opinion poll shows that the president's popularity has improved.*

opium /'əʊpiəm/ *noun* [U] a drug made from the seeds of a poppy (= a red flower)

opponent /ə'pəʊnənt/ *noun* [C] **1** someone who you compete against in a game or competition *He beat his opponent six games to two.* **2** someone who disagrees with an action or belief and tries to change it *an opponent of slavery* ◦ *a political opponent*

opportune /'ɒpətjuːn/ *adjective formal* **an opportune moment/time** a good time for something to happen *His letter arrived at an opportune moment.*

opportunist /ˌɒpə'tjuːnɪst/ *noun* [C] someone who tries to get power or an advantage in every situation • **opportunistic** /ˌɒpətjuː'nɪstɪk/ *adjective* using a situation to get power or an advantage

🧩 WORD PARTNERS FOR *opportunity*

create/have/miss/offer/provide/seize an opportunity • a **golden/good/great/unique** opportunity • **at every** opportunity • an opportunity **for** sth

◦━**opportunity** /ˌɒpə'tjuːnəti/ *noun* **1** [C, U] a situation in which it is possible for you to do something, or a possibility of doing something *a unique opportunity* ◦ *a golden* (= very good) *opportunity* ◦ [+ to do sth] *Everyone will have an opportunity to comment.* ◦ *There are plenty of opportunities for research.* ◦ *Don't miss this opportunity to win a million pounds.* ◦ *She talks about her boyfriend at every opportunity* . **2** [C] the chance to get a job [usually plural] *opportunities for young graduates* ◦ *job/employment opportunities* **3** **take the opportunity to do sth** to use an occasion to do or say something *I'd like to take this opportunity to thank all of you.* ➲See Common learner error at **possibility**.

◦━**oppose** /ə'pəʊz/ *verb* [T] to disagree with a plan or activity and to try to change or stop it *The committee opposed a proposal to allow women to join the club.*

opposed /ə'pəʊzd/ *adjective* **1** **be opposed to sth** to disagree with a plan or activity *We're not opposed to tax increases.* **2** **as opposed to** used to say that two things are very different *I'm talking about English football, as opposed to European football.*

opposing /ə'pəʊzɪŋ/ *adjective* **1** **opposing teams/players, etc** Opposing teams/players, etc are competing against each other. **2** **opposing ideas/beliefs, etc** Opposing ideas/beliefs, etc are completely different. *The book presents two opposing views.*

◦━**opposite**¹ /'ɒpəzɪt/ *adjective* **1** in a position facing or someone but on the other side *on the opposite page* ◦ *in the opposite corner* ◦ *We live on opposite sides of the city.* ◦ *I noticed a gate at the opposite end of the courtyard.* **2** completely different *Police attempts to calm the violence had completely the opposite effect.*

◦━**opposite**² /'ɒpəzɪt/ *adverb, preposition* in a position facing something or someone but on the other side *The couple sat down opposite her.* ◦ *UK She lives opposite* (= on the other side of the road). ◦ *Is there a bakery opposite your house?*

◦━**opposite**³ /'ɒpəzɪt/ *noun* [C] someone or something that is completely different from another person or thing *They're complete opposites.* ◦ *He's the exact opposite of my father.*

the ˌopposite 'sex *noun* someone who is male if you are female, or female if you are male *It's not always easy to meet members of the opposite sex* .

◦━**opposition** /ˌɒpə'zɪʃᵊn/ *noun* **1** [U] strong disagreement *Is there much opposition to the proposed changes?* ◦ *There has been strong opposition from local residents.* **2** **the Opposition/opposition** political parties that are not in power

oppress /ə'pres/ *verb* [T] **1** to treat a group of people in an unfair way, often by limiting their freedom [often passive] *Women were oppressed by a society which considered them inferior.* **2** to make someone feel anxious

oppressed /əˈprest/ *adjective* treated in an unfair way *oppressed minorities*

oppression /əˈpreʃᵊn/ *noun* [U] when people are treated in a way that is unfair and that limits their freedom *political oppression* ○ *the oppression of women*

oppressive /əˈpresɪv/ *adjective* **1** [UNFAIR] cruel and unfair *an oppressive government/regime* **2** [HOT] If the weather or heat is oppressive, it is too hot and there is no wind. *oppressive heat* **3** [NOT RELAXING] not relaxing or pleasant *an oppressive silence*

oppressor /əˈpresəʳ/ *noun* [C] someone who treats people in an unfair way, often by limiting their freedom

opt /ɒpt/ *verb* **opt for sth; opt to do sth** to choose something or to decide to do something *Mike opted for early retirement.* ○ *Most people opt to have the operation.*

  opt out to choose not to be part of an activity or to stop being involved in it *He's decided to opt out of the company's pension scheme.*

optical /ˈɒptɪkᵊl/ *adjective* relating to light or the ability to see *optical equipment/instruments*

optical i'llusion *noun* [C] something that you think you see, but which is not really there

optician /ɒpˈtɪʃᵊn/ *noun* [C] **1** someone whose job is to make eye glasses **2** *UK* a shop where you can have your eyes tested and have your glasses made

---

WORD PARTNERS FOR optimism

express optimism ● cautious/renewed optimism ● cause for/grounds for/reason for optimism ● optimism about sth

---

optimism /ˈɒptɪmɪzᵊm/ *noun* [U] when you believe good things will happen *a mood/spirit of optimism* ○ *There is cause/reason for optimism.* ○ *He expressed cautious optimism about the future.* ⊃Opposite pessimism.

optimist /ˈɒptɪmɪst/ *noun* [C] someone who always believes that good things will happen

optimistic /ˌɒptɪˈmɪstɪk/ *adjective* always believing that good things will happen *We're optimistic about our chances of success.* ○ *[+ (that)] I'm not optimistic that we'll reach an agreement.* ⊃Opposite pessimistic.

optimum /ˈɒptɪməm/ *adjective* [always before noun] *formal* best or most suitable *the optimum temperature*

WORD PARTNERS FOR option

consider/examine the options ● be given/have the option of doing sth ● an attractive/viable option ● an option for sb

---

॰**option** /ˈɒpʃᵊn/ *noun* **1** [C] a choice *That's an option you might like to consider.* ○ *We don't have many options.* ○ *[+ of + doing sth] You always have the option of not attending.* **2** **have no option (but to do sth)** to not have the possibility of doing something else *We didn't want to dismiss him, but we had no option.*

3 **keep/leave your options open** to wait and not make a decision or choice yet ⊃See also: **soft option**.

optional /ˈɒpʃᵊnᵊl/ *adjective* If something is optional, it is available but you do not have to have it. *an optional extra*

opulent /ˈɒpjələnt/ *adjective* Opulent things are expensive and give a feeling of luxury. *an opulent bathroom*

॰**or** *strong form* /ɔːʳ/ *weak form* /əʳ/ *conjunction* **1** [BETWEEN POSSIBILITIES] used between possibilities, or before the last in a list of possibilities *Would you like toast or cereal?* ○ *Is that a boy or a girl?* ○ *You can have beer, wine, or mineral water.* ○ *The house will take two or three years to complete.* **2** [CHANGE] used to change or correct something you have said *We told the truth, or most of it.* **3** [REASON] used to give a reason for something you have said *She must love him or she wouldn't have stayed with him all these years.* **4** [NOT EITHER] used after a negative verb between a list of things to mean not any of those things or people *Tim doesn't eat meat or fish.*

oral¹ /ˈɔːrᵊl/ *adjective* **1** spoken *an oral examination* ○ *an oral agreement* **2** relating to or using the mouth *oral medication* ● **orally** *adverb*

oral² /ˈɔːrᵊl/ *noun* [C] an examination that is spoken, usually in a foreign language

॰**orange¹** /ˈɒrɪndʒ/ *adjective* being a colour that is a mixture of red and yellow *a deep orange sunset* ⊃See colour picture **Colours** on page Centre 12.

॰**orange²** /ˈɒrɪndʒ/ *noun* **1** [FRUIT] [C] a round, sweet fruit with a thick skin and a centre that is divided into many equal parts *orange juice* ⊃See colour picture **Fruit and Vegetables** on page Centre 10. **2** [COLOUR] [C, U] a colour that is a mixture of red and yellow ⊃See colour picture **Colours** on page Centre 12. **3** [DRINK] [U] *UK* a drink made with oranges *Would you like some orange?*

'orange ,juice *noun* [U] a drink made from the juice of oranges

orator /ˈɒrətəʳ/ *noun* [C] *formal* someone who gives good speeches *a brilliant orator*

oratory /ˈɒrətᵊri/ *noun* [U] *formal* when people give good speeches *political oratory*

orbit /ˈɔːbɪt/ *noun* [C, U] the circular journey that a spacecraft or planet makes around the sun, the moon, or another planet *the Earth's orbit* ○ *Two satellites are already in orbit.* ○ *It was the first spacecraft to go into orbit around Jupiter.* ● **orbit** *verb* [I, T] *The moon orbits the Earth.*

orchard /ˈɔːtʃəd/ *noun* [C] a piece of land where fruit trees are grown *an apple/cherry orchard*

orchestra /ˈɔːkɪstrə/ *noun* [C] **1** a large group of musicians who play different instruments together *a symphony orchestra* ○ *a youth orchestra* **2** *US* (*UK* **the stalls**) the seats on the main floor near the front of a theatre or cinema ● **orchestral** /ɔːˈkestrᵊl/ *adjective* [always before noun] Orchestral music is played by or written for an orchestra.

orchestrate /ˈɔːkɪstreɪt/ *verb* [T] to intentionally organize something in order to achieve what you want *a carefully orchestrated demonstration of support*

orchid /ˈɔːkɪd/ *noun* [C] a plant with flowers which are an unusual shape and beautiful colours

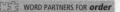
orchid

ordain /ɔːˈdeɪn/ *verb* [T] to officially make someone a Christian priest [often passive] *Dr Coker was ordained by the Bishop of London in 1986.*

ordeal /ɔːˈdiːl/ *noun* [C] a very unpleasant experience *a terrible ordeal* ○ *They feared he would not survive the ordeal.* ○ *She went through the ordeal of being interviewed by a panel of ten people.*

▓ WORD PARTNERS FOR **order**

2 follow/give/ignore/issue/obey orders • clear/strict orders

o→**order¹** /ˈɔːdər/ *noun* **1** [ARRANGEMENT] [C, U] the arrangement of a group of people or things in a list from first to last *in alphabetical order* ○ *in the right/wrong order* ○ *We ranked the tasks in order of importance.* **2** [INSTRUCTION] [C] an instruction that someone must obey *to obey orders* ○ *to give orders* **3 under orders** If you are under orders, someone has told you to do something. [+ to do sth] *Team members are under orders to behave well.* ○ *They claimed they were under orders from the president.* **4** [REQUEST] [C] a request for food or goods in return for payment *Can I take your order now?* **5** [TIDINESS] [U] a situation in which everything is in its correct place *It's nice to see some order around here for a change.* ○ *I want to put all my things in order before I go away.* ⊃Opposite **disorder**. **6 out of order a** [MACHINE] If a machine or system is out of order, it is not working as it should. *The coffee machine's out of order.* **b** [BEHAVIOUR] If someone's behaviour is out of order, it is not acceptable. *What he did was completely out of order.* **7 in order to do/for sth to do sth** with the purpose of achieving something *She worked all summer in order to save enough money for a holiday.* **8** [NO TROUBLE] [U] a situation in which people obey laws and there is no trouble *The army was brought in to restore order to the troubled province.* ⊃Opposite **disorder**. **9 economic/political/social order** the way that the economy, politics, or society is organized *a threat to the established social order* **10** [GROUP] [C] a religious group who live together and have the same rules *an order of nuns* ○ *a monastic order* ⊃See also: **mail order**, **postal order**, **standing order**.

o→**order²** /ˈɔːdər/ *verb* **1** [TELL] [T] to give someone an instruction that they must obey [+ to do sth] *He ordered them to leave.* **2** [REQUEST] [I, T] to ask for food, goods, etc *to order a drink/pizza* ○ *to order tickets* ○ *We've ordered new lights for the kitchen.* ○ [+ two objects] *Can I order you a drink?* **3** [ARRANGE] [T] to arrange a group of people or things in a list from first to last *Have*

you ordered the pages correctly?

order sb about/around to tell someone what they should do all the time *You can't just come in here and start ordering people around.*

orderly¹ /ˈɔːdəli/ *adjective* tidy or organized *an orderly pile* ○ *Please form an orderly queue.* ⊃Opposite **disorderly**.

orderly² /ˈɔːdəli/ *noun* [C] a hospital worker who has no special skills or training

ordinal number /ˌɔːdɪnˈlˈnʌmbər/ (*also* ordinal) *noun* [C] a number such as 1st, 2nd, 3rd, etc that shows the order of things in a list

ordinance /ˈɔːdɪnəns/ *noun* [C] *mainly US* a law or rule which limits or controls something *a tax ordinance*

ordinarily /ˈɔːdᵊnᵊrᵊli/ *adverb* usually *These are people who would not ordinarily carry guns.*

o→**ordinary** /ˈɔːdᵊnᵊri/ *adjective* **1** not special, different, or unusual in any way *ordinary life* ○ *an ordinary day* ○ *I had a very ordinary childhood.* **2** Ordinary people are not rich or famous and do not have special skills. *ordinary people/citizens* ○ *an ordinary man/woman* **3 out of the ordinary** unusual or different *Their relationship was a little out of the ordinary.* ○ *The investigation revealed nothing out of the ordinary.*

ore /ɔːr/ *noun* [U] rock or soil from which metal can be obtained *iron ore*

.org /dɒtˈɔːg/ *Internet abbreviation for* organization: used in some Internet addresses *You can search Cambridge dictionaries online at www.dictionary.cambridge.org*

organ /ˈɔːgən/ *noun* [C] **1** a part of an animal or plant that has a special purpose *reproductive/sexual organs* ○ *The liver is a vital organ* (= you need it to stay alive). ○ *an organ donor/transplant* **2** a large musical instrument that has keys like a piano and produces different notes when air is blown through pipes of different lengths *a church organ*

organic /ɔːˈɡænɪk/ *adjective* **1** [FARMING] not using artificial chemicals when keeping animals or growing plants for food *organic farming/farmers* ○ *organic food/vegetables* **2** [CHEMISTRY] In chemistry, 'organic' describes chemicals that contain carbon. *organic compounds* **3** [LIVING] from a living organism *organic matter/material* ⊃Opposite **inorganic**. • **organically** *adverb* **organically grown** *vegetables*

organism /ˈɔːgənɪzᵊm/ *noun* [C] a living thing, often one that is extremely small *Plants, animals, bacteria, and viruses are organisms.*

organist /ˈɔːgənɪst/ *noun* [C] someone who plays the organ (= an instrument like a piano) *a church organist*

▓ WORD PARTNERS FOR **organization**

a charitable / international / voluntary organization • join/set up an organization

o→**organization** (*also UK* -isation) /ˌɔːgᵊnaɪˈzeɪʃᵊn/ *noun* **1** [GROUP] [C] an official group of people who work together for the same purpose *a charitable/voluntary organization* **2** [ARRANGEMENT] [U] the way that parts of something are arranged *Better organization of the office would improve efficiency.* **3** [PLAN] [U] the planning of an activity or event *Who was responsible for the organization of the conference?* ● **organizational** *adjective* **organizational skills**

○▪**organize** (*also UK* **-ise**) /ˈɔːɡ³naɪz/ *verb* [T] to plan or arrange something *to organize a meeting/wedding*

organized (*also UK* **-ised**) /ˈɔːɡ³naɪzd/ *adjective* **1** An organized person plans things well and does not waste time or effort. **⊃**Opposite **disorganized. 2** [always before noun] involving a group of people who have planned to do something together *organized crime/religion* **⊃**See also: **well-organized.**

organizer (*also UK* **-iser**) /ˈɔːɡ³naɪzə³/ *noun* [C] someone who plans an event or activity *conference/exhibition organizers*

orgasm /ˈɔːɡæz³m/ *noun* [C, U] the time of greatest pleasure and excitement during sex *to have an orgasm*

orgy /ˈɔːdʒi/ *noun* [C] **1** a noisy party at which people have a lot of sex, alcohol, or illegal drugs **2 an orgy of sth** a period when there is too much of an often bad activity *an orgy of destruction*

the Orient /ˈɔːriənt/ *noun old-fashioned* the countries of east Asia

Oriental /ˌɔːriˈent³l/ *adjective* relating or belonging to the countries of east Asia *Oriental art*

orientated /ˈɔːriənteɪtɪd/ *UK* (*UK/US* **oriented**) *adjective* directed towards or interested in something

orientation /ˌɔːrienˈteɪʃ³n/ *noun* **1** [C, U] the type of beliefs that a person has *He's very secretive about his political orientation.* **2** [U] training or preparation for a new job or activity *an orientation session*

oriented /ˈɔːrientɪd/ (*also UK* **orientated**) *adjective* directed towards or interested in something *His new TV series is oriented towards teenage viewers.* ○ *He's very family oriented.*

▨ **WORD PARTNERS FOR** *origin*

sth **has** its origins **in** sth ● the origin(s) **of** sth ● be [Chinese/French, etc] **in** origin

---

origin /ˈɒrɪdʒɪn/ *noun* [C, U] **1** the cause of something, or where something begins or comes from *the origin of the universe* ○ *This dish is Greek in origin.* **2** the country, race, or social class of a person's family *ethnic origin* ○ *She's of Irish origin.*

○▪**original¹** /əˈrɪdʒ³n³l/ *adjective* **1** special and interesting because of not being the same as others *Her essay was full of original ideas.* ○ *He's a highly original thinker.* **2** [always before noun] existing since the beginning, or being the earliest form of something *His original plan was to stay for a week, but he ended up staying for a month.* ○ *Do you still have the original version of this document?*

original² /əˈrɪdʒ³n³l/ *noun* [C] something that is in the form in which it was first created and has not been copied or changed *If the painting were an original, it would be very valuable.*

originality /əˌrɪdʒ³nˈæləti/ *noun* [U] the quality of being interesting and different from everyone or everything else *The judges were impressed by the originality of his work.*

○▪**originally** /əˈrɪdʒ³n³li/ *adverb* at the beginning or before any changes *The bathroom was originally a bedroom.*

originate /əˈrɪdʒ³neɪt/ *verb* [I] **originate from/ in/with, etc** to come from a particular place or person, or to begin during a particular period *Citrus fruits originated in China and Southeast Asia.*

originator /əˈrɪdʒ³neɪtə³/ *noun* [C] *formal* The originator of an idea is the person who first thought of it.

ornament /ˈɔːnəmənt/ *noun* [C] an attractive object that is used as a decoration in a home or garden **⊃**See colour picture **The Living Room** on page Centre 4.

ornamental /ˌɔːnəˈment³l/ *adjective* used for decoration and having no other purpose

ornate /ɔːˈneɪt/ *adjective* decorated with a lot of complicated patterns *ornate wooden doors*

ornithology /ˌɔːnɪˈθɒlədʒi/ *noun* [U] the scientific study of birds ● **ornithologist** *noun* [C] a scientist who studies birds

orphan¹ /ˈɔːf³n/ *noun* [C] a child whose parents are dead

orphan² /ˈɔːf³n/ *verb* **be orphaned** When a child is orphaned, both their parents die. *She was orphaned at the age of six.*

orphanage /ˈɔːf³nɪdʒ/ *noun* [C] a home for children whose parents are dead

orthodox /ˈɔːθədɒks/ *adjective* **1** keeping the traditional beliefs and customs of Judaism or some types of Christianity *an orthodox Jewish family* ○ *the Russian/Greek Orthodox Church* **2** If ideas or methods are orthodox, most people think they are correct, usually because they have existed for a long time. *orthodox medicine* **⊃**Opposite **unorthodox.**

orthodoxy /ˈɔːθədɒksi/ *noun* [C, U] *formal* an idea of a society, religion, political party, or subject that most people believe is correct, or a set of such ideas

orthopaedic *UK* (*US* **orthopedic**) /ˌɔːθəˈpiːdɪk/ *adjective* [always before noun] relating to the treatment or study of bones that have been injured or have not grown correctly *an orthopaedic surgeon*

Oscar /ˈɒskə³/ *noun* [C] *trademark* one of several prizes given to actors and people who make films every year in Hollywood in the US *Who won the Oscar for best actress this year?*

oscillate /ˈɒsɪleɪt/ *verb* [I] *formal* to move repeatedly between two positions or opinions *an oscillating fan* ○ *The story oscillates between comedy and tragedy.* ● **oscillation** /ˌɒsɪˈleɪʃ³n/ *noun* [C, U]

ostensibly /ɒsˈtensɪbli/ *adverb* If something is ostensibly the reason for something else, people say it is the reason, although you do not believe it. *He was discharged from the army, ostensibly for medical reasons.*

ostentatious /ˌɒstenˈteɪʃəs/ *adjective* intended to attract attention or admiration, often by showing money or power *an ostentatious display of wealth* ● **ostentatiously** *adverb*

osteopath /ˈɒstiəʊpæθ/ *noun* [C] someone who treats injuries to bones and muscles by moving and rubbing them ● **osteopathy** *noun* [C]

osteoporosis /ˌɒstiəʊpəˈrəʊsɪs/ *noun* [U] a disease which makes bones weak and makes them break easily

ostracize (*also UK* -**ise**) /ˈɒstrəsaɪz/ *verb* [T] When a group of people ostracizes someone, they refuse to talk to or do things with that person. [often passive] *He was ostracized by the other children at school.*

ostrich /ˈɒstrɪtʃ/ *noun* [C] a very large bird from Africa which cannot fly but can run very fast

ostrich

o╾**other**¹ /ˈʌðəʳ/ *adjective, determiner* **1** [MORE] used to refer to people or things which are similar to or in addition to those you have talked about *I don't like custard - do you have any other desserts? ○ I don't think he's funny, but other people do.* **2** [PART OF SET] used to talk about the remaining members of a group or items in a set *Mario and Anna sat down to watch the other dancers. ○ I found one shoe - have you seen the other one?* **3** [DIFFERENT] different from a thing or person which you have talked about *Ask me some other time, when I'm not so busy.* ⊃See Common learner error at **another**. **4 the other side/end (of sth)** the opposite side/end of something *Our house is on the other side of town.* **5 the other day/week, etc** used to mean recently, without giving a particular date *I asked Kevin about it just the other day.* **6 every other day/week, etc** happening one day/week, etc but not the next *Alice goes to the gym every other day.* **7 other than** except *The form cannot be signed by anyone other than the child's parent. ○* [+ to do sth] *They had no choice other than to surrender.* **8 other than that** *informal* except for the thing you have just said *My arm was a bit sore - other than that I was fine.*

o╾**other**² /ˈʌðəʳ/ *pronoun* **1** used to refer to a person or thing which belongs to a group or set that you have already talked about *Hold the racket in one hand, and the ball in the other. ○ Some of the pieces were damaged, others were missing.* **2 others** used to refer to people or things that are similar to people or things you have already talked about *This is broken - do you have any others?* ⊃See also: **each other**.

o╾**others** /ˈʌðəz/ *pronoun* [plural] other people *Don't expect others to do your work for you.*

otherwise¹ /ˈʌðəwaɪz/ *adverb* **1** except for what has just been referred to *She hurt her arm in the accident, but otherwise she was fine.* **2** different to what has just been stated *I'll meet you there at 6 o'clock unless I hear otherwise. ○ I'd like to help you with any problems,* financial **or otherwise**.

otherwise² /ˈʌðəwaɪz/ *conjunction* used when saying what will happen if someone does not obey an order or do what has been suggested *You'd better phone home, otherwise your parents will start to worry.*

otter /ˈɒtəʳ/ *noun* [C] a small animal with short, brown fur and a long body that swims well and eats fish

ouch /aʊtʃ/ *exclamation* something you say when you experience sudden physical pain *Ouch! This radiator's really hot.*

o╾**ought** /ɔːt/ *modal verb* **1 ought to do sth** used to say or ask what is the correct or best thing to do *You ought to see a doctor. ○ He ought to have told her the truth. ○ Ought I to phone her?* **2 ought to be/do sth** used to say that you expect something to be true or that you expect something to happen *He ought to pass the exam this time.* ⊃See Extra help page **Modal verbs** on page Centre 22.

oughtn't /ˈɔːtᵊnt/ *formal short for* ought not *He oughtn't to have shouted at us.*

ounce /aʊns/ *noun* **1** [C] (*written abbreviation* oz) a unit for measuring weight, equal to 28.35 grams ⊃See Extra help page **Measurements** on page Centre 31. ⊃See also: **fluid ounce**. **2 not have an ounce of sth** to not have any of a quality or emotion *His new novel doesn't have an ounce of originality.* **3 every ounce of sth** all of a quality or emotion that is available *He deserves every ounce of support that we can give him.*

o╾**our** /aʊəʳ/ *determiner* belonging to or relating to the person who is speaking and one or more other people *Janice is our youngest daughter.*

o╾**ours** /aʊəz/ *pronoun* the things that belong or relate to the person who is speaking and one or more other people *Matt's a friend of ours. ○ That's their problem - not ours.*

o╾**ourselves** /ˌaʊəˈselvz/ *pronoun* **1** the reflexive form of the pronoun 'we' *We've promised ourselves a holiday abroad this year.* **2** used for emphasis with the pronoun 'we' or when referring to yourself and at least one other person *John and I arranged the wedding reception ourselves.* **3 (all) by ourselves** alone or without anyone else's help *It's a big garden but we manage to look after it by ourselves.* **4 (all) to ourselves** for our use only *We arrived early this morning and had the swimming pool all to ourselves.*

oust /aʊst/ *verb* [T] to force someone to leave a position of power or responsibility [often passive] *He was ousted from power by a military coup.*

o╾**out**¹ /aʊt/ *adjective, adverb* **1** [AWAY FROM] used to show movement away from the inside of a place or container *He dropped the bag and all the apples fell out. ○ She opened the window and stuck her head out.* **2** [OUTSIDE] outside a building or room *Would you like to wait out here? ○ It's bitterly cold out today.* **3** [NOT THERE] not in the place where you usually live or work, especially for a short time *I came round to see you this morning but you were out.* **4** [FIRE/LIGHT] A fire or light that is out is not burning or shining. *Bring some more wood, the fire's* *gone out.* **5** [AVAILABLE] available to buy or see *When's the new Spielberg film out?* **6** [FASHION] no longer fashionable or popular *Trousers like that **went out** years ago.* **7** [NOT ACCURATE] not accurate *Your figures are out by £300.* **8** [GAME] no longer able to play or take part in a game or competition *Two of the best players were out after ten minutes.* **9** [APPEAR] able to be seen *After a few minutes the sun came out.* **10** [NOT POSSIBLE] not possible or not acceptable *Next weekend is out because we're going away.* **11 be out of sth** to have no more of something left *We're nearly out of petrol.* **12 be out for sth; be out to do sth** to intend to do something, especially for an unpleasant reason *He's only out to impress the boss.* ➲See also: **out of.**

out² /aʊt/ *verb* [T] to report to the public the secret that someone is homosexual [often passive] *He was outed by a tabloid newspaper.*

out- /aʊt-/ *prefix* more than or better than *to outgrow something ○ to outnumber ○ to outdo someone* (= to show that you are better than someone)

out-and-out /ˌaʊtᵊn'aʊt/ *adjective* [always before noun] complete or in every way *an out-and-out lie*

the outback /'aʊtbæk/ *noun* the areas of Australia where few people live, especially the central desert areas

outbid /ˌaʊt'bɪd/ *verb* [T] **outbidding,** *past* **outbid** to offer to pay more for something than someone else *She had to outbid two rivals to buy the business.*

out-box /'aʊtbɒks/ (*also* **outbox**) *noun* [C] **1** the place on a computer which keeps copies of email messages which you have sent **2** *US* (*UK* **out-tray**) a container where you keep letters and documents that you want to send to someone else

outbreak /'aʊtbreɪk/ *noun* [C] when something unpleasant and difficult to control starts, such as a war or disease *an outbreak of flu/fighting*

outburst /'aʊtbɜːst/ *noun* [C] a sudden, forceful expression of emotion in words or actions *an **angry outburst***

outcast /'aʊtkɑːst/ *noun* [C] someone who is not accepted by society because they are different to most other people *a **social outcast***

WORD PARTNERS FOR ***outcome***

announce/await/determine the outcome • the **eventual/final** outcome • the outcome **of** sth

outcome /'aʊtkʌm/ *noun* [C] the final result of an activity or process ***the outcome of** the presidential election*

outcrop /'aʊtkrɒp/ (*also US* **outcropping**) *noun* [C] a rock or group of rocks that sticks out above the surface of the ground *a rocky outcrop*

WORD PARTNERS FOR ***outcry***

cause/provoke/spark an outcry • an **international/national/public** outcry • an outcry **against/over** sth

outcry /'aʊtkraɪ/ *noun* [C] a strong public expression of anger and disapproval about a recent event or decision *There has been a public **outcry against** the new road.*

outdated /ˌaʊt'deɪtɪd/ *adjective* not modern enough *outdated equipment ○ an outdated idea*

outdo /ˌaʊt'duː/ *verb* [T] *past tense* **outdid** *past participle* **outdone** to do something better than someone else *They are always trying to outdo each other with their jokes and funny stories.*

outdoor /ˌaʊt'dɔːʳ/ *adjective* [always before noun] happening, used, or in a place that is outside and not inside a building ***outdoor activities** ○ an outdoor concert ○ an **outdoor swimming pool** ○ **outdoor clothing*** ➲Opposite **indoor.**

outdoors /ˌaʊt'dɔːz/ *adverb* not inside a building *If it's warm this evening, we could eat outdoors.* ➲Opposite **indoors.**

the outdoors /ˌaʊt'dɔːz/ *noun* countryside *He enjoys hunting, fishing, and the outdoors.*

outer /'aʊtəʳ/ *adjective* [always before noun] on the edge or surface of something *Remove the **outer** layers of the onion.* ➲Opposite **inner.**

ˌouter 'space *noun* [U] the universe outside the Earth and its gases where other planets and stars are

the outfield /'aʊtfiːld/ *noun* the outer area of the playing field in sports such as cricket and baseball • **outfielder** *noun* [C] a baseball player who stands in the outfield

outfit¹ /'aʊtfɪt/ *noun* [C] **1** a set of clothes for a particular event or activity *a cowboy outfit* **2** *informal* an organization, company, or any group of people who work together

outfit² /'aʊtfɪt/ *verb* [T] **outfitting,** *past* **outfitted** *US* to provide equipment for something [often passive] *My hotel room was small and outfitted with cheap wooden furniture.*

outgoing /ˌaʊt'gəʊɪŋ/ [US] /'aʊtgəʊɪŋ/ *adjective* **1** [FRIENDLY] Someone who is outgoing is friendly, talks a lot, and enjoys meeting people. **2** [LEAVING POWER] [always before noun] leaving a position of power or responsibility *the outgoing president* **3** [LEAVING A PLACE] [always before noun] going to another place ***outgoing calls/messages***

outgoings /'aʊtˌgəʊɪŋz/ *noun* [plural] *UK* money that you have to spend on rent, food, etc

outgrow /ˌaʊt'grəʊ/ *verb* [T] *past tense* **outgrew,** *past participle* **outgrown 1** to grow too big for something *He's already outgrown these shoes.* **2** to develop so that something is not now suitable *She's outgrown her current job and needs a new challenge.*

outing /'aʊtɪŋ/ *noun* **1** [C] when a group of people go on a short journey for pleasure or education *a **family/school outing** ○ to **go on an outing*** **2** [U] when someone says publicly that someone else is homosexual

outlandish /ˌaʊt'lændɪʃ/ *adjective* very strange and unusual *an outlandish story/idea ○ **outlandish behaviour/clothes***

outlast /ˌaʊt'lɑːst/ *verb* [T] to continue for longer than someone or something else

outlaw¹ /'aʊtlɔː/ *verb* [T] to make something officially illegal *I think all handguns should be outlawed.*

outlaw² /'aʊtlɔː/ *noun* [C] *old-fashioned* a criminal *a dangerous outlaw*

outlay /'aʊtleɪ/ *noun* [C] an amount of money spent by a business or government *The project requires an* **initial outlay** *of $450,000.*

outlet /'aʊtlet/ *noun* [C] 1 [SHOP] In business, an outlet is a shop that sells one type of product or the products of one company. 2 [CHEAP SHOP] *US* a shop that sells goods for a lower price than usual 3 [EXPRESS] a way for someone to express an emotion, idea, or ability *She needs a job that will provide* **an outlet for** *her creative talent.* 4 [WAY OUT] a place where a liquid or gas can flow out of something 5 [CONNECTION] *US* a place where you can connect a wire on a piece of electrical equipment *an electrical outlet*

outline¹ /'aʊtlaɪn/ *verb* [T] to describe only the most important ideas or facts about something *He outlined the department's plans for next year.*

outline² /'aʊtlaɪn/ *noun* [C] 1 a short description of the most important ideas or facts about something *He gave us a* **brief outline** *of the town's history.* 2 the shape made by the outside edge of something

outlive /ˌaʊt'lɪv/ *verb* [T] to continue living or existing after someone or something else has died or stopped existing *She outlived both her children.*

outlook /'aʊtlʊk/ *noun* 1 [no plural] the likely future situation *The outlook for the economy next year is bleak.* 2 [C] the way a person thinks about something *Despite her illness, she has a very positive* **outlook on** *life.*

outlying /'aʊtˌlaɪɪŋ/ *adjective* [always before noun] far from towns and cities, or far from the centre of a place *outlying farms/villages*

outmanoeuvre *UK* (*US* **outmaneuver**) /ˌaʊtmə'nuːvə³/ *verb* [T] to do something clever that gives you an advantage over someone you are competing against *She outmanoeuvred her opponents throughout the election campaign.*

outmoded /ˌaʊt'məʊdɪd/ *adjective* not modern enough *outmoded equipment*

outnumber /ˌaʊt'nʌmbə³/ *verb* [T] to be larger in number than another group *Women now far outnumber men on language courses.*

out of /aʊt əv/ *preposition* 1 [AWAY FROM] used to show movement away from the inside of a place or container *A bunch of keys fell out of her bag.* ○ *She stepped out of the car and walked towards me.* 2 [NO LONGER IN] no longer in a place or situation *He's out of the country until next month.* ○ *I've been out of work for the past year.* 3 [MADE FROM] used to show what something is made from *The statue was carved out of a single block of stone.* 4 [BECAUSE OF] used to show the reason why someone does something *I only gave her the job out of pity.* 5 [FROM AMONG] from among an amount or number *Nine out of ten people said they preferred it.* 6 [NOT INVOLVED] no longer involved in something *He missed the practice session and now he's out of the team.*

out-of-court /ˌaʊtəv'kɔːt/ *adjective* [always before noun] agreed without involving a law court *an out-of-court settlement*

out-of-date /ˌaʊtəv'deɪt/ *adjective* old and not useful or correct any more *I do have a road map but I think it's out-of-date.*

out-of-town /ˌaʊtəv'taʊn/ *adjective* [always before noun] positioned or happening in the countryside or on the edge of a town *an out-of-town supermarket*

outpace /ˌaʊt'peɪs/ *verb* [T] to move or develop more quickly than someone or something else

outpatient /'aʊtˌpeɪʃ°nt/ *noun* [C] someone who is treated in a hospital but does not sleep there at night

outperform /ˌaʊtpə'fɔːm/ *verb* [T] to do something better than someone or something else *Girls are consistently outperforming boys at school.*

outplay /ˌaʊt'pleɪ/ *verb* [T] to play a game or sport better than another player or team

outpost /'aʊtpəʊst/ *noun* [C] a small place that is far from large towns or cities, often where a government or company is represented

outpouring /'aʊtˌpɔːrɪŋ/ *noun* [C] when an emotion is expressed a lot in public *His death provoked a national outpouring of grief.*

output¹ /'aʊtpʊt/ *noun* [U] 1 [AMOUNT] the amount of something that is produced *Over the past year the factory's output has fallen by 15%.* 2 [INFORMATION] information produced by a computer *You can look at the output on screen before you print it out.* 3 [POWER] the power or energy produced by an electrical or electronic system

---

🧩 **WORD PARTNERS FOR outrage**

| cause/express/provoke/spark | outrage |
| • moral/public outrage • outrage at/over sth | |

outrage¹ /'aʊtreɪdʒ/ *noun* 1 [U] a strong feeling of anger or shock *moral outrage* ○ *The scandal caused* **public outrage.** 2 [C] something that causes great anger or shock *a terrorist outrage* ○ [+ (that)] *It's an outrage that these children don't have enough to eat.*

outrage² /'aʊtreɪdʒ/ *verb* [T] to make someone feel very angry or shocked [often passive] *The audience was outraged by his racist comments.* ○ *Local people were* **outraged at** *the bombing.*

outrageous /aʊt'reɪdʒəs/ *adjective* shocking or extreme *outrageous behaviour/clothes* ○ *The prices in that restaurant were outrageous.* • **outrageously** *adverb outrageously expensive*

outran /ˌaʊt'ræn/ *past tense of* outrun

outreach /'aʊtriːtʃ/ *noun* [U] mainly *US* when an organization helps people with their social, medical, or educational problems *an outreach programme* ○ *an outreach worker*

outright /'aʊtraɪt/ *adjective* [always before noun] total, clear, and certain *an* **outright ban** *on smoking* ○ *an* **outright victory** • **outright** /ˌaʊt'raɪt/ *adverb She needs 51% of the vote to* **win outright.** ○ *He was* **killed outright** (= immediately) *when the car hit him.*

outrun /ˌaʊt'rʌn/ *verb* [T] **outrunning** *past tense* **outran** *past participle* **outrun** to move or develop faster or further than someone or something

outscore /ˌaʊt'skɔːr/ *verb* [T] mainly *US* to score more points than another player or team

---

outset /'aʊtset/ *noun* **at/from the outset** at or from the beginning of something *I made my views clear at the outset.*

outshine /ˌaʊt'ʃaɪn/ *verb* [T] *past* **outshone** to be much better than someone else *She easily outshone the other students on the course.*

◦ᴹ**outside**[1] /ˌaʊt'saɪd/ (*also US* **outside of**) *preposition* **1** not in a particular building or room, but near it *She waited outside his room for nearly two hours.* **2** not in a flat just outside Blackpool ○ *You have to phone a different number outside office hours.*

◦ᴹ**outside**[2] /ˌaʊt'saɪd/ *adverb* **1** not inside a building *Go and play outside for a while.* ○ *It's cold outside today.* **2** not in a particular building or room, but near it *She knocked on his bedroom door and left the tray outside.*

outside[3] /ˌaʊt'saɪd/ *adjective* [always before noun] **1** not in a building *an outside light* ○ *outside activities* **2** from a different organization or group of people *outside help* ○ *outside influences* ⊃See also: **the outside world**.

◦ᴹ**the outside**[4] /ˌaʊt'saɪd/ *noun* the outer part or surface of something *The pie was cooked on the outside but cold in the middle.*

ˌ**outside 'chance** *noun* [no plural] when something is not likely to happen *She has an outside chance of reaching the final.*

outsider /ˌaʊt'saɪdər/ *noun* [C] someone who does not belong to a particular group, organization, or place *The villagers are very suspicious of outsiders.* ⊃Compare **insider**.

the ˌoutside 'world *noun* other people in other places *When he was in prison, his radio was his only contact with the outside world.*

outsize /ˌaʊt'saɪz/ (*also* **outsized**) *adjective* [always before noun] larger than usual *an outsize jumper*

the outskirts /'aʊtskɜːts/ *noun* the outer area of a city, town, or village *There are plans to build a new stadium on the outskirts of Liverpool.*

outspoken /ˌaʊt'spəʊkən/ *adjective* expressing an opinion forcefully and not worrying about what other people think *outspoken comments* ○ *He's an outspoken critic of nuclear energy.*

outstanding /ˌaʊt'stændɪŋ/ *adjective* **1** excellent and much better than most *an outstanding achievement* **2** waiting to be paid or dealt with *an outstanding debt*

outstandingly /ˌaʊt'stændɪŋli/ *adverb* used to emphasize how good something is *outstandingly successful*

outstay /ˌaʊt'steɪ/ *verb* ⊃See outstay/overstay your **welcome**[4].

outstretched /ˌaʊt'stretʃt/ *adjective* When a part of your body is outstretched, it is reaching out as far as possible. *He ran towards me with his arms outstretched.*

outstrip /ˌaʊt'strɪp/ *verb* [T] **outstripping**, *past* **outstripped** When one amount outstrips another amount, it is much greater than it. **Demand** *for the toys far outstrips supply.*

outta /'aʊtə/ *informal short for* out of *Let's get outta here!*

out-take /'aʊteɪk/ *noun* [C] a short part of a

film, television programme or music recording that was removed, usually because it contains mistakes *They showed a video with funny out-takes from famous films.*

outward[1] /'aʊtwəd/ *adjective* [always before noun] **1** showing on the outside *He had a serious illness, but there was no outward sign of it.* **2** **outward flight/journey, etc** when you travel away from a place that you will return to ⊃Opposite **inward**.

outward[2] /'aʊtwəd/ (*also UK* **outwards**) *adverb* towards the outside or away from the centre *This door opens outward.*

outwardly /'aʊtwədli/ *adverb* If someone is outwardly calm, confident, etc, they seem to be calm, confident, etc, although they may not feel that way. *She was very nervous, but she remained outwardly calm.* ⊃Opposite **inwardly**.

outweigh /ˌaʊt'weɪ/ *verb* [T] to be greater or more important than something else *The benefits of this treatment far outweigh the risks.*

outwit /ˌaʊt'wɪt/ *verb* [T] **outwitting**, *past* **outwitted** to get an advantage over someone by doing something clever and deceiving them *She outwitted her kidnappers and managed to escape.*

oval /'əʊvəl/ *adjective* in the shape of an egg or a slightly flat circle *an oval face* ○ *an oval table* ● **oval** *noun* [C] an oval shape ⊃See picture at **shape**.

the ˌOval 'Office *noun* the office of the president of the United States

ovary /'əʊvəri/ *noun* [C] the part of a woman or female animal that produces eggs ● **ovarian** /əʊ'veəriən/ *adjective* [always before noun] relating to the ovaries *ovarian cancer*

ovation /əʊ'veɪʃən/ *noun* [C] when a group of people clap for a long time to show that they approve of someone or something ⊃See also: **standing ovation**.

oven /'ʌvən/ *noun* [C] a piece of kitchen equipment with a door which is used for cooking food *an electric oven* ○ *a microwave oven* ⊃See colour picture **The Kitchen** on page Centre 2.

◦ᴹ**over**[1] /'əʊvər/ *adverb, preposition* **1** ABOVE above or higher than something *The sign over the door said "Private, No Entry".* ○ *A fighter plane flew over.* **2** SIDE TO SIDE If you walk, jump, climb, etc over an object or place, you go from one side of it to the other side. *We had to climb over large rocks to get to the beach.* **3** AMOUNT more than a particular amount, number, or age *Over 5,000 Internet users contact our website every year.* ○ *Suitable for children aged 5 and over.* **4** OPPOSITE SIDE on or to the opposite side of a road, bridge, path, etc *The station is over the bridge.* **5** COVER covering someone or something *She placed the quilt over the bed.* **6** DOWN down from a higher to a lower position *The little boy fell over and started to cry.* ○ *She tripped over the rug.* **7** PLACE to a particular place *Could you bring the plates over here* (= bring them to this place). ○ *He was sent over there during the war.* **8** TIME during a particular period of time *I was in Seattle over the summer.* **9** ABOUT connected with or about *It's stupid arguing over something so trivial.* **10** NOT USED not used *There's some food left* *over from the party.* **11** [USING] using the radio or telephone *I made the booking over the phone.* **12 be/get over sth** to feel better after being ill or feeling unhappy about something *It took him months to get over splitting up with his girlfriend.* **13 do sth over** *US* to do something again from the beginning because you did not do it well the first time *You've ruined it! - Now I'll have to do it over.* **14 (all) over again** again from the beginning *It looks all messy. I'm going to have to do it all over again.* **15 over and over (again)** repeatedly *He was whistling the same tune over and over.* **16 roll/ turn, etc (sth) over** to move so that a different part is showing, or to make something do this *She turned the page over.* **17** [CONTROL] in control of someone or something *Her husband has a lot of influence over her.*

☞**over²** /ˈəʊvəʳ/ *adjective* **1** [never before noun] finished *The exams will be over next week.* ○ *It was all over very quickly.* **2 get sth over (and done) with** to do something difficult or unpleasant as soon as you can so that you do not have to worry about it any more

over- /ˈəʊvəʳ/ *prefix* too much *to overeat* ○ *over-populated*

overall /ˈəʊvəˈrɔːl/ *adjective* [always before noun] considering everything or the overall cost of the holiday ○ *the overall effect* ● overall /ˌəʊvəˈrɔːl/ *adverb* How would you rate the school overall?

overalls /ˈəʊvəˈrɔːlz/ *noun* [plural] **1** *UK* (*US* **coveralls**) a piece of clothing that you wear over your clothes to keep them clean while you are working **2** *US* (*UK* **dungarees**) trousers with a part that covers your chest and straps that go over your shoulders

overbearing /ˌəʊvəˈbeərɪŋ/ *adjective* trying to have too much control over other people *an overbearing mother*

overblown /ˌəʊvəˈbləʊn/ *adjective* If something is overblown, it is made to seem more important or serious than it really is.

overboard /ˈəʊvəbɔːd/ *adverb* **1** over the side of a boat and into the water *to fall overboard* **2 go overboard** *informal* to do something too much, or to be too excited about something *I think people go overboard at Christmas.*

overburdened /ˌəʊvəˈbɜːd³nd/ *adjective* having too much to deal with *overburdened with work*

overcame /ˌəʊvəˈkeɪm/ *past tense of* overcome

overcast /ˈəʊvəkɑːst/ *adjective* cloudy and dark *an overcast sky/day*

overcharge /ˌəʊvəˈtʃɑːdʒ/ *verb* [I, T] to charge someone too much money for something *The shop overcharged me by £5.*

overcoat /ˈəʊvəkəʊt/ *noun* [C] a long, warm coat

overcome /ˌəʊvəˈkʌm/ *verb past tense* overcame, *past participle* overcome **1** [T] to deal with and control a problem or feeling *He's trying to overcome his drug addiction and find a job.* ○ *Let's hope she overcomes her shyness.* **2 be overcome by excitement/fear/sadness, etc** to suddenly have too much of a feeling *She was overcome by emotion.* **3 be overcome by smoke/fumes, etc**

to become ill or weak because you have been breathing smoke or poisonous gas *One worker died when he was overcome by chemical fumes.*

overcrowded /ˌəʊvəˈkraʊdɪd/ *adjective* containing too many people or things *an overcrowded classroom/prison* ● **overcrowding** *noun* [U]

overdo /ˌəʊvəˈduː/ *verb* [T] *past tense* overdid, *past participle* overdone to do or use too much of something *I went to the gym yesterday, but I think I overdid it a bit.*

overdone /ˌəʊvəˈdʌn/ *adjective* cooked for too long

overdose /ˈəʊvədəʊs/ *noun* [C] too much of a drug taken at one time *Her daughter died of a drug overdose.* ● **overdose** /ˌəʊvəˈdəʊs/ *verb* [I]

overdraft /ˈəʊvədrɑːft/ *noun* [C] If you have an overdraft, you have taken more money out of your bank account than you had in it. *a £250 overdraft*

overdrawn /ˌəʊvəˈdrɔːn/ *adjective* If you are overdrawn, you have taken more money out of your bank account than you had in it. *We've gone £200 overdrawn!*

overdue /ˌəʊvəˈdjuː/ *adjective* happening later than expected *This decision is long overdue* ○ *We're paying a long overdue visit to Will's mother's this weekend.*

overestimate /ˌəʊvəˈrestɪmeɪt/ *verb* [I, T] to guess or think that something is bigger or better than it really is *They overestimated her ability to do the job.* ⊃Opposite **underestimate**.

over-fishing /ˌəʊvəˈfɪʃɪŋ/ *noun* [U] catching so many fish in a part of the sea that there are not many fish left there *low fish stocks caused by over-fishing*

overflow

overflow /ˌəʊvəˈfləʊ/ *verb* **1** [I] If a container or a place overflows, the thing that is inside it starts coming out because it is too full. *The bath overflowed, and there's water all over the floor!* ○ *The bin was overflowing with rubbish.* **2** [I, T] to come out of a container or a place because it is too full *The river overflowed its banks after the heavy rainfall.* **3 overflow with confidence/happiness/love, etc** to have a lot of a quality or emotion ● **overflow** /ˈəʊvəfləʊ/ *noun* [C, U]

overgrown /ˌəʊvəˈgrəʊn/ *adjective* covered

with plants that have become too big *an over-grown garden*

overhang /ˌəʊvəˈhæŋ/ *verb* [T] *past* **overhung** to hang over something *overhanging branches*

overhaul /ˌəʊvəˈhɔːl/ *verb* [T] to examine a machine or a system carefully and improve it or repair it *to overhaul an engine* ● **overhaul** /ˈəʊvəhɔːl/ *noun* [C]

overhead /ˌəʊvəˈhed/ *adjective, adverb* above you, usually in the sky *overhead power cables* ○ *A police helicopter was hovering overhead.*

overheads /ˈəʊvəhedz/ *UK* (*US* **overhead**) *noun* [plural] money that a company spends on its regular and necessary costs, for example rent and heating

overhear /ˌəʊvəˈhɪəʳ/ *verb* [T] *past* **overheard** to hear what someone is saying when they are not talking to you [+ doing sth] *I overheard him telling her he was leaving.*

overheat /ˌəʊvəˈhiːt/ *verb* [I] to become too hot *The engine keeps overheating.*

overhung /ˌəʊvəˈhʌŋ/ *past of* overhang

overjoyed /ˌəʊvəˈdʒɔɪd/ *adjective* very happy [+ to do sth] *He was overjoyed to hear from his old friend.*

overkill /ˈəʊvəkɪl/ *noun* [U] when something is done too much *Should I add an explanation or would that be overkill?*

overlap /ˌəʊvəˈlæp/ *verb* [I, T] **overlapping**, *past* **overlapped** **1** If two subjects or activities overlap, they are the same in some way. *Although our job titles are different, our responsibilities overlap quite a lot.* **2** If two objects overlap, part of one covers part of the other. ● **overlap** /ˈəʊvəlæp/ *noun* [C, U]

overload /ˌəʊvəˈləʊd/ *verb* [T] **1** to put too many people or things into or onto a vehicle [often passive] *The coach was overloaded with passengers.* **2** to give someone more work or problems than they can deal with

overlook /ˌəʊvəˈlʊk/ *verb* [T] **1** VIEW to have a view of something from above *a balcony overlooking the sea* **2** NOT NOTICE to not notice or consider something *Two important facts have been overlooked in this case.* **3** FORGIVE to forgive or ignore someone's bad behaviour

overly /ˈəʊvəli/ *adverb* in a way that is extreme or too much *overly optimistic* ○ *It wasn't overly expensive.*

overnight /ˌəʊvəˈnaɪt/ *adverb* **1** for or during the night *Sometimes we would stay overnight at my grandmother's house.* **2** very quickly or suddenly *Change does not happen overnight.* ● **overnight** *adjective* [always before noun] *overnight rain* ○ *an overnight* (= sudden) *success*

overpass /ˈəʊvəpɑːs/ *US* (*UK* **flyover**) *noun* [C] a bridge that carries a road over another road

overpower /ˌəʊvəˈpaʊəʳ/ *verb* [T] **1** to defeat someone by being stronger than they are [often passive] *The gunman was overpowered by two security guards.* **2** If a feeling, smell, etc overpowers you, it is very strong and makes you feel weak.

overpowering /ˌəʊvəˈpaʊərɪŋ/ *adjective* unpleasantly strong or powerful *an overpowering smell*

overpriced /ˌəʊvəˈpraɪst/ *adjective* too expensive *an overpriced pair of shoes*

overran /ˌəʊvəˈræn/ *past tense of* overrun

overrated /ˌəʊvəˈreɪtɪd/ *adjective* If something is overrated, it is considered to be better or more important than it really is.

overreact /ˌəʊvəriˈækt/ *verb* [I] to react in a way that is more extreme than you should *She tends to overreact to criticism.*

override /ˌəʊvəˈraɪd/ *verb* [T] *past tense* **overrode** *past participle* **overridden** **1** If someone in authority overrides a decision or order, they officially decide that it is wrong. *I don't have the power to override his decision.* **2** to be more important than something else *His desire for marriage seems to override anything else.*

overriding /ˌəʊvəˈraɪdɪŋ/ *adjective* [always before noun] more important than others *an overriding concern*

overrule /ˌəʊvəˈruːl/ *verb* [T] If someone in authority overrules a decision or order, they officially decide that it is wrong. *Does the judge have the power to overrule the jury?*

overrun /ˌəʊvəˈrʌn/ *verb* **overrunning**, *past tense* **overran**, *past participle* **overrun** **1** [T] If something unpleasant overruns a place, it fills it in large numbers. [often passive] *The house was overrun by rats.* ○ *Troops overran the city.* **2** [I] *UK* to continue for a longer time than planned *Sorry I'm late, but the meeting overran by 20 minutes.*

overseas /ˌəʊvəˈsiːz/ *adjective* [always before noun] in, to, or from another country *an overseas student* ● **overseas** *adverb* *to live/work overseas*

oversee /ˌəʊvəˈsiː/ *verb* [T] **overseeing**, *past tense* **oversaw**, *past participle* **overseen** to watch work as it is done in order to make certain that it is done correctly *A committee has been set up to oversee the project.*

overshadow /ˌəʊvəˈʃædəʊ/ *verb* [T] **1** to cause something to be less enjoyable *The party was overshadowed by a family argument.* **2** to cause someone or something to seem less important or successful

oversight /ˈəʊvəsaɪt/ *noun* [C, U] a mistake that you make by not noticing something or by forgetting to do something

oversleep /ˌəʊvəˈsliːp/ *verb* [I] *past* **overslept** to sleep longer than you had intended *Sorry I'm late, I overslept.*

overstate /ˌəʊvəˈsteɪt/ *verb* [T] to talk about something in a way that makes it seem more important than it really is

overstep /ˌəʊvəˈstep/ *verb* **overstepping**, *past* **overstepped** **overstep the mark** to behave in a way that is not allowed or not acceptable

overt /əʊˈvɜːt/ *adjective* done or shown publicly and not hidden *overt criticism* ● **overtly** *adverb* *overtly racist remarks*

overtake /ˌəʊvəˈteɪk/ *verb* *past tense* **overtook**, *past participle* **overtaken** **1** [T] to become more successful than someone or something else *Tobacco has overtaken coffee to become the country's leading export.* **2** [I, T] to go past a vehicle or person that is going in the same direction

over-the-counter /ˌəʊvəðəˈkaʊntəʳ/ *adjective* [always before noun] Over-the-counter medicines can be bought in a shop without first visiting a doctor. ● **over-the-counter** *adverb Most of these tablets can be bought over-the-counter.*

overthrow /ˌəʊvəˈθrəʊ/ *verb* [T] *past tense* **overthrew**, *past participle* **overthrown** to remove someone from power by using force *They were accused of plotting to overthrow the government.* ● **overthrow** /ˈəʊvəθrəʊ/ *noun* [no plural]

overtime /ˈəʊvətaɪm/ *noun* [U] extra time that you work after your usual working hours *unpaid overtime* ● **overtime** *adverb*

overtones /ˈəʊvətəʊnz/ *noun* [plural] ideas that seem to be expressed but that are not stated directly *His speech had political overtones.*

overtook /ˌəʊvəˈtʊk/ *past tense of* overtake

overture /ˈəʊvətjʊəʳ/ *noun* [C] a piece of classical music that introduces another longer piece such as an opera

overturn /ˌəʊvəˈtɜːn/ *verb* **1 overturn a conviction/ruling/verdict, etc** to officially change a legal decision **2** [I, T] If something overturns or if you overturn something, it turns over onto its top or onto its side. *She overturned her car in the accident.*

overview /ˈəʊvəvjuː/ *noun* [C] a short description giving the most important facts about something *I'll just give you an overview of the job.*

overweight /ˌəʊvəˈweɪt/ *adjective* too heavy or too fat *He's still a few pounds overweight.* ⊃Opposite **underweight**.

overwhelm /ˌəʊvəˈwelm/ *verb* [T] If a feeling or situation overwhelms someone, it has an effect that is too strong or extreme. [often passive] *She was overwhelmed by the excitement of it all.*

overwhelming /ˌəʊvəˈwelmɪŋ/ *adjective* very strong in effect or large in amount *an overwhelming feeling of sadness* ○ *They won by an overwhelming majority.* ● **overwhelmingly** *adverb*

overworked /ˌəʊvəˈwɜːkt/ *adjective* Someone who is overworked has to work too much. *We're overworked and underpaid.*

ovulate /ˈɒvjəleɪt/ *verb* [I] When a woman ovulates, her body produces eggs.

o⟶**owe** /əʊ/ *verb* [T] **1** to have to pay money back to someone [+ two objects] *You still owe me money.* ○ *He owes about £5000 to the bank.* **2 owe sb an apology/favour/drink, etc** to have to give something to someone because they deserve it *I think I owe you an apology.* **3 owe your existence/success, etc to sb/sth** to have something or achieve something because of someone or something else *The museum owes much of its success to the present generation of young British artists.*

owing to /ˈəʊɪŋ tuː/ *preposition* because of *The concert has been cancelled owing to lack of support.*

owl /aʊl/ *noun* [C] a bird that has large eyes and hunts small animals at night

owl

o⟶**own¹** /əʊn/ *adjective, pronoun, determiner* **1** belonging to or done by a particular person or thing *Each student has their own dictionary.* ○ *Petra makes all her own clothes.* ○ *"Is that your mum's car?" "No, it's my own (= it belongs to me)."* **2 of your own** belonging to someone or something *I'll have a home of my own (= home belonging only to me) someday.* **3 (all) on your own a** alone *Jessica lives on her own.* **b** If you do something on your own, you do it without any help from other people. *She's raised three kids on her own.* **4 come into your/its own** to be very useful or successful *By the 1970s, Abrams was starting to come into his own as a soloist.* **5 get your own back (on sb)** UK to do something unpleasant to someone because they have done something unpleasant to you **6 hold your own** to be as successful as other people or things *Alison could always hold her own in political debates.*

o⟶**own²** /əʊn/ *verb* [T] to have something that legally belongs to you *The University owns a lot of the land around here.*

own up to admit that you have done something wrong [+ to + doing sth] *No one has owned up to breaking that window.*

o⟶**owner** /ˈəʊnəʳ/ *noun* [C] someone who legally owns something *a property owner* ● **ownership** *noun* [U] when you own something

ox /ɒks/ *noun* [C] *plural* **oxen** a large, male cow, used especially in the past to pull farm vehicles

oxygen /ˈɒksɪdʒən/ *noun* [U] a gas that is in the air and that animals need to live

oxymoron /ˌɒksɪˈmɔːrɒn/ *noun* [C] two words used together, which mean two different or opposite things, such as 'bitter-sweet' or 'smart casual'

oyster /ˈɔɪstəʳ/ *noun* [C] a sea creature that lives in a flat shell and is eaten as food

oz *written abbreviation for* ounce (= a unit for measuring weight) *an 8 oz steak*

ozone /ˈəʊzəʊn/ *noun* [U] a form of oxygen that has a powerful smell

the ˈozone ˌlayer *noun* the layer of ozone high above the Earth's surface that prevents the sun from harming the Earth

O

Pp

P, p /piː/ the sixteenth letter of the alphabet

p. 1 *written abbreviation for* page *See diagram on p.135*. **2** *abbreviation for* penny or pence (= units of British money) *a 20p coin* ⊃See Common learner error at **pence**.

PA /piːˈeɪ/ *UK abbreviation for* personal assistant: a person who organizes letters, meetings and telephone calls for someone with an important job

WORD PARTNERS FOR *pace***

quicken/slow your pace • at a [blistering/ brisk/leisurely, etc] pace • the pace of sth

pace¹ /peɪs/ *noun* **1** [no plural] the speed at which someone or something moves or does something *We started to walk at a much faster pace.* ○ *the pace of life* **2** [C] a step *Every few paces I stopped to listen*. **3 keep pace with sb/sth** to move or develop at the same speed as someone or something else *We have to keep pace with the changing times*. ⊃See also: at a **snail**'s pace.

pace² /peɪs/ *verb* **1 pace about/up and down, etc** to walk around because you are worried or excited about something *He kept pacing up and down, glancing at his watch.* **2 pace yourself** to be careful not to do something too quickly so that you do not get too tired to finish it

pacemaker /ˈpeɪsˌmeɪkər/ *noun* [C] a small piece of medical equipment in someone's heart that makes it work at the correct speed

pacifier /ˈpæsɪfaɪər/ *US* (*UK* **dummy**) *noun* [C] a small rubber object that you give to a baby to suck in order to make it calm

pacifism /ˈpæsɪfɪzᵊm/ *noun* [U] the belief that war or fighting of any type is wrong • **pacifist** /ˈpæsɪfɪst/ *noun* [C] someone who believes in pacifism

pacify /ˈpæsɪfaɪ/ *verb* [T] to do something in order to make someone less angry or upset *She smiled at Jamie to pacify him.*

○━**pack¹** /pæk/ *verb* **1** [I, T] to put your things into bags or boxes when you are going on holiday or leaving the place where you live *I've got to go home and pack.* ○ *to **pack** your **bags*** ⊃Opposite **unpack**. **2** [T] If people pack a place, there are so many of them in it that it is very crowded. *Thousands of fans packed the club.*

pack sth in 1 *informal* to stop doing something *If this job doesn't get any better I'm going to pack it in.* **2** to manage to do a lot of things in a short period of time *We were only there four days but we packed so much in.*

pack sb off *informal* to send someone away *We were **packed off** to our grandparents' for the summer holidays.*

pack (sth) up to collect all your things together when you have finished doing something *I'm about to **pack** my **things** up and go home.*

pack² /pæk/ *noun* [C] **1** ▢BOX mainly *US* a small box that contains several of the same thing *a pack of cigarettes* **2** ▢BAG mainly *US* a bag that you carry on your back **3** ▢ANIMALS a group of animals that live together, especially those of the dog family *a **pack** of **wolves*** **4** ▢CARDS (*also US* **deck**) a set of playing cards ⊃See also: **fanny pack**.

packages

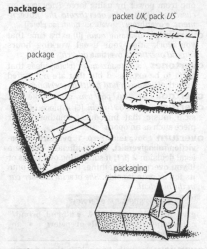

packet *UK*, pack *US*

package

packaging

package¹ /ˈpækɪdʒ/ *noun* [C] **1** ▢PARCEL an object that is covered in paper, inside a box, etc, especially so that it can be sent somewhere **2** ▢GROUP OF THINGS a group of objects, plans, or arrangements that are sold or considered together *a computer package* ○ *This ski package includes hotel, transport, and four days of skiing.* **3** ▢BOX *US* a box or container in which something is put to be sold *a package of raisins/cookies*

package² /ˈpækɪdʒ/ *verb* [T] **1** to put something into a box or container so that it can be sold *It's neatly packaged in a blue and white box.* **2** to show someone or something in an attractive way so that people will like or buy them *What's important is the way we package the programme.*

package 'holiday *UK* (*UK/US* **'package ˌtour**) *noun* [C] a holiday that is arranged for you by a travel company and for which you pay a fixed price before you go

packaging /ˈpækɪdʒɪŋ/ *noun* [U] the paper, box, etc that something is inside so that it can be sold or sent somewhere

packed /pækt/ (*also UK* **packed out**) *adjective* very crowded *The hall was packed.*

packed 'lunch *noun* [C] *UK* food that you put in a bag or box and take to eat at work, school, etc

packet /ˈpækɪt/ *UK* (*US* **pack**) *noun* [C] a small container that contains several of the same thing *a packet of cigarettes/sweets*

packing /ˈpækɪŋ/ *noun* [U] **1** when you put things into bags or boxes in order to take them somewhere *I've got to **do** my **packing** because*

I'm going tomorrow. **2** paper, material, etc that you put around an object in a box so that it does not get damaged

pact /pækt/ *noun* [C] an agreement between two people or groups *We have a pact never to talk about each other.*

pad¹ /pæd/ *noun* [C] **1** (*also US* **tablet**) sheets of paper that have been fastened together at one edge, used for writing or drawing *There's a pad and pencil by the phone.* **2** a small piece of soft material used to protect something or to make something more comfortable *knee/shin pads*

pad² /pæd/ *verb* **padding**, *past* **padded 1 pad about/around/down, etc** to walk somewhere with small, quiet steps *He padded downstairs and out of the front door.* **2** [T] to protect something or make something more comfortable by filling or surrounding it with soft material
pad sth out to make a piece of writing or a speech longer by adding more information to it

padding /'pædɪŋ/ *noun* [U] soft material that is used to fill or cover something to protect it or make it more comfortable

paddle¹ /'pædl/ *noun* **1** [C] a short pole with one flat end that you use to make a small boat move through the water **2** [no plural] *UK* when you walk in water that is not deep *to go for a paddle*

paddle² /'pædl/ *verb* **1** BOAT [I, T] to move a small boat through water with a paddle **2** WALK [I] *UK* (*US* **wade**) to walk in water that is not deep **3** SWIM [I] *US* to swim using short, quick movements with your arms and legs

paddock /'pædək/ *noun* [C] a small field where animals are kept, especially horses

paddy field /'pædi,fiːld/ *UK* (*UK/US* **rice paddy**) *noun* [C] a field in which rice is grown

padlock /'pædlɒk/ *noun* [C] a metal lock with a U-shaped part that is used for fastening bicycles, doors, etc • **padlock** *verb* [T]

paediatrician *UK* (*US* **pediatrician**) /,piːdiə-'trɪʃən/ *noun* [C] a children's doctor

paedophile *UK* (*US* **pedophile**) /'piːdəʊfaɪl/ *noun* [C] someone who is sexually interested in children

pagan /'peɪɡən/ *adjective* relating to religious beliefs that do not belong to any of the main religions of the world *a pagan festival* • **pagan** *noun* [C] someone who has pagan religious beliefs

o→**page¹** /peɪdʒ/ *noun* [C] **1** a piece of paper in a book, magazine, etc, or one side of a piece of paper *The article is on page 36.* ○ *I've only read 50 pages so far.* **2** (*also* **web page**) one part of a website that you can see or print separately ⊃See also: **home page**, the **Yellow Pages.**

page² /peɪdʒ/ *verb* [T] **1** to call someone using a sound system in a public place **2** to send a message to someone's pager (= small piece of electronic equipment)

pageant /'pædʒənt/ *noun* [C] a show that happens outside in which people dress and act as if they are from a time in history

pageantry /'pædʒəntri/ *noun* [U] ceremonies in which there are a lot of people in special clothes

pager /'peɪdʒər/ *noun* [C] a small piece of electronic equipment that you carry which makes a noise or movement when someone sends a message

pagoda /pə'ɡəʊdə/ *noun* [C] a tall religious building in Asia with many levels, each of which has a curved roof

paid /peɪd/ *past of* pay

pail /peɪl/ *noun* [C] a container with an open top and a handle used for carrying liquids

o→**pain¹** /peɪn/ *noun* **1** [C, U] an unpleasant physical feeling caused by an illness or injury *chest/stomach pains* ○ *Are you in pain?* ○ *I felt a sharp pain in my foot.* **2** [U] sadness or mental suffering caused by an unpleasant event *I can't describe the pain I suffered when he died.* **3 be a pain (in the neck)** *informal* to be annoying *My brother can be a real pain in the neck sometimes.* **4 be at pains to do sth; take pains to do sth** to make a lot of effort to do something *He was at great pains to explain the reasons for his decision.*

pain² /peɪn/ *verb* [T] *formal* If something pains you, it makes you feel sad or upset. [+ to do sth] *It pained him to see animals being treated so cruelly.*

pained /peɪnd/ *adjective* appearing to be sad or upset *a pained expression*

o→**painful** /'peɪnfəl/ *adjective* **1** causing physical pain *Recovery from the operation is a slow and painful process.* **2** making you feel sad or upset *a painful memory*

painfully /'peɪnfəli/ *adverb* **1** in a painful way *He landed painfully on his elbow.* **2 painfully clear/obvious, etc** If a problem is painfully clear/obvious, etc, it is embarrassing because it is so clear/obvious, etc. *It was painfully obvious that she didn't like him.* **3** used to emphasize an unpleasant situation or quality *She's painfully thin.*

painkiller /'peɪn,kɪlər/ *noun* [C] a drug which reduces pain

painless /'peɪnləs/ *adjective* **1** causing no physical pain *a painless death* **2** causing no problems or difficulties *There is no painless way of learning a language.* • **painlessly** *adverb*

painstaking /'peɪnz,teɪkɪŋ/ *adjective* done with a lot of care *It took months of painstaking research to write the book.* • **painstakingly** *adverb*

o→**paint¹** /peɪnt/ *noun* [C, U] a coloured liquid that you put on a surface to decorate it *a gallon of*

P

blue paint ○ *The door needs another **coat*** (= layer) *of paint.*

⚬**paint²** /peɪnt/ *verb* **1** [T] to cover a surface with paint in order to decorate it *We've painted the kitchen yellow.* **2** [I, T] to produce a picture of something or someone using paint *These pictures were all painted by local artists.* ➋See also: paint a bleak/rosy, etc **picture¹** of sth.

paintbrush /'peɪntbrʌʃ/ *noun* [C] a brush that is used for painting pictures or for painting surfaces such as walls and doors ➋See picture at brush.

painter /'peɪntə*ʳ*/ *noun* [C] **1** someone who paints pictures **2** someone whose job is to paint surfaces, such as walls and doors *a painter and decorator*

─────────────────────
WORD PARTNERS FOR *painting*

do a painting • a painting **of** sth/sb • a painting **by** sb
─────────────────────

⚬**painting** /'peɪntɪŋ/ *noun* **1** [C] a picture that someone has painted **2** [U] the activity of painting pictures or painting surfaces ➋See also: oil painting.

pair

a pair of trousers   a pair of scissors

a pair of gloves

⚬**pair¹** /peə*ʳ*/ *noun* [C] **1** TWO THINGS two things that look the same and that are used together *a pair of socks/shoes* **2** TWO PARTS something that is made of two parts that are joined together *a pair of scissors* ○ *a new pair of jeans/ trousers* **3** TWO PEOPLE two people who are doing something together *For the next exercise, you'll need to work **in pairs**.*

pair² /peə*ʳ*/ *verb*
pair off If two people pair off, they begin a romantic or sexual relationship.
pair sb off with sb to introduce one person to another because you hope they will begin a romantic relationship *Caroline tried to pair me off with her sister.*
pair up to join another person for a short time in order to do something *I **paired up** with Chris for the last dance.*

pajamas /pə'dʒɑːməz/ *noun* [plural] US spelling of

pyjamas (= shirt and trousers that you wear in bed)

pal /pæl/ *noun* [C] *informal* a friend *He's an old pal of mine.*

⚬**palace** /'pælɪs/ *noun* [C] a large house where a king or queen lives *Buckingham Palace*

palatable /'pælətəbl/ *adjective formal* **1** If food or drink is palatable, it has a pleasant taste. *a palatable local wine* **2** If an idea or plan is palatable, it is acceptable. *They need to make the project more palatable to local people.* ➋Opposite unpalatable.

palate /'pælət/ *noun* [C] **1** the top part of the inside of your mouth **2** the ability to judge and enjoy good food and drink

⚬**pale** /peɪl/ *adjective* **1** pale blue/green/red, etc light blue/green/red, etc *a pale yellow dress* **2** If your face is pale, it has less colour than usual because you are ill or frightened.

pall¹ /pɔːl/ *verb* [I] to become less interesting and enjoyable *The pleasure of not having to work soon began to pall.*

pall² /pɔːl/ *noun* **1** a pall of dust/smoke, etc a thick cloud of dust/smoke, etc **2** cast a pall over sth If an unpleasant situation or piece of news casts a pall over an event, it spoils it. *The news of Nick's accident cast a pall over the celebrations.*

palm¹ /pɑːm/ *noun* [C] **1** the inside surface of your hand ➋See colour picture **The Body** on page Centre 13. **2** a palm tree

palm² /pɑːm/ *verb*
palm sb off to tell someone something that is not true so that they will stop asking questions *He **palmed** me off with an excuse about why he couldn't pay.*
palm sth off as sth to deceive people by saying that something has a particular quality or value that it does not have
palm sth off on sb to give or sell something to someone because you want to get rid of it *He palmed his old computer off on me.*

Palm /pɑːm/ *noun* [C] *trademark* a small computer that you can carry with you

'palm, tree *noun* [C] a tall tree with long leaves at the top which grows in hot countries

palpable /'pælpəbl/ *adjective* very obvious *There was a palpable sense of tension in the crowd.*

paltry /'pɔːltri/ *adjective* A paltry amount of something, especially money, is very small. *a paltry sum of money*

pamper /'pæmpə*ʳ*/ *verb* [T] to treat someone in a kind way and give them everything they want *She pampered herself with a trip to the beauty salon.*

pamphlet /'pæmflɪt/ *noun* [C] a very thin book with a paper cover that gives information about something *The tourist office gave me a pamphlet about places to visit in the city.*

pan¹ /pæn/ *noun* [C] a metal container with a handle that is used for cooking food in ➋See also: a flash² in the pan, frying pan.

pan² /pæn/ *verb* [T] panning, *past* panned *informal* to criticize something severely [often passive] *His last novel was panned by the critics.*

pan out to develop in a particular way *Not all his ideas had panned out in the way he would have liked.*

panacea /ˌpænəˈsiːə/ *noun* [C] something that people believe can solve all their problems

panache /pəˈnæʃ/ *noun* [U] a confident and attractive way of doing things *The orchestra played with great panache.*

pancake /ˈpænkeɪk/ *noun* [C] a thin, flat food made from flour, milk, and egg mixed together and cooked in a pan

panda /ˈpændə/ *noun* [C] a large, black and white animal that lives in forests in China

panda

pandemonium /ˌpændəˈməʊniəm/ *noun* [U] when there is a lot of noise and confusion because people are angry or excited about something that has happened *Pandemonium broke out in the courtroom as they took him away.*

pander /ˈpændəʳ/ *verb*
pander to sb/sth to do what someone wants although it is wrong *He said he would not pander to public pressure.*

pane /peɪn/ *noun* [C] a flat piece of glass in a window or door

panel /ˈpænl/ *noun* [C] 1 PIECE a flat, rectangular piece of wood, metal, etc that forms the surface of a door, wall, etc 2 PEOPLE a group of people who are chosen to discuss something or make a decision about something *a panel of experts* 3 CONTROLS the part of a car, aircraft, etc that the controls are fixed to ⊃See also: solar panel.

panelling UK (US **paneling**) /ˈpænəlɪŋ/ *noun* [U] flat, rectangular pieces of wood that form the surface of walls, doors, etc *carved oak panelling*

panellist UK (US **panelist**) /ˈpænəlɪst/ *noun* [C] one of a group of people who are chosen to discuss something or make a decision about something

pang /pæŋ/ *noun* [C] a sudden, strong feeling of an unpleasant emotion *Bernard felt a sharp pang of jealousy.*

panhandle /ˈpænˌhændl/ *verb* [I] US to ask people for money in a public place • **panhandler** *noun* [C] US

WORD PARTNERS FOR *panic*

be **in a** panic • panic **breaks out** • **absolute/blind** panic • panic **about/over** sth • **do** sth **in** panic • a panic **attack**

panic¹ /ˈpænɪk/ *noun* [C, U] a sudden, strong feeling of worry or fear that makes you unable to think or behave calmly *He was in a panic about his exams.* ○ *She had a panic attack* (= suddenly felt extreme panic) *in the supermarket.*

panic² /ˈpænɪk/ *verb* [I, T] panicking, *past* panicked to suddenly feel so worried or frightened that you cannot think or behave calmly, or to make

someone feel this way *Don't panic, we've got plenty of time.*

panic-stricken /ˈpænɪkˌstrɪkᵊn/ *adjective* extremely frightened

panorama /ˌpænᵊrˈɑːmə/ *noun* [C] a view of a wide area

panoramic /ˌpænᵊrˈæmɪk/ *adjective* A panoramic view is very wide. *a panoramic view of the city*

pansy /ˈpænzi/ *noun* [C] a small garden flower with round petals which can be many different colours

pant /pænt/ *verb* [I] to breathe quickly and loudly because it is hot or because you have been running, etc

panther /ˈpænθəʳ/ *noun* [C] a large, black, wild cat

panties /ˈpæntiz/ *mainly US* (UK **knickers**) *noun* [plural] women's underwear that covers the bottom ⊃See Common learner error at **underwear** ⊃See colour picture **Clothes** on page Centre 9.

pantomime /ˈpæntəmaɪm/ *noun* [C, U] a funny play performed in the UK around Christmas, based on traditional children's stories

pantry /ˈpæntri/ *noun* [C] a small room where food is kept

pants /pænts/ *noun* [plural] 1 US (UK/US **trousers**) a piece of clothing that covers the legs and has a separate part for each leg ⊃See colour picture **Clothes** on page Centre 8. 2 UK (US **underpants**) underwear that covers the bottom ⊃See Common learner error at **underwear**. ⊃See colour picture **Clothes** on page Centre 9.

ˈpant ˌsuit US (UK **trouser suit**) *noun* [C] a woman's jacket and trousers made of the same material

pantyhose /ˈpæntihəʊz/ US (UK **tights**) *noun* [plural] a piece of women's clothing made of very thin material that covers the legs and bottom

papa /pəˈpɑː/ *noun* [C] old-fashioned, another word for father

the papacy /ˈpeɪpəsi/ *noun* the position or authority of the Pope (= leader of the Roman Catholic Church)

papal /ˈpeɪpᵊl/ *adjective* relating to the Pope (= leader of the Roman Catholic Church)

paparazzi /ˌpæpəˈrætsi/ *noun* [plural] photographers whose job is to follow famous people and take photographs of them for newspapers and magazines

o~**paper¹** /ˈpeɪpəʳ/ *noun* 1 MATERIAL [U] thin, flat material used for writing on, covering things in, etc *a piece/sheet of paper* 2 NEWSPAPER [C] a newspaper 3 EXAM [C] UK an examination *Candidates must answer two questions from each paper.* 4 WRITING [C] a piece of writing about a particular subject written by someone who has been studying that subject *She's just published a paper on language acquisition.* ⊃See also: blotting paper, carbon paper, toilet paper, White Paper, wrapping paper.

paper² /ˈpeɪpəʳ/ *verb* [T] to decorate the walls of a room by covering them with paper

paperback /'peɪpəbæk/ *noun* [C] a book that has a soft paper cover

paper ,clip *noun* [C] a small piece of metal used to hold several pieces of paper together ⊃See colour picture **The Office** on page Centre 5.

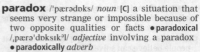

paper clips

papers /'peɪpəz/ *noun* [plural] official documents *I keep all my papers safely locked away.*

paper ,weight *noun* [C] a small, heavy object that you put on top of pieces of paper to stop them from moving

paperwork /'peɪpəwɜːk/ *noun* [U] the part of a job that involves writing letters, organizing information, etc

par /pɑːʳ/ *noun* **1 be on a par with sb/sth** to be the same as or equal to someone or something **2 below par** not as good as usual *I'm feeling a bit below par today.* **3 be par for the course** If a type of behaviour, event, or situation is par for the course, it is not good but it is normal or as you would expect. *"Simon was late." "That's just par for the course, isn't it?"*

parable /'pærəbl/ *noun* [C] a short story, especially in the Bible, that shows you how you should behave

paracetamol /,pærə'siːtəmɒl/ *noun* [C, U] a common drug used to reduce pain and fever

parachute /'pærəʃuːt/ *noun* [C] a large piece of cloth which is fixed to your body by strings and helps you to drop safely from an aircraft ● **parachute** *verb* [I] to jump from an aircraft using a parachute

parachute

parade¹ /pə'reɪd/ *noun* [C] a line of people or vehicles that moves through a public place as a way of celebrating an occasion *a victory parade*

parade² /pə'reɪd/ *verb* **1 parade down/past/ through sth** to walk as a group, usually to show disagreement about something *Thousands of workers paraded through the streets.* **2 parade around/up and down, etc** to walk somewhere so that people will see and admire you *The kids were parading around in their new clothes.* **3** [T] to try to make someone notice something that you are proud of, especially how rich you are or how much you know

paradigm /'pærədaɪm/ *noun* [C] *formal* a typical example or model of something *Career women are establishing a new paradigm of work and family life.*

paradise /'pærədaɪs/ *noun* **1** [no plural] in some religions, a place where good people go after they die **2** [C, U] a perfect place or situation *a tropical paradise* ○ *a shoppers' paradise*

paradox /'pærədɒks/ *noun* [C] a situation that seems very strange or impossible because of two opposite qualities or facts ● **paradoxical** /,pærə'dɒksɪkᵊl/ *adjective* involving a paradox ● **paradoxically** *adverb*

paraffin /'pærəfɪn/ *UK* (*US* **kerosene**) *noun* [U] oil used for heating and lights

paragraph /'pærəɡrɑːf/ *noun* [C] a part of a text that contains at least one sentence and starts on a new line

parallel¹ /'pærəlel/ *adjective* **1** If two or more lines are parallel, the distance between them is the same along all their length. *The streets are parallel.* **2** similar and happening at the same time *Parallel experiments are being conducted in both countries.*

parallel² /'pærəlel/ *noun* [C] a similarity *There are a number of **parallels between** our two situations.* ○ *People are **drawing parallels** (= describing similarities) between the two cases.*

the Paralympic Games /ðə,pærə,lɪmpɪk 'ɡeɪmz/ (*also* **Paralympics**) *noun* [plural] an international sports competition for people who have a disability (= a condition that makes it difficult for a person to do the things that other people do) ● **Paralympic** *adjective* ● **Paralympian** *noun* [C]

paralyse *UK* (*US* **paralyze**) /'pærᵊlaɪz/ *verb* [T] **1** to make someone move all or part of their body [often passive] *He was paralysed from the waist down by polio.* **2** to make something stop working *Rail strikes have paralysed the city's transport system.*

paralysed *UK* (*US* **paralyzed**) /'pærᵊlaɪzd/ *adjective* **1** unable to move all or part of your body because of an injury or illness **2** unable to move or speak because you are so frightened *to be paralysed with fear*

paralysis /pə'rælᵊsɪs/ *noun* [U] **1** being unable to move all or part of your body because of injury or illness *muscular paralysis* **2** not being able to take action *political paralysis*

paralyze /'pærəlaɪz/ *verb* [T] *US spelling of* paralyse

paramedic /,pærə'medɪk/ *noun* [C] someone who is trained to give medical treatment to people who are injured or very ill, but who is not a doctor or nurse

parameter /pə'ræmɪtəʳ/ *noun* [C] a limit that controls the way that you can do something [usually plural] *Before we can start the research we need to **set** some **parameters** (= decide some limits).*

paramilitaries /,pærə'mɪlɪtᵊriz/ *noun* [plural] people who belong to paramilitary organizations

paramilitary /,pærə'mɪlɪtᵊri/ *adjective* [always before noun] organized like an army, but not belonging to an official army *a **paramilitary organization/group***

paramount /'pærəmaʊnt/ *adjective* *formal*

more important than anything else *Safety, of course, is paramount.* ○ *Communication is of* **paramount importance.**

paranoia /ˌpærəˈnɔɪə/ *noun* [U] **1** when you wrongly think that other people do not like you and are always criticizing you *Do you think his boss really hates him or is it just paranoia?* **2** a mental illness that makes people wrongly think that other people are trying to harm them ● **paranoid** /ˈpærənɔɪd/ *adjective* when you have paranoia *Stop being so paranoid - no one's talking about you.*

paraphernalia /ˌpærəfəˈneɪliə/ *noun* [U] all the objects used in a particular activity *the painter's paraphernalia of brushes, paints, and pencils*

paraphrase /ˈpærəfreɪz/ *verb* [I, T] to express something that has been said or written in a different way, usually so that it is clearer ● **paraphrase** *noun* [C]

parasite /ˈpærəsaɪt/ *noun* [C] **1** a plant or animal that lives on or inside another plant or animal in order to get food **2** a lazy person who expects other people to give them money and food

paratrooper /ˈpærətruːpəʳ/ *noun* [C] a soldier who is trained to be dropped from an aircraft using a parachute (= large piece of cloth fixed to the body by strings)

o⊷**parcel** /ˈpɑːsəl/ *noun* [C] something that is covered in paper so that it can be sent by post ⊃See also: **part¹** and parcel.

parched /pɑːtʃt/ *adjective* **1 be parched** *informal* to be very thirsty *I'm going to get a drink - I'm parched.* **2** very dry *a parched desert/land*

pardon¹ /ˈpɑːdən/ *exclamation* **1** (*also US* **pardon me**) a polite way of asking someone to repeat what they have just said *"You'll need an umbrella." "Pardon?" "I said you'll need an umbrella."* **2 Pardon me.** used to say 'sorry' after you have done something rude, for example after burping (= letting air from your stomach out of your mouth)

pardon² /ˈpɑːdən/ *noun* **1** [C] when someone who has committed a crime is officially forgiven and allowed to be free **2 I beg your pardon.** *formal spoken* **a** used for saying 'sorry' when you have made a mistake or done something wrong *I beg your pardon - I thought you were speaking to me.* **b** used to show that you strongly disagree or that you are angry about something that someone has said *I beg your pardon, young man - I don't want to hear you speak like that again!*

pardon³ /ˈpɑːdən/ *verb* [T] to officially forgive someone who has committed a crime and allow them to be free

o⊷**parent** /ˈpeərənt/ *noun* [C] your mother or father *Her parents live in Oxford.* ● **parental** /pəˈrentəl/ *adjective* relating to a parent *parental responsibility*

We spent the holidays visiting all our relatives.
~~We spent the holidays visiting all our parents.~~

ˈparent ˌcompany *noun* [C] a company which controls other smaller companies

parentheses /pəˈrenθəsiːz/ (*also UK* **brackets**) *noun* [plural] two curved lines ( ) used around extra information or information that should be considered as separate from the main part *The age of each student is listed in parentheses.*

parenthood /ˈpeərənthʊd/ *noun* [U] being a parent *the demands of parenthood* ○ *single parenthood*

parenting /ˈpeərəntɪŋ/ *noun* [U] the things that you do during the time when you take care of your baby or child *parenting classes*

parish /ˈpærɪʃ/ *noun* [C] an area that has its own church

parishioner /pəˈrɪʃənəʳ/ *noun* [C] someone who lives in a parish and often goes to church

parity /ˈpærəti/ *noun* [U] *formal* equality, usually relating to the money people earn or their position *The union has also asked for wage parity with similar public-sector workers.* ⊃Opposite **disparity.**

o⊷**park¹** /pɑːk/ *noun* [C] a large area of grass, often in a town, where people can walk and enjoy themselves *We went for a walk in the park.* ⊃See also: **amusement park, car park, industrial park, national park, theme park, trailer park.**

o⊷**park²** /pɑːk/ *verb* [I, T] to leave a vehicle in a particular place for a period of time *I parked the car near the old bridge.* ○ *You can park outside the school.*

parking /ˈpɑːkɪŋ/ *noun* [U] leaving a vehicle in a particular place for a period of time *free/ underground parking*

ˈparking ˌlot *US* (*UK* **car park**) *noun* [C] a place where vehicles can be parked

ˈparking ˌmeter *noun* [C] a device next to a road that you pay so that you can park your vehicle on that road

ˈparking ˌticket *noun* [C] a piece of paper that tells you that you must pay money because you have parked your car where you should not

WORD PARTNERS FOR **parliament**

dissolve/elect a parliament ● **enter** parliament ● **in** parliament

o⊷**parliament** /ˈpɑːləmənt/ *noun* [C, U] in some countries, a group of people who make the laws for the country *the Russian parliament* ● **parliamentary** /ˌpɑːləˈmentəri/ *adjective* [always before noun] relating to a parliament *a parliamentary candidate/election* ⊃See also: **Houses of Parliament, Member of Parliament.**

parlour *UK* (*US* **parlor**) /ˈpɑːləʳ/ *noun* [C] a shop that provides a particular type of goods or services *a beauty/pizza parlour*

parody /'pærədi/ *noun* [C, U] a film, book, etc that copies someone else's style in a way that is funny *It's a parody of a low-budget 1950's horror movie.* • **parody** *verb* [T]

parole /pə'rəʊl/ *noun* [U] when someone is allowed to leave prison early but is only allowed to remain free if they behave well *He's hoping to get released on parole.*

parrot /'pærət/ *noun* [C] a tropical bird with a curved beak and colourful feathers that can be taught to copy what people say

parsimonious /ˌpɑːsɪ'məʊniəs/ *adjective formal* not willing to spend money or give something

parsley /'pɑːsli/ *noun* [U] a herb that is added to food to give it flavour

parsnip /'pɑːsnɪp/ *noun* [C] a long, cream-coloured root that is eaten as a vegetable

⚬**part¹** /pɑːt/ *noun* 1 NOT ALL [C, U] one of the things that, with other things, makes the whole of something *Part of this form seems to be missing.* ○ *I did French as part of my degree course.* ○ *It's all part of growing up.* ○ *You're part of the family.* **2 take part (in sth)** to be involved in an activity with other people *She doesn't usually take part in any of the class activities.* **3** FILM/PLAY [C] a person in a film or play *He plays the part of the father.* **4 have/play a part in sth** to be one of the people or things that are involved in an event or situation *Alcohol plays a part in 60 percent of violent crime.* **5** MACHINE [C] a piece of a machine or vehicle *aircraft parts* ○ *spare parts* **6** HAIR [C] *US* (*UK* parting) the line on your head made by brushing your hair in two different directions **7 the best/better part of sth** most of a period of time *It took the better part of the afternoon to put those shelves up.* **8 in part** *formal* partly *He is in part to blame for the accident.* **9 for the most part** mostly or usually *I enjoyed it for the most part.* **10 look the part** to look suitable for a particular situation *If you're going to be a successful businesswoman, you've got to look the part.* **11 part and parcel** If something is part and parcel of an experience, it is a necessary part of that experience and cannot be avoided. *Stress is part and parcel of the job.*

part² /pɑːt/ *adverb* not completely *She's part Irish and part English.*

part³ /pɑːt/ *verb* 1 SEPARATE [I, T] If two sides of something part, they become separated, and if you part them, you make them separate. *Slowly her lips parted and she smiled.* **2** LEAVE [I, T] *formal* If two people part, or if one person parts from another, they leave each other. *That summer, after six years of marriage, we parted.* ○ *Even after we parted company, we remained in contact.* **3** HAIR [T] to brush your hair in two directions so that there is a straight line showing on your head *In my school days, I had long hair parted in the middle.*

part with sth to give something to someone else, often when you do not want to *You*

know how hard it is to get Simon to part with his money.

partial /'pɑːʃəl/ *adjective* **1** not complete *He made a partial recovery.* **2 be partial to sth** If you are partial to something, you like it. *I'm rather partial to red wine myself.*

partially /'pɑːʃəli/ *adverb* not completely *partially cooked*

participant /pɑː'tɪsɪpənt/ *noun* [C] someone who is involved in an activity *All participants finishing the race will receive a medal.*

participate /pɑː'tɪsɪpeɪt/ *verb* [I] to be involved with other people in an activity *She rarely participates in any of the discussions.* • **participation** /pɑːˌtɪsɪ'peɪʃən/ *noun* [U] *Both shows encourage audience participation.*

participle /pɑː'tɪsɪpl/ ⑳ /'pɑːtɪsɪpl/ *noun* [C] the form of a verb that usually ends with '-ed' or '-ing' and is used in some verb tenses or as an adjective ⊃See also: past participle, present participle.

particle /'pɑːtɪkl/ *noun* [C] a very small piece of something *particles of dust*

⚬**particular** /pə'tɪkjələr/ *adjective* **1** ONE PERSON/THING [always before noun] used to talk about one thing or person and not others *Is there any particular restaurant you'd like to go to?* ○ *"Why did you ask?" "No particular reason."* **2** SPECIAL [always before noun] special *"Was anything important said at the meeting?" "Nothing of particular interest."* **3** NOT EASILY SATISFIED [never before noun] choosing things carefully and not easily satisfied *Teenagers are very particular about the clothes they'll wear.* **4 in particular** especially *Are you looking for anything in particular?*

⚬**particularly** /pə'tɪkjələli/ *adverb* especially *She didn't seem particularly interested.* ○ *"Was the food good?" "Not particularly."*

particulars /pə'tɪkjələz/ *noun* [plural] *formal* details about something or someone *There's a form for you to note down all your particulars.*

parting¹ /'pɑːtɪŋ/ *noun* **1** [C, U] *formal* when you are separated from another person, often for a long time *The pain of parting gradually lessened over the years.* **2** [C] *UK* (*US* part) the line on your head made by brushing your hair in two different directions

parting² /'pɑːtɪŋ/ *adjective* **parting glance/words, etc** something that you do or say as you leave

partisan¹ /ˌpɑːtɪ'zæn/ ⑳ /'pɑːrtɪzən/ *adjective* showing support for a particular political system or leader *partisan politics* ○ *a partisan crowd*

partisan² /ˌpɑːtɪ'zæn/ ⑳ /'pɑːrtɪzən/ *noun* [C] **1** someone who supports a particular political system or leader **2** a member of a group that secretly fights against soldiers who are controlling their country

partition /pɑː'tɪʃən/ *noun* **1** [C] a wall that divides a room into two parts **2** [U] when a coun-

P

try divides into two or more countries or areas of government • **partition** verb [T]

o→**partly** /ˈpɑːtli/ adverb used to show that something is true to some degree but not completely *The house is partly owned by her father.* ○ *He was partly responsible.*

o→**partner**[1] /ˈpɑːtnəʳ/ noun [C] **1** RELATIONSHIP someone that you are married to or having a sexual relationship with *sexual partners* ○ *Are partners invited to the office dinner?* **2** SPORTS/DANCING someone that you are dancing or playing a sport or game with **3** BUSINESS someone who owns a business with another person *a junior/senior partner* ○ *He's a partner in a law firm.* **4** COUNTRY a country that has an agreement with another country *a trading partner* ○ *Britain and its European partners*

partner[2] /ˈpɑːtnəʳ/ verb [T] to be someone's partner in a dance, sport, or game *He looks certain to partner him again in the finals.*

> WORD PARTNERS FOR **partnership**
>
> enter into/go into partnership • be in partnership with sb • a partnership between sb and sb

partnership /ˈpɑːtnəʃɪp/ noun **1** [C, U] when two people or organizations work together to achieve something *She's gone into partnership* (= started to work together) *with an ex-colleague.* **2** [C] a company which is owned by two or more people

part-time /ˌpɑːtˈtaɪm/ adjective, adverb working or studying only for part of the day or the week *a part-time job* ○ *He works part-time as a waiter.*

> WORD PARTNERS FOR **party**
>
> go to/have/throw a party • a birthday/Christmas party • be at a party

o→**party**[1] /ˈpɑːti/ noun [C] **1** EVENT an event where people enjoy themselves by talking, eating, drinking, and dancing *a birthday party* ○ *We're having a party to celebrate the occasion.* **2** POLITICS an organization that shares the same political beliefs and tries to win elections *a political party* **3** GROUP a group of people who are working or travelling together *a party of tourists* **4** LEGAL one of the sides in a legal agreement or disagreement *the guilty party* ○ *We hope to provide a solution that is acceptable to both parties.* ➡See also: the Conservative Party, the Democratic Party, the Green Party, the Labour Party, toe the (party) line[1], the Republican Party, search party, slumber party, third party.

party[2] /ˈpɑːti/ verb [I] to enjoy yourself by talking, eating, drinking, and dancing with a group of people *They were out partying till five o'clock in the morning.*

o→**pass**[1] /pɑːs/ verb **1** GO PAST (*also* **pass by**) to go past something or someone *She passed me this morning in the corridor.* ○ *Cars kept passing us on the motorway.* **2** **pass (sth) over/through, etc** to go in a particular direction, or to cause something to go in a particular direction *Another plane passed over our heads.*

○ *We pass through your village on the way home.* **3** GIVE [T] to give something to someone *Could you pass the salt, please?* ○ *He passed a note to her in the meeting.* **4** TIME [I] If a period of time passes, it happens. *Four years have passed since that day.* **5** **pass (the) time** to spend time doing something *She was eating only to pass the time.* **6** EXAM [I, T] to succeed at a test or an exam, or to decide that someone has been successful *I passed my driving test the first time.* **7** BE MORE THAN [T] to be more than a particular level *Donations have passed the one million mark.* **8** SPORTS [I, T] in sports, to throw or kick a ball to someone else *Edwards passes to Brinkworth.* **9** **pass a law/motion, etc** to officially approve of something and make it into a law or rule *They passed a law banning the sale of alcohol.* **10** GO AWAY [I] If a feeling passes, it goes away. *I know he's angry now but it'll pass.* **11** **pass judgment** to judge someone's behaviour **12** **pass sentence** If a judge passes sentence, they state what the criminal's punishment will be. **13** **let sth pass** to decide not to criticize someone when they say something unpleasant or they make a mistake ➡See also: pass the buck[1].

pass sth around/round to offer something to each person in a group of people *Take a copy for yourself and pass the rest around.*

pass as/for sth/sb If someone or something passes as or for someone or something else, they appear like that person or thing. *She's fifteen but could easily pass for eighteen.*

pass away to die *She passed away peacefully in her sleep.*

pass sth down to teach or give something to someone who will be alive after you have died [often passive] *Folk tales have been passed down from generation to generation.*

pass sth/sb off as sth/sb to pretend that something or someone is different from what they really are *He tried to pass himself off as some sort of expert.*

pass on to die

pass sth on 1 TELL to tell someone something that someone else has told you *Did you pass on my message to him?* **2** GIVE to give something to someone else *Could you pass it on to Laura when you've finished reading it?* **3** DISEASE to give a disease to another person *The virus can be passed on through physical contact.*

pass out to become unconscious *I don't remember any more because I passed out at that point.*

pass sth up to not use an opportunity to do something interesting *It's a great opportunity - you'd be a fool to pass it up.*

pass[2] /pɑːs/ noun [C] **1** TEST a successful result in a test or a course *A pass is above 60%.* **2** DOCUMENT an official document that allows you to do something *a bus/rail pass* ○ *You need a pass to get into the building.* **3** SPORTS in sports, when you throw or kick a ball to someone else **4** PATH a narrow path between two mountains *a mountain pass* ➡See also: boarding pass.

passage /ˈpæsɪdʒ/ noun **1** SPACE [C] (*also*

P

passageway /'pæsɪdzweɪ/) a long, narrow space that connects one place to another *There's a passage to the side of the house, leading to the garden.* **2** [WRITING/MUSIC] **[C]** a short part of a book, speech, or piece of music *She can quote whole passages from the novel.* **3** [TUBE] **[C]** a tube in your body that allows air, liquid, etc to pass through it *the nasal/respiratory passages* **4** [PROGRESS] **[U, no plural]** the movement or progress from one stage or place to another *It's a difficult passage from boyhood to manhood.* **5 the passage of time** *literary* the way that time passes *Love changes with the passage of time.*

passenger /'pæsᵊndʒəʳ/ *noun* **[C]** someone who is travelling in a vehicle, but not controlling the vehicle *a front-seat passenger*

passer-by /ˌpɑːsə'baɪ/ *noun* **[C]** *plural* **passers-by** someone who is walking past something by chance *Police were alerted by a passer-by who saw the accident.*

passing¹ /'pɑːsɪŋ/ *adjective* **[always before noun]** lasting only for a short time and not important *a* ***passing interest***

passing² /'pɑːsɪŋ/ *noun* **1 the passing of time/years** the way that time passes *With the passing of time their love had changed.* **2 in passing** If you say something in passing, you talk about one thing briefly while talking mainly about something else. *She mentioned in passing that she'd seen Stuart.*

passion /'pæʃᵊn/ *noun* **1 [U]** a strong, sexual feeling for someone *She saw the passion in his eyes.* **2 [C, U]** a strong belief in something or a strong feeling about a subject *She spoke with passion about the injustice.* **3 a passion for sth** when you like something very much *a passion for football*

passionate /'pæʃᵊnət/ *adjective* **1** having a strong, sexual feeling for someone *a passionate affair/lover* **2** showing a strong belief in something or a strong feeling about a subject *a passionate speaker* • **passionately** *adverb*

passive /'pæsɪv/ *adjective* **1** letting things happen to you and not taking action *Women at that time were expected to be passive.* **2** A passive verb or sentence is one in which the subject does not do or cause the action but is affected by it. For example 'He was released from prison.' is a passive sentence.

the passive /'pæsɪv/ (*also* **the ˌpassive 'voice**) *noun* the passive form of a verb

ˌpassive 'smoking *noun* **[U]** breathing in smoke from other people's cigarettes

Passover /'pɑːsˌəʊvəʳ/ *noun* **[U]** the Jewish period of religious celebration held in March or April

WORD PARTNERS FOR ***passport***

apply for a passport • **have/hold** a [British/ Japanese, etc] passport • a **valid** passport

⊶**passport** /'pɑːspɔːt/ *noun* **1 [C]** an official document, often a small book, that you need to enter or leave a country *a British passport* **2 a passport to sth** something that allows you to achieve something else *Education is a passport to a better life.*

WORD PARTNERS FOR ***password***

enter/put in your password • a **secret** password • **forget** a password • **change** a password

password /'pɑːswɜːd/ *noun* **[C]** a secret word that allows you to do something, such as use your computer

⊶**past¹** /pɑːst/ *adjective* **1** [BEFORE NOW] **[always before noun]** having happened or existed before now *past relationships* ○ *I know this from* ***past experience.*** **2** [UNTIL NOW] **[always before noun]** used to refer to a period of time before and until the present *It's been raining for the past three days.* **3** [FINISHED] **[never before noun]** Something that is past has now finished. *My student days are past.* **4 past tense** the form of the verb which is used to show what happened in the past

⊶**past²** /pɑːst/ *noun* **1 the past a** the time before the present and all the things that happened then ***In the past*** *people would bathe once a month.* **b** the form of the verb which is used to show what happened in the past **2 sb's past** all of the things that someone has done in their life *I knew nothing about his past.*

⊶**past³** /pɑːst/ *adverb, preposition* **1** [FURTHER] further than *I live on Station Road, just past the Post Office.* **2** [UP TO AND FURTHER] up to and further than someone or something *Three boys went past us on mountain bikes.* ○ *I've just seen the bus go past.* **3** [AFTER HOUR] used to say 'after' the hour when you are saying what time it is *It's five past three.* **4** [AFTER LIMIT] after a particular time or age limit *This bacon is past its sell-by date.* **5 past it** *informal* too old to do something **6 I wouldn't put it past sb (to do sth)** *informal* used to say that you would not be surprised if someone did something, especially something bad, because it is a typical thing for them to do *I wouldn't put it past him to sell her jewellery.*

pasta /'pæstə/ [US] /'pɑːstə/ *noun* **[U]** a food that is made from flour, water, and sometimes eggs and is made in many different shapes ➲See colour picture **Food** on page Centre 11.

paste¹ /peɪst/ *noun* **[C, U]** **1** a soft, wet, sticky substance that is used to stick things together *wallpaper paste* **2** a soft food that spreads easily *tomato/almond paste*

paste² /peɪst/ *verb* **1 [T]** to stick a piece of paper to another piece of paper *The cuttings had been pasted into a scrapbook.* **2 [I, T]** to move a piece of text to a particular place in a computer document ➲See also: **cut and paste.**

pastel /'pæstᵊl/ [US] /pæs'tel/ *adjective* A pastel colour is light. ***pastel colours/shades*** ○ *pastel pink* • **pastel** *noun* **[C]** *The bedroom is decorated in pastels* (= pale colours).

pastime /'pɑːstaɪm/ *noun* **[C]** an activity that you enjoy doing when you are not working *Shopping is one of her favourite pastimes.*

pastor /'pɑːstəʳ/ *noun* **[C]** a priest in some Protestant churches

pastoral /'pɑːstᵊrᵊl/ *adjective* **1** related to giving advice and looking after people *the teacher's* ***pastoral role*** **2** **[always before noun]** *literary* relating to life in the country *a pastoral song/tradition*

ˌpast parˈticiple *UK* (*US* **ˌpast ˈparticiple**) *noun* [C] the form of a verb that usually ends with '-ed' and can be used in the perfect tense, the passive tense, or as an adjective. For example 'baked' is the past participle of 'bake'.

the ˌpast ˈperfect (*also* **the pluperfect**) *noun* the form of a verb that is used to show that an action had already finished when another action happened. In English, the past perfect is made with 'had' and a past participle.

pastry /ˈpeɪstri/ *noun* **1** [U] a mixture of flour, fat, and water that is cooked, usually used to cover or contain other food **2** [C] a small cake that is made with pastry

pasture /ˈpɑːstʃəʳ/ *noun* [C] an area of land with grass where animals can feed

pat¹ /pæt/ *verb* [T] **patting**, *past* **patted** to touch a person or animal with a flat hand in a gentle, friendly way *She stopped to pat the dog.*

pat² /pæt/ *noun* **1** [C] when you pat a person or animal *He gave her an encouraging **pat on** the shoulder.* **2 a pat on the back** praise for something good that someone has done

patch¹ /pætʃ/ *noun* [C] **1** [AREA] a small area that is different from the area around it *a **bald patch*** ○ *There are **icy patches** on the road.* **2** [MATERIAL] a piece of material that you use to cover a hole in your clothes or in other material *He had leather patches sewn on the elbows of his jacket.* **3** [EYE] a small piece of material used to cover an injured eye **4** [LAND] a small area of land used for a particular purpose *a cabbage/vegetable patch* **5 a bad/rough, etc patch** a difficult time *I think their marriage is going through a bad patch.* **6 not be a patch on sb/sth** *UK informal* to not be as good as someone or something else

patch² /pætʃ/ *verb* [T] to repair a hole in a piece of clothing or other material by sewing a piece of material over it *to patch your trousers*

patch sth up to try to improve your relationship with someone after you have had an argument *Has he managed to patch things up with her?*

patchwork /ˈpætʃwɜːk/ *noun* **1** [U] a type of sewing in which a lot of small pieces of different material are sewn together *a **patchwork quilt*** **2 a patchwork of sth** something that seems to be made of many different pieces *We flew over a patchwork of fields.*

patchy /ˈpætʃi/ *adjective* **1** not complete or not good in every way *a **patchy knowledge** of Spanish* **2** existing only in some areas ***patchy clouds/fog***

pâté /ˈpæteɪ/ [US] /pætˈeɪ/ *noun* [U] a soft food, usually made of meat or fish, that you spread on bread, etc *liver pâté*

patent¹ /ˈpeɪtᵊnt, ˈpætᵊnt/ *noun* [C] a legal right that a person or company receives to make or sell a particular product so that others cannot copy it • **patent** *verb* [T] to get a patent for something

patent² /ˈpeɪtᵊnt, ˈpætᵊnt/ *adjective formal* **patent lie/nonsense** something that is obviously false *The explanation he gave - that was patent nonsense.* • **patently** *adverb formal Her claims are patently* (= obviously) *false.*

paternal /pəˈtɜːnᵊl/ *adjective* **1** like a father *paternal affection* **2** [always before noun] A paternal relative is part of your father's family. *He was my paternal grandfather.*

paternity /pəˈtɜːnəti/ *noun* [U] the state of being a father

paˈternity ˌleave *noun* [U] a period of weeks or months that a father spends away from his usual job so that he can look after his baby or child

path /pɑːθ/ *noun* [C] **1** [GROUND] a long, narrow area of ground for people to walk along *There's a path through the forest.* ○ *a **garden path*** **2** [DIRECTION] the direction that a person or vehicle moves in *a **flight path*** **3** [CHOOSING] a particular way of doing something over a period of time *a **career path*** ○ *Whichever path we choose, we'll have difficulties.*

pathetic /pəˈθetɪk/ *adjective* **1** *informal* showing no skill, effort, or bravery *He made a rather **pathetic attempt** to apologize.* ○ *You're too frightened to speak to her? Come on, that's pathetic!* ○ *It was a pathetic performance.* **2** sad and weak *Four times the pathetic little creature fell to the ground.* • **pathetically** *adverb a pathetically small amount of money*

pathological /ˌpæθəˈlɒdʒɪkᵊl/ *adjective* **1** Pathological behaviour or feelings are extreme and cannot be controlled. *a **pathological liar*** ○ ***pathological hatred*** **2** relating to pathology (= the study of disease)

pathologist /pəˈθɒlədʒɪst/ *noun* [C] a doctor who has studied pathology, especially one who tries to find out why people have died

pathology /pəˈθɒlədʒi/ *noun* [U] the scientific study of disease and causes of death

pathos /ˈpeɪθɒs/ *noun* [U] *literary* a quality in a situation that makes you feel sympathy and sadness

WORD PARTNERS FOR ***patience***

have/run out of patience • **lose** (**your**) patience • **test/try** sb's patience • sth **takes** patience • patience **with** sb/sth

⊶**patience** /ˈpeɪʃᵊns/ *noun* [U] **1** the quality of being able to stay calm and not get angry, especially when something takes a long time *Finally, I **lost** my **patience** and shouted at her.* ○ *Making small scale models **takes** a lot of **patience**.* ⊃Opposite **impatience**. **2** *UK* (*US* **solitaire**) a card game for one person

⊶**patient¹** /ˈpeɪʃᵊnt/ *adjective* having patience *You need to be **patient with** children.* • **patiently** *adverb* ⊃Opposite **impatient**.

⊶**patient²** /ˈpeɪʃᵊnt/ *noun* [C] someone who is being treated by a doctor, nurse, etc *a cancer patient*

patio /ˈpætiəʊ/ *noun* [C] an outside area with a stone floor next to a house, where people can sit to eat and relax

patriot /ˈpeɪtriət/ *noun* [C] someone who loves their country and is proud of it

patriotic /ˌpeɪtriˈɒtɪk/ *adjective* showing love for your country and pride in it *patriotic duty* ○ *a patriotic song* • **patriotism** /ˈpeɪtriətɪzm/ *noun*

[U] when you love your country and are proud of it

patrol¹ /pə'trəʊl/ *noun* **1** [C, U] the act of looking for trouble or danger around an area or building *We passed a group of soldiers **on patrol**.* ○ *a patrol boat/car* **2** [C] a group of soldiers or vehicles that patrol an area or building *a border patrol* ○ *an armed patrol*

patrol² /pə'trəʊl/ *verb* [I, T] **patrolling**, *past* **patrolled** to look for trouble or danger in an area or around a building *Police patrol the streets night and day.*

patron /'peɪtrˀn/ *noun* [C] **1** someone who supports and gives money to artists, writers, musicians, etc *a generous patron* ○ *a patron of the arts* **2** a customer at a bar, restaurant, or hotel

patronize (*also UK* **-ise**) /'pætrˀnaɪz/ *verb* [T] **1** to speak or behave towards someone as if you were better than them *Don't patronize me! I know what I'm doing.* **2** *formal* to go to a store, business, etc, especially if you go regularly

patron 'saint *noun* [C] a saint (= a special, famous Christian) who is believed to help a particular place, person, or activity *St. Christopher is the patron saint of travellers.*

🧩 **WORD PARTNERS FOR pattern**

alter/establish/fall into/follow a pattern
• a **consistent/familiar/traditional** pattern

⚬ **pattern** /'pætˀn/ *noun* [C] **1** WAY a particular way that something is often done or repeated *behaviour patterns* **2** DESIGN a design of lines, shapes, colours, etc **3** SHAPE a drawing or shape that helps you to make something *a dress pattern*

⚬ **pause** /pɔːz/ *verb* [I] to stop doing something for a short time *She **paused for** a moment and looked around her.* • **pause** *noun* [C] *There was a short pause before he spoke.*

pave /peɪv/ *verb* [T] to cover a path or road with flat stones, bricks, concrete, etc

pavement
/'peɪvmənt/ *noun* [C]
1 *UK* (*US* **sidewalk**) a path by the side of a road that people walk on *It's illegal to park on the pavement.* **2** *US* the hard surface of a road

pavilion /pə'vɪljən/ *noun* [C] **1** TENT a large tent that is used for outside events **2** SPORTS *UK* a building next to a sports field where players can change their clothes **3** BUILDING *US* one of a group of related buildings, such as a hospital

paw /pɔː/ *noun* [C] the foot of certain animals, such as cats and dogs • **paw** (*also* **paw at**) *verb* [T] to touch something with a paw *I could hear the dog pawing at the door.*

pawn¹ /pɔːn/ *noun* [C] **1** in the game of chess, the smallest piece and the one that has the lowest value **2** someone who does not have

power and is used by other people

pawn² /pɔːn/ *verb* [T] to leave something with a pawnbroker, who gives you money for it and will sell it if you do not pay the money back *She pawned her wedding ring to pay the rent.*

pawnbroker /'pɔːnˌbrəʊkəʳ/ *noun* [C] someone who lends you money in exchange for items that they will sell if you cannot pay the money back

⚬ **pay¹** /peɪ/ *verb* *past* **paid** **1** BUY [I, T] to give money to someone because you are buying something from them, or because you owe them money *Helen **paid for** the tickets.* ○ *Did you **pay** the telephone bill?* ○ *You can pay by cash or credit card.* **2** WORK [I, T] to give someone money for the work that they do *She gets paid twice a month.* ○ *People work for them because they pay well.* ○ *[+ two objects] We **paid** them £600 for the work.* ○ *a paid job* **3** ADVANTAGE [I] to be a good thing to do because it gives you money or an advantage *Crime doesn't pay.* **4** SUFFER [I, T] to suffer because of something bad you have done *He's certainly **paying for** his mistakes.* **5** **pay attention** to look at or listen to someone or something carefully *I missed what she was saying because I wasn't paying attention.* **6** **pay sb a compliment** to tell someone that you admire something about them **7** **pay tribute to sb/sth** to thank someone or say that you admire someone or something, especially in public *He paid tribute to his former teacher.* **8** **pay sb/sth a visit; pay a visit to sb/sth** to visit a place or a person, usually for a short time

---

COMMON LEARNER ERROR

pay for something

Remember that when **pay** means give money to buy something, it is usually followed by the preposition **for**.
Rachel paid for the meal.
~~Rachel paid the meal.~~

---

pay sb/sth back to pay someone the money that you owe them *Only borrow money if you're sure you can pay it back.* ○ *I lent him £10 last month and he still hasn't paid me back.*
pay sth off to pay all of the money that you owe *I'm planning to pay off my bank loan in five years.*
pay (sth) out to spend a lot of money on something, or to pay a lot of money to someone *I've just paid out £700 to get the car fixed.*
pay up *informal* to give someone all of the money that you owe them, especially when you do not want to *Come on, pay up!*

🧩 **WORD PARTNERS FOR pay**

a pay (UK) **cheque/cut/**(US) **raise/**(UK) **rise**
• **rates of** pay

---

pay² /peɪ/ *noun* [U] the money you receive from your employer for doing your job (*UK*) *a **pay** rise/* (*US*) *a **pay** raise* ○ *good **rates of** pay*

pay, wage, salary, or **income?**

Pay is a general word which means the money that you receive for working.
Doctors usually get more pay than teachers.

A **wage** is an amount of money you receive each day or week. It is often paid in cash (= notes and coins).
His weekly wage is $400.

A **salary** is the money you receive each month. A person's **salary** is often expressed as the total amount in a year.
His salary is £20,000.

Your **income** is the total amount of money that you earn by working or investing money.
She has a monthly income of £1,300.

payable /'peɪəbl/ *adjective* **1** describes something to be paid *Rent is payable monthly.* **2** If a cheque (= a piece of paper printed by a bank that you use to pay for things) is payable to a person, that person's name is written on the cheque and the money will be paid to them.

pay-as-you-go /,peɪəzjə'gəʊ/ *adjective* [always before noun] describes a system in which you pay for a service before you use it *a pay-as-you go mobile phone* • **pay-as-you-go** *noun* [U]

'**pay ,channel** *noun* [C] a television channel (= a broadcasting company) that you pay money to watch *Most of the best football matches are on the pay channels.*

'**pay ,check** *noun* [C] *US* pay cheque

'**pay ,cheque** *noun* [C] the amount of money a person earns

payday /'peɪdeɪ/ *noun* [C] the day on which a worker is paid

make/receive payment • a form/method of payment • payment for/of sth

⊶**payment** /'peɪmənt/ *noun* **1** [U] the act of paying *They will accept payment by credit card.* **2** [C] the amount of money that is paid *monthly payments* ⊃See also: **balance of payments, down payment.**

pay-per-view /,peɪpə'vjuː/ *noun* [U] a system in which you choose particular television programmes and then pay to watch them *pay-per-view television/channels*

'**pay ,phone** *noun* [C] a telephone in a public place that you pay to use

PC¹ /,piː'siː/ *noun* [C] **1** a personal computer **2** *UK abbreviation for* police constable (= a police officer of the lowest rank)

PC² /,piː'siː/ *adjective abbreviation for* politically correct (= careful to speak or behave in a way which is not offensive to women, people of a particular race, or people who have physical or mental problems)

PDA /,piːdiː'eɪ/ *noun* [C] *abbreviation for* personal digital assistant: a small computer that you can carry with you

PDF /,piːdiː'ef/ *abbreviation for* **1** [U] portable document format: a system for storing and moving documents between computers that

only allows them to be looked at or printed **2** [C] a document using the PDF system

PE /,piː'iː/ *noun* [U] *abbreviation for* physical education: classes at school where children do exercise and play sport

pea /piː/ *noun* [C] a small, round, green seed that people eat as a vegetable

bring about / establish / restore peace • **keep** the peace • the peace **process** • a peace **agreement/initiative/treaty**

⊶**peace** /piːs/ *noun* [U] **1** when there is no war, violence, or arguing *peace talks* ○ *a peace agreement/treaty* ○ *There seems little hope for world peace.* ○ *The UN sent troops to the region to keep the peace.* **2** when there is quiet and calm *a feeling of peace* ○ *After a busy day, all I want is peace and quiet.* ○ *I wish you'd stop complaining and leave me in peace!* **3** peace of mind a feeling that you do not need to worry about anything *We lock our doors and windows at night for peace of mind.* ⊃See also: Justice of the Peace.

⊶**peaceful** /'piːsfºl/ *adjective* **1** without violence *a peaceful protest* **2** quiet and calm *The churchyard was empty and peaceful.* • **peacefully** *adverb He died peacefully at home.*

peacekeeping /'piːsˌkiːpɪŋ/ *adjective* [always before noun] relating to the activity of preventing war and violence *peacekeeping forces/troops* ○ *a peacekeeping effort/operation* • **peacekeeper** /'piːsˌkiːpər/ *noun* [C] someone, usually a soldier, who tries to prevent war and violence in countries where there is trouble *UN peacekeepers*

peacetime /'piːstaɪm/ *noun* [U] a time when a country is not at war

peach /piːtʃ/ *noun* [C] a soft, sweet, round fruit with red and yellow skin

peacock /'piːkɒk/ *noun* [C] a large, male bird with long tail feathers that it can lift up to show a lot of colours

peak

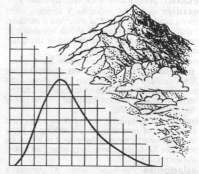

peak¹ /piːk/ *noun* [C] **1** the highest level or value of something *Here we see an athlete at the peak of fitness.* ○ *The price of gold reached its peak during the last recession.* ○ *peak travel* *times* **2** the top of a mountain, or the mountain itself *snow-covered/mountain peaks*

peak² /piːk/ *verb* [I] to reach the highest level or value of something *Her singing career peaked in the 1990s.*

peanut /ˈpiːnʌt/ *noun* [C] an oval-shaped nut with a soft, brown shell *salted peanuts* ○ *peanut oil* ⊃See colour picture **Food** on page Centre 11.

peanut 'butter *UK* (*US* **'peanut ˌbutter**) *noun* [U] a pale brown food made by crushing peanuts *a peanut butter and jelly sandwich*

pear /peəʳ/ *noun* [C] an oval-shaped, pale green or yellow fruit ⊃See colour picture **Fruit and Vegetables** on page Centre 10.

pear

pearl /pɜːl/ *noun* [C] a hard, white, round object that is made inside the shell of an oyster (= a sea creature) and that is used to make jewellery *a string of pearls* ○ *a pearl necklace* ○ *pearl earrings*

pear-shaped /ˈpeəʃeɪpt/ *adjective* **go pear-shaped** *UK informal* If a plan goes pear-shaped, it fails.

peasant /ˈpezᵊnt/ *noun* [C] a poor person who works on the land, usually in a poor country *a peasant farmer*

peat /piːt/ *noun* [U] a dark brown soil made from decaying plants that you can burn as fuel or that you can put around living plants to help them grow

pebble /ˈpebl/ *noun* [C] a small stone

pecan /ˈpiːkæn/ ⑬ /pɪˈkɑːn/ *noun* [C] a nut that grows on a tree, or the tree itself *chopped pecans* ○ *pecan pie*

peck¹ /pek/ (*also* **peck at**) *verb* [T] If a bird pecks something, it lifts or hits it with its beak. *chickens pecking at corn*

peck² /pek/ *noun* [C] **1 give sb a peck on the cheek** to give someone a quick, gentle kiss on the face **2** when a bird pecks something

peckish /ˈpekɪʃ/ *adjective UK* slightly hungry

peculiar /pɪˈkjuːliəʳ/ *adjective* **1** strange, often in an unpleasant way *The wine had a peculiar, musty smell.* **2 peculiar to sb/sth** belonging to or relating to a particular person or thing *Her accent is peculiar to the region.*

peculiarity /pɪˌkjuːliˈærəti/ *noun* [C] **1** something that is typical of a person, place, or thing *Each college has its own traditions and peculiarities.* **2** a strange or unusual characteristic *My mother always hummed - it was one of her little peculiarities.*

peculiarly /pɪˈkjuːliəli/ *adverb* **1** in a way that is typical of someone or something *a peculiarly American sense of humour* **2** in a strange way *The birds were peculiarly quiet just before the earthquake.*

pedagogue /ˈpedəgɒg/ *noun* [C] *formal* a teacher, usually a very strict one

pedal /ˈpedᵊl/ *noun* [C] a part of a machine that you press with your foot to operate or move the machine *bicycle pedals* ○ *a gas/brake pedal*

pedant /ˈpedᵊnt/ *noun* [C] someone who thinks too much about details and rules ● **pedantic** /pɪˈdæntɪk/ *adjective* thinking too much about details and rules *I hate to be pedantic, but Freud was actually Austrian, not German.*

peddle /ˈpedl/ *verb* [T] to sell things, especially drugs or things of bad quality *The shops on the pier peddled cheap souvenirs to the tourists.* ○ *He was arrested for peddling drugs.*

pedestal /ˈpedɪstᵊl/ *noun* [C] **1** the base for a statue (= model of a person or animal) **2 put sb on a pedestal** to believe that someone is perfect

pedestrian¹ /pɪˈdestriən/ *noun* [C] a person who is walking and not travelling in a vehicle *Many streets are reserved for cyclists and pedestrians.* ○ *a pedestrian precinct/crossing*

pedestrian² /pɪˈdestriən/ *adjective formal* ordinary or not interesting *pedestrian ideas* ○ *a pedestrian speech*

peˌdestrian 'crossing *UK* (*US* **crosswalk**) *noun* [C] a special place on a road where traffic must stop if people want to cross

pediatrician /ˌpiːdiəˈtrɪʃᵊn/ *noun* [C] *US spelling of* paediatrician

pedicure /ˈpedɪkjʊəʳ/ *noun* [C, U] when someone makes your feet look attractive by cleaning and cutting your nails ⊃Compare **manicure**.

pedigree¹ /ˈpedɪgriː/ *noun* [C] **1** a list of the parents and other relatives of an animal **2** someone's family history, or their education and experience

pedigree² /ˈpedɪgriː/ *adjective* [always before noun] A pedigree animal has parents and other relatives all from the same breed and is thought to be of high quality. *a pedigree dog*

pedophile /ˈpiːdəʊfaɪl/ *noun* [C] *US spelling of* paedophile

pee /piː/ *verb* [I] peeing, *past* peed *informal* to urinate ● **pee** *noun* [no plural] *informal Do I have time for a pee before we go?*

peek¹ /piːk/ *verb* [I] to look at something for a short time, often when you do not want other people to see you *I peeked out the window to see who was there.*

peek² /piːk/ *noun* **have/take a peek** to look at something for a short time

peel¹ /piːl/ *verb* **1** [T] to remove the skin of fruit or vegetables *Peel and chop the onions.* **2** [I, T] If you peel something from a surface, you remove it and if something peels, it comes away from a surface. *The paint is starting to peel off where the wall is damp.* ⊃See also: keep your eyes (**eye¹**) open/peeled (for sb/sth)

peel sth off to take off clothes, especially wet or tight clothes *We peeled off our muddy socks and left them outside.*

peel² /piːl/ *noun* [U] the skin of fruit or vegetables, especially after it has been removed *Combine nuts, sugar, and orange peel in a small bowl.*

peep /piːp/ *verb* [I] **1 peep at/ through/out, etc** to look at something for a short time, often when you do not want other people to see you *She peeped at them through the fence.* **2 peep through/over/out from, etc** to appear but not be seen completely *The sun peeped out from* *behind the clouds.* • **peep** *noun* **[no plural]** *She* ***took a peep*** *at herself in the mirror.*

peer¹ /pɪəʳ/ *noun* **[C] 1** someone who is the same age, or who has the same social position or abilities as other members of a group *Most teenagers want to be accepted by their peers.* **2** in the UK, a person who has a title and a high social position

peer² /pɪəʳ/ *verb* **peer at/into/through, etc** to look carefully or with difficulty *She peered at me over her glasses.*

ˈpeer ˌgroup *noun* **[C]** a group of people of about the same age, social position, etc *He was the first of his peer group to get married.*

ˈpeer ˌpressure *noun* **[U]** strong influence on a member of a group to behave in the same way as other members in the group, although that behaviour is not good *Many teenagers take drugs because of boredom or peer pressure.*

peg¹ /peg/ *noun* **[C] 1** [ON WALL] an object on a wall or door that you hang things on **2** [ON ROPE] (*also* **clothes peg**) *UK* a short piece of wood, plastic, etc that is used to hold clothes on a rope while they dry **3** [STICK] a stick made of metal or wood that has a sharp end and which is used to fix something somewhere *a tent peg*

peg² /peg/ *verb* **[T] pegging,** *past* **pegged** to fix the cost of borrowing money or the value of a country's money at a particular level **[often passive]** *Interest rates were* ***pegged at*** *8.2 %.*

pellet /ˈpelɪt/ *noun* **[C]** a small, hard ball of metal, grain, etc *shotgun/feed pellets*

pelvic /ˈpelvɪk/ *adjective* **[always before noun]** relating to the area below your waist and above your legs

pelvis /ˈpelvɪs/ *noun* **[C]** the group of bones that forms the area below your waist and above your legs and to which your leg bones are joined

⊶**pen¹** /pen/ *noun* **[C] 1** a long, thin object that you use to write or draw in ink ➲See colour picture **The Classroom** on page Centre 6. **2** a small area with a fence around it that you keep animals in *a pig/sheep pen* ➲See also: **ballpoint pen, felt-tip pen, fountain pen.**

pen² /pen/ *verb* **[T] penning,** *past* **penned** *literary* to write something *sonnets penned by Shakespeare*

pen sb/sth in/up to keep people or animals in a small area **[often passive]** *The soldiers were penned up in their barracks.*

penal /ˈpiːnᵊl/ *adjective* **[always before noun]** relating to the punishment of criminals *a* ***penal code/system***

penalize (*also UK* **-ise**) /ˈpiːnᵊlaɪz/ *verb* **[T] 1** to cause someone a disadvantage *The present tax system penalizes poor people.* **2** to punish someone for breaking a law or a rule *He was penalized early in the match for dangerous play.*

WORD PARTNERS FOR *penalty*

face a penalty • a **heavy/severe/stiff** penalty • a penalty **for** (doing) sth

penalty /ˈpenᵊlti/ *noun* **[C] 1** a punishment for doing something which is against a law or rule *There's a £50* ***penalty for*** *late cancellation of tickets.* **2** in sports, an advantage given to a team when the opposing team has broken a rule *They won a penalty in the first five minutes of the game.* ○ *a* ***penalty goal/kick*** ➲See also: **death penalty.**

penance /ˈpenəns/ *noun* **[C, U]** an act that shows you are sorry for something that you have done

pence /pens/ *noun* plural of British penny; p

COMMON LEARNER ERROR

pence, pennies, or p?

Pence is the usual plural of penny (UK) and is used to talk about amounts of money. In informal UK English you can also say **p**.

Can you lend me 50 pence?
Can you lend me 50p?

The plural form **pennies** is only used to talk about the coins as objects.

He found some pennies in his pocket.

penchant /ˈpɒnʃɒn/ [US] /ˈpentʃənt/ *noun* **have a penchant for sth** *formal* to like something very much *Miguel has a penchant for fast cars.*

⊶**pencil** /ˈpensᵊl/ *noun* **[C, U]** a long, thin wooden object with a black or coloured point that you write or draw with ➲See colour picture **The Classroom** on page Centre 6.

ˈpencil ˌsharpener *noun* **[C]** a tool that you use to make pencils sharp ➲See colour picture **The Classroom** on page Centre 6.

pendant /ˈpendənt/ *noun* **[C]** a piece of jewellery on a chain that you wear around your neck

pending¹ /ˈpendɪŋ/ *preposition formal* used to say that one thing must wait until another thing happens *Several employees have been suspended pending an investigation.*

pending² /ˈpendɪŋ/ *adjective formal* not decided or finished *Their court case is still pending.*

pendulum /ˈpendjᵊləm/ *noun* **[C]** a heavy object on a chain or stick that moves from side to side, especially inside a large clock

penetrate /ˈpenɪtreɪt/ *verb* **1 [I, T]** If something penetrates an object, it moves into that object. *The bullet penetrated his skull.* **2 [T]** If someone penetrates a place or a group, they succeed in moving into or joining it. *No one in our industry has successfully penetrated the Asian market.* • **penetration** /ˌpenɪˈtreɪʃᵊn/ *noun* **[U]**

penetrating /ˈpenɪtreɪtɪŋ/ *adjective* **1** intelligent and full of careful thought *a penetrating discussion/mind* ○ *She wrote a penetrating analysis of Shakespeare's Hamlet.* **2 a penetrating gaze/look/stare, etc** If someone gives you a penetrating look, you feel as if they know what you are thinking. **3** If a sound is penetrating, it is very strong and unpleasant. *a penetrating voice/scream*

penguin /ˈpeŋgwɪn/ *noun* **[C]** a large, black and white sea bird that swims and cannot fly

penicillin /ˌpenɪˈsɪlɪn/ *noun* **[U]** a type of medicine that kills bacteria and is used to treat illness

P

peninsula /pə'nɪnsjələ/
noun [C] a long, thin piece
of land which has water
around most of it *the
Korean peninsula*

peninsula

penis /'pi:nɪs/ *noun* [C] the
part of a man's or male
animal's body that is
used for urinating and
having sex

penitentiary
/ˌpenɪ'tenʃⁿri/ *noun* [C] a
prison in the US

pennant /'penənt/ *noun*
[C] a long, pointed flag

penniless /'penɪləs/ *adjective* having no money

penny /'peni/ *noun* [C] *plural* **pence** or **p** or **pennies**
1 a coin or unit of money with a value of 1/100 of
a pound (= UK unit of money); **p** *There are 100
pence in a pound.* ○ *fifty pence/50p* ⊃See Common
learner error at **pence**. **2** a coin with a value of one
cent (= 1/100 of a dollar) *My dad always let us
have his pennies to buy candy.* **3 every penny** all
of an amount of money *He seemed intent on
spending every penny of his salary.*

WORD PARTNERS FOR ***pension***

get/be on/receive a pension   •   a pension
fund/plan/scheme   •   a **state/private** pension
---

pension¹ /'penʃⁿn/ *noun* [C] money that is paid
regularly by the government or a private company to a person who has stopped working because they are old or ill *a state/private pension* ○ *a pension plan/scheme* • **pensioner** *noun*
[C] *mainly UK* someone who receives a pension
⊃See also: **old-age pension, old-age pensioner.**

pension² /'penʃⁿn/ *verb*
pension sb off *mainly UK* If an organization pensions someone off, it forces that
person to leave their job but pays them a pension.

the Pentagon /'pentəgɒn/ *noun* the department of the US government that controls the
army, navy, etc, or the building where it is
*The Pentagon refused to comment on potential
military targets.*

penthouse /'penthaʊs/ *noun* [C] *plural* **pent-
houses** /'penthaʊzɪz/ an expensive apartment at
the top of a building

pent-up /ˌpent'ʌp/ *adjective* [always before noun]
Pent-up feelings are feelings that you have not
expressed for a long time. *pent-up anger*

penultimate /pə'nʌltɪmət/ *adjective* [always
before noun] *formal* next to the last *Y is the penultimate letter of the alphabet.*

o-**people¹** /'pi:pl/ *noun* **1** [plural] more than one
person *Our company employs over 400 people.*
○ *People live much longer than they used to.*
2 the people all the ordinary people in a country *The rebels have gained the support of the
people.* **3** [C] *formal* all the people of a race
Europe is made up of many different peoples.

people² /'pi:pl/ *verb*
be peopled by/with sb *literary* to be
filled with a particular kind of person *His
novels are peopled with angry young men.*

'people ˌcarrier *UK* (*US* **minivan**) *noun* [C] a
large, high car which can carry more people
than a normal car

pepper¹ /'pepər/ *noun* **1** [U] a black, grey, or red
powder that is made from crushed seeds, used
to give food a slightly spicy flavour *salt and
pepper* **2** [C] a hollow green, red, or yellow
vegetable *green/red pepper* ⊃See colour picture
Fruit and Vegetables on page Centre 10.

pepper² /'pepər/ *verb*
pepper sth with sth to include a lot of
something [often passive] *His speech was
peppered with quotations.*

peppermint /'pepəmɪnt/ *noun* **1** [U] oil from a
plant that is added to food to give it a strong,
fresh taste, or the taste itself *peppermint tea*
2 [C] a small, hard sweet that tastes like
peppermint

per *strong form* /pɜːr/ *weak form* /pər/ *preposition*
for each *Our hotel room costs $60 per night.*
○ *The speed limit is 100 kilometres per hour.*
○ *The wedding dinner will cost £30 per head* (=
for each person).

per annum /pɜːr'ænʌm/ *adverb formal* every
year *a salary of $19,000 per annum*

per capita /pɜː'kæpɪtə/ *adjective, adverb formal*
for each person *This county has the lowest per
capita income in the country.* ○ *Belgians eat
more chocolate per capita than any other nation
in Europe.*

perceive /pə'siːv/ *verb* [T] *formal* **1** to think of
something or someone in a particular way
[often passive] *The British are often perceived as
being very formal.* **2** to notice something that
is not easy to notice *We perceived a faint light
in the distance.*

o-**percent** (*also* **per cent**) /pə'sent/ *adjective, adverb*
for or out of every 100, shown by the symbol %
a 40 percent increase in prices • **percent** (*also* **per
cent**) *noun* [C] *Nearly 70 percent of all cars in the
UK are less than five years old.*

WORD PARTNERS FOR ***percentage***

a **high/large/small** percentage   •   the
percentage **of** sth
---

percentage /pə'sentɪdʒ/ *noun* [C] an amount of
something, often expressed as a number out of
100 *The percentage of women who work has
risen steadily.* ○ *The percentage of people who
are left-handed is small - only about 10%.*

perceptible /pə'septəbl/ *adjective formal* just
able to be noticed *a perceptible difference in
colour* ○ *His pulse was barely perceptible.*

perception /pə'sepʃⁿn/ *noun* **1** [C] what you
think or believe about someone or something
*The public perception of him as a hero is sur-
prising.* **2** [U] the ability to notice something
Alcohol reduces your perception of pain.

perceptive /pə'septɪv/ *adjective* quick to notice
or understand things *a perceptive writer*

perch¹ /pɜːtʃ/ *verb* **1 perch (sth) on/in/above, etc**
to be in a high position or in a position near
the edge of something, or to put something in
this position [often passive] *The village was
perched on the side of a mountain.* ○ *She wore*

glasses perched on the end of her nose. **2 perch on/in, etc** to sit near the edge of something *The children perched on the edges of their seats.*

perch² /pɜːtʃ/ *noun* [C] a place where a bird sits, especially a stick inside a cage

percussion /pəˈkʌʃən/ *noun* [U] musical instruments that make a sound when you hit them with a stick or your hand *Drums, tambourines, and cymbals are percussion instruments.*

perennial¹ /pəˈreniəl/ *adjective* happening again and again, or continuing for a long time *the perennial problem of unemployment*

perennial² /pəˈreniəl/ *noun* [C] a plant that lives for several years

---

OTHER WAYS OF SAYING *perfect*

If something is perfect because it has no mistakes or anything bad, then you can use adjectives such as **faultless**, **flawless**, **immaculate**, and **impeccable**: *They gave a faultless/immaculate performance.* • *His English is impeccable.* • *She has a flawless complexion.*

The adjectives **ideal** and **tailor-made** are sometimes used to describe something that is perfect for a particular purpose: *The book is ideal for children aged between four and six.* • *It sounds as if she's tailor-made for the job.*

In informal situations, if you want to describe something such as a job, house, etc, which is perfect for you, you can use the expression **dream job**, **dream home**, etc: *A pretty cottage in the Suffolk countryside - that would be my dream home.*

---

o→ **perfect¹** /ˈpɜːfɪkt/ *adjective* **1** [WITHOUT FAULT] without fault, or as good as possible *James is a perfect husband and father.* ○ *Her performance was perfect.* **2** [SUITABLE] exactly right for someone or something *You'd be perfect for the job.* ○ *The weather's just perfect for a picnic.* **3** [TO EMPHASIZE] [always before noun] used to emphasize a noun *His suggestion makes perfect sense.*

perfect² /pəˈfekt/ *verb* [T] to make something as good as it can be *I've spent hours perfecting my speech.*

the perfect /ˈpɜːfɪkt/ (*also* the ˌperfect ˈtense) *noun* the form of the verb that is used to show an action that has happened in the past or before another time or event. In English, the perfect is made with 'have' and a past participle. ●See also: **the future perfect**, **the past perfect**, **the present perfect**.

perfection /pəˈfekʃən/ *noun* [U] when someone or something is perfect *She strives for perfection in everything she does.* ○ *chicken legs cooked to perfection*

perfectionist /pəˈfekʃənɪst/ *noun* [C] someone who wants everything to be perfect

o→ **perfectly** /ˈpɜːfɪktli/ *adverb* **1** used to emphasize the word that follows it *To be perfectly honest, I don't care any more.* ○ *I made it perfectly clear to him what I meant.* **2** in a perfect way *The jacket fits perfectly, the skirt not so well.*

perforated /ˈpɜːfəreɪtɪd/ *adjective* **1** Perforated

materials such as paper have small holes in them so that they can be torn or liquid can pass through them. **2** If an organ of your body is perforated, it has a hole in it. *a perforated eardrum* ● **perforate** *verb* [T]

o→ **perform** /pəˈfɔːm/ *verb* **1** [I, T] to entertain people by acting, singing, dancing, etc *She has performed all over the world.* ○ *The orchestra will perform music by Mozart.* **2** [T] *formal* to do a job or a piece of work *In the future, many tasks will be performed by robots.* ○ *Surgeons performed the operation in less than two hours.* **3 perform well/badly, etc** If something performs well, badly, etc, it works that way. *These cars perform poorly at high speeds.*

WORD PARTNERS FOR *performance*

give/put on a performance • a **brilliant/ virtuoso/wonderful** performance

---

o→ **performance** /pəˈfɔːməns/ *noun* **1** [C] acting, singing, or playing music to entertain people *a performance of Shakespeare's Hamlet* **2** [U] how successful someone or something is *The company's performance was poor for the first two years.* ○ *Some athletes take drugs to improve their performance.*

performer /pəˈfɔːməʳ/ *noun* [C] someone who entertains people

the perˌforming ˈarts *noun* [plural] types of entertainment that are performed in front of people, such as dancing, singing, and acting

perfume /ˈpɜːfjuːm/ *noun* [C, U] a liquid with a pleasant smell that women put on their skin ● **perfumed** *adjective* containing perfume

o→ **perhaps** /pəˈhæps/ *adverb* **1** possibly *Perhaps I'll go to the gym after work.* ○ *Ben won't be coming but perhaps it's better that way.* **2** used when you want to suggest or ask someone something *Perhaps you should leave now.*

peril /ˈperəl/ *noun* [C, U] *formal* extreme danger *A shortage of firefighters is putting lives in peril.* ○ *His book describes the perils of war.*

perilous /ˈperələs/ *adjective formal* very dangerous *a perilous journey* ● **perilously** *adverb*

perimeter /pəˈrɪmɪtəʳ/ *noun* [C] the outer edge of an area *the perimeter of the airport*

o→ **period** /ˈpɪəriəd/ *noun* [C] **1** [TIME] a length of time *a 24-hour period* ○ *a period of four months* **2** [SCHOOL/SPORTS] one of the equal parts of time that a school day or sports game is divided into **3** [WOMEN] when blood comes out of a woman's uterus each month **4** [MARK] *US* (*UK* full stop) a mark (.) used at the end of a sentence, or to show that the letters before it are an abbreviation ●See Extra help page **Punctuation** on page Centre 33.

periodic /ˌpɪəriˈɒdɪk/ *adjective* happening regularly *Our sales team makes periodic trips to Asia.* ● **periodically** *adverb*

periodical /ˌpɪəriˈɒdɪkəl/ *noun* [C] a magazine about a particular subject

peripheral /pəˈrɪfərəl/ *adjective* not as important as someone or something else

periphery /pəˈrɪfəri/ *noun* [C] the outer edge of an area *The soldiers were camped on the periphery of the village.*

P

---

perish /'perɪʃ/ verb [I] literary to die Hundreds of people perished in the flood.

perishable /'perɪʃəbl/ adjective Food that is perishable goes bad very quickly.

perjury /'pɜːdʒ³ri/ noun [U] the crime of telling a lie in a court of law The witness was accused of **committing perjury**.

perk¹ /pɜːk/ noun [C] an advantage, such as money or a car, that you are given because of your job [usually plural] A mobile phone is one of the perks of the job.

perk² /pɜːk/ verb
perk (sb) up to start to feel happier, or to make someone feel happier A cup of coffee always perks me up in the morning.

perm /pɜːm/ noun [C] the use of chemicals on someone's hair to make it have curls for several months, or the hair style that is made in this way I'm thinking of **having a perm**. • perm verb [T]

permanence /'pɜːm³nəns/ noun [U] when something continues forever or for a long time

☞**permanent** /'pɜːm³nənt/ adjective continuing forever or for a long time permanent damage ○ a permanent job • permanently adverb He moved here permanently in 1992.

permeate /'pɜːmieɪt/ verb [T] formal to move gradually into every part of something The pungent smell of vinegar permeated the air. ○ Drug dealers have permeated every level of society.

permissible /pə'mɪsəbl/ adjective formal allowed by the rules [+ to do sth] It is not permissible to smoke inside the building.

WORD PARTNERS FOR **permission**

ask for/request/seek permission • give/grant permission • obtain/receive permission

☞**permission** /pə'mɪʃ³n/ noun [U] when you allow someone to do something She **gave** him **permission** without asking any questions. ○ [+ to do sth] He has permission to stay in the country for one more year. ○ They even have to **ask for permission** before they go to the toilet. ○ He took the car **without permission**.

permissive /pə'mɪsɪv/ adjective allowing people to behave in ways which other people may not approve of permissive attitudes

permit¹ /pə'mɪt/ verb permitting, past permitted **1** [T] formal to allow something [often passive] Photography is not permitted inside the museum. ○ [+ to do sth] He permitted them to leave. **2** [I] to make something possible The match starts at 3 p.m., **weather permitting**.

permit² /'pɜːmɪt/ noun [C] an official document that allows you to do something a **work permit** ○ You need a permit to park your car here.

pernicious /pə'nɪʃəs/ adjective formal very harmful

perpendicular /ˌpɜːp³n'dɪkjʊlə³/ adjective at an angle of 90 degrees to something

perpetrate /'pɜːpɪtreɪt/ verb [T] formal to do something very bad [often passive] They heard of torture perpetrated by the army.

perpetrator /'pɜːpɪtreɪtə³/ noun [C] formal someone who has done something very bad There is great public pressure to bring the **perpetrators** of these crimes to justice.

perpetual /pə'petʃuəl/ adjective never ending He seems to be in a **perpetual state** of confusion. • perpetually adverb

perpetuate /pə'petʃueɪt/ verb [T] formal to make something continue, especially something bad People think of him as a cruel man, an image perpetuated by the media.

perplexed /pə'plekst/ adjective confused He seemed a little perplexed by the question. • perplex verb [T]

perplexing /pə'pleksɪŋ/ adjective confusing a perplexing problem

persecute /'pɜːsɪkjuːt/ verb [T] to treat someone unfairly or cruelly because of their race, religion, or beliefs [often passive] He was persecuted for his religious beliefs. • persecution /ˌpɜːsɪ'kjuːʃ³n/ noun [U] political/religious persecution

persecutor /'pɜːsɪkjuːtə³/ noun [C] someone who persecutes people

perseverance /ˌpɜːsɪ'vɪər³ns/ noun [U] when you persevere Hard work and perseverance do pay off in the end.

persevere /ˌpɜːsɪ'vɪə³/ verb [I] to continue to try to do something although it is difficult Despite the difficulties, I decided to **persevere with** the project.

persist /pə'sɪst/ verb [I] **1** If an unpleasant feeling or situation persists, it continues to exist. If symptoms persist, consult a doctor. **2** to continue to do something although it is annoying other people He **persists in** calling me Jane, even though I've corrected him twice.

persistence /pə'sɪst³ns/ noun [U] when someone or something persists

persistent /pə'sɪst³nt/ adjective **1** Something unpleasant that is persistent continues for a long time or is difficult to get rid of. a persistent cough **2** A persistent person continues to do something although other people do not want them to. He can be very persistent sometimes. • persistently adverb He has persistently lied to us.

☞**person** /'pɜːs³n/ noun plural people **1** [C] a human being You're the only person I know here. ○ He is a very dangerous person. **2 in person** If you do something in person, you go somewhere to do it yourself. If you can't be there in person the next best thing is watching it on TV. ⊅See also: the first person, the second person, the third person.

persona /pə'səʊnə/ noun [C] plural personae or personas the way your character seems to other people He's trying to improve his **public persona**.

☞**personal** /'pɜːs³n³l/ adjective **1** RELATING TO A PERSON [always before noun] relating to or belonging to a particular person I can only speak from my own **personal experience**. ○ Please ensure you take all **personal belongings** with you when you leave the train. ○ This is a personal view and not that of the government.

| ɑː arm | ɜː her | iː see | ɔː saw | uː too | aɪ my | aʊ how | eə hair | eɪ day | əʊ no | ɪə near | ɔɪ boy | ʊə poor | aɪə fire | aʊə sour |

2 PRIVATE relating to the private parts of someone's life, including their relationships and feelings *He's got a few **personal problems** at the moment.* ○ *She prefers to keep her personal and professional lives separate.* **3** FOR ONE PERSON [always before noun] designed for or used by one person *a personal computer/stereo* ○ *a personal loan/pension* **4** RUDE rude about or offensive towards someone *I know you're upset, but there's no need to **get personal** (= start making offensive remarks).* **5** BODY [always before noun] relating to your body *personal hygiene*

,**personal ,digital a'ssistant** *noun* [C] (*abbreviation* PDA) a small computer that you can carry with you

o⌐**personality** /ˌpɜːsən'æləti/ *noun* **1** CHARACTER [C] the way you are as a person *She's got a lovely, **bubbly** personality.* **2** FAMOUS [C] a famous person *a well-known TV personality* **3** INTERESTING [U] the quality of having a very strong or interesting character *Sales people need a lot of personality.*

personalized (*also UK* ised) /'pɜːsən'laɪzd/ *adjective* A personalized object has someone's name on it, or has been made for a particular person. *a personalized fitness plan* ● **personalize** *verb* [T]

personally /'pɜːsən'li/ *adverb* **1** done by you and not someone else *I'd like to personally apologize for the delay.* **2** used when you are going to give your opinion *Personally, I'd rather stay at home and watch TV.* **3** **take sth personally** to think that someone is criticizing you when they are not *You mustn't take everything so personally.*

,**personal 'organizer** *noun* [C] a small book or computer containing a calendar, address book, etc ⇒See PDA.

,**personal 'pronoun** *noun* [C] a word that is used to refer to a person in speech or in writing. For example the words 'I', 'you', and 'they' are personal pronouns.

,**personal 'trainer** *noun* [C] a person whose job is to help you improve the shape of your body by showing you what exercises to do

personify /pə'sɒnɪfaɪ/ *verb* [T] If someone personifies a particular quality, they are a perfect example of that quality. *She seems to personify honesty.* ● **personified** *adjective* [always after noun] *Tom was always laziness personified.* ● **personification** /pəˌsɒnɪfɪ'keɪʃən/ *noun* [U]

personnel /ˌpɜːsə'nel/ *noun* **1** [plural] the people who work for an organization *military personnel* **2** [U] the department of an organization that deals with finding people to work there, keeping records about them, etc *I need to speak to someone in Personnel.* ○ *the personnel manager*

perspective /pə'spektɪv/ *noun* **1** [C] the way you think about something *Being unemployed has made me see things **from a** different **perspective**.* **2** [U] when things are drawn so that they appear to be a realistic size and in a realistic position **3** **put sth in/into perspective** If something puts a problem into perspective, it makes you understand how unimportant that problem is.

perspicacious /ˌpɜːspɪ'keɪʃəs/ *adjective formal* quick in noticing, understanding, or judging things accurately

perspiration /ˌpɜːspəˈreɪʃən/ *noun* [U] *formal* the liquid that comes out of your skin when you get hot

perspire /pə'spaɪər/ *verb* [I] *formal* to produce liquid through your skin because you are hot or nervous

o⌐**persuade** /pə'sweɪd/ *verb* [T] to make someone agree to do something by talking to them a lot about it [+ to do sth] *We managed to persuade him to come with us.* ○ [+ (that)] *I persuaded her that it was the right thing to do.* ⊃Opposite dissuade.

persuasion /pə'sweɪʒən/ *noun* **1** [U] when you persuade someone *I'm sure she'll agree, she just needs a little gentle persuasion.* **2** [C] *formal* a political, religious, or moral belief *There were people of all persuasions there.*

persuasive /pə'sweɪsɪv/ *adjective* able to make people agree to do something *It's a very persuasive argument.* ● **persuasively** *adverb*

pertain /pə'teɪn/ *verb*
pertain to sth *formal* to relate to something *Some important evidence pertaining to the case has been overlooked.*

pertinent /'pɜːtɪnənt/ *adjective formal* relating directly to a subject *a pertinent question*

perturbed /pə'tɜːbd/ *adjective* worried or upset *He seemed slightly perturbed by the news.* ● **perturb** *verb* [T]

peruse /pə'ruːz/ *verb* [T] *formal* to look at or read something in order to find what interests you

pervade /pə'veɪd/ *verb* [T] *formal* to move gradually through every part of something *Cheap perfume and tobacco pervaded the room.*

pervasive /pə'veɪsɪv/ *adjective formal* moving into or through everywhere or everything *a pervasive smell* ○ *the **pervasive influence** of television*

perverse /pə'vɜːs/ *adjective* strange and not what most people would expect or enjoy *In a perverse way, I enjoy going to the dentist.* ● **perversely** *adverb*

perversion /pə'vɜːʃən/ *noun* [C, U] **1** getting sexual pleasure in a way that seems strange or unpleasant **2** when something that is right is changed into something that is wrong *the perversion of justice*

pervert¹ /'pɜːvɜːt/ *noun* [C] someone who gets sexual pleasure in a strange or unpleasant way

pervert² /pə'vɜːt/ *verb* [T] to change something that is right into something that is wrong *They were charged with conspiracy to **pervert**

P

the course of justice.

perverted /pəˈvɜːtɪd/ *adjective* relating to getting sexual pleasure in a strange or unpleasant way

pessimism /ˈpesɪmɪzəm/ *noun* [U] when you believe bad things will happen ⟐Opposite optimism.

pessimist /ˈpesɪmɪst/ *noun* [C] someone who always believes that bad things will happen *Don't be such a pessimist!*

pessimistic /ˌpesɪˈmɪstɪk/ *adjective* always believing that bad things will happen *He was feeling pessimistic about the future.* ⟐Opposite optimistic.

pest /pest/ *noun* [C] **1** an animal that causes damage to plants, food, etc *Most farmers think foxes are pests.* **2** *informal* an annoying person

pester /ˈpestəʳ/ *verb* [T] to annoy someone by asking them something again and again [+ **to do sth**] *He's been pestering me to go out with him all week.*

pesticide /ˈpestɪsaɪd/ *noun* [C, U] a chemical that is used to kill insects which damage plants

pet¹ /pet/ *noun* [C] an animal that someone keeps in their home *my pet rabbit*

pet² /pet/ *verb* [T] *petting, past* **petted 1** to touch an animal because you feel affection for them **2** to touch someone in a sexual way

petal /ˈpetəl/ *noun* [C] one of the thin, flat, coloured parts on the outside of a flower *rose petals*

peter /ˈpiːtəʳ/ *verb*
peter out to gradually stop or disappear *The track petered out after a mile or so.*

pet ˈhate *UK* (*US* ˌpet ˈpeeve) *noun* [C] something that annoys you a lot *That's one of my pet hates - people who smoke while other people are eating.*

petite /pəˈtiːt/ *adjective* A petite woman is small and thin in an attractive way.

petition¹ /pəˈtɪʃən/ *verb* [I, T] to officially ask someone in authority to do something [+ **to do sth**] *They are petitioning the government to increase funding for the project.*

░░ WORD PARTNERS FOR **petition**

launch/organize/sign a petition • a petition **against/(calling) for** sth

petition² /pəˈtɪʃən/ *noun* [C] a document that has been signed by a lot of people officially asking someone in authority to do something *Will you sign this petition against experiments on animals?*

petrified /ˈpetrɪfaɪd/ *adjective* extremely frightened *I'm petrified of spiders.*

◦⟳**petrol** /ˈpetrəl/ *UK* (*US* **gas**) *noun* [U] a liquid fuel used in cars *unleaded petrol*

petroleum /pəˈtrəʊliəm/ *noun* [U] thick oil found under the Earth's surface which is used to produce petrol and other substances

ˈpetrol ˌstation *UK* (*US* **gas station**) *noun* [C] a place where you can buy petrol

petticoat /ˈpetɪkəʊt/ *noun* [C] a thin piece of women's clothing worn under a dress or skirt

petty /ˈpeti/ *adjective* **1** [always before noun] unimportant or not serious *petty crime* **2** [never before noun] complaining too much about unimportant things *You can be so petty sometimes!*

petulant /ˈpetʃələnt/ *adjective* behaving in an angry, silly way like a child

pew /pjuː/ *noun* [C] a long seat in a church

pewter /ˈpjuːtəʳ/ *noun* [U] a blue-grey metal

phantom¹ /ˈfæntəm/ *noun* [C] the spirit of a dead person

phantom² /ˈfæntəm/ *adjective* [always before noun] imagined, not real *phantom pains*

pharaoh /ˈfeərəʊ/ *noun* [C] a king of ancient Egypt

pharmaceutical /ˌfɑːməˈsjuːtɪkəl/ *adjective* relating to the production of medicines *a pharmaceutical company* ○ *the pharmaceutical industry* • pharmaceuticals *noun* [plural] medicines

pharmacist /ˈfɑːməsɪst/ *noun* [C] someone who is trained to prepare or sell medicines

pharmacy /ˈfɑːməsi/ *noun* **1** [C] a shop or part of a shop that prepares and sells medicines **2** [U] the study of the preparation of medicines

░░ WORD PARTNERS FOR **phase**

enter/go through a phase • a **passing** phase • a phase **of** sth

phase¹ /feɪz/ *noun* [C] a stage or period which is part of a longer period *The first phase of the project is scheduled for completion next year.* ○ *My younger daughter is going through a phase of only wearing black.*

phase² /feɪz/ *verb*
phase sth in to gradually start using a new system, process, or law *The new tax will be phased in over five years.*
phase sth out to gradually stop using something

PhD /ˌpiːeɪtʃˈdiː/ *noun* [C] an advanced university qualification, or a person who has this qualification *a PhD course/programme* ○ *Maria has a PhD in mathematics.*

pheasant /ˈfezənt/ *noun* [C] *plural* pheasants or pheasant a bird with a long tail that is shot for food

phenomenal /fɪˈnɒmɪnəl/ *adjective* extremely successful or showing great qualities or abilities *The film has been a phenomenal success.* • phenomenally *adverb*

phenomenon /fɪˈnɒmɪnən/ *noun* [C] *plural* phenomena something that exists or happens, usually something unusual *storms, lightning, and other natural phenomena* ○ *Road rage seems to be a fairly recent phenomenon.*

phew (*also* whew) /fjuː/ *exclamation* used when you are happy that something is not going to happen, or when you are tired or hot

philanthropist /fɪˈlænθrəpɪst/ *noun* [C] someone who gives money to people who need help

-phile /-faɪl/ *suffix* makes a noun meaning 'enjoying or liking something' *a Francophile* (= someone who loves France) ○ *a bibliophile* (= someone who loves books)

philosopher /fɪˈlɒsəfəʳ/ *noun* [C] someone who studies or writes about the meaning of life

philosophical /ˌfɪləˈsɒfɪkəl/ *adjective* **1** relating to the study or writing of philosophy *a philosophical problem/question* **2** accepting unpleasant situations in a calm and wise way *She seems fairly philosophical about the failure of her marriage.* • **philosophically** *adverb*

philosophy /fɪˈlɒsəfi/ *noun* **1** [C, U] the study or writing of ideas about the meaning of life, or a particular set of ideas about the meaning of life *Descartes is considered by many to be the father of modern philosophy.* **2** [C] a way of thinking about what you should do in life *My philosophy has always been to give those with ability the chance to progress.*

phishing /ˈfɪʃɪŋ/ *noun* [U] when a person tries to trick you into giving information that would let them take money from your Internet bank account (= an arrangement with your bank to keep your money there and take it out when you need it)

phlegm /flem/ *noun* [U] a thick liquid produced in your lungs, throat, and nose when you have a cold (= common illness that makes you sneeze)

phlegmatic /flegˈmætɪk/ *adjective formal* Someone who is phlegmatic is calm and does not get excited easily.

-phobe /-fəʊb/ *suffix* someone who hates something *a commitment-phobe* (= a person who hates commitment)

phobia /ˈfəʊbiə/ *noun* [C] an extreme fear of something *My mum's got a phobia about birds.*

WORD PARTNERS FOR **phone**

answer/pick up the phone • **put** the phone **down** • a phone **rings** • **by/over** the phone • a phone **bill/company/conversation**

o⌐**phone¹** /fəʊn/ (*also* **telephone**) *noun* **1** SYSTEM [U] a communication system that is used to talk to someone who is in another place *We'll contact you by phone when we get the results.* **2** EQUIPMENT [C] a piece of equipment that is used to talk to someone who is in another place *Would someone please answer the phone?* ○ *I could hear the phone ringing.* **3 on the phone a** USING PHONE using the phone *She's been on the phone all night.* **b** HAVING A PHONE *UK* when you have a phone ⊃See also: **cellular phone, mobile phone, pay phone.**

o⌐**phone²** /fəʊn/ (*also* **phone up**) *verb* [I, T] to communicate with someone by telephone *I tried to phone her last night, but she was out.* ○ *I'm going to phone for a taxi.* ⊃See Common learner error at **telephone.**

COMMON LEARNER ERROR

phone or call?

In British English the verbs **phone** or **call** are used to mean communicate with someone by telephone. You can also use the expressions 'give someone a ring/call' or 'ring (someone)'.

I'll phone you tomorrow.

I'll give you a ring tomorrow.

I'll ring you tomorrow.

In American English **call** is the usual verb which means telephone someone.

Call me later.

I'll call you tomorrow.

'phone ,book *noun* [C] a book that contains the telephone numbers of people who live in a particular area

'phone ,box *UK* (*US* **'phone ,booth**) *noun* [C] a small structure containing a public telephone ⊃See picture at **telephone.**

'phone ,call *noun* [C] when you use the telephone *Will you excuse me, I've got to make a phone call.*

'phone ,card *noun* [C] a small piece of plastic used to pay for the use of some telephones

phone-in /ˈfəʊnɪn/ *UK* (*US* **call-in**) *noun* [C] a television or radio programme in which the public can ask questions or give opinions over the telephone

'phone ,number *noun* [C] the number of a particular telephone

phonetic /fəʊˈnetɪk/ *adjective* relating to the sounds you make when you speak *the international phonetic alphabet* • **phonetically** *adverb*

phonetics /fəˈnetɪks/ *noun* [U] the study of the sounds made by the human voice in speech

phoney¹ *UK* (*US* **phony**) /ˈfəʊni/ *adjective informal* not real *He gave the police a phoney number.*

phoney² *UK* (*US* **phony**) /ˈfəʊni/ *noun* [C] *informal* someone who is not sincere • **phoney** *UK* (*US* **phony**) *adjective informal a phoney smile*

phosphate /ˈfɒsfeɪt/ *noun* [C, U] a chemical that is used in cleaning products and to help plants grow

o⌐**photo** /ˈfəʊtəʊ/ *noun* [C] a picture produced with a camera *a black-and-white/colour photo* ○ *I took a photo of Jack lying on the beach.*

photocopier /ˈfəʊtəʊˌkɒpiəʳ/ *noun* [C] a machine which produces copies of documents by photographing them ⊃See colour picture **The Office** on page Centre 5.

photocopy /ˈfəʊtəʊˌkɒpi/ *noun* [C] a copy of a document made with a photocopier *I made a photocopy of my letter before sending it.* • **photocopy** *verb* [T]

photogenic /ˌfəʊtəʊˈdʒenɪk/ *adjective* Someone who is photogenic has the type of face that looks attractive in a photograph.

o⌐**photograph¹** /ˈfəʊtəgrɑːf/ *noun* [C] a picture produced with a camera *a black-and-white/colour photograph* ○ *He took a lovely photograph of the children in the garden.*

photograph² /ˈfəʊtəgrɑːf/ *verb* [T] to take a photograph of someone or something *They were photographed leaving a nightclub together.*

photographer /fəˈtɒɡrəfəʳ/ *noun* [C] someone whose job is to take photographs

photographic /ˌfəʊtəˈɡræfɪk/ *adjective* [always before noun] relating to photographs *photo-*

P

graphic equipment/film ○ *photographic evidence*

photography /fə'tɒgrəfi/ *noun* [U] the activity or job of taking photographs

phrasal verb /ˌfreɪz³l'vɜːb/ *noun* [C] a verb together with an adverb or preposition which has a different meaning to the meaning of its separate parts. For example 'look up' and 'carry on' are phrasal verbs. ⊃See Extra help page **Phrasal verbs** on page Centre 24 ⊃See colour picture **Phrasal Verbs** on page Centre 16.

○**phrase**¹ /freɪz/ *noun* [C] a group of words which are often used together and have a particular meaning

phrase² /freɪz/ *verb* [T] to express something by choosing to use particular words *It might have been better if he had phrased it differently.*

○**physical**¹ /'fɪzɪk³l/ *adjective* **1** relating to the body *physical fitness/strength* ○ *People put too much emphasis on physical appearance* (= what you look like). **2** [always before noun] relating to real things that you can see and touch *There was no physical evidence linking Jones to Shaw's murder.*

physical² /'fɪzɪk³l/ *US* (*UK* **medical**) *noun* [C] an examination of your body by a doctor to find out if you are healthy

physically /'fɪzɪk³li/ *adverb* in a way that relates to the body *physically attractive/fit*

physical 'therapist *US* (*UK/US* physiotherapist) *noun* [C] someone whose job is to give people physical therapy

physical 'therapy *US* (*UK/US* physiotherapy) *noun* [U] treatment for illness or injury in which you practise moving parts of your body

physician /fɪ'zɪʃ³n/ *noun* [C] *formal* a doctor

physicist /'fɪzɪsɪst/ *noun* [C] someone who studies physics

physics /'fɪzɪks/ *noun* [U] the scientific study of natural forces, such as energy, heat, light, etc

physio /'fɪziəʊ/ *noun* [C, U] *UK informal short for* physiotherapy or physiotherapist

physiological /ˌfɪziə'lɒdʒɪk³l/ *adjective* relating to how the bodies of living things work

physiology /ˌfɪzi'ɒlədʒi/ *noun* [U] the scientific study of how the bodies of living things work

physiotherapist /ˌfɪziəʊ'θerəpɪst/ (*also US* **physical therapist**) *noun* [C] someone whose job is to give people physiotherapy

physiotherapy /ˌfɪziəʊ'θerəpi/ (*also US* **physical therapy**) *noun* [U] treatment for illness or injury in which you practise moving parts of your body

physique /fɪ'ziːk/ *noun* [C] the shape and size of your body *He has a very muscular physique.*

physique /fɪ'ziːk/ *noun* [C] the shape and size of your body *He has a very muscular physique.*

pianist /'piːənɪst/ *noun* [C] someone who plays the piano

piano /pi'ænəʊ/ *noun* [C] a large wooden musical instrument with strings inside and black and white bars that produce sounds

piano

when you press them ⊃See also: **grand piano**.

○**pick**¹ /pɪk/ *verb* [T] **1** CHOOSE to choose something or someone *Do you want to help me pick some numbers for my lottery ticket?* ○ *I was never picked for the school football team.* **2** FLOWERS/FRUIT ETC If you pick flowers, fruit, etc, you take them off a tree or out of the ground. *I picked some apples this morning.* **3** REMOVE to remove small pieces from something with your fingers *You'll have to let the glue dry and then you can pick it off.* **4 pick a fight/argument** to start a fight or argument with someone **5 pick sb's pocket** to steal something from someone's pocket ⊃See also: have a **bone**¹ to pick with sb.

pick at sth 1 to only eat a small amount of your food because you are worried or ill *He picked at his food but had no appetite.* **2** to remove small pieces from something with your fingers *If you keep picking at that scab it'll never heal.*

pick on sb to choose a person and criticize or treat them unfairly *He just started picking on me for no reason.*

pick sth/sb out to choose someone or something from a group of people or things *She picked out a red shirt for me to try on.*

○**pick sth/sb up 1** to lift something or someone by using your hands *He picked his coat up off the floor.* ○ *Just pick up the phone and call him.* ⊃See colour picture **Phrasal Verbs** on page Centre 16. **2** to collect someone who is waiting for you, or to collect something that you have left somewhere *Can you pick me up from the airport?*

pick sth up 1 GET to get something *She picked up some real bargains in the sale.* **2** LEARN to learn a new skill or language by practising it and not by being taught it *He hadn't done any skiing before the holiday, but he picked it up really quickly.* **3** ILLNESS to get an illness from someone or something *She picked up a nasty stomach bug while she was on holiday.* **4** SIGNAL If a piece of equipment picks up a signal, it receives it. *Antennas around the top of the ship picked up the radar signals.* **5** NOTICE to notice something *Police dogs picked up the scent of the two men from clothes they had left behind.*

pick sb up 1 to start talking to someone in order to try to begin a romantic relationship with them **2** If the police pick someone up, they take that person to the police station.

pick up 1 If a business or social situation picks up, it improves. *Business is really starting to pick up now.* **2** If the wind picks up, it becomes stronger.

pick up sth If a vehicle picks up speed, it starts to go faster. *I'll pick up speed on the downhill stretches.*

pick² /pɪk/ *noun* **1** [C] a sharp metal stick used to break hard ground or rocks **2 the pick of sth** the best of a group of things or people **3 have/take your pick** to choose what you want *We've got tea, coffee, or hot chocolate - take your pick.*

picket /'pɪkɪt/ (*also* **'picket ˌline**) *noun* [C] a group of people who stand outside a building in order to show their anger about something and to try to stop people going inside • **picket** *verb* [I, T] *Protesters picketed cinemas across the whole country.*

,picket 'fence *noun* [C] *US* a low fence made from a row of flat sticks that are pointed at the top

pickle /'pɪkl/ *noun* **1** [C, U] *UK* food which has been put into vinegar or salt water for a long time and has a sour taste *cold meat and pickles* **2** [C] *US* a small cucumber (= a green, cylindrical vegetable) that has been put in vinegar or in a liquid containing salt and spices • **pickled** *adjective pickled onions*

pickpocket /'pɪk,pɒkɪt/ *noun* [C] someone who steals things from people's pockets

pickup /'pɪkʌp/ (*also* **'pickup ,truck**) *noun* [C] *US* a small, open truck

picky /'pɪki/ *adjective informal* Someone who is picky does not like many things. *a picky eater*

picnic /'pɪknɪk/ *noun* [C] a meal that you make and take with you somewhere to eat outside *We're going to* **have a picnic** *down by the lake.* • **picnic** *verb* [I] *picnicking past* **picnicked**

pictorial /pɪk'tɔːriəl/ *adjective* relating to pictures or shown using pictures

---

WORD PARTNERS FOR picture

draw/paint a picture • **take** a picture • a picture **of** sb/sth • **in** a picture

---

o↵**picture¹** /'pɪktʃər/ *noun* [C] **1** DRAWING ETC a drawing, painting, or photograph of something or someone *to* **draw/paint a picture** ○ *She's got pictures of pop stars all over her bedroom wall.* ○ *Did you* **take** many **pictures** (= photograph many things) *while you were in Sydney?* ◆See colour picture **The Living Room** on page Centre 4. **2** IDEA an idea of what something is like [usually singular] *I've got a much clearer picture of what's happening now.* **3** TV the image on a television screen *I'm afraid it's not a very good picture.* **4** FILM a film *Could this be the first animated film to win a best picture award?* **5 the pictures** *old-fashioned* the cinema *I really fancy going to the pictures tonight.* **6 get the picture** *informal* used to say that someone understands a situation *Oh right, I get the picture.* **7 paint a bleak/rosy, etc picture of sth** to describe something in a particular way *She paints a rosy* (= happy) *picture of family life.* **8 put/keep sb in the picture** *informal* to explain to someone what is happening *Kenneth had no idea what was going on till I put him in the picture.*

picture² /'pɪktʃər/ *verb* [T] **1** to imagine something in a particular way *The house isn't at all how I had pictured it.* **2** to show someone or something in a picture [often passive] *They were pictured holding hands on the beach.*

'picture ,messaging *noun* [C] sending and receiving pictures on a mobile phone

picturesque /,pɪktʃər'esk/ *adjective* A picturesque place is attractive to look at. *a picturesque cottage on the edge of the Yorkshire Moors*

pie /paɪ/ *noun* [C, U] a type of food made with meat, vegetables, or fruit which is covered in pastry and baked *apple/meat pie* ◆See also: **mince pie.**

pie

o↵**piece¹** /piːs/ *noun* [C] **1** AMOUNT/PART an amount of something, or a part of something *a piece of paper/wood* ○ *She cut the flan into eight pieces.* ○ *Some of the pieces seem to be missing.* ○ *These shoes are* **falling to pieces** (= breaking into pieces). ◆See colour picture **Pieces and Quantities** on page Centre 1. **2** ONE one of a particular type of thing *a useful piece of equipment* **3** SOME some of a particular type of thing *a piece of news/information* ○ *Can I give you a piece of advice?* **4** ART/WRITING ETC an example of artistic, musical, or written work *There was an interesting piece on alternative medicine in the paper yesterday.* **5 ten-/twenty-, etc pence piece** a coin with a value of ten/twenty, etc pence (= British money) **6 be a piece of cake** *informal* to be very easy *The test was a piece of cake.* **7 give sb a piece of your mind** *informal* to speak angrily to someone because they have done something wrong **8 go/fall to pieces** If someone goes to pieces, they become so upset that they cannot control their feelings or think clearly. *He went to pieces when his mother died.* ◆See also: set-piece.

piece² /piːs/ *verb*
piece sth together to try to understand something or discover the truth about something by collecting different pieces of information *Police are trying to piece together a profile of the murderer.*

piecemeal /'piːsmiːl/ *adjective, adverb* happening very gradually *The land is being sold in a* **piecemeal fashion** *over a number of years.*

pier

pier /pɪər/ *noun* [C] a long structure that is built from the land out over the sea and sometimes has entertainments, restaurants, etc on it

pierce /pɪəs/ *verb* [T] **1** to make a hole in something using a sharp point *I'd like to have my ears pierced.* **2** *literary* If a light or a sound pierces something, it is suddenly seen or heard. *A few rays of sunlight pierced the bedroom shutters.*

piercing /'pɪəsɪŋ/ *adjective* **1** A piercing noise, light, etc is very strong and unpleasant. *I heard a loud, piercing scream.* **2** Piercing eyes seem to look at you very closely.

piety /'paɪəti/ *noun* [U] a strong belief in religious morals

๐₋**pig**[1] /pɪg/ *noun* [C] **1** a large pink, brown, or black farm animal that is kept for its meat **2** *informal* someone who is very unpleasant, or someone who eats a lot *He's an ignorant pig.* ⊃See also: **guinea pig.**

pig[2] /pɪg/ *verb* pigging, *past* pigged
  pig out *informal* to eat too much *We pigged out on the cakes and pastries.*

pigeon /'pɪdʒən/ *noun* [C] a grey bird which often lives on buildings in towns

pigeonhole[1] /'pɪdʒənhəʊl/ *noun* [C] one of a set of small open boxes in which letters or messages are left, especially in an office or hotel

pigeonhole[2] /'pɪdʒənhəʊl/ *verb* [T] If you pigeonhole someone, you unfairly decide what type of person they are.

piggyback /'pɪgibæk/ (*also* **piggyback** ,ride) *noun* [C] a way of carrying someone on your back in which they put their arms and legs around you

piggy bank /'pɪgi,bæŋk/ *noun* [C] a small container, often in the shape of a pig, used by children to keep money in

pigheaded /,pɪg'hedɪd/ *adjective* refusing to change your opinion or the way you are doing something although it would be better if you did

piglet /'pɪglət/ *noun* [C] a baby pig

pigment /'pɪgmənt/ *noun* [C, U] a substance that gives something colour ● **pigmentation** /,pɪgmən'teɪʃᵊn/ *noun* [U] the natural colour of a living thing

pigsty /'pɪgstaɪ/ (*also US* **pigpen** /'pɪgpen/) *noun* [C] a place where pigs are kept

pigtail /'pɪgteɪl/ *noun* [C] a hairstyle in which the hair is twisted together and tied [usually plural] *A little girl in pigtails presented the flowers.*

pike /paɪk/ *noun* [C, U] *plural* pike a large river fish with sharp teeth, or the meat of this fish

---

WORD PARTNERS FOR *pile*

a pile of sth ● be in/put sth into a pile

๐₋**pile**[1] /paɪl/ *noun* **1** [C] an amount of a substance in the shape of a small hill or a number of objects on top of each other *a pile of books/ bricks* ○ *a pile of sand/rubbish* ○ *The clothes were arranged in piles on the floor.* **2 a pile of sth/piles of sth** *informal* a lot of something *It's all right for him, he's got piles of money.*

pile[2] /paɪl/ *verb*
  pile in/out *informal* to enter/leave a place quickly and not in an organized way *She opened the door and we all piled in.*
  pile sth up to make a lot of things into a pile by putting them on top of each other *Just pile those books up over there.*
  pile up If something unpleasant piles up,

you get more of it. *My work's really starting to pile up.*

pile-up /'paɪlʌp/ *noun* [C] an accident involving several cars

pilfer /'pɪlfəʳ/ *verb* [I, T] to steal things that do not have much value

pilgrim /'pɪlgrɪm/ *noun* [C] someone who travels to a place which is important in their religion

pilgrimage /'pɪlgrɪmɪdʒ/ *noun* [C, U] a journey to a place which has religious importance *to go on a pilgrimage to Mecca*

pill /pɪl/ *noun* **1** [C] a small, hard piece of medicine that you swallow *a vitamin pill* ○ *I've taken a couple of pills, but my headache still hasn't gone.* ⊃See picture at **medicine.** **2 the pill** a pill which prevents a woman from becoming pregnant ⊃See also: **sleeping pill.**

pillar /'pɪləʳ/ *noun* **1** [C] a tall structure made of stone, wood, etc which supports something above it *The new bridge will be supported by 100 concrete pillars.* **2 a pillar of sth** someone or something who is very important to a place, organization, etc *He was a pillar of the local community.*

pillow /'pɪləʊ/ *noun* [C] a soft object which you rest your head on in bed

pillowcase /'pɪləʊkeɪs/ *noun* [C] a cloth cover for a pillow

pilot /'paɪlət/ *noun* [C] someone who flies an aircraft ● **pilot** *verb* [T]

pimp /pɪmp/ *noun* [C] someone who controls the work and money of a prostitute (= person who has sex for money)

pimple /'pɪmpl/ *noun* [C] a small spot on your skin ● **pimply** *adjective* ⊃See also: **goose pimples.**

pin[1] /pɪn/ *noun* [C] **1** a thin piece of metal with a sharp point used to fasten pieces of cloth, etc together *She pricked her finger on a pin.* **2** a thin piece of metal, wood, plastic, etc that holds or fastens things together *He's had a metal pin put in his leg so that the bones heal properly.* ⊃See also: **drawing pin, pins and needles, rolling pin, safety pin.**

pin[2] /pɪn/ *verb* [T] pinning, *past* pinned **1** to fasten something with a pin *We're not allowed to pin anything on these walls.* ○ *She had a red ribbon pinned to her collar.* **2** pin sb to/ against/under, etc to force someone to stay in a position by holding them *They pinned him to the ground.* ⊃See also: pin your hopes (hope[2]) on sb/ sth.
  pin sb down 1 to make someone give you details or a decision about something *I've been trying to get a decision from Jim, but he's very difficult to pin down.* **2** to force someone to stay in a horizontal position by holding them *They pinned him down on the floor.*
  pin sth down to discover exact details about something *Investigators are trying to pin down the cause of the fire.*
  pin sth on sb *informal* to blame someone for something they did not do *They tried to pin the murder on the dead woman's husband.*
  pin sth up to fasten something to a wall using a pin *The exam results have been pinned up on the noticeboard.*

PIN /pɪn/ (*also* 'PIN ,number) *noun* [C] *abbreviation for* Personal Identification Number: the secret number that allows you to use a bank card in a machine

pinafore /'pɪnəfɔːʳ/ *UK* (*US* jumper) *noun* [C] a loose dress with no sleeves that is worn over other clothes such as a shirt

pincer /'pɪnsəʳ/ *noun* [C] one of a pair of curved hand-like parts of an animal such as a crab (= round, flat sea animal with ten legs)

pinch[1] /pɪnʃ/ *verb* [T] **1** to press someone's skin tightly between your thumb and first finger, sometimes causing pain *One of the kids had been pinching her and she was crying.* **2** *mainly UK informal* to steal something that does not have much value *Who's pinched my ruler?*

pinch[2] /pɪnʃ/ *noun* [C] **1** a small amount of a substance that you pick up between your thumb and your first finger *a pinch of salt* **2** when you press part of the body or an area of skin tightly between your thumb and first finger **3** **at a pinch** *UK* (*US* in a pinch) If something can be done at a pinch, it is possible but it is difficult. *We can fit ten round the table, at a pinch.* **4** **feel the pinch** to have problems because you do not have enough money ⊃See also: take sth with a pinch of salt[1].

pinched /pɪnʃt/ *adjective* A pinched face looks thin and ill.

pine[1] /paɪn/ *noun* **1** [C, U] (*also* 'pine ,tree) a tall tree with long, thin leaves shaped like needles **2** [U] the pale coloured wood from this tree

pine[2] /paɪn/ (*also* pine away) *verb* [I] to be sad because you want someone or something that has gone away *He's pining for his ex-girl-friend.*

pineapple /'paɪnæpl/ *noun* [C, U] a large fruit with thick skin and sharp leaves sticking out of the top which is sweet and yellow inside

pineapple

pinecone /'paɪn,kəʊn/ *noun* [C] a hard, brown, oval object that grows on pine and fir trees (= tall trees which stay green all winter)

ping /pɪŋ/ *verb* [I] to make a short, high noise like a bell *They could hear the microwave pinging in the kitchen.* • **ping** *noun* [C]

pink /pɪŋk/ *adjective* being a pale red colour *pretty, pink flowers* • **pink** *noun* [C, U] ⊃See colour picture Colours on page Centre 12.

pinnacle /'pɪnəkl/ *noun* [no plural] the highest or best part of something *At 35, she is at the pinnacle of her career.*

pinpoint /'pɪnpɔɪnt/ *verb* [T] to say exactly what or where something is *It is difficult to pinpoint the exact time of death.*

,pins and 'needles *noun* **have pins and needles** to feel slight sharp pains in a part of

your body when you move it after keeping it still for a period of time

pint /paɪnt/ *noun* [C] **1** (*written abbreviation* pt) a unit for measuring liquid, equal to 0.568 litres in the UK and 0.473 litres in the US ⊃See Extra help page Measurements on page Centre 31. **2** *UK informal* a pint of beer

pin-up /'pɪnʌp/ *noun* [C] an attractive, famous person who is often in big photographs which people stick to their walls, or the photograph of that person

pioneer /,paɪə'nɪəʳ/ *noun* [C] someone who is one of the first people to do something *one of the pioneers of modern science* • **pioneer** *verb* [T] *He pioneered the use of lasers in surgery.*

pioneering /,paɪə'nɪərɪŋ/ *adjective* [always before noun] starting the development of something important *pioneering work/research on atomic energy*

pious /'paɪəs/ *adjective* having strong religious beliefs, and living or behaving in a way which shows these beliefs

pip[1] /pɪp/ *noun* [C] *UK* a small seed inside fruit such as apples and oranges

pip[2] /pɪp/ *verb* [T] pipping, *past* pipped *UK informal* to beat someone by a very small amount

┌─────────────────────────────────────┐
│ WORD PARTNERS FOR *pipe* │
└─────────────────────────────────────┘

a pipe **leads/runs** [from/to, etc] sth • a pipe **bursts/leaks** • **through** a pipe

pipe[1] /paɪp/ *noun* [C] **1** a long tube which liquid or gas can move through *A water pipe had burst, flooding the basement.* **2** a tube with a bowl-shaped part at one end, used to smoke tobacco *to smoke a pipe* ⊃See also: exhaust pipe.

pipe[2] /paɪp/ *verb* [T] to send something through a pipe *Water is piped from a spring to houses in the local area.*

pipe down *informal* to stop making noise and become quieter

pipe up *informal* to suddenly say something *Then Lydia piped up with her view of things.*

pipeline /'paɪplaɪn/ *noun* [C] **1** a series of pipes that carry liquid or gas over a long distance **2** **be in the pipeline** If a plan is in the pipeline, it is being developed and will happen in the future. *We have several projects in the pipeline.*

piping /'paɪpɪŋ/ *noun* [U] a piece of pipe *copper piping*

,piping 'hot *adjective* Piping hot food is very hot.

piquant /'piːkənt/ *adjective* *formal* having a pleasant, spicy taste

pique[1] /piːk/ *noun* [U] *formal* when someone is annoyed

pique[2] /piːk/ *verb* piquing *past* piqued **pique sb's curiosity/interest, etc** to make someone interested in something

piqued /piːkt/ *adjective* annoyed

piracy /'paɪərəsi/ *noun* [U] **1** attacking and stealing from ships **2** the illegal activity of copying and selling music, films, etc *software/video piracy*

pirate[1] /'paɪərət/ *noun* [C] **1** someone who attacks ships and steals from them **2** someone who illegally copies and sells music, films, etc

P

pirate² /ˈpaɪərət/ *verb* [T] to illegally copy and sell music, films, etc

pirate³ /ˈpaɪərət/ *adjective* **[always before noun]** illegally copied *a pirate CD/DVD*

Pisces /ˈpaɪsiːz/ *noun* [C, U] the sign of the zodiac which relates to the period of 20 February - 20 March, or a person born during this period ➲See picture at **zodiac**.

piss¹ /pɪs/ *verb* [I] *very informal* a very impolite word meaning to pass urine from the body

piss sb off *very informal* to annoy someone

piss² /pɪs/ *noun* **take the piss** *UK very informal* an impolite phrase meaning to make jokes about someone

pissed /pɪst/ *adjective very informal* **1** *mainly UK* an impolite way of describing someone who has drunk too much alcohol **2** *US* an impolite way of describing someone who is angry

ˌpissed ˈoff *adjective very informal* an impolite way of describing someone who is angry

pistol /ˈpɪstᵊl/ *noun* [C] a small gun

piston /ˈpɪstᵊn/ *noun* [C] a part of an engine that moves up and down and makes other parts of the engine move

pit¹ /pɪt/ *noun* [C] **1** [HOLE] a large hole which has been dug in the ground **2** [SEED] *US* (*UK* **stone**) a large, hard seed that grows inside some types of fruit and vegetables **3** [COAL] (*also US* **ˈpit ˌmine**) a place where coal is dug out from under the ground **4 the pits** *UK* (*US* **the pit**) the place where racing cars stop to be repaired or filled with fuel during a race **5 be the pits** *informal* to be very bad *Our hotel was the absolute pits.*

pit² /pɪt/ *verb* **pitting**, *past* **pitted**

pit sb/sth against sb/sth to make someone or something compete against someone or something else *Chelsea will be pitted against Manchester United in the fourth round of the tournament.*

pitch¹ /pɪtʃ/ *verb* **1** [LEVEL] [T] to make something suitable for a particular level or group of people **[often passive]** *His talk was* ***pitched at*** *slightly too high a level for the audience.* **2** [PERSUADE] [I, T] *mainly US* to try to persuade someone to do something *They are* ***pitching for*** *new business at the moment.* **3 pitch (sb/sth) forward/into, etc** to suddenly move in a particular direction, or to make someone or something suddenly move in a particular direction *He braked too hard and the car pitched forward.* **4 pitch a tent** to choose a place for a tent and put it there **5** [BALL] [I, T] in baseball, to throw the ball towards the person who is going to hit it *He used to pitch for the Chicago White Sox.* **6** [SOUND] [T] to make sound at a particular level *The tune was pitched much too high for me.*

pitch in *informal* to help a group of people to do some work that needs to be done *If we all pitch in, we'll get this kitchen cleaned up in no time.*

pitch² /pɪtʃ/ *noun* **1** [SPORT] [C] *UK* an area of ground where a sport is played *a cricket/football pitch* **2** [THROW] [C] in baseball, a throw towards the person who is going to hit the ball *He struck out two batters with six pitches.* **3** [SOUND] [U] how high or low a sound is **4** [PERSUADING] [C, U] the things someone says in order to persuade you to do something *I wasn't very impressed by his* ***sales pitch***. ➲See also: **fever pitch**.

pitch-black /ˌpɪtʃˈblæk/ (*also* **pitch-dark**) *adjective* very dark *Outside it was pitch-black.*

pitcher /ˈpɪtʃəʳ/ *noun* [C] **1** in baseball, someone who throws the ball at the person who is going to hit it ➲See colour picture **Sports 2** on page Centre 15. **2** *US* a container for holding and pouring out liquids *a pitcher of water*

pitfall /ˈpɪtfɔːl/ *noun* [C] a likely mistake or problem in a situation *the pitfalls of buying a house*

pithy /ˈpɪθi/ *adjective* A pithy remark expresses something in a very clear and direct way.

pitiful /ˈpɪtifᵊl/ *adjective* **1** making you feel pity *I didn't recognize him, he looked so pitiful.* **2** very bad *a pitiful excuse* • **pitifully** *adverb*

pittance /ˈpɪtᵊns/ *noun* **[no plural]** a very small amount of money *She works very long hours and yet she* ***earns a pittance***.

WORD PARTNERS FOR ***pity***

feel pity • take pity on sb • pity for sb

⊶**pity¹** /ˈpɪti/ *noun* **1 It's a pity...** used to say that something is disappointing *It's a pity you're not staying longer.* **2** [U] a feeling of sympathy for someone *I was hoping someone would* ***take pity on*** *me* (= help me in a difficult situation) *and give me a lift home.* ➲See also: **self-pity**.

pity² /ˈpɪti/ *verb* [T] to feel sorry for someone *She doesn't want people to pity her.*

pivot /ˈpɪvət/ *noun* [C] **1** a fixed point on which something balances or turns **2** the most important part of something • **pivot** *verb* [I, T]

pivotal /ˈpɪvətᵊl/ *adjective* having a very important influence on something *He has played a* ***pivotal role*** *in the negotiations.*

pixel /ˈpɪksᵊl/ *noun* [C] a small point that forms part of the image on a computer screen

pixie /ˈpɪksi/ *noun* [C] a small imaginary person who can do magic things

pizza /ˈpiːtsə/ *noun* [C, U] a food made from a flat, round piece of bread covered with cheese, vegetables, etc and cooked in an oven ➲See colour picture **Food** on page Centre 11.

placard /ˈplækɑːd/ *noun* [C] a large sign with writing that someone carries, often to show that they disagree with something

placate /pləˈkeɪt/ [US] /ˈpleɪkeɪt/ *verb* [T] *formal* to make someone less angry about something

⊶**place¹** /pleɪs/ *noun* **1** [SOMEWHERE] [C] a position, building, town, area, etc *His leg's broken in two places.* ○ *Edinburgh would be a nice place to live.* ○ *What a stupid place to park.* **2 take place** to happen *The meeting will take place next week.* **3 in place a** [CORRECT POSITION] in the correct position *The chairs are all in place.* **b** [EXISTING] If a rule, system, etc is in place, it has started to exist. *There are now laws in place to prevent this from happening.* **4 out of place a** [WRONG POSITION] not in the correct position *Why are my files all out of place?* **b** [NOT SUITABLE] not right or suitable for a particular situation *Everyone else was wearing jeans and I felt completely out of place in my office clothes.* **5 all over the place** in or to many different places *There was blood all over the place.* ○ *There are clothes all over the place – can you pick them up?* **6 in place of sth** instead of something *Try adding fruit to your breakfast cereal in place of sugar.* **7** [HOME] [C] *informal* someone's home *They've just bought a place in Spain.* ○ *Do you want to come back to my place?* **8** [OPPORTUNITY] [C] an opportunity to take part in something *She's got a place at Liverpool University to do Spanish.* **9 in first/ second/third, etc place** If you are in first/ second, etc place in a race or competition, that is your position. *He finished in fifth place.* **10 fall into place** When events or details that you did not understand before fall into place, they become easy to understand. *At first I was a bit confused about some aspects of the course but it's starting to fall into place.* **11 in the first place** used to refer to the time when something started *How did this error happen in the first place?* **12 put sb in their place** to let someone know that they are not as important as they think they are ⊃See also: **decimal place**, **have/take pride¹ of place.**

place² /pleɪs/ *verb* **1 place sth in/on, etc** to put something somewhere carefully *She placed a large dish in front of me.* **2** [T] to cause someone to be in a situation *One stupid action has placed us all at risk.* **3 can't place sb** to not be able to remember who someone is or where you have met them *I recognize her face, but I can't quite place her.* **4 place an advertisement/ bet/order, etc** to arrange to have an advertisement, bet, order, etc *I've placed an ad in the local newspaper.* **5 place emphasis/importance, etc on sth** to give something emphasis, importance, etc *They place a lot of importance on qualifications.*

placement /'pleɪsmənt/ *noun* **1** [C] *UK* a position that someone has with an organization for a short time in order to learn about the work that is done there *He got a month's placement on a national newspaper.* **2** [U, no plural] when you put something or someone somewhere *the placement of additional police on the streets*

placid /'plæsɪd/ *adjective* A placid person is calm and does not often get angry or excited. *Even Emma, who is a fairly placid character, was furious.* ● **placidly** *adverb*

plagiarism /'pleɪdʒ°rɪz°m/ *noun* [U] when someone copies someone else's work or ideas *He was accused of plagiarism.*

plagiarize (*also UK* -ise) /'pleɪdʒ°raɪz/ *verb* [I, T] to copy someone else's work or ideas ● **plagiarist** /'pleɪdʒ°rɪst/ *noun* [C] someone who plagiarizes

plague¹ /pleɪg/ *noun* [C] **1** a serious disease that spreads quickly and kills a lot of people **2 a plague of sth** a large number of something unpleasant that causes a lot of damage *a plague of rats*

plague² /pleɪg/ *verb* [T] **plaguing** *past* **plagued** to make someone suffer for a long time [**often passive**] *He's been plagued by bad luck ever since he bought that house.*

plaid /plæd/ *noun* [C, U] *US* cloth with a pattern of different coloured squares and crossing lines *a plaid dress*

ᴑᴬ**plain¹** /pleɪn/ *adjective* **1** [SIMPLE] simple and not complicated *plain food* **2** [NOT MIXED] not mixed with other colours, substances, etc *a plain blue carpet* ○ *plain yoghurt* **3** [PERSON] A plain person is not attractive to look at. **4** [OBVIOUS] obvious and clear [+ (that)] *It's quite plain that she doesn't want to talk to me about it.* ⊃See also: be plain **sailing.**

plain² /pleɪn/ *adverb informal* **plain stupid/ wrong, etc** completely stupid/wrong, etc *That's just plain stupid!*

plain³ /pleɪn/ *noun* [C] a large area of flat land

plainclothes /'pleɪn,kləʊθz/ *adjective* [always before noun] Plainclothes police wear normal clothes and not a uniform.

plainly /'pleɪnli/ *adverb* **1** in a simple way that is not complicated *plainly dressed* **2** in a clear and obvious way *This is plainly wrong.*

plaintiff /'pleɪntɪf/ *noun* [C] someone who takes legal action against someone else in a court of law

plaintive /'pleɪntɪv/ *adjective* sounding sad *a plaintive cry*

plait /plæt/ *UK* (*US* **braid**) *verb* [T] to twist three pieces of hair, rope, etc together so that they form one long piece ● **plait** *UK* (*US* **braid**) *noun* [C] *She wore her hair in plaits.*

WORD PARTNERS FOR ***plan***
announce/approve/implement/oppose/ outline/unveil a plan ● an ambitious/ controversial/strategic plan

ᴑᴬ**plan¹** /plæn/ *noun* [C] **1** an arrangement for what you intend to do or how you intend to do something *the country's economic plan* ○ *Do you have any **plans for** the weekend?* ○ *The plan is that we'll buy a car once we're there.* ○ *There's been a **change of plan** and we're going on Wednesday instead.* ○ *Luckily, everything went **according to plan** (= happened the way it was planned).* **2** a drawing that shows how something appears from above or will appear from above when it is built *a street plan.* ○ *We had a designer draw up a plan for the yard.*

ᴑᴬ**plan²** /plæn/ *verb* **planning,** *past* **planned 1** to think about and decide what you are going to do or how you are going to do something *We're just planning our holidays.* ○ *As a manager, you've got to **plan ahead.*** ○ *I'd **planned** the meeting for Friday.* **2 plan to do sth** to intend to do something *He plans to go to college next year.* **3** [T] to decide how something will be built *We got an architect to help us plan our new kitchen.*

plan on doing sth to intend to do something *We're planning on catching the early train.*

plan sth out to think about and decide what you are going to do or how you are going to do something *Have you planned out your journey? ○ I'm just planning out my day.*

WORD PARTNERS FOR ***plane***

board/catch/get on/get off a plane • a plane **gets in/lands/takes off** • **on** a plane • **by** plane

⊶**plane¹** /pleɪn/ *noun* [C] **1** [FLYING] a vehicle that flies and has an engine and wings *What time does her **plane get in** (= arrive)? ○ He likes to watch the **planes taking off** and **landing**. ○ a plane crash* **2** [TOOL] a tool that you use to make wood smooth **3** [SURFACE] in mathematics, a flat surface

plane² /pleɪn/ *verb* [T] to make a piece of wood smooth using a tool called a plane

planet /ˈplænɪt/ *noun* [C] a large, round object in space that moves around the sun or another star *Jupiter is the largest planet of our solar system.* • **planetary** *adjective* relating to planets

planetarium /ˌplænɪˈteəriəm/ *noun* [C] *plural* **planetariums** or **planetaria** a building that has a machine for showing the positions and movements of the stars and planets

plank /plæŋk/ *noun* [C] a long, flat piece of wood *wooden planks*

plankton /ˈplæŋktən/ *noun* [U] very small plants and animals in the sea that are eaten by fish

planner /ˈplænəʳ/ *noun* [C] someone whose job is to plan things, especially which buildings are built in towns *urban planners*

planning /ˈplænɪŋ/ *noun* [U] **1** the activity of thinking about and deciding what you are going to do or how you are going to do something *Events like these take months of careful planning.* **2** control over which buildings are built in an area *town planning* ➲See also: **family planning.**

P

⊶**plant¹** /plɑːnt/ *noun* [C] **1** a living thing that grows in the soil or water and has leaves and roots, especially one that is smaller than a tree *Have you **watered the plants**? ○ tomato plants* **2** a large factory where an industrial process happens *a nuclear power plant* ➲See also: **potted plant.**

plant² /plɑːnt/ *verb* [T] **1** [SEEDS/PLANTS] to put seeds or plants in the ground so that they will grow *to **plant bulbs/seeds/trees*** **2** [SECRETLY] to secretly put something in a place that will make someone seem guilty *She insisted that the drugs had been **planted on** her without her knowledge.* **3 plant a bomb** to put a bomb somewhere so that it will explode there **4 plant sth in/next/on, etc** to put something firmly in a particular place *He planted himself next to me on the sofa.* **5** [IDEA/DOUBTS] to make someone start thinking something *I was confident till you **planted doubts** in my mind.*

plantation /plænˈteɪʃən/ *noun* [C] **1** an area of land in a hot country where a crop is grown *a banana/cotton/sugar plantation* **2** an area of land where trees are grown to produce wood

plaque /plɑːk/ *noun* **1** [C] a flat piece of metal or stone with writing on it which is fixed to a wall, often in order to make people remember a dead person **2** [U] a harmful substance that forms on your teeth

plasma /ˈplæzmə/ *noun* [U] the clear liquid part of blood which contains the blood cells

ˈ**plasma ˌscreen** *noun* [C] a screen for showing very clear words or pictures which uses special gases pressed between two flat pieces of glass

plaster¹ /ˈplɑːstəʳ/ *noun* **1** [U] a substance that is spread on walls in order to make them smooth **2** [C] *UK* (*US* **Band-Aid** *trademark*) a small piece of sticky material that you put on cuts on your body **3 be in plaster** *UK* (*US* **be in a cast**) If your arm or leg is in plaster, it is covered in a hard, white substance to protect a broken bone.

plaster² /ˈplɑːstəʳ/ *verb* [T] **1** to cover most of a surface with something *My boots were **plastered with** mud.* **2** to cover a wall with a substance in order to make it smooth

plastered /ˈplɑːstəd/ *adjective informal* very drunk

⊶**plastic** /ˈplæstɪk/ *noun* [C, U] a light, artificial substance that can be made into different shapes when it is soft and is used in a lot of different ways *Most children's toys are made of plastic.* • **plastic** *adjective a **plastic bag***

plasticity /plæsˈtɪsəti/ *noun* [U] *formal* the quality of being soft enough to make into many different shapes

ˌ**plastic ˈsurgery** *noun* [U] operations on someone's face or body to make them more attractive *to have plastic surgery*

ˈ**plastic ˌwrap** *US* (*UK* **clingfilm**) *noun* [U] thin, transparent plastic used for wrapping or covering food

⊶**plate** /pleɪt/ *noun* **1** [FOOD] [C] a flat, round object which is used for putting food on *a **dinner plate** ○ a plate of biscuits* **2** [METAL/GLASS] [C] a flat piece of metal or glass *I had a metal plate put in my knee after the accident.* **3 gold/silver plate** metal with a thin layer of gold or silver on top **4** [PICTURE] [C] a picture in a book ➲See also: **L-plate, license plate, number plate.**

plateau /ˈplætəʊ/ [US] /plæˈtəʊ/ *noun* [C] *plural UK* **plateaux** or *also US* **plateaus** **1** a large area of high, flat land **2** a period when the level of something stays the same [usually singular] *Sales are still good but they've **reached a plateau**.*

platform /ˈplætfɔːm/ *noun* [C] **1** [RAISED SURFACE] a raised surface for people to stand on, especially when they are speaking to a lot of people *The speakers all stood on a platform.* **2** [TRAIN] the area in a railway station where you get on and off the train *The train for London, Paddington, will depart from platform 12.* **3** [POLITICS] all the things that a political party promises to do if they are elected *They campaigned on a platform of low taxation.* **4** [FOR OPINIONS] a way of telling the public about your opinions *Basically, he uses the newspaper as a **platform for** airing his political views.*

platinum /ˈplætɪnəm/ [US] /ˈplætnəm/ *noun* [U] a silver-coloured metal that is very valuable

platitude /ˈplætɪtjuːd/ *noun* [C] something that

is boring because it has been said many times before

platonic /plə'tɒnɪk/ *adjective* A platonic relationship is friendly and not sexual.

platoon /plə'tuːn/ *noun* [C] a small group of soldiers

platter /'plætər/ *noun* [C] a large plate used for serving food

plaudit /'plɔːdɪt/ *noun* [C] *formal* praise [usually plural] *He has **earned/won** plaudits* (= been praised) *for his latest novel.*

plausible /'plɔːzɪbl/ *adjective* If something that someone says or writes is plausible, it could be true. *a **plausible excuse/explanation*** ⊃Opposite **implausible**. ● **plausibility** /,plɔːzɪ'bɪləti/ *noun* [U] when something is plausible

o╍**play¹** /pleɪ/ *verb* **1** [SPORTS/GAMES] [I, T] When you play a sport or game, you take part in it. *You play tennis, don't you Sam? ○ We often used to play cards. ○ I used to **play** netball **for** my school. ○ I'm playing Tony* (= playing against Tony) *at squash tonight. ○ Newcastle are **playing against** Arsenal tonight.* **2** [CHILDREN] [I, T] When children play, they enjoy themselves with toys and games. *She likes **playing with** her dolls.* **3** [MUSIC] [I, T] to make music with a musical instrument *Tim was playing the piano.* **4** [RECORD/RADIO] [I, T] If a radio, record, etc plays, it produces sounds, or if you play a radio, record, etc you make it produce sounds. *A radio was playing in the background. ○ He plays his records late into the night.* **5** [ACTING] [T] to be a character in a film or play *Morgan played the father in the film version.* **6 play a joke/trick on sb** to deceive someone as a joke *I played a trick on her and pretended we'd eaten all the food.* ⊃See also: play it by **ear**, play games (**game¹**), play (it) **safe¹**, play for **time¹**, play **truant**.

play about/around to behave in a silly way *Stop playing around and get on with your homework!*

be playing at sth UK If you ask what someone is playing at, you are angry because they are doing something silly. *What do you think you're playing at!*

play sth back to listen to sounds or watch pictures that you have just recorded *When I played back our conversation, I realized I hadn't made myself clear.*

play sth down to try to make people think that something is less important or bad than it really is *The government have tried to play down the seriousness of the incident.*

play on sth to use someone's fears in order to make that person do or believe what you want *A lot of marketing strategies just play on your fears and insecurities.*

play up UK **1** If a child plays up, he or she behaves badly. **2** If a machine plays up, it does not work as it should.

play (about/around) with sth 1 to think about or try different ways of doing something *We've been playing around with ideas for a new TV show.* **2** to keep touching or moving something, often when you are bored or nervous *Stop playing with your hair!*

play² /pleɪ/ *noun* **1** [THEATRE] [C] a story that is written for actors to perform, usually in a theatre *We saw a play at the National Theatre. ○ Most schools usually **put on a play** (= perform a play) at Christmas.* **2** [SPORTS/GAMES] [U] the activity of taking part in a sport or a game *Rain stopped play in the Hingis-Davenport match.* **3** [CHILDREN] [U] when children enjoy themselves with toys and games *a **play area*** **4 fair play** behaviour that is fair, honest, and does not take advantage of people **5 a play on words** a joke using a word or phrase that has two meanings ⊃See also: foul **play**, role-**play**.

playboy /'pleɪbɔɪ/ *noun* [C] a rich man who spends his time enjoying himself and has relationships with a lot of beautiful women

o╍**player** /'pleɪər/ *noun* [C] **1** someone who plays a sport or game *football/tennis players* **2** someone who plays a musical instrument *a piano player* ⊃See also: cassette **player**, CD **player**, record **player**.

playful /'pleɪfl/ *adjective* funny and not serious *a **playful** mood/remark* ● **playfulness** *noun* [U] ● **playfully** *adverb*

playground /'pleɪɡraʊnd/ *noun* [C] an area of land where children can play, especially at school

playgroup /'pleɪɡruːp/ *noun* [C] a place where small children go during the day when they are too young to go to school

'playing ,card *noun* [C] one of a set of 52 small pieces of stiff paper with numbers and pictures on, used for playing games

'playing ,field *noun* [C] **1** an area of land used for sports such as football **2 a level playing field** a situation in which everyone has the same chance of succeeding

playoff /'pleɪɒf/ *noun* [C] a game between two teams that have equal points in order to decide which is the winner

playpen /'pleɪpen/ *noun* [C] a small structure with net or bars around the sides that young children are put into so that they can play safely

playroom /'pleɪruːm/ *noun* [C] a room in a house for children to play in

PlayStation /'pleɪˌsteɪʃən/ *noun* [C] *trademark* a machine that you use to play games on your television

plaything /'pleɪθɪŋ/ *noun* [C] someone who is treated without respect and is forced to do things for someone else's enjoyment

playtime /'pleɪtaɪm/ *noun* [C, U] UK a period of time when children at school can play outside

playwright /'pleɪraɪt/ *noun* [C] someone who writes plays

plaza /'plɑːzə/ *noun* [C] US **1** an open, public area in a city or town *Mexico City's main plaza is called the Zocalo.* **2** a group of buildings with shops, often including an open, public area *a shopping plaza*

plc, PLC /,piːel'siː/ *noun* [C] *abbreviation for*

Public Limited Company: used after the name of a large company in Britain whose shares (= equal parts of its total value) can be bought and sold by the public

WORD PARTNERS FOR **plea**

2 issue/make/reject a plea • a **desperate/ emotional /impassioned** plea • a plea **for** sth • a plea **from** sb

plea /pliː/ *noun* [C] **1** when someone says in a court of law if they are guilty or not guilty of the crime they have been accused of *a plea of guilty/not guilty* **2** a strong request *an emotional **plea** for forgiveness* ○ *a plea for information from the police*

plead /pliːd/ *verb past* pleaded *or also US* pled **1** LEGAL [T] to say in a court of law if you are guilty or not guilty of the crime you have been accused of *He **pleaded** not guilty to five felony charges.* **2** ASK [I] to ask for something in a strong and emotional way *He **pleaded** with her to come back.* ○ *She **pleaded** for mercy.* **3** EXCUSE [T] to say something as an excuse *You'll just have to **plead** ignorance* (= say you did not know). **4** plead sb's case/cause to say something to try to help someone get what they want or avoid punishment *I tried to plead Jane's cause with our boss.*

○▪**pleasant** /ˈplezᵊnt/ *adjective* **1** enjoyable or attractive *pleasant weather/surroundings* ○ *We had a very pleasant evening.* **2** A pleasant person has a friendly character. ᕄOpposite **unpleasant**. • **pleasantly** *adverb* *I was **pleasantly** surprised.*

pleasantry /ˈplezᵊntri/ *noun* [C] a polite thing that you say when you meet someone [usually plural] *They **exchanged pleasantries** about the weather.*

please¹ /pliːz/ *exclamation* **1** something that you say to be polite when you are asking for something or asking someone to do something *Could you fill in the form, please?* ○ *Please may I use your telephone?* ○ *Please can I have some sweets?* ○ *Please could you move your bag?* **2 Yes, please.** used to accept something politely *"Would you like a lift home?" "Oh yes, please."*

please² /pliːz/ *verb* **1** [I, T] to make someone happy *the desire to please* ○ *I only got married to please my parents.* ᕄOpposite **displease**. **2 anything/as/what/whatever, etc you please** used to say that someone can have or do anything they want *Feel free to talk about anything you please.* ○ *He can come and go as he pleases.* **3 Please yourself.** a slightly rude way of telling someone that you do not care what they choose to do *"I don't want anything to eat." "Please yourself."*

○▪**pleased** /pliːzd/ *adjective* **1** happy or satisfied *"So how did she react to the news?" "I think she was pleased."* ○ *I wasn't very **pleased** about having to pay.* ○ [+ to do sth] *I'm pleased to be back in England.* ○ [+ (that)] *He was pleased that she had come back.* ○ *I'm really **pleased** with the quality of his work.*

2 Pleased to meet you. a polite way of greeting someone you are meeting for the first time

COMMON LEARNER ERROR

pleased
Be careful to use the correct preposition or verb pattern after this word.
*I'm **pleased with** my new computer.*
*He wasn't very **pleased about** the news.*
*I'm **pleased to be** in London.*
~~I'm pleased for my new computer.~~
~~He wasn't very pleased of the news.~~
~~I'm pleased for being in London.~~

pleasing /ˈpliːzɪŋ/ *adjective* Something that is pleasing gives pleasure. *the most pleasing aspect of her work* ○ *These buildings are very pleasing to the eye.*

pleasurable /ˈpleʒᵊrᵊbl/ *adjective* enjoyable *a pleasurable experience*

WORD PARTNERS FOR **pleasure**

derive/express/give pleasure • **take** pleasure **in** sth • **enormous/great/perverse/ pure/sheer** pleasure

○▪**pleasure** /ˈpleʒᵊr/ *noun* **1** HAPPINESS [U] a feeling of happiness or enjoyment *His visits used to give us such pleasure.* ○ *She seemed to take pleasure in* (= enjoy) *humiliating people.* ○ *It gives me great pleasure to introduce our next guest.* ᕄOpposite **displeasure**. **2** ENJOYABLE EXPERIENCE [C, U] an enjoyable activity or experience *Food is one of life's great pleasures.* ○ *I once had the pleasure of sharing a taxi with her.* **3** NOT WORK [U] If you do something for pleasure, you do it because you enjoy it and not because it is your job. *reading for pleasure* **4 It's a pleasure.; My pleasure.** a polite way of replying to someone who has thanked you *"Thank you for a wonderful evening." "My pleasure."*

pleated /ˈpliːtɪd/ *adjective* A pleated piece of clothing or piece of cloth has regular, vertical folds in it. *a pleated skirt*

pled /pled/ *US past of* plead

WORD PARTNERS FOR **pledge** (*noun*)

break/fulfil/make a pledge • a pledge **on** sth

pledge¹ /pledʒ/ *noun* [C] a serious promise [+ to do sth] *a pledge to create jobs* ○ *He **made** a solemn **pledge** to the American people.*

pledge² /pledʒ/ *verb* [T] to promise seriously to do something or give something *Foreign donors have pledged $550 million.* ○ *He **pledged** his support to Mandela.* ○ [+ to do sth] *He pledged to cut government salaries.*

plentiful /ˈplentɪfᵊl/ *adjective* If something is plentiful, there is a lot of it available. *a **plentiful supply** of meat*

○▪**plenty** /ˈplenti/ *quantifier* **1** easily as much or as many as you need *Don't bring any food - we've got plenty.* ○ *There is **plenty of** evidence* *to support her claims.* ○ *There's plenty of room.* ○ *Help yourself to food - there's plenty more.* **2 plenty big/large/wide, etc enough** easily as big/large/wide, etc as you need something to be *This house is plenty big enough for two families.* **3** a lot *I know plenty of unemployed musicians.* ○ *There's plenty for you to do.*

plethora /'pleθ°rə/ *noun* **a plethora of sth** *formal* a large number of something *There is a confusing plethora of pension plans.*

pliers /plaɪəz/ *noun* [plural] a tool for holding or pulling small things like nails or for cutting wire *a pair of pliers* ➔See picture at **tool**.

plight /plaɪt/ *noun* [no plural] *formal* an unpleasant or difficult situation *the plight of the sick and the poor*

plod /plɒd/ *verb* plodding past plodded **plod along/on/through, etc** to walk with slow, heavy steps *We plodded through the mud.*

plonk¹ /plɒŋk/ *verb UK informal* **plonk sth down/in/on, etc** to put something somewhere quickly and without care *She plonked her bag on the floor.*
plonk yourself down to sit down quickly and without care

plonk² /plɒŋk/ *noun* [U] *UK informal* cheap wine

plop¹ /plɒp/ *noun* [C] the sound made by an object when it falls into water

plop² /plɒp/ *verb* plopping, *past* plopped *US informal* **plop (sth) down/onto, etc** to put something somewhere quickly and without care *She plopped down next to me.*

plot¹ /plɒt/ *noun* [C] **1** STORY the things that happen in a story *I don't like movies with complicated plots.* **2** PLAN a plan to do something bad [+ to do sth] *a plot to blow up the embassy* **3** LAND a piece of land, often for growing food or for building on *a building plot*

plot² /plɒt/ *verb* plotting, *past* plotted **1** [I, T] to plan to do something bad [+ to do sth] *They plotted to bring down the government.* ○ *He fired all those accused of plotting against him.* **2** [T] to make marks on a map, picture, etc to show the position or development of something *This chart plots the position of all aircraft.*

plough *UK*, plow *US*

plough¹ *UK (US plow)* /plaʊ/ *noun* [C] a large tool used by farmers to turn over the soil before planting crops

plough² *UK (US plow)* /plaʊ/ *verb* [I, T] to turn over soil with a plough
plough sth back to spend the money that a business had earned on improving that business *All profits are ploughed back into the company.*
plough into sth to hit something with great force *My car ploughed straight into the car in front.*
plough on to continue doing something, although it is difficult or boring
plough through sth to finish what you are reading, eating, or working on, although there is a lot of it *I had to plough through the whole report.*

plow /plaʊ/ *noun, verb US spelling of* plough

🧩 WORD PARTNERS FOR *ploy*

use a ploy ● a ploy backfires/works ● a clever/cunning/cynical/deliberate ploy ● a ploy by sb

ploy /plɔɪ/ *noun* [C] a slightly dishonest method used to try to achieve something [+ to do sth] *The phone call was just a ploy to get rid of her.*

PLS *informal written abbreviation for* please: used in emails and text messages

pluck /plʌk/ *verb* **1 pluck sth/sb from/out, etc** to quickly pull something or someone from the place where they are *A helicopter plucked him from the sea.* **2** BIRD [T] to pull all the feathers out of a bird before cooking it **3** MUSIC [T] If you pluck the strings of a musical instrument, you pull them with your fingers to make a sound. **4** PLANT [T] *literary* to pick a flower or part of a plant **5 pluck your eyebrows** to pull hairs out of your eyebrows (= lines of hair above your eyes) to make them look tidy ➔See also: pluck up the **courage** (to do sth).

plug

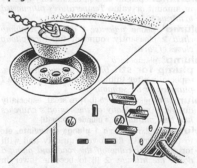

plug¹ /plʌg/ *noun* [C] **1** ELECTRICITY a plastic or rubber object with metal pins, used to connect electrical equipment to an electricity supply *I need to change the plug on my hairdryer.* **2** HOLE something you put in a hole to block it *a bath plug* **3** ADVERTISEMENT when someone talks about a new book, film, etc in public in order to advertise it *She managed to get in a plug for her new book.* **4 pull the plug** to prevent an activity from continuing *They have* *pulled the plug on jazz broadcasts.* ➔See also: spark plug.

plug² /plʌg/ *verb* [T] plugging, *past* plugged **1 plug a gap/hole** *mainly UK* to solve a problem by supplying something that is needed *The new computer system will help to plug the gap in the county's ability to collect taxes.* **2** to talk about a new book, film, etc in public in order to advertise it *He was on TV, plugging his new book.* **3** to block a hole

plug away *informal* to work hard at something for a long time *I'm still plugging away at my article.*

plug sth in to connect a piece of electrical equipment to an electricity supply *Could you plug the iron in for me?* ➔Opposite unplug.

plug sth into sth to connect one piece of electrical equipment to another *You need to plug the speakers into the stereo.*

plughole /'plʌghəʊl/ (*also US* **drain**) *noun* [C] the hole in a bath or sink (= place in a kitchen where dishes are washed) where the water flows away

plug-in (*also* **plugin**) /'plʌgɪn/ *noun* [C] a small computer program that makes a larger one work faster or be able to do more things

plum /plʌm/ *noun* [C] a soft, round fruit with red, yellow, or purple skin and a stone in the middle

plumage /'pluːmɪdʒ/ *noun* [U] a bird's feathers

plumber /'plʌmə^r/ *noun* [C] someone whose job is to repair or connect water pipes and things like toilets and baths

plumbing /'plʌmɪŋ/ *noun* [U] the water pipes in a building

plume /pluːm/ *noun* **1 a plume of dust/smoke, etc** a tall, thin amount of dust/smoke, etc rising into the air. **2** [C] a large feather, often worn for decoration

plummet /'plʌmɪt/ *verb* [I] to fall very quickly in amount or value *Temperatures plummeted to minus 20.*

plump¹ /plʌmp/ *adjective* **1** quite fat *a plump child* **2** pleasantly round or full *nice plump cloves of garlic*

plump² /plʌmp/ *verb*

plump for sth *UK* to choose something, especially after thinking about it for a time *I plumped for the salmon.*

plunder /'plʌndə^r/ *verb* [I, T] to steal, especially during a war *Many of the region's churches had been plundered.* ● **plunder** *noun* [U]

plunge¹ /plʌndʒ/ *verb* **1 plunge down/into, etc** to fall or move down very quickly and with force *The car came off the road and plunged down the hillside.* **2** [I] to become lower in temperature, value, etc very suddenly and quickly *Temperatures plunged below zero.*

plunge sth into sth to push something very hard into something else *He plunged the knife into the man's stomach.*

plunge sb/sth into sth to make someone or something suddenly be unhappy or in an unpleasant situation [often passive] *The country had been plunged into chaos.*

plunge into sth to start doing something with a lot of energy *Trying to forget about her,*

he plunged into his work.

take a plunge ● a plunge in sth ● a **stock market** plunge

plunge² /plʌndʒ/ *noun* **1** [C] a sudden and quick decrease in the value, amount, or level of something *Prices have taken a plunge* (= suddenly become less). **2 take the plunge** to do something important or difficult, especially after thinking about it for a long time *We're finally going to take the plunge and buy a house.*

the pluperfect /,pluː'pɜːfɪkt/ (*also* **the past perfect**) *noun* the form of the verb that is used to show that an action had already finished when another action happened. In English, the pluperfect is made with 'had' and a past participle

plural /'plʊər^əl/ *noun* [C] a word or part of a word which shows that you are talking about more than one person or thing. For example 'babies' is the plural of 'baby'. ● **plural** *adjective* 'Cattle' and 'trousers' are plural nouns.

pluralism /'plʊər^əlɪz^əm/ *noun* [U] the existence in a society of many different types of people with many different beliefs and opinions *political pluralism* ● **pluralist** (*also* **pluralistic** /,plʊərəl'ɪstɪk/) *adjective* relating to pluralism *a pluralist society*

○ **plus¹** /plʌs/ *preposition* **1** added to *Five plus three is eight.* **2** and also *You've won their latest CD plus two tickets for their concert.*

plus² /plʌs/ *adjective* **40 plus, 150 plus, etc** more than the amount stated *temperatures of 40 plus*

plus³ /plʌs/ *conjunction informal* and also *Don't go there in August. It'll be too hot, plus it'll be really expensive.*

plus⁴ /plʌs/ *noun* [C] **1** *informal* an advantage *Well, the apartment has a garden so that's a plus.* **2** (*also* **plus ,sign**) the symbol +, used between two numbers to show that they are being added together

plush /plʌʃ/ *adjective* Plush furniture, buildings, rooms, etc are very expensive and comfortable. *a plush red carpet*

Pluto /'pluːtəʊ/ *noun* [no plural] the planet that is furthest from the Sun, after Neptune

plutonium /pluː'təʊniəm/ *noun* [U] a chemical element that is used in the production of nuclear power and nuclear weapons

ply /plaɪ/ *verb* **1 ply across/between, etc** *old-fashioned* to often make a particular journey *fishing boats plying across the harbour* **2 ply your trade** to work at your job, especially selling things

ply sb with sth 1 to give someone a lot of something again and again *They plied me with food and drink.* **2** to ask someone a lot of questions *They plied him with questions about where he had been.*

plywood /'plaɪwʊd/ *noun* [U] wood that is made by sticking several thin layers of wood together

○ **p.m.** (*also* **pm**) /,piː'em/ used when you are referring to a time after 12 o'clock in the middle of the day, but before 12 o'clock in the middle of the night *Opening hours: 9 a.m. - 6 p.m.*

PM /ˌpiːˈem/ *noun* [C] *abbreviation for* prime minister: the leader of an elected government in some countries

pneumatic /njuːˈmætɪk/ *adjective* filled with air, or operated using air *pneumatic tyres*

pneumonia /njuːˈməʊniə/ *noun* [U] a serious illness in which your lungs fill with liquid and it is difficult to breathe

poach /pəʊtʃ/ *verb* **1** COOK [T] to cook something, especially an egg without its shell, by putting it into liquid that is gently boiling **2** ANIMALS [I, T] to illegally catch or kill animals, especially by going onto land without the permission of the person who owns it **3** PERSON [I, T] to persuade someone to leave a company or team in order to work or play for yours *They can poach experienced people easily because they offer higher salaries.*

poacher /ˈpəʊtʃər/ *noun* [C] someone who illegally catches or kills animals

o-m**pocket¹** /ˈpɒkɪt/ *noun* [C]

pocket

1 BAG a small bag that is sewn or fixed onto or into a piece of clothing, a bag, the back of a seat, etc *a coat/ shirt/trouser pocket* ○ *He was asked to empty his pockets.* ○ *Safety instructions are in the pocket on the seat in front of you.* **2** SMALL AREA/AMOUNT a small area or small amount of something that is different from what is around it *There was real poverty in some pockets of the country.* ○ *small pockets of air trapped inside the glass* **3** MONEY the amount of money that you have for spending *I shouldn't have to pay for travel out of my own pocket* (= with my own money). **4 be out of pocket** to have less money than you should have because you have paid for something *The holiday company cancelled our trip and we were left hundreds of pounds out of pocket.*

pocket² /ˈpɒkɪt/ *verb* [T] **1** to take something, especially money, which does not belong to you *His plan was to pocket the money from the sale of the business and leave the country.* **2** to put something in your pocket *Juan pocketed the knife and walked away.*

pocket³ /ˈpɒkɪt/ *adjective* [always before noun] small enough to fit in your pocket *a pocket dictionary*

pocketbook /ˈpɒkɪtbʊk/ *noun* [C] *US* **1** a woman's bag **2** Someone's pocketbook is their ability to pay for something. *The sales tax hits consumers in the pocketbook.*

pocketful /ˈpɒkɪtfʊl/ *noun* [C] the amount you can fit in a pocket *a pocketful of coins*

pocketknife /ˈpɒkɪtnaɪf/ *noun* [C] *plural* pocketknives a small knife that folds into a case

ˈpocket ˌmoney *noun* [U] an amount of money given regularly to a child by its parents

pod /pɒd/ *noun* [C] the long, flat part of some plants that has seeds in it *a pea pod*

podcast /ˈpɒdkɑːst/ *noun* [C] a recording that you can listen to on your computer or MP3

player from a website. You can also sign up to (= say that you want to receive) a podcast which is then updated (= new information is added to it) through the Internet when you plug your MP3 player into a computer

podiatrist /pəʊˈdaɪətrɪst/ *US* (*UK* **chiropodist**) *noun* [C] someone whose job is to treat problems with people's feet

podium /ˈpəʊdiəm/ *noun* [C] a small, raised area, sometimes with a tall table on it, that someone stands on when they are performing or speaking

WORD PARTNERS FOR *poem*

read/recite/write a poem ● in a poem ● a poem **about** sth ● a poem **by** sb ● a **love** poem

o-m**poem** /ˈpəʊɪm/ *noun* [C] a piece of writing, especially one that has short lines and uses words that sound the same *love/war poems*

poet /ˈpəʊɪt/ *noun* [C] someone who writes poems

poetic /pəʊˈetɪk/ *adjective* **1** Something that is poetic makes you feel strong emotions because it is so beautiful. *To him, life seemed poetic.* **2** relating to poetry *poetic language*

o-m**poetry** /ˈpəʊɪtri/ *noun* [U] poems in general, or the writing of poetry *I enjoy all kinds of poetry, especially love poetry.*

poignant /ˈpɔɪnjənt/ *adjective* making you feel sad *It's a poignant story about a poor family's struggle to survive.* ● **poignancy** /ˈpɔɪnjənsi/ *noun* [U] when something is poignant ● **poignantly** *adverb*

WORD PARTNERS FOR *point*

illustrate/make/prove/raise a point ● take sb's point ● a point **about** sth

o-m**point¹** /pɔɪnt/ *noun* **1** OPINION [C] an opinion, idea, or fact which someone says or writes *Could I make a point about noise levels?* ○ *I take your point* (= I agree with you) *about cycling, but I still prefer to walk.* **2** IMPORTANT OPINION [no plural] an opinion or fact that deserves to be considered seriously, or which other people agree is true *"She's always complaining that the office is cold." "Well, she's got a point."* ○ *"How are we going to get there if there are no trains?" " Good point."* **3 the point** the most important part of what has been said or written *I thought he was never going to get to the point.* ○ *The point is, if you don't claim the money now you might never get it.* ○ *To say his art is simplistic is missing the point* (= not understanding the most important thing about it). **4** SHARP [C] the thin, sharp end of something *the point of a needle* **5** PLACE [C] a particular place *a stopping/fuelling point* ○ *the point where the pipes enter the building* **6** TIME [C] a particular time in an event or process *At this point, people started to leave.* ○ *It has got to the point where I can hardly bear to speak to him.* **7 be at/on the point of doing sth** to be going to do something very soon *Amy was on the point of crying.* **8** REASON [no plural] the reason for or purpose of something *What's the point of studying if you can't get a job after-*

P

wards? ○ There's **no point** inviting her - she never comes to parties. **9 beside the point** not important or not connected with what you are talking about *The fact that he doesn't want to come is beside the point - he should have been invited.* **10 make a point of doing sth** to be certain that you always do a particular thing *He made a point of learning all the names of his staff.* **11 to the point** If something someone says or writes is to the point, it expresses the most important things without extra details. *His report was short and to the point.* **12 up to a point** partly *What he says is true up to a point.* **13** GAME [C] a unit used for showing who is winning in a game or competition *With 3 games still to play, Manchester United are 5 points ahead.* **14** MEASUREMENT [C] a unit used in some systems of measuring and comparing things *The stock exchange fell by five points.* **15 boiling/freezing/melting point** the temperature at which a substance boils, freezes, or melts **16** QUALITY [C] a quality which someone has *I know she's bossy, but she has lots of good points too.* ○ *Chemistry never was my strong point* (= I was never good at it). **17** MATHEMATICS [C] (*also* **decimal point**) the mark (.) that is used to separate the two parts of a decimal *One mile equals one point six* (= 1.6) *kilometres.* **18** DIRECTION [C] one of the marks on a compass (= object used for showing directions) ⊃See also: breaking point, a case in point, decimal point, focal point, moot point, point of view, starting-point, turning point, vantage point.

point

A **point** (.) is used to separate a whole number from a fraction (= number less than 1).
Normal body temperature is 36.9° celsius.

A **comma** (,) is used to divide large numbers into groups of three so that they are easier to read.

28,071,973

1,378

⚬**point²** /pɔɪnt/ *verb* **1** SHOW [I] to show where someone or something is by holding your finger or an object towards it *She pointed at/to a bird flying overhead.* **2** AIM [T] to hold something so that it faces towards something else *She pointed her camera at them.* **3** FACE [I] to face towards a particular direction *The solar panels were pointing away from the sun.*

point sb/sth out to make a person notice someone or something *I didn't think about the disadvantages until you pointed them out to me.*

point sth out to tell someone a fact *If he makes a mistake I always think it's best to point it out immediately.*

point to/towards sth to show that something probably exists, is happening, or is true *All the evidence points to suicide.*

point-blank /ˌpɔɪntˈblæŋk/ *adjective, adverb* **1** If you refuse point-blank, you refuse completely and will not change your decision. **2 at point-blank range** If someone is shot at point-blank range, they are shot from a very short distance away.

pointed /'pɔɪntɪd/ *adjective* **1** If someone says something in a pointed way, they intend to criticize someone. *He made some pointed references to her history of drug problems.* **2** A pointed object has a thin, sharp end. *a pointed chin/beard*

pointer /'pɔɪntə'/ *noun* [C] **1** a piece of information which can help you understand a situation or do something better *I asked for some pointers on applying for jobs.* **2** an object that you use to point at something

pointless /'pɔɪntləs/ *adjective* Something that is pointless has no purpose. *pointless arguments/conflict* ○ [+ to do sth] *It would be pointless to argue with him.* ● **pointlessly** *adverb*

from sb's point of view ● **from** a [political/financial, etc] point of view

‚point of 'view *noun* [C] *plural* **points of view** **1** a way of thinking about a situation *From a medical point of view, there was no need for the operation.* **2** an opinion *You have to be willing to see other people's points of view.* ○ *I can certainly see her point of view.*

point of view or opinion?

When you want to talk about your own opinion, you should say **In my opinion ...**, not 'In my point of view'.

poise /pɔɪz/ *noun* [U] **1** when you behave in a calm and confident way *Recovering his poise, he congratulated his opponent.* **2** when you move or stand in a careful, pleasant way *Ballet is said to give a child poise.*

poised /pɔɪzd/ *adjective* **1** READY [never before noun] ready to do something [+ to do sth] *They have three hundred ships, all poised to attack.* **2** POSITION [never before noun] in a particular position or situation, ready to move or change *a helicopter poised above the crowd* **3** CALM calm and confident *a poised performance*

poison¹ /'pɔɪzᵊn/ *noun* [C, U] a substance that can make you ill or kill you if you eat or drink it *Someone had put poison in her drink.*

poison² /'pɔɪzᵊn/ *verb* [T] **1** KILL to try to kill someone by giving them a dangerous substance to drink or eat *He tried to poison his wife.* **2** MAKE DANGEROUS to put poison or a dangerous substance in something *They poisoned the city's water supply.* **3** SPOIL to make something very unpleasant *These arguments were poisoning his life.* **4 poison sb's mind** to make someone think bad things about someone or something *Her father had poisoned her mind against me.* ● **poisoned** *adjective*

poisoning /'pɔɪzᵊnɪŋ/ *noun* [U] an illness caused by eating, drinking, or breathing a dangerous substance *alcohol/lead poisoning* ⊃See also: food poisoning.

poisonous /'pɔɪzᵊnəs/ *adjective* **1** containing poison *poisonous gas* **2** A poisonous animal uses poison in order to defend itself. *a poisonous snake*

poke

She poked her head
out of the window.

She poked him.

poke¹ /pəʊk/ *verb* **1** [T] to quickly push your
finger or other pointed object into someone or
something *Nell kept poking me in the arm.*
○ *He poked the fire with his stick.* **2 poke (sth)
round/out/through, etc** to appear through or
from behind something, or to make something
do this *Grace poked her head round the door.*
⊃See also: poke/stick your nose¹ into sth.

poke about/around *informal* to look for
something by moving other things *I was
poking around in the garage, looking for a
paint brush.*

poke² /pəʊk/ *noun* [C] when you quickly push
your finger or other pointed object into someone or something *I gave him a poke in the
back.*

poker /ˈpəʊkəʳ/ *noun* **1** [U] a game played with
cards in which people try to win money from
each other **2** [C] a long, metal stick used for
moving the coal or wood in a fire so that it
burns better

poker-faced /ˈpəʊkəˌfeɪst/ *adjective* not showing on your face what you are really thinking
or feeling

poky *informal* (*also* **pokey**) /ˈpəʊki/ *adjective* **1** A
room or house that is poky is unpleasant be-
cause it is too small. **2** *US* too slow

polar /ˈpəʊləʳ/ *adjective* relating to the North or
South Pole

polar ˈbear *UK* (*US* **ˈpolar ˌbear**) *noun* [C] a
large, white bear that lives in the North Pole
(= most northern part of the Earth)

Polaroid /ˈpəʊlərɔɪd/ *noun* [C] *trademark* a
camera that prints a photograph immediately
after you have taken it, or a picture taken with
this type of camera

pole /pəʊl/ *noun* **1** [C] a long, thin stick made of
wood or metal, often used to hold something
up *tent poles* **2 the North/South Pole** the part of
the Earth that is furthest North/South **3 be
poles apart** to be complete opposites

polemic /pəˈlemɪk/ *noun* [C, U] *formal* writing or
speech that strongly criticizes or defends an
idea, a belief, etc

ˈpole ˌvault *noun* [no plural] a sport in which

you use a very long stick to jump over a high
bar

ᵒ⁼**police¹** /pəˈliːs/ *noun* [plural] the official organization that makes people obey the law and
that protects people and places against crime,
or the people who work for this organization *I
heard a gun shot and decided to call the
police.* ○ *A 30-year-old taxi driver is being
interviewed by police.* ○ *a police investigation*

police² /pəˈliːs/ *verb* [T] to make sure that people
obey the law in a particular place or when
they are doing a particular activity *Clubs have
to pay for the cost of policing matches.*

poˌlice ˈconstable *noun* [C] in the UK, a
police officer of the lowest rank

poˈlice deˌpartment *noun* [C] in the US, the
police force in an area or city

poˈlice ˌforce *noun* [C] the police in a country
or area

policeman, policewoman /pəˈliːsmən,
pəˈliːsˌwʊmən/ *noun* [C] *plural* **policemen** or **police-
women** a man/woman who is a member of the
police

poˈlice ˌofficer *noun* [C] someone who is a
member of the police

poˌlice ˈstate *UK* (*US* **poˈlice ˌstate**) *noun* [C] a
country in which the people are not free to do
what they want because the government controls them

poˈlice ˌstation *noun* [C] the office of the
police in a town or part of a city

policy /ˈpɒləsi/ *noun* **1** [C, U] a set of ideas or a
plan of what to do in particular situations that
has been agreed by a government, business,
etc *foreign policy* ○ *It is company policy to
help staff progress in their careers.* **2** [C] an
agreement that you have with an insurance
company (= company that pays the costs if you
are injured, etc)

polio /ˈpəʊliəʊ/ *noun* [U] a serious disease that
sometimes makes it impossible for you to
move your muscles

polish¹ /ˈpɒlɪʃ/ *noun* **1** [C, U] a substance that
you rub on something in order to make it clean
and shiny **2** [no plural] when you rub
something in order to make it clean and shiny
Just give the table a polish. ⊃See also: nail polish.

polish² /ˈpɒlɪʃ/ *verb* [T] to rub something with a
cloth in order to make it clean or to make it
shine *to polish your shoes*

polish sth off *informal* to finish something
quickly *I gave him a bowl of ice cream which
he soon polished off.*

polished /ˈpɒlɪʃt/ *adjective* **1** clean and shiny
after polishing *a polished floor* **2** done with

P

skill and style *He gave a highly **polished** performance.*

The adjectives **courteous**, **respectful**, and **well-mannered** are sometimes used when someone is polite and shows respect for other people: *Although she often disagreed with me, she was always **courteous**.* • *They were quiet, **well-mannered** children.*

A man who is polite to a woman is sometimes described as **chivalrous**: *He held open the door in that **chivalrous** way of his.*

The expression **politically-correct** and its abbreviation, **PC**, are regularly used to show that someone is being polite by speaking in a way which does not offend women, people of a particular race, or people who have physical or mental problems: *'Fireman' has been replaced by the **politically-correct** term 'firefighter'.* • *Calling them 'ladies' - that's not very **PC** of you!*

Conversation which is polite and calm is sometimes described as **civilized**: *Let's discuss this in a **civilized** manner.*

☛**polite** /pəˈlaɪt/ *adjective* behaving in a way that is not rude and shows that you do not only think about yourself *She was too polite to point out my mistake.* • **politely** *adverb He thanked them politely.* • **politeness** *noun* [U]

☛**political** /pəˈlɪtɪkᵊl/ *adjective* relating to or involved in politics *There are two main **political parties** in my country.* ○ *The church has a strong political influence.* • **politically** *adverb*

po,litical a'sylum *noun* [U] protection given by a government to someone whose political activities have made it too dangerous for them to live in their own country

po,litically co'rrect *adjective* careful to speak or behave in a way which is not offensive to women, people of a particular race, or people who have physical or mental problems *It's not politically correct to call women 'girls'.* • **political correctness** *noun* [U]

po,litical 'prisoner *noun* [C] someone who is in prison because their political activities or opinions oppose the government

☛**politician** /ˌpɒlɪˈtɪʃᵊn/ *noun* [C] someone who works in politics, especially a member of the government

politicize (*also UK* **-ise**) /pəˈlɪtɪsaɪz/ *verb* [T] to make something or someone more involved with politics [often passive] *The whole issue has been politicized.* ○ *a highly politicized debate*

WORD PARTNERS FOR *politics*

enter/go into/be involved in politics • **domestic /international/local** politics

☛**politics** /ˈpɒlətɪks/ *noun* **1** ACTIVITIES [U] ideas and activities relating to how a country or area is governed *He has little interest in local politics.* **2** JOB [U] a job in politics *She's planning to retire from politics next year.* **3** *sb's* **politics** someone's opinions about how a country or area should be governed *I don't know what his politics are, but he strongly disagreed with the decision.* **4** RELATIONSHIPS [plural] the relationships in a group which allow particular people to have power over others *I try not to get involved in **office politics**.*

polka /ˈpɒlkə/ *noun* [C] a type of dance, or a piece of music used for this type of dance

polka-dot /ˈpɒlkəˌdɒt/ *adjective* [always before noun] having a regular pattern of small, round spots *a polka-dot bikini*

WORD PARTNERS FOR *poll*

carry out/conduct a poll • a poll **indicates/reveals/shows/suggests** sth • a poll **of** sb

poll[1] /pəʊl/ (*also* **opinion poll**) *noun* [C] when people are asked questions to discover what they think about a subject *A recent **poll indicated** that 77 percent of Americans supported the president.*

poll[2] /pəʊl/ *verb* [T] **1** to ask someone's opinion as part of a study on what people think about a subject [often passive] *Most students polled said they preferred the new system.* **2** to receive a particular number of votes in an election *Labour polled only 45 percent of the Scottish vote.*

pollen /ˈpɒlən/ *noun* [U] a powder produced by flowers, which is carried by insects or the wind and makes other flowers produce seeds

'pollen ,count *noun* [C] the measurement of the amount of pollen in the air

'polling ,day *UK* (*US* **election day**) *noun* [C] the day when people vote in an election

'polling ,station *UK* (*US* **'polling ,place**) *noun* [C] a building where people go to vote in an election

the polls /pəʊlz/ *noun* [plural] voting in an election *The country will **go to the polls** (= vote) on 13 September.*

pollster /ˈpəʊlstəʳ/ *noun* [C] someone who tries to discover what most people think about a subject by asking questions

pollute /pəˈluːt/ *verb* [T] to make water, air, soil, etc dirty or harmful *We need a fuel that won't pollute the environment.* • **pollutant** *noun* [C] a substance that pollutes water, air, etc

pollution /pəˈluːʃᵊn/ *noun* [U] damage caused to water, air, etc by harmful substances or waste *The book shows simple things you can do to reduce pollution from your car.*

polo /ˈpəʊləʊ/ *noun* [U] a game played between two teams who ride horses and hit a ball with long, wooden hammers

'polo ,neck *UK* (*US* **turtleneck**) *noun* [C] a piece of clothing that covers the top part of the body and has a tube-like part covering the neck *a black polo neck sweater*

polo neck

polo neck *UK*, turtleneck *US*

'polo ,shirt *noun* [C] a cotton shirt with

short sleeves, a collar, and buttons at the front

poly- /ppli-/ *prefix* many *polygamy* (= having more than one husabnd or wife at the same time) ○ *a polygon* (= a shape with many sides)

polyester /,ppli'estə^r/ *noun* [U] a type of artificial cloth used for making clothes *a polyester shirt/skirt*

polystyrene /,ppli'stairi:n/ UK (US Styrofoam®) *noun* [U] a light plastic material that is wrapped around delicate objects to protect them, and around hot things to keep them hot *polystyrene packaging/polystyrene cups*

polytechnic /,ppli'teknik/ *noun* [C] a college where students study scientific and technical subjects

polythene /'ppliθi:n/ UK (US **polyethylene** /,ppli'eθəli:n/) *noun* [U] a thin, soft, plastic often used for making bags

pomp /ppmp/ *noun* [U] *formal* special clothes, decorations, and music at an official ceremony

pompous /'ppmpəs/ *adjective* Someone who is pompous is too serious and thinks they are more important than they really are. *He had a very pompous way of talking.* ● **pompously** *adverb* ● **pomposity** /ppm'ppsəti/ *noun* [U] when someone is pompous

pond /ppnd/ *noun* [C] a small area of water, especially one that has been made artificially in a park or garden

ponder /'ppndə^r/ *verb* [I, T] *literary* to think carefully about something [+ question word] *He pondered what might have happened if he hadn't gone home.*

ponderous /'ppnd^ərəs/ *adjective* **1** Ponderous speech or writing is boring or too serious. *I find his prose rather ponderous.* **2** slow because of being very heavy or large *His gait was slow and ponderous.* ● **ponderously** *adverb*

pony /'pəʊni/ *noun* [C] a small horse

ponytail /'pəʊniteɪl/ *noun* [C] hair tied at the back of your head so that it hangs down like a horse's tail

ponytail

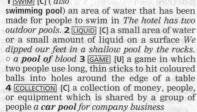

poodle /'pu:dl/ *noun* [C] a type of dog with thick, curly hair

pool¹ /pu:l/ *noun* **1** [SWIM] [C] (*also* **swimming pool**) an area of water that has been made for people to swim in *The hotel has two outdoor pools.* **2** [LIQUID] [C] a small area of water or a small amount of liquid on a surface *We dipped our feet in a shallow pool by the rocks.* ○ *a **pool** of blood* **3** [GAME] [U] a game in which two people use long, thin sticks to hit coloured balls into holes around the edge of a table **4** [COLLECTION] [C] a collection of money, people, or equipment which is shared by a group of people *a car pool for company business*

pool² /pu:l/ *verb* [T] If a group of people pool their money, knowledge, or equipment, they collect it together so that it can be shared or used for a particular purpose. *Several villages*

pooled their resources to set up a building project.

the pools /pu:lz/ *noun* [plural] in Britain, a game in which people try to win a lot of money by guessing the results of football matches

o-**poor** /pɔː^r/ Ⓤ /pur/ *adjective* **1** [NO MONEY] having very little money or few possessions *Most of these people are desperately poor.* ○ *Modern fertilizers are too expensive for poorer countries to afford.* ○ *housing for the poor* **2** [BAD] of very low quality *poor health* ○ *Last year's exam results were poor.* ○ *a poor harvest* ○ *The meeting went smoothly but attendance was poor* (= not many people came). **3** [NO SKILL] not having much skill at a particular activity *She's always been poor at spelling.* **4** [SYMPATHY] [always before noun] used to show sympathy for someone *That cold sounds terrible, you **poor** thing.* **5 be poor in sth** If something is poor in a particular substance, it has very little of the substance. *Avoid foods which are high in calories but poor in nutrients.*

poorly¹ /'pɔːli/ *adverb* badly *poorly educated*

poorly² /'pɔːli/ *adjective* UK *informal* ill *Rosie was feeling poorly so I put her to bed.*

pop¹ /ppp/ *verb* popping, past popped **1** [I, T] to make a short sound like a small explosion, or to make something do this by breaking it *The music played and champagne corks popped.* **2 pop in/out/over, etc** *informal* to go to a particular place *Doug's just popped out for a few minutes.* ○ *I'll pop into the supermarket on my way home.* **3 pop sth in/into/on, etc** *informal* to quickly put something in a particular place *Can you pop the pizza in the oven?* **4 pop out/up** to move quickly and suddenly, especially out of something

pop up *informal* to suddenly appear or happen, often unexpectedly *A message just popped up on my screen.*

pop² /ppp/ *noun* **1** [MUSIC] [U] (*also* 'pop ,music) modern music with a strong beat which is popular with young people **2** [SOUND] [C] a short sound like a small explosion **3** [DRINK] [U] *informal* (*also* US **soda**) a sweet drink with bubbles **4** [FATHER] [no plural] US *informal* father

popcorn /'pppkɔ:n/ *noun* [U] yellow seeds of grain that break open when heated and are eaten with salt, sugar, or butter

Pope /pəʊp/ *noun* [C] the leader of the Roman Catholic Church *Pope John Paul II* ○ *The Pope was due to visit Paraguay in May.*

poplar /'ppplə^r/ *noun* [C, U] a tall tree with branches that grow up to form a thin, pointed shape

popper /'pppə^r/ *noun* [C] UK (US **snap**) a metal or plastic object used to fasten clothing, made of two parts which fit together with a short, loud sound

poppy /'pppi/ *noun* [C] a red flower with small, black seeds

populace /'pppjələs/ *noun* [group] *formal* all the people who live in a particular country or place

o-**popular** /'pppjələ^r/ *adjective* **1** [LIKED] liked by many people *'Jack' was the most popular boy's name.* ○ *The North African coast is becoming*

P

*increasingly **popular with** British tourists.* ⊃Opposite **unpopular. 2** GENERAL [always before noun] for or involving ordinary people and not specialists or people who are very educated *The issue was given full coverage in the popular press.* **3** MANY PEOPLE [always before noun] A popular belief, opinion, etc is one that many people have. *The allegations are false, contrary to **popular belief**.*

WORD PARTNERS FOR **popularity**

gain popularity • be **growing in/increasing in** popularity • sb's/sth's popularity **increases/soars/wanes** • the popularity of sth • sb/sth's popularity **with** sb

popularity /ˌpɒpjəˈlærəti/ *noun* [U] the quality of being liked by many people *the increasing popularity of organic produce* ⊃Opposite **unpopularity.**

popularize (*also* UK **-ise**) /ˈpɒpjəlᵊraɪz/ *verb* [T] to make something become known or liked by many people *It was the World Cup which popularized professional soccer in the United States.* • **popularization** /ˌpɒpjəlᵊraɪˈzeɪʃᵊn/ *noun* [U]

popularly /ˈpɒpjələli/ *adverb* **popularly believed/called/known, etc** believed, called, etc by most people *Los Angeles is popularly known as 'LA'.*

populate /ˈpɒpjəleɪt/ *verb* **be populated** If an area is populated by people or animals, they live in that area. *The countryside is **densely/sparsely populated** (= there are many/few people). ○ The forest was populated by rare and colourful birds.*

WORD PARTNERS FOR **population**

have a population **of** [50 million, etc] • population **growth**

population /ˌpɒpjəˈleɪʃᵊn/ *noun* **1** [C, U] the number of people living in a particular area *What's the **population** of Brazil?* **2** [group] all the people living in a particular area, or all the people or animals of a particular type *a 9% rise in the prison population*

populous /ˈpɒpjələs/ *adjective formal* A populous area has a lot of people living in it. *It's one of the world's most populous cities.*

pop-up /ˈpɒpʌp/ *adjective* [always before noun] **1** A pop-up book is a book which has pictures that stand up from the pages when the book is opened. **2** A pop-up menu is a list of choices on a computer screen which is hidden until you choose to look at it. *Select the option you want from the **pop-up menu**.*

porcelain /ˈpɔːsᵊlɪn/ *noun* [U] a hard, shiny, white substance used to make cups, plates, etc, or the cups and plates themselves *a porcelain dish ○ a fine collection of porcelain*

porch /pɔːtʃ/ *noun* [C] a covered area built onto the entrance to a house

pore¹ /pɔːʳ/ *noun* [C] a very small hole in your skin that sweat (= salty liquid) can pass through

pore² /pɔːʳ/ *verb*
pore over sth to study or look carefully at

something, especially a book or document *Jeremy spent the afternoon poring over his exam notes.*

pork /pɔːk/ *noun* [U] meat from a pig *pork chops*

pornography /pɔːˈnɒgrəfi/ (*also* **porn** *informal*) *noun* [U] magazines and films showing naked people or sexual acts that are intended to make people feel sexually excited • **pornographic** /ˌpɔːnəˈgræfɪk/ *adjective* relating to pornography *pornographic images/videos*

porous /ˈpɔːrəs/ *adjective* allowing liquid or air to pass through *porous rock*

porridge /ˈpɒrɪdʒ/ *noun* [U] a soft, white food made of oats (= type of grain) and water or milk

port /pɔːt/ *noun* **1** SHIPS [C] a town or an area of a town next to water where ships arrive and leave from *a fishing port ○ the Belgian port of Zeebrugge* **2** DRINK [U] a sweet, strong, red wine which is made in Portugal **3** LEFT [U] the left side of a ship or aircraft *the port side*

portable /ˈpɔːtəbl/ *adjective* able to be carried *a portable computer*

portal /ˈpɔːtᵊl/ *noun* [C] a page on the Internet that people use to start searching the World Wide Web

porter /ˈpɔːtəʳ/ *noun* [C] someone whose job is to carry other people's bags in hotels, stations, etc

portfolio /ˌpɔːtˈfəʊliəʊ/ *noun* [C] **1** a collection of designs, pictures, documents, etc that represents a person's work, or the large, flat container that it is carried in **2** a collection of accounts, money, etc that is owned by a person or organization *a stock portfolio*

porthole /ˈpɔːthəʊl/ *noun* [C] a small, round window in the side of a ship or aircraft

portion /ˈpɔːʃᵊn/ *noun* [C] **1** a part of something *A large portion of their profits go straight back into new projects.* **2** the amount of food served to one person, especially in a restaurant

portly /ˈpɔːtli/ *adjective humorous* quite fat *a portly gentleman*

portrait /ˈpɔːtrɪt/ *noun* **1** [C] a painting, drawing, or photograph of someone *a **portrait of** the princess ○ a portrait gallery/painter* **2** a **portrait of sb/sth** a film or book which describes someone or something in detail *His latest film is a portrait of life in the 1920s.* ⊃See also: **self-portrait.**

portray /pɔːˈtreɪ/ *verb* [T] **1** If a book or film portrays someone or something, it describes or shows them. *Both novels portray the lives of professional athletes. ○ In the film he's **portrayed as** a hero.* **2** to act the part of a character in a film or play • **portrayal** *noun* [C, U] when you portray someone or something *He won several awards for his portrayal of the dictator.*

pose¹ /pəʊz/ *verb* **1 pose a danger/problem/threat, etc** to cause a problem *A lot of these chemicals pose very real threats to our health.* **2** [I] to stay in a particular position so that someone can paint or photograph you *The two leaders **posed for** photographs outside the White House.* **3** [I] *mainly UK* to try to make people notice and admire you, especially by looking fashionable *Pascal was posing in his new sunglasses.* **4 pose a question** *formal* to ask a question

pose as sb to pretend that you are someone else *He got into her house by posing as an electrician.*

pose² /pəʊz/ *noun* **1** [C] the position that you stay in while someone photographs or paints you *an elegant pose* **2** [no plural] when someone pretends to be more clever or interesting than they really are *She's not really interested in art, it's just a pose.*

posh /pɒʃ/ *adjective* **1** expensive and used or owned by rich people *a posh hotel/restaurant* **2** *UK* from a high social class *a posh voice*

o─**position¹** /pə'zɪʃ³n/ *noun* **1** [SITTING/STANDING] [C, U] the way someone is sitting, standing, or lying, or if something is pointing up or down, etc *a kneeling position* ○ *I go to sleep on my back but I always wake up in a different position.* ○ *Make sure your chair is in the upright position.* **2** [SITUATION] [C] the situation that someone is in [usually singular] *She's in a very difficult position.* **3 be in a position to do sth** to be able to do something because of your situation *I'm not in a position to talk about this at the moment.* **4** [PLACE] [C] the place where someone or something is *You're in a good position next to the window.* **5 be in position** If someone or something is in position, they are in the place that they should be in. **6 in first/second/third, etc position** in first/second/third, etc place in a race or other competition *She finished the race in third position.* **7** [JOB] [C] *formal* a job *to apply for a position in a company* **8** [OPINION] [C] *formal* a way of thinking about a subject *What's the company's position on recycling?* **9** [GAME] [C] the part that someone plays in a game such as football *What position does he play?* **10** [IMPORTANCE] [C] your level of importance in society *the position of women in society*

position² /pə'zɪʃ³n/ *verb* [T] to put someone or something in a place for a reason [often reflexive] *I positioned myself as far away from her as possible.*

o─**positive** /'pɒzətɪv/ *adjective* **1** [HAPPY] feeling happy about your life and your future *a positive attitude* ○ *I'm feeling much more positive about things now.* **2** [ENCOURAGING] Something that is positive makes you feel better about a situation. *We've shown people samples of the product and had a very positive response.* **3** [CERTAIN] [never before noun] certain that something is true *"Are you sure you saw him?" "Absolutely positive."* ○ [+ (that)] *I'm positive that I switched it off.* **4** [PROOF] [always before noun] showing without any doubt that something is true *positive proof* **5** [MEDICAL TEST] If a medical test is positive, it shows that the person being tested has a disease or condition. *She did a pregnancy test and it was positive.* **6** [NUMBER] In mathematics, a positive number is greater than zero. **7 positive charge** the electrical charge that is carried by protons (= parts of atoms)

positively /'pɒzətɪvli/ *adverb* **1** in a good way

that makes you feel happier *Most children respond positively to praise and encouragement.* **2** used to emphasize something that you say, especially when it is surprising *Our waiter was positively rude.*

possess /pə'zes/ *verb* **1** [T] *formal* to have or own something *He was found guilty of possessing an illegal weapon.* **2 what possessed her/ him/you, etc?** something that you say when someone has done something stupid [+ to do sth] *What possessed you to tell him?*

possessed /pə'zest/ *adjective* controlled by evil spirits

possession /pə'zeʃ³n/ *noun* **1** [C] a thing that you own [usually plural] *personal possessions* ○ *He woke up to discover that all his possessions had been stolen.* **2** [U] *formal* when you have or own something *I have in my possession a photograph which may be of interest to you.* ○ *He was caught in possession of explosives.*

possessive /pə'zesɪv/ *adjective* **1** wanting someone to love and spend time with you and no one else **2** In grammar, a possessive word or form of a word shows who or what something belongs to. For example the words 'mine' and 'yours' are possessive pronouns.

o─**possibility** /ˌpɒsə'bɪləti/ *noun* **1** [C, U] a chance that something may happen or be true *Is there any possibility of changing this ticket?* ○ [+ (that)] *There is a strong possibility that she was lying.* **2** [C] something that you can choose to do *Have you considered the possibility of flying?* ⊃Opposite **impossibility**.

COMMON LEARNER ERROR

possibility, occasion, or **opportunity**?

A **possibility** is a chance that something may happen or be true. **Possibility** cannot be followed by an infinitive.

Is there a possibility of finding a cure for AIDS?

~~Is there a possibility to find a cure for AIDS?~~

An **occasion** is an event, or a time when something happens. **Occasion** does not mean 'chance' or 'opportunity'.

Birthdays are always special occasions.

An **opportunity** is a possibility of doing something, or a situation which gives you the possibility of doing something.

The trip to Paris gave me an opportunity to speak French.

Students had the opportunity to ask questions during the lecture.

I have more opportunity to travel than my parents did.

~~I have more possibility to travel than my parents did.~~

ᵒ⁼**possible** /ˈpɒsəbl/ *adjective* **1** If something is possible, it can happen or be done. [+ to do sth] *The operation will make it possible for her to walk without crutches.* ○ *I'll send it today, if possible.* ⊃Opposite **impossible**. **2** If something is possible, it might or might not exist or be true. *possible safety problems* ○ [+ (that)] *It's possible that the tapes were stolen.* **3 as much/quickly/soon, etc as possible** as much/quickly/soon, etc as something can happen or be done *I'll go as soon as possible.* **4 the best/cheapest/worst, etc possible** the best/cheapest/worst, etc that can happen or exist *the shortest possible time*

ᵒ⁼**possibly** /ˈpɒsəbli/ *adverb* **1** NOT CERTAIN used when something is not certain *Someone, possibly Tom, had left the window open.* **2** EMPHASIS used with 'can' or 'could' for emphasis *We'll do everything we possibly can to help.* ○ *I couldn't possibly ask you to do that.* **3** QUESTIONS used in polite questions *Could I possibly borrow your bike?*

ᵒ⁼**post¹** /pəʊst/ *noun* **1** SYSTEM [no plural] *UK* (*US* mail) the system for sending letters, parcels, etc *Your letter is in the post.* ○ *I'm sending the documents by post.* **2** LETTERS [U] *UK* (*US* mail) letters, parcels, etc that you send or receive *Has the post arrived/come yet?* **3** JOB [C] *formal* a job *a part-time post* ○ *a teaching post* **4** POLE [C] a long, vertical piece of wood or metal fixed into the ground at one end *I found the dog tied to a post.* **5** PLACE [C] a place where someone stands to guard something

ᵒ⁼**post²** /pəʊst/ *verb* [T] **1** *UK* (*US* mail) to send a letter or parcel by post *Did you post my letter?* **2** to leave a message on a website *I posted a query about arthritis treatment.* **3 be posted to France/London/Singapore, etc** to be sent to France/London/Singapore, etc to work, usually for the government or army **4 post a notice/sign, etc** to put a notice/sign, etc somewhere *He posted the message on the noticeboard.* **5 keep sb posted** to make certain that someone always knows what is happening *Keep me posted on anything that happens while I'm away.*

postage /ˈpəʊstɪdʒ/ *noun* [U] money that you pay to send a letter or parcel *first-class postage* ○ *postage and packing*

ˌ**postage and ˈpacking** (*US* ˌshipping and ˈhandling) *noun* [U] money that you pay so that a company will send you something through the post

ˈ**postage ˌstamp** *noun* [C] *formal* a small, official piece of paper that you buy and stick onto a letter or parcel before you post it

postal /ˈpəʊstəl/ *adjective* [always before noun] relating to the system of sending letters and parcels *the postal service/system*

ˈ**postal ˌorder** *UK* (*US* **money order**) *noun* [C] an official piece of paper bought at a post office that you can send instead of money

ˈ**post ˌbox** *UK* (*US* **mailbox**) *noun* [C] a large, metal container in a public place where you can post letters

postcard /ˈpəʊstkɑːd/ *noun* [C] a card with a picture on one side that you send without an envelope *Send me a postcard.*

postcode /ˈpəʊstkəʊd/ *noun* [C] a group of letters and numbers that comes at the end of someone's address in the UK ⊃Compare **zip code**.

poster /ˈpəʊstər/ *noun* [C] a large, printed picture or notice that you put on a wall, in order to decorate a place or to advertise something

posterity /pɒsˈterəti/ *noun* [U] the people who will be alive in the future *These works of art should be preserved for posterity.*

postgraduate /ˌpəʊstˈɡrædʒuət/ (*US* **graduate**) (**postgrad**) *noun* [C] a student who has one degree and now studies at a university for a more advanced degree ● **postgraduate** *adjective a postgraduate degree in mathematics*

posthumous /ˈpɒstjəməs/ *adjective* happening after someone's death *the posthumous publication of her letters* ● **posthumously** *adverb*

posting /ˈpəʊstɪŋ/ *noun* [C] *mainly UK* when you are sent to work in another place *a posting to Madrid*

Post-it (note) /ˈpəʊstɪtˌnəʊt/ *noun* [C] *trademark* a small piece of paper that you can write on and then stick to other papers or surfaces

postman /ˈpəʊstmən/ *UK* (*US* **mailman, letter carrier**) *noun* [C] *plural* **postmen** a man who takes and brings letters and parcels as a job

postmark /ˈpəʊstmɑːk/ *noun* [C] an official mark on a letter or parcel, showing the place and time it was sent

post-mortem /ˌpəʊstˈmɔːtəm/ *noun* [C] a medical examination of a dead body to find out why the person died

ˈ**post ˌoffice** *noun* [C] a place where you can buy stamps and send letters and parcels

postpone /pəʊstˈpəʊn/ *verb* [T] to arrange for something to happen at a later time *The trip to the museum has been postponed until next week.*

postscript /ˈpəʊstskrɪpt/ *noun* [C] extra information at the end of a letter or email, usually added after writing the letters 'PS'

posture /ˈpɒstʃər/ *noun* [U] the position of your back, shoulders, etc when you are standing or sitting *She has very good posture.*

postwar /ˈpəʊstwɔːr/ *adjective* happening or existing in the period after a war *postwar Europe*

pot¹ /pɒt/ *noun* **1** [C] a round container, usually used for storing things or cooking *a flower pot* ○ *a pot of coffee/tea* ○ *pots and pans* **2 go to pot** to be damaged or spoilt because no effort has been made *My diet's gone to pot since the holidays.* ⊃See also: **melting pot**.

pot² /pɒt/ *verb* [T] **potting** *past* **potted** to put a plant into a pot filled with soil

potassium /pəˈtæsiəm/ *noun* [U] a chemical element that combines easily with other elements, often used to help plants grow well

ᵒ⁼**potato** /pəˈteɪtəʊ/ *noun* [C, U] *plural* **potatoes** a round vegetable with a brown, yellow, or red skin that grows in the ground *boiled/fried potatoes* ○ *mashed potato* ⊃See colour picture **Fruit and Vegetables** on page Centre 10 ⊃See also: **couch potato, jacket potato, sweet potato**.

poˈtato ˌchip *US* (*UK* **crisp**) *noun* [C] a very thin, dry, fried slice of potato

potent /'pəʊtᵊnt/ *adjective* very powerful or very effective *a potent drug/weapon* ● **potency** /'pəʊtᵊnsi/ *noun* [U] when something is potent

potential¹ /pəʊ'tenʃᵊl/ *adjective* [always before noun] A potential problem, employer, partner, etc may become one in the future, although they are not one now. *a potential danger/threat* ○ *a potential customer* ○ *A number of potential buyers have expressed interest in the building.* ● **potentially** *adverb a potentially fatal condition*

WORD PARTNERS FOR *potential*

have [enormous/great, etc] potential ● achieve/fulfil/reach/realize your (full) potential ● see/spot sb's/sth's potential ● sb's/sth's potential as sth

potential² /pəʊ'tenʃᵊl/ *noun* 1 [U] qualities or abilities that may develop and allow someone or something to succeed *to achieve your full potential* 2 **potential for sth/doing sth** the possibility that something may happen *There is the potential for some really interesting research.*

pothole /'pɒthəʊl/ *noun* [C] a hole in the surface of a road

potted /'pɒtɪd/ *adjective* 1 planted in a container *potted plants/flowers* ○ *a potted palm* 2 **potted history/version, etc of sth** *UK* a story or report that has been changed to make it shorter and more simple *a potted version of Shakespeare*

potted 'plant (*also UK* 'pot ˌplant) *noun* [C] a plant that is grown in a container, and usually kept inside

potter¹ /'pɒtᵊr/ *noun* [C] a person who makes plates, bowls, etc from clay

potter² /'pɒtᵊr/ *verb*
potter about/around (sth) *mainly UK* to spend time in a pleasant, relaxed way, often doing small jobs in your house

pottery /'pɒtᵊri/ *noun* 1 OBJECTS [U] plates, bowls, etc that are made from clay 2 ACTIVITY [U] the activity of making plates, bowls, etc from clay 3 PLACE [C] a place where plates, bowls, etc made from clay are made or sold

potty¹ /'pɒti/ *noun* [C] a small toilet that young children use

potty² /'pɒti/ *adjective UK informal* crazy or stupid

pouch /paʊtʃ/ *noun* [C] 1 a small, soft bag made of leather or cloth 2 a pocket of skin in which some female animals carry their babies

poultry /'pəʊltri/ *noun* 1 [plural] chickens and other birds that people breed for meat and eggs 2 [U] the meat of chickens and other birds eaten as food

pounce /paʊns/ *verb* [I] to suddenly move towards a person or animal that you want to catch *The police were waiting to pounce when he arrived at the airport.*
pounce on sth/sb to immediately criticize a mistake

pound¹ /paʊnd/ *noun* [C] 1 the unit of money used in the UK and Ireland; £ *a hundred pounds/£100* ○ *a pound coin* 2 (*written abbrevi-*

ation lb) a unit for measuring weight, equal to 453.6 grams or 16 ounces *a pound of potatoes* ○ *The baby weighed just four pounds when she was born* ⊃See Extra help page **Measurements** on page Centre 31.

pound² /paʊnd/ *verb* 1 [I, T] to hit something many times using a lot of force *Someone was pounding on the door.* 2 [I] If your heart pounds, it beats very quickly. *My heart was pounding as I walked out onto the stage.* 3 **pound along/down/up, etc** to run somewhere with quick, loud steps *He pounded up the stairs.*

pour /pɔːr/ *verb* **pour**
1 LIQUID [T] to make a liquid flow from or into a container *I poured the milk into a jug.* ○ [+ two objects] *Can I pour you a drink?* 2 RAIN [I] (*also UK* pour down) to rain, producing a lot of water *We can't go out in this weather - it's pouring!* 3 **pour into/out/from, etc** a LIQUID to flow quickly and in large amounts *Blood was pouring from my leg.* b PEOPLE to enter or leave a place in large numbers *The crowd poured out into the street.*

pour sth out If you pour out your feelings or thoughts, you talk very honestly about what is making you sad. *She listened quietly while he poured out his troubles.*

pout /paʊt/ *verb* [I] to push your lips forward because you are annoyed or because you want to look sexually attractive ● **pout** *noun* [C]

WORD PARTNERS FOR *poverty*

die in/live in poverty ● alleviate/fight/tackle poverty ● abject/extreme poverty

poverty /'pɒvᵊti/ *noun* [U] when you are very poor *to live in poverty*

poverty-stricken /'pɒvᵊtiˌstrɪkᵊn/ *adjective* A poverty-stricken area or person is very poor.

POW /ˌpiːəʊ'dʌbljuː/ *noun* [C] *abbreviation for* prisoner of war: a soldier who is caught by enemy soldiers during a war

powder /'paʊdᵊr/ *noun* [C, U] a dry substance made of many small, loose grains *curry powder* ○ *face powder* ● **powdered** *adjective* in the form of a powder *powdered milk/sugar* ⊃See also: talcum powder.

WORD PARTNERS FOR *power*

come to / devolve / seize / take / wield power ● considerable/enormous power

power¹ /paʊᵊr/ *noun* 1 CONTROL [U] control or influence over people and events *He likes to have power over people.* 2 POLITICS [U] political control in a country *They have been in power too long.* ○ *When did this government come to power* (= start to control the country)? 3 ENERGY [U] energy, usually electricity, that is used to provide light, heat, etc *nuclear power* ○ *Turn off the power at the main switch.* 4 COUNTRY [C] a country that has a lot of influence over others *a major world power*

5 [OFFICIAL RIGHT] [C, U] an official or legal right to do something [+ to do sth] *It's not* ***in my power*** *to stop him publishing this book.* **6** [STRENGTH] [U] strength or force ***economic/military power*** **7** [ABILITY] [U] a natural ability *to lose the power of speech* **8 do everything in your power to do sth** to do everything that you are able and allowed to do *I've done everything in my power to help him.* **9 the powers that be** important people who have authority over others ⊃See also: **balance of power.**

power² /paʊəʳ/ *verb* [T] to supply energy to a machine and make it work [often passive] *The clock is powered by two small batteries.*

ˈpower ˌcut (*also US* **power outage**) *noun* [C] when the supply of electricity suddenly stops

powerful /ˈpaʊəfᵊl/ *adjective* **1** [CONTROL] A powerful person is able to control and influence people and events. *a powerful man/woman* **2** [STRENGTH] having a lot of strength or force *a powerful engine/weapon* **3** [EFFECT] having a strong effect on people *a* ***powerful effect/influence*** • **powerfully** *adverb*

powerless /ˈpaʊələs/ *adjective* not able to control events [+ to do sth] *The police were powerless to stop the fighting.*

power outage /ˈpaʊərˌaʊtɪdʒ/ *US* (*UK/US* **power cut**) *noun* [C] when the supply of electricity suddenly stops

ˈpower ˌstation (*also US* **ˈpower ˌplant**) *noun* [C] a place where electricity is produced

ˈpower ˌtool *noun* [C] a tool that uses electricity

pp *written abbreviation for* pages *See pp 10 - 12 for more information.*

P&P /ˌpiːᵊnˈpiː/ *noun* [U] *UK abbreviation for* postage and packing

PR /ˌpiːˈɑːʳ/ *noun* [U] *abbreviation for* public relations: writing and activities that are intended to make a person, company, or product more popular ***good/bad PR*** ○ ***a PR campaign***

practicable /ˈpræktɪkəbl/ *adjective formal* able to be done successfully *It's just not practicable to travel in this weather.*

practical¹ /ˈpræktɪkᵊl/ *adjective* **1** [REAL] relating to real situations or actions and not to thoughts or ideas ***practical experience*** ○ *They can offer* ***practical help.*** **2** [SUITABLE] suitable or useful for a situation which may involve some difficulty *practical clothes/shoes* ○ *Pale carpets just aren't practical if you have kids.* **3** [POSSIBLE] able to be done successfully *a* ***practical solution*** **4** [GOOD AT PLANNING] Someone who is practical is good at planning things and dealing with problems. *She has a lot of interesting ideas but she's not very practical.* **5** [GOOD WITH HANDS] good at repairing and making things

practical² /ˈpræktɪkᵊl/ *noun* [C] a lesson or examination in which you do or make something instead of only writing

practicalities /ˌpræktɪˈkælətiz/ *noun* [plural] real situations or facts *the* ***practicalities of*** *running your own business*

practicality /ˌpræktɪˈkæləti/ *noun* [U] **1** the possibility that something can be done successfully *I like the idea but I'm not sure about the practicality of it.* **2** how suitable or useful something is for a situation which may involve some difficulty

ˌpractical ˈjoke *noun* [C] a trick using actions and not words to make people laugh ***to play a practical joke*** *on someone*

practically /ˈpræktɪkᵊli/ *adverb* **1** almost *It's* ***practically impossible*** *to get there.* ○ *We see her practically every day.* **2** in a suitable or useful way *We need to think practically.*

practice /ˈpræktɪs/ *noun* **1** [REPEATING] [U] when you repeat an activity to improve your ability *We need a bit more practice before the concert.* ○ *I've got basketball practice tonight.* **2** [ACTIVITY] [C, U] what people do or how they do it ***business/working practices*** ○ [+ of + doing sth] *the* ***illegal practice*** *of copying CDs* ○ [+ to do sth] ***It is common practice*** *to bury waste in landfills.* **3** [WORK] [C] a business in which several doctors or lawyers work together, or the work that they do *a* ***legal/medical practice*** **4 in practice** If something is true in practice, this is the real situation. *In practice, the new laws have had little effect.* **5 be out of practice** to not do something well because you have not done it recently **6 put something into practice** to try a plan or idea *Next month we will have a chance to put these ideas into practice.*

COMMON LEARNER ERROR

practice or practise?

In British English, **practice** is used for the noun, and **practise** for the verb.

He needs more practice before he can sail on his own.

In US English, **practice** is used for the noun and the verb.

practise *UK* (*US* **practice**) /ˈpræktɪs/ *verb* **1** [REPEAT] [I, T] to repeat something regularly in order to improve your ability *You need to practise your pronunciation.* ○ *They're* ***practising for*** *tomorrow's concert.* **2** [WORK] [I, T] to work as a doctor or a lawyer *to* ***practise medicine/law*** **3** [CUSTOM/RELIGION] [T] to do something regularly according to a custom, religion, or a set of rules *to* ***practise a religion*** **4 practise what you preach** to behave as well as you often tell other people they should behave *I'd have more respect for him if he practised what he preached.*

practised *UK* (*US* **practiced**) /ˈpræktɪst/ *adjective* very good at doing something because you have done it so often *She answered the questions with* ***practised ease.***

practising *UK* (*US* **practicing**) /ˈpræktɪsɪŋ/ *adjective* **a practising Catholic/Jew/Muslim, etc** someone who follows the rules of a religion

practitioner /prækˈtɪʃᵊnəʳ/ *noun* [C] *formal* someone who works as a doctor or a lawyer *a medical practitioner* ⊃See also: **general practitioner.**

pragmatic /prægˈmætɪk/ *adjective* doing things in a practical and realistic way and not using only ideas *a* ***pragmatic approach*** *to a problem*

pragmatism /ˈprægmətɪzᵊm/ *noun* [U] when someone is pragmatic • **pragmatist** *noun* [C] someone who is pragmatic

prairie /ˈpreəri/ *noun* [C] a large, flat area of land

P

in North America that is usually covered in grass

o-m**praise¹** /preɪz/ verb [T] **1** to say that you admire someone or something, or that they are very good *He praised the team's performance.* ○ *Residents praised the firemen for their swift action.* **2** to give respect and thanks to a god *Praise God, no one was hurt.*

praise² /preɪz/ noun [U] words you say to show that you admire someone or something *They deserve praise for their achievements.* ○ *Her first novel won a lot of praise from the critics.*

praiseworthy /'preɪz,wɜːði/ adjective formal deserving praise

pram /præm/ noun [C] mainly UK a small vehicle with four wheels for carrying a baby

prance /prɑːns/ verb [I] to walk or dance in a proud way, often because you want people to look at you *She was prancing around in a bikini.*

prank /præŋk/ noun [C] a trick that is intended to be funny

prat /præt/ noun [C] UK very informal a stupid person

prawn /prɔːn/ noun [C] a small sea animal which you can eat, and which has a shell and ten legs

pray /preɪ/ verb [I, T] **1** to speak to a god in order to show your feelings or to ask for something *Let us pray for all the sick children.* ○ [+ that] *She prayed that God would forgive her.* **2** to hope very much that something will happen *We're just praying for rain.*

prayer /preəʳ/ noun **1** [C] the words you say to a god *Shall we say a prayer for him?* **2** [U] when you say words to a god *They knelt in prayer.*

preach /priːtʃ/ verb **1** [I, T] to talk to a group of people about a religious subject, usually as a priest in a church *to preach the gospel* **2** [I] to try to persuade people to believe or support something, often in an annoying way ⊃See also: practise what you preach.

preacher /'priːtʃəʳ/ noun [C] someone who speaks in public about a religious subject, especially someone whose job is to do this

preamble /'priːæmbl/ noun [C] formal an introduction to a speech or piece of writing

precarious /prɪ'keəriəs/ adjective **1** A precarious situation is likely to become worse. *Many illegal immigrants are in a precarious position.* **2** not fixed and likely to fall *That shelf looks a bit precarious.* • **precariously** adverb *Her cup was balanced precariously on the arm of the chair.*

precaution /prɪ'kɔːʃⁿn/ noun [C] something that you do to prevent bad things happening in the future *Driving alone at night can be dangerous, so always take precautions.* ○ *They called the doctor as a precaution.* ○ [+ of + doing sth] *He took the precaution of locking the door.* • **precautionary** adjective **a precautionary measure/step** something that you do in order to prevent something bad from happening

precede /prɪ'siːd/ verb [T] formal to happen or exist before something else [often passive] *The formal ceremony was preceded by a parade.* • **preceding** adjective [always before noun] happening or coming before *the preceding months*

precedence /'presɪdⁿns/ noun [U] when someone or something is considered more important than another person or thing *to give precedence to something* ○ *Quality should take precedence over cost.*

precedent /'presɪdⁿnt/ noun [C, U] an action or decision that is used as an example when someone wants to do a similar thing in the future *This decision has set an important legal precedent for other countries.*

precinct /'priːsɪŋkt/ noun **1** a pedestrian/shopping precinct UK an area in a town where there are shops and no cars are allowed **2** [C] US an area in a city that a particular group of police are responsible for, or the building in which they work *the 45th precinct*

precincts /'priːsɪŋkts/ noun [plural] the area of land around a building, especially a large church *the cathedral precincts*

precious¹ /'preʃəs/ adjective **1** very important to you *His books are his most precious possessions.* **2** rare and very valuable *a precious vase* ○ *a precious metal/stone*

precious² /'preʃəs/ adverb **precious few/little** very little or very few of something *We have precious little money at present.*

precipice /'presɪpɪs/ noun [C] **1** a dangerous situation that could lead to failure or harm *The two countries stood on the precipice of war.* **2** a steep side of a mountain or high area of land

precipitate /prɪ'sɪpɪteɪt/ verb [T] formal to make something happen [often passive] *The war was precipitated by an invasion.*

precipitation /prɪˌsɪpɪ'teɪʃⁿn/ noun [U] In science, precipitation is rain or snow that falls on the ground.

precis /'preɪsiː/ noun [C, U] formal a report giving the main ideas of a piece of writing or speech

o-m**precise** /prɪ'saɪs/ adjective **1** exact and accurate *precise details/instructions* ⊃Opposite imprecise. **2** to be precise used to give exact details about something *We met in 1994 - October first to be precise.* **3** [always before noun] used to emphasize something that you are referring to *At that precise moment, the door opened.*

precisely /prɪ'saɪsli/ adverb **1** EXACTLY exactly *at 6 o' clock precisely* **2** EMPHASIS used to emphasize something *This is precisely the kind of thing I was hoping to avoid.* **3** AGREEMENT used to agree with what someone else says *" It's not the shape I dislike, it's the colour. " " Precisely! "*

precision /prɪˈsɪʒᵊn/ *noun* [U] when something is very exact and accurate *She parked the car with great precision.*

preclude /prɪˈkluːd/ *verb* [T] *formal* to prevent something from happening [+ from + doing sth] *His illness precludes him from taking part in any sports.*

precocious /prɪˈkəʊʃəs/ *adjective* Children who are precocious have the confidence or skill of an adult. *A precocious child, she went to university at the age of 15.*

preconceived /ˌpriːkənˈsiːvd/ *adjective* Preconceived ideas are decided before the facts of a situation are known. ***preconceived ideas***

preconception /ˌpriːkənˈsepʃᵊn/ *noun* [C] what you believe before you know the facts of a situation *People **have** so many **preconceptions about** unmarried mothers.*

precondition /ˌpriːkənˈdɪʃᵊn/ *noun* [C] *formal* what must happen before something else can happen *The ceasefire is a **precondition for** peace talks.*

precursor /ˌpriːˈkɜːsəʳ/ *noun* [C] *formal* something which happens or exists before something else and influences its development *Infection with HIV is a **precursor to** AIDS.*

predate /ˌpriːˈdeɪt/ *verb* [T] to exist or happen before something else *The drinking of alcohol predates the Greeks and Romans.*

predator /ˈpredətəʳ/ *noun* [C] an animal that kills and eats other animals

predatory /ˈpredətᵊri/ *adjective* **1** A predatory person tries to get things from other people in a way that is unfair. **2** A predatory animal kills and eats other animals.

predecessor /ˈpriːdɪˌsesəʳ/ [US] /ˈpredəsesər/ *noun* [C] **1** the person who was in a job or position before *He seems a lot better than his predecessor.* **2** something that existed before another, similar thing *The predecessors to these computers were much larger and heavier.*

predetermined /ˌpriːdɪˈtɜːmɪnd/ *adjective formal* decided before *They met at a predetermined time and place.*

predeterminer /ˌpriːdɪˈtɜːmɪnəʳ/ *noun* [C] a word that is used before a determiner to give more information about a noun. For example 'all' in 'all these children' is a predeterminer.

WORD PARTNERS FOR ***predicament***

face a predicament • **explain** your predicament • be **in** a predicament

predicament /prɪˈdɪkəmənt/ *noun* [C] a problem or a difficult situation *I sympathize with your predicament.*

predicate /ˈpredɪkət/ *noun* [C] the part of a sentence which gives information about the subject. In the sentence 'We went to the airport.', 'went to the airport' is the predicate.

predicative /prɪˈdɪkətɪv/ *adjective* A predicative adjective comes after a verb. In the sentence 'She is happy.', 'happy' is a predicative adjective. ➲Compare **attributive**.

predict /prɪˈdɪkt/ *verb* [T] to say what you think will happen in the future *Companies are predicting massive profits.* ○ [+ (that)] *They predicted that the temperature would reach 80 degrees today.*

predictable /prɪˈdɪktəbl/ *adjective* happening or behaving in a way that you expect and not unusual or interesting *a predictable result* ○ *She's so predictable.* ➲Opposite **unpredictable**.
• **predictably** *adverb*

WORD PARTNERS FOR ***prediction***

make a prediction • an **accurate /gloomy** prediction • a prediction **about** sth • a prediction **of** [disaster/an improvement, etc]

prediction /prɪˈdɪkʃᵊn/ *noun* [C, U] when you say what you think will happen in the future *I wouldn't like to **make** any **predictions about** the result of this match.*

preˌdictive ˈtexting *noun* [U] when your mobile phone suggests words automatically while you use it to write a text message (= a written message sent from one mobile phone to another)

predilection /ˌpriːdɪˈlekʃᵊn/ *noun* [C] *formal* when you like something very much *She **has a predilection for** chocolate.*

predisposed /ˌpriːdɪˈspəʊzd/ *adjective* **be predisposed to sth** to be more likely than other people to have a medical problem or to behave in a particular way *Some people are predisposed to addiction.* • **predisposition** /ˌpriːdɪspəˈzɪʃᵊn/ *noun* [C] when you are likely to have a medical problem or to behave in a particular way *people with a **predisposition to** heart disease*

predominant /prɪˈdɒmɪnənt/ *adjective* more important or noticeable than others *He has played a **predominant role** in these talks.*
• **predominance** /prɪˈdɒmɪnəns/ *noun* [U] when something is more important or noticeable than others *the predominance of English on the Internet*

predominantly /prɪˈdɒmɪnəntli/ *adverb* mostly or mainly *a predominantly Asian community*

predominate /prɪˈdɒmɪneɪt/ *verb* [I] to be the largest in number or the most important *Olive trees predominate in this area.*

pre-eminent /ˌpriːˈemɪnənt/ *adjective* more important or better than others *a pre-eminent artist/scholar* • **pre-eminence** /ˌpriːˈemɪnəns/ *noun* [U] when someone or something is much more important or better than others

pre-empt /ˌpriːˈempt/ *verb* [T] to do something before something else happens in order to prevent it or reduce its effect • **pre-emptive** *adjective* preventing something else from happening *to take **pre-emptive action***

preen /priːn/ *verb* [I, T] **1** If a bird preens or preens itself, it makes its feathers clean and tidy. **2** to try to look attractive [often reflexive] *The actors preened themselves in the dressing room.*

pre-existing /ˌpriːɪgˈzɪstɪŋ/ *adjective* existing before something else *a pre-existing medical condition*

prefabricated /ˌpriːˈfæbrɪkeɪtɪd/ *adjective* **a prefabricated building/home/house, etc** a build-

P

ing that has already been partly built when it is put together

preface /ˈprefɪs/ *noun* [C] a piece of writing at the beginning of a book that explains why it was written

prefect /ˈpriːfekt/ *noun* [C] in the UK, an older student in a school who has special duties and some authority

⊶**prefer** /prɪˈfɜːʳ/ *verb* [T] **preferring**, *past* **preferred** **1** to like someone or something more than another person or thing *I **prefer** dogs **to** cats.* ○ [+ doing sth] *She prefers watching tennis to playing.* **2 would prefer** used to say what you want or ask someone what they want [+ to do sth] *I'd prefer to go alone.* ○ *Would you prefer red or white wine?*

COMMON LEARNER ERROR

prefer

Remember that **prefer** is often followed by **to do sth** or **doing sth**.

I prefer to walk.

I prefer walking.

~~*I prefer walk.*~~

preferable /ˈprefᵊrəbl/ *adjective* better or more suitable *Staying at home is **preferable to** going out with someone you don't like.*

preferably /ˈprefᵊrəbli/ *adverb* if possible *Serve the pudding with ice cream, preferably vanilla.*

WORD PARTNERS FOR ***preference***

express/have a preference • a **clear/marked** preference • a **personal** preference • a preference **for** sth

preference /ˈprefᵊrᵊns/ *noun* **1** [C, U] when you like something or someone more than another person or thing ***personal preferences*** ○ *We have white and brown bread. Do you **have a preference**?* ○ *I have a **preference for** dark-haired men.* **2 give preference to sb** to give special treatment to someone *Hospitals must give preference to urgent cases.*

preferential /ˌprefᵊrˈenʃᵊl/ *adjective* **preferential treatment** If you are given preferential treatment, you are treated in a better way than other people. *There were complaints that some guests had been given preferential treatment.*

prefix /ˈpriːfɪks/ *noun* [C] a group of letters that you add to the beginning of a word to make another word. In the word 'unimportant', 'un-' is a prefix. ➲Compare **suffix**.

pregnancy /ˈpregnənsi/ *noun* [C, U] when a woman is pregnant *a teenage pregnancy*

⊶**pregnant** /ˈpregnənt/ *adjective* **1** A pregnant woman has a baby developing inside her uterus. ***to get pregnant*** ○ *She's five months pregnant.* **2 a pregnant pause/silence** a pause or silence full of meaning that is not said in words

preheat /priːˈhiːt/ *verb* [T] to heat an oven to a particular temperature before putting food in it *Preheat the oven to 180 degrees.*

prehistoric /ˌpriːhɪˈstɒrɪk/ *adjective* relating to a time in the past before there were written records of events *prehistoric remains*

WORD PARTNERS FOR ***prejudice***

encounter / experience / face prejudice • prejudice **against** sb

prejudice¹ /ˈpredʒədɪs/ *noun* [C, U] when someone dislikes a group of people or treats them unfairly because they are a different race, sex, religion, etc *racial prejudice* ○ ***prejudice against women***

prejudice² /ˈpredʒədɪs/ *verb* [T] **1** to influence someone in an unfair way so that they have a bad opinion of someone or something *Her comments may have **prejudiced** the voters **against** him.* **2** to have a harmful effect on a situation *Newspaper reports have prejudiced the trial.*

prejudiced /ˈpredʒədɪst/ *adjective* feeling dislike for a group of people or treating them unfairly because they are a different race, sex, religion, etc *Are the police **prejudiced against** black people?*

preliminary /prɪˈlɪmɪnᵊri/ *adjective* [always before noun] done or happening in order to prepare for the main event or activity *a preliminary discussion/meeting* • **preliminary** *noun* [C] something that you do at the start of an event or activity

prelude /ˈpreljuːd/ *noun* **1 a prelude to sth** something that happens before another event or activity, usually as an introduction to it *There are hopes that the talks are a prelude to an agreement.* **2** [C] a short piece of music that introduces the main piece

premature /ˈpremətʃəʳ/ [US] /ˌpriːməˈtʊr/ *adjective* happening too soon or before the usual time ***premature ageing/death*** ○ ***a premature baby*** ○ [+ to do sth] *It seems a bit premature to start talking about it already.* • **prematurely** *adverb He died prematurely of cancer.*

premeditated /ˌpriːˈmedɪteɪtɪd/ *adjective* If a crime is premeditated, it is planned. ***premeditated murder*** ○ ***a premeditated attack***

premenstrual /ˌpriːˈmenstruəl/ *adjective* relating to the time just before a woman's period (= monthly blood from the uterus) ***premenstrual syndrome/tension***

premier¹ /ˈpremiəʳ/ [US] /prɪˈmɪr/ *noun* [C] the leader of a government *the Chinese premier* • **premiership** *noun* [U] the period in which someone is premier

premier² /ˈpremiəʳ/ [US] /prɪˈmɪr/ *adjective* [always before noun] best or most important *the city's premier hotel*

premiere /ˈpremieəʳ/ [US] /prɪˈmɪr/ *noun* [C] the first public performance of a film, play, etc *a **film premiere*** ○ *the world premiere* • **premiere** *verb* [I, T] [often passive] *The opera was premiered in Paris.*

the Premiership /ˈpremiəˌʃɪp/ *noun* the group of the best English football teams who compete against each other

premise /ˈpremɪs/ *noun* [C] *formal* an idea that you use to support another theory

premises /ˈpremɪsɪz/ *noun* [plural] the land or buildings used by an organization *We're moving to new premises.* ○ *Smoking is not*

P

allowed anywhere on the premises.

premium¹ /'priːmiəm/ *noun* **1** [C] an amount of money you pay for insurance (= payments for an accident or illness) *How much is the monthly premium?* **2** [C] an amount or rate that is higher than average *You pay a premium for apartments in the city centre.* **3 be at a premium** If something useful is at a premium, there is not enough of it. *Time is at a premium just before the start of exams.* **4 place/put a premium on sth** to consider a quality or achievement as very important *She puts a premium on honesty.*

premium² /'priːmiəm/ *adjective* [always before noun] A premium product is of a higher quality or value than others. *premium beer/cigars*

premonition /ˌpremə'nɪʃ°n/ *noun* [C] a feeling that something, especially something unpleasant, is going to happen *to have a premonition* ○ *a premonition of disaster*

prenatal /ˌpriː'neɪt°l/ *US* (*UK* antenatal) *adjective* relating to pregnant women before their babies are born *prenatal care*

preoccupation /priːˌɒkjə'peɪʃ°n/ *noun* **1** [C, U] when you think or worry about something so much that you do not think about other things *a preoccupation with death/food* **2** [C] something that you think or worry about a lot *His main preoccupations are football and women.*

preoccupied /priː'ɒkjəpaɪd/ *adjective* thinking or worrying about something a lot *She's been very preoccupied recently.* ○ *He's far too preoccupied with his own problems to notice mine.* ● **preoccupy** /priː'ɒkjəpaɪ/ *verb* [T] If something preoccupies you, you think or worry about it a lot.

prepaid /priː'peɪd/ *adjective* If something is prepaid, you pay for it before a particular time. *Susan just got prepaid tickets for the show next weekend.*

➤**preparation** /ˌprep°r'eɪʃ°n/ *noun* [U] the things that you do or the time that you spend preparing for something *Did you do much preparation for your interview?* ○ *He's been painting the outside of the house in preparation for winter.* ○ *the preparation of the document*

> **WORD PARTNERS FOR *preparations***
>
> begin/finalize/make preparations ● final/last-minute preparations ● preparations are underway ● preparations for sth

preparations /ˌprep°r'eɪʃ°nz/ *noun* [plural] things that you do to get ready for something *wedding preparations* ○ *We've been making preparations for the journey.*

preparatory /prɪ'pær°t°ri/ *adjective* done in order to get ready for something *preparatory work*

pre'paratory ˌschool *noun formal* a prep school

➤**prepare** /prɪ'peə°/ *verb* **1** [I, T] to get someone or something ready for something that will happen in the future *They're preparing for the big match.* ○ *We're preparing the students for their end-of-year exam.* ○ [+ to do sth] *I was*

busy preparing to go on holiday. **2 prepare yourself** to make yourself ready to deal with a difficult situation *Prepare yourself for a shock.* **3** [T] to make food ready to be eaten *to prepare lunch*

prepared /prɪ'peəd/ *adjective* **1** ready to deal with a situation *I wasn't prepared for the cold.* **2 be prepared to do sth** to be willing to do something *You must be prepared to work hard.*

preponderance /prɪ'pɒnd°r°ns/ *noun formal* a preponderance of sth when there is a larger amount of one thing than of others *There is a preponderance of older people in this area.*

preposition /ˌprepə'zɪʃ°n/ *noun* [C] a word or group of words that is used before a noun or pronoun to show place, direction, time, etc. For example 'on' in 'Your keys are on the table.' is a preposition.

preposterous /prɪ'pɒst°rəs/ *adjective* extremely stupid *That's a preposterous idea!*

prep school /'prepskuːl/ *noun* [C] **1** in the UK, a private school for children aged between 8 and 13 **2** in the US, a private school which prepares students for college

prerequisite /ˌpriː'rekwɪzɪt/ *noun* [C] *formal* something that is necessary in order for something else to happen or exist *Trust is a prerequisite for any sort of relationship.*

prerogative /prɪ'rɒgətɪv/ *noun* [C] *formal* something that you have the right to do because of who you are *Alex makes the decisions - that's his prerogative as company director.*

Presbyterian /ˌprezbɪ'tɪəriən/ *adjective* belonging or relating to a type of Christian church with elected groups of local members involved in the official organization of local churches ● **Presbyterian** *noun* [C]

pre-school /'priːskuːl/ *adjective* [always before noun] relating to children who are too young to go to school *pre-school children/education* ● **pre-school** *noun* [C] a school for children younger than five years old

prescribe /prɪ'skraɪb/ *verb* [T] **1** to say what medical treatment someone needs [often passive] *Painkillers are the most common drugs prescribed by doctors in Britain.* **2** *formal* to say officially what people must do *rules prescribed by law*

prescription /prɪ'skrɪpʃ°n/ *noun* **1** [C] a piece of paper saying what medicine someone needs or the medicine itself *a doctor's prescription* **2 on prescription** *UK* (*US* by prescription) If you get a medicine on prescription, you only get it if you have a written instruction from your doctor.

prescriptive /prɪ'skrɪptɪv/ *adjective formal* saying exactly what must happen *The government's homework guidelines are too prescriptive.*

> **WORD PARTNERS FOR *presence***
>
> the presence of sb/sth ● in the presence of sb/sth

presence /'prez°ns/ *noun* **1** [IN A PLACE] [U] when someone or something is in a place *She signed the document in the presence of two witnesses.*

2 POLICE/SOLDIERS [no plural] a group of police or soldiers who are watching or controlling a situation *a strong **police presence*** **3** QUALITY [U] a quality that makes people notice and admire you **4 presence of mind** the ability to deal with a difficult situation quickly and effectively *She had the **presence of mind** to press the alarm.* **5 make your presence felt** to have a strong effect on other people *The new police chief has really **made his presence felt**.*

∘᪲**present¹** /'prezᵊnt/ *adjective* **1 be present** to be in a particular place *The whole family was present.* **2** [always before noun] happening or existing now *the present situation* ○ *What is your present occupation?* **3 present tense** the form of the verb which is used to show what happens or exists now

---

5🝊 WORD PARTNERS FOR *present*

2 buy/get/give sb/wrap (up) a present • a present for/from sb • a birthday/wedding present

---

∘᪲**present²** /'prezᵊnt/ *noun* **1 the present a** the period of time that is happening now *The play is set **in the present**.* **b** the form of the verb which is used to show what happens or exists now **2** [C] something that you give to someone, usually for a particular occasion *a **birthday/wedding present*** ○ *to give someone a present* **3 at present** now *At present she's working abroad.*

present³ /prɪˈzent/ *verb* [T] **1** GIVE to give something to someone, often at a formal ceremony *to present a prize* ○ *They **presented** her **with** a bouquet.* **2** INFORMATION to give people information in a formal

present

way *He **presented** the report **to** his colleagues.* **3 present a danger/threat/problem, etc** to cause a danger/threat/problem, etc *The final exam may present some problems.* **4** TV/RADIO *UK* (*US* host) to introduce a television or radio programme *He presents a weekly sports quiz.* **5** PLAY/FILM to show a new play or film *The school is presenting 'West Side Story' this term.* **6** INTRODUCE to introduce someone formally *May I present my daughters?* **7** OPPORTUNITY If an opportunity presents itself, it becomes possible. *I'd be happy to go to New York, if the **opportunity presented itself**.*

presentable /prɪˈzentəbl/ *adjective* looking clean and tidy enough *He was looking quite presentable in his jacket and tie.*

presentation /ˌprezᵊnˈteɪʃᵊn/ *noun* **1** SHOW [U] the way something is arranged or shown to people *Presentation is important if you want people to buy your products.* **2** TALK [C] a talk giving information about something *a **sales presentation*** ○ *She gave an excellent presentation.* **3** CEREMONY [C] a formal ceremony at which you give someone something *a presentation ceremony*

present-day /ˌprezᵊntˈdeɪ/ *adjective* existing

---

now *present-day attitudes*

presenter /prɪˈzentəʳ/ *UK* (*US* host) *noun* [C] someone who introduces a radio or television programme

presently /'prezᵊntli/ *adverb* **1** *formal* now *He's presently living with his parents.* **2** *old-fashioned* soon or after a short time *I'll be back presently.*

ˌ**present parˈticiple** *UK* (*US* ˌpresent ˈparticiple) *noun* [C] the form of a verb that ends with '-ing'

the ˌ**present ˈperfect** *noun* the form of the verb that is used to show actions or events that have happened in a period of time up to now. *The sentence 'I have never been to Australia.' is in the present perfect.*

preservation /ˌprezəˈveɪʃᵊn/ *noun* [U] when you keep something the same or prevent it from being damaged or destroyed *the preservation of peace* ○ *the preservation of wildlife*

preservative /prɪˈzɜːvətɪv/ *noun* [C, U] a substance used to prevent decay in food or in wood

preserve¹ /prɪˈzɜːv/ *verb* [T] **1** to keep something the same or prevent it from being damaged or destroyed *to preserve peace* ○ *to preserve the environment* **2** to add substances to something so that it stays in good condition for a long time *to preserve food/wood*

preserve² /prɪˈzɜːv/ *noun* **1** FOOD [C, U] *UK* (*US* preserves) a sweet food made from fruit, sugar, and water *apricot/strawberry preserve* **2** ACTIVITY [no plural] an activity which only a particular group of people can do *Sport used to be a male preserve.* ○ *Owning racehorses is **the preserve** of the rich.* **3** AREA [C] *mainly US* an area where wild animals and plants are protected

preside /prɪˈzaɪd/ *verb* [I] to be officially responsible for a formal meeting or ceremony *An elderly priest **presided at** the marriage ceremony.*
preside over sth to be in charge of a situation, especially a formal meeting or legal trial *The case was **presided over by** a senior judge.*

presidency /'prezɪdᵊnsi/ *noun* **1** [C] the period when someone is president *Her presidency lasted seven years.* **2 the presidency** the job of being president *He **won the presidency** by a wide margin.*

∘᪲**president** /'prezɪdᵊnt/ *noun* [C] **1** the highest political position in some countries, usually the leader of the government *President Kennedy* **2** the person in charge of a company or organization ⊃See also: **vice president**.

presidential /ˌprezɪˈdenʃᵊl/ *adjective* relating to the president of a country *a **presidential** campaign*

∘᪲**press¹** /pres/ *verb* **1** PUSH [I, T] to push something firmly *Press the button to start the machine.* ○ *He pressed his face against the window.* **2** PERSUADE [T] to try hard to persuade someone to do something [+ to do sth] *The committee pressed him to reveal more information.* ○ *They **pressed him for** an answer but he refused.* **3 press charges** to complain officially about someone in a court of law *The family decided not to **press charges against** him.*

P

4 MAKE SMOOTH [T] to make clothes smooth by ironing them *I need to press these trousers.* **5** MAKE FLAT [T] to make something flat by putting something heavy on it for a long time *to press fruit/flowers* **6 press a case/claim** to try to make people accept your demands

press ahead/forward/on to continue to do something in a determined way *They're determined to press ahead with their plans despite opposition.*

press² /pres/ *noun* **1 the press** newspapers and magazines, or the people who write them *the local/national press* ◦ *press reports* **2 good/bad press** praise or criticism from newspapers, magazines, television, etc *She's had a lot of bad press recently.* **3** BUSINESS [C] a business that prints and sells books *Cambridge University Press* **4** PRINT [C] (*also* printing press) a machine used to print books, newspapers, and magazines **5** MAKE FLAT [no plural] when you make cloth flat and smooth with a piece of equipment *Can you give these trousers a press?*

'**press ,conference** *noun* [C] a meeting at which someone officially gives information to the newspapers, television, etc *to call/hold a press conference*

pressed /prest/ *adjective* **be pressed for time/ money** to not have much time/money

pressing /'presɪŋ/ *adjective* A pressing problem or situation needs to be dealt with immediately. *a pressing need for housing*

'**press re,lease** *noun* [C] an official piece of information that is given to newspapers, television, etc

press-up /'presʌp/ *UK* (*US* push-up) *noun* [C] a physical exercise in which you lie facing the floor and use your hands to push your body up

WORD PARTNERS FOR ***pressure***

face/feel pressure • be under/come under pressure • pressure on sb • pressure from sb • pressure for sth

◦-**pressure¹** /'preʃər/ *noun* **1** MAKE SOMEONE DO [U] when someone tries to make someone else do something by arguing, persuading, etc *public/political pressure* ◦ [+ to do sth] *Teachers are under increasing pressure to work longer hours.* ◦ *The government is facing pressure from environmental campaigners.* **2** PROBLEMS [C, U] difficult situations that make you feel worried or unhappy *the pressures of work* ◦ *He's been under a lot of pressure recently.* **3** LIQUID/GAS [C, U] the force that a liquid or gas produces when it presses against an area *water pressure* **4** PUSH the force that you produce when you push something **5 put pressure on sb** to try to force someone to do something [+ to do sth] *They're putting pressure on me to make a decision.* ➔See also: blood pressure, peer pressure.

pressure² /'preʃər/ (*also UK* pressurize, -ise /'preʃəraɪz/) *verb* [T] to try to force someone to do something [often passive, + into + doing sth] *We will not be pressured into making a decision.*

'**pressure ,cooker** *noun* [C] a pan with a lid which you use to cook food quickly in steam

'**pressure ,group** *noun* [C] a group of people who try to influence what the public or the government think about something

pressurize *UK* (*also* -ise) /'preʃəraɪz/ *verb* [T] to try to force someone to do something [often passive, + into + doing sth] *He was pressurized into signing the agreement.*

pressurized (*also UK* -ised) /'preʃəraɪzd/ *adjective* containing air or gas that is kept at a controlled pressure *a pressurized container*

prestige /pres'tiːʒ/ *noun* [U] when people feel respect and admiration for you, often because you are successful *His company has gained international prestige.* • **prestigious** /pres'tɪdʒəs/ *adjective* respected and admired, usually because of being important *a prestigious award* ◦ *a prestigious university*

presumably /prɪ'zjuːməbli/ *adverb* used to say what you think is the likely situation *Presumably he just forgot to send the letter.*

presume /prɪ'zjuːm/ *verb* **1** [T] to think that something is likely to be true, although you are not certain [+ (that)] *I presume that you've done your homework.* **2 be presumed dead/ innocent, etc** If someone is presumed dead/ innocent, etc, it seems very likely that they are dead/innocent, etc. **3 presume to do sth** *formal* to do something that you do not have the right or the skills to do *I certainly wouldn't presume to tell you how to do your job.*

presumption /prɪ'zʌmpʃ°n/ *noun* **1** [C] when you believe that something is true without any proof [+ (that)] *I object to the presumption that young people are only interested in pop music.* **2** [U] behaviour that is rude and does not show respect

presumptuous /prɪ'zʌmptʃuəs/ *adjective* Someone who is presumptuous confidently does things that they have no right to do. *It was a bit presumptuous of her to take the car without asking.*

presuppose /ˌpriːsə'pəʊz/ *verb* [T] *formal* If an idea or situation presupposes something, that thing must be true for the idea or situation to work.

pre-teen /priː'tiːn/ *noun* [C] a boy or girl between the ages of 9 and 12 *a magazine for pre-teens* • **pre-teen** *adjective* *pre-teen fashions*

pretence *UK* (*US* pretense) /prɪ'tens/ *noun* **1** [U] when you make someone believe something that is not true *I can't keep up the pretence* (= continue pretending) *any longer.* ◦ *They made absolutely no pretence of being interested.* **2 under false pretences** If you do something under false pretences, you do it when you have lied about who you are or what you are doing. *The police charged him with obtaining money under false pretences.*

◦-**pretend** /prɪ'tend/ *verb* [I, T] to behave as if something is true when it is not [+ (that)] *I can't pretend that I like him.* ◦ [+ to do sth] *Were you just pretending to be interested?*

pretense /prɪ'tens/ *noun US spelling of* pretence

pretension /prɪ'tenʃ°n/ *noun* [C, U] when you try to seem better or more important than you really are [usually plural] *He seems to be without pretensions of any sort.*

| ɑː: arm | ɜː: her | iː see | ɔː: saw | uː too | aɪ my | aʊ how | eə hair | eɪ day | əʊ no | ɪə near | ɔɪ boy | ʊə poor | aɪə fire | aʊə sour |

pretentious /prɪˈtenʃəs/ *adjective* trying to seem more important or clever than you really are *a pretentious film*

pretext /ˈpriːtekst/ *noun* [C] a false reason that you use to explain why you are doing something *I called her **on the pretext of** needing some information.*

◦━**pretty¹** /ˈprɪti/ *adverb informal* **1** quite, but not extremely *The traffic was pretty bad.* ○ *I'm pretty sure they'll accept.* **2 pretty much/well** almost *We've pretty much finished here.*

◦━**pretty²** /ˈprɪti/ *adjective* **1** If a woman or girl is pretty, she is attractive. *Your daughter is very pretty.* **2** If a place or an object is pretty, it is pleasant to look at. *a pretty little village*

prevail /prɪˈveɪl/ *verb* [I] *formal* **1** to get control or influence *We can only hope that **common sense will prevail**.* **2** to be common among a group of people *The use of guns prevails among the gangs in this area.*
prevail on/upon sb to do sth *formal* to persuade someone to do something that they do not want to do *He was eventually prevailed upon to accept the appointment.*

prevailing /prɪˈveɪlɪŋ/ *adjective* [always before noun] **1** existing a lot in a particular group, area, or at a particular time *a prevailing attitude/mood* **2 a prevailing wind** a wind that usually blows in a particular place

prevalent /ˈprevələnt/ *adjective* existing a lot in a particular group, area, or at a particular time *These diseases are more prevalent among young children.* ● **prevalence** /ˈprevələns/ *noun* [U] when something exists a lot in a particular group, area, or at a particular time *the prevalence of smoking among teenagers*

◦━**prevent** /prɪˈvent/ *verb* [T] to stop something happening or to stop someone doing something *to prevent accidents/crime* ○ [+ from + doing sth] *Members of the public were prevented from entering the building.* ● **preventable** *adjective* If something is preventable, it can be prevented.

COMMON LEARNER ERROR

prevent

Prevent should not be followed by 'to do sth'.
We must prevent such a disaster from happening again.
~~We must prevent such a disaster to happen again.~~

COMMON LEARNER ERROR

protect or prevent?

Protect means to keep someone or something safe from bad things.
You should wear sunscreen to protect your skin.
Prevent means to stop something from happening.
Wearing sunscreen can help prevent skin cancer.

preventative /prɪˈventətɪv/ *adjective* another word for preventive

prevention /prɪˈvenʃən/ *noun* [U] when you stop something happening or stop someone

doing something *crime prevention* ○ *the prevention of diseases*

preventive /prɪˈventɪv/ (*also* **preventative**) *adjective* Preventive action is intended to stop something before it happens. *preventive measures* ○ *preventive medicine*

preview /ˈpriːvjuː/ *noun* [C] **1** an opportunity to see a film, play, etc before it is shown to the public **2** a short film that advertises a film or television programme ● **preview** *verb* [T]

◦━**previous** /ˈpriːviəs/ *adjective* existing or happening before something or someone else *the previous day/year* ○ *a previous attempt* ○ *his previous marriage* ● **previously** *adverb* *He previously worked as a teacher.*

prey¹ /preɪ/ *noun* **1** [U] an animal that is hunted and killed by another animal **2 fall prey to sth** to be hurt or deceived by something or someone bad ⊃See also: **bird of prey**.

prey² /preɪ/ *verb*
prey on sth If an animal preys on another animal, it catches it and eats it. *Spiders prey on flies and other small insects.*
prey on/upon sb to hurt or deceive people who are weak and easy to deceive *These young thieves prey on the elderly.*

🧩 **WORD PARTNERS FOR *price***

charge/increase/pay/put up prices ● prices **fall** ● an **average/exorbitant/high/low/ reasonable** price

◦━**price¹** /praɪs/ *noun* **1** [C] the amount of money that you pay to buy something *high/low prices* ○ *House prices are falling/rising.* ○ *The price of fuel has gone up again.* **2** [no plural] the unpleasant results that you must accept or experience for getting or doing something *Suspension from the club was **a high/ small price to pay** (= very bad/not very bad thing to experience) for his mistake.* **3 at a price** If you can get something at a price, you have to pay a lot of money for it. *False passports are available, at a price.* **4 at any price** If you want something at any price, you will do anything to get it. *She wanted the job at any price.*

COMMON LEARNER ERROR

price or prize?

These two words sound very similar but have different spellings and very different meanings - be careful not to confuse them.
Price means 'the amount of money that you pay to buy something'.
The price of oil has risen by 20%.
Prize means 'something valuable that is given to someone who wins a competition or who has done good work'.
She won first prize in the competition.

price² /praɪs/ *verb* [T] to say what the price of something is [often passive] *The book is **priced** at $40.*

priceless /ˈpraɪsləs/ *adjective* **1** very valuable *a priceless antique/painting* **2** very important or useful *A trip round the world is a priceless opportunity.*

'price ,tag (*also* '**price ,ticket**) *noun* [C] a piece of paper attached to a product that shows the amount a product costs

pricey (*also* **pricy**) /'praɪsi/ *adjective informal* expensive *That jacket's a bit pricey!*

prick /prɪk/ *verb* [T] to make a very small hole in something with a sharp object *Prick the potatoes all over before baking.* ○ *I pricked my finger on a pin.* ●**prick** *noun* [C] *The injection won't hurt - you'll just feel a slight prick.*

prickle¹ /'prɪkl/ *noun* [C] a sharp point on the surface of some plants or the skin of some animals

prickle² /'prɪkl/ *verb* [I] If part of your body prickles, it feels as if a lot of sharp points are touching it because you are frightened or excited. *a prickling sensation*

prickly /'prɪkli/ *adjective* **1** covered with prickles *a prickly bush* **2** *informal* A prickly person or relationship is unfriendly or difficult to deal with.

pricy /'praɪsi/ *adjective* another spelling of pricey

⊶**pride¹** /praɪd/ *noun* [U] **1** SATISFACTION a feeling of satisfaction at your achievements or the achievements of your family or friends *She felt a great sense of pride as she watched him accept the award.* ○ *The whole community takes pride in* (= feels proud about) *the school.* **2** RESPECT the respect that you feel for yourself *Defeat in the World Cup has badly damaged national pride.* **3** IMPORTANCE the belief that you are better or more important than other people *His pride prevented him from asking for help.* **4** sb's **pride and joy** something or someone that is very important to you *He spends hours cleaning that motorcycle - it's his pride and joy.* **5** have/take **pride of place** If something takes pride of place, you put it in the best position so that it can be seen easily. *A photo of her grandchildren took pride of place on the wall.* **6** swallow **your pride** to decide to do something although it will embarrass you *He swallowed his pride and asked if he could have his old job back.*

pride² /praɪd/ *verb*
pride yourself on sth/doing sth to feel satisfaction at a quality or skill that you have *The company prides itself on having the latest technology.*

priest /priːst/ *noun* [C] someone who performs religious duties and ceremonies

the priesthood /'priːsthʊd/ *noun* the job of being a priest

prim /prɪm/ *adjective* Someone who is prim behaves in a very formal way and is easily shocked by anything rude. *Sarah wouldn't find that funny - she's far too prim and proper* (= shocked by anything rude). ● **primly** *adverb*

prima donna /ˌpriːmə'dɒnə/ *noun* [C] someone who behaves badly and expects to get everything they want because they think that they are very important

primal /'praɪmᵊl/ *adjective formal* very basic, or relating to the time when human life on Earth began *primal instincts*

primarily /praɪ'merᵊli/ *adverb* mainly *She's known primarily as a novelist but she also writes poetry.*

primary¹ /'praɪmᵊri/ *adjective* [always before noun] most important *Her primary responsibility is to train new employees.*

primary² /'praɪmᵊri/ *noun* [C] a vote in which people in a political party in the US choose the person who will represent them in an election

,primary 'colour UK (US '**primary ,color**) *noun* [C] one of the three colours, which in paint, etc are red, blue, and yellow, that can be mixed together to make any other colour

'primary ,school (*also* US **elementary school**) *noun* [C] a school for children aged 5 to 11

primate /'praɪmeɪt/ *noun* [C] a member of the group of animals which includes monkeys and people, which have large brains and hands and feet developed for climbing

prime¹ /praɪm/ *adjective* [always before noun] **1** main, or most important *the prime suspect in a murder investigation* **2** of the best quality *The hotel is in a prime location in the city centre.* **3** a **prime example** a very good example of something

prime² /praɪm/ *noun* [no plural] the period in your life when you are most active or successful *At 35, she's in her prime.* ○ *the prime of life*

prime³ /praɪm/ *verb* [T] to prepare someone for an event or situation, often by giving them the information that they need *The president had been well primed before the debate.*

,prime 'minister *noun* [C] the leader of an elected government in some countries

,prime 'time *noun* [U] the time in the evening when the largest number of people watch television *prime-time television*

primeval /praɪ'miːvᵊl/ *adjective* belonging to a very early period in the history of the world *primeval forest*

primitive /'prɪmɪtɪv/ *adjective* **1** relating to human society at a very early stage of development, with people living in a simple way without machines or a writing system *primitive man* ○ *primitive societies* **2** very basic or old-fashioned *The conditions at the campsite were rather primitive.*

primrose /'prɪmrəʊz/ *noun* [C] a wild plant with pale yellow flowers

prince /prɪns/ *noun* [C] **1** the son of a king or queen, or one of their close male relatives *Prince Edward* **2** the male ruler of a small country

princely /'prɪnsli/ *adjective* a **princely sum** a large amount of money *It cost the princely sum of £2 million.*

princess /prɪn'ses/ ⓤⓢ /'prɪnsəs/ *noun* [C] **1** the daughter of a king or queen, or one of their close female relatives **2** the wife of a prince

principal¹ /'prɪnsəpᵊl/ *adjective* [always before noun] main, or most important *Her principal reason for moving is to be nearer her mother.*

principal² /ˈprɪnsəpᵊl/ *noun* [C] the person in charge of a school or college

principality /ˌprɪnsɪˈpæləti/ *noun* [C] a country ruled by a prince

principally /ˈprɪnsəpᵊli/ *adverb* mainly *The advertising campaign is aimed principally at women.*

WORD PARTNERS FOR ***principle***

stick to your principles • a **guiding** principle • be **against** sb's principles • be a **matter of** principle

⊶**principle** /ˈprɪnsəpl/ *noun* **1** [C, U] a rule or belief which influences your behaviour and which is based on what you think is right *He must be punished - it's a **matter of principle**.* **2** [C] a basic idea or rule which explains how something happens or works *The organization works **on the principle that** all members have the same rights.* **3 in principle** If you agree with something in principle, you agree with the idea or plan although you do not know the details or you do not know if it will be possible. *They have approved the changes in principle.* **4 on principle** If you refuse to do something on principle, you refuse to do it because you think it is morally wrong. *She doesn't wear fur on principle.*

principled /ˈprɪnsəpld/ *adjective* showing strong beliefs about what is right and wrong

⊶**print¹** /prɪnt/ *verb* **1** [WRITING/IMAGES] [T] to produce writing or images on paper or other material with a machine *The instructions are printed on the side of the box.* **2** [BOOKS/NEWSPAPERS] [T] to produce books, newspapers, magazines, etc, usually in large quantities, using machines *Fifty thousand booklets have been printed for the exhibition.* **3** [INCLUDE] [T] to include a piece of writing in a newspaper or magazine *They printed his letter in Tuesday's paper.* **4** [WRITE] [I, T] to write words without joining the letters together *Please print your name and address clearly using capitals.* **5** [PATTERN] [T] to produce a pattern on material or paper

print sth out to produce a printed copy of a document that has been written on a computer *Can you print out a copy of that letter for me?*

print² /prɪnt/ *noun* **1** [WORDS] [U] words, letters, or numbers that are produced on paper by a machine **2 in/out of print** If a book is in print, it is possible to buy a new copy of it, and if it is out of print, it is not now possible. **3** [PICTURE] [C] a copy of a picture made using photography or by pressing paper onto a design covered in ink *a print of Van Gogh's 'Sunflowers'* **4** [PHOTOGRAPH] [C] a photograph that is produced on paper **5** [PATTERN] [C] a pattern that is produced on material or paper *a floral print* **6** [HAND] [C] (*also* **fingerprint**) a mark that is left on a surface where someone has touched it *His prints were found all over the house and he was arrested the next day.* **7** [MARK] [C] a mark that is left on a surface where someone has walked *The dog left prints all over the kitchen floor.* ➲See also: **small print**.

printer /ˈprɪntəʳ/ *noun* [C] **1** a machine which is connected to a computer and which produces writing or images on paper *a laser printer* **2** a person or company that prints books, newspapers, magazines, etc

printing /ˈprɪntɪŋ/ *noun* [U] when writing or images are produced on paper or other material using a machine

ˈprinting ˌpress *noun* [C] a machine that prints books, newspapers, magazines, etc

printout /ˈprɪntaʊt/ *noun* [C] information or a document that is printed from a computer *He asked for a printout of the year's sales figures.*

prior /praɪəʳ/ *adjective formal* **1** [always before noun] existing or happening before something else *The course requires no **prior knowledge** of Spanish.* **2 prior to sth** before a particular time or event *the weeks prior to her death*

prioritize (*also UK* **-ise**) /praɪˈɒrɪtaɪz/ *verb* [I, T] to decide which of a group of things are the most important so that you can deal with them first *You must learn to **prioritize** your work.*

priority /praɪˈɒrəti/ *noun* **1** [C] something that is very important and that must be dealt with before other things *My **first/top priority** is to find somewhere to live.* **2 give priority to sth** to consider that something is more important than other things and deal with it first **3 have/take priority (over sth)** to be more important than other things and to be dealt with first *His job seems to take priority over everything else.*

prise /praɪz/ *verb UK* **prise sth apart/off/open, etc** to use force to move, remove, or open something *I prised the lid off with a spoon.*

prism /ˈprɪzᵊm/ *noun* [C] an object made of clear glass which separates the light that passes through it into different colours

WORD PARTNERS FOR ***prison***

go to/be sent to prison • **be released from** prison • **in/out of** prison • a prison **sentence**

⊶**prison** /ˈprɪzᵊn/ *noun* [C, U] a place where criminals are kept as a punishment *He's spent most of his life **in prison**.* ○ *She was **sent to prison** for two years.*

⊶**prisoner** /ˈprɪzᵊnəʳ/ *noun* **1** [C] someone who is being kept in prison as a punishment, or because they have been caught by an enemy **2 hold/keep/take sb prisoner** to catch someone and guard them so that they cannot escape ➲See also: **political prisoner**.

ˌprisoner of ˈwar *noun* [C] *plural* **prisoners of war** a soldier who is caught by enemy soldiers during a war *a prisoner of war camp*

pristine /ˈprɪstiːn/ *adjective* in very good condition, as if new *Her car is **in pristine condition**.*

privacy /ˈprɪvəsi/ [US] /ˈpraɪvəsi/ *noun* [U] when you are alone and people cannot see or hear what you are doing *I hate sharing a bedroom - I never get any privacy.*

⊶**private¹** /ˈpraɪvɪt/ *adjective* **1** [NOT EVERYONE] only for one person or group and not for everyone *Each room has a balcony and a private bathroom.* ○ *You can't park here - this is **private property**.* **2** [NOT GOVERNMENT] controlled by or paid for by a person or company and not by

P

the government *Charles went to a* ***private school****.* **3** SECRET If information or an emotion is private, you do not want other people to know about it. *This is a* ***private matter*** *- it doesn't concern you.* **4 in private** If you do something in private, you do it where other people cannot see or hear you. *I need to talk to you in private.* **5 sb's** ***private life*** someone's personal relationships and activities and not their work **6** QUIET A place which is private is quiet and there are no other people there to see or hear what you are doing. *Is there somewhere private where we can talk?* • **privately** *adverb*

private² /'praɪvɪt/ *noun* [C] a soldier of the lowest rank in the army

the ˈprivate ˌsector *noun* [usually singular] businesses and industries that are not owned or controlled by the government

privatize (*also UK* **-ise**) /'praɪvɪtaɪz/ *verb* [T] If an industry or organization owned by the government is privatized, it is sold to private companies. • **privatization** /ˌpraɪvɪtaɪˈzeɪʃᵊn/ *noun* [U]

privilege /'prɪvᵊlɪdʒ/ *noun* **1** [C, U] an advantage that only one person or group has, usually because of their position or because they are rich **2** [no plural] an opportunity to do something special or enjoyable [+ of + doing sth] *I had the privilege of meeting the Queen.* • **privileged** *adjective* having a privilege *to be in a privileged position*

privy /'prɪvi/ *adjective formal* **privy to sth** knowing information that is not known by many people

◦→**prize¹** /praɪz/ *noun* [C] something valuable that is given to someone who wins a competition or who has done good work *to* ***win*** *a* ***prize*** ○ ***first/second*** *prize* ➾See Common learner error at **price** ➾See also: **booby prize**.

prize² /praɪz/ *adjective* [always before noun] A prize animal or vegetable is good enough to win a competition.

prize³ /praɪz/ *verb* [T] to think that something is very valuable or important *His car is his* ***prized*** *possession.*

prize-winning /'praɪzˌwɪnɪŋ/ *adjective* [always before noun] having won a prize *a prize-winning author*

pro /prəʊ/ *noun* [C] **1** *informal* someone who earns money for playing a sport *a golf/tennis pro* **2 the pros and cons** the advantages and disadvantages of something [+ of + doing sth] *We discussed the pros and cons of buying a bigger house.*

pro- /prəʊ-/ *prefix* supporting or approving of something *pro-European* ○ *pro-democracy demonstrations* ➾Compare **anti-**.

proactive /ˌprəʊˈæktɪv/ *adjective* taking action by causing change and not only reacting to change when it happens

probability /ˌprɒbəˈbɪləti/ *noun* **1** [C, U] how likely it is that something will happen [+ of + doing sth] *What's the probability of winning?* ○ [+ (that)] *There's a* ***high probability*** *that he'll get the job.* **2 in all probability** used to mean that something is very likely *She will, in all probability, have left before we arrive.*

probable /'prɒbəbl/ *adjective* likely to be true or to happen *The* ***probable cause*** *of death was heart failure.* ○ [+ (that)] *It's* ***highly probable*** *that he'll lose his job.*

◦→**probably** /'prɒbəbli/ *adverb* used to mean that something is very likely *I'll probably be home by midnight.*

probation /prəʊˈbeɪʃᵊn/ *noun* [U] **1** a period of time when a criminal must behave well and not commit any more crimes in order to avoid being sent to prison *to be* ***on probation*** **2** a period of time at the start of a new job when you are watched and tested to see if you are suitable for the job • **probationary** *adjective* relating to probation *a* ***probationary period***

proˈbation ˌofficer *noun* [C] someone whose job is to watch and help criminals who have been put on probation

probe¹ /prəʊb/ *verb* [I, T] to ask a lot of questions in order to discover information about something or someone *The interviewer probed deep into her private life.* ○ *probing questions*

probe² /prəʊb/ *noun* [C] **1** when you try to discover information about something by asking a lot of questions *an FBI* ***probe into*** *corruption* **2** a long, thin, metal tool used by doctors to examine parts of the body

OTHER WAYS OF SAYING *problem*

The noun **difficulty** is a common alternative to 'problem': *The company is having some financial* ***difficulties*** *at the moment.*

A small, temporary problem may be described informally as a **hitch** or a **hiccup**: *The ceremony went without a* ***hitch****.*

A **glitch** is a problem that stops something from working properly: *We've had a few technical* ***glitches****, but we'll be ready on time.*

A **hurdle** or **obstacle** is a problem that you need to deal with so that you can continue to make progress: *Getting a work permit is the first* ***hurdle/obstacle****.*

A **pitfall** is a problem that is likely to happen in a particular situation: *It's just one of the* ***pitfalls*** *of buying a house.*

A **setback** is a problem that makes something happen less quickly than it should: *The project has suffered a series of* ***setbacks*** *this year.*

⊶**problem** /ˈprɒbləm/ *noun* **1** [DIFFICULT SITUATION] [C] a situation that causes difficulties and that needs to be dealt with *health problems* ○ *I'm* ***having problems with*** *my computer.* ○ *Drugs have become a serious problem in the area.* ➲See Common learner error at **trouble**. **2** [MATHEMATICS] [C] a question that you use mathematics to solve **3 have a problem with sth/sb** to find something or someone annoying or offensive *Yes, she can smoke in the house - I don't have a problem with that.* **4 No problem. a** [AFTER QUESTION] something that you say to mean you can or will do what someone has asked you to do *"Can you get me to the airport by 11.30?" "No problem."* **b** [AFTER THANKS] something that you say when someone has thanked you for something *"Thanks for taking me home." "No problem."*

problematic /ˌprɒbləˈmætɪk/ *adjective* full of problems or difficulties *He has a very problematic relationship with his father.*

WORD PARTNERS FOR ***procedure***

follow a procedure • correct/proper/standard procedure • a procedure for (doing) sth

procedure /prəʊˈsiːdʒəʳ/ *noun* [C, U] the official or usual way of doing something *The company has new* ***procedures for*** *dealing with complaints.*

proceed /prəʊˈsiːd/ *verb* [I] *formal* **1** to continue as planned *His lawyers have decided not to* ***proceed with*** *the case.* **2 proceed to do sth** to do something after you have done something else *She sat down and proceeded to tell me about her skiing trip.* **3 proceed along/down/to, etc** *formal* to move or travel in a particular direction *Passengers for Sydney should proceed to gate 21.*

proceedings /prəˈsiːdɪŋz/ *noun* [plural] **1** legal action against someone *The bank is threatening to start* ***legal proceedings*** *against him.* **2** a series of organized events or actions *The chairman opened the proceedings with a short speech.*

proceeds /ˈprəʊsiːdz/ *noun* [plural] the money that is earned from an event or activity *All proceeds from the concert will go to charity.*

⊶**process¹** /ˈprəʊses/ [US] /ˈprɑːses/ *noun* [C] **1** a series of actions that you take in order to achieve a result *Buying a house can be a long and complicated process.* **2** [C] a series of changes that happen naturally *the* ***ageing process*** **3 in the process** If you are doing something, and you do something else in the process, the second thing happens as a result of doing the first thing. *She stood up to say hello and spilled her drink in the process.* **4 be in the process of doing sth** to have started doing something *We're in the process of painting our apartment.*

process² /ˈprəʊses/ [US] /ˈprɑːses/ *verb* [T] **1** to add chemicals to a substance, especially food, in order to change it or make it last longer ***processed food*** **2** to deal with information or documents in an official way or by using a computer *Visa applications take 28 days to process.* • **processing** *noun* [U] *data processing*

procession /prəˈseʃᵊn/ *noun* [C] a line of people or vehicles that moves forward slowly as part of a ceremony or public event *a funeral procession*

processor /ˈprəʊsesəʳ/ *noun* [C] the main part of a computer that controls all the other parts ➲See also: **food processor, word processor**.

proclaim /prəʊˈkleɪm/ *verb* [T] *formal* to announce something officially or in public • **proclamation** /ˌprɒkləˈmeɪʃᵊn/ *noun* [C] an official announcement about something important

procrastinate /prəʊˈkræstɪneɪt/ *verb* [I] *formal* to wait a long time before doing something that you must do *I know I've got to deal with the problem at some point - I'm just procrastinating.*

procure /prəˈkjʊəʳ/ *verb* [T] *formal* to obtain something that is difficult to get *I've managed to procure a copy of that document I was telling you about.*

prod /prɒd/ *verb* **prodding** *past* **prodded 1** [I, T] to push someone or something with your finger or with a pointed object *He prodded me in the back and told me to hurry up.* **2** [T] to encourage someone to do something [+ into + doing sth] *We need to prod him into making a decision.* • **prod** *noun* [C] [usually singular] *to* ***give*** *someone a* ***prod***

prodigious /prəˈdɪdʒəs/ *adjective formal* extremely great in size or ability *a prodigious talent* ○ *a prodigious appetite*

prodigy /ˈprɒdɪdʒi/ *noun* [C] a young person who is very good at something *A* ***child prodigy****, she entered university at the age of eleven.*

⊶**produce¹** /prəˈdjuːs/ *verb* [T] **1** [MAKE] to make or grow something *The factory produces about 900 cars a year.* ○ *This plant will produce small yellow flowers in the spring.* **2** [CAUSE] to cause a particular reaction or result *Nuts produce an allergic reaction in some people.* **3** [SHOW] to take an object from somewhere so that people can see it *One of the men suddenly produced a gun from his pocket.* **4** [FILM/PLAY] to control how a film, play, programme, or musical recording is made *He's produced some of the top Broadway shows.* ➲See also: **mass-produce**.

produce² /ˈprɒdjuːs/ *noun* [U] food that is grown or made in large quantities to be sold *dairy produce*

producer /prəˈdjuːsəʳ/ *noun* [C] **1** a company, country, or person that makes goods or grows food *Australia is one of the world's main producers of wool.* **2** someone who controls how a film, play, programme, or musical recording is made *a* ***film/record producer***

⊶**product** /ˈprɒdʌkt/ *noun* [C] **1** something that is made or grown to be sold *They have a new range of skin-care products.* ○ *Does she eat* ***dairy products*** (= things made from milk)*?* **2 product of sth** someone or something that is the result of a particular experience or process *His lack of confidence is the product of an unhappy childhood.* ➲See also: **by-product, end-product**.

P

๐–**production** /prəˈdʌkʃən/ *noun* **1** MAKING [U] when you make or grow something *Sand is used in the* **production of** *glass.* ○ *The new model* **goes into production** (= starts being made) *next year.* **2** AMOUNT [U] the amount of something that is made or grown *We need to increase production by 20%.* **3** PERFORMANCE [C] a performance or series of performances of a play or show *a school production of 'Romeo and Juliet'* **4** ORGANIZING FILM/PLAY [U] when someone controls how a film, play, programme, or musical recording is made *She wants a career in TV production.*

productive /prəˈdʌktɪv/ *adjective* **1** producing a good or useful result *We had a very productive meeting and sorted out a lot of problems.* **2** producing a large amount of goods, food, work, etc *productive land* ○ *a productive worker*

productivity /ˌprɒdʌkˈtɪvəti/ *noun* [U] the rate at which goods are produced *We need to increase productivity by 50%.*

Prof /prɒf/ *noun* [C] *short for* professor *Prof Susan Nishio*

profane /prəˈfeɪn/ *adjective formal* showing no respect for God or for religious or moral rules *profane language* ● **profanity** /prəˈfænəti/ *noun* [U] *formal*

profess /prəˈfes/ *verb* [T] *formal* to express a quality or belief, often when it is not true [+ to do sth] *She professes to hate shopping, but she's always buying new things.*

profession /prəˈfeʃən/ *noun* **1** [C] a type of work that needs special training or education *He's working in a restaurant, but he's a teacher* **by profession** (= he trained to be a teacher). ⊃See Common learner error at **work**. **2** [group] the people who do a type of work considered as a group *The medical profession has expressed concern about the new drug.*

๐–**professional**¹ /prəˈfeʃənəl/ *adjective* **1** JOB [always before noun] relating to a job that needs special training or education *You should get some* **professional advice** *about your finances.* **2** EARNING MONEY Someone is professional if they earn money for a sport or activity which most people do as a hobby. *a professional athlete/musician* ⊃Opposite **amateur**. **3** SKILL showing skill and careful attention *a professional attitude* ○ *He looks very professional in that suit.* ⊃Opposite **unprofessional**.

professional² /prəˈfeʃənəl/ *noun* [C] **1** TRAINED someone who does a job that needs special training or education **2** WITH EXPERIENCE someone who has done a job for a long time and who does it with a lot of skill *She dealt with the problem like a true professional.* **3** SPORTS someone who earns money for doing a sport or activity which most other people do as a hobby *a rugby professional* ⊃Opposite **amateur**.

professionalism /prəˈfeʃənəlɪzəm/ *noun* [U] the skill and careful attention which trained people are expected to have *He complained about the lack of professionalism in the company.*

professionally /prəˈfeʃənəli/ *adverb* **1** WORK in a way that relates to your work *I know him professionally, but he's not a close friend.* **2** WITH TRAINING Work that is done professionally is done by someone who has had special training. *Their house has been professionally decorated.* **3** HIGH STANDARDS in a way that shows high standards or skill *He dealt with the situation very professionally.* **4** SPORT If someone does an activity or sport professionally, they earn money for doing it. *He's good enough at football to* **play professionally**.

professor /prəˈfesər/ *noun* [C] the highest rank of teacher in a British university, or a teacher in an American university or college *a professor of history at Oxford* ○ *Professor Blackman.*

proffer /ˈprɒfər/ *verb* [T] *formal* to offer something to someone *to proffer advice*

proficiency /prəˈfɪʃənsi/ *noun* [U] when you can do something very well *The job requires* **proficiency in** *written and spoken English.*

proficient /prəˈfɪʃənt/ *adjective* very good at something *She's* **proficient in** *two languages.* ○ *I've become quite* **proficient at** *repairing bicycles.*

profile¹ /ˈprəʊfaɪl/ *noun* [C] **1** DESCRIPTION a short description of someone's life, character, work, etc **2** HEAD a side view of someone's face or head *The picture shows him* **in profile**. **3** ATTENTION the amount of attention that something receives *We need to increase our company's profile in Asia.* **4** **high profile** important and noticeable *a high profile job* **5** **keep a low profile** to try not to be noticed

profile

profile² /ˈprəʊfaɪl/ *verb* [T] to describe someone's life, character, work, etc

WORD PARTNERS FOR *profit*

boost/increase profits ● **make** a profit ● profits **fall/rise** ● an **annual/big/gross/healthy/large/small** profit

๐–**profit**¹ /ˈprɒfɪt/ *noun* [C, U] money that you get from selling goods or services for more than they cost to produce or provide *a profit of $4.5 million* ○ *It's very hard for a new business to* **make a profit** *in its first year.*

profit² /ˈprɒfɪt/ *verb*
profit from sth to earn a profit or get an advantage from something *Investors have profited from a rise in interest rates.*

profitable /ˈprɒfɪtəbl/ *adjective* **1** making or likely to make a profit *a profitable business*

2 useful or likely to give you an advantage *a profitable discussion* • **profitability** /ˌprɒfɪtəˈbɪləti/ *noun* [U] • **profitably** *adverb*

profound /prəˈfaʊnd/ *adjective* **1** [EFFECT] If an effect is profound, it is extreme. *The war had a* ***profound impact*** *on people's lives.* **2** [FEELING] If a feeling is profound, you feel it very strongly. *a* ***profound sense of*** *sadness* **3** [UNDERSTANDING] If an idea or piece of work is profound, it shows intelligence or a great ability to understand. *a profound question* ○ *His theories were simple, but profound.* • **profoundly** *adverb*

profusely /prəˈfjuːsli/ *adverb* a lot *He* ***apologized profusely*** *for being late.*

profusion /prəˈfjuːʒən/ *noun* [U, no plural] *formal* an extremely large amount of something *a profusion of wild flowers* ○ *Bacteria grow* ***in profusion*** *in the warm, wet soil.*

prognosis /prɒgˈnəʊsɪs/ *noun* [C] *plural* **prognoses** /prɒgˈnəʊsiːz/ *formal* **1** a judgment that a doctor makes about an ill person's chance of becoming healthy **2** an opinion about the future of someone or something *The prognosis for economic growth is good.*

⊶**program**[1] /ˈprəʊgræm/ *noun* [C] **1** a set of instructions that you put into a computer to make it do something *to write a* ***computer program*** **2** *US spelling of* programme

COMMON LEARNER ERROR

program or **programme**?

In British English , **program** is used for computer instructions, and **programme** for all other meanings. In US English, **program** is used for all meanings.

program[2] /ˈprəʊgræm/ *verb* [T] **programming**, *past* **programmed** **1** If you program a computer, you give it a set of instructions to do something. **2** *US spelling of* programme

⊶**programme**[1] *UK* (*US* **program**) /ˈprəʊgræm/ *noun* [C] **1** [TELEVISION/RADIO] a show on television or radio *a* ***TV programme*** ○ *Did you see that programme about spiders last night?* **2** [PLAN] a plan of events or activities with a particular purpose *a health education programme* **3** [THIN BOOK] a thin book that you buy at a theatre, sports event, etc which tells you who or what you are going to see

programme[2] *UK* (*US* **program**) /ˈprəʊgræm/ *verb* [T] If you programme a machine, you give it a set of instructions to do something. [+ to do sth] *I've programmed the video to start recording at 10 o'clock.*

programmer /ˈprəʊgræməʳ/ *noun* [C] someone who writes computer programs as a job • **programming** *noun* [U] when someone writes computer programs

WORD PARTNERS FOR ***progress***

halt / impede / make / monitor progress • **rapid/real/significant/slow/steady** progress • progress **on/toward** sth

⊶**progress**[1] /ˈprəʊgres/ [US] /ˈprɒgres/ *noun* [U] **1** development and improvement of skills, knowledge, etc ***slow/rapid progress*** ○ *technological progress* ○ *He has* ***made*** *good* ***progress*** *in French this year.* **2 in progress** *formal* happening or being done now *Quiet please - Exams in progress.* **3** movement towards a place

progress[2] /prəʊˈgres/ *verb* [I] **1** to improve or develop in skills, knowledge, etc *Technology has progressed rapidly in the last 100 years.* ○ *Foetal medicine has progressed so much in recent years.* **2** to continue gradually *I began to feel more relaxed as the evening progressed.* ○ *As the course progressed I started to enjoy it.*

progression /prəʊˈgreʃən/ *noun* [C, U] when something or someone changes to the next stage of development *a* ***logical/natural progression*** ○ *Drugs can stop the progression of the disease.*

progressive /prəʊˈgresɪv/ *adjective* **1** thinking or behaving in a new or modern way ***progressive ideas/attitudes*** **2** developing or happening gradually *a progressive disease* • **progressively** *adverb* gradually *My headaches are getting* ***progressively worse.***

the progressive /prəʊˈgresɪv/ *noun* the form of the verb that is used to show that an action is continuing. In English, the progressive is made with 'be' and the present participle.

prohibit /prəʊˈhɪbɪt/ *verb* [T] *formal* to officially forbid something [often passive] *Smoking is prohibited on most international flights.* ○ [+ from + doing sth] *The new law prohibits people from drinking alcohol in the street.* ○ ***a prohibited substance*** • **prohibition** /ˌprəʊhɪˈbɪʃən/ *noun* [U] when something is prohibited *the prohibition against torture*

prohibitive /prəʊˈhɪbətɪv/ *adjective* If the cost of something is prohibitive, it is too expensive for many people. *The cost of flying first class is prohibitive for most people.* • **prohibitively** *adverb For most people the product is* ***prohibitively expensive.***

⊶**project**[1] /ˈprɒdʒekt/ *noun* [C] **1** a carefully planned piece of work that has a particular purpose *a research project* ○ *The new building project will cost $45 million.* ○ *The $240 million project is aimed mainly at improving the quality of drinking water in this city of 12 million people.* **2** a piece of school work that involves detailed study of a subject *We're* ***doing*** *a class* ***project on*** *the environment.*

project[2] /prəʊˈdʒekt/ *verb* **1** [CALCULATE] [T] to calculate an amount or make a guess about the future based on information that you have [often passive, + to do sth] *As people live longer, the demand for health care is projected to increase dramatically.* ○ ***projected costs/growth*** **2** [IMAGE] [T] to show a film or other image on a screen or a wall *Laser images were* ***projected onto*** *a screen.* **3** [QUALITY] [T] If you project a particular quality, that quality is what most people notice about you. *She* ***projected an image*** *of strong leadership.* **4 project from/into/out, etc** *formal* to stick out

projection /prəʊˈdʒekʃən/ *noun* **1** [C] a calculation or guess about the future based on information that you have *government pro-*

jections of population growth **2** [U] when a film or an image is projected onto a screen or wall

projector /prəˈdʒektəʳ/ *noun* [C] a machine that projects films, pictures or words onto a screen or a wall

proliferate /prəˈlɪfʰreɪt/ *verb* [I] *formal* to increase in number very quickly

proliferation /prəˌlɪfʰrˈeɪʃʰn/ *noun* [U] when something increases in number very quickly *the proliferation of new TV channels*

prolific /prəˈlɪfɪk/ *adjective* producing a lot of something *a prolific writer/composer*

prologue /ˈprəʊlɒg/ *noun* [C] an introduction to a book, film, or play

prolong /prəˈlɒŋ/ *verb* [T] to make something last longer *Eating a good diet can prolong your life.*

prolonged /prəˈlɒŋd/ *adjective* continuing for a long time *a prolonged illness*

prom /prɒm/ *noun* [C] in the US, a formal dance party for older students held at the end of the school year *a school prom*

promenade /ˌprɒməˈnɑːd/ *noun* [C] a wide path by the sea

prominence /ˈprɒmɪnəns/ *noun* [U] when someone or something is important or famous *He first came to prominence as a singer in the 1980s.*

prominent /ˈprɒmɪnənt/ *adjective* **1** important or famous *a prominent figure* **2** very easy to see or notice *a prominent feature* • **prominently** *adverb*

promiscuous /prəˈmɪskjuəs/ *adjective* Someone who is promiscuous has sex with a lot of people. • **promiscuity** /ˌprɒmɪˈskjuːəti/ *noun* [U] when someone is promiscuous

promise[1] /ˈprɒmɪs/ *verb* **1** [I, T] to say that you will certainly do something or that something will certainly happen [+ to do sth] *She promised to write to me every week.* ○ [+ (that)] *Paul promised me that he'd cook dinner tonight.* **2** [+ two objects] to say that you will certainly give something to someone *They promised us a reward.* **3** **promise to be sth** If something promises to be good, exciting, etc, people expect that it will be good, exciting, etc.

COMMON LEARNER ERROR

promise

When you use the expression **promise someone something**, no preposition is needed after the verb.

He promised his mum that he would clean his room.

~~He promised to his mum that he would clean his room.~~

☞ **WORD PARTNERS FOR *promise***

break/keep/make/renege on a promise • a broken/rash/solemn/vague promise

promise[2] /ˈprɒmɪs/ *noun* **1** [C] when you say that you will certainly do something *I'm not sure I can do it so I won't make any promises.* **2** **keep/break a promise** to do/not do what you said that you would do **3** **show promise** If

someone or something shows promise, they are likely to be successful. *As a child, he showed great promise as an athlete.*

promising /ˈprɒmɪsɪŋ/ *adjective* likely to be very good or successful in the future *a promising student* ○ *a promising start* to the game

promo /ˈprəʊməʊ/ *noun* [C] *informal* an advertisement, especially a short film

promote /prəˈməʊt/ *verb* [T] **1** [ENCOURAGE] to encourage something to happen or develop *to promote good health/peace* **2** [ADVERTISE] to advertise something *The band is promoting their new album.* **3** [JOB] to give someone a more important job in the same organization [often passive] *She's just been promoted to manager.*

promoter /prəˈməʊtəʳ/ *noun* [C] **1** someone who organizes a large event *a concert promoter* **2** someone who tries to encourage something to happen or develop *a promoter of sexual equality*

☞ **WORD PARTNERS FOR *promotion***

2 gain/get/be given a promotion • promotion to sth

promotion /prəˈməʊʃʰn/ *noun* **1** [ADVERTISEMENT] [C, U] activities to advertise something *a sales promotion* ○ *They're giving away free T-shirts as a special promotion.* **2** [JOB] [C, U] when someone is given a more important job in the same organization *She was given a promotion in her first month with the company.* **3** [ENCOURAGE] [U] when you encourage something to happen or develop *the promotion of a healthy lifestyle*

promotional /prəˈməʊʃʰnʰl/ *adjective* Promotional items or activities are used to advertise something. *a promotional campaign*

prompt[1] /prɒmpt/ *verb* [T] **1** to cause something *His remarks prompted a lot of discussion.* **2** **prompt sb to do sth** to cause someone to do sth *What prompted him to leave?* **3** to help someone, often an actor, remember what they were going to say or do

prompt[2] /prɒmpt/ *adjective* done or acting quickly and without waiting, or arriving at the correct time *a prompt reply* ○ *prompt payment* • **promptly** *adverb*

prone /prəʊn/ *adjective* **1** **be prone to sth/doing sth** to often do something or suffer from something, especially something bad *I'm prone to headaches.* **2** **accident/injury, etc prone** often having accidents/injuries, etc ⊃See also: accident-prone.

pronoun /ˈprəʊnaʊn/ *noun* [C] a word that is used instead of a noun which has usually already been talked about. For example the words 'she', 'it', and 'mine' are pronouns. ⊃See also: personal pronoun, relative pronoun.

pronounce /prəˈnaʊns/ *verb* [T] **1** to make the sound of a letter or word *How do you pronounce his name?* **2** **pronounce sb/sth dead/a success, etc** *formal* to state that something is true in an official or formal way *Doctors pronounced him dead at 12.23 a.m.*

pronounced /prəˈnaʊnst/ *adjective* very easy to

notice *She spoke with a pronounced American accent.*

pronouncement /prəˈnaʊnsmənt/ *noun* [C] *formal* an official announcement *to **make a pronouncement***

pronunciation /prəˌnʌnsiˈeɪʃən/ *noun* [C, U] how words are pronounced *There are two different pronunciations of this word.*

WORD PARTNERS FOR *proof*

have/provide proof   •   conclusive/positive/scientific proof   •   proof of sth

---

o—**proof** /pruːf/ *noun* [U] a fact or a piece of information that shows something exists or is true *She showed us her passport as **proof** of her identity.* ○ [+ (that)] *My landlord has asked for proof that I'm employed.*

-proof /pruːf/ *suffix* used at the end of words to mean 'protecting against' or 'not damaged by' *a bulletproof vest* ○ *a waterproof jacket*

prop¹ /prɒp/ *verb* propping, *past* propped **prop sth against/on, etc** to put something somewhere so that it is supported on or against something *He propped the ladder against the wall.*

prop sth up 1 to lift and give support to something by putting something under it *We had to prop up the bed with some bricks.* **2** to help something to continue *For years the industry was propped up by the government.*

prop² /prɒp/ *noun* [C] an object used in a film or play *a **stage prop***

propaganda /ˌprɒpəˈɡændə/ *noun* [U] information or ideas, which are often false, that an organization prints or broadcasts to make people agree with what it is saying *political propaganda* • **propagandist** *noun* [C] someone who creates, prints, or broadcasts propaganda

propagate /ˈprɒpəɡeɪt/ *verb formal* **1** [I, T] If you propagate plants, you help them to produce new plants, and if plants propagate, they produce new plants. **2** [T] to tell your ideas or opinions to a lot of people in order to make them agree with what you are saying *to **propagate lies/rumours*** • **propagation** /ˌprɒpəˈɡeɪʃən/ *noun* [U] *formal*

propel /prəˈpel/ *verb* [T] propelling *past* propelled **1 propel sb into/to sth** to cause someone to do an activity or be in a situation *The film propelled him to international stardom.* **2** to push or move something somewhere, often with a lot of force *a rocket propelled through space*

propeller /prəˈpelər/ *noun* [C] a piece of equipment made of two or more flat metal pieces that turn around and cause a ship or aircraft to move

propensity /prəˈpensəti/ *noun* [C] *formal* If someone has a propensity for something or to do something, they often do it. *to have a **propensity***

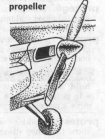
propeller

for violence ○ *a propensity to talk too much*

o—**proper** /ˈprɒpər/ *adjective* **1** [CORRECT] [always before noun] correct or suitable *the **proper way** to do something* ○ *Please put those books back in the **proper place**.* **2** [REAL] [always before noun] mainly UK real and satisfactory *his first **proper job*** ○ *You should eat some proper food instead of just sweets.* **3** [ACCEPTABLE] socially acceptable *It's not proper to interrupt someone when they're speaking.* **4** [MAIN] [always after noun] referring to the main or most important part of something *I live outside Cambridge - I don't live in the city proper.*

o—**properly** /ˈprɒpli/ *adverb* correctly, or in a satisfactory way *She doesn't act properly.*

proper ˈnoun *noun* [C] a word or group of words that is the name of a person or place and always begins with a capital letter. For example 'Tony' and 'London' are proper nouns.

WORD PARTNERS FOR *property*

private property   •   property prices   •   property developer

---

o—**property** /ˈprɒpəti/ *noun* **1** [BUILDING] [C, U] a building or area of land *There are several properties for sale in this area.* ○ *Private property - no parking.* ○ *a property developer* **2** [OBJECT] [U] objects that belong to someone *The police recovered a large amount of **stolen property**.* **3** [QUALITY] [C] a quality of something *the medicinal **properties** of wild plants* ⊃See also: lost property.

the ˈproperty ˌladder *noun* [no plural] a process in which you buy a small house and then sell it to buy a bigger house when you have more money *When house prices are high, it is hard for buyers to **move up the property ladder**.*

prophecy /ˈprɒfəsi/ *noun* [C, U] when someone says that something will happen in the future • **prophesy** /ˈprɒfəsaɪ/ *verb* [I, T] to say that you believe something will happen in the future

prophet /ˈprɒfɪt/ *noun* [C] someone sent by God to tell people what to do, or to say what will happen in the future

prophetic /prəˈfetɪk/ *adjective* saying what will happen in the future *a **prophetic dream/vision*** ○ *Her warnings **proved prophetic**.*

proponent /prəˈpəʊnənt/ *noun* [C] *formal* someone who supports a particular idea or plan of action *a proponent of nuclear energy*

proportion /prəˈpɔːʃən/ *noun* **1** [C] a part of a total number or amount *Children make up a large **proportion** of the world's population.* ○ *The class consists of both men and women in roughly **equal proportions**.* **2 out of proportion** If something is out of proportion, it is much bigger or smaller than it should be, when compared to other things. *The punishment is completely out of proportion to the crime.* **3 in proportion** If something is in proportion, it is the right size or shape when compared to other things. **4 in proportion to** If something changes in proportion to another thing, it changes to the same degree as that thing. *Your tax payment increases in pro-*

portion to your salary. **5 blow/get sth out of proportion** to behave as if something that has happened is much worse than it really is

proportional /prəˈpɔːʃ°n°l/ *adjective* If two amounts are proportional, they change at the same rate so that the relationship between them does not change. *Weight is* **proportional** *to size.*

pro‚portional ‚represen'tation *noun* [U] a system of voting in which the number of a political party's elected representatives is related to the number of votes the party gets

proportionate /prəˈpɔːʃ°nət/ *adjective* If two amounts are proportionate, they change at the same rate so that the relationship between them does not change. *His success was proportionate to his efforts.* ⊃Opposite **dis-proportionate.** • **proportionately** *adverb*

proportions /prəˈpɔːʃ°nz/ *noun* [plural] the size, shape, or level of something *Crime has increased to* **alarming proportions**.

proposal /prəˈpəʊz°l/ *noun* [C] **1** a suggestion for a plan [+ to do sth] *a proposal to raise taxes* ○ *The* **proposal for** *a new sports hall has been rejected.* **2** when someone asks someone to marry them

propose /prəˈpəʊz/ *verb* **1** [T] to suggest a plan or action [+ (that)] *I propose that we delay our decision until we have more information.* ○ *proposed changes* **2 propose to do sth** to intend to do something *They propose to cycle across Europe.* **3** [I] to ask someone to marry you *He proposed to me on my birthday.*

proposition /ˌprɒpəˈzɪʃ°n/ *noun* [C] OFFER an offer or suggestion, usually in business *an attractive/interesting proposition* **2** IDEA an idea or opinion [+ that] *the proposition that all people are created equal* **3** PLAN in the US, a formal plan that people accept or refuse by voting

proprietary /prəˈpraɪət°ri/ *adjective* [always before noun] *formal* owned or controlled by a company *proprietary software*

proprietor /prəˈpraɪətəʳ/ *noun* [C] *formal* the owner of a business such as a hotel, shop, newspaper, etc

propriety /prəˈpraɪəti/ *noun* [U] *formal* socially acceptable behaviour

propulsion /prəˈpʌlʃ°n/ *noun* [U] a force that pushes something forward *jet propulsion*

prosaic /prəʊˈzeɪɪk/ *adjective formal* ordinary and not interesting

prose /prəʊz/ *noun* [U] ordinary written language that is not poetry *He's a wonderful writer - readers love his clear and lively prose.*

prosecute /ˈprɒsɪkjuːt/ *verb* [I, T] to accuse someone of a crime in a law court *No one has been prosecuted for the murders.*

prosecution /ˌprɒsɪˈkjuːʃ°n/ *noun* **1 the prosecution** [group] the lawyers who are prosecuting someone in a court of law *The prosecution will begin presenting evidence today.* **2** [C, U] when someone is prosecuted

prosecutor /ˈprɒsɪkjuːtəʳ/ *noun* [C] a lawyer who prosecutes people

face the prospect **of** sth • **with** the prospect **of** sth • **at** the prospect **of** sth

prospect /ˈprɒspekt/ *noun* **1** [C, U] the possibility that something good might happen in the future *Is there any* **prospect of** *the weather improving?* **2** [no plural] the idea of something that will happen in the future [+ of + doing sth] *We* **face the prospect of** *having to start all over again.* ○ *I'm very excited* **at the prospect of** *seeing her again.* **3 sb's prospects** the possibility of being successful at work *He's hoping the course will improve his* **career prospects**.

prospective /prəˈspektɪv/ *adjective* **prospective buyers/employers/parents, etc** Prospective buyers, employers, parents, etc are not yet buyers, employers, parents, etc but are expected to be in the future.

prospectus /prəˈspektəs/ *noun* [C] a book or magazine which gives information about a school, college, or business for future students or customers

prosper /ˈprɒspəʳ/ *verb* [I] to be successful, usually by earning a lot of money

prosperity /prɒsˈperəti/ *noun* [U] when someone is successful, usually by earning a lot of money

prosperous /ˈprɒsp°rəs/ *adjective* successful, usually by earning a lot of money

prostitute /ˈprɒstɪtjuːt/ *noun* [C] someone whose job is having sex with people • **prostitution** /ˌprɒstɪˈtjuːʃ°n/ *noun* [U]

prostrate /ˈprɒstreɪt/ *adjective* lying flat on the ground with your face pointing down

protagonist /prəʊˈtæg°nɪst/ *noun* [C] *formal* the main character in a play, film, or story

☞**protect** /prəˈtekt/ *verb* [I, T] to keep someone or something safe from something dangerous or bad *It's important to* **protect** *your skin from the harmful effects of the sun.* ○ *Vitamin C may help* **protect against** *cancer.* ⊃See Common learner error at **prevent.** • **protection** /prəˈtekʃ°n/ *noun* [U] *This coat doesn't provide any* **protection against** *the rain.*

protective /prəˈtektɪv/ *adjective* **1** giving protection *protective clothing* ○ *a protective mask* **2** wanting to protect someone from criticism, hurt, danger, etc because you like them *She's fiercely* **protective of** *her children.*

protector /prəˈtektəʳ/ *noun* [C] someone or something that protects

protégé /ˈprɒtəʒeɪ/ *noun* [C] a young person who is helped and taught by an older and usually famous person

protein /ˈprəʊtiːn/ *noun* [U] food such as meat, cheese, fish, or eggs that is necessary for the body to grow and be strong

hold/stage a protest • **do** sth **as** a protest • **in** protest **at** sth • a protest **against/over** sth • a protest **by/from** sb

protest¹ /ˈprəʊtest/ *noun* [C, U] when people show that they disagree with something by standing somewhere, shouting, carrying signs, etc *a protest against the war* ○ *a peaceful/violent protest*

protest² /prəʊˈtest/ *verb* **1** **protest (about/against/at sth)** to show that you disagree with something by standing somewhere, shouting, carrying signs, etc *Students were protesting about cuts to the education budget.* **2 protest sth** *US* to show that you disagree with something by standing somewhere, shouting, carrying signs, etc *Thousands gathered to protest the plan.* **3** [I, T] to say something forcefully or complain about something [+ that] *The girl was crying, protesting that she didn't want to leave her mother.*

Protestant /ˈprɒtɪstᵊnt/ *adjective* belonging or relating to the part of the Christian religion that separated from the Roman Catholic Church in the 1500s ● **Protestant** *noun* [C] ● **Protestantism** *noun* [U] the beliefs of the Protestant Churches

protestation /ˌprɒtesˈteɪʃᵊn/ *noun* [C] *formal* when someone says something forcefully or complains about something *He was arrested despite his protestations of innocence.*

protester (*also* **protestor**) /prəˈtestəʳ/ *noun* [C] someone who shows that they disagree with something by standing somewhere, shouting, carrying signs, etc

protocol /ˈprəʊtəkɒl/ *noun* [C, U] the rules about what you must do and how you must behave in official or very formal situations *royal protocol*

proton /ˈprəʊtɒn/ *noun* [C] a part of an atom with a positive electrical charge

prototype /ˈprəʊtəʊtaɪp/ *noun* [C] the first model or example of something new that can be developed or copied in the future *a prototype for a new car*

protracted /prəˈtræktɪd/ *adjective* If an unpleasant situation is protracted, it lasts a long time. *a protracted dispute/struggle*

protrude /prəˈtruːd/ *verb* [I] If something such as a part of the body protrudes, it comes out from the surface more than usual. *protruding ears/teeth*

WORD PARTNERS FOR *proud*

fiercely/immensely/rightly proud ● proud **of** sth/sb

---

o͎**proud** /praʊd/ *adjective* **1** feeling very pleased about something you have done, something you own, or someone you know *She was so proud of her son.* ○ [+ to do sth] *I'm very proud to be involved in this project.* **2 be too proud to do sth** to not be able to do something, especially ask for help, because you are too embarrassed *He's too proud to ask you for any money.* **3** feeling that you are more important than you really are

proudly /ˈpraʊdli/ *adverb* in a way that shows you are pleased about something you have done, something you own, or someone you know *He proudly showed us a photo of his grandchildren.*

o͎**prove** /pruːv/ *verb* [T] *past* **proved** *past participle mainly US* **proven** **1** to show that something is

true *They knew who had stolen the money, but they couldn't prove it.* ○ [+ (that)] *Can you prove that you weren't there?* ⊃Opposite **disprove**. **2 prove sth/to be sth** to show a particular quality after a period of time *The new treatment has proved to be very effective.* **3 prove yourself** to show that you are good at something *I wish he'd stop trying to prove himself all the time.*

proven /ˈpruːvᵊn/ *adjective* If something is proven, it has been shown to be true. *proven ability/skills*

proverb /ˈprɒvɜːb/ *noun* [C] a famous phrase or sentence which gives you advice *an ancient Chinese proverb* ● **proverbial** /prəˈvɜːbiəl/ *adjective* relating to a proverb

o͎**provide** /prəˈvaɪd/ *verb* [T] to supply something to someone *This booklet provides useful information about local services.* ○ *It's a new scheme to provide schools with free computers.* ● **provider** *noun* [C] someone who provides something *an Internet service provider*

provide for sb to give someone the things they need such as money, food, or clothes *He has a wife and two young children to provide for.*

provided (that) /prəˈvaɪdɪd/ (*also* **providing (that)**) *conjunction* only if *He's welcome to come along, provided that he behaves himself.*

province /ˈprɒvɪns/ *noun* **1** [C] one of the large areas which some countries are divided into because of the type of government they have *the Canadian province of Alberta* **2 the provinces** the areas of a country that are not the capital city and so are not considered exciting or fashionable

provincial /prəˈvɪnʃᵊl/ *adjective* **1** relating to a province **2** relating to or typical of the provinces *a provincial town* ○ *provincial attitudes*

provision /prəˈvɪʒᵊn/ *noun* **1** [U] when something is provided for someone *We need to increase the provision of health care for the elderly.* **2 make provision for sth** to make arrangements to deal with something *He hasn't made any provision for his retirement yet.* **3** [C] a rule that is part of a law or an agreement

provisional /prəˈvɪʒᵊnᵊl/ *adjective* If a situation or arrangement is provisional, it is not certain and might change in the future. *These dates are only provisional at the moment.* ● **provisionally** *adverb*

provisions /prəˈvɪʒᵊnz/ *noun* [plural] supplies of food and other necessary items

proviso /prəˈvaɪzəʊ/ *noun* [C] *formal* something that must happen as part of an agreement *He was released from prison with the proviso that he doesn't leave the country.*

provocation /ˌprɒvəˈkeɪʃᵊn/ *noun* [C, U] when someone makes you angry *He'll start a fight at the slightest provocation.*

provocative /prəˈvɒkətɪv/ *adjective* **1** causing an angry reaction, usually intentionally *a provocative question/remark* **2** Provocative clothes, images, etc are sexually exciting. ● **provocatively** *adverb* *She dresses very provocatively.*

provoke /prəˈvəʊk/ *verb* [T] **1** to cause a strong and usually angry reaction *to provoke an*

---

argument ○ *Her statement has provoked a public outcry.* **2** to intentionally make someone angry so that they react in an angry or violent way *He claimed he was provoked by the victim.*

prowess /ˈpraʊɪs/ *noun* [U] *formal* when you are good at doing something *athletic/sporting prowess*

prowl¹ /praʊl/ *verb* [I, T] to walk around somewhere slowly as if hunting someone or something *to prowl the streets*

prowl² /praʊl/ *noun* **be on the prowl** to be hunting for someone or something *There was a fox on the prowl earlier.*

proximity /prɒkˈsɪməti/ *noun* [U] *formal* when something is near to something else *What's good about this hotel is its proximity to the airport.*

proxy /ˈprɒksi/ *noun* **by proxy** using another person to do something instead of doing something yourself *to vote by proxy*

Prozac /ˈprəʊzæk/ *noun* [U] *trademark* a drug that is used to make people feel happier and less worried *She's on Prozac because of her depression.*

prude /pruːd/ *noun* [C] someone who does not like to hear or see things relating to sex *Don't be such a prude.* ● **prudish** *adjective* a *prudish woman*

prudent /ˈpruːdᵊnt/ *adjective formal* wise and careful [+ to do sth] *I think it would be prudent to leave now before it starts raining.* ● **prudence** /ˈpruːdᵊns/ *noun* [U] *formal* ● **prudently** *adverb*

prune¹ /pruːn/ *verb* [T] If you prune a tree or bush, you cut off some of the branches or flowers to help it grow better.

prune² /pruːn/ *noun* [C] a dried plum (= type of fruit)

pry /praɪ/ *verb* **1** [I] to try to discover private things about people *to pry into someone's personal life.* ○ *She wanted a private holiday away from prying eyes.* **2 pry sth apart/loose/open, etc** to open something with difficulty *She managed to pry open a window and escape.*

PS /ˌpiːˈes/ used when you want to add extra information at the end of a letter or email *PS Give my love to Emma.*

psalm /sɑːm/ *noun* [C] a song or poem from the Bible (= holy book)

pseudo- /sjuːdəʊ-/ *prefix* false *pseudo-academic*

pseudonym /ˈsjuːdənɪm/ *noun* [C] a name used by a writer instead of their own name *He writes under a pseudonym.*

psych /saɪk/ *verb*
psych yourself up *informal* to try to make yourself feel confident and ready to do something difficult

psyche /ˈsaɪki/ *noun* [C] the human mind and feelings *the male psyche*

psychedelic /ˌsaɪkɪˈdelɪk/ *adjective* **1** Psychedelic drugs make you see things that are not really there. **2** Psychedelic colours or patterns are very strong, bright, and strange.

psychiatrist /saɪˈkaɪətrɪst/ *noun* [C] a doctor who is trained in psychiatry

psychiatry /saɪˈkaɪətri/ *noun* [U] the study and treatment of mental illness ● **psychiatric** /ˌsaɪkiˈætrɪk/ *adjective* relating to psychiatry *a psychiatric disorder* ○ *a psychiatric nurse*

psychic /ˈsaɪkɪk/ *adjective* having a special mental ability, for example so that you are able to know what will happen in the future or know what people are thinking *psychic powers*

psycho /ˈsaɪkəʊ/ *noun* [C] *informal* someone who is crazy and frightening

psychoanalysis /ˌsaɪkəʊəˈnæləsɪs/ *noun* [U] the treatment of mental problems by studying and talking about people's dreams, fears, and experiences ● **psychoanalytic** /ˌsaɪkəʊˌænᵊlˈɪtɪk/ *adjective* relating to psychoanalysis

psychoanalyst /ˌsaɪkəʊˈænᵊlɪst/ *noun* [C] someone who treats people using psychoanalysis

psychological /ˌsaɪkᵊlˈɒdʒɪkᵊl/ *adjective* relating to the human mind and feelings *psychological problems* ● **psychologically** *adverb*

psychologist /saɪˈkɒlədʒɪst/ *noun* [C] someone who has studied the human mind and feelings

psychology /saɪˈkɒlədʒi/ *noun* [U] **1** the study of the human mind and feelings *child psychology* ○ *He's studying psychology and philosophy.* **2** the way someone thinks and behaves *the psychology of serial killers*

psychopath /ˈsaɪkəʊpæθ/ *noun* [C] someone who is very mentally ill and usually dangerous ● **psychopathic** /ˌsaɪkəʊˈpæθɪk/ *adjective* a *psychopathic killer*

psychosis /saɪˈkəʊsɪs/ *noun* [C] *plural* **psychoses** /saɪˈkəʊsiːz/ a mental illness that makes you believe things that are not real

psychotherapy /ˌsaɪkəʊˈθerəpi/ *noun* [U] the treatment of mental problems by talking about your feelings instead of taking medicine ● **psychotherapist** *noun* [C] someone who gives people psychotherapy

psychotic /saɪˈkɒtɪk/ *adjective* suffering from a mental illness that makes you believe things that are not true

pt *noun* [C] **1** *written abbreviation for* point (= a unit used for showing who is winning in a game or competition) *Hill 81 pts, Villeneuve 68 pts* **2** *written abbreviation for* pint (= a unit for measuring liquid)

PTO /ˌpiːtiːˈəʊ/ *UK abbreviation for* please turn over: used at the bottom of a page of writing to show that there is more information on the other side

pub /pʌb/ *noun* [C] a place where you can get drinks such as beer and usually food *We're all going to the pub after work.*

puberty /ˈpjuːbəti/ *noun* [U] the time when children's bodies change and become like adults' bodies *to reach puberty* ○ *Puberty is a difficult period for most children.*

pubic hair /ˌpjuːbɪkˈheəʳ/ *noun* [U] the hair that grows around the sexual organs

⚬ **public¹** /ˈpʌblɪk/ *adjective* **1 public awareness/ health/support, etc** the awareness/health/support, etc of all ordinary people *They are trying to raise public awareness of the issue.* ○ *Public opinion has turned against him.* ○ *Is it really* *in the public interest* (= useful for people) *to publish this information?* **2 public parks/toilets/transport, etc** parks/toilets/transport, etc that are for everyone to use and are not private *Smoking should be banned in public places.* **3 a public announcement/appearance/statement, etc** an announcement/appearance/statement, etc that can be seen or heard or known by everyone *The Prime Minister is due to make a public statement later today.* **4 make sth public** to allow everyone to know about something *The government does not plan to make its findings public.* **5 public funds/services/spending, etc** funds/services/spending, etc controlled or supplied by the government and not by a private company

⊶**public²** /ˈpʌblɪk/ *noun* **[group] 1 the (general) public** all ordinary people *a member of the public* ○ *The public has a right to know about this.* ○ *The house is only open to the general public on Sundays.* **2 in public** where everyone can see you *He shouldn't behave like that in public.*

ˌpublic adˈdress system (*also UK* **tannoy**) *noun* **[C]** a system of equipment used in public places that someone speaks into in order to make their voice loud enough to hear

publication /ˌpʌblɪˈkeɪʃən/ *noun* **1 [U]** when a book, newspaper, etc is printed and sold **2 [C]** a book, newspaper, or magazine *a monthly/weekly publication*

publicist /ˈpʌblɪsɪst/ *noun* **[C]** someone whose job is to make people know about someone or something by advertising or giving information in the newspaper, on television, etc

WORD PARTNERS FOR ***publicity***

attract/get/receive/seek publicity • **adverse/bad/good/negative** publicity • publicity **about/for** sth • publicity **surrounding** sth • a publicity **campaign/stunt**

publicity /pʌbˈlɪsəti/ *noun* **[U]** advertising or information about someone or something in the newspaper, on television, etc *a publicity campaign* ○ *to get **bad/good publicity***

publicize (*also UK* **-ise**) /ˈpʌblɪsaɪz/ *verb* **[T]** to make people know about something by advertising or giving information in newspapers, on television, etc *a highly/widely publicized event*

publicly /ˈpʌblɪkli/ *adverb* If you do something publicly, everyone can see it, hear it, or know about it.

ˌpublic reˈlations *noun formal* PR (=writing and activities that are intended to make a person, company, or product more popular)

ˌpublic ˈschool (*US* **ˈpublic ˌschool**) *noun* **[C] 1** in the UK, a school that you pay to go to **2** (*UK* **state school**) in the US, a school that is free to go to because the government provides the money for it

the ˌpublic ˈsector *noun* businesses and industries that are owned or controlled by the government

ˌpublic ˈtransport *noun* **[U]** a system of vehicles such as buses and trains which operate at regular times and that the public use

ˌpublic uˈtility *noun* **[C]** an organization that supplies the public with water, gas, or electricity

⊶**publish** /ˈpʌblɪʃ/ *verb* **[T] 1** [PRINT] to prepare and print a book, newspaper, magazine, article, etc so that people can buy it **[often passive]** *This book is published by Cambridge University Press.* ○ *Did they publish his article?* **2** [WRITE] to write something that is then printed in a book, newspaper, magazine, etc *She works for a small publisher.* ○ *He's published several short stories in national magazines.* **3** [MAKE PUBLIC] to make information available to the public *Are they going to publish the results of the survey?*

publisher /ˈpʌblɪʃəʳ/ *noun* **[C]** a company or person who prepares and prints books, newspapers, magazines, etc

publishing /ˈpʌblɪʃɪŋ/ *noun* **[U]** the business of preparing and printing books, newspapers, magazines, etc *a career in publishing* ○ *the publishing industry*

puck /pʌk/ *noun* **[C]** in ice hockey (= a sport), a small, hard disc that players hit with a stick ➲See colour picture **Sports 1** on page Centre 14.

pudding /ˈpʊdɪŋ/ *noun* **1 [C, U]** in the UK, a sweet dish that is usually eaten as the last part of a meal *We've got apple pie for pudding.* ○ *I'd eaten such a big first course, I didn't have any room for pudding.* **2 [U]** in the US, a soft, sweet food made from milk, sugar, eggs, and sometimes flour *chocolate/vanilla pudding*

puddle /ˈpʌdl/ *noun* **[C]** a pool of liquid on the ground, usually from rain *Milly likes to splash in the puddles.* ○ *I wasn't looking where I was going and stepped in a huge puddle.*

puerile /ˈpjʊəraɪl/ [US] /ˈpjuːərɪl/ *adjective formal* behaving in a silly way like a child *I think they found his sense of humour rather peurile.*

P

puff¹ /pʌf/ *verb* **1 [I]** to breathe fast and with difficulty, usually because you have been doing exercise *I was still puffing from having climbed a flight of stairs.* **2 [I, T]** to smoke something *to puff on a cigarette*

puff sth out to make your chest or your face become bigger by filling them with air

puff up If part of your body puffs up, it becomes larger because it is infected or injured. *Overnight his eyes had puffed up and he couldn't see properly.*

puff² /pʌf/ *noun* **[C] 1** a small amount of smoke, gas, powder, etc *a puff of smoke/air* **2** when someone breathes in smoke from a cigarette *to take a puff on a cigarette*

puffin /ˈpʌfɪn/ *noun* **[C]** a black and white sea bird with a large head and brightly coloured beak

puffy /ˈpʌfi/ *adjective* If the skin around your eyes is puffy, it is slightly swollen. *His eyes were still **puffy** with sleep.* ○ *She had a puffy face, as if she'd been crying.*

puke /pjuːk/ (*also* **puke up**) *verb* **[I, T]** *informal* to vomit *Someone had puked all over the toilet floor.*

pull

🔑**pull**[1] /pʊl/ *verb* **1** **[I, T]** to take hold of something and move it somewhere *If you keep pulling his tail, he'll bite you.* ○ *No wonder it's not working, someone's* ***pulled*** *the plug* ***out***. ○ *He* ***pulled off*** *his boots.* ○ *She bent down and* ***pulled up*** *her socks.* **2 pull a muscle** to injure a muscle by stretching it too much **3 pull a gun/knife, etc on sb** to suddenly take out a weapon *He pulled a gun on us and demanded money.* ➲See also: pull/tear your **hair** out, pull the **plug**[1], not pull any punches (**punch**[2]), pull out all the stops (**stop**[2]), pull strings (**string**[1]), pull your **weight**.

pull sth apart **1** to destroy something by tearing it into pieces **2** to say that something, usually a piece of work, is very bad *The last essay I gave him he really pulled apart.*

pull sb/sth apart to separate two things or people

pull at sth to pull something several times, usually with quick, light movements *Stop pulling at my sleeve.*

pull away **1** If a vehicle pulls away, it starts moving. *I just managed to get on the bus before it pulled away.* **2** If you pull away from someone who is holding you, you suddenly move your body backwards, away from them. *As he went to kiss her she pulled away.*

pull sth down to destroy a building because it is not wanted any more. *They've started pulling down the old cinema.* ○ *Protesters took to the streets and pulled down a statue of the former leader.*

pull in/into sth If a vehicle pulls in or pulls into somewhere, it moves in that direction and stops there. *They pulled in at the side of the road.*

pull sth off to succeed in doing or achieving something difficult *He is about to pull off his biggest deal yet.* ○ *It's a clever idea and if he pulls it off he'll earn a lot of money.*

pull off *UK* If a vehicle pulls off, it starts moving. *The car pulled off and sped up the road.*

pull on sth to put on clothes quickly *I pulled on my jeans and ran downstairs.*

pull out If a vehicle pulls out, it starts moving onto a road or onto a different part of the road. *That car pulled out right in front of me.*

pull over If a vehicle pulls over, it moves to the side of the road and stops. *I was looking for somewhere to pull over so I could read a map.*

pull through to continue to live after you have been badly injured or very ill

pull yourself together *informal* to become calm and behave normally again after being angry or upset *Pull yourself together, now. There's no point in crying.*

pull up **1** If a vehicle pulls up, it stops, often for a short time. *A car pulled up outside the bank and two men got out.* **2 pull up a chair** to move a chair nearer to something or someone *Why don't you pull up a chair and join us?*

pull[2] /pʊl/ *noun* **[no plural]** a strong force that causes something to move somewhere or be attracted to something *the pull of gravity*

pull-down /ˈpʊldaʊn/ *adjective* **[always before noun]** A pull-down menu is a list of choices on a computer screen which is hidden until you choose to look at it. *Choose the desired option from the* ***pull-down menu***.

pulley /ˈpʊli/ *noun* **[C]** a wheel with a rope going round it which is used to lift things

pulley

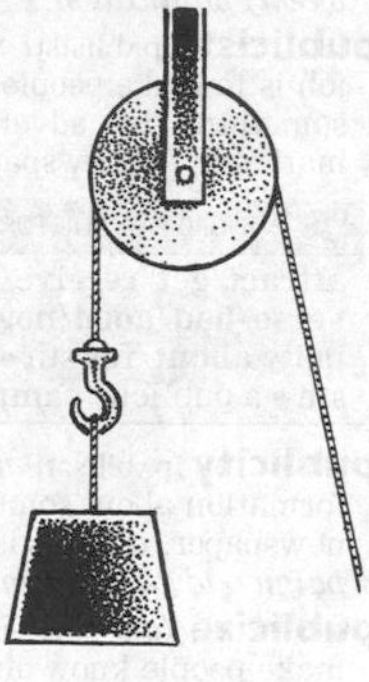

pullover /ˈpʊləʊvə^{r}/ *noun* **[C]** a warm piece of clothing which covers the top of your body and is pulled on over your head *a black woolly pullover*

pulp /pʌlp/ *noun* **[U]** **1** a soft, wet substance made from wood, which is used to make paper **2** the soft part inside a fruit or vegetable *Peel the mangoes and chop up the pulp.*

pulpit /ˈpʊlpɪt/ *noun* **[C]** the raised structure in a church where the priest stands when he speaks to everyone

pulsate /pʌlˈseɪt/ [US] /ˈpʌlseɪt/ *verb* **[I]** to beat or move with a strong, regular rhythm *The whole room was pulsating with music.*

pulse /pʌls/ *noun* **[C]** the regular movement of blood through your body when your heart is beating *She put her fingers on my wrist to* ***take my pulse*** (= count the number of beats per minute). ○ *My* ***pulse rate*** *is 70.*

pulses /pʌlsɪz/ *noun* **[plural]** *UK* seeds such as beans or peas which are cooked and eaten as food *Pulses are a healthy and economical form of protein.*

pump

bicycle pump

petrol pump *UK*,
gas pump *US*

pump¹ /pʌmp/ *noun* [C] a piece of equipment which forces liquid or gas to move somewhere *a **gas/petrol pump** ∘ a **water pump***

pump² /pʌmp/ *verb* [T] to force liquid or gas to move somewhere *Your heart pumps blood around your body.* ∘ *Firemen used powerful hoses to **pump** water **into** the building.*

pump sth into sth to give a lot of money to a plan or organization *They've pumped millions of pounds into the economy.*

pump sth out *informal* to continuously produce a lot of something *a radio pumping out music*

pump sth up to fill something with air using a pump *You should pump your tyres up.*

pumpkin /'pʌmpkɪn/ *noun* [C, U] a large, round vegetable with thick, orange skin

pun /pʌn/ *noun* [C] a joke that you make by using a word that has two meanings

punch¹ /pʌnʃ/ *verb* [T] **1** to hit someone or something with your fist (= closed hand) *He punched me twice in the stomach.* **2** **punch a hole in sth** to make a hole in something with a special piece of equipment

░ WORD PARTNERS FOR **punch**

aim a punch **at** sb • **deliver/land/swing/ throw** a punch

punch² /pʌnʃ/ *noun* **1** HIT [C] when you hit someone or something with your fist (= closed hand) *a punch on the nose* **2** DRINK [U] a sweet, mixed drink made from fruit juice, spices, and usually alcohol **3** HOLE [C] a piece of equipment that makes a hole in something **4 not pull any punches** to speak in an honest way without trying to be kind

punchline /'pʌntʃlaɪn/ *noun* [C] the last part of a joke that makes it funny

punch-up /'pʌntʃʌp/ *noun* [C] *UK informal* a fight in which people hit each other with their fists (= closed hands)

punctual /'pʌŋktʃuəl/ *adjective* arriving at the right time and not too late • **punctuality** /ˌpʌŋktʃu'æləti/ *noun* [U] when you are punctual • **punctually** *adverb*

punctuate /'pʌŋktʃueɪt/ *verb* [T] to add punctuation marks to written words so that people

can see when a sentence begins and finishes, that something is a question, etc

punctuation /ˌpʌŋktʃu'eɪʃ°n/ *noun* [C] the use of punctuation marks in writing so that people can see when a sentence begins and finishes, that something is a question, etc ⊃See Extra help page **Punctuation** on page Centre 33.

punctu'ation ˌmark *noun* [C] a symbol such as a full stop (.) or a question mark (?) used in writing to show where a sentence begins and finishes, etc.

puncture¹ /'pʌŋktʃəʳ/ *noun* [C] **1** a small hole made by a sharp object **2** *UK* a hole in a tyre that makes the air come out *to have a puncture*

puncture² /'pʌŋktʃəʳ/ *verb* [T] to make a hole in something *The knife punctured his lung.*

pundit /'pʌndɪt/ *noun* [C] someone who is an expert in a subject and often gives their opinions on television, radio, etc *a **political pundit***

pungent /'pʌndʒ°nt/ *adjective* A pungent smell is very strong. *the pungent smell of vinegar*

o⌐**punish** /'pʌnɪʃ/ *verb* [I] to make someone suffer because they have done something bad [often passive] *They must be severely **punished for** these crimes.*

punishable /'pʌnɪʃəbl/ *adjective* A crime that is punishable is one that you can be punished for. *Drug dealing is **punishable by death** in some countries.*

punishing /'pʌnɪʃɪŋ/ *adjective* very difficult and making you tired *a **punishing schedule***

░ WORD PARTNERS FOR **punishment**

capital/corporal punishment • an **appropriate/cruel/harsh/severe** punishment • **deserve/escape/impose/inflict/re- ceive** punishment

o⌐**punishment** /'pʌnɪʃmənt/ *noun* [C, U] when someone is punished *He had to stay in his bedroom as a **punishment for** fighting.* ⊃See also: **capital punishment**, **corporal punishment**, be a **glutton** for punishment.

punitive /'pjuːnətɪv/ *adjective formal* given as a punishment or seeming like a punishment *punitive action*

punk /pʌŋk/ *noun* **1** STYLE [U] (*also* ˌpunk 'rock) a style of music and fashion in the 1970s which was wild, loud, and violent **2** PERSON [C] someone who wears punk clothes and likes punk music **3** BAD MAN [C] *US informal* a bad young man

punt¹ /pʌnt/ *noun* [C] **1** a long boat with a flat bottom that you push along the river with a long pole **2** in some sports, a powerful kick which causes the ball to go very far

punt² /pʌnt/ *verb* **1** [I, T] to go or take someone along the river in a punt **2** [T] in some sports, to kick a ball after you have dropped it from your hands and before it touches the ground

punter /'pʌntəʳ/ *noun* [C] *UK informal* someone who is buying something or making a bet (= risking money on a competition)

puny /'pjuːni/ *adjective* very small and weak

pup /pʌp/ *noun* [C] a young dog or other particular type of baby mammal *a seal pup*

P

pupil /ˈpjuːpᵊl/ *noun* [C] **1** a student at school *The school has 1,100 pupils aged 11 to 18.* ➲See colour picture **The Classroom** on page Centre 6. **2** the black, round part in the centre of your eye

puppet /ˈpʌpɪt/ *noun* [C] **1** a toy in the shape of a person or animal that you can move with strings or by putting your hand inside *a **glove puppet*** **2** someone who is controlled by someone else *a political puppet*

puppy /ˈpʌpi/ *noun* [C] a young dog *a litter of puppies*

purchase[1] /ˈpɜːtʃəs/ *verb* [T] *formal* to buy something *Tickets must be purchased two weeks in advance.*

purchase[2] /ˈpɜːtʃəs/ *noun formal* **1** [C, U] when you buy something *the illegal purchase of guns* **2** [C] something that you buy *a major purchase*

⊶**pure** /pjʊəʳ/ *adjective* **1** [NOT MIXED] A pure substance is not mixed with anything else. *pure gold* ○ *pure wool* **2** [EMPHASIS] **[always before noun]** used to emphasize that a feeling, quality, or state is completely and only that thing ***pure coincidence*** ○ *Her face had a look of pure delight.* **3** [CLEAN] clean and healthy ***pure air/water*** **4 pure mathematics/physics, etc** the study of mathematics/physics, etc based only on ideas and not on practical use **5** [GOOD] completely good and not having any bad qualities or bad morals

puree /ˈpjʊəreɪ/ Ⓤⓢ /pjʊəˈreɪ/ *noun* [U] a thick, smooth, liquid food made by crushing and mixing fruit or vegetables *tomato puree*

purely /pjʊəli/ *adverb* only *She married him **purely for** his money.*

purgatory /ˈpɜːgətᵊri/ *noun* [U] **1** in the Catholic religion, a very unpleasant place where you have to go and suffer before you go to heaven **2** a very unpleasant situation *This diet is purgatory.*

purge /pɜːdʒ/ *verb* [T] **1** to get rid of bad feelings that you do not want **[often reflexive]** *She wanted to **purge** herself **of** guilt.* **2** to get rid of people from an organization because you do not agree with them • **purge** *noun* [C]

purify /ˈpjʊərɪfaɪ/ *verb* [T] to remove bad substances from something to make it pure *Plants help to purify the air.* ○ *purified water* • **purification** /ˌpjʊərɪfɪˈkeɪʃᵊn/ *noun* [U]

purist /ˈpjʊərɪst/ *noun* [C] someone who believes in and follows very traditional rules or ideas in a subject

puritanical /ˌpjʊərɪˈtænɪkᵊl/ *adjective* having severe religious morals and not wanting people to enjoy themselves • **puritan** /ˈpjʊərɪtᵊn/ *noun* [C] a puritanical person

purity /ˈpjʊərəti/ *noun* [U] the quality of being pure *air purity*

purple /ˈpɜːpl/ *adjective* being a colour that is a mixture of red and blue *purple pansies* • **purple** *noun* [C, U] ➲See colour picture **Colours** on page Centre 12.

purport /pəˈpɔːt/ *verb*

purport to be/do sth *formal* to pretend to be or do something *a man purporting to be a police officer*

WORD PARTNERS FOR *purpose*

defeat/have/fulfil/serve a purpose • a **clear/good/primary/practical/useful** purpose • the purpose **of** sth

⊶**purpose** /ˈpɜːpəs/ *noun* **1** [C] why you do something or why something exists *The main **purpose of** the meeting is to discuss the future of the company.* ○ *The drug may be legalized for medical purposes.* **2** [U] the feeling of knowing what you want to do *He seems to have lost all **sense of purpose**.* **3 on purpose** intentionally *I didn't do it on purpose, it was an accident.* **4 serve a purpose** to have a use *These small village shops serve a very useful purpose.* ➲See also: **cross purposes**, to/for all intents (**intent**[1]) (and purposes).

purpose-built /ˌpɜːpəsˈbɪlt/ *adjective mainly UK* A purpose-built building has been specially designed for the way it will be used.

purposeful /ˈpɜːpəsfᵊl/ *adjective* showing that you know what you want to do *He has a quiet, purposeful air.* • **purposefully** *adverb*

purposely /ˈpɜːpəsli/ *adverb* intentionally *I wasn't purposely trying to hurt you.*

purr /pɜːʳ/ *verb* [I] **1** [CAT] If a cat purrs, it makes a soft sound in its throat to show pleasure. **2** [PERSON] to talk in a soft, low voice **3** [CAR] If a car purrs, its engine is very smooth and makes a soft sound.

purse[1] /pɜːs/ *noun* [C] **1** *UK* a small container for money, usually used by a woman *a leather purse* **2** *mainly US* (*mainly UK* **handbag**) a bag, usually carried by a woman *I always carry aspirin in my purse.*

purse[2] /pɜːs/ *verb* **purse your lips** to press your lips tightly together, often to show that you are angry

pursue /pəˈsjuː/ Ⓤⓢ /pərˈsuː/ *verb* [T] **pursuing**, *past* **pursued** **1** If you pursue a plan, activity, or situation, you try to do it or achieve it, usually over a long period of time. *She decided to pursue a career in television.* **2** to follow someone or something, usually to try to catch them *The car was pursued by helicopters.* **3 pursue a matter** to try to discover information about something *We will not be pursuing this matter any further.*

pursuit /pəˈsjuːt/ Ⓤⓢ /pərˈsuːt/ *noun* [U] **1** when you try to achieve a plan, activity, or situation, usually over a long period of time *the pursuit of pleasure* ○ *He left his native country **in pursuit of** freedom.* **2** when you follow someone or something to try to catch them *The police are **in pursuit of** a 25-year-old murder suspect.*

pursuits /pəˈsjuːts/ Ⓤⓢ /pərˈsuːts/ *noun* **[plural]** *formal* activities or hobbies *He enjoys climbing and other **outdoor pursuits**.*

purveyor /pəˈveɪəʳ/ *noun* [C] *formal* someone who sells or provides something *a purveyor of antiques*

pus /pʌs/ *noun* [U] a yellow substance that is produced when part of your body is infected

⊶**push**[1] /pʊʃ/ *verb* **1** [MOVE SOMETHING] [I, T] to move someone or something by pressing them with your hands or body *She **pushed** the books **aside** and sat down on my desk.* ○ *We **pushed** the children **down** the slide.* ○ *He **pushed** me violently **out** of the door.* ○ *Someone **pushed** him **into** the river.* ⊃See picture at pull. **2** MOVE YOURSELF [I, T] to move somewhere by moving someone or something away from you *He **pushed** past me.* ○ *He **pushed** his **way** to the front of the crowd.* **3** PRESS [T] to press something *If you **push** this button, your seat goes back.* **4 push (sb) for sth/to do sth** to try hard to achieve something or to make someone else do something *Local residents are **pushing** for the road to be made safer.* **5** ENCOURAGE [T] to try to make someone do something that they do not want to do [+ into + doing sth] *My mother **pushed** me into having ballet lessons.* **6 push yourself** to make yourself work very hard to achieve something ⊃See also: push the **boat** out.

push sb about/around to tell someone what to do in a rude way *I'm fed up with being pushed around.*

push ahead/forward to continue doing something, especially when this is difficult *They have decided to **push ahead** with legal action.*

push sth/sb aside to decide to forget about or ignore something or someone *We can't just push these problems aside - we have to deal with them.*

push in *UK informal* to rudely join a line of people who are waiting for something by moving in front of some of the people who are already there

push on to continue doing something, especially when this is difficult

push sb/sth over to push someone or something so that they fall to the ground

push sth through to make a plan or suggestion be officially accepted *We're trying to push this deal through as quickly as possible.*

push sth up to increase the amount, number, or value of something *If you want to travel on Saturday, it will push the price up a bit.*

push² /pʊʃ/ *noun* **1 a push for sth/to do sth** a big effort to achieve something or make someone do something *a **push** for higher standards in education* **2** [C] when you move someone or something by pressing them with your hands or body [usually singular] *She gave him a little **push** towards the door.* **3 give sb the push** *UK informal* to get rid of someone from a job or relationship **4** [C] encouragement to make someone do something [usually singular] *I'm sure he'll go, he just needs a little **push** that's all.* **5 at a push** *UK* If you can do something at a push, you can do it but it will be difficult. **6 if/when push comes to shove** If you say that something can be done if push comes to shove, you mean that it can be done if the situation becomes so bad that you have to do it. *If push comes to shove, we'll just have to sell the car.*

pushchair /'pʊʃtʃeəʳ/ *UK* (*US* stroller) *noun* [C] a chair on wheels which is used to move small children

pushed /pʊʃt/ *adjective UK informal* **be pushed for sth** to not have much of something *I can't*

stop, I'm a bit pushed for time.

pusher /'pʊʃəʳ/ *noun* [C] someone who sells illegal drugs

push-up /'pʊʃʌp/ *US* (*UK* press-up) *noun* [C] a physical exercise in which you lie facing the floor and use your hands to push your body up *I did forty push-ups yesterday.*

pushy /'pʊʃi/ *adjective* behaving in an unpleasant way by trying too much to get something or to make someone do something *a pushy salesman*

o₋**put** /pʊt/ *verb* [T] putting, *past* put **1 put sth down/in/on, etc** to move something to a place or position *Where have you put the keys?* ○ *She put her bag on the floor.* ○ *You can put your coat in the car.* ○ *He put his arm around her.* **2 put sb in a mood/position, etc** to cause someone or something to be in a particular situation *They'd had an argument and it had put her in a bad mood.* ○ *This puts me in a very difficult position.* **3** to say something using particular words *I don't know quite how to put this, but I'm leaving.* ○ **4** to write something *Please put your name on the list by Monday evening.*

put sth across to explain or express something clearly so that people understand it easily

put sth aside to save something so that you can use it later *I've been putting a bit of money aside every month.*

put sth away to put something in the place where you usually keep it *She folded the towels and put them away in the cupboard.* ⊃See colour picture **Phrasal Verbs** on page Centre 16.

put sth back to put something where it was before it was moved *I put the book back on the shelf.*

o₋**put sth down 1** STOP HOLDING to put something that you are holding onto the floor or onto another surface *I'll just put my bag down for a minute, it's rather heavy.* ⊃See colour picture **Phrasal Verbs** on page Centre 16. **2** TELEPHONE *UK* If you put the phone down, you put the part of the telephone that you speak into back to its usual position. **3** ANIMAL to kill an animal, usually because it is suffering

put sb down 1 to make someone feel stupid or unimportant by criticizing them *I'm tired of him putting me down all the time.* **2** to write someone's name on a list or document, usually in order to arrange for them to do something *I've put you down for the trip to Rome next week.*

put sth down to sth *UK* to think that a problem or situation is caused by a particular thing

put sth forward to state an idea or opinion, or to suggest a plan, so that it can be considered or discussed

put sb/sth in sth to arrange for someone or something to go somewhere *to put someone in prison* ○ *to put some money in the bank* ○ *I'd never put my mother in an old people's home.*

put sth in to fix something into a room or building *I've just had a new kitchen put in.*

put sth into sth/doing sth If you put time, work, or effort into something, you spend a lot of time or effort doing it. *We've put*

P

a lot of effort into this project and we want it to succeed.

put sth off to decide or arrange to do something at a later time *I must talk to her about this, I can't put it off any longer.*

put sb off (sth) to make someone not like someone or something, or not want to do something *Jan was talking about her operation and it put me off my food.*

put sth on 1 [CLOTHES] to put clothes or shoes onto your body *You'd better put your coat on, it's cold outside.* ➲See colour picture **Phrasal Verbs** on page Centre 16. **2** [EQUIPMENT] mainly UK to make a piece of equipment work by pressing a switch *Can you put the light on please?* **3** [BE-HAVIOUR] to pretend to have a particular feeling, or to behave in a way which is not real or natural for you *He's not really upset, he's just putting it on.* **4** [MUSIC/FILM] to put a CD or other recording into a machine so that you can see or hear it *Why don't you put on some music?* **5 put on weight** UK to become fatter and heavier

put sth out 1 [STOP SHINING] mainly UK to make a light stop shining by pressing a switch *Please put the lights out when you leave.* **2** [STOP BURNING] to make something that is burning stop burning *to put out a fire* **3** [PUT OUTSIDE] to put something outside the house *to put out the rubbish/trash*

put sb out to cause trouble or extra work for someone *It would be great if you could help, but I don't want to put you out.*

be put out to be annoyed, often because of something that someone has done or said to you *He seemed a bit put out at not having been invited.*

put sb through sth to make someone experience or do something unpleasant or difficult *Why did they put themselves through this ordeal?*

put sb through to connect someone using a telephone to the person they want to speak to *Can you put me through to customer services, please?*

put sth to sb 1 to suggest an idea or plan to someone so that they can consider it or discuss it **2** to ask someone a question *to put a question to someone*

put sth together 1 to put the parts of something in the correct place and join them to each other *You buy it in a kit and then put it together yourself.* **2** to prepare a piece of work by collecting several ideas and suggestions and organizing them *to put together a plan/ proposal*

put sth up 1 [BUILD] to build something *to put up a tent* ○ *We spent the weekend putting up a fence in the backyard.* **2** [FASTEN] to fasten something to a wall or ceiling *to put up shelves* ○ *I need to put up some curtains in the back bedroom.* **3** [INCREASE] mainly UK to increase the price or value of something *They're going to put up the price of fuel.*

put sb up to let someone stay in your home

for a short period *If you need somewhere to stay, we can put you up for the night.*

put up with sb/sth to accept unpleasant behaviour or an unpleasant situation, although you do not like it *He's so rude, I don't know how you put up with him.*

putrid /'pjuːtrɪd/ adjective decaying and smelling bad *a putrid smell*

putt /pʌt/ verb [I, T] in golf, to hit the ball gently when you are near the hole ● **putt** noun [C]

putty /'pʌti/ noun [U] a soft, grey substance that becomes hard when it is dry and is used to fasten glass into windows or to fill small holes in wood

puzzle¹ /'pʌzl/ noun [C] **1** a game or activity in which you have to put pieces together or answer questions using skill *to do/solve a puzzle* ○ *a crossword puzzle* ○ *a jigsaw puzzle* **2** a situation which is very difficult to understand *Scientists have been trying to solve this puzzle for years.*

puzzle² /'pʌzl/ verb [T] to make someone confused because they do not understand something [often passive] *I was puzzled by what he said.*

puzzle over sth to try to solve a problem or understand a situation by thinking carefully about it

puzzled /'pʌzld/ adjective confused because you do not understand something *He had a puzzled look on his face.*

puzzling /'pʌzlɪŋ/ adjective If something is puzzling, it confuses you because you do not understand it.

PVC /ˌpiːviːˈsiː/ noun [U] a strong material similar to thick plastic

pyjamas UK (US **pajamas**) /pɪˈdʒɑːməz/ noun [plural] shirt and trousers that you wear in bed *a pair of blue pyjamas* ➲See colour picture **Clothes** on page Centre 8.

pyjamas

pylon /'paɪlɒn/ noun [C] a tall structure which supports electrical wires above the ground

pyramid /'pɪrəmɪd/ noun [C] a shape with a square base and four triangular sides that meet to form a point at the top ➲See picture at **shape**.

pyre /paɪəʳ/ noun [C] a pile of wood on which a dead person is burned in some countries

python /'paɪθ°n/ noun [C] a large snake that kills other animals by putting itself tightly around them

Qq

Q, q /kjuː/ the seventeenth letter of the alphabet

QC /ˌkjuːˈsiː/ *noun* [C] *abbreviation for* Queen's Counsel: a lawyer of high rank in the UK

qt *written abbreviation for* quart (= a unit for measuring liquid)

quack /kwæk/ *noun* [C] the sound made by a duck (= water bird) • **quack** *verb* [I]

quadruple /ˈkwɒdrʊpl/ *verb* [I, T] If an amount quadruples, it becomes multiplied by four, or if you quadruple it, you multiply it by four.

quagmire /ˈkwɒgmaɪəʳ/ *noun* [C] **1** a difficult and unpleasant situation *a **legal quagmire*** **2** an area of wet ground that you can sink into

quail /kweɪl/ *noun* [C] *plural* **quail** or **quails** a small bird which is shot for food

quaint /kweɪnt/ *adjective* attractive or unusual in an old-fashioned way *a quaint little village*

quake¹ /kweɪk/ *noun* [C] *US short for* earthquake (= when the Earth shakes)

quake² /kweɪk/ *verb* [I] to shake because you are frightened

WORD PARTNERS FOR ***qualification***

an **academic/basic/formal/recognised** qualification • **gain/get/have/need** a qualification • a qualification **in** sth

qualification /ˌkwɒlɪfɪˈkeɪʃᵊn/ *noun* **1** [EXAMS] [C] *mainly UK* what you get when you pass an exam or a course [usually plural] *legal/medical qualifications* ○ *What qualifications do you need to be a nanny?* **2** [SKILLS] [C] the skills, qualities, or experience that you need in order to do something *The only qualification needed for this job is an eye for detail.* **3** [COMPETITION] [U] success in getting into a competition *England's qualification for the World Cup* **4** [ADDITION] [C, U] an addition to something that is said that makes its meaning less certain

qualified /ˈkwɒlɪfaɪd/ *adjective* **1** having passed exams or courses *a **newly qualified** teacher* **2 qualified to do sth** having the skills, qualities, or experience that you need in order to do something *I think John is the best qualified to make that decision.* **3** If something someone says is qualified, they have added something to it to make it less certain. *The answer was a qualified yes.* ➲Opposite **unqualified**.

qualifier /ˈkwɒlɪfaɪəʳ/ *noun* [C] **1** a game or competition which decides whether you can enter another competition **2** someone who has succeeded in getting into a competition

qualify /ˈkwɒlɪfaɪ/ *verb* **1** [BE ALLOWED] [I, T] If you qualify for something, you are allowed to do it or have it, and if something qualifies you for something, it allows you to do it or have it. *Foreign students no longer **qualify for** grants in the UK.* ○ *To qualify for the competition, you must be over 18.* ➲Opposite **disqualify**. **2** [PASS EXAMS] [I] *mainly UK* to pass exams so that you are able to do a job *He's recently **qualified as** a doctor.* **3** [GET INTO COMPETITION] [I] to succeed in getting into a competition *Nigeria were the first team to **qualify for** the World Cup.* **4** [ADD] [T] to add something to what you say to make its meaning less certain

qualitative /ˈkwɒlɪtətɪv/ [US] /ˈkwɑːlɪteɪtɪv/ *adjective formal* relating to how good something is and not how much of it there is • **qualitatively** *adverb*

WORD PARTNERS FOR ***quality***

affect/enhance/improve/maintain quality • **good/high/inferior/low/poor** quality

⊶**quality¹** /ˈkwɒləti/ *noun* **1** [GOOD OR BAD] [U] how good or bad something is ***good/high quality*** ○ ***poor/low quality*** ○ *The air quality in this area is terrible.* ○ *All we are asking for is a decent **quality of life**.* ○ *The spokeswoman says a **quality control** system is being developed for next year.* **2** [GOOD] [U] when something is very good or well made *A designer label isn't necessarily a guarantee of quality.* **3** [CHARACTER] [C] part of the character or personality of someone or something *leadership qualities*

quality² /ˈkwɒləti/ *adjective* [always before noun] very good *We only sell quality products in this store.*

ˈquality ˌtime *noun* [U] time that you spend with someone when you can give them all of your attention *We've been too busy to give the children much quality time this week.*

qualm /kwɑːm/ *noun* [C] a worry or doubt about something *She **has no qualms about** taking her clothes off in public.*

quandary /ˈkwɒndᵊri/ *noun* [no plural] a situation in which you are trying to make a difficult choice *We're **in a quandary over** which school to send her to.*

quantifier /ˈkwɒntɪfaɪəʳ/ *noun* [C] a word or group of words that is used before a noun to show an amount of that noun. For example the words 'many', 'some', and 'a lot of' are quantifiers.

quantify /ˈkwɒntɪfaɪ/ *verb* [T] to measure or state the amount of something *It is difficult to quantify the damage that this storm has caused.*

quantitative /ˈkwɒntɪtətɪv/ [US] /ˈkwɑːntəteɪtɪv/ *adjective* relating to quantity

WORD PARTNERS FOR ***quantity***

a **huge/large/small/sufficient/vast** quantity • **in** [big/large, etc] quantities

⊶**quantity** /ˈkwɒntəti/ *noun* **1** [C, U] the amount or number of something *A **vast quantity** of information is available on the Internet.* ○ *They are now developing ways to produce the vaccine **in large quantities** and cheaply.* ➲See colour picture **Pieces and Quantities** on page Centre 1. **2 an unknown quantity** someone or something that you do not know and so you cannot be certain about

quantum leap /ˌkwɒntʌmˈliːp/ *noun* [C] a sudden, large increase or improvement in something [usually singular] *a quantum leap in*

Q

information technology

quarantine /'kwɒrᵊntiːn/ *noun* [U] If an animal or person is put into quarantine, they are kept away from other animals or people because they have or might have a disease.

quarrel[1] /'kwɒrᵊl/ *noun* **1** [C] an argument *She walked out after **having a quarrel with** her boss.* **2 have no quarrel with sb/sth** to not disagree with someone or something *We have no quarrel with either of those ideas.*

quarrel[2] /'kwɒrᵊl/ *verb* [I] UK quarrelling *past* quarrelled US quarreling *past* quarreled to have an argument with someone *She'd been **quarrelling with** her mother all morning.*

quarry /'kwɒri/ *noun* [C] a place where stone is dug out of a large hole in the ground *a marble quarry* • **quarry** *verb* [T] to dig stone out of a quarry

quart /kwɔːt/ (*written abbreviation* qt) *noun* [C] a unit for measuring liquid, equal to 1.14 litres in the UK and 0.95 litres in the US

⟳**quarter**[1] /'kwɔːtᵊr/ *noun* **1** EQUAL PART [C] (*also US* **fourth**) one of four equal parts of something; ¼ *Three quarters of the island's residents speak English.* ○ *My house is one and three-quarter miles/a mile and three-quarters from here.* ○ *I waited a quarter of an hour for her.* **2** BEFORE/AFTER HOUR [no plural] a period of 15 minutes before or after the hour *It's (a) **quarter to** three* (= 2.45). ○ (*also US*) *It's **a quarter of** three* (= 2.45). ○ *We're leaving at (a) **quarter past six*** (= 6.15). ○ (*also US*) *We're leaving at (a) **quarter after six*** (= 6.15). **3** BUSINESS [C] one of four periods of time into which a year is divided for financial calculations such as profits or bills (= orders for payment) *I get an electricity bill every quarter.* **4** SCHOOL [C] US one of four periods of time into which a year at college or university is divided **5** SPORT [C] US one of four periods of time into which some sports games are divided **6** PART OF TOWN [C] a part of a town, often where people from a particular country or religion live *the Jewish quarter* **7** COIN [C] a US or Canadian coin with a value of 25 cents, which is a quarter of a dollar

quarter

quarterback /'kwɔːtəbæk/ *noun* [C] a player in American football who controls the attack

quarter-final /ˌkwɔːtə'faɪnᵊl/ *noun* [C] the part of a competition where eight people or teams are left and there are four games to decide who will reach the semi-final (= when only four people or teams are left) *She was knocked out of the competition **in the quarter-finals**.*

quarterly /'kwɔːtᵊli/ *adjective, adverb* produced or happening every three months *Water and*

electricity bills are paid quarterly. ○ *a quarterly magazine/report*

quarters /'kwɔːtəz/ *noun* [plural] rooms to live in or sleep in, usually for people in a military organization

quartet /kwɔː'tet/ *noun* [C] four people singing or playing music in a group

quartz /'kwɔːts/ *noun* [U] a mineral used to make watches and clocks accurate

quash /kwɒʃ/ *verb* [T] **1** *formal* to officially change a legal decision so that it stops existing *His **conviction** was **quashed** last month.* **2** to stop something that you do not want to happen *He appeared on television to **quash** rumours that he was seriously ill.*

quasi- /kweɪzaɪ-/ *prefix* partly *quasi-religious ideas*

quay /kiː/ *noun* [C] a structure built next to water where ships stop and goods are taken on and off

queasy /'kwiːzi/ *adjective* If you feel queasy, you feel slightly ill as if you might vomit.

⟳**queen** /kwiːn/ *noun* [C] **1** FEMALE RULER a female ruler in some countries *Queen Elizabeth II* ○ *God save the Queen!* **2** KING'S WIFE the wife of a king when he is the main ruler in a country **3** PLAYING CARD a playing card with a picture of a queen on it *the Queen of diamonds* **4** INSECT a large female insect which is the most important in a group and which produces all the eggs *queen bee*

queer /kwɪər/ *adjective* **1** *informal* homosexual **2** strange

quell /kwel/ *verb* [T] *formal* to stop something that you do not want to happen *to **quell** a riot* ○ *to **quell** rumours*

quench /kwenʃ/ *verb* **quench your thirst** to drink liquid so that you stop being thirsty

query[1] /'kwɪəri/ *noun* [C] a question *His job is to answer telephone **queries about** airline schedules.*

query[2] /'kwɪəri/ *verb* [T] to ask questions in order to check that something is true or correct [+ question word] *A few students have queried whether exam marks were added up correctly.*

quest /kwest/ *noun* [C] *formal* an attempt to get something or do something difficult *the **quest** for truth* ○ [+ to do sth] *He has begun his **quest** to become the Conservative Party's first Asian MP.*

⟳**question**[1] /'kwestʃᵊn/ *noun* **1** SENTENCE [C] a sentence or phrase that asks you for information *Is it OK if I **ask** you a few **questions**?* ○ *He refused to **answer** my **question**.* ○ *If you have any **questions about** the scheme, do ask me.* ○ *"So where's the money coming from?" "**That's a good question**"* (= I do not know). **2** SITUATION [C] a situation or problem that needs to be considered *This documentary* *raises* important **questions** about the American legal system. ○ *Two important* **questions** *arise* from this debate. **3** [DOUBT] [U] doubt [+ that] *There is* **no question** *that this was an accidental fire.* ○ *His ability as a chef has never been* **in question.** ○ *"So you agree she's the right person for the job." "Yes, absolutely,* **without question."** ○ *The report* **brings/calls into question** (= causes doubts about) *the safety of this drug.* **4 sb/sth in question** the person or thing that is being discussed *He claims that he was in the pub with his girlfriend on the night in question.* **5 be out of the question** If something is out of the question, it is not possible or not allowed. ➞See also: **loaded question, rhetorical question.**

ask a question

Remember to use the verb **ask** with **question**.
We weren't allowed to ask any questions.
~~We weren't allowed to make any questions.~~

question² /'kwestʃən/ *verb* [T] **1** to ask someone questions *Detectives were* **questioning** *a boy* **about** *the murder.* ○ [often passive] *Two out of three people questioned in the survey were non-smokers.* **2** to show or feel doubt about something *I'm not for a moment questioning your decision.* ○ [+ question word] *I'm just* **questioning** *whether we need the extra staff.*

questionable /'kwestʃənəbl/ *adjective* **1** possibly not true or correct [+ question word] *It is highly* **questionable whether** *this drug has any benefits at all.* **2** not honest or not legal *He's being investigated for questionable business practices.*

questioning /'kwestʃənɪŋ/ *noun* [U] when the police ask someone questions about a crime *She was taken in* **for questioning** *by police yesterday morning.*

'question ˌmark *noun* [C] a mark (?) used at the end of a question ➞See Extra help page **Punctuation** on page Centre 33.

complete/fill in a questionnaire • **draw up** a questionnaire • a questionnaire **asks** sth • a questionnaire **about/on** sth

questionnaire /ˌkwestʃə'neər/ *noun* [C] a set of questions asked of a large number of people to discover information about a subject *Residents have been sent* **questionnaires about** *their homes and energy use.*

'question ˌtag *noun* [C] a short phrase such as 'isn't it' or 'don't you' that is added to the end of a sentence to check information or to ask if someone agrees with you. In the sentence, 'It's hot, isn't it?', 'isn't it' is a question tag.

form/be in/join a queue • a queue **stretches** [for miles/around sth, etc] • a **big/long/short/small** queue • a queue **of** [cars/people, etc] • a queue **for** sth

queue /kjuː/ *UK (US* **line)** *noun* [C] **1** a row of people waiting for something, one behind the other *to* **join** the queue ○ *Are you* **in the queue?** **2 jump the queue** to move in front of

queue

people who have been waiting longer for something than you • **queue (up)** *UK (US* **line up)** *verb* [I] to stand in a row in order to wait for something [+ to do sth] *They're queueing up to get tickets.*

quibble /'kwɪbl/ *verb* **quibble about/over/with sth** to argue about something that is not important *They spend far too much time quibbling over details.* • **quibble** *noun* [C]

quiche /kiːʃ/ *noun* [C, U] a dish made of a pastry base filled with a mixture of egg and milk and usually cheese, vegetables, or meat

quick¹ /kwɪk/ *adjective* **1** doing something fast or taking only a short time *I tried to catch him but he was too quick for me.* ○ [+ to do sth] *Publishers were quick to realize that a profit could be made.* **2** lasting a short time *Can I ask you a quick question?*

quick² /kwɪk/ *adverb informal* fast *Come here, quick!*

quicken /'kwɪkən/ *verb* [I, T] to become faster or to cause something to become faster *His breathing quickened.*

quickly /'kwɪkli/ *adverb* fast or in a short time *I quickly shut the door.* ○ *These people need to be treated as quickly as possible.*

quid /kwɪd/ *noun* [C] *plural* **quid** *UK informal* a pound (= UK unit of money) *This bike's not bad for twenty quid.*

quiet¹ /kwaɪət/ *adjective* **1** [NOT NOISY] making little or no noise *Can you* **be quiet,** *please?* ○ *The children are very quiet.* **2** [NOT BUSY] without much noise or activity *I fancy a* **quiet night** *in tonight.* ○ *They found a table in a quiet corner of the restaurant.* **3** [NOT TALKING MUCH] If someone is quiet, they do not talk very much. *He was a shy, quiet man.* **4 keep (sth) quiet** to not talk about something that is secret *It might be wise to keep this quiet for a while.*

quiet or **quite**?

Be careful, these two words look very similar, but they are spelled differently and have completely different meanings.
Quiet means making little or no noise.
The house was very quiet without the children around.
Quite means a little or a lot but not completely.
It's quite cold today.

quiet² /kwaɪət/ *noun* [U] when there is little or no noise *She needs a bit of* **peace and quiet.**

quieten /'kwaɪətᵊn/ *UK (US* **quiet)** *verb* [T] to make someone or something quiet

quieten (sb/sth) down UK (US quiet (sb/sth) down) to become quieter or calmer, or to make a person or animal become quieter or calmer

◦–**quietly** /'kwaɪətli/ adverb **1** making little or no noise "Don't worry," she said quietly. **2** doing something without much noise or activity He sat quietly on the sofa, waiting for her to come home.

quilt /kwɪlt/ noun [C] a cover for a bed which is filled with feathers or other warm material

quip /kwɪp/ verb quipping past quipped to say something in a funny and clever way ●quip noun [C]

quirk /kwɜːk/ noun **1** [C] a strange habit My aunt has a few odd quirks. **2** quirk of fate a strange and unexpected event By some quirk of fate, we came to live in the same town. ●quirky adjective strange a quirky sense of humour

quit /kwɪt/ verb quitting past quit **1** [I, T] to leave your job or school permanently She recently quit her job to spend more time with her family. **2** [T] to stop doing something I quit smoking and put on weight.

◦–**quite** /kwaɪt/ adverb **1** [NOT COMPLETELY] UK a little or a lot but not completely I'm quite tired, but I'm happy to walk a little further. ○ He's quite attractive but not what I'd call gorgeous. **2** [VERY] US very My sister and I are quite different. **3** [COMPLETELY] completely The two situations are quite different. ○ Are you quite sure you want to go? **4 not quite** almost but not completely I'm not quite sure that I understand this. ○ He didn't get quite enough votes to win. **5 quite a bit/a few/a lot, etc** a large amount or number There are quite a few letters for you here. ○ He's changed quite a bit.

quiver /'kwɪvər/ verb [I] to shake slightly ●quiver noun [C]

quiz¹ /kwɪz/ noun [C] plural quizzes **1** a game in which you answer questions a television quiz show **2** US a short test on a subject in school

quiz² /kwɪz/ verb [T] quizzing past quizzed to ask someone questions about something A group of journalists quizzed them about/on the day's events.

quizzical /'kwɪzɪkəl/ adjective A quizzical expression or look seems to ask a question without words.

quota /'kwəʊtə/ noun [C] a limited amount of something that is officially allowed an import quota

quotation /kwəʊ'teɪʃən/ noun [C] **1** a sentence or phrase that is taken out of a book, poem, or play a quotation from Shakespeare/the Bible **2** the amount that a piece of work will probably cost Make sure you get a quotation for all the work before they start.

quot'ation ,marks noun [plural] a pair of marks (" ") or (' ') used before and after a group of words to show that they are spoken or that someone else originally wrote them ⊃See Extra help page Punctuation on page Centre 33.

quote¹ /kwəʊt/ verb **1** [REPEAT] [I, T] to repeat what someone has said or written I was quoting from Marx. ○ Witnesses were quoted as saying there were two gunmen. **2** [GIVE EXAMPLE] [T] to give a fact or example in order to support what you are saying The minister quoted recent unemployment figures. **3** [COST] [T] to say how much a piece of work will cost before you do it

quote² /kwəʊt/ noun [C] short for quotation

quotes /kwəʊts/ noun [plural] short for quotation marks

the Qur'an /kɒrˈɑːn/ noun another spelling of the Koran (= the holy book of Islam)

Q

Rr

R, r /ɑːʳ/ the eighteenth letter of the alphabet

R *informal written abbeviation for* are: used in emails and text messages

rabbi /'ræbaɪ/ *noun* [C] a leader and teacher in the Jewish religion *Rabbi Hugo Gryn*

rabbit /'ræbɪt/ *noun* [C] a small animal with fur and long ears that lives in a hole in the ground

rabble /'ræbl/ *noun* [no plural] a group of noisy, uncontrolled people

rabies /'reɪbiːz/ *noun* [U] a serious disease that people can get if they are bitten by an infected animal

WORD PARTNERS FOR *race*

drop out of/lose/win a race • in a race

ᴏ⌐**race¹** /reɪs/ *noun* **1** COMPETITION [C] a competition in which people run, ride, drive, etc against each other in order to see who is the fastest *a horse race* **2** PEOPLE [C, U] one of the groups that people are divided into according to their physical characteristics *people of many different races* **3** FOR POWER [C] a situation in which people compete against each other for power or control *the race for governor* **4** the races an event when horses race against each other **5** a **race against time/the clock** a situation in which something has to be done very quickly ⊃See also: the human race, the rat race.

COMMON LEARNER ERROR

race or species?

Race is used to talk about one of the groups that people are divided into according to their physical characteristics.

the human race

People of all races and religions live in America.

Species is used to talk about types of animals and plants.

eagles, vultures and other species of bird

race² /reɪs/ *verb* **1** [I, T] to compete in a race *I'll race you to the end of the road.* ○ *I used to race against him at school.* **2 race along/down/over, etc** to move somewhere very quickly *I raced over to see what was the matter.* **3 race sb to/ back, etc** to take someone somewhere very quickly *Ambulances raced the injured to a nearby hospital.* **4** [T] to put a horse, dog, etc in a race

racecourse /'reɪskɔːs/ *noun* [C] *UK* the place where horses, cars, etc race

racehorse /'reɪshɔːs/ *noun* [C] a horse that has been trained to run in races

,race re'lations *noun* [plural] the relationship between people from different races who live together in the same place

racetrack /'reɪstræk/ *noun* [C] the place where horses, cars, etc race

racial /'reɪʃəl/ *adjective* relating to people's race *a racial minority* ○ *racial discrimination/ tension* •**racially** *adverb* a *racially motivated crime*

racing /'reɪsɪŋ/ *noun* [U] the activity or sport in which people, animals, or vehicles race against each other *motor racing* ⊃See also: **horse racing.**

WORD PARTNERS FOR *racism*

combat/encounter/face/tackle racism • a form of racism • racism against sb

racism /'reɪsɪzəm/ *noun* [U] the belief that other races of people are not as good as your own, or the unfair treatment of people because they belong to a particular race

racist /'reɪsɪst/ *noun* [C] someone who believes that other races of people are not as good as their own •**racist** *adjective a* **racist attack**

rack¹ /ræk/ *noun* [C] a type of shelf that you can put things on or hang things from *a magazine/luggage rack*

rack² /ræk/ *verb* **1 be racked with pain/guilt, etc** If someone is racked with pain or an emotion, they suffer a lot because of it. **2 rack your brain/brains** *informal* to think very hard, usually to try to remember something or solve a problem

rack up sth *informal* to get or achieve a lot of something *He's racked up debts of over thirty thousand pounds.*

racket /'rækɪt/ *noun* **1** SPORT [C] (*also* racquet) a piece of equipment that you use to hit a ball in sports such as tennis ⊃See colour picture **Sports 2** on page Centre 15. **2** ILLEGAL [C] *informal* an illegal activity that is used to make money *a drugs smuggling racket* **3** NOISE [no plural] *informal* a loud noise *The neighbours were making such a racket.*

racket

radar /'reɪdɑːʳ/ *noun* [U] a system that uses radio waves to find out the position of something you cannot see

radiant /'reɪdiənt/ *adjective* **1** showing that you are very happy *a radiant smile* **2** very bright •**radiance** /'reɪdiəns/ *noun* [U]

radiate /'reɪdieɪt/ *verb* **1 radiate from/out, etc** to spread out in all directions from a particular point *A number of roads radiate out from the centre.* **2** [T] to show an emotion or quality in your face or behaviour *His face just radiates happiness.* **3** [T] to send out heat or light

radiation /ˌreɪdi'eɪʃən/ *noun* [U] **1** a form of energy that comes from a nuclear reaction and that in large amounts can be very dangerous *dangerously high levels of radiation* ○ *radiation sickness* **2** energy from heat or light that you cannot see *solar/microwave radiation*

radiator /'reɪdieɪtəʳ/ *noun* [C] **1** a metal piece of equipment that is filled with hot water and is used to heat a room ⊃See colour picture **The Living Room** on page Centre 4. **2** a part of a vehicle engine that is used to make the engine cool

radical¹ /'rædɪkəl/ *adjective* **1** A radical change

R

is very big and important. *a **radical** reform*
2 believing that there should be big social and
political changes *a **radical** group/movement* ○
*a **radical** proposal* ● **radically** *adverb The company has **changed radically** in recent years.*

radical² /ˈrædɪkᵊl/ *noun* [C] someone who supports the idea that there should be big social
and political changes

o-**radio¹** /ˈreɪdiəʊ/ *noun* **1** [BROADCASTS] [C] a piece of
equipment used for listening to radio broad-
casts *a car radio* **2 the radio** the programmes
that you hear when you listen to the radio *We
heard him speaking **on the radio** this morning.* **3** [SYSTEM] [U] a system of sending and receiving sound through the air *local radio* ○ *a
radio station* **4** [MESSAGES] [C] a piece of equipment for sending and receiving messages by
sound

radio² /ˈreɪdiəʊ/ *verb* [I, T] **radioing** *past* **radioed** to
send a message to someone by radio *They ra-
dioed for help.*

radioactive /ˌreɪdiəʊˈæktɪv/ *adjective* containing harmful radiation (= energy from a nuclear reaction) *radioactive waste*

radioactivity /ˌreɪdiəʊækˈtɪvəti/ *noun* [U] when
something is radioactive

radish /ˈrædɪʃ/ *noun* [C] a small, round, white or
red vegetable with a slightly hot taste that you
eat in salad

radius /ˈreɪdiəs/ *noun*
[C] *plural* **radii** **1** a certain distance from a
particular point in
any direction *Most
facilities lie **within** a
two-mile **radius** of
the house.* **2** the distance from the centre
of a circle to its edge

radius

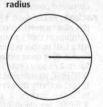

raffle /ˈræfl/ *noun* [C] a
competition in which
people buy tickets with numbers on them and
win a prize if any of their numbers are chosen
raffle tickets ● **raffle** *verb* [T] to offer something
as a prize in a raffle

raft /rɑːft/ *noun* **1** [C] a small, flat boat made by
tying pieces of wood together **2 a raft of sth/sb**
a lot of things or people *a raft of data*

rafter /ˈrɑːftəʳ/ *noun* [C] one of the long pieces of
wood that supports a roof

rag /ræg/ *noun* [C] **1** a piece of old cloth that you
use to clean things **2 be like a red rag to a bull**
UK If a particular subject is like a red rag to a
bull, it always makes someone angry.

rage¹ /reɪdʒ/ *noun* **1** [C, U] strong anger that you
cannot control *a jealous rage* ○ *He **flew into a
rage** (= suddenly became angry) over the
smallest mistake.* **2 be all the rage** *informal old-
fashioned* to be very popular ⊃See also: **road
rage.**

rage² /reɪdʒ/ *verb* [I] **1** to continue with great
force or violence *The battle raged well into the
night.* **2** to speak or behave in a very angry
way

ragged /ˈrægɪd/ *adjective*
1 [CLOTHES] old and torn
ragged jeans **2** [PERSON]
wearing clothes that are
old and torn *a ragged
child* **3** [ROUGH] rough and
not smooth *a ragged
edge*

ragged

rags /rægz/ *noun* [plural]
1 clothes that are old and
torn *an old man dressed
in rags* **2 go from rags to
riches** to start your life
very poor and then later
in life become very rich

WORD PARTNERS FOR **raid**

carry out a raid ● a raid **on** sth ● an **air** raid
● a **dawn** raid

raid¹ /reɪd/ *noun* [C] **1** [SOLDIERS] a sudden attack
on a place by soldiers *an air raid* ○ *a dawn
raid* **2** [POLICE] a sudden visit to a place by
police in order to find someone or something *a
police raid to recover illegal weapons* **3** [STEAL]
when people enter a place by force in order to
steal from it *a bank raid* ⊃See also: **air raid.**

raid² /reɪd/ *verb* [T] **1** [SOLDIERS] If soldiers raid a
place, they suddenly attack it. **2** [POLICE] If the
police raid a place, they suddenly visit it in
order to find someone or something. *Police
raided nine properties in search of the documents.* **3** [STEAL] to steal many things from
somewhere *to raid the fridge*

rail

clothes rail

towel rail *UK*,
towel rack *US*

rail /reɪl/ *noun* **1** [FOR HANGING] [C] *UK* a horizontal
bar on the wall that you hang things on *a cur-
tain rail* **2** [FOR SUPPORTING] [C] a bar around or
along something which you can hold to stop
you from falling *a hand rail* **3** [TRAIN SYSTEM] [U]
trains as a method of transport *rail travel* ○ *a
rail link* ○ *They sent the shipment by rail.*
4 [TRAIN] [C] the metal tracks that trains run on
⊃See also: **towel rail.**

railing /ˈreɪlɪŋ/ *noun* [C] a fence made from posts
and bars *an iron railing*

ˈrailroad ˌtie *US (UK* **sleeper**) *noun* [C] a piece of
wood that is used to support a railway track

railway /ˈreɪlweɪ/ *noun* **1** [C] (*also US* **railroad**
/ˈreɪlrəʊd/) the metal tracks that trains travel
on *Repairs are being carried out on the rail-
way.* **2 the railway(s)** (*also US* **the railroad(s)**) the
organizations connected with trains *He
worked on the railways all his life.*

WORD PARTNERS FOR *rain*

rain **falls** • **heavy/light/pouring/torren-tial** rain • be **pouring with** rain • a **drop of/spot of** rain • **in the** rain

○**rain**¹ /reɪn/ noun **1** [U] water that falls from the sky in small drops *heavy rain* ○ *It looks like rain* (= as if it will rain). **2 the rains** in tropical countries, the time of year when there is a lot of rain *They were waiting for the rains to come.* ⊃See also: **acid rain**.

○**rain**² /reɪn/ verb **it rains** If it rains, water falls from the sky in small drops. *It was raining all weekend.*
be rained off *UK* (*US* **be rained out**) If a sport or outside activity is rained off, it cannot start or continue because it is raining.

rainbow /ˈreɪnbəʊ/ noun [C] a half circle with seven colours that sometimes appears in the sky when the sun shines through rain

'**rain ˌcheck** noun [C] **1** *US* a piece of paper which allows you to buy something at a low price although that thing is now being sold at a higher price **2** *US* a ticket that allows you to see an event at a later time if bad weather stops that event from happening **3 take a rain check on sth** something you say when you cannot accept someone's invitation, but would like to do it at a later time

raincoat /ˈreɪnkəʊt/ noun [C] a coat that you wear when it is raining ⊃See colour picture **Clothes** on page Centre 8.

raindrop /ˈreɪndrɒp/ noun [C] a single drop of rain

rainfall /ˈreɪnfɔːl/ noun [U] the amount of rain that falls in a particular place at a particular time *monthly rainfall* ○ *heavy rainfall*

rainforest /ˈreɪnˌfɒrɪst/ noun [C] a forest with a lot of tall trees where it rains a lot *a tropical rainforest*

rainy /ˈreɪni/ adjective raining a lot *a rainy after-noon* ○ *a rainy day*

○**raise**¹ /reɪz/ verb [T] **1** LIFT to lift something to a higher position *to raise your hand* **2** INCREASE to increase an amount or level *to raise prices/taxes* **3** IMPROVE to improve something *to raise standards* **4** MONEY to collect money from other people *They're raising money for charity.* **5 raise your voice** to speak loudly and angrily to someone **6 raise hopes/fears/doubts, etc** to cause emotions or thoughts *Her answers raised doubts in my mind.* **7 raise a question/subject, etc** to start talking about a subject that you want other people to consider **8** CHILD to look after and educate a child until they have become an adult *Their ideas on how to raise children didn't always agree.* **9** ANIMALS/CROPS to make an animal or crop grow *to raise chickens/sheep* ⊃See Common learner error at **rise** ⊃See also: raise the **alarm**¹.

raise² /reɪz/ *US* (*UK* **rise**) noun [C] an increase in the amount of money that you earn *We usually get a raise at the start of a year.*

raisin /ˈreɪzᵊn/ noun [C] a dried grape (= small round fruit)

rake¹ /reɪk/ noun [C] a garden tool with a long handle that is used for moving dead leaves, grass, etc

rake² /reɪk/ verb [I, T] to use a rake to move dead leaves, grass, etc
rake sth in *informal* to earn a large amount of money. *He's raking it in.*

WORD PARTNERS FOR *rally*

hold/organize/stage a rally • a **mass** rally • **at a** rally

rally¹ /ˈræli/ noun [C] **1** a large public meeting in support of something *an election/campaign rally* **2** a car or motorcycle race *a rally driver*

rally² /ˈræli/ verb **1** [I, T] to come together or bring people together to support something *Her fans rallied behind her from the start.* **2** [I] to get stronger or better after being weak *The stock market rallied late in the day.*
rally around/round (sb) to help or give support to someone *If one of the family has a crisis we rally round them.*

ram¹ /ræm/ verb [T] **ramming**, *past* **rammed** to hit something or push something into something with great force *He had to stop suddenly and a car rammed into him.*

ram² /ræm/ noun [C] a male sheep

RAM /ræm/ noun [U] *abbreviation for* random access memory: a computer's ability to immediately store information

Ramadan /ˈræmədæn/ noun [U] the Muslim re-ligious period in which Muslims do not eat or drink during the part of the day when it is light

ramble¹ /ˈræmbl/ verb **1 ramble along/through, etc** to walk for a long time, especially in the countryside **2** (*also* **ramble on**) to talk for a long time in a boring and often confused way *He rambled on for hours about his time in the army.*

ramble² /ˈræmbl/ noun [C] a long walk in the countryside

rambler /ˈræmblə/ noun [C] someone who walks in the countryside

rambling /ˈræmblɪŋ/ adjective **1** A rambling speech, letter, etc is very long and confused. **2** A rambling building is big and without a regular shape.

ramifications /ˌræmɪfɪˈkeɪʃᵊnz/ noun [plural] the possible results of an action

ramp /ræmp/ noun [C] **1** a sloping surface that joins two places that are at different heights *a wheelchair ramp* **2** *US* (*UK* **slip road**) a short road that is used to drive onto or off a large, fast road

rampage¹ /ræmˈpeɪdʒ/ verb [I] to run around or through an area, making a lot of noise and causing damage *Angry citizens rampaged through the city.*

rampage² /ˈræmpeɪdʒ/ noun [no plural] when a group of people rampage *Rioters went on a rampage through the city.*

rampant /ˈræmpənt/ adjective growing or spreading quickly, in a way that cannot be controlled *rampant corruption/inflation*

ramshackle /ˈræmˌʃækl/ adjective A ram-

R

shackle building is in very bad condition.

ran /ræn/ *past tense of* run

ranch /rɑːnʃ/ *noun* [C] a large farm where animals are kept *a cattle/sheep ranch*

rancher /rɑːnʃəʳ/ *noun* [C] someone who owns or works on a ranch

rancid /ˈrænsɪd/ *adjective* Rancid fat, such as oil or butter, smells and tastes bad because it is not fresh.

random /ˈrændəm/ *adjective* **1** done or chosen without any plan or system *random testing* ○ *a random selection* **2 at random** chosen by chance *Winners will be chosen at random.* ● **randomly** *adverb*

rang /ræŋ/ *past tense of* ring²

WORD PARTNERS FOR *range*

a full/wide range ● a range of sth

---

range¹ /reɪndʒ/ *noun* **1** [OF THINGS] [C] a group of different things of the same general type *a range of colours/patterns* ○ *We discussed a wide range of subjects.* **2** [AMOUNT] [C] the amount or number between a particular set of limits [usually singular] *The price range is from $100 to $200.* ○ *The product is aimed at young people in the 18-25 age range.* **3** [DISTANCE] [U] the distance from which things can be seen, heard, or reached *The soldiers came within firing range.* ○ *He was shot at close range* (= from very near). **4** [MOUNTAINS] [C] a line of hills or mountains **5** [SHOOTING] [C] a place where you can practise shooting a gun *a rifle/shooting range*

range² /reɪndʒ/ *verb* **1 range from sth to sth** to have several different amounts or types *Tickets range from $12 to $35.* ○ *Choose from 13 colours, ranging from classic white to antique blue.* **2** [I] to deal with a large number of subjects *The discussion ranged over many topics.*

ranger /ˈreɪndʒəʳ/ *noun* [C] someone whose job is to look after a forest or a park *a forest ranger*

rank¹ /ræŋk/ *noun* **1** [C, U] a position in society or in an organization, for example the army *He holds the rank of colonel.* **2 the ranks** the ordinary members of an organization, especially the army **3 break ranks** to publicly show that you disagree with a group that you belong to **4 the rank and file** the ordinary members of an organization and not its leaders ➔See also: taxi rank.

rank² /ræŋk/ *verb* [I, T] to have a position in a list which shows things or people in order of importance, or to give someone or something a position on such a list *He ranked number one in the world at the start of the competition.* ○ *The city's canals now rank among the world's dirtiest.*

ransom /ˈrænsəm/ *noun* [C, U] the money that is demanded for the return of someone who is being kept as a prisoner *a ransom note/letter*

rant /rænt/ *verb* [I] to talk a lot about something in an excited or angry way *He was ranting and raving about the injustice of the situation.*

rap¹ /ræp/ *noun* **1** [U] a type of music in which the words are spoken and there is a strong beat *a rap artist* **2** [C] a sudden, short sound made when someone or something hits a hard surface *There was a rap on the window.* **3 a rap on/across/over the knuckles** a punishment that is not severe

rap² /ræp/ *verb* **rapping** *past* **rapped 1** [I, T] to hit a hard surface to make a sudden, short noise *He rapped on the door.* **2** [I] to perform rap music

rape /reɪp/ *verb* [T] to force someone to have sex when they do not want to ● **rape** *noun* [C, U]

rapid /ˈræpɪd/ *adjective* happening or moving very quickly *rapid change/growth* ● **rapidity** /rəˈpɪdəti/ *noun* [U] ● **rapidly** *adverb*

rapids /ˈræpɪdz/ *noun* [plural] a part of a river where the water moves very fast

rapist /ˈreɪpɪst/ *noun* [C] someone who forces another person to have sex when they do not want to

rapper /ˈræpəʳ/ *noun* [C] someone who performs rap music (= a type of music in which the words are spoken and there is a strong beat)

rapport /ræpˈɔːʳ/ *noun* [U, no plural] a good understanding of someone and ability to communicate with them *She has a good rapport with her staff.*

rapture /ˈræptʃəʳ/ *noun* [U] a feeling of extreme pleasure and excitement

⚬ **rare** /reəʳ/ *adjective* **1** very unusual *a rare disease/species* ○ [+ to do sth] *It's very rare to see these birds in England.* **2** If meat is rare, it is still red because it has only been cooked for a short time. *a rare steak*

rarely /ˈreəli/ *adverb* not often *I rarely see her.*

raring /ˈreərɪŋ/ *adjective* **be raring to do sth** *informal* to be very enthusiastic about starting something

rarity /ˈreərəti/ *noun* **1 be a rarity** to be unusual *Genuine enthusiasm is a rarity.* **2** [U] the fact that something is not common *Precious stones are valued for their rarity.*

rascal /ˈrɑːskᵊl/ *noun* [C] **1** *humorous* a person who behaves badly, but who you still like **2** *old-fashioned* a dishonest man

rash¹ /ræʃ/ *noun* **1** [C] a group of small, red spots on the skin *an itchy rash* ○ *Certain foods give him a rash.* **2 a rash of sth** a group of unpleasant events of the same type, happening at the same time *a rash of burglaries*

rash² /ræʃ/ *adjective* done suddenly and without thinking carefully *a rash decision/promise*

rasher /ˈræʃəʳ/ *noun* [C] UK a slice of bacon (= meat from a pig)

raspberry /ˈrɑːzbᵊri/ *noun* [C] a small, soft, red fruit that grows on bushes

rat /ræt/ *noun* [C] **1** an animal that looks like a large mouse and has a long tail *Rats carry disease.* **2** *informal* an unpleasant, dishonest person

rat

WORD PARTNERS FOR **rate**

a **cut in/drop in/increase in/rise in** the
rate ● **at** a rate (of) ● the rate **for/of**

o━**rate**[1] /reɪt/ noun [C] **1** HOW MANY how often
something happens, or how many people
something happens to *the birth rate* ○ *the rate
of unemployment* **2** MONEY a fixed amount of
money given for something *the interest/ex-
change rate* ○ *rates of pay* **3** SPEED the speed at
which something happens *the rate of progress*
4 at this rate used before saying what will
happen if a situation continues in the same
way *At this rate we're not going to be there till
midnight.* **5 at any rate** used before saying one
fact that is certain in a situation that you are
generally not certain about *Well, at any rate
we need her to be there.* **6 first-/second-/third-
rate** very good, bad, or very bad *a first-rate
hotel* ⊃See also: **birth rate, exchange rate.**

rate[2] /reɪt/ verb [T] **1** to judge the quality or ability of someone or something *How do you rate
her as a singer?* **2** to deserve something *The
incident didn't even rate a mention* (= was not
written about) *in the local newspaper.*

o━**rather** /ˈrɑːðəʳ/ adverb **1** slightly or to a degree *I
rather like it.* ○ *I find her books rather dull.*
2 rather than instead of *He saw his music as a
hobby rather than a career.* **3 would rather** If
you would rather do something, you would
prefer to do that thing. *I'd much rather go out
for a meal than stay in and watch TV.* **4** used
to change something you have just said and
make it more correct *I tried writing some
drama, or rather comedy-drama, but it wasn't
very good.*

ratify /ˈrætɪfaɪ/ verb [T] to make an agreement
official *Sixty-five nations need to ratify the
treaty.*

WORD PARTNERS FOR **rating**

give sb/sth/**have** a rating ● sb's/sth's rating
drops/falls/improves/increases ● a **high/
low** rating ● a rating **of** [5/28%, etc]

rating /ˈreɪtɪŋ/ noun **1** [C] a measurement of
how good or popular something or someone is
*A high percentage of Americans gave the Presi-
dent a positive rating.* **2 the ratings** a list of
television and radio programmes showing
how popular they are

ratio /ˈreɪʃiəʊ/ noun [C] the relationship between
two things expressed in numbers to show how
much bigger one is than the other *The female
to male ratio at the college is 2 to 1.*

ration[1] /ˈræʃᵊn/ noun [C] the amount of something that you are allowed to have when there
is little of it available *a food/petrol ration*

ration[2] /ˈræʃᵊn/ verb [T] to give people only a
small amount of something because there is
little of it available *They might have to start
rationing water.*

rational /ˈræʃᵊnᵊl/ adjective **1** based on facts and
not affected by someone's emotions or imagination *a rational argument/debate/explan-
ation* **2** able to make decisions based on facts
and not be influenced by your emotions or
imagination *Look, we've got to try to be ra-

tional about this.* ⊃Opposite irrational. ● **rationally**
adverb

rationale /ˌræʃəˈnɑːl/ noun [C] a group of
reasons for a decision or belief *I don't understand the rationale behind the policy.*

rationalize (*also UK* **-ise**) /ˈræʃᵊnᵊlaɪz/ verb **1** [I,
T] to try to find reasons to explain your be-
haviour or emotions *I can't rationalize the way
I feel towards him.* **2** [T] *mainly UK* to improve
the way a business is organized, usually by
getting rid of people ● **rationalization**
/ˌræʃᵊnᵊlaɪˈzeɪʃᵊn/ noun [C, U]

the 'rat ˌrace noun *informal* the unpleasant
way that people compete against each other at
work in order to succeed

rattle[1] /ˈrætl/ verb **1** [I, T] to make a noise like
something knocking repeatedly, or to cause
something to make this noise *The wind blew
hard, rattling the doors and windows.* **2** [T] to
make someone nervous [often passive] *He was
clearly rattled by their angry reaction.*

rattle sth off to quickly say a list or something that you have learned *She can rattle off
the names of all the players.*

rattle[2] /ˈrætl/ noun [C] a toy that a baby shakes
to make a noise

raucous /ˈrɔːkəs/ adjective loud and unpleasant
raucous laughter

ravage /ˈrævɪdʒ/ verb [T] to damage or destroy
something [often passive] *The whole area has
been ravaged by war.*

ravages /ˈrævɪdʒɪz/ noun **the ravages of dis-
ease/time/war, etc** the damaging effects of dis-
ease/time/war, etc

rave[1] /reɪv/ verb [I] **1** to talk about something
that you think is very good in an excited way
*He went there last year and he's been raving
about it ever since.* **2** to talk in an angry, uncontrolled way

rave[2] /reɪv/ noun [C] an event where people
dance to modern, electronic music

raven /ˈreɪvᵊn/ noun [C] a large, black bird

ravenous /ˈrævᵊnəs/ adjective very hungry
● **ravenously** adverb

ravine /rəˈviːn/ noun [C] a
narrow, deep valley with
very steep sides

ravine

raving /ˈreɪvɪŋ/ adjective
informal completely un-
controlled *He was acting
like a raving lunatic.*

ravings /ˈreɪvɪŋz/ noun
[plural] the strange things
that a crazy person says
the ravings of a madman

ravishing /ˈrævɪʃɪŋ/ adjective very beautiful

o━**raw** /rɔː/ adjective **1** FOOD
not cooked *raw meat/
vegetables* **2** NATURAL in
the natural state *raw
materials* ○ *raw sugar* **3** INJURY If a part of the
body is raw, the skin has come off and it is red
and painful. ● **rawness** noun [U] ⊃See also: hit/
touch a (raw) **nerve.**

ray /reɪ/ noun **1** [C] a narrow beam of light, heat,

R

or energy *an ultraviolet ray* ○ *the rays of the sun* **2 a ray of hope/comfort, etc** a small amount of hope, etc ➔See also: **X-ray**.

razor /'reɪzə^r/ *noun*
[C] a piece of equipment with a sharp blade used for removing hair from the face, legs, etc
➔See colour picture **The Bathroom** on page Centre 3.

'razor ,blade *noun* [C] a very thin, sharp blade that you put in a razor

Rd *written abbreviation for* road *17, Lynton Rd*

re- /riː-/ *prefix* again *to remarry* ○ *a reusable container*

✺**reach**[1] /riːtʃ/ *verb* **1** ARRIVE [T] to arrive somewhere *We won't reach Miami till five or six o'clock.* **2** STRETCH [I, T] to stretch your arm and hand to touch or take something *She reached for a cigarette.* ○ *She reached down to stroke the dog's head.* ○ *He reached out and grabbed her arm.* **3 can reach (sth)** to be able to touch or take something with your hand *Could you get that book down for me - I can't reach.* **4** BE LONG ENOUGH [I, T] If something reaches, or reaches something, it is long enough to touch something. *The rope won't be long enough to reach the ground.* **5** LEVEL [T] to get to a particular level, situation, etc *We hope to reach our goal by May next year.* ○ *I've reached the point where I'm about to give up.* **6 reach a decision/agreement/conclusion, etc** to make a decision, agreement, etc about something **7** TELEPHONE [T] to speak to someone on the telephone *You can reach him at home.*

COMMON LEARNER ERROR

reach

When **reach** means 'arrive somewhere' or 'get to a particular level' it is not normally followed by a preposition.

We finally reached the hotel just after midnight.

The project has now reached the final stage.

~~The project has now reached to the final stage.~~

---

reach[2] /riːtʃ/ *noun* **1 out of/beyond (sb's) reach** too far away for someone to take hold of *I keep the medicines up here, out of the kids' reach.* **2 beyond (sb's) reach** not possible for someone to have *With all this money we can buy things previously beyond our reach.* **3 be within reach (of sth)** to be close enough to travel to *You'll be within easy reach of London.* **4 be within (sb's) reach a** to be close enough for someone to take hold of *The gun lay within reach.* **b** possible for someone to achieve *Winning the championship suddenly seemed within their reach.*

react /ri'ækt/ *verb* [I] **1** SAY/DO [I] to say, do, or feel something because of something else that has been said or done *He reacted angrily to her comments.* **2** BAD EFFECT to become ill because something that you have eaten or used on your body has had a bad effect on you *My skin reacts to most perfumes.* **3** SUBSTANCES In sci-

ence, if a substance reacts with another substance, it changes. *Carbon reacts with oxygen to produce carbon dioxide.*

react against sth to do the opposite of what someone wants you to do because you do not like their rules or ideas

---

🧩 WORD PARTNERS FOR reaction

an **adverse** / **angry** / **immediate** / **initial** / **instinctive** / **negative** / **rapid** reaction ● **gauge/produce/provoke** a reaction ● a reaction **to/towards** sth

---

✺**reaction** /ri'ækʃ^on/ *noun* **1** CAUSED BY SOMETHING [C, U] something you say, feel, or do because of something that has happened *What was his reaction to the news?* **2 reactions** *mainly UK* the ability to move quickly when something suddenly happens *Drivers need to have quick reactions.* **3** CHANGE [no plural] a change in the way people behave or think because they do not agree with the way people behaved or thought in the past *In art, there was a reaction against Realism.* **4** BAD EFFECT [C] an unpleasant feeling or illness caused by something you have eaten or used on your body *A number of people have had a bad reaction to this drug.* **5** SUBSTANCES [C] a change which happens when two substances are put together *a chemical reaction* ➔See also: **chain reaction.**

reactionary /ri'ækʃ^on^ori/ *adjective* being against political or social progress ● **reactionary** *noun* [C] someone who is against political or social progress

reactor /ri'æktə^r/ (*also* **nuclear reactor**) *noun* [C] a large machine which uses nuclear fuel to produce power

✺**read**[1] /riːd/ *verb past* read /red/ **1** WORDS [I, T] to look at words and understand what they mean *What was the last book you read?* ○ *I've been reading about John F Kennedy.* ○ [+ that] *I've read that the economy is going to improve by the end of the year.* **2** SAY [I, T] to look at words that are written and say them aloud for other people to listen to *Do you want me to read it to you?* ○ [+ two objects] *I read him a story at bedtime.* **3** SIGNS [I, T] to look at signs and be able to understand them *Can you read music?* **4** MEASUREMENT [T] to show the temperature, time, etc on a piece of measuring equipment *The thermometer read 20 degrees this morning.* ➔See also: **lip-read.**

read sth into sth to believe that an action, remark, etc has a particular meaning when it has not *Don't read too much into anything he says.*

read sth out to read something and say the words aloud so that other people can hear *He read out the names of all the winners.*

read sth over/through to read something from the beginning to the end, especially to find mistakes *I read over my essay to check for errors.*

read[2] /riːd/ *noun* [no plural] **1** the act of reading something *It's not brilliant but it's worth a read.* **2 a good/easy, etc read** something that is enjoyable, easy, etc to read

readable /'riːdəbl/ *adjective* enjoyable and easy to read

reader /'riːdə^r/ *noun* [C] someone who reads *She's a slow reader.*

readership /'riːdəʃɪp/ *noun* [**no plural**] the number and type of people who read a particular newspaper, magazine, etc *These magazines have a very young readership.*

readily /'redɪli/ *adverb* **1** quickly and easily *Information is readily available on the Internet.* **2** willingly and without stopping to think *He readily admits to having problems himself.*

readiness /'redɪnəs/ *noun* [U] **1** when someone is willing to do something [+ to do sth] *They expressed a readiness to accept our demands.* **2** when someone is prepared for something *It was time to repair their shelters in readiness for the winter.*

o⁻**reading** /'riːdɪŋ/ *noun* **1** ACTIVITY [U] the activity or skill of reading books *I did a lot of reading on holiday.* **2** EVENT [C] an event at which someone reads something to an audience *a poetry reading* **3** MEASUREMENT [C] the measurement that is shown on a piece of measuring equipment *It's best to take a meter reading as soon as you move in*

readjust /,riːə'dʒʌst/ *verb* **1** [I] to change in order to deal with a new situation, such as a new job or home *The children will have to readjust to a new school.* **2** [T] to move something slightly or make a small change to something *He readjusted his tie.*

o⁻**ready** /'redi/ *adjective* **1** [never before noun] prepared for doing something *Give me a call when you're ready.* ○ [+ to do sth] *Are you ready to go yet?* ○ *We're going at eight, so you've got an hour to get ready.* ○ *The army was ready for action.* **2** [never before noun] prepared and available to be eaten, drunk, used, etc *Is dinner ready?* ○ *When will the book be ready for publication?* **3** be ready to do sth to be willing to do something *We are ready to die for our country.* ○See also: **rough**¹ and **ready**.

ready-made /,redi'meɪd/ *adjective* made and ready to use *ready-made meals*

o⁻**real**¹ /rɪəl/ *adjective* **1** NOT IMAGINED existing and not imagined *Romance is never like that in real life.* **2** TRUE true and not pretended *What was the real reason she didn't come?* ○ *Is that your real name?* **3** NOT ARTIFICIAL not artificial or false *real fur/leather* ○ *It's not a toy gun, it's the real thing.* **4** FOR EMPHASIS [always before noun] used to emphasize a noun *She was a real help.* **5** Get real! *informal* used to tell someone that they are hoping for something that will never happen, or that they believe something that is not true ○See also: the real **McCoy**.

real² /rɪəl/ *adverb US informal* very *It's real easy to get there from here.*

'real es,tate *noun* [U] US buildings and land

'real estate ,agent *US* (*UK* **estate agent**) *noun* [C] someone who sells buildings and land as their job

realism /'rɪəlɪz³m/ *noun* [U] **1** when things and people in art, literature, etc are shown as they are in real life **2** when you accept and deal with the true facts of a situation and do not

hope for things that will not happen

realist /'rɪəlɪst/ *noun* [C] **1** someone who accepts the true facts of a situation and does not hope for things that will not happen **2** an artist or writer who shows people and things in their work as they are in real life

realistic /,rɪə'lɪstɪk/ *adjective* **1** accepting the true facts of a situation and not basing decisions on things that will not happen *Let's be realistic - we're not going to finish this by Friday.* **2** showing things and people as they really are, or making them seem to be real *realistic special effects in a film* ○Opposite **unrealistic**. ● **realistically** *adverb*

reality /ri'æləti/ *noun* **1** [U] the way things or situations really are and not the way you would like them to be *Sooner or later you have to face up to reality.* ○ *He may seem charming but in reality he's actually quite unpleasant.* **2** the reality/realities of sth the truth about an unpleasant situation *the harsh realities of life* **3** become a reality to start to happen or exist *New jobs could become a reality by next month.* ○See also: **virtual reality**.

re'ality ,TV *noun* [U] television programmes about ordinary people who are filmed in real situations

realization (*also UK* -isation) /,rɪəlaɪ'zeɪʃ³n/ *noun* **1** [U, no plural] when you notice or understand something that you did not notice or understand before [+ that] *There is a growing realization that education has benefits at many levels.* **2** [U] when you achieve something that you wanted *the realization of an ambition*

o⁻**realize** (*also UK* -ise) /'rɪəlaɪz/ *verb* [T] **1** to notice or understand something that you did not notice or understand before [+ question word] *I didn't realize how unhappy she was.* ○ *I suddenly realized I'd met him before.* ○ [+ (that)] *Some people just don't seem to realize that the world has changed.* **2** realize an ambition/dream/goal, etc to achieve something that you have wanted for a long time *He had realized all his ambitions by the age of 30.*

o⁻**really** /'rɪəli/ *adverb* **1** very or very much *She's really nice.* ○ *I really don't want to go.* ○ *"Did you like it then?" "Er, not really" (= no).* **2** used when you are saying what is the truth of a situation *She tried to hide what she was really thinking.* **3** Really? used when you are surprised at what someone has just said *"Apparently, he's leaving." "Really?"*

realm /relm/ *noun* [C] **1** *formal* an area of knowledge or activity *successes in the realm of foreign policy* **2** *literary* a country that has a king or queen

realtor /'riːltə^r/ *US* (*UK* **estate agent**) *noun* [C] someone who sells buildings or land as their job

reap /riːp/ *verb* **1** reap the benefits/profits/rewards to get something good by working hard for it *Sometimes, this approach can reap* tremendous rewards. **2** [I, T] to cut and collect a crop of grain

reappear /ˌriːəˈpɪəʳ/ verb [I] to appear again or return after a period of time *He reappeared later that day.* • **reappearance** /ˌriːəˈpɪərᵊns/ noun [C, U]

rear¹ /rɪəʳ/ noun **1 the rear** the back part of something *First class accommodation is towards the rear of the train.* **2 bring up the rear** to be at the back of a group of people who are walking or running • **rear** adjective [always before noun] *a rear window/wheel*

rear² /rɪəʳ/ verb **1** [T] If you rear children or young animals, you care for them until they are adults. *In these waters they breed and rear their young.* **2** [I] (also **rear up**) If a horse rears, it stands on its back legs. ⊃See also: raise/rear its ugly **head¹**.

rearrange /ˌriːəˈreɪndʒ/ verb [T] **1** to change the order or position of things *I've rearranged the furniture.* **2** to change the time of an event or meeting *I've rearranged the meeting for Monday.*

rear-view 'mirror noun [C] a small mirror inside a car which the driver looks in to see what is happening behind the car ⊃See colour picture **Car** on page Centre 7.

WORD PARTNERS FOR *reason*

a **compelling/good/obvious/simple** reason • **have/give/understand** a reason • the reason **for** sth • the reason **why** sth happens

---

⊶**reason¹** /ˈriːzᵊn/ noun **1** ⟨WHY⟩ [C] the facts about why something happens or why someone does something *Is there any particular reason why he doesn't want to come?* ○ *He left without giving a reason.* ○ *That was the reason for telling her.* **2** ⟨RIGHT⟩ [C, U] something that makes it right for you to do something [+ to do sth] *There is every reason to believe the project will be finished on time.* **3** ⟨ABILITY⟩ [U] the ability to think and make good decisions *By this time he'd lost his powers of reason.* **4 within reason** If something is within reason, it is acceptable and possible. *You can have as much as you like, within reason.* **5 it stands to reason** If it stands to reason that something happens or is true, it is what you would expect. *It stands to reason that a child who is constantly criticized will have little self-confidence.*

COMMON LEARNER ERROR

reason

Be careful to choose the correct preposition.
*That was the main **reason for** the trip.*
~~That was the main reason of the trip.~~

---

reason² /ˈriːzᵊn/ verb [T] to decide that something is true after considering the facts [+ that] *We reasoned that it was unlikely he would be a serious threat to the public.*
    reason with sb to persuade someone not to do something stupid by giving them good reasons not to

reasonable /ˈriːzᵊnəbl/ adjective **1** ⟨FAIR⟩ fair and showing good judgment [+ to do sth] *It's not*

reasonable to expect people to work those hours. ⊃Opposite **unreasonable**. **2** ⟨BIG ENOUGH⟩ big enough or large enough in number, although not big or not many *There were a reasonable number of people there.* **3** ⟨GOOD ENOUGH⟩ good enough but not the best *I'd say her work is of a reasonable standard.* **4** ⟨CHEAP⟩ not expensive *reasonable prices*

reasonably /ˈriːzᵊnəbli/ adverb **1** in a fair way, showing good judgment *Why can't we discuss this reasonably, like adults?* **2 reasonably good/successful/well, etc** good/successful/well, etc enough but not very good or very well *I did reasonably well at school but not as well as my sister.* **3 reasonably priced** not expensive

reasoning /ˈriːzᵊnɪŋ/ noun [U] the process of thinking about something in order to make a decision *I don't understand the **reasoning** behind this decision.*

reassure /ˌriːəˈʃʊəʳ/ verb [T] to say something to stop someone from worrying [+ that] *He reassured me that I would be paid soon.* • **reassurance** /ˌriːəˈʃʊərᵊns/ noun [C, U] something that you say to make someone stop worrying *Despite my repeated reassurances that she was welcome, she wouldn't come.*

reassuring /ˌriːəˈʃʊərɪŋ/ adjective making you feel less worried *a reassuring smile/voice* • **reassuringly** adverb

rebate /ˈriːbeɪt/ noun [C] an amount of money that is given back to you because you have paid too much *a tax/rent rebate*

rebel¹ /ˈrebᵊl/ noun [C] **1** someone who fights against the government in their country, especially a soldier *Rebels seized control of the airport.* **2** someone who does not like authority and refuses to obey rules

rebel² /rɪˈbel/ verb [I] rebelling, past rebelled **1** to fight against the government **2** to refuse to obey rules because you do not like authority *She rebelled against her family.*

WORD PARTNERS FOR *rebellion*

launch/lead/quash/stage a rebellion • a rebellion **against** sb/sth • a rebellion **by** sb

---

rebellion /rɪˈbeliən/ noun [C, U] when people fight against the government in their country

rebellious /rɪˈbeliəs/ adjective refusing to obey rules because you do not like authority *a rebellious teenager*

rebirth /ˈriːˌbɜːθ/ noun [no plural] when something becomes popular or active for the second time *the rebirth of the women's movement*

rebound¹ /rɪˈbaʊnd/ verb [I] to move back through the air after hitting something *The ball rebounded off the post.*

rebound² /ˈriːbaʊnd/ noun **be on the rebound** to be unhappy because your romantic relationship has ended *She was on the rebound when she met her second husband.*

rebuff /rɪˈbʌf/ verb [T] formal to refuse someone's suggestion or offer, especially in an unfriendly way *The company has rebuffed several buyout offers.* • **rebuff** noun [C]

rebuild /ˌriːˈbɪld/ verb [T] past rebuilt **1** to build something again after it has been damaged

---

R

| ɑː arm | ɜː her | iː see | ɔː saw | uː too | aɪ my | aʊ how | eə hair | eɪ day | əʊ no | ɪə near | ɔɪ boy | ʊə poor | aɪə fire | aʊə sour |

The cathedral was rebuilt after being destroyed by fire. **2** to make a situation succeed again after something bad caused it to fail *The country is still struggling to rebuild its economy.*

rebuke /rɪ'bjuːk/ *verb* [T] *formal* to speak angrily to someone because they have done something wrong • **rebuke** *noun* [C] *formal*

recalcitrant /rɪ'kælsɪtrənt/ *adjective formal* not willing to obey or help someone *recalcitrant schoolchildren*

recall /rɪ'kɔːl/ *verb* [T] **1** to remember something *I don't recall arranging a time to meet.* ○ *I seem to recall that she was going to meet her father.* **2** to order the return of someone or something [often passive] *The ambassador was recalled to London.* • **recall** /'riːkɔːl/ *noun* [U]

recap /'riːkæp/ *verb* [I] recapping, *past* recapped to repeat the most important parts of what you have just said *So, just to recap, we are aiming at a ten per cent increase in sales this quarter.* • **recap** /'riːkæp/ *noun* [C]

recapture /ˌriː'kæptʃə^r/ *verb* [T] **1** to catch a person or animal that has escaped **2** to experience or feel something from the past again *Some men try to **recapture** their youth by going out with younger women.*

recede /rɪ'siːd/ *verb* [I] **1** MOVE AWAY to become further and further away *The coastline receded into the distance.* **2** LESS STRONG If a memory or feeling recedes, it becomes less clear or strong. **3** HAIR If a man's hair recedes, it stops growing at the front of his head. *a **receding** hairline*

receipt /rɪ'siːt/ *noun* **1** [C] a piece of paper that proves that you have received goods or money *Could I have a receipt?* ○ *Remember to keep **receipts** for any work done.* **2** [U] *formal* the act of receiving something *Items must be returned within fourteen days of receipt.*

receipts /rɪ'siːts/ *US* (*UK* takings) *noun* [plural] the amount of money that a business gets from selling things *box-office receipts*

○→**receive** /rɪ'siːv/ *verb* [T] **1** GET to get something that someone has given or sent to you *Occasionally, he receives letters from fans.* ○ *We received a number of complaints.* ○ *I received this email last Monday morning.* **2** REACT to react to a suggestion or piece of work in a particular way [often passive] *His first book was not **well received** (= people did not like it).* **3** WELCOME to formally welcome guests ⊃See also: be on/at the receiving **end**¹ of sth.

receiver /rɪ'siːvə^r/ *noun* [C] **1** TELEPHONE the part of a telephone that you hold in your hand and use for listening and speaking **2** RADIO/TV the part of a radio or television that receives signals from the air **3** PERSON someone who officially deals with a company when it has to stop business because it cannot pay the money it owes

○→**recent** /'riːs^ənt/ *adjective* happening or starting from a short time ago *a recent photo* ○ *In recent years, sales have decreased quite markedly.*

○→**recently** /'riːs^əntli/ *adverb* not long ago *Have you seen any good films recently?* ○ *Until recently he worked as a teacher.*

▓▓▓ **WORD PARTNERS FOR *reception***

3 get/be given/receive a [cool/good, etc] reception • a cool/chilly/frosty/hostile reception • a good/great/rapturous/warm reception • a lukewarm/mixed reception • reception from sb

reception /rɪ'sepʃ^ən/ *noun* **1** HOTEL/OFFICE [no plural] the place in a hotel or office building where people go when they arrive *Ask for me at reception.* ○ *a reception area/desk* **2** PARTY [C] a formal party that is given to celebrate a special event or to welcome someone *a wedding reception* **3** REACTION [no plural] the way people react to something or someone *We were given a very **warm** reception.* **4** RADIO/TV the quality of a radio or television signal

receptionist /rɪ'sepʃ^ənɪst/ *noun* [C] someone who works in a hotel or office building, answering the telephone and dealing with guests *a hotel receptionist*

receptive /rɪ'septɪv/ *adjective* willing to think about and accept new ideas *She's generally very receptive to ideas and suggestions.*

recess /rɪ'ses/ *noun* **1** NOT WORKING [C, U] a time in the day or in the year when a parliament or law court is not working *a parliamentary/congressional recess* ○ *The court is in recess for thirty minutes.* **2** SCHOOL [C, U] *US* (*UK* break) a period of free time between classes at school *At recess the boys would fight.* **3** WALL [C] a part of a wall in a room that is further back than the rest of the wall

recession /rɪ'seʃ^ən/ *noun* [C, U] a time when the economy of a country is not successful *The latest report confirms that the economy is in recession.*

recharge /ˌriː'tʃɑːdʒ/ *verb* [T] to fill a battery (= object that provides a machine with power) with electricity so that it can work again

recipe /'resɪpi/ *noun* **1** [C] a list of foods and a set of instructions telling you how to cook something *a recipe for carrot cake* **2** be a recipe for disaster/trouble/success, etc to be likely to become a disaster, a success, etc

recipient /rɪ'sɪpiənt/ *noun* [C] someone who receives something *a recipient of an award*

reciprocal /rɪ'sɪprək^əl/ *adjective* involving two people or groups that agree to help each other in a similar way *a reciprocal arrangement*

reciprocate /rɪ'sɪprəkeɪt/ *verb* [I, T] to do something for someone because they have done something similar for you

recital /rɪ'saɪt^əl/ *noun* [C] a performance of music or poetry *a piano recital*

recite /rɪ'saɪt/ *verb* [I, T] to say something aloud from memory *She can recite the whole poem.*

reckless /'rekləs/ *adjective* doing something dangerous and not caring about what might happen *reckless driving* • **recklessly** *adverb*

reckon /'rek^ən/ *verb* [T] **1** to think that something is probably true *I reckon he likes her.* ○ [+ (that)] *He reckons that he earns more in a week than I do in a month.* **2** to guess that a particular number is correct *His fortune is*

R

reckoned at $5 million. ⊃See also: a **force**[1] to be reckoned with.

reckon on sth/doing sth to think that something is going to happen and make it part of your plans *We're reckoning on about 200 people for dinner.*

reckon with sb/sth to deal with someone or something difficult

reclaim /rɪ'kleɪm/ *verb* [T] **1** to get something back from someone *You can reclaim the tax at the airport.* **2** to make land good enough to be used for growing crops

recline /rɪ'klaɪn/ *verb* **1** [I] to lie back with the upper part of your body in a horizontal position *I found him reclining on the sofa.* **2** [I, T] If a chair reclines, you can lower the back part so that you can lie in it, and if you recline a chair, you put it in this position. *a reclining chair/seat*

recluse /rɪ'kluːs/ *noun* [C] someone who lives alone and does not like being with other people *For the last twenty years of her life she lived as a recluse.* ● **reclusive** *adjective* living alone and avoiding other people *She led a reclusive life in San Francisco.*

╔═╗ WORD PARTNERS FOR ***recognition***

2 achieve/deserve/gain recognition ● in recognition of sth ● recognition for sth

recognition /ˌrekəg'nɪʃ°n/ *noun* **1** [ACCEPT] [U, no plural] when you accept that something is true or real *There is a growing recognition of the scale of the problem.* ○ [+ that] *There is a general recognition that she's the best person for the job.* **2** [HONOUR] [U] when someone is publicly thanked for something good that they have done *Ellen gained recognition for her outstanding work.* ○ *He was given a medal in recognition of his bravery.* ○ *She is beginning to enjoy international recognition as a writer.* **3** [KNOW] [U] when you know something or someone because you have seen or experienced them before *I waved at her, but she showed no sign of recognition.* ○ *When I next saw her, six years later, she had changed beyond recognition.*

recognizable (*also* UK **-isable**) /'rekəgnaɪzəbl/ *adjective* able to be recognized (= able to be known) *Megan's voice is instantly recognizable.* ○ *She looked a little older but was still recognizable.* ● **recognizably** *adverb* *The foetus is by this stage recognizably human.*

o┅**recognize** (*also* UK **-ise**) /'rekəgnaɪz/ *verb* [T] **1** [KNOW] to know someone or something because you have seen or experienced them before *I recognized her from her picture.* ○ *Doctors are trained to recognize the symptoms of disease.* **2** [ACCEPT] to accept that something is true or real [+ (that)] *She recognized that she had been partly to blame.* ○ *Smoking is recognized as a leading cause of lung cancer.* **3** [SHOW RESPECT] to officially show respect for someone for an achievement *He was recognized by the governor for his work with teenagers.*

recoil /rɪ'kɔɪl/ *verb* [I] to react to something with fear or hate *She recoiled in horror at the thought of touching a snake.*

recollect /ˌrekəl'ekt/ *verb* [T] to remember something *Catherine didn't recollect having seen him.*

recollection /ˌrekəl'ekʃ°n/ *noun* [C, U] when you remember something *He had no recollection of the incident.*

o┅**recommend** /ˌrekə'mend/ *verb* [T] **1** to say that someone or something is good or suitable for a particular purpose *Can you recommend a good wine to go with this dish?* ○ *She has been recommended for promotion.* **2** to advise someone that something should be done *The judge is likely to recommend a long jail sentence.* ○ [+ that] *The report recommended that tourists avoid the region.*

╔═╗ WORD PARTNERS FOR ***recommendation***

accept/follow/implement/make a recommendation ● a recommendation for/on sth

recommendation /ˌrekəmen'deɪʃ°n/ *noun* **1** [C] a piece of advice about what to do in a particular situation *The marketing department made several recommendations to improve sales.* ○ [+ that] *It's my recommendation that this factory be closed immediately.* **2** [C, U] a suggestion that someone or something is good or suitable for a particular purpose *I bought this book on Andy's recommendation.*

recompense /'rekəmpens/ *noun* [U] formal payment that you give to someone when you have caused them difficulty or an injury *Angry soccer fans sought recompense for the cancelled match.* ● **recompense** *verb* [T] formal *He was recompensed for loss of earnings.*

reconcile /'rekənsaɪl/ *verb* [T] **1** to make two different ideas, beliefs, or situations agree or able to exist together *It is sometimes difficult to reconcile science and religion.* ○ *How can you reconcile your love of animals with your habit of eating them?* **2** be reconciled (with sb) to become friendly with someone after you have argued with them

reconcile yourself to sth to accept a situation although you do not like it *Eventually he reconciled himself to living without her.*

reconciliation /ˌrekən,sɪli'eɪʃ°n/ *noun* **1** [C, U] when two people or groups become friendly again after they have argued *to seek a reconciliation* **2** [U, no plural] the process of making two opposite ideas, beliefs, or situations agree *the reconciliation of facts with theory*

reconnaissance /rɪ'kɒnɪs°ns/ *noun* [U] the process of getting information about a place or an area for military use

reconsider /ˌriːkən'sɪdə'/ *verb* [I, T] to think again about a decision or opinion and decide if you want to change it *We've been asked to reconsider the proposal.* ● **reconsideration** /ˌriːkən,sɪd°r'eɪʃ°n/ *noun* [U]

reconstruct /ˌriːkən'strʌkt/ *verb* [T] **1** to create a description of a past event using all the information that you have *The police tried to re-construct the crime using evidence found at the scene.* **2** to build something again after it has been damaged or destroyed

reconstruction /ˌriːkən'strʌkʃ°n/ *noun* [C, U]
1 when you create a description of a past event using all the information that you have *A reconstruction of the crime was shown on TV.*
2 when you build something again after it has been damaged or destroyed

o~**record¹** /'rekɔːd/ *noun* **1** STORED INFORMATION [C, U] information that is written on paper or stored on computer so that it can be used in the future *medical/dental records* ○ *My teacher keeps a record of my absences.* ○ *This has been the hottest summer on record* (= the hottest summer known about). **2** BEHAVIOUR [C] A person's or company's record is their be-haviour or achievements. [usually singular] *She has an outstanding academic record* (= has done very well in school). ○ *Of all airlines they have the best safety record.* **3** BEST [C] the best, biggest, longest, tallest, etc to *set/break a record* ○ *He holds the world record for 100 metres.* **4** MUSIC [C] a flat, round, plastic disc that music is stored on, used especially in the past *to play a record* **5** **off the record** If you say something off the record, you do not want the public to know about it. **6** **put/set the record straight** to tell people the true facts about a situation ⊃See also: **track record.**

o~**record²** /rɪ'kɔːd/ *verb* **1** [T] to write down infor-mation or store it on a computer so that it can be used in the future *He recorded details of their conversation in his diary.* **2** [I, T] to store sounds or pictures using electronic equip-ment, a camera, etc so that you can listen to them or see them again *to record a new album* ○ *a recorded message*

record-breaking /'rekɔːdˌbreɪkɪŋ/ *adjective* [always before noun] better, bigger, longer, etc than anything else before *record-breaking sales of the new video*

recorder /rɪ'kɔːdəʳ/ *noun* [C] **1** a machine for storing sounds or pictures *a video recorder* **2** a long, thin, hollow instrument that you play by blowing into it ⊃See also: **cassette recorder, tape recorder.**

recording /rɪ'kɔːdɪŋ/ *noun* [C, U] sounds or moving pictures that have been recorded, or the process of recording *a recording of clas-sical music* ○ *a new system of digital recording*

'**record** ˌ**label** *noun* [C] a company that records and sells music

'**record** ˌ**player** *noun* [C] a machine that makes it possible to hear the music on a record (= a flat, round disc used especially in the past)

recount¹ /rɪ'kaʊnt/ *verb* [T] *formal* to tell a story or describe an event *He was recounting a story about a woman he'd met on a train.*

recount² /ˌriː'kaʊnt/ *verb* [T] to count something again

recount³ /'riːkaʊnt/ *noun* [C] a second count of votes in an election *They demanded a re-count.*

recoup /rɪ'kuːp/ *verb* [T] to get back money that you have lost or spent *to recoup your losses*

recourse /rɪ'kɔːs/ *noun* [U] *formal* someone or something that can help you in a difficult situ-ation *For many cancer patients, surgery is the only recourse.* ○ *They solved their problem without recourse to* (= without using) *vio-lence.*

o~**recover** /rɪ'kʌvəʳ/ *verb* **1** HEALTH [I] to become healthy or happy again after an illness, injury, or period of sadness *It takes a long time to re-cover from surgery.* ○ *She never recovered from the death of her husband.* **2** SITUATION [I] If a system or situation recovers, it returns to the way it was before something bad hap-pened. *The economy was quick to recover after the election.* **3** BODY [T] to be able to use or feel again part of your body which has been dam-aged *He never fully recovered the use of his legs.* **4** GET BACK [T] to get something back that has been lost or stolen *Police recovered the stolen money.*

recovery /rɪ'kʌv°ri/ *noun* **1** HEALTH [U, no plural] when you feel better or happier again after an illness, injury, or period of sadness *She only had the operation last month but she's made a good recovery.* **2** SITUATION [U, no plural] when a system or situation returns to the way it was before something bad happened *economic re-covery* ○ *The housing industry has made a remarkable recovery.* **3** GET BACK [U] when you get back something that was lost or stolen *the recovery of stolen jewels*

recreate /ˌriːkri'eɪt/ *verb* [T] to make something exist or happen again *They plan to recreate a typical English village in Japan.*

recreation /ˌrekri'eɪʃ°n/ *noun* [C, U] activities that you do for enjoyment when you are not working *Shopping seems to be her only form of recreation.* ● **recreational** *adjective*

recrimination /rɪˌkrɪmɪ'neɪʃ°n/ *noun* [C, U] *formal* the things you say when you blame someone for something, or the act of blaming someone for something

recruit¹ /rɪ'kruːt/ *verb* [I, T] to try to persuade someone to work for a company or to join an organization ● **recruitment** *noun* [U] when you recruit people *graduate recruitment*

recruit² /rɪ'kruːt/ *noun* [C] someone who has re-cently joined an organization *a new recruit*

rectangle /'rektæŋgl/ *noun* [C] a shape with four 90° angles and four sides, with opposite sides of equal length and two sides longer than

R

the other two ➲See picture at **shape**. ● **rectangular** /rek'tæŋgjələʳ/ *adjective* shaped like a rectangle *a rectangular room*

rectify /'rektɪfaɪ/ *verb* [T] *formal* to correct something or change it so that it is acceptable *The government has promised to **rectify the situation**.*

rector /'rektəʳ/ *noun* [C] a priest in some Christian churches

rectum /'rektəm/ *noun* [C] the last part of the body that solid waste travels through before coming out of the bottom

recuperate /rɪ'kuːpəreɪt/ *verb* [I] to become healthy again after an illness or injury *She's still **recuperating from** her injuries.* ● **recuperation** /rɪˌkjuːpəˈreɪʃən/ *noun* [U]

recur /rɪ'kɜːʳ/ *verb* [I] **recurring** *past* **recurred** to happen again or many times *The same ideas recur throughout her books.* ● **recurrence** /rɪ'kʌrəns/ *noun* [C, U] when something recurs *a recurrence of the disease*

recurring /rɪ'kɜːrɪŋ/ (*also* **recurrent**) *adjective* happening again or many times *a **recurring dream***

recycle /ˌriː'saɪkl/ *verb* [I, T] to put used paper, glass, plastic, etc through a process so that it can be used again *We recycle all our newspapers and bottles.* ● **recyclable** /ˌriː'saɪkləbl/ *adjective* able to be recycled *Glass is recyclable.*

recycled /ˌriː'saɪkld/ *adjective* Recycled paper, glass, plastic, etc has been used before and put through a process so that it can be used again.

recycling /ˌriː'saɪklɪŋ/ *noun* [U] when paper, glass, plastic, etc is put through a process so that it can be used again *ways to encourage recycling* ○ *a recycling centre*

⊶**red¹** /red/ *adjective* **redder, reddest 1** [COLOUR] being the same colour as blood *a red shirt* ➲See colour picture **Colours** on page Centre 12. **2** [HAIR] Red hair is an orange-brown colour. **3 go red** *UK* (*US* **turn red**) If someone goes red, their face becomes red because they are embarrassed or angry. **4** [WINE] Red wine is made from black grapes (= small, round, purple fruits). ➲See also: be like a red **rag** to a bull.

⊶**red²** /red/ *noun* **1** [C, U] the colour of blood ➲See colour picture **Colours** on page Centre 12. **2 in the red** If your bank account is in the red, you have spent more money than there was in it. **3 see red** to become very angry

ˌ**red 'card** *noun* [C] in football, a small red card which the referee (= someone who makes sure the players follow the rules) shows to a player to make him stop playing because he has broken a rule

the ˌred 'carpet *noun* special treatment that is given to an important person when they go somewhere *She's given **the red carpet treatment** wherever she goes.*

redden /'redən/ *verb* [I, T] to become red or to make something become red *His face reddened with anger.*

redeem /rɪ'diːm/ *verb* [T] **1** [IMPROVE] to make something seem less bad *He tried to **redeem** his **reputation** by working extra hard.* ○ *a **redeeming feature*** **2 redeem yourself** to do something that makes people have a better opinion of you after you have done something bad *He was two hours late, but he redeemed himself by bringing presents.* **3** [GET SOMETHING] to exchange something for something else **4** [RELIGION] to save someone from evil, especially according to the Christian religion

redemption /rɪ'dempʃən/ *noun* **1** [U] when someone is saved from evil, especially according to the Christian religion **2 be beyond redemption** to be too bad to be improved or saved

redeploy /ˌriːdɪ'plɔɪ/ *verb* [T] to move employees, soldiers, equipment, etc to a different place or use them in a more effective way ● **redeployment** *noun* [C, U] when you redeploy someone or something

redevelop /ˌriːdɪ'veləp/ *verb* [T] to make a place more modern by improving old buildings or building new ones *There are plans to redevelop the city's waterfront area.* ● **redevelopment** *noun* [C, U] when a place is redeveloped

red-handed /ˌred'hændɪd/ *adverb* **catch sb red-handed** *informal* to discover someone doing something wrong *He was caught red-handed trying to steal a car.*

redhead /'redhed/ *noun* [C] someone who has red hair

ˌ**red 'herring** *noun* [C] a fact or idea that takes your attention away from something that is important

red-hot /ˌred'hɒt/ *adjective* extremely hot

redirect /ˌriːdɪ'rekt/ *verb* [T] **1** to send something in a different direction *Traffic should be redirected away from the city centre.* **2** to use money, energy, etc for a different purpose *Money spent on weapons could be **redirected to** hospitals and schools.*

redistribute /ˌriːdɪ'strɪbjuːt/ *verb* [T] to share money, land, power, etc between people in a different way from before *to **redistribute wealth*** ● **redistribution** /ˌriːdɪstrɪ'bjuːʃən/ *noun* [U] the process of redistributing something

ˌ**red 'meat** *noun* [U] meat from animals and not birds or fish

redo /ˌriː'duː/ *verb* [T] to do something again *I'm going to have to redo that report.*

redress¹ /rɪ'dres/ *verb* [T] *formal* to correct something that is wrong, unfair, or not equal *laws aimed at redressing racial inequality*

redress² /rɪ'dres/ [US] /'riːdres/ *noun* [U] *formal* payment for an action or situation that is wrong or unfair

ˌ**red 'tape** *noun* [U] official rules that do not seem necessary and make things happen very slowly

⊶**reduce** /rɪ'djuːs/ *verb* [T] to make something less *to reduce air pollution* ○ *The number of employees was **reduced from** 500 **to** 300.*

reduce sb to sth/doing sth to make someone unhappy or cause them to be in a bad situation *She was **reduced to tears** by his comments.*

reduce sth to sth to destroy something, especially something that has been built *The earthquake reduced the city to rubble.*

WORD PARTNERS FOR *reduction*

a **dramatic/drastic/sharp/significant** reduction • a reduction **in** sth

reduction /rɪ'dʌkʃən/ *noun* [C, U] when something is reduced *She refused to accept a reduction in wages.* ○ *price reductions*

redundancy /rɪ'dʌndənsi/ *noun* **1** [C, U] *UK* when your employer makes you stop working because there is not enough work *There have been a lot of redundancies in the mining industry.* **2** [U] when something is not needed or used because there are other similar or more modern things

redundant /rɪ'dʌndənt/ *adjective* **1** NOT WORK-ING *UK* not working because your employer has told you there is not enough work *Eight thousand people have been made redundant in Britain this year.* **2** NOT NEEDED *UK* not needed or used any more because there are other similar or more modern things *redundant weapons* **3** TOO MUCH more than is needed, especially extra words that mean the same thing

redwood /'redwʊd/ *noun* [C, U] a very tall tree that grows on the west coast of the US, or the wood of this tree

reed /riːd/ *noun* [C] a tall, stiff plant like grass that grows near water

reef /riːf/ *noun* [C] a line of rocks or sand near the surface of the sea *a coral reef*

reek /riːk/ *verb* [I] to have a very unpleasant smell *The whole room reeked of sweat.* • **reek** *noun* [no plural]

reel¹ /riːl/ *verb* [I] **1** to feel very shocked *She was still reeling from the news of his death.* **2** to walk in a way that looks as if you are going to fall over *He came reeling down the street like a drunk.*

reel sth off to say a long list of things quickly and without stopping *She reeled off a list of all the countries she'd been to.*

reel² /riːl/ *noun* [C] an object shaped like a wheel that you can roll film, thread, etc around

re-elect /ˌriːɪ'lekt/ *verb* [T] to elect someone again to a particular position

re-election /ˌriːɪ'lekʃən/ *noun* [C, U] when someone is elected again to the same position *She's (UK) standing for/ (US) running for re-election* (= she wants to be re-elected).

ref /ref/ *noun* [C] *informal short for* referee

refer /rɪ'fɜː'/ *verb* referring, *past* referred

refer to sb/sth 1 to talk or write about someone or something, especially briefly *She didn't once refer to her son.* ○ *He always referred to his father as 'the old man'.* **2** If writing or information refers to someone or something, it relates to that person or thing. *The sales figures refer to UK sales only.*

refer to sth to read something in order to get information *Please refer to your owner's manual for more information.*

refer sb/sth to sb/sth to send someone or something to a different place or person for information or help *My doctor referred me to a specialist.*

referee¹ /ˌrefə'riː/ *noun* [C] someone who makes sure that players follow the rules during a sports game ⊃See colour picture **Sports 2** on page Centre 15.

referee² /ˌrefə'riː/ *verb* [I, T] refereeing *past* refereed to be the referee in a sports game

reference /'refərəns/ *noun* **1** SAY [C, U] when you briefly talk or write about someone or something *In his book, he makes several references to his time in France.* **2** with/in reference to sth *formal* relating to something *I am writing to you with reference to the job advertised in yesterday's newspaper.* **3** LOOK AT [C, U] when you look at information, or the thing that you look at for information *Please keep this handout for future reference* (= to look at in the future). **4** LETTER [C] a letter that is written by someone who knows you, to say if you are suitable for a job or course ⊃See also: **cross reference**.

reference book *noun* [C] a book that you look at in order to find information

referendum /ˌrefə'rendəm/ *noun* [C] an occasion when all the people in a country can vote in order to show their opinion about a political question

referral /rɪ'tɜːrəl/ *noun* [C, U] when someone or something is sent to a different place or person for information or help

refill /ˌriː'fɪl/ *verb* [T] to fill something again *He got up and refilled their glasses.* • **refill** /'riːfɪl/ *noun* [C]

refine /rɪ'faɪn/ *verb* [T] **1** to make a substance pure by removing other substances from it **2** to improve an idea, method, system, etc by making small changes *The engineers spent months refining the software.*

refined /rɪ'faɪnd/ *adjective* **1** PURE A refined substance has been made more pure by removing other substances from it. *refined sugar* **2** POLITE very polite and showing knowledge of social rules **3** IMPROVED improved by many small changes *a refined method*

refinement /rɪ'faɪnmənt/ *noun* **1** IMPROVEMENT [C, U] a small change that improves something *Several refinements have been made to improve the car's performance.* **2** POLITE [U] polite behaviour and knowledge of social rules *a woman of refinement* **3** PURE [U] the process of making a substance pure

refinery /rɪ'faɪnəri/ *noun* [C] a factory where substances, such as sugar, oil, etc are made pure

reflect /rɪ'flekt/ *verb* **1** SHOW [T] to show or be a sign of something *The statistics reflect a change in people's spending habits.* **2** SEND BACK [T] If a surface reflects heat, light, sound, etc, it sends the light, etc back and does not absorb it. **3** IMAGE [I, T] If a surface such as a mirror or water reflects something, you can see the image of that thing in the mirror, water, etc. *He saw himself reflected in the shop window.* **4** THINK [I] *formal* to think in a serious and careful way *In prison, he had plenty of time to reflect on the crimes he had committed.*

reflect on sb/sth If something reflects on someone or something, it affects other people's

R

opinion of them, especially in a bad way. *The whole affair **reflects badly** on the government.*

reflection

reflection /rɪˈflekʃⁿn/ *noun* **1** [C] the image of something in a mirror, on a shiny surface, etc *I saw my reflection in the window.* **2** [C, U] *formal* when you think in a serious and careful way *He paused for reflection before answering my question.* ○ **On reflection** (= after thinking again), *I think I was wrong.* **3 a reflection of sth** something that is a sign or result of a particular situation *His poor job performance is a reflection of his lack of training.* **4 a reflection on sb/sth** something that makes people have a particular opinion about someone or something, especially a bad opinion *Low test scores are a sad reflection on our school system.*

reflective /rɪˈflektɪv/ *adjective* **1** thinking carefully and quietly *a reflective mood* **2** A reflective surface is one that you can see easily when a light shines on it. *a jacket made of reflective material*

reflex /ˈriːfleks/ *noun* [C] a physical reaction that you cannot control *Shivering and blushing are reflexes.* ○ *a reflex action*

reflexes /ˈriːfleksɪz/ *noun* [plural] your ability to react quickly *A boxer needs to have **good reflexes**.*

reflexive /rɪˈfleksɪv/ *adjective* A reflexive verb or pronoun is used to show that the person who does the action is also the person who is affected by it. In the sentence 'I looked at myself in the mirror.', 'myself' is a reflexive pronoun.

reflexology /ˌriːflekˈsɒlədʒi/ *noun* [U] the treatment of your feet by rubbing and pressing them in a special way in order to make the blood flow and help you relax

⚒ WORD PARTNERS FOR **reform**

introduce/propose a reform ● a major/radical/sweeping reform ● reform in/of sth ● economic/political reform

reform¹ /rɪˈfɔːm/ *noun* [C, U] when changes are made to improve a system, organization, or law, or a change that is made *economic/political reform*

reform² /rɪˈfɔːm/ *verb* **1** [T] to change a system, organization, or law in order to improve it *efforts to reform the education system* **2** [I, T] to change your behaviour and stop doing bad

things, or to make someone else do this *a programme to reform criminals* ○ *a reformed drug addict*

reformer /rɪˈfɔːməʳ/ *noun* [C] someone who tries to improve a system or law by changing it *a social reformer*

refrain¹ /rɪˈfreɪn/ *verb* [I] *formal* to stop yourself from doing something [+ from + doing sth] *Please refrain from talking during the performance.*

refrain² /rɪˈfreɪn/ *noun* [C] **1** *formal* a phrase or idea that you repeat often *'Every vote counts' is a familiar refrain in politics.* **2** a part of a song that you repeat

refresh /rɪˈfreʃ/ *verb* **1** [T] to make you feel less hot or tired *A cool drink should refresh you.* **2** [I, T] to make the most recent information on an Internet page appear on your computer **3 refresh sb's memory** to help someone remember something

refreshing /rɪˈfreʃɪŋ/ *adjective* **1** different and interesting *a refreshing change* ○ [+ to do sth] *It's refreshing to see a film that's so original.* **2** making you feel less hot or tired *a refreshing shower/swim* ● **refreshingly** *adverb*

refreshments /rɪˈfreʃmənts/ *noun* [plural] food and drinks that are available at a meeting, event, on a journey, etc *Refreshments are available in the lobby.*

refrigerate /rɪˈfrɪdʒəreɪt/ *verb* [T] to make or keep food cold so that it stays fresh *You should refrigerate any leftover food immediately.* ● **refrigeration** /rɪˌfrɪdʒⁿrˈeɪʃⁿn/ *noun* [U]

refrigerated /rɪˈfrɪdʒəreɪtɪd/ *adjective* **1** A refrigerated container or vehicle keeps the things inside it cold. **2** Refrigerated food or drink is cold because it has been kept in a refrigerator.

refrigerator /rɪˈfrɪdʒəreɪtəʳ/ *noun* [C] a large container that uses electricity to keep food cold ➔See colour picture **The Kitchen** on page Centre 2.

refuel /ˌriːˈfjuːəl/ *verb* [I, T] to put more fuel into an aircraft, ship, etc so that it can continue its journey

refuge /ˈrefjuːdʒ/ *noun* **1** [U] protection from danger or unpleasant conditions *We **took refuge from** the storm in an old barn.* **2** [C] a place where you are protected from danger *a refuge for homeless people*

refugee /ˌrefjʊˈdʒiː/ *noun* [C] someone who has been forced to leave their country, especially because of a war *a refugee camp*

⚒ WORD PARTNERS FOR **refund**

claim/give sb/get a refund ● a **full** refund ● a refund of sth

refund¹ /ˈriːfʌnd/ *noun* [C] an amount of money that is given back to you, especially because you are not happy with something you have bought *The holiday company apologized and gave us a full refund.*

refund² /ˌriːˈfʌnd/ *verb* [T] to give back money that someone has paid to you

refurbish /ˌriːˈfɜːbɪʃ/ *verb* [T] *formal* to repair or improve a building ● **refurbishment** *noun* [C, U] the process of refurbishing a building *The lib-*

rary was closed for refurbishment.

refusal /rɪ'fjuːz°l/ *noun* [C, U] when someone refuses to do or accept something [+ **to do sth**] *his refusal to admit his mistake*

◦ᐟ**refuse**¹ /rɪ'fjuːz/ *verb* [I, T] to say that you will not do or accept something *I asked him to leave but he refused.* ○ [+ **to do sth**] *Cathy refuses to admit that she was wrong.*

refuse² /'refjuːs/ *noun* [U] *formal* waste *a pile of refuse*

refute /rɪ'fjuːt/ *verb* [T] *formal* to say or prove that something is not true or correct *attempts to refute his theory* ○ *She angrily refuted their claims.*

regain /rɪ'geɪn/ *verb* [T] to get something back again *Armed troops have regained control of the capital.* ○ *It was several hours before he regained consciousness.*

regal /'riːg°l/ *adjective* very special and suitable for a king or queen *a regal dress*

regard¹ /rɪ'gɑːd/ *verb* [T] **1** to think of someone or something in a particular way *She is generally regarded as one of the greatest singers this century.* ○ *The plans were regarded with suspicion.* **2** *formal* to look carefully at someone or something

regard² /rɪ'gɑːd/ *noun* **1** [U] respect or admiration for someone or something *I have the greatest regard for her.* ⊃Opposite disregard. **2 in/with regard to sth** *formal* relating to something *I am writing in regard to your letter of 24 June.*

regarding /rɪ'gɑːdɪŋ/ *preposition formal* about or relating to *I am writing to you regarding your application dated 29 April.*

regardless /rɪ'gɑːdləs/ *adverb* **1 regardless of sth** despite something *She'll make a decision regardless of what we think.* **2** without thinking about problems or difficulties *Mr Redwood claimed he would carry on with his campaign regardless.*

regards /rɪ'gɑːdz/ *noun* [plural] friendly greetings *Give/send my regards to your mother when you see her.*

regeneration /rɪˌdʒen°r'eɪʃ°n/ *noun* [U] the process of improving a place or system, especially to make it more active or successful *a programme of urban regeneration* ● **regenerate** /rɪ'dʒen°reɪt/ *verb* [T] to improve a place or system

reggae /'regeɪ/ *noun* [U] a type of popular music from Jamaica with a strong beat

regime /reɪ'ʒiːm/ *noun* [C] a system of government or other control, especially one that people do not approve of *the former Communist regime*

regiment /'redʒɪmənt/ *noun* [group] a large group of soldiers ● **regimental** /ˌredʒɪ'ment°l/ *adjective* relating to a regiment

regimented /'redʒɪmentɪd/ *adjective* too controlled or organized *a regimented lifestyle*

◦ᐟ**region** /'riːdʒ°n/ *noun* **1** [C] a particular area in a country or the world *China's coastal region* **2** [C] an area of the body *pain in the lower abdominal region* **3 in the region of sth** approximately *It probably cost somewhere in*

the region of £900.

regional /'riːdʒ°n°l/ *adjective* relating to a region (= particular area in a country) *a regional dialect/newspaper* ○ *There are very pronounced regional differences in the cuisine.*

register¹ /'redʒɪstəʳ/ *noun* **1** [C] an official list of names *a register of approved builders* ○ *the electoral register* **2** [C, U] the style of language, grammar, and words used in particular situations *a formal/informal register* ⊃See also: cash register.

register² /'redʒɪstəʳ/ *verb* **1** ON A LIST [I, T] to put information about someone or something, especially a name, on an official list *Is he registered with the authorities to sell alcohol?* ○ *Students need to register for the course by the end of April.* ○ *a registered nurse* **2** SHOW A FEELING [T] to show an opinion or feeling *People gathered to register their opposition to the plans.* **3** SHOW AMOUNT [I, T] to show an amount on an instrument that measures something *The earthquake registered 7.3 on the Richter scale.*

registered /'redʒɪstəd/ *adjective* **registered mail/post** a special service that records when a letter or parcel is sent and received

'register ˌoffice *noun* [C] in Britain, a place where births, deaths, and marriages are officially recorded and where you can get married *We got married at the local register office.*

registrar /ˌredʒɪ'strɑːʳ/ *noun* [C] **1** someone whose job is to keep official records, especially of births, deaths, and marriages, or of students at a university **2** *UK* a type of hospital doctor

registration /ˌredʒɪ'streɪʃ°n/ *noun* **1** [U] when a name or information is recorded on an official list **2** [C] (*also* regis'tration ˌnumber) *mainly UK* the official set of numbers and letters on the front and back of a vehicle

registry /'redʒɪstri/ *noun* [C] a place where official records are kept *the land registry*

'registry ˌoffice *noun* [C] in Britain, a place where births, deaths, and marriages are officially recorded and where you can get married

regress /rɪ'gres/ *verb* [I] *formal* to go back to an earlier, less advanced state *I've started playing a lot of games that I played as a child – I think I'm regressing.* ● **regression** /rɪ'greʃ°n/ *noun* [U] *formal* when someone or something regresses

◦ᐟ**regret**¹ /rɪ'gret/ *verb* [T] regretting *past* regretted **1** to feel sorry about a situation, especially something that you wish you had not done [+ doing sth] *I really regret leaving school so young.* ○ [+ (that)] *He began to regret that he hadn't paid more attention in class.* **2** *formal* used to say that you are sorry that you have to tell someone about a situation [+ **to do sth**] *We regret to inform you that the application has been refused.*

R

🧩 WORD PARTNERS FOR **regret**

express regret • **have (no)** regrets • **sb's biggest/only** regret • **with** regret • regret **about/at/over** sth

❍**regret²** /rɪˈgret/ *noun* [C, U] a feeling of sadness about a situation, especially something that you wish you had not done *We married very young but we've been really happy and I've **no regrets**.* ○ *It is **with** great **regret** that I announce Steve Adam's resignation.* ● **regretful** *adjective* expressing regret ● **regretfully** *adverb*

regrettable /rɪˈgretəbl/ *adjective* If something is regrettable, you wish it had not happened and you feel sorry about it. *a deeply regrettable incident* ● **regrettably** *adverb*

❍**regular¹** /ˈregjələ⁽ʳ⁾/ *adjective* **1** [SAME TIME/SPACE] repeated with the same amount of time or space between one thing and the next *a regular pulse* ○ *Plant the seedlings at regular intervals.* **2** [OFTEN] happening or doing something often, especially at the same time every week, year, etc *a **regular occurrence*** ○ *We arranged to meet **on a regular basis**.* **3** [USUAL] *US* usual or normal *I couldn't see my regular dentist.* **4** [SIZE] *informal* being a standard size *a burger and regular fries* **5** [SHAPE] Something that has a regular shape is the same on both or all sides. *She's got lovely, regular teeth.* **6** [GRAMMAR] following the usual rules or patterns in grammar *'Talk' is a regular verb but 'go' is not.* **Ɔ**Opposite **irregular.** ● **regularity** /ˌregjəˈlærəti/ *noun* [U] when something is regular

regular² /ˈregjələ⁽ʳ⁾/ *noun* [C] *informal* someone who often goes to a particular shop, restaurant, etc *Mick was one of the regulars at the local pub.*

❍**regularly** /ˈregjələli/ *adverb* **1** often *Accidents occur regularly on this stretch of the road.* **2** at the same time each day, week, month, etc *They meet regularly - usually once a week.*

regulate /ˈregjəleɪt/ *verb* [T] **1** to control an activity or process, especially by using rules *laws regulating advertising* **2** to control the speed, temperature, etc of something *Babies find it difficult to regulate their body temperature.*

🧩 WORD PARTNERS FOR **regulation**

breach / comply with / enforce / introduce regulations • regulations **governing** sth • **strict/stringent/tough** regulations • **under** a regulation

regulation /ˌregjəˈleɪʃⁿn/ *noun* **1** [C] an official rule that controls how something is done [usually plural] *building regulations* **2** [U] when a process or activity is controlled *government regulation of interest rates*

regulator /ˈregjəleɪtə⁽ʳ⁾/ *noun* [C] **1** someone whose job is to make sure that a system works in a fair way *the water industry regulator* **2** a piece of equipment that is used to control the temperature, speed, etc of something

regulatory /ˈregjələtᵊri/ *adjective* controlling an activity or process, especially by using rules

rehab /ˈriːhæb/ *noun* [U] *informal* treatment to help someone stop drinking too much alcohol or taking drugs *He spent six months **in rehab**.*

rehabilitate /ˌriːhəˈbɪlɪteɪt/ *verb* [T] to help someone live a normal life again after they have had a serious illness or been in prison *a programme to rehabilitate young offenders* ● **rehabilitation** /ˌriːhəˌbɪlɪˈteɪʃⁿn/ *noun* [U]

rehearsal /rɪˈhɜːsᵊl/ *noun* [C, U] a time when all the people involved in a play, dance, etc practise in order to prepare for a performance

rehearse /rɪˈhɜːs/ *verb* [I, T] to practise a play, dance, etc in order to prepare for a performance

reign¹ /reɪn/ *noun* **1** [C] a period of time when a king or queen rules a country *the reign of Henry VIII* **2** [no plural] a period of time when someone controls a sports team, an organization, etc *Christie's reign as captain of the British athletics team* **3** **reign of terror** a period of time when someone uses violence to control people

reign² /reɪn/ *verb* [I] **1** to be the king or queen of a country *Queen Victoria reigned for 64 years.* **2** *formal* to be the main feeling or quality in a situation *Chaos reigned as angry protesters hammered on the doors.*

reigning ˈchampion *noun* [C] the most recent winner of a competition

reimburse /ˌriːɪmˈbɜːs/ *verb* [T] *formal* to pay money back to someone, especially money that they have spent because of their work *Employees will no longer be **reimbursed for** taxi fares.* ● **reimbursement** *noun* [U] *formal* when you reimburse someone

rein /reɪn/ *noun* **1** [C] a long, thin piece of leather that helps you to control a horse [usually plural] *Hold the reins in your left hand.* **Ɔ**See colour picture **Sports 1** on page Centre 14. **2** **free rein** the freedom to do or say what you want [+ to do sth] *The school gives teachers free rein to try out new teaching methods.* **3** **keep a tight rein on sb/sth** to have a lot of control over someone or something *We've been told to keep a tight rein on spending.*

reincarnation /ˌriːɪnkɑːˈneɪʃⁿn/ *noun* [U] the belief that a dead person's spirit returns to life in another body

reindeer /ˈreɪndɪə⁽ʳ⁾/ *noun* [C] plural **reindeer** a type of deer with large horns that lives in northern parts of Europe, Asia, and America

reinforce /ˌriːɪnˈfɔːs/ *verb* [T] **1** to make an existing opinion or idea stronger *to reinforce a view/feeling* **2** to make something stronger *a security door reinforced by steel bars* ○ *reinforced concrete* ● **reinforcement** *noun* [C, U] when you reinforce something

reinforcements /ˌriːɪnˈfɔːsmənts/ *noun* [plural] soldiers who are sent to make an army stronger

reinstate /ˌriːɪnˈsteɪt/ *verb* [T] **1** to give someone the job or position that they had before **2** to cause a rule, law, etc to exist again ● **reinstatement** *noun* [C, U] when you reinstate someone or something

reinvent /ˌriːɪnˈvent/ *verb* **1** [T] to produce

something new that is based on something that already exists *The story of Romeo and Juliet was reinvented as a Los Angeles gangster movie.* **2 reinvent yourself** to change the way you look and behave so that you seem very different ⊃See also: reinvent the **wheel**¹.

reiterate /riː'ɪtᵊreɪt/ *verb* [T] *formal* to say something again so that people take notice of it [+ that] *I must reiterate that we have no intention of signing this contract.* ● **reiteration** /riˌɪtᵊr'eɪʃᵊn/ *noun* [C, U]

o--**reject**¹ /rɪ'dʒekt/ *verb* [T] **1** NOT ACCEPT to refuse to accept or agree with something *The United States government rejected the proposal.* **2** JOB/COURSE to refuse to accept someone for a job, course, etc *I applied to Cambridge University but I was rejected.* **3** PERSON to not give someone the love or attention they were expecting *She felt rejected by her husband.*

reject² /'riːdʒekt/ *noun* [C] a product that is damaged or not perfect in some way

rejection /rɪ'dʒekʃᵊn/ *noun* **1** NOT ACCEPT [C, U] when you refuse to accept or agree with something *Their rejection of the peace plan is very disappointing for the government.* **2** JOB/COLLEGE [C] a letter that says you have not been successful in getting a job, a place at college, etc **3** PERSON [U] when someone does not give someone else the love or attention they were expecting *a feeling of rejection*

rejoice /rɪ'dʒɔɪs/ *verb* [I] *literary* to feel very happy because something good has happened

rejoicing /rɪ'dʒɔɪsɪŋ/ *noun* [U] when people show that they are very happy because something good has happened

rejoin /rɪ'dʒɔɪn/ *verb* [T] to return to a person or place *I was feeling better, so I rejoined the party.*

rejuvenate /rɪ'dʒuːvᵊneɪt/ *verb* [T] to make someone look or feel young and energetic again *You're supposed to come back from a holiday feeling rejuvenated.* ● **rejuvenation** /rɪˌdʒuːvᵊn'eɪʃᵊn/ *noun* [U]

rekindle /ˌriː'kɪndl/ *verb* [T] to make someone have a feeling that they had in the past *The trip seemed to rekindle their love for each other.*

relapse /rɪ'læps, 'riːlæps/ *noun* [C, U] **1** when someone becomes ill again after a period of feeling better *I had a relapse last year and was off work for a month.* **2** when something or someone gets worse again after being better *The company's share prices have suffered a relapse this week.* ● **relapse** /rɪ'læps/ *verb* [I]

relate /rɪ'leɪt/ *verb* **1** [I, T] to be connected, or to find or show the connection between two or more things *How do the two proposals relate?* **2** [T] *formal* to tell a story or describe a series of events
relate to sb/sth to be connected to, or to be about someone or something *Please provide all information relating to the claim.*
relate to sb to understand how someone feels *Most teenagers find it hard to relate to their parents.*

related /rɪ'leɪtɪd/ *adjective* **1** connected *There's been an increase in criminal activity related to drugs.* **2** If two or more people are related,

they belong to the same family. *Did you know that I'm related to Jackie?* ⊃Opposite **unrelated**.

relation /rɪ'leɪʃᵊn/ *noun* **1** CONNECTION [C, U] a connection between two or more things *the relation between smoking and lung cancer* **2** FAMILY [C] someone who belongs to the same family as you *He's called Ken Russell, no relation to* (= he is not from the same family as) *the film director.* ⊃See Common learner error at **parent**. **3 in relation to sth a** COMPARED WITH when compared with something *Salaries are low in relation to the cost of living.* **b** ABOUT about or relating to something *I'd like to ask you something in relation to what you said earlier.*

relations /rɪ'leɪʃᵊnz/ *noun* [plural] the way two people or groups feel and behave towards each other *It was an attempt to restore diplomatic relations between the two countries.* ⊃See also: public relations, race relations.

┌─────────────────────────────────┐
│ 🧩 WORD PARTNERS FOR *relationship* │
└─────────────────────────────────┘

a **close/intimate/personal/loving/stormy** relationship ● **end/forge/form/have** a relationship ● a relationship **between** sb

o--**relationship** /rɪ'leɪʃᵊnʃɪp/ *noun* **1** BEHAVIOUR [C] the way two people or groups feel and behave towards each other *He has a very good relationship with his older sister.* **2** ROMANTIC [C] a sexual or romantic friendship *I don't feel ready for a relationship at the moment.* **3** CONNECTION [C, U] a connection between two or more things *the relationship between sunburn and skin cancer*

┌─────────────────────────────────┐
│ COMMON LEARNER ERROR │
└─────────────────────────────────┘

have a relationship with someone

Be careful to use the correct preposition in this expression.

I have a good relationship with my parents.

~~I have a good relationship to my parents.~~

o--**relative**¹ /'relətɪv/ *noun* [C] a member of your family *a party for friends and relatives* ⊃See Common learner error at **parent**.

relative² /'relətɪv/ *adjective* **1** [always before noun] compared to other similar things or people *the relative prosperity of the West* **2 relative to sth** when compared to something else *The economy has been declining relative to other countries.*

ˌrelative 'clause *noun* [C] a part of a sentence that is used to describe the noun which comes just before it. In the sentence, 'The woman who I saw yesterday wasn't his wife.', 'who I saw yesterday' is a relative clause.

relatively /'relətɪvli/ *adverb* quite, when compared to other things or people *Eating out is relatively cheap.*

ˌrelative 'pronoun *noun* [C] a word such as 'that', 'which', or 'who' that is used to begin a relative clause relative pro...

OTHER WAYS OF SAYING *relax*

The verb **chill** and the phrasal verb **chill out** are very common, informal ways of saying 'relax': *We spent the whole week chilling out on the beach.*

The phrasal verb **wind down** and the verb **unwind** mean 'to start to relax after working or doing something difficult': *It takes me a while to **wind down** when I get back from work.* • *Music helps me to **unwind***.

If a person relaxes so that they don't use up too much energy, the fixed expression **take it easy** is often used: *You'll need to spend a few days **taking it easy** after the operation.*

The fixed expression **put your feet up** is also often used to mean 'sit down and relax': *I'm going to make myself a cup of coffee and **put my feet up** for half an hour.*

⊶**relax** /rɪˈlæks/ *verb* **1** [PERSON] [I, T] to become happy and comfortable because nothing is worrying you, or to make someone do this *I find it difficult to relax.* ○ *The wine had relaxed him and he began to talk.* **2** [LESS STIFF] [I, T] If a part of your body relaxes, it becomes less stiff, and if you relax it, you make it become less stiff. *Try these exercises to relax your neck muscles.* **3** [RULES] [T] to make laws or rules less severe *The government has recently relaxed laws on bringing animals into Britain.* • relaxation /ˌriːlækˈseɪʃən/ *noun* [U]

⊶**relaxed** /rɪˈlækst/ *adjective* **1** feeling happy and comfortable because nothing is worrying you *She seemed relaxed enough.* **2** A relaxed situation is comfortable and informal. *There was a very relaxed atmosphere at the party.*

⊶**relaxing** /rɪˈlæksɪŋ/ *adjective* making you feel relaxed *a relaxing bath*

relay¹ /ˌriːˈleɪ/ *verb* [T] **1** to send a message from one person to another *Cory had an idea which he relayed to his friend immediately.* **2** to broadcast radio or television signals

relay² /ˈriːleɪ/ (*also* 'relay ˌrace) *noun* [C] a race in which each member of a team runs or swims part of the race

⊶**release¹** /rɪˈliːs/ *verb* [T] **1** [PRISONER] to allow a prisoner to be free *A hostage was released before midday.* **2** [STOP HOLDING] to stop holding someone or something *Release the handle.* **3** [INFORMATION] to let the public have news or information about something *Police have not released the dead woman's name.* **4** [RECORD/FILM] to make a record or film available for people to buy or see *The album will be released next month.* **5** [SUBSTANCE] to let a substance flow out from somewhere *Dangerous chemicals were accidentally released into the river.*

WORD PARTNERS FOR *release*

demand/secure sb's release • release **from** sth

release² /rɪˈliːs/ *noun* **1** [FROM PRISON] [C] when someone is allowed to leave prison *1978 saw his release from jail.* **2** [FILM/RECORD] [C] a new film or record that you can buy *Have you*

heard the group's latest release? **3** [SUBSTANCE] [C, U] when a substance is allowed to flow out of somewhere *a release of toxic gas from the factory* ⊃See also: press release.

relegate /ˈrelɪgeɪt/ *verb* [T] to put someone or something in a less important position [often passive] *He'd been relegated to the B team.* • relegation /ˌrelɪˈgeɪʃən/ *noun* [U]

relent /rɪˈlent/ *verb* [I] to allow something that you refused to allow before *The security guard relented and let them through.*

relentless /rɪˈlentləs/ *adjective* never stopping or getting any less extreme *relentless criticism* • relentlessly *adverb*

relevance /ˈreləvəns/ (*also* US relevancy /ˈreləvəntsi/) *noun* [U] the degree to which something is related or useful to what is happening or being talked about *This point has no relevance to the discussion.*

relevant /ˈreləvənt/ *adjective* related or useful to what is happening or being talked about *relevant information* ○ *Education should be relevant to children's needs.* ⊃Opposite irrelevant.

reliable /rɪˈlaɪəbl/ *adjective* able to be trusted or believed *a reliable car* ○ *reliable information* ○ *Andy's very reliable - if he says he'll do something, he'll do it.* ⊃Opposite unreliable. • reliability /rɪˌlaɪəˈbɪləti/ *noun* [U] how reliable someone or something is • reliably *adverb I am reliably informed that the concert has been cancelled.*

reliance /rɪˈlaɪəns/ *noun* reliance on sb/sth when someone or something depends on someone or something else *a total reliance on computers*

reliant /rɪˈlaɪənt/ *adjective* be reliant on sb/sth to depend on someone or something *I don't want to be reliant on anybody.* ⊃See also: self-reliant.

relic /ˈrelɪk/ *noun* [C] a very old thing from the past *an Egyptian relic*

WORD PARTNERS FOR *relief*

a **big/great/tremendous** relief • a **sense** of relief • **to** sb's relief

⊶**relief** /rɪˈliːf/ *noun* **1** [EMOTION] [U, no plural] the good feeling that you have when something unpleasant stops or does not happen *It'll be such a relief when these exams are over.* ○ *"James can't come tonight." "Well, that's a relief!"* **2** [HELP] [U] money, food, or clothes that are given to people because they need help *an international relief operation* **3** [PHYSICAL FEELING] [U] when something stops hurting you *I'd been trying to sleep to find relief from the pain.*

relieve /rɪˈliːv/ *verb* [T] **1** to make pain or a bad feeling less severe *Breathing exercises can help to relieve stress.* **2** to allow someone to stop working by taking their place *The 7 a.m. team arrived to relieve the night workers.*

relieve sb of sth *formal* to take something away from someone *Let me relieve you of your luggage.*

relieved /rɪˈliːvd/ *adjective* feeling happy because something unpleasant did not happen or you are not worried about something any more [+ (that)] *I'm just relieved that she's safe and well.* ○ [+ to do sth] *I heard a noise and was relieved to find that it was only a cat.*

| ɑː arm | ɜː her | iː see | ɔː saw | uː too | aɪ my | aʊ how | eə hair | eɪ day | əʊ no | ɪə near | ɔɪ boy | ʊə poor | aɪə fire | aʊə sour |

> **WORD PARTNERS FOR *religion***
>
> **believe in/practise** a religion • a **major** religion • be **against** sb's religion

⊶**religion** /rɪˈlɪdʒᵊn/ *noun* [C, U] the belief in a god or gods, or a particular system of belief in a god or gods *the Christian religion*

⊶**religious** /rɪˈlɪdʒəs/ *adjective* **1** relating to religion *religious paintings* **2** having a strong belief in a religion *He's a very religious man.*

religiously /rɪˈlɪdʒəsli/ *adverb* **1** regularly *He visited the old woman religiously every weekend.* **2** in a religious way

relinquish /rɪˈlɪŋkwɪʃ/ *verb* [T] *formal* to allow something to be taken away from you *At 80 he still refuses to relinquish control of the company.*

relish¹ /ˈrelɪʃ/ *verb* [T] to enjoy something *I don't **relish the thought** of a twelve-hour flight.*

relish² /ˈrelɪʃ/ *noun* **1** [U] enjoyment *He had baked a cake which the children now ate **with relish**.* **2** [C] a sauce that you put on food to give it more taste

relive /ˌriːˈlɪv/ *verb* [T] to remember something so clearly that you feel as if it is happening now

relocate /ˌriːləʊˈkeɪt/ [US] /riːˈləʊˌkeɪt/ *verb* [I, T] to move to another place *The company **relocated** to Tokyo.* • **relocation** /ˌriːləʊˈkeɪʃᵊn/ *noun* [U] *relocation costs*

reluctant /rɪˈlʌktᵊnt/ *adjective* not wanting to do something [+ to do sth] *Many victims of crime are reluctant to go to the police.* • **reluctance** /rɪˈlʌktᵊns/ *noun* [U] when someone does not want to do something [+ to do sth] *a reluctance to accept changes* • **reluctantly** *adverb*

⊶**rely** /rɪˈlaɪ/ *verb*

⊶**rely on sb/sth 1** to need someone or something in order to be successful, work correctly, etc *Families rely more on wives' earnings than before.* **2** to trust someone or something [+ to do sth] *I know I **can rely on** you to help me.*

⊶**remain** /rɪˈmeɪn/ *verb* **1** [I] to continue to exist when everything or everyone else has gone *Only a few hundred of these animals remain today.* ➲See Common learner error at **rest**. **2 remain calm/open, etc; remain a secret/mystery/prisoner, etc** to continue to be in the same state *The exact date of the wedding remains a secret.* **3 remain at/in/with, etc** *formal* to stay in the same place *She will remain at her mother's until I return.*

the remainder /rɪˈmeɪndəʳ/ *noun* the things or people that are left when everything or everyone else has gone or been dealt with *He drank **the remainder of** his coffee and got up to leave.*

remaining /rɪˈmeɪnɪŋ/ *adjective* [always before noun] continuing to exist when everything or everyone else has gone or been dealt with *Mix in half the butter and keep the remaining 50g for later.*

remains /rɪˈmeɪnz/ *noun* [plural] **1** the parts of something, especially a building, that continue to exist when the rest of it has been destroyed *the remains of a Buddhist temple* **2** *formal* someone's body after they have died

remake /ˈriːmeɪk/ *noun* [C] a film that is the same as one that has been made before *a remake of 'King Kong'* • **remake** /ˌriːˈmeɪk/ *verb* [T] *past* **remade**

remand¹ /rɪˈmɑːnd/ *noun* **on remand** *UK* in prison before your trial (= when a law court decides if you are guilty or not) *He spent two weeks on remand in Bullingdon prison.*

remand² /rɪˈmɑːnd/ *verb* **be remanded in custody** *UK* to be kept in prison on remand *He was charged with murder and remanded in custody.*

> **WORD PARTNERS FOR *remark***
>
> **make** a remark • a remark **about/on** sth

remark¹ /rɪˈmɑːk/ *noun* [C] something that you say *He **made a remark** about her clothes.*

remark² /rɪˈmɑːk/ *verb* [I] to say something [+ that] *He remarked that she was looking thin.*

remark on/upon sth to say something about something that you have just noticed *He remarked on how well you were looking.*

remarkable /rɪˈmɑːkəbl/ *adjective* very unusual or noticeable in a way that you admire *a remarkable woman* ○ *He has a remarkable memory.* ➲Opposite **unremarkable**.

remarkably /rɪˈmɑːkəbli/ *adverb* in a way that makes you feel surprised *She has remarkably good skin for her age.*

remarry /ˌriːˈmæri/ *verb* [I] to get married again

remedial /rɪˈmiːdiəl/ *adjective* [always before noun] **1** intended to help people who are having difficulty learning something *remedial English classes* **2** *formal* intended to improve something ***Remedial action** is needed.*

remedy¹ /ˈremədi/ *noun* [C] **1** something that makes you better when you are ill *a flu remedy* **2** something that solves a problem *The **remedy for** the traffic problem is to encourage people to use public transport.*

remedy² /ˈremədi/ *verb* [T] to solve a problem, or to improve a bad situation *They were able to **remedy the problem** very easily.*

> **OTHER WAYS OF SAYING *remember***
>
> More formal alternatives are verbs such as **recall** and (*UK*) **recollect**: *I don't **recall** arranging a time to meet.* • *I didn't **recollect** having seen him.*
>
> **Remind** means 'to make someone remember something', or 'to make someone remember to do something': *Every time we meet he **reminds** me about the money he lent me.* • *Will you **remind** me to buy some eggs?*
>
> The phrasal verbs **come back to** and **come to** are often used when someone suddenly remembers something: *I'd forgotten his name but it's just **come (back) to** me.*
>
> To **reminisce** is to remember and talk about pleasant things that happened in the past: *We were just **reminiscing** about our school days.*
>
> To **bear** something **in mind** is to remember someone or something that may be useful in the future: *When you book, **bear in mind** that Christmas is the busiest period.*

R

⊶**remember** /rɪˈmembəʳ/ *verb* **[I, T]** **1** If you remember a fact or something from the past, you keep it in your mind, or bring it back into your mind. *I can't remember his name.* ○ **[+ doing sth]** *I don't remember signing a contract.* ○ **[+ (that)]** *Just as the door closed he remembered that his keys were inside the room.* **2** to not forget to do something **[+ to do sth]** *I must remember to send Carol a birthday card.*

COMMON LEARNER ERROR

remember or **memory**?

Remember is a verb. Use **remember** when you think about or bring thoughts into your mind about a person, place, or event from the past.

I can remember when I was at school.

Memory is a noun. Use **memory** to talk about the person, place, or event from the past that you think about.

I have good memories of when I was at school.

remembrance /rɪˈmembrᵊns/ *noun* **[U]** when you remember and show respect for someone who has died *They erected a statue **in remembrance of** him.*

⊶**remind** /rɪˈmaɪnd/ *verb* **[T]** to make someone remember something, or remember to do something *Every time we meet he **reminds** me **about** the money he lent me.* ○ **[+ to do sth]** *Will you remind me to buy some eggs?*

COMMON LEARNER ERROR

remind or **remember**?

If you **remember** a fact or something from the past, you keep it in your mind, or bring it back into your mind.

I can't remember the name of the film.

Did you remember to bring your passport?

When you **remind** someone to do something, you make them remember it.

Can you remind me to phone Anna tomorrow?

~~*Can you remember me to phone Anna tomorrow?*~~

⊶**remind sb of sth/sb** to make someone think of something or someone else *Harry reminds me of my father.* ○ *This song reminds me of our trip to Spain.*

WORD PARTNERS FOR *reminder*

need/serve as a reminder • a **constant/gentle/timely** reminder • a **grim/poignant/sharp/stark** reminder • a reminder **of** sth

reminder /rɪˈmaɪndəʳ/ *noun* **[C]** something that makes you remember something else *For me, ice cream is **a reminder of** happy childhood holidays at the seaside.*

reminisce /ˌremɪˈnɪs/ *verb* **[I]** to talk about pleasant things that happened in the past *We were just **reminiscing about** our school days.* • **reminiscence** *noun* **[C, U]** when you reminisce

reminiscent /ˌremɪˈnɪsᵊnt/ *adjective* **reminiscent of sth/sb** making you think of someone or something that is similar *a smell reminiscent of an old church*

remission /rɪˈmɪʃᵊn/ *noun* **be in remission** to be in a period of time when a serious illness is better *He is in remission at the moment.*

remit¹ /ˈriːmɪt/ *noun* **[no plural]** *UK* the things that you are responsible for in your job

remit² /rɪˈmɪt/ *verb* **[T]** **remitting,** *past* **remitted** *formal* to send money to someone

remnant /ˈremnənt/ *noun* **[C]** a piece of something that continues to exist when the rest of that thing has gone *the remnants of last night's meal*

remorse /rɪˈmɔːs/ *noun* **[U]** the feeling that you are sorry for something bad that you have done *He has **shown** no **remorse for** his actions.* • **remorseful** *adjective* feeling remorse

remorseless /rɪˈmɔːsləs/ *adjective* **1** *UK* never stopping *remorseless pressure to succeed* **2** cruel • **remorselessly** *adverb*

remote /rɪˈməʊt/ *adjective* **1** [PLACE] far away *It was a remote mountain village with no electricity supply.* **2** [TIME] far in time *in the remote past* **3** [SLIGHT] slight *There is a **remote possibility** that it could be cancer.* • **remoteness** *noun* **[U]**

reˌmote conˈtrol *noun* **1** **[C]** (*also* **remote**) a piece of equipment that is used to control something such as a television from a distance ➲See colour picture **The Living Room** on page Centre 4. **2** **[U]** the use of radio waves to control something such as a television from a distance

remote control

remotely /rɪˈməʊtli/ *adverb* **not remotely interested/surprised/possible, etc** not at all interested, surprised, etc *I'm not remotely interested in football.*

removal /rɪˈmuːvᵊl/ *noun* **1** **[U]** when you remove something *stain removal* **2** **[C, U]** *UK* when you remove everything from one house to take to another *a removals firm*

⊶**remove** /rɪˈmuːv/ *verb* **[T]** **1** [TAKE AWAY] to take something away *An operation was needed to **remove** the bullets **from** his chest.* **2** [TAKE OFF] to take something off *Carefully remove the lid, then stir the paint.* **3** [JOB] *formal* to make someone stop doing their job **[often passive]** *He had been **removed from** his job on medical grounds.* **4 be far removed from sth** to be very different from something *The princess's world was far removed from reality.*

remuneration /rɪˌmjuːnᵊrˈeɪʃᵊn/ *noun* **[U]** *formal* when someone is paid for work they have done

renaissance /rəˈneɪsᵊns/ [US] /ˌrenəˈsɑːns/ *noun* **[no plural]** a time when something becomes popular or fashionable again *The British film industry is **enjoying a renaissance**.*

the Renaissance /rəˈneɪsᵊns/ [US] /ˌrenəˈsɑːns/ *noun* the period during the 14th, 15th, and 16th

R

centuries in Europe when there was a lot of interest and activity in art, literature, ideas, etc

rename /ˌriːˈneɪm/ *verb* **[T]** to give something a new name **[+ two objects]** *Siam was renamed Thailand in 1939.*

render /ˈrendəʳ/ *verb* **[T]** *formal* **1** to cause something or someone to be in a particular state or condition *She was rendered speechless upon hearing the news.* **2** to give someone a decision, opinion, help, etc *payment for* ***services rendered***

rendering /ˈrendᵊrɪŋ/ *noun* **[C]** the way that something is performed, written, drawn, etc *a child's rendering of a house*

rendezvous /ˈrɒndɪvuː/ *noun* **[C]** *plural* **rendezvous** an arrangement to meet someone, or the place you have arranged to meet them • **rendezvous** *verb* **[I]**

rendition /renˈdɪʃᵊn/ *noun* **[C]** the way in which a song, piece of music, etc is performed

renegade /ˈrenɪgeɪd/ [US] *noun* **[C]** someone who changes and joins a group that is against their own group *a group of renegade soldiers*

renege /rəˈneɪg/ [US] /rəˈnɪg/ *verb*

renege on sth *formal* to not do what you said you were going to do *to renege on a promise*

renew /rɪˈnjuː/ *verb* **[T]** **1** [OFFICIAL AGREEMENT] to arrange to continue an official agreement that was going to end soon *I've decided not to* ***renew*** *my golf club* ***membership*** *this year.* **2** [BUY] *UK* to get a new one of something that is old *A car isn't the sort of thing you renew every year.* **3** [DO AGAIN] to start to do something again *The next morning enemy war planes renewed their bombing.* • **renewal** *noun* **[C, U]** when you renew something

renewable /rɪˈnjuːəbl/ *adjective* **1** A renewable form of energy can be produced as quickly as it is used. *a* ***renewable energy*** *source such as wind power* **2** A renewable official agreement is one that you can arrange to continue when the time limit is reached. *a 6-month* ***renewable contract***

renewables /rɪˈnjuːəblz/ *noun* **[plural]** types of energy such as wind power and power from the sun that can be replaced as quickly as they are used

renewed /rɪˈnjuːd/ *adjective* starting again in a stronger way than before *He sang now with renewed confidence.*

renounce /rɪˈnaʊns/ *verb* **[T]** to officially say that you do not have the right to something any more, or that you do not want to be involved in something any more *They had renounced all rights to ownership of the land.*

renovate /ˈrenəveɪt/ *verb* **[T]** to repair and decorate a building that is old and in bad condition • **renovation** /ˌrenəˈveɪʃᵊn/ *noun* **[C, U]**

renowned /rɪˈnaʊnd/ *adjective* famous *The Lake District is* ***renowned for*** *its beauty.*

rent¹ /rent/ *verb* **1** [HOME] **[I, T]** to pay money to live in a building that someone else owns *He'll be renting an apartment until he can find a house to buy.* **2** [PAY TO USE] **[T]** *US* (*UK* **hire**) to pay money to use something for a short time *We could rent a car for the weekend.* **3** [RECEIVE MONEY] **[T]** (*also* **rent out**) to allow someone to pay you money to live in your building *I rented out my house and went travelling for a year.*

COMMON LEARNER ERROR

rent and **hire**

In British English you **rent** something for a long time.

I rent a 2-bedroom flat.

In British English you **hire** something for a short time.

We hired a car for the weekend.

In American English the word **rent** is used in both situations.

I rent a 2-bedroom apartment.

We rented a car for the weekend.

WORD PARTNERS FOR ***rent***

pay the rent • the rent **on** sth

rent² /rent/ *noun* **[C, U]** the amount of money that you pay to live in a building that someone else owns *They couldn't afford the rent.*

rental /ˈrentᵊl/ *noun* **[C, U]** an arrangement to rent something, or the amount of money that you pay to rent something *The price includes flights and car rental.*

rented /ˈrentɪd/ *adjective* describes something that you rent ***rented accommodation***

renter /ˈrentəʳ/ *noun* **[C]** *US* someone who pays money to live in a house or an apartment that someone else owns

renunciation /rɪˌnʌnsiˈeɪʃᵊn/ *noun* **[U, no plural]** when you say that you do not want something or believe in something any more *a renunciation of violence*

reorganize (*also UK* **-ise**) /ˌriːˈɔːgənaɪz/ *verb* **[I, T]** to organize something again in order to improve it *He's completely reorganized his schedule for the week.* • **reorganization** /riːˌɔːgᵊnaɪˈzeɪʃᵊn/ *noun* **[C, U]**

rep /rep/ *noun* **[C]** *informal* someone whose job is to sell things for a company *the UK* ***sales rep***

repaid /ˌriːˈpeɪd/ *past of* repay

OTHER WAYS OF SAYING ***repair***

The verbs **fix** and **mend** are common alternatives: *I must get my bike* ***fixed.*** • *Can you* ***mend*** *that hole in my trousers?*

The phrasal verbs **do up** (*UK*) and **fix up** are often used when someone repairs something and improves it: *Nick loves* ***fixing up*** *old cars.* • *They're planning to buy an old cottage and* ***do it up.***

The verb **service** (*UK*) is often used when examining and repairing cars or other machines: *I'm taking the car to the garage to have it* ***serviced*** *this afternoon.*

🔑**repair¹** /rɪˈpeəʳ/ *verb* **[T]** **1** to fix something that is broken or damaged *I must* ***get*** *my bike* ***repaired.*** **2** to improve a bad situation *It will*

R

take a long time to repair relations between the two countries.

WORD PARTNERS FOR ***repair*** *(noun)*

carry out/do repairs • **be in need of** repair • **extensive/major/minor** repairs • the repair **of** sth

repair² /rɪˈpeəʳ/ *noun* **1** [C, U] something that you do to fix something that is broken or damaged [usually plural] *The repairs cost me £150.* **2 be in good/bad repair** to be in good/bad condition

repatriate /riːˈpætrieɪt/ [US] /riːˈpeɪtrieɪt/ *verb* [T] to send someone back to their own country • **repatriation** /ˌriːpætriˈeɪʃᵊn/ [US] /rɪˌpeɪtriˈeɪʃᵊn/ *noun* [U]

repay /ˌriːˈpeɪ/ *verb* [T] *past* **repaid 1** to pay back money that you have borrowed *to **repay** a **loan*** **2** to do something kind for someone who has done something to help you *What can I do to repay you for your kindness?* • **repayment** /rɪˈpeɪmənt/ *noun* [C, U] when you repay someone or the money that you pay back

repeal /rɪˈpiːl/ *verb* [T] to officially make a law end

o‹**repeat¹** /rɪˈpiːt/ *verb* [T] **1** to say or do something more than once *He repeated the number.* ○ *The test must be repeated several times.* **2** to tell someone something that someone else has told you *I've got some news for you but you mustn't **repeat** it **to** anyone.*

repeat² /rɪˈpiːt/ *noun* **1** [no plural] when something happens or is done more than once *Everything is being done to avoid **a repeat of** the tragedy.* **2** [C] *UK* (*US* **rerun**) a television or radio programme that is broadcast again

repeated /rɪˈpiːtɪd/ *adjective* [always before noun] done or happening more than once *He has refused repeated requests to be interviewed.* • **repeatedly** *adverb The victim was stabbed repeatedly.*

repel /rɪˈpel/ *verb* [T] **repelling** *past* **repelled 1** to make someone or something move away or stop attacking you *a smell that repels insects* **2** If someone or something repels you, you think they are extremely unpleasant.

repellent¹ /rɪˈpelᵊnt/ *adjective* extremely unpleasant *I find his views utterly repellent.*

repellent² /rɪˈpelᵊnt/ *noun* [C, U] **insect/mosquito repellent** a substance that you use to keep insects away

repent /rɪˈpent/ *verb* [I, T] *formal* to say that you are sorry for doing something bad • **repentance** *noun* [U] *formal* when someone repents

repentant /rɪˈpentənt/ *adjective formal* feeling sorry about something bad that you have done ➲Opposite **unrepentant**.

repercussions /ˌriːpəˈkʌʃᵊnz/ *noun* [plural] the effects that an action or event has on something, especially bad effects *Any decrease in tourism could have serious **repercussions for** the local economy.*

repertoire /ˈrepətwɑːʳ/ *noun* [C] all the songs, plays, etc that someone can perform

repertory /ˈrepətᵊri/ *noun* **1** [C, U] when a group of actors performs several different plays during a period of time *They have four plays **in repertory** this season.* ○ *a **repertory company/theatre*** **2** [C] all the songs, plays, etc that someone can perform

repetition /ˌrepɪˈtɪʃᵊn/ *noun* [C, U] when something is repeated *We don't want a repetition of last year's disaster.*

repetitive /rɪˈpetətɪv/ (*also* **repetitious** /ˌrepɪˈtɪʃəs/) *adjective* doing or saying the same thing several times, especially in a way that is boring *a repetitive job* • **repetitively** *adverb*

reˌpetitive ˈstrain ˌinjury ➲See RSI.

o‹**replace** /rɪˈpleɪs/ *verb* [T] **1** [USE INSTEAD] to start using another thing or person instead of the one that you are using now *We're thinking of **replacing** our old TV **with** a fancy new one.* **2** [BE USED INSTEAD] to start to be used instead of the thing or person that is being used now *This system will replace the old one.* **3** [GET SOMETHING NEW] to get something new because the one you had before has been lost or damaged *We'll have to replace this carpet soon.* **4** [PUT BACK] *formal* to put something back in the place where it usually is *She picked up the books and carefully replaced them on the shelf.*

replacement /rɪˈpleɪsmənt/ *noun* **1** [C] the thing or person that replaces something or someone *It's not going to be easy to **find** a **replacement for** you.* **2** [U] when something or someone is replaced

replay /ˈriːpleɪ/ *noun* [C] **1** an important part of a sports game or other event on television that is shown again immediately after it has happened **2** *UK* a game of sport that is played again • **replay** /ˌriːˈpleɪ/ *verb* [T] ➲See also: **action replay** *UK*, **instant replay** *US*.

replenish /rɪˈplenɪʃ/ *verb* [T] *formal* to fill something or make it complete again *to replenish supplies* • **replenishment** *noun* [U] *formal* when you fill something or make it complete again

replica /ˈreplɪkə/ *noun* [C] something that is made to look almost exactly the same as something else *a replica of the White House*

replicate /ˈreplɪkeɪt/ *verb* [T] *formal* to make or do something again in exactly the same way • **replication** /ˌreplɪˈkeɪʃᵊn/ *noun* [C, U]

o‹**reply¹** /rɪˈplaɪ/ *verb* [I, T] to answer *"I don't understand," she replied.* ○ *He didn't **reply to** my email.* ○ [+ that] *Henry replied that he had no idea what I was talking about.*

WORD PARTNERS FOR ***reply*** *(noun)*

give/make/send a reply • **get/have/receive** a reply • a reply **to** sth • **in** reply

o‹**reply²** /rɪˈplaɪ/ *noun* [C, U] an answer *Her reply was short and unfriendly.* ○ *Have you had a **reply to** your letter?* ○ *She sent me an email **in reply*** (= as an answer).

o‹**report¹** /rɪˈpɔːt/ *noun* [C] **1** a description of an event or situation *a police report* ○ *an annual report on the economy* **2** *UK* (*US* **reˈport ˌcard**) when teachers write about a child's progress at school for their parents

o‹**report²** /rɪˈpɔːt/ *verb* **1** [DESCRIBE] [I, T] to describe a recent event or situation, especially on television, radio, or in a newspaper *Jo Smith*

reports on recent developments. ○ [+ that] She reported that the situation had changed dramatically. ○ [+ doing sth] A woman outside the shop reported seeing the gun. **2** TELL [T] to tell someone in authority that something has happened, especially an accident or crime He should have **reported** the **accident** immediately. ○ Have you **reported** the fault **to** a technician? **3** COMPLAIN [T] to complain about someone's behaviour to someone in authority. I'm going to **report** him **to** the police. ○ Duncan's been **reported for** smoking.

report to sb/sth to go to someone or a place and say that you have arrived All visitors please report to reception.

reportedly /rɪˈpɔːtɪdli/ adverb If something has reportedly happened or is reportedly a fact, people say it has happened or is true. Two students were reportedly killed and several wounded.

re,ported 'speech noun [U] speech or writing that is used to report what someone has said, but not using exactly the same words

reporter /rɪˈpɔːtəʳ/ noun [C] someone whose job is to discover information about news events and describe them on television, radio, or in a newspaper

repossess /ˌriːpəˈzes/ verb [T] to take back someone's house, car, furniture, etc because they cannot finish paying for them ● **repossession** /ˌriːpəˈzeʃᵊn/ noun [C, U] when someone repossesses something, or the thing that is repossessed

reprehensible /ˌreprɪˈhensəbl/ adjective formal Reprehensible behaviour is extremely bad.

o⌐**represent** /ˌreprɪˈzent/ verb [T] **1** BE to be equal to something In practice the figure represents a 10% pay cut. ○ The cancellation of the new road project represents a victory for protesters. **2** SPEAK FOR to officially speak or do something for someone else because they have asked you to The union represents over 200 employees. **3** COMPETITION to be the person from a country, school, etc that is in a competition **4** SIGN to be a sign or symbol of something The crosses on the map represent churches. **5** SHOW to show someone or something in a particular way

representation /ˌreprɪzenˈteɪʃᵊn/ noun **1** [U] speaking or doing something officially for another person Can he afford **legal** representation? **2** [C, U] the way someone or something is shown an accurate representation of country life ⊃See also: proportional representation.

representative¹ /ˌreprɪˈzentətɪv/ noun [C] someone who speaks or does something officially for another person ⊃See also: House of Representatives.

representative² /ˌreprɪˈzentətɪv/ adjective the same as other people or things in a particular group Are his views **representative of** the rest of the department?

repress /rɪˈpres/ verb [T] **1** to stop yourself from showing your true feelings Brigitta repressed a sudden desire to cry. **2** to control what people do, especially by using force ● **repression** /rɪˈpreʃᵊn/ noun [U] when you repress someone or something

repressed /rɪˈprest/ adjective **1** unable to show your true feelings and emotions a lonely, repressed man **2** A repressed feeling or emotion is one that you do not show. repressed anger

repressive /rɪˈpresɪv/ adjective cruel and not allowing people to have freedom a **repressive** military regime

reprieve /rɪˈpriːv/ noun [C] **1** an official order that stops a prisoner from being killed as a punishment **2** when something happens to stop a bad situation ● **reprieve** verb [T]

reprimand /ˈreprɪmɑːnd/ verb [T] to tell someone in an official way that they have done something wrong [+ for + doing sth] Watts has already been reprimanded for disclosing confidential information. ● **reprimand** noun [C]

reprint /ˌriːˈprɪnt/ verb [T, I] to print a book again

🧩 **WORD PARTNERS FOR reprisal**

fear reprisals ● **in** reprisal for sth ● a reprisal **against/from** sb

reprisal /rɪˈpraɪzᵊl/ noun [C, U] something violent or unpleasant that is done to punish an enemy for something they have done The attack was **in reprisal** for police raids. ○ He did not wish to be filmed because he **feared** reprisals.

reproach¹ /rɪˈprəʊtʃ/ noun [C, U] criticism of someone, especially for not being successful or not doing what is expected There was a hint of reproach in his voice. ○ The article gave the impression that the teachers were **above/beyond** reproach (= could not be criticized). ● **reproachful** adjective showing criticism a reproachful look ● **reproachfully** adverb

reproach² /rɪˈprəʊtʃ/ verb [T] to criticize someone for not being successful or not doing what is expected [often reflexive] You've no reason to reproach yourself.

reproduce /ˌriːprəˈdjuːs/ verb **1** [T] to make a copy of something The diagram is reproduced by permission of the original author. **2** [I] formal If people, animals, or plants reproduce, they produce babies or young animals or plants.

reproduction /ˌriːprəˈdʌkʃᵊn/ noun **1** [U] the process of producing babies or young animals and plants **2** [C] a copy of something, especially a painting

reproductive /ˌriːprəˈdʌktɪv/ adjective [always before noun] relating to the process of producing babies or young animals and plants the reproductive organs

reptile /ˈreptaɪl/ noun [C] an animal whose body is covered with scales (= pieces of hard skin), and whose blood changes temperature, for example a snake ● **reptilian** /repˈtɪliən/ adjective like a reptile, or relating to reptiles

republic /rɪˈpʌblɪk/ noun [C] a country with no king or queen but with an elected government

republican /rɪˈpʌblɪkən/ noun [C] **1** someone who supports the principles of a republic **2** Republican someone who supports the Republican Party in the US the Republican *candidate* • **republican** *adjective* relating to a republic

the Re'publican ˌParty *noun* **[group]** one of the two main political parties in the US

repudiate /rɪ'pju:dieɪt/ *verb* **[T]** *formal* to refuse to accept or agree with something *Cousteau **repudiated** the **criticism/claims**.* • **repudiation** /rɪˌpju:di'eɪʃən/ *noun* **[U]** *formal*

repugnant /rɪ'pʌgnənt/ *adjective formal* extremely unpleasant *She thought the idea **morally repugnant**.* • **repugnance** /rɪ'pʌgnəns/ *noun* **[U]** *formal* when something or someone is repugnant

repulse /rɪ'pʌls/ *verb* **[T] 1** If someone or something repulses you, you think they are extremely unpleasant. *The smell of him repulsed her.* **2** to successfully stop a military attack **[often passive]** *The enemy attack was quickly repulsed.*

repulsion /rɪ'pʌlʃən/ *noun* **[U, no plural]** a strong feeling that someone or something is extremely unpleasant

repulsive /rɪ'pʌlsɪv/ *adjective* extremely unpleasant, especially to look at *a repulsive man with long, greasy hair*

reputable /'repjətəbl/ *adjective* known to be good and honest *a reputable organization* ➲Opposite **disreputable**.

WORD PARTNERS FOR ***reputation***

have a reputation • a reputation **for** sth • a **bad/good** reputation • **acquire/establish/get** a reputation • **damage/destroy/ruin** sb's reputation

⊶**reputation** /ˌrepjə'teɪʃən/ *noun* **[C]** the opinion that people have about someone or something based on their behaviour or character in the past *Both hotels **have a good reputation**.* ○ *He has a **reputation for** efficiency.*

reputed /rɪ'pju:tɪd/ *adjective formal* believed by most people to be true **[+ to do sth]** *The ghost of a young woman is reputed to haunt the building.* • **reputedly** *adverb*

⊶**request¹** /rɪ'kwest/ *noun* **[C, U]** when you politely or officially ask for something *His doctor **made** an urgent **request for** a copy of the report.* ○ *An application form is available **on request*** (= if you ask for it). ○ *A clause was added to the contract **at his request*** (= because he asked).

⊶**request²** /rɪ'kwest/ *verb* **[T]** to politely or officially ask for something *We've requested a further two computers.* ○ **[+ that]** *They requested that no photographs be taken in the church.*

requiem /'rekwiəm/ *noun* **[C]** a Christian ceremony where people pray for someone who has died, or a piece of music written for this ceremony

⊶**require** /rɪ'kwaɪəʳ/ *verb* **[T] 1** to need or demand something *Training to be a doctor requires a lot of hard work.* ○ **[+ that]** *A recent law requires that all programmes are censored.* **2 require sb to do sth** to officially demand that someone does something **[often passive]** *You are required by law to produce a valid passport.*

COMMON LEARNER ERROR

require or request?

The main meaning of **require** is 'need'.

Learning a language requires time and effort.

Request means 'ask for'.

I wrote a letter to request more information.

~~*I wrote a letter to require more information.*~~

requirement /rɪ'kwaɪəmənt/ *noun* **[C]** something that is needed or demanded *college **entrance requirements*** ○ *Valid insurance is a **legal requirement**.*

requisite /'rekwɪzɪt/ *adjective* **[always before noun]** *formal* needed for a particular purpose *I felt that he lacked the **requisite skills** for the job.*

re-release /ˌri:rɪ'li:s/ *verb* **[T]** to make a record or film available for people to buy or see for a second time

rerun /'ri:rʌn/ *US* (*UK* **repeat**) *noun* **[C]** a television or radio programme or film that is broadcast again

reschedule /ri:'ʃedju:l/ [US] /ri:'skedʒu:l/ *verb* **[T]** to agree a new and later date for something to happen

rescue¹ /'reskju:/ *verb* **[T] rescuing**, *past* **rescued** to save someone from a dangerous or unpleasant situation *Fifty passengers had to be rescued from a sinking ship.* • **rescuer** *noun* **[C]**

rescue² /'reskju:/ *noun* **1 [C, U]** when someone is saved from a dangerous or unpleasant situation *an unsuccessful **rescue attempt*** **2 come to the/sb's rescue** to help someone who is in a difficult situation *I forgot my purse but Anna came to the rescue and lent me some money.*

WORD PARTNERS FOR ***research***

carry out/conduct/do research • research **indicates/proves/reveals/suggests** sth • research **into** sth • a research **assistant/institute/programme/project**

⊶**research¹** /rɪ'sɜ:tʃ/ *noun* **[U]** when someone studies a subject in detail in order to discover new information ***research into** language development* ○ *They are **doing research** into the effects of passive smoking.* ○ ***a research project*** ➲See also: **market research**.

research² /rɪ'sɜ:tʃ/ *verb* **[I, T]** to study a subject in detail in order to discover new information about it *He spent several years researching a rare African dialect.* • **researcher** *noun* **[C]**

resemblance /rɪ'zembləns/ *noun* **[C, U]** a similarity between two people or things, especially in their appearance *There's a striking **resemblance between** Diane and her mother.* ○ *He **bears a resemblance to*** (= looks like) *someone I used to know.*

resemble /rɪ'zembl/ *verb* **[T]** to look like or be like someone or something *She resembles her father.*

resent /rɪ'zent/ *verb* **[T]** to feel angry and upset about a situation or about something that someone has done **[+ doing sth]** *I resent having to work late.* ○ *He **resents the fact** that she gets more money than he does.*

resentful /rɪˈzentfᵊl/ *adjective* angry and upset about a situation that you think is unfair *He was bitterly resentful of his brother's success.* ● **resentfully** *adverb* ● **resentfulness** *noun* [U]

resentment /rɪˈzentmənt/ *noun* [U] a feeling of anger about a situation that you think is unfair

reservation /ˌrezəˈveɪʃᵊn/ *noun* **1** [C] an arrangement that you make to have a seat on an aircraft, a room in a hotel, etc *I'd like to make a reservation for Friday evening.* **2** [C, U] a doubt or a feeling that you do not agree with something completely *I still have reservations about her ability to do the job.*

reserve¹ /rɪˈzɜːv/ *verb* [T] **1** to arrange to have a seat on an aircraft, a room in a hotel, etc *I'd like to reserve two seats on the 9:15 to Birmingham.* **2** to not allow people to use something because it is only for a particular person or for a particular purpose *This seat is reserved for elderly or disabled passengers.*

reserve² /rɪˈzɜːv/ *noun* **1** SUPPLY [C] a supply of something that you keep until it is needed *emergency cash reserves* **2 in reserve** ready to be used if you need it *I always keep a little money in reserve.* **3** QUALITY [U] when someone does not show what they are thinking or feeling **4** SPORT [C] in sport, an extra player who is ready to play if one of the other players has an injury **5** AREA [C] an area of land where animals and plants are protected ⊃See also: **nature reserve**.

reserved /rɪˈzɜːvd/ *adjective* not wanting to show what you are thinking or feeling *a quiet, reserved woman*

reservoir /ˈrezəvwɑːʳ/ *noun* [C] an artificial lake where water is stored before it goes to people's houses

'reset (button) *noun* [C] a button or switch on a computer that allows the user to turn the computer off and then on again when a program does not work correctly

reshuffle /ˌriːˈʃʌfl/ *noun* [C] when people in an organization, especially a government are given different jobs to do *a government reshuffle* ● **reshuffle** *verb* [T]

reside /rɪˈzaɪd/ *verb formal* **reside in/with, etc** to live somewhere *The family now resides in southern France.*

residence /ˈrezɪdᵊns/ *noun formal* **1** [C] a building where someone lives *the Queen's official residence* **2** [U] when someone lives somewhere *He took up residence* (= started to live) *in St. Louis.* **3 in residence** living or working somewhere *He was writer in residence with a professional theatre company.* ⊃See also: **hall of residence**.

resident¹ /ˈrezɪdᵊnt/ *noun* [C] **1** someone who lives in a particular place *complaints from local residents* **2** US a doctor who is working in a hospital to get extra training in a particular area of medicine

resident² /ˈrezɪdᵊnt/ *adjective* living in a place *She has been resident in Britain for most of her life.*

residential /ˌrezɪˈdenʃᵊl/ *adjective* **1** A residential area has only houses and not offices or factories. **2** UK A residential job or course is one where you live at the same place as you work or study.

residual /rɪˈzɪdjuəl/ *adjective* remaining *residual value*

residue /ˈrezɪdjuː/ *noun* [C] something that remains after most of a substance has gone or been removed

resign /rɪˈzaɪn/ *verb* [I, T] to officially tell your employer that you are leaving your job *She resigned as headteacher.* ○ *Mr Aitken has resigned from the company.*
resign yourself to sth to make yourself accept something that you do not like because you cannot easily change it *He resigned himself to living alone.*

⎣⎡⎤⎦ WORD PARTNERS FOR ***resignation***

accept/call for sb's resignation ● **announce/hand in/tender** your resignation ● **the resignation of** sb ● sb's resignation **as** [manager/chairman, etc] ● **a letter of** resignation

resignation /ˌrezɪgˈneɪʃᵊn/ *noun* **1** [C, U] when someone tells their employer that they are leaving their job *a letter of resignation* ○ *I handed in my resignation yesterday.* **2** [U] when you accept something that you do not like because you cannot easily change it

resilient /rɪˈzɪliənt/ *adjective* strong enough to get better quickly after damage, illness, shock, etc *Growth figures show that the economy is still fairly resilient.* ● **resilience** /rɪˈzɪliəns/ *noun* [U]

resin /ˈrezɪn/ *noun* [C, U] **1** a thick, sticky substance that is produced by some trees **2** a substance that is used for making plastics

resist /rɪˈzɪst/ *verb* [I, T] **1** AVOID to stop yourself from doing something that you want to do *I can't resist chocolate.* ○ [+ doing sth] *I just can't resist reading other people's mail.* **2** NOT ACCEPT to refuse to accept something and try to stop it from happening *The President is resisting calls for him to resign.* **3** FIGHT to fight against someone or something that is attacking you *British troops resisted the attack for two days.*

resistance /rɪˈzɪstᵊns/ *noun* [U, no plural] **1** DISAGREE when people disagree with a change, idea, etc and refuse to accept it *resistance to political change* **2** FIGHT when someone fights against someone who is attacking them *She didn't put up much resistance* (= fight). **3** ILLNESS the ability of your body to not be affected by illnesses *Cold weather may lower the body's resistance to infection.*

resistant /rɪˈzɪstᵊnt/ *adjective* **1** not wanting to accept something, especially changes or new ideas *They're resistant to change.* **2** not harmed or affected by something *a water-resistant cover* ○ *Bacteria can become resistant to antibiotics.*

resolute /ˈrezᵊluːt/ *adjective formal* determined not to change what you do or believe because you think that you are right *a resolute opponent of the war* ● **resolutely** *adverb*

resolution /ˌrezᵊˈluːʃᵊn/ *noun* **1** DECISION [C] an

official decision that is made after a group or organization have voted *Congress* ***passed a resolution*** *in support of the plan* (= voted to support it). **2** [PROMISE] [C] a promise to yourself to do something *My New Year's* ***resolution*** *is to do more exercise.* **3** [SOLUTION] [U, no plural] *formal* the solution to a problem *a successful* ***resolution*** *to the crisis* **4** [DETERMINATION] [U] *formal* the quality of being determined

resolve[1] /rɪˈzɒlv/ *verb* **1** [T] to solve or end a problem or difficulty *an attempt to resolve the dispute* **2** [I, T] *formal* to decide that you will do something and be determined to do it [+ to do sth] *I have resolved to keep my bedroom tidy.*

resolve[2] /rɪˈzɒlv/ *noun* [U] *formal* when you are very determined to do something

resonant /ˈrezᵊnənt/ *adjective* A resonant sound is loud and clear. *a deep, resonant voice* • **resonance** /ˈrezᵊnəns/ *noun* [U]

resonate /ˈrezᵊneɪt/ *verb* [I] to make a loud, clear sound

resort[1] /rɪˈzɔːt/ *noun* **1** [C] a place where many people go for a holiday *a ski resort* **2 a last resort** something that you do because everything else has failed *Soldiers were given the authority to shoot, but only as a last resort.*

resort[2] /rɪˈzɔːt/ *verb*

resort to sth/doing sth to do something that you do not want to do because you cannot find any other way of achieving something *They should be able to control the riots without resorting to violence.*

resound /rɪˈzaʊnd/ *verb* [I] to make a loud sound, or to be filled with a loud sound *The whole hall* ***resounded with*** *applause.*

resounding /rɪˈzaʊndɪŋ/ *adjective* [always before noun] **1** very loud *resounding applause* **2 a resounding success/victory/failure, etc** a very great success, victory, etc

resource /rɪˈzɔːs, ˈriːsɔːrs/ *noun* [C] something that a country, person, or organization has which they can use [usually plural] ***natural resources*** ➲See also: **human resources**.

resourceful /rɪˈzɔːsfᵊl/ *adjective* good at finding ways to solve problems • **resourcefulness** *noun* [U]

WORD PARTNERS FOR *respect*

command respect • **have/show [great/no, etc]** respect **for** sb • **treat** sb/sth **with** respect

🔑**respect[1]** /rɪˈspekt/ *noun* **1** [POLITE] [U] when you are polite to someone, especially because they are older or more important than you *You should show more* ***respect for*** *your parents.* **2** [ADMIRATION] [U] when you admire someone because of their knowledge, skill, or achievements *She's an excellent teacher and I have the greatest* ***respect for*** *her.* **3** [SHOW IMPORTANCE] [U] when you show by your behaviour that you think something is important or needs to be dealt with carefully *Electricity can be dangerous and should always be* ***treated with respect****.* **4 in this respect/many respects** in a particular way, or in many ways *The school has changed in many respects.* **5 with respect to sth; in respect of sth** *formal* relating to a particular thing *I am writing with respect to your letter of 24 June.* **6 pay your respects a** [VISIT SOMEONE] *formal* to visit someone or go to talk to them **b** [GO TO FUNERAL] (*also* **pay your last respects**) to go to someone's funeral ➲See also: **self-respect**.

🔑**respect[2]** /rɪˈspekt/ *verb* [T] **1** to admire someone because of their knowledge, achievements, etc ***I respect him for his honesty.*** **2** If you respect someone's rights, customs, wishes, etc you accept their importance and are careful not to do anything they would not want.

respectable /rɪˈspektəbl/ *adjective* **1** behaving in a socially acceptable way or looking socially acceptable *a respectable family* ○ *a respectable hotel* **2** large enough or good enough *a respectable income* ○ *There was a respectable number of guests there.* • **respectably** *adverb* • **respectability** /rɪˌspektəˈbɪləti/ *noun* [U]

respected /rɪˈspektɪd/ *adjective* admired by people because of your knowledge, achievements, etc *a highly respected doctor*

respectful /rɪˈspektfᵊl/ *adjective* showing respect for someone or something • **respectfully** *adverb*

respective /rɪˈspektɪv/ *adjective* [always before noun] relating to each of the people or things that you have just talked about *members of staff and their respective partners*

respectively /rɪˈspektɪvli/ *adverb* in the same order as the people or things you have just talked about *Mr Ewing and Mr Campbell gave £2000 and £250 respectively.*

respiration /ˌrespᵊrˈeɪʃᵊn/ *noun* [U] *formal* the process of breathing

respiratory /rɪˈspɪrətᵊri/ [US] /ˈrespərətɔːri/ *adjective* [always before noun] relating to the process of breathing *respiratory illnesses* ○ *the respiratory tract*

respite /ˈrespaɪt/ [US] /ˈrespɪt/ *noun* [U, no plural] a short period of rest from something difficult or unpleasant *The weekend was a brief* ***respite from*** *the pressures of work.*

🔑**respond** /rɪˈspɒnd/ *verb* [I] **1** to say or do something as an answer or reaction to something that has been said or done [+ by + doing sth] *The government has responded by sending food and medical supplies to the region.* ○ *How quickly did the police* ***respond to*** *the call?* **2** to improve as the result of a particular medical treatment *She's* ***responding*** *well* ***to*** *drug treatment.*

respondent /rɪˈspɒndənt/ *noun* [C] someone who has answered a request for information [usually plural] *More than half the respondents were opposed to the new tax.*

WORD PARTNERS FOR *response*

in response **to** sth • sb's response **to** sth • **draw/elicit/provoke** a response • sb's **immediate/initial/instinctive** response

🔑**response** /rɪˈspɒns/ *noun* [C, U] an answer or reaction to something that has been said or done *The President's comments provoked an* ***angry response*** *from students.* ○ *I'm writing* ***in response to*** *your letter of 14 February.* ○ *What was Michael's* ***response to*** *your suggestion?*

abdicate/accept/assume/claim/take/ shirk responsibility • collective/heavy/ huge/total responsibility • responsibility for sth

o-**responsibility** /rɪ,spɒnsə'bɪləti/ *noun* **1** [C, U] something that it is your job or duty to deal with *The head of the department has various additional responsibilities.* ○ [+ to do sth] *It is your responsibility to make sure that your homework is done on time.* **2 take/accept/claim responsibility for sth** to say that you have done something or caused something to happen, especially something bad *No one has yet claimed responsibility for yesterday's bomb attack.*

o-**responsible** /rɪ'spɒnsəbl/ *adjective* **1 be responsible for sb/sth/doing sth** to be the person whose duty is to deal with someone or something *I'm responsible for looking after the children in the evenings.* **2 be responsible for sth/ doing sth** to be the person who caused something to happen, especially something bad *Who was responsible for the accident?* **3** showing good judgment and able to be trusted *a responsible attitude* ○Opposite **irresponsible**. **4** A responsible job is important because you have to make decisions that affect other people. **5 be responsible to sb** If you are responsible to someone at work, they are in a higher position than you and you have to tell them what you have done.

responsibly /rɪ'spɒnsəbli/ *adverb* in a way that shows you have good judgment and can be trusted *to behave/act responsibly*

responsive /rɪ'spɒnsɪv/ *adjective* listening to someone or something and having a positive and quick reaction to them *a wonderfully responsive audience* ○ *They have not been very responsive to the needs of disabled customers.* • **responsiveness** *noun* [U]

o-**rest**[1] /rest/ *noun* **1** the rest the part of something that remains, or the others that remain *I'm not sure I want to spend the rest of my life with him.* ○ *She was slightly older than the rest of us.* **2** [C, U] a period of time when you relax or sleep *Why don't you have a rest?* ○ *I must get some rest.* **3 come to rest** to stop moving ○See also: put/set sb's **mind**[1] at rest.

o-**rest**[2] /rest/ *verb* **1** [I] to relax or sleep because you are tired after doing an activity or because you are ill *Pete's resting after his long drive.* **2 rest your eyes/feet/legs, etc** to stop using your eyes/feet, etc for a while because they are tired **3 rest (sth) on/against, etc** If something rests somewhere, or if you rest it somewhere, it is supported by something else. *She rested her elbows on the table.* ○See also: rest on your **laurels**.

COMMON LEARNER ERROR

rest, stay, or remain?

Rest means to relax or sleep because you are tired or ill. *The doctor told him to rest.*

Stay means to continue to be in the same place, job, or particular state.

It was raining, so we stayed at home.
~~It was raining, so we rested at home.~~

Remain means to continue to be in the same state, or to continue to exist when everything or everyone else has gone.

He remained unconscious for a week after the accident.

After the earthquake, nothing remained of the village.

rest on/upon sth *formal* to depend on something *The whole future of the team rests on his decision.*

restart /,ri:'stɑ:t/ *verb* [T] to start something again that had stopped *They want to restart the talks.*

go to a restaurant • manage/own/run a restaurant • a restaurant offers/serves/ specializes in sth • at/in a restaurant

o-**restaurant** /'restərɒnt/ *noun* [C] a place where you can buy and eat a meal *an Italian/vegetarian restaurant* ○ *We had lunch at/in a restaurant near the station.*

restaurateur /,restərə'tɜ:[r]/ *noun* [C] someone who owns a restaurant

restive /'restɪv/ *adjective formal* unable to be quiet and calm

restless /'restləs/ *adjective* **1** unable to be still or relax because you are bored or nervous *The audience was getting restless.* **2** not satisfied with what you are doing now and wanting something new *After a while in the same relationship I start to get restless.* • **restlessly** *adverb* • **restlessness** *noun* [U]

restore /rɪ'stɔ:[r]/ *verb* [T] **1** MAKE EXIST to make something good exist again *Three wins in a row helped restore the team's confidence.* ○ *Peace has now been restored in the region.* **2** REPAIR to repair something old *to restore antiques* **3** RETURN *formal* to give something back to the person it was stolen from or who lost it *The painting was restored to its rightful owner.* • **restoration** /,restə'reɪʃ°n/ *noun* [C, U] *The building is now closed for restoration* (= repair work). ○ *the restoration* (= return) *of the former government*

restrain /rɪ'streɪn/ *verb* [T] **1** to stop someone doing something, sometimes by using force *He became violent and had to be physically restrained.* ○ [+ from + doing sth] *I had to restrain myself from shouting at him.* **2** to limit something *to restrain arms sales*

restrained /rɪ'streɪnd/ *adjective* calm and not showing emotions *I was expecting him to be furious but he was very restrained.* ○Opposite **unrestrained**.

restraint /rɪ'streɪnt/ *noun* **1** [U] showing control over your feelings **2** [C] control over something *wage restraints*

restrict /rɪ'strɪkt/ *verb* [T] to limit something *They've brought in new laws to restrict the sale of cigarettes.* ○ *I restrict myself to two glasses of wine most evenings.*

restricted /rɪ'strɪktɪd/ *adjective* controlled or limited *a restricted choice of food.*

restriction /rɪ'strɪkʃ³n/ *noun* [C, U] a rule or law that limits what people can do *There are restrictions on how many goods you can bring into the country.* ○ *parking restrictions*

restrictive /rɪ'strɪktɪv/ *adjective* limiting activities too much *restrictive practices*

restroom /'restruːm/ *noun* [C] US a room with toilets that is in a public place, for example in a restaurant ○See Common learner error at **toilet.**

restructure /ˌriː'strʌktʃə³/ *verb* [I, T] to organize a system or organization in a new way ● **restructuring** *noun* [U]

┌─────────────────────────────────┐
│ WORD PARTNERS FOR **result** │
└─────────────────────────────────┘

the result **of** sth ● **as a** result **of** sth ● **with** the result **that** ● **with** catastrophic/disastrous, etc. results ● **excellent/good/disappointing/disastrous** results

o━**result¹** /rɪ'zʌlt/ *noun* 1 [HAPPEN] [C, U] something that happens or exists because something else has happened *Unemployment has risen as a direct result of new economic policies.* ○ *Most accidents are the result of human error.* 2 [COMPETITION] [C] the score or number of votes at the end of a competition or election *The election results will be known by Sunday.* 3 [INFORMATION] [C] information that you get from something such as an exam, a scientific experiment, or a medical test *the results of a blood test*

result² /rɪ'zʌlt/ *verb* [I] to happen or exist because something else has happened *There was a food shortage resulting from the lack of rainfall.*

result in sth to be the reason something happens *The improvements in training resulted in increased wins.*

resultant /rɪ'zʌlt³nt/ *adjective formal* happening as a result of something else

resume /rɪ'zjuːm/ *verb* [I, T] *formal* If an activity resumes, or if you resume it, it starts again. *The talks are due to resume today.* ● **resumption** /rɪ'zʌmʃ³n/ *noun* [no plural]

résumé /'rezəmeɪ/ US (UK CV) *noun* [C] a document which describes your qualifications and the jobs that you have done, which you send to an employer that you want to work for

resurface /ˌriː'sɜːfɪs/ *verb* [I] to appear again after having been lost or forgotten *The story resurfaced in the news again last week.*

resurgence /rɪ'sɜːdʒəns/ *noun* [no plural] when something starts to happen again or people become interested in something again *a resurgence of interest in the game* ● **resurgent** /rɪ'sɜːdʒənt/ *adjective* happening again

resurrect /ˌrez³r'ekt/ *verb* [T] to make something exist again which has not existed for a long time *With this film Dykes hopes to resurrect his career.*

resurrection /ˌrez³r'ekʃ³n/ *noun* [U] 1 when something starts to exist again which has not existed for a long period *the resurrection of a fashion* 2 in the Christian religion, Jesus Christ's return to life after he was killed

resuscitate /rɪ'sʌsɪteɪt/ *verb* [T] to make some-

one breathe again when they have stopped breathing ● **resuscitation** /rɪˌsʌsɪ'teɪʃ³n/ *noun* [U]

retail¹ /'riːteɪl/ *noun* [U] when products are sold to customers from shops *jobs in retail*

retail² /'riːteɪl/ *verb* **retail at/for £50/$100, etc** to be sold to the public for a particular price *This computer retails at $2,000.*

retailer /'riːteɪlə³/ *noun* [C] someone who sells products to the public

retailing /'riːteɪlɪŋ/ *noun* [U] the business of selling products to customers in shops

retain /rɪ'teɪn/ *verb* [T] to continue to keep something *The council will retain control of the school.*

retaliate /rɪ'tælieɪt/ *verb* [I] to do something bad to someone because they have done something bad to you *They have threatened to retaliate against any troops that attack.* ● **retaliation** /rɪˌtæli'eɪʃ³n/ *noun* [U] *They bombed the hotel in retaliation for the arrests.* ● **retaliatory** /rɪ'tæliət³ri/ *adjective retaliatory measures*

retarded /rɪ'tɑːdɪd/ *adjective* less mentally developed than other people of the same age

retention /rɪ'tenʃ³n/ *noun* [U] when something continues to be kept

rethink /ˌriː'θɪŋk/ *verb* [I, T] *past* **rethought** to change what you think about something or what you plan to do *We've had to rethink our strategy.* ● **rethink** /'riːθɪŋk/ *noun* [no plural] *The whole issue needs a fundamental rethink.*

reticent /'retɪs³nt/ *adjective* saying little about what you think or feel *He was reticent about his private life.* ● **reticence** /'retɪs³ns/ *noun* [U]

retina /'retɪnə/ *noun* [C] a part at the back of the eye, which is affected by light and sends messages to the brain

o━**retire** /rɪ'taɪə³/ *verb* [I] 1 to leave your job and stop working, usually because you are old *She retired from the company in 1990.* 2 *formal* to go to another place where you can be alone or more private *After dinner, he retired to his bedroom.*

retired /rɪ'taɪəd/ *adjective* having stopped working, often because you are old *a retired farmer/teacher*

retiree /rɪ'taɪriː/ *noun* [C] US someone who has stopped working, usually because they are old

---

┌─────────────────────────────────┐
│ WORD PARTNERS FOR **retirement** │
└─────────────────────────────────┘

take **early** retirement ● **in** retirement ● retirement **from** sth ● retirement **age**

retirement /rɪ'taɪəmənt/ *noun* [C, U] 1 when you leave your job and stop working, usually because you are old *He's taking early retirement.* 2 the period of your life after you have stopped working *We wish you a long and happy retirement.*

retiring /rɪ'taɪərɪŋ/ *adjective* shy and quiet

retort /rɪ'tɔːt/ *verb* [T] *formal* to answer someone quickly in an angry or funny way *"That doesn't concern you," she retorted sharply.* ● **retort** *noun* [C] *formal*

retrace /rɪ'treɪs/ *verb* **retrace your steps** to go back somewhere the same way that you came *I was lost so I retraced my steps.*

retract /rɪ'trækt/ *verb* [I, T] *formal* to admit that

---

something you said before was not true *Several key witnesses have **retracted** their statements/claims/allegations*.

retrain /riːˈtreɪn/ *verb* [T] to learn a new skill so you can do a different job *Owen used to be an actor but now he's **retraining** as a teacher*.

retraining /ˌriːˈtreɪnɪŋ/ *noun* [U] when someone learns new skills so they can do a different job

retreat¹ /rɪˈtriːt/ *verb* [I] **1** When soldiers retreat, they move away from the enemy, especially to avoid fighting. *The army was forced to retreat*. **2 retreat to/into, etc** to go away to a place or situation which is safer or quieter *She retreated into the bathroom for some peace and quiet*.

retreat² /rɪˈtriːt/ *noun* **1** MOVE [U, no plural] a move away, especially to a place or situation which is safer or quieter *He saw the dog coming towards him and **beat a** hasty **retreat** (= moved quickly away)*. **2** MILITARY [C, U] a move back by soldiers or an army, especially to avoid fighting *a strategic retreat* **3** PLACE [C] a quiet place where you can go to rest or be alone *a mountain retreat*

retrial /ˌriːˈtraɪəl/ *noun* [C] a new trial for a crime that has already been judged in a law court *The judge ordered a retrial*.

retribution /ˌretrɪˈbjuːʃⁿn/ *noun* [U] *formal* punishment for something morally wrong that was done *They're seeking **retribution** for the killings*.

retrieve /rɪˈtriːv/ *verb* [T] to get something after first finding it *I've just **retrieved** the ball **from** the bottom of the pond*. ○ *computer tools for retrieving information* ● **retrieval** *noun* [U] when something is retrieved

retriever /rɪˈtriːvəʳ/ *noun* [C] a large dog with thick black or light brown hair

retro /ˈretrəʊ/ *adjective* looking or sounding like something from the past *His clothes had a retro look*.

retrospect /ˈretrəʊspekt/ *noun* **in retrospect** thinking now about something in the past *In retrospect, I should probably have told her*.

retrospective¹ /ˌretrəʊˈspektɪv/ *noun* [C] a show of work done by an artist over many years

retrospective² /ˌretrəʊˈspektɪv/ *adjective* If a law or decision is retrospective, it affects situations in the past as well as in the future. ● **retrospectively** *adverb*

o-**return¹** /rɪˈtɜːn/ *verb* **1** GO BACK [I] to go or come back to a place where you were before *She returned to America in 1954*. ○ *I won't return from my holiday till May*. **2** GIVE BACK [T] to give, send, or put something back where it came from *He immediately **returned** the records to the files*. **3 return to sth a** START AGAIN to start doing an activity again or talking about something again *I returned to work three months after Susie was born*. **b** AS BEFORE to go back to a previous condition *Life has begun to **return to normal** now that the war is over*. **4** HAPPEN AGAIN [I] If something returns, it happens again. *If the pains return phone the doctor*. **5** DO THE SAME [T] to react to something that someone does or says by doing or saying

the same *I must **return** Michael's **call** (= telephone him because he telephoned me earlier)*. **6 return a verdict/sentence** to announce if someone is guilty or not guilty or what punishment the person will be given in a law court *The jury returned a verdict of guilty*. **7** SPORTS [T] to hit or throw a ball back to someone when playing a sport

return² /rɪˈtɜːn/ *noun* **1** GOING BACK [no plural] when someone goes or comes back to a place where they were before *On his return to Sydney, he started up a business*. **2** GIVING BACK [no plural] when something is given back, put back, or sent back *the return of the stolen goods* **3** ACTIVITY [no plural] when someone starts an activity again *This film marks his **return to** acting*. **4** HAPPENING AGAIN [no plural] when something starts to happen or be present again *What we are seeing here is **a return to** traditional values*. **5** TICKET [C] *UK* (*US* **round-trip ticket**) a ticket that lets you travel to a place and back again, for example on a train **6** PROFIT [C, U] the profit that you get from an investment *This fund has shown **high returns** for the last five years*. **7 in return** in exchange for something or as a reaction to something *I'd like to give them something **in return** for everything they've done for us*. **8** SPORTS [C] when a ball is thrown or hit back to another player in a sports match *She hit an excellent return*. **9** COMPUTER [U] a key on a computer keyboard that is used to make the computer accept information or to start a new line in a document *Type in the password and **press return***. ◐See also: **day return**.

returnable /rɪˈtɜːnəbl/ *adjective* If something is returnable, it can be taken or given back. *a returnable deposit*

reunification /ˌriːjuːnɪfɪˈkeɪʃⁿn/ *noun* [U] when a country that was divided into smaller countries is joined together again as one country *the reunification of Germany*

WORD PARTNERS FOR *reunion*

have/go to a reunion   ● an **emotional** reunion   ● a reunion **of** sb   ● sb's reunion **with** sb   ● a **family/school** reunion

---

reunion /ˌriːˈjuːniən/ *noun* [C] an occasion when people who have not met each other for a long time meet again *a family/school reunion*

reunite /ˌriːjuːˈnaɪt/ *verb* [I, T] to meet again after being apart for a long time, or to bring people together who have been apart for a long time [often passive] *Years later, he was reunited with his brother*.

reuse /ˌriːˈjuːz/ *verb* [T] to find a new use for something so that it does not have to be thrown away *Businesses are finding new ways to reuse materials*. ● **reusable** *adjective*

Rev *written abbreviation for* Reverend (= title of Christian official) *Rev Jo Harding*

rev /rev/ (*also* **rev up**) *verb* [I, T] **revving** *past* **revved** to increase the engine speed of a vehicle *He revved the engine and drove off*.

revamp /ˌriːˈvæmp/ *verb* [T] to change something in order to make it better *They're revamping the restaurant*.

Revd *written abbreviation for* Reverend (= title of Christian official) *the Revd Laurie Clow*

⟳**reveal** /rɪˈviːl/ *verb* [T] **1** to give someone a piece of information that is surprising or that was previously secret [+ that] *It was revealed in this morning's papers that the couple intend to marry.* **2** to allow something to be seen that, until then, had been hidden *His shirt came up at the back, revealing an expanse of white skin.*

revealing /rɪˈviːlɪŋ/ *adjective* **1** showing someone's true character or the true facts about someone or something *a revealing biography/remark* **2** If clothes are revealing, they show a lot of your body.

revel /ˈrevᵊl/ *verb* UK **revelling**, *past* **revelled**, US **reveling**, *past* **reveled**
    revel in sth to enjoy a situation or activity very much *He revelled in his role as team manager.*

revelation /ˌrevᵊlˈeɪʃᵊn/ *noun* **1** [C] a piece of information that is discovered although it was intended to be kept secret *He resigned following revelations about his private life.* **2 be a revelation** to be an extremely pleasant surprise *Anna's boyfriend was a revelation.*

⬚⬚⬚ WORD PARTNERS FOR **revenge**

get/plot/seek/take revenge • **in** revenge for sth • revenge **against/on** sb • **an act of** revenge

revenge /rɪˈvendʒ/ *noun* [U] something that you do to punish someone who has done something bad to you *He's made life very difficult for me but I'll get/take my revenge.* ○ *He was shot in revenge for the murder.*

revenue /ˈrevᵊnjuː/ (*also* **revenues**) *noun* [U] large amounts of money received by a government as tax, or by a company

reverberate /rɪˈvɜːbᵊreɪt/ *verb* [I] If a sound reverberates, it is heard for a long time as it is sent back from different surfaces. *The sound of the shots reverberated around the building.*

revere /rɪˈvɪər/ *verb* [T] *formal* to respect and admire someone very much *a revered religious leader*

reverence /ˈrevᵊrᵊns/ *noun* [U] *formal* a strong feeling of respect and admiration

Reverend /ˈrevᵊrᵊnd/ *adjective* used as a title before the name of some Christian officials *the Reverend Alan Pringle*

reverie /ˈrevᵊri/ *noun* [C] *formal* a pleasant state in which you are thinking of something else, not what is happening around you

reversal /rɪˈvɜːsᵊl/ *noun* [C] when something changes to its opposite *In a reversal of traditional roles, Paul stayed at home to look after the baby and Clare went out to work.*

reverse¹ /rɪˈvɜːs/ *verb* **1** [I, T] to drive a vehicle backwards *I hate reversing into parking spaces.* **2** [T] to change a situation or change the order of things so that it becomes the opposite *It is unlikely that the judge will reverse his decision.*

reverse² /rɪˈvɜːs/ *noun* **1 the reverse** the opposite of what has been suggested *"So, is he happier?" "Quite the reverse - I've never seen him*

look so miserable." **2** [U] (*also* re,verse 'gear) the method of controlling a vehicle that makes it go backwards *Put the car into reverse.* **3 in reverse** in the opposite order or way *Do the same steps but this time in reverse.*

reverse³ /rɪˈvɜːs/ *adjective* [always before noun] opposite to the usual way or to the way you have just described *I'm going to read out the names of the winners in reverse order.*

reversible /rɪˈvɜːsəbl/ *adjective* **1** If something is reversible, it can be changed back to what it was before. *Most of the damage done to the cells is reversible.* ⊃Opposite **irreversible**. **2** Reversible clothes can be worn so that the inside is the outside. *a reversible jacket*

revert /rɪˈvɜːt/ *verb*
    revert to sth/doing sth to go back to how something was before *For a while I ate low-fat food but then I reverted to my old eating habits.* • **reversion** /rɪˈvɜːʃᵊn/ *noun* [U, no plural]

⬚⬚⬚ WORD PARTNERS FOR **review**

carry out a review • a review **of** sth • be **under** review

review¹ /rɪˈvjuː/ *noun* **1** [C, U] the process of considering something again in order to make changes to it *a review of teachers' pay* ○ *The policy is now under review* (= being considered). **2** [C] a report in a newspaper, magazine, or programme that gives an opinion about a new book, film, etc *a book review* ○ *The film has had mixed reviews* (= some good, some bad).

review² /rɪˈvjuː/ *verb* **1** [CONSIDER] [T] to consider something again in order to decide if changes should be made *The courts will review her case.* **2** [REPORT] [T] to give your opinion in a report about a film, book, television programme, etc *He reviews films for the Times.* **3** [STUDY] [I, T] US (UK **revise**) to study a subject before you take a test

reviewer /rɪˈvjuːər/ *noun* [C] someone who writes reviews of a book, film, etc

reviled /rɪˈvaɪld/ *adjective* hated *He is possibly the most reviled man in Britain.*

revise /rɪˈvaɪz/ *verb* **1** [T] to change something so that it is more accurate *a revised edition of the book* **2** [I, T] UK (US **review**) to study a subject before you take a test

revision /rɪˈvɪʒᵊn/ *noun* **1** [C, U] when you change something so that it is more accurate *a downward revision of prices* **2** [U] UK when you study a subject before taking a test

revitalize (*also* UK **-ise**) /ˌriːˈvaɪtᵊlaɪz/ *verb* [T] to make something more active or exciting *attempts to revitalize the city*

revival /rɪˈvaɪvᵊl/ *noun* [C, U] when something becomes more active or popular again *a revival in folk music* ○ *Yoga is enjoying a revival.* **2** [C] a performance of a play, opera, etc that has not been performed for a long time

revive /rɪˈvaɪv/ *verb* **1** [EXIST AGAIN] [T] to make something from the past exist again *to revive memories* ○ *A lot of traditional skills are currently being revived.* **2** [CONSCIOUS] [I, T] to become conscious again or make someone conscious again *A police officer tried unsuccessfully to revive her.* **3** FEEL BETTER **[I, T]** to start to feel healthier and more active again, or to make someone feel this way *A cup of tea and something to eat might revive you.*

revoke /rɪ'vəuk/ *verb* **[T]** *formal* to stop someone having official permission to do something, or to change an official decision *His work permit was revoked after six months.*

revolt¹ /rɪ'vəult/ *noun* **[C, U]** when people try to change a government, often using violence, or when they refuse to accept someone's authority *a slave/peasant revolt*

revolt² /rɪ'vəult/ *verb* **1** **[I]** to try to change a government, often using violence, or to refuse to accept someone's authority *Many were killed when nationalists **revolted against** the new government.* **2** **be revolted by sth** to think that something is extremely unpleasant

revolting /rɪ'vəultɪŋ/ *adjective* extremely unpleasant *The food was revolting.*

revolution /ˌrevəl'uːʃən/ *noun* **1** POLITICS **[C, U]** a change in the way a country is governed, usually to a different political system and often using violence or war *the French Revolution* **2** CHANGE **[C]** a very important change in the way people think or do things *the technological revolution* ○ *This discovery caused a **revolution in** medicine.* **3** CIRCLE **[C, U]** one whole circular movement around a central point, for example one whole movement of a wheel

revolutionary¹ /ˌrevəl'uːʃənʳri/ *adjective* **1** completely different from what was done before *The twentieth century has brought about **revolutionary changes** in our lifestyles.* **2** relating to a political revolution *a revolutionary movement*

revolutionary² /ˌrevəl'uːʃənʳri/ *noun* **[C]** someone who tries to cause or take part in a political revolution

revolutionize (*also UK* **-ise**) /ˌrevəl'uːʃənaɪz/ *verb* **[T]** to change something in every way so that it is much better *This will revolutionize the way we do business.*

revolve /rɪ'vɒlv/ *verb* **[I]** to move in a circle around a central point *A fan was revolving slowly.* ● **revolving** *adjective* [always before noun] *a revolving door*

revolve around/round sth/sb to have as the only interest or subject *Her whole life revolves around her children.*

revolver /rɪ'vɒlvəʳ/ *noun* **[C]** a small gun

revue /rɪ'vjuː/ *noun* **[C]** a show in a theatre with jokes, songs, and dancing

revulsion /rɪ'vʌlʃən/ *noun* **[U]** a strong feeling that something is very unpleasant

WORD PARTNERS FOR *reward*

get/receive a reward ● a big/handsome/ substantial reward ● a reward for sb/sth ● a reward of [$500/$300, etc]

o--**reward¹** /rɪ'wɔːd/ *noun* **1** **[C, U]** something good that you get or experience because you have worked hard, behaved well, etc *There'll be a reward for whoever finishes first.* **2** **[C]** money that the police give to someone who gives

them information about a crime

reward² /rɪ'wɔːd/ *verb* **[T]** to give a reward to someone *She was **rewarded for** her bravery.*

rewarding /rɪ'wɔːdɪŋ/ *adjective* making you feel satisfied that you have done something well *Teaching is hard work but it's very rewarding.*

rewind /ˈriːwaɪnd/ *verb* **[I, T]** *past* **rewound** to make a sound or television recording go back to the beginning

rework /ˌriː'wɜːk/ *verb* **[T]** to change a piece of music or writing in order to improve it or make it more suitable *Elton John reworked his 1974 hit, 'Candle in the Wind', for Princess Diana's funeral.*

rewrite /ˌriː'raɪt/ *verb* **[T]** *past tense* **rewrote** *past participle* **rewritten** to write something again in order to improve it *I had to rewrite my essay.*

rhapsody /'ræpsədi/ *noun* **[C]** a piece of music for instruments

rhetoric /'retʳrɪk/ *noun* **[U]** language that is intended to make people believe things, often language that is not sincere *It was the usual political speech, full of **empty rhetoric**.* ● **rhetorical** /rɪ'tɒrɪkʳl/ *adjective* ● **rhetorically** *adverb*

rhe,torical 'question /rɪˌtɒrɪkʳl'kwestʃən/ *noun* **[C]** a question that is not intended as a real question because you do not expect anyone to answer it

rheumatism /'ruːmətɪzʳm/ *noun* **[U]** a disease in which there is swelling and pain in the joints (= parts of the body where bones join)

rhino /'raɪnəu/ *noun* **[C]** *short for* rhinoceros

rhinoceros /raɪ'nɒsʳrəs/ *noun* **[C]** a large animal from Africa or Asia that has thick skin and one or two horns on its nose

rhubarb /'ruːbɑːb/ *noun* **[U]** a plant that has long, red stems that can be cooked and eaten as a fruit

rhyme¹ /raɪm/ *verb* **[I]** If a word rhymes with another word, the end part of the words sound the same. *'Moon' rhymes with 'June'.*

rhyme² /raɪm/ *noun* **1** POEM **[C]** a short poem that has words that rhyme at the end of each line **2** STYLE **[U]** a style of writing or speaking that uses words which rhyme *The story was written entirely in rhyme.* **3** WORD **[C]** a word that rhymes with another word ⊃See also: nursery rhyme.

rhythm /'rɪðʳm/ *noun* **[C, U]** a regular, repeating pattern of sound *You need a **sense of rhythm** to be a good dancer.* ● **rhythmic** /'rɪðmɪk/ *adjective* with rhythm ● **rhythmically** *adverb*

rib /rɪb/ *noun* **[C]** one of the curved bones in the chest

ribbon /'rɪbʳn/ *noun* **[C]** a long, narrow piece of cloth that is used for tying things or used for decoration

'rib ,cage *noun* **[C]** the structure of ribs (= curved bones) in the chest

o--**rice** /raɪs/ *noun* **[U]** small grains from a plant that are cooked and eaten ⊃See colour picture **Food** on page Centre 11.

'rice ,paddy (*also UK* **paddy field**) *noun* **[C]** a field in which rice is grown

R

The adjectives **wealthy** and **well-off** are common alternatives to 'rich': *Oliver's parents are very wealthy/well-off*.

If someone is very rich, in informal situations you can use the adjective **loaded** or the expression **be rolling in it**: *They don't have any money worries - they're loaded.* • *If he can afford a yacht, he must be rolling in it.*

If someone is richer than they were previously, the adjective **better-off** is often used: *We're a lot better-off now that Jane's working again.*

The adjectives **affluent** and **prosperous** are sometimes used to describe areas where people are rich: *It's a very affluent neighbourhood.* • *In a prosperous country like this, no-one should go hungry.*

✺**rich** /rɪtʃ/ *adjective* **1** [MONEY] having much more money than most people, or owning things that could be sold for a lot of money *She's the third richest woman in Britain.* ○ *These cars are only for the rich.* **2** [CONTAINING A LOT] containing a lot of something that is important or valuable *rich soil* ○ *Both foods are rich in Vitamin C.* **3** [FOOD] Rich food has a lot of butter, cream, or eggs in it. *a rich sauce* **4** [STRONG] A rich sound is low and strong, and a rich colour is bright and strong. • **richness** *noun* [U]

riches /ˈrɪtʃɪz/ *noun* [plural] *literary* a lot of money or valuable objects ⊃See also: go from **rags** to riches.

richly /ˈrɪtʃli/ *adverb* **1 be richly decorated/furnished, etc** to have a lot of beautiful or expensive decoration, furniture, etc *a richly decorated church* **2 be richly rewarded** to be paid a lot of money **3 richly deserve** to very much deserve something *Later that year he received the award he so richly deserved.*

rickety /ˈrɪkəti/ *adjective* likely to break soon *a rickety wooden chair*

ricochet /ˈrɪkəʃeɪ/ *verb* [I] to hit a surface and then be sent back through the air *The bullet ricocheted off the wall.*

✺**rid**¹ /rɪd/ *adjective* **1 get rid of sth a** to throw something away or give something to someone because you do not want it now *We must get rid of some of those old books.* **b** to end something unpleasant *I can't seem to get rid of this headache.* **2 get rid of sb** to make someone leave *She was useless at her job so we had to get rid of her.* **3 be rid of sb/sth** to be without someone or something that you do not like or want *I'd do anything to be rid of him.*

rid² /rɪd/ *verb* ridding, *past* rid

rid sth of sth to remove something unpleasant from somewhere *to rid the world of nuclear weapons*

rid yourself of sth to remove something that you do not want *to rid yourself of a reputation*

riddance /ˈrɪdⁿns/ *noun* **Good riddance!** used to express pleasure when you have got rid of something or someone that you do not want

ridden /ˈrɪdⁿn/ *past participle of* ride

riddle /ˈrɪdl/ *noun* [C] **1** a strange and difficult question that has a clever and often funny answer **2** a situation or event that you cannot understand *Scientists may have solved the riddle of Saturn's rings.*

riddled /ˈrɪdld/ *adjective* **be riddled with sth** to contain a large number of something bad *The wall was riddled with bullets.*

✺**ride**¹ /raɪd/ *verb past tense* **rode**, *past participle* **ridden 1** [I, T] to travel by sitting on a horse, bicycle, or motorcycle and controlling it *I ride my bike to work.* ○ *She taught me to ride* (= to ride a horse). ⊃See Common learner error at **drive**. **2** [T] *US* to travel in a vehicle as a passenger *I've told her not to ride the subway at night.*

ride on sth If something important rides on a situation, it will succeed or fail depending on the situation. *There was $600,000 riding on the outcome of the deal.*

ride out sth to continue to exist during a bad situation *to ride out a recession*

go for/hitch a ride • a ride **in/on** sth • **give** sb a ride

ride² /raɪd/ *noun* [C] **1** [VEHICLE] a journey in a vehicle or train *Can I give you a ride to the station?* **2** [BICYCLE] a journey riding a bicycle, motorcycle, or horse *He's gone out for a ride on his bike.* **3** [PLAYING] a machine at a fair (= event outdoors) which moves people up and down, round in circles, etc as they sit in it

rider /ˈraɪdəʳ/ *noun* [C] someone who rides a horse, bicycle, or motorcycle ⊃See colour picture Sports 1 on page Centre 14.

ridge /rɪdʒ/ *noun* [C] **1** a long, narrow piece of high land, especially along the top of a mountain *a mountain ridge* **2** a narrow, raised line on a flat surface

ridicule¹ /ˈrɪdɪkjuːl/ *verb* [T] to make people laugh at someone in an unkind way *I was ridiculed for saying they might win.*

ridicule² /ˈrɪdɪkjuːl/ *noun* [U] when people laugh at someone in an unkind way

ridiculous /rɪˈdɪkjələs/ *adjective* very silly *I've never heard anything so ridiculous.* • **ridiculously** *adverb* *ridiculously expensive*

riding /ˈraɪdɪŋ/ *noun* [U] the sport or activity of riding horses

rife /raɪf/ *adjective* [never before noun] Something unpleasant that is rife is very common. *Rumours were rife that the band would split up.*

rifle¹ /ˈraɪfl/ *noun* [C] a long gun that you hold against your shoulder when you shoot

rifle² /ˈraɪfl/ (*also* **rifle through**) *verb* [T] to quickly search through things, often in order to steal something *I caught him rifling through my drawers.*

create/heal a rift • a **deep/growing/huge/serious** rift • a rift **with** sb • a rift **between** sb and sb • a rift **over** sth

rift /rɪft/ *noun* [C] **1** a serious disagreement *the deepening rift between the government and the unions* **2** a very large hole that separates parts of the Earth's surface

rig[1] /rɪg/ *verb* [T] **rigging** *past* **rigged** to arrange an election, competition, etc so that the results are not fair or true *He accused the government of rigging the elections.*

rig sth up to quickly make a piece of equipment from any materials you can find

rig[2] /rɪg/ *noun* [C] a large structure for removing gas or oil from the ground or the sea *an oil rig*

rigging /'rɪgɪŋ/ *noun* [U] a system of ropes and chains used to support a ship's masts (= poles)

o-***right**[1] /raɪt/ *adjective* **1** CORRECT correct or true *He only got half the answers right.* ○ *You're right about Alison - she's incredible!* ○ *"You came here in 1979, didn't you?" " That's right."* **2** DIRECTION [always before noun] on or towards the side of your body that is to the east when you are facing north *your right hand* ○ *There's a tree on the right side of the house.* **3** SUITABLE suitable or best in a particular situation *I'm not sure she's the right person for the job.* ○ *Are we going in the right direction?* **4** ACCEPTABLE fair or morally acceptable *It's not right to criticize him behind his back.* **5** put sth right to solve a problem **6** COMPLETE [always before noun] *UK informal* used for emphasizing when something is bad *His house is a right mess.* ⊃See also: all right.

COMMON LEARNER ERROR

right or true?

Right is usually used to say something is correct or to agree with something someone has said.
He gave the right answer.

"That's right, they live in central London."

True is usually used to say something is based on facts.
Is it true that she's leaving?

Everything I've told you is true.

o-***right**[2] /raɪt/ *adverb* **1** EXACTLY exactly in a place or time *He's right here with me.* ○ *I fell asleep right in the middle of her speech.* **2** CORRECTLY correctly *He guessed right most of the time.* **3** DIRECTION to the right side *Turn right after the bridge.* **4** right away/now/after immediately *Do you want to start right away?* **5** ALL all the way *Did you read it right through to the end?* **6** IN SPEECH *UK* used at the beginning of a sentence to get someone's attention or to show you have understood someone *Right, who's turn is it to tidy up?* ○ *Right, so Helen's coming tomorrow and Trevor on Thursday.* **7** Right used in the UK as part of the title of some politicians and Christian officials *Right Honourable/Reverend* **8** It serves her/him/you right! *informal* something you say about a bad thing which has happened to a person and which they deserve *So she left him, did she? Serves him right!* ●**rightness** *noun* [U] ⊃See also: be right up sb's alley, be right up sb's street.

o-***right**[3] /raɪt/ *noun* **1** LAW [C] something that the law allows you to do *the right to free speech* ○ [+ to do sth] *the right to vote* **2** DIRECTION [U] the

right side of your body, or the direction towards this side *You'll find her in the second room on the right.* **3** BEHAVIOUR [U] morally correct behaviour *I've tried to teach them the difference between right and wrong.* **4** have a/no right to do sth to have, or not have, a good reason for something *He has a right to be angry.* ○ *She had no right to speak to me like that.* **5** the Right/right political groups which support capitalism (= a system in which industries and companies are owned by people and not the government) *The right campaigned against the president.*

right[4] /raɪt/ *verb* [T] **1** to put something back in a vertical position, or to return to a vertical position [often reflexive] *The boat righted itself and I rowed us back to the shore.* **2** right a wrong to do something good to make an unfair situation seem better *How can we right the wrongs of the past?*

'**right ,angle** *noun* [C] an angle of the type that is in a square

,**right 'click** *verb* [I] to press the button on the right of a computer mouse (= a small piece of equipment that you move with your hand to control what the computer does)

righteous /'raɪtʃəs/ *adjective* morally right and for good moral reasons *righteous anger/indignation* ●**righteousness** *noun* [U] ⊃See also: self righteous.

rightful /'raɪtfəl/ *adjective* [always before noun] legally or morally correct *The wallet was returned to its rightful owner.*

right-hand /,raɪt'hænd/ *adjective* [always before noun] **1** on the right of something *On the right-hand side you'll see a sign.* **2** sb's right-hand man/woman the person that you most trust and depend on, especially at work

right-handed /,raɪt'hændɪd/ *adjective* Someone who is right-handed uses their right hand to do most things.

rightly /'raɪtli/ *adverb* in a correct way *He is rightly concerned about the situation.*

rights /raɪts/ *noun* [plural] freedom to do and say things without fear of punishment ⊃See also: civil rights, human rights.

right-wing /,raɪt'wɪŋ/ *adjective* supporting the ideas of parties on the political right *a right-wing newspaper* ●**right-winger** *noun* [C]

rigid /'rɪdʒɪd/ *adjective* **1** not able to change or be changed easily *I found the rules a little too rigid.* **2** not able to bend or move easily *a rigid structure* ●**rigidly** *adverb* ●**rigidity** /rɪ'dʒɪdəti/ *noun* [U] being unable to bend or change easily

rigorous /'rɪgərəs/ *adjective* careful to look at or consider every part of something to make sure it is correct or safe *rigorous testing* ○ *a rigorous medical examination* ●**rigorously** *adverb*

rigour *UK* (*US* **rigor**) /'rɪgər/ *noun* [U] when you look at or consider every part of something to make sure it is correct or safe *His arguments lack intellectual rigour.*

rigours *UK* (*US* **rigors**) /'rɪgəz/ *noun* **the rigours of sth** the difficult conditions of a particular situation *the rigours of a harsh winter*

rim /rɪm/ *noun* [C] the edge of something round

R

the rim of a wheel

rind /raɪnd/ *noun* [C, U] the thick skin of fruits such as oranges and lemons and other foods, for example cheese

⚬**ring¹** /rɪŋ/ *noun* [C] **1** JEWELLERY a round piece of jewellery that you wear on your finger *a wedding ring* ○ *a gold ring* ⊃See picture at **jewellery**. **2** CIRCLE something that is the shape of a circle *The children sat in a ring around the teacher.* **3** SOUND the sound a bell makes *The ring of the doorbell woke him up.* **4 a crime/drug/spy, etc ring** a group of people who are involved in an illegal activity together **5 a boxing/circus ring** an area with seats around it where boxers (= people fighting) or people in a circus (= move perform **6 give sb a ring** *UK* to telephone someone *If you want anything, just give me a ring.* ⊃See also: **key ring**.

⚬**ring²** /rɪŋ/ *verb past tense* **rang**, *past participle* **rung** **1** SOUND [I, T] If something rings, it makes the sound of a bell, and if you ring a bell, you cause it to make a sound. *The phone's ringing.* ○ *I rang the doorbell.* **2** TELEPHONE [I, T] *UK* (*UK/US* **call**) to telephone someone *Have you rung your mother?* ○ *I've rung for a taxi.* **3** EARS [I] If your ears are ringing, you can hear a loud sound after the sound has stopped. ⊃See also: ring a **bell**, ring **true**.

ring (sb) back *UK* (*UK/US* **call (sb) back**) to telephone someone a second time, or to telephone someone who rang you earlier *I'm a bit busy - can I ring you back later?*

ring off *UK* (*UK/US* **hang up**) to end a telephone conversation and put down the part of the telephone that you speak into *She'd rung off before I could say goodbye.*

ring³ /rɪŋ/ *verb* [T] to make a circle around something *Dozens of armed police ringed the building.*

ringleader /'rɪŋˌliːdər/ *noun* [C] the leader of a group who are doing something harmful or illegal *the ringleader of a gang of drug smugglers*

'ring ˌroad *noun* [C] *UK* a road built to take traffic around the outside of a city

ringtone /'rɪŋtəʊn/ *noun* [C] the sound that a telephone makes, especially a mobile phone, when someone is calling it

rink /rɪŋk/ *noun* [C] a large, flat surface made of ice or wood where you can skate (= move wearing boots with wheels or a piece of metal) *a roller skating rink* ⊃See also: **ice rink**.

rinse¹ /rɪns/ *verb* [T] to wash something in clean water in order to remove dirt or soap *Rinse the beans with cold water.*

rinse sth out to quickly wash the inside of something with clean water *I'll just rinse these glasses out and leave them to dry.*

rinse² /rɪns/ *noun* [C] **1** when you wash something in clean water to remove dirt or soap *Give it a quick rinse, then squeeze it dry.* **2** a liquid that is used for changing the colour of someone's hair *a dark brown rinse*

riot¹ /raɪət/ *noun* **1** [C] angry, violent behaviour by a crowd of people *a race riot* ○ *Riots started in several cities.* **2 run riot** to behave in a noisy, violent, or wild way without being controlled *They allow their kids to run riot.*

riot² /raɪət/ *verb* [I] to take part in a riot *People were rioting in the streets.* • **rioter** *noun* [C]

rioting /'raɪətɪŋ/ *noun* [U] when a crowd of people riots *There was widespread rioting.*

riotous /'raɪətəs/ *adjective* **1** wild and not controlled by anyone *a riotous party* **2** *formal* violent and not controlled *He was charged with riotous behaviour and jailed for six months.*

rip¹ /rɪp/ *verb* **ripping**, *past* **ripped** **1** [I, T] to tear quickly and suddenly, or to tear something quickly and suddenly *She ripped her dress getting off her bike.* ○ *He ripped open the parcel.* **2 rip sth out/off/from, etc** to remove something by pulling it away quickly *Hedges had been ripped out to make larger fields.* **3** [T] to copy information from a CD onto an MP3 player (= a piece of electronic equipment or a computer program for storing music)

rip sb off *informal* to cheat someone by making them pay too much money for something *We were ripped off by the first taxi driver.*

rip sth off to remove a piece of clothing very quickly and carelessly *I ripped off my clothes and jumped in the shower.*

rip through sth to move through a place or building, destroying it quickly *The bomb ripped through the building, killing six people.*

rip sth up to tear something into small pieces *He ripped up all her letters.*

rip² /rɪp/ *noun* [C] a hole in the shape of a line when cloth or paper has been torn

ripe /raɪp/ *adjective* **1** developed enough and ready to be eaten *ripe bananas* **2 ripe for sth** developed enough to be ready for something *The country is ripe for change.* ○ **The time is ripe for** (= It is the right time for) *investing in new technology.*

ripen /'raɪpᵊn/ *verb* [I, T] to become ripe, or to make something become ripe *The peaches had ripened in the sun.*

rip-off /'rɪpɒf/ *noun* [C] *informal* something that costs far too much money *The drinks here are a complete rip-off.*

ripple¹ /'rɪpl/ *verb* [I, T] to move in small waves, or to make something move in small waves *A field of wheat rippled in the breeze.*

ripple² /'rɪpl/ *noun* [C] **1** a small wave or series of small waves on the surface of water *She dived in, sending ripples across the pool.* **2** something that spreads through a place in a gentle way *a ripple of applause/laughter*

⚬**rise¹** /raɪz/ *verb* [I] *past tense* **rose**, *past participle* **risen** **1** INCREASE to increase in level *rising temperatures* ○ *Prices rose by 10 percent.* **2** GO UP to move up *The balloon rose slowly into the air.* **3** STAND to stand, especially after sitting *He rose from his seat.* **4 rise to/through, etc** to become important, successful, or rich *He quickly rose to stardom.* **5** STRENGTH to become stronger or louder *The wind is rising.* **6** HIGH to be high above something *The bridge rose almost 600 feet above the water.* **7** APPEAR When the sun or moon rises, it appears in the sky. *The sun rises in the East.* **8 rise to the occasion/challenge, etc** to deal with a difficult job or opportunity successfully

rise or **raise**?

Be careful not to confuse these two verbs. **Rise** means to increase or move up. This verb cannot be followed by an object.

The price of petrol is rising.

~~The price of petrol is raising.~~

Raise means to lift something to a higher position or to increase an amount or level. This verb must always be followed by an object.

The government has raised the price of petrol.

~~The government has rised the price of petrol.~~

rise above sth to succeed in not allowing something harmful or bad to affect or hurt you
rise up to try to defeat and change a government

WORD PARTNERS FOR *rise*

a **big/dramatic/massive/sudden** rise • a rise **in** sth • be **on the** rise • the rise **and fall** of sth • a **pay/price** rise

o-**rise²** /raɪz/ *noun* **1** [C] an increase in the level of something *a tax rise* ○ *a rise in interest rates* **2** sb's **rise to fame/power, etc** when someone becomes very famous or powerful **3 give rise to sth** to cause something *The bacteria live in the human body but do not give rise to any symptoms.* **4** [C] *UK* (*US* **raise**) an increase in the amount of money that you earn *a pay rise*

WORD PARTNERS FOR *risk*

carry/increase/pose/minimize/reduce/take a risk • **run** the risk **of** sth • a **great/high/serious/slight/small** risk • the risk **of** sth • **at** risk

o-**risk¹** /rɪsk/ *noun* **1** [C, U] the possibility of something bad happening *the risk of heart disease* ○ *People in the Northeast face the highest risk of being burgled.* ○ [+ (that)] *There is a slight risk that the blood could have become infected.* **2** [C] something bad that might happen *There are more health risks when older women get pregnant.* **3 at risk** being in a situation where something bad is likely to happen *Releasing these prisoners into the community puts the public at risk.* **4 at your own risk** If you do something at your own risk, you are completely responsible for anything bad that might happen because of it. **5 run the risk of sth** to do something although something bad might happen because of it *I think I'll run the risk of hurting her feelings, and tell her the truth.* **6 take a risk** to do something although something bad might happen because of it *This time I'm not taking any risks - I'm going to get insured.*

o-**risk²** /rɪsk/ *verb* [T] **1** If you risk something bad, you do something although that bad thing might happen. [+ doing sth] *I'd like to help you,*

but I can't risk losing my job. **2** If you risk something important, you cause it to be in a dangerous situation where you might lose it. *He risked his life to save me.*

risky /ˈrɪski/ *adjective* dangerous because something bad might happen *Investing in shares is always a risky business.*

rite /raɪt/ *noun* [C] a traditional ceremony in a particular religion or culture *initiation/ funeral rites*

ritual /ˈrɪtʃuəl/ *noun* [C] an activity or a set of actions that are always done in the same way or at the same time, sometimes as part of a religion *Coffee and the paper are part of my morning ritual.* ● **ritualistic** /ˌrɪtʃuəˈlɪstɪk/ *adjective* done as a ritual

rival¹ /ˈraɪvəl/ *noun* [C] someone or something that is competing with another person or thing *business/political rivals* ● **rival** *adjective* [always before noun] *a rival company/gang* ● **rivalry** *noun* [C, U] when two people or things are rivals *There is intense rivalry between the two teams.*

rival² /ˈraɪvəl/ *verb* [T] *UK* **rivalling**, *past* **rivalled**, *US* **rivaling**, *past* **rivaled** to be good enough to compete with someone or something else *Australian wine can now rival the best from France.*

o-**river** /ˈrɪvər/ *noun* [C] a long, natural area of water that flows across the land and into a sea, lake, or another river *the River Thames*

riverside /ˈrɪvəsaɪd/ *noun* [no plural] the area of land at the side of a river *a riverside path*

rivet¹ /ˈrɪvɪt/ *verb* **be riveted** to give something all of your attention because it is so interesting or important *Her eyes were riveted on/to his face.*

rivet² /ˈrɪvɪt/ *noun* [C] a metal pin used to fasten pieces of metal together

riveting /ˈrɪvɪtɪŋ/ *adjective* extremely interesting or exciting *I found the film absolutely riveting.*

roach /rəʊtʃ/ *noun* [C] *plural* **roach** or **roaches** *US* a cockroach (= large insect that sometimes breeds in houses)

o-**road** /rəʊd/ *noun* **1** [C, U] a long, hard surface built for vehicles to drive on *Be careful when you cross the road.* ○ *The journey takes about three hours by road* (= in a car, bus, etc). ○ *Follow the main road* (= large road) *till you come to a church.* **2 Road** (*written abbreviation* **Rd**) used in the name of a road as part of an address *142 Park Road* **3 along/down/up the road** a distance away on the same road *There's a supermarket just down the road.* **4 over the road** *UK* (*UK/US* **across the road**) on the other side of the road *Who lives in that big house over the road?* **5 on the road** driving or travelling, usually over a long distance *We'd been on the road for 48 hours.* **6 down the road** If an event is a particular period of time down the road, it will not happen until that period has passed. *Why worry about something that's 10 years down the road?* **7 go down that road** to decide to do something in a particular way *I don't think we want to go down that road.* ◆See also: **ring road, slip road, trunk road.**

roadblock /'rəʊdblɒk/ *noun* [C] something that is put across a road to stop people who are driving down it *The police had **set up** a road-block and were checking identity papers.*

'road ˌmap *noun* [C] a plan for achieving something *the road map for peace in the Middle East*

'road ˌrage *noun* [U] anger and violence between drivers *a road rage incident*

roadshow /'rəʊdʃəʊ/ *noun* [C] a radio or television programme broadcast from a public place

roadside /'rəʊdsaɪd/ *noun* [C] the area next to a road [usually singular] *They found an injured cat lying **by the roadside**.*

roadway /'rəʊdweɪ/ *noun* [C] the part of the road that the traffic drives on

roadworks /'rəʊdwɜːks/ *noun* [plural] *UK* repairs being done to a road

roadworthy /'rəʊdˌwɜːði/ *adjective* If a car is roadworthy, it is in good enough condition to be safe to drive.

roam /rəʊm/ *verb* [I, T] to move around a place without any purpose *gangs of youths **roaming the street** at night*

roar¹ /rɔːʳ/ *verb* **1** [I] to make a loud, deep sound *We could hear a **lion roaring** from the other side of the zoo.* ○ *She **roared with laughter**.* **2 roar past/down, etc** If a vehicle roars somewhere, it moves fast making a loud noise. *A huge motorcycle roared past.* **3** [I, T] to say something in a very loud voice *"Stop that!" he roared.*

roar² /rɔːʳ/ *noun* [C] a loud, deep sound *a lion's roar* ○ *the roar of a jet engine*

roaring /'rɔːrɪŋ/ *adjective* [always before noun] **1** A roaring fire or wind is very powerful. **2** *informal* used to emphasize a situation or state *The party was a **roaring success**.*

roast¹ /rəʊst/ *verb* [I, T] If you roast food, you cook it in an oven or over a fire, and if food roasts, it is cooked in an oven or over a fire. *Roast the lamb in a hot oven for 35 minutes.* ●**roast** *adjective* [always before noun] *roast beef/pork* ⟳See picture at **cook**.

roast² /rəʊst/ *noun* [C] a piece of roasted meat

rob /rɒb/ *verb* [T] robbing, *past* robbed **1** to steal from someone or somewhere, often using violence *to **rob a bank*** ○ *Two tourists were robbed at gunpoint in the city centre last night.* **2 rob sb of sth** to take something important away from someone *The war had robbed them of their innocence.*

robber /'rɒbəʳ/ *noun* [C] someone who steals *a bank robber* ○ *a gang of armed robbers*

robbery /'rɒbᵊri/ *noun* [C] the crime of stealing from someone or somewhere *a **bank robbery*** ○ *an **armed robbery*** ○ *to **commit a robbery***

robe /rəʊb/ *noun* [C] a long, loose piece of clothing, often something that is worn for ceremonies or special occasions

robin /'rɒbɪn/ *noun* [C] a small, brown bird with a red chest

robot /'rəʊbɒt/ *noun* [C] a machine controlled by a computer, which can move and do other things that people can do ●**robotic** /rəʊ'bɒtɪk/ *adjective* relating to or like a robot

robust /rəʊ'bʌst/ *adjective* strong and healthy *He looks robust enough.* ○ *a robust economy*

◦▪**rock¹** /rɒk/ *noun* **1** SUBSTANCE [U] the hard, natural substance which forms part of the Earth's surface *a layer of volcanic rock* **2** LARGE PIECE [C] a large piece of rock or stone *Huge waves were crashing against the rocks.* **3** MUSIC [U] loud, modern music with a strong beat, often played with electric guitars and drums *hard/soft rock* ○ *rock music* ○ *a rock band/singer* **4 on the rocks a** RELATIONSHIP If a relationship is on the rocks, it has problems and is likely to end soon. **b** DRINK If a drink is on the rocks, it is served with ice in it.

rock² /rɒk/ *verb* **1** [I, T] to move backwards and forwards or from side to side, or to make someone or something do this *She rocked back and forth on her chair.* ○ *He gently rocked the baby to sleep.* **2** [T] to shock a large number of people [often passive] *The country has been rocked by a series of drug scandals.* ⟳See also: rock the **boat**.

ˌrock 'bottom *noun informal* **hit/reach rock bottom** to reach the lowest level possible *The president's popularity has hit rock bottom.*

rocket¹ /'rɒkɪt/ *noun* [C] **1** a tube-shaped vehicle for travelling in space **2** a tube-shaped weapon that carries a bomb

rocket² /'rɒkɪt/ *verb* [I] **1** to quickly increase in value or amount *House prices have rocketed this year.* **2** to make quick progress *She rocketed to stardom after modelling for Vogue last year.*

rock 'n' roll /ˌrɒkən'rəʊl/ *noun* [U] **1** (*also* ˌrock and 'roll) a type of dance music that was especially popular in the 1950s **2 be the new rock 'n' roll** to now be the most fashionable and popular activity

'rock ˌstar *noun* [C] a famous rock musician

rocky /'rɒki/ *adjective* with lots of rocks *a rocky beach*

rod /rɒd/ *noun* [C] a thin, straight pole *a fishing rod* ○ *The concrete is strengthened with steel rods.*

rode /rəʊd/ *past tense of* ride

rodent /'rəʊdᵊnt/ *noun* [C] an animal with long, sharp teeth, such as a mouse or rabbit

rodeo /'rəʊdiəʊ/ *noun* [C] a competition in which people show their skill at riding wild horses and catching cows

roe /rəʊ/ *noun* [U] fish eggs

rogue /rəʊg/ *adjective* [always before noun] not behaving in the way that is expected or wanted *a rogue state* ○ *rogue cells*

◦▪**role** /rəʊl/ *noun* [C] **1** the job someone or something has in a particular situation *This part of the brain **plays an** important **role in** learning.* **2** a part in a play or film *In his latest film, he* *plays the role of a violent gangster.* ⊃See also: title role.

'role ,model *noun* [C] someone you try to behave like because you admire them *Jane is such a good role model for her younger sister.*

role-play /'rəʊl,pleɪ/ *noun* [C, U] pretending to be someone else, especially as part of learning a new skill

roll¹ /rəʊl/ *verb* **1 roll (sth) across/around/over, etc** to move somewhere by turning in a circular direction, or to make something move this way *The ball rolled through the goalkeeper's legs.* ∘ *She rolled over onto her side.* **2 roll down/in/off, etc** to move somewhere smoothly *Tears rolled down her face.* **3** [T] to turn something around itself to make the shape of a ball or tube *to roll a cigarette* **4 roll your eyes** to move your eyes so that they are looking up, usually to show surprise or disapproval **5 be rolling in it** *informal* to be very rich ⊃See also: set/start the **ball** rolling.

roll in to arrive in large numbers *She only set up the business last year and already the money's rolling in.*

roll sth up to fold something around itself to make the shape of a ball or tube, or to make a piece of clothing shorter *to roll up your sleeves/trouser legs* ∘ *to roll up a carpet* ⊃Opposite **unroll**.

roll up *informal* to arrive somewhere, usually late *By the time Jim rolled up, the party had almost finished.*

roll

roll of film   bread roll

roll² /rəʊl/ *noun* [C] **1** ROUND OBJECT something that has been turned around itself into a round shape like a tube *a roll of film* ∘ *a roll of toilet paper* **2** BREAD a small loaf of bread for one person *Would you like a roll and butter with your soup?* **3** LIST a list of names *the electoral roll* **4** SOUND a long, deep sound *a roll of thunder* ∘ *a drum roll* **5 be on a roll** *informal* to be having a successful period *We were on a roll, winning our fourth game in a row.* ⊃See also: rock 'n' roll, toilet roll.

roller /'rəʊlə^r/ *noun* [C] a piece of equipment in the shape of a tube which is rolled around or over something *She uses rollers to curl her hair.*

Rollerblades /'rəʊləbleɪdz/ *noun* [plural] *trademark (also* in-line skates) boots with a single

line of wheels on the bottom, used for moving across the ground • **rollerblading** *noun* [U] *Lots of people go rollerblading in Central Park.* ⊃See colour picture **Sports 1** on page Centre 14.

roller coaster /,rəʊlə'kəʊstə^r/ *noun* [C] an exciting entertainment which is like a fast train that goes up and down very steep slopes

'roller ,skate *noun* [C] a boot with wheels on the bottom, used for moving across the ground • roller skating *noun* [U]

'rolling ,pin *noun* [C] a kitchen tool shaped like a tube that you roll over pastry to make it thinner before cooking ⊃See colour picture **The Kitchen** on page Centre 2.

Roman¹ /'rəʊmən/ *adjective* relating to ancient Rome or its empire *Roman remains*

Roman² /'rəʊmən/ *noun* [C] someone who lived in ancient Rome or its empire

,Roman 'Catholic *adjective* related to the part of the Christian religion that has the Pope (= a very important priest) as its leader • **Roman Catholic** *noun* [C] • **Roman Catholicism** *noun* [U] the beliefs of the Roman Catholic religion

romance /rəʊ'mæns/ *noun* **1** LOVE [C, U] an exciting relationship of love between two people, often a short one *They got married last September after a whirlwind romance.* **2** STORY [C] a story about love **3** EXCITEMENT [U] a feeling of excitement or exciting danger *the romance of the sea*

,Roman 'numeral *noun* [C] a letter that represents a number in the Roman system in which I is 1, II is 2, V is 5, etc

romantic¹ /rəʊ'mæntɪk/ *adjective* **1** LOVE relating to exciting feelings of love *a romantic dinner for two* **2** STORY relating to a story about love *romantic fiction* ∘ *a romantic comedy* **3** IDEAS thinking that things are better than they really are, and that things are possible which are not *a romantic view of the world* • **romantically** *adverb*

romantic² /rəʊ'mæntɪk/ *noun* [C] someone who thinks that things are better than they really are, and that things are possible which are not

romanticize (*also UK* **-ise**) /rəʊ'mæntɪsaɪz/ *verb* [T] to make something seem much better or exciting than it really is *a romanticized image of married life*

romp /rɒmp/ *verb*
**romp around/in/
through, etc** to run
around in a happy,
energetic way *The
children were romp-
ing around in the
garden.* • **romp** *noun*
[C]

roof

o→**roof** /ruːf/ *noun* **1** [C]
the surface that covers the top of a building or

vehicle *a flat/sloping roof* ○ *He climbed onto the roof.* **2 the roof of your mouth** the top part of the inside of your mouth **3 a roof over your head** somewhere to live **4 go through the roof** If the level of something, especially a price, goes through the roof, it increases very quickly. **5 hit the roof** *informal* to become very angry and start shouting *If I'm late again he'll hit the roof.*

roofing /ˈruːfɪŋ/ *noun* [U] material used to make a roof

rooftop /ˈruːftɒp/ *noun* [C] the top of a roof *a view across the city rooftops*

rook /rʊk/ *noun* [C] a large, black bird that lives in Europe

rookie /ˈrʊki/ *noun* [C] *mainly US* someone who has only recently started doing a job or activity and so has no experience *a rookie cop*

WORD PARTNERS FOR ***room***

2 leave/make room • **take up** room • room **for** sb/sth

⊶**room¹** /ruːm, rʊm/ *noun* **1** [C] a part of the inside of a building, which is separated from other parts by walls, floors, and ceilings *a hotel room* **2** [U] space for things to fit into *Is there enough room for all of us in your car?* ○ *Can everyone move up a bit to **make room for** these people?* ○ [+ to do sth] *There's hardly enough room to move in here.* **3 room for sth** a possibility for something to happen *His work isn't bad but there's still some **room for improvement**.* ➲See also: **changing room, chat room, dining room, drawing room, dressing room, elbow room, emergency room, living room, locker room, men's room, operating room, sitting room, waiting room.**

room² /ruːm, rʊm/ *verb* **room with sb** *US* to share a bedroom with someone, usually at college

roommate /ˈruːmmeɪt/ *noun* [C] **1** someone who you share a room with **2** *US* (*UK* **housemate/flatmate**) someone who you share your home with

ˈroom ˌservice *noun* [U] in a hotel, room service is when someone serves you food and drink in your room

roomy /ˈruːmi/ *adjective* having a lot of space *It looks small, but it's really quite roomy inside.*

roost /ruːst/ *noun* [C] **1** a place where birds go to rest or sleep **2 rule the roost** to be the person who makes all the decisions in a group

rooster /ˈruːstəʳ/ *noun* [C] a male chicken

⊶**root¹** /ruːt/ *noun* [C] **1** the part of a plant that grows under the ground and gets water and food from the soil **2** the part of a hair or tooth that is under the skin **3 the root of sth** the cause of something, usually something bad *the root of all evil* ➲See also: **grass roots.**

root² /ruːt/ *verb*

root about/around (sth) to search for something, especially by looking through other things *She was rooting around in her drawer for a pencil.*

root for sb *informal* to show support for someone who is in a competition or who is doing something difficult *Good luck! We're all rooting for you.*

be rooted in sth to be based on something or caused by something *Most prejudices are rooted in ignorance.*

root sth/sb out to find and get rid of the thing or person that is causing a problem *It is our aim to root out corruption.*

roots /ruːts/ *noun* [plural] where someone or something originally comes from *the roots of modern jazz*

rope¹ /rəʊp/ *noun* [C, U] **1** very thick string made from twisted thread **2 be on the ropes** *mainly US* to be doing badly and likely to fail *His career is on the ropes.* **3 learn/know the ropes** to learn/know how to do a job or activity ➲See also: at the **end¹** of your tether, **jump rope, skipping rope.**

rope² /rəʊp/ *verb* [T] to tie things together with rope

rope sb in *informal* to persuade someone to help you with something, especially when they do not want to

rosary /ˈrəʊzəri/ *noun* [C] a string of beads (= small, round balls) that is used to count prayers in the Catholic religion

rose¹ /rəʊz/ *noun* [C] a flower with a pleasant smell and thorns (= sharp points on the stem), that grows on a bush

rose² /rəʊz/ *past tense of* rise

rosé /ˈrəʊzeɪ/ [US] /rəʊˈzeɪ/ *noun* [U] pink wine

rosemary /ˈrəʊzməri/ *noun* [U] a herb that grows as a bush with thin, pointed leaves

rosette /rəʊˈzet/ *noun* [C] **1** *UK* (*US* **ribbon**) a decoration made of coloured cloth, which is given as a prize **2** *UK* a decoration made of coloured cloth in the shape of a rose, worn to show political support for someone

WORD PARTNERS FOR ***roster***

draw up/organize a roster • a roster **of** sth • **on** a roster

roster /ˈrɒstəʳ/ *noun* [C] **1** a plan which shows who must do which jobs and when they must do them *a staff roster* **2** a list of names of people who belong to a team or organization

rostrum /ˈrɒstrəm/ *noun* [C] a raised surface which someone stands on to make a speech or receive a prize

rosy /ˈrəʊzi/ *adjective* **1** Rosy faces are a healthy pink colour. *rosy cheeks* **2** very positive and happy *The future looks rosy.*

rot¹ /rɒt/ *verb* [I, T] **rotting**, *past* **rotted** If vegetable or animal substances rot, they decay, and if something rots them, it makes them decay. *Sugar rots your teeth.* ○ *the smell of rotting fish*

rot² /rɒt/ *noun* [U] **1** decay *There was rot in the woodwork.* **2 the rot sets in** *UK* If the rot sets in, a situation starts to get worse. **3 stop the rot** *UK* to do something to prevent a situation from continuing to get worse

rota /ˈrəʊtə/ *noun* [C] *UK* (*UK/US* **roster**) a plan which shows who must do which jobs and when they must do them

rotary /ˈrəʊtəri/ *adjective* [always before noun] moving in a circular direction

rotate /rəʊ'teɪt/ *verb* [I, T] **1** to turn in a circular direction, or to make something turn in a circular direction *The television rotates for viewing at any angle.* **2** to change from one person or thing to another in a regular order *Farmers usually rotate their crops to improve the soil.* ● **rotation** /rəʊ'teɪʃ³n/ *noun* [C, U] *the rotation of the Earth ○ crop rotation*

rotten /'rɒt³n/ *adjective* **1** Rotten vegetable or animal substances are decaying. *rotten eggs* **2** *informal* very bad *rotten weather*

rottweiler /'rɒtwaɪlə^r/ *noun* [C] a type of large, powerful dog

◦⁻**rough¹** /rʌf/ *adjective* **1** [NOT SMOOTH] A rough surface is not smooth. *rough hands ○ rough ground* **2** [APPROXIMATE] approximate *a rough estimate ○ Can you give me a rough idea of the cost?* **3** [FORCEFUL] If the sea or weather is rough, there is a lot of strong wind and sometimes rain. *The boat sank in rough seas off the Swedish coast.* **4** [ILL] [never before noun] *UK* ill *I feel a bit rough after last night* **5** [DIFFICULT] difficult or unpleasant *She's having a rough time at work.* **6** [DANGEROUS] dangerous or violent *a rough part of town ○ Hockey can be quite a rough game* **7** [NOT PERFECT] quickly done and not perfect *These are just rough sketches.* **8** **rough and ready a** [NOT PREPARED] produced quickly without preparation **b** [NOT POLITE] not very polite or well-educated ● **roughness** *noun* [U]

rough² /rʌf/ *noun* **take the rough with the smooth** *UK* to accept the unpleasant parts of a situation as well as the pleasant parts

rough³ /rʌf/ *adverb* **live/sleep rough** *UK* to live and sleep outside because you have nowhere else to live

rough⁴ /rʌf/ *verb* **rough it** to live in a way that is simple and not comfortable

roughage /'rʌfɪdʒ/ *noun* [U] a substance in fruit and vegetables that helps you to get rid of waste from the body

roughen /'rʌf³n/ *verb* [I, T] to become rough or to make something become rough *Years of housework had roughened her hands.*

roughly /'rʌfli/ *adverb* **1** approximately *There's been an increase of roughly 30% since last year.* **2** forcefully or violently *He pushed us roughly out of the door.*

roulette /ru:'let/ *noun* [U] a game in which a small ball moves around a dish with numbers on it, and people try to win money by guessing where the ball will stop

◦⁻**round¹** /raʊnd/ *adjective* **1** in the shape of a circle or ball *a round table/window ○ round eyes ○ a round face* ➲See picture at **flat**. **2** **round figures/numbers** numbers given to the nearest 10, 100, 1000, etc and not as the exact amounts

◦⁻**round²** /raʊnd/ *UK* (*UK/US* around) *adverb, preposition* **1** [IN A CIRCLE] on all sides of something *We sat round the table. ○ She had a scarf round her neck.* **2** [DIRECTION] to the opposite direction *She looked round. ○ Turn the car round and let's go home.* **3** [TO A PLACE] to or in different parts of a place *He showed me round the flat.* **4** [SEVERAL PLACES] from one place or person to another *Could you pass these forms round,*

please? **5** [VISIT] to someone's home *Wendy's coming round this afternoon.* **6** [NEAR] near an area *Do you live round here?* **7** **round about** at approximately a time or approximately an amount *We'll be there round about 10 o'clock.* **8** **round and round** moving in a circle without stopping *We drove round and round trying to find the hotel.*

round³ /raʊnd/ *noun* [C] **1** **first/second/third/etc, round** a part of a competition *He was beaten in the first round.* **2** [EVENTS] a group of events that is part of a series *a round of interviews ○ a new round of talks between the two countries* **3** [VISITS] *UK* regular visits to a group of people or houses to give them something or to see them *a milk/newspaper round* **4** [DRINKS] drinks that you buy for a group of people *It's your turn to buy the next round.* **5** **round of applause** when people clap *The crowd gave him a huge round of applause.* **6** [BULLETS] a bullet or a set of bullets to be fired at one time from a gun **7** **round of golf** a game of golf

round⁴ /raʊnd/ *verb* [T] to go around something *They rounded the corner at high speed.*

round sth down to reduce a number to the nearest whole or simple number

round sth off to end an activity in a pleasant way *We rounded off the lesson with a quiz.*

round sb/sth up to find and bring together a group of people or animals *The police are rounding up the usual suspects.*

round sth up to increase a number to the nearest whole or simple number

roundabout

roundabout *UK*, traffic circle *US*

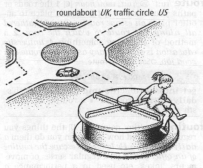

roundabout

roundabout¹ /'raʊndə,baʊt/ *noun* [C] **1** *UK* (*US* traffic circle) a circular place where roads meet and where cars drive around until they arrive at the road that they want to turn into *to go round a roundabout* **2** *UK* an entertainment which goes round and round while children sit on it

roundabout² /'raʊndə,baʊt/ *adjective* [always before noun] A roundabout way of doing something or going somewhere is not the direct way.

rounded /'raʊndɪd/ *adjective* smooth and curved *a table with rounded corners*

rounders /'raʊndəz/ *noun* [U] a British game in

which you try to hit a small ball and then run round all four sides of a large square

roundly /'raʊndli/ *adverb* If you criticize someone or something roundly, you do it very strongly. *The action was roundly condemned by French and German leaders.*

round-the-clock /ˌraʊndðə'klɒk/ *adjective* all day and night *round-the-clock nursing care*

round 'trip *noun* [C] a journey from one place to another and back to where you started

round-trip 'ticket *US* (*UK* return) *noun* [C] a ticket that lets you travel to a place and back again, for example on a train

round-up /'raʊndʌp/ *noun* [C] **1** when a group of people or animals are found and brought together *a police round-up* **2** a short report of all the facts or events relating to a subject *a news round-up*

rouse /raʊz/ *verb* [T] **1** to cause a feeling or emotion in someone *This issue is rousing a lot of public interest.* **2** *formal* to wake someone up *He was roused from a deep sleep.*

rousing /'raʊzɪŋ/ *adjective* making people feel excited and proud or ready to take action *a rousing speech*

rout /raʊt/ *verb* [T] to defeat someone completely ● **rout** *noun* [C] *an election rout*

follow/take a route   ● plan/work out a route   ● along/on a route   ● a route between/from/to

route /ruːt/ Ⓤ /ruːt, raʊt/ *noun* [C] **1** the roads or paths you follow to get from one place to another place *an escape route* ○ *Crowds gathered all along the route to watch the race.* **2** a method of achieving something *A university education is seen by many as the best route to a good job.* ➪See also: **en route.**

get into/have/settle into a routine   ● sb's daily/normal routine   ● a routine of doing sth

routine¹ /ruː'tiːn/ *noun* **1** [C, U] the things you regularly do and how and when you do them *a daily routine* ○ *He longed to escape the routine of an office job.* **2** [C] a regular series of movements, jokes, etc used in a performance *a dance routine*

routine² /ruː'tiːn/ *adjective* **1** done regularly and not unusual *a routine procedure* ○ *routine checks* **2** done regularly and very boring *His job is very routine.*

routinely /ruː'tiːnli/ *adverb* regularly or often

roving /'rəʊvɪŋ/ *adjective* [always before noun] moving around from one place to another place *a roving reporter*

row¹ /rəʊ/ *noun* **1** [C] a straight line of people or things *a row of chairs/houses* ○ *My students sit at desks in rows for most of the time.* **2** [C] a line of seats *to sit on the back/front row* ○ *Isn't that Sophie sitting in the row behind us?* **3 in a row** one after another without a break *He's just won the tournament for the fifth year*

in a row. ➪See also: **death row.**

row² /rəʊ/ *verb* [I, T] to move a boat or move someone in a boat through the water using oars (= poles with flat ends) ● **rowing** *noun* [U]

have a row   ● an almighty/blazing/heated row ● a row about/over sth ● a row with sb ● a row between sb and sb

row³ /raʊ/ *noun UK* **1** ⎡LOUD ARGUMENT⎤ [C] a loud, angry argument *a blazing row* ○ *The couple next door are always having rows.* **2** ⎡DISAGREEMENT⎤ [C] a disagreement about a political or public situation *A row has erupted over defence policy.* **3** ⎡NOISE⎤ [no plural] very loud noise *The kids were making a terrible row upstairs.*

rowdy /'raʊdi/ *adjective* loud and uncontrolled *rowdy behaviour* ○ *rowdy football fans*

row house *US* (*UK* terraced house) *noun* [C] one of a row of houses that are joined together

rowing boat *UK* (*US* rowboat) /'rəʊbəʊt/ *noun* [C] a small boat moved by oars (= poles with flat ends)

royal¹ /'rɔɪəl/ *adjective* **1** relating to a queen or king and their family *the British royal family* ○ *a royal visit* **2 Royal** used in the UK as part of the title of a royal person *His Royal Highness, the Duke of York*

royal² /'rɔɪəl/ *noun* [C] *informal* a member of a royal family *a book about the royals*

royalist /'rɔɪəlɪst/ *noun* [C] someone who supports the principle of having a King or Queen ● **royalist** *adjective*

royalties /'rɔɪəltiz/ *noun* [plural] money that is paid to a writer, actor, etc each time their work is sold or performed *He could receive as much as $1 million in royalties over the next six years.*

royalty /'rɔɪəlti/ *noun* [U] the members of the royal family *There are various rules about how to behave in front of royalty.*

RSI /ˌɑːres'aɪ/ *noun* [C] *abbreviation for* repetitive strain injury: a painful medical condition which can damage the hands, arms and backs of people, especially people who use computers

RSVP /ˌɑːresviː'piː/ used at the end of a written invitation to mean 'please answer' *RSVP by October 9th*

rub¹ /rʌb/ *verb* rubbing, *past* rubbed **1** [T] to press your hand or a cloth on a surface and move it backwards and forwards *She rubbed her hands together to warm them.* ○ *Rub the stain with a damp cloth.* **2 rub sth into/on, etc** to move a substance backwards and forwards over a surface so that it covers it and goes into it *I rubbed some suntan oil on her back.* ○ *Rub the butter into the flour.* **3** [I, T] to touch and move against something, often causing pain or damage *My new boots are rubbing against my toes.* **4 rub it in** *informal* to upset someone by talking to them about something which you know they want to forget *Look, I know what I did was wrong - there's no need to rub it in!* ➪See also: rub shoulders (**shoulder¹**) with sb, rub sb up the wrong **way¹**.

rub off If a quality or characteristic of a particular person rubs off, other people begin to have it because they have been with that person. *His enthusiasm is starting to **rub off** on the rest of us.*

rub sth out *UK* to remove writing from something by rubbing it with a piece of rubber or a cloth

rub² /rʌb/ *noun* [C] when you rub something [usually singular] *Give it a rub and it'll feel better.*

rubber /'rʌbər/ *noun* **1** [U] a strong material that bends easily, originally produced from the juice of a tropical tree, and used to make tyres, boots, etc **2** [C] *UK* (*US* **eraser**) a small object which is used to remove pencil marks from paper ⊃See colour picture **The Classroom** on page Centre 6.

,rubber 'band (*also UK* **elastic band**) *noun* [C] a thin circle of rubber used to hold things together

,rubber 'boot *noun* [C] *US* (*UK* **wellies** [plural]) a large shoe made of rubber that covers your foot and part of your leg

rubber-stamp /,rʌbə'stæmp/ *verb* [T] to officially approve a decision or plan without thinking very much about it

rubbery /'rʌbəri/ *adjective* feeling or bending like rubber *a rubbery piece of meat*

o⟶**rubbish¹** /'rʌbɪʃ/ *noun* [U] *mainly UK* **1** ⟨WASTE⟩ things that you throw away because you do not want them *Our rubbish gets collected on Thursdays.* ○ *a rubbish dump/bin* **2** ⟨NONSENSE⟩ something that is nonsense or wrong *Ignore him, he's talking rubbish.* **3** ⟨BAD QUALITY⟩ *informal* something that is of bad quality *There's so much rubbish on TV.*

rubbish² /'rʌbɪʃ/ *verb* [T] to criticize someone or something *I wish you wouldn't rubbish everything about the concert – I really enjoyed it!*

rubble /'rʌbl/ *noun* [U] pieces of broken bricks from a building that has been destroyed *a pile of rubble*

rubella /ru:'belə/ (*also* **German measles**) *noun* [U] a disease which causes red spots on your skin

rubric /'ru:brɪk/ *noun* [C] a set of instructions or an explanation, especially in an examination paper or book

ruby /'ru:bi/ *noun* [C] a valuable red stone which is used in jewellery

rucksack /'rʌksæk/ *noun* [C] *UK* a bag that you carry on your back ⊃See picture at **bag**.

rudder /'rʌdər/ *noun* [C] a piece of equipment that changes the direction of a boat or aircraft

ruddy /'rʌdi/ *adjective* A ruddy face is red. *ruddy cheeks*

If someone is slightly rude or behaves without respect in a way that is funny, you might describe them as **cheeky** (*UK*): *You asked your teacher how old she was? That was a bit cheeky!*

A more formal alternative to 'rude' is the world **impolite**: *She asks direct questions without being in any way impolite.*

If someone is rude or does not show respect

to a person who is older or has more authority than they do, they might be described as **impertinent** or **insolent**: *It was clear that they found his questions impertinent.*

The adjective **abrasive** describes someone's manner when they are rude and unfriendly: *I found him rather abrasive.*

A person who is rude and unpleasant is sometimes described as **uncouth**: *She found him loud-mouthed and uncouth.*

Language which is rude, referring to the body in an unpleasant way can be described as **vulgar** or **crude**: *He told a rather vulgar joke over dinner.*

o⟶**rude** /ru:d/ *adjective* **1** behaving in a way which is not polite and upsets other people *a rude remark* ○ *He complained that a member of staff had been rude to him.* ○ [+ to do sth] *It would be rude to leave without saying goodbye.* **2** Rude words or jokes relate to sex or going to the toilet. ● **rudely** *adverb* ● **rudeness** *noun* [U] ⊃See also: a rude **awakening**.

rudiments /'ru:dɪmənts/ *noun formal* **the rudiments of sth** the most basic parts or principles of something ● **rudimentary** /,ru:dɪ'mentəri/ *adjective formal* very basic

rueful /'ru:fəl/ *adjective* showing slight sadness about something but not in a serious way *a rueful smile* ● **ruefully** *adverb*

ruffle /'rʌfl/ *verb* [T] If someone ruffles your hair, they rub it gently. *He ruffled my hair and kissed me.*

rug /rʌg/ *noun* [C] **1** a soft piece of material used to cover the floor *The dog was lying on the rug in front of the fire.* ⊃See colour picture **The Living Room** on page Centre 4. **2** *UK* a soft cover that keeps you warm or comfortable

rug
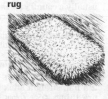

rugby /'rʌgbi/ *noun* [U] a sport played by two teams with an oval ball and H-shaped goals *a rugby player* ⊃See colour picture **Sports 2** on page Centre 15.

rugged /'rʌgɪd/ *adjective* **1** If an area of land is rugged, it looks rough and has lots of rocks. *a rugged coastline* **2** If a man looks rugged, his face looks strong and attractive. *a rugged face*

ruin¹ /'ru:ɪn/ *verb* [T] **1** to spoil or destroy something [often passive] *They were late and the dinner was ruined.* **2** to cause someone to lose all their money or their job *If the newspapers get hold of this story they'll ruin him.*

ruin² /'ru:ɪn/ *noun* **1** ⟨DESTRUCTION⟩ [U] the destruction of something *Fonthill Abbey fell into ruin 10 years after it was built.* **2** ⟨BROKEN BUILDING⟩ [C] the broken parts that are left from an old building or town *Thousand of tourists wander around these ancient ruins every year.* **3** ⟨LOSING EVERYTHING⟩ [U] when someone loses everything such as all their money or their job *The collapse of the bank has left many people in*

R

financial ruin. **4 be/lie in ruins** to be in a very bad state *The war left one million people dead and the country in ruins.*

WORD PARTNERS FOR *rule*

apply/break/enforce/establish a rule ● a rule **forbids/prohibits** sth ● a **strict/unwritten** rule ● a rule **against** sth

○▪**rule**¹ /ruːl/ *noun* **1** [INSTRUCTION] [C] an official instruction about what you must or must not do *to break* (= not obey) *the rules.* ○ *to obey/follow the rules* ○ *You can't smoke at school, it's against the rules* (= not allowed). **2** [LEADER] [U] when someone is in control of a country *military rule* ○ *There have been reports of immense human suffering under his rule.* **3** [USUAL WAY] [no plural] the usual way something is *an exception to the rule* ○ *Workers in the North are, as a rule, paid less than those in the South.* **4** [PRINCIPLE] [C] a principle of a system, such as a language or science *the rules of grammar* **5 a rule of thumb** a way of calculating something, which is not exact but which will help you to be correct enough **6 bend/stretch the rules** to allow someone to do something which is not usually allowed *We don't usually let students take books home, but I'll bend the rules on this occasion.* ⊃See also: ground rules.

rule² /ruːl/ *verb* [I, T] **1** to make an official legal decision [+ (that)] *The judge ruled that it was wrong for a 16-year-old girl to be held in an adult prison.* **2** to be in control of somewhere, usually a country [often passive] *They were ruled for many years by a dictator.* ○ *the ruling party* ⊃See also: rule the **roost**.
rule sb/sth out to decide that something or someone is not suitable for a particular purpose, or to decide that something is impossible *The police have not ruled him out as a suspect.*

ruler /ˈruːlər/ *noun* [C] **1** the leader of a country **2** a flat, straight stick which is used to measure things ⊃See colour picture **The Classroom** on page Centre 6.

ruling /ˈruːlɪŋ/ *noun* [C] an official legal decision, usually made by a judge

rum /rʌm/ *noun* [C, U] a strong, alcoholic drink made from sugar

rumble /ˈrʌmbl/ *verb* [I] to make a deep, long sound *The smell of cooking made his stomach rumble.* ●**rumble** *noun* [no plural] *the distant rumble of thunder*

rumbling /ˈrʌmblɪŋ/ *noun* [C] a deep, long sound *the rumbling of a train passing by*

rumblings /ˈrʌmblɪŋz/ *noun* [plural] signs that people are angry about something *rumblings of discontent*

rummage /ˈrʌmɪdʒ/ *verb* **rummage around/in/through, etc** to search inside something and move things around *I found him rummaging through my drawers.*

ˈrummage ˌsale *US* (*UK* jumble sale) *noun* [C] a sale of old items, especially clothes, usually to make money for an organization

WORD PARTNERS FOR *rumour*

fuel/spark/spread/start rumours ● **deny/dismiss/hear** rumours ● a rumour **circulates/goes around** ● a **persistent/strong/unconfirmed** rumour ● a rumour **about/of** sth

rumour¹ *UK* (*US* rumor) /ˈruːmər/ *noun* [C] a fact that a lot of people are talking about although they do not know if it is true *to spread rumours* ○ *to deny rumours* ○ [+ (that)] *I heard a rumour that you were leaving.*

rumour² *UK* (*US* rumor) /ˈruːmər/ *verb* **be rumoured** If a fact is rumoured, people are talking about it although they do not know if it is true. [+ (that)] *It's rumoured that the company director is about to resign.* ○ [+ to do sth] *The company is rumoured to be in financial difficulty.*

rump /rʌmp/ *noun* [C] the area above an animal's back legs

rumpled /ˈrʌmpld/ *adjective* Rumpled clothes or sheets are untidy because they have folds in them.

○▪**run**¹ /rʌn/ *verb* **running**, *past tense* **ran**, *past participle* **run 1** [MOVE FAST] [I, T] to move on your feet at a faster speed than walking *He ran away when I tried to pick him up.* ○ [+ to do sth] *We had to run to catch up with him.* ○ *I run about three miles every morning.* **2** [ORGANIZE] [T] to organize or control something *She ran her own restaurant for five years.* **3 run sb/sth to/down, etc** to take someone or something somewhere, usually by car *Could you run me to the station this afternoon?* **4** [WORKING] [I, T] If a piece of equipment is running, it is switched on and working, and if you run it, you switch it on and make it work. *The engine is running more smoothly now.* **5** [USE COMPUTER] [T] If you run a computer program, you use it on your computer. *Did you run a virus check this morning?* **6** [TRAVELLING] [I] If trains or buses are running, they are available to travel on. *The buses only run until 11 p.m.* **7** [LIQUID] [I] If liquid runs somewhere, it flows. *Tears ran down her face.* **8** [PUBLISH] [T] to publish something in a newspaper or magazine *All the papers are running this story on the front page.* **9 run a bath** *UK* to fill a bath with water so that it is ready to use **10 run sth along/over/through, etc sth** to move something along, over, or through something else *She ran her fingers through her hair.* **11 run through/down/along, etc** If something long and narrow runs somewhere, it is in that position. *There are wires running across the floor.* **12** [CONTINUE] [I] If a play, film, etc runs for a period of time, it continues that long. **13 run in sb's/the family** If a quality, ability, disease, etc runs in the family, many members of the family have it. *A love of animals runs in our family.* **14** [COLOUR] [I] If a colour runs, it comes out of some material when it is washed. **15 be running at sth** to be at a particular level *Inflation is now running at 5.8%.* ⊃See also: cast/run your/an **eye**¹ over sth, run the **gauntlet**, run **riot**¹, run out of **steam**¹, run **wild**¹.

run across sb to meet someone you know when you are not expecting to *I ran across Jim* *in town the other day.*

run after sb/sth to chase someone or something that is moving away from you

run around to be very busy doing a lot of different things *I'm exhausted, I've been running around all morning.*

run away to secretly leave a place because you are unhappy there *to **run away from home***

run sth by sb to tell someone about something so that they can give their opinion about it *Can I run something by you, Sam?*

run sb/sth down *informal* to criticize someone or something, often unfairly

run for sth to compete in an election *He's running for mayor again this year.*

run into sb to meet someone you know when you are not expecting to *I ran into Emma on my way home.*

run into sth 1 HIT to hit something while you are driving a vehicle *He skidded and ran into a tree.* **2** REACH A LEVEL If an amount runs into thousands, millions, etc, it reaches that level. **3** PROBLEMS If you run into difficulties, you begin to experience them. *to run into trouble*

run off *informal* to leave somewhere unexpectedly *He ran off with all my money.*

run on sth If a machine runs on a supply of power, it uses that power to work. *The scanner runs on mains electricity and batteries.*

run out 1 to use all of something so that there is none left *I've nearly **run out of** money.* **2** If a supply of something runs out, there is none left because it has all been used. *Come on, time is running out.*

run sb/sth over to hit someone or something with a vehicle and drive over them, injuring or killing them *He was run over by a bus as he crossed the road.*

run through sth to repeat something in order to practise it or to make sure that it is correct *I just need to run through my speech one more time.*

run sth up If you run up a debt, you do things which cause you to owe a large amount of money.

run up against sth If you run up against problems or difficulties, you begin to experience them.

o⇥**run²** /rʌn/ *noun* **1** MOVING [C] when you move on your feet at a speed faster than walking as a sport [usually singular] *to go for a run* **2** SCORING [C] in cricket or baseball, a single point to score *a run* **3** a **dummy/practice/trial run** when you do something to practise it before the real time **4** a **run of sth** when something happens several times without something different happening during that period *a run of 10 games without a win* ○ *a **run of good/bad luck* **5** PERFORMANCES [C] a period of performances of a play, film, etc **6** be on the run to be trying to avoid being caught, especially by the police **7** make a run for it *informal* to suddenly run fast in order to escape from somewhere **8** in the long/short run at a time that is far away or near in the future

runaway¹ /ˈrʌnəˌweɪ/ *adjective* [always before

noun] 1 a **runaway success/victory/winner, etc** something good that happens very quickly or easily **2** A runaway vehicle is moving away from somewhere without anyone controlling it. *a runaway car/train*

runaway² /ˈrʌnəˌweɪ/ *noun* [C] someone who has secretly left a place because they are unhappy there *teenage runaways*

run-down /ˌrʌnˈdaʊn/ *adjective* Run-down buildings or areas are in very bad condition. *a run-down housing estate*

rundown /ˈrʌndaʊn/ *noun* [no plural] a report of the main facts relating to a subject *He **gave** us a **rundown on** what happened at the meeting.*

rung¹ /rʌŋ/ *noun* **1** [C] one of the horizontal parts of a ladder (= structure for climbing up) **2** the **first/highest/next, etc rung of the ladder** the first, highest, next, etc position, especially in society or in a job *She's on the bottom rung of the management ladder.*

rung² /rʌŋ/ *past participle of* ring²

run-in /ˈrʌnɪn/ *noun* [C] *informal* an argument *to have a run-in with someone*

runner /ˈrʌnəʳ/ *noun* **1** [C] someone who runs, usually in competitions *a long-distance runner* **2** **drug/gun runner** someone who takes drugs or guns illegally from one place to another ⊃See also: front-runner.

ˌ**runner ˈbean** UK (US ˈrunner ˌbean) *noun* [C] a long, flat, green bean

runner-up /ˌrʌnərˈʌp/ *noun* [C] *plural* **runners-up** someone who finishes in second position in a competition

running¹ /ˈrʌnɪŋ/ *noun* [U] **1** the sport of moving on your feet at a speed faster than walking *I go running three times a week.* ○ *running shoes* ⊃See colour picture **Sports 1** on page Centre 14. **2** the activity of controlling or looking after something *He has recently handed over the **day-to-day running** of the museum to his daughter.* ○ *running costs*

running² /ˈrʌnɪŋ/ *adjective* **1** [always before noun] continuing for a long time *a running battle* ○ *a running joke* **2** **second/third, etc day/week, etc running** If something happens for the second/third, etc day/week, etc running, it happens on that number of regular occasions without changing. *He's won the Championship for the fifth year running.* **3** **running water** If a place has running water, it has a working water system.

runny /ˈrʌni/ *adjective* **1** A runny substance is more liquid than usual. *runny egg* **2** **runny nose** If you have a runny nose, your nose is producing liquid all the time.

run-of-the-mill /ˌrʌnəvðəˈmɪl/ *adjective* ordinary and not special or exciting in any way *He gave a fairly run-of-the-mill speech.*

run-up /ˈrʌnʌp/ *noun* the **run-up to sth** UK the period of time before an event *Sales increased by 15% in the run-up to Christmas.*

runway /ˈrʌnweɪ/ *noun* [C] a large road that aircraft use to land on or to start flying from

rupture /ˈrʌptʃəʳ/ *verb* [I, T] If you rupture something, you break or tear it, and if something ruptures, it breaks or tears. *He fell and rup-*

R

tured a ligament in his knee. ● **rupture** *noun* [C]

rural /'ruərəl/ *adjective* relating to the countryside and not to towns *a rural area*

ruse /ruːz/ *noun* [C] a way of deceiving someone so that they do something that you want them to do [+ to do sth] *The story was just a ruse to get her out of the house.*

o➤**rush¹** /rʌʃ/ *verb* **1** [I, T] to hurry or move quickly somewhere, or to make someone or something hurry or move quickly somewhere *We rushed out into the street to see what all the noise was.* ○ *The UN has rushed medical supplies to the war zone.* ○ [+ to do sth] *We had to rush to catch the bus.* **2** rush to do sth to do something quickly and enthusiastically *His friends rushed to congratulate him after the ceremony.* **3** [T] to make someone do something more quickly than they want to do it [+ into + doing sth] *I refuse to be rushed into making a decision.*

WORD PARTNERS FOR **rush**

2 a **frantic/headlong/last-minute/mad** rush ● a rush **for** sth

rush² /rʌʃ/ *noun* [no plural] **1** MOVEMENT when something suddenly moves somewhere quickly *a rush of air* **2** ACTIVITY a lot of things happening or a lot of people trying to do something [+ to do sth] *There was a mad rush to get tickets for the concert.* **3** HURRY when you have to hurry or move somewhere quickly *I'm sorry I can't talk now, I'm in a rush.*

rushes /rʌʃɪz/ *noun* [plural] tall plants that grow near water

rush ‚hour *noun* [C, U] the time when a lot of people are travelling to or from work and so roads and trains are very busy *the morning/evening rush hour*

rust /rʌst/ *noun* [U] a dark orange substance that you get on metal when it has been damaged by air and water ● **rust** *verb* [I, T]

rustic /'rʌstɪk/ *adjective* simple and old-fashioned in style in a way that is typical of the countryside

rustle /'rʌsl/ *verb* [I, T] If things such as paper or leaves rustle, or if you rustle them, they move about and make a soft, dry sound. *Outside, the trees rustled in the wind.*

rustle up sth to produce something very quickly *I managed to rustle up a meal from the bits and pieces I found in his fridge.*

rusty /'rʌsti/ *adjective* **1** Rusty metal has rust (= an orange substance) on its surface. *rusty nails* **2** If a skill you had is now rusty, it is not now good because you have forgotten it. *My French is a bit rusty.*

rut /rʌt/ *noun* **1** in a rut in a bad situation where you do the same things all the time, or where it is impossible to make progress *He seems to be stuck in a rut at the moment.* **2** [C] a deep, narrow mark in the ground made by a wheel

ruthless /'ruːθləs/ *adjective* not caring if you hurt or upset other people when you try to get what you want *ruthless ambition* ○ *a ruthless dictator* ● **ruthlessly** *adverb* ● **ruthlessness** *noun* [U]

rye /raɪ/ *noun* [U] a plant that has grains which are used to make things such as bread and whisky (= strong alcoholic drink) *rye bread*

R

Ss

S, s /es/ the nineteenth letter of the alphabet

the Sabbath /ˈsæbəθ/ *noun* a day of the week that many religious groups use for prayer and rest

sabbatical /səˈbætɪkᵊl/ *noun* [C, U] a period when a university teacher does not do their usual work and instead travels or studies *He was* ***on sabbatical*** *last year.*

sabotage /ˈsæbətɑːʒ/ *verb* [T] **1** to damage or destroy something in order to prevent an enemy from using it *Rebels sabotaged the roads and bridges.* **2** to spoil someone's plans or efforts in order to prevent them from being successful *She tried to sabotage my chances of getting the job.* • **sabotage** *noun* [U] *an act of sabotage*

saccharin /ˈsækərɪn/ *noun* [U] a sweet, chemical substance that is used in food instead of sugar

sachet /ˈsæʃeɪ/ [US] /sæˈʃeɪ/ *noun* [C] a small bag containing a small amount of something *sachets of sugar and coffee powder*

sack¹ /sæk/ *noun* **1** [C] a large bag made of paper, plastic, or cloth and used to carry or store things **2 the sack** *UK* When someone gets the sack or is given the sack, they are told to leave their job. *He got the sack from his last job.*

sack

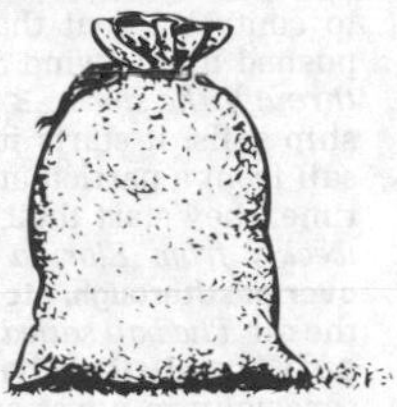

sack² /sæk/ *verb* [T] *UK* to tell someone to leave their job, usually because they have done something wrong *He was sacked for being late.*

sacrament /ˈsækrəmənt/ *noun* [C] an important religious ceremony in the Christian Church *the sacrament of marriage*

sacred /ˈseɪkrɪd/ *adjective* **1** relating to a religion or considered to be holy *sacred music* ○ *a sacred object* **2** too important to be changed or destroyed *I don't work at weekends - my private time is sacred.*

WORD PARTNERS FOR *sacrifice*

make (great/huge) sacrifices • sacrifices **for** sb/sth • the sacrifice **of** sth

sacrifice¹ /ˈsækrɪfaɪs/ *noun* [C, U] **1** something valuable that you give up in order to achieve something, or the act of giving it up *Sometimes you have to* ***make sacrifices*** *to succeed.* **2** something offered to a god in a religious ceremony, especially an animal that is killed, or the act of offering it ⊃See also: **self-sacrifice**.

sacrifice² /ˈsækrɪfaɪs/ *verb* [T] **1** to give up something that is valuable to you in order to achieve something *There are thousands of men ready to* ***sacrifice*** *their lives* ***for*** *their country.* **2** to kill an animal and offer it to a god in a religious ceremony

sacrilege /ˈsækrɪlɪdʒ/ *noun* [U, no plural] when you treat something that is holy or important without respect

sacrosanct /ˈsækrəʊsæŋkt/ *adjective formal* too important to be changed or destroyed *Human life is sacrosanct.*

OTHER WAYS OF SAYING *sad*

Unhappy and **miserable** mean the same as 'sad': *She'd had a very* ***unhappy*** *childhood.* • *I just woke up feeling* ***miserable***.

If someone is **upset**, they are unhappy because something bad has happened: *They'd had an argument and she was still* ***upset*** *about it.* • *Mike got very* ***upset*** *when I told him the news.*

If someone is **broken-hearted** or **heartbroken** they are very sad because someone they love has ended a relationship with them: *She was* ***broken-hearted*** *when Richard left.*

If someone is **devastated** or **distraught**, they are extremely upset: *She was* ***devastated*** *when he died.* • *The missing child's* ***distraught*** *parents made an emotional appeal for information on TV.*

The adjective **depressed** is often used when someone is very unhappy for a long time: *She became deeply* ***depressed*** *after her husband died.*

⊶**sad** /sæd/ *adjective* **sadder, saddest 1** [NOT HAPPY] unhappy or making you feel unhappy *I was very sad when our cat died.* ○ *a sad book/movie* ○ [+ that] *It's a bit sad that you'll miss our wedding.* ○ [+ to do sth] *I was sad to see him go.* **2** [NOT SATISFACTORY] [always before noun] not pleasant or satisfactory *The sad truth is that we've failed.* **3** [NOT FASHIONABLE] *UK informal* boring or not fashionable *You enjoy reading timetables? You sad man!* • **sadness** *noun* [U]

sadden /ˈsædᵊn/ *verb* [T] *formal* to make someone feel sad or disappointed [often passive] *We were saddened by his death.*

saddle¹ /ˈsædl/ *noun* [C] **1** a leather seat that you put on a horse so that you can ride it ⊃See colour picture **Sports 1** on page Centre 14. **2** a seat on a bicycle or motorcycle

saddle

saddle² /ˈsædl/ (*also* **saddle up**) *verb* [I, T] to put a saddle on a horse

saddle sb with sth to give someone a job or problem which will cause them a lot of work or difficulty

saddo /ˈsædəʊ/ *noun* [C] *UK informal* someone, especially a man, who is boring and not fashionable and has no friends

sadistic /səˈdɪstɪk/ *adjective* getting pleasure from being cruel or violent *sadistic behaviour* ○ *a sadistic murderer* • **sadist** /ˈseɪdɪst/ *noun* [C] someone who gets pleasure from being cruel or violent • **sadism** /ˈseɪdɪzᵊm/ *noun* [U]

sadly /ˈsædli/ *adverb* **1** [NOT HAPPY] in a sad way

S

She shook her head sadly. **2** NOT SATISFACTORY in a way that is not satisfactory *Enthusiasm has been **sadly lacking** these past few months at work.* **3** SORRY used to say that you are sorry something is true *Sadly, the marriage did not last.*

sae, SAE /ˌeseɪˈiː/ *noun* [C] *UK abbreviation for* stamped addressed envelope or self-addressed envelope: an envelope that you put a stamp and your own address on and send to someone so that they can send you something back

safari /səˈfɑːri/ *noun* [C, U] a journey, usually to Africa, to see or hunt wild animals *She is **on safari** in Kenya.*

⊶**safe¹** /seɪf/ *adjective* **1** NOT DANGEROUS not dangerous or likely to cause harm *a safe driver* ○ *Air travel is generally quite safe.* ○ *We live in a safe neighbourhood.* ○ [+ to do sth] *Is it safe to drink the water here?* ⊃Opposite **unsafe**. **2** NOT HARMED not harmed or damaged *She returned **safe and sound** (= not harmed in any way).* **3** NOT IN DANGER not in danger or likely to be harmed *During the daylight hours we're **safe from** attack.* **4** **safe to say** If it is safe to say something, you are sure it is correct. *I think it's safe to say that he'll be the next president.* **5** **a safe place; somewhere safe** a place where something will not be lost or stolen *It's very valuable so put it somewhere safe.* **6** **play (it) safe** *informal* to be careful and not take risks ● **safely** *adverb Make sure you drive safely.* ○ *I can safely say* (= I am certain) *I have never met anyone as rude as him.* ⊃See also: a safe **bet²**.

safe² /seɪf/ *noun* [C] a strong metal box or cupboard with locks where you keep money, jewellery, and other valuable things

safeguard¹ /ˈseɪfgɑːd/ *verb* [T] to protect something from harm *a plan to safeguard public health*
safeguard against sth to do things that you hope will stop something unpleasant from happening *A good diet will safeguard against disease.*

safeguard² /ˈseɪfgɑːd/ *noun* [C] a law, rule, or system that protects people or things from being harmed or lost

safe ˈhaven *noun* [C] a place where someone is safe from danger

safe ˈsex *noun* [U] when people have sex using a condom (= a thin rubber covering that a man wears on his penis) so that they do not catch a disease

╔══ WORD PARTNERS FOR **safety**

ensure/guarantee sb's safety ● safety is paramount

⊶**safety** /ˈseɪfti/ *noun* [U] **1** when you are safe *food/road safety* ○ *The hostages were led to safety* (= to a safe place). ○ *a safety valve* **2** how safe something is *Safety at the factory has been improved.* ⊃See Common learner error at **security**.

ˈsafety ˌbelt *noun* [C] a piece of equipment that keeps you fastened to your seat when you are travelling in a vehicle *Please **fasten your safety belt** for take-off.*

ˈsafety ˌnet *noun* [C] **1** a plan or system that

will help you if you get into a difficult situation *Legal aid provides a safety net for people who can't afford a lawyer.* **2** a net that will catch someone if they fall from a high place

ˈsafety ˌpin *noun* [C] a pin with a round cover that fits over the sharp end

saffron /ˈsæfrən/ *noun* [U] a yellow powder that is used as a spice

sag /sæg/ *verb* [I] **sagging** *past* **sagged** **1** to sink or bend down *Our mattress sags in the middle.* **2** *informal* to become weaker or less successful *a sagging economy*

saga /ˈsɑːgə/ *noun* [C] a long story about a lot of people or events

sagacious /səˈgeɪʃəs/ *adjective literary* having or showing understanding and the ability to make good decisions and judgments

sage /seɪdʒ/ *noun* **1** [U] a herb whose leaves are used to give flavour to food **2** [C] *literary* a wise person

Sagittarius /ˌsædʒɪˈteəriəs/ *noun* [C, U] the sign of the zodiac which relates to the period of 22 November - 22 December, or a person born during this period ⊃See picture at **zodiac**.

said /sed/ *past of* say

sail¹ /seɪl/ *verb* **1** TRAVEL [I] to travel in a boat or a ship *We sailed to Malta.* **2** CONTROL BOAT [I, T] to control a boat that has no engine and is pushed by the wind *She sailed the small boat through the storm.* **3** START JOURNEY [I] When a ship sails, it starts its journey, and if people sail from a particular place or at a particular time, they start their journey. *This ship sails weekly from Florida to the Bahamas.* **4** **sail over/past/through, etc** to move quickly through the air *The ball sailed past me.*
sail through (sth) to succeed very easily, especially in a test or competition *She sailed through her exams.*

sail² /seɪl/ *noun* **1** [C] a large piece of material that is fixed to a pole on a boat to catch the wind and make the boat move **2** **set sail** to start a journey by boat or ship

sailboat /ˈseɪlbəʊt/ *noun* [C] *US* a small boat with sails

sailing /ˈseɪlɪŋ/ *noun* **1** [U] a sport using boats with sails *(UK) a sailing boat* **2** **be plain sailing** to be very easy

sailor /ˈseɪləʳ/ *noun* [C] someone who sails ships or boats as their job or as a sport

saint /seɪnt/ *noun* [C] **1** a dead person who has been officially respected by the Christian church for living their life in a holy way *Catherine of Siena was **made a saint** in 1461.* **2** a very kind or helpful person ⊃See also: **patron saint**.

saintly /ˈseɪntli/ *adjective* very good and kind

sake /seɪk/ *noun* **1** **for the sake of sth** for this reason or purpose *For the sake of convenience, they combined the two departments.* **2** **for the sake of sb** in order to help or please someone *He begged her to stay for the sake of the children.* **3** **for God's/goodness/heaven's, etc sake** something you say when you are angry about something *For heaven's sake, stop moaning!*

⊶**salad** /ˈsæləd/ *noun* [C, U] a cold mixture of vegetables that have not been cooked, usually eaten with meat, cheese, etc *I made a big salad for lunch.* ➲See colour picture **Food** on page Centre 11.

salad

salami /səˈlɑːmi/ *noun* [C, U] a spicy sausage (= tube of meat and spices) that is usually eaten cold in slices

salaried /ˈsælᵊrid/ *adjective* receiving a fixed amount of money from your employer, usually every month

WORD PARTNERS FOR ***salary***

earn a salary • a **good/high/top** salary • an **annual** salary • a salary **cut/increase/rise**

⊶**salary** /ˈsælᵊri/ *noun* [C, U] a fixed amount of money that you receive from your employer, usually every month ➲See Common learner error at **pay**.

⊶**sale** /seɪl/ *noun* **1** [SELLING THINGS] [U, no plural] the act of selling something, or the time when something is sold *The sale of alcohol is now banned.* ○ *to **make a sale*** **2 (up) for sale** available to buy *For sale: ladies bicycle - good condition.* ○ *The house next to mine is up for sale.* **3 on sale a** [AVAILABLE] *UK* available to buy in a shop *The video and book are now on sale.* **b** [CHEAP] available for a lower price than usual *This album was on sale for half price.* **4** [EVENT] [C] an event where things are sold *a sale of used books* **5** [CHEAP PRICE] [C] a time when a shop sells goods at a lower price than usual *UK I bought this dress **in the sale**.* ➲See also: **car boot sale, jumble sale**.

saleable /ˈseɪləbl/ *adjective* Something that is saleable can be sold easily. *He's painted some very saleable landscapes.*

sales /seɪlz/ *noun* [plural] **1** the number of items sold *Our sales have doubled this year.* **2** the part of a company that deals with selling things *I used to work **in sales**.* ○ ***a sales department***

ˈ**sales asˌsistant** (*also US* ˈ**sales ˌclerk**) *noun* [C] someone whose job is selling things in a shop

salesman, saleswoman /ˈseɪlzmən, ˈseɪlzˌwʊmən/ *noun* [C] *plural* **salesmen** or **saleswomen** someone whose job is selling things

salesperson /ˈseɪlzˌpɜːsᵊn/ *noun* [C] *plural* **salespeople** someone whose job is selling things

ˈ**sales ˌrep** (*formal* **sales representative**) *noun* [C] someone who travels to different places trying to persuade people to buy their company's products or services

salient /ˈseɪliənt/ *adjective formal* The salient facts about something or qualities of something are the most important things about them.

saline /ˈseɪlaɪn/ [US] /ˈseɪliːn/ *adjective formal* containing salt *saline solution*

saliva /səˈlaɪvə/ *noun* [U] the liquid that is made in your mouth

sallow /ˈsæləʊ/ *adjective* Sallow skin is slightly yellow and does not look healthy.

salmon /ˈsæmən/ *noun* [C, U] *plural* **salmon** a large, silver fish, or the pink meat of this fish *fresh/smoked salmon*

salmonella /ˌsælməˈnelə/ *noun* [U] a type of bacteria which can make you very ill, sometimes found in food that is not cooked enough

salon /ˈsælɒn/ *noun* [C] a shop where you can have your hair cut or have your appearance improved *a **hair salon*** ➲See also: **beauty salon**.

saloon /səˈluːn/ *noun* [C] **1** *UK* (*US* **sedan**) a large car with a separate, closed area for bags **2** *US old-fashioned* a public bar

salsa /ˈsælsə/ *noun* [U] **1** a cold, spicy sauce **2** a type of dance and music from Latin America *a salsa club*

⊶**salt¹** /sɔːlt/, /sɒlt/ *noun* [U] **1** a white substance used to add flavour to food *salt and pepper* **2 take sth with a pinch of salt** *UK* (*US* **take sth with a grain of salt**) to not completely believe something that someone tells you

salt² /sɔːlt/, /sɒlt/ *verb* [T] to add salt to food

ˈ**salt ˌcellar** *UK* (*US* ˈ**salt ˌshaker**) *noun* [C] a small container with holes in for shaking salt on food

saltwater /ˈsɔːltˌwɔːtəʳ/ *adjective* [always before noun] living in or containing water that has salt in it *a saltwater fish*

salty /ˈsɔːlti/ *adjective* tasting of or containing salt *Is the soup too salty?*

salute¹ /səˈluːt/ *noun* [C] a sign of respect to someone of a higher rank in a military organization, often made by raising the right hand to the side of the head *to **give a salute***

salute² /səˈluːt/ *verb* [I, T] to give a salute to someone of a higher rank in a military organization

salvage¹ /ˈsælvɪdʒ/ *verb* [T] **1** to save things from a place where other things have been damaged or lost *gold coins salvaged from a shipwreck* **2** to try to make a bad situation better *an attempt to salvage her reputation*

salvage² /ˈsælvɪdʒ/ *noun* [U] when things are saved from being damaged, or the things that are saved *a salvage company*

salvation /sælˈveɪʃᵊn/ *noun* [U] **1** in the Christian religion, when God saves someone from the bad effects of evil **2** something or someone that saves you from harm or a very unpleasant situation *Getting a dog was Dad's salvation after Mum died.*

salwar kameez /ˌsælwɑːkəmiːz/ (*also* **shalwar kameez**) *noun* [C] a type of suit, worn especially by women in India, with loose trousers and a long shirt ➲See colour picture **Clothes** on page Centre 8.

⊶**same¹** /seɪm/ *adjective, pronoun* **1 the same a** exactly alike *He's **the same** age **as** me.* ○ *We work at the same speed.* ○ *Cars cost **the same** here **as** they do in Europe.* **b** not another different thing or situation *They met at the same place every week.* ○ *You meet the same people at all these events.* **c** not changed *She's the same lively person she's always been.* ○ *He looks exactly **the same as** he did ten years ago.* **2 all/**

just the same despite what has just been said *He doesn't earn much. All the same, he ought to pay for some of his own drinks.* **3 Same here.** *informal* something that you say when something another person has said is also true for you *"I think she's awful." "Same here."* **4 the same old arguments/faces/story, etc** *informal* something or someone you have seen or heard many times before **5 same old same old** *informal* used to say that a situation or someone's behaviour remains the same, especially when it it boring or annoying *Most people just keep on doing the same old same old every day.* ⊃See also: be in the same **boat**, in the same **vein**, be on the same **wavelength**.

o▪**same²** /seɪm/ *adverb* **the same** in the same way *We treat all our children the same.*

sample¹ /'sɑːmpl/ *noun* [C] **1** SHOW a small amount of something that shows you what it is like *a free sample of chocolate* ○ *She brought in some samples of her work.* **2** EXAMINE a small amount of a substance that a doctor or scientist collects in order to examine it *a blood/urine sample* **3** NUMBER a small number of people from a larger group that is being tested *a sample of 500 male drivers*

sample² /'sɑːmpl/ *verb* [T] **1** to taste a small amount of food or drink to decide if you like it *We sampled eight different cheeses.* **2** to experience a place or an activity, often for the first time *an opportunity to sample the local night life*

sanatorium (*also US* sanitarium) /ˌsænə'tɔːriəm/ *noun* [C] *plural* sanatoriums *or* sanatoria a hospital where people go to rest and get well after a long illness

sanction¹ /'sæŋkʃən/ *noun* **1** [C] a punishment for not obeying a rule or a law *economic/trade sanctions against a country* **2** [U] official approval or permission

sanction² /'sæŋkʃən/ *verb* [T] to formally approve of something *He refused to sanction the publication of his private letters.*

sanctity /'sæŋktəti/ *noun formal* **the sanctity of life/marriage, etc** when something is very important and deserves respect

sanctuary /'sæŋktʃʊəri/ *noun* **1** QUIET [C, U] a quiet and peaceful place *After a busy day, I like to escape to the sanctuary of my garden.* **2** PROTECTION [C, U] a place that provides protection *to seek sanctuary* **3** ANIMALS [C] a place where animals are protected and cannot be hunted *a bird/wildlife sanctuary*

o▪**sand¹** /sænd/ *noun* [U] a substance that is found on beaches and in deserts, which is made from very small grains of rock *a grain of sand*

sand² /sænd/ *verb* [T] to make wood smooth by rubbing it with sandpaper (= strong paper with a rough surface)

sandal /'sændᵊl/ *noun* [C] a light shoe with straps that you wear in warm weather ⊃See colour picture **Clothes** on page Centre 9.

sandcastle /'sænd,kɑːsl/ *noun* [C] a model of a castle made of wet sand, usually built by children on a beach

'**sand ,dune** *noun* [C] a hill of sand in the desert or on the coast

sandpaper /'sænd,peɪpəʳ/ *noun* [U] strong paper with a rough surface that is rubbed against wood to make it smooth

sands /sændz/ *noun* [plural] a large area of sand

sandstone /'sændstəʊn/ *noun* [U] rock made of sand

o▪**sandwich¹** **sandwich**
/'sænwɪdʒ/ *noun* [C]
two slices of bread
with meat, cheese,
etc between them *a
cheese/tuna sandwich* ⊃See colour picture **Food** on page Centre 11.

sandwich²
/'sænwɪdʒ/ *verb*
be sandwiched between sth/sb *informal* to be in a small space between two people or things *Andorra is a small country sandwiched between Spain and France.*

sandy /'sændi/ *adjective* covered with or containing sand *a sandy beach*

sane /seɪn/ *adjective* **1** not suffering from mental illness **2** [always before noun] showing good judgment *a sane attitude/decision* ⊃Opposite **insane.**

sang /sæŋ/ *past tense of* sing

sanguine /'sæŋgwɪn/ *adjective formal* positive and full of hope *The director is sanguine about the company's prospects.*

sanitarium /ˌsænɪ'teəriəm/ *noun* [C] *plural* sanitariums *or* sanitaria *another US spelling of* sanatorium (= a hospital where people rest and get well after a long illness)

sanitary /'sænɪtᵊri/ *adjective* relating to preventing disease by removing dirt and waste *sanitary conditions*

'**sanitary ,towel** *UK* (*US* ,sanitary 'napkin) *noun* [C] a thick piece of soft paper that a woman wears to absorb blood from her period (= monthly blood from the uterus)

sanitation /ˌsænɪ'teɪʃᵊn/ *noun* [U] a system for protecting people's health by removing dirt and waste

sanity /'sænəti/ *noun* [U] **1** the quality of behaving calmly and showing good judgment *Jogging helps me keep my sanity.* **2** when you have a healthy mind and are not mentally ill ⊃Opposite **insanity.**

sank /sæŋk/ *past tense of* sink

Santa /'sæntə/ (*also* Santa Claus /'sæntəklɔːz/) *noun* [no plural] a kind, fat, old man in red clothes who people say brings presents to children at Christmas

sap¹ /sæp/ *verb* [T] sapping *past* sapped to gradually make something weak *Ten years of war* *had **sapped** the country's **strength**.*

sap² /sæp/ *noun* [U] the liquid inside plants and trees

sapling /'sæplɪŋ/ *noun* [C] a young tree

sapphire /'sæfaɪə'/ *noun* [C] a bright blue, transparent stone

sarcasm /'sɑːkæzᵊm/ *noun* [U] when you say the opposite of what you mean to insult someone or show them that you are annoyed *"Oh, I am sorry," she said, her voice heavy with sarcasm.*

sarcastic /sɑː'kæstɪk/ *adjective* using sarcasm *a sarcastic comment/remark* ○ *Are you being sarcastic?* • **sarcastically** *adverb*

sardine /sɑː'diːn/ *noun* [C] a small sea fish that you can eat

sari /'sɑːri/ (*also* **saree**) *noun* [C] a dress, worn especially by women from India and Pakistan, made from a very long piece of thin cloth

SARS /sɑːz/ *noun* [U] *abbreviation for* Severe Acute Respiratory Syndrome: a serious disease that makes it difficult to breathe

SASE /ˌeseɪes'iː/ *noun* [C] *US abbreviation for* self-addressed stamped envelope: an envelope that you put a stamp and your own address on and send to someone so that they can send you something back

sash /sæʃ/ *noun* [C] a long, narrow piece of cloth that is worn around the waist or over the shoulder, often as part of a uniform

sassy /'sæsi/ *adjective* US *informal* 1 very energetic and confident *a smart, sassy young woman* 2 slightly rude, but not offensive *a sassy remark*

sat /sæt/ *past of* sit

Sat *written abbreviation for* Saturday

Satan /'seɪtᵊn/ *noun* [no plural] the Devil (= the enemy of God)

satanic /sə'tænɪk/ *adjective* relating to the Devil (= the enemy of God) *a satanic cult/ritual*

satchel /'sætʃᵊl/ *noun* [C] a large bag with a strap that goes over your shoulder, often used for carrying school books ⊃See colour picture **The Classroom** on page Centre 6.

satellite /'sætᵊlaɪt/ *noun* [C] 1 a piece of equipment that is sent into space around the Earth to receive and send signals or to collect information *a spy/weather satellite* 2 a natural object that moves around a planet in space *The moon is the Earth's satellite.*

'satellite ˌdish *noun* [C] a round piece of equipment that receives television and radio signals broadcast from satellites

ˌsatellite 'television (*also* ˌsatellite T'V) *noun* [U] television programmes that are broadcast using a satellite

satin /'sætɪn/ *noun* [U] a smooth, shiny cloth

satire /'sætaɪə'/ *noun* 1 [U] when you use jokes and humour to criticize people or ideas *political satire* 2 [C] a story, film, etc that uses satire • **satirist** /'sætᵊrɪst/ *noun* [C] someone who uses satire

satirical /sə'tɪrɪkᵊl/ *adjective* using satire *a satirical magazine/novel*

satisfaction /ˌsætɪs'fækʃᵊn/ *noun* [U] 1 the pleasant feeling you have when you get something that you wanted or do something that you wanted to do *job satisfaction* ○ *She smiled with satisfaction.* ○ [+ of + doing sth] *I had the satisfaction of knowing that I'd done everything I could.* 2 **to sb's satisfaction** as well as someone wants *He won't get paid until he completes the job to my satisfaction.* ⊃Opposite **dissatisfaction**.

satisfactory /ˌsætɪs'fæktᵊri/ *adjective* good enough *We hope very much to find a satisfactory solution to the problem.* ⊃Opposite **unsatisfactory**. • **satisfactorily** *adverb*

satisfied /'sætɪsfaɪd/ *adjective* 1 pleased because you have got what you wanted, or because something has happened in the way that you wanted *Are you satisfied with the new arrangement?* ⊃Opposite **dissatisfied**. 2 **be satisfied that** If you are satisfied that something is true, you believe it. *The judge was satisfied that she was telling the truth.* ⊃See also: self-satisfied.

satisfy /'sætɪsfaɪ/ *verb* 1 [T] to please someone by giving them what they want or need *They sell 31 flavours of ice cream - enough to satisfy everyone!* 2 **satisfy conditions/needs/requirements, etc** to have or provide something that is needed or wanted *She satisfies all the requirements for the job.* 3 **satisfy sb that** to make someone believe that something is true *I satisfied myself that I had locked the door.*

satisfying /'sætɪsfaɪɪŋ/ *adjective* making you feel pleased by providing what you need or want *a satisfying meal* ○ *My work is very satisfying.*

SATNAV /'sætnæv/ *noun* [U] *abbreviation for* satellite navigation: a system of computers and satellites (– equipment that is sent into space around the Earth to receive and send signals), used in cars and other places to tell a user where they are or where something is

saturate /'sætʃᵊreɪt/ *verb* 1 **be saturated with sth** to be filled with a lot or too much of something *The city is saturated with cheap restaurants.* 2 [T] to make something completely wet *Heavy rain had saturated the playing field.* • **saturation** /ˌsætʃᵊ'reɪʃᵊn/ *noun* [U]

ˌsaturated 'fat *noun* [C, U] a fat found in meat, milk, and eggs, which is thought to be bad for your health

o–**Saturday** /'sætədeɪ/ (*written abbreviation* Sat) *noun* [C, U] the day of the week after Friday and before Sunday

Saturn /'sætən/ *noun* [no plural] the planet that is sixth from the Sun, after Jupiter and before Uranus

o–**sauce** /sɔːs/ *noun* [C, U] a hot or cold liquid that you put on food to add flavour *pasta with tomato sauce* ⊃See also: soy sauce.

saucepan /'sɔːspən/ *noun* [C] a deep, metal pan, usually with a long handle and a lid, that is used to cook food in ➲See colour picture **The Kitchen** on page Centre 2.

saucer /'sɔːsəʳ/ noun [C] a small plate that you put under a cup and saucer

saucy /'sɔːsi/ adjective slightly rude, or referring to sex in a funny way a saucy postcard/joke

sauna /'sɔːnə/ noun [C] **1** a room that is hot and filled with steam where people sit to relax or feel healthy a gym with a pool and a sauna **2** have a sauna to spend time inside a sauna

saunter /'sɔːntəʳ/ verb **saunter into/over/through, etc** to walk in a slow and relaxed way He sauntered through the door two hours late.

sausage /'sɒsɪdʒ/ noun [C, U] a mixture of meat and spices pressed into a long tube

sausages

sauté /'səʊteɪ/ ⓤ /sɔʊ'teɪ/ verb [T] to fry food quickly in a small amount of hot oil

savage¹ /'sævɪdʒ/ adjective **1** extremely violent a savage attack **2** severe savage criticism • **savagely** adverb

savage² /'sævɪdʒ/ verb [T] **1** to attack violently [often passive] A sheep had been savaged by a dog. **2** to severely criticize someone or something [often passive] Her performance was savaged by the critics.

savage³ /'sævɪdʒ/ noun [C] old-fashioned an offensive word for a person from a country at an early stage of development

⚬**save¹** /seɪv/ verb **1** MAKE SAFE [T] to stop someone or something from being killed or destroyed He was badly injured, but the doctors saved his life. ○ She saved the children from drowning. ○ He had to borrow money to save his business. **2** MONEY [I, T] (also save up) to keep money so that you can buy something with it in the future We've saved almost $900 for our wedding. ○ Michael's saving up for a new computer. **3** KEEP [T] to keep something to use in the future I've saved some food for you. **4** save money/space/time, etc to reduce the amount of money/space/time, etc that you have to use **5** save sb (from) doing sth to help someone avoid having to do something We'll eat in a restaurant - it'll save you having to cook. **6** save files/work, etc to store work or information electronically on or from a computer **7** save a goal to prevent a player from scoring a goal He saved two goals in the last minute of the game. ➲See also: save the **day**, lose/save **face¹**.

save on sth to avoid using something so that you do not have to pay for it She walks to work to save on bus fares.

save² /seɪv/ noun [C] when someone prevents a goal from being scored in a sport The goalkeeper made a good save.

saver /'seɪvəʳ/ noun [C] someone who saves money in a bank

saving /'seɪvɪŋ/ noun [C] UK (US savings) when you pay less money than you would usually have to [usually singular] a saving of £20.

savings /'seɪvɪŋz/ noun [plural] money that you have saved, usually in a bank I spent all my savings on a new kitchen. ○ a savings account

savings and 'loan associ,ation US (UK building society) noun [C] a bank that is owned by the people who keep their money in it and that lets them borrow money to buy a house

saviour UK (US savior) /'seɪvjəʳ/ noun **1** [C] someone who saves someone or something from harm or difficulty **2 the Saviour** in Christianity, Jesus Christ

savour UK (US savor) /'seɪvəʳ/ verb [T] to enjoy food or a pleasant experience as much and as slowly as possible to savour a meal ○ I ate slowly, savouring every mouthful. ○ We savoured our moment of victory.

savoury UK (US savory) /'seɪv°ri/ adjective Savoury food is not sweet. savoury biscuits ○ Generally, I prefer savoury to sweet food.

savvy /'sævi/ noun [U] informal practical knowledge and ability business/political savvy • **savvy** adjective informal having knowledge and ability a savvy consumer

saw¹ /sɔː/ noun [C] a tool with a sharp edge that you use to cut wood or other hard material ➲See picture at **tool**. • **saw** verb [I, T] past tense sawed past participle sawn or mainly US sawed to use a saw They sawed the door in half.

saw² /sɔː/ past tense of see

sawdust /'sɔːdʌst/ noun [U] very small pieces of wood and powder that are produced when you cut wood with a saw

saxophone /'sæksəfəʊn/ noun (also sax informal) noun [C] a metal musical instrument that you play by blowing into it and pressing keys to produce different notes • **saxophonist** /sæk'sɒf°nɪst/ ⓤ /'sæksəfəʊnɪst/ noun [C] someone who plays the saxophone

⚬**say¹** /seɪ/ verb [T] says, past said **1** WORDS to speak words "I'd like to go home," she said. ○ I couldn't hear what they were saying. ○ How do you say this word? **2** TELL to tell someone about a fact, thought, or opinion [+ question word] Did she say where she was going? ○ [+ (that)] The jury said that he was guilty. **3** INFORMATION to give information in writing, numbers, or signs My watch says one o'clock. ○ What do the papers say about the election? **4** say sth to yourself to think something but not speak "I hope she likes me," he said to himself. **5** SHOW to show what you think without using words His smile seemed to say that I was forgiven. **6 (let's) say...** used to introduce a suggestion or possible example of something Say you were offered a better job in another city - would you take it? **7 You can say that again!** informal used to show that you completely agree with something that someone has just said "That was a very bad movie!" "You can say that again!" **8 it goes without saying** If something goes without saying, it is generally accepted or understood. It goes without saying that smoking is harmful to your health. ➲See also: Say **cheese!**, easier (**easy²**) said than done.

say or tell?

Say can refer to any type of speech.

"Good night," she said.

She said she was unhappy.

Jim said to meet him here.

Tell is used to report that someone has given information or an order. The verb **tell** is always followed by the person that the information or order is given to.

Simon told me about his new job.

Say is never followed by the person that the information or order is given to.

He told us to stay here.

He said us to stay here.

WORD PARTNERS FOR *say* (noun)

be **given/have** [a/no/some, etc] say • the **final** say • say **in/on** sth

say² /seɪ/ *noun* [U] **1** when you are involved in making a decision about something *We had some say in how our jobs would develop.* **2 have your say** to give your opinion about something

saying /'seɪɪŋ/ *noun* [C] a famous phrase that people use to give advice about life *Have you heard the saying, "misery loves company"?*

sb *written abbreviation for* somebody • sb's *written abbreviation for* somebody's

scab /skæb/ *noun* [C] a layer of dried blood that forms to cover a cut in the skin

scaffolding /'skæfəldɪŋ/ *noun* [U] a temporary structure made of flat boards and metal poles used to work on a tall building

scald /skɔːld/ *verb* [T] to burn something or someone with very hot liquid or steam

WORD PARTNERS FOR *scale*

on a [grand/large/massive/small, etc] scale • the scale **of** sth

scale¹ /skeɪl/ *noun* **1** SIZE [no plural] the size or level of something *We don't yet know the scale of the problem.* ○ *Nuclear weapons cause destruction on a massive scale* (= cause a lot of destruction). **2 large-/small-scale** A large-/small-scale event or activity is large/small in size. *a large-scale investigation* **3** MEASURING SYSTEM [C] the set of numbers, amounts, etc used to measure or compare the level of something *How would you rate her work on a scale of 1-10?* **4** EQUIPMENT [C] *US* (*UK* scales [plural]) a piece of equipment for measuring weight *a bathroom/kitchen scale* ⊃See colour picture **The Kitchen** on page Centre 2, **The Bathroom** on page Centre 3. **5** COMPARISON [C, U] how the size of things on a map, model, etc relates to the same things in real life *a map with a scale of one centimetre per ten kilometres* **6** MUSIC [C] a series of musical notes that is always played in order and that rises gradually from the first note **7** SKIN [C] one of the flat pieces of hard material that covers the skin of fish and snakes

scale² /skeɪl/ *verb* [T] to climb something that is high or steep *to scale a wall*

scale sth back *mainly US* (*UK/US* scale sth

down) to make something smaller than it was or smaller than it was planned to be

scales /skeɪlz/ *noun* [plural] *UK* (*US* scale [C]) a piece of equipment for measuring weight *bathroom/kitchen scales* ⊃See colour picture **The Kitchen** on page Centre 2, **The Bathroom** on page Centre 3.

scallion /'skæliən/ *US* (*UK* spring onion) *noun* [C] a small onion with a white part at the bottom and long, green leaves which is eaten in salads

scallop /'skæləp/ *noun* [C] a small sea creature that lives in a shell and is eaten as food

scalp /skælp/ *noun* [C] the skin on the top of your head under your hair

scalpel /'skælpəl/ *noun* [C] a small, sharp knife that doctors use to cut through skin during an operation

scalper /'skælpər/ *US* (*UK* tout) *noun* [C] someone who unofficially sells tickets outside theatres, sports grounds, etc

scaly /'skeɪli/ *adjective* If your skin is scaly, it is rough and falls off in small, dry pieces.

scam /skæm/ *noun* [C] *informal* an illegal plan for making money

scamper /'skæmpər/ *verb* scamper away/down/ off, etc to run quickly and with small steps, like a child or a small animal

scampi /'skæmpi/ *noun* [U] prawns (= small sea creatures) that have been fried

scan¹ /skæn/ *verb* scanning *past* scanned **1** EXAMINE [T] to examine something with a machine that can see inside an object or body *Airports use X-ray machines to scan luggage for weapons.* **2** COMPUTER [T] to use a piece of equipment that copies words or pictures from paper into a computer *to scan photos into a computer* **3** LOOK [T] to look around an area quickly to try to find a person or thing *She scanned the crowd for a familiar face.* **4** READ [T] (*also* scan through) to quickly read a piece of writing to understand the main meaning or to find a particular piece of information *I scanned the travel brochures looking for a cheap holiday.*

scan² /skæn/ *noun* [C] a medical examination in which an image of the inside of the body is made using a special machine *a brain scan*

WORD PARTNERS FOR *scandal*

a scandal **breaks/erupts** • be **at the centre of/involved in** a scandal • a scandal **surrounding** sth • a **sex** scandal

scandal /'skændəl/ *noun* [C, U] something that shocks people because they think it is morally wrong *a sex scandal*

scandalous /'skændələs/ *adjective* shocking or morally wrong *a scandalous waste of money*

Scandinavian /ˌskændɪ'neɪviən/ *adjective* from or relating to the countries of Sweden, Denmark, Norway, and sometimes Finland and Iceland • Scandinavian *noun* [C]

scanner /'skænər/ *noun* [C] **1** a piece of equipment that copies words or pictures from paper into a computer **2** a piece of medical equipment used to examine images of the inside of someone's body

scant /skænt/ *adjective* [always before noun] very

S

little and not enough *His work has received only scant attention outside this country.*

scantily /'skæntɪli/ *adverb* **scantily clad/dressed** not wearing many clothes and showing a lot of the body

scanty /'skænti/ *adjective* very small in size or quantity *scanty clothing*

scapegoat /'skeɪpɡəʊt/ *noun* [C] someone who is blamed for a bad situation, although they have not caused it *He was made a scapegoat for the disaster.*

scar /skɑːʳ/ *noun* [C] **1** a permanent mark left on the body from a cut or other injury **2** damage done to a person's mind by a very unpleasant event or situation *a psychological scar* • **scar** *verb* [T] **scarring** *past* **scarred** to cause a scar [often passive] *He was scarred for life by the accident.*

scarce /skeəs/ *adjective* rare or not available in large amounts *scarce resources*

scarcely /'skeəsli/ *adverb* **1** only just *They had scarcely finished eating when the doorbell rang.* **2 can scarcely do sth** If you say you can scarcely do something, you mean it would be wrong to do it. *He's only two - you can scarcely blame him for behaving badly.*

scarcity /'skeəsəti/ *noun* [C, U] when there is not enough of something *a scarcity of food/affordable housing*

scare¹ /skeəʳ/ *verb* [T] **1** to frighten a person or animal *Sudden, loud noises scare me.* **2 scare the hell/life/living daylights, etc out of sb** *informal* to make someone feel very frightened ⊃See also: scare/frighten sb out of their **wits**.
scare sb/sth away/off to make a person or an animal so frightened that they go away *She scared off her attacker by screaming.*
scare sb away/off to make someone worried about doing something so that they decide not to do it *The recent bomb attacks have scared away the tourists.*

scare² /skeəʳ/ *noun* [C] **1** a sudden feeling of fear or worry *The earthquake gave us a scare.* **2** a situation that worries or frightens people *a food/health scare*

scarecrow /'skeəkrəʊ/ *noun* [C] a model of a person that is put in a field to frighten birds and stop them from eating the plants

OTHER WAYS OF SAYING *scared*

The adjectives **afraid** and **frightened** are common alternatives to 'scared': *Don't be frightened. The dog won't hurt you.* • *Gerry has always been afraid of heights.*

If someone is extremely scared, then you can use the adjectives **petrified**, **terrified**, **panic-stricken**, or the informal phrase **scared to death**: *I'm petrified/terrified of spiders.* • *She was panic-stricken when her little boy disappeared.* • *He's scared to death of having the operation.*

If someone is scared because they are worrying about something, then you can use ad-

jectives like **afraid** or **worried**: *I'm afraid/worried that something will go wrong.*

o→**scared** /skeəd/ *adjective* frightened or worried *Robert's scared of heights.* ○ *I was scared to death* (= very frightened). ○ [+ (that)] *We were scared that we'd be killed.*

scarf¹ /skɑːf/ *noun* [C] *plural* **scarves** /skɑːvz/ or **scarfs** a piece of cloth that you wear around your neck, head, or shoulders to keep warm or for decoration ⊃See colour picture **Clothes** on page Centre 9.

scarf² /skɑːf/ (*also* **scarf down**) *verb* [T] *US informal* (*UK* **scoff**) to eat a lot of something quickly *Who scarfed all the cookies?*

scarlet /'skɑːlət/ *noun* [U] a bright red colour • **scarlet** *adjective*

scary /'skeəri/ *adjective informal* frightening *a scary place/woman*

scathing /'skeɪðɪŋ/ *adjective* criticizing very strongly *He was scathing about the report.*

scatter /'skætəʳ/ *verb*

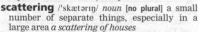

scatter

1 [T] to throw objects over an area so that they land apart from each other *He scattered some flower seeds in the garden.*
2 [I] to suddenly move apart in different directions *The crowd scattered at the sound of gunshots.*

scattered /'skætəd/ *adjective* covering a wide area *His toys were scattered all over the floor.* ○ *There will be scattered showers* (= separate areas of rain) *today.*

scattering /'skætərɪŋ/ *noun* [no plural] a small number of separate things, especially in a large area *a scattering of houses*

scavenge /'skævɪndʒ/ *verb* [I, T] to search for food or for useful things that have been thrown away • **scavenger** *noun* [C] a person or animal who scavenges

scenario /sɪˈnɑːriəʊ/ *noun* **1** [C] a description of a situation, or of a situation that may develop in the future **2 worst-case scenario** the worst situation that you can imagine

scene /siːn/ *noun* **1** PART OF FILM [C] a short part of a film, play, or book in which the events happen in one place *a love scene* ○ *the final scene* **2** VIEW [C] a view or picture of a place, event, or activity *scenes of everyday life* **3** PLACE [C] a place where an unpleasant event has happened *the scene of the crime* **4 the club/gay/music, etc scene** all the things connected with a particular way of life or activity **5** ARGUMENT [C] when people have a loud argument or show strong emotions in a public place [usually singular] *She made a scene when I told her she couldn't come with us.* **6 behind the scenes** If something happens behind the scenes, it happens secretly. *So much happens behind the scenes that we just don't know about.* **7 set the scene for sth** to make an event or situation possible or likely to happen

scenery /'si:n°ri/ *noun* [U] **1** the attractive, natural things that you see in the countryside *The Grand Canyon is famous for its spectacular scenery.* **2** the large pictures of buildings, countryside, etc used on a theatre stage

scenic /'si:nɪk/ *adjective* having views of the attractive, natural things in the countryside *a scenic route* ○ *an area of great scenic beauty*

scent /sent/ *noun* **1** [SMELL] [C] a pleasant smell *the sweet scent of orange blossoms* **2** [LIQUID] [C, U] a pleasant smelling liquid that people put on their skin *What scent are you wearing?* **3** [ANIMAL] [C, U] the smell of an animal or a person that is left somewhere

scented /'sentɪd/ *adjective* having a pleasant smell *a scented candle*

sceptic *UK* (*US* skeptic) /'skeptɪk/ *noun* [C] someone who doubts that a belief or an idea is true or useful

sceptical *UK* (*US* skeptical) /'skeptɪk°l/ *adjective* doubting that something is true or useful *Scientists remain sceptical about astrology.* ○ *She was sceptical of the new arrangement.*

scepticism *UK* (*US* skepticism) /'skeptɪsɪz°m/ *noun* [U] when you doubt that something is true or useful *There was some scepticism about her ability to do the job.*

schedule¹ /'ʃedju:l/ Ⓤ /'skedʒu:l/ *noun* **1** [C, U] a plan that gives events or activities and the times that they will happen or be done *I have a very busy schedule today.* ○ *Will the work be completed on schedule* (= at the expected time)? ○ *The project was finished ahead of schedule* (= earlier than planned). **2** [C] *mainly US* a list of times when buses, trains, etc arrive and leave *Do you have a train schedule I could look at?*

schedule² /'ʃedju:l/ Ⓤ /'skedʒu:l/ *verb* [T] to arrange that an event or an activity will happen at a particular time [often passive] *Your appointment has been scheduled for next Tuesday.* ○ *a scheduled flight*

o┅**scheme¹** /ski:m/ *noun* [C] **1** *mainly UK* an official plan or system *an insurance/savings scheme* ○ *a training scheme for teenagers* **2** a plan for making money, especially in a dishonest way *a scheme to steal money from investors*

scheme² /ski:m/ *verb* [I] to make a secret plan in order to get an advantage, usually by deceiving people *I got the feeling that they were scheming against me.*

schizophrenia /,skɪtsəʊ'fri:niə/ *noun* [U] a serious mental illness in which someone cannot understand what is real and what is imagin-

ary ● **schizophrenic** /,skɪtsəʊ'frenɪk/ *noun* [C] someone who suffers from schizophrenia

schizophrenic /,skɪtsəʊ'frenɪk/ *adjective* relating to schizophrenia *schizophrenic patients/symptoms*

schmooze /ʃmu:z/ *verb* [I, T] *informal* to talk to someone in a friendly, informal way so that they will like you or do something for you *politicians schmoozing with journalists*

scholar /'skɒlə°/ *noun* [C] someone who has studied a subject and knows a lot about it *a legal scholar*

scholarly /'skɒləli/ *adjective* **1** A scholarly article or book is a formal piece of writing by a scholar about a particular subject. **2** If someone is scholarly, they study a lot and know a lot about what they study.

scholarship /'skɒləʃɪp/ *noun* **1** [C] an amount of money given to a person by an organization to pay for their education, usually at a college or university **2** [U] when you study a subject for a long time

scholastic /skə'læstɪk/ *adjective* [always before noun] relating to school and education *scholastic achievements*

o┅**school** /sku:l/ *noun* **1** [PLACE] [C] a place where children go to be educated *Which school do you go to?* ○ *I ride my bike to school.* **2** [TIME] [U] the time that you spend at school *I like school.* ○ *We're going shopping after school.* **3** [PEOPLE] [no plural] all the students and teachers at a school *The whole school took part in the project.* **4 a dance/language/riding, etc school** a place where you can study a particular subject **5** [PART] [C] a part of a college or university *the University of Cambridge Medical School* **6** [UNIVERSITY] [C, U] *US informal* in the US, any college or university, or the time you spend there *Which schools did you apply for?* **7** [FISH] [C] a group of fish or other sea animals **8 school of thought** the ideas and beliefs shared by a group of people ⊃See also: boarding school, elementary school, grade school, grammar school, high school, junior high school, junior school, middle school, night school, nursery school, prep school, preparatory school, primary school, public school, secondary school, state school.

schoolboy /'sku:lbɔɪ/ *noun* [C] a boy who goes to school

schoolchild /'sku:ltʃaɪld/ *noun* [C] *plural* schoolchildren a child who goes to school

schooldays /'sku:ldeɪz/ *noun* [plural] *UK* the period in your life when you go to school

schoolgirl /'sku:lgɜ:l/ *noun* [C] a girl who goes to school

schooling /'sku:lɪŋ/ *noun* [U] education at school

schoolteacher /'sku:l,ti:tʃə°/ *noun* [C] someone who teaches children in a school

o┅**science** /saɪəns/ *noun* **1** [U] the study and knowledge of the structure and behaviour of natural things in an organized way **2** [C, U] a particular type of science *computer science* ○ *Chemistry, physics, and biology are all sciences.* ⊃See also: **natural sciences**, **social science**.

ᵒ⁻**science 'fiction** *noun* [U] stories about life in the future or in other parts of the universe

ᵒ⁻**scientific** /ˌsaɪənˈtɪfɪk/ *adjective* relating to science, or using the organized methods of science *scientific experiments/research* • **scientifically** *adverb a scientifically proven fact*

ᵒ⁻**scientist** /ˈsaɪəntɪst/ *noun* [C] someone who studies science or works in science

sci-fi /ˈsaɪˌfaɪ/ *noun* [U] *informal short for* science fiction

scintillating /ˈsɪntɪleɪtɪŋ/ *adjective* very interesting or exciting *a scintillating performance*

scissors /ˈsɪzəz/ *noun*   **scissors**
[plural] a tool for cutting paper, hair, cloth, etc that you hold in your hand and that has two blades that move against each other *a pair of scissors*

scoff /skɒf/ *verb* **1** [I] to laugh at someone or something, or criticize them in a way that shows you do not respect them *The critics scoffed at his work.* **2** [I, T] *UK informal* (*US* **scarf**) to eat a lot of something quickly *Who scoffed all the chocolates?*

scold /skəʊld/ *verb* [T] *old-fashioned* to speak angrily to someone because they have done something wrong

scone /skɒn, skəʊn/ *noun* [C] a small, round cake *tea and buttered scones*

scoop[1] /skuːp/ *verb* [T] to remove something from a container using a spoon, your curved hands, etc *She scooped the ice cream into the dishes.*
scoop sth/sb up to lift something or someone with your hands

scoop[2] /skuːp/ *noun* [C] **1** a large, deep spoon for lifting and moving an amount of something, or the amount that can be held in it *an ice cream scoop* ○ *a scoop of ice cream* **2** a piece of news discovered and printed by one newspaper before it appears anywhere else

scoot /skuːt/ *verb informal* **scoot along/down/ over, etc** to go somewhere quickly

scooter /ˈskuːtər/ *noun* [C] **1** a small motorcycle **2** a child's vehicle that has two wheels fixed to the ends of a long board and a long handle

scope /skəʊp/ *noun* **1** [no plural] how much a subject or situation relates to *Do we know the full scope of the problem yet?* **2** [U] the opportunity

to do something *There is plenty of scope for improvement.*

scorch /skɔːtʃ/ *verb* [T] to damage something with fire or heat

scorched /skɔːtʃt/ *adjective* slightly burnt, or damaged by fire or heat *scorched earth/fields*

scorching /ˈskɔːtʃɪŋ/ *adjective* very hot *a scorching hot day*

ᵒ⁻**score**[1] /skɔːr/ *noun* **1** [C] the number of points someone gets in a game or test *a high/low score* ○ *What's the score?* **2 scores of sth** a large number of people or things *Scores of teenage girls were waiting to get his autograph.* **3** [C] a printed piece of music **4 on that/this score** about the thing or subject which you have just discussed *The company will pay your travel expenses, so don't worry on that score.*

ᵒ⁻**score**[2] /skɔːr/ *verb* [I, T] to get points in a game or test *He scored just before half-time to put Liverpool 2-1 ahead.*

scoreboard /ˈskɔːbɔːd/ *noun* [C] a large board which shows the score of a game

scorer /ˈskɔːrər/ *noun* [C] a player who scores points in a game *Domingo was Italy's top scorer.*

scorn /skɔːn/ *noun* [U] *formal* the feeling that something is stupid and does not deserve your respect • **scorn** *verb* [T] *formal* to show scorn for someone or something *You scorned all my suggestions.*

scornful /ˈskɔːnfəl/ *adjective formal* showing that you think something is stupid and does not deserve your respect *I'm very scornful of any findings that lack proper scientific data.* • **scornfully** *adverb*

Scorpio /ˈskɔːpiəʊ/ *noun* [C, U] the sign of the zodiac which relates to the period of 23 October - 21 November, or a person born during this period ⊃See picture at **zodiac**.

scorpion /ˈskɔːpiən/ *noun* [C] a small, insect-like creature with a curved, poisonous tail

Scotch /skɒtʃ/ (*also* ˌScotch 'whisky) *noun* [C, U] a type of whisky (= strong alcoholic drink)

ˌ**Scotch 'tape** *US trademark* (*UK* **Sellotape** *trademark*) *noun* [U] clear, thin tape used for sticking things, especially paper, together ⊃See colour picture **The Classroom** on page Centre 6.

the Scots /skɒts/ *noun* [plural] the people of Scotland

Scottish /ˈskɒtɪʃ/ *adjective* relating to Scotland *Scottish history*

scour /skaʊər/ *verb* [T] **1** to search for something very carefully, often over a large area *The police scoured the surrounding countryside for possible clues.* **2** to clean something by rubbing it with something rough

scourge /skɜːdʒ/ *noun formal* **the scourge of sth** something which causes a lot of suffering or trouble *Drug-related crime is the scourge of modern society.*

scout[1] /skaʊt/ *noun* **1** [C] (*also* **Boy Scout**) a member of an organization for young people which teaches them practical skills and encourages them to be good members of society **2 the Scouts** an organization for young people which teaches them practical skills and encourages them to be good members of society **3** [C] someone whose job is to find good musicians, sports people, etc to join an organization *a talent scout*

scout² /skaʊt/ (*also* scout around) *verb* [I] to try to find something by looking in different places *I'm scouting around for somewhere to park.*

scowl /skaʊl/ *verb* [I] to look at someone angrily *He scowled at me from behind his paper.* • **scowl** *noun* [C]

scrabble /ˈskræbl/ *verb*
  scrabble about/around to use your fingers to quickly find something that you cannot see *She scrabbled around in her bag, trying to find her keys.*

scramble /ˈskræmbl/ *verb* **1 scramble down/ out/up, etc** to move or climb quickly but with difficulty, often using your hands *We scrambled up the hill.* **2** [I] to compete with other people for something which there is very little of [+ to do sth] *New teachers scramble to get jobs in the best schools.* • **scramble** *noun* [no plural] *There was a mad scramble for places near the front.*

scrambled 'eggs *noun* [plural] eggs which are mixed together and then cooked

scrap¹ /skræp/ *noun* **1** SMALL PIECE [C] a small piece or amount of something *He wrote his phone number on a scrap of paper.* ○ *I've read every scrap of information I can find on the subject.* **2** OLD [U] old cars and machines that are not now needed but have parts which can be used to make other things *scrap metal* ○ *The car was so badly damaged we could only sell it as scrap.* **3** FIGHT [C] *informal* a fight or an argument, usually not very serious *He was always getting into scraps at school.*

scrap² /skræp/ *verb* [T] scrapping, *past* scrapped **1** *informal* to not continue with a plan or idea *That project has now been scrapped.* **2** to get rid of something which you do not now want

scrapbook /ˈskræpbʊk/ *noun* [C] a book with empty pages where you can stick newspaper articles, pictures, etc, that you have collected and want to keep

scrape¹ /skreɪp/ *verb* [T] **1** to damage the surface of something by rubbing it against something rough *Jamie fell over and scraped his knee.* **2** to remove something from a surface using a sharp edge *The next morning I had to scrape the ice off the car.* **3 scrape a win/draw/pass** *UK* to succeed in a test or competition but with difficulty *France scraped a 3-2 win over Norway.*
  scrape by to manage to live when you do not have enough money
  scrape through (sth) to succeed in something but with a lot of difficulty *I scraped through my exams* (= just passed).
  scrape sth together to manage with a lot of difficulty to get enough of something, often money *I finally scraped together enough money for a flight home.*

scrape² /skreɪp/ *noun* [C] **1** the slight damage caused when you rub a surface with something rough *He suffered a few cuts and scrapes but nothing serious.* **2** *informal* a difficult or dangerous situation which you cause yourself *She's always getting into scrapes.*

scrappy /ˈskræpi/ *adjective* **1** *UK* untidy or organized badly *They won but it was a scrappy match.* **2** *US* determined to win or achieve something *a scrappy competitor*

scratch¹ /skrætʃ/ *verb* **1** RUB SKIN [I, T] to rub your skin with your nails, often to stop it itching (= feeling unpleasant) *He scratched his head.* ○ *Stop scratching! You'll only make it worse.* **2** HURT/DAMAGE [T] to make a slight cut or long, thin mark with a sharp object *The surface was all scratched.* ○ *I scratched myself on the roses.* **3** RUB SURFACE [I, T] to rub a hard surface with a sharp object, often making a noise *I could hear the cat scratching at the door.*

scratch² /skrætʃ/ *noun* **1** [C] a slight cut or a long, thin mark made with a sharp object *I've got all these scratches on my arm from the cat.* **2** [no plural] when you rub your skin with your nails, often to stop it itching (= feeling unpleasant) *Could you give my back a scratch?* **3 from scratch** If you do something from scratch, you do it from the beginning. *She prepared the whole meal from scratch in under an hour.* **4 not be/come up to scratch** *informal* to not be good enough *She told me my work wasn't up to scratch.*

scrawl /skrɔːl/ *verb* [T] to write something quickly so that it is untidy *She scrawled a note, but I couldn't read it.* • **scrawl** *noun* [C, U]

scrawny /ˈskrɔːni/ *adjective* too thin *a scrawny neck* ○ *She's lost so much weight now she's starting to look scrawny.*

o▬**scream¹** /skriːm/ *verb* [I, T] to make a loud, high noise with your voice, or to shout something in a loud, high voice because you are afraid, hurt, or angry *She screamed for help.* ○ *I could hear a woman screaming, "Get me out of here!"*

WORD PARTNERS FOR scream

let out a scream • a blood-curdling/piercing/shrill scream • a scream of [horror/ pain/shock, etc]

---

scream² /skriːm/ *noun* **1** [C] when someone screams *We heard screams coming from their apartment.* ○ *We heard a blood-curdling scream.* **2 be a scream** *informal* to be very funny *You'd love Amanda - she's a scream.*

screech /skriːtʃ/ *verb* **1** [I, T] to make an unpleasant, high, loud sound *A car came screeching around the corner.* ○ *She was screeching at him at the top of her voice.* **2 screech to a halt/ stop** If a vehicle screeches to a halt, it suddenly stops, making an unpleasant, high sound. • **screech** *noun* [C] *We could hear the screech of brakes.*

S

screen

cinema screen *UK,*
movie screen *US*

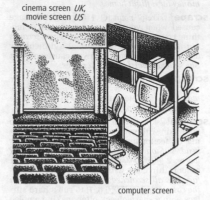

computer screen

⚬ᐟ**screen¹** /skriːn/ *noun* **1** [COMPUTER/TV] [C] the part
of a television or computer which shows
images or writing *I spend most of my day working in front of a computer screen.* **2 on screen**
using a computer *Do you work on screen?*
3 [FILM SURFACE] [C] a large, flat surface where a
film or an image is shown **4** [CINEMA] [U, no plural]
cinema films *an actor of stage and screen* (=
theatre and films) ○ *She first appeared on
screen in 1965.* **5** [NET] [C] a wire net which
covers a window or door and is used to stop
insects coming in **6** [SEPARATE] [C] a vertical
structure which is used to separate one area
from another

screen² /skriːn/ *verb* [T] **1** [MEDICAL] to find out if
people have an illness by doing medical tests
on them *Babies are routinely screened for the
condition.* **2** [GET INFORMATION] to find out information about someone in order to decide if
they are suitable for a particular job *Applicants are screened to ensure that none of them is
a security risk.* **3** [SHOW] to show something on
television or at a cinema [often passive] *The first
episode will be screened tonight.*

screen sth off to separate one area from
another using a vertical structure *Part of the
room is screened off and used as an office.*

screenplay /ˈskriːnpleɪ/ *noun* [C] a story that is
written for television or for a film

'**screen ˌsaver** (*also* screensaver) *noun* [C] a program to protect a computer screen that automatically shows a moving image if the computer is not used for a few minutes

screw¹ /skruː/ *noun* [C] a small, pointed piece of
metal that you turn round and round to fix
things together, especially pieces of wood ⊃See
picture at **tool.**

screw² /skruː/ *verb* **1 screw sth down/to/onto,
etc** to fasten something with a screw *You need
to screw the cabinet to the wall.* **2 screw sth on/
down/together, etc** to fasten something by
turning it round until it is tight, or to be
fastened this way *The lid is screwed on so
tight I can't get it off.* ⊃Opposite unscrew. **3 screw
up your eyes/face** to move the muscles of your

face so that your eyes become narrow *He
screwed up his eyes in the bright sunlight.*

screw (sth) up *informal* to make a mistake,
or to spoil something *I screwed up my exams
last year.*

screw sth up to twist and crush a piece of
paper with your hands *She screwed the letter
up and threw it in the bin.*

screwdriver /ˈskruːˌdraɪvəʳ/ *noun* [C] a tool for
turning screws ⊃See picture at **tool.**

screwed-up /ˌskruːd'ʌp/ *adjective informal* If
someone is screwed-up, they are unhappy and
anxious because they have had a lot of bad experiences.

scribble /ˈskrɪbl/ *verb* [I, T] to write or draw
something quickly and carelessly *She
scribbled some notes in her book.* ● scribble
noun [C, U] something that has been scribbled

script /skrɪpt/ *noun* **1** [C] the words in a film,
play, etc *He wrote a number of film scripts.*
2 [C, U] a set of letters used for writing a
particular language *Arabic/Roman script*

scripted /ˈskrɪptɪd/ *adjective* A scripted speech
or broadcast has been written before it is read
or performed.

scripture /ˈskrɪptʃəʳ/ (*also* the scriptures) *noun*
[U] the holy books of a religion

scriptwriter /ˈskrɪptˌraɪtəʳ/ *noun* [C] someone
who writes the words for films or radio or television programmes

scroll¹ /skrəʊl/ *noun* [C] a long roll of paper with
writing on it, used especially in the past

scroll² /skrəʊl/ *verb* **scroll up/down/through, etc**
to move text or an image on a computer screen
so that you can look at the part that you want

scrollbar /ˈskrəʊlbɑːʳ/ *noun* [C] on a computer
screen, a small rectangle on the side or bottom
that you use to move text or an image

scrooge /skruːdʒ/ *noun* [C] *informal* someone
who spends very little money

scrounge /skraʊndʒ/ *verb* [I, T] *informal* to get
something from someone else instead of
paying for it yourself *He's always scrounging
money off you.*

scrub¹ /skrʌb/ *verb* [I, T] scrubbing, *past* scrubbed to
clean something by rubbing it hard with a
brush *to scrub the floor*

scrub² /skrʌb/ *noun* **1** [U] bushes and small trees
that grow in a dry area **2** [no plural] when you
clean something by rubbing it with a brush *I
gave my hands a scrub.*

scruff /skrʌf/ *noun* **by the scruff of the/your neck**
by the back of the neck *She picked the cat up by
the scruff of its neck.*

scruffy /ˈskrʌfi/ *adjective* dirty and untidy
scruffy jeans ○ *I don't like to look scruffy.*

scruple /ˈskruːpl/ *noun* [C] a belief that something is wrong which stops you from doing
that thing [usually plural] *She has no scruples
about accepting bribes.*

scrupulous /ˈskruːpjələs/ *adjective* **1** very careful and giving great attention to details *He's
very scrupulous about making sure that all the
facts are checked.* **2** always honest and fair
⊃Opposite unscrupulous.

scrutinize (*also UK* -ise) /ˈskruːtɪnaɪz/ *verb* [T] to

S

examine something very carefully *The evidence was carefully scrutinized.*

scrutiny /'skru:tɪni/ *noun* [U] when you examine something carefully *Every aspect of her life came under* public *scrutiny.*

scuba diving /'sku:bə,daɪvɪŋ/ *noun* [U] a sport in which you swim under water using special equipment for breathing

scuff /skʌf/ *verb* [T] to make a mark on your shoes by rubbing them against something rough

scuffle /'skʌfl/ *noun* [C] a short fight in which people push each other *A scuffle broke out* (= started) *behind the courtroom.*

sculptor /'skʌlptəʳ/ *noun* [C] someone who makes sculpture

sculpture /'skʌlptʃəʳ/ *noun* **1** [C, U] a piece of art that is made from stone, wood, clay, etc *a wooden sculpture* ○ *modern sculpture* **2** [U] the art of making objects from stone, wood, clay, etc *She teaches sculpture at an art school.*

scum /skʌm/ *noun* **1** [U, no plural] an unpleasant, thick substance on the surface of a liquid **2** [U] *informal* an offensive way of referring to a very bad person

scurry /'skʌri/ *verb* **scurry along/around/away, etc** to walk quickly or run because you are in a hurry

scuttle /'skʌtl/ *verb* **scuttle across/along/away, etc** to run quickly using short steps *A beetle scuttled across the floor.*

scythe /saɪð/ *noun* [C] a tool with a long handle and a curved blade that is used to cut tall grass and crops

o▪**sea** /siː/ *noun* **1** [C, U] a large area of salt water *I'd like to live by the sea.* ○ *It was our third day at sea* (= travelling on the sea). ○ *It's cheaper to send parcels by sea* (= on a ship). **2 Sea** a particular area of salt water *the North Sea* ○ *the Black Sea* **3 a sea of sth** a large number of something *He looked across the room and saw a sea of faces.*

seabed /'siːbed/ *noun* [no plural] the floor of the sea

seafood /'siːfuːd/ *noun* [U] animals from the sea that are eaten as food, especially animals that live in shells

seafront /'siːfrʌnt/ *noun* [C] *UK* a part of a town that is next to the sea [usually singular] *We walked along the seafront.*

seagull /'siːgʌl/ *noun* [C] a grey and white bird that lives near the sea

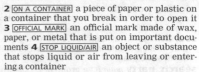
seagull

seahorse /'siːhɔːs/ *noun* [C] a small fish that has a head and neck the same shape as a horse's

seal¹ /siːl/ *noun* **1** ANIMAL an animal with smooth fur that eats fish and lives near the sea

2 ON A CONTAINER a piece of paper or plastic on a container that you break in order to open it **3** OFFICIAL MARK an official mark made of wax, paper, or metal that is put on important documents **4** STOP LIQUID/AIR an object or substance that stops liquid or air from leaving or entering a container

seal² /siːl/ *verb* [T] **1** (*also* **seal up**) to close an entrance or container so that air or liquid cannot enter or leave it *She quickly sealed up the bottle.* **2** to close a letter or parcel by sticking the edges together *to seal an envelope*

seal sth off to prevent people from entering an area or building, often because it is dangerous *Police immediately sealed off the streets.*

'sea ,level *noun* [U] the level of the sea's surface, used to measure the height of an area of land

'sea ,lion *noun* [C] a large seal (= sea animal)

seam /siːm/ *noun* [C] **1** a line of sewing where two pieces of cloth have been joined together **2** a long, thin layer of coal under the ground

seaman /'siːmən/ *noun* [C] *plural* **seamen** a sailor

seance /'seɪɒns/ *noun* [C] a meeting at which people try to communicate with spirits of dead people

o▪**search¹** /sɜːtʃ/ *verb* **1** TRY TO FIND [I, I] to try to find someone or something *I've searched my bedroom but I can't find my watch.* ○ *Police are still searching the woods for the missing girl.* **2** POLICE [T] If the police search someone, they look in their clothes and bags to see if they are hiding anything illegal, such as drugs. *They were searched at the airport.* **3** FIND ANSWER [I] to try to find an answer to a problem *Doctors are still searching for a cure.*

search or **search for**?

If you **search** a place or person, you are looking for something in that place or on that person.

The police searched the man (= looked in his clothes) *for drugs.*

I searched the kitchen (= looked in the kitchen) *for my watch.*

If you **search for** something or someone, you are looking for that thing or that person.

I searched for my watch.

~~I searched my watch.~~

o▪**search²** /sɜːtʃ/ *noun* **1** [C] when you try to find someone or something [usually singular] *Police are continuing their search for the missing girl.* ○ *They went off in search of* (= to find) *a bar.* **2** [no plural] when you try to find an answer to a problem *the search for happiness*

'search ,engine *noun* [C] a computer program which finds information on the Internet by

S

looking for words which you have typed in ⊃See Extra help page **The Web and the Internet** on page Centre 36.

searching /'sɜːtʃɪŋ/ *adjective* A searching question or look is intended to discover the truth about something.

'**search ,party** *noun* [C] a group of people who look for someone who is lost

'**search ,warrant** *noun* [C] an official document that allows the police to search a building

searing /'sɪərɪŋ/ *adjective* [always before noun] extreme and unpleasant *searing pain/heat*

'**sea ,shell** *noun* [C] the empty shell of some types of sea animals

the seashore /'siːʃɔːʳ/ *noun* the area of land along the edge of the sea

seasick /'siːsɪk/ *adjective* feeling ill because of the way a boat is moving

the seaside /'siːsaɪd/ *noun* an area or town next to the sea *We had a picnic at the seaside.* ○ *a seaside resort/community*

◦→**season**¹ /'siːzᵊn/ *noun* [C] **1** PART OF YEAR one of the four periods of the year; winter, spring, summer, or autumn **2** SPECIAL TIME a period of the year when a particular thing happens [usually singular] *the holiday season* ○ *the rainy/dry season* ○ *the football season* **3 in season a** FRUIT/ VEGETABLES If vegetables or fruit are in season, they are available and ready to eat. **b** ANIMALS If a female animal is in season, she is ready to mate. **4 out of season a** FRUIT/VEGETABLES If vegetables or fruit are out of season, they are not usually available at that time. **b** FEW PEOPLE If you go somewhere out of season, you go during a period of the year when few people are there.

season² /'siːzᵊn/ *verb* [T] to add salt or spices to food that you are cooking

seasonal /'siːzᵊnᵊl/ *adjective* happening or existing only at a particular time of the year *a seasonal worker* ○ *the seasonal migration of birds*

seasoned /'siːzᵊnd/ *adjective* [always before noun] having a lot of experience of doing something *a seasoned traveller*

seasoning /'siːzᵊnɪŋ/ *noun* [C, U] salt or spices that you add to food

'**season ,ticket** UK (US ,season 'ticket) *noun* [C] a ticket that you can use many times without having to pay each time

�◻◻◻ WORD PARTNERS FOR *seat*

have/take a seat ● in/on a seat ● the back/ driver's/front/passenger seat

seat¹ /siːt/ *noun* [C] **1** SIT something that you sit on *Please, have/take a seat* (= sit down). ○ *I've booked three seats for the cinema tonight.* ○ *the back/front seat of a car* **2** PART the flat part of a chair, bicycle, etc that you sit on **3** POLITICS a position in a parliament or other group that makes official decisions *a seat in parliament* ○ *a congressional seat*

seat² /siːt/ *verb* **1 seat yourself in/on/next to, etc** to sit somewhere *I seated myself next to the fire.* **2 be seated a** to be sitting down *The director was seated on his right.* **b** used to politely ask a group of people to sit down *Would the people at*

the back please be seated. **3 seat 4/12/200, etc** If a building, room, or vehicle seats a particular number of people, that many can sit in it.

'**seat ,belt** *noun* [C] a strap that you fasten across your body when travelling in a vehicle *to fasten your seat belt* ⊃See colour picture **Car** on page Centre 7

seating /'siːtɪŋ/ *noun* [U] the seats in a public place, or the way that they are arranged

seaweed /'siːwiːd/ *noun* [U] a plant that you find on the beach and that grows in the sea

sec /sek/ *noun* [C] *informal* a very short time *Just a sec - I'm nearly ready.*

secluded /sɪ'kluːdɪd/ *adjective* If a place is secluded, it is quiet and not near people. *a secluded beach/garden*

seclusion /sɪ'kluːʒᵊn/ *noun* [U] when someone lives alone, away from other people *He lived in seclusion for the rest of his life.*

◦→**second**¹ /'sekᵊnd/ *adjective, pronoun* **1** referring to the person, thing, or event that comes immediately after the first *You're second on the list.* ○ *This is my second piece of chocolate cake.* ○ *She didn't win but she did come second* (= was the one after the winner) *in one race.* **2** 2nd written as a word ⊃See also: second best, second-hand, second language, second nature, the second person, second-rate, second thought, second wind.

◦→**second**² /'sekᵊnd/ *noun* [C] **1** TIME one of the 60 parts a minute is divided into **2** SHORT TIME *informal* a very short period of time *I'll be back in just a second.* **3** PRODUCT something that is sold cheaply because it is damaged or not in perfect condition [usually plural] *Some of those towels are seconds.*

second³ /'sekᵊnd/ *verb* [T] to formally support an idea at a meeting [often passive] *The chairperson's proposal was seconded by Ms Jones.*

second⁴ /sɪ'kɒnd/ *verb* [T] UK to send someone to another job for a fixed period of time [often passive] *He was seconded from the police to the Department of Transport.*

secondary /'sekᵊndᵊri/ *adjective* **1** relating to the education of students aged between 11 and 18 *secondary education* **2** less important than something else *What matters is the size of the office. The location is of secondary importance.*

'**secondary ,school** *noun* [C] *mainly UK* a school for students aged between 11 and 18

,**second 'best** *adjective* not the best but the next best *the second best candidate* ● **second best** *noun* [U]

second-class /,sekᵊnd'klɑːs/ *adjective* **1** TRAVEL relating to the less expensive way of travelling in a train, aircraft, etc, that most people use *a second-class carriage/ticket* **2** NOT IMPORTANT less important than other people *Women are still treated as second-class citizens.* **3** UNIVERSITY A second-class university degree is a good degree but not the best possible. ● **second class** *adverb We always travel second class.*

second-guess /,sekᵊnd'ges/ *verb* [T] to guess what someone will do in the future

second-hand /,sekᵊnd'hænd/ *adjective, adverb*

If something is second-hand, someone else owned or used it before you. **second-hand books/clothes** ○ *She buys a lot of clothes second-hand.*

second 'language *noun* [C] a language that you speak that is not the first language you learned as a child

secondly /'sekəndli/ *adverb* used for introducing the second reason, idea, etc *I want two things: firstly, more money, and secondly, better working hours.*

second 'nature *noun* [U] something that you can do easily because you have done it many times before *After a few years, teaching became second nature to me.*

the ,second 'person *noun* the form of a verb or pronoun that is used when referring to the person being spoken or written to. For example 'you' is a second person pronoun

second-rate /,sekənd'reɪt/ *adjective* of bad quality *a second-rate writer*

,second 'thought *noun* **1 on second thoughts** *UK* used when you want to change a decision you have made *I'll have tea, please - on second thoughts, make that coffee.* **2 without a second thought** If you do something without a second thought, you do it without first considering if you should do it or not. *She'll spend a hundred pounds on a dress without a second thought.* **3 have second thoughts** to change your opinion about something or start to doubt it [+ about + doing sth] *I've been having second thoughts about doing the course.*

,second 'wind *noun* [no plural] a return of energy that makes it possible to continue an activity *I was feeling tired, but I got my second wind after lunch.*

WORD PARTNERS FOR *secrecy*

be **shrouded in** secrecy • do sth **in** secrecy • **absolute/strict** secrecy • the secrecy **of/surrounding** sth

secrecy /'siːkrəsi/ *noun* [U] when something is kept secret *Politicians criticized **the secrecy surrounding** the air attack.*

o-=**secret**[1] /'siːkrət/ *adjective* **1** If something is secret, other people are not allowed to know about it. *a secret affair/meeting* ○ *I'll tell you but you must keep it secret.* **2 secret admirer/drinker, etc** someone who does something or feels something without telling other people about it • **secretly** *adverb He secretly taped their conversation.* ⊃See also: **top-secret**.

WORD PARTNERS FOR *secret*

keep a secret • **let sb in on/reveal/tell sb** a secret • a **big/closely-guarded/well-kept** secret

o-=**secret**[2] /'siːkrət/ *noun* [C] **1** something that you tell no one about or only a few people *I'm having a party for him but it's a secret.* ○ *Can you keep a secret?* **2 the secret** the best way of achieving something *So what's the secret of your success?* **3 in secret** without telling other people *For years they met in secret.*

,secret 'agent *noun* [C] someone who tries to

find out secret information, especially about another country

secretarial /,sekrə'teəriəl/ *adjective* relating to the work of a secretary (= office worker who types letters, etc) **secretarial skills** ○ *I'm sure she'll pick up some secretarial work.*

o-=**secretary** /'sekrət³ri/ *noun* [C] **1** someone who works in an office, typing letters, answering the telephone, and arranging meetings, etc **2** (*also* **Secretary**) an official who is in charge of a large department of the government *the Secretary of State*

secrete /sɪ'kriːt/ *verb* [T] to produce a substance *A mixture of substances are secreted by cells within the stomach.* • **secretion** /sɪ'kriːʃ³n/ *noun* [C, U]

secretive /'siːkrətɪv/ *adjective* not willing to tell people what you know or what you are doing *He's very secretive about his relationships.* • **secretively** *adverb*

,secret 'service *noun* [no plural] **1** in the UK, a department of the government that tries to find out secret information about foreign countries **2** in the US, a government organization that protects the president

sect /sekt/ *noun* [C] a group of people with a set of religious or political beliefs, often extreme beliefs *a religious sect*

sectarian /sek'teəriən/ *adjective* relating to the differences between religious groups *sectarian violence*

o-=**section** /'sekʃ³n/ *noun* [C] **1** one of the parts that something is divided into *a non-smoking section in a restaurant* ○ *the business section of a newspaper* ○ *the tail section of an aircraft* **2** a model or drawing of something that shows how it would look if it were cut from top to bottom and seen from the side ⊃See also: **cross-section**.

sector /'sektə³/ *noun* [C] **1** one part of a country's economy *the private/public sector* ○ *the financial/manufacturing sector* **2** one of the parts that an area is divided into *the British sector of the North Sea*

secular /'sekjələ³/ *adjective* not religious or not controlled by a religious group *secular education* ○ *a secular state/government/society*

secure[1] /sɪ'kjʊə³/ *adjective* **1** [NOT FAIL] not likely to fail or be lost *a secure investment/job* **2** [SAFE] safe from danger *I don't feel that the house is secure.* **3** [CONFIDENT] confident about yourself and the situation that you are in *I need to feel secure in a relationship.* ○ *I hope my children feel secure.* **4** [FIXED] firmly fastened and not likely to fall or break *Check that all windows and doors are secure.* ⊃Opposite **insecure**.

secure[2] /sɪ'kjʊə³/ *verb* [T] **1** [ACHIEVE] to achieve something, after a lot of effort *to secure the release of hostages* ○ *We've finally managed to secure funding for the project.* **2** [FASTEN] to fasten something firmly *He secured the bike to the gate.* **3** [MAKE SAFE] to make something safe

securely /sɪ'kjʊəli/ *adverb* If something is securely fastened, it will not fall or become loose.

WORD PARTNERS FOR *security*

lax/tight security • security arrangements/checks • a security breach/guard/lapse/operation/risk • national security

---

security /sɪˈkjʊərəti/ *noun* [U] **1** BEING SAFE the things that are done to keep someone or something safe *airport/national security* ○ *a security alarm* **2** SAFE SITUATION when something is not likely to fail or be lost *financial security* ○ *job security* **3** CONFIDENCE confidence about yourself and the situation that you are in *the security of a long-term relationship* ⊃Opposite **insecurity 4** BORROWING something valuable that you offer to give someone when you borrow money if you cannot pay the money back ⊃See also: **social security**.

COMMON LEARNER ERROR

security or **safety**?

Security means activities or people that protect you from harm, or that try to stop crime.

He works as a security guard.

airport security

Safety is when you are safe or how safe something is.

Remember to wear your safety belt in the car.

Children should have lessons in road safety.

---

sedan /sɪˈdæn/ *US* (*UK* **saloon**) *noun* [C] a large car with a separate, closed area for bags

sedate¹ /sɪˈdeɪt/ *adjective* calm and slow *walking at a sedate pace*

sedate² /sɪˈdeɪt/ *verb* [T] to give a person or animal a drug to make them feel calm • **sedation** /sɪˈdeɪʃᵊn/ *noun* [U] *She had to be put under sedation.*

sedative /ˈsedətɪv/ *noun* [C] a drug used to sedate a person or an animal

sedentary /ˈsedᵊntᵊri/ *adjective* spending a lot of time sitting down or not being active *a sedentary job/lifestyle*

sediment /ˈsedɪmənt/ *noun* [C, U] a solid substance that forms a layer at the bottom of a liquid

seduce /sɪˈdjuːs/ *verb* [T] **1** to persuade someone to have sex with you, especially someone young **2** to persuade someone to do something they would not normally do *I wouldn't have bought it but I was seduced by the low prices.*

seductive /sɪˈdʌktɪv/ *adjective* **1** sexually attractive *a seductive smile/voice* **2** making you want to have or do something *the seductive power of money*

o—**see** /siː/ *verb* seeing, *past tense* **saw**, *past participle* **seen 1** EYES [I, T] to notice people and things with your eyes *Have you seen Jo?* ○ *Turn the light on so I can see.* ⊃See Common learner error at **look. 2** UNDERSTAND [I, T] to understand something *I see what you mean.* ○ *I don't see why I should go.* **3** MEET [T] to meet or visit someone *I'm seeing Peter tonight.* ○ *You should see a doctor.* **4** WATCH [T] to watch a film, television programme, etc *Did you see that film last*

night? **5** INFORMATION [T] to find out information [+ question word] *I'll just see what time the train gets in.* **6** IMAGINE [T] to imagine or think about something or someone in a particular way *I just can't see him as a father.* **7** BELIEVE [T] to believe that something will happen *I can't see us finishing on time.* **8** HAPPEN [T] to be the time or place where something happens *This decade has seen huge technological advances.* **9 see that** If you ask someone to see that something happens, you want them to make sure it happens. *Could you see that everyone gets a copy of this letter?* **10 see sb home/to the station, etc** to go somewhere with someone, especially to make sure they are safe *Let me see you home.* **11 I'll/we'll see** used to say that you will make a decision about something later *"Dad, can I have a guitar?" "We'll see."* **12 see you** *informal* used for saying goodbye ⊃See also: **be glad/happy**, etc to see the **back²** of sb/sth, see **eye¹** to eye (with sb), see **red²**.

see about sth/doing sth to deal with something, or arrange for something to be done *You should see about getting your hair cut.*

see sth in sb/sth to believe that someone or something has a particular quality *I can't understand what you see in her* (= why you like her).

see sb off to go to the place that someone is leaving from in order to say goodbye to them *My parents came to the airport to see me off.*

see sb out to take someone to the door of a room or building when they are leaving *Don't worry, I'll see myself out* (= leave the room/building by myself).

see through sb/sth to understand that someone is trying to deceive you *I saw through him at once.*

see to sth to deal with something *Don't worry, I'll see to everything while you're away.*

seed¹ /siːd/ *noun* **1** [C, U] a small round or oval object produced by a plant that a new plant can grow from *Sow the seeds* (= plant them) *near the surface.* **2 (the) seeds of sth** the beginning of something *the seeds of hope/change* ⊃See also: **sesame seed**.

seed² /siːd/ *verb* **1** [T] to plant seeds in the ground **2 be seeded first/second, etc** in tennis, to be the first/second, etc on a list of players expected to succeed in a competition

seedless /ˈsiːdləs/ *adjective* without seeds *seedless grapes*

seedling /ˈsiːdlɪŋ/ *noun* [C] a young plant that has been grown from a seed

seedy /ˈsiːdi/ *adjective informal* looking dirty or in bad condition and likely to be involved in immoral activities *a seedy bar/hotel*

seeing 'eye dog *US* (*UK/US* **guide dog**) *noun* [C] a dog that is trained to help blind people

seek /siːk/ *verb* [T] *past* **sought 1** to try to find or get something *to seek advice/a solution* **2** to try to do something [+ to do sth] *They are seeking to change the rules.* ○ *to seek re-election* ⊃See also: **hide-and-seek**.

o—**seem** /siːm/ *verb* **seem happy/a nice person, etc;**

---

seem like/as if, etc to appear to be a particular thing or to have a particular quality *She seemed happy enough.* ○ *It seemed like a good idea at the time.* ○ *There doesn't **seem to be** any real solution.* ○ *[+ (that)] It seems that the bars close early here.* ○ *It **seems to me** (= I think) that she's in the wrong job.*

seemingly /'si:mɪŋli/ *adverb* appearing to be something without really being that thing *a seemingly harmless comment*

seen /si:n/ *past participle of* see

seep /si:p/ *verb* **seep from/into/through, etc** to flow very slowly through something *Water was seeping through the walls.*

seesaw

seesaw /'si:sɔ:/ *(also US* **teeter-totter**) *noun* [C] a long board that children play on by sitting at each end and using their feet on the ground to push the board up and down

seethe /si:ð/ *verb* [I] to be very angry, often without showing it *I left him **seething with** anger.*

segment /'seɡmənt/ *noun* [C] one of the parts that something can be divided into *a segment of the population/market* ○ *an orange segment*

segregate /'seɡrɪɡeɪt/ *verb* [T] to separate one group of people from another, especially one sex or race from another *At school the girls were **segregated from** the boys.* ● **segregation** /ˌseɡrɪˈɡeɪʃən/ *noun* [U] *racial segregation*

seismic /'saɪzmɪk/ *adjective* relating to or caused by an earthquake (= when the earth shakes) *seismic activity*

seize /si:z/ *verb* [T] **1** HOLD to take hold of something quickly and firmly *She seized my arm and pulled me towards her.* **2** OPPORTUNITY to do something quickly when you have the opportunity *You need to **seize** every **opportunity**.* **3** PLACE to take control of a place suddenly by using military force *Troops **seized control** in the early hours of the morning.* **4** DRUGS ETC to take away something that is illegal, for example drugs *Officials seized 2.7 tons of cocaine from the ship.*

seize on/upon sth to quickly use something that will give you an advantage *Her story was seized upon by the press.*

seize up If part of your body or a machine seizes up, it stops moving or working in the normal way. *His right leg suddenly seized up during the race.*

seizure /'si:ʒər/ *noun* **1** CONTROL [U] when some-

one takes control of a country, government, etc *a seizure of power* **2** DRUGS ETC [C] when someone in authority takes away something that is illegal, for example drugs *a seizure of heroin* **3** ILLNESS [C] a sudden attack of an illness *an epileptic seizure*

seldom /'seldəm/ *adverb* not often *We seldom go out in the evenings.*

select¹ /sɪ'lekt/ *verb* [T] to choose someone or something *We've selected three candidates.*

select² /sɪ'lekt/ *adjective* consisting of only a small group of people who have been specially chosen *a **select group***

🧩 **WORD PARTNERS FOR *selection***

2 a **good/wide** selection ● a selection **of** sth

selection /sɪ'lekʃən/ *noun* **1** [U] when someone or something is chosen *the **selection** process* **2** [C] a group of people or things that has been chosen *We have a **wide selection** of imported furniture.* ⊃See also: natural selection.

selective /sɪ'lektɪv/ *adjective* **1** careful about what you choose *He's very selective about the people he spends time with.* **2** involving only people or things that have been specially chosen *selective breeding*

self /self/ *noun* [C, U] *plural* **selves** /selvz/ your characteristics, including your personality, your abilities, etc *his true self*

self-assured /ˌselfəˈʃʊəd/ *adjective* confident about yourself

self-catering /ˌselfˈkeɪtᵊrɪŋ/ *adjective UK* describes a holiday in which you have a kitchen so that you can cook meals for yourself *We decided to stay in self-catering accommodation rather than in a hotel.*

self-centred *UK* (*US* **self-centered**) /ˌselfˈsentəd/ *adjective* interested only in yourself

self-confident /ˌselfˈkɒnfɪdᵊnt/ *adjective* feeling sure about yourself and your abilities ● **self-confidence** *noun* [U] being self-confident

self-conscious /ˌselfˈkɒnʃəs/ *adjective* too aware of what other people are thinking about you and your appearance ● **self-consciously** *adverb* ● **self-consciousness** *noun* [U]

self-contained /ˌselfkənˈteɪnd/ *adjective UK* If a flat is self-contained, it has its own kitchen, bathroom, and entrance.

self-control /ˌselfkənˈtrəʊl/ *noun* [U] the ability to control your emotions and actions although you are very angry, upset, etc

self-defence *UK* (*US* **self-defense**) /ˌselfdɪˈfens/ *noun* [U] when you protect yourself from someone who is attacking you by fighting *He claimed he had acted **in self-defence**.*

self-destructive /ˌselfdɪˈstrʌktɪv/ *adjective* A self-destructive action harms the person who is doing it.

self-discipline /ˌselfˈdɪsɪplɪn/ *noun* [U] the ability to make yourself do things that you do not want to do

self-employed /ˌselfɪmˈplɔɪd/ *adjective* working for yourself and not for a company or other organization

self-esteem /ˌselfɪˈstiːm/ *noun* [U] confidence in yourself and a belief in your qualities and abilities *She suffers from* **low self-esteem**.

self-evident /ˌselfˈevɪdᵊnt/ *adjective* obviously true and not needing to be explained

self-explanatory /ˌselfɪkˈsplænᵊtᵊri/ *adjective* easy to understand and not needing to be explained

self-help /ˌselfˈhelp/ *adjective* A self-help book, activity, organization, etc is designed to help you deal with your problems on your own. *a self-help group for alcoholics*

self-indulgent /ˌselfɪnˈdʌldʒᵊnt/ *adjective* doing or having things that you like although they are not necessary or are bad for you • **self-indulgence** /ˌselfɪnˈdʌldʒᵊns/ *noun* [C, U]

self-inflicted /ˌselfɪnˈflɪktɪd/ *adjective* If an injury or a problem is self-inflicted, you have caused it yourself.

self-interest /ˌselfˈɪntrəst/ *noun* [U] interest in what will help you and not what will help other people

selfish /ˈselfɪʃ/ *adjective* caring only about yourself and not other people *It's very selfish of him.* • **selfishly** *adverb* • **selfishness** *noun* [U]

selfless /ˈselfləs/ *adjective* caring about other people and not about yourself

self-made /ˌselfˈmeɪd/ *adjective* rich because you have earned a lot of money yourself *a self-made millionaire*

self-pity /ˌselfˈpɪti/ *noun* [U] sadness for yourself because you think you have suffered so much, especially when this is not true

self-portrait /ˌselfˈpɔːtreɪt/ *noun* [C] a picture that you draw or paint of yourself

self-reliant /ˌselfrɪˈlaɪənt/ *adjective* able to do things yourself without depending on other people

self-respect /ˌselfrɪˈspekt/ *noun* [U] the feeling of pride in yourself and your character • **self-respecting** *adjective*

self-righteous /ˌselfˈraɪtʃəs/ *adjective* believing that you are morally better than other people

self-sacrifice /ˌselfˈsækrɪfaɪs/ *noun* [U] when you do not have or do something so that you can help other people

self-satisfied /ˌselfˈsætɪsfaɪd/ *adjective* too pleased with yourself and what you have achieved

self-service /ˌselfˈsɜːvɪs/ *adjective* A self-service restaurant or shop is one in which you serve yourself and are not served by the people who work there.

self-sufficient /ˌselfsəˈfɪʃᵊnt/ *adjective* having everything that you need yourself and not needing help from others

ᵒᵐ**sell** /sel/ *verb past* **sold** 1 ⌐FOR MONEY¬ [I, T] to give something to someone who gives you money for it *He* **sold** *his guitar* **for** *£50.* ○ *I sold my* bike to Claire. ○ [+ two objects] *I'm hoping she'll sell me her car.* 2 ⌐OFFER¬ [T] to offer something for people to buy *Excuse me, do you sell newspapers?* 3 **sell for**/**at sth** to be available for sale at a particular price *The shirts are selling for £30 each.* 4 ⌐A LOT¬ [I, T] to be bought in large numbers *His last book sold eight million copies.* 5 ⌐MAKE YOU WANT¬ [T] to make someone want to buy something *Scandal sells newspapers.* 6 ⌐IDEA/PLAN¬ [T] to persuade someone that an idea or plan is good *I'm currently trying to sell the idea to my boss.*

sell sth off to sell all or part of a business *The company announced that it would be selling off its hotel business.*

sell out If a shop sells out of something, it sells all of that thing. *They'd* **sold out of** *bread by the time I got there.*

sell up *UK* to sell your house or company in order to go somewhere else or do something else *They sold up and retired to the West Country.*

'sell-by ,date *noun* [C] *UK* the date printed on a food or drink container after which it should not be sold *This meat has* **gone past** *its* **sell-by date.**

seller /ˈseləʳ/ *noun* [C] 1 someone who sells something *a flower seller* 2 a product that a company sells *flower / newspaper / souvenir sellers* ○ *Our* **biggest sellers** *are the calendars.*

Sellotape *trademark* /ˈseləʊteɪp/ *UK* (*US* **Scotch tape** *trademark*) *noun* [U] clear, thin material with glue on it, used to stick things together, especially paper *a roll of Sellotape* ○ *I stuck the note to the door with Sellotape.* ⊃See colour picture **The Classroom** on page Centre 6.

sellout /ˈselaʊt/ *noun* [no plural] 1 a performance or event where all of the tickets have been sold *The concert was a sellout* 2 *informal* when someone does something that is against their beliefs in order to get money or power *Most of the workers see the union agreement as a sellout.*

selves /selvz/ *plural of* self

semantic /sɪˈmæntɪk/ *adjective* connected with the meaning of language *So is there a semantic distinction between the two words?*

semblance /ˈsembləns/ *noun* **semblance of normality/order, etc** a small amount of a quality, but not as much as you would like *Our lives have now returned to some semblance of normality.* ○ *The city has now returned to some semblance of normality after last night's celebrations.*

semen /ˈsiːmən/ *noun* [U] the liquid that is produced by the male sex organs, that contains sperm (= cells that join with female eggs to make new life)

semester /sɪˈmestəʳ/ *noun* [C] *mainly US* one of the two time periods that a school or college year is divided into *The first/second semester* ○ *the spring/fall semester*

semi- /semi-/ *prefix* half or partly *a semicircle* ○ *semifrozen*

semicircle

semicircle /ˈsemɪˌsɜːkl/ *noun* [C] half a circle

semicolon /ˌsemɪˈkəʊlən/ [US] /ˈsemɪˌkəʊlən/ *noun* [C] a mark (;) used to separate parts of a sentence, or items in a list which already has commas ⊃See Extra help page **Punctuation** on page Centre 33.

semi-detached /ˌsemɪdɪˈtætʃt/ *adjective UK* A semi-detached house has one wall that is joined to another house.

semifinal /ˌsemɪˈfaɪnᵊl/ *noun* [C] one of the two games in a sports competition that are played to decide who will play in the final game

seminar /ˈsemɪnɑːʳ/ *noun* [C] a meeting of a group of people with a teacher or expert for training, discussion, or study of a subject

Semitic /sɪˈmɪtɪk/ *adjective* relating to the Jewish or Arab races, or their languages

the Senate /ˈsenɪt/ *noun* [group] a part of a government in some countries

senator /ˈsenətəʳ/ *noun* [C] someone who has been elected to the Senate *Senator Moynihan*

o⁃**send** /send/ *verb* [T] *past* **sent 1** to arrange for something to go or be taken somewhere, especially by post [+ two objects] *I sent him a letter last week.* ○ *Do you think we should send flowers?* **2** to make someone go somewhere *I sent him into the house to fetch some glasses.* **3 send sb to sleep** to cause someone to start sleeping ⊃See also: drive/send sb round the **bend**².

send sth back to return something to the person who sent it to you, especially because it is damaged or not suitable *I had to send the shirt back because it didn't fit me.*

send for sb to send someone a message asking them to come to see you *Do you think we should send for a doctor?*

send (off/away) for sth to write to an organization to ask them to send you something *I've sent off for a catalogue.*

send sth in to send something to an organization *Viewers were asked to send in photographs of their pets.*

send sb in to send soldiers, police, etc to a place in order to deal with a dangerous situation

send sth off to send a letter, document, or parcel by post

send sb off *UK* to order a sports player to leave the playing area because they have done something wrong

send sth out 1 to send something to a lot of different people *to send out invitations* **2** to produce light, sound, etc

send sb/sth up *UK* to make someone or something seem stupid by copying them in a funny way

send-off /ˈsendɒf/ *noun* [C] when a group of people say goodbye to someone at the same time *I got a good* ***send-off*** *at the station.*

senile /ˈsiːnaɪl/ *adjective* confused and unable to remember things because of old age ● **senility** /sɪˈnɪləti/ *noun* [U] the state of being senile

senior¹ /ˈsiːniəʳ/ *adjective* **1** [MORE IMPORTANT] having a more important job or position than someone else *a* ***senior executive*** ○ *We work in the same team but she's* ***senior to*** *me.* **2** [OLDER] older *senior students* **3** [NAME] *mainly US* (*written abbreviation* **Sr**) used at the end of a man's name to show that he is the older of two men in the same family who have the same name *Hello, may I speak to Ken Griffey Senior, please?*

senior² /ˈsiːniəʳ/ *noun* **1 be 20/30, etc years sb's senior** to be 20/30, etc years older than someone *She married a man 20 years her senior.* **2** [C] *US* a student who is in the last year of high school or college

senior ˈcitizen *noun* [C] an old person

seniority /ˌsiːniˈɒrəti/ *noun* [U] the state of being older or of having a more important position in an organization

sensation /senˈseɪʃᵊn/ *noun* **1** [PHYSICAL] [C, U] a physical feeling, or the ability to physically feel things *a burning sensation* ○ *Three months after the accident she still has no sensation in her right foot.* **2** [FEELING] [C] a strange feeling or idea that you can not explain *I had the strangest sensation that I had met him before.* **3** [EXCITEMENT] [no plural] a lot of excitement, surprise, or interest, or the person or event that causes these feelings *Their affair* ***caused a sensation.***

sensational /senˈseɪʃᵊnᵊl/ *adjective* **1** done in a way that is intended to shock people *sensational journalism* **2** very exciting or extremely good *a sensational performance*

sensationalism /senˈseɪʃᵊnᵊlɪzᵊm/ *noun* [U] when a story is told in a way that is intended to shock people

WORD PARTNERS FOR ***sense***

have the sense to do sth ● **good** sense

o⁃**sense**¹ /sens/ *noun* **1** [GOOD JUDGMENT] [U] good judgment, especially about practical things *He had the* ***good sense*** *to book a seat in advance.* **2** [ABILITY] [no plural] the ability to do something *a* ***sense of direction*** ○ *good* ***business sense*** **3** [NATURAL ABILITY] [C] one of the five natural abilities of sight, hearing, touch, smell, and taste *I have a very poor sense of smell.* **4 a sense of humour** *UK* (*US* **sense of humor**) the ability to understand funny things and to be funny yourself **5 a sense of loyalty/responsibility/security, etc** the quality or feeling of being loyal, responsible, safe, etc *He has absolutely no sense of loyalty.* **6** [MEANING] [C] the meaning

S

of a word, phrase, or sentence **7 in a sense/in some senses** thinking about something in a particular way *In a sense, he's right.* **8 make sense a** CLEAR MEANING to have a meaning or reason that you can understand *He's written me this note but it doesn't make any sense.* **b** SHOULD DO to be a good thing to do [+ to do sth] *It makes sense to buy now while prices are low.* **9 make sense of sth** to understand something that is difficult to understand *I'm trying to make sense of this document.* **10 come to your senses** to start to understand that you have been behaving stupidly ⊃See also: **common sense.**

sense² /sens/ *verb* [T] to understand what someone is thinking or feeling without being told about it [+ (that)] *I sensed that you weren't happy about this.*

senseless /'senslas/ *adjective* **1** happening or done without a good reason *senseless violence* **2** not conscious *He was beaten senseless.*

sensibility /ˌsensɪ'bɪləti/ *noun* [C, U] *formal* someone's feelings, or the ability to understand what other people feel

sensible /'sensɪbl/ *adjective* **1** showing good judgment *a sensible decision* ○ [+ to do sth] *Wouldn't it be more sensible to leave before the traffic gets bad?* **2** having a practical purpose *sensible shoes/clothes* • **sensibly** *adverb to eat/behave sensibly*

sensitive /'sensɪtɪv/ *adjective* **1** KIND able to understand what people are feeling and deal with them in a way that does not upset them *I want a man who's kind and sensitive.* **2** EASILY UPSET easily upset by the things people say or do *He was always sensitive to criticism.* ○ *She's very sensitive about her weight.* **3** SUBJECT A sensitive subject or situation needs to be dealt with carefully in order to avoid upsetting people. *Gender is a very sensitive subject.* **4** EASILY DAMAGED easily damaged or hurt *sensitive eyes/skin* **5** EQUIPMENT Sensitive equipment is able to measure very small changes. ⊃Opposite **insensitive.** • **sensitively** *adverb I think she dealt with the problem very sensitively.* • **sensitivity** /ˌsensɪ'tɪvəti/ *noun* [U] when someone or something is sensitive

sensitive or **sensible**?

Remember that **sensible** does not mean 'easily upset' or 'able to understand what people are feeling'. The word you need to express that is **sensitive.**

Don't criticize her too much. She's very sensitive.

sensor /'sensər/ *noun* [C] a piece of equipment that can find heat, light, etc *Sensors detect movement in the room.*

sensual /'sensjʊəl/ *adjective* relating to physical pleasure, often sexual pleasure *a sensual experience* ○ *a sensual mouth* • **sensuality** /ˌsensju'æləti/ *noun* [U] being sensual

sensuous /'sensjʊəs/ *adjective* giving physical pleasure *the sensuous feel of silk sheets*

sent /sent/ *past of* send

◦▪**sentence¹** /'sentəns/ *noun* **1** [C] a group of words, usually containing a verb, that expresses a complete idea **2** [C, U] a punishment that a judge gives to someone who has committed a crime *a 30-year sentence*

sentence² /'sentəns/ *verb* [T] to give a punishment to someone who has committed a crime [often passive] *She was sentenced to six months in prison.*

sentiment /'sentɪmənt/ *noun* **1** [C, U] an opinion that you have because of the way you feel about something *nationalist/religious sentiments* **2** [U] emotional feelings such as sympathy, love, etc, especially when they are not considered to be suitable for a situation *I find her writing full of sentiment.*

sentimental /ˌsentɪ'mentəl/ *adjective* **1** showing kind feelings such as sympathy, love, etc, especially in a silly way *a sentimental song* ○ *The British are very sentimental about animals.* **2** related to feelings and memories and not related to how much money something costs *It wasn't an expensive ring but it had great sentimental value.* • **sentimentality** /ˌsentɪmen'tæləti/ *noun* [U]

sentry /'sentri/ *noun* [C] a soldier who stands outside a building in order to guard it

separable /'sepərəbl/ *adjective* able to be separated ⊃Opposite **inseparable.**

◦▪**separate¹** /'sepərət/ *adjective* **1** NOT JOINED not joined or touching anything else *a separate compartment* ○ *I try to keep meat separate from other food.* **2** NOT AFFECTING not affecting or related to each other *I've asked him to turn his music down on three separate occasions.* ○ *I have my professional life and my private life and I try to keep them separate.* **3** DIFFERENT different *Use a separate sheet of paper.* • **separately** *adverb*

◦▪**separate²** /'sepəreɪt/ *verb* **1** DIVIDE [I, T] to divide into parts, or to make something divide into parts *I separated the class into three groups.* **2** MOVE APART [I, T] to move apart, or to make people move apart *I shall separate you two if you don't stop talking.* **3** HUSBAND/WIFE [I] to start to live in a different place from your husband or wife because the relationship has ended *My parents separated when I was four.* ⊃See Common learner error at **married.**

separation /ˌsepər'eɪʃən/ *noun* **1** [C, U] when people or things are separate or become separate from other people or things *the separation of church and state* ○ *Their working in different countries meant long periods of separation.* **2** [C] a legal agreement when two people stay married but stop living together

◦▪**September** /sep'tembər/ (*written abbreviation* **Sept**) *noun* [C, U] the ninth month of the year

septic /'septɪk/ *adjective* infected by poisonous bacteria (= small living things which cause disease)

sequel /'siːkwəl/ *noun* [C] a film, book, etc that continues the story from an earlier one

S

sequence /'si:kwəns/ noun 1 [C] a series of related events or things that have a particular order *the sequence of events that led to his death* 2 [U] the order that events or things should happen or be arranged in *I got my slides mixed up and they appeared out of sequence*.

sequin /'si:kwɪn/ noun [C] a small, flat, shiny circle that is sewn onto clothes for decoration

serenade /,serə'neɪd/ noun [C] a song, usually about love

serendipity /,serən'dɪpəti/ noun [U] *literary* when you are lucky and find something interesting or valuable by chance

serene /sɪ'ri:n/ adjective calm and quiet *a serene face/smile* • **serenely** adverb

sergeant /'sɑːdʒənt/ noun [C] 1 an officer of low rank in the police 2 a soldier of middle rank in the army or air force

serial /'sɪəriəl/ noun [C] a story in a magazine or on television or radio that is told in separate parts over a period of time

'serial ,killer noun [C] someone who has murdered several people over a period of time

'serial ,number noun [C] one of a set of numbers that is put on an item that is made in large quantities, such as computers, televisions, paper money, etc., so that you can tell one item from another

o→**series** /'sɪəri:z/ noun [C] *plural* series 1 several things or events of the same type that come one after the other *a series of lectures* 2 a group of television or radio programmes that have the same main characters or deal with the same subject *a four-part drama series*

o→**serious** /'sɪəriəs/ adjective 1 [BAD] A serious problem or situation is bad and makes people worry. *a serious accident/illness* ○ *This is a serious matter.* 2 [NOT JOKING] thinking or speaking sincerely about something and not joking *I'm being serious now - this is a very real problem.* ○ *Are you serious about changing your job?* 3 [QUIET] A serious person is quiet and does not laugh often. *a serious child* • **seriousness** noun [U]

o→**seriously** /'sɪəriəsli/ adverb 1 in a serious way *seriously injured* ○ *Smoking can seriously damage your health.* 2 used to show that what you are going to say is not a joke *Seriously though, you mustn't say that.* 3 **take sb/sth seriously** to believe that someone or something is important and that you should pay attention to them *The police have to take any terrorist threat seriously.*

sermon /'sɜːmən/ noun [C] a religious speech given by a priest in church *to deliver/give a sermon*

serotonin /,serə'təʊnɪn/ noun [U] a chemical in your brain which controls your moods

serpent /'sɜːpənt/ noun [C] *literary* a snake

serrated /sɪ'reɪtɪd/ adjective A serrated edge, usually of a knife, has sharp triangular points along it.

serrated

serum /'sɪərəm/ noun [U] a clear liquid in blood that contains substances that stop infection

servant /'sɜːvənt/ noun [C] someone who works and lives in someone else's house doing their cooking and cleaning, especially in the past ⊃See also: civil servant.

o→**serve¹** /sɜːv/ verb 1 [FOOD/DRINK] [I, T] to give someone food or drink, especially guests or customers in a restaurant or bar *We're not allowed to serve alcohol to anyone under 18.* 2 [SHOP] [I, T] to help customers and sell things to them in a shop *Are you being served?* 3 [WORK] [I, T] to do work that helps society, for example in an organization such as the army or the government *to serve in the army* ○ *to serve on a committee/jury* ○ *He served as mayor for 5 years.* 4 [BE USEFUL] [I, T] to be useful as something *It's a very entertaining film but it also serves an educational purpose.* ○ *The spare bedroom also serves as a study.* ○ [+ to do sth] *He hopes his son's death will serve to warn others about the dangers of owning a gun.* 5 [PRISON] [T] to be in prison for a period of time *Williams, 42, is serving a four-year jail sentence.* 6 [SPORT] [I] in a sport such as tennis, to throw the ball up into the air and then hit it towards the other player 7 **serves one/two/four, etc** If an amount of food serves a particular number, it is enough for that number of people. ⊃See also: It serves her/him/you right²!.

serve² /sɜːv/ noun [C] in sports such as tennis, when you throw the ball up into the air and hit it towards the other player

server /'sɜːvər/ noun [C] a computer that is used only for storing and managing programs and information used by other computers *an email/Internet server*

o→**service¹** /'sɜːvɪs/ noun 1 [SHOP] [U] when people help you and bring you things in a place such as a shop, restaurant, or hotel *The food was nice, but the service wasn't very good.* 2 [SYSTEM] [C] a system that supplies something that people need *financial/medical services* ○ *electricity/water services* ○ *They provide a free bus service from the station.* 3 [WORK] [U] the time you spend working for an organization *He retired last week after 25 years' service.* 4 [CEREMONY] [C] a religious ceremony *They held a memorial service for the victims of the bombing.* 5 [CAR/MACHINE] [C] when a car or machine is examined for faults and repaired 6 [SPORT] [C] when you throw a ball up into the air and hit

S

it towards the other player in sports such as tennis ⊃See also: **the Civil Service, community service, lip-service, the National Health Service, national service, secret service.**

service² /'sɜːvɪs/ *verb* [T] to examine and repair a car or machine

serviceable /'sɜːvɪsəbl/ *adjective* able to be used, but not very good or attractive *I have some old but serviceable chairs.*

'service ˌcharge *noun* [C] an amount of money that is added to what you pay in a restaurant for being helped and brought things *a 10% service charge*

serviceman /'sɜːvɪsmən/ *noun* [C] *plural* servicemen a man who is in the army or navy

the services /'sɜːvɪsɪz/ *noun* [plural] the military forces such as the army or navy

'service ˌstation *noun* [C] a place at the side of a road where you can buy fuel for cars, and food

serviette /ˌsɜːviˈet/ *UK* (*UK/US* **napkin**) *noun* [C] a piece of cloth or paper used when you eat, to keep your clothes clean and to clean your mouth and hands

servile /'sɜːvaɪl/ ⑳ /'sɜːrvəl/ *adjective* too willing to do things for other people

serving /'sɜːvɪŋ/ *noun* [C] an amount of food for one person to eat *a large serving of rice*

sesame seed /'sesəmi,siːd/ *noun* [C] a small seed that is used to add a taste to food

session /'seʃən/ *noun* **1** [C] a period during which you do one activity *a weekly aerobics session* ○ *We're having a training session this afternoon.* **2** [C, U] a meeting of an official group of people such as in a court or in the government *The court is now in session.*

⊶**set¹** /set/ *verb* setting, *past* set **1** A TIME [T] to arrange a time when something will happen [often passive] *The next meeting is set for 6 February.* **2** LEVEL [T] to decide the level of something *The interest rate has been set at 5%.* **3** MACHINE [T] to press switches on a machine so that it will start when you want it to *I've set the alarm for 6.30.* ○ [+ to do sth] *Can you set the video to record 'Neighbours' please?* **4 set an example/a record/a standard, etc** to do something in a way that people will copy or try to improve on *She's set a new world record with that jump.* **5 set fire to sth; set sth on fire** to make something start burning **6 set sb free** to allow someone to leave prison, or to allow a person or animal to escape **7 set sth alight** to make something start burning **8 set the table** to put plates, knives, forks, etc on the table before you have a meal **9** SUN [I] When the sun sets, it moves down in the sky so that it cannot be seen. *The sun rises in the East and sets in the West.* **10** BECOME SOLID [I] If a liquid substance sets, it becomes solid. **11** SCHOOL WORK [T] *UK* If you set work or an exam at a school or college, you ask the students to do it. [+ two objects] *Mr Harley forgot to set us any maths homework.* **12 set sth down/on, etc** to put something somewhere *She set the vase down on the table.* **13** BOOK/FILM/PLAY [T] If a book, play, or film is set in a place or period of time, the story happens there or at that time. [often

passive] *It's a historical adventure set in India in the 1940s.* **14 set to work** to start working

set about sth/doing sth to start doing something, especially something that uses a lot of time or energy *I got home and immediately set about cleaning the house.*

be set against sth/doing sth to not want to do or have something *He is dead set against the move.*

set sb/sth apart If a quality sets someone or something apart, it makes them different from and usually better than others of the same type. *It's their intelligence which sets them apart from other rock bands.*

set sth aside to save something, usually time or money, for a special purpose

set sb/sth back to make something happen more slowly or later than it should *The heavy traffic set us back about half an hour.*

set sb back (sth) *informal* to cost someone a large amount of money *A car like that will probably set you back about £12,000.*

set in If something unpleasant sets in, it begins and seems likely to continue. *This rain looks as if it has set in for the rest of the day.*

set off to start a journey *What time are you setting off tomorrow morning?*

set sth off to cause something to begin or happen, especially a loud noise or a lot of activity *He's always burning the toast and setting off the smoke alarm.*

set sb/sth on/upon sb to make a person or animal attack someone *If you come any closer, I'll set the dog on you.*

set out 1 to start doing something when you have already decided what you want to achieve [+ to do sth] *I'd done what I set out to do.* **2** to start a journey

set sth out to give all the details of something, or to explain something clearly, especially in writing *Your contract will set out the terms of your employment.*

set sth up 1 to start a company or organization *A committee has been set up to investigate the problem.* **2** to arrange for something to happen *I've set up a meeting with him for next week.*

set sb up to trick someone in order to make them do something, or in order to make them seem guilty of something that they have not done

set (sth) up to get all the necessary equipment ready for an activity *I need one or two people to help me set up the display.*

⊶**set²** /set/ *noun* [C] **1** GROUP a group of things which belong together *a set of instructions/rules* ○ *a set of keys/tools* **2** FILM/PLAY the place where a film or play is performed or recorded, and the pictures, furniture, etc that are used *They first met on the set of 'Star Wars'.* **3** TENNIS one part of a tennis match *Agassi is leading by four games to one in the third set.* **4** TV/RADIO a television or radio *a TV set* **5** MUSIC a group of songs or tunes that go together to make a musical performance

set³ /set/ *adjective* **1** fixed and never changing *Most people work for a set number of hours each week.* ○ *I have no set routine.* **2 be all set**

to be ready [+ to do sth] *We were all set to go when the phone rang.* ➲See also: On your marks (**mark**[1]). Get set. Go!.

WORD PARTNERS FOR ***setback***

suffer a setback • a **major/serious** setback • a setback **for** sb • a setback **in/to** sth

setback /ˈsetbæk/ *noun* [C] a problem that makes something happen later or more slowly than it should *The project has **suffered** a series of **setbacks** this year.*

set-piece /ˌsetˈpiːs/ *noun* [C] a speech or set of actions that has been carefully planned and practised

settee /setˈiː/ *UK* (*UK/US* **sofa**) *noun* [C] a large, comfortable seat for more than one person

setting /ˈsetɪŋ/ *noun* [C] **1** the place where something is or where something happens, often in a book, play, or film *The house provided the **setting for** the TV series 'Pride and Prejudice'.* **2** a position on the controls of a piece of equipment *Set the oven at the lowest setting.*

settle /ˈsetl/ *verb* **1** ARGUMENT [T] If you settle an argument, you solve the problem and stop arguing. *to **settle a dispute*** **2** LIVE [I] to start living somewhere that you are going to live for a long time *He travelled around Europe for years before finally settling in Vienna.* **3** DECIDE [T] to decide or arrange something [often passive] *Right, that's settled. We're going to Spain.* **4** RELAX [I, T] to relax into a comfortable position [often reflexive] *She settled herself into the chair opposite.* **5** PAY [T] If you settle a bill or a debt, you pay the money that you owe. **6** MOVE DOWN [I] to move down towards the ground or the bottom of something and then stay there *Do you think the snow will settle?* ➲See also: the **dust**[1] settles.

settle down 1 to start living in a place where you intend to stay for a long time, usually with a partner *Do you think he'll ever settle down and have a family?* **2** to start to feel happy and confident with a new situation *Has she settled down in her new job?*

settle (sb) down to become quiet and calm, or to make someone become quiet and calm *Come on children, stop chatting and settle down please!*

settle for sth to accept something, especially something that is not exactly what you want *He wants a full refund and he won't settle for anything less.*

settle in to begin to feel relaxed and happy in a new home or job *Are you settling in OK?*

settle on/upon sth to agree on a decision *We still haven't settled on a place to meet.*

settle up to pay someone the money that you owe them *I need to **settle up with** you for the tickets.*

settled /ˈsetld/ *adjective* **1 be settled** to feel happy and relaxed in a place or situation *He seems quite settled now.* **2** regular and not often changing *The weather's a lot more settled at this time of year.* ➲Opposite **unsettled**.

WORD PARTNERS FOR ***settlement***

agree/negotiate/reach a settlement • a settlement **between** sb and sb • a settlement **over** sth • a **peace** settlement

settlement /ˈsetlmənt/ *noun* [C] **1** an official agreement that finishes an argument *a **peace settlement*** **2** a town or village which people built to live in after arriving from somewhere else *a Jewish settlement*

settler /ˈsetləʳ/ *noun* [C] someone who moves to a new place where there were not many people before *The first European settlers arrived in Virginia in 1607.*

set-top box /ˈsettɒpˌbɒks/ *noun* [C] a piece of electronic equipment that allows you to watch digital broadcasts (= television sounds and pictures sent as signals in the form of numbers) on an ordinary television

set-up /ˈsetʌp/ *noun* [C] *informal* **1** the way that something is arranged or organized *It took me a while to get used to the set-up in my new job.* **2** a plan that is dishonest and is intended to trick someone

⊶**seven** /ˈsevᵊn/ the number 7

⊶**seventeen** /ˌsevᵊnˈtiːn/ the number 17 • **seventeenth** 17th written as a word

seventh[1] /ˈsevᵊnθ/ 7th written as a word

seventh[2] /ˈsevᵊnθ/ *noun* [C] one of seven equal parts of something; 1/7

⊶**seventy** /ˈsevᵊnti/ **1** the number 70 **2 the seventies** the years from 1970 to 1979 **3 be in your seventies** to be aged between 70 and 79 • **seventieth** 70th written as a word

sever /ˈsevəʳ/ *verb* [T] **1** to cut through something, especially a part of the body *to sever an artery* ○ [often passive] *Two of her fingers were severed in the accident.* **2 sever links/ties, etc with sb** to end a relationship with someone

⊶**several** /ˈsevᵊrᵊl/ *pronoun, determiner* some, but not a lot *Several people have complained about the scheme.* ○ ***Several of** my friends studied in Manchester.*

severance /ˈsevᵊrəns/ *noun* [U] when an employer forces an employee to leave a job ***severance pay***

severe /sɪˈvɪəʳ/ *adjective* **1** BAD extremely bad *a severe headache* ○ *severe weather conditions* **2** NOT KIND not kind or gentle *a severe punishment* **3** PERSON A severe person looks unfriendly or very strict. • **severely** *adverb to be severely injured* ○ *She has been severely criticized for the speech.*

severity /sɪˈverəti/ *noun* [U] how severe something is

sew /səʊ/ *verb* [I, T] *past tense* **sewed**, *past participle* **sewn** or **sewed** to join things together with a needle and thread *I need to sew a button on my shirt.*

sew sth up 1 to close or repair something by sewing the edges together **2 have sth sewn up** *informal* to be certain to win or succeed at something

sewage /ˈsuːɪdʒ/ *noun* [U] waste water and waste from toilets *a sewage treatment plant*

sewer /səʊəʳ/ *noun* [C] a large underground

S

system of pipes that carries away sewage

sewing /'səʊɪŋ/ *noun* [U] **1** the activity of join-ing pieces of cloth together or repairing them with a needle and thread **2** the pieces of cloth that you are joining together or repairing with a needle and thread

'sewing ma,chine *noun* [C] a machine that joins pieces of cloth together with a needle and thread

sewn /səʊn/ *past participle of* sew

o→**sex¹** /seks/ *noun* **1** [U] sexual activity between people *to have sex with someone* ○ *sex edu-cation* **2** [U] the fact of being male or female *Do you know what sex the baby is?* ○ *sex dis-crimination* **3** the **female/male/opposite, etc sex** people who are female/male/the other sex from you, etc

sex² /seks/ *verb*
  sex sth up *UK informal* to make something seem more exciting than it really is *It was said that the government had sexed up the report.*

sexism /'seksɪz³m/ *noun* [U] when someone is treated unfairly because they are a woman or because they are a man ● **sexist** *adjective sexist attitudes/jokes*

'sex ,life *noun* [C] a person's sexual activities and relationships

o→**sexual** /'sekʃʊəl/ *adjective* **1** relating to the activity of sex *sexual experiences* ○ *sexual organs* **2** relating to being male or female *sexual discrimination* ○ *sexual equality*

,sexual 'intercourse *noun* [U] *formal* when a man puts his penis into a woman's vagina

sexuality /,sekʃu'æləti/ *noun* [U] the way you feel about sexual activity and the type of sex you prefer

sexually /'sekʃʊəli/ *adverb* in a way that relates to the activity of sex *sexually attractive* ○ *a sexually transmitted disease*

sexy /'seksi/ *adjective* attractive or exciting in a sexual way *sexy underwear* ○ *He's very sexy.*

SGML /esdʒiːem'el/ *noun* [U] *abbreviation for* standard generalized markup language: a system for organizing different parts of a com-puter document

sh (*also* **shh**) /ʃ/ *exclamation* used to tell someone to be quiet

shabby /'ʃæbi/ *adjective* **1** looking untidy and in bad condition *shabby clothes/furniture* **2** Shabby behaviour or treatment is bad and unfair. ● **shabbily** *adverb shabbily dressed* ○ *shabbily treated*

shack¹ /ʃæk/ *noun* [C] a small simple building that has been badly built

shack² /ʃæk/ *verb*
  shack up with sb *very informal* to start living in the same house as someone you are having a romantic relationship with

shackle /'ʃækl/ *verb* [T] **1** to fasten a prisoner's arms or legs together with chains **2** be **shackled by sth** to be prevented from doing what you want to do by something

shackles /'ʃæklz/ *noun* [plural] chains used to fasten together prisoners' arms or legs

shade

shade   shadow

shade¹ /ʃeɪd/ *noun* **1** NO SUN [U] an area where there is no light from the sun and so it is darker and not as hot *I'd prefer to sit in the shade.* **2** COLOUR [C] a colour, especially when referring to how dark or light it is *a pale/dark shade of grey* ○ *pastel shades* **3** COVER [C] a cover that stops too much light coming from the sun or from an electric light *a lamp shade* **4 a shade** a small amount *He's perhaps a shade taller.* **5 a shade of meaning/opinion, etc** a slight difference in the meaning of something

shade² /ʃeɪd/ *verb* [T] to cover something in order to protect it from the sun *He shaded his eyes with his hand.*

shades /ʃeɪdz/ *noun* [plural] *informal* sunglasses (= dark glasses that protect your eyes from the sun)

⟐ WORD PARTNERS FOR **shadow**

sth **casts** a shadow ● a shadow **crosses/falls across** sth ● sth is **in** shadow ● the shadow **of** sth

o→**shadow¹** /'ʃædəʊ/ *noun* **1** [C, U] a dark area made by something that is stopping the light *The tree had cast (= made) a long shadow.* ⟐See picture at shade. **2 beyond/without a shadow of a doubt** If something is true beyond a shadow of a doubt, it is certainly true. **3 cast a shadow over sth** to spoil a good situation with something unpleasant *The bombing has cast a shadow over the Queen's visit.*

shadow² /'ʃædəʊ/ *verb* [T] to follow someone se-cretly in order to see where they go and what they do [often passive] *He was being shadowed by a private detective.*

shadowy /'ʃædəʊi/ *adjective* **1** dark and full of shadows *in a shadowy corner* **2** secret and mysterious *the shadowy world of espionage*

shady /'ʃeɪdi/ *adjective* **1** A shady place is pro-tected from the sun and so it is darker and cooler. *We found a shady spot to sit in.* **2** *in-formal* dishonest and illegal *shady deals*

shaft /ʃɑːft/ *noun* [C] **1** a long, vertical hole that people or things can move through, either inside a building or in the ground *a mine shaft* ○ *a ventilation shaft* **2** the handle of a tool or weapon **3 a shaft of light** a beam of light

shake¹ /ʃeɪk/ *verb*
past tense **shook**, *past participle* **shaken**
1 MOVE [I, T] to make quick, short movements from side to side or up and down, or to make something or someone do this *He was shaking with nerves.* ○ *Shake the bottle.*
2 shake hands to hold someone's hand and move it up and down when you meet them for the first time, or when you make an agreement with them *The two leaders smiled and shook hands for the photographers.* ○ *I shook hands with him.* **3 shake your head** to move your head from side to side to mean 'no' **4** SHOCK [T] to shock or upset someone [often passive] *No one was injured in the crash, but the driver was badly shaken.* **5** VOICE [I] If your voice shakes, you sound very nervous or frightened.

shake *sth* **off** to get rid of an illness or something that is causing you problems *I hope I can shake off this cold before the weekend.*

shake *sb* **off** to succeed in escaping from someone who is following you *He was running after me but I managed to shake him off.*

shake *sth* **out** to hold something that is made of cloth at one end and move it up and down in order to get rid of dirt

shake *sb* **up** If an unpleasant experience shakes someone up, it makes them feel shocked and upset. *The accident really shook him up.*

shake² /ʃeɪk/ *noun* [C] **1** when you shake something *Give it a good shake before you open it.* **2** (*also* **milkshake**) a sweet drink made of milk and chocolate or fruit

shake-up /ˈʃeɪkʌp/ *noun* [C] when big changes are made to a system or an organization *This is the biggest shake-up in the legal system for fifty years.*

shaky /ˈʃeɪki/ *adjective* **1** MOVING making quick, short movements from side to side or up and down *shaky hands* **2** NOT STRONG not physically strong because you are nervous, old, or ill *I felt a bit shaky when I stood up.* **3** LIKELY TO FAIL not working well and likely to fail *They managed to win the game, despite a very shaky start.*

o→**shall** *strong form* /ʃæl/ *weak form* /ʃəl/ *modal verb*
1 shall I/we...? a used to make an offer or suggestion *Shall I cook dinner tonight?* ○ *We'll ask him later, shall we?* **b** used to ask someone what to do *What restaurant shall we go to?* ○ *Who shall I ask?* **2 I/we shall...** *formal* used to say what you are going to do in the future *I shall be talking to her tomorrow.* ○ *I shan't forget to tell them.* ⊃See Extra help page **Modal verbs** on page Centre 22.

COMMON LEARNER ERROR

shall and will

Shall and **will** are both used to talk about what you are going to do in the future. **Shall** is usually used with 'I' or 'we' and is more formal than **will**.

shallot /ʃəˈlɒt/ *noun* [C] a vegetable like a small onion

o→**shallow** /ˈʃæləʊ/ *adjective* **1** not deep *shallow water* ○ *a shallow dish* ⊃See picture at **deep**. **2** not showing any interest in serious ideas

the shallows /ˈʃæləʊz/ *noun* [plural] areas of shallow water

sham /ʃæm/ *noun* [no plural] something that is not what it seems to be and is intended to deceive people *Newspapers have described their marriage as a sham.*

shambles /ˈʃæmblz/ *noun* **be a shambles** *informal* to be very badly organized *The performance was a complete shambles.*

WORD PARTNERS FOR **shame**

2 bring shame **on** sb/sth • **a sense of** shame • **the** shame **of (doing)** sth

shame¹ /ʃeɪm/ *noun* **1 a shame** If you describe something as a shame, you are disappointed that it has happened. [+ to do sth] *It's a real shame to waste all this food.* ○ [+ (that)] *What a shame that they had to destroy such a beautiful building.* **2** [U] when you feel embarrassed and guilty about something bad that you have done *to be filled with shame* **3 have no shame** to not feel embarrassed or guilty about doing bad or embarrassing things **4 put sb/sth to shame** to be much better than someone or something else *Your cooking puts mine to shame.*

shame² /ʃeɪm/ *verb* [T] to make someone feel embarrassed and guilty about something [+ into + doing sth] *His children are trying to shame him into giving up smoking.*

shameful /ˈʃeɪmfəl/ *adjective* Something shameful is bad and should make you feel embarrassed and guilty. *shameful scenes* • **shamefully** *adverb*

shameless /ˈʃeɪmləs/ *adjective* without feeling embarrassed or guilty although you should *shameless behaviour/lies* • **shamelessly** *adverb*

shampoo /ʃæmˈpuː/ *noun* [C, U] a liquid substance that you use to wash your hair *a bottle of shampoo* • **shampoo** *verb* [T] **shampooing** *past* **shampooed**

o→**shan't** /ʃɑːnt/ *mainly UK short for* shall not *I was invited to the party, but I shan't be going.*

shanty town /ˈʃæntiˌtaʊn/ *noun* [C] an area on the edge of a town where poor people live in very simply built houses

WORD PARTNERS FOR **shape**

an irregular/pleasing/strange/unusual shape • **change** shape • **in the** shape **of** sth

shapes

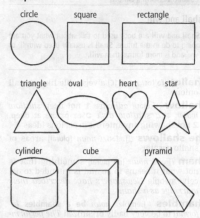

circle   square   rectangle

triangle   oval   heart   star

cylinder   cube   pyramid

o⁻**shape¹** /ʃeɪp/ *noun* **1** [C, U] the physical form of something made by the line around its outer edge *a circular/rectangular shape* ○ *You can recognize trees by the shape of their leaves.* **2 in good/bad/great, etc shape** in good/bad, etc health or condition *She runs every day so she's in pretty good shape.* **3 out of shape** not healthy or physically strong **4 keep in shape** to stay healthy and physically strong **5 take shape** to start to develop and become more clear or certain *The project is slowly beginning to take shape.* **6 all shapes and sizes** many different types of people or things *We saw people there of all shapes and sizes.*

shape² /ʃeɪp/ *verb* [T] **1** to influence the way that something develops [often passive] *Their attitudes were shaped during the war.* **2** to make something become a particular shape *Combine the meat and egg and shape the mixture into small balls.*

shape up *informal* to develop or improve *Things at work seem to be shaping up quite nicely.*

-shaped /ʃeɪpt/ *suffix* used after nouns to mean 'having a particular shape' *a heart-shaped cake* ⊃See also: **pear-shaped**.

shapeless /ˈʃeɪpləs/ *adjective* not having a clear or well designed shape *a shapeless dress*

shapely /ˈʃeɪpli/ *adjective* having an attractive shape *shapely legs*

o⁻**share¹** /ʃeəʳ/ *verb* **1** [I, T] to have or use something at the same time as someone else *She shares a house with Paul.* **2** [I, T] to divide something between two or more people *We shared a pizza and a bottle of wine.* ○ *We shared the cost of the wedding between us.* **3 share an interest/opinion, etc** to have the same interest/opinion, etc as someone else *They share a love of gardening.* **4 share your problems/thoughts/ideas, etc** to tell someone your problems/thoughts, etc

share sth out to divide something into smaller amounts and give one amount to each person in a group *Profits are shared out*

equally among members of the group.

share² /ʃeəʳ/ *noun* [C] **1** one of the equal parts that the value of a company is divided into when it is owned by a group of people *to buy/sell shares* ○ *We own shares in a number of companies.* ○ *Share prices have fallen for the third day running.* **2** a part of something that has been divided [usually singular] *When am I going to get my share of the money?* **3 have your (fair) share of sth** to have a lot of something and enough of it, usually something bad *We've had our fair share of rain already this summer.*

shareholder /ˈʃeəˌhəʊldəʳ/ *noun* [C] someone who owns shares in a company *a shareholders' meeting*

shareware /ˈʃeəweəʳ/ *noun* [U] software that can be used by anyone without having to pay for it

Sharia /ʃəˈriːə/ *noun* [U] the holy law of Islam

shark /ʃɑːk/ *noun* [C]   shark
a large fish with very sharp teeth

o⁻**sharp¹** /ʃɑːp/ *adjective* **1** [ABLE TO CUT] having a very thin or pointed edge that can cut things *a sharp knife* ○ *sharp claws/teeth* **2 a sharp rise/increase/drop, etc** a sudden and very large increase or reduction in something **3 a sharp contrast/difference/distinction, etc** a very big and noticeable difference between two things **4** [QUICK] quick to notice and understand things *a sharp mind* **5 a sharp pain** a sudden, short, strong pain **6** [SEVERE] severe and not gentle *sharp criticism* ○ *She can be a bit sharp with people sometimes.* **7 a sharp bend/turn, etc** a sudden large change in the direction you are travelling **8** [SOUR] A sharp taste is slightly sour. **9** [CLEAR] A sharp image is very clear. *a photograph in sharp focus* **10 a sharp wit** the ability to say things that are funny and clever **11 a sharp tongue** If you have a sharp tongue, you often upset people by saying unkind things to them. **12** [FASHIONABLE] If a piece of clothing or a style is sharp, it is fashionable and tidy. *young men in sharp suits* **13** C sharp/F sharp, etc the musical note that is between the note C, F, etc and the note above it **14** [TOO HIGH] A sharp musical note sounds unpleasant because it is slightly higher than it should be. • **sharply** *adverb* • **sharpness** *noun* [U]

sharp² /ʃɑːp/ *adverb* **3 o'clock/8.30 p.m., etc sharp** at exactly 3 o'clock, 8.30 p.m., etc

sharp³ /ʃɑːp/ *noun* [C] a musical note that is between one note and the note above it

sharpen /ˈʃɑːpᵊn/ *verb* [T] to make something sharper *to sharpen a knife/pencil*

shatter /ˈʃætəʳ/ *verb* **1** [I, T] to break into very small pieces, or to make something break into very small pieces *Someone threw a stone at the car, shattering the windscreen.* **2** [T] to destroy something good, such as your confidence, hopes, or belief in something *The accident completely shattered her confidence.*

shattered /'ʃætəd/ *adjective* **1** very upset **2** *UK informal* very tired

shave¹ /ʃeɪv/ *verb* [I, T] to cut hair off your face or body *to shave your head/ legs* ○ *shaving cream/foam*

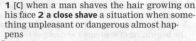
shave

shave sth off to cut a very thin piece off a surface

shave² /ʃeɪv/ *noun*
1 [C] when a man shaves the hair growing on his face **2 a close shave** a situation when something unpleasant or dangerous almost happens

shaven /'ʃeɪv³n/ *adjective* A shaven part of the body has had the hair cut off it. *a gang of youths with shaven heads*

shaver /'ʃeɪvəʳ/ *noun* [C] a piece of electrical equipment used to cut hair off the head or body

shavings /'ʃeɪvɪŋz/ *noun* [plural] very thin pieces that have been cut off something *wood shavings*

shawl /ʃɔːl/ *noun* [C] a piece of cloth that is worn by a woman around her shoulders or used to cover a baby

o--**she** *strong form* /ʃiː/ *weak form* /ʃi/ *pronoun* used as the subject of the verb when referring to someone female who has already been talked about *"When is Ruth coming?" "She'll be here soon."*

sheaf /ʃiːf/ *noun* [C] *plural* **sheaves** /ʃiːvz/ **1** several pieces of paper held together *a sheaf of papers* **2** several pieces of wheat or corn (= plant for grain) tied together

shear /ʃɪəʳ/ *verb* [T] *past tense* **sheared** *past participle* **sheared** or **shorn** to cut the wool off a sheep

shears /ʃɪəz/ *noun* [plural] a cutting tool with two large blades, like a large pair of scissors *a pair of garden shears*

sheath /ʃiːθ/ *noun* [C] a cover for the sharp blade of a knife

o--**she'd** /ʃiːd/ **1** *short for* she had *By the time I got there, she'd fallen asleep.* **2** *short for* she would *She knew that she'd be late.*

shed¹ /ʃed/ *noun* [C] a small building used to store things such as tools *a garden shed*

shed² /ʃed/ *verb* [T] **shedding**, *past* **shed** **1 shed leaves/skin/hair, etc** to lose something because it falls off *A lot of trees shed their leaves in the autumn.* **2** to get rid of something that you do not want or need *A lot of companies are shedding jobs.* **3 shed tears** to cry **4 shed blood** to kill or injure someone ○See also: cast/shed **light¹** on sth.

sheen /ʃiːn/ *noun* [no plural] a smooth shine on a surface

sheep /ʃiːp/ *noun* [C] *plural* **sheep** a farm animal whose skin is covered with wool *a flock of sheep*

sheepish /'ʃiːpɪʃ/ *adjective* slightly embarrassed, usually because you have done something stupid *a sheepish grin/look* ● **sheepishly** *adverb*

sheer /ʃɪəʳ/ *adjective* **1** EXTREME [always before noun] used to emphasize how strong a feeling or quality is *a look of sheer delight/joy* ○ *sheer determination/hard work* **2** LARGE [always before noun] used to emphasize the large size or amount of something *The delays are due to the sheer volume of traffic.* **3** STEEP very steep *a sheer cliff face* **4** CLOTH Sheer cloth is very thin and you can see through it. *sheer tights/nylons*

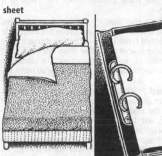
sheet

sheets on a bed   sheet of paper

sheet /ʃiːt/ *noun* [C] **1** a large piece of cloth put on a bed to lie on or under *a double fitted sheet* ○ *to change the sheets* **2 a sheet of paper/glass/ metal, etc** a flat piece of paper/glass, etc *a sheet of yellow paper* ○See also: **balance sheet**.

sheeting /'ʃiːtɪŋ/ *noun* [U] a large flat piece of material, usually used as a cover *plastic sheeting*

Sheikh (*also* **Sheik**) /ʃeɪk/ *noun* [C] an Arab leader

shelf /ʃelf/ *noun* [C] *plural* **shelves** /ʃelvz/ a flat, horizontal board used to put things on, often fixed to a wall or inside a cupboard *a book shelf* ○ *on the top/bottom shelf*

'shelf ˌlife *noun* [C] *plural* **shelf lives** A product's shelf life is the length of time it stays in good condition and can be used. [usually singular] *Fresh fruit has a very short shelf life.*

o--**she'll** /ʃiːl/ *short for* she will *She'll be away until Tuesday.*

shell¹ /ʃel/ *noun* [C]
1 the hard outer covering of some creatures and of eggs, nuts, or seeds *a snail's shell* ○ *an egg shell* **2** a bomb fired from a large gun ○See also: **sea shell**.

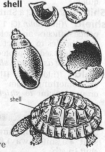
shell

shell

shell² /ʃel/ *verb* [T] to attack a place with bombs

shell out (sth) *informal* to pay or give money for something, especially when you do not want to

shellfish /'ʃelfɪʃ/ *noun* [U] sea creatures that live in shells and are eaten as food

---

🔲 **WORD PARTNERS FOR *shelter***

2 find/provide/seek/take shelter • shelter from sth • under the shelter of sth

---

shelter¹ /'ʃeltə^r/ *noun* **1** [C] a place that protects you from bad weather or danger *a bomb shelter* **2** [U] protection from bad weather or danger *We took shelter from the rain in a doorway.*

shelter² /'ʃeltə^r/ *verb* **1 shelter from/in/under, etc** to go under a cover or inside a building to be protected from bad weather or danger *They went under a tree to shelter from the rain.* **2** [T] to provide cover or protection for someone *Many households are already sheltering refugees.*

sheltered /'ʃeltəd/ *adjective* **1** covered or protected from bad weather or danger *a sheltered spot by the wall* **2 a sheltered existence/life/upbringing, etc** If you have a sheltered life, you are protected too much and experience very little danger or excitement. **3 sheltered accommodation/housing** *UK* houses for old and ill people in a place where help can be given if it is needed

shelve /ʃelv/ *verb* [T] to decide not to continue with a plan [often passive] *The project had to be shelved when they ran out of money.*

shelves /ʃelvz/ *plural of* shelf

shenanigans /ʃɪ'nænɪgənz/ *noun* [plural] *informal* secret or dishonest behaviour *political/sexual shenanigans*

shepherd¹ /'ʃepəd/ *noun* [C] someone whose job is to look after sheep

shepherd² /'ʃepəd/ *verb* [T] to go somewhere with someone in order to guide them or protect them *children shepherded to school by their parents*

sheriff /'ʃerɪf/ *noun* [C] an elected law officer in the US

sherry /'ʃeri/ *noun* [C, U] a strong Spanish wine that is drunk before a meal

she's /ʃiːz/ **1** *short for* she is *She's a very good student.* **2** *short for* she has *She's been working very hard.*

shh /ʃ/ *exclamation* used to tell someone to be quiet

Shia /'ʃiːə/ *noun* [C] a Shiite

shield¹ /ʃiːld/ *noun* [C] **1** a large, flat object that police officers and soldiers hold in front of their bodies to protect themselves **2** a person or thing used as protection *The hostages are being used as **human shields**.*

shield² /ʃiːld/ *verb* [T] to protect someone or something from something dangerous or unpleasant *to **shield** your **eyes** from the sun*

🔲 **WORD PARTNERS FOR *shift***

a dramatic/fundamental/gradual/major shift • a shift (away) from/towards sth • a shift in sth

---

shift¹ /ʃɪft/ *noun* [C] **1** a change in something *There has been a dramatic **shift in** public opinion on this matter.* **2** a period of work in a place such as a factory or hospital *afternoon/night **shift*** ○ *He works an eight-hour shift.*

shift² /ʃɪft/ *verb* **1** [CHANGE] [I, T] to change something *We are trying to **shift** the emphasis **from** curing illness **to** preventing it.* **2** [MOVE STH] [T] to move something to another place *We need to shift all these boxes into the other room.* **3** [MOVE YOURSELF] [I, T] to move into a different position *He shifted uncomfortably in his seat.* **4** [CHANGE SPEED] [T] (*also* shift into) *US* to change the position of the gears (= parts that control how fast the wheels turn) in a vehicle *to **shift gears***

'shift ˌkey *noun* [C] the key on a computer keyboard which allows you to create a capital letter (= a large letter of the alphabet used at the beginning of sentences and names)

shifty /'ʃɪfti/ *adjective informal* Someone who looks shifty looks dishonest.

Shiite /'ʃiːaɪt/ (*also* Shi'ite) *noun* [C] a member of a large group within the Islamic religion • Shiite (*also* Shi'ite) *adjective* describing the Shiites or their type of Islam

shilling /'ʃɪlɪŋ/ *noun* [C] a unit of money used in the past in the UK

shimmer /'ʃɪmə^r/ *verb* [I] to shine gently and seem to be moving slightly *The trees shimmered in the moonlight.*

shin /ʃɪn/ *noun* [C] the front part of a leg between the knee and the foot ⊃See colour picture **The Body** on page Centre 13.

shine¹ /ʃaɪn/ *verb past* shone *or* shined **1** [PRODUCE LIGHT] [I] to produce bright light *The sun was shining brightly through the window.* **2** [POINT LIGHT] [I, T] to point a light somewhere *The car's headlights shone right into my eyes.* **3** [REFLECT] [I, T] If a surface shines, it reflects light, and if you shine it, you make it reflect light. *She polished her shoes until they shone.* **4** [EYES/FACE] [I] If your eyes or face shine, you look happy, healthy, or excited. *His eyes were shining with excitement.* **5** [DO WELL] [I] to do something very well, usually better than other people.

shine² /ʃaɪn/ *noun* **1** [no plural] when something is bright from reflected light on its surface *hair with body and shine* **2 take a shine to sb** *informal* to like someone immediately *I think he's taken a bit of a shine to you.* **3 take the shine off sth** to spoil something pleasant

shingle /'ʃɪŋgl/ *noun* [U] *UK* a lot of very small pieces of stone on a beach

shiny /'ʃaɪni/ *adjective* A shiny surface is bright because it reflects light. *shiny hair*

ship¹ /ʃɪp/ *noun* [C] a large boat that carries people or goods by sea *a cargo ship*

ship² /ʃɪp/ *verb* [T] shipping, *past* shipped to send something from one place to another [often passive] *These vegetables have been shipped halfway around the world.*

shipment /'ʃɪpmənt/ *noun* **1** [C] an amount of goods sent from one place to another *The first shipments of food arrived this month.* **2** [U] when something is sent from one place to another *the shipment of nuclear waste*

| ɑː arm | ɜː her | iː see | ɔː saw | uː too | aɪ my | aʊ how | eə hair | eɪ day | əʊ no | ɪə near | ɔɪ boy | ʊə poor | aɪə fire | aʊə sour |

,**shipping and** '**handling** *noun* [U] *US* postage and packing

shipwreck¹ /'ʃɪprek/ *noun* [C] an accident in which a ship is destroyed at sea

shipwreck² /'ʃɪprek/ *verb* **be shipwrecked** If someone is shipwrecked, the ship they are in is destroyed in an accident.

shipyard /'ʃɪpjɑːd/ *noun* [C] a place where ships are built or repaired

shirk /ʃɜːk/ *verb* [I, T] to avoid doing something because it is difficult or unpleasant *to shirk your duties/responsibilities*

o⊶**shirt** /ʃɜːt/ *noun* [C] a piece of clothing worn on the top part of the body, often made of thin material like cotton and fastened with buttons down the front ➍See colour picture **Clothes** on page Centre 9 ➍See also: **polo shirt, T-shirt.**

shish kebab /'ʃɪʃkə,bæb/ *noun* [C] small pieces of meat or vegetables cooked on a long, thin stick

shit¹ /ʃɪt/ *exclamation very informal* a very impolite word used to show surprise, anger, disappointment, etc

shit² /ʃɪt/ *noun* [U] *very informal* a very impolite word for waste from the body of a person or animal that comes out of their bottom

shiver /'ʃɪvəʳ/ *verb* [I] to shake because you are cold or frightened *She shivered with cold.* ● **shiver** *noun* [C] *He felt a shiver run down his spine* (= He felt afraid).

shoal /ʃəʊl/ *noun* [C] a large group of fish swimming together

┌─────────────────────────────────┐
│ WORD PARTNERS FOR **shock**
└─────────────────────────────────┘

come as a shock   ●   **get/have** a shock   ●   a **big/nasty/real** shock   ● a shock **to** sb   ● **be in** shock

shock¹ /ʃɒk/ *noun* **1** [SURPRISE] [C, U] a big, unpleasant surprise *We got a nasty shock when he gave us the bill.* ○ *Her death came as a terrible shock to him.* ○ *They are still in shock* (= feeling the effect of a shock) *from the accident.* **2** [ILLNESS] [U] a medical condition when someone is extremely weak because of damage to their body *He went into shock and nearly died.* **3** [ELECTRICITY] [C] (*also* **electric shock**) a sudden, painful feeling that you get when electricity flows through your body **4** [MOVEMENT] [C] a sudden movement caused by an explosion, accident, etc ➍See also: **culture shock.**

shock² /ʃɒk/ *verb* [I, T] to surprise and upset someone [often passive] *Many people were shocked by the violent scenes in the film.* ● **shocked** *adjective* [+ to do sth] *We were shocked to find rat poison in our hotel room.*

shocking /'ʃɒkɪŋ/ *adjective* **1** very surprising and upsetting or immoral *shocking news* ○ *This report contains scenes that some people may find shocking.* **2** *UK* very bad *My memory is shocking.* ● **shockingly** *adverb*

shoddy /'ʃɒdi/ *adjective* very bad quality *shoddy goods* ○ **shoddy work/workmanship/treatment**

o⊶**shoe** /ʃuː/ *noun* [C] **1** a strong covering for the foot, often made of leather *a pair of shoes* ○ *to put your shoes on/take your shoes off* **2** **be in**

sb's shoes *informal* to be in the same situation as someone else, especially an unpleasant situation *What would you do if you were in my shoes?*

shoelace /'ʃuːleɪs/ *noun* [C] a long, thin piece of material used to fasten shoes

shoestring /'ʃuːstrɪŋ/ *noun* **on a shoestring** If you do something on a shoestring, you do it using very little money.

shone /ʃɒn/ ⊕ /ʃəʊn/ *past of* shine

shoo /ʃuː/ *verb* shooing *past* shooed **shoo sb away/ off/out, etc** to make a person or animal leave a place by chasing them or shouting 'shoo' at them ● **shoo** *exclamation*

shook /ʃʊk/ *past tense of* shake

o⊶**shoot**¹ /ʃuːt/ *verb past* shot **1** [INJURE] [T] to injure or kill a person or animal by firing a bullet from a gun at them [often passive] *He was robbed and then shot in the stomach.* ○ *An innocent bystander was shot dead in the incident.* **2** [FIRE BULLET] [I, T] to fire a bullet from a gun *Don't shoot!* **3** [SPORT] [I] to try to score points in sports such as football by hitting, kicking, or throwing the ball towards the goal **4** **shoot across/out/up, etc** to move somewhere very quickly *She shot across the road without looking.* **5** [FILM] [T] to use a camera to record a film or take a photograph [often passive] *Most of the film was shot in Italy.*

shoot sb/sth down to destroy an aircraft or make it fall to the ground by firing bullets or weapons at it

shoot up If a number or amount shoots up, it increases very quickly. *Prices have shot up by 25%.*

shoot² /ʃuːt/ *noun* [C] **1** a new branch or stem growing on a plant *bamboo shoots* **2** when someone takes photographs or makes a film *a fashion shoot*

shooting /'ʃuːtɪŋ/ *noun* **1** [C] when someone is injured or killed by a bullet from a gun *a fatal shooting* **2** [U] the sport of firing bullets from guns, sometimes to kill animals

o⊶**shop**¹ /ʃɒp/ (*also US* **store**) *noun* [C] a building or part of a building where you can buy things *a book shop* ○ *a shoe shop* ○ *to go to the shops* ○ *a shop window* ➍See also: **charity shop.**

┌─────────────────────────────────┐
│ **COMMON LEARNER ERROR** │
└─────────────────────────────────┘

shop or **store**?

In **American English** the usual word for shop is **store**. *He went to the store to buy some cookies.*

In **British English** the word **store** is only used to mean a very large shop where you can buy many different things. *Harrods is a famous department store.*

o⊶**shop**² /ʃɒp/ *verb* [I] shopping, *past* shopped to buy things in shops *I'm shopping for baby clothes.* ○ *I usually go shopping on Saturday.*

shop around to compare the price and quality of the same thing from different places before deciding which one to buy *to shop around for a computer*

'**shop as,sistant** *UK* (*US* **sales clerk**) *noun* [C] someone whose job is selling things in a shop

,**shop** '**floor** *noun* [no plural] the part of a factory where things are made and not the part where the managers' offices are

shopkeeper /ˈʃɒpˌkiːpəʳ/ *noun* [C] someone who owns or manages a small shop

shoplifting /ˈʃɒplɪftɪŋ/ *noun* [U] stealing things from a shop ● **shoplifter** *noun* [C] ● **shoplift** *verb* [I]

shopper /ˈʃɒpəʳ/ *noun* [C] someone who is buying things from shops

WORD PARTNERS FOR **shopping**

a shopping **spree/trip** ● to **go** shopping

☞**shopping** /ˈʃɒpɪŋ/ *noun* [U] **1** when you buy things from shops *I love shopping.* ○ *a shopping basket/trolley* **2** the things that you buy from a shop or shops *Can you help me unpack the shopping?* ○ *a shopping bag* ⊃See also: **window shopping**.

'**shopping ˌbasket** *noun* [C] a place on a website where you collect things that you plan to buy from the website ⊃See **basket**.

'**shopping ˌcentre** *UK* (*US* **shopping center**) *noun* [C] a place where a lot of shops have been built close together

'**shopping ˌmall** *noun* [C] a large, covered shopping area

shore[1] /ʃɔːʳ/ *noun* [C, U] the area of land along the edge of the sea or a lake *They had to abandon the boat and swim back to shore.*

shore[2] /ʃɔːʳ/ *verb*

shore sth up to help or improve something that is likely to fail

shorn /ʃɔːn/ *past participle of* **shear**

☞**short**[1] /ʃɔːt/ *adjective* **1** DISTANCE having a small distance from one end to the other *short, brown hair* ○ *short legs* ○ *a short skirt* **2** TIME continuing for a small amount of time *a short visit* ○ *There's a short break for coffee between classes.* **3** BOOK A short book or other piece of writing has few pages or words. *a short article/story* **4** PERSON A short person is not as tall as most people. *She's short and slim with dark hair.* **5** NOT HAVING ENOUGH not having enough of something *I'm a bit short of money at the moment.* ○ *Would you like to play? We're a couple of people short.* ○ *He seemed a bit short of breath* (= having difficulty breathing). **6** be **short for sth** to be a shorter way of saying the same thing *'Mick' is short for 'Michael'.* **7** be **short with sb** to talk to someone quickly in an angry or rude way ● **shortness** *noun* [U] ⊃See also: in the long/short **run**[2].

short[2] /ʃɔːt/ *adverb* **1** short of **doing sth** without doing something *He did everything he could to get the money, short of robbing a bank.* **2** stop **short of sth/doing sth** to almost do something but decide not to do it *She stopped short of accusing him of lying.* **3** fall **short of sth** to not reach a particular level, but only by a small amount *Sales for the first half of this year fell just short of the target.* **4** cut **sth short** to have to stop doing something before it is finished *They had to cut the holiday short when her mother was taken ill.*

short[3] /ʃɔːt/ *noun* **1** in **short** in a few words *In*

short, we need more staff. **2** [C] a short film **3** [C] *UK* a small amount of a strong alcoholic drink like whisky

WORD PARTNERS FOR **shortage**

an **acute/chronic/desperate/serious** shortage ● a shortage **of** sth

shortage /ˈʃɔːtɪdʒ/ *noun* [C] when there is not enough of something *a shortage of nurses* ○ *food shortages*

shortbread /ˈʃɔːtbred/ *noun* [U] a hard, sweet cake

short-circuit /ˌʃɔːtˈsɜːkɪt/ *noun* [C] a fault in an electrical connection ● **short-circuit** *verb* [I, T]

shortcoming /ˈʃɔːtˌkʌmɪŋ/ *noun* [C] a fault [usually plural] *I like him despite his shortcomings.*

shortcut (*also US* ˌshort 'cut) /ˈʃɔːtkʌt/ *noun* [C] **1** a quicker and more direct way of getting somewhere or doing something *I took a shortcut through the car park.* **2** In computing, a shortcut is a quick way to start or use a computer program. *a shortcut key*

shorten /ˈʃɔːtᵊn/ *verb* [I, T] to become shorter or to make something shorter *Smoking shortens your life.*

shortfall /ˈʃɔːtfɔːl/ *noun* [C] the difference between the amount that is needed and the smaller amount that is available *a shortfall in government spending*

shorthand /ˈʃɔːthænd/ *noun* [U] a fast way of writing using abbreviations and symbols

short-haul /ˈʃɔːthɔːl/ *adjective* travelling a short distance *a short-haul flight*

shortlist /ˈʃɔːtlɪst/ *noun* [C] *UK* a list of people who are competing for a prize, job, etc, who have already been chosen from a larger list *to be on the shortlist* ● **shortlist** *verb* [T] *UK* shortlisted candidates

short-lived /ˌʃɔːtˈlɪvd/ *adjective* only lasting for a short time

shortly /ˈʃɔːtli/ *adverb* **1** If something is going to happen shortly, it will happen soon. *Our plans for the next year will be announced shortly.* **2** shortly **after/before sth** a short time after or before something *He left here shortly after midnight.*

short-range /ˌʃɔːtˈreɪndʒ/ *adjective* intended to go a short distance *a short-range missile*

shorts /ʃɔːts/ *noun* [plural] **1** a very short pair of trousers that stop above the knees *T-shirt and shorts* ○ *cycling shorts* **2** *US* men's underwear to wear under trousers ⊃See also: **boxers**.

short-sighted /ˌʃɔːtˈsaɪtɪd/ *adjective* **1** not able to see far without wearing glasses **2** not thinking enough about how an action will affect the future *a short-sighted policy*

short-term /ˌʃɔːtˈtɜːm/ *adjective* lasting a short time *short-term memory*

short-wave /ˈʃɔːtweɪv/ *noun* [U] a system used to broadcast radio signals around the world *short-wave radio*

shot[1] /ʃɒt/ *noun* [C] **1** GUN when a bullet is fired from a gun *Three shots were fired.* **2** SPORT when someone tries to score points in sports such as football by hitting or throwing the ball

Good shot! **3** PHOTOGRAPH a photograph *I got a good shot of them leaving the hotel together.* **4 give sth a shot; have/take a shot at sth** *informal* to try to do something, often for the first time *I've never played football, but I'll give it a shot.* **5** MEDICINE an amount of medicine put into the body with a special needle **6** DRINK a small amount of a strong alcoholic drink *a shot of whisky* **7 like a shot** If someone does something like a shot, they do it quickly and enthusiastically. **8 a shot in the dark** an attempt to guess something when you have no information or knowledge about it ➔See also: **long shot.**

shot² /ʃɒt/ *past of* shoot

shotgun /ˈʃɒtɡʌn/ *noun* [C] a long gun that fires small, metal balls

o⌐**should** *strong form* /ʃʊd/ *weak form* /ʃəd/ *modal verb* **1** BEST used to say or ask what is the correct or best thing to do *He should have gone to the doctor.* ○ *Should I apologize to her?* ○ *You shouldn't be so angry with him.* **2** EXPECT used to say that you expect something to be true or that you expect something to happen *She should be feeling better by now.* ○ *The letter should arrive by Friday.* **3** POSSIBLE *formal* used to refer to a possible event in the future *Should you have any further queries, please do not hesitate to contact me.* **4 why should/ shouldn't...?** used to ask or give the reason for something, especially when you are surprised or angry about it *He told me to forgive her, but why should I?* ➔See Extra help page **Modal verbs** on page Centre 22.

o⌐**shoulder¹** /ˈʃəʊldər/ *noun* **1** [C] where your arm joins your body next to your neck *He put his arm around my shoulder.* **2** [C] *US* (*UK* **hard shoulder**) the area on the edge of a main road, where a car can stop in an emergency **3 rub shoulders with sb** to spend time with famous people **4 a shoulder to cry on** someone who gives you sympathy when you are upset ➔See also: have a **chip¹** on your shoulder.

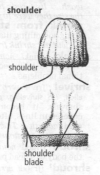

shoulder

shoulder

shoulder blade

shoulder² /ˈʃəʊldər/ *verb* **shoulder the blame/ burden/responsibility, etc** to accept that you are responsible for something difficult or bad

'shoulder ,bag *noun* [C] a bag with a long strap that you hang from your shoulder

'shoulder ,blade *noun* [C] a large, flat bone on each side of your back below your shoulder

shoulder-length /ˈʃəʊldəleŋθ/ *adjective* If your hair is shoulder-length, it goes down as far as your shoulders.

o⌐**shouldn't** /ˈʃʊdənt/ *short for* should not *I shouldn't have said that.*

o⌐**should've** /ˈʃʊdəv/ *short for* should have *She should've finished by now.*

o⌐**shout¹** /ʃaʊt/ *verb* [I, T] to say something very

loudly *"Look out!" she shouted.* ○ *I was angry and I shouted at him.* ○ *I shouted out her name but she didn't hear me.*

> WORD PARTNERS FOR **shout** (*noun*)
>
> give a shout • a shout of [anger, etc] • an **angry** shout

shout² /ʃaʊt/ *noun* [C] when you say something very loudly or make a very loud sound with your voice *He was woken by a loud shout.*

shove /ʃʌv/ *verb* [I, T] **1** to push someone or something in a rough way *He wouldn't move, so I shoved him out of the way.* **2 shove sth into/in/under, etc** to put something somewhere in a quick, careless way *She shoved the suitcase under the bed.* ● **shove** *noun* [C] *to give someone a shove* ➔See also: if/when **push²** comes to shove.

shovel /ˈʃʌvəl/ *noun* [C] a tool with a long handle, used for digging or moving things such as soil or snow ● **shovel** *verb* [I, T] *UK* shovelling, *past* shovelled, *US* shoveling, *past* shoveled

o⌐**show¹** /ʃəʊ/ *verb past tense* showed, *past participle* shown **1** PROVE [T] If numbers, results, facts, etc show something, they prove that it is true. [+ (that)] *Research shows that 40% of the programme's viewers are aged over 55.* ○ *Sales figures showed a significant increase last month.* **2** LET SOMEONE SEE [T] to let someone look at something [+ two objects] *Show me your photos.* ○ *Show your passport to the officer.* **3 show sb what to do/how to do sth** to teach someone how to do something by explaining it or by doing it yourself while they watch *She showed me how to use the new computer system.* ○ *Have you shown him what to do?* **4** EXPRESS [T] to express a feeling so that other people are able to notice it *He hasn't shown any interest so far.* ○ *If she was upset, she certainly didn't show it.* **5** EASY TO SEE [I, T] to be easy to see, or to make something easy to see *The sadness really shows on her face.* ○ *Light-coloured carpets show the dirt.* **6 show sb into/around/round, etc** to take someone to or round a place *She showed me round the factory.* **7** IMAGE [T] If a picture, film, map, etc shows something, that thing can be seen in the picture, film, etc. *A diagram shows the levels of rainfall in different parts of the country.* **8** FILM [I, T] If a cinema shows a film or a film is showing somewhere, you can go and see it there.

show off to try to make people admire your abilities or achievements in a way which other people find annoying *He was the kind of kid who was always showing off to his classmates.*

show sb/sth off to show something or someone you are proud of to other people *I couldn't wait to show off my new ring.*

show up *informal* to arrive somewhere *I waited for nearly half an hour, but he didn't show up.*

show sb up to behave in a way that makes someone you are with feel embarrassed *I didn't want my parents there, showing me up in front of all my friends.*

S

WORD PARTNERS FOR *show* (noun)

host/present a show • a show is broad-cast/screened • be on a show
---

show² /ʃəʊ/ *noun* **1** [C] a television or radio pro-gramme or a theatre performance *He's got his own show on Channel 5.* **2** [C] an event at which a group of similar things are brought together for the public to see *a fashion show* **3 a show of sth** an expression of a feeling which can be clearly seen by other people *Crowds gathered in the central square in a show of support for the government.* **4 for show** for looking at only, and not for using *The cakes are just for show - you can't eat them.* **5 on show** being shown to the public *Her designs are currently on show at the Museum of Modern Art.* ⊃See also: **chat show, game show, talk show.**

'show ,business (*also* **show biz** *informal*) *noun* [U] the entertainment industry, including films, television, theatre, etc

showcase /'ʃəʊkeɪs/ *noun* [C] an event which is intended to show the best qualities of some-thing *The exhibition acts as **a showcase for** British design.*

WORD PARTNERS FOR *showdown*

face/be heading for a showdown • a show-down **between** sb and sb • a showdown **with** sb
---

showdown /'ʃəʊdaʊn/ *noun* [C] an argument or fight that is intended to end a period of dis-agreement *Opponents of the changes are head-ing for **a showdown with** party leaders.*

◦ᴀ**shower**¹ /ʃaʊəʳ/ *noun* [C] **1** ⟨WASH⟩ If you have or take a shower, you wash your whole body while standing under a flow of water. *I got up, **had a shower** and got dressed.* **2** ⟨BATHROOM EQUIPMENT⟩ a piece of bathroom equipment that you stand under to wash your whole body *He likes to sing **in the shower**.* ⊃See colour picture **The Bathroom** on page Centre 3. **3** ⟨RAIN⟩ a short period of rain **4 a shower of sth** a lot of small things in the air, especially falling through the air *a shower of glass*

shower² /ʃaʊəʳ/ *verb* [I] to wash standing under a shower

shower sb with sth to give a lot of some-thing to someone *I was showered with gifts.*

showing /'ʃəʊɪŋ/ *noun* **1** [C] a broadcast of a television programme at a particular time or of a film at a cinema *There's a repeat showing of Wednesday's episode on Saturday morning.* **2 a good/poor/strong, etc showing** how success-ful someone is in a competition, election, etc *She **made** a good **showing** in the world championships.*

showman /'ʃəʊmən/ *noun* [C] *plural* **showmen** someone who is very good at entertaining people

shown /ʃəʊn/ *past participle of* show

show-off /'ʃəʊɒf/ *noun* [C] someone who tries to make other people admire their abilities or achievements in a way which is annoying

showroom /'ʃəʊruːm/ *noun* [C] a large room where you can look at large items for sale,

such as cars or furniture

shrank /ʃræŋk/ *past tense of* shrink

shrapnel /'ʃræpnᵊl/ *noun* [U] small, sharp pieces of metal which fly through the air when a bomb explodes

shred¹ /ʃred/ *noun* [C] **1** a very small piece that has been torn from something [*usually plural*] *She tore the letter **to shreds**.* **2 not a shred of sth** not the smallest amount of something *There is not a shred of evidence to support his story.*

shred² /ʃred/ *verb* [T] **shredding,** *past* **shredded** to tear or cut something into small, thin pieces *shredded cabbage*

shrewd /ʃruːd/ *adjective* good at judging situ-ations and making decisions which give you an advantage *a shrewd businessman* ○ *a shrewd investment* • **shrewdly** *adverb*

shriek /ʃriːk/ *verb* [I, T] to make a sudden, loud, high noise because you are afraid, surprised, excited, etc *to shriek with laughter* ○ *"It's about to explode!" she shrieked.* • **shriek** *noun* [C]

shrill /ʃrɪl/ *adjective* A shrill sound is very high, loud, and often unpleasant. *a shrill voice*

shrimp /ʃrɪmp/ *noun* [C] a small, pink, sea animal that you can eat, with a curved body and a shell

shrine /ʃraɪn/ *noun* [C] a place where people go to pray because it is connected with a holy person or event

shrink¹ /ʃrɪŋk/ *verb* [I, T] *past tense* **shrank,** *past participle* **shrunk** to become smaller, or to make something smaller *My shirt shrank in the wash.* ○ *Its forests have shrunk to almost half the size they were 10 years ago.*

shrink from sth/doing sth to avoid doing something that is difficult or unpleasant *We will not shrink from using force.*

shrink² /ʃrɪŋk/ *noun* [C] *informal* a doctor trained to help people with mental or emo-tional problems

shrivel /'ʃrɪvᵊl/ *verb* [I] *UK* **shrivelling,** *past* **shriv-elled,** *US* **shriveling,** *past* **shriveled** If something shrivels, it becomes smaller, dryer, and covered in lines, often because it is old. • **shriv-elled** *adjective* *There were a few shrivelled apples at the bottom of the bowl.*

shroud¹ /ʃraʊd/ *noun* [C] a cloth used to cover the body of a dead person

shroud² /ʃraʊd/ *verb* **1 be shrouded in dark-ness/fog/mist** to be hidden or covered by the dark/fog, etc *The island was shrouded in sea mist.* **2 be shrouded in mystery/secrecy** to be dif-ficult to find out about or to know the truth about *Details of the president's trip remain shrouded in secrecy.*

shrub /ʃrʌb/ *noun* [C] a large plant, smaller than a tree, that has several main stems

shrubbery /'ʃrʌbᵊri/ *noun* **1** [C, U] an area of a garden with shrubs in it **2** [U] *US* shrubs con-sidered as a group

shrug /ʃrʌɡ/ *verb* [I, T] **shrugging,** *past* **shrugged** to move your shoulders up and down to show that you do not care about something or that you do not know something *I told him we weren't happy with it but he just **shrugged** his*

shoulders. • **shrug** *noun* [C]
shrug sth off to not worry about something and treat it as not important *The team manager shrugged off criticism.*

shrunk /ʃrʌŋk/ *past participle of* shrink

shrunken /'ʃrʌŋkən/ *adjective* having become smaller or having been made smaller *a shrunken old man*

shudder /'ʃʌdəʳ/ *verb* [I] to shake, usually because you are thinking of something unpleasant *I still **shudder at** the thought of the risks we took.* ○ *She **shuddered with** horror.* • **shudder** *noun* [C]

shuffle /'ʃʌfl/ *verb* 1 [WALK] [I] to walk slowly without lifting your feet off the floor *I heard him shuffling around downstairs.* 2 [ARRANGE] [I, T] If you shuffle papers or cards, you mix them or arrange them in a different order. 3 [MOVE] [I, T] to move your body or feet a little because you feel nervous or uncomfortable. *People starting **shuffling** their **feet** and looking at their watches.*

shun /ʃʌn/ *verb* [T] shunning, *past* shunned to avoid or ignore someone or something *He was shunned by colleagues and family alike.* ○ *She has always **shunned publicity**.*

shunt /ʃʌnt/ *verb* [T] to move someone or something from one place to another, usually because they are not wanted *As a teenager he was shunted between different children's homes.*

o→**shut¹** /ʃʌt/ *verb* [I, T] shutting, *past* shut 1 to close something, or to become closed *Shut the door.* ○ *He lay back and shut his eyes.* ○ *The lid shut with a bang.* 2 UK (UK/US **close**) When a shop, restaurant, etc shuts, it stops serving customers and does not allow people to enter. *The museum shuts at 4 o'clock on a Friday.* ○ *Several schools were shut because of the bad weather.*
shut sb/sth away to put someone or something in a place from which they cannot leave or be taken away
shut (sth) down If a business or a large piece of equipment shuts down or someone shuts it down, it stops operating. *Many factories have been forced to shut down.*
shut sb/sth in (sth) to prevent someone or something from leaving a place by shutting a door or gate *We normally shut the dog in the kitchen when we go out.*
shut sth off to stop a machine working, or to stop the supply of something *Shut the engine off.* ○ *Oil supplies have been shut off.*
shut sth/sb out to stop someone or something from entering a place or from being included in something *The curtains shut out most of the light from the street.*
shut (sb) up *informal* to stop talking or making a noise, or to make someone do this *Just shut up and get on with your work!*
shut sb/sth up to keep a person or animal somewhere and prevent them from leaving *You can't keep it shut up in a cage all day.*

shut² /ʃʌt/ *adjective* [never before noun] 1 closed *Her eyes were shut and I thought she was asleep.* 2 UK (UK/US **closed**) When a shop,

restaurant, etc is shut, it has stopped serving customers and does not allow people to enter it.

shutdown /'ʃʌtdaʊn/ *noun* [C] when a business or a large piece of equipment stops operating, usually for a temporary period

shutter /'ʃʌtəʳ/ *noun* [C] 1 a wooden or metal cover on the outside of a window 2 the part at the front of a camera which opens quickly to let in light when you take a photograph

shuttle¹ /'ʃʌtl/ *noun* [C] 1 a bus, train, plane etc which travels regularly between two places, usually a short distance *the London-Glasgow shuttle* ○ *There's a **shuttle service** between the airport and the city centre.* 2 (*also* 'space ,shuttle) a spacecraft which can go into space and return to Earth more than once

shuttle² /'ʃʌtl/ *verb* [I, T] to travel or take people regularly between the same two places *He shuttles between Ireland and England.*

shuttlecock /'ʃʌtlkɒk/ (*also* US birdie) *noun* [C] a small object with feathers that is used like a ball in badminton (= sport like tennis)

shy¹ /ʃaɪ/ *adjective* shyer, shyest not confident, especially about meeting or talking to new people *He was too shy to say anything to her.* • **shyly** *adverb She smiled shyly.* • **shyness** *noun* [U]

shy² /ʃaɪ/ *verb* [I] If a horse shies, it moves backwards suddenly because it has been frightened by something.
shy away from sth to avoid doing something, usually because you are not confident enough to do it *He tends to shy away from public speaking.*

sibling /'sɪblɪŋ/ *noun* [C] *formal* a sister or brother

sic /sɪk/ *adverb* (**sic**) used in writing after a word that you have copied to show that you know it has been spelt or used wrongly

o→**sick¹** /sɪk/ *adjective* 1 ill *He was off work sick for most of last week.* ○ *They provide care for the sick.* 2 **be sick** If you are sick, food and drink comes up from your stomach and out of your mouth. *The baby was sick all down his shirt.* 3 **feel sick** to feel that the food or drink in your stomach might soon come up through your mouth *I was so nervous I felt quite sick.* 4 **be sick of sth** *informal* to be bored with or annoyed about something that has been happening for a long time *I'm sick of people telling me how to run my life.* 5 **It makes me sick.** *informal* something you say when you are jealous of someone *She looks fantastic whatever she wears - it makes me sick.* 6 cruel and unpleasant *He's got a sick mind.* ○ *a sick joke*

COMMON LEARNER ERROR

sick, ill, and be sick

In British English **ill** is the word that is usually used to mean 'not well'. In American English the word for this is **sick**.

He went home early because he felt ill/sick.

In British English to **be sick** is to bring food up from the stomach. Another way of saying this is the word **vomit**, which is used both in British and American English.

sick² /sɪk/ *noun* [U] *UK informal* food or liquid that has come up from someone's stomach and out of their mouth

sicken /'sɪkᵊn/ *verb* [T] to shock someone and make them very angry *Sickened by the violence, she left.*

sickening /'sɪkᵊnɪŋ/ *adjective* causing shock and anger *a sickening act of violence*

sickle /'sɪkl/ *noun* [C] a tool with a round blade used to cut long grass or grain crops

'sick ˌleave *noun* [U] when you are away from your work because you are ill

sickly /'sɪkli/ *adjective* **1** weak and often ill *a sickly child* **2** unpleasant and making you feel slightly ill *a sickly smell*

sickness /'sɪknəs/ *noun* **1** [ILL] [U] when you are ill *She's had three weeks off for sickness this year.* **2** [VOMIT] [U] when the food or drink in your stomach come up through your mouth, or a feeling that this might happen *morning/ travel sickness* **3** [ILLNESS] [C, U] a particular illness *radiation sickness*

WORD PARTNERS FOR *side*

on the [right/left] **side** ● the side **of** sth

◦⁻**side¹** /saɪd/ *noun* [C] **1** [PART OF SOMETHING] one of the two parts that something would divide into if you drew a line down the middle *In most countries people drive on the right side of the road.* ○ *Which side of the bed do you sleep on?* **2** [SURFACE] a flat, outer surface of an object, especially one that is not its top, bottom, front, or back *The ingredients are listed on the side of the box.* ○ *The side of the car was badly scratched.* **3** [EDGE] one edge of something *A square has four sides.* ○ *There were chairs round the sides of the room.* **4** [NEXT TO SOMETHING] the area next to something *trees growing by the side of the road* **5** [PAPER/COIN ETC] either of the two surfaces of a thin, flat object such as a piece of paper or a coin *Write on both sides of the paper.* **6** [ARGUMENT] one of the people or groups who are arguing, fighting, or competing *Whose side is he on?* ○ *Whenever we argue he always takes Alice's side* (= gives support to Alice). **7** [TEAM] *UK* the players in a sports team *He's been selected for the national side.* **8** [PART OF A SITUATION] part of a situation that can be considered or dealt with separately *She looks after the financial side of things.* **9** [CHARACTER] a part of someone's character *She has a very practical side.* **10** [BODY] the two areas of your body from under your arms to the tops of your legs *Stand with your arms by your sides.* ○ *She lay on her side.* **11** [STORY] Someone's side of a story is the way in which they explain how something happened. *I thought I'd better listen to Clare's side of the story.* ○ *So far they'd only heard the story from the wife's side.* **12** [TELE-VISION/RADIO] *UK* a number on a television or radio that you can choose in order to receive a broadcast *Which side is the film on?* **13 from side to side** If something moves from side to side, it moves from left to right

and back again repeatedly. *swinging from side to side* **14 side-by-side** If two things or people are side-by-side, they are next to each other. *sitting side-by-side on the sofa* **15** [RELA-TIVES] the part of your family who are either your mother's relatives or your father's relatives *They tend to be tall on my mother's side of the family.* **16 err on the side of caution** to be very careful instead of taking a risk or making a mistake **17 on the side** in addition to your main job *She does a bit of bar work on the side.* **18 put sth to one side** to not use or deal with something now, but keep it for a later time ➾See also: the flip side.

side² /saɪd/ *verb*

side with sb to support one person or group in an argument *If ever there was any sort of argument, she'd always side with my father.*

sideboard /'saɪdbɔːd/ *noun* [C] a piece of furniture with a flat top and low cupboards and drawers, used for storing dishes and glasses, etc in the room you eat in

sideburns /'saɪdbɜːnz/ *noun* [plural] hair that grows on the sides of a man's face in front of the ear

side effect /'saɪdɪfekt/ *noun* [C] **1** another effect that a drug has on your body in addition to the main effect for which the doctor has given you the drug *Headaches are one side effect of this drug.* **2** an unexpected result of a situation

sidekick /'saɪdkɪk/ *noun* [C] someone who helps, or is friends with, a more powerful and important person

sideline¹ /'saɪdlaɪn/ *noun* [C] a job or business in addition to your main job or business *He works in a bank but teaches English as a sideline.*

sideline² /'saɪdlaɪn/ *verb* [T] to stop someone from being included in an activity that they usually do, especially a sport [often passive] *He's broken his ankle and could be sidelined for weeks.*

sidelines /'saɪdlaɪnz/ *noun* [plural] **1** the outside edge of the playing area of a sport such as football *The coach was shouting instructions from the sidelines.* **2 on the sidelines** not really involved in something

sidelong /'saɪdlɒŋ/ *adjective* **a sidelong glance/ look** a very short look at someone, moving your eyes to the side, and not looking at them directly

'side ˌmirror *US* (*UK* **wing mirror**) *noun* [C] a small mirror on the side of a car or truck ➾See colour picture **Car** at page Centre 7.

sideshow /'saɪdʃəʊ/ *noun* [C] an event or activity that is considered less important than another event or activity

sidestep /'saɪdstep/ *verb* [T] **sidestepping**, *past* sidestepped to avoid talking about a subject, especially by starting to talk about something else *She neatly sidestepped questions about her recent divorce.*

sidetrack /'saɪdtræk/ *verb* [T] to make someone forget what they were doing or speaking about and start doing or speaking about something

---
| ɑː arm | ɜː her | iː see | ɔː saw | uː too | aɪ my | aʊ how | eə hair | eɪ day | əʊ no | ɪə near | ɔɪ boy | ʊə poor | aɪə fire | aʊə sour |

different [often passive] *Sorry, I was talking about staffing and I got sidetracked.*

sidewalk /ˈsaɪdwɔːk/ *US* (*UK* **pavement**) *noun* [C] a path with a hard surface by the side of a road that people walk on

sideways /ˈsaɪdweɪz/ *adverb* in a direction to the left or right, not forwards or backwards *He glanced sideways.*

siding /ˈsaɪdɪŋ/ *noun* **1** [C] a short railway track, connected to a main track, where trains are kept when they are not being used **2** [U] *US* material which covers the outside walls of a building, usually in layers

sidle /ˈsaɪdl/ *verb* **sidle along/over/up, etc** to walk towards someone, trying not to be noticed *He sidled up to her and whispered something in her ear.*

SIDS /sɪdz/ *noun* [U] *US abbreviation for* sudden infant death syndrome: the sudden death of a sleeping baby for no obvious reason ⊃See **cot death**.

siege /siːdʒ/ *noun* [C, U] when an army or the police stand around a building or city to stop supplies from entering it, in order to force the people inside to stop fighting *The city is under siege from rebel forces.*

siesta /siˈestə/ *noun* [C] a short period of rest or sleep in the afternoon

sieve /sɪv/ *noun* [C] a piece of kitchen equipment with a wire or plastic net which separates large pieces of food from liquids or powders *Pass the sauce through a sieve to remove any lumps.* ⊃See colour picture **The Kitchen** on page Centre 2. • **sieve** *verb* [T]

sift /sɪft/ *verb* [T] **1** to put flour, sugar, etc through a sieve (= wire net shaped like a bowl) to break up large pieces *Sift the flour into a large bowl.* **2** (*also* **sift through**) to carefully look at every part of something in order to find something to **sift through evidence**

sigh /saɪ/ *verb* [I, T] to breathe out slowly and noisily, often because you are annoyed or unhappy *He sighed deeply and sat down.* • **sigh** *noun* [C] *a sigh of relief*

o⌐**sight¹** /saɪt/ *noun* **1** [ABILITY] [U] the ability to use your eyes to see *Doctors managed to save his sight.* **2 the sight of sb/sth** when you see someone or something *The sight of so much blood had shocked him.* ○ *(informal) I can't stand the sight of her* (= I hate her). ⊃See Common learner error at **view**. **3** [AREA SEEN] [U] the area that it is possible for you to see *I looked for her but she was nowhere in sight.* ○ *I was able to park within sight of the house.* ○ *Security guards were waiting out of sight* (= where they could not be seen). **4** [VIEW] [C] something which you see, especially something interesting *the sights and sounds of the market* **5 at first sight** when you first see or hear about something or someone *It may, at first sight, seem a surprising choice.* **6 the sights** the beautiful or interesting places in a city or country, that a lot of people visit *He took me around New York and showed me the sights.* **7 lose sight of sth** to forget about an important idea or fact because you are thinking too much

about other, less important things *We mustn't lose sight of the original aims of this project.* **8 set your sights on sth** to decide to achieve something *She's set her sights on becoming an actress.*

sight² /saɪt/ *verb* [T] to see something that it is difficult to see or that you have been looking for [often passive] *The ship was last sighted off the French coast at 8 o'clock yesterday evening.*

-sighted /ˈsaɪtɪd/ used after a word describing a person's ability to see *long-/short-sighted* ○ *partially-sighted*

sighted /ˈsaɪtɪd/ *adjective* A sighted person is able to see.

sighting /ˈsaɪtɪŋ/ *noun* [C] when you see something that is rare or unusual *UFO sightings* ○ *Sightings of these animals are increasingly rare.*

━━━━━━━━ WORD PARTNERS FOR **sightseeing** ━━━━━━━━

do some/go sightseeing • a sightseeing **tour/trip**

sightseeing /ˈsaɪtsiːɪŋ/ *noun* [U] the activity of visiting places which are interesting because they are historical, famous, etc *Did you do much sightseeing while you were in Paris?* ○ *a* **sightseeing tour** *of London* • **sightseer** /ˈsaɪtˌsiːə/ *noun* [C] a person who goes sightseeing *The pavements were crowded with sightseers.*

━━━━━━━━━━ WORD PARTNERS FOR **sign** ━━━━━━━━━━

see/take sth **as a sign** • **show** (no) **signs of** sth • a **clear/sure** sign • a sign **of** sth

o⌐**sign¹** /saɪn/ *noun* [C] **1** [PROOF] something that shows that something is happening *Flowers are the first sign of Spring.* ○ [+ (that)] *It's a sign that things are improving.* ○ *Staff are* **showing signs of** strain. **2** [NOTICE] a symbol or message in a public place which gives information or instructions *a road sign* ○ *a 'no-smoking' sign* **3** [SYMBOL] a symbol which has a particular meaning *a dollar/pound sign* ○ *the sign of the cross* **4** [MOVEMENT] a movement you make to give someone information or tell them what to do ⊃See also: **star sign**.

o⌐**sign²** /saɪn/ *verb* [I, T] to write your name on something to show that you wrote/painted, etc it or to show that you agree to it *He signs his letters 'Prof. James D. Nelson'.* ○ *to sign a contract/treaty*

sign for sth *UK* If a player signs for a football team, he signs a formal agreement saying that he will play for that team. *Fans are hoping Taylor will sign for Blackburn this afternoon.*

sign (sb) in to write your name or someone else's name in a book when you arrive at a building such as an office or hotel *Have you signed in at reception?* ○ *I need to sign you in as my guest.*

sign on 1 to sign a document saying that you will work for someone *She's signed on with a temp agency.* **2** *UK* to sign a form at a government office to say that you do not have a job and that you want to receive money from the government

sign (sb) out to write your name or someone else's name in a book when leaving a building such as an office or factory

sign up to arrange to do an organized activity *I've signed up for evening classes at the local college.*

signal¹ /'sɪgn³l/ *noun* [C] 1 ACTION a movement, light, or sound which gives information, or tells people what to do *Don't move until I give the signal.* 2 WAVE a series of light waves or sound waves which are sent to a radio or television 3 PROOF something which shows that something else exists or is likely to happen *The changing colour of the leaves on the trees is a signal that it will soon be autumn.* 4 TRAINS a piece of equipment which tells trains to stop or to continue 5 VEHICLES/PEOPLE US a piece of equipment that shows people or vehicles when to stop, go, or move carefully *a traffic signal*

signal² /'sɪgn³l/ *verb* [I, T] UK signalling, *past* signalled, US signaling, *past* signaled 1 to make a movement which gives information or tells people what to do *He signalled for them to be quiet.* ○ [+ to do sth] *He signalled the driver to stop.* 2 to show that you intend or are ready to do something [+ (that)] *The US signalled that they were ready to enter talks.*

signatory /'sɪgnət³ri/ *noun* [C] formal a person or country that signs an official document

signature /'sɪgnətʃə'/ *noun* [C] your name written in your own way which is difficult for someone else to copy

██ WORD PARTNERS FOR **significance**

play down /**realize**/**understand** the significance **of** sth ● **have** significance **for** sb ● be **of** [great/little/major/no] significance

significance /sɪg'nɪfɪkəns/ *noun* [U] the importance or meaning of something *I still don't understand the significance of his remark.* ○ *What's the significance of the bird in the painting?*

◦━**significant** /sɪg'nɪfɪkənt/ *adjective* important or noticeable *These measures will save a significant amount of money.* ○ *It is significant that Falkner did not attend the meeting himself.* ⊃Opposite **insignificant.** ● **significantly** *adverb*

signify /'sɪgnɪfaɪ/ *verb* [T] to be a sign of something *Red signifies danger.*

signing /'saɪnɪŋ/ *noun* [C] 1 UK a player who has joined a sports team or a musician who has joined a record company 2 the act of signing something [usually singular] *the signing of the declaration*

'sign ˌlanguage *noun* [C, U] a system of communication using hand movements, used by people who are deaf (= cannot hear)

signpost /'saɪnpəʊst/ *noun* [C] a sign by the side of the road that gives information about routes and distances

Sikh /siːk/ *noun* [C] someone who believes in an Indian religion based on belief in a single god and on the teachings of Guru Nanak ● **Sikh** *adjective a Sikh temple* ● **Sikhism** *noun* [U]

██ WORD PARTNERS FOR **silence**

in silence ● **deafening**/**stunned** silence ● **break** the silence ● **lapse into** silence ● silence **falls**/**descends**/**ensues**

◦━**silence¹** /'saɪləns/ *noun* 1 NO SOUND [U] when there is no sound *The three men ate in silence.* ○ *No sound broke the silence of the wintry landscape.* 2 NO TALKING [U] when someone says nothing about a particular subject *She ended her silence yesterday and spoke to a TV reporter about the affair.* 3 PERIOD OF TIME [C] a period of time when there is no sound or no talking *an awkward/embarrassed silence*

silence² /'saɪləns/ *verb* [T] 1 to stop something making a sound or stop someone from talking, often about a particular subject *He silenced the alarm.* ○ *Opponents of the government would be silenced or thrown into prison.* 2 to stop people from criticizing you by giving a good argument to support your opinion *He seems to have silenced his critics.*

silencer /'saɪlənsə'/ *noun* [C] 1 UK (US **muffler**) a part of a vehicle that reduces noise 2 a piece of equipment that you use on a gun to reduce the sound of it firing

◦━**silent** /'saɪlənt/ *adjective* 1 NO SOUND without any sound *The building was dark and silent.* ○ *At last the guns fell silent.* 2 NO TALKING without talking *He remains silent about his plans.* 3 LETTER If a letter in a word is silent, it is not pronounced. *The 'p' in 'receipt' is silent.* ● **silently** *adverb*

silhouette /ˌsɪlu'et/ *noun* [C, U] the shape of something when the light is behind it so that you cannot see any details *He saw a woman in silhouette.* ● **silhouetted** *adjective the roofs silhouetted against the night sky*

silicon /'sɪlɪkən/ *noun* [U] a chemical element used in making electronic equipment such as computers, and materials such as glass and concrete *a silicon chip*

silk /sɪlk/ *noun* [U] a type of cloth which is light and smooth *a silk dress/shirt*

silken /'sɪlk³n/ *adjective* literary soft and smooth, like silk *her silken skin*

silky /'sɪlki/ *adjective* soft and smooth, like silk *a large, silky, grey cat*

◦━**silly** /'sɪli/ *adjective* 1 stupid *silly games/hats* ○ *I feel silly in this hat.* ○ *It's a bit silly spending all that money on something we don't need.* 2 small and not important *She gets upset over such silly things.* ● **silliness** *noun* [U]

silt /sɪlt/ *noun* [U] sand and clay that has been carried along by a river and is left on land

◦━**silver¹** /'sɪlvə'/ *noun* 1 METAL [U] a valuable, shiny, grey-white metal used to make coins and jewellery *silver and gold* ○ *a solid silver ring* 2 OBJECTS [U] objects made of silver 3 PRIZE [C] a silver medal (= a small, round disc given to someone for finishing second in a race or competition)

◦━**silver²** /'sɪlvə'/ *adjective* 1 made of silver *a silver coin* ○ *a silver necklace* 2 being the colour of silver *a silver sports car*

silver 'medal *noun* [C] a small, round disc

given to someone for finishing second in a race or competition

silverware /'sɪlvəweəʳ/ *noun* [U] *US* (*UK* cutlery) knives, forks, spoons, etc that are used for eating

silver 'wedding anniversary *noun* [C] the date that is 25 years after the day that two people married

silvery /'sɪlvʳri/ *adjective* shiny and pale like silver *a silvery light*

sim card /'sɪm kɑːd/ *noun* [C] a plastic card in a mobile phone that contains information about you and makes you able to use the phone

o--**similar** /'sɪmɪləʳ/ *adjective* Something which is similar to something else has many things the same, although it is not exactly the same. *The two houses are remarkably similar.* ○ *The style of cooking is **similar to** that of Northern India.* ⊃Opposite dissimilar.

similarity /ˌsɪmɪ'lærəti/ *noun* [C, U] when two things or people are similar, or a way in which they are similar *There are a number of **similarities between** the two systems.* ○ *He bears a striking **similarity to** his grandfather.*

similarly /'sɪmɪləli/ *adverb* in a similar way

simile /'sɪmɪli/ *noun* [C] a phrase which compares one thing to something else, using the words 'like' or 'as', for example 'as white as snow'

simmer /'sɪməʳ/ *verb* [I, T] to gently cook a liquid or something with liquid in it so that it is very hot, but does not boil

o--**simple** /'sɪmpl/ *adjective* **1** EASY not difficult to do or to understand [+ to do sth] *It's very simple to use.* ○ *Just mix all the ingredients together - it's as simple as that.* **2** NOT COMPLICATED not complicated or containing details which are not necessary *a simple life* ○ *a simple black dress* (= dress without decoration) **3** IMPORTANT used to describe the one important fact, truth, etc *We chose her for the simple reason that she's the best person for the job.*

simplicity /sɪm'plɪsəti/ *noun* [U] **1** when something is not complicated and has few details or little decoration *I admire the simplicity of his designs.* **2** when something is easy to understand

simplify /'sɪmplɪfaɪ/ *verb* [T] to make something less complicated or easier to do or to understand *We need to simplify the instructions.* ● simplification /ˌsɪmplɪfɪ'keɪʃʳn/ *noun* [C, U]

simplistic /sɪm'plɪstɪk/ *adjective* making something complicated seem simple by ignoring many of the details *a simplistic explanation*

simply /'sɪmpli/ *adverb* **1** EMPHASIS used to emphasize what you are saying *We simply don't have the time.* **2** ONLY only *A lot of people miss out on this opportunity simply because they don't know about it.* **3** NOT COMPLICATED in a way which is not complicated or difficult to understand *simply prepared food*

simulate /'sɪmjəleɪt/ *verb* [T] to do or make something which behaves or looks like something real but which is not real *The company uses a computer to simulate crash tests of its new cars.* ● simulation /ˌsɪmjə'leɪʃʳn/ *noun* [C, U]

simulator /'sɪmjəleɪtəʳ/ *noun* [C] a machine on which people can practise operating a vehicle or an aircraft without having to drive or fly *a flight simulator*

simultaneous /ˌsɪmʳl'teɪniəs/ *adjective* If two or more things are simultaneous, they happen or exist at the same time. *simultaneous translation* ● simultaneously *adverb It was broadcast simultaneously in Britain and France.*

sin[1] /sɪn/ *noun* **1** [C, U] something which is against the rules of a religion *the sin of pride* **2** [no plural] *informal* something that you should not do because it is morally wrong *You've only got one life and it's a sin to waste it.*

sin[2] /sɪn/ *verb* [I] sinning, *past* sinned to do something that is against the rules of a religion ● sinner *noun* [C] someone who does something against the rules of a religion

o--**since**[1] /sɪns/ *adverb, preposition* from a time in the past until a later time or until now *They've been waiting since March.* ○ *The factory had been closed since the explosion.* ○ *I've felt fine ever since.*

since or **for**?

When you talk about the beginning of a period of time, use **since**.

I have lived here since 1997.

When you talk about the whole period of time, use **for**.

I have lived here for five years.

~~I have lived here since five years.~~

o--**since**[2] /sɪns/ *conjunction* **1** from a time in the past until a later time or until now *He's been much happier since he started his new job.* ○ *I've known Tim since he was seven.* **2** because *He drove quite slowly since we had plenty of time.*

sincere /sɪn'sɪəʳ/ *adjective* **1** honest and saying or showing what you really feel or believe *He seems to be sincere.* ⊃Opposite insincere. **2** sincere apologies/thanks, etc *formal* used to add emphasis when you are expressing a feeling *The family wishes to express their sincere thanks to all the staff at the hospital.* ● sincerity /sɪn'serəti/ *noun* [U] *No one doubted his sincerity.*

sincerely /sɪn'sɪəli/ *adverb* **1** in a sincere way *I sincerely hope that this never happens again.* **2** Yours sincerely *formal* used at the end of formal letters where you know the name of the person you are writing to

sinful /'sɪnfʳl/ *adjective* against the rules of a religion or morally wrong *sinful thoughts*

o--**sing** /sɪŋ/ *verb* [I, T] past tense sang, past participle sung to make musical sounds with your voice *They all sang 'Happy Birthday' to him.* ○ *She sings in the church choir.*

singer /'sɪŋəʳ/ *noun* [C] someone who sings *a jazz singer*

singing /'sɪŋɪŋ/ *noun* [U] the activity of singing

S

| j yes | k cat | ŋ ring | ʃ she | θ thin | ð this | ʒ decision | dʒ jar | tʃ chip | æ cat | e bed | ə ago | ɪ sit | i cosy | ɒ hot | ʌ run | ʊ put |

single¹ /'sɪŋgl/ *adjective* **1** ONE [always before noun] only one *There was a single light in the corner of the room.* **2 every single** used to emphasize that you are talking about each one of a group or series *I call him every single day.* **3** MARRIAGE not married *He's young and single.* ⊃See Common learner error at **married. 4** PARENT [always before noun] looking after your children alone without a partner or the children's other parent *a single mother* ○ *a single-parent family* **5** FOR ONE [always before noun] for only one person *a single bed*

single² /'sɪŋgl/ *noun* [C] **1** a record or CD which includes only one main song **2** *UK* (*US* **one-way ticket**) a ticket for a journey that is from one place to another but not back again *Could I have a single to London, please?*

single³ /'sɪŋgl/ *verb*
single sb/sth out to choose one person or thing from a group to criticize or praise them *The report singled him out for special criticism.*

single-handedly /ˌsɪŋgl'hændɪdli/ (*also* **single-handed**) *adverb* on your own, without anyone's help *After his partner left, he kept the business going single-handedly.* ● **single-handed** /ˌsɪŋgl'hændɪd/ *adjective* [always before noun] *a single-handed round-the-world yacht race*

single-minded /ˌsɪŋgl'maɪndɪd/ *adjective* very determined to achieve something *She had a single-minded determination to succeed in her career.*

single 'parent (*UK also* **lone parent**) *noun* [C] someone who has a child or children but no husband, wife or partner that lives with them

singles /'sɪŋglz/ *noun* [U] a game in sports such as tennis, in which one person plays against another *He won the men's singles title two years running.*

singly /'sɪŋgli/ *adverb* separately or one at a time *We don't sell them singly, only in packs of four or ten.*

singular /'sɪŋgjələr/ *adjective* **1** The singular form of a word is used to talk about one person or thing. For example 'woman' is the singular form of 'women'. **2** *formal* very special, or found only in one person or situation *a landscape of singular beauty*

the singular /'sɪŋgjələr/ *noun* the singular form of a word

singularly /'sɪŋgjələli/ *adverb formal* very *Fulbright was singularly uninterested in his comments.*

sinister /'sɪnɪstər/ *adjective* making you feel that something bad or evil might happen *a sinister figure dressed in black*

sink¹ /sɪŋk/ *verb past tense* **sank** (*also US*) **sunk**, *past participle* **sunk 1** WATER [I, T] to go down or make something go down below the surface of water and not come back up *The Titanic sank after hitting an iceberg.* ⊃See picture at **float. 2** SOFT SUBSTANCE [I, T] to go down, or make something go down, into something soft *My feet keep sinking into the sand.* **3** MOVE DOWN [I] to move down slowly *The sun sank below the horizon.*

sink in If an unpleasant or surprising fact

sinks in, you gradually start to believe it and understand what effect it will have on you. *It still hasn't sunk in that I'll never see her again.*

sink sth into sth to spend a large amount of money in a business or other piece of work *Millisat has already sunk $25 million into the Hong Kong project.*

sink into sth to slowly move into a sitting or lying position, in a relaxed or tired way *I just want to go home and sink into a hot bath.*

sink² /sɪŋk/ *noun* [C] a bowl that is fixed to the wall in a kitchen or bathroom that you wash dishes or your hands, etc in ⊃See colour picture **The Kitchen** on page Centre 2, **The Bathroom** on page Centre 3.

sinus /'saɪnəs/ *noun* [C] one of the spaces inside the head that are connected to the back of the nose

sip /sɪp/ *verb* [I, T] **sipping**, *past* **sipped** to drink, taking only a small amount at a time *She sipped her champagne.* ● **sip** *noun* [C] *He took a sip of his coffee and then continued.*

siphon¹ /'saɪfᵊn/ *noun* [C] a piece of equipment for moving liquid from one place to another

siphon² /'saɪfᵊn/ *verb* [T] **1** to remove liquid from a container using a siphon **2** (*also* **siphon off**) to dishonestly take money from an organization or other supply over a period of time

sir /sɜːr/ *noun* **1** (*also* **Sir**) You call a man 'sir' when you are speaking to him politely. *Excuse me, sir, is this seat taken?* **2** You write 'Sir' at the beginning of a formal letter to a man when you do not know his name. *Dear Sir, I am writing to...* **3 Sir** a title used in the UK before the name of a man who has been officially respected or who has a high social rank *Sir Cliff Richard*

WORD PARTNERS FOR **siren**

a siren **goes off/sounds** ● a siren **blares/wails** ● a **police** siren

siren /'saɪərən/ *noun* [C] a piece of equipment that makes a loud sound as a warning *a police siren*

sister /'sɪstər/ *noun* [C] **1** RELATIVE a girl or woman who has the same parents as you *an older/younger sister* ○ *my big/little sister* **2** RELIGION (*also* **Sister**) a nun (= woman who lives in a female religious group) *Sister Bridget* **3** NURSE (*also* **Sister**) a female nurse in the UK who is responsible for a hospital ward (= an area of a hospital containing beds for ill people) **4** MEMBER a woman who is a member of the same race, religious group, organization, etc

sister-in-law /'sɪstᵊrɪnlɔː/ *noun* [C] *plural* **sisters-in-law** the woman married to your brother, or the sister of your husband or wife

sisterly /'sɪstəli/ *adjective* experienced by or for a sister *sisterly love*

sit /sɪt/ *verb* **sitting**, *past* **sat 1** BODY POSITION [I] to be in a position with the weight of your body on your bottom and the top part of your body up, for example, on a chair *Emma was sitting on a stool.* ○ *The children sat at the table by the window.* ○ *We sat by the river and had a* *picnic.* **2** [MOVE BODY] [I] (*also* **sit down**) to move your body into a sitting position after you have been standing *She came over and sat beside him.* ○ *She sat down on the grass.* ⊃See colour picture Phrasal Verbs on page Centre 16. **3 sit sb down/at/in, etc** to make someone sit somewhere *She sat me down and told me the bad news.* ○ *I thought we'd sit the children at the end of the table.* **4** [STAY] [I] to stay in one place for a long time and not be used *He hardly ever drives the car. It just sits in the garage.* **5** [MEETING] [I] If a court, parliament, etc sits, it has a meeting to do its work. *The board will be sitting next week.* **6** [TEST/EXAM] [T] UK to take a test or exam *The changes will affect many students sitting their exams this summer.* ⊃See also: sit on the **fence**[1].

sit about/around to spend time sitting down and doing very little [+ doing sth] *He just sits around all day watching television.*

sit back 1 to relax in a chair so that your back is against the back of the chair *Just sit back and enjoy the show.* **2** to wait for something to happen without making any effort to do anything yourself *You can't just sit back and expect someone else to deal with the problem.*

sit in to go to a meeting or class to watch *I sat in on a couple of classes before choosing a course.*

sit sth out 1 to not do an activity such as a game or dance because you are tired or have an injury *I think I'll sit out the next dance.* **2** to wait for something unpleasant to finish before you do anything *The government is prepared to sit out the strike rather than agree to union demands.*

sit through sth to stay until the end of a meeting, performance, etc that is very long or boring *We had to sit through two hours of speeches.*

sit up 1 to move your body to a sitting position after you have been lying down *I sat up and opened my eyes.* **2** to stay awake and not go to bed although it is late [+ doing sth] *We sat up talking all night.*

sitcom /ˈsɪtkɒm/ *noun* [C, U] a funny television programme that is about the same group of people every week in different situations

site[1] /saɪt/ *noun* **1** [HISTORY] [C] the place where something important happened in the past *a historic site* ○ *the site of a battle* **2** [AREA] [C] an area that is used for something or where something happens *a building site* **3 on site** inside a factory, office building, etc *There are two restaurants on site.* ○ *They provide on-site childcare facilities for employees.* **4** [INTERNET] [C] short for **website** (= an area on the Internet where information about a particular subject, organization, etc can be found)

site[2] /saɪt/ *verb formal* **site sth in/on, etc** to build something in a particular place [often passive] *The company's head office is sited in Geneva.*

sitter /ˈsɪtər/ *noun* [C] *mainly US* a babysitter (= someone who looks after children when their parents go out)

sitting /ˈsɪtɪŋ/ *noun* [C] **1** a meeting of a parliament, court, etc *a late-night sitting of parlia-*

ment **2** one of the times when a meal is served to a large group of people who cannot all eat at the same time

'sitting ˌroom *noun* [C] UK the room in a house where people sit to relax and, for example, watch television

situated /ˈsɪtjueɪtɪd/ *adjective formal* **be situated in/on/by, etc** to be in a particular place *a hotel situated by Lake Garda*

o→ **situation** /ˌsɪtjuˈeɪʃ³n/ *noun* [C] **1** the set of things that are happening and the conditions that exist at a particular time and place *the economic/political situation* ○ *He's **in a** difficult situation.* **2** *formal* the position of a town, building, etc *The park's situation was perfect.*

o→ **six** /sɪks/ the number 6

o→ **sixteen** /ˌsɪkˈstiːn/ the number 16 • **sixteenth** 16th written as a word

sixth[1] /sɪksθ/ 6th written as a word

sixth[2] /sɪksθ/ *noun* [C] one of six equal parts of something; ⅙

'sixth ˌform *noun* [C] in Britain, the part of a school for students between the ages of 16 and 18

o→ **sixty** /ˈsɪksti/ **1** the number 60 **2 the sixties** the years from 1960 to 1969 **3 be in your sixties** to be aged between 60 and 69 • **sixtieth** 60th written as a word

sizable /ˈsaɪzəbl/ *adjective another spelling of* **sizeable**

o→ **size**[1] /saɪz/ *noun* **1** [C, U] how big or small something is *It's an area about the size of Oxford.* ○ *The size of some of these trees is incredible (= they are very large).* **2** [C] one of the different measurements in which things, for example clothes, food containers, etc are made *a size 10 skirt* ○ *What size shoes do you take?* ○ *I usually buy the 1.5 litre size.* ⊃See also: all shapes (**shape**[1]) and sizes.

size[2] /saɪz/ *verb*

size sb/sth up to look at someone or think about something carefully before making a judgment *I could see her trying to size me up.*

sizeable (*also* **sizable**) /ˈsaɪzəbl/ *adjective* quite large *a sizeable crowd*

-sized /saɪzd/ *suffix* used at the end of a word to mean 'of a particular size' *a medium-sized pizza* ○ *a good-sized bedroom*

sizzle /ˈsɪzl/ *verb* [I] to make the sound of food cooking in hot oil

skanky /ˈskæŋki/ *adjective informal* very unpleasant or dirty

skate[1] /skeɪt/ *noun* [C] **1** (*also* **roller skate**) a boot with wheels on the bottom, used for moving

S

across the ground *a pair of skates* **2** (*also* **ice skate**) a boot with a metal part on the bottom, used for moving across ice ➾See colour picture **Sports 1** on page Centre 14. **3 get/put your skates on** *UK informal* used to tell someone to hurry

skate² /skeɪt/ *verb* [I] to move using skates • **skater** *noun* [C] • **skating** *noun* [U]

skateboard /'skeɪtbɔːd/ *noun* [C] a board with wheels on the bottom, that you stand on and move forward by pushing one foot on the ground ➾See colour picture **Sports 1** on page Centre 14.

skateboarding /'skeɪtbɔːdɪŋ/ *noun* [U] the activity of moving using a skateboard ➾See colour picture **Sports 1** on page Centre 14.

skeletal /'skelɪtᵊl/ *adjective* like a skeleton, or relating to skeletons

skeleton /'skelɪtᵊn/ *noun* **1** [C] the structure made of all the bones in the body of a person or animal **2 a skeleton crew/staff/service** the smallest number of people that you need to keep an organization working **3 have a skeleton in the cupboard** *UK* (*US* **have a skeleton in the closet**) to have an embarrassing or unpleasant secret about something that happened in the past

skeptic /'skeptɪk/ *noun* [C] *US spelling of* sceptic

skeptical /'skeptɪkᵊl/ *adjective US spelling of* sceptical

skepticism /'skeptɪsɪzᵊm/ *noun* [U] *US spelling of* scepticism

sketch¹ /sketʃ/ *noun* [C] **1** PICTURE a picture that you draw quickly and with few details *He did a quick sketch of the cat.* **2** ACTING a short piece of acting about a funny situation **3** DESCRIPTION a short description of something without many details

sketch² /sketʃ/ *verb* [T] to draw a sketch *I sketched a map for him on a scrap of paper.*
sketch sth out to give a short description with few details, especially of an idea or plan *I've sketched out some ideas for my new book.*

sketchy /'sketʃi/ *adjective* with few details *Reports about the accident are still sketchy.*

ski¹ /skiː/ *noun* [C] *plural* **skis** one of a pair of long, thin pieces of wood or plastic that you wear on the bottom of boots to move over snow ➾See colour picture **Sports 1** on page Centre 14.

ski² /skiː/ *verb* [I] skiing, *past* skied to move over snow wearing skis • **skier** *noun* [C] • **skiing** *noun* [U] *I'd like to go skiing in Switzerland.* ➾See also: water-skiing ➾See colour picture **Sports 1** on page Centre 14.

skid /skɪd/ *verb* [I] skidding, *past* skidded If a vehicle skids, it slides along a surface and you cannot control it. *The car skidded on ice and hit a tree.* • **skid** *noun* [C]

skies /skaɪz/ *noun* [plural] the sky in a particular place or in a particular state *beautiful, clear, blue skies*

skilful *UK* (*US* **skillful**) /'skɪlfᵊl/ *adjective* **1** good at doing something *a skilful artist* **2** done or made very well *skilful use of language* • **skilfully** *adverb UK*

⚬**skill** /skɪl/ *noun* [C, U] the ability to do an activity or job well, especially because you have practised it *You need good communication skills to be a teacher.*

skilled /skɪld/ *adjective* **1** having the abilities needed to do an activity or job well *a **highly** skilled* (= very skilled) *photographer* ○ *He has become skilled in dealing with the media.* **2** Skilled work needs someone who has had special training to do it. ➾Opposite **unskilled**.

skillet /'skɪlɪt/ *noun* [C] *mainly US* a large, heavy pan with a long handle, used for frying food

skillful /'skɪlfᵊl/ *adjective US spelling of* skilful

skim /skɪm/ *verb* skimming, *past* skimmed **1** MOVE OVER [I, T] to move quickly, and almost or just touch the surface of something *Birds skimmed the surface of the pond.* **2** REMOVE [T] (*also* **skim off**) to remove something from the surface of a liquid *Skim off any excess fat before serving.* **3** READ QUICKLY [T] (*also* **skim through**) to read or look at something quickly without reading all the details *She began skimming through the reports on her desk.*

,**skimmed 'milk** (*also US* '**skim ,milk**) *noun* [U] milk that has had the fat removed from it

skimp /skɪmp/ *verb*
skimp on sth to not spend enough time or money on something, or not use enough of something *We've got plenty of cheese so don't skimp on it.*

skimpy /'skɪmpi/ *adjective* Skimpy clothes show a lot of your body. *a skimpy bikini/dress*

⚬**skin¹** /skɪn/ *noun* [C, U] **1** BODY the outer layer of a person or animal's body *dark/fair skin* **2** ANIMAL the outer layer of a dead animal used as leather, fur, etc *a leopard skin rug* **3** FRUIT the outer layer of a fruit or vegetable *a banana/potato skin* **4** LIQUID a thin, solid layer that forms on the top of a liquid *A skin had formed on the top of the milk.* **5** COMPUTERS the particular way that information is arranged and shown on a computer screen **6 do sth by the skin of your teeth** *informal* to only just succeed in doing something *They held on by the skin of their teeth to win 1-0.* **7 have (a) thick skin** to not care if someone criticizes you

skin² /skɪn/ *verb* [T] skinning, *past* skinned **1** to remove the skin from something **2** (*also UK* **graze**) to injure your skin by rubbing it against something rough *Mary fell and skinned her knees.*

skinhead /'skɪnhed/ *noun* [C] a man who has extremely short hair, especially one who behaves in a violent way

skinny /'skɪni/ *adjective* Someone who is skinny is too thin.

skip¹ /skɪp/ *verb* skipping, *past* skipped **1** MOVE FORWARD [I] to move forward, jumping quickly from one foot to the other *She watched her daughter skipping down the street.* **2** JUMP [I] (*US* ,skip 'rope) to jump over a rope while you or two other people move it over and then under your body again and again *I skip for ten minutes every day to keep fit.* **3** NOT DO [T] to not do something that you usually do or that you should do *I think I'll skip lunch today - I'm not very hungry.* **4** AVOID [T] (*also* skip over) to avoid reading or talking about something by starting to read or talk about the next thing instead *I usually skip the boring bits.*

skip² /skɪp/ *noun* [C] **1** *UK* (*US* Dumpster *trademark*) a very large, metal container for big pieces of rubbish **2** when you jump quickly from one foot to the other

skipper /'skɪpəʳ/ *noun* [C] *informal* the leader of a team, an aircraft, a ship, etc

'skipping ,rope *UK* (*US* jump rope) *noun* [C] a rope that you move over your head and then jump over as you move it under your feet

skirmish /'skɜːmɪʃ/ *noun* [C] a small fight

skirt¹ /skɜːt/ *noun* [C] a piece of women's clothing that hangs from the waist and has no legs ⊃See colour picture Clothes on page Centre 8.

skirt² /skɜːt/ (*also* skirt around) *verb* [T] **1** to avoid talking about something *I deliberately skirted the question of money.* **2** to move around the edge of something *We skirted around the edge of the field.*

skittle /'skɪtl/ *noun* **1** [C] one of a set of bottle-shaped objects that you try to knock down with a ball as a game **2** skittles [U] a game in which you try to knock down bottle-shaped objects with a ball

skive /skaɪv/ (*also* skive off) *verb* [I, T] *UK* to not go to school or work when you should, or to leave school or work earlier than you should ● skiver *noun* [C] *UK informal* someone who skives

skulk /skʌlk/ *verb* skulk about/behind/in, etc to hide somewhere or move around quietly in a way that makes people think you are going to do something bad *I saw a man skulking behind the shed.*

skull /skʌl/ *noun* [C] the part of your head that is made of bone and which protects your brain

'skull ,cap *noun* [C] a small round hat worn especially by some religious men

skunk /skʌŋk/ *noun* [C] a black and white animal that produces a very unpleasant smell in order to defend itself

o▲**sky** /skaɪ/ *noun* [U, no plural] the area above the Earth where you can see clouds, the sun, the moon, etc *a beautiful, blue sky* ○ *The sky suddenly went dark.* ⊃See also: skies.

skydiving /'skaɪ,daɪvɪŋ/ *noun* [U] the sport of jumping out of an aircraft with a parachute (= large piece of cloth that allows you to fall slowly to the ground)

skylight /'skaɪlaɪt/ *noun* [C] a window in the roof of a building

skyline /'skaɪlaɪn/ *noun* [C] the pattern that is made against the sky by tall buildings *the New York skyline*

skyline

'sky ,marshal *noun* [C] a person whose job is to carry a gun and protect the passengers on an aircraft

skyscraper /'skaɪ,skreɪpəʳ/ *noun* [C] a very tall building

slab /slæb/ *noun* [C] a thick, flat piece of something, especially stone *a slab of concrete*

slack¹ /slæk/ *adjective* **1** LOOSE loose or not tight *Suddenly the rope became slack.* **2** BUSINESS If business is slack, there are not many customers. **3** LAZY not trying hard enough in your work *slack management*

slack² /slæk/ *informal* (*also US* slack off) *verb* [I] to work less hard than usual *I'm afraid I haven't been to the gym recently - I've been slacking.*

slacken /'slækən/ *verb* [I, T] **1** to become slower or less active, or to make something become slower or less active *Economic growth is slackening.* **2** to become loose, or to make something become loose *As you get older your muscles slacken.*

slacks /slæks/ *noun* [plural] *mainly US* trousers

slag /slæg/ *verb* slagging, *past* slagged
 slag sb/sth off *UK informal* to criticize someone or something in an unpleasant way

slain /sleɪn/ *past participle of* slay

slalom /'slɑːləm/ *noun* [C] a race in which you go forwards by moving from side to side between poles

slam /slæm/ *verb* slamming, *past* slammed **1** [I, T] to close with great force, or to make something close with great force *Kate heard the front door slam.* **2** slam sth down/onto/into, etc to put something somewhere with great force *She slammed the phone down.* ● slam *noun* [C] [usually singular] *the slam of a car door*

slander /'slɑːndəʳ/ *noun* [C, U] the crime of saying bad things about someone that are not true ● slander *verb* [T] ● slanderous /'slɑːndʳrəs/ *adjective* saying bad things about someone that are not true

slang /slæŋ/ *noun* [U] informal language, often language that is only used by people who belong to a particular group *prison slang*

slant¹ /slɑːnt/ *verb* [I, T] to slope in a particular direction, or to make something slope in a particular direction *Pale sunlight slanted through the curtain.*

slant² /slɑːnt/ *noun* [no plural] **1** a position that is sloping *The road is on/at a slant.* **2** a way of writing about something that shows who or what you support *a political slant* ○ *It's certainly a new slant on the subject.*

slap¹ /slæp/ *verb* [T] slapping, *past* slapped to hit

someone with the flat, inside part of your hand *She slapped him across the face.*

slap sth on to quickly put or spread something on a surface *I'll just slap some make-up on.*

slap² /slæp/ *noun* [C] **1** a hit with the flat, inside part of your hand **2 a slap in the face** something someone does that insults or upsets you *After all that hard work, losing my job was a real slap in the face.*

slapdash /ˈslæpdæʃ/ *adjective* done quickly and without being careful *Her work has been a bit slapdash recently.*

slapstick /ˈslæpstɪk/ *noun* [U] when actors do funny things like falling down, hitting each other, etc to make people laugh

slap-up /ˈslæp.ʌp/ *adjective* **slap-up meal/dinner, etc** *UK informal* a large and very good meal

slash¹ /slæʃ/ *verb* [T] **1** to cut something by making a quick, long cut with something very sharp *His throat had been slashed.* **2** to reduce the amount of something by a lot *to slash prices*

slash² /slæʃ/ *noun* [C] **1** a long, deep cut **2** a mark (/) used in writing to separate words or numbers, often to show a choice or connection

slate¹ /sleɪt/ *noun* [C, U] a dark grey rock that can easily be cut into thin pieces, or a small, flat piece of this used to cover a roof

slate² /sleɪt/ *verb* **1** [T] *UK* to criticize someone or something severely [often passive] *The film had been slated by critics.* **2 be slated** *US* to be expected to be or happen in the future, or to be expected to be or do something in the future [+ to do sth] *Filming is slated to begin next spring.*

slaughter¹ /ˈslɔːtəʳ/ *verb* [T] **1** ANIMAL to kill an animal for meat **2** PEOPLE to kill a lot of people in a very cruel way **3** DEFEAT *informal* to defeat someone very easily

slaughter² /ˈslɔːtəʳ/ *noun* [U] when a lot of people or animals are killed in a cruel way

slaughterhouse /ˈslɔːtəhaʊs/ *noun* [C] *plural* slaughterhouses /ˈslɔːtəhaʊzɪz/ a place where animals are killed for meat

slave¹ /sleɪv/ *noun* **1** [C] someone who is owned by someone else and has to work for them *He treats his mother like a slave.* **2 be a slave to sth** to be completely controlled or influenced by something *You're a slave to fashion.*

slave² /sleɪv/ (*also* slave away) *verb* [I] *informal* to work very hard *Giorgio was slaving away at his homework.*

slavery /ˈsleɪvʰri/ *noun* [U] the system of owning slaves, or the condition of being a slave

slay /sleɪ/ *verb* [T] *past tense* slew, *past participle* slain *literary* to kill someone in a very violent way

sleaze /sliːz/ *noun* [U] political or business activities that are morally wrong

sleazy /ˈsliːzi/ *adjective* unpleasant and morally wrong, often in a way that relates to sex *He spent the night drinking in a sleazy bar.*

sledge¹ /sledʒ/ *UK* (*US* sled /sled/) *noun* [C] a vehicle that is used for travelling on snow

sledge² /sledʒ/ *UK* (*US* sled /sled/) *verb* [I] to travel on snow using a sledge

sleek /sliːk/ *adjective* **1** Sleek hair is smooth and very shiny. **2** A sleek car is attractive and looks expensive.

o⸻**sleep¹** /sliːp/ *verb* *past* slept **1** [I] to be in the state of rest when your eyes are closed, your body is not active, and your mind is unconscious *Did you sleep well?* **2 sleep four/six, etc** If a place sleeps four, six, etc, it is big enough for that number of people to sleep in. **3 sleep on it** to wait until the next day before making a decision about something important so that you can think about it carefully ➾See also: not sleep a wink².

sleep in to sleep longer in the morning than you usually do

sleep sth off to sleep until you feel better, especially after drinking too much alcohol

sleep over to sleep in someone else's home for a night *After the party, I slept over at Tom's house.*

sleep through sth to continue to sleep although there is noise *I don't know how you slept through the storm.*

sleep with sb *informal* to have sex with someone

o⸻**sleep²** /sliːp/ *noun* **1** [U, no plural] the state you are in when you are sleeping, or a period of time when you are sleeping *I haven't had a good night's sleep* (= a long sleep at night) *for weeks.* ○ *You need to go home and get some sleep.* ○ *It took me ages to get to sleep* (= to succeed in sleeping). ○ *He died peacefully in his sleep.* **2 go to sleep a** to begin to sleep *Babies often go to sleep after a feed.* **b** *informal* If part of your body goes to sleep, you cannot feel it. *I'd been sitting on my feet and they'd gone to sleep.* **3 put sth to sleep** to kill an animal that is very old or ill **4 could do sth in your sleep** to be able to do something very easily **5 lose sleep over sth** to worry about something

sleeper /ˈsliːpəʳ/ *noun* **1 a light/heavy sleeper** someone who wakes up easily/does not wake up easily **2** TRAIN [C] a train or a part of a train that has beds in it **3** SUPPORT [C] *UK* (*US* railroad tie) a piece of wood that is used to support a railway track (= the thing a train moves along on) **4** JEWELLERY [C] *UK* a small gold or silver ring worn in the ear

'sleeping ˌbag *noun* [C] a long bag made of thick material that you sleep inside

'sleeping ˌpill *noun* [C] a medicine that you take to help you sleep

sleepless /ˈsliːpləs/ *adjective* **sleepless night** a night when you are not able to sleep *He'd spent a sleepless night worrying about his exam.*
• **sleeplessness** *noun* [U]

sleeping bag

S

sleep-over /ˈsliːpəʊvəʳ/ *noun* [C] a party when a group of young people stay at a friend's house for the night

sleepwalk /ˈsliːpˌwɔːk/ *verb* [I] to get out of bed and walk around while you are sleeping • **sleepwalker** *noun* [C]

sleepy /ˈsliːpi/ *adjective* **1** feeling tired and wanting to go to sleep *The heat had made me sleepy.* **2** quiet and with little activity *a sleepy little town* • **sleepily** *adverb* • **sleepiness** *noun* [U]

sleet /sliːt/ *noun* [U] a mixture of snow and rain • **sleet** *verb* [I] ***It was sleeting** when I looked outside.*

WORD PARTNERS FOR ***sleeve***

long/short sleeves • **roll up** your sleeves

sleeve /sliːv/ *noun* **1** [C] the part of a jacket, shirt, etc that covers your arm *He **rolled up** his **sleeves** to do the dishes.* ➲See picture at **jacket**. **2 have sth up your sleeve** *informal* to have a secret plan *They were worried he might have another nasty surprise up his sleeve.*

-sleeved /sliːvd/ *suffix* **short-sleeved/long-sleeved** having short/long sleeves *a short-sleeved shirt*

sleeveless /ˈsliːvləs/ *adjective* describes a piece of clothing with no sleeves *a sleeveless dress*

sleigh /sleɪ/ *noun* [C] a large vehicle that is pulled by animals and used for travelling on snow

slender /ˈslendəʳ/ *adjective* thin in an attractive way *a slender woman with long, red hair* ○ *The plant's leaves are long and slender.*

slept /slept/ *past of* sleep

sleuth /sluːθ/ *noun* [C] *old-fashioned* a police officer whose job is to discover who has committed a crime

slew /sluː/ *past tense of* slay

slice¹ /slaɪs/ *noun* **1** [C] a flat piece of food that has been cut from a larger piece *a slice of bread/cake/meat* ○ *Would you like another slice of ham/beef?* ➲See colour picture **Pieces and Quantities** on page Centre 1. **2 a slice of sth** a part of something that is being divided *a large slice of the profits* ○ *The film presents us with a fascinating slice of history.* ➲See also: **fish slice**.

slice² /slaɪs/ *verb* **1** [T] (*also* **slice up**) to cut food into thin, flat pieces *Could you slice the tomatoes?* **2 slice into/off/through, etc** [I, T] to cut into or through something with a knife or something sharp *I almost sliced my finger off.* ➲See also: the best/greatest **thing** since sliced bread.

slick /slɪk/ *adjective* **1** done with a lot of skill *a slick presentation* **2** attractive but in a way that is not sincere or honest *He was a bit slick - I didn't trust him.*

slide¹ /slaɪd/ *verb past* **slid 1 slide (sth) across/down/along, etc** to move smoothly over a surface, or to make something move smoothly over a surface *He slid the letter into his pocket.* **2 slide (sth) into/out of/through, etc** to move somewhere quietly, or to make something move quietly *She slid out of the room, being careful not to wake Alan.*

slide² /slaɪd/ *noun* **1** PHOTOGRAPH [C] a small piece of film that you shine light through in order to see a photograph **2** GAME [C] a large object that children climb and slide down as a game **3** GLASS [C] a small piece of glass that you put something on when you want to look at it under a microscope (= equipment used to make things look bigger) **4** LESS/WORSE [no plural] when the level or quality of something gets less or worse *a price slide*

⊶**slight¹** /slaɪt/ *adjective* **1** small and not important *slight differences in colour* ○ *We're having a slight problem with our computer system.* **2** Someone who is slight is thin.

slight² /slaɪt/ *noun* [C] an action or remark that insults someone

slighted /ˈslaɪtɪd/ *adjective* **be/feel slighted** to feel insulted because someone has done or said something which shows that they think you are not important *Annie felt slighted because she hadn't been invited to the meeting.*

slightest /ˈslaɪtɪst/ *adjective* **1 the slightest** [always before noun] the smallest *The slightest movement will disturb these shy animals.* **2 not in the slightest** not at all *"Do you mind if I open the window?" "Not in the slightest."*

⊶**slightly** /ˈslaɪtli/ *adverb* a little *I think I did slightly better in my exams this time.* ○ *I find it slightly worrying.*

slim¹ /slɪm/ *adjective* **slimmer, slimmest 1** Someone who is slim is thin in an attractive way. **2** small and not as much as you would like *There's a **slim chance** he'll succeed.*

slim² /slɪm/ *verb* [I] **slimming**, *past* **slimmed** *UK* to eat less in order to become thinner

slim down to become thinner

slim sth down to reduce the size of something *It is not our intention to slim down the workforce.*

slime /slaɪm/ *noun* [U] a thick, sticky liquid that is unpleasant to touch

slimy /ˈslaɪmi/ *adjective* **1** covered in slime **2** *informal* too friendly in a way that is not sincere

sling¹ /slɪŋ/ *noun* [C] **1** a piece of cloth that you wear around your neck and put your arm into to support it when it is injured **2** a piece of cloth or a strap that you tie around your body to carry things in *She had her baby in a sling.*

sling² /slɪŋ/ *verb past* **slung 1 sling sth over/around/on, etc** to put something in a position where it hangs loosely *He slung his bag over his shoulder.* **2 sling sth into/onto/under, etc** to throw something somewhere in a careless way *She slung her coat onto the bed.*

slingshot /ˈslɪŋʃɒt/ *US* (*UK* **catapult**) *noun* [C] a Y-shaped object with a piece of elastic across it used by children to shoot small stones

slink /slɪŋk/ *verb past* **slunk slink away/off/out, etc** to move somewhere quietly so that no one will notice you *I caught him slinking out of the meeting.*

slip¹ /slɪp/ *verb* **slipping**, *past* **slipped 1** FALL [I] to slide by accident and fall or almost fall *She slipped on the ice and broke her ankle.* **2** OUT OF POSITION [I] to slide out of the correct position

S

The photo had slipped from the frame. **3 slip away/out/through, etc** to go somewhere quietly or quickly *I'll slip out of the room if I get bored.* **4 slip sth into/through, etc** to put something somewhere quickly or secretly *She slipped the letter into an envelope and sealed it.* **5** GIVE SECRETLY [+ two objects] *informal* to give something to someone secretly *I slipped her a five pound note.* **6** GET LESS/WORSE [I] to get less or worse in level or quality *His school grades have slipped recently.* **7 let sth slip** to forget that something is a secret and tell someone about it ⊃See also: slip your mind¹.

slip into sth to quickly put on a piece of clothing

slip sth off to quickly take off a piece of clothing *Slip your shirt off and I'll listen to your heart.*

slip sth on to quickly put on a piece of clothing *I'll just slip my shoes on.*

slip out If a remark slips out, you say it without intending to. *I didn't mean to tell anyone you were getting married - it just slipped out.*

slip out of sth to quickly take off a piece of clothing

slip up to make a mistake

slip² /slɪp/ *noun* [C] **1** PAPER a small piece of paper *He wrote the number on a slip of paper.* **2** FALL when you slide by accident and fall or almost fall **3** WOMEN'S CLOTHING a piece of clothing that a woman wears under a dress or skirt **4** MISTAKE a small mistake **5 give sb the slip** *informal* to escape from someone you do not want to be with **6 a slip of the tongue** a mistake made by using the wrong word

slipper /'slɪpəʳ/ *noun* [C] a soft, comfortable shoe that you wear in the house ⊃See colour picture Clothes on page Centre 8.

slippery /'slɪpʳri/ *adjective* **1** smooth and wet and difficult to hold or walk on *Be careful - the floor's slippery.* **2 a slippery slope** a bad situation that is likely to get worse

'slip ˌroad *UK* (*US* ramp) *noun* [C] a short road that is used to drive onto or off a motorway (= wide, fast road)

slit¹ /slɪt/ *noun* [C] a long, narrow cut or hole in something *Make a slit in the pastry to allow the steam to escape.*

slit² /slɪt/ *verb* [T] slitting, *past* slit to make a long, narrow cut in something *She slit her wrists.*

slither /'slɪðəʳ/ *verb* [I] to move smoothly by twisting and sliding

sliver /'slɪvəʳ/ *noun* [C] a thin piece of something that has come off a larger piece *slivers of glass*

slob /slɒb/ *noun* [C] *informal* a lazy or dirty person

slog¹ /slɒg/ *verb* slogging, *past* slogged *informal* **slog up/down/through, etc** to move forward with difficulty *We slogged up the hill in silence.* **slog away** *informal* to work very hard for a long time *I've been slogging away at this for hours and I'm exhausted.*

slog² /slɒg/ *noun* [U, no plural] *UK informal* a period of hard work *Studying for all the exams was a hard slog.*

slogan /'sləʊgən/ *noun* [C] a short phrase that is easy to remember and is used to make people notice something *an advertising slogan*

slop /slɒp/ *verb* slopping, *past* slopped **slop (sth) about/around/into, etc** If liquid slops about, it moves around or over the edge of its container, and if you slop it about, you make it move around or over the edge of its container. *Her hand shook, making her tea slop into the saucer.*

slope¹ /sləʊp/ *noun* [C] a surface or piece of land that is high at one end and low at the other *There's a steep slope to climb before we're at the top.* ⊃See also: a slippery slope.

slope² /sləʊp/ *verb* [I] to be high at one end and low at the other *The field slopes down to the river.*

sloppy /'slɒpi/ *adjective* **1** CARELESS not done carefully *His work was sloppy and full of spelling mistakes.* **2** CLOTHES Sloppy clothes are loose and untidy. *a girl wearing a sloppy sweater and torn jeans* **3** TOO WET A sloppy substance has too much liquid in it. • **sloppily** *adverb* • **sloppiness** *noun* [U]

slosh /slɒʃ/ *verb* **slosh against/over/around, etc** If liquid sloshes, it moves against or over the edge of its container. *Water sloshed over the edge of the pool as the swimmers dived in.*

sloshed /slɒʃt/ *adjective informal* drunk

slot¹ /slɒt/ *noun* [C] **1** a long, narrow hole that you put something into, especially money **2** a period of time that you allow for something in a plan *The programme is being moved to a later slot.*

slot² /slɒt/ *verb* [I, T] slotting, *past* slotted to fit into a slot, or to make something fit into a slot **slot sb/sth in** to find time for someone or something in a period of time that has already been planned *Dr O'Neil can slot you in around 9.30.*

sloth /sləʊθ/ *noun* **1** [C] an animal that moves very slowly and lives in Central and South America **2** [U] *literary* when someone is lazy

'slot maˌchine *noun* [C] a machine that you put money into in order to try to win money

slouch¹ /slaʊtʃ/ *verb* [I] to stand, sit, or walk with your shoulders forward so that your body is not straight *Stop slouching and stand up straight.*

slouch

slouch² /slaʊtʃ/ *noun* **1** [no plural] the position your body is in when you slouch **2 be no slouch** *informal* to work very hard and be good at something *He's no slouch when it comes to cooking.*

slovenly /'slʌvʳnli/ *adjective* lazy, untidy, and dirty *a slovenly appear-*

ance ○ *I'll have to improve my slovenly habits – my mother's coming to stay.* ● **slovenliness** noun [U]

o→**slow**[1] /sləʊ/ *adjective* **1** NOT FAST moving, happening, or doing something without much speed *I'm making slow progress with the painting.* ○ *He's a very slow reader.* **2 be slow to do sth; be slow in doing sth** to take a long time to do something *The government has been slow to react to the problem.* ○ *The ambulance was very slow in coming.* **3** CLOCK If a clock is slow, it shows a time that is earlier than the correct time. **4** BUSINESS If business is slow, there are few customers. **5** NOT CLEVER not quick at learning and understanding things **6** NOT EXCITING not exciting *I find his films very slow.*

slow[2] /sləʊ/ *verb* [I, T] to become slower or to make something become slower *The car slowed to a halt* (= moved more and more slowly until it stopped).

slow (sth) down to become slower or to make something become slower *Slow down, Claire, you're walking too fast!*

slow down If someone slows down, they become less active. *The doctor told me I should slow down and not work so hard.*

slowdown /'sləʊdaʊn/ *noun* [C] when business activity becomes slower *an economic slowdown* ○ *The figures show a slowdown in retail sales.*

o→**slowly** /'sləʊli/ *adverb* at a slow speed *Could you speak more slowly, please?*

,**slow 'motion** *noun* [U] a way of showing pictures from a film or television programme at a slower speed than normal *They showed a replay of the goal in slow motion.*

sludge /slʌdʒ/ *noun* [U] soft, wet soil, or a substance that looks like this *We seemed to spend the last mile of the walk knee-deep in sludge.*

slug[1] /slʌg/ *noun* [C] **1** a small, soft creature with no legs that moves slowly and eats plants ⊃See picture at **snail. 2** a small amount of a drink, especially an alcoholic drink *He took a slug of whisky from the bottle.*

slug[2] /slʌg/ *verb* [T] **slugging**, *past* **slugged** *informal* to hit someone with your fist (= closed hand)

slug it out *informal* to fight, argue, or compete with someone until one person wins *Federer and Hewitt slugged it out for a place in the final.*

sluggish /'slʌgɪʃ/ *adjective* moving or working more slowly than usual *a sluggish economy* ○ *I felt really sluggish after lunch.*

slum /slʌm/ *noun* [C] a poor and crowded area of a city where the buildings are in a very bad condition *He grew up in the slums of Mexico City.* ○ *slum areas*

slumber /'slʌmbəʳ/ *noun* [C, U] *literary* sleep *She lay down on the bed and fell into a deep slumber.* ● **slumber** *verb* [I] *literary*

'**slumber ,party** *noun* [C] *US* a party when a group of children spend the night at one child's house

slump[1] /slʌmp/ *verb* **1** [I] If a price, value, or amount slumps, it goes down suddenly. *Sales*

have slumped by 50%. **2 slump back/down/over,** etc to fall or sit down suddenly because you feel tired or weak *She slumped back in her chair, exhausted.*

slump[2] /slʌmp/ *noun* [C] **1** a sudden fall in prices or sales *a slump in world oil prices* **2** a period when there is very little business activity and not many jobs *It's been the worst economic slump for 25 years.*

slung /slʌŋ/ *past of* sling

slunk /slʌŋk/ *past of* slink

slur[1] /slɜːʳ/ *verb* [I, T] **slurring**, *past* **slurred** to speak without separating your words clearly, often because you are tired or drunk *He'd drunk too much and was slurring his words.*

slur[2] /slɜːʳ/ *noun* [C] a criticism that will make people have a bad opinion of someone or something *a racial slur* ○ *She regarded it as a slur on her character.*

slurp /slɜːp/ *verb* [I, T] *informal* to drink in a noisy way *He slurped his tea.* ● **slurp** *noun* [C] *informal*

slush /slʌʃ/ *noun* [U] snow that has started to melt

sly /slaɪ/ *adjective* **slyer, slyest 1** deceiving people in a clever way to get what you want **2 sly smile** a smile that shows you know something that other people do not *"I know why Chris didn't come home yesterday," she said with a sly smile.* ● **slyly** *adverb*

smack[1] /smæk/ *verb* **1** [T] to hit someone with the flat, inside part of your hand *Do you think it's right to smack children when they're naughty?* **2 smack sth against/onto/down,** etc to hit something hard against something else *Ray smacked the ball into the net.*

smack of sth If something smacks of an unpleasant quality, it seems to have that quality. *a policy that smacks of racism*

smack[2] /smæk/ *noun* [C] a hit with the flat, inside part of your hand *Stop shouting or I'll give you a smack !*

smack[3] /smæk/ *informal* (*also UK* '**smack ,bang**) (*also US* ,**smack 'dab**) *adverb* **1** exactly in a particular place *She lives smack in the middle of Edinburgh.* **2** suddenly and with a lot of force *He braked too late and ran smack into the car in front.*

o→**small**[1] /smɔːl/ *adjective* **1** LITTLE little in size or amount *They live in a small apartment near Times Square.* ○ *We teach the children in small groups.* **2** YOUNG A small child is very young. *a woman with three small children* **3** NOT IMPORTANT not important or serious *a small mistake* **4 feel small** to feel stupid or unimportant *Simon was always trying to make me feel small.*

Little is a very common alternative to
'small', and can describe things or people:
*I'll just have a **little** piece of cake.* • *She's so
little.*

If someone is extremely small, you can say
that they are **tiny** or **minute**, and if something is extremely small, you can say that it
is **minute**, **tiny**, or, in more formal contexts,
microscopic or **minuscule**: *Inside the pram
was a **tiny** baby.* • *The phone he pulled out of
his pocket was **minute**.* • *The cost of vaccination is **minuscule** compared to the cost of
treatment.*

The adjectives **dwarf** and **miniature** are
sometimes used to describe things that are
smaller than the normal size: *There were
dwarf fir trees in pots on the patio.* • *It's a
miniature bath for the doll's house.*

If a woman or girl is small in an attractive
way, you can use the adjectives **dainty** or
petite: *She had **dainty** feet.* • *Like all his
girlfriends, Emma was dark and **petite**.*

You can use the informal adjective **poky** to
describe a room or other area that is too
small: *They live in a **poky** little flat in south
London.*

The adjective **slight** is sometimes used with
abstract nouns to describe things that are
small and not important: *There was a **slight**
difference in colour.*

COMMON LEARNER ERROR

small or little?

Small refers to size and is the usual opposite of 'big' or
'large'.
*Could I have a hamburger and a small Coke
please?*

Our house is quite small.

Little refers to size but also expresses the speaker's feelings. For example, it can suggest that the speaker likes or
dislikes something.
They live in a beautiful little village.

Rats are horrible little animals.

The comparative and superlative forms of **little** are not
usually used in British English. Use **smaller** or **smallest**
instead.
My car is smaller than yours.

~~My car is littler than yours.~~

---

small² /smɔːl/ *adverb* in a small size *Emma knitted the sweater far too small.*

'small ,ad *noun* [C] *UK* a small advertisement
that you put in a newspaper if you want to buy
or sell something

,small 'change *noun* [U] coins that have little
value

'small ,fry *noun* [U] *informal* people or activities that are not considered important *Compared to companies that size we're just small
fry.*

,small 'print *noun* [U] ⁺the part of a written

agreement that is printed smaller than the
rest and that contains important information
*Make sure you read the small print before you
sign.*

small-scale /ˌsmɔːlˈskeɪl/ *adjective* A small-
scale activity or organization is not big and involves few people.

'small ,talk *noun* [U] polite conversation between people at social events *He's not very
good at making small talk.*

small-time /ˈsmɔːltaɪm/ *adjective* [always before
noun] *informal* not important or successful *a
small-time criminal*

smart¹ /smɑːt/ *adjective* **1** [INTELLIGENT] intelligent
Rachel's one of the smartest kids in the class.
2 [TIDY] If you look smart or your clothes are
smart, you look clean and tidy. *a smart, blue
suit* ○ *I need to look a bit smarter for my interview.* **3** [FASHIONABLE] fashionable and expensive
a smart, new restaurant **4** [MACHINE/WEAPON] A
smart machine, weapon, etc uses computers to
make it work. *smart bombs* • **smartly** *adverb*

smart² /smɑːt/ *verb* [I] **1** to feel upset because
someone has said or done something un-
pleasant to you *The team are still **smarting**
from last week's defeat.* **2** If part of your
body smarts, it hurts with a sharp, burning
pain. *The smoke from the fire made her **eyes
smart**.*

'smart ,card *noun* [C] a small, plastic card that
contains a very small computer and can be
used to pay for things or to store personal information

smarten /ˈsmɑːtᵊn/ *verb*
smarten (sb/sth) up to make a person or
place look more clean and tidy *plans to
smarten up the city centre*

smash¹ /smæʃ/ *verb*   **smash**
1 [I, T] to break into a
lot of pieces with a
loud noise, or to
make something
break into a lot of
pieces with a loud
noise *Thieves
smashed the shop
window and stole
$50,000 worth of com-
puter equipment.*
**2 smash (sth)
against/into/through,
etc** to hit a hard
object or surface
with a lot of force, or
to make something
do this *The car skidded and smashed into a
tree.* ○ *He smashed the glass against the wall.*
3 [T] to destroy a political or criminal organization *attempts to smash a drug smuggling ring*
smash sth up to damage or destroy something *They were arrested for smashing up a hotel
bar.*

smash² /smæʃ/ (*also* ,smash 'hit) *noun* [C] a very
successful film, song, play, etc *the smash hit
movie 'Titanic'*

smashing /ˈsmæʃɪŋ/ *adjective* *UK old-fashioned*
extremely good or attractive *We had a smash-*

ing time at Bob and Vera's party.

smear¹ /smɪəʳ/ *verb* [T] **1** to spread a thick liquid or sticky substance over something *His shirt was **smeared** with paint.* ○ *He **smeared** sun cream **over** his face and neck.* **2** to say unpleasant and untrue things about someone in order to harm them, especially in politics

smear² /smɪəʳ/ *noun* [C] **1** a dirty mark *There was a **smear** of oil on his cheek.* **2** an unpleasant and untrue story about someone that is meant to harm them, especially in politics *a **smear** campaign*

o⌐**smell¹** /smel/ *verb past* smelled *also UK* smelt **1 smell of/like; smell delicious/horrible, etc** to have a particular quality that people notice by using their nose *I've been cooking, so my hands **smell** of garlic.* ○ *That soup **smells** delicious - what's in it?* **2** NOTICE [T] to notice something by using your nose *I think I can **smell** something burning.* **3** UNPLEASANT [I] to have an unpleasant smell *Your running shoes really **smell**!* **4** PUT YOUR NOSE NEAR [T] to put your nose near something and breathe in so that you can notice its smell *Come and **smell** these flowers.* **5** ABILITY [I] to have the ability to notice smells *Dogs can **smell** much better than humans.*

o⌐**smell²** /smel/ *noun* **1** QUALITY [C] the quality of something which you notice by using your nose *The **smell** of roses filled the room.* ○ *There was a delicious **smell** coming from the kitchen.* **2** UNPLEASANT [C] an unpleasant smell *I wish I could get rid of that **smell** in the bathroom.* **3** ABILITY [U] the ability to notice smells *Smoking can affect your **sense of smell**.*

smelly /'smeli/ *adjective* having an unpleasant smell *smelly feet*

smelt /smelt/ *UK past of* smell

o⌐**smile¹** /smaɪl/ *verb* [I] to make a happy or friendly expression in which the corners of your mouth curve up *She **smiled** at me.*

COMMON LEARNER ERROR

smile at someone/something

Be careful to choose the right preposition after the verb smile.

*She **smiled** at the little girl.*

~~She smiled to the little girl.~~

WORD PARTNERS FOR smile (noun)

a **beaming/faint/radiant/rueful/wry** smile • **break into/force/give/wear** a smile • a smile **broadens/flickers across sb's face/fades**

o⌐**smile²** /smaɪl/ *noun* [C] a happy or friendly expression in which the corners of your mouth curve up *"I passed my driving test," she said with a smile.*

smiley /'smaɪli/ *noun* [C] an image such as :-) which looks like a face when you look at it from the side, made using keyboard symbols and used in emails to express emotions ○See Extra help page **Emailing and texting** on page Centre 37.

smirk /smɜːk/ *verb* [I] to smile in an annoying or unkind way *What are you **smirking** at?* • **smirk** *noun* [C]

smitten /'smɪtⁿn/ *adjective* [never before noun] loving someone or liking something very much *He's absolutely **smitten** with this Carla woman.*

smog /smɒg/ *noun* [U] air pollution in a city that is a mixture of smoke, gases, and chemicals

o⌐**smoke¹** /sməʊk/ *noun* **1** [U] the grey or black gas that is produced when something burns **2** [no plural] when someone smokes a cigarette *I'm just going outside for a **smoke**.*

o⌐**smoke²** /sməʊk/ *verb* **1** CIGARETTE [I, T] to breathe smoke into your mouth from a cigarette *Do you mind if I **smoke**?* ○ *She **smokes** thirty cigarettes a day.* **2** MEAT/FISH [T] to give meat or fish a special taste by hanging it over burning wood *smoked ham/salmon* **3** PRODUCE SMOKE [I] to produce or send out smoke *smoking chimneys* ○See also: chain-smoke.

smoker /'sməʊkəʳ/ *noun* [C] someone who smokes cigarettes regularly *He used to be a **heavy smoker** (= someone who smokes a lot).* ○Opposite non-smoker.

WORD PARTNERS FOR smoking

give up/stop/quit smoking • **ban** smoking • **heavy** smoking • the **dangers/effects** of smoking

o⌐**smoking** /'sməʊkɪŋ/ *noun* [U] when someone smokes a cigarette or regularly smokes cigarettes *The new law will restrict smoking in public places.* ○See also: passive smoking.

smoky /'sməʊki/ *adjective* **1** filled with smoke *a smoky bar/room* **2** having the smell, taste, or appearance of smoke *That ham has a delicious, smoky flavour.*

smolder /'sməʊldəʳ/ *verb* [I] *US spelling of* smoulder

o⌐**smooth¹** /smuːð/ *adjective* **1** SURFACE having a regular surface that has no holes or lumps in it *soft, smooth skin* ○ *a smooth wooden table* **2** SUBSTANCE A substance that is smooth has no lumps in it. *Mix the butter and sugar together until smooth.* **3** MOVEMENT happening without any sudden movements or changes *The plane made a smooth landing.* **4** PROCESS happening without problems or difficulties *Her job is to help students make a smooth transition from high school to college.* **5** PERSON too polite and confident in a way that people do not trust *a smooth salesman* • **smoothness** *noun* [U] ○See also: take the rough² with the smooth.

smooth² /smuːð/ (*also* smooth down/out, etc) *verb* [T] to move your hands across something in order to make it flat *He straightened his tie and **smoothed** down his hair.*

smooth sth over to make a disagreement or problem seem less serious, especially by talking to the people involved in it *Would you like me to **smooth** things over between you and Nick?*

smoothie /'smuːði/ *noun* [C, U] a thick cold drink made mainly from fruit, sometimes with milk, cream or ice cream (= cold, sweet food)

smoothly /'smuːðli/ *adverb* **1 go smoothly** to happen without any problems or difficulties

Everything was going smoothly until Darren arrived. **2** without any sudden movements or changes *The car accelerated smoothly.*

smother /'smʌðəʳ/ *verb* [T] **1** KILL to kill someone by covering their face with something so that they cannot breathe **2** LOVE to give someone too much love and attention so that they feel they have lost their freedom *I try not to smother him.* **3** PREVENT to prevent something from happening *I tried to smother my cough.* **4** FIRE to make a fire stop burning by covering it with something

smother sth in/with sth to cover something completely with a substance *She took a slice of chocolate cake and smothered it in cream.*

smoulder *UK* (*US* **smolder**) /'sməʊldəʳ/ *verb* [I] **1** to burn slowly, producing smoke but no flames *a smouldering bonfire* **2** to have a strong feeling, especially anger, but not express it *I could see he was **smouldering** with anger.*

SMS /esem'es/ *noun* [U] *abbreviation for* short message service: a system for sending written messages from one mobile phone to another ● **SMS** *verb* [T, I]

smudge¹ /smʌdʒ/ *noun* [C] a dirty mark *a smudge of ink*

smudge² /smʌdʒ/ *verb* [I, T] If ink, paint, etc smudges, or if it is smudged, it becomes dirty or not clear because someone has touched it. *Be careful you don't smudge the drawing.*

smug /smʌg/ *adjective* too pleased with your skill or success in a way that annoys other people *a smug smile* ● **smugly** *adverb* "*I've never lost a match yet,*" *she said smugly.*

smuggle /'smʌgl/ *verb* [T] to take something into or out of a place in an illegal or secret way *He was arrested for smuggling cocaine into Britain.* ● **smuggler** *noun* [C] *drug smugglers* ● **smuggling** *noun* [U]

WORD PARTNERS FOR *snack*

have a snack ● **a light** snack

snack¹ /snæk/ *noun* [C] a small amount of food that you eat between meals *Do you want a quick snack before you go out?* ○ *snack food*

snack² /snæk/ *verb* [I] *informal* to eat a snack *I've been **snacking on** chocolate and biscuits all afternoon.*

WORD PARTNERS FOR *snag*

hit a snag ● **the (only)** snag **is** ● a snag **in/with** sth

snag¹ /snæg/ *noun* [C] *informal* a problem or difficulty *I'd love to come - **the only snag is** I have to be home by 3 o'clock.*

snag² /snæg/ *verb* [T] **snagging**, *past* **snagged** **1** If you snag something, it becomes stuck on a sharp object and tears. *I **snagged** my coat **on** the wire.* **2** *US informal* to get, catch, or win something *She managed to snag a seat in the front row.*

snail /sneɪl/ *noun* [C] **1** a small creature with a long, soft body and a round shell **2 at a snail's pace** very slowly *There was so much traffic that we were travelling at a snail's pace.*

snail

slug

'**snail ,mail** *noun* [U] *humorous informal* letters or messages that are not sent by email but by post

snake¹ /sneɪk/ *noun* [C] a long, thin creature with no legs that slides along the ground

snake² /sneɪk/ *verb* **snake across/around/through, etc** to follow a route that has a lot of bends *The river snakes through some of the most spectacular countryside in France.*

snap¹ /snæp/ *verb* **snapping**, *past* **snapped** **1** BREAK [I, T] If something long and thin snaps, it breaks making a short, loud sound, and if you snap it, you break it, making a short, loud sound. *The twigs snapped as we walked on them.* **2 snap (sth) open/shut/together, etc** to suddenly move to a particular position, making a short, loud noise, or to make something do this *The suitcase snapped open and everything fell out.* **3** SPEAK ANGRILY [I, T] to say something suddenly in an angry way *I was snapping at the children because I was tired.* **4** LOSE CONTROL [I] to suddenly be unable to control a strong feeling, especially anger *She asked me to do the work again and I just snapped.* **5** PHOTOGRAPH [T] *informal* to take a photograph of someone or something *Photographers snapped the Princess everywhere she went.* **6** ANIMAL [I] If an animal snaps, it tries to bite someone. *The dog was barking and **snapping** at my ankles.* ⊃See also: snap your fingers (finger¹).

snap out of sth *informal* to force yourself to stop feeling sad, angry, upset etc *He's in a bad mood now but he'll soon snap out of it.*

snap sth up *informal* to buy or get something quickly because it is cheap or exactly what you want *The dress was perfect, so I snapped it up.*

snap sb up *informal* to immediately accept someone's offer to join your company or team because you want them very much *She was snapped up by a large law firm.*

snap² /snæp/ *noun* **1** SOUND [no plural] a sudden, short, loud sound like something breaking or closing *I heard a snap as I sat on the pencil.* **2** PHOTOGRAPH [C] *UK informal* (*UK/US* **snapshot**) a photograph *holiday snaps* **3** FASTENING [C] *US* (*UK* **popper**) a metal or plastic object made of two parts which fit together with a short, loud sound, used to fasten clothing **4** GAME [U] a card game in which you say "snap" when you see two cards that are the same **5 be a snap** *US informal* to be very easy *The French test was a snap.*

snap³ /snæp/ *adjective* **snap decision/judgment** A snap decision or judgment is made very quickly and without careful thought.

snappy /'snæpi/ *adjective* **1** written or spoken in a short and interesting way *a snappy title* **2** Snappy clothes are fashionable. *a snappy new suit* **3** **make it snappy** *informal* used to tell someone to hurry

snapshot /'snæpʃɒt/ *noun* [C] a photograph that you take quickly without thinking

snare¹ /sneər/ *noun* [C] a piece of equipment used to catch animals

snare² /sneər/ *verb* [T] **1** to catch an animal using a snare **2** to trick someone so that they cannot escape from a situation *She's trying to snare a rich husband.*

snarl /snɑːl/ *verb* **1** [I, I] to speak angrily *"Go away!" he snarled.* ○ *She snarled at me.* **2** [I] If an animal snarls, it shows its teeth and makes an angry sound. • **snarl** *noun* [C]

snatch¹ /snætʃ/ *verb* [T] **1** to take something or someone quickly and suddenly *Bill snatched the telephone from my hand.* ○ *The child was snatched from his bed.* **2** to do or get something quickly because you only have a short amount of time *I managed to snatch some lunch.*

snatch² /snætʃ/ *noun* [C] a short part of a conversation, song, etc that you hear *I keep hearing* **snatches of** *that song on the radio.*

sneak¹ /sniːk/ *verb past* sneaked *also US* snuck **1 sneak into/out/around, etc** to go somewhere quietly because you do not want anyone to hear you *I sneaked into his bedroom while he was asleep.* **2 sneak sth into/out of/through, etc** to take something somewhere without anyone seeing you *We tried to sneak the dog into the hotel.* **3 sneak a look/glance** at sb/sth to look at someone or something quickly and secretly *I sneaked a look at the answers.*

   sneak up to move close to someone without them seeing or hearing you *Don't* **sneak up on** *me like that - you scared me!*

sneak² /sniːk/ *noun* [C] *informal UK* someone who you do not like because they tell people when someone else has done something bad

sneaker /'sniːkər/ *US* (*UK* trainer) *noun* [C] a soft sports shoe ⟹See colour picture **Clothes** on page Centre 9.

sneaking /'sniːkɪŋ/ *adjective* **1 have a sneaking feeling/suspicion** to think that something is true but not be sure [+ (that)] *I have a sneaking feeling that the English test is going to be very difficult.* **2 have a sneaking admiration/fondness for sb** *UK* to like someone secretly, especially when you do not want to

sneaky /'sniːki/ *adjective* doing things in a secret and unfair way

sneer /snɪər/ *verb* [I] to talk about, or look at someone or something in a way that shows you do not approve of them *Carlos sneered at my attempts to put the tent up.* • **sneer** *noun* [C]

sneeze /sniːz/ *verb* [I] When you sneeze, air suddenly comes out through your nose and mouth. *He had a cold and was sneezing a lot.* • **sneeze** *noun* [C]

snicker /'snɪkər/ *US* (*UK* snigger) *verb* [I] to laugh quietly in a rude way • **snicker** *noun* [C]

snide /snaɪd/ *adjective* A snide remark criticizes someone in an unpleasant way.

sniff /snɪf/ *verb* **1** [I] to breathe air in through your nose in a way that makes a noise *Sam had a cold and she kept sniffing.* **2** [I, T] to breathe air in through your nose in order to smell something *She sniffed the flowers.* • **sniff** *noun* [C]

snigger /'snɪgər/ *UK* (*US* snicker) *verb* [I] to laugh quietly in a rude way *The boys were* **sniggering at** *the teacher.* • **snigger** *noun* [C]

snip¹ /snɪp/ *verb* [I, T] snipping, *past* snipped to cut something using scissors (= tool with two flat blades) with quick, small cuts *She snipped the article out of the magazine.*

snip² /snɪp/ *noun* **1** [C] a small, quick cut with scissors (= tool with two flat blades) **2 be a snip** *UK informal* to be very cheap

snipe /snaɪp/ *verb* [I] **1** to criticize someone in an unpleasant way *I hate the way politicians* **snipe at** *each other.* **2** to shoot people from a place that they cannot see *Rebels were indiscriminately sniping at civilians.* • **sniping** *noun* [U]

sniper /'snaɪpər/ *noun* [C] **1** someone who shoots at people from a place they cannot see **2** on a website, someone who makes an offer for an item just before the end of an auction (= a sale in which things are sold to the person who offers the most money)

snippet /'snɪpɪt/ *noun* [C] a small piece of information, news, conversation, etc *I kept hearing* **snippets of** *conversation.*

snob /snɒb/ *noun* [C] someone who thinks they are better than other people because they are in a higher social position • **snobbery** /'snɒbəri/ *noun* [U] behaviour and opinions that are typical of a snob

snobbish /'snɒbɪʃ/ (*also* snobby) *adjective* like a snob *a snobbish attitude*

snog /snɒg/ *verb* [I, T] snogging, *past* snogged *UK informal* If two people snog, they kiss each other for a long time. • **snog** *noun* [C] *UK informal*

snooker /'snuːkər/ *noun* [U] a game in which two people use long sticks to hit coloured balls into holes at the edge of a table

snoop /snuːp/ *verb* [I] to look around a place secretly in order to find out information about someone *I found her* **snooping around** *in my bedroom.* • **snoop** *noun* [no plural]

snooty /'snuːti/ *adjective* Someone who is snooty behaves in an unfriendly way because they think they are better than other people.

snooze /snuːz/ *verb* [I] *informal* to sleep for a short time, especially during the day *Grandpa was snoozing in his chair.* • **snooze** *noun* [C] *informal Why don't you* **have a snooze**?

snore /snɔːr/ *verb* [I] to breathe in a very noisy way while you are sleeping *I couldn't sleep because my brother was snoring.* • **snore** *noun* [C]

snorkel¹ /'snɔːkəl/ *noun* [C] a tube that you use to help you breathe if you are swimming with your face under water

snorkel² /'snɔːkəl/ *verb* [I] *UK* snorkelling, *past* snorkelled, *US* snorkeling, *past* snorkeled to swim using a snorkel

snort /snɔːt/ *verb* [I, T] to breathe out noisily through your nose, especially to show that you are annoyed or think something is funny *"Stupid man!" he snorted.* ○ *Rosie started snorting with laughter.* ● **snort** *noun* [C]

snot /snɒt/ *noun* [U] *informal* the thick liquid that is produced in your nose

snout /snaʊt/ *noun* [C] the long nose of some animals, such as pigs

WORD PARTNERS FOR *snow (noun)*

snow **falls/melts** ● a snow **flurry/shower** ● **deep/heavy** snow ● [walk/tramp, etc] **through** the snow

∘ₐ**snow¹** /snəʊ/ *noun* [U] soft white pieces of frozen water that fall from the sky when the weather is cold *children playing in the snow*

∘ₐ**snow²** /snəʊ/ *verb* **1 it snows** If it snows, snow falls from the sky. *It snowed all day yesterday.* **2 be snowed in** to be unable to leave a place because there is too much snow *We were snowed in for two days.* **3 be snowed under** to have too much work *I'm snowed under with homework.*

snowball¹ /ˈsnəʊbɔːl/ *noun* [C] a ball made from snow that children throw at each other

snowball² /ˈsnəʊbɔːl/ *verb* [I] If a problem, idea, or situation snowballs, it quickly grows bigger or more important. *The whole business idea snowballed from one phone call.*

snowboard /ˈsnəʊbɔːd/ *noun* [C] a large board that you stand on to move over snow ⊃See colour picture **Sports 1** on page Centre 14.

snowboarding /ˈsnəʊbɔːdɪŋ/ *noun* [U] a sport in which you stand on a large board and move over snow ● **snowboarder** *noun* [C] ⊃See colour picture **Sports 1** on page Centre 14.

snowdrift /ˈsnəʊdrɪft/ *noun* [C] a deep pile of snow that the wind has blown

snowdrop /ˈsnəʊdrɒp/ *noun* [C] a small, white flower that you can see at the end of winter

snowfall /ˈsnəʊfɔːl/ *noun* [C, U] the snow that falls at one time, or the amount of snow that falls *a heavy snowfall* (= a lot of snow)

snowflake /ˈsnəʊfleɪk/ *noun* [C] a small piece of snow that falls from the sky

snowman /ˈsnəʊmæn/ *noun* [C] *plural* **snowmen** something that looks like a person and is made from snow *The kids made a snowman in the garden.*

snowplough UK (US **snowplow**) /ˈsnəʊplaʊ/ *noun* [C] a vehicle used for moving snow off roads and railways

snowstorm /ˈsnəʊstɔːm/ *noun* [C] a storm when a lot of snow falls

snowy /ˈsnəʊi/ *adjective* snowing or covered with snow *a cold, snowy day*

Snr UK (UK/US **Sr**) *written abbreviation for* senior (= the older of two men in a family with the same name) *Thomas Smith, Snr*

snub /snʌb/ *verb* [T] **snubbing**, *past* **snubbed** to be rude to someone, especially by not speaking to them ● **snub** *noun* [C]

snuck /snʌk/ *US past of* sneak

snuff¹ /snʌf/ *noun* [U] tobacco powder that people breathe in through their noses, especially in the past

snuff² /snʌf/ *verb*

snuff sth out 1 *informal* to suddenly end something *England's chances were snuffed out by three brilliant goals from the Italians.* **2** to stop a candle flame from burning by covering it or pressing it with your fingers

snug /snʌg/ *adjective* **1** warm and comfortable *a snug little house* **2** Snug clothes fit tightly. *a pair of snug brown shoes* ● **snugly** *adverb*

snuggle /ˈsnʌgl/ *verb* **snuggle up/down/into, etc** to move into a warm, comfortable position *I snuggled up to him on the sofa.*

∘ₐ**so¹** /səʊ/ *adverb* **1** VERY used before an adjective or adverb to emphasize what you are saying, especially when there is a particular result *I was so tired when I got home.* ○ ○ [+ (that)] *I was so upset that I couldn't speak.* **2** ANSWER used to give a short answer to a question to avoid repeating a phrase *"Is Ben coming to the party?" "I hope so."* **3 so did we/so have I/so is mine, etc** used to say that someone else also does something or that the same thing is true about someone or something else *"We saw the new Star Trek movie last night." "Oh, so did we."* **4** GET ATTENTION used to get someone's attention when you are going to ask them a question or when you are going to start talking *So, when are you two going to get married?* **5** SHOW SOMETHING used with a movement of your hand to show someone how to do something or show them the size of something *The box was so big.* ○ *For this exercise, you have to put your hands like so.* **6 so it is/so they are, etc** used to agree with something that you had not noticed before *"The cat's hiding under the chair." "So it is."* **7 or so** used after a number or amount to show that it is not exact *"How many people were at the party?" "Fifty or so, I guess."* **8 I told you so** used to say that you were right and that someone should have believed you **9 So (what)?** used to say that you do not think something is important, especially in a rude way *"She might tell Emily." "So what?"* **10 and so on/forth** used after a list of things to show that you could have added other similar things *She plays a lot of tennis and squash and so on.* **11 so as (not) to do sth** used to give the reason for doing something *He went in very quietly so as not to wake the baby.* **12 only so much/many** used to say that there are limits to something *There's only so much help you can give someone.* **13 so much for...** *informal* used to say that something has not been useful or successful *"The computer's crashed again." "So much for modern technology."*

∘ₐ**so²** /səʊ/ *conjunction* **1** used to say that something is the reason why something else happens *I was tired so I went to bed.* ○ *Greg had some money so he bought a bike.* **2 so (that)** in order to make something happen or be possible *He put his glasses on so that he could see the television better.* **3** used at the beginning of a sentence to connect it with something that was said or happened previously *So we're not going away this weekend after all?*

so³ /səʊ/ *adjective* **be so** to be correct or true *"Apparently, she's moving to Canada." " "Is that so?"*

soak /səʊk/ *verb* [I, T] **1** If you soak something,

or let it soak, you put it in a liquid for a period of time. *He left the pan in the sink to soak.* ○ *Soak the bread in the milk.* **2** If liquid soaks somewhere or soaks something, it makes something very wet. *The rain soaked my clothes.* ○ *The ink soaked through the paper onto the table.*

soak sth up If a dry substance soaks up a liquid, the liquid goes into the substance. *Fry the potatoes until they soak up all the oil.*

soaked /səʊkt/ *adjective* completely wet *My shirt was soaked.*

soaking /'səʊkɪŋ/ *adjective* completely wet *You're soaking - why didn't you take an umbrella?* ○ *The dog was soaking wet.*

so-and-so /'səʊəndsəʊ/ *noun* [C] **1** used to talk about someone or something without saying a particular name *It was the usual village news - so-and-so got married to so-and-so, and so-and-so's having a baby.* **2** *informal* someone who you do not like *He's a lazy so-and-so.*

o⁻**soap** /səʊp/ *noun* **1** [U] a substance that you use for washing *a bar of soap* ○ *soap powder* ⊃See colour picture **The Bathroom** on page Centre 3. **2** [C] (*also* '**soap ,opera**) a television programme about the lives of a group of people that is broadcast several times every week

'**soap ,opera** (*informal* **soap**) *noun* [C] a series of television or radio programmes that continues over a long period and is about the lives of a group of characters

soapy /'səʊpi/ *adjective* containing soap, or covered with soap *soapy hands*

soar /sɔːr/ *verb* [I] **1** to increase to a high level very quickly *House prices have soared.* **2** to move quickly and smoothly in the sky, or to move quickly up into the sky *The birds were soaring high above.* ● **soaring** *adjective*

sob /sɒb/ *verb* [I] **sobbing** *past* **sobbed** to cry in a noisy way ● **sob** *noun* [C]

sober¹ /'səʊbər/ *adjective* **1** NOT DRUNK Someone who is sober is not drunk. **2** SERIOUS Someone who is sober is serious and thinks a lot. *He was in a sober mood.* **3** NOT BRIGHT UK Clothes or colours that are sober are plain and not bright. *a sober, grey dress* ● **soberly** *adverb*

sober² /'səʊbər/ *verb*
sober (sb) up to become less drunk or to make someone become less drunk *You'd better sober up before you go home.*

sobering /'səʊbərɪŋ/ *adjective* making you feel serious *a sobering thought*

so-called /ˌsəʊ'kɔːld/ *adjective* [always before noun] used to show that you think a word that is used to describe someone or something is wrong *My so-called friend has stolen my girlfriend.*

soccer /'sɒkər/ (*also UK* **football**) *noun* [U] a game in which two teams of eleven people kick a ball and try to score goals ⊃See colour picture **Sports 2** on page Centre 15.

sociable /'səʊʃəbl/ *adjective* Someone who is sociable enjoys being with people and meeting new people.

o⁻**social** /'səʊʃəl/ *adjective* **1** relating to society and the way people live *social problems* ○ *social and political changes* **2** relating to the things you do with other people for enjoyment when you are not working *I have a very good social life.* ● **socially** *adverb* ⊃Compare **anti-social**.

socialism /'səʊʃəlɪzəm/ *noun* [U] a political system in which the government owns important businesses and industries, and which allows the people to share the money and opportunities equally

socialist /'səʊʃəlɪst/ *noun* [C] someone who supports socialism ● **socialist** *adjective* *socialist principles*

socialize (*also UK* **-ise**) /'səʊʃəlaɪz/ *verb* [I] to spend time enjoying yourself with other people *The cafe is a place where students can socialize with teachers.*

,**social 'science** *noun* [C, U] the study of society and the way people live

,**social se'curity** *noun* [U] money that the government gives to people who are old, ill, or not working

'**social ,worker** *noun* [C] someone whose job is to help people who have problems because they are poor, old, have difficulties with their family, etc ● **social work** *noun* [U]

> **WORD PARTNERS FOR *society***
>
> a **democratic** / **free** / **modern** / **multicultural** / **secular** society

o⁻**society** /sə'saɪəti/ *noun* **1** [C, U] a large group of people who live in the same country or area and have the same laws, traditions, etc *The US is a multicultural society.* **2** [C] an organization for people who have the same interest or aim ⊃See also: **building society**.

socio- /səʊʃiəʊ-/ *prefix* relating to society *socio-economic*

sociology /ˌsəʊʃi'ɒlədʒi/ *noun* [U] the study of society and the relationship between people in society ● **sociologist** /ˌsəʊʃi'ɒlədʒɪst/ *noun* [C] someone who studies sociology

sociopath /'səʊʃiəʊpæθ/ *noun* [C] someone who is completely unable to behave in a way that is acceptable to society

sock /sɒk/ *noun* [C] *plural* **socks** *also US* **sox** something that you wear on your foot inside your shoe [usually plural] *a pair of black socks* ⊃See colour picture **Clothes** on page Centre 9.

socket /'sɒkɪt/ *noun* [C] **1** the place on a wall where you connect electrical equipment to the electricity supply **2** a hollow place where one thing fits inside another thing *an eye socket*

soda /'səʊdə/ *noun* **1** [U] (*also* '**soda ,water**) water with bubbles in it that you mix with other drinks **2** [C, U] *US* (*also* '**soda ,pop**) a sweet drink with bubbles *a can of soda*

sodden /'sɒdən/ *adjective* extremely wet *Your shoes are sodden!*

sodium /'səʊdiəm/ *noun* [U] a chemical element that is found in salt and food *a low-sodium diet*

sofa

o⁻**sofa** /'səʊfə/ *noun* [C] a large, comfortable

seat for more than one person ➲See colour picture **The Living Room** on page Centre 4.

⊶**soft** /sɒft/ *adjective* **1** [NOT HARD] not hard, and easy to press *a soft cushion* ○ *Cook the onion until it's soft.* ○ *I like chocolates with soft centres.* **2** [SMOOTH] smooth and pleasant to touch *soft hair/skin* **3** [SOUND] A soft sound is very quiet. *He spoke in a soft voice.* **4** [COLOUR/LIGHT] A soft colour or light is not bright. *soft lilac paint* **5** [PERSON] too kind and not angry enough when someone does something wrong *The kids are naughty because she's too* ***soft on*** *them.* **6** [DRUGS] Soft drugs are illegal drugs that some people think are not dangerous. ● **softness** *noun* **[U]** ➲See also: have a soft **spot¹** for sb.

softball /ˈsɒftbɔːl/ *noun* **[U]** a game that is like baseball but played with a larger and softer ball

ˌ**soft ˈdrink** *UK* (*US* **ˈsoft ˌdrink**) *noun* **[C]** a cold, sweet drink that does not have alcohol in it *Are there any soft drinks for the children?*

soften /ˈsɒfᵊn/ *verb* **[I, T] 1** to become softer or to make something become softer *Heat the butter until it softens.* ○ *These dried apples will soften (up) if you soak them in water.* **2** to become more gentle or to make someone or something become more gentle *Her voice softened.*

softly /ˈsɒftli/ *adverb* in a quiet or gentle way *"Are you OK?" she said softly.*

ˌ**soft ˈoption** *noun* **[C]** *UK* a choice that is easier than other choices *The cookery course is not a soft option.*

soft-spoken /ˌsɒftˈspəʊkᵊn/ *adjective* having a quiet, gentle voice *a small, soft-spoken man*

WORD PARTNERS FOR ***software***

develop/download/install software ● **a piece of** software ● a software **package**

software /ˈsɒftweəʳ/ *noun* **[U]** programs that you use to make a computer do different things *educational software* ○ *We need to install some new* ***software***.

soggy /ˈsɒgi/ *adjective* very wet and soft *soggy ground*

soil¹ /sɔɪl/ *noun* **[C, U]** the top layer of earth that plants grow in *clay/sandy soil*

soil² /sɔɪl/ *verb* **[T]** *formal* to make something dirty ● **soiled** *adjective* dirty *soiled clothes*

solace /ˈsɒləs/ *noun* **[U, no plural]** *formal* comfort when you are feeling sad *Music was a great solace to me.*

solar /ˈsəʊləʳ/ *adjective* relating to, or involving the sun *solar panels*

ˌ**solar ˈenergy** *noun* **[U]** energy that uses the power of the sun

ˌ**solar ˈpanel** *noun* **[C]** a piece of equipment that changes light from the sun into electricity *They have solar panels on the side of the building.*

the ˈsolar ˌsystem *noun* the sun and planets that move around it

sold /səʊld/ *past of* sell

⊶**soldier** /ˈsəʊldʒəʳ/ *noun* **[C]** a member of an army

sole¹ /səʊl/ *adjective* **[always before noun] 1** only *the sole survivor* **2** not shared with anyone else *She has* ***sole responsibility*** *for the project.*

sole² /səʊl/ *noun* **1** [FOOT] **[C]** the bottom part of your foot that you walk on **2** [SHOE] **[C]** the part of a shoe that is under your foot **3** [FISH] **[C, U]** a small, flat fish that you can eat

solely /ˈsəʊlli/ *adverb* only, and not involving anyone or anything else *I bought it solely for that purpose.*

solemn /ˈsɒləm/ *adjective* **1** serious or sad *solemn music* **2** A solemn promise, warning, etc is serious and sincere. ● **solemnly** *adverb* ● **solemnity** /səˈlemnəti/ *noun* **[U]**

solicit /səˈlɪsɪt/ *verb* **1 [T]** *formal* to ask someone for money, information, or help *to solicit donations for a charity* **2 [I]** to offer sex for money, usually in a public place

soliciting /səˈlɪsɪtɪŋ/ *noun* **[U]** when someone offers to have sex for money

solicitor /səˈlɪsɪtəʳ/ *noun* **[C]** in Britain, a lawyer who gives legal advice and help, and who works in the lower courts of law ➲See Common learner error at **lawyer**.

⊶**solid¹** /ˈsɒlɪd/ *adjective* **1** [HARD/FIRM] hard and firm without holes or spaces, and not liquid or gas *solid ground* ○ *solid food* **2** [STRONG] strong and not easily broken or damaged *solid furniture* **3 solid gold/silver/wood, etc** gold/silver/wood, etc with nothing added *a solid silver bracelet* **4** [TIME] continuing for a period of time without stopping *The noise continued for two solid hours/two hours solid.* **5** [INFORMATION] **[always before noun]** Solid information, proof, etc is based on facts and you are certain that it is correct. *This provides* ***solid evidence*** *that he committed the crime.* **6** [PERSON] honest and able to be trusted ● **solidity** /səˈlɪdəti/ *noun* **[U]** ● **solidly** *adverb*

solid² /ˈsɒlɪd/ *noun* **[C] 1** a substance or object that is not a liquid or a gas **2** a shape that has length, width, and height, and is not flat

solidarity /ˌsɒlɪˈdærəti/ *noun* **[U]** agreement and support between people in a group who have similar aims or beliefs

solidify /səˈlɪdɪfaɪ/ *verb* **[I]** If a liquid solidifies, it becomes solid.

solids /ˈsɒlɪdz/ *noun* **[plural]** food that is not liquid *Three weeks after the operation he still couldn't eat solids.*

solipsism /ˈsɒlɪpsɪzᵊm/ *noun* **[U]** the belief that in life you can only really know yourself and your own experiences

solitaire /ˌsɒlɪˈteəʳ/ [US] /ˈsɒləteər/ *US* (*UK* **patience**) *noun* **[U]** a card game for one person

solitary /ˈsɒlɪtᵊri/ *adjective* **1** A solitary person or thing is the only person or thing in a place. *a solitary figure/walker* **2** A solitary activity is done alone. *solitary walks*

ˌ**solitary conˈfinement** *noun* **[U]** when a prisoner is kept in a room alone as a punishment *He was kept in solitary confinement for ten days.*

solitude /ˈsɒlɪtjuːd/ *noun* **[U]** being alone *He*

went upstairs to read the letter in solitude.

solo¹ /ˈsəʊləʊ/ *adjective, adverb* done alone by one person only *a solo performance* ○ *to perform solo*

solo² /ˈsəʊləʊ/ *noun* [C] a piece of music for one person or one instrument

soloist /ˈsəʊləʊɪst/ *noun* [C] a musician who performs a solo

solstice /ˈsɒlstɪs/ *noun* [C] the longest day or the longest night of the year *the summer/winter solstice*

soluble /ˈsɒljəbl/ *adjective* If a substance is soluble, it will dissolve in water. *soluble vitamins* ○ *These tablets are soluble in water.*

WORD PARTNERS FOR *solution*

find/offer/provide/seek a solution • a **diplomatic / good / long-term / peaceful / simple/workable** solution • a solution **to** sth

---

o⌐**solution** /səˈluːʃ⁰n/ *noun* [C] **1** the answer to a problem *There's no easy solution to this problem.* **2** a liquid which a substance has been dissolved into

---

COMMON LEARNER ERROR

solution to a problem

Be careful to choose the correct preposition after **solution.**

This could be one solution to the problem.

~~This could be one solution of the problem.~~

---

o⌐**solve** /sɒlv/ *verb* [T] to find the answer to something *to solve a problem* ○ *to solve a mystery/puzzle* ○ *Police are still no nearer to solving the crime.*

solvent¹ /ˈsɒlvənt/ *noun* [C] a liquid which is used to dissolve other substances

solvent² /ˈsɒlvənt/ *adjective* having enough money to pay your debts

sombre UK (US **somber**) /ˈsɒmbəʳ/ *adjective* **1** sad and serious *a sombre expression/mood* **2** dark and without bright colours *a sombre colour*

o⌐**some¹** *strong form* /sʌm/ *weak form* /s⁰m/ *pronoun, quantifier* **1** UNKNOWN AMOUNT used to refer to an amount of something without saying exactly how much or how many *You'll need a pair of scissors and some glue.* ○ *I can't eat all this chocolate, would you like some?* ○ *Could I have some more* (= an extra amount of) *paper, please?* **2** NOT ALL used to refer to part of a larger amount or number of something and not all of it *In some cases it's possible to fix the problem right away.* ○ *Some of the children were frightened.* **3** UNKNOWN NAME used to refer to someone or something when you do not know the name of it or exact details about it *Some girl phoned for you, but she didn't leave a message.* **4** some **time/distance, etc** a large amount of time, distance, etc *I'm afraid it'll be some time before it's ready.*

COMMON LEARNER ERROR

some or any?

Be careful not to confuse these two words. **Any** is used in questions and negative sentences.

Have you got any friends in America?

I haven't got any money.

Some is used in positive sentences.

I've got some friends in America.

Sometimes **some** is used in questions, especially when the speaker thinks that the answer will be 'yes'.

Have you got some money I could borrow?

The same rules are true for 'something/anything' and 'someone/anyone'.

I didn't see anyone I knew.

I saw someone I knew at the party.

---

some² *strong form* /sʌm/ *weak form* /s⁰m/ *adverb* used before a number to show that it is not the exact amount *He died some ten years ago.*

o⌐**somebody** /ˈsʌmbədi/ *pronoun another word for* someone

someday /ˈsʌmdeɪ/ *adverb* US at an unknown time in the future *We plan to get married someday.*

o⌐**somehow** /ˈsʌmhaʊ/ *adverb* in a way which you do not know or do not understand *Don't worry, we'll fix it somehow.* ○ **Somehow or other** (= I do not know how) *they managed to get in.*

o⌐**someone** /ˈsʌmwʌn/ (*also* **somebody**) *pronoun* **1** used to refer to a person when you do not know who they are or when it is not important who they are *There's someone at the door.* ○ *Will someone please answer the phone?* **2** someone **else** a different person *Sorry, I thought you were talking to someone else.*

someplace /ˈsʌmpleɪs/ *adverb* US used to refer to a place when you do not know where it is or when it is not important where it is *They live someplace in the South.* ○ *If they don't like it here, they can go someplace else* (= to a different place).

somersault /ˈsʌməsɔːlt/ *noun* [C] when you roll your body forwards or backwards so that your feet go over your head and come back down to the ground again • somersault *verb* [I]

o⌐**something** /ˈsʌmθɪŋ/ *pronoun* **1** used to refer to a thing when you do not know what it is or when it is not important what it is *As soon as I walked in, I noticed that something was missing.* ○ *We know about the problem and we're trying to do something about it.* ○ *There's something else* (= another thing) *I wanted to tell you.* **2** or **something (like that)** used to show that what you have just said is only an example or you are not certain about it *Why don't you go to a movie or something?* **3** something **like** similar to or approximately *He paid something like $2000 for his car.* **4** be something *informal* to be a thing which is important, special, or useful *The President visiting our hotel - that would really be something.* **5** something **of a** sth used to describe a person or thing in a way which is partly true but not completely or exactly *It came as something of a* *surprise.* **6 be/have something to do with sth/sb** to be related to something or a cause of something but not in a way which you know about or understand exactly *It might have something to do with the way it's made.*

sometime /'sʌmtaɪm/ *adverb* used to refer to a time when you do not know exactly what it is or when it is not important what it is *sometime before June* ○ *You must come over and visit sometime.*

○━**sometimes** /'sʌmtaɪmz/ *adverb* on some occasions but not always or often *He does cook sometimes, but not very often.* ○ *Sometimes I feel like no one understands me.*

somewhat /'sʌmwɒt/ *adverb formal* slightly *We were somewhat disappointed with the food.*

○━**somewhere** /'sʌmweər/ *adverb* **1** used to refer to a place when you do not know exactly where it is or when it is not important exactly where it is *They had difficulties finding somewhere to live.* ○ *He comes from somewhere near London.* ○ *Can you think of somewhere else* (= a different place) *we could go?* **2 somewhere around/between, etc** approximately *He earns somewhere around £50,000 a year.* **3 get somewhere** to achieve something or to make progress *Right, that's the printer working. Now we're getting somewhere!*

○━**son** /sʌn/ *noun* [C] your male child

sonar /'səʊnɑːr/ *noun* [U] a system, used especially on ships, which uses sound waves to find the position of things in the water

sonata /sə'nɑːtə/ *noun* [C] a piece of music written to be played on a piano or on another instrument and the piano together

⟳ WORD PARTNERS FOR *song*

sing/write a song ● a song about sth ● a love song

○━**song** /sɒŋ/ *noun* [C] words that go with a short piece of music *a folk/love song* ○ *to sing a song*

songwriter /'sɒŋ,raɪtər/ *noun* [C] someone who writes songs

sonic /'sɒnɪk/ *adjective* relating to sound

son-in-law /'sʌnɪnlɔː/ *noun* [C] *plural* sons-in-law your daughter's husband

sonnet /'sɒnɪt/ *noun* [C] a poem with 14 lines, written in a particular pattern *Shakespeare's sonnets*

○━**soon** /suːn/ *adverb* **1** after a short period of time *I've got to leave quite soon.* ○ *It's too soon to make a decision.* ○ *He joined the company soon after leaving college.* **2 as soon as** at the same time or a very short time after *As soon as I saw her, I knew there was something wrong.* ○ *They want it as soon as possible.* **3 sooner or later** used to say that you do not know exactly when something will happen, but you are sure that it will happen *Sooner or later they'll realize that it's not going to work.* **4 would sooner** would prefer *I'd sooner spend a bit more money than take chances with safety.* **5 no sooner ... than** used to show that something happens immediately after something else *No sooner had we got home than the phone rang.*

soot /sʊt/ *noun* [U] a black powder produced

when coal, wood, etc is burnt

soothe /suːð/ *verb* [T] **1** to make something feel less painful *I had a long, hot bath to soothe my aching muscles.* **2** to make someone feel calm or less worried *to soothe a crying baby* ● **soothing** *adjective* making you feel calm or in less pain *soothing music* ○ *a soothing effect/voice*

sophisticated /sə'fɪstɪkeɪtɪd/ *adjective* **1** well-educated and having experience of the world or knowledge of culture **2** A sophisticated machine or system is very advanced and works in a clever way. *a sophisticated computer system* ● **sophistication** /sə,fɪstɪ'keɪʃən/ *noun* [U]

sophomore /'sɒfəmɔːr/ *noun* [C] *US* a student studying in the second year of a course at a US university or high school (= school for students aged 15 to 18)

soprano /sə'prɑːnəʊ/ *noun* [C] a female singer who sings the highest notes

sordid /'sɔːdɪd/ *adjective* unpleasant, dirty, or immoral *a sordid affair*

sore[1] /sɔːr/ *adjective* **1** painful, especially when touched *a sore throat/knee* ○ *Her eyes were red and sore.* **2 sore point/spot/subject** a subject which causes disagreement or makes people angry when it is discussed *Money is a bit of a sore point with him at the moment.* ⊃See also: stick/stand out like a sore thumb[1].

sore[2] /sɔːr/ *noun* [C] an area of skin which is red and painful because of an infection

sorely /'sɔːli/ *adverb formal* very much *to be sorely disappointed/tempted* ○ *He will be sorely missed by everyone.*

sorrow /'sɒrəʊ/ *noun* [C, U] *formal* when someone feels very sad ● **sorrowful** *adjective formal*

○━**sorry** /'sɒri/ *adjective* **1 (I'm) sorry** something that you say to be polite when you have done something wrong, or when you cannot agree with someone or accept something *Sorry I'm late.* ○ *Oh, I'm sorry. I didn't see you there.* ○ *Tom, I'm so sorry about last night - it was all my fault.* ○ *I'm sorry, but I just don't think it's a good idea.* **2** used to show sympathy or sadness for a person or situation *I feel sorry for the children - it must be very hard for them.* ○ *I was sorry to hear about your brother's accident.* ○ [+ (that)] *I'm sorry that things didn't work out for you.* **3 Sorry?** *mainly UK* used as a polite way to say that you did not hear what someone has just said *Sorry? What was that?* **4** used to say that you wish something in the past had not happened or had been different [+ (that)] *I'm sorry that I ever met him.* **5 a sorry sight/state/tale** a bad condition or situation *Her car was in a sorry state after the accident.*

○━**sort**[1] /sɔːt/ *noun* **1** [C] a type of something *We both like the same sort of music.* ○ *What sort of shoes does she wear?* ○ *I'm going to have a salad of some sort.* **2 all sorts of sth** many different types of something **3 sort of** *informal* used to describe a situation approximately *It's a sort of pale orange colour.* **4 (and) that sort of thing** *informal* used to show that what you have just said is only an example from a larger group of things *They sell souvenirs, postcards, that sort of thing.* **5 of sorts** *informal* used to describe something which is not a typical example *He managed to make a curtain of sorts out of an old sheet.*

o--**sort**[2] /sɔːt/ *verb* **1** [T] to arrange things into different groups or types or into an order *They sort the paper into white and coloured for recycling.* ○ *The names are sorted alphabetically.* **2 be sorted/get sth sorted** *UK informal* If something is sorted or you get something sorted, you successfully deal with it and find a solution or agreement. *Did you manage to get everything sorted?*

sort sth out to successfully deal with something, such as a problem or difficult situation *Have you sorted out your schedule yet?*

sort through sth to look at a number of things to organize them or to find something *I had the sad task of sorting through her papers after she died.*

so-so /ˈsəʊsəʊ/ *adjective informal* not very good, but not bad *"Are you feeling better today?" "So-so."*

soufflé /ˈsuːfleɪ/ ⓤ /suːˈfleɪ/ *noun* [C, U] a light food made by baking the white part of eggs *chocolate/cheese soufflé*

sought /sɔːt/ *past of* seek

sought-after /ˈsɔːtˌɑːftəʳ/ *adjective* wanted by lots of people, but difficult to get *a house in a sought-after location*

soul /səʊl/ *noun* **1** [SPIRIT] [C] the part of a person which is not their body, which some people believe continues to exist after they die **2** [MUSIC] [U] (*also* **soul music**) popular music which expresses deep feelings, originally performed by Black Americans **3** [PERSON] [C] *informal* a person *I didn't see a soul when I went out.* ⊃See also: **heart** and soul.

soulful /ˈsəʊlfəl/ *adjective* expressing deep feelings, often sadness *soulful eyes*

soulless /ˈsəʊlləs/ *adjective* without any interesting or attractive characteristics *a soulless housing estate*

soul-searching /ˈsəʊlˌsɜːtʃɪŋ/ *noun* [U] when you think very carefully about something to decide if it is the right thing to do *After much soul-searching, he decided to leave his job.*

o--**sound**[1] /saʊnd/ *noun* **1** [C, U] something that you hear or that can be heard *I could hear the sounds of the city through the open window.* ○ *She stood completely still, not making a sound.* ○ *Can you turn the sound up (= make a radio, television, etc louder)?* **2 the sound of sth** *informal* how something seems to be, from what you have been told or heard *I like the sound of the beef in red wine sauce.* ○ *He's really enjoying college, by the sound of it.*

o--**sound**[2] /saʊnd/ *verb* **1 sound good/interesting/strange, etc** to seem good/interesting/strange, etc, from what you have heard or read *Your job sounds really interesting.* **2 sound like/as if/as though** to seem like something, from what you have heard or read *That sounds like a*

really good idea. **3 sound angry/happy/rude, etc** to seem angry/happy/rude, etc when you speak *You don't sound too sure about it.* **4** [I, T] to make a noise *It looks and sounds like a real bird.* ○ *If the alarm sounds, you must leave the building immediately.*

sound[3] /saʊnd/ *adjective* good or safe and able to be trusted *sound advice/judgment* ○ *The building is quite old, but still structurally sound.* ⊃Opposite **unsound**.

sound[4] /saʊnd/ *adverb* **sound asleep** in a deep sleep

soundbite /ˈsaʊndbaɪt/ *noun* [C] a short statement which is easy to remember, usually used by a politician to get attention on television, in newspapers, etc

ˈsound ˌcard *noun* [C] a small piece of electronic equipment inside a computer that makes it able to record and play sound

soundly /ˈsaʊndli/ *adverb* **1 sleep soundly** to sleep well **2 soundly beaten/defeated** beaten/defeated easily and by a large amount

soundtrack /ˈsaʊndtræk/ *noun* [C] the music used in a film

o--**soup** /suːp/ *noun* [U] a hot, liquid food, made from vegetables, meat, or fish *chicken/tomato soup* ⊃See colour picture **Food** on page Centre 11.

sour[1] /saʊəʳ/ *adjective* **1** having a sharp, sometimes unpleasant, taste or smell, like a lemon, and not sweet *These plums are a bit sour.* **2** very unfriendly or unpleasant *Their relationship suddenly turned sour.*

sour[2] /saʊəʳ/ *verb* [T] to make something unpleasant or unfriendly *This affair has soured relations between the two countries.*

source /sɔːs/ *noun* [C] **1** where something comes from *a source of income/information* ○ *Oranges are a good source of vitamin C.* **2** someone who gives information to the police, newspapers, etc

o--**south, South** /saʊθ/ *noun* [U] **1** the direction that is on your right when you face towards the rising sun **2 the south** the part of an area that is further towards the south than the rest • **south** *adjective the south side of the house* • **south** *adverb* towards the south *Birds fly south in winter.*

southbound /ˈsaʊθbaʊnd/ *adjective* going or leading towards the south

southeast, Southeast /ˌsaʊθˈiːst/ *noun* [U] **1** the direction between south and east **2 the southeast** the southeast part of a country • **southeast, Southeast** *adjective, adverb*

southeastern, Southeastern /ˌsaʊθˈiːstən/ *adjective* in or from the southeast

southerly /ˈsʌðəli/ *adjective* **1** towards or in the south *We continued in a southerly direction.* **2** A southerly wind comes from the south.

o--**southern, Southern** /ˈsʌðən/ *adjective* in or from the south part of an area *the southern half of the country*

S

southerner, Southerner /'sʌðˀnəʳ/ *noun* [C] someone from the south part of a country

southernmost /'sʌðənməʊst/ *adjective* The southernmost part of an area is the part furthest to the south.

south-facing /'saʊθ,feɪsɪŋ/ *adjective* [always before noun] positioned towards the south *a south-facing garden/window*

the ,South 'Pole *noun* a point on the Earth's surface which is furthest south

southward, southwards /'saʊθwəd/, /'saʊθwədz/ *adverb* towards the south ● **southward** *adjective a southward direction*

southwest, Southwest /,saʊθ'west/ *noun* [U] **1** the direction between south and west **2 the southwest** the southwest part of the country ● **southwest, Southwest** *adjective, adverb*

southwestern, Southwestern /,saʊθ-'westən/ *adjective* in or from the southwest

souvenir /,suːvˀn'ɪəʳ/ *noun* [C] something which you buy or keep to remember a special event or holiday *a souvenir shop* ○ *I kept the ticket as a souvenir of my trip.*

sovereign¹ /'sɒvˀrɪn/ *adjective* A sovereign country or state is completely independent. ● **sovereignty** /'sɒvˀrˀnti/ *noun* [U] the power of a country to control its own government

sovereign, Sovereign² /'sɒvˀrɪn/ *noun* [C] *formal* a king or queen

sow¹ /səʊ/ *verb* [T] *past tense* **sowed**, *past participle* **sown** or **sowed** to put seeds into the ground *to sow seeds/crops*

sow² /saʊ/ *noun* [C] a female pig

soya bean /'sɔɪə,biːn/ *UK* (*US* **soybean** /'sɔɪbiːn/) *noun* [C] a bean used to produce oil, and which is used in many foods

soy sauce /,sɔɪ'sɔːs/ *noun* [U] a dark brown sauce made from soya beans, used in Chinese and Japanese cooking

spa /spɑː/ *noun* [C] a place where people go to improve their health by exercising or by having baths in special water *a health spa* ○ *a spa town*

◦▪**space¹** /speɪs/ *noun* **1** [C, U] an empty area which is available to be used *a parking space* ○ *We need more open spaces for children to play in.* ○ *There wasn't enough space for everyone.* ○ [+ to do sth] *We don't have the space to store it all.* **2** [U] the area outside the Earth *They plan to send another satellite into space.* ○ *space travel* **3 in the space of six weeks/three hours, etc** during a period of six weeks/three hours, etc *It all happened in the space of 10 minutes.* ⊃See also: **breathing space, outer space.**

space² /speɪs/ *verb* [T] to arrange things so that there is some distance or time between them [often passive] *They will have to be spaced at least two metres apart.*

spacecraft /'speɪskrɑːft/ *noun* [C] *plural* **spacecraft** a vehicle which can travel outside the Earth and into space

spaceship /'speɪsʃɪp/ *noun* [C] a vehicle which can travel outside the Earth and into space, especially one which is carrying people

'space ,shuttle *noun* [C] a vehicle in which people travel into space (= the area outside the Earth) and back again

spacious /'speɪʃəs/ *adjective* large and with a lot of space *a spacious apartment/office*

spade /speɪd/ *noun* [C] **spade** **1** a tool with a long handle and a flat, metal part at one end used for digging **2 spades** playing cards with black leaf shapes on them *the ace of spades*

spaghetti /spə'geti/ *noun* [U] long, thin pieces of pasta

spam /spæm/ *noun* [U] emails that you do not want, usually advertisements ● **spam** *verb* [T] ● **spammer** *noun* [C] a person who sends spam

span /spæn/ *noun* [C] **1** the period of time that something exists or happens *a short attention span* ○ *an average life span of seventy years* **2** the length of something from one end to the other *a wing span of five metres* ● **span** *verb* [T] **spanning**, *past* **spanned** to exist or continue for a particular distance or length of time *Her acting career spanned almost forty years.*

spaniel /'spænjəl/ *noun* [C] a dog with long hair and long ears

spank /spæŋk/ *verb* [T] to hit someone, usually a child, on their bottom

spanner /'spænəʳ/ *UK* (*US* **wrench**) *noun* [C] a tool with a round end that is used to turn nuts and bolts (= metal objects used to fasten things together) ⊃See picture at **tool.**

spar /spɑːʳ/ *verb* [I] **sparring**, *past* **sparred** to fight or argue with someone in a friendly way

◦▪**spare¹** /speəʳ/ *adjective* **1** If something is spare, it is available to use, because it is extra and not being used. *a spare bedroom* ○ *spare cash* ○ *spare parts* **2 spare time** time when you are not working *I enjoy gardening in my spare time.*

spare² /speəʳ/ *noun* [C] an extra thing which is not being used and which can be used instead of a part which is broken, lost, etc

spare³ /speəʳ/ *verb* **1** [T] to give time or money to someone *I have to go soon, but I can spare a few minutes.* ○ [+ two objects] *Can you spare me some change?* **2** [+ two objects] to prevent someone from having to experience something unpleasant [often passive] *I was spared the embarrassment of having to sing in front of everybody.* **3 to spare** If you have time, money, etc to spare, you have more than you need. *I arrived at the station with more than an hour to spare.* **4 spare no effort/expense, etc** to use a lot of effort/expense, etc to do something [+ to do sth] *We will spare no effort to find out who did this.* **5 spare sb's life** to not kill someone ⊃See also: spare a **thought¹** for sb.

sparingly /'speərɪŋli/ *adverb* carefully using only a very small amount of something *to eat/*

drink sparingly ● **sparing** *adjective*

spark¹ /spɑːk/ *noun* [C] **1** [FIRE] a very small, bright piece of burning material *The fire was caused by a spark from a cigarette.* **2** [ELECTRICITY] a small flash of light caused by electricity **3** [START] a small idea or event which causes something bigger to start *a spark of hope/inspiration*

spark² /spɑːk/ (*also* **spark off**) *verb* [T] to cause an argument, fight, etc to start happening *to spark a debate/protest* ○ *to spark criticism/fears*

sparkle¹ /'spɑːkl/ *verb* [I] **1** to shine brightly because of reflected light *water sparkling in the sun* ○ *Her eyes sparkled with excitement.* **2** to do something in a special or exciting way *The concert gave her an opportunity to sparkle.*

sparkle² /'spɑːkl/ *noun* **1** [C, U] the light from something reflecting on a shiny surface **2** [U] the quality of being special or exciting *The performance lacked a bit of sparkle.*

sparkling /'spɑːklɪŋ/ *adjective* **1** shining brightly because of reflected light **2** special or exciting *a sparkling performance* ○ *sparkling conversation* **3** **sparkling water/wine** water/wine with bubbles in it

'**spark ˌplug** *noun* [C] a part in an engine that makes the fuel burn

sparrow /'spærəʊ/ *noun* [C] a small, brown bird which is common in towns and cities

sparse /spɑːs/ *adjective* **1** existing only in small amounts over a large area *sparse population/vegetation* **2** A room that is sparse contains little furniture and does not seem very comfortable. ● **sparsely** *adverb* **sparsely populated/furnished**

spartan /'spɑːtən/ *adjective* very simple and not comfortable or luxurious *The rooms were clean but spartan.*

spasm /'spæzəm/ *noun* [C, U] when a muscle suddenly gets tight in a way that you cannot control *a back/muscle spasm* ○ *to go into spasm*

spasmodic /spæz'mɒdɪk/ *adjective* happening suddenly for short periods of time and not in a regular way

spat /spæt/ *past of* spit

spate /speɪt/ *noun* **a spate of accidents/crimes/thefts, etc** a large number of bad things which happen at about the same time

spatial /'speɪʃ°l/ *adjective* relating to the position, area, and size of things ● **spatially** *adverb*

spatter /'spætə⁰/ *verb* [T] to cover someone or something with small drops of liquid without intending to [often passive] *His shirt was spattered with blood.*

spatula /'spætjələ/ *noun* [C] a tool with a wide flat blade, used in cooking for mixing, spreading, or lifting food ⊃See colour picture **The Kitchen** on page Centre 2.

spawn /spɔːn/ *verb* [T] to cause a lot of other things to be produced or to exist *Her death spawned several films and books.*

◦**speak** /spiːk/ *verb past tense* **spoke**, *past participle* **spoken** /I/ **1** [I] to say something using your voice *to speak loudly/quietly* ○ *There was complete silence - nobody spoke.* **2** **speak to sb** *mainly UK*

(*mainly US* **speak with sb**) to talk to someone *Could I speak to Mr Davis, please?* ○ *Have you spoken with your new neighbors yet?* **3** **speak about/of sth** to talk about something *He refused to speak about the matter in public.* **4** **speak English/French/German, etc** to be able to communicate in English/French/German, etc *Do you speak English?* **5** [I] to make a speech to a large group of people *She was invited to speak at a conference in Madrid.* **6** **speak for/on behalf of sb** to express the feelings, opinions, etc of another person or of a group of people *I've been chosen to speak on behalf of the whole class.* **7** **generally/personally, etc speaking** used to explain that you are talking about something in a general/personal, etc way *Personally speaking, I don't like cats.* **8** **so to speak** used to explain that the words you are using do not have their usual meaning ⊃See also: speak/talk of the **devil**, speak your **mind¹**.

COMMON LEARNER ERROR

speak or **talk**?

Remember that you **speak** a language. You do not 'talk' it.

She speaks French.

~~She talks French.~~

speak out to give your opinion about something in public, especially on a subject which you have strong feelings about *He decided to speak out against the bombing.*

speak up 1 to say something in a louder voice so that people can hear you *Could you speak up a bit? I can't hear you.* **2** to give your opinion about something, especially about a problem or to support someone else *It's getting bad - it's time someone spoke up about it.*

speaker /'spiːkə⁰/ *noun* [C] **1** the part of a radio, CD player, etc which the sound comes out of ⊃See colour picture **The Living Room** on page Centre 4. **2** **an English/French/German, etc speaker** someone who can speak English/French, etc **3** someone who makes a speech to a group of people *a guest speaker*

spear /spɪə⁰/ *noun* [C] a long weapon with a sharp point at one end used for hunting

spearhead /'spɪəhed/ *verb* [T] to lead an attack or series of actions *to spearhead a campaign*

spearmint /'spɪəmɪnt/ *noun* [U] a type of mint (= a herb used as a flavour for sweets) *spearmint chewing gum*

OTHER WAYS OF SAYING **special**

If someone or something is special because they are better than usual, you can describe them as **exceptional** or **outstanding**: *Their standard of acting was very high but there was one exceptional/outstanding performance.*

The adjective **extraordinary** is sometimes used to describe someone or something that is special in a surprising way: *Her capacity to remember things is extraordinary.* ● *She has an extraordinary talent.*

The adjectives **deluxe** and **superior** are sometimes used to describe things which you can buy which are special because they are particularly good quality: *The shop assistant tried to sell us the deluxe/superior model.*

The adjectives **rare** and **unique** are sometimes used instead of special when it means 'unusual': *This is a rare/unique opportunity to see inside the building.*

If something is special because it is of extremely good quality, you can describe it as **out of this world**: *Their chocolate cake is just out of this world.*

⚬**special**[1] /'speʃ°l/ *adjective* **1** better or more important than usual *things a special friend* ○ *I'm cooking something special for her birthday.* **2 special attention/care/treatment** treatment that is better than usual **3 special offer** *UK* a price which is lower than usual *I bought them because they were on special offer.* **4** different from normal things, or used for a particular purpose *You need to use a special kind of paint.*

special[2] /'speʃ°l/ *noun* [C] **1** a television programme made for a particular reason or occasion and not part of a series *The Christmas special had 24.3 million viewers.* **2** a dish in a restaurant which is not usually available *Today's specials are written on the board.*

,**special ef'fects** *noun* an unusual type of action in a film, or an entertainment on stage, created by using special equipment *The new Harry Potter film includes some very frightening special effects.*

WORD PARTNERS FOR *specialist*

a **leading** specialist • a specialist **in** sth • specialist **knowledge**

---

specialist /'speʃ°lɪst/ *noun* [C] someone who has a lot of experience, knowledge, or skill in a particular subject *a cancer/software specialist* ○ *He's a specialist in childhood illnesses.*

speciality /,speʃi'æləti/ *UK* (*US* **specialty** /'speʃ°lti/) *noun* [C] a product, skill, etc that a person or place is especially known for *We tasted a local speciality made from goat's cheese.*

specialize (*also UK* **-ise**) /'speʃ°laɪz/ *verb* [I] to spend most of your time studying one particular subject or doing one type of business *She works for a company specializing in business law.* • **specialization** /,speʃ°laɪ'zeɪʃ°n/ *noun* [U]

specialized (*also UK* **-ised**) /'speʃ°laɪzd/ *adjective* relating to a particular subject or activity and not general *specialized equipment/language*

⚬**specially** /'speʃ°li/ *adverb* for a particular purpose *They searched the building with specially trained dogs.* ○ *I made this specially for you.*

COMMON LEARNER ERROR

specially or **especially**?

Sometimes these two words both mean 'for a particular purpose'.

I cooked this meal specially/especially for you.

Specially is often used before an adjective made from a

past participle, e.g. specially prepared, specially trained. *He uses a specially adapted wheelchair.*

Especially is used to give emphasis to a person or thing. This word is not usually used at the beginning of a sentence.

I like all kinds of films, especially horror films.

,**special 'needs** *adjective* describes something that is intended for people who have an illness or condition that makes it difficult for them to do the things that other people do *a special needs school*

species /'spiːʃiːz/ *noun* [C] *plural* **species** a group of plants or animals which share similar characteristics *a rare species of bird* ⊃See Common learner error at **race**.

specific /spə'sɪfɪk/ *adjective* **1** used to refer to a particular thing and not something general *a specific purpose/reason* ○ *Could we arrange a specific time to meet?* **2** exact or containing details *Could you be more specific about the problem?*

specifically /spə'sɪfɪk°li/ *adverb* **1** for a particular reason, purpose, etc *They're designed specifically for children.* ○ [+ **to do** sth] *She bought it specifically to wear at the wedding.* **2** exactly or in detail *I specifically told them that she doesn't eat meat.*

specification /,spesɪfɪ'keɪʃ°n/ *noun* [C] *formal* a detailed description of how something should be done, made, etc *They are made exactly to the customer's specifications.*

specifics /spə'sɪfɪks/ *noun* [plural] exact details about something *I can't comment on the specifics of the case.*

specify /'spesɪfaɪ/ *verb* [T] to say or describe something in a detailed way [+ **question word**] *They didn't specify what colour they wanted.*

specimen /'spesəmɪn/ *noun* [C] **1** an animal, plant, etc used as an example of its type, especially for scientific study *This is one of the museum's finest specimens.* **2** a small amount of a substance, such as blood, that is used for a test

speck /spek/ *noun* [C] a very small spot or a very small amount of something *a speck of dirt/dust* ○ *I watched the car until it was just a tiny speck in the distance.*

speckled /'spekld/ *adjective* covered in a pattern of very small spots *a speckled egg*

specs /speks/ *noun* [plural] *informal short for* spectacles

spectacle /'spektəkl/ *noun* [C] **1** an event that is exciting or unusual to watch **2 make a spectacle of yourself** to do something that makes you look stupid and that makes other people look at you *He got drunk and made a real spectacle of himself.*

spectacles /'spektəklz/ *noun* [plural] *old-fashioned* glasses *a pair of spectacles*

spectacular /spek'tækjələr/ *adjective* extremely good, exciting, or surprising *a spectacular success* ○ *a spectacular view* ○ *a spectacular scenery* • **spectacularly** *adverb* *a spectacularly beautiful country*

spectator /spek'teɪtər/ *noun* [C] someone who

watches an event, sport, etc *They won 4-0 in front of over 40,000 cheering spectators.* • **spectate** /spek'teɪt/ *verb* [I] to watch an event, sport, etc

spectre *UK* (*US* **specter**) /'spektər/ *noun* **1 the spectre of sth** the idea of something unpleasant that might happen in the future *This attack raises the spectre of a return to racial violence.* **2** [C] *literary* a ghost (= dead person's spirit)

spectrum /'spektrəm/ *noun* [C] *plural* **spectra 1** all the different ideas, opinions, possibilities, etc that exist *He has support from across the whole political spectrum.* **2** the set of colours into which light can be separated

speculate /'spekjəleɪt/ *verb* [I, T] to guess possible answers to a question when you do not have enough information to be certain *The police refused to speculate about the cause of the accident.* ○ [+ that] *The newspapers have speculated that they will get married next year.*

speculation /ˌspekjə'leɪʃən/ *noun* [U] when people guess about something without having enough information to be certain [+ that] *She has dismissed the claims as pure speculation.*

speculative /'spekjələtɪv/ *adjective* based on a guess and not on information *The article was dismissed as highly/purely speculative.* • **speculatively** *adverb*

sped /sped/ *past of* speed

WORD PARTNERS FOR speech

careful/continuous/human/normal speech • slur your speech

---

o➤**speech** /spiːtʃ/ *noun* **1** [U] someone's ability to talk, or an example of someone talking *His speech was very slow and difficult to understand.* ○ *These changes can be seen in both speech and writing.* **2** [C] a formal talk that someone gives to a group of people *I had to make a speech at my brother's wedding.* **3 free speech/freedom of speech** the right to say or write what you want ➾See also: **figure of speech**, **reported speech**.

COMMON LEARNER ERROR

make/give a speech

Be careful to choose the correct verb.

I have to make a speech.

~~I have to do a speech.~~

He gave a speech at the conference.

~~He said a speech at the conference.~~

---

speechless /'spiːtʃləs/ *adjective* unable to speak because you are so angry, shocked, surprised, etc *I couldn't believe what he was telling me - I was speechless.*

WORD PARTNERS FOR speed

gain/gather/pick up speed • lower / reduce sb's/sth's speed • reach a speed of [100kph/70mph, etc] • at a speed of [100kph/70mph, etc]

---

o➤**speed¹** /spiːd/ *noun* **1** [C, U] how fast something moves or happens *high/low speed* ○ *He was*

travelling *at a speed of 90 mph.* **2** [U] very fast movement *He put on a sudden burst of speed.* **3 up to speed** having all the most recent information about a subject or activity *The course should bring you up to speed with the latest techniques.*

speed² /spiːd/ *verb past* **sped** *or* **speeded 1** **speed along/down/past, etc** to move somewhere or happen very fast *The three men jumped into a car and sped away.* **2 be speeding** to be driving faster than you are allowed to

speed (sth) up to move or happen faster, or to make something move or happen faster *Can you try to speed up a bit please?*

speedboat /'spiːdbəʊt/ *noun* [C] a small, fast boat with an engine

'speed ˌdating *noun* [U] a way to meet people for possible romantic relationships, in which you talk with lots of people for a short amount of time to see if you like them

speeding /'spiːdɪŋ/ *noun* [U] driving faster than you are allowed to *They were stopped by the police for speeding.*

'speed ˌlimit *noun* [C] the fastest speed that a vehicle is allowed to travel on a particular road *to break the speed limit*

speedometer /spiː'dɒmɪtər/ *noun* [C] a piece of equipment in a vehicle that shows how fast it is moving ➾See colour picture **Car** on page Centre 7.

speedy /'spiːdi/ *adjective* done quickly *a speedy recovery* • **speedily** *adverb*

o➤**spell¹** /spel/ *verb past* **spelled** *also UK* **spelt 1** [T] to write down or tell someone the letters which are used to make a word *How do you spell that?* ○ *Her name's spelt S-I-A-N.* **2** [I] If you can spell, you know how to write the words of a language correctly. *My grammar's all right, but I can't spell.* **3 spell disaster/trouble, etc** If something spells disaster, trouble, etc, you think it will cause something bad to happen in the future. *The new regulations could spell disaster for small businesses.*

spell sth out to explain something in a very clear way with details *They sent me a letter, spelling out the details of the agreement.*

spell² /spel/ *noun* [C] **1** a period of time *a short spell in Australia* ○ *a spell of dry weather* **2** a magic instruction *The witch cast a spell over him and he turned into a frog.*

spell-check /'speltʃek/ (*also* **spellcheck**) *noun* [C] a computer program which makes certain that the words in a document have the correct letters in the correct order

o➤**spelling** /'spelɪŋ/ *noun* **1** [C] how a particular word is spelt *There are two possible spellings of this word.* ○ **spelling mistakes 2** [U] someone's ability to spell words *My spelling is terrible.*

spelt /spelt/ *UK past of* spell

o➤**spend** /spend/ *verb* [T] *past* **spent 1** to use money to buy or pay for something *The company has spent £1.9 million on improving its computer network.* ○ *She spends too much money on clothes.* ○ *How much did you spend?* **2** to use time doing something or being somewhere *He spent 18 months working on the project.* ○ *He's*

S

*planning to **spend** some **time** at home with his family. ○ How long did you spend in Edinburgh?*

The most common alternative is the verb **pay**: *When you booked the tickets, how much did you **pay**? • I **paid** an extra £30 to get a double room.*

The verb **invest** is used when someone spends money on something because they hope to get a profit: *She's **invested** all her savings in the business.*

If someone spends a lot of money on something, the phrasal verb **pay out** is sometimes used: *I've just **paid out** $700 to get the car fixed.*

If someone spends a lot of money on something that they want but do not need, you can use the phrasal verb **splash out**: *We've just **splashed out** £12, 000 on a new kitchen.*

The phrasal verb **dip into** is sometimes used when someone spends part of a supply of money that they have been keeping: *We had to **dip into** our savings to pay for the repairs.*

If someone spends money on something when they do not want to, the phrasal verbs **fork out** and **shell out** are often used: *We had to **shell out** two thousand pounds to get the roof fixed. • I'm not going to **fork out** another five hundred quid for their tickets.*

spending /ˈspendɪŋ/ *noun* [U] the money which is used for a particular purpose, especially by a government or organization *government spending on health* ○ ***spending** cuts*

spent¹ /spent/ *adjective* already used, so not useful or effective any more *spent bullets*

spent² /spent/ *past of* spend

sperm /spɜːm/ *noun* [C] *plural* **sperm** a small cell produced by a male animal which joins an egg from a female animal to create a baby

spew /spjuː/ (*also* **spew out**) *verb* [I, T] If something spews liquid or gas, or liquid or gas spews from something, it flows out in large amounts. *The factory spews out clouds of black smoke.*

SPF /ˌespiːˈef/ *noun* [C] *abbreviation for* sun protection factor: the letters and numbers on a bottle of sunscreen (= a substance which protects your skin in the sun) which shows how effective the sunscreen is

in a sphere • a sphere of **activity/influence/life**

sphere /sfɪər/ *noun* [C] **1** a subject or area of knowledge, work, etc *the political sphere* **2** a round object shaped like a ball

spice¹ /spaɪs/ *noun* **1** [C, U] a substance made from a plant, which is used to give a special taste to food ***herbs and spices*** **2** [U] something

that makes something else more exciting *A scandal or two **adds** a little **spice to** office life.*

spice² /spaɪs/ *verb* [T] to add spice to something [often passive] *The apples were **spiced with** nutmeg and cinnamon.*

spice sth up to make something more interesting or exciting *You can always spice up a talk with a few pictures.*

spicy /ˈspaɪsi/ *adjective* containing strong flavours from spice ***spicy** food* ○ *a spicy sauce*

spider /ˈspaɪdər/ *noun* [C] a small creature with eight long legs which catches insects in a web (= structure like a net)

spidery /ˈspaɪdəri/ *adjective* thin and often untidy, looking like a spider ***spidery** handwriting*

spike /spaɪk/ *noun* [C] a long, thin piece of metal, wood, etc with a sharp point at one end • **spiky** *adjective* covered with spikes or having that appearance ***spiky** hair*

o▪**spill** /spɪl/ *verb* [T] *past* **spilled** or *also UK* **spilt** to pour liquid somewhere without intending to *Someone at the party spilled red wine on the carpet.* • **spill** *noun* [C] *an oil spill*

spill out 1 to flow or fall out of a container *The contents of the truck spilled out across the road.* **2** If people spill out of a place, large numbers of them move out of it. *The crowd spilled out onto the street.*

spill over If a bad situation spills over, it begins to have an unpleasant effect on another situation or group of people. *There are fears that the war could spill over into neighbouring countries.*

o▪**spin¹** /spɪn/ *verb* [I, T] **spinning**, *past* **spun 1** If something spins or you spin something, it turns around and around quickly. *The car spun **across** the road.* **2** to make thread by twisting together cotton, wool, etc

spin (sb) around/round If you spin around, or someone spins you around, your body turns quickly to face the opposite direction.

spin sth out to make something such as a story or an activity last as long as possible

spin² /spɪn/ *noun* **1** TURN [C, U] the movement of something turning round very quickly *The skater did a series of amazing spins and jumps.* **2** IDEA [no plural] when an idea is expressed in a clever way that makes it seem better than it really is, especially in politics *This report **puts** a different **spin on** the issue.* **3** CAR [no plural] *informal* a short journey by car

spinach /ˈspɪnɪtʃ/ *noun* [U] a vegetable with large, dark green leaves and a strong taste

spinal /ˈspaɪnəl/ *adjective* relating to the spine *a spinal injury*

'spin ˌdoctor *noun* [C] *informal* someone whose job is to make ideas, events, etc seem better than they really are, especially in politics

spine /spaɪn/ *noun* [C] **1** the long structure of bones down the centre of your back, which supports your body **2** the narrow part of a book cover where the pages are joined together and which you can see when it is on a shelf

spineless /'spaɪnləs/ *adjective* A spineless person has a weak personality and is frightened easily.

spin-off /'spɪnɒf/ *noun* [C] a product that develops from another more important product

spinster /'spɪnstər/ *noun* [C] *old-fashioned* a woman who has never married

spiral /'spaɪərəl/ *noun* [C] **1** a shape made by a curve turning around and around a central point *a spiral staircase* **2 a downward spiral** a situation which is getting worse very quickly, and which is difficult to control

spiral

spire /spaɪər/ *noun* [C] a tall, pointed tower on the top of a building such as a church

spirit¹ /'spɪrɪt/ *noun* **1** FEELING [no plural] the way people think and feel about something *a spirit of optimism* ○ *Everyone soon got into the spirit of* (= started to enjoy) *the carnival - singing, dancing, and having fun.* **2 community/team, etc spirit** when you feel enthusiasm about being part of a group **3 in good/high/low spirits** feeling good/excited/unhappy **4** NOT BODY [C] the part of a person which is not their body, which some people believe continues to exist after they die **5** NOT ALIVE [C] something which people believe exists but does not have a physical body, such as a ghost *evil spirits* **6 the spirit of the law/an agreement, etc** the intended meaning of the law/an agreement, etc and not just the written details **7** DRINK [C] a strong alcoholic drink, such as whisky or vodka [usually plural] *I don't often drink spirits.*

spirit² /'spɪrɪt/ *verb* **be spirited away/out/to, etc** to be moved somewhere secretly *He was spirited away to a secret hide-out in Mexico.*

spirited /'spɪrɪtɪd/ *adjective* enthusiastic and determined, often in a difficult situation *a spirited performance*

spiritual /'spɪrɪtʃuəl/ *adjective* relating to deep feelings and beliefs, especially religious beliefs *a spiritual leader*

spiritualism /'spɪrɪtʃuəlɪzᵊm/ *noun* [U] the belief that living people can communicate with people who are dead ● **spiritualist** *noun* [C] someone who is involved with spiritualism

spit¹ /spɪt/ *verb* [I, T] spitting, *past* spat *also US* spit **1** to force out the liquid in your mouth *I don't like to see people spitting in public.* ○ *He took a mouthful of coffee and then spat it out.* **2 Spit it out!** *informal* used to tell someone to say more quickly what it is they want to say *Come on, spit it out!*

spit² /spɪt/ *noun* **1** [U] *informal* the liquid that is made in your mouth **2** [C] a long, thin stick used for cooking meat over a fire

spite /spaɪt/ *noun* **1 in spite of sth** although something exists or happens *He still smokes, in spite of all the health warnings.* **2** [U] a feeling of anger towards someone which makes you want to hurt or upset them *He hid my new jacket out of spite.*

spiteful /'spaɪtfᵊl/ *adjective* intentionally hurting or upsetting someone *That was a very spiteful thing to do.* ● **spitefully** *adverb*

splash¹ /splæʃ/ *verb* [I, T] **1** If a liquid splashes or you splash a liquid, drops of it hit or fall on something. *The paint splashed onto his new shirt.* ○ *She splashed some cold water on her face.* **2 splash about/around/through, etc** to move in water so that drops of it go in all directions *The children splashed about in the puddles.* **3 be splashed across/all over sth** to be the main story in a newspaper, usually on the front page, which many people will see *His picture was splashed across the front pages of all the newspapers the next morning.*

splash out (sth) *UK* to spend a lot of money on something which you want but do not need *He splashed out on the best champagne for the party.*

splash² /splæʃ/ *noun* [C] **1** a drop of liquid which has fallen on something, or the mark made by it *There were several small splashes of paint on the carpet.* **2** the sound of something falling into or moving in water *They sat listening to the splash of raindrops on the lake.* **3 a splash of colour** a small area of colour which makes something look brighter *The flowers added a splash of colour to the room.* **4 make a splash** *informal* to get a lot of public attention *The film made quite a splash in the US.*

splatter /'splætər/ *verb* [I, T] If a liquid splatters or you splatter it, it falls onto a surface, often in many small drops. [often passive] *His clothes were splattered with blood.*

splendid /'splendɪd/ *adjective* very good or very beautiful, special, etc *a splendid idea* ○ *a splendid view* ● **splendidly** *adverb*

splendour *UK* (*US* splendor) /'splendər/ *noun* [C, U] when something is extremely beautiful or luxurious *Tourists marvelled at the splendour of the medieval cathedral.*

splinter /'splɪntər/ *noun* [C] **1** a small, sharp piece of wood, glass, etc which has broken from a large piece *I've got a splinter in my finger.* **2 a splinter group** a small group of people that forms after leaving a larger organization, such as a political party ● **splinter** *verb* [I] to break into small, sharp pieces

o͟˖**split¹** /splɪt/ *verb* splitting, *past* split **1** BREAK [I, T] If something splits or if you split it, it tears so that there is a long, thin hole in it. *He split his trousers when he bent over.* ○ *Her shoes were splitting apart at the sides.* **2** DIVIDE [I, T] (*also* split up) to divide into smaller parts or groups, or to divide something into smaller parts or groups *The children split up into three groups.* **3** SHARE [T] to share something by dividing it into smaller parts *The cost of the wedding will be split between the two families.* **4** DISAGREE [I, T] If a group of people splits, or something splits them, they disagree and form smaller groups. [often passive] *The government is split on the issue of hunting.* ⊃See also: split hairs (**hair**).

split up If two people split up, they end their relationship. *She split up with her boyfriend.*

S

split² /splɪt/ *noun* [C] **1** BREAK a long, thin hole in something where it has broken apart *There's a split in my trousers.* **2** DISAGREEMENT when a group of people divides into smaller groups because they disagree about something *This issue is likely to cause a major split in the party.* **3** RELATIONSHIP when a marriage or relationship ends *Very few of their friends were surprised when they announced their split.*

split³ /splɪt/ *adjective* **a split second** a very short period of time *It was all over in a split second.* ○ *a split second decision*

splitting 'headache *noun* [C] a very bad pain in your head *I've got a splitting headache.*

splurge /splɜːdʒ/ *verb* [I, T] to spend a lot of money on something which you want but do not need *We could either save the money or splurge on a new car.* • splurge *noun* [C]

◦⁻**spoil** /spɔɪl/ *verb past* spoiled or spoilt **1** MAKE BAD [T] to stop something from being enjoyable or successful *The picnic was spoiled by the bad weather.* **2** CHILD [T] If you spoil a child, you let them have anything they want or do anything they want, usually making them badly behaved. **3** TREAT WELL [T] to treat someone very well, buying them things or doing things for them *He's always sending flowers - he absolutely spoils me!* **4** FOOD [I] *formal* If food spoils, it starts to decay and you cannot eat it.

spoils /spɔɪlz/ *noun* [plural] *formal* things which are taken by the winners of a war *the spoils of war*

spoilt /spɔɪlt/ *adjective* UK (US **spoiled** /spɔɪld/) badly behaved because you are always given what you want or allowed to do what you want *He was behaving like a spoilt child.*

spoke¹ /spəʊk/ *noun* [C] one of the thin pieces of metal which connects the middle of a wheel to the outside edge, for example, on a bicycle

spoke² /spəʊk/ *past tense of* speak

spoken /'spəʊkən/ *past participle of* speak

spokesman, spokeswoman /'spəʊksmən, 'spəʊks,wʊmən/ *noun* [C] *plural* spokesmen or spokeswomen a man/woman who is chosen to speak officially for a group or organization *A spokesman for the company refused to comment on the reports.*

spokesperson /'spəʊks,pɜːsən/ *noun* [C] *plural* spokespeople someone who is chosen to speak officially for a group or organization

sponge /spʌndʒ/ *noun* [C, U] **1** a soft substance full of small holes, which absorbs liquid very easily and is used for washing things **2** (*also* **sponge ,cake**) a soft, light cake • **spongy** *adjective* soft, like a sponge

sponge

sponsor¹ /'spɒnsər/ *verb* [T] to give money to someone to support an activity, event, or organization, sometimes as a way to advertise your company or product *The event is sponsored by First National Bank.* ○ (UK) *a sponsored walk* (= a walk for charity) • **sponsorship** *noun* [U] when someone gives money to support something

sponsor² /'spɒnsər/ *noun* [C] a person or organization that gives money to support an activity, event, etc

spontaneous /spɒn'teɪniəs/ *adjective* happening naturally and suddenly and without being planned *a spontaneous reaction* ○ *The crowd broke into spontaneous applause.* • **spontaneity** /,spɒntə'neɪɪti/ *noun* [U] when something is spontaneous • **spontaneously** *adverb*

spoof /spuːf/ *noun* [C] a funny television programme, film, article, etc that copies the style of a real programme, film, article, etc *They did a spoof of the Oscars, giving awards for the worst films of the year.*

spooky /'spuːki/ *adjective informal* strange and frightening *There's something spooky about that place.*

◦⁻**spoon** /spuːn/ *noun* [C] an object with a handle and a round, curved part at one end, used for eating and serving food *knives, forks, and spoons* • **spoon** *verb* [T] to move or serve food using a spoon *Spoon the sauce over the fish.*

spoonful /'spuːnfʊl/ *noun* [C] the amount of something which can be held on a spoon *Then add a spoonful of yoghurt.*

sporadic /spə'rædɪk/ *adjective* not happening regularly or happening in different places *sporadic violence* • **sporadically** *adverb*

◦⁻**sport¹** /spɔːt/ *noun* **1** [C] a game or activity which people do to keep healthy or for enjoyment, often competing against each other *winter sports* ○ *team sports* ⊃See colour picture **Sports 1 & 2** on pages Centre 14, 15. **2** [U] *UK* all types of physical activity which people do to keep healthy or for enjoyment ⊃See also: **blood sport**.

sport² /spɔːt/ *verb* [T] *humorous* to wear something, especially something which people notice *He turned up sporting a bright red baseball cap and sunglasses.*

sporting /ˈspɔːtɪŋ/ *adjective* relating to sports *a sporting hero*

ˈsports ˌcar *noun* [C] a car designed to go very fast, often with only two seats and an open roof

ˈsports ˌcentre *UK* (*US* **sports center**) *noun* [C] a building with places where you can play different sports

sportsmanship /ˈspɔːtsmənʃɪp/ *noun* [U] behaviour in sport which is fair and shows respect for other players *We hope to teach children good sportsmanship.*

sportsman, sportswoman /ˈspɔːtsmən, ˈspɔːtsˌwʊmən/ *noun* [C] *plural* **sportsmen** or **sportswomen** a man/woman who is good at sport

sportswear /ˈspɔːtsweə^r/ *noun* [U] clothes, shoes, etc for people to wear when they play sports *a sportswear shop*

sporty /ˈspɔːti/ *adjective* **1** Sporty cars, clothes, etc are attractive, comfortable, and stylish. **2** Sporty people are good at sports.

o→**spot¹** /spɒt/ *noun* [C] **1** ROUND MARK a small, round mark which is a different colour to the surface it is on *a blue shirt with white spots* ○ *I noticed a small spot of oil on my jacket.* **2** SKIN *UK* (*US* **pimple**) an unpleasant, small, red mark on your skin *He suffered badly with spots as a teenager.* **3** PLACE a place *We found a good spot to sit and have our picnic.* **4 a spot of sth** *UK old-fashioned* a small amount of something *a spot of lunch/shopping* **5 on the spot a** TIME immediately *I accepted the job on the spot.* **b** PLACE in the place where something happens *The police were called and they were on the spot within three minutes.* **6 have a soft spot for sb** to like someone a lot *I've always had a soft spot for her.* **7 put sb on the spot** to ask someone a question which is difficult or embarrassing to answer at that time ⊃See also: **beauty spot, blind spot**.

spot² /spɒt/ *verb* [T] **spotting**, *past* **spotted** to see or notice something or someone *They were spotted together in London last week.* ○ *She soon spotted the mistake.*

spotless /ˈspɒtləs/ *adjective* completely clean *By the time I'd finished, the whole room was spotless.* ● **spotlessly** *adverb* **spotlessly clean**

WORD PARTNERS FOR *spotlight*
2 be under/come under the spotlight ● the spotlight **falls on/is on** sb/sth ● **put/turn** the spotlight **on** sb/sth ● **in/out of** the spotlight ● the **media/public** spotlight

spotlight /ˈspɒtlaɪt/ *noun* **1** [C] a strong light which can be pointed in different directions **2 the spotlight** when someone gets public

attention by being on television, in the newspapers, etc *to be in the spotlight* ○ *She's rarely out of the media spotlight these days.* ● **spotlight** *verb* [T] *past* **spotlighted** or **spotlit**

ˌspot ˈon *adjective* [never before noun] *UK* exactly correct *Her imitation of Ann was spot on.*

spotty /ˈspɒti/ *adjective* **1** SKIN *UK* having a lot of unpleasant, small, red marks on your skin *a spotty young man with greasy hair* **2** PATTERN *UK* with a pattern of round marks *a spotty dress* **3** NOT GOOD/REGULAR *US* (*UK* **patchy**) If an action, quality, supply, etc is spotty, it is not all good or regular. *Sales of tickets for the concert have been spotty.*

spouse /spaʊs/ *noun* [C] *formal* your husband or wife

spout¹ /spaʊt/ *noun* [C] an opening of a container, in the shape of a tube which liquid flows out through *the spout of a teapot*

spout² /spaʊt/ *verb* [I, T] **1** If a liquid spouts or if something makes it spout, it flows out of something with force. **2** *informal* to talk a lot about something, often when other people are not interested *He was spouting his usual rubbish about politics.*

sprain /spreɪn/ *verb* [T] to injure part of your body by twisting it, but not so badly that it breaks *I slipped on the ice and sprained my ankle.* ● **sprain** *noun* [C]

sprang /spræŋ/ *past tense of* spring

sprawl /sprɔːl/ *verb* [I] **1** (*also* **sprawl out**) to sit or lie in a relaxed, untidy position with your arms and legs stretched out *He sprawled out on the sofa.* **2** to cover a large area, often in a way which is not tidy or not planned *sprawling suburbs* ● **sprawl** *noun* [U] *urban sprawl*

spray¹ /spreɪ/ *noun* **1** [C, U] liquid in a container which forces it out in small drops *hair spray* ○ *spray paint* **2** [U] many small drops of liquid blown through the air *sea spray*

spray² /spreɪ/ *verb* **1** [T] to force liquid out of a container in many small drops *The fields are sprayed with pesticides.* ○ *She sprayed a little perfume on her wrists.* **2** [I, T] If small pieces of something spray somewhere or if something sprays them, they are sent through the air in all directions. *A brick shattered the window, spraying the room with pieces of broken glass.*

o→**spread¹** /spred/ *verb past* **spread 1 spread sth across/over/through, etc** to arrange something so that it covers a large area *He spread the cards out on the table.* **2** TIME [T] (*also* **spread out**) to arrange for something to happen over a period of time and not at once *The payments will be spread over two years.* **3** INCREASE [I] to increase, or move to cover a larger area or affect a larger number of people *The virus is spread by rats.* **4** SURFACE [T] to move a soft substance across a surface so that it covers it *What I really like is hot buttered toast spread with strawberry jam.* ○ *He spread a thin layer of glue on the paper.* **5** INFORMATION [I, T] If information spreads or if someone spreads it, it is communicated from one person to another. *News of his death spread quickly.*

spread out If people spread out, they move from being close together in a group to being in different places across a larger area. *They spread out to search the whole area.*

spread² /spred/ *noun* **1** [MOVEMENT] [U] when something moves to cover a larger area or affect a larger number of people *They are looking for ways to slow down the spread of the disease.* **2** [FOOD] [C, U] a soft food which you put on bread *cheese spread* **3** [NEWSPAPER] [C] an article which covers two or more pages of a newspaper or magazine *a double-page spread*

spreadsheet /'spredʃiːt/ *noun* [C] a computer program which helps you to do business calculations and planning

spree /spriː/ *noun* **a shopping/spending, etc spree** a short period when someone does a lot of shopping/spending, etc

sprig /sprɪg/ *noun* [C] a small piece of a plant with leaves *a sprig of parsley*

sprightly /'spraɪtli/ *adjective* A sprightly person is able to move about easily and quickly although they are old.

○-**spring¹** /sprɪŋ/ *noun* **1** [SEASON] [C, U] the season of the year between winter and summer, when the weather becomes warmer and plants start to grow again *I'm starting a new course in the spring.* ○ *spring flowers/weather* **2** [METAL] [C] a piece of metal which curves round and round and which returns to its original shape after being pushed or pulled *bed springs* **3** [WATER] [C] a place where water comes out of the ground *hot springs* **4** [MOVEMENT] [C, U] when someone or something suddenly moves or jumps somewhere

spring² /sprɪŋ/ *verb past tense* **sprang** *also US* **sprung**, *past participle* **sprung 1 spring back/forward/out, etc** to jump or move somewhere suddenly *The cat sprang onto the sofa.* ○ *I tried to shut the door, but it kept springing open.* **2 spring to life** to suddenly become very active *After about 8 o'clock, the city springs to life.* **3 spring to mind** If a word or idea springs to mind, you suddenly think of it. *He asked if I knew any good places to go, but nothing sprang to mind.*

spring from sth to come from or be the result of something *Many of his problems spring from his strict religious upbringing.*

spring sth on sb to suddenly tell or ask someone something when they do not expect it *I'm sorry to spring this on you, but could you give a talk at tomorrow's meeting?*

spring up to appear suddenly *A lot of new hotels have sprung up along the coast recently.*

,**spring 'clean** *UK* (*UK/US* ,spring 'cleaning) *noun* [no plural] when you clean a place more carefully and using more effort than usual *I gave the kitchen a spring clean at the weekend.* • **spring clean** *verb* [I, T] *UK*

,**spring 'onion** *UK* (*US* scallion) *noun* [C, U] a small onion with a white part at the bottom and long, green leaves, which is eaten in salads

sprinkle /'sprɪŋkl/ **sprinkle**
verb [T] to gently drop small pieces of something over a surface *Sprinkle the cake with sugar before serving.* • **sprinkling** *noun* [no plural] a small amount of a powder or liquid that has been sprinkled on a surface *a sprinkling of pepper/snow*

sprinkler /'sprɪŋkləʳ/ *noun* [C] a piece of garden equipment which automatically spreads drops of water over grass and plants

sprint /sprɪnt/ *verb* [I] to run very fast for a short distance *She sprinted along the road to the bus stop.* • **sprinter** *noun* [C] someone who runs short distances in competitions • **sprint** *noun* [C] *a 100m sprint*

sprout¹ /spraʊt/ *verb* [I, T] If a plant sprouts, or if it sprouts something, it begins to produce leaves, flowers, etc. *The seeds I planted are just beginning to sprout.*

sprout up If a large number of things sprout up, they suddenly appear or begin to exist. *New buildings are sprouting up all over the city.*

sprout² /spraʊt/ *noun* [C] **1** (*also* brussel sprout) a small, green vegetable which is round and made of leaves **2** a part of a plant that is just beginning to grow

spruce /spruːs/ *verb*
spruce sb/sth up to make someone or something cleaner or more tidy [often reflexive] *I'd like to spruce myself up a bit before we go out.*

sprung /sprʌŋ/ **1** *past participle of* spring **2** *US past tense of* spring

spun /spʌn/ *past tense of* spin

spur¹ /spɜːʳ/ (*also* spur on) *verb* [T] spurring, *past* spurred to encourage someone to do something or something to happen *Spurred on by his fans, he won the next three games easily.*

spur² /spɜːʳ/ *noun* [C] **1** a sharp, pointed piece of metal fixed to the boot of someone riding a horse **2 on the spur of the moment** If you do something on the spur of the moment, you do it suddenly, without planning it.

spurious /'spjʊəriəs/ *adjective formal* false and not based on the truth

spurn /spɜːn/ *verb* [T] *formal* to not accept someone or something *He spurned my offer/suggestion.* ○ *a spurned lover*

spurt¹ /spɜːt/ *verb* [I, T] (*also* spurt out) If something spurts liquid or fire, or if liquid or fire spurts from somewhere, it flows out suddenly with force. *Blood was spurting out of his stomach.* **2 spurt ahead/into/past, etc** to increase your speed, effort, or activity *She spurted ahead in the final lap.*

spurt² /spɜːt/ *noun* [C] **1** a sudden, short increase in speed, effort, or activity *He works in short spurts.* **2** a sudden, powerful flow of liquid *The water came out of the tap in spurts.*

sputter /'spʌtər/ *verb* [I] to make several quick, explosive sounds *The car sputtered to a halt.*

spy¹ /spaɪ/ *noun* [C] someone who secretly tries to discover information about a person, country, etc

spy² /spaɪ/ *verb* **1** [I] to secretly try to discover information about a person, country, etc **2** [T] *literary* to see someone or something, often from a distance *I spied him on the dance floor.*
spy on sb to secretly watch someone *He spied on her through the keyhole.*

sq *written abbreviation for* square in measurements *an area of 70 sq km* (= square kilometres)

squabble /'skwɒbl/ *verb* [I] to argue about something that is not important *They're always squabbling over money.* ● **squabble** *noun* [C]

squad /skwɒd/ *noun* [C] **1 bomb/drug/fraud, etc squad** a group of police officers who have special skills to deal with particular problems **2 death/firing/hit, etc squad** a group of people who are trained to kill, usually with guns **3** a sports team *the England rugby squad*

squadron /'skwɒdrən/ *noun* [C] a group of soldiers, ships, aircraft, etc in a military organization *a squadron of fighter jets*

squalid /'skwɒlɪd/ *adjective* **1** very dirty and unpleasant *squalid conditions* **2** morally bad *a squalid affair*

squall /skwɔːl/ *noun* [C] a sudden storm with strong winds

squalor /'skwɒlər/ *noun* [U] extremely dirty and unpleasant conditions *They were found living in absolute squalor.*

squander /'skwɒndər/ *verb* [T] to waste time, money, etc *He squandered all his money on alcohol and drugs.*

o--**square¹** /skweər/ *noun* [C] **1** SHAPE a shape with four equal sides and four 90° angles ⊃See picture at **shape**. **2** PLACE an open area with buildings around it, often in the centre of a town *Trafalgar Square* **3** NUMBER in mathematics, a number that results from multiplying a number by itself *The square of 3 is 9.* **4 back to square one** back to the beginning of a process or piece of work *None of the applicants were suitable, so we had to go back to square one and advertise the job again.* ⊃See also: **fair³** and square.

o--**square²** /skweər/ *adjective* **1** having the shape of a square *a square room* ○ *He has broad shoulders and a square jaw.* **2 square centimetre/ metre/mile, etc** the area of a square with sides that are a centimetre/metre/mile, etc long *3000 square feet of office space* **3 a square meal** a big, healthy meal *You need three square meals a day.*

square³ /skweər/ *verb* **2/3/4, etc squared** 2/3/4, etc multiplied by itself *Four squared is sixteen.*
square off *US* to prepare to fight, compete, or argue with someone *The two teams will square off in the finals next Saturday.*

square up *UK* **1** to prepare to fight, compete, or argue with someone *The players squared up to each other and started shouting.* **2** *informal* to pay someone the money that you owe them *If you pay for it now, I'll square up with you later.*

square with sth to match or to agree with something *Her story doesn't quite square with the evidence.*

squarely /'skweəli/ *adverb* directly *I looked him squarely in the eye.* ○ *The report put the blame squarely on the police.*

square 'root *noun* **the square root of 16/64/ 144, etc** the number you multiply by itself to get 16/64/144, etc *The square root of 144 is 12.*

squash¹ /skwɒʃ/ *noun* **1** SPORT [U] a sport in which two people hit a small rubber ball against the four walls of a room *a game of squash* ○ *a squash court/racket* **2 it's a squash** *UK* used to say that there are too many people or things in a small space *We managed to get in but it was a squash.* **3** DRINK [U] *UK* a sweet drink that tastes like fruit **4** VEGETABLE [C, U] a fruit with hard skin, a soft inside, and large seeds, that you cook and eat as a vegetable

squash² /skwɒʃ/ *verb* **1** [T] to crush something into a flat shape *I stepped on a spider and squashed it.* **2** [I, T] to push someone or something into a small space [often passive] *The kids were all squashed into the back seat.*

squat¹ /skwɒt/ *verb* [I] squatting, *past* squatted **1** (*also* **squat down**) to bend your legs so that you are sitting with your bottom very close to the ground *He squatted down beside me.* **2** to live in an empty building without the owner's permission

squat² /skwɒt/ *adjective* short and wide *a squat little man*

squat³ /skwɒt/ *noun* [C] a building that people are living in without the owner's permission

squatter /'skwɒtər/ *noun* [C] someone who lives in a building without the owner's permission

squawk /skwɔːk/ *verb* [I] If a bird squawks, it makes a loud, unpleasant noise. ● **squawk** *noun* [C]

squeak /skwiːk/ *verb* [I] to make a short, high sound *His shoes squeaked loudly as he walked.* ● **squeak** *noun* [C]

squeaky /'skwiːki/ *adjective* **1** making short, high sounds *a squeaky voice* **2 squeaky clean** very clean

squeal /skwiːl/ *verb* [I] to make a loud, high sound, often because of fear or excitement *She squealed with delight.* ● **squeal** *noun* [C] *squeals of laughter*

squeamish /'skwiːmɪʃ/ *adjective* If you are squeamish about something such as blood, you find it very unpleasant and it makes you feel ill.

o--**squeeze¹** /skwiːz/ *verb* **1** [T] to press something firmly *She squeezed his hand and said goodbye.* **2 squeeze into/through/past, etc** to move somewhere where there is very little space *She squeezed through a narrow gap in the wall.* **3 squeeze a lemon/orange, etc** to press a lemon/orange, etc to get juice from it *freshly* *squeezed orange juice*

squeeze sth/sb in to manage to do something or see someone when you are very busy *The doctor will try to squeeze you in this afternoon.*

squeeze² /skwiːz/ *noun* **1** [C] when you press something firmly *He gave her hand a little squeeze.* **2 it's a squeeze** used to say that there are too many people or things in a small space *We all got in, but it was a tight squeeze.* **3 a squeeze of lemon/orange, etc** a small amount of juice from a lemon/orange, etc

squid /skwɪd/ *noun* [C] *plural* squid a sea creature with a long body and ten long arms

squiggle /'skwɪgl/ *noun* [C] *informal* a short, curly line *Her signature just looks like a squiggle.*

squint /skwɪnt/ *verb* [I] to look at something with your eyes partly closed *She was squinting at her computer screen.*

squirm /skwɜːm/ *verb* [I] to twist your body because you are embarrassed, nervous, etc

squirrel /'skwɪrᵊl/ ⓤ /'skwɜːrᵊl/ *noun* [C] a small animal with a big, fur tail that climbs trees and eats nuts

squirrel

squirt /skwɜːt/ *verb* **1** [I, T] If liquid squirts, it comes out suddenly and with force, and if you squirt liquid, you make it come out suddenly and with force. *Water squirted out all over the floor.* **2 squirt sb with sth** to hit someone with a liquid

Sr (*also UK* **Snr**) *written abbreviation for* senior (= the older of two men in a family with the same name) *Joseph Kennedy, Sr.*

St 1 *written abbreviation for* street (= a road in a town or city that has houses or other buildings) *42 Oxford St* **2** *written abbreviation for* saint (= a dead person who has been officially respected by the Christian Church for living their life in a holy way) *St Patrick*

stab¹ /stæb/ *verb* [T] stabbing *past* stabbed to push a knife into someone *He was stabbed several times in the chest.*

stab² /stæb/ *noun* [C] **1** the act of pushing a knife into someone *He had a deep stab wound in his neck.* **2 a stab of guilt/jealousy/regret, etc** a sudden, unpleasant emotion *She felt a stab of guilt.* **3 have a stab at sth/doing sth** *informal* to try to do something, or to try an activity that you have not done before *She had a stab at solving the problem.*

stabbing /'stæbɪŋ/ *noun* [C] when someone stabs someone *Where were you on the night of the stabbing?* ○ *(US) a stabbing death*

'**stabbing ,pain** *noun* [C] a sudden, strong pain

stability /stə'bɪləti/ *noun* [U] when something is not likely to change or move *political/financial stability* ⊃Opposite instability.

stabilize (*also UK* **-ise**) /'steɪbᵊlaɪz/ *verb* [I, T] If you stabilize something, or if something stabilizes, it stops changing or moving. *The economy has finally stabilized.* ● **stabilization** /ˌsteɪbᵊlaɪ'zeɪʃᵊn/ *noun* [U]

stable¹ /'steɪbl/ *adjective* **1** SITUATION not likely to change or end suddenly *a stable relationship* ○ *The doctor said his condition was stable.* **2** OBJECT fixed or safe and not likely to move *Be careful! That chair isn't very stable.* **3** PERSON mentally calm and not easily upset ⊃Opposite unstable.

stable² /'steɪbl/ *noun* [C] a building where horses are kept

stack¹ /stæk/ *noun* [C] **1** a tidy pile of things *a stack of books/CDs* **2 stacks of sth** *informal* a lot of something *There are stacks of studies linking salt to high blood pressure.*

stack² /stæk/ (*also* **stack up**) *verb* [T] to arrange things in a tidy pile *Can you help me stack these chairs?*

stadium /'steɪdiəm/ *noun* [C] a large, open area with seats around it, used for playing and watching sports *a football/baseball stadium*

o⌐**staff¹** /stɑːf/ *noun* [group] the people who work for an organization *The company has a staff of over 500 employees.* ○ *Please talk to a member of staff.*

staff² /stɑːf/ *verb* [T] to provide workers for an organization [often passive] *The charity was staffed by volunteers.*

stag /stæg/ *noun* [C] a male deer

o⌐**stage¹** /steɪdʒ/ *noun* **1** [C] a period of development, or a particular time in a process *an early stage in his career* ○ *Our project is in its final stages.* ○ *I'm not prepared to comment at this stage.* **2** [C] the raised area in a theatre where actors perform *He's on stage for most of the play.* **3 the stage** performances in theatres *He's written plays for television and the stage.* **4 set the stage for sth** to make something possible or likely to happen *The meeting set the stage for future cooperation between the companies.*

stage² /steɪdʒ/ *verb* **1 stage a demonstration/ protest, etc** to organize and take part in a public meeting to complain about something **2 stage a concert/show, etc** to organize and produce a performance of music or a play, etc *They staged a free concert in Central Park.*

stagger /'stægə/ *verb* **1** [I] to walk as if you might fall *He staggered drunkenly towards the door.* **2** [T] to arrange events so that they do not happen at the same time *We stagger our lunch breaks at work.*

staggered /'stægəd/ *adjective* [never before noun] very shocked or surprised *I was staggered at the prices.*

staggering /'stægərɪŋ/ *adjective* very shocking and surprising *He earns a staggering amount of money.*

stagnant /'stægnənt/ adjective **1** Stagnant water or air does not flow and becomes dirty and smells unpleasant. *a stagnant pond* **2** A stagnant economy, society, or organization does not develop or grow.

stagnate /stæg'neɪt/ ⑳ /'stægneɪt/ verb [I] to stay the same and not grow or develop *He expects the economy to stagnate and unemployment to rise.* • **stagnation** /stæg'neɪʃ³n/ noun [U]

'**stag ,night** noun [C] a night when a group of men go out just before one of them gets married ⊃Compare **hen night.**

staid /steɪd/ adjective serious and old-fashioned *a staid, middle-aged man*

stain¹ /steɪn/ noun **1** [C] a dirty mark on something that is difficult to remove. *a blood/grass stain* ○ *a stain on the carpet* **2** [C, U] a thin, clear paint that you put on wood to make it darker *wood stain*

stain² /steɪn/ verb **1** [I, T] to leave a dirty mark on something which is difficult to remove, or to become dirty in this way *That wine I spilt has stained my shirt.* **2** [T] to paint a wooden surface with a thin paint in order to change its colour *She stained the bookcase to match the desk.*

,**stained 'glass** noun [U] coloured glass that is used to make pictures in windows *a stained-glass window*

stainless steel /,steɪnləs'sti:l/ noun [U] a type of steel (= strong metal) that is not damaged by water

stair /steə²/ noun [C] one of the steps in a set of steps

staircase /'steəkeɪs/ noun [C] a set of stairs and the structure around them *a spiral staircase*

> **WORD PARTNERS FOR stairs**
>
> **climb/fall down/go down/go up** the stairs • the **bottom of/foot of** the stairs • the **head of/top of** the stairs • **on** the stairs • a **flight of** stairs

o→**stairs** /steəz/ noun [plural] a set of steps from one level in a building to another *to climb the stairs* ○ *a flight* (= set) *of stairs*

stairway /'steəweɪ/ noun [C] a set of stairs and the structure around them

stake¹ /steɪk/ noun **1 be at stake** If something is at stake, it is in a situation where it might be lost or damaged. *We have to act quickly - people's lives are at stake.* **2** [C] a part of a business that you own, or an amount of money that you have invested in a business *He has a 30 percent stake in the company.* **3** [C] a strong stick with a pointed end that you push into the ground *a wooden stake*

stake² /steɪk/ verb **stake a/your claim** to say that you want something and that you should have it

stake sth on sth to risk something on the result of a competition or situation *He has staked his reputation on the film's success.*

stake sth out to watch a place in order to catch criminals or to see a famous person *The police are staking out the house where the terrorists are hiding.*

stakes /steɪks/ noun [plural] money or other advantages that you may get or lose in a competition or situation *People get very competitive because the stakes are so high.*

stale /steɪl/ adjective **1** old and not fresh *stale bread* ○ *Cake goes stale quickly if it's not covered.* **2** boring or bored, and not producing or feeling excitement or enthusiasm like before *I'd been too long in the same job and was getting stale.*

stalemate /'steɪlmeɪt/ noun [C, U] a situation in which neither side in an argument can win *The talks ended in a stalemate.*

stalk¹ /stɔːk/ verb **1** [T] to follow a person or animal closely and secretly, often to try to catch or attack them *She claimed that the man had been stalking her for a month.* **2** **stalk out/off, etc** to walk in an angry or proud way *She stalked out of the restaurant.*

stalk² /stɔːk/ noun [C] the main stem of a plant

stalker /'stɔːkə²/ noun [C] someone who follows a person or animal closely and secretly, often to try to catch or attack them

stall¹ /stɔːl/ noun [C] **1**  **stall** mainly UK a small shop with an open front or a table from which goods are sold *a market stall* **2** US a small area in a room for washing or using the toilet *a shower stall*

stall² /stɔːl/ verb **1** [ENGINE] [I, T] If an engine stalls, or if you stall it, it stops working suddenly. *The car stalled when I stopped at the traffic lights.* **2** [STOP] [I] to stop making progress *The peace talks have stalled over the issue of nuclear weapons.* **3** [MORE TIME] [T] to intentionally make someone wait or make something happen later so that you have more time *She wanted an answer immediately, but I managed to stall her.*

stallion /'stæljən/ noun [C] an adult male horse

the stalls /stɔːlz/ UK (US **orchestra**) noun [plural] the seats on the main floor near the front of a theatre or cinema *a seat in the stalls*

stalwart /'stɔːlwət/ noun [C] someone who supports an organization, team, etc in a very loyal way • **stalwart** adjective

> **WORD PARTNERS FOR stamina**
>
> **have** stamina   • **build up/improve/increase** stamina   • **mental/physical** stamina   • stamina **for** sth • a **test of** stamina

stamina /'stæmɪnə/ noun [U] the physical or mental energy that allows you to do something for a long time *Marathon runners need a lot of stamina.*

stammer /'stæmə²/ verb [I] to pause a lot and repeat sounds because of a speech problem or because you are nervous *He blushed and began to stammer.* • **stammer** noun [C] *He has a stammer.*

o→**stamp**¹ /stæmp/ noun [C] **1** (*also* **postage stamp**) a small, official piece of paper that you buy and stick onto a letter or parcel before you post it **2** a tool for putting a special ink mark on something, or the mark made by it *a stamp in a passport* **3 stamp of approval** official, public approval *The president has put his stamp of approval on the proposal.*

stamp² /stæmp/ *verb* **1** [T] to make a mark on something with a tool that you put ink on and press down *She stamped the date on the invoice.* **2** [I, T] to put your foot down on the ground hard and quickly, often to show anger *"No!" she shouted, stamping her foot.* ⊃See also: **rubber-stamp.**

stamp sth out to get rid of something that is wrong or harmful *a campaign to stamp out racism*

stampede /stæm'piːd/ *noun* [C] when a large group of animals or people suddenly move in an uncontrolled way, often in the same direction *Gunfire caused a stampede in the marketplace.* ● **stampede** *verb* [I]

WORD PARTNERS FOR **stance**

take a stance ● change your stance ● a hardline/tough stance ● a stance against sb/sth ● sb's stance on sth

stance /stæns/ *noun* [C] **1** an opinion or belief about something, especially if you say it in public [usually singular] *What's their stance on nuclear energy?* ○ *They are taking a very tough stance against drugs.* **2** *formal* the way that someone stands [usually singular] *an awkward stance*

ꝋ**stand¹** /stænd/ *verb past* stood **1** [ON FEET] [I] to be in a vertical position on your feet *We'd been standing for hours.* **2** [RISE] [I] (*also* stand up) to rise to a vertical position on your feet from sitting or lying down *I get dizzy if I stand up too quickly.* ○ *Please stand when the bride arrives.* ⊃See colour picture **Phrasal Verbs** on page Centre 16. **3 stand in line** US (UK queue) to wait for something as part of a line of people *We stood in line all afternoon.* **4 stand (sth) in/against/by, etc sth** to be in or to put something in a particular place or position *His walking stick stood by the door.* ○ *You'll have to stand the sofa on its end to get it through the door.* **5 can't stand sb/sth** *informal* to hate someone or something *I can't stand him.* ○ [+ doing sth] *She can't stand doing housework.* **6** [ACCEPT] [T] to be able to accept or deal with a difficult situation *She couldn't stand the pressures of the job.* **7 stand at sth** to be at a particular level, amount, height, etc *Inflation currently stands at 3 percent.* **8 where you stand on sth** what your opinion is about something *We asked the senator where she stood on gun control.* **9 where you stand (with sb)** what someone thinks about you, how they expect you to behave, and how they are likely to behave *She said she will never leave her husband, so now at least I know where I stand.* **10** [OFFER] [I] If an offer still stands, it still exists. *You're welcome to visit any time - my invitation still stands.* **11 as it stands** as something is now, without changes in it *The law as it stands is very unclear.* **12 stand trial** If someone stands trial, they appear in a law court

where people decide if they are guilty of a crime. *to stand trial for murder* **13 stand to gain/lose sth** to be in a situation where you can get/lose money or an advantage *He stands to gain a fortune if the company is sold.* **14** [ELECTION] [I] UK (US run) to compete in an election for an official position *to stand for office* ⊃See also: stand your **ground¹**, not have a **leg** to stand on, it stands to **reason¹**, stand on your own two feet (**foot¹**), stand sb in good **stead.**

stand about/around to spend time standing somewhere and doing very little *They stood around waiting for the store to open.*

stand aside to leave a job or position so that someone else can do it instead

stand back to move a short distance away from something or someone *Stand back while I light the fire.*

stand by 1 to be ready to do something or to help *Doctors were standing by to treat the injured passengers.* **2** to do nothing to prevent something unpleasant from happening *We can't stand by while millions of people starve.*

stand by sb to continue to support someone when they are in a difficult situation *She stood by him throughout his troubled career.*

stand by sth If you stand by an agreement, decision, etc, you do not change it. *The government stood by its promise to improve education.*

stand down UK to leave a job or position so that someone else can do it instead *He stood down as party leader.*

stand for sth 1 If a letter stands for a word, it is used to represent it. *UFO stands for 'unidentified flying object'.* **2** If a group of people stand for a set of ideas, they support those ideas. *The party stands for low taxes and individual freedom.* **3 not stand for sth** If you will not stand for something, you will not accept a situation or someone's behaviour. *He can't speak to me like that - I won't stand for it!*

stand in to do something that someone else was going to do because they cannot be there *She stood in for me when I was sick.*

stand out 1 to be very easy to see or notice *The bright blue letters really stand out on the page.* **2** to be better than other similar things or people *His application stood out from all the rest.* ⊃See also: stick/stand out like a sore **thumb¹.**

stand up If an idea or some information stands up, it is proved to be correct.

stand sb up to fail to meet someone when you said you would *He's stood me up twice now.*

stand up for sth/sb to support an idea or a person who is being criticized [often reflexive] *Never be afraid to stand up for yourself.*

stand² /stænd/ *noun* **1** [SHOP] [C] a small shop with an open front or a table from which goods are sold *a hot dog stand* ○ *Visit our stand at the trade fair.* **2** [SPORT] [C] UK (US stands) a structure in a sports ground where people can stand or sit to watch an event **3** [FURNITURE] [C] a piece of furniture for holding things *a music/hat stand* **4 the (witness) stand** (*also* UK **the dock**) the place in a law court where people sit or stand when they are being asked questions *The judge asked her to take the stand* (= go into the witness stand). **5** OPINION [C] an opinion or belief about something, especially if you say it in public [usually singular] *What's the President's* **stand** *on gun control?* **6 take a stand** to express your opinion about something publicly *He refuses to take a stand on this issue.* **7 make a stand** to publicly defend something or stop something from happening

> **WORD PARTNERS FOR *standard***
>
> **come up to** standard • **below/(not) up to** standard • **set** standards • **comply with/conform to/meet** standards • **exacting/high/low/rigorous** standards • standards **of** sth

o̶**standard¹** /'stændəd/ *noun* [C] **1** a level of quality, especially a level that is acceptable *a* **high standard** *of service* ○ *low* **safety standards** ○ *His work was* **below standard** (= not acceptable). ○ *She* **sets** *very high* **standards** *for herself.* **2** a level of behaviour, especially a level that is acceptable [usually plural] *high moral standards* ➔See also: **double standard.**

standard² /'stændəd/ *adjective* usual and not special *standard procedure/practice*

standardize (*also* UK **-ise**) /'stændədaɪz/ *verb* [T] to change things so that they are all the same *I wish someone would standardize clothing sizes.* • **standardization** /ˌstændədaɪ'zeɪʃᵊn/ *noun* [U] *the standardization of computer terms*

ˌ**standard of 'living** *noun* [C] *plural* **standards of living** how much money and comfort someone has *a high standard of living*

standby /'stændbaɪ/ *noun* [C] *plural* **standbys 1** someone or something extra that is ready to be used if needed *We kept our old TV as a standby in case the new one broke.* **2 be on standby** to be ready to do something or to be used if needed *Police were on standby in case there was any trouble after the game.*

stand-in /'stændɪn/ *noun* [C] someone who does what another person was going to do because the other person cannot be there

standing¹ /'stændɪŋ/ *noun* [U] Your standing is the opinion that other people have of you. *Last week's speech has improved the Prime Minister's standing in the polls.*

standing² /'stændɪŋ/ *adjective* [always before noun] **1** permanent and not only created when necessary *a standing committee* ○ *He has a* **standing invitation** *to stay at our house.* **2 a standing joke** a situation that a group of people often make jokes about *The poor quality of his work has become a standing joke in the office.* ➔See also: **long-standing.**

ˌ**standing 'order** *noun* [C] UK an instruction to a bank to pay someone a fixed amount of money at regular times from your account

ˌ**standing o'vation** *noun* [C] when people stand while clapping to show that they have enjoyed a performance very much *She* **got a standing ovation** *for her speech.*

stand-off UK (US **standoff**) /'stændɒf/ *noun* [C] when an argument or fight stops for a period of time because no one can win or get an advantage

standpoint /'stændpɔɪnt/ *noun* [C] a particular way of thinking about a situation or problem *to look at something* **from** *a political/religious* **standpoint**

standstill /'stændstɪl/ *noun* [no plural] a situation in which all movement or activity has stopped *The traffic* **came to a standstill** *in the thick fog.*

stand-up /'stændʌp/ *adjective* [always before noun] A stand-up comedian is someone who stands in front of a group of people and tells jokes as a performance. *stand-up comedy*

stank /stæŋk/ *past tense of* stink

staple¹ /'steɪpl/ *adjective* [always before noun] A staple food, product, etc is basic and very important. *a staple diet of rice and fish*

staple² /'steɪpl/ *noun* [C] a small piece of wire that you put through pieces of paper to join them together • **staple** *verb* [T] to join pieces of paper together with staples

stapler /'steɪplə'/ *noun* [C] a piece of equipment used for putting staples through paper

> **WORD PARTNERS FOR *star***
>
> **2 become/make** sb a star • a **big** star • a **pop** star

star

o̶**star¹** /stɑː'/ *noun* [C] **1** SKY a ball of burning gases that you see as a small point of light in the sky at night **2** FAMOUS PERSON a famous singer, actor, sports person, etc *a* **pop star 3** BEST PERSON someone in a group of people who is the best at doing something *Baggio is one of our* **star players.** **4** SHAPE a shape that has five or more points ➔See picture at **shape. 5 two-star/three-star, etc** used to show how good a restaurant or hotel is *a five-star hotel* **6 sb's stars/the stars** UK *informal* something you read that tells you what will happen to you based on the position of the stars in the sky *My stars said it would be a good month for romance.* ➔See also: **co-star, film star, rock star.**

star² /stɑː'/ *verb* [I, T] **starring**, *past* **starred** If a film, play, etc stars someone, or if someone stars in a film, play, etc, they are the main person in it. *a film starring Meg Ryan* ○ *Tom Hanks* **starred in** *'Sleepless in Seattle'.* ➔See also: **co-star.**

starboard /'stɑːbəd/ *noun* [U] the right side of a ship or aircraft

starch /stɑːtʃ/ *noun* **1** [C, U] a substance in foods such as rice, bread, and potatoes **2** [U] a substance used to make cloth stiff • **starchy** *adjective* containing a lot of starch *I try not too eat too many **starchy foods** such as potatoes and pasta.*

stardom /'stɑːdəm/ *noun* [U] when someone is very famous for acting, singing, etc

stare /steəʳ/ *verb* [I] to look at someone or something for a long time and not move your eyes *Sean was **staring at** me.* • **stare** *noun* [C]

stark¹ /stɑːk/ *adjective* **1** unpleasantly clear and obvious *His death is a **stark warning** to other people about the dangers of drugs.* **2** **stark difference/contrast** a total difference *Jerry is very lazy, in stark contrast to his sister who works very hard.* **3** with a very plain and simple appearance and not very attractive *a stark, snowy landscape* • **starkly** *adverb*

stark² /stɑːk/ *adverb* **stark naked** wearing no clothes

starry /'stɑːri/ *adjective* A starry sky or night is one in which you can see a lot of stars. *She gazed up at the starry sky.*

'star ˌsign *UK* (*US* **sign**) *noun* [C] one of the twelve signs that are based on star positions when you are born, which some people believe shows what type of person you are *"What star sign are you?" "I'm Capricorn."*

start¹ /stɑːt/ *verb* **1** [BEGIN DOING] [I, T] to begin doing something [+ doing sth] *He started smoking when he was eighteen.* ∘ [+ to do sth] *Maria started to laugh.* ∘ *We start work at nine o'clock.* **2** [BEGIN HAPPENING] [I, T] to begin to happen or to make something begin to happen *The programme starts at seven o'clock.* ∘ *Police believe the fire started in the kitchen.* **3** [BUSINESS] [I, T] (*also* **start up**) If a business, organization, etc starts, it begins to exist, and if you start it, you make it begin to exist. *She started her own computer business.* ∘ *A lot of new restaurants have started up in the area.* **4** [CAR] [I, T] (*also* **start up**) If a car or engine starts, it begins to work, and if you start it, you make it begin to work. *The car won't start.* ∘ *Start up the engine.* **5** **to start with** [SITUATION] used to talk about what a situation was like at the beginning before it changed *I was happy at school to start with, but later I hated it.* **b** [LIST] used before saying the first thing in a list of things *To start with, we need better computers. Then we need more training.* **6** [MOVE SUDDENLY] [I] to move suddenly because you are frightened or surprised ⊃See also: set/start the **ball** rolling, get/start off on the wrong **foot¹**.

start (sth) off to begin by doing something, or to make something begin by doing something *She started off the meeting with the monthly sales report.*

start on sth to begin doing something *Have you started on your homework yet?*

start out to begin your life or the part of your life when you work, in a particular way *My dad started out as a sales assistant in a shop.*

start over *US* to begin something again *If you make a mistake, you'll have to start over.*

at the start • **from** the start • the start **of** sth

start² /stɑːt/ *noun* **1** [BEGINNING] [C] the beginning of something [usually singular] *Our teacher checks who is in class **at the start of** each day.* ∘ *Ivan has been involved in the project from the start.* ∘ *The meeting got off to a bad start* (= began badly). **2** **make a start** *mainly UK* to begin doing something *I'll **make a start on** the washing-up.* **3** **for a start** *UK* used when you are giving the first in a list of reasons or things *I won't be going - I've got too much homework for a start.* **4** [ADVANTAGE] [C] an advantage that you have over someone else when you begin something [usually singular] *I'm grateful for the start I had in life.* **5** the start the place where a race begins **6** [SUDDEN MOVEMENT] [no plural] a sudden movement that you make because you are frightened or surprised *Kate sat up **with a start**.* ⊃See also: false start.

starter /'stɑːtəʳ/ *noun* **1** [C] *UK* (*US* **appetizer**) something that you eat as the first part of a meal **2** [C] *US* in sports, a member of a team who is involved in a competition from the beginning *At only 20, he's the team's youngest starter.* **3** **for starters** *informal* used to say that something is the first in a list of things *Try this exercise for starters.* ⊃See also: non-starter.

starting-point /'stɑːtɪŋ.pɔɪnt/ *noun* [C] an idea, subject, etc that you use to begin a discussion or process

startle /'stɑːtl/ *verb* [T] to suddenly surprise or frighten someone *The sound startled me.* • **startled** *adjective a startled expression*

startling /'stɑːtlɪŋ/ *adjective* making you feel very surprised *startling news*

start-up /'stɑːtʌp/ *adjective* [always before noun] relating to starting a business *start-up costs*

starve /stɑːv/ *verb* [I, T] to become ill or die because you do not have enough food, or to make someone ill or die because they do not have enough food *Many people have **starved to death** in parts of Africa.* • **starvation** /stɑː'veɪʃ°n/ *noun* [U] *Children were dying of starvation.*

starved /stɑːvd/ *adjective* **1** **be starved of sth** *UK* (*US* **be starved for sth**) to not have enough of something that you need very much *a child starved of love* **2** *mainly US informal* very hungry

starving /'stɑːvɪŋ/ *adjective* **1** dying because there is not enough food *starving people* **2** *informal* very hungry *I'm absolutely starving.*

stash¹ /stæʃ/ (*also* **stash away**) *verb* [T] *informal* to keep a lot of something in a safe, secret place *His money was stashed away in a cupboard.*

stash² /stæʃ/ *noun* [C] *informal* a lot of something that you keep in a safe, secret place *He had a stash of whisky under the bed.*

state¹ /steɪt/ *noun* **1** [CONDITION] [C] the condition that something or someone is in *the state of the economy* ∘ *The building is in a terrible state.* **2** **in/into a state** *informal* very upset or nervous *Ben was in a real state before the exam.*

3 PART OF COUNTRY [C] (*also* **State**) one of the parts that some countries such as the US are divided into *Washington State* ○ *Alaska is the largest state in the US.* **4** COUNTRY [C] a country *a union of European states* ⮕See Common learner error at **country**. **5 the state** the government of a country *financial help from the state* **6 state visit/occasion, etc** an important visit/occasion, etc involving the leader of a government **7 the States** the United States of America ⮕See also: **police state, welfare state**.

state² /steɪt/ *verb* [T] to officially say or write something [+ (that)] *Two medical reports stated that he was mentally ill.*

stately /'steɪtli/ *adjective* formal and slow *a stately procession through the streets*

,stately 'home *noun* [C] a big, old house in the countryside that people pay to visit in Britain

---
WORD PARTNERS FOR **statement**

issue/make/prepare/release a statement • a **false/joint/public/sworn** statement • a statement **about/on** sth

---

◦▪**statement** /'steɪtmənt/ *noun* [C] **1** something that someone says or writes officially *The pop star is expected to make a statement about his involvement with drugs.* **2** (*also* bank statement) a piece of paper that shows how much money you have put into your bank account and how much you have taken out

,state of a'ffairs *noun* [no plural] a situation *a sad state of affairs*

,state of 'mind *noun* [C] *plural* states of mind how you are feeling at a particular time *to be in a positive state of mind*

state-of-the-art /ˌsteɪtəvðiˈɑːt/ *adjective* using the newest ideas, designs, and materials *a computer system that uses state-of-the-art technology*

,state 'school UK (US public school) *noun* [C] a school that is free to go to because the government provides the money for it

statesman /'steɪtsmən/ *noun* [C] *plural* statesmen an important politician, especially one who people respect

static¹ /'stætɪk/ *adjective* not moving or changing *The number of students on the course has remained static.*

static² /'stætɪk/ *noun* [U] **1** (*also* ,static elec'tricity) electricity that you get when two surfaces rub together **2** noise on a radio or television that is caused by electricity in the air

◦▪**station¹** /'steɪʃən/ *noun* [C] **1** TRAINS a building where trains stop so that you can get on or off them *Dad met me at the station.* **2 bus station** (*also* UK **coach station**) a building where a bus starts or ends its journey **3** SERVICE a building where a particular service is based *(UK) a petrol station/ (US) a gas station* **4** RADIO/TV a company that broadcasts television or radio programmes *a classical music station* ⮕See also: **filling station, fire station, police station, polling station, power station, service station**.

COMMON LEARNER ERROR

station or **stop**?

Station is used for trains.
the train/railway station
the underground/tube station

Stop or **bus stop** is used for buses.
I stood at the bus stop for over half an hour.
Get off at the third stop.

A **bus station** is a place where many buses start or end their journeys.

---

station² /'steɪʃən/ *verb* **be stationed at/in, etc** If someone such as a soldier is stationed somewhere, they are sent there to work for a period of time. *US soldiers stationed in Germany*

stationary /'steɪʃənᵊri/ *adjective* not moving *stationary cars*

stationer's /'steɪʃənəz/ *noun* [C] *UK* a shop where you can buy pens, paper, and other things for writing

stationery /'steɪʃənᵊri/ *noun* [U] things that you use for writing, such as pens and paper

'station ,wagon US (UK estate car) *noun* [C] a big car with a large space for bags behind the back seat

---
WORD PARTNERS FOR **statistic**

collect/gather statistics • statistics **confirm/indicate/reveal/show** sth • **according to** statistics • statistics **on** sth

---

statistic /stə'tɪstɪk/ *noun* [C] a fact in the form of a number that shows information about something [usually plural] *Statistics show that skin cancer is becoming more common.* • **statistical** *adjective* relating to statistics *statistical evidence* • **statistically** *adverb*

statistics /stə'tɪstɪks/ *noun* [U] the subject that involves collecting and studying numbers to show information about something

statue /'stætʃuː/ *noun* [C] a model that looks like a person or animal, usually made from stone or metal

stature /'stætʃəʳ/ *noun* [U] *formal* **1** the importance that someone has because of their work *a scientist of international stature* **2** your height *a man of small stature*

status /'steɪtəs/ *noun* [U] **1** the position that you have in relation to other people because of your job or social position *The pay and status of nurses has improved.* **2** the legal position of someone or something *What's your marital status* (= are you married or not)?

the status quo /ˌsteɪtəsˈkwəʊ/ *noun formal* the situation that exists now, without any changes *They only want to maintain the status quo.*

'status ,symbol *noun* [C] something that someone owns that shows they have a high position in society

statute /'stætʃuːt/ *noun* [C] *formal* a law or rule

statutory /'stætjətᵊri/ *adjective formal* decided or controlled by law *a statutory minimum wage*

staunch /stɔːnʃ/ *adjective* [always before noun] very loyal in your support for someone or your belief in something *a staunch supporter of the Communist party*

stave /steɪv/ *verb*
stave sth off to stop something bad from happening now although it may happen later *He had a bar of chocolate to stave off his hunger.*

○ー**stay¹** /steɪ/ *verb* **1** NOT LEAVE [I] to continue to be in a place, job, etc and not leave *The weather was bad so we stayed at home.* ○ *Do you want to come with me or stay here?* ○ *He stayed in bed all morning.* ○ *Do you want to stay in teaching?* **2** IN A STATE [T] to continue to be in a particular state *The supermarket stays open late.* ○ *I was tired and couldn't stay awake.* **3** VISIT [I, T] to spend a short period of time in a place *We stayed in a hotel.* ○ *We're going to stay with my grandmother.* **4 stay put** *informal* to continue to be in the same place *He told me to stay put while he fetched the car.* ⊅See Common learner error at **rest**.
stay behind to not leave a place when other people leave *I stayed behind after class to speak to the teacher.*
stay in to stay in your home *Let's stay in tonight and watch a video.*
stay on to continue to be in a place, job, or school after other people have left *I stayed on an extra two years at school.*
stay out to not go home at night, or to go home late *He stayed out all night.* ○ *Don't stay out too late.*
stay out of sth to not become involved in an argument or discussion *It's better to stay out of their arguments.*
stay up to go to bed later than usual [+ to do sth] *She stayed up to watch a film.* ○ *We stayed up all night watching the election.*

stay² /steɪ/ *noun* [C] a period of time that you spend in a place *Did you enjoy your stay in Tokyo?* ○ *Our stay in Normandy was the best bit of the holiday.*

stead /sted/ *noun* **stand sb in good stead** to be useful to someone in the future *The course will stand you in good stead.*

steadfast /ˈstedfɑːst/ *adjective formal* refusing to change your beliefs or what you are doing *He is steadfast in his support for political change.* ● **steadfastly** *adverb*

steady¹ /ˈstedi/ *adjective* **1** GRADUAL happening at a gradual, regular rate *steady economic growth* ○ *He has had a steady flow/stream of visitors.* **2** STILL still and not shaking *You need steady hands to be a dentist.* ⊃Opposite **unsteady. 3** NOT CHANGING not changing *She drove at a steady speed.* **4 steady job/work** a job that is likely to continue for a long time and pay you regular money *He's never had a steady job.* ● **steadily** *adverb* ● **steadiness** *noun* [U]

steady² /ˈstedi/ *verb* **1** [T] to make something stop shaking or moving *He managed to steady the plane.* **2 steady yourself** to stop yourself

from falling *She grabbed hold of the rail to steady herself.*

steak /steɪk/ *noun* [C, U] a thick, flat piece of meat or fish *steak and chips*

○ー**steal** /stiːl/ *verb past tense* **stole**, *past participle* **stolen 1** [I, T] to secretly take something that does not belong to you, without intending to return it *Burglars broke into the house and stole a computer.* ○ *stolen cars* **2 steal away/in/out, etc** to move somewhere quietly and secretly

stealth /stelθ/ *noun* [U] secret, quiet behaviour ● **stealthy** *adjective* behaving in a secret, quiet way ● **stealthily** *adverb*

○ー**steam¹** /stiːm/ *noun* **steam**

1 [U] the gas that water produces when you heat it **2 let off steam** to get rid of your anger, excitement, etc by being noisy or using a lot of energy **3 run out of steam** to not have enough energy to finish doing something

steam² /stiːm/ *verb* **1** [T] to cook something using steam *steamed rice* **2** [I] to produce steam *a steaming bowl of soup*
steam (sth) up If glass steams up, or if you steam it up, it becomes covered in steam.

steamer /ˈstiːməʳ/ *noun* [C] **1** a pan used for cooking food using steam **2** a ship that uses steam power

steamy /ˈstiːmi/ *adjective* **1** hot and full of steam *a steamy kitchen* **2** sexually exciting *a steamy love story*

steel¹ /stiːl/ *noun* [U] a very strong metal made from iron, used for making knives, machines, etc ⊃See also: **stainless steel.**

steel² /stiːl/ *verb* **steel yourself** to prepare yourself to do something difficult or unpleasant *He was steeling himself for an argument.*

steely /ˈstiːli/ *adjective* [always before noun] very strong and determined *a steely determination to succeed*

○ー**steep¹** /stiːp/ *adjective* **1** SLOPE A steep slope, hill, etc goes up or down very quickly. *The hill was too steep to cycle up.* **2** CHANGE A steep increase or fall in something is very big and quick. *a steep rise in prices* **3** PRICE *informal* very expensive *Hotel prices are steep at $300 for a room.* ● **steeply** *adverb* *Food prices have risen steeply.* ● **steepness** *noun* [U]

steep² /stiːp/ *verb* **be steeped in sth** to have a lot of something around or to be strongly influenced by something *The town is steeped in history.*

steeple /ˈstiːpl/ *noun* [C] a church tower that has a point at the top

steer /stɪəʳ/ *verb* **1** [I, T] to control the direction of a vehicle *I tried to steer the boat away from the bank.* **2** [T] to influence the way a situation develops *I managed to* ***steer the conversation*** *away from my exam results.* **3** **steer sb into/out of/towards, etc** to guide someone somewhere, especially by putting your hand on their back *He steered me towards the door.* ⊃See also: steer clear³ of sb/sth.

steering /'stɪərɪŋ/ *noun* [U] the parts of a vehicle that control its direction

'**steering ,wheel** *noun* [C] a wheel that you turn to control the direction of a vehicle ⊃See colour picture **Car** at page Centre 7.

stem¹ /stem/ *noun* [C] the long, thin part of a plant that the leaves and flowers grow on

stem² /stem/ *verb* [T] stemming, *past* stemmed to stop something from continuing or increasing *The new procedures are intended to* ***stem the flow*** *of drugs into the country.*

stem from sth to develop as the result of something *Her problems stem from childhood.*

'**stem ,cell** *noun* [C] a cell, especially one taken from a person or animal in a very early stage of development, that can develop into any other type of cell

stench /stenʃ/ *noun* [C] a very unpleasant smell *the stench of rotten fruit*

stencil /'stensəl/ *noun* [C] a piece of paper or plastic with patterns cut into it, that you use to paint patterns onto a surface • **stencil** *verb* [I, T] UK stencilling *past* stencilled US stenciling *past* stenciled to use a stencil to paint patterns onto a surface

---

WORD PARTNERS FOR *step* (noun)

2 take steps to do sth • a **big**/**important**/**major** step • the **first**/**next** step • a step **to-wards** sth • a step **in** (doing) sth

---

o-**step¹** /step/ *noun* [C] **1** MOVEMENT one of the movements you make with your feet when you walk *She* ***took*** *a few* ***steps*** *forward and then started to speak.* **2** METHOD one of the things that you do to achieve something *This meeting is the* ***first step*** *towards a peace agreement.* ○ *The company has* ***taken steps*** *to improve its customer service.* **3** STAIR one of the surfaces that you walk on when you go up or down stairs **4** **in step (with sb/sth)** having the same ideas, opinions, etc as other people *This time, Britain is in step with the rest of Europe.* **5** **out of step (with sb/sth)** having different ideas, opinions, etc from other people *Her views are out of step with government policy.* **6** **be one step ahead (of sb)** to have done something before someone else **7** **watch your step a** WALKING used to tell someone to be careful about where they are walking **b** BEHAVIOUR to be careful about what you say and do

step² /step/ *verb* stepping, *past* stepped **1** **step back/forward/over, etc** to move somewhere by lifting your foot and putting it down in a different place *She stepped carefully over the dog.* **2** **step on/in sth** to put your foot on or in something *I accidentally stepped on her foot.*

step down to leave an important job *He stepped down as manager of the Italian team.*

step in to become involved in a difficult situation in order to help [+ to do sth] *A Japanese bank stepped in to provide financial help.*

step sth up to increase what you are doing to try to achieve something *Police have stepped up their efforts to find the man.*

stepbrother /'step,brʌðəʳ/ *noun* [C] not your parent's son but the son of the person your parent has married

step-by-step /,stepbaɪ'step/ *adjective* [always before noun] A step-by-step method, plan, etc, deals with one thing and then another thing in a fixed order. *a* ***step-by-step guide*** *to buying a house*

'**step ,change** *noun* [C] when a very big change happens *There is a step change taking place in communications technology.*

stepchild /'steptʃaɪld/ *noun* [C] *plural* step-children the child of your husband or wife from an earlier marriage

stepdaughter /'step,dɔːtəʳ/ *noun* [C] the daughter of your husband or wife from an earlier marriage

stepfather /'step,fɑːðəʳ/ *noun* [C] the man who has married your mother but is not your father

stepmother /'step,mʌðəʳ/ *noun* [C] the woman who has married your father but is not your mother

stepping-stone /'stepɪŋstəʊn/ *noun* [C] **1** an event or experience that helps you achieve something else *Education is* ***a stepping-stone*** *to a good job.* **2** one of several stones that you walk on to cross a stream

stepsister /'step,sɪstəʳ/ *noun* [C] not your parent's daughter but the daughter of the person your parent has married

stepson /'stepsʌn/ *noun* [C] the son of your husband or wife from an earlier marriage

stereo /'steriəʊ/ *noun* **1** [C] a piece of equipment for playing CDs, listening to the radio, etc that has two speakers (= parts where sound comes out) *a car stereo* ⊃See colour picture **The Living Room** on page Centre 4. **2** [U] a system for hearing music, speech, etc through two speakers (= parts where sound comes out) *The concert was broadcast* ***in stereo.*** ○ *stereo sound*

WORD PARTNERS FOR *stereotype*

challenge/**fit** a stereotype • a **negative** stereotype • a stereotype **of** sth • a **racial** stereotype

---

stereotype¹ /'steriəʊtaɪp/ *noun* [C] a fixed idea that people have about what a particular type of person is like, especially an idea that is wrong *racial stereotypes* • **stereotypical** /,steriəʊ'tɪpɪkəl/ *adjective* having the qualities that you expect a particular type of person to have *a stereotypical student*

stereotype² /'steriəʊtaɪp/ *verb* [T] to have a fixed idea about what a particular type of person is like, especially an idea that is wrong [often passive] *Young people are often* ***stereotyped*** *as being lazy.*

sterile /'steraɪl/ *adjective* **1** CLEAN completely clean and without any bacteria *a sterile needle*

2 NO CHILDREN unable to produce children **3** NO IDEAS not having enough new ideas *a sterile discussion* • **sterility** /stəˈrɪləti/ *noun* [U]

sterilize (*also UK* -**ise**) /ˈsterᵊlaɪz/ *verb* [T] **1** to make something clean and without bacteria *a sterilized needle* **2** to perform a medical operation on someone to make them unable to have children • **sterilization** /ˌsterᵊlaɪˈzeɪʃᵊn/ *noun* [U]

sterling /ˈstɜːlɪŋ/ *noun* [U] British money

stern¹ /stɜːn/ *adjective* very serious and without any humour *a stern expression/face* ○ *stern criticism* • **sternly** *adverb*

stern² /stɜːn/ *noun* [C] the back part of a ship

steroid /ˈsterɔɪd/ *noun* [C] a drug for treating injuries that some people use illegally in sport to make their muscles stronger

stethoscope /ˈsteθəskəʊp/ *noun* [C] a piece of equipment that a doctor uses to listen to your heart and breathing

stew /stjuː/ *noun* [C, U] a dish made of vegetables and meat cooked together slowly in liquid *beef/lamb stew* • **stew** *verb* [T] to cook food slowly in liquid *stewed fruit*

steward /ˈstjuːəd/ *noun* [C] **1** a man who looks after people on an aircraft, boat, or train *an air steward* **2** someone who helps to organize a race or big event

stewardess /ˈstjuːədɪs/ *noun* [C] a woman who looks after people on an aircraft, boat, or train *an air stewardess*

sth *written abbreviation for* something • **sth's** *written abbreviation for* something's

◦−**stick¹** /stɪk/ *verb past* stuck
1 [I, T] to become joined to something else or to make something become joined to something else, usually with a substance like glue *Anne stuck a picture of her boyfriend on the wall.* ○ *The stamp wouldn't stick to the envelope.*

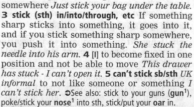

stick

The boy stuck his tongue out.

2 stick sth in/on/under, etc *informal* to put something somewhere *Just stick your bag under the table.* **3 stick (sth) in/into/through, etc** If something sharp sticks into something, it goes into it, and if you stick something sharp somewhere, you push it into something. *She stuck the needle into his arm.* **4** [I] to become fixed in one position and not be able to move *This drawer has stuck - I can't open it.* **5 can't stick sb/sth** *UK informal* to not like someone or something *I can't stick her.* ⮕See also: stick to your guns (**gun¹**), poke/stick your **nose¹** in sth, stick/put your **oar** in.

stick around *informal* to stay somewhere for a period of time *Stick around after the concert and you might meet the band.*

stick at sth to continue trying hard to do something difficult *I know it's hard learning to drive but stick at it.*

stick by sb to continue to support someone when they are having problems

stick out 1 If part of something sticks out, it comes out further than the edge or surface. *His ears stick out a bit.* **2** to be very easy to

notice *She certainly sticks out in a crowd.* ⮕See also: stick/stand out like a sore **thumb¹**.

stick sth out to make part of your body come forward from the rest of your body *The little boy stuck his tongue out.*

stick it out *informal* to continue doing something that is boring, difficult, or unpleasant

stick to sth to continue doing or using something and not change to anything else *I'll stick to lemonade - I'm driving.*

stick together If people stick together, they support and help each other.

stick up to point up above a surface and not lie flat *I can't go out with my hair sticking up like this.*

stick up for sb/sth *informal* to support someone or something when they are being criticized

stick with sb/sth to continue using someone or doing something and not change to anyone or anything else *He's a good builder - I think we should stick with him.*

◦−**stick²** /stɪk/ *noun* [C] **1** a long, thin piece of wood, usually broken or fallen from a tree **2 walking/hockey, etc stick** a long, thin piece of wood that you use when you are walking/playing hockey, etc **3** a long, thin piece of something *a stick of candy/celery* ⮕See also: **carrot** and stick, get (hold of) the wrong **end¹** of the stick.

sticker /ˈstɪkər/ *noun* [C] a piece of paper or plastic with writing or a picture on it that you stick onto a surface *a car sticker* ⮕See also: bumper sticker.

sticky /ˈstɪki/ *adjective* **1** made of or covered with a substance that can stick to other things *sticky fingers* ○ *sticky tape* **2** Sticky weather is unpleasantly hot. **3 a sticky moment/problem/situation, etc** *informal* a moment/problem/situation, etc that is difficult or embarrasses you

◦−**stiff¹** /stɪf/ *adjective* **1** HARD hard and difficult to bend *stiff material* **2** NOT MOVING A door, drawer, etc that is stiff does not move as easily as it should. **3** HURTING If a part of your body is stiff, it hurts and is difficult to move. *I've got a stiff neck.* **4** SEVERE very severe or difficult *stiff competition/opposition* ○ *We need stiffer penalties for drink driving.* **5** FORMAL behaving in a way that is formal and not relaxed **6** THICK A stiff substance is thick and does not move around easily. *Whip the cream until it is stiff.* **7 stiff drink/whisky/vodka, etc** a strong alcoholic drink *I need a stiff brandy.* **8 stiff wind/breeze** a wind that is quite strong • **stiffly** *adverb* • **stiffness** *noun* [U]

stiff² /stɪf/ *adverb* **bored/scared/worried, etc stiff** extremely bored, worried, etc *The lecture was awful - I was bored stiff.*

stiffen /ˈstɪfᵊn/ *verb* **1** [I, T] to become stiff or to make something become stiff **2** [I] to suddenly stop moving because you are frightened or angry *She stiffened at the sound of the doorbell.*

stifle /ˈstaɪfl/ *verb* [T] to stop something from happening or continuing *to stifle a sneeze/*

yawn ○ *Large supermarkets* ***stifle*** *competition.*

stifling /ˈstaɪflɪŋ/ *adjective* extremely hot *a stifling summer in Rome*

> WORD PARTNERS FOR ***stigma***
>
> sth **carries** a stigma • the stigma **attached to/surrounding** sth • sth **loses** its stigma • **a social** stigma • the stigma **of** (doing) sth

stigma /ˈstɪgmə/ *noun* [C, U] when people disapprove of something, especially when this is unfair *There is still **a stigma attached** to being mentally ill.* • **stigmatize** (*also UK* **-ise**) *verb* [T] to treat someone or something unfairly by disapproving of them **[often passive]** *Unmarried mothers are stigmatized by society.*

stiletto /stɪˈletəʊ/ *noun* [C] a shoe with a very high, pointed heel (= part at the bottom and back of a shoe) *a pair of stilettos*

⊶**still¹** /stɪl/ *adverb* **1** [CONTINUING] used to say that something is continuing to happen now or that someone is continuing to do something now *He's still here if you want to speak to him.* ○ *Do you still play basketball?* **2** [POSSIBLE] used to say that something continues to be possible *We could still catch the train if we leave now.* **3** [EMPHASIS] used to emphasize that you did not expect something to happen because something else makes it surprising *He didn't do much work but still came top of the class.* ○ *The weather was terrible. Still, we had a good holiday.* **4 better/harder/worse, etc still** better/harder/worse, etc than something else

⊶**still²** /stɪl/ *adjective* **1 stand/stay/sit, etc still** to stand, stay, sit, etc without moving *Sit still so I can brush your hair.* **2** A still place is calm and quiet. *It was night and the whole village was still.* **3** *UK* A still drink does not have any bubbles in it. • **stillness** *noun* [U]

still³ /stɪl/ *noun* [C] a photograph from one moment in a film

stillborn /ˌstɪlˈbɔːn/ [US] /ˈstɪlˌbɔːn/ *adjective* born dead *a **stillborn baby***

stilt /stɪlt/ *noun* [C] **1** one of two long poles that you can stand on and use to walk above the ground **[usually plural]** *a clown on stilts* **2** one of several poles that support a building above the ground **[usually plural]** *a house on stilts*

stilted /ˈstɪltɪd/ *adjective* talking or writing in a formal way that does not sound natural *a **stilted conversation***

stimulant /ˈstɪmjələnt/ *noun* [C] a drug that makes you feel more active and awake *Coffee contains caffeine which is a stimulant.*

stimulate /ˈstɪmjəleɪt/ *verb* [T] **1** to make something happen or develop more *It stimulates the production of red blood cells.* **2** to make someone feel interested and excited *Colourful pictures can stimulate a child.* • **stimulation** /ˌstɪmjəˈleɪʃən/ *noun* [U]

stimulating /ˈstɪmjəleɪtɪŋ/ *adjective* interesting and making you think *a **stimulating discussion***

> WORD PARTNERS FOR ***stimulus***
>
> **act as/provide** a stimulus • a stimulus **for/** to sth

stimulus /ˈstɪmjələs/ *noun* [C, U] *plural* **stimuli** /ˈstɪmjəlaɪ/ something that makes something else happen, grow, or develop more *The report **provided the stimulus** for more studies.*

sting¹ /stɪŋ/ *verb past* **stung 1** [CAUSE PAIN] [T] If an insect, plant, etc stings you, it causes pain by putting poison into your skin. *He was stung by a wasp.* **2** [FEEL PAIN] [I, T] If your eyes, skin, etc sting, or if something makes them sting, you feel a sudden, burning pain. *That shampoo really made my **eyes sting**.* **3** [UPSET] [T] to upset someone **[often passive]** *She was clearly stung by his criticism.*

sting² /stɪŋ/ *noun* **1** [WOUND] [C] a painful wound that you get when an insect, plant, etc puts poison into your skin *a **wasp/bee sting*** **2** [PAIN] **[no plural]** a sudden, burning pain in your eyes, skin, etc **3** [UPSET] **[no plural]** the feeling of being upset by something *the sting of defeat*

stingy /ˈstɪndʒi/ *adjective informal* not generous *He's too stingy to buy any drinks.*

stink¹ /stɪŋk/ *verb* [I] *past tense* **stank** *also US* **stunk**, *past participle* **stunk 1** to smell very bad *The kitchen **stinks of** fish.* **2** *informal* to be very bad and dishonest *If you ask me, the whole affair stinks.*

stink² /stɪŋk/ *noun* **1 make/cause/create, etc a stink** *informal* to complain about something in a forceful way **2** **[no plural]** a very bad smell

stint /stɪnt/ *noun* [C] a period of time spent doing something *He had a two-year stint as a teacher in Spain.*

stipulate /ˈstɪpjəleɪt/ *verb* [T] *formal* to say exactly what must be done **[+ (that)]** *The rules stipulate that smoking is not allowed.* • **stipulation** /ˌstɪpjəˈleɪʃən/ *noun* [C]

⊶**stir¹** /stɜːʳ/ *verb* **stirring**, *past* **stirred 1** [MIX] [T] to mix food or liquid by moving a spoon round and round in it ***Stir** the **mixture** until it is smooth.* **2** [MOVE] [I, T] to move slightly or make someone move slightly *The baby stirred in its sleep.* **3** [FEEL] [T] to make someone feel a strong emotion *The case has **stirred** great **anger** among the public.*

stir sth up 1 to cause arguments or bad feelings between people, often intentionally *I think she just likes to **stir up trouble**.* **2** If something stirs up memories, it makes you remember events in the past. *The photographs **stirred up** some painful **memories**.*

stir² /stɜːʳ/ *noun* **1 cause/create a stir** to make people excited or surprised *Her new book has caused quite a stir.* **2** **[no plural]** when you mix food or liquid with a spoon *Could you give the soup a stir?*

stir-fry /ˈstɜːˌfraɪ/ *verb* [T] to fry small pieces of vegetable, meat, etc very quickly while mixing them around • **stir-fry** *noun* [C]

stirring /stɜːrɪŋ/ *adjective* making people feel excitement or other strong emotions *a **stirring performance/speech***

stirrup /'stɪrəp/ *noun* [C] one of the two metal parts that support your feet when you are riding a horse

stitch¹ /stɪtʃ/ *noun* 1 ⟨THREAD⟩ [C] a short line of thread that is sewn through a piece of material 2 ⟨WOUND⟩ [C] one of the small pieces of thread that is used to sew together a cut *She needed 50 stitches in her head.* 3 ⟨WOOL⟩ [C] one of the small circles of wool that you make when you are knitting (= making something from wool) 4 ⟨PAIN⟩ [no plural] a sudden pain that you get in the side of your body when you exercise too much *to get a stitch* 5 **in stitches** laughing a lot *He had the whole audience in stitches.*

stitch² /stɪtʃ/ *verb* [I, T] to sew two things together or to repair something by sewing *I need to get my shoes stitched.*
stitch sth up to sew together the two parts of something that have come apart *The nurse stitched up my finger.*

stock¹ /stɒk/ *noun* 1 ⟨SHOP⟩ [U] all the goods that are available in a shop *We're expecting some new stock in this afternoon.* 2 **be in stock/out of stock** to be available/not available in a shop 3 ⟨SUPPLY⟩ [C] a supply of something that is ready to be used [usually plural] *stocks of food/ weapons* 4 ⟨COMPANY⟩ [C, U] the value of a company, or a share in its value *to buy/sell stock* ○ *falling/rising* **stock prices** 5 ⟨LIQUID⟩ [U] a liquid made by boiling meat, bones, or vegetables and used to make soups, sauces, etc *chicken/vegetable stock* 6 **take stock (of sth)** to think carefully about a situation before making a decision ⭢See also: laughing stock.

stock² /stɒk/ *verb* [T] to have something available for people to buy *They stock a wide range of books and magazines.*
stock up to buy a lot of something *We'd better stock up on food for the holiday.*

stock³ /stɒk/ *adjective* **stock answer/phrase, etc** an answer/phrase, etc that is always used and so is not really useful

stockbroker /'stɒk,brəʊkə'/ *noun* [C] someone whose job is to buy and sell stocks and shares in companies for other people

the ˈstock exˌchange (*also* **the ˈstock ˌmarket**) *noun* 1 the place where stocks and shares in companies are bought and sold 2 the value of stocks and shares being bought and sold

stocking /'stɒkɪŋ/ *noun* [C] a very thin piece of clothing that covers a woman's foot and leg *a pair of stockings*

stockpile /'stɒkpaɪl/ *verb* [T] to collect a lot of something, usually so that it can be used in the future *to stockpile food* ● **stockpile** *noun* [C] *a stockpile of weapons*

stocky /'stɒki/ *adjective* having a wide, strong, body *a short, stocky man*

stoic /'stəʊɪk/ *adjective formal* dealing with pain, problems, etc, but never complaining ● **stoically** *adverb* ● **stoicism** /'stəʊɪsɪz²m/ *noun* [U]

stole /stəʊl/ *past tense of* steal

stolen /'stəʊl²n/ *past participle of* steal

stolid /'stɒlɪd/ *adjective* calm and not showing emotion or excitement

ｏ→**stomach¹** /'stʌmək/ *noun* [C] *plural* **stomachs** 1 the organ inside your body where food is digested 2 the front part of your body just below your chest *He punched me in the stomach.* ⭢See colour picture **The Body** on page Centre 13. 3 **have no stomach for sth** to not feel brave enough to do something unpleasant ⭢See also: have butterflies (**butterfly**) (in your stomach).

stomach² /'stʌmək/ *verb informal* **can't stomach sth** to be unable to deal with, watch, etc something unpleasant *I can't stomach horror movies.*

ˈstomach ˌache *noun* [C, U] pain in your stomach *I've got terrible stomach ache.*

stomp /stɒmp/ *verb* [I] to put your foot down on the ground hard and quickly, or to walk with heavy steps, usually because you are angry *He stomped off to his room.*

ｏ→**stone¹** /stəʊn/ *noun* 1 ⟨SUBSTANCE⟩ [U] a hard, natural substance that is found in the ground *a stone wall* 2 ⟨ROCK⟩ [C] a small rock or piece of rock 3 ⟨JEWEL⟩ [C] a hard, valuable substance that is often used in jewellery *precious stones* 4 ⟨WEIGHT⟩ [C] *plural* **stone** *UK* a unit for measuring weight, equal to 6.35 kilograms or 14 pounds *I gained two stone when I was pregnant.* 5 ⟨SEED⟩ [C] the hard seed that is at the centre of some fruits *a cherry stone* ⭢See also: stepping-stone.

stone² /stəʊn/ *verb* [T] to kill or hurt someone by throwing stones (= small rocks) at them, usually as a punishment [often passive] *Two men were* **stoned to death** *by the crowd.*

stoned /stəʊnd/ *adjective informal* 1 relaxed or excited because of the effect of drugs 2 drunk

stonemason /'stəʊn,meɪs²n/ *noun* [C] someone who makes things from stone

stony /'stəʊni/ *adjective* 1 covered with or containing stones (= small rocks) *a stony path/road* 2 not friendly, usually because you are angry *a stony silence*

stood /stʊd/ *past of* stand

stool /stuːl/ *noun* [C] a seat that does not have a back or arms *a piano/bar stool*

stool

stoop¹ /stuːp/ *verb* [I] to bend the top half of your body forward and down *He stooped to pick up the letter.*
stoop to sth/doing sth to do something bad that will give you an advantage *I can't believe he would stoop to blackmail.*

stoop² /stuːp/ *noun* 1 [no plural] when the upper part of your body is bent forwards *He has a slight stoop.* 2 [C] *US* a raised area in front of the door of a house, with steps leading up to it

ｏ→**stop¹** /stɒp/ *verb* **stopping**, *past* **stopped** 1 ⟨FINISH⟩ [I, T] to finish doing something that you were doing [+ doing sth] *Stop laughing - it's not funny.* ○ *He started to say something and then stopped.* ○ *I'm trying to work but I keep having to stop to answer the phone* (= stop so that I can answer the telephone). 2 ⟨FOR A SHORT TIME⟩ [I] to stop a journey or an activity for a short time *He stopped at a pub for lunch.* 3 ⟨NOT OPERATE⟩ [I, T] to not continue to operate, or to make something not continue to operate *My watch has stopped.* ○ *Can you stop the video for a minute?* **4** FINISH MOVING [I, T] to not move any more, or make someone or something not move any more *A car stopped outside the house.* ○ *I stopped someone in the street to ask for directions.* **5** BUS/TRAIN [I] If a bus, train, etc stops at a particular place, it pauses at that place so that people can get on and off. *Does this train stop at Cambridge?* **6** END [T] to make something end *We must find a way to stop the war.* **7** PREVENT [T] to prevent something from happening or someone from doing something [+ from + doing sth] *Health workers are trying to stop the disease from spreading.* **8 Stop it/that!** used to tell someone to finish doing something, usually something annoying *Stop it! I can't concentrate if you keep making a noise.* **9 stop a cheque** *UK* (*US* **stop a check**) to prevent money from being paid from a cheque (= a piece of paper that you sign to pay for things) ➲See also: stop at **nothing**, stop the **rot**².

stop doing something or **stop to do something?**

Stop doing something means 'not continue with an activity'.

Suddenly, everyone stopped talking.

~~Suddenly, everyone stopped to talk.~~

Stop to do something means 'stop one activity so that you can do something else'.

We stopped to look at the map.

stop by (sth) to visit a person or place for a short time *If you're passing our house, why don't you stop by sometime?*
stop off to visit a place for a short time when you are going somewhere else *We stopped off in Paris for a couple of days before heading south.*

o➤**stop²** /stɒp/ *noun* [C] **1** a place where a bus or train stops so that people can get on or off *We need to get off at the next stop.* ➲See Common learner error at **station**. **2 put a stop to sth** to end something unpleasant *We must put a stop to the violence.* **3** a place where you stop on a journey, or the time that you spend there *We had an overnight stop in Singapore.* **4 come to a stop** to stop moving *The car came to a stop in front of an old cottage.* **5 pull out all the stops** to do everything you can to make something succeed ➲See also: bus **stop**, full **stop**.

stoplight /'stɒplaɪt/ *noun* [C] *US* a set of red, green, and yellow lights that is used to stop and start traffic

stopover /'stɒp‚əʊvəʳ/ *noun* [C] a short stop between parts of a journey, especially a plane journey

stoppage /'stɒpɪdʒ/ *noun* [C] when people stop working because they are angry about something their employers have done

stopwatch /'stɒpwɒtʃ/ *noun* [C] a watch that can measure exactly how long it takes to do something and is often used in sports activities

storage /'stɔːrɪdʒ/ *noun* [U] when you put things in a safe place until they are needed *We had to put our furniture into storage.*

o➤**store¹** /stɔːʳ/ *noun* [C] **1** mainly *US* a shop *a book store* ○ *She works at a men's clothing store.* ➲See Common learner error at **shop**. **2** a supply of something that you are keeping to use later *a store of grain* **3 be in store (for sb)** If something is in store for you, it will happen to you in the future. *There's a surprise in store for you!* **4 set great store by sth** *UK* to believe that something is very important *Martina sets great store by physical strength and fitness.* ➲See also: chain **store**, convenience **store**, department **store**, liquor **store**.

o➤**store²** /stɔːʳ/ *verb* [T] **1** (*also* **store away**) to put something somewhere and not use it until you need it *We have a lot of old clothes stored in the attic.* **2** to keep information on a computer *All the data is stored on diskettes.*

storeroom /'stɔːrruːm/ *noun* [C] a room where goods are kept until they are needed

storey *UK* (*US* **story**) /'stɔːri/ *noun* [C] a level of a building *a three-storey house*

stork /stɔːk/ *noun* [C] a large, white bird with very long legs which walks around in water to find its food

o➤**storm** /stɔːm/ *noun* [C] **1** very bad weather with a lot of rain, snow, wind, etc *a snow/thunder storm* **2 a storm of controversy/protest, etc** a strong, negative reaction to something that has been said or done

storm² /stɔːm/ *verb* **1** [T] to attack a building, town, etc, using violence *Armed police stormed the embassy and arrested hundreds of protesters.* **2 storm into/out of, etc** to enter or leave a place in a very noisy way because you are angry *He stormed out of the meeting.*

'storm ‚surge *noun* [C] when a lot of water is pushed from the sea onto the land, usually caused by a hurricane (= a violent storm with very strong winds)

stormy /'stɔːmi/ *adjective* **1** If it is stormy, the weather is bad with a lot of wind and rain. *a stormy night* ○ *stormy seas* **2** A stormy relationship or situation involves a lot of anger and arguments. *a stormy relationship* ○ *a stormy meeting/debate*

o➤**story** /'stɔːri/ *noun* [C] **1** DESCRIPTION a description of a series of real or imaginary events which is intended to entertain people *a horror/detective story* ○ *the story of the revolution* ○ *Tell us a story, Mum.* ○ *She reads stories to the children every night.* **2** REPORT a report in a newspaper, magazine, or news programme *Today's main story is the hurricane in Texas.* **3** EXPLANATION an explanation of why something happened, which may not be true *Did he tell you the same story about why he was late?* 4 BUILDING *US spelling of* storey

stout¹ /staʊt/ *adjective* **1** quite fat *a short, stout man* **2** If shoes or other objects are stout, they are strong and thick.

stout² /staʊt/ *noun* [C, U] a very dark beer

stove /stəʊv/ *noun* [C] **1** a piece of equipment that you cook on *I've left some soup on the stove for you.* ➔See colour picture **The Kitchen** on page Centre 2. **2** a piece of equipment that burns coal, gas, wood, etc and is used for heating a room

stow /stəʊ/ (*also* stow away) *verb* [T] to put something in a particular place until it is needed *Our camping equipment is stowed away in the loft.*

stowaway /'stəʊə,weɪ/ *noun* [C] someone who hides on a ship or aircraft so that they can travel without paying

straddle /'strædl/ *verb* [T] **1** to sit or stand with one leg on either side of something *He straddled the chair.* **2** to be on both sides of a place *Niagara Falls straddles the Canadian border.*

straggle /'strægl/ *verb* [I] **1** to move more slowly than other members of a group *Some runners are straggling a long way behind.* **2** to grow or spread out in an untidy way *I could see a line of straggling bushes.*

straggly /'strægli/ *adjective* growing or spreading out in an untidy way *a straggly beard*

✿**straight¹** /streɪt/ *adjective* **1** NOT CURVED not curved or bent *a straight road* ○ *straight hair* **2** LEVEL in a position that is level or vertical *That shelf's not straight.* **3** IN A SERIES [always before noun] one after another *They've won five straight games so far.* **4** HONEST honest *a straight answer* **5** DRINK An alcoholic drink that is straight is not mixed with water, ice, etc. **6** get sth straight to make sure that you completely understand a situation *Let me get this straight - am I paying for this?* **7** NOT HOMOSEXUAL *informal* not homosexual ➔See also: keep a straight face¹.

✿**straight²** /streɪt/ *adverb* **1** in a straight line *It's straight ahead.* ○ *He was looking straight at me.* **2** immediately *I went straight back to sleep.* **3** sit up/stand up straight to sit or stand with your body vertical **4** not think straight If you cannot think straight, you are not thinking clearly about something. *I was so tired, I couldn't think straight.* **5** tell sb straight (out) to tell someone the truth in a clear way *I told him straight that he wasn't getting a pay increase.* **6** straight away immediately *Go there straight away.*

straighten /'streɪtⁿn/ *verb* [I, T] to become straight or to make something straight

straighten sth out to successfully deal with a problem or a confusing situation *We need to straighten a few things out.*

straighten sth up to make a place tidy *Could you straighten up your room?*

straighten up to stand so that your back is straight

straightforward /,streɪt'fɔːwəd/ *adjective* **1** easy to do or understand *The task looked fairly straightforward.* **2** saying clearly and honestly what you think *She's very straightforward.*

WORD PARTNERS FOR *strain*

feel the strain ● be **under** strain ● the strain of doing sth

strain¹ /streɪn/ *noun* **1** FEELING [C, U] when you feel worried and nervous about something *The strain of the last few months had exhausted her.* **2** put a strain on sb/sth to cause problems for someone or to make a situation difficult *Children put tremendous strains on a marriage.* **3** INJURY [C, U] an injury to part of your body that is caused by using it too much *back strain* **4** STRETCH [U] when something is pulled or stretched too tightly *The rope broke under the strain.* **5** DISEASE/PLANT [C] a type of disease or plant *a new strain of virus*

strain² /streɪn/ *verb* **1** TRY HARD [I, T] to try hard to do something, usually to see or hear something [+ to do sth] *I had to strain to hear the music.* **2** INJURE to injure part of your body by using it too much *I think I've strained a muscle.* **3** CAUSE PROBLEMS [T] to cause problems for a situation or relationship *The incident has strained relations between the two countries.* **4** MONEY [T] to cause too much of something to be used, especially money *The war is straining the defence budget.* **5** SEPARATE [T] to separate solids from a liquid by pouring the mixture into a container with small holes in it *Strain the sauce to remove the seeds and skins.*

strained /streɪnd/ *adjective* **1** showing that someone is nervous or anxious *We had a rather strained conversation.* **2** If a relationship is strained, problems are spoiling that relationship. *Relations are still strained between the two countries.* ○ *They have a rather strained relationship.*

strait /streɪt/ *noun* [C] a narrow area of sea that connects two large areas of sea [usually plural] *the straits of Florida*

strait-jacket /'streɪt,dʒækɪt/ *noun* [C] a special jacket used for mentally ill people that prevents them from moving their arms

strand /strænd/ *noun* [C] **1** a thin piece of hair, thread, rope, etc *She tucked a strand of hair behind her ear.* **2** one part of a story, situation, idea, etc *There are a number of different strands to the plot.*

stranded /'strændɪd/ *adjective* unable to leave a place *We were stranded at the airport for ten hours.*

✿**strange** /streɪndʒ/ *adjective* **1** If something is strange, it is surprising because it is unusual or unexpected. [+ (that)] *It's strange that she hasn't called.* ○ *It's midnight and he's still at work - that's strange.* ○ *What a strange-looking man.* **2** A strange person or place is one that you are not familiar with. *I was stuck in a strange town with no money.* ● **strangely** *adverb* *She's been behaving very strangely* (= in an unusual way) *recently.*

Other ways of saying 'strange' are **odd, bizarre**, and **weird**: *I always thought there was something a bit **odd** about her.* • *I had a really **bizarre/weird** dream last night.*

If something is strange because it is not what you usually expect, you can use the adjectives **curious, funny**, or **peculiar**: *This lemonade tastes **funny**.* • *The chicken had a **peculiar** smell.* • *A **curious** thing happened to me yesterday.*

If someone always behaves strangely, you might describe them as **eccentric**: *The whole family are **eccentric**.*

stranger /ˈstreɪndʒə^r/ *noun* [C] **1** someone you have never met before *I can't just walk up to a complete stranger and start speaking to them.* **2 be no stranger to sth** to have a lot of experience of something *He's no stranger to hard work himself.*

strangle /ˈstræŋgl/ *verb* [T] **1** to kill someone by pressing their throat with your hands, a rope, wire, etc [often passive] *Police believe the victim was strangled.* **2** to prevent something from developing *High-level corruption is strangling the economy.*

stranglehold /ˈstræŋglhəʊld/ *noun* [no plural] a position of complete control that prevents something from developing *Two major companies have a **stranglehold on** the market.*

strap /stræp/ *noun* [C] a narrow piece of material used to fasten two things together or to carry something *a watch strap* ○ *a bru strap* ○ *I want a bag with a shoulder strap.* •**strap** *verb* [T] **strapping**, *past* **strapped** to fasten something using a strap *Have you strapped the children into their seats?*

strategic /strəˈtiːdʒɪk/ *adjective* **1** PLAN helping to achieve a plan, usually in business or politics *strategic planning* **2** WAR related to fighting a war *strategic weapons* **3** POSITION If something is in a strategic position, it is in a useful place for achieving something. •**strategically** *adverb*

adopt/develop/have a strategy • a strategy **for** doing sth • the strategy **of** doing sth • a **long-term/short-term** strategy • a **sales** strategy

strategy /ˈstrætədʒi/ *noun* **1** [C] a plan that you use to achieve something *an economic strategy* ○ *a long-term strategy* **2** [U] the act of planning how to achieve something *military strategy*

straw /strɔː/ *noun* **1** [U] the long, dried stems of plants such as wheat (= plant for grain), often given to animals for sleeping on and eating *a straw hat* **2** [C] a thin plastic or paper tube that you use for drinking through **3 the final/last straw** the last in a series of unpleasant events which finally makes you stop accepting a bad situation

Last week he came home drunk at five in the morning, and that was the last straw.

strawberry /ˈstrɔːb^əri/ *noun* [C] a small, red fruit with a green leaf at the top and small, brown seeds on its surface

stray¹ /streɪ/ *verb* [I] **1** to move away from the place where you should be, without intending to *I suddenly realized that I had strayed far from the village.* **2** to start thinking or talking about a different subject from the one you should be giving attention to *We seem to have strayed from the original subject.*

stray² /streɪ/ *adjective* [always before noun] **1** A stray animal is lost or has no home. *a stray dog* **2** A stray piece of something has become separated from the main part. *a stray hair*

stray³ /streɪ/ *noun* [C] an animal that is lost or has no home

streak¹ /striːk/ *noun* [C] **1** a thin line or mark *She has a streak of white hair.* **2** a quality in someone's character, especially a bad one *Tom has a mean/ruthless streak.* **3 a winning/losing streak** a period of always winning/losing a game *I'm on a winning streak*

streak² /striːk/ *verb* **1 streak across/down/ through**, etc to move quickly *The plane streaked across the sky.* **2 be streaked with sth** to have thin lines of a different colour *His dark hair was lightly streaked with grey.*

stream

stream   stream of water

stream¹ /striːm/ *noun* [C] **1** a small river **2 a stream of sth a** a line of people or vehicles moving in the same direction *a constant stream of traffic* **b** a large number of similar things that happen or appear one after another *He has produced a steady stream of books.* **c** a moving line of liquid, gas, smoke, etc *A stream of smoke was coming from the chimney.*

stream² /striːm/ *verb* **1 stream down/in/through**, etc to move or flow continuously in one direction *Tears were streaming down her face.*

2 [T] to listen to or watch something on a computer directly from the Internet

streamer /'stri:mər/ *noun* [C] a long, narrow piece of coloured paper that you use to decorate a room or place for a party

streamline /'stri:mlaɪn/ *verb* [T] **1** to make an organization or process simpler and more effective *We need to streamline our production procedures.* **2** to give a vehicle a smooth shape so that it moves easily through air or water

๐**street** /stri:t/ *noun* [C] **1** a road in a town or city that has houses or other buildings *We live on the same street.* ○ *a street map* **2 the man/person, etc in the street** a typical, ordinary person **3 be right up sb's street** *UK informal* (*US* **be right up sb's alley**) to be exactly the type of thing that someone knows about or likes to do *I've got a little job here which should be right up your street.* **4 be streets ahead (of sb/sth)** *UK* to be much better or more advanced than someone or something else *American film companies are streets ahead of their European rivals.* ⊃See also: **high street, Wall Street.**

streetcar /'stri:tka:ʳ/ *US* (*UK/US* **tram**) *noun* [C] an electric vehicle for carrying passengers, mostly in cities, which runs along metal tracks in the road

'street ˌlight (*also* **'street ˌlamp**) *noun* [C] a light on a tall post next to a street ⊃See picture at **light.**

streetwise /'stri:twaɪz/ (*US also* **street-smart**) *adjective* Someone who is streetwise knows how to manage dangerous or difficult situations in big towns or cities.

๐**strength** /streŋθ/ *noun* **1** STRONG [U] when someone or something is strong *upper-body strength* ○ *A good boxer needs skill as well as strength.* **2** INFLUENCE [U] the power or influence that an organization, country, etc has *economic strength* **3** BEING BRAVE [U] when you are brave or determined in difficult situations *I think she showed great strength of character.* **4** GOOD QUALITIES [C] a good quality or ability that makes someone or something effective *We all have our strengths and weaknesses.* ○ *The great strength of this arrangement is its simplicity.* **5** STRONG FEELING [U] how strong a feeling or opinion is *There is great strength of feeling against tax increases.* **6** VALUE [U] the value of a country's money *The strength of the dollar has traders worried.* **7 at full strength** with the necessary number of people *Our team is now at full strength.* **8 on the strength of sth** If you do something on the strength of facts or advice, you do it because of them. *On the strength of this year's sales figures, we've decided to expand the business.* **9 go from strength to strength** *UK* to continue to become more successful ⊃See also: **a tower¹ of strength.**

strengthen /'streŋθən/ *verb* [I, T] to become stronger or make something become stronger *exercises to strengthen the leg muscles*

strenuous /'strenjuəs/ *adjective* using or needing a lot of effort *strenuous exercise*

๐**stress¹** /stres/ *noun* **1** WORRY [C, U] feelings of worry caused by difficult situations such as problems at work *work-related stress* ○ *She's been under a lot of stress recently.* **2** IMPORTANCE [U] special importance that you give to something *At school, they laid great stress on academic achievement.* **3** PHYSICAL FORCE [U] physical force on something *Jogging puts a lot of stress on your knee joints.* **4** STRONG PART [U] when you say one part of a word more strongly *In the word 'blanket', the stress is on the first syllable.*

stress² /stres/ *verb* **1** [T] to emphasize something in order to show that it is important [+ (that)] *I stressed that this was our policy.* **2** [I] *US informal* to be worried *Stop stressing about tonight - it'll be fine.*

stressed /strest/ (*also* **stressed out**) *adjective* worried and not able to relax *Tanya's really stressed out about her exams.*

stressful /'stresfʊl/ *adjective* making you stressed *a stressful job*

๐**stretch¹** /stretʃ/ *verb* **1** [I, T] to become longer or wider, or to pull something so that it becomes longer or wider *Don't pull my sweater - you'll stretch it.* **2** [I, T] to make your body or part of your body straighter and longer *Stretch your arms above your head.* **3 stretch away/into, etc** to cover a large area *The fields stretched away into the distance.* **4 stretch into/over, etc** to continue for a long period of time *The discussions will probably stretch into next month.* ⊃See also: stretch your legs (**leg**), bend/stretch the rules (**rule¹**).

stretch out to lie with your legs and arms spread out in a relaxed way

stretch² /stretʃ/ *noun* [C] **1** LAND/WATER an area of land or water *a stretch of coastline* **2** TIME a continuous period of time *He often worked ten hours at a stretch.* **3** BODY when you stretch part of your body *I always do a few stretches before I go jogging.* **4 not by any stretch of the imagination** used to say that something, often a description, is certainly not true *She was never a great player, not by any stretch of the imagination.*

stretcher /'stretʃəʳ/ *noun* [C] a flat structure covered with cloth which is used to carry someone who is ill or injured

stretcher

stricken /'strɪkⁿn/ *adjective* suffering from the effects of something bad, such as illness, sadness, etc *a child stricken by fear* ⊃See also: **panic-stricken, poverty-stricken.**

๐**strict** /strɪkt/ *adjective* **1** PERSON A strict person makes sure that children or people working for them behave well and does not allow them to break any rules. *a strict teacher* ○ *My parents were very strict with us.* **2** RULE If a rule, law, etc is strict, it must be obeyed. *She gave me strict instructions to be there by ten.* **3** BEHAVIOUR [always before noun] always behaving in a particular way because of your beliefs *a strict Muslim* **4** EXACT exactly correct *a strict translation of a text*

strictly /'strɪktli/ *adverb* **1** exactly or correctly *That's not strictly true.* ○ *Strictly speaking* (= The rules say), *we're not allowed to give you any advice.* **2** done or existing for a particular person or purpose *Her visit is strictly business.* **3** strictly forbidden/prohibited used to emphasize that something is not allowed

stride¹ /straɪd/ *verb past* strode stride across/ down/into, etc to walk somewhere with long steps *She strode across the stage.*

stride² /straɪd/ *noun* [C] **1** a long step when walking or running **2** get into your stride UK (US hit your stride) to start to do something well and with confidence because you have been doing it for a period *Once I get into my stride, I'm sure I'll work much faster.* **3** take sth in your stride UK (US take sth in stride) to calmly deal with something that is unpleasant and not let it affect what you are doing *There are often problems at work but she seems to take it all in her stride.*

strident /'straɪdⁿnt/ *adjective* **1** expressed in a strong way *strident criticism* **2** loud and unpleasant *a strident voice*

strife /straɪf/ *noun* [U] *formal* trouble or disagreement between people

o▸**strike¹** /straɪk/ *verb past* struck **1** HIT [T] to hit someone or something *His car went out of control and struck a tree.* ○ *I've never heard of anyone being struck by lightning.* **2** THINK [T] If a thought or idea strikes you, you suddenly think of it. [+ (that)] *It struck me that I'd forgotten to order the champagne.* **3** strike sb as sth If someone strikes you as having a particular quality, they seem to have that quality. *He didn't strike me as a passionate man.* **4** NOT WORK [I] to stop working for a period of time because you want more money, etc *Bus drivers are threatening to strike.* **5** EFFECT [T] If something bad strikes something or someone, it affects them strongly and quickly. *The hurricane struck the coast at about eight in the morning.* **6** ATTACK [I] to attack suddenly *The marines will strike at dawn.* **7** CLOCK [I, T] If a clock strikes, a bell rings to show what the time is. **8** strike gold, oil, etc to find a supply of gold, oil, etc in the ground **9** strike a match to light a match in order to produce fire **10** strike a balance to give two things a same amount of attention *It's important to strike a balance between spending and saving.* **11** strike a deal If two people strike a deal, they promise to do something for each other which will give them both an advantage. *The book's author has struck a deal with a major film company.* ➔See also: strike a chord (with sb), be struck dumb.

strike back to attack someone who has attacked you

strike out 1 to start moving towards somewhere in a determined way *She struck out for the opposite bank.* **2** *US informal* to fail at something *I really struck out with her - she*

wouldn't even let me kiss her goodbye.
strike sth out to draw a line through something wrong that you have written
strike up sth to start a conversation or relationship with someone *I struck up a conversation with a guy who worked behind the bar.*

┌─── WORD PARTNERS FOR **strike** (noun)

be on/go on strike • a strike over sth • strike action

strike² /straɪk/ *noun* **1** [C, U] a period of time when people are not working because they want more money, etc *Teachers are planning to go on strike next month.* **2** [C] a sudden military attack *an air strike* ➔See also: hunger strike.

striker /'straɪkər/ *noun* [C] **1** someone who is on strike **2** a football player whose job is to try to score goals

striking /'straɪkɪŋ/ *adjective* **1** easily noticed *There's a striking resemblance between them.* **2** very attractive *She's very striking.*

string¹ /strɪŋ/ *noun* **1** [C, U] very thin rope used for tying things *a ball of string* **2** [C] a piece of wire that is part of a musical instrument *guitar strings* **3** a string of beads/pearls a set of decorative things joined together on a thread, worn as jewellery **4** a string of sth a number of similar things *a string of questions* ○ *As a writer, she's enjoyed a string of successes.* **5** no strings (attached) If there are no strings attached to an offer or arrangement, there is nothing that is unpleasant that you have to accept. *I'll drive you home - no strings attached.* **6** pull strings to secretly use the influence that you have over important people to get something or to help someone

string² /strɪŋ/ *verb* [T] *past* strung to hang something somewhere with string *They had strung flags across the entrance to welcome us home.*
string sb along to deceive someone for a long time about what you are intending to do
be strung out If a group of things or people are strung out somewhere, they are in a line with spaces between them. *There were chairs strung out across the room.*

stringent /'strɪndʒənt/ *adjective* Stringent controls, rules, etc are very strict or extreme.

the strings /strɪŋz/ *noun* [plural] the people in a musical group who play instruments with strings on them such as the violin

strip¹ /strɪp/ *verb* stripping, *past* stripped **1** [I, T] (*also UK* strip off) to remove all your clothes, or to remove all someone else's clothes *She was stripped and searched by the guards.* ○ *He stripped off his clothes and ran into the sea.* **2** [T] (*also UK* strip off) to remove a covering from the surface of something *to strip paint/wallpaper off the wall*
strip sb of sth to take something important away from someone as a punishment *He was stripped of his gold medal.*

strip² /strɪp/ *noun* [C] **1** PIECE a long, narrow piece of something *a strip of paper/plastic* **2** AREA a long, narrow area of land or water **3** REMOVING CLOTHES entertainment in which someone takes off their clothes in a sexually

S

exciting way *a strip club/show* ⊃See also: **comic strip**.

stripe /straɪp/ *noun* [C] a long, straight area of colour *white with blue stripes* ⊃See picture at **horizontal**.

striped /straɪpt/ *adjective* with a pattern of stripes *a striped shirt*

stripey /ˈstraɪpi/ *adjective another spelling of* **stripy**

stripper /ˈstrɪpəʳ/ *noun* [C] someone who takes off their clothes in a sexually exciting way to entertain people

striptease /ˈstrɪptiːz/ *noun* [C, U] entertainment in which someone takes off their clothes in a sexually exciting way

stripy (*also* **stripey**) /ˈstraɪpi/ *adjective* with a pattern of stripes *stripy trousers*

strive /straɪv/ *verb* [I] *past tense* **strove** *or* **strived** *past participle* **striven** *or* **strived** *formal* to try very hard to do or achieve something *to strive for happiness/peace* ○ [+ to do sth] *We are constantly striving to improve our service.*

strode /strəʊd/ *past of* **stride**

stroke[1] /strəʊk/ *noun* **1** ILLNESS [C] a sudden problem in your brain that changes the flow of blood and makes you unable to move part of your body *to have/suffer a stroke* **2** MOVEMENT [C] a movement that you make against something with your hand, a pen, brush, etc *a brush stroke* **3** SWIMMING [C] a style of swimming **4** SPORT [C] when you move your arm and hit the ball in sports such as tennis, golf, etc **5** **a stroke of luck** something good that happens to you by chance *He had exactly the part that I needed so that was a stroke of luck.*

stroke[2] /strəʊk/ *verb* [T] to gently move your hand over a surface *to stroke a cat/dog* ○ *He stroked her hair.*

stroll /strəʊl/ *verb* **stroll along/down/through,** *etc* to walk somewhere in a slow and relaxed way *They strolled along the beach.* ● **stroll** *noun* [C] *Shall we go for a stroll around the garden?*

stroller /ˈstrəʊləʳ/ *US* (*UK* **pushchair**) *noun* [C] a chair on wheels which is used to move small children

strong /strɒŋ/ *adjective* **1** PHYSICALLY POWERFUL A strong person or animal is physically powerful. *Are you strong enough to lift this table on your own?* **2** NOT BREAK A strong object does not break easily or can support heavy things. *a strong box/chair* **3** QUALITY of a good quality or level and likely to be successful *a strong competitor/team* ○ *a strong economy* **4** FEELING A strong feeling, belief, or opinion is felt in a very deep and serious way. *a strong sense of pride* **5** NOTICEABLE If a taste, smell, etc is strong, it is very noticeable. *There's a strong smell of burning.* **6** PERSONALITY If a person or their personality is strong, they are confident and able to deal with problems well. **7** ALCOHOL containing a lot of alcohol *a strong drink* **8** RELATIONSHIP If a friendship, relationship, etc is strong, it is likely to last for a long time. **9** **strong chance/possibility,** *etc* something that is very likely to happen *There's a strong possibility of rain this afternoon.* **10** **strong opposition/support,** *etc* a lot of opposition/support,

etc **11** **strong language** words that some people might consider to be offensive **12** **sb's strong point** something that someone is very good at *Cooking is not my strong point.* **13** **be still going strong** continuing to be successful after a long time

strongly /ˈstrɒŋli/ *adverb* very much or in a very serious way *He is strongly opposed to violence of any sort.* ○ *I strongly believe that we should take action.*

strong-willed /ˌstrɒŋˈwɪld/ *adjective* very determined to do what you want to do

stroppy /ˈstrɒpi/ *adjective UK informal* angry or arguing a lot *a stroppy teenager*

strove /strəʊv/ *past tense of* **strive**

struck /strʌk/ *past of* **strike**

structural /ˈstrʌktʃərəl/ *adjective* relating to the structure of something *structural damage* ○ *The last five years have seen big structural changes in the company.* ● **structurally** *adverb*

structure[1] /ˈstrʌktʃəʳ/ *noun* **1** [C, U] the way that parts of something are arranged or put together *cell structure* ○ *grammatical structure* **2** [C] a building or something that has been built

structure[2] /ˈstrʌktʃəʳ/ *verb* [T] to arrange something in an organized way *How is the course structured?*

struggle[1] /ˈstrʌɡl/ *verb* [I] **1** to try very hard to do something difficult [+ to do sth] *He's struggling to pay off his debts.* **2** to fight someone when they are holding you *She struggled but couldn't break free.*

struggle on to continue doing something that is difficult

┌───┐
│ 🧩 WORD PARTNERS FOR **struggle** (*noun*) │
└───┘

a **constant/ongoing/uphill** struggle ● a struggle **for** [justice/survival, etc]

struggle[2] /ˈstrʌɡl/ *noun* [C] **1** when you try very hard to do something difficult *It was a real struggle to stay awake during the film.* **2** a fight between people

strum /strʌm/ *verb* [I, T] **strumming,** *past* **strummed** to move your fingers across the strings of a guitar

strung /strʌŋ/ *past of* **string**

strut /strʌt/ *verb* **strutting,** *past* **strutted** **strut along/around/down,** *etc* to walk somewhere with big steps in a proud way ⊃See also: **strut your stuff**[1].

stub[1] /stʌb/ *noun* [C] the short, end piece of something such as a cigarette or pencil that is left after it has been used *There were cigarette stubs all over the floor.*

stub[2] /stʌb/ *verb* **stubbing,** *past* **stubbed** **stub your toe** to hit your toe against a hard surface by accident

stub sth out to stop a cigarette from burning by pressing the burning end against a hard surface

stubble /ˈstʌbl/ *noun* [U] **1** very short, stiff hairs, usually on a man's face **2** the short bits of dried plant stems left in a field after it has been cut

stubborn /'stʌbən/ *adjective* determined not to change your ideas, plans, etc, although other people want you to ● **stubbornly** *adverb* ● **stubbornness** *noun* [U]

stubby /'stʌbi/ *adjective* short and thick *stubby legs/fingers*

stuck¹ /stʌk/ *adjective* [never before noun] **1** not able to move anywhere *My car got stuck in a ditch.* ○ *We were stuck at the airport for twelve hours.* **2** not able to continue reading, answering questions, etc because something is too difficult *I keep getting stuck on difficult words.* **3** be stuck with sb/sth to have to deal with someone or something unpleasant because no one else wants to *Whenever we eat out, I always get stuck with the bill.*

stuck² /stʌk/ *past of* stick

stud /stʌd/ *noun* [C] **1** JEWELLERY a small, metal piece of jewellery that is put through a part of your body such as your ear or nose ⊃See picture at **jewellery**. **2** DECORATION a small piece of metal that is fixed to the surface of something, usually for decoration **3** ANIMALS (*also* '**stud** ,**farm**) a place where horses are kept for breeding

o⊶**student** /'stju:dⁿnt/ *noun* [C] someone who is studying at a school or university *a law student* ○ *a foreign student* ⊃See also: **mature student**.

studio /'stju:diəu/ *noun* [C] **1** ART a room where an artist or photographer works **2** TV/RADIO a room where television/radio programmes or musical recordings are made **3** FILMS a film company or a place where films are made

studious /'stju:diəs/ *adjective* spending a lot of time studying ● **studiously** *adverb*

o⊶**study¹** /'stʌdi/ *verb* **1** [I, T] to learn about a subject, usually at school or university *I studied biology before going into medicine.* ⊃See Common learner error at **learn**. **2** [T] to look at something very carefully *He studied his face in the mirror.*

WORD PARTNERS FOR **study** (noun)

carry out/conduct/undertake a study ● a study **examines/focuses on** sth ● a study **concludes/finds/shows/suggests** sth ● a study **into** sth

study² /'stʌdi/ *noun* **1** FINDING OUT INFORMATION [C] when someone studies a subject in detail in order to discover new information *For years, studies have shown the link between smoking and cancer.* **2** LEARNING [U] when you learn about a subject, usually at school or university *the study of English literature* **3** ROOM [C] a room in a house where you can read, write, etc ⊃See also: **case study**.

o⊶**stuff¹** /stʌf/ *noun* [U] *informal* **1** used to refer to a substance or a group of things or ideas, etc without saying exactly what they are *There's some sticky stuff on the carpet.* ○ *They sell bread and cakes and stuff like that.* ○ *Can I leave my stuff at your house?* **2** know your stuff *informal* to know a lot about a subject, or to be very good at doing something *She's an excellent teacher - she really knows her stuff.* **3** strut your stuff *humorous informal* to dance

stuff² /stʌf/ *verb* [T] **1** stuff sth in/into/behind, etc to push something into a small space, often quickly or in a careless way *He stuffed the papers into his briefcase and left.* **2** FILL to completely fill a container with something *an envelope stuffed with money* **3** FOOD to fill meat, vegetables, etc with a mixture of food before you cook them *stuffed peppers* **4** DEAD ANIMAL to fill the body of a dead animal with special material so that it looks as if it is still alive

stuffing /'stʌfɪŋ/ *noun* [U] **1** a mixture of food which is put into meat, vegetables, etc before they are cooked **2** material which is used to fill the inside of things such as soft chairs, beds, toys, etc

stuffy /'stʌfi/ *adjective* **1** If a room or a building is stuffy, it is hot and unpleasant and the air is not fresh. **2** old-fashioned, formal and boring *a stuffy club for wealthy old men*

stumble /'stʌmbl/ *verb* [I] **1** to step badly and almost fall over *Mary stumbled on the loose rocks.* **2** to make a mistake, such as pausing or repeating a word, while speaking or performing *He kept stumbling over the same word.*

stumble across/on/upon sth/sb to discover something by chance, or to meet someone by chance *I stumbled across these photographs while I was cleaning out my desk.*

'**stumbling ,block** *noun* [C] a problem which makes it very difficult to do something *Lack of money has been the main stumbling block.*

stump¹ /stʌmp/ *noun* [C] **1** the short part of something that is left after most of it has been removed *a tree stump* **2** one of the three vertical wooden sticks that you throw a ball at in the game of cricket ⊃See colour picture **Sports 2** on page Centre 15.

stump² /stʌmp/ *verb* **1** be stumped by sth *informal* to not be able to answer a question or solve a problem because it is too difficult *Scientists are completely stumped by this virus.* **2** [I] *US* to travel to different places to get political support

stump (sth) up *UK informal* to provide money for something, especially when you do not want to

stun /stʌn/ *verb* [T] stunning, *past* stunned **1** to shock or surprise someone very much [often passive] *Friends and family were stunned by her sudden death.* **2** to make a person or animal unconscious, usually by hitting them on the head

stung /stʌŋ/ *past of* sting

stunk /stʌŋk/ **1** *past participle of* stink **2** *US past tense of* stink

stunning /'stʌnɪŋ/ *adjective* very beautiful *stunning views over the city* ○ *She's stunning.* ● **stunningly** *adverb* a **stunningly beautiful** *woman*

stunt¹ /stʌnt/ *noun* [C] **1** when someone does something dangerous that needs great skill, usually in a film *He always does his own stunts.* **2** something that is done to get people's attention *Their marriage was just a cheap publicity stunt.*

stunt² /stʌnt/ *verb* [T] to stop the normal growth or development of something *They say that* *smoking stunts your growth.*

stupefied /ˈstjuːpɪfaɪd/ *adjective* so shocked, tired, etc that you cannot think ● **stupefying** *adjective* making you stupefied ● **stupefy** *verb* [T]

stupendous /stjuːˈpendəs/ *adjective* extremely good or large *a stupendous performance* ● **stupendously** *adverb stupendously successful*

◦⬝**stupid** /ˈstjuːpɪd/ *adjective* **1** silly or not intelligent *That was a really stupid thing to do.* ○ *How could you be so stupid?* **2** [always before noun] *informal* used to show that you are annoyed about something which is causing a problem *I can never get this stupid machine to work!* ● **stupidity** /stjuːˈpɪdəti/ *noun* [U] ● **stupidly** *adverb*

stupor /ˈstjuːpəʳ/ *noun* [no plural] when someone is almost unconscious and cannot think clearly, especially because they have drunk too much alcohol *He staggered into the room in a drunken stupor.*

sturdy /ˈstɜːdi/ *adjective* very strong and solid *sturdy walking boots*

stutter /ˈstʌtəʳ/ *verb* [I, T] to repeat the first sound of a word several times when you talk, usually because you have a speech problem *"C-c-can we g-go now?" she stuttered.* ● **stutter** *noun* [no plural] *He has a really bad stutter.*

WORD PARTNERS FOR **style**

a **distinctive** style ● **in** a style ● a style **of** doing sth

◦⬝**style¹** /staɪl/ *noun* **1** [WAY] [C, U] a way of doing something that is typical of a particular person, group, place, or period *a style of painting/writing* **2** [DESIGN] [C, U] a way of designing hair, clothes, furniture, etc *She's had her hair cut in a really nice style.* **3** [QUALITY] [U] the quality of being attractive and fashionable or behaving in a way which makes people admire you *She's got style.* **4 do sth in style** to do something in a way that people admire, usually because it involves spending a lot of money *If we ever get married we'll do it in style.* **5 cramp sb's style** to prevent someone from enjoying themselves, especially by going somewhere with them

style² /staɪl/ *verb* [T] to shape or design hair, clothes, furniture, etc in a particular way *He spends hours in the bathroom styling his hair.*

-style /staɪl/ *suffix* used at the end of words to mean 'looking or behaving like something or someone' *antique-style furniture* ○ *Japanese-style management* ⊃See also: **old-style**.

stylish /ˈstaɪlɪʃ/ *adjective* fashionable and attractive *a stylish, black suit* ● **stylishly** *adverb stylishly dressed*

Styrofoam /ˈstaɪrəfəʊm/ *US trademark for* polystyrene: a light plastic material that is wrapped around delicate objects to protect them, and around hot things to keep them hot

suave /swɑːv/ *adjective* If someone, especially a man, is suave, they are polite and confident in a way that is attractive but may be false. *suave and sophisticated*

sub- /sʌb-/ *prefix* **1** under or below *substandard workmanship* **2** less important or a smaller

part of a larger whole *a subsection*

subconscious¹ /sʌbˈkɒnʃəs/ *adjective* Subconscious thoughts and feelings influence your behaviour without you being aware of them. *a subconscious fear* ● **subconsciously** *adverb*

subconscious² /sʌbˈkɒnʃəs/ *noun* [no plural] the part of your mind which contains thoughts and feelings that you are not aware of but which influence your behaviour *The memory was buried deep within my subconscious.*

subcontract /ˌsʌbkənˈtrækt/ *verb* [T] to pay someone else to do part of a job that you have agreed to do

subculture /ˈsʌbˌkʌltʃəʳ/ *noun* [C] a group of people with beliefs, interests, etc that are different from the rest of society

subdivide /ˌsʌbdɪˈvaɪd/ *verb* [T] to divide something into smaller parts [often passive] *Each chapter is subdivided into smaller sections.* ● **subdivision** /ˌsʌbdɪˈvɪʒ³n/ *noun* [C, U]

subdue /səbˈdjuː/ *verb* [T] subduing, *past* subdued to start to control someone or something, especially by using force

subdued /səbˈdjuːd/ *adjective* **1** quiet because you are feeling sad or worried *She seemed a bit subdued.* **2** Subdued lights or colours are not bright. *subdued lighting*

WORD PARTNERS FOR **subject**

bring up/broach/raise a subject ● **get onto** a subject ● **change/drop/get off** a subject ● **on** the subject (of sth)

◦⬝**subject¹** /ˈsʌbdʒɪkt/ *noun* [C] **1** [WHAT] what someone is writing or talking about *a series of programmes on the subject of homelessness* **2** [STUDY] an area of knowledge studied in school or university *Chemistry is my favourite subject.* **3** [GRAMMAR] the person or thing which performs the action described by the verb. In the sentence 'Bob phoned me yesterday.', 'Bob' is the subject. **4** [PERSON] someone who is from a particular country, especially a country with a king or queen *a British subject*

subject² /ˈsʌbdʒɪkt/ *adjective* **1 subject to sth a** often affected by something, especially something unpleasant *Departure times are subject to alteration.* **b** only able to happen if something else happens *The pay rise is subject to approval by management.*

subject³ /səbˈdʒekt/ *verb*

subject sb/sth to sth to make someone or something experience something unpleasant *In prison, he was subjected to beatings and interrogations.*

subjective /səbˈdʒektɪv/ *adjective* influenced by someone's beliefs or feelings, instead of facts *a subjective judgment* ● **subjectively** *adverb* ● **subjectivity** /ˌsʌbdʒekˈtɪvəti/ *noun* [U] when someone or something is influenced by beliefs or feelings instead of facts

ˈsubject ˌmatter *noun* [U] what is being talked or written about *I'm not sure whether the subject matter is suitable for children.*

subjunctive /səbˈdʒʌŋktɪv/ *noun* [no plural] the form of the verb which is used to express

doubt, possibility, or wish. In the sentence 'I wish I were rich.', 'were' is in the subjunctive.
● **subjunctive** *adjective*

sublime /sə'blaɪm/ *adjective* extremely good, beautiful, or enjoyable *sublime scenery* ● **sublimely** *adverb*

submarine /ˌsʌbmˀr'iːn/ *noun* [C] a boat that travels under water

submerge /səb'mɜːdʒ/ *verb* [I, T] to cause something to be under the surface of water, or to move below the surface of water *The floods destroyed farmland and submerged whole villages.* ● **submerged** *adjective*

submission /səb'mɪʃˀn/ *noun* **1** [U] when you accept that someone has complete control over you *They tried to starve her into submission.* **2** [C, U] when you send a document, plan, etc to someone so that they can consider it, or the document, plan, etc that you send *The deadline for submissions is 29 April.*

submissive /səb'mɪsɪv/ *adjective* always doing what other people tell you to do *a quiet, submissive wife*

submit /səb'mɪt/ *verb* **submitting**, *past* **submitted** **1** [T] to send a document, plan, etc to someone so that they can consider it *Applications must be submitted before 31 January.* **2** [I] to accept that someone has control over you and do what they tell you to do *He was forced to submit to a full body search.*

subordinate¹ /sə'bɔːdˀnət/ *adjective* less important or lower in rank *a subordinate position/role* ○ *An individual's needs are subordinate to those of the group.*

subordinate² /sə'bɔːdˀnət/ *noun* [C] someone who has a less important position than someone else in an organization

subordinate³ /sə'bɔːdɪneɪt/ *verb* [T] *formal* to put someone or something into a less important position ● **subordination** /səˌbɔːdɪ'neɪʃˀn/ *noun* [U]

sub,ordinate 'clause *noun* [C] in grammar, a clause which cannot form a separate sentence but adds information to the main clause

subpoena /səb'piːnə/ *noun* [C] a legal document ordering someone to go to court ● **subpoena** *verb* [T] to give someone a subpoena

subscribe /səb'skraɪb/ *verb* [I] to pay money to an organization so that you regularly receive a service or product, such as a magazine or newspaper *to subscribe to a magazine/an internet service* ● **subscriber** *noun* [C]
subscribe to sth *formal* to agree with an opinion, belief, etc *I certainly don't subscribe to the view that women are morally superior to men.*

cancel/pay/take out a subscription ● a subscription **to** sth ● an **annual** subscription

subscription /səb'skrɪpʃˀn/ *noun* [C] an amount of money that you pay regularly to receive a product or service or to be a member of an organization *an annual subscription*

subsequent /'sʌbsɪkwənt/ *adjective* [always before noun] happening after something else

The mistakes were corrected in a subsequent edition of the book. ● **subsequently** *adverb*

subservient /səb'sɜːviənt/ *adjective* always doing what other people want you to do

subside /səb'saɪd/ *verb* [I] **1** to become less strong or extreme *The violence seems to be subsiding at last.* **2** If a building subsides, it sinks down to a lower level.

subsidence /səb'saɪdˀns/ *noun* [U] when buildings subside or land sinks down to a lower level

subsidiary /səb'sɪdiˀri/ *noun* [C] a company which is owned by another larger company

subsidize (*also UK* **-ise**) /'sʌbsɪdaɪz/ *verb* [T] If a government or other organization subsidizes something, it pays part of the cost of it, so that prices are reduced. *We have a subsidized restaurant at work.*

subsidy /'sʌbsɪdi/ *noun* [C] money given by a government or other organization to pay part of the cost of something *housing subsidies for the poor*

subsist /səb'sɪst/ *verb* [I] to manage to live when you only have a very small amount of food or money ● **subsistence** *noun* [U]

a **dangerous/hazardous/toxic** substance ● a **powdery/sticky/waxy** substance

o-**substance** /'sʌbstˀns/ *noun* **1** [C] a solid, liquid, or gas *a dangerous substance* ○ *illegal substances* (= illegal drugs) **2** [U] truth or importance *There's no substance to the allegations.* **3 the substance of sth** the most important part of what someone has said or written

substandard /ˌsʌb'stændəd/ *adjective* Something that is substandard is not as good as it should be. *substandard conditions/housing*

substantial /səb'stænʃˀl/ *adjective* **1** large in amount *a substantial change/increase* ○ *a substantial amount of money/time* **2** large and strong *a substantial building* ⊃Opposite **insubstantial**.

substantially /səb'stænʃˀli/ *adverb* by a large amount *House prices are substantially higher in the south.*

substantiate /səb'stænʃieɪt/ *verb* [T] *formal* to provide facts which prove that something is true *His claims have never been substantiated.*

substantive /'sʌbstˀntɪv/ *adjective formal* important or serious *a substantive issue*

substitute¹ /'sʌbstɪtjuːt/ *noun* [C] someone or something that is used instead of another person or thing *Margarine can be used as a substitute for butter.* ○ *a substitute teacher*

substitute² /'sʌbstɪtjuːt/ *verb* **1** [T] to use someone or something instead of another person or thing *You can substitute pasta for the rice, if you prefer.* **2 substitute for sb** to do someone's job because they are not there *I'm substituting for her while she's on holiday.* ● **substitution** /ˌsʌbstɪ'tjuːʃˀn/ *noun* [C, U]

subsume /səb'sjuːm/ *verb* [T] *formal* to include someone or something as part of a larger group [often passive] *The company has been sub-*

sumed by a large US bank.

subterfuge /ˈsʌbtəfjuːdʒ/ *noun* [C, U] *formal* a trick or a dishonest way of achieving something *They obtained the information by subterfuge.*

subterranean /ˌsʌbtəˈreɪniən/ *adjective* under the ground *subterranean passages*

subtitles /ˈsʌbˌtaɪtlz/ *noun* [plural] words shown at the bottom of a cinema or television screen to explain what is being said *It's a French film with English subtitles.*

subtle /ˈsʌtl/ *adjective* 1 [NOT OBVIOUS] not obvious or easy to notice *a subtle change/difference* ○ *a subtle hint* 2 [NOT STRONG] A subtle flavour, colour, etc is delicate and not strong or bright. 3 [CLEVER] clever in a way that does not attract attention *a subtle way of solving the problem* • **subtly** *adverb*

subtlety /ˈsʌtlti/ *noun* 1 [U] the quality of being subtle 2 [C] something that is subtle

subtract /səbˈtrækt/ *verb* [T] to take a number or amount away from another number or amount *You need to subtract 25% from the final figure.* • **subtraction** /səbˈtrækʃən/ *noun* [C, U]

suburb /ˈsʌbɜːb/ *noun* [C] an area where people live outside the centre of a city *a suburb of New York* • **suburban** /səˈbɜːbən/ *adjective* relating to a suburb *a suburban area/home*

suburbia /səˈbɜːbiə/ *noun* [U] the suburbs of towns and cities generally

subversive /səbˈvɜːsɪv/ *adjective* trying to destroy the authority of a government, religion, etc *subversive literature* • **subversive** *noun* [C] someone who is subversive

subvert /səbˈvɜːt/ *verb* [T] *formal* to try to destroy the authority of a government, religion, etc *a plot to subvert the government* • **subversion** /səbˈvɜːʃən/ *noun* [U] *formal*

subway /ˈsʌbweɪ/ *noun* [C] 1 *UK* (*UK/US* **underpass**) a passage under a road or railway for people to walk through 2 *US* (*UK* **underground**) a system of trains that travel underground *We can take the subway to Grand Central Station.* ⊃See Common learner error at **metro.**

sub-zero /ˈsʌbˌzɪərəʊ/ *adjective* Sub-zero temperatures are temperatures below zero degrees.

◦**succeed** /səkˈsiːd/ *verb* 1 [I] to achieve what you are trying to achieve *She has the skill and determination to succeed.* ○ [+ in + doing sth] *He has finally succeeded in passing his exams.* 2 [T] to take an official job or position after someone else *The Queen was succeeded by her eldest son when she died.*

succeed

Remember that **succeed** is often followed by the preposition **in** + doing sth. It is not used with 'to do sth'.
Two prisoners succeeded in escaping.
~~Two prisoners succeeded to escape.~~

achieve/have success • the **key to/secret of** success • success **in** (doing) sth • **without** success

◦**success** /səkˈses/ *noun* 1 [U] when you achieve what you want to achieve *Her success is due to hard work and determination.* 2 [C] something that has a good result or that is very popular *His first film was a great success.*

success

Be careful to choose the correct verb with this noun.
The evening was a great success.
They tried for weeks but had little success.
They are determined to make a success of the scheme.
~~She reached success as a writer.~~

◦**successful** /səkˈsesfəl/ *adjective* 1 [ACHIEVEMENT] achieving what you want to achieve *If the operation is successful, she should be walking within a few months.* 2 [WORK] having achieved a lot or made a lot of money through your work *a successful businessman* 3 [POPULAR] very popular *a successful book/film* ⊃Opposite **unsuccessful.** • **successfully** *adverb*

succession /səkˈseʃən/ *noun* 1 [no plural] a number of similar events or people that happen, exist, etc after each other *to suffer a succession of injuries* ○ *a succession of boyfriends* 2 **in quick/rapid succession** If several things happen in quick/rapid succession, they happen very quickly after each other. *She had her first three children in quick succession.* 3 [U] when someone takes an official position or job after someone else

successive /səkˈsesɪv/ *adjective* happening after each other *He has just won the World Championship for the third successive year.*

appoint/choose/find a successor • a **natural/worthy** successor • a successor **to** sb

successor /səkˈsesər/ *noun* [C] 1 someone who has a position or job after someone else *He is her most likely successor.* 2 an organization, product, etc that follows and takes the place of an earlier one

succinct /səkˈsɪŋkt/ *adjective* said in a very clear way using only a few words *a succinct explanation* • **succinctly** *adverb*

succulent /ˈsʌkjələnt/ *adjective* If food is succulent, it is good to eat because it has a lot of juice. *a succulent piece of meat*

succumb /səˈkʌm/ *verb* [I] *formal* 1 to not be able to stop yourself doing something *I succumbed to temptation and had some cheesecake.* 2 to die or suffer badly from an illness

◦**such** /sʌtʃ/ *pronoun, determiner* 1 used to refer to something or someone that you were just talking about, or something or someone of that type *It's difficult to know how to treat such cases.* 2 used to emphasize a quality of someone or something *She's such a nice person.* ○ *It's such a shame that he's leaving.* **3 such as** for example *She can't eat dairy products, such as milk and cheese.* **4 as such** used after a word or phrase in negative statements to mean in the exact meaning of that word or phrase *There are no rules as such, just a few guidelines.* **5 such...that** used to talk about the result of something *The whole thing was such a worry that I began to lose sleep over it.* **6 there's no such thing/person (as)...** used to say that something or someone does not exist *There's no such thing as ghosts.*

such-and-such /'sʌtʃ°nsʌtʃ/ *determiner informal* used instead of referring to a particular or exact thing *If they tell you to arrive at such-and-such a time, get there a couple of minutes before.*

suck /sʌk/ *verb* **1** [I, T] to have something in your mouth and use your tongue, lips, etc to pull on it or to get liquid, air, etc out of it *to suck a sweet/lollipop* ○ *to suck your thumb* **2 suck sth in/under/up, etc** to pull something somewhere using the force of moving air, water, etc *He was sucked under the boat and drowned.* **3 be sucked into sth** to become involved in something bad when you do not want to **4 he/it/this, etc sucks!** *US very informal* If someone or something sucks, they are bad or unpleasant.

suck up to sb *very informal* to try to make someone who is in authority like you by doing and saying things that will please them

sucker /'sʌkə°/ *noun* [C] **1** *informal* someone who believes everything that you tell them and is easy to deceive **2** something that helps an animal or object stick to a surface

suction /'sʌkʃ°n/ *noun* [U] when something is forced into a container or space by removing air

o→**sudden** /'sʌd°n/ *adjective* **1** done or happening quickly and unexpectedly *a sudden change/increase* ○ *His sudden death was a great shock to us all.* **2 all of a sudden** unexpectedly *All of a sudden she got up and walked out.* ● **suddenness** *noun* [U]

,sudden ,infant 'death ,syndrome *noun* [U] SIDS

o→**suddenly** /'sʌd°nli/ *adverb* quickly and unexpectedly *I suddenly realized who she was.* ○ *It all happened so suddenly that I can't remember much about it.*

Sudoku /,suː'dəʊkuː/ (*also* **Su Doku**) *noun* [C, U] a number game in which you have to write a number between 1 and 9 in each small box of a 9x9 square

suds /sʌdz/ *noun* [plural] small bubbles made from soap and water

sue /suː/ *verb* [I, T] suing *past* sued to take legal action against someone and try to get money from them because they have harmed you *He's threatening to sue the newspaper for slander.*

suede /sweɪd/ *noun* [U] leather that has a slightly rough surface

o→**suffer** /'sʌfə°/ *verb* **1** [I, T] to experience pain or unpleasant emotions *I can't bear to see animals suffering.* **2 suffer from sth** to have an illness or other health problem *She suffers*

from severe depression. **3 suffer a broken leg/a heart attack, etc** to experience an injury or other sudden health problem *He suffered a serious neck injury in the accident.* **4 suffer damage/defeat/loss, etc** to experience something bad such as damage/defeat/loss, etc **5** [I] to become worse in quality *If you're tired all the time your work tends to suffer.*

sufferer /'sʌfərə°/ *noun* [C] someone who suffers from an illness or other health problem *AIDS/cancer sufferers*

WORD PARTNERS FOR **suffering**

create/endure/relieve suffering • human suffering • unnecessary/unspeakable suffering • the suffering of sb

suffering /'sʌfərɪŋ/ *noun* [U] when someone experiences pain or unpleasant emotions *human suffering*

suffice /sə'faɪs/ *verb* [I] *formal* to be enough *You don't need to give a long speech - a few sentences will suffice.*

sufficient /sə'fɪʃ°nt/ *adjective* as much as is necessary *She didn't have sufficient time to answer all the questions.* ⊃Opposite **insufficient**. ● **sufficiently** *adverb I was sufficiently close to hear what they were saying.* ⊃See also: **self-sufficient**.

suffix /'sʌfɪks/ *noun* [C] a group of letters that you add to the end of a word to make another word. In the word 'slowly', '-ly' is a suffix. ⊃Compare **prefix**.

suffocate /'sʌfəkeɪt/ *verb* [I, T] to die because you cannot breathe or to kill someone by stopping them from breathing *He suffocated her with a pillow.* ● **suffocation** /,sʌfə'keɪʃ°n/ *noun* [U]

o→**sugar** /'ʃʊgə°/ *noun* **1** [U] a very sweet substance used to give flavour to food and drinks *coffee with milk and sugar* **2** [C] a spoon of sugar in a cup of tea or coffee *He likes two sugars in his tea.*

o→**suggest** /sə'dʒest/ *verb* [T] **1** IDEA to express an idea or plan for someone to consider [+ (that)] *I suggest that we park the car here and walk into town.* ○ [+ doing sth] *He suggested having the meeting at his house.* **2** ADVICE to say that someone or something is suitable for something *to suggest someone for a job* ○ *Can you suggest a good hotel?* **3** SEEM TRUE to make something seem likely to be true *All the evidence suggests that she did it.*

WORD PARTNERS FOR **suggestion**

bristle at/deny/make/reject/welcome a suggestion • an alternative/constructive/ helpful/ridiculous/sensible suggestion • at sb's suggestion

o→**suggestion** /sə'dʒestʃ°n/ *noun* **1** [C] an idea or plan that someone suggests *to make a suggestion* ○ *Have you got any suggestions for improvements?* **2 a suggestion of/that sth** something that makes something seem likely to be true *There's no suggestion of any connection between the two men.* **3 at sb's suggestion** following the advice that someone has given you *We went to that restaurant at Paul's suggestion.*

A suggestion about what to do is sometimes described as a **thought** or **idea**: *Rebecca has a few **ideas** about how we could improve things.* • *I've had a **thought** about what we might do this summer.*

If someone suggests a plan or action, especially in business, you can use nouns such as **proposal** or **proposition**: *The **proposal** for a new sports hall has been rejected.* • *He wrote to me with a very interesting business **proposition**.*

suggestive /sə'dʒestɪv/ *adjective* **1** making you think about sex *suggestive comments/remarks* **2 suggestive of sth** *formal* similar to something and making you think about it *The shapes are suggestive of human forms.* • **suggestively** *adverb*

suicidal /ˌsuːɪ'saɪdºl/ *adjective* **1** so unhappy that you want to kill yourself *to feel suicidal* **2** likely to have an extremely bad result *a suicidal decision*

suicide /'suːɪsaɪd/ *noun* **1** [C, U] when you intentionally kill yourself *He committed suicide after a long period of depression.* **2** [U] when you do something that will have an extremely bad result for you *political suicide*

'suicide ˌbomber *noun* [C] a person who has a bomb hidden on their body and who kills themselves in the attempt to kill others

○**suit**[1] /suːt/ *noun* [C] **1** a jacket and trousers or a jacket and skirt that are made from the same material *She wore a dark blue suit.* ⊃See colour picture **Clothes** on page Centre 8. **2** one of the four types of cards with different shapes on them in a set of playing cards **3 follow suit** to do the same as someone else has just done *If other shops lower their prices, we will have to follow suit.* ⊃See also: **bathing suit**, **pant suit**, **trouser suit**, **wet suit**.

○**suit**[2] /suːt/ *verb* [T] **1** to make someone look more attractive *Green really suits you.* **2** to be acceptable or right for someone *It would suit me better if we left a bit earlier.* ⊃See Common learner error at **fit**. **3 be suited to/for sth** to be right for someone or something *These plants are better suited to a warm climate.* ⊃See also: suit sb down to the **ground**[1].

○**suitable** /'suːtəbl/ *adjective* acceptable or right for someone or something *a suitable time to call* ○ *This film is **suitable** for children.* ⊃Opposite **unsuitable**. • **suitably** *adverb* *suitably dressed*

A common alternative to 'suitable' is the adjective **appropriate**: *Is this film **appropriate** for young children?* • *You should bring **appropriate** footwear.*

If an action is suitable for a particular situation, you can use the adjectives **apt** or **fitting**: *'Unusual', yes, that's a very **apt** description.* • *The promotion was a **fitting** reward for all his hard work.*

The adjective **right** can also be used to show

that someone or something is suitable for a particular situation: *I'm not sure that she's the **right** person for the job.* • *Is this the **right** way to do it?*

If someone or something is very suitable, you can use the adjective **perfect**: *It's a **perfect** day for a picnic.* • *She'd be **perfect** for the job.*

The expression **in keeping with** is sometimes used when something is suitable for a particular style or tradition: *The antique desk was very much **in keeping with** the rest of the furniture in the room.*

suitcase /'suːtkeɪs/ *noun* [C] a rectangular case with a handle that you use for carrying clothes when you are travelling *to pack your suitcase* ⊃See picture at **luggage**.

suite /swiːt/ *noun* [C] **1** several pieces of furniture which go together *a bedroom suite* **2** a set of hotel rooms which are used together ⊃See also: **en suite**.

suitor /'suːtər/ *noun* [C] *old-fashioned* a man who wants to marry a particular woman

sulfur /'sʌlfər/ *noun* [U] *US spelling of* sulphur

sulk /sʌlk/ *verb* [I] to look unhappy and not speak to anyone because you are angry about something *He's upstairs sulking in his bedroom.* • **sulky** *adjective a sulky teenager*

sullen /'sʌlən/ *adjective* in an unpleasant mood and not smiling or speaking to anyone

sulphur *UK* (*US* sulfur) /'sʌlfər/ *noun* [U] a yellow chemical element that has an unpleasant smell

sultan /'sʌltºn/ *noun* [C] a ruler in some Muslim countries

sultana /sʌl'tɑːnə/ *noun* [C] *UK* a dried grape (= small round fruit) often used in cakes

sultry /'sʌltri/ *adjective* **1** If a woman is sultry, she behaves in a sexually attractive way. *a sultry voice* **2** If the weather is sultry, it is hot and wet. *a sultry summer night*

○**sum**[1] /sʌm/ *noun* [C] **1** MONEY an amount of money *a large/small sum of money* **2** MATHS *UK* a simple mathematical calculation such as adding two numbers together *Kids these days can't do sums without a calculator.* **3** TOTAL the total amount that you get when you add two or more numbers together *The sum of six and seven is thirteen.* ⊃See also: **lump sum**.

sum[2] /sʌm/ *verb* summing, *past* summed

sum (sth/sb) up to describe briefly the important facts or characteristics of something or someone *The purpose of a conclusion is to sum up the main points of an essay.*

sum sth/sb up to quickly decide what you think about something or someone *I think she summed up the situation very quickly.*

summarize (*also UK* -ise) /'sʌmºraɪz/ *verb* [I, T] to describe briefly the main facts or ideas of something

summary[1] /'sʌmºri/ *noun* [C] a short description that gives the main facts or ideas about something *He **gave a** brief **summary of** what happened.*

WORD PARTNERS FOR **summary** (noun)

give/produce/provide a summary • a
brief/quick/short summary • a summary
of sth

summary² /'sʌməri/ *adjective* [always before noun]
formal decided or done quickly, without the
usual discussions or legal arrangements *a
summary arrest/execution*

WORD PARTNERS FOR **summer**

in (the) summer • last/next summer
• early/late summer • the summer **months**

o→**summer** /'sʌmər/ *noun* [C, U] the season of the
year between spring and autumn, when the
weather is warmest *We usually go away in the
summer.* ○ *a long, hot summer* • **summery** *adjective* typical of or suitable for summer

,summer 'holiday (*US* summer vacation) *noun*
[C] the time during the summer when you do
not have to go to school

'summer ,school *noun* [C] an educational
course that happens during the summer when
other courses have finished

summertime /'sʌmətaɪm/ *noun* [U] when it is
summer *In the summertime, we often eat outside.*

summit /'sʌmɪt/ *noun* [C] **1** an important meeting between the leaders of two or more governments *a two-day summit* ○ *a summit meeting*
2 the top of a mountain *The climbers hope to
reach the summit before nightfall.*

summon /'sʌmən/ *verb* [T] **1** *formal* to officially
order someone to come to a place *He was sum-
moned to a meeting.* **2 summon (up) the cour-
age/strength, etc** to make a great effort to do
something [+ to do sth] *He tried to summon up
the courage to speak to her.*

summons /'sʌmənz/ *noun* [C] an official order
saying that you must go to a court of law

Sun *written abbreviation for* Sunday

o→**sun¹** /sʌn/ *noun* **1 the sun** the large, bright star
that shines in the sky during the day and provides light and heat for the Earth **2** [U, no plural]
the light and heat that comes from the sun *I
can't sit in the sun for too long.*

sun² /sʌn/ *verb* sunning, *past* sunned **sun yourself** to
sit or lie in the sun *She was sitting on the deck
sunning herself.*

sunbathe /'sʌnbeɪð/ *verb* [I] to sit or lie in the
sun so that your skin becomes brown • **sun-
bathing** *noun* [U]

sunbed /'sʌnbed/ (*US* tanning bed) *noun* [C] a
piece of equipment with a flat area like a bed
and a strong light, which you lie on in order to
make your skin go darker

sunblock /'sʌnblɒk/ *noun* [C, U] sunscreen

sunburn /'sʌnbɜːn/ *noun* [U] when your skin becomes painful and red from being in the sun
too long • **sunburnt** (*also* sunburned) *adjective*

sundae /'sʌndeɪ/ *noun* [C] a sweet dish made of
ice cream with fruit and nuts

o→**Sunday** /'sʌndeɪ/ (*written abbreviation* Sun)
noun [C, U] the day of the week after Saturday
and before Monday

sundry /'sʌndri/ *adjective* **1** [always before noun] of
different types *sundry items* **2** all and sundry
UK informal (*US* various and sundry) everyone *I
don't want all and sundry knowing about my
problems.*

sunflower /'sʌnflaʊər/ *noun* [C] a tall, yellow
flower with a large, black centre full of seeds

sung /sʌŋ/ *past participle of* sing

sunglasses /'sʌnˌglɑːsɪz/ *noun* [plural] dark
glasses that you wear to protect your eyes
from the sun ⊃See colour picture **Clothes** on page
Centre 9.

sunk /sʌŋk/ **1** *past participle of* sink **2** *US past
tense of* sink

sunken /'sʌŋkən/ *adjective* [always before noun]
1 at a lower level than the surrounding area *a
sunken bath* **2** having fallen down to the
bottom of the sea *a sunken ship* **3 sunken eyes/
cheeks** eyes or cheeks that make you look ill
because they go too far into your face

sunlight /'sʌnlaɪt/ *noun* [U] the light from the sun

sunlit /'sʌnlɪt/ *adjective* [always before noun] A
sunlit place is bright because of light from the
sun. *a sunlit room*

'sun ,lotion *noun* [C, U] sunscreen

Sunni /'sʊni/ *noun* [C] a member of a large group
within the Islamic religion • **Sunni** *adjective* describing the Sunni or their type of Islam

sunny /'sʌni/ *adjective* **1** bright because of light
from the sun *a lovely sunny day* **2** behaving in
a happy way *a sunny smile/personality*

sunrise /'sʌnraɪz/ *noun* [C, U] when the sun
appears in the morning and the sky becomes
light

sunroof /'sʌnruːf/ *noun* [C] part of a roof of a
car which you open to allow air and light from
the sun to come in

sunscreen /'sʌnskriːn/ *noun* [C, U] a substance
that protects your skin in the sun

sunset /'sʌnset/ *noun* [C, U] when the sun disappears in the evening and the sky becomes
dark

sunshine /'sʌnʃaɪn/ *noun* [U] the light from the
sun *Let's sit over there in the sunshine.*

sunstroke /'sʌnstrəʊk/ *noun* [U] an illness
caused by spending too much time in the sun

suntan /'sʌntæn/ (*also* tan) *noun* [C] when your
skin is brown from being in the sun *suntan oil*
• **suntanned** (*also* tanned) *adjective*

super /'suːpər/ *adjective, adverb informal, old-
fashioned* very good *We had a super time.*

super- /suːpər-/ *prefix* extremely or more than
usual *a supermodel* ○ *super-rich*

superb /suː'pɜːb/ *adjective* excellent *a superb
performance/restaurant* • **superbly** *adverb*

superbug /'suːpəbʌg/ *noun* [C] a type of bacteria (= very small living things that cause disease) that is very difficult to destroy

superficial /ˌsuːpə'fɪʃ³l/ *adjective* **1** NOT SERIOUS
If someone is superficial, they never think
about things that are serious or important.
2 NOT COMPLETE not complete and involving
only the most obvious things *superficial
knowledge* ○ *a superficial resemblance*
3 NOT DEEP only on the surface of something

S

superficial damage/injuries ● **superficially** *adverb*

superfluous /suː'pɜːfluəs/ *adjective* not needed, or more than is needed *superfluous details/information*

superhuman /ˌsuːpə'hjuːmən/ *adjective* **superhuman effort/strength, etc** more effort/strength, etc than a normal human being

superimpose /ˌsuːpᵊrɪm'pəʊz/ *verb* [T] to put an image, text, etc over something so that the thing under it can still be seen

superintendent /ˌsuːpᵊrɪn'tendənt/ *noun* [C] **1** in Britain, a police officer of high rank **2** in the US, an official responsible for a place, event, etc

superior¹ /suː'pɪəriər/ *adjective* **1** better than other things *superior quality* ○ *This car is far superior to the others.* **2** thinking that you are better than other people *She has a very superior manner.*

superior² /suː'pɪəriər/ *noun* [C] someone in a higher position than you at work *I will have to report this to my superiors.*

superiority /suːˌpɪəri'ɒrəti/ *noun* [U] **1** when something is better than other things *the superiority of modern design* **2** when you think that you are better than other people *She has an air of superiority.*

superlative /suː'pɜːlətɪv/ *noun* [C] the form of an adjective or adverb that is used to show that someone or something has more of a particular quality than anyone or anything else. For example 'best' is the superlative of 'good' and 'slowest' is the superlative of 'slow'. ⊃Compare **comparative**.

⊶**supermarket** /'suːpəˌmɑːkɪt/ *noun* [C] a large shop that sells food, drink, products for the home, etc

supermodel /'suːpəˌmɒdᵊl/ *noun* [C] a very famous model (= someone whose job is to wear fashionable clothes for photographs)

the supernatural /ˌsuːpə'nætʃᵊrᵊl/ *noun* things that cannot be explained by our knowledge of science or nature ● **supernatural** *adjective* **supernatural forces/powers**

superpower /'suːpəˌpaʊər/ *noun* [C] a country that has great military and political power in the world

supersede /ˌsuːpə'siːd/ *verb* [T] to take the place of someone or something that went before [often passive] *Records were superseded by CDs.*

supersonic /ˌsuːpə'sɒnɪk/ *adjective* faster than the speed of sound *supersonic aircraft*

superstar /'suːpəstɑːr/ *noun* [C] a very famous singer, performer, etc

superstition /ˌsuːpə'stɪʃᵊn/ *noun* [C, U] when someone believes that particular actions or objects are lucky or unlucky

superstitious /ˌsuːpə'stɪʃəs/ *adjective* believing that particular objects or events are lucky or unlucky *Are you superstitious about the number 13?*

superstore /'suːpəstɔːr/ *noun* [C] a very large shop that sells many different things, often outside a town

supervise /'suːpəvaɪz/ *verb* [I, T] to watch a person or activity and make certain that everything is done correctly, safely, etc *Students must be supervised by a teacher at all times.* ● **supervisor** *noun* [C] someone who supervises

WORD PARTNERS FOR **supervision**

be **under** supervision ● **close/constant** supervision ● the supervision **of** sb/sth

supervision /ˌsuːpə'vɪʒᵊn/ *noun* [U] when you supervise someone or something *He needs constant supervision.*

supper /'sʌpər/ *noun* [C] a meal that you eat in the evening *What are we having for supper?*

supplant /sə'plɑːnt/ *verb* [T] *formal* to take the place of someone or something

supple /'sʌpl/ *adjective* able to bend or move easily *a supple body*

supplement /'sʌplɪmənt/ *noun* [C] an extra amount or part added to something *to take a vitamin supplement* ○ *a newspaper with a colour supplement* ● **supplement** /'sʌplɪment/ *verb* [T] *She works part-time to supplement her pension.*

supplementary /ˌsʌplɪ'mentᵊri/ (*also US* **supplemental**) *adjective* added to something *supplementary materials*

supplier /sə'plaɪər/ *noun* [C] someone who provides things that people want or need, often over a long period of time

supplies /sə'plaɪz/ *noun* [plural] the food, equipment, etc that is needed for a particular activity, holiday, etc

⊶**supply¹** /sə'plaɪ/ *verb* [T] to provide things that people want or need, often over a long period of time *to supply food/drugs to people* ○ *This lake supplies the whole town with water.*

WORD PARTNERS FOR **supply** (noun)

a supply **of** sth ● a **constant/endless/plentiful** supply

⊶**supply²** /sə'plaɪ/ *noun* **1** [C] an amount of something that is ready to be used *a supply of water* ○ *food supplies* **2 in short supply** If something is in short supply, there is little of it available. **3** [C] the system of supplying something to people *Someone has turned off the electricity supply.*

⊶**support¹** /sə'pɔːt/ *verb* **1** AGREE to agree with an idea, group, or person *Do you support their views on nuclear weapons?* **2** PROVE to help to show that something is true *There's no evidence to support his story.* **3** HOLD to hold the weight of someone or something *Is this ladder strong enough to support me?* **4** PAY to look after someone by paying for their food, clothes, etc *She has three children to support.* **5** SPORT *mainly UK* to like a particular sports team and want them to win *Who do you support?*

WORD PARTNERS FOR **support** (noun)

enlist/express/give/lose/rally support ● **overwhelming/public/strong/tacit/widespread** support ● support **for** sb/sth o-**support²** /sə'pɔ:t/ *noun* **1** [AGREEMENT] [U] agreement with an idea, group or person *Is there much public support for the death penalty?* **2 in support of sb/sth** agreeing with someone or something *The minister spoke in support of military action.* **3** [HELP] [U] help or encouragement *emotional/financial support* **4** [OBJECT] [C] an object that can hold the weight of something ⊃See also: **child support, income support, moral support.**

> **WORD PARTNERS FOR *supporter***
>
> a **keen/loyal/staunch/strong** supporter • a supporter **of** sth

supporter /sə'pɔ:təʳ/ *noun* [C] **1** someone who supports a particular idea, group, or person *a strong supporter of the government* **2** *mainly UK* someone who likes a particular sports team and wants them to win *English football supporters*

supportive /sə'pɔ:tɪv/ *adjective* giving help or encouragement *a very supportive friend*

o-**suppose** /sə'pəʊz/ *verb* **1 be supposed to do sth a** to be expected or intended to do something, especially when this does not happen *These drugs are supposed to reduce the pain.* ○ *He was supposed to be here by nine.* **b** If you are supposed to do something, the rules say that you should do it. *You're supposed to pay by the end of the month.* ○ *You're not supposed to* (= you should not) *smoke in here.* **2 be supposed to be sth** to be considered by many people to be something *The scenery is supposed to be fantastic.* **3** [T] to think that something is likely to be true [+ (that)] *I suppose that you've already heard the news.* **4 suppose/supposing (that)** used to introduce an idea for someone to consider *Suppose he phones tonight. What should I say?* **5 I suppose** used to show that you are not certain or not completely happy about something *It was quite interesting, I suppose.* **6 I suppose so** used to show agreement to something when you do not really want to *"Can I come with you?" "I suppose so."*

supposed /sə'pəʊzɪd/ *adjective* [always before noun] used to show that you do not believe that someone or something really is what many people consider them to be *a supposed genius* • **supposedly** /sə'pəʊzɪdli/ *adverb The building is supposedly in good condition.*

supposition /ˌsʌpə'zɪʃᵊn/ *noun* [C, U] *formal* when someone believes that something is true although there is no proof

suppress /sə'pres/ *verb* [T] **1** [FEELINGS] to control feelings so that they do not show *I could barely suppress my anger.* **2** [INFORMATION] to prevent information from being known *to suppress evidence/news* **3** [FIGHT] to stop someone or something by using force [often passive] *The rebellion was suppressed by government forces.* • **suppression** /sə'preʃᵊn/ *noun* [U]

supremacy /su:'preməsi/ *noun* [U] when a country or group of people is more powerful, successful, etc than anyone else *a battle/struggle for supremacy*

supreme /su:'pri:m/ *adjective* **1** of the highest rank or greatest importance *the supreme ruler* **2** very great *supreme confidence/effort* • **supremely** *adverb* very *supremely confident*

the su,preme 'court *noun* the court of law that has the most authority in a state or country

surcharge /'sɜ:tʃɑ:dʒ/ *noun* [C] an extra amount of money that you have to pay for something *There is a surcharge for single rooms.*

o-**sure** /ʃɔ:ʳ/ *adjective* **1** [never before noun] certain [+ (that)] *I'm sure that he won't mind.* ○ [+ question word] *She's not sure what she's going to do next.* ○ *I'm quite sure about the second answer.* ⊃Opposite **unsure**. **2 make sure (that)** to take action so that you are certain that something happens, is true, etc *Make sure that you close all the windows before you leave.* **3 be sure of sth** to be confident that something is true *He'll win, I'm sure of it.* **4 for sure** without any doubts *I think he's from Korea but don't know for sure.* **5 be sure of yourself** to be confident of your own abilities, qualities, etc *She's always been very sure of herself.* **6 be sure to do sth a** If you are sure to do something, it is certain that you will do it. *He's sure to go back there again.* **b** used to tell someone what they must remember to do *Be sure to tell her I called.* **7 a sure sign of/that sth** something that makes something seem certain to be true **8 a sure thing** something that is certain to happen *Death is the one sure thing about life.* **9 sure** (*also US* **sure thing**) used to show agreement *"Can I borrow your pen please?" "Sure."* **10 sure enough** as expected *He said the book was on his desk, and sure enough, there it was.*

o-**surely** /'ʃɔ:li/ *adverb* used to express surprise that something has happened or is going to happen *You surely didn't tell him, did you?* ○ *Surely you're not going to go out dressed like that?*

surf¹ /sɜ:f/ *verb* **1** [I] to ride on a wave in the sea using a special board **2 surf the Internet/Net/Web** to look at information on the Internet by moving from one page to another using electronic links (= connections) ⊃See Extra help page **The Web and the Internet** on page Centre 36. • **surfer** *noun* [C] someone who surfs • **surfing** *noun* [U]

surf² /sɜ:f/ *noun* [U] the top of the waves in the sea as it moves onto the coast

> **WORD PARTNERS FOR *surface***
>
> a **flat/hard/level/smooth/uneven** surface • **cover** the surface • **above/below/beneath/on** the surface

o-**surface¹** /'sɜ:fɪs/ *noun* **1** [C] the top or outside part of something *the Earth's surface* ○ *The sun was reflected on the surface of the water.* **2** [no plural] what someone or something seems to be like when you do not know much about them *On the surface he seemed very pleasant.* ⊃See also: **work surface.**

surface² /'sɜ:fɪs/ *verb* **1** [APPEAR] [I] to appear or become public, often after being hidden *This problem first surfaced about two weeks ago.* ○ *So when did these allegations surface?* **2** [RISE] [I] to rise to the surface of water *The submarine surfaced a few miles off the coast.*

3 [COVER] [T] to cover a road with a hard substance

'surface ,mail *noun* [U] letters, parcels, etc that are sent by road, sea, or train and not by aircraft

surfboard /'sɜːfbɔːd/ *noun* [C] a long piece of wood or plastic that you use to ride on waves in the sea

surfeit /'sɜːfɪt/ *noun* [no plural] *formal* too much of something *We've had a surfeit of applications from women for this job.*

surfing /'sɜːfɪŋ/ *noun* [U] **1** the sport of riding on a wave on a special board **2** the activity of looking at a lot of different things on the Internet

surge¹ /sɜːdʒ/ *verb* **1 surge forward/into/ through, etc** to move somewhere with great strength *The crowd surged against the barriers.* **2** [I] to increase very quickly *Prices surged on the stock exchange.*

surge² /sɜːdʒ/ *noun* [C] **1** a large increase in something *a surge in spending* **2** a sudden movement forward

surgeon /'sɜːdʒ³n/ *noun* [C] a doctor who does medical operations ➔See also: **veterinary surgeon.**

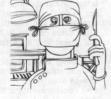
surgeon

surgery /'sɜːdʒ³ri/ *noun* **1** [U] when a doctor cuts your body open and repairs or removes something *to have surgery* ○ *heart/ knee surgery* **2** [C] *UK* a place where doctors or other medical workers treat people ➔See also: **plastic surgery.**

surgical /'sɜːdʒɪk³l/ *adjective* relating to medical operations *surgical instruments/gloves* • **surgically** *adverb*

surly /'sɜːli/ *adjective* unfriendly and rude *a surly teenager*

surmount /sə'maʊnt/ *verb* [T] *formal* to deal successfully with a problem

surname /'sɜːneɪm/ *noun* [C] the name that you and other members of your family all have *His surname is Walker.*

surpass /sə'pɑːs/ *verb* [T] *formal* to be or do better than someone or something else *The book's success surpassed everyone's expectations.*

surplus /'sɜːpləs/ *noun* [C, U] an amount of something that is more than you need *Every year we produce a huge surplus of meat.* • **surplus** *adjective surplus wheat*

o→ **surprise¹** /sə'praɪz/ *noun* **1** [C] an event that you did not expect to happen *I didn't know that my parents were coming - it was a lovely surprise.* ○ *Her resignation came as a complete surprise* (= was very surprising). ○ *a surprise party* **2** [U] the feeling that you get when something

happens that you did not expect *He agreed to everything, much to my surprise.* **3 take/catch sb by surprise** to be unexpected and make someone feel surprise *I wasn't expecting her to be so angry - it took me by surprise.*

surprise² /sə'praɪz/ *verb* [T] **1** to make someone feel surprise *I didn't tell her I was coming home early - I thought I'd surprise her.* **2** to find or attack someone when they are not expecting it

o→ **surprised** /sə'praɪzd/ *adjective* feeling surprise because something has happened that you did not expect [+ **to do sth**] *I'm surprised to see you here.* ○ *She wasn't surprised at his decision.* ○ [+ (that)] *I'm surprised that you've decided to leave.*

o→ **surprising** /sə'praɪzɪŋ/ *adjective* not expected and making someone feel surprised *It's not surprising you're putting on weight, the amount you're eating!* • **surprisingly** *adverb surprisingly good*

surreal /sə'rɪəl/ (*also* **surrealistic** /sə,rɪə'lɪstɪk/) *adjective* strange and not real, like something in a dream *His paintings have a surreal quality.*

surrender /s³r'endə'/ *verb* **1** [I] to stop fighting and admit that you have been beaten *Rebel troops are refusing to surrender.* **2** [T] *formal* to give something to someone else because you have been forced or officially asked to give it to them *He was released on the condition that he surrendered his passport.* • **surrender** *noun* [C, U]

surreptitious /,sʌrəp'tɪʃəs/ *adjective* done secretly so that other people do not see *surreptitious glances at the clock* • **surreptitiously** *adverb*

surrogate /'sʌrəgɪt/ *adjective* [always before noun] used instead of someone or something else *Twenty years older than her, he effectively became a surrogate father.* • **surrogate** *noun* [C] someone or something that is used instead of someone or something else *He seemed to* *regard her as a* **surrogate** *for his dead mother.*

surrogate 'mother *noun* [C] a woman who has a baby for a woman who is not able to have a baby herself

o⤐**surround** /səˈraʊnd/ *verb* [T] **1** to be or go everywhere around something or someone *The house is surrounded by a large garden.* ○ *The police have surrounded the building.* ○ *the surrounding countryside* **2 be surrounded by sb/sth** to have a lot of people or things near you *She's surrounded by the people she loves.* **3** If a feeling or situation surrounds an event, it is closely connected with it. *Mystery still surrounds the exact circumstances of his death.*

surroundings /səˈraʊndɪŋz/ *noun* [plural] the place where someone or something is and the things that are in it *Have you got used to your new surroundings?*

surveillance /sɜːˈveɪləns/ *noun* [U] when someone is watched carefully, especially by the police or army, because they are expected to do something wrong *The police have kept the man under strict surveillance.*

┌─────────────────────────────────┐
│ 🔧 WORD PARTNERS FOR *survey* │
└─────────────────────────────────┘

carry out/conduct/take part in a survey • a survey **finds/reveals/shows/suggests** sth • a survey **of** sth • **in** a survey • **according to** a survey • a **recent** survey

survey[1] /ˈsɜːveɪ/ *noun* [C] **1** [QUESTIONS] an examination of people's opinions or behaviour made by asking people questions *Holidays in the UK are becoming more popular, according to a recent survey.* **2** [BUILDING] *UK* an examination of the structure of a building in order to find out if there is anything wrong with it *The bank have refused a loan until we've had a survey done on the property.* **3** [LAND] when an area of land is looked at, and its measurements and details recorded, especially in order to make a map

survey[2] /səˈveɪ/ *verb* [T] **1** [EXAMINE] to look at or examine something carefully *I got out of the car to survey the damage.* **2** [QUESTION] to ask people questions in order to find out about their opinions or behaviour *75% of midwives surveyed were in favour of home births.* **3** [LAND] to measure and record the details of an area of land **4** [BUILDING] *UK* to examine the structure of a building in order to find out if there is anything wrong with it

surveyor /səˈveɪər/ *noun* [C] **1** *UK* someone whose job is to examine the structure of buildings **2** someone whose job is to measure and record the details of an area of land

survival /səˈvaɪvəl/ *noun* [U] when someone or something continues to live or exist, especially after a difficult or dangerous situation *Flood victims had to fight for survival.*

o⤐**survive** /səˈvaɪv/ *verb* **1** [NOT DIE] [I, T] to continue to live after almost dying because of an accident, illness, etc *He was born with a heart problem and only survived ten days.* ○ *No one survived the plane crash.* **2** [EXIST] [I, T] to continue to exist after being in a difficult or dangerous situation *Only two buildings survived the earthquake.* **3** [LIVE LONGER] [T] If you

survive someone, you continue to live after they have died.

survivor /səˈvaɪvər/ *noun* [C] someone who continues to live after almost dying because of an accident, illness, etc *Rescuers have given up hope of finding any more survivors.*

susceptible /səˈseptəbl/ *adjective* easily influenced or harmed by something *Older people are more susceptible to the virus.* ○ *a susceptible young teenager* • **susceptibility** /səˌseptəˈbɪləti/ *noun* [U] when someone is susceptible

sushi /ˈsuːʃi/ *noun* [U] Japanese food made of cold rice and fish which has not been cooked *a sushi bar*

┌─────────────────────────────────┐
│ 🔧 WORD PARTNERS FOR *suspect* │
└─────────────────────────────────┘

the **chief/main/prime** suspect • a suspect **for/in** sth

suspect[1] /ˈsʌspekt/ *noun* [C] **1** someone who may have committed a crime *He's the prime suspect* (= the most likely suspect) *in the murder case.* **2 the usual suspects** the people you would expect to be present somewhere or doing a particular thing *"Who was at the party?" "Oh, Adrian, John, Dave - the usual suspects."*

o⤐**suspect**[2] /səˈspekt/ *verb* [T] **1** [CRIME] to think that someone may have committed a crime or done something bad *He was suspected of drug dealing.* ○ *suspected terrorists* **2** [THINK LIKELY] to think that something is probably true, or is likely to happen [+ (that)] *They suspected that he was lying.* **3** [NOT TRUST] to not trust someone or something *She suspected his motives for offering to help.*

suspect[3] /ˈsʌspekt/ *adjective* difficult to trust or believe *His explanation was highly suspect.*

suspend /səˈspend/ *verb* [T] **1** to stop something happening for a short time *The semi-final was suspended because of bad weather.* **2 suspend sth from/between, etc** to hang something from somewhere [often passive] *A light bulb was suspended from the ceiling.* **3** to not allow someone to go to work or school for a period of time because they have done something wrong [often passive] *She was suspended from school for fighting.*

suspenders /səˈspendəz/ *noun* [plural] **1** *UK* (*US* garters) pieces of elastic fixed to a belt that hold up a woman's stockings (= very thin pieces of clothing that cover a woman's foot and leg) **2** *US* (*UK* braces) two straps fixed to a pair of trousers that go over your shoulders and stop the trousers from falling down

suspense /səˈspens/ *noun* [U] the feeling of excitement that you have when you are waiting for something to happen *What's your answer then? Don't keep me in suspense.*

suspension /səˈspenʃən/ *noun* **1** [STOP] [U] when someone stops something happening for a period of time *an immediate suspension of all imports and exports* **2** [JOB/SCHOOL] [C, U] when someone is not allowed to go to work or school for a period of time **3** [VEHICLE] [C, U] equipment which is fixed to the wheels of a vehicle in order to make it move more smoothly

S

WORD PARTNERS FOR *suspicion*

2 have a suspicion • **confirm** sb's suspicion
• a **deep/sneaking/strong** suspicion

suspicion /sə'spɪʃⁿn/ *noun* **1** [C, U] a feeling or belief that someone has done something wrong *They were arrested on suspicion of drug dealing.* ◦ *Several members of staff are under suspicion of stealing money.* **2** [C] an idea that something may be true [+ (that)] *I had a sneaking suspicion that the two events might be connected.*

suspicious /sə'spɪʃəs/ *adjective* **1** making you feel that something is wrong or that something bad or illegal is happening *suspicious behaviour/circumstances* ◦ *I called airport security after noticing a suspicious package.* **2** not trusting someone *Many of them remain suspicious of journalists.* • **suspiciously** *adverb She's been acting very suspiciously lately.*

sustain /sə'steɪn/ *verb* [T] **1** to cause or allow something to continue for a period of time *The team may not be able to sustain this level of performance.* **2** to support someone or something so that they can live or exist *The money he received was hardly enough to sustain a wife and five children.* **3 sustain damage/injuries/ losses** *formal* If someone or something sustains injuries, damage, losses, etc, they are injured, damaged, etc.

sustainable /sə'steɪnəbl/ *adjective* able to continue over a period of time *sustainable development/growth*

sustained /sə'steɪnd/ *adjective* continuing for a period of time without getting weaker *a sustained attack* ◦ *sustained pressure*

SUV /ˌesjuː'viː/ *noun* [C] *abbreviation for* sports utility vehicle: a large vehicle with an engine that supplies power to all four wheels, so that the vehicle can travel easily over rough ground

svelte /svelt/ *adjective* thin in an attractive way

swab /swɒb/ *noun* [C] a small piece of material used for cleaning an injury or for taking a small amount of a substance from someone's body so that it can be tested

swagger /'swæɡəʳ/ *verb* [I] to walk in a way that shows that you are confident and think that you are important *A group of young men swaggered around in leather jackets.* • **swagger** *noun* [no plural]

••→**swallow¹** /'swɒləʊ/ *verb* **1** FOOD OR DRINK [T] to move your throat in order to make food or drink go down *The snake swallowed the bird whole.* **2** THROAT [I] to make a movement with your throat as if you are eating, sometimes because you are nervous *Claire swallowed hard, opened the door and stepped inside.* **3** ACCEPT [T] to accept something unpleasant *They found the final decision hard to swallow.* **4** BELIEVE [T] *informal* to believe something, usually something which is not true *I told him we were journalists and he seemed to swallow it.* ⊃See also: swallow your **pride¹**.

swallow sth up to make something disappear *Many small businesses are being swallowed up by large international companies.*

swallow² /'swɒləʊ/ *noun* [C] **1** a small bird with

long, pointed wings and a tail with two points **2** the movement of swallowing

swam /swæm/ *past tense of* swim

swamp¹ /swɒmp/ *noun* [C, U] an area of very wet, soft land

swamp² /swɒmp/ *verb* [T] **1** to give someone more of something than they can deal with [often passive] *The company was swamped with calls about its new service.* ◦ *The market has been swamped by cheap imports.* **2** If an area is swamped, it becomes covered with water. *Heavy rain has swamped many villages in the region.*

swan /swɒn/ *noun* [C] a large, white bird with a long neck which lives on lakes and rivers

swap /swɒp/ *verb* [I, T] swapping, *past* swapped to give something to someone and get something from them in return *Would you mind if Dave swapped places with you for a bit?* • **swap** *noun* [C] *We'll do a swap.*

swarm¹ /swɔːm/ *noun* [C] a large group of things, usually insects, moving together *a swarm of bees*

swarm² /swɔːm/ *verb* [I] to move in a large group *TV reporters swarmed outside the pop star's home.*

swarm with sb/sth If a place is swarming with people, insects, etc, there are a lot of them moving around it. *The house was swarming with police.*

swarthy /'swɔːði/ *adjective* having dark skin

swat /swɒt/ *verb* [T] swatting, *past* swatted to hit something, especially an insect, with a flat object *He swatted a fly with his newspaper.*

sway /sweɪ/ *verb* **1** [I] to move slowly from one side to the other *The trees swayed gently in the wind.* **2** [T] to persuade someone to change their opinion or decision *I think I was swayed by what James said.*

••→**swear** /sweəʳ/ *verb past tense* swore, *past participle* sworn **1** BAD LANGUAGE [I] to use language which people think is rude or offensive *He was sent home because he swore at the teacher.* **2** PROMISE [I, T] to make a serious promise [+ to do sth] *I swear to tell the truth.* ◦ [+ (that)] *She swore that she was at home at the time of the accident.* **3** TRUE [T] used to say that you are sure something is true [+ (that)] *I could have sworn that she said she lived in Canterbury* (= I was sure she lived in Canterbury, but now I have found that it is not true).

swear by sth to believe strongly that something is useful or effective *Have you tried using vinegar to clean windows? My Mum swears by it.*

swear sb in to make someone such as a president, judge, etc officially promise to be honest and responsible when they start their job [often passive] *Mr Stein was sworn in as City Council president yesterday.*

swearing /'sweərɪŋ/ *noun* [U] using rude or offensive language *He was always getting into trouble for swearing.*

'swear ˌword *noun* [C] a word which people think is rude or offensive

sweat /swet/ *verb* [I] to produce liquid through

your skin because you are hot or nervous *I'd been running and I was sweating.* • **sweat** noun [U] *The sweat was running down his face.*

sweat it out *informal* to wait nervously for an unpleasant situation to improve or end *I don't get my exam results till the end of June so I'll just have to sweat it out till then.*

sweat over sth to work hard at something *She's been sweating over the preparations for the party all weekend.*

sweater /'swetəʳ/ (*also UK* **jumper**) *noun* [C] a warm piece of clothing which covers the top of your body and is pulled on over your head ➍See colour picture **Clothes** on page Centre 8.

sweats /swets/ *noun* [plural] *US* a sweatshirt and sweatpants (= loose, comfortable trousers), often worn for exercising ➍See colour picture **Clothes** on page Centre 9.

sweatshirt /'swetʃɜːt/ *noun* [C] a piece of clothing made of soft cotton which covers the top of your body and is pulled on over your head ➍See colour picture **Clothes** on page Centre 9.

sweatshop /'swetʃɒp/ *noun* [C] a small factory where workers are paid very little and work many hours in very bad conditions

sweaty /'sweti/ *adjective* covered in sweat *He was hot and sweaty from working in the garden.*

swede /swiːd/ *noun* [C, U] *UK* a round, yellow vegetable which grows in the ground

sweep[1] /swiːp/ *verb past* swept **1** [I, T] (*also* **sweep up**) to clean the floor using a brush *She's just swept the floor.* ○ *He swept up the pieces of broken glass* (= removed them from the floor with a brush). **2 be swept along/away, etc** to be pushed or carried along, often by something strong which you cannot control *Many trees were swept away in the flood.* **3** [I, T] to quickly affect a large area *The disease is sweeping the country.* ○ *Panic swept through the crowd.* **4 sweep along/into/past, etc** to move quickly, especially in a way that shows you think you are important *She swept past me in the corridor.*

sweep[2] /swiːp/ *noun* [C] **1** a long movement [usually singular] *With a sweep of his arm, he gestured towards the garden.* **2** something shaped in a long curve *a long sweep of sandy beach* ➍See also: **chimney sweep**.

sweeping /'swiːpɪŋ/ *adjective* **1** [always before noun] affecting many things or people *sweeping changes/reforms* **2 sweeping statement/generalization** when someone says something that is very general and has not been carefully thought about

sweepstake /'swiːpsteɪk/ *UK* (*US* **sweepstakes**) *noun* [C] a type of betting (= risking money on a competition) in which the winner receives all the money

o→ **sweet**[1] /swiːt/ *adjective* **1** [TASTE] with a taste like sugar *It was covered in a very sweet chocolate sauce.* **2** [ATTRACTIVE] attractive, often because of being small *Look at that kitten - isn't she sweet?* **3** [KIND] kind and friendly *It was really sweet of you to come.* **4** [SMELL/SOUND] A sweet smell or sound is pleasant. • **sweetness** noun [U]

sweet[2] /swiːt/ *UK* (*US* **candy**) *noun* [C] a small

piece of sweet food, often made of sugar or chocolate *You shouldn't eat so many sweets - they're bad for your teeth.*

sweetcorn /'swiːtkɔːn/ *UK* (*US* **corn**) *noun* [U] the sweet, yellow seeds of maize (= a plant) which are eaten as a vegetable ➍See colour picture **Fruit and Vegetables** on page Centre 10.

sweeten /'swiːtən/ *verb* [T] to make something sweeter, for example, by adding more sugar *She gave me a hot lemon drink, sweetened with honey.*

sweetener /'swiːtənəʳ/ *noun* [C] **1** something which is used to make something taste sweeter *an artificial sweetener* **2** something that is used to persuade someone to do something

sweetheart /'swiːthɑːt/ *noun* [C] You call someone 'sweetheart' to show affection or to be friendly. *Come here, sweetheart.*

sweetly /'swiːtli/ *adverb* in an attractive or kind way *She smiled sweetly.*

,**sweet po'tato** *UK* (*US* **'sweet po,tato**) *noun* [C, U] *plural* **sweet potatoes** a long, red vegetable like a potato but that tastes slightly sweet

swell[1] /swel/ *verb past tense* **swelled**, *past participle* **swollen** or **swelled 1** [I] (*also* **swell up**) to increase in size *One side of his face had swollen up where he'd been stung.* **2** [I, T] to increase in amount because more things are added *The population of the region was swollen by refugees from across the border.*

swell[2] /swel/ *noun* **1** [C, U] the movement of waves in the sea, or the waves themselves *ocean swells* **2** [C] an increase

swell[3] /swel/ *adjective US old-fashioned* good or pleasant *Everyone's having a swell time.*

swelling /'swelɪŋ/ *noun* [C, U] a part of your body which has become bigger because of illness or injury *The doctor gave me drugs to reduce the swelling in my ankle.*

sweltering /'sweltərɪŋ/ *adjective* so hot that you feel uncomfortable *It was a sweltering afternoon in August.*

swept /swept/ *past of* sweep

swerve /swɜːv/ *verb* [I] to change direction suddenly, especially when you are driving a vehicle *He swerved to avoid a cyclist and hit another car.*

swift /swɪft/ *adjective* happening or moving quickly *a swift response* • **swiftly** *adverb*

swig /swɪg/ *verb* [T] swigging, *past* swigged *informal* to drink something, taking a lot of liquid into your mouth at a time • **swig** *noun* [C] *He took a swig of his beer and carried on with the story.*

swill[1] /swɪl/ *verb* [T] **1** (*also* **swill out**) to clean something by making liquid move around it *The dentist handed me a glass of water to swill my mouth out.* **2** to quickly drink a large amount of something, especially alcohol

swill[2] /swɪl/ *noun* [U] waste food that is fed to pigs

o→ **swim**[1] /swɪm/ *verb* **swimming**, *past tense* **swam**, *past participle* **swum 1** [THROUGH WATER] [I, T] to move through water by moving your body *I learnt to swim when I was about 5 years old.* ○ *I* *swim thirty lengths of the pool most mornings.* ⊃See colour picture **Sports** 1 on page Centre 14. **2** [HEAD] [I] If your head swims, you feel confused and are unable to see or think clearly. **3** [SEEM TO MOVE] [I] to seem to move about *I got up suddenly and the room started swimming.* • **swimming** *noun* [U] *I usually go swimming about twice a week.* • **swimmer** *noun* [C] *I'm not a very strong swimmer.*

swim² /swɪm/ *noun* [C] a time when you swim *I went for a swim before breakfast.*

'swimming ,costume *UK* (*US* **bathing suit**) *noun* [C] a piece of clothing that you wear to go swimming ⊃See colour picture **Clothes** on page Centre 9.

'swimming ,pool *noun* [C] an area of water that has been made for people to swim in

'swimming ,trunks *noun* [plural] a piece of clothing that boys and men wear when they swim ⊃See colour picture **Clothes** on page Centre 9.

swimsuit /'swɪmsuːt/ *noun* [C] a piece of clothing that girls and women wear to go swimming ⊃See colour picture **Clothes** on page Centre 9.

swindle /'swɪndl/ *verb* [T] to get money from someone by cheating or deceiving them [often passive] *She was swindled out of thousands of dollars.* • **swindle** *noun* [C] *a multi-million-pound swindle* • **swindler** *noun* [C]

swine /swaɪn/ *noun* **1** [plural] *formal* pigs **2** [C] *informal* an unpleasant person

swing¹ /swɪŋ/ *verb past* **swung 1** [BACKWARDS/FORWARDS] [I, T] to move smoothly backwards and forwards, or to make something do this *She really swings her arms when she walks.* **2** [CURVE] [I, T] to move smoothly in a curve, or to make something do this *The door swung shut.* ○ *Watch the ball as you swing the bat.* **3** [CHANGE] [I] If someone's opinion or their feelings swing, they suddenly change. *Her moods swing with absolutely no warning.*

swing around/round to turn around quickly

swing at sb *informal* to try to hit someone

swing² /swɪŋ/ *noun* [C] **1** [FOR CHILDREN] a chair hanging on two ropes that children sit on and swing backwards and forwards **2** [HIT] an attempt to hit someone *Isn't that the boy Mark took a swing at* (= tried to hit)? **3** [CHANGE] a sudden change *He suffered terrible mood swings.* **4 be in full swing** If an event is in full swing, everything has started and there is a lot of activity. *By ten o'clock, the party was in full swing.*

swipe¹ /swaɪp/ *verb* [T] **1** (*also* **swipe at**) to move your arm in order to try to hit someone or something **2** *informal* to steal something

swipe² /swaɪp/ *noun* [C] an attempt to hit someone

'swipe ,card *noun* [C] *UK* a small piece of plastic that contains electronic information, used to open doors, etc

swirl /swɜːl/ *verb* [I, T] to move around and around quickly, or to make something do this *The mist swirled round the castle.* • **swirl** *noun* [C]

swish /swɪʃ/ *verb* [I, T] to move quickly through the air making a soft sound, or to make something do this • **swish** *noun* [C] *the swish of curtains closing*

○•**switch¹** /swɪtʃ/ *verb* [I, T] **1** to change from one thing to another *We're trying to encourage people to switch from cars to bicycles.* ○ *He's just switched jobs.* **2** to exchange something with someone else *After a couple of months we switched roles.*

switch (sth) off to turn off a light, television, etc by using a switch *Have you switched the computer off?*

switch off *UK* to stop giving your attention to someone or something *I'm afraid I just switch off when she starts telling me about her problems.*

switch (sth) on to turn on a light, television, etc by using a switch

switch over 1 *UK* to change from one television or radio station to another **2** to change from doing one thing to another *We've decided to switch over to low fat milk.*

┌─────────────────────────────────┐
│ ▨ **WORD PARTNERS FOR switch** │
│ **flick/press** a switch • the **on/off** switch │
└─────────────────────────────────┘

○•**switch²** /swɪtʃ/ *noun* [C] **1** a small object that you push up or down with your finger to turn something electrical on or off **2** a change *There has been a switch in policy.*

switchboard /'swɪtʃbɔːd/ *noun* [C] a piece of equipment that is used to direct all the telephone calls made from and to a building

swivel /'swɪvl/ (*also* **swivel around**) *verb* [I, T] *UK* **swivelling**, *past* **swivelled**, *US* **swiveling**, *past* **swiveled** to turn round, or to make something turn round

swollen¹ /'swəʊlən/ *adjective* bigger than usual *a swollen wrist/ankle* ○ *swollen rivers*

swollen² /'swəʊlən/ *past participle of* swell

swoop /swuːp/ *verb* [I] **1** to suddenly move very quickly down through the air *Huge birds swoop down from the sky.* **2** to suddenly attack *The day before police had swooped on his home.* • **swoop** *noun* [C]

swop /swɒp/ *verb* [I, T] **swopping**, *past* **swopped** *another UK spelling of* swap (= to give something to someone and get something from them in return)

sword /sɔːd/ *noun* [C] a weapon with a long, metal blade and a handle, used especially in the past

swordfish /'sɔːdfɪʃ/ *noun* [C, U] *plural* **swordfish** a large fish with a long, pointed part at the front of its head, that can be eaten as food

swore /swɔːʳ/ *past tense of* swear

sworn¹ /swɔːn/ *adjective* **1 sworn statement/testimony, etc** something that you have officially said is true **2 sworn enemies** two people, or two groups of people who are completely against each other

sworn² /swɔːn/ *past participle of* swear

swot¹ /swɒt/ *noun* [C] *UK informal* someone who studies too much

swot² /swɒt/ *UK informal* (*US* **cram**) *verb* [I] swot-

ting, *past* **swotted** to study a lot *I'm swotting for tomorrow's exam.*

swot up (on sth) to learn as much as you can about a subject, especially before an examination

swum /swʌm/ *past participle of* swim

swung /swʌŋ/ *past of* swing

sycamore /ˈsɪkəmɔːr/ *noun* [C, U] a tree with leaves that are divided into five parts and with seeds that turn around as they fall

sycophantic /ˌsɪkəʊˈfæntɪk/ *adjective formal* Someone who is sycophantic praises people in authority in a way that is not sincere, especially in order to get an advantage for themselves. • **sycophant** /ˈsɪkəfænt/ *noun* [C]

syllable /ˈsɪləbl/ *noun* [C] a word or part of a word that has one vowel sound *'But' has one syllable and 'apple' has two syllables.*

syllabus /ˈsɪləbəs/ *noun* [C] *plural* **syllabuses** or **syllabi** a list of the subjects that are included in a course of study

o→**symbol** /ˈsɪmbəl/ *noun* [C] **1** a sign or object that is used to represent something *A heart shape is the symbol of love.* **2** a number, letter, or sign that is used instead of the name of a chemical substance, another number, etc *The symbol for oxygen is O.* ⊃See also: status symbol.

symbolic /sɪmˈbɒlɪk/ *adjective* representing something else *The blue, white and red of the French flag are symbolic of liberty, equality and fraternity.* • **symbolically** *adverb*

symbolism /ˈsɪmbəlɪzəm/ *noun* [U] the use of signs and objects in art, films, etc to represent ideas

symbolize (*also UK* -ise) /ˈsɪmbəlaɪz/ *verb* [T] to represent something *The lighting of the Olympic torch symbolizes peace and friendship among the nations of the world.*

symmetrical /sɪˈmetrɪkəl/ (*also* **symmetric**) *adjective* having the same shape or size on both halves *Faces are roughly symmetrical.*

symmetry /ˈsɪmətri/ *noun* [U] when something is symmetrical

o→**sympathetic** /ˌsɪmpəˈθetɪk/ *adjective* **1** showing that you understand and care about someone's problems *My boss is very sympathetic about my situation.* **2** agreeing with or supporting someone's ideas or actions *He was sympathetic to their views.* ⊃Opposite un-sympathetic. • **sympathetically** *adverb*

COMMON LEARNER ERROR

sympathetic

Be careful not to use **sympathetic** when you simply want to say that someone is **nice**, **friendly**, or **kind**. Remember that if someone is **sympathetic**, they understand your problems.

sympathize (*also UK* -ise) /ˈsɪmpəθaɪz/ *verb* [I] **1** to understand and care about someone's problems *It's a really bad situation - I do sympathize with her.* **2** to agree with or support someone's ideas or actions *I sympathize with the general aims of the party.*

sympathizer (*also UK* -iser) /ˈsɪmpəθaɪzər/ *noun* [C] someone who supports a particular polit-

ical organization, or believes in a particular set of ideas *a communist sympathizer*

WORD PARTNERS FOR *sympathy*

have/express/feel [every/little/no, etc] sympathy **for** sb • **look for** sympathy • **deep/great/heartfelt** sympathy • **words** of sympathy

o→**sympathy** /ˈsɪmpəθi/ *noun* [U] **1** when you show that you understand and care about someone's problems *I have no sympathy for people who say they can't find work but are really just too lazy to look.* **2** agreement with or support for someone's ideas or actions *Scott was in sympathy with this view.*

symphony /ˈsɪmfəni/ *noun* [C] a long piece of music for an orchestra (= large group of different musicians)

symptom /ˈsɪmptəm/ *noun* [C] **1** a physical feeling or problem which shows that you have a particular illness *The inability to sleep is often a symptom of some other illness.* **2** a problem that is caused by and shows a more serious problem *The drinking was just a symptom of his general unhappiness.* • **symptomatic** /ˌsɪmptəˈmætɪk/ *adjective* relating to a symptom

synagogue /ˈsɪnəɡɒɡ/ *noun* [C] a building in which Jewish people pray

sync /sɪŋk/ *noun informal* **1** **be in sync** to be happening at the same time **2** **be out of sync** to not be happening at the same time

synchronize (*also UK* -ise) /ˈsɪŋkrənaɪz/ *verb* [T] **1** to make something happen at the same time as something else *We had a problem synchronizing the music and the images.* **2** **synchronize watches** to make two or more watches show exactly the same time • **synchronization** /ˌsɪŋkrənaɪˈzeɪʃən/ *noun* [U]

syndicate /ˈsɪndɪkət/ *noun* [C] a group of people or companies who join together in order to achieve something *a bank syndicate* ○ *a crime syndicate*

syndrome /ˈsɪndrəʊm/ *noun* [C] a combination of physical problems that often go together in a particular illness

synergy /ˈsɪnədʒi/ *noun* [C, U] when two companies or groups work together and achieve more success than they would separately *a synergy between the two software companies*

synonym /ˈsɪnənɪm/ *noun* [C] a word or phrase that means the same as another word or phrase

synonymous /sɪˈnɒnɪməs/ *adjective* **1** If one thing is synonymous with another, they are very closely connected with each other in people's minds. *It is a country where wealth is synonymous with corruption.* **2** If one word is synonymous with another, they have the same meaning.

synopsis /sɪˈnɒpsɪs/ *noun* [C] *plural* **synopses** a short description of a book, film, etc

syntax /ˈsɪntæks/ *noun* [U] the grammatical arrangement of words in a sentence

synthesis /ˈsɪnθəsɪs/ *noun* [C, U] *plural* **syntheses** /ˈsɪnθəsiːz/ *formal* the mixing of several things to make another whole new thing

S

synthesize (*also UK* **-ise**) /ˈsɪnθəsaɪz/ *verb* [T] to mix several things in order to make something else

synthesizer (*also UK* **-iser**) /ˈsɪnθəsaɪzə^r/ *noun* [C] an electronic musical instrument that can copy the sounds made by other musical instruments

synthetic /sɪnˈθetɪk/ *adjective* not made from natural substances *synthetic rubber* • **synthetically** *adverb*

syphilis /ˈsɪfɪlɪs/ *noun* [U] a serious disease caught during sex that spreads slowly from the sex organs to all parts of the body

syringe /sɪˈrɪndʒ/ *noun* [C] a piece of medical equipment used to push liquid into or take liquid out of someone's body

syringe

syrup /ˈsɪrəp/ *noun* [U] a very sweet liquid

made from sugar and water

०▪**system** /ˈsɪstəm/ *noun* [C] **1** METHOD a way or method of doing things *the American legal system* ○ *the public transport system* **2** EQUIPMENT a set of connected pieces of equipment that operate together *They've had an alarm system installed at their home.* **3** BODY parts of the body that work together in order to make something happen *the body's immune system* **4 the system** the laws and rules of a society **5 get sth out of your system** to get rid of a strong feeling or a need to do something, especially by expressing that feeling or doing the thing you want to do *It's not a bad idea to travel before getting a job - that way you get it out of your system.* ⊃See also: **immune system, nervous system, operating system, public address system, the solar system.**

systematic /ˌsɪstəˈmætɪk/ *adjective* done using a fixed and organized plan *the systematic collection and analysis of information* • **systematically** *adverb*

Tt

T, t /tiː/ the twentieth letter of the alphabet

ta /tɑː/ *exclamation UK informal* thank you

tab /tæb/ *noun* [C] **1** a small piece of paper, metal, etc that is fixed to something and that you use to open it or find out information about it *Pull tab to open.* **2** an amount of money that you owe for something you have bought or for a service you have used *Officials said the tab for the new bridge would be $8 million.* **3 pick up the tab** to pay for something, especially a meal in a restaurant **4 keep tabs on sb/sth** *informal* to watch someone or something carefully to check they do nothing wrong

tabby /ˈtæbi/ *noun* [C] a cat that has stripes in its fur

ˈtab ˌkey *noun* [C] the key on a computer keyboard which allows you to move the cursor (= a symbol which shows you where you are working) forward a few spaces

o-**table¹** /ˈteɪbl/ *noun* [C] **1** a piece of furniture with four legs, used for eating off, putting things on, etc *the kitchen table* **2 lay the table** *UK* (*UK/US* **set the table**) to put plates, knives, forks, etc on the table to prepare for a meal **3** a set of numbers or words written in rows that go across and down the page *The table below shows the results of the experiment.* **4 turn the tables on sb** to change a situation so that you have an advantage over someone who before had an advantage over you ➲See also: put/lay your cards (card) on the table, **coffee table**, **dressing table**.

table

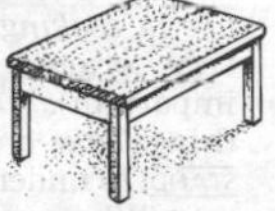

table² /ˈteɪbl/ *verb* [T] **1** *UK* to formally suggest that a particular subject is discussed **2** *US* to decide to discuss something later

tablecloth /ˈteɪblklɒθ/ *noun* [C] a piece of material that covers a table, especially during a meal

tablespoon /ˈteɪblspuːn/ *noun* [C] a large spoon used for measuring or serving food, or the amount this spoon can hold

> WORD PARTNERS FOR ***tablet***
>
> take a tablet • a tablet **for** sth • **sleeping** tablets • **headache** tablets

tablet /ˈtæblət/ *noun* [C] **1** MEDICINE a small, round object containing medicine that you swallow ➲See picture at **medicine**. **2** STONE a square piece of stone that has words cut into it **3** PAPER *US* (*UK/US* **pad**) sheets of paper that have been fastened together at one edge, used for writing or drawing

tablets

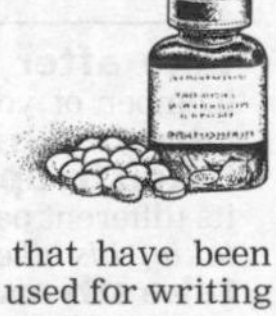

ˈtable ˌtennis *noun* [U] a game in which two or four people hit a small ball over a low net on a large table

tabloid /ˈtæblɔɪd/ *noun* [C] a small newspaper with a lot of pictures and short, simple news stories

taboo /təˈbuː/ *noun* [C, U] something that you should not say or do because people generally think it is morally wrong, unpleasant, or embarrassing *Sex is a taboo in this country.* • **taboo** *adjective Suicide is a taboo subject.*

tacit /ˈtæsɪt/ *adjective formal* understood without being said *a **tacit agreement***

taciturn /ˈtæsɪtɜːn/ *adjective formal* saying very little and not seeming friendly

tack¹ /tæk/ *noun* **1 take/try a different tack** to try to deal with a problem in a different way *I've tried being nice to her and it doesn't work so I might take a different tack.* **2** [C] a small, sharp nail with a flat top *carpet tacks* **3** [C] *US* (*UK* **drawing pin**) a short pin with a flat, round top, used for fastening pieces of paper to the wall

tack² /tæk/ *verb* [T] **1** to fasten something to a wall with a tack **2** to sew something loosely

tack sth on to add something that you had not planned to add

tackle¹ /ˈtækl/ *verb* [T] **1** DEAL WITH to try to deal with a problem *new ways to **tackle crime*** **2** SPEAK TO *UK* to speak to someone about something bad that they have done *I decided to tackle him about his absences.* **3** BALL to try to get the ball from someone in a game such as football

tackle² /ˈtækl/ *noun* **1** [C] an attempt to get the ball from someone in a game such as football **2** [U] all the things you need for a particular activity ***fishing tackle***

tacky /ˈtæki/ *adjective* **1** *informal* cheap and of bad quality *tacky holiday souvenirs* **2** slightly sticky

tact /tækt/ *noun* [U] the ability to talk to people about difficult subjects without upsetting them

tactful /ˈtæktfəl/ *adjective* careful not to say or do anything that could upset someone • **tactfully** *adverb*

> WORD PARTNERS FOR ***tactic***
>
> **adopt/employ/use** tactics • a **change of** tactics • **bullying/underhand** tactics

tactic /ˈtæktɪk/ *noun* [C] a way of doing something that you plan in order to achieve what you want [usually plural] *These bomb attacks represent a **change of tactics** by the terrorists.*

tactical /ˈtæktɪkəl/ *adjective* relating to tactics, or done in order to achieve something ***tactical voting*** ○ ***a tactical error*** • **tactically** *adverb*

tactless /ˈtæktləs/ *adjective* not being careful about saying or doing something that could upset someone

tad /tæd/ *noun informal* **a tad** a little *It was a tad expensive, I thought.*

tadpole /ˈtædpəʊl/ *noun* [C] a small, black animal that lives in water and will become a frog (= green jumping animal)

taffeta /ˈtæfɪtə/ *noun* [U] a stiff, shiny cloth

used in women's formal dresses

TAFN *Internet abbreviation for* that's all for now: used at the end of an email or message

tag¹ /tæg/ *noun* [C] a small piece of paper or plastic with information on it that is fixed to something *a price tag*

tag² /tæg/ *verb* [T] **tagging**, *past* **tagged** to put a tag on something

  tag along *informal* to go somewhere with someone, especially when they have not asked you to

t'ai chi /taɪˈtʃiː/ *noun* [U] a form of Chinese exercise that involves a series of slow movements

tail¹ /teɪl/ *noun* [C] **1** the long, narrow part that sticks out at the back of an animal's body *The dog's pleased to see you - he's wagging his tail.* **2** the back part of something long, such as a plane **3 the tail end of sth** the last part of something *the tail end of the eighties*

tail

tail² /teɪl/ *verb* [T] to secretly follow someone, especially because you think they have done something wrong

  tail off to gradually become quieter, smaller, less frequent, etc *His voice tailed off.*

tailback /ˈteɪlbæk/ *noun* [C] *UK* a line of cars that have stopped or are moving very slowly because of an accident or other problem on the road in front of them

tailcoat /ˈteɪlkəʊt/ *noun* [C] a formal coat that has a short front part and a long back part that is divided in two

tailgate /ˈteɪlɡeɪt/ *verb* [I, T] to drive too closely to the car in front of you ● **tailgating** *noun* [U]

'tail ˌlight *noun* [C] *US* one of the two red lights on the back of a car ⊃See colour picture **Car** on page Centre 7.

tailor¹ /ˈteɪləʳ/ *noun* [C] someone whose job is to make or repair clothes, especially men's clothes

tailor² /ˈteɪləʳ/ *verb* [T] to make or change something so that it is suitable *The kitchen can then be tailored exactly to the customer's needs.*

tailor-made /ˌteɪləˈmeɪd/ *adjective* **1** perfect for a particular person or purpose *It sounds as if you're tailor-made for the job.* **2** Tailor-made clothes are made by a tailor.

tailpipe /ˈteɪlpaɪp/ *US* (*UK* **exhaust pipe**) *noun* [C] the pipe that waste gas from a vehicle's engine flows through ⊃See colour picture **Car** on page Centre 7.

tails /teɪlz/ *noun* [plural] **1** the side of a coin that does not have someone's head on it *Let's toss a coin - heads or tails?* **2** a formal coat that has a short front part and a long back part that is divided in two

taint /teɪnt/ *verb* [T] **1** to spoil people's opinion of someone [often passive] *a government tainted by scandal* **2** to spoil something, especially food or blood, by adding a harmful substance

○ᴡ**take** /teɪk/ *verb* [T] *past tense* **took**, *past participle* **taken 1** CARRY to get and carry something with you when you go somewhere *I always take my mobile phone with me.* **2** GO to go somewhere

with someone, often paying for them or being responsible for them *I took the kids to the park.* ⊃See Common learner error at **bring**. **3** WITH-OUT PERMISSION to remove something without permission *Someone's taken my coat.* **4** GET HOLD to get hold of something and move it *He reached across and took the glass from her.* **5** ACCEPT to accept something *So, are you going to take the job? ○ Do you take credit cards?* **6** NEED If something takes a particular amount of time, or a particular quality, you need that amount of time or that quality in order to be able to do it. [+ to do sth] *It's taken me three days to get here. ○ It takes a lot of courage to stand up and talk in front of so many people.* **7** MEDI-CINE to swallow or use medicine *Take two tablets, three times a day.* **8** MEASURE to measure something *Have you taken her temperature?* **9** CLOTHES to wear a particular size of clothes *I take a size 12 in trousers.* **10** SPACE to have enough space for a particular number of people or things *There's six of us and the car only takes five.* **11** TRAVEL to travel by using a bus, train, car, etc, or by using a particular road *Are you taking the train to Edinburgh?* **12 take a break/rest, etc** to stop working for a period **13 take pleasure/pride/an interest, etc** to have a particular, good feeling about something that you do *I take great pleasure in cooking. ○ These women take their jobs very seriously* (= think their jobs are very important). **14 take a look** to look at something *Take a look at these photos.* **15** UNDER-STAND to understand something in a particular way *Whatever I say she'll take it the wrong way.* **16 I take it (that)** used when you think that what you say is probably true *I take it you're not coming with us.* **17 can't take sth** to not be able to deal with an unpleasant situation *We argue all the time - I really can't take it any more.* **18 take it from me** accept that what I say is true, because I know or have experienced it *You could be doing a much less interesting job, take it from me.* **19 take sth as it comes** to deal with something as it happens, without planning for it **20** BY FORCE to get control of something by force *By morning they had taken the city.*

take part in or **take place?**

If someone **takes part in** something, they join other people in doing it.

All the children took part in the competition.

If something **takes place**, it happens.

The festival takes place every summer in the castle gardens.

take after sb to be similar to an older member of your family *Peter's very tall - he takes after his father.*

take sth apart to separate something into its different parts *He spent the whole afternoon taking his bike apart.*

take sth away 1 to remove something *The waitress took our plates away. ○ Supermarkets are taking business away from small local* *shops.* **2** to subtract a number *Take 3 away from 20.*

take sb away to make someone leave a place and go with you

take sth back **1** to return something to the place you borrowed or bought it from **2** to admit that your opinion was wrong *You're right, he's nice - I take back everything I said about him.*

take sth down **1** to write something *Did you take down the telephone number?* **2** to remove something that is on a wall or something that is temporary *I've taken the pictures down.*

take sth in **1** UNDERSTAND to understand something *It was an interesting lecture but there was just too much to take in.* **2** FILM/BUILDING ETC to go to see a film, visit an interesting building, etc for enjoyment *I thought we might get something to eat and then take in a movie.* **3** CLOTHES to make a piece of clothing narrower

take sb in **1** If the police take someone in, they take that person to the police station. **2** to let someone stay in your house *You could earn some extra cash by taking in foreign students.* **3 be taken in** to be deceived by someone

o—**take sth off** **1** to remove something *If you're hot, take your jacket off.* ⊃See colour picture **Phrasal Verbs** on page Centre 16. **2** to spend time away from your work *I'm taking Friday off to get some things done around the house.*

take off **1** AIRCRAFT If an aircraft takes off, it begins to fly. **2** SUCCESSFUL to suddenly become successful *Her career had just taken off.* **3** LEAVE to suddenly leave without telling anyone where you are going *He took off in the middle of the night.*

take sth on to accept a responsibility *I don't want to take on too much work.*

take sb on **1** to begin to employ someone *We'll be taking on two new members of staff.* **2** to compete against someone *I might take you on at tennis sometime.*

take on sth to begin to have a particular quality *Her voice took on a tone of authority.*

take sth out to remove something from somewhere *He reached into his bag and took out a book.*

take sb out to go somewhere with someone and pay for them *Are you taking her out for her birthday?*

take sth out on sb to unfairly treat someone badly because you are upset *Don't take it out on me!*

take (sth) over to get control of or responsibility for something *They've recently been taken over by a larger company.* ○ *Who'll be taking over from Cynthia when she retires?*

take sb through sth to explain something to someone

take to sb/sth to start to like someone or something *For some reason, I just didn't take to him.*

take to sth/doing sth to start doing something *Dad's taken to swimming every morning.*

take sth up **1** to start doing a particular job

or activity *I thought I might take up cycling.* **2** to use an amount of time or space *This desk takes up too much space.*

take sb up on sth to accept an offer *Could I take you up on your offer of a ride home?*

take sth up with sb to discuss something with someone *You'll have to take the matter up with your manager.*

takeaway /ˈteɪkəweɪ/ UK (US **takeout** /ˈteɪkaʊt/) noun [C] a meal that you buy in a restaurant but eat at home, or a shop that sells this type of meal

take-off /ˈteɪkɒf/ noun **1** [C, U] when an aircraft leaves the ground and begins to fly **2** [C] a film, book, etc that copies someone else's style in a way that is funny

takeover /ˈteɪkˌəʊvəʳ/ noun [C] when a company gets control of another company

takings /ˈteɪkɪŋz/ UK (US **receipts**) noun [plural] all the money that a business gets from selling things

talcum powder /ˈtælkəmˌpaʊdəʳ/ (also **talc**) noun [U] white powder that you put on your skin after a bath

tale /teɪl/ noun [C] a story, especially one which is not true or is difficult to believe *My grandfather used to tell us tales of his time as a pilot during the war.* ⊃See also: **fairy tale**.

> WORD PARTNERS FOR **talent**
>
> **have/show** a talent for sth ● a **natural** talent ● sb's talent **as** sth

o—**talent** /ˈtælənt/ noun [C, U] a natural ability to do something *She showed an early talent for drawing.* ● **talented** adjective showing natural ability in a particular area *a talented young musician*

talisman /ˈtælɪzmən/ noun [C] plural **talismans** an object that people think will make them lucky

o—**talk¹** /tɔːk/ verb **1** [I] to say things to someone *We were just talking about Simon's new girlfriend.* ○ *It was nice talking to you.* ○ *(US) It was nice talking with you.* ⊃See Common learner error at **speak**. **2** [I] to discuss something with someone, often to try to find a solution to a disagreement *The two sides have agreed to talk.* **3 talk about sth/doing sth** to think about or make plans to do something in the future *They're talking about building a new fire station just up the road.* **4 talk business/politics, etc** to discuss a particular subject *I don't like to talk business over lunch.* **5 talking of sth** UK (US **speaking of sth**) used when you are going to start talking about something that is related to what has just been said *Talking of holidays, did you hear about Lesley's skiing trip?* ⊃See also: speak/talk of the **devil**.

talk at sb to talk to someone without letting them say anything or without listening to them

talk back If a child talks back to an adult, they answer them rudely.

talk down to sb to talk to someone in a way that shows you think they are not intelligent or not important

talk sb into/out of (doing) sth to persuade someone to do or not do something *We* *managed to talk Lisa into doing the cooking.*

talk sth over to discuss something with someone, often to find out their opinion or to get advice before making a decision

The most common alternatives are **speak** and **say**: *Could you **speak** more quietly, please?* • *I couldn't hear what they were saying.*

The verb **chat** or the expression **have a chat** are often used if a person is talking with someone in a friendly, informal way: *We were just **chatting** about the party on Saturday.* • *Give me a call and we'll **have a chat**.*

If people talk for a long time about things that are not important, verbs such as **chatter**, **natter** (*UK, informal*), and the expression **have a natter** (*UK, informal*) are sometimes used: *She spent the morning **chattering** away to her friends.* • *We **had a long natter** over coffee.*

If someone talks about something too much in an annoying way, you can use the phrasal verb **go on** (*UK*): *He's always **going on** about how much he hates his work.*

If someone talks quietly so that their voice is difficult to hear, often because they are complaining about something, then the verbs **mumble** and **mutter** are used: *She walked past me, **muttering** to herself.* • *He **mumbled** something about it being a waste of time.*

The verb **whisper** is used when someone talks extremely quietly so that other people cannot hear: *What are you two girls **whispering** about?*

1 have a talk • a talk **with** sb • a talk **about** sth • a **long/serious** talk

๐^ー**talk²** /tɔːk/ *noun* **1** [CONVERSATION] [C] a conversation between two people, often about a particular subject *I **had a long talk with** Chris at the weekend about going to university.* **2** [PEOPLE] [U] when people talk about what might happen or be true *There's been some **talk of** possible job losses.* **3** [TO A GROUP] [C] when someone speaks to a group of people about a particular subject *Someone's coming to the school to **give a talk about** road safety.* **4 be all talk (and no action)** If someone is all talk, they never do the brave or exciting things they often say they will do. ⊃See also: small talk.

talkative /ˈtɔːkətɪv/ *adjective* A talkative person talks a lot.

attend/have/hold/resume talks • talks **break down/take place** • **lengthy/secret/urgent** talks • talks **about/on** sth

talks /tɔːks/ *noun* [plural] formal meetings, especially between political leaders, to discuss a problem and to try to reach an agreement

peace talks ๐ *US officials are **holding talks with** EU leaders over trade.*

ˈ**talk ˌshow** *US* (*UK* **chat show**) *noun* [C] an informal television or radio programme where people are asked questions about themselves and their lives

๐^ー**tall** /tɔːl/ *adjective* **1** having a greater than average height. *He's **tall** and thin.* ๐ *It's one of the tallest buildings in the city.* **2** used to describe or ask about the height of someone or something *How **tall** is she?* ๐ *He's almost 2 metres tall.*

tally¹ /ˈtæli/ *noun* [C] the number of things you have achieved, used, won, etc until now *This adds to his **tally of** 12 race wins so far this year.*

tally² /ˈtæli/ *verb* **1** [I] If two numbers or stories tally, they are the same. **2** [T] (*also* **tally up**) to find out the total number

the Talmud /ˈtælmʊd/ *noun* the ancient Jewish written laws and traditions

talon /ˈtælən/ *noun* [C] a sharp nail on the foot of a bird that it uses to catch animals

tambourine /ˌtæmbᵊrˈiːn/ *noun* [C] a musical instrument with a wooden ring and small metal discs loosely fixed to it which you play by shaking or hitting

tame¹ /teɪm/ *adjective* **1** If an animal is tame, it is not wild and not frightened of people. **2** too controlled and not exciting *His TV show is very tame in comparison with his live performances.*

tame² /teɪm/ *verb* [T] to make a wild animal tame

tamper /ˈtæmpəʳ/ *verb*
tamper with sth to touch or make changes to something which you should not, often in order to damage it

tampon /ˈtæmpɒn/ *noun* [C] a small roll of cotton which a woman puts in her vagina to absorb her monthly flow of blood

tan¹ /tæn/ (*also* **suntan**) *noun* [C] when your skin is brown from being in the sun • **tan** *verb* [I, T] tanning, *past* tanned *I tan quite easily.*

tan² /tæn/ *adjective* **1** being a pale yellow-brown colour *a tan jacket* **2** *US* (*UK/US* **tanned**) having darker skin because you have been in the sun

tandem /ˈtændəm/ *noun* **1 in tandem (with sb)** If someone does something in tandem with someone else, they do it together or at the same time. **2** [C] a bicycle for two people

tangent /ˈtændʒᵊnt/ *noun* [C] **1** a straight line which touches but does not cross a curve **2 go off at/on a tangent** to suddenly start talking about a different subject

tangerine /ˌtændʒᵊrˈiːn/ *noun* [C] a fruit like a small orange

tangible /ˈtændʒəbl/ *adjective* Something which is tangible is real and can be seen, touched, or measured. *tangible benefits/evidence* ⊃Opposite **intangible**.

tangle¹ /ˈtæŋgl/ *noun* [C] several things which have become twisted together in an untidy way *a tangle of hair/wires*

tangle² /ˈtæŋgl/ *verb* [I, T] to become twisted together, or to make things become twisted to-gether ➔Opposite **disentangle, untangle.**

tangled /'tæŋgld/ *adjective* **1** (*also* **tangled up**) twisted together in an untidy way *The wires are all tangled.* **2** confused and difficult to understand *tangled finances* **3 be tangled up in/with sth** to be involved in something unpleasant or complicated that is difficult to escape from

tango /'tæŋgəʊ/ *noun* [C] a South American dance

tangy /'tæŋi/ *adjective* having a strong, sharp but pleasant taste or smell *a tangy lemon drink* • **tang** *noun* [no plural]

tank /tæŋk/ *noun* [C] **1** a large container for storing liquid or gas *(UK) a petrol tank/ (US) a gas tank* ○ *a hot-water tank* **2** a large, strong military vehicle with a gun on it which moves on wheels inside large metal belts ➔See also: **think tank.**

tanker /'tæŋkər/ *noun* [C] a ship or truck used to carry large amounts of liquid or gas *an oil tanker*

tanned /tænd/ (*also US* **tan**) *adjective* having darker skin because you have been in the sun

'tanning ,bed *noun* [C] *US* a sunbed

tannoy /'tænɔɪ/ *UK trademark (UK/US* **public address system**) *noun* [no plural] a system of equipment used in public places that someone speaks into in order to make their voice loud enough to hear

tantalizing (*also UK* **-ising**) /'tæntəlaɪzɪŋ/ *adjective* Something that is tantalizing is very attractive and makes you want it, although often you cannot have it. *a tantalizing glimpse of blue sea*

tantamount /'tæntəmaʊnt/ *adjective* **be tantamount to sth** to be almost as bad as something else *Resignation would be tantamount to admitting he was guilty.*

tantrum /'tæntrəm/ *noun* [C] when someone, especially a child, suddenly shows that they are very angry, usually because they cannot have something *Tom threw a tantrum in the middle of the supermarket.*

> 🧩 **WORD PARTNERS FOR tap**
>
> **turn on/turn off** a tap • a tap is **dripping/running** • the **cold/hot** tap • **under the** tap • tap **water**

tap¹ /tæp/ *noun* [C]
1 [WATER] *mainly UK* (*also US* **faucet**) the part at the end of a pipe which controls the flow of water *the cold/hot tap* ○ *to turn a tap on/off* ○ *She rinsed the cup under the tap.* **2** [KNOCK] a gentle knock or touch, or the noise made by knocking something gently *I felt a tap on my shoulder.* ○ *There*

tap *UK,* **faucet** *US*

was a tap at the door.
3 [TELEPHONE] a small piece of equipment that can be fixed to someone's telephone in order to listen to their telephone calls **4 on tap** easily available *They have all that sort of information on tap.*

tap² /tæp/ *verb* **tapping,** *past* **tapped 1** [KNOCK] [I, T] to knock or touch something gently *I tapped on the window to try and get her attention.* **2** [A SUPPLY] [T] If you tap a supply of something, you use what is available. *There are immense natural resources here waiting to be tapped.* **3** [TELEPHONE] [T] to use a special piece of equipment to listen to someone's telephone calls [often passive] *I think the phone's been tapped.*
tap into sth to use part of a large supply of something for your own advantage

'tap ,dancing *noun* [U] a type of dancing where the dancer wears special shoes with pieces of metal on the bottom which make a noise • **tap dance** *verb* [I] • **tap dancer** *noun* [C]

tape¹ /teɪp/ *noun* **1** [RECORDING] [C, U] a long, thin piece of plastic which is used to store sound, pictures, or information, or a plastic box containing it *I've got the match on tape.* **2** [STICKY] [U] a thin piece of plastic which has glue on one side and is used for sticking things together *adhesive/sticky tape* **3** [MATERIAL] [C, U] a long, thin piece of material used, for example, in sewing or to tie things together ➔See also: **red tape, Scotch tape.**

tape² /teɪp/ *verb* **1** [T] to record something onto tape *I often tape programmes and watch them later.* **2 tape sth to/onto, etc** to stick something somewhere using tape

'tape ,measure *noun* [C] a long, thin piece of cloth, metal, or plastic used to measure lengths

taper /'teɪpər/ *verb* [I, T] to become gradually narrower at one end • **tapered** *adjective*
taper off to become gradually smaller or less frequent *Sales have gradually tapered off.*

'tape re,corder *noun* [C] a machine used to record sound onto tape • **tape recording** *noun* [C] something which has been recorded on tape

tapestry /'tæpɪstri/ *noun* [C] a picture or pattern created by sewing different coloured threads onto heavy cloth

'tap ,water *noun* [U] water which comes out of a tap (= part at the end of a pipe)

tar /tɑːr/ *noun* [U] **1** a thick, black substance that is sticky when hot and is used to cover roads **2** a black, sticky substance that is produced when tobacco burns • **tar** *verb* [T] **tarring** *past* **tarred** to cover something with tar

tarantula /təˈræntjələ/ *noun* [C] a large, hairy spider that is often poisonous

> 🧩 **WORD PARTNERS FOR target**
>
> **attack/hit/miss/strike** a target • an **obvious/prime** target • a target **for** sth

target¹ /'tɑːgɪt/ *noun* [C] **1** [ATTACK] something or someone that you attack, shoot at, try to hit, etc *It's very difficult to hit a moving target.* ○ *Foreign businesses in the region have become a target for terrorist attacks.* **2** [ACHIEVE] something that you intend to achieve *I'm hoping to save £3,000 by June - that's my target.* ○ *If you want to lose weight, you have to* **set** *yourself* (= decide) *a* **target.** **3** BLAME the person or thing that people are criticizing or blaming for something *Such extreme views have recently made him the target of criticism.* **4 be on target** to have made enough progress in order to achieve something that you intended to achieve [+ to do sth] *We're on target to finish the project in June.* **5 target audience/market, etc** the group of people that a programme, product, etc is aimed at

target² /'tɑːgɪt/ *verb* [T] **1** to aim an attack at a particular person or place *They mostly targeted military bases.* **2** to aim advertising, criticism, or a product at someone [often passive] *The products are targeted at people in their late twenties.*

tariff /'tærɪf/ *noun* [C] **1** an amount of money that has to be paid for goods that are brought into a country *import tariffs* **2** a list of prices

tarmac /'tɑːmæk/ *noun trademark* **1** [U] *UK* (*US* **asphalt**) a thick, black substance that is sticky when hot and is used to cover roads **2 the tarmac** the area at an airport where aircraft land and take off

tarnish /'tɑːnɪʃ/ *verb* **1** [T] to spoil the way in which people think of someone so that they do not respect them *to tarnish someone's image/reputation* **2** [I, T] If a metal tarnishes or something tarnishes it, it becomes less bright and shiny.

tarpaulin /tɑː'pɔːlɪn/ (*also US* **tarp**) *noun* [C, U] a large piece of plastic or cloth that water cannot go through which is used to cover and protect things

tart¹ /tɑːt/ *noun* [C]
1 an open pastry case with a sweet filling, often of fruit *an apple tart* **2** *UK very informal* a woman who dresses or behaves in a way to attract a lot of attention from men

tart

tart² /tɑːt/ *adjective* having a sour, bitter taste

tartan /'tɑːtⁿn/ *noun* [C, U] cloth with a pattern of different coloured squares and crossing lines *a tartan kilt*

⚬ **task** /tɑːsk/ *noun* [C] a piece of work, especially something unpleasant or difficult [+ of + doing sth] *I was given the task of sorting out all the stuff in the garage.*

taskbar /'tɑːskbɑːʳ/ *noun* [C] on a computer screen, a set of symbols that shows the programs you are using and allows you to change them

'**task ,force** *noun* [C] a group of people, often a military group, who are brought together in order to do a particular job

tassel /'tæsⁿl/ *noun* [C] a decoration made of a group of short threads tied together which is hung on curtains, furniture, etc

⚬ **taste¹** /teɪst/ *noun* **1** FOOD [C, U] the flavour of a particular food in your mouth *a sweet/bitter taste* ○ *It's got quite a strong taste.* **2** ABILITY [U] the ability to feel different flavours in your mouth *When you've got a cold you often lose your sense of taste.* **3** a taste a small amount of food that you have in order to try it *Could I have just a taste of the sauce?* **4** WHAT YOU LIKE [C, U] the particular things you like, such as styles of music, clothes, decoration, etc *I don't like his taste in music.* ○ *It's okay, but it's not really to my taste.* **5** ART/STYLE ETC [U] the ability to judge what is attractive or suitable, especially in things related to art, style, beauty, etc *Everything in his house is beautiful - he's got very good taste.* **6 be in good taste** to be acceptable in a way that will not upset or anger people **7 be in bad/poor taste** to be unacceptable in a way that will upset or anger people *He told a joke about a plane crash which I thought was in rather poor taste.* **8 a taste for sth** when you like or enjoy something *I've developed a bit of a taste for opera.* **9 taste of sth** when you do or experience something new for a short time *That was my first taste of Mexican culture.*

⚬ **taste²** /teɪst/ *verb* **1 taste funny/nice/sweet, etc** If food tastes a particular way, it has that flavour. *This sauce tastes strange.* ○ *It tastes of chocolate.* **2 can taste sth** to be able to experience a particular flavour in a food *You can really taste the garlic in it.* **3** [T] to put food or drink in your mouth to find out what its flavour is like *I always taste food while I'm cooking it.*

'**taste ,buds** *noun* [plural] the cells on your tongue that allow you to taste different foods

tasteful /'teɪstfⁿl/ *adjective* attractive and chosen for style and quality *a tasteful beige suit* ● **tastefully** *adverb tastefully dressed/decorated*

tasteless /'teɪstləs/ *adjective* **1** UGLY ugly or without style **2** OFFENSIVE likely to upset or anger people *a tasteless joke* **3** FOOD having no flavour *The meat was dry and tasteless.*

tasty /'teɪsti/ *adjective* Food which is tasty has a good flavour and is nice to eat.

tattered /'tætəd/ *adjective* old and badly torn *tattered clothes*

tatters /'tætəz/ *noun* **in tatters** badly torn, damaged, or spoilt *The yacht finally made it to the harbour, its sails in tatters.* ○ *His reputation is in tatters.*

tattoo /tæt'uː/ *noun* [C] a design on someone's skin that is put on using ink and a needle ● **tattoo** *verb* [T] *past* **tattooed**

tattoo

tatty /'tæti/ *adjective UK informal* untidy and in bad condition *He turned up wearing a pair of tatty old jeans.*

taught /tɔːt/ *past of* teach

taunt /tɔːnt/ *verb* [T] to repeatedly say unkind things to someone in order to upset them or make them angry *He was taunted by his class-mates because of his size.* ● **taunt** *noun* [C] *The protesters shouted taunts at the police.*

Taurus /'tɔːrəs/ *noun* [C, U] the sign of the zodiac which relates to the period of 21 April - 22 May, or a person born during this period ➾See picture at **zodiac**.

taut /tɔːt/ *adjective* stretched very tight *My skin feels taut.*

tavern /'tævᵊn/ *noun* [C] *mainly US* a place where people go to drink alcohol

tawdry /'tɔːdri/ *adjective* **1** unpleasant and im-moral **2** cheap and of bad quality

tawny /'tɔːni/ *adjective* being a light yellow-brown colour

⟨WORD PARTNERS FOR **tax**⟩

deduct/increase/pay tax • high/low taxes
• a tax on sth • after/before tax

o→**tax¹** /tæks/ *noun* [C, U] money that you have to pay to the government from what you earn or when you buy things *They're putting up the tax on cigarettes.* ○ *Do you have to pay tax on that?* ➾See also: **income tax**.

tax² /tæks/ *verb* [T] **1** to make someone pay a tax *Goods such as clothes are taxed at 15%.* **2** to need a lot of effort *It's only a short report - it shouldn't tax me too much.*

taxable /'tæksəbl/ *adjective* If something is tax-able, you have to pay tax on it. *taxable income*

taxation /tæk'seɪʃᵊn/ *noun* [U] the system of making people pay taxes

tax-free /ˌtæks'friː/ *adjective* If something is tax-free, you do not pay tax on it.

⟨WORD PARTNERS FOR **taxi**⟩

call/get/hail/order/take a taxi • a taxi
driver/fare/firm

o→**taxi** /'tæksi/ *noun* [C] a car with a driver who you pay to take you somewhere *a taxi driver* ○ *I'll take a taxi to the airport.*

taxing /'tæksɪŋ/ *adjective* difficult and needing a lot of thought or effort to do or understand

'taxi ˌrank *UK* (*US* **'taxi ˌstand**) *noun* [C] a place where you can go to get a taxi

taxpayer /'tæksˌpeɪəʳ/ *noun* [C] a person who pays tax

TB /ˌtiː'biː/ *noun* [U] *abbreviation for* tuberculosis (= a serious infectious disease of the lungs)

tbsp *written abbreviation for* tablespoonful: the amount that can be held by a large spoon used for measuring food

o→**tea** /tiː/ *noun* [C, U] **1** ⟨DRINK⟩ a hot drink that you make by pouring water onto dried leaves, or the leaves that you use to make this drink *herbal teas* ○ *Would you like a cup of tea or coffee?* **2** ⟨AFTERNOON MEAL⟩ *UK* a small afternoon meal of cakes, biscuits, etc and tea to drink *They invited us for afternoon tea.* **3** ⟨EVENING MEAL⟩ *UK* a word used by some people for the main meal that is eaten in the evening

teabag /'tiːbæg/ *noun* [C] a small paper bag with dried leaves inside, used for making tea

o→**teach** /tiːtʃ/ *verb past* taught **1** ⟨GIVE LESSONS⟩ [I, T] to give lessons in a particular subject at a school, university, etc *She taught at Harvard Uni-versity for several years.* ○ *He teaches history.* **2** ⟨SHOW HOW TO⟩ [T] to show or explain to some-one how to do something [+ to do sth] *My dad taught me to drive.* ○ *Can you **teach** me **how to** knit?* **3** ⟨GET KNOWLEDGE⟩ [T] If a situation teaches you something, it gives you new knowledge or helps you to understand something. [+ to do sth] *The whole experience taught him to be more careful with money.* ➾See Common learner error at **learn** ➾See also: teach sb a **lesson**.

o→**teacher** /'tiːtʃəʳ/ *noun* [C] someone whose job is to teach in a school, college, etc *a history/sci-ence teacher* ➾See colour picture **The Classroom** on page Centre 6 ➾See Common learner error at **lecturer**.

teaching /'tiːtʃɪŋ/ *noun* [U] the job of being a teacher *He decided to go into teaching* (= become a teacher).

teachings /'tiːtʃɪŋz/ *noun* [plural] the ideas or beliefs of someone, such as a political or re-ligious leader *the teachings of Martin Luther King*

teacup /'tiːkʌp/ *noun* [C] a cup that you drink tea from

⟨WORD PARTNERS FOR **team**⟩

be in/on a team • join/play for a team
• team captain/coach/member

o→**team¹** /tiːm/ *noun* [group] **1** a group of people who play a sport or game together against an-other group of players *a basketball/football team* **2** a group of people who work together to do something *a management team* ○ *a team of advisers*

team² /tiːm/ *verb*

team up to join someone else and work to-gether with them to do something *I teamed up with Brendan for the doubles tournament.*

teammate /'tiːmmeɪt/ *noun* [C] a member of your team

teamwork /'tiːmwɜːk/ *noun* [U] when a group of people work well together

teapot /'tiːpɒt/ *noun* [C] a container used for making and serving tea, which has a lid, a handle, and a spout (= tube that liquid comes out of) ➾See colour picture **The Kit-chen** on page Centre 2.

teapot

tear¹ /teəʳ/ *verb past tense* tore, *past participle* torn **1** [T] to pull paper, cloth, etc into pieces, or to make a hole in it by accident *The nail had torn a hole in my skirt.* **2** [I] If paper, cloth, etc tears, it becomes dam-aged because it has been pulled. **3 tear sth out of/off/down, etc** to remove something by pulling it

tear

quickly and violently *She tore his picture down from the wall.* **4 tear along/about/past, etc** *informal* to move somewhere very quickly *The kids were tearing around the house.* ○ *He went tearing along the road after the bus.* **5 be torn between sth and sth** to be unable to decide between two choices *I'm torn between the apple pie and the chocolate mousse.* ⊃See also: pull/tear your **hair** out.

tear sth apart 1 to make a group of people argue or fight with each other *The country was torn apart by 12 years of civil war.* **2** to destroy something *The building was torn apart by the bomb blast.*

tear sb apart to make someone very unhappy *Seeing the children suffer really tears me apart.*

tear sb away to make someone stop doing something that they enjoy, in order to do something else *I'll bring Ian, if I can* **tear** *him away from his computer games.*

tear sth down to intentionally destroy a building or structure *They tore down the old hospital and built some offices.*

tear sth off to quickly remove your clothes *He tore off his shirt and jumped into the stream.*

tear sth up to tear paper into a lot of small pieces *He tore up her photograph.*

tear² /teəʳ/ *noun* [C] a hole in a piece of cloth, paper, etc where it has been torn

☞**tear³** /tɪəʳ/ *noun* [C] a drop of water that comes from your eye when you cry *Suddenly he* **burst into tears** (= started crying). ○ *I was in* **tears** (= crying) *by the end of the film.* ● **tearful** *adjective* crying *a tearful goodbye* ● **tearfully** *adverb* ⊃See also: in floods (**flood²**) of tears.

'tear ˌgas *noun* [U] a gas that makes people's eyes hurt, used by the police or army to control violent crowds

tease /tiːz/ *verb* [I, T] to laugh at someone or say unkind things to them, either because you are joking or because you want to upset them *They were* **teasing** *Dara* **about** *her new haircut.* ○ *Don't get upset, I'm only teasing.*

teaspoon /'tiːspuːn/ *noun* [C] a small spoon that is used for mixing drinks and measuring small amounts of food, or the amount this spoon can hold

teatime /'tiːtaɪm/ *noun* [C, U] *UK* the time in the evening when people have a meal

'tea ˌtowel *UK* (*US* **dishtowel**) *noun* [C] a cloth that is used for drying plates, dishes, etc

tech¹ /tek/ *adjective mainly US short for* technical¹ *online tech support*

tech² /tek/ *noun mainly US* **1** [U] *short for* technology *high/low tech* ○ *tech stocks* **2** [C] *informal short for* technician *Bill was a lab tech at NYU.*

techie /'teki/ *noun* [C] *informal* someone who has a strong interest in technology, usually computers

☞**technical** /'teknɪkᵊl/ *adjective* **1** [SCIENCE/INDUSTRY] relating to the knowledge, machines, or methods used in science and industry *We're having a few technical problems.* **2** [SPECIALIZED] relating to the knowledge and methods

of a particular subject or job *There are a few* **technical terms** *here that I don't understand.* **3** [PRACTICAL SKILL] relating to practical skills and methods that are used in a particular activity *As a dancer she had great technical skill.*

technicalities /ˌteknɪ'kælətiz/ *noun* [plural] the exact details of a system or process *the technicalities of photography*

technicality /ˌteknɪ'kæləti/ *noun* [C] a small detail of a law or rule

technically /'teknɪkᵊli/ *adverb* **1** relating to the knowledge, machines, or methods used in science and industry *technically advanced weapons* **2** according to the exact details of a rule, law, or fact *Irvine is technically British but lives in Dublin and races for the Irish team.*

technician /tek'nɪʃᵊn/ *noun* [C] someone whose job involves practical work with scientific or electrical equipment *a lab technician*

☞**technique** /tek'niːk/ *noun* [C, U] a particular or special way of doing something [+ for + doing sth] *Scientists have developed a new technique for taking blood samples.*

techno /'teknəʊ/ *noun* [U] *UK* a type of electronic dance music

techno- /teknəʊ-/ *prefix* relating to technology *a technophile* (= a person who loves technology)

┌─────────────────────────────┐
│ ⚙ WORD PARTNERS FOR *technology* │
└─────────────────────────────┘
advanced/cutting-edge/modern technology ● **develop/harness** technology

☞**technology** /tek'nɒlədʒi/ *noun* [C, U] knowledge, equipment, and methods that are used in science and industry *computer technology* ● **technological** /ˌteknə'lɒdʒɪkᵊl/ *adjective* relating to, or involving technology *technological developments* ● **technologically** *adverb* ⊃See also: information technology.

teddy bear /'tediˌbeə/ (*also UK* **teddy**) *noun* [C] a soft, toy bear

tedious /'tiːdiəs/ *adjective* boring *a tedious job* ● **tediously** *adverb*

tee /tiː/ *noun* [C] a small stick that is used for holding a golf ball

teem /tiːm/ *verb*
be teeming with sb/sth to contain large numbers of people or animals

teeming /'tiːmɪŋ/ *adjective* full of people *the teeming city*

teen¹ /tiːn/ *noun* [C] *mainly US short for* teenager

teen² /tiːn/ *adjective* [always before noun] *informal* relating to, or popular with people who are between 13 and 19 years old *a teen idol*

teenage /'tiːneɪdʒ/ *adjective* [always before noun] aged between 13 and 19 or suitable for people of that age *a teenage daughter* ○ *a teenage disco*

☞**teenager** /'tiːnˌeɪdʒəʳ/ *noun* [C] someone who is between 13 and 19 years old

teens /tiːnz/ *noun* [plural] the part of your life between the age of 13 and 19 *Her youngest daughter is still in her teens.*

'tee ˌshirt *noun* [C] *another spelling of* T-shirt (= a piece of cotton clothing for the top part of the

body with short sleeves and no collar)

teeter /'ti:tə^r/ *verb* **1 be teetering on the brink/edge of sth** to be in a situation where something bad might happen very soon *The economy is teetering on the brink of collapse.* **2 teeter about/across/around, etc** to look as if you are going to fall *She teetered around the room in six-inch heels.*

teeter-totter /,ti:tə'tɒtə^r/ *US* (*UK/US* **seesaw**) *noun* [C] a long board that children play on by sitting at each end and using their feet on the ground to push the board up and down

teeth /ti:θ/ *plural of* tooth

teeth

teethe /ti:ð/ *verb* **1 be teething** If a baby is teething, it is getting its first teeth. **2 teething problems/troubles** problems that happen because something is new and has not been done before

teetotal /,ti:'təʊt^əl/ *adjective* never drinking any alcohol • **teetotaller** *UK* (*US* **teetotaler**) *noun* [C] someone who never drinks alcohol

TEFL /'tefl/ *noun* [U] *abbreviation for* Teaching English as a Foreign Language

tel *written abbreviation for* telephone number *Tel 0113 246369*

tele- /teli-/ *prefix* **1** done using a telephone *telesales* **2** connected with television *telecast* (= something that is broadcast on television) **3** over a long distance *telephoto lens* (= a camera lens that makes distant objects look nearer)

telecommunications /,telɪkə,mju:nɪ'keɪʃ^ənz/ *noun* [U, group] the process or business of sending information or messages by telephone, radio, etc

telecommuting /,telɪkə'mju:tɪŋ/ ⓤ /'telɪkə,mju:tɪŋ/ *US* (*UK* **teleworking**) *noun* [U] working at home, while communicating with your office by computer and telephone • **telecommuter** *noun* [C] *US*

telecoms /'telɪkɒmz/ *noun* [U] *short for* telecommunications

teleconference /,telɪ'kɒnf^ər^əns/ *noun* [C] when people in different places have a meeting using computers, telephones, televisions etc to allow them to talk to each other and see each other

telegram /'telɪgræm/ *noun* [C] a message that is sent by telegraph and printed on paper

telegraph /'telɪgrɑːf/ *noun* [U] an old-fashioned system of sending messages using radio or electrical signals

telemarketing /'telɪ,mɑːkɪtɪŋ/ (*also UK* **telesales**) *noun* [U] the selling of goods or services by telephone

telepathy /tɪ'lepəθi/ *noun* [U] the ability to know what someone is thinking or to communicate thoughts without speaking or writing • **telepathic** /,telɪ'pæθɪk/ *adjective* having or involving telepathy

⟨ ⟩ WORD PARTNERS FOR *telephone*

answer/pick up/put down the telephone • the telephone **rings** • **on** the telephone • a telephone **call**

telephone

telephone

telephone box *UK*,
telephone booth *US*

mobile phone

o←**telephone**[1] /'telɪfəʊn/ (*also* **phone**) *noun* **1** [U] a communication system that is used to talk to someone who is in another place *a telephone call* ○ *I'm sorry, he's on the telephone* (= using the telephone) *at the moment.* **2** [C] a piece of equipment that is used to talk to someone who is in another place *The telephone rang and she hurried to pick it up.* ○ *Could you answer the telephone?*

telephone[2] /'telɪfəʊn/ (*also* **phone**) *verb* [I, T] *formal* to communicate with someone by telephone

COMMON LEARNER ERROR

telephone and **phone**

Telephone and phone mean the same thing, but we usually use **phone** for both the noun and the verb.

I'll phone you this evening.

Can I use your phone, please?

When the phone rings or when you want to make a phone call, you **pick** it **up**.

I picked up the phone and dialled his number.

When you finish a phone call, you **put** the phone **down** or you **hang up.**

Don't hang up - I can explain everything!

She thanked him and put the phone down.

~~She thanked him and hung up the phone.~~

'**telephone di,rectory** *noun* [C] a book that contains the telephone numbers of people who live in a particular area

'**telephone ,number** (*also* **phone number**) *noun* [C] the number of a particular telephone

telesales /'telɪseɪlz/ *UK* (*UK/US* **telemarketing**) *noun* [U] the selling of goods or services by telephone

telescope

telescope /'telɪskəʊp/ *noun* [C] a piece of equipment, in the shape of a tube, that makes things which are far away look bigger or nearer

Teletext /'telɪ,tekst/ *noun trademark* a system that gives written information on many subjects, such as news, on a television screen

televise /'telɪvaɪz/ *verb* [T] to show something on television *The concert will be **televised** live around the world.* ○ *The match will be televised live* (= shown as it is being played) *on BBC Scotland.*

watch television • see/watch sth on television • on television • a television channel/presenter/programme/series

⚬ **television** /'telɪvɪʒ³n/ *noun* 1 [EQUIPMENT] [C] a piece of equipment in the shape of a box, with a screen on the front, used for watching programmes 2 [PROGRAMMES] [U] the programmes that are shown on a television *I mostly **watch** television in the evening.* ○ *I saw it **on** television.* ○ *a television **programme*** 3 [SYSTEM] [U] the system or business of making and broadcasting programmes for television *They both work in childrens's television.* ⊃See also: **closed-circuit television, satellite television.**

COMMON LEARNER ERROR

watch television

Be careful to choose the correct verb with television.
My children watch too much television.
~~My children look too much television.~~

teleworking /'telɪ,wɜːkɪŋ/ *UK* (*US* telecommuting) *noun* [U] working at home, while communicating with your office by computer and telephone • **teleworker** *noun* [C] *UK*

⚬ **tell** /tel/ *verb past* told 1 [SAY] [T] to say something to someone, usually giving them information *He **told** me **about** his new school.* ○ [+ (that)] *Sally **told** me that the play didn't start until 9 o'clock.* ○ *Who **told** you that she was leaving?* ○ *I **told** you he'd be angry.* ○ [+ question word] *Can you **tell** me what time the next bus leaves?* ⊃See Common learner error at **say.** 2 **tell sb to do sth** to order someone to do something *I **told** you to stay here.* ○ *He **told** me to leave the room.* ○ *I **told** her to finish her dinner.* 3 **can tell** to know or recognize something from what you hear, see, etc [+ (that)] *You couldn't **tell** that he was tired.* ○ [+ question word] *You can never **tell** whether Hajime's being serious or not.* ○ *I can't **tell** the **difference** between them.* 4 [UNDERSTAND FROM] [T] If something tells you something, it gives you information. *What does the survey **tell** us about the lives of teenagers?* 5 **(I'll) tell you what** used to suggest a plan *Tell you what, let's go swimming and then get a pizza.* 6 [EFFECT] [I] to have a bad effect on someone *The worry of the last few months was starting to **tell** on him.* 7 **(I) told you so!** *informal* used when someone has caused problems for themselves by doing something that you told them not to *"I think I've taken on too much work." "I **told** you so, didn't I?"* ⊃See also: tell sb's **fortune.**

tell sb/sth apart to be able to see the difference between two things or people that are very similar *It's impossible to **tell** the twins apart.*

tell sb off to tell someone that they have done something wrong and that you are angry about it [+ **for** + doing sth] *Darren **got told off** for talking in class.* ⊃See colour picture **Phrasal Verbs** on page Centre 16.

teller /'telɑʳ/ *noun* [C] *US* someone who works in a bank and gives out or takes in money ⊃See also: **fortune-teller.**

telling /'telɪŋ/ *adjective* showing the truth about a situation, or showing what someone really thinks *a **telling** comment*

telltale /'telteɪl/ *adjective* [always before noun] showing something that someone is trying to keep secret *She was showing all the **telltale** signs of pregnancy.*

telly /'teli/ *noun* [C, U] *UK informal short for* television

temp /temp/ *noun* [C] someone who works in an office for a short time while someone else is away, ill, etc • **temp** *verb* [I] to work as a temp in an office

temper[1] /'tempɑʳ/ *noun* 1 [C, U] when someone becomes angry very easily *He's got a really **bad temper**.* 2 **be in a bad/foul, etc temper** to be feeling angry *I'd avoid her if I were you - she's in a foul temper.* 3 **lose your temper (with sb)** to suddenly become very angry *I **lost** my **temper** with the children this morning.* 4 **keep your temper** to succeed in staying calm and not becoming angry

temper[2] /'tempɑʳ/ *verb* [T] *formal* to make something less strong, extreme, etc *I learnt to **temper** my criticism.*

temperament /'temp³rəmənt/ *noun* [C, U] the part of your character that affects your moods and the way you behave *I don't think he's got the right temperament to be a teacher.*

temperamental /,temp³rə'ment³l/ *adjective* 1 becoming angry or upset very often and suddenly 2 A machine, vehicle, etc that is temperamental does not always work correctly.

temperate /'temp³rət/ *adjective formal* having weather that is not very hot and not very cold *a **temperate** climate*

average/extreme/high/low temperatures • temperatures drop/fall/rise/soar

⚬ **temperature** /'temprətʃɑʳ/ *noun* 1 [C, U] how hot or cold something is *The room's kept at a **temperature** of around 20°C.* 2 **sb's temperature** how hot or cold someone's body is *The doctor examined him and **took** his **temperature** (= measured his temperature).* 3 **have a temperature** to be hotter than usual because you are ill

template /'templeɪt/ *noun* [C] 1 a metal, plastic, etc pattern that is used for making many copies of a shape 2 a system that helps you arrange information on a computer screen

temple /'templ/ *noun* [C] **1** a building where people in some religions go to pray or worship *a Buddhist temple* **2** the area on each side of your head in front of the top of your ear

tempo /'tempəʊ/ *noun* **1** [U, no plural] the speed at which an activity happens *The tempo of the game increased in the second half.* **2** [C, U] *formal* the speed of a piece of music

OTHER WAYS OF SAYING ***temporary***

The phrase **for now** can be used to say that something should happen or be done now but can be changed later: *Just put everything on the table for now - I'll sort it all out later.*

The adjective **disposable** can be used to describe objects which are intended to be used temporarily and then thrown away: *I bought a disposable camera at the airport.*

If something is temporary and low quality, you can say that it is **makeshift**: *We built a makeshift shelter under the trees.*

The adjective **short-lived** can be used instead of 'temporary' when it means 'lasting for a short time': *I had a few relationships at college, most of which were fairly short-lived.*

The expression **acting manager/chairman**, etc is often used to describe someone who does a job temporarily while the person who usually does it is not there: *He'll be the acting director until they appoint a permanent one.*

temporary /'tempər'ri/ *adjective* existing or happening for only a short or limited time *a temporary job* ○ *temporary accommodation/housing* ● **temporarily** *adverb*

tempt /tempt/ *verb* [T] to make someone want to have or do something, especially something that they do not need or something that is wrong [+ to do sth] *She's trying to tempt me to go shopping with her.*

WORD PARTNERS FOR ***temptation***

avoid/resist (the) temptation ● **give in to/succumb to** temptation ● a **strong** temptation ● the temptation **of** doing sth

temptation /temp'teɪʃᵊn/ *noun* **1** [C, U] a feeling that you want to do or have something, although you know you should not [+ to do sth] *I resisted the temptation to* (= I did not) *have another piece of chocolate cake.* **2** [C] something that makes you want to do or have something although you know you should not *He knew crime was wrong but the money was too great a temptation.*

tempting /'temptɪŋ/ *adjective* Something that is tempting makes you want to have or do it. *a tempting invitation/offer*

o→**ten** /ten/ the number 10

tenacious /tɪ'neɪʃəs/ *adjective* very determined to do something and not wanting to stop ● **tenaciously** *adverb* ● **tenacity** /tɪ'næsəti/ *noun* [U]

tenancy /'tenənsi/ *noun* [C, U] the period of time when someone rents a room, house, etc

tenant /'tenənt/ *noun* [C] someone who pays rent to live in a room, house, etc

o→**tend** /tend/ *verb* **1 tend to do sth** to often do a particular thing or be likely to do a particular thing *I tend to wear dark colours.* ○ *July and August tend to be our busiest months.* **2** [T] (*also* **tend to**) *formal* to look after someone or something *He spends most afternoons tending his vegetable garden.*

tendency /'tendənsi/ *noun* [C] something that someone often does, or something that often happens [+ to do sth] *She has a tendency to talk for too long.* ○ *There is a growing tendency for companies to employ people on short contracts.*

tender¹ /'tendə'/ *adjective* **1** GENTLE kind and gentle *a tender kiss/look* **2** FOOD Tender meat or vegetables are soft and easy to cut. *The meat was wonderfully tender and flavoursome.* **3** PAINFUL If part of your body is tender, it is painful when you touch it. **4 at the tender age of 8/17/25 etc** *literary* at the young age of 8/17, etc ● **tenderness** *noun* [U]

tender² /'tendə'/ *verb formal* **1** [I] to make a formal offer to do a job or to provide a service **2** [T] *formal* to formally offer a suggestion, idea, money etc *He tendered his resignation* (= offered to leave his job)

tender³ /'tendə'/ *noun* [C, U] a formal offer to do some work *The work has been put out to tender* (= people have been asked to make offers to do the work).

tenderly /'tendəli/ *adverb* in a kind and gentle way *He looked at her tenderly.*

tendon /'tendən/ *noun* [C] a strong piece of tissue in your body that connects a muscle to a bone

tenement /'tenəmənt/ *noun* [C] a large building that is divided into apartments, usually in a poor area of a city

tenet /'tenɪt/ *noun* [C] a principle or belief of a theory or religion *one of the basic tenets of Islam*

tenner /'tenə'/ *noun* [C] *UK informal* a piece of paper money that has a value of £10 *Could you lend me a tenner?*

tennis /'tenɪs/ *noun* [U] a sport in which two or four people hit a small ball to each other over a net ➔See colour picture **Sports 2** on page Centre 15 ➔See also: **table tennis**.

tenor /'tenə'/ *noun* [C] a male singer with a high voice

tense¹ /tens/ *adjective* **1** FEELING nervous, worried, and not able to relax *The students looked tense as they waited for their exam results.* ○ *Everyone feels tense in an exam situation.* **2** SITUATION A tense situation makes you feel nervous and worried. *There were some tense moments in the second half of the game.* **3** MUSCLE A tense muscle feels tight and stiff.

tense² /tens/ (*also* **tense up**) *verb* [I, T] If your muscles tense, they become tight and stiff, and if you tense them, you make them do this.

tense³ /tens/ *noun* [C, U] the form of a verb which shows the time at which an action happened. For example 'I sing' is in the present tense and 'I will sing' is in the future tense.

WORD PARTNERS FOR **tension**

create/defuse/ease tension ● tension **mounts**
● **growing / increased / mounting** tension
● tension **between** sb and sb ● **ethnic/racial**
tensions

tension /'tenʃªn/ noun **1** NO TRUST [C, U] a feeling
of fear or anger between two groups of people
who do not trust each other ***ethnic/racial tension*** ○ *There are **growing tensions between**
the two countries.* **2** BEING NERVOUS [U] a feeling
that you are nervous, worried, and not relaxed
*You could feel the tension in the room as we
waited for her to arrive.* **3** TIGHT [U] when a
muscle, rope, etc, is tight or stiff

tent /tent/ noun [C] a
structure made of
metal poles and
cloth which is fixed
to the ground with
ropes and used as a
cover or to sleep
under *It only took
twenty minutes to
put the tent up* (= make it ready to use).

tent

tentacle /'tentəkl/ noun [C] one of the long,
arm-like parts of some sea creatures

tentative /'tentətɪv/ adjective **1** A tentative
idea, plan, agreement, etc is not certain. *The
two companies have announced a tentative
deal.* **2** doing something in a way that shows
you are not confident *a child's tentative first
steps* ● **tentatively** adverb

tenth[1] /tenθ/ 10th written as a word

tenth[2] /tenθ/ noun [C] one of ten equal parts of
something; ¹⁄₁₀; 0.1

tenuous /'tenjuəs/ adjective A tenuous connection, idea, or situation is weak and possibly does not exist. *The court is unlikely to
accept such tenuous evidence.* ● **tenuously** adverb

tenure /'tenjəʳ/ noun [U] **1** BUILDING/LAND the
legal right to live in a building or use a piece
of land for a period **2** TIME the period of time
when someone has an important job *his tenure
as president* **3** PERMANENT If you have tenure in
your job, your job is permanent.

tepid /'tepɪd/ adjective A tepid liquid is slightly
warm.

term[1] /tɜːm/ noun **1** WORD [C] a word or phrase
that is used to refer to a particular thing, especially in a technical or scientific subject *a
legal/technical term* **2** TIME [C] the fixed
period of time when someone does an important job or is in a particular place *a prison term*
○ *The government has been elected for another
four-year term.* **3** SCHOOL [C] one of the periods
of time that the school or university year is
divided into *We've got a test at the **end of term**.*
4 in the long/short, etc term a long/short, etc
period of time from now ⊃See also: **half-term**.

term[2] /tɜːm/ verb [T] formal to use a particular
word or phrase to describe something *Critics
termed the movie a 'disaster'.*

terminal[1] /'tɜːmɪnªl/ noun [C] **1** a building
where you can get onto an aircraft, bus, or
ship *a terminal building* **2** a screen and keyboard with which you can use a computer

terminal[2] /'tɜːmɪnªl/ adjective A terminal illness will cause death. *terminal cancer* ● **terminally** adverb **terminally ill**

terminate /'tɜːmɪneɪt/ verb [I, T] formal If something terminates, it ends, and if you terminate
something, you make it end. *His contract has
been terminated.* ● **termination** /ˌtɜːmɪ'neɪʃªn/
noun [C, U]

terminology /ˌtɜːmɪ'nɒlədʒi/ noun [C, U] the
special words and phrases that are used in a
particular subject *medical/scientific terminology*

terminus /'tɜːmɪnəs/ noun [C] the place where a
train or bus finishes its journey

WORD PARTNERS FOR **terms**

agree terms ● **break/meet** the terms **of** sth
● **under** the terms **of** sth

terms /tɜːmz/ noun [plural] **1** the rules of an
agreement *Under the terms of their contract,
employees must give 3 months notice if they
want to leave.* **2 be on good/bad/friendly, etc
terms** to have a good/bad, etc relationship
with someone **3 not be on speaking terms** to
not speak to someone because you have
argued with them **4 in ... terms** (*also* **in terms of**
sth) used to explain which part of a problem or
situation you are referring to *In financial
terms, the project was not a success.* **5 in no uncertain terms** in a direct and often angry way *I
told him to go away in no uncertain terms.*
6 come to terms with sth to accept a sad situation *He still hasn't come to terms with his
brother's death.* ⊃See also: a **contradiction** in terms.

terrace /'terɪs/ noun [C] **1** a flat area outside a
house, restaurant, etc where you can sit **2** UK
a row of houses that are joined together

terraced 'house UK (US **row house**) noun [C]
one of a row of houses that are joined together

the terraces /'terɪsɪz/ noun [plural] in the UK,
wide, concrete steps where people stand to
watch a football game

terrain /tə'reɪn/ noun [C, U] a particular type of
land *rough terrain*

terrestrial /tə'restriəl/ adjective formal relating
to the Earth, not space

☞**terrible** /'terəbl/ adjective very bad, of low quality, or unpleasant *a terrible accident* ○ *The
weather was terrible.*

terribly /'terəbli/ adverb **1** very *She seemed terribly upset.* **2** very badly *I slept terribly last
night.*

terrier /'teriəʳ/ noun [C] a type of small dog

terrific /tə'rɪfɪk/ adjective **1** excellent *a terrific
opportunity* ○ *I thought she looked terrific.*
2 [always before noun] very large, great, or serious *a terrific increase in prices* ○ *a terrific
storm* ● **terrifically** adverb

terrified /'terɪfaɪd/ adjective very frightened
I'm terrified of flying. ○ [+ (that)] *Maggie was
terrified that her parents would discover the
truth.*

terrify /'terɪfaɪ/ verb [T] to make someone feel
very frightened *The idea of parachuting out of
an aircraft terrifies me.* ● **terrifying** adjective *a
terrifying experience*

territorial /ˌterɪˈtɔːriəl/ *adjective* relating to the land that is owned or controlled by a particular country *a territorial dispute*

territory /ˈterɪtᵊri/ *noun* 1 [LAND] [C, U] land that is owned or controlled by a particular country *Spanish territory* 2 [PERSON/ANIMAL] [C, U] an area that an animal or person thinks belongs to them *Cats like to protect their territory.* 3 [AREA OF KNOWLEDGE] [U] an area of knowledge or experience *With this project we'll be moving into unknown territory.*

terror /ˈterᵊr/ *noun* [U] a feeling of being very frightened *There was a look of terror on his face.* ⊃See also: **reign¹** of terror.

terrorism /ˈterᵊrɪzᵊm/ *noun* [U] the use of violence for political purposes, for example putting bombs in public places *an act of terrorism*

terrorist /ˈterᵊrɪst/ *noun* [C] someone who is involved in terrorism *a terrorist attack*

terrorize (*also UK* -**ise**) /ˈterᵊraɪz/ *verb* [T] to make someone feel very frightened by saying that you will hurt or kill them *A gang of young men with knives have been terrorizing local people.*

terse /tɜːs/ *adjective* said or written in a few words, often showing that you are annoyed ● **tersely** *adverb*

tertiary /ˈtɜːʃᵊri/ *adjective UK formal* Tertiary education is education at university or college level. *a tertiary institution*

TESOL /ˈtiːsɒl/ *noun* [U] *abbreviation for* Teaching English to Speakers of Other Languages

WORD PARTNERS FOR *test*

do/sit/take a test ● fail/pass a test ● a test on sth

◦━**test¹** /test/ *noun* [C] 1 [EXAM] a set of questions to measure someone's knowledge or ability *a driving test* ○ *You have to take a test.* ○ *Only two students in the class failed the test.* ○ *Did you pass the biology test?* 2 [MEDICAL] a short medical examination of part of your body *an eye test* ○ *a pregnancy test* 3 [EXPERIMENT] something that you do to discover if something is safe, works correctly, etc *a safety test* 4 [SITUATION] a situation that shows how good something is *This will be a real test of his ability.*

◦━**test²** /test/ *verb* [T] 1 [EXPERIMENT] to do something in order to discover if something is safe, works correctly, etc *None of our products are tested on animals.* 2 [MEDICAL] to do a medical examination of part of someone's body *I'm going to get my hearing tested.* 3 [EXAM] to give someone a set of questions, in order to measure their knowledge or ability *You'll be tested on all the things we've studied this term.* 4 [SITUATION] If a situation tests someone, it proves how good, strong, etc they are.

testament /ˈtestəmənt/ *noun formal* a **testament to sth** *formal* proof of something good *It's a testament to Jane's popularity that so many people are celebrating with her today.* ⊃See also: **the New Testament**, **the Old Testament**.

testicle /ˈtestɪkl/ *noun* [C] one of the two round, male sex organs that produce sperm

testify /ˈtestɪfaɪ/ *verb* [I] to say what you know or believe is true in a law court [+ that] *Elliott testified that he had met the men in a bar.*

testimony /ˈtestɪməni/ *noun* 1 [C, U] a formal statement about what someone knows or believes is true, especially in a law court *the testimony of a witness* 2 **testimony to sth** *formal* proof of something good *The book's continued popularity is testimony to the power of clever marketing.*

'test ,tube *noun* [C] a glass tube that is open at one end and used in scientific experiments

tetanus /ˈtetᵊnəs/ *noun* [U] a serious disease that makes your muscles stiff and is caused by an infection that gets into the body through a cut

tether /ˈteðᵊr/ *verb* [T] to tie an animal to something so that it cannot move away *The goats were tethered to a post.* ● **tether** *noun* [C] ⊃See also: at the **end¹** of your tether.

◦━**text¹** /tekst/ *noun* 1 [WRITING] [C, U] the written words in a book, magazine, etc, not the pictures *a page of text* 2 [BOOK/DOCUMENT] [C] a book or piece of writing that you study as part of a course *'Hamlet' was one of our A level texts.* 3 [MESSAGE] a written message, usually containing words with letters left out, sent from one mobile phone to another

text² /tekst/ *verb* [I, T] to send a text message (= written message from a mobile phone) *Daniel texted me to say he would be late.*

textbook /ˈtekstbʊk/ *noun* [C] a book about a particular subject, written for students *a chemistry/French textbook* ⊃See colour picture **The Classroom** on page Centre 6.

textile /ˈtekstaɪl/ *noun* [C] any type of cloth that is made by weaving (= crossing threads under and over each other)

WORD PARTNERS FOR *text message*

get/send a text message ● a text message saying sth ● a text message from/to sb

'text ,message *noun* [C] a written message, usually containing words with letters left out, sent from one mobile phone to another ● **text messaging** *noun* [U]

texture /ˈtekstʃᵊr/ *noun* [C, U] the way that something feels when you touch it or put it in your mouth *wood with a rough texture* ○ *It's low in fat but it has a nice creamy texture.*

◦━**than** *strong form* /ðæn/ *weak form* /ðᵊn/ *preposition, conjunction* used to compare two different things or amounts *Susannah's car is bigger than mine.* ○ *Tom's a bit taller than Sam.* ○ *It cost less than I expected.*

◦━**thank** /θæŋk/ *verb* [T] 1 to tell someone that you are grateful for something they have done or given you *I haven't thanked her for her present yet.* ○ [+ for + doing sth] *Yu Yin thanked the boys for helping her.* 2 **thank God/goodness/Heavens, etc** something that you say when you are happy because something bad did not happen *Thank goodness you're okay - I was really worried.*

thankful /ˈθæŋkfᵊl/ *adjective* pleased or grateful about something [+ (that)] *We were thankful* *that none of the children saw the accident.*

thankfully /ˈθæŋkfᵊli/ *adverb* used at the beginning of a sentence to show that you are pleased or grateful about something *Thankfully, nobody was hurt.*

thankless /ˈθæŋkləs/ *adjective* A thankless job is difficult or unpleasant and no one thanks you for doing it. *Nursing can be a **thankless job**.* ○ *Keeping the children's rooms tidy is a **thankless task**.*

thanks[1] /θæŋks/ *exclamation informal* **1** used to tell someone that you are grateful because they have given you something or done something for you *Can you pass me the book? Thanks very much.* ○ *Thanks for all your help.* **2 thanks/no, thanks** used to accept or refuse someone's offer *"Would you like a cup of coffee?" "No, thanks."*

o→**thanks**[2] /θæŋks/ *noun* [plural] **1** words that show you are grateful for something someone has given to you or done for you *He sent a message of thanks.* **2 thanks to sb/sth** because of someone or something *I passed my driving test, thanks to the extra help my Dad gave me.* ○ *Its thanks to Sandy that I heard about the job.*

Thanksgiving /ˌθæŋksˈɡɪvɪŋ/ *noun* [C, U] a holiday in the autumn in the US and Canada, when families have a big meal together

o→**thank ,you** *exclamation* **1** used to tell someone that you are grateful because they have given you something or done something for you *Thank you very much for the birthday card.* ○ *"Here's the money I promised you." "Thank you."* **2 thank you/no, thank you** used to accept or refuse someone's offer *"Would you like something to eat?" "No, thank you."*

o→**thank-you** /ˈθæŋkju/ *noun* [C] something that you say or do to thank someone for doing something [+ for + doing sth] *I bought Emma some chocolates as a thank-you for looking after the dog.* ○ *a **thank-you present***

o→**that**[1] /ðæt/ *determiner plural* **those** **1** used to refer to something or someone that has already been talked about or seen *Did you know that woman in the post office?* ○ *How much are those shoes?* **2** used to refer to something or someone that is not near you *He went through that door.* ○ *Have you seen that man over there?* ➾See Common learner error at **this**.

that[2] /ðæt/ *pronoun plural* **those** **1** ALREADY DISCUSSED/SEEN used to refer to something that has already been talked about or seen *That looks heavy.* ○ *You can't possibly wear those!* **2** NOT NEAR used to refer to something that is not near you *What's that in the corner?* **3 that's it a** CORRECT used to say that something is correct *You need to push the two pieces together. That's it.* **b** ENDED used to say that something has ended *Well that's it then, we've finished.* **4 that's that** used to say that something has happened or a decision has been made and there is nothing more to say or do *I won't agree to it and that's that.* **5 that is (to say)** used to correct something you have said or give more information about something *Everybody was at the meeting, well everyone except Jeanne, that is.*

---

this/these or **that/those** ?

Use **this** or **these** to talk about people and things which are close to the speaker.

This is my sister Sarah.

Do you like these earrings I'm wearing?

Use **that** or **those** to talk about people and things which are further away from the speaker.

That girl over there is called Sarah.

I liked those earrings you wore last night.

o→**that**[3] *strong form* /ðæt/ *weak form* /ðət/ *conjunction* **1** used after some verbs, nouns, and adjectives to introduce a new part of a sentence *He said that he'd collect it later.* ○ *Is it true that she's pregnant?* **2** used instead of 'who' or 'which' at the beginning of a relative clause *Have you eaten all the cake that I made yesterday?*

that[4] /ðæt/ *adverb* **1** used when describing the size, amount, or state of something or someone *I've never seen a fish that big before.* **2 not (all) that big/good/warm, etc** not very big, good, warm, etc *It hasn't been all that cold this winter.*

thatched /θætʃt/ *adjective* A thatched building has a roof that is made of straw (= dried grasslike stems). *a thatched cottage*

thaw /θɔː/ *verb* **1** [I, T] (*also* **thaw out**) If something that is frozen thaws, it becomes warmer and softer or changes to liquid, and if you thaw something that is frozen, you make it do this. *Allow the meat to thaw before cooking it.* **2** [I] If a relationship between people thaws, it becomes more friendly after being bad. ● **thaw** *noun* [C]

o→**the** *strong form* /ðiː/ *weak forms* /ði, ðə/ *determiner* **1** ALREADY KNOWN used before nouns to refer to particular things or people that have already been talked about or are already known *Can you pass the salt?* ○ *I'll pick you up at the station.* ○ *That's the new restaurant I told you about.* **2** ONLY ONE used before nouns when only one of something exists *Have you seen the Eiffel Tower?* ○ *I'd love to travel round the world.* **3** SINGULAR NOUN used before a singular noun to refer to all the things or people described by that noun *The Tiger has become extinct in many countries.* **4** ADJECTIVE used before some adjectives to make them into nouns *a home for the elderly* ○ *relatives of the deceased* **5** COMPARE used before each of two adjectives or adverbs to show how one thing changes depending on another *The longer we live here, the more we like it.* **6** EACH used with units or measurements to mean each or every *How many Belgian francs to the pound?* **7** BODY used when referring to a part of the body *He held her tightly by the arm.* **8** TIME used before numbers which refer to dates or periods of time *the sixties* ○ *Thursday the 29th of April* **9** MUSIC used with the names of musical instruments or dances to mean the type of instrument or dance in general *Can you play the violin?*

| ɑː arm | ɜː her | iː see | ɔː saw | uː too | aɪ my | aʊ how | eə hair | eɪ day | əʊ no | ɪə near | ɔɪ boy | ʊə poor | aɪə fire | aʊə sour |

o←**theatre** UK (US **theater**) /'θɪətəʳ/ noun **1** BUILDING WITH STAGE [C] a building with a stage where people go to watch plays *the Arts Theatre* **2** BUILDING FOR FILMS [C] US a building where people go to watch films *a movie theater* **3** WORK [U] the work of writing, acting in, and producing plays **4** MEDICAL [C, U] UK a room in a hospital where doctors do operations

theatrical /θi'ætrɪkəl/ adjective **1** [always before noun] relating to the theatre *theatrical make-up* **2** doing and saying things in a very obvious way that is intended to make people notice you

theft /θeft/ noun [C, U] the action or crime of stealing something *car theft*

o←**their** /ðeəʳ/ determiner **1** belonging to or relating to a group of people, animals, or things that have already been talked about *It was their problem, not mine.* **2** used to refer to what belongs to or relates to a person when you want to avoid saying 'his' or 'her' or when you do not know if the person is male or female *Did this person give their name?*

o←**theirs** /ðeəz/ pronoun the things that belong or relate to a group of people, animals, or things that have already been talked about *I think she's a relation of theirs.*

o←**them** strong form /ðem/ weak form /ðəm/ pronoun **1** used after a verb or preposition to refer to a group of people, animals, or things that have already been talked about *I'm looking for my keys - have you seen them?* **2** used after a verb or preposition to refer to a person when you want to avoid saying 'him' or 'her' or when you do not know if the person is male or female *When each passenger arrives we ask them to fill in a form.*

theme /θiːm/ noun **1** [C] the subject of a book, film, speech, etc *The theme of loss runs through most of his novels.* **2** **theme music/ song/tune** the music that is played at the beginning and end of a particular television or radio programme

'**theme ,park** noun [C] a park with entertainments, such as games, machines to ride on, restaurants, etc, that are all based on one idea

o←**themselves** /ðəm'selvz/ pronoun **1** the reflexive form of the pronoun 'they' *They're both 16 - they're old enough to look after themselves.* **2** used to emphasize the pronoun 'they' or the particular group of people you are referring to *They've decided to run the club themselves.* **3** **(all) by themselves** alone or without anyone else's help *The kids arranged the party all by themselves.* **4** **(all) to themselves** for their use only *They had the whole campsite to themselves.*

o←**then**¹ /ðen/ adverb **1** TIME at that time *Call me tomorrow - I'll have time to speak then.* ○ *Tim and I were at school together, but I haven't seen him since then.* **2** NEXT next, or after something has happened *She trained as a teacher and then became a lawyer.* ○ *Let me finish my drink, then we'll go.* **3** SO so or because of that *Have a rest now, then you won't be tired this evening.* ○ *"My interview's at 9 o'clock." "You'll be catching an early train, then?"* **4** IN ADDITION used in order to add something to what you have just said *I've got two essays to write and then my science project to finish.* **5** **now then/ right then/okay then** used to introduce a question or a suggestion *Right then, what do you want to drink?*

then² /ðen/ adjective [always before noun] used to refer to something which was true in the past but which is not true now *the then Prime Minister Margaret Thatcher*

thence /ðens/ adverb formal from there *The oil is shipped to Panama and thence to Texan refineries.*

theology /θi'ɒlədʒi/ noun [U] the study of religion and religious belief ● **theological** /ˌθiːə'lɒdʒɪkəl/ adjective *theological college*

theoretical /θɪə'retɪkəl/ adjective **1** based on the ideas that relate to a subject, not the practical uses of that subject *theoretical physics* **2** related to an explanation that has not been proved

theoretically /θɪə'retɪkəli/ adverb in a way that obeys some rules but is not likely *It is theoretically possible.*

theorist /'θɪərɪst/ noun [C] someone who develops ideas about the explanation for events *a political theorist*

theorize (also UK **-ise**) /'θɪəraɪz/ verb [I, T] to develop a set of ideas about something [+ that] *Investigators theorized that the crash was caused by engine failure.*

o←**theory** /'θɪəri/ noun **1** [C] an idea or set of ideas that is intended to explain something *Darwin's theory of evolution* **2** [U] the set of principles on which a subject is based *economic theory* **3** **in theory** If something is possible in theory, it should be possible but often it does not happen this way.

therapeutic /ˌθerə'pjuːtɪk/ adjective **1** helping to cure a disease or improve your health *the therapeutic benefits of massage* **2** helping you to feel happier and more relaxed *I find gardening very therapeutic.*

therapist /'θerəpɪst/ noun [C] someone whose job is to treat a particular type of mental or physical illness *a speech therapist*

therapy /'θerəpi/ noun [C, U] the work of treating mental or physical illness without using an operation *cancer therapy* ○ *She's now in therapy to help her deal with her alcohol problem.* ⊃See also: physical therapy.

T

⚬⇥**there¹** *strong form* /ðeəʳ/ *weak form* /ðəʳ/ *pronoun*
There is/are/was, etc used to show that something exists or happens *There are three pubs in the village.* ○ *There's not much room in the back of the car.* ○ *There have been a lot of accidents on this road.* ○ *Is there any milk?*

⚬⇥**there²** /ðeəʳ/ *adverb* **1** PLACE in or at a particular place *We live in York because my wife works there.* ○ *I went to the party but I didn't know anyone there.* ○ *We'll never get there* (= arrive) *in time!* **2** DIRECTION used when you are pointing or looking at something in order to make someone look in the same direction *Put them in that box there.* ○ *Your bag's over there by the door.* **3** AVAILABLE present or available *They were all there - Mark, Jill, and the three kids.* ○ *That money is there for you if you need it.* **4** POINT at a particular point in a process or activity *Do you want to play another game or do you want to stop there?* ○ *Keep on trying - you'll get there* (= succeed) *in the end.* **5 there and then** If you do something there and then, you do it immediately. *I showed James the ring I liked and he bought it there and then.* **6 There you are/go. a** GIVING used when you are giving something to someone *Do you want a tissue? There you are.* **b** EMPHASIZING used to emphasize that you were right *There you go - I told you you'd win!*

thereabouts /ˈðeərəbaʊts/ *adverb mainly UK* near the number, amount, or time that has just been given *For this recipe you'll need 1kg of tomatoes, or thereabouts.*

thereafter /ˌðeəˈrɑːftəʳ/ *adverb formal* after a particular amount, time, or event *Faxes cost $1.20 for the first page, and 60 cents for each page thereafter.*

thereby /ˌðeəˈbaɪ/ *adverb formal* as a result of a particular action or event *The new dam will improve the water supply and thereby reduce hunger and disease.*

⚬⇥**therefore** /ˈðeəfɔːʳ/ *adverb* for that reason *The region has suffered severe flooding and tourists are therefore advised not to travel there.*

therein /ˌðeəˈrɪn/ *adverb formal* **1** in a particular document or place *We recommend that you study the report and the proposals contained therein.* **2 therein lies sth** because of the reason that has just been given *But the medicines are expensive, and therein lies the problem.*

thereof /ˌðeəˈrɒv/ *adverb formal* relating to what has just been said *It's gospel music, traditional country, jazz, and some strange combinations thereof.*

thermal /ˈθɜːməl/ *adjective* [always before noun] **1** relating to heat *thermal energy* **2** Thermal clothes are made to keep you warm. *thermal underwear*

thermo- /ˈθɜːməʊ-/ *prefix* relating to heat or temperature *a thermostat* (= a piece of equipment that controls temperature) ○ *a thermometer*

thermometer
/θəˈmɒmɪtəʳ/ *noun* [C] a piece of equipment that measures the temperature of the air or of your body

thermometer

Thermos /ˈθɜːmɒs/ *noun* [C] *trademark* a container that keeps hot liquids hot or cold liquids cold *(UK) a Thermos flask/ (US) a Thermos bottle* ⊃See picture at **flask**.

thermostat /ˈθɜːməstæt/ *noun* [C] a piece of equipment that controls the temperature of something or of a place *a central heating thermostat*

thesaurus /θɪˈsɔːrəs/ *noun* [C] a book in which words with similar meanings are put together in groups

⚬⇥**these** /ðiːz/ *pronoun, determiner plural of* this ⊃See Common learner error at **that, this**.

thesis /ˈθiːsɪs/ *noun* [C] *plural* theses /ˈθiːsiːz/ **1** a long piece of writing that you do as part of an advanced university course *a master's/PhD thesis* **2** *formal* a theory that is suggested and can then be argued with or agreed with *That is the central thesis of the book.*

⚬⇥**they** /ðeɪ/ *pronoun* **1** GROUP used as the subject of the verb when referring to a group of people, animals, or things that have already been talked about *I saw Kate and Nigel yesterday - they came over for dinner.* ○ *"Have you seen my car keys?" "They're on the kitchen table."* **2** PERSON used to refer to a person when you want to avoid saying 'he' or 'she' or when you do not know if the person is male or female *Someone I met at a party said they knew you.* ○ *"There's someone on the phone for you." "What do they want?"* **3** PEOPLE people in general *They say that breaking a mirror brings you seven years' bad luck.*

⚬⇥**they'd** /ðeɪd/ **1** *short for* they had *They'd just moved in when I saw them.* **2** *short for* they would *They'd like to take us out to dinner.*

⚬⇥**they'll** /ðeɪl/ *short for* they will *They'll be in Scotland next week.*

⚬⇥**they're** /ðeəʳ/ *short for* they are *They're both from Washington.*

⚬⇥**they've** /ðeɪv/ *short for* they have *They've got three children - two girls and a boy.*

⚬⇥**thick¹** /θɪk/ *adjective* **1** DISTANCE Something that is thick is larger than usual between its opposite sides. *a thick slice of meat* ○ *a thick layer of snow* **2 10cm/2m, etc thick** being 10cm/2m, etc thick *a piece of wood 2cm thick* **3** LARGE AMOUNT growing

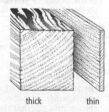
thick

thick   thin

very close together and in large amounts *thick, dark hair* **4** SMOKE Thick smoke, cloud, or fog is difficult to see through. *Thick, black smoke was pouring out of the chimney.* **5** LIQUID A thick substance or liquid has very little water in it and does not flow easily. *Stir the sauce over a low heat until thick.* **6** STUPID *UK informal* not intelligent **7 be thick with sth** If something is thick with a particular substance, it is covered in or full of that substance. *The air was thick with petrol fumes.* **8**

thick and fast quickly and in large numbers *Calls were coming in thick and fast by the end of the programme.* ⊃See also: have (a) thick **skin**¹.

thick² /θɪk/ *noun* **1 be in the thick of sth** to be involved in a situation at the point where there is most activity *He loves being in the thick of the action.* **2 through thick and thin** If you support or stay with someone through thick and thin, you always support or stay with them in easy and difficult situations. *She'd stuck by (= stayed with) Neil through thick and thin.*

thicken /ˈθɪkᵊn/ *verb* [I, T] to become thicker, or to make something thicker *Boil the sauce until it thickens.*

thickly /ˈθɪkli/ *adverb* in thick pieces, or in a thick layer *toast thickly spread with butter*

thickness /ˈθɪknəs/ *noun* [C, U] the distance between the opposite sides of something

thick-skinned /ˌθɪkˈskɪnd/ *adjective* If someone is thick-skinned, they do not get upset when other people criticize them.

thief /θiːf/ *noun* [C] *plural* **thieves** /θiːvz/ someone who steals things *a car thief* ○ *Thieves stole $500,000 worth of computer equipment.*

thigh /θaɪ/ *noun* [C] the top part of your leg above your knee ⊃See colour picture **The Body** on page Centre 13.

thimble /ˈθɪmbl/ *noun* [C] a small metal or plastic object that you use to protect your finger when you are sewing

o⁻**thin¹** /θɪn/ *adjective* **thinner, thinnest 1** DISTANCE Something that is thin is smaller than usual between its opposite sides. *a thin slice of ham* ○ *The walls are very thin.* ⊃See picture at **thick**. **2** PERSON A thin person or animal has very little fat on their body. **3** LIQUID A thin substance or liquid has a lot of water in it and flows easily. *thin soup* **4** AMOUNT having only a small number of people or a small amount of something *His hair is going thin on top.* **5** AIR Thin air does not have enough oxygen in it. **6 wear thin a** ANNOYED If your patience wears thin, you become less and less patient with someone who is annoying you. **b** REPEATED If a joke or explanation wears thin, it becomes less effective because it has been used too much. ⊃See also: disappear/vanish into thin **air**¹, be thin on the **ground**¹, through **thick²** and thin.

thin² /θɪn/ *verb* [T] **thinning,** *past* **thinned** to make a substance less thick, often by adding a liquid to it

thin out If a large number of people or things thin out, they become fewer in number.

o⁻**thing** /θɪŋ/ *noun* **1** OBJECT [C] used to refer to an object without saying its name *How do I switch this thing off?* ○ *I need to get a few things in town.* **2** PERSON [C] used to refer to a person or animal when you are expressing your feelings towards them *You look tired, you poor thing.* **3** IDEA [C] used to refer to an idea, event, or activity *I can't imagine Nick would say such a thing!* ○ *Meeting Nina was the best thing that's ever happened to me.* **4 for one thing** used to give a reason for something *You can't give Amy that shirt - for one thing it's too small for her.* **5 the thing is** *informal* used to introduce a problem which relates to something that you

have just said *I'd love to go out tonight, but the thing is, I've got to finish my report.* **6 a thing** used instead of 'anything' in order to emphasize what you are saying *I haven't got a thing to wear!* **7 have a thing about sth/sb** *informal* to like or dislike something or someone very much *He's got a thing about blonde women.* **8 it's a good thing** *informal* If it is a good thing that something happened, it is lucky that it happened. [+ (that)] *It's a good thing that Jo was there to help you.* **9 first/last thing** *informal* at the beginning/end of the day *I'll phone him first thing and tell him I can't come.* ○ *She likes a glass of milk last thing at night.* **10 be sb's thing** *informal* If an activity or subject is someone's thing, they are very interested in it and like doing it. *Jogging's just not my thing - I prefer team sports.* **11 the best/greatest thing since sliced bread** *humorous* extremely good *When I first got this computer I thought it was the best thing since sliced bread.*

things /θɪŋz/ *noun* [plural] **1** what is happening in your life *Don't worry - things will get better soon.* **2** the objects that you own *I'll just gather my things and then I'll be ready.* **3 be hearing/ seeing things** to imagine that you can hear or see things that do not exist

thingy /ˈθɪŋi/ *noun* [C] *UK informal* used to refer to something or someone when you cannot remember their name *We ate that beef thingy for lunch.*

o⁻**think¹** /θɪŋk/ *verb past* **thought 1** OPINION [I, T] to have an opinion about something or someone *Do you think it's going to rain?* ○ [+ (that)] *I don't think that Emma will get the job (= I believe she will not get it).* ○ *What did you think of the film?* ○ *What do you think about modern art?* **2** CONSIDER [I] to consider an idea or a problem *He thought for a few seconds before answering.* ○ *You should think about where you want to live.* **3** EXPECT [I, T] to believe that something is true, or to expect that something will happen, although you are not sure *I think she's called Joanna.* ○ *"Does this train stop at Oxford?" "Yes, I think so."* ○ [+ (that)] *I never thought that I would see Steven again.* **4 think about/of doing sth** to consider doing something *I'm thinking of moving to Sydney.* ○ *We thought about getting married, but decided not to.* **5 think about/of sb/sth** to use your mind to imagine a situation *I'm sorry I can't be at the wedding, but I'll be thinking of you.* **6 think of sth** to use your imagination and intelligence to produce an idea, a solution to a problem, or an answer to a question *When did you first think of the idea?* **7 think a lot of sb/sth** to admire someone, or to believe that something is good quality *Simon thinks a lot of you, you know.* **8 not think much of sb/sth** to not like someone, or to believe that something is not good quality *I don't think much of the food here.* **9 I think** used to introduce a suggestion or explanation in order to be polite [+ (that)] *It's getting late - I think that we should go.* **10 Who would have thought...?** used to express how surprising something is [+ (that)] *Who would have thought that buying a house could take so long!* ⊃See also: think the **world**¹ of sb. **11 think outside the**

box to use new ideas instead of traditional ideas when you think about something

think about or think of?

Think about someone/something means to have thoughts in your mind about a person or thing, or to consider them.

I was thinking about my mother.

I thought about the question before answering.

I thought the question before answering.

Think of/about something/someone also means to have an opinion about something or someone.

What do you think of/about the colour?

What do you think the colour?

Think of doing something means to consider the possibility of doing something.

We are thinking of having a party.

We are thinking to have a party.

---

think back to remember something that happened in the past *I thought back to the time when I was living in Toronto.*

think sth out to consider all the possible details of something *The scheme was well thought out.*

think sth over to consider an idea or plan carefully before making a decision

think sth through to carefully consider the possible results of doing something

think sth up to produce a new idea or plan *I don't want to go tonight and I'm trying to think up an excuse.*

think² /θɪŋk/ *noun* UK **have a think** to consider something carefully *Have a think about it and then tell me what you've decided.*

thinker /ˈθɪŋkəʳ/ *noun* [C] someone who considers important subjects or produces new ideas *a political/religious thinker*

WORD PARTNERS FOR **thinking**

2 the thinking **behind/on** sth • the **current** thinking

thinking /ˈθɪŋkɪŋ/ *noun* [U] **1** when you use your mind to consider something *This problem requires careful thinking.* **2** someone's ideas or opinions *The book discusses the impact of Christian thinking on western society.* ⊃See also: wishful thinking.

think ˌtank *noun* [C] a group of people who advise the government or an organization about particular subjects and who suggest new ideas

thinly /ˈθɪnli/ *adverb* **1** in thin pieces, or in a thin layer *She sliced the bread thinly.* **2** with only a small number of people or things *thinly populated areas*

third¹ /θɜːd/ 3rd written as a word

o⚊**third²** /θɜːd/ *noun* [C] **1** one of three equal parts of something; ⅓ **2 a third** in the UK, one of the lowest exam results you can achieve at the end of a university course

thirdly /ˈθɜːdli/ *adverb* used in order to introduce the third thing in a list

---

ˌthird 'party *noun* [C] someone who is not one of the two main people or groups that are involved in a situation

the ˌthird 'person *noun* the form of a verb or pronoun that is used when referring to the person or thing being spoken about or described. For example 'she' and 'they' are third person pronouns.

the ˌThird 'World *noun* the countries in Africa, Asia, and South America, which do not have well-developed economies

thirst /θɜːst/ *noun* **1** [U, no plural] the feeling that you want to drink something *I had a long, cold drink to **quench** my thirst* (= stop me feeling thirsty). **2 a thirst for sth** a strong wish for something *a thirst for adventure*

o⚊**thirsty** /ˈθɜːsti/ *adjective* wanting or needing a drink *I felt really hot and thirsty after my run.* • **thirstily** *adverb*

o⚊**thirteen** /θɜːˈtiːn/ the number 13 • **thirteenth** 13th written as a word

o⚊**thirty** /ˈθɜːti/ **1** the number 30 **2 the thirties** the years from 1930 to 1939 **3 be in your thirties** to be between the ages of 30 and 39 • **thirtieth** 30th written as a word

o⚊**this¹** /ðɪs/ *determiner plural* these **1** ALREADY TALKED ABOUT used to refer to something that you have already talked about *Most people don't agree with this decision.* ○ *How did you hear about this course?* **2** NEAR used to refer to something or someone that is near you or that you are pointing to *How much does this CD cost?* ○ *David gave me these earrings for my birthday.* **3** TIME used to refer to the present week, month, year, etc or the one that comes next *I'll see you this evening.* ○ *Kate and Nigel are getting married this June.* **4** NOW TALKING ABOUT *informal* used to refer to a particular person or thing that you are going to talk about *We went to this really great club last night.* ⊃See Common learner error at **that** ⊃See also: be out of this **world¹**.

o⚊**this²** /ðɪs/ *pronoun plural* these **1** ALREADY TALKED ABOUT used to refer to something that you have already talked about *When did this happen?* ○ *This is the best news I've heard all week!* **2** NEAR used to refer to something or someone that is near you or that you are pointing to *Try some of this - it's delicious.* ○ *Are these your keys?* ○ *This is my girlfriend, Beth.* **3** SAY/ASK WHO used to say or ask who someone is when speaking on the telephone, radio, etc *"Hello, is this Julie Hawkins?" "Yes, who's this?"* **4 this and that** different things which are not very important *"What are you doing today?" "Oh, just this and that."*

this/that or these/those?

Remember **this** and **that** are used before a singular noun. **These** and **those** are used before a plural noun.

Look at this photo.

Look at these photos.

Can you pass me that book please?

Can you pass me those books please?

| ɑː arm | ɜː her | iː see | ɔː saw | uː too | aɪ my | aʊ how | eə hair | eɪ day | əʊ no | ɪə near | ɔɪ boy | ʊə poor | aɪə fire | aʊə sour |

⊶**this**³ /ðɪs/ *adverb* used when describing the size, amount, or state of something or someone *I need a piece of wood this big.* ○ *I've never seen her this angry.*

thistle /ˈθɪsl/ *noun* **[C]** a wild plant with purple flowers and sharp points

THNQ *informal written abbreviation for* thank you: used in emails and text messages

thong /θɒŋ/ *noun* **[C]** **1** a piece of underwear or the bottom part of a bikini (= a piece of clothing with two parts that women wear for swimming) which does not cover the bottom **2** *US* a flip flop

thorn /θɔːn/ *noun* **[C]** a small, sharp point on the stem of a plant

thorny /ˈθɔːni/ *adjective* **1** covered in thorns **2** A thorny problem, question, subject, etc is difficult to deal with.

thorough /ˈθʌrə/ [US] /ˈθɜːrəʊ/ *adjective* careful and covering every detail *The government has promised a thorough investigation of the matter.* • **thoroughness** *noun* **[U]**

thoroughbred /ˈθʌrəbred/ *noun* **[C]** a horse especially bred for racing

thoroughly /ˈθʌrəli/ *adverb* **1** very carefully *Wash the spinach thoroughly before cooking* **2** very, or very much *We thoroughly enjoyed ourselves.*

⊶**those** /ðəʊz/ *pronoun, determiner plural of* that ⊃See Common learner error at **that, this.**

⊶**though**¹ /ðəʊ/ *conjunction* **1** used to introduce a fact or opinion that makes the other part of the sentence seem surprising *And though she's quite small, she's very strong.* ○ *Nina didn't phone, **even though** she said she would.* **2** but *They're coming next week, though I don't know when.* ○ *The restaurant serves good, though extremely expensive, food.*

though² /ðəʊ/ *adverb* used to add a new fact or opinion which changes what you have just said *Okay, I'll come to the party - I'm not staying late though.*

WORD PARTNERS FOR ***thought***

give sth **some** thought • **have** a thought • a **secret/sobering/terrible** thought

⊶**thought**¹ /θɔːt/ *noun* **1** [IDEA] **[C]** an idea or opinion *Do you have any **thoughts about/on** where you want to spend Christmas?* ○ **[+ of + doing sth]** *The thought of seeing her again filled him with happiness.* ○ *informal "Why don't we invite Ben?" " **That's a thought*** (= That's a good idea)." **2** [THINKING] **[U]** the activity of thinking, or when you think about something carefully *She sat staring at the picture, **deep in thought**.* ○ *You'll need to **give** the matter **some thought**.* **3** [CARE] **[no plural]** when you do something that shows you care about someone *Thanks for the card - it was a really kind thought.* **4** [SET OF IDEAS] **[U]** a set of ideas about a particular subject *The book examines his influence on recent political thought.* **5 spare a thought for sb** to think about someone who is in a bad situation *Spare a thought for all the people who have lost their homes.* ⊃See also: **school** of thought, **second thought.**

thought² /θɔːt/ *past of* think

thoughtful /ˈθɔːtfᵊl/ *adjective* **1** quiet because you are thinking about something *You look thoughtful.* **2** kind and always thinking about how you can help other people *Thank you for the card - it was very **thoughtful of** you.* • **thoughtfully** *adverb She gazed thoughtfully into the distance.* • **thoughtfulness** *noun* **[U]**

thoughtless /ˈθɔːtləs/ *adjective* not considering how your actions and words might upset someone else *I should have called her to say we'd be late - it was a bit thoughtless of me.* • **thoughtlessly** *adverb*

thought-provoking /ˈθɔːtprəˌvəʊkɪŋ/ *adjective* making you think a lot about a subject *a thought-provoking book/film*

⊶**thousand** /ˈθaʊzᵊnd/ **1** the number 1000 **2 thousands** *informal* a lot *She tried on **thousands of** dresses but didn't like any of them.*

thousandth¹ /ˈθaʊzᵊndθ/ 1000th written as a word

thousandth² /ˈθaʊzᵊndθ/ *noun* **[C]** one of a thousand equal parts of something; ¹⁄₁₀₀₀; .001 *a thousandth of a second*

thrash /θræʃ/ *verb* **1** [HIT] **[T]** to hit a person or animal several times as a punishment **2** [MOVE] **[I]** to move from side to side in a violent way *He was screaming in pain and **thrashing around** on the floor.* **3** [DEFEAT] **[T]** *informal* to win against someone very easily

thrash sth out to discuss a plan or problem in detail until you reach an agreement or find a solution

thrashing /ˈθræʃɪŋ/ *noun* **[C]** **1** *informal* when you win against someone very easily **2** *old-fashioned* when someone hits a person or animal several times as a punishment

thread¹ /θred/ *noun* **1** **[C, U]** a long, thin piece of cotton, wool, etc that is used for sewing *a needle and thread* **2** **[C]** the connection between different events or different parts of a story or discussion *By that point I'd **lost the thread** of the conversation.*

thread² /θred/ *verb* **[T]** **1 thread a needle** to push thread through the hole in a needle **2 thread your way through, between, etc** to move carefully through a crowded place, changing direction in order to avoid people or things

threadbare /ˈθredbeəʳ/ *adjective* Threadbare material or clothes are very thin because they have been used too much. *a threadbare carpet*

WORD PARTNERS FOR ***threat***

2 a threat **to** sb/sth • **pose** a threat • a **potential** threat • a **growing/serious** threat • a **security/terrorist** threat

⊶**threat** /θret/ *noun* **1** [HARM] **[C]** when someone says they will kill or hurt you, or cause problems for you if you do not do what they want *a **death threat*** ○ *I was scared he would **carry out** his **threat*** (= do what he said he would do). **2** [DAMAGE] **[C]** someone or something that is likely to cause harm or damage **[usually singular]** *a **threat to** the environment* ○ *Smoking **poses*** (= is) *a serious **threat** to your health.* **3** [POSSIBILITY] [no plural] the possibility that something bad will happen *the threat of invasion*

☞**threaten** /ˈθretᵊn/ *verb* **1** [HARM] [T] to tell someone that you will kill or hurt them, or cause problems for them if they do not do what you want *He threatened the staff with a gun and demanded money.* ○ [+ to do sth] *He threatened to report her to the police.* **2** [DAMAGE] [T] to be likely to cause harm or damage to something or someone *His knee problem is threatening his cycling career.* **3** [HAPPEN] [I] If something bad threatens to happen, it is likely to happen. [+ to do sth] *The conflict threatened to spread to neighbouring countries.* ● **threatening** *adjective* ● **threateningly** *adverb*

☞**three** /θriː/ the number 3

three-dimensional /ˌθriːdɪˈmenʃᵊnᵊl/ (*also* 3-D /ˌθriːˈdiː/) *adjective* having length, depth, and height *three-dimensional computer graphics*

threshold /ˈθreʃhəʊld/ *noun* **1** [C] the level at which something starts to happen *He had a low boredom threshold.* **2** **on the threshold of sth** at the start of a new and important time or development *We're on the threshold of a new era in European relations.* **3** [C] the floor of an entrance

threw /θruː/ *past tense of* throw

thrift /θrɪft/ *noun* [U] careful use of money so that you do not spend too much ● **thrifty** *adjective*

'thrift ,shop *US* (*UK* **charity shop**) *noun* [C] a shop which sells goods given by the public, especially clothes, to make money for a particular charity

> WORD PARTNERS FOR **thrill**
>
> feel a thrill ● get a thrill from/out of doing sth ● a big/great thrill ● the thrill of (doing) sth ● a thrill seeker

thrill¹ /θrɪl/ *noun* [C] a strong feeling of excitement and pleasure *It was a big thrill meeting the stars of the show.* ○ [+ of + doing sth] *the thrill of winning a competition*

thrill² /θrɪl/ *verb* [T] to make someone feel excited and happy *Ballesteros thrilled the golf world with his performance.*

thrilled /θrɪld/ *adjective* very excited and pleased *She was thrilled with your present.*

thriller /ˈθrɪlər/ *noun* [C] a book or film with an exciting story, often about crime

thrilling /ˈθrɪlɪŋ/ *adjective* very exciting *a thrilling game*

thrive /θraɪv/ *verb* [I] to grow very well, or to become very healthy or successful *The business is thriving.* ○ *He seems to thrive on hard work.* ● **thriving** *adjective a thriving economy*

throat /θrəʊt/ *noun* [C] **1** the back part of your mouth and the passages inside your neck *a sore throat* **2** the front of your neck *He grabbed her round the throat.* ⟳See colour picture **The Body** on page Centre 13. **3 clear your throat** to cough once so that you can speak more clearly

throb /θrɒb/ *verb* [I] throbbing, *past* throbbed **1** If a part of your body throbs, you feel pain in it in a series of regular beats. *My head was throbbing.* **2** to make a strong, regular sound or movement *The whole house throbbed with the music.* ● **throb** *noun* [C] *the throb of the engine*

throes /θrəʊz/ *noun* **in the throes of sth** in a difficult or unpleasant situation *a country in the throes of war*

throne /θrəʊn/ *noun* **1** [C] the special chair that a king or queen sits on **2 the throne** the position of being king or queen *He came to the throne in 1936.*

throng¹ /θrɒŋ/ *noun* [C] *literary* a large group of people

throng² /θrɒŋ/ *verb* [I, T] to be or go somewhere in very large numbers *The street was thronged with shoppers and tourists.*

throttle¹ /ˈθrɒtl/ *verb* [T] to press someone's throat tightly so they cannot breathe

throttle² /ˈθrɒtl/ *noun* [C] the part of a vehicle that controls how much fuel or power goes to the engine

☞**through¹** /θruː/ *preposition* **1** [ONE SIDE TO ANOTHER] from one end or side of something to the other *The River Seine flows through Paris.* ○ *The sun was shining through the window.* ○ *She cut through the wire.* **2** [START TO END] from the start to the end of something *He worked through the night.* ○ *The phone rang halfway through the programme.* **3** [BECAUSE OF] because of someone or something, or with someone's help *I got the job through my mum's friend.* ○ *He became ill through eating undercooked meat.* **4** [UNTIL] *US* (*UK* to) from a particular time until and including another time *The store is open Monday through Friday.*

☞**through²** /θruː/ *adverb* **1** from one end or side to another *He opened the door and walked through.* **2** **read/think/talk, etc sth through** to read, think, talk to someone, etc very carefully about something from the start to the end *I've thought it through and decided not to take the job.* **3** connected to someone by telephone *I tried to phone her but I couldn't get through.* ○ *Can you put me through to her, please?*

through³ /θruː/ *adjective* **1 be through with sth** *informal* to have finished using something or doing something *Let me know when you're through with the iron.* **2 be through (with sb)** *informal* to not have a relationship with someone any more **3** [always before noun] *UK* A through train goes all the way from one place to another place without the passenger having to change trains.

☞**throughout** /θruːˈaʊt/ *adverb, preposition* **1** in every part of a place *The same laws apply throughout much of Europe.* ○ *The house was painted pink throughout.* **2** during the whole of a period of time *He yawned throughout the performance.*

☞**throw¹** /θrəʊ/ *verb* [T] *past tense* **threw**, *past participle* **thrown** **1** [THROUGH THE AIR] to make something move through the air by pushing it out of your hand *Amy threw the ball to the dog.* ○ *He threw the book at the wall.* ○ [+ two objects] *Throw me a chocolate.*

throw

◦ *How far can you throw?* **2 throw sth in/on, etc** to put something somewhere quickly and without thinking about it *He threw his clothes on the floor and got into bed.* **3 throw sth around/down/on, etc** to suddenly and quickly move your body or a part of your body *She threw her arms around the child.* ◦ *Gabriela threw herself onto the bed and started to cry.* **4 throw sb from/forward, etc** to make someone move somewhere suddenly or fall down [often passive] *The bus suddenly stopped and we were thrown forward.* **5** CONFUSE to make someone feel shocked or confused *It threw me completely when he asked me to marry him.* ◦ *The news of the coup threw them into a state of panic.* **6** LIGHT to make light or shadows (= dark shapes) appear on something *The trees threw shadows across the road.* ◦See also: throw **caution**[1] to the wind, throw sb in at the deep **end**[1], throw down the **gauntlet**, throw in the **towel**, throw your **weight** around.

throw sth away 1 to get rid of something that you do not want any more *He read the magazine and then threw it away.* ◦See colour picture **Phrasal Verbs** on page Centre 16. **2** to waste a skill or opportunity *You've spent three years studying – don't throw it all away.*

throw sth in to add something extra when you sell something and not increase the price *They're selling computers with a free printer thrown in.* ◦ *When I bought my glasses, they threw in a free pair of prescription sunglasses.*

throw sth out to get rid of something that you do not want any more *I must throw some of my old clothes out.*

throw sb out to force someone to leave *He was thrown out of school for taking drugs.*

throw (sth) up *informal* to vomit *I spent the night throwing up.*

throw sth up to produce new problems or ideas *The meeting threw up some interesting ideas.*

throw² /θrəʊ/ *noun* [C] when you throw something *a throw of the dice*

throwback /ˈθrəʊbæk/ *noun* [C] something that is like something of the same type in the past *Her style of playing is a throwback to the early days of jazz.*

thru /θruː/ *adjective, adverb, preposition mainly US informal* another spelling of through, used in signs and advertisements

thrust¹ /θrʌst/ *verb past* thrust **thrust sth behind/into/through, etc** to push something somewhere suddenly and with force *She thrust a letter into my hand and told me to read it.*

thrust sth on/upon sb to force someone to accept or deal with something [often passive] *Fatherhood had been thrust on him.*

thrust² /θrʌst/ *noun* **1** [C, U] a strong push or the power used to push something forward **2 the thrust of sth** the main part or ideas of what someone says or does *The main thrust of our work involves helping victims of violent crime.*

thud /θʌd/ *noun* [C] the sound that is made when something heavy falls or hits something else *There was a thud as he fell on the floor.* • **thud**

verb [I] thudding, *past* thudded

thug /θʌɡ/ *noun* [C] an unpleasant person who behaves violently

thumb¹ /θʌm/ *noun* [C] **1** the short, thick finger on the side of your hand that can touch the top of all your other fingers ◦See colour picture **The Body** on page Centre 13. **2 have a green thumb** *US* (*UK* have **green fingers**) to be good at gardening and making plants grow well **3 be under sb's thumb** If you are under someone's thumb, they control you completely. **4 stick/stand out like a sore thumb** to be very different from all the other people or things around *I was the only one in uniform and I stuck out like a sore thumb.* ◦See also: a **rule**[1] of thumb.

thumb² /θʌm/ *verb* ◦See thumb your **nose**[1] at sth/sb.

thumb through sth to quickly turn the pages of a book or magazine

thumbtack /ˈθʌmtæk/ *US* (*UK* **drawing pin**) *noun* [C] a pin with a wide, flat top, used for fastening pieces of paper to a wall

thump /θʌmp/ *verb* **1** HIT [T] *UK* to hit someone with your fist (= closed hand) **2** NOISE [I, T] to hit something and make a noise *She thumped the tambourine.* **3** HEART [I] If your heart thumps, it beats very quickly because you are excited or frightened. • **thump** *noun* [C]

▨ **WORD PARTNERS FOR *thunder***

a **clap/crack/crash/roll/rumble** of thunder • thunder **rumbles/rolls** • thunder **and lightning**

thunder¹ /ˈθʌndəʳ/ *noun* [U] the loud noise in the sky that you hear during a storm *thunder and lightning*

thunder² /ˈθʌndəʳ/ *verb* **1 it thunders** When it thunders during a storm, a loud noise comes from the sky. **2 thunder along/down/through, etc** to move in a way that makes a deep, loud, continuous sound *Traffic thunders through the village all day.*

thunderous /ˈθʌndərəs/ *adjective* extremely loud *the thunderous roar of the aircraft's engine*

thunderstorm /ˈθʌndəstɔːm/ *noun* [C] a storm that has thunder (= loud noise) and lightning (= sudden flashes of light in the sky)

◦⃗ **Thursday** /ˈθɜːzdeɪ/ (*written abbreviation* **Thur, Thurs**) *noun* [C, U] the day of the week after Wednesday and before Friday

thus /ðʌs/ *adverb formal* **1** used after saying a fact to introduce what then happened as a result *The guard fell asleep, thus allowing Bates to escape.* **2** in this way *They limit the number of people allowed into the forest, thus preventing damage to the trails.*

thwart /θwɔːt/ *verb* [T] to prevent someone from doing what they have planned to do

thyme /taɪm/ *noun* [U] a herb used in cooking

thyroid /ˈθaɪrɔɪd/ *noun* [C] an organ in the neck that produces a substance that helps your body to grow and develop

T

TIA *internet abbreviation for* thanks in advance: used in an email when you have asked someone for something

tick¹ /tɪk/ *noun* **1** CLOCK the sound that some clocks or watches make every second **2** MARK *UK* (*US* check) a mark (✓) that shows something is correct or has been done **3** INSECT a small insect that sucks the blood of animals **4** TIME *UK informal* a short time *Wait a tick!*

tick² /tɪk/ *verb* **1** [I] If a clock or watch ticks, it makes a sound every second. **2** [T] *UK* to mark something with a tick **3 what makes sb tick** *informal* the reasons for someone's behaviour

tick away/by If seconds or minutes tick away or by, they pass. *With the final seconds ticking away, Milan scored a goal.*

tick sth off *UK* (*US* check sth off) to put a small mark next to something on a list to show that you have dealt with it

tick sb off **1** *UK informal* to tell someone that they have done something wrong and that you are angry about it *I got ticked off for not going to the meeting.* **2** *US informal* to annoy someone

tick over *UK* If a business or system ticks over, it continues to work but makes little progress. *Carlton managed to **keep** the business **ticking** over.*

o⌐**ticket** /'tɪkɪt/ *noun* [C] **1** a small piece of paper that shows you have paid to do something, for example travel on a bus, watch a film, etc *a lottery ticket* ○ *plane tickets* **2** a piece of paper that orders you to pay money because you have put your car in an illegal place, driven too fast, etc *a parking ticket* ⊃See also: round-trip ticket, season ticket.

tickets

tickle /'tɪkl/ *verb* **1** TOUCH LIGHTLY [T] to touch someone lightly with your fingers, in order to make them laugh **2** PART OF THE BODY [I, T] If a part of your body tickles, or if something tickles it, it feels uncomfortable and you want to rub it. *My nose is tickling.* **3** AMUSE [T] to make someone smile or laugh *I was very tickled by his comments.* ● **tickle** *noun* [C]

tidal /'taɪdl/ *adjective* relating to the regular rising and falling of the sea

'**tidal ,wave** *noun* [C] a very large wave that destroys things, often caused by an earthquake (= when the Earth shakes)

tidbit *US* (*UK* titbit) /'tɪdbɪt/ *noun* [C] a small piece of nice food, or an interesting piece of information

tide¹ /taɪd/ *noun* **1** [C] the regular rise and fall in the level of the sea *high/low tide* **2** [no plural] an increase in something that is developing *the **rising tide** of drug-related deaths*

tide² /taɪd/ *verb*

tide sb over (sth) to help someone through a difficult time, especially by giving them money *I gave her some money to tide her over till she starts earning.*

tidy¹ /'taɪdi/ *adjective* **1** having everything in the right place and arranged in a good order *Her room was clean and tidy.* **2** liking to keep things in the correct place and arranged in a good order *I'm afraid I'm not very tidy.* ⊃Opposite **untidy.** ● **tidily** *adverb* ● **tidiness** *noun* [U]

tidy² /'taɪdi/ (*also* tidy up) *verb* [I, T] *UK* to make a place tidy *I'm tidying up before our guests arrive.*

tidy sth away *UK* to put things back in drawers, cupboards, etc after you have used them *Kids, could you tidy away your toys when you've finished with them?*

tie

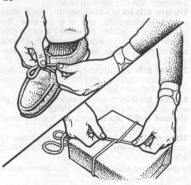

o⌐**tie¹** /taɪ/ *verb* tying, *past* tied **1 tie sth to/together/ around, etc** to fasten something with string, rope, etc *The dog was tied to a tree.* **2** [T] to make a knot in a piece of string, rope, etc *She tied the scarf.* ⊃Opposite **untie. 3** [I] to have the same score as someone else at the end of a competition or game *Sweden **tied with** France in the winter sports competition.* ⊃See also: tie the knot¹.

tie sb down to limit someone's freedom *I don't want to be tied down by having children.*

tie in If one idea or statement ties in with another one, they have some of the same information in them. *His story **ties in with** what Gemma told me.*

tie sb/sth up to tie a part of someone's body with a rope or something similar so they cannot move ⊃Opposite **untie.**

tie sth up to fasten something together using string, rope, etc

be tied up to be very busy and unable to speak to anyone, go anywhere, etc

2 create/forge ties • **cut/sever** (all) ties • **have** ties **with** sb/sth • **close/strong** ties • ties **between** sb and sb • ties **to/with** sb/sth

tie² /taɪ/ *noun* [C] **1** CLOTHES a long, thin piece of cloth that a man wears around his neck with a shirt ⊃See colour picture **Clothes** on page Centre 9. **2** CONNECTION a relationship that connects you with a place, person, etc [usually plural] *The two countries have close ties with each other.* **3** GAME/COMPETITION when a game or competition ends with two people or teams having the same score ⊃See also: **bow tie.**

tie-break /ˈtaɪbreɪk/ *noun* [C] an extra part that is played when a game or competition ends in a tie, to decide who is the winner

tier /tɪəʳ/ *noun* [C] one of several rows or layers *the upper tier of seats in a stadium*

tiger /ˈtaɪgəʳ/ *noun* [C] a large wild cat that has yellow fur with black lines on it

o→**tight¹** /taɪt/ *adjective* **1** FIRM firm and difficult to move *Make sure the knot is tight.* **2** CLOTHES fitting your body very closely *a tight skirt* **3** CONTROLLED controlled and obeying all rules completely *tight security* ○ *They kept tight control of the school budget.* **4** STRAIGHT If cloth, wire, skin, etc is tight, it has been pulled so that it is straight or smooth. **5** NOT MUCH If money, time, or space is tight, there is only just enough of it. *We should get six people into the car but it will be tight.* • **tightly** *adverb* • **tightness** *noun* [U] ⊃See also: keep a tight **rein** on sb/sth.

tight² /taɪt/ *adverb* very firmly or closely *He held her tight.*

tighten /ˈtaɪtᵊn/ *verb* [I, T] to become tighter or to make something become tighter *His hand tightened around her arm.* ⊃See also: tighten your **belt¹.**

tighten sth up to make something become firmer and less easy to move *Tighten up the screws.*

tighten (sth) up to make a rule, system, or law more difficult to avoid *I think they should tighten up the laws on gun ownership.*

tightrope /ˈtaɪtrəʊp/ *noun* [C] a rope high above the ground that a performer walks along at a circus (= show)

tights /taɪts/ *UK (US* **pantyhose)** *noun* [plural] a piece of women's clothing made of very thin material that covers the legs and bottom *a pair of black tights* ⊃See colour picture **Clothes** on page Centre 9.

tile /taɪl/ *noun* [C] one of the flat, square pieces that are used for covering roofs, floors, or walls • **tile** *verb* [T] *a tiled kitchen*

till¹ /tɪl/ *preposition, conjunction* until *The supermarket is open till midnight.* ○ *I lived with my parents till I was twenty.*

till² /tɪl/ *noun* [C] **1** *UK* a machine that holds the money in a shop and shows how much you have to pay **2** *US* a drawer where money is kept in a store

tilt /tɪlt/ *verb* [I, T] to move into a position where one end or side is higher than the other, or to make something move into this position *He tilted backwards on his chair.* • **tilt** *noun* [no plural]

timber /ˈtɪmbəʳ/ *noun* **1** WOOD [U] *UK (US* **lumber)** wood that is used for building **2** TREE [U] *US* trees that are grown to provide wood for building **3** PIECE OF WOOD [C] *UK* a large piece of wood *The roof was supported by timbers.*

o→**time¹** /taɪm/ *noun* **1** HOURS/YEARS ETC [U] Time is what we measure in minutes, hours, days, etc. *He wants to spend more time with his family.* ○ *Time seems to pass so slowly when you're unhappy.* **2** PARTICULAR POINT [C, U] a particular point in the day or night *What time is it?* ○ *What time do you leave for school in the mornings?* ○ *Can you tell me the times of the trains to London, please?* ⊃See Common learner error at **hour.** **3 it's time (for/to do sth)** used to say that something should happen or be done now *It's time to get up.* **4 in (good) time** early or at the right time *We arrived in time to catch the train.* **5 on time** not early or late *I got to school on time.* **6 can tell the time** to be able to know what time it is by looking at a clock or watch **7** PERIOD [no plural] a period of minutes, hours, years, etc *I lived in Switzerland for a long time.* ○ *It takes time* (= takes a long time) *to make friends at a new school.* **8 have time** to have enough time to do something *Do you have time for a cup of coffee?* ○ [+ to do sth] *I never have time to eat breakfast.* **9 in no time** very soon *We'll be home in no time.* **10** OCCASION [C] an occasion when something happens *Give me a call the next time you're in Seattle.* ○ *I can't remember the last time we went away.* ○ *How many times have you been to Germany?* **11 at the same time** If two things happen at the same time, they happen together. *We arrived at the same time.* **12 one, two, six, etc at a time** one, two, six, etc on one occasion *He carried the chairs, three at a time.* **13 time after time** again and again on repeated occasions **14 all the time a** OFTEN very often *"She's been late twice this week." "It happens all the time."* **b** WHOLE TIME during the whole of a period of time *He was ill all the time we were in Spain.* **15 three/eight/nine, etc times** used to say how much bigger, better, worse, etc one thing is than another thing *Ben earns three times more than me.* **16 in a day's/two months', etc time** a week, two months, etc from now *I have to go to the doctor again in a month's time.* **17 at times** sometimes *At times, I wish I didn't have to go to school.* **18 for the time being** for now but not permanently *I'm living with my parents for the time being.* **19** IN THE PAST [C] a period of time in the past *Did you enjoy your time in Japan?* **20 at one time** at a time in the past *At one time, you could drive without taking a driving test.* **21 before sb's time** before someone was born **22 from time to time** sometimes, but not often *I still see my ex-boyfriend from time to time.* **23** RACE [C] the amount of time that someone takes in a race *a winning time of three minutes* **24** IN A PLACE [U] the time in a particular place *The plane arrives at 20.50, New York time.* **25 be ahead of your time** to have new ideas a long time before

T

other people think that way **26 behind the times** not fashionable or modern *Dad's a bit behind the times.* **27 bide your time** to wait for an opportunity to do something *She was biding her time until she could get her revenge.* **28 give sb a hard time** to criticize someone and make them feel guilty about something they have done *Ever since I missed the goal, the other players have been giving me a hard time.* **29 have no time for sb/sth** to have no respect for someone or something *I have no time for people who are racist.* **30 kill time** to do something while you are waiting for something else *I went shopping to kill some time before my job interview.* **31 play for time** *UK* to try to make something happen more slowly because you want more time or because you do not want it to happen **32 take your time** to do something without hurrying ⊃See also: half-time, local time, in the nick² of time, night-time, prime time, a race¹ against time/the clock.

time² /taɪm/ *verb* [T] **1** to decide that something will happen at a particular time *They timed production of the CD so it was in the shops just before Christmas.* ○ *Her comment was well timed.* **2** to measure how long it takes for something to happen or for someone to do something *It's a good idea to time yourself while you do the exercises.* ⊃See also: two-time.

time-consuming /'taɪmkənˌsjuːmɪŋ/ *adjective* needing a lot of time *The legal process was time-consuming and expensive.*

'time ˌframe ⊃See timescale.

time-honoured *UK* (*US* time-honored) /'taɪmˌɒnəd/ *adjective* [always before noun] A time-honoured tradition or way of doing things is one that has been used for a long time.

'time ˌlag *noun* [C] a period of time between two things happening

timeless /'taɪmləs/ *adjective* not changing because of time or fashion *Her clothes have a timeless quality.* ○ *a timeless classic*

timely /'taɪmli/ *adjective* happening or done at exactly the right time ⊃Opposite untimely.

time-out /ˌtaɪm'aʊt/ *noun* [C] a short period during a sports game in which players can rest

timer /'taɪmər/ *noun* [C] a piece of equipment that measures time

times /taɪmz/ *preposition* used to say that one number is multiplied by another number *Two times three is six.*

timescale /'taɪmskeɪl/ (*also* time frame) *noun* [C] the amount of time that something takes or during which something happens

timetable /'taɪmˌteɪbl/ *noun* [C] **1** (*also US* schedule) a list of times when buses, trains, etc arrive and leave **2** a list of dates and times that shows when things will happen ⊃See colour picture **The Classroom** on page Centre 6.

'time ˌzone *noun* [C] one of the areas of the world that has a different time from all the other areas *London and New York are five time zones apart.*

timid /'tɪmɪd/ *adjective* shy and easily frightened *a timid little dog* • **timidly** *adverb* • **timidity** /tɪ'mɪdəti/ *noun* [U]

timing /'taɪmɪŋ/ *noun* [U] **1** the time when something happens *the timing of the announcement* **2** the ability to do something at exactly the right time *You need great timing to be a good football player.*

tin /tɪn/ *noun* **1** METAL CONTAINER [C] *UK* (*UK/US* can) a metal container in which food is sold *a tin of beans/soup* ⊃See picture at container. **2** CONTAINER WITH LID [C] *UK* a metal container with a lid that you keep food or other substances in *a biscuit tin* ○ *a paint tin* **3** COOKING EQUIPMENT [C] (*US* pan) a flat pan that you cook food in *a roasting tin* **4** METAL [U] a soft, silver metal that is often combined with other metals or used to cover them

tinfoil /'tɪnfɔɪl/ *noun* [U] metal made into very thin sheets like paper and used mainly for covering food

tinge /tɪndʒ/ *noun* [C] a small amount of a sad feeling or colour *"Goodbye," he said, with a tinge of sadness.* • **tinged** *adjective* *Her dark hair is now tinged with grey.*

tingle /'tɪŋgl/ *verb* [I] If a part of your body tingles, the skin feels slightly uncomfortable. *My hands are starting to tingle with the cold.* • **tingle** *noun* [C]

tinker /'tɪŋkər/ *verb* [I] to make small changes to something in order to improve or repair it *Tim loves tinkering with car engines.*

tinkle /'tɪŋkl/ *verb* [I] to make a soft, high, ringing sound • **tinkle** *noun* [C]

tinned /tɪnd/ *UK* (*UK/US* canned) *adjective* Tinned food is sold in metal containers.

'tin ˌopener *UK* (*UK/US* can opener) *noun* [C] a piece of kitchen equipment for opening metal food containers ⊃See colour picture **The Kitchen** on page Centre 2.

tinsel /'tɪnsəl/ *noun* [U] long, shiny, coloured string, used as a decoration at Christmas (= a Christian holiday)

tint¹ /tɪnt/ *noun* [C] a particular colour *the yellow and red tints of autumn*

tint² /tɪnt/ *verb* [T] to add a small amount of a colour to something *Do you think he tints his hair?*

tinted /'tɪntɪd/ *adjective* Tinted glass has colour added to it. *tinted sunglasses*

⚬**tiny** /'taɪni/ *adjective* extremely small *a tiny baby* ○ *a tiny little room*

tip¹ /tɪp/ *noun* [C] **1** END the end of something long and narrow *the tips of your fingers* **2** ADVICE a piece of useful advice *gardening tips* ○ *Emma was giving me some tips on how to grow tomatoes.* **3** MONEY an extra amount of money that you give to a driver, someone working in a restaurant, etc to thank them *We*

left a tip because the waiter was so friendly.
4 WASTE *UK (UK/US* **dump)** a place where
people take things that they want to get rid of
We took our old fridge to the tip. **5** UNTIDY PLACE
UK informal (UK/US **dump)** a place that is dirty
and untidy *His bedroom is an absolute tip.* **6 be
on the tip of your tongue** If a word is on the tip
of your tongue, you want to say it but cannot
remember it. **7 be the tip of the iceberg** to be a
small part of a very big problem

tip² /tɪp/ *verb* **tipping,** *past* **tipped 1** [I, T] to move so
that one side is higher than the other side, or
to make something move in this way *The table
tipped and all the drinks fell on the floor.* **2 tip
sth into/onto/out of sth** to make the contents of
a container fall out by holding the container
in a position where this happens *She tipped
the contents of her purse onto the table.* **3** [I, T] to
give an extra amount of money to a driver,
someone working in a restaurant, etc to thank
them **4 be tipped as/to do/for sth** *UK* If someone is tipped to achieve something, most
people say it will happen. *Christie was tipped
to win the race.*

tip sb off to warn someone secretly about
something so that they can take action or prevent it happening ● **tip off** /'tɪpɒf/ *noun* [C] a
piece of information that you give someone secretly, so that they can take action or prevent
something happening

tip (sth) over If something tips over, or if
you tip it over, it falls onto its side.

tiptoe¹ /'tɪptəʊ/ *noun* **on tiptoe** standing on
your toes with the rest of your feet off the
ground

tiptoe² /'tɪptəʊ/ *verb* **tiptoe across/down/
through, etc** to walk quietly on your toes

tire¹ /taɪəʳ/ *noun* [C] *US spelling of* tyre ➲See colour
picture **Car** on page Centre 7.

tire² /taɪəʳ/ *verb* [I, T] to become tired or to make
someone become tired *He tires easily.*

tire of sth/doing sth to become bored
with something *He never tires of playing games
on his computer.*

tire sb out to make someone very tired

OTHER WAYS OF SAYING *tired*

If someone is extremely tired, you can say
that they are **exhausted, worn-out,** or, in
informal situations in the UK, **shattered:**
*I'm too **exhausted** to take the dog for a walk
tonight.* ● *By the time I got home, I was absolutely **shattered.***

You can use the adjectives **burnt-out** and
drained to describe someone who is tired
because they have been working very hard:
*He was **burnt-out** after a full
week of performances.* ● *I'd worked a twelve-
hour day and was absolutely **drained.***

If someone is tired and wants to go to sleep,
you can describe them as **drowsy** or **sleepy:**
*The heat had made me **drowsy/sleepy.***

o╌**tired** /taɪəd/ *adjective* **1** feeling that you want to
rest or sleep *He was **tired out** (= very tired) by
the end of the day.* ○ *She never seems to get
tired.* **2 tired of doing sth** bored or annoyed by

something that has happened too often *I'm
tired of listening to her problems.* ● **tiredness**
noun [U]

COMMON LEARNER ERROR

tired of or **tired from?**

If you are **tired of** something or **of doing** something,
you are bored or annoyed by it.
I'm tired of hearing his awful jokes.

If you are **tired from** something, you want to rest because of it.
I'm tired from the long journey.

tireless /'taɪələs/ *adjective* working very hard at
something and not stopping *He was a **tireless
campaigner/worker** for children's organizations.* ○ *I want to thank James for his **tireless
efforts** on behalf of the company.*

tiresome /'taɪəsəm/ *adjective formal* making
you feel annoyed or bored *a tiresome little boy*

tiring /taɪərɪŋ/ *adjective* making you feel tired *a
long and tiring day*

tissue /'tɪʃuː/ *noun* **1** ANIMAL/PLANT [C, U] the material that animals and plants are made of
human brain tissue **2** FOR YOUR NOSE [C] a soft
piece of paper that you use for cleaning your
nose **3** FOR WRAPPING [U] (*also* '**tissue ,paper)** soft,
thin paper that you cover things with in order
to protect them

tit /tɪt/ *noun* [C] **1** *very informal* a woman's breast
2 tit for tat *informal* when you do something
bad to someone because they have done something bad to you

titbit *UK (US* **tidbit)** /'tɪtbɪt/ *noun* [C] a small
piece of nice food, or an interesting piece of information

WORD PARTNERS FOR ***title***

2 defend/lose/**retain**/take/**win** the title
● the **world** title

o╌**title** /'taɪtl/ *noun* [C] **1** BOOK/FILM ETC the name of
a book, film, etc **2** SPORTS what you get if you
win an important sports competition *He **won**
the 1999 world motor racing **title.*** **3** SOMEONE'S
NAME a word such as 'Lord', 'Dr', etc that is
used before someone's name

titled /'taɪtld/ *adjective* having a title such as
'Lord', 'Lady', or 'Duke' that shows you have a
high social position

title-holder /'taɪtl,həʊldəʳ/ *noun* [C] someone
who has won a sports competition *the World
Grand Prix title-holder*

'**title ,role** *noun* [C] the person in a play or film
who has the same name as the play's or film's
title

titter /'tɪtəʳ/ *verb* [I] to laugh in a nervous way
● **titter** *noun* [C]

T-junction /'tiː,dʒʌŋkʃ°n/ *UK (US* **intersection)**
noun [C] a place where two roads join and
make the shape of the letter 'T'

o╌**to¹** /tə/ **1** used with a verb to make the infinitive
I want to learn Spanish. ○ *He forgot to feed the
cat.* **2** used to give the reason for doing something *I'm just going out to get some milk.*

o╌**to²** *strong form* /tuː/ *weak forms* /tʊ, tə/ *prep-*

osition 1 [DIRECTION] in the direction of somewhere *Dimitri is going to Germany next week.* ◦ *I ran to the door.* **2** [ANOTHER PERSON] used to show who receives something or experiences an action *Could you give these keys to Pete?* ◦ *Anna was speaking to her mother on the phone.* ◦ *I lent my bike to Tom.* **3** [POSITION] almost touching or facing something *She stood with her back to the window.* **4 from ... to ... a** [TIME/DISTANCE] used to give information about periods of time and distances *The museum is open from Monday to Saturday.* ◦ *The bus goes from London to Cambridge.* **b** [INCLUDING] including *The book deals with everything from childhood to old age.* **5** [BEFORE] used to say 'before' the hour when you are saying what time it is *It's five to three.* **6** [COMPARE] used to compare two things *I prefer football to cricket.* **7** [UNTIL] until a particular time or state *It's only two weeks to my birthday.* ◦ *She nursed him back to health.* **8** [SOMEONE'S OPINION] used to say what someone's opinion is *Fifty pounds is nothing to Matthew* (= he would not think it was a lot of money). **9 to sb's disappointment/ relief/surprise, etc** used to say that someone feels surprised, disappointed, etc by something *To Pierre's disappointment, Monique wasn't at the party.* **10** [MEASUREMENT] used to say how many parts make up a whole unit of measurement or money *There are 100 pence to the British pound.* **11** [BELONGING] belonging to or connected with *Can you give me the keys to the car?*

to³ /tuː/ *adverb* **1** *UK* If you push or pull a door to, you close it. **2 to and fro** backwards and forwards *The sign was swinging to and fro in the wind.*

toad /təʊd/ *noun* [C] a small, brown animal with long back legs for swimming and jumping

toadstool /'təʊdstuːl/ *noun* [C] a poisonous fungus (= organism like a plant) with a short stem and a round top

toast¹ /təʊst/ *noun* **1** [U] bread that has been heated to make it brown *a slice of toast* **2** [C] a time when people lift their glasses and drink because they want someone to be successful, happy, etc *At the wedding, there was a **toast to** the happy couple.*

toast² /təʊst/ *verb* [T] **1** to lift your glass and drink with other people because you want someone to be successful, happy, etc **2** to heat bread so that it becomes brown

toaster /'təʊstəʳ/ *noun* [C] a machine that heats bread so that it becomes brown ➌See colour picture **The Kitchen** on page Centre 2.

toasty /'təʊsti/ *adjective* warm and comfortable *It's nice and toasty near the fire.*

tobacco /tə'bækəʊ/ *noun* [U] dried leaves that are inside cigarettes

toboggan /tə'bɒɡ³n/ *noun* [C] a board that you sit or lie on, used for going down a hill on a surface of snow

◦▪**today** /tə'deɪ/ *noun* [U], *adverb* **1** this day, or on this day *It's Johann's birthday today.* ◦ *Today is Friday.* **2** the period of time that is happening now or in this period of time *More young people smoke today than in the past.*

toddle /'tɒdl/ *verb* **toddle down/off/to, etc** *informal* to walk somewhere *Sophie said goodbye and toddled off towards the station.*

toddler /'tɒdləʳ/ *noun* [C] a child who has just learned to walk

toe¹ /təʊ/ *noun* [C] **1** one of the five separate parts at the end of your foot *your **big toe*** (= largest toe) ◦ *your **little toe*** (= smallest toe) ➌See colour picture **The Body** on page Centre 13. **2** the part of a shoe or sock that covers your toes **3 keep sb on their toes** to make sure that someone gives all their attention to what they are doing and is all ready for anything that might happen

toe² /təʊ/ *verb* ➌See toe the (party) **line¹**.

toenail /'təʊneɪl/ *noun* [C] one of the hard, flat parts on top of the end of your toes ➌See colour picture **The Body** on page Centre 13.

toffee /'tɒfi/ *noun* [C, U] a sticky sweet, made by boiling sugar and butter together

tofu /'təʊfuː/ (*also* bean curd) *noun* [U] a soft pale food made from the soya bean plant

◦▪**together¹** /tə'ɡeðəʳ/ *adverb* **1** [WITH SOMEONE] with each other *We went shopping together.* ◦ *They live together.* **2** [CONNECTED] used to say that two or more things are joined to each other, mixed with each other, etc *She tied the two pieces of rope together.* **3** [SAME PLACE] in the same place or close to each other *We all sat together.* **4** [SAME TIME] at the same time *We'll deal with the next two items on the list together.* **5 together with sth** in addition to something *She sent some flowers together with a card.* ➌See also: get your **act²** together, **get-together**.

together² /tə'ɡeðəʳ/ *adjective informal* Someone who is together thinks clearly and organizes their life well.

togetherness /tə'ɡeðənəs/ *noun* [U] a feeling of friendship

toil /tɔɪl/ *verb* [I] *literary* to do difficult work for a long time ● **toil** *noun* [U] *literary*

be on/go to/flush/need the toilet ● toilet **facilities** ● a toilet **seat**

◦▪**toilet** /'tɔɪlɪt/ *noun* [C] **1** a bowl that you sit on or stand near when you get rid of waste substances from your body ➌See colour picture **The Bathroom** on page Centre 3. **2** *UK* (*US* bathroom) a room with a toilet in it

COMMON LEARNER ERROR

toilet

Toilet is the most general word. In **British English** the informal word **loo** is often used. In **American English** the word **bathroom** is often used to mean toilet, especially in the home.

In public places toilets are usually called **the ladies** or **the gents** in Britain and the **men's room, ladies' room**, or **restroom** in America.

The **lavatory** is slightly formal and **WC** is only used in **British English**. These two words are not used much today.

'**toilet ,paper** *noun* [U] paper used for cleaning

your body after you have used the toilet ➲See colour picture **The Bathroom** on page Centre 3.

toiletries /'tɔɪlɪtriz/ *noun* **[plural]** things such as soap, toothpaste (= substance for cleaning teeth), etc that you use for making yourself clean

'toilet ˌroll *noun* **[C]** *UK* paper for cleaning your body after using the toilet that is folded around a tube ➲See colour picture **The Bathroom** on page Centre 3.

token[1] /'təʊkᵊn/ *noun* **[C]** **1** [LOVE/THANKS] something that you give to someone in order to show them love, to thank them, etc *I gave Helen some chocolates as **a token of** thanks for all her help.* **2** [INSTEAD OF MONEY] a round piece of metal or plastic that you put in some machines instead of money *You need a token to get out of the car park.* **3** [PAPER] *UK* (*US* **gift certificate**) a piece of paper that you give someone which they can exchange for a book, CD, etc *a **book/record/gift token***

token[2] /'təʊkᵊn/ *adjective* **[always before noun]** **1** A token person is chosen so that an organization can pretend that they care about that type of person. *a token woman* **2** A token action is small or unimportant and may show your future intentions or may only pretend to. *He made a **token effort** to find a job.*

told /təʊld/ *past of* tell

tolerable /'tɒlᵊrəbl/ *adjective* acceptable but not excellent *The food was just about tolerable but the service was terrible.* ➲Opposite **intolerable.**
• **tolerably** *adverb*

WORD PARTNERS FOR ***tolerance***

show tolerance • tolerance **of/towards** sb/sth • sb's tolerance **level** • **racial/religious** tolerance

tolerance /'tɒlᵊrᵊns/ *noun* **[U]** the quality of allowing people to do or believe what they want although you do not agree with it ***religious/racial tolerance*** ➲See also: **zero tolerance.**

tolerant /'tɒlᵊrᵊnt/ *adjective* allowing people to do what they want especially when you do not agree with it *a tolerant attitude* ○ *I think we're becoming more **tolerant of** children in public places.* ➲Opposite **intolerant.**

tolerate /'tɒlᵊreɪt/ *verb* **[T]** **1** to accept or allow something although you do not like it *We will not tolerate racism of any sort.* **2** to be able to deal with something unpleasant and not be harmed by it *These plants can tolerate very low temperatures.* • **toleration** /ˌtɒlᵊr'eɪʃᵊn/ *noun* **[U]**

toll[1] /təʊl/ *noun* **1** **[C]** money that you pay to use a bridge, road, etc **2** **[no plural]** the number of people who are killed or injured **3 take its toll** to have a bad effect on someone or something, especially over a long period of time *The stress was starting to **take its toll on** him.* ➲See also: **death toll.**

toll[2] /təʊl/ *verb* **[I]** When a bell tolls, it rings slowly, especially because someone has died.

toll-free /ˌtəʊl'friː/ *US* (*UK* **freephone**) *adjective* A toll-free number is a telephone number that you can connect to without paying.

🔑**tomato** /tə'mɑːtəʊ/ [US] /tə'meɪtəʊ/ *noun* **[C, U]** *plural* **tomatoes** a soft, round, red fruit eaten in salad or as a vegetable ➲See colour picture **Fruit and Vegetables** on page Centre 10.

tomb /tuːm/ *noun* **[C]** a place where a dead person is buried, usually with a monument (= stone structure)

tomboy /'tɒmbɔɪ/ *noun* **[C]** a young girl who behaves and dresses like a boy

tombstone /'tuːmstəʊn/ *noun* **[C]** a stone that shows the name of a dead person who is buried under it

tomcat /'tɒmkæt/ *noun* **[C]** a male cat

🔑**tomorrow** /tə'mɒrəʊ/ *noun* **[U]**, *adverb* **1** the day after today or on the day after today *It's my birthday tomorrow.* ○ *Tomorrow is Friday.* **2** the future, or in the future *the children of tomorrow*

ton /tʌn/ *noun* **[C]** *plural* **tons** or **ton** **1** a unit for measuring weight, equal to 1016 kilograms in the UK and 907 kilograms in the US ➲Compare **tonne.** **2 tons of sth** *informal* a lot of something *We've got tons of cheese left.* **3 weigh a ton** *informal* to be very heavy

tone[1] /təʊn/ *noun* **1** [SOUND QUALITY] **[C, U]** the quality of a sound, especially of someone's voice *I knew by her **tone of voice** that she was serious.* **2** [FEELING/STYLE] **[U, no plural]** the general feeling or style that something has *Then the director arrived and the whole tone of the meeting changed.* **3** [TELEPHONE] **[C]** an electronic sound made by a telephone *a dialling tone/an engaged tone* **4** [COLOUR] **[C]** one of the many types of a particular colour

tone[2] /təʊn/ (*also* **tone up**) *verb* **[T]** to make your muscles or skin firmer and stronger *Try these exercises to tone up your stomach muscles.*

tone sth down to make a piece of writing, a speech, etc less offensive or rude *The show was toned down for television.*

tone-deaf /ˌtəʊn'def/ [US] /'təʊndef/ *adjective* unable to sing the correct musical notes or hear the difference between musical notes

tongs /tɒŋz/ *noun* **[plural]** a tool used for picking things up, that has two pieces joined together at one end

🔑**tongue** /tʌŋ/ *noun* **1** [MOUTH] **[C]** the soft thing inside your mouth that you move and use for tasting and speaking **2** [FOOD] **[C, U]** the tongue of some animals that you can eat as meat **3** [LANGUAGE] **[C]** *formal* a language *Japanese is her **native tongue*** (= the language she learnt to speak as a child). ➲See also: **mother tongue**, a **slip**[2] of the tongue, be on the **tip**[1] of your tongue.

tongue-in-cheek /ˌtʌŋɪn'tʃiːk/ *adjective, adverb* said or done as a joke

tongue-tied /'tʌŋtaɪd/ *adjective* unable to say anything because you are nervous

'tongue ˌtwister *noun* **[C]** a phrase or sentence that is difficult to say quickly because it has many similar sounds in it

tonic /'tɒnɪk/ *noun* **1** **[C, U]** (*also* **'tonic ˌwater**) a drink with bubbles in it that has a bitter taste and is often added to alcoholic drinks **2** **[no plural]** something that makes you feel better *Spending time with Leo is always a tonic.*

🔑**tonight** /tə'naɪt/ *noun*, *adverb* **[U]** the night of

T

this day, or during the night of this day *What are you doing tonight?* ○ *I'm looking forward to tonight.*

tonne /tʌn/ *noun* [C] *plural* **tonnes** or **tonne** *UK* a metric ton (= unit for measuring weight, equal to 1000 kilograms) ⊃Compare **ton**.

tonsil /'tɒnsəl/ *noun* [C] one of the two small, soft parts at the back of your mouth

tonsillitis /ˌtɒnsəl'aɪtɪs/ *noun* [U] an illness that makes your tonsils very painful

⚬⁻**too** /tuː/ *adverb* **1 too small/heavy/much,** etc used before adjectives and adverbs to mean 'more than is allowed, necessary, possible, etc' *The film is also far too long.* ○ *There are too many cars on the roads these days.* ○ [+ to do sth] *I decided it was too early to get up and went back to sleep.* **2** also *Do you know Jason too?* ○ *I'll probably go there next year too.* **3 not too** used before adjectives and adverbs to mean 'not very' *"How was your exam?" "Not too bad, I suppose."* ○ *I didn't play too well today.*

took /tʊk/ *past tense of* take

tools

drill

nut

screw   mallet

hammer   saw

bolt   nail

vice *UK,* vise *US*

pliers

spanner *UK,* wrench *US*

chisel

screwdriver

⚬⁻**tool** /tuːl/ *noun* [C] **1** a piece of equipment that you use with your hands in order to help you do something *He keeps his tools in the shed.* **2** something that helps you to do a particular activity *Computers are an essential tool for modern scientists.* ○ *Information technology is an extremely powerful tool.* ⊃See also: **power tool.**

toolbar /'tuːlbɑːʳ/ *noun* [C] on a computer screen, a row of icons (= small pictures that you choose in order to make the computer do something)

'tool ,box *noun* [C] a container in which you keep and carry small tools

toot /tuːt/ *UK (UK/US* **honk)** *verb* **toot your horn** If a driver toots their horn, they make a short

sound with the horn (= thing you press to make a warning noise). ● **toot** *noun* [C]

⚬⁻**tooth** /tuːθ/ *noun* [C] *plural* **teeth 1** one of the hard, white objects in your mouth that you use for biting and crushing food *You should **brush** your **teeth** twice a day.* **2** one of the row of metal or plastic points that stick out from a tool such as a comb (= thing used to make your hair tidy), or saw (= thing used to cut wood) **3 grit your teeth** to accept a difficult situation and deal with it in a determined way ⊃See also: a **kick²** in the teeth, do sth by the **skin¹** of your teeth, **wisdom tooth.**

toothache /'tuːθeɪk/ *noun* [U] a pain in one of your teeth

toothbrush /'tuːθbrʌʃ/ *noun* [C] a small brush that you use to clean your teeth

toothbrush

toothpaste /'tuːθpeɪst/ *noun* [U] a substance that you use to clean your teeth ⊃See colour picture **The Bathroom** on page Centre 3.

toothpaste

toothpick /'tuːθpɪk/ *noun* [C] a small, thin stick that you use to remove pieces of food from between your teeth

⚬⁻**top¹** /tɒp/ *noun* **1** HIGHEST PART [C] the highest part of something *They were waiting for him* **at the top of** *the stairs.* ○ *I want a cake with cherries* **on top. 2** SURFACE [C] the flat, upper surface of something *the table top* **3** LID [C] the lid or cover of a container, pen, etc *Put the top back on the bottle.* **4** CLOTHING [C] a piece of women's clothing worn on the upper part of the body **5** TOY [C] a toy that turns round and round when you move its handle up and down **6 the top** the most important position in a company, team, etc *At forty he was already* **at the top of** *his profession.* **7 at the top of your voice** *UK (US* **at the top of your lungs)** shouting very loudly **8 from top to bottom** completely *I've searched the house from top to bottom and still can't find it.* **9 get on top of sb** *UK* If a difficult situation gets on top of someone, it upsets them. **10 off the top of your head** *informal* If you say a fact off the top of your head, you say it immediately, from memory. *"What date is their wedding?" "I couldn't tell you off the top of my head."* **11 on top of sth** a IN ADDITION in addition to something else that is bad *And then, on top of everything else, her car was* *stolen*. **b** IN CONTROL able to deal with or in control of something *I'm not at all sure that he's on top of the situation*. **12 be on top of the world** *informal* to be very happy **13 over the top** *mainly UK informal* too extreme and not suitable *I thought her performance was way over the top.*

o-**top²** /tɒp/ *adjective* [always before noun] **1** the best, most important, or most successful *He's one of the country's top athletes*. **2** at the highest part of something *I can't reach the top shelf.*

top³ /tɒp/ *verb* [T] **topping**, *past* **topped 1** to be better or more than something *I don't think film makers will ever top 'Gone With The Wind'*. **2 be topped with sth** to be covered with something *lemon tart topped with cream*

top sth off *informal* to finish something in an enjoyable or successful way

top sth up *UK* (*US* **top sth off**) to add more liquid to a container in order to make it full

,**top 'hat** *UK* (*US* 'top ,hat) *noun* [C] a tall, black or grey hat worn by men on some formal occasions

WORD PARTNERS FOR **topic**

cover/discuss/raise a topic • a controversial/hot topic • the (main) topic of sth • a topic of conversation/discussion

topic /'tɒpɪk/ *noun* [C] a subject that you talk or write about

topical /'tɒpɪkəl/ *adjective* relating to things that are happening now

topless /'tɒpləs/ *adjective* without clothes on the upper part of your body

topmost /'tɒpməʊst/ *adjective* [always before noun] highest *the topmost branches of a tree*

topography /tə'pɒgrəfi/ *noun* [U] the shape and other physical characteristics of a piece of land

topping /'tɒpɪŋ/ *noun* [C, U] food that is put on top of other food in order to give it more flavour, or to make it look attractive

topple /'tɒpl/ *verb* **1** [I, T] to fall, or to make something or someone fall **2** [T] to make a leader lose their position of power

top-secret /,tɒp'siːkrət/ *adjective* Top-secret information is very important and must not be told to anyone.

topsy-turvy /,tɒpsi'tɜːvi/ *adjective informal* confused or badly organized

the Torah /'tɔːrə/ *noun* the holy books of the Jewish religion, especially the first five books of the Bible

torch¹ /tɔːtʃ/ *noun* [C] **1** *UK* (*US* **flashlight**) a small electric light that you hold in your hand **2** a long stick with material that burns tied to the top of it

torch² /tɔːtʃ/ *verb* [T] *informal* to destroy something by burning it *A number of houses were torched.*

tore /tɔːr/ *past tense of* tear

torment¹ /tɔː'ment/ *verb* [T] to make someone suffer or worry a lot *All evening the question tormented her*. • **tormentor** *noun* [C]

torment² /'tɔːment/ *noun* [C, U] extreme un-

happiness or pain

torn /tɔːn/ *past participle of* tear

tornado /tɔː'neɪdəʊ/ (*also US* **twister**) *noun* [C] *plural* **tornados** or **tornadoes** an extremely strong and dangerous wind that blows in a circle and destroys buildings as it moves along

torpedo /tɔː'piːdəʊ/ *noun* [C] *plural* **torpedoes** a long, thin bomb that is fired from a ship and moves under water to destroy another ship

torrent /'tɒrənt/ *noun* [C] **1 a torrent of sth** a lot of something unpleasant *a torrent of abuse* **2** a large amount of water that is moving very fast

torrential /tə'renʃəl/ *adjective* Torrential rain is very heavy rain.

torso /'tɔːsəʊ/ *noun* [C] the main part of a human body without its arms, legs, or head

tortilla /tɔː'tiːə/ *noun* [C] a type of thin round Mexican bread

tortoise /'tɔːtəs/ *noun* [C] an animal with a thick, hard shell that it can move its head and legs into for protection

tortoise

tortuous /'tɔːtʃuəs/ *adjective formal* **1** very complicated or difficult *Gaining permission to build was a long and tortuous process*. **2** A tortuous road has many turns in it. *a tortuous path/route*

torture¹ /'tɔːtʃər/ *verb* [T] to cause someone severe pain, often in order to make them tell you something • **torturer** *noun* [C]

torture² /'tɔːtʃər/ *noun* [C, U] **1** when someone is tortured **2** a very unpleasant experience *I had to sit there listening to her for two whole hours - it was torture!*

Tory /'tɔːri/ *noun* [C] someone who supports the Conservative Party in the UK *a Tory voter*

toss¹ /tɒs/ *verb* **1 toss sth away/into/on, etc** to throw something somewhere carelessly *He read the letter quickly, then tossed it into the bin*. **2** [I, T] (*also* **toss up**) to throw a coin in the air and guess which side will land facing upwards as a way of deciding something

toss² /tɒs/ *noun* **1 a toss of a coin** when you throw a coin in the air and guess which side will land facing upwards as a way of deciding something **2 a toss of your head/hair** when you move your head quickly backwards

tot /tɒt/ *noun* [C] *informal* **1** a small child **2** *UK* a small amount of strong alcohol

o-**total¹** /'təʊtəl/ *adjective* [always before noun] **1** including everything *The total cost of the work was $800*. **2** extreme or complete *The whole evening was a total disaster.*

WORD PARTNERS FOR **total** *(noun)*

sth **brings/takes** the total **to** [500/4000, etc] • **reach** a total **of** [500/4000, etc] • the **final/overall/sum** total • [500/4000, etc] **in total**

o-**total²** /'təʊtəl/ *noun* [C] the amount you get when you add several smaller amounts together *In total we made over £3,000.*

total³ /'təʊtəl/ *verb* [T] *UK* **totalling**, *past* **totalled**,

US **totaling**, *past* **totaled** to add up to a particular amount

totalitarian /təʊˌtælɪˈteəriən/ *adjective* belonging to a political system in which the people in power have complete control and do not allow anyone to oppose them • **totalitarianism** *noun* [U]

⊶**totally** /ˈtəʊtəli/ *adverb* completely *They look totally different.* ○ *I totally disagree.*

tote bag /ˈtəʊtˌbæg/ *noun* [C] *US* a large bag with handles and an open top

totter /ˈtɒtəʳ/ *verb* [I] to walk in a way that looks as if you are going to fall *She tottered around the dance floor.*

⊶**touch¹** /tʌtʃ/ *verb* **1** [HAND] [T] to put your hand on something *You can look at them but please don't touch them.* **2** [GET CLOSE] [I, T] If two things touch, they are so close to each other that there is no space between them. *These two wires must not touch.* **3** [EMOTION] [T] If something kind that someone says or does touches you, it makes you feel pleased or a little sad. [often passive] *I was deeply touched by her letter.* **4 not touch sth** to not eat or drink something **5 not touch sb/sth** to not harm someone or not damage something ⊃See also: touch/cover all the bases (base¹), hit/touch a (raw) nerve.

touch down When a plane touches down, it lands.

touch on sth to briefly talk about something *We only touched on the subject.*

touch sth up to improve something by making small changes

touch² /tʌtʃ/ *noun* **1** [HAND] [no plural] when you put your hand on something *I felt the touch of his hand on my face.* **2** [ABILITY] [U] the ability to feel things by putting your hand on them *It was cold* ***to the touch*** (= when I touched it). **3** [DETAIL] [C] a small detail that makes something better *Having flowers on the tables was a* ***nice touch***. **4 a touch** a little *Add a little olive oil and* ***a touch of*** *vinegar.* **5 be/get/keep, etc in touch** to communicate or continue to communicate with someone by telephoning, or writing to them **6 lose touch** to stop communicating with someone, usually because they do not live near you now **7 be out of touch** to know little about what has recently happened

touchdown /ˈtʌtʃdaʊn/ *noun* **1** [C, U] when an aircraft lands **2** [C] when the ball is carried or thrown over a line in order to score points in rugby or American football

touched /tʌtʃt/ *adjective* pleased or a little sad because someone has done something kind *She was touched that he had remembered her birthday.*

touching /ˈtʌtʃɪŋ/ *adjective* making you feel sadness or sympathy *a touching performance*

ˈ**touch ˌscreen** *noun* [C] a screen that works when you touch it

touchstone /ˈtʌtʃstəʊn/ *noun* [no plural] something that other things can be judged against

touchy /ˈtʌtʃi/ *adjective* **1** easily upset *Why are you so touchy today?* **2 touchy subject/issue, etc** a subject that you have to talk about carefully because it is likely to upset someone

⊶**tough** /tʌf/ *adjective* **1** [DIFFICULT] difficult *He's had a* ***tough time*** *at work recently.* ○ *We've had to make some* ***tough decisions***. **2** [SEVERE] Tough rules are severe. ***tough new laws*** *on noise pollution* **3** [STRONG THING] not easily damaged, cut, etc *Children's shoes have to be tough.* ○ *This meat's very tough.* **4** [STRONG PERSON] physically strong and not afraid of violence *a* ***tough guy*** **5** [DETERMINED] determined and not easily upset *You have to be tough to survive in politics.* **6** [UNFAIR] unfair or unlucky *It can* ***be tough on*** *kids when parents get divorced.*

toughen /ˈtʌfən/ (*also* **toughen up**) *verb* [I, T] to become stronger, or to make something or someone stronger *School tends to toughen kids up.*

toupee /ˈtuːpeɪ/ [US] /tuːˈpeɪ/ *noun* [C] a piece of artificial (= not natural) hair worn by a man to cover part of his head where there is no hair

WORD PARTNERS FOR *tour*

be on / go on a tour • a **guided / sightseeing/world** tour • a tour **of** sth

⊶**tour¹** /tʊəʳ/ *noun* [C, U] a visit to and around a place, area, or country *a* ***tour of*** *Europe* ○ *We went on a* ***guided tour*** *of the cathedral.* ○ *The band are* ***on tour*** (= travelling and performing in different places).

tour² /tʊəʳ/ *verb* [I, T] to travel around a place for pleasure *to tour the States*

tourism /ˈtʊərɪzəm/ *noun* [U] the business of providing services for tourists, including organizing their travel, hotels, entertainment, etc

⊶**tourist** /ˈtʊərɪst/ *noun* [C] someone who visits a place for pleasure and does not live there

WORD PARTNERS FOR *tournament*

host/play in/pull out of/take part in/win a tournament • **in** a tournament • a **major** tournament • a **round/stage** of a tournament

tournament /ˈtʊənəmənt/ *noun* [C] a competition with a series of games between many teams or players, with one winner at the end *a golf/tennis tournament*

tourniquet /ˈtʊənɪkeɪ/ [US] /ˈtɜːrnɪkɪt/ *noun* [C] a long piece of cloth that you tie tightly around an injured arm or leg to stop the blood coming out

tousled /ˈtaʊsld/ *adjective* Tousled hair is untidy.

tout¹ /taʊt/ *verb* **1** [T] to praise someone or something in order to make people think that they are important [often passive] *He is being* ***touted as*** *the next big star.* **2** [I, T] *mainly UK* to try to persuade people to buy something *Drug dealers were seen* ***touting for business*** *outside schools.*

tout² /taʊt/ *UK* (*US* **scalper**) *noun* [C] someone who unofficially sells tickets outside theatres, sporting events, etc

tow¹ /təʊ/ *verb* [T] to pull a car, boat, etc, using a rope or chain connected to another vehicle *His car was* ***towed away*** *by the police.*

tow² /təʊ/ *noun informal* **in tow** If you have someone in tow, you have them with you.

T

Shopping can be very stressful with young children in tow.

∘⋆**towards** /təˈwɔːdz/ *mainly UK* (*mainly US* **toward**) *preposition* **1** DIRECTION in the direction of someone or something *She stood up and walked towards him.* **2** POSITION near to a time or place *Your seats are towards the back of the theatre.* ○ *He only became successful towards the end of his life.* **3** FEELING used when talking about feelings about something or someone *His attitude towards work needs to improve.* **4** PURPOSE for the purpose of buying or achieving something *We're asking people for a contribution towards the cost.* ○ *This piece of work counts towards your final mark.*

∘⋆**towel** /taʊl/ *noun* [C] **1** a soft piece of cloth or paper that you use for drying yourself or for drying something *a **bath**/**beach towel*** ○ *a paper towel* ➾See colour picture **The Bathroom** on page Centre 3. **2 throw in the towel** to stop trying to do something because you do not think you can succeed ➾See also: **sanitary towel, tea towel.**

'**towel ,rail** *UK* (*US* '**towel ,rack**) *noun* [C] a horizontal bar on the wall that you hang towels on ➾See picture at **rail.**

tower[1] /taʊəʳ/ *noun* [C] **1** a very tall, narrow building, or part of a building *a church tower* ○ *the Eiffel Tower* **2 a tower of strength** someone who helps you a lot during a difficult time

tower[2] /taʊəʳ/ *verb* **tower over/above sb/sth** to be much taller or higher than someone or something else *David towers over his mother.*

'**tower ,block** *noun* [C] *UK* a very tall building divided into apartments or offices

towering /ˈtaʊərɪŋ/ *adjective* [always before noun] very tall *towering mountains/trees*

go **into** town ● **in** town ● a **part of/side of** town ● (*UK*) the town **centre**

∘⋆**town** /taʊn/ *noun* **1** [C] a place where people live and work, usually larger than a village but smaller than a city *It's a small town in the north of England.* **2** [U] the central area of a town where the shops are *I usually **go into** town on a Saturday.* ○ *Shall I meet you **in** town?* **3 go to town** (**on sth**) to spend a lot of money or time doing something in order to make it special *They've really gone to town on the decorations.* **4 out on the town** *informal* enjoying yourself in bars, restaurants, etc in the evening ➾See also: **ghost town, shanty town.**

,**town 'hall** *noun* [C] a large building where local government is based

township /ˈtaʊnʃɪp/ *noun* [C] in South Africa, an area where only black people live

toxic /ˈtɒksɪk/ *adjective* poisonous *toxic chemicals/fumes* ○ *toxic waste* (= poisonous waste materials produced by industry) ● **toxicity** /tɒkˈsɪsəti/ *noun* [U] *formal* how poisonous a substance is

toxin /ˈtɒksɪn/ *noun* [C] *formal* a poisonous substance

∘⋆**toy**[1] /tɔɪ/ *noun* [C] an object for children to play with *a toy car/train* ○ *He was happily playing with his toys.*

toy[2] /tɔɪ/ *verb*
toy with sth 1 to briefly think about doing something, but not really intend to do it *I've toyed with the idea of going to work abroad.* **2** to move something around in your hands without any clear purpose *He sat toying with his empty glass.*

trace[1] /treɪs/ *verb* [T] **1** FIND to find someone or something that was lost *Police have so far failed to trace the missing woman.* **2** ORIGIN to find the origin of something *She's traced her family **back** to the sixteenth century.* ○ *They were able to trace the **call*** (= find out the number of the telephone used). **3** DEVELOPMENT to describe the way something has developed over time *The book traces the development of women's art since the start of the century.* **4** COPY to copy a picture by putting transparent paper on top and following the outer line of the picture with a pen *tracing paper*

find no/leave no trace (of sth) ● **disappear without/vanish without** trace

trace[2] /treɪs/ *noun* **1** [C, U] proof that someone or something was in a place *There was **no trace** of her anywhere.* ○ *Ships have **disappeared without trace*** (= completely). **2** [C] a small amount of something *They found traces of blood on his clothing.*

track[1] /træk/ *noun* **1** PATH [C] a narrow path or road *We followed a dirt track off the main road.* **2** RAILWAY [C] the long metal lines which a train travels along (*UK*) *a railway track*/ (*US*) *a railroad track* **3** RACE [C] a path, often circular, used for races *a race track* ○ *track events* **4** SPORT [U] (*US*) the sport of running in races around a wide circular path made for this sport **5** MUSIC [C] one song or piece of music on a CD, record, etc **6 keep track** to continue to know what is happening to someone or something *He changes jobs so often - I find it hard to keep track of what he's doing.* **7 lose track** to not know what is happening to someone or something any more *I've lost track of how much we've spent.* **8 on track** making progress and likely to succeed [+ to do sth] *A fighter from Edinburgh is on track to become world heavyweight boxing champion.* **9 a fast track** (**to sth**) a very quick way of achieving or dealing with something *These intensive courses claim to offer a fast track to wealth and success.* **10 off the beaten track** in a place where few people go

track[2] /træk/ *verb* [T] **1** to follow a person or animal by looking for proof that they have been somewhere, or by using electronic equipment *The wolves are tracked by using radio collars.* **2** to record the progress or development of something over a period *The project tracks the effects of population growth on the area.*

track sth/sb down to find something or someone after looking for them in a lot of different places *The man was finally tracked down by French police.*

,**track and 'field** *US* (*UK* **athletics**) *noun* [U] the sports which include running, jumping, and throwing ⊃See colour picture **Sports 1** on page Centre 14.

track 'record UK (US 'track ,record) noun [C] how well or badly you have done in the past *This company has an impressive track record in completing projects on time.*

tracks /træks/ noun [plural] the marks left on the ground by a person, animal, or vehicle *We followed their tracks in the snow.*

tracksuit /'træksu:t/ noun [C] UK loose, comfortable clothes, usually trousers and a top, especially worn for exercising ⊃See colour picture **Clothes** on page Centre 9.

tract /trækt/ noun [C] **1** a system of connected tubes in someone's body which has a particular purpose *the digestive/respiratory tract* **2** a large area of land

tractor /'træktəʳ/ noun [C] a strong vehicle with large back wheels used on farms for pulling things

WORD PARTNERS FOR **trade** (noun)

trade **agreement/deal/policy** • trade **between** [two countries/regions] • trade **with** [a country] • trade **in** sth • a trade **dispute**

⊶**trade**[1] /treɪd/ noun **1** BUYING AND SELLING [U] the buying and selling of large numbers of goods or services, especially between countries *a trade agreement/dispute* ○ *They rely heavily on trade with Europe.* ○ *The laws ban the international trade in ivory.* **2** BUSINESS [C] a particular area of business or industry *the building/tourist trade* **3** JOB [C] someone's job, especially one which needs skill in using their hands *He's a builder by trade.*

trade[2] /treɪd/ verb **1** [I] to buy and sell goods or services, especially between countries *This will increase costs for companies trading with Asia.* **2** [T] mainly US to give something to someone and receive something else in exchange *He traded his guitar for a leather jacket.* • trading noun [U]

trade sth in to give something as part of your payment for something else *He traded his old car in for a new model.*

trademark /'treɪdmɑ:k/ noun [C] the name of a particular company or product which cannot be used by anyone else

trade-off /'treɪdɒf/ noun [C] a situation where you accept something bad in order to have something good *There's always a trade-off between speed and quality.*

tradesman /'treɪdzmən/ noun [C] plural tradesmen UK someone who works in trade or in a trade which needs skill in using their hands, usually in the building industry

trade 'union (also US labor union) noun [C] an organization that represents people who do a particular job

WORD PARTNERS FOR **tradition**

break with/follow/revive/uphold a tradition • an **ancient/old/proud/rich/strong** tradition

⊶**tradition** /trə'dɪʃən/ noun [C, U] a custom or way of behaving that has continued for a long time in a group of people or a society *There is a strong tradition of dance in St Petersburg.* ○ *We decided to break with tradition* (= not behave as usual) *this year and go away for Christmas.*

⊶**traditional** /trə'dɪʃənəl/ adjective following the customs or ways of behaving that have continued in a group of people or society for a long time *traditional Hungarian dress* ○ *traditional farming methods* • **traditionally** adverb

traditionalist /trə'dɪʃənəlɪst/ noun [C] someone who believes in traditional ideas and ways of doing things

WORD PARTNERS FOR **traffic**

reduce/ease/divert/slow down traffic • **bad/heavy** traffic • be **stuck in** traffic • a traffic **accident**

⊶**traffic** /'træfɪk/ noun [U] **1** CARS ETC the cars, trucks, etc using a road *Traffic is heavy* (= there are a lot of cars, etc) *in both directions.* ○ *a traffic accident* ○ *Sorry we're late - we got stuck in traffic.* **2** PLANES AND SHIPS the planes or ships moving around an area *air traffic control* **3** ILLEGAL the illegal buying and selling of goods, such as drugs, weapons, etc *the traffic in illegal drugs*

'traffic ,circle US (UK roundabout) noun [C] a circular place where roads meet and where cars drive around until they arrive at the road that they want to turn into ⊃See picture at **roundabout**.

'traffic ,jam noun [C] a line of cars, trucks, etc that are moving slowly or not moving at all *They got stuck in a traffic jam.*

trafficking /'træfɪkɪŋ/ noun [U] the activity of illegally buying and selling goods, such as drugs or weapons *arms/drug trafficking* • **trafficker** noun [C]

'traffic ,light noun (also lights [plural]) a set of red, green, and yellow lights that is used to stop and start traffic [usually plural] *Turn left at the traffic lights.* ⊃See picture at **light**.

'traffic ,warden noun [C] UK someone whose job is to make sure that people do not leave their cars in illegal places

tragedy /'trædʒədi/ noun **1** [C, U] an event or situation which is very sad, often involving death *the tragedy of their daughter's death* **2** [C] a play with a sad end *a Greek tragedy*

tragic /'trædʒɪk/ adjective very sad, often relating to death and suffering *a tragic accident/death* • **tragically** adverb *He was tragically killed in a flying accident at the age of 25.*

trail[1] /treɪl/ noun [C] **1** a line of marks that someone or something leaves behind as they move *He left a trail of muddy footprints across the kitchen floor.* **2** a path through the countryside, often where people walk *a nature trail*

trail[2] /treɪl/ verb **1** FOLLOW [T] to follow someone, especially without them knowing, in order to watch or catch them *He suspected he was being trailed by undercover police.* **2** HANG DOWN [I, T] UK to hang down and touch the ground, or to make something do this *Your coat's trailing in the mud.* **3** LOWER SCORE [I, T] to have a lower score than someone else, especially in a sport-

| ɑ: arm | ɜ: her | i: see | ɔ: saw | u: too | aɪ my | aʊ how | eə hair | eɪ day | əʊ no | ɪə near | ɔɪ boy | ʊə poor | aɪə fire | aʊə sour |

ing event *City were trailing United 2-1 at half time.*

trail away/off If someone's voice trails away or off, it gradually becomes quieter until it stops.

trailer /'treɪlə^r/ *noun* [C] **1** CONTAINER a container with wheels that can be pulled by a car or a truck **2** HOUSE *mainly US* a house on wheels which can be pulled by a car **3** FILM short parts of a film or television programme which are shown in order to advertise it

'trailer ˌpark *noun* [C] *US* a place where trailers (= vehicles that people live in) can park

o▪**train¹** /treɪn/ *noun* **1** [C] a long, thin vehicle which travels along metal tracks and carries people or goods *a train journey* ○ *We could go by train.* ○ *You'll have to catch/get the next train.* **2** train of thought/events a series of connected thoughts, ideas, or events which come or happen one after the other *I was interrupted and lost my train of thought.*

o▪**train²** /treɪn/ *verb* **1** TEACH [T] to teach someone how to do something, usually a skill that is needed for a job *We are training all our staff in how to use the new computer system.* ○ [+ to do sth] *The aid workers trained local people to give the injections.* **2** LEARN [I] to learn the skills you need to do a job *He trained as a lawyer in Vienna.* ○ *I'm trained in basic first aid.* **3** SPORT [I, T] to practise a sport or exercise, often in order to prepare for a sporting event, or to help someone to do this *He's been training hard for the race for several weeks now.*

trainee /ˌtreɪ'niː/ *noun* [C] someone who is learning how to do something, especially a job *a trainee accountant/teacher*

trainer /'treɪnə^r/ *noun* [C] **1** PERSON someone who trains people *a fitness trainer* **2** ANIMALS a person who trains animals *a racehorse trainer* **3** SHOE *UK* (*US* **sneaker**) a soft sports shoe *a pair of trainers* ➷See colour picture **Clothes** on page Centre 9.

┌─────────────────────────────────┐
│ WORD PARTNERS FOR **training** │
└─────────────────────────────────┘
have/receive/undergo training • give sb/ provide training • training in/on sth • a training course/day/programme/session

o▪**training** /'treɪnɪŋ/ *noun* [U] **1** the process of learning the skills you need to do a particular job or activity *a training course* ○ *computer/ management training* **2** preparation for a sport or competition *weight training* ○ *He's in training for the big match next month.*

trait /treɪt/ *noun* [C] a quality, good or bad, in someone's character *a family trait*

traitor /'treɪtə^r/ *noun* [C] someone who is not loyal to their country or to a group which they are a member of

trajectory /trə'dʒekt^əri/ *noun* [C] *formal* the curved line that something follows as it moves through the air

tram /træm/ *noun* [C] an electric vehicle for carrying passengers, mostly in cities, which moves along metal lines in the road

tramp¹ /træmp/ *noun* [C] someone who has no

home, job, or money and who lives outside

tramp² /træmp/ *verb* [I, T] to walk a long way, or to walk with heavy steps because you are tired *We spent all day tramping around the city looking for somewhere cheap to stay.*

trample /'træmpl/ (*also* **trample on**) *verb* [T] to walk on something, usually damaging or hurting it *She shouted at the boys for trampling on her flowers.* ○ *Two people were trampled to death in the panic.*

trampoline /'træmp^əliːn/ *noun* [C] a piece of sports equipment that you jump up and down on, made of a metal structure with a piece of strong material fixed to it

trance /trɑːns/ *noun* [C] a condition in which you are not completely conscious of what is happening around you or able to control what you are doing *He sat staring out of the window as if in a trance.*

tranquil /'træŋkwɪl/ *adjective* calm and quiet *a tranquil garden* • **tranquility** (*also* **tranquillity**) /træŋ'kwɪləti/ *noun* [U] *I love the tranquility of the woods.*

tranquilizer (*also UK* **-iser**) /'træŋkwɪˌlaɪzə^r/ *noun* [C] a drug which is used to make people or animals sleep or to make them calm

trans- /træns-, trænz-/ *prefix* **1** across *trans-atlantic flights* **2** showing a change *to trans-form* ○ *to translate*

transaction /træn'zækʃ^ən/ *noun* [C] *formal* when someone buys or sells something, or when money is exchanged *a business/financial transaction*

transatlantic /ˌtrænzət'læntɪk/ *adjective* crossing the Atlantic *a transatlantic flight/phone call*

transcend /træn'send/ *verb* [T] *formal* to be better or more important than something else *Somehow her appeal transcends class barriers.*

transcribe /træn'skraɪb/ *verb* [T] to make a written record of something you hear, such as speech or music *I later transcribed the tapes of the interviews.* • **transcription** /træn'skrɪpʃ^ən/ *noun* [C, U] a written record of speech, music, etc, or the process of making it

transcript /'trænskrɪpt/ *noun* [C] an exact written record of speech, music, etc

transfer /træns'fɜː^r/ *verb* transferring, *past* transferred **1** MOVE [T] to move someone or something from one place to another *She was later transferred to a different hospital.* ○ *I'll transfer some money into my other account.* **2** CHANGE JOB/TEAM ETC [I, T] to change to a different job, team, place of work, etc, or to make someone do this *After a year he transferred to University College, Dublin.* **3** CHANGE OWNER [T] to change who owns or controls something *We had all the documents transferred to my name.* • **transfer** /'trænsfɜː^r/ *noun* [C, U] *I'm hoping for a transfer to the Brussels office.*

transfixed /træns'fɪkst/ *adjective* unable to move or stop looking at something because you are so interested, surprised, or frightened *We all sat in silence, transfixed by what we saw on the screen.*

transform /træns'fɔːm/ *verb* [T] to change

T

something completely, usually to improve it
*Within weeks they had **transformed** the area
into a beautiful garden.* ● **transformation**
/ˌtrænsfəˈmeɪʃᵃn/ *noun* [C, U] a complete change
*The company has **undergone** a dramatic
transformation in the past five years.*

transformer /trænsˈfɔːməʳ/ *noun* [C] a piece of
equipment that changes the strength of an
electrical current

transfusion /trænsˈfjuːʒᵃn/ (*also* blood transfusion) *noun* [C] when blood is put into
someone's body

transgress /trænzˈgres/ *verb* [I, T] *formal* to do
something which is against a law or rule
● **transgression** /trænzˈgreʃᵃn/ *noun* [C]

transient[1] /ˈtrænziənt/ *adjective formal* **1** lasting only for a short time *transient pleasures*
2 staying in one place only for a short time

transient[2] /ˈtrænziənt/ *noun* [C] *US* someone
who has no home and stays in a place for only
a short time

transistor /trænˈzɪstəʳ/ *noun* [C] a small piece of
electrical equipment used in radios, televisions, etc

transit /ˈtrænsɪt/ *noun* [U] *formal* the movement
of goods or people from one place to another
Some things got damaged in transit (= while
they were being moved).

transition /trænˈzɪʃᵃn/ *noun* [C, U] *formal* when
something changes from one system or
method to another, often gradually *The country is in the process of **making the transition**
from military rule to democracy.* ● **transitional**
adjective a **transitional period/phase** ○ *a
transitional government*

transitive /ˈtrænsətɪv/ *adjective* A transitive
verb always has an object. In the sentence 'I'll
make a drink.', 'make' is a transitive verb.
⊃See Extra help page **Verb patterns** on page Centre 27.
⊃Compare **intransitive**.

transitory /ˈtrænsɪtᵊri/ *adjective formal* lasting
only for a short time *the transitory nature of
life*

translate /trænzˈleɪt/ *verb* [I, T] **1** to change
written or spoken words from one language to
another *The book has now been **translated** ᵒ╸
from Spanish **into** more than ten languages.* **2**
formal If an idea or plan translates into an
action, it makes it happen. *So how does this
theory **translate into** practical policy?*

translation /trænzˈleɪʃᵃn/ *noun* [C, U] something which has been translated from one language to another, or the process of translating

translator /trænzˈleɪtəʳ/ *noun* [C] someone
whose job is to change written or spoken
words from one language to another

translucent /trænzˈluːsᵃnt/ *adjective* If something is translucent, light can pass through it
and you can almost see through it. *translucent
fabric*

transmission /trænzˈmɪʃᵃn/ *noun* **1** BROADCAST
[C, U] the process of broadcasting something by
radio, television, etc, or something which is
broadcast *radio/satellite transmission*
2 SPREADING [U] the process of passing
something from one person or place to another

*There is still a risk of transmission of the virus
through infected water.* **3** CAR [U] the system in
a car that moves power from its engine to its
wheels *automatic/manual transmission*

transmit /trænzˈmɪt/ *verb* [T] transmitting, *past
tense* transmitted **1** to broadcast something, or to send
out signals using radio, television, etc [often
passive] *The information is transmitted electronically to the central computer.* **2** *formal* to
pass something from one person or place to
another *The **disease** is **transmitted** by mosquitoes.* ● **transmitter** *noun* [C] *a radio/television
transmitter*

transparency /trænˈspærᵊnsi/ *noun* [C] a photograph or picture printed on plastic which you
can see on a screen by shining a light through
it

transparent /trænˈspærᵊnt/ *adjective* If a substance or material is transparent, you can see
through it. *transparent plastic*

transpire /trænˈspaɪəʳ/ *verb formal* **1** It transpires that If it transpires that something has
happened, this fact becomes known. *It later
transpired that he had known about the plan
from the beginning.* **2** [I] to happen *No one is
willing to predict what will transpire as a
result of the policy.*

┌─────────────────────────────────────┐
░░░ WORD PARTNERS FOR **transplant**

have / perform / undergo a transplant ● a
transplant **donor / operation / patient /
surgeon**
└─────────────────────────────────────┘

transplant /ˈtrænsplɑːnt/ *noun* [C] an operation in which a new organ is put into
someone's body *a heart/kidney transplant*
○ *Eventually the organ gives up and a transplant is the only solution.* ● **transplant**
/trænˈsplɑːnt/ *verb* [T] to remove an organ or
other body part from one person and put it
into someone else's body

┌─────────────────────────────────────┐
░░░ WORD PARTNERS FOR **transport**

provide / arrange / improve transport
● **free/cheap** transport ● **public** transport
● the transport **system**
└─────────────────────────────────────┘

ᵒ╸**transport**[1] /ˈtrænspɔːt/ *noun* [U] **1** a vehicle or
system of vehicles, such as buses, trains, aircraft, etc for getting from one place to another
*He can't drive so he has to rely on **public transport**.* ○ *the city's **transport system*** **2** when
people or goods are moved from one place to
another *the transport of live animals*

transport[2] /trænˈspɔːt/ *verb* [T] to move people
or goods from one place to another

transportation /ˌtrænspɔːˈteɪʃᵃn/ *noun* [U] **1**
US (*UK* transport) a vehicle or system of
vehicles, such as buses, trains, etc for getting
from one place to another *Companies are now
encouraging their staff to use alternative means
of transportation.* **2** when people or goods are
moved from one place to another *transportation costs*

transvestite /trænzˈvestaɪt/ *noun* [C] someone,
especially a man, who likes to wear the clothes
of someone of the opposite sex

trap[1] /træp/ *noun* [C] **1** a piece of equipment for catching animals *a mouse trap* **2** a dangerous or unpleasant situation which is difficult to escape from [usually singular] *Such families get caught in the poverty trap.* ⊃See also: **booby trap.**

trap² /træp/ *verb* [T] **trapping**, *past* **trapped**
1 [CANNOT ESCAPE] If someone or something is trapped, they cannot move or escape from a place or situation. *The car turned over, trapping the driver underneath.* **2** [ANIMAL] to catch an animal using a trap **3** [TRICK] to trick someone into doing or saying something that they do not want to

,trap 'door *noun* [C] a small door that you cannot see in a floor or ceiling

trappings /'træpɪŋz/ *noun* [plural] things that you usually get when you are rich and successful, such as a big house and car *the trappings of success/power*

trash¹ /træʃ/ *noun* [U] **1** *US* (*UK* **rubbish**) things that you throw away because you do not want them **2** *informal* something that is of bad quality *It's better than the trash she usually reads.*

trash² /træʃ/ *verb* [T] *informal* to destroy something *Vandals broke in and trashed the place.*

'trash ,can *noun* [C] *US* a container for waste, often one that is kept outdoors ⊃See colour picture **The Office** on page Centre 5.

trashy /'træʃi/ *adjective informal* of very bad quality *a trashy novel/movie*

trauma /'trɔːmə/ *noun* [C, U] severe shock caused by an unpleasant experience, or the experience which causes this feeling *the trauma of marriage breakdown*

traumatic /trɔːˈmætɪk/ *adjective* If an experience is traumatic, it makes you feel very shocked and upset. *His parents split up when he was eight, which he found very traumatic.*

traumatized (*also UK* **-ised**) /'trɔːmətaɪzd/ *adjective* very shocked and upset for a long time *The violence that he witnessed left him traumatized.*

o—**travel¹** /'trævəl/ *verb UK* **travelling**, *past* **travelled**, *US* **traveling**, *past* **traveled 1** [I, T] to make a journey *I spent a year travelling around Asia.* ○ *He has to travel abroad a lot on business.* **2** [I] If light, sound, or news travels, it moves from one place to another. *News of the accident travelled fast.* ⊃See Common learner error at **move**.

travel² /'trævəl/ *noun* **1** [U] the activity of travelling *air/rail travel* ○ *travel expenses/insurance* **2** *sb's* **travels** someone's journey *I meet all kinds of interesting people on my travels.*

COMMON LEARNER ERROR

travel, journey, or trip?

The noun **travel** is a general word which means the activity of travelling.

Air travel has become much cheaper.

Use **journey** to talk about when you travel from one place to another.

He fell asleep during the train journey.

Did you have a good journey?

~~Did you have a good travel?~~

A **trip** is a journey in which you visit a place for a short

time and come back again.

a business trip

a 3-day trip to Spain

'travel ,agency (*also* **'travel ,agent's**) *noun* [C] a company or shop that makes travel arrangements for people

'travel ,agent *noun* [C] someone whose job is making travel arrangements for people

traveller /'trævələʳ/ *noun* [C] **1** (*also US* **traveler**) someone who is travelling or who often travels *We're doing a survey of business travellers.* **2** *UK* another word for gypsy (= a member of a race of people who travel from place to place, especially in Europe)

'traveller's ,cheque *UK* (*US* **traveler's check**) *noun* [C] a special piece of paper which you buy at a bank and exchange for local money when you are in another country

traverse /trəˈvɜːs/ *verb* [T] *formal* to move across something

travesty /'trævəsti/ *noun* [C] *formal* If something is a travesty, it is very badly done or unfair and does not represent how that thing should be. *She described the trial as a travesty of justice.*

trawl /trɔːl/ *verb*

trawl through sth *mainly UK* to look through a lot of things in order to find something *to trawl through data*

trawler /'trɔːləʳ/ *noun* [C] a large ship which is used for catching fish by pulling a large net through the sea behind it

tray /treɪ/ *noun* [C] a flat object with higher edges, used for carrying food and drinks *She came back carrying a tray of drinks.*

treacherous /'tretʃʳrəs/ *adjective* **1** very dangerous, especially because of bad weather conditions *Ice had made the roads treacherous.* **2** *formal* If someone is treacherous, they deceive people who trust them.

treachery /'tretʃʳri/ *noun* [U] *formal* when a person deceives someone who trusts them

treacle /'triːkl/ *UK* (*UK/US* **molasses**) *noun* [U] a sweet, thick, dark liquid used in sweet dishes

tread¹ /tred/ *verb past tense* **trod**, *past participle* **trodden 1** [I, T] *mainly UK* to put your foot on something or to press something down with your foot *I trod on a piece of broken glass.* ○ *David trod in some paint.* ○ *The kids were treading cake crumbs into the carpet.* **2 tread carefully/gently/lightly, etc** to be careful what you say so that you do not upset someone **3 tread water** to float vertically in the water by moving your arms and legs up and down

tread² /tred/ *noun* **1** [C, U] the pattern of lines on the surface of a tyre **2** [no plural] the sound of someone putting their feet down when walking

treadmill /'tredmɪl/ *noun* [C] **1** a machine with a moving part which you walk or run on for exercise **2** a job which is boring because you have to repeat the same thing again and again

treason /'triːzʳn/ *noun* [U] the crime of doing something that harms your country or government, especially by helping its enemies

treasure¹ /'treʒəʳ/ noun **1** [U] a collection of gold, silver, jewellery and valuable objects, especially in children's stories *buried treasure* **2** [C] a very valuable object [usually plural] *art treasures*

treasure² /'treʒəʳ/ verb [T] If you treasure something, it is very important to you and gives you a lot of pleasure. *I shall treasure those memories of her.*

treasurer /'treʒʳrəʳ/ noun [C] someone who is responsible for the money of an organization

treasury /'treʒʳri/ noun [C] the government department which controls a country's money supply and economy

o⊷**treat¹** /triːt/ verb [T] **1** DEAL WITH to behave towards or deal with someone in a particular way *He treats her really badly.* ○ *She felt she'd been unfairly treated by her employer.* ○ *They treat her like one of their own children.* **2** CONSIDER to consider something in a particular way *He treated my suggestion as a joke.* **3** ILLNESS/INJURY to give medical care to someone for an illness or injury *He's being treated for cancer at a hospital in Manchester.* **4** SPECIAL to do or buy something special for someone *I'm going to treat her to dinner at that nice Italian restaurant.* **5** PROTECT to put a substance on something in order to protect it *The wood is then treated with a special chemical to protect it from the rain.*

treat² /triːt/ noun [C] something special which you buy or do for someone else *a birthday treat* ○ *As a special treat I'm taking him out for dinner.* ○ *Annie, put your money away, this is my treat* (= I am paying). ⊃See also: **Trick or treat!**.

treatise /'triːtɪz/ noun [C] a formal piece of writing that examines a particular subject

> 🧩 WORD PARTNERS FOR **treatment**
>
> **get / have / receive / undergo** treatment • **give / provide** treatment • **respond to** treatment • treatment **for** sth

o⊷**treatment** /'triːtmənt/ noun **1** [C, U] something which you do to try to cure an illness or injury, especially something suggested or done by a doctor *She's receiving treatment for a lung infection.* **2** [U] the way you deal with or behave towards someone or something *There have been complaints about the treatment of prisoners.*

> 🧩 WORD PARTNERS FOR **treaty**
>
> **draw up/ratify/sign** a treaty • the **terms of** a treaty • **under** a treaty • a treaty **between** sb and sb • a treaty **on** sth • a **peace** treaty • an **international** treaty

treaty /'triːti/ noun [C] a written agreement between two or more countries *a peace treaty* ○ *an international treaty*

treble /'trebl/ verb [I, T] to increase three times in size or amount, or to make something do this

tree

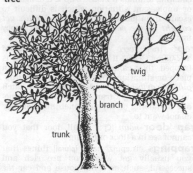

o⊷**tree** /triː/ noun [C] a tall plant with a thick stem which has branches coming from it and leaves ⊃See also: **Christmas tree, family tree, palm tree.**

trek /trek/ noun [C] a long, difficult journey that you make by walking *They started out on the long trek across the mountains.* • **trek** verb [I] trekking, past trekked

trellis /'trelɪs/ noun [C] a wooden structure fixed to a wall for plants to grow up

tremble /'trembl/ verb [I] to shake slightly, especially because you are nervous, frightened, or cold *My hands were trembling so much I could hardly hold the pen.*

tremendous /trɪ'mendəs/ adjective **1** extremely good *I think she's doing a tremendous job.* **2** very large, great, strong, etc *a tremendous amount of money* • **tremendously** adverb very much

tremor /'tremərʳ/ noun [C] **1** a slight earthquake (= when the Earth shakes) **2** a slight shaking of part of your body which you cannot control

trench /trenʃ/ noun [C] a long, narrow hole dug into the ground

trenchant /'trenʃənt/ adjective formal expressing strong criticism *trenchant criticism/ views*

trenchcoat /'trentʃ,kəʊt/ noun [C] a long coat that does not let water through, similar in style to a military coat

trend /trend/ noun [C] a general development or change in a situation *There's a trend towards more locally produced television programmes.* ○ *I'm not familiar with the latest trends in teaching methodology.*

trendy /'trendi/ adjective informal fashionable at the moment *a trendy restaurant* ○ *He writes for a trendy music magazine.*

trepidation /ˌtrepɪ'deɪʃʳn/ noun [U] formal fear or worry about something you are going to do *It was with trepidation that I accepted Klein's invitation.*

trespass /'trespəs/ verb [I] to go on someone's land without their permission • **trespasser** noun [C]

tri- /traɪ-/ prefix three *a triangle* ○ *a tripod*

| ɑː arm | ɜː her | iː see | ɔː saw | uː too | aɪ my | aʊ how | eə hair | eɪ day | əʊ no | ɪə near | ɔɪ boy | ʊə poor | aɪə fire | aʊə sour |

WORD PARTNERS FOR ***trial***

be on/stand trial (for sth) • **be awaiting/be facing** trial • a trial **court/date/judge**

⊶**trial** /traɪəl/ *noun* [C, U] **1** a legal process to decide if someone is guilty of a crime *The two men are now **on trial for** attempted murder.* ○ *He will be taken to the US to **stand trial**.* **2** a test of something new to find out if it is safe, works correctly, etc *The drug is currently undergoing **clinical trials**.* **3 trial and error** a way of learning the best way to do something by trying different methods *There aren't any instructions with it - it's just a matter of trial and error.*

trials /traɪəlz/ *noun* [plural] **1** a sports competition to find out how good a player is **2 trials and tribulations** problems and suffering *the trials and tribulations of growing up*

triangle /ˈtraɪæŋgl/ *noun* [C] **1** a flat shape with three sides ↻See picture at **shape**. **2** a small musical instrument made of a piece of metal with three sides which you hit with a metal bar • **triangular** /traɪˈæŋgjələʳ/ *adjective* shaped like a triangle

tribe /traɪb/ *noun* [C] a group of people who live together, usually in areas far away from cities, and who share the same culture and language and still have a traditional way of life *Native American tribes* • **tribal** *adjective* relating to a tribe *a tribal dance*

tribulations /ˌtrɪbjəˈleɪʃənz/ *noun* [plural] ↻See **trials and tribulations**.

tribunal /traɪˈbjuːnəl/ *noun* [C] an official court or group of people whose job is to deal with a particular problem or disagreement ↻See also: **industrial tribunal**.

tributary /ˈtrɪbjətəri/ *noun* [C] a river or stream which flows into a larger river

tribute /ˈtrɪbjuːt/ *noun* [C, U] **1** something which you do or say to show that you respect and admire someone, especially in a formal situation *The concert was organized as **a tribute to** the singer who died last year.* ○ *The President **paid tribute to*** (= expressed his admiration for) *the brave soldiers who had defended the country.* **2 be a tribute to sb/sth** to show how good someone or something is *It's a tribute to Mark's hard work that the project is finished.*

ˈ**tribute** ˌ**band** *noun* [C] a group of musicians who play the music of a famous pop group and pretend to be that group *a Rolling Stones tribute band*

WORD PARTNERS FOR ***trick***

play a trick (on sb) • a **cheap/cruel/dirty/sneaky** trick • a trick **question**

trick¹ /trɪk/ *noun* [C] **1** [DECEIVE] something you do to deceive or cheat someone, or to make someone look stupid as a joke *a **trick question*** ○ *I wasn't really ill - it was just a trick.* ○ *My little brother liked to **play tricks on** me* (= do things to deceive me as a joke). **2** [METHOD] an effective way of doing something *What's the **trick to** pulling out this sofa bed?* **3** [MAGIC] something that is done to entertain people and that seems to be magic *a card trick* **4 do the trick** If something does the trick, it solves a problem or has the result you want. *If I've got a headache, a couple of aspirins usually do the trick.* ↻See also: **hat trick**.

trick² /trɪk/ *verb* [T] to deceive someone [+ into + doing sth] *They tricked him into signing the papers.*

trickery /ˈtrɪkəri/ *noun* [U] the use of tricks to deceive or cheat people

trickle /ˈtrɪkl/ *verb* **1 trickle down/from/out of, etc** If liquid trickles somewhere, it flows slowly and in a thin line. *She could feel the sweat trickling down her back.* **2 trickle in/into/out, etc** to go somewhere slowly in small numbers *People began to trickle into the classroom.* • **trickle** *noun* [C] *a trickle of blood*

ˌ**Trick or** ˈ**treat!** **1** something that children say on Halloween (= a holiday on 31 October), when they dress to look frightening and visit people's houses to ask for sweets **2 go trick or treating** If children go trick or treating, they visit people's houses on Halloween to ask for sweets.

tricky /ˈtrɪki/ *adjective* difficult to deal with or do *a **tricky question/situation***

tricycle /ˈtraɪsɪkl/ *noun* [C] a bicycle with one wheel at the front and two at the back

trifle /ˈtraɪfl/ *noun* **1 a trifle** *formal* slightly *It does seem a trifle odd.* **2** [C, U] *UK* a cold, sweet dish that has layers of cake, fruit, custard (= sweet, yellow sauce), and cream **3** [C] *formal* something silly or unimportant

trigger¹ /ˈtrɪgəʳ/ (*also* **trigger off**) *verb* [T] to make something begin to happen *His arrest triggered mass protests.*

trigger² /ˈtrɪgəʳ/ *noun* [C] **1** the part of a gun that you pull when you shoot **2** an event or situation that makes something else happen *Stress can be a **trigger for** many illnesses.*

trillion /ˈtrɪljən/ the number 1,000,000,000,000

trilogy /ˈtrɪlədʒi/ *noun* [C] a series of three books, plays, etc with the same characters or subject

trim¹ /trɪm/ *verb* [T] **trimming**, *past* **trimmed** **1** (*also* **trim off**) to cut a small amount from something to make it tidy or to remove parts that you do not need *I've had my hair trimmed.* ○ *Trim the fat off the meat.* **2** to reduce something *to trim costs* **3 be trimmed with sth** to be decorated with something around the edges *a silk dress trimmed with lace*

trim² /trɪm/ *noun* **1** [no plural] when you cut something to make it tidy *The hedge needs a trim.* **2** [U, no plural] decoration that is added to something such as clothes or a car *The car has a stereo, sunroof, and leather trim.*

trim³ /trɪm/ *adjective* looking thin and healthy

trimester /trɪˈmestəʳ/ [US] /traɪˈmestər/ *noun* [C] *mainly US* one of the periods of time that the school or university year is divided into

trimming /ˈtrɪmɪŋ/ *noun* [C, U] decoration on the edge of something such as a piece of clothing

trimmings /ˈtrɪmɪŋz/ *noun* [plural] extra dishes

T

that are often eaten with a main dish *a roast dinner with all the trimmings*

the Trinity /'trɪnəti/ *noun* the existence of God in three forms, Father, Son, and Holy Spirit, in the Christian religion

trio /'triːəʊ/ *noun* [C] a group of three things or people, especially three musicians who play together

> **WORD PARTNERS FOR *trip***
>
> **go on/take** a trip • a **day/two-day/week-end** trip • **on** a trip • a trip **around/to** sth • a **business** trip

oᴟ**trip¹** /trɪp/ *noun* [C] a journey in which you visit a place for a short time and come back again *a business trip* ○ *a day trip to Paris* ○ *We might take a trip to Spain later in the summer.* ⟹See Common learner error at *travel* ⟹See also: round trip.

trip² /trɪp/ *verb* **tripping**, *past* **tripped 1** [I] to fall or almost fall because you hit your foot on something when you are walking or running *Careful you don't trip over the cat!* ○ *He tripped on a stone and hurt his ankle.* **2** [T] to make someone fall by putting your foot in front of their foot

trip (sb) up 1 *UK* to fall because you hit your foot on something, or to make someone fall by putting your foot in front of their foot **2** to make a mistake, or to cause someone to make a mistake *I tripped up on the last question.*

triple¹ /'trɪpl/ *adjective* having three parts of the same type, or happening three times *a triple world champion*

triple² /'trɪpl/ *verb* [I, T] to increase three times in size or amount, or to make something do this *Sales have tripled in the past five years.*

triplet /'trɪplət/ *noun* [C] one of three children who are born to the same mother at the same time

tripod /'traɪpɒd/ *noun* [C] a piece of equipment with three legs, used for supporting a camera

trite /traɪt/ *adjective* A trite remark, idea, etc does not seem sincere or true because it has been used so much before or is too simple.

triumph¹ /'traɪəmf/ *noun* **1** [C] an important success, achievement, or victory *Barcelona's 2-0 triumph over Manchester United* **2** [U] the feeling of happiness that you have when you win something or succeed

triumph² /'traɪəmf/ *verb* [I] to win or succeed *The Democrats once again triumphed in recent elections.*

triumphant /traɪˈʌmfənt/ *adjective* feeling very pleased because you have won something or succeeded *the President's triumphant return to the White House* • **triumphantly** *adverb*

trivia /'trɪviə/ *noun* [U] small facts or details that are not important

trivial /'trɪviəl/ *adjective* small and not important *a trivial matter/offence*

trivialize (*also UK* **-ise**) /'trɪviˀlaɪz/ *verb* [T] to make something seem less important or serious than it really is *I don't mean to trivialize the problem.*

trod /trɒd/ *past tense of* tread

trodden /'trɒdˀn/ *past participle of* tread

trolley

supermarket trolley *UK*, shopping cart *US*

luggage trolley *UK*, luggage cart *US*

trolley /'trɒli/ *noun* [C] **1** *UK* (*US* **cart**) a metal structure on wheels that is used for carrying things *a supermarket trolley* ○ *a luggage trolley* **2** *US* (*UK/US* **tram**) an electric vehicle for carrying passengers, mostly in cities, which runs along metal tracks in the road

trombone /trɒmˈbəʊn/ *noun* [C] a metal musical instrument that you play by blowing into it and sliding a tube up and down

troop¹ /truːp/ *noun* [C] a group of people or animals

troop² /truːp/ *verb informal* **troop into/through/out of, etc** to walk somewhere in a large group *We all trooped into the hall in silence.*

trooper /'truːpəʳ/ *noun* [C] a police officer in the US state police force

troops /truːps/ *noun* [plural] soldiers *UN troops have been sent to help in the rescue effort.*

trophy /'trəʊfi/ *noun* [C] a prize, such as a silver cup, that you get for winning a race or competition

trophy

tropical /'trɒpɪkˀl/ *adjective* from or in the hottest parts of the world *a tropical climate*

the tropics /'trɒpɪks/ *noun* [plural] the hottest parts of the world, near to the Equator (= imaginary line around the Earth's middle)

trot¹ /trɒt/ *verb* **trotting**, *past* **trotted 1** [I] If a horse trots, it runs slowly with short steps. **2** **trot down/up/along, etc** to walk with quick, short steps *The little boy trotted along behind his father.*

trot sth out *informal* to say something that has been said many times before and does not seem sincere *They always trot out the same old statistics.*

trot² /trɒt/ *noun* **1** [no plural] the speed that a horse moves when it trots **2** **on the trot** If you do several things on the trot, you do them one after the other. *They won three games on the trot.*

have trouble **with** sth • **get into/run into** trouble • **the** trouble **is** • **without** any trouble

o←**trouble¹** /'trʌbl/ noun **1** PROBLEMS [C, U] problems, difficulties, or worries [+ doing sth] *We had trouble finding somewhere to park.* ○ *She's been having a lot of trouble with her boss recently.* ○ *I'd like to go to the party, but the trouble is my parents won't let me.* **2 the trouble with sb/sth** used to say what is wrong with someone or something *The trouble with a white floor is that it gets dirty so quickly.* **3** NOT WORKING [U] a problem that you have with a machine or part of your body *back trouble* ○ *car trouble* **4** FIGHTING [U] a situation in which people are fighting or arguing *The trouble started after a group of drunken football fans started to throw bottles.* **5** DIFFICULT SITUATION [U] a difficult or dangerous situation *The company was in trouble and had huge debts.* **6** PUNISHMENT [U] when you have done something wrong and are likely to be punished *Her children are always in trouble.* ○ *They got into trouble with the police.* **7** EXTRA WORK [U] when you use extra time or energy to do something [+ to do sth] *He took the trouble to write to each of them personally.*

COMMON LEARNER ERROR

trouble or **problem**?

Problem means 'a situation that causes difficulties and that needs to be dealt with'. You can talk about **a problem** or **problems**.

Tell me what the problem is.

There's a problem with the engine.

He's having a few problems at work.

Trouble means 'problems, difficulties, or worries' and is used to talk about problems in a more general way. **Trouble** is almost always uncountable so do not use the determiner 'a' before it.

We had some trouble while we were on holiday.

He helped me when I was in trouble.

I had trouble with the car last night.

~~I had a trouble with the car last night.~~

trouble² /'trʌbl/ verb [T] **1** If something troubles you, you think about it a lot and it makes you worry. *The situation has been troubling me for a while.* **2** *formal* used to ask someone politely to help you *I'm sorry to trouble you, but could you tell me how to get to the station?*

troubled /'trʌbld/ adjective worried or having a lot of problems *You look troubled.* ○ *a troubled expression*

troublemaker /'trʌbl,meɪkəʳ/ noun [C] someone who intentionally causes problems

troublesome /'trʌblsəm/ adjective causing a lot of problems, especially over a long period of time *a troublesome knee injury*

trough /trɒf/ noun [C] **1** a long, narrow container that animals eat or drink from **2** *formal* a low point in a series of high and low points

peaks and troughs

troupe /tru:p/ noun [C] a group of singers, dancers, etc who perform together

o←**trousers** /'traʊzəz/ (*also US* **pants**) noun [plural] a piece of clothing that covers the legs and has a separate part for each leg *a pair of trousers* ⊃See colour picture **Clothes** on pages Centre 8, 9.

'**trouser** ,**suit** *UK* (*US* **pant suit**) noun [C] a woman's jacket and trousers made of the same material

trout /traʊt/ noun [C, U] plural trout a type of river fish, or the meat from this fish

truant /'tru:ənt/ noun [C] **1** a child who stays away from school without permission **2 play truant** *UK* to stay away from school without permission • **truancy** /'tru:ənsi/ noun [U] when children are truants

WORD PARTNERS FOR *truce*

agree/call/offer a truce • **a fragile/uneasy** truce • a truce **between** sb and sb • a truce **with** sb

truce /tru:s/ noun [C] an agreement between two enemies to stop fighting for a period of time

o←**truck** /trʌk/ (*also UK* **lorry**) noun [C] a large road vehicle for carrying goods from place to place ⊃See picture at **vehicle.**

trucker /'trʌkəʳ/ noun [C] *mainly US* someone whose job is driving trucks

trudge /trʌdʒ/ verb **trudge along/through/up, etc** to walk slowly with heavy steps, especially because you are tired *We trudged back up the hill.*

o←**true** /tru:/ adjective **1** based on facts and not imagined *a true story* ○ [+ (that)] *Is it true that Martin and Sue are getting married?* ⊃Opposite **untrue** ⊃See Common learner error at **right. 2** [always before noun] real *a true friend* ○ *true love* **3 come true** If a dream or hope comes true, it really happens. **4 be true to sb/sth** to be loyal and sincere even in a difficult situation *It's important to be true to your principles.* **5 ring true** to seem to be the truth *Something about the story didn't ring true.*

truffle /'trʌfl/ noun [C] **1** a soft sweet that is made with chocolate **2** a fungus (= organism like a plant) that you can eat, which grows under the ground

truly /'tru:li/ adverb **1** NOT FALSE used to emphasize that something is true in every way *The project was truly a team effort.* **2** VERY used to emphasize a description of something *It's truly amazing to watch a baby being born.* **3** SINCERE used to emphasize that something is sincere or honest *I truly believe that he is innocent.*

trump /trʌmp/ noun **1** [C] a card that has a higher value than other cards in some card games **2 come/turn up trumps** *UK* to be successful, or provide something that is needed, especially when people do not expect you to *He's really come up trumps with this latest book.*

'**trump** ,**card** noun [C] an advantage that will help you succeed, especially one that other people do not know about

T

trumpet /'trʌmpɪt/ *noun* [C] a metal musical instrument that you play by blowing into it and pressing buttons to make different notes • **trumpeter** *noun* [C]

trumpet

truncheon /'trʌnʃ³n/ *UK* (*US* **nightstick**) *noun* [C] a short stick that police officers carry to use as a weapon

truncheon

trundle /'trʌndl/ *verb* **trundle (sth) along/ down/up, etc** to move slowly on wheels, or to push something slowly on wheels *The bus trundled along the lane.*

trunk /trʌŋk/ *noun* [C] **1** [TREE] the thick stem of a tree that the branches grow from ⊃See picture at **tree**. **2** [CAR] *US* (*UK* **boot**) a closed space at the back of a car for storing things in ⊃See colour picture **Car** on page Centre 7. **3** [NOSE] the long nose of an elephant (= large, grey animal) **4** [CONTAINER] a large box with a lid that you store things in **5** [BODY] the main part of your body, not your head, legs, or arms

'trunk ,road *noun* [C] *UK* a main road across a country or area

trunks /trʌŋks/ *noun* [plural] **1** (*also* **swimming trunks**) a piece of clothing that boys and men wear when they swim **2** underwear worn by men ⊃See colour picture **Clothes** on page Centre 9.

⌐**trust¹** /trʌst/ *verb* **1** [T] to believe that someone is good and honest and will not harm you *My sister warned me not to trust him.* ⊃Opposite **distrust, mistrust. 2 trust sb to do sth** to be sure that someone will do the right thing or what they should do *I trust them to make the right decision.* **3 trust sb with sb/sth** to allow someone to look after someone or something because you believe they will be careful *I wouldn't trust him with my car.* **4 Trust sb (to do sth)!** *mainly UK informal* used to say that it is typical of someone to do something stupid *Trust Chris to leave the tickets at home!* **5 I trust (that)** *formal* used to say that you hope something is true *I trust that you had an enjoyable stay.*

WORD PARTNERS FOR ***trust* (noun)**

have/show trust **in** sb • **earn/gain/win** sb's trust • **betray** sb's trust • **trust between** [two people]

⌐**trust²** /trʌst/ *noun* **1** [U] the belief that you can trust someone or something *a marriage based on love and trust* ○ *They showed a lot of trust in me right from the beginning.* ⊃Opposite **distrust, mistrust. 2** [C, U] a legal arrangement that allows a person or organization to control someone else's money

trustee /trʌs'tiː/ *noun* [C] someone who has legal control over someone else's money or possessions

trusting /'trʌstɪŋ/ *adjective* always believing that other people are good or honest and will not harm or deceive you

trustworthy /'trʌst,wɜːði/ *adjective* Someone who is trustworthy can be trusted.

WORD PARTNERS FOR ***truth***

tell the truth • **discover/find out/learn/ uncover** the truth • the truth **comes out/ emerges** • the **awful/honest/simple** truth • the truth **about** sb/sth

⌐**truth** /truːθ/ *noun plural* **truths** /truːðz/ **1 the truth** the real facts about a situation *Do you think he was telling the truth?* ○ *I don't think we'll ever know the truth about what really happened.* **2** [U] the quality of being true *There may be some truth in their claim.* **3** [C] a fact or idea that people accept is true *moral/religious truths* ⊃Opposite **untruth.**

truthful /'truːθf³l/ *adjective* honest and not containing or telling any lies *a truthful answer* • **truthfully** *adverb* • **truthfulness** *noun* [U]

⌐**try¹** /traɪ/ *verb* **1** [ATTEMPT] [I] to attempt to do something [+ **to do sth**] *I tried to open the window but couldn't.* ○ *Try not to drop anything this time.* **2** [TEST] [T] to do, test, taste, etc something to discover if it works or if you like it *I tried that recipe you gave me last night.* ○ [+ **doing sth**] *Why don't you try using a different shampoo?* **3** [LAW] [T] to examine facts in a court of law to decide if someone is guilty of a crime [often passive] *He was tried for attempted murder.*

try sth on to put on a piece of clothing to discover if it fits you or if you like it *Could I try this dress on, please?*

try sth out to use something to discover if it works or if you like it *We're going to try out that new restaurant tonight.*

try² /traɪ/ *noun* **1** [C] an attempt to do something *She suggested I should have a try.* **2 give sth a try** to do something in order to find out if it works or if you like it **3** [C] when a team scores points in rugby (= game played with an oval ball) by putting the ball on the ground behind the other team's goal line

trying /'traɪɪŋ/ *adjective* annoying and difficult *I've had a very trying day/time.*

tsar *UK* (*UK/US* **czar**) /zɑː^r/ *noun* [C] **1** a male Russian ruler before 1917 **2** a powerful official who makes important decisions for the government about a particular activity

T-shirt (*also* **tee shirt**) /'tiː.ʃɜːt/ *noun* [C] a piece of cotton clothing for the top part of the body with short sleeves and no collar ⊃See colour picture **Clothes** on page Centre 8.

tsp *written abbreviation for* teaspoonful: the amount that can be held by a small spoon used for measuring food

tub /tʌb/ *noun* [C] **1** [LARGE CONTAINER] a large, round container with a flat base and an open top *Outside was a stone patio with tubs of flowering plants.* **2** [FOOD CONTAINER] a small, plastic container with a lid, used for storing food *a tub of ice cream/margarine* ⊃See picture at **container. 3** [BATH] *US* (*UK* **bath**) a large container that you fill with water and sit in to wash ⊃See colour picture **The Bathroom** on page Centre 3.

tuba /'tjuːbə/ *noun* [C] a large, metal musical

instrument that produces low notes, and is played by blowing into it

tube /tjuːb/ noun **1** [C] a pipe made of glass, plastic, metal, etc, especially for liquids or gases to flow through **2** [C] a long, thin container for a soft substance, that you press to get the substance out *a tube of toothpaste* ➾See picture at **container. 3 the Tube** the system of railways under the ground in London *I got the Tube to Oxford Circus.* ➾See also: **test tube.**

tuberculosis /tjuːˌbɜːkjəˈləʊsɪs/ noun [U] (*abbreviation* **TB**) a serious infectious disease of the lungs

tubing /ˈtjuːbɪŋ/ noun [U] a long piece of metal, plastic, etc in the shape of a tube *steel tubing*

tubular /ˈtjuːbjələʳ/ adjective in the shape of a tube

tuck /tʌk/ verb **1 tuck sth into/behind/under, etc** to push a loose piece of clothing or material somewhere to make it tidy *Tuck your shirt in.* **2 tuck sth behind/under/in, etc** to put something in a small place so that it is safe and cannot move *I found an old letter tucked in the back of the book.*

tuck sth away to put something in a safe place *Helen tucked the money away in her purse.*

be tucked away to be in a place that is hidden, or in a place that few people go to *He lives in a cottage tucked away in the Suffolk countryside.*

tuck in/tuck into sth UK *informal* to start eating something, especially with enthusiasm *I was just about to tuck into a huge bowl of pasta.*

tuck sb in/up to make someone, especially a child, comfortable in bed by putting the covers around them

o←**Tuesday** /ˈtjuːzdeɪ/ noun (*written abbreviation* **Tue, Tues**) [C, U] the day of the week after Monday and before Wednesday

tuft /tʌft/ noun [C] a small group of hairs, grass, etc

tug¹ /tʌg/ verb [T] tugging, *past* tugged to pull something suddenly and strongly *Tom tugged at his mother's arm.*

tug² /tʌg/ noun [C] **1** a sudden, strong pull on something **2** (*also* tugboat /ˈtʌgbəʊt/) a boat used for pulling larger ships

tuition /tjuˈɪʃən/ noun [U] **1** the teaching of one person or of a small group of people *French tuition* **2** *mainly US* money that you pay for being taught, especially at college or university

tulip /ˈtjuːlɪp/ noun [C] a brightly coloured spring flower in the shape of a cup

tumble /ˈtʌmbl/ verb [I] **1** to suddenly fall *He tumbled down the stairs.* **2** If the price or value of something tumbles, it suddenly becomes lower. *Share prices tumbled by 20%.* • tumble noun [C]

,**tumble 'dryer** UK (*US* dryer) noun [C] a machine that dries clothes

tumbler /ˈtʌmbləʳ/ noun [C] a glass that you drink out of, that has straight sides and no handle

tummy /ˈtʌmi/ noun [C] *informal* stomach

tumour UK (*US* tumor) /ˈtjuːməʳ/ noun [C] a group of cells in someone's body which are not growing normally

tumultuous /tjuːˈmʌltjuəs/ adjective full of noise and excitement *tumultuous applause* o *a tumultuous reception/welcome*

tuna /ˈtjuːnə/ noun [C, U] *plural* tuna a large sea fish, or the meat from this fish

tune¹ /tjuːn/ noun **1** [C] a series of musical notes that are pleasant to listen to *He was humming a tune as he dried the dishes.* **2 in tune** singing or playing the right notes **3 out of tune** singing or playing the wrong notes *The piano is out of tune.* **4 change your tune** to suddenly change your opinion about something **5 be in tune with sb** to be able to understand what someone wants or needs *The government is not in tune with the voters.*

tune² /tjuːn/ verb [T] **1** to make slight changes to a musical instrument so that it plays the right notes **2** to make changes to a television or radio so that it receives programmes from a particular company *Stay tuned for* (= continue watching or listening for) *more details.* o *The radio is tuned to Radio 5.*

tune in to watch or listen to a particular television or radio programme *Be sure to tune in to next week's show.*

tune (sth) up to make slight changes to a musical instrument before you play it so that it produces the right notes *The orchestra were tuning up.*

tunic /ˈtjuːnɪk/ noun [C] a loose piece of clothing that covers the top part of your body

tunnel¹ /ˈtʌnºl/ noun [C] a long passage under the ground or through a mountain *The train went into the tunnel.* ➾See also: **light¹** at the end of the tunnel.

tunnel

tunnel² /ˈtʌnºl/ verb [I, T] UK tunnelling, *past* tunnelled, *US* tunneling, *past* tunneled to dig a tunnel

turban /ˈtɜːbən/ noun [C] a long piece of cloth that men from some religions fold around their heads

turbine /ˈtɜːbaɪn/ noun [C] a large machine that produces power by using gas, steam, etc to turn a wheel

turbulent /ˈtɜːbjələnt/ adjective **1** A turbulent situation, time, etc is one in which there are a lot of sudden changes, arguments, or violence. *a turbulent relationship* **2** Turbulent air or water moves very strongly and suddenly.

• **turbulence** /ˈtɜːbjələns/ *noun* [U]

turf[1] /tɜːf/ *noun* [U] short, thick grass and the soil it is growing in

turf[2] /tɜːf/ *verb*

turf sb out *UK informal* to make someone leave

turkey /ˈtɜːki/ *noun* [C, U] a bird that looks like a large chicken, or the meat of this bird

turmoil /ˈtɜːmɔɪl/ *noun* [U, no plural] a situation in which there is a lot of trouble, confusion, or noise *The whole region is in turmoil.*

☛**turn**[1] /tɜːn/ *verb* 1 [MOVE YOUR BODY] [I] to move your body so that you are facing a different direction *Ricky turned and saw Sue standing in the doorway.* 2 [CHANGE DIRECTION] [I, T] to change direction when you are moving, or to make a car do this *Turn left at the traffic lights.* 3 [CHANGE POSITION] [T] to move something round so that it faces a different direction *Ella turned the cup to hide the crack in it.* 4 [GO ROUND] [I, T] to move around a central point in a circle, or to make something do this *Turn the steering wheel as quickly as you can.* 5 **turn blue/cold/sour, etc** to become blue, cold, etc *The sky turned black and it started to rain.* 6 **turn 16/21, etc** to become a particular age *He turned 18 last May.* 7 **turn a page** to move a page in a book or magazine in order to see the next one ⊃See also: turn your **back**[2] on sb/sth, turn/put the **clock**[1] back, turn a blind **eye**[1] (to sth), turn over a new **leaf**[1], turn your **nose**[1] up at sth, turn the tables (**table**[1]) on sb, come/turn up trumps (**trump**), turn sth **upside down**[1].

turn sb away to not allow someone to enter a place *By 10 o'clock the club was already full and they were turning people away.*

turn (sb) back to return in the direction you have come from, or to make someone do this *They had to turn back because of the bad weather.*

turn sb/sth down to refuse an offer or request *They did offer me the job, but I turned it down.*

turn sth down to reduce the level of sound or heat that a machine produces *Could you turn the radio down, please?*

turn (sb/sth) into sb/sth to change and become someone or something different, or to make someone or something do this *There are plans to turn his latest book into a film.*

turn off (sth) to leave the road you are driving along and drive on a different road

turn sth off to move the switch on a machine, light, etc so that it stops working, or to stop the supply of water, electricity, etc *How do you turn the computer off?* ⊃See colour picture **Phrasal Verbs** on page Centre 16.

turn sth on to move the switch on a machine, light, etc so that it starts working, or to start the supply of water, electricity, etc *Ben turned the TV on.* ⊃See colour picture **Phrasal Verbs** on page Centre 16.

turn out 1 to happen in a particular way, or to have a particular result *The bomb warning turned out to be a false alarm.* ○ [+ (that)] *I got talking to her and it turned out that we'd been to the same school.* 2 If people turn out for an event, they go to be there or watch. *Over 800 people turned out for the protest.*

turn sth out 1 to produce something *The factory turns out more than 600 vehicles a month.* 2 to move the switch on a light so that it stops working

turn (sth) over *UK* to change to a different television station *Are you watching this or can I turn over?*

turn to sb to ask someone for help or advice *Eventually she turned to her aunt for help.*

turn to sth 1 to find a page in a book *Turn to page 105.* 2 to start to do something bad, especially because you are unhappy *She turned to drugs after the break-up of her marriage.*

turn up 1 *informal* to arrive *Fred turned up late again.* 2 If something that you have been looking for turns up, you find it.

turn sth up to increase the level of sound or heat that a machine produces *I'm cold, could you turn the heating up please?*

turn[2] /tɜːn/ *noun* 1 [TIME] [C] the time when you can or must do something, usually before or after someone else [+ to do sth] *It's your turn to feed the rabbit - I did it yesterday.* ○ *You'll have to be patient and wait your turn.* 2 **take turns** (*also UK* **take it in turns**) If two or more people take turns, one person does something, then another person does something, etc. [+ doing sth] *They all took turns carrying the suitcase.* ○ [+ to do sth] *The children took it in turns to hold the baby.* 3 **in turn** one after another *He spoke to the three boys in turn.* 4 [CHANGE DIRECTION] [C] a change in the direction in which you are moving or facing *a right/left turn* 5 [BEND] [C] a bend or corner in a road, river, etc *Take the next turn on the right.* 6 **turn of events** the way in which a situation develops, especially a sudden or unexpected change 7 **take a turn for the better/worse** to become better or worse suddenly 8 **do sb a good turn** to do something to help someone 9 **the turn of the century** the start of a new century ⊃See also: U-turn.

turnaround /ˈtɜːnəraʊnd/ *noun* [C] when a bad situation changes into a good one

turning /ˈtɜːnɪŋ/ *noun* [C] *UK* a corner where one road meets another *Take the second turning on the left.*

turning point *noun* [C] a time when an important change begins to happen *This event marked a turning point in the country's history.*

turnip /ˈtɜːnɪp/ *noun* [C, U] a large, round, pale yellow vegetable that grows under the ground

turn-off /ˈtɜːnɒf/ *noun* **1** [C] a place where you can leave a main road to go onto another road **2** [no plural] *informal* something which you dislike or which makes you feel less interested, especially sexually *Greasy hair is a real turn-off.*

turnout /ˈtɜːnaʊt/ *noun* [C] the number of people at an event, such as a meeting or election [usually singular] *They blamed the **low turn-out** on the bad weather.*

turnover /ˈtɜːnˌəʊvəʳ/ *noun* **1** [no plural] how much money a business earns in a period of time **2** [U, no plural] the rate at which workers leave an organization and new workers join it *a high turnover of staff*

'turn ˌsignal *US* (*UK* **indicator**) *noun* [C] a light that flashes on a vehicle to show that the driver intends to turn right or left ⊃See colour picture **Car** on page Centre 7.

turnstile /ˈtɜːnstaɪl/ *noun* [C] a gate that only allows one person to go through it at a time

turpentine /ˈtɜːp³ntaɪn/ (*also UK* **turps** /tɜːps/) *noun* [U] a clear liquid that has a strong smell and is used for removing paint

turquoise /ˈtɜːkwɔɪz/ *noun* [U] a blue-green colour ● **turquoise** *adjective*

turret /ˈtʌrɪt/ *noun* [C] a small tower that is part of a building

turtle /ˈtɜːtl/ *noun* [C] an animal with four legs and a hard shell that lives mainly in water

turtleneck /ˈtɜːtlnek/ *US* (*UK* **polo neck**) *noun* [C] a piece of clothing that covers the top part of the body and has a tube-like part covering the neck *a turtleneck sweater* ⊃See picture at **polo neck.**

tusk /tʌsk/ *noun* [C] one of the two long, pointed teeth that come out of the mouth of some animals

tussle /ˈtʌsl/ *noun* [C] a fight or argument, especially between two people who want the same thing

tut /tʌt/ (*also* **tut-tut**) *exclamation* a sound you make when you do not approve of something

tutor /ˈtjuːtəʳ/ *noun* [C] **1** someone who teaches one person or a very small group of people *a private tutor* **2** *UK* a university teacher who is responsible for a small group of students ● **tutor** *verb* [T]

tutorial /tjuːˈtɔːriəl/ *noun* [C] **1** a class in which a small group of students talks about a subject with their tutor, especially at a British university **2** a set of instructions and exercises that teaches you how to use a computer program

tux /tʌks/ *noun* [C] *US short for* tuxedo

tuxedo /tʌkˈsiːdəʊ/ *US* (*UK* **dinner jacket**) *noun* [C] a black or white jacket that a man wears on a very formal occasion ⊃See picture at **dinner jacket.**

o→**TV** (*also* **tv**) /ˌtiːˈviː/ *noun* [C, U] *abbreviation for* television *What's **on TV** tonight?* ○ *We could stay in and **watch TV**.* ⊃See colour picture **The Living Room** on page Centre 4.

twang /twæŋ/ *noun* [C] the sound that is made by pulling a tight string or wire ● **twang** *verb* [I, T]

tweak /twiːk/ *verb* [T] **1** to change something slightly to try to improve it **2** to pull or twist something quickly and suddenly *Dad sat there tweaking his beard.* ● **tweak** *noun* [C]

tweed /twiːd/ *noun* [U] a thick, rough cloth made of wool

tweezers /ˈtwiːzəz/ *noun* [plural] a small tool with two narrow pieces of metal joined at one end, used for picking up or pulling out very small things

tweezers

twelfth¹ /twelfθ/ 12th written as a word

twelfth² /twelfθ/ *noun* [C] one of twelve equal parts of something; ¹⁄₁₂

o→**twelve** /twelv/ the number 12

o→**twenty** /ˈtwenti/ **1** the number 20 **2 the twenties** the years from 1920 to 1929 **3 be in your twenties** to be aged between 20 and 29 ● **twentieth** 20th written as a word

o→**twice** /twaɪs/ *adverb* two times *I've been there twice.* ○ *I have to take the tablets twice a day.*

twiddle /ˈtwɪdl/ *verb* [I, T] to move your fingers around, or turn something around many times, especially because you are bored *Karen just sat there **twiddling with** her hair.*

twig /twɪg/ *noun* [C] a small, thin branch on a tree ⊃See picture at **tree.**

twilight /ˈtwaɪlaɪt/ *noun* [U] the time just before it becomes completely dark in the evening

‌🔲 WORD PARTNERS FOR **twin**

a **set of** twins   ● sb's twin **brother/sister** ● **identical** twins

twin¹ /twɪn/ *noun* [C] one of two children who are born to the same mother at the same time ⊃See also: **identical twin.**

twin² /twɪn/ *adjective* [always before noun] used to describe two similar things that are a pair *twin beds*

twin³ /twɪn/ *verb UK* **be twinned with sth** If a town in one country is twinned with a town in another country, the two towns have a special relationship.

twinge /twɪndʒ/ *noun* [C] **1** a sudden, slight emotion *a twinge of guilt* **2** a sudden, slight pain

twinkle /ˈtwɪŋkl/ *verb* [I] **1** If light twinkles, it shines and seems to be quickly flashing on and off. *The lights of the town twinkled in the distance.* **2** If someone's eyes twinkle, they look bright and happy. ● **twinkle** *noun* [C]

twirl /twɜːl/ *verb* [I, T] to turn around and around quickly, or to make something do this ● **twirl** *noun* [C]

twist¹ /twɪst/ *verb* **1** ⎡TURN⎤ [T] to turn something using your hand *She sat there nervously twisting the ring around on her finger.* **2** ⎡BEND⎤ [T] to bend and turn something many times and change its shape *The wheels of the bike had been twisted in the accident.* **3** ⎡TURN YOUR BODY⎤ [I, T] to turn

twist

part of your body to face a different direction *She twisted her head so she could see what was happening.* **4** [CHANGE DIRECTION] [I] If a road, river, etc twists, it has a lot of bends in it. *The path twisted and turned up the side of the mountain.* **5** [INJURE] [T] If you twist a part of your body, such as your knee, you injure it by turning it suddenly. **6** [CHANGE MEANING] [T] to unfairly change the meaning of something that someone has said *Journalists had twisted his remarks.* ⊃See also: twist sb's **arm**[1].

twist[2] /twɪst/ *noun* [C] **1** [UNEXPECTED CHANGE] a sudden change in a story or situation that you do not expect *The story has an unusual twist at the end.* **2** [MOVEMENT] when you twist something **3** [PART] a part of something that is twisted *There's a twist in the wire.* **4** [SHAPE] a shape that is made by twisting something *Finally, add a twist of lemon for decoration.* **5** [RIVER/ROAD] a bend in a river, road, etc

twisted /'twɪstɪd/ *adjective* **1** Something that is twisted is bent a lot of times and does not have its usual shape. **2** strange and slightly unpleasant or cruel *He'd become **bitter and twisted**.*

twister /'twɪstəʳ/ *noun* [C] *US* another word for tornado (= an extremely strong and dangerous wind that blows in a circle) ⊃See also: tongue twister.

twit /twɪt/ *noun* [C] *informal* a silly person

twitch /twɪtʃ/ *verb* [I] If a part of your body twitches, it suddenly makes a slight movement in a way that you cannot control. *His face twitched nervously.* ● twitch *noun* [C]

twitter /'twɪtəʳ/ *verb* [I] If a bird twitters, it makes a series of short, high sounds.

o--**two** /tuː/ **1** the number 2 **2 in two** into two pieces *She broke the chocolate in two.* **3 put two and two together** to guess the truth from details that you notice about a situation *She didn't tell me she was pregnant - I just put two and two together.* ⊃See also: the **lesser** of two evils, be in two minds (**mind**[1]), stand on your own two feet (**foot**[1]).

two-time /ˌtuːˈtaɪm/ *verb* [T] *informal* If someone two-times their partner, they secretly have a romantic relationship with someone else.

two-way /'tuːˌweɪ/ *adjective* moving, or allowing something to move or work in two directions *a two-way street*

tycoon /taɪˈkuːn/ *noun* [C] someone who is very successful and powerful in business and has a lot of money *a media tycoon* ○ *a property/ shipping tycoon*

tying /'taɪɪŋ/ *present participle of* tie

Tylenol /'taɪlənɒl/ *noun* [C, U] *US trademark* a common drug used to reduce pain and fever

---

WORD PARTNERS FOR *type*

of this type ● **all** types of sth ● **different/ various** types

---

o--**type**[1] /taɪp/ *noun* [C] **1** a person or thing that is part of a group of people or things that have similar qualities, or a group of people or things that have similar qualities *They sell over 20 **different types** of cheese.* ○ *Illnesses of **this type** are very common in children.* **2** someone who has particular qualities or interests *He's the outdoor type* (= enjoys being outside). **3 not be sb's type** *informal* to not be the type of person that someone thinks is attractive *I like Bertrand but he's not really my type.* ⊃See also: blood type.

type[2] /taɪp/ *verb* [I, T] to write something using a keyboard ● **typing** *noun* [U]

typewriter /'taɪpˌraɪtəʳ/ *noun* [C] a machine with keys that you press to produce letters and numbers on paper ● **typewritten** /'taɪpˌrɪtⁿn/ *adjective* printed using a typewriter *a type-written letter*

typhoid /'taɪfɔɪd/ *noun* [U] a serious infectious disease that is caused by dirty water or food

typhoon /taɪˈfuːn/ *noun* [C] a violent storm with very strong winds

o--**typical** /'tɪpɪkⁿl/ *adjective* having all the qualities you expect a particular person, object, place, etc to have *typical German food* ○ *This style of painting is **typical of** Monet.*

typically /'tɪpɪkⁿli/ *adverb* **1** used for saying that something is typical of a person, thing, place, etc *behaviour that is typically English* **2** used for saying what usually happens *Schools in the area typically start at 8.30.*

typify /'tɪpɪfaɪ/ *verb* [T] to be a typical example or quality of something *Emma's opinions typify the attitude of many young people.*

typist /'taɪpɪst/ *noun* [C] *old-fashioned* someone who types (= writes using a machine)

tyranny /'tɪrⁿni/ *noun* [U] when a leader or government has too much power and uses that power in a cruel and unfair way ● **tyrannical** /tɪˈrænɪkⁿl/ *adjective* using or involving tyranny

tyrant /'taɪərⁿnt/ *noun* [C] someone who has total power and uses it in a cruel and unfair way

tyre *UK* (*US* tire) /taɪəʳ/ *noun* [C] a thick, round piece of rubber filled with air, that fits around a wheel *It's got a **flat tyre*** (= tyre with no air in it). ⊃See colour picture **Car** on page Centre 7.

Uu

U, u /juː/ the twenty-first letter of the alphabet

uber- /uːbəʳ-/ *prefix humorous* used before nouns to mean 'extreme' or 'extremely good or successful' *uber-billionaire*

ubiquitous /juːˈbɪkwɪtəs/ *adjective formal* seeming to be in all places *the ubiquitous security cameras*

udder /ˈʌdəʳ/ *noun* [C] the part of a female cow, goat, etc that hangs under its body and produces milk

UFO /ˌjuːefˈəʊ/ *noun* [C] *abbreviation for* unidentified flying object: something strange that you see in the sky that could be from another part of the universe

ugh /ʌɡ/ *exclamation* used to show that you think something is very unpleasant *Ugh! What a smell!*

ugly /ˈʌɡli/ *adjective* **1** unpleasant to look at *an ugly city* **2** An ugly situation is very unpleasant, usually because it involves violence. *There were ugly scenes outside the stadium.* ● ugliness *noun* [U] ⊃See also: raise/rear its ugly head[1].

uh *US* (*UK* er) /ə/ *exclamation* something that you say when you are thinking what to say next *It's not too far - it's about, uh, five miles from here.*

UK /ˌjuːˈkeɪ/ *noun abbreviation for* United Kingdom

ulcer /ˈʌlsəʳ/ *noun* [C] a painful, infected area on your skin or inside your body *a mouth/stomach ulcer*

ulterior /ʌlˈtɪəriəʳ/ *adjective* **ulterior motive/purpose, etc** a secret purpose or reason for doing something

ultimate¹ /ˈʌltɪmət/ *adjective* [always before noun] **1** better, worse, or greater than all similar things *Climbing Mount Everest is the ultimate challenge.* ○ *the ultimate insult* **2** final or most important *the ultimate aim/solution*

ultimate² /ˈʌltɪmət/ *noun* **the ultimate in sth** the best or greatest example of something *It describes the hotel as 'the ultimate in luxury'.*

ultimately /ˈʌltɪmətli/ *adverb* **1** finally, after a series of things have happened *a disease that ultimately killed him* **2** used to emphasize the most important fact in a situation *Ultimately, he'll have to decide.*

WORD PARTNERS FOR ***ultimatum***

deliver/give sb/issue an ultimatum ● an ultimatum demands sth ● an ultimatum from/to sb

ultimatum /ˌʌltɪˈmeɪtəm/ *noun* [C] when someone says they will do something that will affect you badly if you do not do what they want *The children were given an ultimatum - finish their work quietly or stay behind after class.*

ultra- /ʌltrə-/ *prefix* extremely *ultra-modern architecture* ○ *ultra-careful*

ultrasonic /ˌʌltrəˈsɒnɪk/ *adjective* involving ultrasound

ultrasound /ˈʌltrəsaʊnd/ *noun* [U] very high sound waves that are used in medical tests to produce a picture of something inside your body *an ultrasound scan*

ultraviolet /ˌʌltrəˈvaɪələt/ *adjective* Ultraviolet light makes your skin become darker.

umbilical cord /ʌmˈbɪlɪkl̩ˌkɔːd/ *noun* [C] the tube that connects a baby to its mother before it is born

umbrella /ʌmˈbrelə/ *noun* [C] **1** a thing that you hold above your head to keep yourself dry when it is raining **2 umbrella group/organization, etc** a large organization that is made of many smaller organizations

umbrella

umpire /ˈʌmpaɪəʳ/ *noun* [C] someone whose job is to watch a sports game and make sure that the players obey the rules *a tennis/cricket umpire* ● umpire *verb* [I, T]

umpteen /ˌʌmˈtiːn/ *quantifier informal* very many *I've been there umpteen times and I still can't remember the way.* ● umpteenth *I drank my umpteenth cup of coffee.*

the UN /ˌjuːˈen/ *noun abbreviation for* the United Nations: an international organization that tries to solve world problems in a peaceful way

un- /ʌn-/ *prefix* not or the opposite of *unhappy* ○ *unfair* ○ *to unfasten*

○━**unable** /ʌnˈeɪbl/ *adjective* **be unable to do sth** to not be able to do something *Some days he is unable to get out of bed.*

unabridged /ˌʌnəˈbrɪdʒd/ *adjective* An unabridged book, play, etc is in its original form and has not been made shorter.

WORD PARTNERS FOR ***unacceptable***

find sth unacceptable ● completely/totally/wholly unacceptable ● unacceptable to sb

unacceptable /ˌʌnəkˈseptəbl/ *adjective* too bad to be allowed to continue *The water contains unacceptable levels of pollution.* ○ *I find that sort of behaviour completely unacceptable.* ● unacceptably *adverb*

unaccompanied /ˌʌnəˈkʌmpənid/ *adjective* not having anyone with you when you go somewhere *Unaccompanied children are not allowed in the museum.*

unaccountable /ˌʌnəˈkaʊntəbl/ *adjective* **1** impossible to explain *For some unaccountable reason, I've got three copies of the same book.* **2** not having to give reasons for your actions or decisions ● unaccountably *adverb*

unadulterated /ˌʌnəˈdʌltəʳreɪtɪd/ *adjective* **1** complete *I've never heard such unadulterated nonsense in all my life!* **2** pure and with nothing extra added *People using drugs can never be sure that they're using unadulterated substances.*

unaffected /ˌʌnəˈfektɪd/ *adjective* not changed by something *Smaller colleges will be **unaffected by** the new regulations.*

unaided /ʌnˈeɪdɪd/ *adjective, adverb* without help *He's now well enough to **walk unaided**.*

unanimous /juːˈnænɪməs/ *adjective* agreed by everyone *The jury was unanimous in finding him guilty.* ● **unanimity** /ˌjuːnəˈnɪməti/ *noun* [U] when everyone agrees about something ● **unanimously** *adverb* *The members **unanimously agreed** to the proposal.*

unannounced /ˌʌnəˈnaʊnst/ *adjective, adverb* without telling anyone first *an **unannounced** visit*

unappealing /ˌʌnəˈpiːlɪŋ/ *adjective* not attractive or enjoyable *Five hours on a train with Mike is a fairly **unappealing** prospect.* ○ *an **unappealing character***

unarmed /ʌnˈɑːmd/ *adjective* not carrying a weapon

unashamedly /ˌʌnəˈʃeɪmɪdli/ *adverb* in a way that shows you are not embarrassed or worried about what other people think of you *Galliano is unashamedly romantic.*

unassuming /ˌʌnəˈsjuːmɪŋ/ *adjective* not wanting to be noticed *a shy, unassuming man*

unattached /ˌʌnəˈtætʃt/ *adjective* not married or having a romantic relationship *It's hard to find someone who is both eligible and unattached.*

unattended /ˌʌnəˈtendɪd/ *adjective* not being watched or looked after *Passengers should not **leave** bags **unattended**.*

unattractive /ˌʌnəˈtræktɪv/ *adjective* **1** not beautiful or nice to look at *I felt old and unattractive.* **2** not interesting or useful *an unattractive proposition*

unauthorized (*also UK* **-ised**) /ʌnˈɔːθəraɪzd/ *adjective* done without official permission *an unauthorized use of company money*

unavailable /ˌʌnəˈveɪləbl/ *adjective* **1** not able to talk to someone or meet them, especially because you are doing other things *The manager was **unavailable for comment**.* **2** impossible to buy or get *The book is unavailable in Britain.*

unavoidable /ˌʌnəˈvɔɪdəbl/ *adjective* impossible to avoid or prevent *an unavoidable delay* ○ *Most of the problems we've had to deal with have been unavoidable.*

unaware /ˌʌnəˈweər/ *adjective* [never before noun] not knowing about something *He seems totally **unaware of** the problem.*

unawares /ˌʌnəˈweəz/ *adverb* **catch/take sb unawares** If something catches or takes you unawares, it happens when you do not expect it to. *The rain caught me unawares and I didn't have my umbrella.*

unbalanced /ʌnˈbælənst/ *adjective* **1** slightly mentally ill **2** false and not fair *He gave an unbalanced view of the situation.*

unbearable /ʌnˈbeərəbl/ *adjective* too painful or unpleasant for you to continue to experience *The heat was almost unbearable.* ● **unbearably** *adverb*

unbeatable /ʌnˈbiːtəbl/ *adjective* much better than everyone or everything else *We aim to sell the best products at unbeatable prices.*

unbeaten /ʌnˈbiːtən/ *adjective* in sports, having won every game *Manchester United remain **unbeaten** this season.*

unbelievable /ˌʌnbɪˈliːvəbl/ *adjective* **1** extremely bad or good and making you feel surprised *It's unbelievable how lucky she's been.* **2** not probable and difficult to believe ● **unbelievably** *adverb*

unborn /ʌnˈbɔːn/ *adjective* not yet born *the unborn child*

unbreakable /ˌʌnˈbreɪkəbl/ *adjective* impossible to break *unbreakable glass/plastic*

unbridled /ʌnˈbraɪdld/ *adjective* An unbridled feeling is one that you do not try to hide or control. *unbridled enthusiasm/passion*

unbroken /ʌnˈbrəʊkən/ *adjective* continuous and with no pauses *unbroken sunshine*

unbutton /ʌnˈbʌtən/ *verb* [T] to open the buttons on a piece of clothing *He unbuttoned his jacket.*

uncalled for /ʌnˈkɔːldfɔːr/ *adjective* If an action or remark is uncalled for, it is unfair or unkind. *That was uncalled for, Tess - apologize to your brother.*

uncanny /ʌnˈkæni/ *adjective* strange and impossible to explain *an uncanny resemblance* ● **uncannily** *adverb*

uncaring /ʌnˈkeərɪŋ/ *adjective* without sympathy for people with problems *victims of an uncaring society*

uncertain /ʌnˈsɜːtən/ *adjective* **1** not sure or not able to decide about something *Bridie was **uncertain about** meeting him.* **2** not known, or not completely certain *The museum faces an uncertain future.* ● **uncertainly** *adverb* ● **uncertainty** *noun* [C, U]

uncertainty /ʌnˈsɜːtənti/ *noun* [C, U] when something is uncertain *Life is full of uncertainties.*

unchanged /ʌnˈtʃeɪndʒd/ *adjective* staying the same *The area has **remained** virtually **unchanged** in fifty years.*

uncharacteristic /ˌʌnkærəktərˈɪstɪk/ *adjective* not typical ● **uncharacteristically** *adverb*

unchecked /ʌnˈtʃekt/ *adjective* If something bad continues unchecked, it is not stopped.

☞**uncle** /ˈʌŋkl/ *noun* [C] the brother of your mother or father, or the husband of your aunt

unclean /ʌnˈkliːn/ *adjective* morally bad, as described by the rules of a religion

unclear /ʌn'klɪəʳ/ *adjective* **1** not easy to understand *The situation at the moment is unclear.* ○ [+ question word] *It's unclear what actually happened that night.* **2** If you are unclear about something, you do not understand it exactly. *I'm unclear about exactly who's doing what.*

uncomfortable /ʌn'kʌmftəbl/ *adjective* **1** not feeling comfortable and pleasant, or not making you feel comfortable and pleasant *These shoes are really uncomfortable.* **2** slightly embarrassed, or making you feel slightly embarrassed *an uncomfortable silence* • **uncomfortably** *adverb*

uncommon /ʌn'kɒmən/ *adjective* unusual [+ for + to do sth] *It's not uncommon for people to become ill* (= they often become ill) *when they travel.* • **uncommonly** *adverb*

uncompromising /ʌn'kɒmprəmaɪzɪŋ/ *adjective* determined not to change your ideas or decisions *an uncompromising attitude*

unconcerned /ˌʌnkən'sɜːnd/ *adjective* not worried by something *The baby seemed unconcerned by all the noise.*

unconditional /ˌʌnkən'dɪʃənəl/ *adjective* done or given without any limits and without asking for anything for yourself *unconditional love* • **unconditionally** *adverb*

unconfirmed /ˌʌnkən'fɜːmd/ *adjective* An unconfirmed report or story may not be true because there is no proof yet.

unconnected /ˌʌnkə'nektɪd/ *adjective* If two or more things are unconnected, there is no connection between them. *The stomach ailment was unconnected with his cancer.*

unconscious¹ /ʌn'kɒnʃəs/ *adjective* **1** in a state as though you are sleeping, for example because you have been hit on the head *She was knocked unconscious.* **2** An unconscious thought or feeling is one that you do not know you have. *an unconscious fear* • **unconsciousness** *noun* [U]

unconscious² /ʌn'kɒnʃəs/ *noun* [no plural] the part of your mind that contains feelings and thoughts that you do not know about, and that influences the way you behave

unconsciously /ʌn'kɒnʃəsli/ *adverb* If you do something unconsciously, you do it without knowing that you are doing it.

unconstitutional /ˌʌnˌkɒnstɪ'tjuːʃənəl/ *adjective* not allowed by the rules of an organization or political system

uncontrollable /ˌʌnkən'trəuləbl/ *adjective* unable to be controlled *uncontrollable anger* ○ *an uncontrollable desire to cry* • **uncontrollably** *adverb*

unconventional /ˌʌnkən'venʃənəl/ *adjective* doing things in a way that is different from most people *an unconventional lifestyle*

unconvincing /ˌʌnkən'vɪntsɪŋ/ *adjective* not seeming true or real *an unconvincing explanation*

uncool /ʌn'kuːl/ *adjective* embarrassing and not stylish or fashionable

uncountable noun /ʌnˌkauntəbəl'naun/ (*also* **uncount noun**) *noun* [C] a noun which does not have a plural form and cannot be used with 'a'

or 'one'. For example 'music' and 'furniture' are uncountable nouns. ⊃See Extra help page **Countable and uncountable nouns** on page Centre 20.

uncouth /ʌn'kuːθ/ *adjective* behaving in a rude, unpleasant way

---

🔲 WORD PARTNERS FOR *uncover*

uncover **evidence**/a **plot**/a **secret/the truth**
• an **investigation** uncovers sth

---

uncover /ʌn'kʌvəʳ/ *verb* [T] **1** to discover something that had been secret or hidden *The inspectors uncovered evidence of corruption.* **2** to remove a cover from something

undaunted /ʌn'dɔːntɪd/ *adjective* not frightened to do something that is difficult or dangerous *Keiko spoke, undaunted by the crowd.*

undecided /ˌʌndɪ'saɪdɪd/ *adjective* If you are undecided about something, you have not made a decision yet. *I'm still undecided about whether to apply for the job.*

undefeated /ˌʌndɪ'fiːtɪd/ *adjective* in sports, having won every game *Both teams remain undefeated in the final weeks of the season.*

undeniable /ˌʌndɪ'naɪəbl/ *adjective* certainly true *an undeniable fact* • **undeniably** *adverb*

○⇥**under¹** /'ʌndəʳ/ *preposition* **1** BELOW below something *She pushed her bag under the table.* ○ *The children were sitting under a tree.* **2** BELOW THE SURFACE below the surface of something *He could only keep his head under the water for a few seconds.* **3** LESS THAN less than a number, amount, or age *You can buy the whole system for just under $2000.* ○ *We don't serve alcohol to anyone under 18.* **4** CONTROLLED BY controlled or governed by a particular person, organization, etc *a country under military rule* ○ *The restaurant is under new management.* **5** RULE/LAW according to a rule, law, etc *Under the new law, all new buildings must be approved by the local government.* **6** IN A PARTICULAR STATE in a particular state or condition *The President is under pressure to resign.* ○ *Students are allowed to miss school under certain circumstances.* **7** IN PROGRESS used to say that something is happening at the moment but is not finished *A new 16-screen cinema is under construction.* ○ *Several different plans are under discussion.* **8** NAME using a particular name, especially one that is not your usual name *He also wrote several detective novels under the name, Edgar Sandys.* **9** PLACE IN LIST used to say which part of a list, book, library, etc you should look in to find something *Books about health problems are under 'Medicine'.*

under² /'ʌndəʳ/ *adverb* **1** below the surface of something *The child was swimming and suddenly started to go under.* **2** less than a particular number, amount, or age *I want a computer that is £2000 or under.*

under- /ʌndəʳ-/ *prefix* **1** not enough *under-cooked potatoes* **2** below *underwear* ○ *an under-pass*

under-age /ˌʌndər'eɪdʒ/ *adjective* younger than the legal age when you are allowed to do something *under-age drinking/sex*

---

undercover /ˌʌndəˈkʌvəʳ/ *adjective, adverb* working secretly in order to get information for the police or government *an **undercover** police officer*

undercut /ˌʌndəˈkʌt/ *verb* [T] **undercutting**, *past* **undercut** to sell something at a lower price than someone else

the underdog /ˈʌndədɒg/ *noun* the person or team that is expected to lose a race or competition

underestimate /ˌʌndəˈrˈestɪmeɪt/ *verb* [T] **1** to not understand how large, strong, or important something is *Many people underestimate the cost of owning a car.* **2** to not understand how powerful or clever someone is *I thought it would be an easy game but I had underestimated my opponent.* ⊃Opposite **overestimate**.

underfoot /ˌʌndəˈfʊt/ *adverb* under your feet as you walk *Several people were trampled **underfoot** in the rush to escape.*

undergo /ˌʌndəˈgəʊ/ *verb* [T] **undergoing**, *past tense* **underwent**, *past participle* **undergone** to experience something, especially a change or medical treatment *The country is currently **undergoing** major political change.* ○ *He is **undergoing** surgery for a heart problem.*

undergraduate /ˌʌndəˈgrædʒuət/ (*also* **undergrad** /ˈʌndəgræd/ *informal*) *noun* [C] a student who is studying for their first university degree (= qualification)

underground¹ /ˈʌndəgraʊnd/ *adjective, adverb* **1** under the surface of the ground *underground caves* ○ *an animal that lives underground* **2** Underground political activities are secret and illegal. *an underground political organization*

> **WORD PARTNERS FOR *underground* (noun)**
> **take** the underground • **on** the underground • an underground **station** /**train**

underground² /ˈʌndəgraʊnd/ *UK* (*US* **subway**) *noun* [no plural] a system of trains that is built under a city *the London Underground* ⊃See Common learner error at **metro**.

undergrowth /ˈʌndəgrəʊθ/ *noun* [U] short plants and bushes that grow around trees

underhand /ˌʌndəˈhænd/ (*also* **underhanded**) *adjective* secret and not honest *underhand business deals*

underline /ˌʌndəˈlaɪn/ *verb* [T] **1** to draw a line under a word or sentence **2** to emphasize the importance or truth of something *The report **underlines the need** for more teachers in schools.*

underlying /ˌʌndəˈlaɪɪŋ/ *adjective* [always before noun] An underlying reason or problem is the real reason or problem, although it is not obvious. *We need to look at the **underlying** reasons for ill health.*

undermine /ˌʌndəˈmaɪn/ *verb* [T] to make someone less confident or make something weaker *A series of scandals have **undermined** people's **confidence** in the government.*

underneath¹ /ˌʌndəˈniːθ/ *adverb, preposition* under something *Florian was wearing a jacket with a red shirt underneath.* ○ *Deborah pushed her shoes underneath the bed.*

the underneath² /ˌʌndəˈniːθ/ *noun* the bottom part of something

underpaid /ˌʌndəˈpeɪd/ *adjective* not earning enough for your work

underpants /ˈʌndəpænts/ *noun* [plural] a piece of underwear that covers the area between your waist and the top of your legs ⊃See colour picture **Clothes** on page Centre 9 ⊃See Common learner error at **underwear**.

underpass /ˈʌndəpɑːs/ *noun* [C] a road or path that goes under another road

underprivileged /ˌʌndəˈprɪvəlɪdʒd/ *adjective* poor and having fewer opportunities than most people *underprivileged families*

underrate /ˌʌndəˈreɪt/ *verb* [T] to think that someone or something is not as good as they really are *Critics have continued to underrate Sampras.* •**underrated** *adjective* *I think he's really underrated as an actor.* ⊃Opposite **overrated**.

underscore /ˌʌndəˈskɔːʳ/ *verb* [T] *mainly US* to emphasize the importance of something

undershirt /ˈʌndəʃɜːt/ *US* (*UK* **vest**) *noun* [C] a piece of underwear that you wear under a shirt

the underside /ˈʌndəsaɪd/ *noun* the bottom surface of something *There was some damage to the underside of the car.*

⚬▪**understand** /ˌʌndəˈstænd/ *verb* [I, T] *past* **understood 1** KNOW MEANING to know the meaning of something that someone says *I don't understand half of what he says.* ○ *She didn't understand so I explained it again.* **2** KNOW WHY/HOW to know why or how something happens or works [+ question word] *We still don't fully understand how the brain works.* **3** KNOW FEELINGS to know how someone feels or why they behave in a particular way *I don't understand James sometimes.* ○ [+ question word] *I understand why she's so angry.* **4** I/we understand (that)... *formal* used to say that you believe something is true because someone has told you it is *I understand that the school is due to close next year.* **5** make yourself understood to say something to someone in a way that they understand *I had a little difficulty making myself understood.*

understandable /ˌʌndəˈstændəbl/ *adjective* An understandable feeling or action is one that you would expect in that particular situation. *It's understandable that he's angry.* •**understandably** *adverb* *She's understandably upset.*

> **WORD PARTNERS FOR *understanding***
> **develop/gain/have** an understanding (**of** sth) • a **better/clear** understanding • an understanding of sth

understanding¹ /ˌʌndəˈstændɪŋ/ *noun* **1** KNOWLEDGE [U, no plural] knowledge about a subject, situation, etc or about how something works *We now **have a better understanding** of this disease.* **2** AGREEMENT [C] an informal agreement between two people [usually singular, + that] *We **have an understanding** that we*

don't discuss the subject in front of his mother.
3 SYMPATHY [U] sympathy *Thank you for your understanding.* **4 my/her/his, etc understanding** what you thought to be true *It was my understanding that she was coming alone.* **5** ABILITY [U] the ability to learn or think about something

understanding² /ˌʌndəˈstændɪŋ/ *adjective* showing sympathy for someone's problems *Fortunately, she's very understanding.*

understated /ˌʌndəˈsteɪtɪd/ *adjective* simple and attractive in style *an understated tie*

understatement /ˌʌndəˈsteɪtmənt/ *noun* [C, U] when you say that something is less extreme than it really is *'Quite big', did you say? That's an understatement - he's enormous!*

understood /ˌʌndəˈstʊd/ *past of* understand

understudy /ˈʌndəˌstʌdi/ *noun* [C] an actor in the theatre who learns the words and actions of another character so that they can perform if the usual actor is ill

undertake /ˌʌndəˈteɪk/ *verb past tense* **undertook**, *past participle* **undertaken** *formal* **1** [T] to start work on something that will take a long time or be difficult *Max has undertaken the task of restoring an old houseboat* **2 undertake to do sth** to promise to do something

undertaker /ˈʌndəˌteɪkəʳ/ *noun* [C] someone whose job is to organize funerals and prepare dead bodies to be buried or burned

WORD PARTNERS FOR **undertaking**

2 **give/sign** an undertaking • a **written** undertaking • an undertaking **by/from** sb

undertaking /ˈʌndəˌteɪkɪŋ/ *noun* [C] **1** a difficult or important piece of work, especially one that takes a long time [usually singular] *Building your own house is a major undertaking.* **2** *UK* a legal or official promise to do something [usually singular] *The newspaper has given an undertaking not to print the story.*

undertone /ˈʌndətəʊn/ *noun* [C] a feeling or quality that exists but is not obvious *an article with worrying political undertones*

undertook /ˌʌndəˈtʊk/ *past tense of* undertake

undervalued /ˌʌndəˈvæljuːd/ *adjective* If someone or something is undervalued, they are more important or useful than people think they are.

underwater /ˌʌndəˈwɔːtəʳ/ *adjective, adverb* under the surface of water *an underwater camera* ○ *Seals can hear very well underwater.*

underwear /ˈʌndəweəʳ/ *noun* [U] the clothes that you wear next to your skin, under your other clothes

COMMON LEARNER ERROR

types of underwear

Underpants are a piece of underwear that cover the bottom. In British English **underpants** are only worn by men or boys, but in American English they can also be worn by women and girls.

The American English word **panties** is a piece of underwear for women or girls that covers the bottom. The British English word for **panties** is **knickers** or **pants**.

underweight /ˌʌndəˈweɪt/ *adjective* not heavy enough *According to the hospital chart he's four kilos underweight.*

underwent /ˌʌndəˈwent/ *past tense of* undergo

underworld /ˈʌndəwɜːld/ *noun* [no plural] criminals and their activities *the criminal underworld* ○ *the London underworld*

undesirable /ˌʌndɪˈzaɪərəbl/ *adjective formal* Something that is undesirable is not wanted because it is bad or unpleasant. *an undesirable influence*

undeveloped /ˌʌndɪˈveləpt/ *adjective* Undeveloped land has no buildings on it and is not used for anything.

undid /ʌnˈdɪd/ *past tense of* undo

undisclosed /ˌʌndɪsˈkləʊzd/ *adjective* If official information is undisclosed, it is secret. *The meeting between the two leaders is taking place at an undisclosed location.*

undisputed /ˌʌndɪˈspjuːtɪd/ *adjective* If something is undisputed, everyone agrees about it. *an undisputed fact* ○ *the undisputed champion/master*

undisturbed /ˌʌndɪˈstɜːbd/ *adjective* not interrupted or changed in any way *undisturbed sleep*

undivided /ˌʌndɪˈvaɪdɪd/ *adjective* **undivided attention/loyalty/support, etc** complete attention, support, etc *There, now you can have my undivided attention.*

undo /ʌnˈduː/ *verb* [T] **undoing**, *past tense* **undid**, *past participle* **undone** **1** to open something that is tied or fastened *I took off my hat and undid my coat.* **2** to get rid of the effects of something that has been done before *Some of the damage caused by pollution cannot be undone.*

undoing /ʌnˈduːɪŋ/ *noun* **be sb's undoing** to be the thing that makes someone fail *It was a policy that proved to be the President's undoing.*

undone /ʌnˈdʌn/ *adjective* **1** not fastened or tied *Her coat was undone.* **2** not done *I don't think I've left anything undone.*

undoubted /ʌnˈdaʊtɪd/ *adjective* [always before noun] used to emphasize that something is true *The project was an undoubted success.* ○ *her undoubted ability/talent*

undoubtedly /ʌnˈdaʊtɪdli/ *adverb* used to emphasize that something is true *Stress has undoubtedly contributed to her illness.*

undress /ʌnˈdres/ *verb* [I, T] to remove your clothes or someone else's clothes • **undressed** *adjective I got undressed and went to bed.*

undue /ʌnˈdjuː/ *adjective* [always before noun] *formal* more than is necessary *I don't want to cause undue alarm.*

undulating /ˈʌndjəleɪtɪŋ/ *adjective formal* having slight slopes or curves, or moving slightly up and down *undulating roads*

unduly /ʌnˈdjuːli/ *adverb formal* more than necessary *She didn't seem unduly concerned/worried.*

unearth /ʌnˈɜːθ/ *verb* [T] **1** to find something in the ground [often passive] *Thousands of dinosaur bones have been unearthed in China.* **2** to find something that has been secret or hidden

*Reporters **unearthed evidence** of criminal activity.*

unearthly /ʌn'ɜːθli/ *adjective* strange and frightening *an **unearthly light/beauty***

unease /ʌn'iːz/ *noun* [U] when you feel worried because you think something bad might happen

uneasy /ʌn'iːzi/ *adjective* worried because you think something bad might happen *I feel a bit **uneasy about** her travelling alone.*

uneconomic /ʌnˌiːkə'nɒmɪk/ (*also* **uneconomical**) *adjective* **1** using too much money, fuel, time, etc *a car that is uneconomic to run* **2** not making enough profit *plans to close uneconomic factories*

unemployed /ˌʌnɪm'plɔɪd/ *adjective* not having a job *I've been unemployed for six months. ○ The government is helping to create jobs for **the unemployed**.*

🧩 WORD PARTNERS FOR *unemployment*

unemployment **drops/falls/increases/rises**
• **high/low/rising/soaring** unemployment
• the unemployment **rate** • a **drop/fall/increase/rise** in unemployment

unemployment /ˌʌnɪm'plɔɪmənt/ *noun* [U] **1** the number of people who are unemployed *a **rise/fall in unemployment** ○ The unemployment rate has increased to 20 percent.* **2** when you do not have a job

unending /ʌn'endɪŋ/ *adjective* seeming to continue forever *an **unending series** of problems*

unequal /ʌn'iːkwəl/ *adjective* **1** different in size, level, amount, etc **2** unfair *the unequal distribution of wealth* • **unequally** *adverb*

unequivocal /ˌʌnɪ'kwɪvəkəl/ *adjective formal* clear and certain *an unequivocal answer* • **unequivocally** *adverb*

unethical /ʌn'eθɪkəl/ *adjective* morally bad *unethical business methods*

uneven /ʌn'iːvən/ *adjective* not level or smooth *an uneven floor* • **unevenly** *adverb*

uneventful /ˌʌnɪ'ventfəl/ *adjective* without problems or without anything exciting happening *The journey itself was fairly uneventful.*

unexpected /ˌʌnɪk'spektɪd/ *adjective* Something that is unexpected surprises you because you did not know it was going to happen. *His death was completely unexpected.* • **unexpectedly** *adverb*

unfailing /ʌn'feɪlɪŋ/ *adjective* An unfailing quality or ability is one that someone always has. *unfailing support/courtesy* • **unfailingly** *adverb*

unfair /ʌn'feər/ *adjective* **1** not treating people in an equal way *an unfair system ○ The test was unfair because some people had seen it before.* **2** not true and morally wrong [+ to do sth] *It's unfair to blame Frank for everything.* • **unfairly** *adverb* • **unfairness** *noun* [U]

unfaithful /ʌn'feɪθfəl/ *adjective* having sex with someone who is not your wife, husband, or usual sexual partner *She was **unfaithful to** me.*

unfamiliar /ˌʌnfə'mɪljər/ *adjective* **1** not known to you *an unfamiliar face ○ His name was **unfamiliar to** me.* **2** be unfamiliar with sth to not have any knowledge or experience of something *Many older people are unfamiliar with computers.*

unfashionable /ʌn'fæʃənəbl/ *adjective* not fashionable or popular at a particular time

unfasten /ʌn'fɑːsən/ *verb* [T] to open something that is closed or fixed together *to unfasten a seat belt*

unfavourable UK (*US* **unfavorable**) /ʌn'feɪvərəbl/ *adjective* **1** negative and showing that you do not like something *unfavourable publicity* **2** not good and likely to cause problems *unfavourable weather conditions* • **unfavourably** *adverb*

unfeeling /ʌn'fiːlɪŋ/ *adjective* not having sympathy for other people

unfettered /ʌn'fetəd/ *adjective formal* not limited by rules *The UN inspectors were given **unfettered access** to all nuclear sites.*

unfinished /ʌn'fɪnɪʃt/ *adjective* not completed *an unfinished novel/portrait*

unfit /ʌn'fɪt/ *adjective* **1** not suitable or good enough *The food was judged **unfit for** human consumption.* **2** UK not healthy because you do too little exercise

unflattering /ʌn'flætərɪŋ/ *adjective* making someone look less attractive or seem worse than usual *an unflattering photo/dress/colour*

unfold /ʌn'fəʊld/ *verb* **1** [I] If a situation or story unfolds, it develops or becomes known. *The nation watched on TV as the tragic events unfolded.* **2** [I, T] to become open and flat, or to make something become open and flat *I unfolded the map.*

unforeseen /ˌʌnfɔː'siːn/ *adjective* not expected *The concert was cancelled due to **unforeseen circumstances**.*

unforgettable /ˌʌnfə'getəbl/ *adjective* Something that is unforgettable is so good, interesting, etc that you remember it for a long time. *Seeing Niagara Falls was an **unforgettable experience**.*

unfortunate /ʌn'fɔːtʃənət/ *adjective* **1** used to show that you wish something was not true or had not happened *an unfortunate mistake ○ [+ (that)] It was unfortunate that she lost her job just as her husband became ill.* **2** unlucky *One unfortunate person failed to see the hole and fell straight into it.*

⚬**unfortunately** /ʌn'fɔːtʃənətli/ *adverb* used to say that you wish something was not true or that something had not happened *I'd love to come, but unfortunately I have to work.*

unfounded /ʌn'faʊndɪd/ *adjective* not based on facts *unfounded allegations/rumours*

unfriendly /ʌn'frendli/ *adjective* not friendly

unfulfilled /ˌʌnfʊl'fɪld/ *adjective* **1** An unfulfilled wish, hope, promise, etc is one that has not happened or not been achieved. *an unfulfilled ambition/dream ○ unfulfilled potential* **2** unhappy because you think you should be achieving more in your life

ungainly /ʌn'geɪnli/ *adjective* moving in a way

that is not attractive *an ungainly walk*

ungrateful /ʌnˈɡreɪtfəl/ *adjective* not thanking or showing that you are pleased with someone who has done something for you

Sad and **miserable** mean the same as unhappy: *I felt so sad after he left.* ● *I just woke up feeling miserable.*

If someone is **upset**, they are unhappy because something bad has happened: *They'd had an argument and she was still upset about it.* ● *Mike got very upset when I told him the news.*

If someone is **broken-hearted** or **heart-broken** they are very sad because someone they love has ended a relationship with them: *She was broken-hearted when Richard left.*

If someone is **devastated**, or **distraught**, they are extremely upset: *She was devastated when he died.* ● *The missing child's distraught parents made an emotional appeal for information on TV.*

The adjective **depressed** is often used when someone is very unhappy for a long time: *She became deeply depressed after her husband died.*

o-***unhappy** /ʌnˈhæpi/ *adjective* **1** sad *an unhappy childhood* **2** not satisfied *Giorgio was unhappy with his test results.* ○ *I'm unhappy about the situation.* ● **unhappily** *adverb* ● **unhappiness** *noun* [U]

unharmed /ʌnˈhɑːmd/ *adjective* [never before noun] not harmed or damaged *Both children escaped unharmed from the burning building.*

unhealthy /ʌnˈhelθi/ *adjective* **1** ⟨CAUSE ILLNESS⟩ likely to damage your health *Eating too much is unhealthy.* **2** ⟨ILL⟩ not strong, and likely to become ill *She looks pale and unhealthy.* **3** ⟨NOT NORMAL⟩ not normal and slightly unpleasant *an unhealthy interest in weapons*

unheard /ʌnˈhɜːd/ *adjective* not listened to or considered *Her cries went unheard.*

un'heard ˌof *adjective* [never before noun] never having happened before *Thirty years ago the disease was unheard of.*

unhelpful /ʌnˈhelpfəl/ *adjective* **1** not improving a situation *an unhelpful remark* **2** not wanting to help someone, in a way that seems unfriendly *The taxi driver was rude and unhelpful.*

unhurt /ʌnˈhɜːt/ *adjective* not harmed

unicorn /ˈjuːnɪkɔːn/ *noun* [C] an imaginary white horse with a horn growing from the front of its head

unidentified /ˌʌnaɪˈdentɪfaɪd/ *adjective* not recognized *The body of an unidentified woman was found in a field last night.*

unification /ˌjuːnɪfɪˈkeɪʃən/ *noun* [U] when two or more countries join together and become one country *the unification of East and West Germany*

uniform¹ /ˈjuːnɪfɔːm/ *noun* [C, U] a special set of clothes that are worn by people who do a particular job or people who go to a particular school *a school uniform* ○ *a nurse's uniform* ○ *Tom looks completely different in uniform* (= wearing a uniform). ● **uniformed** *adjective* uniformed police officers

uniform² /ˈjuːnɪfɔːm/ *adjective* being the same size, shape, amount, etc *a row of houses of uniform height* ● **uniformity** /ˌjuːnɪˈfɔːməti/ *noun* [U] ● **uniformly** *adverb*

unify /ˈjuːnɪfaɪ/ *verb* [T] to join together two or more countries or groups to make a single one *We need a leader who can unify the party.* ● **unified** *adjective* Many people want a more unified Europe.

unilateral /ˌjuːnɪˈlætərəl/ *adjective* A unilateral action or decision is done or made by one country, group, etc without waiting for others to agree. *unilateral nuclear disarmament* ● **unilaterally** *adverb*

unimaginable /ˌʌnɪˈmædʒɪnəbl/ *adjective* Something that is unimaginable is difficult to imagine because it is so bad, good, big, etc. *unimaginable pain/wealth* ● **unimaginably** *adverb*

unimportant /ˌʌnɪmˈpɔːtənt/ *adjective* not important

uninhabitable /ˌʌnɪnˈhæbɪtəbl/ *adjective* too cold, dangerous, etc to live in

uninhabited /ˌʌnɪnˈhæbɪtɪd/ *adjective* If a place is uninhabited, no one lives there. *an uninhabited island*

uninhibited /ˌʌnɪnˈhɪbɪtɪd/ *adjective* feeling free to behave in any way that you want without worrying about other people's opinions

uninstall /ˌʌnɪnˈstɔːl/ *verb* [T] to remove a computer program from a computer

unintelligible /ˌʌnɪnˈtelɪdʒəbl/ *adjective* impossible to understand

unintentional /ˌʌnɪnˈtentʃənəl/ *adjective* not planned or intended *If I did offend her it was entirely unintentional.*

uninterested /ʌnˈɪntrəstɪd/ *adjective* not interested *He's completely uninterested in politics.*

uninterrupted /ˌʌnˌɪntərˈʌptɪd/ *adjective* continuous *I want a radio station that offers uninterrupted music.*

WORD PARTNERS FOR *union*

join a union ● a union **leader/member/official/representative**

union /ˈjuːnjən/ *noun* **1** [C] (also **trade union**) (also US **labor union**) an organization that represents people who do a particular job *a teachers'/firefighters' union* **2** [U, no plural] when two or more countries, groups, etc join together to make one country, group, etc *a move towards full economic union of EU countries* ⊃See also: the European Union.

ˌUnion ˈJack (also Union flag) *noun* [C] the red, white and blue flag of the United Kingdom

unique /juːˈniːk/ *adjective* **1** different from everyone and everything else *Everyone's fingerprints are unique.* **2** unusual and special *a unique opportunity* **3** be unique to sb/sth to exist in only one place, or be connected with only one person or thing *It's a method of education that is unique to this school.* ● **uniquely** *adverb* ● **uniqueness** *noun* [U]

unique or **only**?

Unique describes something that is special or unusual because only one example of it exists. If something is not special or important, but only one of it exists, you should use **only**.

It is the only bus that goes to the airport.

~~It is the unique bus that goes to the airport.~~

unisex /ˈjuːnɪseks/ *adjective* for both men and women *unisex clothes* ○ *a unisex hairdresser*

unison /ˈjuːnɪsᵊn/ *noun* **in unison** If people do something in unison, they all do it at the same time.

unit /ˈjuːnɪt/ *noun* [C] **1** GROUP a group of people who are responsible for a particular part of an organization *an anti-terrorist unit* **2** MEASURE a measure used to express an amount or quantity *The kilogram is a unit of weight.* **3** SINGLE a single, complete thing that may be part of a larger thing *a French course book with ten units* **4** FURNITURE a piece of furniture that fits together with other pieces *kitchen units* **5** MACHINE a small machine, or part of a machine, that has a particular purpose *a computer's central processing unit* **6** BUILDING a single apartment, office, etc in a larger building

unite /juːˈnaɪt/ *verb* [I, T] to join together as a group, or to make people join together as a group *We need a leader who can unite the party.*

united /juːˈnaɪtɪd/ *adjective* **1** If people are united, they all agree about something. *On the issue of education the party is united.* **2** joined together *a united Germany*

the Un₁ited 'Nations *noun* [group] an international organization that tries to solve world problems in a peaceful way

achieve/maintain/restore unity ● unity **among/between** sb ● **a show of** unity

unity /ˈjuːnəti/ *noun* [U] when everyone agrees with each other or wants to stay together *national unity* ○ *family unity*

universal /ˌjuːnɪˈvɜːsᵊl/ *adjective* relating to everyone in the world, or to everyone in a particular group *Kittens and puppies have an almost universal appeal.* ● **universally** *adverb* *It's a style of music that is universally popular.*

the universe /ˈjuːnɪvɜːs/ *noun* everything that exists, including stars, space, etc *Many people believe that there is life elsewhere in the universe.*

go to university ● **at** university ● **a** university **course**

o▪**university** /ˌjuːnɪˈvɜːsəti/ *noun* [C, U] a place where students study at a high level to get a

degree (= type of qualification) *the University of Cambridge* ○ *I applied to three universities.* ○ *(mainly UK) Sarah studied chemistry at university.* ○ *(mainly UK) I want to go to university when I finish school.*

unjust /ʌnˈdʒʌst/ *adjective* not fair *unjust treatment/laws/sanctions* ● **unjustly** *adverb*

unjustified /ʌnˈdʒʌstɪfaɪd/ *adjective* done without a reason and not deserved *unjustified criticism*

unkempt /ʌnˈkempt/ *adjective* untidy *Her hair was long and unkempt.*

unkind /ʌnˈkaɪnd/ *adjective* slightly cruel *I didn't tell her the truth because I thought it would be unkind.* ● **unkindly** *adverb* ● **unkindness** *noun* [U]

unknown[1] /ʌnˈnəʊn/ *adjective* **1** not known *The cause of his death is still unknown.* **2** not famous *an unknown actor* ⊃See also: an unknown quantity.

unknown[2] /ʌnˈnəʊn/ *noun* **1 the unknown** things that you have not experienced and know nothing about *It's normal to fear the unknown.* **2** [C] someone who is not famous *The game was won by a complete unknown.*

unlawful /ʌnˈlɔːfᵊl/ *adjective formal* illegal *unlawful possession of guns* ● **unlawfully** *adverb*

unleaded /ʌnˈledɪd/ *adjective* Unleaded fuel does not contain lead (= a metal).

unleash /ʌnˈliːʃ/ *verb* [T] to suddenly cause a strong reaction *The newspaper report unleashed a storm of protest from readers.*

o▪**unless** /ənˈles/ *conjunction* except if *I won't call you unless there are any problems.*

unlike /ʌnˈlaɪk/ *preposition* **1** different from someone or something *Jackie's really clever, unlike her sister.* ○ *The furniture was unlike anything she had ever seen.* **2** not typical of someone or something *It's unlike her to be quiet - was there something wrong?*

o▪**unlikely** /ʌnˈlaɪkli/ *adjective* **1** not expected to happen [+ (that)] *It's unlikely that I'll be able to come to the party.* ○ [+ to do sth] *He's unlikely to arrive before midday.* **2** probably not true *an unlikely explanation*

unlimited /ʌnˈlɪmɪtɪd/ *adjective* without any limits *a service that offers unlimited Internet access*

unload /ʌnˈləʊd/ *verb* **1** [I, T] to remove things from a vehicle *Can you help me unload the car?* **2** [I] If a ship, aircraft, etc unloads, goods are taken off it.

unlock /ʌnˈlɒk/ *verb* [T] to open something which is locked using a key

unlucky /ʌnˈlʌki/ *adjective* having or causing bad luck [+ to do sth] *The team played well and was unlucky to lose.* ○ *Some people think it's unlucky to walk under ladders.* ● **unluckily** *adverb*

unmarked /ʌnˈmɑːkt/ *adjective* having no signs or words that show what something is *an unmarked grave*

unmarried /ʌnˈmærɪd/ *adjective* not married

unmatched /ʌnˈmætʃt/ *adjective* better than anyone or anything else *Horses have an athletic beauty unmatched by any other animal.*

unmistakable /ˌʌnmɪˈsteɪkəbl/ *adjective* Something that is unmistakable is very obvious and cannot be confused with anything else. *an unmistakable look of disappointment* ● **unmistakably** *adverb*

unmoved /ʌnˈmuːvd/ *adjective* not feeling any emotion *It's impossible to remain unmoved by pictures of starving children.*

unnamed /ʌnˈneɪmd/ *adjective* An unnamed person or thing is talked about but their name is not said. *The money was given by an unnamed businessman.*

unnatural /ʌnˈnætʃᵊrᵊl/ *adjective* not normal or right *an unnatural interest in death* ● **unnaturally** *adverb unnaturally thin*

unnecessary /ʌnˈnesəsᵊri/ *adjective* **1** not needed *You don't want to make any unnecessary car journeys in this weather.* **2** unkind *Why did she say that? That was unnecessary.* ● **unnecessarily** /ʌnˈnesəsᵊrᵊli/ *adverb*

unnerve /ʌnˈnɜːv/ *verb* [T] to make someone feel nervous or frightened

unnerving /ʌnˈnɜːvɪŋ/ *adjective* making you feel nervous or frightened *He kept looking at me which I found unnerving.*

unnoticed /ʌnˈnəʊtɪst/ *adjective* without being seen or noticed *We managed to slip away unnoticed.*

unobtrusive /ˌʌnəbˈtruːsɪv/ *adjective* not attracting attention *He was quiet and unobtrusive.* ● **unobtrusively** *adverb*

unoccupied /ʌnˈɒkjəpaɪd/ *adjective* An unoccupied building, room, seat, etc has no one in it.

unofficial /ˌʌnəˈfɪʃᵊl/ *adjective* not said or done by the government or someone in authority *Unofficial reports suggest the death toll from the earthquake is around 600.* ● **unofficially** *adverb*

unorthodox /ʌnˈɔːθədɒks/ *adjective* unusual and different from most people's opinions, methods, etc *unorthodox ideas/views* ○ *an unorthodox style of teaching*

unpack /ʌnˈpæk/ *verb*   **unpack** [I, T] to take things out of a bag, box, etc *Bella unpacked her suitcase.* ○ *I haven't had time to unpack yet.*

unpaid /ʌnˈpeɪd/ *adjective* **1** An unpaid debt, tax, etc has not been paid. **2** working without getting any money *unpaid work*

unpalatable /ʌnˈpælətəbl/ *adjective formal* shocking and difficult to accept *an unpalatable fact*

unparalleled /ʌnˈpærᵊleld/ *adjective formal* better, greater, worse, etc than anything else *an act of unparalleled cruelty*

unplanned /ʌnˈplænd/ *adjective* not planned or expected *an unplanned pregnancy*

unpleasant /ʌnˈplezᵊnt/ *adjective* **1** not enjoyable or pleasant *an unpleasant experience/smell* **2** rude and angry *The waiter got quite unpleasant with us.* ● **unpleasantly** *adverb*

unplug /ʌnˈplʌg/ *verb* [T] to stop a piece of electrical equipment being connected to an electricity supply by pulling its plug (= object with pins) out of the wall

unpopular /ʌnˈpɒpjələʳ/ *adjective* disliked by most people *an unpopular idea* ○ *an unpopular teacher* ● **unpopularity** /ˌʌnˌpɒpjəˈlærəti/ *noun* [U]

unprecedented /ʌnˈpresɪdᵊntɪd/ *adjective* never having happened before *The Internet has given people unprecedented access to information.*

unpredictable /ˌʌnprɪˈdɪktəbl/ *adjective* changing so much that you do not know what will happen next *unpredictable weather conditions* ● **unpredictability** /ˌʌnprɪˌdɪktəˈbɪlɪti/ *noun* [U]

unprofessional /ˌʌnprəˈfeʃᵊnᵊl/ *adjective* behaving badly at work *an unprofessional attitude*

unprovoked /ˌʌnprəˈvəʊkt/ *adjective* An unprovoked attack is one in which the person who is attacked has done nothing to cause it.

unqualified /ʌnˈkwɒlɪfaɪd/ *adjective* **1** without the qualifications or knowledge to do something [+ to do sth] *She was totally unqualified to look after children.* **2** [always before noun] *formal* total and not limited in any way *an unqualified success*

unquestionably /ʌnˈkwestʃənəbli/ *adverb* in a way that is obvious and causes no doubt *She is unquestionably the best person for the job.*

unravel /ʌnˈrævᵊl/ *verb* [I, T] UK **unravelling**, *past* **unravelled**, US **unraveling**, *past* **unraveled 1** If you unravel a difficult situation or story, or if it unravels, it becomes clear and easier to understand. *No one has yet unravelled the mystery of his death.* **2** to stop being twisted together, or to move pieces of string, etc so that they are not twisted together

unreal /ʌnˈrɪəl/ *adjective* Something that is unreal seems so strange that it is difficult to believe. *For a while I couldn't believe she was dead - it all seemed unreal.* ● **unreality** /ˌʌnriˈæləti/ *noun* [U]

unrealistic /ˌʌnrɪəˈlɪstɪk/ *adjective* not thinking about what is likely to happen or what you can really do *She has a totally unrealistic view of life.* ○ [+ to do sth] *It's unrealistic to expect their decision before Tuesday.*

unreasonable /ʌnˈriːzᵊnəbl/ *adjective* not fair *unreasonable demands/behaviour* ○ [+ to do sth] *It seems unreasonable to expect one person to do both jobs.* ● **unreasonably** *adverb*

unrelated /ˌʌnrɪˈleɪtɪd/ *adjective* having no connection *Police said his death was unrelated to the attack.*

unrelenting /ˌʌnrɪˈlentɪŋ/ *adjective formal* never stopping or getting any less extreme *unrelenting pressure* ○ *The heat was unrelenting.*

unreliable /ˌʌnrɪˈlaɪəbl/ *adjective* not able to be trusted or depended on *an unreliable witness*

○ *The trains were noisy, dirty, and unreliable.*

unremarkable /ˌʌnrɪˈmɑːkəbl/ *adjective* ordinary and not interesting *an unremarkable town*

unremitting /ˌʌnrɪˈmɪtɪŋ/ *adjective formal* never stopping or getting any less extreme *unremitting hostility/pressure* ○ *unremitting efforts*

unrepentant /ˌʌnrɪˈpentənt/ *adjective* not feeling sorry about something bad that you have done

unreservedly /ˌʌnrɪˈzɜːvɪdli/ *adverb* completely *The minister has apologized unreservedly.*

unresolved /ˌʌnrɪˈzɒlvd/ *adjective formal* If a problem or question is unresolved, there is still no solution or answer. *The question of who owns the land remains unresolved.*

WORD PARTNERS FOR *unrest*

cause unrest ● **continuing/growing** unrest ● unrest **among** sb ● unrest **over** sth ● a **wave of** unrest ● **political/social** unrest

---

unrest /ʌnˈrest/ *noun* [U] when a lot of people are angry about something and are likely to become violent *political/social unrest*

unrestrained /ˌʌnrɪˈstreɪnd/ *adjective* not limited or controlled *unrestrained anger*

unrivalled *UK* (*US* **unrivaled**) /ʌnˈraɪvᵊld/ *adjective* better than any other of the same type *The museum has an unrivalled collection of modern American paintings.* ○ *an unrivalled reputation*

unroll /ʌnˈrəʊl/ *verb* [T] to open something that was rolled into a tube shape and make it flat *He unrolled the carpet.*

unruly /ʌnˈruːli/ *adjective* **1** behaving badly and difficult to control *unruly children* **2** Unruly hair is difficult to keep tidy.

unsafe /ʌnˈseɪf/ *adjective* **1** dangerous *The building is unsafe.* ○ [+ to do sth] *The water was dirty and unsafe to drink.* **2** If you feel unsafe, you feel that you are in danger. *Many women feel unsafe on the streets at night.*

unsatisfactory /ʌnˌsætɪsˈfæktᵊri/ *adjective* not good enough to be acceptable *Many school buildings are in an unsatisfactory condition.*

unsavoury *UK* (*US* **unsavory**) /ʌnˈseɪvᵊri/ *adjective* unpleasant and morally offensive *an unsavoury reputation/incident/character*

unscathed /ʌnˈskeɪðd/ *adjective* [never before noun] not harmed *The driver of the car was killed but both passengers escaped unscathed.*

unscrew /ʌnˈskruː/ *verb* [T] **1** to remove something by twisting it *I can't unscrew the lid.* **2** to remove something by taking the screws (= small, metal pieces) out of it

unscrupulous /ʌnˈskruːpjələs/ *adjective* behaving in a way that is dishonest or unfair in order to get what you want *an unscrupulous financial adviser*

unseat /ʌnˈsiːt/ *verb* [T] to remove someone from a powerful position *Kennedy has a good chance of unseating the President at the next election.*

unseen /ʌnˈsiːn/ *adjective, adverb* not seen or

noticed *an exhibition of previously unseen photographs*

unsettled /ʌnˈsetld/ *adjective* **1** changing often *The weather continues to be unsettled.* **2** anxious and not able to relax or feel happy in a situation *Children tend to get unsettled if you keep changing their routine.*

unsettling /ʌnˈsetlɪŋ/ *adjective* making you feel anxious *an unsettling experience/feeling*

unsightly /ʌnˈsaɪtli/ *adjective* unpleasant to look at *unsightly piles of litter*

unskilled /ʌnˈskɪld/ *adjective* **1** without special skills or qualifications *an unskilled labourer/worker* **2** Unskilled work does not need people with special skills or qualifications.

unsociable /ʌnˈsəʊʃəbl/ *adjective* not wanting to be with other people

unsolicited /ˌʌnsəˈlɪsɪtɪd/ *adjective* not asked for and often not wanted *unsolicited advice/offer*

unsolved /ʌnˈsɒlvd/ *adjective* having no answer or solution *an unsolved mystery/murder/crime*

unsound /ʌnˈsaʊnd/ *adjective* **1** based on ideas, facts, and reasons that are wrong *an unsound practice* **2** in a bad condition *The bridge was structurally unsound.*

unspeakable /ʌnˈspiːkəbl/ *adjective* extremely bad or shocking *unspeakable crimes/suffering* ● **unspeakably** *adverb*

unspecified /ʌnˈspesɪfaɪd/ *adjective* If something is unspecified, you are not told what it is. *The court awarded her an unspecified amount of money.*

unspoiled (*also UK* **unspoilt**) /ʌnˈspɔɪlt/ *adjective* An unspoiled place is beautiful because it has not been changed or damaged by people. *an unspoiled, tropical island*

unspoken /ʌnˈspəʊkᵊn/ *adjective* not said, but thought or felt *unspoken doubts*

unstable /ʌnˈsteɪbl/ *adjective* **1** CHANGE likely to change or end suddenly *an unstable situation* ○ *an unstable economy* **2** PERSON If someone is unstable, their moods and behaviour change suddenly, especially because they are mentally ill. **3** MOVE not fixed or safe and likely to move *That chair looks a bit unstable.*

unsteady /ʌnˈstedi/ *adjective* moving slightly from side to side, as if you might fall *The alcohol had made her unsteady on her feet.*

unstuck /ʌnˈstʌk/ *adjective* **1** **come unstuck a** *UK* If something comes unstuck, it stops being fixed to something. *One of the photos has come unstuck.* **b** *UK informal* to experience difficulties and fail *The negotiations came unstuck at a crucial stage.*

unsuccessful /ˌʌnsəkˈsesfᵊl/ *adjective* not achieving what was wanted or intended *an unsuccessful attempt/effort* ● **unsuccessfully** *adverb*

unsuitable /ʌnˈsuːtəbl/ *adjective* not acceptable or right for someone or something *My parents considered the programme unsuitable for children.*

unsung /ʌnˈsʌŋ/ *adjective* not famous or praised

although you have done something very well *He was the **unsung hero** of the match.*

unsure /ʌnˈʃʊəʳ/ *adjective* **1** not certain or having doubts *I'm a bit **unsure about** what to do.* **2 unsure of yourself** without confidence

unsuspecting /ˌʌnsəˈspektɪŋ/ *adjective* [always before noun] not aware that something bad is happening *an **unsuspecting victim***

unsympathetic /ˌʌnsɪmpəˈθetɪk/ *adjective* **1** showing that you do not understand or care about someone's problems *I told him I'd got a cold but he was completely unsympathetic.* **2** not agreeing with or supporting someone's ideas or actions

untangle /ʌnˈtæŋgl/ *verb* [T] **1** to separate pieces of string, hair, wire, etc that have become twisted together *I'm trying to untangle these wires.* **2** to understand the different parts of a situation that has become confused or very complicated

untapped /ʌnˈtæpt/ *adjective* not yet used *untapped potential*

untenable /ʌnˈtenəbl/ *adjective formal* If an argument, action, or situation is untenable, it cannot be supported or defended from criticism. *an untenable position*

unthinkable /ʌnˈθɪŋkəbl/ *adjective* If something is unthinkable, it is so strange that you can not imagine it will ever happen. *an unthinkable proposition*

untidy

untidy /ʌnˈtaɪdi/ *adjective* not tidy *an untidy room* ○ *She's really untidy at home.*

untie /ʌnˈtaɪ/ *verb* [T] untying, *past* untied to open a knot or something that has been tied with a knot *I untied my shoelaces and kicked off my shoes.*

o─**until** /ənˈtɪl/ (*also* till) *preposition, conjunction* **1** continuing to happen before a particular time or event and then stopping *The show will be on until the end of the month.* ○ *Whisk the egg whites until they look white and fluffy.*

untie

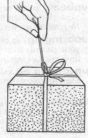

2 as far as *Carry on until you reach the traffic lights and turn right.* **3 not until** not before a particular time or event *It doesn't open until 7.* ○ *We won't start until Jeanne arrives.*

untimely /ʌnˈtaɪmli/ *adjective* happening too soon *her **untimely death** from cancer*

untold /ʌnˈtəʊld/ *adjective* [always before noun] too much to be measured or counted *untold riches* ○ *untold damage* ○ *Words alone cannot convey the untold misery endured by people in these refugee camps.*

untouched /ʌnˈtʌtʃt/ *adjective* **1** not changed or damaged in any way *Most of the island remains untouched by tourism.* **2** If food is untouched, it has not been eaten. *She took a few mouthfuls of soup but left her main course untouched.*

untoward /ˌʌntəˈwɔːd/ *adjective formal* unexpected and causing problems *If nothing untoward happens we should be there by midday.*

untrained /ʌnˈtreɪnd/ *adjective* **1** never having been taught the skills for a particular job *untrained staff* **2 the untrained eye** someone without the skill or knowledge to judge what they see *To the untrained eye, most fake diamonds look real.*

untried /ʌnˈtraɪd/ *adjective* not yet used or tested *new and untried technology*

untrue /ʌnˈtruː/ *adjective* false

untruth /ʌnˈtruːθ/ *noun* [C] *formal* a lie, or something that is not true *It's not the first time that the paper has been in trouble for printing untruths about people's private lives.*

unused¹ /ʌnˈjuːzd/ *adjective* not used now or not used before now *an unused room*

unused² /ʌnˈjuːst/ *adjective* **be unused to sth** to not have experience of something *I was unused to city life.*

unusual /ʌnˈjuːʒuəl/ *adjective* different and not ordinary, often in a way that is interesting or exciting *an unusual name* ○ [+ to do sth] *It's fairly unusual to keep insects as pets.*

unusually /ʌnˈjuːʒuəli/ *adverb* **1 unusually big/ strong/good, etc** bigger, stronger, better, etc than is normal *unusually warm weather* **2 unusually for sb** in a way that is not usual for someone *Unusually for me, I actually couldn't finish my meal.*

unveil /ʌnˈveɪl/ *verb* [T] **1** to tell the public about an idea or plan that was secret before *The new policy is due to be unveiled later this month.* **2** to remove the cover from an object as part of an official ceremony

unwanted /ʌnˈwɒntɪd/ *adjective* not wanted *an unwanted pregnancy*

unwarranted /ʌnˈwɒrəntɪd/ *adjective formal* without a good reason *unwarranted intrusion*

unwary /ʌnˈweəri/ *adjective* not aware of possible dangers *Unwary travellers can easily get lost in these parts.*

unwelcome /ʌn'welkəm/ *adjective* not wanted *unwelcome publicity* ○ *an unwelcome visitor*

unwell /ʌn'wel/ *adjective* [never before noun] *formal* ill *to feel/look unwell*

unwieldy /ʌn'wiːldi/ *adjective* An unwieldy object is difficult to carry because it is heavy, large, or a strange shape.

unwilling /ʌn'wɪlɪŋ/ *adjective* not wanting to do something [+ to do sth] *A lot of people are unwilling to accept change.* ● **unwillingly** *adverb* ● **unwillingness** *noun* [U]

unwind /ʌn'waɪnd/ *verb past* **unwound 1** [I] *informal* to relax, especially after working *Music helps me to unwind.* **2** [I, T] If you unwind something, or if something unwinds, it stops being curled round or twisted round something else and is made straight. *He unwound the bandage.*

unwise /ʌn'waɪz/ *adjective* stupid and likely to cause problems *an unwise decision* ● **unwisely** *adverb*

unwittingly /ʌn'wɪtɪŋli/ *adverb* without intending to do something *I apologized for the chaos I had unwittingly caused.*

unworkable /ʌn'wɜːkəbl/ *adjective* A plan that is unworkable is impossible. *The policy has been described as unworkable.*

unwrap /ʌn'ræp/ *verb* [T] **unwrapping**, *past* **unwrapped** to remove the paper, cloth, etc that is covering something *She carefully unwrapped the present.*

unwrap

unwritten /ʌn'rɪtᵊn/ *adjective* **an unwritten agreement/ law/rule** an agreement, law, etc that is accepted and obeyed by most people but is not formally written

unzip /ʌn'zɪp/ *verb* [T] **unzipping**, *past* **unzipped** to open something by using its zip (= two rows of metal or plastic points that fasten two sides together) *He unzipped his trousers.*

up¹ /ʌp/ *adverb, preposition* **1** HIGHER PLACE towards or in a higher place *He ran up the stairs.* ○ *Pick up your clothes and put them away.* ○ *She looked up and smiled at me.* **2** VERTICAL vertical or as straight as possible *He stood up.* ○ *She opened her eyes and sat up.* **3** INCREASE to a greater degree, amount, volume, etc *Inflation keeps pushing prices up.* ○ *Can you turn up the heat? I'm freezing!* ○ *Please speak up* (= speak louder), *I can't hear you.* **4** COMPLETELY used to emphasize that someone completes an action or uses all of something *I used up all my money.* ○ *Eat up the rest of your dinner.* **5 up the road/street, etc** along or further along the street/road, etc *My best friend lives up the street from me.* ○ *He ran up the path and hugged her.* **6 go/walk, etc up to sb/sth** to walk

directly towards someone or something until you are next to them *He walked straight up to me and introduced himself.* **7** DIRECTION in or towards a particular direction, usually north *We moved from London up to Scotland.* ○ *Chris lives up north.* **8 up and down** If something or someone moves up and down, they move repeatedly in one direction and then in the opposite direction. *The children were constantly running up and down the stairs.* **9 up to 10, 20, etc** any amount under 10, 20, etc *We can invite up to 65 people.* **10 up to** until a particular time *You can call me up to midnight.* **11 up to sth** equal in quality or achievement *His work wasn't up to his usual standard.* **12 up to sth/doing sth** able to do something *It'll be a while before I feel up to walking again.* **13 be up to (sth)** *informal* to be doing or planning something, often something secret and bad *Joe, what are you up to?* **14 be up to sb?** If an action or decision is up to someone, they are responsible for doing or making it. *I can't decide for you Jack, it's up to you.* ○ [+ to do sth] *It's up to her to decide whether she wants to enter the competition.* **15 be up against sb/sth** If you are up against a situation or a person, they make it very difficult for you to achieve what you want to achieve. *We were up against some of the best players in the world.*

up² /ʌp/ *adjective* [never before noun] **1** NOT IN BED not in bed *I was up all night with the baby.* ○ *Is she up yet?* **2 be up and around/about** to be well enough after an illness to get out of bed and move around **3** FINISHED If a period of time is up, it has ended. *My health club membership is up.* **4** INCREASE If a level or amount is up, it has increased. *Profits are up by 26%.* **5** ROAD *UK* If a road is up, it is being repaired. **6** OPERATING If a computer system is up, it is operating. **7** SPORT *US* In baseball and similar sports, if a player is up, they are taking a turn to play. **8 be up and running** If a system, organization, or machine is up and running, it is operating. **9 be up for sth** *informal* to want to do something *We're going clubbing tonight if you're up for it.*

up³ /ʌp/ *verb* [T] **upping**, *past* **upped** to increase something *Dad's upped my allowance by fifty cents a week.*

up-and-coming /ˌʌpᵊn'kʌmɪŋ/ *adjective* [always before noun] becoming popular and likely to achieve success *He's a young, up-and-coming DJ.*

upbeat /'ʌp,biːt/ *adjective informal* positive and expecting a situation to be good or successful *He remains upbeat about the future.*

upbringing /'ʌp,brɪŋɪŋ/ *noun* [no plural] the way your parents treat you when you are growing up *a middle-class/religious upbringing*

upcoming /'ʌp,kʌmɪŋ/ *adjective* [always before noun] An upcoming event will happen soon. *the upcoming elections*

update¹ /ʌp'deɪt/ *verb* [T] **1** to add new information *We've just updated our website.* ○ *I'll update you on* (= tell you about) *any developments.* **2** to make something more modern *They need to update their image.*

get/give an update • an update **on** sth • an update **from** sb

update² /'ʌpdeɪt/ noun [C] **1** new information *I'll need regular updates on your progress.* **2** a new form of something which existed at an earlier time *It's an update of an old 60's movie.*

upfront¹ /ˌʌp'frʌnt/ adjective **1** paid or obtained before work starts *an upfront payment/fee* **2** behaving in a way that makes your beliefs and intentions obvious to other people *She's very upfront about her dislike of men.*

upfront² /ˌʌp'frʌnt/ adverb If you pay someone upfront, you pay them before they work for you.

upgrade /ʌp'greɪd/ verb [T] to improve something so that it is of a higher quality or a newer model *to upgrade a computer* • **upgrade** /'ʌpgreɪd/ noun [C]

upheaval /ʌp'hiːv³l/ noun [C, U] a very big change that causes difficulty or confusion *political/social upheaval*

uphill¹ /ʌp'hɪl/ adjective. **an uphill battle/ struggle/task** something that is difficult to do and needs a lot of effort *I can lose weight but it's a real uphill struggle.*

uphill² /ʌp'hɪl/ adverb towards the top of a hill *We'd walked half a mile uphill.*

uphold /ʌp'həʊld/ verb [T] past **upheld 1** to agree with a decision, especially a legal one, and say it was correct *The court upheld the ruling.* **2** to support a decision, principle, or law *Police officers are expected to uphold the law.*

upholstery /ʌp'həʊlst³ri/ noun [U] the material that covers chairs and other types of seats

upkeep /'ʌpkiːp/ noun [U] the process of keeping something in good condition, or of keeping a person or animal healthy

upland /'ʌplənd/ adjective [always before noun] existing on a hill or mountain *upland areas*

uplands /'ʌpləndz/ noun [plural] high areas of land *the uplands of Nepal*

uplifting /ʌp'lɪftɪŋ/ adjective making you feel happy and full of good feelings *an uplifting film*

upload /ʌp'ləʊd/ verb [T] to copy computer programs or information electronically, usually from a small computer to a larger one or to the Internet ⇨Compare **download**.

upmarket /ˌʌp'mɑːkɪt/ UK (US **upscale**) adjective expensive and used by people who are rich and from a high social class *an upmarket hotel/restaurant*

upon /ə'pɒn/ preposition formal on

upper /'ʌpəʳ/ adjective [always before noun] **1** at a higher position *an upper floor* ○ *the upper lip* ○ *the upper body* **2** of a higher social class **3 the upper limit** the highest amount or level, or the longest time that something is allowed ⇨See also: get/gain the upper **hand¹**.

ˌ**upper 'case** noun [U] letters written as capitals

ˌ**upper 'class** noun [C] the highest social class

of people *members of the upper classes* • **upperclass** adjective *an upper-class accent*

uppermost /'ʌpəməʊst/ adjective **1** highest *the building's uppermost floors* **2 be uppermost in sb's mind** to be the most important thing someone is thinking about *The safety of her children was uppermost in her mind.*

upright¹ /'ʌpraɪt/ adverb vertical and as straight as possible *to sit/stand upright* ⇨See also: **bolt upright**.

upright² /'ʌpraɪt/ adjective **1** straight up or vertical *Please return your seat to an upright position and fasten your seat belt.* **2** honest and morally good *an upright citizen*

uprising /'ʌpˌraɪzɪŋ/ noun [C] when a large group of people try to make political changes or change the government by fighting [usually singular] *a general/popular uprising*

cause/provoke (an) uproar • be (UK) **in**/ (US) **in an** uproar • uproar **among** sb • uproar **at/over** sth

uproar /'ʌprɔːʳ/ noun [U, no plural] when many people complain about something angrily *The book caused an uproar in the United States.* ○ *Local residents are (UK) in uproar/ (US) in an uproar over plans for the new road.*

uproot /ʌp'ruːt/ verb [T] **1** to pull a tree or plant out of the ground *Hundreds of trees were uprooted in the storm.* **2** to make someone leave a place where they have been living for a long time *The war has uprooted nearly half the country's population.*

ˌ**ups and 'downs** noun [plural] the mixture of good and bad things that happen to people *Like most married couples, we've had our ups and downs.*

upscale /'ʌpˌskeɪl/ US (UK **upmarket**) adjective expensive and used by people who are rich and from a high social class *an upscale restaurant/neighbourhood*

o⇥**upset¹** /ʌp'set/ adjective **1** unhappy or worried because something unpleasant has happened *They'd had an argument and she was still upset about it.* ○ *Mike got very upset when I told him the news.* **2 upset stomach/tummy** an illness in the stomach

upset² /ʌp'set/ verb [T] upsetting, past upset **1** to make someone feel unhappy or worried *The phone call had clearly upset her.* **2** to cause problems for something *If I arrived later would that upset your plans?* **3 upset sb's stomach** to make someone feel ill in the stomach

upset³ /'ʌpset/ noun [C] **1** when someone beats the player or team that was expected to win *After Harding won the second set, a major upset seemed likely.* **2 a stomach/tummy upset** UK an illness in the stomach **3** a difficulty or problem *We had the usual upsets but overall the day went well.*

upsetting /ʌp'setɪŋ/ adjective making you feel unhappy or worried *I found the programme very upsetting.*

the upshot /'ʌpʃɒt/ noun the final result of a discussion or series of events *The upshot is* *that we've decided to move to Sydney.*

upside down

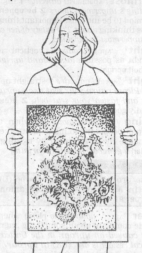

,upside 'down¹ *adverb* **1** turned so that the part that is usually at the top is now at the bottom *One of the pictures had been hung upside down.* ○ *Turn the jar upside down and shake it.* **2 turn sth upside down a** to make a place very untidy while looking for something **b** to change someone's life or a system completely *Their lives were turned upside down when their son was arrested.*

,upside 'down² *adjective* turned so that the part that is usually at the top is now at the bottom *Why is this box upside down?*

upstage /ʌpˈsteɪdʒ/ *verb* [T] to do something that takes people's attention away from someone or something and gives it to you instead *You mustn't upstage the bride.*

upstairs /ʌpˈsteəz/ *adverb* on or to a higher level of a building *He ran upstairs to answer the phone.* ● **upstairs** *adjective* *an upstairs bedroom*

upstart /ˈʌpstɑːt/ *noun* [C] someone who has just started a job but already thinks they are very important

upstate /ˌʌpˈsteɪt/ *adjective* US in the northern part of a US state (= one of the parts into which the country is divided) *upstate New York* ● **upstate** *adverb* *She's taken a trip upstate with some friends.*

upstream /ʌpˈstriːm/ *adverb* along a river in the opposite direction to the way that the water is moving

upsurge /ˈʌpsɜːdʒ/ *noun* [C] a sudden increase *an upsurge in violent crime*

uptake /ˈʌpteɪk/ *noun informal* **be slow/quick on the uptake** to be slow/quick to understand something

uptight /ʌpˈtaɪt/ *adjective informal* worried or

nervous and not able to relax

up-to-date /ˌʌptəˈdeɪt/ *adjective* **1** modern, and using the most recent technology or knowledge **2** having the most recent information *The Internet keeps us up-to-date.*

up-to-the-minute /ˌʌptəðəˈmɪnɪt/ *adjective* most recent *up-to-the-minute news*

uptown /ʌpˈtaʊn/ *adjective, adverb US* in or to the northern part of a city *She lives uptown.*

upturn /ˈʌptɜːn/ *noun* [C] an improvement, especially in economic conditions or a business *There's been a sharp upturn in sales.*

upturned /ʌpˈtɜːnd/ *adjective* pointing up, or turned so the under side faces up *an upturned boat*

upward /ˈʌpwəd/ *adjective* [always before noun] moving towards a higher place or level *an upward glance* ○ *an upward trend in sales*

upwards /ˈʌpwədz/ *mainly UK* (*mainly US* **upward**) *adverb* **1** towards a higher place or level *House prices have started moving upwards again.* **2 upwards of sth** more than a particular amount *Double rooms cost upwards of £70 a night.*

uranium /jʊˈreɪniəm/ *noun* [U] a heavy, grey metal that is used in the production of nuclear power

Uranus /ˈjʊərənəs/ *noun* [no plural] the planet that is seventh from the Sun, after Saturn and before Neptune

urban /ˈɜːbən/ *adjective* belonging or relating to a town or city *urban areas* ○ *urban development*

urbane /ɜːˈbeɪn/ *adjective* confident, relaxed, and polite *With his good looks and urbane manner, he was very popular.*

urge¹ /ɜːdʒ/ *verb* [T] **1 urge sb to do sth** to try to persuade someone to do something *His parents urged him to go to university.* **2** *formal* to strongly advise an action *Financial experts are urging caution.*

urge sb on to encourage someone to do or achieve something *The crowd was cheering and urging her on.*

▸ WORD PARTNERS FOR **urge** (noun)

feel/have/resist/satisfy an urge ● an **irresistible/overwhelming/strong/sudden/uncontrollable** urge

urge² /ɜːdʒ/ *noun* [C] a strong wish or need [+ to do sth] *I resisted a powerful urge to slap him.*

▸ WORD PARTNERS FOR **urgency**

a **matter of** urgency ● a **sense of** urgency ● the **urgency of** sth

urgency /ˈɜːdʒənsi/ *noun* [U] when something is very important and needs you to take action immediately *a matter of great urgency*

urgent /ˈɜːdʒənt/ *adjective* very important and needing you to take action immediately *an urgent message* ○ *The refugees were in urgent need of food and water.* ● **urgently** *adverb* *I need to speak to you urgently.*

urinate /ˈjʊərɪneɪt/ *verb* [I] to get rid of urine from your body

| ɑː arm | ɜː her | iː see | ɔː saw | uː too | aɪ my | aʊ how | eə hair | eɪ day | əʊ no | ɪə near | ɔɪ boy | ʊə poor | aɪə fire | aʊə sour |

urine /'jʊərɪn/ *noun* [U] the liquid that comes out of your body when you go to the toilet

URL /ju:ɑ:'rel/ *abbreviation for* uniform resource locator: a website address

urn /ɜ:n/ *noun* [C] **1** a round container that is used for plants or to store someone's ashes (= the powder that is left after a dead body has been burned) **2** a metal container that is used to make a large amount of coffee or tea and to keep it hot

o⊷**us** *strong form* /ʌs/ *weak forms* /əs, s/ *pronoun* used after a verb or preposition to refer to the person who is speaking or writing and one or more other people *She gave us all a present.* ○ *Would you like to have dinner with us next Saturday?*

USA /ˌju:es'eɪ/ *noun abbreviation for* United States of America

usage /'ju:sɪdʒ/ *noun* **1** [C, U] the way that words are used *a guide to English grammar and usage* **2** [U] the amount of something that is used, or the way that something is used *restrictions on water usage*

o⊷**use¹** /ju:z/ *verb* [T] *past* used **1** PURPOSE If you use something, you do something with it for a particular purpose. *Can I use your pen?* ○ *She uses her car for work* ○ [+ to do sth] *Nick used the money to buy a CD player.* **2** MAKE LESS to take an amount from a supply of something *A shower uses less water than a bath.* **3** PERSON to treat someone badly in order to get what you want *He was just using me to make his girlfriend jealous.* **4** WORD to say or write a particular word or words *'Autumn' is used in British English and 'fall' in American English.* **5 could use sth** *mainly US informal* something that you say when you want or need something *I could use some help with these packages, please.*

use sth up to finish a supply of something *Someone's used up all the milk.*

o⊷**use²** /ju:s/ *noun* **1** USING [U] when you use something, or when something is being used *an increase in the use of mobile phones* ○ *Guests have free use of the hotel swimming pool.* ○ *Turn the machine off when it's not in use* (= being used). **2** PURPOSE [C] a purpose for which something is used *A food processor has a variety of uses in the kitchen.* ○ *Can you find a use for this box?* **3 be (of) any/some use** to be useful *Is this book of any use to you?* **4 be (of) no use** to not be useful *His advice was no use at all.* **5 be no use; be no use doing sth** used to say that trying to do something has no effect *It was no use talking to him - he wouldn't listen.* **6** WORD [C] one of the meanings of a word, or the way that a particular word is used *Can you list all the uses of the verb 'go'?* **7 the use of sth** permission to use something, or the ability to use something *Martin has offered me the use of his car.* **8 make use of sth** to use something that is available *We were encouraged to make use of all the facilities.*

o⊷**used¹** /ju:st/ *adjective* **used to sth/doing sth** If you are used to something, you have done it or experienced it many times before. *He's used to working long hours.* ○ *We've been living here*

for two years and we've (UK) got used to/ (US) gotten used to the heat. ➾Opposite unused.

used² /ju:zd/ *adjective* Something that is used is not new and has been owned by someone else. *a used car* ➾Opposite unused.

o⊷**used to** /'ju:sttu:/ *modal verb* **used to do/be sth** If something used to happen or a situation used to exist, it happened regularly or existed in the past but it does not happen or exist now. *I used to go out every night when I was a student.* ○ *He used to be a lot fatter.* ➾See Extra help page **Modal verbs** on page Centre 22.

COMMON LEARNER ERROR

used to and be used to

Used to + verb is for talking about a situation or regular activity in the past.
My dad used to smoke when he was younger.

I used to live in Italy, but now I live in England.

When you make **used to + verb** into a question or negative using the verb do, the correct form is **use to**.
My dad didn't use to smoke.

Where did you use to live?

~~Where did you used to live?~~

The expression **be used to something/doing something** is for talking about something which you have done or experienced a lot before.
I don't mind the heat. I'm used to hot weather.

He's not used to working long hours.

~~He's not use to working long hours.~~

OTHER WAYS OF SAYING *useful*

If something is useful because it helps you do or achieve something, you can describe it as **helpful** or **valuable**: *They gave us some really **helpful** advice.* ● *He was able to provide the police with some **valuable** information.*

The adjective **invaluable** means 'extremely useful': *The Internet is an **invaluable** resource for teachers.*

An activity which requires a lot of effort but is useful, is sometimes described as **worthwhile**: *It's a difficult course but it's very **worthwhile**.*

Something which is useful because it is simple to use is often described as **handy**: *That's a **handy** little gadget.*

The expression **come in handy** is often used when you think something will be useful in the future: *Don't throw that away - it'll **come in handy** for the party.*

If speech or writing contains a lot of useful information, you can describe it as **informative** or **instructive**: *It's an interesting and highly **informative** book.*

o⊷**useful** /'ju:sfʊl/ *adjective* **1** helping you to do or achieve something *useful information* **2 come in useful** *UK* to be useful and help someone do or achieve something, especially when there is nothing else to help them *You should keep that paint - it might come in useful.* ● **usefully** *adverb*

• **usefulness** *noun* [U]

useless /'juːsləs/ *adjective* **1** If something is useless, it does not work well or it has no effect. *This umbrella's useless - there's a big hole in it.* ○ [+ doing sth] *It's useless arguing with her.* **2** *UK informal* having no skill in an activity *Dave's useless at football.*

user /'juːzər/ *noun* [C] someone who uses a product, machine, or service *drug users* ○ *a new service for Internet users*

user-friendly /,juːzə'frendli/ *adjective* A machine or system that is user-friendly is easy to use or understand. *user-friendly software*

'user ,name *noun* [C] a name or other word that you sometimes need to use together with a password (= secret word) before you can use a computer on the Internet

usher[1] /'ʌʃər/ *verb* **usher sb into/to/across, etc** to show someone where to go or sit *She ushered me into her office.*
usher in sth *formal* to be at the start of a period when important changes happen, or to cause important changes to start happening *His presidency ushered in a new era of democracy.*

usher[2] /'ʌʃər/ *noun* [C] someone who shows people where to sit in a theatre or at a formal event

⊶**usual** /'juːʒuəl/ *adjective* **1** normal and happening most often *I went to bed at my usual time.* ○ *This winter has been much colder than usual.* ⊃Opposite **unusual**. **2 as usual** in the way that happens most of the time *As usual, Ben was the last to arrive.*

⊶**usually** /'juːʒəli/ *adverb* in the way that most often happens *I usually get home at about six o'clock.* ○ *Usually I just have a sandwich.*

usurp /juː'zɜːp/ *verb* [T] *formal* to take someone else's job or power when you should not

utensil /juː'tensəl/ *noun* [C] a tool that you use for doing jobs in the house, especially cooking *wooden cooking utensils* ⊃See colour picture **The Kitchen** on page Centre 2.

uterus /'juːtərəs/ *noun* [C] the organ inside a woman's body where a baby grows

utilitarian /,juːtɪli'teəriən/ *adjective* designed to be useful and not beautiful *utilitarian furniture*

utility /juː'tɪləti/ (*also* **public utility**) *noun* [C] an organization that supplies the public with water, gas, or electricity

utilize *formal (also UK* **-ise**) /'juːtɪlaɪz/ *verb* [T] to use something in an effective way *The vitamins come in a form that is easily utilized by the body.*

utmost[1] /'ʌtməʊst/ *adjective* [always before noun] *formal* used to emphasize how important or serious something is *a matter of the utmost importance* ○ *The situation needs to be handled with the utmost care.*

utmost[2] /'ʌtməʊst/ *noun* **do your utmost** to try as hard as you can to do something [+ to do sth] *We did our utmost to finish the project on time.*

utopia /juː'təʊpiə/ *noun* [C, U] an imaginary place where everything is perfect

utopian /juː'təʊpiən/ *adjective* A utopian idea or plan is based on the belief that things can be made perfect. *a utopian vision of society*

utter[1] /'ʌtər/ *adjective* [always before noun] used to emphasize something *She dismissed the article as utter nonsense.*

utter[2] /'ʌtər/ *verb* [T] *formal* to say something *She left without uttering a word.*

utterance /'ʌtərəns/ *noun* [C] *formal* something that you say

utterly /'ʌtəli/ *adverb* completely *It's utterly ridiculous.*

U-turn /'juːtɜːn/ *noun* [C] **1** a change of direction that you make when driving in order to travel in the opposite direction **2** a complete change from one opinion or plan to an opposite one *the government's U-turn on economic policy*

Vv

V, v /viː/ the twenty-second letter of the alphabet

V *written abbreviation for* volt (= a unit for measuring an electric current) *a 9V battery*

v *UK* (*UK/US* **vs**) /viː/ *preposition abbreviation for* versus (= used to say that one team or person is competing against another) *Germany v France*

vacancy /ˈveɪkənsi/ *noun* **[C]** **1** a room that is not being used in a hotel *Do you have any vacancies?* **2** a job that is available for someone to do *Tell me if you hear of any vacancies for secretaries.*

vacant /ˈveɪkənt/ *adjective* **1** [EMPTY] Somewhere that is vacant is available because it is not being used. *a vacant building* **2** [JOB] A vacant job is available for someone to do. **3** [EXPRESSION] A vacant expression on someone's face shows they are not thinking about anything. • **vacantly** *adverb*

vacate /vəˈkeɪt/ [US] /ˈveɪkeɪt/ *verb* **[T]** *formal* to leave a room, building, chair, etc so that someone else can use it

⊶**vacation¹** /vəˈkeɪʃən/ [US] /veɪˈkeɪʃən/ *noun* **[C, U]** **1** *US* (*UK* **holiday**) a period of time when you are not at home but are staying somewhere else for enjoyment *We're **taking a vacation** in Florida.* ○ *We met Bob and Wendi **on vacation**.* **2** *mainly US* a period of the year when schools or colleges are closed *the summer vacation* ○ *He's **on vacation** for three months.*

vacation² /vəˈkeɪʃən/ [US] /veɪˈkeɪʃən/ *US* (*UK* **holiday**) *verb* **vacation in/on/by, etc** to go on vacation *Sam was vacationing in Guatemala.*

vaccinate /ˈvæksɪneɪt/ *verb* **[T]** to give someone a vaccine to stop them from getting a disease *Have you been **vaccinated against** polio?* • **vaccination** /ˌvæksɪˈneɪʃən/ *noun* **[C, U]**

vaccine /ˈvæksiːn/ *noun* **[C, U]** a substance that is given to people to stop them from getting a particular disease

vacuum¹ /ˈvækjuːm/ *noun* **1** **[C]** a space that has no air or other gas in it **2** **[no plural]** when someone or something important is not now in your life and you are unhappy *When her husband died, it left a big vacuum in her life.*

vacuum² /ˈvækjuːm/ *verb* **[I, T]** to clean somewhere using a vacuum cleaner

ˈvacuum ˌcleaner (*also UK* **Hoover**) *noun* **[C]** an electric machine that cleans floors by sucking up dirt

vagaries /ˈveɪɡəriz/ *noun, formal* **[plural]** sudden changes that are not expected or known about before they happen ***the vagaries of** the English weather*

vagina /vəˈdʒaɪnə/ *noun* **[C]** the part of a woman's body that connects her outer sex organs to the place where a baby grows

vagrant /ˈveɪɡrənt/ *noun* **[C]** *formal* someone who has no job and no home and who lives outside

WORD PARTNERS FOR *vague*

a vague **feeling/idea/impression/memory/promise**

vague /veɪɡ/ *adjective* **1** not clear or certain *I have a **vague idea** of where the hotel is.* ○ *He was a bit vague about directions.* **2** showing that someone is not thinking clearly or does not understand *a vague expression* • **vaguely** *adverb I **vaguely** (= slightly) **remember** meeting her.* • **vagueness** *noun* **[U]**

vain /veɪn/ *adjective* **1 in vain** without any success *I tried in vain to start a conversation.* **2 vain attempt/effort/hope** A vain attempt, effort, etc does not have the result you want. **3** too interested in your own appearance and thinking you are very attractive • **vainly** *adverb*

Valentine /ˈvæləntaɪn/ (*also* **ˈValentine ˌcard**) *noun* **[C]** a card (= stiff, folded paper with a message inside) that you give someone on Valentine's Day

Valentine's Day /ˈvæləntaɪnzˌdeɪ/ *noun* **[C, U]** 14 February, a day when you give a Valentine to someone you have a romantic relationship with or would like a romantic relationship with

valet /ˈvæleɪ/ *noun* **[C]** **1** someone who parks your car when you arrive at a restaurant, hotel, or airport **2** a male servant who looks after a man's clothes and helps him to dress

valiant /ˈvæliənt/ *adjective formal* very brave *a valiant effort* • **valiantly** *adverb*

valid /ˈvælɪd/ *adjective* **1** based on good reasons or facts that are true *a **valid argument*** **2** A valid ticket or document is legally acceptable. *The ticket is valid for three months.* ⮌Opposite **invalid**. • **validity** /vəˈlɪdəti/ *noun* **[U]**

validate /ˈvælɪdeɪt/ *verb* **[T]** *formal* to prove that something is true • **validation** /ˌvælɪˈdeɪʃən/ *noun* **[C, U]**

valley

valley /ˈvæli/ *noun* **[C]** an area of low land between hills or mountains

valour *UK literary* (*US* **valor**) /ˈvælər/ *noun* **[U]** when someone is very brave, especially during a war

⊶**valuable** /ˈvæljuəbl/ *adjective* **1** Valuable objects could be sold for a lot of money. *valuable paintings and antiques* **2** Valuable information, help, advice, etc is very helpful.

OTHER WAYS OF SAYING *valuable*

If something is valuable because it helps you do or achieve something, you can describe it as **helpful** or **useful**: *They gave us some really **helpful** advice.* • *She made a really **useful** contribution to the project.*

Something which is valuable because it produces useful results may be described as **constructive** or **productive**: *It was a very **constructive** discussion.* • *We had a very* *productive meeting and sorted out a lot of problems.*

An activity which is valuable but requires a lot of effort, is sometimes described as **worthwhile**: *It's a difficult course but it's very worthwhile.*

If speech or writing contains a lot of valuable information, you can describe it as **informative** or **instructive**: *It's an interesting and highly informative book.*

valuables /'væljuǝblz/ *noun* **[plural]** small things that you own which could be sold for a lot of money *valuables such as jewellery and watches*

valuation /ˌvæljuˈeɪʃⁿn/ *noun* **[C, U]** when someone judges how much money something could be sold for

⚬**value**¹ /'vælju:/ *noun* **1** **[C, U]** how much money something could be sold for *The new road has affected the **value** of these houses.* ○ *Cars quickly **go down** in value.* **2** **[U]** how useful or important something is *a document of great historical value* **3** **good value (for money)** If something is good value it is of good quality or there is a lot of it so you think the amount of money you spent on it was right. *The meal was very good value.* ⊃See also: **face value**.

value² /'vælju:/ *verb* **[T]** valuing, *past* valued **1** If you value something or someone, they are very important to you. *I always value his opinion.* **2** to judge how much money something could be sold for *The ring was valued at $1000.*

values /'vælju:z/ *noun* **[plural]** your beliefs about what is morally right and wrong and what is most important in life

valve /vælv/ *noun* **[C]** something that opens and closes to control the flow of liquid or gas

vampire /'væmpaɪǝr/ *noun* **[C]** in stories, a dead person who bites people's necks and drinks their blood

van /væn/ *noun* **[C]** a vehicle that is used for carrying things but which is smaller than a truck ⊃See picture at **vehicle**.

vandal /'vændⁿl/ *noun* **[C]** someone who intentionally damages things in public places *Vandals had smashed the shop window.*

vandalism /'vændⁿlɪzⁿm/ *noun* **[U]** the crime of intentionally damaging things in public places

vandalize (*also* UK -ise) /'vændⁿlaɪz/ *verb* **[T]** to intentionally damage things in public places

vanguard /'vænɡɑːd/ *noun* **in the vanguard of sth** involved in the most recent changes in technology and understanding *Libraries are in the vanguard of the electronic revolution.*

vanilla /vǝ'nɪlǝ/ *noun* **[U]** a substance that is used to give flavour to some sweet foods *vanilla ice cream*

vanish /'vænɪʃ/ *verb* **[I]** to disappear suddenly *The sun vanished behind the trees.* ○ *The report mysteriously vanished from the files.* ⊃See also: disappear/vanish into thin **air**¹.

vanity /'vænǝti/ *noun* **[U]** when someone thinks they are very attractive and is too interested in their own appearance

vantage point /'vɑːntɪdʒˌpɔɪnt/ *noun* **[C]** **1** the way you think about a subject when you are in a particular situation *From my vantage point, it is difficult to see how things can improve.* **2** a place from which you can see something very well

vapour UK (*US* vapor) /'veɪpǝr/ *noun* **[U]** many small drops of liquid in the air which look like a cloud

variable¹ /'veǝriǝbl/ *adjective* changing often *The sound quality on the recording is variable.* ● **variability** /ˌveǝriǝ'bɪlǝti/ *noun* **[U]**

variable² /'veǝriǝbl/ *noun* **[C]** something that changes in different situations

variance /'veǝriǝns/ *noun* *formal* **at variance with sb/sth** If two things or people are at variance with each other, they do not agree or are very different. *The statement seems to be at variance with government policy.*

variant /'veǝriǝnt/ *noun* **[C]** something that is a slightly different form from the usual one *There are several variants of the virus.* ○ *spelling variants*

variation /ˌveǝri'eɪʃⁿn/ *noun* **1** **[C, U]** a difference in amount or quality *variations in price* **2** **[C]** something that is slightly different from the usual form *It's a variation on the standard apple pie.*

varied /'veǝrɪd/ *adjective* consisting of many different types of things *a long and varied career*

⚬**variety** /vǝ'raɪǝti/ *noun* **1** **a variety of sth/sb** many different types of things or people *Ben has done a variety of jobs.* **2** **[C]** a different type of something *a new variety of potato* **3** **[U]** a lot of different activities, situations, people, etc *I need more variety in my life.*

⚬**various** /'veǝriǝs/ *adjective* many different *They have offices in various parts of the country.* ○ *I started learning Spanish for various reasons.*

variously /'veǝriǝsli/ *adverb* in many different ways *The event was variously described as "terrible", "shocking", and "unbelievable".*

varnish¹ /'vɑːnɪʃ/ *noun* **[C, U]** a clear liquid that you paint onto wood to protect it and make it shine ⊃See also: nail **polish**.

varnish² /'vɑːnɪʃ/ *verb* **[T]** to put varnish on a surface

vary /'veǝri/ *verb* **1** [BE DIFFERENT] **[I]** If things of the same type vary, they are different from each other. *Car prices vary greatly across Europe.* ○ *Roses vary widely in size and shape.* **2** [CHANGE] **[I]** to change *Temperatures vary* *depending on the time of year.* **3** [INTENTIONALLY CHANGE] [T] to often change something that you do *I try to vary what I eat.*

vase /vɑːz/ [US] /veɪs/ *noun* [C] a container that you put flowers in

vase

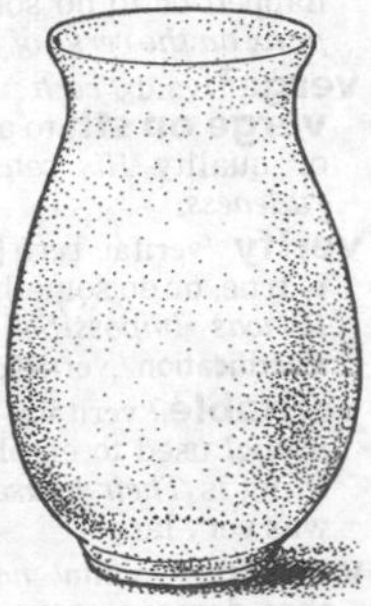

vasectomy /vəˈsektəmi/ *noun* [C] a medical operation that is done to stop a man having children

vast /vɑːst/ *adjective* extremely big *a vast amount of money* ○ *vast forest areas*

vastly /ˈvɑːstli/ *adverb* very much *Life now is vastly different from 100 years ago.*

VAT /ˌviːeɪˈtiː/ *noun* [U] *abbreviation for* value added tax: a tax on goods and services in the UK

vault¹ /vɔːlt/ *noun* [C] **1** a special room in a bank where money, jewellery, and other valuable objects are kept **2** a room under a church where people are buried

vault² /vɔːlt/ *verb* [I, T] to jump over something by first putting your hands on it *Rick vaulted the gate and ran off.* ➲See also: **pole vault**.

VCR /ˌviːsiːˈɑːʳ/ *mainly US* (*UK* **video**) *noun* [C] *abbreviation for* video cassette recorder: a machine that you use for recording television programmes and playing videos (= recorded films or programmes) ➲See colour picture **The Living Room** at page Centre 4.

VDU /ˌviːdiːˈjuː/ *noun* [C] *UK abbreviation for* visual display unit: a machine with a screen that shows information from a computer

've /v/ *short for* have *I've already eaten.*

veal /viːl/ *noun* [U] meat from a very young cow

veer /vɪəʳ/ *verb* **veer across/off/towards, etc** to suddenly change direction *The car veered off the road and hit a tree.*

veg /vedʒ/ *noun* [C, U] *plural* **veg** *UK informal short for* vegetables ***fruit and veg***

vegan /ˈviːgən/ *noun* [C] someone who does not eat meat, fish, eggs, milk, or cheese • **vegan** *adjective*

🔑**vegetable** /ˈvedʒtəbl/ *noun* [C] a plant that you eat, for example potatoes, onions, beans, etc ➲See colour picture **Fruit and Vegetables** on page Centre 10.

vegetarian¹ /ˌvedʒɪˈteəriən/ *noun* [C] someone who does not eat meat or fish

vegetarian² /ˌvedʒɪˈteəriən/ *adjective* not eating, containing, or using meat or fish *All her children are vegetarian.* ○ *a vegetarian restaurant/pizza*

vegetation /ˌvedʒɪˈteɪʃᵊn/ *noun* [U] the plants and trees that grow in a particular area

veggie /ˈvedʒi/ *noun* [C] *UK informal* a vegetarian • **veggie** *adjective*

vehement /ˈviːəmənt/ *adjective, formal* showing strong, often negative, feelings about something *vehement criticism/opposition* • **vehemently** *adverb*

vehicles

🔑**vehicle** /ˈviːɪkl/ *noun* **1** [C] *formal* something such as a car or bus that takes people from one place to another, especially using roads **2 a vehicle for sth/doing sth** something that you use as a way of telling people your ideas or opinions *The paper was merely a vehicle for his political beliefs.*

veil /veɪl/ *noun* **1** [C] a thin piece of material that covers a woman's face **2 draw a veil over sth** *UK* to not talk any more about a subject because it could cause trouble or embarrassment

veiled /veɪld/ *adjective* said so that the true meaning or purpose is not clear ***veiled criticism***

vein /veɪn/ *noun* [C] **1** one of the tubes in your body that carries blood to your heart **2** one of the thin lines on a leaf **3 in the same vein** in the same style of speaking or writing

Velcro /ˈvelkrəʊ/ *noun* [U] *trademark* material that consists of two pieces of cloth that stick together, used to fasten clothes

velocity /vɪˈlɒsəti/ *noun* [C, U] in science, the speed at which something moves

velvet /ˈvelvɪt/ *noun* [U] cloth that has a thick, soft surface on one side *a black velvet jacket*

vendetta /venˈdetə/ *noun* [C] when someone tries to do something bad to someone over a period of time because they have been treated badly by them *He had a **vendetta against** the company after he lost his job.*

vending machine /ˈvendɪŋməˌʃiːn/ *noun* [C] a machine that sells drinks, cigarettes, etc

vendor /ˈvendɔːʳ/ *noun* [C] **1** someone who sells something outside *an ice cream vendor* **2** *formal* a company that sells goods or services

veneer /vəˈnɪəʳ/ *noun* **1** [C, U] a thin layer of wood that covers a piece of furniture that is made of a cheaper material **2 a veneer of sth** *formal* a way of behaving that is not sincere and hides someone's real character or emotions *a thin veneer of calm/respectability*

venerable /ˈvenᵊrəbl/ *adjective* old and very much respected *a **venerable institution**/tradition*

venetian blind /vənˌiːʃᵊnˈblaɪnd/ *noun* [C] a covering for a window that is made from long,

V

flat, horizontal pieces of metal or wood which you can move to let in light

vengeance /ˈvendʒᵊns/ *noun* **1** [U] when you do something bad to someone who has done something bad to you, or the feeling of wanting to do this *an act of vengeance* **2 with a vengeance** If something happens with a vengeance, it happens a lot or in a very strong way. *The disease swept across the country with a vengeance.*

vengeful /ˈvendʒfᵊl/ *adjective formal* wanting vengeance

venison /ˈvenɪsᵊn/ *noun* [U] meat from a deer

venom /ˈvenəm/ *noun* [U] **1** poison that some snakes and insects produce **2** a feeling of extreme anger or hate *Much of his venom was directed at his boss.* • **venomous** *adjective* containing or involving venom

vent¹ /vent/ *noun* [C] a hole in a wall or machine that lets air in and allows smoke or smells to go out

vent² /vent/ *verb* **vent your anger/frustration, etc** to do or say something to show your anger or another strong, bad feeling

ventilate /ˈventɪleɪt/ *verb* [T] to let air come into and go out of a room or building • **ventilation** /ˌventɪˈleɪʃᵊn/ *noun* [U] *a ventilation system*

venture¹ /ˈventʃəʳ/ *noun* [C] a new activity that may not be successful *a* ***business venture*** ➲See also: **joint venture.**

venture² /ˈventʃəʳ/ *verb formal* **1 venture into/out/outside, etc** to leave a safe place and go somewhere that may involve risks *If the snow stops I might venture out.* **2** [T] to be brave enough to say something that might be criticized *I didn't dare* ***venture an opinion.***

venue /ˈvenjuː/ *noun* [C] a place where a sports game, musical performance, or special event happens

Venus /ˈviːnəs/ *noun* [no plural] the planet that is second from the Sun, after Mercury and before the Earth

veranda (*also* **verandah**) /vəˈrændə/ *noun* [C] a room that is joined to the outside of a house and has a roof and floor but no outside wall

⊶**verb** /vɜːb/ *noun* a word that is used to say that someone does something or that something happens. For example the words 'arrive', 'make', 'be', and 'feel' are verbs. ➲See also: **auxiliary verb, modal verb, phrasal verb.**

verbal /ˈvɜːbᵊl/ *adjective* **1** spoken and not written *a verbal promise* **2** relating to words or the use of words *verbal ability/skills* • **verbally** *adverb*

verbatim /vɜːˈbeɪtɪm/ *adjective, adverb* using the exact words that were originally used

WORD PARTNERS FOR ***verdict***

deliver/reach/return a verdict • **a guilty/not guilty** verdict

verdict /ˈvɜːdɪkt/ *noun* [C] **1** a decision in a court of law saying if someone is guilty or not *a* ***guilty verdict*** ○ *The jury took nine hours to* ***reach a verdict.*** **2** someone's opinion about something after experiencing it, often for the first time *You tried out that Italian restaurant? What was the verdict?*

verge¹ /vɜːdʒ/ *noun* [C] **1** *UK* the edge of a road or path that is usually covered in grass **2 be on the verge of sth/doing sth** to be going to happen or to do something very soon *a company on the verge of financial disaster*

verge² /vɜːdʒ/ *verb*

verge on sth to almost be a particular state or quality *His constant questions verged on rudeness.*

verify /ˈverɪfaɪ/ *verb* [T] to prove that something is true, or do something to discover if it is true *It was impossible to verify her statement.* • **verification** /ˌverɪfɪˈkeɪʃᵊn/ *noun* [U]

veritable /ˈverɪtəbl/ *adjective* [always before noun] *formal* used to emphasize how extreme something is *Their house was a veritable palace* (= was very large).

vermin /ˈvɜːmɪn/ *noun* [plural] small animals that damage crops and can give people diseases

versatile /ˈvɜːsətaɪl/ [US] /ˈvɜːrsətᵊl/ *adjective* **1** having many different skills *a versatile player/performer* **2** useful for doing a lot of different things *a versatile tool* • **versatility** /ˌvɜːsəˈtɪləti/ *noun* [U]

verse /vɜːs/ *noun* **1** [C] one of the parts that a song or poem is divided into *I only know the first verse.* **2** [U] words that are in the form of poetry *The story was told in verse.*

WORD PARTNERS FOR ***version***

a new/the latest version • a version **of** sth • the **original** version

⊶**version** /ˈvɜːʃᵊn/ *noun* [C] **1** one form of something that is slightly different to other forms of the same thing *I saw the original version of the film.* **2** someone's description of what has happened *Bates gave his version of events to the police.*

versus /ˈvɜːsəs/ *preposition* **1** used to say that one team or person is competing against another *Tomorrow's game is Newcastle versus Arsenal.* **2** used to compare two things or ideas, especially when you have to choose between them *private education versus state education*

vertical /ˈvɜːtɪkᵊl/ *adjective* pointing straight up from a surface *a vertical line* • **vertically** *adverb* ➲See picture at **horizontal.**

vertigo /ˈvɜːtɪgəʊ/ *noun* [U] when you feel slightly ill because you are in a high place and feel as if you might fall

verve /vɜːv/ *noun* [U] *formal* energy and enthusiasm

⊶**very¹** /ˈveri/ *adverb* **1** used to emphasize an adjective or adverb *She was very pleased.* ○ *Marie speaks very slowly.* ○ *Thank you very much.* **2 not very good/tall/happy, etc** not good, happy, etc *The film wasn't very good.*

very² /ˈveri/ *adjective* [always before noun] used to emphasize a noun *This is the very house where we stayed.*

vessel /ˈvesᵊl/ *noun* [C] **1** *formal* a ship or large boat **2** *old-fashioned* a container for liquids ➲See also: **blood vessel.**

V

vest /vest/ *noun* [C] **1** *UK* (*US* **undershirt**) a piece of underwear that you wear under a shirt **2** *US* (*UK* **waistcoat**) a piece of clothing with buttons at the front and no sleeves, that you wear over a shirt ➲See colour picture **Clothes** on page Centre 9.

vested interest /ˌvestɪd'ɪntrest/ *noun* [C] If you have a vested interest in something, you want it to happen because it will give you advantages.

vestige /'vestɪdʒ/ *noun* [C] a very small amount of something that still exists after most of it has gone *There is still a vestige of hope that she might be found alive.*

vet¹ /vet/ *noun* [C] someone whose job is to give medical care to animals that are ill or hurt

vet² /vet/ *verb* [T] **vetting**, *past* **vetted** to look at details of someone's life, in order to make sure that they are suitable for a particular job [often passive] *Applicants for the job are carefully vetted.*

veteran /'vetᵊrᵊn/ *noun* [C] **1** someone who has been in an army or navy during a war *a veteran of World War Two* **2** someone who has done a job or activity for a long time *a 20-year veteran of BBC news*

veterinarian /ˌvetᵊrɪ'neəriən/ *noun* [C] *US* a vet

veterinary /'vetᵊrɪnᵊri/ *adjective formal* relating to medical care given to animals that are ill or hurt

'veterinary ˌsurgeon *noun* [C] *UK formal* a vet

veto¹ /'viːtəʊ/ *verb* [T] **vetoing**, *past* **vetoed** If someone in authority vetoes something, they do not allow it to happen, although other people have agreed to it. *The plan was vetoed by the President.*

veto² /'viːtəʊ/ *noun* [C, U] *plural* **vetoes** when someone in authority does not allow something to happen

vexed /vekst/ *adjective* **vexed question/issue, etc** a situation that causes problems and is difficult to deal with *the vexed issue of unemployment*

via /vaɪə/ *preposition* **1** going through or stopping at a place on the way to another place *The train to Utrecht goes via Amsterdam.* **2** using a particular machine, system, or person to send or receive something *I receive all my work via e-mail.*

viable /'vaɪəbl/ *adjective* effective and able to be successful *a **viable alternative** to nuclear power* ○ *an economically viable plan* • **viability** /ˌvaɪə'bɪləti/ *noun* [U]

viaduct /'vaɪədʌkt/ *noun* [C] a long, high bridge across a valley

vibes /vaɪbz/ *noun* [plural] *informal* the way a person or place makes you feel *I get **bad/good vibes** from her.*

vibrant /'vaɪbrənt/ *adjective* **1** full of excitement and energy *a vibrant city* ○ *a vibrant, young performer* **2** A vibrant colour is very bright.

vibrate /vaɪ'breɪt/ [US] /'vaɪbreɪt/ *verb* [I, T] to shake with small, quick movements or to make something shake this way *The music was so loud that the floor was vibrating.* • **vibration** /vaɪ'breɪʃᵊn/ *noun* [C, U]

vicar /'vɪkəʳ/ *noun* [C] a priest in some Christian churches

vicarage /'vɪkᵊrɪdʒ/ *noun* [C] the house where a vicar lives

vicarious /vɪ'keəriəs/ *adjective* [always before noun] A vicarious feeling is one you get from seeing or hearing about another person's experiences. *It gives me **vicarious pleasure** to watch him eat.*

vice /vaɪs/ *noun* **1** [BAD HABIT] [C] something bad that someone often does *Smoking is his only vice.* **2** [CRIME] [U] crime that involves sex or drugs **3** [TOOL] [C] *UK* (*US* **vise**) a tool used for holding something tightly while you cut it, make it smooth, etc ➲See picture at **tool**.

ˌvice 'president *noun* [C] **1** the person who is a rank lower than the president of a country **2** *US* someone who is responsible for part of a company *She's vice president of sales and marketing.*

vice versa /ˌvaɪs'vɜːsə/ *adverb* used for referring to the opposite of what you have just said *Never use indoor lights outside and vice versa.*

vicinity /vɪ'sɪnəti/ *noun* **in the vicinity (of sth)** *formal* in the area near a place *A number of buildings in the vicinity of the fire were damaged.*

vicious /'vɪʃəs/ *adjective* **1** violent and dangerous *a vicious attack on a child* ○ *a vicious dog* **2** intended to upset someone *a **vicious rumour*** • **viciously** *adverb*

ˌvicious 'circle (*also* **ˌvicious 'cycle**) *noun* [no plural] when one problem causes another problem which then makes the first problem worse

⊶**victim** /'vɪktɪm/ *noun* [C] someone who has suffered the effects of violence, illness, or bad luck *victims of crime* ○ *hurricane/flood victims*

victimize (*also UK* **-ise**) /'vɪktɪmaɪz/ *verb* [T] to treat someone unfairly because you do not like or approve of them *Ben feels he has been victimized by his teacher.*

victor /'vɪktəʳ/ *noun* [C] *formal* the person who wins a fight or competition

Victorian /vɪk'tɔːriən/ *adjective* from or relating to the period between 1837 and 1901 in Britain *a Victorian house*

victorious /vɪk'tɔːriəs/ *adjective* having won a fight or competition *a victorious army*

WORD PARTNERS FOR ***victory***

claim/secure victory • a **comfortable/easy/impressive** victory • a victory **for/over** sb

victory /'vɪktᵊri/ *noun* [C, U] when you win a fight or competition *Phoenix managed a 135-114 **victory over** Denver.*

⊶**video¹** /'vɪdiəʊ/ *noun* **1** [U] a film or television programme recorded on videotape *'Pride and Prejudice' has just come out **on video**.* **2** [C] something that you have recorded on videotape using a video camera *Caroline and Yann showed us their wedding video last night.* **3** [C] (*also* **VCR**) (*also* **video recorder**) a machine that you use for recording a television programme or watching a video ➲See colour picture **The Living Room** on page Centre 4.

V

video² /'vɪdiəʊ/ *verb* [T] **videoing,** *past* **videoed 1** to record a television program using a video recorder **2** to film something using a video camera

'**video ,camera** *noun* [C] a piece of equipment used to record something onto videotape

'**video ,clip** *noun* [C] a short video recording

'**video ,game** *noun* [C] a game in which you make pictures move on a screen

videophone /'vɪdiəʊ,fəʊn/ *noun* [C] a mobile phone that can record moving pictures

'**video rec,order** *noun* [C] a video machine

videotape /'vɪdiəʊteɪp/ *noun* [C, U] a thin strip of material inside a plastic box that is used for recording television programmes and films

vie /vaɪ/ *verb* [I] **vying,** *past* **vied** to try hard to do something more successfully than someone else *The children were vying for attention.* ○ [+ to do sth] *Film crews were vying with each other to get the best pictures.*

WORD PARTNERS FOR view

express/have/hold a view • strong views • in sb's view • sb's views about/on sth • an exchange of views

---

o⁓**view¹** /vjuː/ *noun* **1** [OPINION] [C] your opinion *We have different views about/on education.* ○ *In her view this is wrong.* **2** [THINGS YOU SEE] [C] the things that you can see from a place *There was a lovely view of the lake from the bedroom window.* **3** [ABILITY TO SEE] [no plural] how well you can see something from a particular place *We had a great view of the procession.* **4** [POSITION] [U] a position from which something can be seen *The house was hidden from view behind a wall.* ○ *He turned the corner and the harbour came into view.* **5 in full view of sb** happening where someone can easily see *All this happened in full view of the cameras.* **6 in view of sth** *formal* because of *In view of recent events, we have decided to cancel the meeting.* **7 with a view to doing sth** *formal* so that you can do something *He's doing some improvements on the house with a view to selling it.* ⊃See also: point of view.

COMMON LEARNER ERROR

view or **sight**?

View means the countryside, buildings, things, etc which you can see from a place, or how well you can see something. A **view** is usually pleasant.

We had a wonderful view from the aircraft.

~~We had a wonderful sight from the aircraft.~~

Sight means when you see something, or the ability to see.

The sight of blood makes me feel sick.

~~The view of blood makes me feel sick.~~

---

view² /vjuː/ *verb* [T] *formal* **1** to have a particular opinion about someone or something *In all three countries he is viewed as a terrorist.* **2** to watch something *They were able to view the city from a helicopter.*

viewer /'vjuːəʳ/ *noun* [C] someone who watches a television programme

viewpoint /'vjuːpɔɪnt/ *noun* [C] a way of thinking about a situation *From his viewpoint the action seemed entirely justified.*

vigil /'vɪdʒɪl/ *noun* [C, U] when people stay somewhere quietly in order to show that they support someone, disagree with someone, etc *an all-night vigil for peace*

vigilant /'vɪdʒɪlənt/ *adjective* watching carefully and always ready to notice anything dangerous or illegal *Police have asked people to be vigilant after yesterday's bomb attack.* • **vigilance** /'vɪdʒɪləns/ *noun* [U]

vigilante /,vɪdʒɪˈlænti/ *noun* [C] a member of a group of people who try to catch criminals and punish them without having any legal authority

vigor /'vɪgəʳ/ *noun* [U] *US spelling of* vigour

vigorous /'vɪgᵊrəs/ *adjective* **1** showing or needing a lot of physical energy *vigorous exercise* **2** showing strong, often negative, feelings about something *a vigorous debate* ○ *He was a vigorous opponent of the government.* • **vigorously** *adverb* *Bates vigorously* (= strongly) *denies murdering his wife.*

vigour *UK* (*US* vigor) /'vɪgəʳ/ *noun* [U] strength and energy *She set about her work with great vigour.*

vile /vaɪl/ *adjective* extremely unpleasant *a vile attack* ○ *The bathroom was vile.*

vilify /'vɪlɪfaɪ/ *verb* [T] *formal* to say bad things about someone so that other people will not like or approve of them

villa /'vɪlə/ *noun* [C] a large house, especially one used for holidays in a warm country

o⁓**village** /'vɪlɪdʒ/ *noun* [C] a place where people live in the countryside that includes buildings such as shops and a school but which is smaller than a town *She lives in a small village outside Oxford.* ○ *a village shop*

villager /'vɪlɪdʒəʳ/ *noun* [C] someone who lives in a village

villain /'vɪlən/ *noun* [C] a bad person in a film, book, etc

vindicate /'vɪndɪkeɪt/ *verb* [T] *formal* to prove that what someone said or did was right after people generally thought it was wrong • **vindication** /,vɪndɪˈkeɪʃᵊn/ *noun* [C, U] *formal*

vindictive /vɪnˈdɪktɪv/ *adjective* intending to harm or upset someone who has harmed or upset you

vine /vaɪn/ *noun* [C] a plant that grapes (= small, green or purple fruit used for making wine) grow on

vinegar /'vɪnɪgəʳ/ *noun* [U] a sour liquid that is used in cooking, often made from wine

vineyard /'vɪnjəd/ *noun* [C] an area of land where someone grows grapes (= small, green or purple fruit) for making wine

vintage¹ /'vɪntɪdʒ/ *adjective* **1** [WINE] Vintage wine is wine of a good quality that was made in a particular year. **2** [VERY GOOD] having all the best or most typical qualities of something, especially from the past *a vintage Hollywood movie* **3** [CAR] A vintage car was made between 1919 and 1930.

vintage² /'vɪntɪdʒ/ *noun* [C] the wine that was

made in a particular year *The 1993 vintage is one of the best.*

vinyl /ˈvaɪnᵊl/ *noun* [U] a type of very strong plastic

viola /viˈəʊlə/ *noun* [C] a wooden instrument, larger than a violin, that you hold against your neck and play by moving a special stick across strings

violate /ˈvaɪəleɪt/ *verb* [T] *formal* **1** to not obey a law, rule, or agreement *Countries that violate international law will be dealt with severely.* **2** to not allow someone something that they should morally be allowed to have *They were accused of violating human rights.* • **violation** /ˌvaɪəˈleɪʃᵊn/ *noun* [C, U] *a violation of privacy*

WORD PARTNERS FOR ***violence***

erupt into/renounce/use violence • **escalating/extreme/gratuitous** violence • violence **against/towards** sb

⊶**violence** /ˈvaɪəlᵊns/ *noun* [U] **1** when someone tries to hurt or kill someone else *an act of violence* ○ *A number of people were killed in the violence.* ○ ***Violence against*** *women has increased in recent years.* **2** extreme force and energy, especially of something causing damage *Such was the violence of the explosion that three buildings collapsed.*

⊶**violent** /ˈvaɪəlᵊnt/ *adjective* **1** [ACTION] involving violence *a victim of* ***violent crime*** ○ *a violent protest* ○ *I don't like violent films* (= films that show violence). **2** [PERSON] likely to hurt or kill someone else *a violent criminal* **3** [DAMAGE] sudden and causing damage *a violent explosion/storm* **4** [EMOTIONS] showing very strong feelings, especially anger *violent emotions* • **violently** *adverb* ➲See also: **non-violent.**

violet /ˈvaɪələt/ *noun* **1** [C] a small plant with a small, purple flower **2** [U] a pale purple colour

violin /ˌvaɪəˈlɪn/ *noun* [C] a wooden musical instrument that you hold against your neck and play by moving a bow (= special stick) across strings • **violinist** /vaɪəˈlɪnɪst/ *noun* [C] someone who plays a violin

violin

VIP /ˌviːaɪˈpiː/ *noun* [C] *abbreviation for* very important person: someone who is famous or powerful and is treated in a special way *The airport has a separate lounge for VIPs.*

viper /ˈvaɪpəʳ/ *noun* [C] a small, poisonous snake

viral /ˈvaɪrᵊl/ *adjective* caused by or relating to a virus (= infectious organism) *a viral infection*

virgin¹ /ˈvɜːdʒɪn/ *noun* [C] someone who has never had sex

virgin² /ˈvɜːdʒɪn/ *adjective* Virgin land, forest, etc has not been used or damaged by people.

virginity /vəˈdʒɪnəti/ *noun* [U] when someone has never had sex *Emma* ***lost her virginity*** (= had sex for the first time) *at sixteen.*

Virgo /ˈvɜːgəʊ/ *noun* [C, U] the sign of the zodiac which relates to the period of 23 August - 22 September, or a person born during this period ➲See picture at **zodiac.**

virile /ˈvɪraɪl/ [US] /ˈvɪrᵊl/ *adjective* A virile man is strong and has sexual energy. • **virility** /vɪˈrɪləti/ *noun* [U]

virtual /ˈvɜːtʃuəl/ *adjective* [always before noun] **1** almost a particular thing or quality *They played the game in virtual silence.* **2** using computer images and sounds that make you think an imagined situation is real *a virtual art gallery*

virtually /ˈvɜːtʃuəli/ *adverb* almost *They're virtually the same.* ○ *I've virtually finished.*

ˌ**virtual reˈality** *noun* [U] when a computer produces images and sounds that make you feel an imagined situation is real

virtue /ˈvɜːtjuː/ *noun* **1** [ADVANTAGE] [C, U] an advantage or useful quality *The great* ***virtue*** *of having a small car is that you can park it easily.* **2** [GOOD QUALITY] [C] a good quality that someone has *Patience is not among his virtues.* **3** [MORAL BEHAVIOUR] [U] behaviour that is morally good **4 by virtue of sth** *formal* because of something *She succeeded by virtue of hard work rather than talent.*

virtuoso /ˌvɜːtjuˈəʊsəʊ/ *noun* [C] someone who is extremely good at doing something, especially playing a musical instrument

virtuous /ˈvɜːtʃuəs/ *adjective* behaving in a good and moral way • **virtuously** *adverb*

virulent /ˈvɪrʊlᵊnt/ *adjective* **1** A virulent disease or poison causes severe illness very quickly. **2** *formal* criticizing or hating someone or something very much *a virulent attack on the government*

WORD PARTNERS FOR ***virus***

carry/contract/have/transmit a virus • a **deadly/rare** virus

⊶**virus** /ˈvaɪərəs/ *noun* [C] **1** an infectious organism too small to be seen that causes disease, or an illness that it causes *The doctor says I've got a virus.* **2** a program that is secretly put onto a computer in order to destroy the information that is stored on it

visa /ˈviːzə/ *noun* [C] an official mark in your passport (= document which proves your nationality) that allows you to enter or leave a particular country *She went to Miami* ***on*** *a* ***tourist visa.***

vis-à-vis /ˌviːzəˈviː/ *preposition* relating to something, or in comparison with something *I have to speak to James vis-à-vis the conference arrangements.*

vise /vaɪs/ *noun* [C] *US spelling of* vice (= a tool used for holding something tightly while you cut it, make it smooth, etc) ➲See picture at **tool.**

visibility /ˌvɪzəˈbɪləti/ *noun* [U] how far or how well you can see because of weather conditions *good/poor visibility* ○ *It was foggy and visibility was down to 50 metres.*

visible /ˈvɪzəbl/ *adjective* able to be seen *The fire* ***was visible from*** *five kilometres away.* ➲Opposite **invisible.** • **visibly** *adverb She was visibly upset.*

vision /ˈvɪʒᵊn/ *noun* **1** [IDEA] [C] an idea or image

V

in your mind of what something could be like in the future *a vision of a better society* **2** [SEE] [U] the ability to see *He has poor vision in his left eye.* ○ *Everyone's vision suffers as they get older.* **3** [ABILITY TO PLAN] [U] the ability to make plans for the future that are imaginative and wise *As a leader, he lacked vision.* **4** [RELIGION] [C] when you see someone or something that no one else can see as part of a religious experience

visionary /ˈvɪʒənəri/ *adjective* able to make plans for the future that are imaginative and wise *a visionary leader* • **visionary** *noun* [C]

⊶**visit**[1] /ˈvɪzɪt/ *verb* [I, T] **1** [SEE A PERSON] to go to someone's home and spend time with them *We have friends coming to visit this weekend.* ○ *We're visiting John's parents next week.* **2** [SEE A PLACE] to go to a place and spend a short amount of time there *Did you visit St Petersburg while you were in Russia?* **3** [INTERNET] to look at a website *Do you know how many people visit the website each month?*

WORD PARTNERS FOR ***visit***

a visit **to** sth • a visit **from** sb • **on** a visit • **pay** sb a visit • **have** a visit **from** sb • **a brief/flying** visit

⊶**visit**[2] /ˈvɪzɪt/ *noun* [C] when you visit a place or a person *the President's **visit to** Hong Kong* ○ *Why don't you **pay** him **a visit*** (= visit him)? ○ *I **had a visit from** an old friend this weekend.*

⊶**visitor** /ˈvɪzɪtəʳ/ *noun* [C] someone who visits a person or place *The museum attracts large numbers of visitors.* ○ *We had a visitor this afternoon.*

visor /ˈvaɪzəʳ/ *noun* [C] **1** [PART OF HAT] the part of a helmet (= hard hat that protects your head) that you can pull down to cover your face **2** [HAT] a hat that has a curved part above your eyes to protect them from the sun ➲See colour picture **Clothes** on page Centre 9. **3** [CAR] the parts in the front window of a car that you pull down to protect your eyes from the sun ➲See colour picture **Car** on page Centre 7.

vista /ˈvɪstə/ *noun* [C] a view, especially a beautiful view that you look at from a high place

visual /ˈvɪʒuəl/ *adjective* relating to seeing *The film has some powerful **visual effects**.* • **visually** *adverb visually appealing*

ˌ**visual ˈaid** *noun* [C] something that helps you understand or remember information, such as a picture or film

visualize (*also UK* **-ise**) /ˈvɪʒuəlaɪz/ *verb* [T] to create a picture in your mind of someone or something *I was very surprised when I met Geoff - I'd visualized someone much older.* • **visualization** /ˌvɪʒuəlaɪˈzeɪʃən/ *noun* [U]

vital /ˈvaɪtəl/ *adjective* **1** necessary *Tourism is **vital to** the country's economy.* ○ [+ (that)] *It's vital that you send off this form today.* **2** *formal* full of energy

vitality /vaɪˈtæləti/ *noun* [U] energy and strength *At 48, he still projects an image of youth and vitality.*

vitally /ˈvaɪtəli/ *adverb* in a very important way *Safety at work is **vitally important**.*

vitamin /ˈvɪtəmɪn/ [US] /ˈvaɪtəmɪn/ *noun* [C] one of a group of natural substances in food that you need to be healthy *Oranges are full of vitamin C.*

vitriolic /ˌvɪtriˈɒlɪk/ *adjective formal* criticizing someone in a very severe and unpleasant way

viva /ˈvaɪvə/ *noun* [C] *UK* a spoken examination at university

vivacious /vɪˈveɪʃəs/ *adjective* A vivacious person, especially a woman, is full of energy and enthusiasm.

vivid /ˈvɪvɪd/ *adjective* **1** Vivid descriptions or memories produce strong, clear images in your mind. *He gave a very **vivid description** of life in Caracas.* **2** A vivid colour is very bright. • **vividly** *adverb I remember my first day at school very vividly.*

vivisection /ˌvɪvɪˈsekʃən/ *noun* [U] when living animals are used in scientific experiments, especially in order to discover the effects of new drugs

vixen /ˈvɪksən/ *noun* [C] a female fox (= wild dog with red-brown fur)

V-neck /ˈviːnek/ *noun* [C] a V-shaped opening for your neck on a piece of clothing, or a sweater, dress, etc with this opening *a V-neck jumper* • **V-necked** /viːˈnekt/ *adjective a V-necked dress*

WORD PARTNERS FOR ***vocabulary***

a **limited/wide** vocabulary • be **in** sb's vocabulary • **widen** your vocabulary

vocabulary /vəʊˈkæbjələri/ *noun* **1** [WORDS] [C, U] all the words you know in a particular language *Reading helps to widen your vocabulary.* **2** [LANGUAGE] [no plural] all the words that exist in a language, or that are used when discussing a particular subject *Computing has its own specialist vocabulary.* **3** [LIST] [no plural] a list of words and their meanings

vocal /ˈvəʊkəl/ *adjective* **1** expressing your opinions in a strong way *She is a **vocal supporter** of women's rights.* **2** involving or relating to the voice, especially singing *vocal music*

ˈ**vocal ˌcords** (*also* **vocal chords**) *noun* [plural] folds of skin at the top of your throat that make sounds when air from your lungs moves over them

vocalist /ˈvəʊkəlɪst/ *noun* [C] the person who sings in a group of people who play popular music

vocals /ˈvəʊkəlz/ *noun* [plural] the part of a piece of music that is sung

vocation /vəʊˈkeɪʃən/ *noun* [C, U] a strong feeling that you are right for a particular type of work, or a job that gives you this feeling *He knew that teaching was his true vocation.*

vocational /vəʊˈkeɪʃənəl/ *adjective* Vocational education and skills prepare you for a particular type of work. *The college offers both vo-*

cational and academic courses.

vociferous /vəʊ'sɪfᵊrəs/ *adjective formal* expressing your opinions in a loud and strong way

vodka /'vɒdkə/ *noun* **[C, U]** a strong alcoholic drink that is popular in Russia and Poland

vogue /vəʊg/ *noun* **[U, no plural]** If there is a vogue for something, it is very fashionable.

WORD PARTNERS FOR ***voice***

a deep/husky/low voice • **lose** your voice • **lower/raise** your voice • **in** a [bored/stern, etc.] voice • your **tone of** voice

🔑**voice¹** /vɔɪs/ *noun* **1** [SOUNDS] **[C]** the sounds that you make when you speak or sing *I could hear voices in the next room.* ○ *Jessie has a beautiful singing voice.* ○ *Could you please **keep your voices down*** (= speak more quietly)? **2 lose your voice** to become unable to speak, often because of an illness *She had a bad cold and was losing her voice.* **3** [OPINION] **[C]** someone's opinion about a particular subject *The programme gives people the opportunity to make their voices heard.* **4** [PERSON] **[no plural]** someone who expresses the opinions or wishes of a group of people *It's important that students have a voice on the committee.* ➲See also: **the passive**.

voice² /vɔɪs/ *verb* **[T]** to say what you think about a particular subject

voice-activated /ˌvɔɪs'æktɪveɪtɪd/ *adjective* A machine that is voice-activated can recognize and follow spoken instructions.

'voice ˌmail *noun* **[U]** an electronic telephone answering system

void¹ /vɔɪd/ *adjective* **1 [never before noun]** not legally or officially acceptable *The contracts were **declared void**.* **2 be void of sth** *formal* to be without something *His last statement was entirely void of meaning.*

void² /vɔɪd/ *noun* **[no plural] 1** when someone or something important is not now in your life and you are unhappy *Her husband's death **left a void** in her life.* **2** a large hole or empty space

vol *written abbreviation for* volume

volcano

volatile /'vɒlətaɪl/ [US] /'vɑːlətᵊl/ *adjective* **1** A volatile person can suddenly become angry or violent. **2** A volatile situation might suddenly change. *a volatile political situation* • **volatility** /ˌvɒlə'tɪləti/ *noun* **[U]**

volcano /vɒl'keɪnəʊ/ *noun* **[C]** *plural* **volcanoes** or **volcanos** a mountain with a large hole at the top which sometimes explodes and produces hot, melted rock and smoke • **volcanic** /vɒl'kænɪk/ *adjective* relating to a volcano *volcanic ash/activity/rock*

vole /vəʊl/ *noun* **[C]** a small animal like a mouse

volition /vəʊ'lɪʃᵊn/ *noun* **[U]** *formal* the power to make your own decisions *He left the firm **of his own volition*** (= because he decided to).

volley¹ /'vɒli/ *noun* **1 [C]** in sports, a kick or hit in which a player returns a ball before it touches the ground *That was a marvellous backhand volley from Andy Murray.* **2 a volley of shots/gunfire, etc** when a lot of bullets are shot at the same time *A volley of bullets ripped through the floorboards.* **3 a volley of abuse/complaints, etc** a lot of insults/complaints, etc said at the same time *I'm afraid my proposal was met with a volley of criticisms.*

volley² /'vɒli/ *verb* **[I, T]** in sports, to return a ball by kicking or hitting it before it touches the ground

volleyball

volleyball /'vɒlibɔːl/ *noun* **[U]** a game in which two teams use their hands to hit a ball over a net without allowing it to touch the ground ➲See colour picture **Sports 2** on page Centre 15.

volt /vɒlt/ (*written abbreviation* **V**) *noun* **[C]** a unit for measuring the force of an electric current *Electricity in Britain is 240 volts, AC.*

voltage /'vəʊltɪdʒ/ *noun* **[C, U]** the force of an electric current, measured in volts

volume /'vɒljuːm/ *noun* **1** [SOUND] **[U]** the level of sound produced by a television, radio, etc *to turn the volume up/down* **2** [AMOUNT] **[U]** the number or amount of something, especially when it is large *the volume of work involved* **3** [SPACE] **[U]** the amount of space inside an object *Which of the bottles has the larger volume?* **4** [BOOK] **[C]** a book, especially one of a set *a new dictionary in two volumes*

voluminous /və'luːmɪnəs/ *adjective formal* very large *voluminous trousers*

voluntary /'vɒləntᵊri/ *adjective* **1** Voluntary work is done without being paid and usually involves helping people. *She does **voluntary work** for the Red Cross.* ○ ***voluntary organizations*** **2** done or given because you want to and not because you have been forced to ***voluntary contributions*** ➲Opposite **involuntary**. • **voluntarily** /ˌvɒlən'teərᵊli/ *adverb She left voluntarily.*

volunteer¹ /ˌvɒlən'tɪəʳ/ *verb* **1** [OFFER] **[I, T]** to offer to do something without being asked or told to do it **[+ to do sth]** *Rob volunteered to look after the kids.* **2** [ARMY] **[I]** to join the army, navy, etc without being officially told to join *In 1939 he **volunteered for** active service.* **3** [INFORMATION] **[T]** to give information without being asked *No one volunteered the truth.*

volunteer² /ˌvɒlən'tɪəʳ/ *noun* **[C] 1** someone who does work without being paid, especially work that involves helping people *a Red Cross volunteer* **2** someone who does or gives something because they want to and not because they have been forced to *Any volunteers to help me move these books?*

V

voluptuous /vəˈlʌptʃuəs/ *adjective* A voluptuous woman has a sexually attractive body, often with large breasts.

vomit[1] /ˈvɒmɪt/ *verb* [I, T] If someone vomits, the food or liquid that was in their stomach comes up and out of their mouth. *She was vomiting blood.*

vomit[2] /ˈvɒmɪt/ *noun* [U] the food or liquid that comes from your mouth when you vomit

voodoo /ˈvuːduː/ *noun* [U] a religion involving magic and praying to spirits

voracious /vəˈreɪʃəs/ *adjective* wanting to do something a lot, especially wanting to eat a lot of food *She has a voracious appetite.* ○ *a voracious reader of historical novels* • **voraciously** *adverb* • **voracity** /vəˈræsəti/ *noun* [U]

o=**vote**[1] /vəʊt/ *verb* [I, T] to show your choice or opinion in an election or meeting by writing a cross on an official piece of paper or putting your hand up *Who did you vote for?* ○ *The unions voted against strike action.* ○ [+ to do sth] *Staff have voted to accept the pay offer.*

> WORD PARTNERS FOR **vote**
>
> **cast** your vote • a vote **against/for** sb/sth • a vote **on** sth

o=**vote**[2] /vəʊt/ *noun* [C] **1** CHOICE when someone shows their choice or opinion in an election or meeting by writing a cross on an official piece of paper or putting their hand up *He lost the election by twenty votes.* **2** DECIDE a way of making a decision by asking a group of people to vote *We called a meeting in order to take a vote on the proposal.* **3 the vote a** NUMBER OF VOTES the total number of votes given or received in an election *The Green party got 10% of the vote.* **b** PERMISSION TO VOTE when someone is officially allowed to vote *In some countries women still don't have the vote.*

voter /ˈvəʊtəʳ/ *noun* [C] someone who votes or who is officially allowed to vote

vouch /vaʊtʃ/ *verb*
vouch for sb/sth to say that you know from experience that something is true or good, or that someone has a good character

voucher /ˈvaʊtʃəʳ/ *noun* [C] a piece of paper that can be used instead of money to pay for goods or services *a discount voucher*

vow[1] /vaʊ/ *verb* [T] to make a serious promise or decision [+ (that)] *She vowed that she would never leave the children again.* ○ [+ to do sth] *I've vowed never to go there again.*

vow[2] /vaʊ/ *noun* [C] a serious promise or decision *marriage vows* ○ *I made a vow that I would write to him once a week.*

vowel /vaʊəl/ *noun* [C] a speech sound that you make with your lips and teeth open, shown in English by the letters 'a', 'e', 'i', 'o' or 'u'

voyage /ˈvɔɪdʒ/ *noun* [C] a long journey, especially by ship, or in space *The ship sank on its maiden voyage* (= first journey).

vs (*also UK* **v**) *preposition written abbreviation for* versus (= used to say that one team or person is competing against another)

vulgar /ˈvʌlgəʳ/ *adjective* **1** rude and likely to upset or anger people, especially by referring to sex and the body in an unpleasant way *vulgar jokes/language* **2** not showing good judgment about what is suitable or pleasant to look at *a vulgar shade of yellow* • **vulgarity** /vʌlˈgærəti/ *noun* [U]

vulnerable /ˈvʌlnərəbl/ *adjective* easy to hurt or attack physically or emotionally *She was a vulnerable sixteen-year-old.* ○ *The troops are in a vulnerable position.* ○ *He's more vulnerable to infection because of his injuries.* • **vulnerability** /ˌvʌlnərəˈbɪləti/ *noun* [U]

vulture /ˈvʌltʃəʳ/ *noun* [C] a large bird with no feathers on its head or neck that eats dead animals

vying /ˈvaɪɪŋ/ *present participle of* vie

V

Ww

W, w /'dʌblju:/ the twenty-third letter of the alphabet

W *written abbreviation for* watt (= a unit for measuring electrical power) *a 40W light bulb*

wacky /'wæki/ *adjective informal* unusual in a funny or surprising way *a wacky sense of humour*

wad /wɒd/ *noun* [C] **1** a thick pile of pieces of paper, especially paper money *a wad of cash* **2** a piece of soft material in the shape of a ball *a wad of UK cotton wool/ US cotton*

waddle /'wɒdl/ *verb* [I] A duck (= water bird) or fat person that waddles walks with short steps, moving from side to side.

wade /weɪd/ *verb* **wade across/through, etc** to walk through water *He waded across the river.* **wade through sth** to read a lot of boring or difficult information

wafer /'weɪfə'/ *noun* [C] a light, thin biscuit

waffle¹ /'wɒfl/ *noun* **1** [U] *informal* speech or writing that says nothing important **2** [C] a square, flat cake with a pattern of holes in it, eaten especially in the US

waffle² /'wɒfl/ (*also* **waffle on**) *verb* [I] *informal* to talk or write a lot and say nothing important

waft /wɒft/ *verb* **waft from/through, etc** to gradually move through the air *The smell of coffee wafted through the room.*

wag /wæg/ *verb* [I, T] **wagging**, *past* **wagged** **1** If a dog wags its tail, it moves it from side to side. **2** If you wag your finger, you move it from side to side, often to tell someone not to do something.

WORD PARTNERS FOR *wage*

earn a wage • a **decent** wage • a wage **increase/rise** • the **minimum** wage

wage¹ /weɪdʒ/ *noun* [no plural] (*also* **wages** [plural]) the amount of money a person regularly receives for their job *weekly wages* ○ *the minimum wage* ⊃See Common learner error at **pay**.

wage² /weɪdʒ/ *verb* **wage a battle/campaign/ war, etc** to fight or organize a series of activities in order to achieve something *They're currently waging a campaign to change the law.*

wager /'weɪdʒə'/ *verb* [T] to risk money on the result of a game, race, competition, etc • **wager** *noun* [C]

wagon /'wægən/ *noun* [C] a large vehicle with four large wheels pulled by horses

wail /weɪl/ *verb* [I, T] **1** to cry loudly because you are very unhappy *"I've lost my mummy," she wailed.* **2** If a siren (= loud noise to warn of danger) wails, it makes a noise. *Somewhere in the distance a police siren was wailing.* • **wail** *noun* [C]

waist /weɪst/ *noun* [C]   waist
1 the part around the middle of your body where you wear a belt *She had a 26 inch waist.* ⊃See colour picture **The Body** on page Centre 13.
2 the part of a piece of clothing that fits round the waist

waistband /'weɪstbænd/ *noun* [C] the strip of material at the top of a pair of trousers or a skirt that goes around the waist

waistcoat /'weɪstkəʊt/ *UK* (*US* **vest**) *noun* [C] a piece of clothing with buttons at the front and no sleeves, that you wear over a shirt ⊃See colour picture **Clothes** on page Centre 9.

waistline /'weɪstlaɪn/ *noun* [C] how big or small your waist is, or the part of a piece of clothing that goes around the waist

o-**wait¹** /weɪt/ *verb* [I] **1** to stay in a place until someone or something arrives or someone or something is ready for you *I'm waiting for Clive.* ○ *How long did you wait for a taxi?* ○ [+ to do sth] *I'm still waiting to use the phone.* **2** to not do something until something else happens *We'll wait till Jane gets here before we start eating.* **3 can't wait** *informal* used to say how excited you are about something that you are going to do [+ to do sth] *I can't wait to see him.* **4 keep sb waiting** to be late so that someone has to wait for you *I'm sorry to have kept you waiting.* **5 wait and see** to wait to discover what will happen *We'll wait and see what she says.* ⊃See also: be waiting in the **wings**.

COMMON LEARNER ERROR

wait or expect?

When you **wait**, you stay somewhere until a person or thing arrives or is ready.

I waited twenty minutes for the bus.

She's waiting for her exam results.

When you **expect** something, you think that it will happen.

I'm expecting the bus to arrive in about 5 minutes.

She expected to do well in the exam.

~~She waited to do well in the exam.~~

COMMON LEARNER ERROR

wait

Wait must always be followed by **for** or **to do sth**. It cannot be followed by the thing you are waiting for.

I am waiting for my mother.

~~I am waiting my mother.~~

wait about/around to stay in a place and do nothing while you wait for someone to arrive or something to happen

wait in *UK* to stay at home because you are expecting someone to visit or telephone you

wait on sb to bring a meal to someone, especially in a restaurant

wait up to not go to bed at night until some-one has come home *I'll be quite late, so don't wait up for me.*

WORD PARTNERS FOR *wait*

face/have a wait • an **agonizing/anxious/long** wait • the wait **for** sth • sth is (well) **worth** the wait

wait² /weɪt/ *noun* [no plural] when you stay in a place until someone or something arrives or someone or something is ready for you *We had a long wait at the airport.*

waiter /'weɪtə'/ *noun* [C] a man who works in a restaurant, bringing food to customers

'**waiting ,list** *noun* [C] a list of people who are waiting until it is their time to have or do something *a hospital waiting list*

'**waiting ,room** *noun* [C] a room in which people wait for something, for example to see a doctor or take a train

waitress /'weɪtrəs/ *noun* [C] a woman who works in a restaurant, bringing food to customers

waive /weɪv/ *verb* [T] **1** to allow someone not to obey the usual rule or not to pay the usual amount of money *He agreed to waive his fee to help us.* **2** to decide not to have something that you are allowed by law to have *She waived her right to have a lawyer representing her.*

○▪**wake¹** /weɪk/ (*also* wake up) *verb* [I, T] *past tense* woke *past participle* woken to stop sleeping or to make someone else stop sleeping *I've only just woken up.* ○ *Could you wake me up before you go?* ○ *You woke me up making so much noise.* ➜See colour picture **Phrasal Verbs** on page Centre 16.
wake up to sth to start to understand something that is important *We need to wake up to the fact that the Earth's resources are limited.*

wake² /weɪk/ *noun* **1** in the wake of sth after something has happened, and often because it has happened *Airport security was extra tight in the wake of last week's bomb attacks.* **2** [C] the waves behind a moving ship **3** [C] when people come together to remember someone who has recently died

'**wake-up ,call** *noun* [C] **1** a telephone call to wake you in the morning, especially when you are staying in a hotel **2** something bad that happens and shows you that you need to take action to change a situation

○▪**walk¹** /wɔːk/ *verb* **1** [I, T] to move forward by putting one foot in front of the other and then repeating the action *She walks to school.* ○ *We walked twenty miles in all.* **2 walk sb home/to sth** to walk with someone in order to guide them or keep them safe *He walked me to my house.* **3 walk the dog** to walk with a dog to give the dog exercise **4 walk all over sb** *informal* to treat someone badly

COMMON LEARNER ERROR

walk or **go on foot**?

The expression **go on foot** means **walk**, usually when you are describing how you get somewhere.

How do you get to school? I go on foot/I walk.

walk into sth to get a job easily
walk off with sth to win something easily *She walked off with the top prize.*
walk out to leave a job, meeting, or performance because you are angry or do not approve of something *He was so disgusted by the film he walked out.*
walk out on sb to suddenly leave your husband, wife, or partner and end your relationship with them *He walked out on his wife and kids.*

WORD PARTNERS FOR *walk*

go for/take a walk • a **brisk** walk • a **long/short** walk

○▪**walk²** /wɔːk/ *noun* **1** [C] a journey that you make by walking, often for enjoyment *We usually go for a walk on Sunday afternoons.* ○ *He took the dog for a walk.* **2 a short/ten-minute, etc walk** a journey that takes a short time/ten minutes, etc when you walk *The station is just a five-minute walk from the house.* **3** [C] a path or route where people can walk for enjoyment *There are some lovely walks in the forest.* **4 walk of life** People from different walks of life have different jobs and different experiences in life.

walker /'wɔːkə'/ *noun* [C] someone who walks for exercise or enjoyment

walkie talkie /,wɔːki'tɔːki/ *noun* [C] a radio that you carry with you and that lets you talk to someone else with a similar radio

Walkman /'wɔːkmən/ *noun* [C] *trademark* a small piece of equipment with parts that you put in your ears which allows you to listen to music that no one else can hear

○▪**wall** /wɔːl/ *noun* [C] **1** one of the vertical sides of a room or building *There were several large paintings on the wall.* **2** a vertical structure made of brick or stone that divides areas that are owned by different people *a garden wall* **3 drive sb up the wall** *informal* to make someone very angry *She drives me up the wall.* ➜See also: **fly²** on the wall, be banging your **head¹** against a brick wall.

walled /wɔːld/ *adjective* **walled garden/city** a garden/city with walls around it

wallet /'wɒlɪt/ (*also US* billfold) *noun* [C] a small, flat container for paper money and credit cards (= plastic cards used for paying with), usually used by a man

wallop /'wɒləp/ *verb* [T] *informal* to hit someone or something hard • **wallop** *noun* [no plural] *informal*

wallow /'wɒləʊ/ *verb* [I] **1** to allow yourself to feel too much sadness in a way that stops people respecting you *There's no use wallowing in self-pity.* **2** to lie or move around in soil or water, especially for pleasure

wallpaper /'wɔːl,peɪpə'/ *noun* [U] paper, usually with a pattern, that you decorate walls with • **wallpaper** *verb* [T]

'**Wall ,Street** *noun* the financial area of New York where shares (= small, equal parts of the value of a company) are bought and sold *The company's shares rose on Wall Street yesterday.*

wally /ˈwɒli/ *noun* [C] *UK informal* a silly person

walnut /ˈwɔːlnʌt/ *noun* **1** [C] a nut that is in two halves inside a brown shell, and whose surface has curves and folds in it **2** [U] the hard wood of the tree that produces walnuts, used to make furniture

walrus /ˈwɔːlrəs/ *noun* [C] a large sea animal that has two tusks (= long, pointed teeth that come out of the mouth)

waltz¹ /wɒls/ *noun* [C] a dance for two partners performed to music that has a rhythm of three beats, or the music for the dance

waltz² /wɒls/ *verb* [I] **1** to dance a waltz **2 waltz in/off, etc** to walk somewhere quickly and confidently, often in a way that annoys other people *You can't just waltz into my bedroom - it's private!*

wan /wɒn/ *adjective* pale and looking ill or tired

wand /wɒnd/ *noun* [C] a thin stick that someone who performs magic tricks holds in their hand

wander /ˈwɒndəʳ/ *verb* **1** [I, T] to walk slowly about a place without any purpose *They wandered aimlessly around the town.* **2** [I] (*also* **wander off**) to walk away from the place where you should be *He was here a moment ago - he must have wandered off.* **3 sb's attention/mind/ thoughts, etc wander** If someone's attention/ mind, etc wanders, they start thinking about one subject when they should be thinking about a different subject. *I was bored and my thoughts started to wander.*

wane /weɪn/ *verb* [I] to become less powerful, important, or popular *Interest in the product is starting to wane.*

wangle /ˈwæŋgl/ *verb* [T] *informal* to succeed in getting something that a lot of people want, by being clever or tricking someone *He managed to wangle an invitation to the party.*

o→**want¹** /wɒnt/ *verb* [T] **1** to hope to have or do something, or to wish for something *He wants a new car.* ○ [+ to do sth] *I don't want to talk about it.* ○ *You can't always do what you want.* ○ *We can go later if you want.* ○ *I want him to explain why.* **2** to need something *This soup wants more salt.* **3 want to do sth** *UK informal* used to give advice to someone *You want to go to bed earlier and then you won't be so tired.* **4 be wanted** to be needed for a particular activity or in a particular place *You're wanted on the phone.*

want something/someone to do something

Be careful to use the correct form after this expression. You cannot say 'that' after **want**.

I just want him to enjoy himself.

~~I just want that he enjoy himself.~~

They don't want the school holidays to end.

~~They don't want that the school holidays end.~~

want² /wɒnt/ *noun* **want of sth** when there is not enough of something *If we fail, it won't be*

for want of effort (= it is not because we have not tried).

wanted /ˈwɒntɪd/ *adjective* If someone is wanted, the police think they have committed a serious crime and are trying to find them. *He is wanted for murder.*

wanton /ˈwɒntən/ *adjective formal* done in order to cause suffering or destruction but with no other reason *wanton cruelty/violence*

wants /wɒnts/ *noun* [plural] the things you want or need

o→**war** /wɔːʳ/ *noun* **1** [FIGHTING] [C, U] fighting, using soldiers and weapons, between two or more countries, or two or more groups inside a country *They've been at war for the past five years.* ○ *He was only a child when the war broke out* (= started). ○ *If this country goes to war* (= starts to fight in a war), *thousands of people will die.* **2** [COMPETING] [C, U] when two or more groups are trying to be more successful than each other *a price war between supermarkets* **3** [TO STOP] [no plural] an attempt to stop something bad or illegal *the war against crime/drugs* ⊃See also: civil war, prisoner of war, world war.

ˈwar ˌcrime *noun* [C] a crime during a war that breaks the international rules of war • **war criminal** *noun* [C] someone guilty of a war crime

ward¹ /wɔːd/ *noun* [C] a room in a hospital where people receiving treatment stay, often for the same type of illness *the maternity ward*

ward² /wɔːd/ *verb*
ward sth off to prevent something unpleasant happening *I take vitamin C to ward off colds.*

-ward, wards /-wəd, -wədz/ *suffix* makes an adverb meaning 'towards a direction or place' *inward* ○ *forward* ○ *homeward*

warden /ˈwɔːdⁿn/ *noun* [C] **1** *US* (*UK* **governor**) someone who is responsible for controlling a prison **2** *UK* someone who is responsible for looking after a particular building or the people in it ⊃See also: traffic warden.

warder /ˈwɔːdəʳ/ *noun* [C] *UK* a prison guard

wardrobe /ˈwɔːdrəʊb/ *noun* **1** [C] *UK* (*US* **closet**) a large cupboard for keeping clothes in **2** [no plural] all the clothes that you own

warehouse /ˈweəhaʊs/ *noun* [C] *plural* **warehouses** /ˈweəhaʊzɪz/ a large building for storing goods that are going to be sold

wares /weəz/ *noun* [plural] *literary* goods that are for sale, especially not in a shop *People were selling their wares at the side of the road.*

warfare /ˈwɔːfeəʳ/ *noun* [U] fighting in a war, especially using a particular type of weapon *chemical/modern warfare*

warhead /ˈwɔːhed/ *noun* [C] the part of a missile (= weapon) that explodes when it reaches the place it is aimed at *a nuclear warhead*

warlord /ˈwɔːlɔːd/ *noun* [C] a military leader who controls a particular area of a country

W

o➤**warm¹** /wɔːm/ *adjective* **1** [TEMPERATURE] having a temperature between cool and hot *It's nice and warm in here.* ○ *Are you warm enough?* ○ *Make sure you keep warm.* **2** [CLOTHES] Warm clothes or covers keep your body warm. *a warm sweater* **3** [FRIENDLY] friendly and showing affection *a warm smile/welcome*

warm² /wɔːm/ *verb* [I, T] to become warm or to make something become warm *She warmed her feet against his.* ○ *I'll warm the soup.*

warm to sb/sth to start to like a person or idea

warm up to do gentle exercises in order to prepare yourself for more energetic exercise *They were warming up before the match.* ● warm-up /ˈwɔːmʌp/ *noun* [C]

warm (sb/sth) up to become warmer or to make someone or something warmer *The house soon warms up with the heating on.*

warmly /ˈwɔːmli/ *adverb* in a friendly way

warmth /wɔːmθ/ *noun* [U] **1** the heat that is produced by something *the warmth of the fire* **2** when someone is friendly and shows affection *There was no warmth in his eyes.*

o➤**warn** /wɔːn/ *verb* [T] **1** to tell someone that something bad may happen in the future, so that they can prevent it [+ that] *I warned you that it would be cold but you still wouldn't wear a coat.* ○ *I've been warning him for months.* **2** to advise someone not to do something that could cause danger or trouble [+ to do sth] *I warned you not to tell her.*

> WORD PARTNERS FOR **warning**
>
> deliver/give/heed/ignore/issue a warning ● a blunt/final/stern warning ● without warning

o➤**warning** /ˈwɔːnɪŋ/ *noun* [C, U] something that tells or shows you that something bad may happen *All cigarette packets carry a warning.* ○ *The bombs fell completely without warning.*

warp /wɔːp/ *verb* **1** [I, T] to become bent into the wrong shape or to make something do this *The window frames had warped.* **2** [T] If something warps your mind, it makes you strange and cruel.

warpath /ˈwɔːpɑːθ/ *noun* **be on the warpath** *informal* to be trying to find someone in order to be angry with them

warped /wɔːpt/ *adjective* strange and cruel *You've got a warped mind!*

warplane /ˈwɔːˌpleɪn/ *noun* [C] an aircraft for carrying bombs

warrant¹ /ˈwɒr³nt/ *noun* [C] an official document that allows someone to do something, for example that allows a police officer to search a building *The police have a warrant for his arrest.* ➤See also: **search warrant**.

warrant² /ˈwɒr³nt/ *verb* [T] to make something necessary *None of her crimes is serious enough to warrant punishment.*

warranty /ˈwɒr³nti/ *noun* [C, U] a written promise made by a company to change or repair one of its products if it has a fault *a five-year warranty*

warren /ˈwɒr³n/ (*also* ˈrabbit ˌwarren) *noun* [C] a group of connected underground holes where rabbits live

warring /ˈwɔːrɪŋ/ *adjective* **warring factions/parties/sides, etc** groups that are fighting against each other

warrior /ˈwɒriə^r/ *noun* [C] a person who has experience and skill in fighting in a war, especially in the past

warship /ˈwɔːʃɪp/ *noun* [C] a ship with weapons, used in war

wart /wɔːt/ *noun* [C] a small, hard lump that grows on the skin

wartime /ˈwɔːtaɪm/ *noun* [U] a period when a country is fighting a war

war-torn /ˈwɔːˌtɔːn/ *adjective* damaged by war *a war-torn country*

wary /ˈweəri/ *adjective* If you are wary of someone or something, you do not trust them completely. *She's still wary of strangers.* ● warily *adverb* ● wariness *noun* [U]

was /wɒz/ *past simple* I/he/she/it *of* be

o➤**wash¹** /wɒʃ/ *verb* **1** [T] to make something clean using water, or water and soap *Dad was washing the dishes.* **2** [I, T] to clean part of your body with water and soap *Have you washed your hands?* ○ *I got washed and dressed.* **3** **be washed away/out/up, etc** If something is washed away/out, etc, it is moved there by water. *A lot of the waste is washed out to sea.* **4** **wash against/on, etc** If water washes somewhere, it flows there. *Waves washed against the base of the cliff.*

wash sth away If water washes something away, it removes that thing. *Floods washed away much of the soil.*

wash sth down to drink something with food or medicine to make it easier to swallow *I had a plate of sandwiches, washed down with a glass of cool beer.*

wash out If a colour or dirty mark washes out, it disappears when you wash something. *Most hair dye washes out after a few weeks.*

wash (sth) up *UK* to wash the dishes, pans, and other things you have used for cooking and eating a meal ➤See colour picture **Phrasal Verbs** on page Centre 16.

wash up *US* to wash your hands, especially before a meal *Go and wash up - your dinner's ready.*

wash² /wɒʃ/ *noun* **1** **a wash a** when you wash a part of your body *Have you had a wash?* **b** *mainly UK* when you wash something *Could you give the car a wash?* **2** [C, U] clothes, sheets, etc that are being washed together *Your jeans are in the wash.*

washable /ˈwɒʃəbl/ *adjective* Something that is washable will not be damaged by being washed.

washbasin /ˈwɒʃˌbeɪs³n/ *UK* (*UK/US* sink) *noun* [C] a bowl in a bathroom that water can flow into, used for washing your face or hands

washcloth /ˈwɒʃklɒθ/ *US* (*UK* flannel) *noun* [C] a small cloth that you use to wash your face and body ➤See colour picture **The Bathroom** on page Centre 3.

W

| ɑː: arm | ɜː: her | iː: see | ɔː: saw | uː: too | aɪ my | aʊ how | eə hair | eɪ day | əʊ no | ɪə near | ɔɪ boy | ʊə poor | aɪə fire | aʊə sour |

washed-out /ˌwɒʃt'aʊt/ *adjective* looking pale and tired

washer /'wɒʃə^r/ *noun* [C] **1** a thin, flat ring that is put between a nut and a bolt (= metal objects used to fasten things together) **2** a machine that washes clothes

washing /'wɒʃɪŋ/ *noun* [U] clothes, sheets, and similar things that are being washed or have been washed, or when you wash these *I'm doing the washing this morning.* ∘ *He does his own washing and ironing.*

'washing ma,chine *noun* [C] a machine that washes clothes

'washing ,powder UK (US **laundry detergent**) *noun* [C] a soap in the form of a powder that is used to wash clothes

washing-up /ˌwɒʃɪŋ'ʌp/ *noun* [U] UK when you wash the dishes, pans, and other things you have used for cooking and eating a meal *He was doing the washing-up.*

,washing-'up ,liquid UK (US **dish soap**) *noun* [C, U] a thick liquid soap used to wash pans, plates, knives and forks, etc

washout /'wɒʃaʊt/ *noun* [no plural] *informal* an event that fails badly *No one came to the fete - it was a complete washout.*

washroom /'wɒʃruːm/ *noun* [C] *mainly US* a room where you can go to the toilet or wash your hands and face

o→**wasn't** /'wɒzᵊnt/ *short for* was not *I wasn't hungry this morning.*

wasp /wɒsp/ *noun* [C] a flying insect with a thin, black and yellow body *a wasp sting*

wasp

wastage /'weɪstɪdʒ/ *noun* [U] when you waste something *fuel wastage*

WORD PARTNERS FOR **waste**

a waste **of** sth • a waste **of effort/money/ time** • **household/nuclear/toxic** waste • waste **disposal** • **go to** waste

o→**waste¹** /weɪst/ *noun* **1** [U, no plural] a bad use of something useful, such as time or money, when there is a limited amount of it *Meetings are a waste of time.* ∘ *They throw away loads of food - it's such a waste.* ∘ *a waste of energy/ resources* **2** [U] things that are not wanted, especially what remains after you have used something *household/nuclear waste* **3** **go to waste** to not be used *I hate to see good food go to waste.*

o→**waste²** /weɪst/ *verb* [T] **1** to use too much of something or use something badly when there is a limited amount of it *I don't want to waste any more time so let's start.* ∘ *Why waste your money on things you don't need?* **2** **be wasted on sb** to be clever or of high quality in a way that someone will not understand or enjoy *Good coffee is wasted on Joe - he prefers instant.*

waste away to become thinner and weaker

waste³ /weɪst/ *adjective* [always before noun] Waste material is not now needed and can be got rid of. *waste paper*

wasteful /'weɪstfᵊl/ *adjective* using too much of

something, or using something badly when there is a limited amount of it

wasteland /'weɪstlænd/ *noun* [C, U] an area of land that cannot be used in any way

'wastepaper ,basket UK (US **wastebasket**) *noun* [C] a container that is used inside buildings for putting rubbish such as paper into

o→**watch¹** /wɒtʃ/ *verb* **1** LOOK AT [I, T] to look at something for a period of time *I watched him as he arrived.* ∘ *The kids are watching TV.* ∘ *I want to watch the news* (= programme on television). ⊃See Common learner error at **look**. **2** BE CAREFUL [T] to be careful about something *She has to watch what she eats.* ∘ *Watch how you cross the road!* **3** GIVE ATTENTION TO [T] to give attention to a situation which is changing *We'll be watching the case with interest.* ⊃See also: **bird-watching**, watch your **step¹**.

watch out used to tell someone to be careful because they are in danger *Watch out! There's a car coming!* ∘ *Drivers were told to watch out for black ice on the road.*

watch over sb to look after someone and protect them if it is necessary

WORD PARTNERS FOR **watch** (noun)

wear a watch • **glance at/look at** your watch

o→**watch²** /wɒtʃ/ *noun* **1** [C] a small clock on a strap that you fasten round your wrist (= lower arm) *I don't wear a watch.* **2** [U, no plural] when you watch or give attention to something or someone, especially to make sure nothing bad happens *We're keeping a close watch on the situation.*

watch

watchdog /'wɒtʃdɒg/ *noun* [C] an organization whose job is to make sure that companies behave legally and provide good services

watchful /'wɒtʃfᵊl/ *adjective* careful to notice things and ready to deal with problems *They were playing outside under the watchful eye of a teacher.*

watchword /'wɒtʃwɜːd/ *noun* [no plural] a word or phrase that describes the main ideas or most important part of something *As regards fashion, the watchword this season is simplicity.*

o→**water¹** /'wɔːtə^r/ *noun* [U] **1** the clear liquid that falls from the sky as rain and that is in seas, lakes, and rivers *hot/cold water* ∘ *a drink of water* **2** (*also* **waters**) an area in the sea or in a river or lake *coastal waters* **3** **be in deep water** to be in a difficult situation which is hard to deal with *They tried to adopt a baby illegally and ended up in very deep water.* **4** **be (like) water off a duck's back** If criticisms, insults, etc are like water off a duck's back to you, they do not affect you at all. *She calls him lazy and useless, but it's like water off a duck's back.* ⊃See also: **drinking water**, **mineral water**, **tap water**.

water² /'wɔːtə^r/ *verb* **1** PLANTS [T] to pour water over plants **2** MOUTH [I] If food makes your mouth water, it makes you want to eat it, sometimes making your mouth produce

W

liquid. *The smells from the kitchen are making my mouth water.* **3** [EYES] [I] If your eyes water, they produce liquid because something is hurting them. *The smoke was making my eyes water.*

water sth down 1 to add water to a drink, especially an alcoholic drink **2** to make a plan or idea less extreme, usually so that people will accept it

watercolour *UK* (*US* **watercolor**) /'wɔːtə,kʌlər/ *noun* [C] a type of paint that is mixed with water, or a picture made with this paint

'**water ,cooler** *noun* [C] a machine for providing cool drinking water, usually in an office or other public place

watercress /'wɔːtəkres/ *noun* [U] a small, strong-tasting plant that is eaten in salads

waterfall /'wɔːtəfɔːl/ *noun* [C] a stream of water that flows from a high place, often to a pool below

waterfront /'wɔːtəfrʌnt/ *noun* [C] a part of a town which is next to the sea, a lake, or a river *waterfront restaurants*

waterhole /'wɔːtəhəʊl/ *noun* [C] a small pool of water in a dry area where animals go to drink

'**watering ,can** *noun* [C] a container used for watering plants in the garden

waterlogged /'wɔːtəlɒgd/ *adjective* Waterlogged land is too wet.

watermark /'wɔːtəmɑːk/ *noun* [C] a pattern or picture on paper, especially paper money, which you can only see when a strong light is behind it

watermelon /'wɔːtə,melən/ *noun* [C, U] a large, round, green fruit that is pink inside with a lot of black seeds

waterproof /'wɔːtəpruːf/ *adjective* Waterproof material or clothing does not let water through. *a waterproof sleeping bag*

waters /'wɔːtəz/ *noun* [plural] the part of a sea around the coast of a country that legally belongs to that country

watershed /'wɔːtəʃed/ *noun* [no plural] an important event after which a situation completely changes *The discovery marked a watershed in the history of medicine.*

water-skiing /'wɔːtəskiːɪŋ/ *noun* [U] a sport in which someone is pulled behind a boat while standing on skis (= long, narrow pieces of wood or plastic fastened to the feet)

watertight /'wɔːtətaɪt/ *adjective* **1** Something that is watertight prevents any water from entering it. **2** A watertight reason or excuse is one that no one can prove is false. *a watertight alibi*

waterway /'wɔːtəweɪ/ *noun* [C] a river or canal (= river made by people, not nature) which people can use to travel along

watery /'wɔːtəri/ *adjective* **1** made with too much water *watery soup* **2** Watery eyes are wet with tears.

watt /wɒt/ (*written abbreviation* **W**) *noun* [C] a unit for measuring electrical power *a 60 watt light bulb*

wave

a wave She's waving.

o-***wave¹** /weɪv/ *verb* **1** [I] to raise your hand and move it from side to side in order to attract someone's attention or to say goodbye *Wave goodbye to Grandma.* ○ *She waved at him.* **2 wave sb in/on/through, etc** to show which way you want someone to go by moving your hand in that direction *The police waved him on.* **3** [I, T] (*also* **wave about/around**) to move from side to side in the air or make something move this way *The long grass waved in the breeze.* ○ *He started waving his arms about wildly.*

wave sth aside to refuse to consider what someone says *She waved aside all my objections.*

wave sb off to wave your hand to someone as they are leaving in order to say goodbye *We went to the station to wave him off.*

o-***wave²** /weɪv/ *noun* [C] **1** [WATER] a line of higher water that moves across the surface of the sea or a lake *I could hear the waves crashing against the rocks.* **2** [GROUP] a group of people or things that arrive or happen together or in a short period of time *There has been a wave of kidnappings in the region.* ○ *Another wave of refugees is arriving at the border.* **3 a wave of hatred/enthusiasm/sadness, etc** when you suddenly feel an emotion *She felt a sudden wave of sadness.* **4** [HAND] when you raise your hand and move it from side to side in order to attract someone's attention or say goodbye *She gave a little wave as the train left.* **5** [ENERGY] a piece of sound, light, or other energy that travels up and down in a curved pattern *a radio wave* ⊃See also: **new wave**, **tidal wave**.

wavelength /'weɪvleŋθ/ *noun* [C] **1** the length of radio wave used by a radio company for broadcasting its programmes **2** the distance between one sound or light wave, etc and the next **3 be on the same wavelength** If two people are on the same wavelength, they have the same way of thinking and it is easy for them to understand each other.

waver /'weɪvər/ *verb* [I] **1** to start to be uncertain about a belief or decision *Her support for him never wavered.* ○ *I'm wavering between the blue shirt and the red.* **2** to shake slightly or lose strength *His voice wavered and I thought he was going to cry.*

wavy /'weɪvi/ *adjective* with slight curves *wavy hair*

| ɑː: arm | ɜː: her | iː: see | ɔː: saw | uː: too | aɪ my | aʊ how | eə hair | eɪ day | əʊ no | ɪə near | ɔɪ boy | ʊə poor | aɪə fire | aʊə sour |

wax¹ /wæks/ *noun* [U] a solid substance that becomes soft when warm and melts easily, often used to make candles

wax² /wæks/ *verb* [T] **1** to put wax on something, especially to make it shiny *They cleaned and waxed my car.* **2** If you wax your legs, you remove the hair from them by using wax.

o‑**way¹** /weɪ/ *noun* **1** METHOD [C] how you do something [+ to do sth] *I must find a way to help him.* ○ [+ of + doing sth] *We looked at various ways of solving the problem.* ○ [+ (that)] *It was the way that she told me that I didn't like.* **2** ROUTE [C] the route you take to get from one place to another [usually singular] *Is there another way out of here?* ○ *I must buy a paper on the way home.* ○ *Can you find your way back to my house?* ○ *I took the wrong road and lost my way* (= got lost). **3 make your way to/through/towards, etc** to move somewhere, often with difficulty *We made our way through the shop to the main entrance.* **4 be on her/my/its, etc way** to be arriving soon *Apparently she's on her way.* **5 in/out of the/sb's way** in/not in the area in front of someone that they need to pass or see through *I couldn't see because Bill was in the way.* ○ *Sorry, am I in your way?* ○ *Could you move out of the way, please?* **6 a third of the way/most of the way, etc** used to say how much of something is completed *A third of the way through the film she dies.* **7 get in the way of sth/sb** to prevent someone from doing or continuing with something *Don't let your new friends get in the way of your studies.* **8 be under way** to be already happening *Building work is already under way.* **9 give way (to sb/sth) a** ALLOW to allow someone to get what they want, or to allow something to happen after trying to prevent it *The boss finally gave way when they threatened to stop work.* **b** TRAFFIC (*US* yield) (*UK*) to allow other vehicles to go past before you move onto a road **10 give way to sth** to change into something else *Her excitement quickly gave way to horror.* **11 give way** If something gives way, it falls because it is not strong enough to support the weight on top of it. *Suddenly the ground gave way under me.* **12 get sth out of the way** to finish something *I'll go shopping when I've got this essay out of the way.* **13** DIRECTION [C] a direction something faces or travels *This bus is going the wrong way.* ○ *Which way up does this picture go* (= which side should be at the top)*?* ○ (*UK*) *He always wears his baseball cap the wrong way round* (= backwards). **14** SPACE/TIME [no plural] an amount of space or time *We're a long way from home.* ○ *The exams are still a long way away/off.* **15 make way** to move away so that someone or something can pass **16 make way for sth** If you move or get rid of something to make way for something new, you do so in order to make a space for the new thing. *They knocked down the old houses to make way for a new hotel.* **17 in a way/in many ways** used to say that you think something is partly true *In a way his behaviour is understandable.* **18 in no way** not at all *This is in no way your fault.* **19 there's no way** *informal* If there is no way that something will happen, it is certainly not

allowed or not possible. *There's no way that dog's coming in the house.* **20 No way!** *informal* certainly not *"Would you invite him to a party?" "No way!"* **21 get/have your (own) way** to get what you want, although it might upset other people *She always gets her own way in the end.* **22 in a big/small way** *informal* used to describe how much or little you do a particular thing *They celebrate birthdays in a big way.* **23 a/sb's way of life** the way someone lives *Violence has become a way of life there.* **24 by the way** used when you say something that does not relate to what is being discussed *Oh, by the way, my name's Julie.* **25 go out of your way to do sth** to try very hard to do something pleasant for someone *He went out of his way to make us feel welcome.* **26 rub sb up the wrong way** *UK* (*US* rub sb the wrong way) *informal* to annoy someone without intending to ⊃See also: the Milky Way.

way² /weɪ/ *adverb informal* used to emphasize how extreme something is *The room was way too hot.* ○ *He's in second place but he's way behind/off.*

,way 'out *noun* [C] **1** *UK* (*UK/US* exit) a door that takes you out of a building **2** a way of avoiding doing something unpleasant *I'm supposed to be going to this meeting at 2.00 and I'm looking for a way out.*

wayside /'weɪsaɪd/ *noun* **fall by the wayside** to fail to complete something or be completed *Many students fall by the wayside during their first year at college.*

wayward /'weɪwəd/ *adjective literary* behaving badly in a way that causes trouble for other people

WC /,dʌblju:'si:/ *noun* [C] *UK abbreviation for* water closet: a toilet, especially in a public place ⊃See Common learner error at **toilet**.

o‑**we** *strong form* /wiː/ *weak form* /wi/ *pronoun* **1** used as the subject of the verb when the person speaking or writing is referring to themselves and one or more other people *My wife and I both play golf and we love it.* **2** people generally *The world in which we live is very different.*

o‑**weak** /wiːk/ *adjective* **1** BODY not physically strong *He felt too weak to sit up.* ○ *The children were weak with/from hunger.* **2** CHARACTER not powerful, or not having a strong character *a weak government/leader* **3** LIKELY TO FAIL likely to fail *a weak economy* ○ *a weak team* **4** LIKELY TO BREAK likely to break and not able to support heavy things *a weak bridge* **5** TASTE A weak drink has little taste or contains little alcohol. *weak coffee/beer* **6** REASON A weak reason or excuse is one that you cannot believe because there is not enough proof to support it. **7** NOT GOOD not good at something *She reads well but her spelling is weak.* **8** SLIGHT difficult to see or hear *He spoke in a weak voice.* ○ *a weak light* ● **weakly** *adverb*

weaken /'wiːkən/ *verb* [I, T] **1** to become less strong or powerful, or to make someone or something less strong or powerful *A number of factors have weakened the economy.* **2** to become less certain or determined about a decision, or to make someone less determined *I told him he wasn't having any more money but then I weakened.*

weakling /'wi:klɪŋ/ *noun* [C] someone who is physically weak

weakness /'wi:knəs/ *noun* **1** [U] when someone or something is not strong or powerful *Asking for help is not a **sign of weakness**.* **2** [C] a particular part or quality of something or someone that is not good *What do you think are your weaknesses as a manager?* ○ *There are a number of weaknesses in this proposal.* **3 have a weakness for sth/sb** to like a particular thing or person very much *She has a real weakness for ice cream.*

wealth /welθ/ *noun* **1** [U] when someone has a lot of money or valuable possessions *He enjoyed his new wealth and status.* **2 a wealth of sth** a large amount of something good *a wealth of experience/information*

wealthy /'welθi/ *adjective* rich *a wealthy businessman/nation* ○ *Only **the very wealthy** can afford to live here.*

wean /wi:n/ *verb* [T] to start to give a baby food to eat instead of its mother's milk *At what age do you wean a baby?*
wean sb off sth to make someone gradually stop using something that is bad for them *I'm trying to wean myself off fatty food generally.*

o⚊**weapon** /'wepən/ *noun* [C] a gun, knife, or other object used to kill or hurt someone *nuclear weapons* ○ *Police have found the murder weapon.* • **weaponry** *noun* [U] weapons

o⚊**wear**[1] /weəʳ/ *verb past tense* **wore**, *past participle* **worn 1** DRESS [T] to have a piece of clothing, jewellery, etc on your body *She's wearing a smart grey suit.* ○ *I wear jeans a lot of the time.* ○ *She wears glasses.* ○ *I don't usually wear make-up for work.* **2** FACE [T] to show a particular emotion on your face. *He was wearing a smile/frown.* **3** HAIR [T] to arrange or grow your hair in a particular way *She usually wears her hair in a ponytail.* **4** SPOIL [I, T] to become thin and damaged after being used a lot, or to make this happen *The carpet is already starting to wear in places.* ○ *He keeps **wearing holes in** his socks.* ◆See also: wear **thin**[1].
wear (sth) away to disappear after a lot of time or use, or to make something disappear in this way *The words on the gravestone had worn away completely.*
wear sb down to make someone feel tired and less able to argue *Their continual nagging just wears me down.*
wear off If a feeling or the effect of something wears off, it gradually disappears. *The anaesthetic is starting to wear off.*
wear on If a period of time wears on, it passes, especially slowly. *As time wore on she became more and more unhappy.*

wear sb out to make someone extremely tired *All this walking is wearing me out.*
wear (sth) out to use something so much that it is damaged and cannot be used any more, or to become damaged in this way *He's already worn out two pairs of shoes this year.*

wear[2] /weəʳ/ *noun* [U] **1** (*also* **wear and tear**) damage that happens to something when it is used a lot *The furniture is already showing signs of wear.* **2** how much you wear a piece of clothing *These clothes are not for everyday wear.* **3 be the worse for wear** to be in a bad state or condition *He looked a little the worse for wear this morning.*

-wear /weəʳ/ *suffix* used at the end of words that describe a particular type of clothes *menswear/swimwear*

wearing /'weərɪŋ/ *adjective* making you tired or annoyed *It's very wearing when the children are so badly behaved.*

weary /'wɪəri/ *adjective* **1** tired *You look weary, my love.* **2 weary of sth/sb** bored with something or someone *She **grew weary** of the children and their games.* • **wearily** *adverb* • **weariness** *noun* [U]

weasel /'wi:zᵊl/ *noun* [C] a small animal with a long body that kills and eats other small animals

o⚊**weather**[1] /'weðəʳ/ *noun* [U] **1** the temperature or conditions outside, for example if it is hot, cold, sunny, etc *The flight was delayed because of bad weather.* **2 be/feel under the weather** to feel ill *She's had a cold and a sore throat and been generally under the weather.*

weather[2] /'weðəʳ/ *verb* [T] to deal with a difficult situation or difficult conditions *to weather criticism/a recession*

weathered /'weðəd/ *adjective* looking rough and old *a weathered face*

'weather ,forecast *noun* [C] a description of what the weather will be like

weave /wi:v/ *verb* **1 weave in and out; weave through** *past* **weaved** to go somewhere by moving around a lot of things *to weave in and out of the traffic* ○ *to weave through the crowd* **2** [I, T] *past tense* **wove**, *past participle* **woven** to make cloth on a machine by crossing threads under and over each other

o⚊**web** /web/ *noun* [C] **1** a type of net made by a spider (= creature with eight legs) to catch insects *a spider's web* **2 the Web** (*also* **the World Wide Web**) the connected pages on the Internet which you can search to find particular information ◆See Extra help page **The Web and the Internet** on page Centre 36.

'web ad,dress (*US* **'web ,address**) *noun* [C] an email or website address

'web ,browser *noun* [C] a computer program which allows you to look at pages on the Internet

webcam /ˈwebkæm/ *noun* [C] a camera which records moving pictures and sound and allows these to be shown on the Internet as they happen

webcast /ˈwebkɑːst/ *noun* [C] a broadcast made on the Internet

ˈweb ˌpage *noun* [C] a part of a website that can be read on a computer screen

⊶**website** /ˈwebsaɪt/ *noun* [C] an area on the Web (= computer information system) where information about a particular subject, organization, etc can be found ➲See study page **The Internet**.

⊶**we'd** /wiːd/ **1** *short for* we had *By the time she arrived we'd eaten.* **2** *short for* we would *We'd like two tickets for the three o'clock show, please.*

Wed (*also* **Weds**) *written abbreviation for* Wednesday

WORD PARTNERS FOR ***wedding***

go to/be invited to/plan a wedding • **at** a wedding • sb's wedding **to** sb • sb's wedding **day** • a wedding **dress/guest/present/reception/ring**

⊶**wedding** /ˈwedɪŋ/ *noun* [C] an official ceremony at which a man and woman get married *We're **going to a wedding** on Saturday.* ○ *a **wedding dress/ring*** ➲See also: **golden wedding**.

wedge[1] /wedʒ/ *noun* [C] a piece of something that is thin at one end and thicker at the other *a big wedge of cheese*

wedge[2] /wedʒ/ *verb* [T] **1 wedge sth open/shut** to use a wedge or similar shaped object to keep a door or window firmly open or closed *The room was hot so I wedged the door open.* **2** to push something into a narrow space *I was wedged between Andy and Pete in the back of the car.*

⊶**Wednesday** /ˈwenzdeɪ/ (*written abbreviation* **Wed, Weds**) *noun* [C, U] the day of the week after Tuesday and before Thursday

wee[1] /wiː/ *noun* [no plural] *mainly UK informal* when you urinate *to have a wee* ○ *I need a wee.* • **wee** *verb* [I] **weeing,** *past* **weed**

wee[2] /wiː/ *adjective* small, usually used by Scottish speakers *a wee girl*

weed[1] /wiːd/ *noun* [C] a wild plant that you do not want to grow in your garden *Dandelions are common weeds.*

weed[2] /wiːd/ *verb* [I, T] to remove wild plants from a garden where they are not wanted

weed sb/sth out to get rid of people or things that you do not want from a group *The government plans to weed out bad teachers.*

weedy /ˈwiːdi/ *adjective UK informal* thin and weak *He looks too weedy to be an athlete.*

⊶**week** /wiːk/ *noun* **1** [C] a period of seven days *last week/next week* ○ *I've got three exams this week.* ○ *We get paid every week.* **2 the week** the five days from Monday to Friday when people usually go to work or school *I don't go out much during the week.*

weekday /ˈwiːkdeɪ/ *noun* [C] one of the five days from Monday to Friday, when people usually go to work or school *This road is very busy on weekdays.*

⊶**weekend** /ˌwiːkˈend/ [US] /ˈwiːkend/ *noun* [C] **1** Saturday and Sunday, the two days in the week when many people do not work *Are you doing anything this weekend?* ○ *I'm going home for the weekend.* **2 at the weekend** *UK* (*US* **on the weekend**) on Saturday or Sunday *He's going to a football match at the weekend.*

weekly /ˈwiːkli/ *adjective, adverb* happening once a week or every week *a weekly newspaper* ○ *We're paid weekly.*

weep /wiːp/ *verb* [I, T] *past* **wept** *literary* to cry, usually because you are sad

⊶**weigh** /weɪ/ *verb* **1 weigh 200g/75 kg/10 stone, etc** to have a weight of 200g/75 kg/10 stone, etc *How much do you weigh?* **2** [T] to measure how heavy someone or something is *Can you weigh that piece of cheese for me?* ○ *She weighs herself every day.* **3** [T] (*also UK* **weigh up**) to consider something carefully, especially in order to make a decision *The jury must weigh the evidence.* ○ *He needs to weigh up the pros and cons of going to college.*

weigh sth against sth to judge which of two things is more important before making a decision *The advantages have to be weighed against the possible disadvantages.*

be weighed down by/with sth 1 to be carrying or holding too much *She was weighed down with shopping bags.* **2** to be very worried about something *be weighed down by problems/debts*

weigh on/upon sb/sth If a problem or responsibility weighs on you, it makes you worried or unhappy. *Problems at work are weighing on me.*

weigh sth out to measure an amount of something *Weigh out 8 ounces of flour.*

WORD PARTNERS FOR ***weight***

gain/lose/put on weight • **carry/lift/support** a weight • **average/excess/heavy/ideal/light** weight

⊶**weight** /weɪt/ *noun* **1** [AMOUNT] [U] how heavy someone or something is *He's about **average** height and **weight**.* **2 lose weight** If someone loses weight, they become lighter and thinner. *I need to **lose** a bit of **weight**.* **3 put on/gain weight** If someone puts on weight or gains weight, they become heavier and fatter. **4** [HEAVINESS] [U] the quality of being heavy *The shelf collapsed under the weight of the books.* **5** [OBJECT] [C] something that is heavy *You're not supposed to lift heavy weights after an operation.* **6 carry weight** to be considered important and effective in influencing someone *His opinions carry a lot of weight with the scientific community.* **7 pull your weight** to work as hard as other people in a group *The rest of the team complained that Sarah wasn't pulling her weight.* **8 throw your weight around** to behave as if you are more important or powerful than other people **9 a weight off your mind** when a problem which has been worrying you stops or is dealt with *Finally selling that house was a weight off my mind.* ➲See also: **paper weight**.

weighted /ˈweɪtɪd/ *adjective* **be weighted in**

W

favour of/towards/against sth to give one group an advantage or disadvantage over other people *The system is weighted in favour of families with young children.*

weights /weɪts/ *noun* [plural] heavy pieces of metal that you lift up and down to make your muscles stronger

weighty /'weɪti/ *adjective* very serious and important *The film deals with the weighty issues of religion and morality.*

weir /wɪəʳ/ *noun* [C] *UK* a low wall built across a river to control the flow of water

weird /wɪəd/ *adjective* very strange *I had a really weird dream last night.*

weirdo /'wɪədəʊ/ *noun* [C] *informal* a person who behaves strangely

welcome¹ /'welkəm/ *exclamation* used to greet someone who has just arrived somewhere *Welcome home! ○ Welcome to the UK.*

o⸳**welcome²** /'welkəm/ *verb* [T] **1** to greet someone who has arrived in a place *Both families were there to welcome us.* **2** to be pleased about something and want it to happen *The decision was welcomed by everybody. ○ I would welcome your advice.*

welcome³ /'welkəm/ *adjective* **1** If something is welcome, people are pleased about it and want it to happen. *a welcome change ○ Your comments are very welcome.* ⊃Opposite **unwelcome**. **2 You're welcome.** used to be polite to someone who has thanked you *"Thank you." "You're welcome."* **3 make sb (feel) welcome** to make a visitor feel happy and comfortable in a place by being kind and friendly to them *They made me very welcome in their home.* **4 be welcome to do sth** used to tell someone that they can certainly do something, if they want to *Anyone who is interested is welcome to come along.* **5 be welcome to sth** used to tell someone that they can certainly have something, if they want it, because you do not

WORD PARTNERS FOR *welcome (noun)*

get/be given a [big/friendly/warm, etc] welcome

welcome⁴ /'welkəm/ *noun* [no plural] **1** when someone is greeted when they arrive somewhere *He was given a warm (= friendly) welcome by his fans.* **2 outstay/overstay your welcome** to stay somewhere too long so that people want you to leave

weld /weld/ *verb* [T] to join pieces of metal together by heating them until they almost melt and then pressing them together

welfare /'welfeəʳ/ *noun* [U] **1** Someone's welfare is their health and happiness. *He is concerned about the welfare of young men in prison.* **2** *US* (*UK* **social security**) money paid by a government to people who are poor, ill, or who do not have jobs *to be on welfare* (= getting welfare)

,**welfare 'state** *UK* (*US* '**welfare ,state**) *noun* [no plural] a system in which the government looks after and pays for people who are ill, old, or who cannot get a job

o⸳**we'll** /wiːl/ *short for* we shall or we will *We'll be home on Friday.*

o⸳**well¹** /wel/ *adjective* [never before noun] better, best **1** healthy *to feel/look well ○ I'm not very well. ○ Are you feeling better now?* ⊃Opposite **unwell**. **2 all is well** everything is in a good or acceptable state *I hope all is well with Jack.* **3 be all very well** used to show that you do not agree with something or that you are annoyed about something *It's all very well for her to say everything's fine, she doesn't have to live here.* **4 be (just) as well** used to say that something might be a good thing to do or happen [+ **(that)**] *It was just as well that you left when you did.* ⊃See also: **be alive and kicking/well**.

o⸳**well²** /wel/ *adverb* better, best **1** in a successful or satisfactory way *I thought they played well. ○ He's doing well at school/work.* **2** in a complete way or as much as possible *I know him quite well. ○ Stir the mixture well.* ⊃See Common learner error at **good**. **3 as well** also *Are you going to invite Steve as well?* **4 as well as sth** in addition to something *They have lived in the United States as well as Britain.* **5 may/might as well do sth** If you may/might as well do something, it will not spoil the situation if you do that thing. *If we're not waiting for Karen, we might as well go now.* **6 may/might/could well** used to say that something is likely to be true *He could well be at Michelle's house.* **7 well above/ahead/below, etc** above/ahead/below, etc by a large amount *It was well after seven o'clock when we got home.* **8 can't/couldn't very well do sth** used to say that something is not a suitable or practical thing to do *I couldn't very well tell her while he was there.* **9 Well done!** used to tell someone how pleased you are about their success *"I passed my exams." "Well done!"*

o⸳**well³** /wel/ *exclamation* **1** used at the beginning of a sentence to pause slightly or to express doubt or disagreement *"You'll go, won't you?" "Well, I'm not sure." ○ "You said the food was bad." "Well, I didn't exactly say that."* **2** (*also* **well, well**) used to express surprise *Well, well, I never expected that to happen.* **3 oh well** used to say that a situation cannot be changed although it might be disappointing *Oh well, it doesn't matter, I can always buy another one.*

well⁴ /wel/ *noun* [C] a deep hole in the ground from which you can get water, oil, or gas

well-balanced /ˌwel'bælənst/ *adjective* **1 a well-balanced diet/meal** food which includes all the different types of food that the body needs to be healthy **2** Well-balanced people are calm and have good judgment.

well-behaved /ˌwelbɪ'heɪvd/ *adjective* behaving in a polite and quiet way *a well-behaved child*

well-being /'welˌbiːɪŋ/ *noun* [U] when someone is healthy, happy, and comfortable

well-built /ˌwel'bɪlt/ *adjective* having a large, strong body

well-connected /ˌwelkə'nektɪd/ *adjective* having important or powerful friends

well-done /ˌwel'dʌn/ *adjective* Meat that is well-done has been cooked completely and is not pink inside.

well-dressed /ˌwel'drest/ *adjective* wearing

attractive, good quality clothes

well-earned /ˌwelˈɜːnd/ *adjective* **well-earned break/holiday/rest, etc** a rest that you deserve because you have been working hard

well-educated /ˌwelˈedʒʊkeɪtɪd/ *adjective* having had a good education

well-established /ˌwelɪˈstæblɪʃt/ *adjective* having existed for a long time *a well-established tradition*

well-fed /ˌwelˈfed/ *adjective* having eaten enough good food *a well-fed cat*

well-heeled /ˌwelˈhiːld/ *adjective* having a lot of money, expensive clothes, etc

wellies /ˈweliz/ *UK informal* (*US* **rubber boots**) *noun* [plural] large rubber boots that you wear outside when the ground is wet and dirty *a pair of wellies*

well-informed /ˌwelɪnˈfɔːmd/ *adjective* knowing a lot of useful information

wellingtons /ˈwelɪŋtənz/ *noun* [plural] *UK* wellies

well-intentioned /ˌwelɪnˈtenʃ⁰nd/ *adjective* trying to be helpful and kind but not improving a situation

well-kept /ˌwelˈkept/ *adjective* **1 a well-kept secret** something that has been carefully and successfully kept secret *The recipe is a well-kept secret.* **2** tidy and organized *a well-kept kitchen*

well-known /ˌwelˈnəʊn/ *adjective* famous *a well-known actor*

well-meaning /ˌwelˈmiːnɪŋ/ *adjective* trying to be helpful and kind but not improving a situation *well-meaning friends*

well-off /ˌwelˈɒf/ *adjective* having a lot of money *His parents are very well-off.*

well-organized (*also UK* **-ised**) /ˌwelˈɔːgⁿnaɪzd/ *adjective* working in an effective and successful way because of good organization

well-paid /ˌwelˈpeɪd/ *adjective* earning a lot of money

well-placed /ˌwelˈpleɪst/ *adjective* in a very convenient position or in a position that gives someone an advantage [+ to do sth] *She's very well-placed to find out what's going on.*

well-read /ˌwelˈred/ *adjective* having read a lot of books on different subjects

well-to-do /ˌweltəˈduː/ *adjective* old-fashioned having a lot of money *a well-to-do family*

well-wisher /ˈwelˌwɪʃər/ *noun* [C] someone who wants another person to be happy, successful, or healthy *A crowd of well-wishers gathered outside the hospital.*

Welsh /welʃ/ *noun* [U] **1** a language that is spoken in some parts of Wales **2 the Welsh** the people of Wales

went /went/ *past tense of* go

wept /wept/ *past of* weep

o⚬**we're** /wɪər/ *short for* we are *Hurry! We're late!*

o⚬**were** /wɜːr/ *past simple you/we/they of* be

o⚬**weren't** /wɜːnt/ *short for* were not *They weren't there.*

o⚬**west, West** /west/ *noun* [U] **1** the direction that you face to see the sun go down **2 the west** the part of an area that is further towards the west than the rest **3 the West** the countries of North America and western Europe ● **west** *adjective* *the west coast of Ireland* ● **west** *adverb* towards the west *They lived in a village four miles west of Oxford.*

the ˌWest ˈEnd *noun* a part of central London that has a lot of shops, theatres, restaurants, etc

westerly /ˈwest⁰li/ *adjective* **1** towards or in the west *Senegal is the most westerly country in Africa.* **2** A westerly wind comes from the west. *westerly breezes*

o⚬**western, Western¹** /ˈwestən/ *adjective* [always before noun] **1** in or from the west part of an area *western France* **2** related to the countries of North America and western Europe *a Western diplomat*

western² /ˈwestən/ *noun* [C] a film or story that happens in the west of the US at the time when Europeans started living there

westerner, Westerner /ˈwestənər/ *noun* [C] someone who is from a country in North America or western Europe

westernized (*also UK* **-ised**) /ˈwestənaɪzd/ *adjective* having a culture like North America and western Europe *Some Asian countries are becoming increasingly westernized.*

ˌWest ˈIndian *adjective* belonging or relating to the West Indies *a West Indian island* ● **West Indian** *noun* [C] someone from the West Indies

the ˌWest ˈIndies *noun* [plural] a group of islands in the Caribbean Sea

westward, westwards /ˈwestwəd, ˈwestwədz/ *adverb* towards the west *They were travelling westward.* ● **westward** *adjective*

o⚬**wet¹** /wet/ *adjective* **wetter, wettest 1** WATER covered in water or another liquid *a wet towel* ○ *We got soaking wet in the rain.* ○ (*UK*) *Look at you - you're wet through* (= very wet)! **2** RAIN raining *a wet and windy day* **3** NOT DRY not dry yet *wet paint* **4** PERSON *UK informal* Someone who is wet has a weak personality.

wet² /wet/ *verb* [T] **wetting**, *past* **wet** or **wetted 1 wet the bed/your pants/yourself, etc** to urinate in your bed or in your underwear without intending to **2** to make something wet

ˈwet ˌsuit *noun* [C] a piece of clothing covering the whole body that keeps you warm and dry when you are under water

o⚬**we've** /wiːv/ *short for* we have *We've bought a house.*

whack /wæk/ *verb* [T] *informal* to hit someone or something in a quick, strong way *She whacked him on the head with her book.* ● **whack** *noun* [C] *informal*

whale /weɪl/ *noun* [C] a very large animal that looks like a large fish, lives in the sea and breathes air through a hole at the top of its head

whale

whaling /ˈweɪlɪŋ/ *noun* [U] hunting whales

wharf /wɔːf/ *noun* [C] *plural* **wharves** /wɔːvz/ an area next to the sea or a river where goods can be put on or taken off ships

◦**what** /wɒt/ *pronoun, determiner* **1** INFORMATION used to ask for information about something *What's this?* ◦ *What time is it?* ◦ *What happened?* ➾See Common learner error at **how**. **2** THE THING used to refer to something without naming it *I heard what he said.* ◦ *Do you know what I mean?* ◦ *What I like most about her is her honesty.* **3** NOT HEARD *informal* used when you have not heard what someone has said and you want them to repeat it. Some people think this use is not very polite. *"Do you want a drink Tom?" "What?"* **4** REPLY *informal* used to ask what someone wants when they call you *"Hey Jenny?" "Yes, what?"* **5** **what a/an ...** used to give your opinion, especially when you have strong feelings about something *What a mess!* ◦ *What an awful day!* **6** **what about...?** used to suggest something *What about asking Martin to help?* **7** **what ... for?** used to ask about the reason for something *What are you doing that for?* ◦ *"We really need a bigger car." "What for?"* **8** **what if...?** used to ask about something that could happen in the future, especially something bad *What if I don't pass my exams?* **9** **what's up (with sb)** *informal* used to ask why someone is unhappy or angry *What's up, Angie? You look troubled.* **10** **what with** *informal* used to talk about the reasons for a particular situation, especially a bad or difficult situation *I'm tired, what with travelling all day yesterday and sleeping badly.* **11** **what's more** used to add something surprising or interesting to what you have just said

COMMON LEARNER ERROR

what

When you have not heard what someone has said and you want them to repeat it, you can say **what?**, but this is not polite. It is better to say **sorry?** or **pardon?**.

"It's 10 o'clock." "Sorry/Pardon?" "I said it's 10 o'clock."

◦**whatever** /wɒt'evəʳ/ *adverb, pronoun, determiner* **1** ANYTHING anything or everything *Do whatever you want.* ◦ *He eats whatever I put in front of him.* **2** NO DIFFERENCE used to say that what happens is not important because it does not change a situation *Whatever happens I'll still love you.* ◦ *We'll support you, whatever you decide.* **3** QUESTION used to ask for information when you are surprised or angry about something *Whatever do you mean?* **4** ANGRY *informal* something that you say when you are angry with someone who is asking you something *'Isabel, will you just listen when I'm talking to you?' 'Whatever.'* **5 or whatever** or something similar *The children are usually outside playing football or whatever.*

whatnot /'wɒtnɒt/ **and whatnot** *informal* and other things of a similar type *They sell cards and wrapping paper and whatnot.*

whatsoever /,wɒtsəʊ'evəʳ/ (*also* **whatever**) *adverb* **no...whatsoever** none at all *There's no evidence whatsoever that she was involved.*

wheat /wiːt/ *noun* [U] a plant whose grain is used for making flour, or the grain itself

◦**wheel¹** /wiːl/ *noun* **1** [C] a circular object fixed under a vehicle so that it moves smoothly over the ground *My bike needs a new front wheel.* **2** **the wheel** a steering wheel (= circular object you turn to direct a vehicle) *You should drive with both hands on the wheel.* ◦ *He fell asleep at the wheel* (= while driving). **3** **reinvent the wheel** to waste time trying to create something that has been done before ➾See also: **Ferris wheel**.

wheel² /wiːl/ *verb* **wheel sth around/into/to, etc** to push something that has wheels somewhere *He wheeled his bicycle into the garden.*

wheel around/round to quickly turn around *She wheeled around to face him.*

wheelbarrow /'wiːl,bærəʊ/ *noun* [C] a big, open container with a wheel at the front and handles that is used to move things, especially around in a garden

wheelchair /'wiːltʃeəʳ/ *noun* [C] a chair with wheels used by someone who cannot walk

wheeze /wiːz/ *verb* [I] to make a noisy sound when breathing because of a problem in your lungs

◦**when¹** /wen/ *adverb* used to ask at what time something happened or will happen *When's your birthday?* ◦ *When did he leave?* ◦ *When are you going away?*

◦**when²** /wen/ *conjunction* **1** used to say at what time something happened or will happen *I found it when I was cleaning out the cupboards.* ◦ *We'll go when you're ready.* **2** although *Why are you doing this when I've asked you not to?*

whenever /wen'evəʳ/ *conjunction* every time or at any time *You can go whenever you want.* ◦ *I try to help them out whenever possible.*

◦**where¹** /weəʳ/ *adverb* used to ask about the place or position of someone or something *Where does she live?* ◦ *Where are my car keys?*

◦**where²** /weəʳ/ *conjunction* **1** at, in, or to a place or position *He's not sure where they are.* ◦ *I know where to go.* **2** relating to a particular part of a process or situation *We've now reached the point where we can make a decision.*

whereabouts¹ /,weərə'baʊts/ *adverb* used to ask in what place or area someone or something is *Whereabouts does he live?*

whereabouts² /'weərəbaʊts/ *noun* **sb's whereabouts** the place where someone or something is *His whereabouts are unknown.*

whereas /weə'ræz/ *conjunction* compared with the fact that *His parents were rich, whereas mine had to struggle.*

whereby /weə'baɪ/ *adverb formal* by which *They've introduced a system whereby people share cars.*

wherein /weə'rɪn/ *adverb formal* in which

whereupon /'weərəpɒn/ *conjunction formal* after which *We decided to have a picnic, where-*

W

upon it started to rain.

wherever¹ /weəˈrevəʳ/ *conjunction* **1** in or to any place or every place *You can sit wherever you like.* **2 wherever possible** every time it is possible *We try to use natural fabrics wherever possible.*

wherever² /weəˈrevəʳ/ *adverb* used to ask in what situation or place something happened, especially when the person asking feels surprised *Wherever did you get that idea?*

wherewithal /ˈweəwɪðɔːl/ *noun* **the wherewithal to do sth** the money, skills, or other things that are needed to do something

o⌐**whether** /ˈweðəʳ/ *conjunction* **1** used to talk about a choice between two or more possibilities *Someone's got to tell her, whether it's you or me.* ○ *I didn't know whether or not to go.* **2** if *I wasn't sure whether you'd like it.*

whew /fjuː/ *exclamation* used when you are happy that something is not going to happen, or when you are tired or hot

o⌐**which** /wɪtʃ/ *pronoun, determiner* **1** CHOICE used to ask or talk about a choice between two or more things *Which of these do you like best?* ○ *Which way is it to the station?* ○ *I just don't know which one to choose.* **2** REFERRING TO SOMETHING used at the beginning of a relative clause to show what thing is being referred to *These are principles which we all believe in.* **3** EXTRA INFORMATION used to give more information about something *The book, which includes a map, gives you all the information you need about Venice.* **4** GIVING OPINION used when you give an opinion about what you have just said *He took us both out for lunch, which I thought was very kind of him.*

COMMON LEARNER ERROR

which or who?

Use **which** to refer to a thing.

The restaurant which is next to the pub is good.

~~The restaurant who is next to the pub is good.~~

Use **who** to refer to a person.

The boy who is wearing the red coat is called Paul.

~~The boy which is wearing the red coat is called Paul.~~

Sometimes it is possible to use 'that' or no word instead of **which** or **who**.

He's the man (that) I saw in the bar.

This is the shirt (that) I bought yesterday.

whichever /wɪˈtʃevəʳ/ *pronoun, determiner* **1** used to say that what happens is not important because it does not change a situation *Whichever option we choose there'll be disadvantages.* ○ *It's a sad situation whichever way you look at it.* **2** any of a group of similar things *Choose whichever bedroom you want.*

whiff /wɪf/ *noun* [no plural] a smell which you only smell for a short time *I just caught a whiff of garlic from the kitchen.*

o⌐**while¹** /waɪl/ (*also UK* **whilst** /waɪlst/) *conjunction* **1** DURING during the time that *I read a magazine while I was waiting.* ○ *I can't talk to*

anyone while I'm driving. ○ *While you're away, I might decorate the bathroom.* **2** ALTHOUGH although *And while I like my job, I wouldn't want to do it forever.* **3** COMPARING used to compare two different facts or situations *Tom is very confident while Katy is shy and quiet.*

⌐◻⌐◻ **WORD PARTNERS FOR while** (*noun*)

take/wait a while • **after/for/in** a while • **quite** a while • a **short** while • a while **ago**

o⌐**while²** /waɪl/ *noun* a while a period of time *a long/short while* ○ *I'm going out for a while.*

while³ /waɪl/ *verb*

while sth away to spend time in a relaxed way because you are waiting for something or because you have nothing to do *We played a few games to while away the time.*

whim /wɪm/ *noun* [C] when you suddenly want to do something without having a reason *We booked the holiday on a whim.*

whimper /ˈwɪmpəʳ/ *verb* [I] to make quiet crying sounds because of fear or pain *The dog was whimpering with pain.*

whimsical /ˈwɪmzɪkəl/ *adjective* unusual in a way that is slightly funny *a whimsical tale*

whine /waɪn/ *verb* [I] **1** to complain in an annoying way *She's always whining about something.* **2** to make a long, high, sad sound *The dog whined and scratched at the door.* • **whine** *noun* [C]

whinge /wɪndʒ/ *verb* [I] whingeing whinging *UK informal* to complain in an annoying way *Oh, stop whingeing!* • **whinge** *noun* [C] *UK He was just having a whinge.*

whip¹ /wɪp/ *noun* [C] a long piece of leather fixed to a handle and used to hit an animal or person

whip² /wɪp/ *verb* whipping, *past* whipped **1** [T] to hit a person or animal with a whip **2** [T] to make a food such as cream more solid by mixing it hard with a kitchen tool **3 whip (sth) away/off/out, etc** *informal* to move or make something move in a fast, sudden way *She opened the bag and whipped out her camera.*

whip up sth 1 to try to make people have strong feelings about something *to whip up enthusiasm/hatred* **2** to prepare food very quickly *I could whip up a plate of spaghetti if you like.*

whir /wɜːʳ/ *noun, verb* whirring, *past* whirred *US spelling of* whirr

whirl¹ /wɜːl/ *verb* [I, T] to move or make something move quickly round and round

whirl² /wɜːl/ *noun* [no plural] **1** when a lot of exciting or confusing things happen at the same time *a whirl of activity* **2** a sudden turning movement **3 give sth a whirl** *informal* to try to do something, often for the first time *I've never danced salsa before but I'll give it a whirl.*

whirlpool /ˈwɜːlpuːl/ *noun* [C] an area of water that moves round and round very quickly

whirlwind¹ /ˈwɜːlwɪnd/ *adjective* a whirlwind **romance/visit/tour, etc** a relationship/visit, etc that only lasts a short time

whirlwind² /ˈwɜːlwɪnd/ *noun* **1** a whirlwind of sth a lot of sudden activity, emotion, etc *a* *whirlwind of activity* **2** [C] a strong wind that moves round and round very quickly

whirr *UK* (*US* **whir**) /wɜːʳ/ *noun* [no plural] a low, continuous sound *the whirr of machinery* ● **whirr** *UK* (*US* **whir**) *verb* [I]

whisk¹ /wɪsk/ *verb* [T] **1 whisk sb away/off/into, etc** *informal* to take someone somewhere quickly *They whisked him off to the police station.* **2** to mix food such as eggs, cream, etc very quickly using a fork or whisk *Whisk the mixture until smooth.*

whisk² /wɪsk/ *noun* [C] a kitchen tool made of wire that is used to mix eggs, cream, etc, or to make such food thicker ⊃See colour picture **The Kitchen** on page Centre 2.

whisker /ˈwɪskəʳ/ *noun* [C] one of the long, stiff hairs that grows around the mouths of animals such as cats

whiskers /ˈwɪskəz/ *noun* [plural] *old-fashioned* hairs growing on a man's face

whiskey /ˈwɪski/ *noun* [C, U] whisky in Ireland or the United States

whisky /ˈwɪski/ *noun* [C, U] a strong, alcoholic drink made from grain

☞**whisper** /ˈwɪspəʳ/ *verb* [I, T] to speak extremely quietly so that other people cannot hear *She whispered something to the girl sitting next to her.* ● **whisper** *noun* [C]

whistle¹ /ˈwɪsl/ *verb* **1** [I, T] to make a sound by breathing air out through a small hole made with your lips or through a whistle *Someone whistled at her as she walked past.* **2** [I] to produce a sound when air passes through a narrow space *He could hear the wind whistling through the trees.*

whistle² /ˈwɪsl/ *noun* [C] **1** a small, simple instrument that makes a high sound when you blow through it *The referee blew the whistle to end the game.* **2** the sound made by someone or something whistling

☞**white¹** /waɪt/ *adjective* **1** [COLOUR] being the colour of snow or milk *a white T-shirt* ○ *white walls* ⊃See colour picture **Colours** on page Centre 12. **2** [PERSON] Someone who is white has skin that is pale in colour. *He's described as a white man in his early thirties.* **3** [OF WHITE PEOPLE] relating to white people *the white community* **4** [FACE] having a pale face because you are ill or you are feeling shocked *He was white with shock.* **5** [COFFEE] *UK* White coffee has milk or cream added to it. *Two coffees please, one black and one white.* **6** [WINE] White wine is a pale yellow colour. ● **whiteness** *noun* [U] ⊃See also: **black¹** and white.

☞**white²** /waɪt/ *noun* **1** [COLOUR] [C, U] the colour of snow or milk ⊃See colour picture **Colours** on page Centre 12. **2** [PERSON] [C] a white person *For a long time, whites controlled the economy here.* **3** [EGG] [C] the part of an egg that is white when it is cooked *Mix the egg whites with the sugar.* ⊃See also: in **black²** and white.

whiteboard /ˈwaɪtbɔːd/ *noun* [C] **1** a white screen on which you can write with a special pen and which allows other people with computers to see what you have written **2** a large board with a white surface that teachers write on ⊃See colour picture **The Classroom** on page Centre 6.

white-collar /ˌwaɪtˈkɒləʳ/ *adjective* relating to work in an office or in a job that needs special knowledge and education *white-collar jobs/workers*

the 'White ,House *noun* **1** the US president and government **2** the building that is the official home and offices of the US president ● **White House** *adjective* *a White House spokesman*

,white 'lie *noun* [C] a lie which is not important and is usually said to avoid upsetting someone

,white 'meat *noun* [U] a meat that is pale in colour, such as chicken

whiten /ˈwaɪtⁿn/ *verb* [I, T] to become white or to make something become white

,White 'Paper *noun* [C] a government report in the UK giving information or suggestions on a subject *a White Paper on employment*

whitewash /ˈwaɪtwɒʃ/ *noun* [no plural] when the truth about a serious mistake, crime, etc is hidden from the public *The newspaper accused the government of a whitewash.* ● **whitewash** *verb* [T]

whizz (*also* **whiz**) /wɪz/ *verb* **whizz by/past/through, etc** *informal* to move somewhere very quickly *She whizzed down the street in her new sports car.*

whizzkid (*also* **whizkid**) /ˈwɪzˌkɪd/ *noun* [C] a young person who is very successful or good at doing something *a computer whizzkid*

☞**who** /huː/ *pronoun* **1** [NAME] used to ask about someone's name or which person or group someone is talking about *Who told you?* ○ *Who's that?* **2** [WHICH PERSON] used at the beginning of a relative clause to show which person or group of people you are talking about *That's the man who I saw in the bank.* **3** [ADD INFORMATION] used to give more information about someone *My brother, who's only just seventeen, has already passed his driving test.* ⊃See Common learner error at **which**.

☞**who'd** /huːd/ **1** *short for* who had *I was reading about a man who'd sailed around the world.* **2** *short for* who would *Who'd have thought we'd still be friends?*

whoever /huːˈevəʳ/ *pronoun* **1** [WHICH PERSON] the person who *Whoever broke the window will have to pay for it.* ○ *Could I speak to whoever is in charge please?* **2** [ANY PERSON] used to say that it is not important which person or group does something *Can whoever leaves last lock up, please?* **3** [SURPRISE] used to ask who a person is when expressing surprise *Whoever could that be phoning at this time?* ○ *Whoever would believe such a ridiculous story?*

☞**whole¹** /həʊl/ *adjective* **1** [always before noun] complete, including every part *She spent the whole afternoon studying.* ○ *The whole family went to the show.* **2** [never before noun] as a single object and not in pieces *The chick swallowed*

whisper

the worm whole. ⊃See also: a whole new **ball game**, the whole **world**¹.

o⁻**whole**² /həʊl/ *noun* **1 the whole of sth** all of something *His behaviour affects the whole of the class.* **2 as a whole** when considered as a group and not in parts *The population as a whole is getting healthier.* **3 on the whole** generally *We've had a few problems, but on the whole we're very happy.*

wholefood /ˈhəʊlfuːd/ *noun* [U] *UK* food that is as natural as possible, without artificial things added to it *a wholefood shop*

wholehearted /ˌhəʊlˈhɑːtɪd/ *adjective* **wholehearted agreement/approval/support**, etc complete agreement/approval/support, etc without any doubts ● **wholeheartedly** *adverb I agree wholeheartedly.*

wholemeal /ˈhəʊlmiːl/ *UK* (*UK/US* **whole wheat**) *adjective* made using whole grains, or made from flour that contains whole grains *wholemeal bread/flour*

wholesale /ˈhəʊlseɪl/ *adjective* **1** relating to products which are sold in large amounts, usually at a cheaper price *wholesale prices* **2** [always before noun] complete or affecting a lot of things, people, places, etc *wholesale changes* ● **wholesale** *adverb*

wholesaler /ˈhəʊlˌseɪlə/ *noun* [C] a company that sells products in large amounts to shops which then sell them to customers

wholesome /ˈhəʊlsᵊm/ *adjective* **1** Wholesome food is good for your health. **2** morally good *wholesome family entertainment*

ˈ**whole** ˌ**wheat** (*also UK* **wholemeal**) *adjective* made using whole grains, or made from flour that contains whole grains *whole wheat bread/flour*

o⁻**who'll** /huːl/ *short for* who will *Who'll be at your party?*

wholly /ˈhəʊlli/ *adverb* completely *His behaviour is wholly unacceptable.*

whom /huːm/ *pronoun formal* used instead of 'who' as the object of a verb or preposition *I met a man with whom I used to work.*

COMMON LEARNER ERROR

whom or **who**?

Whom is very formal and most people use **who** instead.
Whom did you see at the party?
Who did you see at the party?

Whom should be used after a preposition but most people avoid this by putting the preposition at the end of the sentence and using **who**.
With whom did you go to the party?
Who did you go to the party with?

whoop /wuːp/ *noun* [C] a loud, excited shout *He gave a loud whoop of delight.*

whooping cough /ˈhuːpɪŋˌkɒf/ *noun* [U] a serious children's disease in which a cough is followed by a 'whoop' noise

whoops /wʊps/ *exclamation* used when you make a mistake or have a small accident

whopping /ˈwɒpɪŋ/ *adjective* [always before noun]

informal extremely large *a whopping 50 percent increase*

who're /ˈhuːə/ *short for* who are *Who're the people we're going to see?*

whore /hɔː/ *noun* [C] an offensive word for someone whose job is having sex with people

o⁻**who's** /huːz/ **1** *short for* who is *Who's your new friend?* **2** *short for* who has *Who's been using my computer?*

o⁻**whose** /huːz/ *pronoun, determiner* **1** used to ask who something belongs to or who someone or something is connected with *Whose gloves are these?* ○ *Whose car shall we use?* **2** used to say that something or someone is connected with or belongs to a person *She has a brother whose name I can't remember.*

o⁻**who've** /huːv/ *short for* who have *I know people who've bought their homes on the Internet.*

o⁻**why** /waɪ/ *adverb* **1** used to ask or talk about the reasons for something *Why didn't you call me?* ○ *I wonder why he didn't come.* ○ *So that's the reason why he asked her!* **2 Why don't you?/ why not do sth?** used to make a suggestion *Why don't you come with us?* ○ *Why not give it a try?* **3 why not?** *informal* used to agree with something that someone has suggested *"Let's have an ice cream." "Yes, why not?"*

wicked /ˈwɪkɪd/ *adjective* **1** [BAD] extremely bad and morally wrong *a wicked man* **2** [AMUSING] funny or enjoyable in a way that is slightly bad or unkind *a wicked sense of humour* **3** [GOOD] *very informal* extremely good *They sell some wicked clothes.*

wicker /ˈwɪkə/ *adjective* made from thin branches crossed over and under each other *a wicker basket*

wicket /ˈwɪkɪt/ *noun* [C] in cricket, an arrangement of three long, vertical poles with two short poles across the top

o⁻**wide**¹ /waɪd/ *adjective* **1** [LONG DISTANCE] measuring a long distance or longer than usual from one side to the other *a wide river/road* ○ *I have very wide feet.* ⊃See picture at narrow. **2 5 miles/3 inches/6 metres**, etc **wide** having a distance of 5 miles/3 inches/6 metres, etc from one side to the other *The swimming pool is five metres wide.* **3 a wide range/selection/variety**, etc a lot of different types of thing *The library is a good source of a wide range of information.* **4** [EYES] If your eyes are wide, they are completely open. *Her eyes were wide with fear.* **5** [BALL] If a ball, shot, etc is wide, it does not go near enough to where it was intended to go. ⊃See also: be wide of the **mark**¹.

o⁻**wide**² /waɪd/ *adverb* **1 wide apart/open** as far apart/open as possible *The window was wide open.* **2 wide awake** completely awake

wide-eyed /ˌwaɪdˈaɪd/ *adjective* with your eyes completely open because of surprise, fear, happiness, etc *The children looked on, wide-eyed with wonder.*

o⁻**widely** /ˈwaɪdli/ *adverb* **1** including a lot of different places, people, subjects, etc *widely known* ○ *He has travelled widely in Europe.* **2 differ/vary widely** to be very different *Prices vary widely from shop to shop.*

widen /ˈwaɪdªn/ verb [I, T] **1** to become wider or make something become wider *The road is being widened to two lanes.* **2** to increase or make something increase in number or degree *to widen choice*

wide-ranging /ˌwaɪdˈreɪndʒɪŋ/ adjective including a lot of subjects *a wide-ranging discussion/interview*

widescreen /ˈwaɪdskriːn/ adjective describes a very wide cinema or television screen which shows very clear pictures *widescreen TV*

widespread /ˈwaɪdspred/ adjective affecting or including a lot of places, people, etc *a widespread problem* ○ *widespread support*

widow /ˈwɪdəʊ/ noun [C] a woman whose husband has died

widowed /ˈwɪdəʊd/ adjective If someone is widowed, their husband or wife has died.

widower /ˈwɪdəʊəʳ/ noun [C] a man whose wife has died

the width **of** sth • [1 metre/5 feet, etc] **in** width • the **full** width **of** sth

width /wɪtθ/ noun **1** [C, U] the distance from one side of something to the other side *a width of 2 metres* ○ *height, length, and width* ⊃See picture at **length**. **2** [C] the distance across the shorter side of a swimming pool when you swim across it

wield /wiːld/ verb [T] **1** to hold a weapon or tool and look as if you are going to use it *They were confronted by a man wielding a knife.* **2 wield influence/power, etc** to have a lot of influence or power over other people

wiener /ˈwiːnəʳ/ noun [C] US a long thin sausage (= tube of meat and spices) that is usually eaten in bread

⚬**wife** /waɪf/ noun [C] plural **wives** /waɪvz/ the woman that a man is married to *I've never met William's wife.*

wig /wɪg/ noun [C] a covering of real or artificial hair that you wear on your head *She was wearing a blonde wig.*

wiggle /ˈwɪgl/ verb [I, T] to make small movements from side to side or to make something else move from side to side *He was wiggling his hips to the music.* • **wiggle** noun [no plural]

⚬**wild¹** /waɪld/ adjective **1** ANIMAL A wild animal or plant lives or grows in its natural environment and not where people live. *a wild dog* ○ *wild flowers* **2** LAND Wild land is in a completely natural state. *a wild garden* **3** ENERGETIC very energetic and not controlled *a wild party* ○ *wild dancing* **4** WEATHER with a lot of wind, rain, etc *a wild and stormy night* **5** a **wild accusation/guess/rumour, etc** something that you say which is not based on facts and is probably wrong **6 be wild about sth** informal to be very enthusiastic about something *He's wild about jazz.* **7 run wild** If someone, especially a child, runs wild, they behave as they want to and no one controls them. *Their nine-year-old son is left to run wild.* • **wildness** noun [U] ⊃See also: beyond your wildest dreams (**dream¹**).

wild² /waɪld/ noun **1 in the wild** in a natural environment *Animals are better off in the wild than in a zoo.* **2 the wilds** an area which is far from where people usually live *the wilds of Alaska*

wild 'boar noun [C] a wild pig

wild ,card noun [C] someone or something that you know nothing about *a wild-card candidate in the election*

wildcard /ˈwaɪld.kɑːd/ noun [C] in computing, a sign that is used to represent any letter or series of letters *a wildcard search*

wilderness /ˈwɪldənəs/ noun [C] a place that is in a completely natural state without houses, industry, roads, etc [usually singular] *a beautiful mountain wilderness*

wildlife /ˈwaɪldlaɪf/ noun [U] animals, birds, and plants living in their natural environment *a wildlife park*

wildly /ˈwaɪldli/ adverb **1** in a very energetic way and without control *They cheered wildly.* **2** extremely *It hasn't been wildly successful.*

wiles /waɪlz/ noun [plural] tricks or clever ways of making other people do what you want *I'll use my womanly wiles.*

wilful UK (US **willful**) /ˈwɪlfªl/ adjective doing what you want to do, although you are not allowed to or other people tell you not to *wilful disobedience* • **wilfully** adverb

⚬**will¹** strong form /wɪl/ weak forms /wªl, ªl/ modal verb **1** FUTURE used to talk about what is going to happen in the future, especially things that you are certain about *Claire will be five next month.* ○ *I'll see him on Saturday.* ○ *She'll have a great time.* ⊃See Common learner error at **shall**. **2** ABLE/WILLING used to talk about what someone or something is willing or able to do *Ask Susie if she'll take them.* ○ *I've asked her but she won't come.* ○ *The car won't start.* **3** ASK used to ask someone to do something or to politely offer something to someone *Will you give me her address?* ○ *Will you have a drink with us, Phil?* **4** IF used in conditional sentences that start with 'if' and use the present tense *If he's late again I'll be very angry.* **5** HAPPENING OFTEN used to talk about something that often happens, especially something annoying *Accidents will happen.* ○ *He will keep talking when I'm trying to concentrate.* **6 it/that will be** mainly UK used to talk about what is probably true *That will be Helen at the front door.* ○ *That will be his mother with him.* ⊃See Extra help page **Modal verbs** on page Centre 22.

3 make/write a will • **in** sb's will • **leave** sb sth **in** your will

will² /wɪl/ noun **1** MENTAL POWER [C, U] the mental power to control your thoughts and actions or to succeed in doing something difficult *She has a very strong will.* ○ [+ to do sth] *He lacks the will to win.* **2** WANT [no plural] what someone wants *She was forced to marry him against her will.* **3** DOCUMENT [C] a legal document that gives instructions about what should happen to your money and possessions after you die *She left me some money in her will.* ⊃See also: free will, ill will.

W

willful /'wɪlfᵊl/ *adjective US spelling of* wilful

o--**willing** /'wɪlɪŋ/ *adjective* **1 be willing to do sth** to be happy to do something, if you need to *He's willing to pay a lot of money for that house.* **2** wanting to do something *He is a very willing assistant.* ⊃Opposite **unwilling**. ● **willingly** *adverb He would willingly risk his life for her.* ● **willingness** *noun* [U]

willow /'wɪləʊ/ *noun* [C] a tree with long, thin leaves that grows near water

willowy /'wɪləʊi/ *adjective* tall and attractively thin *a willowy blonde*

willpower /'wɪlpaʊᵊr/ *noun* [U] the ability to make yourself do difficult things or to stop yourself from doing enjoyable things that are bad for you *It takes great willpower to lose weight.*

wilt /wɪlt/ *verb* [I] If a plant wilts, it starts to bend because it is dying or needs water.

wily /'waɪli/ *adjective* good at getting what you want, especially by deceiving people

wimp /wɪmp/ *noun* [C] *informal* someone who is not brave and tries to avoid dangerous or difficult situations *I'm too much of a wimp to go rock climbing.* ● **wimpy** *adjective informal*

o--**win**[1] /wɪn/ *verb* winning, *past* won **1** COMPETITION [I, T] to get the most points in a competition or game, or the most votes in an election *Barcelona won the game 6-0.* ○ *Who do you think will win the election?* **2** ARGUMENT [I, T] to be successful in a war, fight, or argument *Protesters have won their battle to stop the road being built.* **3** PRIZE [T] to get a prize in a game or competition *He won $500.* ○ *She won a gold medal at the Olympics.* **4 win approval/respect/support, etc** to get approval/respect/support, etc because of your skill and hard work *Her plans have won the support of many local people.* **5 sb can't win** *informal* used to say that nothing someone does in a situation will succeed or please people *Whatever I do seems to annoy her - I just can't win.*

COMMON LEARNER ERROR

win or beat?

You **win** a game or competition.

Who do you think will win the football game?

You **beat** someone, or a team you are playing against.

We beat both teams.

~~We won both teams.~~

win sb over to persuade someone to support you or agree with you

WORD PARTNERS FOR **win** (noun)

a **comfortable/convincing/emphatic** win ● a win **against/over** sb ● a win **for** sb

win[2] /wɪn/ *noun* [C] when someone wins a game or competition *The Jets have only had three wins this season.*

wince /wɪns/ *verb* [I] to suddenly look as if you are suffering because you feel pain or because you see or think about something unpleasant *It makes me wince just to think about eye operations.*

winch /wɪnʃ/ *noun* [C] a machine with a thick chain, used for lifting heavy things ● **winch** *verb* [T] to lift someone or something with a winch *The injured climber was winched to safety by a helicopter.*

WORD PARTNERS FOR **wind**

the wind **blows** ● a **gust of** wind ● a **biting/light/strong** wind ● **high** winds ● **in** the wind

o--**wind**[1] /wɪnd/ *noun* **1** [C, U] a natural, fast movement of air *The weather forecast said there would be strong winds and rain.* ○ *There isn't enough wind to fly a kite.* **2** [U] *UK* (*US* gas) gas or air in your stomach that makes you feel uncomfortable and sometimes makes noises *I like garlic but it gives me terrible wind.* **3 get wind of sth** to discover something that is intended to be a secret *Dad got wind of our plans for a party.* **4 get your wind (back)** to breathe easily again, for example after you have been running ⊃See also: throw **caution**[1] to the wind, **second wind**.

wind[2] /wɪnd/ *verb* [T] to make someone have difficulty breathing, often by hitting them in the stomach

wind[3] /waɪnd/ *verb past* **wound 1 wind sth around/round, etc sth** to turn or twist something long and thin around something else several times *She wound the rope around the tree.* ⊃Opposite **unwind**. **2 wind (up) a clock/toy/watch, etc** to make a clock/toy/watch, etc work by turning a small handle or button several times *Did you remember to wind the alarm clock?* **3 wind along/down/through, etc** If a river, road, etc winds somewhere, it bends a lot and is not straight. *The path winds along the edge of the bay.*

wind (sth) down to gradually end, or to make something gradually end *to wind down a business*

wind down (*also* unwind) to gradually relax after doing something that has made you tired or worried

wind up to finally be somewhere or do something, especially without having planned it *If he carries on like this, he'll wind up in prison.* ○ [+ doing sth] *I wound up having to start the course from the beginning again.*

wind (sth) up to end, or to make something end *It's time to wind up the game now.*

wind sb up *UK informal* **1** to tell someone something that is not true, as a joke *Have I really won or are you winding me up?* **2** to annoy someone *He keeps complaining and it really winds me up.*

windfall /'wɪndfɔːl/ *noun* [C] an amount of money that you get that you did not expect *Investors each received a windfall of £1000.*

winding /'waɪndɪŋ/ *adjective* a winding **path/road/street, etc** a path/road, etc that bends a lot and is not straight

'wind ,instrument *noun* [C] a musical instrument that you play by blowing into it *A flute is a wind instrument.*

W

| j yes | k cat | ŋ ring | ʃ she | θ thin | ð this | ʒ decision | dʒ jar | tʃ chip | æ cat | e bed | ə ago | ɪ sit | i cosy | ɒ hot | ʌ run | ʊ put |

windmill /'wɪndmɪl/
noun [C] a building
with long parts at
the top that turn in
the wind, used for
producing power or
crushing grain

windmill

⚬ᵂ**window** /'wɪndəʊ/
noun [C] **1** a space
in the wall of a
building or vehicle
that has glass in it,
used for letting
light and air inside
and for looking
through *Open the
window if you're
too hot.* ○ *I could
see the children's
faces at the
window.* ○ *a window frame/ledge* ➪See
colour picture **The Living Room** on page Centre 4.
2 a separate area on a computer screen
showing information and which you can
move around *to minimize/maximize a
window* ➪See also: **French windows**.

windowpane /'wɪndəʊpeɪn/ *noun* [C] a piece of
glass in a window

'**window ,shopping** *noun* [U] when you look
at things in shops but do not buy anything

windowsill /'wɪndəʊsɪl/ *noun* [C] a shelf at the
bottom of a window ➪See colour picture **The Living
Room** on page Centre 4.

windpipe /'wɪndpaɪp/ *noun* [C] the tube that
carries air from your throat to your lungs *She
got a fish bone stuck in her windpipe.*

windscreen /'wɪndskriːn/ *UK* (*US* **windshield**
/'wɪndʃiːld/) *noun* [C] the window at the front
end of a car, bus, etc ➪See colour picture **Car** on
page Centre 7.

'**windscreen ,wiper** *UK* (*US* '**windshield
,wiper**) *noun* [C] one of two long, metal and
rubber parts that move against a windscreen
to remove rain ➪See colour picture **Car** on page
Centre 7.

windsurfing /'wɪndsɜːfɪŋ/ *noun* [U] a sport in
which you sail across water by standing on a
board and holding onto a large sail • **windsurfer**
noun [C] *This part of the coast is very popular
with windsurfers.*

windswept /'wɪndswept/ *adjective* **1** A windswept place often has strong winds. *a remote,
windswept hill* **2** looking untidy because you
have been in the wind *windswept hair*

windy /'wɪndi/ *adjective* with a lot of wind *a
windy day* ○ *Outside it was cold and windy.*

W

⎰⎱⎰⎱ WORD PARTNERS FOR **wine**

a **bottle of/glass of** wine • **dry/red/spark-
ling/sweet/white** wine

⚬ᵂ**wine** /waɪn/ *noun* [C, U] an alcoholic drink that
is made from the juice of grapes (= small,
green or purple fruit), or sometimes other
fruit *a glass of wine* ○ *red/white wine* ○ *Does
he drink wine?* ○ *Should we take a bottle of
wine?*

wing

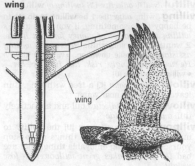

wing

⚬ᵂ**wing** /wɪŋ/ *noun* [C] **1** CREATURE one of the two
parts that a bird or insect uses to fly **2** AIR-
CRAFT one of the two long, flat parts at the sides
of an aircraft that make it stay in the sky
3 CAR *UK* (*US* **fender**) one of the parts at each
corner of a car above the wheels **4** BUILDING a
part of a large building that is joined to the
side of the main part *Their offices are in the
West wing.* **5** POLITICS a group of people in an
organization or political party who have the
same beliefs *the nationalist wing of the party* **6**
take sb under your wing to help and protect
someone who is younger than you or who has
less experience than you

winged /wɪŋd/ *adjective* with wings *a winged
insect*

'**wing ,mirror** *UK* (*US* **side mirror**) *noun* [C] a
small mirror on the side of a car or truck ➪See
colour picture **Car** on page Centre 7.

the wings /wɪŋz/ *noun* [plural] **1** the area
behind the sides of a stage where actors wait
just before they perform **2 be waiting in the
wings** to be ready to do something or be used
at any time

wink

wink¹ /wɪŋk/ *verb* [I] to quickly close and then
open one eye, in order to be friendly or to
show that something is a joke *She smiled and
winked at me.*

wink² /wɪŋk/ *noun* [C] **1** when you wink at someone *He gave me a friendly wink.* **2 not sleep a wink** to not have any sleep *I was so excited last night - I didn't sleep a wink.*

o⁻**winner** /'wɪnəʳ/ *noun* [C] someone who wins a game, competition, or election *the winners of the World Cup*

winnings /'wɪnɪŋz/ *noun* [plural] money that you win in a competition

▓▓▓ WORD PARTNERS FOR *winter*

in (the) winter • a **cold/severe** winter • **last/ next** winter • the winter **months** • a **mild** winter

o⁻**winter** /'wɪntəʳ/ *noun* [C, U] the coldest season of the year, between autumn and spring *We went skiing last winter.* ○ *a mild winter* •**wintry** /'wɪntri/ *adjective* cold and typical of winter *wintry showers* (= snow mixed with rain) ⊃See also: the **dead³** of night/winter.

win-win /'wɪnwɪn/ *adjective* A win-win situation is one in which something good happens to everyone.

wipe¹ /waɪp/ *verb* [T] **1** to clean or dry something by moving a cloth across it *I had a job wiping tables in a café.* ○ *She wiped her hands on the towel.* **2 wipe sth from/away/off, etc** to remove dirt, water, a mark, etc from something with a cloth or your hand *He wiped a tear from his eye.*

wipe sth out to destroy something completely *The earthquake wiped out many villages.*

wipe sth up to remove a substance, usually liquid, with a cloth *Have you got something I could wipe this mess up with?*

wipe² /waɪp/ *noun* [C] **1** when you clean or dry something with a cloth *I'll give the table a wipe.* **2** a thin cloth or piece of paper used for cleaning *baby wipes*

wiper /'waɪpəʳ/ (*also* **windscreen wiper**) *noun* [C] a long, metal and rubber part that removes rain from the front window of a vehicle

o⁻**wire¹** /waɪəʳ/ *noun* **1** [C, U] thin, metal thread, used to fasten things or to make fences, cages, etc **2** [C] a long, thin piece of metal thread, usually covered in plastic, that carries electricity *electrical wires* ⊃See also: **barbed wire**.

wire² /waɪəʳ/ *verb* [T] **1** ELECTRICITY (*also* **wire up**) to connect wires so that a piece of electrical equipment will work *Do you know how to wire a burglar alarm?* **2** JOIN to join two things together using wire **3** SEND *US* to send a message or money using an electrical communication system

wireless /'waɪələs/ *adjective* without a cable

wiring /'waɪərɪŋ/ *noun* [U] the system of wires that carry electricity around a building *The fire was caused by faulty wiring.*

wiry /'waɪəri/ *adjective* **1** Someone who is wiry is strong but quite thin. **2** Wiry hair is thick and stiff, like wire. *a wiry beard*

wisdom /'wɪzdəm/ *noun* **1** [U] the ability to use your knowledge and experience to make good decisions and judgments **2 the wisdom of sth/ doing sth** If you doubt the wisdom of some-

thing, you think it is probably not a good plan. *Many people have questioned the wisdom of spending so much money on weapons.*

'wisdom ˌtooth *noun* [C] *plural* **wisdom teeth** one of the four teeth at the back of your mouth that are the last to grow

wise¹ /waɪz/ *adjective* **1** A wise decision or action shows good judgment and is the right thing to do. *I think we've made a wise choice.* ○ [+ to do sth] *It's always wise to see a doctor if you're worried about your health.* ⊃Opposite **unwise**. **2** A wise person is able to use their knowledge and experience to make good decisions and give good advice. **3 be none the wiser** *informal* to still not understand something after someone has tried to explain it to you •**wisely** *adverb*

wise² /waɪz/ *verb*

wise up *informal* to start to understand the truth about a situation *Employers are starting to wise up to the fact that people want flexible working hours.*

-wise /-waɪz/ *suffix* changes a noun into an adverb meaning 'relating to this subject' *Weather-wise, the holiday was great.* ○ *How are we doing time-wise?*

o⁻**wish¹** /wɪʃ/ *verb* **1 wish (that)** to want a situation that is different from the one that exists *I wish that I didn't have to go to work.* ○ *I wish he would leave.* ○ *I wish I had been there.* **2 wish to do sth** *formal* to want to do something *I wish to speak to the manager.* **3 wish sb luck/success, etc** to say that you hope someone will be lucky, successful, etc *I wished him luck for his test.* **4 I/you wish!** *informal* used to say that you would like something to be true although you know it is not true *"Have your exams finished yet?" "I wish!"*

▓▓▓ WORD PARTNERS FOR *wish* (noun)

ignore/respect sb's wishes • **get** your wish • **have no** wish to do sth • **according to/ against** sb's wishes

o⁻**wish²** /wɪʃ/ *noun* [C] **1** what you want to do or what you want to happen *The hospital always tries to respect the wishes of its patients.* ○ *I have no wish to travel the world.* **2** something that you say secretly to yourself about what you want to have or happen *She closed her eyes and made a wish.* **3 best wishes** something you say or write at the end of a letter, to show that you hope someone is happy and has good luck *Please give her my best wishes when you see her.*

wishful thinking /ˌwɪʃfəl'θɪŋkɪŋ/ *noun* [U] when you want something to happen or be true but it is impossible

wisp /wɪsp/ *noun* [C] **1 a wisp of cloud/smoke/ steam** a small, thin line of cloud/smoke/steam **2 a wisp of hair/grass, etc** a thin piece of hair/ grass, etc •**wispy** *adjective* in the form of wisps *wispy hair* ○ *a wispy cloud*

wistful /'wɪstfəl/ *adjective* slightly sad because you are thinking about something you cannot have *a wistful look/smile* •**wistfully** *adverb*

wit /wɪt/ *noun* [U] the ability to say things that

W

are funny and clever *a woman of great intelligence and wit*

witch /wɪtʃ/ *noun* [C]
in stories, a woman
who has magical
powers that she uses
to do bad or strange
things

witch

witchcraft
/'wɪtʃkrɑːft/ *noun* [U]
the use of magic to
make bad or strange
things happen

witch-hunt /'wɪtʃhʌnt/ *noun* [C] when a group
of people try to blame someone and punish
them for something, in a way that is unfair

☞**with** /wɪð/ *preposition* **1** TOGETHER used to say
that people or things are in a place together or
are doing something together *Emma lives with
her boyfriend.* ○ *Hang your coat with the
others.* **2** HAVING having or including something *a house with a swimming pool* ○ *a
woman with brown eyes* **3** USING using something *She hit him over the head with a tennis
racket.* **4** HOW used to describe the way someone does something *He plays with great enthusiasm.* ○ *She shut the drawer with a bang.*
5 WHAT used to say what fills, covers, etc
something *a bucket filled with water* ○ *shoes
covered with mud* **6** CAUSE because of something *She was trembling with fear.* **7** RELATING
TO relating to something or someone *There's
something wrong with the car.* ○ *The doctors
are very pleased with his progress.* **8** POSITION
used to describe the position of someone's
body *She sat with her legs crossed.* **9 be with
me/you** *informal* to understand what someone
is saying *Sorry, I'm not with you - can you say
that again?*

withdraw /wɪð'drɔː/ *verb past tense* **withdrew,**
past participle **withdrawn 1** MONEY [T] to take
money out of a bank account *She withdrew
$50.* **2** REMOVE [T] to remove something, espe-
cially because of an official decision *This product has been withdrawn from sale.* ○ *He has
threatened to withdraw his support.* **3** MILITARY
[I, T] If a military force withdraws, or if someone withdraws it, it leaves the place where it
is fighting. *The President has ordered troops to
be withdrawn from the area.* **4** COMPETITION [I]
to decide that you will not now be in a race,
competition, etc *Christie was forced to withdraw from the race because of injury.* **5** SOME-
THING SAID [T] *formal* to say that you want
people to ignore something you said before because it was not true *He admitted taking the
money, but later withdrew his confession.*

withdrawal /wɪð'drɔːəl/ *noun* **1** MONEY [C]
when you take money out of a bank account
*This account allows you to make withdrawals
whenever you want to.* **2** STOP [C, U] when someone stops doing something, for example helping someone or giving money [usually singular]
the withdrawal of financial support **3** MILITARY
[C, U] when a military force moves out of an
area [usually singular] *the withdrawal of troops*
4 DRUGS [U] the unpleasant feelings that someone gets when they stop taking a drug that

they have taken for a long time *withdrawal
symptoms* **5** ALONE [U] when someone prefers
to be alone and does not want to talk to other
people *Withdrawal can be a symptom of depression.*

withdrawn /wɪð'drɔːn/ *adjective* [never before
noun] quiet and not talking to other people

wither /'wɪðər/ (*also* **wither away**) *verb* [I] If a
plant withers, it becomes dry and starts to die.

withering /'wɪðərɪŋ/ *adjective* **withering
attack/contempt/look** criticism or an expression that shows that someone strongly
disapproves of someone or something

withhold /wɪð'həʊld/ *verb* [T] *past* **withheld** to
not give someone the information, money, etc
that they want *The company has decided to
withhold payment until the job has been finished.*

☞**within¹** /wɪ'ðɪn/ *preposition* **1** TIME before a
particular period of time has finished *The
ambulance arrived within 10 minutes.* ○ *Consume within two days of purchase.* **2** DISTANCE
less than a particular distance from something
She was born within 20 miles of New York.
○ *The hotel is within easy reach of* (= near)
the airport. **3** INSIDE inside an area, group or
system *a dispute within the department*
○ *There's a pharmacy within the hospital
building.* **4** LIMIT not outside the limits of
something *The project was completed well
within budget.* **5 within the law/the rules/your
rights, etc** allowed according to the law/the
rules/your rights, etc *You're perfectly within
your rights to complain.*

within² /wɪ'ðɪn/ *adverb* inside someone or
something *change from within.*

☞**without** /wɪ'ðaʊt/ *preposition* **1** not having,
using, or doing something *I did the test without
any problems.* ○ *I can't see without my glasses.*
○ *He went to school without eating any breakfast.* **2** when someone is not with someone else
You can start the meeting without me. **3 go/do
without (sth)** to not have something important
They went without sleep for three days.

withstand /wɪð'stænd/ *verb* [T] *past* **withstood** to
not be damaged or broken by something *a
bridge designed to withstand earthquakes*

WORD PARTNERS FOR ***witness***

appeal for a witness ● a witness **to** sth ● a
character/key witness ● a witness **ac-
count/testimony**

☞**witness¹** /'wɪtnəs/ *noun* [C] **1** COURT someone in
a court of law who says what they have seen
and what they know about a crime *The witness
was called to the stand.* **2** SEE someone who
sees an accident or crime *Police are appealing
for witnesses to the shooting.* **3** DOCUMENT
someone who signs their name on an official
document to say that they were present when
someone else signed it

witness² /'wɪtnəs/ *verb* [T] **1** to see something
happen, especially an accident or crime *Did
anyone witness the attack?* **2** to sign your name
on an official document to say that you were
present when someone else signed it

'witness ,box UK (UK/US **'witness ,stand**) noun [C] the place in a court of law where a witness stands or sits when they are answering questions

wits /wɪts/ noun [plural] **1** intelligence and the ability to think quickly **2 keep/have your wits about you** to be ready to think quickly in a situation and react to things that you are not expecting *You have to keep your wits about you when you're cycling.* **3 be at your wits' end** to be very worried about something and not know what you should do next **4 scare/frighten sb out of their wits** to make someone very frightened

witty /'wɪti/ adjective using words in a funny and clever way *a witty comment* ○ *He was witty and charming.*

wives /waɪvz/ plural of wife

wizard /'wɪzəd/ noun [C] **1** in stories, a man who has magical powers **2** informal someone who is very good at something or knows a lot about something *a computer wizard*

WMD /,dʌbəljuːem'diː/ noun [plural] abbreviation for weapons of mass destruction: weapons, such as nuclear bombs, which cause a lot of damage and death when used

wobble /'wɒbl/ verb [I, T] If something wobbles or you make something wobble, it moves from side to side, often because it is not on a flat surface. *The ladder started to wobble.* ○ *Stop wobbling the table.* ● **wobbly** adjective likely to wobble *a wobbly chair*

woe /wəʊ/ noun [U] literary sadness *full of woe*

woeful /'wəʊfᵊl/ adjective very bad and showing no skill *a woeful attempt/performance* ● **woefully** adverb

woes /wəʊz/ noun [plural] formal *your woes* your problems and worries

wok /wɒk/ noun [C] a large, bowl-shaped pan that is used for frying Chinese food

woke /wəʊk/ past tense of wake

woken /'wəʊkᵊn/ past participle of wake

wolf¹ /wʊlf/ noun [C] plural wolves /wʊlvz/ a wild animal like a large dog

wolf² /wʊlf/ (also **wolf down**) verb [T] informal to eat something very quickly *I gave her a plate of pasta and she wolfed it down.*

o-▪**woman** /'wʊmən/ noun [C] plural women /'wɪmɪn/ an adult female person *a 30-year-old woman* ○ *There were two women at the bus stop.* ● **womanhood** noun [U] the state of being a woman

womanly /'wʊmənli/ adjective having the qualities and appearance that people think a woman should have *womanly charms*

womb /wuːm/ noun [C] the organ inside a woman's body where a baby grows

women /'wɪmɪn/ plural of woman

won /wʌn/ past of win

o-▪**wonder¹** /'wʌndər/ verb **1** [I, T] to want to know something or to try to understand the reason for something [+ question word] *I wonder what he's making for dinner.* ○ *I wonder why she left so suddenly.* **2 I/we wonder if/whether ...** used to politely ask someone for something or to

suggest something *I wonder if you could help me?* ○ *We were wondering if you'd like to come over for a meal sometime.*

wonder² /'wʌndər/ noun **1** [U] surprise and admiration *The boys gazed in wonder at the shiny, red Ferrari.* **2** [C] something that makes you feel surprise or admiration [usually plural] *the wonders of modern medicine* **3 no wonder** used to say that you are not surprised about something *No wonder she failed the test if she didn't do any work.* **4 it's a wonder (that)** used to say that you are surprised about something *It's a wonder he's still alive.*

o-▪**wonderful** /'wʌndəfᵊl/ adjective very good *a wonderful idea* ○ *We had a wonderful time in Spain.* ● **wonderfully** adverb

o-▪**won't** /wəʊnt/ short for will not *I won't be home before midnight.*

woo /wuː/ verb [T] **wooing**, past **wooed** to try to persuade someone to support you or to use your business *a political party trying to woo young voters*

o-▪**wood** /wʊd/ noun **1** [C, U] the hard material that trees are made of *a piece of wood* **2** [C] (also **woods**) a large area of trees growing near each other *We went for a walk in the woods.*

wooded /'wʊdɪd/ adjective covered with trees *a wooded area*

wooden /'wʊdᵊn/ adjective made of wood *a wooden chair*

woodland /'wʊdlənd/ noun [C, U] an area of land with a lot of trees

woodwind /'wʊdwɪnd/ noun [U] the group of musical instruments that you play by blowing into them *woodwind instruments*

woodwork /'wʊdwɜːk/ noun [U] **1** the parts of a building that are made from wood **2** the activity of making things from wood

woof /wʊf/ noun [C] the sound made by a dog

o-▪**wool** /wʊl/ noun [U] **1** the soft, thick hair on a sheep **2** thick thread or material that is made from the hair of a sheep *a wool suit* ○ *a ball of wool* ⊃See also: cotton wool.

woollen UK (US **woolen**) /'wʊlən/ adjective made of wool *woollen gloves*

woolly UK (US **wooly**) /'wʊli/ adjective made of wool, or made of something that looks like wool *a green woolly hat*

o-▪**word¹** /wɜːd/ noun **1** [C] a group of letters or sounds that mean something, or a single letter or sound that means something *'Hund' is the German word for 'dog'.* ○ *He has difficulty spelling long words.* **2 not believe/understand/ hear, etc a word** to not believe/understand/ hear, etc anything *I don't believe a word he says.* **3 a word of warning/advice/thanks, etc** something that you say to warn someone, give them advice, thank them, etc *Just a word of warning - he doesn't like people being late.* **4 have a word with sb** to talk to someone for a short time *I'll have a word with Ted and see if he wants to come.* **5 put in a good word for sb** to praise someone, often to someone who might be able to employ them **6 give sb your word** to promise someone something *He gave me his word that he wouldn't tell anyone.* **7 take sb's**

word for it to believe what someone says without any proof **8 in other words** used to explain what something means in a different way *He said he's too busy, in other words, he isn't interested.* **9 in sb's words** used when you repeat what someone said *In the manager's words, the game was 'a total disaster'.* **10 word for word** using the exact words that were originally used *She repeated word for word what he had told her.* **11 have the last word** to say the last thing in a discussion or argument or make the final decision about something **12 not breathe a word** to not tell people a secret *Don't breathe a word about this to anyone.* **13 not get a word in edgeways** UK (US **not get a word in edgewise**) to be unable to say anything because someone else is talking so much ⊃See also: a **play²** on words, **swear word**.

word² /wɜːd/ *verb* [T] to choose the words you use when you are saying or writing something *How should I word this letter?*

change the wording • the **exact** wording • the wording **of** sth • a **form of** wording

wording /'wɜːdɪŋ/ *noun* [U] the words that are used when someone says or writes something

word 'processor *noun* [C] a computer or computer program that you use for writing letters, reports, etc • **word processing** *noun* [U]

wore /wɔːʳ/ *past tense of* wear

⊶**work¹** /wɜːk/ *verb* **1** JOB [I, T] to do a job, especially the job you do to earn money *Helen* **works for** *a computer company.* ○ *He* **works as** *a waiter in an Italian restaurant.* ○ *My Dad works very long hours* (= he works a lot of hours). **2** MACHINE [I] If a machine or piece of equipment works, it is not broken. *Does this radio work?* ○ *The washing machine isn't working.* **3** SUCCEED [I] If something works, it is effective and successful. *Her plan to get rid of me didn't work.* **4 can work sth; know how to work sth** to know how to use a machine or piece of equipment *Do you know how to work the video recorder?* **5** EFFORT [I, T] to do something that needs a lot of time or effort, or to make someone do this [+ to do sth] *He's been working to improve his speed.* ○ *Our teacher works us very hard.* **6 work your way around/through/up, etc sth** to achieve something gradually *I have a pile of homework to work my way through.*

work against sb to make it more difficult for someone to achieve something *Age can work against you when you are looking for a job.*

work at sth to try hard to achieve something [+ doing sth] *You need to work at improving your writing.*

work on sth to spend time repairing or improving something *Tim loves working on old cars.*

work sth out 1 to calculate an amount *I'm trying to work out the total cost.* **2** to understand something or decide something after thinking very carefully [+ question word] *I haven't worked out what to do yet.*

work out 1 If a problem or difficult situation works out, it gradually becomes better. *Don't worry - everything will work out in the end.* **2** to do exercises to make your body stronger *She works out at the gym four times a week.* ⊃See colour picture **Phrasal Verbs** on page Centre 16. **3 work out badly/well, etc** to happen or develop in a particular way *Changing schools worked out really well for me.* **4 work out at sth** to be the result when you calculate something *If we share the costs, it works out at $10 per person.*

work sb out UK to understand the reasons for someone's behaviour *I can't work him out at all.*

work up to sth to gradually prepare yourself for something difficult *I am going to make this phone call – I'm just working up to it.*

do/find/finish/have work • **clerical/dirty/hard/part-time/pioneering** work • **at work**

⊶**work²** /wɜːk/ *noun* **1** EFFORT [U] when you use physical or mental effort to do something *Decorating that room was* **hard work.** ○ *I can certainly do a report for you but it will be a lot of work.* **2** PLACE [U] the place where you go to do your job *He had an accident at work.* **3** JOB [U] something you do as a job to earn money *Has she got any work yet?* ○ *Many young people are* **out of work** (= they do not have a job). **4** ACTIVITY [U] the activities that you have to do at school, for your job, etc *Have you got a lot of work to do?* ○ *The teacher said she was pleased with my work.* ○ *My teacher gives us so much work.* **5 get/set to work (on sth)** to start doing something *I'll just finish this report then I'll set to work on those figures.* **6** ART/MUSIC ETC [C, U] a painting, book, piece of music, etc *The exhibition includes works by Picasso and Klee.* ○ *the* **complete works** *of Shakespeare* **7 do sb's dirty work** to do something unpleasant or difficult for someone else because they do not want to do it themselves *I'm not going to do his dirty work for him!* **8 have your work cut out** to have something very difficult to do *It's a demanding job - she's going to have her work cut out for her.* ⊃See also: **donkey work, work of art.**

work, job or **occupation**?

Work is something you do to earn money. Remember that this noun is uncountable.

She enjoys her work in the hospital.

He's looking for work.

~~He's looking for a work.~~

Job is used to talk about the particular work activity which you do.

He's looking for a job in computer programming.

Teaching must be an interesting job.

~~Teaching must be an interesting work.~~

Occupation is a formal word which means the job that

you do. It is often used on forms. See also: **career** and **profession**.

workable /'wɜːkəbl/ *adjective* A workable plan or system can be used or done easily and is effective. ⊃Opposite **unworkable**.

workaholic /ˌwɜːkə'hɒlɪk/ *noun* [C] *informal* someone who works too much and does not have time to do anything else

workbook /'wɜːkbʊk/ *noun* [C] a book with questions and exercises in it that you use when you are learning something

worked 'up *adjective* very nervous, angry, or excited

worker /'wɜːkəʳ/ *noun* **1** [C] someone who works for a company or organization but does not have a powerful position *an office worker* **2 a quick/slow/good, etc worker** someone who works quickly/slowly/well, etc ⊃See also: **social worker**.

workforce /'wɜːkfɔːs/ *noun* [group] **1** all the people who work for a company or organization **2** all the people in a country who are able to do a job *10% of the workforce are unemployed.*

working /'wɜːkɪŋ/ *adjective* [always before noun] **1** relating to your job *good working conditions* **2 a working man/woman, etc** someone who has a job *a working mother* **3 a working knowledge of sth** knowledge about something which is good enough to be useful *She has a working knowledge of German and Russian.* ⊃See also: **hard-working**.

working 'class *noun* [C] the social class of people who have little money and who usually do physical work ● **working-class** /ˌwɜːkɪŋ'klɑːs/ *adjective a working-class family*

workings /'wɜːkɪŋz/ *noun* **the workings of sth** how something works *the workings of the mind*

workload /'wɜːkləʊd/ *noun* [C] the amount of work that you have to do *Nurses have a very heavy workload* (= they work hard).

workman /'wɜːkmən/ *noun* [C] *plural* **workmen** someone who does a physical job such as building

workmanship /'wɜːkmənʃɪp/ *noun* [U] the skill that is used in making something

work of 'art *noun* [C] *plural* **works of art 1** a very beautiful and important painting, drawing, etc *They stole several valuable works of art.* **2 be a work of art** to be something which is beautiful or needed a lot of skill to create *Have you seen the wedding cake? It's a work of art.*

workout /'wɜːkaʊt/ *noun* [C] when you do a series of exercises to make your body strong and healthy *a daily workout at the gym*

workplace /'wɜːkpleɪs/ *noun* [C] the place where you work *We are trying to get rid of bullying in the workplace.*

worksheet /'wɜːkˌʃiːt/ *noun* [C] a piece of paper with questions and exercises for students

workshop /'wɜːkʃɒp/ *noun* [C] **1** when a group of people meet to learn more about something by discussing it and doing practical exercises *a workshop on crime prevention* **2** a place

where people use tools and machines to make or repair things

workstation /'wɜːkˌsteɪʃᵊn/ *noun* [C] a computer and the area around it where you work in an office

'work ˌsurface (*also* worktop /'wɜːktɒp/) *noun* [C] a flat surface for preparing food in a kitchen ⊃See colour picture **The Kitchen** on page Centre 2.

WORD PARTNERS FOR **world**

travel the world ● **in** the world ● **across/all over** the world

---

o–**world¹** /wɜːld/ *noun* **1 the world** the Earth and all the people, places, and things on it *Everest is the highest mountain in the world.* ○ *She's travelled all over the world.* **2** [C] the people and things that are involved in a particular activity or subject [usually singular] *the entertainment world* ○ *the world of politics* **3 the developing/industrialized/Western, etc world** a particular area of the Earth **4 the plant/animal, etc world** plants/animals, etc as a group **5 your world** your life and experiences *His whole world fell apart when she left.* **6 do sb a/the world of good** *informal* to make someone feel much happier or healthier *That swim has done me a world of good.* **7 be out of this world** *informal* to be of extremely good quality *Their chocolate cake is just out of this world!* **8 think the world of sb** to like and admire someone very much **9 the whole world** *informal* everyone *The whole world knew she was getting married before I did.* ⊃See also: have the **best³** of both worlds, not be the **end¹** of the world, the **Old World**, the **outside world**, the **Third World**, be on **top¹** of the world.

world² /wɜːld/ *adjective* [always before noun] relating to the whole world *world peace* ○ *the world championships*

world-class /ˌwɜːld'klɑːs/ *adjective* one of the best in the world *a world-class swimmer*

world-famous /ˌwɜːld'feɪməs/ *adjective* known by people everywhere in the world *The Eiffel Tower is a world-famous landmark.*

worldly /'wɜːldli/ *adjective* **1 sb's worldly goods/possessions** everything that someone owns *She lost all her worldly possessions in a fire.* **2** having had a lot of experience of life *a worldly woman*

world 'war *noun* [C] a war in which several large or important countries fight

worldwide /ˌwɜːld'waɪd/ *adjective, adverb* in all parts of the world *10 million copies have been sold worldwide.*

the ˌWorld Wide 'Web *noun* part of the Internet that consists of all the connected websites (= pages of text and pictures) ⊃See Extra help page **The Web and the Internet** on page Centre 36.

worm¹ /wɜːm/ *noun* [C] a small creature with a long, thin, soft body and no legs ⊃See also: a **can²** of worms.

worm² /wɜːm/ *verb* **worm your way into sth** to gradually get into a situation by making people like you and trust you, especially by deceiving them *He wormed his way into the family.*

worn¹ /wɔːn/ *adjective*
Worn clothing or objects have been used a lot and show damage. *a worn leather chair*

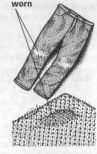

worn

worn² /wɔːn/ *past participle of* wear

worn-out /ˌwɔːnˈaʊt/ *adjective* **1** extremely tired *I was absolutely worn-out after all that dancing.* **2** Something that is worn-out is so old or has been used so much that it is damaged too much to repair. *a worn-out carpet*

o**worried** /ˈwʌrid/ *adjective* anxious because you are thinking about problems or unpleasant things that might happen *She's really worried about her son.* ○ [+ (that)] *I'm worried that she'll tell Maria.*

o**worry¹** /ˈwʌri/ *verb* **1** [I] to think about problems or unpleasant things that might happen in a way that makes you feel anxious *Don't worry - she'll be all right.* ○ *She's always worrying about something.* ○ [+ (that)] *I worry that he might run away.* **2** [T] to make someone feel anxious because of problems or unpleasant things that might happen *It worries me that he hasn't phoned yet.*

COMMON LEARNER ERROR

worry about something or someone
Be careful to use the correct preposition after this verb.
They were worried about the weather.
~~They were worried for the weather.~~

⚃ WORD PARTNERS FOR *worry* (noun)

allay/ease/express a worry • a constant/lingering/nagging/real worry • a worry about/over sth

worry² /ˈwʌri/ *noun* **1** [C] a problem that makes you feel anxious *health worries* **2** [U] when you are anxious about something *She's been sick with worry.*

worrying /ˈwʌriɪŋ/ *adjective* making you feel anxious *a worrying situation* •**worryingly** *adverb She's worryingly thin.*

o**worse¹** /wɜːs/ *adjective* (*comparative of* bad) **1** more unpleasant or difficult than something else that is also bad *The exam was worse than I expected.* ○ *We'll have to stop the game if the rain gets any worse.* **2** more ill *The drugs aren't working, he just seems to be getting worse.* **3** be none the worse for sth to not be harmed or damaged by something *He seemed none the worse for the experience.* **4** worse luck *UK informal* used to show that you are annoyed or unhappy about something *I've got to work on Saturday, worse luck!*

worse² /wɜːs/ *noun* [U] **1** something that is more unpleasant or difficult *It was a nasty*

accident, although I've seen worse. **2** for the worse If a situation changes for the worse, it becomes worse.

worse³ /wɜːs/ *adverb* (*comparative of* badly) less well *He was treated much worse than I was.*

worsen /ˈwɜːsᵊn/ *verb* [I, T] to become worse or to make something become worse *His condition suddenly worsened last week.*

,**worse 'off** *adjective* [never before noun] poorer or in a more difficult situation *If Rick loses his job we'll be even worse off.*

worship /ˈwɜːʃɪp/ *verb* worshipping, *past* worshipped, *also US* worshiping, *past* worshiped **1** [I, T] to show respect for a god by saying prayers or performing religious ceremonies **2** [T] to love and respect someone very much *She worshipped her mother.* •**worship** *noun* [U] *a place of worship* (= a religious building) •**worshipper** *noun* [C]

o**worst¹** /wɜːst/ *adjective* (*superlative of* bad) **the worst** the most unpleasant or difficult *What's the worst job you've ever had?*

worst² /wɜːst/ *noun* **1** **the worst** the most unpleasant or difficult thing, person, or situation *I've made some mistakes in the past, but this is definitely the worst.* **2** **at worst** used to say what the most unpleasant or difficult situation could possibly be *At worst, we might lose our money.* **3** **if the worst comes to the worst** *UK* (*US* if worse/worst comes to worst) if a situation develops in the most unpleasant or difficult way

worst³ /wɜːst/ *adverb* (*superlative of* badly) the most badly *the worst affected area*

o**worth¹** /wɜːθ/ *adjective* **1** **be worth sth** to have a particular value, especially in money *Our house is worth about £600,000.* **2** **be worth doing/seeing/trying, etc** to be useful or enjoyable to do/see/try, etc *It's not as good as his last book but it's definitely worth reading.* **3** **be worth it** to be useful or enjoyable despite needing a lot of effort *It was a long climb up the mountain but the view was worth it.* ○ *Don't bother complaining - it's really not worth it.* **4** **be worth your while** If it is worth your while doing something, it is useful or enjoyable despite needing a lot of effort. *It isn't worth my while going all that way just for one day.*

COMMON LEARNER ERROR

be worth doing something
When **worth** is followed by a verb, the verb is always in the -ing form.
Do you think it's worth asking Patrick first?
~~Do you think it's worth to ask Patrick first?~~

o**worth²** /wɜːθ/ *noun* **1** **£20/$100, etc worth of sth** the amount of something that you can buy for £20/$100, etc *I've put £2 worth of stamps on the letter.* **2** **a month's/year's, etc worth of sth** the amount of something that can be done or used in a month/year, etc *an hour's worth of free phone calls* **3** [U] how important or useful someone or something is *She's finally proved her worth.*

worthless /ˈwɜːθləs/ *adjective* **1** not important

or useful *He made me feel stupid and worthless.* **2** having no value in money *The painting's a fake - it's completely worthless.*

worthwhile /ˌwɜːθ'waɪl/ *adjective* useful and enjoyable, despite needing a lot of effort *It's a difficult course but it's very worthwhile.*

worthy /'wɜːði/ *adjective* **1** deserving respect, admiration, or support *a worthy cause* ○ *a worthy champion* **2 be worthy of attention/respect, etc** to deserve attention/respect, etc

o⟶**would** *strong form* /wʊd/ *weak form* /wəd/ *modal verb* **1** [IF] used to say what might happen if something else happens *What would you do if you lost your job?* **2** [SAID/THOUGHT] used as the past form of 'will' to talk about what someone has said or thought *Sue promised that she would help.* ○ *They thought that she would never recover.* **3** [WILLING] used as the past form of 'will' to talk about what someone was willing to do or what something was able to do *I asked her to talk to him, but she wouldn't.* ○ *The car wouldn't start this morning.* **4 would like/love sth** used to say politely that you want something *I'd (= I would) like a cup of coffee, please.* **5 would you** used to politely ask someone something *Would you like a drink?* ○ *Would you come with me, please?* **6** [IMAGINE] used to talk about a situation that you can imagine happening *It would be lovely to go to New York.* **7 I would imagine/think, etc** used to give an opinion in a polite way *I would imagine she'll discuss it with her husband first.* **8** [OFTEN] used to talk about things that happened often in the past *He would always turn and wave at the end of the street.* **9 She/he/you would!** *mainly UK* used to show that you are not surprised by someone's annoying behaviour *Margot spent £200 on a dress for the occasion but she would, wouldn't she?* ⊃See Extra help page **Modal verbs** on page Centre 22.

o⟶**wouldn't** /'wʊdᵊnt/ *short for* would not *She wouldn't let us watch TV.*

WORD PARTNERS FOR **wound** (*noun*)

inflict/sustain a wound • a wound **heals (up)** • **bullet/gunshot/stab** wounds • a wound **on/to** [sb's arm/back, etc] • an **open** wound

wound¹ /wuːnd/ *noun* [C] an injury, especially one that is made by a knife or bullet

wound² /wuːnd/ *verb* [T] **1** to injure someone, especially with a knife or gun [often passive] *He was badly wounded in the attack.* ○ *wounded soldiers* **2** to upset someone [often passive] *She was deeply wounded by his rejection.*

wound³ /waʊnd/ *past of* wind³

wound 'up *adjective* very nervous, worried, or angry *He gets very wound up before an important match.*

wove /wəʊv/ *past tense of* weave²

woven /'wəʊvᵊn/ *past participle of* weave²

wow /waʊ/ *exclamation informal* something that you say to show surprise, excitement, admiration, etc *Wow! Look at that car!*

WORD PARTNERS FOR **wrangle**

be involved in/get into a wrangle • a **bitter/legal** wrangle • a wrangle **over** sth • a wrangle **between** sb and sb • a wrangle **with** sb

wrangle¹ /'ræŋgl/ *noun* [C] a long and complicated argument *a legal wrangle*

wrangle² /'ræŋgl/ *verb* [I] to argue with someone for a long time *They're still wrangling over money.*

wrap /ræp/ *verb* [T] wrapping, *past* wrapped **1** (*also* wrap up) to cover something or someone with paper, cloth, etc *to wrap a present* ○ *They wrapped him in a blanket.* ⊃Opposite unwrap. **2 wrap sth around sb/sth** to fold paper, cloth, etc around something to cover it *He wrapped a towel around his waist.* **3 wrap your arms/fingers, etc around sb/sth** to put your arms/fingers, etc around someone or something *She wrapped her arms around my neck.*

wrap sth up 1 to fold paper, cloth, etc around something to cover it *Have you wrapped up Jenny's present?* **2** to finish an activity successfully *We hope to have this deal wrapped up by Monday.*

wrap up to dress in warm clothes *Wrap up well - it's cold outside.*

be wrapped up in sth to give so much of your attention to something that you do not have time for other things or people *She's so wrapped up in her work that she hardly sees her kids.*

wrapper /'ræpəʳ/ *noun* [C] a piece of paper or plastic that covers something that you buy, especially food (*UK*) *sweet wrappers/* (*US*) *candy wrappers*

wrapping /'ræpɪŋ/ *noun* [C, U] paper or plastic that is used to cover and protect something

'wrapping ,paper *noun* [U] decorated paper that is used to cover presents

wrath /rɒθ/ *noun* [U] *literary* extreme anger

wreak /riːk/ *verb past* wrought *or* wreaked **wreak havoc** to cause a lot of damage or harm *Floods have wreaked havoc in central Europe.*

wreath /riːθ/ *noun* [C] *plural* wreaths /riːðz/ a large ring of leaves and flowers used as a decoration or to show respect for someone who has died

wreck¹ /rek/ *verb* [T] to destroy something completely *The explosion wrecked several cars and damaged nearby buildings.*

wreck² /rek/ *noun* [C] **1** [VEHICLE] a car, ship, or aircraft that has been very badly damaged **2** [PERSON] *informal* someone who is in a bad physical or mental condition [usually singular] *I was a complete wreck by the end of my exams.* **3** [ACCIDENT] *mainly US* a bad accident involving a car or train *a car/train wreck*

WORD PARTNERS FOR **wreckage**

be cut (free) from/pulled from/recovered from the wreckage • be **trapped in** the wreckage • a **piece of** wreckage • the **tangled** wreckage **of** sth

wreckage /'rekɪdʒ/ *noun* [U] the parts that

W

remain of a car, ship, or aircraft that has been destroyed *Two survivors were **pulled from the wreckage**.*

wren /ren/ *noun* [C] a very small, brown bird

wrench¹ /renʃ/ *verb* [T] **1 wrench sth from/off, etc sb/sth** to pull something violently away from a fixed position *The phone had been wrenched off the wall.* **2** to injure part of your body by turning it suddenly *I wrenched my right shoulder playing tennis.*

wrench² /renʃ/ *noun* **1** [no plural] when you are very sad because you have to leave someone or something *She found leaving home a real wrench.* **2** [C] *US* (*UK* **spanner**) a tool with a round end that is used to turn nuts and bolts (= metal objects used to fasten things together) ⊃See picture at **tool**.

wrestle /'resl/ *verb* [I] to fight with someone by holding them and trying to push them to the ground
wrestle with sth to try very hard to deal with a difficult problem or decision *He's still wrestling with his conscience.*

wrestling /'reslɪŋ/ *noun* [U] a sport in which two people fight and try to push each other to the ground ● **wrestler** *noun* [C]

wretched /'retʃɪd/ *adjective* **1** UNHAPPY very unhappy or ill *I'd been feeling wretched all day so I went to bed early.* **2** BAD very bad or of poor quality *The refugees were living in wretched conditions.* **3** ANNOYED [always before noun] used to show that something or someone makes you angry *This wretched phone won't work!*

wriggle /'rɪgl/ *verb* [I, T] **1** to twist your body or move part of your body with short, quick movements *She wriggled her toes in the warm sand.* **2 wriggle out of sth/doing sth** to avoid doing something that you have agreed to do *Are you trying to wriggle out of going to the meeting?*

wring /rɪŋ/ (*also* **wring out**) *verb* [T] *past* **wrung** to twist a cloth or piece of clothing with your hands to remove water from it *He wrung out his socks and hung them up to dry.* ⊃See also: wring your hands (**hand¹**).

wrinkle /'rɪŋkl/ *noun* [C]
1 a small line on your face that you get when you grow old **2** a small fold in a piece of cloth ● **wrinkle** *verb* [I, T] *a wrinkled face*

wrinkles

wrist /rɪst/ *noun* [C] the part of your body between your hand and your arm

wristband /'rɪstbænd/ *noun* [C] **1** a piece of material which goes around the wrist (= the part of your body between your hand and your arm), for example to hold a watch **2** a piece of material in a particular colour which goes around the wrist and shows that the person wearing it supports a certain charity

wristwatch /'rɪstwɒtʃ/ *noun* [C] a watch which

you wear on your wrist (= the part of your body between your hand and your arm)

writ /rɪt/ *noun* [C] a legal document that orders someone to do something

o▪**write** /raɪt/ *verb past tense* **wrote**, *past participle* **written 1** WORDS [I, T] to produce words, letters, or numbers on a surface using a pen or pencil *Write your name at the top of the page.* ○ *She can't read or write.* **2** BOOK [I, T] to create a book, story, article, etc or a piece of music *He's writing a book on Russian literature.* ○ *She writes for Time magazine.* **3** LETTER [I, T] to send someone a letter [+ two objects] *I wrote her a letter last week.* ○ *Has Bill written to you recently?* **4** DOCUMENT [T] (*also* **write out**) to put all the information that is needed on a document *He wrote out a cheque for £250.*

COMMON LEARNER ERROR

write

Remember to use the correct grammar after **write**.

write to someone
Rachel wrote to me last week.

write someone **a letter**
Rachel wrote me a letter last week.

write someone (American English)
Rachel wrote me last week.

write back to reply to someone's letter
write sth down to write something on a piece of paper so that you do not forget it *Did you write Jo's phone number down?*
write in to write a letter to a newspaper, television company, etc *Lots of people have written in to complain about the show.*
write off to write a letter to an organization asking them to send you something *I've written off for an information pack.*
write sth off 1 to accept that an amount of money has been lost or will never be paid to you *to write off debts* **2** *UK* to damage a vehicle so badly that it cannot be repaired
write sb/sth off to decide that someone or something is not useful or important *They had written him off before they even met him.*
write sth up to write something in a complete form, usually using notes that you made earlier *Have you written up that report yet?*

write-off /'raɪtɒf/ *noun* [C] *UK* a vehicle that is damaged so badly in an accident that it cannot be repaired *I wasn't hurt, but the car was a complete write-off.*

o▪**writer** /'raɪtəʳ/ *noun* [C] someone whose job is writing books, stories, articles, etc

write-up /'raɪtʌp/ *noun* [C] an article in a newspaper or magazine in which someone gives their opinion about a performance, product, etc *The film got a very good write-up in yesterday's paper.*

writhe /raɪð/ *verb* [I] to twist your body in a violent way, often because you are in pain *She lay on her bed, writhing in agony.*

o▪**writing** /'raɪtɪŋ/ *noun* [U] **1** SKILL the skill or activity of producing words on a surface *Teachers focus on reading and writing in the first year.* **2** WORDS words that have been written or printed *The writing was too small to read.* **3** [STYLE] the way that someone writes *You've got very neat writing.* **4** [BOOKS] the books, stories, articles, etc written by a particular person or group of people *She's studying women's writing of the 1930s.* **5** [JOB] the activity or job of creating books, stories, or articles **6 in writing** An agreement that is in writing is official because it has been written and not only spoken. *Please confirm your reservation in writing.*

written¹ /'rɪtᵊn/ *adjective* [always before noun] presented as a document on paper *a written statement/warning*

written² /'rɪtᵊn/ *past participle of* write

o-**wrong¹** /rɒŋ/ *adjective* **1** [NOT CORRECT] not correct *the wrong answer* ○ *We're going the wrong way.* **2 be wrong** to think or say something that is not correct *You were wrong about the party - it's today, not tomorrow.* **3 get sth wrong** to produce an answer or result that is not correct *I got most of the answers wrong.* **4** [PROBLEM] [never before noun] If something is wrong, there is a problem. *There's something wrong with my computer.* ○ *What's wrong?* **5** [NOT MORAL] [never before noun] morally bad [+ to do sth] *It's wrong to tell lies.* **6** [NOT SUITABLE] not suitable *I think she's wrong for this job.* ⊃See also: get (hold of) the wrong **end¹** of the stick, get/start off on the wrong **foot¹**, not put a **foot¹** wrong, rub sb up the wrong **way¹**.

o-**wrong²** /rɒŋ/ *adverb* **1** in a way that is not correct *He always says my name wrong.* **2 go wrong** to develop problems *Something's gone wrong with my computer.* **3 Don't get me wrong.** *informal* used when you do not want someone to think that you do not like someone or something *Don't get me wrong, I like her,*

but she can be very annoying.

wrong³ /rɒŋ/ *noun* **1** [C, U] when something is not morally right *She's old enough to know the difference between **right and wrong.*** **2 be in the wrong** to be responsible for a mistake or something bad that has happened

wrong⁴ /rɒŋ/ *verb* [T] *formal* to treat someone unfairly *a wronged man*

wrongdoing /'rɒŋ,duːɪŋ/ *noun* [C, U] *formal* when someone does something that is illegal or not honest

wrongful /'rɒŋfᵊl/ *adjective* **wrongful arrest/conviction/imprisonment, etc** when someone is accused of something or punished for something unfairly or illegally ● **wrongfully** *adverb* **wrongfully arrested**

wrongly /'rɒŋli/ *adverb* **1** in a way that is not correct *The letter was wrongly addressed.* **2 wrongly accused/convicted/imprisoned, etc** accused or punished unfairly or illegally *She was wrongly convicted of drug smuggling.*

wrote /rəʊt/ *past tense of* write

wrought /rɔːt/ *past of* wreak

,**wrought 'iron** *noun* [U] iron that can be bent into shapes and used to make gates, furniture, etc

wrung /rʌŋ/ *past of* wring

wry /raɪ/ *adjective* A wry expression or remark shows your humour despite being in a difficult or disappointing situation. *a wry smile* ● **wryly** *adverb*

www /,dʌbljuː,dʌbljuː'dʌbljuː/ *noun abbreviation for* World Wide Web (= part of the Internet that consists of all the connected websites) ⊃See Extra help page **The Web and the Internet** on page Centre 36.

Xx

X, x /eks/ **1** LETTER the twenty-fourth letter of the alphabet **2** WRONG used to show that an answer is wrong **3** KISS used to represent a kiss at the end of a letter **4** UNKNOWN used to represent an unknown person or thing

xenophobia /ˌzenəʊˈfəʊbiə/ *noun* [U] extreme dislike or fear of people from other countries ● **xenophobic** /ˌzenəʊˈfəʊbɪk/ *adjective*

XL /ˌekˈsel/ *abbreviation for* extra large: the largest size of clothes

Xmas /ˈkrɪstməs/ *noun* [U] *informal* used as a short way of writing 'Christmas' (= a Christian holiday), mainly on signs or cards *Happy Xmas!*

XML /ˌeksemˈel/ *noun trademark abbreviation for* extensible mark up language: a way of putting symbols into text to make it look right in computer systems

X-ray /ˈeksreɪ/ *noun* [C] **1** a photograph that shows the inside of your body *They took an X-ray of his leg.* **2** a wave of energy that can pass through solid materials ● **X-ray** *verb* [T] to take a photograph that shows the inside of something

xylophone /ˈzaɪləfəʊn/ *noun* [C] a musical instrument consisting of a row of flat, metal bars that you hit with sticks

Yy

Y, y /waɪ/ the twenty-fifth letter of the alphabet

ya /jə/ *pronoun informal* you *See ya later.*

yacht /jɒt/ *noun* [C] a large boat with sails used for pleasure or in races *a luxury yacht*

yacht

Yank /jæŋk/ *noun* [C] *informal* someone from the US, sometimes considered an offensive word

yank /jæŋk/ *verb* [T] *informal* to pull something with a strong, sudden movement *She yanked the drawer open.* ○ *He yanked at the rope.*

yap /jæp/ *verb* [I] yapping, *past* yapped If a small dog yaps, it makes a lot of short, high sounds.

o-◄**yard** /jɑːd/ *noun* [C] **1** UNIT (*written abbreviation* yd) a unit for measuring length, equal to 0.9144 metres or 3 feet *There's a bus stop a few hundred yards up the road.* ⟹See Extra help page **Measurements** on page Centre 31. **2** HOUSE US (*UK* garden) an area of land in front of or behind a house **3** AREA a small area of ground next to a building, often with a fence or wall around it *a school yard*

yardstick /ˈjɑːdstɪk/ *noun* [C] something that you use to judge how good or successful something else is *If popularity is the yardstick of success, he's done very well.*

yarn /jɑːn/ *noun* **1** [U] thread used for making cloth **2** [C] *informal* a long story that is probably not true

yawn /jɔːn/ *verb* [I] to take a deep breath with your mouth wide open, because you are tired or bored ● yawn *noun* [C]

yawn

yawning /ˈjɔːnɪŋ/ *adjective* **a yawning gap** a very big gap (= space or difference)

yd *written abbreviation for* yard (= a unit for measuring length)

yeah /jeə/ *exclamation informal spoken* yes

o-◄**year** /jɪəʳ/ *noun* [C] **1** a period of 12 months, or 365 or 366 days, especially from 1 January to 31 December *last year/next year* ○ *He joined the company a year ago.* **2** the academic/financial,

etc year the period of a year that is used by universities/businesses, etc to organize their activities **3** be two/twelve/37, etc years old to be a particular age *Her son is six years old.* **4** a two-/twelve-/37-, etc year-old someone who is a particular age **5** UK a group of students who start college or a course together *He was in my year at school.* **6** years a long time *I haven't seen Linda for years.* ⟹See also: for **donkey's** years, leap year, new year.

describing age

If you describe someone's age by saying 'Tom is 8 years old', you always write the age as three separate words.

My son is 8 years old.

You can use also use 8-year-old, etc. as an adjective. When you do this, the words are written together using hyphens (-).

I've got a 12-year-old son.

You can also do the same with days, weeks, and months.

I've got a 10-week-old rabbit.

The baby is three months old.

a three-month-old baby

yearbook /ˈjɪəbʊk/ *noun* [C] a book produced every year by a school or organization, containing information about its activities, members, etc

yearly /ˈjɪəli/ *adjective, adverb* happening once a year or every year *a yearly fee* ○ *Interest is paid yearly.*

yearn /jɜːn/ *verb* yearn for sth; yearn to do sth to want something very much with a feeling of sadness *They yearned for peace.* ○ *She yearned to get away.* ● yearning *noun* [C, U]

yeast /jiːst/ *noun* [U] a substance used to make bread rise and to make beer and wine

yell /jel/ *verb* [I, T] to shout something very loudly *The policeman yelled at them to stop.* ● yell *noun* [C]

o-◄**yellow** /ˈjeləʊ/ *adjective* being the same colour as a lemon or the sun *a bright yellow tablecloth* ● yellow *noun* [C, U] the colour yellow ⟹See colour picture **Colours** on page Centre 12.

ˌyellow 'card *noun* [C] in football, a small card shown to a player as a warning that the player has not obeyed a rule ⟹Compare red card

the ˌYellow 'Pages UK *trademark* (*US* the 'Yellow ˌPages) *noun* [plural] a big, yellow book containing telephone numbers of shops and businesses

yelp /jelp/ *verb* [I] If a dog yelps, it gives a sudden cry because of pain or shock.

yep /jep/ *exclamation informal spoken* yes

o-◄**yes¹** /jes/ *exclamation* **1** AGREE used to agree with something, or to give a positive answer to something *"Can I borrow your pencil?" "Yes, of course."* ○ *"Are you feeling better?" "Yes, thanks."* ○ *"Coffee?" " Yes, please."* **2** ANSWER used as an answer when someone calls you *"Jack!" "Yes?"* **3** DISAGREE used to disagree with a negative announcement *"He's not here yet." "Yes he is, I've just seen him."*

yes² /jes/ *noun* [C] a positive reaction or agree-

Y

ment with something *Was that a yes or a no?*

⊶**yesterday** /ˈjestədeɪ/ *noun* [U], *adverb* the day before today *I went to see the doctor yesterday.* ○ *yesterday morning/afternoon*

⊶**yet¹** /jet/ *adverb* **1** before now or before that time *Have you read his book yet?* ○ *"Has he called?" "No, not yet."* **2** now or as early as this time *I don't want to go home yet.* **3 the best/worst, etc yet** the best or worst, etc until now *That was my worst exam yet.* **4 be/have yet to do sth** to not have done something that was expected before this time *They have yet to make a decision.* **5 yet again/another/more, etc** used to show that you are surprised or annoyed that something is being repeated or increased *He's given us yet more work to do.* **6 could/may/might, etc yet** used to say there is still a possibility that something will happen *He may win yet.*

yet² /jet/ *conjunction* used to add something that seems surprising because of what you have just said *simple yet effective*

yew /juː/ *noun* [C, U] a tree with dark, needle-shaped leaves, or the wood of this tree

WORD PARTNERS FOR *yield*

yield **clues/information/a profit/a result**

yield¹ /jiːld/ *verb* **1** [T] to produce or provide something *to **yield a profit*** ○ *The investigation **yielded** some unexpected **results**.* **2 yield to demands/pressure, etc** to be forced to do something **3** [I] *US* (*UK* **give way**) to stop in order to allow other vehicles to go past before you drive onto a bigger road

yield² /jiːld/ *noun* [C] the amount of something that is produced

yo /jəʊ/ *exclamation mainly US informal* used as a greeting

yob /jɒb/ *noun* [C] *UK informal* a rude or violent young man

yoga /ˈjəʊgə/ *noun* [U] a set of exercises for the mind and body, based on the Hindu religion *She does yoga three times a week.*

yoghurt (*also* **yogurt**) /ˈjɒgət/ [US] /ˈjəʊgərt/ *noun* [C, U] a thick, liquid food with a slightly sour taste which is made from milk *a low-fat strawberry yoghurt* ➲See colour picture **Food** on page Centre 11.

yolk /jəʊk/ *noun* [C] the round, yellow part in the middle of an egg

Yom Kippur /ˌjɒmkɪˈpʊəʳ/ *noun* [U] a Jewish holy day in September or October

yonder /ˈjɒndəʳ/ *adverb, determiner literary* in that place or direction

⊶**you** *strong form* /juː/ *weak forms* /ju, jə/ *pronoun* **1** used to refer to the person or people you are talking to *I love you.* ○ *You said I could go with you.* **2** people generally *You learn to accept these things as you get older.*

⊶**you'd** /juːd/ **1** *short for* you had *You'd better go home now.* **2** *short for* you would *I expect you'd like some lunch.*

⊶**you'll** /juːl/ *short for* you will *I hope you'll come again.*

⊶**young¹** /jʌŋ/ *adjective* having lived or existed for only a short time and not old *young children/people* ○ *We were very young when we met.*

young² /jʌŋ/ *noun* [plural] **1 the young** young people generally *It's the sort of music that appeals mainly to the young.* **2 sth's young** an animal's babies

youngster /ˈjʌŋstəʳ/ *noun* [C] a young person, especially an older child *He talked to the youngsters about the dangers of drugs.*

⊶**your** *strong form* /jɔːʳ/ *weak form* /jəʳ/ *determiner* **1** belonging or relating to the person or people you are talking to *Can I borrow your pen?* ○ *It's not your fault.* **2** belonging or relating to people in general *You never stop loving your children.*

⊶**you're** /jɔːʳ/ *short for* you are *You're my best friend.*

⊶**yours** /jɔːz/ *pronoun* **1** the things that belong or relate to the person or people you are talking to *Is this pen yours?* ○ *Our tent's smaller than yours.* **2 Yours faithfully/sincerely, etc** used just before your name at the end of a polite or formal letter **3 yours truly** *humorous* I or me

⊶**yourself** /jɔːˈself/ *pronoun plural* **yourselves** **1** the reflexive form of the pronoun 'you' *Don't cut yourself with that sharp knife.* **2** used to emphasize the pronoun 'you' when talking about the actions of the person you are speaking to *Did you make the dress yourself?* **3 (all) by yourself/yourselves** alone or without anyone else's help *I'm amazed you managed to move those boxes all by yourself.* **4 (all) to yourself** for your use only *So you've got the whole house to yourself this weekend?*

WORD PARTNERS FOR *youth*

3 recapture/relive your youth • **in** sb's youth

youth /juːθ/ *noun* **1** [YOUNG MAN] [C] a young man *gangs of youths* **2** [YOUNG PEOPLE] [group] young people generally *the youth of today* ○ *a youth club* **3 sb's youth** the period of time when someone is young *I was very shy **in my youth**.* **4** [QUALITY] [U] the quality of being young

youthful /ˈjuːθfᵊl/ *adjective* typical of a young person *youthful energy/good looks*

ˈyouth ˌhostel *noun* [C] a cheap, simple hotel, especially for young people who are travelling around

⊶**you've** /juːv/ *short for* you have *If you've finished your work, you can go.*

yo-yo /ˈjəʊjəʊ/ *noun* [C] a small, round toy that you make go up and down on a string that you hang from your finger

yuck /jʌk/ *exclamation informal* used to say that something looks or tastes very unpleasant

yum /jʌm/ (*also* **ˌyum ˈyum**) *exclamation informal* used to say that something tastes very good

yummy /ˈjʌmi/ *adjective informal* If food or drink is yummy, it tastes very good.

yuppie /ˈjʌpi/ *noun* [C] a young person who earns a lot of money and likes expensive things

Y

Zz

Z, z /zed/ the twenty-sixth and last letter of the alphabet

zany /ˈzeɪni/ *adjective* funny in a strange way *zany humour*

zap /zæp/ *verb* **[T] zapping,** *past* **zapped** *informal* to attack or destroy something in a fast and powerful way

zeal /ziːl/ *noun* **[U]** extreme enthusiasm *religious zeal*

zealous /ˈzeləs/ *adjective* extremely enthusiastic • **zealously** *adverb*

zebra /ˈzebrə/ [US] /ˈziːbrə/ *noun* **[C]** an animal like a horse with black and white lines

ˌzebra ˈcrossing *noun* **[C]** *UK* a part of the road painted with black and white lines where people can cross over safely

Zen /zen/ *noun* **[U]** a religion that developed from Buddhism

zenith /ˈzenɪθ/ [US] /ˈziːnɪθ/ *noun* **[no plural]** *literary* the highest or most successful point of something *The city **reached its zenith** in the 1980s.*

WORD PARTNERS FOR ***zero***

sth **drops to/falls to** zero • **above/below** zero

zero /ˈzɪərəʊ/ the number 0

ˌzero ˈtolerance *noun* **[U]** when you do not accept any bad behaviour, often by using laws to prevent it *zero tolerance of crime*

zest /zest/ *noun* **[U] 1** excitement and enthusiasm *a zest for life* **2** the outer skin of a lemon or orange used to give flavour to food

zigzag /ˈzɪgzæg/ *noun* **[C]** a line that changes direction from left to right and back again at sharp angles • **zigzag** *verb* **[I] zigzagging,** *past* **zigzagged** to make a movement or pattern like a zigzag

zillion /ˈzɪljən/ *quantifier informal* a very large number *a zillion times*

zinc /zɪŋk/ *noun* **[U]** a blue-white metal that is used to make or cover other metals

zip¹ /zɪp/ *UK* (*US* **zipper**) *noun* **[C]** a thing for fastening clothes, bags, etc consisting of two rows of very small parts that connect together *Your zip's undone.*

zip² /zɪp/ *verb* **zipping,** *past* **zipped 1 [T]** (*also* **zip up**) to fasten something with a zip *He zipped up his jacket.* **2** (*also* **zip up**) to reduce the size of a computer file (= collection of information) so that it uses less space and can be sent or stored more easily **3 zip along/around/past, etc** *informal* to move somewhere very quickly

ˈzip ˌcode *noun* **[C]** a set of numbers that go after someone's address in the US ⊃Compare **postcode.**

ˈzip ˌdrive *noun* **[C]** part of a computer used for copying large documents onto special disks ⊃See **Memory Stick.**

ˈzip ˌfile *noun* **[C]** a computer file (= collection of information) that has been made smaller so that it uses less space

zipper /ˈzɪpəʳ/ *noun* **[C]** *US* a zip¹

the zodiac

Capricorn
Aquarius
Pisces
Aries
Taurus
Gemini
Cancer
Leo
Virgo
Libra
Scorpio
Sagittarius

the zodiac /ˈzəʊdiæk/ *noun* the twelve signs representing groups of stars which are thought by some people to influence your life and personality *What **sign of the zodiac** are you?*

zombie /ˈzɒmbi/ *noun* **[C] 1** a dead body that walks around because of magic **2 like a zombie** *informal* in a very tired, slow way *The day after the party I was walking around like a zombie.*

zone /zəʊn/ *noun* **[C]** an area where a particular thing happens *a **war zone*** ○ *a nuclear-free zone* ⊃See also: **buffer zone.**

zoo /zuː/ *noun* **[C]** a place where wild animals are kept and people come to look at them

zoological /ˌzəʊəʊˈlɒdʒɪkəl/ *adjective* relating to the scientific study of animals

zoology /zuˈɒlədʒi/ [US] /zəʊˈɒlədʒi/ *noun* **[U]** the scientific study of animals and how they behave • **zoologist** *noun* **[C]** someone who studies zoology

zoom /zuːm/ *verb informal* **zoom along/down/past, etc** to travel somewhere very fast, especially with a loud noise

zoom in to make something appear much closer and larger when using a camera or computer *The TV cameras zoomed in on her face.*

ˈzoom ˌlens *noun* **[C]** a lens (= part of a camera) that can make something appear much closer and larger

zucchini /zʊˈkiːni/ *US* (*UK* **courgette**) *noun* **[C, U]** *plural* **zucchini** or **zucchinis** a long, green vegetable which is white inside

Z

Appendices

Common first names

The names in brackets are short, informal forms of the names.

Male names

Adam /'ædəm/
Alan /'ælən/
Alexander /ˌælɪɡ'zɑːndər/
(Alex) /'ælɪks/
Andrew /'ændruː/
(Andy) /'ændi/
Anthony
UK /'æntəni/
US /'ænθəni/
(Tony) /'təʊni/
Benjamin /'bendʒəmɪn/
(Ben) /ben/
Charles /tʃɑːlz/
(Charlie) /'tʃɑːli/
Christopher /'krɪstəfər/
(Chris) /krɪs/
Daniel /'dænjəl/
(Dan) /dæn/
Darren /'dærən/
David /'deɪvɪd/
(Dave) /deɪv/
Edward /'edwəd/
(Ed) /ed/
(Ted) /ted/
Geoffrey /'dʒefri/
(Geoff) /dʒef/

George /dʒɔːdʒ/
Harry /'hæri/
Jack /dʒæk/
James /dʒeɪmz/
(Jim) /dʒɪm/
John /dʒɒn/
Jonathan /'dʒɒnəθən/
Joseph /'dʒəʊzɪf/
(Joe) /dʒəʊ/
Joshua /'dʒɒʃjuə/
(Josh) /dʒɒʃ/
Ian /'iːən/
Kevin /'kevɪn/
Liam /'liːəm/
Mark /mɑːk/
Martin /'mɑːtɪn/
Matthew /'mæθjuː/
(Matt) /mæt/
Michael /'maɪkəl/
(Mike) /maɪk/
(Mick) /mɪk/
Nicholas /'nɪkələs/
(Nick) /nɪk/
Patrick /'pætrɪk/
Paul /pɔːl/

Peter /'piːtə/
(Pete) /piːt/
Philip /'fɪlɪp/
(Phil) /fɪl/
Richard /'rɪtʃəd/
(Ricky) /'rɪki/
(Dick) /dɪk/
Robert /'rɒbət/
(Bob) /bɒb/
(Rob) /rɒb/
Samuel /'sæmjʊəl/
(Sam) /sæm/
Simon /'saɪmən/
Thomas /'tɒməs/
(Tom) /tɒm/
Timothy /'tɪməθi/
(Tim) /tɪm/
William /'wɪljəm/
(Billy) /'bɪli/
(Will) /wɪl/

Female names

Alice /'ælɪs/
Alison /'ælɪsən/
Amanda /ə'mændə/
(Mandy) /'mændi/
Amy /'eɪmi/
Ann/Anne /æn/
Bridget /'brɪdʒɪt/
Carol /'kærəl/
Caroline /'kærəlaɪn/
Catherine/Kathryn
/'kæθrɪn/
(Kate) /keɪt/
(Katie) /'keɪti/
(Cath) /kæθ/
Charlotte /'ʃɑːlət/
Chloe /'kləʊi/
Christine /'krɪstiːn/
(Chris) /krɪs/
Clare/Claire /kleər/

Deborah /'debrə/
(Debbie) /'debi/
Diane /daɪ'æn/
Elizabeth /ɪ'lɪzəbəθ/
(Beth) /beθ/
(Liz) /lɪz/
Emily /'emɪli/
Emma /'emə/
Hannah /'hænə/
Helen /'helən/
Jane /dʒeɪn/
Jennifer /'dʒenɪfə/
(Jenny) /'dʒeni/
Joanne /dʒəʊ'æn/
(Jo) /dʒəʊ/
Julie /'dʒuːli/
Karen /'kærən/
Laura /'lɔːrə/
Linda /'lɪndə/

Lucy /'luːsi/
Margaret /'mɑːɡərət/
(Maggie) /'mægi/
Mary /'meəri/
Rachel /'reɪtʃəl/
Rebecca /rɪ'bekə/
(Becky) /'beki/
Ruth /ruːθ/
Sarah /'seərə/
Sharon /'ʃærən/
Sophie /'səʊfi/
Susan /'suːzən/
(Sue) /suː/
Tracy /'treɪsi/
Valerie /'væləri/

Geographical names

This list shows the spellings and pronunciations of countries, regions, and continents. Each name is followed by its related adjective. Most of the time you can use the adjective to talk about a person who comes from each place. However, in some cases you must use a special word, which is listed in the column labelled 'Person' (for example, **Finland**, **Finnish**, **Finn**).

To talk about more than one person from a particular place, add 's', except for:

- words ending in 'ese' or 's', which remain the same (**Chinese**, **Swiss**)
- words ending in 'man' or 'woman', which change to 'men' and 'women' (**Irishman**).

This list is for reference only. Inclusion does not imply or suggest status as a sovereign nation.

Name	Adjective	Person (if different from adj)
Afghanistan /æf'gænɪstæn/	Afghan /'æfgæn/	
Africa /'æfrɪkə/	African /'æfrɪkən/	
Albania /æl'beɪnɪə/	Albanian /æl'beɪnɪən/	
Algeria /æl'dʒɪərɪə/	Algerian /æl'dʒɪərɪən/	
Central America /ˌsentrəl ə'merɪkə/	Central American /ˌsentrəl ə'merɪkən/	
North America /ˌnɔːθ ə'merɪkə/	North American /ˌnɔːθ ə'merɪkən/	
South America /ˌsaʊθ ə'merɪkə/	South American /ˌsaʊθ ə'merɪkən/	
Andorra /æn'dɔːrə/	Andorran /æn'dɔːrən/	
Angola /æŋ'ɡəʊlə/	Angolan /æŋ'ɡəʊlən/	
Antigua and Barbuda /æn'tiːɡə æn bɑː'bjuːdə/	Antiguan /æn'tiːɡən/	
Argentina /ˌɑːdʒən'tiːnə/	Argentine /'ɑːdʒəntaɪn/	
Armenia /ɑː'miːnɪə/	Armenian /ɑː'miːnɪən/	
Asia /'eɪʒə/	Asian /'eɪʒən/	
Australia /ɒs'treɪlɪə/	Australian /ɒs'treɪlɪən/	
Austria /'ɒstrɪə/	Austrian /'ɒstrɪən/	
Azerbaijan /ˌæzəbaɪ'dʒɑːn/	Azerbaijani /ˌæzəbaɪ'dʒɑːni/	Azeri /ə'zeəri/
The Bahamas /ðə bə'hɑːməz/	Bahamian /bə'heɪmɪən/	
Bahrain /bɑː'reɪn/	Bahraini /bɑː'reɪni/	
Bangladesh /ˌbæŋɡlə'deʃ/	Bangladeshi /ˌbæŋɡlə'deʃi/	
Barbados /bɑː'beɪdɒs/	Barbadian /bɑː'beɪdɪən/	
Belarus /ˌbelə'ruːs/	Belorussian /ˌbelə'rʌʃən/	
Belgium /'beldʒəm/	Belgian /'beldʒən/	
Belize /be'liːz/	Belizian /bə'liːzɪən/	
Benin /be'niːn/	Beninese /ˌbenɪ'niːz/	
Bhutan /buː'tɑːn/	Bhutanese /ˌbuːtə'niːz/	
Bolivia /bə'lɪvɪə/	Bolivian /bə'lɪvɪən/	
Bosnia-Herzegovina /ˌbɒznɪə,hɜːzəɡɒ'viːnə/	Bosnian /'bɒznɪən/	
Botswana /bɒt'swɑːnə/	Botswanan /bɒt'swɑːnən/	Motswana /mɒt'swɑːnə/
Brazil /brə'zɪl/	Brazilian /brə'zɪlɪən/	
Brunei /bruː'naɪ/	Bruneian /bruː'naɪən/	
Bulgaria /bʌl'ɡeərɪə/	Bulgarian /bʌl'ɡeərɪən/	

Name	Adjective	Person
Burkina Faso /bɜːˈkiːnə ˈfæseʊ/	Burkinabe /bɜːˈkiːnə,bei/	
Burundi /bʊˈrʊndi/	Burundi /bʊˈrʊndi/	Burundian /bʊˈrʊndiən/
Cambodia /ˌkæmˈbəʊdiə/	Cambodian /ˌkæmˈbəʊdiən/	
Cameroon /ˌkæməˈruːn/	Cameroonian /ˌkæməˈruːniən/	
Canada /ˈkænədə/	Canadian /kəˈneɪdiən/	
Cape Verde /ˌkeɪp ˈvɜːd/	Cape Verdean /ˌkeɪp ˈvɜːdiən/	
The Central African Republic /ðə ˈsentrəl ˈæfrɪkən rɪˈpʌblɪk/	Central African /ˌsentrəl ˈæfrɪkən/	
Chad /tʃæd/	Chadian /ˈtʃædiən/	
Chile /ˈtʃɪli/	Chilean /ˈtʃɪliən/	
China /ˈtʃaɪnə/	Chinese /tʃaɪˈniːz/	
Colombia /kəˈlʌmbiə/	Colombian /kəˈlʌmbiən/	
Comoros /ˈkɒmərəʊz/	Comoran /kəˈmɔːrən/	
The Democratic Republic of Congo /ðə ˌdeməˈkrætɪk rɪˈpʌblɪk əv ˈkɒŋgəʊ/	Congolese /ˌkɒŋgəˈliːz/	
The Republic of Congo /ðə rɪˈpʌblɪk əv ˈkɒŋgəʊ/	Congolese /ˌkɒŋgəˈliːz/	
Costa Rica /ˌkɒstəˈriːkə/	Costa Rican /ˌkɒstəˈriːkən/	
Côte d'Ivoire /ˌkəʊt diːˈvwɑː/	Ivorian /aɪˈvɔːriən/	
Croatia /krəʊˈeɪʃə/	Croatian /krəʊˈeɪʃən/	Croat /ˈkrəʊæt/
Cuba /ˈkjuːbə/	Cuban /ˈkjuːbən/	
Cyprus /ˈsaɪprəs/	Cypriot /ˈsɪpriət/	
The Czech Republic /ðə tʃek rɪˈpʌblɪk/	Czech /tʃek/	
Denmark /ˈdenmɑːk/	Danish /ˈdeɪnɪʃ/	Dane /deɪn/
Djibouti /dʒɪˈbuːti/	Djiboutian /dʒɪˈbuːtiən/	
Dominica /ˌdəˈmɪnɪkə/	Dominican /dəˈmɪnɪkən/	
The Dominican Republic /ðə dəˈmɪnɪkən rɪˈpʌblɪk/	Dominican /dəˈmɪnɪkən/	
East Timor /iːst ˈtiːmɔːr/	East Timorese /iːst ˌtiːmɔːˈriːz/	
Ecuador /ˈekwədɔːr/	Ecuadorian /ˌekwəˈdɔːriən/	
Egypt /ˈiːdʒɪpt/	Egyptian /ɪˈdʒɪpʃən/	
El Salvador /ˌelˈsælvədɔːr/	Salvadoran /ˌsælvəˈdɔːrən/	
Equatorial Guinea /ˌekwətɔːriəl ˈgɪni/	Equatorial Guinean /ˌekwətɔːriəl ˈgɪniən/	
Eritrea /ˌerɪˈtreɪə/	Eritrean /ˌerɪˈtreɪən/	
Estonia /esˈtəʊniə/	Estonian /esˈtəʊniən/	
Ethiopia /ˌiːθiˈəʊpiə/	Ethiopian /ˌiːθiˈəʊpiən/	
Europe /ˈjʊərəp/	European /ˌjʊərəˈpiːən/	
Fiji /ˈfiːdʒiː/	Fijian /fɪˈdʒiːən/	
Finland /ˈfɪnlənd/	Finnish /ˈfɪnɪʃ/	Finn /fɪn/
France /frɑːnts/	French /frentʃ/	Frenchman /ˈfrentʃmən/
Gabon /gæbˈɒn/	Gabonese /ˌgæbənˈiːz/	
Gambia /ˈgæmbiə/	Gambian /ˈgæmbiən/	
Georgia /ˈdʒɔːdʒə/	Georgian /ˈdʒɔːdʒən/	
Germany /ˈdʒɜːməni/	German /ˈdʒɜːmən/	
Ghana /ˈgɑːnə/	Ghanaian /gɑːˈneɪən/	
Greece /griːs/	Greek /griːk/	
Greenland /ˈgriːnlənd/	Greenland /ˈgriːnlənd/	Greenlander /ˈgriːnləndər/
Grenada /grəˈneɪdə/	Grenadian /grəˈneɪdiən/	
Guatemala /ˌgwɑːtəˈmɑːlə/	Guatemalan /ˌgwɑːtəˈmɑːlən/	
Guinea /ˈgɪni/	Guinean /ˈgɪniən/	

Name	Adjective	Person
Guinea-Bissau /ˌgɪnɪbɪˈsaʊ/	Guinea-Bissauan /ˌgɪnɪbɪˈsaʊən/	
Guyana /gaɪˈænə/	Guyanese /ˌgaɪəˈniːz/	
Haiti /ˈheɪti/	Haitian /ˈheɪʃən/	
Honduras /hɒnˈdjʊərəs/	Honduran /hɒnˈdjʊərən/	
Hungary /ˈhʌŋgəri/	Hungarian /hʌŋˈgeəriən/	
Iceland /ˈaɪslənd/	Icelandic /aɪsˈlændɪk/	Icelander /ˈaɪsləndər/
India /ˈɪndiə/	Indian /ˈɪndiən/	
Indonesia /ˌɪndəˈniːʒə/	Indonesian /ˌɪndəˈniːʒən/	
Iran /ɪˈrɑːn/	Iranian /ɪˈreɪniən/	
Iraq /ɪˈrɑːk/	Iraqi /ɪˈrɑːki/	
Ireland /ˈaɪələnd/	Irish /ˈaɪrɪʃ/	Irishman /ˈaɪrɪʃmən/
Israel /ˈɪzreɪl/	Israeli /ɪzˈreɪli/	
Italy /ˈɪtəli/	Italian /ɪˈtæliən/	
Jamaica /dʒəˈmeɪkə/	Jamaican /dʒəˈmeɪkən/	
Japan /dʒəˈpæn/	Japanese /ˌdʒæpəˈniːz/	
Jordan /ˈdʒɔːdn/	Jordanian /dʒɔːˈdeɪniən/	
Kazakhstan /ˌkæzækˈstɑːn/	Kazakh /kæˈzæk/	
Kenya /ˈkenjə/	Kenyan /ˈkenjən/	
Kiribati /ˌkɪrəˈbæs/	Kiribati /ˌkɪrəˈbæs/	
North Korea /ˌnɔːθ kəˈriːə/	North Korean /ˌnɔːθ kəˈriːən/	
South Korea /ˌsaʊθ kəˈriːə/	South Korean /ˌsaʊθ kəˈriːən/	
Kuwait /kuːˈweɪt/	Kuwaiti /kuːˈweɪti/	
Kyrgyzstan /ˌkɜːgɪˈstɑːn/	Kyrgyz /ˈkɜːgɪz/	
Laos /laʊs/	Laotian /ˈlaʊʃən/	
Latvia /ˈlætviə/	Latvian /ˈlætviən/	
Lebanon /ˈlebənən/	Lebanese /ˌlebəˈniːz/	
Lesotho /ləˈsuːtuː/	Basotho /bəˈsuːtuː/	Mosotho /məˈsuːtuː/
Liberia /laɪˈbɪəriə/	Liberian /laɪˈbɪəriən/	
Libya /ˈlɪbiə/	Libyan /ˈlɪbiən/	
Liechtenstein /ˈlɪktənstaɪn/	Liechtenstein /ˈlɪktənstaɪn/	Liechtensteiner /ˈlɪktənstaɪnər/
Lithuania /ˌlɪθjuˈeɪniə/	Lithuanian /ˌlɪθjuˈeɪniən/	
Luxembourg /ˈlʌksəmbɜːg/	Luxembourg /ˈlʌksəmbɜːg/	Luxembourger /ˈlʌksəmbɜːgər/
Madagascar /ˌmædəˈgæskər/	Malagasy /ˌmæləˈgæsi/	
Malawi /məˈlɑːwi/	Malawian /məˈlɑːwiən/	
Malaysia /məˈleɪziə/	Malaysian /məˈleɪziən/	
The Maldives /ðə ˈmɔːldiːvz/	Maldivian /mɔːlˈdɪviən/	
Mali /ˈmɑːli/	Malian /ˈmɑːliən/	
Malta /ˈmɔːltə/	Maltese /mɔːlˈtiːz/	
The Marshall Islands /ðə ˈmɑːʃəl ˈaɪləndz/	Marshallese /ˌmɑːʃəˈliːz/	
Mauritania /ˌmɒrɪˈteɪniə/	Mauritanian /ˌmɒrɪˈteɪniən/	
Mauritius /məˈrɪʃəs/	Mauritian /məˈrɪʃən/	
Mexico /ˈmeksɪkəʊ/	Mexican /ˈmeksɪkən/	
Micronesia /ˌmaɪkrəˈniːziə/	Micronesian /ˌmaɪkrəˈniːziən/	
Moldova /mɒlˈdəʊvə/	Moldovan /mɒlˈdəʊvən/	
Monaco /ˈmɒnəkəʊ/	Monégasque /mɒneɪˈgæsk/	
Mongolia /mɒŋˈgəʊliə/	Mongolian /mɒŋˈgəʊliən/	
Morocco /məˈrɒkəʊ/	Moroccan /məˈrɒkən/	
Mozambique /ˌməʊzæmˈbiːk/	Mozambican /ˌməʊzæmˈbiːkən/	

Name	Adjective	Person
Myanmar /'mjænmɑːʳ/	Burmese /bɜː'miːz/	
Namibia /nə'mɪbiə/	Namibian /nə'mɪbiən/	
Nauru /nɑː'uːruː/	Nauruan /nɑːuː'ruːən/	
Nepal /nə'pɔːl/	Nepalese /ˌnepəl'iːz/	
The Netherlands /ðə 'neðələnz/	Dutch /dʌtʃ/	Dutchman /'dʌtʃmən/
New Zealand /ˌnjuː'ziːlənd/	New Zealand /ˌnjuː'ziːlənd/	New Zealander /ˌnjuː'ziːləndəʳ/
Nicaragua /ˌnɪkə'rɑːgwə/	Nicaraguan /ˌnɪkə'rɑːgwən/	
Niger /niː'ʒeə/	Nigerien /niː'ʒeəriən/	
Nigeria /naɪ'dʒɪəriə/	Nigerian /naɪ'dʒɪəriən/	
Norway /'nɔːweɪ/	Norwegian /nɔː'wiːdʒən/	
Oman /əʊ'mɑːn/	Omani /əʊ'mɑːni/	
Pakistan /ˌpɑːkɪ'stɑːn/	Pakistani /ˌpɑːkɪ'stɑːni/	
Palestine /'pæləstaɪn/	Palestinian /ˌpælə'stɪniən/	
Panama /'pænəmɑː/	Panamanian /ˌpænə'meɪniən/	
Papua New Guinea /'pæpuə njuː 'gɪni/	Papua New Guinean /'pæpuə njuː 'gɪniən/	
Paraguay /'pærəgwaɪ/	Paraguayan /ˌpærə'gwaɪən/	
Peru /pə'ruː/	Peruvian /pə'ruːviən/	
The Philippines /ðə 'fɪlɪpiːnz/	Philippine /'fɪlɪpiːn/	Filipino /ˌfɪlɪ'piːnəʊ/
Poland /'pəʊlənd/	Polish /'pəʊlɪʃ/	Pole /pəʊl/
Portugal /'pɔːtʃəgəl/	Portuguese /ˌpɔːtʃə'giːz/	
Qatar /'kʌtɑːʳ/	Qatari /kʌ'tɑːri/	
Romania /rʊ'meɪniə/	Romanian /rʊ'meɪniən/	
Russia /'rʌʃə/	Russian /'rʌʃən/	
Rwanda /ru'ændə/	Rwandan /ru'ændən/	
Saint Kitts and Nevis /seɪnt kɪts ən 'nevɪs /	Kittsian /'kɪtsiən/	
Saint Lucia /seɪnt 'luːʃə/	Saint Lucian /seɪnt 'luːʃən/	
Saint Vincent and the Grenadines /seɪnt 'vɪntsənt ən ðə ˌgrenə'diːnz/	Vincentian /vɪn'sɪntiən/	
Samoa /sə'məʊə/	Samoan /sə'məʊən/	
San Marino /ˌsænmə'riːnəʊ/	Sanmarinese /ˌsænmærɪ'niːz/	
São Tomé and Príncipe /ˌsaʊ tə'meɪ ən 'prɪnsɪpeɪ/	Sao Tomean /ˌsaʊ tə'meɪən/	
Saudi Arabia /ˌsaʊdi ə'reɪbiə/	Saudi /'saʊdi/	
Scandinavia /ˌskændɪˌneɪviə/	Scandinavian /ˌskændɪˌneɪviən/	
Senegal /ˌsenɪ'gɔːl/	Senegalese /ˌsenɪgə'liːz/	
The Seychelles /ðə seɪ'ʃelz/	Seychelles /seɪ'ʃelz/	Seychellois /seɪʃel'wɑː/
Sierra Leone /siˌerəli'əʊn/	Sierra Leonean /si'erə li'əʊniən/	
Singapore /ˌsɪŋə'pɔːʳ/	Singaporean /ˌsɪŋə'pɔːriən/	
Slovakia /slə'vækiə/	Slovak /'sləʊvæk/	
Slovenia /slə'viːniə/	Slovenian /slə'viːniən/	Slovene /'sləʊviːn/
The Solomon Islands /ðə 'sɒləmən 'aɪləndz/	Solomon Islander /'sɒləmən 'aɪləndəʳ/	
Somalia /sə'mɑːliə/	Somali /sə'mɑːli/	
South Africa /ˌsaʊθ 'æfrɪkə/	South African /ˌsaʊθ 'æfrɪkən/	
Spain /speɪn/	Spanish /'spænɪʃ/	Spaniard /'spænjəd/
Sri Lanka /ˌsriː'læŋkə/	Sri Lankan /ˌsriː'læŋkən/	

Name	Adjective	Person
Sudan /suːˈdɑːn/	Sudanese /ˌsuːdəˈniːz/	
Suriname /ˌsʊərɪˈnæm/	Surinamese /ˌsʊərɪnæmˈiːz/	
Swaziland /ˈswɑːzilænd/	Swazi /ˈswɑːzi/	
Sweden /ˈswiːdn/	Swedish /ˈswiːdɪʃ/	Swede /swiːd/
Switzerland /ˈswɪtsələnd/	Swiss /swɪs/	
Syria /ˈsɪriə/	Syrian /ˈsɪriən/	
Taiwan /ˌtaɪˈwɑːn/	Taiwanese /ˌtaɪwəˈniːz/	
Tajikistan /tɑːˈdʒiːkɪˌstɑːn/	Tajik /tɑːˈdʒiːk/	
Tanzania /ˌtænzəˈniːə/	Tanzanian /ˌtænzəˈniːən/	
Thailand /ˈtaɪlænd/	Thai /taɪ/	
Tibet /tɪˈbet/	Tibetan /tɪˈbetn/	
Togo /ˈtəʊɡəʊ/	Togolese /ˌtəʊɡəˈliːz/	
Tonga /ˈtɒŋə/	Tongan /ˈtɒŋən/	
Trinidad and Tobago /ˈtrɪnɪdæd ən təˈbeɪɡəʊ/	Trinidadian /ˌtrɪnɪˈdædiən/	
Tunisia /tjuːˈnɪziə/	Tunisian /tjuːˈnɪziən/	
Turkey /ˈtɜːki/	Turkish /ˈtɜːkɪʃ/	Turk /tɜːk/
Turkmenistan /tɜːkˌmenɪˈstɑːn/	Turkmen /ˈtɜːkmen/	
Tuvalu /tuːˈvɑːluː/	Tuvaluan /ˌtuːvɑːˈluːən/	
Uganda /juːˈɡændə/	Ugandan /juːˈɡændən/	
Ukraine /juːˈkreɪn/	Ukrainian /juːˈkreɪniən/	
The United Arab Emirates /ðə juːˈnaɪtɪd ˈærəb ˈemɪrəts/	Emirian /eˈmɪriən/	
The United Kingdom /ðə juːˈnaɪtɪd ˈkɪŋdəm/	British /ˈbrɪtɪʃ/	Briton /ˈbrɪtən/
The United States of America /ðə juːˈnaɪtɪd steɪts əv əˈmerɪkə/	American /əˈmerɪkən/	
Uruguay /ˈjʊərəɡwaɪ/	Uruguayan /ˌjʊərəˈɡwaɪən/	
Uzbekistan /ʊzˌbekɪˈstɑːn/	Uzbek /ˈʊzbek/	
Vanuatu /ˌvænuˈɑːtuː/	Vanuatuan /ˌvænuɑːˈtuːən/	
Vatican City /ˈvætɪkən ˈsɪti/	Vatican /ˈvætɪkən/	
Venezuela /ˌvenɪˈzweɪlə/	Venezuelan /ˌvenɪˈzweɪlən/	
Vietnam /ˌviːetˈnæm/	Vietnamese /ˌviːetnəˈmiːz/	
Western Sahara /ˌwestən ˌsəˈhɑːrə/	Sahrawian /sɑːˈrɑːwiən/	
Yemen /ˈjemən/	Yemeni /ˈjeməni/	
Yugoslavia /ˌjuːɡəʊˈslɑːviə/	Yugoslav /ˈjuːɡəʊslɑːv/	
Zambia /ˈzæmbiə/	Zambian /ˈzæmbiən/	
Zimbabwe /zɪmˈbɑːbweɪ/	Zimbabwean /zɪmˈbɑːbwiən/	

Regular verb tenses

The simple tenses

Present Simple

used for action in the present, for things that are always true or that happen regularly, and for opinions and beliefs

I/we/you/they	arrive (do not arrive)
he/she/it	arrives (does not arrive)

Past Simple

used for completed actions and events in the past

I/we/you/they	arrived (did not arrive)
he/she/it	arrived (did not arrive)

Future Simple

used for actions and events in the future

I/we/you/they	will arrive (will not arrive)
he/she/it	will arrive (will not arrive)

Present Perfect

used to show that an event happened or an action was completed at some time before the present

I/we/you/they	have arrived (have not arrived)
he/she/it	has arrived (has not arrived)

Past Perfect

used to show that an event happened or an action was completed before a particular time in the past

I/we/you/they	had arrived (had not arrived)
he/she/it	had arrived (had not arrived)

Future Perfect

used to show that something will be completed before a particular time in the future

I/we/you/they	will have arrived (will not have arrived)
he/she/it	will have arrived (will not have arrived)

The continuous/progressive tenses

Present Continuous/Progressive

used for actions or events that are happening or developing now, for future plans, or to show that an event is repeated

I **am** arriv**ing** (**am not** arriving)
we/you/they **are** arriv**ing** (**are not** arriving)
he/she/it **is** arriv**ing** (**is not** arriving)

Past Continuous/Progressive

used for actions or events in the past that were not yet finished or that were interrupted

I **was** arriv**ing** (**was not** arriving)
we/you/they **were** arriv**ing** (**were not** arriving)
he/she/it **was** arriv**ing** (**was not** arriving)

Future Continuous/Progressive

used for actions or events in the future that will continue into the future

I/we/you/they **will be** arriv**ing** (**will not be** arriving)
he/she/it **will be** arriv**ing** (**will not be** arriving)

Present Perfect Continuous/Progressive

used for actions or events that started in the past but are still happening now, or for past actions which only recently finished and their effects are seen now

I/we/you/they **have been** arriv**ing** (**have not been** arriving)
he/she/it **has been** arriv**ing** (**has not been** arriving)

Past Perfect Continuous/Progressive

used for actions or events that happened for a period of time but were completed before a particular time in the past

I/we/you/they **had been** arriv**ing** (**had not been** arriving)
he/she/it **had been** arriv**ing** (**had not been** arriving)

Future Perfect Continuous/Progressive

used for actions or events that will already be happening at a particular time in the future

I/we/you/they **will have been** arriv**ing**
(**will not have been** arriving)
he/she/it **will have been** arriv**ing**
(**will not have been** arriving)

Irregular verbs

This list gives the infinitive form of the verb, its past tense, and then the past participle. If two forms are given, look the verb up in the dictionary to see whether they have a different meaning.

Infinitive	Past Tense	Past Participle	Infinitive	Past Tense	Past Participle
arise	arose	arisen	dream	dreamed, dreamt	dreamed, dreamt
awake	awoke	awoken			
be	was/were	been	drink	drank	drunk
bear	bore	borne	drive	drove	driven
beat	beat	beaten, (also US) beat	dwell	dwelt, dwelled	dwelt, dwelled
			eat	ate	eaten
become	became	become	fall	fell	fallen
befall	befell	befallen	feed	fed	fed
begin	began	begun	feel	felt	felt
bend	bent	bent	fight	fought	fought
bet	bet, betted	bet, betted	find	found	found
bid	bid, bade	bid, bidden	flee	fled	fled
bind	bound	bound	fling	flung	flung
bite	bit	bitten	fly	flew	flown
bleed	bled	bled	forbid	forbade	forbidden
blow	blew	blown	forecast	forecast, forecasted	forecast, forecasted
break	broke	broken			
breed	bred	bred	foresee	foresaw	foreseen
bring	brought	brought	forget	forgot	forgotten
broadcast	broadcast, (also US) broadcasted	broadcast, (also US) broadcasted	forgive	forgave	forgiven
			forgo	forwent	forgone
			forsake	forsook	forsaken
build	built	built	freeze	froze	frozen
burn	burnt, burned	burnt, burned	get	got	got, (also US) gotten
burst	burst	burst			
bust	(UK) bust, (US) busted	(UK) bust, (US) busted	give	gave	given
			go	went	gone
buy	bought	bought	grind	ground	ground
cast	cast	cast	grow	grew	grown
catch	caught	caught	hang	hung, hanged	hung, hanged
choose	chose	chosen	have	had	had
cling	clung	clung	hear	heard	heard
come	came	come	hide	hid	hidden
cost	cost	cost	hit	hit	hit
creep	crept	crept	hold	held	held
cut	cut	cut	hurt	hurt	hurt
deal	dealt	dealt	input	inputted, input	inputted, input
dig	dug	dug			
dive	dived, (also US) dove	dived	keep	kept	kept
			kneel	knelt, kneeled	knelt, kneeled
draw	drew	drawn	know	knew	known

Infinitive	Past Tense	Past Participle	Infinitive	Past Tense	Past Participle
lay	laid	laid	rewrite	rewrote	rewritten
lead	led	led	rid	rid	rid
lean	leaned, (*also UK*) leant	leaned, (*also UK*) leant	ride	rode	ridden
			ring	rang	rung
leap	leapt, leaped	leapt, leaped	rise	rose	risen
learn	learned, (*also UK*) learnt	learned, (*also UK*) learnt	run	ran	run
			saw	sawed	sawn, (*also US*) sawed
leave	left	left	say	said	said
lend	lent	lent	see	saw	seen
let	let	let	seek	sought	sought
lie	lay, lied	lain, lied	sell	sold	sold
light	lit, lighted	lit, lighted	send	sent	sent
lose	lost	lost	set	set	set
make	made	made	sew	sewed	sewn, sewed
mean	meant	meant	shake	shook	shaken
meet	met	met	shear	sheared	sheared, shorn
mislay	mislaid	mislaid	shed	shed	shed
mislead	misled	misled	shine	shone	shone
misread	misread	misread	shoot	shot	shot
misspell	misspelled, (*also UK*) misspelt	misspelled, (*also UK*) misspelt	show	showed	shown, showed
			shrink	shrank	shrunk
mistake	mistook	mistaken	shut	shut	shut
misunderstand	misunderstood	misunderstood	sing	sang	sung
mow	mowed	mown, mowed	sink	sank	sunk
outdo	outdid	outdone	sit	sat	sat
outgrow	outgrew	outgrown	slay	slew	slain
overcome	overcame	overcome	sleep	slept	slept
overdo	overdid	overdone	slide	slid	slid
overhang	overhung	overhung	sling	slung	slung
overhear	overheard	overheard	slink	slunk	slunk
override	overrode	overridden	slit	slit	slit
overrun	overran	overrun	smell	smelled, (*also UK*) smelt	smelled, (*also UK*) smelt
oversee	oversaw	overseen			
oversleep	overslept	overslept			
overtake	overtook	overtaken	sow	sowed	sown, sowed
overthrow	overthrew	overthrown	speak	spoke	spoken
pay	paid	paid	speed	sped, speeded	sped, speeded
plead	pleaded, (*also US*) pled	pleaded, (*also US*) pled	spell	spelled, (*also UK*) spelt	spelled, (*also UK*) spelt
prove	proved	proved, (*also US*) proven	spend	spent	spent
put	put	put	spill	spilled, (*also UK*) spilt	spilled, (*also UK*) spilt
quit	quit	quit	spin	spun	spun
read	read	read	spit	spat, (*also US*) spit	spat, (*also US*) spit
rebuild	rebuilt	rebuilt	split	split	split
repay	repaid	repaid	spoil	spoiled, spoilt	spoiled, spoilt
rethink	rethought	rethought	spread	spread	spread
rewind	rewound	rewound			

Infinitive	Past Tense	Past Participle	Infinitive	Past Tense	Past Participle
spring	sprang	sprung	tread	trod	trodden
stand	stood	stood	undercut	undercut	undercut
steal	stole	stolen	undergo	underwent	undergone
stick	stuck	stuck	understand	understood	understood
sting	stung	stung	undertake	undertook	undertaken
stink	stank, (also US) stunk	stunk	undo	undid	undone
			unwind	unwound	unwound
stride	strode	strode	uphold	upheld	upheld
strike	struck	struck	upset	upset	upset
string	strung	strung	wake	woke	woken
strive	strove, strived	striven, strived	wear	wore	worn
swear	swore	sworn	weave	wove, weaved	woven, weaved
sweep	swept	swept	weep	wept	wept
swell	swelled	swollen, swelled	wet	wet, wetted	wet, wetted
swim	swam	swum	win	won	won
swing	swung	swung	wind	wound	wound
take	took	taken	withdraw	withdrew	withdrawn
teach	taught	taught	withhold	withheld	withheld
tear	tore	torn	withstand	withstood	withstood
tell	told	told	wring	wrung	wrung
think	thought	thought	write	wrote	written
throw	threw	thrown			
thrust	thrust	thrust			

Word beginnings and endings

You can change the meaning of many English words simply by adding a group of letters to the beginning or the ending of a word.

Prefixes

A group of letters added to the beginning of a word is called **prefix**. Here is a list of the most common prefixes and examples of how they are used.

Anglo- relating to the UK or England *an Anglophile* (= someone who loves England)

anti- 1 opposed to or against *anti-racist laws* **2** preventing or destroying *an anti-aircraft missile*

astro- relating to stars or outer space *astronomer • astrophysics*

audio- relating to hearing or sound *audiotape*

auto- 1 operating without being controlled by humans *autopilot* (= a computer that directs an aircraft) **2** self *an autobiography* (= a book that someone writes about their own life)

bi- two *bilingual* (= speaking two languages) • *bimonthly* (= happening twice in a month or once every two months)

bio- relating to living things or human life *biodiversity • bioethics*

centi-, cent- hundred *a centimetre • a century*

co- with or together *a co-author • to coexist*

contra- against or opposite *to contradict* (= say the opposite) • *contraception* (= something that is used to prevent pregnancy)

counter- opposing or as a reaction to *a counter-attack* (= an attack on someone who has attacked you)

cross- 1 across *cross-border* **2** including different groups or subjects *a cross-party committee* (= one formed from many political parties) • *cross-cultural*

cyber- relating to electronic communications, especially the Internet *cyberspace*

de- to take something away *deforestation* (= when the trees in an area are cut down)

deca- ten *decade*

demi- half, partly *demitasse* (= a small coffee cup) • *demigod* (= a creature that is part god and part human)

dis- not or the opposite of *dishonest • disbelief • to disagree*

e- electronic, usually relating to the Internet *email • e-commerce*

eco- relating to the environment *eco-friendly tourism* (= tourism which does not damage the environment)

equi- equal, equally *equidistant* (= the same distance from two or more places)

Euro- relating to Europe *Europop* (= modern, young people's music from Europe)

ex- from before *an ex-boyfriend • an ex-boss*

extra- outside of or in addition to *extracurricular activities* (= activities that are in addition to the usual school work)

geo- of the earth *geothermal* (= of or connected with the heat inside the earth)

hydro- relating to water *hydroponic* (= a method of growing plants in water)

hyper- having a lot of or too much of a quality *hyperactive • hypersensitive* (= more than normally sensitive)

ill- in a way which is bad or not suitable *ill-prepared • an ill-judged remark*

in-, il-, im-, ir- not *incorrect • illegal • impossible • irregular*

inter- between or among *international • an interdepartmental meeting*

intra- within *an intranet*

kilo- a thousand *a kilometre • a kilogram*

macro- on a large scale *macroeconomics* (= the study of financial systems at a national level)

maxi- most, very large *maximum*

mega- 1 *informal* extremely *megarich* (= extremely rich) **2** one million *40 megabytes*

micro- very small *a microchip • microscopic* (= extremely small)

mid- in the middle of *mid-July • a man in his mid-forties • mid-afternoon/-morning*

milli- a thousandth *a millisecond*

mini- small *a miniskirt* (= very short skirt) • *a minibus*

mis- not or badly *mistrust • to misbehave*

mono- one or single *monolingual • a monologue*

multi- many *a multi-millionaire • a multi-storey car park*

nano- 1 one billionth *nanometre* **2** extremely small *nanotechnology*

neo- new *neo-fascists*

non- not or the opposite of *non-alcoholic drinks • non-smokers*

out- more than or better than *to outgrow • to outnumber • to outdo someone* (= to show that you are better than someone)

over- too much *to overeat • overpopulated*

poly- many *polygamy* (= having more than one husband or wife at the same time) • *a polygon* (= shape with many sides)

post- after or later than *postwar • a postgraduate*

pre- before or earlier than *pre-tax profits • pre-school*

pro- supporting *pro-democracy demonstrations*

pseudo- false *a pseudonym* (= false name used especially by a writer) • *pseudo-academic*

quasi- partly *quasi-religious ideas*

re- again *to remarry* • *a reusable container*

semi- half or partly *a semicircle* • *semi-frozen*

socio- relating to society *socio-economic*

sub- **1** under or below *subzero temperatures* **2** less important or a smaller part of a larger whole *a subsection*

super- extremely or more than usual *a supermodel* • *super-rich*

techno- relating to technology *technophile* (=a person who loves technology)

tele- **1** done using a telephone *telesales* **2** connected with television *telecast* (=something that is broadcast on television) **3** over a long distance *telephoto lens* (=a camera lens that makes distant objects look nearer)

thermo- relating to heat or temperature *a thermostat* (= piece of equipment that controls temperature) • *a thermometer*

trans- **1** across *transatlantic flights* **2** showing a change *to transform* • *to translate*

tri- three *a triangle* • *a tripod*

ultra- extremely *ultra-modern architecture* • *ultra-careful*

uber- *humorous* used before nouns to mean 'extreme' or 'extremely good or successful' *uber-billionare*

un- not or the opposite of *unhappy* • *unfair* • *to unfasten*

under- **1** not enough *undercooked potatoes* • *underprivileged children* **2** below *underwear* • *an underpass*

Suffixes

A **suffix** is a group of letters at the end of a word which changes the word's meaning and often its part of speech. Here is a list of the most common suffixes and examples of how they are used.

-able, -ible changes a verb into an adjective meaning 'able to be' *avoid → avoidable* • *admire → admirable* • *like → likeable*

-age changes a verb into a noun meaning 'the action described by the verb or the result of that action' *marry → marriage* • *break → breakage* • *spill → spillage*

-aholic unable to stop doing or taking something *chocaholic* (=someone who cannot stop eating chocolate)

-al **1** changes a noun into an adjective meaning 'relating to' *culture → cultural* • *nation → national* • *nature → natural* **2** changes a verb into a noun meaning 'the action described by the verb' *approve → approval* • *remove → removal*

-an, -ian **1** makes a noun meaning 'a person who does something' *historian* • *politician* **2** makes an adjective meaning 'belonging somewhere' *American*

-ance, -ence, -ancy, -ency makes a noun meaning 'an action, state, or quality' *performance* • *independence* • *preference*

-athon an event or activity that lasts a long time, usually to raise money for charity *a walkathon* (=a long walk)

-ation, -ion changes a verb into a noun meaning 'the process of the action described by the verb, or the result of that action' *educate → education* • *explain → explanation* • *connect → connection*

-ed makes an adjective meaning, 'having this thing or quality' *bearded* • *coloured* • *surprised*

-ee changes a verb into a noun meaning 'someone that something is done to' *employ → employee* • *interview → interviewee* • *train → trainee*

-en changes an adjective into a verb meaning 'to become or make something become' *thick → thicken* • *fat → fatten* • *soft → soften*

-ence, -ency See **-ance**

-er, -or changes a verb into a noun meaning 'the person or thing that does the activity' *dance → dancer* • *employ → employer* • *act → actor* • *cook → cooker* (= a machine for cooking) • *time → timer*

-ese of a place, the language spoken there *Lebanese* • *Chinese*

-esque in the style of *Kafka-esque* (= in the style of writer Franz Kafka)

-est makes superlative adjectives and adverbs *bravest* • *latest*

-ful changes a noun into an adjective meaning, 'having a particular quality' *beauty → beautiful* • *power → powerful* • *use → useful*

-hood makes a noun meaning 'the state of being something and the time when someone is something' *childhood* • *motherhood*

-ian See **-an**

-ible See **-able**

-ical changes a noun ending in **-y** or **-ics** into an adjective meaning 'relating to' *history → historical* • *politics → political*

-ify to produce a state or quality *simplify*

-in an activity in which many people take part *a sit-in*

-ing makes an adjective meaning 'making someone feel something' *interest → interesting* • *surprise → surprising* • *shock → shocking*

-ion See **-ation**

-ise See **-ize**

-ish makes an adjective meaning **1** slightly *a greyish colour* • *a smallish* (= quite small) *house* **2** typical of or similar to *a childish remark* **3** approximately *fiftyish* (= about fifty)

-ist 1 makes a noun meaning 'a person who does a particular activity' *artist* • *novelist* • *scientist* **2** makes a noun and an adjective meaning 'someone with a particular set of beliefs' *communist* • *feminist*

-ive changes a verb into an adjective meaning 'having a particular quality or effect' *attract* → *attractive* • *create* → *creative* • *explode* → *explosive*

-ize, -ise changes an adjective into a verb meaning 'to make something become' *modern* → *modernize* • *commercial* → *commercialize*

-less changes a noun into an adjective meaning 'without' *homeless people* • *a meaningless statement* • *a hopeless situation*

-let small, not very important *piglet*

-like changes a noun into an adjective meaning 'typical of or similar to' *childlike trust* • *a cabbage-like vegetable*

-ly 1 changes an adjective into an adverb describing the way that something is done *She spoke slowly.* • *Drive safely.* **2** makes an adjective and an adverb meaning 'happening every day, night, week, etc' *a daily newspaper* • *We hold the meeting weekly.* **3** changes a noun into an adjective meaning 'like that person or thing' *mother* → *motherly* • *coward* → *cowardly*

-ment changes a verb into a noun meaning 'the action or process described by a verb, or its result' *develop* → *development* • *disappoint* → *disappointment*

-ness changes an adjective into a noun meaning 'the quality or condition described by the adjective' *sweet* → *sweetness* • *happy* → *happiness* • *dark* → *darkness* • *ill* → *illness*

-ology makes a noun meaning 'the study of something' *psychology* (= the study of the mind) • *sociology* (= the study of society)

-or See **-er**

-ous changes a noun into an adjective meaning 'having that quality' *danger* → *dangerous* • *ambition* → *ambitious*

-phile makes a noun meaning 'enjoying or liking something' *a Francophile* (= someone who loves France) • *a bibliophile* (= someone who loves books)

-phobe someone who hates something *commitment-phobe* (= a person who hates commitment)

-ship makes a noun showing involvement between people *friendship* • *a relationship* • *partnership*

-ster a person who is associated with something *gangster*

-ward, -wards makes an adverb meaning 'towards a direction or place' *inward* • *forward* • *homeward*

-wise changes a noun into an adverb meaning 'relating to this subject' *Weather-wise, the holiday was great.* • *How are we doing time-wise?*

-y changes a noun into an adjective meaning 'having a lot of something (often something bad)' *noise* → *noisy* • *dirt* → *dirty* • *smell* → *smelly*

Word Building

It is useful to know how to build up word families using the prefixes and suffixes listed on pages 751–752, and for some exams you need to know these word families. In the list below, words in heavy type are words which have the symbol ⊶ by them in the dictionary, meaning that they are very common and important to learn. The other words on each line are words in the same family, often formed with prefixes and suffixes, or sometimes just a different part of speech (e.g. anger, which is a noun and a verb). All the words in this list have entries in the dictionary except for some beginning with 'un-', 'im-', 'in-' or 'ir-', or ending with '-ly' or '-ily', where the meaning is always regular. Sometimes words in a word family can have meanings which are quite different from others in the group, so you should always check in the dictionary if you are not sure of the meaning.

Nouns	Adjectives	Verbs	Adverbs
ability, disability, inability	**able**, unable, disabled	enable, disable	ably
acceptance, unacceptably	**acceptable**, unacceptable,	**accept** accepted	acceptably,
accident	accidental		accidentally
accuracy, inaccuracy	**accurate**, inaccurate		accurately, inaccurately
accusation, the accused, accuser	accusing	**accuse**	accusingly
achievement, achiever	achievable	**achieve**	
act, **action**, inaction, interaction, reaction, transaction	acting	**act**	
activity, inactivity	**active**, inactive, interactive, proactive	activate	actively
addition	additional	**add**	additionally
admiration, admirer	admirable	**admire**	admirably
advantage, disadvantage	advantageous, disadvantaged		advantageously
advertisement, advertiser, **advertising**			advertise
advice, adviser	advisable, inadvisable, advisory	**advise**	
agreement, disagreement	agreeable	**agree**, disagree	agreeably
aim	aimless	**aim**	aimlessly
amazement	amazed, **amazing**	amaze	amazingly
anger	**angry**	anger	angrily
announcement, announcer	unannounced	**announce**	unannounced
appearance, disappearance, reappearance		**appear**, disappear, reappear	
applicant, application	applicable, applied	**apply**	
appreciation	appreciable, appreciative	**appreciate**	appreciatively
approval, disapproval	approving, disapproving	**approve**, disapprove	approvingly
approximation	approximate	approximate	**approximately**
argument	arguable, argumentative	**argue**	arguably
arrangement		**arrange**, rearrange	
art, **artist**, artistry	artistic		artistically
shame shamelessly	**ashamed**, unashamed, shameful, shameless	shame	shamefully,
attachment	attached, unattached, detachable, detached	**attach**, detach	

Nouns	Adjectives	Verbs	Adverbs
attack, counter-attack, attacker		**attack**, counter-attack	
attention	attentive, inattentive	attend	attentively
attraction, attractiveness	**attractive**, unattractive	attract	attractively
authority, authorization	authoritarian, authoritative, unauthorized	authorize	
availability	**available**, unavailable		
avoidance	avoidable, unavoidable	**avoid**	
awareness	**aware**, unaware		unawares
base, the basics, basis	baseless, **basic**	**base**	**basically**
bearer	bearable, unbearable	**bear**	
beat, beating	unbeatable, unbeaten	**beat**	
beautician, **beauty**	**beautiful**		beautifully
beginner, **beginning**		**begin**	
behaviour/US **behavior**, misbehaviour/US misbehavior	behavioural/US behavioral	**behave**, misbehave	
belief, disbelief	believable, unbelievable	**believe**, disbelieve	unbelievably
block, blockage	blocked, unblocked	**block**, unblock	
blood, bleeding	bloodless, bloody	bleed	
the boil, boiler	boiling	**boil**	
bore, boredom	**bored, boring**	bore	boringly
break, outbreak, breakage	unbreakable, **broken**, unbroken	**break**	
breath, breather, breathing	breathless	**breathe**	breathlessly
brother, brotherhood	brotherly		
build, builder, **building**		**build**, rebuild	
burn, burner	burning, burnt	**burn**	
burial	buried	**bury**	
calculation, calculator	incalculable, calculated, calculating	**calculate**	
calm, calmness	**calm**	calm	calmly
capability	**capable**, incapable		capably
care, carer	careful, careless, caring, uncaring	**care**	carefully, carelessly
celebration, celebrity	celebrated, celebratory	**celebrate**	
centre/US **center**, centralization, decentralization	**central**, centralized	centre/US center, centralize, decentralize	centrally
certainty, uncertainty	**certain**, uncertain		certainly, uncertainly
challenge, challenger	challenging	challenge	
change	changeable, interchangeable, unchanged, changing	**change**	
character, characteristic, characterization	characteristic, uncharacteristic	characterize	characteristically
chemical, chemist, chemistry	chemical		chemically
circle, semicircle, circulation	circular	circle, circulate	
cleaner, cleaning, cleanliness	**clean**, unclean	**clean**	clean, cleanly
clarity, clearance, clearing	**clear**, unclear	**clear**	clear, **clearly**
close, closure	closed, closing	**close**	
closeness	**close**		**close**, closely
clothes, clothing	clothed, unclothed	clothe	
collection, collector	collected, collective	**collect**	collectively
colour/US **color**, colouring/US coloring	coloured/US colored, discoloured/US discolored, colourful/US colorful, colourless/US colorless	colour/US color	colourfully/US colorfully
combination	combined	**combine**	

Nouns	Adjectives	Verbs	Adverbs
comfort, discomfort	**comfortable**, uncomfortable, comforting	comfort	comfortably
commitment	noncommittal, committed	**commit**	
communication, communicator	communicative, uncommunicative	**communicate**	
comparison	comparable, incomparable, comparative	**compare**	comparatively
competition, competitor	competitive, uncompetitive	**compete**	competitively
completion, incompleteness incompletely	**complete**, incomplete	**complete**	**completely**,
complication	**complicated**, uncomplicated	complicate	
computer, computing, computerization		computerize	
concentration	concentrated	**concentrate**	
concern	**concerned**, unconcerned	**concern**	
conclusion	concluding, conclusive, inconclusive	conclude	conclusively
condition, precondition, conditioner, conditioning	conditional, unconditional	condition	conditionally, unconditionally
confidence confidentially	**confident**, confidential	confide	confidently,
confirmation	confirmed, unconfirmed	**confirm**	
confusion	confused, confusing	**confuse**	confusingly
connection	connected, disconnected, unconnected	**connect**, disconnect	
subconscious, unconscious, consciousness, unconsciousness	**conscious**, subconscious, unconscious		consciously, unconsciously
consequence	consequent, inconsequential		consequently
consideration considerately	considerable, considerate,	**consider**, reconsider inconsiderate, considered	considerably,
continent	continental, intercontinental		
continuation, continuity continuously	continual, continued, **continuous**	**continue**, discontinue	continually,
contribution, contributor	contributory	**contribute**	
control, controller	controlling, uncontrollable	**control**	uncontrollably
convenience, inconvenience	**convenient**, inconvenient	inconvenience	conveniently
	convinced, convincing, unconvincing	**convince**	convincingly
cook, cooker, cookery, **cooking**	cooked, uncooked	**cook**	
cool, coolness	**cool**	cool	coolly
correction, correctness	**correct**, incorrect, corrective	**correct**	correctly, incorrectly
count, recount	countable, uncountable, countless	**count**, recount	
cover, coverage, covering	undercover, uncovered	**cover**, uncover	undercover
creation, creativity, creator	creative, uncreative	**create**, recreate	creatively
crime, **criminal**, criminologist	criminal, incriminating	incriminate	criminally
critic, **criticism**	**critical**, uncritical	**criticize**	critically
crowd, overcrowding	**crowded**, overcrowded	crowd	
cruelty	**cruel**		cruelly
cry, outcry	crying	cry	
culture, subculture	cultural, cultured		culturally
cure	cured, incurable	**cure**	
custom, **customer**, customs	customary	accustom	customarily
cut, cutting	cutting	**cut**, undercut	
damage, damages	damaging	**damage**	
danger	endangered, **dangerous**	endanger	dangerously

Nouns	Adjectives	Verbs	Adverbs
dare, daring	daring	**dare**	daringly
dark, darkness	**dark**, darkened, darkening	darken	darkly
date	dated, outdated	date, predate	
day, midday	daily		daily
dead, **death**	**dead**, deadly, deathly	deaden	deadly, deathly
deal, dealer, dealings		**deal**	
deceit, deceiver, deception	deceitful, deceptive	**deceive**	deceptively
decision, indecision	decided, undecided, decisive, indecisive	**decide**	decidedly, decisively, indecisively
decoration, decorator	decorative	**decorate**	decoratively
deep, **depth**	**deep**, deepening	deepen	deeply
defeat, defeatism, defeatist	undefeated, defeatist	**defeat**	
defence/US **defense**, defendant, defender	defenceless/US defenseless, indefensible, defensive	**defend**	defensively
definition indefinitely	**definite**, indefinite	define	**definitely**,
demand, demands	demanding, undemanding	**demand**	
democracy, democrat	democratic, undemocratic		democratically
demonstration, demonstrator	demonstrable, demonstrative	**demonstrate**	demonstrably
denial	undeniable	deny	undeniably
dependant, dependence, independence, dependency	dependable, dependent, independent	**depend**	dependably, independently
description	describable, indescribable, nondescript, descriptive	**describe**	descriptively
desire	desirable, undesirable, desired, undesired	desire	
destroyer, destruction	indestructible, destructive	**destroy**	destructively
determination, determiner	**determined**, predetermined indeterminate	determine	determinedly
developer, **development**, redevelopment	developed, undeveloped, developing	**develop**, redevelop	
difference, indifference, differentiation	**different**, indifferent	differ, differentiate	differently
directness, **direction**, directions, **director**	**direct**, indirect	**direct**, redirect	directly, indirectly
disagreement	disagreeable	**disagree**	disagreeably
disappointment	**disappointed**, disappointing	disappoint	disappointingly
disaster	disastrous		disastrously
disciplinarian, **discipline**	disciplinary, disciplined, undisciplined	discipline	
discoverer, **discovery**		**discover**	
distance	**distant**	distance	distantly
disturbance	disturbed, undisturbed, disturbing	**disturb**	disturbingly
divide, division, subdivision	divided, undivided, divisible, divisive	**divide**, subdivide	
divorce, divorcee	divorced	divorce	
do, doing	done, overdone, undone	**do**, outdo, overdo, redo, undo	
doubt, doubter doubtfully	undoubted, doubtful, doubtless	**doubt**	undoubtedly,
dream, dreamer	dream, dreamless, dreamy	**dream**	dreamily
dress, dresser, dressing	dressed, undressed, dressy	**dress**, redress, undress	
drink, drinker, drinking, drunk, drunkenness	**drunk**, drunken	**drink**	drunkenly
drive, **driver**, driving	driving	**drive**	
due, dues	**due**, undue		due, duly, unduly
earner, earnings		**earn**	
earth	earthy, earthly, unearthly	unearth	
ease, unease, easiness	**easy**, uneasy	ease	**easily**, uneasily, easy

Nouns	Adjectives	Verbs	Adverbs
east, easterner	east, easterly, eastern		east, eastward(s)
economics, economist, **economy**	**economic**, economical, uneconomic(al)	economize	economically
education	educated, uneducated, educational	educate	educationally
effect, effectiveness, ineffectiveness	**effective**, ineffective, ineffectual	effect	effectively, ineffectively
effort	effortless		effortlessly
election, re-election, elector, electorate	unelected, electoral	elect, re-elect	
electrician, **electricity**	**electric**, **electrical**	electrify	electrically
electronics	**electronic**		electronically
embarrassment	**embarrassed**, **embarrassing**	embarrass	embarrassingly
emotion	emotional, emotive		emotionally
emphasis	emphatic	**emphasize**	emphatically
employee, **employer**, **employment**, unemployment	unemployed	**employ**	
encouragement, discouragement	encouraged, encouraging, discouraging	**encourage**, discourage	encouragingly
end, ending	unending, endless	**end**	endlessly
energy	energetic	energize	energetically
enjoyment	enjoyable	**enjoy**	enjoyably
enormity	**enormous**		enormously
entrance, entrant, **entry**		**enter**	
entertainer, **entertainment**	entertaining	entertain	entertainingly
enthusiasm, enthusiast	**enthusiastic**, unenthusiastic	enthuse	enthusiastically, unenthusiastically
environment, environmentalist	environmental		environmentally
equality, inequality	**equal**, unequal	equalize	**equally**, unequally
escape, escapism	escaped, inescapable	**escape**	inescapably
essence, essentials	**essential**		essentially
estimate, estimation	estimated	**estimate**, overestimate, underestimate	
event, non-event	eventful, uneventful, eventual		eventfully, eventually
exam, examination, cross-examination, examiner		examine, cross-examine	
excellence	**excellent**	excel	excellently
excitement	excitable, **excited**, **exciting**, unexciting	excite	excitedly, excitingly
excuse	excusable, inexcusable	**excuse**	inexcusably
existence	non-existent, existing, pre-existing	**exist**, coexist	
expectancy, expectation unexpectedly	expectant, unexpected	**expect**	expectantly,
expenditure, **expense**, inexpensively expenses	**expensive**, inexpensive	expend	expensively,
experience, inexperience	**experienced**, inexperienced	experience	
experiment	experimental	experiment	experimentally
expert, expertise	expert, inexpert		expertly
explaining, **explanation**	unexplained, explanatory, explicable, inexplicable	**explain**	inexplicably
explosion, explosive	exploding, explosive	**explode**	explosively
exploration, explorer	exploratory	**explore**	
expression	expressive	**express**	expressively
extreme, extremism, extremist, extremity	**extreme**, extremist		**extremely**

Nouns	Adjectives	Verbs	Adverbs
fact	factual		factually
fail, failure	unfailing	**fail**	unfailingly
fairness	**fair**, unfair		**fairly**, unfairly
faith, faithfulness	faithful, unfaithful		faithfully
familiarity, **family**	**familiar**, unfamiliar	familiarize	familiarly
fame	famed, **famous**, infamous		famously, infamously
fashion unfashionably	fashionable, unfashionable	fashion	fashionably,
fat	**fat**, fattening, fatty	fatten	
fastener		**fasten**, unfasten	
fault	faultless, faulty	fault	faultlessly
fear	fearful, fearless, fearsome	fear	fearfully, fearlessly
feel, **feeling**, feelings	unfeeling	**feel**	
fiction, nonfiction	fictional		
fill, refill, filling	filling	**fill**, refill	
final, semifinal, finalist	**final**	finalize	**finally**
finish	finished, unfinished	**finish**	
firmness, infirmity	**firm**, infirm		firmly
fish, fishing	fishy	fish	fishily
fit, fittings	fitted, fitting	**fit**	fittingly
fix, fixation, fixture	fixed, transfixed, unfixed	**fix**	
flat	**flat**	flatten	flat, flatly
flower	flowered/flowery, flowering	flower	
fold, folder	folded, folding	**fold**, unfold	
follower, following	following	**follow**	
force	forceful, forcible	**force**	forcefully, forcibly
forest, deforestation, forestry	forested		
forgetfulness	forgetful, unforgettable	**forget**	forgetfully
forgiveness	forgiving, unforgiving	**forgive**	
form, formation, transformation, reformer, transformer	reformed	**form**, reform, transform	
formality	**formal**, informal	formalize	formally, informally
fortune	fortunate, unfortunate		**fortunately**, unfortunately
freebie, **freedom**	**free**	**free**	free, freely
freeze, freezer, freezing	freezing, frozen	**freeze**	
frequency, infrequency infrequently	**frequent**, infrequent	frequent	**frequently**,
freshness, refreshments	**fresh**, refreshing	freshen, refresh	freshly, refreshingly
friend, friendliness	friendly, unfriendly	befriend	
fright frightfully	**frightened**, **frightening**, frightful	**frighten**	frighteningly,
fruit, fruition	fruitful, fruitless, fruity		fruitfully, fruitlessly
fund, refund, funding	funded	fund, refund	
furnishings, **furniture**	furnished, unfurnished	furnish	
garden, gardener, gardening		garden	
generalization	**general**	generalize	**generally**
generosity	**generous**		generously
gentleness	**gentle**		gently
gladness	**glad**	gladden	gladly
glass, glasses	glassy		
good, goodies, goodness, goods	**good**		
government, governor	governmental, governing	govern	governmentally
gratitude, ingratitude	**grateful**, ungrateful		gratefully
greatness	**great**		greatly

Nouns	Adjectives	Verbs	Adverbs
green, greenery, greens	**green**		
ground, underground, grounding, grounds	groundless, underground	ground	underground
grower, **growth**, undergrowth	growing, grown, overgrown	**grow**, outgrow	
guilt, guiltiness	**guilty**		guiltily
habit	habitual		habitually
hair, hairiness	hairless, hairy		
hand, handful	underhand, handy	**hand**	
handle, handler, handling		**handle**	
hanger	hanging	**hang**, overhang	
happiness, unhappiness	**happy**, unhappy		happily, unhapplly
hardship	**hard**	harden	**hard**, hardly
harm	unharmed, harmful, harmless	**harm**	harmlessly
head, heading	overhead, heady	head, behead	overhead
health	**healthy**, unhealthy		healthily, unhealthily
hearing	unheard, unheard of	**hear**, overhear	
heart	heartened, heartening, heartless, hearty		heartily, heartlessly
heat, heater, heating	heated, unheated	heat, overheat	heatedly
height, heights	heightened	heighten	
help, helper, helpfulness, helping	helpful, unhelpful, helpless	**help**	helpfully, helplessly
highness	**high**		high, highly
historian, **history**	historic, prehistoric, historical		historically
hold, holder, holding		**hold**	
home	homeless, homely	home	**home**
honesty, dishonesty	**honest**, dishonest		honestly, dishonestly
hope, hopefulness, hopelessness	hopeful, hopeless	**hope**	**hopefully**, hopelessly
human, humanism, humanity, inhumanity	**human**, inhuman, superhuman, humane		humanly, humanely
hunger	**hungry**		hungrily
hurry	hurried, unhurried	**hurry**	hurriedly
hurt	unhurt, hurtful	**hurt**	hurtfully
ice, icicle, icing	icy	ice	icily
identification, identity	identifiable, unidentified	**identify**	
imagination	imaginable, unimaginable, imaginary, imaginative	**imagine**	unimaginably, imaginatively
importance	**important**, unimportant		importantly
impression	impressionable, impressive	impress	impressively
improvement	improved	**improve**	
increase	increased	**increase**	increasingly
credibility, incredulity, incredulously	**incredible**, credible, incredulous		incredibly,
independence, independent	**independent**		independently
industrialist, industrialization, **industry**	**industrial**, industrialized, industrious		industrially, industriously
infection, disinfectant	infectious	infect, disinfect	infectiously
inflation	inflatable, inflated, inflationary	inflate, deflate	
informant, **information**, informer	informative, uninformative, informed, uninformed	inform, misinform	
injury	injured, uninjured	**injure**	
innocence	**innocent**		innocently
insistence	insistent	**insist**	insistently
instance, instant instantaneously	**instant**, instantaneous		instantly,
instruction, instructor	instructive	instruct	instructively

Nouns	Adjectives	Verbs	Adverbs
intelligence	**intelligent**, unintelligent, intelligible, unintelligible		intelligently
intent, **intention**	intended, unintended, intentional, unintentional	**intend**	intentionally, unintentionally
interest	**interested**, disinterested, uninterested, **interesting**	interest	interestingly
interruption	uninterrupted	**interrupt**	
interview, interviewee		interview	
introduction	introductory	**introduce**	
invention, inventiveness, inventor	inventive	**invent**, reinvent	inventively
invitation, invite	uninvited, inviting	**invite**	invitingly
involvement	**involved**, uninvolved	**involve**	
item	itemized	itemize	
joke, joker		joke	jokingly
journal, journalism, **journalist**	journalistic		
judge, **judg(e)ment**	judgmental	**judge**	
juice, juices	juicy		
keenness	**keen**		keenly
keep, keeper, keeping	kept	**keep**	
kill, overkill, killer, killing		**kill**	
kindness, unkindness	**kind**, unkind		kindly, unkindly
knowledge unknowingly, knowledgeably	knowing, knowledgeable,	**know** known, unknown	knowingly,
enlargement	**large**	enlarge	largely
laugh, **laughter**	laughable	**laugh**	laughably
law, **lawyer**, outlaw	lawful, unlawful	outlaw	lawfully, unlawfully
laziness	**lazy**		lazily
lead, **leader**, leadership	lead, leading	**lead**	
learner, learning	learned, unlearned	**learn**	
legality, illegality, legalization	**legal**, illegal	legalize	legally, illegally
length	lengthening, lengthy	lengthen	lengthily
liar, **lie**	lying	lie	
life	lifeless, lifelike, lifelong		lifelessly
light, lighter, lighting, lightness	**light**	light, lighten	lightly
dislike, liking	likeable	**like**, dislike	
likelihood	**likely**, unlikely		likely
limit, limitation, limitations	limited, unlimited	**limit**	
literature, literacy	literary, literate, illiterate		
liveliness, living	**live**, lively, living	**live**, outlive, relive	live
local, location, relocation	**local**	dislocate, relocate	locally
loser, **loss**	lost	**lose**	
	loud		aloud, loud/loudly
love, lover	lovable, unlovable, loveless, lovely, loving	**love**	lovingly
low	**low**, lower, lowly	lower	low
luck	**lucky**, unlucky		luckily, unluckily
machine, machinery, mechanic, mechanics, mechanism	mechanical, mechanized		mechanically
magic, magician	magic, magical		magically
make, remake, maker, making	unmade	**make**, remake	
man, manhood, mankind	manly, manned, unmanned	man	
management, manager	manageable, unmanageable, managerial	**manage**	
mark, marker, markings	marked, unmarked	**mark**	markedly

Nouns	Adjectives	Verbs	Adverbs
market, marketing	marketable	market	
marriage	**married**, unmarried	**marry**, remarry	
match	matching, unmatched	**match**	
material, materialism, materialist, materials	material, immaterial, materialistic	materialize	
meaning	meaningful, meaningless	**mean**	meaningfully
measure, **measurement**	measurable, immeasurable	**measure**	immeasurably
medical, medication, **medicine**	**medical**, medicated, medicinal		medically
memorial, **memory**	memorable	memorize	memorably
mentality	**mental**		mentally
method, methodology	methodical, methodological		methodically
militancy, militant, the military, militia	**military**, militant		militantly, militarily
mind, minder, reminder	mindless	**mind**, remind	mindlessly
minimum	minimal, **minimum**	minimize	minimally
miss	**missing**	**miss**	
mistake mistakenly	mistaken, unmistakable	mistake	unmistakably,
mix, mixer, **mixture**	mixed	**mix**	
modernity, modernization	**modern**	modernize	
moment	momentary, momentous		momentarily
mood, moodiness	moody		moodily
moral, morals, morality, immorality	**moral**, amoral, immoral		morally
mother, motherhood	motherly		
move, **movement**, removal, remover	movable, unmoved, moving	**move**, remove	movingly
murder, murderer	murderous	**murder**	murderously
music, musical, musician	musical, unmusical		musically
name	named, unnamed, nameless	**name**, rename	namely
nation, national, internationally multinational, nationalism, nationalist, nationality, nationalization	**national**, international, multinational, nationalistic	nationalize	nationally,
nature, naturalist, naturalization, naturalness the supernatural	**natural**, supernatural, unnatural, naturalistic	naturalize	naturally, unnaturally
necessity unnecessarily	**necessary**, unnecessary	necessitate	necessarily,
need, needs	needless, needy	**need**	needlessly
nerve, nerves, nervousness	**nervous**		nervously
news, renewal	**new**, renewable, renewed	renew	newly
night, midnight			overnight, nightly
noise	noisy		noisily
normality/*US* normalcy, abnormality	**normal**, abnormal		**normally**, abnormally
north, northerner	north, northerly, northern		north, northward(s)
notice	noticeable, unnoticed	**notice**	noticeably
number, numeral	innumerable, numerical, numerous	number, outnumber	
nurse, nursery, nursing		nurse	
obedience, disobedience disobediently	obedient, disobedient	**obey**, disobey	obediently,
occasion	occasional		occasionally
offence/*US* **offense**, offender, offensive	offensive, inoffensive	**offend**	offensively
office, officer, official	**official**, unofficial		officially, unofficially
the open, opener, opening, openness	**open**, opening	**open**	openly

Nouns	Adjectives	Verbs	Adverbs
operation, cooperation, operative, cooperative operator	operational, operative, cooperative	**operate**, cooperate	operationally
opposition, opposite	opposed, opposing, **opposite**	**oppose**	opposite
option	optional	opt	optionally
order, disorder	disordered, orderly, disorderly	**order**	
organization, disorganization, reorganization, organizer	organizational, organized, disorganized	**organize**, disorganize, reorganize	
origin, original, originality, originator	**original**, unoriginal	originate	**originally**
owner, ownership		**own**, disown	
pack, package, packaging, packet, packing	packed	**pack**, unpack, package	
pain	pained, **painful**, painless	pain	painfully, painlessly
paint, painter, **painting**		**paint**	
part, counterpart, parting, partition	partial, parting	part, partition	part, partially, **partly**
pass, overpass, underpass, passage, passing	passing	**pass**	
patience, impatience, **patient**	**patient**, impatient		patiently, impatiently
pay, **payment**, repayment	unpaid, underpaid	**pay**, repay	
peace	**peaceful**		peacefully
perfection, imperfection, perfectionist	**perfect**, imperfect	perfect	**perfectly**
performance, performer		**perform**	
permission, permit	permissible, impermissible, permissive	permit	
person, **personality**	**personal**, impersonal, personalized	personalize, personify	personally
persuasion	persuasive	**persuade**, dissuade	persuasively
photo, **photograph**, photographer, photography	photogenic, photographic	photograph	
picture	pictorial, picturesque	picture	
place, placement, displacement, replacement	misplaced	place, displace, replace	
plan, planner, planning	unplanned	**plan**	
plant, transplant, plantation		plant, transplant	
play, interplay, replay, **player**, playfulness	playful	**play**, outplay, replay	playfully
pleasantry, **pleasure**, unpleasantly displeasure	**pleasant**, unpleasant, **pleased**, displeased, pleasing, pleasurable	please, displease	pleasantly,
poem, poet, **poetry**	poetic		
point, pointer	pointed, pointless	**point**	pointlessly
politeness	**polite**, impolite		politely, impolitely
politician, **politics**	**political**, politicized	politicize	politically
popularity, unpopularity, popularization	**popular**, unpopular	popularize	popularly
population	populated, unpopulated, populous	populate	
possibility, impossibility, the impossible	**possible**, impossible		**possibly**, impossibly
post, postage	postal	**post**	
power, superpower	**powerful**, overpowering, powerless	power, empower, overpower	powerfully
practical, practicalities, practicality	practicable, **practical**, impractical		practically

Nouns	Adjectives	Verbs	Adverbs
practice, practitioner	practised/*US* practiced, practising/*US* practicing	**practise**/*US* **practice**	
precision	**precise**, imprecise		precisely
preference	preferable, preferential	**prefer**	preferably
preparation, preparations	prepared, unprepared, preparatory	**prepare**	
presence, **present**, presentation, presenter	**present**, presentable	present, represent	presently
press, **pressure**	pressed, pressing, pressurized	**press**, pressure/pressurize	
prevention	preventable, preventive/preventative	**prevent**	
price	overpriced, priceless, pricey/pricy	price	
print, printer, printing	printed	**print**	
prison, **prisoner**, imprisonment		imprison	
privacy, private, privatization	**private**	privatize	privately
probability	probable, improbable		**probably**, improbably
process, processing, procession, processor	processed	process	
produce, producer, **product**, **production**, reproduction, productivity	productive, counterproductive, reproductive, unproductive	**produce**, reproduce	
profession, professional, professionalism	**professional**, unprofessional		professionally
profit, profitability	profitable, unprofitable	profit	profitably
progress, progression	progressive	progress	progressively
proof	proven, unproven	prove, disprove	
protection, protector	protected, unprotected, protective	**protect**	protectively
provider, provision, provisions	provisional	**provide**	provisionally
public, publication, publicist, publicity	**public**	publicize	publicly
publisher, publishing	published, unpublished	**publish**	
punishment	punishable, punishing	**punish**	
purification, purist, purity, impurity	**pure**, impure	purify	purely
purpose	purposeful		purposefully, purposely
push, pusher	pushed, pushy	**push**	
qualification, disqualification, qualifier	qualified, unqualified	qualify, disqualify	
quarter, quarters	quarterly	quarter	quarterly
question, questioning	questionable, unquestionable	question	unquestionably
quiet, disquiet	**quiet**	quieten/quiet	quietly
race, racism, racist	racial, multiracial, racist		racially
rarity	**rare**		rarely
rate, rating	overrated, underrated	rate, underrate	
reaction, reactor	reactionary	**react**, overreact	
read, reader, readership, **reading**	readable, unreadable	**read**	
readiness	**ready**		readily
realism, realist, reality, realistically unreality, realization	**real**, unreal, realistic, unrealistic	**realize**	real, **really**,
reason, reasoning unreasonably	reasonable, unreasonable	reason	reasonably,
receipt, receipts, receiver, reception	receptive	**receive**	
recognition	recognizable, unrecognizable	**recognize**	recognizably
record, recorder, recording	recorded, unrecorded	**record**	

Nouns	Adjectives	Verbs	Adverbs
referee, reference, referral		**refer**, referee	
reflection	reflective	**reflect**	
regret	regrettable, regretful	**regret**	regrettably, regretfully
regular, regularity, irregularity	**regular**, irregular		**regularly**, irregularly
relation, relations, **relationship**, **relative**	**related**, unrelated, relative	relate	relatively
relaxation	**relaxed**, relaxing	**relax**	
reliability, reliance	**reliable**, unreliable, reliant	**rely**	reliably
religion	**religious**, irreligious		religiously
the remainder, remains	remaining	**remain**	
remark	remarkable, unremarkable	remark	remarkably
repair, disrepair	irreparable	**repair**	irreparably
repeat, repetition	repeated, repetitive/repetitious	**repeat**	repeatedly, repetitively
report, reporter	unreported	**report**	reportedly
representation, representative	representative, unrepresentative	**represent**	
reputation, disrepute	reputable, disreputable, reputed		reputedly
respect, disrespect, respectfully, respectability	respectable, respected, respectful, disrespectful, respective	**respect**	respectably, disrespectfully, respectively
respondent, **response**, responsiveness	responsive, unresponsive	**respond**	
responsibility, irresponsibility	**responsible**, irresponsible		responsibly, irresponsibly
rest, unrest, restlessness	restless	**rest**	restlessly
retiree, retirement	retired, retiring	**retire**	
reward	rewarding, unrewarding	reward	
riches, richness, enrichment	**rich**	enrich	richly
ride, rider, riding	overriding	**ride**, override	
right, rightness, rights, righteousness	right, righteous, rightful	right	**right**, rightly, rightfully
roll, roller		**roll**, unroll	
romance, romantic	**romantic**, unromantic, romanticized	romance, romanticize	romantically
rough, roughage, roughness	**rough**	rough, roughen	rough, **roughly**
round, rounders, roundness	**round**, rounded	round	**round**, roundly
royal, royalist, royalty	**royal**, royalist		royally
rudeness	**rude**		rudely
rule, ruler, ruling	ruling, unruly	rule, overrule	
run, rerun, runner, running	running, runny	**run**, outrun, overrun	
sadness	**sad**	sadden	sadly
safe, **safety**	**safe**, unsafe		safely
satisfaction, dissatisfaction	**satisfactory**, unsatisfactory, **satisfied**, dissatisfied, unsatisfied, satisfying	satisfy	satisfactorily, unsatisfactorily
save, saver, saving, savings, saviour/US savior		**save**	
	scared, scary	scare	
school, pre-school, schooling	pre-school		
science, **scientist**	**scientific**, unscientific		scientifically
score, scorer		**score**, outscore, underscore	
search, research, researcher	searching	**search**, research	
seat, seating	seated	seat, unseat	
secrecy, secret	**secret**, secretive		secretly, secretively
sense, nonsense, sensibility, sensitivity, insensitivity	**sensible**, senseless, sensitive, insensitive	sense	sensibly, sensitively, insensitively
separation	separable, inseparable, **separate**	**separate**	inseparably, separately

Nouns	Adjectives	Verbs	Adverbs
seriousness	**serious**		**seriously**
servant, serve, server, **service**, disservice, the services, serving	serviceable, servile	**serve**, service	
sex, sexism, sexuality	sexist, **sexual**, bisexual, sexy		sexually
shadow	shadowy	shadow, overshadow	
shake	shaky	**shake**	shakily
shape	shapeless, shapely	shape	
(pencil) sharpener, sharpness	**sharp**	sharpen	sharp, sharply
shine	shiny	**shine**, outshine	
shock	shocked, shocking	**shock**	shockingly
shop, shopper, **shopping**		shop	
short, shortage, shortness, shorts	**short**	shorten	short, shortly
shyness	**shy**	shy	shyly
sick, sickness	**sick**, sickening, sickly	sicken	sickeningly
sight, insight, oversight, sighting	sighted, unsightly	sight	
sign, **signal**, signatory, signature, signing	signed, unsigned	**sign**, signal	
significance, insignificance insignificantly	**significant**, insignificant	signify	significantly,
silence, silencer	**silent**	silence	silently
similarity	**similar**, dissimilar		similarly
simplicity, simplification	**simple**, simplistic	simplify	simply
singer, singing	unsung	**sing**	
single, singles	**single**, singular	single	singly
skill	skilful/*US* skillful, skilled, unskilled		skilfully/*US* skillfully
sleep, sleeper, sleepiness, sleeplessness	asleep, sleepless, sleepy	**sleep**	sleepily
slight	**slight**, slighted, slightest		**slightly**
slip, slipper	slippery	**slip**	
smoke, smoker, non-smoker, smoking	smoked, smoking, non-smoking, smoky	**smoke**	
smoothness	**smooth**	smooth	smoothly
society, sociologist, sociology	sociable, unsociable, **social**, anti-social, unsocial	socialize	socially
softness	**soft**	soften	softly
solid, solidarity, solidity, solids	**solid**	solidify	solidly
solution, solvent	soluble, insoluble, unsolved, solvent	**solve**	
south, southerner	south, southerly, southern		south, southward(s)
speaker, **speech**	unspeakable, speechless, outspoken, unspoken	**speak**	unspeakably
special, specialist, speciality/*US* specialty specialization	**special**, specialized	specialize	**specially**
speed, speeding	speedy	speed	speedily
spelling		**spell**, misspell	
spoils	spoilt/spoiled, unspoiled/unspoilt	**spoil**	
sport	sporting, sporty	sport	
spot	spotted, spotless, spotty	spot	spotlessly
stand, standing	standing, outstanding	**stand**	outstandingly
standard, standardization	standard, substandard	standardize	
start, starter, non-starter		**start**, restart	
statement, understatement	understated	state, overstate	
steam, steamer	steamy	steam	
steepness	**steep**		steeply

Nouns	Adjectives	Verbs	Adverbs
sticker	sticky, stuck, unstuck	**stick**	
stiffness	**stiff**	stiffen	stiff, stiffly
stone	stoned, stony	stone	
stop, stoppage	non-stop	**stop**	non-stop
storm	stormy	storm	
	straight	straighten	**straight**
stranger	**strange**		strangely
strength	**strong**	strengthen	strongly
stress	stressed, stressful	stress	
strike, striker	striking	**strike**	
structure, restructuring	structural	structure, restructure	structurally
student, **study**	studious	**study**	studiously
stupidity	**stupid**		stupidly
style	stylish	style	stylishly
substance	substantial, insubstantial, substantive	substantiate	substantially
success, succession, unsuccessfully	**successful**, unsuccessful, successor	**succeed** successive	successfully,
suddenness	**sudden**		**suddenly**
sufferer, suffering	insufferable	**suffer**	insufferably
suggestion	suggestive	**suggest**	suggestively
summer, midsummer	summery		
supplier, supplies, **supply**		**supply**	
support, supporter	supportive	**support**	
supposition	supposed	**suppose**, presuppose	supposedly
surface		surface, resurface	
surprise	**surprised**, surprising	surprise	surprisingly
surroundings	surrounding	**surround**	
survival, survivor		**survive**	
suspect, suspicion	suspect, suspected, unsuspecting, suspicious	**suspect**	suspiciously
swearing	sworn	**swear**	
sweet, sweetener, sweetness	**sweet**	sweeten	sweetly
swim, swimmer, swimming		**swim**	
symbol, symbolism	symbolic	symbolize	symbolically
sympathy, sympathizer	**sympathetic**, unsympathetic	sympathize	sympathetically
system	systematic		systematically
takings, undertaking		**take**, overtake, undertake	
talk, talks	talkative	**talk**	
taste, distaste	tasteful, distasteful, tasteless, tasty	**taste**	tastefully, distastefully
tax, taxation	taxable, taxing	tax	
teacher, teaching, teachings		**teach**	
tear	tearful		tearfully
technicalities, technicality, technician, technique	**technical**		technically
technology	technological		technologically
thanks	thankful, thankless	**thank**	thankfully
theorist, **theory**	theoretical	theorize	theoretically
thick, thickness	**thick**	thicken	thickly
thinness	**thin**	thin	thinly
think, rethink, thinker, thinking	unthinkable	**think**, rethink	
thirst	**thirsty**		thirstily
thought, thoughtfulness thoughtlessly	thoughtful, thoughtless		thoughtfully,
threat	threatening	**threaten**	threateningly
⋯ss	**tight**	tighten	tight, tightly
⋯time, timer, timing	timeless, timely, untimely	time	

Nouns	Adjectives	Verbs	Adverbs
tiredness	**tired**, tireless, tiresome, tiring	tire	tirelessly
title, subtitles	titled	entitle	
top, topping	**top**, topless, topmost	top	
touch	touched, untouched, touching, touchy	**touch**	touchingly
	tough	toughen	toughly
trade, trader, trading		trade	
tradition, traditionalist	**traditional**		traditionally
trainee, trainer, **training**, retraining	untrained	**train**	
transport, transportation		transport	
treat, **treatment**, mistreatment	untreated	**treat**, mistreat	
trick, trickery	tricky	trick	
trouble	troubled, troublesome	trouble	
trust, distrust, mistrust, trustee	trusting, trustworthy	**trust**, distrust, mistrust	
truth, untruth, truthfulness	**true**, untrue, truthful		truly, truthfully
try	trying, untried	**try**	
turn, upturn, turning	upturned	**turn**, overturn	
twist, twister	twisted	**twist**	
type	**typical**	typify	typically
understanding, misunderstanding	understandable, understanding, misunderstood	**understand**, misunderstand	understandably
upset	**upset**, upsetting	upset	
urgency	**urgent**		urgently
usage, **use**, disuse, misuse, usefulness, user	reusable, **used**, disused, unused, **useful**, **useless**	**use**, misuse, reuse	usefully
valuables, **value**, values	**valuable**, invaluable, undervalued	value, devalue	
variable, variance, variant, **variety**	variable, varied, **various**	vary	invariably, variously
view, overview, preview, review, viewer		view, preview, review	
violence	**violent**, non-violent	violate	violently
visit, **visitor**		**visit**, revisit	
vote, voter		**vote**	
want, wants	wanted, unwanted	**want**	
war, warfare, warrior	postwar, warring		
warmth	**warm**	warm	warmly
wash, washer, washing	washable, unwashed	**wash**	
wastage, **waste**	waste, wasteful	**waste**	wastefully
watch	watchful	**watch**	
water, waters	underwater, waterproof, watery	water	underwater
way, subway			midway
weakling, weakness	**weak**	weaken	weakly
wear, underwear	wearing, worn	**wear**	
week, midweek	weekly, midweek		weekly, midweek
weight, weights	overweight, underweight, weighted, weighty	**weigh**, outweigh	
welcome	welcome, unwelcome	**welcome**	
west, western, westerner	westerly, western		west, westward(s)
white, whiteness	**white**	whiten	
whole	**whole**, wholesome, unwholesome		
width	**wide**	widen	**wide**, **widely**

Nouns	Adjectives	Verbs	Adverbs
wild, wildness	**wild**		wildly
willingness, unwillingness	**willing**, unwilling		willingly, unwillingly
win, **winner**, winnings		**win**	
winter, midwinter	wintry		
wire, wireless, wiring	wiry	wire	
woman, womanhood	womanly		
wonder	**wonderful**	**wonder**	wonderfully
wood	wooded, wooden		
wool	woollen/US woolen, woolly/US wooly		
word, wording		word	
work, workaholic, worker, workings	workable, unworkable, overworked, working	**work**, rework	
world, underworld	world, worldly, unworldly, worldwide		worldwide
worry	**worried**, unworried, worrying	**worry**	worryingly
worth	**worth**, worthless, worthwhile, worthy, unworthy		
writer, **writing**	written, unwritten	**write**, rewrite	
wrong	**wrong**, wrongful	wrong	**wrong**, wrongly, wrongfully
year	yearly		yearly
young, youngster, youth	**young**, youthful		